P9-CCM-366

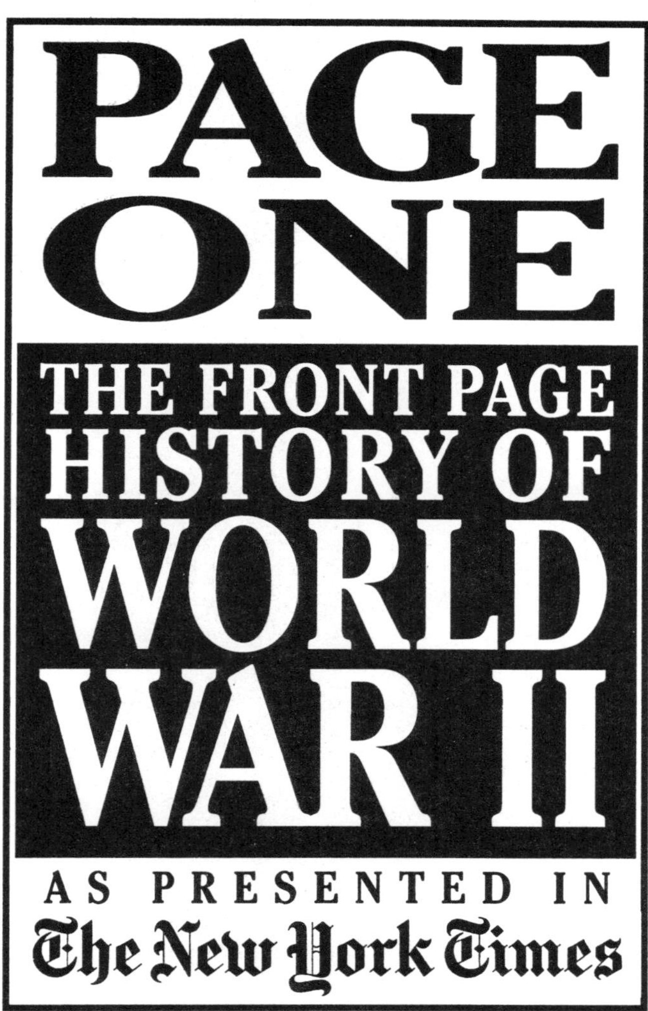
PAGE
ONE
THE FRONT PAGE
HISTORY OF
WORLD
WAR II
AS PRESENTED IN
The New York Times

PAGE ONE

THE FRONT PAGE HISTORY OF WORLD WAR II

AS PRESENTED IN

The New York Times

Galahad Books • New York

First Galahad Books edition published in 1996.

Galahad Books
A division of Budget Book Service, Inc.
386 Park Avenue South
New York, NY 10016

Galahad Books is a registered trademark of
Budget Book Service, Inc.

Published by arrangement with The New York Times Company.

Library of Congress Catalog Card Number: 96-77431

ISBN: 0-88365-962-X

Printed in the United States of America.

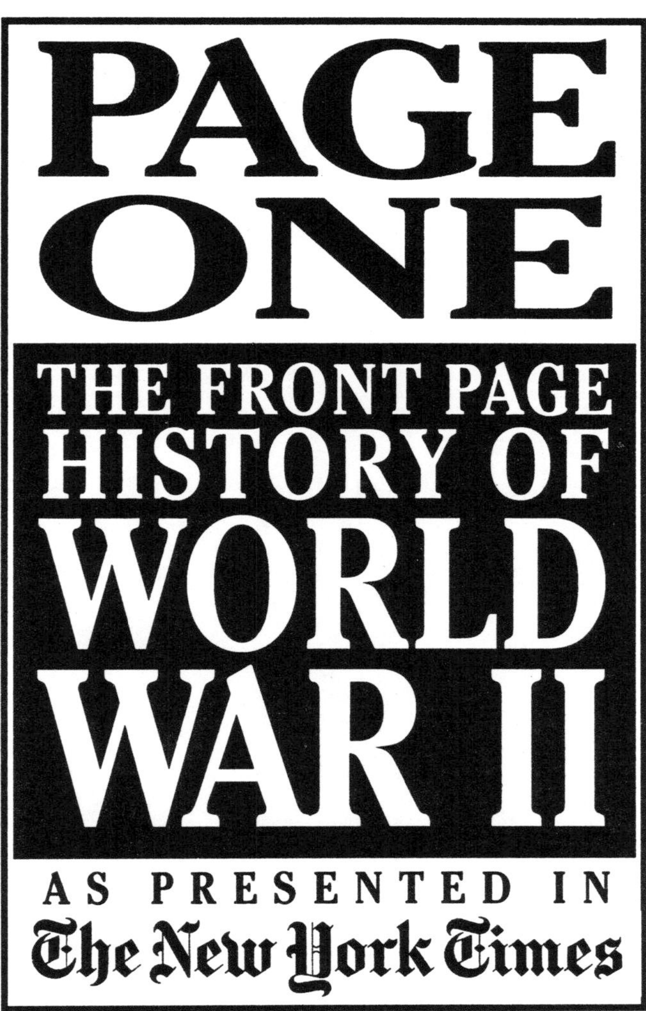
PAGE
ONE
THE FRONT PAGE
HISTORY OF
WORLD
WAR II
AS PRESENTED IN
The New York Times

"All the News That's Fit to Print."

The New York Times.

EXTRA

Partly cloudy and somewhat warmer today. Tomorrow generally fair with moderate temperatures.

Temperatures Yesterday—Max., 67; Min., 61

VOL. LXXXVIII...No. 29,805. Entered as Second-Class Matter, Postoffice, New York, N. Y. NEW YORK, FRIDAY, SEPTEMBER 1, 1939. THREE CENTS NEW YORK CITY and Vicinity | FOUR CENTS Elsewhere Except in 7th and 8th Postal Zones.

GERMAN ARMY ATTACKS POLAND; CITIES BOMBED, PORT BLOCKADED; DANZIG IS ACCEPTED INTO REICH

BRITISH MOBILIZING

Navy Raised to Its Full Strength, Army and Air Reserves Called Up

PARLIAMENT IS CONVOKED

Midnight Meeting Is Held by Ministers—Negotiations Admitted Failure

By The Associated Press.

LONDON, Friday, Sept. 1.—The British Parliament was summoned to meet today at 5 P. M. [12 noon in New York].

British Call Up Forces

By FERDINAND KUHN Jr.

Special Cable to THE NEW YORK TIMES.

LONDON, Friday, Sept. 1.—All attempts to bring about direct negotiations between Germany and Poland appeared to have broken down tonight as Great Britain mobilized her fleet to full strength, stretched her other defensive preparations close to the limit and began moving 3,000,000 school children and invalids from the crowded cities into the safety of the countryside.

Censorship was established over cables after London had been cut off for hours from communication with the Continent.

It was the peak of the crisis, but a day of rumors had not shifted the fundamental issue nor given a conclusive answer to the question of peace or war.

At midnight the British Government was not yet convinced that Germany really intended to attack Poland and provoke a world war.

Terms Called Smoke Screen

All that had happened during yesterday, including the sudden broadcasting of Chancellor Hitler's sixteen-point demands, was interpreted here as a smoke screen rather than as the flash of guns.

After hearing Herr Hitler's "terms" officials here quietly announced tonight that "the government primarily interested in the proposals is, of course, the Polish Government."

Until the Polish Government has had time to consider them, it was said in Whitehall that "it would be highly undesirable for any comment to be made."

It was fully expected that Poland would reject them later today; indeed, Polish circles here were describing them tonight as "utterly unacceptable," for they would involve dismemberment of Poland and loss of Poland's capacity to defend her independence. In any event, there was no sign of any intention here to put pressure on Warsaw to accept.

Much might have been said about the German "proposals" here tonight if the government had not been so anxious to leave the first decision to Warsaw without any prompting. That the British regarded them as artful went without saying, since they conveyed a first impression of reasonableness that was not borne out by the terms themselves.

Until the announcement on the German wireless tonight, the British Government had not been told about them officially, and the Polish Government was not informed until Josef Lipski, Polish Ambassador to Berlin, visited Foreign Minister Joachim von Ribbentrop a few minutes before the broadcast took place.

Shortly after midnight last night, Sir Nevile Henderson, the British Ambassador in Berlin, had heard the "points" read to him by Herr von Ribbentrop, but the reading was so fast that the Ambassador could not even take notes of them in detail. In any event, he was told Herr Hitler's "points" were not being given to him or his government officially, on the ground that it was already too late.

Time Limit Expired

On Tuesday Herr Hitler had asked that a Polish negotiator should arrive in Berlin within twenty-four hours; and as nobody had arrived from Warsaw when the time limit expired, Sir Nevile was told that the "points" could not even be communicated officially to London.

The German time table with the

Continued on Page Four

Bulletins on Europe's Conflict

London Hears of Warsaw Bombing

LONDON, Friday, Sept. 1 (AP).—Reuters British news agency said it had learned from Polish sources in Paris that Warsaw was bombed today.

French Confirm Beginning of War

PARIS, Friday, Sept. 1 (AP).—The Havas news agency said today that official French dispatches from Germany indicated that "the Reich began hostilities on Poland this morning."

The agency also reported that the Polish Embassy here had announced that "Germany violated the Polish frontier at four points."

"German reports of pretended violation of German territory by Poland are pure invention, as is the fable of 'attack' by Polish insurgents on Gleiwitz," the embassy announcement said.

Attack on Entire Front Reported

LONDON, Friday, Sept. 1 (AP).—A Reuters dispatch from Paris said:

"The following is given with all reserve: According to unconfirmed reports received here, the Germans have begun an offensive with extreme violence on the whole Polish front."

First Wounded Brought Into Gleiwitz

GLEIWITZ, Germany, Friday, Sept. 1 (AP).—An army ambulance carrying wounded soldiers arrived at the emergency hospital here today at 9:10 A. M.

The men, carried in a wagon, were on stretchers. One had on a first-aid field bandage. It could not be ascertained where the ambulance came from.

At about 9:30 a half-mile long truck train manned by the engineering corps drove through the heart of the city with pontoon bridge building material. In the train were caterpillar tread, twenty-passenger motor vans.

Obviously the train had been on the road for a considerable time. All equipment was thickly covered with gray mud.

A scouting plane of the air force was patrolling an area over Gleiwitz.

Early today Gleiwitz residents reported that artillery fire

Continued on Page Four

DALADIER SUMMONS CABINET TO CONFER

News of Attack on Poland Spurs Prompt Action—Military Move Thought Likely

By The Associated Press.

PARIS, Friday, Sept. 1.—Edouard Daladier, Premier and War Minister of France, informed that German troops crossed the Polish frontier today, summoned an urgent meeting of his Cabinet for 10:30 A. M.

It was probable that Parliament would be called tomorrow.

Reports of the German invasion came from Berlin and from the Polish Embassy here. The Ministers were called to the Elysee Palace to meet with President Albert Lebrun.

Upon receipt of word of the German operations M. Daladier rushed to the War Ministry and called General Marie Gustave Gamelin, supreme commander of land, sea and air forces, into consultation.

A little later Daladier summoned Foreign Minister Georges Bonnet.

The Polish Embassy said that Germans violated the Polish frontier at four points and at the same time it characterized German charges that Poles had crossed into Germany as "pure invention."

Havas, Frnch news agency, announced that "a German declaration of war against Poland probably will lead France and Great Britain to take new military measures."

Britain and France are committed to aid Poland in any fight to save her independence.

Ministers Stand Firm

By P. J. PHILIP

Wireless to THE NEW YORK TIMES.

PARIS, Aug. 31.—The Cabinet met with President Albert Lebrun for more than two hours this evening at the Elysée Palace. At the close of the meeting Minister of the Interior Albert Sarraut handed the press the following communiqué:

"MM. Edouard Daladier, President of the Council, and Georges Bonnet, Minister of Foreign Affairs, laid before the Cabinet a detailed account of the international situation as a whole.

"The Cabinet was unanimous in formally maintaining the engagements taken by France."

Later M. Daladier had further conversations with M. Bonnet, Fi-

Continued on Page Four

BRITISH CHILDREN TAKEN FROM CITIES

3,000,000 Persons Are in First Evacuation Group, Which Is to Be Moved Today

By FREDERICK T. BIRCHALL

Special Cable to THE NEW YORK TIMES.

LONDON, Friday, Sept. 1.—The greatest mass movement of population at short notice in the history of Great Britain is under way. It is an evacuation, under government order, of little children, invalids, women and old men from congested areas.

From London, Birmingham, Manchester, Liverpool, Edinburgh, Glasgow and twenty-three other cities the great exodus is going on as this dispatch is being written. The numbers are stupendous. More than 3,000,000 of these helpless human beings are being taken out of danger of German bombs.

Nothing like it has ever been attempted anywhere; yet it is going on without mishap—so far, indeed, without serious confusion.

Scenes everywhere were much the same whether in the aristocratic West End or the proletarian East Side, but one that this correspon-

Continued on Page Three

HOSTILITIES BEGUN

Warsaw Reports German Offensive Moving on Three Objectives

ROOSEVELT WARNS NAVY

Also Notifies Army Leaders of Warfare—Envoys Tell of Bombing of 4 Cities

By JERZY SZAPIRO

Wireless to THE NEW YORK TIMES.

WARSAW, Poland, Friday, Sept. 1.—War began at 5 o'clock this morning with German planes attacking Gdynia, Cracow and Katowice.

At Gdynia three bombs exploded in the sea.

The regular German Army started an offensive in the direction of Dzialdowka—in Upper Silesia and Czestochowa. The German plan apparently is to cut off Western Poland along the line of Dzialdowka-Lodz-Czestochowa.

The offensive is developing, from East Prussia, toward Silesia and northwards from Slovakia.

At 9 o'clock an attempt was made to bombard Warsaw. The planes, however, did not reach even the suburbs.

A military attack on the garrison at Westerplatte in the Danzig area was repulsed.

The Foreign Office at 8:45 A. M. issued a communiqué saying that military action had begun in Westerplatte in the Danzig area as well as in Buschkowa near Gdynia, and in Dzialowka, Chojnice and Lowa.

Hostilities have begun and Poland has been attacked, said the communiqué.

Three cities in Upper Silesia suffered artillery bombardment, particulars of which are lacking, it was said.

While this dispatch was being telephoned, the air-raid sirens sounded in Warsaw.

Danzig Fighting Reported

WARSAW, Poland, Friday, Sept. 1 (AP).—It was reported today that Tczew and Czestochowa were bombed by German airplanes early this morning.

There was no official confirmation of the bombing.

Fighting was reported at Danzig.

It was reported officially that German troops had attacked Polish defenses near Mlawa, bordering the southern part of East Prussia. There was no announcement of the damage resulting from the bombing.

Mist and clouds were overhanging the city. A light drizzle apparently afforded momentary protection against air raids. Warsaw went to work as usual.

Roosevelt Warns Navy

WASHINGTON, Friday, Sept. 1 (AP).—President Roosevelt directed today that all naval ships and army commands be notified at once by radio of German-Polish hostilities.

The White House issued the following announcement:

"The President received word at 2:50 A. M. Eastern standard time

Continued on Page Five

Soviet Ratifies Reich Non-Aggression Pact; Gibes at British and French Amuse Deputies

By G. E. R. GEDYE

Special Cable to THE NEW YORK TIMES.

MOSCOW, Aug. 31.—With Premier and Foreign Commissar Vyacheslaff M. Molotoff, working under high pressure—so suddenly applied without any previous indication and contrasting so sharply with earlier delaying tactics this week as to suggest German insistence that the matter be finally settled—the Supreme Soviet [Parliament] tonight unanimously ratified the Russo-German non-aggression pact.

Ratification, which was first foreshadowed at midday, was preceded by a speech by Mr. Molotoff so precise in its definition of Soviet obligations to refrain from participating on the side of Great Britain and France in any war against Germany, so voluble in its defense against charges of inconsistency against Communist Russia for embracing Fascist Germany, and so insistent on the inevitability of friendship between "not merely the governments but also the peoples" of Germany and Russia as to extinguish the last faint hopes of the western democracies that Moscow might yet find loopholes or excuses for joining them at some subsequent date in resisting German aggression against Poland.

Mr. Molotoff's speech contained nothing to justify constantly repeated suspicions of the existence of a secret German-Soviet pact entitling the latter to participate in a partition of Poland.

The Premier's speech contained much trenchant and seemingly irrefutable evidence of blunders by the British and French Governments in handling the question of Soviet cooperation. It was not diffi-

Continued on Page Eight

FREE CITY IS SEIZED

Forster Notifies Hitler of Order Putting Danzig Into the Reich

ACCEPTED BY CHANCELLOR

Poles Ready, Made Their Preparations After Hostilities Appeared Inevitable

Special Cable to THE NEW YORK TIMES.

DANZIG, Friday, Sept. 1.—By a decree issued early this morning Albert Forster, Nazi Chief of State, proclaimed the annexation of the Free City to the Reich, thus settling by a fell stroke the original point of contention in the international crisis.

In a telegram to Chancellor Hitler Herr Forster explained his action as necessary to remove "the pressing necessity of our people and State." Herr Forster also issued a proclamation to the people of Danzig saying the hour awaited for twenty years had arrived because "our Fuehrer, Adolf Hitler, has freed us."

[A NEW YORK TIMES dispatch from Berlin this morning said Herr Hitler telegraphed Herr Forster today thanking him and all Danzigers, and stating:

"The law for reannexation is in effect immediately."

The Chancellor stated, furthermore, that Herr Forster was appointed head of the civil administration of the Danzig area.]

In a four-article decree Herr Forster declared the Constitution of Danzig no longer valid. He declared himself sole administrator of the Danzig part of the German Reich, and he declared that until the Reich's legal system had been introduced by command of Herr Hitler all laws except the Constitution remained in effect. Then Herr Forster immediately wired Herr Hitler of his action, begged the Chancellor to give his approval of the move and through Reich law complete the annexation.

The German flag is now flying everywhere over Danzig, Herr Forster said, and all church bells resound to the event. "We thank God," he declared, "that He gave the Fuehrer the strength and the possibility to free also us from the evil Versailles treaty."

Hitler Accepts Danzig

By The Associated Press.

BERLIN, Friday, Sept. 1.—The German official news agency, D. N. B., announced today that Albert Forster, Nazi Chief of State in Danzig, had proclaimed the reunion of the Free City with the Reich.

Herr Hitler today accepted the Free City of Danzig into the Reich.

"I acknowledge your proclamation of the return of the Free City of Danzig to the Reich," Herr Hitler's telegram said. "I thank you, Gauleiter Forster, and all Danzig men and women, for your loyalty which you have displayed for so many years.

"Greater Germany welcomes you with joy in her heart.

"The law of reunion will be enacted forthwith. I appoint you, Herr Forster, chief of the civil administration in the Danzig territory."

Forster's telegram to Herr Hitler read:

My Fuehrer.

I have just signed and then put into effect the following basic law, concerning the reunion of Danzig with the German Reich.

The basic State law of the Free State of Danzig and the reunion of Danzig with the German Reich is effective Sept. 1, 1939.

To lift the immediate distress of the people and State of the Free City of Danzig, I decree the following basic State law:

ARTICLE I

The Constitution of the Free City of Danzig has been suspended effective immediately.

ARTICLE II

All legal and administrative power will be executed exclusively by the head of State.

ARTICLE III

The Free City of Danzig with its territory and its peoples forms

Continued on Page Five

Hitler Acts Against Poland

The port of Gdynia, north of Danzig (toward top of map), was blockaded this morning. At Gleiwitz (shown by cross) artillery fire was heard after a Polish-German skirmish had been reported there. Cracow, to the east, was among Polish cities said to have been bombed.

Hitler Tells the Reichstag 'Bomb Will Be Met by Bomb'

Chancellor Vows 'Fight Until Resolution' Against Poland—Gives Order of Succession As Goering, Hess, Then Senate to Choose

Chancellor Adolf Hitler of Germany, in a world broadcast this morning, opened "a fight until the resolution of the situation" against Poland, announcing that "from now on bomb will be met by bomb."

At the same time he announced, to face any eventuality, that if anything "happened" to him, Field Marshal Hermann Goering was to be in charge; if to Marshal Goering, Rudolph Hess; if to Herr Hess, the Senate, which he proposes to appoint, will select a successor.

The Chancellor, after attempting to narrow the conflict with Poland by assuring the Western powers that he had no designs on their frontiers, by assuring the neutrality of the sideline powers and by acknowledging the friendliness of Italy and the new relations with Russia, issued a defy to Poland's allies.

Says He Will Carry on

"I shall carry on this fight regardless of against whom I may come," he declared.

At the same time he held the door open for Poland to capitulate to his demands, declaring that he did not intend to make war against women and children. He said that if a solution did not come from the present Polish Government, it would come from a future Polish Government.

The Chancellor expressed confidence, toward the close of his address, that his decision, which was being broadcast over amplifiers hastily erected by electricians at the last moment in the streets of Berlin and the provincial capitals, would be accepted by the German people.

The scene enacted in the Kroll Opera House in Berlin was carried over sound waves to most of the nations of the world. From Berlin hook-ups had been arranged with the three major networks of the United States, and, according to the announcer for the German broadcasting system, over the Italian, Hungarian, Spanish, Norwegian, Swedish, Danish, Yugoslav, British and French national networks.

The summons to the Reichstag, ordered by Herr Hitler himself, had been sent out only a few hours before the meeting. Most of the members had been awaiting the signal, and when the opera house opened shortly before 10 o'clock [5 o'clock, New York time] this morning, they were dressed in the uniforms of their military formations.

After Herr Hitler finished speaking the deputies enacted a law incorporating Danzig into the Reich, declaring Danzig citizens were now Germans, voiding the Constitution of the Free City and extending to its territory the jurisdiction of German law.

At 5:10 A. M., Marshal Goering opened the meeting and turned the floor over to the Chancellor.

In the early part of his address, Herr Hitler electrified his audience with this declaration:

"We have all been suffering under the tortures that the Versailles treaty has been inflicting upon us."

Then, speaking with measured deliberateness of Germany's claims to the pre-war German areas, he announced, as he had on a previous occasion:

"The Treaty of Versailles is, for us Germans, and has been, for us Germans, not a law."

Anticipating what the announcement's reiteration would lead to, the Deputies roared applause. Then Herr Hitler, his indignation rising as he proceeded, set about building up the German case, asserting that his proposals for a peaceful solution of the problem of Danzig and the Polish Corridor had been rejected, and charging that the Poles had visited atrocities on Germans, especially women and children, "killing many of them."

SUMMARY OF SPEECH

A summary of Herr Hitler's speech was translated as follows:

"For months we have been suffering under the burdens of the Treaty of Versailles. Danzig was and is a German city. All these regions have only Germany to thank for their cultural development.

"Minorities in the Polish Corridor have been shamefully mistreated. Here, as in other respects, I have tried to solve the problems by peaceful means. In the fifteen years of National Socialism we have been

Continued on Page Three

HITLER GIVES WORD

In a Proclamation He Accuses Warsaw of Appeal to Arms

FOREIGNERS ARE WARNED

They Remain in Poland at Own Risk—Nazis to Shoot at Any Planes Flying Over Reich

By OTTO D. TOLISCHUS

Special Cable to THE NEW YORK TIMES.

BERLIN, Friday, Sept. 1.—Charging that Germany had been attacked, Chancellor Hitler at 5:11 o'clock this morning issued a proclamation to the army declaring that from now on force will be met with force and calling on the armed forces "to fulfill their duty to the end."

The text of the proclamation reads:

To the defense forces:

The Polish nation refused my efforts for a peaceful regulation of neighborly relations; instead it has appealed to weapons.

Germans in Poland are persecuted with a bloody terror and are driven from their homes. The series of border violations, which are unbearable to a great power, prove that the Poles no longer are willing to respect the German frontier. In order to put an end to this frantic activity no other means is left to me now than to meet force with force.

"Battle for Honor"

German defense forces will carry on the battle for the honor of the living rights of the re-[illegible]kened German people with determination.

I expect every German soldier, in view of the great tradition of eternal German soldiery, to do his duty until the end.

Remember always in all situations you are the representatives of National Socialist Greater Germany!

Long live our people and our Reich!

Berlin, Sept. 1, 1939.

ADOLF HITLER.

The commander-in-chief of the air force issued a decree effective immediately prohibiting the passage of any airplanes over German territory excepting those of the Reich air force or the government.

This morning the naval authorities ordered all German mercantile ships in the Baltic Sea not to run to Danzig or Polish ports.

Anti-air raid defenses were mobilized throughout the country early this morning.

A formal declaration of war against Poland had not yet been declared up to 8 o'clock [3 A. M. New York time] this morning and the question of whether the two countries are in a state of active belligerency is still open.

Reichstag Will Meet Today

Foreign correspondents at an official conference at the Reich Press Ministry at 8:30 o'clock [3:30 A. M. New York time] were told that they would receive every opportunity to facilitate the transmission of dispatches. Wireless stations have been instructed to speed up communications and the Ministry is installing additional batteries of telephones.

The Reichstag has been summoned to meet at 10 o'clock [5 A. M. New York time] to receive a more formal declaration from Herr Hitler.

The Hitler army order is interpreted as providing, for the time being, armed defense of the German frontiers against aggression. The action is also suspected of forcing international diplomatic action.

The Germans announced that foreigners remain in Polish territory at their own risk.

Flying over Polish territory as well as the maritime areas is forbidden by the German authorities and any violators will be shot down.

When Herr Hitler made his an-

Continued on Page Three

CHAMBERLAIN ANNOUNCES BRITAIN IS AT WAR WITH GERMANY

"All the News That's Fit to Print."

NEWS INDEX, PAGE 21, THIS SECTION

The New York Times.

EXTRA

Generally fair, little change in temperature today. Tomorrow cloudy, showers in afternoon or night.

Temperatures Yesterday—Max., 80; Min., 64

Section 1

VOL. LXXXVIII....No. 29,807

Entered as Second-Class Matter. Postoffice, New York, N. Y.

NEW YORK, SUNDAY, SEPTEMBER 3, 1939.

P

Including Rotogravure Picture, Magazine and Book Review. TEN CENTS | TWELVE CENTS Beyond 200 Miles Except in 7th and 8th Postal Zones.

BRITAIN AND FRANCE IN WAR AT 6 A. M.; HITLER WON'T HALT ATTACK ON POLES; CHAMBERLAIN CALLS EMPIRE TO FIGHT

SOVIET IN WARNING

British-French Action to Bring Western Border Revision, Berlin Hears

NAZIS GREET MISSION

Hitler to Receive New Russian Ambassador and General Today

By OTTO D. TOLISCHUS

Wireless to THE NEW YORK TIMES.

BERLIN, Sunday, Sept. 3.—According to well-informed quarters here Moscow is already supposed to have notified Paris and London that if France and Britain join in the present Reich-Polish conflict Russia will find herself compelled to revise her Western borders.

This is tantamount to the threat that any British and French help to Poland will merely hasten the partition of Poland between Germany and Russia. There are hints that Russia might also seek other "compensation" in regions even less convenient to Britain.

As an impressive demonstration of this new cooperation there arrived today by air from Stockholm a new Russian Ambassador and a new embassy secretary, both of whom were said to be very close to Premier Vyacheslaff Molotoff, and a Russian military mission headed by a commanding general.

Officials Greet the Mission

The new Ambassador is Alexander Shkhartzeff, who, it is pointed out here, collaborated with Mr. Molotoff in the Commissariat of Foreign Affairs in Moscow. The new embassy secretary is Vladimir Perloff, up to now Mr. Molotoff's secretary and interpreter.

The military mission consists of General Maxim Purjakoff, designated as the Military Plenipotentiary of the U. S. S. R., and his staff; Brig. Gen. Michael Beljakoff, Colonel Nikolai Skornjakoff, Major Basanoff and Captain Alexander Seditch.

To show the importance of the occasion the members were met at Tempelhof Airfield by Dr. Ernst Woermann, Under-Secretary of State in the Foreign Office; Baron Alexander von Doernberg, Chief of Protocol, and other Foreign Office officials. Lieut. Gen. Seifert, commander of Berlin, headed the list of army officers greeting the Russians. A guard of honor presented arms.

The Russians received an ovation as their automobiles, flying the hammer-and-sickle flag of the Soviet Union, passed the Reich Chancellery. Those assembled along the street gave the Nazi salute.

Hitler to Receive Envoy

Adding importance to all this is the fact that it was announced at midnight that Herr Hitler would receive the new Ambassador, together with the Military Plenipotentiary, for the submission of credentials later today, which sets a precedent for diplomatic speed.

That such a formidable military mission was sent here to work out close collaboration with the German Army is taken for granted now. But German quarters still hold that the consultative clauses of the German-Russian pact are sufficient to cover all the collaboration necessary and a formal military alliance may be signed only as the last trump card to impress London and Paris.

Ambassador Joseph Lipski and his whole embassy staff left Berlin this morning under safe conduct en route to Sweden, which has also taken over the representation of Polish interests. The German Embassy staff was supposed to have left Warsaw at the same time. German interests in Poland are being represented by the Netherlands. Official quarters hold, however, that this merely represents a "cessation of direct diplomatic relations," not a formal break of relations, just as there is no declared state of war.

Meanwhile, since the German-Polish conflict is now being arbitrated by the roar of cannon the re-

Continued on Page Sixteen

Announcement of Final Ultimatum

By The Associated Press.

LONDON, Sunday, Sept. 3.—Following is the text of today's communique revealing the final ultimatum to Germany:

On Sept. 2 His Majesty's Ambassador in Berlin was instructed to inform the German Government that unless they were prepared to give His Majesty's Government in the United Kingdom satisfactory assurances that the German Government had suspended all aggressive action against Poland and were prepared promptly to withdraw their forces from Polish territory, His Majesty's Government in the United Kingdom would without hesitation fulfill their obligations to Poland.

At 9 A. M. this morning His Majesty's Ambassador in Berlin informed the German Government that unless not later than 11 A. M., British Summer time, today, Sept. 3, satisfactory assurances to the above effect had been given by the German Government and had reached His Majesty's Government in London a state of war would exist between the two countries as from that hour.

His Majesty's Government are now awaiting the receipt of any reply that may be made by the German Government.

The Prime Minister will broadcast to the nation at 11:15 A. M.

21 CIVILIANS KILLED IN RAID ON WARSAW

Women, Children Die as Bomb Hits Workers' Apartment—State of War Decreed

By The Associated Press.

WARSAW, Poland, Sept. 2.—Twenty-one dead and more than thirty wounded were counted tonight after German bombs had struck an apartment house in a Warsaw workingmen's quarter.

The bombs tore off the side of the apartment house as if it had been made of paper. Rescue workers still were clearing away the resultant pile of debris in a search for further casualties when this correspondent inspected it.

One of the bombs had dug a crater fully twenty feet in diameter, and the open ground was piled high with furniture and belongings.

In the center of a large park in the southern section of Warsaw, this writer also saw where a bomb had struck a simple wooden dwelling, killing two persons and wounding one. In an open field near the Vistula River, where ten light bombs apparently had been released simultaneously, they had dug craters in a 100-yard circle.

With the writer on this tour of inspection of damage done by the German air bombings were C. Burke Elbrick, secretary of the American Embassy; Clifford Norton, chargé d'affaires of the British Embassy, and officials of the Polish Foreign Office.

During the tour the party twice was forced to take refuge because of air-raid alarms, five of which in all sounded through the city today. Once the party took cover in a shallow dugout filled with working men, their wives and their crying children.

The worst scene of damage was at Kolo, the workingmen's quarter, where, in addition to wrecking one apartment building, the bombs had smashed windows in several others.

An old man gulped back tears as he said his wife and two children were dead. A woman, still staring blankly into space, said:

"My husband is gone."

An official news service communiqué stated that yesterday German raiders dropped 120 bombs on Warsaw and its vicinity, killing ten and wounding twenty-five in Warsaw proper, with the number of casualties in the suburbs still undetermined.

President Ignaz Moscicki declared that Poland was under a "state of war" today as official reports said that Polish forces were resisting German invasion on three fronts.

The "state of war" supersedes the

Continued on Page Fourteen

News dispatches from Europe are now virtually all subject to censorship

PARIS AUTHORIZED WAR DECLARATION

Chamber Voted Credits After Hearing Daladier—New Ultimatum Being Drawn

By The Associated Press.

PARIS, Sept. 2.—Premier Edouard Daladier today received implied authority from the Chamber of Deputies to declare war on Germany.

With that to support them, he and his Cabinet met at the War Ministry at 7:30 tonight to frame a demand that Chancellor Hitler reply to the British-French "last warning" of yesterday.

The power to declare war was vested in a war budget bill of 69,000,000,000 francs, which the sober Deputies, many wearing army uniforms, adopted unanimously by a show of hands after hearing M. Daladier say the government was still willing to negotiate if Germany would cease hostilities in Poland.

Whether the Premier uses the authority vested in him by adoption of the budget depends upon the possibility—frankly viewed as slight—that Herr Hitler would avail himself of a last-minute loophole for peace.

The Premier told the finance committee after the Chamber session that he planned to call the Chamber to approve an actual declaration of war if that became necessary, but he may simply ask for approval after, rather than before, the action is taken.

"The government will take the same chance as Parisians," M. Daladier told a Deputy who asked whether the government planned to leave Paris immediately.

The session was held in a tense atmosphere from 3 to 3:55 P. M.

Continued on Page Seventeen

ROME ASKED PEACE

Pressed Its Proposal for a 5-Power Parley on Britain and France

WAR MEASURES CUT

Press Expressed the Hope Germany Would Win in Poland

By The Associated Press.

ROME, Sept. 2.—Premier Mussolini tonight sought to prevent Polish-German hostilities from spreading into a general European war by arranging a negotiated settlement.

Conferences that the British and French Ambassadors had with Foreign Minister Count Ciano were believed to be connected directly with an Italian proposal of a five-power conference disclosed in London by Prime Minister Neville Chamberlain and Foreign Secretary Viscount Halifax.

The possibility of halting the German-Polish conflict and arranging a peaceable settlement was believed to have been discussed at the diplomatic conferences, but no official information was forthcoming.

Some foreign observers believed, however, that Signor Mussolini had been asked to use his influence on Adolf Hitler to halt fighting in Poland, call his army back and negotiate a settlement of his demands on the Poles.

For Wide Settlement

Here it was regarded as certain that any five-power conference proposed by Premier Mussolini would not be merely for settling the German-Polish conflict but would be aimed at complete revision of the Treaty of Versailles.

Under such a revision Italy and Germany would seek the political and economic concessions that they consider necessary to end European tension once and for all. This has long been Signor Mussolini's idea and Italian newspapers recently have been stressing it as the only real solution. [Italy has been demanding from France concessions concerning Tunisia, the Suez Canal and Jibuti, French Somaliland port.]

While the Ambassadors of France and Britain conferred with Foreign Minister Ciano Italy continued her policy of watchful waiting and avoidance of any military "initiative".

The important commentator, Virginio Gayda, in the Giornale d'Italia noted uneasily that French and British war preparations made it seem that only a miracle could prevent a "more general explosion." Italy, he said, rested on her arms, confident she had done everything possible to avoid war. He said she was following events

Continued on Page Fifteen

NAZIS REPORT GAINS

Hitler's Aims in Corridor Already Won, They Say, Telling of Big 'Trap'

RESISTANCE IS NOTED

But Armies Drive On and Navy Is in Command of Baltic, Germans Hold

Special Cable to THE NEW YORK TIMES.

BERLIN, Sunday, Sept. 3.—Defying the British and French ultimatums, the German armies reported continued advances into Poland yesterday.

By nightfall, it was asserted, not only had they attained the German war aims in the Polish Corridor as outlined in Chancellor Hitler's "sixteen points" but they were pushing forward in a concentric drive toward Warsaw. According to one report, the German forces stood less than fifty miles north of the Polish capital, and a big battle was believed developing along the Narew River.

According to the latest communiqués of the army command, which apparently have already been overtaken by developments, the German armies operating out of East Prussia and Pomerania had virtually cut the Corridor along the Netze and Vistula Rivers, so that all Polish troops remaining in the bottleneck north of it were hopelessly trapped.

Claim Capture of Teschen

In the South the Germans were reported to have taken the heavily fortified Jablunka Pass, the main strategic highway from Slovakia into Poland; to have captured Teschen and Pless [Pszczynya] and to be breaking through the Polish bunker line approaching Biala. This army group apparently has the task of capturing the Upper Silesian industrial section and the Teschen coal mines, taken by Poland from Czecho-Slovakia, and then of advancing along the Vistula toward Sandomierz, the new Polish armament and industrial center.

At the same time two other German Army groups, operating from the north out of East Prussia and from the southwest out of Silesia, apparently were conducting a pincers movement on Warsaw. The southwestern group was declared to have taken Wielun and to be advancing toward Radomsk and Sieradz.

The Northern army group, according to a communiqué, was advancing on Przasnysz, but, according to private reports, is already beyond that town and approaching a larger Polish army that is supposed to have taken a stand on the Narew, where the first real battle of the undeclared war may take place.

Reich Claims "Air" Domination

The communiqué asserted also that the German air force, after many bombing expeditions against air fields, railroads, military transports, retreating marching columns and other military objectives, in which many planes and the munition factory at Skarzysko-Kamienna were destroyed, now has "unchallenged air domination over the entire Polish territory and so is now free for other tasks in protection of the Reich."

In addition, the Germany Navy, which said it had bombed the fortifications and port of Hela and also Gdynia, reported the sinking of a Polish torpedo boat off Hela. It was said to command the Baltic so completely that the fishing embargo was lifted last night.

A communiqué issued by the high command early today, according to the official German News Bureau, declared:

"The German air force yesterday again proved its absolute superiority. The whole air area over the battle zone and the hinterland is completely controlled by the German air force. Attacks were confined exclusively to military objectives.

"After units of German armored cars had reached the Vistula, approximately at noon, the German

Continued on Page Twelve

Fuller Breaks Own Bendix Race Records; Crosses Continent in 8 Hours 58 Minutes

Frank Fuller, San Francisco sportsman pilot, broke his own record in the Bendix Trophy Race from Burbank, Calif., to Cleveland yesterday and then kept on to Bendix, N. J., to break his own record for a transcontinental crossing in the event, opening feature of the National Air Races and the country's outstanding air derby.

Flying a stripped-down Seversky military plane equipped with the same twin Wasp engine he had in the 1937 race, when his earlier records were set, Fuller flew the 2,450 miles from Burbank to Bendix in an elapsed time of 8 hours 58 minutes 8.46 seconds. His average speed was 273.14 miles an hour. His elapsed time in 1937 was 9 hours 23 minutes.

The record for a transcontinental flight is 7 hours 28 minutes, established by Howard Hughes in a specially built plane about two years ago.

In crossing the finishing line at Bendix, Fuller, a wealthy paint manufacturer, won three prizes totaling $12,500. For being the first to reach Cleveland he received a prize of $9,000. As the first to fly over the line at Bendix he won another $1,000, and for breaking his 1937 record he won $2,500.

Fuller reached Bendix at 4:24:53 P. M., Eastern daylight time, and proceeded, without landing, to Floyd Bennett Field, where he brought his plane to earth at 4:35 P. M.

Max Constant of Burbank was the second racer to fly over Bendix, reaching there at 6:13:39 P. M. Arthur C. Bussy of Royersford, Pa., appeared at 7:08:15 P. M.

Although Constant arrived at Bendix ahead of Bussy, he took off from Burbank before him and Bussy was declared the second prize winner and received $5,000 for the flight to Cleveland and an additional $800 for continuing to Bendix and Floyd Bennett Field.

Mrs. Arline Davis of Cleveland landed at Newark Airport at 8 P. M., believing that she had crossed the official marker at Bendix and thereby won the $2,500 prize for the first woman to finish

Continued on Page Three

Text of Chamberlain Address

The following is the text of the address by Prime Minister Chamberlain from 10 Downing Street this morning:

I am speaking to you from the Cabinet Room from 10 Downing Street. This morning the British Ambassador in Berlin handed the German Government the final note stating unless we heard from them by 11 o'clock [6 o'clock New York time] that they were prepared at once to withdraw their troops from Poland a state of war would exist between us. I have to tell you now that no such undertaking has been received and consequently this country is at war with Germany.

You can imagine what a bitter blow it is to me that all my long struggle to win peace has failed. Up to the very last it should have been quite possible to arrange a peaceful settlement between Germany and Poland.

Hitler has evidently made up his mind to attack Poland whatever may happen. Hitler claims that his proposals were shown to Poland and to us. That is not a true statement. The proposals never were shown to the Poles or to us.

The German Government prepared the proposals in German and the same night the German troops crossed the Polish frontier. Germany will never give up force and can only be stopped by force.

We are prepared to uphold our treaty with Poland and to protect them from the wicked and unprovoked attacks on the Polish people. France is joining Britain in fulfillment of her pledges. We have a clear conscience and the situation has become intolerable. Now that we have determined to finish it I know that you will all play your part.

When I have finished speaking several detailed announcements will be made on behalf of the government giving you plans under which it will be possible to carry on the work of the nation in these days of stress which may be ahead, but these plans need your help. You may be taking part in one of the fighting services or one of the other branches.

It is of vital importance that you carry on with your jobs. May God bless you all and may He defend the right for it is the evil things we shall be fighting against—brute force, broken promises, bad faith. But I am certain that right shall prevail.

Bulletins on European Conflict

Air Raid Warning in London

LONDON, Sept. 3 (Sunday).—Air raid sirens sounded an alarm in London today at 11:32 A. M. (5:32 A. M., E.S.T.).

The whole city was sent to shelters by the wail of the alarm but all clear signals were sounded seventeen minutes later.

Ribbentrop Gives Reply to British Envoy

BERLIN, Sunday, Sept. 3 (AP).—German Foreign Minister Joachim von Ribbentrop received British Ambassador Sir Nevile Henderson at 9 A. M. [4 A. M. in New York] today to hand him Germany's answer to the "final warnings" of Britain and France. Herr von Ribbentrop was expected to see the French Ambassador, Robert Coulondre, shortly before noon.

American Diplomats' Families Leave Reich

BERLIN, Sunday, Sept. 3 (AP).—About fifty women and children of the United States Embassy and consular staffs, as well as several other American families, left Berlin today at 8:50 A. M. [3:50 A. M. in New York] for Copenhagen in compartments reserved for them in a regular train.

They were due in Copenhagen at 5:35 P. M. [12:35 A. M. in New York].

War Announced in France

PARIS, Sunday, Sept. 3 (AP).—The radio announced to the French nation today that British Prime Minister Chamberlain had proclaimed Great Britain at war with Germany.

"No News" at the German Embassy

LONDON, Sunday, Sept. 3 (AP).—At the German Embassy in London at 9:30 A. M. today [5:30 A. M., New York], a half hour before the expiration of the British ultimatum, it was said, "There is no news." A spokesman said, "We are in constant communication with Berlin."

Denies Poles Got Five-Power Parley Offer

LONDON, Sunday, Sept. 3 (AP).—Exchange Telegraph Agency, British news agency, said today that Count Edward Raczynski, Polish Ambassador in London, informed it that "the Italian Government did not approach Poland" concerning a reported five-power conference to settle German-Polish issues.

"Apart from the declarations made yesterday in the British Parliament and apart from contradictory reports in the press," the agency quoted him, "the Polish Government has not knowledge of such a scheme."

Exchange Telegraph said the Ambassador declared that "any talk of such a conference" would be "ludicrous and fantastic" as long as "a single enemy soldier stands on Polish soil."

1,000 Americans Sail on French Liner

PARIS, Sunday, Sept. 3 (AP).—The French Line said today that the Ile de France had sailed from Havre with more than 1,000 Americans on board, bound for home.

Heavy Fighting Is Reported in Silesia

WARSAW, Sept. 2 (AP).—Although official information was lacking, it was reported tonight that severe fighting be-

Continued on Page Twelve

TO END OPPRESSION

Premier Calls It 'Bitter Blow' That Efforts for Peace Have Failed

WARNING UNHEEDED

Demand on Reich to Withdraw Army From Poland Ignored

Prime Minister Neville Chamberlain announced to the world at 6:10 o'clock this morning that Great Britain and France were at war with Germany. He made the announcement over the radio, with short waves carrying the measured tones of his voice throughout all continents, from 10 Downing Street in London.

Mr. Chamberlain disclosed that Great Britain and France had taken concurrent action, announcing that "we and France are, today, in fulfillment of our obligations, going to the aid of Poland."

France, however, had not made any announcement beyond stating that the French Ambassador to Berlin would make a final call upon Foreign Minister Joachim von Ribbentrop at 6 o'clock this morning, and it was assumed the French had proclaimed the existence of the state of war.

Speaks With Solemnity

With the greatest solemnity Mr. Chamberlain began his declaration by reporting that the British Ambassador to Berlin had handed in Great Britain's final ultimatum and that it had not been accepted. Without hesitation he announced Britain's decision and, after touching briefly on the background of the crisis, he expressed the highest confidence that "injustice, oppression and persecution" would be vanquished and that his cause would triumph.

Mr. Chamberlain appealed to his people, schooled during the last year as the crisis deepened in measures of defense and offense, to carry on with their jobs and begged a blessing upon them, warning that "we shall be fighting against brute force."

The declaration came after Great Britain had given Chancellor Adolf Hitler of Germany extended time in which to answer the British Government's final ultimatum of Friday. In the final ultimatum Herr Hitler had been told that unless German aggression in Poland ceased, Britain was prepared to fulfill her obligations to Poland.

Warning Was Sharp

Britain's last warning at 4 o'clock this morning, New York time, left no doubt of her stand, for the phrase, "fulfillment of Britain's obligations to Poland," was replaced by a flat statement that a state of war would exist between the two countries as of the hour of the deadline.

After Mr. Chamberlain had finished his statement, which had been introduced as "an announcement of national importance," the announcer warned the British people not to gather together, broadcast an order that all meeting places for entertainment be closed, and gave precautions to prepare the people against air bombings and poison gas attacks.

Mr. Chamberlain began his

Continued on Page Fifteen

"All the News That's Fit to Print."

The New York Times.

LATE CITY EDITION
POSTSCRIPT
Generally fair with showers to-night, continued warm.
Temperatures Yesterday—Max., 79; Min., 64

Copyright, 1939, by The New York Times Company.

VOL. LXXXVIII...No. 29,808. Entered as Second-Class Matter, Postoffice, New York, N. Y. NEW YORK, MONDAY, SEPTEMBER 4, 1939. P THREE CENTS NEW YORK CITY and Vicinity | FOUR CENTS Elsewhere Except in 7th and 8th Postal Zones.

BRITISH LINER ATHENIA TORPEDOED, SUNK; 1,400 PASSENGERS ABOARD, 292 AMERICANS; ALL EXCEPT A FEW ARE REPORTED SAVED

ROOSEVELT IN PLEA

President, on Air, Asks the Nation to Observe True Neutrality

CALLS ALL TO UNITY

Draws Ring Around Americas—'Even a Neutral' May Judge, He Says

By TURNER CATLEDGE
Special to THE NEW YORK TIMES.

WASHINGTON, Sept. 3.—In an extraordinary message broadcast by radio to "the whole of America," President Roosevelt tonight called for an adjournment of all partisanship and selfishness and substitution of complete national unity in the United States to the end that the newest world war may be kept from the Western Hemisphere.

He declared that, as long as it remained within his power to prevent, "there will be no blackout of peace in the United States."

Linking the present European conflagration to the "invasion of Poland by Germany," the President announced that a proclamation of American neutrality was being prepared for issuance under the present Neutrality Act.

"I trust that in the days to come our neutrality can be made a true neutrality," he added.

Would Seek a "Final Peace"

But it seemed clear to him, he said, "even at the outbreak of this great war," that the influence of America should be consistent "in seeking for humanity a final peace which will eliminate, as far as it is possible to do so, the continued use of force between nations."

In his flat declaration that "this nation will remain a neutral nation," the President said he could not ask that every American remain neutral in thought as well. "Even a neutral has a right to take account of facts," he said. "Even a neutral cannot be asked to close his mind or his conscience."

The President gave no inkling of his intentions about calling Congress into special session to revise the stringent Neutrality Law which places certain mandatory obligations upon him. The universal opinion among observers at the capital was that he would issue a call soon, and that it might come upon the heels of the obligatory neutrality proclamation, placing an embargo on arms and munitions of war to Germany, Poland, France and England. White House sources said the neutrality proclamation could be expected within the next forty-eight hours.

Gives Ideas of Safety

Under the law, the neutrality proclamation, which carries with it the proclamation of an arms embargo, is required as soon as the President makes a finding that a state of war exists between two or more countries. Officials were standing today on the technicality that this government had not been officially notified of Britain's and France's declarations. They conceded, however, that this was a mere technicality.

In the course of his message, the President drew a ring around the Western Hemisphere, saying in substance that this was the area which the United States must and would seek to protect and keep neutral.

This country, he said, had certain ideas and ideals of national safety "and we must act to preserve that safety today and to preserve the safety of our children in future years."

That safety, he continued, is and will be bound up with the safety of the Western Hemisphere "and the seas adjacent thereto."

"We seek to keep war from our firesides by keeping war from coming to the Americas," he said.

Recalls Efforts for Peace

He claimed historic precedent, going back to the days of George Washington, for this country's assuming the responsibility of protecting the whole of the Americas. It is serious enough and tragic enough to every American family in every State in the Union to live in a world torn by wars on other continents, he said. Therefore he considered it our national duty to use

Continued on Page Six

Poles Charge Aerial Gas Attacks on Cities As Germany Agrees to 'Humanize' the War

LONDON, Sept. 3 (AP).—The Polish Ambassador to London, Count Edward Raczynski, tonight declared that new German air attacks in all parts of Poland had disclosed that the civilian population was suffering with the Germans using gas in their raids.

WARSAW, Sept. 3 (Polish Telegraphic Agency).—German bombers threw gas bombs on the unfortified village of Grudisk in the county of Ciechanow.

Wireless to THE NEW YORK TIMES.

BERLIN, Sept. 3.—It was announced today that Germany and the Western Powers had agreed to "humanize" the war by not employing poison gas, not bombing open cities from the air, even when in the zone of war operations, and not taking military measures against civilians as long as both sides observed the agreement.

The reported dropping of gas bombs on Polish towns represents the first use of gas from planes in European warfare.

The inauguration of this form of attack recalls that in 1915 the Germans began the use of poison gas on the battlefields and the Allies followed suit.

In 1917 the German General Staff gave consideration to the use of gas from planes in attacking cities, but after a long debate it was decided not to do so. The reason was that the British and French air forces combined were superior to the air force of the Germans, and the fear of what might happen to German cities deterred the Germans from using gas in air attacks at that time.

ITALY FAILS TO ACT AS HER ALLY FIGHTS

Rome Plans to Stay Neutral Unless Attacked—Fascist Moves Kept Secret

By HERBERT L. MATTHEWS
Special Cable to THE NEW YORK TIMES.

ROME, Monday, Sept. 4.—Although Great Britain and France are at war with Germany, Italy has taken no step to join her Axis partner. She remains friendly to Germany but neutral, and she will make no move against the French and British unless attacked. This was made clear in Premier Mussolini's newspaper, the Popolo d'Italia, this morning, which reaffirmed the declaration of neutrality contained in the Council of Ministers' communiqué Friday.

Whether there is any possibility of Italy going beyond that attitude toward one side or the other cannot be stated yet, for the Italians continue to be completely secret. Since history always repeats itself, one may well suppose that the French and British are doing everything they can to win Italian benevolence, if not aid. That is the normal and natural thing for them to do whether they have hopes for success or not. After all, diplomatic relations between Rome and Paris and London continue on a friendly basis, and none need be surprised if André François-Poncet and Sir Percy Loraine, the French and British Ambassadors, who see Count Ciano, the Foreign Minister, so often these days, should be exerting their greatest efforts to win Italy away from Germany. It is their business to do so.

Attitude Is Not Changing

None can say yet what success, if any, they are having. So far as today is concerned there is that Popolo d'Italia article to go upon, which indicates clearly enough that Italy is not changing her attitude because Britain and France have entered the conflict. Although it was printed before those countries acted it was written at a time when there could be no doubt of what was going to happen.

The editorial begins by saying that the Council of Ministers' communiqué should be "re-read and meditated." Its words were "sculpted in stone," says the editorial, meaning that it was meant to last.

From Premier Mussolini's efforts for "peace with justice," two things are to be deduced it continues:

First, that notwithstanding certain foreign interpretations which are too hasty or ingenuous nothing is changed on the plane of Italo-German friendship.

Second, that Signor Mussolini has worked not only for the solution of the German-Polish problem but for all other problems which like this one now being solved by arms, have their origin in the Versailles Treaty.

"It is therefore natural," the article goes on, "that whatever happens, whether the German-Polish conflict remains localized or spreads to a catastrophe, the Duce's work—that is to say the work that

Continued on Page Seven

HITLER WITH ARMY ON EASTERN FRONT

Leaves Berlin After Placing Blame for War on Britain—Allied Envoys Depart

By OTTO D. TOLISCHUS
Wireless to THE NEW YORK TIMES.

BERLIN, Sept. 3.—At 9 o'clock tonight Chancellor Hitler left Berlin, presumably for the Eastern Front. He had previously sent a message to the Eastern Army stating that he was joining them.

He left the city in a heavily guarded special train that mounted anti-aircraft artillery. He was accompanied by his Foreign Minister, Joachim von Ribbentrop, and by Field Marshal Hermann Goering. It was supposed that their destination was Stolp, Pomerania, where the headquarters of the Eastern Army is believed to be located.

The departure of the Chancellor ended a day of proclamations from the chancellery. There was an appeal to the German people, a proclamation to the Nazi party, a message to the soldiers of the East Army and another to the troops manning the Westwall. There was also given out the text of a German memorandum answering the British ultimatum.

Perhaps the most significant feature of all these proclamations and of the memorandum is that they do not mention France, sidetrack

Continued on Page Two

POLES REPORT GAIN

Tell of Fighting on Foe's Soil After Horsemen Retake 2 Towns

SHELL GERMAN AREA

But Invaders Announce Wide Advances—They Capture Rail Center

By The Associated Press.

LONDON, Monday, Sept. 4.—An Exchange Telegraph dispatch from Warsaw reported early today that Polish troops had crossed the German frontier north of Breslau and were fighting on German soil.

Quoting a Polish short-wave radio broadcast, the news agency said the troops had crossed between Rawicz and Leszno. These towns are on the border about twenty-five miles apart and approximately forty-five miles north of Breslau. The report said Polish cavalry was in the action.

[The Polish Telegraphic Agency reported earlier that Polish cavalry had driven German forces from Rawicz and Leszno, which they had captured in surprise attacks on Friday.]

The agency quoted the following communiqué issued last night by the Polish supreme command:

"During the day the German air force carried out raids on numerous unfortified towns, including Warsaw, Deblin, Radom and Cracow. Near Radom and Cracow twenty-six enemy aircraft were brought down. The total number brought down today was sixty-four. The Polish losses amounted to eleven machines. German raiders did not spare the peasant population working in the fields near their villages.

"Considerable enemy forces launched a strong attack in the direction of Silesia and the region of Podhale. Under the pressure of the enemy, Polish forces were compelled to abandon Czestochowa on the Silesian frontier.

"Our lines were slightly pressed in the Silesia sector. In the north Polish troops recaptured Puck and Orlowo."

In an air encounter over Poznan late yesterday, Exchange Telegraph said, six German bombers were shot down near Wolbrom after they had dropped a number of gas bombs.

The agency said that the German radio had announced that a German Army had crossed the Warta [Warthe] River yesterday east of Wielun in Western Poland.

An attempt by Polish troops cut

Continued on Page Nine

The Developments in Europe

Britain and France plunged into war yesterday morning and soon events began to gather momentum.

The most sensational was the torpedoing and sinking of the British liner Athenia off the Hebrides this morning. She was carrying 1,400 passengers, including 292 Americans, from Liverpool to Montreal. The news shocked the White House. [Page 1].

On top of this came charges by Poles that the Germans had dropped gas bombs on towns. [Page 1.]

Britain, following her tactics of the last war, quickly blockaded Germany and closed the entrances to the Mediterranean Sea as well. The British public was calm and grimly determined after it had heard Prime Minister Chamberlain gravely announce on the radio that "this country is at war with Germany." [Page 1.] He made the same announcement in the House of Commons, where he immediately received the support of such former opponents as Winston Churchill and David Lloyd George. In a new War Cabinet Mr. Churchill resumed the post of First Lord of the Admiralty, which he had held in the last war; Lord Hankey, another veteran statesman of that conflict, became Minister Without Portfolio, and Anthony Eden became Secretary for the Dominions. [Page 8; texts of Mr. Chamberlain's addresses and of addresses in the Commons, Page 8.]

In France Premier Daladier, declaring that the responsibility for bloodshed was Chancellor Hitler's, said that France's cause was the cause of justice. [Page 1; text of Daladier's radio speech, Page 8.]

Herr Hitler in a series of statements during the day put the blame for the strife on the British whom he accused of seeking to encircle Germany. He left for the Polish front. [Page 1; texts of these statements, Page 2.]

On that front the Poles were reported to have carried the fighting to German soil in one sector, but were declared to be giving ground in Silesia and at points in Pomorze [Page 1].

Italy still took no step to join her Axis partner in the conflict and it seemed obvious that the British and the French were doing what they could to win her to their side. [Page 1.]

Russia likewise kept a middle-of-the-road position [Page 6.]

President Roosevelt, in an extraordinary message radioed to "the whole of America," called for national unity as a measure for keeping the Western Hemisphere from becoming embroiled. [Page 1; text of the message, Page 6.]

BRITISH NAVY ACTS

It Cuts Off Entrances to the Baltic, North and Mediterranean Seas

LONDON IS UNSHAKEN

Declaration of War Is Met With Resolve—Air Alarm Orderly

Special to THE NEW YORK TIMES.

WASHINGTON, Sept. 3.—The British Government has ordered a naval blockade of Germany, according to information reaching officials here tonight. This government has not been informed officially by the British Government of this fact, however.

It was understood here that the naval blockade went into effect immediately upon the declaration of war and that British naval vessels were blocking the entrance to the Baltic Sea near Skagerrak and were stretched across the North Sea near the Scandinavian peninsula. It was also understood here that the entrances to the Mediterranean at Gibraltar and Suez were being carefully controlled.

Both Britain and France were cloaking their naval and military moves with greatest secrecy and neither the Navy nor the War Department had specific information about them up to 8 o'clock, Eastern standard time, tonight.

Britain Is Determined

By FREDERICK T. BIRCHALL
Special Cable to THE NEW YORK TIMES.

LONDON, Monday, Sept. 4.—At last midnight Great Britain had been at war with Germany for thirteen hours. France had been at war for seven hours—since 5 o'clock.

A darkened London, in which only hooded red and green crosses at the traffic halts, invisible from above, indicate that there are streets, houses and human life below a clear starry sky, awaits calmly the air attacks that it confidently expects despite Chancellor Hitler's professed desire to avoid bombing open cities. Even these tiny indications will be extinguished the moment that sirens hoot their warnings of approaching raiders.

There are few people in the streets because the authorities have broadcast warnings to every one to stay at home and to go out no more than is necessary. Cinemas, theatres and every other form of entertainment likely to draw a crowd have been shut down by order for the time being, at least. Only the churches have held their customary services.

People Grimly Determined

Thus war has come to Britain, to a people grimly determined to meet it and to see it through. The predominating sentiment, if any, is one of relief that the long period of suspense is over. Throughout the land the watchword now is: "Let's get on with it."

War became a reality yesterday morning just after the church bells had ceased ringing. It came in the shape of a sudden interruption of the regular radio program by an announcer:

"The Prime Minister will broadcast an important announcement to the nation."

Then came Mr. Chamberlain's well-known voice, quiet and sad but clear and firm:

"I am speaking to you from the Cabinet room at 10 Downing Street."

Then followed his terse narration of the course of events. That morning (it was actually at 9 o'clock, two hours earlier) the British Ambassador at Berlin had handed Foreign Minister Joachim von Ribbentrop a final note stating that unless the Germans had agreed by 11 o'clock to withdraw their troops from Poland, a "state of war would exist between us."

"I have to tell you now," continued Mr. Chamberlain in the same level tones, "that no such

Continued on Page Four

FIRST SHIP SUNK IN THE WAR

The Athenia, with 1,400 aboard, torpedoed off the Hebrides

Wired Photo—Times Wide World

List of the American Passengers Aboard the Torpedoed Athenia

Special to THE NEW YORK TIMES.

WASHINGTON, Monday, Sept. 4.—The list of American citizens who embarked on the liner Athenia in Liverpool follows; no addresses were given in the cable received at the State Department from Ambassador Joseph P. Kennedy:

Ralph Rufficau
Katheryn McGuire
Hasel Casserly
Charles Grant
Florence Malik
Edith Bridge
Harry Bridge
Robert Harris
Gustaf Petersen
Margaret Buchan
Laura Cattle
Mrs. Thomas Kerr
Kate Hinds
Herbert Spiegelberg
Mrs. Davis
Margaret McGuire
Elizabeth Wise
William Buchanan
Master Charles Grant
Bernice Jansen
Constance Bridge
Sarah Warenreich
John Hughes
Gertrude Reed
George Cattle
Thomas Kerr
Rhoda Thomas
William Hinds
J. Davis
William Peers
Lillian Peers
Charles Prince
Harold Etherington
Ellen Harrington
Jessie Forle
Francis Cooley
Charles Prince (two Charles Princes)
Geoffrey Etherington
R. Casey
George Keliher
Harry Trehearne
Ella Trehearne
Annie Word
Duncan Wood (Two Duncan Woods)
Ernest Ratcliffe
Faith Ratcliffe
Irene de Munn
Edward O'Connell
Aileen Philipsen
Mary Steinberg
Ralph Child
Peter Birchall
Duncan Wood
Ellin Ratcliffe
Donald Gifford
Jozef Karnowski
Dorris O'Connel
John Youngquist
Donald Edwards
John Lawrence
Tryphene Humphrey
Louise Horte
Mary, Dick and Edward Belton
Elsa Philipsen
Adolph Sadowski
John Harju
Charles Stork
Harold Ruggs
Adolph Leocha
Florence Dery
Wiktor Ponjola
Ethel Russell
William Bohn
Ada Bohn
Montgomery Evans
Franklin Dexter
Cathleen Schurr
Agnes Stappel
Lillian Eilstrap
Rose Churchill
Ellen Howland
Miarine Dexter
Maud Shearer
Alexander Sheshunoff
Cosby Eilstrap
Sarah Burdett
Yvette Pepin
Ena Logan
Herbert Bonn
Thomas Quine
Lulu Sweigard
Romona Allen
Gus Anderson
Eleanor Crowley
Harriet Tolley
Janet Elsen
Annie Quine
Carol Allen
Susan Allen

The following Americans boarded the Athenia at Glasgow, the American Consulate there reports:

James Boyle
Cathryn Brennan
Margaret Campbell
Elva Campbell
Agnes Craig
William Diller
Margaret Diller
Louis Diven
Mary Diven
Mary Dowie
Thomas Fielder
John Bernard
Margaret Ford
Cora Gilroy
Don Gilroy
Helen Hannah
Jan Hannah
Florence Hargreave
Selena Isaacs
Jeanette Jordan
Margaret Little
Harriet McFadzean
Mary McKellar
Alexander Nichol
Edith Nichol
Marion Nichol
Alice Tocklington
John Pringle
Lottie Tringle
Katherine Scott
Essie Mallery
William Mallery
Helen Stewart
Edgar Wilkes
Margaret Wilkes
Donald Wilkes
William Wilkes
Myrtle Barber
Barbara Bradfield
Joan Outhwaite
Alberta Wood
Lucile Lucas
Elizabeth Martin
Gertrude Martin
Ila Vincent
Michael Flynn
Alice Robinson
Robert Townsend
Bainbridge Hayden
Dirus Ekaube
Doris Elaine Kent
William Ralph Singleton
Margaret Moore
Sarah Bloom
Olive Bloom
Fred Tinney
Madeline Tinney
Charles Cotterman
Benson Price
Elizabeth Alton (two listed)
Louis Burns
Mary Burns
Harriette Jones
Joan Moffett
Elsie Moffett
Joseph MacDonald
Elmetta MacDonald
Harriet Roney
Wendell Sherk
Nicola Lubitsch
Henry Smith
Ellen Smith
Jeannette Smith
Caroline Stuart
Frieda Windmann
Matthew Brown
Mary Brown
Elizabeth Brown
James Curran
Isobel Bruce
Betsy Brown
Dorothy Fox
W. E. MacBain
Marjorie MacBain
Gus Anderson
Caroline Rice
William Bown
Ada Bown
Elizabeth Lewis
May Lewis
Donald Lewis
William Aitken
Anne Baker
Alma Bloom
Dorothy Feder
Martha Bonnet
William Brown
George Calder (Two listed)
Margaret Calder
Alice Chalmers
William Chalmers
Margaret Doggett
Eileen Duncombe

The names of the Americans who boarded the Athenia at Belfast could not be obtained up to 5 o'clock this morning.

News dispatches from Europe and the Far East are now virtually all subject to censorship.

HIT OFF HEBRIDES

Ship Bound for Canada Carried Some Children Among Americans

CAPITAL IS SHOCKED

President's Aide Notes Liner Had Refugees, Not Munitions

By The Associated Press.

BELFAST, Northern Ireland, Monday, Sept. 4.—All persons aboard the sunken British liner Athenia, except some killed by a German torpedo, were reported saved today.

An agent of the ship's owners here issued the report. He said all survivors had been picked up by other vessels.

By The Associated Press.

LONDON, Monday, Sept. 4.—The British Liner Athenia, with ~~246~~ United States citizens among her 1,400 passengers, was torpedoed and sunk 200 miles west of the Hebrides, the British Ministry of Information announced early today. [Washington reports said 292 Americans were aboard the Athenia.]

The United States Embassy, checking on the departures of Americans hurrying home in flight from the European war, said 101 boarded the ship at Liverpool and 145 at Glasgow. [Forty-six more Americans boarded the vessel at Belfast, Washington was informed.]

The Athenia sailed Saturday from Liverpool.

The British Ministry of Information said the 13,581-ton ship reported to the Admiralty she had been torpedoed 200 miles off the Hebrides, west of Northern Scotland.

The Ministry of Information said the last official information received by the Admiralty from the ship was that she was sinking "rapidly." Since there were no further advices, it was then assumed she had gone down.

[Stephen Early, secretary to President Roosevelt, said in Washington that official reports indicated the Athenia was carrying "mostly Canadians and some Americans."

["I'd like to point out," he said, according to The Associated Press, "that, according to official information, the ship had gone from Glasgow to Liverpool and was bound for Canada, bringing refugees.

["I point this out to show that there was no possibility, according to official information, that the ship was carrying any munitions or anything of that kind."]

292 Americans Were Aboard

WASHINGTON, Monday, Sept. 4 (AP).—Dispatches to the State Department indicated today that at least 246 [later news brought the figure to 292] Americans were aboard the liner Athenia, torpedoed in the North Atlantic.

White House Is Informed

Special to THE NEW YORK TIMES.

WASHINGTON, Monday, Sept. 4.—Information received here last night that the Cunard White Star liner Athenia had been torpedoed off the coast of Ireland while en route to the United States brought a prompt statement from the White House acknowledging receipt of the news and information from the State Department that it had received eighteen long-distance calls within a few minutes of a radio broadcast of the news. The calls appealed for information about relatives aboard.

The White House said that the vessel was bound from Glasgow and Liverpool to Montreal with a large group of Canadian passengers and with an undetermined number of Americans among them.

At 6 A. M., British Summer Time [1 A. M. in New York] Ambassador Joseph P. Kennedy cabled the State Department as follows:

"Admiralty unable as yet to indicate whether Athenia has sunk or rescue arrangements; 101 American citizens embarked on her at

Continued on Page Five

"All the News That's Fit to Print."

The New York Times.

LATE CITY EDITION
Generally fair and cooler today and tonight. Tomorrow fair with moderate temperature.
Temperatures Yesterday—Max., 84; Min., 64

Section 1

NEWS INDEX, PAGE 51, THIS SECTION

VOL. LXXXVIII....No. 29,821 — Entered as Second-Class Matter, Postoffice, New York, N. Y. — NEW YORK, SUNDAY, SEPTEMBER 17, 1939. — PPP — Including Rotogravure Picture, Magazine and Book Review. TEN CENTS | TWELVE CENTS Beyond 200 Miles Except in 7th and 8th Postal Zones.

SOVIET TROOPS MARCHED INTO POLAND AT 11 P. M.; NAZIS DEMAND WARSAW GIVE UP OR BE SHELLED; FIERCE BATTLE IS RAGING ON WESTERN FRONT

2 SENATORS BLAST EMBARGO REPEAL AS LEADING TO WAR

Clark, Disavowing Filibuster, Asks Prolonging of Session to Curb Rule by Decree

DEFENDS 'INSULATIONISTS'

Vandenberg Calls Favoring Any Belligerent 'Unneutral' and Urges 'Middle Ground'

By TURNER CATLEDGE
Special to THE NEW YORK TIMES.

WASHINGTON, Sept. 16—The fight over lifting the embargo against export of arms was intensified further today as Senators Clark of Missouri and Vandenberg of Michigan aimed new blasts at the Administration's program to alter the Neutrality Act at the special session of Congress.

Following upon the radio address last night of Colonel Lindbergh, the Senators, a Democrat and a Republican, took up Senator Borah's thesis—that the issue was more of intervention or non-intervention in the affairs of Europe than of mere methods of neutrality.

Senator Clark's remarks were contained in a statement telegraphed from his home in St. Louis for release at the capital.

Senator Vandenberg made his plea to his own constituents at a Republican rally at Grand Rapids, telling them not to allow their minds to be taken off domestic problems by the agitation over the conflict abroad.

In his address, Senator Vandenberg declared that the arms embargo should not be repealed by a revision of the present neutrality laws.

"In my view," he said, "it is not 'neutrality' for us to change that code today to make it fit some favored belligerent, no matter what our sympathies. In my view, that is unneutrality. It is trying to be half in this war and yet to safely stay out. I do not believe there can be any such middle ground."

Clark for Check on Executive

"I welcome the President's call for an extraordinary session of the Congress," Senator Clark said in his statement.

"Since the President has by proclamation declared the existence of a national emergency, it is the duty of the Congress to remain in session and share fully in the responsibilities of government during the duration of the national emergency. This is and should remain a government by law and not by decree.

"So far as the Neutrality Act is concerned there has been no suggestion of a 'filibuster' on the part of any of the Senators who oppose the emasculation and perversion of the whole neutrality policy heretofore adopted by the Congress and approved by the President by the repeal of the provision for a mandatory arms embargo.

"The suggestions of a 'filibuster' have been put out in inspired articles from Washington and Hyde Park designed to promote gag rule and stifle free and fair discussion of perhaps the most important question of public policy which has confronted the Congress of the United States since that tragic day in 1917 when the decision was made to throw the United States into the World War.

Sees Decision on "Taking Sides"

"We are now to determine whether or not we have learned anything from that awful experience by deciding whether by repealing the arms embargo we shall again deliberately set our feet on the path which inevitably leads to war.

"Those of us who oppose the abandonment of a bona fide neutrality policy stand precisely where President Roosevelt stood in his eloquent Chautauqua speech in 1936 when he was a candidate for reelection when he said in defending the law containing a mandatory arms embargo:

"'We are not isolationists except in so far as we seek to isolate ourselves completely from war.'

"My friend, Senator Elbert Thomas of Utah, one of the leading revisionists, let the cat out of the bag the other night as to the real posi-

Continued on Page Thirty-seven

White House Gate Closed To Keep Out Trysting Cars

Special to THE NEW YORK TIMES.

WASHINGTON, Sept. 16—Neither wars nor rumors of wars, but the popularity among motorists of the White House grounds on Summer nights is the reason one of the iron gates on Pennsylvania Avenue is now closed after dark and a guard stands at the other, day and night, to tell all comers that only those having appointments may park their cars inside.

People have been driving in, especially at night, and parking there, Mrs. Roosevelt revealed at a press conference today. And though it is a pleasant place to sit, under the trees, the White House driveway is really not a good trysting place, she said. Too many motorists were attracted by it.

As the number of parking parties increased, so did the problem of keeping the driveway open and free of obstruction. Now an extra all-night guard is on duty, from dark to dawn, to keep it so.

LATIN TRIP FOR FAIR PLEDGED BY MAYOR

'If They Want Me to Go, I Am Going,' He Says—Crowds Set New Record for Saturday

By SIDNEY M. SHALETT

Clarifying his position as the possible World's Fair ambassador of good-will to South America, Mayor La Guardia, in two statements yesterday, agreed that he would go "if necessary," but hinted that the trip might not take place for at least several months.

There was even a third statement issued by Stanley Howe, the Mayor's executive secretary, to settle the "incident" created Friday night when Grover A. Whalen, Fair president, announced in the Mayor's absence that Mr. La Guardia would fly "at an early date" to sell the United States' neighbors to the South on the idea of participating in the 1940 exposition.

As Mr. Howe viewed it, the Mayor would like, with permission of the State Department, to make a trip both to sell South American nations on the 1940 Fair and to "unsell" them on any totalitarian ideas that may have crept in.

These matters yesterday were exceedingly important to the administrators who run the Fair, but despite all the flurry about South American envoys and European participation the Fair itself was entertaining the biggest Saturday crowd in its history. From early morning on thousands of visitors streamed past the turnstiles, and early in the evening it became evident that a new record for a Saturday would be set.

The Mayor issued his first statement shortly after noon, after a hurried dash from the World's Fair City Hall to Hoboken to see Mr. Whalen off on the Statendam. The Fair president, who had made the announcement Friday in which the Mayor did not fully concur, was sailing for Europe as salesman for the 1940 Fair.

Boat Held Up for Mayor

Arriving at the dock only four minutes before sailing time, Mayor La Guardia induced the captain to hold up the boat until he could hurry aboard, have a word with Mr. Whalen and pose with him for a farewell picture. It was such an eleventh-hour affair that the last gangplank was partly dismantled and had to be made secure again before the Mayor and his retinue could leave the ship.

Then, on the pier, the Mayor gave out the following statement concerning his South American plans:

"There are a great many preliminaries. If it can do the Fair any good, and if these necessary preliminaries can be made, and if there is a real need, I'll go. But there is nothing definite yet."

Then he whisked off in his car. His next appearance, late in the afternoon, was at a ceremony of the United Spanish War Veterans in the Court of Peace at the Fair. There he was asked again if he would fly south, and this time he made it a little stronger.

"I'll do anything that is helpful and necessary for the World's Fair," the Mayor said. "If they want me to go, I am going. Of course, that requires a good deal of preliminary preparation and is al-

Continued on Page Forty-eight

6 U. S. SHIPS KEPT IN PORT AS SEAMEN HOLD OUT FOR PAY

Stalemate Results Over War Risk Insurance Demands—No Solution Seen Near

FRIED CALLS 12 SAILORS

Plans Inquiry on Tie-Up of American Trader—Owners Say Capital Must Act

American merchant shipping was badly hampered in New York harbor yesterday when the crews of six vessels refused to sail their ships, insisting on concrete concessions to their demands for extra compensation for entering European waters affected by the war.

With Federal agencies already overburdened by the unusual duties laid on them as a result of the war, confusion reigned on the waterfront, and at a late hour there appeared to be little chance of solution or compromise.

Two of the ships, one with passengers, were to have sailed Friday afternoon but their crews staged a sit-down strike after signing the ship's articles. In other cases, the men declined to sign the articles, leaving vessels with no manning force.

Fried Sends Out Summonses

On the United States liner American Trader, which was at the Chelsea piers of the company with passengers and cargo, twelve union men received summonses from the office of Captain George Fried, supervising inspector of the Bureau of Marine Inspection and Navigation.

The summons in each case was returnable immediately at 45 Broadway, but a representative of the National Maritime Union appeared in the men's stead and received an adjournment until 10 A. M. tomorrow, allowing the union time to obtain counsel for them.

Captain Fried had boarded the American Trader on Friday night and had been at the piers yesterday, but he declined to reveal the nature of the charges to be filed against the men, saying that the public would be admitted to the hearing.

He also declined to explain why only twelve of the seventy seamen had been called, or to say how they had been selected.

Will Set Up Special Board

He planned to constitute a "C" board to preside at the inquiry, headed by himself and including Captain Karl Nielsen and Howard C. Bridges, inspectors of the district. The "C" board would sit in the same manner as a grand jury, to determine if charges should be filed against the men.

The National Maritime Union, which has disclaimed responsibility for the strike on Friday, issued a

Continued on Page Forty-six

Blast Shakes Offices Of Reich Air Ministry

By The Associated Press.

BERLIN, Sunday, Sept. 17—An explosion occurred in the Air Ministry headquarters on the Leipzigerstrasse early today. Firemen and police closed off an extensive area around the building.

The Propaganda Ministry acknowledged that there had been an explosion, but no immediate explanation was forthcoming. It was reported that no one had been injured. There was shattered glass in the street, but the extent of the damage was not immediately apparent.

The Propaganda Ministry refused to speculate whether the blast might have been caused by a bomb. It said merely that an investigation was under way.

"The persons responsible are being sought energetically," a Propaganda Ministry spokesman declared.

The blast came during the regular nightly blackout and the streets were deserted.

TOKYO MINIMIZES SOVIET AGREEMENT

Denies Non-Aggression Pact Is to Follow Truce—Policy on Russia Is Held Unchanged

By HUGH BYAS
Wireless to THE NEW YORK TIMES.

TOKYO, Sept. 16—Japanese officials emphatically deny and characterize as "absolute nonsense" reports that a non-aggression pact with Russia is under negotiation or is contemplated. They also deny that Germany had a hand in arranging the armistice on the Manchukuoan-Mongolian border or that German influence could induce Japan to change her policy toward the Soviet.

The Japanese Government regards the armistice as a means of terminating the border fighting. It is part of the new Cabinet's policy for a speedy settlement of the China "incident." Not only does it assure peace on the Mongolian frontier, it is asserted, but it shows Generalissimo Chiang Kai-shek that he cannot expect further diversions in the north, and it helps demonstrate that the Soviet has lost faith in the possibility of a Chinese victory.

According to Domei, the Japanese news agency, the armistice is a definite help toward a settlement in China by enabling Japan to devote her entire energy to the impending peace moves. When asked what Russia receives, the Japanese answer is that she wins a cessation of potentially serious disputes with Japan and possibly certain territorial concessions during the frontier adjustment.

On the broader question whether the armistice is a first step toward a revolutionary realignment of world forces, officials suggest that the move is adequately explained

Continued on Page Thirty-two

Major Sports Yesterday

BASEBALL

The Yankees clinched their fourth consecutive American League pennant under Manager Joe McCarthy and equaled the record set by John McGraw's Giants of 1921 to 1924. It was the eleventh flag victory for the New Yorkers, who beat the Tigers at the Stadium, 8—5. The second-place Red Sox lost. In Cincinnati the Reds halted the Giants, 6—1, and maintained their lead of three and a half games over the victorious Cards.

GOLF

Marvin (Bud) Ward of Spokane defeated Ray Billows of Poughkeepsie, N. Y., 7 and 5, to win the national amateur championship on the North Shore Country Club links, Glenview, Ill. Ward is the first Pacific Coast golfer to take the title.

TENNIS

Welby Van Horn upset John Bromwich, 2—6, 4—6, 6—2, 6—4, 8—6, to gain the final of the national singles championship with Robert L. Riggs, who eliminated Joe Hunt, 6—1, 6—2, 4—6, 6—1. Miss Alice Marble and Miss Helen Jacobs entered the women's final.

HORSE RACING

Hash won the Edgemere Handicap at Aqueduct, where Merry Knight annexed the Junior Champion Stakes. At Chicago, Challedon captured the Hawthorne Gold Cup. Farndale took the Foxcatcher National Cup Steeplechase at Fair Hill, Md.

POLO

The Bostwick Field four beat Westbury, 9—8, in the first match of the national open tournament.

(Complete Details of These and Other Sports Events in Section 5.)

GERMANS SET BACK

Heavy Counter-Attacks Repulsed by the French Drive

NAZIS BLAST TOWNS

Gamelin Hits at Three Points in Saar Area, Hardest on Moselle

By G. H. ARCHAMBAULT
Wireless to THE NEW YORK TIMES.

PARIS, Sept. 16—The Germans are bringing up more and more troops on the western front, where the fighting grows fiercer daily. That is the salient point in the French headquarters communiqués today. This morning's bulletin, Communiqué 25, said:

"There was a restless night on numerous parts of the front. Enemy artillery was very active in the region south of Saarbruecken.

"Our troops made some progress east of the Moselle.

"A strong enemy counter-attack, following artillery preparation, was driven back in the region near the lower valley of the Nied River."

This evening Communiqué 26 announced:

"There was great activity on both sides on the part of artillery and of first-line troops on the entire front.

"The enemy is constantly reinforcing before us.

"At several points the enemy abandoned and destroyed several of his villages from which he retreated."

Battle West of Saarbruecken

The heaviest fighting at present is on that portion of the front running some twenty miles west of Saarbruecken. The object is the possession of observation points dominating not only the Saar Valley but also certain parts of the Westwall.

The specific purpose of the German attack near the River Nied, which is a tributary of the Saar, was to regain a number of observation points along the plateau from which the town of Saarlautern can be brought under the fire of French guns.

After artillery preparation the German infantry left its cover for a swift attack. The duration of this preparation, however, had sufficiently indicated its purpose. The French guns came into action as soon as the infantry got on the move and the attack was soon stopped. It is reported that the Germans employed a relatively large force for this attempt.

There is also heavy fighting for the establishment of the Saar bridgeheads. The possession of the banks of the river at divers points is important for the bringing up of heavy tanks.

That the Germans should be bringing up reinforcements continuously, as reported in the evening communiqué, may imply the intention of attempting stronger counter-attacks than any hitherto. It may even suggest an endeavor to wrest the initiative from the French. It is manifest that important developments may be expected soon.

Three Main Sectors

As the second week of the war ends, the operations on the west front are clearly divided into three main sectors. These are, reading the map from the east to the west:

1. From the Rhine, in the vicinity of Lauterbourg to the highway from Zweibruecken to Bitche.

2. From this highway to a point on the Saar north of Forbach, taking in Saarbruecken, the industrial heart of the Saarland.

3. From this point west of Saarbruecken to the Moselle River in the vicinity of the village of Perl.

In each of these three sectors French troops are operating on German soil.

At the beginning of the hostilities the eastern sector was the most active, with the French occupation of the forest called Bienwald, in order to gain ground at the point where the Maginot Line and the Westwall describe a right angle before following the Rhine Valley southward. In that valley itself scarcely a shot has been fired as yet; the garrisons of the respective fortified lines are merely sentries.

Continued on Page Forty-two

The International Situation

A Poland already tottering under the blows of the German military machine was subjected to another invasion last night, this time by Soviet forces, according to an official announcement in Berlin.

It was declared that the Russian Government had informed the Polish Ambassador it was marching in "to protect its own interests and to protect the White Russian and Ukrainian minorities."

Nevertheless, Moscow said, Soviet neutrality is being maintained. Berlin said the action had German sanction. [Page 1.]

The German sweep in Poland was unabated. Kutno, Bialystok and Przemysl fell. But at Warsaw the invaders were still encountering furious resistance. As a result they issued an ultimatum to the Poles to quit Warsaw within twelve hours on pain of bombardment of the entire city. [Page 1.] The effects of previous bombardments and air raids on the Polish countryside were described by a correspondent, who found towns in flames, inhabitants wailing over ruins of homes and chaos everywhere. [Page 28.] In general, military experts found that Poland's despair was undermining her resistance. [Page 40.]

Meanwhile, the "Battle of the Saar," snowballing daily into a major engagement, was being fiercely fought. The French reported that after a heavy artillery exchange the Germans had destroyed and abandoned several villages and had retreated. [Page 1.]

In the face of continued harrying of commerce by German submarines, which yesterday sank two more British ships, the Admiralty set up convoy service for merchant vessels. [Page 1.] Three South American countries, Argentina, Brazil and Uruguay, fearing violations of their neutrality by belligerent warships, were negotiating to pool their naval strength for protection of the entire coast of South America. [Page 31.]

The full significance of the Russo-Japanese truce on the Mongolian border was still unclear, as was Germany's role, if any, in its conclusion. Japanese officials emphatically denied reports that a non-aggression pact with Russia would follow, insisting that Japan remained an anti-Comintern power. [Page 1.] But one result of the new truce emerged in the form of reports that the Japanese, freed of fears for the Manchukuoan border, had launched a general offensive in Central China. [Page 30.] In London news of the truce was received with equanimity; statesmen there had become accustomed to surprises from Moscow. [Page 34.]

In this country Senators Clark and Vandenberg rallied to Senator Borah's fight against alteration of the Neutrality Act. [Page 1.]

MERCHANT CONVOYS SET UP BY BRITAIN

Guard Pressed After Her Loss of 21 Ships—Three More Vessels Are Victims

By The Associated Press.

LONDON, Sept. 16—The British Admiralty pressed into service tonight convoys for merchant shipping after it was disclosed authoritatively that enemy craft had sunk twenty-one British ships, involving a tonnage of 122,843, during the first two weeks of the war.

The use of convoys was not instituted by the British in the last war until 1917.

While slim cruisers and racing destroyers roved and struck on the shipping lanes, planes of the Royal Aircraft patrolled the skies around the United Kingdom in redoubled efforts to halt the persistent shipping losses to U-boats or mines.

Despite the casualties, naval quarters expressed optimism about the situation at sea.

Understatement in Reports

Increasing patrol activity and the Admiralty's cautious announcement that "a number of U-boats have been destroyed," was taken by naval authorities to tell a story of far greater successes than the guarded statement indicated.

Britain placed responsibility on Germany for the sinking last night of the 8,000-ton Belgian motorship Alex Van Opstal in the Channel off Weymouth, asserting she was sunk by mine or torpedo in violation of international law.

[In Brussels, Belgian authorities refrained from lodging a protest, pending a report from the master of the vessel as to whether she was sunk by torpedo or mine.]

A British communiqué said there were no British mines in the neighborhood, that Germany had sent no notification of German mines there and that attack without warning was in violation of the submarine protocol to which Germany subscribed.

[The Alex Van Opstal left New York on Sept. 6 for Antwerp with eight passengers and 3,400 tons of grain.]

The latest ship to be added to the list of British losses was the tanker Cheyenne of the Anglo-American Oil Company, which was announced officially to have been attacked and sunk by a submarine off the southwest coast of Ireland.

[The Anglo-American Oil Company, according to Poor's Man-

Continued on Page Forty-six

Dispatches from Europe and the Far East are now subject to censorship.

ORDER GIVES POLES 12 HOURS TO LEAVE

Nazis Say Citizens Will Have to Take 'Consequences' Today Since Army Is Defiant

Wireless to THE NEW YORK TIMES.

BERLIN, Sept. 16—The German Army High Command has given Warsaw until 3:10 o'clock tomorrow morning to decide whether or not to surrender. In the event the Polish capital does not give in to the German troops now surrounding it on all sides, the city will "take the full consequences of being regarded as a military sector."

[The German High Command reported at 4:30 o'clock this morning, an hour and twenty minutes after expiration of the ultimatum, that its army in the field had had no word from the Polish authorities, The Associated Press reported.]

The notice was served in the form of a double ultimatum: First, a military ultimatum expiring at 3:10 o'clock tomorrow morning, and the second ultimatum to the civilian population to leave the city by 3:10 o'clock in the afternoon [10:10 A. M. New York time].

A German officer entered Warsaw with a white flag at 8 o'clock this morning to demand the surrender of the city. According to the report of the official German News Agency the commandant of the city refused to see him or accept a written demand for the surrender of the city.

The officer, it is stated, thereupon returned to the German lines and this afternoon a squadron of the German air force distributed the pamphlets.

Nazis Cite Law Violation

Warsaw already has been subjected to a partial bombardment by the German air force and artillery but, according to German report, only objects of a military nature have been fired upon. Preparations for defense by the civilian population, however, are regarded by the German High Command as being a "violation of international law depriving the city of its character as an open city." German shells and German bombs will crash into the city tomorrow afternoon unless it is "surrendered without resistance" by dawn tomorrow.

"The patience of the German Army is now exhausted," states the official news agency. "The German Army is no longer willing to observe inactively these conditions which are a slap in the face of all international law, but is determined to put an end to these activities of the Warsaw power holders which, though of no importance whatever in a military sense, constitute a

Continued on Page Forty

FRONTIER CROSSED

Reich Ministry States That Invasion Has German Sanction

ENVOY IS NOTIFIED

Soviet Pleads Need to Aid Minorities, but Claims Neutrality

By The United Press.

BERLIN, Sunday, Sept. 17—A spokesman for the Propaganda Ministry announced that Russian troops had marched into Poland today at 4 A. M. Moscow time [11 P. M. Saturday in New York].

The Soviet troops entered Poland with the full knowledge and approval of the German Government, he said.

The spokesman made his statement after D. N. B., the official German news agency, had reported from Moscow that the Soviet Government had informed the Polish Ambassador, Dr. Waclaw Grzybowski, Saturday night that Soviet troops were about to cross the frontier.

The agency said that the note handed to the Ambassador informed the Poles that the troops would cross the frontier along its entire length from Polosk in the north to Kamenets-Podolski in the south "in order to protect our own interests and to protect the White Russian and Ukrainian minorities."

The Soviet Government, the agency said, told the Poles that it maintained its neutrality despite its military action, but added that its treaties with the Polish State could be regarded as canceled because the Polish State could no longer be regarded as existing.

To Occupy Two Districts

MOSCOW, Sunday, Sept. 17 (AP).—Soviet Russia has decided to send her army across the Polish frontier today and to occupy the Polish Ukraine and White Russia.

The government was understood unofficially to have sent a note last night to the Polish Ambassador here saying that the Red Army would enter the Polish Ukraine and White Russia today from Polosk to Kamanets-Podolski.

Copies of this note were said also to have been sent simultaneously to all diplomatic representatives here saying the action was taken because Poland no longer exists. It was said to have declared there no longer is a Polish Government because its whereabouts are unknown.

The note was said to have declared that "the Soviet Union will retain neutrality, but feels it necessary to protect White Russian and Ukrainian minorities in Poland and will do everything to keep peace and order."

[Poland not only has a non-aggression pact with Russia but in mutual assistance treaties by which the British and French are pledged to aid Poland in defense of her independence against any aggression. Polish invocation of this treaty brought Great Britain and France into war against Germany on Sept. 3, two days after a German army invaded Western Poland.]

Covers Entire Frontier

The scene of the Russian action would extend across the whole of Russia's Polish frontier.

It would increase considerably Russia's frontier with Rumania. Rumania holds Bessarabia, wrested from Russia after the World War, and the Soviet Government never has relinquished its claims on this territory.

Russia's decision to act came after she had sent a vast number of men to her western frontier in semi-mobilization and had followed with her "peace" with Japan.

It was believed here that the Polish Embassy in Moscow would leave and that, possibly, the British also would leave, since they are allies of Poland.

Man Power Is Threat

If necessary, Soviet Russia could throw nearly 2,000,000 trained soldiers against the struggling Poles.

The official Communist party newspaper Pravda this Spring estimated Russia's peacetime army at 1,800,000. This estimate did not include the millions of semi-trained

Continued on Page Thirty-six

"All the News That's Fit to Print."

The New York Times.

LATE CITY EDITION
Generally fair and warmer today. Tomorrow cloudy, continued warm, showers in afternoon or night.
Temperatures Yesterday—Max., 66; Min., 55

Copyright, 1939, by The New York Times Company.

VOL. LXXXIX...No. 29,832. Entered as Second-Class Matter, Postoffice, New York, N. Y. NEW YORK, THURSDAY, SEPTEMBER 28, 1939. PP THREE CENTS NEW YORK CITY and Vicinity | FOUR CENTS Elsewhere Except in 7th and 8th Postal Zones.

ESTONIA REPORTED READY TO YIELD AS RUSSO-GERMAN PARLEYS BEGIN; WARSAW, A SHAMBLES, SURRENDERS

PITTMAN PREDICTS 'CASH-CARRY' LAW; SUPPORT GROWING

Senator Says on Radio Plan to Repeal Embargo Is Surer Way to Avoid War

SPEEDY ACTION IS CERTAIN

O'Mahoney Approves the New Neutrality Program—Foes Arrange for Mass Meeting

By TURNER CATLEDGE
Special to THE NEW YORK TIMES.

WASHINGTON, Sept. 27—A plea to the country to study closely the new neutrality resolution, to see if it is not in fact a stronger guarantee that America will not be involved in the European war than the present arms embargo, was broadcast tonight by Senator Pittman on the eve of the Foreign Relations Committee's formal consideration of the measure.

The Senator, who is chairman of the committee, coupled with his plea a prediction that the new resolution, repealing the embargo on arms and munitions and substituting a mandatory "cash-and-carry" system for all commerce between the United States and warring nations, would become law. He spoke over a network of the National Broadcasting Company.

Mr. Pittman's forecast as to the outcome was being adopted by more and more observers in Washington with each new addition to the "paper" majority which the Administration has claimed for embargo repeal from the start. The prediction was made on all sides tonight, even among opponents of repeal, that the resolution would be reported favorably by the Foreign Relations Committee tomorrow or Friday and that debate would start in the Senate early next week.

Opponents Keep On Fighting

In the face of appeals and predictions of the Administration forces, opponents of the resolution continued to insist that they would win in their efforts to retain the arms embargo, maintaining that the issue was at bottom one of peace or intervention by the United States.

Arrangements were completed tonight for a mass meeting of pro-embargo forces to be held Friday night at the Belasco Theatre, under the auspices of various peace and religious societies. Speakers scheduled for the meeting, described as "America's Town Meeting Against War," are Senators Capper of Kansas, Clark of Missouri and Nye of North Dakota; the Rev. Ernest Fremont Tittle of Chicago; Norman Thomas, former Socialist candidate for President; John T. Flynn, economist, and Roland Hayes, Negro concert singer.

Among the sponsors of the meeting are the Women's International League for Peace and Freedom, the National Council for Prevention of War, the Fellowship of Reconciliation, the War Resisters League, the Keep America Out of War Congress, the Youth Committee Against War, World Peace Ways, the World Peace Commission of the Methodist Church and the Church of the Brethren.

Heavier Guard to Capitol

Meanwhile arrangements for a heavier guard at the Capitol were made today after a conference between Kenneth Romney, sergeant at arms of the House; Chesley Jurney, sergeant at arms of the Senate; J. Edgar Hoover, head of the Federal Bureau of Investigation, and Colonel E. W. Starling, head of the White House Secret Service detail.

This was another step in a movement growing quite general in Washington for extra precautions around government buildings. This already has meant the closing of the White House grounds to visitors. Special restrictions also will be invoked governing admissions to the galleries when the Senate starts debate on the neutrality resolution.

Senator Pittman contended in his radio address that many of the petitions and communications which had deluged members of the Senate against repeal of the embargo demonstrated that they were based upon ignorance of the intent of Congress or were the result of "vicious organized foreign propaganda."

Plans for Permanent Law

He emphasized that the proposed resolution did not repeal all neutrality legislation, but asserted that on the contrary it vitally strengthened the neutrality legislation.

The Senator took up each section of the resolution, asserting that it was broader, deeper and more definite than the provisions of present law. The major intent of the authors, he said was to leave as little as possible to the discretion of the President and write a law

Continued on Page Ten

Total of Idle in U. S. Lowest Since End of '37

A 4.3 per cent decline during August brought national unemployment to the lowest point since December, 1937, according to statistics made public yesterday by the National Industrial Conference Board. The number of jobless persons dropped from 9,852,000 in July to 9,424,000 last month, a reduction of 428,000.

Total employment in the United States rose from a July figure of 44,782,000 to 45,263,000 in August. Agriculture and manufacturing showed the greatest advances, with more than 200,000 additional employes recorded in each field.

The government's emergency labor force declined to 2,169,000 workers, a drop of 16.6 per cent from July. This was the sixth consecutive monthly cut in the emergency work force, and brought the total to the lowest point in twenty months.

BERGDOLL HID IN U. S. 7 YEARS, HE SWEARS

Returned Twice While Nation Thought He Was in Reich—Got 'Pot of Gold'

While the army, G-men and indignant patriots believed Grover Cleveland Bergdoll was a fugitive in Germany for nineteen years, the World War draft evader slipped back into this country twice and led a shadowy existence in his Philadelphia mansion for seven years, according to his story yesterday before a general court-martial.

The long, bizarre story of the Philadelphia millionaire, whose escapades stirred a storm of notoriety around his name and family and provoked a string of prosecutions and a Congressional investigation, was further enriched as Bergdoll told a variation of his pot-of-gold story.

Bergdoll was on his way to Maryland hills to dig up his pot of gold, with permission of the War Department, when he broke away from two sergeants and fled to Germany in 1920. But yesterday he said the $150,000 "pot" was sealed in concrete, right in his own home. He came back for it in the depression year, 1929, and stayed for four years. Then he returned again in 1935 and stayed until last October, he said.

The faces of the thirteen officers of the military court seemed to freeze as Bergdoll admitted passport irregularities, false statements to consular agents and fictitious names to dupe immigration officials.

Loses First Bout With Law

Bergdoll lost his first bout with military law when the court, with Brig. Gen. Irving J. Phillipson as president, refused to mitigate the first charge from "desertion in time of war" to "desertion in time of peace." This was important, inasmuch as the three-year statute of limitation applies to the peacetime offense. No time lapse in prosecution can invalidate a charge of wartime desertion.

It became apparent as the trial moved on, with Bergdoll's aged mother and other relatives as witnesses, that his testimony of clandestine sojourns in his native land was intended to pry Bergdoll loose from the military authorities by virtue of the time question.

Harry Weinberger, the prisoner's lawyer, asserted that a three-year limit applied to the desertion charge and two years to escape. When he was overruled he nevertheless pressed the question in the hope that a military reviewing authority might later decide otherwise. In that case Bergdoll's presence in this country, within reach of the authorities, would tend to make the statute of limitation applicable.

It was understood, however, that the military prosecutors will contend that even if Bergdoll returned he did so surreptitiously to outwit the authorities. Thus the charges would stand.

May Get Six Years More

Bergdoll is now serving the remainder of the five-year prison term imposed for desertion by a court-martial in 1920, three months before he escaped. For the new charge of desertion and escape in conspiracy he may get six years more.

Last evening, as the first session of the trial ended in the Y. M. C. A. gymnasium on Governors Island, a warrant was being prepared for the arrest of Bergdoll's brother, Erwin Bergdoll, who also is a convicted draft dodger. The warrant was to be based on his alleged evasion of subpoena servers seeking him as a witness.

Bergdoll, who returned to this country on May 25 finally to "face the music," took the stand at noon and within a few minutes told his first sensation—that he came back in June, 1929. The ship was the Duchess of Bedford out of Liverpool, and Bergdoll used the name and passport of Joseph Amann, porter of his hotel in Germany.

He landed in Montreal, said the

Continued on Page Eighteen

DEMOCRATS VOTE BENCH NOMINATION TO JUDGE LEHMAN

State Committee in Resolution Voices Hope for Nonpartisan Choice for Appeals Chief

LABOR TO ACT SATURDAY

Endorsement by Republicans Now Seen Likely—Jurist's Record Is Praised

Acting under authority delegated by the last State Convention of the party, the Democratic State Committee yesterday nominated Irving Lehman, senior Associate Judge of the Court of Appeals, for chief judge of that court. The meeting was held at the National Democratic Club.

Postmaster General James A. Farley, who presided as chairman of the committee, expressed the hope that the other major parties would endorse Judge Lehman.

The State Committee of the American Labor party will meet Saturday at the Hotel Commodore and endorse Judge Lehman. Whether the Republican State Committee at its meeting at the Hotel Ten Eyck in Albany next Tuesday will do so is uncertain.

Republican Action Awaited

A few days ago it seemed likely that the Republican committee would nominate a Republican and Supreme Court Justice Edmund H. Lewis of Syracuse was mentioned as a probability. Word has been received here that Justice Lewis does not wish the nomination, and the up-State pressure for the nomination of a Republican was said to have been reduced considerably.

The sentiment of up-State lawyers is reported to be for the endorsement of Judge Lehman by the Republican State Committee.

Judge Lehman's nomination for Chief Judge has been urged by the State Bar Association, the Association of the Bar of the City of New York, the New York County Lawyers Association and the Federation of Bar Associations of Western New York. Belief was expressed by Republican leaders here that the chances favored the endorsement of Judge Lehman by the Republican committee.

Nominating Resolution

Judge Lehman was placed in nomination by Howard Wilbur of Catskill, who offered the following resolution:

Whereas we note Judge Irving Lehman has served the people of the State of New York as a judge for thirty-one years since his first election to the Supreme Court in 1908.

Judge Lehman has long been recognized as one of the ablest, most conscientious and fairest judges in the history of our State judiciary. His high character and knowledge of the law, his broad vision, his independence and his unflagging devotion to duty have often been commended by bench and bar. He has received the un-

Continued on Page Nineteen

Report Thaelmann Freed To Attest Nazi-Soviet Tie

By The Associated Press.

BERLIN, Sept. 27—An unofficial but trustworthy source said tonight that Ernst Thaelmann, former Communist chieftain in Germany, and others associated with him had been released from prisons and concentration camps as a result of the new-found German-Soviet Russian cooperation.

Likewise, placards and books attacking communism have been removed from public view.

Herr Thaelmann, twice a candidate for President of Germany, was arrested March 3, 1933, slightly more than a month after Adolf Hitler, whom he bitterly opposed, became Chancellor.

No formal charges were ever placed against him. As the months passed without any formal accusation, Dr. Hans Frank, Reich Justice Commissioner, indicated it still would be a long time before "we can have the case fully ready for court."

In his first campaign for President in 1925 Herr Thaelmann, who boasted that he was once a hobo in the United States, placed fourth.

MEDIATION BY U. S. SUGGESTED IN CHINA

Basis for Peace Would Be the Return to 9-Power Treaty, Says Foreign Minister

Copyright, 1939, by United Press

CHUNGKING, China, Sept. 27—Chinese Foreign Minister Wang Chung-hui, in an interview today, said emphatically that the National Government would continue resistance against Japan until "final victory," but suggested that the United States, if that country were willing to act as mediator, was in a favorable position to bring the undeclared Chinese-Japanese war to an early end.

The Foreign Minister outlined the basis on which an honorable peace was possible. He said that China's foreign policy was not fettered by the events in Europe or elsewhere and added:

"Chinese policy is based on treaties, principally the Nine-Power Treaty. [That treaty is designed to protect the rights of foreign nations in China and China's territorial integrity.]

"The first point of our policy is the enforcement of these treaties for the preservation of our independence and integrity.

"Secondly, we favor economic cooperation with all friendly nations and this will apply to Japan as soon

Continued on Page Three

Pope Said to Seek Peace and a Free Poland, Protected Against Communism and Atheism

By Telephone to THE NEW YORK TIMES.

ROME, Sept. 27—Pope Pius has been working diplomatically through neutral States to get Britain and France to agree to a peace conference that would end with the creation of a Polish buffer State on ethnic lines, it is reported here.

This report has been current since last Friday but has not been confirmed. Your correspondent has received it from three different sources. Today an Italian correspondent repeats it from Berlin, so there seems to be something in it.

It is said the Pontiff feels that the great menace to Christian civilization comes from Russia and her recent eruption into Central Europe and that all States, including Germany, ought to get together to prevent the spread of communism and the atheism that accompanies it.

At the same time the Pope feels that anything is better than a continuation of the war, particularly as the worst effects of it are yet to be felt. Consequently, say these reports, he would be willing to accept, although not to condone, Germany's conquest of Poland if a settlement were arranged that would guarantee Europe a lasting peace and the Polish Catholics a State of their own which protected them from communism and the neo-paganism of Germany.

The diplomatic manoeuvre involved would be a delicate one since it presupposes the possibility of separating Germany and Russia. Otherwise, the Vatican would be ranged against Germany and Russia combined, which, in effect, would mean that it would be taking sides in the war. This is something the Pontiff has carefully avoided doing.

It should be noted that this supposed proposal by the Pope parallels Premier Mussolini's peace move. He has suggested a cessation of hostilities in acceptance of the German conquest and, indirectly, the formation of a purely Polish State.

It has not been suggested, however, that the Premier has been taking advice from the Vatican, for the Italian line of policy has been consistent in that regard ever since the war started and even before. Behind that openly declared policy there has been and still is intense diplomatic activity by the Italian Government to bring pressure on Britain and France, which is what the Pope is supposed to be doing.

If Premier Mussolini is really being backed by the Pontiff it would help to explain Rome's hopes that the British and French will yield. It also gives a clue to the extent of the pressure to which London and Paris are being subjected.

One thing does seem certain: that the Vatican is forming an organization to give religious aid to prisoners and probably to handle mail for them. Later there may be a supplementary organization to arrange for the exchange of prisoners.

This has been foreshadowed for several weeks. It is understood that the Vatican is almost ready to put the plan into operation. Similar work was done by the Vatican dur-

Continued on Page Five

20-DAY SIEGE ENDS

Polish Defenders Yield Last Stronghold to Nazi Invaders

3,000 SLAIN IN 24 HOURS

Blazing Capital Faced Famine and Pestilence—Occupation Is Set for Tomorrow

By The United Press.

BUDAPEST, Hungary, Sept. 27—The city of Warsaw surrendered unconditionally tonight, the German High Command announced, after twenty days of siege that saw the Polish capital bombed and burned "into an unspeakable inferno" with thousands of civilian dead.

Complete destruction of at least half of the once magnificent city on the Vistula, exhaustion of its defenders' ammunition, starvation and pestilence brought capitulation long after Polish resistance had been virtually wiped out in the rest of the nation.

For days the city had stood alone in defiance of the German conquest from the West and the Soviet Russian invasion from the East, fighting off German troops and tanks in the outskirts in hand-to-hand fighting while German long-range guns and bombing planes systematically wrecked the capital.

500 Fires Sweep City

In the last twenty-four hours of Warsaw's defense more than 3,000 persons, mostly women and children, were reported to have been killed. The Polish Transcontinental Press said 500 fires were sweeping what had been magnificent buildings, parks and homes.

The announcement of Warsaw's unconditional surrender was made by the German High Command in Berlin, but Polish radio dispatches confirmed the capitulation. The Berlin radio announced the surrender at 8:10 P. M. [2:10 P. M. New York time], then struck up "Deutschland ueber Alles" and the "Horst Wessel Lied."

The German High Command said actual surrender of the city to the German forces encircling it on all sides—in some places they have been within four miles of the center of the city for four days—probably would occur Friday.

The Germans estimated that 100,000 ragged and weary Polish troops of the Warsaw garrison would surrender and hand over their arms along with the civil administration headed by Mayor Stefan Starzynski, who has come to be known as "Stefan the Stubborn" because of his rejection of every German ultimatum during the twenty days of siege.

Formal Surrender Delayed

The German High Command's communiqué, announcing the end of what even the Germans admit was a heroic defense, said:

"The High Command announces that Warsaw has capitulated unconditionally. The formal surrender of the city to the German High Command is expected to occur on Sept. 29. The military garrison consists, according to present estimates, of more than 100,000 men."

Polish refugees here were fearful of the fate of Mayor Starzynski, assailed by the Nazis because he rallied men and women civilians to take up arms and beat off the Germans in the suburbs.

After agreeing to negotiate the city's surrender with the Germans, the Warsaw defenders designated their commander to negotiate with General Johannes Blaskowitz of the German Army on the terms.

The German radio, describing the Nazi decision of last Friday to bomb and shell Warsaw into submission after rejection of repeated German ultimatums, insisted that Warsaw had been respected as an open city as long as possible.

Poles Proposed Surrender

"But Warsaw was transformed into a fortress by measures of the Polish commander, who restored the old forts and armed part of the civilian population," the Berlin radio said.

"Our attack yesterday brought into German hands the first line of defense north of the city and the second line in the south and as a result of these attacks the Polish commander today offered to surrender the city and garrison to the German Commander in Chief."

Although surrounded, Warsaw held out longer against the Ger-

Continued on Page Six

The International Situation

A Russian ship was torpedoed off the Estonian coast yesterday and with it, possibly, Estonia's hopes of escaping Soviet domination. With Moscow's ominous announcement of the sinking, pressure on the little Baltic country was increased to a point where it was believed ready to yield to Russian demands. This development coincided with the arrival of Estonian Foreign Minister Selter and German Foreign Minister von Ribbentrop in Moscow. Herr von Ribbentrop conferred with Joseph Stalin for several hours. [Page 1.]

Just what the Moscow discussions were all about was still a matter of speculation, but Berlin argued that not only Russia and Italy but also Turkey were now siding with the Reich, warned that a Russo-German military alliance was possible and told the Allies to end the war "while there is still time." [Page 4.]

In Bucharest it was generally believed that Turkey had been lost to the Allies and that Russia and Germany were laying out spheres of influence. In Rome the Russian intrusion into the Balkans was found disturbing. [Page 4.] Paris thought the Moscow conversations might prove a turning point in Chancellor Hitler's course, leading to sensational peace offers or a check on German expansion eastward. [Page 7.]

Warsaw's twenty days of heroic resistance ended in unconditional surrender, resulting from death, devastation, disease and a shortage of food and ammunition. [Page 1.] In the east of Poland the Red Army, harassed by guerrillas, continued its march and occupied the entire Galician oil fields, but found wells had been dynamited. [Page 5.]

Hopes that in the final disposition of Poland a buffer State would be set up were attributed to Pope Pius, who was understood to be working to get Britain and France to agree to a peace conference. [Page 1.]

Comparative peace seemed to have descended on the Western Front, where positions remained unchanged, but German guns were dropping shells in the French rear areas around Wissembourg. [Page 2.]

At sea Germany made her first attempt to break the British blockade with airplanes. Twenty of them attacked a British squadron in the North Sea. According to Berlin, an aircraft carrier was "destroyed," a battleship was hit and all the planes returned safely. According to London, no British ship was hit, no casualties were suffered, one German flying boat was shot down, another was damaged and a third came down on the sea, where its occupants were captured. [Page 1.]

This British report was made before a House of Commons session that voted without protest a schedule of drastic wartime taxes that include a basic income levy of 37½ per cent. [Page 1.]

A controversial note was injected into the Pan-American meeting at Panama by a Chilean proposal that the American nations refuse to recognize as contraband anything except actual articles of war. Argentina and Uruguay favored merely refusing to recognize as contraband foodstuffs and clothing. United States support for the latter idea was indicated. [Page 9.]

BRITISH TAXED 37½% OF INCOME FOR WAR

Levy on $10 Weekly Earnings and Surtaxes Up to 80% Voted Without Protest

By FERDINAND KUHN Jr.
Special Cable to THE NEW YORK TIMES.

LONDON, Sept. 27—The staggering cost of fighting this war was brought home to the British people today by imposition of the highest income tax in history and by new charges of all kinds that may leave their mark on British economy for generations to come.

Even in the darkest days of the World War and in the financial crisis of 1931 there never was anything like the tax program that Sir John Simon, Chancellor of the Exchequer, coolly announced in the House of Commons today.

The income tax was boosted mercilessly to a new record of seven shillings six pence in the pound, a basic rate of 37.5 per cent, more than six times what the British taxpayer had to bear at the end of 1914. To soften the blow slightly, a lower rate of seven shillings, or 35 per cent, will be charged for the remaining six months of this fiscal year, but after next April 1 the full rate will be in force, and there is no guarantee that it will not go higher as the war drags on.

Exemptions Are Slashed

Exemptions were slashed all along the line so that a single man earning the equivalent of $10 a week was brought into the income-tax-paying class. At the other end of the scale the surtax was raised so steeply that a capitalist earning £100,000 a year must surrender four-fifths of his entire income to the government.

No Labor Cabinet bent on equalizing distribution of wealth would have dared submit such a budget; but even the higher income tax was not the whole story. A universal excess profits tax of 60 per cent was substituted for the existing tax that applied only to armament firms. Nothing was said today about a capital levy, but the Chancellor of the Exchequer warned that at the end of the war the government might move toward "conscription of wealth" by tapping unearned war profits, such as those produced by increase in real estate values.

The estate duty was raised by 10 per cent at one stroke to help pay for Great Britain's colossal expenditure of £2,000,000,000 in a single year. Finally, a whole series of in-

Continued on Page Eight

NAZI PLANES RAID THE BRITISH FLEET

One Shot Down, Says Churchill—Reich Claim of Hits on Warships Disputed

Wireless to THE NEW YORK TIMES.

LONDON, Sept. 27—Germany's first attempt to break the British blockade from the air has failed, Winston Churchill, First Lord of the Admiralty, told the House of Commons in a statement which indicated that a fast and well-armed battleship is still a match for a bomber.

[Berlin announced that a second British aircraft carrier had been "destroyed" and a British battleship crippled by a number of Nazi planes in what was described as "the first successful action of its kind in military history."]

Replying to the German claims that they had sunk a British aircraft carrier and successfully bombed several battleships in a North Sea battle, Mr. Churchill produced a radio message from Sir Charles Forbes, Commander-in-Chief of the Home Fleet, which read:

"Yesterday afternoon in the middle of the North Sea a squadron of British capital ships, together with an aircraft carrier, cruisers and destroyers, were attacked by about twenty German aircraft.

"No British ship was hit and no British casualties were incurred. One German flying boat was shot down and another is reported to be badly damaged."

House Cheers Statement

The First Lord of the Admiralty, who has been sweeping gloom out of the House with his eloquent and confident statements on naval warfare, read this radiogram with ill-concealed delight. When he had finished he looked up and smiled broadly. The House roared.

When they quieted down Mr. Churchill, who never fails to hold back a little information for a rebound, said:

"I might have added that another German aircraft came down in the North Sea. We sent a destroyer to collect her, and her crew of four have been brought in as prisoners."

Mr. Churchill also entered the dis-

Continued on Page Six

Dispatches from Europe and the Far East are subject to censorship.

SOVIET SHIP IS SUNK

Moscow Reports Vessel Torpedoed Off the Estonian Coast

SHARP DEMANDS EXPECTED

Ribbentrop Talks With Stalin on Questions Relating to Developments in Poland

By G. E. R. GEDYE
Wireless to THE NEW YORK TIMES.

MOSCOW, Thursday, Sept. 28—Ominous news of the sinking of a Soviet steamer was issued here last night. At 6 P. M. yesterday, it was stated officially, a submarine of unidentified nationality torpedoed and sank the Soviet steamer Metallist, 968 tons, in Narva Bay, off the coast of Estonia.

A Soviet naval patrol vessel in the neighborhood rescued nineteen members of the Metallist's crew; twenty-four others are missing, the statement said. This, following last night's hostile Soviet communiqué concerning Estonia, doubtless is a prelude to grave developments for the Baltic States.

The description "Narva Bay" may indicate Soviet territorial waters outside the town of Narva just south of the Gulf of Finland opposite the Estonian coastline.

Protests Soviet Flights

Later it was reported here that the Estonian Government had protested through its Foreign Minister, Karl Selter, who returned to Moscow yesterday, against the alleged violation of Estonian frontiers by Soviet airplanes and had denied all suggestions of connivance in the escape of a Polish submarine from Tallinn last week, but had nevertheless decided to yield to Soviet demands in view of the impossibility of obtaining any help in resisting any Soviet invasion.

While Lithuania was reported in the Soviet press to have decreased her military precautions, Latvian circles on the other hand were greatly alarmed by the hostile tone of Soviet references to Estonia. In view of the extremely short Estonian frontier any Soviet move against Estonia, the Latvians felt, would inevitably involve them.

It was thought possible yesterday that the Soviet demands on Estonia might not include actual occupation of Tallinn, but that the Soviets might content themselves with the installation of Soviet Army garrisons on certain Estonian islands commanding Tallinn, coupled with special privileges for the use of Tallinn as a port.

Joachim von Ribbentrop, German Foreign Minister, arrived in Moscow yesterday. The planes that brought him and his party were soon followed by another machine, from which Mr. Selter stepped. And during the day Premier and Foreign Minister Vyacheslaff Molotoff conferred with Shukru Saracoglu, Turkish Foreign Minister, also a guest here.

Von Ribbentrop Meets Stalin

In the small hours of this morning the Soviet Government issued a communiqué on Herr von Ribbentrop's visit—which was brief and unexpectedly noncommittal. Questions connected with developments in Poland, it stated, were discussed during a midnight interview. Count Friedrich Werner von der Schulenburg, German Ambassador to Moscow, and Alexander Shkhartseff, Soviet Ambassador to Berlin, were present at the conversations, which took place in the presence of Joseph Stalin. The conversations lasted more than two hours, the communiqué said. [The talk lasted four and one-half hours, an Associated Press dispatch from Moscow said.]

Nothing was announced concerning new agreements or a date for renewal of the conversations. It is assumed, of course, that they will be resumed later today.

Shigenori Togo, Japanese Ambassador, upon his own urgent demand, saw Mr. Molotoff Tuesday night. Nothing was revealed concerning the purpose or result of the interview, but Japanese here do not conceal their alarmed feeling that the visit of Herr von Ribbentrop may result in a full Russo-German military alliance, so it is safe to assume that Mr. Togo requested full information for his government concerning the object of this visit, of which the Japanese learned in advance only through a Soviet radio broadcast.

One curious thing about this visit

Continued on Page Four

"All the News That's Fit to Print."

The New York Times.

LATE CITY EDITION
Cloudy and warmer today, showers tonight or tomorrow; cooler tomorrow afternoon and night.
Temperatures Yesterday—Max., 74; Min., 58

VOL. LXXXIX...No. 29,833. Entered as Second-Class Matter, Postoffice, New York, N. Y. NEW YORK, FRIDAY, SEPTEMBER 29, 1939. PPPP THREE CENTS NEW YORK CITY and Vicinity | FOUR CENTS Elsewhere Except in 7th and 8th Postal Zones.

REICH AND SOVIET JOIN FOR PEACE--OR WAR; NO BUFFER STATE; NEW PACT WARNS ALLIES; ESTONIA GIVES MOSCOW SEA AND AIR BASES

COMMITTEE VOTES 'CASH-CARRY' BILL TO END ARMS BAN

Eases Curbs on Air and Sea Lines Serving Americas and Tightens Credits

APPROVES PLAN BY 16 TO 7

Senate Starts Debate Monday —Pittman Predicts Decision in Three Weeks

By TURNER CATLEDGE
Special to THE NEW YORK TIMES.

WASHINGTON, Sept. 28—Administration forces won an opening skirmish today in the neutrality fight when the Foreign Relations Committee, by a vote of 16 to 7, approved and sent to the Senate the Pittman resolution repealing the arms embargo and substituting a strict "cash-and-carry" system for all American commerce with warring nations.

The committee adopted only two substantial changes in the resolution as drafted last week-end. One was designed to give some relief to American ships and airlines serving British and French possessions in the Western Hemisphere and to transpacific air lines flying between American ports and similar possessions in the Orient. The other aimed to tighten the provision for ninety-day short-term commercial credits to belligerent purchasers of goods in this country.

The committee's action, taken one week almost to the hour after President Roosevelt convened Congress in special session to buttress America's neutrality in the new European war, made it certain that the prospectively historic debate on foreign policy would begin next Monday. Despite the favorable committee report, the measure faces a "hell-to-breakfast" fight from the Senate isolationists who are intent upon retaining the arms embargo against all countries at war.

Committee to Meet Today

Senator Barkley of Kentucky, majority leader, obtained the Senate's consent at a brief session this noon for Senator Pittman, chairman, to file the committee's official report during the week-end recess. The committee has been called to meet again tomorrow to polish up the language of the resolution, which will go before the Senate as a substitute for the Bloom bill passed by the House at the last session.

Four of the committee majority which gave the favorable report reserved the right to seek amendment or vote against the resolution on the floor. Even with these exceptions the Administration gained a distinct advantage in avoiding further delay or an adverse recommendation in committee.

The isolationists did not make a stand in the committee room. They made no motions and offered no amendments. They hardly raised a voice in protest, preferring simply to record their votes and then wait for open battle on the Senate floor where they propose to make a last-ditch fight against repeal of the mandatory embargo. Except for the proposed embargo repeal, the isolationists look upon the Pittman resolution with great favor, particularly because of the mandates it puts upon the President and Executive departments to maintain this country's neutrality.

Line-up of the Committee

The vote on reporting the measure, which came after three hours' deliberation, was as follows:

For reporting—Pittman of Nevada, Harrison of Mississippi (by proxy), George of Georgia, Wagner of New York, Connally of Texas, Thomas of Utah, Van Nuys of Indiana, Pepper of Florida, Murray of Montana, Schwellenbach of Washington, Green of Rhode Island, Barkley of Kentucky, Reynolds of North Carolina, Guffey of Pennsylvania, Gillette of Iowa, Democrats; White of Maine, Republican.

Against reporting—Clark of Missouri, Democrat; La Follette of Wisconsin, Progressive; Shipstead of Minnesota, Farmer-Laborite; Borah of Idaho, Johnson of California, Vandenberg of

Continued on Page Eleven

The International Situation

Germany and Russia, in a pact announced early this morning, drew a line through Poland considerably to the east of Warsaw and said that was their frontier. Then, declaring that peace in Eastern Europe was thus settled, they warned Britain and France to make peace in the West, saying that otherwise they would "consult each other regarding necessary measures" The nature of such measures was forecast by a provision in the agreement that Russia would supply Germany with materials to be paid for "over a long time." [Page 1; text of the pact and supplementary documents begins on Page 1.]

Overshadowed by this development was the virtual disappearance last night of another European State. Estonia signed a mutual assistance pact with Russia; to be sure, it guaranteed the "sovereign rights" of both countries, but more significantly it granted Russia the right to sea and air bases on Estonian territory and the right to maintain armed forces—put by one source at 25,000 men—in the country. [Page 1; text of the pact, Page 8.]

Although the signing of this agreement coincided with the visit of the German Foreign Minister to Moscow, Berlin circles denied that the Russian move was part of the Nazi-Soviet understanding. [Page 4.]

As the last Polish fortress—that at Modlin—fell to the German Army, which advanced to its new "border" with Russia, Reich military circles were saying that their country must now be stronger than ever to be ready for an "inevitable dispute" with the Soviet some day. [Page 1.]

Berlin again claimed a success at sea, saying its planes had scored a hit on a British cruiser. The British again promptly disputed the claim; they said it probably arose from an unsuccessful attempt the day before to bomb a destroyer. [Page 1.] Nevertheless, the Germans did seem to be organizing a large-scale sea and air attack on British ships, bases and ports to break the blockade and impose one of their own. [Page 2.]

As part of this campaign, a German submarine sank another neutral freighter, a Swedish ship, whose captain was held aboard the U-boat for seven hours and whose crew was rescued. [Page 2.]

But Britain's success in countering the undersea menace was shown by news from Montreal that the convoy system was working. Fifteen freighters loaded with grain, constituting the first convoy of the war, reached Britain safely, and there have been others since that one. [Page 1.]

The Administration in Washington won the first round in the Neutrality Bill controversy when the Senate Foreign Relations Committee voted 16 to 7 to report out the Pittman resolution. Only two changes were made. [Page 1; text of the bill as approved by the committee, Page 10.]

NAVY RAIDED AGAIN

British Cruiser Bombed 'Successfully,' Berlin Version Declares

LONDON DENIES HITS

Plane Reported to Have Aimed at Destroyer but Missed

Conflicting claims on the results of a new battle between warship and plane were made by London and Berlin yesterday. Germans said they had "successfully attacked" a British heavy cruiser off the coast of Scotland. The British said a plane had aimed bombs at a destroyer in those waters but missed.

Wireless to THE NEW YORK TIMES.

BERLIN, Sept. 28—Following the success claimed yesterday in the German air attack on a squadron of the British fleet in the North Sea, the German High Command announced today that a heavy British cruiser of "the Washington type" was successfully attacked by airplanes near the Isle of May off the coast of Scotland not far from Edinburgh.

A German "fighting squadron" is alleged to have struck the fore portion of a 10,000-ton British cruiser with a 500-pound bomb. What happened to the ship after this is not reported.

[The "Washington-type" cruisers are the 10,000-ton vessels built after the Washington arms limitation treaty, which banned construction of larger ships of this type.]

Replying to the British denial of German success in the North Sea battle between British ships and German planes, a communiqué today repeats the assertion that a British airplane carrier and a battleship were hit by bombs. This attack was made by fourteen German land bombers, it is said. Fearing no resistance, such as would be anticipated in a land attack, the German planes are said to have been unaccompanied by pursuit planes.

A Foreign Office spokesman this afternoon suggested the British send neutral representatives of the foreign press stationed in Great Britain to see the squadron involved.

Chancellor Hitler meanwhile today unexpectedly went to Wilhelmshaven with Grand Admiral Erich Raeder, commander of the German Navy. He personally congratulated the commanders and crews of returned submarines on their "great successes."

Hint Ark Royal Was Hit

BERLIN, Sept. 28 (UP)—Still insisting that a British aircraft carrier was "reduced to a wreck" and that a British battleship was damaged when a fleet of planes attacked a large British naval squadron in the middle of the North Sea Tuesday, the German wireless broadcast a sarcastic statement to-

Continued on Page Two

TALLINN GIVES WAY

Capitulates to Demands as Russian Planes Fly Over the City

MUTUAL AID PROMISED

Trade Treaty Signed by Selter and Molotoff—Nazis Are Pleased

By G. E. R. GEDYE
Special Cable to THE NEW YORK TIMES.

MOSCOW, Friday, Sept. 29—Without its necessitating any immediate change in the uncertain map of Europe the Estonian Republic virtually ceased to exist in the early hours of today.

By the signature of two treaties, labeled "mutual assistance" and "trade agreement," the little Baltic republic passed under the full domination of the Soviet Union and yielded to Russia naval bases and airdromes and the right to maintain military forces in Estonian territory.

She fully accepted the implications of Soviet assertions about the operations of mysterious, unidentified submarines in Estonian waters and handed to Moscow the keys to her security and national existence, which she had held since the collapse of Russian Czarism and the formation of the Soviet Union.

The "mutual assistance" pact is to come into force upon the exchange of ratifications at Tallinn, the capital of Estonia, within six days. The pact is concluded for ten years. Unless it is denounced by either party within a year from the date of expiration, it is to continue for another five years.

It was signed by Premier and Foreign Commissar Vyacheslaff M. Molotoff of Russia and Foreign Minister Karl Selter of Estonia.

Negotiated in Kremlin

The final form of Estonia's political eclipse was "negotiated" within the walls of the Kremlin with the hapless Estonian Foreign Minister.

While Germany's Foreign Minister, Joachim von Ribbentrop, after a banquet at the Kremlin, sat watching the Russian Ballet in the Moscow Theatre, the little anti-communist state, which until now had been the playground of the Nazi forces, was handed over to the Russian colossus within a few months after her rejection of proposals to guarantee her frontiers against German aggression in the attempted Anglo-Franco-Russian peace front.

It was rumored that Estonia had made a vain appeal to Germany at the eleventh hour.

Estonia's "alliance" with Russia refers to the possible event of aggression by a "great power." Whether or not the Soviet Union's action is part of an agreement with Germany the fact remains that the only great power capable at the moment of adopting an aggressive attitude toward Estonia is Germany herself.

By secret agreement or by acceptance of a development she has been unable to hinder after having launched a new war, Germany has had to yield this northern zone of influence to the country against whom her influence was long exercised. Whether connivance or surrender flavored this dessert in Herr von Ribbentrop's banquet, it can hardly have been a particularly palatable dish.

The pact, the official communiqué says, was negotiated from Sept. 22 to 28 between Mr. Molotoff and Mr. Selter with the assistance of Joseph Stalin, Vice Premier A. I. Mikoyan, the Estonian Minister to Moscow, Alexandre Rey and others. The pact and the trade agreement were signed Sept. 28.

Terms of the Agreement

Article I of the Soviet-Estonian pact says the two contracting parties will give each other every assistance, including military, if direct aggression occurs on the part of any great European power against their respective frontiers in the Baltic Sea or their land frontiers or across the territory of the Latvian Republic, as well as against the bases in Estonia, that are granted to the Soviet Union,

Continued on Page Eight

Russo-German Agreements

By German Transocean Wireless.

MOSCOW, Friday, Sept. 29—The following are texts of the German-Soviet frontier and friendship agreement signed here early this morning and accompanying documents.

The German Reich Government and the Government of Soviet Russia, after the disintegration of the former Polish State, consider it their task to restore in this region law and order and to insure nationals living there an existence corresponding to their national character. With this aim in view they have agreed as follows:

Article I

The German Reich Government and the Government of the Soviet Republics lay down as the frontier of their respective spheres of interests in the region of the former Polish State the line which is drawn on the attached map and which will be described in detail in a supplementary protocol.

Article II

Both parties recognize the frontier laid down in Article I of the interest spheres of both States as definite and will decline interference of any kind by a third power with this settlement.

Article III

The necessary new political regulation is undertaken by the German Reich Government in districts west of the line laid down in Article I and by the Government of the Soviet Republic in districts east of this line.

Article IV

The German Reich Government and the Government of the Soviet Republic regard the before-mentioned settlement as a foundation for progressing development of friendly relations between their peoples.

Article V

This treaty will be ratified, and ratification documents will be exchanged in Berlin as soon as possible. The agreement comes into force on the day of its signature.

VON RIBBENTROP
MOLOTOFF

Protocol Statement

The following statement by the German Reich Government and the Government of the Soviet Russian Republic of Sept. 28, 1939, is attached to the protocol:

After the German Reich Government and the Government of the Soviet Russian Republic have definitely settled by the treaty signed today the question resulting from disintegration of the Polish State, thus creating a safe foundation for lasting peace in Eastern Europe, they unanimously express the opinion that it would correspond to the true interests of all peoples and make an end to the war existing between Germany on the one hand and England and France on the other hand. Therefore, both governments, if necessary in conjunction with one of the befriended nations, will direct their joint efforts toward searching this aim as soon as possible. But should the efforts of both governments fail, then the fact would be estab-

Continued on Page Four

THREATEN 'STEPS'

Berlin and Moscow Will Act if Britain, France Reject Peace Move

FRONTIER IS FIXED

Russia Agrees to Give Germany Supplies on Extended Time

By The United Press.

LONDON, Friday, Sept. 29—The Moscow radio broadcast at 6:40 A. M. today made an official announcement that Russia and Germany had signed an agreement in Moscow fixing the German-Russian frontier and revealed that no Polish State would be formed.

The broadcast said that the Russian Premier and Foreign Commissar, Vyacheslaff M. Molotoff, and German Foreign Minister Joachim von Ribbentrop issued a joint statement that, after the liquidation of Poland, there was no necessity for a continuation of hostilities.

The joint statement added that if Britain and France, however, continued hostilities, then the responsibility rested with them, and Germany and Russia then would consult each other about "necessary steps."

The joint statement also said that the Soviet Government agreed to supply Germany with all necessary raw materials in exchange for German goods, which would be delivered over a longer period.

Reich Confirms Pact

BERLIN, Friday, Sept. 29 (UP)—The Foreign Office today announced the signing in Moscow during the night of a "frontier and friendship" treaty with Russia, liquidating Poland as a nation and creating a "secure foundation for permanent European peace."

"The German Reich Government and the Government of the U. S. S. R., by signing the treaty, finally regulated the question arising from the collapse of the Polish State and thus created a secure foundation for permanent European peace," the announcement said.

"They thus express agreement that it would be in the true interests of all peoples to put an end to the state of war between the Reich and Britain and France. The two governments will, therefore, make mutual efforts if necessary with other friendly powers to attain this end as soon as possible.

"Should, however, the two governments' efforts be unsuccessful, the fact would thus be established that France and Britain were responsible for continuation of the war, in which event the German and U. S. S. R. governments would consult regarding necessary measures."

Banquet for Ribbentrop

By G. E. R. GEDYE
Wireless to THE NEW YORK TIMES.

MOSCOW, Friday, Sept. 29—Following Wednesday night's Russo-German talks in the Kremlin—which, it was learned later, lasted not two hours, as the communiqué said, but five and a half hours—the conversations were resumed at 3 o'clock yesterday afternoon. For 7 P. M. a banquet was arranged at the Kremlin in honor of Joachim von Ribbentrop German Foreign Minister; Count Friedrich Werner von der Schulenburg, German Ambassador here, and several members of Herr von Ribbentrop's suite.

In German circles the banquet was described as extremely cordial in tone. Herr von Ribbentrop sat down to the table not only with Joseph Stalin, Premier Vyacheslaff Molotoff and War Commissar Klementy Voroshiloff, but also with Lazar M. Kaganovitch, Commissar of Heavy Industry and Fuel, who happens to be Jewish, and with Vice Premier Anasthasius I. Mikoyan and Lorenti Beria, Commissar of Internal Affairs.

3 Vice Commissars Present

Three Soviet Vice Commissars of Foreign Affairs—Vladimir Potemkin, S. A. Losovsky and V. G. Dekanosoff—the Soviet Ambassador to Berlin, Alexander Shkhartsaff; the Soviet Trade Commissioner to

Continued on Page Four

HAMILTON OPPOSES 'PARTISANSHIP' BAN

Republican Chairman 'Resents' Plan to Make Party 'Rubber Stamp' in War Crisis

Expressing disagreement with President Roosevelt's suggestion for an "adjournment of partisanship" during the present European crisis, John D. M. Hamilton, chairman of the Republican National Committee, opposed last night such a move on the eve of the 1940 Presidential campaign.

Mr. Hamilton, who spoke at the organization meeting of the New York County Republican Committee at Manhattan Center, 311 West Thirty-fourth Street, declared that he resented any attempt in the name of emergency to stampede the Republican party into becoming a mere rubber stamp for Administration proposals. He said there had been an "adjournment of politics" in the name of emergency in 1933, with the result that millions of unemployed still walked the streets, and that the national debt had reached an all-time high.

"Should Not Be Diverted"

"Nothing would be more disastrous to this nation than an adjournment of politics which would permit a blackout of urgent domestic problems," Mr. Hamilton asserted. "As a party we would be faithless to our trust if we permitted what is happening in Europe to divert us from the task that is ours of correcting the errors of the last six and a half years and of redirecting our energies toward a useful and permanent recovery.

"We need to reorder our finances and we need to consider some of the ill-advised legislation that still remains on the statute books. There are many other vital domestic issues about which we need to think and to think deeply."

Mr. Hamilton asked what was the nature of the "limited emergency" proclaimed by the President, saying that no guns were leveled at the United States, that no threatening demands on the government had been made and that the nation was at peace and would remain at peace, if the will of the people was allowed to prevail.

With obvious reference to the differences of opinion regarding President Roosevelt's proposal for repeal of the embargo provision of the Neutrality Act, which cut across party lines, Mr. Hamilton said:

"There is no obligation or com-

Continued on Page Thirteen

CANADIAN CONVOYS ELUDE SUBMARINES

Cargoes of Vital Resources, Some From New York, Are Crossing Atlantic Unscathed

Special to THE NEW YORK TIMES.

MONTREAL, Sept. 28—The regulations of censorship heretofore have barred from the newspapers one of the greatest Canadian stories of the European war, the story of how the senior dominion of the British Commonwealth of Nations is supplying the motherland with resources with which to defeat nazism.

At regular intervals convoys are leaving the Atlantic coast escorting vessels laden with wheat, metal, manufactured goods and other products, and every ship is arriving safely in British ports.

The grain movement is perhaps the most important. During the first week or two of the war, wheat and corn from Great Lakes ports piled up in Montreal, jammed the elevators and made it necessary for laden lakers to anchor in the river to await unloading.

But Britain quickly organized her convoy system, and it was learned here today that the first successful convoy, comprising fifteen freighters with cargoes aggregating 500,000 bushels of grain, had reached England.

Since then other convoys have

Continued on Page Eight

British Flying Boat Escapes From Iceland; Danes Protest, Alleging Breach of Parole

Wireless to THE NEW YORK TIMES.

REYKJAVIK, Iceland, Sept. 28—Count Eduard Reventlow, Denmark's Minister to London, today protested to the British Government against the departure of a British naval plane from Iceland this morning.

The plane landed Tuesday evening at the lonely trading post of Raufarhofen in Northern Iceland, lost in the fog. The naval plane, with nine aboard, anchored in the harbor, and the commander was said to have given his word that he would submit to the government's orders.

It had been planned to fly the plane to Reykjavik at 8 o'clock this morning. The British plane, however, departed at 6 A. M. and disappeared at sea.

LONDON, Sept. 28 (UP)—The British Admiralty tonight ordered a service inquiry into charges by the Iceland Government that nine members of the crew of a Royal Air Force flying boat broke their parole after being interned by Iceland authorities.

It was announced earlier in the day that the nine fliers and the flying boat had returned to Britain after being forced down by fog near Raufarhofen in Northern Iceland. The fliers and the ship were interned by Icelandic authorities.

The Danish Minister in London, acting on behalf of the Reykjavik government, protested to the British Government tonight against the alleged action of the British fliers in breaking their parole and the inquiry was ordered.

If violation of parole is proved, "appropriate action" will be taken by the British Government, it was said.

LAST WARSAW FORT YIELDS TO GERMANS

Modlin Surrenders and Nazis Achieve War Aims in East—Distrust of Soviet Seen

By OTTO D. TOLISCHUS
Wireless to THE NEW YORK TIMES.

WITH THE GERMAN ARMY, Before Warsaw, Poland, Sept. 28—The German campaign in Poland came to an end today when the fortress of Modlin followed Warsaw in surrendering unconditionally at 7 o'clock this morning. At the same time the bulk of the German Army had returned to the western side of the German-Russian demarcation line, which army circles regard as the new Reich border.

With that surrender of the last fort defending the city, Germany has attained her war aims in the East, namely, the partition of Poland, in exactly four weeks. She is already at work organizing the newly won territory in order to enhance its agricultural and industrial resources.

Again Chancellor Hitler has proved himself the "Mehrer" or aggrandizer, of the Reich. To his political triumph he has added an unprecedented military triumph as well.

But German Army quarters are perfectly well aware that this new aggrandizement has been obtained at a high price that is not measured by German casualties, which are comparatively small, but by the fact that, in place of weak Poland, Germany has again put powerful Russia on her eastern flank. Army circles are so aware of this new situation that they frankly declare:

"Germany must now be stronger than ever, not only to win the conflict with France and Britain but also to prepare for the inevitable dispute with Soviet Russia that must come some day."

Consolation for the Conquered

In fact that is the consolation the German Army offers the conquered foe remaining on the German side of the demarcation line who still fear National Socialist Germany less than they do Bolshevist Russia.

The final dramatic scenes of Warsaw's and Modlin's surrender were witnessed by this writer together with a group of other foreign correspondents who arrived at the German front line on the edge of the capital yesterday afternoon to find Warsaw in flames and Modlin still being bombed and shelled to pieces.

We stood at the same spot on the Warsaw-Modlin road where General

Continued on Page Four

GERMAN ATTACKS IN WEST REPULSED

Heavy Guns Reported Active —Allied Air Forces Bring Down Nazi Planes

By G. H. ARCHAMBAULT
Wireless to THE NEW YORK TIMES.

PARIS, Sept. 28—The comparative lull continues on the West Front, with occasional raids. The French took a number of prisoners in a raid this afternoon in the sector nearest the Moselle River. There is also much firing of heavy guns. The weather now is becoming cold and it is very trying for men in the first lines, especially at night. But with the experience gained during the four Winters of the World War the Quartermaster Corps is ready to meet the emergency.

Today's General Headquarters communiqués follow:

"No. 49 [morning]. It was a quiet night on the whole.

"An enemy attack west of Saarbruecken failed.

"At sea commercial navigation returned to normal conditions, thanks to the organization of convoys and aerial patrols.

"Yesterday afternoon our air force, operating in conjunction with the British air force, brought down several enemy pursuit planes.

"During the night our reconnoissance planes were active."

"No. 50 [evening]. The local attack by our troops in the region immediately east of the Moselle River is proceeding favorably. Some prisoners were taken."

War Limited to One Front

With Warsaw fallen, the war has now become restricted to a single front where both sides can concentrate all their forces, for it is supposed here that the German High Command will leave in Poland only policing units—the partly trained Landwehr, Gestapo and detachments of Storm Troops. The Poles' gallant stand lasted only one month, but it has been invaluable.

It has enabled French mobilization and concentration to proceed unimpeded, as well as British concentration to begin in normal conditions. It has also enabled the allied High Command not only to enter German territory but to oc-

Continued on Page Five

Dispatches from Europe and the Far East are subject to censorship.

"All the News That's Fit to Print."

The New York Times.

LATE CITY EDITION
POSTSCRIPT
Mostly cloudy, mild temperatures today, followed by light rain.
Temperatures Yesterday—Max., 51; Min., 39

VOL. LXXXIX...No. 29,895. Entered as Second-Class Matter, Postoffice, New York, N. Y. NEW YORK, THURSDAY, NOVEMBER 30, 1939. P THREE CENTS NEW YORK CITY and Vicinity | FOUR CENTS Elsewhere Except in 7th and 8th Postal Zones.

RUSSIANS START THEIR INVASION OF FINLAND; PLANES DROP BOMBS ON AIRFIELD AT HELSINKI; WAR STARTS AS U. S. MOVE FOR PEACE IS MADE

KUHN FOUND GUILTY ON ALL FIVE COUNTS; HE FACES 30 YEARS

Leader of the Bund Here Will Be Sentenced Tuesday as Thief and Forger

JURY OUT FOR 8½ HOURS

Defense Counsel Rebuked by the Court as Clashes Mark Final Day of Trial

Fritz Kuhn, the leader of the German-American Bund, was convicted shortly after 10 o'clock last night of grand larceny and forgery in General Sessions Court.

He stood up, with only his forefinger on his left hand waving along the side seam of his trousers, and heard without a blink the verdict of a jury that had deliberated eight and a half hours. The maximum sentence he can receive is thirty years, and the day on which he will hear his fate was set by Judge James G. Wallace as Tuesday.

Pending the sentence Judge Wallace told Peter L. F. Sabbatino, the counsel who had defended Kuhn during his trial in General Sessions Court, that action on a promised contempt of court would be suspended until then. He gave Mr. Sabbatino leave to make any motions he desired in the intervening time.

Kuhn marched off to the Tombs with the stoical attitude of a good German soldier, which he says he once was. There was no tremor on his face, and the three courtroom bailiffs who surrounded him when Morris C. Bullock, the foreman of the jury, pronounced him guilty, had only to tug at his sleeve to lead him away to prison. There was not even an interchange of glances between him and Mr. Sabbatino or Wilbur V. Keegan, associate counsel.

What the Verdict Meant

The verdict was that he was guilty of grand larceny in the first and second degree in the theft of $717 from the bund to pay for the transportation of the furniture of Mrs. Florence Camp across the country, and of second degree larceny and two counts of forgery in the "Murray transaction."

The Murray transaction was a $500 item which Kuhn listed on the bund books of record and told the bund members that he had paid to James D. C. Murray for legal services. These two items, totaling $1,217, were all that the jury had to pass on of an indictment which originally charged thefts amounting to more than $14,000.

One pair of counts, dealing with more than $8,000 charged against Kuhn as a theft had been eliminated before the trial began and Judge Wallace knocked out another pair charging that he had stolen $4.424 of the bund funds because, the judge ruled, the prosecution had not proved this beyond a reasonable doubt.

During a long afternoon and early evening while the jury was out, Kuhn sat in the court room talking to his counsel. He had sandwiches brought in to him and munched on them while Assistant District Attorney Herman J. McCarthy, who prosecuted him, walked the corridors of the Criminal Courts Building.

Part of Charge Is Re-read

After seven and a half hours the jury came in shortly before 9 P. M. to ask Judge Wallace for a re-reading of a part of his charge dealing with the Camp transactions.

When the verdict finally did come in a half-hour later he stood up again. But this time the bailiff who was behind him asked him to step outside the rail enclosing the space for the attorneys, and as he stood there two other bailiffs came up behind him.

The precaution of three men surrounding the man who says his war record covered service as a machine gunner in Alpine service during the World War was not necessary. He made no move and there was no sign of emotion on his face.

The index finger of his left hand wiggled spasmodically. But he did not even move his hand.

Then, in a voice that was not even audible a few feet away, he gave his "pedigree" to a bailiff. He said he was born in Germany forty-two years ago and revealed

Continued on Page Twelve

Must Stay Day in Mexico Or Pay San Diego Duties

Special to THE NEW YORK TIMES.

WASHINGTON, Nov. 29—The twenty-four hour limit goes into effect Friday on the Mexican border in the San Diego Customs District and persons wishing to avail themselves of the $100 customs exemption on goods brought into this country must stay in Mexico at least twenty-four hours.

Collectors have been instructed that in their discretion they may permit tourists staying a shorter time to bring in goods with an aggregate value of not more than $5 without paying duty.

The unusual situation in the San Diego district is created by the proximity of the Free Port of Tijuana, into which European merchandise may enter duty-free. Large retail establishments there maintain billboards along the roads to Tijuana advertising bargains on selected European imports.

CITY WILL SET UP A 'BOOSTER' BUREAU

Mayor Reveals Plans for New Department to Attract More Business Here

Reviewing the accomplishments of his administration before a gathering of merchants and property owners yesterday, Mayor La Guardia disclosed plans for still another project for the betterment of the city—a Department of Commerce—to bring more business and industry here.

He told the Central Mercantile Association at its Fall luncheon in the Hotel Pennsylvania that he had often boosted New York on his frequent flights out of town and that now he would have a municipal organization for this purpose, "and I am going to out-small-town the smallest town in the country."

The Mayor had reviewed the difficulties of city finance, education costs, the new pension plan for policemen and firemen, the Sixth Avenue improvement, transit unification, plans for Ninth and Second Avenues, the North Beach Airport and the new information bureau under the Park Avenue ramp in Pershing Square, not mentioning other accomplishments.

Will Combat Adverse Reports

"We have been confronted with a lot of small-town stuff about business in New York being more costly than elsewhere," he then went on. "I am going to out-small-town the smallest town in the country. I am going to establish a Department of Commerce which will have the function of providing information and advice to business men interested in coming to New York."

The Mayor's bureau will add no cost to the city government, he said, because he will "pick up employes from various city departments to do the work." He also will invite business and labor here to cooperate, he said, adding that "labor will have to assume its responsibility and I expect it to do its part."

The first step in the functioning of such a new program, the Mayor said, has already been taken in his invitation to the film industry to return to New York. He said there was no reason why this industry should be centered in one city "but we should have our share." He reported that, "notwithstanding ridicule and opposition, we are making progress."

Ryan Seen as Likely Head

A report that a municipal department of commerce would be established was published last Sunday but had not been publicly acknowledged by the Mayor until yesterday. The report said that Clendenin J. Ryan, Deputy Commissioner of Sanitation, would head the new department and would be sworn in as its first Commissioner this week.

In his address, which lasted for more than an hour, the Mayor dwelt particularly on his new pension plan for policemen and firemen. The establishment of the plan was prompted by the fact that any pension plan in existence July 1, 1940, will, under constitutional amendment, become a contractual obligation of the city.

The Mayor noted that the Legislature had failed to put the policemen and firemen pension system on

Continued on Page Twelve

DIES AT RALLY HERE WARNS U. S. TO STOP ITS 'APING' OF EUROPE

10,000 Cheer His Plea for National Unity and a Fight on All Alien Forces

HE PLEADS FOR TOLERANCE

Calls on Administration to Provide Funds to Continue Work of His Committee

Speaking last night in Madison Square Garden before an enthusiastic throng estimated at 10,000 to 12,000 persons, representing many patriotic and religious organizations, Representative Martin Dies of Texas denounced communism, fascism and nazism as alien forces tearing at American unity. He made a strong plea also for racial and religious tolerance.

Asserting that there was an organized campaign to discredit the work of the Congressional Committee Investigating un-American Activities which he heads, Mr. Dies made a demand for public funds with which to continue hearings on subversive groups next year. He also called on the Administration, which he implied was opposed to the committee, to come out openly and say whether or not it favored the drive against foreign "isms."

On this question Mr. Dies got strong support from the audience and from the other speakers, who urged those present to demand from Congress an appropriation that would preserve the committee as it is.

The husky, 6-foot Representative who has achieved national prominence since he was named chairman of the committee in 1938 was escorted to the platform by a guard of American Legionnaires while the drums of the Seventh Regiment band announced him with a fanfare.

Mr. Dies's fellow-speakers were Colonel George U. Harvey, Borough President of Queens; Joseph P. Ryan, president of the International Longshoremen's Association; Jeremiah Cross, past State commander of the American Legion; Laurens Hamilton, president of the New York State chapter, Sons of the American Revolution, and Jean Mathias, New York State commander, Jewish War Veterans of the United States.

As chairman of the meeting, Merwin K. Hart, president of the New York State Economic Council, opened the meeting at 8:30 P. M. Frederick Jagel of the Metropolitan Opera sang the "Star-Spangled Banner," although he advocates the adoption of a new anthem for the United States.

Among those who attended, it was reported but not confirmed, were

Continued on Page Thirteen

Intelligence Chief Quits; Dutch Blame Venloo Case

Wireless to THE NEW YORK TIMES.

AMSTERDAM, the Netherlands, Nov. 29—Major Gen. J. W. van Oorschot, 64-year-old head of the Netherlands intelligence service, resigned today. He had headed the department since 1919.

Observers are inclined to link his resignation with the Venloo frontier incident.

THE HAGUE, the Netherlands, Nov. 29 (UP)—The Venloo incident involved the shooting of a Netherlands intelligence officer, Lieutenant Klop, and the kidnapping of two British intelligence agents and a chauffeur by German Gestapo [secret police] agents. General J. W. van Oorschot, who resigned today, was responsible for sending Lieutenant Klop to Venloo.

The British version of the incident was that two British intelligence officers, Sigismund Payne Best and Captain Richard Henry Stevens, went to Venloo to investigate presumably legitimate German peace talk on Nov. 9.

REICH OIL SITUATION VIEWED AS CRITICAL

Germany Isolated From Great Sources of Supply—Imports From U. S. Virtually Ended

Special to THE NEW YORK TIMES.

WASHINGTON, Nov. 29—The oil situation in Germany, especially the Reich's reserve of fuel oils, is the most serious problem facing the Hitler government today, in the opinion of American naval and military experts. Export data in the Department of Commerce appear to substantiate this opinion.

Germany is one of the few great nations without oil resources and since the war started she has received virtually no crude, lubricating or gasoline supplies from the United States the one market that under normal conditions would be in a position to make up at least part of the deficit.

Official statistics, plus reports considered reliable, all indicate that Germany is completely isolated from the great oil markets of the world. So grave is the situation that Germany is making frantic efforts to develop synthetic gasoline plants, which, it is hoped, may be in partial operation by the middle of 1940. Even the Germans do not expect the plants to be operating to capacity before the end of 1941.

Any hopes the Germans might have of getting appreciable quantities of oil from the Russian fields are dispelled, according to official information, by the fact that Russia is having a hard time producing enough for her own needs. This is

Continued on Page Seven

Unofficial Thanks to Be Given Here Today By Irreconcilables Clinging to 'Old Style'

It will be just another day on New York's official calendar today, but half the nation, led by New England, will observe Thanksgiving with a determination to make the celebration of the traditional date outshine the "new Thanksgiving" fixed by President Roosevelt and marked by the other half of the country a week ago.

They will be joined here in unofficial joy by those New York irreconcilables who refuse to eat turkey on any but the last Thursday of November, by those who have children coming home from school or college in "old-style" States, and by those who feel that any holiday is worth celebrating again even if it did occur only seven days before. These double celebrators will be following the example of Colorado, Mississippi and Texas, which are observing a second holiday in addition to the one last week.

Including these three, twenty-six States have proclaimed today as Thanksgiving Day. Americans in Sao Paulo, Brazil, dissenting from their fellows in Rio de Janeiro, and most other Americans abroad also will observe the day—which has been termed the "Republican Thanksgiving" in contrast to the "New Deal Thanksgiving" on Nov. 23.

In New York many theatres are giving special matinees, and numerous restaurants will have turkey dinners for those who wish to partake. Private clubs are in some cases holding special events which were scheduled for today before the President changed the date. The Volunteer Rescue Army, which fed turkey to 2,018 unemployed last week, will give the same menu today for 3,000 at its chapel at 379 First Avenue.

Magistrate Henry H. Curran, sitting in Felony Court yesterday, declared he would observe the holiday today to "give thanks for the twenty-three States that didn't fall for this tyrannical novelty which came out of Washington." But he will eat chicken because "it's not fair to make the turkeys suffer on two days."

In Highland Park, N. J., a suburb of New Brunswick, school pupils will be dismissed at 1 P. M. as a "gesture toward those who believe the day is still the oldtime Thanksgiving."

Rutgers University, in New Brunswick, will observe its second Thanksgiving today to permit students to go to Providence, R. I., to the Brown-Rutgers football game. Mayor C. D. White of Atlantic City has also proclaimed today as a second Thanksgiving.

The nation's principal observance

Continued on Page Fifteen

HULL ACTS QUICKLY

Offer of Good Offices in Ending Dispute Sent to Finland and Russia

HELSINKI LIKELY TO AGREE

But Moscow's Reaction Is Held to Be Highly Problematical —Pittman Assails Soviet

U. S. Offer Received

By The United Press.

MOSCOW, Thursday, Nov. 30—The United States' offer to mediate in the Soviet-Finnish dispute was received at the American Embassy here at 10:30 A. M. (3:30 A. M. Eastern Standard Time).

The offer will be presented or delivered to the Soviet Foreign Office some time this morning by Walter Thurston, Chargé d'Affaires.

By BERTRAM D. HULEN

Special to THE NEW YORK TIMES.

WASHINGTON, Nov. 29—The increasingly serious developments in relations between Russia and Finland led the United States today to proclaim her readiness to extend good offices for a pacific adjustment of the points at issue, if that should be agreeable to both parties.

The move was made in an effort to leave no stone unturned that would prevent a spread of European hostilities. It was in the form of a statement issued by Secretary of State Cordell Hull after several telephone conversations with President Roosevelt. In particular, it represented their views of a way in which the American Government could throw its weight into the scales for peace after consideration had been given in the State Department to possible courses of action.

The text of the statement follows:

This government is following with serious concern the intensification of the Finnish-Soviet dispute. It would view with extreme regret any extension of the present area of war and the consequent further deterioration of international relations.

Without in any way becoming involved in the merits of the dispute, and limiting its interest to the solution of the dispute by peaceful processes only, this government would, if agreeable to both parties, gladly extend its good offices.

Text Is Cabled to Envoys

The force of a diplomatic appeal was given the statement when Secretary Hull late today cabled the text to the United States Legation in Finland and the United States Embassy in Russia with instructions that it be delivered to the Foreign Offices.

The statement was issued at 3:05 P. M., one hour before word was received of Russia's severance of diplomatic relations with Finland, and an hour and a half before the press carried reports of the speech of Vyacheslaff M. Molotoff, Soviet Premier and Foreign Commissar.

In comment on the statement the State Department said it did not constitute intervention, nor did it necessarily mean mediation. It simply meant, it was stated, that this government is using what efforts it can to help Russia and Finland settle the dispute themselves.

Although Secretary Hull merely expressed a readiness to extend good offices if Russia and Finland are agreeable, his action threw open the possibility of an adjustment that might be worked out along any one of several lines. An offer of good offices, mediation and arbitration are the three recognized methods for pacific adjustment of disputes under The Hague conventions of 1907 and have been utilized by the United States on many occasions, particularly in Latin America.

In the case of an offer of good offices the country making the tender sets no limitations upon the form that will be used in seeking to facilitate an adjustment. It could be by diplomatic conversations, mediation, arbitration reference to a commission of inquiry or any other method. The country making the tender, moreover, usually does not figure in the ad-

Continued on Page Six

The International Situation

Soviet Russia severed diplomatic relations with Finland last night and this morning the Red Army crossed the border while Soviet planes bombed the airfield at Helsinki. Explaining the break over the radio, Premier Molotoff said that Finnish hostility had become "unbearable," and virtually demanded that a different government be set up in Helsinki. He also indicated rejection to a tender of good offices by the United States. [Page 1.] This offer had been made by Secretary Hull after he had been in touch with President Roosevelt. [Page 1.]

Finland, meanwhile, revealed that the Russian action had been taken before she had delivered a note to the Kremlin offering to withdraw forces from the border and suggesting conciliation. [Page 1.]

London evinced friendliness for the Finns and welcomed the news of the American offer. [Page 6.] Likewise Italy, fearing that near-by Rumania might next claim Russia's attention, expressed through her press sympathy for the Finns. [Page 7.] Germany, on the other hand, supported Russia, although she indicated that her attitude if a conflict began would be one of "benevolent neutrality." [Page 4.]

The Reich's most serious problem of the moment, according to Washington experts, is its critical oil situation. Germany was revealed as completely isolated from the world's oil markets. [Page 1.]

There was little actual war activity during the day. The British reported having driven off two German air raid attempts. [Page 2.] The French said one of their patrols had penetrated deep into German territory in the Vosges sector and had brought back valuable information. [Page 8.] And at sea two more British ships were sunk. [Page 3.]

Japan, a possible sufferer from the hostilities at sea, studied measures of reprisal against the Anglo-French blockade of German exports. It was reported that such measures might include seizure of Allied cargoes in the Orient. [Page 1.]

In the Balkans the Rumanian Foreign Minister turned down Hungary's revisionist demands, but at the same time invited her to help improve relations between the two countries. [Page 10.]

Today Premier Daladier will go before the French Parliament and ask, with every expectation of success, that his emergency powers be continued. [Page 9.]

JAPAN MAY SEIZE CARGOES OF ALLIES

Studies Plan for Reprisals if Anglo-French Ban on Reich Exports Continues

By HUGH BYAS

Wireless to THE NEW YORK TIMES.

TOKYO, Thursday, Nov. 30—The Japanese Government is considering retaliatory measures against Great Britain's two-way blockade of Germany. These may include seizure of Anglo-French ship cargoes in Far Eastern waters.

This threat appears in the newspaper Nichi Nichi this morning as part of its report of a conference held at the Foreign Office yesterday to discuss the British reply to Ambassador Mamoru Shigemitsu's protest against the Order in Council for seizure of German exports on neutral ships.

Reports from other sources indicate that interference with Anglo-French shipping in the Far East still is a somewhat distant possibility, depending on the British response to Japan's demand for special consideration of her German imports. Asahi says that Mr. Shigemitsu has been instructed to press the British Government to give assurances that Japanese trade will receive special consideration in enforcement of the blockade.

The Foreign Office conference in which Foreign Minister Kichisaburo Nomura, Vice Foreign Minister Masayuki Tani and several bureau chiefs participated, found the British order had been formulated in flexible terms so that its effect could not be ascertained until it has been enforced. It was decided to await the text and to continue the policy of pressing Britain to give consideration to Japan's "important" imports from Germany.

If the Japanese representations to Britain are disregarded, a further measure will be considered in the terms of Japan's original protest, which threatened appropriate counter-measures.

Norway Adds Her Protest

OSLO, Norway, Nov. 29 (UP)—Foreign Minister Halvdan Koht announced today that the Norwegian Government has made representations to the Allied Governments regarding their decision to seize German exports.

The Norwegian Government, Mr. Koht said, "fails to see how such a move can be in accord with international law." He added that Norway claimed the right to demand compensation for any losses involved, and urged Great Britain to reconsider her decision. Norway is

Continued on Page Three

Dispatches from Europe and the Far East are subject to censorship.

FINLAND IS BLOCKED IN MEDIATION PLEA

Note Delivered After Rupture Offers to Recall Troops—Soviet Move Awaited

The text of the last Finnish note appears on Page 5.

By The Associated Press.

HELSINKI, Finland, Thursday, Nov. 30—Profoundly disturbed by Moscow's action rupturing diplomatic relations, but still determined to stand fast, Finns uneasily awaited developments today, fearing the beginning of hostilities at any time. But early this morning officials said there had been no troop movements across the borders so far as they could learn.

It was all the more shocking to the Finns because the Moscow action came before they could deliver a note to the Kremlin offering to withdraw Finnish defense forces from the frontier as a gesture toward settling their quarrel.

The offer was made by Foreign Minister Eljas Erkko in his reply to Russia's denunciation of the 1932 Finnish-Soviet non-aggression treaty.

"My government is ready to settle with the Soviet Government the question of the removal of Finnish defense forces on the Karelian Isthmus, with the exception of frontier customs guard forces, to such a distance from Leningrad that it could not even be alleged that they threaten its security," Mr. Erkko's note said.

Making a Sincere Effort

He prefaced this statement with the explanation that Finland was motivated by a desire "to prove emphatically that there is a sincere effort to reach an accord with the Soviet Government and refute the Soviet Government's allegations that Finland has adopted a hostile attitude toward the U.S.S.R. and is desirous of threatening the security of Leningrad."

Despite the breaking off of diplomatic relations, and despite the midnight broadcast of Soviet Premier Vyacheslaff M. Molotoff, who announced the action, Finland's note answering Moscow's denunciation of their non-aggression pact was delivered to the Kremlin at 1:10 A. M., Moscow time.

This was almost three hours after the Vice Commissar of Foreign Affairs, Vladimir Potemkin, had notified the Finnish Minister that relations were broken.

The Finnish answer said the Helsinki Government thought Russia unjustified in denouncing the non-aggression pact and suggested that a conciliation commission be named to examine the controversy.

The news from Moscow spread rapidly through Helsinki. Grim Finns gathered in clusters to discuss the situation. Government of-

Continued on Page Five

BORDER IS CROSSED

Soviet Artillery Opens Fire as Troops March in Karelian Sector

AIR RAID WARNING SOUNDED

People Run to Shelters as the Capital Sees Russian Planes —Five Bombs Are Dropped

Special Cable to THE NEW YORK TIMES.

COPENHAGEN, Denmark, Thursday, Nov. 30—At 9:15 A. M. today the first Russian troops crossed the Karelian frontier into Finland. At 9:20 o'clock an air raid warning was sounded in Helsinki, causing panic in the streets.

At 9:25 o'clock Russian bombers flew over the Finnish capital.

Five Bombs Dropped

HELSINKI, Finland, Nov. 30 (UP)—Five bombs were dropped on the city's airfield today. A report from the border station at Terijoki said Russian troops had opened artillery fire against the Finns early this morning.

Terijoki is on the Karelian Isthmus, twenty-two miles from Leningrad.

The bombing of Helsinki occurred a few minutes after a Russian two-motored airplane flew over the city, driving people to shelter.

Earlier, a squadron of six Russian airplanes had been sighted over the Gulf of Finland, approaching the city.

Finnish anti-aircraft guns fired on the squadron as well as on the single plane over the capital.

Finnish anti-aircraft batteries fired on the plane here and coastal batteries attacked the Russian squadron in the gulf.

Molotoff Proclaims Split

By G. E. R. GEDYE

Wireless to THE NEW YORK TIMES.

MOSCOW, Thursday, Nov. 30—Premier Vyacheslaff M. Molotoff announced in a thirteen-minute radio speech last midnight the breaking off of diplomatic relations with Finland by the Soviet Union through the recall of all Soviet diplomatic, consular and economic representatives in Finland. At the same time he warned all units of the Red Army and Red Navy to stand ready for every emergency.

In contrast to the last Soviet note to Finland and in glaring contrast to the abusive violence of the inspired press and radio campaign, Mr. Molotoff's speech, except for one important particular, conformed entirely to international usage.

Although it accepted, of course, without any effort to substantiate their accuracy, all the Soviet charges concerning the alleged extraordinary violations of the frontier by the Finns in the last few days, the language was restrained and contained indications that the Soviet was prepared to grant concessions to reach a settlement—with the "Finnish people." In that, however, lay the important exception to conformity with international usage.

Appeals to "Finnish People"

Despite the sentences asserting no desire to interfere in internal Finnish affairs and that the Finnish regime's relations with other States was exclusively the affair of Finland, the speech directly appealed over the heads of the present Finnish Government "to the Finnish people." Thus it confirmed the belief expressed more than once that the Soviet Union intended to try to force the surrender of the bases demanded from Finland through a change in the Finnish Government rather than through involving the Soviet Union in an invasion of Finnish territory.

By these passages of his speech Mr. Molotoff would seem to have confronted the Finnish Government with the alternatives of immediately recalling its diplomatic mission from Moscow at the peril of a still further increase in Soviet military pressure, if not of invasion, or of resignation. If the latter alternative were chosen, it would open the

Continued on Page Four

"All the News That's Fit to Print."

The New York Times.

LATE CITY EDITION
Cloudy and colder today. Tomorrow partly cloudy with slowly rising temperatures.
Temperatures Yesterday—Max., 43; Min., 31

Copyright, 1939, by The New York Times Company.

VOL. LXXXIX...No. 29,909. Entered as Second-Class Matter, Postoffice, New York, N. Y. NEW YORK, THURSDAY, DECEMBER 14, 1939. PP THREE CENTS NEW YORK CITY and Vicinity | FOUR CENTS Elsewhere Except in 7th and 8th Postal Zones.

BRITISH DEFEAT NAZI RAIDER IN ALL-DAY FIGHT; SHE RUNS TO MONTEVIDEO WITH 36 DEAD, 60 HURT; U-BOAT SUNK, REICH CRUISER HIT IN NORTH SEA

A. F. L. LEADER SAYS NLRB 'PLAN' SAVED LEWIS' COAL UNION

Area Jurisdiction Ruling Led Thousands to Quit the Rival P.M.W., Ozanic Tells Inquiry

'SHOOTING' ORDER CHARGED

NLRB Report Said U. M. W. Officer Urged This Treatment for Progressive Miners

By The Associated Press.

WASHINGTON, Dec. 13—Joe Ozanic, young leader of the Progressive Mine Workers (A. F. L.), charged before a House investigating committee today that the National Labor Relations Board had followed a "plan" to give the United Mine Workers (C. I. O.) "a way out" in the desperate rivalry between the two unions.

The "plan," as he described it, was embodied in a controlling decision, which certified the C. I. O. union as the bargaining agent for all the coal mines in a specified geographic area. This was done, he said, despite provable majorities for the Progressives in individual mines affected.

As a result, he asserted, the United Mine Workers and employers in the field had forced thousands of Progressive members to switch to the C. I. O. union, and pay its dues, regardless of their own desires in the matter.

In one instance which he cited, that of the Acme Semi-Anthracite Coal Company of Williams, Okla., members of the Progressive union were unemployed, he said, because their jobs had been taken by miners imported by the United Mine Workers.

Bitterness of Feud Evidenced

All the accumulated bitterness of the fierce battle between the C. I. O. and the American Federation of Labor was epitomized for the committee in the day's testimony. Mr. Ozanic spoke repeatedly of "Dictator John L. Lewis," and of alleged "coercion" by C. I. O. members against his own followers.

At one point Edmund M. Toland, the committee's counsel, introduced a memorandum from Philip G. Phillips, the West Virginia regional director of the Labor Board, which quoted "Van Bitner" as having advised United Mine Workers' organizers to shoot Progressive organizers "faster than they would shoot a rabbit."

"Who is Van Bitner?" Chairman Smith, Democrat of Virginia, inquired.

"Van Bitner," Mr. Ozanic replied, "why, he's the provisional district president for District 17 of the United Mine Workers. He was appointed by Dictator John L. Lewis and never in his life elected by the United Mine Workers. That, gentlemen, is Mr. Bitner."

Later Van A. Bittner, who spells his name with two "t's" and is president of District No. 17, and also a member of the U. M. W. International Board, denied that he had ever made the shooting statement.

Denial by U. M. W. Official

"That statement of Phillips is absolutely untrue and made out of whole cloth," he told reporters. The memorandum mentioned that "Bitner" spoke at a Labor Day meeting in Charleston, W. Va., but the U. M. W. official said that the union held no Labor Day meeting in Charleston in 1938.

When Mr. Ozanic took the stand he told the committee that he started work as a coal miner at the age of 15 and was a member of the United Mine Workers of America.

After twenty-two years in that union, he said that he and fellow-miners in the Illinois fields "seceded" because of the U. M. W.'s dictatorial policies" and formed the Progressive Mine Workers of Illinois in 1932.

The new union soon recruited 35,000 of the State's 42,000 miners, he said, and, he added, still had them. After the Progressives received an international charter from the A. F. L. in 1938, Mr. Ozanic said, it recruited an additional 80,000 workers in coal fields outside Illinois. To the latter, however, rec-

Continued on Page Eighteen

Revolutionary Landmark In Queens Being Razed

The old frame building in Elmhurst, Queens, used during the Battle of Long Island as the headquarters of the British Army, was being razed by its present owner yesterday despite efforts of Borough President George U. Harvey to have the property purchased by the city and restored as a historic landmark.

The building, which stands at what is now Fifty-seventh Avenue and Queens Boulevard, was erected in 1762. On Sept. 3, 1776, General William Howe, commanding the British forces, wrote his official report to the King on what happened during the Battle of Long Island six days before, while using the house as his headquarters.

The present owner, Dr. Hevia, Cuban tobacco planter, who has a home in Richmond Hill, decided to raze the building when it became in need of repair. He has no plans for future use of the land.

RALLY HERE SCORES REICH AND SOVIET

Hoover, Landon, La Guardia and Green Are Heard by 20,000 in Garden

Before a mass meeting of more than 20,000 persons who filled every seat in Madison Square Garden last night, former President Herbert Hoover, former Governor Alf M. Landon of Kansas, Mayor La Guardia and William Green, president of the American Federation of Labor, headed prominent Christian and Jewish speakers who joined in protest against the persecution of Jews by Nazi Germany and in an appeal for the mobilization of the moral forces of the world against Hitlerism and Stalinism.

The meeting, held under the auspices of the American Jewish Congress and the Jewish Labor Committee, unanimously adopted by rising vote a resolution asking President Roosevelt to convey American condemnation of the persecution of the Jews in Nazi Poland to the German Government and to use every possible means to succor the victims of the oppression. It was decided to appoint a committee representing the two organizations to take the resolution to Washington.

Hitler and Stalin Booed

Cheering every reference to President Roosevelt's neutrality program, the audience booed equally every mention of Hitler and Stalin. They laughed loudly when speakers ridiculed Nazi and Communist propaganda that Hitler and Stalin are working for peace against the imperialistic war aims of England and France.

They also applauded statements that the real issue was the defense of democracy against totalitarianism, whether its label was Nazi, Fascist or Communist, and that anti-Semitism was only the first step toward the destruction of all religions, labor unions and civil liberties. Many in the audience came in delegations from New York labor unions in which Jewish membership predominates.

The speakers and the audience made it clear that their protests were aimed at the Russian invasion of Finland as well as German aggression in Poland, and that their appeals for help were directed in behalf of the Finns as well as the Jews in Poland, Austria Czecho-Slovakia and Germany.

It was announced that part of a collection taken up at the meeting to defray its expenses and to help Jewish victims of Hitlerism would be turned over to former President Hoover's Finnish relief fund if the collection was large enough. The total was not announced, as the contributions were not to be counted until today.

About seventy policemen were stationed outside the Garden in case of disturbances, but there was no trouble.

Several hundred persons were turned away when the gates of the Garden were closed by Fire Department order at 8:35 P. M., half an hour after the meeting opened. About 200 clustered outside the police lines, despite the rain.

Mayor La Guardia received the biggest ovation of all the speakers when he arrived on the platform after flying in from Chicago on a night plane. He expressed his "horror" at what is taking place in Europe and said he hoped that what

Continued on Page Eight

RUSSIA CONDEMNED

League Certain to Expel Her as Committee of 13 Calls Her Aggressor

PLANS AID TO FINNS

U. S. Will Be Invited to Help—Victim One of Invader's Judges

Text of League report on Russia is on Page 6.

By P. J. PHILIP
Wireless to THE NEW YORK TIMES.

GENEVA, Dec. 13—Soviet Russia, it is now considered certain, will be thrust forth from the company of the League of Nations, having, in the opinion of her fellow-members, by her own acts placed herself outside the Covenant.

A report by thirteen of them—the committee appointed by the Assembly to consider Finland's appeal—held today that Russia has been the aggressor and called on member States to lend all possible aid to the victim. It also offered the facilities of the League to coordinate such help and suggested that non-members be invited to cooperate.

The report was drafted by a subcommittee composed of the representatives of Great Britain, France, Sweden, Bolivia and Portugal.

In the public meeting of the Assembly during the morning Argentina demanded the expulsion, declaring that she would no longer remain a member of the League if the Soviet Union continued to enjoy that title.

Russia Not Represented

The Russian Government was not there to defend itself and no one cared to assume its defense. Jacob Suritz, Soviet Ambassador to France, anticipating events, had left Geneva on the morning train.

Alternative suggestions to that of expulsion proposed by Argentina were invited. It was stipulated that they should be heard in private committee so as to avoid embarrassment to those who feel that their geographic position as Russia's neighbors affects their judgment of both the legal and moral aspects of the question.

Cuba wanted to speak after Argentina in the Assembly, but was overruled as Mexico and India already had agreed to submit their proposals in private.

The Assembly then prepared one more step on the way to expulsion by electing the Union of South Africa and Finland to the council in the place of New Zealand and Sweden, re-electing Bolivia and shelving until after the council shall have taken its decision on the Russian issue the re-election of

Continued on Page Six

Liner Columbus Cleared For Transatlantic Dash

By The Associated Press.

VERACRUZ, Mexico, Dec. 13—Port authorities disclosed tonight that the 32,581-ton German liner Columbus had obtained clearance papers for a transatlantic voyage and was prepared to sail without further notice.

All crew members on shore leave have been ordered to report aboard to prepare for a "long voyage."

The ship's representatives said her destination was Oslo, Norway.

It was believed that the Columbus would slip from port shortly, but in view of persistent rumors of British warships in the Gulf of Mexico and Caribbean she was expected to sail as secretly as possible, probably at night without lights.

The same agency also arranged for the departure of the German freighter Arauca, also here since the start of the war. The crew was busy this afternoon painting the vessel black.

VALPARAISO, Chile, Dec. 13—The 4,930-ton German steamer Dusseldorf sailed from this Pacific Ocean harbor today, the fourth to sail of five German ships here at the outbreak of war. The only remaining one is the school ship Velero Priwall.

FINNS REPORT GAIN IN COUNTER-THRUST

Say Russians Are Hurled Back as Major Battle Impends—Soviet Is 'Invaded'

By The United Press.

COPENHAGEN, Denmark, Thursday, Dec. 14—Heavily reinforced Finnish troops early today were reported to be laying siege to the strategic town of Salla, just above the Arctic Circle, where the Russians were said to have lost 7,000 men.

The Finns, concentrating large forces in an effort to prevent the Red Army from reaching the Gulf of Bothnia and cutting Finland in two, hoped to recapture Salla today, frontier dispatches said.

Salla is about 125 miles northeast of the top of the Gulf of Bothnia at the Swedish-Finnish border and slightly northeast of the town of Kemijaervi, where fierce fighting was reported.

Thrust Into Russia Reported

[Finnish forces had carried the war to Russian soil in a strong drive north of Lake Ladoga, according to unofficial reports in Helsinki. This followed closely the reported bombing of the Soviet's Leningrad-Murmansk railway, which was said to have halted an attempt to transport submarines to the Arctic.]

Against the Russians' reported losses of 7,000 men in the new Finnish counter-offensive, the Finns claim to have lost only 230 men.

Continued on Page Nine

Davies Will Resign as Envoy to Belgium To Become an Adviser on Europe to Hull

By FELIX BELAIR Jr.
Special to THE NEW YORK TIMES.

WASHINGTON, Dec. 13—Joseph E. Davies is soon to give up his post as Ambassador to Belgium and take a place in the special division of the State Department dealing with war emergencies.

The Ambassador's resignation is lying on the President's desk. Whether it was offered when Mr. Davies called on the President today or was sent ahead of his return to the United States was not ascertained. The resignation was technical, in any event. Arrangements for the transfer were completed several weeks ago.

The duties to be assigned to Mr. Davies will be similar to those now being performed by Hugh R. Wilson, who recently resigned as Ambassador to Germany, and Breckenridge Long, former Ambassador to Italy. President Roosevelt is said to be desirous of putting the details of the emergency situations abroad in the hands of diplomats who have had experience in the field.

Mr. Davies entered the diplomatic service as Ambassador to Russia and later was transferred to Brussels. He has been credited at various times with an ambition to represent this country in London. He returned to this country yesterday, ostensibly to participate in negotiations over revision of the reciprocal trade agreement with Belgium.

As he left the Executive Office today after conferring with the President, Mr. Davies said that he wanted to be on record as having stated that he was not a candidate for the Secretaryship of the Navy, a post with which his name had been connected in recent rumors.

Mr. Davies will probably go back to Brussels to wind up the affairs of his ambassadorship and also to participate in official activities incident to the start of operation of the trade agreement.

After it became known that information regarding Mr. Davies's resignation had been obtained by THE NEW YORK TIMES, a spokesman of the State Department said that Mr. Davies had been instructed to return here and that he reported today to the President, Secretary Hull and Under-Secretary Welles. The spokesman issued this statement:

"No decision has been reached as to what his future duties will be either in Washington or in the event that he returns to Belgium.

Continued on Page Sixteen

NORTH SEA SUCCESS

British Submarine That Spared Bremen Said to Have Scored Twice

NEW TACTICS IN AIR

Planes Patrol Nazi Base to Prevent Laying of Mines at Night

Special Cable to THE NEW YORK TIMES.

LONDON, Dec. 13—The British Admiralty announced tonight that the British submarine that sighted and spared the German liner Bremen a few days ago had sunk a German U-boat and torpedoed a German cruiser in the North Sea.

The announcement marked the first time that any British submarine had been in action against enemy seacraft. Details of the British submarine's exploit were not given and officials would not make any comment on the identity of the German cruiser involved.

When asked whether the cruiser had sunk after the torpedoing the officials pointed out that the communiqué specified sinking in the case of the U-boat but used the word "torpedoed" in the case of the cruiser. This was taken to mean the cruiser had been damaged. When the action took place was not revealed.

New Air Patrol Fixed

The Air Ministry issued today a statement hinting at new tactics in the evolving strategy of war in the air and on the sea. British planes, it was said, had maintained an all-night watch over the German seaplane bases at Sylt, Borkum and Norderney in Helgoland bight.

The official announcement indicated that a new arm of defense against air attack had been formed and that it was its duty to squelch attacks from the air on enemy territory instead of awaiting the arrival of Nazi air armadas.

Hindsight is sometimes helpful in interpreting the mysterious diplomatic manoeuvring in these uncertain times, but yesterday's announcement that a British submarine failed to sink the Bremen and the latest announcement that British planes roared harmlessly over German naval bases last night do not help much in understanding the way this strange war is developing.

Presumably, the British Admiralty thinks more was gained diplomatically by the strict observance of international law than could have been gained by the sinking of the queen of Germany's merchant navy. Likewise, it may be presumed the British feel there is more to be gained by sending planes to hover over the nests of Germany's mine-laying flying boats than by bombing their bases and that it is better to hold the threat of attack above the Nazi fliers' heads than to try to drive them from British coasts with all the advantage that falls to the fighter who rises fresh to the fray.

Nazis Scoff at Statement

The Germans, of course, scoff at the British statement that they could have sunk the Bremen but did not think it sporting or legal. The truth is, the Germans say, that the British are just trying to put the best face possible on their naval impotence.

The official announcement of the new patrols over the German bases in Helgoland Bight said they were "continuously maintained." Their purpose, it was said, was "to interrupt the activities of mine-laying aircraft operating from these bases." Despite anti-aircraft opposition "the operations were successfully carried out."

Today's Air Ministry statement indicated that Britain's method of meeting the new magnetic mine menace included not only some method of sweeping up the destructive eggs laid by planes and submarines in coastal shipping channels but also contemplated measures to prevent their being laid at all. Aviation experts said there was much about the establishment of what already have been dubbed "security patrols" that is mysterious.

It was pointed out, for instance, that the official statement rather indicated that bombing planes were used, that they circled more or less

Continued on Page Three

The International Situation

Britain's far-flung sea power caught up with a raiding German pocket battleship yesterday in the Western Hemisphere.

A running battle was fought during the day and last night off the Uruguayan coast between the Nazi craft, identified as the Admiral Graf Spee, and two small British cruisers, the Ajax and the Achilles. The cruiser Exeter had also been in the battle, but was damaged and forced to drop out. The pursuit continued with hits scored on both sides until the pocket battleship raced into neutral Montevideo harbor badly damaged and with thirty dead aboard. The Ajax and the Achilles followed and lay outside the harbor. Page 1.]

Under international law Uruguay must now determine the minimum repairs needed to make the German ship seaworthy, and when these repairs have been made the vessel must either put to sea or be interned for the duration of the war. [Page 4.]

London claimed another naval success, reporting that the British submarine that had sighted the liner Bremen on her dash to Germany had sunk a U-boat and torpedoed a German cruiser. At the same time the Air Ministry indicated a new policy of an all-night air patrol over German seaplane bases to frustrate aerial mine-laying. [Page 1.]

Following his adventurous voyage homeward, the Bremen's commander declared at a reception that he believed the liner had been held up in New York last August to help the British. [Page 3.]

While the Finns reported having thrown the Russians back in counter-offensives and were unofficially said to have carried the war to Russian soil [Page 1], a League of Nations committee condemned Russia as an aggressor, called for all possible aid to the Finns by members and non-members alike and suggested expulsion of the Soviet, a development that now seems certain. [Page 1.]

What the League was doing was still kept from the Soviet people. [Page 8.] But a hint that Moscow was not insensitive to criticism was seen in the hasty summoning home of the new Russian Ambassador to Rome, who had not yet had time to present his credentials. [Page 1.]

While the British House of Commons in its first secret session since the World War debated Opposition charges of government bungling on supplies [Page 11], peace talk in the House of Lords by a few members caused Foreign Secretary Halifax to characterize the debate as "unfortunate." [Page 1.]

SOVIET CALLS HOME NEW ROME ENVOY

Italians Believe He Will Be Asked How Seriously They Mean Balkan Warning

By HERBERT L. MATTHEWS
By Telephone to THE NEW YORK TIMES.

ROME, Dec. 13—Nikolai Gorelchin, the new Russian Ambassador, who has not yet had time to present his credentials, was hastily summoned back to Moscow by telegram and left Rome on Monday, it was learned today. The Russian Embassy claims it is a mere informative visit without particular significance and that Mr. Gorelchin, who saw Count Ciano, the Foreign Minister, last week, will return to Rome shortly.

However, it is at least a coincidence that his sudden recall should come at a time when there are almost daily hostile demonstrations against Russia and when the Fascist Grand Council, to say nothing of the entire Italian press, has been issuing warnings to Moscow to keep out of the Balkans. One is entitled to suppose that Joseph Stalin wants to know just what the Italians mean and how serious they are with their threats.

Italy's Earnestness Clear

If that is what his visit is about, Mr. Gorelchin will doubtless inform his government that Italy means business, for genuinely strong measures are being taken to parry the expected Russian thrust, should it try to go beyond Bessarabia. On the other hand, the Soviet Government may have become sensitive about criticism and hostility and may not intend to send Mr. Gorelchin back here.

In connection with the press criticism, Roberto Farinacci's newspaper, the Regime Fascista, offers a novel explanation for the Russo-German alliance. After saying that Finnish resistance has proved Russian weakness, the writer concludes:

"So when England, France and the Osservatore Romano [the Vatican City newspaper] speak of the Russian peril, it is in bad faith. Russia preferred the German alliance because she thought that if she had to fight Germany she would be beaten."

Premier Georges Kiosseivanoff of Bulgaria, in an interview with the Giornale d'Italia's correspondent today, says that while Bulgaria has not renounced "the realization of

Continued on Page Seven

Dispatches from Europe and the Far East are subject to censorship.

BRITISH PEERS URGE NEW PEACE MOVES

Mediation Call Hurts Nation, Halifax Replies—Commons Holds Secret Session

Special Cable to THE NEW YORK TIMES.

LONDON, Dec. 13—The question of making peace now and without military victory arose in the House of Lords today in a debate described by Foreign Secretary Viscount Halifax as "unfortunate because it would create a wrong impression abroad that Britain was not united in her determination to fulfill her war aims."

The debate centered around the problem of whether a lasting peace could be obtained at this time and whether a long war would not mean that the country paid a terrible price in vain.

[Meanwhile the House of Commons in its first secret session since the last war debated for seven hours and a half Opposition charges that the government is bungling the production of vital war supplies.]

The debate was precipitated by a suggestion from the Earl of Darnley that Britain take up the Belgian and Netherland proposal for mediation, which, he said, still is open. Supported by Lord Arnold and the Bishop of Chichester, he said Britain had not done enough after the Versailles treaty to conciliate Germany and warned against a "revenge-producing victory."

Three Peers Reply

Lord Balfour, Viscount Samuel and Lord Snell opposed the Earl amid cheers. Lord Balfour declared there was a reign of violence and terror in Germany, "and as long as that persisted any idea that there was a change of heart or that a freely negotiated peace was possible was illusory."

Lord Darnley maintained that Chancellor Hitler's actions were aimed partly to make Germany free and prosperous but chiefly to make her free from any danger in the future, and every threat made against him made him think aggression more necessary.

Lord Arnold said it was unfortunate the Earl's proposal could not be discussed at a secret session. He contended that laying down peace conditions in advance did not help negotiations, but hindered them. He added:

"If a satisfactory peace could be secured in other respects, this country would not wish to continue the war on account of Austria."

Lord Arnold believed that if the war continued until Herr Hitler was overthrown by revolution, Germany would become Communist and enter into an alliance with Russia. He feared that communism might spread over Eastern Europe and "not only would any peace at the end of a long war be

Continued on Page Twelve

PREY OF 3 CRUISERS

Pocket Battleship Puts In South America Port After 18-Hour Fight

EXETER FORCED OUT

Foe Badly Damaged 1 Ship, but Two Others Continue Chase

By JOHN W. WHITE
Special Cable to THE NEW YORK TIMES.

BUENOS AIRES, Argentina, Thursday, Dec. 14—The German pocket battleship Admiral Graf Spee struggled into Montevideo harbor shortly before last midnight with thirty-six of her crew dead, sixty wounded and the ship badly damaged as the result of an eighteen-hour running battle with the British cruisers Exeter, Ajax and Achilles.

Shortly after the Graf Spee's arrival two British cruisers, the Ajax and the Achilles, arrived in the outer roads off Montevideo, but at an early hour this morning had not reported to the authorities ashore regarding their casualties.

[Returning from a visit aboard the Admiral Graf Spee, the German Minister to Uruguay, Otto Langman, said that the dead included a lieutenant and the wounded the commander of the ship, The Associated Press reported. His statement that the ship was the Spee and not the Admiral Scheer as reported at first was the first indication that the Graf Spee had been operating in the Atlantic.

[The spokesman for the German Legation at Montevideo said that "there are thirty-six dead and sixty wounded aboard the Graf Spee, mostly because the British used mustard gas shells," The United Press reported. The spokesman said that the damage to the battleship was insignificant.

[Captains of six British ships captured by the Graf Spee off the South American and South African coasts will be landed at Montevideo, the spokesman added.]

Open Fire on the Spee

The British squadron was under the command of Commodore H. H. Harwood.

Contact with the Graf Spee was established six times during the morning when the pocket battleship attacked the Ajax while the latter was convoying the French passenger liner Formosa from Rio de Janeiro to Montevideo. The Ajax called for help and the Exeter and Achilles arrived at full speed and opened fire on the battleship.

The four warships fought an intense artillery duel from 6 o'clock until 10. Despite the Admiral Spee's speed and heavier armament she was repeatedly hit by shells from the British cruisers, especially the Exeter. The Spee, accordingly, directed her main efforts to putting the Exeter out of commission. By this time all four warships were running southward, the Formosa having dropped back for safety.

The Exeter, finally disabled, was forced to drop out of the battle but by this time the Spee was so badly damaged that the commander began running at full speed for the River Plate, closely followed by the Ajax and Achilles.

The battle apparently lasted on and off all day, as the firing was renewed twice after the warships were within sight of the Uruguayan shore. Just after the warships passed Punta del Este, which projects far out to sea, the two British cruisers turned westward toward the shore to take advantage of the setting sun by getting the Graf Spee silhouetted against the reflected light in the eastern sky while they were protected by the shadow of the land.

Spee Changes Her Course

This forced the Spee to change her course disadvantageously to the southeast. Then the British warships renewed their heavy firing, which continued until well after dark. Under cover of night the Graf Spee changed her course and finally reached the refuge of Montevideo,

Continued on Page Four

"All the News That's Fit to Print."

The New York Times.

LATE CITY EDITION
POSTSCRIPT
Cloudy, preceded by rain today, slightly colder tonight.
Temperatures Yesterday—Max., 51; Min., 44.

VOL. LXXXIX...No. 30,026. Entered as Second-Class Matter, Postoffice, New York, N. Y. NEW YORK, TUESDAY, APRIL 9, 1940. P THREE CENTS NEW YORK CITY and Vicinity | FOUR CENTS Elsewhere Except in 7th and 8th Postal Zones.

GERMANS OCCUPY DENMARK, ATTACK OSLO; NORWAY THEN JOINS WAR AGAINST HITLER; CAPITAL IS REPORTED BOMBED FROM AIR

HOUSE TO CONSIDER WAGE ACT CHANGES EARLY NEXT WEEK

Leaders in Surprise Moves Also Slate Bill for Court Review of Agency Rulings

LABOR LAW ACTION LIKELY

Proponents of Amendments Expect Drive to Dispose of All Labor Legislation

House consideration next week was slated for the bill to amend the Wages and Hours Act and for the Logan-Walter bill to provide for a court review of decisions by governmental agencies. [Page 1.]

A refusal by the Supreme Court to review the Labor Board's order in the Republic Steel case sustained the reinstatement of 5,000 C. I. O. strikers with $5,000,000 back pay. [Page 20.]

The Socialist party convention, at Washington, stated in a resolution that "the interests of American working men and women will best be served by the making of an immediate peace between the C. I. O. and A. F. L." [Page 1.]

Colonel Harrington, WPA Administrator, will be questioned Thursday by the House Appropriations Subcommittee on evidence gathered by its investigators bearing on the 1941 relief outlay. [Page 20.]

The NLRB refused to relieve Mrs. Elinore M. Herrick of further responsibility in connection with the election of employes of the Consolidated Edison Company of New York after a charge of collusion with the company. [Page 20.]

Two Revision Bills Slated

By HENRY N. DORRIS
Special to THE NEW YORK TIMES.

WASHINGTON, April 8—House leaders decided today on consideration early next week of the Barden bill to amend the Wages and Hours Act, a decision which occasioned surprise in labor quarters since it had been assumed this measure would follow the Smith or Norton amendments to the National Labor Relations Act.

But this was not the only surprise, because the tentative calendar for next week also contained a place for the Logan-Walter bill providing court review of any decision of a governmental agency which has the force of law.

When these two measures are out of the way, proponents of amendments to the Wagner Act expect to win consideration of their measures. Just how they will manage this was not revealed, but it was said by one member that the procedure was for a "Bang! Bang! Bang!" program that would wipe the House calendar clean of labor legislation that has "plagued" it for more than a year.

The Barden bill has been pending since last August, when a rule was granted for its consideration. It was never considered, however, because of the "compromise" by which the lending-spending and United States Housing Authority bills—desired by the Administration—were taken up. Both of these failed to obtain consideration, but they served to crowd out the Barden bill, which primarily aims at a redefinition of the "area of production" provision of the Wages and Hours Act.

Would Remove "Ambiguities"

The amendment proposed by Representative Barden of North Carolina, a member of the House Labor Committee, proposes to remove the "ambiguities" of the "area of production" clause and the ruling subsequently made on it by the former Wages and Hours Administrator, Elmer F. Andrews.

Under that ruling processing plants located within ten miles of the area where agricultural products are grown or harvested are exempt from the provisions which require them to pay a minimum wage of thirty cents an hour or work their employes not to exceed forty-two hours per week without overtime pay of time and a half. The Barden amendment proposes

Continued on Page Twenty

The International Situation

War caught up two more countries in its clutches today as the Germans invaded Denmark and attacked Norway.

In the early morning Nazi troops crossed the southern border of Denmark, landed on Danish soil from warships and occupied the Danish capital, Copenhagen—all apparently without resistance. [Page 1.]

Almost at the same time a diplomatic dispatch to Washington announced that Norway was at war with Germany. [Page 1.] This development followed an attempt by German warships—more than 100 of which had been sighted last night moving northward in the Kattegat—to force an entry, with aerial support, into Oslo Fjord. At latest reports German troops were debarking on the Norwegian coast and had entered Navik, Bergen and Trondheim, while the Norwegians were said to have moved their capital, which was reported bombed.

Berlin explained it was taking Denmark and Norway under its "protection" to prevent any hostile attack upon them. [Page 4.]

There had been at least one suggestion yesterday of German troop movements in Scandinavia. A Nazi transport had been torpedoed off Southern Norway with a loss of 150 out of some 300 uniformed men aboard. In the same neighborhood a large German tanker was sent to the bottom. [Page 1.]

The mining of Norwegian waters had taken Norway completely by surprise and eight German freighters were apparently in the same predicament, as they were trapped in those waters and unable to get home. With British warships patrolling the mine fields the ore traffic at Narvik was halted and it seemed likely that Swedish iron shipments would be halved. [Page 3.] Norway protested to both Britain and France against the mining, terming it "an open breach of international law" and demanding that the mines be removed. [Page 1.] London had expected the protest and discounted it. But the British were believed to be ready to go to Norway's aid against the Germans. [Page 2.]

With a loophole in the blockade apparently plugged in Scandinavia the British gave some of their attention to the Balkans; their envoys to the countries of that region began their conferences. [Page 9.] At the same time Southeastern Europe was startled by Rumania's detention of a fleet of British barges carrying dynamite, which, according to the Germans, was to have been used for blocking the Danube. British quarters insisted the explosives were to have been used only for destroying river craft in the event of a German invasion of Rumania. [Page 1.]

ROOSEVELT EFFIGY 'FRONT' GUN TARGET

Healy Also Swears Cassidy Wanted 12 in Congress Shot in Capital as Gesture

Denis A. Healy, star prosecution witness in the trial of seventeen men indicted for conspiring to overthrow the United States Government, testified yesterday in the Brooklyn Federal Court that some of the defendants had used a likeness of President Roosevelt's head as a target during rifle practice.

He swore that John F. Cassidy, a defendant who was prominent in the Christian Front, had favored "going to Washington and shooting twelve Congressmen to show that the Christian Front means business," and he testified that William Gerald Bishop, another defendant, wanted to place Major General Van Horn Mosely, U. S. A. retired, at the head of a dictatorship after overthrowing the present government.

Telling of how members of the group practiced making crude bombs out of empty beer cans, Healy said that they had discussed committing acts of sabotage here if the United States entered the war. He declared that Bishop had boasted to him of knowing who was responsible for an explosion he said had occurred on an oil tanker in the lower bay a few days earlier.

Cross-Examination Begun

Healy finished his direct testimony at 2:30 P. M. yesterday after having been on the witness stand for five hours, beginning Friday afternoon. He began at once a hammering cross-examination at the hands of defense counsel, which two estimated would last for at least two full court days in their effort to discredit his story of having posed as one of the plotters, meanwhile keeping the Federal Bureau of Investigation informed of every development.

He was forced to admit that he had lied on numerous occasions, that he had pretended to be anti-Semitic in order to "carry out my role"; that he had once approached Bishop for aid in smuggling a relative into this country from Canada, and that he had once been convicted of street fighting, for which he received a suspended sentence.

Conceding that he had testified for the government in a previous case, Healy denied that he was a "professional witness," as was charged by former Magistrate Leo J. Healy, counsel for eleven of the defendants. He said the government had arranged a leave of absence for him from the New York Central Railroad, and was paying him the same salary while he was

Continued on Page Sixteen

BRITISH EXPLOSIVES HELD BY RUMANIANS

Fleet of Barges Detained at Danube Port—Nazis Charge Plot to Block River

By The Associated Press.

BUCHAREST, Rumania, April 8—Detention of a fleet of dynamite-laden British barges, said by Germans to be designed to blow up a narrow Danube gateway and block a German supply line, today electrified Southeastern Europe with the fear war soon might spread to this quarter of the world.

Rumanian police, acting on a tip said to have been supplied by the pro-Nazi Iron Guard, halted the fleet near Giurgiu, Danube River port whence Germany ships much-needed Rumanian oil supplies. Aboard were tons of dynamite.

Germans alleged the British planned to blockade the spot in the Danube known as the Iron Gate by sinking the barges and wrecking the narrow channel where the river cuts through the Carpathian barrier between high cliffs. The Iron Gate is 280 miles up river from Giurgiu.

Official British quarters, acknowledging the barges were loaded with explosives, insisted they were to be used only for destroying Allied river craft in case of a German invasion of Rumania.

The only official British statement on the matter was a communiqué saying merely that Rumanian authorities had seized two cases of firearms which a British barge captain had neglected to declare in passing customs.

Troops Guard Gateway

The British aim was reported in Germany to be the blocking of the Iron Gate with sunken barges and blasting of the narrow artificial channel through which all river shipping must pass.

Two hundred Rumanian and Yugoslav soldiers armed with machine guns tonight were guarding the gateway where the Danube forms the boundary between Rumania and Yugoslavia. Giurgiu was turned into a military zone by the Rumanian Army, which banned all entries without special permits.

The German version of the seizure, said to have taken place Saturday, reported more than 100 British Army, Navy and Air Force men, who were to have participated in the coup, had been arrested.

Both the Rumanian Foreign Office and British quarters, however, insisted there was no basis to the German reports that Britons had been seized aboard the barges, and official London sources declined to

Continued on Page Eight

REICH SHIP IS SUNK

150 Lost Off Transport Torpedoed by British Off South Norway

ALL MEN IN UNIFORM

Large Nazi Tanker Also Sunk by Allies, but Crew Is Rescued

Special Cable to THE NEW YORK TIMES.

OSLO, Norway, April 8—A British submarine torpedoed and sank the German troop ship Rio de Janeiro today off Lillesand, on the south coast of Norway. At least 150 German soldiers are believed to have perished.

It is reported here that the German transport, formerly a freighter on the South American run, had at least 300 men aboard and that fewer than 150 are accounted for. The ship, of 5,261 tons, was out of Hamburg and was classified here as a transport because all the men aboard were in uniform.

Another large German vessel, the tanker Posidonia, was also reported torpedoed today off the south Norwegian coast, but without loss of life.

[Lloyd's Register of Shipping does not list a German tanker Posidonia. The Associated Press, in recording the report of still a third sinking, that of the German tanker Kreta, indicated that there might be some confusion over the Posidonia's case, since the Kreta, apparently to conceal her identity, had sent out the call letters of the Posidonia. Other reports said that the Posidonia used the Kreta's signals.]

The report of the torpedoing of the Rio de Janeiro received here states that the British submarine intercepted the transport off the Norwegian coast, hailed her and fired a warning shot across her bows. This was disregarded and the troopship altered her course, speeding toward land or territorial waters. The submarine then fired a torpedo.

Some Jump Overboard

With the explosion some of the Germans immediately jumped overboard. A Norwegian fishing vessel was near by and went to the rescue, taking these men out of the water.

As the transport appeared to be settling, the submarine fired a second torpedo, with terrific result. An iron bar from the ship was hurled 150 feet and struck the rescuing fishing vessel, killing three of the Germans who had been taken aboard.

The fishing vessel continued its work of rescue and was aided by other fishing craft that hurried out when an alarm was sounded along the coast. These ships took a total

Continued on Page Five

NAZIS IN NORWAY

Troops Debark at Ports —Government Leaves Oslo for Hamar

NARVIK IS OCCUPIED

Air Attacks on Capital Reported—Civilians Are to Be Evacuated

Sweden Is Mobilizing

By The United Press.

STOCKHOLM, Sweden, April 9—The Swedish radio announced today that the government had ordered general mobilization.

Wireless to THE NEW YORK TIMES.

LONDON, Tuesday, April 9—The Paris correspondent of Reuters, British news agency, reported this morning that the Oslo radio had announced that German troops had debarked in Norwegian ports at 3 A. M.

[Mrs. J. Borden Harriman, United States Minister to Norway, notified the State Department early this morning that she had been informed by the Foreign Minister that Norway considered herself at war with Germany.

[Mrs. Harriman also reported that at 5:30 A. M. Norwegian shore batteries were still engaged in battle with four invading German warships that were trying to force entry into Oslo Fjord.]

It was also announced that the Norwegian Government had left Oslo for Hamar, in Central Norway.

Reuters further reported that the Germans had occupied the cities of Bergen and Trondheim.

[The Oslo radio announced this morning that the Norwegian Government had ordered general mobilization after an all night session of the Cabinet, The Associated Press reported.]

Reuters also reported from Paris that the Oslo radio announced this morning that the Germans had occupied Narvik.

The Norwegian legation here issued the following communiqué this morning:

"The German Minister in Oslo saw the Norwegian Foreign Secretary at 4:30 o'clock this morning and demanded that Norway should be handed over to the German administration. If this was not done all resistance would be defeated. This demand was refused and hostilities have started."

LONDON, Tuesday, April 9 (AP) —A Reuters, British news agency,

Continued on Page Two

Canadian Premier to See Roosevelt Soon, Stopping Off En Route South for a Vacation

By FREDERICK T. BIRCHALL
By Telephone to THE NEW YORK TIMES.

OTTAWA, April 8—Prime Minister W. L. Mackenzie King will leave Ottawa in a few days for a short holiday in the South of the United States. On his way through Washington he will pay a visit to President Roosevelt at the White House.

This will be Mr. Mackenzie King's first visit to Washington since war was declared. There are several questions he would like to take up with Mr. Roosevelt. There are doubtless also matters the President will be glad to discuss with the Canadian Prime Minister.

While there is no information here as to the precise subjects that may figure in the conversation, some of those ripe for discussion are well known. Among these are the progress of the St. Lawrence Waterway project, continuance of the trade agreements renewed last year and the extent to which the United States can aid Canada's war effort.

As to the St. Lawrence project, it is known that both administrations are anxious to have the treaty signed with as little delay as possible so that it may be submitted to Congress in time for consideration before adjournment. Since the project again came up opposition to it has developed in both countries. It will not have easy sailing.

Among matters even more pressing are the exemption of Americans resident in Canada from the conditions affecting the ownership of foreign currency and securities and the status of American fliers who desire to come here and enlist under the Air Training Plan and for overseas service.

It has been strongly urged that Canada modify for these the oath of allegiance now required from all who join her forces, which does not automatically give them Canadian citizenship, while causing them to lose their own.

Another point of interest is Canada's desire to obtain from the United States more airplanes for use in the initial stages of the commonwealth air training plan. The present prospect is that there will be a shortage of planes until Canadian plants, now in receipt of about $40,000,000 worth of orders, can reach the stage of advanced production.

Any or all of these topics may be profitably discussed between the

Continued on Page Five

NEW THEATRE OF WAR IS OPENED

German troops invaded Denmark at 5 A. M. today. A few hours previously German warships attempted to force an entry into Oslo Fjord (cross). This action, which brought Norway into the war against the Reich, followed the sighting last night of a German armada steaming northward off Lessoe (3). Near Lillesand (1) a German troop transport was torpedoed by a British submarine and a U-boat was rumored to have been sunk. Off Faerder Light (2) one and perhaps two German tankers were sent down. The Allied mine fields off Norway are indicated by arrows.

NORWAY DECLARES WAR ON GERMANY

Washington Notified of Action by U. S. Minister at Oslo—Warships Sent There

Special to THE NEW YORK TIMES.

WASHINGTON, Tuesday, April 9—Norway is at war with Germany. This was the word received soon after 1 o'clock this morning by the State Department from Mrs. J. Borden Harriman, the American Minister at Oslo.

The startling information was received less than two hours after equally disturbing intelligence had been received of the German occupation of Denmark.

[President Roosevelt, at Hyde Park, kept in close touch with the State Department and his special train was held ready for a quick return to Washington, The United Press reported.]

The State Department announced the state of war in the following communique:

"The American Minister at Oslo, Mrs. J. Borden Harriman, telegraphed the Department tonight that the Foreign Minister had informed her that the Norwegians had fired on four German warships coming up Oslo Fjord and that Norway was at war with Germany. In response to a request by the British Minister to Norway the American Legation at Oslo has been authorized to take over British interests in Norway in case he is forced to leave."

Envoy's Request Explained

State Department officials, in answer to queries regarding the apparently ambiguous last paragraph of Mrs. Harriman's cable, said that there could be no doubt that Norway was at war against Germany. They pointed out that the Norwegians were firing on German warships and the British envoy was considering the possibility that he might have to evacuate, although he was not certain he would have to do so.

[The United Press said Mrs. Harriman reported that she had taken charge of the British and French Legations.]

It was reported on usually good authority that American warships in European waters had been ordered to proceed northward so they could take part in the evacuation of American citizens in Denmark,

Continued on Page Four

ALLIED MINES BRING A PROTEST BY OSLO

Breach of International Law Charged by Koht—Sweden Takes Defense Measures

By The Associated Press.

OSLO, Norway, April 8—Foreign Minister Halvdan Koht told Parliament today that Norway had protested to Paris and London against the mining of her waters at dawn, a sudden move by which the Allies hope to cut off Germany's Swedish ore shipments through Norway's western coastal waters.

In a public statement Mr. Koht charged the Allies with an "open breach of international law" and demanded that the mines "be removed at once and that the guard by foreign warships cease." Britain was patrolling Norway's waters near the new mine fields, stating such action would be for forty-eight hours to warn away neutral vessels.

In all Scandinavia statesmen, in realization that the dreaded day had arrived bringing the European war to the north, gathered to discuss the cloudy future and await a feared retaliation from Germany.

Leaders of the Norwegian Parliament, which was called into special session, said they were behind the government's action in the crisis. A Cabinet meeting was held in Oslo, which military and naval leaders attended.

Political Leaders Meet

Leaders of all of Denmark's political parties met in Copenhagen, and in Stockholm Swedish leaders watched gravely. The Swedish Foreign Office announced there had been no violation of Swedish waters, but officials admittedly were worried.

The Oslo newspaper Arbejderbladet, a government organ, said that "the situation is particularly grave for our country, but in such times we must keep our heads cool."

"Any tendency toward nervousness or panic would only make it worse," the paper said. "Norway naturally will protest in a most emphatic way against any closing of her waters and demand respect for international laws. But it is a ques-

Continued on Page Four

Dispatches from Europe and the Far East are subject to censorship at the source.

COPENHAGEN TAKEN

Troops Cross Border as Ships Debark Others in Sudden Nazi Blow

DANES FALLING BACK

Germans Say They Act to Forestall Foe and Protect Neighbor

By SVEND CARSTENSEN
Wireless to THE NEW YORK TIMES.

COPENHAGEN, Denmark, Tuesday, April 9—German troops crossed the Danish frontier at 5 o'clock this morning.

Three German cruisers arrived at that same hour at Middelfart and troops immediately occupied streets of the town.

Copenhagen was also occupied by German troops this morning.

The invasion came without warning. For some hours before the crossing of the border reports had circulated here that the Germans of South Jutland were expecting German troop trains carrying 45,000 men to arrive at the town of Flensburg during the night. That German town on the border was characterized as a convenient port for shipping troops northward, and although Danish border guards had been put in the highest state of preparedness it was not thought that there would be any threat to Denmark.

This belief had been bolstered by the fact that the fleet of more than a hundred German warships that passed through the Great Belt into the Kattegat and Skagerrak yesterday and early today included troopships—and it was presumed that this fleet was on the way to Norway to retaliate against the British Navy.

More Centers Seized

Mr. Carstensen left Copenhagen after the entry of German forces and went to Kolding, where he filed the following dispatch:

Special Cable to THE NEW YORK TIMES.

KOLDING, Denmark, Tuesday, April 9—The German occupation continues here. It is reported that two ferry points on the Great Belt—Nyborg and Korsoer—have been occupied.

Troops have landed at Middelfart on a large scale. A Little Belt bridge has been reported seized and the city of Aalborg in North Jutland has been occupied.

Although there were no reports of clashes between Danish troops and the invaders today, military resistance was expected at Haderslebem, about thirty miles north of the German border. The placing of guns and erection of barricades were reported from that town.

After leaving Copenhagen I observed from my automobile swarms of fast German planes flying over towns dropping badly printed leaflets that laid responsibility for Germany's invading Denmark and Norway to what was termed a British intention to make Scandinavia a theatre of war.

The leaflets termed Winston Churchill, Britain's First Lord of the Admiralty, "the century's greatest warmonger," who planned to police Norwegian and Danish waters against the wills of the two countries.

The statement said that, since Norway and Denmark were unable to resist effectively, Germany had resolved to act in advance of a British attack and by her own forces take over "protection" of Danish and Norwegian neutrality and "guard" the countries during the war. It was asserted that Germany did not intend to obtain bases for her fight against Britain but solely aimed at preventing Scandinavia from being a battlefield for "British expansion of the war."

According to the statement, negotiations were going on between the German and Danish Governments to make Denmark "secure" and assure that her army and navy were maintained and the Danish people's freedom respected. The country's independence, it was said, is fully secured. The proclamation

Continued on Page Two

"All the News That's Fit to Print."

The New York Times.

LATE CITY EDITION
POSTSCRIPT
Fair, not much change in temperature today. Tomorrow cloudy.
Temperatures Yesterday—Max. .. ; Min. ..

VOL. LXXXIX...No. 30,057. Entered as Second-Class Matter, Postoffice, New York, N. Y. NEW YORK, FRIDAY, MAY 10, 1940. THREE CENTS NEW YORK CITY and Vicinity | FOUR CENTS Elsewhere Except in 7th and 8th Postal Zones.

NAZIS INVADE HOLLAND, BELGIUM, LUXEMBOURG BY LAND AND AIR; DIKES OPENED; ALLIES RUSH AID

U. S. FREEZES CREDIT

President Acts to Guard Funds Here of Three Invaded Nations

SHIP RULING TODAY

Envoy Reports to Hull on Germany's Attacks by Air and Land

Special to THE NEW YORK TIMES.

WASHINGTON, Friday, May 10—President Roosevelt early today ordered the freezing of all credits held by Belgium, the Netherlands and Luxembourg in this country.

He called a conference for 10:30 A. M. of heads of the State, War and Navy Departments to consider pressing problems of neutrality.

The President acted swiftly after news of Germany's invasion of the three European neutral countries reached Washington and galvanized high officials into action. His order with regard to the freezing of all the invaded countries' credits and cash balances here was a counterpart of the action taken after Germany invaded Norway and Denmark.

Congress this week completed action on legislation that specifically authorizes the President by decree to freeze all such cash and credits of any belligerent. The object is to prevent these resources from falling into the hands of the invading power.

Ships to Be Considered

The President's order directed Secretary of the Treasury Henry Morgenthau Jr. to freeze all Belgian, French and Luxembourg credits before the markets open this mo. ing.

It was announced also that the conference to be held at 10:30 will consider the question of Belgian and Netherland ships that may be in United States ports. Attorney General Robert H. Jackson also will attend this conference.

The White House, meanwhile, indicated some skepticism of the official explanation of the invasion given by German Propaganda Minister Joseph Goebbels, who was reported to have said that the Germans moved because of inforr that Great Britain and Fr tended to invade the co volved.

"Nevertheless," saic .. pnen T. Early, Presidential secretary, after he had quoted the Goebbels statement, "it remains to be seen who invaded who."

It was announced that the President would remain awake throughout the night, if necessary, to receive reports and consult with officials. Sumner Welles, Under-Secretary of State, at 1:45 A. M. joined the group of State Department officials who remained on duty at the department.

Report From Ambassador

A general invasion of the three neutrals by heavy German land and air forces was reported to the State Department and Mr. Roosevelt early today by Ambassador John J. Cudahy at Brussels.

After trying vainly to re-establish telephone connection with Secretary of State Cordell Hull, over which he had relayed a "blow-by-blow" description of developments several hours earlier, the Ambassador got through the following terse message:

"German planes continue to cross the border and are bombing the airport near Brussels. It seems to be a general attack on all three countries."

A State Department press liaison officer who was relaying latest diplomatic bulletins to reporters as they came in by transatlantic telephone, dropped the cryptic remark:

"As the American Ambassador spoke from Brussels, an embassy military attaché stood at his elbow."

After relaying the information to the President that the Belgian Government had ordered all hands to stand by, Ambassador Cudahy again called Secretary Hull between 10 and 11 o'clock and said he had been informed by officials in Brussels that one German and

Continued on Page Two

The International Situation

In the midst of Britain's Cabinet crisis Germany struck another powerful blow early this morning by invading the Netherlands, Belgium and Luxembourg.

After swarms of planes had engaged in air fights over Amsterdam, parachute troops, some of them clad in Netherland uniforms, descended at strategic points while planes bombed air fields. The Netherlands resisted the incursion and promptly opened the dikes that are part of her water defense system. [Page 1.]

Parachute troops likewise made surprise landings in Belgium and bombs from 100 planes blasted the Brussels airport. [Page 1.]

Appeals for help were dispatched to the Allies by the invaded countries and it was understood that machinery of assistance was being set in motion. Queen Wilhelmina in a proclamation issued at The Hague declared, "I and my government will do our duty." [Page 1.]

As in the case of Norway, Berlin explained that the German action had been taken to forestall the Allies; an announcement said that an attack on Germany had been planned through the territory of the Low Countries. What the Reich was doing, it was declared, was safeguarding the neutrality of those countries. [Page 1.]

President Roosevelt lost no time in acting on the new situation. After night conferences he ordered the freezing of credits of the three invaded countries. Further measures are to be taken today. [Page 1.]

London, meanwhile, announced that British troops had occupied Iceland to prevent a possible German seizure of that former Danish possession. [Page 1.]

Before all these happenings Neville Chamberlain had appeared to be on his way out as Prime Minister, but today it was expected the new developments might save him.

Following upon his relatively narrow escape in the House of Commons vote on Wednesday night, Mr. Chamberlain set about yesterday to see what could be done to satisfy his critics. He offered Cabinet posts to two leaders of the Labor Opposition, but they refused to serve under him. As to whether they would serve under another Conservative, they delayed their reply. If Mr. Chamberlain steps out of office, it is thought probable his place will be taken by the present Foreign Secretary, Viscount Halifax, with Winston Churchill acting as government spokesman in the Commons, from the floor of which the peer would by tradition be barred. [Page 1.]

A new offset to the Norwegian reverses was a London announcement that British submarines had attacked three German convoys and scored eleven torpedo hits, in addition to destroying two ships sailing home. [Page 6.]

Moreover, the Allies' Narvik campaign seemed to be making progress. From that far northern area it was reported that two Allied columns closing in on the railway to the port were within ten miles of each other near the Swedish border: their intention apparently was to join and drive westward along the railroad to Narvik itself, which is held by the Nazis. The Germans, in their effort to thwart the besiegers, were said to be landing parachute troops and supplying them by air. [Page 4.]

In the aftermath of the campaign in the south of the country Foreign Minister Koht disclosed that four of Norway's six divisions had been lost—killed, wounded or captured by the Nazis or interned by Sweden. [Page 6.]

Bombs Drop on Swiss Soil

By The United Press.

BERNE, Switzerland, Friday, May 10—The army staff announced today that foreign airplanes had dropped bombs in the Berne Jura Alpine district between Delemont, near the frontier, and Mount Terr, damaging a railroad.

Traffic continued over the road, the army staff said. It added that other foreign planes were flying over Swiss territory near Basle but that no details had been received.

MUSSOLINI TO LET 'ONLY FACTS' SPEAK

Press Assures Yugoslavia, but Reminds Her of Fate of Poland and Norway

By HERBERT L. MATTHEWS

By Telephone to THE NEW YORK TIMES.

ROME, May 9—The fourth anniversary of the founding of the new Italian Empire was celebrated today in an atmosphere of warlike preparation. The army was honored, Italian armed strength was glorified and the country was told by its leading commentators that the empire would soon earn that "freedom of the seas" which to Italians means domination of the Mediterranean.

Rome, like every other city in the empire, resounded today to martial music while thousands of soldiers paraded through streets from whose buildings hung innumerable flags. The great ceremony was at the Piazza Venezia this morning. Premier Mussolini awarded gold and silver medals to the kin of soldiers fallen in Fascismo's three wars in Ethiopia, Spain and Albania. Later, responding to the insistent appeal of the thousands of men massed below his balcony, he spoke very briefly, only to say that he was resuming his cloak of silence.

"May 9, 1936, was a great day in the history of the country, a day of solar victory," he said. "After my speeches, you must accustom yourself to my silence. Only facts will break it."

Small groups in the crowd thereupon began yelling "Tunisia!" and "Malta!" but the cries were not general.

At the same time this morning

Continued on Page Seven

ICELAND OCCUPIED BY BRITISH FORCE

Secret Expedition Is Justified as Thwarting Action There by Germany

By JAMES MacDONALD

Special Cable to THE NEW YORK TIMES.

LONDON, Friday, May 10—Forestalling a possible German swoop on the strategically valuable former Danish dominion of Iceland, the British have landed an expeditionary force there, it was announced this morning by the Foreign Office here.

Neither the size of the British contingent, which was sent out in the deepest secrecy, nor its place of landing was revealed in the official communiqué.

The landing of the expeditionary force was still going at an early hour this morning. Observers guessed that the landing place must be Reykjavik.

TEXT OF COMMUNIQUE

The official announcement read as follows:

Since the German seizure of Denmark it has become necessary to reckon with the possibility of a sudden German descent on Iceland.

It is clear that in the face of an attack on Iceland, even on a very small scale, the Icelandic Government would be unable to prevent their country from falling completely into German hands.

His Majesty's Government have accordingly decided to preclude this possibility which would de-

Continued on Page Three

ALLIED HELP SPED

Netherland and Belgian Appeals Answered by British and French

TACTICS ARE WATCHED

London Thinks Move an Effort to Get Bases to Attack Britain

Italians Reported Massing

By The United Press

BUENOS AIRES, Argentina, Friday, May 10—The Madrid radio was heard broadcasting today that the British had closed the Strait of Gibraltar and that Italy was massing troops on the French frontier.

Special Cable to THE NEW YORK TIMES.

LONDON, Friday, May 10—The British Government received appeals for help early today from both the Netherlands and Belgium.

The British and French reply to the Netherland-Belgian appeals was prompt. Representatives of the respective governments here were told by 8:30 A. M. (3:30 A. M. New York time) they could expect all the help Britain could give them.

The Netherland Legation here received assurance that its country and Belgium were now regarded as Allies of Britain and France.

Within a few minutes after receipt of official news of the invasion of the Low Countries, the British Cabinet was called to 10 Downing Street and was in session with Prime Minister Neville Chamberlain.

According to information here, the Belgian Cabinet was in Brussels and Premier Hubert Pierlot conferred with King Leopold.

The German invasion of the Low Countries had been expected in London, and it must be presumed the Allies were ready for it to some extent.

Allies Visible to Planes

The biggest handicap to the British and French was in the timing of the German thrust at dawn. This prevented the Allies moving troops under cover of darkness, and since hundreds of German planes already had flown over practically all of Netherland and Belgian territory for some hours, the disposition of Allied troops and their every movement must have been known to the German High Command.

While the Netherlanders and Belgians had taken every precaution

Continued on Page Four

BRUSSELS IS RAIDED

400 Reported Killed—Troops Cross Border at Four Points

PARACHUTE INVASION

Mobilization Is Ordered and Allied Aid Asked—Luxembourg Attacked

Wireless to THE NEW YORK TIMES.

BRUSSELS, Belgium, Friday, May 10—The invasion Belgium had feared since the outbreak of the European war came before dawn this morning. About a hundred German planes flew over this city and bombed the airport.

The airfield at Antwerp also was bombed. Parachute troops were landed at Hasselt in Eastern Belgium. Artillery fire was reported heard along the German and Luxembourg frontiers.

Anti-aircraft guns at the airport commenced firing with the appearance of the first invaders and kept up a steady barrage. Those in the center of the city went into action at 5:30 A. M.

Above the drone of airplane engines could be heard the staccato of machine guns. Bombs wrecked many houses in the vicinity of the airport and caused some loss of life. [Exchange Telegraph (British news agency) said 400 persons had been killed in the first raid.]

Reports from Antwerp and other parts of the country said German planes had flown constantly over since 4:30 A. M., keeping anti-aircraft batteries steadily in action.

Premier Hubert Pierlot and Foreign Minister Paul-Henri Spaak conferred with King Leopold and then called an emergency meeting of the Cabinet. The radio broadcast repeated summonses to all soldiers to join their units at once. A "state of alarm" was decreed throughout the country with the appearance of the first planes.

The Belgian radio also stated German parachute troops had fluttered down at Nivelles, less than twenty miles south of Brussels, and at Saint Trond, about thirty-five miles east of the capital.

The broadcast stated that Germany had made no demarche in Brussels before the invasion.

Wireless to THE NEW YORK TIMES.

LONDON, Friday, May 10—The Germans crossed the Belgian frontier at four points this morning, according to an announcement over

Continued on Page Two

Chamberlain Saved by Nazi Blow In Low Countries, London Thinks

By RAYMOND DANIELL

Special Cable to THE NEW YORK TIMES.

LONDON, Friday, May 10—The first effect of the German attack on the Low Countries is expected to be that Prime Minister Chamberlain will be saved just when it looked as if he was sure to fall.

It was believed that the Labor party, which so far has refused to serve under him in a truly national government, and only yesterday rejected a formal offer to do so, will now close ranks, forget political difficulties and take any Cabinet job offered to its leaders. Furthermore, the Labor party conference, which was supposed to start at Bournemouth on Monday, now will probably be called off.

There is just a possibility that Mr. Chamberlain may quit immediately and turn his seals of office over to First Lord of the Admiralty Winston Churchill. This was a strong but unconfirmed rumor as a Cabinet meeting held this morning came to an end.

In addition, it was said that under Mr. Churchill, Alfred Duff Cooper would receive the Admiralty post, Anthony Eden the War Office and that Viscount Halifax would remain at the Foreign Office.

Until the invasion of the Low Countries was known, the consensus of political observers here had been that the end of the Chamberlain Government could not be long delayed.

The two questions uppermost were how soon it would take place and who would succeed him at No. 10 Downing Street. The betting had been that it would be sooner rather than later and that Foreign Secretary Viscount Halifax would be the next Prime Minister, with Mr. Churchill serving as his spokesman in the House of Commons, from whose floor the present Foreign Secretary, as a peer, is barred by tradition.

The troubles of the 71-year-old Prime Minister, who struggled vainly to maintain Europe's peace by appeasement and who was accused in the House of Commons of bungling the business of war-making, increased rather than diminished during the day. However, the House, despite the gravity of the internal crisis and perils abroad, decided to take its usual twelve-day Whitsuntide holiday, subject to recall in the event of major developments, which followed promptly.

Mr. Chamberlain's efforts to broaden the base of his Cabinet by

Continued on Page Five

NAZIS SWOOP ON THE LOW COUNTRIES

By land and air German troops descended this morning upon the Netherlands, Belgium and Luxembourg. The principal land incursion into the Netherlands was at Roermond.

Ribbentrop Charges Allies Plotted With the Lowlands

By GEORGE AXELSSON

Wireless to THE NEW YORK TIMES.

BERLIN, Friday, May 10—Foreign Minister Joachim von Ribbentrop at 9 o'clock this morning announced that Reich forces had launched military operations against Holland, Belgium and Luxembourg to "protect their neutrality."

Earlier it was reported that German troops had occupied Maastricht, the Netherlands, and had "landed" contingents in Brussels, probably meaning parachute troops.

Herr von Ribbentrop said that Germany had received unimpeachable proof that the Allies were engineering an imminent attack through the Lowlands into the German Ruhr district wherefore the Germans felt compelled to take corresponding measures. He said the time had come for settling the final account with the "Franco-British leaders."

And thus the war to a decisive finish has at last started in the West. This was the assumption when Herr von Ribbentrop informed the world through newspaper men that the German action meant that she had decided to settle all accounts with the Allies.

"France and Britain dropped their mask," said Herr von Ribbentrop. "The alarm in the Mediterranean was a feint behind which the Allies were preparing an onslaught on German territory which the Reich could not tolerate."

The notes—handed to The Hague and Brussels simultaneously with a shorter note to the Grand Duchy of Luxembourg just prior to their invasion by Germany—accused the Lowlands with having been overwhelmingly partial toward the Allies, adding that the attitude of the press was objectionable to the Reich.

A memorandum similar in tone to that handed to Denmark and Norway last month stated:

"In the life-and-death struggle thrust upon the German people, the government does not intend to await an attack by Britain and France inactively allowing the war to be carried through Belgium and Holland onto German soil. The government, therefore, has issued orders to safeguard the neutrality of the two countries with all the military means of the Reich."

Ribbentrop Reads Statement

In eight points the memorandum outlines the German argument that Belgium and Holland had not observed the strictest neutrality upon which German respect for their territories was founded. The document accuses them with having even supported Germany's enemies in their hostile intentions. Belgium fortified exclusively her Eastern frontier against Germany, leaving the French frontier unfortified, one argument reads.

Berlin slept peacefully unaware

Continued on Page Four

HOLLAND'S QUEEN PROTESTS INVASION

Wilhelmina Vows She and the Government Will Do Duty—Bars Negotiation With Foe

By The United Press.

THE HAGUE, the Netherlands, Friday, May 10—Queen Wilhelmina said today in a statement on the German invasion of the country that "I and my government will do our duty."

The Queen, in a proclamation addressed to "my people," said:

"After our country, with scrupulous conscientiousness, had observed strict neutrality during all these months, and while Holland had no other plan than to maintain strictly this attitude, Germany last night made a sudden attack on our territory without any warning.

"This was done notwithstanding a solemn promise that the neutrality of our country would be respected so long as we ourselves maintained that neutrality.

"I herewith direct a flaming protest against this unprecedented violation of good faith and violation of all that is decent in relations between cultured States.

"I and my government now will do our duty.

"Do your duty everywhere and under all circumstances. And let every one go to the post to which he has been appointed and, with the utmost vigilance and with that inner calm and serenity which comes from a clear conscience, do his work."

The Netherland general military headquarters in a communiqué said:

"Never will the High Command or government enter into negotiations with the enemy."

Dispatches from Europe and the Far East are subject to censorship at the source.

AIR FIELDS BOMBED

Nazi Parachute Troops Land at Key Centers as Flooding Starts

RIVER MAAS CROSSED

Defenders Battle Foe in Sky, Claim 6 Planes as War Is Proclaimed

First Bombing in France

Special Cable to THE NEW YORK TIMES.

PARIS, Friday, May 10—The Bron airdrome, a big airport near Lyon, was bombed by German planes today. One German aircraft was shot down. The alarm was first given at 4:25 A. M. The all-clear signal was given at 6:45 A. M.

WASHINGTON, Friday, May 10 (AP)—United States Ambassador William C. Bullitt telephoned the State Department from Paris at 4 A. M. today that the Germans had bombed a number of fortified towns in France, "such as Dunkerque and Calais."

By The United Press.

AMSTERDAM, The Netherlands, Friday, May 10—Germany invaded the Netherlands early today, land troops being preceded by widespread air attacks on airdromes and by the landing of parachute troops.

The Netherlands resisted and announced she was at war with Germany. Anti-aircraft batteries and fighter planes engaged swarms of German aircraft when they appeared simultaneously over a score of Netherland cities.

An official proclamation said:

"Since 3 A. M. German troops have crossed the Netherland frontier and German planes have tried to attack airports. Inundations are effective according to plans. The army anti-aircraft batteries were found prepared. So far as is known six German planes have been shot down."

[French, Belgian and British planes were sighted over the Netherlands this morning, a Reuters (British news agency) dispatch said in quoting the Netherland radio station at Hilversum, near Amsterdam.

German troops were first reported crossing the Netherland frontier near Roermond, eight miles north of the Belgian frontier. German planes landed troops by parachute at strategic points near Rotterdam, The Hague, Amsterdam and other large cities.

A large number of the German troops landed by parachute were said to be dressed in Netherland military uniforms.

Other Germans crossed the Maas River in rubber boats to Netherland territory. They were said to be reaching the Netherland side in "considerable numbers."

A fierce air battle raged over Amsterdam as Netherland fighter planes dived repeatedly on German bombers and troop transport planes with chattering machine guns.

Schiphol Airdrome outside Amsterdam, the nation's largest, was heavily bombed. Military authorities immediately threw a heavy guard around the airdrome in an effort to defend it against German parachute troops.

Planes identified as German Heinkels bombed Schiphol Airdrome repeatedly, loosing some thirty heavy caliber bombs on the landing field between 5:15 and 5:30 A. M.

Reports poured in of planes in great numbers over a score of Netherland cities. Netherland authorities, hurriedly organizing defense, flashed orders to the whole country to be on the alert against parachute troops.

Fifty planes were over Nijmegen, sixty miles southeast of Amsterdam on the German border.

A number of parachute troops reportedly landed at Sliedrecht, Delft and several other points. Delft is twelve and a half miles from The Hague. About 100 parachute troops

Continued on Page Three

"All the News That's Fit to Print."

The New York Times.

Copyright, 1940, by The New York Times Company.

LATE CITY EDITION
Partly cloudy, little change in temperature today. Tomorrow fair, temperature unchanged.
Temperatures Yesterday—Max., 79; Min., 49

VOL. LXXXIX...No. 30,058. Entered as Second-Class Matter, Postoffice, New York, N. Y. NEW YORK, SATURDAY, MAY 11, 1940. PPP THREE CENTS NEW YORK CITY and Vicinity | FOUR CENTS Elsewhere Except in 7th and 8th Postal Zones.

DUTCH AND BELGIANS RESIST NAZI DRIVE; ALLIED FORCES MARCH IN TO DO BATTLE; CHAMBERLAIN RESIGNS, CHURCHILL PREMIER

COALITION ASSURED

Labor Decides to Allow Leaders to Join New National Cabinet

OLD MINISTERS STAY

Churchill Asks Them to Remain Until They Can Be Replaced

The text of Chamberlain's statement is printed on Page 9.

By RAYMOND DANIELL

Special Cable to THE NEW YORK TIMES.

LONDON, May 10—In the gravest crisis Great Britain has faced since the World War, Winston Churchill became Prime Minister tonight as Allied armies raced across Belgium again for a death grapple with invading German armies.

Neville Chamberlain, who had headed the government since just after King George VI ascended the throne, resigned early in the evening after convincing himself that it was impossible to remain and give the country the truly national government that the people want.

A genuine coalition Cabinet was assured when the executive committee of the Labor party declared that it would accept a share in a government headed by a new Prime Minister who had the nation's confidence. This is expected also to result in the entry of Liberals into the government.

Invasion Fails to Save Cabinet

The German invasion of Belgium, the Netherlands and Luxembourg, which transformed the static conflict of the West into a total European if not yet World War, had been expected throughout the day to "freeze" Mr. Chamberlain in his job for a short time at least, despite the poor showing in Wednesday's division when the government's majority in the House of Commons was cut from 200 to eighty-one.

That Mr. Chamberlain would have to relinquish his high office became apparent last night when Clement R. Attlee and Arthur Greenwood, the Opposition Labor leaders, informed him to his face that they would not consent to serve in a Cabinet that he headed. Thus they provided the cue for the undecided Liberals and Conservatives who were critical of the government.

Without these dissidents, it was felt it would be impossible for the man who brought back "peace in our time" from Munich to establish a government satisfactory to the disturbed Members of Parliament and their worried constituents. These were too angry at the let-down to their hopes of the Allied withdrawal from Norway after the optimistic build-up their press had given them about the success of operations across the North Sea.

Demand for Coalition

After the acrimonious debate that followed the Prime Minister's admission that the campaign in Central and Southern Norway was at an end, it was apparent that the country demanded a new administration in which the Opposition would share the responsibilities of leadership.

Early this evening Mr. Chamberlain drove to Buckingham Palace and told the King he thought the time had come for him to relinquish his seals of office. Soon afterward Mr. Churchill, who has been the nearest approach to a war leader this country has had since the conflict began, went to the Palace also and accepted an invitation to form a government.

This came as something of a surprise, for it was known that as late as last night, Mr. Chamberlain favored Foreign Secretary Viscount Halifax as his successor. A small crowd was waiting at Whitehall when the following announcement was issued from there:

"The Right Hon. Neville Chamberlain, M. P., resigned the office of Prime Minister and First Lord of the Treasury this evening, and the Right Hon. Winston Churchill, M. P., accepted His Majesty's invitation to fill the position.

"The Prime Minister desires that all Ministers should remain at their posts and discharge their functions with full freedom and responsibility while the necessary arrangements

Continued on Page Nine

The International Situation

The War in the Low Countries

The Netherlands—The defenders claimed to be holding the Germans along the lines of the Yssel and Maas Rivers. At Delfzijl, across the River Eems from the German stronghold of Emden, the Netherland troops appeared still to be in command, despite strong German attacks. [Page 1.] German troops, landed by air transports and parachute at Rotterdam, did not succeed in seizing the city; Rotterdam officials said the invaders there had been pressed into dangerous positions. [Page 6.] The Netherland Commander in Chief summed up: "The surprise attack is a failure." [Page 1.]

Belgium—Although dispatches agreed that in most places the Belgians had stopped the Germans at the frontier, it was reported that Limburg Province, in the northeast, had been overrun. Brussels, Antwerp and other important centers were bombed; in Greater Brussels forty-one persons were reported killed, eighty-two wounded. German troops were landed by parachutes extensively in the eastern part of the country, but no accounts of outstanding success at this kind of Blitzkrieg were received. The attitude in Belgium was that the army could hold out for a time, but help was needed quickly. King Leopold was at the front. [Page 1.]

Luxembourg—This small and armyless duchy was overrun by the Germans.

Allied Help—Paris emphasized that two hours after German troops had crossed neutral borders, meeting strong resistance, French and British troops had crossed into Belgium, receiving enthusiastic welcome.

Battle was engaged at many points. The French put the German attacking force at twenty-nine divisions. On both banks of the Moselle, which separates Luxembourg from Germany, a German operation was under way which, the French said, might be the beginning of a large-scale attack. French air fields, railways, coal mines and factories were attacked by air raiders. Generalissimo Gamelin said: "Germany has engaged us in a struggle to the death. The watchword is: 'For France and all her Allies: Courage, energy, confidence.'" [Page 1.]

Germany — Berlin made no great claims of immediate victory, aside from the general statement that enemy resistance in the border region had been broken. [Page 1.] In an Order of the Day to his troops, Chancellor Hitler said: "The fight beginning today decides the fate of the German nation for the next 1,000 years. Do your duty now!" [Page 4.]

The War Elsewhere

Britain changed pilots, Neville Chamberlain stepping down in response to popular demand, and Winston Churchill taking over. Mr. Churchill is expected to have full Labor and Liberal support; he asked all Ministers to carry on until he could form a new government. It was believed that Sir John Simon and Sir Samuel Hoare, Mr. Chamberlain's closest advisers, would lose their portfolios. [Page 1.]

In France political differences were composed under the pressure of the invasion. Louis Marin and Jean Ybarnegaray, who were leaders of the opposition to the inclusion of Socialists in the Cabinet, took portfolios as Ministers of State. [Page 10.]

At Rome, closely watched by Allied diplomats, there was no hint that Mussolini would enter the war. [Page 5.]

At Vatican City the Pope was reported deeply shocked at the German invasion. He is expected to issue a formal condemnation today. [Page 4.]

At Washington President Roosevelt, in a public address, said that the American people were "shocked and angered by the tragic news from Belgium and the Netherlands and Luxembourg." He added that it would be a "mistaken idea" to believe the Americas safe from would-be conquerers because of geographical distance. [Page 1.] The American Red Cross started a drive for a European war relief fund of at least $10,000,000. [Page 1.]

AMERICA ANGERED, SAYS ROOSEVELT

Citing 'Cruel Invasions' to Science Congress, He Warns of Danger to Americas

The President's address before Science Congress, Page 10.

By FELIX BELAIR Jr.

Special to THE NEW YORK TIMES.

WASHINGTON, May 10—President Roosevelt twice today condemned Germany's invasion of Belgium, Holland and Luxembourg as an unwarranted aggression on neutral countries and as threatening the cultural and scientific civilization of the world. Speaking indirectly but with obvious reference to developments of the past twenty-four hours, the Chief Executive pictured Nazi aggression as a definite threat to the security of the Americas.

On both occasions the President impressed his determination to keep America at peace and safeguard the nation's neutrality. But each time he raised a question whether the country could long stand idly by "if all the other continents embrace by preference or by compulsion a wholly different principle of life."

As a self-styled "pacifist," in common with citizens of the twenty-one American republics, President Roosevelt told the eighth American Scientific Congress in an internationally broadcast address that the time had come to apply commonsense principles to the situation now confronting the Americas. After emphasizing the pacific instincts of all Western Hemisphere republics, he said:

"But I believe that by overwhelming majorities in all the Americas, you and I, in the long run and if it

Continued on Page Ten

RED CROSS APPEAL SEEKS $10,000,000

President Says 'We Will Not Fail' Latest War Victims—$2,000,000 Quota Here

Special to THE NEW YORK TIMES.

WASHINGTON, May 10—The American Red Cross started a drive today for a European war relief fund of "at least" $10,000,000 to which "all sympathetic Americans" were urged to contribute generously and at once. The appeal was made by Norman H. Davis, National Chairman, under the authority voted by the Red Cross convention which ended a three-day session here Wednesday, and was supported by a special message issued from the White House by President Roosevelt this afternoon.

"I urge all Americans who have a feeling of deep sympathy for the peoples of those unfortunate countries who today have been added to the long list of those who are suffering the horrors of invasion and aerial bombardment to respond quickly and generously to this appeal," the President said.

"The American Red Cross, our official national volunteer relief agency, is efficiently organized to answer such emergency calls. It is, therefore, the logical agency through which our citizens can express their compassion for the innocent victims of the wars that rage overseas. I am confident we will not fail them."

In using the discretion conferred on him to call for war relief funds "if and when necessary," Mr. Davis said that "the invasion today of three small neutral nations and the spread of death and devastation among their innocent civilian populations" had created a situation requiring immediate action.

"The hour has struck, with a

Continued on Page Eight

AID IS SENT AT ONCE

French Enter Belgium—Britons Cross Sea to Netherlands

CONTACT SOON MADE

AlliesHelpLowCountries Meet First Thrust of 29 German Divisions

By G. H. ARCHAMBAULT

Wireless to THE NEW YORK TIMES.

PARIS, May 10—Two hours after the Germans invaded the Low Countries, French and British forces were crossing the border to help the Netherland and Belgian Armies withstand the shock of at least twenty-nine German divisions. Contact was made without delay, and by nightfall the battle had been engaged at many points.

[The landing of British troops by transport at Netherland ports was reported by The Associated Press from Amsterdam.]

On broad lines both the Netherlanders and the Belgians are resisting with determination on positions already prepared. Farther south, what may turn out to be an operation on a large scale, in its preliminary phase on both banks of the Moselle River.

The Germans also made a demonstration in the extreme north at the mouth of the Ems River. Progress thence southward through the Netherlands would be impeded by marshes.

von Epp Plan Believed Used

The Germans apparently are putting into execution the von Epp plan, a modification of the famous Schlieffen plan. The French military authorities are very cautious in their commentaries, but it is pointed out that the von Epp plan foresaw disposing of the Netherlands in twenty-four hours.

This is France's battle. She has been waiting for it for eight months. Her army leaders have prepared for it in every detail. Every soldier knows what is at stake. It will be a fight to the finish.

General Maurice Gustave Gamelin gave the keynote when he sent the following general order to all troops:

"The attack which we have been anticipating since October was launched this morning.

"Germany has engaged against us in a struggle to the death.

"The watchword is 'For France and all her Allies: Courage, energy, confidence.'"

Although in their scrupulous regard for their duty as neutrals, the Netherlands and Belgium declined to hold conferences with the British and French general staffs before Germany showed her hand, and although King Leopold, like his father before him in 1914, has taken active command of the Belgian Army, it is understood that a general plan of action is being coordinated and that General Gamelin, virtually if not in name, becomes the supreme director of military operations. All information on military movements consequently is

Continued on Page Six

THE FIRES OF WAR LEAP ACROSS THE LOW COUNTRIES

Following upon Germany's lightning invasion there were no connected battle fronts yesterday, but many scattered points of major fighting. The main battle sectors in the Netherlands were at Delfzijl (1) and along the Yssel River (2) and the Maas River (4), while a struggle raged in the city of Rotterdam (3). In Belgium the Germans claimed to have advanced to the Albert Canal and taken Maastricht fortress (6), although there was stiff fighting along the canal. Brussels and Antwerp (5) were both attacked by Nazi bombers. Luxembourg (7) was overrun by the invaders, but the Allies were apparently engaging the Germans west of the Moselle River.

BELGIUM REPORTS NAZIS ARE HALTED

Leopold Is at Front as Active Commander—41 Killed, 82 Wounded in Brussels Raid

Wireless to THE NEW YORK TIMES.

BRUSSELS, Belgium, May 10—King Leopold today assumed command of the Belgian armies and is directing the resistance to the Nazi invasion as Allied forces are being rushed to their assistance. While Belgium was gathering her forces to resist this lightning attack, Brussels, Antwerp and numerous other points in the country had to withstand air raids.

Most of these attacks were directed against airports, but in most cases Belgian aviation had foreseen the attacks and the planes had been removed. The exception was the capital, which, according to an announcement by the government, contains no military centers.

This little country, twice invaded by German armies in the last twenty-five years, went methodically about insuring its defense and quickly became part of the Allied defense. The government issued an appeal to the population to preserve calm and assist in that way the military measures for defense. The people were asked to spot German saboteurs and German troops in Belgian and Allied uniforms while mobilization is taking place.

Bridges and roads were being blown up to prevent the first German advance and the Belgian system of sluices for flooding were being put into service.

BRUSSELS, Belgium, May 10 (UP)—The Belgian Army, with King

Continued on Page Eight

Bulletins on European Conflict

Special Cable to THE NEW YORK TIMES.

AMSTERDAM, the Netherlands, Saturday, May 11—Amsterdam was bombed shortly after dawn today. The raid lasted twenty-five minutes, during which a number of heavy bombs fell. No casualties were immediately reported. Another wave of German bombers passed over the city a half hour later.

Widespread French Air Alarms

PARIS, Saturday, May 11 (AP)—Widespread air alarms sounded throughout France this morning. The alert in central-eastern France ended after thirty-two minutes.

Allies Recapture Airports

The British wireless said this morning in a broadcast received by the Columbia Broadcasting System that "with the exception of one," all airports in Belgium and the Netherlands occupied by the Germans "have now been recaptured by us."

Bomb Hits Argentine Legation

BUENOS AIRES, Argentina, May 10 (UP)—Foreign Minister José Marie Cantilo announced tonight that he had been informed by Carlos Brebbia, Argentine Minister to the Netherlands, that the Argentine Legation in The Hague had been struck directly by a powerful bomb.

Grounded Plane's Bombs Kill Many

PARIS, May 10 (UP)—A German bomber was brought down today in the town square of a Northern French village. The two German fliers, injured, attempted to flee but were caught by villagers. The entire village was gathered around the wrecked plane when its bomb cargo suddenly exploded, killing many.

EAST INDIES COLONY GETS MARTIAL LAW

Germans Interned and Ships Seized—Tokyo Announces Status Quo Policy

Special Cable to THE NEW YORK TIMES.

SINGAPORE, May 10—News of the German invasion of the Netherlands reached the Netherlands Indies by wireless. The Governor General issued a proclamation similar in terms to that of Queen Wilhelmina and announced that all Germans of military age, from 16 upward, would be interned immediately.

All the German merchant ships that have been lying in Netherlands Indies harbors since the outbreak of war were seized and other precautions were taken.

Within three hours it was announced that the majority of the Germans in Batavia, Sourabaya and other important towns were detained. Later in the evening the Governor General again went on the radio, reporting the latest developments and confirming the internment of the Germans.

According to the newspaper, The Straits Times, the Governor's resident authorities throughout the Netherlands Indies today received a telegram marked "Berlin" and acted according to previous instructions. They were required to report to the Governor General by noon tomorrow the situation regarding the internment of Germans.

While there is natural excitement among the Netherlanders through-

Continued on Page Ten

BORDER RESISTANCE BROKEN, NAZIS SAY

'Furious Attacks' Reported in Cooperation With Fliers Over a Broad Front

By GEORGE AXELSSON

Wireless to THE NEW YORK TIMES.

BERLIN, May 10—For the second time in little more than a quarter of a century the field gray columns of the German Army have been set marching "Nach Paris." Obviously aiming to flank the Maginot Line to stab the Allied armies from the rear the German troops crossed the frontiers into the Netherlands, Belgium and Luxembourg at 5:30 o'clock this morning establishing contact with the enemy along what the General Headquarters communiqué terms a broad front.

Even before this early hour, at the first gleam of dawn, Germany's mighty air armadas launched assaults upon enemy territory which now also include the Low Countries.

[Chancellor Hitler, in an order to his troops, declared that the "fate of the German nation for the next thousand years is at stake."]

German headquarters has chosen to reveal but little of what were the results of the first day of this "major war," upon the outcome of which hangs Europe's destiny. But from the scanty official information so far available observers feel justified in believing that the procedure successfully used in the Polish campaign is once more being

Continued on Page Four

Fair Will Open at 10 A. M. With Balmy Day Forecast

The New York World's Fair, 1940 edition, will open at 10 o'clock this morning, dedicated, in the words of its officials, to a good time for every one who comes.

The opening had the blessing of the United States Weather Bureau, which predicted partly cloudy skies, with little change from yesterday's balmy temperatures. This led to high hopes of a better "break" than the Fair received on the opening day on April 30, 1939. The forecast for tomorrow was "fair with little change in temperature."

In contrast with last year, when predictions of 1,000,000 visitors for the first day were freely made, estimates of probable attendance were lacking yesterday. Harvey D. Gibson, chairman of the board, declared he would be satisfied "if every one who comes to the Fair has a good time."

There were, however, many indications of keen public interest, including a 200,000 increase in advance ticket sales.

Mr. Gibson's brief statement was viewed by Fair planners as sounding the keynote of the entire 1940 exposition, which has been dedicated to fun and informality rather than to pomp and ceremony. Last year Grover A. Whalen, Fair president, enthusiastically predicted a crowd of 1,000,000 on opening day, and it was a post-mortem verdict that the idea of such a big crowd actually kept people away. This year Mr. Gibson, at the helm of the exposition, has refused firmly to talk of big crowds, but lays the emphasis rather on "lots of fun for little money."

"We feel," Mr. Gibson's statement said, "that we will have a happy, carefree crowd at the Fair on opening day. We are more in-

Continued on Page Twelve

HOLLANDERS FIRM

Report 100 Nazi Planes Shot Down as Troops Strike at Invaders

BOMBERS RANGE LAND

Air Attacks Continuous —Parachutists Land at Strategic Spots

By OSCAR MOHR

Wireless to THE NEW YORK TIMES.

AMSTERDAM, the Netherlands, May 10—The German invaders of the Netherlands are being held in check and the surprise element of their attack can be considered a failure, Lieut. Gen. Henri Gerard Winkelman, the Netherland supreme commander, declared tonight.

"In all parts of the country our forces stand firm in their positions as far as this is required by orders," General Winkelman said in an order to his troops, "and they even attack the enemy intrepidly and successfully where necessary for preventing execution of the enemy's plans."

General Winkelman's statement followed a High Command communiqué declaring that the Netherland forces were offering "serious resistance" along the Maas and Yssel Rivers and were maintaining their positions at Delfzijl "in spite of strong German attacks."

Heavy Toll of Planes Claimed

At least seventy German airplanes were shot down during the day as they attacked airdromes or attempted to land, the communiqué said. [A later communiqué raised the number to more than 100, The Associated Press and The United Press reported.] Four German armored trains were declared to have been blown up, one of them with the railway bridge at Venlo, along the German border.

The statement added that small German units that had landed in the interior were being "fiercely attacked" and it charged that Netherland prisoners of war were being used by the Germans as shields.

In declaring that "the strategic surprise attack can be regarded as a failure," General Winkelman expressed Queen Wilhelmina's "high satisfaction" over the quality of the resistance and said that "the firm attitude of our troops is reflected in the attitude of our people, who give proof of calm determination."

German bombers ranged over the country during the day.

In one of their earliest attacks they dropped more than 300 bombs on the Schiphol Airdrome outside Amsterdam and destroyed the landing field along with several buildings. The number of casualties in the first attack was reported to be surprisingly low—three persons wounded and two firemen shot dead by machine-gun fire.

Aerial Thrusts Combated

AMSTERDAM, the Netherlands, Saturday, May 11 (UP)—A Netherland communiqué early today said the number of German planes shot down over the Netherlands now exceeded 100, in addition to fourteen captured at reconquered airdromes.

With one exception, all the airports temporarily taken by the Germans now have been recaptured, the communiqué said.

Last night Germans bombed The Hague, governmental seat of the invaded nation, and one explosive fell close to the United States Minister, George A. Gordon. There were air alarms all evening at half-hourly intervals.

One German transport plane, carrying nineteen soldiers, plunged through the roof of a house in The Hague when it was shot down. The falling soldiers all wore Netherland uniforms.

The Germans succeeded in landing troops at two small fields near The Hague and gained control of them. They were at Okkenburg and Ypenburg. But the Germans were small units and were immediately surrounded.

Many small towns in the southern

Continued on Page Three

Dispatches from Europe and the Far East are subject to censorship at the source.

"All the News That's Fit to Print."

NEWS INDEX, PAGE 51, THIS SECTION

The New York Times.

LATE CITY EDITION
Fair, slowly rising temperature today. Tomorrow increasing cloudiness and warmer.
Temperatures Yesterday—Max., 66; Min., 44

Section 1

VOL. LXXXIX....No. 30,059. Entered as Second-Class Matter, Postoffice, New York, N. Y. NEW YORK, SUNDAY, MAY 12, 1940. F+ Including Rotogravure Picture, Magazine and Book Review. TEN CENTS | TWELVE CENTS Beyond 200 Miles, Except West of Pa.—South of Md.—North of Mass.

GERMANS CLAIM A LIEGE FORT, GAIN IN HOLLAND; ROTTERDAM FIGHTS PARACHUTISTS, FIRES RAGE; ALLIES BOMB KRUPP WORKS AND RHINE AREAS

'40 FAIR GETS OFF TO LIVELY START; 191,196 ON HAND

Carefree, Informal Atmosphere Dominates Scene Despite Specter of the War

PRESIDENT SENDS MESSAGE

Calls Exposition Symbol of Common Sense—Governor, Mayor Decry Invasions

Roosevelt message, Lehman and La Guardia speeches, Page 43.

By RUSSELL B. PORTER

Rededicated to a New World of peace and freedom, while the Old World is being racked by war and bondage, the New York World's Fair reopened yesterday for its second season as the greatest and most magnificent exposition in history.

For 170 days and 170 nights, until the end of October, it will continue as a symbol of the culture and progress of democratic civilization, and of individual rights to the pursuit of life and happiness under free government, in contrast to the new dark age and human wretchedness brought upon mankind by dictatorship.

President Roosevelt, who opened the 1939 Fair in person with an invitation to all the world to attend, sent a message that was read at the dedication ceremonies in the Court of Peace and Freedom, hailing the "Forty Fair" as "a symbol of international common sense" that "deserves to have every success."

Invasions Are Denounced

Governor Lehman and Mayor La Guardia delivered addresses at the same exercises in which they denounced the Nazi and Soviet invasions of small countries. The Governor, warning of the dangers of isolationism, urged the United States to abandon its "smugness" and "complacency," and to arm itself so strongly that no aggressor would dare attack us. Only thus, he said, can American democracy be preserved.

The Mayor cautioned Germany and Russia that the entire American people support President Roosevelt's foreign policy. Neither of the aggressor nations was represented at this year's Fair, he added, because "no international rogues' gallery" was wanted.

Speaking on behalf of the foreign nations participating in the Fair, Y. A. Paloheimo, Commissioner General of Finland, asserted that their presence was proof of their devotion to the same ideals of peace and freedom for which this country stands.

Cool, cloudy weather kept down the day's attendance, but 191,196 paid admissions had been recorded at midnight, according to the final official figures.

The day was clear and warm about noon time, but during the afternoon clouds partly obscured the sun from time to time and a strong wind set in late in the day that caused the air to become decidedly chill as evening came on. The temperature had dropped to 46 at 12:30 A. M. today.

Rain Begins at 7 P. M.

Shortly after 7 P. M. a drizzle began falling, but failed to dampen the festive atmosphere. However, about three hours later, the rain came down heavily and the crowds began leaving. The rain forced the cancellation of all outdoor shows, including the late performances of "American Jubilee" and the Aquacade.

The formal opening took place against a background of patriotic music, marching troops, bands, waving flags and with army warplanes, navy blimps and huge transport planes circling the Fair grounds. No matter how much this military display may have reminded one of the sinister nature of similar scenes going on across the seas at the same moment, on the peaceful Flushing Meadows it was only a colorful and stirring piece of pageantry.

Instead of dropping explosive bombs or parachute troops to wreak death and destruction upon the land below, the planes merely roared past and dipped their wings in salute. The transport planes carried not soldiers but prominent women who came to visit the Fair from all over the country under the

Continued on Page Forty-two

The International Situation

The War in the Low Countries

Germany — The Germans claimed yesterday to have captured Eben Emael in Belgium, key fort in the defenses of Liége, which would give them control of the junction of the Meuse River and Albert Canal. Liége guards one of the historic routes to France, last used in 1914. The Germans also said they had crossed the Yssel River in the Netherlands, along which the Netherland army had taken a strong stand. They claimed air mastery in both the Netherlands and Belgium. [Page 1.]

Belgium—The Belgians contended that their positions around Liége were still intact, but admitted the enemy had gained a foothold farther north. Heavily equipped French and British troops were reported moving through Belgium to undisclosed positions. [Page 1.]

The Netherlands—Amsterdam dispatches said the army had withdrawn from the frontier as the Germans landed thousands of parachutists behind the lines. The forcing of the Yssel south of Arnhem was admitted; it was acknowledged that the Germans (as they claimed) had recaptured Waalhaven Airport near Rotterdam. Both Amsterdam and Rotterdam were bombed several times. Numerous fires were reported in Rotterdam, and the liner Statendam was reported ablaze in the harbor. "Fifth Column" activity in Amsterdam and The Hague was reported wiped out. [Page 1.]

Britain—London said the Royal Air Force was carrying the war to German territory by bombing troop concentrations in the Rhineland. Allied aircraft also were doing their utmost to disrupt communications immediately to the rear of the invading Germans. [Page 1.]

Repercussions Elsewhere

In London Winston Churchill named a Cabinet of national unity. It includes a "War Cabinet" of five, headed by Mr. Churchill as Prime Minister and Defense Minister. Others are Clement R. Attlee and Arthur Greenwood, representing Labor; Viscount Halifax, who remains as Foreign Secretary, and Neville Chamberlain. Anthony Eden became War Secretary. [Page 1.]

In London it was reported that Allied forces had landed at two Netherlands West Indies points to prevent possible sabotage by German residents. [Page 1.]

In Washington the State Department made clear that it did not look upon the landing of these Allied forces as infringement of the Monroe Doctrine. No change of sovereignty was involved, it was pointed out. [Page 29.]

In Tokyo the government notified the belligerents, the United States and Italy that it was deeply concerned about possible spread of the war to the Netherlands East Indies. Newspapers emphasized Japan was ready "to take positive means" to prevent anything of the sort. [Page 28.]

In Rome there were evidences of mounting anti-British feeling. Anti-British posters appeared in many parts of the city, and the British Ambassador was reported to have protested. Objections to the Allied contraband control were voiced in the Senate, whereupon Premier Mussolini applauded. [Page 1.]

At the Vatican the Pope sent his blessing to the rulers and peoples of Belgium, the Netherlands and Luxembourg. [Page 36.]

In Washington President Roosevelt sent a message to King Leopold expressing American sympathy for Belgium and the hope that "policies which seek to dominate peaceful and independent peoples through force and military aggression may be arrested." [Page 1.]

ITALY CHALLENGES ALLIED BLOCKADE

Terms It 'Intolerable'—British Envoy Mauled in Street—Pope Decries Invasion

By HERBERT L. MATTHEWS

By Telephone to THE NEW YORK TIMES.

ROME, May 11—A strong report—so strong as to constitute a genuine challenge to the Allies—has just been made by the Italian Foreign Office to Premier Mussolini on the workings of the Allied blockade.

Phrases like "literally intolerable," "gravity of this situation" and "clumsy functioning" are used freely in this thirteen-page report, which was made public tonight in such a way as to show that it is a gage thrown down to the Allies.

To make the situation even more serious, it so happens that there have been anti-Allied demonstrations by young Fascisti, in one of which the British Minister, Sir Noel Charles, was mauled and insulted. Moreover, all Rome was plastered with posters during last night that were intended to make the Allies look ridiculous. The British Embassy has made a protest to the Italian Government.

[Sharp condemnation of the latest German invasions was implied by Pope Pius in messages he sent to the rulers of Belgium, the Netherlands and Luxembourg.]

Rome Step Unprecedented

The report to Premier Mussolini was made by Luca Pietromarchi, chief of the "economic war" office of the Ministry of Foreign Affairs, and it is quite unprecedented that anything of the sort should be made public. Foreign correspondents were called to the Press Ministry to receive copies.

This follows up the protest made directly to London by the Italian Government on March 3, which was also in strong terms. The British rejected that, and here is the second Fascist move coming at an extraordinarily critical time.

"The machinery of control," says the report, "through its complicat-

Continued on Page Thirty-seven

CHURCHILL NAMES WAR CABINET OF 5

Attlee, Greenwood, Halifax and Chamberlain in It—Eden and Sinclair Get Posts

By RAYMOND DANIELL

Special Cable to THE NEW YORK TIMES.

LONDON, May 11—Winston Churchill, Great Britain's new Prime Minister, selected his War Cabinet tonight. It was a real coalition government of five, and it met the popular demand that those who guide the destinies of the nation in the realm of higher strategy be spared the routine tasks of running departments.

Of those charged with departmental duties Foreign Secretary Viscount Halifax, who until the German invasion of the Low Countries was Neville Chamberlain's choice as his successor, alone has a place in the inner circle of Cabinet Ministers.

The new Prime Minister reserved for himself the portfolio of Minister of Defense—a post he had been expected to get under Mr. Chamberlain ever since the then War Secretary, Leslie Hore-Belisha, retired from the Cabinet last Winter.

Mr. Chamberlain, who resigned because the country had lost patience with his efforts to make war as it had lost faith in his attempts to maintain peace, was made Lord President of the Council, a post of vaguely defined duties.

Posts for Opposition

Clement R. Attlee, who as leader of His Majesty's Opposition received an honorarium of £2,000 a year, became Lord Privy Seal, another post of variable responsibility. Arthur Greenwood, deputy leader of the Opposition since 1935, became Minister Without Portfolio.

Lord Halifax remained in charge of foreign affairs and naturally retained his place in the inner circle.

Such was the War Cabinet Mr. Churchill selected. In his old place as First Lord of the Admiralty, he

Continued on Page Thirty-four

OUR FEELING VOICED

Roosevelt Tells Leopold America Hopes Nazis Will Be Halted

SEEK NEW STATUS

Americas May Amend Neutrality Stand to Non-Belligerency

By FRANK L. KLUCKHOHN

Special to THE NEW YORK TIMES

WASHINGTON, May 11—President Roosevelt declared in a message to King Leopold of Belgium today that he and the people of the United States hoped that "policies which seek to dominate peaceful and independent peoples through force and military aggression may be arrested."

Mr. Roosevelt's message was sent in reply to one from King Leopold in which the King stated that Belgium had been "brutally attacked by Germany, which had entered into the most solemn engagements with her." King Leopold asked for the support of Mr. Roosevelt's "moral authority" in the Belgians' resistance to invasion.

President Roosevelt in his reply reiterated the statement he made in his address last night that the "cruel invasion" of the Low Countries had "shocked and angered" the people of the United States.

King Leopold's cablegram was as follows:

His Excellency the President of the United States of America:

Brutally attacked by Germany, which had entered into the most solemn engagements with her, Belgium will defend herself with all of her strength against the invader.

In these tragic hours which my country is undergoing I am addressing myself to Your Excellency, who so often has demonstrated toward Belgium an affectionate interest, in the certainty that you will support with all of your moral authority the efforts which we are now firmly decided to make in order to preserve our independence. LEOPOLD.

The President's reply read:

His Majesty Leopold III, King of the Belgians.

I have received Your Majesty's telegram. As I stated in an address which I delivered last night to representatives of the twenty-one American republics, the cruel invasion by force of arms of the independent nations of Belgium, Netherlands and Luxembourg has shocked and angered the people of the United States and, I feel sure, their neighbors in the Western Hemisphere.

The people of the United States hope, as do I, that policies which seek to dominate peaceful and independent peoples through force and military aggression may be arrested, and that the government and people of Belgium may

Continued on Page Thirty-three

SNIPING IN SEAPORT

Liner Statendam Said to Be Afire as Rotterdam Combats '5th Column'

BORDER UNITS RETIRE

Swarms of Parachutists Provide Major Problem as Nazis Push Attacks

By The United Press.

ROTTERDAM, the Netherlands, May 11—Tremendous fires blazed in this beleaguered city tonight as the defenders strove to dislodge attacking Germans from the right bank of the Maas River.

The Germans were reported to be making no progress, but apparently they were holding their position.

The Rotterdam water tower was blazing and huge fires were visible elsewhere in the city, which was without drinking water. On the right bank of the Maas the 28,291-ton Holland-America liner Statendam was reported on fire and many other blazes lighted the sky.

The police were searching out apparent "Fifth Column" elements in the city. Shooting was audible everywhere. These groups had been sniping intermittently at Netherland troops from the roofs of private houses.

The city was alive with unconfirmed rumors, one of which was that the Netherland destroyer Jan van Gelder had been sunk in the Maas.

Netherland Forces Retire

AMSTERDAM, the Netherlands, May 11 (UP)—Netherland troops withdrew from the frontier tonight as German planes landed thousands of parachutists behind the fighting lines in a determined drive against The Hague and Rotterdam.

The Netherland High Command reported that the Germans had succeeded in fording the Yssel River, south of Arnhem, and said frontier troops had been ordered to withdraw after four hours of sharp fighting. The High Command said the Netherlanders were making a stand at Pannerden Fortress, ten miles southeast of Arnhem.

[French military advices said the Germans had captured Arnhem, The Associated Press reported.]

Before withdrawing, the High Command said, the troops threw back a German detachment and destroyed a German armored train and all the troops it was carrying.

Strategic Town Recaptured

By OSCAR MOHR

Wireless to THE NEW YORK TIMES.

AMSTERDAM, the Netherlands, May 11—Apart from the facts stated in the High Command communiqués, no details about the strategic situation can be given with any certainty. But it is obvious that the Netherland troops in the first defensive lines are doing their job

Continued on Page Thirty

British Airmen Hit Nazi Columns; Raid Is Reported at Essen in Ruhr

French Planes Join in Blasting Rhineland Concentrations to Hamper Drive Westward —Germans Strike at Bases in France

By The Associated Press.

LONDON, Sunday, May 12—A German radio broadcast heard here early today said Essen, where the great German Krupp arms works are situated, and two other German towns had been bombed by Allied planes.

Essen is about fifty miles from the Netherland frontier in the rich Ruhr coal fields.

The Royal Air Force, following up morning raids, again attacked German mechanized forces advancing from the Rhine toward the Meuse River late yesterday afternoon, the Air Ministry announced.

[The Air Ministry said direct hits were scored on a German column that included tanks and armored cars a few miles from Maastricht in the Netherlands.]

The Air Ministry previously reported that R. A. F. planes had blasted away at German troop concentrations in the Rhineland and between the Rhine and Meuse [Maas] Rivers.

It announced that "hits were obtained on a bridge over the Rhine near Wesel and one line of traffic at its approaches."

At least fifty German planes were reported destroyed and many others put out of action by the R. A. F. in yesterday's raids in the Netherlands and Belgium.

"The enemy's advance was further hampered by a series of operations in which bombs were seen to hit important railways and road junctions and bridges at Alderkerke, Geldern, Rees and Goch," the Ministry said.

"Some twenty of our aircraft are missing."

Fresh from the lesson of Norway, where lack of air support in part cost the Allies the rich south and center regions, the Royal Air Force led the campaign to hold flying bases in the Low Countries at all costs and delay Germany's land power until Allied troops could take up positions alongside the Netherlanders and Belgians.

British fliers also scouted the whole battle area for a hint of where Germany's strongest blows likely would fall and patrolled rear areas to hunt out German columns moving toward the Netherlands.

PARIS, May 11 (AP)—France counted her civilian dead in two days of air raids at 148 tonight, reports from various towns swelling the first total of more than 100 persons killed.

The report indicated that air fields, railway centers and stations appeared to be the principal objectives of the Nazi Air Force.

Other reports said German planes

Continued on Page Thirty-two

ALLIES LAND FORCE IN THE WEST INDIES

Act to Prevent Nazi Sabotage—Washington Says Monroe Doctrine Is Not Infringed

By JAMES B. RESTON

Special Cable to THE NEW YORK TIMES.

LONDON, May 11—The Foreign Office announced tonight that Allied troops had landed in the Netherlands West Indies Islands of Curacao and Aruba, forty miles from the north coast of Venezuela and 750 miles from the Panama Canal, in order to "prevent possible German attempts at sabotage in the important oil refineries of these islands."

This action followed consultation with the Netherland authorities and the communiqué states that "the United States Government has been kept informed of the position by the Allied diplomatic representatives in Washington."

[The State Department, in commenting on this development, made it clear that it did not regard the landing of Allied troops in the Netherlands West Indies as an infringement of the Monroe Doctrine since no change in sovereignty was involved. There was no question, the State Department added, of the friendly nature of the troop landings; that the aid was of a temporary nature and that Netherland authorities would still be in control of the islands.]

Troops Cordially Welcomed

It was emphasized here that these troops, who, it was said, had been cordially welcomed both at Curacao and Aruba, were ordered there merely "to cooperate with the local administration in the execution of necessary measures for the security of the islands."

Since the Anglo-French troops were merely acting at the request of the Netherland Government it was pointed out that no question of any change in the sovereignty of the islands could arise.

It was not made clear here whether the British and French Governments discussed the occupation of the islands with the United States State Department before it took place or whether they merely advised Washington of their intention to take action. There is some reason for believing, however, that they discussed the question prior to reaching a final decision.

In the British view the Allies are merely taking the same kind of precaution with the Netherlands West Indies as the United States was taking with the Netherlands Indies. There is, of course, as little question of the Germans being able to occupy Curacao and Aruba as that the Japanese could occupy the Netherlands Indies, but the Allies

Continued on Page Twenty-seven

BRUSSELS ADMITS BREAK IN DEFENSES

Says Germans Got a 'Foothold' in Maastricht Region—Other Lines Firm

By The Associated Press.

BRUSSELS, Belgium, May 11—Supported by planes and armored cars, powerful German forces won a foothold in Belgian defense positions near the Netherland city of Maastricht today.

But a government communiqué tonight reported the Nazis had suffered "heavy losses" in attacks on Belgian fortifications, and said "Our positions remained intact" around the fortified town of Liége, which was heavily bombed.

[The German High Command claimed capture of Eben Emael, a fort in the Liége chain commanding the crossing of the Albert Canal and the Meuse River fifteen miles north of Liége. D. N. B., official German news agency, said another Liége fort fell into German hands yesterday.]

Tonight's communiqué said:

"During the day important enemy forces, with the aid of incessant bombardments, carried out by powerful aerial units and supported by armored cars, attacked in the Maastricht region. They succeeded in getting a foothold in our defense line.

"Our troops in Luxembourg continued their operations following a preconceived plan and vigorously held their own against the invaders.

"Around Liége our positions remain intact. The enemy has suffered heavy losses before certain of our fortifications.

"The enemy aviation has carried out systematic bombardments, attacking numerous localities over a great part of our territory."

Air Defenses Are Active

An earlier communiqué said Belgian troops in the first line of defense had established contact with German advance units "in several sectors" of the front, and reported at least fifteen German planes were shot down. Operations of Belgian fliers and anti-aircraft batteries were "very active."

The chief points of contact between the Belgian and German forces were said to be along the Albert Canal and the Meuse River and in the Ardennes Mountains facing German-occupied Luxembourg.

Heavily equipped British and

Continued on Page Thirty-six

Dispatches from Europe and the Far East are subject to censorship at the source.

BERLIN LISTS GAINS

Taking of Defense Key Laid to 'New Type' of Air-Land Blow

BIGGER DRIVE HINTED

Nazis View Invasion as Curtain-Raiser for Vast Offensive

By GEORGE AXELSSON

Wireless to THE NEW YORK TIMES.

BERLIN, May 11—The first concrete news of the German Army's progress in its drive into the Low Countries is contained in a special bulletin released late tonight by General Headquarters on the capture of Eben Emael, a fort outside of Liége, where the commandant and 1,000 men are said to have surrendered this afternoon. The fort is said here to be one of the strongest in the vast Liége chain of fortifications, since Eben Emael controls passage across the Meuse River and the Albert Canal and to the west dominates the city of Maastricht.

Yesterday the Germans unofficially reported the capture of an unnamed Liége fort with 1,200 men, and if this is not the same fort—army circles here say they are two different forts—the Reich's army already has made a serious dent in Liége, where twenty-five years ago it arrived three days after the invasion started.

Eben Emael was put of commission yesterday, the communiqué significantly claims, by the use of a "new means of attack" and the cooperation of the air force. Attackers surrounding the fort evidently had become isolated during the manoeuvre, for the bulletin says it was only when a unit driving from the north had succeeded in re-establishing connections after furious fighting that the Belgian force surrendered.

Bigger Air Drive Hinted

With military progress in the West predestined to be slow while the offensive is still in the preliminary stage, in which air force activities are predominating, the army command stresses destructive raids against Allied airfields and other missions that should for the present occupy a considerable part of the Reich's aerial fleet and are considered a curtain-raiser for what bids fair to become history's biggest and most fateful battle.

An indication that the air offensive is about to be intensified further is seen in a short official announcement that Field Marshal Hermann Goering has left for his air headquarters. Meanwhile the Germans claim to have bombed in their first major attack seventy-two flying fields in the Netherlands, Belgium and France, destroying 400 enemy planes on the ground.

Audacious expeditions landing troops from planes by parachute are said to have resulted in the occupation of several enemy fields, chiefly in the Netherlands. Neutral military observers here are attentively watching this novelty in German strategy to see if it turns out to have any more than nuisance value.

The German Army's past performances would seem to justify the assumption that land operations, when they begin in earnest, will be just as energetic as the air fighting is now. Meanwhile, there is little definite news on the accomplishments of the land forces except in the Luxembourg sector, where it is claimed the German Army easily overran the Grand Duchy and now is believed to stand in the proximity of Arlon on the Belgian-Luxembourg border.

Here it faces the strong French system of forts from Longwy, past Montmedy and Sedan to Hirson and Maubeuge, that prolongs the Maginot Line, and as in the north it must force the Ardennes and the combined Belgian-Netherland defense lines.

Minor Resistance Indicated

It is still too early to tell the extent of the initial German moves in the border districts. Beyond the capture of one of the outworks of the Liége forts, where allegedly heavy-caliber bombs dropped by dive bombers decided the issue, it must be assumed in the absence of definite news that such incursions as occurred up to the time of this

Continued on Page Forty

Major Sports Yesterday

HORSE RACING

Colonel E. R. Bradley's Bimelech led from start to finish in winning the fiftieth running of the Preakness Stakes before a record-breaking crowd of 50,000 at the Pimlico track. Favored at 9 to 10 in the betting, Bimelech triumphed by two lengths over Mioland, with third going to the Kentucky Derby winner, Gallahadion. The victor's share of the $73,365 purse was $53,230, this being the third Preakness success for Colonel Bradley, whose colt was second to Gallahadion in the Derby the preceding Saturday. At Jamaica the closing-day feature, the Excelsior Handicap, went to Maxwell Howard's The Chief after Fighting Fox, who finished first, was disqualified along with his stablemate, Isolater, who ran third. In the revised placing Sandy Boot was second and Anthology third back of The Chief.

BASEBALL

Scoring two runs in the eleventh inning, the Red Sox won at the Stadium, 9—8, to hand the Yankees their eighth successive defeat. At Ebbets Field the Dodgers were downed by the Phillies, 5—4. The setback, coupled with the Reds' victory over the Cardinals in St. Louis, dropped the Dodgers to second place in the National League and put the Reds on top. The Giants routed the Bees, 10—2.

ROWING

Columbia's varsity, junior varsity and freshman eight-oared crews scored a sweep in the Childs Cup regatta on the Schuylkill. Pennsylvania was second and Princeton third in the varsity race. Yale's varsity beat M. I. T. and Syracuse at Derby, Conn.

(Complete Details of These and Other Sports Events in Section 5.)

"All the News That's Fit to Print."

The New York Times.

LATE CITY EDITION
Mostly cloudy, temperatures unchanged today; showers tonight and tomorrow; cooler tomorrow.
Temperatures Yesterday—Max., 70; Min., 51

VOL. LXXXIX...No. 30,061. Entered as Second-Class Matter, Postoffice, New York, N. Y. NEW YORK, TUESDAY, MAY 14, 1940. P THREE CENTS NEW YORK CITY and Vicinity | FOUR CENTS Elsewhere Except in 7th and 8th Postal Zones.

GERMANS GAIN IN SAVAGE ATTACKS IN BELGIUM; REACH ROTTERDAM, CUTTING HOLLAND IN TWO; FRENCH MEET NAZIS IN CLASH OF 1500 TANKS

ROOSEVELT TO ASK INCREASE IN FUNDS FOR DEFENSE USES

Consults With Army and Navy Heads and Legislators and Studies Reports on War

MAY SEEK $500,000,000

White House Warns on Guesses Before Estimates Are Made—Rise in Debt Limit Is Likely

Special to THE NEW YORK TIMES.

WASHINGTON, May 13—President Roosevelt will send a message to Congress this week, probably on Thursday, asking a substantial increase in appropriations for the national defense. Army and navy officials are making a survey of their pressing needs. Secretaries Morgenthau and Woodring, Assistant Secretary Johnson and General George C. Marshall conferred with the President today.

Later the President talked with Secretary Edison and Assistant Secretary Compton, regarding the navy's program.

Pending a decision on the amount of additional funds which he will ask (generally estimated at $500,000,000), the President was concentrating on defense matters to the exclusion of other official business.

After the President's customary meeting with Democratic leaders of Congress, Senator Barkley said that no mention was made of special taxes to meet an increase in defense appropriations. He said that Congress might have to delay adjournment, but predicted winding up early in June.

Guided by reports from United States military observers who have watched the Nazi war machine function since the invasion of Poland, Mr. Roosevelt expects to decide in a few days on the amount which can be spent effectively in the next fiscal year over and above the $2,000,000,000 already appropriated.

In making known the President's decision to request more funds, Stephen T. Early, White House secretary, said that the Chief Executive's message would emphasize "defense purposes for which the money would be spent."

Expanded Manoeuvres an Aim

Soon after returning to the War Department from the White House conference, Secretary Woodring stated that the army hoped to expand its August manoeuvres to include 310,000 regular, reserve and National Guard troops in view of "the present state of the world." He said that it was planned to stage the manoeuvres in each of the four army corps areas, instead of only one.

"The War Department said that Major General Henry H. Arnold, Chief of the Army Air Corps, had cut short a two weeks' inspection tour of Caribbean defenses and would return to this country tonight. He will assist in drafting army expansion plans.

News of the sudden return of the Army Air Chief coincided with estimates of War Department officials that not more than eighty-seven military planes were being delivered to the army in any month and that even that figure sometimes was not reached.

The War Department's estimate did not include production for the navy, for commercial purposes or for foreign governments, it was explained. Officials estimate that Germany has produced as many as 2,300 planes a month, although the average is believed to be considerably lower.

Senate Gets Demands for Funds

Demands for large increases in military and air defenses, meanwhile, were heard in the Senate. Senators Lodge, Tydings, Barkley and Lee championed them after Senator Lodge introduced a resolution to set up a joint committee of the House and Senate to study the defense situation and draft a plan for submission to Congress.

Senator Lodge said that studies by an Appropriations subcommittee had indicated that this country could not put more than 75,000 fully equipped troops into the field in an emergency. To obtain weapons for the regular army and National Guard, he said, would take more than a year.

Senator Vandenberg wanted to

Continued on Page Thirteen

The International Situation

The War in the Low Countries

Germany's war for the Low Countries developed yesterday into a series of violent attacks along a 200-mile front from the Netherlands to the Moselle River. It was a full Blitzkrieg effort, utilizing armored columns and airplane bombers and strafers. The Allies met it with delaying actions. Paris military authorities emphasized main bodies were not yet engaged. [Page 1.]

A three-pronged thrust into Belgium was being carried out from the "appendix" of the Netherlands, between the German and Belgian frontiers, which was overrun the first day of the war. One drive was to the northwest, to separate Belgium from the Netherlands. Another was southwest, against the Liége defenses. The third pierced the Albert Canal line near Hasselt on the route to Brussels. Berlin dispatches spoke of a clash between a mechanized column and enemy armored forces near St. Trond, forty miles east of Brussels. [Follows the above.]

According to a Paris dispatch, this action involved 1,500 to 2,000 tanks and was the greatest tank engagement ever fought; the French claimed to have won it. [Page 1.]

Chief success of the offensive was the splitting of the Netherlands in two. An Amsterdam dispatch admitted that the Germans had taken Moerdyk Bridge across Hollandsch Diep, one of the outlets of the Maas (Meuse) River. This bridge, the largest in Europe, is the main artery for motor and rail traffic between North and South Netherlands. In North Netherlands defending troops withdrew to the main water defenses protecting the nation's "stronghold," which includes Amsterdam, Rotterdam and The Hague. [Page 1.]

Queen Wilhelmina, Crown Princess Juliana and the Princess's two daughters and husband, Prince Bernhard, took refuge in England. [Page 1.]

In Belgium the Germans claimed to have occupied Liége just one day behind their 1914 timetable. But the protecting Liége fortresses had not been reduced. [Page 1.]

Repercussions Elsewhere

At London Prime Minister Churchill, predicting a testing period of "blood, toil, tears and sweat," received overwhelming votes of confidence from both Houses of Parliament. [Page 1.]

At Rome and throughout Italy there were new demonstrations of anti-British feeling. British residents were being advised by their consulates to go home. But the Italians still had no blackout or air-raid practice, dug no bomb shelters, took no steps to protect their art treasures. [Page 1.]

At Berlin the High Command announced that ten French prisoners of war would be executed for every German parachutist shot by the French "in violation of international law." Germany persisted in her denial that such troops were disguised in Allied uniforms and hence subject to execution as spies. [Page 10.]

At Washington military experts expressed doubts that Germany had developed any new weapon of general efficacy that would win the war. [Page 6.]

President Roosevelt will shortly send to Congress a request for additional defense funds (probably $500,000,000) to be added to the $2,000,000,000 already appropriated for the next fiscal year. [Page 1.]

At New York pessimism in Wall Street over the war's progress brought leading stocks down $2 to nearly 10 points in the widest decline since Nov. 19, 1937. [Page 35.]

NAZIS CLAIM LIEGE

But Berlin Admits Some Forts in Belgian Ring Still Hold Out

'THREAT' TO BRUSSELS

Thrust as in 1914 Held Likely to Force New Stand at Antwerp

By GEORGE AXELSSON

Wireless to THE NEW YORK TIMES.

BERLIN, May 13—The Germans tonight were well on their way into the heart of Belgium; they claimed to have successfully turned the Liége defenses and to have captured the city itself. A lightning and spectacular advance across dykes and flooded areas had carried them almost to Rotterdam to the relief of their "suicide battalions" of aerial shock troops, landed by parachute and troop transport planes since the beginning of the invasion.

Both these claims are made in a General Headquarters communiqué issued today, which also speaks of an intensified air offensive that has cost the Allies 320 planes shot down in the last twenty-four hours.

If the generally reliable German General Headquarters' claims are correct, the conflict, which is beginning to be called a second installment of the World War, repeats some of the early features of its predecessor as well as having some sensational features of its own, such as the use of parachute troops and dark hints of secret weapons.

Situation Similar to 1914

The German assertion that the swastika flag flies tonight from the citadel of Liége, although some of the forts of the ring about the city are holding out, recalls 1914, when a German brigade penetrated between the forts and occupied the city through the initiative of a then little-known staff officer, Eric von Ludendorff. Then as now, the forts offered stubborn resistance.

At that time heavy howitzers, whose destructive power was the first World War surprise, finally overcame the resistance, but now it is believed the Germans no longer need be immediately worried about these "islands," which they have surrounded, the better to attend to exploitation of their breach in the Liége-Maastricht-Hasselt line.

Through this breach they have been able to pour great numbers of swift motorized units that are believed to have reached Tirlemont, well on the way to Louvain and Brussels. Also in the World War German advance guards were pressing against that same line long before the Liége forts fell.

The threat to Brussels is considered immediate, in which case the Belgians are expected to fall back on Antwerp, as in 1914. The Germans are expected to continue pushing westward in an effort to cut Belgium in two, squeezing the northern part and the unconquered part of the Netherlands between two German armies.

Assuming that they successfully reach the sea, they are expected even before that time to turn south on Namur and the defense line running westward from there by way of Charleroi, Mons, Tournai and

Continued on Page Eight

NAZIS ATTACK IN BELGIUM AND SLICE ACROSS NETHERLANDS

The northern country has been virtually bisected by German forces that advanced from the east, passed the important bridge at Moerdyk (3), which is the main north-south line, and closed in on Rotterdam. Other German contingents have thrust across the northern provinces (1) to Yssel Lake, while still others are fighting on the west bank of the Yssel River (2). In Belgium the Nazis claimed the citadel of Liege (4), north of which 1,500 tanks waged a furious battle. A detailed map of this region appears in the inset. In Luxembourg (5) the invaders were apparently fighting a holding action, attacking toward the near-by French border.

PARIS IS CONFIDENT

Fighting Fierce on 200-Mile Front—Liege Held by Allies, It Is Said

NAZIS RUSH UP UNITS

Major Battle Still to Be Fought, but Intensity of Action Increases

By G. H. ARCHAMBAULT

Wireless to THE NEW YORK TIMES.

PARIS, May 13—With the utmost violence of which they are capable and making full use of armored columns and airplanes, the German armies today began a mass attack from Arnhem in the Netherlands to the Moselle River, a front of approximately 200 miles. At all points fighting has been exceedingly fierce.

Nevertheless, the great battle has not yet been engaged. The enemy is still bringing up his main bodies, while French, British, Netherland and Belgian troops are fighting delaying actions at some points and rear-guard engagements at others. The line the Allied High Command has set as the limit of its retirement has not yet been reached. Then, and then only, will the issue be joined between the two armies.

Here tonight there is calm confidence. According to all accounts, Generalissimo Maurice Gustave Gamelin remains as cool as did Marshal Joffre during the Battle of the Marne, at which time the present generalissimo was his trusted aide.

From the latest reliable information available here tonight no line can yet be drawn even approximately to show the respective positions. The fighting still consists of a series of local actions, which, however, is increasing both in extent and importance. For full comprehension they should be considered from north to south.

THE NETHERLANDS

The Germans have pushed westward of Arnhem in the general direction of Amersfoort. They have also crossed the Yssel and the Maas [Meuse] Rivers at several points. The Netherland Army is resisting stubbornly on the Grebbe River and since the battle began is winning high praise in French military circles.

[The Netherland High Command in a communiqué, issued last night admitted that German motorized troops had cut the Netherlands in two when they captured Moerdyk Bridge and crossed the Hollandsch Diep, just south of Rotterdam, The United Press reported. It was also admitted that the main water defense system, the Grebbe Line, had been penetrated.]

The second water line begins in the region of Amersfoort. The Netherland plan of defense foresees ultimate resistance in an area marked by The Hague, Amsterdam, Utrecht and Dordrecht, which can be surrounded by floods. The Nazis seem likely to seek passage across the Grebbe River, and if successful, push toward Zeeland Province by a route south of the water line.

Both British and French troops are now in complete liaison with the Netherlands.

In the interior the Netherlanders have succeeded in rounding up more detachments of German air infantry.

BELGIUM

In the north, Liége is seriously threatened despite the brilliant counter-attack by French armored columns described in another dispatch. [At this point, twenty-nine words were censored.]

All the forts forming the defense of Liége were attacked today by heavy artillery. The Berlin radio claims that the Germans have taken several, but information here is that none had fallen when the latest reports were received this evening. Berlin speaks of having taken the "Citadel" but it is explained here that Liége Citadel does not form part of the ring of forts. Eben Emael, a fort taken during the night, is outside the fortified belt. It was built to defend the Albert Canal at its point of junction

Continued on Page Four

Dispatches from Europe and the Far East are subject to censorship at the source.

HATRED OF BRITISH IS FANNED IN ITALY

Student Demonstrators in a Dozen Cities Dispersed by Complacent Police

By HERBERT L. MATTHEWS

By Telephone to THE NEW YORK TIMES.

ROME, May 13—There were demonstrations all over Italy this morning under the Fascist party's direction to arouse patriotic sentiments for war and hatred for Great Britain.

The reason given is popular reaction to the publication of the Foreign Office report showing how the British blockade is harming Italian trade. In Rome the hostility toward the British has become even more manifest, with an attempted demonstration against the British Embassy and another protest by the embassy to the Italian Government.

British tourists and visitors are being advised by their consulates to leave Italy whenever they ask for guidance. Residents, one of the consuls told your correspondent today, "are not discouraged from going if it suits their convenience."

Britons in Rome and Florence are naturally nervous these days, for to a certain class of young Fascisti there has obviously been given a free hand to bait them. The British Military Attaché's chauffeur was ordered to take the British flag off his automobile, but the attaché refused to let him. Lady Loraine, wife of the British Ambassador, Sir Percy Loraine, is understood to have taken hers off her own car, although the Ambassador continues to display his.

University Students Active

Most of the work of this sort is done by students of the "Guf," the disciplined Fascist university organizations. They demonstrated in many parts of Rome this morning, finally converging on the street leading toward the British Embassy. The police, with remarkable prescience, had been placed on guard on every street leading toward the building. The good-natured youngsters, who were generally in groups of about fifty, were shooed away by equally good-natured policemen. It all ended happily.

Nevertheless, the fact of the dem-

Continued on Page Ten

CHURCHILL BACKED BY 'FULL WAR' VOTE

New British Prime Minister Meets Commons—Lloyd George Rallies Support

Text of Churchill's statement will be found on Page 6.

By RAYMOND DANIELL

Special Cable to THE NEW YORK TIMES.

LONDON, May 13—To a Parliament summoned into session secretly lest the gathering tempt German bombers, Winston Churchill made today his first speech as Prime Minister, predicting victory, but warning that evil days lay immediately ahead.

The House of Commons presented a new aspect when Mr. Churchill rose to apologize for the unceremonious way the new government was formed and to move himself for the vote of confidence that was given him overwhelmingly.

Mr. Churchill defined the aim of his government as "victory at all costs."

"I have nothing to offer but blood,

Continued on Page Six

British Fliers Smash Into Nazis; Aim at Air Mastery in Belgium

By HAROLD DENNY

Wireless to THE NEW YORK TIMES.

WITH THE BRITISH ARMY, in Belgium, May 13—A battle such as the world has never seen before is now beginning just inside Belgium's eastern border, where invading Germans have smashed in the first serious barrier of this country. The battle is not going too well from the standpoint of the Allies, and the situation today can only be described as grave, though it is not hopeless.

Yesterday's reports that the Germans had penetrated the Belgian line in the Maastricht region are now confirmed. The Belgians have been forced to retire along a ten-mile front to an already prepared second line, which, however, has the advantage of being shorter.

The Germans were able to cross the River Meuse on two bridges that should have been demolished but were not. British bombing planes took terrible chances in diving low to bomb these bridges in an attempt to destroy them before the Germans got over but were unsuccessful. The Germans poured in by these avenues and then mushroomed out, catching the Belgian elements flankwise and forcing them hastily to withdraw.

At the present stage the battle is a race between Belgians endeavoring to establish themselves in a new line farther east and Germans striking with ground troops and aviation in an effort to widen the breach and exploit the initial gain into a major break-through.

The Germans are employing heavily motorized units and bringing into play tanks and all the vast war

Continued on Page Five

NAZIS CROSS BRIDGE BELOW ROTTERDAM

Sever Main North-South Link of Netherlands—Also Cut Through Grebbe Line

By The United Press.

AMSTERDAM, May 13—German motorized forces today cut the Netherlands in two when they struck sixty miles across the nation's river belt to Moerdyk Bridge and crossed the Hollandsch Diep, just south of Rotterdam, the Netherland High Command admitted in a communiqué tonight. It revealed that the swift-striking Nazi army had achieved one of the chief aims of its invasion of the Netherlands.

The Germans, on reaching Moerdyk Bridge, the largest in Europe, came to within thirty miles of the Netherlands capital at The Hague.

Earlier in the day it had been admitted that the German mobile forces, led by tanks and armored cars, had reached the industrial center of Langstraat, east of Moerdyk Bridge along the southern extension of the Maas River.

Tonight's communiqué said:

"From Langstraat the enemy reached Moerdyk Bridge and crossed the Hollandsch Diep."

Rotterdam Fighting Continues

In Rotterdam, fifteen miles north of the Hollandsch Diep, German detachments still were fighting in parts of the city, the communiqué said.

Tonight's communiqué said that in the Grebbe sector the Netherlanders recaptured one position, but were unable to hold it against Nazi counter-attacks and finally retreated.

The Moerdyk Bridge is sixteen miles southeast of Rotterdam, which was under intermittent aerial bombings throughout the day, while fires set by incendiary bombs continued to burn.

Netherland forces were described earlier by the High Command as fighting fiercely to stem the powerful Nazi advance westward from Langstraat, which actually is a nest of small industrial villages on the southern branch of the Maas River called the Berschemaas.

Military leaders then said that the Germans, by their rushing drive, ran the risk of being bogged down and perhaps isolated in a region of dykes, canals and low-lands. Many sluice gates of the area had been opened so wide, it was said, that the country was half inundated.

Moerdyk Bridge, spanning the Hollandsch Diep, which leads into the North Sea, was circled by Ger-

Continued on Page Four

Warships of Land Charge In Epic Battle Near Liege

Wireless to THE NEW YORK TIMES.

PARIS, May 13—For the first time in the history of warfare tanks have met tanks in a terrific clash of steel—between 1,500 and 2,000 of them. The clash was epic, surpassing anything the human brain had ever conceived. The fight lasted hours as more and more French armored columns rushing to the aid of Belgian infantry made headlong for the German tanks as soon as they were sighted.

The struggle began yesterday and continued for the greater part of today north of Liége in the vicinity of Tongres, Waremme and Saint Trond. Never had there been such a fray. For hours the scene was hell itself with tanks engaging at close range, charging one another, belching projectiles on all sides and some catching fire and exploding.

When the roar of battle ceased the French were masters of the situation, according to word received here, and many derelict enemy tanks dotted the field.

Called a "Brilliant Action"

It is described officially as a "brilliant action" that proved the high value of French materiel. This news has been received here with great gratification as confirmation of the belief that most French tanks are superior to the German, weight for weight. Moreover it indicates that tank tactics have been well studied by the French.

The conditions of the battle make it clear that the tanks on both sides were light tanks. Possibly they included on the French side a unit that this correspondent visited behind the Belgian frontier not very long ago. On that occasion a sham fight was organized, in the course of which was revealed remarkable mechanical suppleness and immediate response to commands.

The methods employed cannot be revealed but they are so efficient that the tanks manoeuvred with as much ease as cavalry and their evolutions left the spectators marveling.

What occurred near Tongres may be gathered from the following indications then given the correspondent by a senior officer:

"We shall go into action just as if we were light cruisers at sea sighting an enemy. Our tactics are summarized in the words 'immediate attack and rapidity of fire.'

"This means, of course, highly trained crews and the prompt decision on the part of their leaders. A battle between tanks will be short and the formation adopted at the outset will be decisive because there will be no opportunity to correct mistakes. The clash will be mighty and the outcome of that first battle will prove whether our tactics are right. I believe they are. May the day come soon when we shall see."

QUEEN WILHELMINA GOES TO ENGLAND

Arrives on British Warship—Juliana and Children Precede Her to London

By JAMES B. RESTON

Wireless to THE NEW YORK TIMES.

LONDON, May 13—Queen Wilhelmina of the Netherlands has arrived in London, a refugee. She came from the Netherlands to England aboard a British warship.

Europe's last remaining reigning Queen, who last week completed the forty-second year of her reign, stepped off her heavily guarded royal train at the grimy Liverpool Street Station tonight. There she was met by King George VI and taken immediately to Buckingham Palace.

Earlier in the day Princess Juliana arrived here with her consort, Prince Bernhard zu Lippe-Biesterfeld, and their two daughters, Princess Beatrix, 2 years old, and Princess Irene, 9 months old.

Greeted by Royal Guard

When the Queen's train stopped at the station, Netherland soldiers and officers of the Royal Guard in gray-blue uniforms and steel helmets leaped to the platform and stood at attention. British soldiers in khaki battle dress saluted as Wilhelmina, dressed in a navy blue coat and skirt and with a gas mask slung across her shoulder stepped from her car.

King George, in the uniform of an admiral of the fleet, walked across the barricaded section of the platform to greet the refugee Queen. He shook her hand and kissed her on both cheeks.

Crown Princess Juliana and Prince Bernhard also greeted the Queen. For a few minutes they stood conversing on the platform, watched by a silent crowd. Then King George led the way to the royal automobile outside the station.

Before departing Queen Wilhelmina shook hands with her Minister to London, Count Johan Paul van Limburg Stirum, and his predecessor, Jonkheer de Marees van Swin-

Continued on Page Four

"All the News That's Fit to Print."

The New York Times.

LATE CITY EDITION
Fair, continued cool today. Tomorrow increasing cloudiness, slightly warmer.
Temperatures Yesterday—Max., 64; Min., 53

VOL. LXXXIX...No. 30,065. Entered as Second-Class Matter, Postoffice, New York, N. Y. NEW YORK, SATURDAY, MAY 18, 1940. PPPP THREE CENTS NEW YORK CITY and Vicinity | FOUR CENTS Elsewhere Except in 7th and 8th Postal Zones.

NAZIS PIERCE FRENCH LINES ON 62-MILE FRONT; TAKE BRUSSELS, LOUVAIN, MALINES AND NAMUR; WASHINGTON SPEEDS ITS BIG DEFENSE PROGRAM

ROOSEVELT IS BUSY

Calls Parley on Great Air Force, Considers Bigger Sea Patrol

UNITY IN CONGRESS

Partisanship Shelved in Drive—Midwest May Get Arms Plants

By FELIX BELAIR Jr.
Special to THE NEW YORK TIMES.

WASHINGTON, May 17—National defense preparations were begun by government agencies today on a scale unapproached since the World War.

In response to President Roosevelt's preparedness message calling for an impregnable America, first steps were taken toward proposed far-reaching undertakings, such as construction of airplane and munitions factories in the Middle West, out of reach of possible quick bombing raids.

The President followed his request to Congress for a goal of 50,000 first-line fighting planes by calling a conference of aviation industry leaders with army, navy and Treasury officials to be held in the office of Secretary Morgenthau Monday morning. Earlier in the day he disclosed plans to recommission thirty-five more World War destroyers for emergency patrol duty at a cost of $6,000,000.

Developments of the Day

As the executive and legislative branches gave evidence of the "partnership" for which the President appealed in his $1,182,000,000 national defense message yesterday, the preparedness campaign brought the following developments:

1. The House Military Affairs Committee began hearings on the President's defense program envisaging an army nucleus of 750,000 regulars and 250,000 reserves, fully equipped for active service by June 30, 1941.

2. Military authorities shaped plans calling for a $300,000,000 outlay to bring actual aircraft production up to 30,000 planes a year as quickly as possible under a program specifying a number of factories between the Allegheny and Rocky Mountains capable of producing a hundred planes a month, the government to build the plants and rent them on a "fixed-fee basis."

3. House leaders organized a drive for modification of the Walsh-Healey Act to permit the President to waive forty-hour week limitations governing shipbuilding to speed up the present expansion program.

4. Mr. Roosevelt made known plans to call to Washington soon several recognized industrialists to speed industrial mobilization required to carry out his unprecedented peacetime defense program.

5. The White House placed its stamp of approval on plans of Colonel Frank Knox, Chicago publisher, to sponsor the creation of a chain of aviation training camps throughout the country to supplement the military and naval training facilities.

6. The Navy Department considered proclaiming all industrial navy yards, air bases and fields as restricted areas and sought ways and means of increasing the number of its skilled mechanics from 75,000 to 150,000 or 200,000 men. The President's defense plan included the placing of the navy's expansion program on a twenty-four-hour basis instead of eight hours as at present.

Leaders Discard Partisanship

Political leaders, meanwhile, declared a moratorium on partisanship to expedite early enactment of legislation carrying out the President's plan to make our defenses invulnerable. The statement of former President Hoover endorsing Mr. Roosevelt's message to Congress was received by the White House as "an indication of national unity which we welcome and that political differences are being cast aside in the emergency."

The President, apparently convinced of Republican good will for his program, invited Alfred M. Landon to a White House luncheon conference next Wednesday.

In announcing the President's endorsement of the aviation training plan suggested by Colonel Knox, Stephen T. Early, White House

Continued on Page Six

The International Situation

The War in the West

German arms struck yesterday along the whole Western Front from the Netherland border to the northern anchor of the Maginot Line at the Luxembourg corner. As night fell the situation was as follows:

The Nazis claimed that on the northern wing against the British and Belgians they had penetrated to the outlying forts of Antwerp and occupied Malines and Louvain and that advance units were in Brussels, the Belgian capital. On the southern wing, against the French, the German High Command said it had broken through the fortifications along the Belgian-French border for a distance of 100 kilometers (62 miles) from just south of Maubeuge to Carignan, south of Sedan, and had penetrated into France as far as Le Cateau, La Capelle and to a point north of Rethel. The communiqué admitted, however, that the lines were changing hourly. The Germans claimed 12,000 French prisoners, including two generals. On the central Belgian front advances were reported at Namur and Wavre. [Page 1.]

The Allies did not deny that the situation was critical. General Gamelin, supreme commander of the Allied forces, issued a general order to all troops stating that the "fate of our country, of our Allies, the destiny of the world depend on the battle now being fought." The command was, "Conquer or die." The order recalled Marshal Joffre's famous message to the French Armies before the 1914 First Battle of the Marne, where the "taxicab army" from Paris stopped the Kaiser's legions, and saved Paris. A communiqué said that the Germans had penetrated as far as Avesnes and Vervins, about fifteen miles into France along the Belgian border. It estimated the Germans had engaged the "greatest part" of their heavy tank divisions in the attack. Attacks south of Sedan in the vicinity of Montmedy and Sedan were said to have been repulsed. Allied bomber and fighter squadrons were reported carrying out their missions of harassing enemy troop concentrations and rear lines of communication. [Page 1.]

While London admitted a withdrawal of its forces to a new defense line behind Brussels, advices from field headquarters in Belgium indicated the retreat had been orderly and that British air forces were more than holding their own in harassing the enemy and protecting their own rear from German bombing and machine-gunning attacks on communication lines. [Page 1.]

The Air Ministry at London said the German advance was not being made without cost. It estimated German plane losses in the last seven days at 1,000. However, it said, large reserves (estimated at 23,000 planes) made it probable the German air effort could be sustained for some time. [Page 4.]

Tragic victims of the horror were uncounted numbers of refugees who choked all roads in Belgium not already filled with troops and guns moving up to the fighting lines, homeless, unfed, many wounded, seeking a sanctuary which appeared not to exist. [Included in the above.]

King Leopold of the Belgians, his capital lost, moved his government to Ostend. [Page 1.]

Repercussions Elsewhere

Scenes in government departments reminiscent of World War days were seen in Washington as the Federal agencies involved moved to put into effect the needed defense measures outlined by President Roosevelt in his speech to Congress Thursday. The President called a conference of Army, Navy and Treasury officials and aviation leaders to discuss his program to build up the United States air force to 50,000 planes. [Page 1.]

War fever mounted in Rome. Premier Mussolini's newspaper, Popolo d'Italia, thundered: "The Italian people must now or never achieve their Mediterranean destiny." The Senate, in an atmosphere of war hysteria, heard a budget report with a record deficit and warning of more taxes; the stock market suffered another "Black Friday" recession. [Page 1.]

On the Balkan diplomatic front Russia was reported bringing pressure on all interested countries to retain the status quo there under threat of forming an alliance with Yugoslavia and Bulgaria and reviving the idea of a union of all the Slavs in Europe. [Page 5.]

COL. KNOX TO FORM AIR 'PLATTSBURGS'

Roosevelt Authorizes Civilian Groups to Promote Training of Students as Pilots

Special to THE NEW YORK TIMES.

CHICAGO, May 17—With the authorization of President Roosevelt, Colonel Frank Knox, publisher of The Chicago Daily News and Republican Vice Presidential nominee in 1936, stated here today that a civilian group would be formed to cooperate with the government in training 10,000 pilots at volunteer camps this Summer in the nine army corps areas. Colonel Knox discussed the project in a White House conference yesterday with the President.

The training camps will be opened about July 1, Colonel Knox said, and will be designed primarily to accommodate 10,000 college students who have been receiving preliminary training through the Civil Aeronautics Authority.

"What we are undertaking," Colonel Knox said, "is not to replace any of the present activities, but to extend and increase them. We can turn out airplanes rapidly, but not top pilots, and we need at least two pilots for each plane."

World War Comparison

Colonel Knox described the new organization as a parallel to the army training camps of the last World War, such as Plattsburg, N. Y.

The cost of promoting the volunteer enlistments in the camps will be financed privately, he continued. The army has agreed for its part to provide tents, reserve officers for training, cooks and camp sites.

"Most of all," Colonel Knox said,

Continued on Page Seven

WAR BASIS EVIDENT IN ITALIAN BUDGET

With Record Deficit Figures, Senators Cheer Belligerent Speeches of Leaders

By HERBERT L. MATTHEWS
By Telephone to THE NEW YORK TIMES.

ROME, May 17—While nothing startling happened in Italy today, there have been a number of minor developments to drive home further the feeling that Italian intervention in the European war is not very far off.

The Senate held a session in the morning full of genuine war fervor. The Minister of Finance, Count Paolo Thaon di Revel, presented what amounts to a war budget and admitted a deficit for this year of more than 26,000,000,000 lire. Premier Mussolini's own newspaper, in a highly significant editorial, as good as told the nation that it was about to enter the conflict. The Stock Exchanges had a singularly black day; the great successes claimed by Germany on the French front provided a temptation of the first magnitude for the Fascist leaders.

The temperature in the Senate session was feverish. Every time the name of King Victor Emmanuel or of Premier Mussolini was mentioned there was a remarkably emotional reaction. Count Suardo, the President of the Senate, spoke words like these:

"The Italian people press around you, Duce, to form an iron block of energy and will, ready for your orders wherever you wish to guide them, because they know that the road you will take at their head to preserve our vital rights has just one goal—the grandeur and power of Italy."

At the end of Count Suardo's

Continued on Page Five

GAMELIN IN APPEAL

Says Fate of Nation and World's Destiny Hang on Present Conflict

FIGHTING IS AT PEAK

Full Air Forces Battle—Attacks at Sedan and Montmedy Repulsed

By G. H. ARCHAMBAULT
Wireless to THE NEW YORK TIMES.

PARIS, May 17—"The fate of our country and that of our allies and the destiny of the world depend on the battle now being fought."

Thus begins a general order to all troops issued this evening by General Maurice Gustave Gamelin, supreme Allied commander.

Taken in conjunction with the communiqué issued from General Headquarters tonight, it reveals the situation as tragic.

"Today the German attack developed on a massive scale," the communiqué stated, "not only in Belgium but in the region of Avesnes and Vervins. On those fronts the enemy engaged the greater part of his heavy tank divisions. The battle took the form of a veritable melee."

Avesnes and Vervins are in the North of France, the latter some fifteen miles from the Belgian border.

[Cannonading was heard today on the outskirts of Paris, according to The Associated Press. It was not learned whether this was anti-aircraft or other fire.]

All United in Battle

General Gamelin's order adds that British, Belgian and Polish soldiers are fighting by the side of the French, together with foreign volunteers. The British Air Force, he added, like the French, is fighting to the last man.

Every troop that cannot advance, the general asserted, must die where it stands rather than abandon the portion of national soil entrusted to it. Concluding, he said:

"As always in the critical hours of our history, the watchword is 'Conquer or die.' We must conquer."

This general order so reminiscent of that issued by Marshal Joffre in 1914 on the first day of the Battle of the Marne tells the story. There are no details. A terrific struggle is being fought for the future of mankind. All else is of no moment.

That the Allied General Headquarters has not departed from its calm is indicated in the remainder of the communiqué, which proceeds to refer to minor incidents as follows:

"Further to the east the enemy attacked in the region of Sedan and Montmedy without success.

Aviation Continues Activity

"In close collaboration with the Royal Air Force our aviation continued its energetic and efficacious action against ground troops, crossroads and railways. While assuring the protection of our troops our fighters engaged in numerous encounters. Many enemy planes were brought down. In the present conditions of open warfare it is not possible to know the exact number."

Nor is it of moment to refer to this morning's news relating to the actions on the Meuse. They all pale into insignificance with the day's developments. Since the outline of the pocket formed by the Germans was indicated by a spokesman for the general staff that pocket has been burst.

Any appreciation of the situation, any comment would be mere guesswork utterly out of place in the circumstances.

Decisive Victory Sought

PARIS, May 17 (AP)—The French armies, under orders from General Maurice Gustave Gamelin to "die on the spot rather than give further ground," battled a massive German tank drive into Northern France tonight in a clash described by the high command as "a veritable melee."

Adolf Hitler's fighters carried their week-old offensive on the Western Front to a peak during the day with violent blasts both in Belgium and France in a desperate effort to drive home a decisive victory.

The German thrust through Bel-

Continued on Page Three

GERMANY'S SWIFT COLUMNS SWEEP TO NEW SUCCESSES

Nazi forces, breaking through the extension of the Maginot Line in Northern France across the Belgian border, have reached the vicinity of Avesnes (4) and Vervins (5) and are reported north of Rethel (6) in a thrust toward Laon. The Allies claim to have halted a further attempt to widen the gap south of Sedan (7). In Belgium the Germans occupied Louvain and Malines (1) and claim to have reached the outer fortifications of Antwerp; they also crashed through the Dyle River defenses and marched into Brussels (2) as British forces withdrew to the west, and reported the capture of Namur (3). The dotted line indicates approximate Allied fixed positions.

Gamelin, 1940; Joffre, 1914

Gamelin Order

By The United Press.

PARIS, May 17—Following is the text of General Maurice Gustave Gamelin's order of the day to the French armies:

"The fate of our country and that of our Allies and the destiny of the world depend on the battle now being fought.

"English, Belgian and Polish soldiers and foreign volunteers fight at our side.

"The British Air Force is engaged up to the hilt like ours.

"Every unit that is unable to advance must accept death rather than abandon that part of the national territory entrusted to it.

"As always in the critical hours of our history the watchword today is 'Conquer or die.' We must conquer."

Joffre Order

Following is the text of the order addressed by Marshal Joffre to all army headquarters and to troops on Sept. 6, 1914:

"We are about to engage a battle on which the fate of our country depends and it is important to remind all ranks that the moment has passed for looking to the rear; all our efforts must be directed to attacking and driving back the enemy.

"Troops that can advance no further must, at any price, hold on to the ground they have conquered and die on the spot rather than give way. Under the circumstances which face us, no act of weakness can be tolerated."

BELGIANS REMOVE CAPITAL TO OSTEND

Vacating of Brussels Laid to 'Obvious Necessity'—U. S. Envoy Remains at Post

Wireless to THE NEW YORK TIMES.

PARIS, May 17—The removal of the Belgian capital from Brussels to another point in Belgian territory was announced today in a broadcast from Brussels by M. Vanderpoorten, Minister of the Interior, speaking for Premier Hubert Pierlot.

[The Belgian Government is now established at Ostend, on Belgium's North Sea coast, The Associated Press reported in a dispatch from Ostend.]

"This painful decision," he said, "has been forced upon us by obvious necessity. The Allied troops are defending themselves step by step, but the rapidity of movement that armies have today causes events to transpire with greater rapidity than ever. After a few days of war we find ourselves in a situation which, without being so grave, recalls in certain respects what it was after the first weeks of war in 1914. We shall soon witness, we firmly believe, the same recovery which took place then."

The Minister praised the courage of the Belgian Armies and people, and added:

"The Premier yesterday after-

Continued on Page Four

FRANCE PAYS PRICE FOR SHIFTING UNITS

Penetration by Nazi Armored Forces Laid to Fact Aid Had to Be Rushed to Neutrals

Wireless to THE NEW YORK TIMES.

PARIS, May 17—Outside military circles, the public mind not only here but seemingly all over the world is much exercised over the swift advance of German armored columns into French territory. The briefest explanation is that the Allies have paid that price for moving immediately to the aid of Belgium and the Netherlands despite the fact that both countries steadfastly refused to consider any joint plan of campaign in the event of invasion.

Apparently what seems most inexplicable to the layman is that the line of defenses along the French frontier should have been penetrated. The answer is twofold:

First, these defenses were not the Maginot Line of solid permanent concrete works that extends only from Montmedy eastward to the Rhine, but field fortifications—trenches, ditches, pits and the like—reinforced since the war by pill boxes and blockhouses.

Second, that the value of field works is determined by the forces behind them.

Since the Allied High Command decided early in the campaign to

Continued on Page Four

BRITISH FALL BACK BEHIND BRUSSELS

'Adjustment' West of City Is Announced—Troops Steady Against Nazi Blows

Special Cable to THE NEW YORK TIMES.

LONDON, May 17—The War Office announced tonight that the British Army in Belgium had retired the night before to positions west of Brussels, "certain adjustments at the front having become necessary."

"This readjustment," the communiqué said, "was carried out without interference. There is no question of any collapse or break through in this sector as suggested by the German communiqué."

By HAROLD DENNY
Wireless to THE NEW YORK TIMES.

WITH THE BRITISH ARMY IN BELGIUM, May 17—The Germans renewed today their assaults on the British positions, hurling tanks supported by airplanes with especial severity on the right side of the British line.

The British are withstanding these terrific mechanized assaults with great steadiness and can be counted upon to continue doing so. The British Expeditionary Force is fighting under the French High Command, and its employment is governed by the working out of the grand battle plan. The British are playing the role assigned to them no matter what their local situation. Should the French be hard pressed in the Sedan area—enough, that is, to threaten the splitting of the Allied general line—a realignment of the British forces might be necessary.

British Staff Pleased

British staff officers are pleased with the fine qualities their troops are exhibiting against attacks such as soldiers never had encountered before this war. They are equally confident of the ability of the French High Command to meet any situation presented by the German drive. The French must have foreseen every emergency which could develop and devised effective counter-measures. The French seem to have the gift of choosing the exact moment to strike most effectively.

The British now are fighting side by side with the Belgians, who made contact with them in the vicinity of Malines.

British resistance to the German

Continued on Page Three

Dispatches from Europe and the Far East are subject to censorship at the source.

NAZIS REPORT ROUT

Allies 'in Full Retreat' Westward Into France, Germans Declare

AIR VICTORIES NOTED

Sedan Prisoners Said to Total 12,000, Among Them 2 Generals

By GEORGE AXELSSON
Wireless to THE NEW YORK TIMES.

BERLIN, May 17—Brussels, Malines and Louvain have fallen to the relentlessly advancing Germans, who also claim to have broken into France across the defenses of the Maginot Line extension on a wide front, standing not more than ninety miles from Paris at the nearest point.

The German High Command today broke a three days' silence on its Western Front operations to announce two major successes. First was the driving of a sixty-two-mile wedge into the French lines from south of Maubeuge to Carignan, southeast of Sedan. Second was a break through the Belgian Dyle line positions south of Wavre, along with the capture of Namur.

The spearhead of the German advance into France—where, a General Headquarters communiqué significantly says, "Our infantry units and air force are pursuing the enemy in full retreat westward"—is tonight said to be in the vicinity of La Capelle and Le Cateau, halfway between Maubeuge and St. Quentin.

In the sector southeast of Sedan the Germans, according to their communiqué, have taken 12,000 prisoners, including two generals, and also captured abundant war material.

British Throw in Tank Units

In Belgium, the Germans early this morning already had advanced their lines to Malines, the vicinity of Louvain and south of Brussels in the Waterloo area, making the military situation of the capital seem hopeless for the defenders.

Here, it is admitted, the British had thrown in particularly powerful tank units in a desperate attempt to stem the German advance to the coast. The lines were swaying back and forth along this entire sector, with tank meeting tank and infantry against infantry in vicious hand-to-hand encounters of a ceaseless attack and counter-attack.

The Germans evidently were following the Polish campaign method of launching giant tanks in wild forward lunges fanwise, as though along the fingers of an outspread hand, and trusting to skill and chance to hold the spearheads and eventually close the gaps between.

With Paris and the English Channel coast directly threatened, the military plight of the Allies appears most grave, as seen from Berlin. The British, it is said, must now devote every ounce of their resources to saving the coast, while the French must be equally occupied with the defense of their capital, rendering mutual aid difficult if not impossible.

French Attacks Said to Fail

The Germans admit violent French attacks on their south flank, presumably in the Longwy sector, but say these attempts to relieve the main fronts met with no success. Instead, it is claimed, the Germans gained further ground in their counter-attacks.

That the struggles in Belgium and France have changed their aspect in the last forty-eight hours is asserted by military observers here. Only Wednesday the two battle zones, that in front of Brussels and that to the south in France, formed one connected front from Antwerp by Charleville to Sedan.

The German break through between Namur and Givet and into the Maginot Line across the Meuse was thrust at the point where the south flank of the Belgian battle zone joined the northern flank of the French. Widening of the breach between Namur and Givet and the rapid German push westward in the Maubeuge sector are said to have separated the two battle lines and doubled over the flanks.

The Belgian front is now reported turned back on the Sambre River westward where, according to the Germans, the Allied forces now are threatened with a flanking move-

Continued on Page Two

"All the News That's Fit to Print."

The New York Times.

LATE CITY EDITION
Cloudy, little change in temperature today. Tomorrow rain, not much change in temperature.
Temperatures Yesterday—Max., 70; Min., 58

VOL. LXXXIX No. 30,069. Entered as Second-Class Matter, Postoffice, New York, N. Y. NEW YORK, WEDNESDAY, MAY 22, 1940. THREE CENTS NEW YORK CITY and Vicinity | FOUR CENTS Elsewhere Except in 7th and 8th Postal Zones.

NAZIS AT CHANNEL, TRAP ALLIES IN BELGIUM; CROSS AISNE RIVER 60 MILES FROM PARIS; FRANCE CAN'T DIE, REYNAUD TELLS PEOPLE

PRESIDENT SPEEDS DEFENSE PROGRAM; APPEALS FOR UNITY

At Press Talk He Condemns Nazis as Machine-Gunning Fleeing French Civilians

MOVES ON 'FIFTH COLUMN'

New Reorganization Order Will Put Immigration Bureau in Justice Department

As President Roosevelt outlined yesterday at his press conference further details of plans for the nation's defense [Page 1] various departments of the government took action to speed up preparedness. The navy submitted to Congress a program calling for 10,000 planes and 16,000 pilots. It also ordered a forty-eight-hour work week in navy yards and the hiring of 15,000 more civilian employes. [Page 13.]

Senator Pepper offered a resolution authorizing the President to sell to any invaded country any of the army's or navy's airplanes. The Senate sped action on the War Department Appropriation Bill, now increased to almost $1,500,000,000 in cash grants and close to $325,000,000 in contract authorizations. [Page 10.]

The President asked the House to lift its $50,000 limit on WPA grants, because such a restriction would hamper projects for defense. [Page 8.] He also vetoed a $109,985,450 Rivers and Harbors bill in order to give preference to military projects. [Page 11.]

States 3-Point Plan

By FELIX BELAIR Jr.

Special to THE NEW YORK TIMES.

WASHINGTON, May 21—President Roosevelt today coupled an appeal for national unity behind his preparedness drive with the grimmest picture of German military tactics yet painted in any official American quarter—a picture of the deliberate machine-guning of millions of fleeing French women, children and old men by Nazi war planes. He said Americans well understood the implications of such ruthless methods and would be guided accordingly.

Then the President, employing the gravest tone he has used in referring to the war in Europe, outlined the following three-point policy which he said would govern the nation's defense preparations:

Not a single war millionaire will be created in this country as a result of the war disaster.

Labor will not attempt to take advantage of its collective power to foment strikes and interfere with the national defense program to squeeze higher wages from employers in the so-called war industries.

Under no circumstances will the Administration sanction a weakening of the social legislative gains attained during the last seven years. Labor standards prescribed in the Walsh-Healey act and the Wage-Hour Law must not be relaxed in the name of the national defense.

Plans Attack on "Fifth Column"

As the President gave further impetus to the preparedness drive there were the following developments in his national defense program:

1. Mr. Roosevelt sought to strengthen the country against "fifth column" activities by providing for an early transfer of the Bureau of Immigration and Naturalization from the Labor Department to the Department of Justice. He said he would send to Congress tomorrow another reorganization plan giving effect to the transfer proposal.

2. With full Administration backing, chairmen of the Senate and House Naval Affairs Committees introduced companion bills to spend an additional $124,000,000 for a naval air armada of 10,000 planes and 16,000 pilots. Introduced by Senator Walsh and Representative Vinson after a White House conference, the proposed legislation would increase the navy's authorized aerial fleet by 7,000 units, of

Continued on Page Ten

The International Situation

On the Battle Fronts

Eleven days after the start of their offensive on the Western Front, the Germans yesterday drove a spearhead to the English Channel, cutting off the Allied troops in Belgium and the northwest tip of France from the main body of the French Army. The German command estimated that half a million to a million men had thus been trapped between a steadily pressing mass of German attackers and the North Sea. [Page 1.]

The German thrust, described by Berlin as "the greatest attack of all time," swept sixty miles along the Valley of the Somme, reaching Abbeville, on the estuary of that river. Amiens and Arras fell. The Germans claimed that their air force, aided by submarines and torpedo-carrying mosquito boats, was in command of the Channel. However that may be, French and Belgian ports, from which the British must embark if all effort to hold the northern line is abandoned, were being unmercifully bombed last night. Despite all this activity in the west, the Germans did not let up in the southern part of their huge salient. The push toward Paris continued, with semi-official sources in Berlin saying the invaders had crossed the Aisne at Soissons, sixty miles from the capital. [Included in foregoing.]

Paris contended that only motorcycle troops had reached Abbeville. Despite the break-through, French authorities said, there still was furious fighting in the neighborhood of Cambrai, far to the German rear, where the invaders had not yet succeeded in consolidating their positions. But there was as yet no sign of large-scale counter-attack. [Page 1.]

The French admitted that the Somme Valley above St. Quentin was in chaos. Parachutists set hundreds of fires around Arras and Amiens; in the triangle between the Belgian border, Amiens and the Channel, not one railway station stood intact. [Page 1.]

The Germans apparently had succeeded in capturing the commander of the French Ninth Army, General Henri Honoré Giraud. A Berlin dispatch said the capture had been "half-tragic, half-comic"—that the general had walked into his headquarters and found German officers there. Paris admitted there had been no communication with the general for forty-eight hours. [Page 1.]

Early this morning waves of Allied fliers bombed Aachen (Aix-la-Chapelle), on the west border of Germany. Bombs showered on the city and on Westwall fortifications. This raid was outstanding among many aimed at the German rear. The British Air Ministry announced that during the night German planes had dropped bombs on two districts in Southeastern England; no damage or casualties were reported. [Page 1.]

Alfred Duff Cooper, British Minister of Information, warned his countrymen by radio that they might expect invasion at any time. Volunteer "parashoots" were rushed to positions guarding points vulnerable to attack by German soldiers floating down from the skies. [Page 3.]

Premier Reynaud, addressing the French Senate, said the inefficient training and handling of General André Georges Corap's army was responsible for France's plight. "Unbelievable faults" would be punished, he declared. The Premier said the classic French conception of war had been demolished by armored divisions, fighting planes and disorganization of the rear by parachutists. He emphasized his faith in France to surmount her period of trial, and asserted: "Abroad they are beginning to understand * * * that what is happening affects them and their children. Let them not come to this understanding too late." [Page 1.]

Repercussions Elsewhere

Italy, which is expected shortly to join the German side, closed the border between Italian-owned Albania and Yugoslavia, where Allied sentiment has been strong. There were reports in Yugoslavia that munitions were being rushed in below the border and that barrack and other military construction work was being pressed in twenty-four-hour shifts. [Page 5.]

President Roosevelt, at a press conference in Washington, appealed for national unity in preparedness. He set forth three points to govern policy in building up our defenses: (1) No war millionaires will be created; (2) labor must not take advantage of its collective power to foment strikes interfering with the defense program; (3) there must be no weakening of social legislation of the last seven years, notably laws affecting labor standards. [Page 1.]

HENDRICKSON LEADS IN JERSEY PRIMARY

Willkie Gets Surprise Write-In Vote Against Dewey in Presidential Contest

A write-in vote for Wendell L. Willkie in the New Jersey primaries yesterday disclosed surprising strength for the utilities executive as a candidate for President. State Senator Robert C. Hendrickson of Gloucester County was leading former Governor Harold G. Hoffman for the Republican nomination for Governor.

A total of 2,395 election districts out of 3,631 in the State gave 165,650 votes to Mr. Hendrickson and 144,290 to Mr. Hoffman, a commanding lead of 21,360 for Mr. Hendrickson.

Contrary to pre-election predictions, Hendrickson carried Bergen and Union Counties on the basis of incomplete returns. His margin in both counties was small, however. His plurality in Essex County was larger than had been expected.

State Senator Winant Van Winkle, a Hendrickson supporter, was defeated for renomination in Bergen County by a Hoffman candidate, Lloyd L. Schroeder. Complete returns gave Schroeder 27,386 votes to 26,251 for Van Winkle.

District Attorney Thomas E. Dewey entered the Republican primary as a preferential candidate

Continued on Page Sixteen

ALLIES FIGHT BACK AT FURIOUS DRIVES

Admit Penetration of Nazis to Abbeville, but Look for Re-forming of Lines

By The Associated Press.

PARIS, May 21—The Allies, with their backs to the English Channel, tonight fought against a new German advance that spread a path of fire across Northern France and threatened to isolate England.

The French High Command's night communiqué admitted the Germans had driven their advance guard to Amiens and Arras, on the edge of the coastal plain leading to the English Channel.

A War Ministry spokesman added that German motorcycle troops had pushed on to penetrate the outskirts of the Abbeville region. The city of Abbeville is on the Somme estuary, twelve miles from the Channel's open waters, and about twenty-five miles west of Arras and Amiens. The War Ministry spokesman said he believed the French still held Abbeville itself, but that he could "give no official confirmation."

German motorcycle units thrust along roads to the west of Arras and Amiens behind advance bombardments and machine gunning from Nazi planes. Other roads radiating from the French towns, filled with refugees, were reported strafed by the Germans from the

Continued on Page Four

PREMIER IS CANDID

'Unbelievable Faults' in Allied Defense to Be Punished, He Says

'DISASTER' ADMITTED

But France Is Told Hope and Savage Energy Can Still Bring Victory

The text of Premier Reynaud's address is on Page 6.

By P. J. PHILIP

Wireless to THE NEW YORK TIMES.

PARIS, May 21—Announcing quietly, amid a chilly silence, that since 8 o'clock this morning the advancing German forces had occupied Amiens and Arras, Premier Paul Reynaud in the Senate this afternoon called on the people of France, soldiers and civilians alike, to be worthy of the "grandeur of the hour in which we are living" and to "rise to the height of the misfortunes of our country."

Succinctly, sparing no one, he told the tragic story of the mistakes that had been made in the Belgian campaign, of the lack of preparation, of the miscalculations, of the terrible exactness of the German calculations and their consequences.

The Germans had broken the hinge on which the whole left wing of the Allied armies swung, the Premier explained. They had pounded through the breach and driven forward with their armored divisions and airplanes far behind the French northern defense line. The French classic conception of war had been utterly routed by this new conception which disorganized the country behind the lines while it piled hammer blow on hammer blow at strategic points.

Cites "Unbelievable Faults"

There had been, he went on, "unbelievable faults which will be punished." Bridges over the Meuse that should have been destroyed had not been destroyed. Describing what happened to General André Corap's army, he called it a "disaster" and "total disorganization."

M. Reynaud seems not to have given up hope. He demanded that that hope should be backed by confidence and savage energy on the part of all who are fighting and working for the salvation of the country.

This new method of war must be met by new methods of defense, he held. France had in the past repeatedly overcome such initial mistakes and miscalculations; she had risen from the pit of defeat to victory under Marshal Henri Philippe Petain and Marshal Foch's lieutenant, General Maxime Weygand, in the past and could do so again.

There was an indirect word directed toward America and all the peoples far removed from the struggle. They were beginning to understand and to see that their future also was involved, M. Reynaud de-

Continued on Page Six

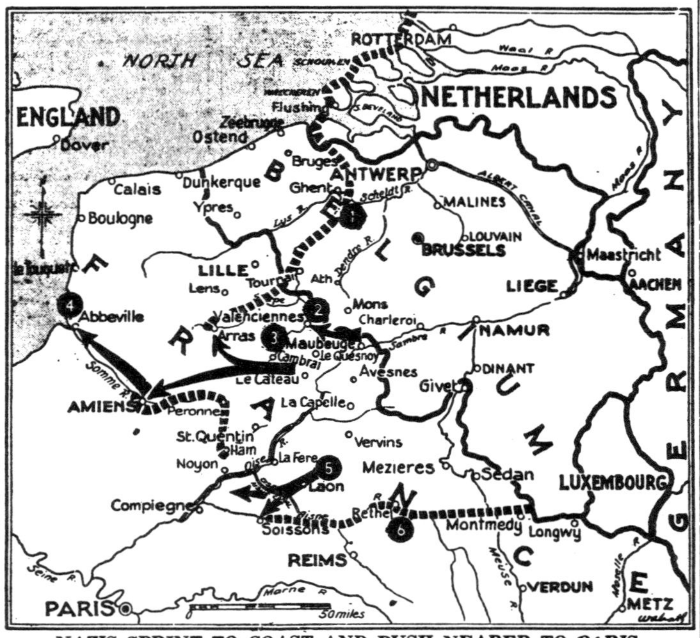

NAZIS SPRINT TO COAST AND PUSH NEARER TO PARIS

Allied forces have been put in peril by a German spearhead driven between French and Belgian troops at Valenciennes (2) and by the westward push of the German right wing in Belgium, where the Belgians were engaged east of Ghent (1). Even more serious, however, was the advance to Abbeville (4) near the shore of the English Channel. As fighting raged north of Cambrai (3) motorized units swept south of that town and then, while some of them moved northwest to Arras, the rest raced along the Somme valley, took Amiens and continued on to the coast. Nor was the threat to Paris lessened. At Amiens the Nazis claimed to have a bridgehead across the Somme, while to the east the German advance beyond Laon (5) was semi-officially declared to have resulted in the capture of Soissons, within sixty miles of Paris, and threats to both Noyon and Compiegne. At Rethel (6), however, the French said they were clinging to the south bank of the Aisne. The approximate limit of the German advance is shown by the broken line, which is based on dispatches received from both Berlin and Paris.

'Chutists and Cyclists Set Fires Behind Allied Lines

By The United Press.

PARIS, May 21—Germany unleashed the full fury of "total war" on Northern France today, dropping parachutists with torches to set fire to wide areas around Arras, Amiens and other cities in the Nazi drive to the English Channel.

Hundreds of German planes rained incendiary bombs on every city, village and community in the Picardy and Flanders lowlands, military dispatches said.

At the same time giant air transports unloaded aerial incendiaries who were instructed to race through the countryside and set fire to or dynamite factories, railway stations, munitions and fuel dumps and other such objectives in scores of cities between Cambrai and the sea.

In the triangle between the Belgian frontier, the Channel and Amiens, not one railway station stood intact tonight, military spokesmen said.

Property losses were tremendous. Spokesmen said they could be figured in tens of billions of francs along a corridor of destruction thirty-five miles wide in which not a building stood undamaged and

Continued on Page Two

Women, Children Begin Evacuation of Gibraltar

Wireless to THE NEW YORK TIMES.

GIBRALTAR, May 21—Women and children are being evacuated from Gibraltar. The first batches left today for French Morocco. Others will follow tomorrow and subsequent days.

The action follows an official announcement today that the Governor of Gibraltar, Lieut. Gen. Sir Clive Liddell, had received instructions from the War Cabinet that owing to the international situation the evacuation of women and children from Gibraltar would be compulsory immediately.

AACHEN IS BOMBED HEAVILY BY ALLIES

Troop Concentrations There—German Bombs Dropped in Southeast England

By The United Press.

AACHEN, Germany, Wednesday, May 22—Waves of Allied bombing planes early today attacked this German city along the German Westwall fortifications, bombing and battling Nazi Messerschmitt fighters.

The first air raid alarm was sounded at 12:45 A. M., when the first enemy bombers appeared over the city and began dropping bombs. The attack was met by anti-aircraft fire for fifteen minutes, and Messerschmitt fighters went into the sky to battle the raiders. From then on the Allied planes came in waves and were still sweeping upon the city at 1:05 A. M.

[Aachen, also known as Aix-la-Chapelle, lies at the point of the German, Netherland and Belgian borders and was the "jumping off" place for the German in-

Continued on Page Four

Dispatches from Europe and the Far East are subject to censorship at the source.

Nazis Report Capture of Giraud; Say General Walked Into a Trap

Wireless to THE NEW YORK TIMES.

BERLIN, May 21—The Germans told an astounding story today of how General Henri Giraud, commander of the French Ninth Army, was captured. In a lightning advance in the Cambrai sector, Nazi forces occupied the château headquarters of the French Ninth Army. Here they learned that the commanding general had left, having been relieved by order of the new Commander in Chief, General Maxime Weygand, by General Giraud, who had been head of the Seventh Army.

According to accounts here, the Germans set their trap by merely remaining and taking General Giraud and his staff into custody as they arrived to take charge, ignorant of the situation. The story of the capture leaked out in Berlin yesterday, but the High Command did not want it spread, hoping that dispatch riders and others attached to the Ninth Army headquarters, uninformed of the change, would fall into the net.

BERLIN, May 21 (UP)—General Henri Honore Giraud, commander of the French Ninth Army, which had struggled to stem the German tide for eleven days, was said to have been taken prisoner in a "half-tragic, half-comic manner" when he walked into his headquarters and found German officers there.

General Giraud, 61 years old and one of France's most famous strategists, had been placed in command of the main Allied defense along the German "bulge" front in Northern France and Southern Belgium only on Saturday, it was said by German officials.

As a captain in the World War, he was captured by the Germans two weeks after the outbreak of the conflict and finally escaped through Belgium and the Netherlands to

Continued on Page Five

BRITISH FIGHT HARD TO AVOID DISASTER

Their Whole Force in Belgium Is Trapped in Untenable Position, Allies Admit

By The United Press.

LONDON, May 21—The lightning German thrust to the English Channel has separated the main French and British armies and trapped the entire British expeditionary force in an untenable position, the Allied High Command recognized tonight.

The writer left one of the Channel ports today when the German drive was reaching its peak. It was directly menaced by advancing German mechanized units.

The British have their choice of attempting evacuation under a rain of German bombs over the entire Channel area or facing the enemy in a last-ditch effort to hold the only avenue of escape left to them—the Channel ports of Calais, Boulogne, Ostend and Blankenberge.

In either event, the B. E. F. is fighting desperately to escape annihilation.

[In Berlin it was said that the British had received orders to embark for England and that "our planes are bombing embarkation centers."]

Le Touquet Threatened

The Germans are completing encircling tactics in their drive on the coast between Abbeville and Le Touquet, which they are due to reach at any hour.

[Le Touquet is about twenty miles north of Abbeville, from which a double-trunk railroad line runs to the French resort.]

German mechanized divisions were rumbling along roads leading to the principal ports. Allied forces were rushing to oppose them, but the Nazis were flushed with victory and no obstacle seemed capable of checking them.

The roads were crowded with refugees from Northern France, Belgium and the Netherlands. They blocked the roads and made Allied military manoeuvres more difficult.

The B. E. F. at present is awaiting the order of the Commander in Chief to make a terrific last stand in which it would throw all it possesses of gun power, tanks, infantry divisions and aircraft.

The French, on the other (southwestern) flank of the German columns, have been assembling for

Continued on Page Four

500,000 'ISOLATED'

Swift Thrust to Coast Cuts Off Huge Force, Berlin Claims

SOISSONS 'TAKEN,' TOO

Invaders Stab at Paris as Threat to Britain Progresses

By GEORGE AXELSSON

Wireless to THE NEW YORK TIMES.

BERLIN, May 21—In a crowning series of staggering blows dealt to the Allies in the last few days, the Germans claim tonight to have reached Abbeville on the Picardy coast, fifteen miles from Le Treport on the English Channel. Thus they have now virtually achieved their aim to isolate the combined Allied armies in the western corner of Belgium and the northwestern tip of France. Unless they can fight their way out, this should seal the fate of the Belgian Army and numerous divisions of the French, altogether totaling perhaps between 500,000 and 1,000,000 men, including whatever British forces are left in this area.

[The German thrust toward Paris has reached the region of Reims, it was said in official German circles early today, according to an Associated Press dispatch from Berlin.]

In an apparently masterful enveloping movement rapidly closing in, the Germans claim to have definitely broken up the entire French Ninth Army, taking prisoner its commander, General Henri Giraud, with his complete staff. The mission of the Ninth Army was to insure liaison between the strong Allied units in Belgium and the Maginot Line south of Sedan.

En route to Abbeville, the Germans say, they occupied Amiens and Arras. The River Somme up to the estuary that the Germans tried in vain to reach in their "risk it all" drive in March, 1918, should thus be in their hands after brisk fighting that apparently lasted fewer hours than it did months during the World War.

Soissons Reported Taken

At the same time they are pushing toward Paris, and it is semi-officially said here tonight that they have taken the city of Soissons, a bare sixty miles by air from the French capital. Noyon and Compiègne, in this same area, appear to be seriously endangered and likely to be occupied at one moment or another.

With perhaps 1,000,000 Allied troops hopelessly cut off and squeezed by powerful German armies between the mouths of the Rivers Scheldt and Somme, the question arises here in the minds of neutral military observers: How could the Allied Army leaders have permitted a situation threatening such a major disaster?

One explanation is that it is perhaps the outcome of a desperate French attempt at a counter-offensive aimed at the flank of the German right wing without having sufficiently insured the rear lines of communication. It is suggested that German tanks of the mastodon type may have charged the French laterally, cutting off their supply lines and forcing the bulk of the attackers clear through the fronts into the jaws of German tongs as flocks of Nazi dive-bombers efficiently supported the deadly ground work of the tank divisions.

French Effort Criticized

In this connection, it is asked here: What has happened to the French artillery? It is a matter of record that the French have the most efficient artillery, from light field pieces including the famous 75's up to railway and other heavy long-range guns.

None of these, any more than French supertanks reputedly weighing in the neighborhood of fifty tons, have figured in reports of the fighting available here. The superiority of the German tank and of the German plane seems definitely established, in the eyes of observers here.

With the Channel ports from Ostend to Boulogne strongly compromised, a powerful German bid for final victory seemingly enters a decisive stage. As seen from here, the Allied position is not altogether

Continued on Page Two

"All the News That's Fit to Print."

NEWS INDEX, PAGE 37, THIS SECTION

The New York Times.

Copyright, 1940, by The New York Times Company.

LATE CITY EDITION
Mostly cloudy today and tomorrow; occasional light showers with little change in temperature.
Temperatures Yesterday—Max., 61; Min., 53

Section 1

VOL. LXXXIX..No. 30,073. Entered as Second-Class Matter, Postoffice, New York, N. Y. NEW YORK, SUNDAY, MAY 26, 1940. Including Rotogravure Picture, Magazine and Book Review. TEN CENTS | TWELVE CENTS Beyond 200 Miles, Except West of Pa.—South of Md.—North of Mass.

GERMANS PUSH DRIVE TO TRAP ALLIES IN NORTH; TAKE GHENT, VIMY; PRESS ON CALAIS, BOULOGNE; FRENCH STILL FIGHT IN GAP; 15 GENERALS OUT

PRESIDENT TO FORM A DEFENSE BOARD OF ALL SEGMENTS

Experts From Industry, Labor, Consumers, Etc., Will Work With Federal Officials

TO COORDINATE PROGRAM

Roosevelt Seeks 'to Avoid Upsetting American Life,' to Prevent 'Highs and Lows'

By FRANK L. KLUCKHOHN
Special to THE NEW YORK TIMES.

WASHINGTON, May 25—President Roosevelt will form a special emergency body of government officials and private individuals representing the various segments of national life to coordinate the national defense program, the White House announced today.

It is the President's present intention to call experts in transportation, communication, industrial, production, finance, labor and consumers "so that all groups that go to make up the pattern of American life will be represented," Stephen Early, secretary to the President, said.

The President has decided to keep "flexible" the plan for coordinating preparedness efforts so that it can be modified in the light of changing conditions. He has not yet decided upon details, offices, or names, Mr. Early said. He added that people outside as well as inside the government were making suggestions regarding the coordination body and its personnel. The projected organization was referred to by the President's secretary as a "national defense emergency coordination group."

Would Avoid "Highs and Lows"

It was made clear that the President did not regard the White House announcement today as marking a change of defense plans to meet criticism of his refusal to appoint a war industries board to direct industrial mobilization. On the contrary, Mr. Early said the outside experts invited to Washington "will not supersede any one in the government but will work with them."

"The President is very anxious to avoid any upsetting of American life and, as far as possible, to prevent the highs and lows that prevailed during the World War," Mr. Early stated.

"In other words, he wants to keep prices from soaring, to give the producers a reasonable profit and to prevent the consumers from having to pay unreasonably high prices—that applies to foodstuffs, housing problems and the necessities of life.

"Through these gentlemen whom the President expects to invite to come in and take their part with the government will come about the coordination of government and American life both as a whole and as it divides itself through the representatives whom he will select.

"The President is working personally on the plan and various persons are providing memoranda for him. The plan itself has to be very carefully coordinated. People outside the government are giving the President advice and he is receiving many suggestions through telegrams and the mails."

President Works on Address

Mr. Roosevelt canceled all engagements today and isolated himself in the oval White House study to work on his "fireside chat" on national defense to be delivered to the nation over major broadcasting networks at 10:30 P. M. Eastern daylight-saving time tomorrow.

Progress was reported on various fronts in speeding the national defense program and in strengthening the power of the "sixth column" being formed to block "fifth-column" activities in this country. Principal developments were as follows:

1. A Senate judiciary subcommittee unanimously approved a bill to require the fingerprinting and registration of aliens in the United States and to penalize subversive activities in the Army, Navy and Coast Guard.

2. A group of twenty-five government officials, Army officers and prominent citizens headed by Colonel Frank Knox of Chicago con-

Continued on Page Three

The International Situation

On the Battle Fronts

The Battle of Flanders, as seen by the Germans, moved yesterday into a new phase. Berlin contended that the bottling up of Allied elements north of the German spearhead to the Channel had been completely accomplished; the next objective was to cut the trapped forces into small detachments and to dispose of them piecemeal. In two sectors this process of division already was under way. [Page 1.]

One German thrust was aimed northward from Vimy Ridge, a proving ground of Canadian valor in the last war. Berlin claimed that this push had carried the attackers along the heights to Lillers and St. Omer and had reached the Channel at Gravelines, midway between Dunkerque and Calais. A second attack, Berlin reported, was launched to the north on both sides of Douai, the objective being to join forces with a third thrust to the west from the region of Tournai. As these interior columns sought to hack the Allied-held territory into small segments, other German forces pushing down from the northeast claimed Ghent and Courtrai. If verified, these victories would mean that the line of the Lys River had been turned; the Germans predicted that the defenders would soon fall back to the Yser Canal. Units of the Channel spearhead forces, the Germans said, have taken Boulogne and encircled Calais. [Included in foregoing.]

The French, denying the loss of Boulogne and Calais, concentrated their attention on the narrow corridor north of the Somme through which the Germans still supplied and reinforced their units near the Channel. Allied counter-attacks in this region, Paris reported, were frequent and intense, but the breach was still unclosed. That breach—which may well measure the infinity between victory and defeat for the Allies in the Battle of Flanders—was the object of pressure from the north by the British, from the south by the French. [Page 1.]

General Weygand sacked fifteen French generals, offering no explanation. Speculation about this greatest mid-battle shake-up in French history centered on the theory that the purpose was to get rid of the followers of General Gamelin who had accepted his concept of defense warfare, and to put the army under men saturated in the Foch principle of attack. [Page 1.]

While British fliers reported continued destructive bombing, England got a very small foretaste of Blitzkrieg. German bombers visited a 200-mile strip of the east coast from the North Riding of Yorkshire to East Anglia. Eleven civilians were injured. British spokesmen said that in the north the Germans aimed at steel mills, in the south at civilian morale. [Page 1.]

Repercussions Elsewhere

Britain pressed ahead with her counter-offensive against fifth columnists. Many arrests were made; many more were scheduled, some of them to affect persons in high places. One suspect already arrested was identified as an American citizen connected with the United States Embassy; about this development Secretary of State Hull would make no comment. London heard reports, based on papers taken from an arrested officer of the outlawed Irish Republican Army, that an uprising in Ireland, possibly with German help, was scheduled for this week-end. [Page 1.]

Diplomats accredited to the Holy See were sounded out by the Papal Secretary of State on whether, in the event of war between their home governments and Italy, they would ask for sanctuary at the Vatican. This move was taken as an index of the Vatican's belief that Italy would soon intervene. [Page 1.]

The White House announced that President Roosevelt would form a defense emergency coordination group to handle all problems arising from this country's preparedness program. Officials now in the government and outside experts will make up the board. They will represent transportation, communications, industrial production, finance, labor and similar sectors of the national life. [Page 1.]

CONTROL OF ALIENS NEARS SENATE VOTE

Subcommittee Approves Their Registration or Deportation Within Four Months

Special to THE NEW YORK TIMES.

WASHINGTON, May 25—A subcommittee of the Senate Judiciary Committee recommended this action today:

That all aliens in the United States be required to register at postoffices and be fingerprinted within four months, with automatic deportation as the penalty for failure so to register. The number of aliens is estimated at 4,000,000.

The compulsory deportation of aliens who have knowingly encouraged other aliens to enter the United States illegally, or who have been convicted of carrying or possessing arms, and certain other crimes and misdemeanors, or who advocate the overthrow of the United States Government by violence. The term "alien" would attach to every foreigner who has not actually completed his naturalization.

That the publication or distribution of books, pamphlets or other literature advising the nation's armed forces to disobey their superiors or advocating the violent overthrow of government be made unlawful. The penalty would be ten years in prison, or $10,000 fine or both.

That all aliens seeking entry into the United States be fingerprinted.

The measure would also make it illegal for any person to advocate "by word of mouth or in writing, or by transmission by radio, to knowingly or willfully advocate, abet, advise or teach the duty, necessity, desirability or propriety of overthrowing or destroying the Gov-

Continued on Page Six

VATICAN PREPARES TO SHELTER ENVOYS

Offer Interpreted as a Sign Italy Is Ready to Enter War—Propaganda Unabated

By CAMILLE M. CIANFARRA
By Telephone to THE NEW YORK TIMES.

ROME, May 25—As the officially promoted campaign for Italian intervention in the European conflict reached a new high today, the Vatican made clear that it regarded Italy's entrance into the war as probable. Luigi Cardinal Maglione, Papal Secretary of State, invited all diplomats accredited to the Holy See whose countries "may find themselves at war with Italy to give immediate answer as to whether they intend to return home or take up residence in the Vatican."

"In the latter case," Cardinal Maglione advised, according to a semi-official announcement, "the Holy See will house only the head of the mission and a secretary."

Diplomatic circles pointed out that an invitation of this kind implied the Pope's conviction that Italy was on the verge of taking the plunge or, at best, that the situation was so grave as to induce him to take all precautions for such eventuality.

The Vatican's step added to the general pessimism caused in foreign circles by other indications that the campaign for intervention continued unabated. All newspapers today printed a manifesto addressed to the "Corsican irredentists." Responsible spokesmen and publications bluntly stated that the Italians were awaiting only Premier Mussolini's command to "break their chains" and achieve "real independence."

The manifesto, signed by a Corsican political exile, proclaims to

Continued on Page Thirty-two

PARIS CLAIMS TOLL

German Losses Heavy as Main Allied Forces Hold, French Say

RESERVES GATHERING

Weygand Seen Bringing Armies Together for Counter-Attack

By G. H. ARCHAMBAULT
Wireless to THE NEW YORK TIMES.

PARIS, May 25—The breach is still unfilled that separates the Belgian and British Armies in the north from the main French body in the south. And through that breach the Germans still send armored columns—and to a lesser degree motorized infantry units—in an endeavor to cut the northern armies both from the French and from the sea.

Consequently the northern armies are now fighting facing east, south and west. Such is the situation tonight on the plains of Flanders.

In any war, initial mistakes take time to retrieve: in a war waged at such a speed as this one, the time factor has added importance. Yet undue haste on the part of the Allies might jeopardize all.

Without presuming to penetrate General Maxime Weygand's intentions, the Allied commander's preliminary task was obvious. First of all, he must regroup his forces and then distribute them for the purposes of the manoeuvre that he intends to attempt.

Must Concentrate Reserves

Above all, he must concentrate his reserves in the zones of his choice, to be brought into play once he has decided on wresting the initiative from his enemy. Obviously, pending that moment, the Germans' interest is never to relax their pressure.

At this stage, therefore, much depends on the resistance of the Allied troops engaged. The communiqué issued this evening from French General Headquarters says in this connection:

"Our troops are fighting with an energy and a determination demonstrated by the efforts exerted by the enemy, and in all encounters they are inflicting heavy losses on the Germans."

Reports reach here that the Belgians are holding their ground admirably and fighting with the greatest gallantry at the extreme north of the front between the Scheldt and the sea.

After the Allied withdrawal in that zone—described here as relatively small—the Germans attacked with violence as soon as contact was re-established. At several points today, especially in the region of Courtrai, they have been repeatedly counter-attacked.

Equally strong is the pressure on the British lines slightly to the south, while the main battle around Cambrai, Arras and Valenciennes has never ceased to rage.

The French communiqué says that "in the north the situation has undergone no important change." It is added in authorized quarters

Continued on Page Twenty-nine

GAP IN ALLIED LINES STILL UNCLOSED AND NAZIS PUSH ON

The situation at Boulogne (1) was still uncertain, with the Germans claiming to have taken the Channel port and the French admitting the possibility there was fighting there. The French asserted they held Calais, however, although the Germans said they had thrust from Vimy Ridge (2), which they had captured, through Lillers and St. Omer to Gravelines on the coast. This slant, taken together with a further westward advance in Belgium, where Courtrai (4) and Ghent, to the north, were reported captured, and with a German attack between Roubaix and Valenciennes (5), made the position of the trapped Allied armies more precarious. But the British continued to hammer southward around Bapaume (3), while the French pounded northward between Amiens and Ham (6) in an effort to join forces. South of Sedan (7) the French admitted the Germans had made a gain, but said the lost ground had been recovered. The approximate battle-fronts are shown by the heavy broken lines on the map.

BRITISH AND IRISH ON ALERT FOR COUP

U.S. Embassy Employe Among Many Seized — De Valera Warns Countrymen of Peril

By The United Press.

LONDON, May 25—Documents seized from an arrested officer of the outlawed Irish Republican Army tonight gave rise to reports that this week-end had been set as the zero hour for an uprising in Ireland, possibly with German aid, as a preliminary to a blow at England.

Every precaution was being taken both here and in Ireland against any week-end move by fifth columnists.

A vast round-up was going forward in which it was estimated that hundreds will be arrested. Already prominent persons have been taken into custody, as well as a person connected with the United States Embassy here. It was learned that this person is an American citizen.

Guards were being increased at all public buildings, power plants and bridges. Barbed wire barricades were being erected along highways and barricades already in place were being strengthened.

The danger of a German stroke in Ireland was suddenly presented to the public in vivid terms. Docu-

Continued on Page Thirty

French Shake Up Command As a 'Penalizing' Measure

Unprecedented Move During Battle Is Taken by Weygand—Aggressive Generalship Is Believed to Be the Aim

Wireless to THE NEW YORK TIMES.

PARIS, May 25—Changes in the French High Command were announced here tonight in the following official statement:

"In consequence of the military operations in progress, which have already resulted in the nomination of General Weygand as Commander in Chief on the whole of the theatres of operations, important changes have been made in the High Command.

"As of today fifteen general officers have been relieved of their commands. They include army and corps commanders, several divisional commanders and several heads of services in large units."

"Penalties" Announcement

PARIS, May 25 (AP)—General Maxime Weygand tonight summarily dismissed fifteen generals who figured in the French rout from the Meuse front and injected fresh blood into his Allied High Command for the decisive phase of the battle for the English Channel.

A War Ministry communiqué, published under the heading of "Penalties," said the fifteen commanders of full armies, corps, divisions and other army services had been removed from their posts. Their names were not announced.

Their commands already have been taken over by new men chosen by General Weygand in his flying trips to the front to lead the campaign against the German corridor to the sea.

Seven infantry colonels were promoted to be major generals to fill the places of those ousted. Promoted are Henri Martin, Jean Besse, André Durand, Charles Mast, Charles de Gaulle, Gustave Mesny and Louis Buisson.

After the announcement of the changes Premier Paul Reynaud conferred with César Campinchi, Navy Minister; Laurent Eynac, Air Minister; Raoul Dautry, Minister of Armament, and Louis Frossard, Minister of Information.

Move Causes Sensation

PARIS, May 25 (UP)—The announcement today of the ousting of fifteen French generals gave notice of the greatest shake-up the French

Continued on Page Twenty-nine

BOMBERS HAMMER AT NAZIS' COLUMNS

R.A.F. Fliers on Offensive Near Boulogne—11 Civilians Hurt in Air Attack on Britain

By HAROLD DENNY
Special Cable to THE NEW YORK TIMES.

LONDON, Sunday, May 26—British bombers directed heavy attacks from morning to dusk yesterday against German motorized columns on the French coast roads near Boulogne, the Air Ministry reported. The bomber attacks began early Friday, when nine Blenheims dropped repeated salvos of heavy and light bombs on forty German motor vehicles standing in a field near a crossroads just off a main road. German anti-aircraft fire from many batteries struck British planes, but brought none down.

Other German motorized columns were attacked in the same way repeatedly throughout the day in "almost continuous offensive," the Air Ministry said.

Many hits were reported on German tanks and other vehicles on the road, on Nazi anti-aircraft batteries and other objectives. All the British aircraft in these attacks returned, according to the official reports, although bearing some battle scars, and only one airman was slightly wounded.

New Air Raid Warning in Kent

Following German air raids early yesterday over the east coast of Britain from the North Riding of Yorkshire southward to East Anglia, in which eleven civilians were injured, an air raid warning was sounded in East Kent, southeast of London, early today.

[British fighter planes and anti-aircraft guns met a German raid on the East Kent coast near Dover early today, news service dispatches indicated. One Nazi

Continued on Page Thirty-one

Dispatches from Europe and the Far East are subject to censorship at the source.

Major Sports Yesterday

HORSE RACING

Third Degree, owned by Mrs. Payne Whitney and ridden by Eddie Arcaro, easily won the forty-seventh running of the Metropolitan Handicap at Belmont Park as Eight Thirty, the odds-on favorite, finished fourth. Second to the line, four lengths behind the winner, was Can't Wait. Third place went to War Dog.

BASEBALL

Rain and wet grounds forced curtailment of the major league program in the East, the Giants, Dodgers and Yankees being held idle. The Dodgers, nevertheless, went into undisputed possession of first place in the National League when the Reds, who had been tied with them for the lead, were beaten in the second game of a double-header. The Reds won the opener, 7—2, but then lost to the Cardinals, 5—1.

ROWING

Cornell snapped Harvard's long string of victories by taking the varsity race in the regatta on Cayuga Lake. Harvard lost by a length and a half, with Syracuse third.

GOLF

Craig Wood, Winged Foot pro, added a 66 to his first-round 64 at the Forest Hill Field Club, Bloomfield, N. J., for a total of 130 and a five-stroke lead at the half-way mark in the metropolitan open. Ben Hogan of the Century Club is in second place.

(Complete Details of These and Other Sports Events in Section 5.)

RING IS TIGHTENED

Nazis Move West in Belgium, Northwest From Vimy Ridge

BOULOGNE CLAIMED

Neutral Zone to Spare Trapped Civilians Is Weighed in Berlin

By GEORGE AXELSSON
Wireless to THE NEW YORK TIMES.

BERLIN, May 25—The battle in which the Germans are trying to wipe out some 1,000,000 Allied troops pocketed between Abbeville and Ghent increased further in fury today as fresh German infantry units reached the fronts and were thrown into the fray. The cities of Ghent, Courtrai and Boulogne now are claimed to be in German hands and it was semi-officially intimated tonight that more cities in the interlying area had been taken during the day, although for military reasons their names could not be announced.

Calais is still held by the Allies, but the Germans say they have completely surrounded it and made it useless to the Allies as a military base.

Inside the sack rapidly being compressed by the Germans are understood to be shut in the entire Belgian Army, a large part of the British Expeditionary Force and the First and Seventh as well as remnants of the Ninth French Armies, in all upward of 1,000,000 men.

Civilian Haven Weighed

It was reported in Berlin tonight that German military authorities, moved by humanitarian reasons, contemplated an appeal to the Allies within the sack to herd some 5,000,000 civilians similarly trapped thereabout into a separate sector from which the military operations could be kept by mutual agreement.

The situation for these civilians, among whom are 2,000,000 refugees from occupied Belgian provinces, hourly is becoming more desperate. With every avenue of escape closed by the German Army, they are in the midst of the battle zone, fully exposed to all the horrors of modern warfare with its artillery and air bombardments and tank fire. Hunger is worsening the predicament, especially of those practically besieged populations of Lille, Douai, Tourcoing, Roubaix and other towns in this district.

Since the Germans first ringed this area at the beginning of the week, these cities could obtain no new provisions, road transport having become next to impossible through the action of bombers, or by the fact that the highways were primarily needed for troop transport or manoeuvring. Herding them into a "neutral zone" will not solve the food problem, but at least it would save them from death or mutilation.

The city of Ghent, which finally fell after having been doggedly defended by the Allies, reportedly was taken without a fight. When the Germans flanked it by crossing the Lys River north and south, the city became undefendable.

Tanks Also Flank Douai

Douai seems similarly flanked by German tank divisions dashing past it on both sides in the direction of the Channel ports. A series of ridges from Vimy past Lillers and St. Omer to Gravelines, halfway between Calais and Dunkerque, was taken by the Germans, according to a High Command communiqué.

Fighting still rages furiously around Arras, Cambrai and Valenciennes all the way down to Amiens in such a multitude of engagements and encounters within encounters that observers find it difficult to understand how the combatants themselves know who is who. The Germans, of course, have driven or are trying to drive a number of smaller wedges to separate Allied detachments within the big sack and thus facilitate gaining their main objective—crushing all resistance therein.

The Germans say they are now attacking French frontier fortifications between Roubaix and Valenciennes, but the outcome of this

Continued on Page Thirty-one

"All the News That's Fit to Print."

The New York Times.

LATE CITY EDITION
Mostly cloudy with occasional showers and slightly warmer today and tomorrow.
Temperatures Yesterday—Max., 69; Min., 51

VOL. LXXXIX..No. 30,074. Entered as Second-Class Matter, Postoffice, New York, N. Y. NEW YORK, MONDAY, MAY 27, 1940. THREE CENTS NEW YORK CITY and Vicinity | FOUR CENTS Elsewhere Except in 7th and 8th Postal Zones.

ALLIES REPULSE SAVAGE ATTACKS, LINES HOLD; ADMIT LOSS OF BOULOGNE; NAZIS CLAIM CALAIS; DEFENSE OF BRITAIN ENTRUSTED TO IRONSIDE

PRESIDENT ASSURES NATION OF SAFETY; DECRIES PANIC TALK

He Declares All Needed Will Be Done to Build and Keep Adequate Defenses

WARNS ON FIFTH COLUMN

Replying to Critics, He Says Armed Forces Are at Peak for Peacetime Service

Text of President Roosevelt's address is printed on Page 12.

Special to THE NEW YORK TIMES.

WASHINGTON, May 26—President Roosevelt assured the nation tonight that whatever may be needed will be done to secure the armed defenses of the United States at this time, when the world "is threatened by forces of destruction." We shall build our defenses, he said, to whatever heights the future may require.

"We shall rebuild them swiftly, as the methods of warfare swiftly change," he added.

The President addressed the nation over a combined network of the National Broadcasting Company, the Columbia Broadcasting System and the Mutual Broadcasting System. He spoke from the diplomatic cloak room in the basement of the White House.

The President's statements on building our defenses came toward the end of an address in which he counseled the people against panic, defended the armament program of the last few years, confirmed the White House announcement of yesterday that leading industrialists were to be called to help plan and coordinate the defense program, reiterated his determination to see that the social reforms of the last few years are not sacrificed, and that no "war millionaires" are created in the rush to rearm, and warned the people against a new technique for "weakening a nation at its very roots."

Warns on "Foreign Agents"

The Trojan horse, or fifth column device, which may be called on in an attempt to harm America, is simple, the President said. First, he went on, discord is sown, a group, sectional, racial or political in character, is encouraged to exploit prejudices through false slogans and emotional appeals. The aim of those who deliberately incite various groups, he said, is "to create confusion of counsel, public indecision, political paralysis and eventually a state of panic."

"Sound national policies come to be viewed with a new and unreasoning skepticism, not through wholesome political debates of honest and free men, but through the clever schemes of foreign agents," the President added.

"As a result of these new techniques, armament programs may be dangerously delayed. Singleness of national purpose may be undermined. Men can lose confidence in each other, and therefore confidence in the efficacy of their united action. Faith and courage can yield to doubt and fear. The unity of the State can be so sapped that its strength is destroyed."

He Appeals For Red Cross

The President began with an appeal for support of the Red Cross in its drive for funds for relief of civilians in war-stricken Europe. He pictured the scene abroad, of once peaceful roads of Belgium and France along which millions of people were "running from their homes to escape bombs and shells and fire and machine-gunning, without shelter and almost wholly without food."

"They stumble on, knowing not where the end of the road will be," the President said. "I remind you of these people because each one of you that is listening to me tonight has a way of helping them. The American Red Cross, that represents each of us, is rushing food, clothing and medical supplies to these destitute civilian millions. Please, I beg you, give to your nearest Red Cross chapter, give as generously as you can. I ask this in the name of our common humanity."

The President recalled that the happenings of the last two weeks

Continued on Page Twelve

The International Situation

On the Battle Fronts

The French lost Boulogne, important Channel port, yesterday, but claimed elsewhere to be holding their own, and even to be inching into the Peronne-Bapaume gap, which is the lifeline of the German forces in the coastal area north of the Somme. Paris dispatches spoke repeatedly of the heavy price in dead and wounded the Germans were paying to keep the offensive going, but it was admitted that the German pressure was not lessening. [Page 1.]

Paris reported four major German drives: one in the north near Courtrai, which was said to have failed to break Belgian positions on the Lys; twin thrusts south of Courtrai, in which there was much hand-to-hand fighting; and a fourth attack near Valenciennes, in which the French claimed to have driven back repeated German assaults. In still another part of the front—along the eastern side of the big German bulge into France—French guns "mowed down in their tracks" whole platoons of German infantry which, Paris said, were caught pouring through to reinforce German forces to the west. [Included in foregoing.]

The Germans presented a different picture of the front. They claimed the capture of Calais (denied by the French) and emphasized the possibility of a quick offensive against England from what they called their seventy-five-mile hold on the Channel. They also reported progress in their manoeuvres designed to cut into isolated units the Allied forces encircled near the Belgium border. One German force drove northward from Vimy Ridge, another southward from Courtrai. According to the Germans, these two columns were within nineteen miles of each other. If they got together, they would cut off all the Allied troops within the area bounded by Arras, Cambrai, Valenciennes, Courtrai, Roubaix and Lille. In trying to carry out this high plan the Germans admitted they were encountering desperate resistance. [Page 1.]

London reported a four-hour air battle over the French coast between Dunkerque and Calais, as well as the bombing of German columns near Boulogne and in the Lys sector. Berlin claimed that bombs dropped on Southeastern England Friday night had landed "with good effect" on numerous airports; the British had previously reported those raids, but said they accomplished virtually nothing. [Page 1.]

Repercussions Elsewhere

The British replaced General Sir Edmund Ironside, Chief of the Imperial Staff, with Lieut. Gen. Sir John Greer Dill, an exponent of tank and bomber warfare. Sir Edmund becomes Commander in Chief of the Home Forces, responsible for taking all measures against invasion. British spokesmen said the change reflected concern about the home front rather than about the conduct of the British Armies in the field. [Page 1.]

Premier Reynaud conferred in London with Prime Minister Churchill, crossing the Channel and returning by airplane. The French Government announced the dismissal of police officers in several cities, including the chiefs in Lille and Valenciennes in the Flanders battlefield area. Charges were not made public. [Page 3.]

Italy, still on the fence, decreed that after June 1 no more gasoline be burned up in civilian automobiles, motorcycles or boats, except by special permit. Premier Mussolini conferred with his high army officers and with munitions manufacturers; he ordered a program of artillery construction. The word heard on every side in Rome was that Italy would take the plunge between June 10 and 20, when, it was said, the Germans will have under way their major offensives against England and Paris. [Page 1.]

In a radio address to the nation President Roosevelt voiced confidence that the United States would not have to abandon its democratic way of life to match the strength of the aggressors. He reported on the state of the national defense, asserting that the Navy was "stronger today than it was during the World War"; he warned against sectional, racial or political prejudices, which might be exploited by fifth columnists and traitors; he said business men were being called to Washington to insure "maximum speed and efficiency" in the operation of defense industries, and he ruled out any "breakdown or cancellation of any of the great social gains" of recent years on the ground that underlying all defense efforts were "the spirit and morale of a free people." [Page 1.]

FIRST LADY'S PLEA IGNORED BY YOUTH

Attack on Defense Program Allowed to Stand After Her Warning Lives Are at Stake

Mrs. Franklin D. Roosevelt, who many times has defended the American Youth Congress against attack, told its newly organized affiliate, the New York Youth Congress, at Mecca Temple last night, that it was making a tragic mistake in opposing present American defense measures. The advice of the youth group, if followed, might needlessly sacrifice many American lives, she declared.

"You don't want to go to war," she told the 1,100 delegates and visitors in the closing session of the three-day congress. "I don't want to go to war. But war may come to us."

And when and if it comes, she said, courage would not be enough, mere men would not be enough, as had been proved in Europe. Defense of this country would take the most modern machines of war and that is what the defense appropriations now sought are intended to provide, she said. In adopting resolutions on such subjects, she declared, youth was talking about something it could not hope to understand even if it studied the question every day for years as Army and Navy experts had studied it.

The President's wife said she was in favor of a defense program that would include, in addition to armaments, more and better housing, ex-

Continued on Page Eleven

ITALY'S WAR ENTRY AFTER JUNE 10 SEEN

Growing Signs Held to Point to a Step Then—Mussolini Confers on Readiness

By HERBERT L. MATTHEWS

By Telephone to THE NEW YORK TIMES.

ROME, May 26—The signs of approaching intervention by Italy on the side of Germany were stronger than ever today. The circulation of all vehicles using gasoline, including private automobiles, motor cycles and motor boats, is to cease on June 1 except for those with special permits. Premier Mussolini held two highly significant conferences at the Palazzo Venezia.

The first was with four generals—Camillo Grossi, Alfredo Guzzoni, Bergia and Angelo Rossi—as well as Lieut. Col. Renato Piacentini of the War Ministry's mobilization department. The second was with the heads of the Odero, Terni and Ansaldo armament works, to whom the Premier "laid down a program of artillery construction."

Marshal Rodolfo Graziani, Chief of Staff of the Italian Army, and General Ubaldo Soddu, Under-Secretary of War, were present at both conferences.

Ansaldo Still Belligerent

Giovanni Ansaldo's weekly broadcast to the armed forces was another sign of the times, for he said the Italians would "break through the circle of steel that encloses them in the Mediterranean" just as the Germans broke through the Maginot Line. Virginio Gayda, in his

Continued on Page Four

COMMAND SHIFTED

Sir John Dill Becomes Chief of All British Fighting Forces

NOTED FOR ATTACK

Belgian Cabinet Heads and Reynaud Confer With Halifax

By RAYMOND DANIELL

Special Cable to THE NEW YORK TIMES.

LONDON, May 26 — Important changes were announced tonight by the British Army High Command. They reflected the growing concern of the government of this country over the defense of the homeland against invasion rather than any dissatisfaction such as was responsible for last night's "purge" of the French generals.

Under a decree issued by the King, acting on the advice of the new Churchill government, General Sir Edmund Ironside, who has been Chief of the Imperial Staff, relinquishes that office to become Commander in Chief of the home forces. He will be succeeded by Sir John Greer Dill who was recently recalled from France to become Vice Chief of the Imperial Staff. General Sir Walter Kirke, who has been commander of the home forces, was retired after forty-five years of service.

The announcement of the shift in commands was made early this evening after Paul Reynaud, the French Premier, had journeyed across the Channel today to confer with Prime Minister Winston Churchill and other members of the war Cabinet on the military and strategic situation confronting the Allies. This is held to be changed by the fact that the German Army has broken through the West Front defenses and has established itself at Boulogne, only twenty-six miles across the narrow waters that have been this country's moat for centuries.

Situation Taken Seriously

Barbed wire barricades along the beaches, the organization of home defense battalions to repel parachute troops, and the machine-gun nests in Whitehall and around the Admiralty give dramatic evidence of the seriousness with which the danger of invasion is regarded.

Before the arrival of M. Reynaud, who returned to Paris this evening, Hubert Pierlot, Belgian Premier; Paul-Henri Spaak, Minister of Foreign Affairs; Defense Minister Lieut. Gen. Henri Denis and M. van den Poorten, Minister of the Interior of Belgium, arrived in London and consulted with Viscount Halifax, the Foreign Secretary. They were met, upon their arrival, by Camille Gutt, the Belgian Minister here, who accompanied them to the Foreign Office.

Among the many problems discussed by the Allied war leaders, in addition to the strategic ones

Continued on Page Five

DRIVE NEAR DOVER

Berlin Sees Its Channel Forces in Position to Attack Britain

LILLE IS ENDANGERED

2 German Spearheads 19 Miles Apart Aim to Divide Allies

By PERCIVAL KNAUTH

Wireless to THE NEW YORK TIMES.

BERLIN, May 26—The fall of Calais, reported in a special bulletin of the German High Command tonight, presages the beginning of the long prophesied German attack on the British Isles. With this second and most important Channel port in their hands, the Germans now are directly opposite Dover, with their guns not only able to cover a landing of German troops on British soil, but also in a position to ward off an attack by the only hindrance still standing between them and England, the British fleet.

Special significance attached by authorized German military circles to bombing by German planes of numerous airports in Eastern and Southeastern England, moreover, indicates that Germany has launched a drive for air superiority over Britain, which is the most vital prerequisite for a modern offensive.

Increasing activity in the war on British shipping, in which the long quiescent German U-boat arm is expected to play a major role, as predicted by authorized military circles tonight, strengthens a general belief that England is the next goal of the German armies now marching up the Channel coast.

Aim to Divide Allies

The Germans now consider the fate of the trapped Allied armies in Artois and Flanders definitely sealed. With Calais captured, they are further cut off from England, their only remaining source of supply.

The German armies southwest and northeast of Lille have started a drive that, if successful, would cut the Allied forces in two. Though the trapped armies are fighting with desperation and putting up strongest resistance, the time is drawing near when their ammunition will give out and they will be forced to surrender, officials here assert.

There still are three possibilities for the continuation of German operations in the west. One is an attack against England, which is now believed imminent. The second is a further southward drive on Paris. The third is an offensive from Luxembourg with the purpose of turning the Maginot Line. These three possibilities, it was authoritatively said tonight, remain open, but it was emphasized that "the

Continued on Page Two

NAZIS GAIN ON COAST AND STRIKE AT LILLE

Paris acknowledged that Boulogne (1) had been taken and Berlin claimed the capture of Calais (2) as well and an advance to Gravelines (3), probably from the southeast. The Germans appeared to be weaving a net around Lille to confine the Allied forces still further. From Courtrai (4) the Nazis advanced to Iseghem and at the same time apparently moved southwest to within nineteen miles of a column that had pushed north from Vimy (5). The broken lines represent the approximate stabilized battle lines, although, of course as in the case of the Lille operations, there is fighting behind these lines.

ADMIRALTY ADMITS LOSS OF TWO SHIPS

Destroyer Bombed by Nazi Fliers Off France—Mine Sinks a Sweep-Trawler

Special Cable to THE NEW YORK TIMES.

LONDON, May 26—The British Admiralty announced tonight that the 1,100-ton destroyer Wessex had been sunk off the French coast by German planes and the 290-ton mine-sweeping trawler Charles Boyes had been lost after hitting a German mine.

On the Wessex, six members of the crew were reported killed and fifteen wounded. The destroyer's normal crew consisted of 134 officers and men. The vessel was built under the World War emergency program and was completed in March, 1918. Her commander was Lieut. Comdr. W. A. R. Cartwright.

Two officers, including the commander, and thirteen men were believed killed or drowned when the Charles Boyes sank. All other members of the crew, whose total was not given, were injured, but were picked up by other vessels and brought to shore.

The Wessex was the fifth British destroyer lost by Nazi airplane bombs since the war began and the fifteenth lost from all causes.

Germans Report Narvik Action

BERLIN, May 26 (UP)—A British aircraft carrier has been bombed and sunk off the Norwegian port of Narvik and two other Allied warships have been bombed and set on fire there, official German statements today claimed.

The aircraft carrier, which was not identified, was said to have been bombed and hit Friday in Ofot Fjord and was attacked again Saturday in the fjord, where it was hit by three bombs, one of which was of "heaviest caliber."

"On May 25 German fighting planes achieved an additional major success in the sea area around Narvik," the D. N. B. agency said. "After an enemy airplane carrier received a heavy bomb hit on May 24 in Ofot Fjord the same vessel on May 25 was struck by three bombs, one of which was of the heaviest caliber. As a result of this heavy damage the aircraft carrier had to be given up and sank."

The German High Command in its communiqué said that a battleship and a cruiser were heavily hit by air bombs off Narvik and that "fire was seen to break out."

[The German communiqué of Saturday reported attacks in the Narvik area on an aircraft carrier, a battleship and a criuser or destroyer. The British aircraft carrier Courageous, 22,500 tons, was sunk last Sept. 17.]

The German High Command announced that additional parachute troops of the German Alpine units had been landed at Narvik.

The High Command also told of bomb hits on two large merchant ships of 5,000 tons, two smaller merchant ships and a warship off Calais in the English Channel.

R. A. F. LISTS VICTORY IN 4-HOUR AIR DUEL

40 Nazi Bombers Crippled in Battle Over French Coast, Ministry Declares

By HAROLD DENNY

Wireless to THE NEW YORK TIMES.

LONDON, May 26—The chief British military activity again has been in the air where Royal Air Force planes, based both on the Continent and in England, in innumerable daring attacks regardless of odds, have brought down scores more of German planes, wrecked German troop-supply trains, bombed troop columns along the roads and blown up munitions and gasoline dumps, destroying bridges and even raiding repeatedly far into Germany in efforts to cause damage and confusion behind the lines.

British aviators, according to Air Ministry reports, continue to inflict losses on Germans all out of proportion to their own losses. Yesterday, because of cloudy weather, British fighters brought down only twenty German planes with an attendant loss of four attacking British planes.

Today, however, British fighter pilots regained their recent average of forty German planes shot down. Four British fighters were lost in so doing. British bombing planes, operating both from France and England, paid for the damage they inflicted with the loss of six of their own number. However, four British fighter planes reported missing Thursday have since returned safely.

[The Air Ministry reported yesterday, according to The United Press, that in a four-hour air battle over the French coast between Calais and Dunkerque British planes shot down at least twenty Nazi bombers and put another twenty out of action. Two R.A.F. squadrons attacked a large formation of German bombers guarded by a strong escort of Nazi fighter planes, and for hours the air was filled with fighting craft, with one German plane after another being brought down, the Ministry stated.]

Heroic Exploits Numerous

The past two days of fighting have been filled with heroic personal exploits although the names of pilots have been withheld.

One of the most exciting was that of a young New Zealander who, with all the instruments of his Hurricane plane except the compass and the oil temperature and pressure gauges shot out in a dogfight with German fighters, his gunsights gone and his starboard gasoline tank leaking, was about to land at an airdrome in France to

Continued on Page Four

Dispatches from Europe and the Far East are subject to censorship at the source.

ALL FRONTS ACTIVE

Despite Severe Losses Nazis Continue Drives in Flanders Battle

4 ATTACKS LAUNCHED

Allied Planes Drop Tons of Bombs on German Units Along Coast

By G. H. ARCHAMBAULT

Wireless to THE NEW YORK TIMES.

PARIS, May 26—Despite severe losses, the Germans have not ceased their pressure in Flanders. Apart from the loss of Boulogne the Allies have withstood it everywhere, according to the latest reports received tonight. On broad lines that is the day's story. But it needs analysis for comprehension of its significance.

The Germans have not ceased their pressure because they must not lose the initiative if their object is to be attained. They have staked so much on this offensive and they have won such an initial success that they cannot change their plans.

[General Maxime Weygand, Commander in Chief of the Allied land forces, flew over the Allied troops in the North yesterday and it was reported that they were being well supplied through the strip of coast south of Zeebrugge and north of German-held Boulogne, The Associated Press reported.]

The Germans now seem to be totally disregarding the cost in human life. All Allied reports agree on the heavy casualties inflicted in the course of four attacks on the Flanders plain, wave upon wave being brought down by automatic weapons and quick-firing guns.

German Losses Cited

The French communiqué tonight refers to equally great losses in recent actions between the Aisne and the Meuse Rivers. It says that it is confirmed, notably by prisoners' statements, that the losses inflicted on the Germans by artillery and automatic weapons are very high. During the actions it was found that entire platoons of German infantry were mowed down where they stood, the communiqué stated.

Frequently in war the change from defensive to offensive comes very swiftly. The genius of a great captain lies in timing it exactly. So that for the Allies it is heartening news that "from a defensive point of view the last twenty-four hours marked a real success," in the words of a spokesman for the General Staff.

This success was all the greater because the Nazi attacks were fierce. There were four of them and on wide fronts—some eight miles in each case—with intensive use of tanks, airplanes, artillery and infantry—attacks "in the grand manner," as the French say.

The first was launched on the extreme north of the front against the Belgians in the neighborhood of Courtrai. It lasted many hours, with the Belgians defending their soil "with admirable determination."

Attack at Two Points

South of Courtrai the Germans attacked the French at two points with very considerable forces. Here also the fighting was prolonged and much of it was hand to hand, the French infantry frequently halting German assaults at the point of the bayonet.

The fourth attack began at dawn against Valenciennes; it took the form of a double action, east and west. It was still raging at dusk after the Germans had been driven back time after time only to return despite the many dead left on the ground.

West of this field of carnage—that is to say, in the region of the Channel coast—the principal event was the fate of Boulogne. For two days there had been fighting in the streets. This morning the French defenders were still in the citadel, but during the day heavy reinforcements were brought up by the Germans and the town had to be abandoned.

The French communiqué mentions "ruthless street fights." The main German thrust is now directed at Calais, and there has been sharp fighting some distance to the south of that port. It was reported tonight that all the harbors to the

Continued on Page Four

Extra Police on Guard at La Guardia Field; Move Believed Made to Forestall Sabotage

Extra policemen have been assigned to La Guardia Field, the city airport at North Beach, Queens, to tighten the control of the large number of visitors to the field, it was learned yesterday.

Although the extra guard was generally believed to have been ordered to forestall any possibility of sabotage, officials at the airport did not express any fear of sabotage. One of them merely remarked that "after all, the airport is one of the city's most vital points."

The order for a more strict surveillance over visitors was reported to have come from Dock Commissioner John McKenzie, in charge of the airport, directly from Mayor La Guardia. But it was not learned whether the order originated with the Mayor or had been requested by the Federal Government.

Visitors henceforth will be barred from the six large hangars on the field and will not be allowed on the third floor of the Administration Building where the government Weather Bureau and airway traffic control are located, or the field control tower on top of the building. The control tower has not been open to the public since the field opened, but from now on passes to enter the tower will be restricted.

Relatively few of the many thousands of visitors to the field have sought entrance to the hangars, but with policemen now on guard at the entrance to each hangar, all visitors will be required to have special passes.

There will be no restrictions on visitors in the public rooms of the Administration Building, and the public can still go on the elevated walk, where for 10 cents one may watch the planes arriving and departing.

The new order will cancel plans for guided tours through the hangars this Summer. The tours, it was estimated, would have brought about $75,000 to the city.

Major Elmer Haslett, manager of the airport, said yesterday that on Saturday he had notified the six airlines operating at the field of the new rule restricting visitors. The new rule also applies to the Marine Terminal from which Pan American Airways operates its transatlantic services, but the Pan American hangar has always been closed to visitors.

"All the News That's Fit to Print."

The New York Times.

EXTRA

Mostly cloudy, with scattered showers and little change in temperature today and tomorrow.
Temperatures Yesterday—Max., 65; Min., 52

VOL. LXXXIX—No. 30,075. Entered as Second-Class Matter, Postoffice, New York, N. Y. NEW YORK, TUESDAY, MAY 28, 1940. THREE CENTS NEW YORK CITY and Vicinity | FOUR CENTS Elsewhere Except in 7th and 8th Postal Zones.

LEOPOLD ORDERS BELGIAN ARMY TO QUIT; ALLIES FORCED BACK IN FLANDERS POCKET; FRENCH GAIN IN ATTACKS ON THE SOMME

NEW TAX TO MEET COSTS OF DEFENSE PLANNED IN CAPITAL

Congress Leaders Lay Basis for Measure in Line With President's Program

NO OPPOSITION EXPECTED

Toolmakers Marshaled for Expansion—Training of 45,000 Fliers Asked by Roosevelt

Congress leaders began shaping defense tax legislation yesterday in response to manifested readiness of the country to bear the cost. [Page 1.]

Action for control of aliens came in the House, which approved the President's order transferring the Immigration Service to the Justice Department, and in a Senate committee, which reported favorably a House bill to fingerprint and register all non-citizens. [Page 9.]

The Senate passed the La Follette Civil Liberties Bill, outlawing strike-breakers and labor espionage, after revamping it and adding a defense clause. [Page 1.]

The formation of a war industries board, responsible to the President, to supervise industrial preparation for defense, was recommended in a secret report by the Stettinius advisory board, disbanded after the war began in the Fall. [Page 13.]

Machine tool spokesmen received assurances from Secretary Morgenthau and Army and Navy experts that the defense program would mean $200,000,000 in orders for the industry. [Page 11.]

Tax Legislation in View

By TURNER CATLEDGE

Special to THE NEW YORK TIMES.

WASHINGTON, May 27—A move to enact a defense tax bill at this session of Congress took sudden and definite form today as Administration authorities and Congressional revenue leaders reached a tentative conclusion to act at once upon the country's evident willingness to bear directly the added burdens necessary to preparedness.

President Roosevelt was reported to have turned his attention seriously to the question of new taxes in week-end discussions with Secretary Morgenthau.

The question was being revived from a dormant state at the Capitol this afternoon by Representative Doughton of North Carolina, chairman of the Ways and Means Committee; Representative Cooper of Tennessee, chairman of the Ways and Means tax subcommittee, and Senator Harrison of Mississippi, chairman of the Senate Finance Committee.

Draft of Basis Ordered

The three leaders conferred at length with Colin F. Stam, chief of staff of the joint committee on internal revenue taxation, and were understood to have commissioned him to work out a defense tax program to be used as a basis for further discussion with the President and Treasury officials.

They also started a check of their colleagues in the House and Senate to determine in advance the chance for putting such a program quickly through Congress. Declining to comment on the progress of their discussions, they simply said it was obvious from their meeting that the subject of tax legislation again had become a live one.

Agitation continued in Congress, meanwhile, for a straightforward approach to the revenue problem as made more acute by the defense program.

It was becoming increasingly apparent that the debt limit of $45,000,000,000 would be reached early in the new year—much sooner than expected when the budget was submitted last January—and the demand was growing that the two main revenue questions, debt-limit increase and taxation, be met at the same time, and at this session, despite the presence of an election year.

As the word got around that a

Continued on Page Twelve

The International Situation

On the Battle Fronts

Premier Reynaud of France announced in an early morning broadcast that the Belgian Army had collapsed and that King Leopold had given up the struggle. He said, however, that France would continue to fight and that the line along the Somme was intact. The Belgian King's action was taken without consultation with his allies and against the advice of his Ministers. The latter, now in England, will continue resistance and raise a new army, Premier Reynaud said. [Page 1.]

The area held by the isolated Allied Army on the Franco-Belgian border was further constricted yesterday as the Germans, undeterred by their own heavy casualties, used everything they had to force a quick decision. Paris admitted two Allied withdrawals, one from the salient at Valenciennes, the other from the northern side of the "Artois Gap," which connects the German forces in the Channel area with the main body of the invading army. [Page 1.]

An almost unceasing attack was being pressed by the Germans against the Northern flank of the bottled-up Allied forces. Paris reported that they had even resorted to mass formation attacks, such as had not been seen since early in 1914, when the machine gun demonstrated what it could do to concentrated human targets. German units from the Swiss border and the Westwall had appeared in the line, the French said. The area of battle—a triangle based on the Channel north from the Calais region, its apex near Cambrai—had become a second Verdun, Paris reported; it was marked by the same significance and by the same determination on the part of the defenders. Farther to the south, the French said they had taken several villages above the Somme, in a movement evidently aimed at closing the "Artois Gap," but that gap was being widened on the Northern side by the Germans. [Included in foregoing.]

Berlin claimed success in the opening stages of a drive to cut the pocketed Allied forces in two. This drive started in the Courtrai region and was aimed at Ypres: it had resulted, the Germans said, in a deep dent in the Allied positions. But the defenders admittedly were standing their ground resolutely, and progress was only step by step. Obituaries of German soldiers who had died on the Western Front were beginning to appear in German newspapers. [Page 1.] One of those who fell was Prince Wilhelm of Prussia, eldest son of the former Crown Prince and favorite grandson of the former Kaiser. [Page 4.]

London, admitting that the situation in Northern France was of increasing gravity, reported that German bombers were attacking Channel shipping and were causing serious loss of life. These air attacks were designed to slash to pieces British supply lines to the Flanders battlefield — or evacuation lines from the Flanders battlefield. [Page 1.]

An excerpt from a letter written home by a French soldier gave an inkling of the fury of the battle in Flanders: "We know nothing, understand nothing, but keep fighting, fighting; eating when we can, how we can; and no one has thought of sleep for these past ten days." [Page 3.]

The Germans reported early this morning that waves of British planes were bombing Duesseldorf, near Germany's west border. This was one of many air forays at communication centers and airdromes in the German rear. [Page 1.]

Repercussions Elsewhere

A French airman arrived in Paris from the front with a story that an American hospital in Ostend had been destroyed by German bombers, who killed virtually the entire medical staff and the patients. [Page 5.]

The Allied courting of Italy continued, London reporting that Italian ships would be exempt from blockade search under an agreement by which no goods received in Italy would be re-exported to Germany. But the Italians went on openly preparing for war against the Allies. [Page 1.]

The British Board of Trade, moving to save dollar exchange and shipping space, prohibited the importation of cotton from non-Allied countries, including the United States, except by special license. [Page 14.]

ACTS TO BAR JOBS TO REDS, BUNDISTS

Senate Also Votes to Outlaw Strike-Breakers and Use of 'Munitions' by Industry

Special to THE NEW YORK TIMES.

WASHINGTON, May 27—The La Follette Civil Liberties Bill was passed by the Senate late today, 47 to 20, but only after being amended to a fragment of its original form and turned into something of a "defense" measure by the inclusion of provisions to limit the employment of aliens in industry.

The bill primarily forbids the use of oppressive practices over labor by employers doing business in interstate commerce. If approved by the House, it would outlaw the use of strike-breakers and labor spies in labor disputes and the possession or use of firearms, tear gas or other "munitions" by any industry except banks and trust companies.

That part of the bill survived Senate consideration, but otherwise the Senate deleted much of the measure and added amendments undreamed of a month ago, prior to European war developments, which suddenly made the Congress defense conscious.

The Senate approved without record votes two amendments by Senator Reynolds which injected the defense picture into the bill. The first amendment would provide that no industry covered by the measure should employ aliens to an extent greater than 10 per cent of its total personnel. By the other one, it forbade the employment of any Nazi or Communist, without exception.

Senator Reynolds's 90-10 amend-

Continued on Page Twelve

LABOR LOSES FIGHT ON ANTI-TRUST ACT

But the Supreme Court Bars Damages to Apex, Holding State Has Jurisdiction

Summary of the court's decision will be found on Page 21.

By LOUIS STARK

Special to THE NEW YORK TIMES.

WASHINGTON, May 27—The Supreme Court today denied organized labor's contention that it was wholly excluded from prosecution under the Sherman Anti-Trust Act but refused the Apex Hosiery Company of Philadelphia the right to collect $711,932 in damages from Local 706, American Federation of Full-Fashioned Hosiery Workers, a Congress of Industrial Organizations affiliate, because of a seven-week sit-down strike in 1937.

In line with its policy of thirty-two years, the court ruled that the words of the anti-trust act "do embrace to some extent and in some circumstances labor unions and their activities."

As to the damages, the majority, composed of Justice Stone and the five Roosevelt appointees, upheld the Third Circuit Court in ruling that the union had violated the laws of Pennsylvania, where it could be compelled to answer for damages in the State courts.

From the provision respecting damages Chief Justice Hughes and Justice McReynolds and Roberts sharply dissented. They maintained that once it was agreed that the anti-trust act does not except labor unions the Supreme Court had no option but to apply the Sherman

Continued on Page Twenty-one

NAZIS DRIVE WEDGE

Thrust Toward Ypres Aims to Cut Allies' Pocket in Two

SENEGALESE ATTACK

Berlin Reports Colonial Troops Hurled Back in Fierce Battle

By GEORGE AXELSSON

Wireless to THE NEW YORK TIMES.

BERLIN, May 27—Fighting with their backs to the sea, the Allied troops pocketed in Belgian and French Flanders were pressed harder than ever today by the Germans, who admit they are throwing in all forces at their command to gain a decision in this vital sector. A new danger to the defenders is seen here in what looks like a German effort to drive a wedge into the pocket, cutting it in two, by a thrust from the direction of Courtrai to Ypres and Dunkerque.

The Allies still hold a considerable part of the coast line, based on German statements, from Gravelines to Hoofdplaat on the south shore of the Scheldt estuary, which is the only piece of Netherland territory still in Allied hands. They seem to stand their ground resolutely in this area despite the ferocity of the German ground and air onslaughts, although the Germans claim to have dented the line deeply north of Menin toward Ypres.

In trying to save themsIves from complete encirclement the Allies are offering desperate resistance, with the Germans seemingly able to gain ground only step by step. This is making the present battle comparable with the bloodiest ever fought during the World War and with the most furious fighting at the time Field Marshal Sir Douglas Haig issued his famous "backs to the wall" order of the day in the Spring of 1918 to men standing off what turned out to be Germany's final and greatest bid for victory in the drive on Arras and Amiens, aiming to reach the Channel ports.

Civilian Slaughter Feared

Tens of thousands of tons of high explosive and incendiary bombs are being dropped from planes on the area, which has been narrowing from day to day. The artillery rains innumerable shells along the entire width of the front and thousands of tanks are charging one another in the midst of a man-made inferno that may by now have laid in ruins such cities as Douai, Lille, Roubaix, Dunkerque and Ostend, prosperous communities only three short weeks ago.

What has become of the civilian population of these cities and interlying villages and farm lands, caught in crossfire from both sides, it is generally feared, will reveal one of the biggest tragedies of modern times. Five million men, women and children, including 2,000,000 refugees who had fled from the occupied provinces of Belgium, are

Continued on Page Four

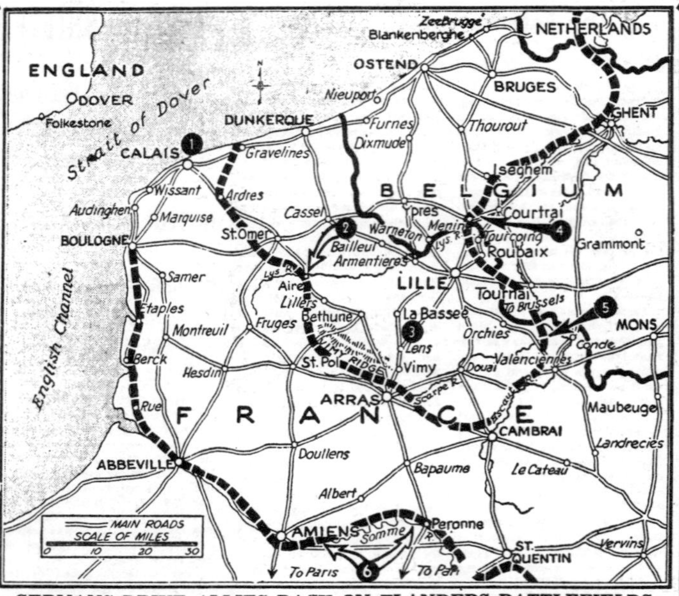

GERMANS DRIVE ALLIES BACK ON FLANDERS BATTLEFIELDS

Nazi forces concentrated yesterday on smashing the troops held in the roughly triangular salient extending from the region of Calais (1)—the fall of which was still not conceded by the French—down to the Arras-Cambrai area and back up to the Netherlands border. British troops counter-attacked at Aire (2) and French Senegalese troops counter-attacked near Lens (3), presumably against a German column operating within the main lines. Between Menin and Courtrai (4), however, the Nazis struck across the Lys River in the direction of Ypres. They also struck in the neighborhood of Valenciennes (5) and the Allies fell back along the Escaut River. The Allies likewise had apparently retired in the region east of Arras, at the southern extremity of the salient; this movement widened the Germans' gap, which formerly had extended from Bapaume to Peronne. On the southern edge of the gap, however, the French reported the recapture of several villages along the Somme (6). The broken line represents the approximate battlefronts.

DUESSELDORF IS HIT BY ALLIED BOMBERS

R. A. F. Reports More Raids on Airdromes and German Rear Positions

By The United Press.

BERLIN, Tuesday, May 28—The city of Duesseldorf, just over the German frontier from Belgium, was bombed repeatedly by waves of planes that came over from 12:30 to 2:30 A. M. today, telephone messages from Duesseldorf stated.

Special Cable to THE NEW YORK TIMES.

LONDON, May 27—Last night and today British aviators, as every day since the Germans launched the invasion of the Low Countries, again carried out daring bombing raids behind the German lines in an effort to slow up the German drive and to relieve pressure on ground troops.

They attacked German lines of communications and motorized columns, bridges, supply depots, anti-aircraft batteries and similar objectives in Belgium and Western Germany and attacked airdromes used by the Germans at Flushing, Brussels, Antwerp, Venlo and Charleroi. It is reported that hits were made on many of these objectives. It is believed that British aviators did considerable damage to a concen-

Continued on Page Six

Partial Reynaud Text

By The United Press.

PARIS, Tuesday, May 28—A partial text of Premier Paul Reynaud's broadcast on the Belgian surrender follows:

A grave event occurred in the course of the night. France can no longer count on the Belgian Army.

We knew dark days were coming. They have come. We will hold the Somme-Aisne line, and because we hold it we will win!

The Belgian Army has laid down its arms on orders of its King—the same King who appealed to the Allies to come to his help, the same King who in December last year refused to have any staff talks with the Allies, the same King who up to May 10 professes to have equal faith in the word of Germany as in the word of the Allies.

This same King, without a word of gratitude or admiration for the soldiers of the Allies, has now handed the Belgian Army over to the invader.

This decision was taken in strict contradiction of the feeling of his country and of the soldiers, who had been putting up a magnificent effort.

France and Britain alone will have to carry on the struggle which they had taken upon themselves together with the Belgians May 14.

You know what the position is in the South. The French armies are holding successfully the lines of the Somme and Aisne and the Maginot Line.

In the North the Belgian Army, the British Expeditionary Force and some of our troops have been engaged in the defense of Belgium.

I am told by the Belgian Government that the King's decision was taken against the wish of Belgians and that the government intends to go on fighting and form a new army which will stand beside the French.

This is without precedent in history.

Our faith in victory is intact. We shall hold on to the Somme and Aisne, and as we hold on we shall conquer.

Editor Asks Unstinted U. S. Aid for France; Planes, Food and Medicine Immediate Needs

By HAMILTON FISH ARMSTRONG
Editor of Foreign Affairs

Wireless to THE NEW YORK TIMES.

PARIS, May 27—Today in France there is no "political situation" to be analyzed and described.

French policy can be stated in one sentence: The army, the government and the people intend to win this great battle in the north at any and every cost and then at any and every cost to hold out through the battles of the Summer until planes and supplies from America and from the British and French Empires enable them to face the German Armies with something like equality of number in aviation and matériel.

If they can win through to that point they can win through to final victory.

Every single American plane will count. Every day earlier that it can reach the French pilot waiting to take it into battle will count. Perhaps it will help turn the scales at some vital point at some vital moment. If there is a single reserve American Army plane that can be spared, it ought to be flown or shipped across the Atlantic tomorrow.

Since this ferocious struggle began in Belgium and Flanders, civilian refugees have been flooding down across the country, making every crossroads, every village and every railway junction a station of misery. They arrive in boxcars, bundled in the straw. They come by road in every conceivable sort of vehicle.

In the Bordeaux region three days ago I saw two fire engines that had come through from Brussels. Baby carriages, a sewing machine and bundles of every shape were piled on one. Ten or fifteen persons were packed into the other, the women,

Continued on Page Eight

WAR PREPARATIONS GO AHEAD IN ITALY

But Blockade Talks With the British Continue—500 Americans Stranded

By HERBERT L. MATTHEWS

By Telephone to THE NEW YORK TIMES.

ROME, May 27—Italy went on openly preparing for war against the Allies today, but no vital step was taken.

Except for the constant calling up of individuals, which is taking place on a fairly large scale but without real mobilization, there is no sign of imminent military action. The preparations are still predominantly psychological, but from that viewpoint they could not be stronger.

As far as the Germans are concerned, they insist here, as they do in Berlin, that no pressure is being brought on Italy and even that they have no particular desire for Italian intervention now. They claim to be convinced that Premier Mussolini will give the order to march very soon. But if he does so, it will be on his own initiative and in Italy's particular interest.

The situation is complicated by

Continued on Page Nine

BRITAIN PREPARED AS WAR IS NEARER

News of Nazi Drive Toward Channel Ominous—British Flank Now Exposed

Special Cable to THE NEW YORK TIMES.

LONDON, Tuesday, May 28—The gravity of the British official spokesmen's statements last night on the military situation around Courtrai and the position of the towns mentioned in the communiqués as showing the German occupation ever nearer the English Channel had to a great extent prepared the British public to hear the bad news of French Premier Paul Reynaud's broadcast today. But the complete collapse of the Belgian Army was unexpected.

In British military circles here the news of King Leopold's capitulation came as a staggering shock. Instantly it was realized that the

Continued on Page Six

Dispatches from Europe and the Far East are subject to censorship at the source.

CABINET TO FIGHT

Leopold's Ministers Say They Will Raise a New Army

KING ACTED ALONE

Allies Not Consulted, Reynaud Declares, Predicts Victory

By The Associated Press.

PARIS, Tuesday, May 28—Capitulation of the Belgian Army before the German advance on orders of King Leopold III after eighteen days of fighting was announced today by Premier Paul Reynaud of France.

King Leopold ordered the Belgian Army to lay down its arms, M. Reynaud said, without consulting the French or British Governments "which went to the aid of Belgium."

The French Premier made his announcement in a radio broadcast at 8:30 A. M. (2:30 A. M., E. S. T.), hastily arranged after an emergency meeting of the French Cabinet, which lasted until the early hours of this morning.

M. Reynaud said that King Leopold had made the decision to capitulate against the unanimous advice of his Ministers.

Some hours before the Premier's announcement Premier Hubert Pierlot of Belgium had anounced in Paris, after a meeting with his refugee Cabinet, that his government had decided to continue in the war on the side of the Allies. The Premier said that Belgium would triumph sooner or later and called upon all Belgians to remain confident of victory.

Ministers to Fight On

M. Reynaud followed that up today with the announcement that the Belgian Government, in opposition to its King's orders, would continue to function and would "raise a new army."

He said the Belgian capitulation had failed to lower French and British hopes for victory against the German invaders.

M. Reynaud prefaced his announcement of the capitulation with the words: "I must announce a grave event to the nation."

"The Belgian Army," he said, "has just brusquely capitulated in the field on the order of its King."

The King, he asserted, had issued the order without consulting "the responsible government."

He explained that the three Allied armies fighting in Belgium were under the command of General Georges Blanchard.

As the battle continued, he said, troops were sent supplies via Dunkerque.

Speaks With Sarcasm

The French Premier spoke with extreme sarcasm when he referred to King Leopold.

He said the action of the King of the Belgians was "without precedent in history."

M. Reynaud told his countrymen, however, that France's "faith in victory is still intact."

"The French troops are holding now along the line of the Somme River," he said.

His speech lasted less than five minutes.

The Premier said that "all France is thinking of her soldiers at this extremely grave hour."

"The French people and her soldiers make one solid block," he said, declaring that the French Army was holding

Continued on Page Two

"All the News That's Fit to Print."

The New York Times.

LATE CITY EDITION
Partly cloudy today, showers tonight, little change in temperature. Tomorrow showers.
Temperatures Yesterday—Max.,64; Min.,53

Copyright 1940, by The New York Times Company.

VOL. LXXXIX...No. 30,077. Entered as Second-Class Matter, Postoffice, New York, N. Y. NEW YORK, THURSDAY, MAY 30, 1940. THREE CENTS NEW YORK CITY and Vicinity | FOUR CENTS Elsewhere Except in 7th and 8th Postal Zones.

ALLIES ABANDONING FLANDERS, FLOOD YSER AREA; A RESCUE FLEET AT DUNKERQUE; FOE POUNDS PORT; ONE FORCE CUT OFF FROM THE SEA AS LILLE FALLS

PRESIDENT TO ASK $750,000,000 MORE FOR ARMY PROGRAM

Nazi Blitzkrieg Held to Show the $3,300,000,000 Allotted Fails to Meet Needs

FOR TANKS, GUNS, PLANES

Tax Bill to Be Offered in House Today—D. M. Nelson Named Procurement Director

By FELIX BELAIR Jr.
Special to THE NEW YORK TIMES.

WASHINGTON, May 29—On the eve of his first meeting with the reconstituted Council of National Defense, President Roosevelt was putting finishing touches today on a new request for $750,000,000 as a supplemental appropriation for further expansion and mechanization of the military establishment to take account of European war developments since he sent his preparedness message to Congress two weeks ago.

The projected increase in funds for the Army, over and above the omnibus $3,300,000,000 defense program already pending, was mapped by the President in a White House conference with Treasury and War Department officials.

It was the President's plan to send up the supplemental request in a few days. Subject to additions, the new program contemplates placing orders immediately for the following:

About 3,000 new pursuit and bombing planes.

Between 1,500 and 2,000 tanks.

About 500 heavy howitzers.

A supply of aerial bombs of various sizes, to cost between $20,000,000 and $30,000,000.

Other modern weapons of war which have been developed in Army laboratories, but not yet put into actual production.

German Drive Appraised

There was no official announcement on the results of the meeting, and Secretary Woodring, who acted as spokesman for the group, said only that they had reviewed "the whole military situation."

From others present, however, it was learned that the nation's military establishment had been reappraised in the light of Germany's advances in Western Europe since the President's preparedness message was first submitted to Congress.

Other developments in the national defense program were:

1. The Senate Naval Affairs Committee brought out a measure increasing the air force limit of the Navy to 10,000 planes and 16,000 pilots, with a report warning that the "country at this time is facing the possibility that the Allies may be defeated and that we may have to defend ourselves in both oceans at the same time."

2. Senate leaders were planning to take up tomorrow the $1,500,000,000 bill providing an 11 per cent increase in under-age surface tonnage, with indications that the measure would be disposed of without delay.

Procurement Officer Named

3. Secretary Morgenthau named Donald M. Nelson, executive vice president of Sears, Roebuck & Co., as director of the Treasury's Procurement Division, thereby adding another business executive to the list of those on whom the administration is relying for the success of the defense program.

4. Administration—Congressional plans for placing emergency rearmament financing on a "pay-as-you-go" basis gathered momentum, with an announcement by Representative Doughton, chairman of the House Ways and Means Committee, that he would introduce tomorrow a measure raising the statutory debt limit by $3,000,000,000 and imposing upward of $656,000,000 in new defense taxes.

5. Secretary Hull modified aviation restrictions under the Neutrality Act to permit the delivery of American planes by American pilots to Halifax, N. S., thereby removing the ban on through deliveries over the Maritime Provinces.

6. White House sources explained that there would be the closest possible relations between Presi-

Continued on Page Eight

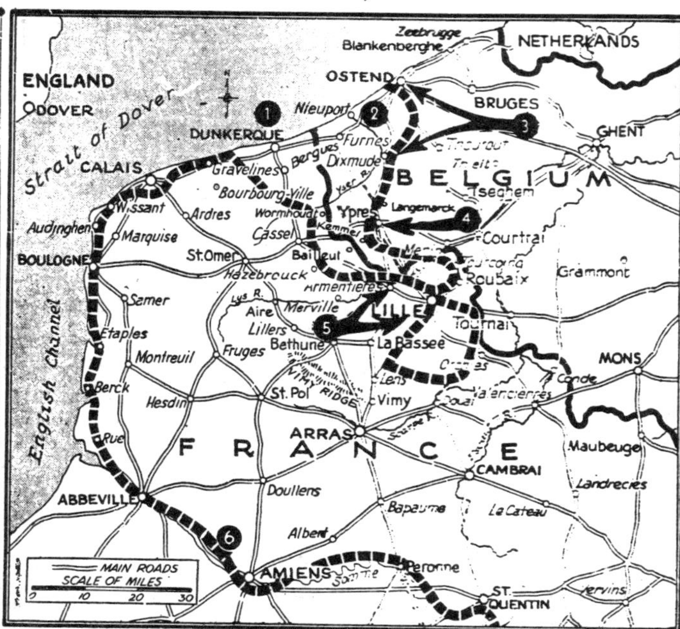

ALLIES STRIKE FOR COAST IN EVER-TIGHTENING POCKET

To keep the exit at Dunkerque (1) open French and British sea, land and air forces were waging a furious struggle yesterday; to retard the German advance the Allies were understood to have opened sluice gates on the Yser to flood the region below Nieuport (2). In the sector that had been held by the Belgians the Nazis pushed to Ostend and Dixmude (3). Farther south they were reported to have taken Ypres (4). Their most important operation of the day, however, was the bisecting of the pocket by the capture of Lille and Armentieres (5), thus cutting off from the sea the Allied forces in the lower section. Along the Somme the French eliminated a German bridgehead west of Amiens (6). The broken lines show the approximate battlefronts.

HULL ORDER SPEEDS PLANES TO ALLIES

Allows Our Pilots to Fly Craft Over Three Canadian Maritime Provinces

Special to THE NEW YORK TIMES.

WASHINGTON, May 29—The way was opened today for expediting deliveries of American airplanes to the Allied fighting lines when Secretary Hull modified regulations of the Neutrality Act to permit the delivery of such aircraft by American pilots to ports in the three eastern Canadian Provinces.

The step was designed to facilitate deliveries to the Allies because of the urgency of their military situation. It was taken at the request of the French Government.

Mr. Hull ruled that "American nationals may travel in belligerent aircraft over the Canadian Provinces of New Brunswick, Nova Scotia and Prince Edward Island."

This means that pilots from the United States may fly new planes to Halifax, whence they will be flown across the Atlantic by pilots of the Allies or sent across by ship.

American pilots have been delivering planes in Ottawa and other Canadian cities. As before, they must still conform under the new order to regulations by pushing planes over the Canadian border from the United States.

Previously, while American pilots could fly planes over Canadian territory, once they were pushed over the border the fliers could not enter the three eastern maritime Provinces because American ships are barred from them and aircraft regulations conform to shipping rules. Newfoundland was excluded from the modification today because there was no actual need for including it.

The Department of Commerce announced that April shipments of aircraft and equipment to the Allies included 195 planes and 285 engines.

Of the planes, France received seventy completely powered craft and ninety-eight in a knock-down condition. The United Kingdom obtained twenty-three assembled and powered and Canada four.

Of the engines, 230 went to France, forty-three to Canada and twelve to the United Kingdom. The French plane acquisitions were valued at $9,176,538, those of the United Kingdom at $3,139,000 and those of Canada at $388,398.

With a variety of other equipment included, French purchases for the month totaled $14,443,071; those of the United Kingdom $3,906,671 and those of Canada $728,929.

The Department of Commerce announced that total exports of aero-

Continued on Page Ten

Berlin Exchange Slumps As Optimism Is Decried

Wireless to THE NEW YORK TIMES.

BERLIN, May 29—In what was apparently a strong reaction to warnings against over-optimism, which have been circulated generally among the population following the German victories in the West, the Berlin Boerse today took a sudden nose dive.

Most issues dropped between 1 and 2 per cent. In shipping, Hapag dropped 5 per cent and North German Lloyd dropped 3 per cent. Fixed interest securities were quiet and generally unchanged. The close was irregular, with call money at 1½-2%.

Utilities, motor works and other heavy industries led the recession, while metal works in the Rhineland were among those that showed the maximum decline.

URUGUAY ON GUARD FOR FIFTH COLUMN

Check on Assembly, Increase in Army Urged—Nazis Take Bold Tone in Ecuador

Special Cable to THE NEW YORK TIMES.

MONTEVIDEO, Uruguay, May 29—The Uruguayan Government is frankly alarmed over Nazi fifth column activities.

After several Cabinet meetings at which the problem was closely studied, President Alfredo Baldomir has sent to Congress, with a request for urgent action, two bills. One provides for general rearmament and the other modifies Article 38 of the Constitution, which guarantees the right of assembly.

It has been rumored in well-informed diplomatic circles in more than one South American capital yesterday and today that Uruguay fears an invasion of Nazi fifth columnists from Southern Brazil. Official circles tonight emphatically denied any such fear and also denied that Uruguay had requested assistance from any other government.

The President's office earlier in the day, however, had published the details of the plans for rearmament and for modifying the constitutional guarantees.

Article 38 of the Constitution says that "all persons have a right to form themselves into associations, whatever may be the object sought, except they do not constitute an association declared by law to be illicit.

Since the law doesn't define what constitutes an illicit association, the bill that President Baldomir sent to Congress yesterday defines such il-

Continued on Page Six

ITALY BARS IMPORTS EXCEPT BY BARTER

Cancels Permits to Bring In Goods or to Buy Exchange for Payments Abroad

By HERBERT L. MATTHEWS
By Telephone to THE NEW YORK TIMES.

ROME, May 29—The Ministry of Foreign Exchange issued an order today to all banks and industrial firms canceling permits for importation and permission to acquire foreign currency to pay for imports. Thus Italy cuts herself off commercially from the world, except for barter agreements, and even there Italian ships coming in are not departing to bring back further imports.

This is the most serious indication yet given of the expectation of war, certainly as serious as the postponement of the sailing of Italian vessels announced last Friday.

The Conte di Savoia is due back from New York Sunday. No one expects her to depart, even on June 23, when she is scheduled to go. That will leave only the Conte Grande out of the Mediterranean among the large Italian ships. She sailed for South America a week ago.

[The steamship Roma arrived yesterday at Naples, according to The Associated Press, and is now expected to remain there instead of proceeding to Genoa, as scheduled. The Roma was to have left Genoa for New York June 29.]

Trade with the United States will suffer most heavily by the decision taken today. It has been possible for importers to acquire dollars at

Continued on Page Four

11,000 Times Speedier Way Found To Obtain Atomic Power Element

By WILLIAM L. LAURENCE

Development of a process that speeds up by 11,000 times the extraction of U-235, the element recently discovered to possess 5,000,000 times the power output of coal, promising to make it possible to utilize atomic energy as a new source of enormous power for all purposes, and to place in the hands of the nations at war, especially Germany, the most powerful fuel ever to be discovered, is to be announced in the forthcoming issue of Nature, leading British scientific weekly, advance proofs of which have reached THE NEW YORK TIMES. Germany, more than any other European nation, has been concentrating on developing this power. If the tests succeed the Allied blockade could be materially offset.

The new process for extracting U-235 that promises to revolutionize methods of power production and to usher in a new civilization based on the utilization of atomic power, was developed by Professor Wilhelm Krasny-Ergen of the Wenner-Grens Institute, Stockholm, Sweden, one of the leading scientific research institutions in Europe.

On May 5 it was announced that a tiny amount of U-235, a relative of uranium, had been isolated at the University of Minnesota and at the General Electric Company, and that pioneer experiments at the physics laboratories at Columbia University, under the direction of Professor

Continued on Page Eighteen

NAZIS TIGHTEN TRAP

They Drive a Line Across Pocket, Encircling Foes in South

SAY YPRES IS TAKEN

Zeebrugge and Ostend Fall—Large Stores Are Reported Seized

By GEORGE AXELSSON
Wireless to THE NEW YORK TIMES.

BERLIN, May 29—Remnants of the Allied Armies cut off in Flanders came a step nearer to being wiped out today when the Germans, simultaneously pressing from east and west toward the middle, managed to drive a wedge right across the pocket, thus separating the French and British divisions north of Lille from those in the south, who now are surrounded on all sides, no longer having access to the sea.

The Germans tonight claim to be in the city of Lille, in Ypres and Armentières and to have burned Dunkerque under heavy artillery bombardment. The Belgian capitulation permitted the Germans to take Bruges, Zeebrugge, Ostend and Thourout without a struggle.

Piercing the Allied lines at Lille, where, however, fortifications still seem to hold out, permitted the Germans to make two pockets out of the big one. The smaller of these, south of Lille, is square with the sides between nine and twelve miles long, and inside this narrow space are compressed the French divisions that only a few days ago tried to break the strong German hold at Valenciennes, as well as British contingents that figured in desperate resistance in the sector between Arras and Cambrai.

Refugees Also in Trap

Hemmed in with these troops is an incalculable number of refugees and other civilians, who are exposed to bombs and shell fire on the same terms as the soldiers fighting one another in this area.

The larger northern pocket reaches from Lille to the sea, and although it is some thirty miles wide the situation of the troops enclosed in it appears to be hardly more enviable than that of their comrades surrounded to the south. They are being hard pressed on three sides by withering German fire as well as from the air.

Their only chance of retreat, should they choose this way out, seems to be the narrow strip of coast between Dunkerque and Nieuport, but the Germans are said to be continuously shelling and bombing this district, making an exit, even if protected by Allied warships, seem most difficult.

Crowded together in an area bounded by Dixmude, Ypres—which the Germans claim to have taken by storm tonight—Armentières, Bailleul and Bergues, remnants of the British Expeditionary Force and whatever French and Belgians remain thereabout appear to have a choice only between death or surrender.

The situation up there, according to latest reports received in Berlin, indicates that the Allies have chosen to fight to the last. The Germans stand before Dixmude, where the British are holding them, and a similarly bitter struggle is raging at

Continued on Page Four

The International Situation

On the Battle Fronts

The Battle of Flanders became yesterday a wholly rear-guard action, with the Allies trying to evacuate as many as possible of the troops caught in the German pocket. The trapped men fought on "desperately but not despairingly," Paris reported. [Page 1.]

The port of Dunkerque was still in Allied hands (although the Germans reported its embarkation area in ruins), as was Nieuport, just above the Belgian border. Ships were said to be waiting at the coast to take off the men who could get to them, although how they stayed afloat in the torrent of German bombing seemed a mystery. The British and French fleets were furiously bombarding German forces on the Channel, hoping to cover the withdrawal. The task of evacuation was made doubly difficult by a German force that, Paris reported, had straddled the Franco-Belgian border near Cassel and Mount Kemmel. The French said that defense floodgates had been opened, inundating part of the area west of the Yser. On other fronts the French asserted that they had eliminated a German bridgehead on the Somme west of Amiens, and had repulsed a German thrust near Rethel, on the left flank of the invaders. [Included in the foregoing.]

The desperate situation of the Allied army of the north was made evident by Berlin dispatches telling of the success of the German effort to cut the opposing forces in two. The invaders drove a wedge between the two Allied wings to the north of Lille. Thus there are now two pockets; the forces south of Lille are completely surrounded, in a square-shaped area whose sides measure only nine to twelve miles. The pocket above Lille was greatly reduced by German advances pressing down from the north and up from the south. [Page 1.]

Early this morning shattered remnants of the British Expeditionary Force began arriving at British ports. Most of them were wounded. To the survivors still in Flanders King George sent a message saying they had displayed "gallantry that has never been surpassed in the annals of the British Army." [Page 1.]

The Allies recorded a victory in Norway. They took Narvik, and the Germans admitted its loss. The British said their warships had sunk seven German troop transports in the Narvik area in the last three days. [Page 1.]

Repercussions Elsewhere

Britain took drastic measures to guard against possible fifth column activities on the part of aliens. Beginning June 3, all aliens must be in their "ordinary place of residence" from 10:30 P. M. to 6 A. M.; they are forbidden to own bicycles, boats or aircraft without special permission. [Page 3.]

Italy, by decreeing an end to import and foreign currency permits, cut herself off from the world commercially, except for her barter arrangements. And even they have ceased to mean anything, as Italian vessels no longer are being sent abroad for cargoes. The new regulations gave the strongest indication yet of Italy's intention to join Germany in the field soon. [Page 1.]

Because Russia had refused to accept Sir Stafford Cripps, Left-Wing Labor member of the British Parliament, as a "special trade envoy," London conferred Ambassadorial status on him. Sir Stafford is in Athens, en route to Moscow. With offers of improved trade with Britain, he will seek to woo Russia away from Germany. [Page 4.]

The Nazi fifth-column technique stirred fears in South America. Uruguay's Congress received from President Baldomir two bills, one of which would provide for rearmament, the other modifying the Constitution to deny the right of assembly to anti-democratic organizations with foreign connections. [Page 1.]

What has happened in Flanders impelled a reappraisal in Washington of American defense plans, with the result that President Roosevelt decided to ask Congress for $750,000,000 (in addition to the $3,300,000,000 already projected) to be used to buy 3,000 pursuit and bombing planes, 1,500 tanks, 500 heavy howitzers and at least $20,000,000 in aerial bombs. [Page 1.] The Senate Naval Affairs Committee, recommending House-adopted bills to speed air and naval preparedness, said the country's defense plans must be based on the possibility of defeat for the Allies. [Page 9.]

ALLIES GET NARVIK IN LAND-SEA FIGHT

Warships Support Troops in Final Thrust From Beis and Rombaks Fjords

By JAMES MacDONALD
Special Cable to THE NEW YORK TIMES.

LONDON, May 29—Narvik, Norway's important iron ore port, the prize of an unrelenting struggle ever since Germany invaded Norway on April 9, has been captured by Allied forces, the War Office and Admiralty announced in a joint communiqué today. The communiqué also announced the capture of Fagernaes, on the shore of Narvik Harbor, and Forsneset, five miles east of Narvik on the railway line over which Swedish iron ore reaches Narvik for shipment to Germany.

Fierce fighting by Norwegian, French, British and Polish forces continues in the district. An unofficial report received here today said British naval forces had sunk seven German troop transports in Narvik waters since Sunday.

British warships are reported high up in Rombaks Fjord, shelling German positions on the Ofoten railway. In a narrow part of the fjord the Germans have sunk four ships in an attempt to block off the British naval vessels.

Other reports reaching London today said German planes had raided Bodoe, at the entrance to Vest Fjord, about ninety miles south of Narvik, last evening, dropping 200 bombs and machine-gunning the town. Of the population of 6,000, it is said at least 5,000 are now

Continued on Page Five

HARRIED B. E. F. MEN ARRIVING IN BRITAIN

Many of Wounded Had to Wade Out to Boats Under Constant Fire of German Forces

By The United Press.

LONDON, Thursday, May 30—Shattered remnants of the British Expeditionary Force—blood-stained, muddy and walking like men asleep—began arriving in British ports early today.

Most of the first arrivals were wounded. They described a constant, pitiless German bombing and strafing bombardment of the French ports from which Viscount Gort is attempting to save his trapped divisions.

They said the shattered British forces were "sliding off a stretch of coast thirty miles long."

German bombs rained down continually, even on hospital ships, they said. Quays and harbor works of the French ports were under terrific German air attack, which went on all through last night.

Allied warships and the Royal Air Force worked and fought like beavers to aid the rescue of the battered armies of Flanders whose fate was teetered on the Channel's brink. Under a screen of intense curtain fire from long-range naval guns, the B. E. F. was backing out through the Dunkerque area.

Continued on Page Five

Dispatches from Europe and the Far East are subject to censorship at the source.

COAST FIGHT RAGES

Communications Lines and Bases Bombarded Constantly by Nazis

DUNKERQUE SHELLED

Allies Inflicting Heavy Losses as They Battle in Rear-Guard Actions

By G. H. ARCHAMBAULT
Wireless to THE NEW YORK TIMES.

PARIS, May 29—The full import of the Belgian defection during the course of the battle in Flanders may be gathered from the indication given tonight by a spokesman for the General Staff that King Leopold's army represented about half the Allies' forces engaged on that front.

French and British in that area continue to fight desperately, though not despairingly yet, with the knowledge that at present at least little help can be given them. Their valor is described as very comforting in the circumstances, and it is added that whatever happens their honor will be safe.

Breaking the anonymity rule that has prevailed hitherto, it is announced this evening that, under General Georges Maurice Jean Blanchard's direction, General René-Jacques-Adolf Prioux is striving to fight his way to the coast in the general direction of Dunkerque, where Vice Admiral Jean Marie Abrial of the French Navy is cooperating and is holding that base, where he has organized a service of supplies with vessels of all kinds of tonnage.

Prioux a Cavalry Man

General Prioux was a corps commander at the beginning of the war; he is sixty-one years of age and comes from the cavalry arm.

No one has yet come from that inferno in Flanders to describe the scene; doubtless it baffles the imagination. For the battle is being waged on land, in the air, on the sea and under the sea. Every engine of death yet devised by man is in action and the fight never ceases day or night. Nor is it confined to the actual battlefield. All bases, all lines of communication are bombed continually by the Germans, with the Germans concentrating a great effort on Dunkerque.

The communiqué issued from French General Headquarters this morning said that "information from accurate sources warrants the affirmation that the losses suffered by the Germans in the engagements yesterday and last night were particularly high."

The French and British are fighting mostly rear-guard actions against very superior numbers, but whenever any unit finds itself in approximately equal strength it counter-attacks "to progress over the enemy dead."

Position Very Critical

Nevertheless despite heroic deeds it cannot be gainsaid that the position of the Allied division is very critical.

The exact position of General Blanchard's forces is not known; his front in any case must be very fluid. Doubtless he has shortened his lines in order to constitute a sort of mobile fortress moving toward the sea and fighting every inch of the way. The tragic aspect of his situation lies in the fact that the prime task of Leopold's army was to cover the coast.

It is revealed today in this connection that it was at the Belgian King's repeated insistence that the Allies took up positions on the Scheldt to protect Antwerp and also that the order to retreat was deferred until May 15, although the Allied High Command had urged withdrawal on the eleventh or twelfth.

There is confirmation today of the indication given yesterday in these dispatches that before the capitulation there were French detachments between the Belgians and the sea. It is hoped that though relatively small they may have acted effectively along the coast. It is believed, moreover, that it has been possible to flood part of the country west of the Yser River. Water lines of this sort proved of great value in the last war in this very region.

On the coast the Allies have lost Ostend. They hold Nieuport and

Continued on Page Two

"All the News That's Fit to Print."

The New York Times.

LATE CITY EDITION
Cloudy with showers and little change in temperature today and tomorrow.
Temperatures Yesterday—Max., 65; Min., 57

Copyright, 1940, by The New York Times Company.

VOL. LXXXIX..No. 30,089. Entered as Second-Class Matter, Postoffice, New York, N. Y. NEW YORK, TUESDAY, JUNE 11, 1940. THREE CENTS NEW YORK CITY and Vicinity | FOUR CENTS Elsewhere Except in 7th and 8th Postal Zones.

ITALY AT WAR, READY TO ATTACK; STAB IN BACK, SAYS ROOSEVELT; GOVERNMENT HAS LEFT PARIS

NAZIS NEAR PARIS

Units Reported to Have Broken Through Lines to West of Capital

SEINE RIVER CROSSED

3 Columns Branch Out From Soissons—Enemy Held, French State

By The Associated Press.

PARIS, June 10—Marauding German tanks were reported tonight to have reached the Paris region itself as the government left the capital.

While some German armored advance guards were said to have penetrated to the environs of Paris in isolated raids through the French lines, the main front was about thirty-five miles west and northeast of the capital. Although steadily approaching, the battle's roar still could not be heard here.

[The German High Command has no knowledge that Nazi tank units have reached the Paris region, The United Press reported.]

The battle, which had been waged heretofore on familiar World War territory for the most part, swung into virgin soil as the Germans advanced west of Paris.

In the triangle bounded by Amiens on the Somme, Rouen, seventy miles west of Paris on the Seine, and Vernon, forty miles west on the Seine, the Germans redoubled their attacks, crossing the river at several points. An armored column, which crossed the Bresle last week, led the assault.

The French took their main stand west of Paris all along the Seine in an effort to prevent the Germans from effecting further passages and taking the capital from the rear.

In the central sector of the Oise Valley, directly north of Paris where the Germans had suffered tremendous losses, they held back their infantry and sent out dive bombers in an effort to break down French resistance.

They broadened their salient, however, farther east, where they had crossed the Aisne. Three columns fanned out from Soissons through La Ferte Milon and Fere en Tardenois and toward Fismes.

Hold Firm on East Flank

They were just north of Chateau-Thierry and the Marne, where they were stopped in their 1918 thrust by Americans fighting with the French.

On the east flank, where the French have been holding firm, fresh German infantry, tanks and planes battered the French lines, but with small gains.

But France, besieged on two sides by Germans driving on Paris from the north and the Italians entering the war on the south, proclaimed her grim determination to carry on the fight.

The main combats were centered in the Seine Valley to the west of Paris, with the High Command declaring that some German elements had crossed the Seine River at certain points, and in the Ourcq River Valley to the northeast of the capital.

The communiqué, however, said the "enemy is held everywhere by vigorous counter-attacks."

The French communiqué was filed from Paris, but was issued "Somewhere in France." The regular press conference of the War Office was not held this morning, as only a few attachés were in the office.

The High Command reported that the German break-through to the Seine resulted from increased pressure applied by the Nazis between the route from Amiens to Rouen and from Amiens to Vernon as far as the lower Seine.

In the other principal area of combat, east of the Oise River, German columns coming down from the region of Soissons have resumed their attack toward the Ourcq River.

The German offensive in the

Continued on Page Two

The International Situation

On the Battle Fronts

Italian guns will speak today in Europe. Italy's declaration of war against France and Britain became effective at 12:01 A. M., Rome time. Before 100,000 men and women, packed in the Piazza Venezia and near-by streets, Premier Mussolini yesterday announced his decision. It was war against "the plutocratic and reactionary democracies of the West." For the present that does not include the United States, but Rome reports that few Italians, from Signor Mussolini down, believe they will see the end of this war without having America against them.

The Italian Premier specifically excluded Turkey, Switzerland, Yugoslavia, Greece and Egypt from his military designs. Rome hoped Turkey would fail to keep her agreement to support the Allies in a Mediterranean war.

Demonstrators in Rome carried placards naming Italian objectives in the war—Tunisia, Jibuti, Corsica, Suez, Malta, Cyprus. There were reports that action against some of these places already had started. But Rome was convinced that nothing big would get under way until today. [All the foregoing, Page 1, Column 8.]

The sixth day of the Battle of France brought the German invaders still closer to Paris; at one point—south of Beauvais—they were said to be within twenty-five or thirty miles of their goal. On the French left wing the Germans crossed the Seine at several points in a dangerous advance that threatened to envelop the capital. In the center, they pushed through to the Ourcq Valley, a movement that similarly threatened to flank Reims. On the French right wing the German pressure was furiously increased; but the French said no great gains had resulted. Information from the French side was less complete than usual because the government press bureau was evacuated from Paris and had not yet established a stable headquarters. [Page 1, Column 1.]

The French Government moved, apparently to the neighborhood of Tours. An exodus of civilians from Paris got under way. [Page 1, Column 2.]

Berlin analyzed the front thus: A semicircle had been thrown around Paris, from which three wedges were being driven into the defense lines. The first, in the lower Seine Valley, succeeded in cutting off the extreme left of the French Army, which can now be pushed to the coast. The second was progressing toward the Marne from the Aisne below Soissons. The third, on the French right, had pierced the Aisne and was headed toward Reims. [Page 1, Column 5.]

London admitted the loss of the airplane carrier Glorious, two destroyers, a transport and an oil tanker—totaling 50,706 tons—in an engagement in the North Sea. King Haakon of Norway arrived in Britain with his government. Some Norwegian troops also were carried off and will continue the war on the Western Front. [Page 16, Column 3.]

Repercussions Elsewhere

President Roosevelt, in a broadcast speech, termed Italy's entry into the war a threat to the American way of life. "The hand that held the dagger has struck it into the back of its neighbor," he said. Declaring it an "obvious delusion that we of the United States can safely permit the United States to become a lone island in a world dominated by the philosophy of force," he advocated all possible material aid to the Allies. [Page 1, Column 4.]

The Canadian Parliament declared war against Italy; Prime Minister Mackenzie King denounced Premier Mussolini as "a carrion bird waiting for brave men to die." [Page 4, Column 5.]

Premier Reynaud, broadcasting to the French people after Italy's announcement, said France had won out over greater difficulties in the past. He asserted France always had been willing to negotiate Italian demands peaceably. [Page 12, Column 1.]

Berlin, jubilant over the entry of the Italians, expressed the belief that Premier Mussolini's military effort would be concentrated in the Mediterranean. It was said that no immediate Italian land attack on France was expected. [Page 5, Column 1.]

Switzerland reported much military activity, but no rumble of guns, in mountain passes between France and Italy. The Swiss were concerned about rumors that there were new German troop concentrations on the country's northern frontier. [Page 5, Column 5.]

Turkey stood ready to fulfill her engagements to the Allies under the mutual-assistance pact of last October. It was believed that the first step, once Italy made that pact operative by an aggressive move in the Mediterranean, would be the placing of Turkish ports and air fields at the disposal of the Allies. [Page 1, Column 7.]

Belgrade heard reports that the Italians had landed troops and much mechanized equipment at the Italian-owned port of Zara, which is on the Yugoslav coast, and on the Italian-owned island of Lagosta, nearby. [Page 1, Column 6.]

OUR HELP PLEDGED

President Offers Our Full Material Aid to Allies' Cause

AMERICA IN DANGER

Fate Hangs on Training and Arms, He Says at Charlottesville

The text of the President's speech will be found on Page 6.

By FELIX BELAIR Jr.

Special to THE NEW YORK TIMES.

CHARLOTTESVILLE, Va., June 10—"On this 10th day of June, 1940, the hand that held the dagger has struck it into the back of its neighbor." In these words tonight President Roosevelt condemned the decision of Premier Mussolini which took Italy into the war on the side of Germany.

The remark was interpolated by the President in an address at the graduation exercises of the University of Virginia here. There could be no missing the depth of his feeling, since he put into the words all the emphasis at his command.

Italy's intervention was denounced furthermore as a definite threat to the way of life and the trade and commerce of the Americas. This government, he said, would give all material aid to France and Great Britain as "opponents of force."

The Chief Executive of the United States spoke to the nation and to the world only a few hours after Premier Mussolini announced his decision to join hands with Chancellor Hitler and unleashed his fascist legions against France and Great Britain. More details were revealed by Mr. Roosevelt of his correspondence with the Italian dictator in an effort to keep Italy at peace and to prevent the spread of war to the Mediterranean basin.

"To the Regret of Humanity"

"Unfortunately—unfortunately, to the regret of all of us and to the regret of humanity—the chief of the Italian Government was unwilling to accept the procedure suggested, and he has made no counter proposal," the President said.

And a moment later:

"The Government of Italy has now chosen to preserve what it terms its freedom of action and to fulfill what it states are its promises to Germany. In so doing it has manifested disregard for the rights and security of other nations, disregard for the lives of the peoples of those nations which are directly threatened by the spread of this war, and has evidenced its unwillingness to find the means, through pacific negotiation for the satisfaction of what it believes are its legitimate aspirations."

The President bespoke the prayers and hopes of this nation for those peoples beyond the seas who were battling for their freedom.

"In our American unity," he

Continued on Page Six

Nazi Tide Laps at Paris as Italy Joins War

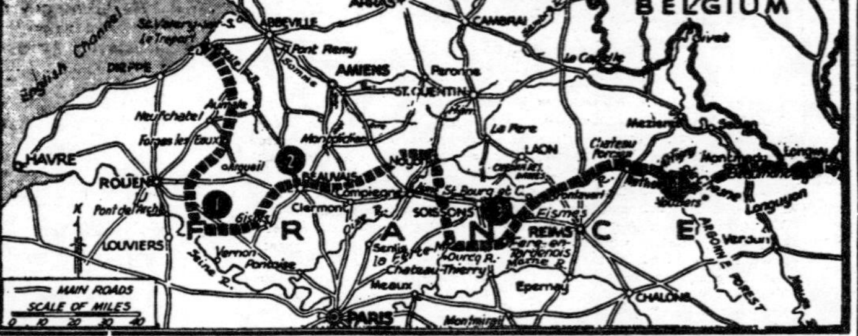

On the western end of the line the Germans pushed a wedge to the Seine southeast of Rouen (1) and struck mighty blows in the region of Beauvais (2). In the center they reached the Ourcq River below Soissons (3). To the east they crossed the Aisne at two points near Vouziers (4).

Italy's announcement of her entry into the war was accompanied by no attack anywhere. One report had Italian troops invading the French Riviera (1), but this was unsupported. Rome's troops landed at two Italian-owned points on the Yugoslav coast: Zara (2) and Lagosta (3). In Albania (4) Italian military preparations were accelerated.

DUCE GIVES SIGNAL

Announces War on the 'Plutocratic' Nations of the West

ASSURES 5 NEUTRALS

Bid Is Made to Russia, But Rome Has No Pledge of Aid

'Hostilities' Are Reported

"Hostilities were started four hours ago, Central European time," Radio Roma, the official Italian short-wave radio, said last night at 11 o'clock Eastern daylight time in a broadcast recorded by Columbia Broadcasting System's short-wave listening station.

"The first Italian war bulletin is expected to be issued within a few hours."

At 2:18 A. M. today, however, the official British wireless said that "there have been no reports as yet of any engagements growing out of Italy's entrance into the war," Columbia's listening station reported.

By HERBERT L. MATTHEWS

By Telephone to THE NEW YORK TIMES.

ROME, Tuesday, June 11—Italy declared war on Great Britain and France yesterday afternoon, to take effect at one minute past midnight. The land, air and sea forces of the Italian Empire were already in motion.

It is a war, as Premier Benito Mussolini announced to the people from his balcony at the Palazzo Venezia at 6 in the evening, against the "plutocratic and reactionary democracies of the West." For the moment that does not include the United States, but few Italians believe that they will see the war to a finish without having the Americans against them.

Signor Mussolini expressly excluded Turkey, Switzerland, Yugoslavia, Greece and Egypt as enemies unless they attacked Italy or the Italian possessions.

Turkey provides the burning question of the day. Italians are absolutely convinced that the Turks will not move against them and will not honor their agreement with the Allies. It is hoped to confine Italian activity to France, Great Britain and the Mediterranean and to keep the Balkans tranquil. If that can be done, Italians think, the Turks will remain quiet.

Soviet Action Discounted

Russia has washed her hands of the struggle. The Italians know that any disturbance in the Balkans will immediately bring her in; but as long as the struggle is confined to the west and south the Soviet will do nothing either to hinder or help. This was told to your correspondent a few hours ago by a very authoritative source.

It was emphasized there were no engagements about furnishing material or anything else, nor any threats or promises.

The Italian Ambassador, Augusto Rosso, left in the morning for Moscow and Ivan Gorelkin, Soviet Ambassador, is coming back to Rome, thus ending a long period without such representation. The Italians were anxious to restore full diplomatic relations in this critical period, according to this writer's informant, and the Russians agreed, but without compromising themselves.

It thus appears that Premier Mussolini has embarked on this dangerous venture without really knowing what Soviet Russia will do in the long run.

President Roosevelt's speech clearly has come too late. There was nothing that the United States could do to halt this conflict, the Italians say. Whatever brake Mr. Roosevelt may have exercised was overcome by the momentum of the whole Fascist policy. Once it was set in motion, nothing could stop it.

The Italians do not believe that the United States can affect the issue, whatever it does. They see

Continued on Page Four

FRENCH MINISTRIES MOVED SOUTHWARD

Tours Is Believed New Capital, but Reynaud Goes to Army —No Civilian Panic

By The Associated Press.

PARIS, June 10—The French Government left Paris tonight.

"Paul Reynaud, Premier, has gone with the armies," said a communiqué, which also declared:

"The High Command asked the Ministers to effect their withdrawal to the provinces in conformity with established dispositions. This withdrawal has been effected."

The announcement of the departure of the Ministers was made only after they were safely installed "somewhere in France" in the southern provinces.

The government transfer at General Maxime Weygand's request was approved last night at a Cabinet meeting.

Under cover of darkness the Ministers drove to their new offices

Continued on Page Ten

BRITISH NAVY GUNS HAMMER AT NAZIS

Shelling From Sea, Rushing of Troops and Planes Mark London's Share in Battle

By HAROLD DENNY

Special Cable to THE NEW YORK TIMES.

LONDON, June 10—Britain was rushing all available forces today into the battle in France, which was officially called here the "Battle of Paris and London" because of the Nazi threat to England. This reinforcement across the English Channel will continue, it was stated, "despite the imminent danger of German invasion of the United Kingdom."

The guns of British warships pounded the Germans to support Allied troops near the coast.

"Important contingents" of new troops have already gone to France, it was announced.

Even closer cooperation of the

Continued on Page Twelve

La Guardia Warns of Strict Neutrality Here; Consuls Told to 'Adhere to Consular Duties'

Mayor La Guardia went on the air over WNYC, the city broadcasting station, yesterday afternoon with a strong plea to the million persons of Italian blood in this city to preserve strict neutrality in the face of Italy's declaration of war.

Moving with characteristic rapidity, the Mayor telephoned the city broadcasting studio in the New York City Building at the World's Fair and said he would be on the air ten minutes later. He thought over the message he wanted to deliver while driving over from the World's Fair City Hall, and was prepared to speak immediately upon his arrival. Meantime, Morris S. Novik, director of the station, had made arrangements to rebroadcast the Mayor's talk over five commercial stations at intervals later in the day.

Speaking slowly and impressively, the Mayor stated his policy that the European war must be fought on the battlefields of Europe and not on the sidewalks of New York.

Recalling his war service as an ally of the Italian forces in Italy, the Mayor said he fully realized that the Italian entry into the war on the opposite side must be as painful to others of Italian blood as it was to him. Nevertheless, he insisted that the national policy of neutrality must be observed in the city. While he pledged full protection to consular officers of various European governments in the city, the Mayor made clear that these officials must stay within the bounds of their consular duties.

The Mayor's speech follows:

This is F. H. La Guardia, Mayor of the City of New York, talking. On Sept. 3, 1939, when the Nazi

Continued on Page Eight

NAZIS CLAIM BREAK IN SUPPLY ARTERY

Paris Cut Off From Havre by Thrust to Seine East of Rouen, Berlin Says

By C. BROOKS PETERS

Wireless to THE NEW YORK TIMES.

BERLIN, June 10—German forces in Northern France were fighting tonight to shorten the radius of a semicircle they are drawing about Paris, according to reports received here. Apparently they are attempting to drive three wedges into the remaining French territory north of the capital.

The first is on the Germans' extreme right wing, which is reported to have reached the lower Seine east of Rouen and therewith cuts off Paris from Havre. Mass tank formations, assisted by light motorized units, are claimed here to have made more than a sixty-mile ad-

Continued on Page Eleven

Three Italian Freighters Are Scuttled by Crews

By The Associated Press.

LA LINEA, Spain, Tuesday, June 11—Two Italian merchant ships, the 10,000-ton Chelina and the 2,000-ton Numbolia, were scuttled by their crews in Gibraltar waters late yesterday [Monday] when their crews heard the radio news that Italy had gone to war.

RIMOUSKI, Que., June 10 (UP)—The 3,921-ton Italian freighter Capo Noli was set afire by her crew tonight as she proceeded down the St. Lawrence, but the scuttling attempt failed.

The Marine Department said the Canadian pilot grounded the freighter near the Father Point pilot station. A naval control boat extinguished the flames.

The government salvage boat Lord Strathcona left Quebec tonight for the site with a large derrick in tow. The Capo Noli will be taken over by the Canadian Government and her crew probably will be interned.

TURKEY PREPARES UNDER ALLIED PACT

Partial Mobilization Expected Today—Troops Are on Move —Precautions in Balkans

By J. W. KERNICK

Special Cable to THE NEW YORK TIMES.

ISTANBUL, Turkey, June 10—Turkey, speeding her military preparations as a result of Italy's entry into the war, stood ready tonight to fulfill her obligations under her mutual-assistance agreement with Britain and France.

That accord, concluded last October, stipulates that Turkey will lend the Allies every assistance in her power in the event of hostilities in the Mediterranean as a result of aggressive action by a European power. Hence Turkish aid can be invoked as soon as the first shot is fired.

The Italian action has already resulted in the calling of several classes to the colors by the Turkish Government. It is believed that the next move will be to place ports and airfields at the disposal of the Allies.

[The Turkish Cabinet met last night to consider the question of war or peace, The Associated Press reported, but it was believed that Turkey's entrance into the war would be by gradual steps, not immediately.]

Italy's declaration of war caused neither surprise nor excitement in Turkey. The Turks had suspected for some time and lately became certain that Premier Mussolini could not forever remain an onlooker while Chancellor Hitler marched.

Premier Mussolini's assurances that he did not intend to attack Yugoslavia, Turkey, Greece, Switz-

Continued on Page Two

ITALIANS REPORTED ON YUGOSLAV COAST

Said to Have Landed at Two Places Controlled by Rome— Mass on Greek Border

By The United Press.

BELGRADE, Yugoslavia, Tuesday, June 11—Large numbers of Italian troops were reported early today to have been landed along the Yugoslav coast at two Italian points as the Yugoslav Government prepared to fight in defense of its territory if necessary.

[It was reported from Berlin yesterday that Italian forces had invaded France through the Riviera, but this was denied in Rome, and German military quarters said later that they had no knowledge of any such movement.]

Reports from Split on the Adriatic coast said that large forces of Italian troops had been landed at

Continued on Page Four

Dispatches from Europe and the Far East are subject to censorship at the source.

"All the News That's Fit to Print."

The New York Times.

LATE CITY EDITION
Fair and cooler today and tonight. Tomorrow fair with slowly rising temperatures.
Temperatures Yesterday—Max., 89; Min., 68

Copyright, 1940, by The New York Times Company.

VOL. LXXXIX No. 30,092. Entered as Second-Class Matter, Postoffice, New York, N. Y. NEW YORK, FRIDAY, JUNE 14, 1940. THREE CENTS NEW YORK CITY and Vicinity | FOUR CENTS Elsewhere Except in 7th and 8th Postal Zones.

BULLITT REPORTS NAZIS INSIDE PARIS GATES; REYNAUD ASKS U. S. FOR 'CLOUDS OF PLANES'; BRITISH GIVE FRENCH NEW PLEDGE, RUSH AID

CONGRESS TO STAY IN CAPITAL IN FEAR OF NEW WAR CRISIS

Democratic Leaders Abandon Plans to Adjourn—Recess Is Considered Instead

SENATE VOTES WAR RELIEF

Approves $50,000,000 Fund—Tax Bill Pushed—Industry Coordination Speeded

By TURNER CATLEDGE
Special to THE NEW YORK TIMES.

WASHINGTON, June 13—The drive to adjourn Congress by June 22 was abandoned today by the Democratic leadership as growing apprehension over the fast-spreading war in Europe increased the demands that the legislative branch remain at the capital to meet new emergencies that might arise.

A proposal to recess during political conventions, possibly from June 22 to Aug. 1, was being considered favorably by the leaders, but a final decision will be dictated largely by influences originating overseas.

Collapse of adjournment plans featured a series of Washington developments in foreign affairs and national defense, chief among them being:

Publication by the White House of an appeal from Premier Reynaud of France to President Roosevelt, asking all possible American aid to the Allies short of an expeditionary force, and pledging France to continue its fight against Germany even if it had to do so eventually from its American possessions.

Introduction in the House by Representative Celler of New York of a bill repealing the Neutrality Act.

Monroe Doctrine Move Speeded

Granting of a special order by the Rules Committee for early consideration in the House of the Pittman-Bloom resolution putting the world on notice that this country will never recognize the change of sovereignty among European powers of territory in the Western Hemisphere.

Passage by the House of a bill instructing the Attorney General to deport Harry Bridges, a native of Australia and West Coast C. I. O. leader, "whose presence in this country the Congress deems hurtful."

Announcement by Finland, through its Minister, that she would pay the June 15 installment on her old Allied war debt, as usual.

Acceleration of activity in the process of coordinating the elements involved in the new national defense program, under the guidance of the National Defense Advisory Commission.

Announcement by Paul V. McNutt, Federal Security Administrator, that no general labor shortage exists at present, but that efforts will be necessary to meet temporary gaps in specialized skills needed in defense preparations.

Unanimous approval by the Senate of the $50,000,000 war relief fund requested by President Roosevelt.

Tax Revision Gains Force

The most immediate reaction to the abandonment of adjournment of plans was new vigor behind the movement for a more fundamental revision of the tax laws, as a substitute for the $1,004,000,000 Defense Financing Bill already passed by the House and now pending in the Senate.

At the second day's hearing on the tax measure before the Finance Committee Senators asked Treasury officials for estimates on levies which if adopted would increase the annual yield of the bill by upward of $300,000,000.

These requests indicated probable attempts to broaden the income tax base still further by lowering personal exemptions for married persons from $2,500 to $1,800, instead of $2,000; revival of the World War tax of one cent a bottle on soft drinks; an increase in the Federal gasoline tax from 1 to 2 cents a gallon, instead of 1½ as carried in the House bill, and generalization of the impost on theatre

Continued on Page Thirteen

French Fight With No Relief And No Sleep, 24 Hours a Day

Some Soldiers Have Been in the Thick of It for Ten Days With No Let-Up—Losses Are Admittedly Serious

Wireless to THE NEW YORK TIMES.

TOURS, France, June 13—Following Premier Paul Reynaud's letter to President Roosevelt, if the average French soldier had read Shakespeare he would thus paraphrase King Henry V's famous monologue: "You gentlemen of America, now abed, may think yourselves accursed if you do not help us with material to fight here."

But certainly he would not have time to describe the nature of that fighting.

From accounts reaching here, only veterans of the last war can conceive the conditions. On some portions of the front men have been in the thick of it for ten days and ten nights with no prospect of being relieved, no possibility of injecting new units into the firing line, because the actions are rearguard actions, no let-up in the twenty-four hours, no rest, no sleep and few occasions to eat or drink—men with a ten-day growth of beard, unwashed, unkempt, grimy, many bleeding from minor wounds, but still fighting.

Divisions are reduced to even smaller proportions. An officer of the General Staff today admitted that the French losses are serious, but he added that notwithstanding this fact small individual units continue to attack the Germans on their own initiative without waiting for orders.

Answering a query from this correspondent, the officer indicated that by small units he meant battalions and companies — even platoons. This sufficiently described the undaunted spirit of the French soldier in this emergency.

When a second lieutenant or a first sergeant charges into the Nazi masses at the head of some hundred men or so there can be no greater example of courage or devotion. For the Germans they thus attack have never been in the line more than three or four days on end—the German numerical superiority permits regular relief of divisions.

It is scarcely conceivable that such men could ever be beaten but there comes a time when even they cannot continue to face odds rising in some places to as much as ten to one.

For be it remembered that the German soldier is a good fighter, as the French have always recognized; indeed, that very fact increases their valor. The same view does not hold good of the Italians. The average French soldier has nothing but contempt for Premier Mussolini's troops. It has been instilled in their minds by the stories of veterans who crossed the Alps to retrieve the rout from the Piave—for despite official euphemisms it was indeed a rout.

Signor Mussolini's action has increased that contempt a hundredfold. If the Italians ever decide to pit their infantry against the French they will receive a taste of their metal from the very first minute.

ITALIAN CONSULATE CHARGED WITH PLOT

Police Documents Report Official Guidance of Fascist Propaganda Here

The Italian Consulate General in New York, working under orders from Mussolini, according to documents disclosed yesterday, is seeking to promote fascism in this country by ideological propaganda in schools, newspapers, magazines and through radio. A campaign to enroll members in fascist and profascist organizations of various kinds, open and camouflaged, is being conducted as part of the consuls' activities, the document charged.

Police Commissioner Valentine distributed yesterday morning copies of a twenty-five-page mimeographed confidential memorandum to the borough commanders and inspectors of the criminal alien, sabotage and bomb squads. The distribution, with instructions to act and make arrests wherever and whenever necessary, was made at a conference of police officials in the office of Assistant Chief Inspector John J. Ryan at Police Headquarters, immediately after the regular line-up. Inspector Ryan warned each of his subordinates against making the contents of the memorandum public. Severe penalties, he said, would result from disobedience of instructions.

Part of Nation-Wide Drive

The latest step to combat subversive activities was taken at the request of the Federal authorities and was approved by the Mayor. Police action here was said to be part of a nation-wide drive to check anti-national defense moves.

The memorandum gave in detail the results of a lengthy investigation into Fascist activities carried on in this city and elsewhere. According to the authorities, these activities were carried on with the approval of the Italian Consulate officers, the latter working under the mantle of "diplomatic immunity."

It was said that the investigators were able to obtain copies of governmental instructions to the consulate on the dissemination of propaganda and through what channels. Attachés of the consulate, and through them, various Italian organizations, each named in the memorandum, were instructed to preach fascism, enlist all possible aid for it, and try as effec-

Continued on Page Ten

NAZI BODY DISBANDS AS URUGUAY ACTS

Reich Legation Takes Over the Party's Property—Trick to Balk Inquiry Seen

By JOHN W. WHITE
Wireless to THE NEW YORK TIMES.

MONTEVIDEO, Uruguay, June 13—The German Minister, Otto Langmann, informed Foreign Minister Alberto Guani last night that the Nazi party and German Labor Front in Uruguay had been dissolved, their leaders removed from office, membership cards recalled and organization property turned over to the German Legation.

This action was taken at a moment when a Congressional investigation had accumulated evidence on which it was proposed to ask the Prosecuting Attorney to dissolve German organizations and institute criminal proceedings against their leaders.

The German Minister's note makes no mention of a dozen lesser organizations affiliated with the Nazi party and the Labor Front. It is not known yet whether the dissolution extends to them.

The note was described by semi-official sources today as one of the most cynical actions ever taken by any foreign diplomat in Uruguay. It denied there were any secret groups in the Nazi organizations or any groups carrying on secret work and insisted that the Nazi party in Uruguay was concerned only with the social welfare of its members, who at no time mixed in the internal affairs of Uruguay.

Move Viewed as a Trick

The dissolution is regarded by the Uruguayan authorities as an attempt to save the Nazi leaders from criminal proceedings and place Nazi party property under diplomatic immunity to prevent further search and seizure by police operating under instructions from the Congressional investigating committee.

Members of the investigating committee said Herr Langmann's note would intensify rather than retard their investigation. They said the committee expected to present its report to the Chamber of Deputies Monday.

The German Minister's action was believed in well-informed circles to be an effort to save Julius Dalldorf, Nazi leader in Uruguay, from the consequences of any responsibility that the investigating com-

Continued on Page Eight

NEW GERMAN DRIVE

Chalons Reported Taken and Maginot Line Said to Be Endangered

FORTS HELD CUT OFF

Gains Between Argonne Wood and Meuse River Claimed in Berlin

By C. BROOKS PETERS
Wireless to THE NEW YORK TIMES.

BERLIN, June 13—After having made a gala appearance yesterday, the communiqué of the German High Command retired again today behind a curtain of generalities which shields the advances of the Reich's invading armies in France.

"On the entire attacking front," it declared, "operations are in rapid advance."

In Champagne, furthermore, it alleges that Châlons-sur-Marne was taken.

What has happened to Paris, twelve and a half miles from the point German divisions were reported to have reached about midnight Tuesday, remains, so far as Berlin is concerned, a mystery.

The only thing the Germans say about the French capital is that they hope the French do not make it a point of resistance in spite of the French declaration that it is an "open city." For, if they do, the Germans frankly point out, the Reich's armies will have no other choice but to break that resistance with all the means at their command. They do not fail, furthermore, to point to the example of Warsaw, to which might be added that of Rotterdam.

Peril to Maginot Line Seen

The capture of Châlons may be highly significant. For the armies of the German left wing appear to be moving in a southeasterly direction. At Châlons they have left behind them the forts of Verdun and Metz and are almost due west of Nancy.

With increased activity along the Upper Rhine front—between Karlsruhe and the Swiss border—and hints in military quarters here that a crossing of the Rhine in the face of the Maginot Line is not an impossible task for an army like Germany's, a large scale encirclement action by German forces seems a possibility, albeit an improbable one.

None the less, the Maginot Line appears threatened, at least from the rear, by the German advance in this sector. For railway connections between Metz, Nancy and Paris for all practical purposes, Germans declare, have been cut. In this sector, furthermore, where Germans claim they are "pursuing enemy troops," the High Command asserts that further ground has been won between the Argonne Forest and the Meuse River.

With the capture of Châlons, the Germans proudly point out they are leaving the battlefields of 1915 behind them and the High Command adds that already they have crossed the Marne in several places,

Continued on Page Five

URGENT PLEAS TO US

Premier Says Battle Is Lost and France Needs Quick Help to Go On

NOTE TO ROOSEVELT

White House Announces 'Everything Possible Is Being Done' to Aid

The texts of Premier Reynaud's appeals are printed on Page 6.

By P. J. PHILIP
Wireless to THE NEW YORK TIMES.

TOURS, France, June 13—In terribly significant phrases Premier Paul Reynaud made an urgent "final" appeal to the United States for "clouds" of war planes in a broadcast this evening and thereby he laid bare the tragic situation of France at the end of one month of Blitzkrieg.

This appeal was made a few hours after it had been disclosed that M. Reynaud had sent a pressing appeal to President Roosevelt on Monday, the day that Italy entered the war, for all help short of an expeditionary force.

The first of the Premier's significant phrases tonight was: "In losing this battle."

The second was: "Our struggle, which is every day more dreadful, has henceforth no more meaning unless in waging it we can see even from far away the growing hope of a common victory" of the democratic countries.

The third was: "We must prevent Hitler from suppressing the legal government and declaring to the world that France has no other government than one of these puppet governments in his pay like those he has tried to constitute in so many places."

Hope Wanes, Fear Rises

The whole story of this moment and of what may happen tomorrow was told in these three sentences by the Premier. The anguish of it all to those Frenchmen who were listening was indescribable. It was a story not only of a lost battle but of a waning hope and a growing fear.

M. Reynaud called on the United States to make good on its past history, for "despite our reverses, the power of the democracies remains immense."

"We have the right to hope that the day is nearing when all this power will be set to work," he declared. "That is why we hold hope in our hearts. It is why also that we have wishes that France should keep a free government and why we have left Paris.

"Wounded France has the right to turn toward the other democracies and say to them: 'I have claims on you.' No one who has any feeling of justice can say that she is wrong.

"But it is one thing to approve and another thing to act. We know what a high place ideals hold in the life of the great American people. Will they hesitate still to declare

Continued on Page Six

35,000-Ton Battleship Is Launched Here; North Carolina Held Warning to Dictators

Mud boiled from the bottom of Wallabout Basin yesterday; tugboat captains in the East River held down their whistles and 50,000 persons cheered as the battleship North Carolina slid down greased ways at the navy yard in Brooklyn to her first taste of the salt.

The 35,000-ton ship—newest and greatest of the world's ships of the battle line—was only about 75 per cent completed as to hull, less than that as to machinery, at her launching, and it will require more than a year to complete her. But there was grace in her long lines, and a tremendous impression of strength in the huge bulk of her, and, as Governor Clyde R. Hoey of North Carolina said, she "speaks a language that even a dictator can understand."

And it was evident, too, that she speaks a language that naval architects in all countries will some day understand, for there are many innovations in her construction—most of them still closely guarded naval secrets.

Secretary of the Navy Edison, Governor Hoey, whose daughter, Miss Isabel Young Hoey, broke a bottle of champagne against the ship's bulbous bow and said: "I christen thee North Carolina"; Mayor La Guardia, Lieut. Gen. Hugh A. Drum, a Congressional delegation from Washington and other distinguished military, civic and government officials attended the ceremonies.

Those ceremonies closely followed the brief, traditional pattern of the Navy, but they were preceded by almost twenty-four hours of hard work to make the ship ready for her launching. Several hundred men, under Captain C. A. Dunn

Continued on Page Fourteen

The International Situation

On the Battle Fronts

United States Ambassador Bullitt reported from Paris early today that the German Army was "inside the gates" of the city. While the French admitted the situation was desperate, General Weygand was said to have his armies still in order, although the pressure was increasing every hour. The French communiqué estimated the attacking enemy forces at 120 divisions—the maximum number the General Staff had foreseen as possible for the Germans to throw into the conflict. France saw the German drive as having a threefold object: to cut all communication between England and France, to encircle Paris for the moral effect, and to separate the forces along the Maginot Line from those in the West. [Page 1, Column 8.]

Premier Reynaud went on the air to tell the French nation he had sent a "final desperate appeal" for help to the United States. If France is to survive, he said, she must have "clouds of war planes from across the Atlantic to crush the evil force that dominates Europe." In Washington a formal statement from the White House said "everything possible" was being done to expedite war supplies. Previously, Secretary Early had said President Roosevelt felt he had fully answered the earlier appeal of the French Premier—forwarded June 10 but just made public—in his radio address of the same date pledging all material aid to the Allies and condemning Italy's war entrance. [Page 1, Column 5.]

The French sent word to Germany through Ambassador Bullitt that Paris was an open city and would not be defended. Whatever the city's fate, the American Ambassador will remain there with nine of his aides to represent his own country and the interests of whatever others request it, Washington said. [Page 5, Column 3.]

The Germans announced that their drive was continuing. The High Command communiqué did not go into much detail on the day's advances, but said the campaign was progressing on the whole front. Its most important claim was that the German Armies had captured Chalons-sur-Marne, threatening the Maginot Line from the rear. Other gains between the Argonne Wood and the Meuse were reported. [Page 1, Column 4.]

With the battle cry "Death or Victory!" Britain continued pouring every available man and piece of war equipment she could across the Channel. Many of those sent had been pulled out of home-defense positions. London said fresh British troops already had been thrown into the front lines along the Seine, heartening the French. [Page 1, Column 7.]

Rome said Italy's part in the war was still in its preliminary stages. Its communiqué reported air attacks on Toulon and Bizerte and the torpedoing of a cruiser and an oil tanker by a submarine, but no land actions. Allied attacks on Tobruk in Libya and several places in Ethiopia were acknowledged. The casualties in the Allied air attack on the "open city" of Turin were officially listed as fourteen dead and thirty-seven injured. [Page 1, Column 6.]

Repercussions Elsewhere

With the situation in Europe becoming more critical by the hour, plans to adjourn Congress by June 22 were abandoned. It appeared a recess would be taken for the two major political conventions. One of the considerations working against adjournment was said to be a growing desire for more fundamental tax revision to finance defense. Representative Celler of New York introduced a bill in the House to repeal the Neutrality Act. [Page 1, Column 1.]

Documents in the hands of the New York police are reported to show that Fascist propaganda in the United States is being promoted by the Italian Consul General in New York through Italian-American societies, being distributed in the schools, over the radio and through newspapers and periodicals. [Page 1, Column 2.]

Turkey, non-belligerent ally of France and Britain, signed a trade treaty with Germany providing for the exchange of goods to the value of 21,000,000 Turkish pounds [$14,280,000 at yesterday's New York quotations]. Some quarters interpreted this as indicating Turkey's intention not to enter the conflict. Others saw it as a necessity for Turkey because the spread of the war had shut off many sources of supply and markets. [Page 5, Column 1.]

ITALIANS INCENSED BY TURIN AIR RAID

Threaten Reprisal for Killing of 14—Toulon Is Bombed—Malta Raided 5 Times

By HERBERT L. MATTHEWS
By Telephone to THE NEW YORK TIMES.

ROME, June 13—The war today, as far as Italy is concerned, was still in its preliminary stage of attacks on naval and air bases all the way from Ethiopia to France. During last night's raids Italian planes attacked Toulon, France, and Bizerte, the French naval base in Tunisia. The British went for Tobruk, Italy's naval base in Libya.

This war will not be as slow in development as Germany's, but one must expect some days, if not weeks, to pass before the full weight of the forces involved is thrown into the balance.

The Allied air raid on Turin Tuesday night remains the most serious development of the conflict for Italy. Fourteen persons were killed, according to the official communiquè, and thirty-seven wounded.

This morning's war bulletin said, "The bombs that fell on Turin, which is an open city, caused little damage." Later a statement was issued listing the dead and wounded. It said that thirty bombs were dropped, of which ten failed to explode. Five of the bombs struck a market place, it was stated, and others fell in the streets.

Commenting on the statement,

Continued on Page Six

BRITISH VOW UNITY IN FRANCE'S CAUSE

Government Sends Message—Isles' Defenses Cut to Rush Men to the Seine

By The Associated Press.

LONDON, Friday, June 14—The British Government sent a message to the French Government today pledging that "Great Britain will continue to give the utmost aid in her power."

The message followed information last night that Britain was reducing her home defenses to rush all available men and weapons to the Seine River line in France.

To the French Government the message said:

"In this solemn hour for the Br-
ish and French nations and
cause of freedom and democracy
which they have vowed themse-
His Majesty's Government d-
to pay to the Government o-
French Republic the tribute
is due to the heroic fortitu-
constancy of the French ar-
battle against enormous

"Their efforts are worth-
most glorious traditions
and have inflicted deep
lasting injury upon th-
strength.

"Great Britain will
give the utmost aid
We take this oppor-
claiming the indisso-
our two peoples an-
pires.

"We cannot me-

Continued o-

PARIS IS OPEN CITY

French Rule Out Fight in Capital, but Carry on With Aid of British

FORCES STILL INTACT

But Germans Pour Over Bridgeheads in Effort to Hem in Defenders

By The Associated Press.

WASHINGTON, Friday, June 14—The German Army is "inside the gates of Paris," Ambassador William C. Bullitt informed the State Department early today.

"The city is quiet," Mr. Bullitt's message said.

He had telephoned Anthony J. Drexel Biddle, United States Ambassador to the Polish Government now at Tours, France, and Mr. Biddle relayed the message t-
Washington.

Mr. Bullitt, who has remained
his post in Paris, sent the notifi-
tion at 7 P. M., Paris time, Thu-
day (2 M., New York ti-
Thursday), but it was nearly
A. M. Eastern Standard time,
day before Mr. Biddle got wor-
the State Department. Mr. B-
gave no indication of wha-
meant by "inside the gates."

No Confirmation in Lond-

LONDON, Friday, June 14
spokesman at the French E-
said at 8 A. M. [3 A. M., Ne-
time] today that he had
firmation of United States
sador Bullitt's report that
man Army had reached a-
side the gates of Paris.

Nazis Pour Over Brid-

By G. H. ARCHAM-
Wireless to THE NEW YO-

TOURS, France, J-
though the general figh-
not altered very much
the salient point of
day resided in the
Germans began to po-
bodies beyond the
and bridgeheads est-
day and the day be-

Equally salient w-
the French armies
and homogeneous;
Weygand contin-
forces in hand, a-
armies are in bei-
time.

It is made cle-
the French High
intend to wage
confines of Pa-
battle progres-
ern limits of
pression mus-
meaning to
the French
west until
integrated

This me-
destructio-
cause the
ly decid-

[The
today
Gove-
Brit-
utm-
act-
no
o-

"All the News That's Fit to Print."

The New York Times.

LATE CITY EDITION
Partly cloudy, warmer today, followed by showers tonight. Tomorrow fair, temperature unchanged.
Temperatures Yesterday—Max., 78; Min., 65

VOL. LXXXIX...No. 30,093. Entered as Second-Class Matter, Postoffice, New York, N. Y. NEW YORK, SATURDAY, JUNE 15, 1940. THREE CENTS NEW YORK CITY and Vicinity | FOUR CENTS Elsewhere Except in 7th and 8th Postal Zones.

GERMANS OCCUPY PARIS, PRESS ON SOUTH; CAPTURE HAVRE, ASSAULT MAGINOT LINE; FRENCH ARMY INTACT; SPAIN SEIZES TANGIER

HITLER IS DOUBTED

Roosevelt Skeptical of Pledge He Will Not Cross Atlantic

HAS RECOLLECTIONS

U. S. Doing All It Can for Allies, He Asserts of French Appeal

By FELIX BELAIR Jr.
Special to THE NEW YORK TIMES.

WASHINGTON, June 14—President Roosevelt replied today to ...olf Hitler's reported denial of ...itorial aspirations in the West... Hemisphere with a reference to ...erman Chancellor's record of ... pledges to respect the in... of European nations over a ...ble period of time.

...rt of the same answer the ... said the United States ... and would continue to ...g in its power to give ...ies. He said, in effect, ...or Hitler's statement ... that he would con... ...s to Europe was to ...onsiderable quanti...

...followed up this ...ent of plans to ...cientific genius ...tional defense. ...ections," the ...sked at his ... reaction to ...

The International Situation

On the Battle Fronts

Paris was taken over yesterday by the German war machine.

Led by dust-stained tanks, followed by motorized divisions and then by infantry, the German Army marched down the Champs Elysées. Tense, grim-faced Parisians—the few who had remained behind—stood silently on the curbs as a hostile force marched through the famous boulevards of the "City of Light" for the first time since 1871. Shops were closed and shuttered. [Page 1, Column 7.]

In Berlin there were scenes of wild rejoicing. On Chancellor Hitler's orders church bells were rung for a quarter of an hour and the Nazi flag was ordered displayed for three days. [Page 2, Column 2.]

Berlin said that the fall of Paris—described as "catastrophic" morally and economically for the French—had completed the second phase of the war. The first was the Battle of Flanders. The third, the High Command communiqué said, was pursuit and "final destruction" of all the French forces. The chief drive of this "final" phase appeared to be directed against the flank of the Maginot Line through Champagne and the Argonne Forest—famous World War battlefield of American troops. Montmédy, western anchor of the line, was reported conquered. Spearheads had driven as far east as Vitry-le François, between Paris and Nancy. Verdun was said to be threatened. On the coast Havre's fall was claimed. [Page 1, Column 8.]

Hitler's personal press representative in the field with him said that the German leader considered the fall of Paris only an incident on his road of conquest and that he was not interested in peace now. [Page 2, Column 8.]

The French High Command said it had abandoned Paris because there was no "valuable strategical reason" why it should be defended and it did not want the city devastated. The communiqué said the French Army was retreating in good order. A slackening of the German drive was reported at several points, but the heavy push in Champagne, threatening the rear of the Maginot Line, was still in progress. The armament of the line is useless against an attack from the rear. A frontal attack on the line west of the Saar was reported repulsed. [Page 1, Column 5.]

High sources in London said that Britain had agreed to accept any military or political decision the French Government might make but would fight on whatever it was. [Page 1, Column 6.] If the war is to be waged successfully, however, informed sources said, every available piece of war material in the United States must be sent to the Allies at once. [Page 1, Column 4.]

The war appeared to be developing for Italy. First reports of action on her Alpine frontier were reported in a communiqué. It was divulged for the first time, too, that the Italian fleet was at sea in force. [Page 1, Column 3.] Attacks in Africa were reported both by the Italian air arm and by Allied troops against Libya, Eritrea and Ethiopia. Successes were claimed by the Italians in all actions. [Page 4, Column 1.]

The French Government abandoned Tours as its provisional capital and started southward, apparently for the port of Bordeaux. It was the seat of the French Government for a short time in 1914. [Page 1, Column 6.]

Repercussions Elsewhere

Spanish troops yesterday took over control of Tangier, the small internationally-policed territory in Northern Africa fronting on the Straits of Gibraltar. Madrid said the action had been taken to "guarantee its neutrality" and had been done with the ... consent of the other three ...rantors—Britain, France and ... Berlin said the consent of ...llies was given after the ...turn of Tangier has been ... the most frequently expressed ...rritorial demands of ...in. That of British ...tar is the other. ...mn 4.] In Washington ...y Hull said the ...uld insist on its extraterritorial rights in Tangier under the treaty of 1906. [Follows the foregoing.]

"That brings up recollections," President Roosevelt said at his press conference when a purported interview with Chancellor Hitler was shown to him quoting the German leader as saying he had no aspirations in this hemisphere. The President's reference was to similar statements made about European countries. Driving ahead with the American defense program, the President announced the appointment of a scientific research commission to work with the defense advisory commission. [Page 1, Column 1.]

...ROTESTS ...IAN CHARGES

...ull—Inquiry Here ...German Agent to ...s of Reprisals

MOROCCANS MOVE IN

Spanish Troops Take Over Zone in Which U. S. Has Rights

'GIBRALTAR' NOW CRY

Madrid Students Parade and Shout for Return of the Famous Rock

By T. J. HAMILTON
Special Cable to THE NEW YORK TIMES.

MADRID, June 14—The Spanish Government announced early this afternoon that with the object of guaranteeing "the neutrality of the international zone" in Morocco, Moroccan troops entered Tangier this morning.

It was stated officially that the action had been taken in agreement with Great Britain, France and Italy, who are other guarantors of the zone under a convention of 1903. The United States, which is also a signatory to the convention, received a copy of the announcement in a note delivered to the United States Embassy here at 11 A. M.

The text of the communiqué follows:

"With the object of guaranteeing the neutrality of the international zone and the city of Tangier, the Spanish Government has decided to take charge provisionally of the surveillance, police and public safety services of the international zone; forces of Moroccan troops entered this morning with this object.

"All existing services are assured and they continue functioning normally."

Coveted by the Spanish

Next to Gibraltar, Tangier occupies the front rank in Spanish territorial aims. In the last few days newspapers have devoted special attention to it among African territories that the French, assertedly with the connivance of the British, took away from Spain.

Although the first extra newspapers did not appear on the streets until 4 P. M., word that Tangier had been occupied spread quickly. By noon flags were appearing on houses throughout Madrid and members of the Falange youth movement were marching in uniform through the streets.

The news helped to bring an extra welcome for General Franco when he arrived late in the afternoon to open an exposition showing accomplishments of the government in rebuilding devastated regions. The press confined itself to printing the text of the government communiqué and relating the history of the international zone.

However, there were four demonstrations during the day, in which university student Falangistas predominated, all shouting, "Tangier is ours!" Some of these demonstrations passed the French and British Embassies.

British circles emphasized tonight that the occupation of Tangier had taken place with the complete agreement of Britain and France, who along with Italy and Spain were guarantors of the interna-

Continued on Page Six

ITALIANS IN CLASH ON FRENCH BORDER

Report Attack Repulsed—Fleet Action Revealed—Coast Is Shelled

By HERBERT L. MATTHEWS
By Telephone to THE NEW YORK TIMES.

ROME, June 14—The war began to develop for Italy on land, sea and air, according to this morning's communiqué, with the first activity on the Italo-French frontier and an indication that the Italian Fleet was on its way on some great mission.

The taking of Tangier by the Spaniards is considered a first-rate victory for the Axis, but, of course, the fall of Paris dominates everything else.

Among Fascisti here there is rejoicing over the fate of Paris. The newspaper Lavoro Fascista cheers ... an eight-column box whose sentiments are typical.

"C'est Paris," it says. "Capitalists, Jews, Masons and snobs all the world are in mourning. ... spiritual capital of all the old ... has fallen. Paris has ... Paris itself 'la ville lumière' ..."

... war shapes up, even this ... Mediterranean seems ... certain to become ... theatre of operations. ... there was some activity ... time yesterday on ... There were ... and "enemy, at-

Continued on Page Four

FRENCH NOTE LULL

Battle Continues Along Front—At Some Points Its Violence Abates

ATTACK IS REPULSED

Nazi Losses Are Heavy in Maginot Assault—Loire Next Barrier

By G. H. ARCHAMBAULT
Wireless to THE NEW YORK TIMES.

TOURS, France, June 14—Is there any significance in the fact that although the battle continued to be waged today all along the front from the coast to the Argonne, it was notable that at certain points its violence was abating?

That question is in every mind tonight, for it may contain confirmation of the belief that the Germans have now engaged the maximum of their available forces.

The communiqué issued tonight gives little information on the day's operations, but it implies that all the retreating French forces continue to fight rear-guard actions and that at several parts of the front they have, in addition, counter-attacked the advancing Germans.

The only reference to Paris is as follows: "The prescribed withdrawal has been effected in conformity with our plans."

But if there has been a relative lull on the main line of battle the Germans were very active in front of the Maginot Line, especially west of the Saar River. Early in the morning they launched a violent attack with the now customary accompaniment of tanks and dive-bombing planes. The French claim to have thrown back the attacking force, on which they inflicted heavy losses.

Present Front Uncertain

Manifestly this attack must be considered in correlation with the fighting in the Argonne, farther to the west.

It is impossible tonight to indicate the present front even approximately. It is really one long line of pockets and salients, a situation calling for great qualities of generalship in order to preserve cohesion of the French forces.

Meanwhile, with the withdrawal of the French troops charged with the defense of Paris the first phase of the Battle of France was ended in defeat. It may be called the Battle of the Seine. The next phase may be the Battle of the Loire.

The issue was clear from the moment it was decided to declare Paris an open city and the news of withdrawal cannot have surprised many. A communiqué issued this morning from French General Headquarters explained that there were insufficient strategic reasons for defending the capital to justify risking destruction of France's very heart.

From the military point of view it is clear now that a battle for Paris would merely have immobilized troops, added to the loss of life and brought about no com-

Continued on Page Three

Will Fight On, British Insist, Even if the French Capitulate

London Letting Ally Make Decision on the Immediate Course as Help Is Speeded—New Nazi Peace Offensive Expected

By The United Press.

LONDON, June 14—Britain has agreed to accept any decision France may make regarding military and political policy, but if France is lost as an ally the British will fight on alone against Chancellor Hitler's war machine, it was understood tonight.

The British Government was understood to have agreed this week to any choice the French Government might make in regard to these military and political matters, which weigh more heavily with each hour of Germany's increased drive, provided the choice had the approval of Generalissimo Maxime Weygand.

Foreign observers in London today regarded the German assault against the Maginot Line, particularly the strong flanking attack south of Montmedy around Vitry-le-François, as of far greater strategic importance than yesterday's German occupation of undefended Paris. Nevertheless, the psychological importance of the fall of Paris and the effect on French morale are not underestimated.

The impression prevails in foreign embassies in London that Herr Hitler would respond affirmatively to any possible French peace overture, but would impose harsh conditions as his price for ending the war in France. These conditions, it was felt, might range from dismantling the $500,000,000 Maginot Line to the return to Germany of Alsace-Lorraine and other territorial and economic and financial concessions.

There are strong indications, however, that Herr Hitler would refuse to negotiate with Britain, since he is intent on smashing Britain's financial and industrial power.

How far Germany would be prepared to bid for a completely Nazi-dictated peace presumably would depend upon the extent of the German losses suffered in the war.

If Britain should be compelled to fight on alone without France as an ally she would be able, it is felt in British quarters, to carry on until Autumn with United States aid. The British Navy is relatively intact despite Germany's claims to the contrary. Then, it is asserted, starvation might seriously menace Germany and Italy during the Winter, impairing their military strength and the security of their home fronts.

British morale appears to be firm,

Continued on Page Five

TOURS ABANDONED AS FRENCH CAPITAL

Government Is Expected to Make Seat at Bordeaux—U. S. Move Is Awaited

By P. J. PHILIP
Wireless to THE NEW YORK TIMES.

TOURS, France, June 14—Tours has ceased to be the substitute capital of France after a brief three-day career. Premier Paul Reynaud's speech last night and other symptoms showed clearly before we went to bed that that would be so.

There were already signs of packing up again in different administrations. Sleep seemed, however, more urgent than flight, especially as we ourselves had just obtained a bed—the first we had slept in since Sunday. In that we were luckier than most, although it does seem expensive to have had only one night's sleep in a two-room apartment rented for a month. However, it permitted a proper wash and a change of linen.

And now we and everybody else are on our way again. We don't know what is happening because the information service installed here with so much trouble on Monday has opened its wings and fled with a part of the censorship service. Press Wireless is functioning for a few hours and then good-bye to Tours.

Avalanche Advancing

The morning communiqué told the story of why this should be so—in part at least. The avalanche is advancing from all sides, closing around Paris and pushing forward in Champagne. The problem is where to go to escape it.

During the day, while we are on the road, things are likely to happen that will change the whole situation. It is too much now to hope that they will change it in any way that can be counted as satisfactory.

Along the roads through here the stream of civilian and military cars has recommenced. The embassies and legations have already pulled out. Wherever we go is going to be so congested that the remnants of that camping outfit with which we started are going to be invaluable.

Only 5,000 American bombers and fighters flying across the Atlantic in response to Premier Reynaud's desperate appeal could restore to the French people their belief that they are not alone in this terrible fight. Words and promises and the complicated explanation of political circumstances will not suffice. They will serve only to break further the dying hope there is today in every French heart.

For the British all the French feeling is as if they were of the

Continued on Page Three

REICH TANKS CLANK IN CHAMPS-ELYSEES

Berlin Recounts Parade Into Paris—Third of Citizens Reported Remaining

By The United Press.

BERLIN, June 14—German tanks today clanked across the Seine bridges, past the Arc de Triomphe and down the tree-lined Champs Elysées into the heart of Paris at the head of the first cavalcade of invaders to enter the French capital in nearly seventy years.

Flanked by armored cars, the dust-stained tanks swung triumphantly into Paris from the northwest at the head of Nazi units occupying the "City of Light," German accounts of the event said.

It was the ninth recorded invasion of Paris and the first since Bismarck's legions trod the broad boulevards in 1871. The jubilant German press proclaimed the fall of Paris to be the "symbol of decision" in Chancellor Adolf Hitler's Western offensive.

[Berlin Nazis expected Adolf Hitler to visit Paris June 21, the twenty-first anniversary of Germany's acceptance of the Treaty of Versailles, an Associated Press dispatch said.]

Entry From Northwest

The advance into Paris, through the suburbs of Argenteuil and Neuilly and into the aristocratic western part of the city began early in the morning, the Germans said. It was exactly five weeks after the massive western offensive began with the German drive into the Netherlands and Belgium.

The tanks rumbled between thin lines of tense and silent Parisians, the Germans said. Reports from the French capital estimated that probably a third of the city's normal population of 2,800,000 had remained in Paris.

Behind the tanks rolled anti-tank units, still dusty and laden with evidence of the furious fighting in which they had taken part to the north.

As the long shadows of the early morning retreated, more and more Nazi contingents streamed into the capital, evacuated by French Armies hoping to save their beloved Paris from the fate of Warsaw.

Motorized infantry, riding in steel-shielded trucks mounting machine guns to command the broad streets, converged from the Seine bridges to the Place de l'Etoile.

In that hub from which radiate eleven streets stands the Arc de Triomphe and its tomb of the Unknown World War Soldier, where flickers the Eternal Flame.

German reports indicated that the parade through Paris swung around

Continued on Page Two

2 FORCES TAKE CITY

Berlin Says Industrial Losses May Be Worst Feature for French

MONTMEDY CAPTURED

Anchor of Maginot Line Lost—Nazis Report Foe Is Routed

By C. BROOKS PETERS
Wireless to THE NEW YORK TIMES.

BERLIN, June 14—Today, for the third time within the last century and a quarter, victorious German troops marched into Paris. This time, however, the legions, the clatter of whose hobnailed boots resounds throughout Paris and the entire world, are more than just German soldiers. They are the bearers of a proposed new order for Europe and perhaps the world, a major tenet of which is to destroy the old one.

With the capitulation of Paris, the Germans claim that the destruction of the remaining French forces is but a matter of "the shortest time." Well-informed quarters in Berlin put that time at two weeks at most.

For the German High Command announced today that the second phase of the western campaign has been completed successfully, the resistance of the French northern fronts has been broken and the enemy is "in full retreat along the entire front from Paris to the Maginot Line near Sedan."

Retreat Called Rout

If the statements of German military officials in Berlin are correct, this "full retreat" is really a rout. For the French, forced from their positions, have had no time to construct new ones but are being constantly harassed by German tanks, other motorized units and planes as they move southward, it is reported.

Early this morning, the Germans declare, they unleashed a frontal attack on the Maginot Line along the entire Saar front. Farther east, the fall of Montmedy, "anchor" of the Maginot Line, was claimed as well.

The extreme right wing of the German forces was not idle either. For yesterday it captured Havre, Berlin heard, and thus added approximately another hundred miles to the stretch of French coast that already is in German hands.

Advance on Cherbourg

The lower Seine, moreover, according to the High Command, was crossed on a wide front. The extreme right wing, it is believed, now is advancing on Cherbourg further to cut France off from Great Britain and provide the Germans with still another base for a future raid on the British Isles.

The front is now about 300 miles long as the crow flies, Germans declare, from Havre to the Rhine.

Although no information has been officially released here relative to the progress of the attack on the Maginot Line, it was said in usually accurately informed quarters tonight that the force of the German drive in this sector already has borne fruit and that Reich troops have broken through in several places.

Escape Held Impossible

Forces of the German left wing are reported pushing forward in a southeasterly direction in what now appears to be a plan to storm the triangle of the Maginot fortifications from several sides, while an advance west of the fortifications to Belfort—southern tip of the Maginot Line—would cut off the avenue of escape for the French troops manning the line.

This German left wing yesterday was said to have captured Vitry-le Francois and crossed the Marne-Rhine Canal, which connects that town with Strasbourg. Still farther west another tentacle of the German left wing last evening was reported to have stormed the famous Hill 304 (Dead Man's Hill) northwest of Verdun, in which sector in 1916, Germans say, they lost 80,000 men.

The southern tip of the Argonne Forest also has been reached, Germans declare.

The Meuse defenses and Verdun

Continued on Page Two

British Call on U. S. for Munitions at Once; French Order 120 Bombers Here for 1941

By RAYMOND DANIELL
Special Cable to THE NEW YORK TIMES.

LONDON, June 14—In circles close to the government it was said today that every gun, every ounce of war materials that the United States can spare was needed urgently and needed quickly if the cause for which the Allies were fighting was not to be lost on the battlefields of France. It is not a matter of months but of weeks, even days, it was added by those in a position to know the facts, of which the ordinary people in this country only now are becoming dimly aware.

Withdrawal of the battered French armies behind their abandoned capital and contemplation of the possibility that the Government of France may be forced to withdraw from Europe to Africa, led to expressions that made increasingly apparent the extent to which the

Continued on Page Four

After the Anglo-French Purchasing Commission yesterday had announced that French purchases of war material in the United States were being stepped up, the French signed a contract at 7 P. M. for 120 "flying fortresses" to be delivered in the second and third quarters of 1941. The planes are to be built by the Consolidated Aircraft Corporation.

In an interview earlier in the day a spokesman for the Anglo-French commission said that contracts for "many millions of dollars" had been placed during the day.

Instead of curtailing purchases following the capture of Paris by the Germans, France is sending more purchasing experts, this spokesman said. In response to a question relative to the ability to pay cash for purchases, he added:

"There is no immediate end of our

Continued on Page Four

"All the News That's Fit to Print."

NEWS INDEX, PAGE 33, THIS SECTION

The New York Times.

Copyright, 1940, by The New York Times Company.

LATE CITY EDITION
Cloudy today with little change in temperature. Tomorrow cloudy and slightly warmer.
Temperatures Yesterday—Max., 72; Min., 52

Section 1

VOL. LXXXIX. No. 30,101. Entered as Second-Class Matter, Postoffice, New York, N. Y. NEW YORK, SUNDAY, JUNE 23, 1940. Including Rotogravure Picture, Magazine and Book Review. TEN CENTS | TWELVE CENTS Beyond 200 Miles, Except West of Pa.—South of Md.—North of Mass.

FRENCH SIGN REICH TRUCE, ROME PACT NEXT; BRITISH BOMB KRUPP WORKS AND BREMEN; HOUSE QUICKLY PASSES 2-OCEAN NAVY BILL

REPUBLICAN FIGHT LOOMS ON WAR ISSUE AT THE CONVENTION

Dewey, Taft and Willkie Reach Philadelphia to Appeal to the Delegates

NO GROUP HAS CONTROL

Rival Candidates Make Ballot Claims—Willkie Stronger—Hoover Possibility Seen

A battle between divergent views on the war and peace issue loomed yesterday among delegates to the Republican National Convention, opening tomorrow. Messrs. Dewey, Taft and Willkie, rival candidates for the Presidential nomination, reached Philadelphia to press their campaigns. No leader or group of leaders was in a position to dominate the proceedings or the committee on resolutions. The effect of a speech by Mr. Hoover to the convention Tuesday night is expected to decide what, if any part, he will play as a Presidential nominee. [All the foregoing Page 1, Column 1.]

In press conferences Mr. Dewey declared for aid to the Allies without violating international or domestic law or entering the war; Mr. Willkie for aid to the Allies without going to war, and for reciprocal trade treaties. [Page 2, Column 1.]

The national committee approved a change in the rules under which districts which fail to show a poll of 1,000 Republicans would be deprived of representation at future conventions. Other rules changes approved would ease penalties on States which do not give a majority for the national ticket. [Page 2, Column 4.]

Drafters of the platform, split over aid to the Allies, hinted that a stand on the foreign policy plank might be left largely to the decision of the Presidential nominee. [Page 3, Column 1.]

Convention Unbossed

By JAMES A. HAGERTY
Special to THE NEW YORK TIMES.

PHILADELPHIA, June 22—The Republican National Convention, which will convene here Monday in the Municipal Auditorium, will open without a boss or even under the control of any particular group of minor bosses.

This was the indication, today, when District Attorney Thomas E. Dewey of New York, Senator Robert A. Taft of Ohio and Wendell L. Willkie, president of the Commonweath and Southern Corporation, just now regarded as the three leading candidates for the Presidential nomination, arrived in the convention city to make direct appeals to the delegates.

With no leader or group of leaders in a position to dominate either the convention or the committee on resolutions, the delegates face the prospect of a hotly contested fight for the nomination for President, and an equally bitter floor contest on the resolution on foreign relations.

Little difficulty is expected in putting through the rest of the platform which is expected to follow the recommendations of the program committee of the National Committee, headed by Dr. Glenn Frank.

Alfred M. Landon, nominee for President in 1936, who is chairman of the subcommittee on foreign relations of the committee on resolutions, continued today his efforts to get a plank that would be satisfactory both to the isolationists and those favoring a declaration of aid to the Allies, but the formula, so far as could be learned, had not been found tonight.

Candidates Give Views

Mr. Dewey, Mr. Willkie and Senator Taft each had a press conference. Mr. Dewey declared for aid for the Allies without violating international or domestic law or getting into the war. Mr. Willkie, who was nearly mobbed by supporters in the Bellevue-Stratford Hotel, also declared for aid to the Allies without going to war and

Continued on Page Two

Major Sports Results

BASEBALL

New York's major league teams all met defeat yesterday. The Reds downed the Giants, 3—1, on Ernie Lombardi's homer with one man on base, the Pirates beat the Dodgers, 7—2, and the Tigers won from the Yankees, 3—2. Despite the setback, the Dodgers stayed in first place in the National League.

RACING

Your Chance won the $13,350 Dwyer Stakes at Aqueduct after Snow Ridge, first past the finish line, was disqualified for bumping in the stretch. Gen'l Manager was placed second and Andy K. third. The crowd of 20,520 bet $1,076,417 on the seven races, this being Aqueduct's first million-dollar day.

TRACK AND FIELD

The University of Southern California won its sixth successive National Collegiate A. A. championship in the meet at Minneapolis. The New York A. C. easily retained the metropolitan A. A. U. senior title.

(Complete Details in Section 5.)

CITY WPA TO PURGE 1,000 NAZIS, REDS

Signing of Affidavits to Be Started Tomorrow—FBI to Aid in Investigations

Without waiting for President Roosevelt to sign the new Relief Appropriations Act, Colonel F. C. Harrington, National Work Projects Commissioner, set in motion yesterday the machinery for purging the WPA rolls of Communists and Nazis by July 1.

The purge in this city will begin tomorrow, and the local administrator, Lieut. Col. Brehon B. Somervell, estimated that at least 1,000 WPA workers would lose their jobs before it was completed. All of the 101,000 persons on the rolls here, and 1,700,000 in other parts of the country, will be required to sign affidavits disavowing Communist or Nazi affiliations. The maximum penalty for false statement will be $2,000 fine and two years' imprisonment.

Colonel Somervell made clear that his office would not rely on affidavits alone in carrying out the mandate of the new law. The registration lists of the Board of Elections will be compared with the WPA payroll to turn up the names of Communists. The full facilities of the Federal Bureau of Investigation, the Police Department and the WPA's own Bureau of Investigation will be invoked as a further means of identification.

Dies Records to Be Used

Still another source of data, Colonel Somervell revealed, will be the reports and testimony gathered by the Dies committee and the record compiled in the recent trial of Fritz Kuhn, leader of the German-American Bund.

Because of "the well-known practice of Communists to deny membership in the party and to use false names in enrollment with the WPA," the administrator called upon all "responsible citizens" to make available any information they had on subversive activities among Federal relief employes. He said he expected at least 50,000 letters, and he promised that "grudge letters would be carefully sifted out from those submitting authentic information."

Although Congress did not complete action on the new Relief Act until yesterday morning, WPA officials in this city have been collecting material on Communists and Nazis on their rolls for several weeks. More than 1,000 names of persons tentatively identified as members of un-American groups are now under scrutiny, it was learned.

Under the wording of the law, Colonel Somervell said, a person does not have to be a member of the Communist party to be ineligible for WPA employment. He said he regarded Trotskyists as Communists within the meaning of the law, and indicated that other "splinter groups" would be subject to a similar interpretation. The administrator said he would function as the court of last resort in determining whether a person entertained subversive views.

The WPA purge creates a problem for municipal relief authorities.

Continued on Page Thirteen

FOR 200 NEW SHIPS

70% Increase in Fleet Authorized as Congress Recesses Till July 1

TO COST 4 BILLIONS

Chambers Enact Tax, Defense and Relief Fund Measures

Special to THE NEW YORK TIMES.

WASHINGTON, June 22—Congress took a recess at 9:10 o'clock tonight, adopting a resolution to reassemble on July 1 after the Republican National Convention at Philadelphia, and to take a similar week's recess during the Democratic National Convention at Chicago.

As a night session began to clear the decks for the recess, the House gave a dramatic flourish to a day devoted to pressing legislation by passing and sending to the Senate the "two-ocean" navy bill. No dissent was heard in the voice vote.

Within less than two hours, the House thus gave its approval to the construction of the world's mightiest navy, designed for defense of the United States and the Western Hemisphere. The Senate did not have time to act.

The "two-ocean" navy bill would authorize about 200 warships, a 70 per cent increase in the nation's fleet, or an expansion of 1,325,000 tons of combatant and auxiliary vessels to be built in the next six years at an estimated cost of $4,000,000,000.

Naval Air Force Augmented

Besides the increase in ship tonnage, the two-ocean navy measure also would increase the naval air force authorized strength from 10,000 to 15,000 planes.

It provides for $25,000,000 for "mosquito" torpedo boats, and authorizes an appropriation of $150,000,000 to expand shipbuilding facilities at government and private yards.

It provides also for the expenditure of $20,000,000 for expansion of facilities for armor plate manufacture and $50,000,000 for added facilities for construction of guns.

In calling for enactment of the bill, as recommended by Admiral Harold R. Stark, Chief of Naval Operations, Chairman Vinson of the House Naval Affairs Committee said that when the bill became law the Administration would ask for $175,000,000 for an immediate start on the program.

Mr. Vinson and Representative Maas of Minnesota, ranking minority member on the committee, led the brief debate by asserting that the United States should not depend upon the Navy of any other power for its defense.

"The time has come to realize that if the United States is to remain free and independent it must depend upon itself," Mr. Maas said. "It is foolish to risk our defense on the thin thread of a (the Panama) canal."

The Navy now has 307 ships in

Continued on Page Fourteen

$5,377,552,058 Voted For Defense This Year

By The Associated Press.

WASHINGTON, June 22—Here are the defense appropriation totals, including contract authorizations, which Congress has approved thus far this session:

*Regular Army bill	$1,823,254,624
*Regular Navy bill	1,492,542,750
Supplemental defense	1,768,913,908
Urgent deficiency	28,000,000
Emergency deficiency	252,340,776
Strategic materials (in Treasury appropriation)	12,500,000
Total	$5,377,552,058

*To which supplemental sums were added by the Senate.

There are also items intended for defense in the Civil Aeronautics Authority, Civilian Conservation Corps, WPA and the Army Civil Functions Supply Bills.

COMMITTEE LEANS TO KNOX REJECTION

But Senate Naval Group Votes to Hear Him July 1—Stimson Will Testify Next Day

By HAROLD B. HINTON
Special to THE NEW YORK TIMES.

WASHINGTON, June 22—Confirmation of Colonel Frank Knox as Secretary of the Navy probably will be opposed by the Senate Naval Affairs Committee, according to some members questioned after a stormy executive session today. If members maintain the opposition shown today, an adverse report will be made to the Senate, it was said.

The Naval and the Military Affairs committees, to which the nominations of Colonel Knox and of Henry L. Stimson as Secretary of War have been referred, will hear the nominees in person during the week of July 1, when Congress reassembles after its recess for the Republican National Convention.

There is no indication that the Military Affairs Committee will recommend rejection of Colonel Stimson, although he will probably be closely questioned by such isolationists members as Senators Reynolds and Lundeen.

The Naval Affairs Committee will give Colonel Knox a more searching examination, it was believed. Some members, it was reported, favored rejecting the nomination today, but counsel prevailed that no nominee should be disapproved without having a chance to be heard.

Senator Walsh, its chairman, announced after the meeting that Colonel Knox would be invited to appear on July 1. In other quarters it was said that eleven members attended today's meeting and that most of those who spoke were opposed to the nomination. Only Senators Hale and Barbour took no part in the discussions.

The most outspoken opponents, according to these reports, included Senators Walsh, Tydings, Smith of South Carolina, Byrd, Holt and Gillette, all Democrats. Senator Johnson of California, a Republican, also indicated his opposition. Others attending the meeting were

Continued on Page Fifteen

British Torpedo and Bomb the Scharnhorst; Submarine, Planes Waylay Nazi Battleship

By HAROLD DENNY
Special Cable to THE NEW YORK TIMES.

LONDON, June 22—The Germans' 26,000-ton battle cruiser Scharnhorst has been seriously damaged by a British submarine and airplanes off the Norwegian coast, according to reports given out tonight by the Admiralty and the Air Ministry.

The Scharnhorst was believed to be lying at bay with German destroyers and war planes clustering about her protectively, awaiting further attack by British naval units summoned by the Royal Air Force bombers.

The battle with the Scharnhorst and her escorting forces was the most important of three attacks on German and Italian naval craft reported in London.

The other incidents were the almost unbelievable exploit of the capture of an Italian submarine by a British trawler in the Gulf of Aden opposite British Somaliland and the sinking by an airplane of a German supply ship in the North Sea.

The Scharnhorst, with her sister ship the Gneisenau, the most powerful of German war vessels, had previously taken severe punishment. She was heavily pummeled in April by the British battleship Renown off Narvik, Prime Minister Winston Churchill then reported.

On June 13 she was reported here to have been badly bombed, with one—perhaps two—British bombs making direct hits on the center of the ship when she was in Trondheim Fjord.

"One of our submarines sighted the Scharnhorst soon after she left Trondheim Fjord," the day's reports said. "The battle cruiser was clearly on passage to a safe port where she could repair damage sustained when hit by at least one heavy bomb during an attack by the aircraft of the fleet arm on June 13."

This latest encounter with the Scharnhorst touched off an excep-

Continued on Page Twenty-one

ARMS PLANT IS HIT

R.A.F. Raiders Continue Assault Upon Nazis' Bases of Supply

SCORE NEAR BERLIN

Plane Factory Is Target —Germans Retaliate Along English Coast

By JAMES MacDONALD
Special Cable to THE NEW YORK TIMES.

LONDON, June 22—Royal Air Force bombers pounded the big Krupp arms works at Essen and important aircraft factories and military stores at Bremen, Kassel, Rothenburg and Goettingen and a big naval depot at Willemsoord in German-occupied Netherlands in a heavy series of air raids last night, according to the Air Ministry's communiqué today.

As against their boast of heavy damage done to the Nazis, British officials insisted that Nazi airmen had accomplished little in their retaliatory raids in this country this morning and last night.

Three persons were killed in a Suffolk town and three wounded elsewhere, it was announced. It was declared that bombs burst sporadically in "several counties on the east coast," but that most of them fell in open country, causing small damage. The German raids, it was said, were less intense than those of Tuesday and Wednesday nights. The Ministry did not state whether or not any Nazi planes were shot down, or if any defending fighter machines were lost.

All Appears Quiet

Meanwhile all appeared quiet on the British home air front tonight. There were no unwelcome noises of purring enemy motors that were picked up by the sensitive sound-detecting devices on the ground.

[Alexandria, Egypt, fought off three Italian air raids yesterday, the first of the war. British fliers attacked Tobruk, Libya, and reported hitting a large warship. Rome said bombers had destroyed a British naval base in Egypt and raided Marseille and Bizerte, Tunisia.]

Many sections of British planes are reported to have taken part in widespread raids on German objectives last night, but only one was shot down and only two are reported missing.

The plane that was shot down was one of several that subjected Willemsoord to a terrific aerial bombardment.

Almost five tons of high explosive and incendiary bombs were dropped in less than a minute. During that lightning stroke oil tanks were set afire, naval storehouses blown to rubble, two unidentified ships sunk, another badly damaged, "and German machine-gunners received a dose of their own medicine," the Air Ministry said. American built Lockheed-Hudson planes were used in that sortie.

Two Planes Missing

Many planes were engaged in the big raids over Germany. They returned with only two missing.

British raiders over Bremen directed their attack against the large Focke-Wulf airplane factory. They made direct hits with incendiary and explosive bombs in the middle of the factory buildings. Two violent explosions were seen by the British fliers after their bombs burst.

The airfield adjoining the factory was also bombed and one hangar was badly damaged, according to assertions made here.

Another section of the raiders reported that they had hit several buildings of the Krupp plant at Essen as well as railroad sidings near by. The exact extent of the damage done there, however, was not disclosed in London.

The objective at Kassel was the Fieseler aircraft factory and it was said that several bombs were seen exploding directly on the target.

Airplane hangars were damaged at Rothenberg, where also military buildings and the air field were hit. Another attacking force dropped bombs on the aircraft storage depot

Continued on Page Twenty-six

The International Situation

In Europe and Africa

An armistice between Germany and France was signed in the Forest of Compiegne yesterday at 6:50 P. M. German time (12:50 P. M. New York time). Immediately after the signing the French representatives left by a German plane, German-piloted, for Rome, where they will sign a companion document with Italy. Six hours after the signatures have been appended to the Italian armistice the order to cease fire will become effective. The terms of the armistice are still withheld; in Bordeaux they were described as "hard but honorable." London reported, without confirmation, that these were the principal provisions: (1) Occupation of France by Germany and Italy for the duration of the war with Britain; (2) surrender of all war stores; (3) surrender of all gold and foreign currency reserves; (4) delivery of coal and other raw material supplies to Germany for a fixed period. [Page 1, Column 8.]

Prime Minister Churchill said he had heard "with grief and amazement" of the French acceptance of terms that, to his mind, would mean that France and her empire would be entirely at the mercy of the dictators. He called on the French people to continue resistance. This call was reiterated by General Charles de Gaulle, former French Under-Secretary of War, who broadcast from London, calling on all French people not under Axis guns to mobilize to carry on the war. [Page 1, Column 6.]

The French negotiators arrived in Rome by plane from Compiègne. [Page 27, Column 1.]

Berlin announced that 500,000 French soldiers, encircled in Alsace-Lorraine, had surrendered, among them three army commanders. Only isolated resistance was left in that part of France. The Germans took the port of Lorient, on the southern coast of Brittany. According to Swiss reports, the French repulsed a German attack on L'Ecluse Fort, which dominates the Rhone at the Swiss border. [Page 22, Column 1.]

British bombers struck at the famous Krupp armaments works at Essen and at aircraft factories at several other points in Germany. In a raid on Willemsoord, German-held base in the Netherlands, the British said they had sunk two ships, set one afire and destroyed naval storehouses. Berlin reported that nearly 100 planes took part in Friday night's bombing of Britain. The Germans said that in recent actions they had sunk two British transports, one of 11,000 tons, the other of 32,000, the latter carrying about 5,000 men who were lost. British bombers reached the Berlin area Friday night, the Germans admitted, injuring seven persons and damaging buildings. [Page 1, Column 5.]

The British reported that the German battleship Scharnhorst, 26,000 tons, had been both torpedoed and bombed, with "considerable damage" resulting. The action took place off the Norwegian coast. A destroyer was torpedoed in the same fight, London said. The British trawler Moonstone informed the Admiralty that it had captured a large Italian submarine in the Gulf of Aden. Depth charges forced the submarine to the surface, where guns were brought into play. The Italian commander and several officers were reported killed; three officers and thirty-seven men were captured. [Page 1, Column 3.]

Three groups of Italian bombers attacked the Allied naval base at Alexandria, Egypt, early yesterday. They were driven off, the British reported, by the combined fire of both French and British naval units, and no warships were hit. Rome claimed to have sunk three enemy ships in the Mediterranean. [Page 1, Column 7.]

By the emphatic means of an official government statement, Russia denied that troops were being concentrated on the German frontier. [Page 22, Column 7.]

Developments Elsewhere

Within less than two hours, the House of Representatives adopted the "two-ocean" navy bill, which will give the United States the most powerful navy in the world—a navy 70 per cent greater than the present one. [Page 1, Column 3.]

After a stormy session of the Senate Naval Affairs Committee, it appeared in Washington that Colonel Frank Knox, Republican, would not be approved by the committee for Secretary of the Navy. Colonel Henry L. Stimson, Republican, nominated for Secretary of War, also faces hard going before the Military Affairs Committee. But confirmation of both appointments is expected when the issue gets to the floor. [Page 1, Column 4.]

In Hyde Park, where he was spending the week-end, President Roosevelt contemplated the possibility that the United States might have to shift the fleet to the Atlantic to face a superior sea power of the totalitarian nations. [Page 16, Column 1.]

GENERAL SUMMONS FRENCH TO RESIST

De Gaulle Offers to Organize Fight Abroad—Churchill Supports His Stand

By RAYMOND DANIELL
Special Cable to THE NEW YORK TIMES.

LONDON, Sunday, June 23—A broadcast to the French people by one of their own military leaders calling on them to continue the fight against Germany by every means in their power was made from here last night.

General Charles de Gaulle, assistant and adviser to Paul Reynaud when the former Premier was also War Minister, told his countrymen the proposed armistice would be not only capitulation but "submission and slavery."

[The general undertook to organize such French resistance as was possible himself and urged French fighting men and technicians everywhere to join him in the task, according to The United Press.]

General de Gaulle's arguments were reinforced early this morning by Prime Minister Winston Churchill in a statement expressing "grief and amazement" at the terms. He indicated they would transform France into an active enemy, and he too urged French-

Continued on Page Twenty-seven

ALEXANDRIA FIGHTS FIRST ITALIAN RAIDS

20 Bombs Fall in 3 Attacks—Warship Reported Fired by R. A. F. at Tobruk

By JOSEPH M. LEVY
Wireless to THE NEW YORK TIMES.

CAIRO, Egypt, June 22—Alexandria experienced its first bombing this morning when twenty bombs were dropped in three Italian air raids. Two persons were killed; twenty-three were injured.

The dead were a native woman, who was killed when bombs hit among palm trees growing in a village close to the city, and a man who was killed by a bomb that demolished four Alexandria houses. Here nineteen persons were injured.

[Another air raid warning sounded in Alexandria early today, but no planes appeared, The Associated Press reported, and the all-clear signal was given in fifteen minutes.]

Bombs were reported dropped indiscriminately on the city, harbor and native villages, the bombers flying high and dodging in their attempt to avoid anti-aircraft fire. Two Italian planes were reported badly damaged. It is not certain whether either was shot down.

Only a few bombs fell in the city.

Continued on Page Twenty-three

NAZI TERMS SIGNED

But Hostilities Persist as French Fly to Get Italy's Demands

SEVERITY PROTESTED

Huntziger Voices View at Close of 27-Hour Compiegne Parley

By GUIDO ENDERIS
Wireless to THE NEW YORK TIMES.

BERLIN, June 22—The armistice treaty between Germany and France was signed today in the forest of Compiègne at 6:50 P. M. German Summer time [12:50 P. M. New York time]. Col. Gen. Wilhelm Keitel, Chancellor Hitler's plenipotentiary, signed for Germany and General Charles Huntziger for France.

Its contents will not be made public for the present, but it is announced that the agreement does not provide for immediate cessation of hostilities. The fighting is to end six hours after the Italian Government has notified the German High Command of the signing of an armistice treaty between Italy and France.

As the latter is now believed to be a mere formality, already agreed upon by the leaders of the Axis Powers in their discussion in Munich last Tuesday, its conclusion is expected within the next forty-eight hours. The French delegation that conferred at Compiègne also will negotiate with Italy. Such procedure, it is predicted, will end the war on the Continent early in the coming week.

Scene in Car Dramatic

The French delegation returned to Compiègne from Paris at 10 A. M. and continued its deliberations throughout the day, during which it was in constant communication with the Bordeaux government. To expedite contacts, German military authorities installed a direct telephone wire connecting the armistice car with Bordeaux.

The German radio broadcast announcing the signing of the treaty closed with the words, "We thank our Fuehrer." There was a dramatic scene in the armistice car at Compiègne before the formalities were completed. General Huntziger, in a choked voice, announced that his government had ordered him to sign.

"Before carrying out my government's order," he said, "the French delegation deems it necessary to declare that in a moment when France is compelled by fate of arms to give up the fight, she has a right to expect that the coming negotiations will be dominated by a spirit that will give two great neighboring nations a chance to live and work once more. As a soldier you will well understand the onerous moment that has now come for me to sign."

After the signatures were affixed, General Keitel requested all present to rise from their seats, and then said:

"It is honorable for the victor to do honor to the vanquished. We have risen in commemoration of those who gave their blood to their countries."

Talks With Italy Speeded

The French delegation left Compiegne for Paris tonight and is expected to take up negotiations with Italy without further delay to bring the hostilities to a quick close.

With an Italian-French armistice in imminent prospect, military activities are now expected to give way to diplomatic negotiations and it is not improbable that Germany, Italy, France and possibly also Belgium will meet in conference soon in some German city to discuss steps for an approach to honorable peace.

Meanwhile there is no indication in German official or press utterances to suggest that Germany is not grimly determined to prosecute her war on Britain with all possible speed, and this determination has received fresh impetus through uninterrupted attacks by British bombers on German objectives.

With French Channel ports now [illegible] German air bases [illegible] coastal points also [illegible] in recent days and [illegible] liquidation of the [illegible]

Continued on Page Twenty-[illegible]

"All the News That's Fit to Print."

The New York Times.

LATE CITY EDITION
Rain this morning, clearing and slightly warmer this afternoon; fair tonight and tomorrow.
Temperatures Yesterday—Max.,74; Min.,61

Copyright, 1940, by The New York Times Company.

VOL. LXXXIX..No. 30,112. Entered as Second-Class Matter, Postoffice, New York, N. Y. NEW YORK, THURSDAY, JULY 4, 1940. THREE CENTS NEW YORK CITY and Vicinity | FOUR CENTS Elsewhere Except in 7th and 8th Postal Zones.

BRITISH FORCIBLY SEIZE FRENCH WARSHIPS; U-BOAT TORPEDOES PRISON SHIP, 1,068 LOST; GERMAN AIRPLANES BOMB BRITAIN ALL DAY

ROOSEVELT TO ASK $5,000,000,000 MORE IN DEFENSE OUTLAY

Seeks $4,000,000,000 for Army, $1,000,000,000 for Navy in Ten Billion Plan

LARGE SUM FOR PLANES

Congress to Get Message Monday—Senate Committee Approves Knox, 9-5

President Roosevelt prepared yesterday for submission to Congress Monday a supplemental defense program calling for $5,000,000,000 more, $4,000,000,000 to go to the Army and $1,000,000,000 to the Navy. If this amount is granted it will raise the nation's defense fund to $10,000,000,000. [Page 1, Column 1.]

The House bill to authorize a 70 per cent expansion of the Navy in six years was endorsed by the Senate Naval Affairs Committee. [Page 7, Column 1.]

Mass production of Rolls-Royce engines by the Packard Motor Car Company was virtually assured. [Page 7, Column 3.]

General Pershing in a letter to the Senate Military Affairs Committee said compulsory military training was essential in view of "great threats" to American security. The committee is considering legislation to establish such training. [Page 9, Column 1.]

Nine members of the Senate Naval Affairs Committee voted for confirmation of Frank Knox as Secretary of the Navy; five members voted against it. [Page 8, Column 1.]

Near All-Time High

Special to THE NEW YORK TIMES.

WASHINGTON, July 3—President Roosevelt was putting the finishing touches tonight on a new $5,000,000,000 supplemental program for further expansion of the military and naval forces which will be urged on Congress in the form of a special message early next week. White House sources indicated that the message would go in soon after the President's return from his Hyde Park home for which he departed tonight, on Monday.

With the $5,082,210,080 already voted for defense at the present session of Congress, the added $5,000,000,000 will bring the estimated cost of the defense preparations now planned to more than $10,000,000,000.

This nearly equals the all-time record of $11,011,387,000 appropriated for the World War fiscal year of 1918.

The new program, contemplating a huge expansion of production facilities by manufacturers of planes, guns, tanks and other essential material, proposes to allow $4,000,000,000 to the Army. Of this about $1,500,000,000 would be used for the production of military planes. At least $1,000,000,000 would go to the Navy for ships, planes and munitions.

50,000 Planes Is Goal

One of the primary objectives was understood to be to put the aviation industry well on the way toward the Administration's goal of an annual output of 50,000 fighting planes.

The War Department under the expansion program based on the $4,000,000,000 supplemental request is understood to be counting on at least 3,000 tanks and 25,000 first-line fighting planes by the end of 1941, including those now available. An early increase in enlisted strength to 750,000 men also is contemplated, although officials are reluctant to predict when that will be attained.

President Roosevelt had at his conference Acting Secretaries Louis Johnson and Lewis Compton of the War and Navy Departments; William S. Knudsen, production chief of the Defense Advisory Commission, and Harold D. Smith, Director of the Budget. Mr. Smith indicated after the meeting that about half of the $5,000,000,000 outlay to be asked by the President would be in cash and half in the form of authorizations.

Aim at Mass Production

One of the conferees explained that the primary purpose of the supplemental program was to make possible the mass production of tanks, guns, planes, troop vehicles and other heavy equipment by next August.

Until the President broadened the supplemental program to include about $1,000,000,000 more for the Navy it was indicated that his message would go to Congress before his departure for Hyde Park, either in the form of a special message or letters to the Vice President and the Speaker of the House.

The latter alternative was said to have been abandoned in view of the magnitude of the program. It

Continued on Page Seven

Strato Planes to Cut Flight Time to Coast

Special to THE NEW YORK TIMES.

LOS ANGELES, Calif., July 3—High-altitude passenger service will be started between Los Angeles and New York Monday, when T. W. A.'s thirty-three-seat "Stratoliner" leaves on its first 13 hour 40 minute flight east.

Two hours and two minutes will be slashed from the best schedules by this service in four-motored transports, it was stated. One round-trip flight daily will be made by T. W. A.'s fleet of five such planes.

By The Associated Press.

MIAMI, Fla., July 3—The nation's first fleet of strato-Clippers will go into service tomorrow between Miami and Latin America, providing faster passenger service and serving six-day-a-week mail service to every capital in South America.

LINER FIRE AT PIER THREATENS TUNNEL

The Algonquin, Ablaze, Sinks Near Holland Tube, but Officials Say It Is Safe

A stubborn five-hour fire of undetermined origin which swept the after holds of the Clyde Mallory liner Algonquin yesterday, two hours before the vessel was to have sailed with 160 vacation-bound passengers, resulted in the injury of twenty-four firemen, tied up holiday traffic in lower New York and caused fears for the safety of the Holland Tunnel. The 5,945-ton coastwise vessel was docked at Pier 34, North River, at a point less than fifty feet south of the tunnel, and as the liner began to founder by the stern after tons of water had been poured into her holds, concern was felt for a time that the tunnel might be damaged.

A spokesman for the Port of New York Authority said later, however, that the Holland Tunnel would not be closed. An engineer is watching the situation, he explained, but added that the tunnel appeared to be in no danger. The tunnel tubes are protected at that point by a heavy blanket of clay and crushed rock, it was explained, and even if the stern of the Algonquin is resting in the mud, there is no reason to fear damage to the tunnel.

Three Alarms Sounded

The fire, which necessitated three alarms and brought hundreds of firemen and twenty-six pieces of apparatus, including two fireboats, to the scene, was discovered by the crew at about 10 A. M. Police Commissioner Lewis J. Valentine, Fire Chief John J. McElligott and several other high officials of the Police and Fire Departments responded to the final alarm.

Suggestions of sabotage were discounted by Fire Marshal Thomas P. Brophy, who said the fire probably had been caused by "spontaneous ignition." The police of the waterfront, sabotage and criminal alien squads reported that they had found nothing suspicious about the fire.

The liner, which was to have sailed at noon for Miami, Fla., and Houston, Texas, had a general cargo. In the holds 3, 4 and 5, penetrated by the flames, were bales of feather quilts, flax, insulating material, old rags, pipe calking and lubricating oil. The 125 members of the crew, under command of Captain P. G. Gerhard, were on board when the fire was discovered, but the passengers were in the waiting room on the pier, at the foot of Spring Street.

Most of the passengers thought the fumes which penetrated the waiting room had been caused by a minor blaze and they awaited word that they could embark. At 12:30 P. M., however, H. G. Wenzel, passenger agent of the line, announced that the sailing had been canceled. The carnival spirit which had been prevalent up to that time, came to an abrupt end, and exclamations of disappointment were heard.

Mr. Wenzel said no substitute sailing would be arranged, but added that persons going to Miami could sail on the Shawnee on Saturday and those bound for Houston, might leave on the Seminole next Wednesday. A majority of the passengers cashed in their tickets. Martin Alexander, an advertising manager, and his fiancée, Miss Marian Gordon, who had planned to be married aboard the Algonquin, refused to let the fire thwart them: They were married in the offices of the line on the pier.

Almost immediately after their arrival the firemen who answered the first alarm were affected by the smoke. Wearing gas masks, they descended deep into the holds. For nearly five hours the two fireboats, John J. Harvey and Firefighter, as well as the land apparatus poured water into the ship. The liner soon began to list to starboard and aft. About 3 o'clock, after Mr. McElligott arrived, the stern settled so that the open deck was covered with water to a depth of nearly two feet. It was only then that the

Continued on Page Thirty-two

RAIDS IN WIDE AREA

Many Civilian Casualties as Bombs Fall in City and Country

SIX OF ATTACKERS DOWNED

British Strike Back—Berlin Reports 19, Mostly Children, Killed in Hamburg

By JAMES MacDONALD

Special Cable to THE NEW YORK TIMES.

LONDON, Thursday, July 4—Nazi air attacks against Great Britain took on new boldness yesterday with sporadic daylight raids on Scotland, England and Wales lasting from morning until evening. Scores of bombs were dropped: seven civilians were killed and seventy-seven injured: private property was damaged and six German planes were shot down and four damaged.

Some of the raiders came in pairs but most of them singly, dropping anywhere from two to nineteen bombs at widely scattered points. The Air Ministry's communiqué did not say whether any military targets were hit, but did tell of damage to houses and stores. Residents of one southeast coast town declared that a German raider, not content with dropping bombs, deliberately machine-gunned the civilian population.

Troops on a south coast beach also were machine-gunned.

[Berlin reported that nineteen civilians were killed in a British raid on Hamburg and that a total of 448 civilians had been killed by British bombers up to the end of June.]

Raiders at Great Heights

The raids kept anti-aircraft batteries and Royal Air Force fighters busy throughout the day all along the east coast and at points inland, where the angry roar of ground batteries brought war to what is normally a smiling English countryside.

The Nazi planes mostly flew at great altitudes, sometimes 25,000 feet or more—too high for accurate aim, whatever targets they were seeking. Their incendiary, explosive and delayed action bombs fell haphazard among shoppers and workmen in towns and farmers in their fields. Some bombs thudded harmlessly in marshlands.

The Germans lost their first plane during the morning, when the pilots of three Spitfires patrolling the east coast of England sighted two Dornier "flying pencils" five miles away. The British closed in on the nearest of the Dorniers, giving it a full blast of their machine guns. Instantly the plane burst into flames, turned on its back and hurtled into the sea.

The Spitfires then turned their attention to the other Dornier. They damaged it badly, according to Air Ministry reports, but not

Continued on Page Six

Argentina Drops 5 Nazis From Army College Staff

Wireless to THE NEW YORK TIMES.

BUENOS AIRES, Argentina, July 3—The Argentine Ministry of War issued this afternoon a brief communiqué announcing termination of the services of the German military mission that for several years has been instructing in the Argentine Army Technical College. The communiqué merely stated that the contract of these instructors had expired and that therefore their services had come to an end.

The German Embassy stated that the chief of the mission, Gen. Guenther Niedenfughr, had been appointed German Military Attache at Rio de Janeiro and that the next in rank, Lieut. Col. Frederich Wulf, had been appointed Military Attache at Santiago, Chile.

The embassy said the destination of three other officers on the mission had not been decided.

CHAMPLAIN IS SUNK BY MINE, NAZIS SAY

French Liner Is Said to Have Gone Down on Eve of Her Departure for U. S.

Wireless to THE NEW YORK TIMES.

BERLIN, July 3—The French liner Champlain, according to a German news agency report from Geneva, struck a mine at la Pallice, France, seventy-five miles north of Bordeaux, a few days ago and sank. She was ready to leave for the United States with a large number of passengers and a heavy cargo, it was stated, when a sudden explosion occurred. The ship quickly took on a heavy list and in a short time disappeared beneath the waves.

Thanks to efforts of the officers and crew, who were said to have preserved complete calm, all the passengers were saved, the report said. The waters of the bay were quiet, making rescue work less difficult than usual under such circumstances. However, some stokers and several stewardesses were drowned.

It apparently is not quite clear whether the explosion occurred when the ship ran onto a mine or whether a drifting mine struck her. The report concludes, however, that a mine was responsible for the disaster. The German agency report originated from a report in the Petit Dauphinois, sent by that paper's correspondent in La Rochelle, France.

First Voyage in 1933

When the Champlain began her maiden voyage to this country from Havre in June, 1932, her owners contended that the 28,124-ton ship was the largest, fastest and most luxurious vessel of her type. Her rakish bow was first seen in New York on June 25, 1932, when she completed the crossing at an average speed of 19.5 knots.

The Champlain had accommoda-

Continued on Page Four

Ortiz, Ill, Leaves Argentine Presidency; Vice President Castillo Temporary Head

By The Associated Press.

BUENOS AIRES, July 3—President Roberto M. Ortiz of Argentina relinquished tonight the duties of his office temporarily because of ill health. He has long been a sufferer from diabetes. He took office Feb. 20, 1938.

He issued a decree announcing he was leaving office for an indefinite period on the advice of three physicians.

The Argentine Constitution provides that during absence of the Chief Executive the work of the Presidency shall fall upon the Vice President.

The transfer of Presidential power to Vice President Ramon S. Castillo may be significant because Señor Castillo and Señor Ortiz differ widely in their concept of the powers of the State and those of the Provinces. They were elected in 1938 for six-year terms.

The decree, signed by President Ortiz, as required by the Constitution, came unexpectedly for Argentina. It had not been known widely that the Chief Executive's condition had become more serious.

Born of Basque stock and with neither military, social nor political background, President Roberto M. Ortiz served his political apprenticeship in the municipal and Federal Legislatures of Argentina. He first became prominent through his activities as an importer and lawyer, then as Administrator of Internal Revenue and Minister of Public Works.

It was not until his term of office as Finance Minister under the "New Deal" administration of Augustin Justo in 1933, however, that he became internationally known as a public administrator. The financial success of the Justo administration served to mark Señor Ortiz for the Presidency, which he won in the elections of 1938.

He is regarded as a man of unusual determination and has striven to bring to every community of Argentina a system of fair and impartial elections.

Ramon S. Castillo served successively in the Justo administration as Minister of the Interior, Minister of Justice and Minister of Public Education. As Acting Foreign Minister he urged the Madrid Government in October, 1936, to spare the life of José Antonio Primo de Rivera, captive Fascist sympathizer and son of the former Spanish dictator.

Last December Señor Castillo and four other members of the Argentine Cabinet were reported on the verge of resigning over differences with President Ortiz regarding the allegedly fraudulent elections in the province of Catamarca.

FIGHT AS SHIP SINKS

Germans and Italians Killed in Battle for Places in Lifeboats

RAIDER GIVES NO WARNING

Passengers Asleep as Torpedo Struck—Strife Is Revived Aboard Rescue Vessel

By JAMES B. RESTON

Special Cable to THE NEW YORK TIMES.

LONDON, July 3—Zigzagging westward across the Atlantic with 1,640 German and Italian prisoners sleeping down below and armed British soldiers patrolling her decks, the British prison ship Arandora Star, 15,501 tons, was torpedoed by a German submarine shortly after dawn yesterday morning. She went down with half of her company of prisoners battling along the rails for places in lifeboats.

It is believed 1,068 of the prisoners drowned or were killed in the battle for boats. About 1,000 survivors were landed today at a Scottish port, including 572 prisoners in addition to most of the crew of 300 and the 200 British soldier guards.

At the port where they were landed fighting broke out again among the battered German and Italian survivors.

Prisoners Mostly Merchants

Most of the prisoners aboard the Arandora Star were German and Italian merchants who were doing business in Britain when the war broke out. At first they were put behind barbed wire in prison camps here, but fear of what might happen if Nazi parachute troops succeeded in landing near these internment camps led British officials to decide that these prisoners should be transferred to Canada.

They were placed aboard the former Blue Star luxury cruise liner at the beginning of this week. The ship immediately headed through the North Channel and had got west of Ireland when a U-boat picked her up and blasted her with a torpedo.

As the survivors reconstructed their experience today, the explosion of that torpedo was terrific. It staggered the liner from stem to stern, and the sea poured in on men sleeping in bunks and hammocks swung in the holds.

The ship's lighting plant was immediately crippled by the explosion, and this added to the confusion. At first there was a terrific scramble by men to get on deck during which many were killed, survivors related, but it was when they got on deck that the real fighting started.

Apparently the British guards did their best to maintain order. The prisoners were directed to line up at boat stations but, according to survivors, the Germans refused and started a rush for the boats. This developed into a mad scramble during which many men were killed before they even had a chance to get away from the sinking ship.

"Fought Like Brutes"

One soldier who was aboard the ship said tonight:

"The Germans fought on the decks like brutes. They punched and kicked their way past the Italians.

"The scramble for boats was sickening. At one time I saw thirty of them fighting to slide down a rope into one of the lifeboats.

"The pity of it is that some of our lads were killed trying to lower boats for them."

The soldier and crew members, helped in some cases by prisoners, succeeded in floating life rafts and getting most of the lifeboats into the water. The fighting on the decks apparently hampered this, however, as not enough rafts and boats were floated to take care of all those in the water.

From the lifeboats the scene around the sinking liner was unbelievable, according to one ship's officer. To every man aboard, he said there had been issued a lifebelt, but the ship was attacked without warning and most of them either jumped or were thrown overboard without anything to hold them afloat.

Men clung onto the wreckage of the ship and the edges of boats and rafts as long as they could. The sea, fortunately, was not rough.

"After two hours in the water, swimming and resting on planks that had been blown from the ship," said a British soldier, "we saw a

Continued on Page Four

The International Situation

The British Navy is forcibly taking control over French naval ships in British ports, it was announced in London this morning. No details of the operation were made public except that "casualties" already had resulted—indicating that at least some French commanders were resisting the attempt to make them disobey the orders of the French Government that has surrendered. The British also are taking steps against French warships in French North African ports. [Page 1, Column 8.]

The British liner Arandora Star, en route from Britain to Canada with 2,000 persons aboard, most of them Germans and Italians bound for internment camps, was torpedoed by a German submarine off Ireland, it was disclosed yesterday. About 1,000 survivors reached one Scottish port, and others may turn up. Many of the lost were killed in a wild rush for lifeboats, British survivors said. [Page 1, Column 5.]

The French liner Champlain, formerly in the transatlantic service, was reported to have been sunk by a mine several days ago north of Bordeaux. She was about to leave for the United States with a large number of passengers, all of whom were saved. [Page 1, Column 4.]

German airmen started raiding Britain yesterday morning and kept it up almost all day. This stepped-up air activity was interpreted by the British as preparation for the impending German attempt to invade the country; there was much German reconnaissance over coast defenses. Tuesday night British airmen in American-made bombers dropped loads on German bases in the Netherlands. Other British bombers visited Western Germany. [Page 1, Column 3.]

The attack on Britain is a matter of "days if not hours," newspapers and military commentators in Rome agreed. [Page 2, Column 2.]

France will shortly call a National Assembly to approve a new constitution. According to Berlin dispatches, that constitution will eliminate "unwieldy democratic procedure." [Page 3, Column 8.]

The Russians completed their occupation of ceded provinces of Rumania at noon yesterday. Later in the day the Rumanian Parliament met; it had been expected to ratify the cession of Bessarabia and Northern Bukovina, but no such action was taken. In some quarters fears were expressed that the Russians eventually would extend their occupation to take in the entire Danube delta. Rumania hoped to make an arrangement by which Germany would guarantee her frontiers, but Germany appeared not to be interested. Hungarian troops, poised on the frontier of Transylvania, the former Hungarian province that Hungary wants returned to her, were reported to have been withdrawn. [Page 1, Column 7.]

Hungary, it was reported in Budapest, was ready to negotiate, rather than fight, with Rumania over her claim to Transylvania. [Page 4, Column 8.]

Cairo reported that the British Air Force had destroyed three Italian planes in a raid into Italian East Africa, bringing to sixty the total of Italian craft shot down since the war in the Near East started. Rome declared that a British attack in Ethiopia had been beaten off, sixty British dead being left on the field. [Page 4, Column 1.]

The British reply to Japan's demand that the road from Burma be closed to supplies for China probably will be a polite refusal. London reported that the British might sweeten the refusal with an offer to give up the British Concession at Shanghai. In Hong Kong the Japanese Consul-General denied that Japan intended to blockade that colony; it had been reported that such a blockade was projected as pressure to force the closing of the Burma road. [Page 1, Column 6.]

BRITAIN EXPECTED TO REBUFF JAPAN

Will Not Surrender on Issue of Burma Road—Pact With United States Denied

Special Cable to THE NEW YORK TIMES.

LONDON, July 3—The British reply to the Japanese request for the closing of the Burma road into China is now being prepared and may be sent in the next few days. The nature of the reply is not known yet, but the British are expected to refuse very politely.

The British have not yet abandoned their sympathy for the Chinese or their desire to help them. They have been unable to send the Chinese any supplies for several months. Most of the supplies for the Chinese Government, headed by Generalissimo Chiang Kai-shek, that have gone over the Burma road, have come, recently at least, from either the United States or Russia.

The British apparently are not willing to cut this source of supply from the Chinese Government. At the same time, however, it is possible that the British may offer an alternative suggestion to the Japanese. This might perhaps take the form of an offer to give up the British interest in the International Settlement, and British influence at Shanghai.

Obviously, the British are not in a position to defend the Shanghai Concession, where they have only troops with rifles and machine guns behind barbed wire. If the British deserted Shanghai they would probably concentrate the troops now there at Hong Kong, in great force, and use the others wherever they might be most needed. It is possible that any British offer to pull out of Shanghai may be conditioned upon the willingness of the Axis powers, with any interests there, to do the same.

But in all relations with Japan the British have faced an almost insoluble dilemma. Japan can fight, and under the present circumstances it is difficult to see just how Britain can produce either the ships or the men and guns to meet her. In addition, the British atti-

Continued on Page Six

CHANGES IN REGIME IN BUCHAREST SEEN

Military Dictatorship Held a Possibility—New War Steps Taken by Government

By C. L. SULZBERGER

By Telephone to THE NEW YORK TIMES.

BUCHAREST, Rumania, July 3—At noon today the Russian occupation of Bessarabia and Northern Bukovina was completed and the last Rumanian soldiers had withdrawn from the ceded territories. One hour later the loss was observed by one minute of silence imposed throughout the country. Black-trimmed flags were displayed everywhere and many people wore in mourning.

Five hours after the final stage of the cession Parliament met in special assembly. After a brief acknowledgment of Rumania's misfortune the Deputies and Senators stood silent for a minute and the sitting ended.

There had been many reports that Parliament would ratify the deed of the lost territories to Russia and that speeches on the government's policy would be heard. The Grand Rabbi was expected to utilize his position as a Senator to condemn the attitude of those Jews who hailed the Soviet and to reaffirm the loyalty of the bulk of his coreligionists to the regime.

That the session lasted only five minutes and that none of these anticipated events took place gave rise to many rumors to the effect that the ratification had been postponed in order to avoid speeches that might be considered provocative by Moscow, or in order to prevent opponents of the government's recent policy from airing their views.

These reports appear to be unfounded. What would seem to be the truth is that the government decided yesterday to refrain from ratifying the loss of the territories so that Rumanian admission of their new status would never be historically recorded except as the de facto result of forceful occupation. Such a course of action was recommended in the Iorga memorandum received yesterday. This

Continued on Page Five

SOME UNITS RESIST

2 Casualties Reported—One French Admiral Refuses Conditions

CLASH CONTINUES AT ORAN

London Says It Is Essential to Keep These Vessels Out of Enemy Hands

Special Cable to THE NEW YORK TIMES.

LONDON, Thursday, July 4—All units of the French Fleet in British ports were put under British control yesterday, the Ministry of Information revealed in a sudden announcement early this morning.

At the same time, the Ministry said, "certain conditions" were offered to French vessels in North African ports, designed to keep these ships out of German hands.

The French Admiral at the port of Oran, in Algeria, refused to accept these conditions and "action had to be taken," it was announced. Those operations are still proceeding, and Prime Minister Winston Churchill will make a statement concerning them to the House of Commons today, the announcement concluded.

Lack of Confidence

The British action, the communiqué stated, was based upon the fact that no confidence could be placed in the German and Italian assurances that the French vessels would not be used against Britain. At the same time, however, it was declared that Britain was animated by the desire to restore the independence of France and the integrity of the French Empire.

It was declared that this action had to be taken "before it was too late" and this phrase is thought to be significant here.

The success of the operation, presumably that of putting all French ships now in British ports under British control, was announced, and it was stated that two casualties that occurred had been the result of a misunderstanding.

Action Is Continuing

The second part of the communiqué, however, referred to vessels in the North African ports, upon which "conditions" were imposed, and apparently this operation, which the communiqué described as "taking action," had not been concluded when the statement was issued.

How large a part of the powerful French Navy is now at the disposal of the British is not known, and it was not even hinted in the statement. It was assumed, however, that the action announced covered not only such French men-of-war as might be in ports in Great Britain, but also French vessels in other British ports throughout the world.

The exact disposition of the French fleets has been kept a closely guarded secret since the Pétain Government in France signed the armistice with Germany. However, it is known that a number of units are at Casablanca.

On an officially conducted visit to one British naval base in home waters last week, American newspaper men saw a number of small French naval craft and were told that others were anchored at another British home base.

Circumstances Not Revealed

The circumstances of the clash in which the two casualties occurred and the details concerning the difficulties encountered by the French admiral's attitude at Oran were not forthcoming. British naval officials firmly declined to elaborate on the communiqué of the Ministry of Information, pointing out that Mr. Churchill would make a fuller statement in the House of Commons today.

It is believed that there are at least 120 small French craft, such as submarine chasers, torpedo boats and the like, in English waters.

The French Fleet has been working in close cooperation with the British Navy since the outbreak of the war. In this connection, it will be recalled that before the war began the British and French Governments agreed that in the event of European hostilities the French Fleet would operate under the general command of the British Admiralty, although functioning as the French Fleet and not as part of the British, while the British Army would be under the orders of the French High Command.

With Italy's entry into the war and the consequent necessity for the French to give added protection to their African colonies in the Medi-

Continued on Page Two

"All the News That's Fit to Print."

NEWS INDEX, PAGE 27, THIS SECTION

The New York Times.

LATE CITY EDITION
Fair today, not much change in temperature. Tomorrow cloudy with showers at night.
Temperatures Yesterday—Max., 80; Min., 60

Section 1

Copyright, 1940, by The New York Times Company.

VOL. LXXXIX..No. 30,115. | Entered as Second-Class Matter, Postoffice, New York, N. Y. | NEW YORK, SUNDAY, JULY 7, 1940. | Including Rotogravure Picture, Magazine and Book Review. | TEN CENTS | TWELVE CENTS Beyond 200 Miles, Except West of Pa.—South of Md.—North of Mass.

ROOSEVELT URGES MONROE DOCTRINES FOR EUROPEAN AND ASIATIC CONTINENTS; BRITISH PLANES BOMB THE DUNKERQUE

WILLKIE WILL SHUN ANY 'BRAIN TRUST' OR 'GHOST' SPEECHES

Determined to Write His Own Addresses on Problems of Nation, Friends Say

DEFERS CAMPAIGN PLANS

Will Fly to Capital Tomorrow for a Talk With McNary—Going to Colorado Tuesday

Wendell L. Willkie, Republican Presidential nominee, has turned "thumbs down" on the formation of any "brain trust" and is determined during the coming campaign to present his position on problems confronting the nation in speeches that he has personally written, it was learned authoritatively yesterday.

While the candidate has always been willing to listen to suggestions and advice from all possible sources, it is known that he has proudly told persons close to him that "I have never in my life delivered a speech which I haven't written myself and I am not going to change my habits now."

Meanwhile Mr. Willkie deferred any formal announcement of his campaign organization plans until after a conference with United States Senator Charles L. McNary, his running mate, in Washington tomorrow afternoon.

Following a second day meeting with the subcommittee of the Republican National Committee at the Waldorf-Astoria Hotel, Mr. Willkie announced that no definite action had yet been taken on the appointment of his proposed three-man campaign board.

Will Fly to Washington

He said he was leaving the city tomorrow afternoon at 2 o'clock by plane from La Guardia Airport and would "talk over" the entire campaign set-up with Senator McNary, whom he will be meeting for the first time, before making any decision concerning the board, which is to include the Republican national chairman, a campaign manager and a personal representative of the candidate.

Under the plans announced yesterday, Mr. Willkie is scheduled to arrive in Washington shortly after 3 o'clock, and will confer in private with Senator McNary during the rest of the afternoon. In the evening he will be the guest of honor at a dinner given by Representative Joseph W. Martin Jr., minority leader of the House, and Representatives Frank O. Horton and Charles A. Halleck. The dinner will be attended by Republican members of Congress, John D. M. Hamilton, Republican national chairman; the staff of the Congressional campaign committee and the eleven members of the subcommittee who have been conferring with Mr. Willkie here.

On Tuesday morning Mr. Willkie will hold another meeting with the subcommittee at the Willard Hotel, at which time, it is expected, he will formally announce his campaign organization appointments.

Immediately following the Tuesday morning meeting Mr. Willkie is scheduled to leave the Capital by plane for Colorado, where he and Mrs. Willkie and their son, Philip, will spend a vacation of at least two weeks. The exact location of the Willkie vacation spot has not yet been determined, but Mr. Willkie will be the guest of Governor and Mrs. Ralph Carr of Colorado.

Plans for Acceptance Speech

It was disclosed that during his vacation in Colorado Mr. Willkie intended to draft his acceptance speech, which is scheduled to be made in his home town of Elwood, Ind., around Aug. 1. This speech, like the rest of the speeches during the campaign, it was said, will be written personally by Mr. Willkie.

While it was announced that no final decision would be reached on the proposed three-man campaign board until after the conference between the two Republican standard bearers in Washington tomorrow, it was believed that some opposition within the Republican ranks was developing against the appointment of a campaign manager as well as national chairman. It was believed that some Republican leaders felt that the appointment of a campaign manager would relegate the national chairman to a subordinate position.

It was thought likely that a solution to the problem might be reached by the appointment of the person Mr. Willkie wanted as campaign manager as national chairman and the retention of Mr. Hamilton as executive assistant to the chairman. It was pointed out that the Democratic National Committee had done this when John J. Raskob served as national chairman and Jouett Shouse acted as executive assistant and attended to the many organizational matters devolving upon a chairman.

If this plan were to be carried

Continued on Page Two

Farley Is Quitting Politics To Head Yankee Ball Club

Leader to Leave Cabinet After Convention and Decline to Run Campaign but May Keep State Post for a Time

By JAMES A. HAGERTY

Postmaster General James A. Farley will not accept re-election as chairman of the Democratic National Committee and shortly after the Democratic National Convention will become the head of the Yankee baseball team and its chain of clubs.

Mr. Farley also will resign as Postmaster General soon after the convention. He probably will retain his post as Democratic State chairman for the present, largely because of his friendship for United States Senator James M. Mead, whom he wishes to see renominated and re-elected, but his decision not to run another Presidential campaign marks the beginning of his withdrawal from active participation in politics to enter business.

James M. Cox, former Governor of Ohio, is Mr. Farley's principal backer in the purchase of the Yankee baseball empire from the Ruppert estate at a price said to be between $3,500,000 and $4,000,000. Edward Barrow, who now heads the baseball system, will be retained to perform his present duties, with the title of vice president. Mr. Barrow, it was learned, will continue to have full authority in directing the Yankees and subsidiary clubs.

Definite knowledge that Mr. Farley will not run another national campaign came simultaneously with announcement at Hyde Park that he had been invited to confer there today with President Roosevelt. The information concerning Mr. Farley's plans did not come directly from him, and he could not be reached for discussion of them after his intention to quit politics for business became known.

Although Mr. Farley is known to have been opposed in principle to a third term for any President, he is said by friends to believe that President Roosevelt has created a situation in which it will be virtually impossible for the Democratic National Convention to nominate any other candidate. Approximately three-fourths of the delegates have been instructed for President Roosevelt and it is understood to be Mr. Farley's belief that there would not now be a chance to build up any one else into a winning candidate.

Originally in favor of the nomination of Secretary of State Cordell Hull for President, with some hope that he himself might be named for second place on the ticket, Mr. Farley now is understood to feel that Mr. Roosevelt must head the Demo-

Continued on Page Two

$130,907,034 PLAN OF WPA WORK HERE FOR YEAR DRAFTED

Somervell Discloses Program Drawn Up With Mayor and Federal, State Aides

COST TO CITY $30,583,800

$90,680,100 Is Allocated to Construction, $31,655,200 to White-Collar Projects

A program calling for the expenditure of $130,907,034 on WPA projects in New York City in the next twelve months and providing employment throughout that period for 105,000 relief workers has been drawn up by Lieut. Col. Brehon B. Somervell, local Work Projects Administrator, in cooperation with Mayor La Guardia and representatives of State and Federal agencies.

More than 95 per cent of the work is to be done under the sponsorship of city departments, with the municipal park system as the principal potential beneficiary. Colonel Somervell disclosed last night. The entire program was prepared, however, with the understanding that its execution depended on the amount of WPA funds actually allocated to this city.

The city is to assume $30,583,800 of the $122,335,300 total cost of the projects to be undertaken at its request. The State, with projects involving an outlay of $1,087,671, is to put up $307,200 and Federal departments, sponsoring work with an aggregate cost of $7,484,063, are to contribute $723,170. The cost to the WPA of the full program will be $99,292,864.

Bulk Is Construction Work

The bulk of the work sponsored by the Mayor is in the construction field. The contemplated expenditure on projects of this type is $90,680,100, with the remaining $31,655,200 set aside for white-collar and professional enterprises.

Included in the $24,276,400 park construction program are plans for new play areas at various points along the Belt Parkway in Brooklyn and Queens. The total cost of these undertakings will exceed $9,000,000, according to the program.

A total of $10,365,500 is allocated to Borough President James J. Lyons of the Bronx for the building of highways and sewers. Repaving of Eastern Boulevard is the largest project listed for the borough. Borough President George U. Harvey of Queens is to receive $6,833,000, Stanley H. Isaacs of Manhattan $6,491,700, John Cashmore of Brooklyn $5,648,700 and Joseph A. Palma of Richmond $2,555,300.

Renovations and repairs to public school buildings will take $5,771,900 of the WPA outlay and $169,600 more will be spent on landscaping and repair work at the four city colleges. Slum clearance activities in Manhattan, Brooklyn and the Bronx will cost $2,424,300, and the Department of Water Supply, Gas and Electricity will get $5,735,700, most of which is to be used for extension and improvement of the municipal water supply system.

Hospitals throughout the city will benefit from the expenditure of $5,403,300 on repairs, alterations and new construction. Other engineering projects will be carried on for the city on bridges, public markets, warehouses, incinerators and sanitation depots, libraries and public buildings of all kinds.

The largest single item in the white-collar and professional program is $5,357,395 for the maintenance of WPA sewing shops. These shops produce clothing, towels and bedding for the city's 140,000 home relief families.

A WPA allowance of $1,793,471 is made for the commodity distribu-

Continued on Page Four

YOUTH CONGRESS BARS LIBERTY PLEA

Refuses to Consider Suppression of Civil Status in Totalitarian States

By FRANK S. ADAMS

Special to THE NEW YORK TIMES.

COLLEGE CAMP, Wis., July 6—A new challenge to the American Youth Congress to go on record against the suppression of civil liberties by totalitarian States, including Soviet Russia, rose from within its own ranks late today.

After Gene Tunney, former heavyweight prizefight champion of the world, had made known his support of plans for a rival youth organization, and had started back for New York, the issue was brought up anew by Franklin Kramer, delegate to the Congress from the All-Campus Peace Federation of the University of Wisconsin.

Mr. Kramer at a meeting of the Commission on Civil Liberties of the Congress offered a resolution which would have placed the Congress on record as condemning the suppression of civil liberties under the totalitarian governments of Germany, Italy, Russia and Spain.

The resolution was ruled out of order on the ground that the commission was constituted to consider only civil liberties in the United States, but Mr. Kramer announced he would offer it later tonight at a general session of the Congress.

"I'd like to see a little deviation from the Communist party line," Mr. Kramer told reporters. "I don't want to kick out the Communists or the Fascists either, but there should be a stand against the party line.

Raises Issue of Finland

"We never can attack the sacred cow of Russia or of Communism. We can criticize England for her colonies and tell the United States to keep out of South America, but we can't say anything about Russia going into Finland or Poland."

Mr. Kramer said that he had no desire to split the Congress and did not believe the majority of the delegates were Communists. However, he said, the Communists in the Congress were able to control the other delegates by "rolling the bandwagon of ridicule."

"I don't care what the Communists say, it's what they leave out," he went on. "On Russia and communism there is always silence. I'm not anti-congress and I would hate to be called anti-Communist. I think this resolution is pretty futile now, although I didn't when I came here."

Mr. Kramer said that he had talked to Murray Plavner of New York, leader of the "pro-American" bloc of foes of the congress, but that he was not convinced of Mr. Plavner's sincerity.

Earlier in the day the Youth Congress had staged an elaborate mock-reception for Mr. Tunney, who had ignored its invitation to speak before it.

While 500 or more delegates and observers howled with glee, a committee of six girls escorted the imaginary figure of the former prizefighter to the platform and grouped about his empty chair. James B. Carey, secretary of the Congress of Industrial Organizations and a vice president of the Youth Congress, offered to shake hands

Continued on Page Twenty-six

MEXICO IS TENSE ON EVE OF VOTING

Almazan Supporter Is Killed in Capital—Bridges to the United States Closed

By ARNALDO CORTESI

Wireless to THE NEW YORK TIMES.

MEXICO CITY, July 6—Tomorrow the Mexican people, tense with excitement, will be called to the polls to decide by their votes who shall compose the new Congress, which is to be completely renewed on Sept. 1, and who shall be the new President to sit in the National Palace for a six-year period beginning Dec. 1.

Though the campaign was fought with considerable bitterness on both sides, everything points to the conclusion that tomorrow's election will be comparatively peaceful. There will certainly be plenty of local clashes between the supporters of the two candidates, but no general upheaval on a national scale is expected.

One newsboy, supporting General Almazan, was killed and two other persons were wounded here today.

A fight is expected to occur especially in the early morning, when the contest begins between the two opposing parties to gain control of the polls. The Mexican electoral law provides that the polls shall be run by a committee of citizens selected by themselves among the first to reach voting places. As control of the polls gives an opportunity for chicanery, the election of these committees always gives rise to keen rivalry.

Police Precautions Taken

The authorities have taken every possible precaution to maintain order. All troops and police will be confined to barracks tonight and will be distributed among the polls tomorrow. According to law they are not allowed to stay inside the voting places, but will be kept in the vicinity in case of trouble.

The police have been busy in the last few days rounding up all bricks, stones, clubs and other objects that might be used as missiles or weapons. Strict orders have

Continued on Page Fifteen

Major Sports Yesterday

RACING

Myron Selznick's Can't Wait, paying $11.90 for $2, won the $29,850 Butler Handicap by a length and a half from War Dog before 21,460 persons, who wagered $1,034,972 at Empire City. Eight Thirty, the favorite, was third. Kantar Run returned $233.60, a record price for the New York season, by capturing the first race.

BASEBALL

The Dodgers maintained their one-game lead over the Reds by shutting out the Bees, 2—0, behind Tot Pressnell's three-hit pitching at Boston. However, the Giants were routed by the Phils, 8—2, at the Polo Grounds and the Yankees dropped an 8-7 decision to the Athletics on Frank Hayes's safety in the tenth at Philadelphia.

GOLF

Frankie Strafaci, twice metropolitan champion, and the three players who tied for the medal, Charley Newman, Aquila C. Giles and Bob Sweeny, were eliminated in the Long Island amateur.

TENNIS

Frank Kovacs and Elwood Cooke reached the final of the Nassau invitation tourney. Kovacs beat Joe Hunt, 6—2, 6—1, 2—6, 6—3, and Cooke halted Hal Surface, 4—6, 6—3, 6—0, 6—1.

(Complete Details of These and Other Sports Events in Section 5.)

6 HITS ON WARSHIP

British Make Sure Pride of French Navy Will Not Fight Again

FLEET IN EGYPT GIVES UP

Destroyer and Escort Vessel Reported Sunk, Former After 2-Hour Battle

Special Cable to THE NEW YORK TIMES.

LONDON, July 6—The bombing by British naval planes of the already crippled French battleship Dunkerque to complete the task of making her permanently unfit to fight against this country, a task begun in the Battle of Oran Wednesday, was announced by the Admiralty today.

The raid on the powerful battleship cost the British two planes, but they scored six direct hits.

[The sinking of a French destroyer by British warships in a two-hour battle off Crete and of a French escort vessel near Algiers was announced by the French, according to The Associated Press. London sources called the story of the destroyer's loss false "propaganda," The United Press reported.]

The Admiralty reported that planes of the fleet air arm dropped the six bombs on the Dunkerque as the once-proud vessel lay grounded on the coast of Algeria where she was driven ashore in flames after the Battle of Oran.

Wednesday's Task Completed

Officials explained that the extent of the damage done to the Dunkerque during the battle was not known. Therefore, today's bombing attack was made because "it was considered essential that the ship should be in no condition to take part in the war in case she should fall under enemy control."

The communiqué said that at the end of the naval engagement between the British ships and their former Allies at Oran French Admiral Marcel-Bruno Gensoul, the commander, had signaled that his warships were "hors de combat" and that he was ordering the crews to evacuate their vessels.

In view of this, the British Admiralty said, it was not considered necessary to send out any warnings before making further attacks on the Dunkerque.

The Admiralty did not say whether the two British planes that failed to return from the raid on the battleship were shot down as a result of opposition fire.

Alexandria Fleet Demobilized

Special Cable to THE NEW YORK TIMES.

CAIRO, Egypt, July 6—Demobilization of that part of the French fleet that has been in Alexandria has been carried out without difficulty, Colonel Salisbury Jones, former head of the British military mission in Syria, said in a broadcast speech today.

Addressing his former comrades-in-arms, Colonel Jones said that the demobilization had been effected in a spirit of complete understanding. [According to The United Press, the French ships at Alexandria include the battleship Lorraine, four cruisers and several minor vessels.]

200 Dead on 3 French Ships

LONDON, Sunday, July 7 (AP)—A Reuters dispatch from Vichy, France, today quoted an Algiers dispatch as saying the French battleships Dunkerque and Provence and the destroyer Mogador lost 200 killed and 150 seriously wounded in the naval battle with British warships last Wednesday.

The dispatch also said there were only 200 survivors from the French battleship Bretagne. Her normal complement was 1,133, but she was in port at the time of the battle and probably many of the crew were ashore on leave.

The four ships were reported ashore as a result of the fight. It was said engineers were studying means of refloating them.

Sinking of Destroyer Denied

LONDON, July 6 (UP)—An authoritative source here today denied reports that British cruisers had sunk the French destroyer Frondeur off Crete.

"There is no fragment of truth in this report, which must be regarded as a particularly unscrupulous example of propaganda," it was stated.

A German report said that forty-two members of the Frondeur's crew had been rescued by a Greek

Continued on Page Twenty-two

The International Situation

American Developments

President Roosevelt yesterday reiterated his warning to non-American nations to stay out of this hemisphere. What happens to the American possessions of conquered countries is a matter for the American republics alone to decide, he held. He added that, under a similar principle of regional consultation and decision, Europe and Asia might well apply "Monroe Doctrines" of their own. The President's position, expressed through a White House secretary, was re-emphasized one day after it became known that a previous warning to stay out of this hemisphere, transmitted through diplomatic channels three weeks ago, had been rejected by Germany as pointless. [Page 1, Column 8.]

Five United States destroyers reached the vicinity of Martinique, French West Indies, where the French aircraft carrier Béarn, with 150 American military planes aboard, is in harbor. The mission of the destroyers is observation only; they are to determine whether British warships are blockading the island. Washington reported that the United States was as anxious as the British about the possibility that the planes might fall into German hands via the French. [Page 1, Column 7.]

In Europe and Africa

The British attempted to give the coup de grace to the 26,500-ton French battleship Dunkerque. In Wednesday's French-British naval battle off Oran, Algeria, the Dunkerque, heavily damaged, was run ashore. Yesterday, London announced, planes were sent in after her; they scored six hits with big bombs. Two of the planes failed to return, possibly indicating French resistance.

Commanders of French naval units with the British Fleet at Alexandria, Egypt, were reported to have agreed to a program by which their vessels would be immobilized, staying there indefinitely. [All the foregoing, Page 1, Column 5.]

Count Ciano, Italy's Foreign Minister, confers in Berlin today with Chancellor Hitler. Rome asserts that the fate of Southeastern Europe will be decided at that meeting. The Italians analyze the situation thus: Russia has advanced into the Balkans, and may advance farther; Hungary and Bulgaria are clamoring for pieces of Rumania; it is imperative, as far as the Germans and Italians are concerned, that the Balkans remain quiet during the attack on Britain. How that quiet can be achieved is the first topic for discussion between Count Ciano and the Chancellor. Rome also reported that attempts were being made to get a totalitarian France to join in the attack on Britain. [Page 19, Column 1.]

Chancellor Hitler returned to Berlin from the west, and received a triumph. Bands played, church bells rang, crowds in the streets shouted "Sieg Heil!" and flowers were strewn in his path by white-bloused Hitler Maidens. [Page 1, Column 6.]

British raiders reported bombing German naval bases at Kiel and Wilhelmshaven and docks at Cuxhaven and Hamburg. German raiders reported bombing harbors, railways and oil tanks in South and Central England. The Germans said their airmen had sunk one British submarine and damaged another in the North Sea. [Page 21, Column 1.]

The German Propaganda and War Ministries took a group of foreign correspondents on a tour of the Ruhr and Rhine Valleys to display the effects of nightly British air raids. No evidence of damage to military objectives was shown the visitors; it is the German contention that no such damage has been inflicted. The correspondents did not see Essen, home of the Krupp works, which Britain claims to have bombed. They reported that residents of the industrial areas were evidencing the physical and nervous effects of nightly trips to bombproof shelters. [Page 21, Column 2.]

The Germans admitted that they were having trouble with the conquered Netherlanders. The German military command in Amsterdam issued a communiqué saying that the character of British air raids proved the British were getting information from within the Netherlands. The persons responsible were threatened with death. [Page 22, Column 6.]

A "successful action" against Italian warships in Tobruk Harbor, Libya, was credited to British naval and air force planes by the London Admiralty. The Italian High Command said that strong British attacks on two North African forts had been repulsed. [Page 23, Column 4.]

HITLER WELCOMED BY FRENZIED BERLIN

Thousands Cheer Chancellor on Flower-Covered Route in Conqueror's Triumph

By PERCIVAL KNAUTH

Wireless to THE NEW YORK TIMES.

BERLIN, July 6—Adolf Hitler, "field lord," "guider of battles," "victor of the greatest campaign in history" rode triumphant into Berlin today over a carpet of flowers.

The mile-long route from the Anhalter station to the Chancellery was a perfumed avenue of greens, reds, blues and yellows flanked by cheering thousands who shouted and wept themselves into a frantic hysteria as the Fuehrer passed.

Whatever price in misery and sorrow Germany paid for her defeat twenty-two years ago was forgotten today in the frenzied joy of victory. Caesar in his glory was never more turbulently received and Adolf Hitler, one-time corporal in the Kaiser's army, was indeed accorded a Caesar's welcome.

Eight weeks of warfare, moreover, had changed him. The spirit that had animated him to snap his fingers in glee when he received the news that the French had asked for an armistice was evident today in the beaming smiles and the frank delight he showed at his reception.

He was greeted at the station by Field Marshal Hermann Goering and nearly every military, government and party functionary of high rank in the Reich.

Dr. Hjalmar Schacht, former President of the Reichsbank, who recently has been rarely seen at official public receptions, was present, sharing a car with Dr. Alfred

Continued on Page Twenty

U. S. NAVAL VESSELS WATCH MARTINIQUE

Hull Studies Data With Other American States on British Blockade of French Isle

Special to THE NEW YORK TIMES.

WASHINGTON, July 6—Five destroyers of the American neutrality patrol were said in informed quarters here to be lying tonight off Martinique, French island in the West Indies, to observe the reported British blockade.

It was stressed that the duty of this flotilla, which left St. Thomas, Virgin Islands, yesterday, according to press reports, was merely to observe and report, in line with the usual policy of ships on neutrality patrol, and not to take any direct action.

Secretary of State Cordell Hull indicated during the day that this government was not planning any immediate steps with regard to the Martinique situation, when he remarked that, while United States patrols here and there were seeking to assemble full information, it took a little time to do this.

As to Other American Nations

When asked whether conversations had been instituted with Latin-American governments about the danger of bringing actual warfare into the bounds of the Pan-American neutrality zone, the Secretary of State remarked that he guessed other American nations had not had time to get the facts either.

Mr. Hull said that there was no United States consul nearer to Martinique than Trinidad, British West Indies.

Although London raised the technical point that a blockade did not exist, it was conceded privately by

Continued on Page Sixteen

PLAN OF PRESIDENT

All the Nations in Each Sphere Would Decide Territories' Fate

NOT JUST A CONQUEROR

Thus Americas Will Act, Chief Executive Says, Renewing Warning to Germany

From a Staff Correspondent

HYDE PARK, July 6—President Roosevelt suggested today that Europe and Asia each apply the principles of the Monroe Doctrine to its own territories. Under these principles all of the European and Asiatic nations would confer and "make the decision—not just one conquering power."

"Let all of them settle their disputes in Asia and Europe and let all the Americas settle the question of disposition, administration and supervision of such islands or other territorial possessions which belonged to nations conquered by Germany and which lie properly within this hemisphere," said Stephen T. Early, White House secretary, who spoke for the President.

This renewed warning to European and Asiatic powers to keep out of the Western Hemisphere, coming on the heels of Germany's former rejections as "pointless," of the United States' "hands off" notice to the Reich, was regarded as sounding the keynote of the Pan-American conference scheduled for Havana this month. It had the effect of investing other Western Hemisphere nations with a proprietary interest in the Monroe Doctrine.

"We Seek No Expansion"

The President, in effect, told outside countries to mind their business as this nation proposed to mind its own. But he withdrew nothing from his statement yesterday that freedom of cultural and commercial intercourse between nations was necessary for enduring world peace.

Mr. Early was careful to point out that the Chief Executive had discussed the subject at length with Secretary Hull during a telephone conversation last night.

"There is an absence of any intention on the part of this government," Mr. Early said for the President, "to interfere in any territorial problems in Europe or Asia. This government would like to see and thinks there should be applied 'a Monroe Doctrine' for each of those continents.

"The United States is not out to gain any new territorial possession; it does not contemplate any territorial expansion.

Question for Americas

"But, for example, should a victorious Germany lay claim to territories of conquered nations in this hemisphere, we hold that the issue comes within the province of the Monroe Doctrine. We hold that it works in this way: The United States does not take over the islands or territorial possessions of the conquered nations but it believes and holds the position that their disposition and administration should be decided among and by all of the American republics."

As an example of the practical application of the policy he said the President had outlined a short time before, Mr. Early said this government would ask no voice in the disposition of French Indo-China because of its place in the sphere of Asiatic influence.

"For instance," said Mr. Early, "in the case of French Indo-China, we think the disposition should be decided among the Asiatic countries."

It was recalled in connection with the President's latest interpretation of the Monroe Doctrine that the Cuban Government recently proposed that the American republics should take joint action to "hold in trust" the Western Hemisphere possessions of conquered European nations.

However, Mr. Early frowned on the interpretation that, according to the President's policy, this country would have nothing to say about the disposition of the Dutch East Indies.

This was taken to mean that national defense considerations made it necessary to consider the Dutch East Indies within the sphere of American influence. Mr. Early, apparently, thought it unnecessary

Continued on Page Fourteen

"All the News That's Fit to Print."

The New York Times.

LATE CITY EDITION
Fair and continued warm today and tomorrow.
Temperatures Yesterday—Max., 90; Min., 69

VOL. LXXXIX...No. 30,128. Entered as Second-Class Matter, Postoffice, New York, N. Y. NEW YORK, SATURDAY, JULY 20, 1940. THREE CENTS NEW YORK CITY and Vicinity | FOUR CENTS Elsewhere Except in 7th and 8th Postal Zones.

FARLEY WILL QUIT IN MONTH; BOARD TO NAME SUCCESSOR; 3D TERM FIGHT IS ORGANIZING

FARLEY EXPLAINS

Says Financial Reasons Impel Him to Retire as Party Pilot

WILL RETAIN STATE POST

He Pledges Roosevelt Full Support, but Many Leave Chicago Disgruntled

By JAMES A. HAGERTY
Special to THE NEW YORK TIMES.

CHICAGO, July 19—As delegates to the Democratic National Convention, many of them disgruntled, were leaving town today, the new Democratic National Committee re-elected Postmaster General Farley chairman to serve until Aug. 17 and appointed a subcommittee of five with power to select Mr. Farley's successor.

The subcommittee, composed of Edward J. Flynn of New York, chairman; David Fitzgerald Sr. of Connecticut, William W. Howes of New York, Mrs. Mildred Jasper of Ohio and Miss Beatrice Cobb of North Carolina, was directed to confer with President Roosevelt and Secretary Wallace, nominee for the Vice Presidency, before naming the new chairman. The effect of this action was to put it up to the President to name the man to conduct his campaign.

Senator James F. Byrnes of South Carolina and Frank G. Walker of New York continued to be about the only two under serious consideration for the chairmanship, although Mr. Farley when asked, said he had heard suggestions of Harry L. Hopkins, Secretary of Commerce, and Leo Crowley, chairman of the Federal Deposit Insurance Corporation. Senator Byrnes and Mr. Walker each has said that he would not accept the chairmanship.

Dissatisfaction Indicated

Selection of a new chairman may be difficult for the President, as men of Mr. Farley's ability as a campaign manager are few, and there are indications, not only that Wendell L. Willkie, Republican Presidential nominee, will make a fighting campaign, but that there are many Democrats who are not satisfied with their party's ticket and may bolt.

Mr. Farley, whose ability as a political prognosticator was proved by his success in predicting the results of the 1932 and 1936 Presidential campaigns, declined to give any advance prediction of the result of this year's election.

"I don't think I'll do any predicting," he said. "That's a matter the new fellow will have to reckon with."

The feeling of dissatisfaction among Democrats was shown plainly by many delegates as they prepared to depart for their homes. There was in the convention a considerable sprinkling of Democrats who were opposed to the third term nomination on principle, and who believed, despite the President's assertion that he had been reluctant to run, that Mr. Roosevelt had so handled the situation as to leave the convention no alternative but to renominate him.

Objection to Wallace

There was a much larger number of delegates who were strongly opposed to the nomination of Secretary Wallace, a former Republican and ardent New Dealer, for second place on the ticket. This was shown by the groans and boos which followed the casting of votes for Mr. Wallace in the balloting last night.

President Roosevelt, it was learned, was informed by telephone that he was in error if he thought the nomination of Secretary Wallace would add strength to the ticket in the farm States and also was told that the nomination would be resented by old-line Democrats, to whom loyalty to their party is a fetish.

It was noteworthy that the nomination of Secretary Wallace, even with the weight of the President's authority behind his candidacy, could hardly have been brought about without the support of the party leaders of the large cities. Large blocks of needed votes were thrown to Mr. Wallace in Illinois by Mayor Kelly of Chicago, in Pennsylvania by Senator Guffey and others, and in New York by Mr. Flynn.

Mr. Farley said in a statement read at a press conference immediately after the national committee meeting in the Stevens Hotel that he was retiring as national

Continued on Page Seven

Burke Predicts Organized Drive By Anti-Third-Term Democrats

He Tells of Offers of Aid for Campaign—Ex-Legion Head Shifts to Willkie and Senator Smith Bolts President

Special to THE NEW YORK TIMES.

WASHINGTON, July 19—Formation of a national organization of anti-third-term Democrats to support Wendell L. Willkie for the Presidency in November was predicted today by Senator Burke, who bolted his party yesterday in protest against the nomination of President Roosevelt as a violation of American political tradition.

Senator Burke, who was defeated for the Democratic Senatorial nomination in the Nebraska primary in April, made his prediction as Senator Vandenberg described the Democratic convention as "totalitarian" and warned against "an American political dictatorship such as obviously reduced the Chicago convention to the status of a ditto mark."

Senator Burke told reporters during an interview that his denunciation of the third term effort yesterday had prompted many telegrams of congratulation and offers to help him create a pro-Willkie organization of anti-third-term Democrats. He said the extent of this sentiment in the Middle West was "tremendous."

He cited one telegram from James W. Mellen, chairman of the Jeffersonian Democrats of California, in which it was suggested that "all our kind of Democrats" meet at some central point to form a national organization with purposes similar to his own.

"The many Democrats who feel as I do will undoubtedly get together," he added.

Senator Burke further declared that he would oppose in the coming national election in his own State of Nebraska or elsewhere any candidate who expressed approval of a third term for Mr. Roosevelt and predicted that unless checked by unforeseen circumstances, anti-third-term sentiment would be more than enough to defeat the President for re-election.

Commenting on the President's address last night, he added:

"It was an able and well delivered speech as the President's usually are but altogether unconvincing as to the main issue involved. I do not see that the President offered any reason why he should not go ahead with the private life which he said was his all-consuming desire."

In his statement on the Democratic convention, Senator Vanden-

Continued on Page Eight

WALLACE DEFERS CAMPAIGN PLANS

Course to Be Mapped After He Talks to Roosevelt Thursday in Washington, He Says

By WARREN MOSCOW
Special to THE NEW YORK TIMES.

CHICAGO, July 19—Henry A. Wallace, nominated early this morning for Vice President on the Democratic ticket, will confer with President Roosevelt in Washington on Thursday regarding his campaign plans.

Secretary Wallace, at a press conference in his rooms in the Palmer House, said that he did not know what those plans would be until he had talked to the President. The President, he said, suggested that he curtail a vacation which he had planned and return to Washington next week. Mr. Wallace will spend the interval at his home in Iowa.

"I will do anything the President wants me to do in the way of campaigning," Mr. Wallace declared.

In view of the President's speech to the delegates, that he would attempt nothing in the way of a campaign tour, it was suggested to Mr. Wallace that this might fall on his shoulders. He laughingly said that he would try to carry the load, if necessary.

Mr. Wallace, who has never run for public office, was questioned about his former political affiliations, and his answers emphasized his lack of close connections with the Republicans. His nomination had been attacked on the convention floor because he was registered Republican until 1936.

"My father was a Republican," Mr. Wallace began. "As you know, he served as Secretary of Agriculture in the Harding and Coolidge Administrations, dying in office in 1924. He worked for the farmer, as I have always tried to work for the farmer, but he did not get any place with the Republican high command.

Broke With Republicans in 1924

"By 1924, I was convinced of that, but my father was a Republican and I was loyal to him. When he died, I no longer felt bound by that loyalty and I did not vote for Coolidge in 1924.

"In 1928, I had some feeble hopes that Frank Lowden might be nominated by the Republicans, but I went to the convention, not as a delegate, took a look around, and knew it was no use. They nominated Hoover and when the Democrats nominated Smith, I supported Smith, making speeches around Iowa.

"By 1932, of course, I was speaking for Roosevelt under Democratic auspices, while in 1928 I had been speaking on my own."

Asked why he had delayed enrolling as a Democrat until 1936, Mr. Wallace said that failure to change the enrollment was an oversight. He did not vote often in party primaries, he said.

Mr. Wallace revealed how, when

Continued on Page Seven

'I SOUGHT TO RUN,' WILLKIE ASSERTS

Makes 'No Pretense of Noble Motive,' He Says in Referring to Roosevelt Speech

By JAMES C. HAGERTY
Special to THE NEW YORK TIMES

DENVER, July 19—Declaring that he had "frankly sought the opportunity to run for President," Wendell L. Willkie today took President Roosevelt to task for his address last night to the Democratic National Convention.

Coming here this morning from his Colorado Springs hotel to confer with stockmen and beet sugar producers in the Rocky Mountain region, Mr. Willkie, in a brief speech to about 500 persons at the Denver Union Stock Yards, referred to the President's speech by saying:

"I shall make no pretense of noble motives.

"I am not going to tell you of my unselfish sacrifices in seeking to be President of the United States.

"I frankly sought the opportunity to run for President on the Republican ticket because I have some deep-seated convictions I want to present to the American people and which, if I am elected, I want to carry into execution."

Continuing, Mr. Willkie chided the President for the fear expressed in Mr. Roosevelt's speech last night that the election of his opponent might endanger the continuation of the American democratic system.

Says He Learned the Hard Way

"I know something about the democratic way of life, not from books or theorists, but from experience," the Republican nominee asserted.

"I know the democratic way of life as an experience. I have worked on the ranges and the farms. I learned about civil liberties, not in textbooks, but in the hard struggle for survival.

"I know your aspirations and your hopes. I know your resolve that this great democracy shall be preserved at all hazards.

"If you elect me President you will have some one who understands the everyday problems of everyday people. I have lived them and glory in it. My route was the hard route, not the soft route."

Mr. Willkie's speech indicated the manner in which he will reply to attacks during the campaign. He has expressed pride in having come up "the hard way," asserting that he has a better understanding of the problems of the "common people" for that reason.

Mr. Willkie left his Colorado Springs hotel early this morning to fly here for his meeting with the stockmen. Arriving here shortly after 10:30 A. M., he held a private conference with cattlemen at a hotel and then came out to the Denver Union Stock Yards.

Cheered on his arrival at the yards, Mr. Willkie gave his speech from a hay-covered truck in front

Continued on Page Eight

BRITAIN PROMISES TREASURY TO ABIDE BY MONETARY PACT

Phillips Tells Morgenthau War Will Not Undo Accord on Freedom of Exchange

DISCUSS FRENCH ASSETS

How to Keep Them Out of Hands of Nazis Is a Point Urged by the Visiting Official

Special to THE NEW YORK TIMES.

WASHINGTON, July 19 — The principle of freedom of trade and of exchange laid down in the Tri-Partite Monetary Agreement of 1936 was reaffirmed today in a joint statement by Secretary Morgenthau and Sir Frederick Phillips, British Under-Secretary of Treasury, at the end of five days of conferences.

Attention was given to the methods of controlling assets of invaded countries held in the United States and Great Britain. Although the disposition of French assets, valued at from $1,500,000,000 to $2,000,000,000, held in the United States under embargo was not mentioned specifically in a joint statement, it was regarded as certain that this aspect of the "frozen" credit problem, involving possible recognition of the Nazi conquest of France, was thoroughly discussed.

Sir Frederick said that he told Secretary Morgenthau:

"We don't want these assets to get into the effective control of Germany."

He made it clear to reporters, however, that he could not speak for the United States Treasury. He could not say what the United States would do in regard to the assets of invaded countries. As for Britain, "We will continue the control."

Sir Frederick, who came here from England at Secretary Morgenthau's request, left the capital to return by way of Canada. A short time before Sir Frederick's departure, William C. Bullitt, Ambassador to France, arrived in the United States for talks with President Roosevelt on American recognition of the French Government headed by Marshal Petain.

TEXT OF STATEMENT

The text of the statement issued by Secretary Morgenthau and Sir Frederick follows:

Conferences during the past week between Sir Frederick Phillips, Under-Secretary of the British Treasury, and Secretary Morgenthau have provided an opportunity for the discussion of questions of mutual interest to the British and American Treasuries.

The British Under-Secretary was able to assure Secretary Morgenthau that, while Great Britain is now obliged by the exigencies of war to resort to exchange control and other temporary measures affecting international transactions, his government plans to return to liberal monetary and trade policies as soon as possible after hostilities cease. Such temporray measures include the arrangement between the financial centers of London and New York inaugurated on July 18 for a system of registered sterling accounts, which should tend toward stabilizing the sterling rate and help proetct the American market.

Prospective British purchases in the United States were considered in detail, and their effects on the balance of payments between the two countries during

Continued on Page Thirty

YIELD OR FACE RUIN, HITLER DEMANDS; LONDON IS SCORNFUL OF HIS THREAT; ITALIAN CRUISER SUNK; WIDE AIR RAIDS

BRITAIN IS DEFIANT

Hitler's Peace Offer Not Worthy of Comment, Officials State

BUT CHURCHILL MAY REPLY

Talk Taken as Indication That Blitzkrieg Is Near—Press Pledges Fight to End

By RAYMOND DANIELL
Special Cable to THE NEW YORK TIMES.

LONDON, July 19—Chancellor Hitler's speech tonight left official Britain unmoved. The attitude of Whitehall officialdom, with ears glued to radios, was that "we have heard all this before."

To British ears there was discernible in Herr Hitler's speech the usual attitude of injured innocence and plausible expressions of peaceful intent, coupled with threats of dire consequences to follow the flouting of his will. It was this part of the speech in which Herr Hitler declared his recognition that the belligerents were engaged in a life or death struggle, which aroused the chief interest here, and this was taken as an indication that the long anticipated and long delayed Battle for Britain may not be far off.

The Nazi leader's words were interpreted here as designed for domestic consumption and indicative of a desire to get the struggle over with quickly before another Winter.

Already "Ancient History"

The official reaction was that Herr Hitler's speech deserved no comment, inasmuch as it dealt with what is counted in these swift-moving days as ancient history and with threats that had been anticipated by Prime Minister Winston Churchill, who has said repeatedly that in the battle for this island there will be no surrender.

The whole speech, it was said, was barren of all ideas save abuse of Mr. Churchill, Alfred Duff Cooper, Minister of Information, and Anthony Eden, Secretary for War. It was intimated that Mr. Churchill would find an opportunity to reply before Commons next week.

The Prime Minister, it was pointed out, has said already that this country is prepared to face extermination rather than surrender. It was suggested that Herr Hitler was in the position of a highwayman who, having robbed all the victims but the one who still had a gun, was proposing that the last opponent connive with him in crime and escape with his own possessions or be murdered. This victim, it was said, prefers to shoot it out.

To officials here the most interesting passage in Herr Hitler's speech was his statement that he could see no reason why the war should go on and his assertion that this was his last appeal to the "common sense" of the one nation still in being on this side of the Atlantic and east of Russia that opposes his domination. That was interpreted as the ultimatum for which this country, armed to the teeth, has been waiting.

However, there was nothing in the speech of the Nazi dictator, who taunted Mr. Churchill for al-

Continued on Page Two

The International Situation

Developments in Europe

Chancellor Hitler made "one more and final appeal to reason in England" last night. He warned that if it was rejected and Britain did not sue for peace the result would be war to the death, with the annihilation of one or the other.

"Churchill may believe it will be Germany," he said. "I know it will be Britain."

Accusing the British of deliberately bombing German civilians, Herr Hitler declared that Germany up to now had made no answer. "When we do answer," he said, "nameless suffering will descend upon millions of people."

The speech was delivered before the Reichstag in the Kroll Opera House in Berlin and broadcast from there to Britain and all the world. [All the foregoing, Page 1, Column 8.]

Official Britain met the Nazi ultimatum with silence. Unofficially, the reaction was that Herr Hitler had said nothing new, nothing that would tend to dissuade the government from its announced policy of extermination rather than surrender. It was generally believed that the German onslaught now could not be far off. [Page 1, Column 5.]

Coincidentally with the speech, British and German airmen intensified their aerial attacks after two days of comparative quiet. The biggest battle was over the English Channel, where German bombers attacked a British convoy and were met by British fighters. More than 150 planes were engaged. The British said the toll of the day's raids was eleven German planes shot down, five of their own lost. The Germans said the score was fifteen British planes and only two German. The British claimed destructive bomb hits on a Krupp munitions plant at Essen, the naval base at Emden, an aircraft factory at Bremen and various other German air and supply concentrations. [Page 1, Column 6.]

In preparation for the expected invasion Britain promoted a B. E. F. veteran, Lieut. Gen. Sir Alan Brooke, to Commander-in-Chief of the defense force, replacing General Sir Edmund Ironside. General Brooke commanded the Second British Corps in Flanders. [Page 3, Column 8.]

A major British success in the war at sea was reported. Off the Island of Crete in the Eastern Mediterranean the Australian cruiser Sydney and an accompanying flotilla of destroyers engaged and sank Italy's 40-knot cruiser, the Bartolomeo Colleoni, believed to be one of the fastest warships of her size in the world. [Page 1, Column 7.]

Disquieting for British merchant shipping, however, was the report of the rescued crews of two British freighters that another German raider was on the high seas. They were sunk by the roaming successor to the Admiral Graf Spee 400 miles east of the Lesser Antilles, which lie along the eastern fringe of the Caribbean Sea. [Page 1, Column 4.]

Alleging mistreatment of German nationals in the Netherland East and West Indies, a Nazi spokesman in Amsterdam said reprisals were to be made against prominent Netherland citizens. The mistreatment alleged was the continued holding of Germans in concentration camps in the Netherland overseas empire, which remains loyal to the Queen and has never recognized the German conquest of the homeland. [Page 2, Column 1.]

In America and Asia

Secretary Hull, en route with his aides to the Pan-American Conference at Havana, announced to the world that the American nations were meeting solely to develop common interests, had no thought of conquest or domination of other peoples and were not unfriendly to other governments. The chief economic hope of the conference is that some solution may be worked out for the problems posed in the Americas by the European conflict. [Page 7, Column 1.]

Complete agreement on the policies that Japan's new government would pursue was announced after a four-hour meeting of Premier-designate Konoye, Foreign Minister Matsuoka, War Minister Tojo and Navy Minister Yoshida. No details were given. It was believed that Prince Konoye sought guarantees of Army support. [Page 6, Column 5.]

SPEAKS AS A VICTOR

Hitler Denies He Had Any Intention to Destroy the British Empire

SEES NO REASON FOR WAR

But He Warns Churchill of the Fate Facing Millions if the Struggle Is Continued

Text of Chancellor Hitler's address, Pages 4 and 5.

By GUIDO ENDERIS
Wireless to THE NEW YORK TIMES.

BERLIN, July 19—Confronting Prime Minister Winston Churchill with the choice between continuing the war or concluding a peace for which Britain must make overtures, Chancellor Hitler tonight told the British statesman that the continuation of hostilities could end only with the complete annihilation of one or the other of the two adversaries. The vanquished in that event, Herr Hitler predicted, would be Britain.

The Chancellor's speech was regarded in German circles as a bold appeal to reason in Britain as much as elsewhere, but Herr Hitler said it was not an appeal of the vanquished—that he was speaking as a victor in the name of "common sense."

He saw no reason, he said, why the war must go on.

"Churchill ought, for once, to believe me when I prophesy that a great empire will be destroyed—an empire which it was never my intention to destroy or even harm. I do, however, realize that this struggle, if it continues, can end only in the complete annihilation of one of the two adversaries. Churchill may believe it will be Germany, I know it will be Britain."

The prediction came at the close of a speech chiefly devoted to a review of Germany's military operations in the war up to the defeat of France. It was a serious speech and its gravity centered on the brief closing reference to the outlook for bringing the conflict to an end.

No Ultimatum Involved

Yet Herr Hitler left no doubt that the conditions under which he would consider a peace step from Britain presupposed some other spokesman than Mr. Churchill.

Herr Hitler's speech was anything but an ultimatum with a time limit. It was, he declared, an appeal to reason, and he expsessed the hope that it would provoke a positive reply from Britain, which he considers to be in a position of the vanquished, toward whom he is willing to adopt a magnanimous attitude. That he is in a receptive mood to such a response was indicated quite as decisively as was his readiness to settle the issue through a recourse to destructive methods.

Today's Reichstag was decidedly a war Reichstag. Its meeting was guarded as closely as a military secret. Its convocation was announced only a few hours before it sat, but that did not prevent the Kroll Opera House from holding a capacity audience. Herr Hitler, who wore his field gray tunic, was vociferously cheered when he entered the chamber accompanied by Field Marshal Hermann Goering and Rudolf Hess, his deputy party leader.

The guest of honor was Count Ciano, the Italian Foreign Minister, who flew from Rome, arriving shortly before the session opened. No less than 100 generals and admirals occupied a large section of the balcony and they liberally applauded Herr Hitler's speech, which was largely in the nature of a review of the military campaigns in Norway, Belgium and France.

Politics Plays Minor Role

Politics played a minor role in Herr Hitler's speech today and his reference to the outlook for peace with Britain came at the close. There was not a single reference to United States foreign policy or President Roosevelt, in contrast with Herr Hitler's former practice, and the omission is interpreted as an official desire to disregard the familiar strictures on "aggressor nations."

Russo-German relations, Herr Hitler said, were firmly established and their respective spheres of interest had been clearly defined, despite alleged British attempts to disturb existing relations between Berlin and Moscow.

The customary cordial reference to Italo-German relations provoked loud applause, which evidently

Continued on Page Five

Nazi Raider Sinks 2 British Ships Off West Indies; Sea Hunt Begins

Special Cable to THE NEW YORK TIMES.

LONDON, July 19—The Admiralty sent out tonight a radio warning to all ships in the Atlantic to look out for an armed German commerce raider that had already sunk two British merchant vessels, the King John of 5,228 tons, and the Davisian, 6,433 tons.

Both ships, the message said, were sunk somewhere in the vicinity of the West Indies.

British warships are already operating according to a plan to deal with the Nazi raider, which "is believed to be a converted merchant vessel," the Admiralty said. Details of the sinkings are being studied by Admiralty officials.

British seamen from the King John and the Davisian were picked up and landed at the French island of St. Bartholomew. They immediately were shipped to the British island of St. Kitts, from where their reports of the attacks by the raider were sent to the Admiralty.

It is believed here that the Germans gathered some ships they had seized after their attacks on Denmark and Norway, outfitted them with guns and sent them to raid on vessels bringing war supplies from the United States to Britain.

Such operations by the Germans had been expected here. It was anticipated that German raiders would become active again when the supplies of war material ordered in America last Autumn began to cross the Atlantic in large quantities.

It has not been difficult for the Germans to equip ships in Norwegian ports and send them toward the Western Hemisphere around the north of Iceland. The British have sowed mines between Iceland and Greenland, evidently to discourage just such movements.

The Germans thus far have apparently not made use of commerce raiders to the extent they did in the World War, nor so much as the British expected them to use raiders. It is seven months since the German pocket battleship raider Admiral Graf Spee came to a dramatic end by battle in the River Plate estuary after several successful attacks on British shipping in the Indian and South Atlantic Oceans.

At that time the Admiralty dis-

Continued on Page Three

150 PLANES BATTLE OVER BRITISH COAST

R. A. F. in Huge Dogfight With Nazis to Save Ships—Hits on Krupp Works Claimed

By JAMES MacDONALD
Special Cable to THE NEW YORK TIMES.

LONDON, Saturday, July 20—Raiding Nazi planes tore at widely separated parts of this country this morning after a day of fierce aerial attacks and counter-attacks by the British and German air forces yesterday and Thursday night.

Unofficially it was reported bombs were dropped at points in Southwest and Southeast Scotland and Northeast and Southwest England, but no account of casualties or damage was given.

Civilans in a Scottish town said they saw a fire in the distance and they were sure it was a German plane that had been shot down. A railroad employe in Southwest England said Nazi fliers sprayed machine gun bullets over a station while many people were waiting for a train.

Continuing their dogged defiance of Germany's vaunted air strength, Royal Air Force bombers rained destruction on the Krupp Works at Essen, the naval base at Emden, an oil refinery and an aircraft factory at Bremen and various German air bases and communications systems, according to the Air Ministry. Three British planes were announced as lost during these large-scale operations.

On the other hand Nazi airmen made mass daylight attacks against Great Britain, concentrating mostly on shipping in the English Channel where two furious sky battles occurred with more than 150 British fighter planes and German bombers trying to kill each other off.

Eleven German planes were shot

Continued on Page Three

SEA BATTLE FOUGHT IN MEDITERRANEAN

Fast Italian Warship Sunk by British Cruiser, Destroyers —250 of Crew Saved

By JAMES B. RESTON
Special Cable to THE NEW YORK TIMES.

LONDON, July 19—Britain scored her first naval victory of the war over Italy today when the 6,830-ton cruiser Sydney and a small force of destroyers sank the fast 5,069-ton Italian cruiser Bartolomeo Colleoni in a running battle northwest of the island of Crete in the Mediterranean.

Contact was made by the Sydney early this morning when the Bartolomeo Colleoni and another Italian cruiser were sighted between Crete and the southern tip of Greece. In the ensuing battle the other Italian cruiser, the name of which is not known, withdrew, and the last message received by the Admiralty stated that the Sydney and her destroyers had taken up the chase.

One of the British destroyers went immediately to the spot where the Bartolomeo Colleoni was abandoned and picked up about 250 members of her crew. Nothing is known, however, about what happened to the other 250 men who are believed to have been aboard the Italian cruiser when she foundered.

The Bartolomeo Colleoni, which was the third of the Condottieri class of cruisers to be put into service in 1932, was one of the fastest cruisers in the world. She was built, like seven others of her class, to make thirty-seven knots, but the official Italian press reported she made forty knots in her trials.

Her primary armament, the same as the Sydney's, was eight 6-inch guns, though her anti-aircraft and torpedo armaments were inferior.

Because of the danger of radioing

Continued on Page Three

"All the News That's Fit to Print."

NEWS INDEX, PAGE 31, THIS SECTION

The New York Times.

LATE CITY EDITION
Mostly cloudy and continued warm today. Tomorrow fair and continued warm.
Temperatures Yesterday—Max., 90; Min., 74

Section 

VOL. LXXXIX..No. 30,129. Entered as Second-Class Matter, Postoffice, New York, N. Y. NEW YORK, SUNDAY, JULY 21, 1940. Including Rotogravure Picture, Magazine and Book Review. TEN CENTS | TWELVE CENTS Beyond 200 Miles, Except West of Pa.—South of Md.—North of Mass.

REED CALLS PARLEY OF NEW DEAL FOES FOR 3D-TERM FIGHT

Invites Burke to Meeting of His Democratic Group, With Wide Drive Possible

THOUSANDS WRITE WILLKIE

Republican Says Messages Are Flooding In From Anti-Third Term Democrats

Special to THE NEW YORK TIMES.

KANSAS CITY, July 20—A group of anti-Roosevelt third-termers, of whom former Senator James A. Reed is a leader, are preparing to consider possible action in the Presidential campaign.

Mr. Reed, chairman of the Democratic Executive Committee of the Jeffersonian movement, has called a meeting for Thursday in Chicago. He has invited Senator Burke, Democrat of Nebraska, who recently bolted to support Wendell L. Willkie, to be present.

"I have simply issued a call for the members of that committee, numbering five or six, to see what ought to be done," former Senator Reed said today. "Just what course will be pursued will be discussed then."

The movement, it was said, might cover the country. The committee of which Mr. Reed is the head was set up in the campaign of 1936 when President Roosevelt was nominated for a second term.

Ely and Colby on Committee

In addition to Mr. Reed the committee includes Joseph B. Ely, Colonel Henry Breckinridge, Bainbridge Colby, former Secretary of State; Graham Wright of Georgia and Joseph W. Bailey of Texas, former member of the House of Representatives.

Mr. Reed said that he did not know what form the possible nation-wide activities of anti-third-term and anti-New Deal Democrats would take.

Anti-third-termers say that many delegates at the party's Chicago convention were not sympathetic to a third term, and assert that this sentiment was emphasized when President Roosevelt let it be known that he desired Secretary Wallace as his running mate.

Mr. Reed has long opposed the New Deal and its policies. He has not yet proclaimed his personal opinions of the ticket named by the Chicago convention, but his friends said that he had expressed views indicating that he was not satisfied and that he had evidenced a high regard for Wendell L. Willkie, the Republican nominee.

Willkie Tells of Support

Special to THE NEW YORK TIMES.

COLORADO SPRINGS, July 20—Wendell L. Willkie told a press conference here today that thousands of letters and telegrams of support were pouring in from all parts of the country, with many of them coming from Democrats opposed to a third term for President Roosevelt.

At the press conference, Mr. Willkie made public a letter from Booth Tarkington in which the author stated that the Republican nominee would have "the vote of every intelligent adult who does profitable work."

"My phone hasn't stopped ringing since the close of the Democratic convention and my secretarial staff has been flooded with telegrams from Democrats all over the country," Mr. Willkie asserted. "These Democrats are for me and I am sure that in the next few days you will see that many others will publicly announce themselves."

The text of the Tarkington letter, sent to Russell Davenport, Mr. Willkie's personal representative in the Republican campaign organization, read:

"'What ought Willkie to do?' He ought to do what he is. That is, he mustn't lose anything of what makes us say, 'A man has arisen.'

"Why did we say that? Because he was the visible strong destroyer of a lie that was leading our bowed and unwilling selves into slavery.

"What lie? That it is odious to succeed in business. What slavery? State socialism—obedience to the successful politician—or to the philanthropic yearner.

"New Deal politics had been working Jacob's time—Hitler's time—seven years—adroitly saturating American minds with that lie, and it was working delightfully for the crowd that put it over, horribly for all the rest of us who labor.

"Willkie A Visible Shining Hope"

"I saw the best group of business and professional men in Indianapolis rise to Willkie: for that moment they were all coming out of the slough of despond with a leap—the burden gone. Willkie was a visible shining hope. After he'd gone, the old depression settled down on some of 'em again—the machine would never allow old common sense to sit in the saddle again.

"We'd have to take some slickster who'd enlarge promises to the

Continued on Page Two

Major Sports Yesterday

BASEBALL

Detroit's Tigers tightened their grip on first place in the American League by defeating the Yankees, 3—1. Harold Newhouser, 19-year-old left-hander, pitched for the winners. In the National League the Cincinnati Reds added to their lead by downing the Giants, 5—1, as Bucky Walters pitched his fourteenth victory of the season. The St. Louis Cardinals beat the second-place Dodgers, 3—2, and Brooklyn is now four games behind the Reds.

HORSE RACING

Sirocco, 13-to-1 shot, captured the $50,570 Arlington Classic as Gallahadion, Kentucky Derby winner, finished second and Bimelech, the favorite, ran third. Sirocco triumphed by seven lengths. At Empire City the $6,925 Fleetwing Handicap went to He Did, the favorite, who carried 132 pounds in racing to a half-length victory. Omission captured the $7,725 East View Stakes at the Yonkers track.

TENNIS

Donald McNeill, Oklahoma star, defeated John Kramer of Montebello, Calif., 9—7, 6—3, 6—2, in the Maryland State final. Miss Alice Marble and Miss Mary Arnold, California duo, won the women's doubles title. Frank Parker and Frank Kovacs reached the final of the Eastern clay-court tournament.

(Complete Details of These and Other Sports Events in Section 5.)

WILLKIE AND PEEK TALK FARM PLANS

Ex-Head of AAA Gives Views to Nominee, Assailing the New Deal Trade Policy

By JAMES C. HAGERTY

Special to THE NEW YORK TIMES.

COLORADO SPRINGS, July 20—Wendell L. Willkie conferred here today on agricultural and foreign trade problems with George N. Peek, first administrator of the New Deal's AAA, and former special foreign trade adviser to President Roosevelt.

Mr. Peek's visit with the Republican nominee was in line with Mr. Willkie's announcement that he was planning to get "all possible viewpoints" on national problems before drafting his acceptance speech which he is to give at his birthplace, Elwood, Ind., about August 10.

Mr. Peek came here from a vacation in California after Mr. Willkie had accepted a suggestion by Senator Vandenberg of Michigan that he should get the farm economist's viewpoint on agricultural and trade problems. The nominee and Mr. Peek conferred in private for more than two hours.

Following the conference, Mr. Willkie called reporters into his suite and told them that he had been getting Mr. Peek's views, making it clear that he was not committing himself to Mr. Peek's program.

"As I have told you boys before I am trying to get viewpoints on all the various national problems," the nominee said.

"I hope to get all sides of each question and then determine myself what my course on them will be."

Peek Hits New Deal Policies

Mr. Peek, an opponent of the reciprocal trade treaties who ended his Administration connections in 1935, outlined an eight-point agricultural and a four-point foreign trade program.

In general, Mr. Peek's farm program accused the New Deal of "restrictive policies," while his foreign trade plans opposed the Administration's programs, especially the reciprocal trade agreements.

During the reading of these points, Mr. Willkie appeared to disagree on many of them. When Mr. Peek assailed the Administration's reciprocal trade program, the nominee interrupted to remind the reporters:

"This is only Mr. Peek's viewpoint."

Mr. Peek nodded and replied:

"I am not trying to commit you on anything, Mr. Willkie."

Among the points advocated by Mr. Peek on the agricultural program were the continuance of commodity loans to farmers on "a sound basis"; the encouragement of farmer cooperatives; the continuation of all "desirable features" of existing farm legislation with emphasis, however, put on control of trade rather than on control of production; the development of new uses for American agricultural products in industry, and the securing of protection and "full price benefits" to the American farmer in an American market through a limitation of competitive farm imports.

For Foreign Trade Board

As to the foreign trade question, Mr. Peek advocated the replacement of the Tariff Commission by a Foreign Trade Board which would determine American foreign trade policies in the light of American "domestic interests"; the ratification by Congress of all present and future trade treaties; the establishment of a "system of national bookkeeping" to keep trade figures "straight," and the adoption by the government of a "realistic policy of trade for the national interest."

Earlier in the day Mr. Willkie said that he would formally announce on Monday the plans for his acceptance speech when Representative Charles A. Halleck, who has been handling the acceptance speech details, will arrive here for a conference.

HEAT OF 90° DRIVES THRONGS FROM CITY

Humidity Reaches 84% but Falls as Mercury Rises—Six Dead in the Midwest

New York City experienced the second day of its heat wave yesterday as the temperature climbed to 90 degrees, but elsewhere in the nation, particularly in the Midwest, the thermometer registered temperatures of more than 100 and six persons were killed by the heat.

Thousands fled from the city to near-by beaches and other resorts, clogging the main traffic arteries. Traffic became particularly heavy during the afternoon as many local residents took advantage of the half-holiday. The police reported that, although traffic was abnormal even for Saturday, no serious accidents were reported.

With no relief in sight, according to the Weather Bureau, the police predicted that today the roads would have to carry the heaviest automobile traffic of the year.

Heat Aggravated by Humidity

The city's heat was aggravated by humidity that reached 84 per cent. However, the humidity declined as the temperature rose. Thus at 2 P. M., when the maximum temperature of 90 was recorded, the humidity was at its lowest for the day—41 per cent.

The prediction for today was partly cloudy and continued warm, and for tomorrow fair and continued warm. Yesterday's average temperature was 82 degrees, eight degrees above normal. A fifteen-mile-an-hour northwest wind blew throughout the day.

There was one heat prostration and one drowning in the city and another drowning in New Jersey. David Ferguson, 24 years old, of 314 Clifton Place, Brooklyn, was overcome while walking along Atlantic Avenue near Van Sicklen Avenue, Brooklyn. He was treated by an ambulance doctor and taken to Beth El Hospital, where his condition was said to be good.

The death of a 50-year-old man late last night was attributed to a heart attack induced by the heat. The man was James Bello of 949 Grand Street, Brooklyn, a laborer at the plant of the Gergory Galvanizing Company, 4900 Grand Avenue, Ridgewood, Queens. He collapsed outside the plant and died before medical aid reached him.

The city drowning occurred at Broad Channel in the Rockaways. The dead man was identified as Charles Rosen, 42, of 371 Marcy Avenue, Brooklyn.

Reaches for Oar, Drowns

Mr. Rosen rented a rowboat early in the day with George Heck of 118 Java Street, Brooklyn. While the men were fishing in the channel off West Tenth Road, Jamaica, Queens, Mr. Rosen lost an oar. He reached to grab it and fell into the water.

A 12-year-old girl was drowned and her brother and sister were rescued in Leonardo, N. J., when they stepped from a shallow sand bar into a deep channel that conects the Leonardo Yacht Club Harbor with Sandy Hook Bay. The dead girl was Angela Earley of North Newark, N. J. Three older girls rescued two of the children.

The crowd at Coney Island was held down by threatening weather. Nevertheless, about 400,000 persons visited that beach. Once at the beach the people remained, although it rained there for a few minutes during the afternoon.

The Rockaways had their biggest Saturday crowd of the season, with an estimated 450,000 visitors. At this resort the police reported 305 first aid cases, forty-eight rescues and forty-one lost children. The crowd there was said to be greater than many Sunday crowds this season.

Fishing enthusiasts were unusually numerous at the Rockaways. At one fishing station, where 100 boats are available for renting, there was none left by 3 P. M. This in spite

Continued on Page Five

ROOSEVELT SIGNS 2-OCEAN NAVY BILL; START NOW SOUGHT

Knox to Ask House Tomorrow for $1,000,000,000 at Once to Get Program Under Way

ARMY TO STRESS INDUSTRY

Stimson, Explaining Arms Need, Will Push Plant Expansion, an Aid to Britain

By FRANK L. KLUCKHOHN

Special to THE NEW YORK TIMES.

WASHINGTON, July 20—President Roosevelt signed today the $4,000,000,000 bill, authorizing construction of a giant two-ocean navy as Navy officials, including Secretary Knox, prepared to testify Monday before the House Appropriations Committee on a program for immediate expenditure of almost $1,000,000,000 under this authorization to get the six-year program rapidly under way.

On Tuesday Henry L. Stimson, Secretary of War, will lead Army officials to Capitol Hill to explain the Army's need for nearly $4,000,000,000 additional for thousands of tanks, airplanes, anti-aircraft guns and other modern equipment fully to supply an army of 1,200,000 men and to furnish 800,000 reserves with "critical" weapons.

Of this sum about $1,500,000,000 will be requested for airplanes to bring this country's force to 26,000 planes.

Plant Expansion Aiding Britain

The stress in Army testimony, it is learned, will be upon plans for swiftly expanding facilities for production of all types of weapons for modern warfare, and, in addition to a long itemized list of weapons and supplies to be presented, about $400,000,000 will be requested as part of the $4,000,000,000 appropriation for the sole purpose of plant expansion.

In addition, officials revealed, the Reconstruction Finance Corporation will lend $72,000,000 for aircraft plant expansion and about $100,000,000 for general expansion.

If Great Britain can withstand Nazi attempts at conquest in the coming weeks until uncertain weather begins, United States production of all types of materiel and munitions for modern warfare will be sufficiently increased by Spring to give the British tremendous, and perhaps decisive, supply aid, high Administration circles stated today.

In equipping a large American defensive army at top speed, American plant output will be stepped up to a point where, by May 10 of next year, it will be possible to sell the British enough to meet their needs without interfering with supplying needs at home, it was asserted.

Details Ready for Congress

A rather astonishing picture of what War Department officials believe to be possible in rapidly utilizing American productive capacity and potential capacity is promised to Congress next week.

Although the general objectives sought under the proposed expenditures and the time limits set for the program will be outlined, a strong effort will be made to have Congress keep the detailed information secret to prevent its reaching the hands of potential enemies.

Whereas heretofore foreign attachés had been able to obtain information merely by reading the records of Congressional hearings, officials said that the time had come when detailed plans must be closely guarded.

With the Nazis threatening Great Britain, this country must spend

Continued on Page Twelve

BULLITT, BACK, SAYS FRANCE OF PETAIN IS NO FASCIST STATE

Ambassador, Here on Clipper, Praises Marshal, Denies Laval Is Real Leader

FALL OF PARIS DESCRIBED

German Entry, Peaceful and Orderly, Envoy Declares—Tells of Wide Chaos

William C. Bullitt, American Ambassador to France, returned to the United States yesterday with praise for Marshal Henri Philippe Pétain and the French people, and with disbelief that the government of Premier Pétain rightly could be called a fascist State. He also refused to put any faith in the suggestions that Vice Premier Pierre Laval was the real head of France's reconstruction administration.

Mr. Bullitt returned on the Dixie Clipper of the Pan American Airways after a delay of four days at Horta, the Azores, because of engine difficulty. He came as a courier to President Roosevelt and Secretary of State Cordell Hull, with whom, he said, his confidential communications had been cut off since June 12. He left Vichy on July 11, the day Marshal Pétain assumed the dictatorial rule of the new French State.

Silent on French Errors

Waiving his customary practice of being uncommunicative to reporters, Mr. Bullitt granted a twenty-minute interview, during which he drew the line at two kinds of questions. He did not want to talk about the mistakes that France had made in the past—leading to the German victory—nor was he willing to make any prediction as to the future, either of France or of Britain.

He talked of the German entry into Paris and of the air bomb that narrowly missed taking his life; of the choked conditions in Vichy, where four telegraph operators tried vainly to keep up with the cable business of a national capital, and of the colossal task the Pétain government faces in trying to restore system out of "desperate disorder."

He left La Guardia Field to spend the week-end at the home of his brother, Orville Bullitt, in Pennsylvania and planned to go to Washington tomorrow.

"The French people," Mr. Bullitt said, "have all the magnificent qualities they always had. The soldier of 1940 was fully the equal of the soldier of 1914. I don't want to go into the mistakes that led to the downfall of France, but I want to say that the French people are intact.

"In France today there are 10,500,000 people on the roads, refugees from their homes. Bridges are gone, roads are choked, communications are poor or non-existent, there is no gasoline. France faces a problem of reconstruction that is one of the most difficult that ever confronted any nation.

Pétain Widely Respected

"Marshal Pétain is universally respected in France, as he is throughout the world. He is doing his best to bring order out of desperate disorder—and I do not mean that the people are disorderly. As for the future, I do not want to say anything. First, I must speak to the President and to the Secretary of State."

In a question a reporter referred to France as a "fascist State."

"I don't know if it is right to call

Continued on Page Twenty-five

U. S. Seeks to Adjust Dispute at Martinique; Hears British, French Claims to 100 Planes

Special to THE NEW YORK TIMES.

WASHINGTON, July 20—The State Department is endeavoring to facilitate an amicable adjustment between Great Britain and France over the approximately 100 American-made airplanes on the French aircraft carrier Bearn at Fort de France, Martinique, but with what promise of success officials did not reveal today.

The Department's interest was manifested this morning when Sumner Welles, Acting Secretary of State, conferred separately with Count Rene Doynel de Saint-Quentin, the French Ambassador, and the Marquess of Lothian, British Ambassador.

The former Allies are at loggerheads over the planes, each claiming title to them, while the State Department is active in the case because of apprehensions lest the British should be tempted to defy the Pan-American safety belt and other considerations and attempt to seize the planes forcibly. The Department shudders when it thinks of the possibility of another Oran, this time in West Indian waters, according to diplomats.

The planes had been taken on the Bearn for delivery in France when the German victory forced the aircraft carrier to head for Martinique. Since then she has remained in port, with British warships reported to be watching offshore but the British government denying that there is a blockade.

The French say they bought and paid for the planes, and so own them. The British contend that just before the Franco-German armistice an arrangement was made whereby they assumed French assets and liabilities in connection with the purchase of war supplies in this country, that the planes were bought through the Allied Purchasing Board, and that they now own them.

Neither Ambassador would discuss the matter, and Mr. Welles described their conversations as routine. The Ambassadors, though they followed each other into the office of the acting Secretary of State, did not meet.

BRITISH BEAT OFF MASS RAIDS BY SWARMS OF NAZI PLANES; R. A. F. BOMBS GERMAN BASES

The International Situation

In Europe and Africa

German daylight raids were widespread in Britain again yesterday. Some of the raids brought German planes into action in mass, notably an assault on a convoy in the English Channel. In this engagement shore batteries and the anti-aircraft guns of escort ships, as well as British fighter craft, participated. The British said the Germans were driven off; no details of what they had accomplished were revealed. London reported that since June 18 German raiders had killed 336 British civilians and injured seriously 476. British raids on German military and industrial centers on the Continent were carried on as usual Friday night. [Page 1, Column 8.]

Berlin was displeased with the British press reaction to Chancellor Hitler's "final appeal" of Friday. That reaction, which was generally scornful, was held by the Germans to have been inspired by "higher quarters." [Page 1, Column 7.]

Rome newspapers indicated that the Italians would not—as had been previously expected—participate in the Battle of Britain. They will concentrate on Africa and the Mediterranean. Commentators agreed that the attack on Britain was a matter of days. [Page 27, Column 5.]

In anticipation of the war budget to be brought in on Tuesday, London heard predictions that the basic income-tax rate would be raised from 37½ per cent to 45 per cent and that capital might be conscripted through forced loans. [Page 23, Column 1.]

British military authorities in Cairo said their planes had successfully raided Italian bases in Ethiopia, Eritrea and Libya, setting many fires. The Italians asserted that they had done serious d mage to British warships in an engagement Friday off Crete, in which they admitted that the British had sunk the cruiser Bartolomeo Colleoni. [Page 27, Column 1.]

The German authorities in the Netherlands made their first inroads into the legal system of that conquered nation. They decreed the establishment of German courts to try Netherlanders accused of acts against the German nation, people, individuals or property. Several Netherland colonial officials were arrested in reprisal for alleged mistreatment of Germans interned in the Netherlands Indies. [Page 22, Column 1.]

American Developments

President Roosevelt signed the $4,000,000,000 two-ocean navy bill. Administration officials said that if Britain could hold off the Germans through the Winter she would be able to obtain vast and perhaps decisive war supplies in the United States by next Spring. [Page 1, Column 4.]

Secretary of State Hull, arriving in Havana for the Pan-American Conference of Foreign Ministers to discuss military and economic problems brought on by the war, said the meeting would provide "a new demonstration of the vigor and vitality of the American Republics." [Page 1, Column 6.]

Arriving in New York by air from Europe, William C. Bullitt, United States Ambassador to France, expressed doubt that France had turned into a Fascist State. [Page 1, Column 5.]

HULL IS ACCLAIMED BY HAVANA THRONG

Secretary Starts Preliminary Talks With Other Delegates on Americas' Problems

Wireless to THE NEW YORK TIMES.

HAVANA, July 20—The Pan-American Conference of Foreign Ministers, which opens here tomorrow, "will be a new demonstration of the vigor and vitality of the American republics when they work jointly for their common interest," Secretary of State Cordell Hull declared upon his arrival here this morning.

The Secretary, accompanied by Mrs. Hull and fifteen members of the American delegation, arrived at 10 o'clock on the steamship Florida from Miami. As the boat came in a crowd at the dock cheered the Secretary and Mrs. Hull, who were on the deck, and later they received an ovation as they descended the gangplank.

Mr. Hull was met by Dr. Miguel Angel Campa, Cuban Secretary of State, and other Cuban State Department officials, and George Messersmith, United States Ambassador, and members of the embassy and consulate staffs.

In a press conference at his hotel Mr. Hull expressed his pleasure at again visiting Cuba, where he served in the United States Army during the Spanish-American War, and voiced his appreciation for the hospitality of the Cuban Government.

Hull to Speak Tomorrow

Concerning the problems facing the conference, Mr. Hull limited himself to stating that "we are meeting to discuss problems essential to the life of the Americas." He said that he would address the conference Monday on present conditions and problems. Then he added:

"There are a number of important considerations to keep in mind. First is the exceedingly important issue of full and free interchange of information in order that the particular situation of each country represented may be known."

Later Mr. Hull started to talk with other delegates.

More representatives of the American nations arrived at Havana tonight. The delegates of Argentina and Uruguay reached Santiago de Cuba today and are expected to arrive here tomorrow morning by train. President

Continued on Page Seventeen

NAZIS AGAIN WARN BRITONS TO GIVE UP

Press and Radio Urge Ousting of Churchill So Peace Can Be Reached Immediately

By PERCIVAL KNAUTH

Wireless to THE NEW YORK TIMES.

BERLIN, July 20—The British press reaction to Chancellor Hitler's speech yesterday left authoritative German quarters unconcerned. The German Government, it was stated authoritatively, saw no need for further statements on its part, but was "awaiting unconcernedly the final reaction of official British circles."

The immediate rejection by the British press of Herr Hitler's hint of peace if Britain got rid of Prime Minister Winston Churchill, it was stated here, failed to portray the true popular sentiment in England and London's comments bore obvious earm ks of being inspired by "higher quarters."

The hastiness and superficiality of the British retorts, it was asserted, showed they were not the result of cool consideration nor born of a true feeling of responsibility. They showed all too readily, in the opinion of German quarters, a desire to influence public opinion.

[News service dispatches from Berlin reported a Nazi radio drive at the British people, with the Germans broadcasting Adolf Hitler's "last appeal to reason" and warning against Prime Minister Churchill.]

Last Words Spoken, Says Berlin

So far as Germany is concerned, the Nazi press reiterated, the last words have been spoken.

"It is 1 minute before 12," one commentator remarks; at 12, it is inferred, the full fury of German military might will start to accomplish what the "reason" of Herr Hitler's final statement to the British may have failed to effect.

How long the Germans will await an official British response or something tantamount to it has not been revealed. But there is a unanimity of opinion in the German press comment that the time left for the British to arrive at decisions is not long.

The "generous" offer by Herr Hitler, as victorious field lord of one of the greatest German armies in history, it is asserted in one editorial, gives the enemy, Britain, an opportunity to realize her sorry state before it is too late to save the far-flung reaches of her em-

Continued on Page Twenty-six

SKY BATTLES FIERCE

British Fliers Blast at Reich Oil Stores and Aircraft Factory

100 PLANES IN ONE FIGHT

London Declares 12 Raiders Were Downed—Attacks Go On Early Today

By JAMES MacDONALD

Special Cable to THE NEW YORK TIMES.

LONDON, Sunday, July 21—Great Britain's air forces shot down twelve German war planes over British waters and territory yesterday, repelled a mass aerial attack on a convoy in the English Channel and inflicted heavy damage during counter-raids on Nazi oil plants, air bases, harbors and communication lines, according to Air Ministry communiqués.

The unremitting air exchanges continued early today, when Nazi raiders droned over Northwest and Southeast England. British fighter planes drove them back from Wales.

In the northwest area a German plane dropped bombs that killed at least one person, injured others and demolished houses and shops.

Everywhere throughout the areas where alarms were sounded hidden guns split the blackout with lurid flashes of anti-aircraft fire and British defender machines sparked aloft, determined to have it out with the aerial trespassers.

Several hours after midnight officials here said reports coming to London were not complete enough to show the extent of casualties or damage.

Major Fight Over Channel

The English Channel was once again the scene of the hottest part of yesterday's air struggle, but, as usual, officials would not state whether any ships were destroyed or harbors damaged for fear the Germans might learn information that would be to their advantage.

Early in the evening big squadrons of German dive bombers swooped down on a convoy manoeuvring through the Channel. As soon as they were sighted, escorting warships and shore batteries frantically sent up blistering anti-aircraft fire. Meanwhile British fighter pilots who had been waiting watchfully ashore jumped into their cockpits, gave their machines "the gun" and streaked into the sky.

Soon more than 100 war planes were dipping and wheeling above the Channel waters, all belching deadly machine-gun fire. Men and women on shore ran for cover, lest the whipping hail of spent bullets should hit them.

Two British Planes Lost

Official reports said the German attackers fled, many of them badly damaged.

Regarding plane losses, the Air Ministry communiqué said at least eight Nazi planes were shot down during the coastal attacks and four others elsewhere during the day. Only two British planes failed to return home, it was said, and the pilot of one of them managed to land safely.

Parts of Scotland, England and Wales suffered bombing attacks early yesterday morning and later in the day, casualties being reported and damage done to school buildings and houses.

One of the four German planes shot down inland crashed to earth in Southwest England. Its crew of four, one of whom was wounded after a fight with defending planes, were taken prisoner. At another point in England a lone parachutist was seen fluttering down from an altitude of 8,000 feet, but whether he was from a German plane or an R. A. F. machine was not stated and his fate was a mystery.

Figures released by the Ministry of Home Security yesterday showed that since June 18, when large-scale German bombing raids against the United Kingdom began, 336 civilians have been killed and 476 seriously injured. The largest number killed in any one locality on a single raid was thirty-two.

Points in Germany Bombed

Bremen, Emden and Wilhemshaven were among the many points that came in for severe R. A. F. bombing attacks, according to Air Ministry officials.

Just when the Bremen and Hamburg radio stations were due to broadcast later at night another résumé of Chancellor Hitler's Reichstag speech, they went off the air. The usual reason for any sud-

Continued on Page Twenty-seven

"All the News That's Fit to Print."

The New York Times.

LATE CITY EDITION
Fair, continued warm today. Tomorrow cloudy and continued warm with thunder showers.
Temperatures Yesterday—Max., 93.4; Min., 76

VOL. LXXXIX..No. 30,137. Entered as Second-Class Matter, Postoffice, New York, N. Y. NEW YORK, MONDAY, JULY 29, 1940. THREE CENTS NEW YORK CITY and Vicinity | FOUR CENTS Elsewhere Except in 7th and 8th Postal Zones.

BERLIN SEES DRIVE ON BRITAIN MATTER OF DAYS, IF NOT HOURS; RAIL TRAFFIC IN FRANCE IS CUT

HEAT WAVE DRIVES MILLIONS FROM CITY; RELIEF NOT YET DUE

93.4° Is Recorded on the Third Successive Day of Above-90 Temperatures

HUMIDITY CLIMBS HIGHER

Promised Cold Mass From West Gets Hot Before It Can Help—Day Is Windless

With more than a third of its population seeking refuge at near-by beaches and other resorts and most of the remaining residents relaxing at home, New York City seemed almost like a lifeless metropolis yesterday as the temperature rose above 90 degrees for the third consecutive day.

In the Midwest, which had believed the heat wave broken by rains and cool winds on Saturday after more than a week of suffering, the hot weather returned yesterday and no relief was in sight in that area.

The prospects for relief here were no better than they were in the Midwest or in Maryland, the Virginias and the Carolinas.

Toll Heavy in Nation

Two persons were killed by the heat and two others were prostrated in the city. Another person died from the heat in New Jersey. A man was killed by lightning during a storm near Camden, N. J., last night. There was one drowning in the city and another in New Jersey. There were 590 deaths in the entire country attributed to the current heat wave, 304 of them due to drowning.

The forecast for today by the local Weather Bureau was for fair and continued warm weather.

Furthermore, with the return of abnormally high temperatures in the Central States, the last hope of New York for immediate relief faded.

Until yesterday it was believed that the cool air mass that was drifting toward New York from the Great Lakes region might break through the layer of hot air around the city and bring the heat wave to an end.

However, the air mass has moved eastward so slowly, according to the Weather Bureau, that by the time it gets here it will have become as warm as the rest of the atmosphere in the Midwest.

Yesterday's highest temperature was 93.4 degrees, recorded at 1:50 P. M., compared with 98.6 degrees on Saturday, but the humidity was higher yesterday than on the preceding day. Whereas on Saturday the humidity between 1 and 5 P. M. fluctuated between 42 and 48 per cent, yesterday during the same hours it was 50 to 58 per cent. The highest humidity of the day was 82 per cent at 8 A. M. Yesterday's mean temperature was 84 degrees, 9 degrees above normal.

Virtually No Wind

Another factor that aggravated the heat yesterday was the lack of wind. Most of the day southerly breezes drifted over the city at a velocity of only three to four miles an hour. The velocity increased to eleven miles an hour about 5 P. M.

Yesterday was the fifth time in the last ten days that the thermometer has registered 90 degrees or more. Except for last Tuesday and Wednesday, when the temperature was 81 and 80, respectively, there has been no day when the mercury did not touch 87 degrees.

The Weather Bureau gave the following figures for temperature and humidity yesterday:

	Tem.	Hu.		Tem.	Hu.
Midnight.	77	..	3 P.M...	91	56
1 A.M...	77	..	4 P.M...	90	57
2 A.M...	79	..	5 P.M...	89	58
3 A.M...	78	..	6 P.M...	84	59
4 A.M...	78	..	7 P.M...	82	60
5 A.M...	77	..	8 P.M...	80	65
6 A.M...	80	..	9 P.M...	78	75
7 A.M...	79	81	10 P.M...	77	..
8 A.M...	76	82	11 P.M...	76	..
9 A.M...	82	69	11:30 P.M.	78	..
10 A.M...	87	65	12:30 A.M.	77	..
11 A.M...	88	61	1:30 A.M.	76	..
Noon.....	90	55	2:30 A.M.	76	..
1 P.M...	91	50	3:30 A.M.	76	..
2 P.M...	92	56			

Between 5 and 9 P. M. the temperature dropped from 89 degrees to 78, but the humidity rose to 75 per cent.

With beaches drawing crowds as large as and larger than the huge attendance of last Sunday, the highways were jammed during the early part of the day, while buses, subways and other trains had one of the busiest days of the year.

After sundown New Yorkers began returning and the main roads leading from beaches were jammed. Traffic was particularly heavy on the Triborough Bridge, the George Washington Bridge and along the Henry Hudson Parkway's southbound lanes.

Coney Island was again the greatest magnet for New York's heat-stricken people. The police estimated that more than 1,000,000 persons visited that resort. Several thousand had slept on the beach overnight.

Bathhouses were filled there and

Continued on Page Nine

New Fight in Labor Party Starts; May Affect Senatorial Election

Right-Wingers Bid for Convention Control, Plan to Back Mead—Foes Would Split Vote by Naming an Independent

By WARREN MOSCOW

A second primary fight within the American Labor party, which will have an important bearing on the election of a United States Senator from this State in November, was started yesterday when the right-wing element in the party issued an appeal for support for its candidates for delegates to the State convention.

The first primary fight, last Spring, resulted in right-wing control of the State committee, which nominates Presidential electors, and thereby insured endorsement of the Roosevelt-Wallace Democratic electors by the Labor party. Had the left-wingers won the Spring primary, a third slate of electors, pledged to some independent, was planned.

Much the same situation exists now with regard to the State convention delegates. If the right-wingers, led by Luigi Antonini, Sidney Hillman, Alex Rose and Paul Blanshard, win control of the convention, the Labor party will endorse James M. Mead, Democratic Senator slated for renomination.

If the left-wingers win control, they are expected to nominate an independent candidate for Senator, thereby improving the chances of the Republican nominee, to be picked from a list headed by Bruce Barton and William F. Bleakley.

In the matter of actual political procedure and manipulation, the right-wingers in the Labor party for a long time have been close to the Democratic command in the State, despite their split with the Democrats on city politics, and the left-wingers have been close to the Republican organization headed by Kenneth F. Simpson.

The left-wing dealings with Mr. Simpson have come about because the group, headed by Hyman Glickstein, Eugene P. Connolly and Morris Watson, have control of the New York County organization, and local dickerings on endorsements, started when the Rose faction was in control in the county, have been continued.

Uncertain factors in the fight for delegates to the State convention are the amount of funds available to the left-wing group, on one hand, and the amount of work the right-wingers are willing to devote to the primary campaign. The right-wingers should start the delegate fight with an advantage, as delegates are apportioned, within the Labor party, on the basis of one delegate for each 600 votes cast for Governor under the Labor emblem in 1938.

The left-wing stronghold is New York County, where the Labor party polled only 73,000 votes in

Continued on Page Seven

PORT TO WELCOME THE AMERICA TODAY

Stedman Turns Liner at 24 Knots in Demonstration for 900 Guests on Board

By Radio to THE NEW YORK TIMES.

ABOARD THE S. S. AMERICA at Sea, July 28—A cooling northeast breeze refreshed 900 guest passengers of the United States lines today as the America, new queen of the American merchant marine, slipped through the pond-like sea toward New York on her maiden passenger-carrying run. She will reach New York tomorrow.

[The America is scheduled to arrive in the harbor at noon today, where she will be met by an escort of Coast Guard, police and fireboats, Army and Navy airplane formations and many private craft. She is to dock at Pier 59, at the foot of West Eighteenth Street, at 1:20 P. M., and the ceremonies of welcome to Captain Stedman and the officials aboard are scheduled to begin at 1:30.]

Captain Giles C. Stedman, the master, called her "the most beautifully performing ship I have ever commanded" and he proceeded to demonstrate her responsiveness, playing with the 35,000-ton luxury liner with the enthusiasm of a boy with a new toy.

With several shipping executives and United States Senators standing with him on the bridge as the trim vessel raced through the water at 24 knots, her maximum speed for the run, Captain Stedman ordered the helm to full port, and the great liner listed slightly as she slid into a sharp circular turn.

Circles in 5½ Minutes

In 5½ minutes the America had completed the circle with the helm hard over to port. The diameter of the circle was 850 yards, considered unusually small for a vessel of 723 feet going at such speed. She listed only 8 degrees in making the turn.

Proudly the master then ordered the helm to full starboard and again the America turned sharply with the same results except that the list owing to the wind factor was only 6 degrees. Steering a course generally northeast on her departure last night from Newport News, Va., the America was not expected to attain a distance of more than 200 miles from the coast.

A school of whales was sighted this morning and one barely missed a head-on collision with the liner.

The executives of the shipping and allied industries who are aboard the America heard Ambassador Joseph P. Kennedy, in a two-way broadcast from London to the ship, spur them to new endeavors in the work of rebuilding the United States merchant marine.

Speaking to Max O'Rell Truitt, member of the United States Maritime Commission who is one of the government officials on board, Ambassador Kennedy declared that the United States needed as many new units for the merchant marine as it could get, and it needed them as soon at it was possible to build them.

Mr. Kennedy, former chairman of the Maritime Commission, commented on the fact that it took almost three years to build this new

Continued on Page Nine

WILLKIE DEVOTES 'DAY OFF' TO SPEECH

Starts Dictating Acceptance Text as He Gets His First Respite From Parleys

By JAMES C. HAGERTY

Special to THE NEW YORK TIMES.

COLORADO SPRINGS, Col., July 28—Wendell L. Willkie today started dictating the first draft of his formal acceptance speech, to be delivered at Elwood, Ind., on Aug. 17.

For the first day since his arrival here three weeks ago the Republican Presidential nominee had no engagements, but remained in his hotel suite throughout the day and evening.

In the morning Mr. Willkie rested and read the morning newspapers, and in the afternoon called in Miss Grace Grahm, his secretary, and made a start on his acceptance speech, using an outline he has made since he has been here. He plans to continue dictating the draft during the early part of this week.

Claude Chandler for Him

After having lunch, the nominee made public the text of a telegram from Claude Chandler of San Diego, pledging support to his candidacy. Mr. Chandler has been active in Southern California Democratic circles and in 1932 was an "original" Roosevelt supporter, running as delegate at large on the Roosevelt ticket to the Democratic National Convention. The Roosevelt ticket was defeated by the Garner ticket in California in that year.

The telegram from Mr. Chandler read as follows:

"President Roosevelt's acceptance of the nomination for a third term has shocked and disappointed me. I could not believe it possible that any American holding that high and exalted office would thus violate the trust placed in him to guard and protect our sacred liberties and democratic institutions.

"As delegate at large on the Roosevelt ticket in the California Presidential primary in 1932 I led the campaign for him in San Diego. At that convention I worked day and night to bring about his nomination.

"I actively campaigned for his election in 1932 and again in 1936. Now I shall support your candidacy, knowing in my heart that I will be aiding in the election of a President who has a better understanding of the patriotic duty of all true Americans."

Mr. Willkie, who has been making speaking appearances throughout Colorado and a two-day trip into Utah and Wyoming during his "vacation" stay here, seemed to enjoy thoroughly his "day off" today.

With no conferences or interviews scheduled for the day, Mr. Willkie loafed around his suite in the morning and then started to dictate his speech in the afternoon.

No "Outside Trips" This Week

It was announced that no "outside trips" had been arranged for this week and that the nominee, although working on the draft of his speech, expected to continue during the week his conferences here with leading Republicans, independents and anti-New Deal

Continued on Page Seven

CONGRESS CLEAN-UP OF DEFENSE BILLS SOUGHT BY SEPT. 1

Drive to Start Tomorrow With Report of Training Bill to Senate for Debate

PASSAGE IN 2 WEEKS IS AIM

Guard Call, Huge Army-Navy Fund Bill, Profits Tax Slated —Recess May Follow

By HENRY N. DORRIS

Special to THE NEW YORK TIMES.

WASHINGTON, July 28—A drive aimed at completing national defense legislation by Sept. 1 will start Tuesday in Congress. Leaders entertain hopes that when that is done either adjournment or a long recess can be taken.

The immediate program in what may be one of the busiest weeks of the session so far contemplates starting debate Wednesday in the Senate over the Burke-Wadsworth Selective Compulsory Military Training Bill. House consideration of bills to provide funds for starting new power facilities for the Tennessee Valley Authority and construction of new shore facilities for the Navy.

Although both the Senate and House meet tomorrow, the sessions are expected to be perfunctory since many members of both were guests of the United States Maritime Commission on the cruise of the new liner America and will not return to Washington until tomorrow night.

Items on Defense Program

The remaining items in the national defense program, in the probable order of their consideration, are:

1. The Burke-Wadsworth bill.

2. The $25,000,000 appropriation for construction of a new dam and steam plant for the TVA, to provide power for manufacture by the Aluminum Company of America of aluminum sheets for plane wings.

3. The Vinson bill to authorize expenditure of $50,000,000 for construction of naval shore establishments.

4. The bill requested by President Roosevelt for authority to call out the National Guard, which will be heeded to train, in cooperation with the Regular Army, the men who will be called if the Burke-Wadsworth bill is enacted.

5. The $4,848,000,000 appropriation bill to pay for equipment for an army of 1,500,000, and for new Navy construction.

6. An excess profits tax bill, designed to recapture unreasonable profits on defense contracts and to be substituted for the 8 per cent profit limitation on defense contracts imposed by the Vinson-Trammell act.

If the Burke-Wadsworth bill is enacted, the War Department is expected to ask for some additional legislation, but its nature will depend upon the final terms of the Burke-Wadsworth measure.

Ten-Day Debate Expected

The Senate Military Affairs Committee is expected to report the Burke-Wadsworth bill to the Senate on Tuesday. It already has approved the bill section by section.

There was some sentiment among Senate Republicans to defer the opening of debate until Aug. 5, but Senator Barkley, the majority leader, will offer it Wednesday in the hope that the "extended discussion" will not take more than ten days. Should the debate extend beyond that period, the Army might have to defer its plans for calling into service 400,000 men on Oct. 1, with prior registration of the estimated 42,000,000 men between 18 and 64 who would be re-

Continued on Page Six

HULL PLAN STANDS AS MINOR CHANGES WIN WIDER BACKING

Pan-American Declaration for Ban on Foreign Intrusion Merges Viewpoints

AVOIDS BLANKET REMEDIES

Problems Likely to Arise Soon to Be Placed Foremost in Formal Action Today

By HAROLD B. HINTON

Wireless to THE NEW YORK TIMES.

HAVANA, July 28 — The Pan-American Foreign Ministers put in a hard Sunday today working in committees and subcommittees that are trying to include the last-minute ideas of the lesser lights, intended to improve the general agreement reached by their leaders yesterday, but the prospects were that the second consultative meeting since the outbreak of the European war would confine its concrete conclusions to the problems most likely to arise in the next few weeks.

These problems obviously depend on military developments in Europe more than on the volition of the American republics. For instance, the Chilean delegation is convinced that the Economic Committee on Hemisphere Defense must include machinery that could quickly expropriate public utilities owned by non-American nationals in the event of the capture of the governments heretofore protecting those investments.

No doubt this viewpoint takes in the possibility of an emergency that might arise if, for example, shares now owned by British individuals in an Argentine railroad were suddenly declared to belong to the German Economic Ministry. The Argentine Government would have to review the situation, since the public interest obviously would be affected differently where shares were distributed among individuals, trust funds and bank portfolios in England and Scotland, and where they were concentrated in the hands of the German Government.

Blanket Solution Avoided

The Chileans suggested that a common policy should be worked out to cover such contingencies, which might be common to most Latin-American countries. The Economic Committee, however, scenting possible unforeseen complications from an attempt to evolve a blanket solution, has merely recommended further study of means of orderly repatriation of all foreign-owned shares in Latin-American public utilities through purchase from nationals of the affected countries.

A similar thought has resulted in a milder watering down of the United States' proposal for taking over European possessions in the Western Hemisphere in the event of an attempted change of sovereignty as a result of the European war. Secretary of State Cordell Hull's plan, setting forth precise machinery leaping automatically to action as soon as an emergency arises, has been diluted by the addition of declarations of principles that do not harm the general objective, according to United States experts, but tend to give the effect of a championship baseball team scattering its hits.

On the credit side, Mr. Hull has obtained approval of an emergency scheme for establishing a committee made up of representatives of the United States, Venezuela, Ecuador, the Dominican Republic and either Cuba or Brazil to function for the possessior from now until the permanent arrangement, as outlined by the convention and requiring ratification by the home con-

Continued on Page Five

C.I.O. Auto Union Will Act on Communists; Delegates Hit Forced Defense Training

By LOUIS STARK

Special to THE NEW YORK TIMES.

ST. LOUIS, July 28—Meeting today on the eve of the opening of the fourth constitutional convention of the United Automobile Workers of America (C. I. O.), the constitution committee discussed several far-reaching proposals which would not only constitutionally bar Communists, Nazis and Fascists from holding office in the union, but from membership as well.

Although no action was taken by the committee on these resolutions, as it will meet again to discuss them, it was reported that strong sentiment had developed for the affirmative submission of a substitute for the various resolutions dealing with subversive influences in the union.

One suggestion for rewriting the resolution on subversive influences was that it should be shown that the union strongly opposed any one who was aligned with a political or other group controlled by a foreign government. It is regarded as unlikely that a form of resolution barring a Communist from membership in the union would be passed because the Communist party is a legal organization and because Communists are employed in the industry and the union cannot exclude those who are hired by the employers.

A copy of the resolutions offered by locals and referred to committees for action disclosed today strong sentiment for approving national defense and a preparedness program, but at the same time opposing conscription and retaining beneficial labor and social legislation and civil liberties.

Coupled with defense proposals are strong expressions against American intervention in the European war and the favoring of an isolation position for the United States.

One argument used against com-

Continued on Page Eight

The International Situation

The War in Europe and Africa

Recent intensification of the German sea and air war on Britain was interpreted yesterday in Berlin as portending the approach of zero hour for a mass invasion. The attempt was believed there to be a matter of only days, perhaps hours. A sign of the increased tempo of the war was discernible in German High Command communiqués claiming the sinking of British shipping at a rate twice that of the worst period of the World War. [Page 1, Column 8.]

An indication that some major action might be impending was an order halting all railroad traffic between the occupied and unoccupied areas of France. Observers in the provisional French capital of Vichy had no information as to the reason but pointed out that just before the invasion of the Low Countries on May 10 the German military took over all transport in the Reich. It was learned that two areas in the occupied zone, one of them along the Channel coast, had been closed for some time. [Page 2, Column 2.]

In Rome an editorial in Foreign Minister Ciano's newspaper said the answer to the question, "When will the war start against England?" was that it had begun Friday. [Page 2, Column 6.]

German planes raided Wales for three hours, the longest attack of the war, early today. Yesterday a mass air assault on the southeast coast was beaten off in a dog fight involving at least seventy planes. The R.A.F. also was on the offensive, the Air Ministry said, with waves of bombers raining destruction on naval bases and German airdromes. [Page 1, Column 7.]

The British also apparently carried the war to Italy in the Adriatic. Reports from near-by Yugoslav cities said that bombers had attacked the important Italian port of Trieste for three hours and had raided Pola and Udine. The Yugoslavs heard that one of three British submarines had been sunk in that sea during the day. Rome made no mention of any action there, but said its bombing planes had attacked British fleet units in the Eastern Mediterranean and again had raided the British naval bases of Malta and Alexandria. Land action along the Sudan and Libyan borders also was reported. [Page 3, Column 6.]

Repercussions Elsewhere

Agreement having been reached on formation of a solid front against any threat from abroad, the Havana conference of the twenty-one American republics devoted itself to working out the details of economic and trusteeship plans that had been agreed on in principle. One issue not yet settled was enunciation of a formula to handle foreign holdings in public utilities such as large British investments in Argentine railways. [Page 1, Column 5.]

The Italian press was scornful of the work of the conference. Premier Mussolini's paper said the results had been "perfectly nil" and that the only facts emerging were Argentine and Guatemalan claims on British possessions—the Falkland Islands and British Honduras—and a strong anti-British antipathy among the Latin nations. [Page 5, Column 6.]

The unexplained arrest in Japan of twelve prominent Britons, including C. H. N. James, chief representative in Japan of the British Federation of Industries, was disclosed in Shanghai. [Page 1, Column 6.]

BRITONS ARRESTED SECRETLY IN JAPAN

Seizure of 11 Business Leaders, Besides News Man, Linked to New Tokyo Policy

By The Associated Press.

SHANGHAI, Monday, July 29—It was learned from private advices today that eleven prominent British business men in Japan have been arrested by Japanese authorities in five cities. Previous reports had listed nine men.

All were said to have been arrested Saturday in sudden raids without warning. The Japanese censorship suppressed all news on the subject.

Reasons for the arrests were not disclosed, but British circles believed that pressure from Germany on Japan was at least partly responsible.

One of those held was said to be E. W. James of Kobe, who had returned from Canada only last Friday.

The arrests were apparently at the same time as the seizure in Japan—as disclosed here late Saturday—of Melville James Cox, Reuters (British news agency) correspondent in Tokyo, who was reported taken into custody for "military reasons."

Nine of the business men arrested were identified as:

C. H. N. James, retired naval officer and chief representative in Japan of the British Federation of Industries; J. F. Drummond, F. M. Jonas, E. W. James, J. F. James, two brothers named Ringer, R. A. Holder, president of the British Association, and H. M. McNaughton, honorary Greek consular representative.

C. H. N. James was said to have been arrested at Tokyo; Messrs. Drummond, Jonas, Holder and E. W. James at Kobe, J. F. James and one of the Ringer brothers at Shimonoseki, Mr. McNaughton at Osaka, and the second Ringer at Nagasaki.

Reuters said British Ambassador Sir Robert Leslie Craigie was to attempt to obtain the release of Mr. Cox through Japanese Foreign Minister Yosuke Matsuoka.

Tokyo Moves Worry London

Wireless to THE NEW YORK TIMES.

LONDON, July 28—To say that there is disappointment here regarding the results of successive British gestures toward conciliation with Japan would be an understate-

Continued on Page Six

R. A. F. FIGHTS RAIDS, POUNDS NAZI BASES

Reports Downing 10 of Foe—70 Craft Clash Over Channel —Wales Heavily Bombed

By JAMES MacDONALD

Special Cable to THE NEW YORK TIMES.

LONDON, Monday, July 29—Swarms of German bombing planes growled over widely separated parts of Britain early today, following all-day air activity yesterday, when, according to official announcement, British fliers shot down ten Nazi planes, five of them during a series of fierce fights over the English Channel.

Two British planes were lost during yesterday's operations, that included not only defense of the homeland and coastal waters but also air thrusts at the Germans. Royal Air Force pilots bombed two supply ships, eight air bases, naval dockyards and lines of communication.

During Nazi attacks from the sky this morning, a large number of Germans gave one Welsh district its longest air raid thus far, lasting more than three and a half hours. Many British fighter planes roared aloft to engage the Nazis.

In Wales and elsewhere bombs crashed on the ground and searchlights raked the skies as anti-aircraft guns bellowed and defending machines streaked after the invaders.

Results of Attacks Unchecked

Reports early in the morning did not say what damage had been done or whether there were any casualties.

In yesterday's air operations Germany lost four planes at inland points in Britain, and another off the Norwegian coast besides the five during the Channel engagements.

One of the Channel fights occurred in thin air at an altitude of 30,000 feet, where a group of Messerschmitts was caught flying in a line abreast. One German fighter plane was sent into the sea in a six-mile death dive.

At least seventy planes engaged in the series of fights that raged over many miles of Channel sky during the day. The Germans introduced something new in their aerial warfare by using single-engine Messerschmitt 109 fighters, each of which carried one medium-size bomb.

Whether the German fighters

Continued on Page Two

ATTACK INTENSIFIED

'Softening Up' of Britain From Sea and Air Now Starts in Earnest

NAZIS DRIVE ON SHIPPING

Communiques of 2 Days Claim Sinking of 166,000 Tons—South of England Bombed

By GEORGE AXELSSON

Wireless to THE NEW YORK TIMES.

BERLIN, July 28—The process of "softening up" Britain by means of dive bombers, submarines and torpedo-carrying mosquito craft seems now to have begun in earnest and a big landing attempt may be only a matter of days, if not hours.

[All railroad service between the German-held and unoccupied areas of France was halted yesterday without any official explanation. The brief communiqué issued by the Pétain government indicated that travel by road was also prohibited. This action recalled similar German moves the day before the invasion of the Low Countries on May 10.]

From all German sources come reports of intensified air attacks on British military airdromes, ports and rail junctions, as well as ship convoys and armaments factories, and that sort of activity in this war has always been a sure forerunner of a big German onslaught.

The communiqués of the last two days speak of a total of 166,000 tons of British merchant tonnage being sunk by submarines, speedboats and dive bombers, in addition to three destroyers, including the Whirlwind of 1,100 tons. If this rate can be maintained the British stand to lose tonnage at the rate of more than 2,000,000 tons monthly, which the Germans claim to be murderous.

South of England Bombed

The indications are now, say the Germans, that this rate will not only be kept up but will be substantially bettered. Nazi dive bombers in the last few days, it is said here, have been peppering the entire south of England all the way from Hastings westward to Cardiff and Swansea, as well as air fields in Cornwall.

It is reported that the attacks at times reached the intensity of waves of a hundred each.

Judging from reports here the Royal Air Force so far has been unable to do much to hinder these raids, which are directed as much against open sea shipping as they are against fixed land objectives, so that the German Rear Admiral Gadow may be right when he claims that the only access to Britain's west coast for sea borne trade at present is the approach through the North Channel between Belfast and the Scottish coast.

One of Germany's "fighting" war correspondents, Fritz Mittler, who serves aboard one of the dive bombers assigned to English Channel objectives and whose members have humorously nicknamed themselves the "Channel workers," tells how he participated in a dive-bombing raid Thursday against a Channel convoy in which his squadron allegedly scored hits on eight ships out of twenty.

Herr Mittler's colleagues were peacefully playing cards on their side of the Channel when reconnaissance planes brought word of the presence of a convoy. Hastily donning their parachutes, lifebelts and leather helmets, the men jumped into their Junkers 87's.

After flying over Eastbourne, Hastings, Dungeness, Littletown and Dover he and his comrades, he writes, flew up the Thames to London in the face of furious anti-aircraft fire from the ground and ships. Herr Mittler says he dove his plane onto what he judged to be a 5,000-ton ship to within a few hundred feet when he released a bomb and, he adds, as he turned up he heard a mighty detonation and saw flames and smoke shoot to the sky from the freighter. He says that British anti-aircraft fire did not greatly bother his squadron.

While waiting for the heralded big drive against Britain to commence the Germans "behind the lines," that is, civilians and a great number of the armed forces on leave from France and Norway, take things easy.

Sea Blockade Pushed

BERLIN, July 28 (UP)—Pushing her air and sea blockade of the British Isles, Germany tonight

Continued on Page Two

"All the News That's Fit to Print."

The New York Times.

LATE CITY EDITION

Local thunder showers, continued warm today. Tomorrow local showers and not quite so warm.

Temperatures Yesterday—Max., 88; Min., 71

Copyright, 1940, by The New York Times Company.

VOL. LXXXIX...No. 30,138. Entered as Second-Class Matter, Postoffice, New York, N. Y. NEW YORK, TUESDAY, JULY 30, 1940. THREE CENTS NEW YORK CITY and Vicinity | FOUR CENTS Elsewhere Except in 7th and 8th Postal Zones.

ROOSEVELT ASKS A YEAR'S TRAINING OF NATIONAL GUARD

Requests Congress to Enact Law Authorizing Him to Call Troops to Colors

QUICK ACTION IS URGED

Grenville Clark, on Radio, Says Selective Service Will Give Inventory of Our Skills

Text of President Roosevelt's letter to the Senate, Page 11.

By FRANK L. KLUCKHOHN

Special to THE NEW YORK TIMES.

WASHINGTON, July 29—President Roosevelt asked Congress today for prompt action on legislation to permit him to order out the National Guard for a year's training, and for possible service in the Western Hemisphere and the Territories and possessions of the United States, including the Philippine Islands.

The President announced that he plans to call the National Guard to service in successive increments.

"The security of the nation demands that this component of our Army be brought to the highest possible state of training efficiency more rapidly than its present program permits," he said.

Reserve officers also would be called to service for training.

Mr. Roosevelt made his request in a letter to the President of the Senate, with which he transmitted a brief proposed joint resolution.

In modern warfare, he remarked, "only the seasoned and highly trained troops can hope for success in combat."

"Our citizen soldiery, no matter how willing and earnest," the letter said, "cannot possibly attain the necessary degree of efficiency through their normal training activities.

"This group of men, who of necessity must be the first to fight in the nation's defense have a right to the best preparation that time and circumstance permit."

For Period Ending June 30, 1942

Recognizing the personal sacrifices that long service would entail, the President promised to release the National Guard from service as rapidly as possible, but, he said, he could not, "with clear conscience, longer postpone this vitally essential step in our progress toward adequate preparedness." The proposed resolution would limit to June 30, 1942, the period in which the authority could be exercised.

Army plans call for placing the National Guard in training by Sept. 15, if possible, so that the 300,000 to 400,000 men who will be called to colors Oct. 1, if the Burke-Wadsworth Bill is passed by Congress, may train with the Guard and Regular Army.

As isolationist Senators become increasingly vocal in opposition to compulsory selective service measures and a mild move developed with their backing to at least narrow the age limits of those to be registered, Grenville Clark, representing the Military Training Camps Association, sponsor of the bill, explained the reasons for the provision to register all males between the ages of 18 and 65. The explanation was made in a speech broadcast nationally over the National Broadcasting Company system.

Mr. Clark said that besides the definite practical advantages of listing all males between the ages of 18 and 64, "we see also a great moral value in listing our full man power, thereby telling the world that we do not propose to permit our institutions and way of life to be destroyed and that we don't intend to be pushed around."

"The wide registration," he said, "makes for national unity and morale and makes it clear that, if necessary, all ages and not only the youth will take part."

Cites Danger if Britain Loses

In amplifying his remarks about the value, particularly from a practical viewpoint, in registering all males from 18 to 64 years of age, Mr. Clark said:

"The registration of all men between these ages will give us an inventory of our nation's manpower and enable the country to make the best use of each man's ability and experience if and when necessary. This registration is a vital feature of the bill.

"In order to spread the load and carry out the selective system, large numbers must be listed in the pool, even though most of them may never be called. The actual numbers to be called for training at any time will depend upon the decisions of the President, with the advice of the War and Navy Departments, subject always to ap-

Continued on Page Eleven

New U. S. Queen of Seas Receives Tumultuous Welcome in Harbor

Liner America Greeted From Sky, Land and Water—300 Join Mayor and Other Officials in Reception at Pier

By JOHN H. CRIDER

From the land, from the sky and from the water New York extended an enthusiastic welcome yesterday to the liner America, new queen of the American merchant marine, as she sailed rakishly into her home port on her first passenger-carrying run.

Welcomers spared nothing in noise, color and energy to make it perfectly clear that they were proud to have the nation's biggest, costliest and safest liner make her home in New York.

Far from the destruction of a European war, the giant ship has a peaceful mission of commerce before her, but Mayor La Guardia, in his welcome at her berth in flag-draped Pier 59, North River, served notice to the world that the America was potentially a valuable naval auxiliary.

"There are many more from whence she came," he shouted to the crowd on the pier.

The din of whistles and sirens as the America reached the Battery at 12:28, with her own deep-throated whistles contributing to the welcoming chorus, caused many of the newcomer's 900 passengers to clap hands to their ears. The deafening noise lasted several minutes.

The $17,500,000 America, new flagship of the United States Lines, came alongside the Riverside, carrying the Mayor's official welcoming committee, at noon, and, after reaching her pier at about 1:15, she was easily docked in fifteen minutes in the favorable tide.

If it had not been for the mad cheering of 300 welcomers on the end of the bunting-draped United States Lines pier, and the playing of "God Bless America" by the ship's band and the Fire Department Band on the pier, the ease of the docking might have suggested this initial berthing was a routine affair.

Harbor veterans said it was the noisiest reception since the Normandie, French luxury liner, entered the bay on June 3, 1934, to win the North Atlantic speed pennant.

Not since the Queen Mary completed her maiden voyage on June 1, 1936, had New York had occasion to pay harbor honors to a new transatlantic liner, and it was seven years ago, on April 30, 1933, that it last had occasion to extend the traditional welcome to a liner of American construction. That was the Washington, her sister ship.

The 900 passengers aboard the America, including fifteen Senators and eighty-seven Representatives, many of whom had never before seen New York Harbor go wild in honor of a newcomer to the nation's greatest port, were as curious about the reception as the welcomers were about the America.

Continued on Page Twenty-one

ROOSEVELT VIEWS OUR NEW DEFENSES

Inspecting Speeding of Work at Norfolk, He Says We Will Feel Safer in a Year

By CHARLES W. HURD

Special to THE NEW YORK TIMES.

NORFOLK, Va., July 29—A long and energetic day spent in inspecting the network of defense works and defense-building operations that honeycomb this Virginia peninsula gave President Roosevelt confidence tonight that "a year from now we can feel a lot better" about the invulnerability of the United States against invasion by any foreign power.

He made this observation after a tour such as few individuals besides himself or persons traveling with him would be permitted to take in the present emergency.

"I should say this is a good eye demonstration," the President said at the end of his tour, "of what we have been doing for national defense since last Summer. At the airport they have quadrupled their facilities, at the fleet base I should say they have increased operations by 50 per cent, and about the same thing is true at the Navy Yard. We are going to see a lot more before we get through."

"Do you think Washington could be invaded again?" he was asked. This was a reference to the British invasion in the War of 1812.

"That would depend," the President answered, "entirely on where it came from and who it was. A year from now we can feel a lot better."

Sees Building at Close Range

Accompanied by a few of the key men involved in the defense effort, Mr. Roosevelt saw battleships towering in their ways, watched the latest-type aircraft roar through manoeuvres, witnessed effective anti-aircraft operations, saw great coast defense guns cradled in their carriages at Fort Monroe and glimpsed the intricate operations necessary to turn an arms program from paper work into trained men and the highly complex tools of war.

For the first time he viewed some of the physical work which has sprung from Administration and Congressional action in spurring, through authorization and appropriation, the greatest arms program ever undertaken by the country in peace time. It is manifested here in almost every phase.

Incidentally, this trip was the first by Mr. Roosevelt to a city since he was nominated for a third term. In drives of about 100 miles, taken in temperatures that approached 100 degrees, with 99 degrees officially recorded while he was at Langley Field, he was greeted by cheering crowds that lined literally miles of streets. This community is consistently Democratic and Mr. Roosevelt is a popular figure. Also, this was his first visit since he came here as Assistant Secretary of the Navy more than twenty years ago.

The President's tour embraced the Navy Yard at Portsmouth; the naval operating base south of Norfolk, on the Elizabeth River; Fort Monroe, at Old Point Comfort; Langley Field, one of the major flying bases maintained by the

Continued on Page Twelve

'ECONOMIC FRONT' URGED BY FARRELL

Ex-Head of Steel Corporation Says British Might Join Us —Barter Plan Held Likely

By The Associated Press.

SAN FRANCISCO, July 29—Prospects for an "economic front" made up of the American nations and the countries of the British Empire were discussed today by James A. Farrell, chairman of the National Foreign Trade Council and former head of the United States Steel Corporation, as a means of combating a prospective totalitarian bloc in Europe.

"Whatever the outcome of the military struggle, it is likely that efforts will be made at its close to establish an economic bloc in Europe," he said. "With Europe under a dictatorship, we would have to match the power of a European economic union with the combined power of this Western Hemisphere in bargaining our way through to a reciprocal commercial understanding."

Mr. Farrell discussed the outlook for trade with other countries in an address opening the convention of the National Foreign Trade Council.

"The uncertainty of our trade relations with the Orient, due to the Sino-Japanese war and the trade effects of the Philippine Independence Act, if carried through in its present form, calls for serious consideration of the direction in which we should look for a strengthening of our bargaining power with a European economic bloc comprising our former leading markets," he went on.

"In these circumstances, with

Continue on Page Thirteen

WILLKIE COUNTS ON WILSON DEMOCRATS AND THOSE OF 1932

Says He Sees No Reason Why They Should Not Back Him Instead of Roosevelt

NEW DEAL CALLED ISSUE

Nominee Asserts Party Lines Will Be Broken—Predicts Cracking of the South

By JAMES C. HAGERTY

Special to THE NEW YORK TIMES.

COLORADO SPRINGS, Col., July 29—Wendell L. Willkie predicted today that traditional Democratic and Republican party allegiances would be overturned in this year's campaign and that a new political alignment, centering around approval or disapproval of the New Deal, would be the demarcation line for the vast majority of American voters.

This belief has been strengthened considerably during his stay here by telegrams and letters from all parts of the country, expressing opposition to the third-term nomination of President Roosevelt and pledging support to Mr. Willkie.

As each day brings an increasing volume of offers of support from anti-New Deal Democrats and independents, as well as Republicans, Mr. Willkie's confidence in his ultimate victory at the polls in November increases in a like proportion. This has led to his belief that he will be able to crack the "solid South" better than any previous Republican Presidential nominee has, and to his emphasis on the formation of an independent Democratic movement throughout the country.

Hopes for Democrats of '32

Today, at his press conference, Mr. Willkie, elated over completion of half of the first draft of his acceptance speech, brought his theory of political realignment into the open, when, in reply to a question as to how much he was counting on Democratic support, he stated:

"I do not know of any reason why any Democrat who subscribed to and believed in the 1932 Democratic platform or believes in the historic principles of the Democratic party, or who was a Woodrow Wilson Democrat, should not vote for me in preference to the President—not at all on the basis of personality, but on the basis of what he and I respectively believe and advocate."

Asked how he thought the Republican voters would react to this statement, Mr. Willkie continued:

"I think the Republican party, through me, is likewise advocating the cause that represents the viewpoint of the Republicans of the country, namely, opposition to the policies and practices of the Roosevelt administration, particularly with reference to domestic questions."

Pausing for a minute, Mr. Willkie, speaking slowly and with emphasis, then summed up his contention that he would receive support from all voters except those believing in or committed to the New Deal.

"In other words," he added, "both Republicans and Democrats have a common viewpoint. The people who should not vote for me are those who believe in the New Deal and those bound by rigid party ties or those controlled by the corrupt and nauseating party machines that are

Continued on Page Fourteen

Heat in City at 88.3° as the Humidity Rises; Breezes From Ocean Bring Slight Relief

The heat wave's grip on the city was loosened slightly yesterday by breezes that drifted in from the ocean, but New Yorkers, unable to get away to the beaches as on Sunday, hardly noticed the wind as a rise in the humidity made the day uncomfortable.

In parts of the Midwest, as well as in the Virginias and the Carolinas, relief came through rains and cool winds. However, in most of the Ohio and Mississippi Valleys as well as in some of the Central States, the temperature was in the nineties.

The local Weather Bureau predicted that, although thunder showers were expected here this afternoon, the average temperature would be as high as yesterday, with the thermometer reaching at least 90 degrees, as compared with yesterday's high mark of 88.3 degrees at 12:50 P. M. There was no sign of relief in other stricken sections of the nation.

In the metropolitan area five persons were drowned and one died of the heat and one was prostrated. A youth was killed by lightning in New Jersey. The number of deaths in the entire country attributed to the heat wave rose to 717, of which 364 were due to drowning, according to the Associated Press.

The mean temperature in the city yesterday was 82 degrees, two degrees less than on Sunday but seven degrees more than the normal mean. The record high for the date is 96 degrees, which was set in 1892.

According to the local Weather Bureau, the temperature in the city was cooled somewhat by the shifting of easterly breezes to a southeasterly direction. As the wind shifted it gained in velocity, attaining a speed of twelve to fifteen miles an hour.

The change in the direction of the wind was caused by the arrival of a high pressure area from the Great Lakes region. On Friday, when this high-pressure area first began to move toward the city, the Weather Bureau had hoped it would break the heat wave here.

On Sunday the high-pressure area was moving so slowly over a warm area that the Weather Bureau announced it would afford no relief to New York when it got here. However, the pressure area, when it arrived yesterday, was sufficiently high to cause the land breeze to shift to a sea breeze from the east early yesterday. The shift was completed during the afternoon when the wind became southeast.

Yesterday was the ninth day since

Continued on Page Twenty

3 CHIEF PROJECTS OF U. S. APPROVED AT HAVANA PARLEY

Plan for Administration of Colonies Is Adopted at Night Plenary Session

ECONOMIC EFFORT UNIFIED

United Stand Taken on Fifth-Column Activity—Hull Is Pleased With Results

Texts of agreements reached at Havana will be found on Page 6.

By HAROLD B. HINTON

Special Cable to THE NEW YORK TIMES.

HAVANA, July 29—Detailed methods by which the American republics may best defend themselves against the possible consequences of the European war were formally approved tonight at a closed plenary session of their foreign ministers.

Although the general outlines of the agreed measures had been known for several days, texts of the approved projects revealed minor but interesting modifications resulting from conferences over the week-end. Not all texts were available tonight, but those made public gave the general impression that informal conversations between the delegates had resulted in greater flexibility and perhaps greater practicability than in the original Washington drafts.

Nazi Acquisitions Banned

One example is the treatment of the emergent question of transfer of the sovereignty of European possessions in this hemisphere. This problem was treated extensively in a formal convention, but its urgency was recognized in an instrument known as the Act of Havana, which sets forth the unanimous determination of the American republics that Germany shall not control any terrritory in this hemisphere.

[Members of the Argentine delegation said that any signature put on the document here would have to be approved finally by the Congress in Buenos Aires.]

This document, as well as the formal convention, operates on the principle of insurance underwriters in guaranteeing severally and collectively the status quo of the American dependencies of European governments as constituted before the European war pending either their return to their former sovereigns or their agreed ability to assert and preserve their independence.

Both instruments recognize a possible emergency in which a single republic might act in behalf of all, acting first and consulting afterward. For example, the Act of Havana recites:

"Should the need for emergency action be so urgent that the action of the committee cannot be awaited, any of the American republics, individually or jointly with others, shall have the right to act in a manner which its own defense or that of the continent requires. Should this situation arise, the American republic or republics taking action shall place the matter before the committee immediately."

The emergency conditions foreseen are described as European possessions being "in danger of becoming the subject of barter of territory or change of sovereignty."

Committee of 14 States

The committee to which reference is made consists of representatives of fourteen of the twenty-one republics as a minimum. This principle of two-thirds consent in urgent matters runs through the entire machinery, replacing the customary unanimous concurrence.

This committee may be called into session at the request of any signatory, but any country could take what it deems appropriate action pending the committee call, but subject to subsequent validation.

In this clause Argentina interposed a reservation to the effect that the Malvinas [Falkland] Islands could not be considered as falling within the purview of the instrument because they were now considered under Argentine sovereignty.

This reference to a long-standing dispute with Great Britain has been sanctioned at previous Pan-American gatherings, as has the controversy of Guatemala over British Honduras.

The permanent arrangement embodied in the convention requiring parliamentary ratification by the individual republics recites that, as a result of the European war, situations may develop regarding the territories of belligerents in this hemisphere "which may extinguish or materially impair the sovereignty which they exercise over them or leave their government without a leader," by which the peace of this hemisphere is threatened.

The convention reserves to the American republics "the right to

Continued on Page Six

BRITISH REPEL MASS AIR RAIDS OVER DOVER, DOWN 20 PLANES; BOMB CHERBOURG OIL TANKS

The International Situation

The War in Europe and Africa

Germany launched the greatest mass airplane attack of the war on Great Britain yesterday. More than eighty bombers and fighters roared across the English Channel against the port of Dover. What damage they did was not divulged, but an official British report said seventeen of the raiders were shot down. Unofficial estimates were as high as twenty-seven. There were other raids by smaller groups. The British themselves continued attacks on German oil dumps and airdromes, seventeen objectives being bombed during the night. Destruction of oil stores at Cherbourg was claimed. [Page 1, Column 8.]

Berlin listed 78,750 more tons of British shipping destroyed by air, submarine or torpedo boat attack. It raised the total claimed in the last three days to more than 200,000 tons. The Germans say that is at a pace that will soon starve out Britain. [Page 5, Column 1.]

Gibraltar fortress again was bombed by the Italians. The principal damage, however, according to Spanish reports, was caused by the careless handling of a hand grenade, which detonated a dump of anti-aircraft shells. Four British soldiers were reported killed. British aviation also was active. Two big Sunderland flying boats, in separate patrols over the Mediterranean, were attacked by Italian fighters. The crew of one British plane said they shot down two planes, the other claimed one. The Italians again bombed Malta, and there was air activity along both the Ethiopian and Libyan borders. [Page 1, Column 7.]

Rumania's Premier and Foreign Minister returned to Bucharest from visits to Salzburg and Rome. Shortly thereafter it was announced that Rumania was prepared to cede some disputed territory to Hungary and Bulgaria, whose representatives also recently consulted Adolf Hitler. [Page 1, Column 6.]

Repercussions Elsewhere

The Havana conference of the twenty-one American republics unanimously adopted last night the United States-sponsored collective trusteeship plan for possessions in this hemisphere of European nations whose sovereignty is endangered. To implement immediately the work of the conference, pending ratification by the various legislatures, an act was adopted that sets up machinery for interim application of the principles of the convention. This was done to meet any sudden change in the European situation. [Page 1, Column 5.]

President Roosevelt asked Congress to grant him authority to call out the National Guard and Army Reserve Officers if necessary to defend the United States and its possessions. "I cannot, with clear conscience, longer postpone this vitally essential step," he said in his message. It was believed in Washington that Congress would quickly give him the authority he sought. [Page 1, Column 1.]

Japanese-British relations, already strained, became even more so with the announcement by the Japanese Foreign Office that the arrest of twelve British citizens Saturday was for espionage and that one of them, a veteran newspaper correspondent, had committed suicide in apparent fear of being found guilty. The British Ambassador asked for a full investigation. London was angry. It was believed the incident would prove embarrassing to the Churchill Government, which has been trying to placate Japan. [Page 10, Column 1.]

Sources in Hong Kong close to the Chiang Kai-shek Government said that China had unconditionally refused a Japanese peace offer. These sources said the peace offer—apparently a blue print of the "New Order in East Asia"—demanded outright cession by China of five northern provinces and formation of a new Chinese Republic, which would include British Burma, French Indo-China and independent but weak Thailand (Siam). The plan apparently took for granted a German victory in Europe. The new China would be governed by the puppet regime Japan set up in Nanking. [Page 10, Column 2.]

RUMANIA REPORTED READY TO CEDE LAND

Agreement 'in Principle' Said to Have Been Reached With Hungary and Bulgaria

By The United Press.

BUCHAREST, Rumania, July 29—Rumania is "willing and ready" to cede territory to Hungary and Bulgaria, it was stated in official quarters tonight.

These quarters, following a government announcement that Rumania has agreed "in principle" to come to an understanding with her neighbors, disclosed that Rumania is reconciled to the necessity of acceding to the demands of Hungary and Bulgaria for Transylvania and Dobruja, respectively.

Rumania sees in this, it was said, the most effective means of preventing the spread of communism in the Balkans and of insuring the maintenance of peace in Southeastern Europe.

This viewpoint tends to confirm reports that Chancellor Hitler and Premier Mussolini, permitting Russia to occupy Bessarabia and Northern Bukovina unopposed, have now called a halt to further westward expansion of the Soviet and are asking the cooperation of all Danubian States in constructing an unbreakable barrier against further penetration from the East.

Rumania, Bulgaria and Hungary will hold a series of consultations soon to discuss territorial demands and come to an understanding, a government statement said.

Further Cessions Opposed

BUCHAREST, Rumania, July 29 (AP)—Germany has given Rumania until Sept. 15 to settle her territorial differences with Hungary and Bulgaria by direct negotiation, it was reported tonight in authoritative quarters.

If there is no agreement then, it was said, the Axis powers plan to

Continued on Page Eight

GIBRALTAR BLAST KILLS 4, WOUNDS 7

Shell Magazine Explodes—British Claim to Have Shot Down 5 Italian Planes

By The Associated Press.

LA LINEA, Spain, July 29—Four British soldiers were reported killed and seven injured today in the explosion of an ammunition dump in Britain's great rock fortress at Gibraltar.

Reports reaching here said a carelessly handled grenade set off a magazine of anti-aircraft shells. British officials would not discuss the blast.

The final removal of all civilians from Gibraltar was reported in Madrid.

Unidentified planes flew over Gibraltar last night and drew heavy anti-aircraft fire.

Unconfirmed reports received at La Linea said several members of an anti-aircraft battery had been court-martialed for delay in manning their guns during a heavy raid on July 26.

British Claim Five Foes Downed

Wireless to THE NEW YORK TIMES.

CAIRO, Egypt, July 29—A British Sunderland flying boat, attacked by three formations of Italian monoplanes after it had bombed and strafed Italian ships, shot down two Fascist fighters yesterday in a thrilling running battle, it was reported today.

The Sunderland crew sighted three Italian ships while patrolling the Mediterranean and immediately dived to the attack. Suddenly a large flight of Italian warplanes appeared and the Sunderland was forced to retreat. After a brief gun battle one formation consisting of three Fascist planes followed the Sunderland, attempting to prevent it from reaching its base. The flying boat's gunners held the Italians at bay, while the pilot skillfully manoeuvred the huge craft to prevent the Italians from getting in a

Continued on Page Five

NAZIS BEATEN OFF

80 Craft Attack Port in Fiercest Assault of the War

GERMAN BASES POUNDED

Berlin Claims 200,000 Tons of British Shipping Lost in Three-Day Period

By JAMES B. RESTON

Special Cable to THE NEW YORK TIMES.

LONDON, July 29—A few hours after the German radio announced that mass air attacks on Britain were about to start, more than eighty Nazi bombers and fighters made a surprise dive-bombing raid on the port of Dover today, but were beaten off in the fiercest air battle of the war.

In thirty minutes of spectacular fighting above the Channel, the Air Ministry said, not a single bomb landed on shore, seventeen German planes were shot down and only one British fighter failed to return safely. [British communiqués said twenty German planes in all were shot down.]

[A British communiqué early today reported German air bombing in Northeast and Southwest England during the night. It said "anti-air defenses went into action early this morning and brought down an enemy bomber over Southeast England."]

German Bases Bombed

While this and other attacks were taking place British bombers were not idle. They attacked military objectives all the way from Northwest Germany to Northern France, battering seventeen airports in Germany, the Low Countries and France and damaging oil depots, docks and freight yards.

A pilot of the Coastal Command reported that his colleagues had successfully fired German oil tanks at Cherbourg last night, though no details of this attack were given.

Today's raids appeared to be Germany's first real test of the British coastal defenses in a mass attack on a port, and it started innocently enough with a single German reconnaisance plane rising through a great cumulus cloud into the blue and circling at well over 20,000 feet just outside the port.

Anti-aircraft guns took a few potshots at it just to make it keep its distance, but before they could do much more the first formation of bombers appeared. All guns then began to bark and fighters spiraled up to meet the raiders.

Keeping the sun at its back and forcing the anti-aircraft gunners to fire into the glare, the first formation waited until it was about a quarter of a mile out of the town and then went into a roaring dive. As it did so two bombers were hit by flying shrapnel from anti-aircraft shells and went down in a smoking spiral into the sea, but the six others kept going and dropped their bombs on the harbor.

Barrage Mars Bombers' Aim

Great spouts of water went up and scores of little sailboats and fishing smacks bobbed about in the harbor. In the face of rapid fire from the pom-poms, however, the bombing was erratic.

By the time the second formation of German planes approached the harbor British Hurricane and Spitfire fighters were high in the sky ready to intercept them. They got above and kept swooping down on them, then climbing up again to take another crack at them with their eight machine guns.

Whenever possible, Messerschmitt fighters stayed above the German bombers in the hope of preventing these British attacks, but in a few minutes, as wave after wave of bombers arrived in flying triangles, the sky above the port was filled with diving planes of every description.

In most cases the Germans managed to keep their formations, but the nearer they got to shore the heavier the fire became and they obviously were unable to bomb with any accuracy.

Spitfires from one squadron alone destroyed four Messerschmitts and a bomber and a Hurricane of another squadron accounted for four Junkers and a fighter. Near the end of the fight, twelve bombers, chased by fighters, came right down almost to sea level in an attempt to escape, but at the end of the terrific dive the Hurricanes pumped the rear bomber full of lead and it dove into the Channel with a great splash.

An Air Ministry statement said

Continued on Page Four

"All the News That's Fit to Print."

The New York Times.

LATE CITY EDITION

Fair, with little change in temperature today and tomorrow.

Temperatures Yesterday—Max., 80; Min., 63

Copyright, 1940, by The New York Times Company.

VOL. LXXXIX..No. 30,174. Entered as Second-Class Matter, Postoffice, New York, N. Y. NEW YORK, WEDNESDAY, SEPTEMBER 4, 1940. THREE CENTS NEW YORK CITY and Vicinity | FOUR CENTS Elsewhere Except in 7th and 8th Postal Zones.

ROOSEVELT TRADES DESTROYERS FOR SEA BASES; TELLS CONGRESS HE ACTED ON OWN AUTHORITY; BRITAIN PLEDGES NEVER TO YIELD OR SINK FLEET

R. A. F. REPELS RAIDS

Fliers Turn Back Three Drives on London—Reich Perfecting Technique

PLANES REACH BERLIN

2½-Hour Alarm in City—British Hit Hard at French Coast

By JAMES B. RESTON

Special Cable to THE NEW YORK TIMES.

LONDON, Wednesday, Sept. 4—German bombers started ringing that big London doorbell early yesterday morning. They rang it again in the afternoon while Prime Minister Winston Churchill and his Ministers were commemorating the first anniversary of the war, and they kept ringing it right up till last midnight, when the third "all clear" of the day was sounded over the capital.

It was a day of fierce air battles, fought at great height in blue and silver sky all over Southeast England, and at the end, though Reich Marshal Hermann Goering's night shift was still operating all over the island, the British Air Ministry announced that twenty-five Nazi planes had been shot down to fifteen of Britain's. Eight British pilots were said to be safe, though it is not known whether they are in condition to fly.

[British bombing planes flew high over Berlin shortly after last midnight. Berlin spokesmen were quoted as saying that most of the Royal Air Force planes were turned back by severe anti-aircraft fire between Wittenberg and Magdeburg, but several planes escaped through the anti-aircraft barrage and reached Berlin, where they were again met with anti-aircraft fire.]

These German bombers, which have already overwhelmed five countries in the past twelve months, have now perfected a technique in attacking this vast, sprawling city, and they tried to work it again yesterday morning in the first raid.

Two Formations Meet

Just at 10 o'clock, timed to perfection, one wave of bombers approached the Thames Estuary from their bases in Belgium. Simultaneously, another formation, flying high through a light haze, came up from bases in France and met them over the Kentish coast. Altogether they were about 250 of them, and defying anti-aircraft batteries at first they started along the banks of the Thames toward London.

As they came inland, however, they met first one, then a second squadron of British fighters, who dived through Nazi fighter patrols into the bombers, broke up the formation and then attacked them singly and drove them back over the coast.

Some German bombers dropped their dynamite in Kent and Essex, but all that is said about the effect of these bombs is that they caused few casualties and little damage.

What can be said is that, if these bombers were trying to get into the heart of London to attack objectives here, they certainly failed, for while sirens were sounded everywhere in Greater London nobody in the heart of the city saw any fighting.

There was an interesting sidelight to the second mass raid of the day. At 2:45 P. M. Mr. Churchill, who somehow contrives to look more confident every day, walked into Westminster Abbey to attend the special service in commemoration of the day a year ago when Britain declared war on Germany. Alongside him walked tall, gaunt Viscount Halifax, Foreign Secretary; dapper Arthur Greenwood, Minister without portfolio; Sir Kingsley Wood, Chancellor of the Exchequer; Anthony Eden, War Secretary, and Joseph P. Kennedy, United States Ambassador to Great Britain.

They took their places in the cool church beside a great audience. At 2:50 P. M., as they were sitting there waiting for the service to start, air-raid sirens started echoing through the great cathedral.

Mr. Churchill got up, walked over to the cloisters and had a long talk with the Dean. In a few minutes he returned and took his place beside his Ministers in the chancel. It was announced that the service would proceed.

Around the city the British fight-

Continued on Page Three

The International Situation

Destroyer-War Base Deal

Completion of a deal by which the United States will transfer to Britain fifty over-age destroyers and obtain ninety-nine-year leases on eight shore and island bases stretching from Newfoundland to British Guiana was announced by President Roosevelt yesterday in a message to Congress. Coincidentally, the British Government pledged not to scuttle or surrender its fleet under any conditions. [Page 1, Column 8.]

The objective of the arrangement with Britain is to build a 4,500-mile iron fence in the Atlantic to assure this country's safety for a century, an authoritative State Department source said. To attain this, any interpretations of international law and parts of treaties in conflict must be subordinated, he said. Since this country's purpose is its defense, no well-intentioned nation can call the move a hostile act, he declared. [Page 1, Column 7.]

President Roosevelt, en route to Washington, disclosed that he looked upon the agreement as a means of keeping an enemy from the country's front door. Listing it as in some ways more important for defense than Jefferson's Louisiana purchase, he hinted there might be other similar arrangements. [Page 1, Column 6.]

The President had acted on an opinion from Attorney General Jackson, who held that the Executive had the right to negotiate the transfer without Senate consent and the constitutional power to dispose of the vessels. [Page 1, Column 5.]

Wendell L. Willkie, Republican Presidential nominee, said the country would undoubtedly approve the arrangement, but criticized Mr. Roosevelt's failure to obtain Congress's approval. [Page 1, Column 3.]

London rejoiced. A Foreign Office spokesman described the agreement as a practical method for each nation to contribute to the other's defense requirements. [Page 1, Column 4.]

Axis spokesmen did not challenge the deal's legality under neutrality laws. In Berlin it was belittled as unlikely to affect the war's outcome. It was said to be a bargain for the United States and evidence that Britain was "cracking up." In Rome it was expected the Italians would be embittered. [Page 15 Column 1.]

Developments in Congress

The House opened debate on the Selective Service Training Bill, the discussion following the lines of the Senate's deliberation. Indications were that the bill would pass by a good margin, the principal controversy centering on the question of industrial conscription. Leaders planned for final action Friday. [Page 17, Column 1.]

The Senate Finance Committee opened hearings on the excess profits tax and defense expansion amortization bill. The probability of changes in the measure increased as witnesses hit at its effects on business. [Page 10, Column 1.]

The War in Europe, Asia and Africa

German bombers hammered at Britain's airfields, harbors and naval bases, engaging the Royal Air Force in battles all over Southern England. Three raids on London were repelled. [Page 1, Column 1.]

Several R. A. F. bombers reached Berlin early today to provoke violent anti-aircraft fire after the British had loosed a powerful aerial counter-offensive in which their planes had bombed German industrial centers, the French coast and Italian power stations. [Page 3, Column 1.]

In the central Mediterranean, new type Italian bombers scored a victory, damaging a British battleship, an aircraft carrier, a cruiser and a destroyer, the Rome High Command announced. The R. A. F. again pounded Assab, port in Italian Eritrea. [Page 4, Column 6.]

Led by Tahiti, France's most important colony in Oceania, the French-protected Society Islands have voted to throw in their lot with Britain, repudiating Vichy, it was reported. [Page 6, Column 1.]

A virtual Japanese ultimatum demanding a military base and passage for troops was reported to have been rejected by French Indo-China and conflict there was believed inevitable. [Page 6, Column 3.]

In an attempted Iron Guard coup three gunmen broke through King Carol's palace guard and fired several shots into the air. Others equally vainly besieged a radio station, fought with troops. [Page 1, Column 2.]

A clash between Hungarian and Rumanian troops over the occupation of Transylvania was reported at Bucharest. [Page 4, Column 1.]

BRITISH JUBILANT

Destroyers Strengthen Their Fleet at Point of Greatest Strain

MORAL EFFECT GREAT

But Press Warns People Gesture Does Not Mean U. S. Will Enter War

By RAYMOND DANIELL

Special Cable to THE NEW YORK TIMES.

LONDON, Sept. 3—It would be impossible to overstate the jubilation in official and unofficial circles caused today by President Roosevelt's announcement that fifty United States destroyers were coming to help Great Britain in her hour of peril. They will be manned by British crews and will fly the white ensign of the Royal Navy, it is true, but they are coming, nevertheless.

It was tangible proof that American talk of giving "all aid short of war" was more than idle chatter and that this country's friends across the Atlantic, despite German propaganda and the heavy bombardment of British cities and towns, had decided there was still lots of fight left in the British lion and that it was not too late to help turn the tide against totalitarian domination of Europe.

Destroyer Losses Offset

Under the arrangement, it was pointed out by authoritative sources, the United States gained security against future aggression, while the British fleet at one stroke acquired fifty 1,200-ton destroyers as an offset to the thirty lost since the beginning of hostilities.

These destroyers are badly needed at this stage of the war with British seapower engaged in a death grapple with the German Empire. Since the French were knocked out as an ally, the whole job of protecting convoys and maintaining the lifelines of the Empire against the new enemy in the Mediterranean has fallen upon the British fleet, while the air force has concentrated chiefly on destroying the enemy's supplies and defending the homes of the people of this island, which is under repeated bombardment from the air throughout its length and breadth.

Added to this multiplication of the navy's duties has been the necessity of blockading the whole Continent of Europe while standing by to resist the very real threat of a German invasion which, as War Secretary Anthony Eden warned today, still hangs over this country.

As great as was Britain's need the material gain by today's transaction was matched in British minds by the intangible implications of most open indication yet of Anglo-American cooperation for defense against the Nazi threats.

The Times, London, will point out editorially tomorrow that such cooperation between a belligerent and a neutral is "a new departure" but one that is dictated by the necessities of modern war. The editorial goes on to say:

"The tragic fate of some of the smaller peoples of Europe might have been averted if they had not been restrained from planning for

Continued on Page Fifteen

RULING BY JACKSON

Opinion Holds Transfer by President Needs No Senate Action

AN 'EXECUTIVE' DEAL

Opponents in Congress Seek to Find Means of Obstructing It

Attorney General Jackson's opinion is printed on Page 16.

By LEWIS WOOD

Special to THE NEW YORK TIMES.

WASHINGTON, Sept. 3—President Roosevelt has unqualified power to exchange fifty over-age destroyers for British naval and air bases in the Western Hemisphere without Senate consent, in the opinion of Attorney General Jackson, made public today, but, while Mr. Jackson asserted the Executive's right to dispose of naval vessels, he again refused to sanction the legality of delivery of "mosquito boats" now under construction.

Under a World War law the Attorney General ruled that it would be entirely proper to transfer the destroyers, since these were not built "with the intent that they should enter the service of a belligerent," but turning over the uncompleted mosquito boats, he argued, would be impossible, as this would legally mean that they were intended for a belligerent.

Opponents of the British-American deal sought tonight to find means of obstruction and delay, but this seemed to hinge upon the extent to which the direct interest of a taxpayer could be proved and the general opinion here was that the adversaries were blocked from court action and could depend only upon sufficient massing of public opinion. Apparently the Administration felt legally secure.

Writing his opinion to President Roosevelt last Tuesday, Mr. Jackson went into detail as to constitutional power and especially stressed the responsibility of the Executive to use every authority for national defense at a time when "present world conditions forbid him to risk" any constitutionally avoidable delay.

"No Future Commitments"

The Attorney General conceded that the wide Presidential power over foreign relations was not unlimited, but in this case, Mr. Jackson contended, there were no promises or future commitments by the United States which would require Senate consent or, indeed, any Congressional action. The agreement provided an opportunity to establish naval and air bases for coastline defense, he maintained, but needed no appropriation of money. Thus it was unnecessary for the Senate to ratify "an opportunity that entails no obligation," he declared.

Alluding to precedents, Mr. Jackson remarked that the "proposition falls far short" of the acquisition of the Louisiana Territory by President Jefferson from a belligerent during a European war. Outside of constitutional power, he went on,

Continued on Page Sixteen

UNITED STATES ACQUIRES DEFENSE BASTIONS

Bases at the places indicated by circled dots are being leased by Great Britain to this country for ninety-nine years. The leases for those in Newfoundland and Bermuda are in effect outright gifts; the leases for the others are in exchange for fifty over-age United States destroyers. The bases in the Caribbean area will supplement present American defense centers (black diamonds) in guarding approaches to the Panama Canal.

LINE OF 4,500 MILES

Two Defense Outposts Are Gifts, Congress Is Told—No Rent on Rest

FOR 50 OLD VESSELS

President Holds Move Solely Protective, 'No Threat to Any Nation'

Texts of messages on leasing of naval bases, Page 10.

By FRANK L. KLUCKHOHN

Special to THE NEW YORK TIMES.

WASHINGTON, Sept. 3—President Roosevelt informed Congress today that he had completed an arrangement by which the United States will transfer to Great Britain fifty over-age destroyers and obtain from Britain ninety-nine-year leases for sea and air bases at eight strategic continental and island points in the Western Hemisphere.

The new American defense line thus established will stretch 4,500 miles from Newfoundland to British Guiana and include other bases on the islands of Bermuda, the Bahamas, Jamaica, St. Lucia, Trinidad and Antigua.

It is intended to make difficult, if not impossible, naval and air attacks upon the United States and much of the New World. The exact sites of the bases will be determined later by the two governments.

A solemn pledge by the British Government to the United States not to scuttle or surrender the British fleet under any conditions was revealed coincidentally by the State Department's publication of correspondence between Secretary Hull and the British Ambassador, the Marquess of Lothian.

Secretary Hull was informed that it represented the "settled policy" of His Majesty's Government not to "surrender or sink" the British fleet.

Reshaping of Naval Defense

The deal, carrying with it far-flung international as well as domestic defense implications, was hailed by President Roosevelt as the most important since the Jefferson Administration completed the Louisiana Purchase in 1803.

Informed official circles contended that it assured the British Fleet as an Atlantic sea-screen for the United States and made it possible for the American Fleet to remain in the Pacific.

Some thought it might lead to an informal defensive alliance between this country and Australia similar to the arrangement recently completed administratively with Canada, although others disagreed on this point.

President Roosevelt informed Congress that the British Government had given the right to bases in Newfoundland and Bermuda as an outright gift, "generously given and gladly received," but that "the other bases mentioned have been acquired in exchange for fifty of our over-age destroyers."

Previously, the President had insisted that the destroyer and base deals were separate.

Legal Basis for Procedure

Mr. Roosevelt explained in his message that he had acted upon a legal opinion by Attorney General Jackson which held that the Chief Executive had the right to dispose of the destroyers and complete the deal without consultation with the Senate and without its approval.

The President made clear that he would not seek the Senate's endorsement by remarking that he sent his statement merely "for the information of Congress."

Chairman Walsh of the Senate Naval Affairs Committee and several other Senators publicly condemned the proposed deal as illegal under domestic and international law when it was reported in the press some weeks ago that President Roosevelt had agreed to give Britain fifty destroyers after pleas from Prime Minister Winston Churchill.

In view of Senator Walsh's stand, some Senators privately expressed the opinion that there might be an attempt to have the Naval Affairs Committee open an investigation of the whole transaction.

After the President's message was

Continued on Page Twelve

BUCHAREST CHECKS IRON GUARDS' COUP

Shots Fired in Front of Royal Palace—Handbills Call on Carol to Abdicate

By EUGEN KOVACS

Wireless to THE NEW YORK TIMES.

BUCHAREST, Rumania, Sept. 3—A group of the Iron Guards, dissatisfied with the conduct and policy of other Iron Guards who are Ministers and who participated in the Crown Council, organized and carried out several attempts tonight against different public buildings in Bucharest. All these attacks failed.

A small group consisting of three persons appeared in an automobile this evening at 8:30 before the Royal Palace and one of them fired two shots in the air. A policeman on duty in front of the gates of the palace fired at the car but failed. The man who fired the shots tried to escape, however, but was arrested, while the car disappeared.

The regular news bulletin broadcast at 10 o'clock was canceled.

A second group, consisting of young men wearing military uniforms and disguised as Iron Guards, attacked the Bucharest radio station. The guard fired and succeeded in repelling the attacking group.

At the cabin of transmission of the Central Telephone Exchange a man was found who cut off some lines so that the telephone connection with abroad was cut off for a while. At the State Railway repair works in the suburb of Grivitza an-

Continued on Page Four

WILLKIE FOR PACT, BUT HITS SECRECY

Regrets President Did Not Put Deal With Britain Before Congress and People

By JAMES A. HAGERTY

Special to THE NEW YORK TIMES.

RUSHVILLE, Ind., Sept. 3—Asked today to comment on President Roosevelt's announcement of the agreement to turn over to Great Britain fifty over-age destroyers in return for air and naval bases in British Western Hemisphere areas, Wendell L. Willkie, Republican nominee for President, declared that the country undoubtedly would approve the program, but criticized the President's failure to obtain prior approval of Congress as smacking of totalitarianism.

In a statement prepared with care and with realization that it might have important foreign repercussions, Mr. Willkie said:

"The country will undoubtedly approve of the program to add to our naval and air bases and assistance given to Great Britain. It is regrettable, however, that the President did not deem it necessary in connection with this proposal to secure the approval of Congress or permit public discussion prior to adoption.

"The people have a right to know of such important commitments prior to and not after being made. We must be extremely careful in these times when the struggle in the world is between democracy and to-

Continued on Page Fourteen

Writer on British Destroyer Sees U-Boats in Raids and One Sunk

By BRYDON TAVES

ABOARD A BRITISH DESTROYER, in the North Atlantic, Sept. 3 (UP)—Germany is shooting the works to make good the threat of total blockade of the British Isles, but after eight days aboard a little British flotilla leader I can say that hundreds of ships are entering and leaving British ports each week.

German submarine and air attacks marked my voyage. Not one day passed without action. The British crew was either manning gun and depth-charge stations to fight off a U-boat or manning anti-aircraft stations to fight attacking planes.

I saw one British merchantman take a long-range torpedo squarely amidships and sink within a half hour. The next day our destroyer evened the score.

A "tin fish," meant for us, missed by a scant thirty feet as we whipped around. Then we rocked from the concussion of our own depth charges and I saw an oil patch spread slowly over the surface, marking that U-boat's end.

The destroyer was engaged in a typical convoy job, and its duties were something between those of a conscientious sheep dog and a sister of charity leading a bunch of orphans across Times Square.

We were one destroyer and one smaller warship escorting a thirty-ship convoy spread over fifteen square miles of ocean. Watching the line of hulls stretching out behind us, I remembered what a naval officer in a convoy control room in a West coast port told me just before I sailed.

"Give me fifty over-age American destroyers," he said, "and I will

Continued on Page Four

ROOSEVELT HAILS GAIN OF NEW BASES

Exchange of Over-Age Ships for British Leases Offers Outer Defense Line, He Says

By CHARLES HURD

Special to THE NEW YORK TIMES.

ON BOARD ROOSEVELT TRAIN, Sept. 3—President Roosevelt indicated that the chief value of the trade with Great Britain of fifty over-age destroyers for naval and air base sites in British crown colonies in the Western Hemisphere lay in the fact that this outer line of defenses would keep any enemy away from this country's front door.

For that reason, he said, his agreement with the British Government was more important for the defense of this country than anything since the Louisiana Purchase in 1803, which assured American military control over the Mississippi River.

There may be other similar negotiations, he added, but he cautioned newspaper reporters not to try to guess where they would be, listing the odds at 10 to 1 that such guesses would be wrong.

The President did not deny a suggestion made by a reporter that perhaps Greenland might be the site for another base. He merely renewed his caution against speculation.

The President's view of the agreement, which has been known to be in progress for several weeks, was given at a special press conference on his private train at the same hour that his offices in Washington sent to Congress a message that the exchange was accomplished.

A dozen newspaper reporters heard Mr. Roosevelt read the text of the message to Congress, which he completed during a trip from Hyde Park, N. Y., to Tennessee, North Carolina and West Virginia. He read the message, after laughingly telling them that there was no story. While the document, with supporting papers, was being made public in Washington at noon, he began his press conference at 11:50 A. M. Eastern time.

Mr. Roosevelt called the press conference to meet in the tiny vestibule of his private car forty-five minutes after he departed from South Charleston, W. Va., where he inspected work being done to restore to high productivity a long abandoned Navy ordnance plant built in 1917-18 to construct armor plate and shells.

Among the statements he made

Continued on Page Ten

SHIP TRADE IS HELD NOT HOSTILE ACTION

State Department Stresses Defense Phase of Exchange of Vessels for Bases

Special to THE NEW YORK TIMES.

WASHINGTON, Sept. 3—No country could consider the transfer of fifty United States destroyers to Great Britain and the obtaining by this country of naval and air bases in British New World territory as a hostile act, an informed State Department source said today.

Only a nation seeking world conquest could use this as a pretext for belligerent action, the source asserted.

The intention of this government in completing the agreement was merely to strengthen its own defenses and no other considerations were entertained, State Department officials said, in insisting that the United States had the opportunity to obtain a 4,000 or 5,0000 mile ring of steel around the eastern part of the hemisphere on terms unequaled since the Louisiana Purchase. They added that the protection would last for 100 years.

It was made clear that it was no time to consider any technical provisions which might be sought in international law by opponents of the agreement but that in these dangerous days, when the world is almost literally on fire, defense considerations must come first.

This view was expressed in answer to questions of correspondents about the Second Hague Convention of 1907, of which the United States and Germany are signatories, but Great Britain is not.

Hague 1907 Convention Is Quoted

Article VI of this convention asserts:

"The supply in any manner, directly or indirectly, by a neutral power of a belligerent power, by warships, ammunition or war material of any kind whatever, is forbidden."

Article VIII says:

"A neutral government is also bound to display the same vigilance to prevent the departure from its jurisdiction of any vessel intended to cruise, or menace in hostile operations, which had been adapted entirely or partly within the said jurisdiction for use in war."

Article XXVIII, however, states: "The provisions of this present convention do not apply except to the contracting powers and then only if all the belligerents are parties to the convention."

One could accurately visualize a

Continued on Page Sixteen

"All the News That's Fit to Print."

The New York Times.

LATE CITY EDITION
Fair and cooler today. Tomorrow fair and continued cool.
Temperatures Yesterday—Max., 72; Min., 64

VOL. LXXXIX..No. 30,181. Entered as Second-Class Matter, Postoffice, New York, N. Y. NEW YORK, WEDNESDAY, SEPTEMBER 11, 1940 THREE CENTS NEW YORK CITY and Vicinity | FOUR CENTS Elsewhere Except in 7th and 8th Postal Zones.

BRITISH BOMB BERLIN, HIT REICHSTAG BUILDING AND OTHER LANDMARKS IN CENTER OF THE CITY; GERMANS POUND AT LONDON IN 8-HOUR ATTACK

ROOSEVELT TO TALK 'POLITICS' TONIGHT BEFORE TEAMSTERS

First Avowed Campaign Talk Will Be a Paid Broadcast Over Two Networks

'HISTORY' WILL BE A TOPIC

President Professes Not to Know if 8-Year Survey Would Be Political or Historical

By CHARLES HURD
Special to THE NEW YORK TIMES.

HYDE PARK, N. Y., Sept. 10—President Roosevelt dropped tonight the nonpolitical attitude which he has heretofore adopted. He will deliver tomorrow night a major speech in Washington before the annual convention of the Brotherhood of Teamsters, Chauffeurs, Stablemen and Helpers, A. F. of L.

He will speak over two nation-wide radio networks on broadcast time to be paid for by the Democratic National Committee, instead of getting facilities free from all four networks available.

The decision was announced by Stephen T. Early, White House secretary, who told news correspondents:

"I expect that President Roosevelt in all probability will deliver the labor speech of the campaign."

The decision that this speech would be Mr. Roosevelt's first bid for re-election apparently was made at the last minute. The President at a press conference earlier indicated that he did not consider the speech to be political.

Mr. Early, who acted as Presidential spokesman later, said that the decision was dictated to some extent by a desire not to burden the radio circuits by carrying the talk as an unpaid news service by all the radio companies and thereby making them liable for granting equal facilities and time to Wendell L. Willkie.

New Phase of the Campaign

The White House announcement, made only a few hours before the President left on his train for the capital, opened a new phase of his activities as they concern this election year. Heretofore he has insisted that his inspection trips and his talks were made as duties of the President.

He will speak nonpolitically in Philadelphia on Sept. 20, when he receives a degree from the University of Pennsylvania, and here on Oct. 5, when he dedicates in one ceremony a new high school and two grade schools.

This attitude also will characterize other similar trips and talks in the future, but White House sources recalled that Mr. Roosevelt made for himself a loophole in the non-campaign rule in his radio address to the Democratic National Convention at Chicago, on July 19.

In that speech he said:

"Since last Summer I have been compelled to abandon proposed journeys to inspect many of our great national projects from the Alleghanies to the Pacific Coast. Events move so fast in other parts of the world that it has become my duty to remain either in the White House itself or at some near-by point where I can reach Washington and even Europe and Asia by direct telephone.

"I do expect, of course, during the coming months, to make my usual periodic reports to the country through the medium of press conferences and radio talks. I shall not have the time or the inclination to engage in purely political debate, but I shall never be loath to call the attention of the nation to deliberate or unwitting falsifications of fact which are sometimes made by political candidates."

Early Recalls President's Stand

On returning from a work session with the President at the Hyde Park house in late afternoon, Mr. Early gathered reporters in his office and recalled that statement by Mr. Roosevelt, laying emphasis on the President's earlier stipulation that he would use the press conferences and radio speeches to reply to political attacks.

"The address tomorrow night will be on radio time to be paid for by the Democratic National Committee," Mr. Early said, and he added, "That is all."

This announcement served to lift the proposed speech, which Mr.

Continued on Page Fifteen

La Guardia to Reveal Choice for President

Special to THE NEW YORK TIMES.

WASHINGTON, Sept. 10—Mayor La Guardia will announce his choice for President in a nation-wide radio broadcast Thursday evening over the NBC Red Network, he announced here today.

The Mayor, here as chairman of the United States section of the United States-Canadian Joint Defense Commission, issued a typewritten announcement to this effect. It has been reported that the Mayor would work for President Roosevelt's re-election, but he refused to go beyond his formal announcement.

The Democratic National Committee will pay the bill for Mayor La Guardia's broadcast tomorrow evening, Edward J. Flynn, chairman of the committee, said yesterday. The speech will be delivered from 7:15 to 7:30 P. M. and will be repeated later from 11:15 to 11:30 P. M. for Pacific Coast listeners.

Mr. Flynn said that the Mayor had suggested the broadcast to him several days ago.

LEHMAN DEPLORES STATE TAX CURBS

Asserts Attempts at 'Economic Isolation' Are a Threat to Democratic Way of Life

Charging that several States have deliberately attempted a policy of "economic isolation" in recent years, Governor Lehman warned last night that their efforts to "stifle the flow of trade across State lines" might eventually threaten our democratic way of life.

Governor Lehman, Governor A. Harry Moore of New Jersey and Governor Raymond E. Baldwin of Connecticut spoke at the annual dinner of the National Tax Association, which is holding its thirty-third annual conference at the Hotel Pennsylvania. Their addresses followed a day of discussion of current tax problems by many governmental and university specialists in the field.

Governor Moore pointed out that at present three-quarters of the cost of government in New Jersey is defrayed by taxes on real property, and he contended that this is too narrow a tax base. In working out replacement taxes, however, he said, care must be taken not to impose taxes that would harm the State's industries in their competitive position with other States.

Governor Baldwin, pointing out that Connecticut has a balanced budget without a sales tax or a State income tax, said that in his State an indicated deficit of $1,500,000 when he took office in January, 1939, has been changed to a surplus of $1,000,000 by a policy of government "friendly" to business, labor and agriculture, with resultant increased production.

Sees Struggle by States for Gain

In his assault on State tax policies that are creating interstate trade barriers, Governor Lehman said that over a period of years there has arisen "a shameless struggle for gain at the expense of sister States." He said that these policies were of "questionable material benefit" to the States that employ them.

"Laws have employed the power of government not for purposes of revenue but rather to stifle the flow of trade across State lines in behalf of domestic interests and enterprises," Governor Lehman said. "The net result has been to limit open competition, raise prices, lower standards of quality and, finally, to affect adversely the national income."

Turning to the "political and social implications" of this trend, Governor Lehman said that "while our democratic way of life is being challenged more fiercely than at any recent stage of our national history, we quibble among ourselves over questionable material benefit."

"If the time ever arrives when boundary lines of the forty-eight States assume greater significance than as mere geographic borders, our democracy is doomed," Governor Lehman continued. "National strength and solidarity in times of crisis are strongly dependent upon singleness of purpose, absolute

Continued on Page Twenty-nine

WILLKIE OPPOSES DELAYING OF DRAFT DESPITE PRESSURE

Hopes the Senate and House Conferees Will Eliminate the Fish Amendment

HE REBUFFS ISOLATIONISTS

Takes Stand in Face of 140 House Republicans Who Voted to Wait

By JAMES A. HAGERTY
Special to THE NEW YORK TIMES.

RUSHVILLE, Ind., Sept. 10—Disregarding strong pressure from members of the Republican organization, Wendell L. Willkie came out today against the House amendment to the Burke-Wadsworth selective service bill, which, if accepted by the Senate, would delay the draft until after the November election.

"I hope that, as a result of the conference between House and Senate conferees on the selective service bill, the Fish amendment is eliminated," Mr. Willkie said in a formal statement.

In opposing any delay in the draft, or selective service for national defense as Mr. Willkie prefers to phrase it, the Presidential nominee ran counter to 140 Republicans in the House who voted for the amendment, including Representative Joseph W. Martin Jr., chairman of the national committee. Only twenty-two Republicans voted against the amendment.

Resists Isolationist Pressure

Mr. Willkie's declaration confirmed the assertion he made in his speech Saturday night that never during his campaign would he take any position in which he did not believe. He is known to regard the international situation as so serious that there should be no avoidable delay in any of the preparations for national defense. He declared for "selective service" in his acceptance speech and explained afterward that he meant selective service now, not later.

Since that time he has resisted pressure from leading members of his party to modify his position and take more of an isolationist stand. He has been frank at all times regarding his views on foreign policy.

He has said frequently that he favored aid to Great Britain, short of war, adding that when he said "short of war" he meant "short of war." In criticizing President Roosevelt's exchange of over-age destroyers for defense bases in British possessions, he favored the trade but attacked the method used by the President as dictatorial.

Research Aides Arrive

Members of the research staff which will accompany Mr. Willkie on his trip to the Pacific Coast arrived here today. Among them were Russell W. Davenport, who resigned as managing editor of Fortune to join the movement to nominate Mr. Willkie; Raymond Leslie Buell, former director of The Foreign Policy Association, and Elliott

Continued on Page Seventeen

Ford's Party Leaves $46 As Tip After Luncheon

By The Associated Press.

DETROIT, Sept. 10—Ethel Gaff, 19-year-old Fort Wayne (Ind.) hotel waitress, need not worry about the $46 left on the table after Henry Ford and his party ate a $4 luncheon. It was the change from a $50 bill which paid for the luncheon.

Miss Gaff was reported in doubt as to whether the money was a tip or whether the automobile manufacturer had forgotten it in his hurry to resume his motor trip.

"I paid the check, and I left the money purposely as a tip for the young lady," Harry Bennett, personnel director of the Ford Motor Company, said today. "She did a very good job in taking care of us, and particularly in keeping curiosity seekers away from Mr. Ford."

PLANE PRODUCTION HAILED BY KNUDSEN

He Says in Buffalo Interview We Will Have 11,000 Combat Craft by April, 1942

By The Associated Press.

BUFFALO, Sept. 10—In nineteen months the Army and Navy will have about 11,000 combat airplanes, fighters and bombers, William S. Knudsen of the National Defense Commission said today as he approached the end of a nation-wide tour of aircraft plants with Major Gen. H. H. Arnold, chief of the Army Air Corps.

"We know the United States is making the best airplanes," he said, and added:

"I believe that presently we can say we are making the most airplanes."

The figure of 11,000 was based on a total production by April 1, 1942, of 33,000 planes, 14,000 destined for Great Britain and 19,000 for the armed services of the United States. General Arnold said that of those to be delivered to the Army and Navy, about 60 per cent would be so-called combat types.

Mr. Knudsen said the current American airplane production of 900 a month, including both military and large commercial types, would be doubled in twelve months. Seated in the office of Burdette S. Wright, president of the Curtiss Aeroplane Division of the Curtiss-Wright Corporation, he fixed at three a day the delivery of new Curtiss P-40 fighter planes to the Air Corps.

General Arnold added that 524 P-40's, one of the newest types of American fighters, were on order for the Air Corps, and that 140 had been delivered.

The visitors saw two of these fighter planes, the American counterpart of British and German pursuit craft, streak at 320 miles an hour across Buffalo's Municipal Airport in a rare public demonstration of the progress of the nation's air rearmament drive.

Delivery of P-40's to both the Air Corps and to Great Britain's Royal Air Force has been slowed down by the limited manufacture of engines by the Allison Engineering Corporation, a General Motors subsidiary at Indianapolis, but Mr.

Continued on Page Fourteen

Italians Jail Prince Doria as Anti-Fascist; Prince Torlonia Also Reported Arrested

By CAMILLE CIANFARRA
Wireless to THE NEW YORK TIMES.

ROME, Sept. 10—Prince Filippo Andrea Doria-Pamaphili-Landi, 54-year-old head of an Italian princely family, has been put in a concentration camp, it is learned.

It is also reported, but without confirmation, that 28-year-old Prince Alessandro Torlonia, whose mother was Elsie Moore of New York and who married a daughter of the King of Spain, also has been arrested.

Circles close to the government emphatically denied this evening that the "alleged" arrests of two Roman princes were part of a round-up of anti-Fascisti.

"No such round-up has taken place," they stated, "and all reports to the contrary are completely unfounded."

Prince Doria's arrest is stated to have been caused by remarks unfriendly to the Fascist regime, which he made publicly less than a fortnight ago. At present, according to friends of the family, he is doing manual labor. Since it is feared he is affected by heart trouble and rheumatism, there is considerable apprehension for his life among his friends.

Prince Doria, after the death of his first wife, married his English nurse, Gesina Mary Dyckes, who is generally credited with having kept him alive with her constant care.

His anti-Fascist feelings are well known in Rome. He heartily disapproved the Ethiopian campaign.

On Dec. 18, 1935, the "day of the faith," when, following the adoption of sanctions against Italy by the League of Nations, Italian women were asked to donate their wedding rings to increase Italy's gold reserves, Prince Doria refused to display the Italian flag on the balcony of his beautiful eighteenth century palace in the Corso Umberto, Rome's main street.

This gesture did not escape a

Continued on Page Six

LONDON IS HARRIED

Night Invaders Resume Bombing After 4 Raids by Day Are Repelled

BRITONS CARRYING ON

People Now Sleep in the Shelters—Water and Gas Impaired

By RAYMOND DANIELL
Special Cable to THE NEW YORK TIMES.

LONDON, Wednesday, Sept. 11—As darkness fell last night a waxing moon rose above the smoldering embers of the previous night's great fires, which threatened for a time to destroy the beautiful St. Paul's Cathedral and St. Mary-le-Bow Church, whose sweet-toned chimes for generations have lulled the Cockney children to sleep. The German Air Force then returned in force to London to continue the attack that has made life in this capital a nightmare since Saturday.

The all clear was sounded at 4:39 this morning, after the raid had been in progress for eight hours and twenty-four minutes.

[Nazi bombers smashed at London with increasing violence early today, The Associated Press reported. Until early this morning, it was stated, the attack was much less ferocious than the previous three. Then the pace stepped up until four separate squadrons were wheeling about the capital at the same time at opposite points of the compass.]

The screams of their bombs, the earth-shaking crashes, the blazes that lit the sky, the clangor of fire engines and ambulances, the bark of anti-aircraft guns and nerve-racking hum of engines droning like a mosquito that does not bite, brought another sleepless and hideous night to 7,000,000 harried persons who are trying to carry on in the face of an attack that spares neither humble workmen's homes nor the homes of the nobility.

Bombing Is at Random

For nine hours last night explosive-laden planes roared overhead, dropping high explosive and incendiary bombs apparently whenever the spirit moved the man in charge of the bomb racks to press the button. They released death and destruction upon helpless civilians who shuddered each time the ground shook beneath them.

Two hospitals, one filled with ailing children and the other a maternity hospital, suffered heavy damage. It is not accurately known at present, while the raid is still going on, how many homes were wrecked or persons killed, for the rescue workers are still digging among the ruins.

It was estimated, however, that Sunday night's raid caused at least 286 deaths and sent 1,400 persons, including the lame, halt and blind, into hospitals, seriously injured.

Question of Morale

But it is not the dead or the injured, or even the extensive property damage that really counts in this battle for London, which is a mere prelude to the Battle for Britain. It is what is happening to the city's life and the nerves of its people that matters the most.

They are standing up to the punishment that is being rained on them from the skies with a courage that makes the eyes of a neutral observer smart at times. There is no doubt about their bravery, but one cannot help but wonder how long any people's nerves can stand up under this kind of bombardment, in which every one knows that each breath may be the last one, and in which the suspense is awful.

That does not mean that a defeatist attitude is growing. Far from it. These people are getting madder by the minute.

Many homes are without gas and tea. Citizens are forced to undergo tremendous inconveniences in getting to and from the places where they earn their livelihood, and their ingrained politeness to one another is becoming a little strained.

There is hardly any one who has not a friend who has been bombed out of his home or has had a narrow escape from death or injury.

Monday night bombs dropped on every section of London. Slum hovels, wealthy homes, warehouses and luxury apartments, all felt the

Continued on Page Two

The International Situation

The War in Europe and Africa

Berlin last night suffered the most intense raid yet inflicted by Royal Air Force planes. Earlier British craft had ranged over Northwestern Germany, Belgium, the Netherlands, France and the Norwegian coast, raiding twenty-five places. Relays of planes blasted Hamburg wharves, a Berlin power plant, docks, factories, barges and supplies at Continental ports. Four bombers failed to return, the Air Ministry reported. [Page 1, Column 8.]

With fires from Monday's attack still smoldering, Nazi bombers swooped down upon London again last night to give the harassed city its fourth sleepless night. The crash of descending bombs started at dusk, when the air-raid sirens sounded the fifth warning of the day. Previous raids had been limited apparently to reconnaissance flights and the planes had been driven off by British fighters. The early alarms were so timed that they drove workers to air-raid shelters at lunch time, at tea time, and again at the height of the evening rush hour with people jammed around crippled transit facilities. Though harassed at their daily tasks after a sleepless and strained night Londoners' morale was unbroken and they were getting "madder by the minute." [Page 1, Column 5.]

Women and children, many dazed from shell shock, jammed the railroads, begged rides from motorists and pleaded with the authorities to find havens for them in an exodus from battered London. The menfolk were carrying on. The Minister of Transport asked that every one refrain from unnecessary travel; the Minister of Health broadcast a plea for aid to the homeless and warned of increasing destitution as a result of bombing. [Page 3, Column 1.]

Announcing more raids against the British capital, Berlin official sources said that new waves would strike London until the British people bring to power a government willing to accept German terms. The present havoc being wrought in London, German papers said, is not the Battle of Britain but merely the Battle of London, and they promised that the Battle of Britain would follow when London, as the nerve-center of the British Isles and an important military objective, had been destroyed. [Page 1, Column 7.].

London and Berlin reports told of a new secret British weapon, a "self-igniting leaf" of cardboard and phosphorus, that had started fires in Germany. [Page 1, Column 6.]

In what was reported to have been the worst raid in the Middle East, Italian fliers bombed Tel Aviv, Palestine, killing 150 civilians. British claimed there were no military objectives there. Rome reported bombing of the Jaffa harbor, the Alexandria-Matruh Railroad and Port Sudan. [Page 6, Column 3.]

Prince Filippo Andrea Doria-Pamphili-Landi, 54-year-old head of an Italian princely family, is now doing manual labor in a concentration camp for remarks unfriendly to the Fascist regime, it was learned in Rome. Reports that Prince Alessandro Torlonia, whose mother was Elsie Moore of New York and who married a daughter of the King of Spain, had also been arrested were unconfirmed. The government denied that there had been a round-up of anti-Fascisti. [Page 1, Column 3.]

American Developments

The American Red Cross sped plans to provide relief for victims of German air raids in London and other British cities. The Washington office of the Red Cross ordered 500,000 garments shipped from its New York warehouses, made preparations to send additional medical supplies, and cabled funds for purchase in London of twelve mobile canteen units of eight vehicles each for feeding homeless civilians. [Page 14, Column 4.]

House and Senate conferees on the conscription bill spent the day tabulating the differences between the two adopted versions of the measure without conclusive result. Washington opinion is that the final version will accept the House age limits of 21 to 45 and that the Fish amendment to delay the draft sixty days will be dropped. [Page 12, Column 3.]

The Senate agreed to limit debate on the Export-Import Bank Bill to ten minutes today after spending yesterday in fruitless debate. Senator Taft has offered the only amendment, restriction of loans to help Latin-American production of strategic, critical or non-competitive products. [Page11, Column 1.]

INCENDIARY 'CARDS' A BRITISH WEAPON

Damp Discs, Dropped by R.A.F. by Thousands, Dry and Ignite—Nazis Incensed

By The Associated Press.

LONDON, Sept. 10—Britain disclosed tonight a new "secret weapon" in the form of innocent-looking bits of chemically treated cardboard dropped by the millions on Germany as delayed fire-bombs that burst into flame in unexpected quarters.

Germany, in first making public the new British tactics, acknowledged that the fire-secreting "calling cards" carried something more than a mere nuisance threat.

British authorities, in subsequently admitting use of the new weapon, described it only as a "self-igniting leaf," and declined to furnish details.

But the authentic German description, given after chemical analysis, sounded like a sequence from some fertile adventure cartoon or a passage from a detective thriller.

The cards, composed of guncotton and phosphorus, are carried in a moist state, the Germans said. Scattered over the countryside in lots of a quarter-million from a single plane, they dry out naturally and spring suddenly into flames about eight inches high when warmed by natural processes to a moderate temperature.

Implying that the cards may bear a printed message, the Germans said they were particularly dangerous because people had been pick-

Continued on Page Twelve

NAZIS SEE BATTLE AS FIGHT TO FINISH

Air Attacks on London Will Be Pressed Till British Yield, It Is Said in Berlin

By The United Press.

BERLIN, Sept. 10—Nazis, angered by British bombing of Berlin and other cities, reported tonight that the German Air Fleet was roaring against London again in an offensive that would be pressed relentlessly until the British capitulate.

New waves of German bombers flying against London will carry out remorseless and incessant warfare, Nazis said, until "the smoking ruins of industrial and military objectives, decimation of the British Air Force and shattered morale of the British people bring into power a government that will accept German terms."

The German terms were regarded here as unconditional capitulation.

Official German quarters were silent regarding any peace terms, but there were many unofficial suggestions that the collapse of Britain is "only a matter of weeks."

The Nazi press said that "now it is an eye-for-an-eye and a tooth-for-a-tooth" battle and said that "the sword of the German air force strikes pitilessly."

"What effects the heavy caliber bombs have were clearly revealed by Warsaw and Rotterdam," one newspaper said. "If London wishes to taste a similar fate to the full extent, then let Herr Churchill and his criminal clique continue to send pirates at night to Germany."

The Propaganda Ministry said

Continued on Page Four

RAID NAZI CAPITAL

Miss U. S. Embassy, Hit Brandenburg Gate, Germans Say

AIM HELD DELIBERATE

R. A. F. Hammers 25 Vital Points to Weaken Foe's Offensive

By PERCIVAL KNAUTH
Wireless to THE NEW YORK TIMES.

BERLIN, Wednesday, Sept. 11—The Royal Air Force this morning attacked the heart of Berlin's governmental center, dropping explosive and incendiary bombs in the immediate vicinity of the Wilhelmstrasse and the Reich's Chancellory. Appearing over the capital a few minutes after midnight with the moon nearly at full to guide them, the British fliers steered their course straight down "Via Triumphalis" bisecting Berlin from east to west and dropped a veritable hail of incendiary bombs on the famous Unter den Linden and Brandenburg Gate.

Two houses away from the American Embassy incendiary bombs set a small fire. Three hundred yards up the "East-West Axis" a bomb estimated at between 500 and 1,000 pounds in weight smashed into the broad asphalt speedway, rocking buildings in a half-mile radius. Incendiary bombs splattered on the rooftops, on the Brandenburg Gate, the Academy of German Art, the House of German Engineers and the old Reichstag building, setting small fires, which, however, were said to have been quickly extinguished.

In THE NEW YORK TIMES office near the Wilhelmplatz detonations of half a dozen explosive bombs in the vicinity of the cellar were heard in the underground air-raid shelter. Incendiary bombs were said to have set small fires in a Jewish hospital, close to the university buildings, and the Charite Hospital.

The Catholic Saint Hedwig's Hospital, second largest in Berlin, likewise was said to have been struck by incendiary bombs which started several fires.

Two Injured by Bombs

In the Invalidenstrasse, close to the central business section, explosive bombs injured two persons and blasted the front of an apartment house as well as part of another house. In Dorotheenstrasse, which runs parallel to Under den Linden, a dud bomb buried itself many feet deep in the street, while another ripped a wide hole in the office building.

An American news agency, with offices on the top floor of a building on this street, had a narrow escape when a bomb struck a house next door.

The British apparently attacked in four waves coming from the west. German military observers estimated the altitude of the first wave at about 18,000 feet, with each successive wave flying at a lower height, the last dropping its bombs from an altitude of about 6,000 feet. They flew straight into the city and when over the governmental district dropped numerous flares, which were followed by both explosive and incendiary bombs.

Some planes were reported to have flown low and machine-gunned anti-aircraft, artillery and searchlight batteries. The ground defenses followed the planes with a steady barrage, which was louder over the center of the capital than ever heard before.

Official German quarters asserted the attack on the governmental district were obviously premeditated and designed to destroy government buildings. R. A. F. fliers, it is asserted, had every opportunity of sighting their objectives both in the light of the great number of flares and the bright moon. It is concluded here, therefore, that the order had been given in London to attack the governmental district, for it is claimed that "all military objectives whatever were strictly avoided."

What form the German retaliation for this attack will take cannot as yet be said. However, German quarters always have been very clear in stating that retaliation will follow a hundred thousandfold in the same manner as the British attack. Never before have governmental districts in Berlin

Continued on Page Four

"All the News That's Fit to Print."

The New York Times.

LATE CITY EDITION
Fair and warmer today and tomorrow.
Temperatures Yesterday—Max., [illegible]; Min., 46

Copyright, 1940, by The New York Times Company.

VOL. XC...No. 30,198. Entered as Second-Class Matter, Postoffice, New York, N. Y. NEW YORK, SATURDAY, SEPTEMBER 28, 1940. THREE CENTS NEW YORK CITY and Vicinity | FOUR CENTS Elsewhere Except in 7th and 8th Postal Zones.

JAPAN JOINS AXIS ALLIANCE SEEN AIMED AT U. S.; ROOSEVELT ORDERS STUDY OF THE PACT'S EFFECT; BRITISH DOWN 130 RAIDERS, BLAST NAZI BASES

REPUBLICANS MAKE 3D TERM THE ISSUE; PICK STATE SLATE

BARTON IS CHOSEN

Leaders at Convention Turn Fire on the New Deal and Roosevelt

DEWEY SEES MENACE

Keynoter Assails 'One-Man Power'—Party Hears Willkie Tonight

Text of platform and Dewey and Barton addresses, Page 8.

By WARREN MOSCOW
Special to THE NEW YORK TIMES.

WHITE PLAINS, Sept. 27—The Republican campaign in New York State was started today at the Republican State Convention here, when the party organization nominated a strong slate headed by Bruce Barton for United States Senator, heard State and national leaders unite in a stinging castigation of the New Deal and adjourned until tomorrow evening to hear Wendell L. Willkie make his bid for New York support in a speech at the Empire City race track.

The delegates to the convention heard Thomas E. Dewey, National Chairman Joseph W. Martin Jr., State Senate Leader Joe R. Hanley and Mr. Barton unite in an onslaught on the New Deal's foreign and domestic policies as menacing our safety from within and from without. They spared neither the President nor his family as they tried to drive home the meaning of the violation of the anti-third term tradition.

Members of the Ticket

The ticket, nominated without opposition, is as follows:

For United States Senator: Bruce Barton of New York.

For Judges of the Court of Appeals: Benjamin B. Cunningham of Rochester, Edmund H. Lewis of Syracuse and Albert Conway of Brooklyn.

For Representatives at Large: Messmore Kendall of Westchester and Miss Mary Donlon of Oneida and New York.

Judges Lewis and Conway, Republican and Democrat respectively, are on the bench by appointment and will get an endorsement from the Democratic State Convention on Monday.

Justice Cunningham, now a member of the Appellate Division of the Fourth Department, was picked as a compromise nominee at a conference of party leaders during a convention recess and Judges James P. Hill of Norwich and Christopher J. Heffernan of Amsterdam, who had been deadlocked in a behind-the-scenes battle, both withdrew to make way for Justice Cunningham. The latter probably will get a Democratic endorsement, in view of the fact that he was appointed to the Appellate Division by Governor Lehman and won his last election to the Supreme Court with a bi-partisan endorsement. He is a Republican.

Starts on Fighting Key

The convention started on a fighting key with Mr. Dewey's speech, in the morning, as temporary chairman, and it came to a climax with an equally strong speech by Representative Barton, selected for the nomination yesterday at the insistence of Wendell L. Willkie.

"In the next six weeks the American people must decide whether to cast away the tradition which for 150 years has stood between them and the menace of one-man power; whether they will gamble with their liberties by electing a President for the third term," Mr. Barton told

Continued on Page Eight

Tonight Will Bring End Of Daylight Saving Time

With daylight saving time ending at 2 A. M. tomorrow, most New Yorkers were expected to turn their clocks back one hour tonight before retiring—thus regaining the hour of sleep lost when the Summer time became effective on April 28.

The New York Central Railroad is adding a new train to its Chicago-to-New York fleet. To be known as the Grand Central, the train will leave Chicago at 2:30 P. M., Central Standard time, and arrive in New York at 8:30 A. M., Eastern Standard time.

The Pennsylvania Railroad and the New York, New Haven & Hartford Railroad also are providing a new train from the Pennsylvania Station to Boston and New England points. It will be called the Bay State and, starting from Philadelphia, will depart from New York at 9:45 A. M. and arrive at Boston at 2:40 P. M.

WILLKIE DEMANDS OUR SYSTEM STAND

Change of Administration Is Needed to Save Democracy, He Says in Wisconsin

By JAMES A. HAGERTY
Special to THE NEW YORK TIMES.

MADISON, Wis., Sept. 27—Wendell L. Willkie ended his 6,000-mile Western trip tonight with a speech in the Field House of the University of Wisconsin to about 15,000 persons. He was introduced by Dean Christian Christiansen of the College of Agriculture.

Mr. Willkie criticized the President for trying to enlarge the Supreme Court on the ground that some of its members were too old.

"And yet," he continued, "the President recently appointed to a most important position, Secretary of War, a man older than the age he fixed as too old to render proper judicial decisions."

The candidate also recalled that President Roosevelt had tried to "purge" members of Congress of his own party who did not agree with him, offering another instance in which the Executive tried to infringe upon the powers of the other two departments of the Federal Government.

'Must Make System Work'

He declared that the present Administration had preserved the form but not the substance of democracy and had concentrated power in the Chief Executive.

"That is the road by which every ancient and every modern democracy has died," he added.

"Do you know that in Germany there is still a Reichstag and in Italy a parliament? There is still the form of democracy, but the substance is gone.

"You must take the American system of government and make it work, with its coordinate branches, as it is, or you must admit that it is a failure. I repudiate the latter notion with all the vigor of my being.

"This American system of government can be made, and will be made, if you put another Administration into power, the most effective and most pleasant way of life."

Mr. Willkie brought laughter by saying that Thomas Jefferson, sponsor after Washington of the anti-third-term tradition, was the founder of the party which President Roosevelt, "in part," now leads.

He added that every attempt so far to violate the anti-third-term tradition had been defeated, and cited that in 1928 the United States Senate adopted a resolution against the third term. Although Madison is the home of Senator Robert M. La Follette, author of that resolution, Mr. Willkie did not mention him.

On his entrance to Wisconsin, the

Continued on Page Seven

LONDON BADLY HIT

Capital and Its Suburbs Bear Brunt of Heavy German Attacks

OTHER AREAS RAIDED

Coastal Towns Pounded—600 Planes Used in Daylight Assaults

By ROBERT P. POST
Special Cable to THE NEW YORK TIMES.

LONDON, Saturday, Sept. 28—The Germans changed their recent air-raid tactics yesterday and sent over by daylight wave on wave of bombers with fighter as chaperones above.

It is estimated that at least 600 Germans crossed the coast before dark, and of these the latest figures show 130 shot down for certain. The British loss at the time of writing is put at thirty-four fighters. Fifteen of the downed British pilots are safe.

This is a preliminary count. The figures may be higher when all precincts have reported. In any case it is probable that the number of German planes that will never fly again is considerably bigger than the British announce.

From all reports on the daylight raiding, it would appear that the Germans once again were testing the British fighter defenses and paying heavily for it. Some German planes flew "cloud hopping" over London, which had five air-raids during the day. They dropped bombs that did some damage, but the worst destruction done in England before dark was on the outskirts of London and in certain coastal towns where the Germans, chased by Spitfires and Hurricanes, jettisoned their loads while trying to escape.

One of Worst Night Raids

At night the siren again wailed and the night raiders again came over to take advantage of a cloudy sky. And again the attack was directed mainly at the London area.

Several bombs crashed in the central area of London in the early morning as German planes continued to hum over the metropolis. A good many fires were started, but they were quickly extinguished.

[By early this morning, the attack had developed into one of the worst raids the capital has experienced in many nights, according to The Associated Press, with heavy bombs falling and anti-aircraft fire heaviest in the center of the city.]

But the rest of the country did not go free either by day or night. Two separate waves estimated at fifty each crossed the Dorset coast and went after the Bristol area. At night planes were reported over other towns. During the day, too, the countryside saw planes overhead. At Seven Oaks a big Junkers bomber dived to its death, narrowly missing the City Hall in High Street.

The raiders visited Northwest and Southeast England during the night, scattering explosives and incendiaries.

Big formations could be seen plainly over London during the day. In one police station a man

Continued on Page Four

New Air Defense Devices Reported Used in London

By The Associated Press.

LONDON, Sept. 27—New secret devices with which to combat night raiders were reported today in use in the London area, which last night had one of the lightest night raids in three weeks.

The devices were said to have been developed by British scientists, and observers declared there was a chance that, used together, two of the devices might make night bombing as hazardous as raiding by day.

In a gradual lifting of the curtain of censorship, British correspondents were permitted to comment upon new air-raid noises heard by Londoners in the last few nights. These were a heavy single explosion disintegrating into staccato cracks high up in the heavens, a flat roar that seems to strike a ceiling several miles up and bump its way clamorously along the top of the sky, and a muffled rattling like a "carpet slipper machine-gun."

"These queer noises are in fact caused by new types of weapons, or by well tried weapons adapted to new uses," said one observer.

R.A.F. RAKES NAZIS ON 500-MILE COAST

Pounds Invasion Fleet, Bombs Kiel Anew—Raids Gun Sites After Cross-Channel Duel

By JAMES B. RESTON
Special Cable to THE NEW YORK TIMES.

LONDON, Sept. 27—British bombers raided the German invasion fleet along 500 miles of European coast last night, bombed lines of communication deep in Nazi territory and penetrated the fortified naval base at Kiel, where the 26,000-ton German battleship Scharnhorst was said to be anchored, it was announced here today.

This afternoon, during a duel between German and British long-range guns, British bombers flew across the English Channel and attacked Nazi gun emplacements in France near Cap Gris Nez. In the artillery duel, which lasted an hour, shells fell in the Dover area, but there were no casualties and no serious damage was reported.

In the persistent night raids on Germany the British have three main objectives—to harass ships, men and supplies gathered along the coast for a possible invasion of this country, to cripple transportation and industrial production inside Germany and to carry the war to the German people. Last night's raid conformed to this general pattern, but whereas in the preceding few nights the Bomber Command centered its attention on communications and industrial plants, last night the British tried first of all to knock out the Scharnhorst.

When the first relays of bombers approached the naval basin at Kiel German guns immediately opened fire. Flying high, the raiders were able to stay out of range. They opened the attack by dropping incendiary bombs around the edge of the base and then, by the light of fires, hurled several sticks of high-explosive bombs into the basin, where two large ships were clearly seen.

An Air Ministry statement here

Continued on Page Five

Jersey Poll Books Burned, Senators Hear; Charge of Move to Block Inquiry Renewed

Special to THE NEW YORK TIMES.

WASHINGTON, Sept. 27—Poll books in Hudson County, depended upon to show padded registry, have been destroyed, according to word received today by Senator Guy M. Gillette of Iowa, chairman of the Senate committee investigating election expenditures. Similar information was conveyed to Senator Charles W. Tobey of New Hampshire, one of the subcommittee authorized to inquire into the alleged election frauds.

Senator Tobey, who caused a sensation yesterday by asserting that pressure had been exerted to stop the hearing, planned in Jersey City, renewed his charges today in the Senate. He read into the record a dispatch printed in The Newark Evening News to the effect that Representatives Edward J. Hart and Mrs. Mary T. Norton of New Jersey had exerted pressure to delay or prevent the inquiry. Mrs. Norton said that she had never approached any Senator on the subject, while Representative Hart declined to discuss the question.

Senator Gillette later exonerated both New Jersey House members from any ulterior activities. He said that Mrs. Norton had never seen him about the situation in Hudson County, while Representative Hart had asked him when the hearing would begin, but had not suggested that it be delayed or stopped.

Renewing his charges of alleged pressure, Senator Tobey, speaking in the Senate, said:

"I charged in my statement yesterday that pressure had been applied on Senators to postpone in-

Continued on Page Seven

HULL SEES NO SHIFT

Holds Accord Does Not Substantially Alter Recent Situation

DEFENSE AIDES MEET

Notables Ask President to Rush Increased Aid to Britain

By CHARLES HURD
Special to THE NEW YORK TIMES.

WASHINGTON, Sept. 27—President Roosevelt quickly directed today a sweeping search into the possibilities in the new German-Italian-Japanese alliance, but the Administration adopted an official attitude that the alliance momentarily creates little change in a situation that already existed.

Mr. Roosevelt declined to make any comment at the regular press conference in his office this morning. He merely told reporters that he had received no official notification of the conclusion of the accord.

However, while Secretary of State Cordell Hull gravely acknowledged the pact's existence at a State Department press conference, the President undertook studies involving every major branch of the government.

[A group of Americans prominent in business and political affairs called at the White House to urge that aid to Britain be increased and speeded in every form possible. They reported later that they were "enthusiastically encouraged" by the President's response, though they were unable to divulge what he said.]

Cabinet Studies Situation

A Cabinet meeting, regular scheduled for this afternoon, was devoted exclusively during a ninety-minute session to discussion of the latest developments in the foreign situation. It was preceded by a long conference in the President's office, to which were invited all the ranking officials of the War and Navy Departments.

These conferences were reported to have been concerned not only with political implications in the expanded Rome-Berlin Axis but also with economic possibilities, both from the standpoint of potential effects on American sources of commodities such as tin and rubber and a possible advancement from Oct. 16 of the effective date for the embargo on exports of scrap iron and steel, ordered yesterday.

There also was informal discussion, without conclusive decision, of a possible extension of the embargo on scrap exports to exports of pig iron and steel which currently can be sent to Japan without restriction.

It was obvious that the government's attitude was based largely on the expectation that Britain would be able to hold her line against the German attack. A collapse of Britain would create an entirely new situation.

The President's refusal to comment at his press conference came about two hours after news services had first reported the new treaty. He declined smilingly but persistently to make any statement, saying all that he had heard thus far had been a rumor, that he had nothing official. When he was asked if the news was unexpected he replied, Well, yes and no, and referred inquirers to the State Department.

Hull Expresses Official View

At the State Department, where a press conference was held soon afterward, Secretary Hull did express the viewpoint of this government in phrases which he permitted to be quoted directly.

Speaking slowly and with care and marking his words by an unusually grave countenance, he summed up the official attitude as follows:

"The reported agreement of alliance does not, in the view of the government of the United States, substantially alter a situation which has existed for several years. Announcement of the alliance merely makes clear to all a relationship which has long existed in effect and to which this government has repeatedly called attention.

That such an agreement has

Continued on Page Two

The International Situation

The German-Italian-Japanese Pact

Japan yesterday formally allied herself with Germany and Italy for the task of establishing a "new order" in Europe and East Asia by signing in Berlin a mutual assistance pact, by all indications aimed at the United States.

The three bound themselves for a period of ten years to come to the aid of any one of the others attacked by a power not at present involved in the European or Chinese-Japanese conflicts. Although political commitments of the three with Soviet Russia were specifically exempted by Article V of the six-article pact, a veiled threat to Moscow was seen.

By the terms of the pact, Japan recognized German-Italian hegemony in Europe. The two dictator nations in turn recognized Japanese hegemony in the Far East, apparently leaving to her determination of the fate of British, French and Netherland possessions there. [All the foregoing Page 1, Column 8.]

The official attitude of the United States, as stated by Secretary of State Hull, was that the announcement of the alliance merely publicly confirmed a relationship already existing. President Roosevelt began a study of the pact's possible effects by conferring with the Cabinet, War, Navy and Defense Commission officials but had no public comment. Possibility of quicker invocation of the embargo on scrap steel and iron to Japan, now scheduled to go into effect Oct. 16, and its possible extension to other war materials was reported discussed. [Page 1, Column 5.] The President was visited during the day by a group of prominent Americans asking more war aid for Britain. The British Ambassador made a similar plea. [Page 2, Column 1.]

Yakichiro Suma, Japanese Foreign Office spokesman, said the alliance did not mean abandonment of Japan's attitude toward the United States and that hope still was held for a betterment of relations. Observers in Tokyo construed the formal junction with the Axis as a desperate gamble that Germany and Italy would defeat Britain before the United States was prepared to give effective aid. The benediction on the pact of Emperor Hirohito—spiritual as well as political leader of Japan—was broadcast to the nation. [Page 1, Column 7.]

Italians were surprised that Japan and not Spain proved the third party to the pact, but quickly recovered and immediately grasped its significance as a warning to the United States to keep out of the conflict. It also was accepted there as a challenge to Soviet Russia. [Page 3, Column 1.]

Information in Shanghai was that Germany was attempting to promote a rapprochement between Moscow and Tokyo, but that the Soviet had set a high price, including abrogation of most of the Portsmouth treaty, which ended the Russo-Japanese War in 1905. A Russian source in London said the pact placed the Soviet in a "dangerous and very grave" situation. [Page 1, Column 6.]

The London reaction was that the publicly announced alliance had served to clear the atmosphere, had brought Britain and the United States even closer together and had removed any brake on all possible aid to China. [Page 3, Column 8.]

The War in Europe and Africa

The Germans yesterday and last night launched the heaviest attacks in several days on London and other key cities in England. Heavy daylight raids on London and Bristol were reported turned back with a cost to the Germans by early evening of at least 130 planes against thirty-four British defenders, from which fifteen of the pilots jumped to safety. It was estimated at least 600 German planes engaged in the day raids. The day rounded out three weeks of aerial siege of the British capital. [Page 1, Column 3.]

The R. A. F. again Thursday night made devastating attacks on German invasion bases and canals, arterial highways, industrial plants and harbors in Germany proper, the Air Ministry said. The principal attack, a communiqué stated, was launched on the German naval base at Kiel, where the battle-scarred German battleship Scharnhorst is under repair. One raiding pilot said he had never seen such fires as he and his fellow fliers set there. A daylight bombing attack was made on German big gun emplacements at Cap Gris Nez after a short artillery duel with British batteries at Dover. [Page 1, Column 4.]

Both the British and Italians reported air attacks on the other's supply and military bases in Africa. Otherwise all was quiet on that front. [Page 5, Column 6.]

STALIN'S DEMANDS SAID TO BE LARGE

Reported Seeking to Cancel Many Tokyo Gains as Price of Accepting Axis Pact

By HALLETT ABEND
Wireless to THE NEW YORK TIMES.

SHANGHAI, China, Sept. 27—The immediate future of the international situation in the Far East now depends to a great extent upon what degree of understanding the Germans will be able to arrange between Japan and Russia.

It is understood that Max Stahmer, private emissary from Chancellor Hitler, having concluded the alliance satisfactorily, now is acting as go-between for Moscow and Tokyo.

[In Tokyo it was said Japan already had the assurances she required from Russia. Up to last evening, the Russian people had not been allowed to hear of the conclusion of the Axis-Japanese pact, according to The Associated Press.]

Joseph Stalin's terms as reported here, however, are extremely harsh from the Japanese viewpoint. He is said to demand [illegible] of all abrogation of the [illegible]smouth treaty, except that portion ceding the southern half of Sakhalin Island to Japan. This would cancel Japan's immensely valuable fishing concessions off the Siberian coast, which not only furnish an important por-

Continued on Page Four

WARNING TO U. S. IS SEEN IN TOKYO

Spokesman of Foreign Office Declines to Say Whether New Pact Affects Us Now

By HUGH BYAS
Wireless to THE NEW YORK TIMES.

TOKYO, Sept. 27—The forces driving Japan forward have finally decided to take all risks in pursuit of their Greater East Asia policy, formally allying Tokyo with Berlin and Rome. They gamble on Germany's winning the war before the United States is ready.

Any power not presently involved in the European War is menaced by their joint action if it attacks any of the contracting parties. Though no country is specified, the pact is an unmistakable warning to the United States.

The point of the document lies in Article III, which in the Foreign Office translation reads: "Japan, Germany and Italy undertake to assist one another with all political, economic and military means when one of the three contracting parties is attacked by a power not presently involved in the European War or the Sino-Japanese conflict."

Yakichiro Suma, Foreign office spokesman, declined to say whether United States assistance to Britain "short of war" would constitute an "attack" in the terms of the treaty.

Neither the word "attack" nor Greater East Asia are defined, he said. He added that Japan was not

Continued on Page Four

RUSSIA REASSURED

Accord Viewed as Threat to Soviet, in Spite of Safeguard Clause

WASHINGTON WARNED

Interference Barred With 'New Order' in Europe and Eastern Asia

Text of treaty and statements for three nations, Page 3.

By GUIDO ENDERIS
Wireless to THE NEW YORK TIMES.

BERLIN, Sept. 27—By another of those bold forays into the realm of "Blitz diplomacy" with which the world has now become familiar, the Reich's Chancellery at noon today became the birthplace of a tripartite military alliance linking Germany, Italy and Japan. Its implications seem designed to have a profound effect not only on the further course of Europe's war but more directly on the world situation in general.

It is expressly specified that the commitments assumed today shall not affect the political status existing between each of the three signatories and Soviet Russia.

Opinion in neutral diplomatic quarters tonight appears to concur on two points, one being by implication that the pact contains a veiled threat to Russia, while that to the United States is decidedly less obscure.

On the latter point advance press comment leaves no doubt, and opinions gathered in informed quarters also frankly suggest that the pact may be interpreted as being directed against "certain groups in the United States who are trying to disrupt relations between peoples and nations."

Ten-Year Pledge Given

In a highly ceremonial setting in the Chancellery's reception chamber, the German and Italian Foreign Ministers and the Japanese Ambassador pledged their respective countries for ten year to cooperation in the interest of lasting peace and to "the creation of the preconditions necessary to that new order that will promote the welfare and prosperity of their peoples."

The signing formalities occupied just about two minutes, after which Chancellor Hitler joined the scene, entering the chamber through a door opening from his private working apartments. It was the same chamber in which the German-Italian military pact was signed in 1939, but today's audience did not include the diplomatic corps. Those who witnessed the formalities comprised government officials, Nazi party leaders and representatives of the German and foreign press.

The pact negotiated today consists of a brief preamble and six articles. By its terms Japan recognizes Germany's and Italy's leadership in constituting "a new order in Europe." The Axis powers, for their part, recognize and respect Japan's priority rights in the establishment of "a new order in Eastern Asia." It was authoritatively stated that the Russian Government had been duly apprised of the impending conclusion of the three-power pact and informed that the signatory powers were in accord on this point.

Total Aid Promised

On the basis of these premises, the partners to the pact agree to support one another in fulfillment of their tasks and to throw their complete political, economic and military resources into the defense of any of the partners who may be attacked by any power not at present involved in the European war or in the Chinese-Japanese conflict.

In pronouncing his benediction on the pact after signing formalities were concluded, Foreign Minister Joachim von Ribbentrop declared: "Organized warmongers in the Jewish capitalistic democracies have succeeded in plunging Europe into a new war which was not wanted by Germany. Our fight is not directed against other peoples, but against the existence of international plotters who once before succeeded in plunging Europe into a sanguinary war."

The German Foreign Minister

Continued on Page Three

"All the News That's Fit to Print."

The New York Times.

LATE CITY EDITION

Occasional light rain and slightly warmer today. Tomorrow rain, followed by colder at night.
Temperatures Yesterday—Max.,53; Min.,38

VOL. XC...No. 30,242. Entered as Second-Class Matter, Postoffice, New York, N. Y. NEW YORK, MONDAY, NOVEMBER 11, 1940. THREE CENTS NEW YORK CITY and Vicinity | FOUR CENTS Elsewhere Except in 7th and 8th Postal Zones.

$65,000,000 ROADS PROPOSED BY MOSES FOR CITY'S DEFENSE

He Urges U. S. Financing of 4 Express Links to Close 'Vital Gaps' in the System

SPEED IS HELD A FACTOR

Pelham-Port Chester, Harlem River, Brooklyn-Queens and Canal St. Drives Asked

A plan for immediate construction of four major new highways in the metropolitan area costing $65,000,000, which would facilitate the defense of New York City in war, was submitted to Mayor La Guardia yesterday by Robert Moses as chairman of the Triborough Bridge Authority.

The four proposed roads are a Pelham-Port Chester express highway costing $16,300,000, a Brooklyn-Queens connecting highway costing $12,100,000, an elevated highway across lower Manhattan costing $19,100,000, and a Harlem River Drive costing $17,500,000.

According to Mr. Moses, the nearly half-billion dollars worth of tunnels, bridges, highways and parkways that have been built in and adjacent to New York City since the World War could not adequately cope with both military and essential civilian requirements in wartime without the four proposed highways to fill the "vital gaps" in the city's road system.

Congressional Aid Asked

Because the four projects have been planned mainly in the interests of national defense, Mr. Moses suggested that the entire $65,000,000 be defrayed by the Federal Government out of Congressional defense appropriations.

He assumed that a nation-wide road program of this kind will soon be adopted.

Those parts of the city's modern arterial system built in the past few years have been financed through city, county, State and inter-State bonds, grade-crossing elimination appropriations, parkway funds, local borough assessments and direct Federal subsidy.

Speed in planning and construction were dominant factors in the selection of the four new roads now put forward, according to Commissioner Moses. All of the work laid out, he held, could be completed in one year on a three-shift design and construction basis under emergency orders, land acquisition being speeded up to fit into the period of design. Construction, Mr. Moses estimated, could begin "immediately" by distributing the responsibility for the engineering design and letting of contracts among the several agencies of the city equipped for the work.

The emergency highway transportation problem, the Commissioner explained, in view of present conditions, has gone beyond the stage of merely making travel on the open road more comfortable, and is concerned with breaking bottlenecks in strategically situated cities where traffic has increased faster than the construction of pavements and roads to accommodate it.

European War a Guide

"Our arterial highways already built, under construction, or scheduled for early construction will meet normal demands," Mr. Moses said, "but we have learned from the European war that motor traffic arteries designed for peacetime use cannot absorb the added burden of mass military manoeuvres and transportation of defense material by truck.

"The seven and one-third million people who live in New York and travel around it, not to speak of those in the suburbs, cannot be evacuated during military defense movements. They must be fed and their food must be hauled over roads within the city. If the streets are to be kept open for the inhabitants to survive, they cannot be commandeered for military use and defense transportation without disaster.

"It is evident from the large-scale production of machines for military defense that emphasis is being placed upon motorized military equipment. If ponderous units of mobile war machines must come into New York or move around within the city, there are vital gaps in the arterial system that should be filled immediately as aids to national defense."

Construction of the Pelham-Port Chester express highway would be designed to relieve congestion on the Boston Post Road and the Hutchinson River Parkway leading to New England. The new artery would be about fifteen miles long, paralleling the New Haven Railroad. On the north it would join the Boston Post Road at the Connecticut State line near the Merritt Parkway and on the south it would connect with Eastern Boulevard

Continued on Page Twenty-one

Rumanian Quake Kills 1,000, Sets Oil Afire, Cuts Railways

Bucharest and Other Cities Badly Damaged, Entire Villages Razed—300 Buried as Big Apartment House Falls

By The Associated Press.

BUCHAREST, Rumania, Monday, Nov. 11—The most destructive earthquake in Rumanian history killed and injured thousands over the week-end, leveled whole villages, set raging fires in rich oil fields and caused millions to flee to open fields. New tremors overnight added to the terror early today.

Between 1,000 and 2,000 persons were believed killed outright when the most violent quake struck at 3:39 A. M. yesterday. Thousands were injured and made homeless. The majority of buildings in 5,000 square miles of thickly populated areas were damaged. Tens of millions of dollars in property damage resulted. Hardly a house in Bucharest was untouched.

Officials estimated that 300 men, women and children were trapped in a ten-story apartment structure, Bucharest's newest and most modern, which was reduced to a pile of rubble amid screams of the dying. [The United Press identified this building as the Carlton, some parts of which are thirteen stories high.] More than 100 convicts were killed in a destroyed penitentiary.

Campina, a thickly populated oil town about 100 miles northwest of the capital, was reported in ruins, with refinery chimneys toppled and fierce fires started in plants, including those of Romano-Americana, a subsidiary of the Standard Oil Company of New Jersey. Ploesti, another oil production center closer to Bucharest, was hard hit.

[Oil fields in the Ploesti region were badly damaged by the quake, with nearly half the oil wells set on fire, the British Broadcasting Corporation said last night in a broadcast heard here by the National Broadcasting Company, quoting dispatches from Rumania. It also said damage was much greater than believed at first.]

Hospital trains moving over a dislocated railway system sought to reach Focsani and Galati, two of the hardest hit cities, where death tolls were believed considerable. Focsani, about 100 miles from Bucharest, was the epicenter of the quake.

A report from Brasov, historic German Transylvania city, said hundreds of roofs and large build-

Continued on Page Three

WILLKIE TO OUTLINE HIS PLANS TONIGHT

Expected to Pledge All Aid to Defense But Call for a Strong Opposition Party

By JAMES C. HAGERTY

Wendell L. Willkie will address the nation tonight in a radio speech from 10:30 to 11 o'clock on the course he believes he and his supporters should follow during the next four years of President Roosevelt's third term administration.

The speech of the defeated Republican Presidential nominee will be made from his personal headquarters at the Hotel Commodore and will be broadcast nationally by the major networks, which have donated the time to permit Mr. Willkie to express his views.

It is expected that Mr. Willkie, who received about 22,000,000 votes in the election, will call upon his supporters to cooperate completely with the Administration in the building of a national defense program and the granting of all possible aid to Britain. But the Republican standard-bearer is also expected to issue a call for a strong opposition party to represent the minority who voted the Republican Presidential ticket and to act as a check, under the two-party system, on any possible assumption of unlimited power by the New Deal.

Works on His Speech

During the day Mr. Willkie spent most of his time putting the finishing touches on his speech. In the morning and early afternoon he worked on the address at his home, 1010 Fifth Avenue, and at 4 P. M. went to his hotel headquarters for some further work on it.

While at his headquarters he also went over some of the flood of 30,000 letters and telegrams he has received from his supporters in all sections of the country since his defeat. These messages, virtually all of which urge him to continue his "crusade for American principles," have had a profound effect on Mr. Willkie and were primarly responsible for his decision to go on the air tonight and give his opinion on the national situation.

These messages constitute a cross-section of the popular vote cast for the Republican candidate and come from every part of the country. They are from children, laborers, housewives, business and professional men, lawyers, school teachers—from persons in practically every walk of life.

And while the wording of each message is different, the same general theme runs through them all—"What are we to do now? Tell us, Mr. Willkie."

Urged to Head Opposition

Many of the messages are from members of the Associated Willkie Clubs of America informing Mr. Willkie that the clubs in the various parts of the country have decided to continue as organizations to "keep your fight going." Others are from members of the Democrats-for-Willkie and Republicans telling him the same thing. And others are from independents urging Mr. Willkie to take the lead in the formation of a strong opposition party to the New Deal.

A great many of the letters expressed concern over the speculation that Mr. Willkie may be offered a Federal position by the New Deal and appealed to him to refuse any offer that might be made and lead the opposition party.

Those letters that were written

Continued on Page Ten

SENATOR PITTMAN DIES UNEXPECTEDLY

Foreign Relations Committee Head Stricken in Nevada—George Slated for Post

By The Associated Press.

RENO, Nev., Nov. 10—Senator Key Pittman, 68, chairman of the Senate Committee on Foreign Relations, died at the Washoe General Hospital at 12:35 A. M. (3:35 A. M. Eastern standard time) today. He had suffered a heart attack early yesterday and several hours before his death he was put in an oxygen tent.

Senator Pittman, first elected to the United States Senate in 1912 for an unexpired term of four years, defeated Samuel Platt, Republican, in last Tuesday's election—his sixth successive victory for that office.

Although Senator Pittman was not in vigorous health when he came home to campaign successfully for re-election, it was not until last Saturday, when he failed to appear at a political rally here, that his illness became known publicly.

Monday night—election eve—he was taken to the hospital and his physician, Dr. A. J. Hood, disclosed that he had been in bad health throughout the campaign.

Governor Expresses Sorrow

Governor E. P. Carville, expressing regret at the Senator's death, said he had made "no commitments and will take no action" in naming a successor until after funeral services Thursday. Mr. Pittman's unexpired term ends in January.

"The nation and our State," said the Governor, "have lost a faithful and tireless statesman."

The Senator's wife, Mimosa Gates Pittman, was at his bedside when death came. His brother, Dail Pittman of Ely, Nevada, newspaper publisher, arrived here today.

The body with a guard of honor from the Nevada National Guard will lie in state Thursday in the State Building, where Episcopalian funeral services will be conducted. The body will be placed in a vault here pending Mrs. Pittman's decision for final disposition.

Governor Carville said he would issue a proclamation Tuesday designating Thursday a day of mourning and ordering all State offices closed during the afternoon

As chairman of the Foreign Affairs Committee, Senator Pittman was a constant opponent of appeasement and an advocate of a strong foreign policy for the United States, both with European totalitarian governments and in the Far East. He also was active in behalf of Pan-American solidarity.

Senate Group to Attend Funeral

By The Associated Press.

WASHINGTON, Nov. 10—From Uvalde, Texas, Vice President Garner telegraphed Chesley W. Jurney, Senate Sergeant at Arms, instructing him to make arrangements for a delegation to attend funeral services in Nevada for Senator Pittman. Mr. Jurney said it was probable that the twenty-two members of the Foreign Relations Committee would be appointed as delegates and asked to meet in Nevada, since few of them now are in Washington.

The Senate was in recess until Tuesday but those attending the funeral were expected to leave here tomorrow and arrive in Reno, Nev., Thursday, Mr. Jurney said.

The entire membership of the Senate was invited to the funeral

Continued on Page Twelve

CHAMBERLAIN DIES; BRITAIN MOURNING HER FORMER CHIEF

Death at 5:30 P. M., Saturday, Not Announced to Country Till Sunday Forenoon

LEADERS VOICE TRIBUTES

Ex-Prime Minister 71—Led in Effort to Appease Hitler and Thus Avert War

By RAYMOND DANIELL

Special Cable to THE NEW YORK TIMES.

LONDON, Nov. 10—In a low rambling farmhouse among tall larches in the heart of Hampshire Neville Chamberlain, former Prime Minister, lies dead tonight. The man who thought by trade with the dictators at Munich he could assure "peace in our time" was not permitted to see even the outcome of the war to which he reluctantly committed his country after his efforts at appeasement failed.

The Birmingham business man who was one of the most controversial figures of his time died at 5:30 yesterday afternoon, but it was not until 10:20 this morning that the news of his passing was disclosed to the public. Many dwellers in the straggling cottages near the quiet house where Mr. Chamberlain passed his last days learned of his death through the official announcement in the noon news broadcast from London.

Adjoining the grounds of Heckfield House, within whose camouflaged walls Mr. Chamberlain sank into a coma yesterday with his wife and sisters at his bedside, is the fine old Norman Church of St. Michael. The Vicar, the Rev. H. R. P. Tringham, and the members of the congregation who attended the morning service were as ignorant of what had happened among them as the rest of the country.

Prayer Offered After Death

Just before the beginning of his sermon the Vicar suggested a prayer for Mr. Chamberlain, "who is very, very seriously ill."

It was Armistice Sunday and the church was fairly well filled with veterans of the war and soldiers and home guards serving in this one. At vespers, attended by a small number of countryfolk, the Vicar paid a tribute to the memory of the man for whom they had prayed earlier in the day. Mr. Tringham said:

"The first thought that comes to one referring to Mr. Chamberlain is, 'Blessed are the peacemakers, for they shall be called the children of God.' No one could have worked harder for our peace and although it seemed a failure it was a grand failure. The man, because of his ideals and unselfishness, was an inspiration not only to us but also to generations to come and probably what he has done was as great a work as that of people who had easy success."

It is expected the body will be brought to London for a state funeral.

Soon after the announcement of Mr. Chamberlain's death was received in his home city, Birmingham, where he had served as Lord Mayor and where his father and brothers had rendered distinguished civic service, flags on public buildings were lowered to half staff. Some followers in his constituency, Edgbaston, wore mourning brassards.

The Rev. Noel Hutchcroft, head of the Methodist Mission in Birmingham, expressed the feelings of has fellow-citizens when he said:

"His loyalty to his beliefs defied the material danger to which his

Continued on Page Four

DE GAULLE VICTORY IN GABON REPORTED; GREEKS COUNTER-ATTACK ON 3 FRONTS; NAZIS INTENSIFY AIR RAIDS ON LONDON

FASCISTI FALL BACK

Evzones in Epirus Sector Push Foe to Position Held Six Days Ago

ITALIANS GET NEW LEADER

Soddu, War Under-Secretary, Assumes Albanian Command—Storms Hamper Planes

By C. L. SULZBERGER

By Telephone to THE NEW YORK TIMES.

ATHENS, Nov. 10—Under cover of a continued blanket of rain which has hampered the activities of the Italian Air force in the northern and northeastern mountain regions and held up the mechanized attack in the west, the Greek Army has followed up its dramatic success of yesterday with a series of small but strong counter-attacks on all three fronts.

In the Epirus coastal region the Greek lines have been straightened in the vicinity of the Kalamas River and, following a sharp push forward with bayonets and hand grenades, Evzone units have shoved the Italians back to a bridgehead position they held six days ago.

In the Pindus section the Greeks have recaptured a bridge on the crossing of a road between Argyrokastron and Yanina and new strongholds north and northeast of Konitza have been occupied.

Koritza Still Under Fire

On the border of Macedonia Greek troops continued to shell Koritza and a few peaks have been occupied.

Italy's difficulties appear to be becoming increasingly serious. The official spokesman tonight pointed out that Rome had placed a new general—General Ubaldo Soddu, Under-Secretary of War—in charge of Albanian operations, and added that it could not be considered a good sign to change direction in the middle of a battle.

The spokesman also brought attention to the fact that today's Italian communiqué is remarkably scarce of information, claiming only the capture of a gun and munitions during a cavalry reconnaisance.

More detailed information about the military situation cannot at this time be given, although it is generally known. But if one sticks to the word of government statements in describing it as highly satisfactory, one is being unduly modest.

The most outstanding success has been that of the Pindus battle in the Aoos River Valley, where Alpini mountain troops, and reinforcements from the crack Third Division have been annihilated and the main thrust into Greece destroyed. [In Albania the Aoos River is called the Viosa.]

Tonight's communique confirms first reports of this victory, saying that the Third Division, which was familiar with the terrain of these regions and which included seasoned Alpini, Bersaglieri and Fascist militia troops, were surrounded and broken up in the Pindus sector around Smolika and Grammos.

Enemy losses in men and material were heavy and reinforcements rushed up from Valona were beaten back.

As details of this combat reach

Continued on Page Two

The International Situation

A broadcast from the Belgian Congo yesterday said that the "Free French" forces of General Charles de Gaulle had captured Libreville and now controlled all of the French colony of Gabon, on the West African coast. London heard that Vichy had ordered the loyal French garrison to cease useless resistance. At the provisional French capital, however, Governor General Tenu of Gabon was quoted as saying that resistance continued, but that Libreville was short of food and medical supplies because of the British sea blockade. [Page 1, Column 8.]

The Italian High Command reported the recapture of Gallabat, in the Sudan, just across the border from Ethiopia. For the first time it was acknowledged that the Italian troops had been driven out of the town by the British last Wednesday. Cairo said only that the fighting went on. [Page 6, Column 4.]

New Greek successes were reported on all sectors of the 100-mile fighting line along the Albanian border yesterday, with continued "mopping up" in the Pindus Mountains of the remnants of the crack Italian division that was surrounded and cut to pieces there. Additional artillery was moved up for the siege of Koritza. Fog and rain again shielded Greek troops and cities from the Italian Air Force. Rome said little on the Greek campaign, but reported an air attack on a British naval force in the Central Mediterranean. Acknowledgment was made of British bombing raids in Italy. [Page 1, Column 5.]

Official announcement that General Ubaldo Soddu, Italian Under-Secretary for War and an expert on infantry tactics, had been placed in charge of the campaign in Greece was made in Rome. An observer said reinforcements had been poured into Albania and predicted a renewed Italian attack. [Page 2, Column 2.]

"General Fate" appeared to have enlisted on the side of Britain and Greece when a devastating earthquake shook German-dominated Rumania, disrupting rail traffic and doing probably heavy damage to the oil fields that help supply the Axis war machine. Half of the oil wells in the Ploesti fields were said to have been set afire. Thousands were killed or injured. [Page 1, Column 2.]

The British and the Germans exchanged new air blows. The Royal Air Force struck at the submarine base at Lorient, the Channel ports of Boulogne and Calais and eighteen German airdromes. The German Air Force centered its attention on London. There were no successful day raids on the city, but the night attack was heavy and lasted eleven hours. [Page 1, Column 7.]

A newspaper account, which, in Germany, amounts to an official statement because of strict control of the press, said the attitude of pro-British Turkey lay within the scope of the Berlin conference to which Soviet Premier Molotoff is en route. Britain's Near Eastern nonbelligerent ally also is friendly with Russia. Much pomp marked the Soviet Premier's departure from Moscow, where it was said he was returning the visit made to Russia a year ago by German Foreign Minister von Ribbentrop [Page 1, Column 6.]

Some new military adventure by Japan in East Asia may be forced soon by the Axis and Tokyo extremists, it was believed by observers in Singapore, especially if Britain should grant the United States use of her Singapore naval and air base. Withdrawal of Japanese troops from South China and their concentration at Hainan was believed possibly to foreshadow a drive to the south against the rich East Indies. [Page 8, Column 2.]

Two men who had important parts in shaping the foreign policies of Britain and the United States during the last few years died yesterday, Neville Chamberlain in England [Page 1, Column 4.] and Senator Key Pittman, chairman of the Senate Foreign Relations Committee, in Reno, Nev. [Page 1, Column 3.] It was believed in Washington that Senator George of Georgia, an "unreconstructed rebel" who, however, is a supporter of the Roosevelt foreign policies, would succeed Senator Pittman. [Page 12, Column 3.]

TURKEY TO BE ISSUE IN NAZI-SOVIET TALK

Goering's Paper Hints Japan Will Also Be Discussed—Molotoff En Route

By The Associated Press.

BERLIN, Nov. 10—The newspaper Essener National Zeitung, organ of Reich Marshal Hermann Goering, boldly stated tonight that the Turkish problem lay within the scope of the Russian-German conference opening early this week in Berlin with the arrival of Premier and Foreign Commissar Vyacheslaff M. Molotoff from Moscow.

Considering the nature of the German press such an assertion took on the appearance of a semi-authorized statement that Germany intended to have the conferees do something about Turkey, which is pro-British in sentiment.

Every statement of the press about what would evolve from the conference was tempered, however, by the cautionary suggestion that nothing too revolutionary in nature should be expected. Rather, it declared, there should emerge a strengthening of the already "warm relations" between Germany and Russia.

Press Is Optimistic

Press statements concerning the subject-matter of the Russian Premier's visit grew more optimistic as the day arrived when Mr. Molotoff with thirty-two aides actually had left Moscow.

The National Zeitung asserted that the smoothly working nature of the Russian-German agreements had also extended to the Far East. There, it pointed out, Russian-Japanese relations were improving.

Such a situation, it was added, has given greater freedom to action to both Russia and Japan, enabling both powers to pull away from Britain.

"The statesman Stalin," said the paper, "has seen through to their final consequences the English plans to have Russia play the same

Continued on Page Six

NEW AIR BLOW SEEN AS HITLER REVENGE

Bombs, Gunfire Light London Following the Munich Raid—R. A. F. Hammers Back

By JAMES MacDONALD

Special Cable to THE NEW YORK TIMES.

LONDON, Monday, Nov. 11—Fresh bomb craters pitted districts of Britain and of Germany and Nazi-occupied territory today following a vigorous exchange of aerial hammer blows by the German Air Force and the British Royal Air Force.

Once again German fliers concentrated on London, seemingly seeking revenge for the R. A. F. raid on Munich Friday night when, according to British officials, one bomb hit the beer cellar where Adolf Hitler had just made his speech on the anniversary of the Nazis' 1923 Putsch.

[British planes attempted to attack Berlin last night, but were turned back by "an energetic defense" before they could drop bombs, according to a German communiqué early today as reported by The United Press.]

Outbursts of fighting between enemy aviators and London's defending gun crews punctuated the night until the "all clear" came about two hours before dawn. German planes were either over the city or hovering on the outskirts for nearly eleven hours.

While London is bearing the brunt of the latest raids, other parts of Britain were also affected during the night. Enemy planes coming over singly or by twos, were reported in southwest, southeast and northwest districts.

Meanwhile the British announced a new series of R. A. F. attacks on the Channel "invasion" ports, the U-boat base at Lorient, France, and eighteen air bases from which Nazi and Fascist airmen take off for their attacks on Britain.

From daybreak until just after nightfall London enjoyed a peace-

Continued on Page Seven

COLONY IS CLAIMED

'Free French' Reported to Have Captured the Port of Libreville

VICHY SAYS BATTLE IS ON

Defenders of African Region's Capital Held to Be Resisting 'British-Aided' Attack

Special Cable to THE NEW YORK TIMES.

LONDON, Monday, Nov. 11—The "Free French" forces of General Charles de Gaulle have captured the port of Libreville in Gabon, French Equatorial Africa, according to a report received from Leopoldville, Belgian Congo, by the British Broadcasting Corporation and broadcast here at midnight.

No details were given beyond the statement that there had been only "slight losses on both sides" and that General de Gaulle had appointed one of his officers as Governor of the colony.

The British Admiralty on Saturday denied reports that British ships had shelled Libreville and stated that the French submarine Poncelet, damaged in an attack on a British warship, had been scuttled.

Official circles here said there was no indication that British forces had been involved in the latest action at Libreville.

[The National Broadcasting Company said here yesterday that the British broadcast had stated that Gabon was taken over by the de Gaulle forces after the Vichy government had ordered the defenders of Libreville to cease "useless" resistance. "All Gabon is united under the standard of 'Free France'," according to reports quoted in the British broadcast.]

Fight Still On, Vichy Says

VICHY, France, Nov. 10 (UP)—Loyal French forces at Libreville, capital of Gabon, French Equatorial Africa, were reported today to be holding out against intensified British air bombing and land attacks from two directions by "Free French" followers of General Charles de Gaulle. British cruisers were reported to be continuing offshore surveillance, taking no part in the attack on the capital.

The Ministry of Colonies said that the "Free French" forces had landed yesterday on either side of Libreville. Today they were reported to be attacking simultaneously from north and south. Reports to Vichy said that the attacking forces consisted chiefly of French Colonial troops, from garrisons in Equatorial Africa, leading bands of armed natives.

The capital was reported to be blockaded by land and sea and running perilously low on medicines and food.

"Reports reaching us in recent hours of operations in Gabon confirm the dramatic situation in which the colony finds itself, as well as the odious character of the civil war brought on by criminal former officers," a statement by the Ministry of Colonies said.

Quoting a message from French officials in Libreville on events leading up to the attack, the Ministry said that the bombardment of Libreville was continuing under "unbelievable conditions of savagery and inhumanity."

Called "Full-Fledged" War

VICHY, France, Nov. 10 (AP)—The "Free French" forces of General Charles de Gaulle are fighting a "full-fledged" war in Gabon, French Equatorial Africa, it was officially reported here today.

The report on conditions in Gabon came from General Tenu, Commander in Chief of the French forces at Libreville, who assured the government that "nothing" would make the besieged capital of Gabon surrender.

[A radio report received in London from the Belgian Congo said that General Tenu was among the prisoners taken when "Free French" forces captured Libreville. The de Gaulle followers also were said to have seized a large quantity of war materials, according to The United Press.]

General Tenu declared in his message that the de Gaulle forces, who are pledged to carry on the war against the Axis powers, were being aided by the British in a "full-fledged" war against the French colony.

"Do the British people know that their ships, planes, bombs and gold are being used by General de Gaulle

Continued on Page Six

French-German Peace Negotiations Barred Until War Against Britain Has Terminated

By LANSING WARREN

By Telephone to THE NEW YORK TIMES.

VICHY, France, Nov. 10—There will be no negotiations for peace between France and Germany until the war with Britain has terminated.

This became known here tonight following the return of Vice Premier Pierre Laval from a trip to Paris in the course of which he conferred with Reich Marshal Hermann Goering. In their talk they discussed the whole range of collaboration which had been outlined between Reichsfuehrer Hitler and Marshal Henri Philippe Pétain, French Chief of State, at Montoire.

M. Laval had not been expected to return to Vichy until Tuesday, but he left in Paris Fernand de Brinon, who ranks as Ambassador, and Minister of Finance Marcel Bouthillier, who are continuing the economic conversations.

As long as the war continued with Britain, it was said here, the Continent of Europe would remain disturbed at many points that would enter the treaty and that it would, therefore, have to be revised. The situation was too complicated now by the war between Italy and Greece, it was said, and the Gaulist [General Charles de Gaulle, leader of the "Free" French forces] agitation in France and the empire added to the complexity of the case.

Postponement of the idea of peace negotiations does not, however, necessarily mean the abandonment of efforts for French-German collaboration.

A note issued tonight by the Agence Havas—which will soon be an official government news agency—points out that it is now important to "create an atmosphere of mutual understanding between the two countries and have it ratified by public opinion."

The principle of collaboration has been accepted by both parties in the meeting at Montoire, and on both sides it has now been decided to bring an understanding of the situation home to both populations. This is the sole policy open to the French Government, the Havas note concludes.

"All the News That's Fit to Print."

The New York Times.

LATE CITY EDITION
Rain today, little change in temperature; rain turning to snow and colder late tonight or tomorrow.
Temperatures Yesterday—Max., 48; Min., 44

Copyright, 1940, by The New York Times Company.

VOL. XC..No. 30,246. Entered as Second-Class Matter, Postoffice, New York, N. Y. NEW YORK, FRIDAY, NOVEMBER 15, 1940. THREE CENTS NEW YORK CITY and Vicinity | FOUR CENTS Elsewhere Except in 7th and 8th Postal Zones.

GREEKS START GENERAL ADVANCE; VICHY PROTESTS NAZI EXPULSIONS; MOLOTOFF QUITS BERLIN WITH PLAN

TRANSIT WORKERS WARNED BY CITY STRIKE IS ILLEGAL

Board, in Reply to Threat, Tells Men They Would Lose Their Civil Service Status

LEWIS'S AID IS EXPECTED

Union Charges Failure to Keep Promises on Collective Bargaining Contracts

In swift response to an implied threat of a strike on the unified transit lines that it operates for the city, the Board of Transportation warned all employes yesterday that those who left their jobs without official sanction would be subject to charges, dismissal and loss of service rights and status.

Notices posted last night at various points on the New York City Transit System, including subway, elevated, street car and bus lines, declared that the Board of Transportation was a governmental agency; that its employes were under civil service; that the right to strike was not recognized, and that all employes leaving their jobs without the board's approval would be subject to charges, dismissal and loss of civil service status.

The veiled threat of a strike was made Wednesday night in resolutions adopted at a membership meeting of the Transport Workers Union, the C. I. O. affiliate, that has a membership of about 27,000 on the I. R. T. and B. M. T. divisions of the city system, as well as some strength on the IND division.

Other membership meetings, to be held in Brooklyn today and tomorrow, are scheduled to ratify the action already taken. The union claims about 50,000 members among the employes of subway, elevated, street car and bus lines in the New York area.

Sees Failure to Keep Promise

The union based its veiled threat of strike upon the alleged failure of the Board of Transportation to keep its promise to observe the terms of the collective bargaining contracts between the union and the managements of the I. R. T. and B. M. T. systems. These contracts were taken over by the city in connection with transit unification last June.

On April 2 a threatened strike of the 27,000 employes of the two systems was averted, when Mayor La Guardia and John L. Lewis, chairman of the C. I. O., agreed that the contracts would be taken over and their terms observed by the Board of Transportation, pending final judicial decision on all disputed questions of law. Among these questions were the right of civil service employes to strike, the validity of a "union shop" clause and several other provisions considered important by the union.

As part of the settlement Mayor La Guardia handed to Lee Pressman, general counsel for the C. I. O., a letter declaring, in effect, that the agreement meant that the terms of the contracts between the union and the I. R. T. and B. M. T. managements would be observed by the Board of Transportation, pending final judicial decision, even if the board should hold, as to any specific provision, that it was contrary to the State Constitution or the State statutes.

Ever since unification there have been a number of clashes between the union and the Board of Transportation over alleged non-observance of the contracts, and in at least one instance union members have walked out on their jobs for a brief period to stress a grievance.

Lewis Aid Expected

That the Transport Workers Union believes that Mr. Lewis may again take part in the transit situation was indicated at the membership meeting on Wednesday by the unanimous adoption of a resolution calling for his continuance as leader of the C. I. O. despite his pre-election statement that he would resign if President Roosevelt was re-elected.

In its resolution the union charged that the Board of Transportation had, since unification, "repeatedly and persistently endeavored to break the labor contracts which it solemnly undertook to abide by."

The implied threat of strike was contained in the declaration in the resolution that notice was served on the members of the Board of Transportation that "organized transit labor would not tolerate any tampering with their labor contracts or with their rights as American workers." Elsewhere in the text of the resolution the union asserted that "we warn the Board of Transportation that failure on its part to deal honorably with the employes and their union will meet with unanimous and vigorous protest on our part and that the commissioners shall be held responsible before the public for the consequences of their

Continued on Page Fifteen

Netherlands Indies Plans A Base for Capital Ships

By The Associated Press.

BATAVIA, Java, Nov. 14—The Commander in Chief of the Netherlands Indies Navy announced today that enlargement of the works at the Surabaya naval base, on Java's northern coast, was continuing and indicated that the base would be large enough to accommodate capital ships.

The Commander in Chief said work on the base was proceeding just as if construction of capital ships already had commenced.

BANDOENG, Java, Nov. 14 (UP)—The government of the Netherlands Indies today abandoned plans to build three battlecruisers for this colony's navy because of a shortage of materials.

The Netherlands' largest warships are two 8,350-ton cruisers based in the Netherlands Indies.

8 DRAFT OBJECTORS GET PRISON TERMS

Divinity Students Sentenced to Year and a Day—Refuse Final Chance to Register

Eight young divinity students were in jail last night, starting to serve prison terms incurred by their refusal to register under the Selective Service Act. None could have been called for service under the draft law, but all had maintained that their consciences prevented them even from complying with the procedure of registration. Each was sentenced to a year and a day.

They persisted in their refusal to register yesterday morning, as they stood in a group before the bench in the crowded Federal courtroom. Each told Judge Samuel Mandelbaum that he found it impossible to register. They all knew that Judge Mandelbaum wanted to set them free, if only they would at last comply with the law.

They knew that United States Attorney John T. Cahill, while he recommended the sentence of a year and a day, still hoped they would relent. But none did, and one even rebuked the Federal officials for the "stress upon leniency" which he said he and his fellow defendants "did not particularly like."

All Pleaded Guilty

All the students, whose studies at Union Theological Seminary are being interrupted by the prison sentence, had pleaded guilty. They all were willing to accept the penalty for their action.

The story of their activities was explained to the court by Mr. Cahill, as follows:

"These eight defendants are charged with a violation of the Selective Service and Training Act of 1940. Their violation constitutes a deliberate refusal to register as required by the Act. All of the defendants are divinity students and as such are exempt from military service under the Act, but not from registration.

"The defendants place their refusal to register upon grounds of conscience. The 1940 Selective Service Act makes specific provision for conscientious objectors and exempts them from military service. These provisions have been pointed out to the defendants and they have been urged to register and thereafter note their conscientious objection in the manner and form provided by the law. This they have refused to do.

"After the day fixed for registration had passed and prior to their indictment, these defendants were again urged to register by the United States Attorney's office and by the grand jury itself. Right up until the last minute before they were indicted, they were offered the opportunity of complying with the law, even at that late date. They have, however, persisted and they continue to persist in their refusal to register."

Court Term "Kept Open"

Mr. Cahill asked that the "term of the court be kept open," a technical move that will make it possible for Judge Mandelbaum to free the young men at any time that they agree to register. This request was readily granted by the court.

Even if they do not register, however, the youthful prisoners may be released on parole at the end of four months.

Kenneth Walser, a lawyer, accompanied the young men at their arraignment, but even he said that he had not received a single request for leniency. He pointed out that the object of the registration was identification of all men of draft age. He said that the young men had identified themselves by leaving signed statements with an assistant United States attorney at the place of registration.

He pleaded for a suspended sentence, declaring that the defendants were in a class by themselves. Any impression that draft dodgers were being treated too easily could

Continued on Page Twenty-three

KNOX IN WARNING OF PERILOUS TIMES DENOUNCES HITLER

We Will Appease No One on Earth, Declares Secretary, Assailing 'Greedy Fanatic'

HE CALLS FOR SACRIFICES

Tells New England Meeting That We Will Send Britain Everything We Can Spare

The text of Secretary Knox's speech appears on Page 12.

By HUGH O'CONNOR
Special to THE NEW YORK TIMES.

BOSTON, Mass., Nov. 14—A conference of 750 of the leading business men of New England, led by the Governors or the Governors-elect of the six New England States, today heard Frank Knox, Secretary of the Navy, declare in an extemporaneous address that the United States would not "appease anybody on earth."

At the opening of the annual New England Conference at the Hotel Statler here, Secretary Knox asserted:

"It doesn't fit the American spirit, the American purpose, or the American security to talk appeasement in a world like this where force and force alone determines the fate of nations."

In his speech, broadcast both nationally and internationally, Secretary Knox denounced Adolf Hitler as "a fanatic, greedy for world domination," who was "likely in the very near future" to attack Gibraltar by going through Spain.

"We are reliably informed," he said, "that Germany has a whole division in civilian clothes in Spain itself."

Upholds the British Blockade

It had now become apparent, Colonel Knox told the session, that the attempt to invade England had failed. He then laid down the policy that the British blockade of Europe must be respected despite "the ghastly conditions that we read about in Europe this Winter, black starvation for helpless, innocent peoples."

Emphasizing the belief that an Axis success in the Mediterranean would "go a long way toward achieving victory in this war," Secretary Knox said:

"Consequently you can imagine the relief in military circles when the news came to us only yesterday of the victory of the British air force in destroying a large part of the Italian fleet while it clung to its bases behind the shelter of its shore defenses."

In addition to all possible aid for Britain "short of leaving ourselves defenseless," Secretary Knox said:

"I hope we will soon come to have as unanimous a public opinion in favor of helping China."

The interest of the United States in helping China, he asserted, was to prevent "some fresh excursions to the South" by Japan, which he described as "that nation now dominated by a secret cabal of military officers who rule it."

"For your reassurance," he told his audience, "I am glad to tell you as the Chief of the Navy that we have the strongest fleet today that floats the seven seas. It is not only stronger, but thank God it's ready."

Secretary Knox warned business that profits would necessarily "have

Continued on Page Twelve

Hitler Says Reich Must Be Model 'Socialistic' State

By The Associated Press.

BERLIN, Nov. 14—Reichsfuehrer Adolf Hitler told behind-the-lines workers today that Germany's greatest post-war duty would be to serve the world as a "model" socialistic State.

Wireless to THE NEW YORK TIMES.

BERLIN, Nov. 14—Reichsfuehrer Hitler this noon received eighty-five "soldiers of labor," workers from the armaments industries and behind the front, and forty women workers from munitions industries, all of whom had been decorated with the Cross for Distinguished War Service. He expressed his and the Reich's thanks for services "which gave our soldiers the best arms in the world and unlimited amounts of munitions, built the steel-like Westwall and donated their labor so that Germany today has the best anti-aircraft defenses of the world."

Victory, he said, would be attained the more quickly the more united and determined the German nation was and the more its enemy "recognizes that every thought of the Germany of 1918 is in vain."

R. A. F. RAIDS POUND BERLIN REPEATEDLY

Waves of Bombers Met by Nazi 'AA' Fire—5 Are Reported Downed in City, 3 Outside

Special Cable to THE NEW YORK TIMES.

LONDON, Friday, Nov. 15—The British Air Ministry announced this morning that Royal Air Force bombers in the past twelve hours had completed "heavy, successful" raids on Berlin and industrial targets elsewhere in the Reich and on enemy-occupied airfields.

[The British Government announced that Nazi raiders during the night had made "a very heavy attack on one Midland town" and that it was feared the casualties were "heavy." Attacks on other Midland towns caused some fatalities, it was said. London escaped with relatively light raids.]

Four Berliners Reported Killed

BERLIN, Friday, Nov. 15 (UP)—The British Air Force, making what appeared to be one of its most intensive attacks on Berlin last night, suffered the loss of eight planes during the raid, according to an official communiqué.

Informed Nazis said that four persons were killed and one injured in the raid, during which the capital's defense forces appeared to give the R. A. F. the strongest resistance it has received in the many attacks here.

Informed persons said one apartment house was demolished by a direct bomb hit.

A number of attic fires broke out in Berlin due to incendiary bombs.

Two British planes, in crashing, caused a big fire, but it was claimed

Continued on Page Six

5 New Battleships, Threat to Nazi Raiders, Believed Added Recently to British Navy

Special Cable to THE NEW YORK TIMES.

LONDON, Nov. 14—The British have been and still are maintaining silence about their five new 35,000-ton battleships of the King George V class, laid down in 1937 and launched last year. [The five were originally scheduled for completion in 1940 and 1941.]

Last Spring it was reported by Hector C. Bywater, naval expert, that these ships had undergone their trials. The Admiralty spokesman said tonight that whether or not they had joined the fleet nothing would be said about them until an encounter with an enemy disclosed their completion.

Prime Minister Churchill and other government leaders have spoken repeatedly of accretions soon coming to the navy's strength through new building far more extensive than is represented by the five capital ships begun before the war broke out. However, it has been said repeatedly that Great Britain's greatest need in this war is small ships like the fifty destroyers recently obtained from the United States.

Lack of these guardians of merchant ships compelled the British to use the Jervis Bay, a converted liner lightly armed, to guard the big convoy attacked by a raider in mid-Atlantic. Although the commissioning of five new capital ships this early in the war would be spectacular, completion of a score of destroyers would be more important when Germany and Italy are trying desperately to destroy the commerce that feeds these islands.

The commissioning of five 35,000-ton battleships would give Great Britain pineteen capital ships as well as a potent challenge to the extensive raiding activities of the two German pocket battleships still believed to be in service—the Admiral Scheer and the Luetzow.

Before the construction of the King George V class, the Admiralty had only three capital ships considered capable of catching and outgunning either the Admiral Scheer or the Luetzow. These are the 42,100-ton Hood, Britain's largest man-of-war, the Repulse and the Renown.

The five latest additions to the navy constitute a serious threat to the roaming Nazi raiders in that they are better equipped for battle and for speed. Each is armed with ten 14-inch and sixteen 5.25-inch guns, as against the Germans' six 11-inch and eight 5.9-inch guns. The new British vessels, furthermore, are capable of thirty knots, four more than the Germans.

LORRAINE 'PURGED'

French-Speaking People Sent to Unoccupied France or Poland

FLEET LEAVES TOULON

Clash Between Petain and the Apostles of Vengeance Is Believed Near Showdown

By G. H. ARCHAMBAULT
Wireless to THE NEW YORK TIMES.

VICHY, France, Nov. 14—This date may prove memorable in France, both as regards relations with the German victor and as regards the internal situation.

Marshal Henri Philippe Pétain's government has taken a very firm stand against the expulsion of French-speaking residents of Lorraine by the German authority. It implies that this action goes far beyond the negotiations for "collaboration." Furthermore, it invokes the armistice convention with the implication that that convention represents the fundamental basis of relations between victor and vanquished.

[A dispatch from Berne, Switzerland, stated that the French Fleet had left Toulon yesterday afternoon for an unannounced destination.]

In any case, it has been a day of excitement in unoccupied France, after an unexpected and in one sense unusual communiqué was issued this morning, following a meeting of the Cabinet presided over by Marshal Pétain and attended by Vice Premier Pierre Laval, who had been summoned back from Paris especially for the meeting.

TEXT OF COMMUNIQUE

The communiqué follows:

The German authorities in Lorraine have just requested French-speaking inhabitants of the region to choose between their transfer to Poland or their departure for unoccupied France. Our compatriots decided for France.

Since Monday, Nov. 11, 1940, their expulsion has been taking place at the rate of five to seven trainloads per day.

They have unquestionably been told by persons without proper authority that this measure was taken in conformity with an accord reached between the French Government and the Government of the Reich.

The French Government issues the most formal denial to this imputation.

No measure of this kind was ever under discussion at the Franco-German meetings.

As concerns the facts themselves, the French Government has applied [The Associated Press translated this word as "protested"] to the German armistice commission.

[If the procedure is being applied to all of Lorraine, it will affect roughly 800,000 persons.]

Situation Held Critical

Today's announcement was made in the form of "a communiqué from the government" without reference to the Cabinet meeting. The key sentence seems to be the one referring to "persons without authority." Manifestly these persons cannot be other than German.

The fact that the French Government "issues the most formal denial to this imputation" is pregnant with possibilities.

It is understood the refugees receive only a few hours' notice and that none is permitted to take more than 2,000 francs and a small grip. Many of them doubtless come from the iron-mining districts. The Germans have laid much store by Lorraine ore in contemporary times.

Refugee trains pass through Lyon, where nurses and social workers have volunteered their services day and night. Thence they proceed south to regions in the Rhone Valley.

It is no secret that Marshal Pétain feels wholehearted sympathy for the refugees. Last evening he conferred with Prefect Schmidt of the Meurthe et Moselle Department of Lorraine.

Possibly he may be going to Lyon himself in the course of his trips of inspection, inaugurated by his recent visit to Toulouse. If so, he would be able to inform himself on the spot, as is his determination. In this connection these words of the marshal are being recalled tonight:

"We must know how to wait, and how to suffer."

While on the subject of refugees,

Continued on Page Four

The International Situation

Attacking at dawn all along the 100-mile battlefront, the Greek Army, ably supported by its own and British air units, was reported in Athens to have driven the Italians from all but a small part of Greek territory. A Greek communiqué indicated a major battle was under way. The invaders were said to have been driven back across the Kalamas River, to be still in full retreat in the center and to have been unsuccessful in an attempt to send a relief force to besieged Koritza in the northeast. Wide destruction in British bombing raids on Albanian ports was reported. [Page 1, Column 8.]

New British bombing raids on the Italian home front in which further destruction was done at Taranto and other naval bases were reported by London. Fires and explosions followed the attacks, the British fliers reported. The decisive Taranto action of Monday, where important units of the Italian fleet were severely damaged, will have far-reaching political effects, the British anticipated, not only among European neutrals, including the Soviet Union, but perhaps in Italy. [Page 1, Column 7.]

The British claims of destruction at Taranto evoked a special communiqué in Rome calling Prime Minister Churchill's report to the House of Commons Wednesday a "fantastically distorted version." To answer the British claims, a detailed account not only of the Taranto action but of the whole aero-naval situation in the Mediterranean may be issued soon, the official Italian news agency said. [Page 3, Column 1.]

The British also continued to carry the air war to the Axis in the north, Berlin being bombed again last night by waves of R. A. F. planes. Eight of the attackers were shot down, the Germans said, acknowledging that at least some had penetrated the city's defenses. Previously the Air Ministry in London had told of a raid on Berlin the night before in which a railway station, the Grunewald rail storage yards and railway yards in the Tempelhof section had been hit. Other industrial objectives, the Channel ports and German airdromes also were attacked. [Page 1, Column 4.]

At home the Royal Air Force had a big day, the Air and Home Security Ministries said, bagging nineteen German planes, against a loss of only two of their own, from both of which the pilots jumped to safety. The German raids were widespread, with the industrial Midlands apparently getting most of the bombs, but were relatively light on London. [Page 5, Column 1.]

Soviet Premier Molotoff left Berlin after two days of conferences with Adolf Hitler and German Foreign Minister von Ribbentrop, with whom he was reported to have discussed the full range of German-Soviet relations, political and economic. The communiqué issued by the Germans said merely that there had been an exchange of views and "agreement of both parties on all questions of importance which are of interest to Germany and the Soviet Union." No new commitments by Russia were sought or given, Nazi sources said. Further talks were expected. [Page 1, Column 6.]

Coincident with Mr. Molotoff's departure from Berlin, Spain's Foreign Minister, Ramon Serrano Suñer, left Madrid for Paris, presumably for a talk with Axis spokesmen. There was no indication in the Spanish press, however, that any decisive developments were impending, such as a German drive on Gibraltar. [Page 7, Column 1.]

Forced evacuation of French-speaking residents of the province of Lorraine in the German-occupied part of France was announced in Vichy in a communiqué that, because of its strong language, was interpreted as perhaps portending a decided change in French-German relations. The communiqué made a most formal denial" that the forced evacuation was in conformity with any agreement yet made. The evacuation began last Monday with only a few hours' notice. The Frenchmen received their choice of being sent to unoccupied areas of France or to Poland. [Page 1, Column 5.]

In neutral Berne it was believed a showdown was imminent between Marshal Pétain on the one hand and Vice Premier Laval and Admiral Darlan on the other. The reported sailing from Toulon of the French fleet was believed to have been instigated by the latter two, as its presence at an African base would serve as a threat to the British there even if it was not used offensively. [Page 4, Column 2.]

Secretary of the Navy Knox, addressing a New England defense conference in Boston, declared in a broadcast address that the United States "will not appease anybody on earth." He foresaw a German drive on Gibraltar as a likely development soon, and urged the giving of as much aid to China as we now are giving to Britain. He charged that Japan was ruled by a "secret cabal of military officers." [Page 1, Column 3.]

NAZIS NOW AWAIT STALIN'S REACTION

Molotoff Leaves Berlin With Hitler's Proposals—Makes No Commitments There

Wireless to THE NEW YORK TIMES.

BERLIN, Nov. 14—The state visit to Berlin of Premier and Foreign Commissar Vyacheslaff Molotoff of Russia ended at 11 o'clock this morning, when a special train bearing the visitor and his associates back to Moscow pulled out of Anhalter Station.

The concluding communiqué, summing up the diplomatic activities of the Russian Premier during the last two days, was as terse as had been expected. It read:

"During his presence in Berlin on Nov. 12 and 13 of this year, President of the Council of People's Commissars, and Foreign Commissar Molotoff had conversations with the Fuehrer and with Reich Foreign Minister von Ribbentrop.

"The exchange of views was conducted in an atmosphere of mutual trust and led to agreement of both parties on all questions of importance that are of interest to Germany and the Soviet Union."

Germans declined to go beyond the scope of this official communiqué in commenting on the results of Mr. Molotoff's visit. It is learned, however, that in the exhaustive conversations, in which conferences between Reichsfuehrer Hitler and Mr. Molotoff occupied more than seven hours, the entire range of Russo-German relations was discussed and that not a

Continued on Page Eight

NEW TARANTO RAID IS MADE BY BRITISH

Docks and Oil Tanks Reported Ablaze in Sequel to Attack That Crippled Fleet

By RAYMOND DANIELL
Special Cable to THE NEW YORK TIMES.

LONDON, Nov. 14—While military experts weighed the results of the Fleet Air Arm's success against the Italian Navy in Taranto, news reached London today that British planes had followed up with a series of telling blows against that and other Italian bases.

The opinion of military observers here is that events of the last few days may have a marked effect on future strategy in the Mediterranean. Egypt, it was believed, might show the effects most quickly. Until now, Egypt's chief concern has been the western frontier. A little while ago the threat to Alexandria appeared immediate but has not materialized.

Not only in the air and on the sea have there been signs of a shift in the fortunes of war. The Alpini and Centauri divisions which Premier Mussolini sent against Greece were said now to be retreating through the Pindus gorges, very vulnerable to air attack if the weather permits one to be made. Whether or not the Greeks can continue their local successes and capture Koritza, the situation in the Adriatic sector has altered in favor of the Allies.

The same is held to be true in Africa where the fall of Gallabat

Continued on Page Two

BIG BATTLE RAGING

Fighting on Four-fifths of Front Is Reported in Italian Territory

R. A. F. HITS FOE'S BASES

11 Fascist Planes Downed, It Is Said—A Second Italian Division Is Smashed

By C. L. SULZBERGER
By Telephone to THE NEW YORK TIMES.

ATHENS, Greece, Nov. 14—The Greek Army today began what appeared to be a coordinated general advance and tonight along four-fifths of the Albanian front it was fighting in Italian territory. Three localized Italian counter-attacks were repulsed without slowing up the Greek forces, and it is clear that the initiative is now coming from this side.

From the wording of tonight's communiqué it is indicated that a major battle is under way, and there is mention of "great infantry, artillery and aircraft action" along the entire extent of the front.

Already considerable new materiel has been captured, and the small Greek Air Force came into prominence as an offensive element for the first time while bombing Argyrokastron and Koritza, destroying enemy planes on the ground and attacking columns of troops. It is declared that eleven Italian planes were brought down in battle and ten more damaged, while only one Greek aircraft failed to return.

From the swampy banks of Lake Presba to the Drinos River Evzone troops are leading the push in advance of the old frontier posts, and in the Epirus sector the Italians are retiring to avoid difficulties resulting from the badly exposed eastern flank. They have now withdrawn to considerably north of the Kalamas River, although on this sector they are still on Greek soil.

Koritza Partly Surrounded

In the Lake Presba region the Greeks occupied new heights north of Koritza, and that city is now partly surrounded by a series of positions shaped in the form of a half-moon. On the Epirus front there appears to have been heavy air action, and it is reported that ten Italian planes were brought down.

The Athens radio announced that fifteen Fascist planes were destroyed near Koritza. A dispatch from Yanina stated that north of the Pindus range Greek troops continued to penetrate farther into Albania, occupying one by one fortified positions that enable them to threaten enemy communication lines.

While Greek infantry and mountain artillery units pressed home their counter-attack, the British Air Force continued to harass the Italian Army at its Albanian bases behind the line.

With British air and sea forces hammering away at Italian sea and land communications, it appears that the Greek Army is availing itself of the opportunity to strike back at Fascist land units, forcing them back on their disorganized bases. How extensive this manoeuvre will be remains to be seen, but there are many who anticipate great developments in the near future. The Greek Premier, General John Metaxas, knows well the Greek temperament, which is better suited to attack than to a defensive inactivity.

Italy Increases Forces

The main thrust seems to be aimed at cutting off Southern Albania and it may be pointed out that both the Porto Edda and Argyrokastron Roads are scarcely fortified. On the other hand, the strengthening of positions already dominating Koritza seriously handicaps any possible future drives by the Italian commander, General Ubaldo Soddu, from this region in the direction of Kastoria and Florina, where many people think the next big Italian attack will come when the army is reorganized.

The official spokesman said tonight that Italy now has 300,000 soldiers in Albania, and it is stated that the Berlin Boersen Zeitung said that the Eleventh Army Corps was there. This correspondent estimated fourteen divisions were there two days ago and efforts were being made to send two more divisions immediately.

Enemy air activity was moderately extensive within the country today, but according to the communiqué of the Ministry of Public Security the damage was not heavy. Italian bombers raided the harbor

Continued on Page Two

"All the News That's Fit to Print."

The New York Times.

LATE CITY EDITION
Partly cloudy and colder today. Tomorrow fair and slightly warmer.
Temperatures Yesterday—Max., 49; Min., 40

VOL. XC...No. 30,247. Entered as Second-Class Matter, Postoffice, New York, N. Y. NEW YORK, SATURDAY, NOVEMBER 16, 1940. THREE CENTS NEW YORK CITY and Vicinity | FOUR CENTS Elsewhere Except in 7th and 8th Postal Zones.

COVENTRY WRECKED IN WORST RAID ON ENGLAND, WITH 1,000 CASUALTIES; BRITISH SMASH BERLIN RAIL DEPOTS

ROOSEVELT NAMES DR. MILLIS TO NLRB, REPLACING MADDEN

Witt, Board Secretary, and 2 Others Quit as Shake-Up Looms in 'Leftist' Group

LEISERSON HAILS CHOICE

End of Deadlock Between Him and Smith Forecast—Madden Nominated for Claims Bench

By CHARLES HURD
Special to THE NEW YORK TIMES.

WASHINGTON, Nov. 15—President Roosevelt today appointed Dr. Harry A. Millis of Chicago to succeed J. Warren Madden, former chairman of the National Labor Relations Board. Dr. Millis, who is 67, served on the old NRA Labor Board in 1934 and 1935, prior to its reconstitution under the Wagner act.

This appointment of a man whose nomination was expected to result in considerable shuffling in the board personnel, especially its "left wing" element, was followed within a few hours by the resignation of three important aides of the board, including Nathan Witt, the secretary.

The appointment broke an impasse which has existed since Aug. 27, when Mr. Madden's term expired and his necessary retirement left the board consisting only of Dr. William Leiserson and Edwin S. Smith, whose opposing views made it impossible for them to reach agreements on many controversies before them.

Mr. Smith had voted much of the time with Chairman Madden, just as Dr. Leiserson is expected hereafter to vote generally with Dr. Millis. Dr. Leiserson called selection of Dr. Millis a "splendid appointment."

Madden Named for Court Post

Coincident with appointment of Dr. Millis, Mr. Roosevelt sent to the Senate a nomination of Mr. Madden to fill a vacancy on the United States Court of Claims, where he would receive $12,500 a year as contrasted with his former $10,000 NLRB post. Mr. Smith immediately wrote to Mr. Madden expressing regret that he had not been reappointed to the NLRB.

The appointment of Dr. Millis was expected to receive quick confirmation by the Senate.

The President, in nominating Dr. Millis, did not indicate whether he would be designated as chairman of the board, but this was the assumption in well-informed circles.

Dr. Millis is a Professor of Economics at the University of Chicago and has been acting as labor relations conciliator for the General Motors Corporation and the C. I. O. United Automobile Workers. Prior to his call to the University of Chicago he was on the faculties of Stanford University and the Universities of Arkansas and Kansas. His long experience in labor affairs includes various temporary appointments by the Federal Government. Recently he has made studies on collective bargaining for the Twentieth Century Fund.

Activities in the offices of the NLRB as a result of the appointment gave graphic indication of the changes anticipated there, as well as the division of feeling within the board.

Mr. Witt submitted his letter of resignation addressed to the board and made it public together with a somewhat longer letter to Mr. Madden, complimenting the latter's work.

Pay Tribute to Ex-Chairman

Soon after Mr. Witt took this step, Alexander B. Hawes, chief administrative examiner, and Thomas I. Emerson, associate general counsel, filed their own resignations. Both also paid tribute to Mr. Madden.

Mr. Emerson's principal work, in his five-year association with the NLRB, has been to direct the work of lawyers in the Review Section who passed upon examiners' reports. This Review Section was sharply criticized for its alleged collective lack of experience by the special House committee that studied the NLRB a year ago, and Dr. Millis was expected to overhaul its organization.

All three officials asked that their resignations be effective immediately. Mr. Hawes wrote to the board that he had served for three years under the "fearless and able chairmanship" of Mr. Madden and "I do not wish to remain with the board, now that he has not been reappointed."

Mr. Emerson publicly announced that, concerning Mr. Madden, "I have supported his policies throughout," and that it was difficult for him to see "how the members of the board could have performed a more courageous, competent and worth-while public service."

Mr. Witt's letter to the board based his resignation on failure to reappoint Mr. Madden. His person-

Continued on Page Twenty

Hull Decides to Remain In Cabinet, Friends State

Special to THE NEW YORK TIMES.

WASHINGTON, Nov. 15—Cordell Hull has reached a decision to continue as Secretary of State in the third Roosevelt administration, according to officials who said today that he has so informed friends. Mr. Hull is in Augusta, Ga., on a vacation and President Roosevelt is cruising on the Presidential yacht Potomac, consequently no comment was available from either official.

The decision turned upon the international situation, it was said. It was understood that Secretary Hull would have preferred to retire to private life. The war emergency and his familiarity with United States foreign policy for eight years induced him to remain in office, it was explained.

Mr. Hull will be the first Secretary of State to serve more than eight years. Only four have served that long, the last being Hamilton Fish, sixty-four years ago.

C. I. O. STRIKE SHUTS WAR PLANES PLANT

5,200 Vultee Workers Idle—Hillman Voices Hope for Quick Wage Accord

Special to THE NEW YORK TIMES.

LOS ANGELES, Nov. 15—Work on $80,000,000 worth of military aircraft production, described in Washington as "vital to our national defense," came to a halt today as members of the C. I. O. United Automobile Workers went on strike at the Downey plant of Vultee Aircraft, Inc., fourth largest plane producer on the West Coast.

Early this morning hundreds of pickets drew up across the huge plant's entrances. The last outgoing night shift came out with tool kits in hands. The first ingoing day shift stopped short before such picket line banners as "They Shall Not Pass!" and "Keep Out! This Means You!"

The plant, where top-speed wheels had long hummed twenty-four hours a day, was hushed and 5,200 workers found themselves idle.

Agents of the War Department, National Defense Commission and Labor Department were at work on a remedy for a situation causing the greatest interruption to date in defense production.

Secretary Perkins assigned Edward H. Fitzgerald, one of the department's veteran labor conciliators, to help Lyman Sisley, first department conciliator in the situation. Mr. Sisley has spent night and day working toward a solution since the matter was put up to him by the disputants Wednesday night.

Seek New Conversations

Upon Captain Fitzgerald's arrival from San Francisco, he and Mr. Sisley, who long have teamed together in West Coast conciliation endeavors, outlined a new peace plan which, they said, they were seeking to lay before the union leaders. The aim, it was understood, was to bring company and union negotiators around one table. Company officials said they would attend.

Company representatives charged that Vultee was being used by the union as a guinea pig for a nation-wide drive to bring all airplane manufacture under the C. I. O. banner.

The union has control only in one other West Coast airplane plant, that of North American Aviation, Inc., a much smaller establishment.

Union representatives assert that all they are after is an increase to 75 cents an hour from the present 50 cents an hour minimum wage at the Vultee plant, where they claim a large majority of the 3,800 production workers among the 5,200 total employes.

They want the rate to be retroactive to Oct. 11. They point out that they have a 75-cent minimum in local automobile manufacturing plants.

The company has offered to increase the minimum to 55 cents after three months of employment and 60 cents after six months, asserting that it takes six months to train a beginner.

Agreement on Other Points

All other points in a proposed contract between the company and the union, both sides state, have been agreed on.

Vultee is producing military planes exclusively, basic trainers for the United States Army, Vanguard pursuit planes for foreign account and a new secret type combat plane.

Highways to and from the plant were choked today with automobiles of idle workers, many bearing out-of-State license plates. Two cars, one with an Ohio license plate, were rigged up with loud-speakers to address union messages. A field kitchen with soup kettles was set up for picketers.

Police reported no disorder, but disruption of traffic. Union agents questioned persons who approached

Continued on Page Twenty

$58,000,000 TUNNEL TO QUEENS OPENED; 3,000 AT CEREMONY

Officials Praise New Unit of City's Interborough Arteries—Mrs. Harvey Cuts Tape

DRIVERS QUICK TO USE IT

Long Line Waits at Manhattan End, but a 'First' Has to Be Drafted at the Other

The $58,000,000 Queens Midtown Tunnel under the East River was opened to the public at 1:20 P. M. yesterday, nearly an hour after the close of dedicatory exercises held under lowering skies in the presence of 3,000 guests of the New York City Tunnel Authority, assembled in the traffic plaza at the Queens end of the new tube.

It was 12:36 P. M. when Council President Newbold Morris, acting in the absence of Mayor La Guardia, formally accepted the new traffic artery for the city. The acceptance came at the end of a speaking program in which city and Federal officials took part. Afterward there was a motor parade of guests through the tunnel to Manhattan and return, followed by a motorcade along the new Midtown Highway in Queens to its intersection with the Connecting Highway between Queens and Brooklyn.

At the start of the trip along the Midtown Highway that traffic artery, reached by a ramp from the Queens portal of the new tunnel, was opened to public use by Borough President George U. Harvey after Mrs. Harvey had cut a ribbon stretched across the highway.

"First" Has to Be Hunted

Not until the motor parades were over was the new tunnel ready for public use, and even then it was necessary for a police motorcyclist to scurry out into the streets of Long Island City to find a "first car" to make the crossing to Manhattan.

Harry E. Sochovit, gasoline station operator, of 585 East Sixteenth Street, Brooklyn, was the first motorist to pay a toll for use of the tunnel. It was just 1:20 P. M. when he drove his tan coupé up to a toll booth, handed over his quarter, posed for photographers and sped on toward Manhattan.

At 1:30 P. M., with a crowd of 4,000 persons watching, John Topf, a chauffeur of 26-13 Jackson Avenue, Long Island City, entered the Manhattan end of the tunnel bound for Queens, where he paid his quarter on leaving the traffic plaza. There was a long line of cars waiting to enter the Manhattan portal of the tunnel, some having arrived as early as 9 A. M. The absence of a waiting line at the Queens portal was explained by the fact that the available space was pre-empted by guests' cars taking part in the opening ceremonies and the parades that followed.

Head of Authority Presides

Alfred B. Jones, chairman of the Tunnel Authority, presided at the dedicatory exercises and introduced a group of speakers that included Senator Robert F. Wagner, Mr. Morris, Borough President Stanley M. Isaacs of Manhattan, Borough President Harvey, Maurice E. Gilmore, Regional PWA Director, and George McAneny, president of the Regional Plan Association. Jesse H. Jones, Secretary of Commerce and chairman of the Reconstruction Finance Corporation, was unable to be present but sent a telegram. John J. Carmody, PWA Administrator, was also unable to attend and sent a telegram.

Deputy Mayor Rufus E. McGahen read a letter from Mayor La Guardia voicing his regret at not being able to be present. Regret at the Mayor's absence was also expressed by Chairman Jones, who added that

Continued on Page Nineteen

Helgoland, German Ship, Reported Caught, Sunk

Shipping circles received reports yesterday that the 2,927-ton German freighter Helgoland, which fled from Barranquilla, Colombia, Oct. 28, had been cornered and sunk in the Caribbean by British warships, according to The Associated Press.

The Hamburg-American line freighter, built in 1939, was reported to be carrying pilots of Scadta, German air line in South America, when she slipped out of port at night. She was reported to have put to sea to refuel a raider attacking South Atlantic shipping.

SPAIN IMPOSES GAG ON U. S. REPORTERS

Forbids Them to Send News, Charging We Refuse to Admit Spanish Writer

By T. J. HAMILTON
Special Cable to THE NEW YORK TIMES.

MADRID, Nov. 15—The Spanish Government today forbade all representatives of American newspapers and news agencies in Spain to send out any dispatches after a time to be fixed within a day or two.

It was stated that the action was taken in reprisal for the alleged refusal of the United States to grant a visa to the recently appointed Washington correspondent of E. F. E. [the foreign service of the official Spanish news agency, E. F. E.-Cifra.] Unofficially, however, it was understood that the United States had not refused a visa to the E. F. E. correspondent, but that it was merely a matter of Spain's expecting the wheels of the State Department in Washington to grind faster than usual.

The following communiqué was issued by the Press Bureau tonight:

"It is authorized to file stories to America declaring that, since the American authorities have not permitted the entry into the United States of a representative of the E. F. E. agency and the setting up of an office of said agency in said country, The United Press and The Associated Press agencies in this country will be abandoned."

Later an official spokesman said this order would apply also to The International News Service and to the Madrid correspondents of The Chicago Tribune and THE NEW YORK TIMES.

A spokesman for the director general of the Press Bureau at first stated that American correspondents would not be permitted to file dispatches after midnight Sunday night. Later, however, the correspondents were informed that they would be notified either directly by the Press Bureau or through their embassy when the prohibition would take effect.

Weddell to Ask Information
Special to THE NEW YORK TIMES.

WASHINGTON, Nov. 15—The State Department today cabled Alexander W. Weddell, the United States Ambassador in Madrid, requesting information concerning the suspension by the Spanish Government of American newspaper and news agency correspondents and their services.

The department denied, as alleged in Madrid, that it had refused visas for correspondents of E. F. E., the official Spanish news agency, or

Continued on Page Five

Hoover Urges Aid to 5 Little Democracies; Says Famine and Disease Peril War Victims

Special to THE NEW YORK TIMES.

POUGHKEEPSIE, N. Y., Nov. 15—Former President Herbert Hoover in an address at Vassar College tonight renewed his plea for international assistance to the conquered nations of Europe, with a warning that famine and its accompanying epidemic diseases would reach an acute stage there this Winter or next Spring.

Mr. Hoover named specifically "the five little democracies" of Finland, Norway, Holland, Belgium and Central Poland, and asserted that the United States had a moral responsibility toward these nations, all of which, he said, "sacrificed and fought against overwhelming odds to maintain freedom and their democratic ideals."

"I am not making any proposals as to the French, although they are indeed suffering, because of the present obscurity of their food and political situation," he added.

Reiterating his proposal for a lifting of the British blockade to permit the passage of shiploads of food to be distributed under German guarantees and neutral control, Mr. Hoover emphasized the increased urgency of the situation since he first advanced the program three months ago.

"The people of Brussels are already on a ration of seven ounces of bread a day," he pointed out. "Typhus already rages in Warsaw. Holland is killing its animals for lack of feed."

Though lives and "infinite suffering" still could be saved, Mr. Hoover asserted, no time should be lost in the effort, for three months would be required to set up the necessary organization.

At the same time he discussed arguments that Germany would ben-

Continued on Page Seven

R.A.F. STRIKES AGAIN

Returns to Berlin After Losing Ten Planes in Raids on Reich

HAMBURG ALSO BATTERED

Bremen Attacked and 26 Nazi Airports From Norway to Brittany Bombed

By JAMES MacDONALD
Special Cable to THE NEW YORK TIMES.

LONDON, Saturday, Nov. 16—The heavy Royal Air Force bombers that battered Berlin railroad stations and freight yards for several hours yesterday morning and Thursday night carried out only one phase of widespread raids that had for their objectives twenty-six Nazi air bases and harbors and shipping all the way from Stavanger, Norway, to Lorient, Brittany, according to an Air Ministry announcement.

[Another British raid on Berlin last night was announced by the German radio in a broadcast heard here by the National Broadcasting Company. Six raiders were reported downed as soon as they crossed the Channel, and only twelve penetrated to the Berlin area, three of them being shot down in the city and three in the outskirts, according to The United Press, however, Berlin enjoyed a raidless night.]

London officials would not disclose the size of their fleet of night raiders, but it was believed to have been large because the attack embraced so many points and was declared to have entailed heavy bombardments, particularly of Berlin.

The Air Ministry announced the loss of ten of the British raiders, which is a greater number than usual.

Cross-Channel Gun Duel

Meanwhile freakish weather entered the war picture again. After a spell of brilliant sunshine over the Strait of Dover in the forenoon, when British and German long-range gunners had a hot argument, a southwesterly gale, which is unwelcome news for German strategists who may still be clinging to plans for the invasion of Great Britain, sprang up last night. Heavy rain clouds scudded across the sky, while the wind churned up a rough sea.

The cross-Channel shelling began just before daybreak yesterday and lasted several hours. Big shells screeched angrily in both directions, but as far as the English side of the strait is concerned there was comparatively small damage and no casualties whatever, it was said, despite the fierceness of the barrage.

The British raiders who flew to Berlin during the night had the advantage of a full moon and perfect weather, according to the Air Ministry. The first wave is said to have reached the Nazi capital two hours after dark and was followed by other waves for several hours thereafter.

The reason for bombing Berlin's various large railroad terminals and extensive freight yards, it was pointed out here, is that Berlin is the most important focal point for the railroads of Central Europe. Whatever damage is done to them would affect not only Germany herself but also her transport to the adjacent countries she has conquered.

Power Plants Bombed

Targets in Berlin included the Stettiner Station, the Schlesischer Station and Anhalter Station, the Tempelhof railroad yards and freight yards between the Potsdamer and Anhalter Stations. Other Berlin objectives were the power station in the Charlottenburg district and the Wilmersdorf power station in the heart of the German capital.

One pilot who took part in the Berlin raid said he witnessed a terrific explosion which momentarily drowned out the city's guns. He told of seeing a big building go "sky high" and several fires breaking out all around.

Hamburg suffered a British bombardment that was said to have lasted nearly an hour. The principal goal there was the Rhenania Ossag Mineral Oil Works where fifteen bomb bursts were seen, according to R. A. F. reports.

Shipping and docks at Ostend, Havre and Lorient also were raided during the early hours of the morning as well as late Thursday night, it was added. Heavy attacks

Continued on Page Two

The International Situation

The compact industrial city of Coventry, lying northwest of London in the geographical heart of England, was devastated Thursday night by an estimated 500 German planes raining incendiary and demolition bombs on it for ten and a half hours. Casualties totaled at least 1,000 persons, many of them firemen, policemen and air-raid precaution workers who went about their jobs regardless of the storm of death from the skies. The bombing was done from a high altitude, the British said, the German planes dumping their loads indiscriminately over the city, and vital manufacturing plants suffered less than churches, schools, hospitals and the homes of the workers. [Page 1, Column 8.]

The Nazis boasted that it was the "greatest attack in the history of aerial warfare" and said it had crippled British aviation production. They said the raid was in retaliation for the British attack on Munich Nov. 8 while the Brown Shirts were celebrating the seventeenth anniversary of their beer hall revolt. [Page 3, Column 2.]

They were back over England again last night, subjecting some London areas to what was described as one of the heaviest raids of the war. Many fires were started. During the day the Royal Air Force took a measure of revenge for Coventry by shooting down eighteen planes with the loss of only one of their own, the Air Ministry said. [Page 1, Column 6.]

While the Germans were over Coventry, the Royal Air Force was giving Berlin what apparently was its heaviest attack, the Air Ministry reporting that the German capital's railway yards and stations—nerve center of the transportation system of Central Europe—were heavily and effectively attacked under perfect weather conditions. Power stations also were reported hit. Berlin said the raid was the heaviest of the war. Another attack was in progress last night. Hamburg, the German base at Stavanger, in Norway, and twenty-six Nazi airdromes were other objectives of the British pilots. [Page 1, Column 5.]

The Greeks continued to drive the Italian invaders before them all along the front, reports from Athens said, shock troops advancing to within a few miles of Koritza, and the defenders of Yanina, in the southwest, driving toward the border to threaten the Albanian port of Porto Edda. The Italians were reported in disorderly retreat in the latter area, where they previously had made their greatest advance into Greece. The land actions were supported by British and Greek bomber and fighter planes, harassing the Italian rear and attacking the ports through which reinforcements and supplies from Italy must come. [Page 1, Column 7.]

The Yugoslav border city of Bitolj was bombed again by three unidentified planes, the fourth time its neutrality had been invaded since the start of the Grecian campaign. The first bombing was Nov. 5, when three planes, unofficially identified as Italian, dropped bombs on the city, killing nineteen persons and wounding many others. Belgrade already was tense with reports of German troop concentrations along the Yugoslav-Rumanian border and the continued evacuation of German nationals from Greece. [Page 4, Column 5.]

That some new Axis military move was imminent seemed apparent with the announcement in Berlin and Rome of a conference at Innsbruck, Austria, of General Field Marshal Wilhelm Keitel, Chief of the German High Command, and Marshal Pietro Badoglio of Italy. The official Germany agency said it was a natural development, military action always following political action. The probability that what they discussed was a German-Italian attack on Gibraltar was seen in some quarters, who read that significance into the trip to Paris and Berlin of Spain's Foreign Minister, Ramon Serrano Suner. [Page 4, Col. 1.]

A Spanish ban on United States reporters was interpreted by some observers as another indication of impending military action against Gibraltar. The Spanish explanation of the order was that it was in retaliation for the refusal of Washington to grant a visa to a correspondent for the official Spanish news agency, EFE, or to allow it to operate in this country. State Department officials in Washington denied that any such refusal had been made. Not even an application has been made, they said. [Page 1, Column 4.]

The United States, however, did follow Britain in protesting to Spain against seizure of the former international zone of Tangier in Africa, which is on the Atlantic side of the Strait of Gibraltar and control of which would aid any attack on that British fortress. [Page 5, Column 1.]

BOMBING OF LONDON HEAVIEST IN MONTH

200 Planes Raid Capital, 80 in One Formation—Damage Is Reported Widespread

By The United Press.

LONDON, Saturday, Nov. 16—More than 200 German raiders, taking advantage of a full moon, a cloudless sky and a slight haze, last night and early today gave London its heaviest and most protracted pounding in a month.

Large formations of as many as eighty Nazi planes swept the capital and maintained a Blitzkreig intensity for several hours after midnight and then dwindled to the customary parade of nuisance raiders until dawn. [The "all clear" sounded shortly before 7 A. M., according to The Associated Press.]

Two of the night raiders were reported to have been shot down.

Bombs damaged two hospitals. Incendiaries penetrated the dispensary of one hospital but were doused quickly by the staff before the flames reached medical supplies, some of an explosive nature. At the second hospital, two explosives landed on the grounds but did not cause any casualties.

Scores of Fires Started

LONDON, Saturday, Nov. 16 (AP)—German raiders during the night have started scores of fires, leveled apartment houses and buried civilians in the wreckage.

One whole block of apartments caved in, and the casualties were believed to be heavy. Sweating rescuers toiled in the ruins amid falling anti-aircraft shrapnel and bomb explosions. Firemen working their

Continued on Page Three

700 ITALIANS TAKEN AS GREEKS PUSH ON

Drive Is Aimed at Cutting Off Fascisti in South Albania—Koritza Again Bombed

By C. L. SULZBERGER
By Telephone to THE NEW YORK TIMES.

ATHENS, Greece, Nov. 15—Slashing its way further into Albania, the Greek Army completed its second day of full-fledged offensive action tonight by capturing 700 more Italian soldiers and forcing enemy units to retreat on at least two sectors.

Major encounters are obviously occurring, and once again the military communiqué refers to intensive infantry, artillery and aerial action. Three Italian planes were shot down and two Greek aircraft failed to return to their bases, it was said.

The Greek drive is aimed in two directions. The forces on the Epirus and the Pindus fronts are seeking to cut off Italian troops in Southern Albania. These units were heavily concentrated between Porto Edda and Konispolis when the war started. They launched the original attack, the impetus of which carried them considerably south of the Kalamas River.

Having cleaned up the Pindus sector and eliminated the remaining Italian outposts around Mount Smolika, the Greek Army is pushing down the Albanian side of Mount Grammos, north of Konitza, and fighting through Albania westward in the direction of Porto Edda.

This action is supported by another push from the region of Kalpaki and the march north by the units stationed near the Kalamas

Continued on Page Four

'REVENGE' BY NAZIS

Industrial City Bombed All Night in 'Reply' to R. A. F. Raid on Munich

CATHEDRAL IS DESTROYED

Homes and Shops Bear Brunt of Mass Assault—Military Damage Is Minimized

By RAYMOND DANIELL
Special Cable to THE NEW YORK TIMES.

LONDON, Nov. 15—Daybreak today unveiled scenes of devastation wrought in another night of widespread air raids, but there was nothing to match the bruised and battered face of Coventry, a little Midlands city that was the victim of one of the worst bombardments from the air since the Wright brothers presented wings to mankind.

There the Nazi bombers accomplished what they tried to do to this capital in the early days of the Battle of London, by using as big a force of sky marauders against that compact city of 250,000 as they used against London with its 8,000,000 inhabitants. The tons of bombs they dropped caused at least 1,000 casualties, wrecked countless homes and destroyed the lovely fourteenth-century St. Michael's Cathedral, one of the finest examples of perpendicular architecture left in these islands.

To accomplish the full purpose of the assault, which the Germans said was intended as revenge for the Royal Air Force bombing of Munich while Reichsfuehrer Hitler was speaking there last Friday, Nazi raiders made repeated feints against London to keep the defenders busy while the main body of attackers roared over Midlands industrial centers and concentrated the fury of their bombings on Coventry.

Debris Marks Cathedral Site

Visitors to Coventry today found a scene of devastation where the cathedral once stood. The blackened arches and window faces of fretted stone, for all their disfigurement, still retained traces of their stately grace. But blocks of masonry, heavy pieces of church furniture and plaques commemorating the lives of famous men merged in the common dust heaped up between the teetering walls.

Elsewhere in the city other buildings had been severely damaged. Throughout the day business men and shopkeepers salvaged what remained of their possessions by grubbing among shattered timber and piled-up bricks. Some shopkeepers were doing business on the sidewalks. On roads leading away from the city could be seen a pitiful parade of refugees who were trying to reach billets in the countryside before black-out time.

Coventry lies in the very heart of England, almost equidistant, about ninety miles, from four great ports—Liverpool, Bristol, London and Hull. An industrial center specializing in the manufacture of motor cars and cycles, Coventry is an important cog in Britain's war machine.

But it was not Coventry's factories that took the worst punishment from the raiders, but human life, little homes, churches and hospitals—as it has been everywhere in Britain since the Nazis, forced to fly high above barrage balloons and anti-aircraft guns, began their concentrated bombings.

Scenes of Damage Everywhere

It was impossible today to stroll through many of the streets of the ancient city, where Lady Godiva is said to have made her famous ride, without seeing tragic evidence of the hell loosed from the skies through the night, when bombs crashed at intervals of one or two minutes.

Coventry is now like a city that has been wrecked by an earthquake and swept by fire. Its people looked dazed today as they poked about the ruins of their homes and surveyed the wreckage of the downtown business section, and they laughed bitterly at the chalked mottoes of defiance to Hitler scrawled on pavements and buildings.

The local authorities lost no time in starting to repair the damage and in caring for the injured, homeless and hungry. Herbert Morrison, the Minister of Home Security, was on the scene directing relief operations. Orders were issued for the release of stores of emergency food if necessary, and shopkeepers and wholesalers who normally compete against one another cooperated to assure the distribution of essential supplies.

There was much to be done. Tele-

Continued on Page Three

"All the News That's Fit to Print."

The New York Times.

Copyright, 1940, by The New York Times Company.

LATE CITY EDITION

Increasing cloudiness, somewhat warmer today. Tomorrow rain at night, temperature unchanged

Temperatures Yesterday—Max., 49; Min., 35

VOL. XC...No. 30,251. Entered as Second-Class Matter, Postoffice, New York, N. Y. NEW YORK, WEDNESDAY, NOVEMBER 20, 1940. THREE CENTS NEW YORK CITY and Vicinity | FOUR CENTS Elsewhere Except in 7th and 8th Postal Zones.

BIRMINGHAM ATTACKED ALL NIGHT IN A RAID LIKE THAT ON COVENTRY; HUNGARY DUE TO JOIN AXIS TODAY

HOUSE BY 191 TO 148 BEATS MOVE TO END CONGRESS SESSION

44 Democrats Join With Solid Republican Line-Up to Upset Administration Leaders

ON JOB REST OF THE YEAR

Action on Walter-Logan Bill Up to Senate—Civil Service Measure Is Adopted

By HENRY N. DORRIS
Special to THE NEW YORK TIMES.

WASHINGTON, Nov. 19 — The House refused today to adjourn for the session, voting 191 to 148 to keep its machinery in readiness for any emergency that may confront the nation.

The outcome was a defeat for the Administration at the first convening of the whole Congress since the election, and was accomplished by a solidly voting Republican minority, to whose 144 votes were added forty-four votes from the Democratic side, two from the Progressives and one American-Laborite. Six voted present, making the total number present 345. Aside from three vacancies, eighty-seven members were absent.

The result surprised the Senate, which had been half-heartedly debating whether to bring up the controversial Walter-Logan Bill while awaiting House action on the adjournment resolution. The Senate now probably will proceed to a decision on that legislation.

Meanwhile both chambers adopted the conference report on the Ramspeck Civil Service Bill and sent that legislation to the White House.

Likely to Stay Rest of Year

The House action will serve to keep Congress in session probably for the rest of the year, since Speaker Sam Rayburn and Representative McCormack, the majority leader, said they would not offer another resolution of that kind "very soon." Each took the defeat smilingly. They said the decision means there probably will be day-to-day sessions until a new program is formulated, which may be a resumption of the three-day recesses which have been in order since three weeks before the election.

Mr. Rayburn said the House had no program, and indicated that the only business likely to be presented would be relatively minor bills.

President Roosevelt, when asked at his press conference whether it made any difference to him that the House had refused to adjourn, said that it did not. Later he was asked whether he had any further work for Congress to do, since it appeared it would be in session the rest of the year. Mr. Roosevelt replied that there were more Army and Navy promotions all the time. He indicated that he had no further defense legislative recommendations at this time.

Mr. McCormack said he knew of no legislation to present now.

"You don't expect me to bail them out, do you?" he asked when questioned as to whether some of the bills on the calendar might not be called in order to give the House members something to keep them busy.

Martin Hails the Result

Representative Joseph W. Martin Jr. of Massachusetts, the minority leader, who was one of the combination of "Martin, Barton and Fish" referred to by Mr. Roosevelt during his campaign, said that the House vote "reflected the real sentiment of the country in this crisis."

"It is that they wish Congress to remain in session, not so much as to what it does, but to be on hand if necessary," he said. "Mr. Roosevelt said in recent weeks that he could not go outside a twelve-hour traveling radius of Washington. If that is the proper course for the President, then it is the proper course for Congress."

Representative Martin indicated the House action would give the Senate an opportunity to consider the Walter-Logan bill, which would subject the rules and regulations of government agencies to judicial review, and to the Smith amendments modifying in several particulars the terms of the National Labor Relations Act.

He also said a start should be made immediately by the Ways and Means Committee on a study of new tax legislation to be considered next session.

"We have to have tax legislation," he said. "It seems to me to be good sense to start the study now, so we will have a program worked out early in the new session."

Mr. Martin said he would not insist on daily sessions of the House; only that Congress remain in a "stand-by status."

Republicans, jubilant over their victory, gibed at the Democrats, saying that it had been accom-

Continued on Page Twelve

Orders Justices to Warn Drivers on Guilty Pleas

By The United Press.

ALBANY, Nov. 19—The Court of Appeals ruled today that magistrates and peace justices must inform vehicle law violators that suspension or revocation of driving licenses may result from guilty pleas.

The court upheld Leonard Demartino in an order voiding revocation of Demartino's license. He contended a police justice told him that if he pleaded guilty the only penalty would be a small fine. After he paid the fine, the Motor Vehicle Bureau revoked his license for having more than three speeding convictions within eighteen months.

ROOSEVELT URGES A.F.L. TO SEEK PEACE

In Appeal Read by Green He Asserts 'Men of Honor' Can Settle Differences

The Roosevelt and Green messages are printed on Page 17.

By A. H. RASKIN
Special to THE NEW YORK TIMES.

NEW ORLEANS, Nov. 19—President Roosevelt appealed to the American Federation of Labor today to promote national unity and national defense by making "an unselfish, a far-sighted and a patriotic effort to bring about a just and honorable peace" within the ranks of labor.

"Peace may not be easy to achieve and the intricate problems involved may not be easy to solve," the President declared, "but when men of honor and good intentions sit down together they can work out a solution which will restore the much-needed harmony either by unity or by a sensible working arrangement."

Mr. Roosevelt sent a message to William Green, president of the federation, which was read at the group's convention. The delegates applauded at many points in the reading.

Mr. Green replied to the President that the federation was ready at any time to discuss plans for peace with the Congress of Industrial Organizations.

Despite their willingness to negotiate, A. F. L. leaders admitted tonight that the position enunciated by John L. Lewis, president of the C. I. O., in his address to the group's convention in Atlantic City today, precluded any real possibility of a general peace between the federation and the C. I. O.

Lewis a "Dictator," Says Green

Mr. Green told reporters that he regarded Mr. Lewis's talk as an invitation to the Amalgamated Clothing Workers and other right-wing C. I. O. unions to "get out" of the C. I. O. He said these unions would find "the door of the house of the American Federation of Labor open to receive them if they decided to come back home."

"Mr. Lewis has revealed himself as a real dictator," Mr. Green declared.

The continued influence of Mr. Lewis in the C. I. O. and the presence of Communists in positions of leadership in many of its unions were cited by federation officers as major obstacles to unity. They renewed their charge that Mr. Lewis had "vetoed" an agreement reached between A. F. L. and C. I. O. negotiators in 1937 and that he had broken off the conferences begun a year ago at the request of President Roosevelt.

The left-wing elements in the C. I. O. were depicted by the A. F. of L. leaders as "panicky" at the prospect of labor peace because they expected to be deprived of all authority if their organizations should enter the federation. The strength of these left-wingers would be thrown against the resumption of peace negotiations, the federation leaders said.

Mr. Roosevelt's plea for labor peace was accompanied by a warning that the interest of the nation demanded "intense and sustained cooperation" from all groups of citizens and that sacrifices might be required of every one.

Among the contributions labor could make to the preparedness program he listed the avoidance of strikes in defense industries, assistance in the planning of programs for labor supply and industrial efficiency, promotion of sound employer-employe relations and preservation of social gains.

He expressed certainty that labor leaders, with "the interest of the nation at heart and the advantage of their followers in mind," could find a road to peace in their own ranks.

Mr. Green, replying to Mr. Roosevelt, said that the negotiating committee established by the A. F. L. a year ago was prepared to meet with a C. I. O. committee at any time to seek a settlement of the differences which have split labor into two camps since 1935.

The Federation committee consists of these four vice-presidents: Harry C. Bates of the Bricklayers Union, Matthew Woll of the photo-

Continued on Page Seventeen

LEWIS SHUTS DOOR TO UNITY OF LABOR; MURRAY WON'T RUN

C. I. O. Head Suggests Hillman Union, Advocate of Peace, Join the A. F. L.

HEAPS SCORN ON CRITICS

His Choice for New President Declines—Inaction on Red Issue Believed Reason

By LOUIS STARK
Special to THE NEW YORK TIMES.

ATLANTIC CITY, N. J., Nov. 19—John L. Lewis slammed the door to labor unity for the present in an impassioned address today before the convention of the Congress of Industrial Organizations, virtually demanding that the Amalgamated Clothing Workers of America, chief exponent of peace "explorations," clear out and follow David Dubinsky's International Ladies Garment Workers Union and Max Zaritsky's Hat, Cap and Millinery Workers Union back into the American Federation of Labor.

The C. I. O. president poured ridicule, irony and scorn on the heads of Sidney Hillman, president of the men's clothing workers union and labor member of the National Defense Advisory Commission; William Green and other A. F. of L. figures. The audience, with the exception of the Amalgamated union delegates and their allies, responded by applauding and cheering over and over again and laughing uproariously when the bellowing voice of the C. I. O.'s dominating figure made his opponents the butts of his jokes and his sarcasm.

Heated Debate on Peace Issue

The Lewis speech was the climax of an afternoon of heated debate on a committee report that proposed to continue the C. I. O. peace negotiating committee but that did not include the Amalgamated delegates' proposal seeking immediate resumption of the peace parleys with the A. F. of L. The report was adopted unanimously.

Delegates who had read reports of a peace message sent to the A. F. of L. convention by President Roosevelt expected to have a similar message read to their gathering. Mr. Lewis, according to a press aide, said he had not received a labor peace message from the White House by this afternoon.

Philip Murray, vice president of the C. I. O., at this morning's session declined to stand for the candidacy for the presidency of the organization, and immediately evoked a flood of speculation, as it had been expected by many delegates that he would accede to the importunities of Mr. Lewis and take the retiring president's place.

The Scottish-born chairman of the Steel Workers Organizing Committee, however, declined after considering Mr. Lewis's suggestion for nine days. He did not give the reasons for his decision, but it was understood by some of his associates that he felt impelled to withdraw when he saw no possibility of the convention taking some action on the communism issue. The Amalgamated Clothing Workers have proposed a resolution barring from office or employment in the C. I. O. any persons subscribing to the Communist, Nazi or Fascist philosophy. Mr. Lewis declared emphatically yesterday that nobody holding these philosophies had anything to do with the C. I. O.

Mr. Murray denied rumors of a rift between him and Mr. Lewis. Pointing to his heart he exclaimed with emotion, "The hot spot has been here for a few days. I owe it to you and to the nation and to my colleagues to give to you what is beating within my bosom. I lay myself naked that you may have the truth. I disdain hypocrisy. I

Continued on Page Sixteen

Canada Plans Navy School As Aid in Joint Defense

By Telephone to THE NEW YORK TIMES.

OTTAWA, Nov. 19—The establishment of a Canadian naval college and the building of destroyers and perhaps cruisers in Canadian naval yards in the near future were announced today by Navy Minister Angus L. Macdonald as measures already decided and necessary in the joint defense scheme with the United States of the North American Continent.

As her contribution to the war, he said, Canada had raised her naval strength to a grand total of 13,273 men of all ranks on active service, or nearly eight times the pre-war number.

Since the war began, he said, 3,500 ships, carrying 21,000,000 tons of cargo, have sailed from Canadian ports. No single troopship had been lost and, despite enemy claims, the convoy system of merchant shipping was working so well that within a single week last month 775 convoyed ships reached British ports and only five convoyed ships were lost.

GREEK PLEA FOR AID IS STUDIED BY U. S.

Appeal to Rush Planes Put Up to Our Defense Priority Chiefs and Britain

Special to THE NEW YORK TIMES.

WASHINGTON, Nov. 19—The Defense Commission and other government agencies entrusted with problems of munitions and war materials have under consideration a request from the Greek Government for aviation and other military supplies, it was announced today by Sumner Welles, Acting Secretary of State.

The announcement was made only after the Press Minister in Athens, warning that the "free countries" should not be misled by Greek successes in the field, appealed publicly to Great Britain and the United States to send the greatest possible number of planes to Greece.

His warning synchronized with advices received through official channels here that reports of Greek successes against Italy, while true in the main, had been exaggerated. It is understood that Greece especially desires fighter planes with which to meet Italian bombers, and bombers with which to attack.

Washington Studies Plea

The appeal for an opportunity to purchase war materials was made several days ago. It was made to the United States through the American Legation in Athens and Simon P. Diamontopoulos, the Greek Minister here, in conversations with Mr. Welles. He reiterated the plea in another conversation with the Acting Secretary of State late yesterday.

Mr. Welles said at his press conference today that he had told the Minister that the request would receive the most sympathetic consideration of this government, but the question would have to be determined by other branches of the government, to whom it was being referred for decision. President Roosevelt had no comment to make on it at his press conference.

From what Mr. Welles said, the inference was drawn that no decision had been reached. It was said by other officials that the answer would turn upon whether priorities could be so arranged that Greek

Continued on Page Four

Vatican Says Nazism Is Foe of Christianity; Lists Persecutions in Reich to Support Charge

The Vatican radio yesterday denied an assertion by the Spanish newspaper Alcazar that national socialism was not contradictory to Christian ideals, according to the British Broadcasting Corporation's report, recorded here by the Columbia Broadcasting System.

The British broadcast was quoted as follows:

"A remarkable broadcast by Vatican City radio has summarized the Catholic Church's attitude toward Nazi Germany in no uncertain terms. The broadcast was in reply to an assertion published by the Spanish newspaper Alcazar that German Nazi socialism was not contradictory to Christian ideals.

"It was only necessary to scrutinize nazism over the past eight years, the broadcast said, to see that the assertion was false. 'Nazi literature,' says the Vatican, 'has attacked Christianity and the Catholic Church as a whole, as well as its personnel and its institution, and has even attacked the most essential dogmas of the church. The attack has been carried out with the greatest possible efficiency.'

"As to the educational situation, continues the Vatican broadcast, 'if national socialism is a Christian movement, as the Alcazar alleges it to be, how can it be explained that in 1933 almost the entire Catholic youth was educated in Catholic schools, whereas now that magnificent school organization is practically non-existent.

"'In view of these two facts how can any one assert, as the newspaper does, that both within and without the Reich national socialism has shown its respect for religion?'

"The Vatican City radio spoke of the closing down of monasteries in Austria and the deportation of

Continued on Page Three

PACT READY TO SIGN

Vienna Meeting Today to Bring Budapest In Seen as a Formality

COALITION IS ANTI-BRITISH

Spain and Russia Believed to Acquiesce in 'New Order' for Continental Europe

Wireless to THE NEW YORK TIMES.

VIENNA, Nov. 19—Traveling by train from Salzburg, Foreign Ministers Joachim von Ribbentrop of Germany and Count Ciano of Italy arrived at 6 P. M. for their third "Belvedere conference." They were welcomed by Baldur von Schirach, Reich Governor and Nazi Gauleiter for Vienna.

Here, together with the Hungarian Foreign Minister, Count Stephen Csaky, they are scheduled to arrange tomorrow for the ceremonious incorporation of Hungary in "the new order" now being established in the Old World by Nazi Germany and Fascist Italy, and possibly also the cooperation of Hungary formally with the Far Eastern partner of Berlin-Rome-Tokyo pact.

Agreement Already Reached

Full agreement between Berlin, Budapest and Rome as to Hungary's role in "the new order" already has been settled through normal diplomatic channels. Tomorrow's conference is expected to be devoted, therefore, to consideration of final details, drafting the treaty that will record the agreement in the language of diplomacy and signing the treaty.

It is assumed the treaty will be in the form of a three-power pact, the first of a series between the Axis powers and their smaller neighbors of Southeastern Europe. It is further assumed in diplomatic and political quarters in Vienna that the basis of these pacts will be a military guarantee by the Axis powers of each small nation's continued existence, in return for which the guaranteed States will pledge their loyal cooperation with the Axis in foreign affairs, as well as consolidation of the new social and political order in Continental Europe west of Russia.

Some observers expect that as a result of tomorrow's conference a close bond will be formally established between Europe's smaller States and Japan. The majority opinion, however, is that such is not the case, although the spirit of the three-power pact of Berlin, Rome and Tokyo undoubtedly will gradually be extended in Axis treaties with all other European States.

Each State's Role Fixed

Each State's position in the new order, as foreseen by Berlin and Rome, will depend on several factors. Among these are not only the speed and willingness with which each government accepts "the new order," but also the ability of each State to carry a proportionate part of the load in the task of establishing and maintaining "the new order."

This was revealed recently in an editorial in the Vienna newspaper Neuer Wiener Tagblatt by Dr. Rudolf Fischer, one of the most authoritative writers in Greater Germany on international affairs. That editorial is generally interpreted as a sort of introduction to tomorrow's conference, as the Tagblatt has a special position and a mission with regard to Southeastern Europe that is unique among Germany's dailies and one of Dr. Fischer's nicknames is "Hitler's schoolmaster for the Balkans."

In an editorial entitled "Political Blockade," Dr. Fischer wrote:

"In the great political movement of the Continent Great Britain's exclusion already is complete. There is not one State whose leadership wishes to exclude or even isolate itself from the efforts to establish peace now and at the same time to prepare means to defend it in the future.

"The expulsion of Great Britain from the Continent is not only the building material available for the new structure. Even more important is realization of the facts for which the war's progress has paved the way in Europe.

"In the first place the attitude toward the functions and possibilities of the medium and smaller States has altered. Much that yesterday appeared obvious in the maintenance cost of these States will tomorrow be viewed as a purposeless luxury.

"German diplomacy's primary ef-

Continued on Page Six

The International Situation

Nazi raiders last night and early this morning dropped thousands of bombs on Birmingham in a systematic fury of destruction, reported in Berlin to be even more complete than the wrecking of Coventry last week. Raids were also made on other Midlands industrial centers, including another one on Coventry. London confirmed the severity of the attack on several Midlands cities and said casualties were expected to be heavy. The capital was also raided. [Page 1, Column 8.]

British planes in turn bombed the 150 buildings of the Leuna synthetic oil plant for three hours Monday night, severely damaging that nerve center of German industry, the Air Ministry reported. The Europa, pride of the German merchant marine, was squarely hit by a bomb at her Bremen dock; production at the Fokker airplane plant in Amsterdam was halted by a hit on the power plant and the Union chemical factory at Stettin was wrecked, the Air Ministry said. Repeated British bombing has cut the Krupp armament output in Essen to half, according to reports from Germany to the Air Ministry. [Page 1, Column 7.]

In the Greek-Italian hostilities Koritza was still besieged by the Greeks with neither side gaining conclusive advantage. The Italians were said to have captured British troops brought from Egypt. The Athens radio reported the taking of Herseg, severing a main supply line south of Koritza, although Rome merely acknowledged loss of a town in that area. In the south the Greeks were said to have forced an Italian retreat at the Kalamas River. [Page 1, Column 6.]

The Greek Government has appealed to this country for aviation and military supplies and Sumner Welles, Acting Secretary of State, declared the appeal would receive sympathetic consideration. Final decision is said to depend on Great Britain's willingness to relinquish prior orders. [Page 1, Column 4.]

The Axis diplomatic offensive was taking the form of a drive to coalesce all European States except Greece into a united front against Britain. Foreign Ministers Ciano of Italy and von Ribbentrop of Germany arrived in Vienna for their conference today with Hungarian Foreign Minister Csaky and Premier Teleki at which Hungary's incorporation into the "new order" is expected to be completed. Unconfirmed Berlin reports told of a meeting of Belgian King Leopold and Reichsfuehrer Hitler. [Page 1, Column 5.]

Rome observers expected not only Hungarian adherence to the tripartite Axis but also Rumanian adherence after the visit of General Antonescu of Rumania to Berlin Friday. Rumania's decision was made last week after talks by him with Premier Mussolini, Rome reported. Spain is cooperating with the Axis, but is not expected to move on the military front at this time because of vulnerability to British blockade, according to Italian sources. [Page 6, Column 2.]

The Vatican City radio attacked Nazism as contradictory to Christian ideals in a summary of the Catholic Church's position. [Page 1, Column 3.]

Premier Eamon de Valera declared in an interview that Eire had determined to remain neutral and would not surrender ports for British use, which, he said, would "involve us in war and all its consequences." [Page 2, Column 2.]

GREEK GAINS WIDEN IN ALBANIAN DRIVE

Two Towns Reported Taken—Italians Fight Furiously to Hold Koritza Base

By C. L. SULZBERGER
Wireless to THE NEW YORK TIMES.

ATHENS, Greece, Nov. 19—Again relying chiefly on their courage and upon advances covered by nightfall, culminating in swift bayonet attacks, Greek Evzone troops won their breach in the Italian lines on the central front and took the village of Herseg on the Argyrokastron-Koritza road, it was reported here today.

It is also reported that Leskovik has been taken and that part of the Italian counter-attacks have been beaten back, and tonight's communiqué says there have been successful new offensives on the Morova Mountain ranges. Eleven Fascist planes were downed in front-line fighting and no Greek planes were lost."

This, in brief, describes the results of another hard day's fighting. The battle for Koritza continues, and it is understood that the Greek Army has improved its attacking positions both east and southwest of that strategically important town, inching along the heights without risking a descent to the plains except for reconnaissance by engineering units.

Wide Advance Reported

It would seem that Mount Ivan, with its strong artillery positions, is for the moment being relatively ignored—despite previous intimations that it had been taken—and that the idea is to render this height untenable by advances in other regions. Progress continues along the Koritza-Pogradec road, which links with the ancient Roman Via Aegnatia. The advance by way of Herseg toward Moschopol and Berat seems to be moving with greatest speed. For the first time in three days the activity of Italian aviation seems to be reduced.

The Athens radio reports that a "general advance" has been under way all day, but its extent is not delineated. The military situation is described as "very favorable." It is said that there have been new successes around Koritza and that the only road along which retreat is possible is under heavy Greek artillery fire.

The radio mentions foreign reports that fleeing Italians crossing the Yugoslav frontier surrendered quantities of arms, including 1,600

Continued on Page Four

3-HOUR R. A. F. RAID BLASTS OIL PLANT

British Claim Hit on the Liner Europa at Dock—Say Krupp Output Has Been Halved

By JAMES MacDONALD
Special Cable to THE NEW YORK TIMES.

LONDON, Nov. 19—A heavy Royal Air Force bombing attack was made last night on the important synthetic oil factory at Leuna, Air Ministry officials said today.

They also described damage done recently by British attacking planes to the Krupp works and other German targets, including the 49,746-ton transatlantic liner Europa, which was reported hit amidships while docked at Bremerhaven.

Leuna in Central Germany, not far from Leipzig, was the only target singled out by the R. A. F. last night. It is one of the most sensitive nerve centers of Germany's industrial and military networks. The oil plant there produces 400,000 tons annually.

German long-range guns along Cap Gris Nez on the German-occupied French coast sprang to life this forenoon. This habit of revealing anger whenever the R. A. F. does an unusual amount of damage is now an old story to the British.

The German guns on the other side of the Channel fired across the misty Strait of Dover for nearly an hour, beginning shortly before noon. Two salvos were followed by a succession of single shots. Neither casualties nor damage was reported.

Light showers drizzled over the Strait of Dover throughout the day and a cutting wind came out of the northwest. The sea was calm but the mist limited visibility to mid-channel.

The R. A. F. delivered a three-hour attack, lasting until just before midnight, on the Leuna synthetic oil plant, which consists of about 150 manufacturing buildings that make not only synthetic gasoline but also chemical fertilizer and other by-products. Its many pipe lines are highly vulnerable and if one bomb hit an essential part of the factory such as a gas or hydrogenation plant it would disorganize the whole concern for a considerable time.

On the raid last night waves of British bombers found increasingly bad weather as they flew over Germany but they managed to find the Leuna target with its long rows of high chimneys.

The first arrival made a glide bombing attack and the pilot re-

Continued on Page Two

MIDLAND CITY FIRED

Nazi Bombers Fly in Waves to Hammer at Industrial Center

HEAVY DAMAGE IS FEARED

British Defenses Said to Be Helpless Against Technique of Night Mass Assault

By PERCIVAL KNAUTH
Wireless to THE NEW YORK TIMES.

BERLIN, Wednesday, Nov. 20—German bombers, taking off from bases in France, Belgium and the Netherlands, launched an all-night attack on Birmingham last night and this morning, which is believed here to have ravaged that city even more fiercely than Coventry was damaged a few nights ago, it is reported in Berlin. The attack was carried out by massed formations of bombers, it is stated; they dropped thousands of bombs on armament factories and public utility works throughout the city.

[Britain reported an exceptionally severe attack on a West Midlands city, which was not named. Early this morning the authorities in London stated that the heavy property damage done had been chiefly to non-military objectives, The United Press reported.]

British anti-aircraft defenses were reported to be helpless against a steady stream of German planes that attacked in waves from different points at varying heights. The planes, it was announced, were able clearly to see their targets in the light of numberless fires blazing throughout the city.

Weather Proves Favorable

The attack was started just after dark, it is stated, when clearing skies gave promise of favorable weather throughout the night. Flying into England on a wide front, the German planes converged on their objective, the reports here state, attacking in mass, while behind them new formations followed.

The first wave dropped numerous incendiary bombs, it is said, which started more than twenty huge fires. From then on the city was brilliantly illuminated so that the following formations were easily able to spot their burning target and drop their bombs in full flight.

At 4 o'clock this morning the attack was declared to be still in progress. Its destructive effect was held in German quarters to be greater than that of the raid on Coventry last week. No estimate was made of the number of planes involved, but the operation was called a "large scale attack," which is a superlative in German military phraseology.

Mass Attack Reported

Waves of German bombers are reported to have attacked "concentrically in mass and stepped at various altitudes." The weather was reported to have cleared up entirely as the night wore on so that "all the squadrons reached their objective."

The first reports mentioned only "a city in central England" and were far more cautious in their estimates of damage inflicted.

The phrase, "to Coventrize," meaning to wipe a town from the face of the earth, as was Coventry, was used to describe the objective of the raid. That objective, German quarters indicate, has now been attained.

Other points in England, among them London, were likewise reported to have been attacked in the course of the night. Raids on the capital, as well as on objectives in the southern counties, were stated to have been "successful."

Attack on Midlands

By RAYMOND DANIELL
Special Cable to THE NEW YORK TIMES.

LONDON, Wednesday, Nov. 20—Waves of Nazi bombers crossed the east coast last night in the face of heavy bombardment. They swarmed like bees over three Midland cities. Over one city in that section the planes arrived at the rate of one each minute.

Liverpool had three raids and reports of Nazi air activity have been received from towns in the northwest and southeast of England, northeast of Scotland, Wales, northeast of England and East Anglia.

After one vicious cut at London, the German raiders last night and this morning switched their most powerful assault against the Midland towns.

One of these was subjected to a methodical blasting, only less se-

Continued on Page Two

"All the News That's Fit to Print."

The New York Times.

LATE CITY EDITION
Fair today, little change in temperature. Tomorrow cloudy, followed by rain.
Temperatures Yesterday—Max., 46; Min., 39

Copyright, 1941, by The New York Times Company.

VOL. XC..No. 30,293. Entered as Second-Class Matter, Postoffice, New York, N. Y. NEW YORK, WEDNESDAY, JANUARY 1, 1941. THREE CENTS NEW YORK CITY and Vicinity | FOUR CENTS Elsewhere Except in 7th and 8th Postal Zones.

HITLER SEES VICTORY IN 1941, DISAVOWS WORLD CONQUEST; 2 ITALIAN TRANSPORTS SUNK

NEW YEAR REVELRY DOWNS WAR GLOOM; TIMES SQ. JAMMED

Pleasure-Bent Crowds Swarm Into Night Clubs, Trying to Forget Blackouts Abroad

1,489 POLICEMEN ON DUTY

Hotels Report Reservations 50 Per Cent Above Last Year —Champagne Is Scarce

The thousands of bulbs and miles of neon lights in Times Square glittered and blinked down last night on one of the largest and most pleasure-bent crowds that ever greeted a new year.

While the surging merrymakers in midtown jammed to a full stop at the breathless moment before midnight, millions of others, at hotels, restaurants and private homes throughout the city, were celebrating.

And there was the note of solemnity, too, in the glowing Watch Night services in the city's churches. It was suggested as well before countless firesides—or their city equivalents—as fathers, mothers and children ushered in 1941 according to their particular wont.

For everywhere—even in the most hectic whirlpools of the downtown throng—there hovered the realization that London, Rome, Berlin were blacked out; that smoke still rose from the ruins of British buildings; that there were more dark days ahead for countless human beings in other countries, even if this one was fortunate enough to continue at peace.

Escape Motif Evident

The escape motif clearly keyed the Times Square demonstration to its high pitch of jubilation. Soldiers and sailors dotted the mob; young men who may be soldiers or sailors before next year shouldered along with them. When, at 12 sharp the 300-pound luminous ball atop the Times Building slid its 60-foot course and proclaimed the evening's climax, they joined with every one else in the building up a crescendo that brooked no competition.

At the temporary police headquarters at Forty-sixth Street, between Times and Duffy Squares, Chief Inspector Louis F. Costuma and Deputy Chief Inspector John J. De Martino were in hearty agreement that the throng was virtually unprecedented.

"It's bigger, better and more joyful than ever," the chief repeated. "I candidly say a million people and that's without exaggeration."

"Over a million," the Deputy Chief commented. "Over a million."

But Chief Inspector Costuma carefully qualified his estimate as taking in the area between Fifth and Eighth Avenues, Forty-second and Fifty-ninth Streets, and between 11 and 12 P. M. That took in every one in hotels, restaurants and theatres, and every horn-tooting pedestrian who manoeuvred himself to the heart of the congestion within that hour.

Efforts to establish the exact number of people between Forty-third and Forty-seventh at the moment Electrician Thomas Ward caused the big ball to fall for the twenty-seventh consecutive year were futile. But both police executives laughed at the meek suggestion that it might be restricted to from 30,000 to 50,000.

"Bigger Than Ever Before"

"It's bigger than ever," Chief Inspector Costuma insisted. "We never shut down so early."

He meant that never before had all vehicular traffic in the area been rerouted as early as 10:55, when the word went out last night that those who liked to swap "Happy New Years" on foot had captured Times Square completely.

Throughout the area 1,489 policemen were on duty. They had the assistance for the first time of a new mechanical device, tried experimentally on the four corners of Forty-fifth Street.

It was a pedestrian signal box, affixed either to regular lampposts or to shorter special posts. Glaringly illuminated, each box told persons facing east or west to "Stop" or "Walk" in harmony with the regular traffic lights.

An officer in the police information booth at Forty-third Street explained the boxes were experimental.

"They're good things if people pay attention to them," he said. Then, after a pause, "but they won't."

The boxes seemed hardly to get a fair test last night because there were so many patrolmen on duty at intersections that signals were hardly necessary.

Unquestionably, the relative mildness of the weather had a lot to do with the size and exuberance of the crowd. Last year, midnight found the thermometer at 22; mounted

Continued on Page Twenty-six

ASCAP Radio Contract Expires; Society Begins Check on Programs

Action to Protect Copyrights on at Midnight —$1,000,000 Insurance Will Indemnify BMI Advertiser or Station if Sued

The bulk of music written in the last half century was withdrawn last midnight from three-quarters of the nation's radio stations, including the three major networks. As the old year passed, the American Society of Composers, Authors and Publishers and the National Association of Broadcasters formally severed contractual relations and prepared to do battle with words and lawsuits over the method and amount of future payment for songs heard on the air.

Finally plunged into a controversy that both factions had long doubted would ever reach the point of affecting the musical fare for millions of Americans owning radio sets, leaders of the broadcasters and songwriters accused each other of blocking negotiations that might have prevented the drastic upheaval in the radio and music worlds. There was no sign of any immediate peace and the holiday eve was devoted to the perfection of last-minute strategies.

At midnight employes of ASCAP in thirty-one cities started machines to record musical programs played on the radio, the purpose being to catch any infringement of copyright. In addition to its vast American catalogue, ASCAP controls, through foreign affiliates, much of the contemporary music of Finland, France, the British Empire, Yugoslavia, Bulgaria, Portugal, Switzerland, Sweden, Spain, several South American countries and the nations overrun by Germany.

Broadcast Music, Inc., the music publishing house organized by the radio industry to compete with ASCAP, announced that it had taken out $1,000,000 insurance, a fourth of it written by Lloyd's, London, to indemnify any station or advertiser that is sued by ASCAP as a result of the use of the new BMI catalogue.

The Department of Justice moved to hasten action on its anti-trust suit against ASCAP, BMI and the National Broadcasting Company and the Columbia Broadcasting System, which might possibly force some break in the deadlock. According to The Associated Press, the government will ask the Federal court in Milwaukee to allow filing of an information detailing the basis of the action instead of the usual presentment to the grand jury. The procedure would obviate the need of calling witnesses, it was said.

The last direct effort between ASCAP and the broadcasters to negotiate a truce was made three weeks ago, it was disclosed last night, when John Paine, general manager of ASCAP, and Irving Berlin and Billy Rose conferred with Neville Miller, president of the National Association of Broadcasters. Mr. Paine said that ASCAP then agreed to negotiate on the terms proposed by the NAB. He

Continued on Page Twenty-eight

HOPSON CONVICTED IN $20,000,000 FRAUD

Found Guilty on 17 Counts, but Cleared of Conspiracy—Two Lawyers Acquitted

The methods followed by Howard C. Hopson in puffing up the Associated Gas and Electric system to the billion-dollar organization it was before its collapse in bankruptcy were branded fraudulent yesterday by a jury in Federal court, which found him guilty of having cheated the system of nearly $20,000,000. It became known that the jurors had agreed on Hopson's guilt of mail fraud almost immediately after receiving the case at noon Monday.

The announcement of the verdict was delayed, according to members of the jury, by debate over the charges against Charles M. Travis and Garrett A. Brownback, lawyers who spent virtually all of their time working on legal matters of the system. These two were acquitted.

The verdict against Hopson means that he may be sentenced to serve as much as five years in prison, and pay a fine of $1,000. Although there were seventeen counts in the indictment, every precedent calls for a sentence not greater than the maximum for one count.

Tons of Records Studied

The case was prepared and prosecuted by Hugh A. Fulton, as special assistant to Attorney General Robert H. Jackson. Assigned to the case last February, Mr. Fulton examined literally tons of records of the system and of Hopson's personal corporations. He was assisted by Rudolph Halley and Samuel H. Reis of the United States Attorney's staff, and Eugene O'Dunne of the Treasury Department.

Hopson and Brownback face another indictment alleging income tax frauds, but there was some question yesterday whether these charges would be pressed.

About 1 P. M. yesterday a deputy United States marshal tapped on the door of an anteroom, where Hopson was awaiting the jury's verdict. With him was the male nurse who had accompanied him to court and sat beside him during every day of the eight weeks of trial.

Short, bald and colorless, Hopson shuffled back into the high-ceilinged courtroom, for almost the last time—he will have to return at 1 P. M. on Jan. 9, for sentencing. He slumped into the red leather-covered chair inside the court railing. Judge Alfred C. Coxe took his seat at the bar, and the eleven men and one woman on the jury filed in. Hopson scratched his head, and crossed and uncrossed his legs.

Then came the ritual of announcing the verdict—the clerk's question whether a verdict had been reached, the foreman's reply that it had, the clerk's question what it was, and the announcement.

Hopson was found guilty on all seventeen counts of mail fraud, not guilty of conspiracy. The two lawyers were cleared of all the charges.

Hopson scratched his head again, let it loll back, and without opening his lips emitted the moaning sound that had come from him frequently during the trial.

Travis is a square-shouldered

Continued on Page Twenty-one

FORD ACCUSES NLRB, ASKS RULING ON 'BIAS'

Wants Court to Decide if He Must 'Sit Idly By' and Let Union Try to Seize Plant

Special to THE NEW YORK TIMES.

WASHINGTON, Dec. 31—The Ford Motor Company asked the Supreme Court today to decide whether an employer could legally discharge members of a union when that union was committed to a sit-down strike policy, "or whether he must sit idly by and permit the union to attempt the seizure of his plant by force and violence."

"The right of an employer to take precautions against violent seizure of his property or the use of sit-down or slow-down strikes inside the plant is of particular importance in the present national emergency," said the Ford company in a petition for review of a decision by the Sixth Circuit Court of Appeals.

Frederick H. Wood, who signed the brief, asked the high court to review the Circuit Court's findings upholding a National Labor Relations Board order growing out of the disturbances in 1937 in Detroit. The events dealt with in the board's ruling, Mr. Wood stated, took place between February and June, during and soon after the United Automobile Workers sitdown strikes at the General Motors and Chrysler plants in Michigan from December, 1936, to April, 1937.

Ford Feared Same Thing

These strikes and "repeated public threats of U. A. W. and C. I. O. leaders" during and after them "presaged a like violent and lawless seizure of petitioner's (Ford) plant," he added. He quoted Justice Murphy, then Governor of Michigan, as saying that the strikes were part of "the greatest industrial conflict of all time."

According to Mr. Wood, the strikes and threats "demonstrated, as the court below recognized, that a small minority of employes could, with the aid of invaders from outside, forcibly take control of an industrial plant, with resultant stoppage of production and unemployment for all employes, and that regular law-enforcement agencies would be unwilling to take the drastic measures necessary to evict the sit-downers."

The Labor Board found that the Ford company had been "unfair" in respect to allegations that it, the company, had caused assaults on U. A. W. organizers; distributed two pamphlets, criticizing and disparaging labor organizations; circulated a "vote of confidence" at the River Rouge plant, and discharged twenty-four of the 80,000 employes at the River Rouge and Highland Park plants because of U. A. W. activities or sympathy.

The Circuit Court upheld the board except as to the charge that distribution of statements of Henry Ford's labor views to his workers was an unfair practice. It is understood that the government may appeal from that part of the Circuit Court's decision.

Much of the brief was devoted to that part of the board's decree which ordered reinstatement of the discharged men, whom the Circuit Court fixed at twenty-three. The

Continued on Page Twenty

ALL NAVY 'GAMES' OFF FOR THIS YEAR; FLEET KEPT A UNIT

Battle Force Now in Hawaiian Waters Will Remain Intact for First Time in 20 Years

SHIPS IN FIGHTING TRIM

Gunnery Practice and Exercises Simulating War Conditions Are Almost Continuous

By LELAND C. SPEERS

Special to THE NEW YORK TIMES

WASHINGTON, Dec. 31—For the first time in more than twenty years the United States Fleet will not engage in large-scale manoeuvres this year. Instead the fleet is being held as a unit in Hawaiian waters and, according to good information, will remain there until the existing international situation is definitely improved.

The manoeuvres of 1940 which involved the solution of what was known as "Fleet Problem 21," were held last Spring and lasted from the first week in April until the latter part of May. The exercises covered a wide area in the Eastern Pacific. The problem was designed "to increase the effectiveness of all types of surface ships, submarines and aircraft, and to cover as far as practicable some of the special naval situations that have occurred during the current European conflict."

The 1940 manoeuvres were among the most extensive ever carried out by the fleet and involved about 130 fighting units manned by about 2,500 officers and 40,000 enlisted men. In 1939, practically the same number of ships and men were used in manoeuvres held in the Atlantic. They covered an area extending from the Caribbean to the waters off Northern Brazil.

Gunnery Practice Continuous

This year, although no manoeuvres will be held, the fleet is kept busy. Gunnery practice, involving all guns from the giant turret guns of the battleships to the smaller calibers on destroyers, is practically continuous. The divisions of the fleet are engaged in exercises, simulating battle conditions, the purpose being to make the fleet the most efficient naval fighting force in the world.

Every battle unit in the fleet has been overhauled and is ready for instant action in an emergency, no matter how sudden. In the overhauling of the battle force of the fleet the ships were quietly transferred to the West Coast in three sections. As fast as one section was overhauled and had rejoined the fleet another section was ready to head for the West Coast. The result is that all battle units are considered ready to fulfill any mission that may be assigned them.

For many years it has been the rule in the Navy to make changes in the flag commands of the fleet. These changes as a rule affected a majority of the high commands. This year, however, Admiral James O. Richardson is expected to remain in supreme command with Admiral C. P. Snyder, commanding the battle force, continuing as second in command.

Twenty-four in Flag Commands

There are two admirals, three vice admirals and nineteen rear admirals at present exercising flag commands in the fleet, while Major General W. P. Upshur is in command of the Marines on duty with the fleet.

Vice Admiral Adolphus Andrews commands the Scouting Force; Vice Admiral W. S. Pye, Battleship Di-

Continued on Page Six

'RIGHTEOUS PEACE' PRESIDENT'S WISH TO THE ITALIAN KING

Hopes for This Blessing for Monarch's People in '41 Voiced in New Year's Greeting

SPECULATION IS AROUSED

Payment in Raw Materials One of Means Weighed in Lease-Lend Aid for Britain

Special to THE NEW YORK TIMES.

WASHINGTON, Dec. 31—In a New Year's greeting to King Victor Emmanuel III of Italy, President Roosevelt expressed the hope that the Italian people may be enabled to enjoy the "blessing of a righteous peace" during the coming year.

Despite Administration warnings against any unusual interpretation of the message, Washington classed it among the moves to drive a wedge between Italy and the other partners in the totalitarian Axis.

This view was the more persistent because of two developments in the last week: (1) the speech of Prime Minister Churchill of Great Britain, directed to the Italian people and calling upon them to repudiate the regime of Premier Mussolini, which had dragged them into the war, and, (2) Sunday night's radio address by President Roosevelt in which he again pledged all possible assistance to Britain (short of war) in her struggle with the Axis powers.

King's Message Is Customary

The President's message technically was in reply to one received by him from King Victor Emmanuel. It is not a general custom for the President to exchange New Year's greetings with heads of States, but for years the Italian King has followed the practice and the President has responded in kind.

The King continued the custom this year and Mr. Roosevelt, in his reply, used such language as opened the way for the interpretations reported above.

Following is a translation of the message from the King to the President, dated at Rome, Dec. 23:

His Excellency,
President Roosevelt,
Washington

On the approach of the New Year I wish to express to you, Mr. President, all my most cordial good wishes for the people of the United States and for you personally.

VITTORIO EMANUELE.

The President's reply, dated at the White House Dec. 30, was as follows:

His Majesty
Vittorio Emanuele III
King of Italy
Rome

I greatly appreciate Your Majesty's cordial message. I extend to Your Majesty my most sincere wishes for your personal welfare and my hope that during the year to come the Italian people may be enabled to enjoy the blessing of a righteous peace.

FRANKLIN D. ROOSEVELT.

Hidden Meaning Disclaimed

Administration spokesmen insisted there was no hidden meaning in the President's message; that it was prompted by and framed in conformity with diplomatic protocol.

President Roosevelt intimated at his press conference in the afternoon that means for aiding the democracies in their fight against the Axis powers along the line of policy emphasized in his Sunday night address were proceeding. He disclosed that his plan to lend or lease

Continued on Page Eleven

500 Victims of Nazi Sea Raiders Rescued By Australians From a South Pacific Island

By The Associated Press.

SINGAPORE, Wednesday, Jan. 1—Five hundred men, women and children who had been landed by German commerce raiders Dec. 21 on Emirau Island, in the Bismarck Archipelago, northeast of New Guinea, have been rescued by an Australian ship and taken to Australia, it was announced officially today.

The rescued persons included British, French and Norwegian citizens. There were seventy women and seven children in the group.

Admiral Sir Geoffrey Layton, commander in chief of Britain's China Station, said the situation was not as alarming as it first appeared because the survivors had come from ships sunk over several months and not from a sudden wave of sinkings within the last few weeks.

The passengers and crew members were from the following ships: Rangitane, Holmwood, Notou, Ringwood, Triona, Triadic, Triaster, Vinni, Turakina and Komata, it was said.

The Admiral said both the British and Australian Navies were "well aware of the activities of the raiders and appropriate measures are being taken."

He said that in view of the vast expanse of ocean to be covered it might take some time to bring the raiders "to book" but that they would be accounted for eventually.

The Bismarck Archipelago is a former German colony in the South Pacific, consisting of a group of islands inhabited by Papuans, who formerly were cannibals. Emirau Island is given as Squally Island on some maps.

Reports have been received from the Orient in recent days of intensive German raider activity in the South Pacific. A Shanghai dispatch to The United Press last Saturday reported that the German steamer Scharnhorst had been in use as a prison ship for seamen captured by German raiders.

According to Lloyd's Register of Shipping, the Rangitane was the largest of the vessels named. A 16,712-ton liner, the Rangitane was owned by the New Zealand Shipping Company, Ltd., and registered out of Plymouth, England. The Tura-

Continued on Page Five

The International Situation

An Axis victory in 1941 was predicted yesterday by Reichsfuehrer Hitler in two proclamations, one to the German armed forces and the other to the German people. In the second proclamation he made what appeared to be a reference to President Roosevelt's fireside chat when he declared it was a lie to assert that Germany and Italy wanted to conquer the world. [Page 1, Column 8.]

That assertion by the President was also attacked in German official and press comment as one of two falsehoods allegedly underlying his argument, the other being that Germany planned to attack the United States after this war. The heaviest Nazi propaganda guns were trained on Mr. Roosevelt's broadcast. He was said to have shown irritability and to have misled American opinion. [Page 16, Column 2.]

That there was no Axis threat to the United States was echoed in the Italian press, which again described the President as a warmonger. [Page 15, Column 1.]

Unmindful of Axis strictures, the President pursued the shaping of his policy. For one thing he indicated at his press conference that he had no idea of sending United States warships or Marines abroad to fight. For another thing he sent a New Year's message to the King of Italy expressing hope that the Italian people might during the coming year enjoy the "blessing of a righteous peace"—a message that was cautiously interpreted as an effort to pry Rome from the tripartite front. [Page 1, Column 5.]

Such an effort was finding reinforcement in the field of battle. From Yugoslavia it was reported that two more armed Italian merchantmen carrying war supplies across the Adriatic had been sunk by unidentified warships in two engagements, raising to five the total of Italian vessels sunk in that area within a week. [Page 1, Column 7.]

In snowy Albania, according to Athens, Greek troops struggling toward Valona captured heights near Klisura along with 500 Italian reinforcing troops. [Page 2, Column 2.]

Besieged Bardia in Libya was reported by British sources to be "passively undergoing continued bombardment." [Page 3, Column 3.]

Rome's version of its two campaigns was different. It said that Italian warships had intensively shelled bases on the Greek-Albanian coast while Italian bombers raided seaports and airdromes, and that Bardia was fighting off the besiegers. [Page 2, Column 4.]

Apparently accepting the view that the war will be a long one, Italy extended rationing control over foodstuffs to apply similarly to industrial raw materials. [Page 2, Column 3.]

Puzzling moves continued in the Balkans. Reports of German concentrations along the Southern Hungarian frontier disturbed Yugoslavia and other concentrations on the Southern Rumanian border caused renewed fears of a move through Bulgaria. [Page 4, Column 5.]

Air activity over British and German areas was virtually at a standstill. But London, taking stock of Sunday night's destructive fire-bomb raid, was planning to invoke compulsory powers to provide fire-fighters for every building. [Page 3, Column 1.]

The menace to British shipping showed a sharp reduction for the week ended Dec. 23, during which eighteen vessels totaling 43,300 tons were reported lost, but Food Minister Woolton warned that Britain's larder was growing leaner and urged food economy. [Page 4, Column 1.]

That the sea menace is potent in the Pacific was demonstrated by news that 500 passengers and crew members from ten sunken ships had been rescued from a tiny island in the Bismarck Archipelago, where they had been deposited by raiders. [Page 1, Column 4.]

Another phase of the situation in the Pacific was brought out by the disclosure in Washington that no American fleet manoeuvres would be held in that ocean this year. Likewise no major changes are to be made in the Fleet High Command. [Page 1, Column 4.]

MARSHALL DEFIES U. S. TO BARE DATA

Insists We Could Have Aided Peace—Senator Lee Calls No-War Group 'Betrayers'

Verne Marshall, head of the No Foreign War Committee, hotly repeated yesterday his challenge to the Administration to make public the "agenda" brought to the United States from Germany in October, 1939, by William Rhodes Davis, oil man. This "agenda," Mr. Marshall contended in an interview in Washington on Monday, might have served as the instrument for a White House conference to end the war in Europe.

Mr. Davis, in a statement issued yesterday, did not disclose the exact nature of the "agenda." He described it merely as "information" and said he had supplied information to the government from time to time as a loyal American.

"Such information as I have transmitted to our government," his statement said, "I believe can best be utilized by officials of the different departments at Washington who carry responsibility for the protection of our national security.

"I am confident that when, in the opinion of the present Administration, the best interests of our country can be served by making public the information which I have from time to time delivered to it, that information will be made public."

Endorses Committee's Work

Mr. Davis closed his statement by saying:

"It is with emphasis that I endorse all the purposes of the No Foreign War Committee in its vigorous effort to keep the United States out of unnecessary wars. That committee stands for America, first, last and forever."

Mr. Marshall seemed upset by the Davis statement. He spoke of it at the press interview in the No Foreign War Committee suite at 100 East Forty-second Street.

"Some misguided but well-inten-

Continued on Page Fourteen

NEW ADRIATIC RAIDS PREY ON CONVOYS

War Craft Send More Fascist Troopships to Bottom Near Coast of Yugoslavia

By Telephone to THE NEW YORK TIMES.

BELGRADE, Yugoslavia, Dec. 31—Two Italian merchantmen were sunk in the Adriatic today by unidentified warships, according to word reaching here.

[Reuters, British news agency, said the sinking of four Italian transports by a British warship in the Adriatic had been reported in Belgrade. A week ago, according to the Greek Admiralty, the submarine Papanicolis sank three fully loaded transports en route to Valona.]

In one incident an armed Italian merchantman was destroyed in the morning near the Southern Yugoslav Adriatic coast in a running fight. The Italian vessel sank near Bar, according to reports from Cetinje, in Montenegro.

An unidentified torpedo boat or submarine sank the Italian vessel, loaded with troop trucks, according to her crew, after a chase down the coast toward Bar. The attacking vessel fired fifteen shells, most of which took effect on the Italian merchantman, which had time only for three bursts from her aft gun before she began to sink.

Cannonading off the coast awakened the population in the little seacoast village of Vulojitsa, near Bar, at 7:45 this morning. Coast Guardsmen and fishermen rushed to the waterfront and saw a huge pall of smoke rising from the listing freighter, lying about half a mile offshore.

The attacking warship, farther at sea, sent home the last of her fifteen shots and disappeared as the Italian ship began to go under. The crew took to life rafts and life belts and Yugoslav fishermen and coast guards attempted to rescue them in small boats, which were swamped in the heavy sea. Most of the Italian crew swam ashore. There is no re-

Continued on Page Two

HITS DEMOCRACIES

Nazi Chief Reviles Them and Their Leaders as Responsible for War

EXHORTS ARMED FORCES

Hitler Says This Year Will See the Consummation of the Reich's Greatest Victory

By C. BROOKS PETERS

Wireless to THE NEW YORK TIMES.

BERLIN, Dec. 31—Adolf Hitler, in a New Year's proclamation to the "National Socialist Armed Forces," declared today:

"The year 1941 will bring consummation of the greatest victory in our history."

Not only have German soldiers by the force of their weapons defeated their enemies, Herr Hitler declared, but the occupied countries have been "morally conquered through your noble conduct and exemplary discipline." Then he paid tribute to both German and the allied Italian "comrades" who fell in the struggle.

In another proclamation addressed to the German people Herr Hitler made several other caustic remarks about the democracies and their present champions in the world. He said it was "a dumb and infamous lie" to maintain that Germany and Italy wanted to conquer the world "while the actually existing world conquerors require war in order to realize higher interest on their capital."

Then, seemingly with direct reference to the United States, Herr Hitler asserted:

"In States which have scarcely ten persons per square kilometer to nourish and which have all the raw materials of the world at their disposal there are ten to twelve million unemployed—that is to say, people expelled from human happiness—and all that not only because of a lust for profit, corruption and indolence, but also because the stupidity of the rulers in these plutocratic democracies rejected all methods and measures that could put brakes on the limitless egoism of the individual in favor of the life of all."

TEXT OF ORDER OF THE DAY

The text of Herr Hitler's proclamation to the armed forces follows:

Soldiers: The National Socialist Armed Forces of the Greater German Reich in the war year 1940 attained glorious victories without parallel. With extraordinary daring you defeated the enemy on land, at sea and in the air.

All the tasks that I placed before you were solved by your heroism and soldier ability. You defeated the fighting power of our enemies through the might of your weapons.

The territories that you occupied have now been morally conquered through your noble conduct and exemplary discipline. Thanks to your soldiery, we have succeeded in a few months of world-historical fighting in bringing the unsuccessful heroic fighting efforts of the World War to the final point of success. The shame of the surrender of the Forest of Compiegne has been eliminated forever.

I thank you, my soldiers of the army, navy and air force as your supreme commander for your unparalleled achievements, and also thank you in the name of the entire German nation. We remember our comrades who gave their lives for the future of our people. We also think of the heroic soldiers of our allied Fascist Italy.

The war must be continued as a result of the will of democratic warmongers and Jewish capitalists. The representatives of a breaking world believe that they may achieve in 1941 what they were unable to do in 1940.

We are ready and armed as never before. We are now standing on the threshold of a new year. I know every one will do his duty. Almighty God will not leave those who, threatened by the world, with their courageous hearts are helping themselves.

Soldiers of the National Socialist armed German forces of the Greater German Reich! The year 1941 will bring consummation of the greatest victory in our history.

Blames War Profiteers

It was the second time today that Herr Hitler prophesied victory for German arms in 1941. When after the successful campaign in the West last Summer he offered peace to the British, Herr Hitler said in the proclamation to the German people

Continued on Page Sixteen

"All the News That's Fit to Print."

The New York Times.

Copyright, 1941, by The New York Times Company.

LATE CITY EDITION
Light snow today, somewhat colder in afternoon and night. Tomorrow fair and continued cold.
Temperatures Yesterday—Max., 38; Min., 30

VOL. XC...No. 30,303. Entered as Second-Class Matter, Postoffice, New York, N. Y. NEW YORK, SATURDAY, JANUARY 11, 1941. THREE CENTS NEW YORK CITY and Vicinity | FOUR CENTS Elsewhere Except in 7th and 8th Postal Zones.

BILL GIVES PRESIDENT UNLIMITED POWER TO LEND WAR EQUIPMENT AND RESOURCES; BRITISH POUND PORTS IN MASS DAY RAIDS

PLANES FOR BRITAIN SAVED IN FIRE HERE ON LOADED VESSEL

But Blaze in Hold of Freighter at Brooklyn Pier Destroys Red Cross Supplies

INQUIRIES BY CITY AND FBI

Mayor at Scene Says Welding Spark Might Be the Cause—Sailing Time Not Delayed

A fire of undetermined origin was discovered at 5:30 o'clock last night in a hold of the British freighter Black Heron at her berth at Pier 8 at the foot of Pineapple Street, Brooklyn, on the eve of the ship's sailing for an undisclosed port with a large cargo of war materials and Red Cross supplies.

The blaze menaced three Douglas bombers fastened to the decks of the freighter, which were part of her cargo, but the flames were extinguished in an hour before they reached the expensive planes. Mattresses and medical supplies were destroyed by the fire, which sent dense clouds of smoke over the Brooklyn waterfront, but it was not expected to delay the vessel's departure.

No estimate of the loss was made by officials but representatives of insurance interests said it would amount to between $50,000 and $100,000 in fire and water damage to mattresses, second-hand clothing and bundles of medical supplies in the hold, which was entirely devoted to a Red Cross shipment. Crates of plane parts in another hold were undamaged, they said. Officials said the ship carried no explosives.

After firemen under Deputy Fire Chief Raymond George had brought the blaze under control, Mayor La Guardia, who was at the scene, inspected the ship and conferred with her officers and with city officials aboard the vessel. The Mayor had heard of the fire over the police radio as he was driving home.

Had Been Welding at Scene

He said it was too early to give an opinion on the cause of the blaze, but an investigation was being made by Fire Marshal Thomas P. Brophy and other officials. Late in the afternoon, he said, workers had been welding iron shackles about the Douglas bomber fastened to the deck above Hold 3, the hold in which the blaze occurred, and the inquiry would seek to discover if the blaze had been set by sparks showered on the deck in the course of welding.

The Black Heron is one of four ships sold by the Black Diamond Steamship Company, an American concern, to the Cunard Line. The sale was approved by the United States Maritime Commission last Dec. 3. Built in 1918, the freighter is 392 feet long and has a gross tonnage of 4,926. She was rebuilt three years ago. She was docked at the south side of the pier, which is leased by the New York Dock Company.

The fire was discovered at 5:30 P. M. Timothy Scott, Second Officer of the Black Heron, summoned Patrolman Frank McKay of the Poplar Street station, on pier duty. An alarm brought fire engineers, two fireboats, the Coast Guard cutter Hudson, marine launches, police emergency squads and radio cars and a squad of special agents of the Federal Bureau of Investigation.

Hole Broken in Deck

With the bomber secured above the battened-down hatch, the firemen had to break a hole in the deck to get at the blaze. Afterward, however, they had no difficulty in extinguishing the flames with chemicals. A second alarm was turned in as a precautionary measure because of the nature of the cargo.

Fifty detectives and the squad of Federal agents carried on the investigation last night at the pier to establish whether the blaze may have been caused by sabotage. They learned that eighty longshoremen had been loading the ship with munitions, medical supplies and foodstuffs until 5 P. M. and when they quit work only 300 tons of steel remained to be put aboard.

The freighter is manned by forty-two officers and crew, all British.

No chance was taken of losing the warplanes while the fire was still burning. A Merritt, Chapman & Scott Company wrecking tug was summoned on the first alarm. The tug stood by throughout, ready to remove the planes from the deck with a derrick if necessary.

Fire Marshal Brophy said last night that he was convinced there was nothing suspicious about the origin of the blaze but that he would continue the investigation to establish whether there was any negligence. He said he found a hole the size of a pencil in the deck above where the fire started in mattresses and he believed this was caused by a red-hot fragment cast off in welding, burning through the deck and igniting the cargo.

Continued on Page Seven

Chinese Finds U. S. Navy Excels Japan's 322 Times

By The Associated Press.

CHUNGKING, China, Jan. 10—The newspaper Takung Pao did some figuring today and decided that "the United States Navy is 322 times more powerful than the Japanese Navy."

The editorial writer figured that the present United States naval budget is 322 times the Japanese naval budget, based on the rate of unofficial dealings in the yen.

"The fate of the Japanese Empire lies in President Roosevelt's hands," the writer elaborated. "The Japanese Navy can be wiped out when he decides."

NAZI CHIEFS CACHED MILLIONS ABROAD

Story Comes Out in Court Here as Agent, Rumanian, Gets 2 Years in Passport Fraud

Reich Marshal Hermann Goering and other high Nazi officials have smuggled millions of dollars out of Germany, to be deposited for their personal use in banks here and in other countries, it was confirmed here yesterday. The cash was transported by a Rumanian, who used a fraudulently obtained United States passport in his trips back and forth across the German border, it was shown.

Rumors that Marshal Goering and others who would have much to lose if the Nazi government failed were secreting nest eggs outside their own country were prevalent soon after the war broke out in the Fall of 1939. Adolf Hitler was the only one not mentioned in such stories, and he was not included yesterday.

The story came out in Federal Court, where the Rumanian received a prison term of two years and a fine of $2,500 for his admitted frauds in connection with the passport. The culprit is Isidore Lazarus, a former confidence man who though known among the Nazis as Lee Lane is a Jew.

Got Refugees' Property

Richard J. Burke, assistant United States attorney, told Judge Vincent L. Leibell the story as it had been pieced together from information obtained by an unnamed foreign agency, the United States Department of State and other investigators. He said Lazarus had caused refugees to transfer their property, in cash, to him before they left Germany. Through arrangements with Marshal Goering, Dr. Hjalmar Schacht, Dr. Joseph Goebbels, Propaganda Minister, Dr. Robert Ley, head of the Labor Front, and others, Lazarus saw to it that the refugees got a small part of the value of their belongings when they reached other countries, while the rest, amounting to vast sums, went to the account of the Nazi officials, Mr. Burke said.

He added that part of the money Lazarus smuggled out was used for propaganda and espionage in the countries where it was deposited.

Mr. Burke read the following extract from a letter from an important official of the Department of State, whom he did not identify:

"According to his own admission to me, he [Lazarus or Lane] not only made these arrangements between oppressed persons and high ranking members of the government—for which he received a commission—but he also acted as the intermediary through which these high ranking members of the German Government transferred the money they received from this traffic to banks in other countries. Lane admitted to me that he made many trips from Germany to other countries carrying money for deposit outside of Germany. . . . Lane himself has admitted that he could reopen these connections with high ranking members of the German Government at any time."

Sums Small, Prisoner Said

Lazarus admitted that he had got money out of Germany for the Nazi officials, but said it was in small amounts. He confirmed the statement of Mr. Burke that the cash was for the personal use of these officials. He maintained, however, that he was violently anti-Nazi, and had kept in with the German leaders only so that he could help those "poor devils" who were finding it hard to get out of Germany with their belongings.

Judge Leibell listened for nearly an hour and a half while Lazarus and Moses Sachs, his attorney, argued for a light sentence. Lazarus is a tall man, well dressed, with white hair that is sparse on top. He smiled reassuringly at Judge Leibell as he tried to explain away Mr. Burke's charges, but gradually, as it became apparent that he was not to be let off with a fine, he became more and more agitated.

He groped for letters that he said would show his high purposes and protested again and again that he had been trying to help those "poor devils." At last he attacked the accusations by declaring:

"It's inconceivable!"

Judge Leibell calmly replied that it was not inconceivable.

Lazarus's own story was that he

Continued on Page Seven

NAZI AIR BASES HIT

Calais Area Blasted in R. A. F.'s Biggest Day Attack of War

RUHR IS BOMBED AT NIGHT

London Reports All Raiders Safe—Berlin Claims 8—Sicily Heavily Pounded

By JAMES MacDONALD
Special Cable to The New York Times.

LONDON, Saturday, Jan. 11—In a swift, hard-hitting aerial attack marking their biggest daylight raid thus far strong forces of Royal Air Force bombers guarded by an escort of 100 fighter planes smashed Nazi-occupied air bases at midday yesterday, destroying three German machines that tried unsuccessfully to chase them off and damaging others on the ground, it was announced here.

All the British planes engaged in the "full dress" exploit of this country's growing air strength returned home safely, according to Air Ministry officials.

[The Germans asserted they shot down eight British planes and repulsed the entire formation. The Associated Press stated.]

Last night R. A. F. bombers again attacked the German-held naval base at Brest, the Air Ministry reported early today.

The daylight raid on the Pas-de-Calais Department in France was the immediate aftermath of widespread forays Thursday night, in which British bombers struck at Brest for the third time this week and hammered docks in Flushing, Dunkerque and Calais, oil depots in Rotterdam, Gelsenkirchen and other points in the Ruhr and objectives in Norway.

Success Reported Everywhere

Everywhere they went they scored successes, British officials said.

[R. A. F. headquarters in Cairo announced that during a heavy raid on Messina, Sicily, several tons of bombs had been dropped among cruisers and other naval vessels. It also was reported that an Italian battleship of the Littorio class probably had been hit during an R. A. F. attack on Naples.]

Residents of a southeast coast town cast questioning eyes skyward shortly after noon, when the loud drone of airplane motors hit their eardrums. They saw many British planes flying in close formation as they headed for France at low enough altitude to make their markings reassuringly distinguishable.

Shortly afterward the planes disappeared in the obscurity of the French coast. Then residents of the town heard the muffled sound of anti-aircraft fire and the all-too-familiar "crumping" of bombs.

According to later announcements British raiders were diving through a big barrage of German anti-aircraft guns at Calais and Cap Gris Nez, bombing and machine-gunning every air base assigned to them. In the forests of Guines, near Calais, explosive and incendiary bombs started fires in the woods and enveloped a near-by railroad station in a pillar of white smoke. One low-level attack was made on gun positions and troops in the vicinity of Wissant.

German planes on the ground at

Continued on Page Seven

Aid Bill Is Number 1776; Is Called a Coincidence

Special to The New York Times.

WASHINGTON, Jan. 10—The "all-out" Aid to Britain bill took the number HR1776 today when it reached the bill clerk's office. The fact that the number coincides with the year of our declaration of independence was pointed out to officials, who said it was purely coincidental.

"The last bill bore the number 1775," a clerk said, "and as this bill was the first to reach this office today it was designated 1776 as a matter of routine. There was no request from any source that it be especially numbered."

KLISURA CAPTURED IN GREEK ADVANCE

Fall of Vital Albanian Base Is Held One of Most Significant Successes of the War

By A. C. SEDGWICK
By Telephone to The New York Times.

ATHENS, Jan. 10—What may be regarded as one of the most significant successes achieved by Greek arms since the start of the Albanian campaign was announced here today—the fall of Klisura.

Engagements in this all important sector have been reported during the last few weeks, but only in a general fashion, with all details reserved as military secrets. However, it became known that the Greeks were performing extremely difficult feats, seizing high mountain peaks and capturing enemy strongholds one after the other. All operations were conducted under appalling conditions in the bitterest cold.

Time and again in history armies have fought for this village only to be hurled back. In itself, Klisura is unimportant and might be described as little more than a hamlet inhabited by Albania peasantry, but as a strategic position upon a naturally-fortified line it is of the utmost significance.

The Greeks did not attempt a frontal attack but instead bided their time, methodically taking heights to the east, and then after they once dominated Klisura, attacked it upon its more vulnerable flanks.

Church Bells Start Ringing

The long-hoped-for victory of Klisura was announced in the early afternoon, and immediately, as if its importance were recognized by all, the bells of Athens churches started to ring. In less than five minutes all the streets of the city became a mass of blue and white bunting and Union Jacks. Military bands blared out martial music, intermingled with popular airs, the words to which are satirical commentaries upon Premier Mussolini and his Fascisti.

The actual entry into Klisura, it is believed, took place early this morning after a night of ferocious fighting in which the Italians, as if realizing fully how costly would be the loss of this key position in terms of general strategy and prestige, held out as long as possible, capitulating only when the Greeks attacked with fixed bayonets.

The General Headquarters communiqué stated that 600 men and 20 officers were captured during the course of the battle. Matériel, including four guns and an unspecified number of tanks, trench mor-

Continued on Page Eight

Soviet and Reich Make Enlarged Trade Deal; New Frontier Treaty Also Signed in Moscow

By The Associated Press.

MOSCOW, Jan. 10—Soviet Russia agreed today to send to warring Germany quantities of food, especially grains, in a significant collaboration officially described as "an enlarged economic agreement."

[With announcement in Berlin of the signing at Moscow of the new Soviet-German agreement, D. N. B., the official German news agency, called it the "greatest grain deal in history," The Associated Press reported. D. N. B. was quoted as saying the arrangement could be called "an economic plan."]

The trade agreement was in fact one of five compacts signed here today. The others dealt with such subjects as mutual border revisions and settlement of property claims and migrations connected with Russia's absorption of Latvia, Estonia and Lithuania.

Tass, official Soviet news agency, said the new agreement "constitutes a further stage in the execution of the economic program outlined by the two governments in 1939."

It said the negotiations "passed in the spirit of mutual understanding and confidence conforming to the friendly relations existing between the U. S. S. R. and Germany," and added, "All economic problems, including those which arose in connection with incorporation of new territories in the U. S. S. R., were solved in conformity with the interests of both countries."

Russia also will furnish industrial raw materials and oil products in exchange for German industrial equipment under the new treaty, which runs until Aug. 1, 1942.

Amounts were not specified, but Tass said the new pact provided for "deliveries considerably exceeding

Continued on Page Eight

Communiqué on German-Russia agreement, Page 8.

OPPOSITION STARTS

Bill Called Monstrous and Totalitarian Too by Hiram Johnson

'STREAMLINED WAR' SEEN

But Administration Forces Voice Confidence in Quick Adoption by House

Special to The New York Times.

WASHINGTON, Jan. 10—Although there was considerable outspoken criticism of the Administration's bill to aid the democracies after it was introduced in Congress today, it was impossible to gauge the strength of the opposition in Senate or House with accuracy.

Some members who pride themselves on their ability to sense the trend in their branches of Congress confessed their inability to predict the fate of the measure, and the estimates of some who ventured predictions varied widely.

Expressions of direct opposition came for the most part from members identified with the anti-Administration isolationist group. Some conservative Democrats who usually have supported the Administration's foreign policy questioned the wisdom, however, of granting to the President the broad authority which the legislation would convey.

One isolationist Senator said there would be no more than a dozen votes against the bill in the Senate, while another predicted that it would be amended beyond recognition before it could win a majority.

Administration leaders in the House said they were confident that the measure would pass with a safe margin. Yet another usually reliable forecaster was equally certain that the House would not accept the bill in the form in which it was introduced.

Two Suggestions for Changes

An indication of the views expressed may be gained from two changes which were suggested in different quarters as desirable. They were:

1. An ironclad requirement that the Chief of Staff or the Chief of Naval Operations certify to the advisability of conveying military or naval equipment to foreign hands.

2. That a proviso be attached requiring from Great Britain the transfer of full title in fee simple to the Atlantic and Caribbean bases recently leased to the United States for ninety-nine years in exchange for fifty destroyers.

The outcome will be in the hands of the middle-ground members, who, for the most part, withheld comment. They wanted more time for consideration and to hear the Administration's case.

Opposition was clearly stated by Senator Hiram W. Johnson of California, author of the law prohibiting the extension of credits to debt-default nations and a leader in the Senate fight against entry into the League.

"I am neither an appeaser nor a Hitlerite," Senator Johnson said. "I want to see Hitler whipped and Britain triumphant. But I regard the bill as presented today as monstrous. I decline to change the whole form of my government on the specious plea of assisting one belligerent.

Says Test Is Up to Congress

"The bill presents squarely to Congress whether it shall create a dictatorship. It confers extraordinary powers on the President and, in the last clauses, as I read it, authorizes him to promulgate 'such rules and regulations as may be necessary and proper to carry out any provisions of this act.'

"It is up to Congress now to determine whether our government shall be as ordained or become a member of the totalitarian States. So far as I am concerned, and I speak for myself alone, I shall oppose it."

Senator Ellison D. Smith, Democrat, of South Carolina had this to say of the President's bill:

"We are about to give him absolute power over the purse and the people, but not with my consent."

Senator Taft of Ohio, a contender for the Republican Presidential nomination last Spring, denounced the measure.

"The proposed bill combines all the faults of the worst New Deal legislation," he said, "including unlimited delegation of authority and blank-check appropriations. In addition it authorizes the President to make war on any nation in the world and to enter the present war

Continued on Page Five

Text of Lease-Lend Bill

By The Associated Press.

WASHINGTON, Jan. 10—The text of the measure introduced in Congress today to effect President Roosevelt's plan of lending or leasing military equipment to "democracies" was as follows:

A Bill

To further promote the defense of the United States, and for other purposes.

Be it enacted by the Senate and House of Representatives of the United States of America in Congress assembled, that this act may be cited as "an act to promote the defense of the United States."

SECTION II

As used in this act:

(A) The term "defense article" means:

1. Any weapon, munition, aircraft, vessel, or boat;

2. Any machinery, facility, tool, material, or supply necessary for the manufacture, production, processing, repair, servicing, or operation of any article described in this subsection:

3. Any component material or part of or equipment for any article described in this subsection:

Defense Articles Described

4. Any other commodity or article for defense. Such term "defense article" includes any article described in this subsection: Manufactured or procured pursuant to Section 3 or to which the United States or any foreign government has or hereafter acquires title, possession or control.

(B) The term "defense information" means any plan, specification, design, prototype, or information pertaining to any defense article.

SECTION III

(A) Notwithstanding the provisions of any other law, the President may, from time to time, when he deems it in the interest

Continued on Page Three

The International Situation

A bill conferring on President Roosevelt virtually unlimited personal authority to have manufactured or procured any war materials and to transfer such materials to any nations of the world in the interest of American defense was introduced into the Congress yesterday. Washington observers predicted that a stiff fight would develop over the proposed legislation. [Page 1, Column 8.]

At his press conference the President declared that he realized the extent of the unprecedented request but added that some one had to have such authority in the interest of speed. [Page 1, Column 7.]

Britain's growing air strength was indicated by the heaviest daytime mass bombing raid ever carried out by the R. A. F. Approximately fifty bombers, plus 100 fighters, savagely struck at the "invasion ports" of France in broad daylight. Thursday night, London revealed, widespread R. A. F. raids damaged Brest, the Ruhr valley, Netherland ports, Gelsenkirchen, the Krupp works at Essen and Nazi-held French harbors. [Page 1, Column 3.] German fliers made a furious attack on a town on the south coast of England. [Page 7, Column 7.]

Announcement of the Greek capture of Klisura, strongly held Italian base, led to rejoicing in Athens. The early fall of near-by Tepeleni and a strong Greek drive on Valona were foreseen. [Page 1, Column 4.]

As British forces continued moving into position around Tobruk, their heavy guns started shelling the besieged Italian garrison, British field headquarters stated. The R. A. F. again bombed airfields at Benina, Bengazi and Tobruk. Far to the south British South African forces captured Buna, in Kenya, and El Wak, on the Kenya-Italian Somaliland frontier. [Page 8, Column 5.]

British Middle East headquarters also announced that Thursday night R. A. F. planes severely bombed Italian warships at Messina, Sicily, and raided Palermo again. Rome declared Italian explosives had fallen on a British battleship during an Italian raid on an enemy squadron in the Mediterranean. [Page 8, Column 1.]

German and Russian economic and diplomatic representatives signed "an extended trade agreement" in Moscow, providing for heavy shipments from the Soviet Union to Germany of grain, fodder and oil in the coming year in return for German finished goods. [Page 1, Column 3.]

From Thailand came reports that air raids against the French Indo-Chinese capital of Saigon and two other cities had been ordered in retaliation for the bombing of Bangkok, the Thailand capital. [Page 6, Column 8.]

BILL INTERPRETED BY TWO LEADERS

Barkley and McCormack Explain Provisions of Measure for Aiding Britain

Special to The New York Times.

WASHINGTON, Jan. 10—Following is an official interpretation of President Roosevelt's aid-Britain bill prepared by Senator Barkley and Representative McCormack, majority leader, who introduced it today:

"The attached bill giving effect to President Roosevelt's lend-lease proposals will be introduced simultaneously when Congress meets at noon today by Senator Barkley and Representative McCormack, the two majority leaders.

"The bill simply translates into legislative form the policy of making this country the arsenal for the democracies, and seeks to carry out President Roosevelt's pledge to these countries, 'in ever-increasing numbers, ships, planes, tanks, guns.'

"It follows the precedent established by Congress last June when the President was empowered to authorize the Secretaries of War and Navy to manufacture, purchase and repair war materials for the American republics. Under the present bill, this country is enabled to furnish war materials of every kind to any country whose defense

Continued on Page Three

PRESIDENT CALLS FOR SWIFT ACTION

Democracies Will Survive Only if Congress Speeds Aid, He Tells Newspaper Men

Special to The New York Times.

WASHINGTON, Jan. 10—President Roosevelt called today for swift action upon the bill granting him "blank-check" powers to obtain and transfer war supplies to Britain and her allies. Speed, he said, was essential if the democracies are to survive.

The President made the statement at a forenoon press conference before the measure was introduced in Congress. While the legislation would grant him very broad powers, he said, some one had to have authority to act quickly in this world crisis. Thus every week of delay by Congress meant a week's delay in production.

In asking utmost speed, the President made it clear that he would leave the method of obtaining it to Congress. He asked the newspaper men to point out to the country, however, the difference between the authorization to act contained in the bill introduced today and actual appropriations for executing its provisions which, he emphasized, could not be sought from Congress until the authorization was obtained.

The President said he did not intend to ask Congress at one time

Continued on Page Three

GOES TO CONGRESS

Measure Would Allow British Naval Repair in Our Ports

QUICK ACTION IS URGED

Aim Is 'to Do the Job Right' in Aiding Allies—Line-Up Points to Bill's Passage

By TURNER CATLEDGE
Special to The New York Times.

WASHINGTON, Jan. 10—A bill to confer upon President Roosevelt practically unlimited personal power to place American war equipment, new and old, at the disposal of foreign nations in the interest of the defense of the United States was introduced in Congress today amid signs of a brewing legislative storm.

Presented as an Administration proposal by the majority leader in each house, and intended solely to implement the policy of "all out" aid to the non-Axis powers now under attack, the bill carries one of the greatest grants of authority ever extended by Congress to the President, either in peace or war.

As interpreted by authorities, including some who helped frame the measure, the President would be empowered, under its terms, to transfer the whole or any part of the Navy or Army equipment to other countries and place new defense production at their disposal—all upon such terms and under such conditions as he himself might determine. The sole limitation would be that the transfer of materials should be deemed by the President to be in the interest of American defense.

Powers Held Needed for Speed

Administration spokesmen scouted as "ridiculous" any suggestion that the President would use the bill's powers to these possible limits. The whole purpose, they said, was to do the job of aid-to-the-Allies which the country seems to be demanding and "do it right."

The President himself urged the quickest possible action on the bill, saying at his press conference that speed was the most vital element in translating the Allied-aid policy into action. He had no personal desire to have the vast powers conferred by the measure, he said, but they were needed to avoid delays.

The Capitol appeared somewhat surprised by the nature and extent of the bill, although its terms had been discounted by advance publication. Administration leaders laid plans immediately for pushing it through Congress as rapidly as possible, with hearings to start next week before the Senate and House committees dealing with foreign affairs. They want to rush it through ahead of any possible reactions which might make more bitter the fight they expect.

Stormy Debate Is Expected

The extent of opposition can hardly be gauged at this time. Enough was seen today to indicate that the measure will have a stormy legislative course whatever the result. Signs of disapproval came not alone from the "noninterventionist" group which would have fought any Allied-aid proposal, but from some others who, although they were unwilling to speak out because of the peculiar nature of the subject and the times, were nonplused at the magnitude of executive authority proposed in the bill.

Resistance to additional grants of executive powers has been mounting steadily over the last few years, but how much it has been softened under the urgency of the foreign situation with repeated underscorings by the President and other advocates of aid to the Allies is something yet to be seen.

The bill was introduced by Senator Barkley in the Senate and Representative McCormack of Massachusetts in the House. No drama attended its presentation in either body.

Shortly before introducing it the two leaders issued a joint statement explaining its terms. The major purpose was simply to translate into legislative form the policy of making this country "the arsenal of democracy," the leaders said, and to carry out President Roosevelt's pledge to send to beleaguered democracies "in ever-increasing numbers, ships, planes, tanks, guns." They explained the bill in detail, which, briefly, provides the following:

The President is empowered, "notwithstanding the provisions of any other law," when he deems

Continued on Page Three

"All the News That's Fit to Print."

The New York Times.

LATE CITY EDITION
Rain with slowly rising temperatures today. Tomorrow cloudy, moderate temperatures.
Temperatures Yesterday—Max., 35; Min., 23

VOL. XC..No. 30,309. Entered as Second-Class Matter, Post Office, New York, N. Y. NEW YORK, FRIDAY, JANUARY 17, 1941. THREE CENTS NEW YORK CITY and Vicinity | FOUR CENTS Elsewhere Except in 7th and 8th Postal Zones.

ILLUSTRIOUS BOMBED AGAIN; CRUISER SOUTHAMPTON SUNK; R.A.F. BLASTS NAZI NAVY BASE

NAZIS CLAIM 3 HITS

Report New Damage to Carrier at 'Fortress'—Malta Tells of Raids

CRUISER WAS ABANDONED

Fire Set by Nazi Dive Bombers Forced British to Sink Her—Catania Pounded Anew

By The Associated Press.

BERLIN, Friday, Jan. 17—Informed sources said early today that German dive bombers had attacked the 23,000-ton British aircraft carrier Illustrious yesterday for the second time in seven days and scored three direct hits. The attack was said to have taken place "in a British naval fortress in the Mediterranean, where a number of bombs were dropped."

[Apparently the attack was carried out at Valletta, Malta, which reported prolonged dive-bombing attacks both Wednesday night and yesterday. As another aftermath to last Friday's German-Italian dive-bombing attack in which the Illustrious was damaged along with the British cruiser Southampton and the destroyer Gallant, London reported yesterday that the damage to the 9,100-ton Southampton had been so severe that she had to be abandoned by her crew and sunk by other British warships.]

One heavy bomb and two medium bombs hit the Illustrious in yesterday's attack, the Germans said, and "despite fierce anti-aircraft fire, only one German bomber has failed to return." It was declared that the Illustrious probably would not be fit for action for the rest of the war.

The Germans added that they had made a direct hit on a steamer in the same engagement.

Long Attacks on Malta

VALLETTA, Malta, Jan. 16 (AP)—Dive bombers attacked Valletta Harbor and the town this afternoon in a prolonged assault. There was a continuous explosion of bombs, and guns of all calibers roared at the persistent invaders.

Yesterday a hostile plane, curiously marked with a red cross, made a long reconnaissance over the island. Last night there was more reconnaissance and then a prolonged attempt to bomb selected targets. The night's alerts covered almost four hours—a record here.

In both attacks—those of last night and today—there were an undetermined number of casualties. British sources said that the raiders' losses had been "substantial" and that Royal Air Force fighters had suffered no damage.

Hit on Another Carrier Claimed

ROME, Jan. 16 (AP)—The report of the Axis on its bomb and torpedo offensive against British sea power in the Mediterranean was further filled in today by the assertion of a Rome newspaper that the 22,600-ton aircraft carrier Eagle had been torpedoed.

At the same time the High Command acknowledged a new night attack by British planes on Catania, Sicily [supposed to be the main base for the German dive bombers now cooperating with the Italian Air Force]. The damage was minor, the High Command communiqué said, and "a few" persons were killed or injured.

[Catania was bombed also last Sunday night, according to the British. In that attack, the Royal Air Force reported yesterday at Cairo, between thirty and forty aircraft were either destroyed or severely damaged.]

The Giornale d'Italia, reporting the attack on the Eagle, a converted battleship, asserted that a wave-skimming Italian torpedo plane had scored a hit on her recently between Tobruk, Libya, and the Greek island of Crete.

At the same time the Italians credited two of their submarines with the torpedoing of a British light cruiser in the Mediterranean and the sinking of a British merchant ship in the Atlantic.

The cruiser, which was reported to have been attacked Friday night, was not identified, but the sunken merchant vessel was said to have been the Ardabham. [The communiqué presumably referred to the 4,980-ton freighter Ardanbhan, from which Mackay Radio intercepted a message last Dec. 27 saying she had been torpedoed about 600 miles off Scotland.]

CATANIA, Sicily, Jan. 16 (UP)—Funeral services were held today

Continued on Page Three

The International Situation

FRIDAY, JAN. 17, 1941

The Administration brought another "big gun" to bear yesterday on potential Congressional opposition to its pending lend-lease arms bill. Secretary of War Stimson warned that the United States stood in real danger of aerial invasion should the British Navy be destroyed or surrendered. The Secretary also said this country faced an acute emergency in the time element involved in producing arms for ourselves and for Britain. [Page 1, Column 8.]

Under questioning Secretary Stimson told members of the House Foreign Affairs Committee that by June 1 the United States would have an Army of 1,400,000 men, fully housed, with complete personal equipment and much basic fighting material, but Under-Secretary of War Patterson emphasized that this Army would not be able to take the field fully equipped until 1942. [Page 9, Column 2.]

Indicating that the American merchant marine, too, was being rapidly expanded to meet any crisis, President Roosevelt asked Congress for an added appropriation of $350,000,000 for construction of 200 new cargo ships and urged that authority be given the Maritime Commission to construct new shipyards. [Page 1, Column 6.]

Reaction in the controlled press of the Axis capitals was bitter and Axis organs attacked this country from varying angles. In Berlin the press accused the United States of violating the rights of the South American nations by aiding Britain in blocking them from European markets [Page 6, Column 5]; the Rome press warned that Anglo-American attempts to separate Italy from Germany were "doomed to failure" [Page 6, Column 3], and a Tokyo organ termed Secretary Hull's statements before Congress a "clear challenge short of an ultimatum to the Axis." [Page 5, Column 1.]

London was reported to be considering requesting acquiescence of the Americas in the installing of a contraband control station in the West Indies to examine shipping passing through the Panama Canal for Vladivostok, Russian Pacific port. London has contended such goods eventually reach Germany. Washington circles took the position that this passage of goods would "keep Russia quiet" and would not grow too serious for Britain. [Page 1, Column 3.]

The French freighter Mendoza, which has tried to cross the Atlantic from Uruguay to unoccupied France with food but has been turned back several times by the British merchant cruiser Asturias, was reported slipping up the coast of Brazil just inside the three-mile limit, with the Asturias in close attendance. [Page 4, Column 2.]

Germany's challenge to British domination of the Mediterranean continued as German dive-bombers, Berlin said, scored three more hits on the British aircraft carrier Illustrious at a British "naval fortress" in the Mediterranean. From Malta, where the Illustrious was believed to be, came word of a violent dive-bombing attack. [Page 1, Column 1.] London announced the sinking of the cruiser Southampton in the Mediterranean after fires started by German dive-bombers off Sicily last Friday had grown beyond control. The British, however, again raided Catania, Sicily, where German planes are based and the R. A. F. said that thirty to forty aircraft had been damaged on the previous raid there. [Follows the foregoing.]

British bombers in North Africa also spattered Italian Libyan airports with explosives as British big guns kept up their hammering of the Italian garrison in Tobruk, which has constructed a tank trap around the town, indicating an intention to defend it bitterly. [Page 3, Column 1.]

The R. A. F. unleashed one of the most violent air raids of the war Wednesday night and yesterday morning against much-bombed Wilhelmshaven. The first wave of planes hovered over the German naval base continually from 8 P. M. to midnight and returning pilots told of "shoveling bombs" into the fires below and watching the flames grow larger. The second raid lasted from 5 A. M. to 6 A. M. and London said, added to the havoc. Another heavy raid on Wilhelmshaven was carried out last night. [Page 1, Column 2.] London itself received Nazi air attention but the night assault was lighter than usual. [Page 2, Column 2.]

LAKE OF FIRE SEEN IN WILHELMSHAVEN

British Planes Bomb German Docks and Shipyards on Successive Nights

By RAYMOND DANIELL
Special Cable to THE NEW YORK TIMES.

LONDON, Friday, Jan. 17—The British carried out heavy concentrated raids Wednesday night on the big shipbuilding yards and drydocks in Wilhelmshaven, main base of the German North Sea fleet.

Bombers of the Royal Air Force had been there thirty-nine times before, but never in such force. It was a sort of double-header raid, for it was carried out by two separate waves of attackers, one of which plastered the objective from 8 P. M. to midnight and the other from 5 to 6 A. M. yesterday.

Another heavy bombing attack on Wilhelmshaven was carried out by the R. A. F. during the past night, according to a brief statement early today. This second raid on successive nights was called "very successful."

The chief point of attack Wednesday night was the Bauhafen, a great basin joined by the Hafen Canal to the outer harbor and the sea. Around this protected basin are crowded slipways, docks, engineering works of all kinds, storehouses, assembling sheds, armorplate shops, foundries, iron works and a gun store.

In the docks of the Marinewerfte to the north twenty-four submarines could be built at one time and the harbor itself with its great floating cranes is designed to accommodate the largest warships. The main railway station of Wilhelmshaven lies a few hundred yards to the southwest. There are power stations closer by, both north and south of the harbor, while to the east are many naval barracks.

This whole section was set afire

Continued on Page Two

BASE FOR BLOCKADE IN TRINIDAD SOUGHT

Britain May Ask Americas for Contraband Control Area to Halt Russian Trade

Special Cable to THE NEW YORK TIMES.

LONDON, Jan. 16—The possibility of asking the Americas for permission to establish some sort of contraband control at a West Indies base, such as Trinidad, is being considered here.

The reason for this is the growing worry over Russian help to Germany, which is reaching such proportions that Russia may prove to be a dangerous loophole in the British blockade. Most of this aid comes from the United States and South America and goes through the Panama Canal. It does not go direct to Germany. Instead it goes to Vladivostok and reaches Germany by delayed action.

The Russians are not acting as a direct channel for goods for Germany. But they are replacing their own stocks west of Vladivostok with goods that arrive there, releasing those stocks for use in Germany. For example, according to the British, Russia received within the last three months more cotton from the United States than her previous yearly averages. Germany has more cotton than she should have, considering the British blockade.

The same thing applies to oil. Russia can feed her needs in Siberia by importing, thereby diverting to the west oil that ordinarily would go to the east. The same thing applies to oil-drilling machinery, of which the United States is practically the sole world producer.

The British, therefore, suspect that the Germans have developed a

Continued on Page Four

EAST HIT BY GALE, SNOW, SLEET, RAIN; WIDE ICE DAMAGE

Storm Like That of March, 1940. Feared as Power Lines and Traffic Are Disrupted

MANY INJURED IN CITY

Freezing Crust Covers Roads, Causing Many Auto Crashes —Planes Are Grounded

Indications multiplied last night that the New York area and adjacent parts of the Northeast were being revisited by an ice storm similar to the destructive one of March 3 and 4, 1940.

With reports coming in from up-State, Southern New England, New Jersey, Pennsylvania, Maryland and Delaware telling of roads made treacherous by ice, of sagging, icicle-laden utility wires, crashing tree branches and a mounting toll of automobile accidents and pedestrian fatalities and injuries, confirmation of the seriousness of conditions came from the local Weather Bureau.

The bureau said that heavy rains, general on the Eastern seaboard as far south as Charleston, S. C., were freezing as they reached the surface nearly everywhere from Washington, D. C., to Boston. At Boston and beyond it was snowing.

Moisture in Air Blamed

The rains, following a fall of about half an inch of snow late Wednesday night and early yesterday, were described as the result of a secondary disturbance off the Virginia Capes, which caused masses of warm, moisture-laden air to flow northward and overrun this frozen area.

The resulting clash precipitated the rain from clouds about 1,500 feet up, where 38 or 40 degrees were the prevalent temperatures. This phenomenon was immediately reported at La Guardia Field, where the icing conditions nearer the surface were so severe all day that a mere handful of planes came and left.

The greatest activity noted at the field was that of crowds of boys skating on adjoining highways, a condition paralleled at Wilmington, Del., where The Associated Press reported that the surest means of travel was by ice skates.

Early today the temperature had risen to 36 degrees and the Weather Bureau said the forecast was for rain and slowly rising temperatures.

Staten Island Is Hit

In Staten Island the storm was called the worst in many years. By 9:30 P. M. nearly every town on the island was in either partial or total darkness, due to failure of the power lines when trees fell on them. Two-thirds of the fire alarm system was out of commission for more than an hour and a half. The bus system was severely disrupted, automobiles were stalled in ditches all over the island and train service was considerably slowed. Many streets were strewn with the limbs of trees.

More than 750 ambulance calls were reported in Manhattan and the police said the majority were for persons injured in falls on ice.

In Brooklyn nearly 600 ambulance calls were reported throughout the day. Delays in bus service and an acute shortage of taxicabs in the borough was reported. Nassau County, L. I., reported many automobile accidents.

From Seventy-second Street north as far as 125th Street the West Side Highway was strewn with stalled automobiles by 10 P. M. Many others ploughed on through several inches of water at the dips in the roadway.

Westbound commuting service on

Continued on Page Thirty-six

STIMSON SEES DANGER OF INVASION IF BRITISH NAVY BE BEATEN OR TAKEN; HOOVER URGES DEFINITION OF POWERS

WOULD AMEND BILL

Action Asked of Bloom to End Bitterness and Foster Unity

IS FOR SHORT-OF-WAR AID

Impairment of Defense and Sending of U. S. Ships Into War Zones Feared

Early amendment of the lend-lease bill to define positively what powers it would confer upon the President was urged by former President Herbert Hoover in a letter to Representative Sol Bloom, chairman of the House Foreign Affairs Committee, which Mr. Hoover made public yesterday.

Such clarification of the bill's powers, he said, should enable concrete debate, eliminate much controversy and greatly contribute to national unity.

Mr. Hoover reiterated his position in favor of all possible aid to Britain, short of war, but said he did not approve of our joining in the conflict.

The former President said his letter was inspired by the statement of Mr. Bloom in Washington Tuesday that the committee would be glad to hear the views of Mr. Hoover and other prominent persons. He did not indicate whether he intended to ask for such a hearing or intended to let his letter stand as the answer to the invitation.

Growing Bitterness Seen

"There is unfortunately growing up in the country a bitterness of discussion which it seems to me in the interest of national unity could be allayed by the committee," his letter said. "This division lies largely in the interpretations and implications in respect to the powers proposed to be conferred in this bill and its meaning.

"For example, citizens of high patriotic thought and experience, who desire to support the President, believe that under the bill and even without any supplemental action by the Congress:

"That battleships and other naval vessels could be given away;

"That our defense could be vitally impaired by giving away Army equipment;

"That equipment and materials provided in the bill could be transported through the war zone in American ships convoyed by the American Navy;

"That commodities and articles could be purchased in other countries with our money;

"That alien ships now in sanctuary in our harbors could be seized;

"That it opens American ports to repair of belligerent vessels and makes such ports bases for belligerent operations and may become the objective of them;

"That the program of gifts to Britain could begin before the very considerable resources now available to the British Government in the United States have been first called upon as payment or collateral;

"That the bill could cancel parts of the labor laws, the Johnson act, the neutrality acts, The Hague conventions and possibly other laws;

"That it empowers involvement

Continued on Page Seven

President Asks 200 Cargo Ships; House Speeds New Naval Funds

Message to Congress Calls for $350,000,000 to Protect Us Against World Ship Shortage—Steps Already Taken

By HENRY N. DORRIS
Special to THE NEW YORK TIMES.

WASHINGTON, Jan. 16—President Roosevelt asked Congress today for immediate funds for 200 new cargo vessels "to protect against the effect upon the United States of a possible world shortage of such ships." The Naval Affairs Committee at the same time rushed to the House bills calling for emergency authority for more naval ships, shipyards, armor and gun factories, and for protection of the fleet against air attacks.

The President's request for a total of $350,000,000 for new cargo vessels and new shipyards was referred to the House Appropriations Committee.

Representative Woodrum of Virginia, chairman of the subcommittee which will consider it, said the request would be taken up early next week, with the probability it will be reported to the House for action late in the week.

The House will be occupied the first part of the week in considering the bills unanimously reported by the Naval Affairs Committee, which would authorize a total of $1,209,000,000 in expenditures as follows:

1. Construction of 400 vessels of various types for the Navy, 280 of which are to be undertaken immediately, and the other 120 when shipyards are available.

2. Expansion of shipyards, or construction of new ones, for which $315,000,000 in authorizations were voted by the committee. This expenditure is expected to push the construction of the two-ocean Navy and deliver many of the new vessels months, and in some cases years, ahead of schedule.

3. An authorization of $194,000,000 for doubling the Navy's ordnance facilities, for the manufacture of guns of all classes, particularly, of "pompoms" and other anti-aircraft equipment.

4. An authorization of $300,000,000 for equipping the fleet with the latest anti-aircraft equipment.

The President's message gave the details of the cargo ship construction program, which he stated some time ago would be submitted to Congress.

TEXT OF THE MESSAGE

The text of President Roosevelt's message was as follows:

I am convinced that the national interest demands that immediate steps be taken upon an emergency basis to provide against the effect upon the United

Continued on Page Seven

KENNEDY TO URGE OUR 'STAYING OUT'

Says After White House Call He Will Speak Own Mind 'for Once' Tomorrow

Special to THE NEW YORK TIMES.

WASHINGTON, Jan. 16—Joseph P. Kennedy, retiring Ambassador to Great Britain, conferred with President Roosevelt unexpectedly today. As he left the White House he said that his radio speech on Saturday night would accent "staying out of war."

Mr. Kennedy added that the speech would touch upon the lend-lease bill now before Congress and that it was written before he talked with the President and other officials.

"For once, I am going to say for myself what I have in my mind," the Ambassador said.

"Why don't you ask the President?" he replied when asked what Mr. Roosevelt thought of this plan.

Successor's Name a Secret

The Ambassador said that he had discussed with the President the subject of a successor at London. It was understood that the Chief Executive's choice for the post was not absolutely final, and Mr. Kennedy refused to tell the name of the man under consideration.

Mr. Kennedy confirmed the fact that he would appear before the House Foreign Affairs Committee on Tuesday to give his views on the Administration's lend-lease measure. He declined to discuss Secretary Morgenthau's statement yesterday outlining Great Britain's difficulties concerning dollar exchange. The Ambassador said that he had not read the statement.

To give him more time to work on his inaugural address, the President held his weekly Cabinet meeting today instead of Friday. The President had not yet put his address on paper but it would probably not take more than twenty minutes to deliver, according to Stephen Early, White House secretary.

The President also conferred jointly today with Secretaries Hull, Stimson and Knox, and General George C. Marshall, the Army's Chief of Staff, and Admiral Harold Stark, Chief of Naval Operations. The foreign situation in general was discussed.

Knudsen Also a Caller

William S. Knudsen, director of the Office of Production Management, called on the Chief Executive, accompanied by John Biggers, production chief of the OPM, and laid before Mr. Roosevelt a chart showing in detail the organization of the new defense super-council.

At Mr. Knudsen's office it was said that President Roosevelt probably would make the chart public next week.

Miss Anne Morgan, a leader in relief work in France and an advocate of more American relief for

Continued on Page Five

Auto Show Here This Year Is Abandoned To Let Manufacturers Push Defense Task

By The Associated Press.

DETROIT, Jan. 16—Because of the demands of the national defense program there will be no National Automobile Show this year.

In making this announcement today, Alvan Macauley, president of the Automobile Manufacturers' Association, said the decision was reached by the association's board of directors after consulting with all car producing companies.

Mr. Macauley added that cancellation of the show, held annually in New York, usually in Grand Central Palace, would not affect plans which the individual manufacturers may have made to introduce new models as usual next Fall. There will be new models, he added, but explained that the industry had pledged its whole support to the defense program, and the model changes will be regulated by the requirements of the rearmament task.

The National Automobile Show, which has been held annually since 1900, first as a combined bicycle and automobile presentation, is the only showing sponsored exclusively by the automobile manufacturers. Other local shows are staged by local dealers' organizations.

Apparently in anticipation of a curtailment of car and truck production because of the defense program requirements, the industry has been operating at high levels almost since the introduction of 1941 models last Fall.

The factories turned out more than 1,500,000 units during the final quarter of 1940 and have accumulated a field stock estimated in some quarters at close to 500,000 vehicles. It was back at high level output again last week after the Christmas and New Year's holiday week curtailment. Ward's reports estimated last week's assemblies at 115,935 vehicles, while other trade sources reported today that this week's assemblies would be in excess of 120,000.

AID BILL IS VITAL, WILLKIE DECLARES

Talk Won't Keep Us Out of War, Resources to Britain Will, He Says at Town Hall

Making an unscheduled appearance last night at Town Hall to participate with 1,000 fellow-Americans in the weekly Town Hall of the Air radio program, Wendell Willkie declared that if the American people believed, "as I believe," that the collapse of Britain would mean the passing of a free way of life from America, then they would grant to President Roosevelt the extraordinary powers he has asked in the lease-lend bill.

"We shall not keep America out of war by mere strong statements that she is to stay out of war," he declared. "We will keep America out of war if we supply to the fighting men of Britain sufficient resources so they may crush and defeat the ruthless dictatorship of Hitler."

Shaking the same unruly lock of curly hair which became so familiar to the United States during the last campaign and speaking in the same husky voice, the defeated Republican Presidential candidate declared:

"I, who opposed Franklin Roosevelt, call upon all Americans to give him such power in this most severe crisis, I believe, in the history of America, so that we can debate with him again in another election."

Heard Thomas in Debate

Mr. Willkie had driven through the storm from his Fifth Avenue apartment to Town Hall, in West Forty-third Street, and sat quietly with Mrs. Willkie in a mezzanine box while Norman Thomas, the Socialist leader, and Dr. Frank Kingdon, New York chairman of the Committee to Defend America by Aiding the Allies, had debated the issue of the lease-lend bill.

During this debate Mr. Thomas charged that neither the President nor Mr. Willkie, during the campaign, had raised the issue presented by the introduction of the bill and for that, he said, "there is no justification." He called the bill a "mad grant of dictatorial power."

As the hour program, broadcast over the NBC network, was nearing its end, George V. Denny Jr., president of Town Hall and moderator of the program, asked Mr. Willkie if he would like to reply to Mr. Thomas's charge, or if he had any remarks to make.

"I would like to remind you," Mr. Willkie said, as he rose, smiling, waving his hand in answer to the cheers and handclapping which greeted him, "that when Mr. Thomas says that the American people had no choice except to vote for Mr. Roosevelt or myself, they also had

Continued on Page Eight

'CRISIS EXCEEDS '17'

Secretary of War Holds Lend-Lease Measure an Urgent Need

FOR UNIFYING DEFENSE

Favors 'Transfer' of Part of Our Navy to Others, if Advantageous to Us

The text of Mr. Stimson's statement is on Page 7.

By TURNER CATLEDGE
Special to THE NEW YORK TIMES.

WASHINGTON, Jan. 16—The United States stands today in real and great danger of invasion by air in the contingency that the British Navy should be destroyed or surrendered, Secretary Stimson told the House Foreign Affairs Committee today in urging the speediest possible enactment of the principle of President Roosevelt's lend-lease bill for aid to the nations resisting the Axis powers.

The War Secretary said, moreover, that this country is faced with a more acute emergency with reference to the time element in production of munitions for defense than it was when we entered the first World War in 1917. In that former crisis, he pointed out, there was a "stable front line" in France. Italy and Japan were arrayed on the side of Britain and France against Germany. The British, French, Italian and Japanese fleets were in almost complete control of all the oceans of the world.

Munitions factories and production of Great Britain and France in 1917 were so abundant, Mr. Stimson continued, that they were able to supply, and did supply, the United States the great bulk of weapons it needed. In other other words, those countries constituted our principal arsenals.

Urgency of Situation Stressed

Today, he said, the situation is almost reversed. Italy and Japan are members of the German-dominated Axis. France has been conquered and her fleet made incapable of opposing the Axis powers. The arsenals of conquered countries, such as France, are at the service of the Axis nations, and Great Britain, far from being able to come to the assistance of this country, "is compelled to enter our markets for a substantial quantity of weapons for her own use."

"Instead of being able leisurely to pick and choose and deliberately to arm ourselves, relying upon the then existing stability on the other side of the Atlantic, we are not only compelled to arm ourselves entirely by our own efforts but to do so at the very time when it is imperative that our American industry and plants should be working at top speed to furnish vital weapons of defense to Great Britain in order that she may meet the crisis which is confronting her this Spring and Summer, and thus preserve her fleet as a bulwark in the Atlantic Ocean," Mr. Stimson said.

He considered it manifest in such a situation, he said, that every possible effort be made to simplify all steps in production of the munitions which are to constitute our defense.

He also thought it patent that expeditious means and clear authority must be provided to "assure the prompt distribution of munitions to countries whose defense is important to us." And he regarded the President's bill as a "forthright and clear grant of power which will enable the President to place in operation the best and simplest plan to carry out a national policy many times stated and endorsed."

Stimson to Return to Stand

Mr. Stimson was the only witness before the Foreign Affairs Committee today. He will go on the stand again tomorrow to submit to further questioning by committee members and then will be followed in turn by Secretary Knox and William S. Knudsen, director of the Office of Production Management.

Secretary Stimson's warning of the danger of aerial attack from the totalitarian powers should the British Navy go under came during a brush between him and Mr. Fish. The New York Representative, leader of the House forces opposed to the President's bill, was insisting that the Secretary tell the committee where the dangers were that demanded such a drastic step as proposed in the legislation.

"Does the Secretary believe any foreign nation could land troops on

Continued on Page Six

"All the News That's Fit to Print."

The New York Times.

LATE CITY EDITION
Fair with slowly rising temperature today. Tomorrow increasing cloudiness and warmer.
Temperatures Yesterday—Max.,29; Min.17

Copyright, 1941, by The New York Times Company.

VOL. XC..No. 30,313. Entered as Second-Class Matter, Postoffice, New York, N. Y. NEW YORK, TUESDAY, JANUARY 21, 1941. THREE CENTS NEW YORK CITY and Vicinity | FOUR CENTS Elsewhere Except in 7th and 8th Postal Zones.

ROOSEVELT INAUGURATED FOR THE THIRD TIME; WINANT TO BE NAMED AMBASSADOR TO LONDON; BRITISH INVADE ERITREA; DICTATORS SET COURSE

FASCISTI IN FLIGHT

Desert Fighters Driving Italians Toward Vital Red Sea Port

R. A. F. BOMBS BASES

Clashes on Kenya Front Widen New Threat to African Colonies

Wireless to THE NEW YORK TIMES.

CAIRO, Egypt, Jan. 20—Italian troops continued an orderly retreat from Kassala into Eritrea today, closely followed by British mobile forces, which continually harassed the Fascist rear guard. Fortifications around Sabderat and Tessenei were occupied yesterday without opposition, thus again making the results of many months' labor useless to the Italians.

The advancing British forces now are more than thirty miles inside Eritrea, headed east through foothills along the southern section of a road that makes a flat loop south from Sabderat, which is ten miles inside the border, to the Tessenei area, about twenty miles inside. The road then turns east and then north again directly south of Agordat, where it meets the railway from the Red Sea port of Massawa.

The railway extends west from Agordat to within sixty miles of Kassala, but the road in that region is not comparable with the southern route.

Supply Problem Difficult

The British units are now somewhat reinforced, but all the action thus far has been a mere series of patrol forays. The Italians apparently are withdrawing according to plan in good order. It is possible that they will retreat to Agordat to eliminate the extremely difficult problem of supplying a rather large force over rough and rutty roads under frequent bombing and subject to daily attacks of British patrols, which had continually threatened to isolate Kassala.

From Agordat the Italians will have the advantage of easy supplies unless the R. A. F. destroys the railway. The British, on the other hand, will be forced to supply their forces over the road previously used by the Italians, should they decide to penetrate that far.

This action on the part of the Italians is strangely similar to that of the British last Summer when they withdrew to the railhead at Matruh, forcing the Italians to lengthen their lines of communication. However, it is likely that the British also learned a lesson from the subsequent events and that they are unlikely to take such chances as those that made the Italians a prey to flanking movements.

R. A. F. Hampers Retreat

Early yesterday morning R. A. F. bombers attacked gun positions southeast of Tessenei and further hampered the Italian retreat by bombing and machine-gunning truck concentrations in the same area. Massawa, Assab and Hargeisa also were bombed. The attackers braved an intensive antiaircraft fire at Massawa, setting many fires at this port, where supplies going inland to Agordat must be landed.

Blinding sand storms again swept Northern Libya yesterday, considerably hampering air activity, but R. A. F. patrols were carried out in the Tobruk area.

On the Kenya front British motorized units continued their offensive patrol activities, which are steadily reducing the Italian gains made last Summer.

Clashes on Kenya Border

NAIROBI, Kenya, Jan. 20 (UP)—South African forces, part of the southern jaw of a British pincer campaign against the Italians in East Africa, reported today the capture of prisoners in clashes on the Kenya-Italian Somaliland and Kenya-Ethiopian borders.

Prisoners were taken in the El Yibo area, near Lake Rudolf along the border between Kenya and Western Ethiopia, said a communiqué, and eleven dead, including two European officers, were left behind by the dispersed Fascist unit.

In a patrol clash on the El Wak road, near the Kenya-Italian So-

Continued on Page Ten

The International Situation

TUESDAY, JAN. 21, 1941

President Roosevelt took office for his tradition-breaking third term in a historic inaugural ceremony on the Capitol steps yesterday. In an address broadcast throughout the world he considered the status, the strength and the future of free democracies in the present menaced world. As to this nation, he said: "We do not retreat. We are not content to stand still. As Americans, we go forward, in the service of our country, by the will of God." The speech and the occasion were marked by a solemnity that seemed to reflect the grave international events. [Page 1, Column 8.]

The inaugural parade foreshadowed the new military role that this country is preparing to play in defense of the democracies. Instead of the panoply of floats, and the colorful uniforms of club and fraternal organizations, it was primarily a military spectacle, which some 500,000 persons viewed from every available vantage point. [Page 1, Column 6.]

As if further to emphasize the international wartime aspect of the occasion, the members of the diplomatic corps attending included representatives of nations that are fighting each other, as well as those of nations that have been occupied or overrun. [Page 4, Column 6.]

The next United States Ambassador to London to succeed Joseph P. Kennedy, who is retiring, will be John Gilbert Winant, former Governor of New Hampshire and former Director of the International Labor Office at Geneva, it was learned in London. It is understood he will be accompanied by a business man having the rank of Minister who will serve as liaison officer to handle United States supplies to Britain. [Page 1, Column 4.]

Reichsfuehrer Hitler and Premier Mussolini have held their meeting, but just when, or where, or what was discussed has not been disclosed. The official German news agency said merely that the leaders had met in the presence of their Foreign Ministers and "had a comprehensive exchange of views relative to the situation." [Page 1, Column 2.] The Italian communiqué was identically worded. It was thought in Rome that the obvious matters discussed were Axis policy regarding the Balkans, the Mediterranean, Britain and developments in the United States and France. [Page 11, Column 3.]

Colonel William J. Donovan arrived in Sofia, Bulgaria, to be received by King Boris. Although he has no official rank, it was believed in diplomatic circles in Sofia that his mission was to provide information concerning the help the United States was prepared to give Britain, and that King Boris's decision regarding any future German pressure might be guided by what the Colonel had to say. [Page 10, Column 2.]

The "dissipation of all misunderstanding" between Marshal Pétain and Pierre Laval was explained in Vichy as a move initiated by the Marshal to curb a violent press campaign in Paris against the Vichy government and to unify French opinion. The step will not alter French policy and France will not turn over her immobilized fleet to Germany for use against Britain, an official spokesman said. [Page 1, Column 3.]

Italian forces retreating from the Kassala area withdrew into Eritrea, Italian East Africa, followed by pursuing British mobile units, according to Cairo. The British already were more than thirty miles inside Eritrea. [Page 1, Column 1.]

Italian air formations dropped tons of explosives on the Athens district and on Crete, but without doing much damage, according to Athens reports. The Greeks reported having sunk an Italian submarine. [Page 11, Column 1.]

Bad flying weather over the Strait of Dover prevented German bombers from getting through to England last night. There were a few scattered daylight attacks, which caused only slight damage. [Page 9, Column 1.]

Communiqués of the belligerents are on Page 10

AXIS CHIEFS DRAFT NEXT MOVE IN WAR

Quick New Action Is Expected After Hitler-Mussolini Talk —U. S. Believed a Topic

By C. BROOKS PETERS

Wireless to THE NEW YORK TIMES.

BERLIN, Jan. 20—The veil of secrecy that shrouded the movements of Reichsfuehrer Hitler and Premier Mussolini for forty-eight hours was lifted slightly this afternoon when the official German news agency released a communiqué declaring that a meeting between the two leaders and their Foreign Ministers had taken place.

The communiqué did not reveal when or where the conversations had been held nor what decisions had been reached. It said merely:

"On the occasion of a meeting in the presence of the Foreign Ministers of the Axis, the Fuehrer and the Duce had a comprehensive exchange of views relative to the situation. This exchange took place in the spirit of the hearty friendship between the two government heads and of the intimate comradeship in arms between the German and Italian peoples. It resulted in complete agreement of mutual opinions on all questions."

The issuance of this communiqué was somewhat surprising, for two hours earlier—shortly after 1 o'clock—three score foreign correspondents had been informed in a press conference that reports of a meeting between Herr Hitler and Signor Mussolini could be categorically denied.

Later the semi-official commentary Dienst aus Deutschland declared that the meeting had taken place over the week-end, but it did not say where. Since the previous meeting between the two men was held in Florence, Italy, when Herr Hitler learned of the Italian ultimatum to Greece, and since the German communiqué today was released before the Italian announce-

Continued on Page Twelve

VICHY INSISTS REICH WILL NOT GET NAVY

Petain Held Still Master—Talk With Laval Termed Merely a Move for Unity

By The United Press.

VICHY, France, Jan. 20—France refuses to turn over her immobilized fleet to Germany for use against Great Britain and insists upon full observance of the French-German armistice, despite the reconciliation of Marshal Henri Philippe Pétain and Pierre Laval, an official spokesman said today.

The "dissipation of all misunderstandings" between Marshal Pétain and the man he ousted as Vice Premier on Dec. 13 was undertaken by the 84-year-old marshal in a move to curb a violent campaign in the Paris press against the Vichy government, it was stated.

"France lives in the same regime as before and France's policy consists of respecting to the letter every line of the armistice convention," said a spokesman.

"It must be perfectly understood that our fleet will not be used against our former allies, just as it must be understood that we will continue to assure and safeguard our empire overseas.

"Marshal Pétain remains the chief of all France—free France, occupied France and overseas France," the spokesman continued.

"He remains the man who represents integral authority. Tomorrow, the same as today and yesterday, his Ministers, whoever they may be, will be responsible only to him. To use his own words, it is he whom history must judge."

The official French radio today broadcast the following explanation of the meeting of Marshal Pétain and M. Laval:

"It was for imperious reasons of domestic policy that Marshal Pétain decided to deprive himself on Dec. 13 of the aid of M. Laval, as

Continued on Page Twelve

ENVOY IS SELECTED

Former Head of World Labor Office Picked to Succeed Kennedy

BUSINESS MAN TO AID

Will Be Named Minister for Liaison in Supply of U. S. War Goods

By DAVID ANDERSON

Special Cable to THE NEW YORK TIMES.

LONDON, Jan. 20—John G. Winant will be the next United States Ambassador to the Court of St. James, it was learned today. He is expected to be accompanied by a business man who will have the rank of Minister and liaison duties in connection with the United States' production of war materials, which is becoming more essential to Great Britain daily.

The former Governor of New Hampshire has been mentioned often by the British press as a possible successor to Ambassador Joseph P. Kennedy since the latter faded from the scene. His appointment will cause little surprise and will be received with pleasure by his many friends here.

Mr. Winant entered the European picture in 1935 when he became assistant director of the International Labor Office at Geneva, moving up to the directorship two years ago. His record as an administrator, coupled with his personality, stamped on the minds of influential Britishers a most favorable impression.

The Foreign Office here would not discuss the Ambassadorship until the appointment had passed through. It would not even confirm that its assent had been asked to Mr. Winant's appointment.

With Viscount Halifax, Foreign Secretary until he was named Ambassador to the United States, expected in Washington soon, it was a question of absorbing interest here who would be his opposite number in London. Since Lord Halifax has been selected to carry on the mission of his predecessor, the Marquess of Lothian, in explaining to Americans what their stake is in Britain's battle, it is safe to assume that the selection of Mr. Winant means that he will carry on President Roosevelt's policy whereby arms and machines will be hastened to this country.

A Liberal Republican

John Gilbert Winant is a liberal Republican whose humanitarian principles have far transcended party or class lines. As a prominent member of the Republican party, he has been a staunch supporter of President Roosevelt's New Deal program, and as a wealthy New England aristocrat he has devoted his mature years to an intensive study of labor and social welfare problems.

Tall, deliberate and earnest, "an aristocratic version of Abraham Lincoln," he has often been mentioned as a possible Presidential candidate on a liberal Republican platform. He was mentioned as a

Continued on Page Nine

AGAIN THE NATION'S CHIEF EXECUTIVE

Franklin Delano Roosevelt taking the oath from Chief Justice Charles Evans Hughes

Times Wide World

Hull to Refuse to Disclose Envoys' Data to Congress

He Will Reject Demands for Access to Reports by Bullitt and Kennedy on European Affairs

By The Associated Press.

WASHINGTON, Jan. 20—The State Department will reject legislative demands that the department make public the diplomatic reports of Joseph P. Kennedy and William C. Bullitt, according to rumors on Capitol Hill. Mr. Kennedy, who will retire soon as Ambassador to Great Britain, and Mr. Bullitt, former Ambassador to France, were said by Senator Wheeler of Montana to have disagreed sharply on the course the United States should pursue in the European war.

One legislator told reporters that the State Department would decline to release the reports, even to congressional committees, on the ground that they were confidential documents of the Executive branch of the government.

This informant said that Administration officials believed publication of the documents would shed little light on the lend-lease legislation and might create an unnecessary side issue in the fight over the program.

Mr. Kennedy is scheduled to testify before the House Foreign Affairs Committee tomorrow.

Representative Fish, ranking minority member of the committee, said today that opposition witnesses "definitely will answer the absurd charges made by Government officials that we are in danger of immediate invasion and that this bill has something to do with a crisis in England in sixty or ninety days."

Fish declared it was "absurd" to talk of aiding Britain in a period of sixty to ninety days because, he added, none of the equipment leased or loaned to the British would reach them during that period.

There were reports on the Senate side today that opposition members were seeking to draft a substitute for the lend-lease legislation which would provide an outright cash gift to Britain of $1,000,000,000 to $2,000,000,000.

Indications that this "gift" strategy would be employed in the determined fight for defeat of the lease-lend legislation served to give notice that inauguration day signified

Continued on Page Eight

DEFENSE PROGRAM IS PARADE KEYNOTE

Mechanized Units, Coast Guard and Soldiers, Sailors and Marines Salute President

Special to THE NEW YORK TIMES.

WASHINGTON, Jan. 20—The inaugural parade which marched "the historic mile" down Pennsylvania Avenue today and past the White House to salute President Roosevelt for the third time provided a dramatic foretaste of things to come in the military program of the United States.

Soldiers on foot and on wheel, airplanes in mass formations and sailors and marines marching with fixed bayonets, these component parts of the parade virtually swamped the few civilian units, which themselves were barely sufficient to represent the civilian activities of the Federal Government.

This was an inaugural parade without floats, without civilian drum and bugle corps, without drum majors or "drum majorettes," without club and fraternal bands and without the delegations of silk-hatted marchers whom States have sent to the Capitol ever since Thomas Jefferson was first inaugurated here in 1801.

Even the tempo was different, for the mechanized mass of the parade, the gigantic wheel and tractor implements of mechanized warfare roared past the reviewing stand at forty miles an hour.

There were only two bits of color in the whole parade. The first was furnished by the Marine Band, which wore the traditional scarlet coats with blue trousers and yellow chevrons and stripes. The other was provided by a National Youth Administration unit, dressed in Russian-type blouses colored bright red or bright blue, accompanied by a band wearing flowing capes.

Otherwise the military and naval display was characterized by khaki or blue or gray uniforms, by riflemen marching with fixed bayonets and soldiers equipped for field service, including steel helmets.

About thirty Governors had a prominent place in the parade, each having three small sedans for his official party. The rest of the parade was confined to the preparedness program which formed the

Continued on Page Seven

'New World Order' Only a Matter of Time, Says Matsuoka, Urging U. S. to 'Allay' Crisis

By The Associated Press.

TOKYO, Tuesday, Jan. 21—Foreign Minister Yosuke Matsuoka told the Japanese Diet today that Japan, Germany and Italy certainly would accomplish their goal of a new world order "if only given time" and expressed hope that the United States "will bend her utmost efforts to allay the impending crisis of civilization."

Should both the United States and Japan become involved in a new world war because of the triple military alliance, he said "no one could guarantee that it could not develop into a war spelling the downfall of modern civilization."

United States trade embargoes against Japan, he said, left his country no alternative save to build up a self-sufficient trade sphere in "Greater East Asia" and he declared that the United States "has evinced no adequate understanding" that such a sphere "is truly a matter of vital concern to Japan."

"British dominions and colonies are in various ways interfering with Japan's shipping," he said.

He represented the military alliance with Germany and Italy as a device designed to "prevent further extension of present disturbances," and declared that Germany and Italy shared his country's desire to remove mutual Japanese-Russian misunderstandings.

"Some of those pending issues [with Russia] are now well on the way to settlement," he said.

"Establishment of a new world order, the goal of the powerful triple pact, if only given time, will surely be accomplished," he continued.

"There is no room for doubt that it will be crowned with brilliant success. If the Japanese people are fully and firmly prepared for this task, the future of our empire will indeed be great and glorious."

"The United States," the Foreign Minister said in his lengthy foreign

Continued on Page Fourteen

PRESIDENT FINDS IT EXHILARATING DAY

Attends the Many Ceremonies in High Spirits, His Mien Turning Grim at Times

By FRANK L. KLUCKHOHN

Special to THE NEW YORK TIMES.

WASHINGTON, Jan. 20 — One word describes the way the first American President to win a third term felt on the first day of his third Administration—exhilaration.

It was with obvious zest and joy that President Roosevelt went through a long day of ceremonies which began with a church service at 10:30 A. M., came to a climax with the precedent-shattering taking of his third oath of the office at 12:11 P. M. and, after a colorful parade, an air demonstration by 235 planes and various receptions, ended with a family dinner at the White House at 8 P. M.

The President clearly was in high spirits as he drove down Pennsylvania Avenue to the Capitol in an open car. He chatted animatedly with Speaker Rayburn, who sat next to him, and waved his tall silk hat with his right hand to the crowds, smiling and nodding to those thousands upon thousands lining the streets whose eyes were focused upon him.

He was in just as happy a mood when he drove back to the White House with Mrs. Roosevelt beside him amidst the same acclaim.

Face Shows Solemnity, Too

There were grim moments and solemn moments during the day, and these were reflected in Mr. Roosevelt's face, such as when he prayed in church, delivered his philosophical inaugural address, and alertly watched mechanized equipment, including light tanks and scout cars, future officers in the form of West Point and Annapolis cadets, fighting contingents and uniformed NYA and CCC boys parade by him after luncheon.

By and large, however, the President appeared to enjoy keenly the glittering display and pageantry of the day, the color of foreign and American uniforms of many hues and the good-fellowship involved in lunching with 1,200 dignitaries and other guests, receiving Governors and members of the Electoral College and meeting 2,000 more guests at a 5 o'clock tea. His enjoyment was manifested by his frequent smile, his eagerness and his constant conversation.

The services at St. John's Episcopal Church this morning were brief, but to some extent they set the tone of the day. There were three hymns, "O God, Our Help in Ages Past," "America," and "Faith of Our Fathers." The Rev. Frank R. Wilson of the Roosevelts' home church, St. James of Hyde Park, read a general confessional; the Rev. Howard S. Wilkinson of St. Thomas's Church of Washington read the Twentieth Psalm and the Rev. C. Leslie Glenn of St. John's read from II Kings 6:8-17. There was no sermon.

As the President's mother, Captain James Roosevelt of the Marines, Crown Prince Olaf and Crown Princess Martha of Norway and the other members of the President's personal party, as well as the Cabinet members and dignitaries in the congregation knelt, the clergyman, standing before the

Continued on Page Six

NO RETREAT HERE

Democracy Won't Die and Nation Proves It, President Asserts

INACTION A DANGER

Sacrifices Justified, He Adds, if Spirit of the Land Is Saved

Text of the President's speech will be found on Page 2.

By TURNER CATLEDGE

Special to THE NEW YORK TIMES.

WASHINGTON, Jan. 20—On the exact spot on the Capitol steps where, with few exceptions, Presidents have taken the oath since the time of James Monroe, Franklin Delano Roosevelt was inaugurated again today as President of the United States. While one tradition was thus observed, another was shattered, for Mr. Roosevelt was the first person in American history to win or accept more than two terms in the White House.

The Constitutional oath was intoned by Chief Justice Hughes, and with his hand on an opened page of an old family bible, Mr. Roosevelt turned to an immense crowd shivering in the bright cold sunshine, and to them and millions listening in on the radio throughout the world he voiced the challenge:

"We do not retreat. We are not content to stand still. As Americans, we go forward, in the service of our country, by the will of God."

After uttering these words, interpreted here as summing up the aspirations represented in the domestic and foreign policies of his Administration, Mr. Roosevelt, as Commander in Chief of the Army and Navy, reviewed a military parade intended to impress upon the visiting multitudes the results of their own efforts toward national defense.

Against Disruption From Without

The President made it clear that he considered it an historic occasion.

In his clear, modulated voice, the President likened the trials now before the country to those of the times of Washington and Lincoln. In Washington's day the task of the people was to create and weld together a nation. In Lincoln's, it was to preserve the nation from disruption from within.

"In this day," he said, "the task of the people is to save that nation and its institutions from disruption from without."

Although conceived and delivered under the stress of the international crisis, the address did not chart by specification the future course of the Administration. Rather, it was a philosophic dissertation on the status and strength of free institutions in this troubled world—a prelude to a declaration that "our strong purpose is to protect and perpetuate the integrity of democracy."

The inauguration ceremony in itself was over in less than half an hour. Mr. Roosevelt took the oath at 12:11 P. M., and sixteen and one-half minutes later he had completed his address, one of the shortest on record.

Wallace Takes the Oath

Five minutes before the President faced Chief Justice Hughes, Henry Agard Wallace took the oath as Vice President, receiving it at the hands of his predecessor, John Nance Garner. Incidentally, one of Mr. Roosevelt's first acts in his new Administration was to turn and embrace his former team-mate whom he once referred to as "Old Man Commonsense," and to bid him God's speed on his journey back to Texas and retirement.

After the ceremony at the Capitol the President rode to the White House with Mrs. Roosevelt down lanes of cheering thousands along Constitution and Pennsylvania Avenues. After an inaugural luncheon at the White House, attended by more than 1,000 guests, the President reviewed the troops as they passed through a Court of Freedom in front of the Executive Mansion.

Nearest the President at this function were Vice President Wallace, Mrs. Roosevelt and the Presi-

Continued on Page Three

"All the News That's Fit to Print."

NEWS INDEX, PAGE 35, THIS SECTION

The New York Times.

LATE CITY EDITION
Partly cloudy and continued warm today and tomorrow.
Temperatures Yesterday—Max., 91; Min., 75

Section 1

Copyright, 1941, by The New York Times Company.

VOL. XC. No. 30,465. Entered as Second-Class Matter, Postoffice, New York, N. Y. NEW YORK, SUNDAY, JUNE 22, 1941. Including Rotogravure Picture, Magazine and Book Sections. TEN CENTS New York City and Vicinity

HITLER BEGINS WAR ON RUSSIA, WITH ARMIES ON MARCH FROM ARCTIC TO THE BLACK SEA; DAMASCUS FALLS; U. S. OUSTS ROME CONSULS

MUST GO BY JULY 15

Ban on Italians Like Order to German Representatives

U. S. DENIES SPYING

Envoys Told to Protest Axis Charges—Nazis Get 'Moor' Text

By BERTRAM D. HULEN
Special to THE NEW YORK TIMES.

WASHINGTON, June 21—The Italian Embassy was directed by the State Department in a note published today to close all its consular offices and other agencies in this country having connections with the Italian Government by July 15. This was the reply to the Italian demand for the closing of all American Consulates in Italy.

At the same time Sumner Welles, Under-Secretary of State, announced that he had sent to Dr. Hans Thomsen, the German Chargé d'Affaires, the text of President Roosevelt's message to Congress yesterday denouncing the sinking of the American freighter Robin Moor in the South Atlantic on May 21.

This message, which accused Germany of being an international outlaw, engaging in piracy and attempting to intimidate the United States by the sinking and to drive American commerce from the seas, contained notice that this country would not yield before such measures and stated that compensation would be sought for the sinking.

It was transmitted "for the information" of the German Government, but constituted in effect a note of protest. A further communication will be sent asking damages when a final determination has been reached of the extent of damages that should be sought.

Will Deny Improper Acts

In addition, the State Department instructed the American Embassies in Berlin and Rome to inform the respective governments that the United States objects to all allegations of improper acts by American consular officials in those countries and to complete arrangements for the withdrawal of the consular officials and their staffs by July 15, the limit set by the German and Italian Governments.

The Axis governments had charged that the American Consuls had spied for the British. No reply has been made by the State Department to the German protests against the order closing Nazi consulates in this country, but the protest will be rejected. The United States alleged subversive activities as the reason for the demand for them to be closed by July 10.

The notes to the German and Italian Embassies were sent by messenger last night. However, no direct charge of improper activities was made against the Italian consuls in the note Mr. Welles sent to Don Ascanio dei principi Colonna, the Italian Ambassador. He merely stated that the continued functioning of Italian consular establishments within United States territory "would serve no desirable purpose."

In addition, the closing of Italian agencies having connections with the Rome government was requested. The Italian Embassy, as in the earlier case of the German Embassy, was exempted, but the closing of the office of the Italian Commercial Counselor in New York was demanded, along with the consulates.

Welles Note to Colonna

The note from Mr. Welles to Prince Colonna follows:

June 20, 1941

His Excellency
Don Ascanio dei principi Colonna
Royal Italian Ambassador

Excellency:

I have the honor to inform Your Excellency that the President has directed me to request that the Italian Government promptly close all Italian consular establishments within United States territory and remove therefrom all Italian consular of-

Continued on Page Two

Hope Dims for Submarine; Diver Balked at 370 Feet

Knox Believes All 33 Are Dead on the O-9 and Expects Rites at Scene for Navy 'Heroes'—Pressure Halts Descent

By RUSSELL PORTER
Special to THE NEW YORK TIMES.

PORTSMOUTH, N. H., June 21—As hope faded rapidly for the crew of the Submarine O-9, which failed to rise after submerging yesterday morning twenty-four miles east of this city, it became known tonight that the Navy might be unable to complete its salvage operations, and might be compelled to leave the bodies entombed where they lie—440 feet below the surface of the Atlantic.

This theory was based upon the assumption that the two officers and thirty-one men must already be given up as lost, but that assumption has become stronger with every new development since the submarine was reported missing.

Last night cork insulation from the interior of the hull was picked up, showing that at least part of the submarine had collapsed, and early today, after fourteen hours of dragging, grapnels located an object believed to be the sunken craft. Since then no signals from the O-9 have been received on the sensitive sound-detection devices on the salvage ships in response to their repeated messages.

The view that the O-9's fate was sealed was strengthened this afternoon when reporters and photographers, visiting the scene in a Navy press boat, saw one of the Navy's most experienced divers fail in an attempt to reach the O-9 after descending 370 feet, or within seventy feet of where the Navy believes it has located the submarine with grapnel lines.

The diver, George Crocker, 31 years old, of Seattle, asked to be hauled up when he became convinced that he was not getting enough air pressure from his life lines of helium-oxygen mixture to overcome the increasing sea pressure as he went lower and lower.

A message from the Falcon said: "Diver descended 370 feet. Had difficulty in breathing. Brought to surface. Will continue attempts by varying diving techniques."

On the salvage ship the dive was called "the most dangerous in submarine history." It was pointed out that no one had ever made a successful "working" dive at 440 feet and that any diver who went down so far, where he would have to grope his way in complete darkness under terrific sea pressure, 195.8 pounds to the square inch, could do so only at extreme risk to his life.

Colonel Frank Knox, Secretary of the Navy, returning tonight on

Continued on Page Thirty

ARMY ASKS GUARD BE KEPT IN SERVICE

Recommends Congress Act to Hold State Troops, Reserve Officers Indefinitely

By HALLETT ABEND
Special to THE NEW YORK TIMES.

WASHINGTON, June 21—Members of the National Guard and Reserve Officers Corps will be kept in active service beyond the single year planned when they were called, if a recommendation made today by the War Department is approved by President Roosevelt and Congress.

Instead of a return to civilian life, starting Sept. 15, their terms of service in uniform may be extended indefinitely, or at least until the Army selectees have been sufficiently trained in ample numbers to permit the Guardsmen to be demobilized. The recommendation to the President does not specify any limit to the proposed extension of service.

At present there are 289,800 National Guardsmen, including their 21,800 officers, on active duty with the Federal Army. They were inducted into service in increments beginning Sept. 15 of last year. Some went into uniform as late as March of this year. Their terms of service, at time of induction, were limited to twelve months, which may not be extended except by act of Congress.

341,300 Would Be Affected

In addition to the National Guardsmen, who comprise eighteen divisions and one cavalry brigade now on active service, the government has called up 51,500 Reserve officers under the same terms, making collectively 341,300 officers and men who would be affected.

Today's War Department recommendation to the President that steps be taken to retain in the service these Guardsmen and Reserve officers was taken, according to the official announcement, because "the War Department has been flooded with queries from the field" as to whether or not the specified one-year limit of service would hold good or be changed.

"These queries are to be expected," continues the announcement, "because whatever the decision, there are many adjustments which the citizen-soldier must make in his affairs."

As yet no decision has been reached in the War Department whether or not to seek authority to retain selectees in the Army beyond the one-year training period specified in the Selective Service Act, but presumably such a step

Continued on Page Nineteen

NAVY MAY REPLACE SHIPYARD STRIKERS

Weighs Putting Own Machinists to Work to End Long Tie-Up in San Francisco

By The Associated Press.

SAN FRANCISCO, June 21—Striking A. F. L. machinists in a $300,000,000 defense program have come to a showdown with the United States Navy and their own international officers.

Reliable reports, not officially denied, indicated that the Navy might install its own machinists in the huge Bethlehem shipyards Monday if the local union did not heed the order of its international president to call off the strike by that time.

The same reports indicated that the Army also might be on hand

Continued on Page Twenty-eight

R. A. F. BLASTS FOE

Bags 26 Nazi Planes in Record Day Raids on Invasion Coast

GERMANY IS BOMBED

British on 11th Straight Night Offensive Into Western Reich

Special Cable to THE NEW YORK TIMES.

LONDON, Sunday, June 22—Twenty-six Nazi fighter planes were destroyed in daylight yesterday by Royal Air Force fliers on their fifth straight day of raiding the Germans' invasion coast and air bases in Northern France.

Twice before dark, waves of R. A. F. warcraft—reportedly numbering at least 150 planes each—swept over the Channel in offensive operations.

Bombers attacked the Nazi's airdromes on each occasion while strong forces of fighters blasted the way for the big planes through formations of German defense fighters. While the major raids were going on, other strong R. A. F. units patrolled over the French coast and battled Messerschmitts.

Attack Goes On; Big Bombs Used

Last night and early this morning the R. A. F. was still attacking the invasion coast, using some of the latest type of high-powered bombs.

Explosions rolled across the Channel like peals of thunder, shaking the ground and rocking buildings for miles along the Kentish coast, observers there reported.

A night curtain of fog hung over the Strait of Dover and little could be seen of the raids. The latest British attacks were apparently being made in the Boulogne area, where some of the heaviest daylight bombing was carried out.

Meanwhile R. A. F. bomber forces were again attacking Western Germany, officials here said briefly early today. The attacks marked the eleventh consecutive night in which the British have bombed industrial centers and war bases in the Reich.

Two Nazi bombers were shot down during the night in small scattered enemy raids on the east and southeast coasts of England. A few German bombs were reported dropped there; there were no accounts of casualties or damage.

The R. A. F. coastal patrol squadrons reported destroying at least two enemy planes and one Nazi

Continued on Page Eighteen

SYRIAN CITY TAKEN

French Withdraw After a Hard Fight—British Closer to Beirut

TADMUR PUSH IS ON

Allied Planes Harassing Vichy Troops, Whose Defense Falters

By C. L. SULZBERGER
By Telephone to THE NEW YORK TIMES.

ANKARA, Turkey, June 21—French troops evacuated the city of Damascus today after a persistent bombardment by British artillery and withdrew to new positions outside the Syrian capital, according to official advices from Beirut. Early in the afternoon it was learned that the Allied vanguard was already beginning to enter the city. This evening the British reported complete occupation.

The Damascus airport at Mezze has been taken by Indian detachments of the Allied forces and one of the key points east of Damascus has been surrounded by Druz tribesmen fighting on the side of the British.

The Beirut radio announced tonight that a British motorized column pushing westward from Iraq was now heading toward Tadmur. The British column, it was said, has been bombed constantly by the French Air Force, which has just been reorganized and reinforced by French squadrons coming from North Africa. Some German planes also were said to have arrived in Syria.

Advance in High Gear

It is clear that the Allied advance is beginning to move into high gear. Unconfirmed reports that the British forces have reached Beirut indicate that it may also fall soon. Beirut's fate depends largely on whether the British will call in their superior naval forces to shell the city proper. So far this has been avoided in order to keep damage and casualties at a minimum.

[A dispatch from Cairo said that Australian forces had been progressing toward Beirut for two days and had passed Ras Damour.]

The Allies, convinced of the seriousness of the French resistance, evidently have begun to fight this undeclared war in earnest and intend to get it over with fast at any cost. The main center of French resistance in the east has been Damascus, and the capture of the city is of great importance.

The Allied counter-move to the French attack in the south, which developed earlier in the week, is now proceeding with dispatch in the Merdjayoun district. The fortress of Merdjayoun is in Allied hands and it is obvious that the region is being rapidly cleared, since the coastal advance is dependent to a large degree on a corollary advance in the center.

Considerable concentrations of French artillery had been brought up around Damascus. The French dug in and placed batteries in many of the villas and gardens in the outer sections of the city. These batteries were slowly picked off by British gunners with Royal Air Force support, but the principal British effort was artillery shelling. The British sought to avoid excess damage by aerial bombardment, which is less accurate than artillery fire.

Tadmur Believed in Peril

The French admission that a British column is pressing toward Tadmur would seem to indicate that perhaps the town is endangered. Several days ago reliable sources here reported the existence of the column, but this was steadfastly denied by Beirut.

While there have been new reports that the trouble for the British in Iraq is far from over, the fact that they are able to spare considerable forces from there would indicate that everything is under control. It is known that British forces also are working westward along the North Syrian frontier toward Aleppo, but the exact strength of these units is not known here.

British military circles admit that the Syrian adventure can no longer

Continued on Page Twelve

The International Situation

SUNDAY, JUNE 22, 1941

At 5:30 o'clock this morning, Berlin time, two statements were read over the German radio that constituted a declaration of war upon the Soviet Union by Germany. A proclamation of Adolf Hitler, read by Propaganda Minister Goebbels, said that Russia, with Britain and the United States, had sought to "throttle" Germany and that he had therefore decided to put the fate of the German people in the hands of the army. A statement by Foreign Minister von Ribbentrop contained the actual declaration of war. The Finns and the Rumanians were mentioned as allies. Berlin reported subsequently that troops were on the march in East Prussia. [Page 1, Column 8; with map.]

Yesterday was a good day for British arms.

In the Syrian campaign Damascus was occupied. The British announced its capture and Vichy reported its evacuation to avoid street fighting and destruction of the city. Another British force was pushing nearer Beirut, supported by the fleet and the air arm, while a third column was moving toward Tadmur. [Page 1, Column 5; Map on Page 12.]

No less encouraging to the British was a victory much closer to home in the largest British daylight air attack of the war. In a sweep two waves of 150 planes each pounded the French Channel coast, going particularly for airdromes, and engaged German air defenses. The British reported downing twenty-six Nazi planes in these attacks for a loss of five of their own. Late last night the British were continuing their attacks across the Channel. [Page 1, Column 4; Map, Page 18.]

The Libyan theatre was quiet, but British pressure in East Africa was indicated by a protest from Vichy against what was declared to be a virtual ultimatum from General Wavell to French Somaliland to join the Free French or suffer an intensified blockade. London confirmed the representations of General Wavell. [Page 14, Column 1.]

Washington continued the accelerated pace of its anti-Axis diplomatic offensive. The Italian Embassy was instructed to close the forty-nine Italian consulates and seven agencies in this country before July 15. President Roosevelt's message to Congress on the Robin Moor was handed to the German Embassy while the State Department instructed the United States embassies in Berlin and Rome to inform those governments that the United States objected categorically to any allegations of improper acts by United States consuls. [Page 1, Column 1.]

Italian consular circles here were silent concerning the Washington order, but Italian anti-Fascist quarters expressed jubilation. [Page 3, Column 1.]

WHERE GERMAN ARMIES MARCH ON RUSSIA

Shown on the map is the western frontier of the Soviet Union, a battle line of more than 2,000 miles. Berlin indicated an attack from Norway to Rumania.

The Hitler Proclamation

The text of Adolf Hitler's proclamation, as recorded here by Columbia Broadcasting System, follows:

It was a difficult step for me to send my Minister to Moscow in order to attend to work against the policy of encirclement of Britain.

I hoped that at last it would be possible to put away tension.

Germany never intended to occupy Lithuania. The defeat of Poland induced me to again address a peace offer to the Allies. This was declined because Britain was still hoping to bring about European coalition.

That is why Cripps [Sir Stafford Cripps, British Ambassador] was sent to Moscow. He was commissioned under all circumstances to come to an agreement with Moscow. Russia always put out the lying statement that she was protecting these countries [evidently Lithuania, Estonia and Latvia, the Baltic States].

The penetration of Russia into Rumania and the Greek liaison with England threatened to place new, large areas into the war. Rumania, however, believed she was able to accede to Russia only if she received guarantees from Germany and Italy for the remainder of the country. With a heavy heart, I did this, for if Germany gives guarantees, she will fulfill them. We are neither Englishmen nor Jews.

I asked Molotoff [Soviet Foreign Commissar V. M. Molotoff] to come to Berlin, and he asked for a clarification of the situation. He asked, "Is the guarantee for Rumania directed also against Russia?"

I replied, "Against every one."

And Russia never informed us that she had even more far-reaching intentions against Rumania.

Molotoff asked further, "Is Germany prepared not to assist Finland, who was again threatening Russia?"

My reply was that Germany has no political interests in Finland, but another attack on Finland could not be tolerated, especially as we do not believe that Finland is threatening Russia.

Molotoff's third question was, "Is Germany agreeable that Russia give guarantees to Bulgaria?"

My reply was that Bulgaria is a sovereign State and I did not know that Bulgaria needed guarantees. Molotoff said Russia needed a passage through the Dardanelles and demanded bases in the Bosporus.

A few days later she [Russia] concluded the well known friendship agreement which was to incite the Serbs against Germany. Moscow demanded the mobilization of the Serbian Army.

When I still was silent, the men in the Kremlin went one step further. Russia offered to deliver war material against Germany. This was at the same time that I advised Matsuoka [Japanese Foreign Minister Yosuke Matsuoka] to bring about a lessening of the tension with Russia.

Serbian officers flew to Russia, where they were received as allies. Victory of the Axis in the Balkans at first foiled the plan to involve Germany in a long war and then, together with England and with the hope of American supplies, to throttle Germany.

Now the moment has come when I can no longer look at this development. Waiting would be a crime against Germany.

For weeks the Russians have been committing frontier violations. Russian planes have been crossing the frontier again and again to prove that they are the masters. On the night of June 17 and again on June 18 there was large patrol activity.

The march of the German Armies has no precedent. Together with the Finns we stand from Narvik to the Carpathians. At the Danube and on the shores of the Black Sea under Antonescu [Rumanian Dictator Ion Antonescu], German and Rumanian soldiers are united.

The task is to safeguard Europe and thus save all.

I have therefore today decided to give the fate of the German people and the Reich and of Europe again into the hands of our soldiers.

BAD FAITH CHARGED

Goebbels Reads Attack on Soviet—Ribbentrop Announces War

BALTIC MADE ISSUE

Finns and Rumanians Are Called Allies in Plan of Assault

Statement by von Ribbentrop is printed on Page 6.

By C. BROOKS PETERS
By Telephone to THE NEW YORK TIMES.

BERLIN, Sunday, June 22—As dawn broke over Europe today the legions of National Socialist Germany began their long-rumored invasion of Communist Soviet Russia. The non-aggression and amity pact between the two countries, signed in August, 1939, forgotten, the German attack began along a tremendous front, extending from the Arctic regions to the Black Sea. Marching with the forces of Germany are also the troops of Finland and Rumania.

Adolf Hitler, in a proclamation to the German people read over a national hook-up by Propaganda Minister Dr. Joseph Goebbels at 5:30 this morning, termed the military action begun this morning the largest in the history of the world. It was necessary, he added, because in spite of his unceasing efforts to preserve peace in this area it had definitely been proved that Russia was in a coalition with England to ruin Germany by prolonging the war.

Saw Stalemate in West

Herr Hitler, in his proclamation as reported here, made one vitally interesting statement, namely, that the supreme German military command did not feel itself able to force a decisive victory in the West—apparently on the British Isles—when large Russian troop concentrations were on the Reich's borders in the East.

The Russian troop concentrations in the East began in August, 1940, Herr Hitler asserted. "Thus, there occurred the effect intended by the Soviet-British cooperation," he added, "namely, the binding of such powerful German forces in the East that a radical conclusion of the war in the West, particularly as regards aircraft, could no longer be vouched for by the German High Command.

[The German radio announced early today that documentary proof would shortly be given of a secret British-Russian alliance, made behind Germany's back.]

Designed "to Save Reich"

The German action, Herr Hitler explained to his fellow-National Socialists, is designed to save the Reich and with it all Europe from the machinations of the Jewish-Anglo-Saxon warmongers.

The German Foreign Minister, Joachim von Ribbentrop, followed Dr. Goebbels on the air with a declaration of the Reich Government read before the foreign correspondents in the Foreign Office. Herr von Ribbentrop said he received V. G. Dekanozoff, the Russian Ambassador, this morning and informed him that in spite of the Russian-German non-aggression pact of Aug. 23, 1939, and an amity pact of Sept. 28, 1939, Russia had betrayed the trust that the Reich had placed in her.

"Contrary to all engagements which they had undertaken and in absolute contradiction to their solemn declarations, the Soviet Union had turned against Germany," the Reich note asserted. "They have first not only continued, but even since the outbreak of war intensified their subversive activities against Germany in Europe. They have second, in a continually increasing measure, developed their foreign policy in a tendency hostile to Germany and they have third massed their entire forces on the German frontier ready for action."

The Soviet Government, it was charged, had violated its treaties

Continued on Page Seven

"All the News That's Fit to Print."

The New York Times.

LATE CITY EDITION
Scattered showers and somewhat cooler today and tomorrow.
Temperatures Yesterday—Max., 94; Min., 75

VOL. XC...No. 30,466. Entered as Second-Class Matter, Postoffice, New York, N. Y. NEW YORK, MONDAY, JUNE 23, 1941. THREE CENTS NEW YORK CITY and Vicinity

SMASHING AIR ATTACKS ON SIX RUSSIAN CITIES, CLASHES ON WIDE FRONT OPEN NAZI-SOVIET WAR; LONDON TO AID MOSCOW, U. S. DELAYS DECISION

R. A. F. BAGS THIRTY

Downs 57 Nazis in Two Days of Attacks Over Bases in France

BOMBERS DO WORK

British Believed Curbing Enemy Raids at Start—London Has Alarm

By CRAIG THOMPSON
Special Cable to THE NEW YORK TIMES.

LONDON, Monday, June 23—In another series of big daylight sweeps over the German-occupied territory of Northern France yesterday, the Royal Air Force shot down thirty German fighters, many of the new Messerschmitt 109-F type, with a loss of only two of their own planes.

Strong forces of Hurricanes and Spitfires worked destruction on the Nazi defenders, while smaller numbers of Blenheim bombers that they escorted rained high explosives on the Germans' airfields.

Repeating their smashing offensives over and behind the invasion coast on Saturday—when the R. A. F. bagged twenty-seven Nazi fighters—the British airmen forced the battles over the enemy's bases.

[British bombers attacked points in Northwest Germany again last night—their twelfth raid into the Reich in as many nights—according to an Associated Press report from Berlin.]

London Hears Guns Again

Early this morning an air raid alarm sounded in London for the first time since June 14. The "all clear" came some time later, with no reports of bombing.

[Intermittent gunfire was heard in London some time after the air raid sirens sounded early today, The Associated Press reported. German aircraft were reported to have attacked shipping off the Northeast Coast of England during the night and one coastal town reported the sight and sound of explosions and gunfire at sea. No bombs were dropped on land in that area.]

Yesterday's daylight raids followed up a long attack over Saturday night by a heavy force of British bombers on Dunkerque and Boulogne.

Simultaneously, in the hours before dawn yesterday, the industrial areas of Western Germany around Duesseldorf and Cologne were bombed by R. A. F. squadrons.

Persons on the Kentish coast described the Dunkerque and Boulogne attacks as "the heaviest yet." They said bombs falling across the Channel rocked the earth on the English side. The Air Ministry said the attacks on the two ports were made by lighter forces than those that struck over Western Germany.

Night Vigil Over Nazi Air Bases

While the British were bombing Western Germany and the invasion ports, offensive patrols of R. A. F. night fighters maintained a vigil over the Nazis' aerodromes in Northern France. The purpose is to detect enemy bomber squadrons taking off for England and try to knock them down, while giving warning to Britain by radio.

This method of intercepting the Nazis' bombers at the start has been found increasingly effective. It is one more step in Britain's aggressive bid for control of the air, not only over the British Isles and the Channel but over Northern France as well.

The day's R. A. F. offensive included a hard bombing of freight yards at Hazebrouck, used by the Germans to handle traffic to Channel ports, the Air Ministry reported.

The two-day totals of fifty-seven German fighters shot down in these sweeps to British losses of seven planes are considered remarkable, and are the highest in terms of ratio of any comparable operations of the war.

Over the last six days in constant raiding of the German-held area of Northern France, the R. A. F. has shot down ninety-eight Nazi planes and lost twenty-three of its own, making the ratio for the week's

Continued on Page Eleven

The International Situation

MONDAY, JUNE 23, 1941

Three large battle zones—north, middle and south—appeared to be developing yesterday in the first day of Germany's invasion of Russia. In the north reports were vague; in the middle the Germans were driving ahead and in the south the Russians were reported to be holding well.

On the Finnish-Baltic front there were exchanges of bombing, with the Russians attacking Aabo in Finland and a fort in the Aaland archipelago and with the Germans striking at Russian airdromes. Stockholm reports said German troops were attacking on the Karelian Isthmus. From East Prussia the main German attack was delivered across Poland. Russian "strategic withdrawals" were reported toward Bialystok and Lwow after a surprise attack. In the Bessarabian-Black Sea sector a three-pronged drive was directed northward up the Sereth River, across the Pruth toward Jassy and up the Black Sea coast toward Odessa. The Russians, well fortified, were reported to be holding their own there. [Page 1, Column 8; Maps, Pages 1 and 6.]

In Moscow, Foreign Commissar Molotoff, speaking six hours after the invasion had started, ordered the "repulse" of this "predatory assault" and called the German justification for it a "sheer lie and provocation" that had been "belatedly concocted." [Page 1, Column 7.] Martial law was declared in all the Soviet border areas and popular enthusiasm was reported. [Page 10, Column 1.]

Italy, stressing the anti-Bolshevist idea, joined Germany's declaration of war. Active Italian intervention was not expected, but preparation for a long conflict with Britain, Russia and the United States was predicted. [Page 5, Column 1.]

In Berlin, where the taboo on mentioning German-Russian relations was lifted, the public was reported to be calm and unconcerned. Many Russians were arrested. [Page 3, Column 1.]

Britain's position in relation to the conflict and a promise of economic and technical support for Russia were set forth by Prime Minister Churchill in a broadcast to the world. "Any man or State who fights against nazism will have our aid," he declared. "Any man who fights with Hitler is our foe." Mr. Churchill recalled his own opposition to communism, which he did not recant, but named the defeat of Hitler as the first objective for both Britain and the United States. [Page 1, Columns 6 and 7.]

That part of Mr. Churchill's speech that conveyed a warning to the United States was supported in Washington, where the only official reaction to the Nazi-Soviet war was an informal statement by the State Department that the German attack on Russia was regarded there as convincing proof that Adolf Hitler planned to dominate the world. The question of lend-lease aid was deferred and Congressional opinion was divided upon it. [Page 1, Column 4.]

Washington was watching the Far East quite as closely as the European scene, however, for repercussions from the Nazi attack. There were suggestions that Japan might use this occasion for a drive on the Netherlands Indies, but other quarters forecast a possible swing by Japan away from the Axis. [Page 11, Column 1.]

This same division of opinion existed in Tokyo, where in an atmosphere of stunned surprise a series of governmental conferences was called to discuss Japanese policy. [Page 1, Column 5.]

Britain continued to take advantage, meanwhile, of Germany's diversion of strength to press the aerial hammering of Northern France and Western Germany. There was another big daylight battle yesterday and the British reported the destruction of thirty Nazi planes with a loss of only two of their own. [Page 1, Column 1.]

On the Syrian front, also, Britain continued to be victorious. Ankara sources reported that the French commander faced encirclement as the British force from Iraq had entered Tadmur. There was fighting in the outskirts of Beirut and the fall of that city was expected shortly. [Page 9, Column 1.]

SENATOR HARRISON DIES IN WASHINGTON

President Pro Tem of Upper House Is Stricken at 59—Body Lies in State Today

Special to THE NEW YORK TIMES.

WASHINGTON, June 22—Senator Byron Patton Harrison of Mississippi, who was always known as Pat Harrison, died at 6:30 o'clock this morning in the Emergency Hospital, where he underwent an operation a week ago for removal of an intestinal obstruction. The operation followed an illness which had seriously impaired his health. His age was 59.

At the bedside were the Senator's wife, the former Mary Edwina McInnis of Leakesville, Miss., and his son, Byron Patton Jr. of Gulfport, Miss.

Also surviving are two daughters, Mrs. James W. Cummings of Bethesda, Md., and Mrs. Irvin Miller of Nashville, Tenn.; a brother, Burroughs Harrison of Kilmichael, Miss., and a sister, Mrs. C. E. Saunders of Crystal Springs, Miss.

The esteem in which Senator Harrison was held was attested by the fact that Senate colleagues began immediate preparation for a special train to convey his body to Gulfport for burial. All members of the Senate who could arrange to attend and members of the Mississippi delegation of the House were designated as a committee to attend the rites, which will be held at Gulfport at 2:30 P. M. Wednesday.

Body Lies in State Today

The Senator's body will lie in state at the Capitol from 2 to 6 P. M. tomorrow. His family withstood the urging of his friends for a state funeral. Mr. Harrison often had said that he would not wish his passing to be marked by such a ceremony if he were still in public life at the time.

The special train bearing the body

Continued on Page Seventeen

REDS HERE DEMAND FIGHT ON HITLERISM

'Criminal Attack on Greatest Champion of Peace' Scored in Party Manifesto

The Communist party of the United States issued last night a statement that termed the German war on Russia "an unprovoked criminal attack upon the greatest champion of peace, freedom and national independence."

The statement couched in the terms of Communist ideology, called for "full support and cooperation with the Soviet Union in its struggle against Hitlerism."

Thus the "party line" of association with the Germans, which had existed since the signing of the Nazi-Soviet pact shortly before the war started in September, 1939, was broken.

But the statement did not associate the party either with the war aims of the Churchill government of Britain or with the aims of American policy as enunciated by President Roosevelt, except in the call for the defeat of the Germans.

"Imperialist" War Emphasized

The manifesto spoke of the European conflict as the "second imperialist world war," and declared that the Russians had "liberated the peoples of the Western Ukraine, White Russia, Bessarabia and the Baltic States."

It argued, moreover, that the "reactionaries and imperialists of both sides" had conspired against the peace and neutrality of the Soviet Union. And it declared that the rulers of Fascist Germany were now engaged in a "desperate struggle with their imperialist rivals in England and the United States."

The statement was signed by William Z. Foster, chairman of the party, and Robert Minor, acting secretary. Mr. Minor succeeded Earl Browder, who is in Federal

Continued on Page Eleven

WASHINGTON WAITS

But State Department Says Hitler Reveals Aim to Rule World

AID IS A PROBLEM

Few Vessels Available to Carry It Even if Approval Comes

By BERTRAM D. HULEN
Special to THE NEW YORK TIMES.

WASHINGTON, June 22—Germany's attack on Russia is regarded by the State Department as convincing proof that Reichsfuehrer Hitler plans to dominate the world.

This much was said today as officials conferred on the sensational turn of the European war and prepared to take up for decision the question of whether the United States, like Great Britain, would offer material aid to the Soviet Union as a victim of aggression.

If anybody needs further proof that Herr Hitler has planned domination of every country in the world, the department said, the attack on Russia should be sufficient to convince such persons, and that force is his instrument for carrying out his plans. It is another indication, the department asserted, that a non-aggression pact with Germany means simply an opportunity for Germany, if and when she desires to attack the other party to the non-aggression pact.

This informal statement served to reinforce contentions long made by President Roosevelt and Secretary of State Cordell Hull that Germany was bent upon world conquest. But the department was less definite concerning the prospects of lease-lend aid to Russia. That was left for future determination.

Warns of Slackened Effort

No official communication has been received from Russia, the department said, consequently any questions regarding lease-lend aid need not be discussed at this time.

Viscount Halifax, the British Ambassador, conferred during the day with Sumner Welles, Under-Secretary of State, but no comment was made afterward. Presumably they touched upon Prime Minister Churchill's promise of assistance to the Soviet Union. There are many who believe that if Britain wants the United States to extend lease-lend aid the attempt will be made.

Senator Walter F. George of Georgia, chairman of the Committee on Foreign Relations, said it was clear that Germany had undertaken to obtain food, oil and mineral supplies from Russia to enable her to carry on a long war, and that she wanted to secure the Eastern door because she never had really trusted Russia.

He thought the danger, from the American standpoint, might be found in a general feeling of relief that would tend to slow down the defense effort. This undoubtedly, he said, would be encouraged by foreign propaganda.

On the other hand, Representative Hamilton Fish of New York, ranking Republican member of the House Committee on Foreign Affairs, said the Russo-German war

Continued on Page Three

AREA OF MAIN ATTACKS IN RUSSO-GERMAN HOSTILITIES

As Soviet fliers reportedly bombed a fort in the Aaland Archipelago and the port of Aabo (1), the Nazis were said to have attacked on the Karelian Isthmus (2) and across the border of East Prussia (3). Northeast of Lyck (3) the Germans occupied Kalvarija, it was acknowledged by Moscow. A map showing the entire German-Soviet theatre of war appears on Page 6.

JAPAN IS WORRIED BY GERMAN ATTACK

Some Believe Tokyo Will Seek Rapprochement With United States and Britain

By OTTO D. TOLISCHUS
Wireless to THE NEW YORK TIMES.

TOKYO, June 22—The outbreak of war between Germany and Russia despite the Russian-German nonaggression pact froze official Japan into icy silence. The only official comment was that there would be no comment.

The Cabinet spokesman maintained that the Japanese Government was not taken by surprise but the press says the government views the new development "with serious concern." To the unprepared public, which sees the European war rapidly developing into a world war affecting Japan's own fate, it came as a stunning blow.

[Russia is preparing to ask Japan for assurances of neutrality, while German sources in Japan said Berlin does not intend to request Japanese intervention, the United Press reported from Tokyo this morning.]

Immediately after receiving the announcement of the outbreak of the new war from Ambassador Hiroshi Oshima in Berlin, Foreign Minister Yosuke Matsuoka reported to Emperor Hirohito. An extraordinary liaison conference between the Cabinet and High Command is scheduled for tomorrow.

According to the newspaper Asahi, the Japanese Government "is giving careful consideration to counter measures to cope with the situation, taking into account all conceivable possibilities." But the general impression is that Japan will adopt a policy of watchful wait-

Continued on Page Eleven

Churchill Promises to Aid All Who Are Hitler's Foes

He Declares Britain Has a Single Purpose, to Destroy 'Bloodthirsty Guttersnipe' and His Entire Nazi Regime

By ROBERT P. POST
Special Cable to THE NEW YORK TIMES.

LONDON, June 22—As this country rocked under the impact of this morning's announcement that Russia and Germany were at war, Prime Minister Winston Churchill went to the microphone tonight to tell his countrymen and the world that Germany was the enemy and that Britain was not going to take her eyes off the main target.

[*The text of Mr. Churchill's address appears on Page* 8.]

Mr. Churchill, who declined to take back a single word of all his vitriolic attacks on communism in the past, said nevertheless that Britain was prepared to give any aid to the Russians within her power. He carefully avoided any mention of the word "alliance."

"We have but one aim and one single, irrevocable purpose," the Prime Minister said, and his words obviously were directed as much at the United States as at Britain. "We are resolved to destroy Hitler and every vestige of the Nazi regime. From this nothing will turn us. Nothing."

Then Mr. Churchill declared:

"We shall fight him by land; we shall fight him by sea; we shall fight him in the air, until, with God's help, we have rid the earth of his shadow and liberated its people from his yoke. Any man or State who fights against nazism will have our aid. Any man or State who fights with Hitler is our foe.

Allies Also Urged to Aid

"That is our policy and that is our declaration. It follows, therefore, that we will give whatever help we can to Russia and to the Russian people. We will appeal to all our friends and allies in every part of the world to take the same course and pursue it as we shall, faithfully and steadfastly to the end.

"We have offered to the government of Soviet Russia any technical or economic assistance which is in our power and which is likely to be of service to them."

Thus did Mr. Churchill voice the official British attitude and thus did he remind Britain and the United States that this latest development in this crazy war must not divert their eyes from the target, which in Mr. Churchill's view and in that of responsibe people here is Nazi Germany.

If ever Mr. Churchill had reason to rejoice, if ever the British had reason to rejoice, they did tonight. Germany is again embroiled with Russia. Reichsfuehrer Hitler has returned to the original ideas of "Mein Kampf" and has repudiated all the things he said from the time he signed a treaty with Russia until he sent his divisions crashing into Russia. Anti-bolshevism has been revived, and the Nazis fight on two fronts.

But no hats went into the air

Continued on Page Eight

MOSCOW PREDICTS CRUSHING OF NAZIS

Molotoff in Broadcast Says Hitler Will Meet Doom Like Napoleon's in Russia

The text of Molotoff's statement is printed on Page 10.

By The Associated Press.

MOSCOW, June 22—As Germany struck at Russia by land and air in a dawn invasion today the Soviet Government immediately accepted the challenge, hurling the might of its Red Army against the Nazis with orders to "repulse this predatory assault," which Moscow's spokesman said was started under a pretext that "is a sheer lie and provocation."

Foreign Commissar Vyacheslaff Molotoff, broadcasting on behalf of Premier Joseph Stalin six hours after the invasion started, expressed confidence that the Soviet forces would inflict a "crushing blow" to Russia's non-aggression pact partner.

In this first word to the Soviet public that Russia was at war with Germany, Mr. Molotoff announced that the Red Army, Fleet and Air Force already had been ordered to move against Adolf Hitler's forces.

The German invasion, Mr. Molotoff asserted, was started without declaration of war. He said no demands had been made.

"This unheard-of attack upon our country is perfidy unparalleled in the history of civilized nations," Mr. Molotoff cried. "The attack on our country was perpetrated despite the fact that a treaty of non-aggression had been signed between the U. S. S. R. and Germany and that the Soviet Government most faithfully abided by all provisions of this treaty."

During the entire life of the German-Russian pact, the Foreign Commissar told the people, "the German Government could not find grounds for a single complaint against the U. S. S. R. as regards observance of this treaty."

"The entire responsibility for this predatory attack upon the Soviet Union," he went on, "falls fully

Continued on Page Ten

Navy Sea Burial Given to Men of O-9 After Divers Confirm Death of All

By RUSSELL B. PORTER
Special to THE NEW YORK TIMES.

PORTSMOUTH, N. H., June 22—After the Navy Department officially abandoned all hope of rescuing the two officers and thirty-one men of the training submarine O-9 this afternoon, impressive funeral services were held aboard another submarine near the place where the O-9 went down Friday morning

The area where the O-9 lies 440 feet below the surface is beyond the Isles of Shoals and Boon Island Light, twelve miles off the Maine coast and twenty-four miles east of Portsmouth Navy Yard.

Colonel Frank Knox, Secretary of the Navy, delivered a eulogy of the crew members, and all the military rites of a naval burial at sea were performed in the presence of 1,000 officers and men on the twelve ships of the salvage fleet drawn in a circle.

A full Presidential salute of twenty-one guns was fired by the submarine tender Vixen, flagship of the fleet, during the ceremony, which included three volleys from a Marine guard of honor and the playing of taps, as well as religious services. Flowers were strewn on the calm surface of the sea and floated away in a light breeze under clear sunny skies in a last tribute to the dead.

The decision to cease all salvage attempts was announced at 2:30 o'clock this afternoon, following unprecedented descents this morning by two Navy divers. For the first time it had ever been done, they went down 440 feet in "working" dives in rubber canvas diving suits.

They stayed only a minute under the terrific pressure on the muddy bottom of the Atlantic Ocean, and could see very little in the rays of

Continued on Page Thirty-four

RUSSIANS HIT BACK

Reported Holding Nazis Despite Fierce Raids on Vital Bases

WITHDRAW IN NORTH

Huge Air Fleets Battle on Far-Flung Front—Finns Hit Plane

By DANIEL T. BRIGHAM
By Telephone to THE NEW YORK TIMES.

BERNE, Switzerland, June 22—Military and diplomatic quarters here tonight, basing their opinions on meager details that began filtering through the gradually settling fog of first-day military operations, declared the struggle at the end of the first eighteen hours of fighting between Russia and Germany virtually a draw. The Russian troops were believed to be holding surprisingly well in the district around Cernauti, in Bukovina where they were encountering a double offensive from German motorized columns and intensive bombing by Stuka formations that had been attacking almost incessantly since dawn.

In the north certain "strategic withdrawals" had been reported, notably southward along the road from Lyck, East Prussia, to Bialystok and eastward from a point just south of Przemysl toward Lwow—in which region occurred the serious frontier "incident" referred to in these dispatches on June 19 and by Reichsfuehrer Hitler in his proclamation this morning.

Finnish Ports Bombed

Farther north, according to a communiqué from Helsinki to the Finnish Legation here this evening, "small" Russian bomber formations attacked the harbor of Aabo [Turku] on the Gulf of Bothnia twice this morning, dropping bombs close to Finland's two largest "battleships"—the Vainamoinen and the Ilmarinen, both of 3,900 tons, which were lying in the harbor. No damage was done, the report said, but one of the two-pound anti-aircraft guns on the former warship reportedly scored a direct hit on one of the bombers.

Elsewhere Russian bombers were reported to have attacked Finnish fortifications at Alskaer [in the Aaland Archipelago] but without causing any damage or casualties.

[Revolt in Estonia against Soviet overlordship was reported by the Stockholm representative of Tass, the official Russian news agency. The revolt was still in progress at a late hour, the report said, and added that several Soviet ships in Tallinn harbor had been seized by the rebels.]

On the eastern Finnish front, intensive aerial reconnaissance was carried out all day by the Russians, apparently in an attempt to locate concentrations of German troops, which, Helsinki sources asserted, were not there. At a late hour this evening there were no authoritative reports from Finland of movements of Finnish troops against Russian forces at any point.

Nazis Raid Soviet Bases

Both sides reported intensive aerial activity over the whole front, with frequent sallies by bombers of both sides to break up troop concentrations and smash communication centers. In these operations, Russian bombers are not believed to have fared so well, but their chasers are reported to have given a good account of themselves, repeatedly breaking up vastly stronger formations of German bombers before they could reach their objectives.

The German aerial effort in the north seems to have concentrated on Russian airdromes in the Baltic States. German observers declared "more than 100 first-line planes," hangars and immense stocks of gasoline were destroyed in these raids, from which the Russians could not "be expected to react immediately." The Russian Foreign Commissar, Vyacheslaff M. Molotoff, announced heavy damage and hundreds of casualties in German air raids on Sevastopol, Kiev, Zhitomir and Kaunas. [Odessa and

Continued on Page Two

"All the News That's Fit to Print."

The New York Times.

LATE CITY EDITION
Fair with moderate temperatures today and tomorrow.
Temperatures Yesterday—Max., 82; Min., 61

VOL. XC...No. 30,468. Entered as Second-Class Matter, Postoffice, New York, N. Y. NEW YORK, WEDNESDAY, JUNE 25, 1941. THREE CENTS NEW YORK CITY and Vicinity

TURKS MASS ON SYRIAN LINE, MENACING FRENCH; SOVIET FLIERS BLAST WARSAW AND CONSTANTA; ROOSEVELT TO GIVE ALL POSSIBLE AID TO RUSSIA

TAX CUT $3,300,000 FOR UTILITY USERS; SALES LEVY STANDS

Reduction on Telephone, Gas and Electric Services Is Approved by City Boards

MAYOR OPPOSED ACTION

Program to Get $71,575,000 for Relief Voted—Basic Rate for City Set at $2.80

Tax reductions amounting to $3,300,000 for users of telephone, gas and electric service were approved by the City Council and the Board of Estimate yesterday as both bodies adopted an emergency relief tax program for next year designed to raise a total of $71,575,000.

The Democratic-controlled Council voted the tax cut in the face of opposition by Mayor La Guardia and Controller Joseph D. McGoldrick, who contended that the tax program should be re-enacted without change. Because of the Mayor's opposition, Councilman Joseph E. Kinsley, chairman of the Council finance committee, reported that the Council would be unable to reduce the city sales tax from 2 to 1 per cent. The Citizens Budget Commission, the Merchants Association and a number of other organizations had asked for the sales tax cut in view of the present surplus in relief tax funds.

The $3,300,000 reduction voted by the Council will benefit householders who have been paying a city relief tax of 3 per cent on their bills for telephone, gas and electric service. The new rate is 2 per cent and the expected revenue from this source during the next fiscal year is $6,700,000, against more than $10,000,000 raised in the fiscal year now expiring. Controller McGoldrick's figures showed that relief taxes on electricity in the current fiscal year raised $4,980,156, taxes on gas consumption produced $918,287, users of steam paid $243,171, telephone users paid $3,151,009 and taxes on telegraph and cable service amounted to $76,683. Relief taxes on other utility services brought the total above $10,000,000.

Stockbrokers Aided

Stockbrokers also received a benefit in the new tax program through the elimination of double taxation on brokerage transactions. Under the former tax bill principals and brokers both paid a city tax on the same transaction. The new set-up assesses only one tax on each transaction.

After taking the first step toward reducing the tax burden on city residents, the Council adopted the relief tax program without further change. It also fixed the basic tax rate for the next fiscal year at $2.80 on each $100 of assessed valuation, the figure named last week by Controller McGoldrick. In submitting the report of the finance committee, Councilman Kinsley, a Bronx Democrat, said:

"Under the terms of the charter the Council is mandatorily required to fix the tax rate at the figure computed by the Controller, based on estimates furnished by him and the Department of Taxes.

"Inclusive of the $6,500,000 yield of the proposed business tax, he estimates the general fund revenues at $118,746,327.51—a figure $5,846,327.51 in excess of his estimates for the present year. In arriving at this figure the Controller has made some startling reductions in his estimates of revenues paid into the general fund.

"The reductions total $3,900,000. If the estimates of these funds had been maintained at their present level, the tax rate could be reduced by almost 3 points below the point suggested by the Controller.

New Business Tax

"There has evidently been serious error in either the computation made for the present year or that for the forthcoming year. Though this is almost self-evident, the Council is powerless to correct the mistake.

"Your committee must therefore recommend that the tax rate proposed by the Controller be adopted."

The taxes adopted yesterday include a renewal of the 2 per cent sales tax with an estimated yield of

Continued on Page Fifteen

Group Here Repudiates Support of Reds in U. S.

Holding that a Soviet pattern for a new world order is no more acceptable than that of the Nazis, Fight for Freedom, Inc., of which United States Senator Carter Glass is honorary chairman, yesterday released a statement repudiating any support of the Communist party in the United States.

"We are fighting for freedom," read the statement. "In such a struggle those who advocate totalitarian doctrines for this country can, of necessity, have no part in our movement. We believe firmly in the four freedoms which President Roosevelt has outlined. This includes freedom of religion. When we have succeeded in crushing Hitler's Germany we do not expect the new world order to be patterned upon the models of the Nazi Reich or Soviet Russia."

R. A. F. HAMMERS ON, BAGS 13 MORE NAZIS

Margin of 5 to 1 Claimed in Pilots—Offensive Enters 14th Day Savagely

By DAVID ANDERSON
Special Cable to THE NEW YORK TIMES.

LONDON, Wednesday, June 25—Hammering Germany's industrial centers in the northwest and her fighting aircraft over France, the British Royal Air Force yesterday kept up its prolonged campaign of attrition, bagging nine enemy fighters. Four more German bombers were reported shot down over Britain.

[A United Press dispatch stated that the Royal Air Force had loosed one of the greatest attacks of the current offensive against the French "invasion coast" early today. The explosions of their super bombs could be heard for many miles and the flames of fires set in the attack cast a glare along a 20-mile front, the dispatch added.]

It is hoped that the continual blows delivered now for thirteen successive nights along the Rhineland and the seaports of the Reich will sap the enemy's strength while production in Britain drives ahead unimpeded by raiders. The greatest effect of the current harvest of Messerschmitts reaped daily in the offensive sweeps across the English Channel seems to be lying in the shock it will have on the foe's morale, coupled with a rise of confidence here.

Early yesterday morning British bombers in force attacked factories at Cologne and Duesseldorf and once more, also, the naval base at Kiel. Secondary targets blasted with high explosives were Wilhelmshaven, Emden and Hanover and various unspecified places in occupied territories. One British plane was reported by the Air Ministry to be missing.

Haze Hampers Bombers

Despite the prevailing good weather, the conditions were not ideal for raiding, owing to a ground haze which obscured the vision of pilots and made accurate bombing and observation results most difficult. Fires and explosions caused at Kiel were said to "suggest" that munitions had blown up. Numerous large fires were said to have been seen through the mists.

Last evening's sweep over the invasion ports and inland points accounted for nine German fighters at a cost of two British planes escorting the bombers, according to reports received to date. The raiders attacked a power station at Comines near Lille, which is a part of France noted for its heavy industries.

The latest recapitulation of the successes attained by the R. A. F. Fighter Command for Saturday, Sunday and yesterday is as follows:

Enemy fighters destroyed, twenty-eight, thirty and twenty; British fighters lost, four, two and three; British bombers shot down, one, none and two; British pilots saved, two, one and one.

Germans Dispute Claims

In the last eight days more than 100 German machines have been destroyed against thirty British planes missing. The press of Britain today is featuring the contrast between the London and Berlin communiqués covering these air battles. Whereas the R. A. F. sets German

Continued on Page Six

RED CREDITS FREED

President Says Extent of Our Aid Hinges on British Demands

MOSCOW IS SILENT

No Move Will Be Made Till Soviet Can Tell What Is Needed

By FRANK L. KLUCKHOHN
Special to THE NEW YORK TIMES.

WASHINGTON, June 24—President Roosevelt pledged today that the United States would give all possible aid to Soviet Russia in its defense against Nazi Germany. The Treasury, acting upon his orders, released $40,000,000 in Soviet credits, frozen June 14.

At his press conference the President revealed that he was prepared to implement the policy implied yesterday by Sumner Welles, Under-Secretary of State, of giving material assistance to any country fighting Germany, but indicated that American help could not be effective unless the Nazi-Soviet war is a long one. He emphasized that Britain has first lien on exportable planes, tanks and munitions of war.

When the President met the press in his office he was frank to admit that he not only was lacking in any information as to what the Stalin government felt it needed from this country, but that diplomatic reports were so scant that he probably knew less of what was going on in Moscow at this time than any desk man in a newspaper office.

Doubts That Oumansky Knows

Until this government obtained a list of what Russia needed from the United States, Mr. Roosevelt emphasized, no moves could be made toward supplying her wants. Even after a list is obtained, he added, it would be impossible merely to go to a department store and buy what was needed. War supplies for export were pledged a long way ahead and could not be released to Russia except by agreement, apparently with Britain.

Asked whether he would call in Constantine Oumansky, the Soviet Ambassador in Washington, to obtain an idea of what his government needed, the Chief Executive remarked that he did not believe the Ambassador knew any more

Continued on Page Seven

Ankara Radio 'Jammed' In Pro-British Broadcast

The British Broadcasting Corporation report heard last night at the Columbia Broadcasting System's listening station said London had heard "a remarkable comment" from the Ankara radio, giving a decidedly pro-British slant on the Russo-German war.

The Turkish radio commentator was quoted as saying:

"The German military onslaught on Russia became an urgent necessity because in the West Germany was unable to defeat Great Britain and the war seemed to be unending. Great Britain was also successful in insuring American aid, and the day of a clash between an Anglo-Saxon bloc and Germany was fast approaching."

At this point "the Turkish broadcast was interrupted by severe jamming, presumably by German transmitters," London stated.

RUSSIA WELCOMES AID FROM BRITAIN

Eden Also Tells the Commons of Optimism Regarding the Pact With Turkey

By ROBERT P. POST
Special Cable to THE NEW YORK TIMES.

LONDON, June 24—Russia has accepted the British offer of aid and military and economic missions will leave shortly for Moscow, Foreign Secretary Anthony Eden announced in the House of Commons today.

Regarding Turkey, Mr. Eden acknowledged that the British would have preferred that the Turkish agreement with Germany had not been signed, but he said that the agreement puts the British-Turkish agreement in the forefront of Turkish foreign policy and that the British within the last twenty-four hours had received assurances that it was still there.

[When members voiced criticism of Turkey, Prime Minister Churchill closed this phase of discussion, according to The Associated Press. "It would not be in the public interest," Mr. Churchill said, "for the discussion to continue along these lines. This really is a case of the least said the soonest mended."]

Prime Minister Winston Churchill disappointed the Commons by refusing to discuss the war situation, leaving Mr. Eden to talk of political and diplomatic situations. What

Continued on Page Eight

The International Situation

WEDNESDAY, JUNE 25, 1941

The spotlight of war swung to another potential front yesterday. Turkey was said to be massing troops on her Syrian frontier possibly in preparation for cooperation with the British and Free French. Ankara reported that a special mission was en route to Turkey from Vichy to ask for the evacuation of French troops through Turkey, indicating that the campaign was near its conclusion. Wider implications than that were hinted, however, as Turkey studied the Nazi-Soviet conflict. The British forces, meanwhile, received instructions to proceed with dispatch in the Syrian clean-up and they appeared to be carrying out their orders. [Page 1, Column 8.]

An intimation that political as well as military developments might be expected on this front was given in the House of Commons by Foreign Secretary Eden when he stated that the Turco-German pact had put the Anglo-Turkish agreement in the forefront of Turkish foreign policy and that the British, within the last twenty-four hours, had received assurances that it was still there. Mr. Eden also announced that military and economic missions would shortly start for Moscow. [Page 1, Column 4.]

A somewhat similar assurance of aid to Russia was given in Washington by President Roosevelt, although he made it plain that the form had not been determined and that Britain had priority on war materials. There was, however, the release of $40,000,000 in Soviet credits from the freezing order. [Page 1, Column 3.]

The degree and success of Russian military resistance was still obscure. From Berne, Switzerland, it was reported that the main forces had not yet come in contact. Nevertheless, the German movement in the south was believed to have crossed Bessarabia and reached the Dniester line, where very heavy fighting was reported. A Moscow communiqué announced devastating air raids on Constanta, Warsaw, Koenigsberg and Lublin, and claimed the sinking of a German submarine. [Page 1, Column 5.]

In the north the German forces were reported to have swept into Kaunas, Lithuania, aided by an anti-Soviet revolt. Tallinn, Estonia, was reported in flames. [Page 1, Column 7.]

Moscow and Berlin told opposite stories of the fighting. Moscow shouted its defiant patriotsim and declared that the invaders were being repulsed. [Page 4, Column 2.] Berlin stated that the Nazis were advancing in all sectors with great success and that Adolf Hitler was on the Eastern front in command. [Page 1, Columns 6 and 7.]

The British continued their smashing offensive in the air against the Continent. After a daylight sweep yesterday they carried one of their heaviest attacks of the war forward into the night. They announced a three-day total of seventy-eight Nazi planes shot down as against twelve British lost. [Page 1, Column 2.]

RED ARMY STRIKES

Nazi Mechanized Force Reported Defeated in Lithuanian Fight

U-BOAT IS CLAIMED

Reich Soldiers in South Said to Have Reached the Dniester River

By The Associated Press.

MOSCOW, Wednesday, June 25—Russia, meeting the German onslaught with "stiff resistance," announced officially early today that her armies had annihilated a Nazi mechanized regiment and that her bombers had started great fires in Warsaw, Constanta and other German-occupied cities.

Reporting great damage to military objectives, the Red Army said that gasoline dumps were burning in Warsaw and that the Rumanian Black Sea port of Constanta was ablaze after three bombings by Soviet planes.

In addition to Warsaw and Constanta the Russian Air Force bombed Danzig, which the Germans seized in 1939, the East Prussian city of Koenigsberg and Lublin, about 100 miles southeast of Warsaw. Each of these cities was subjected to three attacks, the communiqué declared.

U-Boat Is Reported Sunk

In the Gulf of Finland, the Russians reported, a German submarine was sunk by units of the Red Fleet.

The war report revealed that the Germans had brought their parachute troops into play in the all-out assault on Russia. The Red Army charged that the Germans wore Soviet uniforms.

"The Germans are dropping parachutists for the interruption of communications in batches of five or ten clad in the uniform of Soviet militiamen," the communiqué declared. "Units for the destruction of these parachutists have been created behind the front line. The NKVD [Russian secret police] is entrusted with the direction of the operations of these units."

On the long battle line, the Russians declared, the German offensive in the Shavli area of Lithuania has been repulsed with heavy losses to the Nazis. Fierce fighting was in progress in defense of Kaunas, Lithuania; Grodno, Poland, and Vilna, the Russians said. Large tank formations were battling in the Brody area.

It was in the Shavli fighting that mechanized units of the Russian Army met and destroyed German tank formations and a mechanized German regiment, the report stated.

Successes in Air Claimed

The Red Army High Command said that its air force was cooperating with the army in the field and had dealt "crushing blows to the airdromes and important military targets of the enemy." The communiqué reported that the air force had brought down thirty-four aircraft during the day and that 381 German planes had been destroyed since the war began—161 by Russian aircraft in air battles and 220 on the airdromes of the Luftwaffe.

The communiqué then turned to Finland, declaring that German soldiers quartered in that country had been beaten back in an attempt to cross the Soviet border.

"Finland has lent her territory to the German Army and Air Force," the communiqué said. "For the past ten days concentrations of German troops and planes have been proceeding on the borders of the U.S.S.R. On June 23 six German aircraft flying from Finnish territory attempted to bomb the Kronstadt region. These aircraft were repelled."

The Red Army report went on to say that "Rumania has put her territory at the complete disposal of the German armies." Repeated attempts by the German-Rumanian armies to capture Cernauti, in the Bukovina territory yielded to Russia last year by Rumania, have failed, it was stated.

Nazis Push Two Drives

By DANIEL T. BRIGHAM
By Telephone to THE NEW YORK TIMES.

BERNE, Switzerland, Wednesday, June 25—It is becoming increasingly apparent that the main fighting

Continued on Page Four

NAZI MOVES FORECAST PINCER STRATEGY

The Germans bombed the Soviet naval base at Hangoe (1) and the Russians reported the sinking of a U-boat in the Gulf of Finland. While the Nazis were said to have entered Kaunas (2) and to have taken Shavli, to the north, Moscow reported fighting around both these places. The main German offensives were apparently taking the shape of converging drives from the Bialystok and Brest-Litovsk areas (4) in the direction of Minsk and from the Lublin and Cernauti areas (5) in the direction of Kiev, but the progress of these drives was uncertain. To the south the Germans were reported to have reached the eastern frontier of Bessarabia (6). Soviet fliers pounded Danzig and Koenigsberg (3), Warsaw (west of 4) and the Black Sea ports of Sulina and Constanta (7).

Hitler Goes to Soviet Front; Reports Invasion 'Success'

By C. BROOKS PETERS
By Telephone to THE NEW YORK TIMES.

BERLIN, June 24—Adolf Hitler has joined his troops on the Eastern Front. At the same time, Berlin reports say, the German armies are advancing with great success in the sectors along which their invasion is concentrated. Herr Hitler's presence on the Eastern Front was indicated by the dateline of today's German High Command communiqué, which, contrary to those of the first two days of this campaign, "emanated from the Fuehrer's headquarters."

All the German communiqué issued today had to say about the fighting against the new Russian Army was that "in the east operations are proceeding with great success according to plan."

A Russian division is reported by a German front correspondent to have been taken by surprise by Nazi forces and destroyed after its tanks had been dispersed by the German Air Force.

The reports furnished by the official news agency and those of the front-line war correspondents provide much color, but virtually no facts that may be used in reporting to foreign countries. These reports suggest that the German Air Force is vastly superior in quality to the Russian and that terrific losses have been inflicted on this Russian war arm.

Even in Spain, the Germans remark, Russian planes proved inferior to the German, although the Russians showed that they had excellent fliers. Since then, however, the German air force is said to have been greatly improved and to have benefited from the experience in battle gained since Sept. 1, 1939.

The Russian high seas fleet is old, in the German view, and of the modern Russian submarines many are stationed in the Far East. One Russian submarine is reported to have been sunk by a German U-boat off Ventspils, Latvia, yesterday, while one Russian destroyer is said to have run on a German mine and sunk, also in the Baltic.

The official news agency announced that Slovakia had declared war on Russia and that Slovak forces had crossed the border to join the German forces on Russian territory.

Other than the communiqué, not a word about the progress of the German legions was released in official quarters. Correspondents were sternly warned, moreover, that speculation about the direction being taken by the German drive, as well as the mention of specific geographical localities, how long the

Continued on Page Five

KAUNAS IS CLAIMED BY BALTIC REBELS

Nazis Said to Hold Lithuanian Capital With Insurgent Aid —Tallinn Reported Afire

By Telephone to THE NEW YORK TIMES.

STOCKHOLM, Sweden, June 24—Tallinn was reported in flames tonight, and German troops were said to be in Kaunas.

From Helsinki the correspondent of Aftonbladet announced that from the tower of the Olympic stadium in the Finnish capital observers with field glasses had seen extensive fires reflected in the skies above Tallinn, Estonian capital across the Gulf of Finland, "which has apparently been submitted to German bombing and is now one great sea of flame."

Without indicating the origin of the report, the Nya Dagligt Allehanda reports that at noon today the Kaunas radio announced that German troops were in the city. A German officer, says the newspaper, declared on the same broadcast that units of the Red Army still held positions in certain suburbs of the Lithuanian capital, but that some of the Red Army soldiers gave themselves up to the Lithuanian insurgents.

The German officer also appealed to German troops not to confuse the Lithuanian insurgents and the Red troops. The Lithuanians, he said, were armed with weapons taken from Russian prisoners.

In Vilna, also, says the same article, street fights between Russian soldiers and the Lithuanian insurgents were in progress. Allehanda adds that it is proved that at least Vilna's broadcast was a genuine one, because the broadcaster's voice was recognized as belonging to a well-known Lithuanian poet.

It must be added, however, that

Continued on Page Three

DENTZ HELD BEATEN

Ankara Awaits Mission to Arrange Retreat Through Turkey

ALLIES PRESS AHEAD

Two Columns Expected to Converge for Drive Up Coast to Beirut

By G. H. ARCHAMBAULT
By Telephone to THE NEW YORK TIMES.

VICHY, France, June 24—News reaches here that in Turkey the dispositions taken by the High Command have been modified in the last few days, and that bodies of troops have been moved south close to the Syrian border.

This adds force to an impression that has been gaining ground here: namely, that what was at first a sort of colonial operation between the French on the one side and the British and de Gaullists on the other, is developing in importance in view of the extension of the general conflict in Russia. [An Associated Press dispatch from Vichy said "informed sources" there believed the Turks might be trying to help the British by threatening the French mandates while the Germans were preoccupied with their Russian campaign.]

A War of Many Phases

Competent observers here insist that a true appreciation of the situation cannot be obtained by considering each theatre of operation separately, as they are only phases of a general battle on a varying scale, and Syria has its part therein.

From the outset of the Syrian campaign, the French announced their determination of meeting the attack with their own forces only. It is known now that offers of aid were made from the German side; they were all declined. Yet the French admit that they are inferior both in numbers and in matériel. Hitherto the only reinforcements they have been able to send have been by air in the form of planes from France and North Africa.

There is reason to believe that there is considerable diplomatic activity in Ankara. This is normal, in view of the fact that the Turks have just signed an accord with Berlin and Turkey represents a gap in the line of battle in the Near East.

In connection with this diplomatic activity, "authorized French circles refuse to comment on certain foreign broadcasts regarding a trip to the Near East made by Jacques Benoist-Mechin, Secretary of State attached to the Vice Premier's office." Mr. Benoist-Mechin recently was appointed negotiator with the German authorities in Paris as direct delegate of Vice Premier François Darlan.

As regards the fighting in Syria, little change is reported in any sectors except near Damascus, where the British-de Gaullist forces that occupied the city are now debouching in two columns, one along the road eastward leading to Beirut and the other along the road northward leading to Homs and thence to Aleppo, near the Turkish border.

Vichy forces are reported to be in contact with both columns, the first in the narrow gorges and the second in the desert.

Tadmur, it is asserted, is still holding out, defended by troops of the Foreign Legion.

A new sector is said to have developed in the Jebel Druz, where French detachments are declared holding well, although all their communications by land are cut.

French Retreat Hinted

By C. L. SULZBERGER
Special Broadcast to THE NEW YORK TIMES.

ANKARA, Turkey, June 24—A special mission of six representatives of the Vichy government, headed by Jacques Benoist-Mechin, is expected to arrive in Turkey soon from France to discuss the possibility of evacuating through this country the armies now fighting under General Henri Fernand Dentz against the Allies in the French-mandated territories of the Levant.

However, the aircraft bringing the mission from Vichy is now twenty-four hours overdue, and considerable worry is evident in

Continued on Page Four

"All the News That's Fit to Print."

The New York Times.

LATE CITY EDITION
Increasing cloudiness with rising temperature today. Tomorrow cloudy, somewhat colder.
Temperatures Yesterday—Max.,34; Min.,25

Copyright, 1941, by The New York Times Company.

VOL. XCI No. 30,634. Entered as Second-Class Matter, Postoffice, New York, N. Y. NEW YORK, MONDAY, DECEMBER 8, 1941. THREE CENTS NEW YORK CITY and Vicinity

JAPAN WARS ON U. S. AND BRITAIN; MAKES SUDDEN ATTACK ON HAWAII; HEAVY FIGHTING AT SEA REPORTED

CONGRESS DECIDED

Roosevelt Will Address It Today and Find It Ready to Vote War

CONFERENCE IS HELD

Legislative Leaders and Cabinet in Sober White House Talk

By C. P. TRUSSELL
Special to THE NEW YORK TIMES.

WASHINGTON, Dec. 7—President Roosevelt will address a joint session of Congress tomorrow and will find the membership in a mood to vote any steps he asks in connection with the developments in the Pacific.

The President will appear personally at 12:30 P. M. Whether he would call for a flat declaration of war ag-in Japan was left unannounced tonight. But leaders of Congress, shocked and angered by the Japanese attacks, were talking of a declaration of war on not only Japan but on the entire Axis.

The plans for action tomorrow were made tonight in a White House conference at which the President, surrounded by his Cabinet and by Congressional leaders of both parties, went through reports, some official, some unconfirmed, of the continued assaults of the Japanese upon American Pacific outposts.

Meet Far Into Night

The conference lasted until after 11 o'clock and at its close an official statement was issued. This said that the President had reviewed for his conferees the latest advices from the Pacific and declared:

"It should be emphasized that the message to Congress has not yet been written and its tenor will, of course, depend on further information received between 11 o'clock tonight and noon tomorrow. Further news is coming in all the time."

Congressional leaders asserted as they left the White House that they did not know what the President would say tomorrow.

"Will the President ask for a declaration of war?" Speaker Rayburn was asked.

"He didn't say," answered the Speaker.

Asked whether Congress would support a declaration of war, Mr. Rayburn observed:

"I think that is one thing on which there would be unity."

Politics Declared Dropped

"There is no politics here," said Representative Joseph W. Martin Jr., Minority House Leader. "There is only one party when it comes to the integrity and honor of the country."

"The Republicans," said Senator Charles L. McNary of Oregon, the Senate minority leader, "will all go along, in my opinion, with whatever is done."

Unless international developments and plans changed overnight, it was indicated, the Presidential recommendations would be directed for the present, at least, at Japan only. This was asserted authoritatively in the face of widespread expectation that any

Continued on Page Six

TOKYO ACTS FIRST

Declaration Follows Air and Sea Attacks on U. S. and Britain

TOGO CALLS ENVOYS

After Fighting Is On, Grew Gets Japan's Reply to Hull Note of Nov. 26

By The Associated Press.

TOKYO, Monday, Dec. 8—Japan went to war against the United States and Britain today with air and sea attacks against Hawaii, followed by a formal declaration of hostilities.

Japanese Imperial headquarters announced at 6 A. M. [4 P. M. Sunday, Eastern standard time] that a state of war existed among these nations in the Western Pacific, as of dawn.

Soon afterward, Domei, the Japanese official news agency, announced that "naval operations are progressing off Hawaii, with at least one Japanese aircraft carrier in action against Pearl Harbor," the American naval base in the islands.

Japanese bombers were declared to have raided Honolulu at 7:35 A. M., Hawaii time [1:05 Sunday, Eastern standard time].

Premier-War Minister General Hideki Tojo held a twenty-minute Cabinet session at his official residence at 7 A. M.

Soon afterward it was announced that both the United States Ambassador, Joseph C. Grew, and the British Ambassador, Sir Robert Leslie Craigie, had been summoned by Foreign Minister Shigenori Togo.

The Foreign Minister, Domei said, handed to Mr. Grew the Japanese Government's formal reply to the note sent to Japan by United States Secretary of State Cordell Hull on Nov. 26.

[In the course of the diplomatic negotiations leading up to yesterday's events, the Domei agency had stated that Japan could not accept the premises of Mr. Hull's note.]

Sir Robert was summoned by

Continued on Page Five

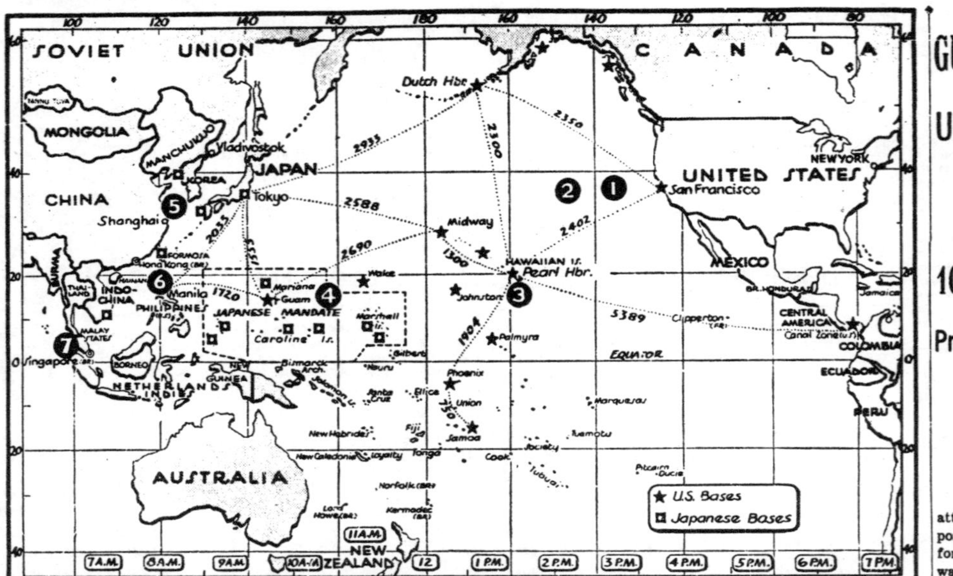

PACIFIC OCEAN: THEATRE OF WAR INVOLVING UNITED STATES AND ITS ALLIES

Shortly after the outbreak of hostilities an American ship sent a distress call from (1) and a United States Army transport carrying lumber was torpedoed at (2). The most important action was Hawaii (3), where Japanese planes bombed the great Pearl Harbor base. Also attacked was Guam (4). From Manila (6) United States bombers roared northward, while some parts of the Philippines were raided, as was Hong Kong, to the northwest. At Shanghai (5) a British gunboat was sunk and an American gunboat seized. To the south, in the Malaya area (7), the British bombed Japanese ships, Tokyo forces attempted landings on British territory and Singapore underwent an air raid. Distances between key Pacific points are shown on the map in statute miles.

GUAM BOMBED; ARMY SHIP IS SUNK

U. S. Fliers Head North From Manila—Battleship Oklahoma Set Afire by Torpedo Planes at Honolulu

104 SOLDIERS KILLED AT FIELD IN HAWAII

President Fears 'Very Heavy Losses' on Oahu—Churchill Notifies Japan That a State of War Exists

By FRANK L. KLUCKHOHN
Special to THE NEW YORK TIMES.

WASHINGTON, Monday, Dec. 8—Sudden and unexpected attacks on Pearl Harbor, Honolulu, and other United States possessions in the Pacific early yesterday by the Japanese air force and navy plunged the United States and Japan into active war.

The initial attack in Hawaii, apparently launched by torpedo-carrying bombers and submarines, caused widespread damage and death. It was quickly followed by others. There were unconfirmed reports that German raiders participated in the attacks.

Guam also was assaulted from the air, as were Davao, on the island of Mindanao, and Camp John Hay, in Northern Luzon, both in the Philippines. Lieut. Gen. Douglas MacArthur, commanding the United States Army of the Far East, reported there was little damage, however.

[Japanese parachute troops had been landed in the Philippines and native Japanese had seized some communities, Royal Arch Gunnison said in a broadcast from Manila today to WOR-Mutual. He reported without detail that "in the naval war the ABCD fleets under American command appeared to be successful" against Japanese invasions.]

Japanese submarines, ranging out over the Pacific, sank an American transport carrying lumber 1,300 miles from San Francisco, and distress signals were heard from a freighter 700 miles from that city.

The War Department reported that 104 soldiers died and 300 were wounded as a result of the attack on Hickam Field, Hawaii. The National Broadcasting Company reported from Honolulu that the battleship Oklahoma was afire. [Domei, Japanese news agency, reported the Oklahoma sunk.]

Nation Placed on Full War Basis

The news of these surprise attacks fell like a bombshell on Washington. President Roosevelt immediately ordered the country and the Army and Navy onto a full war footing. He arranged at a White House conference last night to address a joint session of Congress at noon today, presumably to ask for declaration of a formal state of war.

This was disclosed after a long special Cabinet meeting, which was joined later by Congressional leaders. These leaders predicted "action" within a day.

After leaving the White House conference Attorney General Francis Biddle said that "a resolution" would be introduced in Congress tomorrow. He would not amplify or affirm that it would be for a declaration of war.

Congress probably will "act" within the day, and he will call the Senate Foreign Relations Committee for this purpose, Chairman Tom Connally announced.

[A United Press dispatch from London this morning said that Prime Minister Churchill had notified Japan that a state of war existed.]

As the reports of heavy fighting flashed into the White House, London reported semi-officially that the British Empire would carry out Prime Minister Winston Churchill's pledge to give the United States full support in case of hostilities with Japan. The President and Mr. Churchill talked by transatlantic telephone.

This was followed by a statement in London from the Netherland Government in Exile that it considered a state of war to exist between the Netherlands and Japan. Canada, Australia and Costa Rica took similar action.

Landing Made in Malaya

A Singapore communiqué disclosed that Japanese troops had landed in Northern Malaya and that Singapore had been bombed.

The President told those at last night's White House meeting that "doubtless very heavy losses" were sustained by the Navy and also by the Army on the island of Oahu [Honolulu]. It was impossible to obtain confirmation or denial of reports that the battleships Oklahoma and West Virginia had been damaged or sunk at Pearl Harbor, together with six or seven destroyers, and that 350 United States airplanes had been caught on the ground.

The White House took over control of the bulletins, and the Navy Department, therefore, said it could not discuss the matter or answer any questions how the Japanese were able to penetrate the Hawaiian defenses or appear without previous knowledge of their presence in those waters.

Administration circles forecast that the United States soon might be involved in a world-wide war, with Germany supporting Japan, an Axis partner. The German official radio tonight attacked the United States and supported Japan.

Axis diplomats here expressed complete surprise that the Japanese had attacked. But the impression gained from their attitude wa that they believed it represented a victory for the Nazi attempt to divert lease-lend aid from Britain, which has been

Continued on Page Four

JAPANESE FORCE LANDS IN MALAYA

First Attempt Is Repulsed—Singapore Is Bombed and Thailand Invaded

By The Associated Press.

SINGAPORE, Monday, Dec. 8—The Japanese landed in Northern Malaya, 300 miles north of Singapore, today and bombed this great British naval stronghold, causing small loss of life among civilians and property damage.

About 300 Japanese troops landed on the east coast of Malaya and began filtering through jungle-fringed swamps and rice fields toward Kota Bahru airdrome, which is ten miles from the northern terminus of a railroad leading to Singapore.

An official report from the

Continued on Page Two

Tokyo Bombers Strike Hard At Our Main Bases on Oahu

By The United Press.

HONOLULU, Dec. 7—War broke with lightning suddenness in the Pacific today when waves of Japanese bombers attacked Hawaii this morning and the United States Fleet struck back with a thunder of big naval rifles. Japanese bombers, including four-engined dive bombers and torpedo-carrying planes, blasted at Pearl Harbor, the great United States naval base, the city of Honolulu and several outlying American military bases on the Island of Oahu. There were casualties of unstated number.

[The United States battleship Oklahoma was set afire by the Japanese attackers, according to a National Broadcasting Company observer, who also reported in a broadcast yesterday that two other ships in Pearl Harbor were attacked.

[The Japanese news agency, Domei, reported that the battleship Oklahoma had been sunk at Pearl Harbor, according to a United Press dispatch from Shanghai.

[Governor Joseph B. Poindexter of Hawaii talked with President Roosevelt late yesterday afternoon, saying that a second wave of Japanese bombers was just coming over, and the Gov-

Continued on Page Thirteen

ENTIRE CITY PUT ON WAR FOOTING

Japanese Rounded Up by FBI, Sent to Ellis Island—Vital Services Are Guarded

The metropolitan district reacted swiftly yesterday to the Japanese attack in the Pacific. All large communities in the area, including New York City, Newark, Jersey City, Bayonne and Paterson, went on immediate war footing.

One of the first steps taken here last night was a round-up of Japanese nationals by special agents of the Federal Bureau of Investigation, reinforced by squads of city detectives acting under FBI supervision. More than 100 FBI men, fully armed, were assigned to the detail.

The prisoners were sent to Ellis Island, where they will be held pending action at Washington. It was indicated hundreds would be detained.

Earlier Mayor La Guardia had convened his Emergency Board and directed that Japanese nationals be confined to their homes pending decision as to their status and had their clubs and other meeting places closed and put under police guard.

A police sergeant and five policemen immediately went to the Japanese Consulate at 630 Fifth Avenue in Rockefeller Center where the Consul General, Morito Morishima, and his staff were preparing to leave, and posted a guard there. The Consul General and his staff were escorted to their homes when they left. They were not to move about the city without police in attendance.

Rear Admiral Adolphus Andrews, commander of the North Atlantic Squadron, held reporters at a conference in the Federal

Continued on Page Three

HULL DENOUNCES TOKYO 'INFAMY'

Brands Japan 'Fraudulent' in Preparing Attack While Carrying On Parleys

Texts of Secretary Hull's note and Japan's reply, Page 10.

By BERTRAM D. HULEN
Special to THE NEW YORK TIMES.

WASHINGTON, Dec. 7—Japan was accused by Secretary of State Cordell Hull today of making a "treacherous and utterly unprovoked attack" upon the United States and of having been "infamously false and fraudulent" by preparing for the attack while conducting diplomatic negotiations with the professed desire of maintaining peace.

But even before he knew of the attack, Mr. Hull had vehemently brought the diplomatic negotiations to a virtual end with an outburst against Admiral Kichisaburo Nomura, the Japanese Ambassador, and Saburo Kurusu, special envoy, because of the insulting character of the reply they deliv-

Continued on Page Eleven

The International Situation

MONDAY, DEC. 8, 1941

Yesterday morning Japan attacked the United States at several points in the Pacific. President Roosevelt ordered United States forces into action and a declaration of war is expected this morning. [Page 1, Columns 7 and 8.] Tokyo made its declaration as of this morning against both the United States and Britain. [Page 1, Column 2.] The first Japanese assault was directed at Pearl Harbor Naval base in Hawaii. Many casualties and severe damage resulted. [Page 1, Columns 4 and 5; Map, Page 13.] United States Army aircraft took off from the Philippines this morning and some points in the Archipelago were bombed. [Page 8, Column 2.] Singapore and Hong Kong were bombed and a Japanese landing in Northern Malaya and a move on Thailand were reported. [Page 1, Column 3.] In Shanghai, Japanese marines occupied the waterfront; a British gunboat was sunk, a United States gunboat seized. [Page 9, Column 1.]

Factional lines dissolved as an angered Congress prepared to meet this morning. [Page 1, Column 1.] Secretary of State Hull accused Japan of having made a "treacherous and utterly unprovoked attack" after having been "infamously false and fraudulent." [Page 1, Column 6.] He released the text of diplomatic exchanges with Japan [Page 10], while the President gave out the text of his fruitless appeal to the Japanese Emperor. [Page 12.] The White House was the hub of Washington activity and news bulletins were released there. [Page 12, Column 3.]

The Federal Bureau of Investigation was ordered to begin a round-up of some Japanese in this country. [Page 6, Column 8.] As New York City went on a war footing and public precautions were taken, the FBI began the detention of Japanese nationals. [Page 1, Column 4.]

The unification of the country under the impact of the attack was swift. [Page 6, Column 6.] Formerly conspicuous isolationists indicated full support for the war effort. [Page 6, Column 4.]

Prime Minister Churchill notified Tokyo that a state of war existed. [Page 4, Column 1.] Declarations were made last night or early today by Australia, Canada [Page 14 Column 1], the Netherlands Indies [Page 7, Column 2] and Costa Rica. [Page 15, Column 1.]

Libya was the scene of a renewed tank battle and the Tobruk corridor was reported again clear of Axis forces. [Page 20, Column 2, with map.] On the Moscow front the German line was broken at two places, said Soviet sources. [Page 17, Column 2.]

Lewis Wins Captive Mine Fight; Arbitrators Grant Union Shop

The three-man arbitration board appointed by President Roosevelt to arbitrate the union shop dispute in the captive coal mines last night reversed the decision of the National Defense Mediation Board and ruled that all workers in the captive mines should be required to join John L. Lewis's United Mine Workers as a condition of employment.

The decision was made by a two to one vote, with Benjamin F. Fairless, president of the United States Steel Corporation, dissenting. Dr. John R. Steelman, who took a leave of absence from his post as director of the United States Conciliation Service to serve as chairman of the arbitration panel, and Mr. Lewis voted in favor of extension to the captive mines of the union shop provision of the standard Appalachian agreement.

Despite his dissent, Mr. Fairless promised that the coal mining subsidiaries of United States Steel would put the ruling into effect. All eight steel companies operating captive mines had given formal assurances before the decision was reached that they would accept it as binding.

The arbitration award ended a dispute in which Mr. Lewis had repeatedly defied the President by calling strikes that menaced the production of steel and that had had its repercussions in the enactment by the House of the Smith anti-strike bill.

In explaining his vote for the union shop, Dr. Steelman pointed out that 95 per cent of the 53,000 captive miners had voluntarily assumed membership in Mr. Lewis's C. I. O. union and that 99.5 per cent of all the miners in the nation were now members of the union.

Since the bulk of the industry, including many owners of captive mines, was already operating under the union shop, it could not be argued that the United Mine Workers was endeavoring to take

Continued on Page Forty-three

NEWS BULLETINS

are broadcast by The New York Times every hour on the hour over Station WMCA—570 on the dial.

WEEKDAYS
8 a. m. through 11 p. m.
SUNDAYS
9 a.m., 1 p.m., 5 p.m., 11 p.m.

"All the News That's Fit to Print."

The New York Times.

LATE CITY EDITION
Cloudy followed by clearing and colder today. Tomorrow fair and moderately cold.
Temperatures Yesterday—Max., 44; Min., 25

Copyright, 1941, by The New York Times Company.

VOL. XCI..No. 30,635. Entered as Second-Class Matter, Postoffice, New York, N. Y. NEW YORK, TUESDAY, DECEMBER 9, 1941. THREE CENTS NEW YORK CITY and Vicinity

U. S. DECLARES WAR, PACIFIC BATTLE WIDENS; MANILA AREA BOMBED; 1,500 DEAD IN HAWAII; HOSTILE PLANES SIGHTED AT SAN FRANCISCO

TURN BACK TO SEA

Two Formations Neared City on Radio Beams, Then Went Astray

ALARM IS WIDESPREAD

Whole Coast Has a Nervous Night—Many Cities Blacked Out

By LAWRENCE E. DAVIES
Special to THE NEW YORK TIMES.

SAN FRANCISCO, Dec. 8—Two formations of "many planes," described as undoubtedly enemy aircraft, flew over the San Francisco Bay area tonight, it was announced officially by Brig. General William O. Ryan, commander of the Fourth Interceptor Command, after a progressive blackout had blotted out naval and military establishments and whole cities along the Pacific Coast.

Conflicting reports spread, contributing to the "war of nerves," as the sirens wailed and broadcasting were silenced.

After another spokesman, through an error, had declared the blackout to be an air raid test, General Ryan said at the Presidio that it was no test but "the real thing."

The ships were detected first about 100 miles at sea, he said. In two formations they headed for the Monterey Peninsula, about eighty miles south of this city, and for San Francisco Bay itself.

Radio detectors plotted their course, bringing one formation in just north of the Golden Gate and the other to a point near Fort Barry, at the south end of the Golden Gate Bridge.

Planes Turn Back to Sea

After flying northward for some distance the planes turned south to a point thirty-five or forty miles below the peninsula section below San Francisco. Apparently trying to orient themselves, they flew about a while longer and then headed southwest to sea, General Ryan said.

The commanding officer, whose station is at Riverside and who said he just "happened" to be at the Presidio tonight, declared that the planes followed radio beams to these shores. When radio stations on the West Coast were silenced as part of the blackout the enemy craft apparently were not sure of their position.

No American planes were sent to the attack, he said, because "you don't send planes up unless you know what the enemy is doing and where he is going and you don't send planes up in the dark unless you know what you are doing."

Although there was no official explanation for the absence of anti-aircraft fire, it was indicated that the planes were hardly close enough for effective use of the guns.

Plane Carriers Rumored

Although General Ryan had no information, he said, as to the presence of enemy aircraft carriers hovering off the Pacific Coast, rumors of their presence had been broadcast during the day and this, it was acknowledged, would be the logical explanation for the appearance of the planes.

Lieut. Gen. John L. Dewitt,

Continued on Page Twenty-eight

NEWS BULLETINS

Please do not telephone The New York Times for war news. Every hour on the hour news bulletins are broadcast over Station WMCA—570 on the dial.

WEEKDAYS
8 a. m. through 11 p. m.
SUNDAYS
9 a.m., 1 p.m., 5 p.m., 11 p.m.

Philippines Pounded All Day As Raiders Strike at Troops

Air Base Near Capital Among Targets Hit by Japanese—Landing on Lubang With Aid of Fifth Columnists Reported

By H. FORD WILKINS
Wireless to THE NEW YORK TIMES.

MANILA, Tuesday, Dec. 9—After a day of widespread aerial attacks throughout the Philippines, Japanese bombers swept in over Manila Bay early this morning and attacked Nichols Field, the United States Army air base on the outskirts of this capital, and simultaneously reports were received of a Japanese landing on Lubang Island, off the northwestern tip of Mindoro.

This morning's attack, which began shortly after 3 o'clock, was the first in the Manila area. The damage was believed to have been slight, but some casualties were reported. [A National Broadcasting Company correspondent reported that an official statement issued in Manila after the raid said: "In the raid on Nichols Field, which was conducted by approximately ten Japanese bombers, one hangar was damaged and one officers' quarters was burned. The casualty list consists of one soldier killed and twelve wounded—all Americans."]

The reported landing on Lubang, sixty miles southwest of Manila, was not officially confirmed, but the reports received credence here. [Other unconfirmed reports, relayed by the Columbia Broadcasting System, told of landings in the Davao region, on the southern island of Mindanao.]

The Manila area's first experience with bombs was a climax to a day and night of tension and activity. The explosions could be

Continued on Page Nine

1 BATTLESHIP LOST

Capsized in Pearl Harbor, Destroyer Is Blown Up, Other Ships Hurt

FLEET NOW IS FIGHTING

Aid Rushed to Hawaii—Some Congressmen Sharply Critical

By CHARLES HURD
Special to THE NEW YORK TIMES.

WASHINGTON, Dec. 8—The Battle of the Pacific spread tonight over a 5,000-mile "front" from Hawaii to the Philippines while a badly battered United States Fleet fought back at Japanese sea and air forces that launched severe attacks yesterday afternoon.

Tonight the Japanese were reported to be launching their main attack at the Philippines, particularly at Palawan, the greatest natural harbor in the archipelago. That attack was preceded today, according to reports from Manila, by an onslaught against the United States military air fields there, which put these out of commission for the time being and set fire to storage tanks containing vital gasoline for air operations.

The Japanese Sunday attack on Hawaii was reported in informed quarters to have been launched from the mandated islands, rather than from Japan proper, and aircraft carriers apparently approached undetected within 250 or 300 miles of Pearl Harbor.

3,000 Casualties on Oahu

The White House announced officially that the attack on the Island of Oahu, site of Honolulu and the Pearl Harbor naval base, probably has cost about 1,500 lives and resulted in an equal number of wounded persons.

To the toll of lives announced for this region, and undisclosed casualties in the Philippines and at other points, was added official word that one "old battleship" had capsized in Pearl Harbor, a destroyer had exploded and that several other

Continued on Page Four

The President signs the declaration of war — Associated Press Wirephoto

UNITY IN CONGRESS

Only One Negative Vote as President Calls to War and Victory

ROUNDS OF CHEERS

Miss Rankin's Is Sole 'No' as Both Houses Act in Quick Time

By FRANK L. KLUCKHOHN
Special to THE NEW YORK TIMES.

WASHINGTON, Dec. 8—The United States today formally declared war on Japan. Congress, with only one dissenting vote, approved the resolution in the record time of 33 minutes after President Roosevelt denounced Japanese aggression in ringing tones. He personally delivered his message to a joint session of the Senate and House. At 4:10 P. M. he affixed his signature to the resolution.

There was no debate like that between April 2, 1917, when President Wilson requested war against Germany, and April 6, when a declaration of war was approved by Congress.

President Roosevelt spoke only 6 minutes and 30 seconds today compared with Woodrow Wilson's 29 minutes and 34 seconds.

The vote today against Japan was 82 to 0 in the Senate and 388 to 1 in the House. The lone vote against the resolution in the House was that of Miss Jeanette Rankin, Republican, of Montana. Her "No" was greeted with boos and hisses. In 1917 she voted against the resolution for war against Germany.

The President did not mention either Germany or Italy in his request. Early this evening a statement was issued at the White House, however, accusing Germany of doing everything possible to push Japan into the war. The objective, the official statement proclaimed, was to cut off American lend-lease aid to Germany's European enemies, and a pledge was made that this aid would continue "100 per cent."

A Sudden and Deliberate Attack

President Roosevelt's brief and decisive words were addressed to the assembled representatives of the basic organizations of American democracy—the Senate, the House, the Cabinet and the Supreme Court.

"America was suddenly and deliberately attacked by naval and air forces of the Empire of Japan," he said. "We will gain the inevitable triumph, so help us God."

Thunderous cheers greeted the Chief Executive and Commander in Chief throughout the address. This was particularly pronounced when he declared that Americans "will remember the character of the onslaught against us," a day, he remarked, which will live in infamy. "This form of treachery shall never endanger us again," he declared amid cheers. "The American people in their righteous might will win through to absolute victory."

Then, to the accompaniment of a

Continued on Page Five

PLANES GUARD CITY FROM AIR ATTACKS

Army Interceptors Join the Navy Patrols—Anti-Aircraft Apparatus Set Up Here

While long lines of men of fighting age waited impatiently outside of every Army, Navy and Marine Corps recruiting office in the city yesterday, representatives of the city, State and Federal Governments went ahead with the grim business of making New York City ready for war.

Beginning at dawn yesterday Army fighting planes took off at regular intervals from Mitchel Field to maintain, in conjunction with a Navy patrol, a constant fighting force in the air, so there could be no repetition here of the surprise in Hawaii. At the same time the First Interceptor Command called to active duty 40,000 volunteer civilian aircraft spotters at 1,300 posts scattered through thirteen eastern coastal States and the District of Columbia.

Anti-Aircraft Guns Set Up

The Sixty-second Coast Artillery of Fort Totten, Bayside, Queens, set up anti-aircraft apparatus at vantage points around the city. One base was in Prospect Park, Brooklyn.

Air raid wardens went on duty at midnight in every part of the city, as a result of a series of conferences among Police and Fire Department officers and representatives of the Board of Education and the Department of Housing, at which it was agreed that air raid warnings would be broadcast by the blowing of the sirens of all police radio cars and emergency trucks and all Fire Department apparatus.

Alternating long and short blasts of the sirens will be sounded from the moment the Army notifies the Police and Fire Departments of the approach of an enemy and will be continued throughout the duration of the raid. The all-clear signal will be given by a series of short blasts from the sirens, it was agreed.

Teachers to Be Warned

The Police and Fire Departments, with their network of communications reaching into every neighborhood in the city, also undertook to advise the 800 public schools of an impending raid when the alarm is sounded, so the teachers can shepherd their pupils to their homes in accordance with plans already made.

Precautions against sabotage of bridges, tunnels, railroads, reservoirs, dams, power plants and other points of key importance throughout the city also were discussed at conferences of high police officials with Commissioner

Continued on Page Twenty-six

MALAYA THWARTS PUSH BY JAPANESE

Thailand Capitulates and Is Seen Virtually in Axis—Two Raids on Singapore

By F. TILLMAN DURDIN
Wireless to THE NEW YORK TIMES.

SINGAPORE, Dec. 8—The Japanese in the first eighteen hours of their attack on the Malaya peninsula have forced Thailand to capitulate, but do not now appear to have achieved any appreciable success in an invasion of British Malaya.

There was an air raid on Singapore this morning. Prai, on the mainland opposite Georgetown, more commonly known as Penang from the name of the island on which it is located, was also bombed, but damage was said to be slight.

[Bombs again started dropping on Singapore at 4 A. M. today, The Associated Press re-

Continued on Page Ten

The International Situation

TUESDAY, DECEMBER 9, 1941

The United States yesterday made a formal declaration of war on Japan after President Roosevelt had addressed a joint session of Congress. [Page 1, Column 8.] The Senate approved by unanimous vote [Page 6, Column 1] while one woman in the House of Representatives dissented. [Page 6, Column 4.]

In the national effort the Supply, Priorities and Allocations Board mapped expanding production [Page 36, Column 1], leaders of organized labor pledged support [Page 36, Column 4], and Mayor La Guardia issued a proclamation giving air raid defense instructions [Page 34, Column 1.]

In San Francisco two formations of enemy aircraft were sighted over the city, which was blacked out. [Page 1, Column 1.]

White House announcements indicated that the battle of the Pacific was raging with the United States still on the defensive. [Page 1, Column 4; Map, Page 4.] There were extensive air attacks in the Philippines [Page 1, Columns 2 and 3; Map, Page 9], raids on Hong Kong [Page 11, Column 1] and a Tokyo report that both Guam and Wake had been put under the Japanese flag. [Page 12, Column 1; with map.] The British were mopping up on a Japanese landing party in Malaya, but Thailand had yielded. [Page 1, Column 3; Map, Page 10.]

The small detachment of United States Marines at Tientsin and Peiping was disarmed and detained by the Japanese and they closed the United States Consulate in Shanghai [Page 3, Column 1.] Imperial Headquarters in Tokyo made sweeping claims of victory in the battle of the Pacific, listing great damage to the United States forces. [Page 1, Column 5.]

In London, Prime Minister Churchill announced Britain's declaration of war to Parliament and made a stirring address to the world. [Page 14, Column 1.]

The American nations began to line up behind the United States. A conference will be held, but seven countries have already declared war on Japan, two have broken diplomatic relations and several others are preparing to act. [Page 22, Column 3.] China decided to declare war not merely on Japan but on Germany and Italy as well. [Page 9, Column 4.] The various European governments in exile also supported the United States. [Page 18, Column 1.] Russia's position is obscure. [Page 2, Column 2.]

The United States accused Germany of having egged Japan on; said lease-lend aid would continue. [Page 1, Column 6.]

Berlin gave out word that Winter had stopped the Germans short of Moscow and that the capture of the Russian capital had been put off until Spring. [Page 1, Column 7.]

In Libya, the Axis armored forces were attacked from three directions by the British and what was expected to be a major engagement was eventually merely a rearguard action. [Page 24, Column 3.]

LARGE U. S. LOSSES CLAIMED BY JAPAN

Tokyo Lists 2 Battleships, 1 Mine-Sweeper Sunk, 4 Capital Ships, 4 Cruisers Damaged

TOKYO, Tuesday, Dec. 9 (From Official Broadcasts, Distributed by The Associated Press)—Japanese Imperial Headquarters announced last night the sinking of two United States battleships and a mine-sweeper, severe damage to four other American capital ships and four cruisers and the destruction of about 100 American planes in Japan's surprise blows at Hawaii, the Philippines and Guam.

The official news agency, Domei, quickly interpreted "these magnificent early gains" as giving Japan naval mastery over the United States in the Pacific, and said that any force that the United States could muster now "would be regarded as utterly inadequate to accomplish any successful outcome in an encounter with the thus-far-intact Japanese fleet."

In addition, "many enemy merchant ships were captured" in the Pacific, it was announced, and the communiqué listed an unconfirmed report that a Japanese submarine had sunk an American aircraft carrier off Honolulu.

"No Japanese ships were lost during the fighting," it added.

Domei said today it was "understood that Japanese forces had destroyed more than 300 American planes, including 200 in dogfights and on the ground in Hawaii. The others, it said, were "believed" destroyed in the Philippines. Of the total, the news agency said, thirty were Fortress planes and thirty long-range bombers.

Japanese newspapers identified the two American battleships declared sunk Sunday at Pearl Harbor, Hawaii, as the 31,800-ton West Virginia, and the 29,000-ton Oklahoma. [An Italian broadcast, however, quoted Domei as listing the Oklahoma and the 33,100-ton Pennsylvania as lost. In Berlin, D. N. B. said in a Tokyo dispatch that an American transport ship carrying 350 men had been sunk off Manila.]

Japanese planes were reported to have again attacked the Philippines and British Hong Kong yesterday, inflicting "heavy damage" in a follow-up of the raids launched Sunday. "Twelve out of fourteen enemy planes on the ground were

Continued on Page Thirteen

The President's Message

Following is the text of President Roosevelt's war message to Congress, as recorded by THE NEW YORK TIMES *from a broadcast:*

Mr. Vice President, Mr. Speaker, members of the Senate and the House of Representatives:

Yesterday, Dec. 7, 1941—a date which will live in infamy—the United States of America was suddenly and deliberately attacked by naval and air forces of the empire of Japan.

The United States was at peace with that nation, and, at the solicitation of Japan, was still in conversation with its government and its Emperor looking toward the maintenance of peace in the Pacific.

Indeed, one hour after Japanese air squadrons had commenced bombing in the American island of Oahu the Japanese Ambassador to the United States and his colleague delivered to our Secretary of State a formal reply to a recent American message. And, while this reply stated that it seemed useless to continue the existing diplomatic negotiations, it contained no threat or hint of war or of armed attack.

Attack Deliberately Planned

It will be recorded that the distance of Hawaii from Japan makes it obvious that the attack was deliberately planned many days or even weeks ago. During the intervening time the Japanese Government has deliberately sought to deceive the United States by false statements and expressions of hope for continued peace.

The attack yesterday on the Hawaiian Islands has caused severe damage to American naval and military forces. I regret to tell you that very many American lives have been lost. In

Continued on Page Six

U. S. TO CONTINUE AID TO BRITAIN

White House Charges Nazis Sought Pacific War, but Will Fail to Gain Ends

Special to THE NEW YORK TIMES.

WASHINGTON, Dec. 8—A statement accusing Germany of having done everything in her power "to push Japan into the war" was issued this evening at the White House.

The statement declared that Germany's objective was "to put an end to the lease-lend program," which has aided the European enemies of Germany, including Britain and Russia and their allies and Turkey. It added that this program would continue "in full operation" and that the German attempt to end lease-lend shipments was "100 per cent" mistaken.

This statement took full cognizance of the belief in diplomatic circles here that Germany would carry out its pledges to Japan, its Axis ally, by declaring war on the United States and that Italy would

Continued on Page Seventeen

NAZIS GIVE UP IDEA OF MOSCOW IN 1941

Winter Forces Abandonment of Big Drives in North Till Spring, Berlin Says

By The Associated Press.

BERLIN, Dec. 8—Winter has stopped the Germans short of Moscow and the capture of the Soviet capital is not expected this year, a military spokesman declared tonight.

[A surprise Russian attack on Eastern Crimea from the Caucasus was revealed in a Moscow broadcast. A counter-attack from Sevastopol also was reported. The Soviet claimed important progress around Taganrog and on Moscow's defense lines.]

It seemed likely from the spokesman's statement that until Spring there could be no further major German offensive except along the extreme southern front. This word reduced the Russian campaign to secondary interest for the Germans for the first time, and attention focused instead on Ja-

Continued on Page Twenty-five

President to Talk On Radio Tonight

By The Associated Press.

WASHINGTON, Dec. 8—President Roosevelt will make a radio address to the nation tomorrow night at 10 P. M., Eastern standard time, at which time the White House said he would make "a more complete documentation" of the Japanese attack than has yet been possible.

Stephen Early, Presidential secretary, announced that the Chief Executive would speak for half an hour and that the address would be carried by all networks.

Mr. Roosevelt began dictating the speech tonight in his White House study.

"All the News That's Fit to Print."

The New York Times.

LATE CITY EDITION
Fair, slowly rising temperature today. Tomorrow cloudy, moderately cold, occasional snow.
Temperatures Yesterday—Max., 34; Min., 24

VOL. XCI..No. 30,638. Entered as Second-Class Matter, Postoffice, New York, N. Y. NEW YORK, FRIDAY, DECEMBER 12, 1941. THREE CENTS NEW YORK CITY and Vicinity

U.S. NOW AT WAR WITH GERMANY AND ITALY; JAPANESE CHECKED IN ALL LAND FIGHTING; 3 OF THEIR SHIPS SUNK, 2D BATTLESHIP HIT

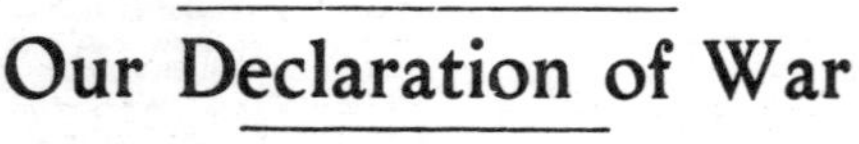

Left: The President set his signature to the act against Germany. Center: He checked the time with Senator Tom Connally. Right: After that he placed the United States officially at war with Italy.

Associated Press Wirephotos

BLOCKED IN LUZON

But Japanese Put Small Force Ashore in South of Philippine Island

SABOTEURS ARE HELD

Some in Manila Seized for Spreading Rumor About City Water

By H. FORD WILKINS

Wireless to THE NEW YORK TIMES.

MANILA, Friday, Dec. 12—The United States Army Far East headquarters announced today that a small Japanese invasion force was reported to have pushed ashore at Legaspi, Southern Luzon, and "the enemy has improved his strength in Northern Luzon," where, however, the situation remains unchanged materially. The announcement added that the report of the Legaspi landing was still unconfirmed and there were no details.

[Small forces of Japanese apparently have been landed at Legaspi, it was said officially three hours after the morning communiqué had said merely that the Legaspi development had not yet been confirmed, a United Press dispatch from Manila said.]

There was no further indication of the progress of the sea war. The office of Admiral Thomas C. Hart, commander in chief of the United States Asiatic Fleet, remained silent.

One Japanese plane was shot down by an American fighter near Bancayan, in the mountain mining district.

2,000 Families Are Moved

Manila took further emergency measures to evacuate portions of the old walled city. The Red Cross supervised the removal of 2,000 families, loading them into buses and trucks and taking them to safety zones considerably removed from the city. Identification cards were issued and checked as the evacuees lined up for removal

With Lieut. Gen. Douglas MacArthur's United States Far Eastern forces fully in control of the North Luzon invasion threat and his air force sufficiently active to disperse Japanese raiders headed for Manila, his intelligence service turned yesterday to mopping up fifth columnists.

Their latest trick was to circulate rumors that the city water supply had been poisoned. Army, city and government officials quickly scotched the rumors with assurances and proof that nothing whatever was wrong with the water supply. Several persons were arrested, including air-raid wardens, on a city-wide house-to-house campaign warning the people against "impure water."

Several persons entered hospitals asserting that they had been poisoned, but examination disclosed that nothing was wrong with them but upset stomachs and fear. Elaborate analysis proved that the water they drank was not contaminated.

The official communiqué asserting that mopping-up operations were progressing heightened the morale of the nation, suddenly plunged into total war and its first taste of conflict in forty years.

The sinking of a United States Army transport in Manila Bay, as announced by Tokyo, was denied officially here yesterday.

Interned Japanese, numbering around 2,000, were revealed to be extremely uncomfortable under the threat of bombs from Japanese planes, recognizing that bombs do not distinguish nationalities.

Legaspi Move Discounted

MANILA, Friday, Dec. 12 (U.P.)—The small Japanese landings at Legaspi, a port of about 36,000

Continued on Page Eight

Line-Up of World War II

THE ALLIES

Australia
†Belgium
Canada
China
Costa Rica
Cuba
†Czecho-Slovakia
Dominican Republic
*El Salvador
Free France
Great Britain
†Greece
Guatemala
Haiti
*Honduras
Netherlands Indies
New Zealand
Nicaragua
†Norway
*Panama
†Poland
South Africa
†Soviet Union
United States
†Yugoslavia

THE AXIS

Finland
Germany
Hungary
Italy
Japan
Manchukuo
Rumania
Slovakia

*Have declared war on Japan only.

†At war only with Germany, Italy and their European allies.

CITY CALM AND GRIM AS THE WAR WIDENS

Loyalty and a Determination to Win Are Evident in Every Class and National Group

The people of New York City received the news that we are at war with Germany and Italy as well as Japan with profound calm and a quiet, stern determination to see it through, no matter how long it takes. Patriotism and loyalty were the spontaneous order of the day in every household, every business office, every factory, every school and every institution. The whole city rallied in support of the war.

All over the city the Stars and Stripes flew proudly from public and private buildings, and those in charge of Army, Navy, Coast Guard and civilian defense organizations swung promptly and forcefully into action to protect the city

Continued on Page Twenty-one

U. S. FLIERS SCORE

Bombs Send Battleship, Cruiser and Destroyer to the Bottom

MARINES KEEP WAKE

Small Force Fights Off Foe Despite Loss of Some of Planes

By CHARLES HURD

Special to THE NEW YORK TIMES.

WASHINGTON, Dec. 11—A Japanese battleship, a cruiser and a destroyer have been sunk in the Pacific and a second battleship badly damaged by bomb hits, the United States forces announced in communiqués today recording their first major victories in the warfare that began last Sunday with surprise Japanese attacks.

Damage to the second battleship was revealed tonight in a Navy communiqué, which said a man-of-war of the Kongo class had been hit by Navy patrol planes off the coast of Luzon. This was "the second battleship to be bombed effectively by United States forces," the communiqué asserted.

The battleship sunk, also of the Kongo class, was believed to have been the 29,330-ton Haruna. She went down after having been set afire by aerial bombardment north of Luzon. She had been supporting an attack in which the Japanese effected a landing at Aparri, a remote village on the northern Philippine coast, separated from Manila by mountains and forests.

The cruiser, unidentified except that it was of the light class, and the destroyer were sunk also by fliers who took off from Wake

Continued on Page Six

The International Situation

FRIDAY, DECEMBER 12, 1941

The United States declared war yesterday on Germany and Italy. Congress acted swiftly without a dissenting vote. [Page 1, Column 8.] Then, without debate, it passed a bill to permit the use of all United States land forces anywhere in the world. [Page 1, Column 7.]

This action coincided with good news from the Pacific. Washington announced the sinking of a Japanese battleship, a cruiser and a destroyer and reported severe damage to a second battleship by bomb hits. [Page 1, Column 3, Map, Page 6.]

The American declaration came within a few hours after Germany and Italy had declared war on the United States. The Reich's declaration was made in a diplomatic note and in a Reichstag address by Adolf Hitler. [Page 4, Column 1.] Benito Mussolini proclaimed Italy's declaration. [Page 4, Column 5.]

In London, where news of America's full entry into the world war brought predictions of an Allied grand strategy [Page 13, Column 5], Prime Minister Churchill declared that the Allies would win ultimately at any cost. [Page 1, Column 4.] Mexico broke off relations with Germany and Italy, while ten other Latin-American nations declared war on those countries or prepared to take that step. [Page 9, Column 1.]

The Soviet radio asserted that any Axis hopes for a separate peace with Russia were in vain. The radio declared that Russia was determined to fight alongside the United States and Britain until the Allies won. [Page 19, Column 1.]

In all of yesterday's land fighting, Japan was checked. In the Philippines, attempts to win a firm foothold on Luzon appeared smashed, except for a landing of parachutists at an airport 180 miles northeast of Manila and another small landing on the southeastern coast of the island. [Page 1, Column 1; Map, Page 2.] The British reported a slow-down of Japanese attacks in Malaya. [Page 13, Column 1.] While British forces fought off new assaults on Hong Kong, a two-day Chinese offensive to relieve pressure there was reported to have inflicted 15,000 casualties. [Page 11, Column 1, with map.]

Tokyo claimed the destruction of an American destroyer, a submarine and eighty-one planes, in addition to the capture of 350 Americans on Guam. [Page 8, Column 5.] With the commander of Britain's Far Eastern Fleet among 595 men still missing in the sinking of the Prince of Wales and the Repulse, the British named a new commander. [Page 14, Column 3.]

Amid debate in Washington over a proposed investigation of what happened at Pearl Harbor Sunday [Page 10, Column 1], Secretary of the Navy Knox arrived in Honolulu, presumably to seek first-hand information on that attack. [Page 1, Columns 5 and 6.]

President Roosevelt called upon industrial and labor representatives to meet next week and reach a voluntary agreement to end labor disputes for the duration. [Page 29, Column 2.] It was revealed also that the Administration was considering the registration of all men between the ages of 18 and 65 for military and civilian service. [Page 34, Column 1.]

On the European fighting front the Russians reported further gains against German forces. [Page 18, Column 3.] The Berlin radio revealed that the Nazis had replaced their commander on the Moscow front. [Page 19, Column 3.] In Libya, the main Axis forces were still withdrawing westward, Cairo announced. [Page 17, Column 1.]

AXIS TO GET LESSON, CHURCHILL WARNS

He Announces Replacement of Libyan General—Upholds Phillips's Judgment

Text of Mr. Churchill's speech will be found on Page 16.

By CRAIG THOMPSON

Special Cable to THE NEW YORK TIMES.

LONDON, Dec. 11—Prime Minister Winston Churchill delivered a review of the war in the Pacific, North Africa, Russia and the Atlantic today that contained a compound of gloom and of optimism, but he ended with this ringing declaration:

"Just handfuls and cliques of wicked men and their military or party organizations have been able to bring these hideous evils upon mankind. It would indeed bring shame upon our generation if we did not teach them a lesson which will not be forgotten in the records of a thousand years."

Precedes Declarations

He spoke to the House of Commons before the Axis war declarations and the United States' reply.

Mr. Churchill gave hitherto unpublished details about the sinkings of the Prince of Wales and the Repulse, which made plain that the British had lost the use of airdromes on the Malay Peninsula and that the ships had had to rely solely on their anti-aircraft guns for protection against the attacking planes. In so doing he stoutly defended the judgment whereby Vice Admiral Sir Tom S. V. Phillips, who appeared tonight to have been lost, undertook an attack on Japanese transports that resulted in the sinkings of the warships.

Mr. Churchill announced that Lieut. Gen. Sir Alan Gordon Cunningham had been replaced in Libya by Major Gen. Neil Methuen Ritchie, adding that General Cunningham "has been reported by medical authorities to be suffering from serious overstrain and was granted sick leave."

General Ritchie, the new commander of the Eighth Army, is 44 years old. His was one of three "young-men" appointments to the General Staff that were made last June. In the last war he was commissioned a second lieutenant in the Black Watch at the age of seventeen and was a captain when he was twenty. He fought in France, Mesopotamia and Palestine, and received the Distinguished Service Order and the Military Cross.

Mr. Churchill gave an indication of the size of British and Allied losses in merchantmen in the Battle of the Atlantic for November that would, from his statement, appear to have been no greater than 100,000 tons. This would be a

Continued on Page Seventeen

Our Declaration of War

Special to THE NEW YORK TIMES.

WASHINGTON, Dec. 11—Following are the texts of the documents wherein the President asked a war declaration against Germany and Italy, and Congress acted:

The President's Message

To the Congress of the United States:

On the morning of Dec. 11 the Government of Germany, pursuing its course of world conquest, declared war against the United States.

The long-known and the long-expected has thus taken place. The forces endeavoring to enslave the entire world now are moving toward this hemisphere.

Never before has there been a greater challenge to life, liberty and civilization.

Delay invites great danger. Rapid and united effort by all of the peoples of the world who are determined to remain free will insure a world victory of the forces of justice and of righteousness over the forces of savagery and of barbarism.

Italy also has declared war against the United States.

I therefore request the Congress to recognize a state of war between the United States and Germany, and between the United States and Italy.

FRANKLIN D. ROOSEVELT.

The War Resolution

Declaring that a state of war exists between the Government of Germany and the government and the people of the United States and making provision to prosecute the same.

Whereas the Government of Germany has formally declared war against the government and the people of the United States of America:

Therefore, be it

Resolved by the Senate and House of Representatives of the United States of America in Congress assembled, that the state of war between the United States and the Government of Germany which has thus been thrust upon the United States is hereby formally declared; and the President is hereby authorized and directed to employ the entire naval and military forces of the United States and the resources of the government to carry on war against the Government of Germany; and, to bring the conflict to a successful termination, all of the resources of the country are hereby pledged by the Congress of the United States.

(An identic resolution regarding Italy was adopted)

Secretary Knox Visits Honolulu; Bases There Were Raided 5 Times

Special to THE NEW YORK TIMES.

WASHINGTON, Dec. 11—The Navy Department announced tonight that Secretary Frank Knox had arrived in Honolulu this afternoon.

There was no previous announcement that he had left for Hawaii, nor was there any intimation of the specific purpose of his visit.

WASHINGTON, Dec. 11 (U.P.)—Delegate Samuel W. King of Hawaii disclosed tonight after a telephone conversation with Governor Joseph B. Poindexter that twenty Japanese planes were shot down during the Sunday raid on Pearl Harbor.

Mr. King said the information was authorized for release in Hawaii by Lieut. Gen. Walter C. Short and that Mr. Poindexter was permitted to make the disclosure by transpacific radio-telephone.

Mr. Poindexter told Mr. King that "civilian morale is 100 per cent throughout the territory.

"Civilian defense measures are working without a hitch," he added.

HONOLULU, Dec. 11 (U.P.)—In addition to two deadly attacks on the United States naval base at Pearl Harbor last Sunday, Japanese bombers followed with a third attack later that day and with a fourth Monday morning, it is possible to disclose today for the first time.

Censorship permits a cautious description of the attack. A few seconds after the first bombers came over, with the rising sun insignia of Japan on their wings, defending anti-aircraft batteries sent up a heavy barrage.

Within a few minutes heavy clouds of black smoke began rolling up from Pearl Harbor, fourteen miles from Honolulu.

Planes roared in over the harbor, dropping bombs on navy centers and ships. Torpedo planes splashed

Continued on Page Eleven

CONGRESS KILLS BAN ON AN A. E. F.

Swift Action Without Debate—Service Terms Are Extended to Six Months After War

Special to THE NEW YORK TIMES.

WASHINGTON, Dec. 11—Congress swiftly eliminated prohibitions against American expeditionary forces today and continued terms of enlistment or induction to a date six months after hostilities end. Acting without debate, the two houses dropped the A. E. F. ban by removing restrictions in the Selective Service Act on the use of troops outside the Western Hemisphere.

The Senate Appropriations Committee, meanwhile, added an undetermined sum to the $8,246,000,000 third supplemental national defense appropriation bill as passed by the House. This change was said to have raised the bill's total above $10,500,000,000.

A ranking member of the committee was unable to say tonight what the exact amount of the bill was, but he said he was "satisfied it is above $10,500,000,000." He added that the amendments approved by the committee were mostly for new items, regarded as emergency ones by the Army and the Navy and Coast Guard. If approved, the measure would set a record for the size of a single appropriation bill.

Fund for Army Pay Specified

Among the amendments approved by the committee was one setting at $314,000,000 the supplemental item for pay of the Army, but immediately following it was a proviso that this amount should not be taken to mean the limit if the Army inducted or enlisted thousands of new personnel. If this took place, under the amendment practical authority would be granted for pay of the personnel under Congressional promise to pass deficiency bills to whatever extent was necessary.

Some $390,000,000 was added to the bill for military air construction. The Signal Corps also received a sizable increase for construction and equipment, while to the Navy were granted increases of many millions for landing fields, yards and docks. The Coast Guard received $4,750,000 for extraordinary expenses and $8,743,000 for new equipment.

The Army Chief of Staff received $125,000,000 as an emergency fund, to be accounted for to Congress every three months, and various sums were voted for additions to forts and posts within the United States.

The measure changing the Selective Service Act regarding the tenure of service and the extent of service came on the heels of action by both houses in declaring war on Germany and Italy, follow-

Continued on Page Thirty-four

WAR OPENED ON US

Congress Acts Quickly as President Meets Hitler Challenge

A GRIM UNANIMITY

Message Warns Nation Foes Aim to Enslave This Hemisphere

By FRANK L. KLUCKHOHN

Special to THE NEW YORK TIMES.

WASHINGTON, Dec. 11—The United States declared war today on Germany and Italy, Japan's Axis partners. This nation acted swiftly after Germany formally declared war on us and Italy followed the German lead. Thus, President Roosevelt told Congress in his message, the long-known and the long-expected has taken place.

"The forces endeavoring to enslave the entire world now are moving toward this hemisphere," he said.

"Never before has there been a greater challenge to life, liberty and civilization."

Delay, the President said, invites great danger. But he added:

"Rapid and united effort by all of the peoples of the world who are determined to remain free will insure a world victory of the forces of justice and righteousness over the forces of savagery and barbarism."

For the first time in its history the United States finds itself at war against powers in both the Atlantic and the Pacific.

Quick and Unanimous Answer

Congress acted not only rapidly but without a dissenting vote to meet the Axis challenge. Within two and three-quarters hours after the reading of Mr. Roosevelt's message was started in the Senate and House at 12:26 P. M., the President had signed the declarations against Germany and Italy. Seventy-two hours previously the Japanese attack on Hawaii had brought about the declaration of war against the other Axis partner.

Congress also quickly completed legislation to allow selectees and National Guardsmen to serve outside the Western Hemisphere and set the term of service in the nation's forces until six months after the termination of the war.

In the Senate the vote was 88 to 0 for war against Germany and 90 to 0 for war against Italy. The vote in the House was 393 to 0 for war against Germany and 399 to 0 for war against Italy. The larger Congressional vote against Italy was attributable to the fact that some members reached the floor too late to vote on the declaration against Germany.

In the House, Miss Jeannette Rankin, Republican, of Montana, who cast the lone dissenting vote on Monday against declaring war on Japan, today voted a non-committal "present" with regard to Germany and Italy.

Ignoring Hitler's declarations before the Reichstag today regarding American policy, and Mussolini's to a crowd before the Palazzo di Venezia in Rome, Congress adopted identical resolutions against Germany and Italy. It merely noted that their governments had thrust war upon the United States.

Grim Mood in Congress

Congress acted in a grim mood, but without excitement. Not only on the floors of the Senate and House, but in the galleries the grim mood prevailed. President Roosevelt, busy at the White House directing the battle and production effort as Commander in Chief, did not appear to read his message, as he did when war was declared upon Japan.

There was a deeply solemn undernote as the members assembled at noon. Senator Walsh, chairman of the Senate Naval Affairs Committee, had announced that the

Continued on Page Five

"All the News That's Fit to Print."

The New York Times.

LATE CITY EDITION
Snow probably turning to rain, slowly rising temperatures today. Tomorrow rain.
Temperatures Yesterday—Max., 32; Min., 21

Copyright, 1941, by The New York Times Company.

VOL. XCI..No. 30,639. Entered as Second-Class Matter, Postoffice, New York, N. Y. NEW YORK, SATURDAY, DECEMBER 13, 1941. THREE CENTS NEW YORK CITY and Vicinity

JAPANESE POUNDED IN LUZON, WARSHIPS CHASED; RUSSIANS ROUT NAZI ARMIES ON MOSCOW FRONT; HOUSE GETS BILL TO REGISTER ALL MEN 18 TO 64

GERMANS SMASHED

85,000 Die, Vital Points Retaken in Debacle, Soviet Claims

END OF MENACE SEEN

Pockets Trap Invaders in Drives North and South of Capital

By DANIEL T. BRIGHAM
By Telephone to THE NEW YORK TIMES.

BERNE, Switzerland, Saturday, Dec. 13—Eighty-five thousand killed, recapture of most of the strategic points around Moscow from which the German forces were menacing it, seizure of quantities of matériel and a rout of the German Army in the central sector comparable only with that inflicted on it in the Rostov battle—these were among the claims made in a special communiqué issued by the Soviet High Command early this morning.

The announcement gave the first details of the progress of fighting on the central front since the Russian troops launched their wide counter-offensive in that sector at dawn last Saturday.

[Berlin again announced briefly that operations on the eastern front had been confined to local activity.]

Klin Reported Ringed

At midnight Thursday, the communiqué declared, the line around Moscow had been altered as follows:

1. Troops under General Leliuchenko, attacking northward from the neighborhood of Dmitrov, had taken Pogaceva. Then they had pivoted westward and, attacking on a wide front, advanced across the Sestra River and encircled Klin.

2. Troops under General Kousnetzoff, from Dmitrov itself, had struck southwest and still were progressing southwest of Klin. The objective of this offensive appeared to be to support another one pushing against Istra and driving on Volokolamsk, the recapture of which the Russian military spokesman announced as imminent.

3. Troops under General Vakhoff had pushed northward from Krjukova and retaken Solnechnogorsk, south of Klin. This action made possible a triple offensive that menaced with encirclement all German troops left in the "Dmitrov pocket," which at one time had progressed as far east as the Volga-Moscow Canal and threatened the capital with encirclement from the north.

Menace to Moscow Ended

4. Russian forces under General Rokossovsky had pushed up the Moscow-Volokolamsk road to throw the Germans out of Istra, their nearest point of approach to the capital and the location of the first major frontal thrust to reach the capital's outskirts on Dec. 5.

5. Troops under General Govoroff in the south-central sector had retaken Koulebiakine Lokatnya and were continuing their advance at a rapid pace.

6. Forces under General Bourgoineff were developing their offensive northeast of Tula, where a German pocket had included the towns of Kriukovo and Venev. Considerable advances had been made in this sector in the last week, and to these troops went the credit, according to the communiqué, for having liberated the northeastern defenses of Tula from immediate menace.

7. The First Cavalry Corps of the Guard, under General Bieloff, had retaken Venev and Stalinogorsk and was participating from the southern edge of the "Venev pocket" in a terrific squeeze to break the German thrust toward Ryazan, which is now declared to be ended.

8. South of the Stalinogorsk theatre, troops under General Golikoff had retaken the strategically important towns of Michailovsk

Continued on Page Seven

The Normandie: Tricolor to Stars and Stripes
The New York Times

U. S. Seizes the Normandie And 13 Other French Ships

Fourteen French freighters, tankers and passenger vessels were seized by the United States Government yesterday as armed Coast Guardsmen moved quietly and swiftly on the waterfronts of five ports in the United States and one in the Canal Zone. Including the fast superliner Normandie, registered at 83,423 gross tons, the seizures aggregated more than 150,000 tons of shipping, most of it modern and fairly fast.

Five of the ships were taken in New York by Coast Guard details under Captain John S. Baylis, who himself boarded the Normandie at West Forty-eighth Street.

Members of the skeleton crew of the Normandie, which has numbered about 125 men since the ship laid up here at the outbreak of war in 1939, were relieved of their posts by Coast Guardsmen and were held in custody by the Department of Justice.

Crews of other ships in San Pedro and San Francisco, in Mobile, New Orleans and at the Canal Zone also were taken into custody

Continued on Page Ten

14 CONVICTED HERE AS GERMAN SPIES

Verdict, Read After 8 Hours, Also Finds Agents Guilty of Failure to Register

All fourteen men accused of espionage and failure to register as agents of a foreign government, namely Germany, were found guilty on both counts a little before midnight last night by a jury of nine men and three women in United States District Court in Brooklyn that had deliberated about eight hours.

The defendants, charged specifically with conspiracy to evade registration as alien agents and to transmit abroad information about the United States defense effort, face maximum jail sentences of twenty-two years.

Judge Mortimer W. Byers, after thanking the jurors for their verdict, ordered the prisoners remanded to jail until Monday, which he fixed as the "record" date for sentence. The court announced, however, that the sentencing would be adjourned until probation reports on the prisoners were prepared.

19 Others to Be Sentenced

Also facing sentence at that time will be the nineteen other persons, including three women, who pleaded guilty to the original indictment and have been awaiting sentence.

In dismissing the jurors, Judge Byers said: "It will readily appear that you have rendered a very substantial contribution to the welfare of the country which you and I hold very dear."

T. Vincent Quinn, Assistant United States Attorney, who played a prominent part in the conviction of the defendants, told the jury that it had "done a hard job very well."

List of Convicted Spies

Those found guilty were:

Frederick Joubert Duquesne, 63 years old, described as a "soldier of fortune," veteran spy for more than forty years, and an inveterate Anglophobe.

Edmund Carl Heine, 50, former $30,000-a-year foreign sales agent for the Ford and Chrysler motor companies.

Herman Lang, former inspector for the C. L. Norden Company,

Continued on Page Ten

19-44 FOR FIGHTING

Rest Will Be Listed for Defense Survey of U. S. Man Power

QUICK PASSAGE IS DUE

Legislation for Support of Wives of Service Men Is Weighed

The text of the Registration Bill appears on Page 14.

By HENRY N. DORRIS
Special to THE NEW YORK TIMES.

WASHINGTON, Dec. 12—Legislation to require all men from 19 to 44 years old inclusive to register for training and service in the land or naval forces, and all other men from 18 to 64 inclusive to register for whatever defense duties might be assigned them, was introduced in the House today after a conference between officials of the War Department and the House leaders.

To hasten consideration of the legislation, hearings will be started tomorrow before the Military Affairs Committee, with Brig. Gen. Lewis B. Hershey, Selective Service Administrator, as the first witness.

Representative May of Kentucky, chairman of the committee, introduced the bill after a conference in the office of Speaker Rayburn. In addition to Mr. May, Mr. Rayburn and General Hershey, Secretary of War Henry L. Stimson, and Representatives John W. McCormack, the majority leader; James W. Wadsworth and Walter G. Andrews, Republicans of New York, were present.

A Survey of Man Power

Mr. Rayburn said after the conference that the ages, 18 to 64 inclusive would be registered for the purpose of obtaining an accurate survey of American man power.

He said also that the "proper committees" would begin immediately to consider revival of the

Continued on Page Fourteen

ATTACK ON PHILIPPINES PRESSED FROM MANY DIRECTIONS

At Aparri (1) and Vigan (2) the Japanese strengthened their forces. Parachutists were said to have landed near Tuguegarao and Ilagan (3). Around Lingayen (4) the defending forces were holding firmly. Japanese concentrations were reported off Zambales Province (5) and at Legaspi (8). Aerial raids were made on Olongapo naval base and Clark Field (6) and on a field at Batangas (7). The inset map shows the region surrounding the Philippines.

AID TO DEFENDERS

Reinforcements Rushed to Troops Battling the Invaders on Luzon

ARIZONA IS CLAIMED

Tokyo Says Battleship Was Sunk in Raid on Hawaii Sunday

By The United Press.

MANILA, Saturday, Dec. 13—American armed forces battled Japanese attacks on three sides of Luzon Island, chased enemy warships from Philippine coastal waters and fought aerial raiders until heavy storms last night disrupted operations.

A driving rain—rare for mid-December in these islands—bolstered the spirits of the defenders of the Philippines and provided a respite for weary military and civilian populations after five days of desperate fighting.

[Lieut. Gen Douglas MacArthur, commander in chief of the United States Forces of the Far East, announced today that the Japanese bombed Clark Field, 40 miles north of Manila, this morning, an Associated Press dispatch from Manila said. No important ground action was reported.

[The naval section of Imperial Headquarters at Tokyo issued the following communiqué this [Saturday] afternoon at 3 o'clock, according to Transocean German News Service:

["It has now been confirmed that, in addition to two previously named United States battleships, the American battleship Arizona, 32,600 tons, was sunk in Battle of Hawaii [presumably last Sunday]. It is also confirmed that in recent battle off Malaya one British destroyer of large-sized class was sunk in addition to two battleships Prince of Wales and Repulse."

[The United States Navy Department in Washington said, "No comment."]

Japanese Fliers Captured

One Japanese plane shot down near Clark Field yesterday morning fell in the mountains. Natives captured the crew of three and brought them to town trussed up like wild pigs.

[Fifth columnists set off red flares in Manila last night in a new outbreak of such activity but were answered by the blazing rifles of sentries acting under orders to "shoot to kill," an Associated Press dispatch said. Several houses in which lights could be seen were fired upon, and all on the streets who failed to respond to challenges likewise drew rifle shots.]

Reinforcements Cheered

The civilians remaining here appeared calmer than at any time since hostilities were opened by the Japanese. Along the downtown streets yesterday the crowds cheered loudly as reinforcements moved northward in "blitz-buggies"—commandeered buses. From among the watchers, the shout arose:

"Give 'em hell!"

[General MacArthur announced "with great sorrow" the death of Captain Colin P. Kelly Jr. of the Army Air Corps, who scored three direct hits on the Japanese battleship Haruna. The general also reported "with pride" that Lieutenant Boyd Wagner had distinguished himself by shooting down two Japanese planes and machine-gunning twelve others on the ground. Lieutenant Wagner returned to his base only because his gasoline was running low. Navy fliers were commended by Admiral Hart for daring and valor in pressing home attacks on Japanese warships.]

People in the streets yesterday,

Continued on Page Six

The International Situation

SATURDAY, DECEMBER 13, 1941

American forces defending Luzon, aided by a heavy downpour of rain, were fighting Japanese attacks on three sides of the island last night after they had brought down eleven enemy planes during the day and chased Japanese naval units away from Philippine coastal waters. [Page 1, Column 8.] The defense there was strong, and Wake and Midway Islands also were holding out against the Japanese, the Navy announced. A late communiqué said there was no confirmation of Tokyo reports that Guam had fallen. [Page 1, Columns 6 and 7.]

British bombers struck hard at Japanese forces massed in Southern Thailand as the enemy penetrated British lines at some points in Northern Malaya in heavy fighting. [Page 2, Column 2, with map.] The Japanese were using tanks in the jungle warfare, but British resistance was vigorous. [Page 1, Column 7.]

Japanese artillery on the Chinese mainland fought a duel with British ships off the coast and with land guns based on an island off Hong Kong. Two more assaults caused a British withdrawal from advanced mainland positions defending the crown colony. [Page 4, Column 5, with map.] The Japanese said that their troops had occupied Kowloon on the mainland facing Hong Kong and were preparing to attack the island. Tokyo also reported gains in the Philippines. [Page 4, Column 1.]

While Russia's official Communist newspaper Pravda declared that Japan was doomed to defeat in the Pacific [Page 3, Column 6]. Soviet communiqués announced a decisive victory before Moscow. They reported the recapture of more than 400 towns and villages and the defeat of a German Army of 750,000 north and south of the capital, with 85,000 killed and nearly half of the Nazis' original fifty-one divisions smashed, encircled or in retreat. [Page 1, Column 1; Map, Page 7.] In Libya, Cairo announced, the British advance westward swept forty miles beyond Tobruk past El Gazala, which is still held by the Axis. [Page 8, Column 5, with map.]

The United States seized fourteen French ships in American ports, including the liner Normandie here. All crews were removed and held. Officials gave no reason for the seizures and declined to comment on private advices that Germany was poised to take over French West Africa. [Page 1, Columns 2 and 3.]

These were other American developments:

A bill was introduced in the House to require registration of all men from 19 to 44 years of age, inclusive, for military service and of all other men 18 to 64 for civilian defense duties. Hearings will begin today. [Page 1, Column 4.]

While the Senate passed an appropriation of $10,500,000,000 more for defense, the Navy asked Congress to authorize a 30 per cent increase in naval combat strength. [Page 1, Column 5.]

It was disclosed that the United States would set up "an arsenal of the democracies" in Eritrea, East Africa, to equip and service the Near Eastern war effort for the duration. [Page 1, Columns 6 and 7.]

10 BILLION VOTED TO PUSH DEFENSE

Senate Raises House Bill—Navy Also Asks Funds for 166 More Fighting Ships

By W. H. LAWRENCE
Special to THE NEW YORK TIMES.

WASHINGTON, Dec. 12—While the Senate was passing a $10,572,350,705 supplemental defense appropriation, including funds to strengthen the Army and naval air arms for all-out war with the Axis, the Navy asked Congress today to authorize an increase of 30 per cent in its combat strength through the addition of 166 fighting vessels, including seven or eight 45,000-ton battleships.

The huge defense measure which went through a war Senate in less than five hours of debate was boosted $2,325,809,000 above the House-approved total, and the lower chamber promptly sent the measure to conference with an understanding that differences would be ironed out over the week-end so that final action might be taken on Monday.

In passing a measure providing more than $10,500,000,000 in cash and contract authorizations, the Senate brought the total budget cost of national defense thus far to $70,772,563,270, amid predictions by some Senators that the final cost of the war may exceed $200,000,000,000.

The Navy's statement that it wanted the still uncompleted two-ocean fleet increased by 30 per cent, or 900,000 tons, was made by Senator Walsh, chairman of the Naval Affairs Committee. He interrupted discussion of the $10,500,000,000 bill to obtain unanimous consent for introduction of the naval authorization measure.

Walsh Presents Navy Bill

"Mr. President, with the permission of the Senator from Tennessee, I should like to depart from the appropriation bill under consideration and make what I think is a very important announcement to the Senate," Senator Walsh said.

"I am about to introduce, by unanimous consent, a bill sent me by the Navy Department to authorize the composition of the United

Continued on Page Eleven

Wake and Midway Hold Out, U. S. Communiques Reveal

By CHARLES HURD
Special to THE NEW YORK TIMES.

WASHINGTON, Dec. 12—Small garrisons of United States troops continued a determined defense of Wake and Midway Islands in the Pacific Ocean and the forces in the Philippines repulsed still greater attacks on the island of Luzon, according to brief communiqués issued by the War and Navy Departments today.

These communiqués hinted at heavy action in all these quarters but vouchsafed no details of these segments of the Battle of the Pacific. Of naval operations at sea there was no word whatever, except that our naval units were participating in the defense of Luzon.

There was no positive word about Guam, but the Navy reported that "there is no confirmation of the alleged occupation of Guam by the Japanese."

With Hawaii quiet after the smashing attack on Pearl Harbor last Sunday, the communiqués drew a picture indicating that the Japanese had concentrated their forces in the western reaches of the Pacific.

This area embraces considerably more than half of the distance from Southern Asia to the North American Continent. Midway Island, of which today's announcement gave the first official word, is 1,300 miles northwest of Hawaii

Continued on Page Three

TOKYO TANKS ROLL IN MALAY JUNGLE

British Counter Vigorously—Dutch Submarine Sinks 4 Loaded Troopships

By F. TILLMAN DURDIN
Wireless to THE NEW YORK TIMES.

ADVANCED ARMY HEADQUARTERS, British Malaya, Dec. 12 — Vigorous counteraction by British forces is steadily stabilizing the war situation in Northern Malaya after the initial successes the Japanese achieved by their surprise tactics.

[Netherlands submarines sank four Japanese troopships off Patani in southern Thailand, not far from the Malayan frontier, a Singapore communiqué said

Continued on Page Three

U. S. to Build 'Arsenal' in Eritrea To Arm Allied Forces in Near East

By The Associated Press.

CAIRO, Egypt, Dec. 10 (Delayed) — The United States will virtually take over Eritrea for the duration of the war and convert it into an arsenal of the democracies in the Near East under an arrangement with Great Britain made known here today.

Title to this strip of land along the Red Sea, which was wrested from Italy by British forces, will remain with Britain, and its administration will continue to be British. But the United States will pour thousands of technicians and workmen into it to erect factories, assembly plants and other establishments.

It will be the powerhouse behind combat troops in this part of the world. Well out of enemy bombing range, airplanes, tanks and other equipment will be assembled there and minor manufacturing will be carried on. American materials will pour into Eritrea and come out as the implements of war, ready for the battlefield.

Other more extensive measures that cannot be disclosed now are also on the program.

Towns situated in regions enjoying salubrious climatic conditions will spring up, linked to the coast by new railroads.

The task of converting this land into an enormous supply base, although staggering, will be carried out with lightning speed. It is an undertaking unparalleled in world history. Plans include using available Italian labor in East Africa.

"All the News That's Fit to Print."

The New York Times.

LATE CITY EDITION
Partly cloudy, slightly warmer today. Tomorrow mostly cloudy, moderate temperature.

Copyright, 1941, by The New York Times Company.

VOL. XCI..No. 30,642. Entered as Second-Class Matter, Postoffice, New York, N. Y. NEW YORK, TUESDAY, DECEMBER 16, 1941. THREE CENTS NEW YORK CITY and Vicinity

KNOX REPORTS ONE BATTLESHIP SUNK AT HAWAII, 5 OTHER CRAFT LOST, BUT MAIN FLEET IS AT SEA; PRESIDENT LAYS PERFIDY TO JAPAN'S EMPEROR

AIR WARDEN ORDERS WILL BE BACKED UP BY $500 PENALTIES

Alternate Jail Sentences Are Provided in Bill Council Will Act Upon Today

5 NEW SIRENS DELIVERED

Devices May Be Heard One to Two Miles—Tests Tomorrow —School Rules Unchanged

Failure to obey civil defense regulations or refusal to comply with the orders of air raid wardens would be made punishable by a jail term of not more than six months or a fine of not more than $500 by a local law to be introduced at this afternoon's meeting of the City Council by majority leader Joseph T. Sharkey of Brooklyn.

The measure, which was requested yesterday by Mayor La Guardia, also provides that during an air raid all except duly authorized persons must immediately leave streets, parks and open spaces and proceed to the nearest cover, and that vehicles must be parked immediately and their passengers take to the nearest shelter.

After the air-raid alarms last Tuesday and Wednesday many air-raid wardens complained that crowds thronged into the streets to see what was going on and ignored their directions to seek shelter. The legislation sought by the Mayor is intended to correct this condition and to give the wardens legal authority to disperse crowds which might be subject to heavy casualties in an actual raid.

Warden Cards Printed

The Police Department has completed the printing of 200,000 identification cards for air-raid wardens, it was learned last night at the office of the Coordinator of Civilian Defense at Police Headquarters, and is about to begin issuing them to qualified wardens. Zone wardens will receive white cards, sector wardens yellow cards and post wardens salmon-colored cards.

Each warden must affix a photograph of himself, chauffeur size, to his card and return it to the police through his local precinct. A Police Department seal will then be placed over his picture and signature to guarantee the validity of the card, and then it will be returned to the holder. The cards will be two by three inches in size.

Five big "siro-drones," the first of seventy to be delivered this week, arrived yesterday at the office of Thomas W. Rochester, chief engineer of the Police Department. The five included two different types, one of which is supposed to be audible within a radius of two miles and the other with a range of one mile.

Can Be Heard Mile

Both sirens are about three feet high, with horns twenty inches in diameter, and are electrically operated. The type with a radius of one mile is operated by a two-horsepower motor and the louder horn by a five-horsepower motor. They are ordinarily used as factory whistles and fire alarms in small towns and are manufactured by the H-O-B Company, Inc., of Stapleton, S. I.

Mayor La Guardia, Police Commissioner Valentine, and other local officials and civilian defense leaders will attend tests of both types of the new "siro-drones" tomorrow afternoon. The Mayor's party is to arrive at Spring and Lafayette Street, near Police Headquarters, at 4:30 P. M. to try out the sirens after they have been placed on a Police Department tower truck.

Earlier tomorrow afternoon, at 4 o'clock the Mayor and his entourage will visit the building of the New York Edison Company at Fortieth Street and the East River for a trial of the big whistle, operated by steam and electricity, that is mounted on the structure.

Continued on Page Twenty-four

'Keep Flag Flying,' MacArthur's Order

Wireless to THE NEW YORK TIMES.

MANILA, Dec. 15—Morale at headquarters of the United States Army's Far Eastern Forces is above par.

An officer on the staff of General Douglas MacArthur, Commander in Chief, suggested to him that the American flag atop the bastion that marks the headquarters might serve as a target for Japanese planes. General MacArthur laughed and said:

"Take every other normal precaution for the protection of the headquarters, but let's keep the flag flying."

18-64 AGE LISTING FOR DRAFT RUSHED

House Committee for Military Service at 21, Senate Group for Minimum of 19

By HENRY N. DORRIS
Special to THE NEW YORK TIMES.

WASHINGTON, Dec. 15—Congressional committees speeded legislation today to give full wartime powers to the President and extend the registration requirements of the Selective Service Act to all men from 18 to 64, inclusive.

The House Military Affairs Committee gave final approval to a bill carrying the Selective Service changes. The Senate Military Affairs Committee gave tentative approval to a bill, withholding full approval pending testimony in executive session tomorrow by Brig. Gen. Lewis B. Hershey, Selective Service Administrator.

The bills as they stood tonight differed on the ages subject to military service. The Senate bill contains tentatively the War Department recommendation for the age brackets 19 to 44, inclusive. The House committee approved the bracket 21 to 44, inclusive.

About 41,000,000 men would be affected by the overall registration requirement, which is planned not only to provide an army of 2,800,000 to 7,500,000 but to ascertain

Continued on Page Thirty-one

RUSSIANS TAKE KLIN

Vital Rail Point in Center Seized as Push Gains on Every Front

NAZIS FLEE IN NORTH

Lose 3 Towns in Tula Area—Soviet Claims Crimean Advance

By DANIEL T. BRIGHAM
By Telephone to THE NEW YORK TIMES.

BERNE, Switzerland Tuesday, Dec. 16—Smashing through ever-weakening German lines of defense, Soviet troops continued their brilliant operations in the fighting yesterday, recapturing Klin, important rail point on the Moscow-Leningrad line, and three communications centers south of Moscow.

The Red Army also advanced in the Volkhov area, southeast of Leningrad, and in Crimea the Germans were pushed back to the outskirts of Balaclava by Russian troops from Sevastopol, a Russian military spokesman announced on the Moscow radio this morning.

In operations intended to disengage the entire Leningrad-Moscow rail line, the Russians carried out encircling movements north of the Valdai Heights that enabled them to smash the German Thirty-ninth Army Corps. According to the spokesman, 20,000 Germans were killed or wounded in this action.

The remainder of the German force was reported to be fleeing in a southwesterly direction in an attempt to rejoin a "fairly large German force" with its back to Lake Ilmen. However, a Russian column threatens the Germans' southern wing on that sector.

On the Leningrad end of the front Red Army troops began a wide-scale operation southwestward from Tosna. It is understood that the main objective is to straighten out a deep salient that the Germans have held for more

Continued on Page Fifteen

U. S. 'WHITE PAPER'

President in Message Reveals How Tokyo Hid Treacherous Aims

AS HITLER DID LATER

Tyrants Will Fall in End to the Free Peoples, He Says on Radio

The President's message to Congress is on Page 6.

Special to THE NEW YORK TIMES.

WASHINGTON, Dec. 15—Emperor Hirohito was accused today by President Roosevelt, in effect, of personal complicity in Japan's course of carrying on peace negotiations with the United States while putting into operation the plan for a treacherous attack upon this country.

The Emperor is regarded by most Japanese as a divinity whose personal honor must be above reproach, and diplomatic circles here expressed the opinion today that the revelation of perfidy might have serious repercussions within Japan later.

The President revealed in a message transmitted to Congress the details of the reply from the Emperor to his personal appeal to peace on Dec. 6. The message, which was looked upon as the equivalent of an American White Paper, outlined the whole course of American-Japanese relations and of step-by-step execution of the joint German-Japanese-Italian plan for world conquest.

"The issue of the war is whether a revival of barbarism is to be forced on the self-respecting peoples of the world by tyrants, President Roosevelt declared last night in his radio address on the 150th anniversary of the ratification of the Bill of Rights. Whereas Hitler's idea is that the individual has no rights whatsoever under an absolute master, the state, the President pledged that this nation will not lay down arms until "liberty is once again secure in the world we live in."]

Talked Peace After War Started

The President emphasized that Hirohito's reply to his peace appeal was delivered orally to Ambassador Joseph C. Grew in Tokyo three hours and forty minutes after Japanese planes and submarines had started the war by a surprise attack on Pearl Harbor.

The full text of the Emperor's reply was not made public, but he was quoted as saying, in part, after Japan had begun the war:

"Establishment of peace in the Pacific, and consequently of the world, has been the cherished desire of His Majesty, for the realization of which he has hitherto made his government to continue its earnest endeavors."

Japan's real reply, the President stressed, had been given earlier by the long-prepared attack without warning on American bases in the Pacific. "There," he said, "is the record, for all history to read in amazement, in sorrow, in horror and disgust."

After outlining the attempt by the United States to maintain friendly relations with the Japanese from the time Commodore Perry opened Japan to the outside world in 1853, and telling of continued American efforts to maintain a peace based on justice and fair-dealing in the Orient, the President stated that Japan openly entered a league of fascism against the free world under the pretext of signing the anti-Comintern Pact in 1936.

Tells of Axis Accord Against Us

He offered evidence to show that Japan, Germany and Italy arranged together to time their blows against free nations in the best manner to effect joint plans for world dominance, and mentioned how the three finally and openly concluded last year "a treaty of

Continued on Page Six

The International Situation

TUESDAY, DECEMBER 16, 1941

Secretary of the Navy Knox yesterday reported losses to the United States Fleet in the Pearl Harbor attack as one battleship, a target ship, a minelayer and three destroyers. Casualties, as he gave them out, were heavier than had been previously reported. He said that defense forces were "not on the alert" and that the Japanese had been aided by a great "fifth column." An investigation is going forward. [Page 1, Column 8.]

The situation in the Philippines appeared to be stabilized, with an air raid on the naval station at Olongapo the only major operation. Midway, as well as Wake, was said in reports from Washington to be still holding out. [Page 1, Column 5; Map, Page 2.] British troops, resisting a Japanese attack in force on the Malay Peninsula, were declared to have dug in on a stronger defense line in southern Kedah and to have abandoned the southern tip of Burma. [Page 14, Column 3.] British and Netherland air units fought off strong Japanese forces. [Page 1, Column 5 and 6.] At Hong Kong the British had retired from the mainland and were strongly defending the island. The Chinese thrust in relief was gaining momentum. [Page 10, Column 2.]

Tokyo's Premier pictured his foes in collapse, but warned of a long war. [Page 1, Columns 6 and 7.]

President Roosevelt, in a message to Congress outlining the events leading up to the war, laid stress on the Japanese bad faith, in which, he implied, the Emperor himself was involved. [Page 1, Column 4.] In a broadcast to the nation on the anniversary of the ratification of the Bill of Rights, he made Adolf Hitler the chief object of his attack and pledged our victory for the sake of liberty. [Page 30, Column 2.]

The President also made his quarterly report to Congress on lease-lend aid and emphasized that our entrance into the war increased its necessity. [Page 4, Column 1.] Military Affairs Committees of the Senate and House approved bills to register all males between 18 and 65 years, but differed slightly on the age for military service. [Page 1, Column 2.]

Moscow reported the recapture of the city of Klin and said the drive around Tula was successful; indeed, there were continued victories of the Russian offensive on all fronts. [Page 1, Column 3; Map, Page 15.]

The Axis also continued to give ground in Libya and the Nazis were reported to be throwing their last tank and infantry strength into a desperate delaying action. [Page 16, Column 1.] Their supply lines were said to have been further impaired with the sinking in the Mediterranean of a large supply ship and the sinking or damaging of half a dozen smaller vessels. [Page 17, Column 1.]

Vichy heard of fresh attacks on Nazis in Paris, including the bombing of a restaurant. There were reports that Marshal Pétain had refused the Germans the use of the French fleet and bases in Tunisia. [Page 18, Column 3.] Secretary of State Hull expressed friendly and encouraging sentiments toward the French people at his press conference. [Page 19, Column 1.]

As the American republics took further actions in support of the United States, Argentina contemplated instituting a state of siege to curb Axis activities. [Page 9, Column 3.]

ENEMY MAKES SOME GAINS IN MALAYA AND SOUTH BURMA

British defenders of Victoria Point (1) were reported to have withdrawn as a Japanese force pushed westward across the Kra Isthmus. An announcement of fighting in Southern Kedah (2) indicated that the Japanese had made progress in that area. "Some activities" were reported in Kelantan (3). Ipoh (4) had an air raid alarm. Frame on inset shows the area covered by large map.

Allied Fliers Match Japan's In North Malaya Fighting

By F. TILLMAN DURDIN
Special Cable to THE NEW YORK TIMES.

SUNGEI PATANI, North Malaya, Dec. 14 (Delayed)—Against Japanese based on airdromes in Thailand that apparently had been prepared for them long before the attack on Malaya began, British, Australian and Netherland air units in this region are putting up courageous and effective opposition. One Royal Air Force source told me that the Japanese were operating from five different airfields in Southern Thailand within forty-eight hours after the war broke out.

[Japanese forces pushed into the southern part of the State of Kedah, Northern Malaya, and took Victoria Point, the tip of Southern Burma, the British announced. The Japanese, however, moved at a heavy cost in lives, it was said. The defenders were entrenched on the eastern side of the peninsula south of Kota Bharu. Penang was not raided yesterday, but Japanese bombers attacked Ipoh, tin mining center.]

The Japanese at present are using planes chiefly for bombing Malayan airdromes. The city on Penang Island, off the west coast of Malaya, is the only civilian center

Continued on Page Fourteen

FILIPINOS BEAT OFF 154 ENEMY BOATS

Lingayen Guns Blast Japanese for 3 Days—Invading Planes Bomb Olongapo Naval Base

By The United Press.

MANILA, Tuesday, Dec. 16—First details reached here today of an engagement at Lingayen Beach, 110 miles northwest of Manila, where a Filipino Army division, lining the shore with artillery, blasted 154 motorboat loads of invading Japanese soldiers without letting one of them reach land alive.

The fighting lasted three days. It began last Wednesday night and at last report the Filipinos were holding the beach. The colonel in command sent word to Manila that his force would stand their ground "to the last man."

Details were brought here by a correspondent of The Philippines Herald. He quoted the colonel, whom he did not identify, as having said:

"We eagerly awaited the Japanese attempt to land. The enemy showed up Wednesday night. I counted 154 motorboats in all. We held our fire until they were near.

"Then our artillery roared into action. Most of the boats were destroyed. A few managed to escape to warships which must have been anchored far beyond the horizon. Since then the enemy has attempted to land, but each time he has been frustrated."

The correspondent reported that when the colonel promised to fight to the last man "he was merely voicing the sentiments of men of all ranks whom I interviewed." The colonel was said to be con-

Continued on Page Six

Knox Statement on Hawaii

By The Associated Press.

WASHINGTON, Dec. 15—The text of Secretary Knox's statement detailing losses in the Japanese attack on Pearl Harbor follows:

My inspection trip to the island enables me to present the general facts covering the attack which hitherto have been unavailable.

1. The essential fact is that the Japanese purpose was to knock out the United States before the war began. This was made apparent by the deception practiced, by the preparations which had gone on for many weeks before the attack, and the attacks themselves, which were made simultaneously throughout the Pacific. In this purpose the Japanese failed.

2. The United States services were not on the alert against the surprise air attack on Hawaii. This fact calls for a formal investigation, which will be initiated immediately by the President. Further action is, of course, dependent on the facts and recommendations made by this investigating board. We are all entitled to know it if (a) there was any error of judgment which contributed to the surprise, (b) if there was any dereliction of duty prior to the attack.

3. My investigation made clear that after the attack the defense by both services was conducted skillfully and bravely. The Navy lost:

(a) The battleship Arizona, which was destroyed by the explosion of, first, its boiler and then its forward magazine due to a bomb which was said to have literally passed down through the smokestack;

(b) The old target ship Utah, which has not been used as a combatant ship for many years, and which was in service as a training ship for anti-aircraft gunnery and experimental purposes;

(c) Three destroyers, the Cassin, the Downes and the Shaw;

(d) Minelayer Oglala. This was a converted merchantman, formerly a passenger ship on the Fall River Line and converted into a minelayer during the World War.

The Navy sustained damage to other vessels. This damage varies from ships which have been already repaired and are ready for sea, or which have gone to sea, to a few ships which will take from a week to several months to

Continued on Page Seven

HEROIC ACTS CITED

2,897 Defenders Killed in Gallant Battle—Base Not 'on Alert'

FIFTH COLUMN ACTIVE

2-Man Submarine Used —Roosevelt to Name Inquiry Board

By CHARLES HURD
Special to THE NEW YORK TIMES.

WASHINGTON, Dec. 15—Japan did not administer a knockout blow or destroy the effectiveness of American naval forces in the Pacific when she attacked at Pearl Harbor, Hawaii, at dawn on Dec. 7, and thus failed to achieve her objective, Secretary of the Navy Frank Knox reported today on his return from a flight to Hawaii to investigate the attack.

High Japanese official had asserted that the blow struck at Pearl Harbor destroyed American naval supremacy in the Pacific. Mr. Knox evidenced a different view when he said:

"The Japanese failed to knock out the United States before the war began."

Fleet Now Hunts Enemy

The Secretary said the United States Army and Navy forces in Hawaii "were not on the alert against the surprise attack" of the Japanese and in consequence losses had been heavy. After the action started, however, he said, our soldiers and sailors fought bravely, and he added that all remaining effective units of the Pacific Fleet "are at sea seeking contact with the enemy."

He listed the destroyed vessels as the battleship Arizona, the destroyers Cassin, Downes and Shaw; the minelayer Oglala and the target and training ship Utah. In addition, he said that the battleship Oklahoma had capsized and that an unannounced number of vessels had been damaged.

The Navy casualties in this action were given by Mr. Knox as 91 officers and 2,638 men killed and 20 officers and 636 men wounded. Late this evening the Army announced that its losses in this engagement totaled 168 officers and men, bringing the aggregate service losses to 2,897.

Attack's Objective Failed

Mr. Knox gave his report at a special press conference a few hours after his return from Honolulu. He supplemented a prepared statement by replies to questions that emphasized the fact that the Japanese, launching their attack with carrier-borne planes and submarines, eluded the naval patrols at sea, caught the Army Air Force on the ground and destroyed the great majority of planes there, and showed a detailed knowledge of objectives.

Against these adverse reports, Mr. Knox reported that the sailors and soldiers fought bravely and well after the action started, and he told reporters that the Japanese failed in their objective, which was to knock out the Pacific fleet before the war started.

Responsibility for the errors committed, he said, will be investigated immediately by a Presidential commission. He declined to anticipate the results of such an investigation. After calling on President Roosevelt this evening, Mr. Knox said the President would name the inquiry board tomorrow.

The Japanese losses for this engagement were listed by the Secretary as three submarines, including one large and one small one destroyed and a small one captured, and forty-one planes.

One reason for the success of the Japanese, he asserted, was cooperation from the Hawaiian Islands themselves.

"The most effective fifth-column work in this war was done in Hawaii, with the exception of Norway," Mr. Knox said.

He declined to elaborate on stage

Continued on Page Seven

Tokyo Premier Claims Triumph, Then Warns of War to Be Fought

By The Associated Press.

TOKYO, Tuesday, Dec. 16 (From Japanese Broadcast) — Premier Hideki Tojo, addressing an extraordinary session of the Japanese Diet, today reiterated his assertions that Japan had declared war on the United States only after trying all means of peaceful settlement. He declared:

"Our fighting services have speedily broken through the enemy key positions within less than ten days. The bulk of the American Fleet which had been at Hawaii is destroyed: the main body of the British Far Eastern Fleet is crushed; the encircling front against Japan, the strength of which the enemy has exaggerated and given wide publicity in an attempt to intimidate Japan, is shattered at various places.

"The anti-Japanese encircling front already is on a fair way to collapse."

He nevertheless cautioned the Japanese that "a war remains waiting to be fought."

Japanese Imperial Headquarters reported that Japanese expeditionary forces had landed on British Borneo at dawn today despite a heavy gale.

The headquarters also reported that Japanese Army and Navy forces completed occupation of the island of Guam last Friday.

A joint communiqué of the army and navy sections of Imperial Headquarters warned Japanese yesterday "against the lurking danger of enemy submarines" off Japan's island coasts and urged them to

Continued on Page Thirteen

"All the News That's Fit to Print."

The New York Times.

LATE CITY EDITION
Occasional rain and somewhat warmer today.
Temperatures Yesterday—Max., 50; Min., 34

VOL. XCI No. 30,650. Entered as Second-Class Matter, Postoffice, New York, N. Y. NEW YORK, WEDNESDAY, DECEMBER 24, 1941. THREE CENTS NEW YORK CITY and Vicinity

JAPANESE LAND STRONG FORCE SOUTH OF MANILA; ROOSEVELT, CHURCHILL WORK ON PACIFIC ACTION; PETAIN REPORTED OUT UNDER GERMAN PRESSURE

PRESIDENT SETS UP LABOR PEACE PLAN THAT BARS STRIKES

Amicable Settlement of All Disputes and Board to Handle Them Also in Formula

INDUSTRY 'TAKES ORDERS'

But Leaders Reiterate Stand That Closed Shop Should Not Be Issue for Arbitration

By W. H. LAWRENCE
Special to THE NEW YORK TIMES.

WASHINGTON, Dec. 23—President Roosevelt promulgated today a three-point formula designed to guarantee uninterrupted production during the war by providing final arbitration of all disputes between employers and employes. He turned down industry's demand that the closed shop be ruled out as an arbitrable question.

Mr. Roosevelt acted as it became apparent that the industry-labor conference, convened by him, could never reach the unanimous accord he desired, due to the deadlock between the twelve industrialists and the twelve leaders of labor on the question of extending the closed shop to factories now operating under the open shop.

The final agreement on basic war labor policy was forced by the President when he accepted the three points on which industry and labor generally were in accord, and ignored the fourth and final proposition of industry, dealing with the closed shop.

The industry-labor conference was called to meet this afternoon after William H. Davis, its moderator, and Senator Elbert Thomas, Democrat, of Utah, associate moderator, had reported to the President the deadlock upon the union shop question.

TEXT OF PRESIDENT'S LETTER

Mr. Davis read this letter from the President:

"Gentlemen of the conference:

"Moderator Davis and Senator Thomas have reported to me the results of your deliberations. They have given me each proposition which you have discussed. I am happy to accept your general points of agreement as follows:

"1. There shall be no strikes or lockouts.

"2. All disputes shall be settled by peaceful means.

"3. The President shall set up a proper War Labor Board to handle these disputes.

"I accept without reservation your covenants that there shall be no strikes or lockouts and all disputes shall be settled by peaceful means. I shall proceed at once to act on your third point.

"Government must act in general. The three points agreed upon cover of necessity all disputes that may arise between labor and management.

"The particular disputes must be left to the consideration of those who can study the particular differences and who are thereby prepared by knowledge to pass judgment in the particular case. I have full faith that no group in our national life will take undue advantage while we are faced by common enemies.

"I congratulate you—I thank you, and our people will join me in appreciation of your great contribution.

"Your achievement is a response to a common desire of all men of good-will that strikes and lockouts cease and that disputes be settled by peaceful means.

"May I now wish you all a Merry Christmas.

"Very sincerely yours,
"(Signed)
"FRANKLIN D. ROOSEVELT."

Industrialists "Stunned"

The industrialists were stunned, as one of them put it, by the President's letter. They had expected an opportunity to present to the

Continued on Page Thirty-two

Darlan Said to Take Over; Nazi Move in Spain Rumored

Some Reports Declare Germans Are Merely Sending Arms Into Africa, but Others Tell of Movements by Troops

By CRAIG THOMPSON
Special Cable to THE NEW YORK TIMES.

LONDON, Dec. 23—Reports originating "somewhere in Europe" and received here tonight said that Marshal Henri Philippe Pétain had resigned as the French Chief of State, as a protest against German pressure, and that he had been succeeded by Admiral François Darlan, the Vice Premier. The reaction here was that the reports, relayed by the Reuter news agency, were "entirely likely."

There is, however, little additional information. Marshal Pétain's alleged refusal to continue to lead unoccupied France was attributed to his unwillingness to carry out the terms of the Saint-Florentin agreement, which he and Reich Marshal Hermann Goering entered into less than a month ago. But the terms of this arrangement are still unknown.

The reports that Marshal Pétain had resigned were coupled with insistent reports that the Germans had started moving toward Spain. These latter reports open up speculation as to provisions in the Saint-Florentin agreement at which Marshal Pétain might have balked.

Britain, like the United States, has long continued a conciliatory attitude toward Vichy because she believed that Marshal Pétain and unoccupied France could be used at least as a buffer against a German movement across the country. If Marshal Pétain's reported resignation proves to be a fact, a change in that attitude is very probable, because Admiral Darlan is completely untrusted.

There has been continuous concern that Vichy might be persuaded to use the now immobilized French Fleet against Britain in the Mediterranean. There is a pos-

Continued on Page Seven

CHURCHILL TALKS

With President at Side, He Says Knockout Is Way to Win War

CERTAIN OF VICTORY

Our Entry and Turning of the Tide in Russia Basis of Faith

By FRANK L. KLUCKHOHN
Special to THE NEW YORK TIMES.

WASHINGTON, Dec. 23—Sitting at President Roosevelt's right in an extraordinary dual press conference at the White House today, Prime Minister Churchill declared that anti-Axis war plans must be based upon defeating Germany by military knockout blows from outside.

Answering blunt questions with equal bluntness, employing American slang in parrying searching inquiries and obviously enjoying himself, Mr. Churchill sat with the President behind his desk as he outlined general Allied policies and discussed the situation on far-flung world battlefields.

The general answers made by the Prime Minister to his questioners were as follows:

1. As far as the Far East was concerned, the strategical importance of Singapore was obvious, and it would be defended until an offensive in the Pacific was again possible. In Europe, Soviet Russia was giving Germany a bad beating and inflicting heavy losses, but the Allies must be prepared to go on from year to year until ultimate victory, in which Mr. Churchill reiterated supreme confidence.

2. Nevertheless, the turning point in the war may have been reached, with Russia smiting the Germans and Great Britain and the United States at last standing shoulder to shoulder.

As to Problem of Supplies

3. As far as supplies were concerned, the belief was expressed that production would be stepped up to the point where quantity and quality were not the prime problems, but rather those of getting them to the right front at the most effective time.

Both the Prime Minister and the President emphasized that the current conferences—which started with both military-naval and diplomatic joint conversations today—were dedicated to the grave war emergency and not to post-war problems, which could be dealt with later. With reference to the latter, Mr. Churchill said there was no desire at this time to go into complicated, entangled and not too attractive jungles.

President Roosevelt talked for eight minutes before he introduced the Prime Minister, who answered questions for twelve. The President emphasized that Australia and New Zealand were both in the danger zone—as was Canada on both her coasts—and that the British dominions as well as Russia, China, the Netherlands and other countries fighting the Axis powers eventually would be brought into the conferences.

Working on Unity in Pacific

The President said that the meetings were proceeding well, and that he and the Prime Minister were working on definite unity of action in the Southwestern Pacific. Whether this meant joint action at Singapore was not disclosed.

Mr. Churchill threw cold water on any project for a supreme allied general staff, asserting that the leaders of the anti-Axis nations would block out the broad outlines of war policies and that the staffs of the various countries could work out details.

Emphasizing that this war against Germany, Japan and Italy was being fought out all over the world—on land, sea and in the air—the Prime Minister expressed doubt that any one man knew

Continued on Page Four

NEW LANDING INDICATES A TWO-WAY DRIVE ON MANILA

Heavy fighting raged in the Lingayen Gulf area (1), where the Japanese used tanks in vigorous attacks south of Agoo. North of this place they continued to put troops ashore. Enemy fliers hit a vital bridge at Villasis (2). The new landing was made in the vicinity of Atimonan (3) by a heavy force. The position of this whole Luzon area in the Philippine archipelago is shown at (A) on the inset. Tokyo reported the capture of Davao (B), but American reports spoke of continued fighting there. Off the port Netherland fliers attacked Japanese transports.

NEW THRUST BY FOE

40 Vessels Land Men at Atimonan—Fighting Heavy at Lingayen

LONGEST BRIDGE HIT

Defenders Push Repairs on the Villasis Span—Enemy Claims Davao

By The Associated Press.

MANILA, Wednesday, Dec. 24—Official Army reports today said that greatly outnumbered American and Filipino troops were battling valiantly against a Japanese invasion force that landed from forty transports at Atimonan, 135 miles by air southeast of Manila, during the night.

Observers here interpreted the Atimonan thrust as an attempt to force General Douglas MacArthur to split his forces and thus weaken resistance on the vital northern front, where his men were reported standing off another invading army "against great odds."

Before landing at Atimonan, which is on the Luzon east coast, the Japanese attempted a landing on the southwest coast of the island, near Batangas, but were beaten off.

[Japanese planes raided the Manila area twice today, causing fires that Filipino firemen fought without regard to their own danger, The United Press reported.]

Hard Fighting in North

"Heavy fighting continues in the north," said an earlier bulletin from General Douglas MacArthur's headquarters, referring to the Lingayen Gulf area, where the Japanese for the past two days have been engaged in a major push on the beaches against American and Filipino troops, who were declared to be holding them firmly.

"The enemy is exerting great pressure," an Army spokesman said of the Lingayen battle. "The enemy is particularly active aerially at many points throughout the bay."

One Japanese aerial blow of late yesterday was the heavy damaging of the big steel bridge at Villasis. The bridge, the longest in the Philippines, is a vital link in the highway from the Lingayen area. A United States Army spokesman said the damage already was being repaired.

It was the first Japanese hit on any of the innumerable bridges they have sought to smash in these islands.

Troopships Reported Sunk

There were no official reports from the Davao area, where the Japanese landed on the southern island of Mindanao, but press reports quoted refugees from other Mindanao points as saying that seven Japanese troopships had been sunk in Davao Harbor and that defense forces were taking a heavy toll of the Japanese who got ashore.

Another press report said four Japanese members of a patrol were killed in the Legaspi sector on the extreme south of Luzon Island.

The landing at Atimonan is the sixth the Japanese have attempted in these islands. The Army spokesman declined to estimate the total force involved.

Atimonan is a small seacoast town known chiefly as a rendezvous for deep-sea fishermen. The region has foothills reaching almost down to the sea and is sparsely populated. Northwestward of the town are rugged mountains blocking the path to Manila.

There is just one mountain highway, easily blocked, which leads directly from Atimonan to Manila.

General MacArthur's headquarters announcement that a heavy force of invaders had landed at the town indicated that there were sufficient Japanese troops to afford a real striking power and probably

Continued on Page Two

RAID PRECAUTIONS HIT TRAFFIC LIGHTS

Signals Badly Confused on Some Streets—Police Forbid Wardens to Touch Them

Efforts to place the city's 16,000 traffic lights under some form of central control for air raid emergencies have disrupted the system in some parts of Manhattan and Brooklyn, it was disclosed yesterday as Police Commissioner Valentine forbade air raid wardens to touch the lights in the future.

At the same time, majority members of the City Council criticized Mayor La Guardia anew for ambiguities in his air raid precautions bill and for his refusal to accept clarifying amendments to the bill.

Councilman Walter R. Hart,

Continued on Page Eleven

CITY SHERIFF PLAN UPHELD ON APPEAL

Highest State Court Includes Single Register in 5-2 Opinion Validating Referendum

Special to THE NEW YORK TIMES.

ALBANY, Dec. 23—By a vote of 5 to 2 the Court of Appeals upheld today the city referendum that abolished the offices of county Sheriffs and Registers and replaced them with a city-wide Sheriff and a city-wide Register. The prevailing opinion, written by Judge Finch, held that the county officers who were elected the same day the referendum was passed did not have any "vested rights" to the offices.

The case involving the Sheriffs' offices was the action of Harold J. and Viola Burke against Paul J. Kern, president of the Municipal

Continued on Page Eighteen

The International Situation

WEDNESDAY, DECEMBER 24, 1941

Forty Japanese transports landed troops 135 miles southeast of Manila during the night, while other invaders exerted "great pressure" in the Lingayen area to the north. Thus emerged a pincer strategy against Manila. On the northern arm of the pincers the Japanese reinforced their landings and used light tanks, but American bombers, tanks and big guns were reported taking a heavy toll. Tokyo claimed the capture of Davao, but this was disputed. [Page 1, Column 8.]

Hitting at enemy ships at Davao, Netherland planes set a tanker ablaze, and west of Borneo a Netherland submarine sunk three Japanese transports and a tanker, Batavia announced. [Page 1, Columns 5 and 6.]

Enemy forces made a landing on Wake Island after having battered the garrison from the air for sixteen days, but the Marine and naval defenders continued to resist, it was announced in Washington. [Page 1, Columns 6 and 7.] Resistance continued also at Hong Kong. A dispatch direct from the British colony said the invaders had suffered great casualties. [Page 7, Column 1, with map.] In Malaya the British held their lines and apparently prepared for a big offensive. [Page 5, Column 5.]

A disclosure that unity of action in the Southern Pacific was being worked out in the conferences between President Roosevelt and Prime Minister Churchill was made by the President as the two men held a joint press conference in the White House. Mr. Churchill, who said the war's turning point might now have been reached, declared that Allied plans must be based on crushing Germany from the outside by military action. He dashed cold water on any project for a supreme Allied general staff. [Page 1, Column 4.]

The prospect of a new German military move—expected by Mr. Churchill—was reflected in rumors that fifteen to twenty Nazi divisions were moving into Spain from occupied France, but London was skeptical of the story. In France, according to a Reuter dispatch, Marshal Pétain has resigned, refusing to execute an agreement made with Germany Dec. 1. The agreement was said to call for German use of African bases. [Page 1, Columns 2 and 3.]

On the Russian front Soviet sources reported important new gains for their forces southwest of Moscow and at other points along the battle line, but Sevastopol in Crimea was acknowledged menaced by great enemy pressure. [Page 1, Column 5.] In Libya the British announced they had cut off part of the Axis forces retreating toward Tripoli and said their advance had carried to the coastal plain south of Bengazi, where a battle loomed. [Page 1, Column 7; Map, Page 8.] The British also reported the sinking of three Axis supply ships and probably three others in the Mediterranean. [Page 8, Column 2.]

Japanese submarines attacked three more American ships off the California coast, sinking one of them, but there was no loss of life. [Page 5, Column 1.]

NEW RUSSIAN GAINS SMASH NAZIS' LINES

Dnieper Set as Goal of Drive—Tula Push Menaces Orel—Leningrad Ring Dented

By DANIEL T. BRIGHAM
By Telephone to THE NEW YORK TIMES.

BERNE, Switzerland, Wednesday, Dec. 24—German lines before the Moscow front collapsed at several points during yesterday's fighting to give the Soviet forces one of their most fruitful days of gain since they retook Klin, according to the Russian military spokesman this morning.

Yesterday's gains, according to the midnight communiqué, included Gorbachevo, an important railway junction midway between Tula and Orel, and Odoevo, to the northwest of Gorbachevo, and Ko-zelsk, possession of which will flank the Germans' north-south communications between Kaluga

Continued on Page Six

Foe Lands on Wake Island; Garrison Continues Battle

By CHARLES HURD
Special to THE NEW YORK TIMES.

WASHINGTON, Dec. 23—The Japanese forces that have been battering a small Navy garrison on Wake Island since Dec. 7 effected a landing there on "the morning of the twenty-third," the Navy Department reported today, but it appeared that the garrison still was fighting back at its attackers tonight.

The landing came twenty-four hours after a strong air attack on the garrison, in the course of which "several enemy planes were shot down."

[Wake Island was "completely occupied" yesterday morning, according to a Tokyo broadcast recorded by The United Press. Two destroyers were lost in the attack, it was said.]

Lack of news concerning Midway Island, northeast of Wake Island, which also has been under almost constant attack, was taken to indicate that the garrison there still held its ground.

Wake Island is about 2,000 miles

Continued on Page Four

BRITISH UNITS BAR EXIT FROM BENGAZI

Reach Plain at Gulf of Sidra as Planes Deal Blows to Axis in Air and on Land

By JOSEPH M. LEVY
Wireless to THE NEW YORK TIMES.

CAIRO, Egypt, Dec. 23—British mobile columns, slashing ahead of the main body of the British advance, reached the coastal plain of the Gulf of Sidra yesterday and, possibly, cut off at least part of the Germans who are retreating from Bengazi in the direction of Tripoli. Northeast of Bengazi British reinforcements added strength to the attacks on the enemy's covering positions there.

Operations are in such a fluid state at this stage it is unlikely that the Germans are completely blocked by the British thrust to the coastal plain south of Bengazi, but it is certain that many of the Germans, at least, will be forced to strike with all their remaining power if they seek a way out.

[An authoritative military commentator in London said, according to The Associated Press, that the remnants of the Axis force probably would attempt a final stand in the region of Bengazi because General Erwin Rommel, the German commander, "cannot help it." He said

Continued on Page Eight

Dutch Submarine Sinks 4 Ships; Fliers Bomb Japanese at Davao

By The Associated Press.

BATAVIA, Netherlands Indies, Dec. 23—Three big Japanese transports and a tanker have been sunk west of Borneo by a Netherlands submarine, the Commander of the Netherlands Navy was informed tonight.

[A British broadcast received in New York Sunday night quoted Batavia sources as saying Netherland naval forces had sunk two Japanese transports off Borneo and that a Netherland torpedo plane had sunk a third, bringing the destruction of Japanese troop or supply ships by American and Netherland forces to a total of thirteen. These were not confirmed by Batavia. If the newest announcement is additional it brings the total to seventeen.]

Strong forces of Netherland naval planes swept over Davao Harbor today and aided the American and Filipino forces resisting a Japanese invasion of that Mindanao Island point by pressing home a heavy attack upon enemy vessels.

A 440-pound bomb squarely hit a 10,000-ton Japanese tanker and left her exploding in flames, it was announced. Other ships in the southern Philippine post also were attacked.

Japanese raids on a Netherland

Continued on Page Nine

"All the News That's Fit to Print."

The New York Times.

LATE CITY EDITION
Continued cold today.
Temperatures Yesterday—Max., 43; Min., 26

VOL. XCI...No. 30,690. Entered as Second-Class Matter, Postoffice, New York, N. Y. NEW YORK, MONDAY, FEBRUARY 2, 1942. THREE CENTS NEW YORK CITY and Vicinity

U. S. PACIFIC FLEET BATTERS JAPANESE BASES IN MARSHALL AND GILBERT ISLES; 11 PLANES LOST; CORREGIDOR'S GUNS SMASH INVASION FLOTILLA

AUTO PLANTS' SPEED ON ARMS MENACED BY WAGE DISPUTE

C. I. O. Demands Double Pay for Sunday Be Kept in Change-Over, but Manufacturers Balk

UNION ASKS WLB STEP IN

Deadlock Threatens to Delay Start of Seven-Day Week on 9 Billions in War Orders

By A. H. RASKIN

Special to THE NEW YORK TIMES.

DETROIT, Feb. 1—With automobile production halted and the government calling for around-the-clock activity in plants converted to the manufacture of guns, tanks and planes, a dispute over double pay for Sunday work threatened today to delay the introduction of the seven-day week in factories with a backlog of $9,000,000,000 in war orders.

Under the program developed by the War Production Board for the shutting down of passenger car and light truck production, it had been hoped that all the energies of the auto industry would be poured into the task of arms manufacture with no loss of time because of Sunday lay-offs.

In a last-minute effort to break the wage deadlock, the international executive board of the United Automobile Workers, C. I. O., appealed to the War Labor Board to intervene. The union promised to put a seven-day schedule into effect at once if the manufacturers agreed to make retroactive any decision handed down by the board.

Agreement on 4-Shift Plan

The controversy centers around the union's demand for retention of a contract clause under which its members receive double pay for Sunday work, whether or not they work more than forty hours a week. The manufacturers have asked that this clause be waived and that Sunday be treated as a normal work day under a four-shift operating schedule. This schedule would make it possible to keep plants fully-manned on a twenty-four hour basis, seven days a week, without having any individual worker put in more than five days of eight hours each.

The union is in favor of the four-shift plan, but it refuses to accept the industry's argument that there is no justification for continuing a system of premium payments for Sunday work at a time when such work is essential to speed the all-out war effort.

The C. I. O. point of view, as set forth by Walter P. Reuther, author of the much-debated Reuther plan for turning auto factories into arsenals, is that the abandonment of extra compensation for Sundays would not advance the output of arms but would simply increase the margin of profit for the companies holding government contracts.

Unwilling to Surrender Gain

"We are willing to give up anything necessary for the security of our country, but we are not willing to surrender any of our hard-won gains just to enrich the corporations," Mr. Reuther said.

In urging abandonment of the extra-pay clause, the manufacturers emphasized that they did not object to paying time and one-half for work in excess of forty hours a week. They said the clause calling for additional compensation on Sundays was written into the contract in a period when the industry's attention was devoted almost exclusively to the making of passenger cars and commercial vehicles and the clause was frankly intended to discourage plants from staying open on Sundays or holidays. Now that it had become a patriotic necessity to continue work throughout the week, the idea of a penalty for Sunday work should be dropped, the manufacturers contended.

Announcement of the union's ap-

Continued on Page Eight

Democrats Will Hold Fund Dinners Feb. 23

By The Associated Press.

WASHINGTON, Feb. 1—Edward J. Flynn, chairman of the Democratic National Committee, said today that the annual fund-raising dinners of the party would be held Monday night, Feb. 23, when President Roosevelt will make a Washington's Birthday fireside address.

Democratic party dinners have been held on the anniversary of Andrew Jackson's victory in the Battle of New Orleans, Jan. 8. They were deferred this year because of the war.

"Parent dinners" will be held here, with other dinners in practically all of the States, Mr. Flynn said. His announcement said nothing about prospective charges. Diners at Jackson Day dinners have paid $100 to attend the Washington gatherings and lower prices elsewhere.

"The occasion will afford the opportunity to lift the burden of debt that hangs over the Democratic National Committee—the residue of the deficit left over from the campaign that resulted in the re-election of Franklin D. Roosevelt," Mr. Flynn said, adding that the debt totals $600,000.

MAYOR 'EXPECTS' TO RESIGN OCD JOB

Says He Will 'Relinquish' It After Settling Pending Items —Warden Staff to Be Cut

Mayor La Guardia announced yesterday at City Hall that he "expects to relinquish" his Federal post of Director of the Office of Civilian Defense as soon as he has disposed of several matters now pending in the organization of that agency. Although he did not say how long it would take to clear up these loose ends, it was hinted that formal announcement of his resignation might be expected soon.

The Mayor's announcement was made at the end of one of his Sunday "Talks to the People," broadcast over WNYC, the municipal radio station, from his desk in City Hall. Although the Mayor had indicated on several earlier occasions that he intended to give up either his defense post or his post as Mayor, this was the first public declaration that he had decided to

Continued on Page Ten

CITY ASSESSMENTS DOWN $45,814,255 TO $16,177,322,971

$51,110,155 Is Off Ordinary Realty, While $5,295,900 Is Added on Utility Holdings

MANHATTAN CUTS HIGHEST

8,350 New Buildings Added to Rolls, With Valuation Placed Tentatively at $116,174,025

Showing a tentative net decrease of $45,814,255 from the final figures for 1941-42, taxable real estate and special franchises in New York are tentatively assessed at $16,177,322,971 on the assessment rolls for 1942-43, released yesterday. The final figures for 1941-42 totaled $16,223,137,226.

When he made public the tentative rolls for the next fiscal year, which begins July 1, Joseph Lilly, president of the City Tax Commission, pointed out that the net decrease was only a fraction of the city-wide reductions made on real estate.

"Reductions in the assessed valuations of existing properties for 1942-43," Mr. Lilly explained, "were recommended by the assessors and adopted by the Tax Commission, amounting to $230,740,715. This total reduction is offset by an approved increase amounting to $39,424,830, leaving a net field reduction for equalization of $191,345,885."

Against this stood increases of $132,929,300 for new buildings.

Manhattan, with a tentative reduction of $95,311,400, fared better with the tax assessors than any other borough, although the utility companies in Manhattan provide an exception. Their realty has been tentatively assessed at an aggregate increase of $12,144,460.

Changes in the borough-wide assessments on ordinary real estate are as follows:

Manhattan	—$93,311,400
The Bronx	— 15,139,505
Brooklyn	— 15,506,985
Queens	— 42,716,190
Richmond	— 1,852,535
Total	—$51,110,155

Borough decreases or increases

Continued on Page Six

The War Summarized

MONDAY, FEBRUARY 2, 1942

United States naval and air forces have made a smashing raid on Japanese naval and air bases in the Marshall and Gilbert Islands in mid-Pacific, sinking many Japanese naval auxiliaries, bombarding shore installations and destroying Japanese planes, the Navy Department announced yesterday. The Japanese put up a strong resistance. Eleven United States planes were lost. [1:8.]

General MacArthur's heavy artillery on forts in Manila Bay also gave the Japanese a setback by crushing an effort to take the Corregidor fortress and other strongholds by surprise. The Japanese had assembled a force with barges and launches at Ternate, on the south side of the bay opposite Corregidor; the shellfire destroyed the expedition. [1:5-6; map, P. 3.]

Meanwhile the great crisis of the Southwest Pacific front continued to develop actively in the Netherlands Indies and quietly, for the moment, before Singapore and in Burma.

British artillery on the north shore of Singapore Island opened fire across Johore Strait on the advancing Japanese forces. Governor Sir Shenton Thomas appealed to Singapore's inhabitants to stand firm. King George sent a message of sympathy and good cheer. The Tokyo radio claimed that cutting off of the mainland water supply had sealed the fate of the island. [1:4.]

In the Netherlands Indies Japanese bombers attacked a port on the Netherland part of Timor, southernmost island of the archipelago. Netherland troops were reported fighting the Japanese in the Pontianak area on the west coast of Netherland Borneo, 475 miles northeast of Batavia, although Tokyo claimed that Pontianak had fallen. Fighting also continued at Amboina, naval base between Celebes and New Guinea. [1:7; Map, P. 2.] Farther east Australian bombers struck again at the Japanese invasion fleet in the harbor of Rabaul on New Britain Island, and Japanese bombers continued raiding the near-by New Guinea coast. [2:2.]

In Burma the British have stabilized their new front along the west bank of the Salween River, it was announced in Rangoon. But, the Japanese were reported to be trying to cross the river just north of Moulmein. A Chungking newspaper disclosed that the British command had not yet thrown Chinese troops into the Battle of Burma. [4:1.]

Russian reports said that a Soviet drive on the Ukraine front was getting closer to Dniepropetrovsk on the great bend of the Dnieper. In two sectors farther south in the Ukraine drives developed in the same general direction [1:5.]

From Libya came the news that British troops had withdrawn again, this time to the vicinity of Maraua, eighty miles northeast of Bengazi, recently captured by the Germans. [5:5, with map.]

BLOWS BY THE AMERICAN NAVY MARK DEVELOPMENTS IN THE PACIFIC WAR

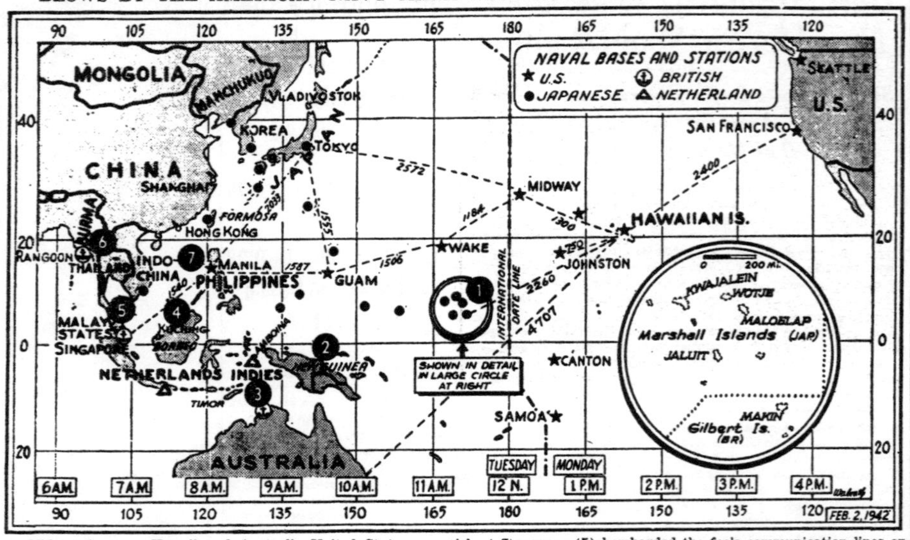

Midway between Hawaii and Australia United States warships and planes attacked Japanese bases in the Marshall and Gilbert Islands (1), sinking fleet auxiliaries and destroying planes and shore establishments. Enemy fliers raided points on New Guinea (2) and Timor (3), while on Borneo (4) ground forces widened their footholds. (Detailed map, Page 2.) The besieged British at Singapore (5) bombarded the foe's communication lines on the Malayan mainland. In Burma (6) the British reported the battlefront stabilized. General MacArthur not only hurled back thrusts at his lines near Manila (7) but also destroyed by artillery a flotilla gathered by the Japanese presumably for an invasion of the island forts of Manila Bay. (Detailed map, Page 3.)

SINGAPORE'S GUNS LAUNCH DEFENSE

Japanese Attacked as They Seek to Establish Line Opposite Island

By The Associated Press.

SINGAPORE, Feb. 1—Singapore's guns along the low north shore today opened fire for the first time in direct defense of this principal Far Eastern British base, sending their shells screaming across the Strait of Johore.

The shells were aimed at Japanese communications where the invaders were drawing up their forces to positions looking across the mile-wide water barrier, presumably for a direct assault on this fortress that was once considered impregnable largely because of 400 to 500 miles of protecting jungles to the north.

The battered and bruised defenders of the long retreat from the Thai border since Dec. 8 through Malaya, numbering 60,000 by official announcement, meanwhile heard the first government report that long-needed reinforcements had arrived.

[Tokyo broadcast yesterday that the fate of Singapore was sealed. The report said the mainland water supply was cut off and 3,000,000 persons were on the besieged island of 220 square miles. There has been no British statement of the number of persons under siege. The normal population of the island was less than 800,000, but there has been a huge influx of refugees since the invasion of Malaya began. There are two water reservoirs on the island and this is the season of monsoon rains.]

Thomas Issues Statement

Sir Shenton Thomas, Governor of Singapore, said substantial aid already had reached the island in the last few days. The nature of the reinforcements was not officially disclosed.

"We have been told by Mr. Churchill and others that help is being sent as quickly as possible," he said in a broadcast. "I can tell you now that in the last few days substantial reinforcements have been received.

"The battle of Singapore is now beginning. It will be grim, no doubt, but not more so than in Britain, Russia and China. And if the people of those countries can stand up to total war so can the people of Singapore."

He said as many women and

Continued on Page Four

Manila Bay Forts Destroy Assembled Troops, Barges

Special to THE NEW YORK TIMES.

WASHINGTON, Feb. 1—Long-range American guns, barking salvos some ten miles across the water from four fortresses in Manila Bay, have blasted and destroyed a Japanese concentration of men and boats, caught by surprise in apparent preparation for an attempted mass invasion of Corregidor and other Manila Bay strongholds, the War Department announced today.

Sighted at the port of Ternate, on the south side of the bay, were "numerous" launches and barges, the War Department announced, clustered for a projected expedition. The big batteries of Corregidor and Forts Drum, Frank and Hughes, let loose full force.

"The surprise was complete," the communiqué stated, "and the force and its equipment were destroyed."

Simultaneously the Army reported that General Douglas MacArthur, during the last twenty-four hours, had repelled several strong thrusts at his American-Filipino lines stretched across the Bataan Peninsula.

"The fighting was heavy," the communiqué declared, "but all of our positions were firmly held.

"Enemy losses were relatively large."

Thus was begun the ninth week of war against overwhelming odds in the Philippines.

For the present, at least, it appeared, today's long-range breaking up of a concentration for invasion had protected effectively General MacArthur's forces from enemy assault and pocketing from the rear, and at the same time had again kept the Japanese forces from acquiring use of Manila Bay.

As the situation stood at 1 P. M.

Continued on Page Three

RUSSIANS ADVANCE UPON DNIEPER CITY

Fighting Nineteen Miles From Dniepropetrovsk Reported —Other Drives Gain

By DANIEL T. BRIGHAM

By Telephone to THE NEW YORK TIMES.

BERNE, Switzerland, Monday, Feb. 2—After three days of fighting in which they crushed imposing German rear-guard forces in quick succession, Russian troops from Lozovaya, in the Donets Basin, succeeded yesterday in making contact with what were described as the main German lines nineteen miles northeast of Dniepropetrovsk, it was reported this morning by a commentator on the Moscow radio. A battle was said to be under way.

The Soviet spokesman also said that strong Russian formations southeast of Dniepropetrovsk had driven wedges into a German line. These formations were declared to be concentrating their main mechanized forces for an all-out offensive.

A little farther to the south, the

Continued on Page Three

Rios, Leftist, Wins in Chilean Vote; President-Elect Favors Aid to U. S.

By THOMAS J. HAMILTON

Special Cable to THE NEW YORK TIMES.

SANTIAGO, Chile, Feb. 1—Juan Antonio Rios, Popular Front candidate, who has promised to press the policy of collaboration with the United States pursued by the late President Pedro Aguirre Cerda, today defeated General Carlos Ibanez del Campo, Rightist, by a decisive majority of more than 55,000 votes in Chile's Presidential election.

The Ministry of the Interior announced just before midnight that, with 9,000 votes still to be accounted for, Señor Rios received 257,980 votes, to 202,035 for General Ibanez.

This was a considerably larger majority than Señor Aguirre Cerda received when he defeated the Rightist candidate in 1938.

Not only did Señor Rios pile up large leads in the mining and industrial centers, but he also led in South Chile, where it had been assumed the considerable German population would swing the vote to General Ibanez.

President-elect Rios was supported by his own Radical party and by the Socialists, Communists and other Left Wing groups.

The election passed off with only three or four cases of disorder throughout the country. The news of Señor Rios's victory was received with complete calm in Santiago.

Mounted police had been stationed in the square around the Ministry of the Interior, but the evening was quiet here.

Domestic issues, such as the increased cost of living under the Popular Front government were

Continued on Page Five

JAPANESE IN RAID NEAR AUSTRALIA

Ten Planes Bomb Kupang on Timor—Foes Press Dutch at Four Strongholds

By The United Press.

BATAVIA, Netherlands Indies, Feb. 1—Japanese bombers struck today at Netherland Timor, southernmost of the Indies, only 310 miles from the Australian coast, while Netherland troops battled landing parties at four points, including the Amboina naval base.

In their deepest air raid yet made into the Indies Japanese planes attacked Kupang on Timor and shipping south of there in the strait between Timor and the small island of Samau. There was said to have been no damage or casualties. There were ten planes in the raiding force.

Kupang, with its important airfield, is a stop on the air line between Australia and Java. Darwin, naval base on the north coast of Australia, is 570 miles to the southeast. Surabaya, main Netherland naval base, is 830 miles to the northwest. Amboina, now under heavy Japanese attack, is 580 miles northeast of Kupang.

The latest reports from Amboina said the Japanese had pushed close to the airport.

Australia Issues Reports

Confirmation of these developments in the parts of the Netherlands Indies of most vital importance to Australia came from Melbourne, where they were announced in a Royal Australian Air Force communiqué. Australian planes were stationed at Amboina and other airfields in the Netherland islands, possibly including Kupang, soon after the Pacific war started.

Stiff Netherland resistance was being offered also to a two-pronged Japanese drive to grab the Pontianak area, on the west coast of Netherland Borneo, only 475 miles northeast of Batavia, capital of the Netherlands Indies.

The Netherland Air Force, together with United States and Australian planes under United Nations command, appeared to control the air, at least temporarily, for a communiqué said that "enemy air activity has been less than during the foregoing days."

Japanese planes attacked Netherland naval planes on reconnaissance flights, without result, it added.

The communiqué was the first in some days to give no place names

Continued on Page Two

MANY SHIPS SUNK

Severe Aircraft Losses Inflicted on Japanese in Raid on Isles

KEY POINTS SHELLED

Planes Back Up Assault by War Vessels—U. S. Casualties Slight

By C. P. TRUSSELL

Special to THE NEW YORK TIMES.

WASHINGTON, Feb. 1—Warships and planes of the United States Pacific Fleet have delivered smashing assaults with shell, bomb and torpedo against the strategically situated and powerfully armed and manned Japanese-mandated Marshall Islands and against a Japanese-occupied island in the Gilbert group, the Navy Department announced today.

Surface and air units of Admiral Chester W. Nimitz's forces, operating in perfect coordination, sank many Japanese fleet auxiliaries, destroyed many enemy planes, on the ground and in the air, and inflicted heavy damage on Japanese military installations and air bases. Many of the enemy's key positions were battered by bombardments from American warships. The American raiding forces found no large Japanese combatant vessels.

"Two of our surface vessels," the Navy's communiqué said, "received minor damage from near bomb misses. Eleven American aircraft failed to return from the attack. Our total personnel losses are not yet known, but are believed to have been slight."

Enemy Caught Unawares

Taking the Japanese wholly unawares, the American units poured their shells, launched their torpedoes and hurled their bombs on the Japanese bases on Jaluit, Wotje, Kwajalein and Roi and on Tarao, in the Maloelap Atoll, all in the Marshall group, which is some 2,000 miles southwest of Pearl Harbor. Makin Island, in the British-owned Gilbert group, also was attacked. It had been seized by the Japanese early in the war.

The news, received in official Washington with great satisfaction, was regarded in many quarters as an answer—and probably only a preliminary and token answer—to the question long raised and repeated frequently by critics: "Where is our Navy?"

Although no large enemy combatant vessels were found by the attacking forces of Admiral Nimitz, the Japanese Fleet apparently suffered seriously under the blows from the sea and air. Not only were many Japanese naval auxiliaries—smaller craft upon which the combatant units must depend for fuel, supplies, repairs, minesweeping and so on—sunk, but

Continued on Page Three

Seas Near Singapore Made Perilous by Foe

By F. TILLMAN DURDIN

Wireless to THE NEW YORK TIMES.

BATAVIA, Netherlands Indies, Feb. 1—Departure from Singapore these days is an exciting, perilous and uncertain enterprise because of Japanese air and sea raiders. I have just arrived in Batavia after running the gantlet of Japanese airplane and submarine activity.

The ship aboard which I made the trip was bombed three times by Japanese planes, but they scored no hits.

When I left Singapore Thursday the naval base had been damaged somewhat by Japanese bombings, but still was a going concern.

Our ship was bombed at points where the Japanese are now making routine daily attacks on United Nations shipping. We fired everything we had at the Japanese, who visibly had as narrow an escape as we had had from their bombs.

"All the News That's Fit to Print."

The New York Times.

LATE CITY EDITION
Rain and mild today.
Temperatures Yesterday—Max., 41; Min., 33

VOL. XCI...No. 30,695. Entered as Second-Class Matter, Postoffice, New York, N. Y. NEW YORK, SATURDAY, FEBRUARY 7, 1942. THREE CENTS NEW YORK CITY and Vicinity

KERN IS SUSPENDED WITH ENTIRE BOARD IN ROW WITH MAYOR

Order Calls for Civil Service Members to Show Cause Why They Should Not Be Ousted

COURT DEFIANCE CHARGED

Ousting 'Politically Appointed' Employes Is Blamed by Head of Commission

Mayor La Guardia laid the groundwork yesterday for the speedy removal of Paul J. Kern, president of the Municipal Civil Service Commission, and Wallace S. Sayre and Ferdinand Q. Morton, its other members, when he suspended the entire commission and ordered the three officials to show cause at 11 o'clock Monday morning why they should not be removed from office.

The Mayor ordered the suspensions early yesterday morning from his home, prior to his departure from La Guardia Field at 9 o'clock for Washington. At the airport the Mayor said he could not tolerate the attack launched by Mr. Kern and his colleagues against Corporation Counsel William C. Chanler.

Mr. Kern complained last Thursday that the corporation counsel had refused to represent him in an appeal from a Supreme Court order directing payment of salaries to four employes of the City Register's office. Contending that the four were political appointees, Mr. Kern and his colleagues decided to appeal from the decision and at the same time began court action against Mr. Chanler to force him to represent the commission in the action.

Mayor Gives Explanation

Despite his publicly announced decision on Thursday against speaking to newspaper men, the Mayor explained his position freely to reporters at the airport.

"I have suspended the entire Civil Service Commission," he said. "I sent the papers to City Hall this morning from my home. They will be served shortly after 9 o'clock and order the commission members to show cause why they should not be removed from office, and are returnable at 11 o'clock on Monday.

"My action speaks for itself. One agency of government cannot attack another agency and not impair its usefulness. No executive can stand for this type of action."

William B. Herlands, Commissioner of Investigation, served the order personally upon Mr. Kern and Mr. Sayre yesterday morning. Mr. Morton, Negro member of the commission, was ill yesterday and was served at his home, 152 West 131st Street. At the same time Mr. Herlands posted members of his staff in the commission offices with orders to prevent the destruction or removal of records. The investigators searched every package that left the offices yesterday.

Text of Mayor's Order

Mayor La Guardia's order read:

"Pursuant to the authority vested in me by the law of the State of New York and the Charter of the City of New York, you are hereby suspended from office and will show cause on Monday, Feb. 9, 1942, at 11 A. M., why you should not be removed from office for conduct unbecoming a Civil Service Commissioner and making a deliberately false statement concerning official matters and insubordination—all to the injury of civil service and contrary to the interest of the City of New York and the duties which you are by law charged to perform."

Under the law, the three Commissioners must receive a public hearing and have the right to be represented by counsel. The hearing will be held in the Mayor's office at City Hall.

The "insubordination" specified by the Mayor concerned the Commission's refusal to follow his policy of making no objection to the retention of the four employes on the Register's staff. Their retention has been approved by the State Civil Service Commission and payment of their salaries was ordered recently by Supreme Court Justice Carroll G. Walter. The Commission's attack on Corporation Counsel Chanler and Mr. Kern's characterization of the Corporation Counsel as a politically minded lawyer also figured in the Mayor's specifications.

In contrast to the issue defined by the Mayor, Mr. Kern contended yesterday that the whole issue involved was whether four politically

Continued on Page Nine

Tammany Ousts Sullivan As Leader by 145 to 136

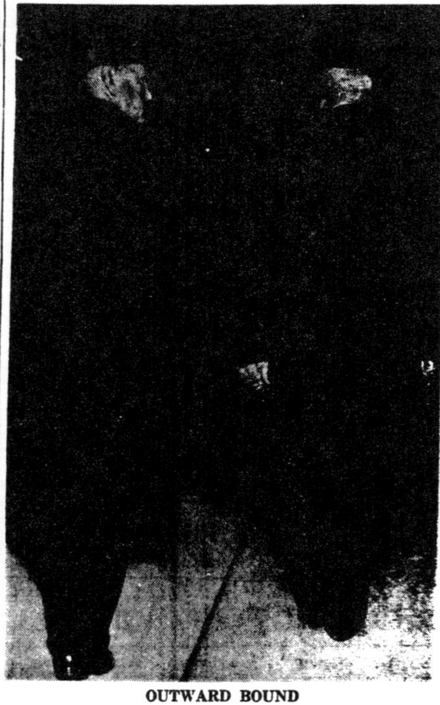

OUTWARD BOUND

Mr. Sullivan leaves the Hall, his companion being Daniel E. Finn Sr., a Sachem, who is shown at the left. The New York Times (by Brewer)

The Tammany executive committee last evening ousted Christopher D. Sullivan as leader by a vote of 145 to 136 and named Charles H. Hussey, chairman of the executive committee, to act as temporary leader until Feb. 27, when another meeting of the committee will be held to elect a permanent leader.

In view of the criticism to which Mr. Sullivan has been subjected since the overwhelming defeat of Tammany at the last election, the closeness of the vote was unexpected. By a new method of voting, each Assembly district was allotted twelve votes divided among the leaders and co-leaders, of whom there are as many as six in some districts, and in addition twelve

Continued on Page Eight

House Forbids OCD Funds For 'Dancers,' Donald Duck

By The Associated Press.

WASHINGTON, Feb. 6—In an upsurge of revolt against the appointment of Melvyn Douglas, screen actor, and Mayris Chaney, Mrs. Roosevelt's dancer-protege to high civilian defense posts, the House voted, 88 to 80, today to forbid use of civilian defense funds for "instructions in physical fitness by dancers, fan dancing, street shows, theatrical performances or other public entertainment."

During an angry discussion that preceded the vote, Representative Hoffman, Republican, of Michigan, suggested that a "Bundles for Eleanor" movement be started in tribute to Mrs. Roosevelt's ability to get jobs for her friends. He referred to Miss Chaney and others.

Equally severe were the Repre-

Continued on Page Nine

TEACHERS TO ISSUE ALL SUGAR BOOKS

Henderson Tells Limit of About 12 Ounces a Week and Curb Proposed for Hoarders

By CHARLES E. EGAN
Special to The New York Times.

WASHINGTON, Feb. 6—The duty of issuing sugar rationing books to every man, woman and child in the country was entrusted tonight to public school teachers. They were instructed to deal firmly with hoarders until the secreted supplies are exhausted.

Formal rationing will start, Leon Henderson, Price Administrator said, as soon as the enormous job of printing and distributing "War Ration Book No. 1" has been completed. Local rationing boards, which have been handling the distribution of tires, will have general supervision of consumers and of the issuance of the books.

According to OPA officials, the allotment for each citizen will probably be three-quarters of a pound of sugar a week. The exact amount is still to be fixed because the War Production Board has not determined how much is to be made available each week for thousands of retail stores in the country.

One book of sugar stamps will be printed for each person in the country, regardless of age, the OPA stated. It will carry twenty-eight stamps, each numbered and restricted to a designated week. When sugar is bought the corresponding stamp will be torn from the book. Each stamp will entitle the bookholder to purchase the weekly allowance.

"When buying sugar, the storekeeper will be required to tear the proper stamp out of the buyer's book," the statement said. "These stamps will then be pasted on a card by the storekeeper. These cards will then be turned in to the supplier of sugar for the store in

Continued on Page Seven

PRESIDENT REJECTS A PARTISAN STAND IN CONGRESS RACE

We, in War, Need Lawmakers, Regardless of Party, Who Back Government, He Says

THEIR RECORDS THE GUIDE

Willkie Hails This, Calling It 'Repudiation' of Flynn, and Urges World Vision

By W. H. LAWRENCE
Special to The New York Times.

WASHINGTON, Feb. 6—President Roosevelt declared today that the United States at war needed Congressmen regardless of party who will back up their government and who had a record of backing up the country in an emergency regardless of party.

Mr. Roosevelt thus chose for himself a role in the 1942 elections different from that adopted in 1918 by President Wilson, who asked the country to return a Democratic House of Representatives and Senate—an appeal which was turned down by the voters.

Some political observers regarded the President's press conference remark as a toning down of the Monday speech by Edward J. Flynn, Democratic National chairman, who said that "no misfortune except a major military defeat could befall this country to the extent involved in the election of a Congress hostile to the President."

"Vast confusion," Mr. Flynn added, "would inevitably result if we had a President of one party and a House of Representatives, for example, of the opposition party."

Non-Partisan Stand Stressed

The President laid emphasis on the phrase, regardless of party, and he used it not once but twice in replying to a newspaper man's request for comment on Mr. Flynn's declaration, which had aroused considerable criticism by Republicans, who accused him of breaking the political truce which had been in effect since the United States entered the war.

None among his auditors believed that the President was counting himself out of participation in the Fall election campaign, and his statement suggested that he might throw his influence against any Senator or Representative up for re-election whose record would not satisfy the President as to his readiness to support the Administration in emergency matters.

The President has scheduled a nation-wide broadcast for Feb. 23, when he will report to the nation on progress of the war effort, and the Democratic National Committee is using this speech as a rallying point for dinners across the

Continued on Page Nine

The War Summarized

SATURDAY, FEBRUARY 7, 1942

The Japanese, apparently halted for the time being everywhere but in the Netherlands Indies, came up against a double rebuff yesterday in the Philippines.

Enemy gun emplacements on the southeastern shore of Manila Bay, presumably set up for an attack on Corregidor Island, received a destructive storm of shellfire from American fortifications, while a Japanese propaganda barrage by radio and pamphlets encountered only "amusement" among the defenders of Bataan Peninsula. The propaganda employed General Emilio Aguinaldo, who led the Filipino Insurrection in 1899, as a "Quisling." [1:8; map, P. 4.]

In Burma, American and British fliers scored their most spectacular success when they broke up bombing attacks on Rangoon by downing at least ten and probably twenty of thirty Japanese raiders. The British prevented any major crossing of the Salween River and appeared to be standing firm on its west bank. [1:7.]

But the Japanese seized the East Borneo river port of Samarinda, sixty miles north of Balik Papan, and their planes scouted Java, where Netherland forces prepared for a parachute invasion. [2:2, with general map.]

Singapore Island, in its seventh day of siege, underwent more aerial attacks and traded new artillery blows with the Japanese, silencing additional enemy batteries. Japanese parachute tactics seemed a strong prospect here, too. [3:5.]

Pacific War Councils of the United Nations were revealed by President Roosevelt to have been set up in Washington, and the War Department announced that a "combined Chiefs of Staff" board had been established there, with the United States and Britain each represented by four ranking officers. [1:6-7.]

From the Russian front came reports of growing German resistance, bolstered by air-borne reinforcements, particularly in the southern sectors. For the first time in weeks Soviet dispatches spoke of battles in which the Russians were outnumbered. However, the Red Army was said to be moving ahead after having inflicted almost 10,000 casualties in the three-day period ended Thursday. [6:2.]

A British stand in Libya, along the rugged approaches to Tobruk, "from a line which can be defended and defended successfully," was predicted by highly placed informants. The British appeared to be organizing for such a stand as they held their ground some fifty-five miles west of Tobruk. The R. A. F. pounded Axis transport columns effectively. [5:1.]

The sinking of another American tanker off the New Jersey coast was revealed by the Navy Department, and British officials disclosed that losses in the Battle of the Atlantic had gone up sharply, with more U-boats operating off the Atlantic seaboard than ever before. [1:5.]

26 ON TANKER LOST AS U-BOAT STRIKES; 12 ADRIFT 36 HOURS

The India Arrow Sinks in an Inferno of Blazing Oil, the Twelfth in U. S. Waters

SHIPS IGNORE SURVIVORS

Wary of Attack, They Refuse to Answer Signal—London Views Situation Gravely

In a grim continuation of the warfare that already has claimed thirteen announced victims in United States waters, another American tanker has been picked off by an enemy U-boat operating off the New Jersey coast. Twenty-six of her crew of thirty-eight are missing, the Navy Department disclosed yesterday.

The 8,327-ton tanker India Arrow sank in a sea of blazing oil after she had been torpedoed and shelled by a submarine that struck without a second's warning early Wednesday evening. The twelve survivors, picked up by a fishing boat, were brought into Atlantic City yesterday morning after spending two nights and a day in a wave-tossed lifeboat.

The ship, owned by the Socony-Vacuum Oil Company, New York City, was the twelfth sunk and the thirteenth attacked in American waters since Jan. 14, according to Navy announcements. In addition, a dispatch from an Eastern Canadian port last night told of the landing of survivors from a torpedoed British tanker, the fifth sinking off the Canadian coast that has been revealed during the same period. This brings the known total of U-boat victims off the Canadian-American coast to eighteen in all.

London Takes Grave View

The seriousness of the situation on this side of the Atlantic was emphasized yesterday in an official disclosure from London. Declaring that sinkings in the Battle of the Atlantic, including the American victims, had gone up sharply, the official sources asserted that a considerable portion of the Nazi U-boat pack undoubtedly was hunting off the United States coast and that there unquestionably "are more U-boats operating in the Western Atlantic than ever before."

Landing in Atlantic City after their harrowing experience, the captain and eleven others of the India Arrow's crew revealed a new horror of the submarine warfare in home waters. Their stories indicated that prevalence of enemy raiders apparently has made merchant ships extremely wary of all signals, and it has become increasingly difficult for survivors of a sunken ship to reach a rescue ship at night. Several times during the black hours of the first night out, the men from the India Arrow had the heart-rending experience of sighting ships that might have rescued them, but, according to one of the survivors, they all steered clear when the lifeboat's crew signaled with flashlights.

Captain Johnson, a gray-haired, 48-year-old sea veteran, told how one lifeboat jammed with officers and seamen went down when debris from the ship's shelled bridge struck it. He soberly said:

"I am doubtful if any others survived."

Bringing Oil Here

The India Arrow, a 468.3-foot tanker, built in 1921 at Quincy, Mass., was sailing from Corpus Christi, Texas, to her home port of New York City with a cargo of oil when the torpedo struck her at 7 o'clock Wednesday evening. Her exact location off the New Jersey coast was not revealed in the Navy announcement.

Captain Johnson, who lives at New Dorp, S. I., with his wife and three young children, told the story of how it happened.

"I was on the bridge," he said. "There was a loud report, and the torpedo lammed into the starboard side, to the fore of the engines. The ship caught fire and started sinking in about five minutes. Oil from the No. 10 cargo tank, which was punctured, leaked onto the water and caught fire, too."

The ship started to list, the shelling from the submarine's deck gun began, the bridge collapsed and the captain fell off the bridge, he related. Almost miraculously, he was "washed into a lifeboat" that had been launched successfully from the starboard side—he still is

Continued on Page Three

M'ARTHUR BLASTS FOE'S GUNS, IGNORES PLEA BY AGUINALDO; MORE INVADERS REACH LUZON

Capital Is Made War Center For Effort of United Nations

War Department and the President Reveal Setting Up of New 'Combined Chiefs of Staff Group'

By FRANK L. KLUCKHOHN
Special to The New York Times.

WASHINGTON, Feb. 6—Washington will be the military staff headquarters for the United Nations, especially the Pacific War Councils dealing with the Southwestern Pacific area, according to announcements made today by President Roosevelt and the War Department.

The War Department said that the "Combined Chiefs of Staff Group" of the United States and Britain were established here, with four ranking officers representing each country. This was announced soon after President Roosevelt told his press conference that action problems involving Pacific strategy would be settled in Washington, in close cooperation with officials in London who, he indicated, would handle broad political matters. General Sir Archibald Wavell of Britain will handle all tactical problems in the Pacific area, the President emphasized.

This apparently was the broad solution of the problem created by Australia's expressed desire to cooperate more closely with the United States, although many details still remained to be filled in. The United States lies between the Pacific and European theatres of war. From the purely geographic viewpoint, therefore, Washington offers advantages over London as a strategic center.

The Anglo-American staff meeting here is the only such body in existence but indications were strong that problems involving the conduct of the war in Europe and the Near and the Middle East still would be settled by the United Nations in London. Soviet Russia, for instance, was not mentioned in the War Department announcement, although it was said that the combined staffs would assist in adjusting joint operations involving

Continued on Page Four

The text of the War Department's statement, Page 4.

Avalanches of Mud Kill Two Californians in Homes

By The United Press.

SAN FRANCISCO, Feb. 6—Avalanches of mud loosed by heavy rains tumbled down the slopes of Mount Davidson in the heart of San Francisco late today, crushing six homes and killing at least one person. The walls of mud were advancing 400 feet an hour toward other homes in the neighborhood. The mud and rocks struck the first home on the mountainside without warning. Police hastily evacuated hundreds of residents from the Mission and Sunnyside residential districts as their frame dwellings were ground into the debris.

Mrs. Dora Krammer, middle-aged housewife, was swallowed by the muck, as firemen attempted to rescue her from the kitchen of her home. Muriel Swanfelt, 17, was killed when an avalanche swept away the home of her parents, north of San Francisco.

Firemen rescued Thomas Hill, 65, a brother-in-law of Mrs. Krammer, from five feet of mud. Hill clung to a wall, protecting his face, until rescue workers dug down to him, slipped a rope under his armpits and raised him to the top of the house.

Firemen arrived in time to hear Mrs. Krammer's muffled cries, but new slides poured down on them before they could reach her. A large tree crashed through the kitchen roof, and workers were forced to abandon their rescue attempts.

Hundreds of residents barely escaped from their homes before they were surrounded by the soggy earth. Scores were treated for shock and minor injuries.

Three ambulances and emer-

Continued on Page Five

RANGOON FIGHTERS BREAK UP BIG RAID

Americans and R.A.F. Destroy 10 to 20 of 30 Japanese Planes—Salween Line Held

By The Associated Press.

RANGOON, Burma, Feb. 6—In a swift and effective shift from offense to defense fighter pilots of the American Volunteer Group and the Royal Air Force broke up a chain of vicious Japanese raids on the Burma Road port today by destroying at least ten and probably twenty raiders, up to two-thirds of the attacking force.

Their victory came in daylight, after Rangoon had been pounded all night by waves of enemy raiders in the third consecutive overnight attack.

The last raid, at 9:50 A. M., was the seventh wave, involving thirty enemy planes. When it was over—with no Allied losses—the official score for the defenders was: A. V. G.—seven Japanese bombers certainly shot down, five more probably; R. A. F.—three Japanese

Continued on Page Three

Britain Issues Pikes (Yes, Pikes) To Defenders Against Invasion

By The Associated Press.

LONDON, Feb. 6—Prime Minister Winston Churchill declared recently that the British would defend vital airfields even if they had to do it with pikes—and now, to the amazement of some quarters, the War Office actually has issued spiked poles to Home Guard units.

The five-foot four-inch weapons are not considered a joke, at least by the War Office, but the press has been quick to hoot at the return to equipment that medieval foot soldiers found useful for poking armored horsemen.

A cartoonist of The Daily Mail suggested revival of the bow, with arrows tipped with explosive "Molotoff cocktails," and the use of rock-tossing catapults against tanks.

An editorial in The Daily Mirror said:

"You never know. The pole-axe may return. Crossbowmen of the thirteenth century might be useful behind the hedges. Archers with poisoned arrows might take tips from Harold at Hastings. The War Office may be found studying reproductions of Bayeux tapestry and using medieval manuscripts as military manuals. It is not so absurd as it sounds. Did not head-piece armor return in the last war?"

Lord Croft, Under-Secretary of War, who received credit for the idea, was quoted as having said that "after members of the Home Guard have attacked with grenades, and mainly at night, the pike is a handy weapon for mopping-up operations."

An army officer engaged in Home Guard training said the

Continued on Page Six

ENEMY PLAN FOILED

Japanese Emplacements on Manila Bay Shore Wrecked by Shells

A NEW 'QUISLING' ARISES

Aguinaldo's Plea to MacArthur to Surrender Stirs Amusement —Foe Prepares a Drive

Special to The New York Times.

WASHINGTON, Feb. 6—General Douglas MacArthur again upset plans of the Japanese in the Philippines when his artillery destroyed enemy gun emplacements on the southeastern shore of Manila Bay, which apparently had been designed for an attack on the island fortress of Corregidor, the War Department announced today.

It revealed, however, that nine Japanese transport ships were unloading Japanese troops at ports on Lingayen Gulf, about 100 miles north of Bataan Peninsula, where the United States-Filipino forces have been enjoying a lull recently.

The department also disclosed that the Japanese were resorting once again to futile propagandistic weapons. In the person of General Emilio Aguinaldo the enemy has found "a sort of Philippine Quisling," the department said in a communiqué released this evening. General Aguinaldo in 1899 led the Filipino insurrection against the United States.

A Laugh for Defenders

In a radio broadcast addressed to General MacArthur from Manila, General Aguinaldo urged the immediate surrender of the American forces. His appeal, the War Department asserted, was, of course, ignored by the United States general. In the last few days the enemy has unleashed a barrage of propaganda designed to lower the morale of our troops. Besides radio broadcasts, there have been pamphlets dropped from the skies. In all these propagandistic assaults the Japanese have been calling upon General MacArthur's men to surrender.

"These appeals have occasioned considerable amusement for the troops," the War Department asserted.

It is believed that the 12-inch guns on Corregidor Island contributed substantially to putting the new enemy emplacements out of commission. Apparently the Japanese gun emplacements were destroyed before the batteries had ever been in action.

Yesterday comparative quiet again reigned on the Bataan front. The Japanese did engage in bombing attacks on our troop positions. These attacks began early in the day, but they decreased in intensity as the day progressed. They did no damage.

There was also intermittent artillery fire by the enemy in the center of the front. It appears to have been mostly in the nature of range finding. Scouting operations were greater than in the preceding forty-eight hours, but they also were concentrated in the center sector, with quiet reported from both flanks.

Foe's Forces "Very Large"

The nine Japanese transports on Lingayen Gulf were reinforcing what the War Department termed "the already very large enemy concentrations in Bataan and other points on the Island of Luzon." There was no indication in the official communiqué, however, that General MacArthur's army had sufficient air strength attached to it to do more than engage in reconnaissance flights over this concentration of enemy ships and men.

A renewed assault, this time heavily reinforced in men and equipment, and thus tremendously more powerful than General MacArthur's defending force, thus appears inevitable in the near future.

In choosing General Aguinaldo as "a sort of Philippine Quisling" the Japanese are following the example of their German Axis partners in Norway. They evidently believe that the reputation of the 72-year-old Philippine general will

Continued on Page Four

"All the News That's Fit to Print."

The New York Times.

LATE CITY EDITION
Cold and windy today.
Temperatures Yesterday—Max., 30; Min., 19

Copyright, 1942, by The New York Times Company.

VOL. XCI..No. 30,697. Entered as Second-Class Matter, Postoffice, New York, N. Y. NEW YORK, MONDAY, FEBRUARY 9, 1942. THREE CENTS NEW YORK CITY and Vicinity

JAPANESE LAND ON SINGAPORE ISLE; OPEN ALL-OUT DRIVE ON M'ARTHUR; U-BOAT SINKS ANOTHER U. S. TANKER

FORCED FARE RISE BY SEPT. 10 FEARED UNDER STATE LAWS

Muzzicato Warns of Mandate Unless Amendments Are Voted at This Session

TRANSIT EXPERTS QUOTED

Needed Proviso in His Bill to Freeze 5-Cent Rate, but It Is Not Backed by City

Because of legislation enacted at Albany in 1940 and 1941 there is a real danger that the Board of Estimate will be under a mandate to increase the fare on the city's subway and elevated lines after next Sept. 10, State Senator Charles Muzzicato, Manhattan Republican, declared yesterday.

Senator Muzzicato, whose bill to freeze the fare at 5 cents for the duration of the war will be up for public hearing in Albany Feb. 17, said several transit experts, including two who have served the city in that capacity, have assured him that the danger is real and that it can be averted only by amending the law to make it clear that the city will have the power, should it decide to retain the 5-cent fare, to use tax funds to meet any deficit in fixed charges.

The unified transit lines, including the subways and elevated routes, now earn a surplus over operating expenses but fall far short of paying interest and amortization on the bonds issued to finance their construction.

$5,000,000 Less for Budget

Point was given to Senator Muzzicato's warning by the disclosure that the unified system's earnings would contribute $5,000,000 less to the 1942-43 city budget for application to reduction of debt service charges than they did to the budget for 1941-42.

"The fact is," Senator Muzzicato declared, "that I have been advised by competent transit lawyers that the city actually had no legal right to resort to tax funds in 1941 to make good the deficit on fixed charges of the subway lines. Unless this power to use tax funds to meet such deficits is clarified by State law the city may find itself compelled, after Sept. 10, to get the funds by raising the fare."

Conceding that competent counsel have held that the city, by virtue of provisions in the State Constitution, had the obligation to make good the deficit on the interest on all of its outstanding bonds, Senator Muzzicato insisted that litigation after Sept. 10 might result in a court ruling that the proper method of making good in the case of transit issues would be to get the needed revenue out of operation of the lines and not through taxation.

"Why take that chance," he said, "when it would be so simple to give the city the express power to cover deficits by means of tax funds?"

Bill Contains Needed Proviso

The bill sponsored by Senator Muzzicato contains such a provision. It has not received, however, the support of the La Guardia Administration, whose transit advisers are of the opinion that such power exists in the present state of the law.

Lawyers familiar with the recent history of transit legislation hold varying views on the necessity for giving the city the express power to resort to tax funds to make up transit deficits. That power was contained in the bill sponsored by the La Guardia Administration in 1940 and enacted after introduction by Senator Frederic Coudert Jr. and Assemblyman Abbott Low Moffat. It is omitted, however, in the Rapid Transit Law of 1941, a recodification sponsored by the La Guardia Administration, that repealed parts of the Rapid Transit Act and the Public Service Commission Law, including a section of the latter statute to which the Coudert-Moffat bill was an amendment.

The Rapid Transit Law of 1941, which is now the controlling legislation, has this to say about the fare in Section 36:

"If the Board of Transportation shall undertake or engage in public or municipal operation pursuant to the authority of this chapter the rate of fare shall not be more than 5 cents for a period not to exceed ten years from Sept. 10, 1932. The Board of Estimate of any city engaged in public or municipal operation and maintaining

Continued on Page Eleven

Clocks Put Ahead As War Time Begins

Those who have not advanced their clocks one hour are hereby reminded that since 2 o'clock this morning War Time has been in effect throughout the country.

Signed by President Roosevelt on Jan. 20, the daylight saving act is aimed at speeding up the country's war output, and is expected to save 736,282,000 kilowatt-hours of electricity. All transportation companies and railroads have begun operating on the new time, which will be in effect until six months after the cessation of hostilities.

Unlike regular daylight saving time, which was observed last Summer in seventeen States in whole or in part, War Time will be uniform for the entire country.

HOUSE FIGHT LOOMS ON 'FRILLS' FOR OCD

Leaders of Both Parties Call In Absent Members for Vote Today on Stage Activities

By C. P. TRUSSELL
Special to THE NEW YORK TIMES.

WASHINGTON, Feb. 8—So-called frills and furbelows of the National Civilian Defense program, as disclosed and attacked in the wake of appointments to high OCD posts of friends and protégés of Mrs. Eleanor Roosevelt, Assistant Director, have created a situation in the House which prompted urgent telegraphic summonses today to all absent members to rush back to Washington for a final and significant showdown tomorrow.

Administration leaders, conceding the fearful of embarrassing potentialities of the satirical restrictions inserted tentatively into the OCD appropriation bill Friday as House members revolted bitterly against the more "artistic" of the OCD innovations, sent out wires to all missing Democrats.

It was admittedly their hope that responding members of the majority would vote against and kill the amendment, now in the bill, which would prohibit the use of any of the OCD's $100,000,000 for instructions in physical fitness by dancers, fan dancers, street shows, theatrical performances or other public entertainment.

Douglas Denies He Will Be Paid

This ban was directed particularly at the physical fitness phase of the Civilian Defense program, placed in charge of Miss Mayris Chaney, dancer protégée of Mrs.

Continued on Page Nine

MOVIES ARE PUT IN ESSENTIAL CLASS BY DRAFT RULING

Hershey Finds Industry Aid to the Morale of Civilians and Also to War Production

FEW DEFERMENTS SEEN

Ruling Covers Actors, Writers, Directors and Other Key Men if They Can't Be Replaced

The motion picture industry is "an activity essential in certain instances to the national health, safety and interest, and in other instances to war production," according to a ruling by Brig. Gen. Lewis B. Hershey, Director of Selective Service, which was revealed yesterday through the war activities committee of the industry.

In accordance with this ruling, instructions have been sent to Selective Service officials in California to grant deferment to "actors, directors, writers, producers, camera men, sound engineers and other technicians" who cannot be replaced because of "the shortage of persons of their qualifications and skill" and whose removal "would cause a serious loss of effectiveness."

No Blanket Requests

George J. Schaefer, chairman of the war activities committee, declared that the industry "would not think of asking for blanket deferments," but that the ruling would give it the right to "apply for the retention of indispensable individuals from time to time."

"In my opinion," he added, "deferment will be sought only for a negligible number of persons engaged in motion-picture production."

William A. Brady, veteran theatrical producer, who at one time made silent films, attacked General Hershey's ruling. Mr. Brady said: "I don't think either screen people or theatre people can be termed essential. They weren't in the First World War, nor have they been in England during the progress of this war."

Balaban Tells of Work

Replying to Mr. Brady's attack, Barney Balaban, president of Paramount Pictures, said the motion picture industry was helping to win the war both here and in England in many ways.

"Within the last two weeks," he declared, "our government has

Continued on Page Nine

The War Summarized

MONDAY, FEBRUARY 9, 1942

The long-expected crisis of the Pacific war has apparently arrived with the British announcement that Japanese troops have landed in some force on Singapore Island and are being stubbornly fought. Previous reports had referred to Japanese occupation of Ubin Island in the Strait of Johore, but the position of the Singapore defenders has apparently taken a turn for the worse. The holding of Singapore is regarded as vital for the defense of both Burma and the Netherlands Indies. [1:8; map, P. 4.]

In the Philippines Japanese land and air forces launched a general attack against General MacArthur's whole position on the Bataan Peninsula and against the forts at the entrance to Manila Bay. Shore artillery pounded the forts, bombers joined the attack on all points and Japanese infantry assaults came on both the right and the left of the Bataan line. [1:4.]

Surabaya in the Netherlands Indies, last remaining important naval base of the United Nations in the Southwest Pacific, was again attacked by Japanese bombers, but only slight damage was reported. Japanese bombers also visited Palembang, Sumatra; Banka Island, off Sumatra, and a port of New Guinea. [3:1; general map, P. 2.] Observers in Batavia believed that the Japanese were concentrating on nipping the growing air power of the United Nations. [1:6-7.]

No new activity of any significance was reported from Burma. Activity on the Salween River line was limited to patrol skirmishing. It was disclosed that General Wavell, United Nations Commander in Chief for the Southwest Pacific, had recently visited Rangoon and expressed a moderate degree of optimism.

Arrival of strong reinforcements on the Salween front was also reported. [1:7.]

Dispatches from Russia reported that a deep wedge had been driven into the German lines below Leningrad and it was indicated that the siege of the city might soon be completely broken. Lesser advances on other fronts were claimed. [7:1.]

British headquarters in Cairo said that the Axis advance in Libya had been halted at the distant western approaches to Tobruk; that El Gazala, 40 miles west of Tobruk, was still in British hands, contrary to Axis claims, and that British forces were sweeping the desert south and west of El Gazala unopposed. [6:2.]

Berlin announced the death in an airplane accident of a great engineer and administrator, Major Gen. Fritz Todt, builder of the Nazi regime's super-highways and of the Westwall fortifications on the French frontier. He met death "while carrying out a military mission." [4:6.]

Sir Stafford Cripps, former British Ambassador to Moscow, said in a speech that Germany could be defeated by this time next year if the British went all out in their war effort and if both Britain and the United States gave all possible aid to Russia. [3:5.]

London sources asserted that Friday's explosion and Saturday's rioting at Tangier, Spanish Morocco, were part of an Axis effort to drag Spain into the war by creating an incident. [6:3.]

The United States Navy Department announced that the Socony Vacuum tanker China Arrow, 8,403 tons, had been sunk last Thursday morning by an enemy submarine off the Atlantic coast. [1:5.]

2 FLANKS ATTACKED

MacArthur Combats Big Thrusts at Right and Left of His Line

'ALL-OUT' PUSH IS SEEN

Forts at Entrance to Manila Bay Escape Serious Harm in Two-Hour Shelling

By C. BROOKS PETERS
Special to THE NEW YORK TIMES.

WASHINGTON, Feb. 8—The anticipated Japanese attack on the mountainous defense positions on Bataan Peninsula in the Philippine theatre held by General Douglas MacArthur and his relatively small force of American and Filipino soldiers was unleashed between 4 P. M. yesterday and 1 P. M. today, a War Department communiqué of the war indicated.

At the same time Japanese resumed their bombardment of fortifications at the entrance of Manila Bay. The shells were fired every four minutes, the War Department said, from concealed batteries on the Cavite shore, on the southeastern shore of Manila Bay. For two hours the enemy fired at Fort Mills, Fort Hughes and Fort Frank. No serious damage was caused by the thirty shells fired, the War Department said.

The assault to which General MacArthur's forces are subjected appears to be the most intense they have had to withstand. The terse phraseology of the communiqué suggests that it is an "all-out" enemy attack.

Three Types of Attack

The Japanese thrust is three-dimensional. Enemy bombers are engaging in twenty-four-hour raids on Bataan positions. Long-range artillery attacks daily and on the ground Japanese infantry launched attacks on General MacArthur's right and left.

On the right flank the Japanese engaged in an "infiltration thrust," the War Department communiqué disclosed. This thrust was repulsed by a sharp counter-attack carried out by American and Filipino troops.

On the left flank of General MacArthur's forces, however, the enemy may have gained some advantage. The War Department asserts that fighting in this sector is increasing in intensity. Since the American and Filipino forces there are of necessity fighting a defensive action this appears to indicate that Japanese assaults on General MacArthur's left flank are becoming more serious.

The War Department revealed yesterday that the Japanese were laying a heavy artillery barrage along the entire Bataan front. This barrage, apparently designed to weaken defense positions before the present assault, was accompanied by raids of enemy dive-bombers.

Recent War Department communiqués have emphasized that the enemy has succeeded in landing large-scale reinforcements on the island of Luzon. Specific mention has also been made of the arrival of fresh Japanese troops on the fighting front in the battle of Bataan.

Several days of quiet preceded the assault that is in progress. It is thought here that the enemy may have had sufficient time to prepare a large-scale action.

Big Attack Is Expected

WASHINGTON, Feb. 8 (UP)—For the last several days the pattern of the Japanese attacks on the defenders of the Philippines and their stepped-up tempo have suggested that the Japanese were preparing for an all-out assault on the last remaining centers of organized resistance, determined to end the Philippines campaign quickly, whatever the cost.

A week ago today General Douglas MacArthur reported that his Manila Bay fortifications had smashed what appeared to be enemy preparations to attempt to take

Continued on Page Two

THE A. E. F. IN IRELAND LINES UP FOR REVIEW

At an unidentified base the United States contingent stands ready for inspection by Major Gen. Russell P. Hartle, commander. Associated Press Radiophoto, passed yesterday by British censor

ALL ON SHIP SAVED AS U-BOAT SINKS HER

Tanker China Arrow Is Victim of a Daylight Attack—37 Drift 57 Hours in Boats

Another victim of Nazi submarines—the fifteenth attack acknowledged to have taken place in United States Atlantic waters since Jan. 14—was revealed yesterday when the Navy announced that the 8,403-ton oil tanker China Arrow had been sunk 100 miles off the coast in a bold daylight attack last Thursday morning.

A cheering note in the latest disaster was the fact that there was no loss of life. All thirty-seven members of the crew of the China Arrow, a sister ship to the 8,327-ton India Arrow that went down off New Jersey the day before, were picked up Saturday night after nearly fifty-seven hours at sea in three lifeboats, and were landed safely yesterday morning at Lewes, Del.

At the Lewes Coast Guard station Captain Paul Hoffman Browne, 46-year-old master of the Socony-Vacuum Oil Company tanker, and other survivors told the story of how the China Arrow met her end at an undisclosed position in the Atlantic.

Two Torpedoes Strike

At 11:15 A. M. Thursday two torpedoes struck the unarmed vessel almost simultaneously. The crew left the listing ship, but the captain and a 20-year-old radio operator, Kenneth W. Maynard, stayed aboard, hoping that help might come before the submarine struck a death blow.

Just before noon, however, the U-boat came to the surface 500 feet away from the China Arrow.

Continued on Page Eight

Japanese Striving to Crush Growing Allied Air Power

By F. TILLMAN DURDIN
By Telephone to THE NEW YORK TIMES.

BATAVIA, Netherlands Indies, Feb. 8—The continued Japanese air raids on Java and neighboring islands, coupled with the absence of any new sea-borne attacks on the Netherlands Indies in the last few days, are indicative of the carefulness with which the Japanese are conducting their campaign in Indonesia.

Mindful of the severe losses that their last big invasion convoy suffered under attacks by Netherland and American forces in the Strait of Macassar, the Japanese now appear to be attempting to facilitate their next move forward by crippling United Nations aviation and wrecking the main United Nations naval base at Surabaya.

The present lull in the Japanese offensive doubtless will be utilized to the fullest by a superior Japanese air force to inflict the greatest possible losses, both on the ground and in the air, on United Nations aviation and to cause the utmost damage to United Nations ships and naval establishments, in the hope that the Strait of Macassar blow cannot be repeated when a new Japanese convoy sets forth for Indies objectives.

The Japanese are well aware that the United Nations' air strength is steadily mounting in the Far East.

Allied Effort Intensified

Meanwhile, the United Nations are intensifying their efforts to add power of all kinds to the solid foundation represented by Netherland military strength in Java and other unoccupied Indies islands. Observers here liken the situation to that in Britain in early 1940, when the construction of a fortress and the acquisition of supplies from overseas had to be achieved in a period of time that seemed all too short.

Fortunately for the United Na-

Continued on Page Four

U. S. Generals' Daring on Bataan Improves Their Troops' Morale

By NAT FLOYD
Wireless to THE NEW YORK TIMES.

ON THE BATAAN PENINSULA, Feb. 6 (Delayed)—The high example of their officers and their experience in difficult jungle warfare for almost two months have tempered the spirit and improved the individual fighting technique of General Douglas MacArthur's forces.

A recent bitterly contested though small engagement in the jungle showed how the defenders are earning the title of veterans. Two brigadier generals, studying battle conditions at close range, calmly continued their work under fire. Although separated in time by two days the incidents occurred on the same battlefield within a space of 100 feet.

After a Japanese landing party of 200 to 300 men had been cut off, American and Filipino units established a line to contain the invaders. The ground was relatively level but was covered with tropical trees twenty to fifty feet high. Heavy underbrush and vines made progress virtually impossible without the use of bolo knives. Visibility was only twenty to twenty-five feet.

The only entrance to the area was a narrow dirt road at a corner at which the Japanese had established a strong point with one 47 mm. cannon, one heavy machine gun, eight machine guns and automatic rifles, all of which were dug in.

Various types of weapons were used against the unflankable strong point with the result that guns and

Continued on Page Three

WAVELL IN BURMA SEES FOE CHECKED

He Is Optimistic After Visit to Front—British Heavily Raid Foe Near Moulmein

By The Associated Press.

RANGOON, Burma, Feb. 8—Stanch British defenders of Burma and its vital gateway to China have checked the Japanese along the Salween River to the satisfaction of the United Nations Commander, General Sir Archibald P. Wavell, who visited the front a second time recently.

General Wavell's visit, disclosed today, spotlighted the Burma front as potentially perhaps the most important in opposing Japan's drive for hegemony over all of Eastern Asia.

General Wavell spoke with officers and men on the Moulmein front within sound of opposing artillery and was understood to have expressed "reasoned optimism" regarding the United Nations' position in the Southwest Pacific. He flew from Java, his headquarters in the threatened Netherlands Indies.

[British Blenheim bombers, escorted by R. A. F. and American volunteer fighter planes, have staged a heavy attack on Japanese positions on Kado Island in the mouth of the Salween River just north of Moulmein, The United Press reported today from Rangoon. The Japanese recently occupied the island as a stepping stone across the river to Martaban, but this port is still held by the British. All the United Nations planes returned safely from the raid.]

Meanwhile Sir Archibald Clark Kerr, recently transferred from Chungking to Moscow as British Ambassador, envisioned over the Calcutta radio a "big push" by American, British and Chinese troops against the Japanese, who are striking in from puppetized Thailand.

He did not explain his reference to American troops. He paid warm tribute to General Chiang Kai-shek, the Chinese leader, saying "China is safe in his hands."

"China has fought the Japanese to a standstill and will continue to fight like demons, putting their deep hatred into the conflict," the Ambassador said.

Air activity over Rangoon, chief

Continued on Page Six

STRAIT IS CROSSED

Foe Drives From Johore on West Coast After Move in East

BRIDGEHEAD ESTABLISHED

British Garrison Battles a Large Force of Invaders After Artillery Barrage

By The United Press.

SINGAPORE, Monday, Feb. 9—Japanese invasion troops in "some force" crossed the Strait of Johore last night and have established a bridgehead on the west coast of Singapore Island, it was announced officially today.

Imperial forces immediately engaged the invaders and fighting continued, the announcement said.

A hail of shells from British batteries mounted in the jungles and swamps of this beleaguered fortress was believed to have exacted a heavy toll among the invaders.

The enemy landing was effected under the protection of an earth-shaking barrage by Japanese siege guns drawn up on the Johore shore of the narrow strait that separates the island from the mainland. [Tokyo broadcasts claimed some Japanese tank units had landed on Singapore.]

British, Australian and Indian troops went into action as soon as outposts had flashed the alarm and reports from the front said merciless fighting was in progress in the jungle and swamps.

Artillery Duel Through Day

The landing came ten days after British Imperial forces had withdrawn from the Malayan mainland and less than twenty-four hours after a Japanese force had landed on Ubin Island, a scant half mile off the northeast coast of Singapore Island.

The invasion of Singapore itself was preceded by a lull in an artillery duel that had raged throughout yesterday between British guns on the northern shore of the island and Japanese batteries near Johore Bahru.

But early this morning every gun which the Japanese had been able to get within range of the island opened up with a tremendous roar that brought every man of the island garrison to the alert and put civilians of the 751,000 population into the front line of a grim and merciless fight.

As the guns blazed, an air raid alert sounded, then another. Japanese planes were flying over the island, close to the city, trying to observe the effect of the cannonading.

The city of Singapore is situated on the island's southeast shore, at least fifteen miles from the probable invasion point.

Blow Struck at Danger Spot

Under pre-arranged plans, the island garrison went into action and reserves moved up to the fighting lines where the advanced units were fighting with every weapon they could muster, hunting out the Japanese attackers in the thick jungle of the west coast swamps.

The west coast had been recognized as the great danger spot. It is less than a mile from the Johore short, it is the widest part of the island, and its terrain is admirably suited to the tactics of the Japanese infiltration troops who had crept down on Singapore from the top of Malaya.

The cannonading diminished somewhat about 8 A. M. as the invaders and the Imperial forces came to close fighting.

All over the island the Imperial troops were awaiting the alarm which would tell of another landing attempt, possibly from Ubin Island within striking distance of the dismantled naval base, a big Royal Air Force airdrome and heavily fortified Changi on the island's northeast tip.

Throughout yesterday small parties of Japanese had felt out the island defenses by making suicide sorties in various types of small craft across the strait.

Patrols had dealt with them

Continued on Page Four

"All the News That's Fit to Print."

The New York Times.

LATE CITY EDITION
Rain and warmer today.
Temperatures Yesterday—Max., 35; Min., 28

Copyright, 1942, by The New York Times Company.

VOL. XCI..No. 30,703. Entered as Second-Class Matter, Postoffice, New York, N. Y. NEW YORK, MONDAY, FEBRUARY 16, 1942. THREE CENTS NEW YORK CITY and Vicinity

SINGAPORE SURRENDERS UNCONDITIONALLY; CHURCHILL ASKS UNITY IN HOUR OF DEFEAT; FOE POURS INTO SUMATRA, STRIKES IN BURMA

78% REGISTERED HERE ON FIRST DAY OF THE THIRD DRAFT

Estimates Place Those Enrolled at 468,000, With 7,020,000 Listed in the Nation

ROLLS TO CLOSE TONIGHT

20-44 Age Group Brings Out Many Middle-Aged Men Who Are Nationally Known

List of registration places will be found on Page 13.

The third registration under the Selective Service Act went into full swing yesterday, particularly in cities, and when the books closed for the day at 9 P. M., indications were that perhaps 7,020,000 men in the United States and 468,000 in New York City had been written into the record of the nation's man-power.

Exact figures, in accordance with an Army announcement ten days ago, will not be made public. But reasonably accurate estimates were made possible by the statement of Colonel Arthur V. McDermott, director of the New York City draft system, that about 78 per cent of those required to register this time had done so by closing time last night.

It has been generally believed that the current "T" or father-and-son draft would affect 9,000,000 men throughout the country and 600,000 within the five boroughs. The assumption that the local turnout would apply on a percentage basis from coast to coast seemed reasonable because of the sleety weather here; which some officials felt would mean that if the percentage differed elsewhere, it would be greater, but surely not less.

Every Class Is Tapped

Regardless of figures, the third draft, like the first two, tapped every stratum of American life. Applying to the 20-44-year age group, but not including those who signed up on either Oct. 16, 1940 or July 1, 1941, it dipped into the large group of men in early middle life that includes some of the nation's best known names in all fields of endeavor.

Many of them may not register until today — when registration centers will be open from 7 A. M. to 9 P. M. throughout the land. But today will be the last chance, and by tonight the roll of potential draftees will have been expanded to take in the following, including several who appeared yesterday:

Former Colonel Charles A. Lindbergh, 40 years old on Feb. 4; former District Attorney Thomas E. Dewey and his successor, Frank S. Hogan, both 39; Acting Governor Charles Poletti, 38; Council President Newbold Morris, 40; John Barbirolli, conductor, 42; Controller Joseph D. McGoldrick, 40; President R. M. Hutchins of the University of Chicago, 43, and Carl Hubbell, veteran baseball pitcher, 39.

Celebrated entertainers, writers, business men, educators and scientists also were on the list.

But the drama of the father-son draft lay not in the "big names" involved so much as in it bridging of two generations; and its reaching out to touch thousands of Americans whose national and racial backgrounds were as diffuse as their idiosyncrasies and their incomes.

Fathers literally appeared with sons, and in at least one case, a father was registrar while the son was registrant. Veterans who bore the scars of World War I appeared, ready to join the list of potential eligibles for World War II; a good example was Andrew W. Knebel of Addison, N. Y., State com-

Continued on Page Three

Australia Arrests Aliens Along Coast

By The Associated Press.

BRISBANE, Australia, Monday, Feb. 16—Hundreds of enemy aliens, mostly Italian sugar-field workers, were arrested in a widespread round-up Friday night and Saturday in North Queensland. The sugar belt lies along the coast where Japanese could land in an attempted invasion.

A special barred and guarded train is taking the aliens southward for internment at Townsville. The Italians had been boasting, according to newspapers, that "the Japanese won't touch us." Many had hidden firearms.

SYDNEY, Australia, Feb. 15 (From Australian broadcast recorded by The United Press in New York)—The government completed plans today for the registration of all male aliens tomorrow and Tuesday

HEATING WITH GAS CURTAILED BY WPB

New York Is Among Seventeen States Named in Order to Supply War Industries

Special to The New York Times.

WASHINGTON, Feb. 15—Curtailment in the consumption of natural and mixed natural and manufactured gas was ordered by the War Production Board today to assure adequate supplies for war production activities.

Curtailment is necessary, the board said, because of increased gas requirements for both war purposes and civilian use, coupled with the scarcity of materials that would be required if existing systems were expanded.

One of increased war production uses of natural gas will be the program to manufacture 400,000 tons of synthetic rubber, the major part of which will be made from butadiene, which is produced from natural gas.

Part of the WPB's order becomes effective on March 1 and applies to seventeen States, including New York and the District of Columbia "where the need for curtailment is greater." Other parts

Continued on Page Ten

PREMIER IS SOMBER

Calls Singapore Military Disaster, but He Warns Against Weakness

ACCLAIMS U. S. ENTRY

Lists It as Dream 'Come to Pass'—Gives Russia as Example in Peril

The text of Mr. Churchill's address is on Page 6.

By ROBERT P. POST

Wireless to The New York Times.

LONDON, Feb. 15—The entrance of the United States into the war is a fact that cannot be compared with anything else "in the whole world." Prime Minister Churchill said in a world broadcast tonight.

When he surveyed the power of the United States and its resources and felt that they were now in it "with the British Commonwealth of Nations, all together, however long it lasts, till death or victory." Mr. Churchill said that this was the first and greatest event he had to report to the British people.

"That is what I have dreamed of, aimed at and worked for and now it has come to pass," Mr. Churchill said.

But at the same time he balanced the good of the latest war developments—in which he included the efforts of Russia—against the heavy and grave events elsewhere. And frankly telling the people throughout the world that he spoke "under the shadow of a heavy and far-reaching military defeat," the loss of Singapore, Mr. Churchill went on to call for a spirit of unity and new exertions in this dark hour.

Adverse news "of many misfortunes and gnawing anxieties lie before us," Mr. Churchill said, but from that very fact he invoked a new spirit of toughness from the people who march against the Axis.

Perhaps with reference to the widespread spirit of uneasiness that has covered this country and

Continued on Page Six

SINGAPORE SURRENDERS: WHERE TERMS WERE SET AND 2 SIGNATORIES

The Ford Motor Company plant where commanding officers of British and Japanese armies conferred

Associated Press

Lieut. Gen. Tomoyuki Yamashita

Lieut. Gen. Arthur E. Percival

2-WAY BURMA DRIVE AIMS AT RAIL TOWN

Japanese Strike for Thaton on Line to Rangoon—R. A. F. Bombs Supplies

By The Associated Press.

RANGOON, Burma, Feb. 15—Japanese forces struck from two directions tonight at Thaton, forty miles northwest of Martaban on the Rangoon railroad, and the battle for the east coast of the Gulf of Martaban neared its climax.

The invaders are attacking from seaside landing points above captured Martaban as well as from a deep salient thrust from their Salween River bridgehead at Paan, unofficial reports said.

The Army communiqué merely said:

"There were no further attacks on the Salween front but reports indicate the enemy is preparing for an attack in the area of Duyinzaik-Thaton."

British bombers, accompanied by American fighters, heavily bombed enemy supply dumps at Paan and Martaban and swept wide over enemy-occupied territory on reconnaissance flights. Canadians piloted two of the Blenheim bombers that blasted and machine-gunned a Japanese troop camp at Martaban and river craft and motor vehicles.

The Blenheims flew with a fighter screen of American and British fighters and pressed home two heavy attacks yesterday. Some defense fire was encountered but all Allied planes returned safely.

The Japanese have established bridgeheads over the Salween at Paan and Martaban and it was there that the British bombers concentrated.

The front flared into battle today; twenty-four hours after bombers had thinned the enemy lines so

Continued on Page Two

Ships Land Foe in Sumatra; Dutch Blow Up Oil Property

By F. TILLMAN DURDIN

By Telephone to The New York Times.

BATAVIA, Netherlands Indies, Monday, Feb. 16—The Japanese, having opened their drive on Sumatra with a parachute attack Saturday on the Palembang oil region, continued their campaign yesterday with a large-scale landing of troops from ships on the coast about sixty miles from Palembang. The landing was made in an area of marshes and mangrove swamps along the muddy banks of the Musi River, which leads to Palembang.

The Indies defense forces in the Palembang region have started the destruction of one of the world's greatest oil fields, together with refineries and other installations.

The Japanese parachute-troop attack on Saturday, made in an attempt to forestall the destruction, has failed, and it was announced in Batavia yesterday that the wrecking of all "vital points" in the vicinity of Palembang began Saturday night.

The destruction of the Palembang oil fields, stores and machinery will represent a loss of properties worth more than $100,000,000. However, it is a move that will ultimately be a major contribution to the fight against the Japanese. It denies to the enemy more than 50 per cent of the oil production of the Netherlands Indies.

Enemy Aim Frustrated

Nearly all the other oil-producing areas of the Indies already have been destroyed and thus the main aim of the Japanese attack on Indonesia—to obtain oil quickly—has been frustrated.

The Netherlanders reported that nearly all the Japanese parachute troops who landed Saturday, in the vicinity of the refineries of the Socony-Vacuum and Netherland companies, had been counted for. Of an estimated 700 soldiers

Continued on Page Two

M'ARTHUR EXPECTS BIG ENEMY ATTACK

Reports Japanese Regrouping on Bataan for a Resumption of Their Offensive

By C. BROOKS PETERS

Special to The New York Times.

WASHINGTON, Feb. 15—General Douglas MacArthur reported from his Philippine stronghold on the Island of Luzon today that enemy preparations for the long-anticipated all-out Japanese offensive against the American and Filipino positions in the Battle of Bataan were visibly under way. He suggested that the attack was imminent.

General MacArthur said that the enemy was regrouping his forces. The evident objective of such a regrouping, he added, would be "a resumption of the offensive."

Now that the mighty British bastion of the East, Singapore, has fallen, the Bataan front remains the only theatre of the war in which the Japanese have been unable to advance almost at will and achieve their objectives.

It may be that, regardless of the sacrifices in men and equipment that a devastating assault would cost, the enemy will consider an overpowering attack justified to

Continued on Page Four

Bataan 'One-Man Army' Kills 116 On Raids Behind Japanese Lines

By CLARK LEE

Associated Press Correspondent

ON THE BATAAN PENINSULA, Feb. 13 (Delayed)—Captain Arthur W. Wermuth of Chicago, who has killed 116 Japanese and captured many more, is America's No. 1 one-man army to his fellow-officers of the Fifty-seventh Filipino Scout Regiment.

He "absolutely accounted" for at least 116 Japanese with his 45-caliber tommy-gun and Garand rifle, his fighting companions said today. He has won the silver star for gallantry, the Distinguished Service Cross for extraordinary heroism, and the Purple Heart with two clasps.

Thrice wounded, he spent more than two weeks in January more behind the Japanese lines than in the American line. He has led so many scouting raids he has lost count. His actions have forestalled many enemy attacks and prepared the way for American counter-attacks.

I finally located him today, just out of the hospital and on his way to battle. At dinner, I got part of his story and other officers gave me the rest.

Captain Wermuth, who is from Chicago, fights the war as he played football for Northwestern Military Academy at Lake Geneva, Wis.—fearlessly and for keeps. This 190-pounder with a Van Dyke beard is at home in the Bataan Mountains, where he has spent many years. He knew life in the open before he saw Bataan. His

Continued on Page Four

WASHINGTON SEES DIRE BLOW IN EAST

Sumatra Is Expected to Fall, Cutting Off Allies' Main Oil Supply in the Indies

By JAMES B. RESTON

Special to The New York Times.

WASHINGTON, Feb. 15—The considered judgment of responsible officials in Washington is that the fall of Singapore marks the darkest moment of the war for the United Nations. Even the anticipation of the event and the rhetoric of Winston Churchill did not minimize the feeling that this blow may be decisive in the Southwest Pacific and may vitally affect the outcome of the conflict in China and the Middle East.

If there was any confidence in the fate of Sumatra, with its rich oil fields and coast line bordering the Malacca Strait, the feeling here would not be so pessimistic, but it is virtually conceded that Sumatra, too, must inevitably fall, cutting the United Nations off from their main supply of oil in the Southwest Pacific and leaving the Japanese free passage into the Indian Ocean from where they can raid the Allied supply lines to China, Suez and the Persian Gulf.

The only bright spot in this dreary picture is some indication that more United States aircraft have arrived in Java, though deliveries to the Netherlands Indies from the United States are only about one-quarter of what the Dutch have ordered. The number of aircraft involved in these recent deliveries cannot be disclosed, but there is reason to believe that enough were landed to give the Dutch some chance of sending a few planes into the air against the invaders.

Also, there was confidence among United Nations' representatives here that the battle of production will bring the tools of war

Continued on Page Five

BRITISH CAPITULATE

Troops to Keep Order Until Foe Completes Occupation of Base

3 DRIVES HEM CITY

Tokyo Claims Toll of 32 Allied Vessels South of Singapore

By JAMES MacDONALD

Special Cable to The New York Times.

LONDON, Feb. 15—Singapore has fallen.

The long dreaded news that the key British base of the Pacific and Indian Oceans would be captured by the Japanese—a major reverse clearly foreseen many days ago—was announced tonight by Winston Churchill, a few hours after dispatches from Vichy and Tokyo reported that Lieut. Gen. Arthur E. Percival's forces had surrendered unconditionally at 3:30 P. M. today British daylight saving time [9:50 P. M. Sunday Singapore time and 10:30 A. M. Eastern war time].

London officials naturally declined to disclose what plans had been made or were perhaps in the making for establishing a naval base elsewhere to meet the grave emergency arising from the loss of Singapore. They could not or would not divulge how many Imperial troops were taken prisoner or how many got away.

Commanders Meet

According to the official Tokyo announcement, fighting ceased along the entire front three hours after a meeting between General Percival and the Japanese Commander in Chief, Lieut. Gen. Tomoyuki Yamashita, in the Ford motor plant at the foot of Timah Hill, where the documents of surrender were signed. The terms were not disclosed here, but a Japanese Domei Agency dispatch late tonight said that under the capitulation up to 1,000 armed British soldiers would remain in Singapore City to maintain order until the Japanese Army completed occupation.

Similar terms, it is recalled, were contained in the surrender of Hong Kong on Christmas Day.

The Tokyo radio said the Japanese had constantly kept pouring in fresh troops to make up for losses from the fierce resistance of British Imperial troops.

In the final battle, three Japanese columns were said to have advanced on the city. Yesterday the central column completed occupation of the water reservoirs and a part of this column reached the northern outskirts of the city on a six-mile front. Another column bypassed the reservoirs, crossed the Kranag River and cut the road from Singapore to the civil airport. The third column reached Alexandria Road in the western part of the city.

Some Resisting, Tokyo Says

[Japanese units left the main island in barges and seized Blakang Mati, the island opposite Keppel Harbor, thereby gaining control of the sea approach to Singapore from the south, according to a Tokyo broadcast recorded by The United Press.

[Japanese troops entered Singapore City today under the terms of the surrender by the British, but a Domei dispatch said some of the defending forces and "other hostile elements" still were resisting, another Tokyo broadcast heard by The United Press stated.]

The Berlin radio, quoting the Japanese newspaper Asahi, said the largest part of the British and Australian forces "obviously" left Singapore Friday for Sumatra.

Unofficial reports reached London late tonight that 2,000 persons

Continued on Page Four

The War Summarized

MONDAY, FEBRUARY 16, 1942

Japan became the master of Singapore yesterday. At Rangoon, back door to China, civilian evacuation went on. Japanese troops were invading Southern Sumatra, stepping stone to Java.

In London Winston Churchill warned the British people to remain united behind their government, but expressed no word of optimism regarding the immediate future in the Far Eastern war theatre.

Prime Minister Churchill announced the fall of Singapore a few hours after the Tokyo radio had announced that hostilities ceased. The British Army, according to the Tokyo report, surrendered unconditionally. The surrender came one week after the Japanese had started to storm the island. [1:8; map, p. 4.] Official Washington called the fall of Singapore the darkest moment of the war. [1:7.]

The British Prime Minister's broadcast drew Britain's attention to Russian firmness in supporting the government in the hour of peril and emphasized the great importance of American entry into the war. [1:3].

The invaders that landed in Southern Sumatra apparently intended to drive on the Palembang oil center. Netherland bombers attacked Japanese transports and scored hits. Fewer than 100 of 700 Japanese parachutists who had landed in the Palembang zone Saturday escaped, according to Batavia; the Tokyo radio claimed, however, that the parachutists had occupied several important positions. [1:5-6; map, p. 2.]

In Burma the Japanese were developing drives from two directions toward Thaton on the Martaban - Rangoon Railway. Landing parties were moving inland from the seacoast above Martaban and the Japanese were moving out from their Salween River bridgehead up the river at Paan. Protected by American fighter planes, British bombers attacked enemy supply dumps at Paan and Martaban. [1:4; map, p. 2.]

General MacArthur's report from the Philippines indicated that the Japanese were advancing preparations for another full-fledged offensive against his Bataan positions. Enemy front-line forces, which had suffered heavy casualties, were being relieved by fresh troops. [1:5.]

Germany was reported to be drawing on her "Spring offensive" reserves for the campaign in Russia, but without, as yet, halting the Russian advance. Moscow said Soviet columns at one point were about seventy-five miles from the former Polish frontier. [8:2.]

British and Australian pilots flying planes made in the United States smashed a formation of thirty of the Axis' dive-bombers and fighters in Libya near El Gazala. Twenty of the enemy planes were shot down. In the Mediterranean, submarines sank two Axis supply ships and probably a third. A fourth ship was set afire by British bombers. On land the Germans seemed to be attempting to flank the British lines before Tobruk. [7:1]

"All the News That's Fit to Print."

The New York Times.

LATE CITY EDITION
Mild and windy today.
Temperatures Yesterday—Max., 49; Min., 37

Copyright, 1942, by The New York Times Company.

VOL. XCI—No. 30,734. Entered as Second-Class Matter, Postoffice, New York, N. Y. NEW YORK, WEDNESDAY, MARCH 18, 1942. THREE CENTS NEW YORK CITY and Vicinity

M'ARTHUR IN AUSTRALIA AS ALLIED COMMANDER; MOVE HAILED AS FORESHADOWING TURN OF TIDE; THIRD NATIONAL ARMY DRAFT BEGINS IN CAPITAL

PRESIDENT WARNS AGAINST RUSHING ANTI-STRIKES LAW

No Problem Exists at Present and Things Are Going Along Pretty Well, He Cautions

HE EXPLAINS 40-HOUR ACT

But Bill to Ban It Is Pushed to Hearings in House—Senate Also Swept by Debate

By W. H. LAWRENCE
Special to THE NEW YORK TIMES.

WASHINGTON, March 17 — President Roosevelt, at the moment when Congressional sentiment for anti-strike legislation became accentuated, stated today that there was no strike problem at the present moment and cautioned against rushing labor legislation to enactment when things were going along pretty well.

Congress, Mr. Roosevelt told his press conference this afternoon, could not pass a law that would make a man turn out more work. That, he observed, was up to the enthusiasm of the individual. More parades, band playing and flag waving, he suggested, would stir up enthusiasm more than restrictive law.

Organized labor, meanwhile, reported that the President was in agreement that the performance of labor was "exceptional, and, of course, satisfactory." It was agreed, spokesmen said, that voluntary action on the part of labor to yield its right to strike was a more satisfactory answer to the production problem than resort to legislation such as has been presented to the House in the last twenty-four hours.

Action Demanded in Congress

On Capitol Hill, however, steps toward legislative action persisted.

On the House side plans were made to go ahead with almost immediate hearings on a bill which would suspend the forty-hour week for the duration, would freeze open and closed shop conditions, and also clamp ceilings upon industry's profits on war contracts. Demands for Congressional action, which centered in the House yesterday, swept across the Capitol today to the Senate, where, for more than four hours, they displaced other thought and business.

Mr. Roosevelt told the press conference that he favors continuance of time-and-a-half pay for work over forty hours a week, but revealed that he had called upon the "combined Labor War Board," composed of six representatives of the American Federation of Labor and Congress of Industrial Organizations, to give up union contract rules which require double pay for work on Sundays. William Green, president of the A. F. of L., and Philip Murray, president of the C. I. O., and other representatives of both labor organizations visited the White House a few hours before the press conference.

Advocating continuous operation of plants to speed up the production of war materials, the President in his press conference remarks urged plant management to adopt a staggered shift system under which workers would receive double pay only if they worked seven consecutive days.

Says Law Is Misunderstood

Decrying "an amazing state of public misinformation," which he blamed in part upon the newspapers and irresponsible speeches in Congress, the President told of receiving a letter from a professional economist, who drew the conclusion that Japan would not have declared war and the United States would not have lost the Philippines or the Dutch East Indies if 30,000,000 man-days had not been lost by strikes in the first twenty-one months of the defense program.

The President said, with a smile,

Continued on Page Twenty

Gen. Homma Suicide Confirmed by Chilean

By The United Press.

SANTIAGO, Chile, March 17—The suicide of General Masahara Homma, commander of the Japanese forces in the Philippines, as reported by General Douglas MacArthur, was confirmed today by Carlos Barry, a Chilean journalist stranded in Japan, in a report to his newspaper, the Chileno.

Señor Barry and five other Chilean newspaper men, guests of the Japanese Government on a visit to Japan and Manchuria, were on their way home on a Japanese steamer when the Japanese bombed Pearl Harbor. Their ship turned about and landed them again at Yokohama. They now await passage on a vessel returning exchanged Western Hemisphere diplomats.

50% AIRPLANE RISE REPORTED BY NELSON

He Warns Three-Month Gain Is Not Enough—K. T. Keller Asked to Head Output

Text of Mr. Nelson's address is printed on Page 18.

Special to THE NEW YORK TIMES.

WASHINGTON, March 17—Plane production has been stepped up 50 per cent since Pearl Harbor, Donald M. Nelson, chairman of the War Production Board, said tonight in a radio address. He warned, however, that there was no reason for complacency, because the country was nowhere near its goals.

"We need more and forever more of these weapons and we need them now," he said. "We have got to realize the value of time."

It was learned tonight that K. T. Keller, president of the Chrysler Corporation, had been strongly urged by the War Production Board to direct the agency's airplane production program and to effect "short cuts" which will make possible the production of a greater

Continued on Page Eighteen

3,485 FIRST NUMBER

All Night Is Required for Drawing That Affects 9,000,000 Men

USE IN NAVY IS URGED

Hershey Also Suggests Assigning Some Labor for War Projects

List of the draft numbers drawn is on Pages 12, 13 and 14.

Secretary of War Stimson drew the first number—3,485—from the famous goldfish bowl in Washington at 6:05 o'clock last night to begin America's third draft lottery in seventeen months, although its first in wartime since 1918.

The drawing continued throughout the night. By 6 A. M. 6,000 of the 7,000 numbers had been listed and it was expected that the lottery would be completed by 8 o'clock.

Green capsules containing the serial numbers of those who registered last month, drawn in this St. Patrick's Day lottery, gave to 9,000,000 men between 20 and 44 years of age the green light to go ahead in the tasks to which they may be assigned in total war against Hitler and the Japanese. Green cards will be used in Selective Service headquarters to record the order of their liability to military service.

In a brief introductory address Brig. Gen. Lewis B. Hershey, Director of Selective Service, urged conscription of men for the Navy as well as the Army and suggested that at least on some war projects labor also should be "selected."

The No. 1 boy of the draft in New York City, just as on the two previous occasions, was a Chinese—Chin Fong Ho, a 20-year-old waiter born in China, now living in New York's Chinatown and

Continued on Page Fifteen

M'ARTHURMEN: ON THE ALERT EN ROUTE TO AUSTRALIA

Gun crew manning a mobile anti-aircraft gun on one of the transports—the fighters and the gun are now on the island-continent
Additional photographs appear on Page 3.
The New York Times (official U. S. Navy)

NAZIS CLOSE PORTS OF NORTH NORWAY

Reported Adding to Forces—British Say Tirpitz Eluded Torpedo-Plane Attack

By The Associated Press.

LONDON, March 17—All Norway's ports from North Cape to Aalesund had been closed by the Germans today, presumably to screen stealthy marshaling of German military and naval forces that indicated that those far-northern waters were about to become a newly active major war theatre.

Speaking just after a disclosure that the mighty German battleship Tirpitz "appears to have avoided" a recent British torpedo-plane attack off Narvik, and thus even now is presumably loose upon the high seas, a responsible London informant speculated that the Germans were preparing attempts to isolate Russia's Arctic ports, cut her supply lines from her allies or even move against United States-garrisoned and British-garrisoned Iceland.

Another View Suggested

Another informant, who is in constant communication with the Norwegians, suggested a second possible interpretation—that the Germans were worried about the possibilities of United Nations response to Russian calls for the opening of a second front.

And in that connection he declared that Norway was seething against the Germans.

Among the day's accumulating incidents that pointed to major action in the north, the sharpest and most alarming in British eyes was the news that the Tirpitz had not been run to cover.

The British source who said that the Tirpitz "appears to have avoided" attacks in the vicinity of Narvik March 9 added that he had "no information" about her present whereabouts. After the torpedo-plane attack, he said, the Tirpitz retired to the coast under a smoke screen and was lost there among the fjords.

When the attack on the Tirpitz was made, he continued, she probably was within cover of fighter protection, but "the attacks were pressed home under rather difficult weather conditions."

He said that the Tirpitz and the German 10,000-ton cruiser Prinz Eugen had been located in a fjord near Trondheim before the Tirpitz had sailed, that the Prinz Eugen had been torpedoed on the passage to Trondheim, and that thus the three ships that made a dash recently through the English Channel—the Prinz Eugen and the Ger-

Continued on Page Nine

MacArthur Party in 2 Planes Soars Over Japanese Fronts

By BYRON DARNTON
Wireless to THE NEW YORK TIMES.

UNITED STATES ARMY HEADQUARTERS, in Australia, Wednesday, March 18—General Douglas MacArthur flew over some of the hottest fighting areas in the Southwestern Pacific on his journey of more than 2,000 miles from the Philippines to assume supreme command of the United Nations' forces in this area, it was revealed this morning when news of the general's arrival with his family and staff was made public.

Two United States Army planes were used for the journey. General MacArthur has not yet arrived at headquarters, although he is in Australia and has assumed command. Some of his officers are here, and they are in the best of health. It is understood that General MacArthur and his family are resting after their journey, but that he will arrive at headquarters soon. He is tired.

It was officially disclosed that the appointment of General MacArthur had been made with the "most enthusiastic" approval of Australia. American correspondents here have heard repeatedly from Australian civilians and soldiers the question, "Why don't you send us MacArthur?"

Details of the general's journey have not yet been fully revealed, but it was explained that the long flight had taken the party over the areas of the heaviest recent Japanese activity. Whether the planes used by the MacArthur party had been dispatched from Australia for that purpose or already were in the Philippines was not disclosed. But the feat demonstrates that communications exist between the

Continued on Page Five

URUGUAYAN VESSEL, TWO OTHERS SUNK

Nation Seizes German Ship in Retaliation—Fourth Craft Feared Lost in Bahamas

The sinking of at least three, and possibly four, ships by Axis submarines operating off our Atlantic coast was disclosed yesterday. The victims were a medium-sized merchant ship of United States registry, a 5,785-ton Uruguayan vessel, an unidentified vessel from which fifty-seven survivors were landed in Nassau, and possibly a large United States tanker reported sunk in the Bahamas.

Most important from the standpoint of international relations was the Uruguayan ship Montevideo, which was sent to the bottom with seventeen of her crew off Jeremie, Haiti. Her loss brought the number of South American republics that have suffered submarine sinkings to three. Four Brazilian ships have been torpedoed and on Monday the sinking of the Chilean freighter Toltén was announced.

In swift retaliation the Uruguayan Government seized the 8,268-ton German ship Tacoma, which had been interned in Uruguayan waters ever since the destruction of the pocket battleship Graf Spee in December, 1939.

Uruguay, which had already broken off relations with the Axis powers, ordered the suspension of further sailings of her ships until arrangements could be made to safeguard them. It was expected, according to The Associated Press, that the government would arm them. In view of the public indignation caused by the announcement of the sinking, the Uruguayan Government placed guards over the property of Axis nationals.

Previously 200 rioting students had stoned a toy shop operated by a Spaniard believed to be a member of the pro-Fascist Falangists and called for the imprisoning of a Uruguayan nationalist leader.

Foreign Minister Alberto Guani

Continued on Page Seventeen

PLEASED AUSTRALIA GREETS A 'FIGHTER'

MacArthur Warmly Welcomed—British Expect That Policy of Defense Will End

By The Associated Press.

MELBOURNE, Australia, Wednesday, March 18 — General Douglas MacArthur's arrival to assume the United Nations command in the Southwestern Pacific was hailed jubilantly by the Australian press today as the most important and most welcome move thus far in the defense of this Commonwealth.

"It will be regarded as the best single piece of news since the outbreak of the Pacific war," said one editorial. "His gallant stand in the Philippines has fired the imagination of Australians, who love a fighter, and his command of Australians in addition to American troops will be an inspiration to the fighting forces."

[In London it was suggested that the appointment of General MacArthur, which was highly approved, meant that the United Nations intended to substitute offense for defense in the Far East.]

The selection of so high a United States officer for the important post, it was pointed out, gives emphasis to the statement by Secretary of War Henry L. Stimson that "considerable" American forces are here.

"It is also an indication," the newspaper added, "of President Roosevelt's realization of how important is the Southwest Pacific in this global war and of what aid the

Continued on Page Five

Bill for Women's Auxiliary Corps Of 150,000 Passed by the House

By NONA BALDWIN
Special to THE NEW YORK TIMES.

WASHINGTON, March 17—The House passed today a bill creating a volunteer Women's Army Auxiliary Corps, whose members, by taking over duties now performed behind the lines by enlisted men, would release many men for combat duty. The roll-call vote was 249 to 86.

The bill, sponsored by Representative Edith Nourse Rogers of Massachusetts, was passed with two amendments, the major one limiting the strength of the corps to 150,000. The other permits Army nurses to enroll in the corps.

The bulk of the four-hour discussion on the measure revolved around the extent to which Army discipline and military law would apply to members of the WAAC. Reading Section 2 of the Articles of War, Chairman May of the Committee on Military Affairs expressed the opinion that members of the WAAC would be subject to court-martial.

The issue was raised by Representative Nichols of Oklahoma in proposing an amendment to entitle members of the corps to the same compensation, pensions and disability claims that are extended to soldiers. The amendment was rejected by a standing vote of 70 to 30, but his contention that, under the

Continued on Page Twenty-one

GENERAL FLIES OUT

Wife, Child Accompany Him on Trip From Philippine Post

ORDER BY PRESIDENT

Roosevelt Asserts All Americans Back It—Expect Action Now

By CHARLES HURD
Special to THE NEW YORK TIMES.

WASHINGTON, March 17 — General Douglas MacArthur today became Supreme Commander of the United Nations forces in the Southwestern Pacific.

This dramatic shift of command and promotion for the dashing officer who has held the Japanese at bay on the Island of Luzon for three months and ten days was announced by the War Department simultaneously with his arrival in Australia. Traveling by plane, he arrived with his staff and his wife and child.

A few hours after announcement of the action, President Roosevelt told a press conference that he was "sure that every American" agreed with his decision to take General MacArthur out of the Philippines.

He recognized, he said, that Axis propaganda agents would see in this move abandonment of the Philippines, but this is not the case. General MacArthur will command everything, including sea and air forces, east of Singapore in the Southwestern Pacific, the President added, and will be more useful in Australia than on Bataan Peninsula.

President's Statement

Finally, the President authorized quotation of the following statement:

"I know that every man and woman in the United States admires with me General MacArthur's determination to fight to the finish with his men in the Philippines. But I also know that every man and woman is in agreement that all important decisions must be made with a view toward the successful termination of the war. Knowing this, I am sure that every American, if faced individually with the question as to where General MacArthur could best serve his country, could come to only one answer."

[Lieut. Gen. George H. Brett, United States Army, is Deputy Supreme Commander of the United Nations Forces in the Southwest Pacific and is in command of all the United Nations air forces in the region, according to a United Press dispatch from Melbourne, Australia.]

No move made by the United States Government since the war began has had a more vivid or optimistic reaction than this one. Officials in and out of Congress rushed to commend the action, and reports from New York indicated that the Stock Exchange immediately registered higher prices.

In the reaction manifested here were two indicated causes for optimism. One was the feeling that General MacArthur was equal to the task of stemming the Japanese advance southward, in view of his record in the Philippines, and of planning future offensive operations. The other was a belief that perhaps he had not been assigned to the High Command until United Nations intelligence officers felt that there was a good chance of changing the tide of battle.

On Washington's Birthday

In any event, he landed somewhere in Australia not long after the arrival of heavy United States air and ground forces, sent to augment the Australian troops. The action, in which Australia endorsed the choice of General MacArthur, has been a closely guarded secret since Feb. 22, when President Roosevelt ordered General

Continued on Page Three

The War Summarized

WEDNESDAY, MARCH 18, 1942

General Douglas MacArthur assumed command of the United Nations forces in Australia and the Southwest Pacific yesterday at a moment when both sides in the war were evidently devoting themselves principally to preparations for offensives later in the Spring. Only in Russia was there heavy action, with Soviet forces pounding furiously at the Staraya Russa sector and at Kharkov.

Washington announced that General MacArthur had already arrived in Australia by order of President Roosevelt. He has assumed command by request of the Australian Government. His command will include the Philippines, where he has been succeeded by Major Gen. Wainwright. Although the President announced that General MacArthur's withdrawal did not mean the Philippines were to be abandoned, the Japanese yesterday staged their first assault since March 8 on the Bataan defense line. They were sharply repulsed. [1:8.]

At the United States Army Headquarters in Australia it was disclosed that two Army planes had been used for General MacArthur's flight and that they had passed through areas of the most intense Japanese activity. The greatest secrecy was observed, and not even Premier Curtin of Australia was informed until the flight had been completed. [1:5-6.]

High officials of the government in Washington and Congressional leaders were unanimous in praising Mr. Roosevelt's decision to send General MacArthur to Australia. [4:4.]

In Britain General MacArthur's appointment was hailed as a demonstration of the coordination existing between the Empire and the United States. [4:1.]

Australians called the selection the best news since the outbreak of the war in the Far East. [1:7.]

In Burma Chinese troops on the Allied left flank routed Japanese-officered Thai troops. [8:1; with map.]

During a British parliamentary debate the assertion was made that the thirteen United Nations naval ships destroyed off Java had had to oppose a force of ninety-nine Japanese war vessels. [8:5.]

A possible new development in the European sphere was foreshadowed by a German order closing all Norway's ports from North Cape to Aalesund. The order suggested that German troop and naval movements of some importance were being screened. [1:4; map, P. 9.]

The Soviet reports indicated that the Germans were being forced back northwest and west of Kharkov in fierce hand-to-hand fighting. Advance units appeared to have broken through the surrounding fortifications at one point and to be engaged in a house-to-house battle. [7:1.]

Germany's increasing grip on French North Africa was demonstrated by a Vichy order for the internment of all Britons between the ages of 18 and 50 living on the coast of Morocco. [9:1.]

The sinking of three and possibly four vessels in our Atlantic waters was disclosed, including one Uruguayan ship. Uruguay promptly seized the German ship Tacoma, lying in Montevideo harbor. [1:5.] In Santiago, Chile, anti-Axis rioting broke out because of the sinking last Friday off New York of the Chilean ship Toltén. [17:1.]

"All the News That's Fit to Print."

The New York Times.

LATE CITY EDITION
Rain today and not much change in temperatures.
Temperatures Yesterday—Max., 53; Min., 35

Copyright, 1942, by The New York Times Company.

VOL. XCI..No. 30,757. Entered as Second-Class Matter, Postoffice, New York, N. Y. NEW YORK, FRIDAY, APRIL 10, 1942. THREE CENTS NEW YORK CITY and Vicinity

JAPANESE CAPTURE BATAAN AND 36,000 TROOPS; SINK TWO BRITISH CRUISERS; ITALIANS LOSE ONE; INDIA REPORTED AGREEING ON NATIVE COUNCIL

SENATOR AND JONES CLASH OVER ATTACK ON WAR PLANT DEAL

Bunker Charges DPC Condones 'Unconscionable Profits' for Nevada Magnesium Plant

UNTRUE, SAYS SECRETARY

Fees Paid to 9 Contractors, He Adds, Will Be Less Than 2% of Cost of 70 Millions

Special to THE NEW YORK TIMES.

WASHINGTON, April 9—Senator Bunker, Democrat, of Nevada, today attacked the Defense Plant Corporation, an RFC subsidiary, charging that the terms of its contract with Basic Magnesium, Inc., for a plant at Las Vegas, Nev., meant "unconscionable profits." Secretary Jones, as head of the RFC, immediately replied that the charges were misleading and untrue, and, in effect, challenged Senator Bunker to press them without benefit of Senatorial immunity.

The Secretary of Commerce replied to Senator Bunker in a statement.

"Senator Bunker's statements accusing RFC officials of wrongdoing," he said, "are unworthy of a United States Senator and cannot go unchallenged. The Senator must know these statements are untrue.

"The magnesium plant that is being built by the government near Las Vegas, Nev., will cost approximately $70,000,000 and have an estimated annual capacity of 112,000,000 pounds of metallic magnesium.

Says Fees Total Less Than 2%

"Nine separate contractors are participating in the construction. The fees to be paid the nine contracting and engineering firms, together with the fee to Basic Magnesium, Inc., for its engineering plans, supervision and 'know-how,' will aggregate less than 2 per cent of the total cost of the plant.

"The operating or management fee of the plant is to be half cent per pound of magnesium produced, which is approximately 2 per cent of the estimated cost.

"The royalty for the ores will not exceed ¼ cent per pound of magnesium metal produced.

"No irregularities have been discovered in the construction of the plant that would warrant the irresponsible statements made by Senator Bunker. The plant is wholly owned by the government and will be operated for its account. All expenditures in connection with the construction of the plant as well as its operation are carefully audited as the work progresses.

"Defense Plant Corporation contracted with Basic Magnesium, Inc., for the construction of this plant at the request of OPM and the War Department, and the government's interest is fully protected.

"Senator Bunker's speech contains many false and misleading statements, which it takes no courage to make under his cloak of immunity."

"Sinister," Bunker Contends

In his speech in the Senate the Nevada Senator said:

"Those individuals who have participated in unconscionable profits in America and who have slowed down our war production are worthy of the disgust and contempt of every American."

He contended that the data he presented were sufficient "to warrant the conclusion that the Defense Plant Corporation has entered into an agreement that is so sinister as to indicate that some officials in our government are guilty of malfeasance in the performance of their duties."

"If the agreement between the Defense Plant Corporation and Basic Magnesium, Inc., represents a cross-section of conduct on the part of the Defense Plant Corpora-

Continued on Page Eighteen

Cripps Said to Have Accord On National Regime in India

Plan Is Reported to Envisage Rule by a Council With Briton Directing Army and Native in Defense Ministry

By The United Press.

NEW DELHI, India, April 9—Great Britain and India are in general agreement on a self-government plan that will establish the first all-Indian national government in two centuries and provide for an executive council of fifteen members, all but one of them to come from the various political parties, it was learned tonight.

The plan was reported to be acceptable, with the exception of a few minor adjustments, to the two major political groups—the All-India Congress party and the Moslem League.

Under the plan a native government Minister will handle all Indian defense matters except war strategy and tactics, which a British military chief will control.

With only final details to be smoothed out, formal announcement of the settlement was predicted for late tomorrow or Saturday.

Inquiries late tonight revealed that under the agreement reached between the Congress party and Sir Stafford Cripps, British negotiator, the new national government would be directed not by a Cabinet but by the Executive Council of the Viceroy of India, the Marquess of Linlithgow.

The importance of that point in the agreement, it was said, was the fact that a Prime Minister would not be appointed and asked to form a Cabinet—the usual constitutional procedure—but that the Viceroy would appoint members to the council, after receiving the names of nominees by the various Indian parties.

Under the new government, the country will be mobilized to resist the Japanese, who are pressing closer.

It was learned that an executive

Continued on Page Six

2 Police Officials Suspended On Amen's Charges of Graft

In an unexpected move that may present a test case of far-reaching effect in the Police Department, Special Prosecutor John Harlan Amen's two extraordinary grand juries returned supplemental presentments yesterday against two high-ranking police officers who had sought retirement while under investigation in connection with alleged police protection of a $100,000,000 city-wide gambling racket.

The two, Inspector Camille C. Pierne of the Tenth Division in Brooklyn and Lieutenant Terence J. Harvey of the Brooklyn Borough headquarters squad, were named in Wednesday's presentments that bared the existence of police graft estimated at more than $1,000,000 a year, but no specific charges were lodged against them on the theory that a mere application for retirement was sufficient to preclude the prosecution of departmental charges against them.

However, Police Commissioner Valentine, after conferring behind closed doors with his aides and later in the afternoon with Mayor La Guardia, issued a statement Wednesday night asserting that he had notified Mr. Amen that inasmuch as the retirement applications of several police officers had not been acted upon by the Police Pension Fund he regarded them as members of the uniformed force and would like to be advised if the grand jury had made any charges against them so that he could be "guided accordingly."

Mr. Amen's reply yesterday was to send a letter to Commissioner Valentine asserting that it was because of his understanding of Mr. Valentine's earlier advice that he had not filed charges against men

Continued on Page Thirty-eight

GASOLINE SUPPLIES CUT AGAIN BY WPB

Deliveries to East and 2 States in Northwest Will Be Reduced From 80 to 66⅔ Per Cent

Special to THE NEW YORK TIMES.

WASHINGTON, April 9—The War Production Board issued today an order further curtailing gasoline deliveries to filling stations and bulk consumers in seventeen Eastern States, the District of Columbia and Oregon and Washington.

Effective April 16, deliveries of gasoline to filling stations and bulk consumers in curtailment areas will be cut to 66 2-3 per cent of average deliveries in December, January and February, adjusted for seasonal variations. Deliveries have been reduced 20 per cent since March 19.

Secretary Ickes, Petroleum Coordinator, discussing the WPB order, said at his press conference:

"If this curtailment proves satisfactory, we may go to Leon Henderson and tell him we see no need for rationing."

Mr. Ickes added that the matter

Continued on Page Twenty-six

Jesse Jones Shakes Eugene Meyer; Eye-Glasses Broken in Encounter

Special to THE NEW YORK TIMES.

WASHINGTON, April 9—Jesse Jones, Secretary of Commerce, and Eugene Meyer, editor and publisher of The Washington Post, were participants in a fistic encounter at the annual dinner of the Alfalfa Club at the Hotel Willard tonight.

A sharp verbal exchange arising from resentment by the Secretary of an editorial in which his testimony before the Senate's Truman committee investigating the rubber situation was criticized preceded the encounter, club members said.

As told by eyewitnesses, Secretary Jones was approached by Mr. Meyer, a long-time critic of the banker, as Mr. Jones entered the small ballroom of the hotel. Accounts of witnesses vary as to the words which immediately preceded the encounter, but most members agreed that Secretary Jones grasped Mr. Meyer by the coat and started to shake him. As Mr. Meyer wrenched himself free his eyeglasses fell to the floor and were smashed.

Mr. Meyer, the accounts continue, swung at the Secretary but friends, including John J. O'Connor, former New York Representative, pushed them apart. Secretary Jones left immediately after the fight, while Mr. Meyer stayed for a time chatting with friends.

The men have been frequent adversaries since the Hoover Administration, when both served with the Reconstruction Finance Corporation, of which Mr. Meyer was then chairman. Mr. Jones is also a publisher, owning The Houston Chronicle.

Today's editorial asserted that Mr. Jones had shielded himself behind the President, the British and the Netherlanders in defending his handling of the rubber situation.

PLANES GET SHIPS

Japanese Sink Big Naval Units in Bay of Bengal, Blast Base in Ceylon

BRITISH RAID CARRIER

Score Near-Misses, Get 4 Aircraft—2 Fleets Massing for Battle

By RAYMOND DANIELL
Wireless to THE NEW YORK TIMES.

LONDON, April 9—The Japanese have struck a heavy blow against the British Navy in the struggle for mastery of the Bay of Bengal, which is the key to the Indian Ocean, in sinking by air attack the heavy cruisers Dorsetshire and Cornwall. In return, near-misses were scored by bombers in an attack on a Japanese aircraft carrier in the Bay of Bengal.

Full enemy control of the Bay of Bengal, the eastern half of which the Japanese command already, would lay the eastern coast of India open to invasion. Renewed aerial attacks today on Trincomalee, the main British naval base on the island of Ceylon, off the south coast of India, made it more apparent than ever that the Japanese were seeking to extend their domination westward.

1,100 Are Rescued

News of the sinking of the 10,000-ton Cornwall and 9,975-ton Dorsetshire was given in an Admiralty communiqué, which placed the encounter with the Japanese planes in the Indian Ocean. The announcement said 1,100 survivors, —including the commanders, Captain A. W. S. Agar of the Dorsetshire and Captain P. C. W. Manwaring of the Cornwall—had been picked up. The Dorsetshire was the ship whose torpedoes administered the coup de grace to the German battleship Bismarck in the Atlantic last year.

The attack on the Japanese aircraft carrier was announced in a communiqué received tonight from Colombo, Ceylon. In the action, which followed today's attack on Trincomalee, four Japanese planes were shot down. Some of the attacking planes did not return, but their number was not disclosed. While Trincomalee was being raided a couple of Japanese planes appeared over Colombo, but dropped no bombs.

[The Colombo communiqué also revealed that in the attack on Trincomalee the Japanese damaged harbor and airdrome facilities and caused a few casualties among dockyard personnel. The Associated Press reported. Six of the Japanese planes were shot down, six others were probably destroyed and two were listed as damaged. The Japanese, who attacked with "a large force of bombers and fighters," caused no damage in the town of Trincomalee.]

Allied Cargo Ships Sunk

The loss of the Cornwall and the Dorsetshire, coupled with an official statement from New Delhi, India, that several merchantmen have been sunk in recent enemy air and naval attacks in the Bay of Bengal, represents a serious blow not only at British naval strength in that area but against United Nations lines of communication.

The number of merchant vessels lost was not announced, but the total of survivors from them—between 400 and 500, who have landed on the coast of Orissa in India—indicates a considerable number. Tokyo said today that the number of ships sunk was twenty-one, with twenty-three others so severely damaged that they must be regarded as lost.

The Japanese naval force in the Bay of Bengal area is operating hundreds of miles from its presumed base in the Andaman Islands. The distance from the Andamans to Ceylon is more than 1,000 miles. Before the occupation of

Continued on Page Six

IN THE FOX HOLES OF BATAAN

U. S. Troops in action on the Philippine peninsula, the fall of which was announced yesterday
Associated Press Wirephoto (U. S. Army Signal Corps)

ITALIAN CRUISER SUNK BY BRITISH

10,000-Ton Vessel Destroyed by Submarine—Foes Spar in Libyan Fighting

By ROBERT P. POST
Wireless to THE NEW YORK TIMES.

LONDON, April 9—A 10,000-ton eight-inch-gun Italian cruiser has been sunk in the Central Mediterranean by torpedoes from a British submarine, the Admiralty announced today.

The cruiser, which may have been convoying reinforcements for Marshal Erwin Rommel in Libya, was accompanied by destroyers and aircraft when Lieut. Comdr. E. P. Tomkinson, who received the Distinguished Service Order with bar in December for his work on submarine patrol, ordered the attack. Eight minutes after his torpedoes struck home, the commander risked attack by the cruiser's escort to show his periscope. The cruiser was heard to break up and sink while the destroyers picked up survivors.

Lieut. Commander Tomkinson's earlier exploits were carried out with the Urge, one of the smallest British submarines. Last April he sank a heavily laden oil tanker of more than 10,000 tons. For this he

Continued on Page Eight

Sacred Saffron of Priests Aids Foe's Burma Advance

By HARRISON FORMAN
Wireless to THE NEW YORK TIMES.

CHUNGKING, China, April 9—Clad in the sacred saffron robes of the Poongee—literally meaning "great glory"—the fifth column in Burma is taking advantage of the historic sanctuary provided by Burmese Buddhism. In the past the Poongees have included, besides the genuinely devout, many thieves, bandits and general malcontents, and they have always been a major problem for British administration.

Unlike most other priesthoods, the Poongees require no special training or lifelong vows. Any man may in practice become a Poongee for any period desired, days or years, by the simple procedure of shaving his head, donning a saffron robe, formally renouncing all things worldly before a temple and thereafter living solely by begging, which is not permitted for more than daily needs.

In practical example, a business man may welch on a contract or a debt by simply becoming a Poongee, and he thereby is cleansed of all worldly obligations and responsibilities. The Poongees are arrogant and sacrosanct in so far as the police are concerned. The Poongees are publicly regarded as holy men who can do no wrong, and the British military confess they are practically helpless in the face of such fanaticism.

An eyewitness on the Burma front reports that at a certain supposedly secret airport there ap-

Continued on Page Five

AMERICANS BAG TEN IN BURMA AIR FIGHT

A. V. G. Routs Twenty of Foe Without One Loss—Lull in Land Fighting Continues

By The United Press.

CHUNGKING, China, April 9—Reinforced American Volunteer Group fliers have roared back into the Battle of Burma, destroying ten planes and damaging two others in a mass dogfight with twenty Japanese Zero fighters in which one American plane was lost but its pilot saved, an A. V. G. communiqué announced tonight.

The battle was fought over the Burmese town of Loi-Win, the communiqué said. [An Associated Press dispatch from Chungking, based on the same official source, said the encounter took place Wednesday over Leiyun in the south of China's Yunnan Province. Neither Loi-Win nor Leivun appears on available maps.]

Week of Inaction Ended

This was the first challenge to Japanese air superiority over Burma battlegrounds since the invaders launched their all-out offensive against cities and airports in that theatre early last week. The strength of the A. V. G. force—American-made and American-flown planes fighting under the Chinese banner—was not disclosed.

Official Chinese dispatches disclosed that German officers were mapping the Japanese drive against Chinese lines north of Toungoo in Central Burma. One German officer was reported captured by the defenders and reconnaissance revealed that the Japanese were massing troops in Thailand to the east for a possible envelopment move against the Chinese on the Nazi model.

Chinese spokesmen said the Japanese concentrations in the Chiengmai area across the Thailand border not only menaced the Chinese positions around Toungoo but enabled the invaders to threaten a diversion drive into China's Kwangsi and Yunnan Provinces.

The Toungoo front—one-third of the way to bombed-out Mandalay from captured Rangoon—has been fairly static for a week. A belated Chinese communiqué reported the Japanese attacked south of Yedashe, eighteen miles north of Toungoo, on Monday and that fighting continued after dark that night. Subsequent communiqués

Continued on Page Five

War News Summarized

FRIDAY, APRIL 10, 1942

Rocky Bataan Peninsula, the finger of land that still defied the Japanese after they had conquered most of the Southwest Pacific, finally succumbed yesterday. Its 36,853 remaining American and Filipino defenders—drained by hunger, exhaustion and disease—could no longer rally to beat off an enveloping movement that broke their lines on the east flank. For three months they had fought against ever-growing odds. Although Corregidor Island and the other forts in Manila Bay stayed in American hands, it was questionable how long they could hold out. [1-8; map, P. 2.]

The United Nations suffered a probably greater strategic setback in the Bay of Bengal. Japanese planes sank two British 10,000-ton cruisers, the Dorsetshire and the Cornwall, and a great naval battle loomed with the coast of India at stake. Allied bombers attacked a Japanese naval squadron and scored near-misses on an aircraft carrier. In this Allied attack and in a raid on the Ceylon naval base of Trincomalee, the Japanese lost at least ten planes. [1:4; map, P. 6.]

Allied aerial successes were reported from Burma and Australia. Reinforced American volunteer pilots in the Burma theatre shot down ten enemy fighters and damaged two others without a loss of their own. [1:7.] United Nations bombers blasted planes and military targets in a surprise raid on Rabaul, New Britain. [3:1.]

With the threat to India growing daily, the drawn-out negotiations in New Delhi appeared nearing a successful compromise—the establishment of an Indian national government in which the defense minister would share responsibility with General Wavell. [1:2-3.]

The naval defeat in the Indian Ocean was offset somewhat by the sinking of a 10,000-ton Italian cruiser by a British submarine in the Mediterranean. In Libya, the British were jockeying for position against strong Axis forces, whose movements no longer seemed to indicate a large-scale offensive. [1:5.]

Germany flung large units of tanks and planes into the Russian front to feel out the Red Army's strength in virtually every sector, Moscow reports said, but the reinforced Soviet forces broke up their attacks and clung to the initiative. [11:1, with map.]

In occupied Europe, the embittered Norwegian people observed the second anniversary of the German invasion with a "strike" of silence as Quislingists and German troops marched in the streets. [9:1.]

DEFENSE CRUSHED

Stimson Reveals Defeat Followed Failure to Get in More Food

CORREGIDOR IS HELD

Wainwright on the Isle Free to Set Course, Roosevelt Tells Him

What Tokyo Reports

By The Associated Press.

TOKYO, Friday, April 10 (From Japanese broadcasts recorded in New York)—The Domei news agency said today that "60,000 Filipino and American troops resisting the Japanese on Bataan Peninsula have begged for a halt in hostilities after six days of fierce Japanese assault."

"Details of the conditions of surrender are not yet disclosed," said the Domei dispatch, "nor is it known yet whether the Japanese forces have decided to accept the terms."

Corregidor was raided twice yesterday by Japanese bombers and tons of explosives were unleashed on military installations, Domei reported.

By CHARLES HURD
Special to THE NEW YORK TIMES.

WASHINGTON, April 9—An overwhelming Japanese Army, aided by the allies of hunger, fatigue and disease, today crushed the small mixed force that had held Bataan Peninsula since December.

Japanese forces, heretofore estimated at 200,000 men, including fresh assault troops, and supported by tanks, artillery, bombers and attack planes in profusion, enveloped an exhausted defending army of 36,853 men, as counted officially yesterday afternoon.

The defeat of the American and Filipino forces was officially announced as a "probability" in a War Department communiqué issued as of 5:15 A. M. today. A few hours later Secretary of War Henry L. Stimson announced the defeat at his regularly scheduled weekly press conference. He already had carried the word to President Roosevelt.

Reveals Supplies Were Sent In

When Secretary Stimson met reporters in his conference room he paid the highest praise to the spirit of the defenders in a fight recognized as hopeless from the beginning had pledged that the Philippines would be reconquered. In the same talk he described extraordinary efforts made to provision the garrison, saying that "several shiploads of supplies" were sent into the Philippines, "but for every ship that arrived safely we lost nearly two."

As far as was known here today the rocky fortress of Corregidor Island still held its own astride the entrance to Manila Bay and other troops held adjacent fortified islands. The decision as to whether they should continue fighting was laid squarely on Lieut. Gen. Jonathan M. Wainwright, to whom President Roosevelt dispatched yesterday a message giving him absolute authority to continue the fight or make terms, as he might see fit.

Army Records Position

This responsibility is a heavy one for General Wainwright, for it is assumed here that he lacks transport to take more than a handful of the Bataan forces across the four miles of water that separates Bataan Peninsula from Corregidor. Even so his food is desperately short, Secretary Stimson having said this morning that every man in Bataan had been on short rations since Jan. 11. This was a primary reason for the collapse of the defense after five days of savage hand-to-hand fighting.

The long-expected defeat, which by its deferment wrote an epic in American military history, was officially indicated in War Depart-

Continued on Page Two

"All the News That's Fit to Print."

The New York Times.

LATE CITY EDITION
Slightly cooler today.
Temperatures Yesterday—Max., 65; Min., 44

Copyright, 1942, by The New York Times Company.

VOL. XCI No. 30,765. Entered as Second-Class Matter, Postoffice, New York, N. Y. NEW YORK, SATURDAY, APRIL 18, 1942. THREE CENTS NEW YORK CITY and Vicinity

JAPAN REPORTS TOKYO, YOKOHAMA BOMBED BY 'ENEMY PLANES' IN DAYLIGHT; CLAIMS 9; BIG RAIDS OVER FRANCE; LEAHY IS RECALLED

FARM LEADERS ASK CONGRESS TO CURB LEWIS DAIRY DRIVE

House Group Is Told He Aims at Control of Nation'` Food and Imperils War Program

RACKET LAW AID IS SOUGHT

Action Is Urged to Put Unions Under Trust Act—Vinson Labor Measure Hits Snag

By C. P. TRUSSELL
Special to THE NEW YORK TIMES.

WASHINGTON, April 17—Congressional attention to proposals for suspension of the forty-hour week, freezing of open and closed shop conditions and related war labor issues were turned sharply today to the unionization of the farmer, a fast-spreading movement that brought leaders of agricultural organizations before a House Judiciary subcommittee in mass protest.

Declaring that the "Food for Freedom" program faced danger if John L. Lewis's new Dairy Farmers' Union and other active groups attained their organizational objectives, witnesses urged the enactment of legislation that would put labor unions under the anti-racketeering law of 1934, and subject them to prosecution under anti-trust statutes.

"If Lewis succeeds in his organizational program," W. P. Davis, manager of the New England Milk Producers Association, told the subcommittee, "it will give him power to paralyze the food supply of the nation."

The Lewis union, an affiliate of his United Mine Workers, is driving now for a closed shop for New York City that would reach from the producer on the farm, through the handler and processor and to home deliveries in the city. In the Flint (Michigan) area, where it started, it claims about 85 per cent unionization.

Remedial Bills Considered

There are three bills before the subcommittee, all designed to give the Federal courts jurisdiction in cases involving work stoppage for non-labor purposes and to tighten up statutes dealing with interference of interstate commerce by violence, threats, coercion or intimidation. Sponsoring the measures are Representative Monroney of Oklahoma, Walter of Pennsylvania and Hobbs of Alabama, all Democrats.

As this hearing progressed the forty-hour week legislation sponsored by Representatives Vinson of Georgia and Smith of Virginia ran into a snag before the House Committee on Naval Affairs, which Mr. Vinson heads. Only a tie vote of

Continued on Page Nine

'No. 1 Bank Robber' Is Seized in Jersey

Special to THE NEW YORK TIMES.

NEWARK, N. J., April 17—Agents of the Federal Bureau of Investigation swarmed into a tavern in Long Branch, N. J., last night and arrested Ralph Greco, 35 years old, of Hoboken, who was described by Federal authorities as the "No. 1 bank robber fugitive" of the nation.

Greco, who had boasted that he would never be taken alive, surrendered meekly when the agents caught up with him in Wilson's bar after a three-year search, it was announced this afternoon by E. E. Conroy, in charge of the Newark office of the F. B. I. Unarmed, he was seated with his wife and a group of friends. The prisoner, owner of a long police record, is held in connection with the theft of $76,000 last August from the First Stroudsburg (Pa.) National Bank and of $11,500 from the First National Bank of Suffield, Conn., in 1938.

No Convoys Lost As Blimps Guard

By The United Press.

MOFFETT FIELD, Sunnyvale, Calif., April 17—Rear Admiral John Wills Greenslade said today that the Navy's use of blimps for convoy protection and submarine patrol has been so effective that "to date on both coasts no convoy has been successfully attacked while under lighter-than-air convoy."

Admiral Greenslade spoke at the formal commissioning of the Moffett Field air base as a naval air station, to serve as operating headquarters for blimps being used in coastal patrol.

STATE SENATE BARS REAPPORTIONMENT

Legislative and Congressional Redistricting Both Beaten—Republicans Cold to Change

By WARREN MOSCOW
Special to THE NEW YORK TIMES.

ALBANY, April 17—Both Legislative and Congressional reapportionment legislation met defeat in the Senate today, thus ending for some time plans for a more even distribution, according to population, of representation in the Legislature and in Congress. There is little likelihood that either measure will be brought up again in the present session.

Arguments as to constitutionality, equity and necessity dominated two hours of debate, but the defeat lay in matters not mentioned, such as the feeling among up-State Republicans that the urban areas would control their party as well as the Legislature; the hesitancy to vote to unseat a friend, if the legislator himself were not affected; fear of loss of Republican control of the Assembly in a bad year and similar intangibles. This is not new or unusual, since Tammany blocked a legislative reapportionment in 1935, when the Democrats controlled both houses, because it would have lost its dominant position in relation to the other Democratic counties.

All of this was reflected in the

Continued on Page Sixteen

WAR PRODUCTION OF ALLIES EXCEEDS AXIS, NELSON SAYS

WPB Chief Predicts That by End of Year We Can Overcome Foes' Accumulated Reserve

BUT WARNS OF LETDOWN

MacLeish Chides Editors for Failing to 'Police' Spread of 'Defeatist Propaganda'

The United States is "over the hump" on war production, Donald M. Nelson, chairman of the War Production Board, declared at the annual dinner last night of the American Society of Newspaper Editors in the Hotel Waldorf-Astoria.

"We can see daylight ahead in our whole war production effort," he added.

Combined production of the United States, Russia and England, he asserted, today is much greater than that of the Axis nations, and by the end of the year, he said, "it is safe to predict" that we shall have overcome the accumulated reserve built up by Japan since 1930 and by Germany since 1933.

From then on, he promised, we shall "have our enemies at an increasing disadvantage."

Nearly 500 members and guests of the society received Mr. Nelson's address with enthusiastic applause. He was introduced as a man who is doing a "whale of a job" by Dwight Marvin of The Troy (N. Y.) Record, retiring president of the society, who announced that last night's was the largest dinner ever held by the society. Editors attended from all parts of the country.

Chinese Envoy a Speaker

Dr. Hu Shih, Chinese Ambassador at Washington, also addressed the gathering. He said that China, like the United States, is "fighting a war to preserve a peaceful way of life against a militaristic Japanese dictatorship." Another speak-

Continued on Page Thirteen

ENVOY SUMMONED

Roosevelt Directs Him to Report on Outlook Facing France

EMBASSY TO REMAIN

Diplomatic Tie Is Kept—Laval Still Trying to Form Cabinet

By BERTRAM D. HULEN
Special to THE NEW YORK TIMES.

WASHINGTON, April 17—Admiral William D. Leahy, the United States Ambassador to France, was directed by President Roosevelt today to return to this country in view of the return to power of Pierre Laval.

The announcement was made by Sumner Welles, acting Secretary of State. The technical reason given was that Admiral Leahy's return was ordered for consultation, which means that if events should turn more favorably in the future, he would be in a position to return to his post.

But it amounts at the present juncture to a recall because of the turn of affairs in France. Whether that will have its effect on the French people and result in internal political pressure against the retention of M. Laval in power, or increased German pressure on France for all-out collaboration with the Axis, is a question that it is assumed will soon be answered.

Laval's Domination Cited

Mr. Welles, in making the announcement, said Admiral Leahy had been requested to return immediately for consultation in view of the events of the last few days in France and in view of information received that the new government of France is composed of elements dominated by M. Laval and all that implies. A more complete statement of American policy may be forthcoming soon.

[In Vichy, Pierre Laval was reported to be having difficulty in forming a Cabinet. After the resignation of the Darlan Cabinet, the French Government was informed that Admiral Leahy had been called to Washington.]

Admiral Leahy will not leave immediately because Mrs. Leahy is recovering from an operation performed a week ago and is not yet in condition to travel. Mr. Welles said this would delay their departure for at least a brief period. According to Vichy reports, this may be two or three weeks.

The United States Embassy staff and consuls, under present plans, will remain in France after Admiral Leahy leaves. They will be under the direction of S. Pinkney Tuck, counselor of the Vichy embassy, as chargé d'affaires. They would have had to leave with the Ambassador had the United States action been extended to a severance of diplomatic relations.

As matters now stand, the plan has been abandoned, or is being held in abeyance indefinitely, of sending limited quantities of food, clothing and essential economic supplies to French North Africa from the United States, as well as food and clothing for children in France.

Henry-Haye Rebuffed

Mr. Welles disclosed at his press conference that he had refused yesterday to receive from Ambassador Gaston Henry-Haye the French rejection of his note of April 13 because this had been submitted for approval to German authorities before being transmitted here.

In his note of April 13 Mr. Welles rejected a Vichy protest over the establishment of an American consulate general at Free French Brazzaville, in Equatorial Africa, without consulting Vichy. The French rejection charged that the note of Mr. Welles was "injurious," not "insulting," as first reported.

Mr. Welles said he told the

Continued on Page Two

FLYING GENERAL IS DECORATED

Brig. Gen. Ralph Royce, who hopped 4,000 miles to bomb Japanese bases in the Philippines, receives the Distinguished Service Cross from Major Gen. Rush Lincoln, somewhere in Australia. Lieut. Col. J. H. Davies, who was on the flight, is at the right. He, too, won the D. S. C. This picture was radioed from Australia to San Francisco.
Associated Press Wirephoto

War News Summarized

SATURDAY, APRIL 18, 1942

Bombs fell on Tokyo in daylight today, it was announced by Japanese Imperial Headquarters. The Tokyo radio said that "enemy planes" had inflicted "telling damage" on "schools and hospitals" without causing damage to military establishments. Another broadcast said that nine of the raiders had been brought down. No confirmation of the attack came from any United Nations source. [1:8.]

Secretary of War Stimson disclosed that the United States Army was "getting pretty near to the stage of being ready for an offensive." He said the offensive would be taken at the earliest possible moment. [1:5.]

On the Far East's crucial Burma front the British abandoned Magwe, gateway to the Yenangyaung oil fields, and applied the scorched-earth policy to oil wells that produce 1,000,000 gallons a day. They retreated slowly under severe pressure. [1:7; map, P. 4.]

In the Philippines, the War Department announced, 35,000 combatant troops were in Japanese hands on Bataan Peninsula, together with several thousand non-combatant and supply troops and about 25,000 civilians. Sixteen of the captives were generals. [4:5.]

On the diplomatic front, President Roosevelt ordered Ambassador Leahy to return from Vichy in a swift aftermath to a French Cabinet resignation that left the ultra-collaborationist Pierre Laval to form a new government.

Admiral Leahy's virtual recall was officially described as a return for consultation—a loophole that would enable him to take up his post again if events should change for the better. Of this there seemed little likelihood. Acting Secretary of State Welles accused Vichy of having submitted one of its diplomatic notes for German approval. [1:4.]

M. Laval had not yet completed his Cabinet late last night after a day of conferences. Under the developing new governmental set-up, Admiral Darlan, retiring Vice Premier, remained head of France's land, sea and air forces through a political device apparently designed to allay American qualms about the French Fleet. [2:2.]

France's coast reverberated for the sixth consecutive day to the crash of British bombs as more than 600 planes engaged in sweeps against German targets. The day's operations, following night raids on enemy airdromes and a U-boat base, included the longest daylight raid yet reported—an assault on a plant at Augsburg, Germany, thirty-five miles short of Munich. [1:5-6.]

On Europe's land front, the Russians were advancing against strong resistance in the area of Demidov, forty miles northwest of Smolensk, the Moscow radio reported. [6:2.]

An Italian communiqué reported a futile British attempt to land troops on an island south of Crete—an attempt of which the British said they knew nothing. The Italians also told of the sinking of a British submarine, while London announced the sinking of a large Italian transport. [5:5.]

600 R. A. F. Planes Attack; Reich City Bombed in Day

Wireless to THE NEW YORK TIMES.

LONDON, Saturday, April 18—For the sixth successive day—and using an increased number of planes, estimated at more than 600 fighters and fast bombers during the day—the Royal Air Force continued its large-scale offensive sweeps over Northern France yesterday. The day-long attacks followed a night in which the big planes of the Bomber Command rained huge missiles on the docks at Havre again, on the Nazis' submarine base at Lorient, France, and on German stations in the Netherlands.

With the continually growing intensity of the R. A. F. raids, the Air Ministry made public an estimate that the Germans were now being forced to keep an army of 1,500,000 men tied up in defensive positions along the coast of Western Europe.

To add to the British operations, heavy bombers of the R. A. F. went out during the last hours of daylight and blasted an important factory at Augsburg, Southern Germany, the Air Ministry announced early today.

Augsburg, about thirty-five miles northwest of Munich, is an important aircraft manufacturing center for the Germans and is also the site of a large chemical works.

The raid meant a round-trip flight over 1,000 miles of enemy country, and the target was one of the most

Continued on Page Five

STIMSON PLEDGES EARLY OFFENSIVE

Army Is 'Pretty Near' Striking Stage, He Says—Belittles Confusion on MacArthur

Special to THE NEW YORK TIMES.

WASHINGTON, April 17—The American Army is "getting pretty near to the stage of being ready for an offensive," and will take that offensive "at the earliest practicable moment," Secretary of War Henry L. Stimson said at a press conference today.

[A War Department communiqué issued by Mr. Stimson yesterday said that an estimated 25,000 civilians and 35,000 United States and Filipino combatant troops and sixteen generals were now presumably in Japanese hands as a result of the fall of Bataan. A communiqué on the latest military action said that three Japanese batteries had been silenced by the Manila Bay forts and that "fierce fighting" was going on in Panay Island, which the Japanese invaded Thursday.]

Mr. Stimson described as "a tempest in a teapot" recent reports that General Douglas MacArthur had been unable to appoint a staff for his new command because he never had received an official directive delineating the extent of his authority in the Southwest Pacific.

The geographical boundaries of General MacArthur's command are a military secret, Mr. Stimson declared. None the less, he added, General MacArthur's command closely approximates that which the United Nations gave General Sir Archibald P. Wavell in much the same area.

"The practical coordination of effort and its strategic direction," Mr. Stimson stated, "is a matter for General MacArthur and General MacArthur alone."

Mr. Stimson's assertion that an

Continued on Page Seven

BRITISH BLOW UP BURMA OIL WELLS

Defenders Abandon Magwe but Fight to Protect Chinese Flank North of Toungoo

By CRAIG THOMPSON
Wireless to THE NEW YORK TIMES.

LONDON, April 17—Destruction of the oil fields at Yenangyaung—most important of Burmese producing centers with an output of 1,000,000 gallons daily—was reported here today as the British fell back to north of Magwe, twenty miles south of Yenangyaung.

Communiqués and other information received here show the Japanese have not yet reached the oil fields, but their destruction indicates that the British forces plan to continue their retreat. Meanwhile the Chinese were fighting above Myohla about thirty miles north of Toungoo.

[The Burma oil fields were the last source of supply for the United Nations in the Pacific and Eastern Indian Ocean area. The United Press said it would require from six months to a year for the Japanese to recondition and operate the wells destroyed. Six thousand of 8,000 wells are said to have been blast-

Continued on Page Four

Writer Tells of Philippine Escape And Stay at Secret U. S. Air Base

By NAT FLOYD
Wireless to THE NEW YORK TIMES.

SOMEWHERE IN AUSTRALIA, April 17—After watching America's planes going and coming on secret fields during our initial offensive blow at the Japanese deep in the Philippines I was permitted to make the long hop to Australia in the plane that carried Brig. Gen. Ralph Royce, the commander of the flight.

I had become acquainted with the athletic, hard-hitting General during his stay at the air fields, which I had reached almost a month earlier after a series of dashes from island to island. I shall never forget the uplift of morale when the long-expected planes came sailing in and settled on those fields.

During the succeeding days and nights the temporary operating headquarters was a busy place. General Royce and his officers were continually planning raids and dispatching planes upon their distant missions in large and small groups. In the afternoon General Royce would eat and rest briefly while awaiting the return of the planes.

He sat deep in a comfortable chair. I thought he would take a needed siesta, but a few minutes later when he heard a Flying Fortress land he sat up and said:

"I know how I am going to spend the afternoon. I'm going to take that plane out and bomb * * *"

He started briskly toward the field, but he turned back later after he had met the pilot, who told him a Japanese missile had caused enough damage to require several hours for repairs.

Later in the day I talked with the co-pilot of one of the B-25s [medium bombers], who was en-

Continued on Page Four

DAMAGE IS 'LIGHT'

Japanese Say Raiders Hit Schools, Hospitals, Not War Objectives

THEIR PUBLIC 'ANGRY'

No Confirmation of the Tokyo Radio Report Is Given in Washington

By The Associated Press.

SAN FRANCISCO, April 17—The Tokyo radio announced tonight that "enemy bombers" had attacked Tokyo, the Columbia Broadcasting System's listening station reported. The Tokyo broadcast said:

"Enemy bombers appeared over Tokyo for the first time in the current war, inflicting damage on schools and hospitals. The raid occurred shortly past noon on Saturday [Tokyo time].

"Invading planes failed to cause any damage on military establishments, although casualties in the schools and hospitals were as yet unknown.

"This inhuman attack on these cultural establishments and on residential districts is causing widespread indignation among the populace."

Communiqué Claims Planes

"It is confirmed that three enemy aircraft were shot down when hostile planes attacked the Tokyo-Tosamo region this afternoon for the first time since the war [started]," said a communiqué issued by Japanese Imperial Headquarters. "The enemy planes approached from several directions." Later another Tokyo radio broadcast reported that nine of the raiders had been shot down.

This later broadcast said that none of the hostile planes had penetrated to the heart of the city. It was said that they had released "a few bombs on the outskirts" and that "Japanese interceptor planes immediately took chase."

The Columbia Broadcasting System said the first announcement of the bombing was in an English-language broadcast. The announcement was repeated a few minutes later in a Japanese-language broadcast, which injected a new angle that "the enemy planes did not attempt to hit military establishments."

Raid "Just After Noon"

The Japanese-language broadcast said:

"Just after noon on the 18th the first enemy planes appeared over the city of Tokyo. A number of bombs were dropped. The enemy planes did not attempt to hit military establishments and only inflicted damage on grammar schools, hospitals and cultural establishments.

"These planes were repulsed by a heavy barrage from our defense guns.

"The previous training of the Tokyo populace for air raid defense was put into immediate practice. I wish to reveal that our losses were exceedingly light."

Tokyo Radio Interrupts Itself

TOKYO, Saturday, April 18 (From Japanese broadcast recorded by The United Press in San Francisco)—Enemy airplanes bombed Tokyo today, it was announced officially.

The Tokyo radio, in giving the announcement, interrupted another program "to give you this flash." The announcement said:

"Enemy bombers appeared over Tokyo for the first time since the outbreak of the current war of Greater East Asia. The bombing inflicted telling damages on schools and hospitals."

Yokohama Also Reported Hit

BERLIN, Saturday, April 18 (From German broadcasts recorded by The Associated Press)—

Continued on Page Three

"All the News That's Fit to Print."

The New York Times.

LATE CITY EDITION
Warmer with showers today.
Temperatures Yesterday—Max., 52; Min., 43

Copyright, 1942, by The New York Times Company.

VOL. XCI. No. 30,776. Entered as Second-Class Matter, Postoffice, New York, N. Y. NEW YORK, WEDNESDAY, APRIL 29, 1942. THREE CENTS NEW YORK CITY and Vicinity

SALES PRICES, RENTS, SERVICE CHARGES FROZEN; ROOSEVELT SEES AXIS CRACKING, PLEDGES FIGHT TO VICTORY THROUGH 'WORK, SORROW AND BLOOD'

AURORA OF LIGHTS DIMS OUT IN CITY FOR THE DURATION

Skyscrapers Lost in Low Haze as Famed Display Here Is Darkened by Army

STREET BULBS GLOW DULLY

Great Signs in Times Square Found to Illuminate the Mist Lying Over the Area

New York City's neon aurora and skyscraper diadem were dimmed for the war's duration after sundown yesterday. Along with the rest of the Eastern seaboard the City of Light's nocturnal display was reduced by Army order to dispel sky glow that has brought our ships far at sea into sharp silhouette in Axis gunsights.

Skyscraper clocks—as in the Metropolitan, Paramount and other city towers—vanished from New York's evening skyline as dusk settled. Rockefeller Center, the Empire State Building, Wall Street's towers, the Chrysler Building and other great monoliths were lost in low haze even under the yellow moon.

Seen from the 102d floor of the Empire State Building after 8 o'clock the city's streets were squares of brooding shadow rimmed by sidewalk lamps and by red neon signs that bloomed like poppies. Red neon, incidentally, gave off the most glow. This was particularly noticeable over Times Square.

Commissioner Valentine was asked late yesterday afternoon whether Times Square's numerous spectacular signs would be dimmed. In a written answer he cited a passage from the Army's official orders: "Exterior illumination used for advertising * * * that cannot be shaded shall be extinguished." Most of the square's great signs are unshaded and last night they illuminated low-lying haze banks but kept burning just the same.

Charwomen Have to Learn

Toward the shank end of the evening skyscrapers that had been hidden in darkness began to show lights, high up, at different floors. It turned out, in most cases, that the offenders were charwomen come to do office floors. They were warned to pull the shades. In some hotels new guests who had not seen the newspapers also turned on lights without drawing shades, but were warned against repeating the offense.

Army observers stood out to sea to watch the effect of the dimming. Their report may not be ready until today. Major Gen.

Continued on Page Ten

President Included In Jersey Blackout

Special to THE NEW YORK TIMES.

MADISON, N. J., April 28—Plans for a practice blackout tonight in this Morris County community of 8,000 were so complete that even the President's radio speech was blacked out from 10 to 10:15 P. M.

When a practice darkening of Western and Southern New Jersey was ordered for tonight two weeks ago the Town Council decided to put it into effect by throwing a switch at the municipal power station, cutting off radios as well as electrical ice boxes. The town buys current from a power company and distributes it through one central station.

Frank Waters, superintendent of the distributing plant, was flooded with telephone calls today from residents who pointed out that the time for the blackout was the same as the time for the President's speech. Mr. Waters replied, however, that as the time for the President's speech was announced only yesterday it was too late to change the blackout plans.

Japanese Drive for Lashio With 5,000 Men; City Afire

Burma Road Terminus Blasted by Bombers —Chinese Fight Desperately to Turn the Tide in the Vicinity of Taunggyi

By DAVID ANDERSON
Wireless to THE NEW YORK TIMES.

LONDON, April 28—More than 5,000 Japanese have knifed through the northern Shan States in the direction of the Lashio terminus of the Burma Road. The invaders are reported to have re-entered Taunggyi, some 110 miles southeast of Mandalay, which was captured by the Chinese under United States Lieut. Gen. Joseph W. Stilwell with heavy losses four days ago.

The Chinese were making a desperate attempt to stem the tide by turning the Taunggyi force east toward Loilem to cut off the enemy from the rear. This is viewed here as a forlorn hope.

The main body of the invading force, slashing its way forward after what might prove to be a knockout blow to Burma, consists of 3,000 troops moving north toward Konghaiping, according to a Chungking report. Allied reconnaissance planes have sighted another enemy column of at least 2,000 men closing in on Kehsi Mansam, about seventy miles almost due south of Lashio. A third column of 2,000 is sweeping east toward Kunhing.

The two northbound columns are believed aiming to cut the Mandalay-Lashio railroad or to capture Mandalay. [A United Press dispatch from Chungking described the opposing forces as racing for Bhamo, about 100 miles north of Lashio, from which a good secondary road connects with the Burma Road. The German - controlled Paris radio broadcast a "Tokyo report" that the Japanese had taken Lashio, The Associated Press reported from London.]

The eastward Japanese advance presumably has the twofold objec-

Continued on Page Three

TAXI ARMY SPEEDS TO 'PROTECT' CITY

5,000 State Guardsmen Free Army's Mobile Units in First Cooperative Manoeuvre

Five thousand soldiers from the twelve metropolitan regiments of the New York Guard were mobilized at their armories last night and transported in a fleet of fifty buses and 200 taxicabs to 100 strategic points throughout the city in an emergency test of their readiness to deal with concerted city-wide sabotage by enemy agents and fifth columnists.

Railroad stations, airports, bridges, tunnels, ferry terminals and other "sensitive" spots in the life of the city were covered by the regiments of the First, Second and Fifth Brigades of the only military force authorized for the State of New York now that the National Guard has been incorporated into the Army.

The manoeuvres were staged as a joint Army and State Guard operation under secret orders issued

Continued on Page Eight

R. A. F. RAINS BOMBS ON TRONDHEIM BASE

Blasts Nazi Threat to Supply Line to Russia—Cologne and Norwich Also Suffer

By RAYMOND DANIELL
Wireless to THE NEW YORK TIMES.

LONDON, April 28—Norwich, with its vestiges of Roman and Norman culture, was selected last night by the Germans for their retaliation for British raids on German cities.

While the German bombers were trying to destroy that ancient city in East Anglia, 110 miles northeast of London, British bombers pounded Cologne, the third largest city in Germany, and carried out a heavy attack on Trondheim fjord in Norway, which the Germans have been building into a naval base for attacks on the Allied supply line to North Russia.

[German planes bombed two towns in Eastern England early today, The United Press reported, causing a number of casualties. The Berlin radio said one

Continued on Page Five

War News Summarized

WEDNESDAY, APRIL 29, 1942

President Roosevelt turned the thoughts of the people of the United States to the present need for uncompromising sacrifice and toward the future last night as the war picture in Burma became darker and the British stepped up their all-out air offensive over Europe.

The President in a broadcast to the nation pledged offensive war against the Axis in many parts of the world and suggested that Germany and Italy were beginning to crack. He warned that the United States would take measures to prevent Axis use of French territory for military purposes. He said the United States would use its air force in Europe and take the offensive from Australia and New Zealand and that aid would be sent to the Chinese even if Burma fell. [1:4.]

Japanese forces continued their advance through the Northern Shan States toward the Mandalay-Lashio railway and Lashio itself, gateway to the Burma Road. The columns driving through the mountains in Eastern Burma were said to have 2,000 to 3,000 men each. The Japanese also pushed on northward along the north-south railway. [1:2-3; map, P. 2.]

United Nations headquarters in Australia reported the Japanese had lost seven planes in a raid on Darwin and also announced raids on enemy shipping at New Ireland and in the Solomon Islands. A Japanese transport was sunk. [4:1.]

British air squadrons bombed Cologne, Trondheim Fjord, Norway, and points in Northern France. One observer reported a square mile of planes had gone over the Channel in a single raiding formation. The Germans bombed Norwich. The British acknowledged the loss of twenty-three planes. [1:3; map, p. 5.]

Russian reports suggested that a Soviet Spring offensive was starting in the Kharkov-Bryansk sector, threatening the Germans in the Northern Donets. It was asserted that two important positions had been taken. A Soviet advance had been made near Orel, but checked, according to German reports. [7:1.]

The British Admiralty announced the sinking of two heavily laden Axis supply ships and a minesweeper in the Mediterranean. [6-1.]

In France the Germans ordered the execution of five French hostages for the wounding of a German soldier at Rouen last Friday. [6:4.]

The Swiss heard that the famous General Giraud, who had escaped from a German prison camp, had been in France for some days and had seen Marshal Pétain. [6:2-3.]

BIG FORCES ABROAD

President Says 'Several Hundred Thousand' Are on Foreign Soil

A WARNING TO VICHY

Reveals Our Navy Is in Mediterranean and Indian Ocean

By FRANK L. KLUCKHOHN
Special to THE NEW YORK TIMES

WASHINGTON, April 28—President Roosevelt gave a pledge tonight of offensive action by the United States in Europe and the Far East and called upon the American public to help win the war by sacrifices on the home front as its fighting men are beginning to turn the tide in battle.

In a nation-wide broadcast which was re-broadcast all over the world, he declared that our civilization would be saved and that we were willing to pay the cost in "hard work and sorrow and blood."

He interpolated that "several hundred thousands" of American Army and Navy forces already had been transported to "bases and battlefields thousands of miles from home." This was the first indication that such large operations had been effected. He also revealed American naval vessels were in the Mediterranean and Indian Ocean.

The President asserted that he would use his executive powers to the full to assure "total war," and attacked minority elements within the United States which are hampering the war effort.

Warning on French Territory

He indicated a belief that Germany and Italy were beginning to crack from within. He said emphatically that the United Nations would prevent the use of French territory by the Axis, that American flying fortresses soon would be in action over Europe and that Australia and New Zealand, where Japan's advance appeared to be checked, would be used as offensive bases.

Conceding that the situation in Burma appeared critical, he pledged that airplanes and munitions would be delivered to China by different routes. He paid high tribute to Russia's war effort.

He remarked that if "somebody" had dropped bombs on Tokyo, "it is the first time in history that Japan has suffered such indignities."

The President called for civilians at home, even those not engaged in defense industries, to look upon sacrifice as a privilege and pointed out that the "home front" civilian-soldier can play as great a part in winning the war as the heroes he cited for their extraordinary deeds on the battle lines.

He sharply attacked those Americans who approve self-denial for others but not for themselves; the "faint of heart" experts, "self-styled," in both the military and economic fields; "bogus patriots," using the freedom of the press to propagandize for Berlin and Tokyo, and most energetically of all, the "handful of noisy traitors," themselves would-be dictators, who have yielded to Hitlerism in their hearts and would yield the republic also.

Fliers Active in All the World

"This great war effort must be carried through to its victorious conclusion by the indomitable will and determination of the people," the President declared.

It was to the war fronts that the Executive turned first, remarking that American troops had taken up positions all over the world and that "American planes, manned by Americans, are flying in actual combat over all the continents and oceans."

The President then hinted at offensive action in the Mediterranean area, remarking that, while surface aspects seemed the same,

Continued on Page Fourteen

ANNOUNCING REGULATIONS OF PRICE-CONTROL PROGRAM

Price Administrator Leon Henderson and Donald Gordon, chairman of the Canadian Wartime Prices and Trade Board, discussing phases of the new rules. Associated Press Wirephoto

The President's Broadcast

Following is the text of President Roosevelt's broadcast last night as recorded and transcribed by THE NEW YORK TIMES:

My Fellow Americans:

It is nearly five months since we were attacked at Pearl Harbor. For the two years prior to that attack this country had been gearing itself up to a high level of production of munitions. And yet our war efforts have done little to dislocate the normal lives of most of us.

Since then we have dispatched strong forces of our Army and Navy, several hundred thousand of them to bases and battle fronts thousands of miles from home. We have stepped up our war production on a scale that is testing our industrial power, our engineering genius and our economic structure to the utmost. We have had no illusions about the fact that this would be a tough job—and a long one.

American warships are now in combat in the North and South Atlantic, in the Arctic, in the Mediterranean, in the Indian Ocean and in the North and South Pacific. American troops have taken stations in South America, Greenland, Iceland, the British Isles, the Near East, the Middle East and the Far East, the continent of Australia and many islands of the Pacific. American war planes, manned by Americans, are flying in actual combat over all the continents and all the oceans.

On the European front the most important development of the past year has been, without question, the crushing counter-offensive on the part of the great armies of Russia against the powerful German Army. These Russian forces have destroyed and are destroying more armed power of our enemies—troops, planes, tanks and guns—than all the other United Nations put together.

In the Mediterranean area matters remain, on the surface, much as they were. But the situation there is receiving very careful attention.

Recently we have received news of a change in government in what we used to know as the Republic of France—a name dear to the hearts of all lovers of liberty—a name and an institution which we hope will soon be restored to full dignity.

Throughout the Nazi occupation of France we have hoped for the maintenance of a French Government which would strive to regain independence to re-establish the principles of "liberty, equality and fraternity," and to restore the historic culture of France. Our policy has been consistent from the very beginning. However, we are now greatly concerned lest those who have recently come to power may seek to force the brave French people to submission to Nazi despotism.

The United Nations will take measures, if necessary, to prevent

Continued on Page Fourteen

Price Order Will Ruin Grocers By Thousands, Protest Declares

Special to THE NEW YORK TIMES.

WASHINGTON, April 28 — Sharp protests against the Office of Price Administration's action in making March the governing period in fixing both retail and wholesale prices under today's universal price ceiling order will be registered this week by independent retail grocers, spokesmen indicated tonight. Grocers have contended that a time lag of at least sixty days should have been allowed for the proper adjustment of retail to wholesale prices.

Officials of the National Association of Retail Grocers will gather in Chicago tomorrow for a meeting to set a policy toward the price order.

Mrs. R. M. Kiefer, secretary, said that leaders of the association spent much time here last week trying to convince OPA officials that some provision for adjusting retail prices to replacement costs should be included in the order.

By telephone from Indianapolis she declared that unless the order is changed "thousands upon thousands of retail grocers who cooperated with the government in keeping prices at low levels will be ruined in the next few months."

The organization, she added, would call protest meetings in cities and towns through the country, with the grocers asked at these meetings to appeal to Congressional delegations to demand reconsideration of the order.

In another reaction to the order, the Retailers Advisory Committee called for rigid obedience to the order, asserting that adjustments

Continued on Page Seventeen

BUYING SUSPENDED BY RETAILERS HERE

Wholesalers Get No Orders as Storekeepers Lament Lag of 11% in Price Rise

Retailers, manufacturers and wholesalers began preparations yesterday to write a new page in American business history in the controlled economy to be established by the nation's first over-all price ceiling covering millions of merchandise items.

New orders at wholesale came virtually to a standstill yesterday as industry awaited details of the price regulations. Retail trade was reported to be fairly active, but volume in the last week or so has been showing smaller sales gains over a year ago as shoppers tapered off buying to gauge the effects of the impending price order.

Numerous "squeeze" adjustments involving many branches of production and distribution were foreseen as business moves to hold prices in retail and wholesale channels to the highest levels quoted by individual sellers in March. While most retailers did not base their prices in March or this month on wholesale replacement costs, some price advances did occur.

The result, when the order governing retailers goes into effect on May 18, will be to move these prices back to the levels in March. Retail quotations in that month, despite the lag between wholesale and retail price advances, were at their highest levels since the start of the war. They showed an average increase of 18.7 per cent over March, 1941, according to the Fairchild Index.

Retailers' Time Lag

Retailers were disappointed that the price-control order made no provision for a roll-back of manufacturers' or wholesalers' prices to take care of the retailers' time lag, estimated at about 11 per cent at the end of March.

In some quarters, however, attention was called to Section 4 of the price order, dealing with supplemental regulations, as "holding out the possibility of future adjustments for the retailer's time lag." This section, it was pointed out, provides that if the maximum prices established for any commodity fail equitably to distribute returns from the sale at retail among producers, manufacturers, wholesalers and retailers "the Price Administrator will by supplementary regulation establish such maximum prices for different classes of sellers, or fix such base periods for the determination of their maxi-

Continued on Page Eighteen

MARCH PRICES TOP

Practically Every Item in Cost of Living Put Under OPA Curb

LICENSING SYSTEM

Retailers Must Act May 18, Wholesalers and Factories May 11

The text of the order on price regulation, Pages 15, 16.

By CHARLES E. EGAN
Special to THE NEW YORK TIMES.

WASHINGTON, April 28—Prices of every major item affecting living costs were ordered frozen today by the Office of Price Administration.

Acting to halt inflationary spiralling which had carried the cost of living 15 per cent above pre-war levels, the OPA called upon retailers, wholesalers and manufacturers of all essential products to freeze their selling prices at March levels. In companion regulations the Federal agency fixed a ceiling on rents.

A licensing system under which retailers and wholesalers who violate terms of the orders can be deprived of the right to do business was set up to enforce compliance with the ceiling levels. Powers granted to the Price Administrator under the Emergency Price Control Act of 1942 were held sufficient to compel compliance with the rental order.

The price control measures, together with an expansion of rationing will assure families in the low and middle-income brackets of an equal opportunity with those of greater income to buy available goods, Leon Henderson, the Federal Price Administrator, said in announcing the orders.

Can't See All Ramifications

At a press conference where he outlined the inflationary influences which compelled aggressive action by the government, Mr. Henderson admitted that the orders are more comprehensive than many had expected.

"They are of such magnitude," he said, "that even we who have been busy framing them for the last few weeks, cannot fully visualize their ramifications."

Under the order on retail prices, stores are called upon, beginning May 18, to hold prices for goods they sell at the highest levels they charged during March. Beginning May 11, wholesalers and manufacturers prices likewise are frozen at the "highs" of last month.

Service industries, such as laundries, garages and so forth come within the scope of the order and go under price ceilings July 1, with

Continued on Page Fourteen

Limit on Delivery Of Papers Likely

By The Associated Press.

WASHINGTON, April 28—Deliveries of newspapers will be restricted to one edition a day at any one point beginning May 15, an Office of Defense Transportation official said today in an informal explanation of the ODT's April 20 order to eliminate special trips and reduce local trucking mileage.

Newspapers now deliver each edition to sales points or redistribution points, the number of such deliveries running as high as twenty-five a day in one instance, the official said.

The order to local delivery carriers applies to every type of commercial enterprise and to governmental agencies, including those of the Federal Government.

It was explained that some hardships of the order might be relieved by pooling arrangements or by special exemption upon application to the ODT.

"All the News That's Fit to Print."

The New York Times.

LATE CITY EDITION
Mild today.
Temperatures Yesterday—Max., 74; Min., 52

Copyright, 1942, by The New York Times Company.

VOL. XCI..No. 30,783. Entered as Second-Class Matter, Postoffice, New York, N. Y. NEW YORK, WEDNESDAY, MAY 6, 1942. THREE CENTS NEW YORK CITY and Vicinity

CORREGIDOR SURRENDERS UNDER LAND ATTACK AFTER WITHSTANDING 300 RAIDS FROM THE AIR; BRITISH HIT MADAGASCAR BASE; VICHY RESISTS

CHARGE ACCOUNTS ARE DUE IN 40 DAYS AS INFLATION CURB

Reserve Board's Regulation, in Effect Today, Is First Check on Such Retail Customers

Bringing retail charge accounts under control for the first time and ruling that installment purchases must be liquidated in twelve months the Federal Reserve Board promulgated yesterday amendment No. 4 to its consumer credit regulation W, carrying into effect the seventh point in President Roosevelt's anti-inflation program.

Under the amendment, which is effective today, charge account customers of retail stores will be required to speed up their payments to complete them within forty days after the end of the month in which purchase is made. If this is not done the account will be transferred to an installment basis requiring liquidation within six months and no further charge account purchases will be permissible until the items in default are paid for.

The amendment also tightened substantially the earlier restrictions on installment sales and broadened the scope of the merchandise covered to forty-six listed classifications, including almost every item used in the American home, and clothing and jewelry as well. The down payment was generally raised to 33 1/3 per cent and the payment period to twelve months.

Explains Aim of Rules

Allan Sproul, president of the Federal Reserve Bank of New York, in announcing the amendment here, said:

"As amended, the regulation is extended to cover a comprehensive list of durable and semi-durable goods for civilian consumption and contemplates that the volume of outstanding consumer credit, already substantially diminished, will be further contracted in keeping with the government's purpose to prevent the rapid bidding up of prices.

"The purpose of this revision is to help make effective the last point in the seven-point program which the President set forth in his special message to Congress of April 27, 1942, as follows: 'To keep the cost of living from spiraling upward, we must discourage credit and installment buying, and encourage the paying off of debts, mortgages and other obligations; for this promotes savings, retards excessive buying and adds to the amount available to the creditors for the purchase of war bonds.' "

With respect to charge accounts, the regulation, in effect and depending upon the date of the purchase, provides for a forty to a seventy day payment period, similar to that in effect in Canada. The average period for payment of

Continued on Page Fourteen

Nazis' War Industry Spurs Plane Output

By Telephone to THE NEW YORK TIMES.

BERNE, Switzerland, May 5—German war industry has been ordered to devote all its attention henceforth to turning out airplanes, even to the detriment of tanks and other matériel. This news from Berlin tonight confirms indications reaching foreign circles here that mastery of the air is the paramount consideration for the moment.

Figures declared to be trustworthy indicate that the peak of plane production in the Reich was reached in June, 1941, when 3,300 were turned out. Now it has fallen to between 2,700 and 2,800. Italy's contribution does not exceed 700 machines a month.

It is understood the Germans' estimate of their opponents' production is: United States, 3,300 planes a month; Britain, 2,400; Russia, 2,600 to 2,900. But the Nazis can draw upon considerable reserves.

WPB CUTS GASOLINE 50 PER CENT IN EAST

Non-Essential Users May Be Down to 5 Gallons a Week After May 16 Order

By The Associated Press.

WASHINGTON, May 5—Gasoline consumption in the East will be slashed 50 per cent below normal starting May 16, the War Production Board said tonight. This means that many of the area's 10,000,000 motorists probably will have to get along with as little as five or six gallons a week.

The reduction will become effective the day the seaboard area begins using ration cards.

[In New York motorists will register for gasoline rationing next Tuesday, Wednesday and Thursday. Rationing will begin on May 15.]

While the overall curtailment will be one-half, informed sources explained that it would amount to about a 60 per cent cut for non-essential users of automobiles, since necessary vehicles will continue to receive their full requirements of fuel.

Action Recommended by Ickes

The WPB action, taken on recommendation of Harold L. Ickes, petroleum coordinator, came shortly after Joseph B. Eastman, defense transportation director, declared "every owner of a motor vehicle in public or private service should realize that he holds this vehicle in trust for the national war effort and that it should be used only for purposes of necessity."

This statement of Mr. Eastman's applied to the whole country, not merely to the East.

Simultaneously with the gasoline order, WPB directed that de-

Continued on Page Thirteen

BRONX GRAND JURY CLEARS EVERYONE IN THE FLYNN CASE

County Is 'Singularly Free of Fraud and Corruption,' Presentment Says

The Bronx County grand jury that has been hearing evidence on the paving with city materials and labor of a courtyard on the Lake Mahopac estate of Edward J. Flynn, chairman of the Democratic National Committee, as well as other irregularities in the Bronx, handed up a seventeen-page presentment yesterday, finding that Bronx County is "singularly free of fraud and corruption," but that many irregularities are prevalent.

The grand jury declared that after hearing all the evidence submitted, it did not find that the facts warranted the indictment of any one.

Work on Flynn Estate Reviewed

In discussing the work done on the Flynn estate on Nov. 14, 15, 17 and 18 of last year, the presentment said city employes had been transported to the estate from the city by city-owned station wagons and that the work had consisted of laying 8,000 second-hand granite blocks.

The city employes, the presentment said, were paid in full for their services; 8,000 blocks were returned to the city and the gasoline and oil issued to the city station wagons for the Mahopac trip were returned in full. The cost of trucking the blocks by private concerns was paid by Mr. Flynn. The courtyard was only part of a general alteration on the estate, with the total job to cost more than $30,000.

The evidence adduced, it continued, showed that Mr. Flynn had never expressed any desire that the work be done under city auspices or by city employes and without expense to him, but that the job would be done by a private contractor and paid for by Mr. Flynn. The work done by city employes was under the supervision of Robert L. Moran, Bronx Commissioner of Public Works.

Paul J. Kern, deposed president of the Civil Service Commission, who conducted an investigation in the paving job while still in office, was severely rebuked by the grand jury for hampering the investigation conducted by William B. Herlands, Commissioner of Investigation.

No Conspiracy Found

"In respect to the second phase of the investigation," the presentment said, "the alleged conspiracy between Mayor La Guardia, Mr. Flynn and Commissioner Herlands to suppress the Kern investigation, the charge was entirely without foundation and we feel that it never would have been made but for the fact that Mr. Kern is greatly influenced by what he terms 'his intuition.' "

Mr. Kern had charged that Mayor La Guardia was trying to suppress his investigation in Mr. Flynn's behalf, and that in return Mr. Flynn was to obtain for the Mayor the Democratic nomination for United States Senator.

The grand jurors found that the records of the Department of Highways and Sewers under Commissioner Moran were in a "deplorable condition." They said they believed Borough President James J. Lyons when he testified that he was ignorant of the Mahopac paving job, and "we strongly condemn that ignorance." Commissioner Moran, they said, was Mr. Lyons's appointee and the Borough President could not avoid responsibility for the manner in which any subordinate conducted a department.

The Grand Jury's Presentment

In its presentment the grand jury said.

"The subject matter of our investigation resolved itself naturally, into three phases; 1, the Maho-

Continued on Page Twenty-eight

Direct Hit on Tirpitz By British Reported

By Telephone to THE NEW YORK TIMES.

STOCKHOLM, Sweden, May 5—British Royal Air Force bombs scored a direct hit on the battleship Tirpitz when she was in Kiel harbor prior to her transfer to her present anchorage at Trondheim, Norway, according to an eyewitness account by a Swedish seaman published in Ny Dag. The observer also reported a great change of morale among German civilians.

"Although the British attacks on Kiel were usually made from a great height, sometimes from 20,000 feet," he is quoted as saying, "the bombs hit their targets with astonishing precision. Thus in every bombing the biggest wharf in Kiel was regularly set ablaze, and on one occasion a British bomber scored a direct hit on the Tirpitz."

FOE ENTERS CHINA ACROSS BURMA LINE

Advance Units Over Border While Main Columns Wait—Planes Aid British Retreat

By DAVID ANDERSON
Wireless to THE NEW YORK TIMES.

LONDON, May 5—The Japanese have entered Yunnan Province in China via the Burma Road, it was announced today. Their vanguards reached the suburbs of Wangting, which is on a small river dividing Burma and China, and Chungking said the Japanese were being engaged by Chinese troops in the hills. The main enemy column was waiting within Burma at Chukok, near by.

The invading force must have made a detour around the Chinese fighting at Kutkai because the battle there was reported still going on. Other Chinese units were believed holding out north of Mandalay on the banks of the Irrawaddy River. British soldiers were continuing their slow retreat west of Mandalay.

"At times their [the Japanese]

Continued on Page Four

BRITISH ADVANCING

Landing Force Reported Within Four Miles of Madagascar Base

'CHUTISTS ARE USED

Warships and Aircraft Make Frontal Assault to Help Troops

By RAYMOND DANIELL
Wireless to THE NEW YORK TIMES.

LONDON, May 5—Small units of British Commandos and regular troops won a bridgehead at Courier Bay in the action against Madagascar and were reported tonight to be fighting their way across a ten-mile-wide isthmus toward the important naval base of Diego Suarez.

[A London dispatch of The Associated Press quoted Vichy reports that waves of British parachutists had been landed at the outset of a double attack in which warships and squadrons of aircraft made a frontal thrust from the sea timed to coincide with the overland assault on the rear of the base by British light armored units landed at Courier Bay.

[The Associated Press said that, according to advices released by Vichy sources, the British occupying forces had reached Andrakaka, four miles from Diego Suarez. The French estimated that the attacking forces numbered 20,000 and the French and native defenders about 7,000.]

There were only sketchy accounts of the battle for the big French island, which lies athwart vital United Nations supply routes. However, a joint Admiralty-War Office communiqué issued this afternoon clearly indicated that opposition had been offered by the Vichy French garrison. The capture of a defending battery was reported.

A communiqué issued late to-

Continued on Page Two

War News Summarized

WEDNESDAY, MAY 6, 1942

Corregidor, the island fortress at the entrance to Manila Bay, was surrendered to the Japanese after a furious assault. The British were engaged in breaking French resistance to their landing in Madagascar. Japanese forces reached and crossed the Burma-China frontier. Other war fronts were largely unchanged.

The surrender of Corregidor and other island bases was announced by United Nations Headquarters in Australia, following an earlier Washington communiqué stating that the Japanese had started landing operations. The defenders were reported to be short of both food and ammunition. [1:8.]

British landing forces on Madagascar were reported to be within four miles of the Diego Suarez naval base at the northern extremity of the island. The French garrison was resisting, but Vichy reported that some 20,000 British had landed or were preparing to land. London said the Commandos had encountered little resistance. [1:5; map, P. 2.]

The Vichy regime ordered the garrison at Madagascar to resist. Pierre Laval in a note to the United States Government rejected Washington's warning against French belligerent action, but he insisted his government would not be the first to take measures to break relations with the United States. Admiral Darlan, chief of the Vichy military forces, expressed extreme bitterness toward Britain. [1:6-7.]

Secretary of State Hull indicated clearly at his press conference that the United States would adhere to a policy of full support of British occupation of Madagascar. [3:1.]

Meanwhile, Japanese forces in Burma had reached the Chinese frontier in the Burma Road sector and had penetrated a slight distance into China. A battle was raging on the frontier, and the Japanese had been halted, according to Chungking. United States bombers from India attacked successfully Mingaladon airport north of Rangoon. The Japanese said their planes had set on fire the Chinese city of Yungchang, 120 miles inside China in Yunnan Province. [1:4, map, P. 4.]

Chungking said that Chinese guerrillas in Eastern China had raided fifteen Japanese-occupied cities during the past two weeks and destroyed power plants and communications. [6:3, with map.]

The United Nations Australian Headquarters announced successful air attacks on Lae, New Guinea, and Rabaul, New Britain. A Japanese air attack on Port Moresby was repulsed. [4:4.]

On the other side of the world, London announced Royal Air Force attacks on the Skoda munitions plant in Czechoslovakia and factories at Stuttgart in Southwestern Germany. The Germans raided points on the British south coast. [10:2.]

The story was heard in London that a group of German generals had informed Adolf Hitler that if the campaign in Russia this year should fail, they would seek to abolish the National Socialist system. [8:4-5.]

Moscow reported an offensive in the south against German-held Kharkov, Kursk and Taganrog. [1:7.]

Washington disclosed the sinking of three more merchant vessels off the United States east coast. [5:1.]

JAPANESE FINALLY TAKE CORREGIDOR

Japanese forces attacking from the Bataan Peninsula have forced the surrender of Corregidor and other United States island fortresses at the entrance to Manila Bay.

Laval Protests 'Aggression' But Won't Seek U. S. Break

By LANSING WARREN
By Telephone to THE NEW YORK TIMES.

VICHY, France, May 5—Replying to the American note expressing approbation of the British occupation of Madagascar, Pierre Laval as Chief of the French Government and Foreign Minister, tonight protested the move as an aggression. He rejected as inadmissible the "pretension of the Government of the United States to forbid France to defend her territory when attacked," and declared that he leaves "to President Roosevelt the share of responsibility that may fall to him in consequence of this aggression."

[In Washington, Secretary Hull made it clear that there would be no deviation from the approval of the British action at Madagascar. After a White House session, Pacific War Council members praised the move.]

M. Laval, in handing his note to the American Chargé d'Affaires, S. Pinckney Tuck, recalled the long record of friendship between France and the United States and added:

"You were present at my recent interview with your Ambassador, Admiral Leahy, and I wish again to repeat to you what I said to him, that no definitive gesture leading to a break will be initiated by France."

Indicates Grave Situation

M. Laval read his reply to the assembled French and foreign press in a salon of the Hotel du Parc, and completed it with comments that indicated the full seriousness for French-American relations because the United States for the first time was directly involved in diplomatic controversy with France.

Following is the text of the note as read to the correspondents by M. Laval:

In replying to the note handed in today by the Chargé d'Affaires of the United States of America, the French Government raises the most energetic protest against the aggression of which Madagascar has just been the object on the part of British forces.

It notes the assurance given that Madagascar will be returned to France some day.

It rejects as inadmissible the pretension of the Government of the United States to forbid France to defend her territory when attacked.

The French Government is the sole judge of the obligations imposed by its honor. In that manner, the defenders of Madagascar have understood correctly their duties. They have not hesitated, despite their numerical inferiority, to carry out their duties according to the most noble tradition of the French Army.

England so often since the Armistice has manifested hostility to France and the aggression

Continued on Page Two

RED ARMY ATTACKS KEY GERMAN BASES

Timoshenko Smashes at Kursk, Kharkov and Taganrog to Forestall Nazi Drivé

By The Associated Press.

MOSCOW, May 5—Stealing the jump on Reichsfuehrer Hitler, hundreds of thousands of Russian soldiers, tanks and planes smashed head-on today at three key German bases from which it was believed the Nazi leader was planning his Spring or Summer drive.

Under command of Marshal Semyon Timoshenko, the first Russian general to turn back the German military machine with the recapture of Rostov last November, the Red Army struck at Kharkov, Kursk and Taganrog in the strongest Nazi-held section of the long battle line.

Action was also stepped-up in the northern sectors, particularly the hard-fought Kalinin area northwest of Moscow. The army newspaper Red Star said the Germans were

Continued on Page Ten

OTHER FORTS FALL

American Soldiers Had Held Out in Spite of Supply Shortage

COURAGE IS PRAISED

Roosevelt Views Their Example as Guarantee of Final Victory

By The Associated Press.

AT UNITED NATIONS HEADQUARTERS, Australia, Wednesday, May 6—The American fortress of Corregidor and the other fortified islands in the entrance to Manila Bay surrendered today, it was officially announced here.

Besides the rock that is Corregidor, the United States forts that had held out were Fort Hughes, Fort Drum and Fort Frank.

The end came in the second day of the final Japanese assault, launched at midnight Tuesday, Manila time, with landings from Bataan Peninsula after Corregidor had been pounded again and again by Japanese big guns and aerial bombs. Corregidor alone had had 300 air raids since Dec. 29, when thirty-five Japanese bombers attacked for three hours.

A spokesman for General Douglas MacArthur, who led the brilliant defense of Bataan and the forts at the mouth of Manila Bay until ordered to Australia, made this announcement:

"General Wainwright has surrendered Corregidor and the other fortified islands in Manila Harbor."

There were believed to be about 7,000 men and women altogether on Corregidor and the other fortified islands. Besides the original garrisons, there was a naval detachment consisting originally of some 3,500 Marines and bluejackets who were removed to Corregidor when fighting ceased April 9 on Bataan Peninsula. A group of Army nurses also reached Corregidor.

Troops Half-Starved

By CHARLES HURD
Special to THE NEW YORK TIMES.

WASHINGTON, May 5—The fortified island of Corregidor in Manila Bay, last bastion of the American defenders of the Philippine Island, Luzon, was fighting a landing attack by Japanese troops today.

The issue of the fighting was not known in Washington at 5 P. M., when the War Department issued a communiqué, but two factors indicated grave concern over the outcome of a contest in which the defenders are outnumbered,

Continued on Page Five

Mrs. Rosenberg in 2 Federal Jobs While Making $22,500 on the Side

By LOUIS STARK
Special to THE NEW YORK TIMES.

WASHINGTON, May 5 — Some members of the House Appropriations Committee asserted today that they were determined to write into all future supply bills a provision prohibiting Federal administrative officials from accepting employment outside the government. This came following the disclosure at a closed meeting of an appropriations subcommittee today that Mrs. Anna M. Rosenberg of New York, regional director of the Social Security Board, receives a large income from private industry and also draws pay from another agency.

Mrs. Rosenberg's Social Security Board post pays $7,500 on a full time basis. Besides this Federal position she revealed to the subcommittee today that she received $20,000 a year for part time work as public and labor relations consultant to the Macy-Bamberger stores in New York and Newark, and $2,500 a year for similar services performed for I. Miller, New York shoe dealer.

In addition, Mrs. Rosenberg is a consultant on the staff of Nelson Rockefeller, coordinator of American Affairs. For this service she receives $6,000 a year. Her total earnings therefore are $36,000 a year, $13,500 paid by two government agencies and $22,500 by industry.

Arthur J. Altmeyer, chairman of the Social Security Board, who accompanied Mrs. Rosenberg to the committee meeting today, revealed that when the regional directorship was offered to her six years ago Mrs. Rosenberg made it a condition that she be permitted to continue her work as labor consultant for private concerns. Correspond-

Continued on Page Twenty-eight

G. M. Defies WLB on Double Pay; Hearing Will Take Up Issue Today

Special to THE NEW YORK TIMES.

DETROIT, Mich., May 5—On the eve of the start of negotiations before a panel of the National War Labor Board between the General Motors Corporation and the United Automobile Workers, C. I. O., C. E. Wilson, president of the corporation, revealed today that it had defied the board on the issue of double-time pay for Sunday and holiday work.

The disclosure came in the release by Mr. Wilson of the texts of exchanges of correspondence among the corporation, the board and the union. The correspondence dated from April 27. It included a copy of the order by the board to Mr. Wilson May 1 that double-time pay for Sunday work be continued by the company to May 18.

In reply to the order, the releases by Mr. Wilson showed, H. W. Anderson, vice president of General Motors, sent the board on May 2 a telegram which said that "we protest and do not agree to comply with your directive order."

The hearings before the NWLB panel are scheduled to open in Washington tomorrow morning. They aim at a renewal of the union contract which expired April 28. The contract has been continued in effect except for a stipulation by General Motors April 27 that "pending a final adjustment," double time "will not be paid for Sunday and holiday work." It has been agreed that when a new agreement is reached all its terms will be retroactive to April 28.

Walter P. Reuther, director of the General Motors division of the union, has made known that the union wished to have the Washington hearing open to the public, including the press. Mr. Wilson, in a telegram to the board today,

Continued on Page Fourteen

"All the News That's Fit to Print."

The New York Times.

LATE CITY EDITION
Moderate temperature today.
Temperatures Yesterday—Max., 80; Min., 63

VOL. XCI..No. 30,809. Entered as Second-Class Matter, Postoffice, New York, N. Y. NEW YORK, MONDAY, JUNE 1, 1942. THREE CENTS NEW YORK CITY and Vicinity

1,000 BRITISH BOMBERS SET COLOGNE ON FIRE; USE 3,000 TONS OF EXPLOSIVES IN RECORD RAID; GERMANS ARE HURLED BACK IN BID FOR TOBRUK

NEAR 'MIRACULOUS,' IS MAYOR'S RETORT TO ARMY ON DIMOUT

'Good Job Is Being Done,' He Insists, Taking Issue With Report of Air Survey

HE INVITES AN INSPECTION

Westchester, Other Sections Say They Are Observing Regulations Strictly

Great progress has been made in dimming out the lights of New York City, Mayor La Guardia declared yesterday in his weekly radio broadcast over WNYC, the municipal radio station. He maintained that considering the extent and population of the city and its normal illumination the success of the dimout "borders on the miraculous."

Mayor La Guardia took issue with the report released Saturday by Major Gen. T. A. Terry, commanding the Second Corps Area, which characterized the observance of dimout regulations throughout the metropolitan area as "in general disappointing." He stoutly maintained that the dimout "has been very successful" and he invited an inspection of Broadway or any other thoroughfare of the city.

"Oh yes, I read the papers this morning," the Mayor said. "I read the report and I am quite certain that Major Gen. Terry regrets the characterization and the description in that report as much as I do. I say I am sure that Major Gen. Terry regrets it, because he told me so this morning."

Says "Good Job Is Being Done"

Mayor La Guardia contended that "if you will strip the report of its characterizations and descriptions, using diamonds very profusely, it will be seen that a good job is being done."

The Mayor announced that arrangements had been made to dimout the Lewisohn Stadium at City College for the usual Summer season of symphony concerts and that the series would start this year on June 17.

When General Terry was informed of the Mayor's remarks about the Army report, he merely said:

"The city, so far as I know, is cooperating splendidly in the dimout effort, but it is a big job and it has quite a way to go."

Persons familiar with General Terry's struggle to reduce the sky glow over the metropolitan area explained that the report was meant to be helpful and not to be critical, and that the difference between the general and the Mayor was simply a difference of opinion as to literary style. The Mayor did not like the way the report was written, they said, but the general did. They denied that the general had expressed regret at the language of the report; they said he had merely expressed regret that the Mayor didn't like it.

Colonel Frederick L. Devereux, chief director of civilian protection of Westchester County, made a personal inspection yesterday to make sure that Westchester communities obeyed the blackout regu-

Continued on Page Eight

If in Doubt, Put It Out

Army officials are still perturbed over many "flagrant" instances of non-compliance with the dimout regulations and are continuing their efforts to educate citizens to the vital importance of extinguishing all unnecessary lights and shielding all those that are necessary.

Pointing out that the massed effect of countless thousands of lights in New York City and its surrounding area is to create a sky glow that silhouettes ships for enemy submarines far at sea, they are endeavoring to drive home to the public the slogan of the Second Corps Area: "If in doubt, put it out."

Swedish Ship Brings 908 From War Zone

The Swedish-American liner Drottningholm, bringing 908 citizens of the United States and other American republics from the war zones in Europe, arrived in the Narrows at 7 o'clock last evening and anchored to wait until this morning. According to the Navy Department, she will dock at 8 A. M. today at Pier F, Jersey City.

Her passenger list includes many diplomats and consular officials with their families, war correspondents from Africa, Egypt, Italy and other countries in Europe and the East.

G. Hilmer Lundbeck, managing director of the Swedish-American Line, who will meet the Drottningholm at the pier, said the ship would leave again on June 3 or 4 for Lisbon and make a return trip to New York bringing back more American citizens.

DECEPTION IS LAID TO STANDARD OIL

Arnold in New Complaint Says Firm Misled Senators on Buna Rubber and Plane Gasoline

By C. P. TRUSSELL
Special to THE NEW YORK TIMES.

WASHINGTON, May 31—The Standard Oil Company of New Jersey "covered up" and "distorted facts" in its rebuttal to charges that the company's cartel arrangement with I. G. Farbenindustrie of Germany had hampered the development of synthetic rubber in the United States, Thurman Arnold, assistant attorney general, asserted today.

The head of the Anti-Trust Division of the Department of Justice accused the company of similar misrepresentations about the effect of the cartel on aviation gasoline for the United States and about the company's sale of gasoline to Axis airlines and negotiations with Matsui, a Japanese firm, before the war.

Mr. Arnold will present tomor-

Continued on Page Seven

NAZIS HELD IN LIBYA

British Hammer Enemy by Land and Air With Hint at Offensive

R. A. F. RAIDS FURIOUS

Rommel Force Reported in Trap Facing Flight or Annihilation

By JOSEPH M. LEVY
Wireless to THE NEW YORK TIMES.

WITH BRITISH FORCES in the Western Desert, May 31—After four days of miscalculated Blitzkrieg, Field Marshal Erwin Rommel and his Axis armored forces, together with reinforcements that he had rushed through gaps forced in mine fields in a vain effort to solve his supply problem, were making a last attempt today to achieve their original objective—Tobruk.

As the British Eighth Army continued to batter the enemy in the fighting in Eastern Libya, it seemed most probable that the British commander, Lieut. Gen. Neil Methuen Ritchie, would turn from the defensive to the offensive.

Credit for the decisive turn in the battle goes jointly to the Royal Air Force, which cut the German supply columns to pieces, and to the British armored forces, which, with the help of United States-built tanks, attacked the Axis armored elements.

Enemy Gets Panicky

Although the German moves, in the main, were orderly, around Harmat, about eighteen miles northeast of Bir Hacheim, the Nazis were so bewildered that they destroyed or abandoned thirty-five of their own tanks, while at a few other points they showed similar signs of nervousness.

Magnificent fighting by the British and the Free French, coupled with the ceaseless attacks by the R. A. F. that previously had blocked the German bid for Tobruk, turned the enemy westward. Thus, for all their efforts the Ger-

Continued on Page Seven

War News Summarized

MONDAY, JUNE 1, 1942

Britain's Air Force subjected Cologne, Germany's third city, early yesterday to the heaviest single air raid ever undertaken, while the situation on the world battle fronts changed little, though there was heavy fighting in Libya.

A thousand or more bombers participated in the great raid on Cologne and in all 1,250 planes took part in the operation. Some 3,000 tons of bombs were dropped on the city in ninety minutes, according to the British, and returning pilots said they had seen a cloud of smoke 15,000 feet high rising above Cologne. The smoke remained visible as far as the Netherland coast, 135 miles away. Forty-four British planes failed to return. [1:8; map, P. 2.]

Pilots who gave a more detailed picture of the raid said that they had left Cologne a sea of flame. One of the returning pilots said that seven-eighths of Cologne had been set afire. [1:7.]

The great assault involved elaborate planning. At least thirteen different types of planes were used. They took off from sixty different airfields and had to go in over the objective at six-second intervals. [1:6.]

The German High Command granted that the British had done "great damage" to Cologne in the "terror raid," but alleged that it was mostly in residential sections. German broadcasts also claimed that only seventy British planes had taken part and that the figure given by the British was fantastic. [3:1.]

The Prague radio announced that eighteen more Czechs had been executed, raising to eighty-one the total since the attack on Reinhard Heydrich, the notorious deputy chief of the Gestapo. Herr Heydrich was believed to be near death. [4:1.]

Vichy reported that two policemen had been killed and three others wounded in a food riot in Paris. [1:5.]

British forces in Libya were battering at the Axis troops making a last attempt to get at their objective, Tobruk. The battle appeared to have taken a decisive turn in favor of the British. [1:3; map, P. 7.]

The Russians claimed to have taken important enemy lines on the Kalinin front northwest of Moscow. Only local encounters were reported from the Kharkov front. [1:4.]

United Nations Headquarters, Australia, announced that three Japanese midget submarines probably had been destroyed during a wholly unsuccessful Japanese mass submarine attack on Sydney harbor. [1:5-6.]

Chungking announced attacks on eight Japanese positions in Anhwei Province some 200 miles west of Shanghai. The Japanese were making a new landing on the coast of Chekiang Province and pressing their attack in that region. [6:3-4.] The Chinese military attaché at Washington urged the United Nations to strike quickly at Japan from air bases in the Chinese coastal region now threatened by the Japanese. [6:[illegible].]

The United States Navy released the news of the sinking of three United States merchant vessels in the Caribbean and one Norwegian vessel in the Gulf of Mexico. [6:7.]

TEA AFTER THE GREATEST AIR RAID IN HISTORY

A warming cup from an American-donated canteen is welcomed by Canadian bombers

Associated Press Radiophoto, passed yesterday by British censor

NAZIS' LINES SEIZED IN KALININ FIGHTING

Red Army Takes the Initiative After Repelling Heavy Blows —Izyum Barrier Holds

By RALPH PARKER
Wireless to THE NEW YORK TIMES.

MOSCOW, May 31—While fighting on the Kharkov front subsides, action on other fronts is characterized by reconnaissance in considerable force by both sides. This reconnaissance, when challenged by one side or the other, leads to sharp and bitter fighting.

Action of this sort has developed on the largest scale on what the Russians still call the Kalinin front, although Red Army troops are fighting far from the city of Kalinin itself. Kalinin Province is large, stretching from the Latvian border to a point east of Moscow.

The army newspaper Red Star reports that several days ago the Germans showed considerable activity in several sectors of this front, starting frequent attacks after having accumulated heavy forces. The failure of these local attacks seems to have discouraged them from persisting and their activities have decreased. But in several areas the Russians now have taken the initiative and have captured lines described as highly favorable for future action.

[A Russian communiqué said, according to The Associated Press, that Soviet forces had seized important lines after three days spent in repulsing German counter-attacks. The Germans left 1,100 dead or wounded on the field, it was added.]

Von Leeb Forces Routed

It also is reported that two battalions of the German 254th Division, which is part of General Field Marshal Wilhelm Ritter von Leeb's army on the Leningrad front, were routed in an attempt to advance through swampy country. Russian artillery checked German tanks using a road, but German flanking movements through swamps made some progress until the enemy forces were trapped. The Germans fled after severe hand-to-hand fighting with Russian grenadiers. The Russians are constantly improving their positions on this front, Red Star says.

On the Kharkov front the Russian river barrier in the Izyum-Barvenkova sector, southeast of Kharkov, was firmly held against new German attempts to cross it. Reports reaching Moscow from the

Continued on Page Five

3 Midget Submarines Raid Sydney; All Believed Sunk

By The United Press.

MELBOURNE, Australia, Monday, June 1—Three Japanese midget submarines penetrated the great harbor at Sydney, Australia's largest city, last night, but they were believed to have been destroyed after they had damaged one small vessel, it was announced today.

The raid, first threat to this part of Australia, was thought to indicate the presence of at least a small Japanese naval force off the southeastern—and most populous—section of the country. Midget submarines, which have only a short range, operate from a mother ship and it was felt that such a vessel hardly would travel unescorted.

The first submarine was sighted moving slowly along the main harbor channel, its periscope and upper conning tower exposed. It passed close to a harbor ferry loaded with passengers. Depth charges, released by naval vessels soon afterward, rocked waterfront buildings, and gunfire echoed across the harbor.

Announcement of the raid by the two-man submarines—of the type used in the attack on Pearl Harbor last Dec. 7—was made in a special communiqué issued by General Douglas MacArthur's headquarters.

"The enemy's attack was completely unsuccessful," the communiqué said. "Damage was confined to one small harbor vessel of no military value."

One of the submarines was believed to have been destroyed by

Continued on Page Six

2 POLICEMEN SLAIN IN PARIS FOOD RIOT

More Wounded in Bitter Clash —Gang Raids Shop, Throws Goods to Waiting Queue

By LANSING WARREN
By Telephone to THE NEW YORK TIMES.

VICHY, France, May 31—Crowds mobbed a food store in Paris today and in the clash that followed two policemen were killed and three wounded. A considerable number of other persons were injured.

The trouble started when persons inside the store began looting supplies and throwing foodstuffs and canned goods from the windows to those who were waiting in the food lines outside. The police were called and met with armed resistance from the rioters.

Arrests were made after the riot, showing, according to the police, that the incident had been organized by "Communist agitators." Those accused will be brought before the special court-martial.

The store where the clash took place is located on the left bank of the river, on the Rue de Seine.

In another quarter of Paris youths of a political organization during the night overturned the statue of Edward VII. The statue to the founder of the Entente Cordiale was located in the small

Continued on Page Four

FINE TIMING USED IN R. A. F. ASSAULT

Coordination at Home Fields Sends a Plane Over Reich City Every 6 Seconds

Wireless to THE NEW YORK TIMES.

LONDON, May 31—A vast amount of intricate planning and preparation preceded last night's attack on Cologne by more than 1,000 bombers. The operation, the first in which all Royal Air Force commands were concerned in one night's activity, called for perfect timing and perfect coordination. At least thirteen different types of aircraft were used—the greatest assortment ever engaged together.

More than 1,000 bombers had to be got into the air from scores of fields in a very short space of time at exactly regulated intervals. Each plane had to have a bomb load appropriate to its type and suitable for the part it was to play in the great raid.

The nicest timing was required of the "intruder" squadrons, whose task it was to keep German fighters busy while the bombers slipped through the defenses and attacked the objectives. Another bit of fine timing was required to arrange the bombers' arrival so that they would be coming in from all direc-

Continued on Page Three

COLOGNE 'INFERNO' ASTONISHES PILOTS

Defenses Overwhelmed, British Fliers Say—Germans on Air Describe Horrors

By The United Press.

LONDON, May 31—Seven-eighths of Cologne, a city the size of Boston, was in flames, an inferno "almost too gigantic to be real," when the history-making raid was over last night, pilots who took part in it said tonight.

"When we got there, I almost felt like leaving and trying to find another target. It didn't seem possible to do more damage than had already been done," Wing Commander Johnny Fauquier, Canadian pilot officer, related.

"Cologne was just a sea of flames," said Squadron Leader Len Frazer of Winnipeg, one of the more than 1,000 Canadian airmen who had a hand in the epic raid.

"I saw London burning during the Battle of Britain, and it was nothing compared with Cologne," Pilot Officer H. J. M. Lacelle of Toronto, gunner in the tail of a Canadian bomber, contributed.

Their reports were typical of the thousands being sifted tonight and compiled into a record of the mightiest piece of destruction ever devised by man.

Defenses Overwhelmed

The lurid sky over Cologne for ninety minutes was as busy as Piccadilly Circus as the great Lancasters and Halifaxes, Stirlings and Manchesters, streaked in at the rate of one every six seconds to unload their total cargo of steel-cased death.

Before the overwhelmed and bewildered German defenses could focus on one plane, it was zooming away and another was on its tail. The Royal Air Force plan of supersaturating the enemy's target field was described as an absolute success. German fighter planes were there, but not enough to interfere seriously with the attack.

"It was almost too gigantic to be real," said the pilot of one Halifax. "But it was real enough when we got there. Below us in every part of the city buildings were ablaze. Here and there you could see their outlines, but mostly it was just one long stretch of fire.

"It was strange to see the flames reflected on our aircraft. It looked at times as if we were on fire ourselves, with the red glow dancing up and down our wings."

"I could identify every type of

Continued on Page Three

A 90-MINUTE RAID

R. A. F. Causes Havoc in the Rhine City—Nazis Admit 'Great Damage'

COST IS 44 PLANES

250 Extra Aircraft Hit Foe's Bases—Attack a Start, Says Churchill

By RAYMOND DANIELL
Wireless to THE NEW YORK TIMES.

LONDON, Monday, June 1—More than 1,000 British bombers dumped 3,000 tons of high explosive bombs Saturday night on Cologne and elsewhere in the Rhineland and in the Ruhr.

"Cologne was the main objective," the Air Ministry said, and British officials asserted the raid was the biggest air attack in the history of warfare.

Prime Minister Winston Churchill, congratulating Air Marshal A. T. Harris, chief of the Bomber Command of the Royal Air Force, who planned and directed the devastating attack on one of Germany's largest and industrially most important cities, described it as "a herald of what Germany will receive city by city from now on."

Losses Relatively Slight

It was indeed the heaviest blow the R. A. F. has delivered yet in its promised air offensive against the Nazis, and it will not be long now before the American Air Force joins the British. The shadow that two years ago was no bigger than a man's hand has grown to a huge cloud threatening the whole Reich.

Forty-four British planes failed to return to their bases from the Saturday night operations, which included heavy attacks on Nazi coastal bases and airfields and fighter action against enemy interception.

This was the largest number of planes the British have ever lost in one raid, but it was still little more than 4 per cent of all the planes that were used.

That the losses for an assault upon a German city defended, as Cologne was, by 120 searchlights and at least 500 anti-aircraft guns and big Nazi night fighter forces, were not heavier was due largely to new tactics used by the R. A. F.

Tactics Counter Nazi Defenses

The bombers went in over their target at the rate of one every six seconds to distract and confuse the searchlight operators and the German gun crews and prevent their concentrating long on any single plane.

At the same time at least 250 other planes were drawn from every command of the R. A. F. and swarmed over the Nazi airports, from which enemy fighters might have been drawn to intercept the Cologne attackers.

[The Germans claimed to have shot down forty-seven British planes, thirty-six over Cologne and eleven near the coast. Berlin, while reporting "great damage" at Cologne, tried to discount the size of the raid by saying only seventy R. A. F. bombers were over the city. At the same time, Nazi officials talked of "reprisals."

[British bombers were over Western Germany again last night, according to a Berlin broadcast recorded by The Associated Press early today.]

Offensive Goes on During Day

Saturday night's supreme effort by no means exhausted the R. A. F. In daylight yesterday British fighters made several sweeps over Nazi-occupied France and Belgium. They shot down four Nazi fighters and lost eight of their own planes.

Off the Netherland coast British planes set afire and sunk a German armed trawler and two other vessels were driven aground, ac-

Continued on Page Two

"All the News That's Fit to Print."

The New York Times.

LATE CITY EDITION
Showers and slightly warmer today.
Temperatures Yesterday—Max., 62; Min., 54

Copyright, 1942, by The New York Times Company.

VOL. XCI..No. 30,810. Entered as Second-Class Matter, Postoffice, New York, N. Y. NEW YORK, TUESDAY, JUNE 2, 1942. THREE CENTS NEW YORK CITY and Vicinity

COLOGNE DEATH TOLL PUT AS HIGH AS 20,000, WITH 54,000 HURT; NAZIS RAID CANTERBURY; AXIS TANKS STRUGGLE TO ESCAPE IN LIBYA

NEW DIMOUT ORDER SAYS ALL LIGHTING MUST BE SCREENED

Shades Required for Windows and Skylights Unless Lamps' Direct Rays Are Cut Off

ADVERTISING SIGNS BANNED

Rulings by Army, Effective at Once, to Apply in New York, Jersey and Delaware

The text of the new dimout regulations, Page 12.

All windows and skylights in a wide area along the seaboard must be shaded or screened to prevent escape through them of direct rays of light, according to new and more stringent dimout regulations announced last night by the Army. As an alternative, the interior lights of the rooms concerned must be shaded individually to prevent rays from shining through the windows, it was said. All illuminated exterior advertising signs were banned.

Major Gen. T. A. Terry, commanding the Second Corps Area, promulgated the new regulations, which will become effective at once and apply from sundown to sunrise for the duration of the war. He announced that copies of the rules had been sent to the Governors of New York, New Jersey and Delaware and that State and local authorities would be expected to enforce them.

Area Covered by Rules

The regulations apply to all New York City; to Nassau and Suffolk Counties and that part of Westchester County south of Mount Pleasant Township in New York State; to all or part of twelve New Jersey counties, including Hudson, Essex and Union, Passaic County southeast of the Passaic River and Bergen County south of Route 4, and to the counties of Kent and Sussex in Delaware.

The rules provide that all street and traffic lights and all lights used for outdoor protection, manufacture, storage or shipping of war materials, such as floodlights in freight yards, docks and shipyards, must be reduced in volume, number or wattage to "a minimum consistent with their purpose" and must be shaded to prevent their rays from shining above the horizontal.

Exterior lights used in such places as parking lots, playgrounds, marquees, sidewalk cafes and places of amusement must be shaded to prevent their rays from shining above the horizontal, and the combined lighting of such areas may not exceed an average of one-quarter watt a square foot. No individual light of more than 100 watts may be used for such purposes.

Business Displays

Shop and display windows, open lobbies and business places must be shaded by opaque material to prevent the direct rays of lights within from being visible without, and the total lighting must not exceed one-half watt a square foot of window opening. If a display window is not shielded from the interior of the store by a protective backdrop, the interior lighting must not exceed one-quarter watt a square foot of floor space.

Automobiles must use only their parking lights in areas where their headlights might be visible at sea. All lights normally visible from the sea must be dimmed or shaded so that they will not be visible more than a mile from shore. Bonfires for burning brush or rubbish must be extinguished an hour before sundown.

General Terry explained that

Continued on Page Twelve

If in Doubt, Put It Out

The most recent foot-lambert measurements taken off the coast here show that the land horizon brightness is still eight times as great as the sea horizon brightness, a spokesman for the Second Corps Area disclosed yesterday as part of the campaign for stricter observance of the dimout regulations in the metropolitan and adjacent areas.

Pointing out that a ratio of two to one in land horizon brightness over sea horizon brightness is all that is required to silhouette a ship for an enemy submarine, he declared that a great improvement in conditions would have to be effected. The Army is still urging the public to observe the Second Corps Area slogan: "If in doubt, put it out."

Mexico Now at War With 3 Axis Nations

Special Cable to THE NEW YORK TIMES.

MEXICO CITY, June 1—Foreign Minister Ezequiel Padilla tonight notified Germany, Italy and Japan that Mexico was at war with them.

He handed the representatives here of Sweden, Switzerland and Portugal, acting for the three Axis Powers, the proclamation by President Manuel Avila Camacho at 6:20 P. M.

The proclamation will be published in the official journal tomorrow, when the extraordinary powers conferred on the President and the suspension of constitutional guarantees will take effect.

The first war declaration in Mexico's history aligns her as the twenty-eighth of the United Nations belligerents.

STORE DELIVERIES CUT DRASTICALLY

Bread, Laundry, Newspapers, Other Daily Services Reduced to Save Rubber and Oil

The highly organized delivery services of milk companies, department stores, laundries, newspapers, bakeries and dozens of other services all suffered drastic wartime curtailment yesterday under the new order of the Office of Defense Transportation diminishing delivery mileage by 25 per cent.

The curtailment measure, designed to conserve rubber and gasoline, appeared to meet with general compliance. Most of the concerns employing large fleets of trucks reorganized delivery schedules both by eliminating some deliveries and by contracting delivery areas, but in most cases, it was said, the prudent householder in the city need suffer no serious inconvenience. Summer resorts and outlying communities served by metropolitan fleets will be hardest hit by the restricted deliveries.

Milk Program to Begin

The every-other-day plan for the delivery of milk, which received official approval from the ODT yesterday, will begin today when the first one-half of those consumers who enjoy home delivery of milk will receive a two-day supply. Milk deliveries, both wholesale and retail, will begin from now on in the early daylight hours instead of before dawn, and "call-back" deliveries will be eliminated entirely. There will be no curtailment, however, in milk deliveries to Army, Navy and hospital services.

Newspapers, by way of complying with the delivery order, reduced the number of editions in some cases from seven to four, combined editions, changed press deadlines and made plans for the consolidation of routes and deliveries. These measures were said to assure a saving of truck mileage well above the 25 per cent required by the order. The plan for consolidation of routes awaits a decision expected today by Raymond P. McNulty, impartial chairman of the newspaper industry of New York, in a dispute between the publishers and the Newspaper and Mail Deliverers Union, which had objected to proposals to combine routes and deliveries.

Department store delivery services had already been largely reorganized and the campaign to persuade customers to carry their own parcels had met with such success that no drastic changes in these delivery schedules were needed yesterday. In general the stores have eliminated such luxury services as

Continued on Page Fifteen

'DIPLOMAT SHIP' IN

92 of Her Passengers Are Unscheduled Refugees From Nazi Prisons

IMMIGRATION MEN WARY

75 Are Held for Questioning—Leahy Returns, Worn and Sad, With Wife's Body

The Swedish American liner Drottningholm, gaudily painted and marked as a "diplomat ship" entitled to safe passage in the Atlantic, docked in Jersey City yesterday morning with 908 passengers, including the first American diplomatic party to be exchanged since the United States entered the war.

Escorted by patrol craft and cutters, the 11,055-ton liner came up the bay as thousands of ferry commuters crossed the harbor and the Hudson. Her bright blue and yellow markings were clearly visible to them despite heavy rain squalls. She is one of the few neutral liners of her size remaining in service, and she stood out in sharp contrast amid a harbor company of dull gray ships.

Those on board, some of them recently out of concentration camps and prisons, told harrowing stories of privation and cruelty in Nazi Europe, reiterating the accounts given by thousands of refugees who have preceded them in recent years.

A Strange Shipload

Veteran port officials who have been meeting ships regularly for many years said the voyage of the Drottningholm was unlike any they could remember. In addition to United States diplomats returning to Washington from the closed embassies and legations, there were Americans who could not speak English, elderly Americans who had not seen this country since childhood, and some with American papers who had never been here.

For hours after the ship docked, workers of the Travelers Aid Society and other welfare agencies were busy with puzzled adults, obviously alien to their native land, and with children traveling on citizen passports. There were fifty-two children less than 8 years old on the ship.

Though she was an American refugee ship, chartered by the Maritime Commission for the Department of State, the Drottningholm actually brought only 480 United States citizens, so that nearly half of those on board were aliens.

An air of mystery surrounded ninety-two non-Americans, most of whom came from the German women's concentration camp at Liebenau and the men's camp at Laufen, Upper Bavaria. The circumstances of their presence on the ship were not exactly clear, but ship officers and others said they had been interned when the war began and that they appeared at the last moment on the diplomat

Continued on Page Five

RETREAT IN DESERT

Rommel's Chief Aide Is Captured as British Pursue Enemy

FOE FIGHTS FOR WAY WEST

Posts Guns to Hold Gaps in Mine Fields—R. A. F. Aids Battle to Close Exits

By The United Press.

CAIRO, Egypt, June 1—Field Marshal Erwin Rommel's battered Axis tank army sought today to fight its way back westward through two gaps in the British mine fields between El Gazala and Bir Hacheim, and his tank commander, General Ludwig Cruewell, was a prisoner in British hands, front reports said tonight.

Under merciless attack from British infantry, artillery and planes, the Germans were burning their stranded tanks as they retreated.

Nazi prisoners were quoted as saying that Adolf Hitler had sent a message to Marshal Rommel that "Tobruk must fall by June 1," but when Marshal Rommel had seen his offensive breaking down he had flown to a rear base to try to reorganize his mauled forces.

Battle on for Exits

The German and Italian spearheads that broke through the British desert defense line last week were scrambling toward the mine-field gaps through which they had intended to run their supply lines. One of these gaps is at Mteifel es-Seghir, about forty miles southwest of Tobruk. The other is at Taleb, about ten miles farther south.

"The enemy," said a British communiqué, "though attacked continuously by our armored forces and the Royal Air Force, has partially succeeded in his purpose and has established a considerable force of anti-tank artillery in a position covering the gaps with the object of preventing their being closed by our armored forces. The gaps are under continuous artillery fire and R. A. F. attack. A large proportion of remaining enemy tanks and transports is still east of the mine fields and is being attacked by our troops and air forces."

The heaviest fighting was centered around Knightsbridge, desert crossroads about twenty-eight miles southwest of Tobruk, where British tanks and artillery were "smothering the enemy in massed fire," according to a front-line dispatch.

The R. A. F., master of the desert skies ever since Marshal Rommel struck last Wednesday, was concentrating its attacks on Axis tanks and supply vehicles, but today's R. A. F. communiqué also reported four more German planes shot down, three of them dive-bombers.

There also was a heavy R. A. F. raid on the Axis coastal base at Derna last night. A communiqué reported large fires set among parked German and Italian planes. Nineteen R. A. F. planes were reported missing by the British today.

General Cruewell was captured when his reconnaissance plane was shot down in the British lines, a British communiqué announced.

Error Traps Cruewell

WITH BRITISH FORCES IN Libya, May 31 (Delayed) (AP)—General Ludwig Cruewell, a commander of the German Africa Corps, who was captured May 26, said tonight that he had been taken prisoner because his pilot had landed in the midst of British desert troops in the mistaken belief that they were Italians.

British sources disclosed that Field Marshal Erwin Rommel, commander of the German Africa Corps, had sought shelter in a British Red Cross station last Friday while his motorized troops were fighting unsuccessfully against a British tank attack. He entered the dressing station after his troops had taken possession of it and chatted with soldiers and patients. After four hours he

Continued on Page Ten

Windsor Suddenly Cuts U. S. Stay; Labor Strife in Nassau Reported

By The United Press.

WASHINGTON, June 1—The British Embassy announced tonight that the Duke of Windsor would leave shortly—tonight or tomorrow morning—to return to Nassau, the Bahamas, "on urgent business," which was not explained.

The Duke will cut short his visit here, which had been planned to last for several days. The embassy did not indicate whether he would return soon. The Duchess will remain here, at least for a few days.

The change in the Duke's plans was unexpected. A few hours before the announcement of his plans to leave at once, the British press service had released his itinerary for tomorrow.

By The Associated Press.

WASHINGTON, June 1—A member of the Duke of Windsor's party said tonight he understood there had been "some sort of labor disturbance" at Nassau, capital of the Bahama Island group governed by the Duke.

Sidney Farrington, an aide to the Duke, said members of the party had talked with officials at Nassau and were assured that the situation was not serious. The character of the labor disturbance was not explained.

Special to THE NEW YORK TIMES.

WASHINGTON, June 1—The Duke and Duchess of Windsor had luncheon today at the White House as guests of the President and Mrs. Roosevelt. Stephen T. Early, Presidential secretary, said the luncheon was strictly a "family" affair and that no guest list would be issued.

"The President and Mrs. Roose-

Continued on Page Twenty-five

VICHY AMBASSADOR RETURNS TO WASHINGTON

Admiral William D. Leahy (center) is greeted by Ray Atherton (left), Acting Chief of the Division of European Affairs of the State Department, and Major General Blanton Winship, former Governor General of Puerto Rico.

Associated Press Wirephoto

BLACKOUT COVERS ALL OF NEW JERSEY

First State-Wide Test in East Reported by OCD Official as '93% Perfect'

With no moon to aid the mock raiders and rain helping to keep people at home in many sections, New Jersey staged from 10:10 to 10:40 last night the first Statewide surprise blackout in the East.

Pending a more comprehensive report by Major Gen. Thomas A. Terry, commandant of the Second Corps Area, who with Leonard C. Dreyfuss, head of the State Defense Council, and others observed the test from a naval craft cruising offshore, the demonstration appeared successful.

Harry A. Neuberger, director of civil protection, said at his Newark headquarters after the all-clear:

"Colonel Walter W. Metcalf, regional director of civil defense, and his aide, Major William Cullen, ob-

Continued on Page Twelve

Arnold Sees Early U. S. Aid In Irresistible Air Offensive

By RAYMOND DANIELL

Wireless to THE NEW YORK TIMES.

LONDON, June 1—Unless skilled observers have misread the signs, the great striking force that the Royal Air Force demonstrated in its ninety-minute raid with more than 1,000 bombers on Cologne Saturday night, will be doubled this Summer. Except for a few Bostons among the 250 other planes used to disrupt Nazi interceptor stations, not a single aircraft of American manufacture participated in the Cologne attack.

But Lieut. Gen. Henry H. Arnold, chief of the United States Army Air Corps, made if clear here today that before very long, not only American planes but American bomber crews flying under their own command would join the R. A. F. in "an air offensive against the enemy which he cannot meet, defeat or survive."

That, General Arnold disclosed, was the immediate purpose of his mission here.

[British bombers with fighter escorts struck throughout yesterday at port works, bases and factories used by the Nazis from Flushing to Cherbourg and in-

Continued on Page Four

War News Summarized

TUESDAY, JUNE 2, 1942

Reports of the staggering effect of the huge Cologne raid on the Rhineland population and additional reports that the Germans were in trouble in Libya indicated that Adolf Hitler was not doing too well yesterday. Other war fronts were relatively quiet, though the Japanese were developing an important complex of drives in East Central and Southern China.

Private information reaching New York from Europe indicates that deaths at Cologne may have totaled 20,000 and the wounded 54,000. The Germans claimed officially that there were only 111 dead. There were reports of mass migrations from Rhineland cities. [1:8.]

General Arnold, Chief of the United States Army Air Forces, now in London, followed up the great raid on Cologne with the statement that United States Army planes would soon join the British in an air offensive that the enemy would not be able to "meet, defeat or survive." [1:6-7.]

The Royal Air Force resumed the bombing offensive upon Germany last night. In daylight yesterday the R. A. F. attacked German bases and factories from Flushing to Cherbourg on the coast and various points inland in Belgium and France. [3:2.]

Historic monuments and other buildings in the town of Canterbury were wrecked by the Germans' "vengeance raid" early yesterday, but the British left the Germans guessing as to the cathedral there. [1:7.]

The Prague radio announced the execution of twenty-seven more Czechs, including four women, in connection with the attempted assassination of Reinhard Heydrich. This brought the total since the attack on the Protector to 108. [8:5.]

Marshal Rommel's attacking force in Libya was evidently attempting yesterday to withdraw westward under difficulties. The British announced the capture of General Cruewell, German second in command. Axis anti-tank guns had been placed to cover the line of retreat through the British land-mine fields. [1:4; map, P. 10.]

There was a lull on all Russian fronts, where the Germans were mobilizing new tank forces. [8:2.]

Japanese forces in China opened a three-pronged drive in Southern Kwangtung Province, evidently intended to open up the Hankow-Canton railway line. A new drive out of Nanchang southward and the continued drive through Chekiang Province in the direction of Nanchang indicated there was also an effort to open up the Hangchow-Canton railway connection. [2:2, with map.]

United States bombers based on India again pounded Japanese bases in Burma. [2:7.]

The liner Drottningholm docked yesterday with 908 passengers, of whom 480 were United States citizens repatriated from Europe. [1:3.]

REPRISAL DIRECTED AT CATHEDRAL CITY

Historic Canterbury Buildings Damaged in 25-Plane Raid —Casualties Are Light

By ROBERT P. POST

Wireless to THE NEW YORK TIMES.

CANTERBURY, England, June 1—About twenty-five German planes swept down last night on this ancient and famous cathedral city in what surely was a reprisal for the Royal Air Force raid on Cologne. But if the Germans fancied that it was an effective reprisal their fancy was ridiculous.

It is true that the Germans scored hits on their targets—old schools, churches and other medieval relics, some of which were irreparably damaged. It also is true that they killed a small number of civilians and a few soldiers. But it was not an effective reprisal, for Canterbury is a small and sleepy city, without a single factory or industry in it.

Whether or not the Germans hit Canterbury Cathedral is information that the censor will not permit to be disclosed. It would be of value to the enemy. But the Germans, coming in low by bright moonlight, certainly aimed for the cathedral.

[Although Canterbury had undergone no previous large-scale bombing, the Germans claimed to have attacked an airfield there in August, 1940, and they dropped about twenty bombs on the town on Oct. 17, 1940, but without damaging the cathedral.]

Morale Is Not Impaired

The raid seems to have been totally useless except as a vehicle of vengeance. It did not further the Nazis' plan for winning the war and it did not impair at all the morale of the people of Canterbury. If Canterbury is the first to pay for the raid on Cologne, then Canterbury is willing to pay.

"It was a bad raid for a small town," Mayor William Lefevre said today. "But if it was a reprisal, then every person in Canterbury would be willing to take this and much worse in return for such achievements as that of the R. A. F. over Cologne."

The newly enthroned Archbishop of Canterbury, Dr. William Tem-

Continued on Page Three

RHINELAND EXODUS

Mass Abandonment of Cities Reported After Battering of Cologne

R. A. F. RESUMES ATTACK

Another Great Raid on Reich Is Made—Germany Claims Felling of 29 Planes

Private advices from competent neutral observers in Berlin, relayed from Europe to THE NEW YORK TIMES last night, estimated the number killed in the Cologne raid as "in the neighborhood of 20,000." The total population is roughly 800,000.

British bombing forces resumed the heavy offensive over Germany last night, after a Sunday night interruption because of bad weather, London officials said today, according to The Associated Press. A Berlin broadcast, recorded by The United Press at London, said "strong forces" of the R. A. F. bombed towns in Western Germany. Berlin claimed twenty-nine of the raiders had been shot down.

So serious is the situation said to be in Cologne, in view of the warm weather that special detachments of the German Army sanitary forces have been dispatched to aid the local services in preventing the spread of disease. In addition to those killed, 54,000 were said to have been wounded, about 20 per cent critically.

The impression on the Rhineland population is said to have been such that, despite official restrictions on traveling and all attempts by the local authorities to put a stop to the exodus, the entire population of Aachen, Duesseldorf, Wuppertal, Mainz and other cities has started a mass migration from the Rhineland to avoid further bombardment. Three-fifths of the inhabitants of Cologne are being officially evacuated, mostly to the area of Munich, where they will be housed in emergency barracks erected during the last twenty-four hours.

Cathedral Is Not Damaged

Confirmation has also been received that the world-famous Cathedral of Cologne was unscathed, despite the 3,000 tons of incendiary and explosive bombs rained down during Saturday night's raid.

The Germans in a special communiqué issued yesterday afternoon "admitted" the death list had risen to "111 killed and some wounded." Later the Berlin radio said "139 civilians" had been killed. The word "terroristic" was used frequently in comment by official German quarters. In the past when that word has been employed it has often turned out to be an admission that damage was great. Although details are lacking, it is understood from Berlin neutral quarters that roughly five-sevenths of Cologne's chemical and fine machine-tool industries have been completely wrecked.

In European capitals last night, neutral as well as belligerent, the massive bombardment of Cologne by the British caused the deepest interest. It raised the question of mastery in the air and suggested that, contrary to views accepted hitherto in military quarters, this mastery may decide the final issue. Moreover, there was every indication that henceforth reprisal would follow upon reprisal.

"Women and Children" Is Cry

One German reaction, based in part on the reception of the news in the United States, suggested that the British intention was to wage war "exclusively on women and children" and to destroy civilian quarters and public monuments. As to the raid itself, the tendency in Berlin was to paint a dreadful picture of British losses. D. N. B., official German news agency, for instance, described "the wreckage of British planes brought down during the terroris-

Continued on Page Four

"All the News That's Fit to Print."

The New York Times.

LATE CITY EDITION
Warmer with gentle winds today.
Temperature Yesterday—Max., 69; Min., 52

Copyright, 1942, by The New York Times Company.

VOL. XCI..No. 30,812. Entered as Second-Class Matter, Postoffice, New York, N. Y. NEW YORK, THURSDAY, JUNE 4, 1942. THREE CENTS NEW YORK CITY and Vicinity

JAPANESE BOMB DUTCH HARBOR, ALASKA, TWICE; R. A. F. HAMMERS RUHR AND NORTHERN FRANCE; ROMMEL DRIVES WIDE WEDGE IN LIBYAN LINE

HOUSE BODY VOTES TO ELIMINATE CCC, SAVING $75,818,000

Appropriations Committee Cuts Item From Labor-Security Bill and Leaves $1,058,451,660

DIVIDES 15 TO 12 ON CAMPS

Scarcity of Farm Labor Cited, but Foes of Abolition Move to Take Fight to Floor

Special to THE NEW YORK TIMES.

WASHINGTON, June 3—Abolition of the Civilian Conservation Corps was voted by the House Committee on Appropriations today when it struck from the Labor Department-Federal Security Agency supply bill for the coming fiscal year the entire $75,818,000 with which the Administration sought to continue the CCC at 350-camp strength. The committee sent to the House a bill totaling $1,058,451,660.

This year the corps has been operating under a $246,960,000 fund, appropriated by Congress without contest.

The 15-12 vote for abolition came suddenly today, just before the committee reported the measure, with thirteen of its forty members absent. A fight for restoration of the much-reduced operating fund was begun immediately and will be carried to the House floor, probably tomorrow.

Committee action followed a tie vote of 3 to 3 in the subcommittee which handled the Labor-Security measure, when the issue of continuing or shutting down the nine-year-old project was taken to its first test.

Several factors entered into the voting of the committee members today.

Boys Needed Badly on Farms

The CCC, it was found, was drawing enrollees heavily from areas where farm labor was so scarce that warnings had been sounded that the "food-for-freedom" program was endangered.

In 1940, committeemen were told in executive session, recruitment from farm areas constituted about 19 per cent of the corps' strength. Last year, it was asserted, 43 per cent of the enrollees came direct from farms, and an additional 20 per cent from small towns in agricultural districts.

Meanwhile, from a peak of about 1,500 camps and 300,000 enrollees, the CCC had been reduced to 400 camps with 80,000 members and dropped further, as of the day before yesterday, to the 350 camps which, it was decided, were to be continued.

About 200 of the remaining camps are on military reservations and 150 on forest-protection projects, including forty-eight in national park areas.

Congressional approval of the Appropriations Committee's action, it was learned, would wipe out a personnel of 40,000 enrollees working on military reservations

Continued on Page Twelve

If in Doubt, Put It Out

The Army is trying to discourage the use of blue electric lamps in such places as theatre marquees, open lobbies, and amusement places because scientific measurements have shown they are not effective in reducing the amount of light contributed to the glow over the metropolitan area, it was learned yesterday at the headquarters of the Second Corps Area.

As a substitute Army experts recommend the use of red bulbs of low wattage, which contribute little if any light to the city's sky glow. In its campaign to reduce land horizon brightness to a point where it will no longer silhouette ships at sea for Axis submarines, the Army urges the public to remember the slogan of the Second Corps Area: "If in doubt, put it out."

West Coast Radios Off in 'Precaution'

Special to THE NEW YORK TIMES.

SAN FRANCISCO, Calif., June 3—Radios were silenced along the West Coast from the Canadian frontier to the Mexican border tonight at the direction of the Fourth Fighter Command.

The action was described as "merely a precautionary measure in view of the situation earlier today"—a reference, presumably, to the Japanese raid on Dutch Harbor, Alaska.

While radios were off the air a "blue" alert signal was sounded at 10:28 P. M., but the "all clear" came nine minutes later. There was no actual blackout, but the radios continued silent even after the alert period ended.

Headquarters of the Western Defense Command and Fourth Army announced afterward that an "unidentified target" that was "later identified" led to the alert. The statement did not say whether or not the "target" had been identified as "friendly."

A. F. L. UNION STRIKES AT BENNETT FIELD

Jurisdictional Dispute Over $3,000 Cables Hampers Navy $8,120,000 Program

A strike of 250 electricians, growing out of a jurisdictional conflict affecting $3,000 worth of work installing telephone cables, has tied up all electrical work on the Navy's $8,120,000 program for the expansion of Floyd Bennett Field since last Friday, it became known yesterday.

Because of the interdependence of the various construction crafts, the electrical tie-up has impeded other phases of construction on the Brooklyn naval air base, a vital link in the nation's coast defense, but officials were hopeful that operations would be resumed in time to prevent a full shutdown.

The strike was called by Local 3 of the International Brotherhood of Electrical Workers, A. F. of L.,

Continued on Page Fourteen

500 FIGHTING SHIPS TO COST 8 BILLIONS ASKED IN NEW BILL

Huge Aircraft Carrier Program Dominates, and Not a Single Battleship Is Called For

1,000 WARSHIPS NAVY'S AIM

As Vinson Presents New Measure, House Votes 3 Billion Bill —It Adds 100 Submarines

By C. P. TRUSSELL

Special to THE NEW YORK TIMES.

WASHINGTON, June 3—The greatest of the nation's new naval building programs, to add 500 fighting ships and 800 patrol, mine-laying and tending craft to the fleet and double its striking power as a completed two-ocean Navy in twenty-four months, was presented to the House today. It was sponsored by the chairman of the Naval Affairs Committee, Representative Vinson, after consultations with the Navy High Command.

The estimated expenditure of $8,300,000,000 would carry the defense and war commitments of the last three years past $170,000,000,000.

Even as the record-setting measure was introduced, the House, by a separate bill, voted $2,797,499,740 to the Navy in direct supplemental appropriations and contract powers, largely for the high-speed construction of more than 100 submarines and 500,000 more tons of auxiliary vessels to operate "in connection with the submarine program."

Though explanations were guarded as the latter appropriations measure was called up, it was indicated that the $1,115,000,000 of new auxiliary craft to be constructed, purchased or converted, might be used to service long-range operations of our submarines in the Pacific and other far-flung waters.

To avoid any delay, the House waived the rules by unanimous consent and voted the money even

Continued on Page Eleven

Commandos in Raid On Boulogne Area

By The United Press.

LONDON, Thursday, June 4—Special Service troops landed on the coast of Northern France early today and made a "reconnaissance raid" on the Boulogne-Le Touquet area, a special communiqué announced today. The troops obtained valuable information, the communiqué said.

The British Navy escorted and re-embarked the raiding force, while the Royal Air Force Fighter Command provided a protective "umbrella" for the operations.

Boulogne lies directly across Dover Strait from the southeast coast of England and is about thirty-two miles from Folkestone. Le Touquet is twelve miles south of Boulogne and also on the coast.

FASCIST PRESSURE ON VATICAN FAILS

Mussolini Unable to Bring Pope to Take a Stand on Axis Side in the War

The following article is by a former Rome correspondent of THE NEW YORK TIMES *who has just arrived in this country.*

By CAMILLE M. CIANFARRA

Since Italy's intervention in the war the relations between the Vatican and the Fascist Government have become increasingly strained as a result of Premier Benito Mussolini's policy of curbing the temporal activity of the Pope.

It would be an exaggeration to say that the Pope today is a prisoner in the Vatican, as was Pope Benedict XV during the first World War. Yet the fact remains that many important clauses of the 1929 Lateran Treaty between the Holy See and Italy that were drawn with the specific aim of safeguarding the temporal independence of the Pontiff were systematically violated when they did not fit in with Signor Mussolini's plans.

The geographical position of the Vatican State, in the heart of Italian territory, makes this policy easy to pursue. Signor Mussolini has many means with which to disturb the temporal life of the tiny State and is taking full advantage of them to apply pressure to the Pontiff in an effort to win the moral support of the Catholic Church for the Axis.

Yugoslav Minister Ousted

When Italy and Germany invaded Yugoslavia in April, 1941, the Yugoslav Minister to the Holy See was ordered to leave Italy. He protested that he intended to take up residence in the Vatican, where quarters were already being prepared for him. He pointed out that an article of the Concordat clearly specified that members of the diplomatic corps accredited to the Holy See might reside within the Vatican grounds. In reply, the Italian Government ordered him to leave Italy within twenty-four hours. A strong protest by the papal secretariat of State failed to alter this decision.

Another example of Fascist tactics occurred soon after Italy's intervention in the war. The Vatican newspaper Osservatore Romano was limited by Signor Mussolini almost exclusively to religious news. The fault of that newspaper, in the eyes of Fascisti, was the printing of impartial dispatches which, by their very fairness, contradicted those appearing in the Italian press.

For a few days the Osservatore Romano continued its editorial policy of absolute impartiality. As a result every issue was seized as soon as it came out, and Italians who asked for it at news stands found waiting Blackshirts who clubbed them on the charge of being traitors.

The church has been humiliated in Italy, its clergy having the

Continued on Page Ten

War News Summarized

THURSDAY, JUNE 4, 1942

Japanese planes raided the United States base at Dutch Harbor in Alaskan waters yesterday, the Axis somewhat strengthened its position in Libya, and Essen, Germany, was bombed again. There was some sharp but indecisive fighting on the Russian and Chinese fronts.

Dutch Harbor was raided twice, the second raid coming six hours after the first, in which four Japanese bombers and about fifteen fighters took part. In the first attack little damage was done. [1:8.]

Japanese forces in Chekiang Province continued to push toward Chuhsien, site of an important air base on the Hangchow-Nanchang railway, according to Chungking reports. There was also heavy fighting in Kiangsi Province south of Nanchang, where the Japanese had started southward in the general direction of the Hankow-Canton railway. [6:3, with map.]

From the European front the British reported that Tuesday night R. A. F. bombers returned to Essen to follow up the preceding night's raid. A few hundred aircraft took part in the latest raid on the Ruhr region, but the affair was described in London as a routine attack. [1:5.]

Stockholm heard from Berlin that several first-aid trains and strong Gestapo detachments had been sent to bombed Cologne and the Ruhr. [1:5-6.]

In Libya Marshal Rommel succeeded in making a larger breach in the British-mined and semi-fortified Bir Hacheim line and securing a better connection with his forces to the west of that line and then turned to strike back at the British. Meanwhile the British seized a position well to the west, from which they can harass German communications. [1:6-7; map, P. 4.]

Moscow announced that Russian shock troops in a surprise attack on the Kalinin front had created a strategically important salient. The Germans claimed to have crushed an encircled Russian force on the central front. [8:2.]

Twenty-five more Czechs have been executed, according to the Prague radio, bringing the total to 133 since the attempt to assassinate the notorious Gestapo leader, Reinhard Heydrich. [9:3.]

Vichy accused Britain and Russia of attempting to provoke civil war in France. The statement was read to the press by Pierre Laval's chief of press and propaganda, Paul Marion. [4:1.]

In Washington the House of Representatives adopted three resolutions declaring war on Bulgaria, Hungary and Rumania without a dissenting vote. Little interest was displayed in the routine proceedings since the three States are merely minor instruments of Berlin. [9:1.]

Legislation was introduced in the House for construction of 500 new warships to cost a total of $8,300,000,000. [1:3.]

The Navy announced three new sinkings of United Nations merchant vessels. [11:1.] The sinking of eighteen United Nations cargo ships in the Bay of Bengal last April 6 was also disclosed. Among them was one United States vessel. [6:4.]

BRITISH RAIDS GO ON

Ruhr Area Again Is Hit, Though Scale of Blow Is Not So Large

ATTACK IN DAYLIGHT

Fighters Sweep Coastal Areas—Nazis Claim 58 British Planes

By RAYMOND DANIELL

Wireless to THE NEW YORK TIMES.

LONDON, Thursday, June 4—Essen, home of the Krupps, and the industrial region around it with homes and factories still smoldering after the raid by 1,036 heavy and medium bombers Monday night, was attacked again Tuesday night by "strong" forces of the Royal Air Force, it was announced yesterday.

While the German Propaganda Ministry sought desperately to minimize the British raids on Cologne and Essen and to magnify their own reprisal attacks on British cathedral cities, including Canterbury, the British made no attempt to present Tuesday night's operations as anything more than they were—a routine assault by a few hundred aircraft.

That it was on a large scale, however, was indicated by the fact that the British revealed the loss of fourteen planes. British bombers shot down two enemy fighters that tried to destroy them in the Ruhr raid. It was not certain that the full strength of the British raiding force was directed against Essen again, but on the contrary it was indicated that the attacks were spread out over the Ruhr and German-occupied France.

Royal Air Force bombers again struck at Germany during the night, it was authoritatively learned today, an Associated Press dispatch from London said.]

[The Berlin radio reported this morning that British planes attacked several towns in the Northwest German coastal area, damaging business and residential quarters. German night-fighter planes and anti-aircraft batteries shot down ten of the raiders, the broadcast said, an indication that the British forces may have been numerous.]

Dampens Expectations

A Royal Air Force commentator yesterday took up the same line as Prime Minister Winston Churchill when he warned in the House of Commons against the expectation that the great feat of the Bomber Command in concentrating more than 1,000 aircraft over a single objective in a short space of time could or would be duplicated every night.

The Air Ministry's commentator said that, now the practicability and advantage of sending huge air armadas over targets to the point at which sheer numbers "saturate" defenses had been demonstrated, there was every intention of repeating and increasing the "dose."

Continued on Page Four

ENEMY BOMBS FALL IN ALEUTIAN ISLANDS

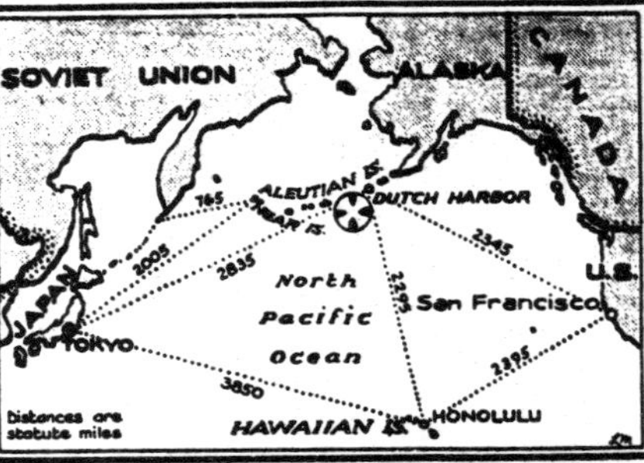

Four Japanese bombers escorted by fifteen fighters conducted a fifteen-minute raid on Dutch Harbor (cross on upper map) yesterday. Six hours later a second raid was made. The position of Dutch Harbor on Unalaska Island is shown on the lower map.

Battle in Desert Is Centered On Axis Salient in Mine Field

By JOSEPH M. LEVY

Special Cable to THE NEW YORK TIMES.

CAIRO, Egypt, June 3—With a wedge driven into the British mine fields that extend from El Gazala to Bir Hacheim, and with guns placed to protect their flanks, Axis forces in Libya engaged today in a threefold task—fighting off British attempts to isolate that part of the German armored corps that was operating well east of the mine-field gap, protecting communications in the Axis rear areas from British advances and making preparations for another effort of their own.

The first phase of the Axis offensive now seems to be definitely over. Its results for the Axis appear to be that the Germans and Italians failed in every aim, although they did stave off disaster and greatly improve their situation by forcing two small gaps about nine miles apart in the British mined area and then squeezing out those British forces that were between the gaps—forces that endeavored in vain to prevent the Axis units from consolidating those avenues for supplies into a single, rather broad thoroughfare.

The Germans have not had a single moment of real rest, however. And the second phase of this campaign opens with all observers—and, perhaps, even participants—in doubt regarding who is on the defensive and who is on the offensive.

The Germans undoubtedly expect and hope to make another bid

Continued on Page Four

ROMMEL LECTURED BRITONS ON TACTICS

Writer, Captured in Libya, Tells How the German General Twitted Prisoners

The following is the second of a series of articles by a correspondent of THE NEW YORK TIMES *who was captured in Libya six months ago and has just returned to this country:*

By HAROLD DENNY

When something occurs as drastic as capture in battle, one cannot quite grasp it at first. It is one of those things that can happen to other persons, but never to oneself.

We correspondents had all accepted the possibility of being killed or wounded, though the mathematical chance of being hit really was small. But we had hardly thought of being captured.

"I don't believe it," said Edward Ward, the B. B. C. correspondent, as we trotted along, our upraised arms flopping ridiculously. "These things just don't happen. This is a dream."

We half expected to be disposed of with machine guns, for a large group of prisoners is a hindrance to a flying column in the desert. But we were not. To give the devil his due, the German troops behaved honorably in that battle. There was no unnecessary shooting. Once the Germans had conquered British resistance the killing ceased.

But before we got off that battlefield there was another flurry of firing from somewhere. A few shells burst fairly close and some machine gun bullets whistled by us. But we had been through so much that day that they hardly registered on our minds.

Groups of prisoners, flushed from their various coverts, were gradu-

Continued on Page Five

U. S. BASE IS TARGET

Both Raids on Navy and Air Establishments Made by Daylight

FIRST ATTACK IS LIGHT

Four Bombers, Fifteen Fighters Set Fire to 'a Few Warehouses'

Special to THE NEW YORK TIMES.

WASHINGTON, June 3—The Japanese air force today made two daylight raids on the important American Naval and Air Base at Dutch Harbor, Alaska.

The first attack occurred at 6 A. M., Alaskan time [noon, E. W. T.]. The second attack took place six hours later, at noon Alaska time [6 P. M., E. W. T.].

The Naval communiqué announcing the second raid was released here at 9 P. M. It stated merely that "a brief report just received in the Navy Department" told of the attack "but no further details are available at this time."

The Navy released three communiqués in all this afternoon and evening recounting the enemy activity over Alaska. The first announced merely that a raid on Dutch Harbor had occurred. The second said that "there were but few casualties" and that "a few warehouses were set on fire but no serious damage was suffered."

None of Foe Reported Downed

The Navy made no mention of the effect of the second aerial assault. None of the Navy's communiqués recorded that any of the enemy planes was shot down in either attack.

Only a small Japanese force took part in the first raid. The Navy said there were only four enemy bombers and approximately fifteen fighter planes. On the basis of this early information it was not thought in local naval circles that the Dutch Harbor base could have been greatly injured by an attack on this scale.

The first attack was said to have lasted for fifteen minutes. The duration of the second attack was not announced.

Both attacks carried new significance in that they opened a new battle zone, removed by 2,000 miles from any other place where Japanese and American forces have clashed. They also marked the first occasion enemy bombs have been dropped on the North American Continent.

On the basis of the first advices to reach Washington of the initial assault on Dutch Harbor, it was not felt that this attack alone could be construed as representing the Japanese response to the American attack of April 18 on Tokyo and other Japanese cities. To regain face, in the words of Secretary of War Henry L. Stimson, it was thought the enemy would have to embark on a more important project than attacks on a distant outpost of the continental United States.

Dutch Harbor is on Unalaska, one of the Aleutian Islands, about 2,000 miles northwest of San Francisco and 2,835 miles northeast of Tokyo. It is just about due north of Hawaii, where the Japanese began the war with their devastating surprise raid on Dec. 7.

What forces and equipment are based at Dutch Harbor is a military secret, but they are probably large. Great efforts are known to have been made to fortify this area since the beginning of the "emergency" that preceded entry of the United States into the war.

For many years the Dutch Harbor establishment represented the northern end of a naval patrol line that extended roughly southward to the Hawaiian Islands and southwestward to the Panama Canal. More recently, however, it has become also a vital air link along the northern route to Asia.

In considering the extension of

Continued on Page Three

Havoc in Essen Bad as in Cologne; Rescue Trains Off to Bombed Cities

By GEORGE AXELSSON

By Telephone to THE NEW YORK TIMES.

STOCKHOLM, Sweden, June 3—Several first-aid trains of the N. S. V., the Nazi party social welfare organization, have left for Cologne and the Ruhr, according to news from Berlin today. Strong Gestapo detachments have also been dispatched to West Germany, as there appears to be much looting in the bombed area. As the seat of the organized Catholic opposition, the Ruhr district has never been on the party's good books, anyway.

Essen, Duisburg and Oberhausen have been badly hit by the Royal Air Force raids. The damage done is every bit as considerable as that inflicted Sunday morning on Cologne, according to fragments of news received here from Berlin permitting this deduction.

Essen newspapers have also been added to the list of publications "missing" on the Berlin newsstands. Cologne newspapers were missing following the first R. A. F. mammoth raid. This does not necessarily mean that the newspapers have stopped publishing, but it proves conclusively that at least the damage caused by the raids was widespread.

The Berlin news agency, Dienst aus Deutschland, said tonight that the Royal Air Force raids constituted a new problem for the Reich,

Continued on Page Four

"All the News That's Fit to Print."

The New York Times.

LATE CITY EDITION

Scattered showers and somewhat warmer today.

Temperatures Yesterday—Max., 64; Min., 59

VOL. XCI. No. 30,813. | Entered as Second-Class Matter, Postoffice, New York, N. Y. | NEW YORK, FRIDAY, JUNE 5, 1942. | THREE CENTS NEW YORK CITY and Vicinity

JAPANESE BATTLESHIP AND CARRIER DAMAGED, MANY PLANES SHOT DOWN IN RAID ON MIDWAY; BIG R. A. F. FORCES BOMB FRANCE, FIRE BREMEN

TWO 'GAS' ORDERS TIGHTEN RATIONING FOR NATIONAL PLAN

OPA Bids Local Boards Re-examine All Cards, Require Proof of Car Pool Pleas

SYSTEM SPLITS SENATORS

Revenue Depletion, Bootleg Peril Argued—House Group Seeks Delay for Inquiry

By FREDERICK R. BARKLEY
Special to THE NEW YORK TIMES.

WASHINGTON, June 4—Two indications were given today that the government is going to "get tough" in the administration of gasoline rationing, both under the present temporary plan and the permanent one going into effect on July 1.

First, the Office of Price Administration gave specific authority to local rationing boards to call in holders of all rationing cards to determine whether they had obtained the cards by mistake or fraud.

Under an amendment to the regulations, the boards may also require the surrender of unlimited "X" cards if found to have been wrongfully obtained or to be now used illegally for purposes other than the use for which they were issued.

Secondly, the OPA directed that Atlantic Seaboard motorists applying for supplemental gasoline rations under the permanent plan be required to prove statements that they are members of car-sharing or pooling groups.

End of Privilege as Penalty

The first OPA order of the day gave power to local boards to prohibit the obtaining of any gasoline rationing card or book, under any plan in effect now or later, by persons who refuse to appear for questioning when summoned, unless with good cause, or who refuse to surrender any cards now held.

Such action by a board, it was explained, could be appealed to the OPA State director, who has authority to reverse a local decision.

The new punitive procedure, it was stated, would be additional to any other actions which might be taken against violators of the rationing regulations. It also permits any board to review a card which it believes was improperly issued by a board in another area.

Strict Rules for Driving Pools

Regarding the second order, Joel Dean, chief of the OPA fuel rationing branch, said that "it will not be sufficient for motorists applying for more than the basic ration (under the permanent plan) merely to state that they transport other people to work."

Every applicant also would have to show that he has made every effort to form a club of at least four members, including himself, he said, and would have to supply their signatures together with their occupations and mileage.

He urged motorists contemplat-

Continued on Page Fourteen

If in Doubt, Put It Out

Windows in private homes must be shaded or screened in conformity with the Army's new dimout regulations, it was emphasized yesterday at the headquarters of the Second Corps Area. It was explained that some citizens were under the misapprehension that the new regulations applied only to offices, business establishments and factories.

Steps to prevent direct rays of light escaping from windows and skylights throughout the metropolitan area and along the New Jersey and Delaware shores are necessary to prevent building up the sky glow that has proved of assistance to enemy submarines by silhouetting our shipping for attack. Army officers attached to the Second Corps Area headquarters call upon the public to remember the slogan: "If in doubt, put it out."

'Neutral' Japanese Want Soviet Beaten

By The Associated Press.

TOKYO, June 4 (From Japanese broadcast)—The Diplomatic Review, closely connected with the Foreign Office, said today that Japan was conforming to the spirit of her neutrality pact with Soviet Russia and yet, as Germany's ally, "desires the complete success of German forces against Russia."

ROOSEVELT BACKING TO BAR FISH SOUGHT

Entering Coalition Candidate in His Home District to Be Asked at Week-End Parley

By JAMES C. HAGERTY

Friends of President Roosevelt, faced with the possibility that Representative Hamilton Fish Jr. might be successful in his fight for re-election in the President's home Congressional district, will confer over the week-end with the Chief Executive in an attempt to gain his support in a move to align the Democratic county organizations in the district behind a single "coalition" anti-Fish candidate, it was learned here yesterday.

These friends of the President at present regard Mr. Fish as an almost certain winner in the coming Republican primaries in August, despite the open opposition to his candidacy by Thomas E. Dewey, probable Republican nominee for Governor, and Wendell L. Willkie. They point to the recent 190-26 endorsement of Mr. Fish by the Orange County Republican Committee and the 41-to-2 support given by the Putnam County organization as an indication of Mr. Fish's strength.

While the President's friends admit that the Republican nomina-

Continued on Page Fifteen

FIGHT TO DROP CCC WIDENS INTO MOVE TO KILL NYA ALSO

House Votes Scheduled Today on Abolishing Two Agencies, Following Sharp Attacks

NYA DECLARED NEEDLESS

Duplicates Work of Office of Education, Says Dirksen—CCC's Friends Cite Fire Peril

By C. P. TRUSSELL
Special to THE NEW YORK TIMES.

WASHINGTON, June 4—The House fight over the Appropriation Committee's decision to abolish the Civilian Conservation Corps broadened today into a movement to deny further operating funds to the National Youth Administration also and force the transfer of its war-worker training program, virtually its only remaining activity under present plans, to the Office of Education.

A showdown by vote on the future of the CCC, created by Presidential executive order in 1933, and the NYA, established two years later, was scheduled for tomorrow. The House was called in an hour earlier than the usual meeting time in anticipation of a long struggle.

To continue the NYA, Representative Dirksen of Illinois, a member of the Appropriations body, told the House today, would be to finance the duplication of work now being done on a larger scale by the Office of Education. Both the NYA and the Office of Education function under the Federal Security Agency, he pointed out.

The abolition of the NYA and the transfer of its war functions,

Continued on Page Thirty-eight

War News Summarized

FRIDAY, JUNE 5, 1942

The Japanese, on the heels of their "feeler" air raid on Dutch Harbor, Alaska, carried their assault 1,900 miles to the southwest yesterday with an attack on Midway Island, farthermost outpost of the United States in the Northern Pacific.

A Japanese battleship and an aircraft carrier were damaged, a "heavy toll" was taken of enemy bombers and "our attacks on the enemy are continuing," said Honolulu headquarters of Admiral Nimitz, in command of the United States Pacific Fleet. A Navy communiqué in Washington said Japanese planes in their second flight over Dutch Harbor on Wednesday dropped no bombs. [All the foregoing, 1:8; maps, P. 2 and 3.]

The underscored threat of Japanese air raids spurred a redoubling of civilian defense vigilance along the Pacific Coast, where a precautionary radio silence lasted more than eight hours last night. [3:4.]

From the Southwest Pacific theatre of war General MacArthur's headquarters reported the sinking of a Japanese transport and two supply ships and heavy damage to a third supply vessel in attacks by a lone submarine along enemy shipping lanes. The transport carried possibly 12,000 Japanese troops. [1:7.]

In China's coastal Chekiang Province, the defenders gained in a three-sided drive against Japanese-occupied Kinhwa and held a firm grip on Chuhsien, strategic railway city and air base about 700 miles from Japan. [4:1.]

Generalissimo Chiang Kai-shek, in the Chinese capital, held war councils with the ranking American commanders in Southeast Asia—Lieut. Gen. Stilwell, Major Gen. Brereton and Brig. Gen. Chennault. The capital buzzed with talk of a Japanese drive on Siberia. [4:2.]

Whatever the threat to their Far Eastern flank, the Russians were still striking at the German invaders. Although the lull in the ground fighting continued, Soviet planes bombed and machine-gunned Axis troops and supplies behind the lines in various sectors. [7:1.]

Amid furious sandstorms on the Libyan battlefront, the British recaptured Tamar, the point of easternmost Axis penetration through the nine-mile gap in their lines. They failed to narrow that gap, but brisk R. A. F. attacks and a mechanized assault against the Axis rear in the Bir Hacheim area frustrated Field Marshal Rommel's efforts to advance. [1:6-7; map, P. 8.]

In Western Europe, the R. A. F. kept up a round-the-clock tempo of attack with night raids centering on the German port of Bremen and daylight sweeps in which more than 1,000 fighters were reported to have given Northern French targets their heaviest battering. [1:4; map, P. 6.]

Britain's Commando raid between Boulogne and Le Touquet, which gained valuable information and rattled the German defenders, was followed by a French assault on a German post at Hazebrouck, according to Vichy dispatches. [1:5-6.]

Reinhard Heydrich, "the hangman" of the Gestapo, died painfully in Prague eight days after the Czech patriot attack on him. The Germans shot twenty-four more Czechs in their campaign of reprisal, bringing the official death toll to 178. [1:5.]

In Washington, the Senate voted unanimously to complete Congressional action on the declaration of war against Hungary, Rumania and Bulgaria. [12:1.]

Another Axis satellite nation, Finland—still at peace with the United States—received a state visit from Adolf Hitler, who presented a medal to Field Marshal Mannerheim. [7:3-4.]

NAZI BASES STRUCK

1,000 British Fighters Sweep Across Channel in All-Day Attack

REICH PORT SEARED

Night Offensive Covers Bremen Shipyards and Factories With Flames

By JAMES MacDONALD
Wireless to THE NEW YORK TIMES.

LONDON, Friday, June 5—Flying right around the clock, the Royal Air Force kept up an almost incessant attack against the Nazis Wednesday night and all day yesterday.

British planes subjected Bremen to a heavy bombing raid, blasted the docks at Dieppe, attacked hostile air bases in occupied France and the Low Countries and laid mines in enemy waters. Other bombers and many squadrons of R. A. F. fighters swept over Northern France again throughout daylight and during last evening.

[More than 1,000 British fighter planes went across the Channel yesterday in what observers reported was the largest force yet used in daylight attacks, according to a United Press dispatch from London.]

The day offensive was directed chiefly against the Cherbourg region in the morning, against Boulogne and the Pas de Calais in the afternoon and against the port of Dunkerque last evening, the Air Ministry said.

Nazis Report Raid on Poole

The Germans sent what British officials said was a "small number" of planes over Britain during Wednesday night. The Nazi raiders made a sharp attack on one English South Coast district, causing some casualties and property damage. [The Berlin radio said "the British naval base of Poole" was attacked.]

In all the Wednesday night operations, British officials said, the R. A. F. lost ten bombers and two fighters. They reported two Nazi bombers destroyed over Britain and four other German planes shot down in fights over the Nazis' airfields.

The Air Ministry reported three R. A. F. fighters lost in daylight yesterday and one German fighter destroyed on the sweeps.

The size of the R. A. F. raid on Bremen was not anywhere near that of the raids on Cologne and Essen on Saturday and Monday nights. But the British loss of ten bombers Wednesday night would seem to indicate that the "strong force" mentioned in yesterday's communiqué covered—on the ratio of losses of less than 4 per cent that the week's raids have cost the R. A. F.—more than 200 bombers dispatched over that second largest port of Germany.

Nearly 3,000 British bombers, it is estimated, have pounded various points in Germany since Saturday night, when more than 1,000 planes attacked Cologne.

Weather Aids Bremen Bombing

The Bremen attack was the ninety-fourth time the R. A. F. has raided that city, where there are shipyards for building U-boats, factories producing Nazi dive bombers and long-range Focke-Wulf and Kondor planes, a big oil-refining plant and important railroad terminals and freight yards. All these were targets of the British bombers.

Aided by a clear sky the raiders found no difficulty in reaching Bremen. A slight ground haze obscured the factories and shipyards, but the fliers met this obstacle by dropping many flares, by the glaring light of which they dropped their loads of explosives.

The attack lasted only about half an hour, in accordance with the R. A. F.'s latest technique of

Continued on Page Six

COMMANDOS RETURN AFTER RAID ON BOULOGNE

Wading ashore after surprise visit to the French coast

New York Times Radiophoto, passed yesterday by British censor

Commandos Rattle Nazis; French Blow Up Munitions

By RAYMOND DANIELL
Wireless to THE NEW YORK TIMES.

LONDON, June 4—The British made another jab early today at German defenses on the French coast. A small party of Commandos, supported by the Royal Air Force and the Royal Navy, landed on a beach between Boulogne and Le Touquet, tossed grenades at and exchanged rifle fire with the defenders, and retreated under a smoke screen with light casualties.

It was purely a reconnaissance raid, and the British are saying that "valuable information" was gained and that they are well satisfied.

While the British Special Service troops, commanded by Major K. R. S. Trevor, were ashore, light naval forces under Lieut. Comdr. T. N. Cartwright engaged two enemy patrol boats, sank one and damaged the other. The British craft suffered neither damage nor casualties.

[Vichy dispatches said French patriots stormed a strong German military guard at Hazebrouck, forty-two miles east of Boulogne, and exploded a German Army munitions depot, according to a London United Press report.]

Wearing shorts, stockings and soft woolen hats and with blackened faces a party of Britain's rough and tumble troops slipped ashore at 3 A. M. today and established themselves behind their own guns on the beach before Nazi troops opened fire. According to a newspaper correspondent who was permitted to accompany them, the defenders were so badly rattled that part of the time they were firing at each other.

Some of the raiders, it was said, managed to cut through the barbed-wire defenses and penetrate some distance inland. One pillbox at the edge of the dunes opened heavy fire upon the hit-and-run invaders, but the anti-tank guns and the Bren guns that the Com-

Continued on Page Six

HEYDRICH IS DEAD; CZECH TOLL AT 178

Gestapo Official Succumbs in Prague—Fatality Laid to Attack by Parachutists

By DANIEL T. BRIGHAM
By Telephone to THE NEW YORK TIMES.

BERNE, Switzerland, June 4—Reinhard Heydrich, deputy Gestapo chief and former Reich Deputy Protector of Bohemia-Moravia, died early this morning in Prague Hospital one week and one day after the attack on his automobile by two Czech patriots at Rokitzan last Wednesday afternoon.

A fourth blood transfusion, attempted shortly after 4 o'clock this morning, failed to rally the Gestapo official, who succumbed "in considerable pain," according to a Berlin radio report this afternoon. No date has been set for the funeral.

A blackout of information over the Czech and German radios concerning what was going on inside Czechoslovakia was not lifted until late this evening, when the executions of twenty-four more persons were listed. Six of them were women.

Slaying in Prague and Bruenn

Thirteen were condemned in Prague and eleven in Bruenn. Five in Prague and three in Bruenn were charged with "approving the attack on the Gestapo chief and encouraging by their utterances the protection of the two culprits." Four others in each group were executed for "lying to the police or not telling all they knew." The remainder were executed for "harboring persons guilty of anti-German acts or utterances and possessing arms."

While the total of executed persons reached the official figure of 178 for a crime they were in the main guilty only of "approving," the Prague radio set another precedent early this afternoon, between broadcasts repeating Deputy Reich Protector of Bohemia-Moravia Kurt Daluege's proclamation of martial law, by announcing in one bulletin that forty-six persons had been executed during the day yesterday instead of twenty-five as announced shortly before midnight last night. No explanation was given for the new figure.

Neutral reports from Berlin, where commentary tonight was scarcely encouraged, managed to speculate on the imminence of the "execution of the Fuehrer's orders" announced by Herr Daluege on assuming power last week. It was recalled by one authoritative

Continued on Page Thirteen

SUBMARINE SINKS 3 JAPANESE SHIPS

Transport Carrying Possibly 12,000 Troops and 2 Supply Vessels Are Victims

By The Associated Press.

AT UNITED NATIONS HEADQUARTERS, Australia, June 4—A United Nations submarine, presumably American, on cruise somewhere in the Japanese ship lanes, was credited officially tonight with the destruction or damaging of four enemy ships totaling 29,000 tons—one of them an overloaded troopship that went down with possibly as many as 12,000 Japanese soldiers.

[General Douglas MacArthur's headquarters reported this morning that United Nations bombers yesterday rained explosives on the Japanese-held airdrome at Koepang, Timor, and the docks at Rabaul, New Britain, The Associated Press reports.]

An armed transport of 6,000 tons and two jammed supply ships of 10,000 tons and 6,000 tons, respectively, were torpedoed and sunk, and a 7,000-ton supply ship was badly damaged.

Implying that the better part of a division might have perished aboard the transport, United Nations headquarters said all aboard probably were lost, and added:

"The Japanese are notorious for overloading troop transports. It is known that they put more than 12,000 soldiers on some 6,000-ton ships."

It was indicated that the submarine had made its attacks well beyond Australian waters, somewhere on the seas between Japan's numerous Southwestern Pacific bases.

The news had a tonic effect on Australians, who had been sobered earlier today by Japanese submarine attacks on southeastern coastal

Continued on Page Two

Planes Pound Axis Units in Libya; British Recapture a Strong Point

By JOSEPH M. LEVY
Special Cable to THE NEW YORK TIMES.

CAIRO, Egypt, June 4—Sandstorms so terrible that they choked men's throats and buried vehicles hub-deep forced a comparative lull yesterday in the great Libyan tank battle that has been raging with only brief let-ups for more than a week, but whenever there was even a slight easing in the blow Royal Air Force planes continued their attacks on the enemy fighting forces and supply columns.

Italian troops, with a slight stiffening of German tanks, made a half-hearted attack on British positions around Bir Hacheim, but the combination of bad weather and fierce bombing and machine-gunning attacks by low-flying British planes apparently helped to discourage the Axis force. Meeting firm resistance, it did not press home the attack, and meanwhile British forces in the vicinity attacked from the rear.

Apparently to support the Axis assault, a force of enemy dive-bombers attempted to raid British troops in this area, but were driven off by an R. A. F. squadron, which shot down seven Stukas.

It is now reported that British armored forces late Tuesday drove a Nazi armored column out of Tamar, a strong point about six miles west of Knightsbridge, and destroyed at least fourteen Axis tanks. However, sporadic fighting continued yesterday in the Knightsbridge area whenever the weather permitted.

Although still closely pressed, the Germans east of the minefield gap were able to protect their flanks, and British drives from the north and south did not

Continued on Page Eight

U. S. ISLE IS BOMBED

Defenders Repel Heavy Assault by Navy Planes From Strong Flotilla

FOE IS UNDER ATTACK

Carriers and Battleships Are Pursued—Damage to Outpost Is 'Minor'

By ROBERT TRUMBULL
Special Cable to THE NEW YORK TIMES.

HONOLULU, June 4—A heavy attack on Midway Island this morning by planes from Japanese carriers accompanied by battleships, cruisers and destroyers has been repulsed with damage to a battleship, a carrier and possibly other enemy vessels, Admiral Chester W. Nimitz, Commander in Chief of the Pacific Fleet, announced this evening.

Admiral Nimitz said that all branches of United States armed forces participated in the defense. A "heavy toll' was taken of the raiding planes. Damage to material and installations on Midway was "minor."

No reports have been received of casualties among the defenders. The statement said that the battle was continuing.

TEXT OF STATEMENT

The text of the statement follows:

At 6:35 A. M. Midway time that island was heavily raided by Japanese carrier-based planes. The attack was repulsed by the local defenders, in which all armed services are represented.

A heavy toll of attacking planes was taken. The damage to installations at Midway was reported as minor. No report of personnel casualties has been received.

The Japanese carriers were accompanied by battleships, cruisers and destroyers. One battleship and one carrier have been definitely damaged and other vessels are believed to have been hit. Our attacks on the enemy are continuing.

Midway had been attacked five times previously since the war began, but never so heavily as today.

First Attack on Dec. 7

HONOLULU, June 4 (AP)—The five previous attacks on Midway were repulsed by naval and marine forces. The first and heaviest attack was the Dec. 7 raid by Japanese cruisers and destroyers. The second attack, on Jan. 2, likewise was driven off. The third attack was on March 10, when aerial forces were repulsed by Marine Corps fighters commanded by Captain James L. Neefus.

Admiral Nimitz last month flew to Midway and decorated four naval and Marine officers. He likewise commended Commander Cyril T. Simard of the Midway Naval Air Station and Lieut. Col. Harold Shannon, commanding the Marine defense units.

The admiral said excellent coordination of ground and air forces under Commander Simard had demonstrated that the efficiency was most commendable. He praised Colonel Shannon for the excellent manner in which the defense of Midway was conducted.

Follows Dutch Harbor

By CHARLES HURD
Special to THE NEW YORK TIMES.

WASHINGTON, June 4—Japanese bombers today struck at Midway Island, lying northwest of Hawaii on the route to Japan, within twenty-four hours after the foray against Dutch Harbor, in the Aleutian Islands, and a later reconnaissance flight over that base.

The report of the new attack on Midway was given out coincident with a positive denial by a Navy spokesman of reports, emanating from Canada, that there had been a third flight over Dutch Harbor.

Midway Island lies 1,300 statute miles northwest of Hawaii. It is

Continued on Page Two

"All the News That's Fit to Print."

The New York Times.

LATE CITY EDITION
Continued warm today and probably scattered showers or thunderstorms in the afternoon.
Temperatures Yesterday—Max., 83; Min., 66

Copyright, 1942, by The New York Times Company.

VOL. XCI...No. 30,820. Entered as Second-Class Matter, Postoffice, New York, N. Y. NEW YORK, FRIDAY, JUNE 12, 1942. THREE CENTS NEW YORK CITY and Vicinity

SOVIET AND BRITAIN SIGN WAR AND PEACE PACT; MOLOTOFF AND ROOSEVELT PLAN FOR 2D FRONT; ARMY FLIERS BLASTED TWO FLEETS OFF MIDWAY

BIG BOMBERS WON

Routing Japanese Task Force June 4 Vital in Pacific Victory

CARRIERS TARGETS

Enemy's Invasion Ships Met and Pounded First Far West of Island

By ROBERT TRUMBULL
By Telephone to THE NEW YORK TIMES.

WITH UNITED STATES ARMY AIR FORCES, Hawaii, June 11—Officers of the United States Army Air Forces disclosed today some of the carnage spread by their high altitude bombers in conjunction with the Navy among the Japanese invasion fleet that massed off Midway last week in futile effort to take this vital island in the American Pacific defense chain.

The Army fliers who actually dropped the bombs reported personally that they made hits on three Japanese carriers, one cruiser and one other large vessel that may have been either a cruiser or a battleship, one destroyer and one large transport. The Air Forces' reports on the battle are still incomplete.

American gunners aboard the planes shot down an undetermined number of Japanese Zero fighters. Two United States Army planes were lost out of a large force in the operations.

Army airmen interviewed here emphasized that their operations against the enemy fleet were just one phase of a well-coordinated attack involving the Army, Navy and Marines. Their stories revealed the accuracy of Japanese anti-aircraft fire, which they said heretofore had been underestimated, and they spoke highly of the Japanese Zero fighters, which are manned by expert pilots.

Flying Fortresses Did Job

Another emphasis was on the power of the American B-17 bomber, the Flying Fortress. It was clear in several accounts of the action that the Japanese fighter planes were not anxious to tangle with these aerial dreadnoughts.

The introduction to the story was given by Brig. Gen. Willis H. Hale of Colorado Springs, Col., who is in charge of all the Army bombers in the Hawaiian area. Every squadron under General Hale's command participated in the action, which stretched over the two days of June 3 and 4.

General Hale expressed the belief that the Battle of Midway was primarily won in the blasting by the Flying Fortresses of a Japanese naval task force, including carriers, off the island on the morning of June 4.

Midway was pounded by Japanese planes from the carriers the previous afternoon and again that morning while the Flying Fortresses were away. Later all the American planes were gathered

Continued on Page Nine

If in Doubt, Put It Out

The advent of warm weather had brought a new problem to complicate the observance of the Army's dimout regulations, it was said yesterday by civilian lighting experts who have been working with the Army on the matter. They said many persons, particularly small shopkeepers, who have carefully shielded their windows in the prescribed manner are now thoughtlessly leaving outside doors open.

Pointing out that light streaming through these openings helps to build up the loom over the city that aids enemy submarines at sea to spot shipping of the United Nations, the experts said that when doors are left open for ventilation a screen should be placed where it can cut off direct rays of light from the interior. The general rule for lights should remain: "If in doubt, put it out."

'Gas' Ration Unit Is Doubled To Tide Over 2 Weeks More

Emergency Period Is Extended From June 30 to July 15—OPA Says Time Is Needed to Train for Permanent Plan

Special to THE NEW YORK TIMES.

WASHINGTON, June 11—The gasoline ration unit of "A" and "B" cards in the seventeen East Coast rationed States was increased by the Office of Price Administration today from three to six gallons, effective after midnight Sunday, to tide drivers over a two-week extension of the temporary rationing plan which was originally set to expire June 30. The present ration cards, with whatever units are left on them, must last through to July 15.

The two weeks extension is needed, the OPA said, to train registrars and members of rationing boards in handling the permanent rationing system scheduled now to go into effect July 15 instead of July 1.

Card holders who have exhausted their card units by Monday may apply to local rationing boards for additional ration cards, but these will be effective only for the

Continued on Page Fifteen

Jones Beach Buses Not Curbed by ODT

Special to THE NEW YORK TIMES.

WASHINGTON, June 11—A recent order of the Office of Defense Transportation calling for elimination of unnecessary intercity bus transportation, particularly to "places conducted primarily for purposes of amusement and entertainment" has "no direct application" to transport of recreation seekers to Jones Beach on Long Island, the ODT announced today.

The policy was set forth in a telegram from Joseph B. Eastman, ODT director, to Robert Moses, president of the Long Island State Park Commission and the Jones Beach State Parkway Authority.

The order, Mr. Eastman said, does not apply to Jones Beach inasmuch as it is less than fifteen air miles from New York's boundaries. His telegram, however, added rather cryptically:

"Because of the rubber situation we believe that parks such as Jones Beach should be served by rail to the fullest extent possible."

HOUSE COMMITTEE RAISES TRAVEL TAX

Doubles Transport Impost, Adds to Cigarette and Cigar Levies—125 Million Gained

Special to THE NEW YORK TIMES.

WASHINGTON, June 11—The Ways and Means Committee voted today to double the present 5 per cent transportation tax, voted increases in cigar, tobacco and cigarette levies and postponed until tomorrow final action on other excise tax changes recommended by the Treasury.

The net additions to present revenue were estimated at $125,800,000. The transportation tax increase was estimated to yield an additional $35,000,000. It would provide for a flat 10 per cent tax

Continued on Page Twenty-eight

YOUNG DECK CREW DESTROYS U-BOAT

Freighter Gets 3d, Perhaps 5th, Raider Sunk in Caribbean—2 Allied Vessels Lost

By The United Press.

HAVANA, June 11—The gun crew of an American merchant ship, most of them youths of 20 or less, has sunk an Axis submarine after a brief running gun fight, thus raising the total of enemy U-boats sunk in recent weeks in waters of the Greater Antilles to three—and possibly five—authoritative but unofficial sources said tonight.

Braving withering bursts of machine-gun fire that swept the decks of their vessel, the gunners fired at the submarine until it was

Continued on Page Twelve

War News Summarized

FRIDAY, JUNE 12, 1942

The United States, Soviet Russia and Great Britain stood last night in full agreement on the question of opening a second front in Europe this year and on the fundamental problems of building a post-war era of peace and security.

Russia and Britain had entered a close war alliance and a twenty-year pact of mutual assistance and cooperation. The historic document, whose wording guarded the Soviet Union from any commitment against Japan, banned a separate peace with Germany and her European satellites and pledged common action to preserve peace and resist aggression in the future. Both countries agreed not to seek "territorial aggrandizement" nor to interfere in the "internal affairs" of other nations. [1:8.]

The Soviet Union reached an unwritten agreement with the United States on the "urgent" matter of a second front, on measures for increasing war shipments to Russia and on post-war cooperation. In addition, the Russians signed a master lease-lend agreement providing for mutual defense aid. The decision on the second-front question was not disclosed. [1:4.]

The three-power understanding, announced in London and Washington, evolved from secret flying visits to those capitals by Russia's Foreign Commissar, Vyacheslaff M. Molotoff. [1:6:7.]

The Soviet-British treaty evoked cheers in Moscow, where hope rose for a continental invasion in the West. [2:2.] Diplomats from the Baltic States pinned their faith on the Atlantic Charter for the restoration of their governments—a question skirted by the pact. [4:5.]

On the Russian war front, German tanks and infantry advanced in the Kharkov area against fierce resistance. Their immediate aim, Berlin conceded, was to straighten their dented lines. Sevastopol's defenders reported they had killed 15,000 Germans in three days. [1:5.]

In Libya, a battered Free French-British garrison withdrew from Bir Hacheim, southern anchor of the defense line, after a sixteen-day siege. The withdrawal eased the Axis supply problem and presaged a drive on Tobruk. [1:5-6; map, P. 2.]

In China's Kiangsi Province three Japanese columns moved swiftly eastward, threatening to outflank Chinese defenders along the Nanchang-Hangchow railroad and to make a juncture with westbound Japanese forces around Chuhsien. [7:1.]

The American victory at Midway Island loomed even larger as Army fliers turned in reports—still incomplete—of their blows to two Japanese invasion armadas—a battle fleet and a group of transports. [1:1.] A Japanese naval expert confirmed the loss of two aircraft carriers, rather than one, as Tokyo had announced Wednesday [8:3.]

U. S., SOVIET AGREE

Russian, Here Secretly, Maps War Action in 1942 With President

LEASE PACT SIGNED

Provides Reciprocal Aid and Plans for a 'Better World'

Text of White House statement will be found on Page 6.

By W. H. LAWRENCE
Special to THE NEW YORK TIMES.

WASHINGTON, Friday, June 12—The United States and Russia have reached a full understanding on the "urgent tasks of creating a second front in Europe in 1942," and have signed a master lease-lend agreement providing reciprocal defense aid and designed to create "a new and better world" after victory is won, it was announced officially yesterday.

A White House announcement at midday was the first public revelation that Vyacheslaff M. Molotoff, Soviet Foreign Commissar, had flown secretly to the United States and in several conferences with President Roosevelt and other political and military leaders of the United States Government between May 29 and June 4 had achieved unity on these three main propositions:

1. The urgent tasks of creating a second front in Europe in 1942.
2. Measures for increasing and speeding up the supplies of planes, tanks and other kinds of war materials from the United States to the Soviet Union.
3. Fundamental problems of cooperation of the Soviet Union and the United States in safeguarding peace and security to the freedom-loving peoples after the war.

"Link in Solidarity Chain"

At midnight the State Department announced that Secretary of State Cordell Hull and Maxim Litvinoff, the Soviet Ambassador, had signed a master lease-lend pact, which was described as "an additional link in the chain of solidarity being forged by the United Nations in their twofold task of prosecuting the war against aggression to a successful conclusion and of creating a new and better world."

"The agreement reaffirms this country's determination to continue to supply in ever-increasing amounts aid to the Soviet Union in the war against the common enemy," the State Department announcement said. "The agreement also provides for such reciprocal aid as the Soviet Union may be in a position to supply. But no matter how great this aid may prove to be, it will be small in comparison with the magnificent contribution of the Soviet Union's armed forces to the defeat of the common enemy."

Washington's two agreements with the Soviet Union were disclosed shortly after similar pacts between the Russians and the British had been announced to the House of Commons by Anthony Eden, British Foreign Secretary, with whom Mr. Molotoff had negotiated secretly before visiting the United States. The Anglo-Soviet agreements included an identical reference to the establishment of a second front and a twenty-year mutual assistance pact against "Hitlerite Germany."

Japan Not Mentioned

Neither announcement in Washington mentioned discussions of Russian cooperation in the war of the United States and Great Britain against Japan, with whom Soviet Russia remains at peace, but it was pointed out that no announcement would have been likely under the circumstances even if

Continued on Page Six

THE SOVIET FOREIGN COMMISSAR AT THE WHITE HOUSE

Vyacheslaff M. Molotoff with President Roosevelt at the recent historic conference.
Associated Press Wirephoto

STRONG NAZI DRIVE FOUGHT IN UKRAINE

Russians Report Fierce Battle at Kharkov—Sevastopol Siege Gains Little

By The Associated Press.

MOSCOW, Friday, June 12—The Germans have thrown strong tank and infantry forces against Russian defense positions on the Kharkov front, and fierce battles have developed, the government announced today.

Stubborn fighting continued in the Crimea, where the Germans were smashing against the Soviet naval fortress of Sevastopol. The Red Army was reported inflicting heavy losses on the Nazis in repulsing their attacks.

In three days of fighting there alone, the midnight Soviet communiqué declared nearly 15,000 German officers and men were killed. The Nazis lost more than fifty tanks and sixty planes in the same period.

[The German High Command reported that Soviet counter-attacks at Sevastopol had been unsuccessful. Semi-official sources described the Sevastopol and Kharkov actions as preliminary to "the coming great offensive."

The communiqué said there were no significant changes in other sectors, although earlier bulletins had reported action over a wide front that, combined with the great land battles of the Crimea and the Ukraine, brought the war on the Russian front to the highest pitch of the year.

There was mass aerial combat

Continued on Page Nine

Molotoff's London-U. S. Trip Was Best-Kept War Secret

Special Cable to THE NEW YORK TIMES.

LONDON, June 11—The secrecy surrounding the visit here of Soviet Foreign Commissar Vyacheslaff M. Molotoff, which was imposed at the request of the Russians on the grounds of security, was lifted today and the general public was at last told the details. Though diplomatic circles and many other persons in London knew he was here, it was not a matter of general knowledge even after he was accompanied by Anthony Eden and Ivan M. Maisky to call on the King at Buckingham Palace.

Mr. Molotoff's first visit lasted one week and was supplemented on his return from the United States by another stay of two days, during which military matters were discussed.

The usual formalities of signing an important treaty were adhered to, but nothing was allowed to be published about it until today.

Mr. Molotoff made all trips between here, Russia and the United States in a big Russian plane with an all-Russian crew. All members of the crew have been decorated in this war.

Mr. Molotoff arrived somewhere in Britain on May 20. With him were Arkady Soboleff of the Soviet Foreign Office, General Shelovski, and General Feodor Issayeff, who has already been wounded in this war. There was also his interpreter and party assistants, including two women typists.

The British Government gave the Russian party a special train to London, which stopped at a suburban station. There were few people on the platform and practi-

Continued on Page Four

Special to THE NEW YORK TIMES.

WASHINGTON, June 11—The flying visit of Vyacheslaff M. Molotoff from Moscow to London, then to Washington and back to London and Moscow, was one of the best kept secrets of the war.

Only a few high government officials, diplomats and newspaper men pledged to secrecy knew that Mr. Molotoff, after signing a twenty-year pact with Britain, had flown to Washington in a Soviet bomber, accompanied by Arkady Soboleff, Secretary General of the Foreign Office; V. Lapshoff, Chief of Chancellery for the Deputy Prime Minister; S. P. Kozyreff, Chief of Chancellery of the Foreign Office, and a group of technical advisers.

The Russian party arrived here late Friday afternoon and was taken immediately to the White House, where Mr. Molotoff was the guest of President Roosevelt. The discussions continued through Mon-

Continued on Page Four

Bir Hacheim Falls to Axis in Libya; Free French Retire After 16 Days

By JOSEPH M. LEVY
Special Cable to THE NEW YORK TIMES.

CAIRO, Egypt, June 11—Although the gallant Free French defenders of Bir Hacheim had repulsed for sixteen days constant attacks by German tanks, guns, infantry and dive-bombers, they were finally forced to withdraw from that outpost in the Libyan defense line last night, it was announced today. The French troops inflicted heavy losses on the Axis attackers and made it necessary for them to use a heavy concentration of their best armor to obtain final success.

Despite the effectiveness of their own arms, the French had not been left alone, for British armored and motorized forces had been doing their best to relieve the garrison by attacking the rear and flank of the Axis forces. The defenders also had extensive air support, which seems to have caused the German Air Force and ground units considerable trouble. Captured German prisoners, some of whom saw service in Russia, complained that it was the weakness of the German air support that had made them unable to overrun the Bir Hacheim positions sooner.

The fall of Bir Hacheim is a step for the Nazis in securing their southern flank. They will be in a slightly better position to thrust northeast toward Tobruk, fifty miles away, or toward El Gazala, on the Mediterranean coast fifty miles to the northwest, but there is no guarantee that their communications will be safe in any event. British mobile columns can continue to swing around the Axis southern positions to attack German supply routes.

The occupation of Bir Hacheim will absorb infantry that the Axis needs elsewhere. Moreover, if the

Continued on Page Two

NO SECRET IN PACT, BRITISH ARE TOLD

Commons Cheers the News of Open Treaty—Agreement Is Hailed as Peace Safeguard

By ROBERT P. POST
Special Cable to THE NEW YORK TIMES.

LONDON, June 11—The loudest cheers—or rather a loud but gentlemanly "Hear, hear!"—greeted Secretary Anthony Eden's announcement in the House of Commons today that there were no secrets in the British-Russian treaty and no commitments not made public. The cheers were an indication of the Members' relief on learning that Britain was not going to be drawn into any possible Continental demands on the part of Russia.

The second loudest response came when Mr. Eden announced that there had been complete agreement on a second European front in 1942.

The immediate Parliamentary reaction came from Arthur Greenwood, official leader of the Labor Party outside the Government, who said the House had received the statement with the most profound satisfaction "that we are working together as comrades in the war, and would be working together in times of peace."

Then came a little surprise as David Lloyd George rose amid another Parliamentary chorus.

"As one who has labored over twenty years to establish good understanding between Soviet Russia and this country," he said, "I

Continued on Page Two

A 20-YEAR TREATY

Mutual Aid Agreement Bars Separate Peace and Annexations

JAPAN NOT COVERED

Pact Based on Atlantic Charter Is Hailed by King and Kalinin

Text of White Paper, treaty and Eden's speech, Page 3.

By RAYMOND DANIELL
Wireless to THE NEW YORK TIMES.

LONDON, June 11—A treaty has been signed binding Russia and Great Britain in close alliance in the war against Nazi Germany and the countries "associated with her in acts of aggression in Europe" and pledging cooperation and mutual assistance for twenty years on the principles of the Atlantic Charter.

This momentous announcement was made by Foreign Secretary Anthony Eden in the House of Commons late this afternoon. He introduced the White Paper containing the text of the treaty and the speeches made by him and by Soviet Foreign Commissar Vyacheslaff M. Molotoff when they affixed their signatures to the historic document May 26 at the Foreign Office.

The White Paper also included the texts of the messages exchanged between King George VI and President Mikhail I. Kalinin, in which the alliance between this democratic nation and the world's first Communist State was hailed as the foundation on which the post-war world would be built.

Prime Minister Winston Churchill, in a message to Premier Joseph V. Stalin, said he thought the treaty would go far toward "overcoming barriers" between the two countries and expressed "the conviction that victory will be ours."

Mr. Stalin in reply said he hoped the treaty would strengthen relations not only between the Soviet Union and Britain but also with the United States, whose close collaboration is sought "after the victorious conclusion of the war."

Accord on Second Front

A Foreign Office communiqué issued at the same time as the White Paper was presented said that during the visit of Mr. Molotoff, which was kept a closely guarded secret until he had returned safely to Moscow after visiting President Roosevelt in Washington, "a full understanding was reached between the two parties with regard to the urgent task of creating a second front in Europe in 1942." Mr. Molotoff, Soviet Ambassador Ivan M. Maisky, Major Gen. Issayeff, Rear Admiral Kharlamoff, Mr. Churchill, Deputy Prime Minister Clement R. Attlee, Mr. Eden and the British Chiefs of Staff all took part in the discussions of this subject, the communiqué disclosed, although naturally it did not reveal what decisions were taken. Obviously it is just as possible to agree not to do things as to do them.

By inserting the words "in Europe," Russia limited her commitment so that she is not bound to lift a finger against the other enemy of Britain and the United States, Japan, except in the unlikely event that her armies or navy should enter this war-torn Continent. This limitation is cheerfully accepted here, for it is felt that the Russians have their hands full already.

There was considerable relief in parliamentary and diplomatic circles that the treaty contained no reference to post-war boundaries. One section of the treaty that Mr. Eden read to the Commons pledged both countries not to seek "territorial aggrandizement" and held a promise not to interfere in "the

Continued on Page Three

"All the News That's Fit to Print."

The New York Times.

LATE CITY EDITION
Warm today.
Temperatures Yesterday—Max., 80; Min., 60

Copyright, 1942, by The New York Times Company.

VOL. XCI...No. 30,827. Entered as Second-Class Matter, Postoffice, New York, N. Y. NEW YORK, FRIDAY, JUNE 19, 1942. THREE CENTS NEW YORK CITY and Vicinity

CHURCHILL HERE FOR TALKS ON SECOND FRONT; BRITISH RETIRE IN LIBYA, TOBRUK AGAIN IN PERIL; SEVASTOPOL THROWS BACK NEW NAZI ATTACKS

TRUMAN CHARGES WPB AIDES CAUSED WAR WORK DELAYS

Attack on 'Dollar-a-Year' Men as Slowing Conversion Spurs Defense of Nelson

CONNALLY, LUCAS HAIL HIM

Report Urges Posts for Labor, Small Business—Nelson Asked It Be Held Up

By JAMES B. RESTON
Special to The New York Times.

WASHINGTON, June 18—In a special report which Donald M. Nelson regarded as a reflection on his policy and which some Senators declared should not be published, the Truman committee charged today that the War Production Board had not fully measured up to its responsibility of converting the nation's industry to war production, and called on Mr. Nelson to demote some dollar-a-year men and promote labor and small business in the battle of production.

The report, which Mr. Nelson urged the special committee investigating the national defense program to withhold, was sharply criticized in the Senate on the ground that it tended to obscure and distort recent production progress which Senator Truman himself admitted had been made.

The Truman committee, voting 9—1 to publish the document, conceded that a satisfactory program of curtailing civilian production was "at last under way," but asserted that there was still no satisfactory program for attaining maximum war production.

Group Sets Responsibility

Responsibility for this failure was blamed in part on some dollar-a-year men whose integrity was said to be unquestioned but who were accused of being "unable to divorce themselves from their subconscious gravitation to their own industries."

Senator Lucas of Illinois, Senator Connally of Texas and Senator Burton of Ohio, all members of the committee, sought in the debate to distinguish between the situation which existed several months ago and the situation now existing. Senator Lucas said the WPB was doing "a magnificent job." Senator Connally stated that mistakes had been made but noted that conversion of the country's industry to war production was a little harder than pressing a button for a Senate page. Mr. Burton stressed that the committee wanted to commend Mr. Nelson for increasing national production and merely hoped that by pointing out mistakes production could be increased even more. Mr. Truman agreed with Mr. Burton's observation.

Speaking to Senator Truman, Mr. Lucas said:

"I doubt if a man could be found

Continued on Page Twelve

If in Doubt, Put It Out

Among the enemies of the dimout are reflections from polished surfaces, civilian lighting experts who have been cooperating with the Army pointed out yesterday. Even though a street light or parking lot light is properly shaded to throw its rays downward, an automobile thoughtlessly parked underneath it may reflect them toward the sky and thus defeat the precautions that have been taken.

Untiring vigilance is necessary in the campaign to reduce the amount of light above the metropolitan area, which has been so helpful to U-boat captains in spotting our shipping along our coast. Full compliance with the dimout regulations from an hour after sundown, which is at 8:31 o'clock tonight, is a distinct help to the war effort. The Army continues to exhort all citizens to bear in mind the slogan: "If in doubt, put it out."

Queen Wilhelmina Flies to Canada; Visits Daughter and Grandchildren

Netherland Sovereign to Stay With Juliana at Her Summer Home in Lee, Mass.—Will Pay Visit to the Roosevelts

Special to The New York Times.

OTTAWA, June 18—Queen Wilhelmina of the Netherlands arrived in Ottawa today by plane from Great Britain. She will remain only a few days before going to Lee, Mass., where her daughter, Princess Juliana, has rented a home for the Summer.

During her stay in Ottawa Queen Wilhelmina will be a guest at Government House with the members of her party.

It is stated that she will visit Washington as a guest of President and Mrs. Roosevelt. No other announcement has yet been made with regard to her itinerary, however.

Princess Juliana and her two children, accompanied by Canadian Prime Minister W. L. Mackenzie King and by representatives of the

Continued on Page Four

ROYAL VISITOR

Queen Wilhelmina
Monkmeyer

WILLKIE CAUTIONS HIS PARTY ON HASTE

Advises Careful Weighing of Candidates' Records on War and World Affairs

Wendell L. Willkie urged the Republican party in New York State yesterday to maintain an open mind in its selection of a State ticket in the Fall elections and to study the records of all available candidates to choose the strongest possible slate.

Holding that any Republican ticket, if it is to be successful, must, of necessity, be one that would attract support from a "large number" of supporters of the war and post-war programs throughout the State as well as gain the confidence of labor, Mr. Willkie, in a press interview at his office at 15 Broad Street, demanded that all candidates for State-wide office in the Republican ranks make "clear and unequivocal statements" as to how they stand "toward the interests of American labor and toward the international situation."

He declared that he "earnestly" hoped that the Republicans would be victorious in the State elections and expressed the conviction that such a victory would strengthen greatly "our democratic two-party system and give an enormous impetus to the war effort of the United Nations." But he declared that the hopes for such a Republican sweep would be harmed if the party attempted to push through any slate without thoroughly considering the potentialities of all candidates.

He revealed that in the last few

Continued on Page Twenty-four

COURT RULE SAVES 3,000 TEACHER JOBS

Right of Board of Education to Hire Out-of-License Instructors Is Upheld

Special to The New York Times.

ALBANY, June 18—Modifying an order of the Appellate Division, first department, the Court of Appeals ruled today that the New York City Board of Education had the right to assign out-of-license teachers to conduct junior high school classes. The effect of the court's decision is that some 3,000 teachers in the New York City school system are assured of their positions.

The board was challenged by Nathan Davis of the Bronx, who stood fifth on an eligible list for appointment to a position as a teacher of mathematics. He contended that the board had no right to appoint an out-of-license teacher, but the modification order of the court pointed out that the board may do so until July 1, 1943.

Mr. Davis, who argued his own case before the court, contended there were twenty-one vacancies in the mathematics teaching force. The board insisted there were no vacancies and that there was a plentiful supply of teachers, who, although not licensed to teach mathematics, could be assigned to teach that subject and thus fill the mathematics needs of the school system.

The court's opinion stated that Mr. Davis was entitled to the relief which the appellate division accorded him when it reversed an order of the Bronx County special term dismissing the complaint.

"After that order was made the

Continued on Page Eighteen

Soviet Ratifies Pact With Britain; Molotoff Pledges 'Mighty' Blows

By RALPH PARKER
Wireless to The New York Times.

MOSCOW, June 18—The Supreme Soviet, Russia's Parliament, at its first meeting since the war began, tonight formalized the people's acceptance of the treaty with Britain and, linked with it, the agreements documented in the Washington and London pronouncements.

In the presence of Premier Joseph Stalin, the agreements negotiated by Foreign Commissar Vyacheslaff M. Molotoff with Britain and the United States were rubber-stamped in the name of the workers, peasants and fighting men of the entire Soviet Union. In factories and farms, dugouts and barracks, these momentous understandings already had received the seal of popular approval.

There were few vacant seats in the great hall of the Kremlin when the people's representatives assembled. Each constituent republic of the Soviet Union, including those that adhered to it in 1939 and 1940, was represented. Thousands of spectators were massed in the gallery. Sir Archibald Clark Kerr, the British Ambassador, was one of the few foreign diplomats present.

The deputies, representing 180,000,000 persons, of whom a considerable proportion are under Adolf Hitler's yoke, presented a somewhat somber sight in the brilliantly lighted hall as they sat with head-phones clamped over their heads. A surprising number were the little skullcaps of the mid-Asian republics. Some were women, and many of these had

Continued on Page Six

CRIMEA CITY HOLDS

People Vow Not to Yield as Red Army Keeps Besiegers Off

UKRAINE LINE IS FIRM

Nazis Halted at River—Berlin Claims Bastion Near Naval Base

By The United Press.

MOSCOW, Friday, June 19—Russian armies fighting from recaptured trenches repulsed fresh attacks at Sevastopol and inflicted new heavy losses in German ranks yesterday, it was announced today as the city's besieged people flashed word to the outside world that they would "die to the last soul" before surrendering.

The midnight Soviet communiqué had little to report beyond the assertion that new attacks were hurled back at the Crimean naval base and that no material changes had taken place in other sectors.

Reports from the front said the Russians also had thwarted mass German attempts to cross a strategic Ukraine river—evidently the Donets—near Kharkov, killing 3,000 more Germans there and at Sevastopol. "Huge" forces of German infantry, tanks and artillery tried repeatedly to storm across the river, only to be beaten back from the bank, Pravda reported.

Siege Fails, Russians Say

The German offensive against Sevastopol has failed, the Moscow News asserted. It said the Germans had lost so many planes in the fourteen-day assault that air attacks on the beleaguered Black Sea base had been reduced sevenfold.

[The German High Command said German and Rumanian troops, in fierce hand-to-hand fighting, stormed into Sevastopol's main northern fortifications, captured the Maxim Gorki Fort, "the most modern and strongest bastion of the whole fortress," and carried the attack to within less than two miles of the harbor. Air attacks destroyed matériel depots and supply transports in the harbor area, the communiqué said.]

A unanimous resolution from the people of Sevastopol was sent by Fedor Menshikoff, secretary of the Crimean Communist party, saying that despite the attacks of hundreds of dive-bombers, artillery and ten divisions of infantry numbering some 150,000 troops, the city would never yield.

"Hundreds of thousands of bombs and shells only serve to inspire heroic efforts of soldiers and civilians alike," the resolution said. Mr. Menshikoff also reported that hundreds of girls were enlisting for army training, learning how to fight under actual fire, against the day when they might be called into battle.

Russians in Counter-Blows

Pravda's correspondent reported from Sevastopol that hordes of German tanks and motorized infantry repeatedly charged the northern and southern approaches to the city, but were beaten back in mangled disorder at a cost of another 1,500 killed.

Vicious Soviet counter-attacks in one Sevastopol sector drove the Germans from an outer line of trenches that they had managed to seize but were unable to consolidate, the army newspaper Red Star reported.

At the same time Red Fleet marines, equipped with hand grenades and combustible bottles, hurled themselves at German tanks that had punched into the Soviet positions and destroyed them.

Sevastopol anti-aircraft gunners and fighter pilots downed seven German planes and damaged three Wednesday, Pravda reported. It

Continued on Page Six

DESERT UNITS SPLIT

British Fall Back Toward Egypt, but Some Take Up Posts in Tobruk

NAZIS AMID DEFENSES

Drive Into Rezegh and El Adem, in Outer Rim—Coast Road Still Open

By JOSEPH M. LEVY
Wireless to The New York Times.

CAIRO, Egypt, June 18—Onslaughts by Axis armored forces in the battle in Libya have forced the British to evacuate Rezegh and El Adem, strong points in the perimeter defenses of Tobruk, it was announced today. This retirement allowed the Axis forces to get within a few miles of the sea and made the isolation of Tobruk a possibility that had to be faced, although the British still clung to the coastal road to the east.

British mobile forces were still fighting south and west of Tobruk, giving the Germans some trouble to their flank and rear, but it appeared that the Nazis had succeeded in establishing a salient through the British defensive area south of Tobruk. Rezegh is twenty miles southeast of Tobruk and El Adem is eighteen miles south of the port. The position today was thus roughly analogous to that of a few days ago, when the Germans developed the so-called Cauldron salient through the British defenses south of El Gazala.

Can Withstand Siege

Tobruk now occupies a position relative to the German thrust similar to that of El Gazala a few days before its evacuation this week—with two important differences. Tobruk has a far better harbor, which keeps it in close touch with the sea, and its defenses and living quarters are permanent, permitting it to stand a much longer siege than El Gazala could have stood. Whether the British will find it necessary or advisable to hold out there for a long period remains to be seen.

The present German position is not regarded here as unduly strong, despite the apparent success of the Axis armored forces, for their salient is threatened from north and south by strong British positions. Thus if the Nazis have any hope of reaching Egypt they must first surround or storm Tobruk and the British strong points to the south.

A storming of Tobruk still appears a most unpromising procedure for any army, but the Nazis might try to repeat their success at Bir Hacheim by similar tactics on British fortifications still standing south of the new Axis salient. Further progress by the Germans depends not only on their ability to push on against determined resistance by British forces of tanks

Continued on Page Three

War News Summarized

FRIDAY, JUNE 19, 1942

For the second time since the United States entered the war, Prime Minister Winston Churchill arrived in this country yesterday for conferences with President Roosevelt which, it was hinted, are to deal in part with the opening of a second front in Europe. Military aides accompanied the Prime Minister, and the official announcement of his presence said his meetings with the President would concern "the war, the conduct of the war and the winning of the war." [1:8.]

In Moscow, Foreign Commissar Molotoff, also a recent visitor to Washington, announced that plans worked out during his stay there called for the dispatch of $3,000,000,000 worth of fighting material from the United States to the Soviet Union. The Supreme Council of Soviets ratified the Anglo-Soviet agreement and approved the government's foreign policy. [1:2-3.]

On the Soviet fighting front, the Russians reported the recapture of outer trenches before beleaguered Sevastopol and the repulse of a German attempt to cross a strategic river in the Ukraine, evidently the Donets. The German High Command, however, claimed the capture of Maxim Gorki Fort, Sevastopol's "strongest bastion," within two miles of the harbor entrance. [1:4; map, P. 6.]

In Libya, the British evacuated El Adem and Rezegh, making the isolation of Tobruk a possibility, although they still clung to the coastal road east of the stronghold. [1:5; map, P. 3.]

The American heavy bombers that attacked the Italian fleet in the Mediterranean last Monday scored repeated direct hits on the battleships Littorio and Conte di Cavour, Washington announced. [1:7.]

The Nazi-controlled Prague radio in a communiqué announced the capture and execution of "the assassins" of Reinhard Heydrich, Gestapo Protector of Bohemia-Moravia. Captured in hiding in a Prague church, the men proved to be Czechs "dropped over the Protectorate by British planes" to make the attack, the communiqué said. [1:5-6.]

Secretary of War Stimson declared that the Japanese threat to the Pacific Coast was "temporarily much less" as a result of the naval battles in the Pacific. [8:3.]

In China Chungking revealed the existence of a United States Army bomber command, announcing the appointment of Colonel Caleb V. Haynes as its commander. [9:3.]

HERE AGAIN

Winston Churchill
The New York Times, 1941

British Link Churchill Trip To Shifts in War Situation

By RAYMOND DANIELL
Special Cable to The New York Times.

LONDON, Friday, June 19—Strategic problems of the greatest possible import were believed here to lie behind Prime Minister Winston Churchill's second visit to the United States since the country entered the war. That much seemed indicated by the fact, as officially announced here early today, that he was accompanied by General Sir Alan Brooke, Chief of the British Imperial General Staff, and Major Gen. Sir Hastings Ismay, chief of Mr. Churchill's personal staff as Defense Minister.

And it is perhaps significant that the Prime Minister's transatlantic trip came at a time when apparently events in the Middle East have taken a turn for the worse.

News of Mr. Churchill's safe arrival in the United States was released here long after early editions of the London morning papers had gone to press, so there was little opportunity given the newspapers for comment or speculation.

The general line that was indi-

Continued on Page Three

U. S. NAMES 2 SHIPS HIT IN ITALY'S FLEET

Battleships Littorio and Conte di Cavour Struck by Our Fliers, Army Reveals

By CHARLES HURD
Special to The New York Times.

WASHINGTON, June 18—The American heavy bombers that attacked the Italian fleet in the Mediterranean on June 15 in cooperation with Royal Air Force units scored repeated direct hits on the Italian battleships Littorio and Conte di Cavour, the War Department reported here tonight.

The American four-engined bombers, of the Consolidated B-24 type, weathered a "considerable amount of anti-aircraft fire," which did no serious damage to them.

This was the gist of a communiqué based upon preliminary reports from Colonel Harry A. Halverson, commander of one bombing force that flew to the attack from a base in North Africa. Damage to the two battleships, coincident with extensive damage done by R. A. F. bombers to cruisers and destroyers in the Italian fleet, caused it to turn back from its apparent object of attacking an important British convoy.

The American bombers went out with R. A. F. planes early on Monday morning and found their target at 8 A. M., local time, the communiqué stated.

The ineffective anti-aircraft fire of the Italians apparently left them a clear field for bombing opera-

Continued on Page Four

Heydrich Killers Slain, Say Nazis, As Ultimatum to Czechs Expires

By DANIEL T. BRIGHAM
By Telephone to The New York Times.

BERNE, Switzerland, June 18—The German Gestapo vigilantes announced tonight that they had succeeded "in the early hours of this morning" in capturing and killing the authors of the fatal attack upon Deputy Reich Protector Reinhard Heydrich. Their principal accomplices were captured, it was said.

The actual "arrest" was carried out in a Prague church by the "Prague section of the State Police," according to the German communiqué.

This announcement came just after the expiration of the "last chance" accorded the Czech populace to deliver the guilty parties at 8 o'clock this evening, failing which the reprisals were definitely going to take a serious turn, according to official German announcements. The communiqué issued before 10 o'clock tonight and read over the Prague radio, follows:

"The murderers of the Deputy Reich Protector of Bohemia-Moravia, S. S. [Elite Guard] Obergruppenfuehrer and General of Police Heydrich, were discovered in a church of Prague in which they had taken refuge for some time, during the early hours of the morning of June 18. They were shot immediately on arrest.

"Their delivery was due to the vast searches undertaken to this end by the direction of the State Police of Prague. On the same occasion the principal accomplices were also discovered. All the criminals were of Czech nationality and had been dropped over the Protec-

Continued on Page Seven

PREMIER'S 2D VISIT

Visitor to See President on 'Winning the War,' Says Early

SECRECY IS IMPOSED

Arrival First Hint of Trip—No Further Statement Expected This Week

By FRANK L. KLUCKHOHN
Special to The New York Times.

WASHINGTON, June 18—Prime Minister Winston Churchill of Great Britain arrived in the United States today for conferences with President Roosevelt on "the war, the conduct of the war and the winning of the war," the White House announced shortly after 8 o'clock tonight.

Speculation that the talks would cover the task of opening a second front in Europe would be "perfectly justified," a spokesman affirmed.

Mr. Churchill was scheduled to begin his conferences with President Roosevelt "immediately." It was said at the White House that no further statements on his visit should be expected this week.

The Prime Minister was accompanied by ranking British staff officers and two personal aides. It was apparent that considerable secrecy would be maintained until the talks were completed. No information was vouchsafed as to how Mr. Churchill reached here for his unannounced visit.

Follows Molotoff Visit

The arrival of the British Prime Minister, who had spent late December and early January in this country soon after its entry into the war, followed by only a few days the visit of Vyacheslaff M. Molotoff, Soviet Foreign Commissar. The latter led to a full understanding between the United States and Soviet Russia on "the urgent tasks of creating a second front in Europe in 1942."

It was thought natural here that the Roosevelt-Molotoff conferences would be followed by others between the President and Mr. Churchill. It was noted that the talks between the American and British leaders followed visits of ranking United States Army, Navy and Air officers to London and of British military and supply leaders here. It was thought in diplomatic circles that final policy might be determined in the talks that began today.

Although it had been known since early afternoon that Mr. Churchill was arriving, it was only about fifteen minutes before the announcement that reporters were called to the White House. Stephen Early, Presidential secretary, dictated the following informal statement to reporters in his office without referring to notes:

"Mr. Winston Churchill, Prime Minister of Great Britain, is again in the United States. The Prime Minister will confer while here with the President.

"The conferences will begin immediately. The subject of the conferences will be, very naturally, the war—the conduct of the war and the winning of the war.

"With the Prime Minister when he arrived were General Sir Alan Brooke [Chief of the British Imperial General Staff]; Major General Sir Hastings Ismay [Secretary of the Imperial Defense Council]; Brig. Gen. G. M. Stewart [Director of Plans of the War Office]; Sir Charles Wilson [Mr. Churchill's personal physician]; Commander C. V. R. Thompson, secretary and aide, and Mr. John Martin, private secretary to the Prime Minister.

"I do not anticipate any further statements by the President or Prime Minister this week."

A reporter asked Mr. Early whether the discussions would deal with the opening of a second front. The Presidential aide replied, "I

Continued on Page Two

"All the News That's Fit to Print."

The New York Times.

LATE CITY EDITION
Little change in temperature today.
Temperatures Yesterday—Max., 85; Min., 69

Copyright, 1942, by The New York Times Company.

VOL. XCI. No. 30,830. Entered as Second-Class Matter, Postoffice, New York, N. Y. NEW YORK, MONDAY, JUNE 22, 1942. THREE CENTS NEW YORK CITY and Vicinity

TOBRUK FALLS, AXIS CLAIMS 25,000 PRISONERS; GERMANS DRIVE WEDGE INTO SEVASTOPOL LINES; JAPANESE ASHORE ON KISKA IN THE ALEUTIANS

'GAS' DROUGHT CUTS HOLIDAY PLEASURE AS CITY SWELTERS

New Yorkers Stay at Home or Drive Only to Suburbs—Many Avoid Main Roads

CROWDS AT SOME RESORTS

Others Are Hard Hit as Travel Is Spotty—Humidity Soars and Mercury Reaches 84°

New Yorkers, afflicted with the first sweltering Sunday of the season under the gasoline shortage, stayed at home yesterday, sitting on the sidewalks or in penthouse or roof gardens, or went to near-by parks and beaches. Pleasure driving was only half of normal, by and large, and the resorts, particularly the distant ones, bore the brunt of the decline. Relatives and friends in the suburbs apparently had many visitors.

The heat was not record-breaking. Temperatures rose from a low of 69 degrees at 8:45 A. M. to a high of 84 degrees at 5:30 P. M. The humidity, however, remained at 75 per cent, which the Weather Bureau said was extremely high for such high temperatures. In the morning two-tenths of an inch of rain fell and skies were overcast long after, accounting for many of the stay-at-homes in the city.

Brooklyn's first heat prostration of the season was reported last night when John Chambers, 45 years old, of 244 West End Avenue, Coney Island, collapsed as he was walking in Flatbush Avenue near East Twenty-sixth Street, Brooklyn. He was removed to Coney Island Hospital, where his condition was described as fair.

Motoring Is Spotty

The drop in pleasure driving, although marked as far as resorts were concerned, and severe if parkway use was an accurate indication, did not fully reflect the gasoline supply situation. With many stations dry, traffic on the George Washington Bridge was reported normal for a Sunday, through the Holland Tunnel a third off, and over other bridge and tunnel exits the reduction was not significant.

Yet on the Westchester parkways motor traffic was 30 per cent of normal and on the Long Island parkways about 60 per cent of normal. Police traffic experts believed that this reflected the spotty character of the gasoline shortage, which was acute in Westchester and near-by Long Island and some sections of New Jersey, but not serious in others.

Those who had gasoline in their tanks apparently went pleasure driving in spite of the appeals to save gasoline, but avoided the parkways and resorts, where they would be conspicuous. Many, the traffic experts thought, must have gone to visit friends and relatives

Continued on Page Nine

If in Doubt, Put It Out

Carelessness remains the greatest enemy of the Army's dimout regulations, it was said yesterday by civilian lighting experts who have been working with the Army on ways of cutting down the nightly illumination over the city that is used by enemy submarines in spotting shipping off our coast.

Windows and doors thoughtlessly opened for relief from the heat continue to loose light rays that help build up the sky glow over the metropolitan area, these experts said. They urged that whenever a window or door is opened for this purpose, it should be properly shaded or screened to prevent direct rays of light from emerging. These and other precautions should be placed in effect by one hour after sundown, which is at 8:31 P. M. tonight.

Meanwhile, the Army adjures all citizens: "If in doubt, put it out."

Peter of Yugoslavia Reaches Washington

Special to THE NEW YORK TIMES.

WASHINGTON, June 21—King Peter of Yugoslavia arrived here by airplane today. He was accompanied by M. Nincitch, the Yugoslav Foreign Minister.

They will discuss with President Roosevelt and other officials their country's continued opposition to the Axis. One of their objectives, it is understood, will be to obtain lease-lend aid for the guerrilla forces resisting the Nazis in Yugoslavia.

The King and his entourage will spend tonight at Blair House and will leave tomorrow to spend a few days in the country. He is traveling incognito until Wednesday, when he will return to Washington to begin the official program of his visit to the United States.

DIMOUT 'FAILURE' IS LAID TO MAYOR

Defense Council Members Say He Has Not Ordered Police to Enforce Army Rules

Charges that Mayor La Guardia has failed to give the Police Department orders to enforce the Army's dimout regulations, but has endeavored unsuccessfully to get the Army to modify its specifications, were advanced yesterday by two members of the executive board of the Lower West Side Defense Council, acting as a special committee in behalf of the council.

Howard Mulligan, a lawyer, of 103 Waverly Place, and J. B. C. Woods of 38 Perry Street, made public copies of a letter they had sent to the Mayor charging that conditions in their area were "deplorable." Mr. Mulligan explained that he and Mr. Woods had been authorized to take this action at a meeting at the council's headquarters, 27 Barrow Street, last Tuesday evening.

"Nightly, men are dying and ships are being sunk by the enemy off our coast because you, sir, prefer not to carry out the Army's orders," the letter charged.

In his weekly radio broadcast on June 7 Mayor La Guardia an-

Continued on Page Thirteen

RED ARMY RETIRES

Paris Radio Says Nazi Troops Have Reached Town of Sevastopol

AXIS LOSSES SEVERE

Placed at 7 Divisions—Germans Repelled on Kharkov Front

By RALPH PARKER
Wireless to THE NEW YORK TIMES.

MOSCOW, Monday, June 22—The Russian High Command acknowledges in its communiqué this morning that the Germans have succeeded, at a high cost in lives lost, in driving a wedge into the defenses of Sevastopol. But the bulletin also reports the repulse of numerous severe German assaults on the Sevastopol front.

[The German-controlled Paris radio said today that German troops had reached the town of Sevastopol after breaking through the Russian inner defense lines, The United Press reported from London. German sappers smashed their way through the final defense line outside the town with flame throwers, the Paris broadcast claimed.]

[The Germans reported the Red Army forces on the Kharkov front, where fighting on any considerable scale appears to be confined to one narrow sector, are said to have achieved an important success. After two enemy regiments had crossed a river barrier and advanced on the eastern bank, the Russians struck back, driving the Germans into and across the river. The Russians themselves then crossed the river and captured points on the western bank.

Press reports yesterday indicated that the Germans were continuing to pour troops into the Sevastopol fighting and that the situation there was grave. These reports said that waves of German and Rumanian infantry, attacking Russian lines in the southern sector of the Crimean base's defenses while planes dive-bombed Soviet artillery positions, had

Continued on Page Five

NEW LANDING MADE

Japanese Cruiser Is Hit in Army Air Blow at Kiska's Harbor

TRANSPORT IS SUNK

U. S. Fliers See Enemy's Temporary Buildings on Aleutian Isle

By C. BROOKS PETERS
Special to THE NEW YORK TIMES.

WASHINGTON, June 21—The Japanese forces that have been operating in the western Aleutian Islands since June 3 have succeeded in occupying Kiska, 650 miles west of Dutch Harbor, strategic American operations base, the Navy Department announced today.

Enemy occupation of Attu, westernmost island of the American chain and some 275 miles northwest of Kiska, was acknowledged in a Navy announcement on June 12.

Flying conditions in the Aleutian region—in which "foul weather and fog" are the general rule, the Navy reported recently—were sufficiently satisfactory in the last few days to permit "some restricted air operations against Kiska," today's Navy communiqué asserted.

Long-range Army aircraft attacked a small force of Japanese ships in Kiska's harbor and reported hits on a cruiser, the Navy announced. An enemy transport was sunk.

Tents of Japanese Seen

The American planes that finally were able to penetrate to the remote island of Kiska, where until the Japanese occupation the United States Navy maintained a weather station, observed that the enemy had set up tents and "minor temporary structures on land."

The communiqué added that operations in that area continued to be restricted "by considerations of weather and great distances."

Last Monday the Navy Department reported that Army and Navy planes were continuing air assaults "against the Japanese forces which recently were reported to have landed on western islands of the Aleutian group." At that time the Navy asserted that at least three Japanese cruisers, one destroyer, one gunboat and one transport had been damaged, "some of them severely," by air attacks.

Since the announcement on June 12 of the occupation of Attu naval circles in Washington have minimized the seriousness of Japanese landings in the western Aleutians, characterizing them as having been inspired primarily by a desire "to save face" after the defeat administered by American Army and Navy forces in the Coral Sea and off Midway Island.

Supply Problem Difficult

Military experts here have stated that supply would be a major problem for any enemy forces that endeavored to establish themselves in the Aleutians. The distance from bases in Japanese territory to the Aleutian Islands is so great, these circles have contended, that aerial transport is not feasible, particularly in view of the uncertain weather conditions. Therefore, supplies must be transported by surface craft, which are constantly exposed to attack by American submarines.

There is, however, a possibility that in the Rat Island group, of which Kiska is one island, the Japanese could conceal submarine mother ships and perhaps even small aircraft carriers, the experts here said. Submarines from such bases might prove effective should Japan attack Russia, they added.

But for the most part, according to the opinion conveyed to reporters in Washington by military circles, the enemy will have to be

Continued on Page Four

War News Summarized

MONDAY, JUNE 22, 1942

Tobruk fell yesterday, and the resultant threat to Egypt and the British position in the Eastern Mediterranean changed the war picture drastically, while the Russians acknowledged a significant German advance at Sevastopol, though at the cost of heavy enemy losses.

Tobruk fell to a smashing blow delivered by waves of German tanks according to London reports. The Germans claimed that 25,000 prisoners had been taken. In London the opinion prevailed that there had not been time to lay minefields around Tobruk before the Axis attack. [1:8.]

Military observers in London referred to the fall of Tobruk as an "incontestable disaster." The Germans were believed to have obtained a large quantity of stores. General Rommel was expected to drive on Suez. [2:2.]

British bombers attacked Emden, German submarine base, for the second successive night, airfields in the Netherlands and enemy shipping off the Netherland coast. Heavy air attacks were also made on the French and Belgian coasts. [1:5.]

Moscow granted that the defenders of Sevastopol had been forced to fall back as the enemy forced a wedge in their lines, but declared that the action had crippled five German and two Rumanian divisions. Sharp activity was reported in the Kharkov and Leningrad sectors. [1:3.]

President Kalinin of the Soviet Union, in a review of a year of war, stated that the Germans no longer were capable of a general offensive. [5:5; map, P. 5.]

Lord Beaverbrook, addressing a "Salute to Russia" meeting in Britain, again urged the United Nations to open a second front. He asserted that the British Army was now sufficiently prepared. [3:1.]

Chungking reported that the Japanese had been halted in Kiangsi and had lost 1,300 troops in Honan. The Minister of War asserted that the Japanese soon would be so bogged down in China that they would not be able to attack Russia with full strength. [4:1.]

The United States Navy announced that Japanese forces in the Aleutians had succeeded in occupying the island of Kiska, 650 miles west of Dutch Harbor. Bomb hits were made on a Japanese cruiser and a Japanese transport was sunk. [1:4; map, P. 4.]

Colonel J. L. Ralston, Canadian Defense Minister, disclosed that a government telegraph station at Estevan Point, Vancouver Island, had been shelled by a submarine Saturday night, but no damage was done. [1:5-6.]

As President Roosevelt and Prime Minister Churchill continued their conversations yesterday Washington reported that the fall of Tobruk and Russian withdrawals at Sevastopol had checked "second front speculation." Concern was being shown over the necessity for holding the present front in Egypt. [1:7.]

ROMMEL'S FORCES TAKE IMPORTANT PORT IN LIBYA

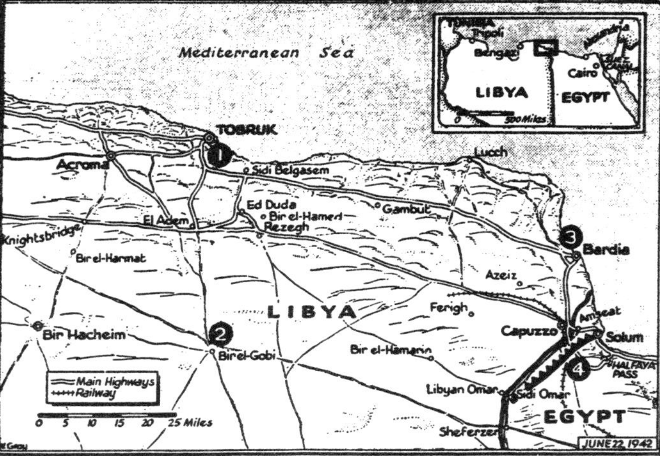

Tobruk (1) has been overwhelmed and captured with its garrison by the Axis, which also claimed the capture of Bir el-Gobi (2) and the minor port of Bardia (3). There were indications that the Germans were working their way from Bardia southward to Capuzzo for an assault across the border into Egypt. Here they will find defenses between Solum and Sidi Omar (4).

Vancouver Island Shelled; Northwest Coast Dims Out

By P. J. PHILIP
Special to THE NEW YORK TIMES.

OTTAWA, June 21—Estevan Point on Vancouver Island was shelled by an enemy submarine at 10:35 o'clock, Pacific time, last night (1:35 A. M., Sunday, Eastern war time), Colonel J. L. Ralston, the Defense Minister, announced here today. The submarine was presumed to be Japanese.

The enemy's objective was the government wireless and telegraph station there. No damage was done, said a report from Lieut. Gen. Kenneth Stuart, Canadian Chief of Staff and acting Commander in Chief of the West Coast defenses.

[Coastal dimouts in the States of Washington and Oregon were put into effect last night, following the shelling of Estevan Point, which is about 125 miles north of the United States border.]

There is an airfield near Estevan Point, but no report has come through as to whether action was taken against the attacking submarine.

The attack was the first against Canadian soil in the history of Canada as a Dominion. Last month two ships were torpedoed and sunk in the Gulf of St. Lawrence.

The Defense Minister's announcement said:

"The Commander in Chief, West Coast defenses, reported that the Dominion Government telegraph station at Estevan Point, Vancouver Island, was shelled by a submarine at 10:35 P. M. (Pacific time) on Saturday night. No damage resulted."

Estevan Point lies halfway along the western shore of Vancouver Island, about 150 miles northwest of Victoria. Its only importance seems to be the estab-

Continued on Page Four

R. A. F. PAYS EMDEN 2D VISIT IN 2 NIGHTS

Also Hammers Other Targets in Northwest Reich—Hits Ship Off Dutch Coast

By JAMES MacDONALD
Wireless to THE NEW YORK TIMES.

LONDON, June 21—A large number of British bombers hammered Emden, Germany, last night for the second night in succession and also other objectives in Northwest Germany and air bases in the Netherlands.

At the same time American-built Hudson planes of the Coastal Command, ever on the lookout for enemy shipping, searched waters off the Netherland coast, where a Canadian flying crew dropped two bombs on a medium-sized cargo vessel.

The communiqué announcing these operations did not divulge the number of planes engaged, but said the raids cost the Royal Air Force six bombers and one Coastal Command plane. The R. A. F. losses were increased today when one fighter plane failed to return home from a daylight attack on Dunkerque.

[The Berlin radio went off the air at 1:50 A. M. today, a possible sign that British bombers were again over Germany, The United Press reported from London.

[German planes dropped bombs early today in a sharp attack on the south coast of England, The Associated Press reported. Two of the raiders were shot down and two more Nazi planes destroyed over Europe.]

As in the case of the R. A. F. raids on Emden late Friday night and early yesterday morning, the Air Ministry did not go into details about the targets for the night or indicate the extent of damage.

While patrolling along the Netherland coast during the night Coastal Command fliers caught up with an enemy convoy of three ships. The rear gunner on a Canadian-manned plane said on his return to his base that he saw two bombs hit one vessel amidship, hurling debris high in the air in the resulting explosions. Whether the vessel sank was not determined. What became of her two companion ships was not learned here.

Although the sky was clear, there was less daylight activity to-

Continued on Page Five

'Never a Dull Moment' at Midway, Reporter Watching Battle Found

The following account of the Battle of Midway is by a correspondent of THE NEW YORK TIMES who was aboard one of the United States warships.

By FOSTER HAILEY
Special to THE NEW YORK TIMES.

WITH THE PACIFIC FLEET, at Sea, June 4 (Delayed)—Today is the day. Mark it on your calendar in red ink, Thursday, June 4. It may be the one on which the tide definitely turned in the battle of the Pacific.

This morning at dawn the Japanese launched planes from a strong striking force northwest of Midway. We are in a position to strike them on the flank. If our planes can only get to their carriers before the Japanese planes attacking Midway car return, the result may be a naval disaster for the Japanese.

White water is curling away from the clipper bows of the cruisers and the big carriers, whose escort we are, as we drive on at high speed with the destroyers ahead and on the flanks. It is a relief for the nerves when the first alarm is sounded. It turns out to be false, but the activity has eased the tension.

There is another spurt of activity as another air contact is reported, but it turns out to be a big patrol plane from Midway that joins the force to act as an anti-submarine guard.

"Midway was attacked at 8:48 A. M.," our Admiral and Chief of Staff says crisply when an inquiry on the situation is made.

"We should be in launching distance soon."

The dawn was a gloomy one, but now the clouds are breaking up.

Continued on Page Four

NEWS PUTS DAMPER ON CHURCHILL VISIT

But Washington Sees Mid-East Crisis as Incidental in His Planning With Roosevelt

By JAMES B. RESTON
Special to THE NEW YORK TIMES.

WASHINGTON, June 21—Washington was in a sober and realistic mood tonight. The fall of Tobruk and the situation of the Russians at Sevastopol have put a damper on the unrestrained second-front speculation that has surrounded the Roosevelt-Churchill talks. The chief immediate concern was viewed as the holding of the second front the United Nations now have in Egypt, rather than opening up new fronts on the European Continent.

The President and Mr. Churchill continued their talks during the day, and the chiefs of staff of the United States and Britain, General George C. Marshall and General Sir Alan Brooke, who came to the United States with Mr. Churchill, continued their exchange of information and their planning for the future.

The plain and simple truth about these important discussions is that only a few persons know what has gone on since Mr. Churchill arrived, and they are not telling what they know.

The purpose of the conversations is much less complicated, dramatic and urgent than one would tend to deduce from the secrecy with which they have been surrounded.

It is undoubtedly true, as Stephen Early, White House secretary, has said, that they are dealing with the future plans of the

Continued on Page Eight

NAZIS NEAR EGYPT

British Are on Border as Rommel Presses On After Victory

PORT'S LOSS SERIOUS

Plan for a Second Front Seen Upset by Need to Hold New Line

By DAVID ANDERSON
Special Cable to THE NEW YORK TIMES.

LONDON, June 21—A smashing blow delivered yesterday by waves of German tanks, heavily supported from the air, crushed the defenses of Tobruk in Libya. The War Office tonight confirmed the loss of the town, already claimed by the enemy, who said 25,000 prisoners, including "several generals" had been captured.

The story of what happened, as given by both German and Italian sources, appears to cover the battle fairly fully, but the accuracy of these reports cannot be checked at present. Briefly, it can be said Field Marshal Erwin Rommel's armored units that had passed Tobruk in pursuit of the British Eighth Army did so to make certain whether the British showed any signs of preparing a counter-attack.

When the German Marshal was satisfied this was not the case he reversed his forces, bringing back tanks against Tobruk from the south, driving from the vicinity of Ed Duda, and did this fiercely with every ounce of power at his command. At the same time the Luftwaffe began intensive bombing of Tobruk's defenses. Within a matter of hours the battle was over.

Tobruk Long in Battle

Tobruk must have been softer in its last moments than during the many other attacks it beat off during the last seventeen months since it was captured from the Italians on Jan. 22, 1941. It has been on the fringe of the Libyan battlefield for some weeks with inevitable strain as strategy wavered between one of concentration of strength there and one of evacuation.

Despite the presence of a large garrison when Tobruk fell it is believed there was not time to lay minefields on its perimeter or otherwise strengthen its defenses to face an immediate storming.

A Cairo communiqué, released here at noon today, paved the way for the worst. It read:

"Yesterday the enemy attacked the perimeter of Tobruk in great strength. In spite of most determined resistance by our forces the enemy succeeded in penetrating the defenses and in occupying a considerable area inside them."

Twelve strong points in the defenses were taken by the first wave of enemy tanks, according to Berlin. This made a wedge two and a half miles wide, and German sources state the British defenders then realized that further resistance was useless.

Bombers Blast Defenses

But they had other reasons for weighing most seriously the advantages of carrying on the fight. The Germans said today that "numerous bombers' ceaseless attack wrought great destruction in the fortifications and other military works of the port and town."

It was not long after noon yesterday when large formations of German bombers swooped down on a group of four anti-aircraft batteries, all of which were silenced, it was reported by Berlin. Still more of the Luftwaffe's heavy aircraft, laden with high explosives, cruised over a column of twenty tanks, setting many of them ablaze.

Finally, the German radio said, "About 2 P. M. another great attack was made on Tobruk, which lasted three hours without interruption and caused numerous fires.

Continued on Page Two

"All the News That's Fit to Print."

NEWS INDEX, PAGE 35, THIS SECTION

The New York Times.

LATE CITY EDITION
Somewhat warmer today.
Temperatures Yesterday—Max., 70; Min., 61

Section 1

VOL. XCI—No. 30,836. Entered as Second-Class Matter, Postoffice, New York, N. Y. NEW YORK, SUNDAY, JUNE 28, 1942. Including Magazine and Book Sections. TEN CENTS New York City and Vicinity

FBI SEIZES 8 SABOTEURS LANDED BY U-BOATS HERE AND IN FLORIDA TO BLOW UP WAR PLANTS; ALLIES PLEDGE MOVES TO RELIEVE RUSSIANS

PRICE OF GASOLINE GOES UP 2½ CENTS IN EAST TOMORROW

OPA Also Orders Increase of 2 Cents on Oils, Including Four of the Fuel Types

LACK OF SUBSIDY DECRIED

Henderson Calls Higher Costs Unfair to Public—Wider Ration Area Expected

Special to THE NEW YORK TIMES.

WASHINGTON, June 27—Gasoline will cost Eastern motorists 2½ cents a gallon more beginning Monday.

Increases of 2 cents a gallon, effective at the same time, also were ordered by the Office of Price Administration today for range oil, kerosene, tractor fuel, distillate Diesel fuel oils, gashouse oils and Nos. 1, 2, 3 and 4 fuel oils. Residual fuel oils are not affected.

The increases, third allowed by the OPA on gasoline and other oils since the beginning of the year, were made necessary, Leon Henderson, Price Administrator, said, by increased costs of moving petroleum to the East Coast by means other than tanker.

Word came also that when permanent gasoline rationing goes into effect in the East July 22 the boundaries of the affected area will in all probability be extended to include the ninety-three counties in Western New York, Pennsylvania, West Virginia, Maryland and Virginia which have been exempt to date.

OPC Approval Reported

According to reports here tonight, the Office of Petroleum Coordinator favors such an extension, and it is said to have gained favor with the Office of Price Administration because of a view that the problem of rationing administration would be greatly simplified by having the area bounded by State lines.

The plan would carry rationing to Buffalo and other important cities which have been exempt.

The ninety-three counties were exempted when emergency rationing became effective May 15, because the Office of Petroleum Coordination found that they had sufficient supplies of gasoline to take care of demand. Officials warned at that time, however, that the exemption might be only temporary.

In a special statement accompanying his announcement of the price increases on gasoline and other oils, Mr. Henderson declared that it was unfair to make Eastern consumers shoulder the expense of moving gasoline by means other than by tanker, but that for the time there was nothing that could be done about it in the absence of arrangements for subsidies.

"The Office of Price Administration," he said, "is keenly aware of the inequity of making consumers of petroleum products bear the entire cost of the submarine warfare

Continued on Page Twenty-eight

If in Doubt, Put It Out

The outdoor weenie roast and the beach fire are out for the duration, civilian defense offficials said yesterday as a reminder for picnickers. Sings, story-telling and hayrides are among the outdoor pastimes in which groups of people can join after dark without adding to the sky glow that helps enemy submarines find our ships. Vacationists are learning that a darkened circle is just as conducive to sociability as a blazing fire that shoots sparks into the skies.

All dimout regulations go into effect one hour after sunset. Tonight the sun sets at 8:22 o'clock. Don't take a chance with any outdoor light. Play safe and remember the Army's admonition: "If in doubt, put it out."

Major Sports Results

RACING

Whirlaway won the Brooklyn Handicap by two lengths from Swing and Sway on Aqueduct's closing day, which netted a minimum of $100,000 for Army-Navy relief. Warren Wright's thoroughbred thereby boosted his earnings to $404,486, only $33,244 less than Seabiscuit's all-time record.

BASEBALL

The Reds upset the Dodgers, 3—1, on Pinch-hitter Ray Lamanno's three-run homer with two out in the ninth. The Giants defeated the Pirates, 5—2, behind Bob Carpenter. At Chicago, Joe DiMaggio and Buddy Hassett led the Yankees to a 7-3 triumph over the White Sox.

GOLF

Frank Tatum Jr. of Stanford captured the N. C. A. A. golf title by downing Manuel De La Torre of Northwestern, 5 and 4, at South Bend. Vincent Raskopf vanquished Olin P. Boone, 2 up, in Long Island junior final at Cherry Valley. Miss Betty Jameson of San Antonio won the women's Western open at Chicago.

(Complete Details in Section 5.)

WILLKIE DEMANDS 'MEN OF FORESIGHT'

Backing Baldwin for Post in Connecticut, He Says Party Must Have Such Leaders

By JAMES C. HAGERTY

Special to THE NEW YORK TIMES.

WESTPORT, Conn., June 27—Wendell L. Willkie, speaking here this afternoon at a luncheon meeting sponsored by the Fairfield County Republican Women's Association, threw the full weight of his position as titular leader of the Republican party behind the candidacy of Raymond E. Baldwin as the party's nominee for Governor of Connecticut.

In supporting Mr. Baldwin, who served as Governor from 1938 to 1940 and who acted as one of the Willkie floor managers at the 1940 Republican National Convention, the former Republican Presidential candidate declared that he favored Mr. Baldwin because he represented the type of leadership so urgently needed in the Republican party. He said that his action was

Continued on Page Thirty-one

ROMMEL PUSHES ON

Enemy Units in Egypt Slow Down 15 Miles From Matruh

BRITISH HARRY FOE

Two-Week Halt in Axis Supplies to Bengazi Reported Forced

By DAVID ANDERSON

Special Cable to THE NEW YORK TIMES.

LONDON, June 27—General Field Marshal Erwin Rommel's Axis war machine was reported tonight to be slowly rolling toward a standstill in front of the British line that extends from Matruh, Egypt, to a point some forty miles inland.

Cairo gives little sign of knowing when or where the enemy will strike, but has issued reports of heavy aerial activity against advancing German supply columns and of delaying actions fought by British mechanized units.

The latest definite information from Cairo is that Marshal Rommel's forces are about fifteen miles from Matruh and apparently are tending to bear somewhat in the direction of the seacoast.

Opinion in London

Prudent observers here believed tonight that it would be safer to assume that the pace of the invasion of Egypt had slowed down of its own accord than to indulge in wishful thinking that the enemy had been checked.

[The Associated Press reported from Cairo that the British Eighth Army stood reinforced at full strength against a powerful Axis striking force, and, in a dispatch from Alexandria, said it had been learned unofficially that, with British submarines blasting away at Axis supply vessels, not a single enemy convoy had reached Bengazi, Libya, in the past fortnight.]

Speculation concerning the anticipated battle has not yet entirely ruled out the possibility that Marshal Rommel may risk the great gamble of attempting to swing southward of the Qattara Depression.

Fierce running fights have been going on along the tracks of the

Continued on Page Six

REPORT ON PARLEYS

Roosevelt and Churchill Say Germans Will Be Diverted by Push

STATEMENT HOPEFUL

Cuts in Shipping Losses, Blows at Japan, Help for China Projected

By W. H. LAWRENCE

Special to THE NEW YORK TIMES.

WASHINGTON, June 27—Coming operations by the military forces of the United Nations "will divert German strength from the attack on Russia," it was announced today by President Roosevelt and Prime Minister Churchill in a final communiqué on their week-long series of conferences in which the offensive strategy of the war was mapped.

For obvious reasons, the two leaders offered no more enlightenment on the methods they had agreed upon to carry out a previous British-Soviet-American understanding on the "urgent tasks of creating a second front in Europe in 1942."

They left the leaders of Germany and Italy with only a guess as to when, where and how the operations would be begun that would require the diversion of Axis man power now pressing against the Soviet armies on the eastern front.

Churchill Left Thursday

The second-front declaration, purposely vague, was the high point of the joint statement issued simultaneously at 11:30 A. M. here and in London after Prime Minister Churchill had arrived safely home by airplane from the United States, which he left secretly Thursday night.

Other major strategy decisions indicated by the joint statement were:

New plans for using the naval forces of the United Nations to reduce the toll of merchant shipping were made. In recent months losses have outstripped ship building.

Measures against Japan have been prepared.

New methods to relieve sorely pressed China will be undertaken.

Statement Is Optimistic

The Roosevelt-Churchill statement was optimistic. They reviewed the circumstances of their meeting in August, 1941, when the Atlantic Charter was drawn at sea before the United States entered the war, and again in late December, 1941, after the attack on Pearl Harbor. They declared their belief that "the over-all picture is more favorable to victory than it was either in August or December of last year."

But they warned against complacency. The task ahead, they said, must not be underrated and the conferences here have been conducted "with the full knowledge of the power and resourcefulness of the enemy."

Nowhere in the statement did the two leaders mention the sharp British reverses in the North African campaign, which took place while Mr. Churchill was en route here and during his stay in this country. These have aroused considerable criticism of the Prime Minister in Britain, but Mr. Churchill assured a Congressional delegation on Thursday that Egypt would be held and he minimized the advances of the Axis armies led by General Field Marshal Erwin Rommel.

Big Production Stressed

Mr. Roosevelt and Mr. Churchill said that their survey of the production of munitions of all kinds disclosed "an optimistic picture" on the whole, and that the arsenals of the two countries were approaching maximum production "on schedule." This was borne out by the President's special production report yesterday, which dis-

Continued on Page Two

War News Summarized

SUNDAY, JUNE 28, 1942

In New York last night J. Edgar Hoover announced the arrest of eight Nazi saboteurs, who were landed from submarines on Long Island and the Florida coast with TNT, maps, $150,000 in cash and instructions for blowing up such objectives as Hell Gate Bridge, the Aluminum Company of America, vital rail terminals and major war plants. [1:8.]

President Roosevelt and Prime Minister Churchill issued yesterday a joint statement asserting that the military forces of the United Nations would engage in operations that would divert German strength from the attack on Russia. The statement indicated decisions had been reached calculated to lower the submarine toll of shipping and to expedite aid to China. It was issued after the safe arrival of Prime Minister Churchill in Britain. [1:4.]

The Prime Minister returned to face political difficulties arising from the defeat in Libya, but it was still indicated that there was no serious challenge to his leadership. [2:2.]

A large vanguard of the United States Army Air Forces has been established in the British Isles and is making preparations to engage soon in mass attacks on Germany, coordinated with those of the Royal Air Force, according to London reports. Friday night there were a number of British attacks on German-occupied regions, and the Germans attacked fairly severely the city of Norwich. [1:7.]

Moscow granted that Soviet troops were being slowly pushed back in portions of the Kharkov front but said that the Germans were making no rapid advances and had gained no immediate military advantage except the capture of Kupyansk. The Sevastopol front was holding under the same sort of heavy German pressure. [1:5.]

Cairo announced that the main Axis forces were only fifteen miles west of Matruh, major British base on the Egyptian coast. A big battle seemed imminent and may have begun. [1:3; map, P. 6.]

British submarines were reported to have attacked many Axis supply vessels in the Mediterranean, and it was said in Alexandria that not an enemy convoy had reached Bengazi in the past two weeks. [6:5.]

The Chinese admitted the loss of Lishui, last of three major air bases in the Eastern Kiangsi-Chekiang area from which Japan could be bombed. The Japanese recapture of Kweiki on the Hangchow-Nanchang railway also was acknowledged. [12:3, with map.]

At Atlanta, Ga., it was disclosed that the first major expeditionary force of the United States Marine Corps had landed at a South Pacific base with a formidable arsenal of modern equipment. [1:5-6.]

EXPLOSIVES HIDDEN BY NAZI SABOTEURS ON FLORIDA BEACH

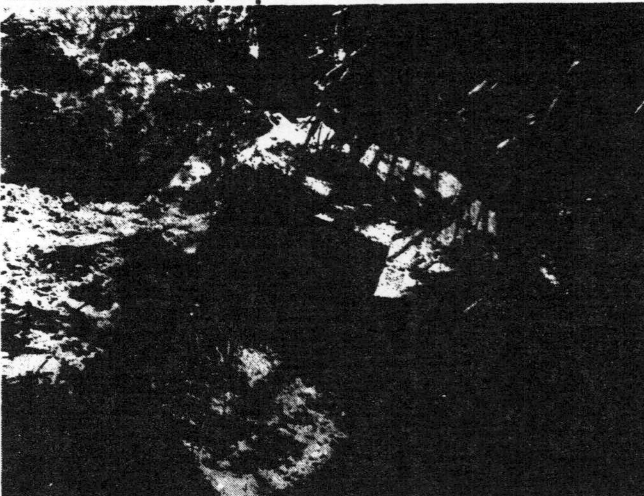

Four boxes containing TNT which was to have been used to destroy war plants

The New York Times (FBI)

First Major Marine A. E. F. Reaches South Pacific Port

By The Associated Press.

ATLANTA, June 27—This war's first major expeditionary force of United States marines has landed at a South Pacific port apparently equipped for offensive landing in that theatre of war. The far-off arrival of "transports swarming with marines" was revealed here today by Major Meigs O. Frost, Southern public relations chief for the Marine Corps.

Accompanying the announcement that the convoy carried the Marines' biggest overseas contingent of the war was the first story to be released as written by one of the Marines' own war correspondents assigned to combat forces.

The story told merely of the human side of life aboard the transports during the voyage from an unrevealed American port to the undisclosed destination, but contained clear implications of the job ahead of the task force.

With a number of Southern leathernecks known to have been included, first official advice regarding the force was relayed here from Washington by Brig. Gen. Robert L. Denig, Marine Headquarters Public Relations Director, in line with an effort to bring Marine news close to home.

The anonymous sergeant correspondent related how some of the Marines enjoyed the tropical nights by sleeping in Higgins landing boats aboard their ships.

The sergeant's story recorded no attacks on the convoy.

Recalling blacked-out nights, band concerts and swing sessions, the sergeant decided that the trip was far from dull and "living conditions aboard ship weren't as bad as anticipated."

"Most popular place aboard ship was the soda fountain, where Marines and sailors relaxed on cokes and ice cream.

"The chaplain's library was pop-

Continued on Page Eleven

RED ARMY CHECKING NAZI UKRAINE PUSH

Axis 'Fist' Kept From Spreading Out Beyond Kupyansk—Sevastopol Gain Slow

By RALPH PARKER

Wireless to THE NEW YORK TIMES.

MOSCOW, June 27—Though yielding ground slowly in fierce rear-guard fighting, Marshal Semyon Timoshenko has prevented the Germans from taking immediate or spectacular advantage of the capture of Kupyansk.

Russian dispatches from the southwestern front describe the fighting as of exceptional fierceness, but though it is apparent that General Field Marshal Fedor von Bock is trying to widen the battle front, the stubbornness of the Russian defense in depth has prevented his powerful armored force, attacking in a narrow sector, from ripping open the Russian lines and causing confusion.

The "fist" that struck is, as it were, still clenched, with its tanks and motorized infantry bunched together, though after the capture of Kupyansk it probably was the German plan to thrust probing fingers into various sectors of the Russian resistance.

[The midnight Soviet communiqué said Sevastopol's defenders had repulsed more attacks that cost the Axis heavily, while on the other fronts there were no significant changes. Berlin reported that a new Russian attempt to land at Kerch had been frustrated and said additional positions had been captured at Sevastopol.]

At Sevastopol yesterday a dangerous German wedge was driven into the northeastern sector. Though the pressure now is heavy on all fronts as new German regiments hastily brought from other fronts come into line, Col. Gen. Fritz Erich von Mannstein's gains are measured in yards. Small groups of shock troops succeeded in skirting through in the southern sector, where three enemy divisions now are believed to be operating, but these in no way represent any general advance and are vigorously engaged in hand-to-hand combat.

Much of the fighting now is described as a close-quarter struggle in trenches and gun emplacements, and here the Red Army men and

Continued on Page Nineteen

U. S. AIR ACTIVITIES IN BRITAIN RUSHED

Increasing Forces Arrive to Join From Own Bases in Offensive Against Nazis

Special Cable to THE NEW YORK TIMES.

LONDON, June 27—With preparations of the British Royal Air Force about complete for continuing—or rather, doubling in power—its attacks against Germany, such as that on Thursday night, which left still-smoking ruins at Bremen, authoritative sources here directed attention today to the important part predicted for the United States Army Air Forces in the offensive over Europe.

A great deal has been said about the arrival of tens of thousands of American soldiers in the British Isles; but little or nothing has been permitted to be published hitherto about the large number of United States Air Forces personnel now reaching here.

These American airmen have been taking over flying fields in the United Kingdom, studying the operational systems of the R. A. F. and working on plans for close coordination with the British.

The preparations indicated the establishment of United States air bases in Britain from which American units would bomb Germany in joint operations with the R. A. F.

[The R. A. F. bombed Germany again last night and a Berlin broadcast heard at London said Bremen had been attacked once more, according to a United Press dispatch.]

The time is rapidly approaching when the Liberators, Flying Fortresses and other giant United States bombers will be augmenting the R. A. F.'s Stirlings, Halifaxes,

Continued on Page Fifteen

Japan Bombed With 20-Cent Sight; Arnold Gives D. F. C. to 23 Raiders

By C. BROOKS PETERS

Special to THE NEW YORK TIMES.

WASHINGTON, June 27—The American B-25 bombers that carried out the daring surprise attack on Tokyo and other Japanese objectives last April 18 were equipped with improvised bombsights that cost about 20 cents each.

This and other interesting details of the aerial assault carried out by a force under the command of Brig. Gen. James H. Doolittle were revealed by the War Department today as the Distinguished Flying Cross was pinned on twenty-three members of the Army Air Forces who participated in the raid.

Because the raid on Japan was planned as a low-altitude operation, "with the planes' wings barely skimming the treetops as they flew toward their objective," it seemed inevitable that some of the planes might fall into Japanese hands (not one did, however), which would have given the enemy an opportunity to become familiar with the Norden bombsight.

But low-altitude bombing does not, in the Army's opinion, require the extreme accuracy of the Norden bombsights and they were not used in the planes participating in the attack. Major Charles R. Greening, armament officer of the squadron and one of the officers decorated today, improvised the 20-cent bombsights.

Five Japanese cities were marked for bombing in the April 18 raid: Tokyo, Yokohama, Nagoya, Kobe and Osaka. Objectives were tank, armament and aircraft

Continued on Page Eighteen

INVADERS CONFESS

Had TNT to Blast Key Factories, Railroads and City Water System

USED RUBBER BOATS

Carried $150,000 Cash—All Had Lived in U. S.—Face Death Penalty

By WILL LISSNER

Two groups of saboteurs, highly trained by direction of the German High Command at a special school for sabotage near Berlin, carrying cases of powerful explosives and nearly $150,000 in cash, were landed on the Long Island and the Florida coasts from submarines in the last fortnight with orders to blow up certain key plants and to cause panics in large cities, it was disclosed last night.

Despite their training the two gangs of four men each fell afoul of special agents of the Federal Bureau of Investigation almost immediately and the arrest of all eight was announced last evening by J. Edgar Hoover, director of the Bureau. They were in custody within a month after they had shipped on their expedition out of a submarine base on the French coast.

Mr. Hoover reported the arrests to President Roosevelt and released full biographies of the men, which showed that they were former waiters, machinists and German-American Bund agitators, long resident here and fluent in English, who were repatriated by the German Embassies in the United States and Mexico to be recruited for the sabotage school.

Carried List of Objectives

In the possession of the men was a list of special assignments of industrial plants they were to sabotage and department stores in which they were to create panics. The plants were the following:

Aluminum Corporation of America, Alcoa, Tenn.

Aluminum Corporation of America, Massena, N. Y.

Aluminum Corporation of America, East St. Louis, Ill.

Aluminum Corporation of America, Cryolite (aluminum base) plant, Philadelphia.

Chesapeake & Ohio Railroad (around industrial areas.)

Pennsylvania Railroad (at Newark, N. J.)

Hell Gate Bridge (railroad bridge from Astoria, Queens, to the Bronx.)

Canals and locks of the Ohio River from Cincinnati to St. Louis. (St. Louis, contrary to German geography, is not connected with the Ohio River.)

Specified department stores and

Continued on Page Thirty

Spy Crew Escaped From a Coast Guard

A story was told in Amagansett, L. I., last night that purported to give details of the landing of the sabotage crew there. According to this version, when the gang had finished burying its cases of equipment on the beach, the saboteurs were discovered by a young Coast Guardsman on shore patrol. He challenged them and the spies attempted to bribe him with some of their large store of money. He spurned the bribe and they fled.

Unable to round the men up single-handed, the Coast Guardsman ran back to his station, gave the alarm and called out patrols. The Army sent a detail to the scene and, together with the Coast Guard, the Army men searched the area, but the saboteurs had made good their escape, temporarily.

"All the News That's Fit to Print."

The New York Times.

LATE CITY EDITION
Continued warm and humid, probably scattered showers and thunderstorms today.
Temperatures Yesterday—Max., 78; Min., 72

Copyright, 1942, by The New York Times Company.

VOL. XCI...No. 30,866. Entered as Second-Class Matter, Postoffice, New York, N. Y. NEW YORK, TUESDAY, JULY 28, 1942. THREE CENTS NEW YORK CITY and Vicinity

RUSSIANS EVACUATE ROSTOV, WITHDRAW SOUTH OF THE DON; RAID LEAVES HAMBURG AFIRE

SOVIET CITIES FALL

Novocherkassk Is Lost—Nazis Push Across Don Farther East

RUSSIANS EXACT BIG TOLL

Germans Claim a Town South of Rostov on Oil Pipeline—Gain Near Stalingrad

By The Associated Press.

MOSCOW, Tuesday, July 28—Red Army troops have withdrawn from Rostov and from Novocherkassk, twenty miles to the northeast, before the steady German drive into the Caucasus, the Soviet High Command announced today. After fighting grimly in the streets of the shell-wrecked cities, which are north of the Don River, the Russians retreated to positions south of the river.

[The German High Command, which had claimed the two cities last week, reported yesterday the capture of Bataisk, five miles south of Rostov on the railway and oil pipeline from Baku. The Germans also reported southward advances east of Rostov and said that Axis troops in the Don bend had reached the river on a broad front in a push toward Stalingrad.]

The Russians also were imperiled all along the lower Don River, as far east as Tsimlyansk, 120 miles from Rostov. In that sector the Germans continued to throw pontoon bridges across the Don faster than the Russians could smash them.

Russians Counter-Attack

This morning's bulletin described the Tsimlyansk action as follows:

"The enemy repeatedly attempted to cross the river. Fighting is going on with fluctuating successes. In one sector the Germans succeeded in pushing forward, but were stemmed by a counter-attack by Soviet troops and lost during this engagement 350 officers and men killed."

The phrase "fluctuating successes" bore out press dispatches that acknowledged that the Germans were flowing across the Don despite the wrecking of numerous pontoon spans by Soviet airmen and artillery.

According to the dispatches, the Don was crossed between Rostov and Tsimlyansk only at terrific cost to the Germans. Thousands of dead Germans littered the banks of the river or slipped downstream along with smashed pontoons, the dispatches said. But long lines of German reserves always were ready to take the place of the fallen.

Last November a civilian army of men, women and children at Rostov joined hands with the Red Army to repulse huge German forces that had entered the city. The German withdrawal from Rostov was the turning point in Ger-

Continued on Page Three

Credit Rules Eased On Heating Change

By The Associated Press.

WASHINGTON, July 27—To facilitate the conversion of oil-burning heating equipment on the East Coast to coal because of the expected oil shortage this Winter, the Federal Reserve Board liberalized credit restrictions today.

The board will no longer require down payments or repayments within a limited term of months in connection with the conversion of heaters, installation of weatherstripping or insulation or other devices to conserve fuel. Dealers and contractors will be at liberty to establish whatever requirements they choose.

Under previous Federal Reserve regulations, if conversion were financed on the installment plan it would have to be paid for one-third down and the balance in twelve months.

The board also removed credit restrictions on the repair or replacement of property damaged or lost in a flood.

600 R. A. F. Planes Strike Searing Blow at Reich Port

175,000 Incendiaries and Many 2-Ton Bombs Loosed in 50-Minute Attack—London's Guns Active as Nazis Hit Back in Britain

By RAYMOND DANIELL

Wireless to THE NEW YORK TIMES.

LONDON, Tuesday, July 28—For fifty minutes Sunday night British bombers to the number of about 600 dumped fire and explosives on Hamburg, Germany's largest port and most heavily defended submarine building center.

For the first thirty-five minutes of the concentrated attack two waves of the big Royal Air Force planes unloaded about 175,000 incendiary bombs and regular high explosives upon Hamburg's yards and industries.

Then a third wave of bombers followed up entirely with high explosives, including many of the 4,000-pound missiles that have a terrific blasting power.

Yesterday afternoon, the Air Ministry reported many of the R. A. F.'s Wellington bombers struck again in Northwestern Germany.

London's antiaircraft guns went into action early today and the city had a raid alarm as Nazi planes, hitting back apparently in more force than on recent enemy raids, went overhead. Some German bombs were reported to have fallen in the Home Counties outside London, but none in the city itself. The all-clear sounded after an hour or so of intermittent gunfire.

The heaviest German attack was on a town in the West Midlands. Nazi planes were reported over Northern Ireland, where United States troops are stationed, but no bombing there was indicated. Eight Nazi planes were downed in Britain during the night, officials said.

Air Marshal Sir Arthur T. Harris, chief of the Bomber Command, declared the Sunday-night raid on Hamburg "one of the outstandingly successful attacks" of the war.

British officials reported the loss of twenty-nine big planes in the night's operations, including bomb-

Continued on Page Four

PATROLS MEET FOE IN NEW GUINEA PUSH

Contact Shows Enemy Gain of 55 Miles From His New Landing Point in Papua

By The United Press.

AT UNITED NATIONS HEADQUARTERS, Australia, Tuesday, July 28—Allied patrols have made contact with Japanese forces near Oivi, fifty-five miles inland from Japanese-held Gona Mission on the northeast coast of New Guinea, where Allied bombers have blown up an ammunition dump in a new raid, a United Nations communiqué disclosed today.

Oivi is east of Kokoda, half-way point on the 110-mile overland road from Gona Mission to the Allied base of Port Moresby on the south coast. The Japanese had thus penetrated fifteen miles farther inland from the Awala area, where they were reported yesterday to be in contact with United Nations patrols.

The communiqué said a lone Japanese flying boat raided Townsville, on the northeast coast of Australia, which also was attacked ineffectively early last Sunday, but caused no damage.

[The Australian radio, heard by The United Press in San Francisco, yesterday said Allied dive bombers are continuing their attacks against Japanese forces in New Guinea and carried out two strong night assaults on the Timor Island stronghold of Kupang, where hits were scored on the airdrome and nearby barracks, according to the United Nations headquarters communiqué. A small Japanese raiding force of about five planes twice raided Port Darwin, but there were no casualties or damage, the communiqué added.]

Australia Warns of Spies

Wireless to THE NEW YORK TIMES.

CANBERRA, Australia, July 27—"Almost positive evidence" of activities of enemy agents is causing anxiety in governmental circles today.

The possibility of landings of spies for the Japanese from submarines at infrequent spots along Australia's long and lonely coastline is not discounted in view of recent revelations in the United States. It is also considered possible that the enemy governments may have planted agents in Australia before the war who have succeeded in disarming suspicion and making Australian friends, from whom they obtain information.

The existence of illegal radios in the Commonwealth has long been

Continued on Page Three

U. S. AIRMEN ROUT RAID ON CHUNGKING

Only 4 of 50 Enemy Planes Reach Chinese Capital for First Attack in 11 Months

By The United Press.

CHUNGKING, China, July 27—United States Army fighter planes, battling beneath a full moon, routed fifty Japanese bombers that took off from Hankow to make their first raid of the year on Chungking tonight, letting only four of them get through to attack the outskirts of this Chinese capital.

Pilots of the American Twenty-third Pursuit Group soared into the sky from a West China base as soon as advance observation posts sounded the alarm that the Japanese were on the way from Hankow, 460 miles to the northeast, at 6:30 P. M.

An air defense headquarters communiqué announced that the Americans intercepted the raiding party and blazed into combat over Eastern Szechwan Province, some 120 miles from Chungking. Except for the few American Volunteer Group veterans, these Americans were having their first big crack at the enemy since their arrival in China.

Only Four Reach Capital

Observers said that twenty-seven Japanese planes got as far as Kiangpei, across the Kialing River just north of Chungking, but only four actually flew over the capital at 3:30 P. M.

The raiders left Hankow for the first attack on Chungking in eleven months with the advantage of bright moonlight, but low clouds had gathered by the time the four bombers reached their objective. They dumped their bombs far from any important target at a point well outside the city. The communiqué said the raid was a complete failure.

The defense authorities, remembering how large numbers of enemy planes had bombed the city in daylight throughout the Summers of 1939, 1940 and 1941, could hardly believe that the disappearance of the four bombers was the end of the raid. The all-clear signal was delayed another hour until 9:30 P. M.

The communiqué said that "the extreme calmness and best order maintained in dugouts by the citizens of this city were admirable, indeed." One reason for the calmness was the confidence manifested when word spread that the Americans were out to intercept the Japanese.

It was virtually a three-hour tea party for the people gathered in the bomb-proof dugouts, which had

Continued on Page Six

A. L. P. RIGHT WING IS OUT FOR MEAD; 3D PARTY SHELVED

But It Retains Right to Run Own Man if Bennett Is Named for Governor

KELLY CENTER OF INTEREST

Brooklyn Chief May Be Called to White House in Move to Get Him to Back Senator

The right wing of the American Labor party last night endorsed the candidacy of Senator James M. Mead for Governor and withdrew in his favor its threat of a third-party ticket. This wing controls the party's State Committee, has controlled all State conventions in the past, and represents to a larger degree than the left wing the last-ditch New Deal vote in the State.

The threat, made a week ago, was conditioned on the then expected nomination by the Democrats of Attorney General John J. Bennett Jr., who is not acceptable to the American Labor party. The action last night was taken by the State Executive Committee, meeting at the Hotel Claridge. The full State Committee will meet next Monday and will set Saturday, Aug. 22, as the date of the party's State convention, two days after the end of the Democratic session.

The action by the executive committee does not bind it to support the nominee of the Democratic convention should it turn out to be Mr. Bennett, who still maintained yesterday his pledged majority to the Democratic convention, despite the continuance of the New Deal drive for Mr. Mead.

If Mr. Bennett is nominated, the A. L. P. still plans to run its third-party candidate on the theory that it will be the Old Guard of the Democratic party, rather than the New Deal, that will meet consequent defeat in the November elections. On the other hand, there is no bar to the support by the A. L. P. of some New Deal candidate other than Mr. Mead, should some such candidate emerge as the eventual nominee of the Democratic convention.

Text of the Resolution

The resolution adopted unanimously by the Labor party committee follows:

"The State Executive Committee of the A. L. P. has gone on record repeatedly as urging the Democratic party of the State of New York to nominate for Governor a candidate who would unite behind him all the New Deal and labor forces of New York State.

"The candidacy of United States Senator James M. Mead—declared in response to public appeal—presents both the Democratic party and the A. L. P. with just such a candidate. In Senator Mead we have an outstanding candidate

Continued on Page Eighteen

SENATORS REJECT TAX EXEMPTS LEVY AND JOINT RETURNS

Committee Cuts 400 Millions From Treasury's Request for $2,400,000,000 Rise in Bill

10% ON ALL INCOME ASKED

M. L. Seidman of Board of Trade Denounces Bill—Ruml Urges Current Tax Collection

By THOMAS J. HAMILTON

Special to THE NEW YORK TIMES.

WASHINGTON, July 27—Disregarding Secretary Morgenthau's plea for action against two "special privileges, the Senate Finance Committee today rejected his recommendations for mandatory joint income returns and the taxation of income from outstanding issues of State and municipal securities.

The committee's vote, which, according to Senator George, the chairman, was taken earlier in order to "confine our hearings to subjects that possibly will be included in the tax bill," eliminated $400,000,000 of the $2,400,000,000 additional revenue which Secretary Morgenthau asked for last week.

Senator George emphasized that the question of taxing income from future issues of State and municipal securities had been "left open," but remarked that if this plan were adopted it would bring virtually no money into the Treasury during the current year.

Also left open was the question of abolishing percentage depletion allowances on mines and oil wells, the third of the "special privileges" which Mr. Morgenthau asked to be abolished. Each of these, the Treasury says, costs it $200,000,000 a year.

George Says Action Is Final

The House had already disregarded Mr. Morgenthau's recommendations with regard to these three types of exemption, and Senator George said that the committee's action meant there was no chance of including in the bill mandatory joint returns or taxation of income from existing State and municipal securities.

He explained, however, that the committee had left undecided the question of taxing income of families in the "community property" States on the same basis as those in the rest of the country. If this plan were adopted, he said, it would yield between $85,000,000 and $87,000,000 more. Mr. George recalled that a similar provision was voted by his committee last year, but was rejected in the Senate.

In the community property States husband and wife share their income equally, and by submitting individual returns they have been able to avoid the higher rates in the upper brackets.

Mandatory joint returns, which were intended primarily to stop this practice, would have yielded $420,-

Continued on Page Eight

War News Summarized

TUESDAY, JULY 28, 1942

The Germans appeared yesterday to be on the verge of establishing strong positions south of the lower Don, but suffered a heavy British aerial attack on the important city of Hamburg.

Moscow acknowledged that Rostov and neighboring Novocherkassk had been evacuated and that the Soviet forces in the sector had withdrawn south of the Don. The Germans were said to be seeking to multiply their bridgeheads, notably in the Tsimlyansk sector, some 120 miles up-river from Rostov. Soviet gains near Voronezh and near Bryansk were claimed again. [1:1; map, P. 2.]

Berlin claimed that Bataisk, five miles south of Rostov on the railway to Baku, had been captured. Farther east on the lower Don front the Germans were also advancing southward, according to Berlin. German troops were said to have reached the river on a broad front in the great Don bend west of Stalingrad. [3:1.]

British troops in Egypt resumed their attacks and some Axis prisoners were taken. Royal Air Force planes again bombed Tobruk successfully Sunday night after an attack by United States and R. A. F. bomber crews Saturday night that caused large fires. [4:1.]

London announced that about 600 R. A. F. bombers had dropped many two-ton bombs and 175,000 incendiaries on Hamburg Sunday night. Air Marshal Harris called the raid one of the most successful of the war. London had an air raid alarm early today as Nazi planes, attacking in the Midlands, went overhead. [1:2-3.]

Allied patrols made contact with Japanese forces near Oivi, in Papua, fifty-five miles inland from Gona and half-way point on the road toward Port Moresby, United Nations base on the south coast of Papua, on the Island of New Guinea. [1:2.]

Witnesses who have reached London reported the destruction of the Norwegian village of Televaag near Bergen in revenge for the killing of two Gestapo agents. According to the report, eighteen hostages were killed and the rest of the male population was sent to work in Germany. [3:2.]

United States fighter planes routed forty-six of fifty Japanese bombers bound for a raid on Chungking. The four raiders that got through to the outskirts of the Chinese capital were unable to hit any important target. [1:3.]

The German Transocean News Agency broadcast a report asserting that Premier Tojo of Japan had told an audience of 20,000 at Osaka that "Japan is determined to destroy the United States and Great Britain." [6:7.]

SUPREME COURT IS CALLED IN UNPRECEDENTED SESSION TO HEAR PLEA OF NAZI SPIES

RECALLED FROM ARMY TO JUDICIAL DUTY

Supreme Court Justice Murphy, now a lieutenant colonel in the Army, was reached at Dilworth, N. C., over a field telephone for tomorrow's special session to consider Nazi saboteur case.

The New York Times (U. S. Army)

TO SIT TOMORROW

Full Bench to Decide if It Will Hear Saboteurs' Habeas Corpus Petition

CIVIL TRIAL SEEMS AIM

Military Proceedings Halted Until Thursday—Justices Are Hastily Summoned

By LEWIS WOOD

Special to THE NEW YORK TIMES.

WASHINGTON, July 27—A history-making special session of the Supreme Court will be held on Wednesday to consider whether the highest tribunal shall receive petitions to file writs of habeas corpus from the eight Nazi saboteurs now on trial before a military commission.

In a startling move Chief Justice Stone called the special session with the approval of his eight colleagues. All will be here, even Associate Justice Douglas, now speeding east from Oregon, and Associate Justice Murphy, now a lieutenant colonel in the Army on manoeuvres in North Carolina.

Possibly the court will decide that same day whether to reject or receive the petition to file the writs; possibly it will take the motions under consideration. At any rate, Attorney General Francis Biddle and Major Gen. Myron C. Cramer, judge advocate general, the prosecutors of the Nazis, will resist the proposal in every way possible.

Move Entirely Unexpected

The astonishing announcement that the court would meet in special session came without the slightest advance indication. Shortly after the Army colonels named by President Roosevelt to represent the saboteurs closed their case newspaper men received word to be at the Supreme Court Building at 5:45 P. M. There, Charles Elmore Cropley, clerk of the court, handed this statement to them:

"The Chief Justice directs that it be announced that the Supreme Court will convene a special term of the court on Wednesday, July 29, at noon, in order that petitions for writs of habeas corpus, on behalf of certain persons now being tried by a military commission appointed by the President, may be submitted to it.

"The petitions will be presented by counsel on July 29, and the prisoners will not be present at the bar of the Supreme Court on that day."

Neither Mr. Cropley, any of the defending Army colonels, nor, in fact, any one connected with the case, would speculate upon the moves of the defense. Nevertheless, it was believed their arguments would attack perhaps the Presidential order creating the military commission, and, most of all, the accompanying petition spe-

Continued on Page Ten

Last Extra Session Was Held in 1920

Special to THE NEW YORK TIMES.

WASHINGTON, July 27—Only once before in contemporary times has a special session of the Supreme Court been called, but ample authority exists in Section 338 of the Judicial Code, which says:

"The Supreme Court shall hold at the seat of government one term annually commencing on the first Monday in October and such adjourned or special terms as it may find necessary for the dispatch of business."

The only other instance of modern annals when the court met suddenly in a special term was on April 13, 1920, in connection with a dispute over oil flowing from the famous Burk-Burnett properties in the Southwest. The court had appointed Jacob G. Dickinson as receiver in a title controversy between Oklahoma and Texas over the oil. He refused to serve, and the court, then in a three-week recess, was hurriedly summoned to name Frederic A. Delano, the uncle of President Roosevelt.

Downpour Halts Railroads; Two Die in Storm in City

A series of violent rainstorms that began early yesterday morning and continued in various parts of the city and suburbs most of the day disrupted commuter service between Westchester and Manhattan in the early rush hour and led to two deaths in the metropolitan area.

Thousands of residents of Southern and Central Westchester got to their jobs late, while others did not get to work at all. Those who remained at home found their county flooded in many sectors, with hundreds of small boats waterlogged along the shore, cellars and everything in them ruined and, in Bronxville, the high school isolated by a temporary lake.

The storm also produced several lightning scares, although tumbling bricks and one slight fire were the worst effects. It turned main highways into quagmires, spread a coating of mud on the Bronx's Webster Avenue, marooned automobiles, turned the meandering little Bronx River into a miniature Mississippi on a rampage and led to some unprecedented commuter routes to New York.

Shunted Onto Freight Line

One of the most unusual of those which became one of the most common during the worst of the morning, began with the harassed passengers on the New York, New Haven & Hartford shore line being shunted just below New Rochelle into the Harlem River Branch, which takes freight into New York via Hell Gate Bridge.

Had the trains been able to proceed to the bridge and into the city via Queens and Pennsylvania Station, the rain-weary passengers would have been relatively lucky, though late. As it turned out, they were taken only to the vicinity of the Westchester Avenue station, in a section of the East Bronx of which many of them had barely heard. It was a long, muddy trek in most cases to the nearest subway, bus or cab connection to Manhattan.

The freakish weather, while helping the city's water supply and coming when most needed by Suffolk County vegetable growers, also caused emergency scheduling and delay on the Bronx division of the Eighth Avenue-Independent subway—and turned into a dreary morass the thriving eight-acre farm of Mrs. Rose Falasca at Morris Park Avenue and Eastchester Road. Her chickens and a German

Continued on Page Eleven

WLB REFUSES RISE, CITES PAY FORMULA

Reasoning as in Steel Case, It Finds 1,200 Rand Workers Already Have Increase

By LOUIS STARK

Special to THE NEW YORK TIMES.

WASHINGTON, July 27—The National War Labor Board refused today to give a general wage increase to 1,200 employes of the Remington-Rand Company and in doing so applied the wage stabilization formula used in the recent "little steel" case.

The United Radio, Electrical and Machine Workers, C. I. O., representing the employes in the plants at Tonawanda and North Tonawanda, N. Y., had requested an increase of 10 cents an hour.

The vote of the board was 4 to 2, the public and industry members joining together, while the labor representatives dissented. The board, however, made one adjustment by adding 2½ cents an hour to the wage of female employes on an incentive basis in order to iron out an inequality resulting from a growing disparity between wages paid to men and women working in the company's plants.

The board asserted that the "little steel" formula has already served as a decelerator and stabilizer of the wage movement.

Previous Rises Are Noted

Wayne Lyman Morse, dean of the University of Oregon Law School, who wrote the board's opinion, said that the Remington-Rand employes had received two wage increases since Jan. 1, 1941, totaling 18 cents an hour for men and 11 cents for women.

Since these increases exceeded the 15 per cent rise in the cost of living during the Jan. 1, 1941-May, 1942, period, he concluded that "the employes are not entitled to a further wage increase at this time on the basis of any change in the cost of living since Jan. 1, 1941, in view of the wage stabilization formula laid down by the board in

Continued on Page Nine

"All the News That's Fit to Print."

The New York Times.

LATE CITY EDITION
Continued cool today.
Temperature Yesterday—Max., 71; Min., 61

Copyright, 1942, by The New York Times Company.

VOL. XCI..No. 30,894. Entered as Second-Class Matter, Postoffice, New York, N. Y. NEW YORK, TUESDAY, AUGUST 25, 1942. THREE CENTS IN NEW YORK CITY

REPUBLICANS NAME DEWEY UNANIMOUSLY FOR GOVERNOR; WILLKIE PLEDGE IN PLATFORM

ACTION IS SPEEDY

Delegates Acclaim Him After Seeing a Film of His Career

WAR DIRECTION ASSAILED

Candidate Pledges Loyalty of Party to President, Keeps the Right of Criticism

Keynote, Dewey's acceptance, Page 12; platform Page 13..

By WARREN MOSCOW
Special to THE NEW YORK TIMES.

SARATOGA SPRINGS, N. Y., Aug. 24—Thomas E. Dewey, nominated without opposition tonight as the candidate of the Republican party for Governor, pledged his own and his party's loyalty to the nation's Commander in Chief in wartime, but reserved the right of free criticism to maintain democracy on the home front.

To a cheering gathering in the convention hall Mr. Dewey demonstrated the type of criticism he thought was proper, even in wartime.

He denounced those who asserted that a Republican victory in the State might be hailed by our enemies abroad as evidence of internal disunity; he declared that the Democratic convention in Brooklyn last week "smacks only of the arrogance and degeneracy of a political machine which asks that it be in office forever."

After paying casual respect to Edward J. Flynn's "antique paving blocks," he charged that the Democrats had shown that they had more interest in controlling the Democratic national convention in 1944 than in picking the best qualified man for Governor.

Would Serve Only the State

For his own part, Mr. Dewey announced his disinterest in the national political picture, declaring that, if elected, he would devote the next four years "exclusively to the service of the people of the State of New York."

This declaration was in contrast with the admitted concern of Mr. Dewey's supporters over the selection of a candidate for Lieutenant Governor, who would serve the State for two years should Mr. Dewey be nominated and elected President in 1944.

Mr. Dewey's nomination, in the making since his first and almost successful race against Governor Lehman in 1938, became official at exactly 8:45 P. M. It came about in an unorthodox manner. The Dewey managers decided to scrap all real nominating speeches and give their audience instead a newsreel made up of pictures, with appropriate commentary, of various aspects of Mr. Dewey's career, from racket-buster to party statesman.

Kenneth S. Macaffer, Albany County chairman, announced the newsreel. When it ended he said:

"I nominate Thomas E. Dewey."

Dewey Is Cheered 15 Minutes

Then came a fifteen-minute demonstration, aided by three bands, which played "Roll Out the Barrel," "Auld Lang Syne" and "Working on the Railroad," among other tunes.

This was followed by seconding speeches by Mrs. Jessica McWeis of Monroe, Meyer Goldberg of New York, Mrs. Bertha J. Digges of Buffalo, Thomas B. Rudd of Oneida, George A. Arkwright of Kings, Jean A. Martin of the Young Republicans and Charles M. Harrington of Clinton County. All of the seconding speeches were very short, clear and businesslike.

Judge Harrington said that he believed, despite the cry he said would be raised by the Democrats that Mr. Dewey should be in the Army rather than running for public office, that the candidate's opportunity for public service was greater on the home front. The opposition, before the campaign is over, will wish Mr. Dewey was any place but in the campaign, he declared.

Chairman Ives called for further nominations. There was none, and

Continued on Page Twelve

THE CANDIDATE

Mr. and Mrs. Thomas E. Dewey in their hotel suite at Saratoga
The New York Times

VOTES 9 TO 7 TO TAX NEW PUBLIC BONDS

Senate Group Cuts Dependent Credit to $300, but Allows Relief on Doctor Bills

By THOMAS J. HAMILTON
Special to THE NEW YORK TIMES.

WASHINGTON, Aug. 24—The Senate Finance Committee "tentatively" voted 9 to 7 today to tax the income from future issues of State and local bonds.

Little more revenue during the current fiscal year is expected if the proposal is adopted by Congress, but it would have the effect of gradually drying up the last means of avoiding heavy taxation. The removal of tax exemption on the income from new issues of Federal securities became effective last year.

The Finance Committee also voted "tentatively" to reduce the individual income tax allowance for each dependent from the present $400 to $300. Revenue of $220,000,000 is expected from this reduction.

Earlier, a finance subcommittee, headed by Senator Clark of Missouri, approved the pay-as-you-go income tax plan presented by Beardsley Ruml, treasurer of R. H. Macy & Co., despite a protest by Randolph E. Paul, general counsel of the Treasury, declaring that the proposed bookkeeping shift represented in the cancellation of taxes due on 1941 income would be "a pure windfall" for those who had large incomes that year.

The committee agreed to allow some relief for individual taxpayers who have to meet heavy medical expenses. Under the provision approved today, all such expenditures in excess of 5 per cent of net

Continued on Page Eleven

PRICE PLOT CHARGED ON CABLE FOR NAVY

U.S. Jury Indicts Nine Concerns and Six Officials—Profit Is Put at 35 to 70%

Attorney General Francis Biddle announced yesterday in Washington that a Federal grand jury in Newark had indicted nine corporations supplying all of a special patented electric cable designed to resist flame, shock and water, and used in the complex wiring systems of the fighting ships of the Navy.

Together with six presidents or responsible officers of their organizations, the nine corporations are charged with "conspiring to make identical bids at unreasonably high prices." According to Mr. Biddle, they sold $55,000,000 of this cable to the government since 1939 and made profits ranging from 35 to 70 per cent. He said the government was now buying $6,000,000 of it each month.

The indictment declares that the patent-owning corporation gave the Navy an unrestricted license to use the patented cable in 1933 and came to an understanding with the eight other defendant corporations and their heads, as manufacturers under the patent, that their mutual agreement to sell at a uniform price to the public would not apply to the government's calls for competitive bids.

Thereafter, however, the indictment sets forth, the eight licensed corporations continued to receive copies of each bid prepared by the patent-owning corporation and to copy out the figures identically and to submit them as their own competitive bids.

In advance of arraignment next Monday, statements were issued on

Continued on Page Seventeen

Hillman Union Not in the Line-Up Of Backers of Alfange Candidacy

Sidney Hillman's union, the Amalgamated Clothing Workers of America, which was one of the founders of the American Labor party and which has been one of the party's chief financial supporters, may withhold its support of Dean Alfange, the party's candidate for the Governorship, it was indicated yesterday.

This attitude was disclosed when union officials were questioned concerning the dropping of all Amalgamated representatives from the Labor party State Executive Committee and the failure of any Amalgamated representative to take any part in the conferences that preceded Mr. Alfange's selection.

What stand, if any, the union will take in the forthcoming campaign will depend largely on what views President Roosevelt expresses on the subject, one official said. The Amalgamated, it was pointed out, always has been a New Deal union and a consistent backer of the President.

Mr. Hillman shared the direction of the Office of Production Management with William S. Knudsen until that agency was superseded by the War Production Board.

The elimination of all Amalgamated representatives from the Labor party executive committee was described as a "coincidence" and not the result of union policy. It just happened, it was said yesterday, that none of the Amalgamated officials cared to serve. The absence of Amalgamated officials from the conferences, it was added, was just another "coincidence."

Mayor La Guardia's attitude on

Continued on Page Thirteen

BAHR IS CONVICTED AS A GERMAN SPY; HEARS FATE SEPT. 2

Jury, Out 2 Hours, Brings in Verdict Against Man Sent Back to U. S. by Gestapo

HIS WIFE SOBS AT TRIAL

He Faces Long Term or Death —Von Clemm Gets 2 Years as Nazi Gem Importer

From a Staff Correspondent

NEWARK, N. J., Aug. 24—Herbert Karl Friedrich Bahr, 29-year-old German-born, American-educated engineer, was found guilty of being a Nazi spy by a jury of housewives and business men in Federal Court here today. He took the news with a blink and a dazed shake of his head. On Sept. 2 at 10 A. M. he will learn whether he is to die or spend a long time in prison.

The jury deliberated two hours. After being charged by Judge William F. Smith, who, calling their attention to the circumstance that the crime was a capital offense in wartime, told them to weigh their judgment carefully, the jurors filed out of the court room at 3:55 P. M. At 5:55 P. M. they signified they had reached a verdict.

During that two-hour interim Bahr's young wife, Mrs. Ruth Bahr of Buffalo, sat on a front bench in the court room. She had not seen her husband, until this trial opened a week ago, since the time in 1938 when he went to Germany to pursue his engineering studies under an international scholarship. She left her 4-year-old son in Buffalo.

Bahr's Wife Disturbed

She took a seat in the center of a group of women, and after a few minutes of stony silence buried her face in her hands. When she lifted it again her nose was red and she was snuffling, but within a few minutes she was in an animated conversation with the women around her. There came, after about an hour of this, word that the jury was returning. The room filled up, the jurors filed in, her husband, dressed in the $100 suit he bought in Portugal with the money the Gestapo had given him, was led in, flanked by two bailiffs.

He sat down next to Frederick M. P. Pearse, the attorney who had defended him without fee, and for a second the long-separated couple stared fixedly at each other. In the face of neither was there a flicker of exchanged emotion.

The clerk asked the jurors if they had reached a verdict. A wave of nodding heads answered him. He called for it, and Mrs. C. M. Schmidt, plump, gray, pleasant-faced housewife of Elizabeth, N. J., stood up. "We find the defendant guilty," she said. Her voice had a nervous quaver, and on the last word it bounced up almost to a stifled cry. The little wife in the front row sobbed and Bahr blinked. Mr. Pearse asked that the jury be polled. Twelve times, then, the word "guilty" filled the room as each juror affirmed the verdict.

Sentence Date Is Set

Judge Smith dismissed the jury, and said in answer to a question by Assistant District Attorney Thorn Lord that he would pass sentence on Sept. 2. Bahr cast one quick glance at the bench, shook his head, took Mr. Pearse's hand in a quick wordless clasp, and walked out flanked by his bailiffs. On the front row his wife sobbed quietly, her face once again buried in her hands. By twos and threes the women who had been talking to her got up and went away in silence, leaving her alone.

The case had lasted six days. The backbone of the prosecution was a long detailed statement that Bahr had given to the Federal Bureau of Investigation on July 7, eight days after reaching Jersey City on the diplomatic exchange ship Drottningholm. In this Bahr said he had received $7,000 and had been sent to the United States as an agent of the Nazis. He supplied two pieces of cotton, each of which, when soaked in water, produced an invisible ink he was to use in sending back to Germany information obtained here.

It was his defense that he never intended to do any of the things the Nazis instructed him to do, that he permitted them to believe he was willing to work for them in order to get back to the United States. It was the lag of time between his arrival and his telling of the story that Mr. Lord emphasized

Continued on Page Ten

NAZIS MAKE 50-MILE GAIN IN CAUCASUS; TWIN DRIVES CLOSING IN ON STALINGRAD; FORTRESSES RAID FRANCE WITHOUT LOSS

ENEMY HAMMERS RUSSIANS IN ALL SOUTHERN SECTORS

Germany's twin drives in the region of Stalingrad apparently were crunching steadily onward. Southeast of Kletskaya (1) the defenders battled to pinch off the spearhead of tanks that had crossed the Don forty miles from Stalingrad. Northeast of Kotelnikov (2) the Nazis had driven a large wedge into the defense lines. In the Krasnodar area (3) the Russians were pressed back. Another long German stride toward the Grozny oil fields was disclosed in a Moscow announcement of fighting near Prokhladnaya (4), eighty-five miles from the fields.

BRAZIL SEIZES SHIPS AND BANKS OF AXIS

Argentina, Chile, Peru, Bolivia and Paraguay Grant Her Non-Belligerent Rights

By FRANK M. GARCIA
Special Cable to THE NEW YORK TIMES.

RIO DE JANEIRO, Brazil, Aug. 24—Confiscation measures against Axis assets in Brazil were enforced today as a reprisal for losses suffered through sinkings of Brazilian ships by Axis submarines.

Affected were three large Axis banks, which remained closed today, and Axis ships that had previously been seized by Brazil.

[In Washington the Inter-American Defense Board adopted a unanimous resolution of "adherence and friendship" on

Continued on Page Five

U. S. Bombers Strike Blow At U-Boat Yards on Seine

By FRANK L. KLUCKHOHN
Wireless to THE NEW YORK TIMES.

LONDON, Aug. 24—The American Flying Fortresses proved their durability again today when, escorted by United States, British, Canadian and Polish fighters, they bombed the Nazis' western communications system, striking at Le Trait, on the Seine estuary midway between Rouen and Havre, and dropping heavy explosive missiles on the shipyards there, where U-boats are built. All of the big planes, twelve in number for this fourth daylight attack over France in eight days, again returned safely.

[British bombers, probably hundreds strong, raided Germany last night, The United Press reported from London early today. A Berlin broadcast said the Rhine-Main River area, of which Frankfort is the center, was attacked and that fifteen R. A. F. planes were shot down.]

All of the Fortress planes went

Continued on Page Four

War News Summarized

TUESDAY, AUGUST 25, 1942

The war centered almost exclusively yesterday in the colossal struggle in Southern Russia, except for a significant Chinese victory.

Moscow acknowledged that German armored forces had reached the outskirts of the Grozny oil fields, eighty-five miles northwest of Grozny in the vicinity of Prokhladnaya, after a fifty-mile drive down the Rostov-Baku railway. The Germans engaged in a pincers drive on Stalingrad were fighting in force in the plain between the Don and Volga Rivers after having driven a wedge into Soviet defense positions southwest of Stalingrad. [1:8.]

Prime Minister Churchill returned to Britain from his Moscow mission together with W. Averell Harriman, President Roosevelt's representative. [4:2.]

Twelve United States Flying Fortresses bombed U-boat yards at Le Trait, near Rouen, France, by daylight with an Allied fighter escort. Last night British bombers raided Germany, apparently on a heavy scale; Berlin said the Rhine-Main area was attacked. [1:6-7; map, P. 4.]

Vichy protested to the United States over the fortress attack on Rouen last week, the Laval regime announced. It was maintained that though Rouen was under German occupation, non-military installations must be considered as being under Vichy's protection. [4:6.]

Adolf Hitler appointed Otto Thierack, President of the notorious People's Tribunal, as Minister of Justice and empowered him to "deviate from existing laws" in building up a "National Socialist justice." London saw in the appointment evidence of Herr Hitler's fear of internal trouble in Germany in the event of a military setback. [1:7.]

Argentina and Chile joined Peru, Bolivia and Paraguay in deciding to extend non-belligerent rights to Brazil. [6:3.]

Brazil closed German and Italian banks and incorporated into the State-operated merchant fleet German and Italian vessels caught in Brazilian ports at the outbreak of the war in 1939. The sinkings of the United States tanker Louisiana and a Swedish vessel were disclosed in Rio de Janeiro. [1:5.]

From Chungking came the announcement that Chinese forces had captured Linchwan, second largest Japanese base in Kiangsi Province, and had advanced to within thirty miles of Japanese-held Nanchang. [7:1, with map.]

HITLER TIES COURTS CLOSE TO THE PARTY

Names Thierack, a Tried Nazi Henchman, Justice Minister —Anxiety Held Indicated

By Telephone to THE NEW YORK TIMES.

BERNE, Switzerland, Aug. 24—A sweeping reorganization of the administration of justice and judiciary procedure in the Nazi Reich was implicit in the appointment today by Adolf Hitler of Dr. Otto Georg Thierack, formerly President of the People's Court, to the vacant post of Reich Minister of Justice. He succeeds the late Dr. Franz Guertner.

A number of other key positions in the Reich judiciary also have been filled by "regular" Nazi party members, and the shift in policy suggests that the machinery of the law now has come more directly under the control of Herr Hitler and the party.

Herr Hitler's instructions to Dr. Thierack implied mandatory powers of an exceptional character. The decree announcing his appointment empowers him to provide for a "forceful administration of justice" in order that the problems confronting the great German Reich may be fulfilled. The Minister is instructed to conform to Herr Hitler's directives and instructions to adopt measures for the establishment of National Socialist judiciary administration. To achieve these ends he may, if necessary, deviate from existing laws, says Herr Hitler's decree.

Dr. Roland Feisler, who was State Secretary in the Ministry of Justice and is a promient Nazi party man, succeeds Dr. Thierack as President of the People's Court. Dr. Hans Frank, president of the German Academy of Law, has asked to be relived of that post in order to be able to devote himself exclusively to his duties as Gov-

Continued on Page Two

RED ARMY RETIRES

Nazis Closer to Grozny Oil—Also Advance in Krasnodar Area

CROSS THE DON IN FORCE

Break-Through on East Bank Made by Troops Driving on Stalingrad, Foe Says

By The United Press.

MOSCOW, Tuesday, Aug. 25—German forces have reached the gates of the Grozny oil fields after a fifty-mile sweep down the Caucasus railroad and are pounding toward Stalingrad after having crossed the Don River in force to the northwest and wedged into Soviet defenses southwest of the city.

The Soviet High Command announced today the new Russian setback in the Caucasus, revealing that Red Army defenders of the Grozny oil were fighting German tanks and infantry in the area of Prokhladnaya. That rail junction is fifty miles below Pyatigorsk and eighty-five miles northwest of Grozny, in the heart of the oil fields.

In the Krasnodar area of the Caucasus, where the Germans are driving toward the Black Sea port of Novorossiisk, the Red Army yielded two more places.

[The Germans reported continued advances in the Caucasus. In their drive for Stalingrad, it was said, German divisions crossed the Don and broke through strong Russian positions on the eastern bank.]

Driving Toward Railroad

On the Stalingrad front, semi-official Soviet sources conceded, German tanks and motorized infantry have stormed across the Don bend in force southeast of Kletskaya. These forces were reported to be driving on toward the Moscow-Stalingrad railroad.

The Soviet High Command reported violent fighting against enemy tanks and infantry on the eastern bank of the Don. In a struggle for one fortified place the Russians destroyed eight German tanks and killed at least 400 troops, it was said.

In the region of Kletskaya, which is on the western bank, Russian troops were engaged in active operations, one unit driving the enemy out of a fortified position, according to the communiqué.

Southwest of Stalingrad, in the Kotelnikov area, the Russians fought hard against large enemy armored and infantry forces that had pushed a wedge into the Soviet defenses. A counter-attack by one Red Army unit was said to have destroyed eleven tanks, eight anti-tank guns and 300 soldiers.

In fighting at a railway station, the Soviet communiqué stated, two companies of Rumanian infantry that attempted to attack the Russian line were wiped out by machine-gun and mortar fire.

Wireless to THE NEW YORK TIMES.

MOSCOW, Aug. 24 — General Field Marshal Fedor von Bock's

Continued on Page Two

Soviet Bombers Raid Helsinki in 8 Waves

By The United Press.

HELSINKI, Finland, Tuesday, Aug. 25—Eight waves of Russian planes attacked Helsinki late last night and early today.

The planes ran into heavy anti-aircraft fire.

The air raid warning first was sounded at 11 P. M., and was renewed at short intervals as successive waves of bombers approached the city.

Up to early this morning no bomb explosions had been heard in Central Helsinki. Reports from outlying districts were not received immediately. [At this point the Finnish censor cut the telephone line between Helsinki and Stockholm, over which the correspondent was reading his dispatch, The United Press reported.]

"All the News That's Fit to Print."

The New York Times.

LATE CITY EDITION
Somewhat warmer today.
Temperatures Yesterday—Max., 74; Min., 59

VOL. XCI..No. 30,896. Entered as Second-Class Matter, Postoffice, New York, N. Y. NEW YORK, THURSDAY, AUGUST 27, 1942. THREE CENTS IN NEW YORK CITY

U. S. BLASTS 6 SHIPS IN SOLOMONS; FOE LANDS AT TIP OF NEW GUINEA; NAZIS DRIVEN BACK NEAR MOSCOW

RUML PLAN BEATEN; COMMITTEE VOTES A WITHHOLDING TAX

Senators Back Treasury 13-3, Saying Income Year Shift Might Mean Windfalls

COUNTER PLAN REJECTED

Payroll Work Is Simplified—Bond Coupon Payments Are Exempted at Source

By THOMAS J. HAMILTON
Special to THE NEW YORK TIMES.

WASHINGTON, Aug. 26—The Senate Finance Committee rejected today by a vote of 13 to 3 the Ruml "pay-as-you-go" income tax plan, under which taxes on 1941 incomes would be canceled or "skipped" in order to put taxpayers on a current basis.

Senator George, the chairman, said:

"It was felt that it would offer a windfall to those who had large incomes in 1941 and very low incomes subsequently."

The plan was sponsored by Beardsley Ruml, treasurer of R. H. Macy & Co. and chairman of the Federal Reserve Bank of New York.

The committee also rejected by 11 votes to 6 an amended version, submitted by the Treasury, to limit the benefits received by persons with large incomes.

The committee afterward approved by 10 to 6 the 5 per cent withholding tax voted by the House to eliminate gradually the present lag of a year in paying income taxes. In order to reduce the burden of collecting it, however, certain small dividends and other forms of income were removed from the withholding levy provision, and a simplified method of computing the tax on wages and salaries was approved.

Treasury Opposed Plan

In announcing the committee's defeat of the Ruml plan, Mr. George said that the Treasury had "strenuously opposed" the proposal, and added that the majority of committee members agreed with the objections presented by Randolph H. Paul, Treasury general counsel.

In explaining the view of the committee that the Ruml plan also would not immediately put individual income tax payments on a current basis, Mr. George said adjustments by means of refunds or additional payments by taxpayers still would be necessary at the end of the year, and it would take four or five years to put taxpayers on a pay-as-you-go basis.

"The committee," Mr. George continued, "also was hesitant about it because the matter had not been thoroughly explored."

In presenting his plan to the committee last month Mr. Ruml emphasized the difficulties taxpayers would have next year in paying both the 5 per cent withholding tax, which is to be credited against payments made on 1943 income when the regular quarterly payments become due the following year, and the regular payments due on this year's income. The minimum rate for the latter, as fixed by the House bill, is 19 per cent, and he pointed out that this would mean a minimum of 24 per cent on net taxable income next year.

Wanted Tax Clock Moved Ahead

"We are now paying a tax in 1942," Mr. Ruml said in explaining his plan. "It is considered a tax on 1941 income. Suppose we move the tax clock ahead, suppose we redefine our tax and say that the tax we are paying in 1942 represents a tax on our income for 1942. In 1943 we continue to pay a tax which becomes a tax paid with respect to income which will be received in 1943.

"Although the tax on 1941 income drops out of existence, the Treasury continues to receive its revenue and the taxpayer continues to pay his tax. But when he dies or ceases to receive income he does not owe a tax as he does under the present system."

Mr. Ruml said that as a result the loss to the Treasury would occur only when a taxpayer died and the "reduction" would be "spread over the lifetime of the present income-tax paying generation."

In attacking the proposal, Mr. Paul said it would be inacceptable unless relief from taxation was confined to the normal tax and the first bracket of surtax. The Treasury also proposed that 1942 instead

Continued on Page Twelve

Nazis Assert Raiders Had Big Fins on Feet

German newsreel shots of prisoners taken in the Dieppe raid showed members of a special unit who were said to have swum ashore with the aid of huge fins on their feet, according to a broadcast last night by Transocean, German news agency.

The newsreel was shown to foreign correspondents in Berlin last night.

By Telephone to THE NEW YORK TIMES.

BERNE, Switzerland, Aug. 26—The German Foreign Office, according to dispatches received here tonight, believes the Allied raid at Dieppe brought French opinion closer to Axis policies.

Presumably this view is based in part on reports that the Chief of State, Marshal Henri Philippe Pétain, and the Chief of Government, Pierre Laval, congratulated the German Army on its "success" at Dieppe.

MORE WAR ORDERS PROMISED TO CITY

Mayor Tells Conference of Plans to Get Jobs for Many of 400,000 Now Idle

The prospect of more war work for New York City in the near future, with jobs for many thousands of the city's 400,000 idle, was held out by Mayor La Guardia, Senator Robert F. Wagner and Representative Emanuel Celler of Kings in addresses before a conference of labor union delegates and employer representatives held yesterday in the Hotel Commodore under the auspices of the State Federation of Labor and the City Central Trades and Labor Council.

Represented at the conference were spokesmen of the construction, garment, printing, shipbuilding and other trades suffering from unemployment arising from the dislocations and displacements caused by the war production program.

The Mayor asserted that one of the largest aluminum plants in the country would be completed "just across the river" in December, giving employment to thousands of New Yorkers. Contracts were awarded last March for a government-financed aluminum plant in this area and in May construction plans for an aluminum plant were filed in Queens.

Upon the suggestion of Mayor La Guardia, the conference adopted a resolution providing for the creation of a permanent joint commit-

Continued on Page Seventeen

MEATLESS PERIODS, LIVESTOCK CEILING DRAFTED IN CAPITAL

OPA Is Working Out Top Prices for Hogs and Cattle With Producers' Groups

REVISING RETAIL LEVELS

Food Committee Has a Plan to Ask Public to Forego Meat One Day in Each Week

Special to THE NEW YORK TIMES.

WASHINGTON, Aug. 26—Meatless days, the imposition of price ceilings on live hogs and cattle, and the ironing out by the Office of Price Administration of inequalities caused by taking Lenten prices as the basis for the ceilings put on meat at the retailer's level, are the measures with which it is proposed to end the meat shortage, it was learned today.

The OPA announced that plans were being made to put a price ceiling on live hogs. It indicated that similar action would be taken soon on cattle prices.

J. K. Galbraith, OPA deputy administrator, told a delegation of livestock producers that the ceilings would be worked out in conjunction with representative groups of producers and would be submitted to Secretary Wickard for his approval. At the Agriculture Department it was said that there was little doubt of the plan's approval.

Western Cattlemen Protest

The OPA ceiling on livestock prices is planned despite the protests of a score of Western cattlemen, who told Price Administrator Leon Henderson this afternoon that imposition of the ceiling would reduce production and cause "chaos" in the livestock industry.

Mr. Henderson replied that, while he appreciated hearing their viewpoint, it was the conviction of OPA that livestock prices must be lowered.

On Friday the Food Requirements Committee will meet to discuss the establishment of meatless days, among other measures. The idea is to appeal to the public to go without meat one day a week in September and October. The committee also will work out plans for better distribution of the available meat supply by means of allocation.

The OPA will do its part, it was learned, by leveling out some of the inequities in the ceiling prices for pork and beef. In March, which is taken as the base, meat

Continued on Page Thirteen

War News Summarized

THURSDAY, AUGUST 27, 1942

Hard pressed Russia appeared yesterday to have launched a second front of her own northwest of Moscow while Japan, dangerous to both Russia and India, was becoming increasingly involved in operations northeast of Australia growing out of the American offensive in the Solomon Islands.

Moscow announced that the Red Army, in a fifteen-day offensive northwest of Moscow on a seventy-two mile front, had advanced twenty-five to thirty miles, killed 45,000 Germans, recaptured 610 populated places and routed or defeated fourteen German divisions. Meanwhile, however, huge German forc were pressing fiercely on the defenders of Stalingrad, and Moscow acknowledged a retreat in the Caucasus to the edge of the Grozny oil fields. [1:5; map P. 7.]

From Cairo it was reported that New Zealand troops had routed an Italian division on the Egyptian front and that United States bombers had attacked shipping in Suda Bay, Crete, and in the Corinth Canal. [1:6-7; map, P. 2.]

The Navy Department at Washington disclosed that six more Japanese vessels engaged in the offensive against United States positions in the Solomon Islands had been successfully bombed, including two destroyers. Five of the ships were damaged when an enemy striking force attempted to approach Guadalcanal Island. Fourteen more Japanese planes were shot down when they raided the United States held air base on Guadalcanal. According to the Navy spokesman, "the results, to date, of the battle for the retention of our foothold in the Solomons are encouraging." [1:8.]

General MacArthur's Australian headquarters acknowledged that the Japanese had made a landing on Milne Bay at the strategic southeastern tip of New Guinea but reported that Allied bombers had sunk a transport and damaged two warships. Defending troops gave battle. [1:5.]

Chungking reports indicated that the Chinese expected soon to recapture Chuhsien and Lishui, two advantageous positions for air raids on Japan. The Japanese retreats in Chekiang and Kiangsi Provinces were said to continue. [1:7.]

Brazil announced that more than a thousand Germans and Italians had been arrested in Rio de Janeiro and neighboring States, and other thousands were believed to have been arrested elsewhere. Venezuela granted Brazil non-belligerent rights. [5:2.]

Brig. Gen. Barnes, United States Assistant Chief of Ordnance, disclosed after a tour of British arms plants that the United States and Britain had some surprise weapons for the Germans and said that the Germans enjoyed no superiority in equipment. [3:1.]

Russian planes raided Eastern, Northeastern and Central Germany and one reached the outskirts of Berlin, the Germans announced. The R. A. F. hit two German ships. German planes dropped bombs in East Anglia. [1:5-6.]

The Vichy regime ordered a round-up of all foreign Jews who had entered France since 1936, despite a reported plea from the Pope for moderation in dealing with refugees. [3:5.]

RUSSIAN PUSH IS ON

3 Towns Captured, 14 Nazi Divisions Beaten on 70-Mile Front

BUT FOE GAINS IN SOUTH

Germans Reach Grozny Region—Tank and Air Battles for Stalingrad Raging

By RALPH PARKER
Wireless to THE NEW YORK TIMES.

MOSCOW, Thursday, Aug. 27—On Aug. 11, on a seventy-mile front embracing the Kalinin and western zones in the directions of Rzhev, Gzhatsk and Vyazma, General Gregory K. Zhukoff and Colonel Gen. Ivan S. Koneff gave orders to their generals to open an offensive.

A special communiqué issued here last night sums up the Red Army's successes to date in this drive. It shows a general advance of twenty-five to thirty miles, destruction of many hundreds of enemy tanks, capture of three towns among 610 populated points liberated and the defeat of fourteen divisions, including crack Axis troops.

The special announcement said the battle was raging unabated on the outskirts of Rzhev. Among the places reported recaptured were Zubtsov, about thirteen miles southeast of Rzhev; Pogoryaloe Gorodishche, farther east on the Moscow rail line, and Karmanovo.

Grozny Oil Region Reached

In the Caucasus the battle area shifted into the Grozny oil fields by reaching the region of Mozdok, thirty miles east of Prokhladnaya. Mozdok has few wells, but lies on the verge of a richer-yielding area. No further German advance on Stalingrad was reported, though the enemy continued to drive frenziedly against the Russian defenses.

[The German communiqué said Russian troops had been thrown back farther toward Stalingrad and that German Alpine units had made additional progress in the Caucasus. It mentioned strong Red Army attacks near Rzhev and southwest of Moscow, but said they had been repulsed.]

The lower prong aimed against Stalingrad was reported to have lost sixty-two tanks yesterday, while the destruction of forty-two was mentioned in descriptions of fighting in individual sectors of the northern prong, now established in great force across the Don.

Defense System Pierced

The capture of Zubtsov removes one of the most important pins in the elaborate German defense system that defied General Koneff's Kalinin-front armies throughout the Winter and the deep penetration along the whole front means that elsewhere, too, the Russian armies have battered their way through one of the most powerfully constructed stretches of the great "Ostwall," of which German prisoners have been boasting so much lately.

"Grinding down the man power of the German Fascist divisions, destroying and capturing a large part of their equipment, our troops continue to engage the enemy in fierce battles," the special communiqué said.

It listed nine German divisions that had been routed and five others on which heavy losses had been inflicted. A long list of material captured included 250 tanks and 757 guns, and the tally of equipment destroyed included 324 tanks and 343 guns. In air combat 250 German planes were said to have been shot down, and 296 others were listed as destroyed or damaged on enemy territory.

The operational generals mentioned in the communiqué include three not before prominent in any accounts of operations, Generals Polyenoff, Reiter and Shvetzoff, but Lieut. Gen. D. V. Lelushenko is known as the victor at Klin and Rogachev during the battle for Moscow; Lieut. Gen. Fediuninsky led the Fifty-fourth Army to vic-

Continued on Page Seven

LANDING IS COSTLY

Transport Sunk, Cruiser and Destroyer Hit at Milne Bay

ALLIED TROOPS IN ACTION

Battle Small Force After Our Planes Pound Convoy—Six Zeros Bagged at Buna

By BYRON DARNTON
Wireless to THE NEW YORK TIMES.

AT UNITED NATIONS HEADQUARTERS, Australia, Thursday, Aug. 27—The Japanese have made another landing in New Guinea. This one is at Milne Bay, on the southeastern tip of the island, and United Nations ground forces already are in contact with the enemy there. The landing was not a surprise to our ground forces.

These facts were revealed today in a communiqué from General Douglas MacArthur's headquarters and by a headquarters spokesman. There is no word as to whether the ground action has assumed any significant proportions, but there is no doubt about the importance of the Milne Bay position to the United Nations forces.

The bay is 225 miles southeast of Port Moresby, New Guinea, and about 400 miles from the big Japanese base at Rabaul, New Britain. A successful incursion by the Japanese would mean that they would have a strategically located airfield from which to break up United Nations air raids on Rabaul. Also, they would have another strong point from which to attack the United Nations base at Port Moresby.

The Japanese landed from a small convoy, which was attacked several times by our air force from low altitudes in extremely bad weather. Flying Fortresses sank one enemy transport, heavily damaged and probably sank one cruiser and damaged one destroyer. B-26 medium bombers and P-40 fighters heavily bombed and strafed Japanese barges, supplies and troops who had got ashore. Many fires were started, the communiqué said, and six landing barges were destroyed.

Move Was Anticipated

This convoy was the one that had been attacked Tuesday night near the Trobriand Islands, about 100 miles north of Milne Bay. On that occasion our planes sank a Japanese gunboat and strafed two transports. This correspondent would like to emphasize the official statement that "our ground forces anticipated this movement and are in contact." This statement should be compared with the situation when the Japanese made a surprise landing in the Buna-Gona area of New Guinea a month ago.

The communiqué that told of the Milne Bay developments also reported a successful air attack on Buna, where the Japanese have established an air strip. Despite bad weather our fighters destroyed six and damaged two of ten Zero

Continued on Page Eight

'ENCOURAGING' NEWS FROM THE PACIFIC

It appeared from yesterday's reports that two Japanese striking forces have been involved in the Solomon Islands action. One, composed of transports, cruisers and destroyers, descended on Guadalcanal Island from the north (1), probably steaming through Indispensable Strait (inset). Five vessels in this force were damaged by American planes based on the island. The second armada approached from the northeast (2). Two carriers, a battleship and several cruisers of this force were hit, and presumably it is still being engaged. To the west the Japanese landed at Milne Bay (3) at a cost of one transport sunk and two warships damaged. Allied troops promptly went into action against the enemy.

Italians Routed in Egypt; U. S. Fliers Raid Axis Ships

By The United Press.

CAIRO, Egypt, Aug. 26—New Zealand troops routed an Italian division west of El Alamein, and United States bombers blasted at Axis shipping in Suda Bay, Crete, and on the Corinth Canal in Greece today as the Allies lashed out to break up General Field Marshal Erwin Rommel's preparations for a new offensive in Egypt.

The New Zealanders, aided by a terrific barrage and spearheaded by Maoris, attacked the Bologna Division to break the long desert lull, front dispatches said. The Italians were said to have been surprised and terrified. Some of them fled, many were killed, and others were taken back as prisoners when the New Zealanders returned to their original positions, it was reported.

The New Zealanders' sortie appeared to have been in the nature of a reconnaissance.

Imperial artillery trapped Italians in advanced positions with a box barrage, front reports said, and the Maoris pounced on them with bayonets as they were preparing new positions, placing mines and stringing barbed wire.

The United States bombers dropped more than 50,000 pounds of bombs on objectives on the Corinth Canal and in Suda Bay in a dawn foray.

"The exact damage has not been ascertained, but the bombing accuracy of this squadron has been displayed in the past," a report said. "It may well be assumed that damage was heavy."

Other United States bombers raided El Daba, Axis base west of El Alamein, starting a number of fires, the report said, and "all planes returned safely from all missions." Axis fighters were seen, but they made no attacks.

Royal Air Force medium bombers and British naval aircraft, it was disclosed, carried out strong

Continued on Page Two

Red Planes Range Over Reich; One Reaches Berlin, Nazis Say

German broadcasts recorded in New York this morning by The Associated Press said Russian warplanes attacked Eastern, Northeastern and Central Germany during the night and that one of the raiders succeeded in reaching the outskirts of Berlin.

High explosives and incendiaries were dropped at random, but no noteworthy damage was caused, the German broadcast said.

By The Associated Press.

LONDON, Thursday, Aug. 27—German raiders showered fire bombs early today on several points in East Anglia. Two persons were injured in one town.

Wireless to THE NEW YORK TIMES.

LONDON, Aug. 26—There was a lull in the air activity in this theatre last night and today, but that is not say there was no raiding by both British and Germans, for a day never goes by on either side without the dropping of a few bombs and the killing of a few persons.

At least one German plane was shot down and another probably destroyed by Private S. Johnson Manning with a Bren gun during an attack on a South Coast English town. One German Focke-Wulf-190 crashed into a ditch outside Eastbourne, its bombs still in its racks, and another was seen falling into the sea in this action.

The Air Ministry laconically reported that there were "a small number of casualties" and that some damage had been done.

A German report said Ipswich was bombed last night and that a

Continued on Page Three

CHINA NEAR GAINING TWO BIG AIRFIELDS

Some Chungking Officials Say Chuhsien and Lishui Will Be Recaptured Soon

By The Associated Press.

CHUNGKING, China, Aug. 26—Chuhsien, site of the biggest air field in China and the best base for bombings of Japan, is under attack by Chinese forces in the big drive against the Japanese invaders in Chekiang and Kiangsi Provinces.

The Chinese have taken a point four and one-half miles south of the strategic city in Western Chekiang and also are attacking Japanese forces directly to the westward, the Chinese High Command said.

Some quarters in Chungking expressed confidence that the Chinese soon would recapture Chuhsien and Lishui, second-best site from which to launch air attacks against Japan. The Chinese, who have Lishui under siege, said tonight that Japanese troops who tried to push south from Sungyang in Chekiang Province had been defeated and were fleeing back toward Lishui, twenty-five miles to the east.

Other Japanese forces were declared by the Chinese command to have been crushed fifteen miles northwest of Sungyang five days ago.

Chinese soldiers who reached the southwestern suburbs of Chuhsien by the railway from Kiangshan could see flames in the city, a front line dispatch to the Central Daily News reported. It added that the fires set by the Japanese indicated their withdrawal was imminent.

Another Chinese column striking eastward across the country from Changshan occupied Chaohsien, about fifteen miles west of Chuhsien, Monday and continued its advance toward the city, Chinese reports said.

The Central Daily News, in a review of the war, apparently inspired by official quarters, said the offensive in the Solomons and the Chinese counter-offensive in Chekiang and Kiangsi would force the Japanese to revise plans for their continental advance. Hitherto most

Continued on Page Seven

ISLES FIRMLY HELD

One Fleet Beaten Off by U. S. Planes Based on Guadalcanal

BATTLE IS 'ENCOURAGING'

Japanese Lose Twelve More Aircraft—Main Struggle Is Raging Off Solomons

By C. BROOKS PETERS
Special to THE NEW YORK TIMES.

WASHINGTON, Aug. 26—United States aircraft based on Guadalcanal Island have damaged six more Japanese ships, including two destroyers, and have repulsed what apparently was a smaller striking force of the powerful Japanese armada striving to dislodge our forces from their recently won bases in the southeastern Solomon Islands.

In addition, the Navy Department announced today in a communiqué reporting "encouraging" results in the Solomons struggle, seven Japanese bombers and five Zero fighters were shot down yesterday during an enemy raid on Guadalcanal. In a previous raid on the island the Japanese had lost twenty-one planes. Our losses in the two actions were four fighter planes, the Navy revealed.

Our forces at Guadalcanal continue to hold their positions in spite of strong enemy thrusts, and have made the enemy pay heavily for each attack, the Navy said. However, "it is still too early to estimate the outcome of the battle at sea being fought off the Solomon Islands," the communiqué declared.

Enemy Force Withdraws

That battle was separate from the action that resulted in the repulse of the smaller enemy striking force, which had approached Guadalcanal from the north, probably through Indispensable Strait, and which was compelled to make a full withdrawal.

The major battle at sea, in which the main enemy fleet was involved, still was raging. When it had been joined, and whether surface vessels were within range of each other, was not disclosed. The participation of our carrier-based naval planes and Army Flying Fortresses—the latter probably based on New Caledonia—had been revealed yesterday, when it was reported that they had damaged two Japanese aircraft carriers, a battleship and several cruisers.

Although today's communiqué gave no further information concerning this struggle at sea, or any indication of losses we might have suffered, it suggested strongly that the Japanese might have suffered another naval defeat comparable to that off Midway. The communiqué said that "the results, to date, of the battle for the retention of our foothold in the southeastern Solomons are encouraging."

Emanating from the conservative Navy Department, this statement appeared to confirm what unofficial military circles had indicated yesterday: That the attempt of the Japanese to retake the Solomons bases recently occupied by United States Marines was doomed to failure.

Progress of the Battle

On the basis of the Navy announcements issued yesterday and today, it is possible to reconstruct in part the progress of the Battle of the Solomons since Sunday.

During the afternoon of Sunday (Washington time) the enemy unleashed a strong air attack against Guadalcanal Island, where, the Navy revealed today, we have land-based Marine and naval aircraft, including dive-bombers. These planes' bases had been constructed by the enemy after his capture of Guadalcanal in May. They were taken over and put into commission by the American landing forces that occupied Guadalcanal, Tulagi and perhaps several other islands in operations that began Aug. 7.

The obvious objective of the Japanese air attack on Sunday was to put our planes and the airfields

Continued on Page Eight

"All the News That's Fit to Print."

The New York Times.

LATE CITY EDITION
Showers today in early morning; cooler in afternoon.
Temperatures Yesterday—Max., 77; Min., 60
Sunrise, 6:19 A. M.; Sunset, 7:35 P.M.

Copyright, 1942, by The New York Times Company.

VOL. XCI. No. 30,898. Entered as Second-Class Matter, Postoffice, New York, N. Y. NEW YORK, SATURDAY, AUGUST 29, 1942. THREE CENTS IN NEW YORK CITY

R. A. F. BOMBS WIDELY IN GERMANY; FORTRESSES RAID FRENCH PLANT; REDS STIFFEN AROUND STALINGRAD

ASSOCIATED PRESS IS SUED AS TRUST; DIRECTORS TO FIGHT

U. S. Seeks Order to Compel It to Sell News and Picture Services to Any Paper

CHICAGO SUN CASE CITED

Robert McLean Says Action Is 'Without Merit in Either Law or Fact'

By RUSSELL B. PORTER

The United States Government filed suit in the Federal district court here yesterday in a civil action against The Associated Press, charging it with violating the Sherman and Clayton anti-trust acts. Under the direction of Assistant Attorney General Thurman Arnold, who is in charge of anti-trust prosecutions, Charles H. Weston, a special assistant to the Attorney General, came here from Washington to file the 14,000-word complaint.

On his arrival here shortly after noon, Mr. Weston said he had been told to delay filing of the suit until he heard further word from Washington. Some time later he received instructions which caused some last-minute changes to be made in the petition. He then filed the complaint with Herbert Charlson, deputy United States court clerk, at 3:03 P. M. A summons was issued and handed to United States Marshal James E. Mulcahy for service. The answer is returnable within twenty days.

Citing the refusal of the AP members at their last annual meeting to grant a membership to Marshall Field for his new morning newspaper, The Chicago Sun, which is in competition with Colonel Robert R. McCormick's Chicago Tribune, an old established member, the government asked for a court order to compel the AP to supply its news and picture services to any newspaper willing to pay the cost.

Membership By-Law Attacked

The government asked that the AP be permanently enjoined against further enforcement of by-law provisions which deal with the admission of new members, and that it be required to divest itself of stock in Wide World Photos, Inc., a news picture service formerly owned by THE NEW YORK TIMES, which the AP acquired last year.

The complaint charges that the by-laws illegally restrain and monopolize interstate commerce in news and illegally restrain the interstate commerce of newspapers which are prevented from obtaining AP news as competitors of existing members. It also alleges that the requirement in the by-laws that the 1,300 members supply their local news exclusively to the AP is an illegal restraint and monopoly of interstate commerce in news. The purchase of Wide World by the AP is called an illegal acquisition of the stock of a competing corporation.

Besides the AP as an association, the defendants named in the suit include the eighteen members of the board of directors, the publishers of the newspapers with which the directors are affiliated and all AP members in the continental United States as a group.

AP to Contest Action

Robert McLean, publisher of The Philadelphia Evening Bulletin and president of The Associated Press, issued a statement on behalf of the board of directors, asserting the intention of the AP to fight the suit, which he characterized as "without merit in either law or fact." Holding that the operation and practice of the AP comply fully with all the laws of the United States, the statement also said:

"The Associated Press has invaded the lawful rights of no one in the great and unsurpassed service that it has rendered to the reading public for the last forty-two years. What is charged against it is no more, at bottom, than this: that it seeks to protect its members who have invested their skill, their work and their money in its growth."

Commenting in his own behalf, Mr. McLean added:

"The Associated Press has made every effort to meet the legal views of the government, culminating in the action of the annual meeting last April at which the membership adopted radical revisions of the by-laws. The membership was, however, unwilling to

Continued on Page Eight

11 in Dieppe Shot, Many Reported Held

By Telephone to THE NEW YORK TIMES.

STOCKHOLM, Sweden, Aug. 28—Rhyming ill with the Germans' loud public praise of the population of Dieppe for its attitude during the recent raid, second-hand reports received here from Dieppe via Paris show that the Germans actually shot eleven Dieppe civilians, in addition to imprisoning several hundred immediately after the raid.

In all cases the victims were chosen from previously prepared lists of persons "likely to sympathize actively with the enemy." Because it was politically inexpedient to announce the executions as such, they were called "civilian casualties" and added to the list of the few innocent bystanders who were killed largely through their own curiosity.

The casualties of the Germans in the engagement are estimated by the same sources at around 600 killed and missing and about 2,000 wounded.

ROOSEVELT MEETS WITH WAR CHIEFS

Production-Strategy Link Is Believed Topic of Army, Navy, Air and WPB Heads

Special to THE NEW YORK TIMES.

WASHINGTON, Aug. 28—President Roosevelt held two important war production conferences at the White House today.

He talked jointly with Admiral William D. Leahy, his Chief of Staff; General George C. Marshall, Army Chief of Staff; Admiral Ernest J. King, commander in chief of the fleet; Lieut. Gen. Henry H. Arnold, Army Air Force commander; Donald N. Nelson, War Production Board chairman, and Harry L. Hopkins, White House adviser.

None of them would comment, but it was believed that the conferees were concerned with tying war production more closely to a strategy for victory.

Before the conference, the President had lunched with Mr. Hopkins and General Marshall, who had been mentioned in dispatches from both Washington and abroad as a probable choice for supreme commander of the forces of the United Nations in undertaking offensive operations designed to open a second front against the Germans.

Earlier in the day the President learned from leaders of the C. I. O. United Automobile Workers of a threat to continuous war production resulting from failure to apply universally the waiver of extra compensation, usually double time,

Continued on Page Seven

PRESIDENT TALKS OF MEATLESS DAYS TO SAVE SHIPPING

He Estimates One a Week Might Release 30 to 40 Vessels for Transporting Arms

INDUSTRY ASSAILS IDEA

Spokesman Asserts Plan Failed to Work in First World War and Proposes Rationing

Special to THE NEW YORK TIMES.

WASHINGTON, Aug. 28—The American people may be asked to observe one meatless day a week in the near future, to save shipping space needed for the movement of war weapons to fighting fronts, President Roosevelt said today.

Thirty to forty ships, now engaged in carrying meat to the United Nations from Argentina, New Zealand and Australia, he estimated, could be released for the transport of guns and munitions if this country supplied the meat and shipped it over the relatively more direct routes. He conceded that the program would bring about a heavier drain on domestic meat supplies for civilians, but said this could be balanced by requiring citizens to do without meat in their diet once a week.

Members of the Food Requirements Committee named by the Department of Agriculture, at a meeting today estimated that at least one-fourth of the United States meat supply would be required to meet military and lease-lend use in the near future. The committee is studying the probable meat requirements with a view to recommending steps to guarantee military supplies and to distribute the civilian supply equitably by regions and among individuals.

Ships Topic in Fraser Talks

It was while answering questions about his conferences with Prime Minister Peter Fraser of New Zealand that the President said his talks with Mr. Fraser as well as studies he had made of the shipping problem, had established that a meatless day a week in this country would release thirty to forty ships now hauling meats from distant points.

He said the primary question in the whole situation was one of shipping rather than who should ship meat and where it should be shipped. The effect of a change in shipping rates and in supply sources he conceded would cause a drop in meat shipments from such countries as Argentina but he maintained it would not bring

Continued on Page Ten

NAZI TANKS HALTED

Spearhead Is Smashed in Russian Ambush North of City

RZHEV ATTACK IS PRESSED

New Soviet Gains Reported on Moscow Front—Firm Stand in Caucasus Continues

By RALPH PARKER

Wireless to THE NEW YORK TIMES.

MOSCOW, Saturday, Aug. 29—While General Gregory K. Zhukoff's offensive on the front west of Moscow continued to develop satisfactorily with the capture of more inhabited points, the great battle northwest of Stalingrad raged throughout yesterday without any further appreciable German gains, according to the Soviet communiqué issued early today. Great losses were inflicted on the armored spearhead of General Field Marshal Fedor von Bock's attack.

The High Command reported that Soviet counter-attacks continued northwest of Stalingrad and that a force of German tommy-gunners was wiped out to the last man after it had advanced dangerously close to the defenders' positions. Southwest of the city, however, the Germans drove a further salient into the Russian lines after having been held for some days.

It is clear from Russian reports from the Stalingrad front that the first German attempt to storm the city by a surprise blow of mechanized forces strongly supported from the air ended in failure, and that in some sectors the vanguard is in considerable difficulties, locked in the Russians' deep defenses. The second attempt, already well under way, lacks the surprise element and is likely to prove costlier than the first.

Pressure on Rzhev Grows

The Russian offensive under General Zhukoff and Col. Gen. Ivan S. Koneff is reported to be proceeding according to plan. While Rzhev itself is being stormed by General Lelyushenko, other powerful Russian forces are pressing on against the city's line of communications with Vyazma. No significant changes are reported from the Caucasus, where battles are being waged both in the mountains and on the plains.

[The Germans claimed unspecified gains before Stalingrad and in the Caucasus, but emphasized the Russians' growing resistance. The Berlin radio reported the capture of a town forty miles southwest of Astrakhan. Continued Russian attacks in the Rzhev and Voronezh regions were acknowledged, as well as a new Soviet offensive southeast of Leningrad.]

While there is no doubt that Stalingrad has suffered severely from the reported German air Blitz, the new city is planned on the open system with much green space around the buildings and the immense factory that dominates the place. The Germans' comparisons with their Rotterdam raid are misleading, for, whereas Rotterdam's center was built up, Stalingrad's is exceptionally open. Many of the bombs probably fell in roads, gardens and parks.

Tank Spearhead Smashed

About a division of tanks with armored-car support appears to have been the strength of the first thrust toward the northwest approaches of Stalingrad. While a large bomber force sought to blast a lane to the city and by systematic raids on its center to disorganize the resistance, about 120 tanks in three columns pierced the defenses. The central column made a direct assault in a crucial sector and the others circled about it in an enveloping move.

At first only guns and anti-tank rifles opposed them, but then Soviet tanks entered the battle decisively, checked the dangerous thrust, gripped one of the flanking columns in firm pincers and caused the other to disperse and scatter over the steppe, where special anti-tank units lay in ambush.

About ninety German tanks at-

Continued on Page Six

War News Summarized

SATURDAY, AUGUST 29, 1942

The United Nations flung their growing air might against Germany and German-occupied soil in the last forty-eight hours. Last night the R. A. F. struck at Southern Germany. The Nazis assert they shot down thirty-two planes. On the previous night a strong force of heavy British bombers, estimated at 600, dumped tons of high explosives and incendiaries on the Baltic part of Gdynia in Poland and the Prussian industrial center of Kassel, eighty miles beyond the Ruhr Valley. Thirty of the raiders did not return. In daylight United States Flying Fortresses subjected the Meaulte aircraft factory, one of the largest in France, to a precision bombing and maintained their record of no losses. [1:8.]

British sources estimated that this year's aerial campaign against Germany had knocked out at least 500 war factories and had made at least 1,000,000 persons homeless. [4:1.]

Russia's defenders of Stalingrad and the Caucasus held German forces to a virtual standstill, inflicting grievous losses on an armored spearhead trapped in the defenses northwest of the Volga city. A Moscow communiqué reported 2,800 enemy troops killed in that sector. The Soviet counter-offensive on the central front swept the Germans out of several more localities. [1:4; map, P. 6.]

The Egyptian land front saw only patrol and artillery action, but Allied planes bombed Axis supply convoys in the southern sector, and British aircraft, striking at Mediterranean supply lines, torpedoed an Italian cruiser northwest of Crete. [5:1.]

In the Far East China's counter-offensive rolled up its most impressive gains thus far. The Chinese forces overran Chuhsien and Lishui, air bases in Chekiang within bombing range of Japan. With the Japanese in a vast withdrawal, the Chinese were only a few miles from Nanchang, main enemy base in the Kiangsi area. [1:5; map, P. 4.]

As for Japanese naval activity in the Solomon Islands area, a United States Navy spokesman revealed there had been "no reports" of new clashes for more than two days. A high government authority declared that the withdrawal of Japanese naval forces from the area represented no major American victory, since the enemy action had been only a reconnaissance in force. [1:7.]

An eyewitness account of the seizure of five islands in the Solomons by United States Marines revealed that the Americans had won their prescribed objectives within forty-eight hours of the surprise aerial and naval attack. [1:6-7.]

Heavy fighting raged between Allied troops and Japanese invaders around Milne Bay, at the tip of New Guinea, with Allied bombers flying low to give effective support. [3:1.]

In Washington, President Roosevelt disclosed a plan, based on the assumption of Spain's continued neutrality, to rehabilitate Spanish cultural life under the sponsorship of the twenty-one American republics and to encourage the post-war movement of tourists to Spain from the Western Hemisphere. [1:5-6.]

MOVE AND COUNTERMOVE IN THE BATTLE OF THE SOLOMONS

0 MILES 500
Rabaul
NEW BRITAIN
Gasmata
BOUGAINVILLE
Kieta
SOLOMON IS.
Buna
MALAITA
Port Moresby
Milne Bay
GUADALCANAL
Coral Sea
AUSTRALIA
Cape Esperance
Marovo
SAVO I.
BUENA VISTA I.
Indispensable Strait
Sandfly Passage
OLEVUGA I.
Rara
Nago
FLORIDA I.
TULAGI I.
Tulagi Harbor
Gavutu Hbr
Longapolo
reefs and rocks
NUSU I.
Sealark Channel
Domma
Lunga Bay
Kukum
Lunga
Berande
Densely Wooded
Lapo
GUADALCANAL I.
0 5 10 15 20 25 Miles
AUG. 29, 1942

United States Marines who landed on Tulagi and the adjoining islands of Tanambogo, Gavutu Makambo and Mbangai on Aug. 7 and 8 encountered heavy resistance, according to a correspondent accompanying them, but finally accounted for most of the Japanese, who fought to the end from caves. Simultaneous landings on Florida Island, to the east, and Guadalcanal, to the southwest, met with little opposition. On the night of Aug. 20 some 700 Japanese attempted a landing on Guadalcanal, but 670 were killed, according to our Navy's communiqué, and the remnant captured. Another Navy communiqué last Tuesday told of "a large-scale battle" raging at sea "in an attempt to repel a strong Japanese striking force." The following day the Navy recorded bomb hits on two enemy carriers, a battleship and several cruisers. With reference to the actions of the past ten days, a high Washington official now cautions that the Japanese moves should be regarded not as a full offensive, but rather as a reconnaissance in force. The inset shows the relation of the Solomon Islands to Australia and neighboring regions.

TWO BIG AIRFIELDS SEIZED BY CHINESE

Chuhsien and Lishui Are Again Available for Raids on Japan by American Bombers

By HARRISON FORMAN

Wireless to THE NEW YORK TIMES.

CHUNGKING, China, Saturday, Aug. 29—Chinese troops yesterday recaptured Chuhsien and Lishiu and their major airfields, located about 800 miles by bombing flight from Japan, the Chinese Army Command announced today.

With the recent recapture from the Japanese of Yushan, in the same Chekiang Province area, China now has possession again of the "big three" bomb-Japan air bases that the Japanese themselves avowed were primary objectives of their seaboard campaign.

In occupying Chuhsien the Chinese Army also completed control of about 200 miles of the Chekiang-Kiangsi railway, all but a small stretch of which only a fortnight ago was in Japanese hands. At the western end of the line the Chinese are now driving close to Nanchang, the enemy's chief North Kiangsi base.

[A heavy United States Army bombing raid yesterday on the Hanoi-Laokai railway and Japanese bases along that Indo-

Continued on Page Four

Tulagi Won in 48 Hours; T. N. T. Buried Foes in Caves

By ROBERT C. MILLER

United Press Correspondent

MARINE HEADQUARTERS, Guadalcanal Island, the Solomons, Aug. 8 (Delayed)—The Marines have landed and Old Glory is flying today over the first Japanese-conquered territory retaken by the United Nations in the Pacific War. Less than forty-eight hours after the United States armada drove undiscovered to the very flank of Japan's newly created empire and opened a surprise naval and aerial attack on the Solomons, the Marines, backed up by the fleet and units of the Australian Navy and supported by Navy, Army and Australian bombers and fighter planes, accomplished all their prescribed objectives.

I went ashore with a Marine landing party and witnessed the operation from the beginning. The Japanese strongholds of Tulagi, Tanambogo, Gavutu, Mbangai and Makambo were captured and objectives controlling the larger Guadalcanal and Florida Islands were occupied according to plan.

Japanese casualties suffered in the battle far exceeded those of the United Nations.

The resistance encountered by the Marines varied. On Tulagi, Tanambogo and Mbangai Islands, it was very bitter. On Guadalcanal and Florida Islands, the Marines encountered little opposition.

Japanese bombing raids on the invasion fleet were beaten off by anti-aircraft fire and an umbrella

Continued on Page Three

PUBLIC IS WARNED ON SOLOMONS FIGHT

High U. S. Official Says Enemy Was Not Engaged in Decisive Battle—New Move Awaited

By C. BROOKS PETERS

Special to THE NEW YORK TIMES.

WASHINGTON, Aug. 28—A high government authority today cautioned the American press and the American public against interpreting the withdrawal of Japanese naval forces from the Solomon Islands area as a major victory for the United States.

The enemy action, he said, did not represent a major offensive. It was merely a reconnaissance in force. It is not advisable in any way, he added, to convey the impression to the American people that a major enemy offensive has been repulsed or that our forces have won a major victory.

It is lamentable, this high authority continued, for any newspaper to overemphasize what are essentially minor victories.

No New Action in Area

This evening, meanwhile, a Navy spokesman stated that "up to 5:40 P. M. no reports had been received in the Navy Department to indicate there have been any new actions in the Solomons area." The Navy statement obviously was designed to contradict flatly dispatches which have been received and widely circulated in the United States alleging that a new action in the Battle of the Solomons has been joined and that its outcome might prove decisive in the Pacific.' These reports emanated from Auckland, New Zealand, and London.

There have been no engagements between Japanese and American forces in the Solomons area for more than forty-eight hours, the Navy made clear.

The admonition from the high government official came less than twenty-four hours after the issuance by the Navy of a communiqué disclosing that the Japanese attacking force appeared to have

Continued on Page Three

Roosevelt Outlines Plan for Aid From Americas to a Neutral Spain

Special to THE NEW YORK TIMES.

WASHINGTON, Aug. 28—A plan to rehabilitate the art treasures, the manuscripts, literature and famous buildings of Spain and to encourage the movement of tourists from the twenty-one American republics to Spain after the war was outlined today by President Roosevelt, who said it was predicated on the Spanish Government's remaining neutral in this war, as this country hoped it would remain.

Rehabilitation of Spanish cultural life, damaged to some extent by the violent civil war, and improvement of her railway system and other tourist accommodations to encourage an influx of North, Central and South American tourists after the war were discussed in some detail by the President at his press conference.

The plan would be financed, he said, by contributions from individuals, groups and foundations within the Americas under the sponsorship of the individual governments, but it would not, so far as the United States was concerned, include a Federal appropriation.

The President said that the plan was now being explained to the Latin-American governments by Nelson A. Rockefeller, Coordinator of Inter-American Affairs.

Mr. Roosevelt waived aside a suggestion as to whether this form of aid was not calculated to influence Spain to be neutral in the war. To say that, he told an inquiring reporter, would be to impugn the motives of a project dedicated to the finer things of life.

Another reporter asked the President whether he anticipated opposition from persons who would object to any kind of assistance to the government of Generalissimo Francisco Franco, who won power by a rebellion assisted by the German and Italian Governments.

President Roosevelt replied that he did not think there would be

Continued on Page Five

SOUTH REICH IS HIT

British Attack Again in Force After Blows at Kassel and Gdynia

U. S. RAID OVER MEAULTE

Nazi-Used Aircraft Factories Blasted in Day—Allied Fighters Swarm at Foe

By The United Press.

LONDON, Saturday, Aug. 29—Another huge force of British long-range bombers, probably numbering at least 650, was believed to have smashed last night for the second straight night at German war factories, less than twelve hours after an American Flying Fortress assault on a French aircraft works.

British officials said briefly that the Royal Air Force attacked Germany during the night.

The Berlin radio, heard here, said the R. A. F. bombed South and Southwest Germany, where Mannheim has been a target for British raiders. Berlin claimed that Nazi night fighters and anti-aircraft batteries shot down thirty-two of the British planes.

British losses in recent night raids have averaged about 5 per cent, and if the German figure were correct it would indicate that more than 600 R. A. F. bombers took part.

A report from Zurich said that air raid alarms were sounded in Northern Switzerland and Southwestern Germany during the night.

German bombers made scattered raids last night and early today on Northeastern England and East Anglia, causing some damage and a few casualties. Two Nazi bombers were shot down.

Allied Offensive Grows

By MEYER BERGER

Wireless to THE NEW YORK TIMES.

LONDON, Aug. 28—The tempo of the Allied air offensive against Germany and German-held territory in Western Europe was stepped up a bit higher through last night and today.

Planes of the Royal Air Force and the United States Army Air Forces swarmed in constant streams over enemy regions. As major blows, American Flying Fortresses—striking again without the loss of any of the big bombers—blasted an airplane factory at Meaulte, France, in a late-afternoon raid.

Before dawn a "strong force"—meaning several hundred—of R. A. F. bombers ranged far across Germany and raided the Baltic port of Gdynia and the Central German industrial city of Kassel.

R. A. F. and American fighter and fighter-bomber squadrons struck across the Channel against Nazi coastal shipping and the foe's bases in occupied France during darkness and daylight, engaging in many dogfights with German defense fighters.

R. A. F. Raid on Kassel Heavy

The British bombing of German factories at Kassel was emphasized in an Air Ministry communiqué, which described the attack as "concentrated and effective."

The greater part of the R. A. F. night raiding force roared through the clear moonlight to Kassel, eighty miles east of the Rhine-Ruhr confluence, and loosed bombs in a swift assault.

The R. A. F. losses for the night, covering the Gdynia and Kassel attacks and widespread operations over the Nazi-held coast, were put at thirty bombers and two fighters. [An Associated Press estimate from London was that about 600 British bombers were engaged in the attacks.]

Late in the afternoon the air waves from Europe thickened with heavier explosions as the Flying Fortresses, escorted by Spitfires, roared over Northern France and smashed at the factories in Meaulte, near Albert. Again having laid their deadly eggs in high-level precision bomb-

Continued on Page Four

"All the News That's Fit to Print."

The New York Times.

LATE CITY EDITION
Moderately warm today.
Temperature Yesterday—Max., 77; Min., 63
Sunrise, 6:31 A. M.; Sunset, 7:51 P. M.

Copyright, 1942, by The New York Times Company.

VOL. XCI..No. 30,900. Entered as Second-Class Matter, Postoffice, New York, N. Y. NEW YORK, MONDAY, AUGUST 31, 1942. THREE CENTS IN NEW YORK CITY

JAPANESE FORCES AT MILNE BAY CRUSHED, TRAPPED ENEMY BEING DRIVEN INTO SEA; REDS ATTACK AT STALINGRAD, BOMB REICH

CITY ENFORCEMENT OF AUTO DIMOUT TO BEGIN TONIGHT

La Guardia Issues Detailed Regulations and Promise of Drastic Police Action

UTILITIES ARE INCLUDED

Mayor Says Prospects for Adequate Fuel Oil Supply for Winter Are Brighter

The detailed regulations for the dimming out of vehicle headlights were made public yesterday by Mayor La Guardia as he announced that rigid enforcement of the rules by the Police Department would begin tonight. The regulations apply to street cars, interstate and intrastate buses and the city's franchised bus lines as well as to private motor cars and trucks.

"The police have been very patient in conducting a campaign of education, and from Monday on the law will have to be enforced," the Mayor said in his weekly radio "Talk to the People" from his desk at City Hall. Announcement of the enforcement policy, involving the serving of summonses upon violators, will be made today by Commissioner Valentine.

The Specific Regulations

Following are the specific regulations, effective from one-half hour after sunset to one-half hour before sunrise:

1. Drivers of buses operating only within the city shall use parking lights or headlights. Where headlights are used they shall be operated on the dim or low beam. The lenses of the headlights shall be shielded, hooded or painted three-quarters down from the top.

2. Drivers of interstate or intrastate buses while operating within the city shall either comply with the above requirements or use the white or yellow marker lights attached to the front of their buses.

3. Operators of street cars shall operate with the lenses of the headlight shielded, hooded or painted half-way down from the top.

4. Drivers of all other motor vehicles with parking lights contained separate from or outside of the headlights shall use their parking lights only.

5. Drivers of vehicles with parking lights contained inside of the headlights, or drivers of vehicles which have no parking lights, shall use the lowest candle power units in the headlights. The lenses of the headlights shall be shielded, hooded or painted half-way down from the top of the lenses.

6. If headlights are painted, black paint shall be used.

Most Cars Meet Requirements

Most of the vehicles to which the new rules apply have already met the requirements, it was said.

In connection with the automobile dimout rules the Mayor expressed agreement with a suggestion made to him by a parent who pointed out the increased need of careful watching of children in the streets, now that automobile headlights are to remain dimmed at night. The Mayor, acting on a suggestion from George Mand of the Bronx Board of Trade, warned drivers of buses and taxicabs that they must not attempt to drive too fast while ordinary motor vehicles were driving slowly because of the dimming of their lights.

Mayor La Guardia welcomed the ruling of the Office of Defense Transportation barring taxicab cruising throughout the United States. New York has been studying this problem and has been prepared for it for two years, he said. The Mayor expressed special pleasure at that part of the ODT order that forbids any increase in the number of cabs now operating in any given community.

"That is very wholesome," the Mayor declared. "It will permit the taxicab drivers to make a decent and good living and we expect full and complete cooperation from the taxi industry."

The Mayor predicted that the city would have no trouble in reconciling the ODT rules with conditions existing here. The city, he said, has been trying for two years to apply the same sort of regulation and has been taken to the courts two or three times because of its efforts.

The city's prospects for getting an adequate supply of fuel oil for the Winter are a bit brighter, the

Continued on Page Eighteen

Women on Trucks Join Tin Can Drive

When the 300 trucks of the Department of Sanitation make their tin can collection tours on Wednesday there will be a woman volunteer worker on every truck, seated next to the driver, Mayor La Guardia announced yesterday in his radio "Talk to the People" from City Hall.

"Women will ride the trucks," the Mayor declared. "The women's salvage division will be represented by one of its members on each truck and the American Women's Voluntary Services will also take part. So on Wednesday, when the tin can brigade goes out and the batteries move, you will find one of these fine women volunteers right on the job next to the driver's seat."

One of the functions of the volunteers, it was indicated, would be to advise tenants, superintendents and others how to put tin cans in proper shape for collection.

TREASURY TO OFFER SPENDING TAX PLAN

Acts Tomorrow With Dual Aim, to Curb Inflation and Add 4 to 5 Billion Revenue

By The Associated Press.

WASHINGTON, Aug. 30—Treasury proposals for a new wartime tax on individuals, a "spending tax" calculated to yield $4,000,000,000 to $5,000,000,000 annually, will be laid before the Senate Finance Committee Tuesday, Chairman George said today.

Designed to tighten the brakes on inflation and raise revenues substantially beyond the estimated $24,000,000,000 yearly total reached under the bill voted by the House, the proposals would impose additional taxes on virtually all persons with more than $1,000 annual income.

As outlined by Senator George to reporters, the spending tax would apply on all money paid out by an individual in the course of the year in excess of certain specified exemptions.

Although Senator George said he was not conversant with all the details, there were indications that the rate might be as high as 10 per cent, possibly with graduated increases in the higher brackets of expenditures. The tax would be imposed over and above all other taxes now in effect and proposed in the new bill.

Procedure to Find Tax

To compute his spending liability, a taxpayer would figure his net income for the year, taking into account all the deductions and exemptions customarily allowed to him in determining his income tax. When this amount had been arrived at he then could make

Continued on Page Ten

Berlin, Baltic Ports Raided In Biggest Soviet Air Attack

Fires Set in German Capital, Koenigsberg, Danzig, Stettin, Without Loss of Plane, Moscow Says—R. A. F. on Day Sweeps

By The United Press.

LONDON, Aug. 30 — Russian bombers, lashing out at least 900 miles from the Eastern Front in heavy raids over Germany, set ninety-one fires in Berlin, Koenigsberg, Danzig and Stettin last night, the Moscow radio announced today. It warned the German people that they could expect long nights of terror from mighty Allied air raiding forces this Winter.

Moscow said great fires and explosions marked the course of the Red bombers' flight across the Reich, and it claimed once again that not a Russian plane was lost in the raid.

The Berlin radio acknowledged that explosive and incendiary bombs crashed into the outer districts of the German capital. It asserted that the Russian raiders went over at great height and dumped their bombs at random over a wide area of East and Central Germany.

Berlin insisted that damage done was small. It did not claim that any Russian planes were shot down.

[The British Royal Air Force, grounded by bad weather Saturday night, continued in daylight yesterday its offensive against the Nazis on the occupied European coast, The Associated Press reported from London.]

The Soviet bombing attack apparently was the heaviest of a series of raids the Russians have made on Northeastern German cities.

Moscow said forty-eight focuses of fire were started in Berlin, seventeen of which were large ones.

Continued on Page Six

GREW TELLS NATION OF JAPAN'S POWER

There Is No Room in Pacific for Ourselves and a 'Swashbuckling' Tokyo, He Warns

The text of Mr. Grew's address is printed on page 4.

By THOMAS J. HAMILTON

Special to THE NEW YORK TIMES.

WASHINGTON, Aug. 30—Joseph C. Grew, Ambassador to Tokyo for ten years, warned the American people tonight that war production and fighting spirit must be increased, and that unless we abandoned the hope of leading normal lives, "leaving the spirit of self-sacrifice to our soldiers and sailors," we risked the danger of a stalemate in the war with Japan.

Mr. Grew emphasized "the offensive spirit which permeates all of the armed forces of the Empire and the belief of the Japanese that we are 'constitutional weaklings,' unwilling to make the sacrifices

Continued on Page Four

CHINESE STORMING NANCHANG SUBURBS

Japanese Are Pushed Back to Line They Held Before Drive Started Last May

By The Associated Press.

CHUNGKING, China, Aug. 30—Chinese soldiers are storming the suburbs of Nanchang, Japan's major base in Kiangsi Province for twenty-nine months, and have recaptured Lungyu in their eastward pursuit of the Japanese in Chekiang Province, the Chinese reported tonight.

A High Command communiqué stated that the Chinese began attacks on the Nanchang outskirts after pursuing enemy units northward from Likiatu, forty miles south of Nanchang. Heavy fighting was reported in progress near Lientang, nine miles south of Nanchang, which the Chinese captured Thursday. Japanese reinforcements launched a counter-attack.

Thus the Chinese were presenting their greatest threat to Nanchang since the Japanese captured it, March 27, 1939.

All Lost Positions Retaken

The Chinese High Command announced the capture of the village of Liangkiatu, about twelve miles south of Nanchang, and indicated that the Chinese thus had pushed the Japanese back to the area they held around Nanchang before they began their "disastrous" campaign last May to take Eastern China airfields and seize a railroad route to Singapore.

The High Command has not announced the capture of Lungyu but a Central News Agency dispatch said the city was occupied by the Chinese this morning after fighting during the night. Lungyu is twenty miles east of Chuhsien, site of the biggest air base in China, and twenty-five miles northwest of Kinhwa, former capital of the province.

It was also reported unofficially that the Chinese had occupied Lanchi, twenty miles northwest of Lungyu and terminus of a branch rail line from Kinhwa. The Japanese captured Lanchi May 30, fifteen days after launching the drive that resulted in occupation of wide areas of Chekiang and Kiangsi Provinces and the capture of the 450-mile Hangchow-Nanchang railway.

The reoccupation of Lanchi would endanger Kinhwa and possibly expedite the withdrawal of Japanese troops from the railway between Lungyu and Kinhwa.

China's offensive has recaptured nearly 350 miles of the Hangchow-Nanchang railway and most of the territory Japan gained this Summer in the two provinces.

Not Defeat, Says Tokyo

A Tokyo report broadcast to the United States yesterday by Berlin

Continued on Page Three

War News Summarized

MONDAY, AUGUST 31, 1942

Yesterday's war news appeared to balance up once more in a manner generally favorable to the United Nations despite the perilous situation in Southern Russia.

General MacArthur's Australian headquarters announced that the Japanese force that had landed at strategic Milne Bay on the southeastern tip of New Guinea had been defeated and driven back into a narrow and difficult position after it had suffered heavy losses in men and equipment. [1:8.]

The United States Navy disclosed that seven of twenty-four Japanese planes that had attacked our forces on Guadalcanal Island in the Solomons had been shot down without American losses. This raised to 111 at least the total of enemy planes destroyed in the Solomons campaign. [3:4.]

Chungking reported that Chinese troops were fighting in the suburbs of Nanchang, chief Japanese base in Kiangsi Province for the last twenty-nine months. The recapture of Lungyu in Chekiang was also announced. [1:4.]

The former United States Ambassador to Tokyo, Joseph C. Grew, warned the people of the United States that there was danger of a stalemate in the war with Japan unless greater sacrifices were made by the American people. He prophesied that Japanese morale would not break even under great reverses. [1:3.]

Moscow reported that the massed Germans before Stalingrad were still being held off and were even being counter-attacked in some sectors. In the Caucasus a counter-thrust on the edge of the Grozny oil fields was reported to have pushed back a German spearhead. The Soviet position in the Rzhev sector, where the Russians are attacking, was said to have improved again. [1:5.]

The Russians announced that Soviet bombers had started forty-eight fires, seventeen of them large, and caused nine explosions in a night raid on Berlin. Stettin, Danzig and Koenigsberg were also raided, Moscow said. [1:3-4.]

A correspondent reported from a key city in India that thousands of United States soldiers posted there had built up its defenses and that more men and matériel were arriving. [1:5-6.]

In the Mediterranean British forces were exceptionally active. Rome reported a British Commando-style raid on the island of Anticythera, between Greece and Crete. A force of British destroyers was reported to have shelled Marshal Rommel's base at El Daba and several air attacks were made on military objectives in Sicily. [1:7; map, p. 2.]

Travelers arriving in Stockholm from Paris said that 100,000 German civilians now working there were being trained on Sundays to take part in putting down a possible French uprising. [1:6-7.]

NAZIS DRIVEN BACK

Marines and Peasants Aid in Advance in Some Stalingrad Sectors

PUSH AT GROZNY HALTED

Russians Gain on the Moscow Front—Germans Say They Paid With Big Losses

By The Associated Press.

MOSCOW, Monday, Aug. 31—The Russian defenders of Stalingrad have hurled back all German attacks and struck counter-blows in some sectors, a communiqué said today, while the Red Army made new gains on the Moscow front and in a new offensive pushed back the German spearhead aimed at the Grozny oil fields in the Caucasus.

Soviet troops, supported by Volga Marines and armed peasants, launched counter-attacks northwest and southwest of Stalingrad, inflicting heavy losses on the enemy, particularly on an Italian battalion, which was said to have lost 70 per cent of its men.

The Moscow radio announced that Soviet troops had recaptured one populated place northwest of Stalingrad after they had fought the Germans "street by street and house by house."

"Toward the end of the day," the announcer continued, "the Hitlerites began to retreat, leaving hundreds of officers and men in the streets. Another unit of the Red Army drove the Germans from near-by hills, thus obtaining a commanding position over the whole locality."

Two Settlements Regained

The communiqué did not claim any gains in these attacks, but earlier reports said the Russians had driven the Germans from two settlements on distant approaches to the city.

On the Moscow front, which extends about seventy miles from Rzhev to the north, the Russians said their forces had made a new crossing of a river—presumably the Volga—and were fighting on the west bank. Another crossing was announced yesterday.

In the Caucasus, where the Germans had pushed a slender wedge along the railway to the area of Prokhladnaya, about fifty miles from the Grozny oil fields, the Russians also counter-attacked and recaptured an unidentified village.

Whether this was a general offensive or a local attack was not indicated. The communiqué merely said that "as a result of stubborn fighting our troops broke the resistance of the enemy and occupied an inhabited locality." It added that nine German tanks were destroyed and about a battalion of German infantry killed.

Announcing the new gains northwest of Moscow, the High Command said:

"On the Western Front, Soviet troops fought for river crossings. By the end of the day our troops

Continued on Page Two

NEW SETBACKS FOR FOE IN THE PACIFIC

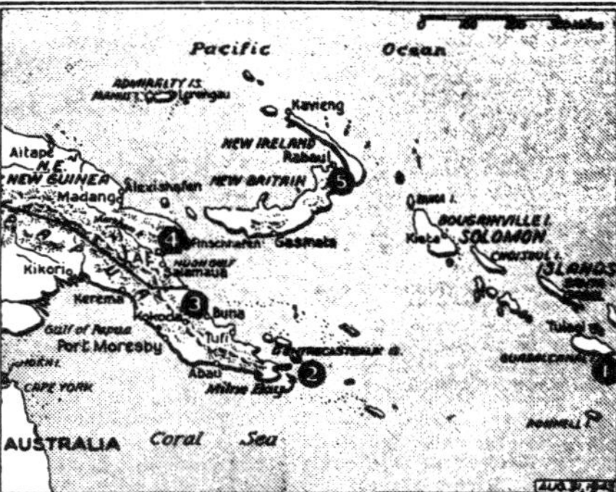

In the Solomon Islands two enemy air attacks on American positions on Guadalcanal (1) were repulsed. At the tip of New Guinea, directly west, the Japanese who had landed around Milne Bay (2) were smashed back to the little peninsula north of the bay. Thus the new threat to the Allied base at Port Moresby on the southern coast has been largely removed. A first threat had come with the occupation by the Japanese of Lae and Salamaua (4); then an effort to approach the base from the rear was defeated in the Battle of the Coral Sea; next the Japanese landed at Buna and worked their way inland to Kokoda (3), where they have just suffered another repulse. The main base for these operations is believed to be Rabaul (5), target of many air attacks.

100,000 Nazi Civilian Aides Train to Fight Paris Rising

By GEORGE AXELSSON

By Telephone to THE NEW YORK TIMES.

STOCKHOLM, Sweden, Aug. 30—One hundred thousand German civilians, holding positions in various Reich departments in the former French capital, are being trained on Sundays in street fighting and other forms of partisan warfare, according to reliable persons who left Paris last Thursday and have now arrived here.

Standard French Army rifles are being used for the training, which aims at shaping the German civilian into a valuable adjunct to the army against the day of a possible general French uprising, these informants said. Suspecting that the French had hidden formidable quantities of arms at the time of the collapse, to be drawn upon when the hour comes, the Germans are providing their civilians with the opportunity of familiarizing themselves with French weapons.

Exercises Held in Open

These exercises are being held openly in the Boulogne and Vincennes parks, the informants said, and with the idea of impressing the French population Parisians are encouraged to attend as spectators.

The SS [Elite Guard] and Gestapo now reign supreme in Paris and the public posters giving the names of those who face firing squads are signed by the SS chief instead of by the officer commanding, General Otto von Stuelpnagel, they reported.

Far from being impressed by the German reign of terror, the French, these sources said, are ever devising new means of showing their hatred of their oppressors. Open hostility to the Germans is on the increase, they said, and the campaign of Chief of Government

Continued on Page Eight

BRITISH POUND FOE IN MEDITERRANEAN

Troop Thrust at Isle Reported —Sicilian Bases Raided —Ships Shell El Daba

By The Associated Press.

LONDON, Aug. 30—A mysterious, Commando-style raid on the tiny island of Anticythera, between Greece and Crete, and twenty-four hours of intense air action against Sicily from Malta indicated today that the British were striking strongly once more for the initiative in the Mediterranean.

British submarines were reported to be taking a heavy toll in attacks on convoys that were trying to carry reinforcements, oil and ammunition to General Field Marshal Erwin Rommel's Axis forces in North Africa.

A Reuter (British news agency) dispatch from "aboard a British destroyer in the Eastern Mediterranean" reported that yesterday morning a force of British destroyers rained shells on Marshal Rommel's tank-repair shops and stores at El Daba, on the Egyptian coast.

Rome Reports Island Raid

The first word of the raid on Anticythera—the Italians call the island Cerigotto—came from the Italian High Command, which said that a "small enemy unit" made a landing attempt Friday night, but "fled on the quick intervention of our defenses."

An authoritative source here said "it is not unlikely that some sort of landing was made," but added that he would not be surprised "if we never heard of it officially."

"There may have been something there that our forces wished to destroy, but if the report is true, and whatever the nature of the landing, it doubtless was of minor importance, corresponding to little more than patrol activity," he said.

The Italians naturally would wish to make the most of it if British forces had landed and then withdrawn, he added.

The raids on Sicily started Wednesday night, the Air Ministry announced today, when a small number of Axis planes tried to pierce Malta's defenses. Two of

Continued on Page Two

Key Town in India Is Fortified By Thousands of American Troops

By HERBERT L. MATTHEWS

Wireless to THE NEW YORK TIMES.

A TOWN IN INDIA, Aug. 26 (Delayed)—Americans have invaded this town in force and it is trying with unequal success to turn into a proper melting pot.

This has become one of the key points of India, what with the Germans advancing in the Caucasus and the Japanese on the Burma frontier. It is natural, therefore, that American efforts should be concentrated on pouring men and material into it and developing its resources.

In the last five months there has been an amazing growth in the size and the facilities of the American force, under a fiery, tough American commander.

It is hard going here, as everywhere in the world, and it would not fool the enemy or serve any purpose to deny that there is still a long way to go and lots needed from home. Miracles have been performed here on a shoestring, showing what the United Nations are going to be able to do when material really starts rolling. Curiously enough, the only abundance here is an enormous quantity of precious material booked for China under lease-lend that cannot get to China now that the Burma Road is closed and that cannot be used by the Americans and the British because of that technicality.

However, right now this town can take anything that the enemy might throw at it. No time is being lost, and whatever happens this place will be prepared for it.

There are thousands of Americans here now and they are providing the town with many problems, some pleasant and some wor-

Continued on Page Eight

ALLIES MOPPING UP

Japanese Losses Heavy as Australians Take Back Vital Area

FOE REPELLED AT KOKODA

His Casualties Severe There Also—Our Forces Down 7 Aircraft in Solomons

By BYRON DARNTON

Wireless to THE NEW YORK TIMES.

AT UNITED NATIONS HEADQUARTERS, Australia, Monday, Aug. 31—General Douglas MacArthur's headquarters issued this morning a special communiqué announcing that the Milne Bay area, on the southeastern tip of New Guinea, where the Japanese had made a landing that seriously threatened all United Nations positions in New Guinea, was "rapidly being cleared of the enemy."

The Japanese have been pushed back to the narrow confines of the peninsula north of the bay, the communiqué says, and there Australian troops are battling to thrust the enemy into the sea. Headquarters also reports that the evacuation of remnants of the Japanese force probably was carried out by naval vessels under the cover of darkness last night.

[In the Solomon Islands the Japanese lost seven of twenty-four planes during two ineffective attacks against American-held Guadalcanal, the Navy Department announced in Washington yesterday.]

Foe's Move Anticipated

The communiqué gives every assurance that all danger from the Milne Bay area has definitely been ended. Thus there was one occasion on which a Japanese move had been anticipated and prepared for. Coming on the heels of the Solomons battle, it makes the situation in this area much brighter.

It was reported yesterday that one Japanese cruiser and eight destroyers had made their way into the bay on Friday night, and it was feared that these warships were bringing important reinforcements. The belief at headquarters now is that these ships were used for evacuation.

It has been a closely guarded secret for some time that we were preparing new installations in the Milne Bay area, which is important to us not only in the defense of the Port Moresby area, where there are several airfields, but also offensively. The base at Milne Bay makes the bombing of the enemy base at Rabaul, on New Britain, much easier. In view of these considerations the installations were made at Milne Bay and a considerable body of Australian troops was placed there to guard those installations.

Led by General Clowes

These troops, including units seasoned in the Libyan and Syrian campaigns, are led by Major Gen. Cyril Clowes, Australian veteran of the fighting in the Middle East. General Clowes is complimented in the communiqué by General MacArthur for having "ably commanded" the Australian force. There are a few American service troops serving in the Milne Bay area under General Clowes.

The communiqué reveals for the first time that the Japanese landed tanks at Milne Bay. The enemy, says the bulletin, lost "all his heavy supplies and equipment, including tanks." It is known that not many tanks were taken ashore by the Japanese. Persons familiar with the country have been mystified by the attempt to use this weapon, for the terrain is wholly unsuited for tank warfare.

Japanese forces landed last Wednesday on the northern shore of the bay, about eight miles from our installations. In that area there is only a narrow beach and it is deep mud at this season of the year, when the rains are heaviest.

Milne Bay has cost the Japanese heavily in more ways than one. They moved a considerable number of Zero fighter planes to the air

Continued on Page Three

"All the News That's Fit to Print."

The New York Times.

LATE CITY EDITION
Scattered showers today; moderate temperatures.
Temperatures Yesterday—Max., 74; Min., 59
Sunrise, 6:26 A. M.; Sunset, 7:10 P. M.

Copyright, 1942, by The New York Times Company.

VOL. XCI..No. 30,908. Entered as Second-Class Matter, Postoffice, New York, N. Y. NEW YORK, TUESDAY, SEPTEMBER 8, 1942. THREE CENTS IN NEW YORK CITY

PRESIDENT TO CONGRESS: CURB PRICES OR I WILL; WILL TAKE WAR TO GERMANY, HE TELLS NATION; NAZIS GAIN IN FRONTAL ATTACK ON STALINGRAD

BATTLE IS WIDENED

Red Army Retires West of Volga City—Line to Southwest Holds

FOE HIT IN CAUCASUS

Defenders of Road to Oil Wells of Grozny Put Nazis to Flight

By RALPH PARKER
Wireless to The New York Times.

MOSCOW, Tuesday, Sept. 8—General Field Marshal Fedor von Bock attacked Stalingrad yesterday on a new line, west of the city, and made some progress against stiff Red Army resistance. A Soviet communiqué issued today says, in announcing the shift in the battle, that Soviet troops in one western sector withdrew to new positions after they had repelled four German attacks.

Russian forces southwest of Stalingrad are reported to have hurled back several violent German attacks of great strength. The Germans suffered heavy losses, it is said, and in close-range fighting in one sector Red Army men destroyed eight of thirty German tanks that were carrying out an assault.

The Russian bulletin also reports hard fighting in the Novorossiisk region of the Black Sea coast, where the Russians again lost ground, and on the southern bank of a river near Mozdok, where the German invaders of the Caucasus are attempting to advance to the Grozny oil fields. In the Mozdok area, the communiqué states, the Germans were counter-attacked successfully.

[The Germans, who claimed Novorossiisk on Sunday, said nothing more yesterday about the fighting in the Caucasus, but they reported an advance at Stalingrad. The city's defenders were said to have lost 108 tanks in futile counter-attacks.]

Nazi Wedge Pushed Out

Enemy attacks southwest of Stalingrad were increasing in fury. According to reports received yesterday, German tanks managed to advance into the Russian lines Sunday night. Russian machine-gunners and mortar detachments made a flank attack on the intruders and the salient was forced out.

The Russians were reported yesterday to have regained ground northwest of Stalingrad, and the situation there appears today to be unchanged. The enemy's northern flank is somewhat exposed as a result of his failure to take Voronezh and of the initiative shown by the Russians in the Kletskaya sectors.

The German Air Force continues to play an important part in the operations near Stalingrad, and although the Soviet Stormovik assault planes—whose designer received a high decoration yesterday—are giving valuable support to Red Army troops, the German dive-bombers appear to have the ascendancy. A new type of Messerschmitt fighter plane, with an

Continued on Page Two

U. S. Troops at Bases In Ecuador and Isles

By The United Press.

QUITO, Ecuador, Sept. 7—United States troops have taken over bases on the Santa Elena Peninsula, westernmost area of Ecuador, and in Ecuador's Galapagos Islands, 650 miles to the west, Defense Minister Colonel Carlos Guerrero disclosed at a secret session of Congress tonight.

Colonel Guerrero said the action was taken with the full approval of the Defense Ministry as a step in continental defense.

Ecuador has broken off diplomatic relations with the Axis countries, but has not declared war.

U. S. Fliers Smash Japanese Returning to Solomon Isles

Enemy Suffers Severe Losses in Troops and Boats—Small Units Believed Ashore—Raid on Guadalcanal Is Ineffective

Special to The New York Times.

WASHINGTON, Sept. 7—Several small Japanese detachments attempting landings on the swampy western reaches of Guadalcanal Island, in the Solomons have suffered heavy losses in attacks by United States planes, it was announced by the Navy tonight.

The Navy's communiqué did not say whether all the enemy landing forces had been repulsed, and it was assumed that small parties had made their way to shore in an attempt to reinforce the isolated Japanese patrols that had withdrawn to the mountains and jungles of the island when United States forces first occupied the Guadalcanal-Tulagi area. United States Marine forces are hunting down the scattered Japanese units.

This latest report on the efforts of the Japanese to regain a foothold on what had been their southernmost base was released a few hours

United States planes have attacked enemy landing operations off San Jorge Island (1) and near the western end of the island of Guadalcanal (2).

after a Navy announcement that American fighter planes had shot down two Japanese bombers and one fighter out of a group of forty-six planes that raided Guadalcanal shortly after noon on Saturday (Solomon Islands time). The raiders—twenty-six bombers with an escort of twenty Zero fighters—inflicted only minor damage.

On the same day the Japanese

Continued on Page Five

PRESIDENT SPEAKS

Vital Decisions Made on Taking the Offensive, He Says on Radio

'RUSSIA WILL HOLD'

New Japanese Blows Are Predicted—Hopeful on the Near East

The text of the President's speech will be found on Page 17.

Special to The New York Times.

WASHINGTON, Sept. 7 — The United States and Great Britain, confident that Soviet Russia will hold out despite serious setbacks, have made vital military decisions designed to put their armies on the offensive against Germany at one or more of a dozen different points in Europe, President Roosevelt told the country and the world by radio tonight.

"The power of Germany must be broken on the battlefields of Europe," he said.

The Chief Executive, after explaining why he had called upon Congress again for legislation to hold down living costs, reviewed the progress of the war to date. He was cautiously optimistic in his appraisal of the future for the United Nations as he warned again that great sacrifices of blood, treasure and convenience must be expected before victory over the Axis powers can be assured.

Situation on Four Fronts

He gave the world this sketch of the developments to date on the four major battle fronts:

The Russian Front: A smashing victory still eludes Hitler and, though he has captured important territory, he still has been unable to accomplish his major objective—the destruction of a single Russian army. Millions of Germans seem doomed to spend another cruel and bitter Winter on the Russian Front, while Soviet forces continue to kill more Nazis and destroy more airplanes and tanks than are being smashed on any other front. In spite of any setbacks, Russia "will hold out and, with the help of her Allies, will ultimately drive every Nazi from her soil."

The Pacific Ocean Area: One major Japanese offensive was stopped at Midway, with heavy losses to the Japanese fleet, but the enemy still possesses great strength and "will undoubtedly

Continued on Page Seventeen

REPORTS ON HOME AND OVERSEAS FRONTS

The President addressing the nation last night

Associated Press Wirephoto

War Spurring Discoveries 20 Years Ahead of Peace

By WILLIAM L. LAURENCE
Special to The New York Times.

BUFFALO, Sept. 7—In a thousand and one chemical laboratories throughout America chemists are discovering new continents of matter at such a rapid pace under the pressure of war that "the world of 1940 has already become an antiquity," Dr. Charles M. A. Stine said tonight at the opening general session of the American Chemical Society's meeting.

Dr. Stine is a vice president of E. I. du Pont de Nemours & Co. Inc., and its adviser on research and development.

"The inconceivables of only two years ago are today's realities," he said. "War is compressing into the space of months developments which might have taken us half a century to realize if necessity had not forced the pace.

"These pressures are unprecedented. The developments are unprecedented. Give us a victorious peace and the freedom of enterprise it should guarantee, and our progress will be unprecedented. Let our swords be mighty and mighty indeed will be our plowshares."

When the war is won, he said, we will have at our command ten to a hundred times what we had before in new materials. These new materials are not mere predictions, but are actually on the way, he added.

The newest models of our motor cars, frozen in dealers' storehouses, have aged two decades since their creation, and developments which would not have come until 1960 could be incorporated in the automobile of today, were production to be resumed.

Dr. Stine enumerated many sci-

Continued on Page Twenty-one

AXIS IS REINFORCING ITS FRONT IN EGYPT

Rommel Is Preparing Stand Under Harrying Attacks—British Hit 12 Enemy Ships

By A. C. SEDGWICK
Wireless to The New York Times.

WITH THE BRITISH EIGHTH ARMY, in Egypt, Sept. 7—The enemy force that fought a delaying, rearguard action in the southern sector while the main body of the German Africa Corps was withdrawing under British pressure appears to have "thickened" during the last twenty-four hours. The bringing up of reinforcements no doubt made this process possible.

Although the British light armored units are harrying the enemy flanks, he has now taken up positions in the Qaret el Himeimat area as well as an area about seven miles to the north. The high ground of the former area is particularly well worth his while to hold. For this purpose he has some tanks, although not many,

Continued on Page Nine

NEW FORTRESS RAID AVENGES U. S. LOSS

Rotterdam, Utrecht Bombed, 12 Nazis Downed—R. A. F. Hits Duisburg and Ports

By FRANK L. KLUCKHOHN
Special Cable to The New York Times.

LONDON, Tuesday, Sept. 8—The United States Flying Fortresses yesterday bombed shipyards at Rotterdam and rail yards at Utrecht in the Netherlands and more than paid back the Nazis for the enemy's destruction of two Fortress planes Sunday by shooting down, with the aid of Allied fighter escorts, at least twelve Nazi planes at the cost of one Allied fighter.

The four-motored American bombers, with the swarms of Allied fighters around them, were seen going out by watchers on British beaches.

A few moments later they were over Rotterdam and Utrecht. There, taking advantage of clear visibility, they pounded the Schiedam shipyards at Rotterdam and the Utrecht rail objectives.

Amid air fighting in which Reich Marshal Hermann Goering's fliers tried vainly to repeat their first

Continued on Page Eight

Roosevelt Stirs Congress By Threat to Act on Prices

By FREDERICK R. BARKLEY
Special to The New York Times.

WASHINGTON, Sept. 7—The few members of Congress who were in Washington today received President Roosevelt's anti-inflation message and demand for new farm ceiling legislation with pretty general agreement that inflation must be prevented, with less general agreement that farm prices must be kept from going up and with several vigorous expressions of alarm over the President's assertion that, if Congress did not act by Oct. 1 to block the inflationary threat, he had the power to do so and intended to use that power.

Senator Taft asserted that if the President could take such action, Congressional elections might as well be suspended, "because Congress would become "a shell of a legislative body."

Senator La Follette declared that the President virtually "placed a pistol at the head of Congress." Both he and Senator McNary, the minority leader, voiced doubt that the President had the constitutional power he threatened to use.

The general view, however, was that Congress would buckle down to the task of revising farm legislation to permit the placing of price ceilings no higher than parity instead of the 110 per cent of parity to which farm prices may go under existing law before controls can be imposed.

The office of Speaker Rayburn announced that he would leave his Texas home for Washington tonight and that he wanted all members of the House back by next

Continued on Page Fifteen

RAID ALARM CAUSED BY A U. S. BOMBER

Army Admits Lag in Explaining the Alert—Protective Units' Turnout Gratifies Mayor

An unidentified plane sighted off the coast caused the sounding of an air raid alarm in New York City and parts of Westchester, Long Island and New Jersey early yesterday morning. Later it was identified as an Army bomber. At 2:32 A. M., nine minutes after the first preliminary signal and only one minute after the sirens actually began to wail, the Army ordered the all-clear sounded because the plane had been recognized as a friendly one.

In that brief space of time, however, two persons died from the alarm—one of a heart attack and the other of a fall in the dark—a third was probably fatally injured; millions of slumberers were roused from their sleep by the eerie sound of the sirens; radio stations went

Continued on Page Eighteen

TIME ULTIMATUM

President Sets Limit of Oct. 1 to End 110% Farm Parity Law

HE TO CURB WAGES

Quick Tax Bill Action Is Asked in Message—For $25,000 Income Top

Text of the message to Congress is printed on Page 14.

By W. H. LAWRENCE
Special to The New York Times.

WASHINGTON, Sept. 7—President Roosevelt sent to Congress today an ultimatum on anti-inflation controls, calling for enactment by Oct. 1 of legislation authorizing the stabilization of farm prices at parity or present levels. He warned that if the Congress fails to act in the next twenty-three days he will put the program into effect, along with wage stabilization, under his wartime powers as Commander in Chief despite the restrictions of the present Price Control Act.

Having laid his demands before Congress, the President spoke to the country by radio tonight. He told the people that two legislative steps which he had called for in his original anti-inflation program, were vital if the perilous price spiral already noted was to be checked. These two legislative actions were, one, the grant of power to control farm prices now restricted by the 110 per cent price-parity law and, two, increased taxation. At the same time the President reviewed the progress of the war.

In his bristling message to Congress, reminiscent of the bold action he asked for and received in the "first 100 days" of his first term, the President said that he was determined to check the rising cost of living with or without Congressional sanction because "a vicious spiral of inflation" would stagger the whole economic system and make it more difficult to win the war.

He took the unprecedented step of establishing a definite deadline for the independent legislative branch, with the explanation that "we cannot hold the actual cost of food and clothing down to approximately the present level beyond Oct. 1."

No Word on Super-Board or 'Czar'

Contrary to expectations in some official quarters, the President took no steps to set up an economic "czar" or to create a super-board which would coordinate Federal policy on prices, wages, taxes, credits and savings. He asked nothing of Congress which had not been requested in his seven-point anti-inflation program of April 27, but he demanded speed in carrying out his proposals for removing restrictions on farm price control and for increasing taxes.

The message, sent to the Capitol at noon, brought mixed reactions from the few members of Congress who stayed in Washington during the semi-recess of Congress.

Administration leaders, calling the membership back to begin consideration of the message next Monday, were confident that it would be approved by Congress, since many who opposed the President's tactics in threatening to act independently were, themselves, in favor of removing Price Control Act restrictions which forbid the setting up of farm commodity ceilings no lower than 110 per cent of parity, below the highest price from 1919 to 1929, or below the prices prevailing on Oct. 15 or Dec. 15, last year.

Aim Favored, Method Criticized

Among those who favored the President's objectives, but criticized his methods, were the Republican floor leader, Senator McNary, who was the Republican

Continued on Page Fourteen

174 Ships Launched in One Day And Keels Are Laid for 49 More

Labor in the nation's shipyards spent its traditional holiday at work yesterday, setting a record of 223 ships launched or begun. The metropolitan area about New York contributed its share, while in a lunch-hour speech to the workers in the busy Navy Yard in Brooklyn Rear Admiral E. J. Marquart, congratulating the men, described the achievements since Pearl Harbor as a "staggering total almost beyond the belief of one's own eyes."

The launchings totaled 174—consisting of naval craft of many types, as well as a number of 10,-500-ton Liberty ships—while keels were laid for forty-nine more.

For the New York area Admiral Marquart sounded the note that echoed through all the shipyards everywhere in the nation. Speaking into a microphone on his desk, knowing that his words were carried to the ears of every one of thousands of men in the yard, his and their observance of Labor Day was without ceremony. Work was too urgent for display; they listened as they munched their lunches.

"As we in the Navy look back on the past nine months," he said, "we—you and I—can take pride in our recovery from the treacherous blow we received at Pearl Harbor.

"The battles at Midway Island and in the Coral Sea; at Alaska and at the Solomon Islands just one month ago today; the clashes with enemy undersea fighters right here in our own watery front yard, the Atlantic, all testify that you have worked thoroughly and well. Ship for ship, just as man for man, we are faster and tougher than the enemy. If our foes still harbor any doubts on that score we of the Navy still invite battle; we seek out the chance to convince

Continued on Page Three

War News Summarized

TUESDAY, SEPTEMBER 8, 1942

German troops, checked northwest and southwest of Stalingrad, have begun a direct frontal assault from the west, according to Moscow, and have made some progress. The Russians acknowledged that the Germans had penetrated their lines near Novorossiisk, Black Sea Caucasus port, but did not concede that it had fallen, as claimed by Berlin. [1:1.]

United States Flying Fortresses with fighter escort attacked successfully Rotterdam's shipyard area and Utrecht in the Netherlands, shooting down twelve German planes and losing none of their own. This followed a heavy night attack by the Royal Air Force on Duisburg and the Ruhr region. Single R. A. F. bombers attacked Emden and Bremerhaven in daylight. [1:5.]

In Egypt Marshal Rommel's defeated force was braced by reinforcements after it had been pressed back, in some areas, beyond the starting point of its recent offensive, according to Cairo reports. British naval headquarters at Alexandria announced that British submarines had sunk five large and two medium-sized Axis ships recently on the Italy-to-Libya supply route. [1:2.]

After sending a message to Congress with an ultimatum on the matter of inflation control, President Roosevelt reviewed the war in a broadcast in which he said that the United States and Britain were preparing offensive action at one or more of a dozen points in the European area. He expressed confidence that Russia would hold out despite setbacks. [1:4.]

A Navy Department communiqué suggested that small parties of Japanese had landed on United States-held Guadalcanal Island in Solomons after suffering heavy casualties. A force of twenty-six Japanese bombers and twenty Zero fighters also attacked positions on Guadalcanal, but with little effect. Two enemy bombers and one fighting plane were shot down. [1:2-3.]

A United Nations Headquarters communiqué from Australia disclosed that Japanese forces had advanced in the Kokoda-Myola sector in New Guinea but with estimated casualties of 1,000. [5:1.]

Nation Travels Without Its Cars And Saves Lives on Labor Day

The railroads, buses and the subways bore the brunt yesterday of transporting what was pretty strictly a pedestrian throng of Labor Day holidaymakers. By contrast, the bridges and tunnels leading into the city carried a flow of vehicular traffic that was less than that of a normal weekday.

Acting Police Commissioner Louis F. Costuma put 4,000 extra men on duty, 2,000 of them detailed to handle traffic at tunnels and bridges. They were almost idle, but the men stationed at the rail and bus terminals had plenty of work. Through most of the day, and particularly in early evening, the sidewalks of New York were jammed from building line to curb in the midtown amusement area, while the streets were comparatively empty.

In New York and throughout the nation the day proved one fact—a sure way to reduce traffic fatalities is to take the automobiles off the highways. A compilation by The Associated Press of fatal highway accidents in the nation from Friday at 6 P. M. until mid-afternoon yesterday showed 164, as compared to 423 for the same period last year. Adding the violent deaths from other causes, the week-end total was brought to 255, as compared to 626 in 1941. The rationing of rubber and gasoline was credited with this result.

With the largest population, New York was in third place in the number of traffic fatalities by States with twelve. California recorded the largest number with 18, Michigan had fourteen and Illinois had eleven. Gasoline rationing applies only to the Eastern States.

In the big rail terminals here, Pennsylvania Station and Grand Central, it was said that peak travel loads were handled smooth-

Continued on Page Thirteen

"All the News That's Fit to Print."

The New York Times.

LATE CITY EDITION
Somewhat cooler today.
Temperatures Yesterday—Max., 65; Min., 56
Sunrise, 7:04 A. M.; Sunset, 6:20 P. M.

VOL. XCII...No. 30,943. Entered as Second-Class Matter, Postoffice, New York, N. Y. NEW YORK, TUESDAY, OCTOBER 13, 1942. THREE CENTS NEW YORK CITY

PRESIDENT FOR DRAFTING YOUTHS AT 18 YEARS; SAYS OUR OFFENSIVES WILL AID RUSSIA, CHINA; 3 U. S. CRUISERS SUNK IN EARLY SOLOMONS FIGHT

JEFFERS HITS BACK AT SENATE CRITICS; HE'LL RUN OWN JOB

Cotton Group Is Defied to Stop Him if Army Wants to Use Rayon in Heavy-Duty Tires

'GAMBLING TOO LONG' NOW

Let's Win War First, He Says, and Denounces Interference by Pressure Groups

Special to THE NEW YORK TIMES.

WASHINGTON, Oct. 12—William M. Jeffers, rubber administrator, told the Senate Agriculture Committee today that if the Army wanted to substitute rayon for cotton as a base for its heavy duty rubber tires the Army would get rayon regardless of the protests of any Congressional group or any one else.

His response to cotton State Senators who had asked him to appear in order to quiz him on the rayon substitution report was blunt.

"We have been gambling with this war too damned long," he said. "I don't intend to be influenced by anybody, any time or anywhere."

In rapid exchanges with his questioners, Mr. Jeffers said that the War Production Board had approved expansion of the rayon manufacturing industry to help provide fabric for the Army's tire needs. The questions came so fast that the witness at times had three or more before him almost simultaneously.

Agreeing with Senator Stewart of Tennessee that the Army had not yet completed its tests of rayon as a tire fabric, Mr. Jeffers said that nevertheless these tests already had proved that rayon-base tires for big Army trucks had higher tensile strength and a greater resistance to deterioration from heat.

Bombarded With Questions

"But why should we embark on an untried scheme in the middle of the war?" Senator McKellar of Tennessee demanded.

"Didn't representatives of the big rayon companies on the WPB have a voice in reaching this decision to use rayon?" asked Senator Stewart.

"What about the charge that seven of the nine WPB officials who recommended this change have financial interests either in rayon companies or big tire companies?" asked Senator ("Cotton Ed") Smith, the committee chairman.

Mr. Jeffers finally managed to interpose that he understood that

Continued on Page Fourteen

Declares Picketing Intolerable in War

By The United Press.

DETROIT, Oct. 12—Lieut. Gen. William S. Knudsen told the Economic Club today that Detroit would not long tolerate picket lines at its war plants.

"We cannot afford to lose an hour for any reason whatever," he said.

"I can't for the life of me think of a picket line with banners on a battle front in Europe or the Solomon Islands. The boys who are there have only one thing to fight with. That is what Detroit's brains, hands and manhours can give them."

MAYOR IN CAPITAL TO FIGHT JUNK MEN

Will Try to Break Bottleneck in Scrap Movement—Bronx Collection Is On Today

The collection of scrap metal for the great and growing war machine of the United States will begin in the Bronx this morning at 7 A. M. while Mayor La Guardia, in Washington, will seek to break the bottleneck that is threatened by the attitude of junk dealers.

Borough President James J. Lyons of the Bronx predicted yesterday that the Bronx would yield more than 50,000 tons of scrap metal. With 72,175 tons already collected, this figure would push the city total well above its quota of 100,000 tons.

Six hundred trucks, 570 of them from the Department of Sanitation and 30 from the office of the Borough President, will begin rolling this morning. Already the citizens of the Bronx have piled their offerings on the sidewalks for the collectors. Five dump plots have been designated: at Goulden Avenue and 200th Street, 150th Street and Exterior Street, Zerega and Lafayette Avenues, the Baychester land fill at Bartow Avenue and a lot at Metcalf Avenue and Eastern Boulevard.

Lyons to Lead the Way

Ahead of the trucks, Mr. Lyons will leave the Goulden Avenue dumping ground at 6:30 A. M. to lead in the gathering of the first truckload. Each of the trucks will have a woman member of the Bronx Civilian Defense Volunteer Office or other civic organization to guide the drivers to collections.

To preserve the piles for the collectors—against the possible depredations of unauthorized junkmen—the police had instructions to maintain special watch through last night and to prohibit junkmen from entering areas where scrap had been piled on the streets.

Although it was believed that the Mayor looked somewhat favorably upon the plan offered by Samuel Bassow, head of Bassow

Continued on Page Fifteen

U. S. ITALIANS AIDED

Biddle Announces Lifting of the 'Alien Enemy' Stigma on Monday

PRESIDENT APPROVES

Loyalty of 600,000 in Nation Said to Have Been Demonstrated

The text of Mr. Biddle's address is on Page 12.

Six hundred thousand unnaturalized Italians living in the United States will be freed from the stigma of being alien enemies of this country, beginning next Monday, it was announced last night by Attorney General Francis Biddle in a speech at a Columbus Day celebration at Carnegie Hall. His address was carried over a nationwide radio hook-up of the Mutual Broadcasting System.

This action, which Mr. Biddle said was taken with the approval of President Roosevelt, will free these Italians from many restrictions that have hampered them until now. It will permit them to travel freely, to possess cameras and firearms except where local regulations forbid, to remain out after the curfew now prescribed for alien enemies on the West Coast, and will free them from the necessity of carrying identification cards.

Mr. Biddle declared that this exoneration of Italians living in this country has been well earned by their loyalty to the United States.

Only 228 Italians Interned

In ten months of unprecedented wartime vigilance, he said, during which the government has acted on a policy of taking no chances with any one who might be dangerous, it has been necessary to intern only 228 Italians, or fewer than one-twentieth of 1 per cent.

The Attorney General also declared he had asked Congress to change the naturalization laws in a way that would make it possible for 200,000 of the older Italians living in this country to become citizens. This would be done by eliminating the necessity for taking a literacy test in the case of persons who are 50 years old or more, and have lived in this country continuously since before July 1, 1924.

Because of the obvious value to this country to be derived from spreading the news of the government's action through Axis Europe, Mr. Biddle's speech was carried last night on virtually all the short-wave radio stations now under government control. It was understood also that the British Broadcasting Corporation and the

Continued on Page Twelve

SEA BATTLE IN DARK

Quincy, Vincennes and Astoria Lost While Shielding Marines

FLARES GUIDED FOE

Guns, Torpedoes Fired at Close Range—Most of Crews Saved

By CHARLES HURD

Special to THE NEW YORK TIMES.

WASHINGTON, Oct. 12—The American Navy paid three heavy American cruisers—the Quincy, Vincennes and Astoria—as part of the price for successful occupation of the Japanese air field on Guadalcanal Island in the Solomons, the Navy revealed tonight.

The Quincy and the Vincennes were sunk in action and the Astoria succumbed to fire a few hours after a large Allied naval force had engaged in an old-fashioned gun and torpedo clash at close range with a Japanese battle force as searchlights and star shells lit the early morning darkness of Aug. 9.

"The enemy fire was heavy and accurate," said a communiqué announcing the loss of these vessels.

The Navy previously had announced the loss of two destroyers and four transports in the Solomons, while stating that one unidentified American cruiser had been sunk and two others damaged. The actual announcement of the loss of the 10,000-ton fighting ships was withheld until replacements could be sent into the Southwestern Pacific for them and for the Canberra, an Australian cruiser sunk in the same engagement and earlier announced as lost.

The "majority" of the personnel of the three American cruisers was saved, the Navy stated, but many men were lost. Among those definitely known to have died in action was Captain Samuel N. Moore of the Quincy. There was no word of the fate of Captain F. L. Riefkohl of the Vincennes or of Captain William G. Greenman of the Astoria.

Almost 3,000 men were known to have been aboard the cruisers when they were destroyed. There were

Continued on Page Four

SCENE OF ACTION IN WHICH ALLIED CRUISERS WERE LOST

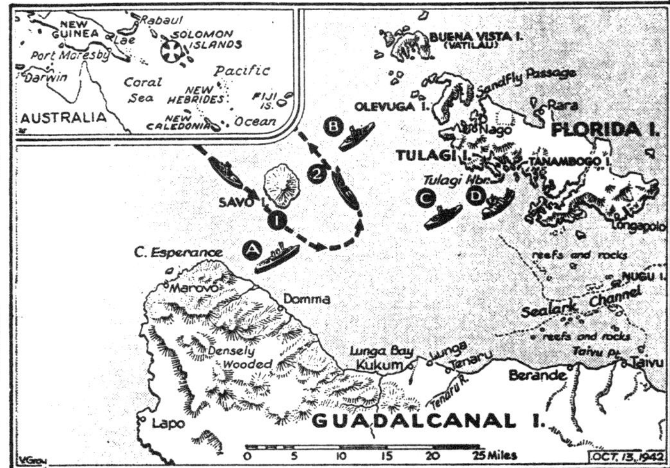

When the foothold on Guadalcanal and Tulagi was being strengthened Aug. 9 Allied screening forces of cruisers and destroyers were placed on both sides of Savo Island (A and B) and an additional screening force (C) was placed near the transports and supply ships (D). By the dark of early morning Japanese cruisers and destroyers sped past Savo (1) and, on sighting covering unit A, opened fire, hitting the Australian cruiser Canberra, which later sank. The enemy then swung to the northeast of Savo and a close-range battle was fought at (2) with covering unit B. There the American cruisers Quincy and Vincennes were sunk and the Astoria was set afire; she later sank, too. The enemy withdrew northwest. Inset shows the surrounding region.

CHURCHILL TALLIES NEW ALLIED GAINS

Stresses Increases in Ships, Bombing of Germany, U. S. Arrivals and Air Power

The text of Mr. Churchill's speech is on Page 8.

By RAYMOND DANIELL

Special Cable to THE NEW YORK TIMES.

LONDON, Oct. 12—Reviewing the progress of the war when he received the freedom of the city of Edinburgh today, Prime Minister Churchill declared that the last two months were the "least bad" since January in the battle of the Atlantic.

"The months of August and September have been—I will not say the best but the least bad months since January," he said. "They have seen new building of merchant ships that substantially out-

Continued on Page Eight

U. S. Rebuke to Chile Based On Proof of Nazi Spy Haven

By HAROLD CALLENDER

Special to THE NEW YORK TIMES.

WASHINGTON, Oct. 12—It was learned authoritatively here today that the references to Axis influence and espionage in Chile and Argentina, embodied in the speech that Sumner Welles, as acting Secretary of State, delivered at Boston last Thursday were made because this government had proof that Axis agents in those countries had transmitted information that has led to the sinkings of ships in American waters.

The reason Mr. Welles spoke out at that moment, it was explained, was that this government desired to remove the impression that the then projected visit to Washington of the President of Chile, Juan Antonio Rios, would signify that the United States was satisfied with Chile's policies—the facts being precisely the contrary.

In consequence of Mr. Welles's speech, the Chilean Ambassador, Rodolfo Michels, notified Mr. Welles today of the "postponement" of President Rios's visit.

In its protest Saturday against Mr. Welles's charges, the Chilean Government, quoted Admiral Julio Allard, commander of the Chilean Fleet, as saying that no ships had been sunk in the Pacific south of Panama and that information originating in Chile could not be responsible for sinking of ships "several thousand miles from Chile."

To this the reply made here today was that an Axis agent whom the Chilean authorities themselves had arrested in Sep-

Continued on Page Ten

NAZIS AGAIN STRIKE INSIDE STALINGRAD

But Make Only Slight Gain—Russians in Mozdok Region of Caucasus Advance

By The United Press.

MOSCOW, Tuesday, Oct. 13—German armored and infantry forces resumed attacks in the Stalingrad area yesterday after a short lull, and in one sector of the city the Russian defenders were pressed back slightly, the Soviet High Command announced today.

The Russian communiqué, bearing out earlier front reports that the Red Army was taking the initiative in the Caucasus, also said that Russian troops had advanced in some sectors of the Mozdok area and had counter-attacked successfully southeast of Novorossiisk, in the Black Sea coastal region.

In its report on Stalingrad, the Soviet bulletin said that a regiment of German troops, led by

Continued on Page Three

War News Summarized

TUESDAY, OCTOBER 13, 1942

The United States Navy disclosed the loss of three heavy cruisers on Aug. 9 in the opening phase of the battle for the Southern Solomons. All three were sunk by the fire of Japanese war vessels during a night engagement in which the enemy was forced to withdraw without attacking United States transports landing troops and equipment. The previously announced sinking of the Australian cruiser Canberra occurred in the same battle. Japanese losses in the engagement were not known. [1:4.]

From Russia came the news that the Germans had resumed heavy fighting inside Stalingrad and that one regiment had gained slightly in one block with the aid of fifty tanks. In the Caucasus the Russians advanced in a number of sectors, according to Moscow. The Germans also claimed gains in the Caucasus. [1:7; map, P. 3.]

Malta announced that the Axis air forces had resumed heavy raiding and had suffered the loss of at least thirty-seven planes without accomplishing much in the way of damage. It was noted that such heavy assaults on Malta had generally accompanied the movement of important Axis convoys toward Africa. United Nations bombers were reported to have scored hits on two freighters, a destroyer and a schooner in the Eastern Mediterranean. [3:1.]

Prime Minister Churchill, speaking in Edinburgh, said that the last two months had shown less relative loss than any since January in the battle of the Atlantic and stressed the series of effective raids on Germany recently. [1:5.]

In Washington it was explained that Under-Secretary of State Sumner Welles's Boston speech on Axis activity in Argentina and Chile was meant to show that Chilean President Rios's contemplated visit to the United States did not involve United States acceptance of the Chilean policy of neutrality. [1:6-7.]

At the Columbus Day celebration in New York commemorating the four hundred and fiftieth anniversary of the discovery of America Attorney General Biddle announced that the 600,000 Italian citizens living in the United States would no longer be regarded as enemy aliens or treated as such. [1:3.]

From Washington President Roosevelt broadcast a recommendation that 18 and 19-year-old youths be drafted for military service and indicated that a general labor draft might become necessary to keep up production. [1:8.]

Wendell Willkie, returning from his world tour of United Nations battle fronts, reached Canada by plane via Siberia from Chungking. [1:6-7.]

Willkie in Canada, Starting East; Explains Second Front Stand

By The Associated Press.

EDMONTON, Alberta, Oct. 12—Wendell Willkie, arriving here tonight from Fairbanks, Alaska, on his globe-girdling flight, said he thought it inappropriate while abroad to reply to "flippant statements made by certain public officials concerning the expression of my opinion in Russia on the question of a second front."

Mr. Willkie arrived here about 7:30 P. M., mountain daylight time, and will leave by plane tomorrow morning for Minneapolis.

In a prepared statement he said:

"The last lap of the flight around the world, from China through the republic of Mongolia, Siberia and Alaska, was among the most fascinating experiences of the whole trip. All members of the party and the crew performed marvelously in this undertaking, which involved flying over some wide areas never before traveled by civilians and by few, if any, military air men.

"Some several months ago I decided I could be helpful to the war effort if I visited various fighting fronts, some of our Allied countries and some of the countries in the Middle East which have not yet decided officially on their course of action in this war.

"My objectives were several—to give encouragement to our Allies, to give an impetus to action by the undecided countries and to report to the American people on the facts I found and the conclusions I reached.

"I asked the President for the necessary consent now required to travel abroad. After we had discussed the subject on several occasions he said it would be satisfactory for me to go, provided in addition I did some specific jobs

Continued on Page Six

MAY DRAFT LABOR

President in Radio Talk Warns That Legislation May Be Necessary

SHIPS OUTPACE FOE

He Found People in High State of Morale on His War Plants Tour

The text of the President's address is on Page 5.

By W. H. LAWRENCE

Special to THE NEW YORK TIMES.

WASHINGTON, Oct. 12—President Roosevelt recommended tonight the drafting of 18 and 19 year old youths for military service as an essential measure to speed victory, and indicated that it may become necessary to draft labor for mine, mill, factory and farm to meet the country's huge war production commitments.

In a confident 30-minute multi-topic speech to the nation and the world by radio, the President renewed his pledge of offensive action by the United States to relieve the pressure on Russia and China, but, of course, refrained from giving any indication as to when, where and how these new fronts would be opened.

We are getting ahead of our enemies in "the bitter battle of transportation," and in "the battle of production," he declared. The United Nations are going to win the war "and do not let any one tell you anything diffe:ent." The Axis leaders, Mr. Roosevelt continued, know their defeat is inevitable.

Tells of His War Plant Tour

Reporting on his recent two-week tour of war production and armed forces' establishments from coast to coast, the President praised the spirit of the people, rebuked the critics of the censorship he ordered and of the limited press coverage permitted, and announced that he would make other trips for similar purposes in the same way.

He had a good word for Congress, declaring that its "prompt and effective" action against inflation "was a splendid example of the operation of democratic processes in wartime."

He was scornful of the "typewriter strategists" for newspapers and radio stations who furnish military commentaries. Their trouble, he said, is that, "while they may be full of bright ideas, they are not in the possession of much information about the facts or problems of military operations."

Faith was affirmed in the war planning by the military leadership. The President mentioned Admiral William D. Leahy, his own Chief of Staff; General George C. Marshall, Army Chief of Staff; Admiral Ernest J. King, Chief of Naval Operations and Commander in Chief of the United States Fleet, and Lieut. Gen. H. H. Arnold, Chief of the Army Air Forces.

These officers, he said, have con-

Continued on Page Five

U. S. Discloses Bases In Fijis and Hebrides

Special to THE NEW YORK TIMES.

WASHINGTON, Oct. 12—The existence of American bases in the New Hebrides and the Fiji Islands became officially known tonight with mention of these island groups in a Navy communiqué on the sinking of the cruisers Quincy, Vincennes and Astoria near Guadalcanal Island on Aug. 9.

There was no information about the size or type of these bases, but the communiqué named them as among the points that would have been threatened by the enemy if development of Japanese bases on the Solomons had not been checked.

1917 Shell Casing To Go to War Again

The casing of the first shell fired into Germany by United States forces in the last war is going back at Hitler's legions. Max Weinstein, president of Russeks Fifth Avenue, said yesterday that it would be turned into Manhattan's scrap drive on Thursday. In the last war he obtained it from Arthur Guy Empey, Canadian author of "Over the Top," by buying a $50,000 Liberty Bond. It has been on his desk since. Mr. Weinstein is also going to throw into the heap a pair of bronze doors designed by Stanford White, originally valued at $5,000.

In the Hunter College contribution, two tons in all, to be given today to Borough President Edgar J. Nathan Jr., will be two stoves from the homes of President Roosevelt and his mother, Sara Delano Roosevelt, at 47 and 49 East Sixty-fifth Street. The houses have been bought for the college for extra-curricular activities and named the Sara Delano Roosevelt Memorial House.

Chicago Court Backs Petrillo; Dismisses U. S. Injunction Suit

Special to THE NEW YORK TIMES.

CHICAGO, Oct. 12—The government lost its anti-trust suit against James C. Petrillo and his American Federation of Musicians today when Judge John P. Barnes of the Federal District Court dismissed the Department of Justice petition for an injunction to end the union's ban on the recording of music for radio, juke boxes, and other public reproductions. Judge Barnes held that the dispute was essentially a labor dispute and did not come under the anti-trust laws.

Immediately afterward Mr. Petrillo, in triumphant vein, announced that his ban on canned music "still stands."

Thurman Arnold, head of the anti-trust division of the Department of Justice, who had come to Chicago from Washington to argue for the injunction, said merely, "The government will appeal the case."

The suit was based on Mr. Petrillo's order, effective Aug. 1, barring union musicians from making "canned music" not for home use.

In the nation-wide controversy which followed, union spokesmen argued that their action was a case of self-preservation, that the "canned music" which musicians made actually tended to destroy their own livelihood as live musicians.

Against this, radio spokesmen and others, including the government, contended that the ban had the earmarks of a monopoly, and threatened to put many small radio stations and other businesses out of existence. These points were argued today in the hearing before Judge Barnes.

Last week both the government and Joseph Padway, attorney for

Continued on Page Seventeen

"All the News That's Fit to Print."

The New York Times.

LATE CITY EDITION
Warm today.
Temperatures Yesterday—Max., 65; Min., 49
Sunrise, 7:13 A. M.; Sunset, 6:08 P. M.

Copyright, 1942, by The New York Times Company.

VOL. XCII..No. 30,951. Entered as Second-Class Matter, Postoffice, New York, N. Y. NEW YORK, WEDNESDAY, OCTOBER 21, 1942. THREE CENTS IN NEW YORK CITY

9 BILLION TAX BILL VOTED IN CONGRESS; NEW LEVIES LIKELY

PRESIDENT TO SIGN

Action Today Will Put Excise Rate Rise Into Effect on Nov. 1

LARGEST TAX IN HISTORY

Addition to Current Revenue Will Take Net of 25 Billions Out of National Income

By The Associated Press.

WASHINGTON, Oct. 20—Congress sent its largest tax bill in history to the White House today and President Roosevelt said he would sign it tomorrow to make higher excise levies on a long list of items effective Nov. 1.

Unprecedented individual income taxes will be levied on this year's incomes. Payroll deductions will start Jan. 1 for collecting the 5 per cent Victory tax levied on next year's incomes. The latter is in addition to the individual income tax.

Geared to produce new revenue estimated at $6,881,000,000 net by the Treasury and $7,900,000,000 by Congressional committees, the new bill would increase collections of direct taxes close to $25,000,000,000 yearly. In addition, about $1,750,000,000 would be taken from taxpayers and returned to them in the form of current credits for debt payments or in post-war rebate. Nevertheless, the measure went to the White House labeled "inadequate" by the Treasury.

Secretary Morgenthau recently called for another tax bill to yield an additional $6,000,000,000. Congress leaders were uncertain when a start would be made on the new bill but it was generally thought that action would be deferred until after Jan. 1.

Two Dissenters in House

The present bill, molded to compromise form by conferees of the House and Senate, received its final Congressional approval today in short order. The House discussed the measure briefly and approved it by a standing vote of 130 to 2. The two dissenters were Representatives Hinshaw, Republican, of California, and Robsion, Republican, of Kentucky. Mr. Hinshaw disliked the Victory tax and Mr. Robsion thought several items could have been improved.

The Senate talked the measure over for an hour, heard some sharp criticism of the 3 per cent tax on freight bills and then approved the bill by a voice vote which sounded unanimous.

The measure raises income tax rates to their highest level yet. The normal individual income tax rate is increased from 4 to 6 per cent. To that is added a graduated surtax starting at 13 per cent and increasing to 82. At present the surtax ranges from 6 to 77 per cent. Personal exemptions have been lowered.

The result is that the taxpayer will pay 19 per cent on his first dollar of taxable income, with the total percentage to be paid rising sharply as income increases.

Under the Victory tax's terms all individuals will be taxed a flat 5 per cent of income in excess of

Continued on Page Ten

Save Middle Class, Congress Is Urged

By The Associated Press.

WASHINGTON, Oct. 20—Representative Andresen of Minnesota told the House today that America's "middle class, backbone of the nation," was threatened with liquidation by current and impending taxes, and suggested that Congress "do something about it."

Speaking of millions of Americans with fixed incomes, Mr. Andresen said:

"These men and women are needlessly being put out of business and profession, and something must be done before it is too late. When the middle class is liquidated, American democracy is destroyed."

Mr. Andresen said that Department of Commerce authorities had predicted that more than 300,000 independent merchants and small manufacturers would be out of business by next July as a result of wartime conditions.

MEATLESS TUESDAY GOES WELL IN CITY

Eating Places Offer a Wide Choice of Substitutes and Report No Complaints

With the innovation of "meatless Tuesdays" yesterday, hotel and restaurant patrons began changing their eating habits for the duration to conserve red meats for the armed forces and for lend-lease.

Customers of all types of eating establishments accepted the new and substitute dishes offered on meatless Tuesday with patriotic good grace. Managements of hotels and restaurants were unanimous in reporting that they heard no complaints and that their clientele contented themselves with "ordering what's on the menu."

When Mayor La Guardia requested restaurants to serve no beef, lamb, pork or veal on Tuesday, he placed no prohibition on poultry, liver, kidney, hearts, sweetbreads, tripe and fish. No lid was clamped on eating places specializing in hamburgers and frankfurters, but the Mayor had urged that sales of those items on Tuesday be discouraged. Nedick's, specializing in fruit drinks, hot dogs and hamburgers, displayed a sign at its stands reading:

"Sorry. No hamburgers. Tuesday, you know. Thank you."

The standard breakfast dish of ham and eggs or bacon and eggs vanished from Tuesday menus.

The Automat chain of restaurants displayed a sign that read:

"Tuesday only. In cooperation with the Mayor's request to restaurants, meat is omitted from the menu."

Fish cake and poached egg was

Continued on Page Seventeen

HOUSE GROUP URGES SINGLE WAR AGENCY FOR ALL-OUT EFFORT

Tolan Report Scores Present Policy as 'Drift,' in Guiding Men and Materials Uses

ORDERS CALLED CONFUSED

Draft, WPB, Military and Lend-Lease Procurement Would Be Under the One Direction

By LOUIS STARK
Special to THE NEW YORK TIMES.

WASHINGTON, Oct. 20—Declaring that current proposals for compulsory service in war production are merely "tinkering with the program for mobilizing America's economic resources," the House committee investigating national defense migration, of which Representative John H. Tolan of California is chairman, proposed today the statutory creation of an Office of War Mobilization as supreme authority for directing the war economy, military and civil.

In a twenty-four page report, which is highly critical of the War Production Board, the War Manpower Commission, the Selective Service System, the committee maintained that "despite numerous realignments, ten months after Pearl Harbor, business as usual considerations still permeate the Washington war production agencies."

"War production is treated as a salesman's proposition, rather than as the mobilization of our entire national plant for total war," the report stated.

"Contract-letting still is the responsibility of the military services that continue to confuse assigning of contracts with productive activity itself. The armed services are also nominally responsible for the scheduling of production, while raw materials, whose proper distribution is so critical to maximizing production, are nominally under the War Production Board.

"The equally fundamental task of mobilizing manpower is nominally the responsibility of still other agencies. Even the organization charts show no provision for the coordinated use of the basic factors of production."

Absence of Program Is Scored

In assailing "the absence of a program of production and an organization to coordinate it," the report said that the nation merely has "a series of individual competing production projects."

"At virtually every point where coordination and planning should be exercised we find competition and manoeuvring," the report added. "There is competition among the major branches of the military services.

"There is competition between the military services and the industry branches of the WPB. There is endless jockeying between the individual industry branches.

"By default the individual prime contractors have been left with the responsibility for planning and scheduling production. Instead of an even flow of materials, manpower and other resources to these contractors and their subcontractors, according to a comprehensive production program, each contractor strives to complete his job ac-

Continued on Page Seventeen

PRESIDENT TELLS PLAN TO FURLOUGH OLDER ARMY MEN

He Says Soldiers 35 to 40 Might Better Serve Manpower Need in Munition Factories

TO CUT LUXURIES OUTPUT

Action on Full Mobilization Is Deferred Until McNutt Board Makes Its Report

By W. H. LAWRENCE
Special to THE NEW YORK TIMES.

WASHINGTON, Oct. 20—President Roosevelt indicated today that some older men would be furloughed from the Army to return to farm and factory jobs essential to the war effort as soon as younger men, especially the 18 to 19 year old youths, were available for induction into the military forces.

In a general and extended discussion of the manpower problem at his press conference, the President said that he was awaiting a report from a Labor-Management Advisory Committee before deciding what over-all legislation, if any, was necessary to mobilize the full power of the nation.

He made it clear, however, that the government already has decided to curtail more drastically the production of luxury goods in order to free workers for essential jobs. He indicated that officials are seriously considering a compulsory savings plan to drain off an estimated $5,000,000,000 in excess purchasing power.

As the Senate prepared to take up tomorrow the House-approved measure lowering the draft age from 20 to 18 years, the President was asked whether older men considered by military officials unsuitable for combat duty might not be deferred to relieve critical manpower shortages in factories, mills, mines and on farms.

Saw for Himself on Tour

The President replied that on his recent tour of the country he had seen men of 35 to 40 in Army camps who would have been much better off in munitions factories. They were too old to march twenty-five or thirty miles with full equipment, he said. He supposed that some of them would be furloughed, especially if they were fitted for some particular trade or occupation in which there was a manpower shortage.

Asked if the law might be changed to exempt older men from the draft, he replied that he thought they would continue to draft older men who were physically fit.

Mr. Roosevelt introduced the manpower problem into the press conference by remarking that he had received a number of letters and telegrams concerning the critical farm labor shortage, and especially raising the question of why much-needed laborers from Mexico were not being brought in to help in the harvest.

3,000 Mexicans Brought In

He said that he had asked the State Department for a report, and had been advised that on Aug. 4 an agreement was reached with the Mexican Government to bring in 3,000 agricultural workers. Several hundred already have been brought in, he said, and taken to California and Arizona.

The Mexicans, he continued, showed marked enthusiasm at the chance to help serve the democratic cause by saving crops vital to the United Nations, and several thousand others have signified a willingness to come.

With an eye to the "Good Neighbor" policy, the President observed that this was an eloquent demonstration of the important role our Mexican allies can and are taking in the war effort of the United Nations.

In the beet fields of Montana, he continued, some Japanese labor already has been brought from concentration camps. In response to a question about whether the Japanese would receive regular wages, he said that they would be paid but he did not know whether they would get regular wages.

Asked about his conference today with Paul V. McNutt, War Manpower Commission Chairman, he said that they had talked about the general situation, and that Mr. McNutt had advised him he expected to have by next week the report of the Labor-Management Advisory Committee.

A reporter asked the President what he thought of proposals to

Continued on Page Seventeen

U. S. FLIERS HAMMER JAPANESE TROOPS; LAND AND SEA BATTLES STILL DELAYED; RUSSIANS BEAT OFF STALINGRAD BLOWS

FOCUS OF ACTION IN STRUGGLE OF THE SOUTHWEST PACIFIC

On Guadalcanal—the center of the concentric circles on the map—Army, Navy and Marine planes bombed the Japanese over a two-day period, and at Rekata Bay, just to the north, Flying Fortresses set fires in a raid on Monday. Aside from these actions, the Allied and Japanese naval forces appeared to be jockeying for position. The circles provide a guide to the distances between Guadalcanal and the principal bases in this region, which are indicated by flags.

BOMBINGS KEPT UP

Army, Navy and Marine Planes Make Attacks on Guadalcanal

REKATA BAY ALSO RAIDED

Large Japanese Naval Force Is Still in Solomons—Knox Expects Foe to Strike

By CHARLES HURD
Special to THE NEW YORK TIMES.

WASHINGTON, Oct. 20—Army, Navy and Marine Corps planes bombed Japanese troop concentrations and supply dumps on Guadalcanal Island on Sunday and Monday (Solomon Islands time), the Navy announced this evening, but otherwise a lull seems to have settled over that tropical battle front.

In the Navy's communiqué, which said that the Japanese had made no further landings on Guadalcanal, there was only one other report of Solomons action. That was a report of a raid on Rekata Bay, carried out by Army Flying Fortresses on Monday. The raiders started fires.

The communiqué stated that large numbers of Japanese warships and auxiliary vessels still were in the Solomons area, and while the Navy necessarily gave no indication of the deployment of our own sea and air forces, the impression in informed circles here was that both sides might be jockeying for position in what might well be the decisive contest in the battle of the southwestern Pacific.

No Thrust by Japanese

The Japanese troops that landed on Guadalcanal last Thursday have made no offensive thrust against American positions on the island. At least, the Navy Department has received no report of such a thrust. Yet no one in authority here assumes for a minute that the contest has gone to a stalemate. Secretary Frank Knox himself emphasized this at a press conference this morning.

"It is still a good, stiff, hard fight," he told reporters, "and, as my own judgment, the Japs by no means have yet exercised their maximum force."

A compilation of reports received here—and Secretary Knox again emphasized that all news received from the Solomons area was being made public, unless it was directly helpful to the enemy—indicates that the Japanese naval forces probably are concentrated to the north and west of Guadalcanal, principally around New Georgia Island. Some units, but not large ones, have been reported occasionally near Savo Island, less than twenty-five miles north of Guadalcanal.

The region between New Georgia and Rabaul, on New Britain, a principal Japanese base, is one from which the enemy could steam overnight to the battle area of Guadalcanal. At the same time ships in that region are too far away for steady attacks by the American aircraft based on Guadalcanal and are quite a distance

Continued on Page Three

RED ARMY CRUSHES NAZI MASS ATTACKS

70 Tanks Fail to Penetrate New Lines as Losses Mount —Germans Claim a Block

By The Associated Press.

MOSCOW, Wednesday, Oct. 21—The Russians announced today that their Stalingrad garrison had repulsed two furious German attacks supported by seventy tanks inside the city yesterday and quoted Nazi captives as saying their divisions had lost 70 per cent of their effectives in the last few days.

[The Germans claimed another block of houses in northern Stalingrad and said the mopping up of the Red October factory area was proceeding. In Stockholm it is believed the Russians still hold about seven miles of the city's river bank, from the southern part of the Red October works to the middle of the Dzherzhinsky plant, a Reuter dispatch reported.]

The Soviet midnight communiqué told of the continuing successful Russian defense, now in its ninth week, after dispatches disclosed that the Red Army was

Continued on Page Nine

Laval Tells French Labor It Must Serve in Germany

By LANSING WARREN
By Telephone to THE NEW YORK TIMES.

VICHY, France, Oct. 20—In a radio broadcast addressed to French workers, whom he asked four months ago to volunteer for labor in Germany, Chief of Government Pierre Laval, France's unshakable guide toward collaboration with the Nazis, told them tonight that they must go to work in the plants of the Reich on government orders.

"You must obey," he said, "for yourselves, for the prisoners and for France." He added that the superior interests of the country would require an understanding with Germany.

[The hour for resistance has come, General Charles de Gaulle, Fighting French leader, told France by radio from London shortly after M. Laval's speech.]

Toward the end of the speech M. Laval told the workers to consider the alternative before them: Making a contract with material advantages or facing enforced labor in Germany.

One new point in M. Laval's address was the announcement that, "if a few more than 100,000 skilled workers agree to expatriate themselves, the wives of French prisoners will be permitted to go to Germany and work near the places

Continued on Page Four

DARNTON OF TIMES IS KILLED AT FRONT

Accident Victim in Operational Area in New Guinea— A Vivid Reporter

By The United Press.

AT UNITED NATIONS HEADQUARTERS, Australia, Wednesday, Oct. 21—Byron Darnton, a war correspondent of THE NEW YORK TIMES, was killed accidentally Sunday in an advanced operational area in New Guinea, it was announced today.

Born in Michigan in 1897

Byron Darnton was born in Adrian, Mich., on Nov. 8, 1897, the son of the late Robert Darnton and the late Lucy Creighton Darnton. He attended public school and high school in Adrian. While he was still a freshman in high school he came to New York to visit his uncle, Charles Darnton, who was then dramatic critic for The Evening World.

Under his uncle's kindly tutelage he saw the sights of New York and got his first glimpse of the inside of a newspaper office. In later years he often laughingly remarked to his friends that he had never got over the itch for news that he acquired then.

He had just finished high school when this country declared war on Germany in 1917. He enlisted at once in the Thirty-third Infantry, Michigan National Guard and was sent to Camp MacArthur at Waco, Texas, for training. In January, 1918, he sailed for France as a member of the Red Arrow Division.

Saw Much Hard Fighting

Between May and November, 1918, he saw plenty of hard fighting. His division was the first American outfit to set foot on German territory, in Alsace in May, 1918. He took part in the battles of the Oise, the Aisne, the Meuse-Argonne, and in the attack on the Kriemhilde-Stellung line. He rose from private to line sergeant and just before the armistice was selected for officers' training school.

The armistice put a stop to his training, but while he was on his way back to this country his commission as a second lieutenant caught up with him.

He entered the University of Michigan after his discharge from

Continued on Page Three

War News Summarized

WEDNESDAY, OCTOBER 21, 1942

United States planes based on Guadalcanal pounded Japanese concentrations Sunday and Monday, the Navy disclosed yesterday, but ground operations of any importance did not develop. Large numbers of Japanese warships and auxiliaries were still in the vicinity, however, and Secretary of the Navy Knox said that the affair was a good, hard fight and that the enemy had not yet employed his maximum force. [1:8.]

In another Pacific war theatre General MacArthur disclosed the accidental death of Byron Darnton, correspondent of THE NEW YORK TIMES, at the front in New Guinea. [1:7.]

Moscow reported that the Stalingrad garrison had repulsed two heavy German attacks supported by seventy tanks on a workers' settlement. German captives were quoted as saying their divisions had lost 70 per cent of their effectives in the last few days. The Russians claimed recapture of a community in the Mozdok region in the Caucasus. [1:5.]

British Mosquito bombers, flying singly, attacked enemy targets at Hanover, Wilhelmshaven and Bremen in low level daylight raids. The Air Ministry disclosed that American-built Mustang fighters had destroyed nineteen railway engines, seven tugs and numerous barges in last week's operations. [5:4.]

The First Lord of the Admiralty announced that 530 Axis submarines had been sunk or damaged in the war by the British and American Navies. The Admiralty also disclosed that two new 35,000-ton battleships, the Anson and the Howe, were now with the fleet, restoring British sea strength to the pre-war total of fifteen battleships and battle cruisers. [1:2-3.]

Pierre Laval, Vichy chief of government, broadcast to French workers a warning that they must be prepared to work in Germany either under voluntary contract or by compulsion. [1:6-7.]

From London General de Gaulle, chief of the Fighting French, broadcast to his countrymen a declaration urging resistance to the labor draft. [4:3.]

London heard that an Italian Alpini regiment at Gorizia in Northern Italy had mutinied on being ordered to Russia. It was also reported that Albanian mountaineers had proclaimed an independent Albania and were fighting on several fronts. [5:1.]

In Latin America the Chilean Cabinet resigned as the result of a political crisis precipitated by Sumner Welles's statement that Chile and Argentina were permitting Axis spies to report movements of Allied shipping. [6:1.]

530 U-Boats Bagged, Briton Says; Two Battleships Join Royal Navy

By DREW MIDDLETON
Special Cable to THE NEW YORK TIMES.

LONDON, Oct. 20—More than 530 German, Italian and Japanese submarines have been sunk or damaged by the British and United States Navies in the long, bitter battle to maintain the United Nations' sea-borne communications in the face of enemy attacks "enormously increased" over those of World War I, A. V. Alexander, First Lord of the Admiralty, revealed today.

Soon after his declaration in a speech at Caxton Hall that the opening of a second front depended as much on control of the sea as of the air, the Admiralty announced that two important instruments for maintenance of that control had joined the fleet. They are the battleships Anson and Howe, 35,000-ton giants mounting ten 14-inch guns to hurl tons of explosive against German fortifications in support of Allied landings on the Continent.

With the submarine menace checked, if not wholly defeated, Mr. Alexander indicated, the United Nations appear to be moving from the phase of greatest danger for their control of the seas toward one in which their navies are gathering strength to shield and sustain the largest amphibious operation of the war.

His impressive tally of Axis losses, which averages three U-boats sunk or damaged each week, did not appear to include those sunk or damaged by the Royal Air Force's Coastal Command and its American counterpart. The British force, operating since the first days of the war, has greatly increased in number, range and striking power in the past six months. Axis submarines operating from French ports in the Bay of

Continued on Page Seven

Willkie's Broadcast Is Set for Monday

Wendell L. Willkie, who recently returned from a round-the-world tour of fighting fronts in Europe and Asia, will broadcast his report to the American people over the major networks in a half-hour talk on Monday from 10:30 to 11 P. M., according to an announcement yesterday.

Mr. Willkie conferred with President Roosevelt last week on the impressions he received during his tour and has since been working on a speech to the American public. During his visit to Russia, in which he conferred with Premier Stalin, he was outspoken in urging the opening of a second front to relieve the Soviet armies.

MacArthur Praises Darnton's Devotion

By Wireless to the Editor of THE NEW YORK TIMES.

SOMEWHERE IN AUSTRALIA, Wednesday, Oct. 21—It is my painful duty to inform you of the accidental death in New Guinea of Byron Darnton.

He served with gallantry and devotion at the front and fulfilled the important duties of war correspondent with distinction to himself and THE NEW YORK TIMES and with value to his country.

I had but recently conferred with him at Port Moresby and had been gratified by his comprehensive grasp of the battle situation.

I deeply regret his death. Please inform his family and convey to them my sincerest sympathy.

MACARTHUR.

"All the News That's Fit to Print."

The New York Times.

LATE CITY EDITION
Cooler today.
Temperatures Yesterday—Max., 74; Min., 60
Sunrise, 7:15 A. M.; Sunset, 6:05 P. M.

VOL. XCII. No. 30,953. Entered as Second-Class Matter, Postoffice, New York, N. Y. NEW YORK, FRIDAY, OCTOBER 23, 1942. THREE CENTS IN NEW YORK CITY

AMERICANS REPEL JAPANESE TEST PUSH, BOMB FOE'S POSITIONS ON GUADALCANAL; RUSSIANS RIP INTO TWO GERMAN FLANKS

SENATE BY 49 TO 25 SHUNTS DRY RIDER OUT OF 18-19 DRAFT

Lee Amendment Is Sent Back to Committee to Cool Until After the Elections

ADVOCATES SEE DEFEAT

Chavez Chides Chamber on Not Facing Issue Now—Knox Opposes the Proposal

By C. P. TRUSSELL
Special to THE NEW YORK TIMES.

WASHINGTON, Oct. 22—The Senate, by a vote of 49 to 25, today shunted the hotly contested "prohibition" amendment out of the bill proposing to lower the draft age to 18 years, and sent it to its military committee for hearings and recommendations which are expected to come, if at all, long after election on Nov. 3.

Advocates of the amendment regarded the Senate's stand as a definite defeat. The amendment, which would prohibit the sale of all alcoholic beverages, including wines and beer, in communities adjacent to military or naval posts, was suspected widely of being a first step toward country-wide prohibition.

The Senate's method of disposing of the issue without indefinite postponement of final action on the draft measure was adopted eagerly upon the motion of Senator Barkley, the majority leader. The Senate was chided by Senator Chavez of New Mexico, however, for acting as if it feared to "face the music."

Though individual Senators had asserted frankly that the best "political" vote on the dry amendment, which was sponsored by Senator Lee of Oklahoma, was "aye," spirited and at times bitter debate indicated that open opposition to it was stronger than calculations had indicated.

Say Law Would Dry Up Cities

While Senator Lee contended that his amendment proposed to do no more than was written into the first World War Draft Act of 1917, opponents insisted that its effect would be so sweeping as to dry up not only communities adjoining military reservations, but large metropolitan areas as well.

Army forces, they recalled, had moved into some of the largest hotels in cities such as Chicago, had taken over beach resorts, and had been so deployed, in fact, that posts had been established in many cities around utilities installations, public institutions and at other points. The drying up of adjacent areas, it was held, would bring prohibition back on a large scale.

If such steps were required for protection of the armed forces, it was suggested, the War Department has power to declare objectionable areas "out of bounds," an authority which may even prescribe specific establishments which service men may not enter.

Before the side-tracking vote was taken, the formal opposition of the War and Navy Departments to the amendment were read to the Senate.

Supplementing yesterday's communication from Secretary Stimson were two more, one from Secretary Knox of the Navy Department and the other from Robert Patterson, Under-Secretary of War. Both agreed with Secretary Stimson that the amendment if adopted would be destructive rather than constructive to service morale and would disrupt the present program for enforcing temperance which, they emphasized, had proved effective.

Way Is Cleared for Draft Bill

The principal question of lowering the draft age to include youths of 18 and 19 held Senate attention through the earlier part of the day until Senator Lee pressed for consideration of his amendment. The rest of the session was concentrated upon that.

Now, with the road cleared for consideration of the draft itself, predictions were made that the bill could be passed by the upper house before the end of this week.

Senator Gurney of South Dakota, author of the draft bill, told the Senate that speed was essential.

"Our enemies' best divisions are made up of younger men," he said, "they are the elite troops, and the Panzer divisions, if you please. To

Continued on Page Eleven

First Daytime Air Raid Drill Ties Up City for 24 Minutes

Mayor Says the Results Are Splendid in Some Respects, but He Is 'Not Satisfied'—Especially Chides Idle Onlookers

For twenty-four minutes yesterday afternoon, from 2:30 to 2:54 P. M., New York City's normal pursuits were almost completely suspended by the first daytime air raid drill since the war began. It was ordered by Major Gen. William N. Haskell, State director of Civilian Protection, with the approval of the Army.

"The drill was a purely civilian defense function and its purpose was to test the reaction of the New York City population to a real surprise alert," said a statement issued through the headquarters of the Eastern Defense Command in behalf of the Second Service Command, which is under the command of Major Gen. Thomas A. Terry.

Mayor La Guardia, who took personal charge of mobilizing the city's protective and emergency services, said that while the drill showed splendid results in many respects, he was "not satisfied" with it on the whole. He was especially critical of the number of pedestrians who remained on the streets and the number of persons in buildings who rushed to the windows.

"Whether it is a drill or a bombing, people must get away from windows," the Mayor told reporters after the all-clear had sounded. "We will have enough to do to handle injuries and bombs without having a lot of unnecessary casualties. This is no child's play. It is a very serious business. We do not have to wait until bombs drop to realize that."

He was so irked at the number of pedestrians he saw on the streets while he was speeding to an "incident" at Astor Place and Fourth Avenue that he called Police Headquarters by radio telephone from his car and had an order broadcast to all cruising radio patrol cars to have the police assist air raid wardens in clearing the streets.

Eight persons were arrested throughout the city during the

Continued on Page Thirteen

OLD TROLLEY RAILS IN NASSAU SEIZED

Government Takes Possession of Abandoned Trackage in Seven Communities

The Federal Government, invoking the requisitioning powers granted the President by Congress last year, has taken possession of seven parcels of abandoned street car trackage in Nassau County to speed another 500 tons of steel to the mills, it was announced yesterday by the special projects section of the War Production Board. The rails are in Glen Cove, Roslyn, Freeport, Hempstead, Floral Park, Lynbrook and Elmont.

The move, which gives the government immediate access to the materials, with compensation to the owners to be decided later, is understood to presage similar action in New York City. The War Production Board, having completed its surveys of many such projects, is reported ready now to seize heavy scrap metal wherever technicalities or other obstacles might protract negotiations in advance of acquisition.

It was explained at the regional WPB office here that the requisitioning powers were invoked in the Nassau street rails case not because of any unwillingness by the owners but as a result of technical complications as to ownership. Without a clear, warrantable title, the firm of H. E. Salzberg, Inc., which had bought the rails several years ago from traction companies which have since dissolved, was unable to make the rails available to the government, except through court action, WPB officials said.

Title to the rails has been vested in the Metals Reserve Company, a subsidiary of the Reconstruction Finance Corporation. Metals Reserve, through another RFC subsidiary, War Materials, Inc., will now advertise for bids for removal of the rails. In its announcement

Continued on Page Thirteen

2 BOARDS TO PASS ON NEW BUILDINGS

Federal, State, City, Private Construction Made Subject to Double Review

Special to THE NEW YORK TIMES.

WASHINGTON, Oct. 22—Formation of two boards of review, which will pass on construction projects whether military or civilian, was reported today by the War Production Board to administer the construction order which it issued yesterday curbing construction by governmental projects and to handle the combined work of five governmental agencies which have been passing upon construction.

Ferdinand Eberstadt, WPB vice chairman in charge of program determination and materials allocation, has been made chairman of the Facility Clearance Board, which will pass on all new projects, military or civilian, whether publicly or privately financed, and which cost $500,000 or more.

A second committee, which will report to Mr. Eberstadt, was set up under Colonel Gordon E. Textor, an Army engineer associated with WPB. It will pass judgment on new projects costing $100,000 to $500,000. In addition, the agency, which is to be known as the Facility Review Committee, will review all projects under way or approved, regardless of cost.

The two committees will take over the work formerly done by the Plant Site Board and of the Facility Committee of the Requirements Committee, both of WPB; the Facilities Clearance Committee of the Army and Navy Munitions Board, the Special Committee of Facilities of the War Department and the Facilities Cutback Committee of WPB.

At his press conference this morning Donald M. Nelson, WPB chairman, made it clear that the new committees will have authority over State and municipal con-

Continued on Page Seventeen

Annapolis Gets Army-Navy Game; Outsiders Barred to Reduce Travel

Special to THE NEW YORK TIMES.

WASHINGTON, Oct. 22—This year's Army-Navy football game will be played at Annapolis and tickets to it will be available only to residents of that city, the White House announced tonight.

President Roosevelt, the announcement said, has given general approval to plans for playing the game at the capital of Maryland.

Mr. Roosevelt has also given explicit instructions, through Secretaries Knox and Stimson, to the officials of the West Point and Annapolis academies whose duty it will be to work out arrangements for the game.

These directions were given:

"Since no railroad facilities afford means of transportation to Annapolis on regularly operated lines and since there is compelling need to save gasoline and rubber, tickets will be issued only to residents of Annapolis—not to outsiders.

"That only members of the Army team and such other officials whose presence is needed for the actual playing of the game will go from West Point to Annapolis.

"That every precaution be taken to prevent persons living outside of Annapolis—in Washington or Baltimore or other near-by places—from securing tickets of admission to the game."

The White House announcement said that it was the President's opinion that the exigencies of the war with their needs for economy and sacrifice could be served "only by the imposition this year of these unusual limitations."

"The fact that the game was scheduled before war was declared and its cancellation at this late date undoubtedly would cause great disappointment throughout the armed forces, in and out of the United States, was discussed at

Continued on Page Twelve

NEW CEILINGS PUT ON WHEAT AND PORK TO CURB PRICE RISE

OPA and Wickard Disclose Plan Designed Also to Get More Equitable Distribution

'LOAN' GRAIN TO MILLERS

Dollars-and-Cents Values Are Set for 90 Cuts of Pork at Wholesale in 3 Zones

Special to THE NEW YORK TIMES.

WASHINGTON, Oct. 22—New moves to keep down the prices of bread, flour and pork to the consumer have been made by the Office of Price Administration and the Department of Agriculture.

Leon Henderson, Price Administrator, balked by Congress of his desire to use subsidies to maintain food ceiling prices, has found a way with the Agricultural Department's assistance to grant an indirect subsidy to wheat producers which will bring cheap wheat on the market.

Mr. Henderson announced a program today to make wheat available to flour millers at prices approximating the levels which prevailed from Sept. 28 to Oct. 2. This is to be achieved by the release of government-loan wheat back to farmers by the Commodity Credit Corporation for sale in the market.

The release price for the wheat will be less than the government's loan per bushel, plus accumulated carrying charges, by an amount sufficient to enable the farmer to sell the wheat again at prices in line with the ceiling prices on flour. The farmer's selling price will be at a level which will enable millers to buy wheat and produce and sell flour under OPA's ceiling for flour and bread.

Millers Saved From "Squeeze"

This will remove any danger of flour millers being "squeezed" between advancing wheat prices and a flour ceiling or of a similar squeeze developing between flour and bread.

The Commodity Credit Corporation, which lends farmers 85 per cent of the parity price for their wheat, will announce the release prices of loan wheat at such time as its marketing becomes necessary to achieve the purposes of the program. Secretary Wickard emphasized today that farmers cooperating in the farm programs of the department received in any case full parity for their wheat as a result of the Commodity Credit Corporation's loans and the payments made to bring total returns up to parity by the Agricultural Adjustment Agency.

As an example of how its program would operate OPA offered a

Continued on Page Seventeen

NAZI LINES DENTED

Red Army Hacks Gaps in Ring Above and Below Stalingrad

WINTRY WEATHER SPREADS

Nazi Attacks in City Costly—Berlin Reports Slow Gains Against Stiff Defense

By The United Press.

MOSCOW, Friday, Oct. 23—Russian troops tore into the German flanks above and below Stalingrad yesterday, capturing two lines of trenches to the northwest and wiping out a Nazi unit to the south, while twelve tanks were destroyed and a battalion [1,000 men] of shock troops annihilated inside the city, the High Command reported today.

"In the Stalingrad area our troops engaged in repelling attacks of enemy infantry and tanks," the midnight communiqué said. It followed dispatches that reported Winter settling heavily over the Volga and Caucasus fronts, with snow, rain and blizzards impeding operations.

The Red Army was reported hacking gaps in the German lines on both sides of Stalingrad, while in the Volga city weakening Nazi attacks were warded off for the fourth straight day.

Unit Wiped Out in South

The High Command, in one of its rare reports on fighting south of Stalingrad, said a Red Army detachment wiped out more than a company of German infantry and destroyed five guns and twenty mortars.

[The German communiqué reported the capture of "stubbornly defended pillboxes and barricades" in Stalingrad, and for the second successive day mentioned strong Soviet flank attacks northwest of the city, claiming they were repelled from the air. Continued progress in the Western Caucasus, despite torrential rain, also was reported.]

Marshal Semyon Timoshenko's reinforced relief drive toward Stalingrad from the northwest appeared to be gathering momentum steadily. The Soviet communiqué

Continued on Page Six

War News Summarized

FRIDAY, OCTOBER 23, 1942

United States forces have thrown back the first reported ground attack against their positions on Guadalcanal Island since the Japanese poured troops ashore under a shield of bombs and shells, the Navy announced yesterday. The enemy assault, a "minor" thrust against the defenders' western flank on Tuesday, was apparently intended only to test the American lines. The Navy communiqué on action in the Solomons reported also that American airmen were maintaining their raids on Japanese troop and supply concentrations on the island. [1:8.]

Northwest of Guadalcanal, at the scene of a reported enemy naval concentration, bombers under General MacArthur's command loosed ten tons on Japanese shipping in a raid on Buin, near Shortland Island. [4:7.]

A military observer, after a 14,000-mile tour of the Pacific war front, found that American forces in that theatre, although finally on the offensive with the aid of qualitative air superiority, were handicapped by inexperienced leadership and service rivalries. [1:6-7.]

Japan's claim to have captured four American fliers who bombed Tokyo received credence from Secretary of War Stimson, who said that some of the crews taking part in that raid might have been forced down in Japanese-controlled China. [5:1.]

Shackling of German prisoners of war in Canada in retaliation for Nazi measures was revealed to have resulted in violence at one Ontario camp, where guards and resisting prisoners suffered injuries. [1:6-7.]

Russia's Stalingrad front, lashed by snow and rain, saw the Soviet defenders wresting two lines of trenches from the Germans above the city. South of it the Russians wiped out a Nazi company, while within its battered streets they killed 1,000 more invaders in repulsing attacks. The Germans penetrated Soviet forward positions around Mozdok at a cost of another 1,000 killed. [1:5.]

Bombers from Britain struck over Northern Italy last night in the first such raid since April. In daylight the Royal Air Force sent single-flying bombers over the Ruhr and other industrial parts of Germany and its fighters hit Nazi rail and other targets in North France. American Flying Fortresses were revealed to have downed nine Nazi fighters over Lorient on Wednesday. [3:2.]

Refusal of French workers to report for departure to German war factories led the Nazi authorities in Paris to warn that occupying troops would resort to force against future offenders. [1:7.]

Admiral Darlan, chief of Vichy's armed forces, reached Dakar to inspect land, sea and air units that Swiss reports said had been recently reinforced. He broadcast a message from Marshal Pétain warning that "new threats" faced the West African base and likening its situation to that of Madagascar before the British invasion. [1:6-7.]

Japan's Hold on West Pacific Not Broken in Almost a Year

Times Writer After Tour Notes First U. S. Offensive Step in Solomons, but Finds Costly Errors—Weighs Two Sides

Following is the first of a series of articles by the military editor of THE NEW YORK TIMES, who has just returned from a Pacific tour.

By HANSON W. BALDWIN

Japanese domination of most of the Western Pacific and much of Eastern Asia has not yet been seriously challenged in almost a year of war.

But the United States, aided by a clear-cut qualitative air superiority, has assumed the offensive. And if we can hold our Solomons foothold, we shall have taken the first small step in a campaign that may some day lead to the gates of Tokyo.

The struggle in the Pacific, as viewed by this correspondent during the course of a 14,600-mile flight over the Pacific from San Francisco to Hawaii to the Solomons and return, is a bitter, relentless "no-quarter" war that cannot be won quickly or easily. In the opinion of most of the men who are fighting this war the Japanese are more dangerous foes than the Germans, and they consider Japan, rather than Germany, the primary adversary. Others, with a broader global view of the world conflict, agree with the prevailing strategic concept that our main effort must first be directed against Hitler-dominated Europe, but emphasize that the Pacific cannot safely be considered a secondary, or minor, "front."

Most of our leaders and observers in the Pacific believe that the European and Pacific wars are, in a military sense two separate wars that coincide strategically only at those points and in those areas where Japanese and German ambitions and self-interest happen to coincide. In other words, Japan will conduct operations and make moves that will help Germany only

Continued on Page Four

Darlan, at Dakar, Summons Base to Meet 'New Threats'

By LANSING WARREN
By Telephone to THE NEW YORK TIMES.

VICHY, France, Oct. 22—Admiral François Darlan, Commander in Chief of the French armed forces, has flown to Dakar from Vichy, it became known today when he broadcast to the West African colony a message from Marshal Henri Philippe Pétain, Chief of State, telling it to resist any attack as it did that of the British and de Gaullists in September, 1940. Marshal Pétain's message spoke of threats to Dakar, which, he said, were "without the shadow of a pretext."

Newspapers in both zones of France have been devoting much attention to empire defense. The Paris press, particularly, has been talking much of British menaces and of the concentrations of British and American troops in colonies near French West Africa.

In his broadcast to French workers on Tuesday, Chief of Government Pierre Laval went out of his way to mention the fact that he was thinking much about the empire and announced that he would shortly make a special talk on that subject.

M. Darlan's visit to Dakar was decided upon after the government had denied charges that Dakar had been used to aid Axis submarines. An Admiralty statement said that France could not deny all the rumors and misrepresentations that found credit abroad, but, in the presence of the widespread false reports of the past few days, it declared that no French ship

Continued on Page Eight

FRENCH LABOR GETS A THREAT OF FORCE

Nazis Warn Those Who Fail to Report in Occupied Zone for Work in the Reich

By Telephone to THE NEW YORK TIMES.

VICHY, France, Oct. 22—German officials in Paris tonight issued a warning to French workers that, unless they reported for departure to Germany at the hour assigned, the occupation authorities would be obliged to take measures of force.

The notice was issued by General Otto von Stuelpnagel, Nazi Commander for Greater Paris, after it was learned that a number of workers ordered to report at the Gare de l'Est yesterday and today had failed to appear.

Under the present system French workers designated for service in the Reich receive instructions from the Laval govern-

Continued on Page Eight

War Prisoners in Canada Fought Shackling, Several Hurt in Riot

By The Associated Press.

OTTAWA, Oct. 22—Defense Minister James L. Ralston announced tonight that prisoners of war in Canada forcibly resisted shackling on Oct. 10, and that prisoners and guards received injuries, most of them of a minor character.

The government issued the following statement:

"The Minister of National Defense tonight stated that when prisoners of war at Bowmanville, Ont., forcibly resisted shackling on Saturday, Oct. 10, both prisoners of war and guards received injuries, the majority of a minor character.

"Refusing to obey orders, prisoners of war barricaded themselves in their barracks. It was necessary to fire four warning shots by rifle, three in the air and one toward the ground which ricocheted and wounded one of the prisoners in the leg. This took place at a time when the prisoners seized and brutally assaulted an officer of the guard. Two other prisoners received light bayonet wounds. There were no fatalities.

"At another point a hole was chopped through the roof and a fire hose was used to help quell the disorder. Considerable furniture was smashed and windows were broken.

"No machine-gun fire was used nor was there tear gas or any other form of gas resorted to throughout the trouble. Food was prepared and served to the prisoners, some of whom went on a hunger strike which lasted for two days. The shackling at Bowmanville prisoners of war camp was proceeded with. Normal prisoner of war camp life was resumed after the guard was reinforced by detachments from a near-by military camp. All has been quiet in the Bowmanville camp since a few days after the encounter.

"Except for mild resistance at

Continued on Page Five

THRUST IS 'MINOR'

U. S. Planes Seek Out and Bomb Foe on Isle—Enemy Craft Felled

FLEETS EYE EACH OTHER

Japanese Navy Believed to Be Reluctant to Close While Weather Favors Bombers

By CHARLES HURD
Special to THE NEW YORK TIMES.

WASHINGTON, Oct. 22—The first known effort by the Japanese to thrust forward by land on Guadalcanal Island in the Solomons—a "minor" action on Tuesday (Guadalcanal date)—was repulsed by the Marine and Army defenders in the American positions, the Navy reported in a communiqué issued today.

The communiqué made clear that this was not an important attack in any sense of the word, but it was noteworthy only as a test of strength that would have been important had it succeeded and opened the path for a stronger movement by the enemy.

[Allied bombers yesterday dropped ten tons of bombs on ships at Buin, Bougainville Island, in the Solomons, while three Japanese bombers raided Port Moresby without causing casualties or damage, General MacArthur's headquarters in Australia announced today.]

The patrol operation came almost a week after the Japanese landed on Guadalcanal west of the airfield and positions held by the Americans. This landing was opposed by our bombers and fighters, but there was no clash of ground forces. Otherwise, all activity on the island itself has consisted of exchanges of bombings and shellings, in which barrages by naval vessels of the opposing sides against island targets have been interspersed between bombing missions.

Our Planes Harass Foe

"Our aircraft continue active," the communiqué said, "in seeking out and bombing enemy troops and supply concentrations on Guadalcanal Island."

On the night of Monday-Tuesday (Guadalcanal time), the communiqué added, "an enemy bomber was shot down over Guadalcanal." The bomber, it added, "is believed to have been on a reconnaissance mission and was destroyed by anti-aircraft fire."

Informed observers here read in today's communiqué confirmation of an opinion that appears to be held pretty generally in quarters

Continued on Page Four

U. S. Transport Loss In Atlantic Is Denied

Wireless to THE NEW YORK TIMES.

LONDON, Oct. 22—Lieut. Gen. Dwight D. Eisenhower, commanding United States forces in the European theatre, tonight emphatically denied Axis claims to have sunk transports heavily laden with American troops during the latter part of September.

In repeated attempts to convince the world that they had torpedoed a number of transports, the Nazis had a U-boat commander broadcast a description of one attack on a convoy, in which he said he had observed through his periscope direct torpedo hits on several liners.

General Eisenhower said formal denial had been withheld "until every American soldier that was on the Atlantic at the time of the German announcement was landed safely in the United Kingdom and we could assure ourselves of the complete falsity of the German claims."

He declared that the navies whose task it was to escort continuous troop movements to the European war theatre "have been and are daily according magnificent protection, a fact which every soldier in our Army clearly appreciates and gratefully acknowledges."

"All the News That's Fit to Print."

NEWS INDEX, PAGE 47, THIS SECTION

The New York Times.

LATE CITY EDITION
Cold this morning.
Temperatures Yesterday—Max., 63; Min., 50
Sunrise, 7:17 A. M.; Sunset, 6:03 P. M.

Section 1

VOL. XCII..No. 30,955. Entered as Second-Class Matter, Postoffice, New York, N. Y. NEW YORK, SUNDAY, OCTOBER 25, 1942. Including Magazine and Book Sections. TEN CENTS New York City and Vicinity

ALLIES GAIN IN BIG NORTH AFRICAN OFFENSIVE; BRITISH BOMBERS BATTER MILAN, TURIN, GENOA; HALSEY REPLACES GHORMLEY IN THE SOLOMONS

YEAR OF TRAINING OF 18, 19-YEAR-OLDS IS VOTED BY SENATE

Bill Is Then Passed After Final Plea by Army's Chief Fails to Avert the Restriction

HELP FOR FARMS ORDERED

Amendment, Adopted by 62 to 6, Provides for Deferring Workers Now Employed

By C. P. TRUSSELL
Special to THE NEW YORK TIMES.

WASHINGTON, Oct. 24—By a vote of 58 to 5 the Senate passed tonight, after eight hours of controversy and clashes with the Administration and Army command, its own bill to lower the Selective Service minimum age to 18 years, but provided especially that no inductee under 20 years of age should be sent into actual combat overseas without a full year of training.

In the face of renewed protest and warning from General Marshall, Chief of Staff, with President Roosevelt entering his personal appeal against restrictions, the Senate, by 39 to 31, wrote into its measure this provision:

"No person under 20 years of age inducted under this act shall be placed in actual combat duty beyond the territorial boundaries of continental United States until after he has had at least one year's training following his induction."

This amendment, sponsored by Senator O'Daniel of Texas, shunted aside another proposal offered previously by Senator Norris which would have prohibited the sending of inductees under 19 years of age into combat zones unless the same training had been received. Two hours after the O'Daniel provision was adopted, Senator Lucas, who had voted for it, urged the Senate to provide that any inductee under 20 who volunteered for foreign combat service might do so, provided he had received "adequate" training. The Senate voted this down, 32—33.

The Senators who voted against final passage of the bill were Bulow and Clark of Idaho, Democrats; Johnson of California, Nye and Shipstead, Republicans.

Induction After 45 Banned

Just before the bill was passed this evening, the Senate, with a voice vote, adopted the Ellender amendment under which no Selective Service registrant would be inducted for training or service after he had attained the age of 45.

It provided, too, by a 62-to-6 record vote, for the holding of labor on the farms. Under the amendment, sponsored by Senator Tydings, a bona fide farm worker, so engaged regularly, would be deferred from training or service in the land or naval forces so long as he remained on his job, or until replaced. The amendment, Mr. Tydings, said, had been prepared at his request by the Selective Service System, which entered no objections to it.

For months, farm State Senators and Representatives had warned against the depletion of farm labor by enlistment, the draft and the lure of wartime industrial wages, and had worked for such a provision of law as the Senate accepted late today.

With a voice vote, the Senate later rejected a second O'Daniel amendment which would have barred the payment of overtime to workers in industry for the duration of the war, existing law to the contrary notwithstanding. In effect, it would have suspended the 40-hour week.

As to the educational status of the new inductees, the Senate stood by the original form of its own bill, which would permit students in high schools or similar institutions to complete their academic year before induction, pro-

Continued on Page Thirty

Pacific Command Shake-Up Is Laid to Guadalcanal Crisis

Shift to Offensive Is Seen in Washington in Selection of 'Fighting' Admiral Halsey as Commander in the South Pacific

By CHARLES HURD
Special to THE NEW YORK TIMES.

WASHINGTON, Oct. 24—The Navy has relieved Vice Admiral Robert L. Ghormley of command of the Solomon Islands action and replaced him with Vice Admiral William F. Halsey Jr., it was announced here today. Admiral Halsey distinguished himself last Spring in conducting the notable hit-and-run air and sea raid on Japanese installations in the Gilbert and Marshall Islands in the Japanese-controlled region southwest of Hawaii.

The change in command was made public without other official comment by the Navy, but surprise that might have been occasioned by a shift in the midst of battle was somewhat tempered by reports in recent weeks indicating that the occupation of key points in the Solomon Islands had become a stalemate if not a critical defensive situation.

Admiral Chester W. Nimitz, Commander in Chief of the Pacific Fleet, continues in supreme command of naval operations in the Pacific area, except for Australia and New Guinea, where General Douglas MacArthur controls, but Admiral Halsey, as the new commander of naval forces in the South Pacific area, now inherits direct responsibility for pursuing the Solomons attack.

The view expressed in informed quarters here was to the effect that the new Solomons commander would be expected to turn that venture from a currently defensive operation into an aggressive fight such as first characterized the occupation.

Admiral Ghormley's future was left in doubt, the Navy announcement stating only that his "new duties will be announced at a later date."

Coincident with this major change the Navy also announced relief of Vice Admiral William S. Pye as commander of a Pacific

Continued on Page Forty-one

FRICTION MARRING PACIFIC TEAM-WORK

Times Writer Finds It Behind Lines, Though the Services Cooperate Well at Front

Following is the third of a series of articles by the military editor of THE NEW YORK TIMES, *who has just returned from a Pacific tour.*

By HANSON W. BALDWIN

Army, Navy and Marine ground and air forces are working together in close harmony in combat areas in the Pacific, but behind the lines there is some friction and considerable mutual criticism.

In the Solomons area, where elements of all three services have been in action, the cooperation appeared to this correspondent to be close and successful. There was good-natured joshing between the services, but little criticism. Each expressed an admiration for the other's commander; most personnel submerged their differences in the common good.

From one important air strip in the New Hebrides, carved out of the jungle at record speed, great four-motored B-17's and Army and Navy and Marine Corps fighters were operating; there was no bick-

Continued on Page Thirty-nine

SEAPLANE TENDER BOMBED AT RABAUL

Heavy Allied Planes May Have Sunk 17,600-Ton Vessel in New Attack on Harbor

By The Associated Press.

AT UNITED NATIONS HEADQUARTERS, Australia, Sunday, Oct. 25—A large Japanese seaplane tender was believed destroyed at Rabaul, New Britain, by Allied bombers, the High Command announced today.

The tender was one of the targets picked out by heavy bombers that struck again at the harbor of Rabaul, where Japanese ships have been concentrated, presumably for an impending assault on American-held Guadalcanal in the Solomon Islands to the southeast. An assault the day before resulted in the sinking or damaging of ten Japanese ships, including a cruiser and a destroyer.

[An American naval force raided the Gilbert and Ellice Islands, sank two small patrol boats and damaged a destroyer and a merchantman, Washington reported yesterday.]

Today's communiqué said that the second assault, made at night, had resulted in a hit with a 500-pound bomb amidships of a sea-

Continued on Page Forty

Major Sports Yesterday

FOOTBALL

Paced by two freshman backs, Yale achieved its first major victory since 1940 at the expense of Dartmouth. Notre Dame, though trailing at half-time, stopped previously undefeated Illinois. Penn and Army flashed powerful running attacks to down Columbia and Harvard, respectively. Manhattan toppled Duquesne on a field goal. Princeton crushed Brown and unbeaten Georgia Tech routed Navy. Scores of leading games:

Alabama	14	Kentucky	0	Nebraska	7	Oklahoma	0
Amherst	27	Wesleyan	0	Notre Dame	21	Illinois	14
Army	14	Harvard	0	Ohio State	20	Northwest'n	6
Baylor	6	Texas A.&M.	0	Penn.	42	Columbia	12
Boston Coll.	27	Wake Forest	0	Penn State	13	Colgate	10
Brooklyn	38	N. Y. Aggies	0	Princeton	32	Brown	13
California	19	Washington	6	S. M. U.	21	Corp. Christi	6
Detroit	6	Georgetown	0	Stanford	14	So. Calif.	6
Duke	28	Pittsburgh	0	Susquehanna	6	C. C. N. Y.	0
Georgia	35	Cincinnati	13	Syracuse	12	Cornell	7
Ga. Tech	21	Navy	0	Tennessee	52	Furman	7
Holy Cross	28	N. C. State	0	Texas	12	Rice	7
Iowa	14	Indiana	13	T. C. U.	21	Pensacola N'l.	0
Lehigh	28	Rutgers	10	Tulane	29	No. Carolina	14
Manhattan	10	Duquesne	7	U. C. L. A.	14	Santa Clara	6
Mich. State	14	Great Lakes	0	Wash. State	26	Oregon St.	13
Minnesota	16	Michigan	14	Williams	47	Tufts	6
Miss. State	26	Florida	12	Wisconsin	13	Purdue	0
Missouri	45	Iowa State	6	Yale	17	Dartmouth	7

HORSE RACING

Boysy won the Scarsdale Handicap by a neck from Spiral Pass at Empire City, where 27,126 racegoers wagered $1,661,293, a record for the track. At Laurel, Md., Whirlaway took the Washington Handicap and Askmenow captured the Selima Stakes.

(Complete Details of These and Other Sports Events in Section 5.)

ITALY UNDER RAIDS

R. A. F.'s Lancasters Hit Milan in Low-Level Daylight Attack

NIGHT BLOWS GO ON

Genoa Fires Rekindled, Other Ports Pounded—Fighters Harry Nazis

By RAYMOND DANIELL
Special Cable to THE NEW YORK TIMES.

LONDON, Sunday, Oct. 25—The Royal Air Force's biggest bombers from Britain are giving Northern Italy a severe pounding by day and night.

A large force of the powerful four-motored Lancasters attacked Milan by daylight yesterday.

Three bombers were lost in the Milan attack, the Air Ministry said. Preliminary reports showed the raid was successful; the attack was pressed home at a low level as the Lancasters went under clouds to loose their bombs.

[A Vichy report, transmitted by The Associated Press via London last night, said fifty four-motored British bombers flew over unoccupied France in daylight and that one of them machine-gunned a barracks and railway station at Montluçon, west of Vichy.]

Last night, indicating that the R. A. F. was at it again, air raid alarms sounded at Berne, Switzerland, at 9:05 o'clock, according to a Reuter report from the Swiss capital.

Genoa Raids Cut Rommel's Supply

Genoa was raided Friday night for the second night in a row by "another strong force" of British bombers, and other squadrons of the big planes bombed the Italian industrial center of Turin and the port of Savona, twenty miles west of Genoa.

In the Friday night operation, almost at the hour when the British Eighth Army in Egypt, supported by the British Navy and Allied air forces, was beginning its offensive for Allied mastery of North Africa and the Mediterranean, Lancaster, Stirling and Halifax bombers and two-motored Wellingtons roared over the Alps and unloaded hundreds of tons of incendiary and demolition missiles on blazing and battered Genoa, major port from which Field Marshal Erwin Rommel has drawn a large part of his Axis reinforcements and supplies.

By daylight yesterday also the R. A. F.'s Spitfires and Mustang fighters of the Army Cooperation Command went on with their offensive against the Nazis over the French and Netherland coasts—without losing a plane.

The fighters shot up enemy military buildings, ships and trains, rounding off one of the most intensive weeks of daylight air blows at the Germans that saw R. A. F. bombers make thrusts over the Reich on four successive days.

Milan a Center of Axis Industry

The Milan raid was carried out before dusk presumably on lines similar to those used in the R. A. F. attack at Le Creusot in occupied France on Saturday, Oct. 17, when ninety-four Lancasters blasted the Schneider armament plants there.

Milan is about seventy-five miles northwest of Genoa and is an important industrial city. The Caproni bomber plants are located there.

The weather for Friday night's raid on Genoa was not as good as on Thursday night, when the whole "strong force"—usually meaning many more than 100 planes—of R. A. F. bombers that made the attack then returned safely. In the Friday night attack, the Air Ministry reported, three bombers were lost.

Men of the crews that participated in the new blasting of Genoa

Continued on Page Four

NEW YORK OBSERVES WARTIME NAVY DAY

Sailors passing the reviewing stand on Fifth Avenue — The New York Times

300,000 ACCLAIM NAVY DAY PARADE

10,000 March Down 5th Ave. in 2-Hour Demonstration—British Seamen in Line

The Navy took over on Fifth Avenue between Eighty-seventh and Sixty-second Streets for nearly two hours yesterday and a throng estimated by the police at 300,000 obviously had a fine time watching and cheering the 10,000 marchers.

It was the city's first Navy Day parade since the attack on Pearl Harbor and accordingly was replete with unprecedented features. There were nearly as many uniformed women as swung down the avenue in the all-women's parade of April 11. There were British seamen and marines. And there was the weather itself, more like an early April day than one on the rim of November.

The demonstration was unusual even in its lacks. Mayor La Guardia, usually a fixture in the reviewing stand at Sixty-seventh Street, was out of town. The scheduled grand marshal, Rear Admiral Edward J. Marquart, was prevented from appearing by illness and his place was taken by Rear Admiral Lamar R. Leahy.

And there was a noticeable absence of one naval group whose nonparticipation provoked this exchange between two women spectators just south of the reviewing stand:

"Say, I wonder what happened

Continued on Page Thirty-eight

U. S. Soldiers' Gifts Are Sunk in Atlantic

By The Associated Press.

WASHINGTON, Oct. 24—The Army Postal Service said today that 4,986 sacks of United States mail bound for American armed forces in the British Isles had been lost in the sinking of a United Nations cargo ship.

Much of the shipment was parcel post and represented one of the first parcel shipments of Christmas mail.

The War Department said that the lost mail was deposited in the United States during the latter part of September. Mails reaching the New York Port of Debarkation Army Postoffice later than Oct. 3 were not included in this shipment.

FLIERS STILL HUNT FOR RICKENBACKER

Long-Range Patrol Craft of Navy Find No Trace of Lost Army Plane in Pacific

Special to THE NEW YORK TIMES.

WASHINGTON, Oct. 24—Long-range naval patrol planes that are considered ideally suited for searches at sea have joined in the hunt for the United States Army plane in which Captain E. V. Rickenbacker was a passenger, the Navy Department announced today. They are operating from an island base southwest of Honolulu.

No word of the missing craft

Continued on Page Forty-one

War News Summarized

SUNDAY, OCTOBER 25, 1942

Britain's Eighth Army, strongly supported by both British and United States air units, struck yesterday before dawn to open the third British North African offensive and cracked through the Axis positions. United Nations airmen had clear-cut superiority. The land attack was frontal on the German line between the sea and the Qattara Depression. Axis airfields and bases behind the lines were bombed incessantly. [1:8; map, P. 3.]

American-built light naval vessels of unusual speed shelled the Axis supply port of Matruh on the Egyptian coast during the night and got away safely without loss of a ship, despite a three-hour Axis air counter-attack. [5:1.]

London announced that Genoa and Turin had been attacked for the second successive night and Milan also bombed by day in a third raid. Rome acknowledged notable damage at Savona, a shipbuilding center twenty-five miles west of Genoa. [1:4.]

Moscow stated that reinforced German troops had been thrown back inside Stalingrad after hard fighting. The Germans had made a slight advance toward Tuapse, on the Black Sea coast, from their inland positions in the Caucasus. [1:7.]

United Nations Headquarters, Australia, reported that bombers attacking Japanese vessels in the harbor of Rabaul, New Britain Island, were believed to have destroyed a seaplane tender of 17,600 tons. [1:3.] No action was reported in the Solomon Islands. Washington disclosed that a naval expedition to the Gilbert and Ellice Islands, between Hawaii and the Solomons, had sunk two small Japanese patrol boats and damaged a destroyer and a merchant ship. [40:1; map, P. 40.]

The Navy Department announced that Vice Admiral Robert L. Ghormley had been relieved of command of the Solomon Islands action, being replaced by Vice Admiral William F. Halsey Jr., who conducted the successful hit-and-run raid in the Gilbert and Marshall Islands last Spring. [1:2-3.]

MORE NAZI THRUSTS FAIL IN STALINGRAD

German Losses Mount Rapidly in Several Volga Sectors—Berlin Claims Gains

By The Associated Press.

MOSCOW, Sunday, Oct. 25—The Germans threw two freshly reinforced infantry divisions, eighty tanks and "large" air forces against Russian positions in Stalingrad yesterday, a Soviet communiqué said today, but after bitter hand-to-hand fighting the Nazis were thrown back with heavy losses.

The new attack, launched after fresh troops were brought in to replace nearly 10,000 that the Russians said they had killed in two days, was directed at the factory district in the northern part of the battle-torn city. In this area alone, the communiqué said, more than 1,500 Germans were killed yesterday and seventeen tanks destroyed.

[The Germans reported new gains in Stalingrad's Red October factory and for the third time officially claimed to have reached the Volga. A dominating mountain northeast of Tuapse in the Caucasus was captured in a hard battle, Berlin said.]

The heaviest German losses were in a southern sector of the Stalingrad front, where one Soviet formation was said to have killed 7,000 men, destroyed fifty-seven tanks, 100 guns and twenty-six planes. The Russians also captured 150 German tanks that had been disabled in previous engagements and were being used as firing positions.

Heavy fighting was continuing both northwest of Stalingrad and south of the city. In one sector northwest of the city, the Russian communiqué said, Soviet troops "made a slight advance, overcame enemy minefields and barbed-wire entanglements and broke into enemy positions." The Germans launched four counter-attacks, but were forced to fall back after losing about 250 men.

Farther south in the Caucasus the Russians were on the defensive both in the Mozdok area and along the Black Sea. The communiqué said, however, that all attacks were repulsed and that the positions remained unchanged.

Strong Nazi Attacks Fail

By RALPH PARKER
Wireless to THE NEW YORK TIMES.

MOSCOW, Oct. 24—The German Air Force resumed its activity at Stalingrad yesterday, operating in force to support ground forces numbering 7,000 to 8,000 men, which with tanks maintained their attacks in the northern part of the city. It is estimated that 1,500 bombs were dropped on the Russian lines and behind them. Coordinated with this, heavy artillery and

Continued on Page Eighteen

AXIS LINES DENTED

Allied Troops Reported Pouring Through Gap Ripped From the Air

TANKS ARE CLOSING IN

British General's Order to the Troops Is to 'Destroy Rommel'

Special Cable to THE NEW YORK TIMES.

LONDON, Oct. 24—In an offensive against the enemy in the Alamein sector of the Egyptian Western Desert battlefront, Britain's Eighth Army has smashed through Axis defenses at several points, according to latest press reports reaching London tonight from Cairo. Security reasons make it impossible to specify the objectives reached.

That the attack is important was emphasized by Lieut. Gen. Bernard L. Montgomery's order of the day, issued on the eve of the attack, calling on the British forces to "destroy Rommel and his army" and adding:

"Victory should swing our way."

General Montgomery is field commander of the Eighth Army.

The land fighting that has so far developed is described as fierce because of the narrow nature of the present front, which measures only forty miles, from El Alamein to the Qattara Depression, although the lines themselves twist and wind over a greater length. The attack, which was preceded by the heaviest air offensive yet seen in Egypt, indicates that the Allies won the battle that had been going on over the last eight weeks for effective building up of supplies.

Rommel Held Worried

There are indications that General Field Marshal Erwin Rommel is having worries over his supply lines—worries largely created by Allied airmen, who over the last fortnight have been playing havoc not only with Axis supplies going to the front but to Marshal Rommel's ports as well. It is believed that he has two German armored divisions, two Italian armored divisions, one German motorized division; the 164th German Infantry Division, which is partly motorized, and about a half-dozen Italian infantry divisions that are probably not up to half strength.

Failure to get sufficient arms and ammunition for these forces may lose Marshal Rommel the battle. But for weeks the enemy has been strengthening his lines and extending their defense in depth, and it is remarked that no sensationally rapid advance can be expected on the part of the Allied forces.

Italian newspaper comment this week-end showed how worried the Italians were getting over the arrival of American troops in Africa and the growing strength of the Allied air forces in the Middle East. These newspapers paint a gloomy picture for their readers. They hint

Continued on Page Three

King Christian X In Serious Relapse

By The Associated Press.

STOCKHOLM, Sweden, Sunday, Oct. 25—A special bulletin issued in Copenhagen early today said King Christian X, who was injured last week when he fell from a horse, had taken a sudden change for the worse and was in a serious condition.

The 72-year-old monarch had been reported improving rapidly since the accident, but about 7 P. M. Saturday night his heart developed an abnormal action.

His physician administered a stimulating treatment which resulted in a slight recovery.

Queen Alexandrine, Crown Prince Frederik and Prince Knud were summoned to the hospital last evening and spent the night there.

"All the News That's Fit to Print."

The New York Times.

LATE CITY EDITION
Colder today.
Temperatures Yesterday—Max., 61; Min., 43
Sunrise, 7:19 A. M.; Sunset, 6:09 P. M.

Copyright, 1942, by The New York Times Company.

VOL. XCII..No. 30,957. Entered as Second-Class Matter, Postoffice, New York, N. Y. NEW YORK, TUESDAY, OCTOBER 27, 1942. THREE CENTS IN NEW YORK CITY

JAPANESE OPEN MAJOR ATTACK ON GUADALCANAL; HIT CARRIER, SINK DESTROYER; WASP LOST SEPT. 15; WILLKIE DEMANDS SECOND FRONT, BURMA DRIVE

COFFEE RATIONING ON CUP-A-DAY BASIS ORDERED ON NOV. 29

Limitation Applies to Every Person in the Country, With None for Those Under 15

SUGAR BOOK TO BE USED

WPB Tells OPA to Act as Stock Dwindles—Retailers to Stop Selling Nov. 22 for Week

Special to THE NEW YORK TIMES.

WASHINGTON, Oct. 26—The OPA announced today that it will start rationing coffee to civilians starting at midnight Nov. 28, and will grant an allowance of one pound every five weeks to every individual in the country 15 years old or over. As worked out unofficially by government men and those in the coffee trade here, the ration will provide slightly more than one cup a day to each individual.

In giving warning of the impending rationing, the OPA departed from the policy of secrecy it has followed heretofore in dealing with any product capable of being hoarded. Leon Henderson, Federal Price Administrator, cautioned, however, that "there is no reason for any one to run to the corner grocer, put the 'squeeze' on him and try to force him to help a hoarder. There is absolutely no excuse for hoarding coffee at this time."

Consumers will get their coffee ration by surrendering the last stamp of War Ration Book No. 1, the book now used only for sugar rations. The stamps which will be used for coffee rationing are those numbered from 28 down to and including 19, but because of the make-up of the book the first stamp to be detached for the coffee allowance will be Stamp No. 27, followed by No. 28, No. 25, No. 26, etc.

None for Those 14 Years Old

No book on which the age of the holder is stated at 14 years or younger will be valid for the coffee ration. Use of the book for sugar will continue exactly as in the past. Those who did not obtain the sugar ration books, it was added, may do so now by applying to their War Price and Ration Boards.

Estimates of the number of cups of coffee to be obtained from a pound varied from thirty-five to forty-five among OPA officials, but on the basis of forty cups the new ration will work out to slightly more than a cup a day for consumers.

"We're announcing the forthcoming rationing now because we're going to have to talk to a lot of people in the coffee industry and elsewhere about the administration of the rationing program," Mr. Henderson said.

"Naturally stories and rumors will be creeping around about what we propose to do. Most of them will be entirely garbled and thus create more confusion and hysteria than even now exists on the subject of coffee. We are therefore stating what we plan to do so that the public can get the story straight and from an official source.

"The coffee story is this: For ten years before 1941 we consumed about thirteen pounds of coffee per capita per year. Last year, due to abnormal demands, this figure jumped to about sixteen pounds. Thus far in 1942 we have consumed coffee at the rate of about 12.5 pounds annually. Therefore, a ration of one pound each five weeks a person over 15 certainly is not a drastic reduction."

Retailers' Supplies Dwindled

OPA was directed to undertake the rationing program by the War Production Board after it became apparent that the available coffee supply in retail stores—65 per cent of normal—was not sufficient to meet current demand. This, the

Continued on Page Eighteen

Chilean Fisticuffs Debate Axis Break

By Reuter.

SANTIAGO, Chile, Oct. 26—Two groups of about 400 persons, some demonstrating for a break with the Axis and some against it, came to blows here today. The police intervened immediately and arrested ten persons. Several were injured.

SANTIAGO, Oct. 26 (UP)—Joaquin Fernandez y Fernandez took up his duties as Chile's new Foreign Minister today amid a clamor throughout the country for breaking relations with the Axis.

Mass meetings sponsored by the democratic parties and organized labor were held throughout the nation calling for rupture of diplomatic ties with Germany, Italy and Japan.

VALPARAISO, Chile, Oct. 26 (UP)—Eight persons, including two women, were arrested by police today on suspicion of Axis espionage activities and authorities said they believed that a German shipping agency, fully staffed although it has handled no shipping for the past three years, is the center of a local spy ring.

ACTION ON DRAFT SNAGGED IN HOUSE

Move to Accept Year's Training Imposes Delay Past Election —Hershey Urges Wider Call

By FREDERICK R. BARKLEY
Special to THE NEW YORK TIMES.

WASHINGTON, Oct. 26—Postponement of final action on the teen-age draft bill until after the election a week from tomorrow appeared almost certain today as the House ran into a snag in attempting to send the differing House and Senate versions to conference.

Representative Rankin of Mississippi moved to instruct the House conferees to approve a Senate amendment requiring that these youths receive a full year's training in the United States before being sent to combat duty abroad.

This proposal, adopted by the Senate, 39 to 31, despite opposition of Administration and Army leaders, is believed to have considerable support in the House.

Mr. Rankin's motion came after Representative Thomason, ranking Democrat on the Military Affairs Committee, said that he could not pledge that his conferee group would assure a separate vote on the training plan.

Speaker Rayburn then directed withdrawal of Mr. Thomason's motion to send the bills to conference by unanimous consent, pointing out that the House was acting under an informal agreement not to handle any controversial questions until after the election, and that with many members absent for the final week of the campaign a quorum for a vote would not be available.

However, the House will meet

Continued on Page Nineteen

QUICK AID IS URGED

RepublicanLeaderWould Relieve Pressure on Russia and China

FOR PACIFIC CHARTER

Millions Said to Look to U. S. for Liberty Now and After the War

The text of Mr. Willkie's report is on Page 8.

In his promised report to the American people on his recently completed trip to the Middle East, Russia and China, Wendell L. Willkie renewed last night his demand for the establishment of a second fighting front in Europe, and added to it an expression of hope that our forces in India could soon begin an all-out attack on Burma.

"Thus we will relieve the pressure of our enemies on China and Russia, those two superb fighting allies," Mr. Willkie declared.

Declaring that the era of imperialism had ended, Mr. Willkie said that our Allies in the East expected us "now—not after the war—to use the enormous power of our giving to promote liberty and justice." The peoples of the East, he said, want the United States to join them in "creating a new society, global in scope, free alike of the economic injustices of the West and the political malpractices of the East."

The 1940 Republican Presidential nominee spoke to the nation over the combined networks of the Columbia Broadcasting System, the National Broadcasting Company, the Mutual Broadcasting System and the Blue Network, from 10:30 to 11:07 P. M. He made his address from the CBS studio at 49 East Fifty-second Street.

Believed Heard by 36,320,000

Broadcasting officials, on the basis of one of the commercial surveys used to check the response to programs, estimated last night that 36,320,000 persons had tuned in on Mr. Willkie's broadcast. This figure, it was said, represented about twice the normal listener response to a topnotch commercial broadcast, and compared with the record of 62,100,000 auditors reached by President Roosevelt's address on Dec. 9, 1941, just after Pearl Harbor.

Although we are on the road to winning the war, Mr. Willkie said, we are running a grave risk of spending far more in men and materials than is necessary. We are also in danger of losing the friendship of half of our allies before the war is over, and then of losing the peace, he warned, unless we recognize that "in many important respects we are not doing a good job," and correct our errors.

He hotly assailed the contention that private citizens, particularly those not expert in military affairs

Continued on Page Eight

DESERT ARMY FIRM

Allies Consolidate Their Successes—Tanks in Minor Clashes

1,450 OF FOE SEIZED

Our Air Forces Deliver More Heavy Blows at Front and at Sea

By DAVID ANDERSON
Special Cable to THE NEW YORK TIMES.

LONDON, Oct. 26—Striving to gain elbow room in which to fight on the scale and in the fashion that the occasion demands, the British Eighth Army in Egypt spent the third day of battle in consolidating its initial successes and in inching forward wherever possible. Tanks at last made their appearance in minor clashes.

Laconic reports from Cairo reaching here indicate the wish to save comment until later, when there should be something substantial to put in the communiqués.

Today it was announced that 1,450 Axis troops had been captured up to last evening. There were no important advances by British troops, although the Allied air forces kept up their all-out offensive.

No Dislodging by Axis

The statement that the Eighth Army is holding on to its new positions is not as defensive as it sounds, for the enemy is expected to achieve local success from time to time. But lately there have been no counter-attacks with sufficient weight to dislodge the advancing Allied troops.

The job of pushing General Field Marshal Erwin Rommel's defenses aside is bound to be a long one, especially as the attackers have for their plan the paving of avenues over which British tanks can roll. Days of tedious fighting are seen to be ahead before sappers and infantry can hack their way into the open.

Indeed, there is some support here for the belief that the Eighth Army may have to resort to dull pounding tactics, with a column of supplies lying in the rear and the soundness of supply lines being the final margin for British victory. That could go on for weeks.

Nothing coming in from the battlefront suggests that the main German defenses have been breached or, for that matter, even

Continued on Page Five

THE WASP AFIRE AFTER BEING STRUCK BY TORPEDOES

Smoke rises from U. S. aircraft carrier following a Japanese submarine attack in South Pacific

Associated Press Wirephoto (U. S. Navy)

RED ARMY HOLDING IN SEESAW COMBAT

Germans in Stalingrad Drive In Wedge but Are Thrust Back by Counter-Blow

By The Associated Press.

MOSCOW, Tuesday, Oct. 27—The Red Army maintained its lines in Stalingrad yesterday in a seesaw battle in which the Germans drove a wedge into Russian positions in one sector and then were forced to withdraw, the Soviet High Command announced today.

The main fighting took place in a factory area in the northern part of the city—presumably around the Red October foundry works—where attacking German tank and infantry forces lost three tanks and 750 men killed in a five-hour combat.

"The Germans succeeded in driving a wedge into the Soviet defenses," the Soviet communiqué said, "but were attacked from the

Continued on Page Three

Japanese Bomb East India; Say Allies Plan Burma Push

By HERBERT L. MATTHEWS
Wireless to THE NEW YORK TIMES.

NEW DELHI, India, Oct. 26—The long-expected Japanese air attacks on our bases in East India began yesterday, it was announced in today's British General Headquarters communiqué. "Chittagong and some airdromes in Northeast Assam" were involved. Chittagong is in Bengal on the Bay of Bengal, not far from the Burma border, while Assam is a province in Northeast British India, adjacent to Burma.

More detailed information is expected later, but preliminary reports, according to the communiqué, indicate that civilian and military casualties "were extremely light and damage was small."

"Civilian labor employed in the areas attacked," the communiqué said, "displayed extremely high morale and their devotion to routine duties was most marked."

[Domei stated yesterday that the Japanese air attack on air bases in East India on Sunday was a preventive measure against a contemplated major-scale United Nations offensive against Burma, according to Tokyo broadcasts recorded by The Associated Press. The Associated Press reported that the Japanese raids were renewed yesterday on the Assam objectives.]

The reference to civilians in the British communiqué was an important one, for much depends on the Bengalis holding firm.

The reference to Northeastern Assam—as a glance at the map will show—also is most significant. That means the Japanese are aiming at bases of British Army forces

Continued on Page Nine

FIRES IN HONG KONG GUIDE A NEW RAID

Americans Also Blast Enemy's Airfield Near Canton—23 Japanese Planes Downed

By HARRISON FORMAN
Wireless to THE NEW YORK TIMES.

CHUNGKING, China, Oct. 26—All Chungking was electrified by the news that American bombers with fighter escorts Sunday afternoon and again early this morning dumped twenty tons of bombs on Hong Kong's docks, shipping and warehouses, blowing up the power station and shooting down ten and probably five more of eighteen Zeros and I-45's.

The Japanese planes attempted to intercept the returning American formation, which suffered one bomber lost. One American fighter plane was forced down, but the pilot was reported safe.

A terrific scare was thrown into the Japanese throughout North China, Manchuria, Korea and Japan proper only four days ago by the blasting by American bombers

Continued on Page Nine

ALL-OUT PUSH IS ON

Naval Shelling Supports Japanese Attack on U. S. Flank on Isle

ENEMY CRUISERS HIT

2 of Foe's Carriers Hurt in Naval Clash—Wasp Victim of Torpedoes

By CHARLES HURD
Special to THE NEW YORK TIMES.

WASHINGTON, Oct. 26—The Japanese have launched a massive air, land and sea attack against the American forces on Guadalcanal, in the Solomon Islands, the Navy announced in a communiqué issued tonight.

Word of this long-expected attack came a few hours after the Navy had announced that the aircraft carrier Wasp had been sunk on Sept. 15, as the result of a Japanese submarine attack, while engaged in covering the movement of reinforcements and supplies to Guadalcanal. About 90 per cent of the Wasp's personnel were saved.

In the current fighting, the latter Navy announcement said, the Navy has suffered "severe damage" to another carrier and has lost the destroyer Porter. In addition, "other United States vessels have reported lesser damage."

The shock of the announcement of the loss of the Wasp, quickly manifested in official circles here, was overshadowed by the later announcement of news that had been expected here for almost a month, but that none the less came as a dramatic climax to the venture that began on Aug. 7, when American forces smashed their way onto Guadalcanal.

A Decisive Engagement

No one in authority would hazard a guess as to the outcome of the current engagement, but there was a general agreement in informed circles that the engagement probably would be fought to a decisive finish. On it, most authorities agreed, probably will depend the course of the war in the southwestern Pacific for the next year.

The Japanese are believed to have thrown into the fight the bulk of their sea power, as well as air power, which has continued to function despite the enemy's loss of about 400 planes in the Solomons. What forces the United States Navy carried into the fight to support the Marine and Army troops on land necessarily was not announced.

The Navy's communiqué on the new Japanese attack was unequivocal in picturing the seriousness of the enemy's effort to wrest from American hands the small airfield hewn out of the jungle on

Continued on Page Six

Byrnes Turns Down Farm Bloc; Roosevelt Ceiling Basis Stands

By W. H. LAWRENCE
Special to THE NEW YORK TIMES.

WASHINGTON, Oct. 26—An angry Senate farm bloc, demanding revisions in Federal price policies which would permit prices paid to farmers for their products to go higher, was turned down today by James F. Byrnes, Economic Stabilization Director; Leon Henderson, Federal Price Administrator, and Secretary Wickard.

Mr. Henderson, denouncing an attempt to "gun" him out of his job and to "sabotage" the Office of Price Administration, estimated that granting of farm bloc demands would add $100,000,000 annually to the price of bread alone. He offered no estimates of the over-all increase in living costs which would result from the proposed revision.

The basic issue debated before the Senate Agriculture and Forestry Committee was whether President Roosevelt had authority of Congress to direct Messrs. Byrnes, Henderson and Wickard to "consider present governmental payments to agricultural producers, and subsidy payments, in arriving at the minimum ceiling prices."

The farm bloc contended that he did not have such authority, and Senator Reed of Kansas charged flatly that the President's execu-

Continued on Page Nineteen

War News Summarized

TUESDAY, OCTOBER 27, 1942

The United States Navy Department disclosed that a major land, sea and air battle was under way in the Solomon Islands, with both United States and Japanese warships suffering. The action started with a coordinated Japanese attack on Guadalcanal Island positions Sunday morning. In a sortie carried out by the United States planes from the carriers of a task force two Japanese carriers were damaged. The United States destroyer Porter was sunk and a carrier damaged. [1:8; map, P. 6.] Loss of the carrier Wasp Sept. 15 by submarine torpedoes was disclosed [6:1.]

In Eastern India Japanese planes bombed British air bases. Chittagong and points in Eastern Assam were attacked. Casualties and damage were reported to have been light. Domei, Japanese news agency, claimed that three planes were shot down and thirty-nine destroyed on the ground and called the attacks a preventive action to check a move on Burma. [1:6-7; map, P. 9.]

United States fliers again bombed Hong Kong, destroying a power station. At Canton an airfield was bombed successfully. Ten Japanese planes were shot down. One United States bomber was lost during the operations in the sector yesterday and the day preceding. [1:7.]

On the Egyptian battlefront United Nations troops were swarming through widening gaps in the Axis defensive line and 1,450 prisoners had been taken. Four Junkers troop-carrying planes were shot down and a munitions ship was blown up in the harbor of Tobruk. [1:4.]

A German spokesman placed the United Nations force in Egypt at 1,000,000 men and 1,000 tanks. Berlin claimed that all attacks on the Axis line had been repulsed. [4:5.]

An Italian communiqué stated that 3½ persons had been killed and more than 3,000 injured during the week-end bombings of Genoa. Most of the deaths were understood to have occurred when the crowd in a large air raid shelter broke in panic. [5:1.]

Wendell L. Willkie, reporting in a national broadcast on his recent tour, renewed his demand for a second front in Europe and expressed hope that an offensive would be undertaken in Burma. He warned that the United States stood to lose half its friends abroad if it did not start making a better job of the war. [1:3.]

Wasp Crew's Battle With Fires To Save Carrier Told by Skipper

By FOSTER HAILEY
By Telephone to THE NEW YORK TIMES.

HONOLULU, Oct. 26—The last hours of the aircraft carrier Wasp as her heroic officers and crew fought to save her and then, hopes of that gone, swam to each other in the water and gave life belts to those who could not swim, were described today by her skipper, Captain Forrest P. Sherman.

Already back in an active post as Chief of Staff to Vice Admiral John H. Towers, commander of Naval Air Forces in the Pacific, Captain Sherman laid aside his work for a few minutes to tell newspaper men of the loss of his ship.

Time and again in his recital of the desperate hours after 2:44 P. M., Sept. 15, when three Japanese torpedoes hit the Wasp, he returned to the heroism shown by his officers and men in fighting the fires that finally ravaged her and led to the decision to abandon ship and sink her.

"I can't say too much for the spirit of the men of the Wasp from the time we first went down there until I saw them last," Captain Sherman said. "I visited every injured man on the hospital ship before I left and there wasn't a one that didn't want to get out of there and back on a ship after the Japs. That was the only request I got—to go with me on another carrier."

Captain Sherman singled out for

Continued on Page Six

Roosevelt Confers With Naval Chiefs

By The Associated Press.

WASHINGTON, Oct. 26—President Roosevelt called the Naval High Command into conference late today as the defenders of Guadalcanal, in the Solomons, apparently faced one of the most terrific ordeals in American history.

With reinforced Japanese obviously bent on throwing everything they have into the drive to overwhelm the Marines and Army men, an atmosphere of tense expectation was apparent in some Washington quarters.

Conferring with the President were Admiral Ernest J. King, Commander in Chief of the Fleet, and Mr. Roosevelt's personal Chief of Staff, Admiral William D. Leahy. The conferees said nothing to newspaper men, but it was considered probable that the conference dealt with strategic and combat problems in the Southwest Pacific, particularly the Solomon Islands.

"All the News That's Fit to Print."

NEWS INDEX, PAGE 55, THIS SECTION

The New York Times.

LATE CITY EDITION
Continued cool today with light winds.
Temperatures Yesterday—Max., 57; Min., 45
Sunrise, 7:34 A. M.; Sunset, 5:45 P. M.

Section 1

VOL. XCII—No. 30,969. Entered as Second-Class Matter, Postoffice, New York, N. Y. NEW YORK, SUNDAY, NOVEMBER 8, 1942. Including Magazine and Book Sections. TEN CENTS New York City and Vicinity

AMERICAN FORCES LAND IN FRENCH AFRICA; BRITISH NAVAL, AIR UNITS ASSISTING THEM; EFFECTIVE SECOND FRONT, ROOSEVELT SAYS

U.S. DRIVES ON BUNA

American Troops Flown to Area Closing In on Big Japanese Base

PAPUA IS OVERRUN

All Except Beachhead of Buna-Gona Seized in New Guinea Push

By The Associated Press.

AT UNITED NATIONS HEADQUARTERS, Australia, Sunday, Nov. 8—American combat troops are in action near Buna, vital Japanese base on the north New Guinea coast, General Douglas MacArthur disclosed today.

Simultaneously, General MacArthur disclosed that the Allies have occupied Goodenough Island to the northeast of New Guinea, off Collingwood Bay, in an obvious flanking movement.

[American Army troops on Guadalcanal advanced on Friday (Solomons time) in the area to the west of Henderson airfield, the Navy reported yesterday. They crossed the Malimbui River a few miles south of Koli Point, where the Japanese recently landed reinforcements, but met little opposition.]

It was from Buna, in midsummer, that the Japanese began a drive across tortuous trails of the Owen Stanley Mountains which carried to within thirty-two miles of Port Moresby, Allied base on the south coast, before it was stalled. Late in September the Allies began encircling and infiltration movements which rolled the Japanese back and yesterday's communiqué had mentioned bitter fighting at Oivi, which is fifty-five miles south of Buna.

Japanese Resist at Oisi

"American ground troops in force, transported by air from Australia during the last month, have penetrated Central and Northern Papua to the vicinity of Buna," a communiqué stated.

"The Allied forces now control all of Papua except the beach head in the Buna-Gona area."

The surprising development came as a thrust around the eastern end of New Guinea from Milne Bay where Japanese troops landed in July only to be pinned against the sea and slain or forced to their ships.

"Units from Milne Bay," the communiqué said, "have now completed clearing remnants of hostile forces from the islands to the north and have occupied adjacent strategic points."

While this disclosure was being made, Australian ground forces still were meeting fierce resistance at Oivi where the retreating Japanese are making a stand. Today's communiqué said the Australians maintained constant pressure and were resorting to their hitherto successful tactics of local encircling movements in efforts to dislodge the defenders.

The Allied air force continued to support the overland drive with strafing attacks on the Japanese troops.

Island Attacked Oct. 22

AT UNITED NATIONS HEADQUARTERS, Australia, Sunday, Nov. 8 (U.P.)—The announcement of sweeping Allied gains in New Guinea came as a surprise to observers here, although an Australian offensive through mountainous central New Guinea had been making steady progress toward the north coast for the past five weeks.

[Delayed dispatches from Harold Guard, United Press staff correspondent in New Guinea, revealed that the Americans had

Continued on Page Forty-five

LEADS IN AFRICA

Lieut. Gen. Dwight Eisenhower
Associated Press

R.A.F. ROCKS GENOA; U.S. RAID ON BREST

Bombers From Britain Pound North Italy 2 Nights in Row—Hit Nazis on Coast

Special Cable to THE NEW YORK TIMES.

LONDON, Sunday, Nov. 8—Bombers from Britain struck a heavy blow at Northern Italy over Friday night, blasting the port of Genoa again in support of the Eighth Army's battling of the Nazis and Italians in the African desert.

Again last night the Royal Air Force sent its big bombers over Northern Italy, British officials reported briefly early today. The announcement meant that the R.A.F. from here was seeing to it that the Axis forces in Africa got no help from home.

American heavy bombers, both Flying Fortresses and Liberators, escorted by Allied fighters, carried out a smashing attack on the docks and U-boat pens at Brest in occupied France yesterday afternoon, United States Army headquarters here announced.

Bombs were seen to strike the targets at Brest. The communiqué stressed that sharp Nazi anti-aircraft fire and enemy fighter opposition were encountered over the coast of Brittany.

The Brest raiders shot down four Nazi fighters. All the United States bombers returned, but one Allied fighter was lost.

The R. A. F.'s fighter squadrons

Continued on Page Twenty-one

NAZIS NEAR LIBYA

British Drive Out to Bar New Stand by Enemy or Reinforcements

FOE BOMBED ALL NIGHT

Pursuers Reported to Be Within 40 Miles of Halfaya Pass

By The United Press.

CAIRO, Egypt, Nov. 7—The British Eighth Army under Lieut. Gen. Bernard L. Montgomery hurled armored forces, motorized infantry and swarms of planes tonight at the remnants of German General Field Marshal Erwin Rommel's once-proud Afrika Korps—possibly only 25,000 out of an original 140,000—now trying to brace for a stand at Halfaya [Hellfire] Pass on the Libyan frontier, 240 miles west of the Alamein battleground.

The main body of the British forces was reported to be well west of Matruh, 110 miles west of El Alamein, and advance striking forces were believed to be as far as 200 miles west of El Alamein, or close to the Egyptian-Libyan frontier, 240 miles west of El Alamein.

How many men Marshal Rommel had left in the Halfaya area could not be established. Already 20,000 prisoners have been counted in British hands. Marshal Rommel's desert casualties were estimated at approximately 20,000 more. In addition, 75,000 Italian troops had been left far behind the swirling battleground, ready to surrender when the British could find time and men to round them up.

Marshal Rommel entered the battle with a maximum of 140,000 troops in the forward area. It was doubted whether he had more than one or two divisions left to attempt another stand at Halfaya unless he had been able to rush large reinforcements from the rear.

It appeared possible tonight that the Axis forces might not even attempt to stand at Halfaya, but would, instead, continue their headlong flight as deeply as possible into Libya in an effort to open a gap between themselves and the Eighth Army.

Such a manoeuvre, however, may already be doomed to failure. General Montgomery has ordered that every attempt be made to cut off Marshal Rommel's retreat. It was believed that he might have sent a hard-hitting, fast-moving

Continued on Page Four

SHOCK TROOPS LEAD

Simultaneous Landings Made Before Dawn at Numerous Points

PLANES GUARD SKIES

An Armada Pours Men on the Beaches—Early Actions Satisfactory

By WES GALLAGHER
Associated Press Correspondent

ALLIED HEADQUARTERS IN NORTH AFRICA, Sunday, Nov. 8—American soldiers, marines and sailors from one of the greatest armadas ever put into a single military operation swarmed ashore today on the Vichy-controlled North Africa shore before dawn, striking to break Hitler's hold on the Mediterranean.

[Reports reaching Allied headquarters in North Africa today disclosed that successful landings had been made by American assault parties on beaches of North Africa near two main objectives outlined in operational plans, an Associated Press dispatch stated.

[British forces reported attemping a landing at Algiers after a bombardment were said by the Vichy radio to have been "beaten off."]

Tall, decisive Lieut. Gen. Dwight D. (Ike) Eisenhower, supreme commander of the huge forces involved in the operation, worked throughout the night directing the first great American blow at the Axis.

Included in the forces were crack combat troops, Rangers (airborne units) and the cream of America's airmen.

British naval and air force units supported the American landing forces, who were preceded by a snowstorm of leaflets and a radio barrage promising the French that the United States had no intention of seizing French possessions and only sought to prevent Axis infiltration.

It undoubtedly was the longest over-water military operation ever attempted, with hundreds of ships in great convoys coming thousands of miles under the protection of British and American sea and air might.

I came on one of these big convoys.

Fighting-fit American soldiers

Continued on Page Five

WHERE THE UNITED STATES PREPARES FOR NEW FRONT

As the survivors of Marshal Rommel's beaten German legions fled westward toward the Libyan border (1), powerful American land, sea and air forces landed behind them at various places in Vichy France's colonies along the Mediterranean (2) and on the shores of the Atlantic, apparently in Morocco (3). British naval and aerial units are assisting them. There was no indication of military action against Vichy's possessions on the western bulge of the Atlantic (4). A large and comprehensive map of the African and Mediterranean theatre of war will be found on Page 1 of Section 4 of this issue of THE TIMES. However, Section 4 had gone to press before the announcement last night of the landing of American troops.

LANDING PLAN KEPT SECRET BY WRITERS

Americans Selected for Duty, Bureaus Sworn to Silence—Eisenhower Slipt Away

By RAYMOND DANIELL
Special Cable to THE NEW YORK TIMES.

LONDON, Sunday, Nov. 8—For weeks American newspaper men have been the custodians of one of war's biggest secrets. It was not an easy secret to keep because through all that time they had to improvise excuses for the absence of a large number of the members of their London staffs to conceal the fact that they had gone with the expeditionary forces.

Most London offices of Amer-

Continued on Page Fourteen

President's Statement

Special to THE NEW YORK TIMES.

WASHINGTON, Nov. 7—President Roosevelt's statement announcing the opening of a second front in French North and West Africa follows:

In order to forestall an invasion of Africa by Germany and Italy, which, if successful, would constitute a direct threat to America across the comparatively narrow sea from Western Africa, a powerful American force equipped with adequate weapons of modern warfare and under American command is today landing on the Mediterranean and Atlantic coasts of the French colonies in Africa.

The landing of this American Army is being assisted by the British Navy and air forces, and it will, in the immediate future, be reinforced by a considerable number of divisions of the British Army.

This combined Allied force, under American command, in conjunction with the British campaign in Egypt is designed to prevent an occupation by the Axis armies of any part of Northern or Western Africa and to deny to the aggressor nations a starting point from which to launch an attack against the Atlantic coast of the Americas.

In addition, it provides an effective second-front assistance to our heroic allies in Russia.

The French Government and the French people have been informed of the purpose of this expedition and have been assured that the Allies seek no territory and have no intention of interfering with friendly French authorities in Africa.

The government of France and the people of France and the French possessions have been requested to cooperate with and assist the American expedition in its effort to repel the German and Italian international criminals, and by so doing to liberate France and the French Empire from the Axis yoke.

This expedition will develop into a major effort by the Allied Nations and there is every expectation that it will be successful in repelling the planned German and Italian invasion of Africa and prove the first historic step to the liberation and restoration of France.

U.S. MEETS 'THREAT'

Big Expeditions Invade North and West Africa to Forestall Axis

EISENHOWER AT HEAD

President Urges French to Help, Calls Move Aid to Russia

Roosevelt's appeal to French people and Eisenhower's message to North Africans, Pg. 8.

By C. P. TRUSSELL
Special to THE NEW YORK TIMES.

WASHINGTON, Nov. 7—Powerful American forces, supported by British naval and air forces, landed simultaneously tonight at numerous points on the Mediterranean and Atlantic coasts of French North Africa, forestalling an anticipated invasion of Africa by Germany and Italy and launching effective second-front assistance to Russia, President Roosevelt announced tonight.

Lieut. Gen. Dwight D. Eisenhower is in command.

The President made the announcement even as the American forces, equipped with adequate weapons of modern warfare, he emphasized, were making the landings.

President Speaks to France

Soon he was speaking direct to the French Government and the French people by short-wave radio and in their own tongue, giving assurances that the Allies seek no territory and have no intention of interfering with friendly French, official or civilian. He called upon them to cooperate in repelling "the German and Italian international criminals."

By doing so, he said, they could help liberate France and the French Empire.

[United States and British planes dropped leaflets in France and French Africa containing messages to the people from President Roosevelt and General Eisenhower, London reported.]

General Eisenhower himself, the White House let it be known, also spoke by radio to the French people, explaining the purposes of the invasions.

His proclamation, delivered while the American troops were making their landings, gave specific directions to French land, sea and air forces in North Africa as to how they could avoid misunderstanding and prevent action against them by a system of signals. This is a military operation, General Eisen-

Continued on Page Three

Major Sports Yesterday

FOOTBALL

Making both touchdowns in the second half, Notre Dame defeated Army before 75,142 spectators at the Yankee Stadium. With a scoring pass in the first period and several goal-line stands, Navy thrilled 74,000 fans at Philadelphia by upsetting Penn. Both Fordham and Columbia lost free-scoring contests here and the Big Three—Princeton, Yale and Harvard—all went down to defeat. Iowa toppled hitherto unbeaten Wisconsin. Scores of leading games:

Alabama	29	So. Carolina	0
Amherst	35	Trinity	6
Boston Coll.	28	Temple	0
Brown	20	Holy Cross	14
Colgate	35	Columbia	26
Cornell	13	Yale	7
Dartmouth	19	Princeton	7
Duke	42	Maryland	0
Duquesne	7	St. Mary's	7
Georgia	75	Florida	0
Ga. Pre-Fl.	41	Auburn	14
Ga. Tech	47	Kentucky	7
Great Lakes	42	Purdue	0
Illinois	14	Northwestern	7
Indiana	7	Minnesota	0
Iowa	6	Wisconsin	0
La. State	26	Fordham	13
Michigan	35	Harvard	7
Miss. State	7	Tulane	0
Missouri	26	Nebraska	6
Moravian	32	C. C. N. Y.	0
Navy	7	Penn	0
Notre Dame	13	Army	0
Ohio State	59	Pittsburgh	19
Oklahoma	76	Kan. State	0
Oregon	14	U. C. L. A.	7
Penn State	18	Syracuse	13
Rice	40	Arkansas	9
So. Calif.	21	California	7
Stanford	20	Washington	7
Texas	20	Baylor	0
Tex. A. & M.	27	S. M. U.	20
Texas Tech	13	T. C. U.	6
Vanderbilt	19	Mississippi	0
Wash. State	25	Mich. State	13
Williams	31	Wesleyan	6

HORSE RACING

Good Morning won the Florence Nightingale Purse by half a length from Too Timely on the war-relief program before 22,099 racegoers who bet $1,550,089 at Belmont Park. Aonbarr defeated Riverland by a neck in the Grayson Handicap at Pimlico.

HOCKEY

The New York Rangers downed the Montreal Canadiens, 4—3, in the overtime opening game at Madison Square Garden.

(Complete Details of These and Other Sports Events in Section 5.)

War News Summarized

SUNDAY, NOVEMBER 8, 1942

The White House announced last night that powerful American forces were landing on the Atlantic and Mediterranean coasts of French North Africa to forestall a German invasion. The announcement stated that the landing was to prevent the creation of an Axis threat to the Atlantic coast of the Americas across the narrow sea in Western Africa. France has been assured that the Allies seek no territory. [1:8.]

American correspondents with the African expeditionary force told of simultaneous landings by the United States troops at many points hundreds of miles apart. [1:4.]

Britain's Eighth Army continued its pursuit in North Africa of Marshal Rommel's shattered army. Twenty thousand prisoners had been taken, according to Cairo. British columns were said to be 200 miles west of El Alamein, close to the Libyan border. [1:3; map, P. 4.]

London announced that British heavy bombers had launched a "concentrated and effective" attack on Genoa Friday night and again raided Northern Italy last night. United States bombers attacked the U-boat base at Brest, France, and other planes from Britain pounded Nazi targets from the Netherlands to the Bay of Biscay. [1:2; map, P. 21.]

Moscow reported that the Soviet armies held on all fronts and killed some 1,800 of the enemy on the Stalingrad and Caucasus fronts. The German advances in the Nalchik region had apparently been halted. [38:4-5.]

General Douglas MacArthur's headquarters announced that American troops in force had been transported by air to New Guinea and had penetrated to the vicinity of Buna, Japanese base on the north coast. [1:1; map, P. 45.]

The United States Navy announced that Army forces on Guadalcanal Island in the Solomons had attacked Japanese troops to the east of the airfield Nov. 6 and had encountered little opposition. Announcement was also made that at least 5,188 Japanese had been killed in land fighting on Tulagi and Guadalcanal since the United States occupation Aug. 7. [46:1 with map.]

United States bombers attacked successfully the docks at Rangoon, Burma, and returned to their bases in India. [46:8.]

Blow to Knock Italy Out of the War Called Goal of American Invasion

Special Cable to THE NEW YORK TIMES.

LONDON, Sunday, Nov. 8—Allied Army, Navy and air forces commanded by Lieut. Gen. Dwight D. Eisenhower, commander of all American forces in the European theatre, have struck a powerful blow to free the Mediterranean from Axis control and knock Italy out of the war. That, in the opinion of military observers here, the meaning of the movement of United States forces that now become part of the gigantic pincers with which it is expected that the last vestiges of the German and Italian forces in North Africa will be annihilated.

The movement now under way called for the finest timing. It was essential that, before that huge armada of whose presence at Gibraltar the Nazis were aware got under way, Britain's Eighth Army in Egypt should break through Marshal Erwin Rommel's defenses and start the westward push that is fast becoming a rout. Now United States soldiers swarming ashore at many points in French North Africa are closing Marshal Rommel's back door.

The first stage of the battle just beginning will be a struggle for the control of roads, railways and airfields in Algeria and the neighboring colony of Tunisia. Once the control of these has been won, Allied reinforcements and supplies will be able to dispense with the long journey around the Cape of Good Hope that has been one of

Continued on Page Thirteen

Petain Says Vichy Will 'Defend' Lands

By The Associated Press.

LONDON, Sunday, Nov. 8—The Vichy radio said today that Marshal Henri Philippe Pétain had sent President Roosevelt a message expressing his "astonishment and sadness" at learning of "the aggression of your troops against North Africa."

Marshal Pétain said that the reasons given by the President for the landings failed to justify them and added:

"France and its honor are involved. We are attacked and we will defend ourselves."

The Vichy government issued a communiqué opening with an "appeal to Frenchmen not to allow yourselves to be swayed by foreign broadcasts."

"All the News That's Fit to Print."

The New York Times.

LATE CITY EDITION
Much colder today with diminishing winds.
Temperatures Yesterday—Max., 65; Min., 50
Sunrise, 7:30 A. M.; Sunset, 5:13 P. M.

Copyright, 1942, by The New York Times Company.

VOL. XCII...No. 30,972. Entered as Second-Class Matter, Postoffice, New York, N. Y. NEW YORK, WEDNESDAY, NOVEMBER 11, 1942. THREE CENTS IN NEW YORK CITY

HITLER TO TAKE OVER ALL FRANCE AND CORSICA; OUR TROOPS IN ORAN, SPEEDING TOWARD LIBYA, TANKS IN CASABLANCA; ROOSEVELT TELLS PLANS

ALLIES IN ACCORD

President Reveals Stalin Was Informed of Plan by Churchill

'NOW IT CAN BE TOLD'

How Decision on Second Front Move Was Made Is Described

By W. H. LAWRENCE
Special to THE NEW YORK TIMES.

WASHINGTON, Nov. 10—Declaring that a second front has to be tailor-made and custom-built and cannot be purchased ready made in a department store, President Roosevelt gave his press conference today a detailed account of the months of planning that preceded the French North African expedition and the limiting factors that made impossible a large-scale Allied offensive across the English Channel before the middle of 1943.

In excellent humor, Mr. Roosevelt leaned back in his chair, puffing on a cigarette and described tersely how Prime Minister Winston Churchill and he had decided on the African offensive as early as the end of June, but had to take it on the chin in silence when ignorant outsiders, who could not have been cognizant of the fact, were demanding something—a second front—that had already been decided upon by the two governments after consultation with their principal fighting allies.

Chronology of Planning

The President's chronology of offensive planning, with the first decision to attack across the English Channel being changed to an expedition into French North Africa, cleared up a major change in language relating to a second front from the June 12 joint communiqué issued by Mr. Roosevelt and Vyacheslaff M. Molotoff, Soviet Foreign Commissar, and the June 27 joint statement of the President and Prime Minister Churchill.

On June 12, when the President and Commissar Molotoff said that the United States and Russia had reached a full understanding on the "urgent tasks of creating a second front in Europe in 1942," a final decision to abandon the Channel offensive in favor of the North African attack had not yet been made, it appeared from the President's recital.

But on June 27, when the President and Prime Minister said simply that coming operations by the military forces of the United Nations would "divert German strength from the attack on Russia," this government and Great Britain already were in agreement on shifting the offensive to North Africa.

The final decisions on the North African move, including the points of attack, the number of men to be employed and the problems of transport and naval protection, were settled toward the end of July at the London conferences of the Prime Minister and British military and naval leaders with General George C. Marshall, Army Chief of Staff; Admiral Ernest J. King, Commander in Chief of the United States Fleet and Chief of Naval Operations, and Harry L. Hopkins, personal representative of the President. The actual date of attack was decided by the end of August, he said.

As the President explained it, in response to a request for a "now it can be told story," the inception of the offensive action in which the American and British armies are engaged in North Africa goes back to about two weeks after Pearl Harbor, when the President invited Prime Minister Churchill and his joint staff to come to Washington just before Christmas. The time had come, he said,

Continued on Page Seven

Thanksgiving Feast Is Set for Army

Here is the menu, announced yesterday by the War Department, for the Thanksgiving dinner on Nov. 26 to be served to American soldiers in all parts of the world as well as in the United States:

Fruit Cup
Roast Turkey — Dressing and
Cranberry Sauce — Giblet Gravy
Mashed Potatoes
Corn — Peas
Stuffed Celery — Tomato Salad
Assorted Pickles
Bread — Butter
Pumpkin Pie
Apples — Grapes
Coffee
Candies — Nuts

MANPOWER DRAFT OPPOSED IN REPORT

Management and Labor in WMC Policy Group Join in Backing Voluntary Plan

The war manpower report is printed on Page 21.

Special to THE NEW YORK TIMES.

WASHINGTON, Nov. 10—A Management-Labor Policy Committee, unanimously opposing enactment of a national war service act for the conscription of labor at this time, has submitted a broad-scale voluntary program designed to eliminate serious manpower problems which now threaten successful prosecution of the war, it was announced today.

After the White House had made public the report submitted Friday, President Roosevelt told his press conference that, while he had been giving considerable study to the recommendations, he had not yet decided whether to put any of them in effect. He said there was no immediate emergency which would require executive action or a request for executive action at once, but added that the problem would grow increasingly serious in the months ahead and that something would be done in a few weeks.

In response to a question, the President said he had not yet decided whether to shift the selective Service system, which handles the drafting of men for the Army, from its present independent status to the War Manpower Commission, which was one of the recommendations of the Management-Labor Policy Committee.

Major Policy Changes Proposed

Warning that "major weaknesses exist in the present approach to the over-all manpower situation, weaknesses that require immediate attention and correction, and which, if not corrected, will seriously impede the war effort," the committee suggested these major changes in governmental policy if an industrial and military force of 62,500,000 men

Continued on Page Twenty-one

ORAN BATTLE BRIEF

500 Miles of Africa's Coastline Now in Hands of Allies

PLANES, SHIPS HELP

New Assault Southeast of Algiers Reported by Paris Radio

By The Associated Press.

LONDON, Nov. 10 — United States expeditionary armies wiped out effective resistance along 500 miles of Africa's Western Mediterranean coast today with the conquest of Oran, Algeria's second city, and a German report said that the Bey of Tunis had granted President Roosevelt's request for the passage of American troops to Libya.

[In Washington, President Roosevelt said yesterday that he had received no reply to his message to the Bey of Tunis.]

On the Atlantic coast, the resistance of Casablanca, the chief city of Morocco, was fast crumbling under all-out naval and air assault by United States Rear Admiral Henry K. Hewitt's heavy warships and dive-bombers as American armored columns infiltrated the city's eastern suburbs with tanks.

Rabat, the normal seat of French power in Morocco, on the coast above Casablanca, evidently was isolated and evacuated by the Vichy commander, General Charles Nogues.

Broad Victory Seen Near

Hence it appeared that in a matter of hours the United States armies commanded by Lieut. Gen. Dwight D. Eisenhower would be in effective control of all French North Africa save for Eastern Algeria and Tunisia.

[Yves Chatel, Governor General of Algeria, has moved his headquarters to Constantine, in the east, and reassumed his administration there, the Vichy radio announced last night, according to The Associated Press in New York.

[In London The United Press recorded a Paris broadcast saying that American forces were advancing from Algiers in the direction of Bou Saada, 120 miles southeast.]

American contingents evidently were well on their way to Libya, either through Tunisia or around it. The report of the Bey's acquiescence was received with some reserve here lest it be merely an attempt to justify the movement of Axis troops into Tunisia.

Time and time again today Vichy's radio insisted that "all is calm" in Eastern and Central Algeria and Tunisia. Some broadcasts, however, reported fighting at Blida, twenty-five miles inland from Algiers.

Official Allied Headquarters as-

Continued on Page Four

AMERICAN OPERATIONS IN AFRICA PROCEED SMOOTHLY

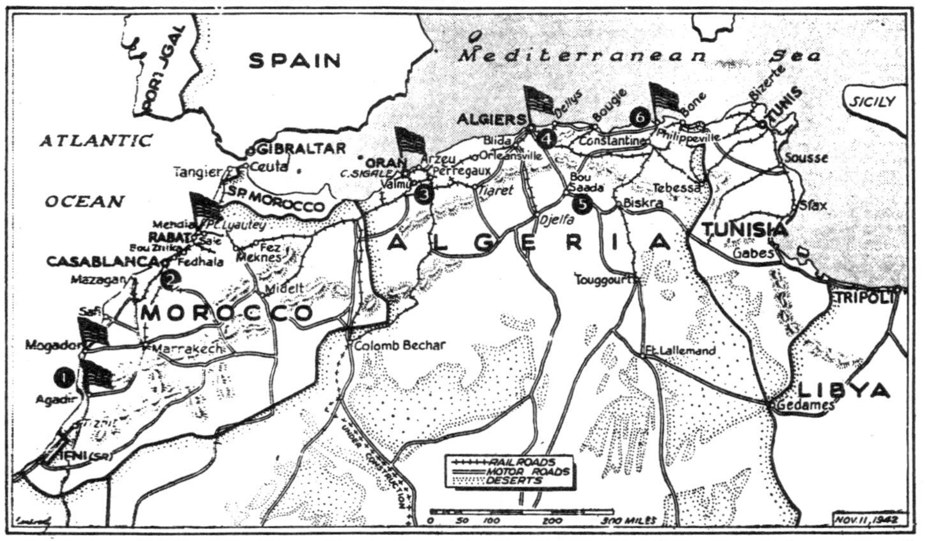

Tangier reports had United States troops still going ashore at Agadir and Mogador (1). The principal, almost the only, center of resistance was at Casablanca (2), where the United States Navy largely subdued Vichy naval opposition and three American tank columns were said to have smashed into the outskirts. Oran (3) fell to an American pincers manoeuvre and one occupying force moved east to deal with a Vichy counter-attack near Orleansville. Land operations had ceased at captured Algiers (4), but there was some resistance at Blida, to the south. From Algiers the Americans were reported to have struck southeastward toward Bou Saada (5), and from Philippeville (6) they were said to be moving eastward in the direction of the frontier of Tunisia.

CHURCHILL CREDITS PLAN TO PRESIDENT

His Own Role That of 'Active and Ardent Lieutenant' in African 'Second Front'

The text of Mr. Churchill's address is on Page 4.

By RAYMOND DANIELL
Wireless to THE NEW YORK TIMES.

LONDON, Nov. 10—The first public utterance by Prime Minister Winston Churchill since General Sir Bernard L. Montgomery's victory in Egypt and the landing of Lieut. Gen. Dwight D. Eisenhower's American Army in French Colonial Africa was made today at Mansion House. It was a renunciation of any Allied territorial aims, a pledge that France should rise again, and a flat declaration that the sole purpose of the Allied landings in Morocco and Algeria was

Continued on Page Four

Tanks Batter Casablanca; Battleship Afire in Harbor

By The United Press.

LONDON, Nov. 10—Vichy broadcasts recorded here reported today that three United States tank columns had crashed into Casablanca, Morocco, and that the city was under heavy attack by superior American forces and was being bombarded violently. Governor General Charles Nogues of Morocco has fled from Rabat to the interior, the radio added.

The broadcasts said that "our troops still are holding out east of Casablanca," while coastal artillery and field guns were resisting vigorously.

Three tank columns closed in on Casablanca, the French said, and swarmed into its outskirts.

A Tangiers dispatch revealed that Fighting French forces were in action at Casablanca against the Vichy troops. It said the Fighting French were battling in the old part of the city, where they were encircled. Americans held the Casablanca reservoir, enabling them to cut off the city's water

Continued on Page Eight

NEW ALLIED FLEET REPORTED MASSING

Concentration of Warships and Transports Noted in Gibraltar Harbor

By The Associated Press.

LONDON, Nov. 10 — Reports from France tonight said another powerful fleet of United Nations warships and a great number of merchantmen were gathering at Gibraltar, while throughout European waters and in the Atlantic naval activities were reported on a vast scale.

Reports from the Continent said some of the vessels of that portion of the French fleet stationed at Toulon had slipped off into the Mediterranean. There was speculation as to whether they were heading for the vicinity of Bizerte, Tunisia, through which American land forces proposed to advance on what is left of German Field Marshal Erwin Rommel's force in Libya.

The German High Command made an unsupported announce-

Continued on Page Six

HITLER, MUSSOLINI, LAVAL IN A PARLEY

Rome Reported Scene of Talks—Duce Said to Ask Nazis for Aid in Crisis

By DANIEL T. BRIGHAM
By Telephone to THE NEW YORK TIMES.

BERNE, Switzerland, Nov. 10—Negotiations for an alliance of Germany, France and Italy against the United Nations were reported under way "somewhere in Europe" tonight.

Most indications pointed to the scene as Rome, although Balkan speculation suggested Munich and other sources hinted at Salzburg. The Brenner Pass, in view of the reported presence of Adolf Hitler and Pierre Laval, Vichy Chief of Government, with their suites at the conferences, is not regarded as sufficiently equipped to house such a parley.

The negotiations and discussions of the future agreement are understood to be in the hands of Herr Hitler, who is accompanied by Reich Marshal Hermann Goering and General Field Marshal Wilhelm Keitel, for the Germans. M. Laval is attended only by his envoy to the Vatican, Leon Berard, and Premier Mussolini is being advised by General Ugo Cavallero, on the military side, and Count Ciano, Italian Foreign Minister.

Asked at his usual press conference for foreign newspaper men today for confirmation on denials of the reports of such a gathering

Continued on Page Ten

LETTER TO PETAIN

Hitler Says Occupation of Whole Country Is Made Necessary

HE SOLICITS ACCORD

Versailles to Be Seat of Puppet Regime Under Nazi Soldiery

By The United Press.

LONDON, Wednesday, Nov. 11—Adolf Hitler has ordered German troops to occupy the remainder of France and the Mediterranean island of Corsica, 300 miles north of the coast of Africa, to counter the United States invasion of French possessions in Northern Africa, the Paris radio announced today.

The Paris radio said Hitler announced his decision was to "prevent further British-American aggression against French territory."

[A wireless dispatch to THE NEW YORK TIMES this morning from Berne, Switzerland, said five German divisions entered the Northern Doubs Valley as the Nazis began the occupation of all of France.]

A letter from Hitler to Marshal Henri Philippe Pétain, read by an official German Army spokesman over the Paris station, announced that Hitler had decided to lift armistice restrictions forcing the French Government to be located in the previously-unoccupied zone of France.

[The French Government will be moved from Vichy to Versailles, said a Paris broadcast recorded by The Associated Press.]

"I have given orders to the German Army to advance through the unoccupied zone to take up positions in order to safeguard the zone against Anglo-American attack," said Hitler's announcement to the French people.

The United States and Britain, after various attempts to carry the war into Europe, "now have proceeded to attack the territories of the French Empire, thereby threatening Corsica as well as the south coast of France," Hitler said.

HITLER LETTER TO PETAIN

LONDON, Nov. 11 (UP)—German troops were reported speeding through unoccupied France today toward a Mediterranean area at which Adolf Hitler said American and British troops proposed landings as a sequel to the American coup in North Africa.

A Paris broadcast quoted Hitler as saying "we have known for twenty-four hours" that Allied attacks were planned upon the French fleet, Corsica and the French mainland coast. He said British and American strategists had "regard to the weakness of the French forces in those parts."

"In these circumstances," Hitler said, "I felt compelled to order the German Army immediately to march through the unoccupied zone—and this is now being done—and to march to the point aimed at by the Anglo-American landing troops."

The letter from Hitler to Marshal Pétain said:

"We have known for twenty-four hours that it is the intention of our enemies to direct the next attack against Corsica, which island they will occupy, and against the south of France."

"I have given this (order) with one single aim, and that is to repel an American and British landing."

"I have given the order to the troops to look after the interests of France," Hitler's letter went on. "The German Government desires as far as possible in collaboration with the French army to protect

Continued on Page Five

War News Summarized

WEDNESDAY, NOVEMBER 11, 1942

The Paris radio reported early today that Adolf Hitler had ordered his army to march into unoccupied France "to repel a possible American or British landing." In a letter to Marshal Pétain, Hitler said that he wished "as far as possible, in collaboration with the French Army, to protect the African possessions of European powers." [1:8.]

United States forces eliminated major resistance along the greater part of the Mediterranean coast of French North Africa yesterday with the fall of Oran. [1:3.]

General Eisenhower, Allied commander in North Africa, told correspondents that he expected the fall of Oran would be the signal for the cessation of organized resistance in the French colonies. [7:1.]

United States troops supported by tanks were reported to have entered the outskirts of Casablanca, Morocco, and a British broadcast said that all resistance of the Vichy naval forces at Casablanca had ceased. An Allied headquarters communiqué disclosed that the new French battleship Jean Bart, was out of action and burning in the harbor. [1:5-6.]

There were reports that a United States column had struck out eastward in Algeria in the direction of Tunisia. President Roosevelt said that no reply had been received to his notification to the Bey of Tunis that United States troops would be sent through the protectorate. [2:2.]

Vichy reported that another powerful Allied convoy had reached Gibraltar. Berlin announced destruction of two Allied cruisers and a transport by Axis submarines and planes. London told of the torpedoing of an Italian cruiser off the north coast of Sicily. [1:6.]

Berne heard that Adolf Hitler, Benito Mussolini and Pierre Laval were in conference "somewhere in Europe." [1.7.]

President Roosevelt disclosed that the decision to open a North African front this year had been made last Summer after it had been decided that it would be impossible to open an effective second front in the northern portion of the European continent this year. [1:1.]

Prime Minister Churchill said that the landings in Africa were the prelude to a new front against Hitler and declared that the plan had been devised by President Roosevelt. [1:4.]

Action on the Egyptian-Libyan front was limited to minor rearguard activity at Sidi Barrani and Solum. The enemy's position was apparently becoming increasingly catastrophic. [3:2.]

Soviet troops registered some small successes at Stalingrad and near Tuapse on the Black Sea. German assaults were repulsed. [13:1.]

East Faces Gasoline Ration Slash And Possible 5% Fuel Oil Cut

By CHARLES E. EGAN
Special to THE NEW YORK TIMES.

WASHINGTON, Nov. 10—Faced with increasing difficulties in maintaining petroleum supplies on the East Coast, the government plans a further slash in the amount of gasoline to be allowed civilian motorists in this area.

Suggestions to cut the fuel-oil allowance to householders have been studied but, according to reports, there is strong opposition to any substantial cut, on the ground that the health hazards created by reducing allowable home temperatures below 65 degrees are too great to justify more than a slight decrease.

A formal announcement on both these proposals is expected later in the week from the War Production Board.

Official concern over the difficulties in transporting petroleum to the Atlantic Coast area, where gasoline rationing is in effect, was evident in many quarters here today. Shipments by railroad tank car, which have exceeded 800,000 barrels a day in some weeks, declined to 733,594 barrels a day last week, and averaged 759,233 the week before. This fact was called to the attention of the WPB at its regular weekly meeting today, along with a request that it authorize a reduction in gasoline rations.

Although no official announcement of the WPB's action was made, one report was that the board had actually approved a proposed slash of one-fourth in the gasoline allowance to be given "A" card holders in the seventeen Eastern States.

In addition, it was stated, the

Continued on Page Eleven

Darlan in U. S. Hands at Algiers; Petain 'Commands' Vichy's Forces

By DAVID ANDERSON
Wireless to THE NEW YORK TIMES.

LONDON, Nov. 10—Admiral François Darlan, chief of Vichy's armed forces, is now in Allied hands at Algiers "being entertained by one of our American generals with the respect and dignity due an officer of his rank," London headquarters of the Allied force announced tonight. No detail was given as to how and when Admiral Darlan got into his present situation.

Ever since his presence in French North Africa was confirmed soon after American operations began—he had gone ostensibly for a check-up on Vichy's defenses—it was suspected here that Admiral Darlan might permit himself to be caught or might voluntarily walk into General Dwight D. Eisenhower's camp.

Admiral Darlan has never been one to carry resistance to extremes, especially when there is something to gain by following the opposite course. He has long been known for his marked dislike of the British, however, and that has been given as an explanation of many of his actions at Vichy.

Many observers here feel that Admiral Darlan would not be able to re-establish his fortunes just by joining the United Nations, as did General Henri Giraud. The admiral is considered too unreliable.

LONDON, Nov. 10 (UP)—With Admiral Darlan definitely a prisoner of General Eisenhower at Algiers, old Marshal Henri Philippe Pétain, stubbornly repeating his order for resistance, took over the disorganized and melancholy defense of all

Continued on Page Four

"All the News That's Fit to Print."

The New York Times.

LATE CITY EDITION
Rain and moderately cool today
Temperatures Yesterday—Max., 50; Min., 40
Sunrise, 7:14 A. M.; Sunset, 5:30 P. M.

VOL. XCII...No. 30,986. Entered as Second-Class Matter, Postoffice, New York, N. Y. NEW YORK, WEDNESDAY, NOVEMBER 25, 1942. THREE CENTS IN NEW YORK CITY

NAZIS' GRIP ON STALINGRAD BROKEN; 15,000 SLAIN AS SOVIET PUSH GAINS; BRISK FIGHTING SPREADS IN TUNISIA

EXTORTION CHARGED BY MAYOR IN ROW OVER STIRRUP PUMPS

Herlands Says Effort Was Made to 'Shake Down' a Dealer by Promise to 'Fix' Council

REPORT HELD 'RECKLESS'

Solomon, Ex-Deputy Controller, Modell, La Guardia Critic, Deny the Accusations

Mayor La Guardia and William B. Herlands, Commissioner of Investigation, charged yesterday that an attempt had been made to "shake down" a stirrup-pump distributor on the claim that a proposed local law could be killed by the City Council as the result of "influence."

The Mayor said that he learned of the "crude and brazen attempt of a shakedown" from Commissioner Herlands on Saturday and that it was for this reason that he announced on Sunday his plans to have the city sell stirrup pumps directly to consumers.

Copies of Mr. Herlands' official report supplying details of the alleged extortion attempt were given yesterday afternoon to District Attorney Frank S. Hogan and to the grievance committee of the Association of the Bar of the City of New York.

Modell Called "Contact Man"

Named as principals in the Herlands' report were:

Henry Modell, president of Modell's, a sporting goods and uniform store at 198 Broadway, described as "the contact man."

Milton Solomon, an attorney with offices at 165 Broadway, former Deputy City Controller and one-time Democratic candidate for President of the Board of Aldermen, listed as the "alleged fixer."

Maurice Holt, owner of the Triangle Appliance Corporation of 11 West Forty-second Street, which is said to have a stirrup pump distribution monopoly. Although he appeared cast in the role of victim, the report indicated he went through with the deal on the advice of the Department of Investigation.

"Stated baldly, this is the case of a lawyer trying to obtain a large sum of money from a business man by assuring him that he, the lawyer, had the 'influence' to 'kill' certain legislation which was objectionable to said businessman," Commissioner Herlands' report said.

"Outrageous," Says Solomon

Mr. Solomon described the charges as "outrageous" and "reckless" when informed of the contents of the report at his home, 9 Prospect Park West, Brooklyn, last night.

Mr. Modell declared that the accusations were "a dastardly lie" and a "red herring," and declared that he would not allow the Mayor "to get away with it." On Sunday Mr. Modell had assailed the Mayor for putting the city into the pump-selling business, declaring this municipal venture to be unfair competition with business men who were selling the equipment at retail at a small profit.

Councilman Walter R. Hart, chairman of the City Council Defense Committee, declared that he was surprised and astounded by the charges. The report quoted Mr. Solomon as boasting to Mr. Holt that Mr. Hart was his "man" and could kill the pending bill.

According to Commissioner Herlands's report, Mr. Holt was disturbed over the prospect of enactment of a local law sponsored by Councilman Hugh Quinn, Queens Democrat. This measure, still pending before the Council, eliminates stirrup pumps from the list of fire fighting weapons that building owners or tenants must have under the Air Raid Law. As the law now stands they may be used as an alternative to rubber hose under certain conditions.

Mayor Charges Shakedown

"When I made my statement Sunday announcing my decision to give the consumers the benefit of direct sale of stirrup pumps as provided by the Office of Civilian Defense, I did so because it was the only way to put an end to the crude and brazen attempt at a shakedown," the Mayor told reporters yesterday afternoon after he had conferred with Commissioner Herlands.

"I received Saturday a report from the Commissioner of Investigation. That report was given to District Attorney Hogan this after-

Continued on Page Thirty

Two Thanksgivings For Pacific Troops

Wireless to THE NEW YORK TIMES.

WELLINGTON, N. Z., Nov. 24—There will be two Thanksgiving Days this year—one on the western side of the International Date Line as well as that on the American side.

For the first time, Thanksgiving Day will be nationally celebrated in the Antipodes wherever United States troops are now stationed. In the Fiji and Samoan Islands it may cause a headache. The date line bisects these islands and forces in American Samoa will mark the continental American day, but in Fiji it will be a day earlier if Americans are there.

WAR POWERS BILL STRIKES NEW SNAG

House Group Considers Repeal of Income Curb, Calling It Invasion of Rights

Special to THE NEW YORK TIMES.

WASHINGTON, Nov. 24—New manifestations against "government by bureaucracy" became plain in Congress today, leaving the future of the Third War Powers Bill in doubt and suggesting that moves were afoot for application of brakes to administrative authorities when the new session begins in January.

Only a technicality prevented what was viewed as an almost certain insertion into the powers-granting measure by the Ways and Means Committee of a provision which would nullify by statute President Roosevelt's recent executive order limiting annual salaries to $25,000 net.

Sponsors of the proposed "repealer" said they had sufficient committee votes in sight to write it into the bill, if Representative Doughton, the chairman, had not ruled it not germane, and thus out of order. Further attempts will be made, it was asserted, when and if the legislation reaches the Senate, if not before.

During two executive sessions, lasting most of the day, the Ways and Means body dealt with protests by members against Executive Department interpretations of limitations written into previously enacted power-giving legislation by the Congress, it was reported later.

No Decision as to Hearings

The salary limiting order, it was brought out, was only one of many administrative actions drawing the fire of members as allegedly having gone beyond the intent of Congress in the carrying out of its directives.

The Ways and Means Committee refused to write the $25,000 limitation into the tax bill when the proposal was made specifically. Mr. Roosevelt acted under a clause in the anti-inflation price and wage control bill.

At the end of the day no decision had been reached even as to the holding of hearings on the modified draft of the powers program, which was approved unanimously by a subcommittee Saturday after the committee had rejected the Administration's sweeping draft. Doubt was expressed by members that the legislation could get through both the House and Senate before Congress adjourned.

Committee members insisted, however, that further hearings should be held before any bill was reported, and a decision on this phase may be made tomorrow. They maintained further, that

Continued on Page Thirteen

PRESIDENT WARNS PRODUCTION CHIEFS TO RECONCILE AIMS

If They Can't Agree He Will Put Them in Foodless Room Until They Reach Solution

NEW CONTROL PLAN DENIED

WPB-Armed Services Dispute on Aircraft Brushed Aside at Press Conference

By W. H. LAWRENCE
Special to THE NEW YORK TIMES.

WASHINGTON, Nov. 24—With reports current in the capital of a growing crisis within the Administration on the issue of civilian versus military control of the country's economy, President Roosevelt today brushed aside questions as to whether the War Production Board or the armed forces have the final authority on war production problems.

While Washington speculated about a possible Presidential move to break the stalemate between the civilian and military leaders, now manifested in a quarrel over a new master production set-up, the Chief Executive, at his press conference, said that WPB, Army and Navy officials are supposed to agree, and, when they do not, he will lock them in a room and tell them they will get no food until they come out with an agreement.

Denying reports that he was working on plans for a new one-man control of production, supply, manpower and related wartime problems, the President said that on the whole, the present system is working very well.

WPB Circles Apprehensive

The President's optimism was not shared in well informed WPB circles, which apprehensively heard reports that the Army was attempting to take control of manpower and looked upon the aircraft stalemate as the first challenge to Donald M. Nelson's authority to take back powers over production which he himself delegated to the Army and Navy last March. The WPB official said, half seriously and half jokingly, that he feared "quasi-martial law" was ahead for the country.

Persons familiar with the views of the armed services denied, however that there was any challenge to Mr. Nelson in the dispute revolving around the creation of a new aircraft production committee, representing the Army and Navy and headed by Charles E. Wilson, former president of the General Electric Corporation. These persons, expressing the highest admiration for Mr. Wilson's production abilities, were confident of a compromise solution which would give influence in aircraft matters to Lieut. Gen. William S. Knudsen, former OPM head and now War Department Production Director, and would eliminate Harold E. Talbott of WPB from the committee.

While the aircraft production fight may be settled amicably without a definite test of authority, there was no doubt in informed quarters, where production authorities have been discussed with the civilian and military leaders, that there is a conflict between the services and Mr. Nelson over how much authority he should exercise over such matters as production scheduling.

The armed services feel that WPB should give its major atten-

Continued on Page Twelve

Valtin Arrested for Deportation; Board Cites 'Wavering Loyalties'

Special to THE NEW YORK TIMES.

WASHINGTON, Nov. 24—Jan Valtin, author of "Out of the Night," was arrested today in Bethel, Conn., on a warrant issued by the Immigration and Naturalization Service and held for deportation to Germany. The arrest was announced here soon afterward by Attorney General Biddle.

Valtin, who is 37 years old and whose real name is Richard Julius Herman Krebs, had been the subject of extended hearings before the Board of Immigration Appeals. The deportation order is not expected to be carried out until after the war, and Valtin probably will be interned meanwhile.

The board found that Krebs entered this country illegally after once having been arrested and deported and after committing a crime involving moral turpitude, in this case perjury. Technically, the board unanimously voted to order the deportation after first denying an application for suspension of deportation proceedings on the ground that Krebs had not been "a person of good moral character for the past five years, as required by law, and that he was otherwise deportable."

Within the last five years, the board asserted, Krebs "has been considered an agent of Nazi Germany."

The board minced no words in ordering the deportation. Unanimously, said Thomas G. Finucane, chairman, the members found the author's life "so marked with violence, intrigue and treachery that it would be difficult, if not wholly unwarranted, to conclude

Continued on Page Fifteen

ALLIES' GAIN SLOW

Attack of Axis Armored Unit Broken Up by Chutist Forces

MORE CLASHES IN SOUTH

New Landings Reported at Sfax and Gabes as U. S. Planes Shoot Up Troop Train

By RAYMOND DANIELL
Special Cable to THE NEW YORK TIMES.

LONDON, Nov. 24—Sharp fighting took place today in several sectors of Tunisia, where the Allied forces are advancing on Axis-held Tunis, the capital, and Bizerte, the vital naval base. There has been no major clash yet, however, although air activity is increasing as the opposing forces manoeuvre for positions.

The official Allied communiqués continued to be as uninformative as the Axis radios were misleading. However, the communiqués contained enough information to indicate that the Allies were advancing on a broad front while the Axis continued its hasty preparations to make the Tunis-Bizerte corner a sort of Tobruk.

Tonight's communiqué from headquarters, mentioning "local engagements" of Allied forward units, gave few details. Continued activity was reported from the southern sector, where French patrols are operating. A unit of Allied paratroopers repulsed an enemy mechanized column, taking prisoners, according to the communiqué. Unofficial sources reported that British troops advancing eastward along the coastal road had engaged in several minor brushes with enemy patrols.

Four enemy aircraft were shot down by British and American fighters, which also attacked an enemy troop train near Gabès, while heavy bombers raided Bizerte and Tunis. All the bombers and fighters returned safely to their bases, the communiqué said.

[The Vichy radio said that the Axis had landed large troop formations on the Tunisian east coast at Sfax and Gabès, far below Bizerte and Tunis, The Associated Press reported from London. Another Associated Press dispatch, from Allied Headquarters in North Africa, said that British troops had driven back a German advance screen in Northern Tunisia while the

Continued on Page Six

U. S. BOMBERS SCORE BULL'S-EYE IN TRIPOLI HARBOR

Smoke (arrow) marks direct blast on the Spanish Mole during a raid on the Libyan port

Associated Press Radiophoto (U. S. Army Air Forces)

BRITISH PUSH FOE TOWARD AGHEILA

Take Oasis Far to Southeast as Axis Forces Continue Retreat Across Libya

Special Cable to THE NEW YORK TIMES.

CAIRO, Egypt, Nov. 24—If there is to be a battle at El Agheila it is likely to begin soon, for the German rear guard is moving southwestward from Agedabia toward there, putting up only enough of a fight to keep from being overrun.

Agedabia is now in British hands. The need for consolidation and building of supply services is undoubtedly a greater factor in determining the British rate of advance in that area now than are any efforts of the weak rear guard screens.

The Germans have few tanks left and not too many guns. But they must cast the die one way or the other soon. They must either rush back to Tripoli or fight desperately at El Agheila.

It is regarded as a question whether the present members of the German Africa Corps will be anxious to fight a hopeless battle

Continued on Page Six

War News Summarized

WEDNESDAY, NOVEMBER 25, 1942

Adolf Hitler's forces in the Stalingrad salient of the eastern front appeared to be on the verge of total disaster yesterday. The situation on the African fronts was little changed and activity in the Pacific war theatre was limited.

West of Stalingrad the Russian Army was reported to be advancing on a 200-mile front and to have penetrated as deep as twenty-five miles into enemy-held territory, while other Soviet troops drove down into the city from the north through the encircling German lines. Another 15,000 German soldiers were reported killed and 12,000 more taken prisoner. [1:8.]

Berlin acknowledged that the Russians had penetrated the German defensive line in the Don bend region. [8:2.]

Rumanian troops, fighting with the Germans in the region, were said to be surrendering in masses and apparently the Germans were retreating and leaving them to their fate. [1:6-7.]

It still seemed doubtful that Marshal Rommel's forces in Libya would give battle at El Agheila. The Axis rear guard was approaching El Agheila rapidly and was offering little opposition. [1:5.]

Sharp clashes took place in Tunisia between Axis forces and Allied troops advancing out of Algeria, but battle had not yet been joined and the Germans and Italians continued to strengthen their positions around Bizerte and Tunis. [1:4; map, P. 6.]

In London a Labor member of Parliament asserted that Prime Minister Churchill had suppressed a broadcast scheduled by the chief of the Fighting French, General de Gaulle, after Foreign Secretary Anthony Eden had approved it. A charge that "reactionary tendencies" were gaining the upper hand was raised in connection with the incident. [6:1.]

The Polish Government in Exile announced that the German Gestapo Chief, Heinrich Himmler, had ordered half the Jews in Poland killed by the end of this year in preparation for the eventual slaughter of all Jews in the country. [10:1.]

Secretary of the Navy Knox told reporters that Japanese reinforcements had not been landed recently on Guadalcanal and that the island could probably be kept isolated from further Japanese infiltration. United States troops advanced farther west of Henderson Field. [1:7.] The situation of the Japanese defending Buna in Northeastern New Guinea remained desperate. [3:1.]

United States bombers based on India raided the railway installations at Mandalay, Burma, again Sunday and reported that the previous raid last Friday had been very effective. [4:1.]

Nazis Retreat, Some in Panic, Leaving Rumanians in Lurch

By RALPH PARKER
Wireless to THE NEW YORK TIMES.

MOSCOW, Nov. 24—While the Red Army's two-barbed thrust was plunging deeper into the enemy's flanks, Stalingrad's defenders grasped the initiative and, exactly three months after the city was first assaulted, began to clear the Germans systematically from fortresses and cellars. Continuing their gradual advance last night, the Russians took blockhouses by storm and broke resistance in both the northern factory and southern regions of the impregnable city.

On the Don steppes, on the western slopes of the Ergeni Hills and southwestward along the main highway and railroad toward the Kuban, the counter-offensive is maintaining its tempo and proceeding according to a careful strategic plan to undermine the entire position of the German armies in the south. This is a reward, the newspaper Izvestia asserts, for the heroic resistance of the Red Army, the skillful training of its commanders and other tireless work in the rear.

Russia's allies, too, had a share in it, the paper adds, for the Germans' strategic difficulties were aggravated by the Allies' operations in Africa and the threatening prospect of a continental invasion. It is understood that British and American-built tanks are being used in the present offensive.

No attempt is made to minimize the stern tasks ahead of the Red Army on the Don-Volga front. The Germans' resilience and power in defensive fighting are known from bitter experience, reserves are being accumulated hastily to meet the Red Army's advance and time is reducing the advantages gained by the element of surprise—prisoners' testimony agree that the

Continued on Page Eight

GUADALCANAL FOES CUT OFF, KNOX SAYS

Secretary Asserts Enemy Can Not Send In Aid—Nimitz Denies Naval Battle

By CHARLES HURD
Special to THE NEW YORK TIMES.

WASHINGTON, Nov. 24—The Navy believes it has closed the routes by which the Japanese may reinforce their garrisons on Guadalcanal Island, Secretary of the Navy Frank Knox said today. This result was credited to the naval victory recently won by American sea forces against "seemingly hopeless odds" in the waters around the Solomon Islands.

[Admiral Chester W. Nimitz, Commander in Chief of the Pacific Fleet, said yesterday that, so far as he knew, there was no naval action going on in the Solomons area such as had been reported by the Japanese radio Monday night.]

Secretary Knox expressed the belief that our own soldiers and marines now face a straitened enemy, while further dispatches from Guadalcanal reported that the Americans there were extending

Continued on Page Four

Chicago Trio Get Death Penalty For Treason, Wives Prison Terms

Special to THE NEW YORK TIMES.

CHICAGO, Nov. 24—Three German-Americans who aided and sheltered Herbert Hans Haupt, executed Nazi saboteur and spy, were sentenced to death for treason today by Federal Judge William J. Campbell "as a timely and solemn warning to all who would attempt the smallest act of sabotage." Their wives, who were convicted of the same crimes, were ordered to prison for twenty-five years and fined $10,000 each.

"The sentence must serve notice upon the enemy that the cunningly devised scheme for the use of American citizens of German birth as pawns in the game of sabotage and espionage in this country is doomed to failure," the judge asserted.

The men are Hans Max Haupt, father of Herbert, who was captured with seven other saboteurs after they had landed in June from German submarines on the Long Island and Florida coasts; Walter Wilhelm Froehling, uncle of Herbert, and Otto Walter Wergin, close friend of the Haupts and Froehlings. Their wives are Erna Emma Haupt, Lucille Froehling and Kate Martha Wergin. All had been convicted by a jury of eight women and four men on Nov. 14.

Judge Campbell set Jan. 22 as the execution day, but the defense filed an appeal this afternoon, and Paul A. F. Warnholtz, chief counsel, said he would fight the sentences to the Supreme Court.

If the death sentences are sustained the three men will be executed at either the Cook County jail in Chicago or at the States-

Continued on Page Fifteen

12,000 MORE TAKEN

Russians Smash Ahead, Capture Many Places in Multiple Drive

HELP REACHES VOLGA CITY

Column Arrives From North—Three Divisions With Generals Among Forces Encircled

By The Associated Press.

MOSCOW, Wednesday, Nov. 25—The three-month-old Nazi grip on Stalingrad was weakening today after a swiftly advancing Red Army had killed 15,000 more Germans yesterday and captured 12,000, including three divisional generals, in a great Winter offensive rolling so fast that some Nazi units were cut down from behind in panicky retreat.

Russian official announcements raised the toll of Nazis to 77,000 dead or captured, not counting huge numbers of wounded who apparently are freezing to death on the frozen steppes, as did other German units last Winter in the rout from Moscow.

The Red Army's effort to encircle the entire Nazi army stalemated before Stalingrad, estimated at 300,000, clearly was gaining in power. Two communiqués told of vast stocks of war equipment falling to the Soviet tide, of at least one enemy airdrome being seized so swiftly that scores of German planes were unable to take to the air.

Stalingrad Defenders Gain

Inside Stalingrad the Russians in frontal assaults also were gaining against Nazi detachments whose rear communications had been slashed by Russian flanking armies sweeping across the Don River far to the west.

[The German High Command admitted the gravity of the situation by acknowledging the penetration of Nazi defenses southwest of Stalingrad. But it said "countermeasures" were under way and reported "savage battles" in the Don bend region. The London Express quoted a Stockholm report that the Germans had "begun to pull out of Stalingrad."]

The midnight Soviet communiqué said 900 Germans were killed and dozens of enemy blockhouses occupied in a slow but steady advance inside Stalingrad, while in the Caucasus Red Army units cut down additional hundreds of Nazis in successful stands in the Nalchik and Tuapse sectors.

This bulletin added some details to the striking Russian successes above and below Stalingrad and inside the Don River bend, as announced in a special communiqué. One Red Army unit captured a Nazi airdrome so swiftly, it said, that forty-two enemy planes did not have time to take to the air. Twenty-five of these planes were destroyed and the seventeen others were captured intact.

In some sectors there was evident Axis demoralization, because hundreds of fleeing Germans were being struck down from behind as

Continued on Page Eight

Daladier and Others Seen in Nazi Hands

Wireless to THE NEW YORK TIMES.

ON THE SPANISH FRONTIER, Nov. 24—France's former leaders who had been held at the Pourtalet prison in the Pyrenees, including former Premiers Paul Reynaud, Edouard Daladier and Léon Blum and General Maurice Gustav Gamelin, are reported to have been moved to Bordeaux in the last forty-eight hours to be sent to Germany, according to a statement here today by a Frenchman who has just crossed the frontier.

The informant said the dossiers for the Riom war-guilt trials had been demanded by the German Ministry of Justice for study and that Vichy officials had surrendered them to the Germans.

"All the News That's Fit to Print."

The New York Times.

LATE CITY EDITION
Continued moderately cold and windy today.
Temperatures Yesterday—Max., 48; Min., 30
Sunrise, 8:12 A. M.; Sunset, 6:06 P. M.

Copyright, 1943, by The New York Times Company.

VOL. XCII..No. 31,049. Entered as Second-Class Matter. Postoffice, New York, N. Y. NEW YORK, WEDNESDAY, JANUARY 27, 1943. THREE CENTS IN NEW YORK CITY

ROOSEVELT, CHURCHILL MAP 1943 WAR STRATEGY AT TEN-DAY CONFERENCE HELD IN CASABLANCA; GIRAUD AND DE GAULLE, PRESENT, AGREE ON AIMS

15,000 QUIT WORK IN DRESS PAY ROW; PEACE MOVES START

85,000 in 2,000 Shops Here Due to Be Out This Week Unless U. S. Calls Halt

STEELMAN AIDE ARRIVES

But Need for WLB Action Is Seen—Mayor Asks OPA to Modify Price Order

Between 15,000 and 20,000 dressmakers, members of the International Ladies Garment Workers Union, quit their jobs yesterday in what the union called a "spontaneous" stoppage to enforce demands for wage readjustments after the breakdown of negotiations with employers on Monday. No war production is involved.

Both employers and union spokesmen predicted that all 85,000 workers in the industry, affecting 2,000 shops in New York City and vicinity, would be tied up by the end of the week if the stoppage was not arrested. Spokesmen for five employer associations charged the stoppage was in violation of the current agreement in the industry, which does not expire until Jan. 31, 1944.

While David Dubinsky, president of the I. L. G. W. U., reaffirmed the union's willingness to abide by arbitration or to call off the stoppage if the War Labor Board assumes jurisdiction in the controversy efforts to settle the dispute were begun by the United States Conciliation Service and Mayor La Guardia.

Complaint Filed Against Union

Upon complaint filed with Harry Uviller, impartial chairman of the dress industry, charging violation of contract by the union, Mr. Uviller will confer with employer and union representatives in his office at 1440 Broadway this morning. He too, however, expressed the belief that the dispute could be settled through action by the War Labor Board.

Involved in the controversy is the declaration by Mr. Dubinsky that the union would oppose the application of the War Labor Board's Little Steel formula in the dress stoppage on the ground that it had been voided by the rise in the cost of living. Acceptance of the union's position would invalidate for all industries subject to President Roosevelt's wage stabilization order the board's criterion of measuring the justification of wage increases on the basis of living costs as they stood in May, 1942.

The position taken by the employers in the dress industry is that while they are cognizant of the justice of the union's demand for a wage equalization because of the rise in living costs, they are unable to grant it as long as prices remain frozen under OPA order.

Mayor Seeks OPA Order Change

Efforts to bring about modification of the OPA order were being pressed by Mayor La Guardia yesterday, as Bernard J. Forman, Federal conciliator, acting on instructions of Dr. John R. Steelman, director of the United States Conciliation Service, arrived in the city and met representatives of the employers and the union. Both employers and union officials were of the opinion that Mr. Forman's intervention was not likely to succeed and that Dr. Steelman would have to ask Frances Perkins, Secretary of Labor, to certify the dispute to the War Labor Board.

After conferring yesterday afternoon at City Hall with George A. Sloan, City Commissioner of Commerce, Mr. La Guardia disclosed that he had recommended to Prentiss Brown, OPA administrator in Washington, that OPA order 287, which fixes maximum prices for the dress industry, be modified. In

Continued on Page Eighteen

Rationalizing of Industry Undertaken in War Drive

WPB Officials Outline Steps Purposing to Make Entire Lines of Enterprise Act as a Single Manufacturer

By The Associated Press.

WASHINGTON, Jan. 26—A far-reaching plan to "rationalize" a vast segment of American industry—to end duplication of effort and other practices described as wasteful—is in the final stages of consideration in the War Production Board, high officials disclosed tonight.

The aim, the officials said, was to increase war production, but they predicted that in peace years the plan would mean more goods for consumers at cheaper prices.

These officials, who prefer to remain unidentified at this time, said the immediate objective was to solve the crucial problem of "components"—the valves, engines, heat exchangers, instruments and other bottleneck items for which many of the "must" war production programs are competing.

The net result, if carried through as contemplated, would be to make an entire industry function as a single manufacturer, ending what is termed the "wasteful" use of critical machines, equipment, manpower and transportation.

Inefficiency results when each of several companies in an industry is making a score of different objects, it was explained. The WPB idea is that total output can be increased if each company is concentrated on a few products. Similarly, the effort will be made to get rid of the waste motion involved when several companies are making several versions of the same product.

WPB intends to attack the problem, it was disclosed, by going direct to industry, bringing leaders from each industry to Washington—probably as WPB employes on a "without compensation" basis—

Continued on Page Fifteen

E. J. FLYNN QUITS PARTY COMMITTEE

Move Apparently Spells Favorable Vote by Senate Group on His Nomination

By W. H. LAWRENCE
Special to The New York Times.

WASHINGTON, Jan. 26—Edward J. Flynn resigned today as a Democratic National Committeeman from New York and this step apparently cleared the way for a close but favorable vote by the Senate Foreign Relations Committee on his nomination to be Minister to Australia.

The resignation was announced by Frank C. Walker, who succeeded Mr. Flynn as chairman of the national committee.

The Senate Foreign Relations Committee will meet in executive session tomorrow morning to vote on recommending Mr. Flynn's nomination. While most observers believed that he would win approval by a very slender margin, opponents were still hopeful that they could deadlock the committee by a tie vote in the absence of favorable proxy from Senator Glass of Virginia, who is ill at his Lynchburg home.

Senate to Vote Monday

The Senate itself will consider the nomination on Monday and a vigorous floor fight is expected.

Mr. Flynn's resignation of all party political positions assured him the vote of Senator Clark of Missouri, who had made this action the price of his support and who had told Democratic leaders that if it were not forthcoming he and Senator Hatch of New Mexico would wage an intensive campaign among Senate Democrats to block Mr. Flynn's confirmation.

Although Mr. Flynn had said when he quit as national chairman that he would retain his committee membership, administration leaders felt that they needed the support of Senators Clark and Hatch and persuaded the New Yorker to reconsider this decision, although it meant, in all probability, that the New York place on the national committee would go to James A. Farley, who now is counted among the anti-New Dealers and an opponent of any effort to win a fourth term for the President.

If Mr. Farley doesn't take the job himself, he is expected to dictate the selection of Mr. Flynn's successor by the New York Democratic Committee

"With full appreciation of his great services both as chairman and New York National Committeeman, I feel the exercise of his duties in the post to which the President has appointed him and the implied absence from the

Continued on Page Forty-two

250 SLAIN RESISTING NAZIS IN MARSEILLE

Seventy Women Victims of the Fighting as 40,000 Are Ousted From Port Area

By MILTON BRACKER
Special Cable to The New York Times.

LONDON, Jan. 26—One hundred and eighty men and seventy women have been shot in connection with the round-up of what the Germans term "subversive elements" and evacuation of the Old Harbor area of Marseille, according to Swiss reports.

The occupation authorities have reiterated their warning that whoever enters the forbidden area, now under a state of siege, will be executed.

Although naturally more concerned with the return of General Charles de Gaulle from his conference, Fighting French circles in London have closely followed reports from France's greatest seaport, hitherto not regarded as a

Continued on Page Ten

NAZI RING IS CUT UP

Only 12,000 of Foe Left in Stalingrad Force—'Liquidation' Near

RAIL LINES CLEARED

Red Army's Offensives Increase in Violence, Berlin Reports

By The Associated Press.

LONDON, Jan. 26—Russian troops have killed or captured all but 12,000 German troops of the huge forces trapped at Stalingrad and have freed the three main railways radiating westward for the continuing offensive that has carried the Red Army forward 245 miles, Moscow announced tonight in a special communiqué recorded by the Soviet monitor here.

[Soviet troops have entered Stalingrad from the west through the former Nazi seige lines, said a Moscow broadcast recorded by The United Press at London early today.]

Since Jan. 10, the Russians said, they have killed more than 40,000 Germans and captured 28,000, leaving 12,000 split there in two pockets yet to be liquidated.

Two Groups Isolated

"We have not yet liquidated two small enemy groups, separated and isolated from each other, totaling in all no more than 12,000 men, one to the north of Stalingrad and the other nearer to the central part of the town," the communiqué continued. "Both these groups are doomed and their liquidation is only a question of two or three days."

[The Germans said their remaining troops in Stalingrad were concentrated in a narrow space and were continuing their "heroic resistance" under the command of their generals. The Soviet onslaught on large parts of the front were said to have increased in violence.]

Twenty-two Nazi divisions of some 220,000 men had been reported encircled in the Don-Volga pocket before Stalingrad after the Russians began their November offensives above and below the Volga River city.

The Russians threw a cordon

Continued on Page Twelve

War News Summarized

WEDNESDAY, JANUARY 27, 1943

President Roosevelt and Prime Minister Churchill, together with their joint chiefs of staff and other military and civil officials, have concluded a ten-day conference at Casablanca, Morocco, in which a general program of military strategy for 1943 was worked out. The President said that the United Nations would be satisfied with nothing short of the enemy's unconditional surrender. He said the objectives for the year would be to maintain and extend the initiative won late in 1942, to dispatch all possible aid to Russia and to give assistance to the Chinese armies. General Giraud and General de Gaulle met during the conference and reached an agreement to cooperate in the prosecution of the war. [1:8.]

Washington believed that the conference would result in a continuing planned offensive on all fronts and observers were struck by the fact that the aim to win an unconditional surrender of the enemy excluded the possibility of a negotiated peace. [1:5.]

Other dispatches concerning the conference appear on Pages 1 to 6.

United States troops supported by other units broke through a pass northwest of Kairouan in Tunisia and recaptured considerable territory seized by the Germans in a recent clash. Britain's Eighth Army captured Ez Zauia, thirty miles west of Tripoli. [9:1, with map.]

A report was heard in London that the Germans had killed 250 French inhabitants of Marseille, including seventy women, during resistance to their effort to clear the Old Harbor district. Some 40,000 persons were moved out of the area, according to the Vichy radio. [1:3.]

A Soviet special communiqué announced that the Russians had killed or captured all but 12,000 of the Axis soldiers trapped at Stalingrad. Three main railway lines leading out of the city were reported freed. [1:4.] Reports from Berlin reaching Switzerland indicated that the force trapped at Stalingrad had been written off. [12:1.]

President Ryti of Finland, in closing the session of Parliament, expressed the hope that friendly relations would be restored with the United States. [12:1.]

From Australia came a protest by Prime Minister Curtin in an Australia Day broadcast. He said that the Pacific area was too important to be left to a force of "caretakers." [13:2.]

A large force of Japanese planes approaching Guadalcanal was driven off by United States planes and four Zeros were shot down without loss to the Americans. United States ground forces consolidated their position at Kokumbona village. [13:4.]

CAPITAL SEES PLAN

Offensive With Common Strategy Is Viewed by Washington as Key

FRENCH UNION A GAIN

Bar Upon a 'Negotiated Peace' Cited as Blow to Hopes of Axis

By HAROLD CALLENDER
Special to The New York Times.

WASHINGTON, Jan. 26—The meeting at Casablanca of President Franklin D. Roosevelt and Prime Minister Winston Churchill was regarded in official circles here as a council of war designed to clear the way for Allied unity and a common strategy on all fronts, and to plan a continuing offensive whose object is, not the negotiated peace for which the Axis has at times angled and may angle again, but "unconditional surrender" of the enemy. It was the first time this phrase had been used in an official definition of the war aims of the United Nations.

As an expression of the common strategy that is being worked out, it was expected by many that a war council of the "big four"—Britain, Russia, China and the United States—would emerge, and that the mutual aid and coordinated purposes of the United Nations would receive increasing emphasis in the form of more inclusive consultations on all major aspects of the war and on the distribution of the sinews of war in the future.

This was the interpretation placed by observers here tonight upon those words of the official announcement concerning efforts to include Premier Joseph Stalin and Generalissimo Chiang Kai-shek in the dramatic meeting on the coast of Morocco, which symbolized the growing offensive power of the Allies on the southern margin of the European war theatre and the alignment of the bulk of the French Empire on the side of the United Nations.

Parley Essentially Military

It was emphasized in official circles here that the gathering at Casablanca was essentially military, as indicated by the presence there of the highest American and British strategists of the navies, armies and air forces, including the commanders of the North African operations, and that the major preoccupation was the winning of the war rather than political issues, save as they directly affected the grand strategy of the Allied coalition.

Tonight's announcement from Casablanca cleared up some of the mystery that has surrounded the proceedings since Jan. 9, when the press was informed by the Office of Censorship that President Roosevelt was going on a trip and the attention of correspondents was drawn to the code of voluntary censorship, which forbids publication of any hints or speculation about the President's movements.

In the seventeen-day interval of silence that followed, private guesses had placed the President at numerous widely separated spots all the way from Alaska to Moscow. One rumor was that he had gone to London; others had him at intervening points; but most guesses were warm in that they pointed to the coast of Africa as the probable place of his rendezvous with Mr. Churchill and the leaders of the Allied fighting services.

Rumor About Stalin

Some expected that Mr. Stalin and the Chinese Generalissimo would turn up at the appointed meeting place to personify, with the American and British leaders, the over-all unity lately discussed.

It was generally assumed that, wherever the meeting, the question of union of the French forces on a military rather than a political basis and the formulation of

Continued on Page Two

President Pays Surprise Visit To U. S. Troops in Morocco

Roosevelt Reviews Soldiers at Base Outside Casablanca—Visits Graves of Americans Who Fell During Landings

By WALTER LOGAN
United Press Correspondent

CASABLANCA, French Morocco, Jan. 21 (Delayed)—President Roosevelt inspected American troops in French Morocco today, surprising them by his presence and leaving their faces wreathed in smiles.

The President reviewed the troops from a jeep driven by Staff Sergeant Oran Lass of Kansas City, Mo., who was the proudest soldier in the United States Army but maintained an air of impeccable dignity throughout.

In the jeep with the President were Lieut. Gen. Mark Clark, Commander of the United States Fifth Army; Charles Fredericks, the President's personal bodyguard, and the general officer

Continued on Page Five

HONORED BY PRESIDENT

Brig. Gen. William H. Wilbur, who received from Mr. Roosevelt in Africa the Congressional Medal of Honor. Associated Press Wirephoto [Story on Page 5]

The Official Communique

By The Associated Press.

CASABLANCA, French Morocco, Jan. 26—Following is the text of the official communiqué on the conference of President Roosevelt and Prime Minister Churchill:

The President of the United States and the Prime Minister of Great Britain have been in conference near Casablanca since Jan. 14.

They were accompanied by the combined Chiefs of Staff of the two countries; namely,

FOR THE UNITED STATES:

General George C. Marshall, Chief of Staff of the United States Army; Admiral Ernest J. King, Commander in Chief of the United States Navy; Lieut. Gen. H. H. Arnold, commanding the United States Army Air Forces, and

FOR GREAT BRITAIN:

Admiral of the Fleet Sir Dudley Pound, First Sea Lord; General Sir Alan Brooke, Chief of the Imperial General Staff, and Air Chief Marshal Sir Charles Portal, Chief of the Air Staff.

These were assisted by:

Lieut. Gen. B. B. Somervell, Commanding General of the Services of Supply, United States Army; Field Marshal Sir John Dill, head of the British Joint Staff Mission in Washington; Vice Admiral Lord Louis Mountbatten, Chief of Combined Operations; Lieut. Gen. Sir Hastings Ismay, Chief of Staff to the Office of the Minister of Defense, together with a number of staff officers of both countries.

They have received visits from Mr. Murphy [Robert Murphy, United States Minister in French North Africa] and Mr. Macmillan [Harold Macmillan, British Resident Minister for Allied Headquarters in North Africa]; from Lieut. Gen. Dwight D. Eisenhower, Commander in Chief of the Allied Expeditionary Force in North Africa; from Admiral of the Fleet Sir Andrew Cunningham, naval commander of the Allied Expeditionary Force in North Africa; from Major Gen. Carl Spaatz, air commander of the Allied Expeditionary Force in North Africa; from Lieut. Gen. Mark W. Clark, United States Army [commander of the United States Fifth Army in Tunisia], and, from Middle East Headquarters, from General Sir Harold Alexander, Air Chief Marshal Sir Arthur Tedder and Lieut. Gen. F. M. Andrews, United States Army.

The President was accompanied by Harry Hopkins [chairman of the British-American Munitions Assignment Board] and was joined by W. Averell Harriman [United States defense expediter in England].

With the Prime Minister was Lord Leathers, British Minister of War Transport.

For ten days the combined staffs have been in constant session, meeting two or three times a day and recording progress at intervals to the President and Prime Minister.

The entire field of the war was surveyed theatre by theatre throughout the world, and all resources were marshaled for a more intense prosecution of the war by sea, land, and air.

Nothing like this prolonged discussion between two allies has ever taken place before. Complete agreement was reached between the leaders of the two countries and their respective staffs upon war plans and enterprises to be undertaken during the campaigns of 1943 against Germany, Italy and Japan with a view to drawing the utmost advantage from the markedly favorable turn of events at the close of 1942.

Premier Stalin was cordially invited to meet the President and Prime Minister, in which case the meeting would have been held very much farther to the east. He was unable to leave Russia at this time on account of the great offensive which he himself, as Commander in Chief, is directing.

The President and Prime Minister realized up to the full the enormous weight of the war which Russia is successfully bearing along her whole land front, and their prime object has been to draw as much weight as possible off the Russian armies by engaging the enemy as heavily as possible at the best selected points.

Premier Stalin has been fully informed of the military proposals.

The President and Prime Minister have been in communication with Generalissimo Chiang Kai-shek. They have apprised him of the measures which they are undertaking to assist him in China's magnificent and unrelaxing struggle for the common cause.

The occasion of the meeting between the President and Prime Minister made it opportune to invite General Giraud [General Henri Honoré Giraud, High Commissioner of French Africa] to confer with the Combined Chiefs of Staff and to arrange for a meeting between him and General de Gaulle [General Charles de Gaulle, Fighting French Commander]. The two generals have been in close consultation.

The President and Prime Minister and their combined staffs, having completed their plans for the offensive campaigns of 1943, have now separated in order to put them into active and concerted execution.

LEADERS GO BY AIR

Aim at 'Unconditional Surrender' by Axis, President Says

MILITARY AIDES TALK

French Chiefs Declare Groups Will Unite to Liberate Nation

By DREW MIDDLETON
Special Cable to The New York Times.

CASABLANCA, French Morocco, Jan. 24 (Delayed)—President Roosevelt and Prime Minister Churchill today concluded a momentous ten-day conference in which they planned Allied offensives of 1943 aimed at what the President called the "unconditional surrender" of the Axis powers.

The President flew 5,000 miles across the Atlantic with his Chiefs of Staff to confer with Mr. Churchill and British military, naval and air chieftains in a sun-splashed villa within sound of Atlantic breakers. Every phase of the global war was discussed in conferences lasting from morning until midnight. Both war leaders emphasized that the conference was wholly successful and that complete agreement had been reached on great military enterprises to be undertaken by the United Nations this year.

General Henri Honoré Giraud, High Commissioner for French North Africa, and General Charles de Gaulle, leader of Fighting France, met at the conference and found themselves in accord on the primary task of liberating France from German domination. President Roosevelt predicted that French soldiers, sailors and airmen would fight beside the Allied armies in the liberation of France.

Stalin Kept Informed

The President and Mr. Churchill expressed regret for Premier Joseph Stalin's inability to leave the Russian offensive, which he is directing personally, but emphasized that all results of the conferences had been reported to the Soviet leader. [Generalissimo Chiang Kai-shek was similarly advised, The Associated Press reported.]

Assurance of future world peace will come only as a result of the total elimination of German and Japanese war power, the President declared. He borrowed a phrase from General Grant's famous letter to the Confederate commander at Forts Donelson and Henry—"unconditional surrender"—to describe the only terms on which the United Nations would accept the conclusion of the war.

He emphasized, however, that

Continued on Page Six

Trondheim Blasts Heard in Sweden

By The United Press.

STOCKHOLM, Sweden, Jan. 26—Residents of the Swedish frontier area tonight reported having heard thunderous explosions throughout the day from the direction of Trondheim on the Norwegian coast.

[Trondheim Fjord, reputed still the berth of important German warships, including the battleship Tirpitz, extends inland from Trondheim to within thirty miles of the Swedish border.]

The explosions were described as of an intensity comparable with those of last Spring when British planes bombed the Trondheim area.

Border district residents at first thought the explosions were from gunfire, but later thought it more likely an air raid was under way, advices reaching here said.

However, no planes were visible and the explosions resounded steadily from 10:30 A. M. to 5 P. M. except for brief intervals an unusually long period for an air attack.

"All the News That's Fit to Print."

The New York Times.

LATE CITY EDITION
Slightly warmer today with moderate winds.
Temperatures Yesterday—Max., 41; Min., 27
Sunrise, 7:37 A. M.; Sunset, 6:34 P. M.

VOL. XCII..No. 31,063. Entered as Second-Class Matter. Postoffice, New York, N. Y. NEW YORK, WEDNESDAY, FEBRUARY 10, 1943. THREE CENTS IN NEW YORK CITY

PRESIDENT ORDERS 48-HOUR WEEK IN WAR EFFORT; GREAT 'INVASION OF EUROPE' IN 1943 THE GOAL; GUADALCANAL IS OURS; RUSSIANS TAKE BELGOROD

FOE QUITS ISLAND

Japan Abandons Few Troops Remaining on Guadalcanal

SETS NEW STRATEGY

Enemy Hopes to Hold Isles to North—Knox Weighs Moves

By CHARLES HURD
Special to The New York Times.

WASHINGTON, Feb. 9—The long and hard-fought battle for the island of Guadalcanal in the Solomons apparently has ended, Secretary of the Navy Frank Knox said here today. His declaration, made at a press conference, was the first authoritative statement of a United States victory that has been indicated by the Navy communiqués for the past two or three weeks.

The conquest of this island, or specifically a few square miles of territory around Henderson Airfield on its northern shore, gives American forces undisputed possession both of the airfield and an excellent harbor near by, which becomes a threat to Japan's major bases in the South Pacific. This conclusion was voiced by Secretary Knox.

The Secretary's comment was inspired by a broadcast Japanese communiqué, which announced that units of troops had been withdrawn from Guadalcanal. Mr. Knox said this appeared to be correct. He added the speculative statement that possibly the sea action that was announced as occurring last week and the previous week in the Solomons, with some loss for our Navy, might have been precipitated by the Japanese to cover withdrawal of troops rather than as an attack on our forces.

Question on Resistance

"Has all enemy resistance on the island ceased?" a reporter asked Mr. Knox.

"It has apparently ceased," the Secretary replied, noting that some isolated groups of Japanese still remained there.

The Japanese announcement stated that certain units had been transferred from Guadalcanal and New Guinea early in February.

Secretary Knox told those present at his conference that when he returned from a recent tour of the South Pacific, including a visit to Guadalcanal, he had then stated the opinion that significant Japanese opposition on Guadalcanal had collapsed. He quoted Major Gen. Alexander D. Patch, Army commander on Guadalcanal, as having estimated at the time of his visit (Jan. 21-22) that there were 4,000 to 6,000 enemy troops still on Guadalcanal.

Small Groups Surrounded

"We are satisfied by our air and ground reconnaissance," Mr. Knox said, "that there is no large number of Japanese in one group. Several small groups have been surrounded and cut off from supplies and reinforcements."

When he gave the opinion today that perhaps the recent Japanese naval action, as yet not reported in any detail, may have covered withdrawal efforts, he emphasized that this was only speculative and "we will have to await confirmation."

The isolated groups still on the island, Mr. Knox went on, now face "either death or surrender as their only alternative." The Navy Secretary, speaking in response to questions, said that the conquest of the tiny battlefield has "both positive and negative value."

"The negative value," he explained, "is that it denies to the Japanese an opportunity for raids on our communications. Affirmatively, it has brought us up to where we are in striking distance of some of their most important bases."

His statement obviously referred

Continued on Page Four

RADIATION CENTER OF AMERICAN POWER IN THE PACIFIC

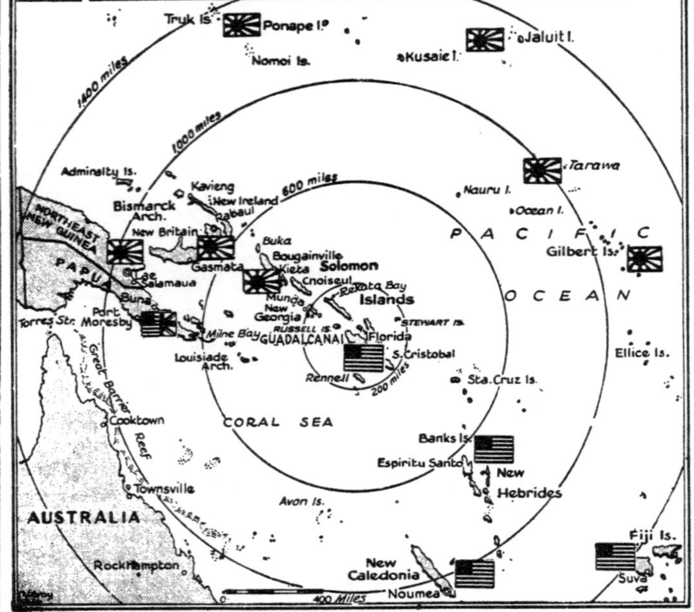

Conquest of Guadalcanal and abandonment of the island by the Japanese have put our forces "in striking distance of some of their most important bases," according to Secretary Knox. Japanese flags on the map show enemy bases in this region and circles indicate distances from Guadalcanal.

NAZI LINE TOTTERS

Kharkov's Peril Grows as Rail Junction Falls in Three-Way Drive

ROSTOV FIGHT RAGES

Counter-Attacks Holding Russians Below Don, Berlin Claims

By The Associated Press.

LONDON, Feb. 9—The entire German line in Southern Russia appeared to be caving in tonight as the Russians, in a special communiqué recorded here by the Soviet monitor, announced the capture of Belgorod with a smashing Red Army blow that further imperiled Kharkov, chief Nazi base east of the Dnieper River.

Belgorod was the second huge German base and railway center, held tenaciously through all the Russian counter-offensives of the Winter of 1941-42 and the Spring of 1942, to fall to the Red Army in forty-eight hours. The city is only fifty miles northeast of Kharkov, industrial center of the Ukraine, and is seventy-eight miles southeast of Kursk, the big defense center that fell only yesterday.

Along with Belgorod, the Russians took Shebekino, only forty miles northeast of Kharkov's city limits and twenty miles southeast of Belgorod. Belgorod is at the junction of the Kursk-Kharkov line and a handy railway that runs northwest to Gomel and the central front. One of Kharkov's strongest outer defenses, it was a nut that Russian armies tried in vain to crack a year ago.

Nazi Supply Lines Tangled

The speed with which the Russian forces were toppling strong German defense centers one after another apparently had tied German communications and transportation into knots, and everywhere along a 500-mile snowy front, from Novorossisk in the Caucasus to north of Orel, the Red Army was reporting mounting successes.

[The German communiqué reported heavy defensive battles "against enemy attempts to break though and outflank German positions, conducted with large forces." German counter-attacks in defense of Rostov were reported. On the lower Don, in the entire Donets area and west of the Oskol River, Soviet attacks on a broad front were said to have been repulsed in fierce fighting or checked by counter-attacks.]

Orel, at the top of the line, 200 miles south of Moscow, appeared to be left dangerously suspended by the fall of Kursk to the south and a massive thrust past that former German bastion toward Lgov

Continued on Page Eight

WLB Denies Pay Increase In 'Big Four' Packers Case

Industry and Public Members Outvote Labor Group on Cost-of-Living Plea and Hold to the 'Little Steel' Formula

By LOUIS STARK
Special to The New York Times.

WASHINGTON, Feb. 9—Refusing to modify its "Little Steel" formula, the War Labor Board denied a wage increase to 180,000 employes of the "Big Four" meat packing companies today and thus presaged a showdown between the Administration and John L. Lewis.

Wage demands of the packing house employes and those of the 450,000 bituminous coal miners are parallel inasmuch as both groups of employes have received wage increases above the 15 per cent rise in living costs between January, 1941, and May, 1942.

The WLB's 7-to-4 decision, concurred in by public and employer members while labor members dissented, stood squarely behind the anti-inflation act of Congress of Oct. 2, 1942, and President Roosevelt's executive order the next day naming James F. Byrnes as Director of Economic Stabilization.

The board granted to the unions maintenance of membership and the check-off. The industry members dissented on these provisions and also on those providing retroactive overtime pay, termination of the contract date and premium for night work.

In a concurring opinion on the wage question, the industry members urged that extension of the present forty-hour work week to forty-eight hours would permit many workers, including packing-house employes, to increase their "take home" earnings while, at the same time the longer work week would ease pressure on the board for wage increases to influence the flow of manpower.

The dissent of labor members will not be made public for a day or two.

Among the wage cases, besides that of the miners, which will be affected by the packing house decision are the recommendations for

Continued on Page Seventeen

SHARP RISE IN PAY

Overtime Rates Stand for Those Now on 40-Hour Basis

NOT EFFECTIVE HERE

Order Applies at Start to 32 Areas—Plan Detailed by Byrnes

Byrnes's speech and the 48-hour week order appear on Page 18.

Special to The New York Times.

WASHINGTON, Feb. 9—A minimum wartime work week of forty-eight hours was decreed tonight by President Roosevelt. Paul V. McNutt, War Manpower Commission chairman, announced that it would apply immediately to thirty-two labor shortage areas, not including New York City.

Making public the Presidential order in a nation-wide broadcast, James F. Byrnes, Director of Economic Stabilization, pictured it as one step in general preparations for an Allied invasion of Europe "within a measurable period of time," presumably in 1943.

To prepare the way, prices and wages must be kept down, Mr. Byrnes said, asserting that the Administration would stand pat on the "Little Steel" wage formula and other wage and price control measures.

His position on wages was supported by a War Labor Board decision denying employes of the "Big Four" packing companies an increase in pay, holding it would be a violation of that formula.

Weekly Wage Earnings to Rise

For workers who heretofore have been on a forty-hour week, the President's executive order ultimately will result in a 30-per-cent increase in pay at time and one-half for the additional eight hours under the Forty-Hour Week Act, which was not affected by the order.

For the 15,434,000 workers in manufacturing industries who put in an average of forty-four hours a week in November, the order will eventually mean an average increase of 13.6 per cent in weekly wages.

The President's order and Mr. Byrnes's speech marked the opening of a government campaign to win support from the people in anticipation of a showdown fight with John L. Lewis, president of the United Mine Workers of America, who has demanded a $2 per day wage increase for 450,000 soft-coal miners.

Under the "Little Steel" formula, which limits general pay increases to a total of 15 per cent since Jan. 1, 1941, in order to compensate for increased living costs up to May, 1942, the bituminous miners would not be entitled to any further increase.

The 48-hour order, which applies to all war and non-war

Continued on Page Eighteen

PEYROUTON SETS UP ECONOMIC COUNCIL

Group Including Arabs Will Be Elected by Leaders of Various Elements Involved

Wireless to The New York Times.

ALLIED HEADQUARTERS IN NORTH AFRICA, Feb. 9—Marcel Peyrouton, Governor General of Algeria, created a Permanent Council of War Economy today to tackle the complex Algerian economic situation.

The creation of the council also marks the first step toward a rebirth of representative government here, for its members will be elected by various economic groups. This carries out the prediction of the American Minister, Robert Murphy, that General Henri Honoré Giraud, the French civil and military commander in chief, would move "slowly but surely" toward

Continued on Page Seven

Tunisia Air Offensive Grows, Raises Losses of Axis to 625

By DREW MIDDLETON
Wireless to The New York Times.

ALLIED HEADQUARTERS IN NORTH AFRICA, Feb. 9—American air power struck heavily at vital Axis air bases, shipping and docks in widespread and successful air assaults over Tunisia yesterday. Eighteen enemy fighters were shot down, increasing the Axis losses since the opening of the North African campaign to 625 aircraft.

At the same time, the astounding story of the one-day toll of the British submarine P-211, revealed today, vividly demonstrated the Royal Navy's part in the offensive against Field Marshal General Erwin Rommel's communications with Italy and Sicily, an offensive that is gaining in weight with each passing week. The P-211 sank three ships and destroyed another in one day of patrol in the Tyrrhenian Sea.

[American Liberator raids on Sicily, reported from Cairo, gave rise to the belief in London that the augmented air warfare

Continued on Page Six

CLOTHING IN PLENTY, NEEDS NO RATIONING

WPB and OPA Assure Country There Is No Shortage as Shoes Order Starts Buying

By CHARLES E. EGAN
Special to The New York Times.

WASHINGTON, Feb. 9—As a step to halt any rush of consumers to buy clothing on the theory that it would follow shoes in the list of rationed articles, Donald M. Nelson, chairman of the War Production Board, and Prentiss M. Brown, Federal Price Administrator, asserted in a joint statement today that there was no shortage of clothing and therefore no need of rationing.

The statement read as follows:

"Announcement of shoe rationing appears to have stimulated scare buying in some parts of the country. Such buying is unnecessary.

"Supplies of wool in the United States are larger by several hundred million pounds than they were when the Japs struck at Pearl Harbor.

"The War Production Board has not directed the Office of Price Administration to undertake the rationing of clothing.

"The Office of Price Administration has set up no machinery for rationing clothing.

"A continuance of overbuying can create temporary maldistribution of clothing stocks, and its only effect is to handicap persons with a legitimate need for new clothing. It is contrary to the best interest of the war program, and is totally unnecessary for the protection of the individual."

Washington merchants who sold four times the normal amount of apparel items and had to contend with clamoring throngs who sought to stock up on topcoats, suits and accessories were caustic in criticism of the manner in which the government had handled the announcement of the shoe rationing order Sunday. Merchants insisted

Continued on Page Nineteen

War News Summarized

WEDNESDAY, FEBRUARY 10, 1943

Major news from the battlefronts yesterday concerned the continued rapid Soviet advance and the final defeat of the Japanese land forces on Guadalcanal Island.

Moscow announced the capture of Belgorod, fifty miles northeast of Kharkov, one of the important strong points on the German defense line in Russia, and of Shebekino, forty miles northeast of Kharkov. Russian armies were advancing on Kharkov from three directions. They were also pounding at the outer defenses of Rostov and from Kramatorsk in the Ukraine they continued to thrust southward in an effort to trap the Germans in the Rostov and Taganrog regions. [1:5; map, P. 9.]

Secretary of the Navy Knox announced that serious enemy land resistance had ceased on Guadalcanal. [1:1.] Japanese Imperial Headquarters broadcast an announcement that Japanese forces on Guadalcanal had been evacuated to other points. [4:1.]

Before the House Foreign Affairs Committee the Secretary of the Navy suggested that in connection with lend-lease arrangements the United States should negotiate to acquire after the war a string of naval and air bases reaching across the Pacific into Asiatic waters. [3:1.]

Chungking announced that a major battle was under way on the Yunnan-Burma frontier. The largest number of United States bombers sent against Rangoon in a single day to date heavily bombed the docks and railway facilities. [4:6.]

United States bombers struck heavily at various points in Tunisia and attacked Messina, Sicily. [1:3-4.]

In Algeria Governor General Peyrouton established an economic war council that is to be elected by various economic groups. [1:2.]

General de Gaulle, chief of the Fighting French, told correspondents in London that an agreement with General Giraud's regime in North Africa was impossible until the laws of the French Republic had been reestablished there. [7:1.]

German planes killed two children and two teachers when they bombed schools in Southeastern England. There was a certain amount of air activity on both sides of the Channel. [3:2.]

Prime Minister Churchill, appearing in Parliament after his trip, said that Britain was dipping into her food reserves, but the situation was not crucial. [3:5.]

VOTE PAY INQUIRY ON SUBVERSIVES

Members of House Adopt Cannon Resolution for Hearings on Charges

By HENRY N. DORRIS
Special to The New York Times.

WASHINGTON, Feb. 9—By an overwhelming voice vote House Democrats and Republicans joined today in adopting the Cannon resolution to investigate charges of radicalism in the Federal Government personnel.

A five-man subcommittee of the Appropriations Committee, to be appointed tomorrow by its chairman, Representative Cannon, was instructed under the resolution to accord hearings to all government employes accused by the Dies committee or other groups of communistic affiliations. Mr. Cannon promised that these hearings would be conducted promptly, so that the House could determine whether to strike at "convicted" radicals by cutting them off the Federal payroll through riders to appropriation bills as they come up.

After adopting the resolution the House agreed by a roll-call vote of 267 to 136 to strike out of the Treasury-Postoffice supply bill an amendment by Representative Hendricks, previously adopted, denying further pay to William

Continued on Page Seventeen

48-HR. WORK AREAS LIMITED AT FIRST

WMC Aide Doubts It Will Ever Be Applied Here Unless Situation Gets 'Tighter'

By The Associated Press.

WASHINGTON, Feb. 9—Paul V. McNutt, War Manpower Commissioner, said tonight that "until further notice" the executive order establishing the 48-hour week would apply only to thirty-two "labor shortage" areas listed by him.

In those areas, it will apply to all employment, covering retail stores, newspapers and even domestic servants, Deputy Commissioner Fowler V. Harper said, and will be mandatory rather than be merely a statement of policy which they may follow or disregard.

While the order is to take effect immediately in these areas, employers will receive time to attain a 48-hour week gradually over a period of several weeks.

Mr. McNutt, in a statement, made this comment on the President's order.

"The purpose of the executive order is to make more manpower available as needed and to increase production. It is imperative that this be done in an orderly manner.

"Those establishments in which the minimum work week is less than forty-eight hours are to stop recruiting (labor) at once unless they can go to a forty-eight-hour week without need for releasing workers or due to expansion or production schedules still need more workers.

"They will go on a forty-eight-hour week in such a manner as will assure orderly absorption of surplus workers by absorption or transfer within the employers' operations.

"No employer should prior to March 31 release workers for the purpose of attaining the forty-eight-hour week. If by March 31, 1943, an employer has not attained a forty-eight-hour week without the need for releasing workers for other employment, he will advise the area representative of the War Manpower Commission of what number need be released to attain a forty-eight-hour week. The employer will at that time present a proposed schedule for release of workers for further absorption within his own plant in order to attain the forty-eight-hour week. The area director will then authorize a proper schedule of release or

Continued on Page Eighteen

Labor Party Bill in State Senate Is Backed by Democratic Leader

Special to The New York Times.

ALBANY, Feb. 9—Senator John J. Dunnigan, Democratic minority leader, appeared today as the sponsor of the first program bill submitted by the American Labor party. The bill, sent up by the State Committee of the Labor party, would make the State and all its agencies the enforcement officers for Federal price-fixing regulations for protection of the consumer.

The political significance of Senator Dunnigan's sponsorship of the measure lies in the fact that never before, in the six sessions that the American Labor party has existed as a recognized political group, has any Democratic leader appeared as sponsor for any of its measures.

Senator Dunnigan made his move with the background of the last election in mind. He is convinced, it was learned, that the Democratic party in the city and the State must work with the Labor party, if it is to win the Mayoralty or the Governorship the next time either is at stake.

Senator Dunnigan, it was learned, made the move on his own responsibility, after consultation with leaders of the American Labor party. The Assembly sponsor of the measure was Assemblyman Crews, Brooklyn Republican, who has already introduced some of the Labor party's measures.

Governor Dewey has conferred with Labor party leaders over the telephone and presumably would not be adverse to winning the group to his support. He has had under consideration for some time the appointment of a man from that party to his Cabinet.

There were two other signs in the Legislature today of activity and alertness on the Democratic side, which up to now had been quiescent to the point of arousing comment.

Senator Gutman of Brooklyn

Continued on Page Forty-six

Churchill on Radio Soon About His Trip

By The Associated Press.

LONDON, Wednesday, Feb. 10—London's morning newspapers said today that Prime Minister Winston Churchill would discuss his recent travels in a broadcast to the nation, scheduled tentatively for next Sunday or the following Sunday, Feb. 21.

"He will deal at length with his recent travels and talks with President Roosevelt and warn the country that in spite of our successes there are hard days ahead," said The Daily Mail.

The Prime Minister, who returned Sunday from his trip to North Africa and the Middle East, told the House of Commons yesterday that he would make a statement soon on the war situation.

"All the News That's Fit to Print."

The New York Times.

LATE CITY EDITION
Continued cold and windy t·‑ay.
Temperatures Yesterday—Max., 54; Min., 32
Sunrise, 7:55 A. M.; Sunset, 6:36 P. M.

VOL. XCII..No. 31,065. Entered as Second-Class Matter, Postoffice, New York, N. Y. NEW YORK, FRIDAY, FEBRUARY 12, 1943. THREE CENTS IN NEW YORK CITY

CHURCHILL PLEDGES INVASION WITHIN 9 MONTHS; SEES GAINS AT SEA; SAYS 500,000 ARE IN AFRICA; EISENHOWER, PROMOTED, IN SUPREME COMMAND

50 CITY BUILDINGS NOW FACE CLOSING IN FUEL SHORTAGE

Court in Brooklyn Must Shut Down and Others Are Said to Be 'in a Bad Way'

GOVERNOR CONFERS HERE

Seeks to Build Up Reserves in State—Fire Houses, Police Stations Are Affected

The Pennsylvania Avenue Court House in Brooklyn, which houses both Magistrate's and Municipal Courts, will definitely have to shut down and about ten other courts will have to curtail their activities because they have burned their fuel oil rations too fast, City Fuel Oil Administrator Edwin A. Salmon declared yesterday.

The restaurant in the Bronx Terminal Market must close "immediately" for the same reason, according to Mr. Salmon, who said that about fifty of the 650 public buildings in this city which burn oil were "in a bad way." Most of the fifty buildings, Mr. Salmon said, would have to operate at lower temperatures.

It was in Pennsylvania Avenue Court that the leaders of the Brooklyn murder syndicate were first brought to book and held on vagrancy charges, while Kings County District Attorney William O'Dwyer built up the murder cases which later led to smashing of the racket ring.

Although the city will not appeal to the Office of Price Administration for extra rations for any of the buildings that have been unable to budget their three-month allowance so that it will reach to March 31, when the next period begins, an appeal has been made to the Petroleum Administrator for War in behalf of the municipal fireboats, Mr. Salmon said.

Listing Called "Oversight"

The appeal, said Mr. Salmon, was made necessary by "an oversight" through which PAW failed to list fireboats among the essential users exempt from the 40 per cent cut in fuel oil rations for purposes other than heating.

"It is impossible to cut the rations of fireboats," he said. "They must keep steam up at all times. The city's appeal has been made for restoration of that cut, and it will be granted."

Four fire houses which have been burning fuel oil faster than their rations warrant will, however, have to get along until March 31 on what is left of their current allotment, Mr. Salmon said. The houses are in the Bronx, Brooklyn and Queens.

While the municipal administration wrestled with its own heating problem, Governor Dewey, in the city for a short visit, conferred yesterday at the Hotel Roosevelt with PAW officials and petroleum industry representatives on steps that might be, taken during the warm months to build up fuel oil reserves throughout the State.

Transportation and storage and the possibility of making greater use of the State Barge Canal for bringing in petroleum supplies were discussed.

Distribution Gains Seen

The petroleum experts and the Governor also took up the recent critical distribution situation that led Mr Dewey to order an investigation by Attorney General Nathaniel L. Goldstein. Mr. Dewey was told that while the fuel oil shortage was still serious, the distribution problem had been greatly improved and that holders of ration coupons could, in most cases, redeem them for fuel oil without difficulty.

Among those at the conference with Mr. Dewey were Walter P. Heddon, director of port development of the Port of New York Authority; William C. Eberle, director of the district PAW transpor-

Continued on Page Thirty-eight

Victory Bond Drive in April Will Seek $12,906,000,000

Morgenthau Hopes New Appeal Will Yield at Least as Much as the Sum Obtained in December and Hails Small Investors

By FREDERICK BARKLEY
Special to THE NEW YORK TIMES.

WASHINGTON, Feb. 11—Secretary Morgenthau disclosed today that the next large financing operation of the Treasury Department would come in April and that it would seek to get "at least as much as and probably more than" the record-breaking $12,906,000,000 obtained from individual and corporate investors in the December Victory Loan drive.

The Secretary, just returned from a vacation in Cuba, told his first press conference since December that he expected to spend most of his time between now and April working on plans for the second Victory Loan campaign planned for that month.

Although he voiced hope for larger returns to the Treasury than were yielded in the first drive, he said that the amount which would be asked from investors had not yet been decided. In the first drive the goal was set at $9,000,000,000 and this objective was exceeded by more than 35 per cent. This permitted postponement of the second drive until April, whereas the Treasury's original plan was to hold one either in late February or early March.

At the same time Mr. Morgenthau released statistics which he said showed that voluntary war-bond investments in the present war exceeded any previous government financing in world history, both as to dollar volume and the number of people participating therein.

From the inception of the war-bond program in May, 1941, through December, 1942, the statement said, nearly 50,000,000 Americans bought the $25 maturity value war-savings bonds at a cost price of more than $7,000,000,000.

Continued on Page Thirty-two

ARNOLD NOMINATED FOR CIRCUIT COURT

President Names 'Trust Buster' to Succeed Rutledge on Washington Bench

Special to THE NEW YORK TIMES.

WASHINGTON, Feb. 11—Thurman Arnold, familiarly known as the "trust buster" of the Department of Justice, was named by President Roosevelt today as an associate justice of the Circuit Court for the District of Columbia, to take the place of Wiley B. Rutledge, recently confirmed by the Senate for a Supreme Court seat.

The Arnold nomination came as no surprise, for when President Roosevelt chose Mr. Rutledge for the highest court, on Jan. 11, it was indicated that the assistant attorney general could have the appellate court vacancy if he desired.

Washington has been filled with stories of Mr. Arnold's being "kicked upstairs" in order to call

Continued on Page Thirty-eight

HOUSE TAKES STEPS TO RECLAIM POWERS

Adopts, 294 to 50, Move to Set Up Executive Agencies Study —Funds Inquiry Voted

By HENRY N. DORRIS
Special to THE NEW YORK TIMES.

WASHINGTON, Feb. 11—The House moved in two new directions today toward reclaiming some of the power it delegated to the executive department, and halting alleged abuses of the powers, by adopting resolutions to set up a new investigating committee and giving subpoena powers to the Appropriations Committee.

The first resolution, adopted by a roll-call vote of 294 to 50, was offered by Representative Smith of Virginia. It would set up a seven-man committee to investigate government agencies and bureaus to determine whether they have exceeded delegated authority.

The second resolution, giving

Continued on Page Thirty-eight

War News Summarized

FRIDAY, FEBRUARY 12, 1943

Prime Minister Churchill delivered yesterday his anticipated report on the Casablanca conference to the House of Commons. He declared that the meeting had laid out United Nations offensive plans for the next nine months and that there were almost 500,000 Allied troops in Africa now. He was optimistic about the war against the U-boats, disclosing that sinkings of them had reached a new peak and that Allied ship losses caused by them during the last two months had been the lowest in a year. [1:8.]

Another repercussion of the Casablanca conference came with the announcement of a unified command in North Africa. General Eisenhower will be the commander in chief. Next under him will be General Sir Harold Alexander, Air Marshal Sir Arthur Tedder and Admiral of the Fleet Sir Andrew Cunningham. The North African commander was promoted by President Roosevelt to the temporary rank of full general. [1:6-7.]

It was also announced that Lieut. Gen. Arnold, chief of the United States Army Air Forces, and Field Marshal Dill had visited India and China to discuss war plans with Field Marshal Wavell and Generalissimo Chiang Kai-shek. [1:7.]

The British Eighth Army had its first clash of any importance with Marshal Rommel's troops in Tunisia when the enemy threw tanks into an engagement east of Ben Gardane. In Northern Tunisia Allied forces were said to have passed to the attack in the Mateur area, about fifteen miles south of Bizerte, but the report was not confirmed. According to the dispatch, the Allied troops advanced eight miles and gained their primary objectives. [1:5.]

General Juin, French commander in North Africa, in an order of the day to his troops announced that some of his forces were being withdrawn from action to be re-equipped and trained by the Allies under his supervision. [6:3.]

Meanwhile, in a smashing thirty-five-mile advance from Barvenkova, Russian forces seized the town of Lozovaya in the Ukraine, cutting the main railroad from Kharkov to the Crimea. This push put the Red Army only sixty-five miles east of Dniepropetrovsk and the Dnieper River. Before Rostov the Russians continued to advance. [1:4, Map, P. 8.]

General MacArthur's headquarters reported that the Japanese had been decisively defeated in the Wau region of New Guinea and were retiring toward Mubo, twelve miles from the big enemy base at Salamaua. Two hundred more enemy dead were said to have been counted following recent fighting. [1:5-6.]

RUSSIANS SWEEP ON

Cut Key Kharkov Line at Lozovaya in Drive Toward Dnieper

ROSTOV RING TIGHTER

Red Army Takes Towns North of City, Widens Grip on Black Sea

By The Associated Press.

LONDON, Feb. 11—The Red Army, in its smashing semi-encirclement of Kharkov, has cut the Ukraine bastion's main railway to the south and the Crimea by capturing the key rail junction of Lozovaya, the Moscow radio announced tonight in a special communiqué recorded here by the Soviet monitor.

The capture of Lozovaya apparently represented a thirty-five-mile advance westward from Barvenkova by a force that, threatening at any moment to turn southward toward the Sea of Azov, is menacing from the rear hundreds of thousands of German troops in the area of Rostov.

Kharkov, which has been the Germans' strongest position in all Russia east of the Dnieper, already has had the main railway from the north cut and is engulfed by Red Army troops on a fifty-mile arc reaching as close as twenty-two miles.

Thrust Aimed for Dnieper

The Red Army's westward push to Lozovaya brings it within sixty-five miles of the great Dnieper River, along which many observers believe the Germans are planning to make a stand in retreat. From Lozovaya, which is seventy-five miles south of Kharkov, the nearest point on the Dnieper is the city of Dniepropetrovsk, site of the great hydro-electric dam that the Russians destroyed in their retreat more than a year ago.

[The Germans intend to withdraw their line to the Dnieper and Dvina Rivers if their present positions prove untenable, The United Press reported from Stockholm on "good authority." Such a withdrawal would mean abandonment of Estonia and half of Latvia. The German communiqué reported "considerable defensive successes" with increasing counter-attacks.]

By knifing through to the Kharkov-Crimean railway at Lozovaya the Russians have cut off the German armies at Kharkov from direct communication with those in the Donets Basin. Lozovaya was taken by the Germans in their initial push through this area in the Fall of 1941, was recaptured by the Russians on Jan. 30, 1942, in the Red Army's first Winter offensive, and then was won back by the Germans in their Summer offensive of 1942.

Rostov Ring Contracts

While General Kulagin's forces in this action further increased the threat to the German forces at Rostov, other Russian forces in the immediate vicinity of the Caucasus gateway drove in still closer. The official German agency D. N. B. acknowledged a Red Army flank attack across the ice of the Sea of Azov in the area of the Don estuary, but said it collapsed under Nazi artillery fire.

The Germans also told of Russian pressure on the Nazi Caucasus forces surrounded in the vicinity of the Black Sea naval base of Novorossiisk, reporting that Soviet reinforcements had landed during the night near the base.

[The London radio reported that Novorossiisk was "to a great extent in the hands of the Russians," according to the Office of War Information.]

A Moscow broadcast, also re-

Continued on Page Eight

FIGHT BY ROMMEL

German Tanks and Guns Battle 8th Army Units— Ben Gardane the Prize

GAIN BY ALLIES CITED

British-French Thrust of Eight Miles in Mateur Area Is Reported

By Reuter.

WITH THE BRITISH EIGHTH ARMY in Tunisia, Feb. 11—Field Marshal General Erwin Rommel is showing fight at last. In the biggest action since his belated stand at El Agheila, Libya, he has thrown tanks, infantry and artillery against forward forces of the British Eighth Army in the marshy frontier area of Tunisia.

The fight has developed into a battle for the mud tracks that lead directly to the northwest—to the important center of Ben Gardane. Both sides are deploying light mobile forces.

Use of tanks usually foreshadows withdrawal by Marshal Rommel, but on this occasion it is prompted not only by anxiety for his forces on the coast, which are likely to be cut off, but also by the threat to Ben Gardane with its promise of easier movements on better tracks.

Tanks also have been put in to counterbalance the growing grip by units of the British Seventh Armored Division, which have thrust across the frontier south of the great marshes of Marset El Briga.

This move apparently took the Germans by surprise. They never believed that the British could move so quickly in heavy going after rains.

Eight-Mile Drive Reported

LONDON, Feb. 11 (AP)—British and French troops were reported tonight by a field correspondent in the Mateur area to have set the long-dormant northern front in Tunisia into action with a continuing attack that had advanced them about eight miles.

The report came from a Reuter correspondent in the Mateur sector—fifteen to twenty miles south of Bizerte—who declared that Allied forces, including British and French Commando troops, had attacked the Italian-held line in the northern area at dawn yesterday.

The smash carried eight miles deep over an area of about 100 square miles, he said, adding:

"By evening the men reached their primary objectives.

"According to information so far available, the operation has gone well, but full results will not be known until the second sweep now in progress has been completed."

There was no word of the attack immediately from any other source.

Wireless to THE NEW YORK TIMES.

ALLIED HEADQUARTERS IN NORTH AFRICA, Feb. 11—The

Continued on Page Two

Japanese Smashed in Wau Area; Flee Toward Base Near Salamaua

By The United Press.

AT UNITED NATIONS HEADQUARTERS, Australia, Friday, Feb. 12—The Japanese have been "decisively defeated" in the Wau sector of New Guinea on the approaches to enemy-held Salamaua in a twelve-day encounter that cost them nearly 1,000 dead and many more wounded, the Allied command announced today.

The Japanese, whose main lines were pushed back six miles on Wednesday by Australian jungle fighters, are retreating toward the village of Mubo, only twelve miles southwest of the port of Salamaua, which the Japanese have held since March, 1942. The Wednesday fighting was outside the former gold-mining town of Wau, which is thirty-five miles southwest of Salamaua.

The communiqué announced that an additional 200 Japanese dead had been counted in the area, most of which were counted yesterday after the ferocious Australian attack cracked the enemy lines on Wednesday after they began their drive on Tuesday.

The estimated 1,000 killed since Jan. 30 ran the total Japanese dead in the Wau Mubo area for this year to about 1,500. A total of 416 was reported killed during January, according to Allied communiqués which recorded two Allied raids lasting three days each, the last of which ended on Jan. 29.

A headquarters spokesman added

Continued on Page Ten

THE NEW UNITED NATIONS SET-UP IN AFRICA

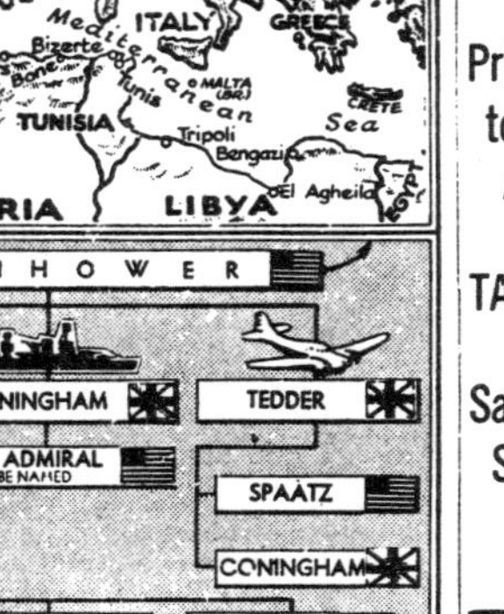

Feb. 12, 1943

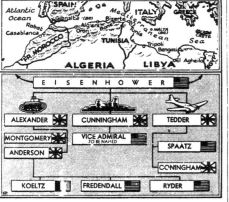

The map shows General Eisenhower's command, stretching from the west coast of Africa to the Egyptian border. The chart depicts the organization of his staff. How French General Giraud fits into this picture was not disclosed in yesterday's announcements.

British Land, Air, Sea Chiefs To Serve Under Eisenhower

By DREW MIDDLETON
Wireless to THE NEW YORK TIMES.

ALLIED HEADQUARTERS IN NORTH AFRICA, Feb. 11—The strongest possible team of Allied commanders, including what General Dwight D. Eisenhower called "the three stars of the British Empire," has been formed under the direct command of General Eisenhower for the final drive against the Axis forces in Tunisia. The Britons are General Sir Harold R. L. G. Alexander, Admiral Sir Andrew Browne Cunningham and Air Marshal Sir Arthur Tedder.

This group, serving under its American commander, will probably also be the directing body of the first great Allied attack into Europe, for which the clearing of Tunisia is prerequisite. The British Eighth and First Armies and their American comrades of the Fifth Army and other forces probably provide the spearhead for that attack.

[The advancement of the American commander to the temporary rank of full general was announced by President Roosevelt yesterday.]

Command Area Defined

The Allied North African theatre, of which General Eisenhower is Commander in Chief, extends in theory from Casablanca, French Morocco, east to the Tripolitanian frontier as a result of the command changes announced today. For practical purposes, however, it extends farther east to the British Army's supply bases in Tripolitania and Libya.

General Alexander, a hard-bitten veteran of Dunkerque and Burma, is to have command under General Eisenhower of all British, American and French ground forces east of Algiers. General Sir Bernard L. Montgomery's veteran British Eighth Army and Lieut. Gen. Kenneth A. N. Anderson's British First Army come under General Alexander's immediate di-

Continued on Page Three

ALLIED GENERALS SEE CHIANG, WAVELL

Gen. Arnold and Marshal Dill Visit China and India to Press War on Japan

By The Associated Press.

NEW DELHI, India, Feb. 11—American and British generals have concluded ten days of conferences in India and in China, where they consulted Generalissimo Chiang Kai-shek on ways to press home the battle to Japan.

A joint war communiqué today said "a complete accord was reached in coordination of offensive plans and signifying the united determination of the powers concerned to insure full cooperation and mutual assistance against the Japanese."

The presence of the war leaders in India and China gave rise to the belief that the Oriental theatre would blaze with new Allied offensive action. One immediate result is expected to be an increase in supplies to China.

Confer With Wavell

Field Marshal Sir John Dill, British joint staff mission member, and Lieut. Gen. Henry H. Arnold, United States Army Air Chief, reached India with their staffs about ten days ago from the unconditional surrender conference at Casablanca. Representing Prime Minister Churchill and President Roosevelt, they conferred with Field Marshal Sir Archibald P. Wavell. After inspecting military installations in Eastern India, Marshal Dill and General Arnold flew over the Himalayas for discussions with General Chiang.

Brig. Gen. A. C. Weddemeyer, representing the United States Chief of Staff General George C. Marshall, accompanied them.

In Chungking the conference was joined by Lieut. Gen. Joseph W. Stillwell, General Chiang's American chief of staff, and General Ho Ying-ching, Chinese Minister of War. After leaving Chungking, the Dill-Arnold party returned to India for final conferences with Marshal Wavell.

The communiqué said that subsequent conferences would be held between Marshal Wavell and General Douglas MacArthur, United

Continued on Page Two

TO BLEED GERMANY

Prime Minister in Talk to Commons Declares Aim to Smash Nazis

TALKS OF LANDINGS

Says Fight on U-Boats Shows Steady Gain Since Start of War

The text of Mr. Churchill's address in Commons, Page 4.

By The Associated Press.

LONDON, Friday, Feb. 12—Prime Minister Winston Churchill, disclosing that nearly half a million Allied troops were now in Africa at the great bridgehead to Europe and that the Casablanca parleys had produced an immense and detailed Allied offensive pattern for the next nine months, solemnly proclaimed yesterday the Allied resolve to make the Nazis "burn and bleed" on other fronts as they had already over the length of Russia.

In an exuberant appearance before the House of Commons, where, as he looked out upon the grand vista of the war, he found obvious difficulty in adhering to what he called "the strictest standards of anti-complacency opinions," the Prime Minister made these disclosures:

First—"We have now a complete plan of action which comprises apportionment of forces as well as their direction, and this plan we are going to carry out according to our policy during the next nine months, before the end of which we [Mr. Churchill and President Roosevelt] will make efforts to meet again. * * * Everything in human power is being done and will be done to bring British and American forces into action against the enemy with the utmost speed and energy and on the largest scale."

Battle Against U-Boat Vital

Second, that the Allies were drawing steadily ahead toward winning the greatest of all battles of this war, a battle that stood at the forefront of every other discussion at Casablanca—the battle against the submarine.

Third, that the supreme commander of the Allied armies of North Africa was General Dwight D. Eisenhower, U. S. A. ("one of the finest men I ever knew," Mr. Churchill observed) and that Britain would gladly and loyally go forward as subordinates to this essentially American enterprise.

"Great Britain and the United States," the Prime Minister told the House proudly, "are now warrior nations, walking in fear of the Lord, very heavily armed and

Continued on Page Five

President Reports On Africa Tonight

Special to THE NEW YORK TIMES.

WASHINGTON, Feb. 11—President Roosevelt will report to the country by radio at 9:30 o'clock, E. W. T., tomorrow night on his Casablanca war conferences with Prime Minister Churchill, the White House stated.

The President's speech, which is to be broadcast by all radio networks, probably will deal also with problems of the home front, including the fight against inflation and the effort to keep both wages and prices stabilized, it was indicated.

The speech will take up about twenty minutes, according to Stephen T. Early, White House press secretary.

Mr. Early said also that the President would make a speech on Feb. 22 to the country and celebrants at Washington Day birthday dinners sponsored by the Democratic National Committee as a means of raising funds for party activities.

"All the News That's Fit to Print."

The New York Times.

LATE CITY EDITION
Slightly warmer today with gentle to moderate winds.
Temperatures Yesterday—Max., 32; Min., 21
Sunrise, 7:34 A. M.; Sunset, 6:27 P. M.

Copyright, 1943, by The New York Times Company.

VOL. XCII..No. 31,066. Entered as Second-Class Matter, Postoffice, New York, N. Y. NEW YORK, SATURDAY, FEBRUARY 13, 1943. THREE CENTS IN NEW YORK CITY

PRESIDENT PLEDGES MANY INVASIONS IN EUROPE, OUSTING FOE FROM CHINA AND ATTACK ON JAPAN; RUSSIANS TIGHTEN TWO TRAPS, TAKE KRASNODAR

RULING HITS SPORTS IN COLLEGES PICKED FOR ARMY TRAINING

Chief of Special Courses Says Soldiers Will Have No Time for Varsity Teams

PROGRAM BEGINS MARCH 1

Athletic Officials, Surprised by Ban, Hope to Carry On for Those Not in Service

By The United Press.

WASHINGTON, Feb. 12—The Army today struck a heavy blow at football and other major college sports when it ruled that students under its new specialized training program at colleges and universities could not participate in intercollegiate athletics.

Colonel Herman Beukema, director of the program, said at a press conference that the intensity of the Army's heavy training schedule would preclude participation in such activities.

He said the schools would decide whether they could maintain a normal athletic program with civilian students only, but the ruling appeared to presage difficult sledding for football particularly, inasmuch as selective service "rejects" and youths under 18 soon will comprise the greater part of the civilian student body.

The Navy, a joint participant with the Army in the college training program, has not disclosed whether it will follow the Army's lead.

Several hundred colleges and universities will feel the impact of the decision. The War Manpower Commission already has announced 271 schools at which certain advanced Army and Navy courses will be given under the program, and another long list of institutions eligible to give more elementary courses will be issued shortly.

Beukema said the first courses under the Army phase of the program would begin March 1 and that the program would be in full swing by April 1. No contracts with institutions have been signed by the Army or Navy, but they will be shortly.

50,000 Graduates This Year

Apart from aviation cadets, the Army program will turn out approximately 50,000 students this year and in 1944 probably about 150,000.

Officer candidate schools generally will have first claim on college youths on completion of their basic training at Army camps, Beukema said. Youths of sufficient maturity and qualifications will go directly to such schools.

Those who need further development and others with special technical qualifications who require additional specialized training will be assigned to colleges and universities under the plan.

Selection of candidates for the first courses—advanced engineering in at least one university in each service command—will begin in a few days at Army camps, Beukema said. Initial candidates all will be chosen from men already on active duty or about to finish basic training. The entire list of eligibles is more than ample to fill the first contingents.

Beukema said the training program would include twenty-four or twenty-five hours a week in classroom and laboratory, additional outside studies, five hours a week of military training and an hour daily for physical training. Competitive intramural sports will be part of this schedule.

Approximately 29,000 enlisted Army reservists now in college who are not in certain special categories are subject to call for active duty at the end of the first college term ending after Dec. 31, 1942. For some, this will mean the end of the Fall semester and for others the end of the Winter quarter. Many of these will be returned to schools under the new

Continued on Page Sixteen

Eisenhower Is Told By Wife of New Rank

Wireless to THE NEW YORK TIMES.

ALLIED HEADQUARTERS IN NORTH AFRICA, Feb. 12—A cablegram from his wife last night made the promotion to full general "official" for General Dwight D. Eisenhower, Allied Commander in Chief in North Africa.

The first news of his promotion—he is the youngest American full general—came from a naval officer who heard it on the ship's radio.

The official notice came through this morning just as an enterprising French jeweler appeared at headquarters bearing twelve hand-made silver stars for the general.

PETRILLO PROPOSES FEES FOR RECORDS

Levy to Go to a Union Fund Not to Musician Asked as Basis of Peace Plan

A new type of union demand, under which the employe would not receive a wage increase, but the employer would pay a fixed amount directly to the union itself, was announced yesterday by James C. Petrillo, president of the American Federation of Musicians, as a proposed basis for settlement of the controversy over recordings.

Mr. Petrillo said that the money received from the record manufacturers and "juke-box" operators, in the form of a fee on each disk sold and on each phonograph in operation, would go into a special fund administered by the union's national headquarters and would be spent as follows:

"For the purpose of reducing unemployment which has been created in the main by the use of mechanical devices, and for fostering and maintaining musical talent and culture and musical appreciation, and for furnishing free, live music to the public by means of symphony orchestras, bands and other musical combinations."

While the plan would improve the economic position of the musicians as a group, Mr. Petrillo said that he had been advised by his lawyers that it did not conflict with the wage stabilization act as administered by the War Labor Board. His chief attorney is Joseph A. Padway, general counsel for the American Federation of Labor.

"It is no wage increase," Mr. Petrillo said. "We discussed it with our attorneys, and they say we're all right. There's no precedent for it. This is something absolutely new."

Beyond stating specifically that the individual musician who made a record would not benefit financially from the plan, Mr. Petrillo declined to discuss details of administering the special fund.

"First, we've got to get the fund," he remarked.

Mr. Petrillo said that he had in-

Continued on Page Twenty-four

DEWEY PROMISES MOVE TO END CRISIS ON FARMS OF STATE

Will Summon Thousands of Volunteers to Work as a Patriotic Duty

STUDENTS ARE SINGLED OUT

Governor at Lincoln Dinner Says the People Need No Directive to Win War

Warning that there was a critical shortage of farm labor in New York, Governor Dewey declared last night that the State had a plan to meet the emergency and keep up food production.

The Governor, who spoke at the fifty-seventh annual Lincoln dinner of the National Republican Club at the Waldorf-Astoria Hotel, disclosed that this plan contemplated the use of students in the high schools and women's colleges and the aid of persons in business who ordinarily work in other occupations in community efforts throughout the State in harvesting and processing the crops.

"Within ten days," Governor Dewey said, "I expect to be able to go on the radio to talk to all the people of the State—the farmers, the men and women of the cities and the small towns, the high school boys and college girls, and tell them in detail what they can do to meet the food crisis. I am confident that when they know what they can do they will need no orders or directives from any one. They will rally to the job and do it."

Other speakers were Mgr. Fulton J. Sheen of the Catholic University, Washington, who said that the young men in the armed services on their return from the war would want jobs and would be entitled to them, whether they were members of a union or not, and United States Senator Albert W. Hawkes of New Jersey, who asserted that the United States was headed straight for "state socialism" and that only vigorous action could change this course.

Bishop William T. Manning offered the invocation and Rabbi Jonah B. Wise of the Central Synagogue pronounced benediction. Secretary of State Thomas J. Curran, president of the club, presided. Charles H. Tuttle, chairman of the dinner committee, was toastmaster. The attendance was more than a thousand.

Recalling that during his campaign for election he had urged action to meet the impending food shortage, Governor Dewey said there was no use in complaining that something should have been done a year ago.

"We are in a war and we cannot stop to argue about the failures and the lack of foresight of others," he said. "We have to save the situation as far as possible.

"Whatever the difficulty, we

Continued on Page Seven

Landon Assails 'Nazi New Dealers'; Likens Wallace Aims to Hitler's

By The Associated Press.

OMAHA, Feb. 12—Former Governor Alfred M. Landon of Kansas urged tonight "a coalition of real Democrats and the Republican party" as a guarantee that Vice President Wallace "and his fellow-travelers will not lead us down the same disastrous primrose path in which Hitler has led his people."

In a speech at a Republican Lincoln Day banquet the former Presidential nominee asserted that "at last the practical progressives and the real liberals of the Democratic party are awake to the fact that by use of Trojan horse methods a small but dominant group of Nazi New Dealers who seek to establish here what Hitler described in his early days as the National Socialistic state have seized control of their party."

"The tangle of domestic policies and managing bureaucracy which prevented our return to prosperity under the Roosevelt Administration," he went on, "is preventing an efficient prosecution of the war.

"We are being compelled to fight on two fronts—one a global war, the other a Nazi bureaucratic war. Instead of leadership uniting us with 'an eye single to the task' on the war front we have a bureaucratic leadership in Washington thirsting for power and just as obviously determined to establish a permanent control of our lives, thus creating a second front at home."

Referring to President Roose-

Continued on Page Seven

NAZIS' PERIL GROWS

Encircling of 500,000 Threatened in Fall of Donets Rail Key

KUBAN UNITS PENNED

Loss of Caucasus Base Drives Them to Sea—Rostov Pressed

By The Associated Press.

LONDON, Feb. 12—The Red Army of the Ukraine was reported officially tonight to have captured Krasnoarmeisk, a main rail junction twenty-five miles northwest of Stalino, thus threatening to trap some 500,000 Axis troops already hard pressed by other Russian units attacking in the Donets Basin and Rostov areas to the east.

A special Russian communiqué, recorded by the Soviet monitor here, told of the cutting of the main Dniepropetrovsk-Stalino railway at Krasnoarmeisk.

Other important developments included the capture of Krasnodar, Kuban Cossack capital in the Western Caucasus; Shakhty, a railroad town forty-five miles above Rostov, and Voroshilovsk, twenty-five miles southwest of Voroshilovgrad, Donets Basin industrial center.

Nazis Penned in Caucasus

The capture of Krasnodar left other sizable German forces based at Novorossiisk, on the Black Sea coast, stranded. Their best hope appeared to be an attempted flight by sea to the Crimea. But Moscow has reported that the Soviet Black Sea Fleet's big guns already are in action off Novorossiisk and the Germans have told for days of fighting Red marines landing along the coast to prevent a Nazi evacuation by boat.

German announcements, indicating that the Nazis were in trouble at Novorossiisk, said the Black Sea Fleet had tried to batter its way into the port and that a German tank division had frustrated Russian outflanking efforts on land. The Nazi communiqué appeared to be contradictory or at least confused. After saying Russian attacks had abated, it added that "mobile defense battles are, however, continuing with undiminished force."

Shakhty fell to the Russians striking southward toward Rostov, where, unofficial estimates say,

Continued on Page Six

RUSSIAN STEAMROLLERS CONTINUE TO CRUSH RESISTANCE

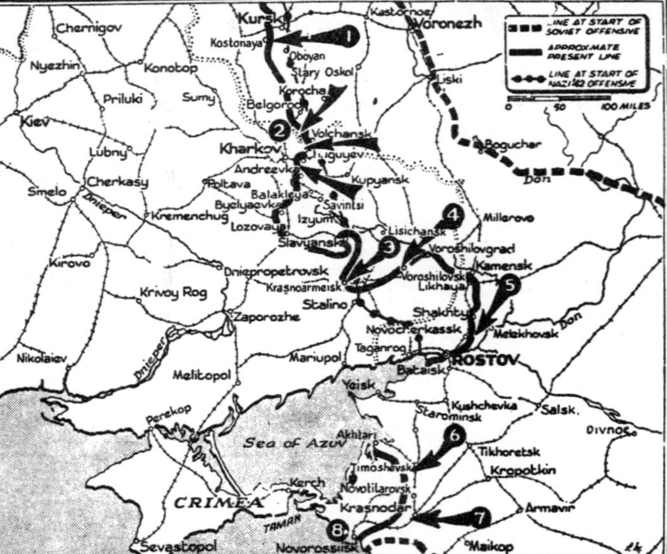

Soviet forces took more places south of Kursk (1) and closed in on Kharkov (2). They captured the railway junction of Krasnoarmeisk (3), threatening to trap 500,000 Axis troops, and also gained Voroshilovsk (4). Shakhty (5) was seized, but the German defenders of Rostov stiffened. In the Caucasus, Timoshevsk (6) and Krasnodar (7) fell to the Russians. The Nazis claimed to have driven off Soviet warships trying to penetrate the harbor of Novorossiisk (8).

TERRITORY CLAIMS LISTED BY RUSSIAN

Pravda Editor Says Estonia, Latvia, Lithuania, Bessarabia Are Part of Soviet Union

By BERTRAM D. HULEN

Special to THE NEW YORK TIMES.

WASHINGTON, Feb. 12—The latest and most emphatic assertion of the claim of the Soviet Union to Bessarabia, Estonia, Latvia and Lithuania on the ground that they are legally a part of Russia is contained in an editorial in Pravda, which was circulated in English translation today by the Soviet Embassy in its information bulletin.

It aroused deep interest in diplomatic circles because the claim has heretofore been asserted only by implication.

The editorial was written by David Zaslavsky, one of the editors of the newspaper, and appeared on

Continued on Page Six

War News Summarized

SATURDAY, FEBRUARY 13, 1943

President Roosevelt, in a broadcast speech last night, announced that operations to "drive our enemies into the sea" in Tunisia would not be long delayed. He said the Allies would gain control of the strait across the Mediterranean, and would invade Europe at more than one point. He warned the nation that the battles to come would be costly and appealed for calm courage on the home front. He promised action to drive the Japanese from China. Speaking of the post-war world, he said that every nation would be completely free but no Fascist governments would be permitted. [1:8.]

The Russians continued to advance unchecked in the Ukraine and the Caucasus. Krasnoarmeisk, a rail junction between Stalino and Dniepropetrovsk, fell to the Soviet forces, as well as Voroshilovsk, twenty-five miles southwest of Voroshilovgrad. In the Caucasus the rail center of Krasnodar was retaken. [1:4.]

The Soviet Embassy in Washington gave wide circulation to a Pravda editorial that was interpreted in diplomatic circles as a Russian claim on Bessarabia and the Baltic States. [1:5.]

In Tunisia, as ground activity was restricted by snow and the main air action was an attack on Sened, details were revealed of a successful Allied Commando raid on the Bizerte area Tuesday night. [3:1.]

On the political scene in North Africa it was announced that Charles Brunel, an ardent de Gaullist, had been put in charge of the important new Algerian Council of War Economy. [2:2.]

Britain's Air Force resumed its aerial offensive in Europe Thursday night with a raid on the naval base of Wilhelmshaven. Yesterday raids were made on targets in Northwestern Germany, the Netherlands, Belgium and Northern France. [1:6-7.]

General MacArthur's headquarters reported that the retreat of the Japanese from the Wau region of New Guinea was continuing. [1:7.]

Heavier fighting was reported from Burma, where the Japanese launched a series of sharp counter-attacks above Akyab. A British communiqué said that the assaults had been repelled with heavy enemy losses. [5:1, with map.]

Premier Mussolini made more changes in the Italian Cabinet. Six Under-Secretaries and three Ministers were replaced by men believed to be more loyal to Il Duce. [4:1.]

Wilhelmshaven Raided Hard By R. A. F. in War on U-Boats

By JAMES MacDONALD

Special Cable to THE NEW YORK TIMES.

LONDON, Feb. 12—Resuming its around-the-clock offensive, the Royal Air Force bombed the German naval base of Wilhelmshaven last night and carried out many attacks during daylight today over Northwestern Germany, the Netherlands, Belgium and Northern France. The night and day attacks across the North Sea struck new blows in the anti-submarine warfare.

British aerial activity seemingly continued tonight because Nazi broadcasting stations that usually shut down during R. A. F. raids went off the air just after 5:30 o'clock and remained dead for some time. The Hilversum station in the Netherlands was silent for three and a half hours and the Friesland and Bremen stations, also on the North Sea coast, were off the air for ninety minutes.

Many R. A. F. heavy bombers dropped two and four-ton missiles on Wilhelmshaven in a raid concentrated into twenty minutes of attack that cost three British planes.

Fast Mosquito bombers were over the same area in the daylight offensive and returned without loss. One R. A. F. fighter was missing from the hundreds of sorties over German-occupied territory.

Airmen in the night raid reported a terrific explosion set off by their missiles at Wilhelmshaven, an important U-boat building center that was pounded by Flying Fortresses and Liberators on Jan. 27 in the first raid made by the United States Army Air Forces on Germany proper. The R. A. F. at-

Continued on Page Two

JAPANESE CONTINUE NEW GUINEA FLIGHT

Seek Refuge Near Salamaua—135 More Killed in Papua—Allies Batter Rabaul

By The United Press.

AT UNITED NATIONS HEADQUARTERS, Australia, Saturday, Feb. 13—The Japanese retreat is continuing northeast of Wau on the approaches to the New Guinea port of Salamaua, the Allied command announced today in a communiqué which also said that 225 more enemy troops had been killed or found dead in Papua.

"The enemy continues his withdrawal," the bulletin said in reference to the situation at Wau, thirty-five miles southwest of Salamaua, where the Japanese have been defeated decisively after a twelve-day encounter that cost them nearly 1,000 killed and many more wounded.

The Japanese were reported retreating toward the village of

Continued on Page Four

Canterbury Rebuked by Manning For Note Favoring Church Union

Bishop William T. Manning, head of the Protestant Episcopal Diocese of New York, made public last night a letter to the church press protesting against the "ecclesiastical intrusion" of the Archbishop of Canterbury (William Temple) in the controversy now going on in the Episcopal Church in this country over a proposed organic union with the Presbyterian Church.

In church circles here it was said it was unprecedented for an American Episcopal Bishop to administer a public rebuke to an Archbishop of the Church of England. The action with which Bishop Manning took issue was the writing of a letter by the Archbishop last October to Bishop Edward L. Parsons, retired, of California, chairman of the Commission of Approaches to Unity of the Episcopal Church, saying that success of the union movement would be "a very great contribution to the cause we all have at heart."

The Archbishop gave Bishop Parsons permission to publish his letter, and it was published recently in the Episcopal Church press, together with a statement by Bishop Parsons noting the interest shown by Americans in the Archbishop's utterances.

Bishop Manning's letter follows:

Bishop Parsons, the retired Bishop of California and chairman of our commission, a majority of which proposes to unite the Episcopal Church with one

Continued on Page Fourteen

HARD BLOWS IN '43

Roosevelt Promises 'Bad News' for Nazis, Italians and the Japanese

AIR-LAND AID TO CHINA

Executive, on Radio, Tells World Quislings and Lavals Must Go

The Text of the President's address appears on Page 8.

By W. H. LAWRENCE

Special to THE NEW YORK TIMES.

WASHINGTON, Feb. 12—President Roosevelt declared tonight that great Allied operations designed to drive the enemy into the Mediterranean Sea were imminent in Tunisia and would be followed by "actual invasions of the Continent of Europe."

The Commander in Chief not only pledged more than one invasion of Europe but also promised that "great and decisive action against the Japanese will be taken to drive the invader from the soil of China." In addition to great land and air actions in China, he said, there would be air action against Japan itself.

Speaking to 700 members and guests at the annual dinner of the White House Correspondents Association here, and by radio over all networks to the entire country, Mr. Roosevelt expressed confidence in the success of military operations planned at the Casablanca war conferences with Prime Minister Churchill and looked ahead to complete victory over all the Axis nations—"to the day when United Nations forces march in triumph through the streets of Berlin, Rome and Tokyo."

He pictured a post-war world in which nations, while free to determine their own form of government as assured by the Atlantic Charter, would in no instance be permitted to choose "the fascist form of government or the Nazi form of government or the Japanese war-lord form of government." His warning appeared directed at those in France who remained loyal to the Vichy regime and was in part a reply to critics here of collaboration with former Vichy men. He said he was sure that France would never select any totalitarian form of government by free will.

Although he declared that "we do not expect to spend the time it would take to bring Japan to final

Continued on Page Three

Spellman Reported Arriving at Madrid

By Reuter.

LONDON, Feb. 12—A German news agency report says that the Catholic Archbishop of New York today arrived at Madrid airdrome from Lisbon, Portugal. He was met by the United States Ambassador in Madrid, and the Papal Nuncio to Spain. It is supposed that the Archbishop will shortly proceed to Rome by air.

Special to THE NEW YORK TIMES.

WASHINGTON, Feb. 12—It was learned from official sources here tonight that Archbishop Spellman of New York recently was planning a trip to the "Iberian Peninsula." These sources believed it to be purely a church matter.

Mgr. John J. Casey, secretary of the Archdiocese of New York, said last night that Archbishop Francis J. Spellman was making a tour of Army camps and visiting Catholic chaplains in his capacity of Military Vicar for the Armed Forces of the United States. Mgr. Casey said he did not know whether or not the Archbishop was at present outside the continental United States.

"All the News That's Fit to Print."

The New York Times.

LATE CITY EDITION
Warmer today with moderate winds.
Temperatures Yesterday—Max., 46; Min., 26
Sunrise, 6:45 A. M.; Sunset, 7:17 P. M.

VOL. XCII—No. 31,[illegible]. Entered as Second-Class Matter, Postoffice, New York, N. Y. NEW YORK, TUESDAY, MARCH 30, 1943. THREE CENTS IN NEW YORK CITY

ROMMEL FLEES AS BRITISH BREAK MARETH LINE; WARSHIPS SHELL GABES, WITH FOE RACING THERE; R. A. F. AGAIN HITS BERLIN, RUHR AND ST. NAZAIRE

MEAT STOCK FREED BY ARMY AND NAVY TO HELP CIVILIANS

Lend-Lease Also Cooperating With OPA to Give Temporary Relief in Shortage Areas

TO REPLACE SUPPLY LATER

Clamor for Meat Dies Down Here—Coupons Treasured as Rationing Starts

The Army, Navy and Lend-Lease Administration agreed yesterday to cooperate with the Office of Price Administration to provide meat supplies for relieving acute shortages which may develop in any district in the first few days of coupon rationing. Slaughterers were permitted for two weeks to cease setting aside specified percentages of their output for war purposes. [1:1.]

New York City received its first emergency supplies of meat, but there was almost no retail buying on the first day of meat rationing. [12:1.]

Most of the nation's cities had little demand for meat. Supplies were in most cases adequate, but Detroit, Birmingham and some others had acute shortages. The OPA released large emergency stocks for Chicago. Poultry wholesalers in Cleveland and Detroit closed to enforce a demand on the OPA for a chance to make a profit. [14:1.]

Chester C. Davis appointed Jesse W. Tapp, another banker, as his assistant in the War Food Production Office. He conferred with Secretary Wickard and indicated they were in agreement that there should be no delay. [13:3.]

Action in Washington

By CHARLES E. EGAN

Special to THE NEW YORK TIMES.

WASHINGTON, March 29—Cooperation has been promised by the Army, Navy and Lend-Lease Administration to relieve any unusually acute meat shortages which may develop during the next few days, the Office of Price Administration stated today.

According to government officials the meat earmarked for other uses will be made available to civilians on a temporary basis, insuring that it will be replaced as rapidly as improvement in shipments into a given area permits.

The arrangement was only one phase of a general move to ease the meat shortage as point-rationing went into effect today. It was a companion piece to the announcement by the Department of Agriculture that the order requiring livestock slaughterers to set aside certain percentages of their production for direct war purposes has been suspended for two weks.

This action was taken, department officials said, to enable wholesalers and retailers to build up their inventories after last week's unprecedented rush, so that meat will be available to retailers to meet consumer demand under the rationing program.

Says Several Days Are Needed

Prentiss M. Brown, OPA Administrator, in announcing the cooperative agreement his office has reached, said that the buying policies of the Army, Navy and Lend-Lease Administration were being adjusted temporarily to help meet the initial civilian demands as housewives began buying meat under rationing.

"Supplies throughout the nation are believed adequate to meet the civilian demand under rationing, but several days may be needed to get meat in sufficient varieties and quantities into all areas," Mr. Brown said.

"Therefore, it behooves every housewife to bear with her local butcher and the government in this initial period.

"I am particularly gratified at

Continued on Page Twelve

Soft Coal Strike Is Averted By New Presidential Move

White House Sends Dr. Steelman Here as 'Personal Representative' and Southern Operators Agree to Continue Talks

By JOSEPH SHAPLEN

President Roosevelt intervened again in the soft coal wage dispute yesterday and averted the threatened strike in the Southern area of the Appalachian region.

As a consequence of the President's new action the Southern Coal Producers Association, employing 135,000 men and representing a third of the nation's bituminous output, agreed to a thirty-day extension of the current agreement with the United Mine Workers, expiring at midnight Wednesday, with continuance of collective bargaining.

The operators of the Northern Appalachian region, employing 172,000 of the nation's 450,000 bituminous coal diggers, had signed an agreement with the union last week providing for extension of the old contract until May 1. Extension of the agreement for thirty days in both the Southern and Northern sections as proposed by the union assures uninterrupted operation of the mines after April 1.

The principal points at issue in the wage negotiations are the demands of the union for a basic increase of $2 a day, computation of a day's work from portal to portal, and unionization of some 50,000 minor bosses. The Northern operators have rejected these demands as unacceptable for financial and managerial reasons, but have expressed willingness to discuss them. By their action yesterday the Southern operators have followed suit.

The President's renewed intervention came in the form of the arrival here yesterday morning of Dr. John R. Steelman, director of the United States Conciliation Service of the Department of La-

Continued on Page Ten

MME. CHIANG PUTS WAR TO WORKERS

2,000 on Coast Cheer Clenched-Fist Demand for Ceaseless Production to End Conflict

By LAWRENCE E. DAVIES

Special to THE NEW YORK TIMES.

SAN FRANCISCO, Calif., March 29—With clenched fists which she pounded on a table to give emphasis to fighting words, Mme. Chiang Kai-shek exhorted workers of America tonight to increase industrial production to end the war "at the earliest moment possible."

At an unscheduled meeting which was unprecedented on her transcontinental tour, Mme. Chiang spoke in the C. I. O. hall to 2,500 union members, chiefly longshoremen, with leaders of American Federation of Labor, Congress of Industrial Organizations and Railroad Brotherhoods on the platform. She told them that what she was going to say was "meant for all workers in America."

"Your cause is China's cause," she said. "Because my own people have suffered and bled for six long years I have a message I'd like to bring to you.

"That is: Unity is strength.

"I've often said we must not only win the war, we must also win the peace. But in order to win the peace we must first win the war and that at the earliest moment possible.

"Your task is not one whit less important than that of the fighting forces at the front. You must

Continued on Page Fourteen

WLB EXTENDS RULE OVER LABOR FIELD

Morse Opinion Asserts Power Covers Disputes Regardless of Direct War Tie-Up

By LOUIS STARK

Special to THE NEW YORK TIMES.

WASHINGTON, March 29—The National War Labor Board claimed today jurisdiction over all labor disputes, large and small, whether in war industries or not, whether they are disputes affecting intrastate commerce or interstate commerce, whether they involve strikes or threats of strikes in hotel barbershops, in laundries or cleaning and dyeing establishments or elsewhere.

Wayne Lyman Morse, public member, who wrote the board's opinion in a case affecting 100 salesmen who solicit advertising for classified telephone directories published in New York by the Reuben H. Donnelley Corporation, said:

"After more than a year's experience in finally determining a large number of wartime labor disputes involving all sorts of issues and almost every conceivable type of dispute, the WLB takes judicial notice of the fact that any labor dispute of whatever nature which threatens to result in a strike or lockout does, in fact, affect the prosecution of the war on the home front."

The WLB had taken formal jurisdiction of the Donnelley case on Jan. 23 unanimously and had designated Mr. Morse, dean of the University of Oregon Law School, to write the opinion. The case af-

Continued on Page Ten

Mayor to Join Protest Tonight Against 2 Executions by Russia

Mayor La Guardia entered yesterday the battle between rights and lefts in the labor movement over the execution by the Soviet Government of Henryk Ehrlich and Victor Alter, when it was announced that he would be a speaker at the memorial protest meeting for the two Polish labor leaders at Mecca Temple tonight.

The announcement was made by the Committee of 250, headed by David Dubinsky, president of the International Ladies Garment Workers Union. Mr. Dubinsky will preside at the meeting, which will be addressed, among others, by William Green, president of the American Federation of Labor; James B. Carey, secretary-treasurer of the Congress of Industrial Organizations; Senator James M. Mead of New York and Representative Jerry Voorhis of California.

Speaking as president of the New York State Federation of Labor, with a membership of 1,500,000, Thomas J. Lyons addressed the following message to Mr. Dubinsky:

"The American people are in the midst of a great struggle for self-preservation, for the survival on this continent and everywhere in this world of the undying principles of humanity without which life is worthless.

"We in America do not intend to dictate domestic policies to any of our friends or allies, but we cannot fail in our duty to protest from the depth of our hearts when we see the principles of humanity for which we are fighting trampled under foot by those with whom we are engaged in a struggle against a common enemy.

"That is why I join with you in

Continued on Page Eight

AIR BLOWS 'HEAVY'

British Bomb German Capital for Second Time in 3 Nights

U-BOAT BASE FIRED

Day Raiding Pressed on Nazis in North France and Netherlands

By The Associated Press.

LONDON, Tuesday, March 30—The Royal Air Force bombed Berlin last night for the second time in three nights and also attacked targets in the Ruhr Valley, British officials announced today.

The raid on the German capital, which was subjected Saturday night to an assault more devastating than any it had undergone before, followed a series of daylight attacks by squadrons of the British Bomber Command on targets in France and the Netherlands.

Sunday night, in the interlude between the raids on Berlin, heavy British bombers blasted the great German submarine base at St. Nazaire, leaving fires from which smoke still was coiling 15,000 feet into the air yesterday afternoon.

The Air Ministry, in describing Sunday night's forty-sixth raid on St. Nazaire as "heavy and concentrated," indicated that the attack probably was as destructive as that of Feb. 28, when 1,000 tons of Britain's heaviest bombs shattered and burned the same target.

Visibility for the all-out bombing assault on the big U-boat nest was excellent, and R. A. F. crewmen said their bombs struck squarely on the docks and left large fires raging which were visible long after they left the target.

"There were seven large fires merging together," one pilot related. "They seemed to be bubbling and seething. The whole attack was remarkably concentrated."

Many crews described a huge explosion at the southern end of the docks, accompanied by a burst of orange flame and clouds of black smoke, indicating that a bomb had found its mark on a torpedo depot or ammunition dump.

The fifth bombing attack there this month fell on the first anni-

Continued on Page Eight

RETREAT IN TUNISIA: ROMMEL STARTS ON HIS WAY

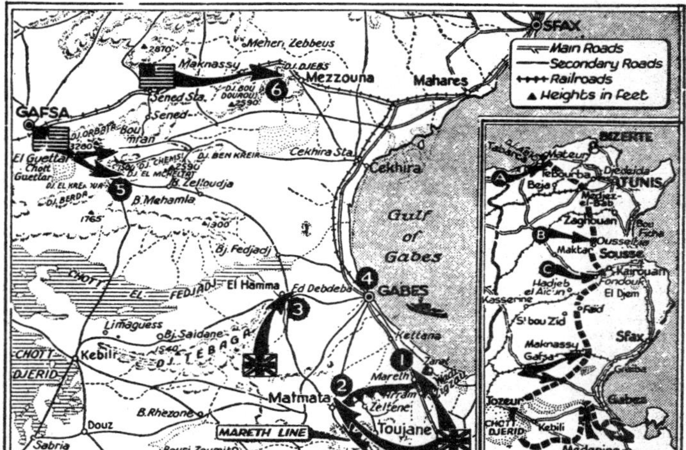

March 30, 1943

Britain's Eighth Army captured the Mareth Line defenses and the strong points of Mareth (1), Toujane and Matmata (2) after the flanking column's seizure of El Hamma (3) had made the Axis position to the south untenable. The enemy started falling back on Gabès (4), which was bombarded from the sea. If Marshal Rommel seeks to escape northward along the coast he must run an Allied gantlet: Americans are pressing forward east and southeast of El Guettar (5), east of Maknassy (6) and east of Fondouk (C on inset); French forces are holding a salient near Ousseltia (B) and British and French troops are pushing out east of Djebel Abiod (A).

U. S. STRATEGY SET FOR PACIFIC 'ACTION'

Joint Staff Chiefs and Top Aides of MacArthur, Nimitz and Halsey Map Offensive

By SIDNEY SHALETT

Special to THE NEW YORK TIMES.

WASHINGTON, March 29—Future fighting plans for every area of the Pacific Ocean were outlined in Washington at a series of "post-Casablanca" conferences just concluded between the Joint Chiefs of Staff and fifteen top-ranking representatives of Admiral Chester W. Nimitz, General Douglas MacArthur and Admiral William F. Halsey Jr., the War Department revealed today.

The War Department itself described the meetings as "important," and said that the plans discussed concerned "future actions" in the various Pacific theatres.

Among the conferees who came

Continued on Page Five

'Impossible' Waste Crossed By British Flanking Column

By DON WHITEHEAD

Associated Press Correspondent

WITH THE BRITISH EIGHTH ARMY, West of Gabès, March 28 (Delayed)—In his biggest gamble of the entire African campaign General Sir Bernard L. Montgomery has outfoxed the "Fox of the Desert" by one of the boldest and most daring manoeuvres accomplished by the British Eighth Army in its campaign to drive Field Marshal Erwin Rommel out of North Africa.

Strong elements of British troops outflanked the Mareth Line through a wild, sandy, dust-blown fringe of the Sahara across country that seemed impossible for an army to move over. I have just come across this waterless wasteland, which Marshal Rommel apparently thought could never be crossed by armor. Never in the almost 2,000 miles of advance from El Alamein, Egypt, have I seen country that punishes men and machines more than this land does. But the Eighth Army accomplished the final phase of the move in a spectacular dash at almost unbelievable speed.

It was not a case of playing safe and taking no chances—not this move. It was the greatest gamble that General Montgomery had taken—a cool, calculated gamble that forced Marshal Rommel to divide his army into two parts in Southern Tunisia.

Three weeks ago a force went around the Matmata hills and then toward Gabès, pioneering the wasteland. When the Germans repulsed the break-through in the

Continued on Page Four

YANKS SCALE PEAK UNDER GERMAN FIRE

Djebel el Mcheltat, in Central Tunisia, Is Captured After Day-Long Hammering

By The United Press.

BEYOND EL GUETTAR, Tunisia, March 29—American infantry, hammering ahead through fierce mortar and artillery fire, captured the German stronghold of Djebel el Mcheltat, a 1,500-foot hill, during the night after attacking it throughout yesterday.

The enemy is now entrenched on Djebel Chemsi, twelve miles east of El Guettar. Another American column on the right of the Gabès road is still attacking the east slopes of Djebel Berda, in the low hills overlooking the road.

All day yesterday our boys crept forward over hills and through ravines, slowly gaining ground in a tough, slugging battle that de-

Continued on Page Three

War News Summarized

TUESDAY, MARCH 30, 1943

The British won one of the war's major battles when, after eight days of relentless struggle, General Montgomery's Eighth Army brought about the collapse of the Mareth Line in Tunisia.

A combined frontal and flanking attack overwhelmed the key points of Mareth, Toujane and Matmata. Marshal Rommel was retreating yesterday over low country toward Gabès through an ever-narrowing gap and under attack from the air. Gabès itself was bombarded from the sea. The Americans pushed ahead east of El Guettar over difficult terrain and against strongly entrenched German positions in Central Tunisia, while in the north the British First Army advanced near Djebel Abiod. [1:8.]

A correspondent with the Eighth Army said that General Montgomery took the greatest military gamble of his career in moving the armor of his flanking column across the fringe of the Sahara and in doing so outfoxed Marshal Rommel, who apparently thought such a feat was impossible. [1:6-7.]

The Axis also suffered in Europe. The R. A. F. bombed Berlin again last night and hit in the Ruhr Valley, after a heavy, concentrated raid Sunday night on the U-boat base at St. Nazaire that left a fourth of the French port afire. In daylight yesterday British bombers were over the Netherlands and France. [1:4.]

Action in Russia was limited, with Soviet troops advancing slowly toward Smolensk and holding the Germans on the Donets. [1:6-7.]

Japan received her share of attention at Washington, where a three weeks' conference ended after having outlined Allied fighting plans in the Pacific. The United Nations Joint Chiefs of Staff and fifteen ranking officers from the Pacific theatre participated in the sessions. [1:5.]

Accord between pro-Allied French forces is believed near, reports from Algiers said. General Catroux, who as General de Gaulle's representative has been conferring with General Giraud, will hold a press conference today. [4:1.]

Post-war problems were other subjects of discussion in Washington as well as in London. A United States Treasury spokesman said a full-dress international conference on post-war monetary stabilization would be held soon to clear up Anglo-American differences. [6:3.]

An Allied high commissioner for education in Germany was suggested at a conference of educators in London, to undo the domestic effects of Nazi propaganda. [6:4.]

Russians Gain Toward Smolensk; Tanks and Infantry Hit Defenses

By The United Press.

LONDON, Tuesday, March 30—Russian tanks and infantry shock troops, fighting their way into the main German defense system before Smolensk, have smashed a series of enemy pill boxes and captured three inhabited places, the Soviet Monday midnight communiqué said today.

Moscow dispatches said that the Russians had been slowed by the mud as well as by the formidable defenses of one of the largest fortification systems on the entire Eastern Front, and Axis broadcasts said that the Red Army had opened a new and heavy attack in the north, trying to free the main communications of Leningrad before the ice melted on Lake Ladoga, across which they had moved supplies all Winter.

The midnight Red Army communiqué, recorded here from the Moscow radio, reported that on the Smolensk and Donets River fronts the Russians were fighting in territory dotted by German pill boxes, blockhouses and dugouts.

In their two-pronged drive on Smolensk the Russians yesterday engaged in fighting largely of local importance, the midnight bulletin said. But announcement that pillboxes as well as fortified villages had started to fall meant that the Red Army had begun its task of driving into thick defense belts, preparing for a Spring drive after the thaw.

In one Smolensk sector the Russians stormed a German strong point, killing 160 Germans, and Red Army tanks smashed three German tanks and a trench mortar battery. One of the tank crews de-

Continued on Page Seven

MAIN FORTS TAKEN

Attackers Pour Through Breaches—Gain on Flank Reported

ALLIES PERIL ROAD

Strong Forces in Center and North Drive for Coastal Highway

By C. L. SULZBERGER

Wireless to THE NEW YORK TIMES.

ALLIED HEADQUARTERS IN NORTH AFRICA, March 29—The British Eighth Army under General Sir Bernard L. Montgomery has outflanked and occupied the main positions of the Mareth Line after a brilliant enveloping move across the fringe of the Sahara, it was officially announced today. Bearing down hard on the enemy's right wing after having encountered difficulties in his smashing frontal attack, General Montgomery has scored a decisive strategic victory.

The strong-points of Mareth, Toujane and Matmata have been overwhelmed and Field Marshal General Erwin Rommel's Africa Corps is now withdrawing across the low-lying plains toward the Gabès gap under fiercely incessant Allied air attacks. The Gabès area is under heavy naval bombardment.

[The Axis-controlled "Voice of the Arab World" said in an Arabic broadcast heard by The United Press in London, that "we have received news that the English have occupied Gabès."]

Spitfires and Airacobras swept over the Gabès-Mezzouna communications lines while Kittyhawk bombers shattered the Gabès-El Hamma road.

British Pour Through Breaches

After days of battle in which the veteran British and German armies had been standing almost toe to toe along the stark ridges bordering the gates to Central Tunisia, the British desert fighters are now pouring through the breaches in the best prepared positions on the Southern Mediterranean shore. The Western Desert Air Force, despite high winds screaming out of the south with swirling dust-clouds, is hammering the withdrawing enemy formations as they approach the sixteen-mile Gabès-El Hamma region through which they are being herded. [This gap has been narrowed to fourteen miles by a British advance beyond El Hamma, according to an Algiers broadcast recorded by Reuter.]

The British have won one of the decisive battles of the war by sheer staying power, excellence and quantity of equipment, supreme cooperation between ground and air units and generalship of the first order. There is no indication where Marshal Rommel's battered forces may again seek to make a stand. By sound strategic and tactical concepts, General Montgomery has again succeeded in smashing a skilled opponent by a combination of frontal and flanking attacks. Every success has been fuller than that initially achieved at El Alamein, Egypt. Not only has Marshal Rommel been forced to withdraw in the Mareth Line area but the formidable triangular range of mountains between Zeltene, Toujane and Matmata has been entirely abandoned.

[The Algiers radio, according to Reuter, said tonight that it was generally believed in military circles that Marshal Rommel would retreat to a line north of Sousse, since the positions in the plains bounded by Chott Djérid, Kairouan, Sousse and Gabès are untenable.

[Reports from Algiers to Madrid said that Marshal Rommel had established headquarters in the region of El Djem, forty-two miles north of Gabès, The United Press reported. He was arranging Axis withdrawals and counter-attacks along his flanks to

Continued on Page Four

"All the News That's Fit to Print."

The New York Times.

LATE CITY EDITION
Scattered showers with moderate winds today.
Temperature Yesterday—Max., 56; Min., 37
Sunrise, 6:10 A. M.; Sunset, 7:46 P. M.

VOL. XCII..No. 31,133. Entered as Second-Class Matter, Postoffice, New York, N. Y. NEW YORK, WEDNESDAY, APRIL 21, 1943. THREE CENTS IN NEW YORK CITY

ROOSEVELT, ON TOUR, VISITS MEXICAN PRESIDENT; THEY PLEDGE FIGHT FOR 'GOOD NEIGHBOR WORLD'; BRITISH 8TH ARMY CRACKS AXIS ENFIDAVILLE LINE

TAX BILL FRAMERS VIRTUALLY AGREED ON 50% ABATEMENT

Ways and Means Chiefs of Both Parties Hold Night Parley to Whip Out a Compromise

REPORT TO RAYBURN TODAY

Payroll Withholding Levy of 20% Is Said to Be One Phase of the Accord Reached

By JOHN H. CRIDER
Special to THE NEW YORK TIMES.

WASHINGTON, April 20—Virtual agreement on a pay-as-you-go tax bill was reported reached tonight by leading members of the Ways and Means Committee, who have been conferring almost continuously since last Friday in an effort to end the tax stalemate.

Chairman Doughton and colleagues of both parties who comprised the conferring group will report their findings to Speaker Rayburn and House leaders at a conference tomorrow morning.

While the conferees were pledged to secrecy, pending their report to the Speaker, every indication pointed to agreement on "forgiveness" of somewhere in the neighborhood of 50 per cent of the 1942 tax liability.

One likely feature of the compromise is the non-controversial 20 per cent withholding provision contained in the major pay-as-you-go bills and the former Ways and Means bill. This would become effective July 1, from which date 20 per cent of taxable income would be withheld from the pay of all wage and salary earners.

Knutson Promises Statement

The conferees, following the "do or die" meeting behind closed doors, admitted reporters and explained, in the words of Representative Knutson, ranking Republican conferee, that "we will have something very definite to tell you tomorrow."

A colloquy, which seemed most significant, came when Mr. Knutson, explaining to reporters that there would be something "very definite tomorrow," was interrupted by Chairman Doughton, who asked whether he meant to imply by the statement that "we have reached a definite agreement here tonight."

Mr. Knutson replied that he "did not mean to imply that we have not come to an agreement either."

Chairman Doughton, acting as spokesman for the Democrats, and Mr. Knutson for the Republicans, made it clear that they had agreed with Speaker Rayburn not to disclose their findings before reporting back to him.

"We would feel fine, wouldn't we," Mr. Knutson asked, "to have the Speaker read about this in the papers tomorrow morning?"

Apparently Not Entirely Agreed

The little light that the conferees shed on their findings indicated that there was still a small area of disagreement between the Republicans and Democrats, but that it was narrowed to such small proportions that a night's sleep, plus the conciliation of the Speaker and the party leaders tomorrow, would close the gap.

When he emerged from a meeting of the group this afternoon for a recess before the night session, Representative Disney, Democrat of Oklahoma, said:

"It begins to look like 50 per cent forgiveness. I personally think it is a crime, but that is the way it looks now."

When reporters entered the Ways and Means Committee office tonight after what was described as the "final" conference of the group, Chairman Doughton had lost some of his buoyancy of the last few days, but Representative Knutson seemed in high spirits.

Some were inclined to draw from this that Mr. Doughton had yielded entirely to the Republican point of view, but those familiar with the elderly chairman were in-

Continued on Page Nineteen

The Hornet Was 'Shangri-la' For Doolittle's Tokyo Raid

War Department Reveals All but One of 16 Bombers Crashed, 64 of 80 Men Returned —8 Believed to Be Prisoners

By SIDNEY SHALETT
Special to THE NEW YORK TIMES.

WASHINGTON, April 20—The secret of "Shangri-la," from which Major Gen. James H. Doolittle and his boys flew to rain bombs on Tokyo on April 18, 1942, was finally unveiled by the War Department tonight. The bombers' starting point was the U. S. S. Hornet, the gallant aircraft carrier since lost in the epic battle of Santa Cruz in the South Pacific.

Eighty Americans, flying in sixteen North American B-25 medium bombers, took off from the decks of the Hornet to bomb selected objectives—armament plants, dockyards, railroad yards and oil refineries—in Tokyo, Yokohama, Nagoya, Kobe and Osaka, the War Department revealed.

The bomber that landed in Russian territory was the only one to reach a destination safely, the announcement revealed. All the others made forced or crash landings and all these were wrecked.

Of the eighty Americans, sixty-four came back. They found their way to camps of the Chinese Army and from there returned to the American forces. Five of the eighty landed in Russia. They are interned. Two others are missing. One American was killed.

The eight others who did not come back, the War Department said, are prisoners—or "presumed to be prisoners"—of the Japanese.

It was an audacious raid, and one that took the Japanese by surprise. At that stage of the war no one had dreamed—or at least had not executed the dream—of sending big land bombers careening off

Continued on Page Three

The official story of the Tokyo raid is on Page 4.

HEIGHT IS STORMED

Moonlight Attack Opens New Drive on Enemy's Tunisian Position

PLANE TOLL NOW 112

French Hold Newly Won Gains Despite Foe's Counter-Attack

By FRANK L. KLUCKHOHN
Special Broadcast to THE NEW YORK TIMES.

ALLIED HEADQUARTERS IN NORTH AFRICA, April 20—The British Eighth Army has initiated the "big drive" toward Tunis by attacking in force northwest of Enfidaville and has "penetrated" the enemy position, it was announced officially tonight.

Just how far it has penetrated this position, lying just fifty miles south of Tunis, and how far this advance can be exploited is, as yet, undisclosed. But heavy fighting continues and the German forces are obviously trying their best to stem this onslaught on the eastern end of their thirty-three-mile mountain bridgehead. Today's communiqué reported that there had been "active patrols" yesterday on the whole 120-mile line that the Germans are trying to defend.

[The British have seized mountain heights dominating the coastal road to Tunis, while a flanking force operating somewhat west of the main battle area has smashed ahead three miles to capture Djebel Garci, a 1,200-foot height commanding the area twelve miles inland from the sea, front dispatches said, according to The Associated Press.

[While the Algiers radio, heard by the Columbia Broadcasting System, said that the French were pushing forward toward Pont du Fahs and farther north the British First Army was advancing steadily on Tebourba, eighteen miles west of Tunis, a Paris broadcast recorded in London reported that two Anglo-American attacks in the region of Medjez-el-Bab and Bou Arada, northwest of Enfidaville, had been repulsed.]

As General Sir Bernard L. Montgomery attacked, the Allied air force maintained its heavy bomb-

Continued on Page Nine

PRESIDENT RECEIVES A MODEL OF A LIGHT BOMBER

Mr. Roosevelt accepts a miniature of a new attack craft from a representative of the workers at the Douglas Aircraft Company in Tulsa, Okla., during a visit to the plant on his tour.
Associated Press Wirephoto

(Other pictures of President's tour on Page 11)

MEET IN MONTERREY

Urge World in Which No People Is Exploited to Benefit Another

ARGENTINA A TARGET

Roosevelt Criticizes Her —President Made War Plant Tour

The texts of the Presidential addresses are on Page 10.

By W. H. LAWRENCE
Special to THE NEW YORK TIMES.

MONTERREY, Mexico, April 20—President Franklin D. Roosevelt of the United States and President Manuel Avila Camacho of Mexico jointly pledged tonight to fight the war through to final and complete victory over the Axis so that the Good Neighbor policy of the Americas can be extended to a whole world in which there will not be exploitation of the resources and people of one country for the benefit of any group in another.

They met in this Northern Mexican industrial city in the first face-to-face conference of the Presidents of the two neighbor countries since Oct. 16, 1909, when President William Howard Taft of the United States and President Porfirio Diaz of Mexico met at El Paso, Texas, and Ciudad Juarez, Mexico, to participate in ceremonies opening the International Bridge linking the two countries.

That meeting was a peaceful one, with commerce as the keynote, but the conference today was against a background of war, which made it necessary for President Roosevelt to come here secretly during a tour of inspection of American war factories and camps training members of the armed forces.

Review Mexican Troops

Together, President Roosevelt and President Avila Camacho this afternoon reviewed a motorized Mexican division, and the Mexican Chief Executive was host at a state dinner tonight at which both Presidents spoke, one in Spanish and the other in English.

A highlight of Mr. Roosevelt's prepared address was his declaration that the governments of the United States and Mexico "recognize a mutual interdependence of our joint resources" and "know that the day of the exploitation of the resources and the peoples of one country for the benefit of any group in another country is definitely over." This was regarded as his assurance to the American republics that the financial practices of which they had complained in the past would not be renewed and, possibly, as a declaration that might have important bearing upon post-war peace terms, particularly as they affect the British Empire.

For Complete Victory

Both Presidents were specific in their demand for complete victory and recognition of essential steps to remove the seeds of future wars, and some believed that the statements were, in part at least, a response to reported recent peace "feelers" from the Spanish Government headed by Generalissimo Francisco Franco.

President Roosevelt said:

"In the shaping of a common victory our peoples are finding that they have common aspirations. They can work together for a common objective. Let us never lose our hold upon that truth. It contains within it the secret of future happiness and prosperity for all of us on both sides of our unfortified border.

"Let us make sure that when our victory is won, when the forces of evil surrender—and that surrender shall be unconditional—then we, with the same spirit and with the same united courage, will

Continued on Page Eleven

CIVILIAN SUPPLY PUT UP TO SENATE

Committee Reports Maloney Bill to Divorce OCS and WPB for a Separate Agency

Special to THE NEW YORK TIMES.

WASHINGTON, April 20—Brushing aside the War Production Board's opposition and its reorganizational steps designed to discourage Congressional action, the Senate Banking and Currency Committee approved unanimously and reported out today the Maloney bill which would take the Office of Civilian Supply away from the WPB and establish it as an independent administration with coordinate, rather than subordinate, powers.

The measure, which would give a $12,000-a-year administrator authority to determine the needs and call for allocations of manpower and material "to keep the civilian population healthy and functioning effectively," and even to make decisions regarding the rationing of goods and services, is scheduled to be presented to the Senate Thursday, with floor action possible next week. Predictions were widespread that the bill would be adopted.

Tomorrow, when Arthur D. Whiteside, new WPB vice chairman in charge of civilian requirements, takes his post, the WPB itself will undertake to give the civilian population a larger part in supply programs. Donald M. Nelson, WPB chairman, is reported planning to form two committees

Continued on Page Twenty

CITY SUMMONS 625 AS PRICE VIOLATORS

OPA Also Accuses 63 Pork Retailers—Woolley Warns All Ceilings Must Be Observed

By JEFFERSON G. BELL

The two-pronged drive by city and Federal authorities against alleged violators of food price ceilings and other rationing regulations was broadened considerably yesterday.

Mayor La Guardia announced that 625 summonses had been served on retail food merchants in the Markets Department campaign, while the district Office of Price Administration said that in its drive to enforce consumer maximum pork price ceilings it had prepared summonses for sixty-three pork retailers. These summonses, returnable within a week or ten days, are to be mailed out today, when the list is to be made public.

Grocers Meet With Woolley

Meanwhile, spokesmen for thousands of the city's smaller food merchants who say they are so bewildered they cannot understand OPA regulations and who are threatening to stop selling eggs met with Markets Commissioner Daniel P. Woolley. They tried to dissuade the city authorities from pushing prosecutions of alleged ceiling violators under the Code of Administrative Procedure provisions covering short weights and short measures.

After the meeting Mr. Woolley

Continued on Page Thirty-three

Senators to Open OWI Inquiry As Witnesses at Press Parley

Special to THE NEW YORK TIMES.

WASHINGTON, April 20—Congressional investigation of the operations of Office of War Information will start tomorrow when Elmer Davis, director, stages a press conference for the benefit of the Senate Judiciary Committee. Only members of Congress and reporters will be admitted.

Judiciary Committee members explained that they had asked Mr. Davis to hold his regular press meeting at the Capitol instead of at the Social Security Building, OWI headquarters.

As the inquiry seems to be aimed at ascertaining whether Mr. Davis and his aides have been "propagandizing," or have made any "commitments" for the United States in the foreign field, questions along these lines are expected. Further, some of the Senators expressed curiosity over the recent resignation of fifteen writers from OWI.

The appearance of Mr. Davis in the Senate Office Building caucus room will not be his only one before a Congressional body. Today the Senate Agriculture subcommittee decided to summon both Mr. Davis and William M. Jeffers to explain their sharp clash over publicity regarding the rubber program.

Voting to call the two witnesses, Senator Wheeler said he would be glad to see OWI eliminated, for this "would be a blessing to the country."

Mr. Wheeler held that in view of the "wide discrepancy of views" of Mr. Davis and Mr. Jeffers over the rubber program, both should testify.

"Jeffers," the Senator stated

Continued on Page Twelve

RED ARMY ATTACKS ON KALININ FRONT

New Drive Indicated in Capture of Strong Point—Germans Repulsed in Caucasus

By The United Press.

LONDON, Wednesday, April 21—A Soviet communiqué, in the first reference in weeks to the Kalinin front, said today that a Russian detachment there made a surprise attack on strong fortified enemy positions, captured a dominating height and held it against six enemy counter-attacks. The Germans left 400 killed at the approaches to the height, it was said.

The Kalinin front is so called because it is a command area. Kalinin is 100 miles northwest of Moscow. Actually the fighting line is about 180 miles west of Kalinin, in the vicinity of Kholm, where it was assumed the action took place.

General Ivan Purkaeff, who was Russian military attaché in Berlin when the Germans attacked Russia, has been commanding the Kalinin front.

In the Kuban valley of the West-

Continued on Page Eight

Germany's Gamble on Tank And Dive-Bomber Held Lost

By C. L. SULZBERGER
Wireless to THE NEW YORK TIMES.

CAIRO, Egypt, April 20—The tank and dive-bomber—the two chief offensive weapons that the Germans developed before this war and on which they banked largely to win the "lightning war" begun almost four years ago—have now been outclassed and virtually rendered useless, according to gratified British artillery and air experts.

The heavy concentration of fire-power of field pieces and anti-aircraft, as well as the effective use of attack and fighter planes, has made old-fashioned the German armored spearhead covered by dive-bomber waves, these experts say. The Royal Air Force insists that the dive-bomber is now a "dead pigeon." In ground attacks, the Royal Artillery considers that guns are already so far ahead of tanks that no new armored vehicle can be satisfactorily developed during this war that could regain superiority.

Thus the main arm of the German offensive threat is done for, in the British view. As a result, the Germans, who had neglected other military techniques, such as artillery, to gamble on these surprise weapons employed in vast quantities, are now falling behind not only in the armament race with the Allies but in actual types and usage of general military equipment. This, it must be emphasized, is the British opinion and not necessarily that of the United States Army experts, but it is based on long experience, sound study and considerable logic.

The artillery piece, they say, has completely gained the whip-hand over the tank. The armored vehicle is helpless in the face of a properly handled gun. This superiority has come to stay. The German Army

Continued on Page Nine

FLIERS IN PACIFIC HOLD 5-TO-1 EDGE

128 Planes, 19 Ships Destroyed or Damaged in 15 Days for Loss of 8 Aircraft

Special to THE NEW YORK TIMES.

WASHINGTON, April 20—Fifteen days of aerial dueling in the Southwest Pacific, scene of the current bitter struggle between the Japanese and the Allies for supremacy of the skies, has cost the enemy 128 planes destroyed or damaged, nineteen warships and cargo vessels damaged or sunk and twelve other ships possibly damaged, the War Department announced today.

The cost to the Allied air forces, under American command, for the heavy Japanese toll was eight planes destroyed and seventeen damaged, the War Department said.

It was regarded here as significant that the War Department compared the Japanese and American scores at a time when the Southwest Pacific air power situation was in the limelight. There has been evidence of growing Japanese air strength and General

Continued on Page Five

War News Summarized

WEDNESDAY, APRIL 21, 1943

The British Eighth Army celebrated Adolf Hitler's birthday yesterday by announcing that an offensive opened by moonlight had penetrated Marshal Rommel's Enfidaville defense line in Tunisia. West of the main action, other elements captured Djebel Garci, dominating one of the roads leading to Tunis. [1:4, map P. 9.]

British landing parties seized the Kerkennah Islands in the Gulf of Gabès east of captured Sfax, which are stepping stones to Sicily. [1:6-7, map P. 9.]

Two London districts received a few Nazi bombs yesterday, but heavy anti-aircraft fire drove off the enemy planes. The R. A. F. kept up its day raids in Western Europe and was over Germany again last night. [14:1.]

Persistent charges by tanks, planes and infantry failed to dislodge the Red Army from its positions in the Kuban, Western Caucasus, Moscow said. On the Kalinin front, northwest of Moscow, the Russians captured a height and killed 3,000 Germans who had sought to retake it. [1:5.]

The Army published a summary showing that, at the cost of eight planes lost and seventeen damaged, Allied fliers in the Southwest Pacific from April 11-15 had destroyed or damaged 128 Japanese planes, nineteen ships, including nine warships, and probably damaged twelve more vessels. [1:7.]

The Japanese Cabinet underwent a drastic shake-up when the former pro-Allied diplomat, Marmoru Shigemitsu, replaced the pro-army Foreign Minister Tani. Three others were dropped from Premier Tojo's cabinet. [6:3.]

The aircraft carrier Hornet, since lost, was the "Shangri-la" from which eighty American fliers in sixteen B-25 bombers raided Japan under General Doolittle last year, the War Department announced. Sixty-four of the men returned through China, five were interned in Russia, two are missing, one was killed and eight are believed prisoners of the Japanese [1:2-3.]

President Roosevelt, after touring American military camps for a week, spoke with President Avila Camacho of Mexico at a dinner in Monterrey last night. Both Executives stressed the importance of the Good-Neighbor policy, which they held out as a pattern for the world after the war. Mr. Roosevelt urged a world in which the people and resources of a country would not be exploited by others. [1:8.]

General Draja Mikhailovitch, Yugoslav Chetnik leader, said in a prepared statement that he had spurned frequent Axis proposals to lay down his arms, and assured the United Nations he would be at their side when they invaded the Balkans. [6:5.]

British Occupy Kerkennah Islands In Gulf of Gabes Without a Shot

By The United Press.

SFAX, Tunisia, April 15 (Delayed)—British Army assault parties landed on the Kerkennah Islands, in the Gulf of Gabès east of Sfax, early yesterday and occupied them without firing a shot, giving the Allies control of two of the six island stepping-stones between Tunisia and Sicily.

Enemy forces stationed on the two French islands, mostly populated by Arabs friendly to the French, were reported to have left about four days before the British paddled ashore in small boats at Rharbi, sixteen miles from Sfax.

Reports reaching here from a signalman after the return of the naval force said that the natives had been extremely friendly and that the head man at Melita, the capital and only town of Rharbi, southernmost of the two islands, had given the British the keys to the Italian barracks.

The assault parties were composed of a special service detachment that had received commando-like training. Crossing at night from Sfax, the troops put ashore in landing boats launched from naval craft that anchored until all were successfully ashore, then put back to Sfax. There was no opposition.

Another naval force brought in stores and equipment to facilitate the occupation of the northern island, Chergui.

The islands are rich in groves of olive, fig and date trees and possess large fields of barley and pasture land for sheep. Their occupation leaves the Axis with four islands between Tunisia and Sicily. They are Pantelleria, Lampedusa, Linosa and Lamione.

"All the News That's Fit to Print."

The New York Times.

Copyright, 1943, by The New York Times Company.

LATE CITY EDITION
Moderately cold with gentle winds today.
Temperatures Yesterday—Max., 47; Min., 40
Sunrise, 6:09 A. M.; Sunset, 7:41 P. M.

VOL. XCII..No. 31,134. Entered as Second-Class Matter, Postoffice, New York, N. Y. NEW YORK, THURSDAY, APRIL 22, 1943. THREE CENTS IN NEW YORK CITY

JAPANESE EXECUTE OUR AIRMEN; U. S. WILL PUNISH ALL RESPONSIBLE; 8TH ARMY CAPTURES ENFIDAVILLE

TAX COMPROMISE FAILS AND 2 BILLS WILL GO TO HOUSE

Collapse of Truce Overnight Puts Both Parties Back of Own Abatement Plans

TEST DUE IN TWO WEEKS

Democrats Would Apply 1941 Rates to 1942 Income and Adopt Withholding Levy

By JOHN H. CRIDER
Special to THE NEW YORK TIMES.

WASHINGTON, April 21—The House will get another chance to vote on pay-as-you-go tax bills within the next two weeks as the paradoxical result of the inability of members of the Ways and Means Committee, who have tirelessly sought a compromise since last Friday, to reach an agreement.

An overnight change of attitude on the part of some of the Republican conferees was reported by members of both parties to have ended the hope of obtaining a single bill upon which Democrats and Republicans in the House might agree.

Out of the "agreement to disagree" comes not only another chance for members to express themselves on the floor, but what was advanced as a much more generous proposal by the Democratic majority, which heretofore has rejected any cancellation of 1942 liability.

The least amount of 1942 taxes "forgiven" under the plans to go before the House would be between 40 and 50 per cent, or from $4,000,000,000 to $5,000,000,000.

Two Proposals Advanced

The majority appeared ready to throw its full support behind a bill to be introduced by Chairman Doughton of Ways and Means. It embodies what was described as the final proposal of the Democratic conferees in the now terminated series of conferences aimed at compromise.

The bill would apply rates of the 1941 revenue act to 1942 income, thereby forgiving the difference between taxes under the lower 1941 rates and rates of the 1942 act, which would automatically eliminate about 7,000,000 new taxpayers from any 1942 liability. Their payments would immediately become current.

The Republicans will offer the House their final compromise proposal, which would "forgive" 75 per cent of the 1942 liability on the first $5,000 of income and whatever additional income up to $20,000 might also be "earned income," and 50 per cent of all income over $20,000.

Each plan also incorporates bonus features to encourage advance payment of taxes. The Democratic proposal would "forgive" roughly 40 per cent of the 1942 liability, while the Republicans would abate somewhere between 50 and 75 per cent of that liability. Chairman Doughton said that, including discounts allowed for advance payments of future liability, the Democratic scheme would abate about 50 per cent.

The attempt at compromise broke down on the question of how to treat the taxpayers with less than $20,000 income, and spokesmen for each side made claims for the superiority of his manner of providing for the small taxpayers.

Democrats Explain Plan

The Democrats explained their final proposal as follows.

"Adopt pay-as-you-go taxation in 1943 and subsequent years, including withholding at source on salaries and wages effective July 1.

"Forgive the approximate difference between the 1942 tax and the tax computed at 1941 rates and exceptions. To avoid administrative difficulties, a formula will be used for the computation of the amount forgiven.

"Spread the unforgiven part of the 1942 liability over a period of three years, but give the Commissioner of Internal Revenue authority to extend the payment over a longer period, in the case of hardship, upon the payment of interest during the period of the extension. Provide for some discount if payment of unforgiven 1942 liability is made within the two-year period. If payments are made on or before the following dates,

Continued on Page Twenty-six

Don't Buy Bonds, Nazis Ask by Radio

By The United Press.

The Berlin radio advised the American people to refuse to buy war bonds and decline to pay taxes, according to a broadcast heard in New York yesterday by the Columbia Broadcasting System.

The Nazi broadcaster asserted that in the United States there was a "mad scramble on to see who pays the least of the bill, which group of the community gets out of the mess with the least sacrifice."

"The best and wisest thing people can do who did not want this war is to prepare for the worst," said the Berlin speaker. "They can begin by not subscribing to the present loan of $13,000,000,000 to help pay for the war.

"You cannot win this war, anyway, and would probably be worse off if you did. So anything that brings it to an end quickly is good. Let the banks buy the loan and let them keep it."

WORLD FOOD SHIFTS IN MIND FOR PARLEY

Free Flow of Surpluses Is on Tentative Agenda Set for Hot Springs May 18

By JOHN MacCORMAC
Special to THE NEW YORK TIMES.

WASHINGTON, April 21—The tentative agenda for the international food conference, scheduled to open May 18 at Hot Springs, Va., and the hopes of its United States organizers call for worldwide regulation of the food supply of the globe in the interests primarily of human health, secondly as an economic measure which would lay the foundation for healthy national economies and free international trade, and thirdly as a preservative of peace.

Food will be considered as a basis for sound minds and healthy bodies, and thus as the chief ingredient in the fulfillment of the "freedom from want" clause of the Atlantic Charter; as a basis for prosperity, since sixty per cent of those who work in the world work at agriculture; and as a preventive and even as a weapon of war.

The conference will presuppose the establishment of world security, a reasonably free world trade, and a world economic agreement and currency stabilization. Food itself is an important element in all three.

Forty nations have been invited to send delegates to the conference. A notable exception is Argentina, one of the world's greatest producers of wheat, corn and meat.

Production Shifts Suggested

What will be suggested to them and by them could be described as a world Agricultural Adjustment Administration, with the shifting of world production out of such permanent surplus commodities as cotton, coffee, sugar and perhaps wheat; as a world-wide surplus commodities disposal or food stamp plan, with two world prices for wheat, one to the prosperous nations and another to the hungry millions of, say, China, a world-wide ever-normal granary to be operated by the accumulation of "buffer stocks" of basic foods, which would be used to regulate supply and stabilize price.

The basis from which the subject is to be approached is that human beings, to be healthy, need three

Continued on Page Sixteen

APRIL PLANE OUTPUT 7,000, NELSON SAYS, AND STILL GAINING

He Tells Publishers Hitler's Big Error Was Underestimating U. S. Productive Speed

DEAR CALLS FOR VIGILANCE

A. N. P. A. Head Declares It Is Price of Liberty Against Government Restrictions

The text of Mr. Nelson's address is printed on Page 20.

Declaring that Adolf Hitler had made his "one great miscalculation" in failing to count on the ability of American industry to swing into war production as quickly as it has, Donald M. Nelson, chairman of the War Production Board, revealed yesterday that United States airplane production probably would reach the 7,000-a-month rate this month, or come close to it, and promised it would keep on growing until it was as large as needed.

The last previous figure on airplane production was released by Under-Secretary of War Robert P. Patterson last month, when he said it had reached the 5,500 mark in February and that more than 65 per cent of our total production in January had been combat planes.

Mr. Nelson made his announcement at yesterday afternoon's session of the fifty-seventh annual convention of the American Newspaper Publishers Association at the Waldorf-Astoria Hotel.

In response to the presentation of a souvenir brochure that contained a report on the nation-wide metal-scrap collection conducted by the newspapers last Fall to keep the steel mills running and war production going at top speed, Mr. Nelson commended the newspaper industry for having done one of the most successful jobs that any industry has done for the war program.

Lauds Power of Free Press

Testifying to the power of the press as he had observed it in the scrap drive, he said it had strengthened his belief in a free press as a fundamental without which democracy could not be maintained.

He said that the many fine jobs done by American industry in the war under the free enterprise system had taught him "one great lesson," which should be valuable to posterity in future emergencies —that free industry, having the best brains in the United States, "the brains that built up the country," can do any production job that is clearly stated and put up to it, no matter how impossible it may seem.

The great strength and virility being shown by American industry on the production front, plus the virility shown by American youth on the battle front, he went on, guarantee not only victory in the war but the future of America. If the problems of post-war peace are presented to American industry as clearly as the problems of war have been, he said, it can solve them just as well—in a practical way, beneficial to the country.

Mr. Nelson defended his associates in WPB, many of whom have been under criticism, and said they are "just as representative of the best i. the country as we can possibly find."

Although the tone of his speech

Continued on Page Twenty

Secret Polish Radio Asks Aid, Cut Off

By The Associated Press.

STOCKHOLM, Sweden, April 21—The secret Polish radio appealed for help tonight in a broadcast from Poland and then suddenly the station went dead.

The broadcast, as heard here, said:

"The last 35,000 Jews in the ghetto at Warsaw have been condemned to execution. Warsaw again is echoing to musketry volleys.

"The people are murdered. Women and children defend themselves with their naked arms.

"Save us..."

A United Press dispatch from Stockholm quoted the broadcast as speaking of "the last thirty-five Jews in Warsaw," while London listeners reported that the broadcast had said that "the last 35,000 Jews in Warsaw's ghetto" had been sentenced to death.

NAVY CALLED SLOW IN SUBMARINE WAR

Truman Report Says Tardiness Caused Tonnage Loss Equal to New Ships

By C. P. TRUSSELL
Special to THE NEW YORK TIMES.

WASHINGTON, April 21—The Truman committee, reporting to the Senate its findings after extensive investigations into the Navy and merchant marine ship construction programs, declared today that the Navy had done "a magnificent job" in building a first-class fighting fleet, but it held that in doing so it sacrificed protection of vessels carrying vital cargoes to overseas battlefronts.

The Navy, the committee charged, was "slow to realize" the menace of the Axis submarines, although the history of the last war and the improvements made in our own submersibles indicated the danger. It found that the destroyer escort and corvette programs were tardy in getting under way and were delayed months because of a diversion of valves to other uses.

While lost time was being made up, the committee reported, German submarines were taking a toll of 1,000,000 tons of shipping a month and, in the aggregate, wiping out a total of tonnage that

Continued on Page Fourteen

BRITISH DRIVE ON

Eastern Anchor of Foe's Southern Line Taken in Encirclement

ADVANCE IN MOUNTAINS

Troops Push Past Djebel Garci as First Army Takes Point Above Medjez-el-Bab

By FRANK L. KLUCKHOHN
Wireless to THE NEW YORK TIMES.

ALLIED HEADQUARTERS IN NORTH AFRICA, April 21—In a two-pronged drive the British Eighth Army has captured Enfidaville, on the eastern end of the thirty-three-mile southern Axis line, and has driven nearly two miles into the towering hills beyond Djebel Garci, fourteen miles west of this key town, it was announced tonight.

[The Eighth Army also stormed and took Takrouna, which lies between Enfidaville and Djebel Garci, official reports said.]

Enfidaville itself was captured by a minor splitting of the right wing of the attackers. One column thrust ahead on the east, the other on the west, to meet beyond the town, which was encircled and then taken.

Here, as in the Djebel Garci area, General Sir Bernard L. Montgomery employed his usual tactics of forcing the enemy to meet him at two main points while he had the initiative. This time, however, because of the rugged terrain, he split his men into small groups, which advanced under the protection of heavy mortar and machine-gun fire from their comrades. Despite its relatively speedy initial advances against vicious fighting, the Eighth Army knows that the enemy has even stronger positions farther back in the hills. Four desperate counter-attacks by the best German units, however, failed to dislodge the British from their new positions.

First Army Also Gains

As the Eighth Army struck, British First Army forces occupied Smidia, about three miles north of Medjez-el-Bab. [The name "Smidia" does not appear on detailed maps but it may be a local topographical designation.] The First Army thus improved its position near the vital Medjez-el-Bab-Tebourba road, in

Continued on Page Eight

Britain Warns Nazis on Gas; Hears They Plan to Use It

'Several Sources' Report Hitler Is Ready to Employ Lethal Fumes in Russia—Instant Reprisals Promised

By MILTON BRACKER
Special Cable to THE NEW YORK TIMES.

LONDON, Thursday, April 22—An almost unprecedented communiqué issued shortly before midnight by 10 Downing Street declared that reports were coming in from "several sources" that Reichsfuehrer Adolf Hitler was preparing to use poison gas against the Russian Army. The communiqué reiterated Great Britain's intention to retaliate immediately if the report proved correct.

"His Majesty's Government take early occasion," the statement said, "to renew the warning which the Prime Minister gave last year—namely, that any use of poison gas against their Russian allies by the Nazis or their satellites will immediately be followed by the fullest possible use of this process of war upon German munitions centers, seaports and other military objectives throughout the whole extent of Germany."

The spokesman was not willing to specify what made up the "several sources," but the wholly unexpected announcement lent emphasis to several recent hints that the long-dreaded use of gas in World War II was likely to begin.

Only on Tuesday Home Affairs Secretary Herbert Morrison reminded the nation that there still was danger of a chemical attack and that it would be "dangerous and foolish" to ignore the possibility or to let gas masks deteriorate.

Also, Minister of Information Brendan Bracken suggested recently that Herr Hitler might go down like Samson pulling down the pillars of civilization with him.

And German reports regarding the campaign in South Russia have

Continued on Page Five

U. S. and Mexican Presidents Visit an Air Station in Texas

By W. H. LAWRENCE
Special to THE NEW YORK TIMES.

CORPUS CHRISTI, Texas, April 21—President Roosevelt of the United States and President Avila Camacho of Mexico ended twenty-four hours of conferences today after a luncheon at the naval air training station here at which Mr. Roosevelt declared the training programs of the United States armed forces for officers of Latin-American countries were a wide and long step forward for continental defense and unity of purpose.

Two hundred naval aviation cadet officers, eating their regular mess in Hall No. 143, cheered lustily as they realized that their surprise guests were the Presidents whose meeting at Monterrey, Mexico, yesterday was the first in thirty-four years between the heads of the two countries.

[President Avila Camacho returned to Mexico during the evening, The United Press reported].

What the two Presidents talked about privately, and the steps that they may have decided upon to speed the prosecution of the war, were not revealed publicly, but Mr. Roosevelt told the naval cadets that his meeting with President Avila Camacho was one of the high points of his life.

The visiting Chief Executive shook hands with the Mexican cadets in training here as they left the luncheon hall, and it was in reference to this act that the President mentioned the training programs which are being conducted in this country for army and naval officers from the Central and South American countries.

"From the point of view of continental defense and unity of purpose this kind of mutual training that we are doing both in the Army

Continued on Page Five

ALLIED RAIDS SEAR NAZI SUPPLY LINES

British Bomb Stettin, Rostock and Berlin as Russians Set New Fires in Tilsit

By The Associated Press.

LONDON, April 21—Sweeping out in force in perfect flying weather, British bombers last night blasted manufacturing and other war installations in the Baltic ports of Stettin and Rostock, left Berlin alight with fires and ranged widely over other sections of occupied Europe today in one of the war's biggest air assaults on German communications.

Simultaneously, a mass raid by Russian bombers on the East Prussian railway center of Tilsit last night started fires visible nearly 100 miles away, Moscow announced.

The broadcast said the fires merged into "one huge conflagration" at Tilsit and that big explosions were particularly numerous near munitions dumps, among railroad installations and around the harbor and airfield. All Soviet planes were said to have returned safely from the raid, the fifth big Russian attack on the Northeast

Continued on Page Two

PRESIDENT AGHAST

He Says Civilized People Will Share Horror at Act of Japanese

DOOLITTLE FLIERS VICTIMS

Some of 8 Captured Men Slain as Bombers of Civilians—Congress Members Angry

Text of the President's statement will be found on Page 4.

By BERTRAM D. HULEN
Special to THE NEW YORK TIMES.

WASHINGTON, April 21—The Japanese Government has barbarously executed some of the eight American aviators captured from Major Gen. James H. Doolittle's raid on Japan, April 18, 1942, on the grounds that they intentionally bombed non-military installations and deliberately fired on civilians. The exact number is not known here.

This was announced by President Roosevelt today in a statement issued from the White House "with a feeling of deepest horror." The feeling "will be shared by all civilized peoples," the President stated.

The remaining aviators apparently have received prison terms under unstated conditions. Evidently all of the men were tortured.

The President served notice in his statement and in a protest through the State Department to the Japanese Government that "the American Government will hold personally and officially responsible for these diabolical crimes all of those officers of the Japanese Government who have participated therein and will in due course bring these officers to justice."

Futile Effort to Frighten

"This recourse by our enemies to frightfulness is barbarous," the President declared in his statement, which he sent to the White House from Corpus Christi, Texas. "The effort of the Japanese war lords thus to intimidate us will utterly fail. It will make the American people more determined than ever to blot out the shameless militarism of Japan."

In her treatment of the aviators Japan flagrantly violated the Geneva Prisoners of War Convention, to which she had subscribed, as well as flouted all civilized practice.

The State Department in its protest warned Japan "that for any other violations of its undertakings as regards American prisoners of war or for any other acts of criminal barbarity inflicted upon American prisoners in violation of the rules of warfare accepted and practiced by civilized nations as military operations now in progress draw to their inexorable and inevitable conclusion, the American Government will visit upon the officers of the Japanese Government responsible for such uncivilized and inhumane acts the punishment they deserve."

The note denounced Japan for descending to acts of "barbarity and manifestations of depravity" by "the murder in cold blood" of the Americans.

Members of Congress Horrified

The announcement was received with horror in Congress, where members denounced the Japanese as "savages" and called for more vigorous prosecution of the war. But there were members who advised against retaliating in kind on Japanese prisoners in our hands.

General Henry H. Arnold, commander of the Army Air Forces, said in a statement that this was an example of what to expect, warned his men to be prepared for such savagery and advised them to give the Japanese all they had.

There are relatively few Japanese prisoners in our hands, for they usually choose death to surrender. No figures have been

Continued on Page Three

Black Market in Gasoline Raided; 30 Arrested, Fake Stamps Seized

The United States Secret Service announced yesterday that thirty men had been arrested and more would be, and that counterfeit gasoline ration stamps with a face value of 2,500,000 gallons had been seized, with printing plates, during a ten-day offensive against a huge black market ring of dealers in this city.

A check-up on hundreds of thousands of ration stamps in the city's banks, where they were deposited by dealers under the ration banking system that went into effect early this year, gave Office of Price Administration investigators their first clues to the identity of the black market dealers handling the counterfeit stamps.

It became known last night that a similar check-up had been started on food rationing stamps but that so far no counterfeits had been found.

The Secret Service men entered the case at the request of Secretary of the Treasury Henry Morgenthau Jr., to whom OPA officials had reported their findings.

James J. Maloney, supervising agent of the Secret Service in the New York area, who announced the arrests and seizures, said that 500,000 spurious T stamps, each with a face value of five gallons, had been confiscated. He quoted Mr. Morgenthau as having told him:

"These counterfeit T stamps are fighting on the side of Rommel against our boys on the battle front."

Those under arrest include nineteen garage and service station

Continued on Page Fifteen

War News Summarized

THURSDAY, APRIL 22, 1943

Japan has executed at least some of the eight United States fliers who bombed that country in General Doolittle's raid last year. This was admitted by the Japanese Government, and President Roosevelt yesterday announced the fact "with a feeling of deepest horror."

The State Department made public its note of protest and promised that the responsible officials would be brought to justice. It was indicated that all the Americans had been tortured and any survivors had been sentenced to prison. [All the foregoing, 1:8.]

General Arnold, commanding the United States Air Forces, pledged those forces to the utter destruction of Japan's "inhuman war lords" and asked his men to retaliate for the execution of their comrades by destroying the Japanese air force. [4:5.]

Army bombers attacked Kiska in the Aleutians fifteen times Monday and left great fires burning on the nearly completed Japanese air base there. Multiple raids were also carried out in the Solomons area. [7:1.]

The British Eighth Army captured Enfidaville in the new Tunisian drive and beat off four Axis counter-attacks. Takrouna, between Enfidaville and Djebel Garci, taken Tuesday, was stormed and captured. Allied aviators destroyed twenty-seven enemy planes and lost only eight in another day of intense activity. [1:5; map, P. 8.]

The R. A. F. bombed the Baltic port of Stettin, the port and Heinkel aircraft plant at Rostock, and Berlin, while the Russians paid another visit to Tilsit. Other Allied planes based in Britain swept over Western Europe. [1:7; map, P. 2.]

While the Russians were beating off more determined German attacks around Novorossisk on the Black Sea [9:1], the British Government issued an unexpected statement saying it had received numerous reports that the Nazis were soon to use poison gas against the Red Army. Britain repeated her promise to retaliate immediately and fully against Germany itself. [1:6-7.]

The Truman committee, reporting to the Senate, said that this country had failed to build sufficient escort vessels and that U-boats were sinking 1,000,000 tons of shipping a month. [1:4.]

President Roosevelt and President Avila Camacho of Mexico continued their discussions at Corpus Christi, Texas. [1:6-7.]

General de Gaulle issued a memorandum listing objections to General Giraud's proposals for French unity. The Fighting French leader asked representation of the underground movement, curtailment of the military commander's authority and removal of Vichy collaborationists in North Africa. [10:1.]

WLB Threatens to Ask for Troops To Rout Lewis Pickets in Newark

Special to THE NEW YORK TIMES.

WASHINGTON, April 21—The War Labor Board threatened tonight, in effect, to ask President Roosevelt to order troops to break up the picket line which John L. Lewis's District 50, United Mine Workers, has thrown around the Celanese Corporation of America's plant at Newark, N. J.

"Unless the picket line is removed at once so that patriotic American workers may have free and unhampered access to employment * * * your government is left with no other course but to provide that necessary protection to the company and workers which will permit of full production at the plant, unhampered by interference by pickets from your union," the board warned in telegrams to Mr. Lewis, U. M. W. president, and District 50 officials.

It was said unofficially that this meant the board was prepared to ask for troops.

The telegram was composed by Wayne L. Morse, public member, after a meeting of the board which adjourned shortly before midnight. In addition to Mr. Lewis, it was addressed to Edward Hekelbeck, regional director of District 50; Royal Dugan, District 50 organizer, and Michael Widman, organizing director of District 50.

It was the second appeal telegraphed to the union leaders since District 50 members threw a picket line around the plant in protest against the NLRB's refusal to hold a collective bargaining agent elec-

Continued on Page Thirty-four

"All the News That's Fit to Print."

The New York Times.

LATE CITY EDITION
Warmer today with moderate winds.
Temperatures Yesterday—Max., 54; Min., 41
Sunrise, 6:27 A. M.; Sunset, 7:43 P. M.

VOL. XCII..No. 31,135. Entered as Second-Class Matter, Postoffice, New York, N. Y. NEW YORK, FRIDAY, APRIL 23, 1943. THREE CENTS IN NEW YORK CITY

BRITISH SMASH ROMMEL ATTACKS; GAIN IN HILLS ABOVE ENFIDAVILLE; TOKYO WARNS U. S. AGAINST RAIDS

COAL TIE-UP LOOMS AS WLB INTERVENES IN WAGE DISPUTE

Lewis Asserts That Miners Consider Negotiations Ended and Men Free to Act

MAKES NO REPLY TO BOARD

Two Operator Groups Accept Bid to Capital Hearing—Row Certified by Miss Perkins

The threat of a stoppage of soft coal mines employing 450,000 men became acute yesterday as the War Labor Board intervened in the deadlocked bituminous negotiations after Frances Perkins, Secretary of Labor, had certified the dispute to the board.

Invitations addressed to John L. Lewis, president of the United Mine Workers, and spokesmen of the operators asking both sides to appear at a preliminary hearing in Washington tomorrow morning were telegraphed by the board.

The operators, who have requested the board's intervention repeatedly, let it be known that they would respond to its invitation. No such statement came from Mr. Lewis, however. Instead, he declared that abrupt termination of the negotiations at this time would be a violation of the thirty-day extension under which the negotiations have been proceeding and would relieve the miners of their obligations under the extension agreed upon separately with the operator groups of the Northern and Southern Appalachian regions.

Lewis Warning Seen

Mr. Lewis has denounced the labor board as "a court packed against labor" and has hinted that the miners would refuse to appear before it. His statement yesterday bearing upon the meaning, as understood by the union, of the extension agreements, was regarded as a warning that with the intervention of the War Labor Board the union considered that the old contracts have expired and the miners were free of any obligation not to stop work. The principle repeatedly proclaimed by Mr. Lewis has been that "the miners do not work without a contract or the equivalent thereof." In the current negotiations the "equivalent" was supplied by the extension agreements.

The operators and miners are scheduled to meet again this morning when Mr. Lewis may clarify further the union's position.

With the mine chieftain presiding, the union's scale committee met last night at the Hotel Roosevelt to discuss the situation arising from the War Labor Board's intervention. It was believed likely that before making public the union's reply to the board Mr. Lewis would call a meeting of the international policy committee of the union to approve the reply. Union spokesmen declared that with the collective bargaining negotiations under the extended agreements ended, it would be difficult to restrain miners in all parts of the country from remaining away from the mines.

Miss Perkins's View

In announcing her certification of the soft coal dispute to the WLB Miss Perkins said in Washington:

"In peacetime I should have been inclined to wait patiently for the members of this conference to work out something constructive, but coal is essential to the prosecution of the war, and because chances cannot be taken on so vital a matter I am certifying this case to the National War Labor Board."

While announcing her certification of the dispute to the board, Miss Perkins at the same time asked the miners and operators to continue their negotiations. This request, made before the board had sent its invitations to both sides for the hearing tomorrow morning, was transmitted to the conferees through Dr. John R. Steelman, director of the United States Conciliation Service and President Roosevelt's representative in the negotiations, who had tried in vain to bring about a settlement. The conferences of the miners and operators scheduled for this morning—the Northern meeting at the Hotel Biltmore and the Southern at the Hotel Commodore—were in response to this request. In view

Continued on Page Eleven

Stassen Is Ordered To Active Naval Duty

By The Associated Press.

WASHINGTON, April 22—The Navy announced tonight that Governor Harold E. Stassen of Minnesota, a lieutenant commander in the Naval Reserve, has been ordered to active duty, effective April 29.

After reporting to the Great Lakes Naval District office at Chicago for temporary duty Mr. Stassen will go to a naval training school at Fort Schuyler, N. Y., on May 28 for indoctrination.

TAX FIGHT DELAYED; HOUSE GOES HOME

Doughton and Knutson Plans Seem Leading Contenders in New Battle May 3

By JOHN H. CRIDER

Special to The New York Times.

WASHINGTON, April 22—The House took an Easter recess tonight, with pay-as-you-go legislation scheduled as the first order of business when it meets again May 3. The Senate did not recess. The issues when the battle is resumed will be the Doughton, Carlson, Knutson and Forand - Robertson bills.

As the Representatives started for home there was considerable expectancy that the impact of home views might somewhat alter the alignments recorded in the last floor fight on pay-as-you-go March 30.

But they went home assured by events of the last forty-eight hours that they could promise their constituents some kind of pay-as-you-go bill. Also, they felt they could tell wage and salary earners that 20 per cent of taxable income would be withheld from pay checks beginning July 1.

Since the failure of Speaker Rayburn's efforts to obtain a bipartisan compromise resulted in an agreement to let the matter be fought out on the floor, the consequences were generally interpreted as a victory for the House Republicans, whose leader, Representative Martin, has insisted that the only way to end the stalemate was to let the House write its own bill.

No Limit on Amendments

Speaker Rayburn said that although he would like to see the tax debate limited to two bills, one for each party, he did not see how he could limit amendments when he had ruled last time that the legislation was privileged and therefore open to amendment.

The commanders of the opposing forces were busier today getting their legislation in order than in seeking recruits. Chairman Doughton of the Ways and Means Committee introduced his new bill late tonight and will meet with the committee tomorrow afternoon to report it. Representative Knutson, who will sponsor the new Republican bill, had not even reached the drafting stage.

The Carlson bill, embodying the principal features of the Ruml pay-as-you-go plan, which was defeated on the floor March 30 by the narrow margin of 198 to 215, still figured conspicuously in the legislative line-up, and its Kansas Republican author expressed confidence that it had a better chance than ever of passage.

Representative Carlson said he would change his bill by lowering the barrier line from $20,000 to $5,000 as a further guarantee against "windfalls." Under his original bill all taxpayers earning

Continued on Page Thirty-eight

BOND SALES SOAR AFTER EXECUTIONS; CITY OVER QUOTA

$3,475,000,000 Bought Here by Investors Other Than Commercial Banks

CAMPAIGN WILL CONTINUE

Nation Shows Its Resentment of Tokyo's Action—Goals Topped at Many Points

As a nation-wide wave of anger at the revelation that the Japanese had executed some of the American fliers who bombed Tokyo sent war bond sales bounding upward yesterday, the Second Federal Reserve District, consisting of New York State, Northern New Jersey and Fairfield County, Conn., went over the top with total sales of $3,475,000,000 to investors other than the commercial banks. This was $475,000,000 more than the quota set when the drive opened.

In Washington, Secretary of the Treasury Henry Morgenthau Jr. announced that subscriptions totaling $11,322,000,000 had been received up to Wednesday night, leaving only $1,678,000,000 to be obtained to fill the second war loan drive quota of $13,000,000,000. But press dispatches from Chicago, Omaha, Rochester, Des Moines and other cities reported that sales had taken a big jump in response to the shocking news.

Mr. Morgenthau disclosed at his press conference that the Twelfth Federal Reserve District, with headquarters at San Francisco, was "at the bottom of the barrel" in the drive. He said this was "peculiar," because "the West Coast is closer to the front than any other part of America, and has always led the way heretofore." He predicted that resentment against the Japanese would stimulate the drive there, and elsewhere throughout the country.

The record-breaking success of the drive here was announced by Allan Sproul, chairman of the War Finance Committee of the Second Reserve District, at a rally on the steps of the Subtreasury Building at Broad and Wall Streets. A crowd of 5,000 in the streets cheered his announcement and his promise that the campaign would be continued here with vigor.

Full Limit of Buying Asked

"Now let us forget our quota and think of our goal," Mr. Sproul declared. "Our goal is to $3,000,000,000. Our real goal is the maximum amount which each individual in the district can buy. No quota is high enough which falls short of that maximum. In terms of dollars in this district, in this Second War Loan, we shall be disappointed if we do not top $4,000,000,000."

Mayor La Guardia called upon the crowd at the rally to show their indignation over the executions of the fliers by making additional purchases. The Mayor then purchased a $1,000 bond.

"In the last twenty-four hours we learned of something that happened several months ago," the Mayor said in angry tones. "There is indignation in the hearts of all Americans at what happened to some of our aviators who took part in General Doolittle's raid on Japan.

"We know what war is, and we are prepared for its horrors. We have no illusions about war, but we protest with all the energy that is in us against the cold-blooded

Continued on Page Eight

MacArthur to Keep Post After He Is 64

Special to The New York Times.

WASHINGTON, April 22—The War Department has no intention of retiring General Douglas MacArthur from active service when he reaches the retirement age of 64 next year, Robert P. Patterson, Under-Secretary of War, declared at a press conference today.

"There is no such plan," he asserted. "General MacArthur's services have been of extraordinary value to this country. There is no reason to warrant any opinion that this country will not continue to avail itself of his services."

NAZIS FAIL TO GAIN IN KUBAN THRUSTS

Russians Claim Continued Toll as Germans Pound at Lines —Novorossiisk Pierced

By The Associated Press.

LONDON, Friday, April 23—Soviet troops mowed down hundreds of Germans still attacking their Kuban valley lines above the enemy bridgehead at Novorossiisk in the Caucasus, and the Red Air Force made mass raids on Nazi military formations and other targets, Moscow announced early today.

Three hundred Germans were killed in attempting to take one hilltop and hundreds fell in another sector, said the midnight communiqué, recorded here by the Soviet monitor.

[Berlin reports said the fighting for Novorossiisk had entered its final stage, according to a Reuter dispatch from Stockholm. The Russians were said to have penetrated the city at several points.]

The Soviet Baltic Fleet's air force, attacking enemy ports in that area, was said to have caused serious damage to installations, shot down thirteen planes and destroyed a patrol ship and three troop landing craft.

Finns Report Raid Repulsed

This presumably referred to the attack on Kotka on the Finnish coast midway between Leningrad and Helsinki. A Finnish communiqué had reported earlier that a Soviet assault on that port was repelled by Finnish anti-aircraft artillery.

On the front west of Moscow, the Russian communiqué said, an enemy infantry company was annihilated and three artillery and mortar batteries were silenced by

Continued on Page Three

THREAT TO FLIERS

Tokyo Says All Who Raid Japan Hold 'One-Way Ticket to Hell'

U. S. REJECTS REPRISALS

Patterson, Under-Secretary of War, Declares Officials Will Pay—Nazis Back Killings

Every American flier participating in future bombing raids on Japan has a "one-way ticket to hell," a Japanese propaganda broadcast to the United States declared yesterday in an obvious attempt to intimidate the United States air forces and prevent a repetition of the American attack on the island empire, The Associated Press said.

The broadcast, recorded by the Federal Communications Commission, followed a Domei news agency broadcast beamed at the United States on Tuesday that referred to the execution of some of Major Gen. James H. Doolittle's companions and said "this same policy will continue to be enforced in the future."

Stressing ominously that Japan would "leave nothing undone" to prevent future aerial attacks, the latest English-language warning from Tokyo said:

"And by the way, don't forget, America—make sure that every flier that comes here has a special pass to hell, and rest assured it's strictly a one-way ticket."

Executions Held Justified

President Roosevelt's protest against the execution of some of General Doolittle's men was countered by Domei with the assertion that "the Japanese were perfectly justified in severely punishing American fliers who were found guilty of purposely carrying out wanton attacks on innocent civilians, hospitals and schools."

The Japanese home and empire broadcasts did not include the President's denunciation of the executions as "an act of barbarity," nor did it mention his solemn promise that all officials connected with the crime against military law would be punished. Instead, they called Mr. Roosevelt's statement a "protest full of complaints" and said it was made to "provoke the fighting spirit of the American people."

The broadcast said the President was "completely ignoring the inhuman deeds of this Air Force unit of his own nation" in a "desperate attempt to unify the national ef-

Continued on Page Four

Doolittle Pledges New Blows To Make Japan Beg Mercy

U. S. Fliers Soon Will Make Heavier Attacks in Memory of Slain Comrades, General Says, Reviling Foe's Barbarity

By The United Press.

ALLIED HEADQUARTERS IN NORTH AFRICA, April 22—Major Gen. James H. Doolittle called on the United States today to bomb Japan until the empire crumbles and it begs for mercy, to show that it failed in its aim when it executed some of the fliers who accompanied him on the first raid in history on Tokyo.

General Doolittle said that he and the men who, with him, bombed Japan a year ago want to go back and do it again on a devastating scale.

"We will drop each bomb in memory of our murdered comrades," General Doolittle said. "Our bombs will not miss their mark. We do not seek revenge, but we do want to have a fighting part in correcting a situation that threatens everything we hold dear.

"Our job is to utterly and completely defeat the Japanese nation and everything its war lords stand for. This can only be accomplished by striking at the heart of Japan itself.

"We started it last year. Soon our bombers will be there again—not last year's limited effort, but a devastating attack that will continue until the Japanese Empire crumbles and they beg for mercy."

He promised that Americans would never forget the Japanese murders and that they would only work harder to defeat Japan.

Two other of the Tokyo fliers were present when General Doolittle made his statement.

"The day will come when these atrocities will be avenged, and I hope I am among the avengers," said Captain Howard A. Sessler of Arlington, Mass.

"All I can say of the fate of my buddies is that now the people of the United States should realize

Continued on Page Five

Only Military Targets Hit, Tokyo Raid Fliers Declare

By SIDNEY SHALETT

Special to The New York Times.

WASHINGTON, April 22—Their voices a little shaky as they commented on the execution of their comrades by the Japanese, two of Major Gen. James H. Doolittle's fliers revealed here today that so faithfully did they carry out their orders to bomb only pre-selected objectives they even passed up such legitimate military targets as an unprotected aircraft carrier and a line of pursuit ships parked on an enemy airport.

The fliers, Captains Ted W. Lawson and Harold S. Watson, told how General Doolittle had a premonition of how the Japanese would react, for every day he lectured his "family" on the importance of hitting nothing except the targets. His instructions, they declared, were carried out religiously and they agreed that the Japanese accusation that the Americans deliberately bombed nonmilitary objectives and machine-gunned civilians was simply "a damn lie."

Captains Lawson and Watson, both young, extremely modest men, told the story of the memorable raid of April 18, 1942, when, for the first time in history, big land bombers left the deck of an aircraft carrier to carry out a raid on enemy shores. Because they had to leave their "Shangri-la"—since identified as the aircraft carrier Hornet—ten hours ahead of schedule, none of the eighty Americans ever expected to reach safety in China, but there was not the slightest hesitation about taking off, the young officers disclosed.

There were courage, drama, humor and later tragedy in their stories, but the fliers were as matter-of-fact as if they were describing an interesting chess game. Only when they were asked about

Continued on Page Four

U.S. FORCE BOMBS NAURU IN PACIFIC

Japanese Island Base, 780 Miles From Guadalcanal, Is Again Attacked

Special to The New York Times.

WASHINGTON, April 22—The Navy announced today that Army bombers had carried out a large-scale daylight bombing attack on Nauru, an island west of the Gilbert group, inflicting considerable damage and shooting down five to seven Zeros that sought to stop them, with no losses to the American planes. The island had been bombed March 26 by Liberators.

Numa Numa harbor, on the northeast coast of Bougainville, also was raided. In the North Pacific, Kiska had ten more attacks.

A "large force" of Army bombers carried out the bombing of Nauru yesterday and, despite heavy anti-aircraft fire and fighter plane action, administered considerable punishment to Japanese installations, the communiqué said.

Nauru—also known as Pleasant Island—is about 780 miles northeast of the Guadalcanal air field,

Continued on Page Four

ALLIED RING HOLDS

Germans Lose 27 Tanks in Furious Lunge at British in North

8TH ARMY PUSHES 3 MILES

Grenades and Bayonets Win Ground in Hills—U. S. and French Patrols Busy

By DREW MIDDLETON

Wireless to The New York Times.

ALLIED HEADQUARTERS IN NORTH AFRICA, April 22—A desperate German attempt to forestall the opening of a final Allied offensive in Northern Tunisia was frustrated Tuesday night when veteran infantry and artillery of the British First Army broke an attack launched on an eight-mile front south of Medjez-el-Bab.

Twenty-seven enemy tanks, including two huge Mark VIs, of sixty to eighty tanks employed by the enemy were destroyed by British gunners yesterday morning when German armor attempted to screen the withdrawal of five crack enemy infantry battalions. These had been badly mauled by British shell, machine-gun and rifle fire and 500 prisoners were rounded up by First Army units.

The Eighth Army's infantry, fighting its way through the rugged country northwest of Enfidaville, was set upon in two counterattacks by strong German forces yesterday. These assaults, which the communiqué classed as "major," were halted by heavy artillery fire that inflicted serious losses on the enemy.

Germans Strongly Entrenched

British riflemen advanced three miles north through the quadrilateral of mountainous wooded country northeast of Enfidaville. German soldiers were fighting for every inch of this strong natural position, which extends westward for about twelve miles and northward for about ten, and the battle there has been costly and severe, with the British rooting out the Germans from cleverly concealed machine-gun and artillery positions in sudden rushes.

Late reports from the Eighth Army describe heavy fighting throughout this area today. There was much hand-to-hand fighting, with the British infantry "feeling" for the enemy in roughly wooded hills and breaking up German strong points with cold steel, clubbed rifles and grenades.

Patrols were active on the fronts of the Second United States Army Corps and Nineteenth French Corps.

Bombers and fighters of the Tactical Air Force kept up the pounding of enemy airfields within the contracting semicircle of Allied manpower in Tunisia. Axis ground positions and routes of reinforcement also were strafed and bombed. Ten enemy aircraft were destroyed in fighting throughout the day, in which, it now can be officially disclosed, new and powerful Spitfires of the Royal Air Force were engaged.

Fighting on the Sea

The gradual encirclement of the enemy progressed by sea as well as by land. A light coastal force of the Royal Navy damaged a number of enemy E-boats in a clash near Bizerte. One German ship was badly hit. There was an explosion aboard and she retired under cover of the remainder of the flotilla, which was peppered by British gunfire.

Light naval forces sank a small enemy supply ship northwest of Sicily Tuesday night.

The enemy hurled five of his strongest and freshest infantry battalions and one of his best tank battalions into his attack on the First Army positions. This assault evidently was a continuation of old German tactics aimed at keeping the Allies off balance and preventing them from massing a heavy attack. Successful during

Continued on Page Two

War News Summarized

FRIDAY, APRIL 23, 1943

The British First Army in Tunisia was reported yesterday to have delivered a stunning defeat to the Germans Tuesday night when General von Arnim launched a strong attack on an eight-mile front south of Medjez-el-Bab. The enemy lost twenty-seven tanks and 500 men taken prisoner. The Eighth Army, meanwhile, moving slowly in the area above Enfidaville, advanced three miles and continued the arduous task of dislodging the enemy from strongly entrenched positions. [1:8; map, P. 2.]

Under-Secretary of War Patterson told reporters in Washington that the Axis was losing at least 50 per cent of its ships and transport planes operating between Italy and Tunisia. [3:1.]

Allied air activity over Europe was on a much reduced scale, the only raids of consequence being fighter sweeps by the R. A. F. over Belgium and Northern France. The Luftwaffe raided a city in Scotland, which Berlin identified as Aberdeen, Wednesday night. [8:2.]

Moscow reported that the Germans had lost hundreds more men in fruitless attacks against the Soviet lines in the Kuban Valley. [1:4.]

Replying to Prime Minister Churchill's warning against the use of gas on the Eastern Front, the Berlin radio said Germany intended to abide by her pledge of last year. The British statement was termed "provocative" in the broadcast. [1:6-7.]

New Delhi headquarters reported the third raid of the war on Bangkok, the capital of Thailand, by American planes. British and American aircraft continued active over Burma. [6:6.]

The Navy announced that Army bombers had carried out a large-scale raid on Nauru Island west of the Gilbert group. Kiska in the Aleutians was raided ten more times. [1:7; map, P. 4.]

The Japanese radio issued a warning that any American fliers who attempted another raid on Japan would be certain to have a "one-way ticket to hell." [1:5.] Two of the men who took part in last year's attack on Tokyo told reporters they had obeyed to the letter orders to bomb specific military targets only. [1:6-7.] General Doolittle in North Africa said we should strike again and again until the Japanese Empire was crushed. [1:6-7.] Under-Secretary Patterson declared we would take our revenge against the enemy's leaders and not against prisoners in our hands. [5:1.]

Nelson Asks New Rubber Survey By Baruch to Settle Conflict

By CHARLES E. EGAN

Special to The New York Times.

WASHINGTON, April 22—A move has been started here to reconvene the Baruch committee, which mapped out the nation's wartime rubber program, for a study of the current synthetic rubber situation and settle once and for all whether the program should be cut back.

According to authoritative reports tonight, Donald M. Nelson, chairman of the War Production Board, has urged a resurvey by the committee in talks with Bernard M. Baruch, its chairman, and with James F. Byrnes, Director of Economic Stabilization.

The same reports indicate that Mr. Baruch has been reluctant to call his committee into session again and has taken the stand that the WPB has power to investigate the synthetic rubber program and to compel a curtailment if convinced that production will exceed expectations.

Because of the scarcity of materials, the WPB is seeking to keep output of synthetic rubber to levels necessary to meet only essential requirements.

WPB officials, including Mr. Nelson, are said to take the attitude that recommendations as to curtailment of production will find readier acceptance by the public if made by the Baruch committee, which never had any disputes with the armed services over the rubber question.

In January, when the armed

Continued on Page Twelve

Nazis Reiterate Vow Not to Use Gas Unless Their Enemies Do So First

By The Associated Press.

LONDON, April 22—The Berlin radio, replying to the British statement warning of gas war reprisals, quoted German Foreign Office circles as saying that Germany would stand by a pledge given last year that she would use poison gas only if her enemies used it first. The broadcast, recorded by The Associated Press, said Berlin political circles termed Prime Minister Winston Churchill's declaration "provocative."

The British Broadcasting Corporation today beamed short-wave broadcasts to Germany, directly informing the German people that they could expect if their leader should order the use of gas. The broadcasts emphasized the United Nations' air superiority and quoted Prime Minister Churchill's comment that "British resources and scale of delivery [of gas warfare facilities] have greatly increased since last year."

Mr. Churchill's statement said the reports of Germany's "intentions had come from "several sources." A Soviet official, meanwhile, declared that "we have passed on to the British Foreign Office information that supplies of gas recently have been reaching the German armies on the Russian front."

LONDON, April 22 (UP)—American forces in Great Britain will join in blanketing war objectives in Germany with gas if the Germans resort to gas warfare on the Russian front, it was indicated tonight.

It was revealed here that Major

Continued on Page Three

"All the News That's Fit to Print."

The New York Times.

LATE CITY EDITION
Rain today with little change in temperature; fresh winds.
Temperatures Yesterday—Max., 56; Min., 50
Sunrise, 5:48 A. M.; Sunset, 8:02 P. M.

Copyright, 1943, by The New York Times Company.

VOL. XCII..No. 31,154. Entered as Second-Class Matter, Postoffice, New York, N. Y. NEW YORK, WEDNESDAY, MAY 12, 1943. THREE CENTS IN NEW YORK CITY

CHURCHILL ARRIVES FOR TALK WITH ROOSEVELT; FOE CUT OFF ON CAP BON PENINSULA COLLAPSING; GERMANS IN SOUTH SURRENDER TO THE FRENCH

ANTI-STRIKE BILL RECAST, TIGHTENED BY HOUSE GROUP

Connally Measure Shifted to Punishment for Leaders and Union Members

SMITH'S IDEAS ARE PUT IN

Word That WLB Members Felt Satisfied Fails to Stop Committee's Action

By C. P. TRUSSELL
Special to THE NEW YORK TIMES.

WASHINGTON, May 11—Brushing aside the protests of organized labor and holding that the Senate-adopted Connally bill was inadequate for strike control in time of war, the House Military Affairs Committee, in executive session, completely rewrote that legislation today, converting it into a measure directed more at punishment for strikers, their leaders and their unions than at government seizures of property.

By a vote of 21 to 0, the committee left only basic provisions of the Connally plant-seizure legislation, avoided giving the President new, specific powers for taking over strike-bound factories and mines, and substituted virtually all the stringent provisions of a bill, sponsored by Representative Smith of Virginia, which the House passed a few days before Pearl Harbor but which died in the Senate. The legislation will be reported formally to the House as soon as the official draft can be made ready.

WLB Message of No Avail

The committee's action was taken in the face of a unanimous agreement by the National War Labor Board, to which the pending legislation would give more authority to settle management-labor disputes and enforce its decisions, that the Connally bill met with its general approval. This decision was communicated to the House committee in the midst of its deliberations.

When it had completed its revisions and substitutions, the committee sought to make it unlawful, under penalties of loss of union status under the National Labor Relations Act, for workers to strike in a war production plant until the expiration of the thirty days from the date on which written notice of intent was given the Secretary of Labor. It would be unlawful also for management to effect a lockout within such a period.

Those inducing and leading strikes in plants held by the government would face the severe penalties of the Connally bill, including fines and imprisonment.

It would be unlawful, under terms of the legislation, for employes in a war plant to strike until after the Secretary of Labor had directed the United States Conciliation Service to take a secret ballot of the workers and the results of this voting had been published.

No person who refused to strike, the bill provides, could be deprived of his union benefits.

No Outsiders as Pickets

Further, it would be unlawful for any one, by force or violence, to prevent another from accepting employment or continuing employment under any war contractor, whether or not the plant involved had been seized by the government. Permission for picketing would be restricted to those who had been bona fide employes of a strike-bound plant when the management-labor dispute developed.

Also, it would be unlawful for any person or group to stage a strike in a plant, whether it was on war production or not, in order to induce or attempt to induce or require a war contractor to recognize, deal with, or employ members of any labor union.

As in the Connally bill, the

Continued on Page Sixteen

Pact in Hard Coal Likely; Lewis Promises a Statement

Optimism Grows as Talks Continue Here and Chairman of WLB Panel Suspends Hearings on Dispute in Washington

By JOSEPH SHAPLEN

Prospect of an agreement between the United Mine Workers and anthracite operators before expiration of the fifteen-day truce under which the entire coal industry is now operating appeared yesterday, together with a possibility that the threatened resumption of the recent coal stoppage upon expiration of the truce may be averted in both the anthracite and bituminous fields.

The situation looked brighter in the anthracite than in the bituminous dispute, however. The truce now in effect in the industry expires at midnight next Tuesday.

John L. Lewis, president of the United Mine Workers, may cast light on the situation when he makes a statement at 4 o'clock this afternoon at the union's headquarters in the Hotel Roosevelt, breaking a silence of more than a week.

Mr. Lewis announced that he would make such a statement as another session of anthracite operators and miners ended at the Waldorf-Astoria yesterday.

Hope of a direct agreement for the anthracite industry was seen in the unexpected announcement in Washington yesterday by Morris L. Cooke, chairman of the War Labor Board's panel considering the coal crisis, that the anthracite hearings of the panel have been indefinitely postponed because negotiations between hard coal operators and miners were proceeding in New York.

Mr. Cooke's statement was fol-

Continued on Page Fifteen

250 POULTRY SHOPS IN CITY ON STRIKE

Dealers Suspend Business to Break 'Black Market'—Fish Wasted Off Jersey

By JEFFERSON G. BELL

Hundreds of New York City food merchants are refusing to handle poultry and fish under conditions established by Office of Price Administration regulations, it was learned yesterday.

As the revolt of food purveyors gained momentum 250 poultry dealers, organized as Chicken Dealers of the Lower East Side, closed their doors and went on "strike," to the dismay of thousands of customers. Along the New Jersey seacoast fishermen began dumping hundreds of thousands of pounds of fresh whiting back into the sea from their nets because Manhattan dealers will not handle whiting under the OPA ceiling of 4 cents a pound.

The strike of the East Side poultry dealers has unusual features because it is aimed at what some of the strikers call the black market and because it has left three local unions of the Amalgamated Meat Cutters, American Federation of Labor, virtually helpless to act even in self-defense. The unions do not know whether it would do any good to establish a picket line, because their members are not on the payrolls of the employers on strike.

The strike of the poultry dealers began on Monday and continued yesterday. The three unions of poultry workers dressing the poultry normally supplied to the striking shopkeepers anxiously are

Continued on Page Thirty-three

BUCK'S RE-ELECTION DEFIES THE MAYOR

Unanimously Returned, School Board Head Scores 'Attacks' and 'Unwarranted Slander'

By unanimous vote the Board of Education re-elected Ellsworth B. Buck, Staten Island member, as its president yesterday, thus ignoring the recent warning of Mayor La Guardia that he would "fire" Mr. Buck the first chance he got.

In accepting the nomination Mr. Buck assailed those who attack the schools and warned that freedom from political control was essential. Without mentioning the Mayor by name, he asserted that while the board and the city must operate harmoniously, they must remain separate entities. Mr. Buck told his colleagues he would not accept a third term as board president.

The board's action was in direct defiance of the Mayor, who declared on April 12, after the vote against Mark Starr, that he had "lost confidence" in Mr. Buck. No other candidate was nominated for president yesterday, and the members joined in praising Mr. Buck for his "integrity" and his "independence and sound judgment."

Fackenthal Is Vice President

Joseph D. Fackenthal, Brooklyn member, was elected vice president, succeeding Dr. Alberto C. Bonaschi of the Bronx. A holdover member since May, 1942, Dr. Bonaschi was renominated for the post of vice president but declined, explaining that he did not expect to remain on the board much longer, and that his health did not permit him to take on additional responsibilities. Mayor

Continued on Page Forty-eight

President Says Our Plane Output Exceeds That of Rest of World

Special to THE NEW YORK TIMES.

WASHINGTON, May 11—President Roosevelt announced today that production of airplanes by the United States now exceeded that of all other nations combined, with emphasis being placed on the four-engined bomber to carry out plans for greater offensives against the Axis.

Converting airplane production statistics into the weight of planes instead of their number as a better test of output, the President told his press conference that United States factories turned out 87,000,000 pounds of airplanes in 1941, 291,000,000 pounds in 1942 and were expected to produce 911,000,000 pounds in 1943 and 1,417,000,000 pounds in 1944.

Declaring that our war plans called for this country and its allies to go more and more on the offensive, the President said that the four-engined bomber, a prime attack weapon, now was being produced at a rate six months ahead of the schedule set in December. The modern four-engined bomber, he said, weighed ten times as much as a single-engined fighter plane.

Not only had the number of airplanes produced in this country greatly increased since 1941, he continued, but the type of plane had changed radically. In the beginning, he said, we concentrated on defense airplanes, including fighters, light bombers and dive-bombers. Now, he said, our emphasis was on four-engined bombers, two-engined heavy bombers, long-range fighters and cargo planes.

'LAST TANK BATTLE'

Armor Clashes at Base of Peninsula—British Race Up Coasts

100,000 PRISONERS

Enemy in Zaghouan Area Told to 'Surrender Unconditionally'

By FRANK L. KLUCKHOHN
Wireless to THE NEW YORK TIMES.

ALLIED HEADQUARTERS IN NORTH AFRICA, May 11—British armored forces and troops were advancing far up the coast roads on either side of the Cap Bon Peninsula today after having closed its mouth. Thus far they have taken about 20,000 new prisoners, who are being concentrated near Beni Aïchoun, on the south coast.

Organized enemy resistance has collapsed and there will be no Axis "Bataan" on this peninsula. Elements of the British Sixth Armored Division are destroying the remaining tanks of the German Tenth Armored Division near Grombalia, at the peninsula's base, in what it is hoped will be the last tank battle of the campaign. The war in Africa now seems to be within hours of its close.

Already almost 100,000 Germans and a few Italians have been captured. When the remaining pocket of resistance inland collapses, as it must, the complete destruction of Germany's and Italy's African armies is expected to result in a total of about 150,000 prisoners.

Germans Yield to French

In the inland bulge of about 650 square miles opposite the Cap Bon Peninsula, where large enemy forces are trapped in a hopeless position, the Germans east of Zaghouan and on Djebel Zaghouan, southwest of the town, asked the French for an armistice. The French replied with a demand for unconditional surrender and the turning over of all matériel intact.

[The Germans accepted the French ultimatum, The Associated Press reported.]

Earlier French reports had said that large numbers of German

Continued on Page Two

MR. CHURCHILL BACK IN WASHINGTON FOR WAR TALKS

The British Prime Minister driving to the White House with President Roosevelt last night
Associated Press Wirephoto

FLOW OF CAPTIVES TAXES FIRST ARMY

Prisoners of Cap Bon Action Pour In Too Fast for Questioning—Many Shed Uniforms

By DREW MIDDLETON
Wireless to THE NEW YORK TIMES.

BRITISH FIRST ARMY HEADQUARTERS, Tunisia, May 10 (Delayed)—Strong tank and infantry formations of the British First Army cut down behind the Axis forces facing the British Eighth Army and continued to mop up the enemy positions at the base of the Cap Bon Peninsula today as the campaign in Tunisia moved rapidly toward its close.

West of Tunis all the enemy forces have been "bagged." The First and Thirty-fourth Divisions of the Second United States Corps and the British forces are working in the closest cooperation.

Continued on Page Three

War News Summarized

WEDNESDAY, MAY 12, 1943

Prime Minister Winston Churchill arrived in Washington last evening for his fifth war conference with President Roosevelt. He was accompanied by a staff of military and naval experts and was preceded by Lord Beaverbrook.

It was believed in Washington that Mr. Churchill and Mr. Roosevelt would discuss world-wide strategy of the United Nations and closer cooperation with the Soviet Union. The opening of a second front in Europe and shipment of increased supplies were considered the best aid to Russia. [All the foregoing, 1:8.]

London interpreted the presence of Lord Beaverbrook in Washington as evidence that a serious move would be made to heal the breach between Russia and Poland. He was said to have a plan to bring the two nations together. If it meets with President Roosevelt's approval, he may proceed to Moscow to present it to Joseph Stalin. [3:1.]

Organized Axis resistance in the Tunisian fighting was said to have crumbled. Prisoners were surrendering in droves. East of Zaghouan a French commander had the distinction of imposing terms of unconditional surrender on a German general for the first time in this war. Mopping up operations were proceeding on most fronts, and the British were advancing up both sides of the Cap Bon Peninsula after having closed its mouth. [1:4; map, P. 2]

Nearly 200 American bombers escorted by more than 100 fighters raided Marsala in what appeared part of a campaign to destroy the airfields, harbors and other military installations of Sicily. In the North African campaign the Allies had destroyed 3,000 Axis planes and lost 679. [1:6-7; map, P. 4.]

Italy was reported to have decreed a "state of emergency" in the Calabrian Peninsula as part of the defense against anticipated Allied invasion. Civilians throughout Italy were said to be fleeing for safety to the center of the country. [1:7]

A German High Command communiqué asserted Marshal Rommel had been ill in Germany for two months. [4:2.] But a report from the Near East said the erstwhile "Desert Fox" had paid a visit to Crete as part of his new job of strengthening Axis defenses in the Balkans. [4:6.]

On the Russian front the Red Army announced capture of a strong point near Novorossiisk and destruction of fifty-six Nazi planes. German railroad communications behind the lines were heavily raided. [6:5.]

British troops were reported arriving in Dominica from Barbados "in connection with the Martinique situation." There was no comment from Washington. [1:6-7; map, P. 3.]

300 Planes Bomb Marsala; Pantelleria Attacked Twice

Special Broadcast to THE NEW YORK TIMES.

ALLIED HEADQUARTERS IN NORTH AFRICA, May 11—The United States Army Air Force continued the destruction of Sicily's airfields, harbors and installations today by attacking Marsala on the west coast, leaving fires the smoke of which was visible over the African coast. Almost 200 bombers and more than 100 fighters took part in this all-American raid.

The harbor, railroad, yard and warehouses at Marsala were special objectives. Flying Fortresses, Mitchells and Marauders went in in waves, with Lightnings darting about to give them protection. The smoke of numerous fires rose to a height of 10,000 feet, casting a pall over the whole area.

Two Airfields Bombed

Yesterday Flying Fortresses dealt further punishing blows to the Axis air force by bombing the Sicilian airfields of Milo and Borizzo. Strings of bombs fell on a line of thirty to forty aircraft at Milo, leaving half of them aflame. Two other large fires were started.

Four large fires threw smoke 5,000 feet high after the Borizzo raid. The Fortresses and their Lightning escorts were attacked over the latter target by German and Italian fighters. Two Messerschmitts were shot down.

It was also announced that Wellingtons had dropped two-ton bombs on the docks, industrial areas and power stations at Palermo, Sicily, the night of May 9-10, after the big daylight Fortress raid of May 9.

[Malta-based planes bombed airfields, railway stations and power plants at Biscari, Marsala and Porto Empedocle in Sicily,

Continued on Page Four

'TOE' OF ITALY PUT IN STATE OF ALERT

Many Families Said to Flee From Calabria and Even Rome—Fortifications Lacking

By DANIEL T. BRIGHAM
By Telephone to THE NEW YORK TIMES.

BERNE, Switzerland, May 11—Dropping secrecy regarding the seriousness of the situation following the latest developments in North Africa, the Italian Government tonight decreed a "state of emergency" for the Calabrian Peninsula—the southern tip of Italy, forming the toe of the boot.

This measure, it is learned, was decided upon following an alleged British broadcast early yesterday morning warning Sicilians "to make their choice," according to Italian sources. Long since this choice appears to have been made for them, for all of the port material that could be spared had been transferred to the mainland "for other uses." For days past arms and munitions sent to the island in preparation for reshipment to Tunisia have been in the process

Continued on Page Four

British Send Troops to Dominica, Cite U. S.-Martinique 'Situation'

The British radio announced last night that a British West Indian detachment had embarked for little Dominica Island, a British possession that lies between Martinique and Guadeloupe in the French West Indies.

About the same time, according to The United Press, Germany reported that United States naval forces were moving against Martinique and Guadeloupe.

Officials at both Washington and London declined all comment on the reports.

Early today a United Press dispatch from San Juan, P. R., a United States naval base, said a high-placed source there characterized the German radio report that United States vessels were moving to the occupation of Martinique as "pure baloney." Informed sources at San Juan, the dispatch went on, said the next move in the Caribbean area probably would be directed against Guadeloupe.

The German report was broadcast by the German Transocean agency. It said that it was "reported" that American naval forces were on the way to Martinique and Guadeloupe, intending to "capture" both islands.

The strength of the United States forces was not reported, Transocean said, but the enemy agency "assumed" that they would be supported by the American warships "at present blockading Martinique."

"The French islands will hardly

Continued on Page Three

INVASION ONE TOPIC

Prime Minister's Party Includes High Army and Navy Experts

COMMAND AN ISSUE

White House Talks May Cover Leadership of Armies in Europe

By W. H. LAWRENCE
Special to THE NEW YORK TIMES.

WASHINGTON, May 11—Prime Minister Winston Churchill arrived in Washington late today for conferences with President Roosevelt relative to preparations for a second front in Europe and other offensive actions against the Axis around the world.

The official announcement that Mr. Churchill, accompanied by a staff of military and naval experts, had reached Washington and had been met by the President was released by the White House at 6:48 P. M., E.W.T.

The White House statement was confined to the bare announcement of his arrival and the fact that he would be the guest of the President for the duration of his stay. But the timing of the visit, coming as it did just at the climax of the Allied operations in North Africa, and the military character of Mr. Churchill's traveling companions made it obvious that the two leaders were ready to talk about the next moves necessary to achieve the "unconditional surrender" goal they set at their last meeting in Casablanca in January.

Broad Survey Indicated

It was expected that the President and Prime Minister would survey the war situation in every world theatre and make plans for Anglo-American operations in each of them in cooperation with the other United Nations.

It was considered certain that high on the agenda was a series of steps to aid the Russian armies battling against the Germans in Eastern Europe, including a second front or series of fronts in Western and Southern Europe, as well as measures to speed up the movement of supplies.

Secretary of the Navy Frank Knox said today that the liquidation of the Axis armies in Africa would reopen the Mediterranean to

Continued on Page Three

Hitler Tours West, Ousts Paris Chief

By The Associated Press.

LONDON, May 11—A German broadcast recorded by Reuter tonight said that Adolf Hitler, whose headquarters had been long described as on the Eastern Front, now is at an unspecified point in the West. There was no immediate elaboration.

Wireless to THE NEW YORK TIMES.

BERNE, Switzerland, Wednesday, May 12—Back in Paris after a two-day inspection tour of his "Atlantic wall" defenses, Adolf Hitler late yesterday ousted Col. Gen. Ernst von Schaumburg as commander of the occupation forces in the Paris region and appointed 52-year-old General von Beulenburg-Wehrfeldt as commander of all forces in the "northwestern region," according to a Berlin announcement received here early today.

The move followed long conversations with his military advisers, during which the Reichsfuehrer "acted on the latest reports from Tunisia." A usually well-informed Berlin source reported that Herr Hitler intends to extend his shake-up of the Western command to all ranks. Col. Gen. Dietloff von Arnim has been mentioned as a possible appointee, though it is still doubted here whether he escaped the Allied ring in Tunisia.

"All the News That's Fit to Print."

The New York Times.

LATE CITY EDITION
Moderate temperatures and moderate winds today.
Temperatures Yesterday—Max., 81; Min., 61
Sunrise, 5:24 A. M.; Sunset, 8:27 P. M.

Copyright, 1943, by The New York Times Company.

VOL. XCII..No. 31,185. Entered as Second-Class Matter, Postoffice, New York, N. Y. NEW YORK, SATURDAY, JUNE 12, 1943. THREE CENTS IN NEW YORK CITY

PANTELLERIA YIELDS, CONQUERED BY AIR MIGHT; ROOSEVELT INVITES ITALY TO OUST MUSSOLINI; 200 U. S. PLANES HAMMER REICH U-BOAT YARDS

ODT RULE CAUSES POTATOES TO ROT EN ROUTE TO CITY

Refrigeration Barred on Cars From South, Huge Quantities Arrive Badly Spoiled

LOSSES 10 TO 80 PER CENT

California Shipments, Iced at Start and Twice in Transit, Reach Here Undamaged

By JEFFERSON G. BELL

Huge quantities of new potatoes shipped here from the South to relieve New York City's recent potato famine have rotted in transit, it was learned yesterday, because they were shipped without refrigeration in accordance with orders of the Office of Defense Transportation.

The loss of precious potatoes while the nation's food situation daily becomes more alarming is the subject of adverse comment in the food trade. Spokesmen for the food industry conceded it was logical to expect a shortage of refrigerator cars, but some of them would not agree that it was necessary to eliminate refrigeration altogether.

The first indication of a shocking loss of potatoes was found in "Miscellaneous Fruit and Vegetable Report No. 103," issued as of Thursday by the local office of the Food Distribution Administration of the United States Department of Agriculture. The report on shipments from Florida and other parts of the South cited "many showing considerable decay."

Large Quantities Rot

Inquiries made to F. H. Vahlsing, wholesale produce, 127 Warren Street, one of the largest potato dealers in the city, revealed that new potatoes shipped here from the South were rotting in large quantities, while potatoes from California were arriving in good condition.

California potatoes are iced before shipment and twice in transit. Shipments from the South come through without refrigeration. According to a Vahlsing spokesman, the percentage of rotten potatoes runs as high as 75 to 80 per cent in some cars and from 10 to 20 per cent in others. The Atlantic Commission Company, 102 Warren Street, buying for the A. & P. chain, reported that it had been compelled to reject "many carloads" of potatoes because of decay.

H. P. Schwarzman, director of purchases for the non-profit Joint Purchasing Corporation, which buys for many of New York City's voluntary hospitals and other charitable institutions, likewise reported that new potatoes arriving here were in badly rotted condition.

Employes of the fruit and vegetables division of the Food Distribution Administration of the United States Department of Agriculture reported that fifty-nine carloads of new potatoes had arrived yesterday, that eighty-five carloads had been unloaded and that sixty-nine cars remained on track.

Decayed Stock "Dull and Weak"

The fruit and vegetable report for June 10, citing new potatoes, declared that the market for the best quality was "unsettled with weaker feeling," and that stock showing decay was "dull and weak." Florida, 100-pound sacks, Katahdins, Sebagos, U. S. No. 1, were quoted at $4.75 to $5, while the "slightly decayed" were quoted at $4 to $4.50.

The report added that "many showing considerable decay, including some Bliss Triumphs, B size, and commercials," had been sold at $1.50 to $3.75.

Out of this situation have developed the so-called "victory grades," according to the report, which showed that prices ranged from $3.75 to $4, while prices ranging as low as 75 cents to $3.50 were paid for "many showing considerable decay, including some Sebagos and Bliss Triumphs."

Fund to Aid Schools Urged by Senators

By The Associated Press.

WASHINGTON, June 11—Legislation to authorize $300,000,000 of Federal aid to education annually was approved today by a Senate Labor subcommittee.

Offered by Senators Lister Hill, Democrat, of Alabama, and Elbert D. Thomas, Democrat, of Utah, the bill would authorize allocation of $200,000,000 a year to the States on a school-attendance basis during the war for payment of increased teachers' salaries and other unusual expenses.

In addition, it proposes the setting up of a permanent annual fund of $100,000,000 for allocation to States on the basis of financial need to equalize teachers' salaries and strengthen the school systems of the poorer States.

ROOSEVELT DENIES SHIFT ON SAVINGS

He Says He Does Not Endorse Compulsory Plan to Help Close Inflationary Gap

By JOHN H. CRIDER

Special to The New York Times.

WASHINGTON, June 11—President Roosevelt denied today that he endorsed compulsory savings at his Tuesday press conference. He explained that if he gave that impression it was because he was discussing the theory of taxation.

The President's apparent change in position was of great importance because the technical staffs of the Treasury and the Budget Bureau and the Director of Economic Stabilization are at work on a fiscal program against inflation which the Chief Executive may convey to Congress in a message soon.

The President said on Tuesday in a general discussion of the tax situation that the inflationary gap could be closed in one way or another. One way, he said, was compulsory savings and the other was taxes—probably a combination of the two.

President Explains Views

He added that this was just as necessary now as when he asked Congress in January to legislate an additional $16,000,000,000 of revenue by taxes, savings or both, to be effective during the fiscal year 1944, which starts July 1.

After the President explained that he did not mean on Tuesday to endorse compulsory savings, a reporter asked him a question which ended with Mr. Roosevelt making the statement that it was possible to legislate what the reporter called "voluntarism."

Recalling that in his budget message the President had asked Congress for $16,000,000,000 more in taxes, savings or both, the reporter asked:

"Now what kind of legislation could there be, sir, on savings,

Continued on Page Six

GERMANY HIT AGAIN

American Big Bombers Pound Wilhelmshaven and Cuxhaven

EIGHT ARE MISSING

'Large Number' of Nazi Fighters Bagged—RAF Makes Night Attack

By The Associated Press.

LONDON, Saturday, June 12—A formation of more than 200 American heavy bombers renewed the Allied aerial offensive against Western Europe yesterday by smashing at German shipyards and port installations at Wilhelmshaven and Cuxhaven.

The big four-motored bombers flew a round trip of more than 600 miles without a fighter escort. A United States Eighth Air Force communiqué said eight of them failed to return.

One large section of the American sky fleet smashed through swarms of Nazi fighters to blast the submarine yards at Wilhelmshaven. The communiqué said the bombers shot down a "large number" of challenging enemy planes.

U-boat yards and harbor installations were the objectives at Cuxhaven. Bomb bursts were seen on the targets at both Reich ports, the communiqué said.

Royal Air Force heavy bombers kept up the renewed offensive with an attack in Germany last night, British officials announced today.

First U. S. Raid on Cuxhaven

The Wilhelmshaven - Cuxhaven raid was the first concentrated attack on Hitler's European fortress by heavy bombers from British bases since May 29, when American Flying Fortresses and Liberators struck a triple daylight blow at St. Nazaire, La Pallice and Rennes in France and the Royal Air Force followed up with a devastating night assault on Wuppertal in Germany.

Yesterday's raid was the fifth by American heavy bombers on Wilhelmshaven but their first on Cuxhaven, thirty miles away to the northeast. It was the sixty-second air attack of the war for American bombers.

It was the seventy-ninth Allied attack on Wilhelmshaven, which last was raided May 21, also by American heavy bombers. Wilhelmshaven was the first target in Germany to be hit by the Americans last Jan. 27.

Cuxhaven, formerly Hamburg's pleasure resort and a nest for submarines, has been attacked seventeen times by the R. A. F., the last time on Nov. 9, 1941.

The R. A. F. added to the renewal of Allied aerial blows with daylight sweeps in which fighters attacked enemy targets in France and the Netherlands and Ventura bombers battered the coke ovens

Continued on Page Three

ALLIES PLANT FLAG ON FIRST MEDITERRANEAN STEPPING-STONE

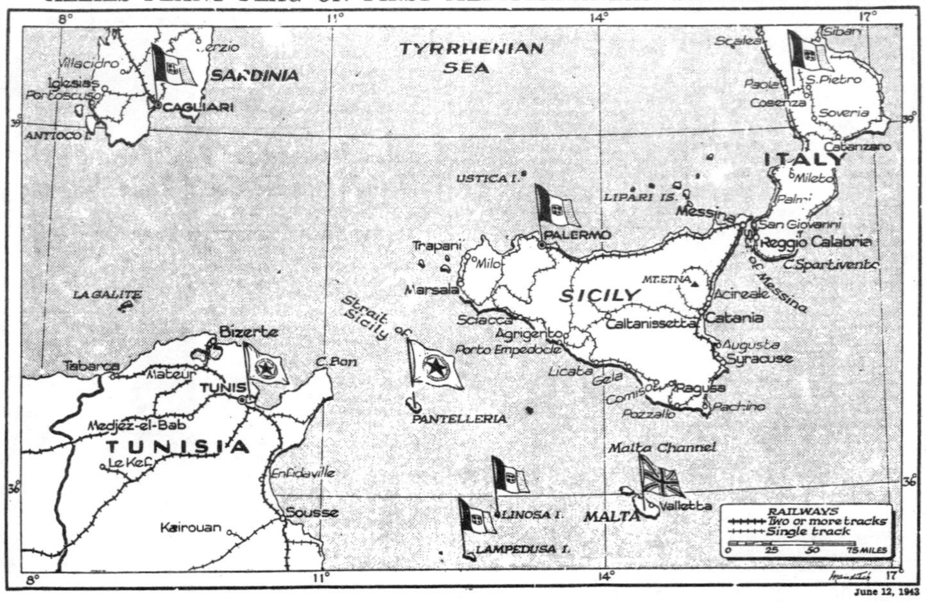

June 12, 1943

Pantelleria surrendered yesterday and with its occupation other Italian territory was placed in greater jeopardy. (United Nations holdings are indicated by the arbitrary star-in-circle flags.) Lampedusa (bottom of map) is now virtually isolated by the Allied arc of Tunisia-Pantelleria-Malta. An unconfirmed report told of another Commando sortie on the island. Sicily, where new raids were made on Gela and Pozzallo, on the southeastern coast, is now brought within easier fighter-plane range through possession of the airfield on the Italian "Gibraltar." A detailed map of the island of Pantelleria will be found on Page 2.

STRIKE BILL VOTED BY HOUSE, 219-129

Conference Compromise Wins Bipartisan Backing—Vote in Senate Due Today

Special to The New York Times.

WASHINGTON, June 11—The House, by a bipartisan vote of 219 to 129, adopted today a compromise version of the Strike and Labor Control Bill, but Senate efforts to complete legislative action went over until tomorrow when the debate turned to the terms of the compromise, which was developed in conference.

House action came early in the day after an hour's debate. The Senate took up the compromise at 5 P. M. after disposing of the Agriculture Department Appropriation Bill, but abandoned efforts to act on it just before 6 o'clock despite the hope voiced yesterday by Senator Tom Connally, Democrat, of Texas, author of the Senate version, that the measure could be

Continued on Page Seven

President Warns Italians After Pantelleria Victory

By W. H. LAWRENCE

Special to The New York Times.

WASHINGTON, June 11—Hailing the surrender to Allied forces of the Mediterranean island of Pantelleria as a portent of things to come, President Roosevelt openly invited the Italian people today to overthrow Premier Benito Mussolini and the Fascist party and to expel the Germans so that they could be restored to a respected position in the European family of nations.

As long as Premier Mussolini and the Germans dominated Italian life, the President said, the United Nations had no alternative but to prosecute the war against Italy to a complete victory.

Mr. Roosevelt's bid for an Italian revolt was predicated on his declaration that the Italian people were, by and large, a peace-loving people, who would not be subjected to the horrors of war had they not been betrayed by Premier Mussolini.

The present effects of the British-American campaign against Italy, he continued, were the perfectly logical and inevitable result of the ruthless course that had

Continued on Page Three

War News Summarized

SATURDAY, JUNE 12, 1943

The white flag of surrender rose over Pantelleria shortly before noon yesterday, ending the fiercest aerial blitz in history. Within twenty-two minutes Allied landing parties completed occupation of the Italian "Gibraltar." They found an estimated 8,000 fear-stunned, thirsty soldiers huddled in the ruins of the island on which Allied planes had cascaded a greater tonnage of bombs from May 29 to June 10 than had been unloaded in the entire remainder of the Mediterranean theatre in May. [1:8; maps, pages 1 and 2.]

Some details of the assault that overwhelmed Pantelleria came from jubilant, air-minded officers in Washington, who hailed it as the first example of conquest of territory primarily by air attack. They said that since the beginning of June 3,500 tons of bombs had blanketed the island, with 1,000 planes joining in throwing the "Sunday punch." Our plane losses during the entire operation were less than one-half of 1 per cent. [3:1.]

President Roosevelt utilized the Allied victory to call upon the Italian people to oust their German-dominated government. The President urged Italians to depose Premier Mussolini and make peace with Allies. [1:5-6.]

More than 200 bombers of the United States Air Force in Britain swept over Northwestern Germany to strike at the submarine bases of Wilhelmshaven and Cuxhaven. It was the first large-scale attack by British-based planes since May 9. The RAF struck in Germany last night. [1:3.]

Aerial warfare got top billing on the Russian front, too. Seven hundred Soviet planes attacked enemy airports, destroying or damaging more than 150 enemy aircraft on the ground, and shooting down ten others. [4:1.]

A significant chorus of editorial praise was accorded the United States and Great Britain by the Russian press on the first anniversary of the Russian-American agreement. This unanimous outburst was believed to have been approved if not inspired by the Kremlin and was said to mark the beginning of a new Russian policy of fuller collaboration with Britain and the United States. [1:6.]

Among the French factions in North Africa, Generals de Gaulle and Giraud were still at loggerheads. General de Gaulle was insisting on the immediate removal of high French officers who had opposed the Fighting French, but his letter of resignation was rejected. [3:5.]

SOVIET EXTOLS U. S. AS POST-WAR ALLY

Lavish Praise of Our War Role Predicts 'Protracted Peace' Based on Firm Accord

By C. L. SULZBERGER

By Wireless to The New York Times.

MOSCOW, June 11—To the accompaniment of the most lavish and enthusiastic praise of the United States ever promulgated in the Soviet Union, the Russian people were informed today that British-Russian-American cooperation, cemented in blood, would lead to the complete smashing of the European Axis, abetted by a direct Allied assault on the Continent. They were also told that increased understanding and collaboration between the three great powers would facilitate the establishment of a "just and protracted peace" in which the free nations of the world could live in an atmosphere "of creative labor for the good of humanity."

The occasion for these pronouncements was the first anni-

Continued on Page Four

AIR WAR LANDMARK SEEN BY DOOLITTLE

He Links First Conquest Due to Aviation Alone to Events Facing Germany and Japan

By The Associated Press.

STRATEGIC AIR FORCE HEADQUARTERS IN NORTH AFRICA, June 11—Major Gen. James H. Doolittle, in a statement tonight, declared that the conquest of Pantelleria by air power "is definitely a landmark in the history of military aviation."

General Doolittle's statement follows:

"This is no surprise to us whatsoever. If the Italians had not capitulated it would have surprised us and we would have to be thinking up a lot of alibis. But the way it worked out was only what we planned and expected. That's the way any airman would look at it.

"This is the first time in the history of warfare that territory has been conquered, as far as I know, by air power alone without occupation. Crete was subdued by air power, but occupied by accompanying forces landed by parachute, gliders and crash-landed transports.

"It was merely a proposition of steadily increasing the Pantelleria bombardment to a point at which it was physically impossible for them to stand up under it.

"At that point they capitulated. This was brought about by Royal Air Force night bombers

Continued on Page Two

ISLAND IS OCCUPIED

The Italian 'Gibraltar' Is Knocked Out by Record Avalanche of Bombs

ALL GUNS SILENCED

Troops Take Over in 22 Minutes as New Design in Warfare Emerges

By DREW MIDDLETON

By Wireless to The New York Times.

ALLIED HEADQUARTERS IN NORTH AFRICA, June 11—Blasted into ruins by hundreds of tons of bombs, the Italian island of Pantelleria, the last Axis stronghold in the Sicilian Strait, surrendered to overwhelming Allied air power this morning rather than endure another day of death and destruction under the most concentrated aerial attack in the history of warfare.

Allied assault craft darted ashore at noon soon after air crews had sighted a white cross of surrender on the airfield and cruisers and destroyers that supported the landing had spied a white flag flying from Semafore Hill, 2,000 yards from the Harbor of Pantelleria. There was slight resistance from Axis troops, dazed by thirteen days of continuous bombing, and all primary objectives were reached by 12:22 P. M. [London estimates placed the garrison at 8,000 Italians, The Associated Press said.]

It was evident that the island was so disorganized by the bombing and frequent shelling by British cruisers and destroyers that news of the surrender had failed to reach all the enemy troops on the island although the commander had surrendered by displaying the white flag and white cross.

German Dive-Bombers Routed

British troops scrambled up the rocky beaches past wrecked gun batteries—the last enemy gun was silenced by dusk yesterday—and the people of the island crept from shelters to watch with eyes dulled by fear.

[Within an hour after the surrender of Pantelleria, fifty to sixty German dive-bombers attempted to break up the landing forces, but Americans in Lightning fighters routed the Germans, forcing them to jettison their bombs haphazardly in flight, The Associated Press reported. An Algiers broadcast said that naval and infantry casualties in the occupation were negligible.]

The major share of credit for opening the first breach in Italy's chain of island strongholds goes to air power, such air power as never before had been concentrated on a target of similar size.

The climax came yesterday when more bombs were dropped on the island than were dropped in the entire month of April on all targets in Tunisia, Sicily, Sardinia and Italy.

As great a weight of bombs was unloaded on the island in the intensified aerial offensive from May 29 to June 10 as was dropped on all targets in the African theatre in the month of May. And this round-the-clock assault was preceded by six days of heavy intermittent attacks.

Yielded After Third Demand

The capitulation in the form of the white cross on the airfield came as formations of Flying Fortresses, Mitchells and Marauders were over the island. Two previous requests to surrender were ignored by the commander of the Axis garrison. Once emblems of surrender were sighted by the Allied air and naval forces [at 11:40 A. M., according to The Associated Press], the Allied military commander started occupation of the island.

[The surrender also was made known by Admiral Pavesseni, senior Italian officer on the island, in a message to an American air base, saying, "Beg sur-

Continued on Page Two

Senate 'Holds Line' on Prices, Balking Plan to Bar Roll-Backs

By C. P. TRUSSELL

Special to The New York Times.

WASHINGTON, June 11—The Senate shunned today the responsibility for a possible "breaking of the price line," and declined, by a vote of 36—37, to suspend its rules and adopt legislation concededly designed to prevent roll-backs of food costs. A two-thirds vote was required.

By its action the upper house appeared to follow the advice of Senator Bennett C. Clark, Democrat, of Missouri, who urged that a "club" be kept "in the closet" while the legislative branch waited to see what the Administration did to hold the line on the coal-strike front.

Mr. Clark predicted that if the Administration yielded to John L. Lewis, this "club," in the form of the vetoed Bankhead bill to prohibit the deduction of any farm benefits in the fixing of price ceilings, would be wielded promptly to override the President's veto.

The Bankhead bill was recommitted to the Agricultural Committee in April, after Mr. Roosevelt had returned it to Congress, pronouncing it a measure that would give farmers "an unwarranted bonus at the expense of the consumers" and set off "an inflationary tornado."

Although the Senate had passed it originally by a vote of 78—2, it then lacked the votes to pass it over the veto, so it was left in a state of suspended animation until "a more propitious time."

The issue was brought to a new

Continued on Page Six

Daily Gasoline for 1,000 Bombers Cut Off by Texas Refinery Strike

Special to The New York Times.

WASHINGTON, June 11 — Advised by the War Department of an unauthorized strike closing a Shell Oil Company refinery near Houston, Texas, where high-octane aviation gasoline sufficient to fuel a bomber mission of 1,000 planes a day over Europe is produced every twenty-four hours, Secretary Harold L. Ickes, Solid Fuels Administrator for War, said today he would take all possible steps to bring the walkout to an end.

Efforts were made by Federal officials to reach Philip Murray, president of the Congress of Industrial Organizations. The strike was called by a local of that organization's Oil and Refinery Workers International Union.

Robert P. Patterson, Under-Secretary of War, was understood to be deeply disturbed by the strike, which was caused by a dispute between a supervisor at the Deer Park Refinery and an employe who had been discharged for intoxication.

Dr. R. H. Waser, manager of the plant, said that the employe assaulted the supervisor. The local union version was that the employe had been assaulted by the supervisor before his dismissal. Thus the union demanded that the supervisor also be dismissed. The company refused, offering to suspend the supervisor until the dispute was settled, but this was rejected by the union.

War Department officials felt that at this stage of the war the no-strike pledge made by labor leaders following Pearl Harbor

Continued on Page Seven

"All the News That's Fit to Print."

The New York Times.

LATE CITY EDITION
Continued cool with moderate winds today.
Temperatures Yesterday—Max., 68; Min., 60
Sunrise, 5:27 A. M.; Sunset, 8:31 P. M.

Copyright, 1943, by The New York Times Company.

VOL. XCII—No. 31,204. Entered as Second-Class Matter, Postoffice, New York, N. Y. NEW YORK, THURSDAY, JULY 1, 1943. THREE CENTS IN NEW YORK CITY

M'ARTHUR STARTS ALLIED OFFENSIVE IN PACIFIC; NEW GUINEA ISLES WON, LANDINGS IN SOLOMONS; CHURCHILL PROMISES BLOWS IN EUROPE BY FALL

MAYOR FACES FIGHT WITH OPA ON PLAN FOR HANDLING MEAT

Gives Approval for Sales by Slaughterers to Retailers on Consignment Basis

FEDERAL ACTION LOOMS

Price Agency Director Here Promises Move Should Violation Be Found

A direct conflict between Mayor Fiorello H. La Guardia and the Office of Price Administration appeared inevitable last night, after the Mayor had announced that he had approved, on his own responsibility, a plan for independent slaughterers to sell meat to the public at consumer ceiling prices through consignments to retailers, despite the OPA's objections to the plan.

"If they go ahead with a plan that is in violation of the regulations, OPA will be forced to take action," Frank C. Russell, district OPA director, retorted when informed of the Mayor's decision. "Apparently, the Mayor has given his permission for something which the OPA legal department has turned down."

Former Municipal Court Justice Nathan Sweedler of 225 Broadway, who, as counsel for the Eastern States Independent Meat Packers and Slaughterers, proposed the plan approved by the Mayor after the OPA had turned it down, announced that his organization hoped to have meat on sale in some retail shops today and expected to have a large quantity available by Saturday.

Sees Quick Meat Supply

Mr. Sweedler has estimated that his group could provide 25,000 pounds of beef within twenty-four hours after the Mayor gave his approval to the plan and eventually could gear its output to 1,000,000 pounds a week, but the Mayor was even more optimistic. He said that the plan might provide the city with 1,000,000 pounds a week "and it may be 5,000,000 pounds."

Under the plan the meat would be sold on consignment, the retailer keeping 21 per cent of the selling price. According to Mr. Sweedler, the remaining 79 per cent would pay for the cost of livestock, freight and slaughtering. He contends that under his plan meat could be sold at the consumer ceiling prices, and any butcher violating the ceiling would be deprived of meat through a voluntary policing system.

The Mayor announced his approval of the plan to reporters at City Hall and then released a letter to Commissioner of Markets Daniel P. Woolley in which he argued that the plan did not conflict with any existing regulations and that it should be accepted as a temporary measure.

Holds Plan Feasible

"I have carefully studied the report you submitted to me with plan for direct consignment of food from the original processor to retailer direct, and selling by such retailer to consumer at ceiling prices or lower," the Mayor said in his letter. "I do not see how any such plan could conflict with any existing rules or regulations of any Federal agency, provided the producer, farmer or livestock man is paid the market price and the retailer sells at ceiling prices or lower.

"The whole purpose of food control is to make food available and fix ceiling prices. There is nothing in the rules that prevents anyone from selling below ceiling prices. Surely, in the protection of the consumer, we could not or would not prosecute a retailer for selling below ceiling prices provided his food is wholesome and complies with all health requirements and government inspection.

"In fact, if an original processor or retailer wanted to give food

Continued on Page Seventeen

OWI Closes Twelve Regional Branches

By The Associated Press.

WASHINGTON, June 30 — Twelve regional and thirty-six branch offices of the Office of War Information throughout the country began closing at midnight tonight as the fiscal year ended.

The OWI said an official would remain in each of the twelve regional offices for a few days to liquidate the affairs of both the regional and branch offices.

The shutdown was made necessary, the OWI said, because the Senate voted to appropriate only $3,000,000 for the domestic branch of the organization and earmarked the amount, allowing none for maintaining the regional and branch offices. The House had voted to abolish the domestic service entirely.

"It isn't likely that the Congressional conference committee, which has yet to act finally, would go above the Senate's $3,000,000, so we are closing down the offices," an agency spokesman said.

CONGRESS CRUSHES SUBSIDY PROGRAM

Ban on Payments to Cut Prices Stays in CCC Bill Passed by Overwhelming Majorities

By The Associated Press.

WASHINGTON, June 30 — Congress, handing the Roosevelt Administration another legislative setback, today forbade use of subsidies to push down retail food prices and ordered the meat-butter price "roll back" ended by Aug. 1.

The ban was incorporated in legislation extending the life of the Commodity Credit Corporation for two more years from midnight tonight and adding $750,000,000 to its present $2,650,000,000 lending powers. Both Senate and House approved the measure by far more than the two-thirds majority which would be necessary to override a veto. The House vote was 160 to 32, and the Senate vote, 62 to 13.

Less restrictive than the original House measure, the bill permits continued use of subsidies, up to $150,000,000 to meet increased transportation costs such as are now being paid on the movement of oil to the East Coast and on coffee imports, and to promote production of critical metals and war-essential foods. It also allows incentive payments on canning and specialty crops, price support for domestic vegetable oils and fats, and payments for sale of wheat for feeding purposes. However, no subsidies could be paid simply to reduce prices.

Before final passage, a provision prohibiting Government agencies from deducting farm benefit payments in calculating agricultural price ceilings was stricken out.

Just before final Congressional action, Lou R. Maxon, deputy administrator of the Office of Price

Continued on Page Seventeen

WALLACE AND JONES RENEW THEIR ROW AFTER 2-HOUR TALK

Conference Called by Byrnes Fails 'to Resolve and Determine' Controversy

SHARP STATEMENTS ISSUED

Secretary Says Charge of Delay by RFC in War Effort Is 'Dastardly' and 'Untrue'

By JOHN H. CRIDER

Special to The New York Times.

WASHINGTON, June 30—An attempt by the War Mobilization Director, James F. Byrnes, to harmonize the differences between Vice President Henry A. Wallace and Secretary of Commerce Jesse H. Jones, failed today after he had summoned them to his office for a two-hour discussion this afternoon.

Tonight the Vice President issued a statement which somewhat tempered his bitter accusations against Mr. Jones made yesterday but said the fundamental differences remained.

To this the Secretary replied:

"Mr. Wallace in his statement tonight repeats that delays of the RFC have retarded the war effort. This dastardly charge is as untrue as when he first made it. As for the rest of his statement, Mr. Wallace was not authorized to speak for me. I will continue to speak for myself, and as previously stated, I shall insist upon a Congressional investigation."

The Vice President's statement made it clear that the basic differences between himself and Mr. Jones had been altered only to the extent that "Mr. Jones did not object" to Mr. Wallace's plan to ask Congress after its recess for funds for foreign procurement which would make it independent of the Reconstruction Finance Corporation, headed by the Secretary of Commerce.

There was no mention of Mr. Byrnes in the Vice President's statement, although it was the fruit of the War Mobilization Director's efforts to play the role of peacemaker for the Federal Bureaucracy cast for him by President Roosevelt's Executive Order of May 28 calling upon him to "resolve and determine controversies between such agencies or departments."

Meanwhile, the Senate, showing little indication at this point of being in a mood to grant the broad authority over foreign procurement expenditures sought by Mr. Wallace, inserted in the War Agencies Appropriation Bill an amendment by Senator Kenneth McKellar, Democrat, of Tennessee, providing that BEW could not use for foreign purchases any of the $36,000,000 appropriated without approval of a majority of the

Continued on Page Eleven

UNITED NATIONS FORCES MOVE FORWARD IN THE SOUTHWEST PACIFIC

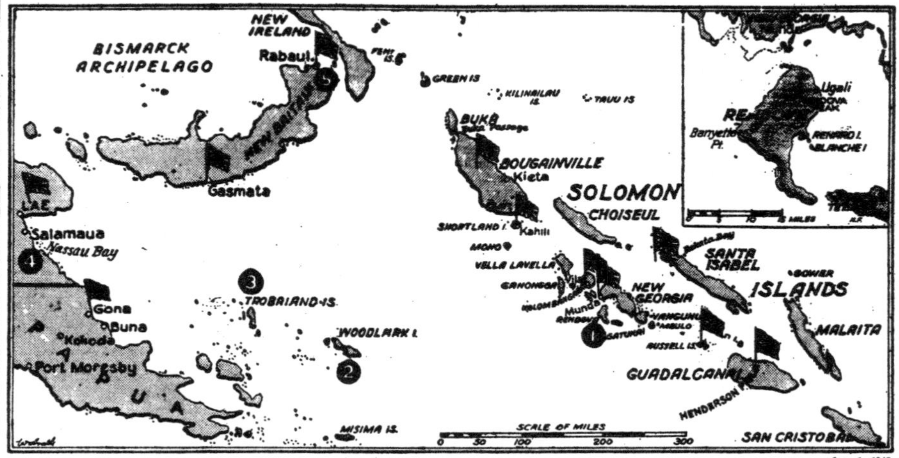

American troops landed on Rendova and New Georgia Islands (1), in the vicinity of the enemy air base at Munda, and engaged the Japanese. The inset shows this area in detail. To the west the Allies occupied Woodlark Island (2) and the Trobriand Islands (3) without opposition. In New Guinea they occupied Nassau Bay (4), just below Salamaua; the landing craft encountered only slight resistance. Apparently these widespread operations have as their ultimate goal the reduction of Rabaul (5), which was bombed.

76 BILLIONS SPENT IN U.S. FISCAL YEAR

71 of the Total Were for War —Public Debt Up to 140 Billions, Deficit to 55

Special to The New York Times.

WASHINGTON, June 30 — The United States ended its fiscal year tonight with a record of expenditures of more than $76,000,000,000, receipts of more than $21,000,000,000, a gross public debt of more than $140,000,000,000 and a deficit of more than $55,000,000,000.

The latest figures available at the Treasury were for June 26, four days before the actual end of the fiscal year. On that date total war expenditures for the year were $71,014,000,000, as against $25,515,000,000 on the same date in 1942.

Spending for civilian purposes was $5,375,000,000, as compared with $5,800,000,000 on the same day a year earlier. The War Department spent $41,690,000,000 and the Navy $20,513,000,000. War expenditures of the Agriculture Department totaled $2,005,000,000. The Maritime Commission spent $2,733,000,000.

In one year the public debt increased from $76,560,000,000 to $140,028,000,000 and the deficit advanced from $19,152,000,000 to $55,242,000,000.

Receipts of $21,625,000,000 up to

Continued on Page Twelve

Prime Minister Warns Axis Allied Attacks Are Imminent

By RAYMOND DANIELL

By Cable to The New York Times.

LONDON, June 30—Prime Minister Churchill warned the Axis today that the Allies were preparing heavier blows on land and sea and by air from east, south and west to bring about the unconditional surrender that he and President Roosevelt declared at Casablanca was the price of peace.

The text of Mr. Churchill's address is printed on Page 4.

In the Mediterranean and "elsewhere," he said, heavy fighting probably would develop "before the leaves of autumn fall," but he added that large-scale amphibious operations take months to prepare.

Significantly, he dwelt at length and in considerable detail upon the growing scale and intensity of the British-American air offensive against Germany from this island, and indicated that Russian air power, long tied down to the battle lines, would soon be able to join in the attack on Nazi industry from the east.

A Major Victory at Sea

Reviewing the Battle of the Atlantic, he said a victory had been won at sea against the submarines two months ago comparable with the Allied conquest of Africa with the capture of 350,000 German and Italian prisoners and vast quantities of war material. He likened the victory in Tunisia to the Russian triumph at Stalingrad.

The Prime Minister was speaking in the ancient Guildhall, where he received freedom of the City of London, that square mile of the British capital that still bears the

Continued on Page Four

BERLIN EVACUATION REPORTED PLANNED

Swedes Hear Exodus Is to Start in Fall—Wuppertal Held Beyond Rebuilding

By GEORGE AXELSSON

By Telephone to The New York Times.

STOCKHOLM, Sweden, June 30 —Berlin will evacuate in the Fall women and children not engaged in the war industries, according to reliable information received here today through private channels.

Fear of heavier and more frequent Allied air raids with the coming of longer nights has prompted this decision, and authorities have already begun the preliminary arrangements, it is stated.

The extent to which the Ruhr has been hit by the RAF raids is indicated by a statement by Adolf Hitler's chief city planning consultant, Armaments Minister Albert Speer, just back from a tour of inspection of the devastated area.

He said it was not worth while to try to rebuild Wuppertal.

Continued on Page Three

MARTINIQUE YIELDS, ASKS TERMS OF U.S.

Robert, 'to Avoid Bloodshed,' Ready to Accept Change of French Authority

The Martinique radio broadcast a statement last night by Admiral Georges Robert, Vichy's High Commissioner on the island, asserting that he had asked the United States Government to dispatch a "plenipotentiary to fix the terms for a change of French authority."

The broadcast said that Admiral Robert had taken the action "to avoid bloodshed." It was recorded by Federal Communications Commission monitors, The United Press said.

The admiral has, since the fall of France, stood firm in his determination to hold Martinique and nearby French islands in the Caribbean under his own rule, loyal to Marshal Henri-Philippe Pétain, French Chief of State.

The reception of the broadcast was marred by technical difficulties, but those portions of the broadcast that could be heard said:

"Communiqué to the population:

"In order to avoid bloodshed between the French and * * * I have asked the Government of the United States, under the double condition of its renewing the guarantee to maintain French sovereignty in these islands and of the nonintervention of American forces, to send a plenipotentiary to fix the terms for a change of French authority. "* * * my duty to the people and the Marshal * * *

"Admiral Robert."

Recently there have been unconfirmed reports of clashes between the Admiral's troops and elements favoring the rule of the islands by

Continued on Page Eight

2-PRONGED DRIVE

Americans Battle Enemy on New Georgia and Rendova Islands

SALAMAUA IN PERIL

Allies Seize Trobriand and Woodlark Isles—Rabaul Pounded

By SIDNEY SHALETT

Special to The New York Times.

WASHINGTON, Thursday, July 1—Combined Army and Navy forces under General Douglas MacArthur have opened the long expected offensive against the Japanese in the south and southwest Pacific.

Fighting was in progress on Rendova and New Georgia islands, which were hit by ground, naval and air forces in "closest synchronization," a communiqué from General MacArthur's headquarters in Australia reported today. Nassau Bay, ten miles south of the big Japanese base of Salamaua in New Guinea, fell to the Allies after a slight skirmish, and the Trobriand and Woodlark island groups, 300 to 400 miles west of the New Georgia group, were occupied without opposition.

The Allied push—aimed, observers here believe, at the major Japanese base of Rabaul, on New Britain Island—got under way yesterday, Solomons time, which was Tuesday here.

Nutcracker Move Seen

It was believed here, on the basis of early reports, that the fighting and occupations reported so far were preliminary to major actions to come. If bases in the New Georgias are consolidated, a two-way push against Rabaul might be developing, with one arm advancing northwestward from the Central Solomons and the other swinging across eastward from new bases in New Guinea.

United States heavy bombers carried out an attack on Rabaul during the night, dropping nearly twenty-three tons of high-explosive, fragmentation and incendiary bombs throughout the dispersal areas at the Vunakanau and Lakunai airdromes, the communiqué from Australian headquarters reported. "Several explosions" and "numerous fires" were observed, one of which was visible for 100 miles, the announcement said.

The big bombers, which have punished Rabaul extensively in recent weeks, ran into heavy Japanese anti-aircraft fire and interference from some enemy night fighters. One American bomber was missing after the raid.

The Tobriand and Woodlark islands will be valuable as stepping-stones in a chain of fighter-plane bases from the Allied stronghold of Milne Bay, on the tip of New Guinea. Japanese-held Gasmata and Rabaul may be raided with comparative ease with the aid of these bays.

Navy Gives First News

The first report of landing actions came early yesterday when the Navy announced here in a communiqué that combined United States forces had landed June 30 (Solomons time) on Rendova Island, in the New Georgia group, which is only five miles from the important Japanese air base of Munda, on New Georgia Island, but that communiqué said, "No details have been received."

A hint that the fighting had extended came later from Secretary of the Navy Frank Knox in Los Angeles, where he is inspecting Pacific Coast installations. The Secretary declared that the Rendova attack was the beginning of "an offensive against the Japanese base at Munda and surrounding bases." Navy officials in Washington yesterday declined, however, to con-

Continued on Page Three

Cattle Grower Says 'Policymakers' Are to Blame in Meat Shortage

By JAY G. HAYDEN

North American Newspaper Alliance.

WASHINGTON, June 30—Joseph G. Montague, general counsel for the Texas and Southwestern Cattle Raisers Association, put the blame for the meat shortage today on "the unofficial policy-makers close to the President," thereby bringing into the open a charge which figured behind the scenes in the Congressional rejection of food subsidies and the retirement of Chester C. Davis as Food Administrator.

Speaking before the Senate Agricultural Committee, Mr. Montague said:

"Surrounding the President are a group of people who have no responsibility, yet determine policy and cause confusion in the meat situation. They are entrenched in power and determined to change the economic and social order."

Mr. Davis is believed to have had substantially this same thought in mind when he gave as his first reason for resignation that "I find I have assumed a public responsibility while the authority, not only over broad food policy, but day-to-day actions, is being exercised elsewhere."

Mr. Davis, according to his close friends, became convinced that the real policy-makers were the same old New Deal inner cabinet, including particularly Harry L. Hopkins, Associate Justice Felix Frankfurter and Judge Samuel Rosenman, which has functioned prominently throughout the Roosevelt Administration. Whether he was speaking of his own knowledge or merely

Continued on Page Seventeen

War News Summarized

THURSDAY, JULY 1, 1943

The Allied Southwest Pacific and South Pacific Commands have started a broad offensive against Japanese positions. The first results of the combined naval, air and land operations are:

Landings on Rendova and New Georgia Islands in the Central Solomons, where fighting is going on.

Occupation, without opposition, of the Trobriand Islands and Woodlark Island off the southeastern tip of New Guinea at the north end of the Coral Sea.

A landing at Nassau Bay, ten miles south of Salamaua in New Guinea.

Heavy aerial bombardment of the big Japanese base at Rabaul, New Britain.

Gen. Douglas MacArthur is in general command of the combined operations, with Admiral William F. Halsey Jr. directing the offensive of the South Pacific forces. The battle area extends 500 miles north of Guadalcanal to Rabaul and 750 miles northwest to Salamaua [All the foregoing, 1:8.]

In London, Prime Minister Churchill pledged that after Hitler's defeat "every man, every ship and every airplane in the King's service that can be moved to the Pacific will be sent and there maintained in action * * * for as many years as are needed to make the Japanese, in their turn, submit or bite the dust."

Mr. Churchill then announced that "very probably there will be heavy fighting in the Mediterranean and elsewhere before the leaves of autumn fall." He characterized Tunisia and the campaign against the U-boat as the two greatest Allied victories of the war, and promised that every corner of Germany would be bombed as thoroughly as the Ruhr had been. [All the foregoing, 1:5-6.]

On the other war fronts, Flying Fortresses raided Le Mans in France and the RAF hit targets in western Europe [5:2-3], Reggio Calabria and Messina were bombed in the Mediterranean [6:2], and Russian troops captured a strong position on the Velikiye Luki front. [7:1.]

Admiral Robert, Vichy's High Commissioner in Martinique, asked the United States for terms under which the West Indies islands could be transferred to other French authority. [1:7.]

Laundry Workers Held Essential But the WMC Restricts Services

Special to The New York Times.

WASHINGTON, June 30 — The War Manpower Commission extended to the country's laundries today the same preferential treatment in the allocation of manpower as is given to essential war industries.

Laundries classified as "locally needed" by regional directors of the WMC will be supplied with workers by the United States Employment Service, will be protected from labor piracy and will have their existing labor force stabilized, except that there will be no occupational deferment under the Selective Service Act. They will receive this aid only if they discontinue luxury services to their patrons.

To be classified as "locally needed" they must meet standards agreed upon by the War Labor Board's Office of Civilian Requirements and the WMC. These standards are designed to enable the laundries to give adequate essential service to more people than they are now doing with their available labor force and to put maintenance services on a "rock-bottom, first-things-first basis."

Under the new ruling hand ironing, the retouching of all flat work and the retouching of wearing apparel by hand after pressing, except for a bare minimum required to make it presentable; fancy packaging and unnecessary folding are eliminated, and customers will be limited to one grade of starching of their shirts and other wearing apparel.

Laundries are expected to cooperate in inducing hotels, boarding houses and tourist homes to change bed linen only once a week for any one patron; limit each patron to one face towel and one bath towel

Continued on Page Ten

"All the News That's Fit to Print."

The New York Times.

LATE CITY EDITION
Showers, warm and humid today; moderate winds.
Temperatures Yesterday—Max., 79; Min., 66
Sunrise, 5:35 A. M.; Sunset, 8:29 P. M.

VOL. XCII..No. 31,213. Entered as Second-Class Matter, Postoffice, New York, N. Y. NEW YORK, SATURDAY, JULY 10, 1943. THREE CENTS IN NEW YORK CITY

ALLIED TROOPS START INVASION OF SICILY; NAVAL ESCORTS BOMBARD SHORE DEFENSES; LANDINGS PRECEDED BY SEVERE AIR ATTACK

ROOSEVELT VOICES DOUBT ON MAKING LEWIS OBEY WLB

He Asks at Press Conference How to Force Someone to Sign Against His Will

ORDER TO WARD IS CITED

He Declares He Could Take Property but Probably Could Not Seize Union

By SAMUEL B. BLEDSOE
Special to THE NEW YORK TIMES.

WASHINGTON, July 9—President Roosevelt indicated today that he had no intention of taking action to force John L. Lewis, head of the United Mine Workers, to obey the War Labor Board's directive that he sign an agreement with the bituminous mine operators.

Asked at his press conference whether he intended to reaffirm the board's order in the mine union case, the President said that, after all, the order was that of a quasi-judicial body and spoke for itself. He asked what action he could take—send a little polite note on pink paper and say, "Dear Mr. Lewis, I hope you will sign the contract"?

Pressed to say what he would do if Mr. Lewis did not sign, the President inquired in turn what the reporter would do and got the reply, "I don't know. I'm not President." The President then commented upon the difficulty of forcing some one to sign something against his will.

Montgomery Ward Case Cited

A reporter reminded that Sewell Avery, head of Montgomery Ward & Co., had been directed by the President to sign a wage agreement which provided for a maintenance of membership clause and check-off of union dues after the company had defied a WLB order.

President Roosevelt said that, although he did not want to take over Montgomery Ward, he had authority to do so, but doubted that he had similar authority to take over the mine union.

Asked if he felt he needed some sanction of law to deal with recalcitrant miners, Mr. Roosevelt replied that there was Section 8 of the Smith-Connally Anti-Strike Act and the first seven sections of the bill. He suggested that these sections be examined.

War Labor Board officials refused to be quoted on Mr. Roosevelt's statements. They said they still were hoping that the President intended to crack down on Mr. Lewis, but they also disclosed that they feared the board had been left high and dry.

Interpretation of WLB Order

They said that while the directive of June 18 did not specifically order Mr. Lewis to sign an agreement with the operators, such action clearly was implied by the directive. Although the matter had been put up to President Roosevelt, there was no indication, they stated, that the President had asked Mr. Lewis to obey the directive and no indication that he intended to do so.

One official declared that the real issue in the Lewis case was whether an individual, or pressure group, could continue in wartime to defy a Government directive intended to further prosecution of the war.

If President Roosevelt does not intend to take further action in the Lewis case, but continues to operate the mines under the direction of Secretary Ickes, some officials here declared, a good deal will be heard about the differences in handling a situation when an employer defies the WLB and when a union defies it.

Obedience by Ward Forced

Acting as "Commander in Chief in time of war," the President issued the order to Montgomery Ward & Co. last December. The company had objected strenuously to the maintenance-of-membership

Continued on Page Seven

Cripps Bids Workers Back New Air Phase

By Wireless to THE NEW YORK TIMES.

LONDON, July 9—Appealing for maximum production and the cessation of absenteeism and strikes among aircraft workers, Sir Stafford Cripps, Minister of Aircraft Production, declared in a radio broadcast tonight that this country has entered a new and more intensive phase of the war "and almost at any moment there may be a great intensification" of the present offensive.

He asked the workers to support this offensive to their utmost.

"An assault upon the Axis powers in Europe and the Far East," Sir Stafford said, "entails dislodging them from occupied territories. That will be a costly task. Our casualties will inevitably be heavy but we can help to keep down those losses."

PRESIDENT BARS DATA FOR INQUIRY

On His Order Army, Navy, Budget Bureau Deny Radio Committee's Request

By WINIFRED MALLON
Special to THE NEW YORK TIMES.

WASHINGTON, July 9—Acting on the order of President Roosevelt, the War and Navy Departments refused today to transmit information requested by the House committee investigating the Federal Communications Commission.

Their reply stated that production of documents and testimony of witnesses relative to the proposed executive order transferring to the War and Navy Departments the radio intelligence activities of the commission had been forbidden by the President as "contrary to the public interest."

In a letter to the committee, James V. Forrestal, Under-Secretary of the Navy, wrote:

"The President of the United States authorized me to inform the committee that he, the President, refuses to allow the documents described in your letter to be delivered to the committee, as such delivery would be incompatible with the public interest.

"I must decline to permit the appearance of naval officers, active or inactive, before your committee, as such appearance would be incompatible with the public interest."

A letter to the same effect was received from Robert P. Patterson, Under-Secretary of War.

On similar ground Harold D. Smith, Director of the Budget, declined to testify at today's hearing of the committee and refused to deliver Budget Bureau data.

James Lawrence Fly, chairman of the FCC, appearing as chairman of the Board of War Communications, also declined to answer questions, declaring himself bound

Continued on Page Seven

RUSSIANS STIFFEN

Red Army Repels Heavy Attacks in Orel and Kursk Sectors

AXIS LOSSES SOAR

Both Sides State Fight Grows in Intensity—Nazis Win 'Inches'

By The Associated Press.

LONDON, Saturday, July 10—The Russian armies of the center bloodily beat off savage German attacks all along the Orel and Kursk fronts yesterday, held their own in the Belgorod sector to the south, and destroyed 193 Nazi tanks and 94 planes in the great battle of attrition, the Soviet command announced early today.

The German dead, in two battle areas specifically mentioned, were nearly 5,000 for the day, Moscow declared in the regular midnight communiqué recorded here by the Soviet monitor, thus bringing to about 40,000 the total German casualties for five days of violent action.

German losses in matériel also were rising to tremendous proportions

Yesterday's destruction raised to 2,036 the number of enemy tanks thus far listed as knocked out, and to 904 the number of Nazi planes smashed since the beginning of the offensive.

In the Orel-Kursk sector, said the bulletin, the Nazis after four days of heavy losses had "gained no success" and had been forced to shift the weight of attack to other areas, reinforcing their "battered troops" by nine infantry divisions and one tank division.

Twenty Attacks Beaten Back

A score or more of German attacks were beaten off—thirteen of them in a single area of action—and fighting at times was hand-to-hand.

Fifteen hundred Nazis were wiped out in these actions, said the Soviet command, as was most of a German battalion in a near-by action.

About Belgorod—scene of four previous German penetrations against which the Russians had battered all day—no further Nazi progress was reported, although it was declared the invaders were "bringing into battle all their reserves, striving at any cost to achieve success."

In the Belgorod sector 2,000 Germans were killed during the day; in a near-by action 1,000 more fell. But it was in the Kursk-Orel sector where the supreme Nazi efforts were being made.

The Germans themselves, in a long broadcast propaganda report, spoke of "ferocious fighting" south of Orel, where Nazi troops "could gain ground only inch by inch."

Further German advances—

Continued on Page Four

MUNDA HAMMERED

Planes, Warships, Guns Batter Japanese at New Georgia Base

GROUND PUSH GAINS

Enemy's Counter-Blows to Ward Off Assault Are Declared Weak

By TILLMAN DURDIN
By Wireless to THE NEW YORK TIMES.

ALLIED HEADQUARTERS FOR THE SOUTHWEST PACIFIC, Saturday, July 10—American planes unloosed the most terrific aerial attack yet made on Japanese positions on New Georgia Island yesterday. More than a hundred bombers escorted by fighters pounded Munda and the Bairoko Harbor areas early in the morning. At the same time United States destroyers shelled Munda.

Seventy tons of bombs, including two thousand-pounders, were used to blast the camp areas, supply dumps and anti-aircraft positions. The biggest group of bombers concentrated on the area between Munda Point and the Lamberti coconut plantation, where part of the main Japanese defenses around the Munda airdrome are located.

While dive bombers and level bombers were circling and hurling their bombs in this area American artillery from across Blanche Channel on Rendova shelled Japanese anti-aircraft sites. Other groups of bombers pounded the Japanese at Bairoko harbor, port across the peninsula from Munda and Enogai inlet, three miles north of Bairoko Harbor.

Heavy Damage Done

There is every reason to believe that the combined aerial, naval and land artillery bombardment of yesterday morning heavily damaged the Japanese defenses. It was one of the most devastating artillery and air attacks ever made in the Pacific on a land target. The destroyers shelled the base before dawn.

Forty-five Japanese fighters attempted to intervene in the battle for Munda early yesterday afternoon. They appeared over Rendova Island, where they were intercepted by patrolling American fighters. Four were shot down in the

Continued on Page Five

ISLAND OF SICILY IS INVADED BY ALLIED FORCES

July 10, 1943

General Eisenhower announced that his troops had debarked at various points on Sicily early today. The landings were preceded by furious air assaults and warships accompanying the transports shelled the coastal defenses. Troops got ashore at the western tip of the island (cross), according to the Algiers radio. Strong forces of tanks were reported being used. The invasion had been preceded by heavy bombings of a variety of targets (bomb devices).

SEVERAL LANDINGS

American, British and Canadian Troops Carry Out the Attack

A 'LIBERATION' START

But Eisenhower Urges French Be Calm Till Their Hour Strikes

By DREW MIDDLETON
By Wireless to THE NEW YORK TIMES.

ALLIED HEADQUARTERS IN NORTH AFRICA, Saturday, July 10—Allied infantry landed at a number of places on the rocky Sicilian coast under a canopy of naval gunfire early this morning as the long-awaited invasion began.

Gen. Dwight D. Eisenhowed, Allied Commander in Chief, speaking to the people of metropolitan France, called the attack "the first page in the liberation of the European Continent," and promised "there will be others."

Allied headquarters announced the invasion in the following communiqué:

> Allied forces under command of General Eisenhower began landing operations on Sicily early this morning.
>
> The landings were preceded by Allied air attack.
>
> Allied naval forces escorted the assault forces and bombarded the coast defenses during the assault.

[The Algiers radio, in an English-language broadcast to North America at 12:40 A. M. today, said that Allied forces had landed on the rocky western tip of Sicily, 260 miles from Rome. The broadcast was recorded by United States Government monitors.

[The broadcast said the landings were made in good weather, with German and Italian air forces providing "fierce" opposition. In anticipation of the assault, the island's Italian-German defenders blew up harbor installations, the broadcast said]

"Softened Up" By Air Attack

A heavy attack was carried on by planes of the Northwest Africa Air Force and the Middle East Air Command for nearly two weeks, reaching blitz proportions in the last week, when a round-the-clock assault blasted Axis air bases and communication centers with hundreds of tons of bombs. This came to a furious climax yesterday and last night.

The Allied naval force that escorted the invading troops pounded the formidable defenses of Sicily with salvos of shells while infantrymen, their bayonets twinkling in the starlight raced ashore from landing crafts. Many tanks were landed.

Sicily, largest island in the Mediterranean, has a population of just under 4,000,000 persons and has been strongly fortified, specially along the southern coast, since 1939. The coasts are heavily mined and beaches are covered by batteries of artillery that fire from hills.

French Urged to Be Calm

General Eisenhower's announcement to the French people, which was sent by radio, asked them to remain calm and not to expose themselves to reprisals through "present rash actions."

Many of the troops involved in the invasion of Sicily are veterans of the Tunisian campaign.

Military men here expect very heavy fighting. The Germans are known to have reinforced the island comparatively recently, and despite the prolonged aerial bombardment strong fortifications remain to be overcome.

Many military objectives were hit by American and British bombers during the two weeks' attack on the island. The main weight of the bombing at night was directed against the airfields, particularly

Continued on Page Two

PRESIDENT PARRIES FRENCH BIAS QUERY

There Is No France Now, He Explains—Giraud Wins Arms for 300,000

By HAROLD CALLENDER
Special to THE NEW YORK TIMES.

WASHINGTON, July 9—Commenting upon the accusation that the United States was interfering in French affairs, President Roosevelt at his press conference today said that 95 per cent of the French people were still under the German heel and that there was no France now.

When a correspondent remarked that, at any rate, there was a French committee, and asked whether this Government would recognize it, the President said that question had not arisen.

Regarding the visit here of General Giraud, who is also Commander in Chief of the French forces in North and West Africa, Mr. Roosevelt said merely that at lunch yes-

Continued on Page Four

RAF Pounds Cologne Again In 1,000-Ton 'Repeat' Attack

By FREDERICK GRAHAM
By Cable to THE NEW YORK TIMES.

LONDON, July 9—Cologne, which was the first city to feel the weight of a 1,000-plane raid in the British attack of May 30, 1942, was plastered again last night by the Royal Air Force with more than 1,000 tons of bombs. The raid was the 119th of the war on the Rhine city, and it was described by officials here as effecting "a crushing setback to the German attempts to revive the skeletonized industrial life of the town."

Despite an intense Nazi anti-aircraft barrage and severe icing conditions and electrical storms, the heavy British and Canadian bombers pressed home an "effectively concentrated" attack at a cost of only eight planes, the Air Ministry reported.

[British heavy bombers raided Germany again last night, said a brief London announcement early today, reported by The Associated Press.

[RAF fighters and light bombers raided northern France in force by daylight yesterday and attacked German shipping along the coast. The St. Omer airfield was bombed and Mustang fighters punished Nazi traffic.

[Nazi raiders attacked the London area yesterday afternoon, two of the about ten attackers being shot down. Bombs caused casualties in the suburbs. In a southeast English town an enemy raider landed a bomb in a movie theatre filled with children and at least twelve persons were reported killed and injured.]

Authoritative comment on the

Continued on Page Three

BOMBS TORE SICILY BEFORE INVASION

Allied Fliers Ripped Airfields, Communications and Plants in Week-Long Blitz

By Wireless to THE NEW YORK TIMES.

ALLIED HEADQUARTERS IN NORTH AFRICA, July 9—Swarms of Allied bombers maintained their round-the-clock pounding of Axis air bases in Sicily, and formations of fighter bombers, including new A-36's, which are also fitted as dive-bombers, hammered transport, communications and industrial plants on the besieged island yesterday as the great Allied aerial offensive centered on Sicily for the sixth straight day.

The new A-36 fighter-bomber, which was developed from North American's P-51 Mustang fighter, is the newest "plane of all work." It is used as both a dive and glide bomber and takes part in strafing missions as well. The Mustang is supposed to be the world's most effective fighter under 15,000 feet,

Continued on Page Two

War News Summarized

SATURDAY, JULY 10, 1943

American, British and Canadian troops landed early this morning on Sicily, the last-stepping stone to Italy. While the size of the invasion force was not known, the War Department said naval forces had escorted the invasion troops and bombarded Sicilian coast defenses. The enemy is believed to have between eleven and thirteen divisions on the rugged island, of which nine or ten are Italian and the rest German.

As the Allies struck, General Eisenhower broadcast an appeal to the French people warning them against rash actions that would bring upon them reprisals from the Nazis. He urged them to listen to Allied broadcasts. "When the hour of action strikes," he declared, "we will let you know." [All the foregoing, 1:8.]

The invasion came on the heels of six consecutive days of powerful Allied air assaults on Sicily, during which air bases, communications centers and industrial plants had been pounded almost incessantly. During the last day twenty-one enemy planes had been destroyed and a quarter of a million pounds of bombs had been dropped on Catania alone. [1:7.]

The German offensive along the Orel-Kursk-Belgorod front increased in fury yesterday as the Nazis threw ten more divisions against the Russians near Belgorod. But the Russians said their forces were holding at all points and had destroyed another 193 tanks and ninety-four planes and had slain 5,000 men. In the four days since the Germans opened their drive the Russians claim to have killed 40,000 men and knocked out 2,036 tanks and 904 planes. [1:3.]

Germany, too, was blasted as the RAF inflicted another powerful blow on Cologne. Making their 119th raid on the Ruhr city, the fliers lost only eight bombers as they dropped more than a thousand tons of bombs in what was termed "a crushing setback to German attempts to revive the skeletonized industrial life" of Cologne. [1:6-7.]

More than 100 Allied bombers joined warships and artillery in launching the strongest barrage to date against the Japanese base of Munda. The Japanese sent forty-five Zeros over Rendova Island, but they were dispersed and four were destroyed. The enemy also tried, with small success, a dive-bombing attack on our base at Nassau Bay, New Guinea. [1:4; map, P. 5.]

A joint American-British announcement said that Allied and neutral shipping losses from U-boat attacks during June were the smallest since the United States entered the war. [1:6-7.]

Son-in-Law Held in Oakes' Murder; Bahaman Police Cite Fingerprints

By The United Press.

NASSAU, Bahamas, July 9—Alfred de Marigny, 36, was booked at the police station here tonight on a charge of killing his father-in-law, the multimillionaire British baronet, Sir Harry Oakes.

A formal charge of murder was placed against the bearded accused, who denied any connection with the slaying.

Sir Harry was known to have been unhappy over the marriage of his eldest daughter, Nancy, then 17 years old, to M. de Marigny at New York in May, 1942. It was the second marriage for the Count, who had been divorced in Miami, Fla., in 1937.

He was arrested at 6 o'clock tonight by Lieut. Col. R. A. Lindop and Major Embert Pemberton of the Nassau constabulary.

Capt. E. W. Melchen of the Miami Police Department, summoned by airplane to aid in the investigation after Sir Harry's body was found on a bed that had been set afire Thursday morning, said the arrest and charge were based on "hair analysis, fingerprints and interrogation."

Attorney General Eric Hallinan reported that Sir Harry had been bludgeoned to death. There were four severe head wounds, he said, as well as burns on the body.

Officers believed an electric fan had blown out the flames before they had destroyed the bed.

The charge against Count de Marigny came as a sensational climax to the death of Sir Harry, one of the world's richest men, with a fortune unofficially estimated to be as great as $200,000,000.

Until the announcement came, details of the slaying had been

Continued on Page Twenty-six

June Losses to U-Boats Lowest Since We Entered the Conflict

Special to THE NEW YORK TIMES.

WASHINGTON, July 9—Intimations that the United Nations have been winning the war against the submarine were confirmed by a joint statement issued today by the British and United States Governments.

June losses of Allied and neutral ships by submarine attack, said the report, were the lowest since this country entered the war, sinkings of Axis submarines were substantial, and the main transatlantic convoys were now proceeding practically unmolested.

The statement was as follows:

1. In June the losses of Allied and neutral merchant ships from submarine attacks were the lowest since the United States entered the war. The losses from all forms of enemy action were the second lowest recorded since the war between Britain and Germany began.

2. The number of targets offered to the anti-submarine vessels and aircraft of the United Nations was not as great in June as previously, but the sinkings of Axis submarines were substantial and satisfactory.

3. The heavy toll taken of the U-boats in May showed its effect in June in that the main transatlantic convoys were practically unmolested, and the U-boat attacks on our shipping were in widely separated areas. However, every opportunity was taken of attacking U-boats leaving and returning to their bases on the west coast of France.

4. The merchant shipping ton-

Continued on Page Three

"All the News That's Fit to Print."

The New York Times.

LATE CITY EDITION
Moderately warm today with moderate winds.
Temperatures Yesterday—Max.,83; Min.,70
Sunrise, 5:40 A. M.; Sunset, 8:23 P. M.

Copyright, 1943, by The New York Times Company.

VOL. XCII..No. 31,223. Entered as Second-Class Matter. Postoffice, New York, N. Y. NEW YORK, TUESDAY, JULY 20, 1943. THREE CENTS IN NEW YORK CITY

ALLIED BOMBS BLAST ROME MILITARY AREAS; TIMES MAN FROM AIR SEES SHRINES SPARED; AXIS FORCES STEADILY FALL BACK IN SICILY

REPUBLICAN GROUP WARNS ISOLATION MEANS '44 DEFEAT

Post-War Conference Holds Such a Stand Would Force Voters to Favor 4th Term

PLATFORM ADOPTED HERE

Conference Calls on Spangler to Have His Appointees Adopt Its Proposals

The most determined drive yet seen to force the Republican party into a vigorous policy of international collaboration manifested itself yesterday at the Hotel Commodore, as 300 delegates attended the eastern regional conference of the unofficial Republican Post-War Policy Association.

With supporters of Wendell L. Willkie dominating the proceedings, the kid gloves of diplomacy were taken off, and notice was served that unless the Republican party drops "narrow nationalism," the voters will have to choose a fourth term for Roosevelt in preference to what the Republicans will be offering.

While prominent speakers stressed the need for Republican leadership in international affairs, and argued that Republican traditions called for this leadership, the real keynote was sounded by Mayo Shattuck, president of the Massachusetts Bar Association and chairman of the conference's committee on resolutions.

Warns Party on Isolationism

Mr. Shattuck, in presenting the platform, unanimously adopted a few minutes later, said:

"We believe that the Republican party is about to be given its chance again for leadership and for power in the United States. But our people are not fools. Just as they are intelligent enough to have decided long ago that the so-called New Deal is nothing but a hopeless mess, from the standpoint of domestic policy, so they have sense enough to believe that another return to normalcy—and, incidentally, to smug isolationism—would be worse yet. If they have to make that choice, they will make what I believe to be the intelligent choice, as between them. They will continue to take the New Deal.

"I, for one, without warning that I would be standing here, am so glad that some of the intelligent, hard-hitting members of my party have sensed this problem and intend to do something about it, that I hardly know how to express my joy.

"Gentlemen, Mr. Chairman, if you will show the people of the United States that the election of a Republican administration does not mean another gang of inward-turning, narrow-minded isolationist stuffed shirts—if you will present to the people a big and broad-gauge man who will undertake to define and to pursue a problem for the participation by our fraction of the human race in such affairs as affect all of the human race, you will be given power just as surely as you are in this room, and what an opportunity and what a world stand before us! We are on the threshold of magnificent plenty and great, enlightened human cooperation, and we are just fumbling with the key to the lock.

"So, Mr. Chairman, don't falter in any respect. The failure, if it is a failure, may be the end of our party, and, what is more important, it could mean the end of our Republic in anything like the form which we have come so to love."

Action by Party Group Demanded

His remarks, because of their bluntness, overshadowed a drive at the conference to take over the official Republican post-war policy committee named by the Republican national chairman, Harrison Spangler.

At the request of Deneen Watson, chairman of the unofficial group, Mr. Watson was authorized to call on Mr. Spangler and demand action by the Spangler group on the platform adopted by the conference. Mr. Spangler was in New York yesterday, but had no comment to make on the demand. Since political leaders believe that the Spangler group was appointed to head off the Willkie group, a showdown in the near future seems likely.

Those attending the conference included organization Republicans from Connecticut and Vermont in force and a generous leavening of leading Republican figures from

Continued on Page Nine

'Dud' Enemy Bombs Make China's Dyes

So many of the Japanese bombs dropped in China's northwest territories have failed to explode that the picric acid taken from them has been found sufficient to dye this year's entire Chinese blanket supply, the New York Committee of the National War Fund revealed yesterday.

"Word to this effect reached the committee yesterday through United China Relief," the committee spokesman said. "In addition, the committee learned, the Japanese bomb canisters are being melted down and recast into farm implements.

"The blankets for which the Japanese are supplying the dye in this unintentional way are produced locally by the Chinese spinning and weaving cooperatives, which, with similar industrial cooperatives throughout free China, have proved a mainstay in China's fight."

PRICES ARE FROZEN IN EATING PLACES

April 4 to 10 Base Period for Fixing Charges in 250,000 Hotels and Restaurants

Restaurant and hotel prices of food and beverages were ordered frozen yesterday by the Office of Price Administration at the levels prevailing April 4 to 10, inclusive. The order was signed by Sylvan L. Joseph, regional administrator, and becomes effective next Monday. Two hundred and fifty thousand eating places from New York to Washington, D. C., are said to be affected.

Promulgation of the freeze order yesterday morning represented an abandonment of the attempt to hold restaurant and hotel food prices at the April scale entirely through voluntary cooperation by the trade. In a "statement of considerations" issued simultaneously with the order, Mr. Joseph said that "since April 10, 1943, restaurant prices have continued to rise and are threatening to rise further."

Area Reductions Coming

The statement said also that the OPA soon would begin the issuance of supplemental orders directing reductions in restaurant prices in special areas and by specified operators.

"Records of many operators showed wider gross operating margins in February, March and April, 1943, than in the corresponding period of 1942, together with very substantial increases in net operating costs," Mr. Joseph said.

The order applies to Region II of the OPA, which covers New York, New Jersey, Pennsylvania, Delaware, Maryland and the District of Columbia.

"In some areas within the region and for some operators there is every indication that the April 4-10 prices are excessive and should be rolled back," Mr. Joseph said. "As soon as further data are collected on these areas and operators, the necessary corrective action will be taken."

At the regional OPA offices it was indicated that restaurant prices in the New York City area were not as far out of line as in other sections. Washington and Baltimore were specifically cited by Mr. Joseph as areas in which there should be substantial roll-backs in eating place prices when

Continued on Page Thirteen

SOVIET SWEEPS ON

Red Army Captures 130 Populated Places in Advance on Orel

RUSSIANS 12 MILES AWAY

3 Prongs Closing on Nazi Base Despite Stubborn Fight—Axis Loses Rail City

By The Associated Press.

LONDON, Tuesday, July 20—Russian armies pounding on a semi-circle around Orel captured 130 villages and populated places in advances from four to six miles yesterday to the north, east and south of the great German base 200 miles south of Moscow, the Soviet command announced today.

Earlier reports from Moscow had placed the Red Army within twelve miles of Orel and said the Russians were wheeling up artillery within range of the city. Berlin reported the whole Russian front ablaze with Red Army attacks all the way from Leningrad to Novorossiisk in the western Caucasus.

Among the towns captured was Malo Arkhangelsk, twenty-five miles south of Orel, on the railway running to Russian-held Kursk.

Another seventy-two German tanks and ninety-six planes were destroyed, running the toll of attrition exacted from the Germans since their attack of July 5 to 3,516 tanks and 2,094 planes. These latest reported German losses were suffered Sunday.

The midnight communiqué, recorded by the Soviet monitor from the Moscow radio, said the Germans were fighting back stubbornly, mounting a dozen counter-attacks during Monday. All were declared repulsed with heavy losses.

Troops pounding down from the north achieved the greatest successes, scooping up seventy populated places, the communiqué said. Troops pressing up from the south toward a junction with the column atop and behind Orel were said to have captured twenty populated places. A junction of these columns would pinch off the Orel salient and trap large German forces in the base.

Other troops moving in frontally from the east were credited with seizing forty places.

Front Is "S"-Shaped

The 255-mile front from Belgorod to Sukhinichi is formed like an "S," with a German bulge in the Russian lines around Orel and with a Russian bulge pointing out from Kursk. It was in the Kursk area that the battle was joined July 5, when the Nazis opened their offensive.

The communiqué said only patrol activities had been reported from the Belgorod area at the extreme southern end of the front. It was near Belgorod that the Germans achieved some penetration early in the month, but were unable to exploit it.

[The Germans have brought

Continued on Page Five

RAID IS EXPLAINED

Axis Troops Were Using Rome Railways to Rush Aid to Sicily

BOMBERS ARE ACCURATE

Press Observers in the Planes See No Damage to Sacred Centers in the City

By HERBERT L. MATTHEWS

By Wireless to THE NEW YORK TIMES.

ALLIED HEADQUARTERS IN NORTH AFRICA, July 19—The last of the capitals of the warring powers in Europe to remain untouched today shook under the impact of one of the heaviest bombing raids yet launched in the Mediterranean theatre. Hitherto inviolate because it was the sacred city of Catholicism and all Christendom, it could no longer be ignored in the military strategy of the war, for it is the chief bottleneck for supplies from Germany and northern Italy.

It had to be bombed, but Catholics everywhere may rest assured that most extraordinary precautions were taken to avoid hitting Vatican City, any of the four ancient basilicas with which Christian history is linked or any other sacred targets. St. John Lateran was a mile and a half away. With precision bombing there was no possibility of coming anywhere near that "mother church" of the Catholic world.

The Vatican and St. Peter's were four miles away and their windows probably did not even rattle. In Pantellaria our planes dropped bombs within 1,000 yards of Allied troops quite safely, and any good bombardier can guarantee to leave unscathed anything half that distance from his target.

Three Military Targets Hit

Three highly important military targets, the San Lorenzo freight yards just outside the main railway station in the southeastern part of Rome, the Littorio freight yards on the northern edge and the Ciampino airfield four miles southeast of the city, received tremendous punishment in daylight today. No other parts of Rome were damaged.

I know because I was over Rome

Continued on Page Four

CIVILIANS IN SICILY SURRENDER THEIR ARMS

Turning in their weapons after our men captured Comiso

The New York Times Radiophoto, passed yesterday by censor

U. S. TROOPS PRESS MUNDA FROM EAST

Kill 179 Japanese in Advance—Salamaua Gain Made as Planes Aid Both Attacks

By TILLMAN DURDIN

By Wireless to THE NEW YORK TIMES.

ALLIED HEADQUARTERS IN THE SOUTHWEST PACIFIC, Tuesday, July 20—Allied ground forces made gains on both the Munda and Salamaua fronts yesterday against sharp fighting by the Japanese, Gen. Douglas MacArthur's communiqué today reported.

In the battle for Munda airdrome on New Georgia Island of the Central Solomons American troops enlarged a beachhead recently established at Lilio, about two and a half miles east of the enemy's airfield after a fierce engagement. One hundred and seventy-nine Japanese dead were counted in the sector the United States soldiers took over after the battle.

Punching into the Japanese defenses around Munda the Ameri-

Continued on Page Six

Americans Close In on Enna; Axis Center Is Breaking Up

By Wireless to THE NEW YORK TIMES.

ALLIED HEADQUARTERS IN NORTH AFRICA, July 19—Bronzed veterans of the British Eighth Army have hammered their way to within three miles of Catania, key to the defense of eastern Sicily, while in the center of the Allied advance American and Canadian forces have dashed through feeble Italian resistance to points ten miles from Enna, center of the island's road and railroad system.

The Americans stormed and captured Caltanissetta yesterday while to the southeast the Canadians drove the Italians out of Piazza-Armerina on the main road from the coast to Enna. Each of these towns is thirteen miles from Enna, whose possession will give the Allies control of transportation in central Sicily.

[American and British troops have reached Enna, the Moroccan radio reported. The Algiers radio said that aerial reconnaissance had noted the enemy's "general movement of retreat" toward Messina in northeastern Sicily. "By road and rail enemy forces are falling back on Messina with heavy and light equipment," it stated. The broadcasts were reported by the United States Foreign Broadcast Intelligence Service.

[The Algiers radio also broadcast a report that Axis headquarters in Sicily had been moved to Reggio Calabria in Italy. The Associated Press said.]

The Axis situation resembles a rout in the central sector, where Italians are surrendering by companies to the onrushing tide of khaki. The Allies have now captured 35,000 prisoners. The Americans have taken 23,000 of these, while the Eighth Army and Canadians have sent 12,000 back to their cages.

Only in the extreme east, in front of Catania, has resistance been stiff. The Germans have

Continued on Page Three

NOTED CHURCH HIT, ITALIANS REPORT

Stefani and Vatican Radio Say Pope Visited the Damaged San Lorenzo Basilica

By DANIEL T. BRIGHAM

By Telephone to THE NEW YORK TIMES

BERNE, Switzerland, July 19—Casualties in the bombing of Rome, according to Italian semi-official sources, were heavy. No official statement has been made.

The greatest damage was inflicted in the Prenestena workers' suburb, where, according to the Stefani news agency, civilian residences were pulverized. Stefani said damaged places included the Basilica of San Lorenzo fuori le Mura, property of the Vatican less than 500 yards from the San Lorenzo freight yards; the cemetery of Campo Verano, University City, the Polyclinic and the working-class quarters of San Lorenzo and Tiburtino.

The air-raid alarm lasted three hours, during most of which the bombers were overhead.

To counteract the effect of the Allied leaflets, warning of the bombing, fascist militiamen throughout the afternoon handed out leaflets reading:

"Italians! Allied planes have dropped leaflets over Italy calling on you to accept a dishonorable peace. While they drop these leaflets, however, those same Allied

Continued on Page Two

RAIL CENTERS HIT

San Lorenzo, Littorio Yards and Ciampino Airfield Targets

NO U. S. PLANES LOST

Religious Edifices Marked in Red on Fliers' Maps to Be Avoided at All Cost

By DREW MIDDLETON

By Wireless to THE NEW YORK TIMES.

ALLIED HEADQUARTERS IN NORTH AFRICA, July 19—Waves of Allied bombers pounded sprawling freight yards and other industrial military objectives at Rome this morning in the first air assault ever made on the capital of crumbling Italy.

[Most of the planes were American, manned by Americans. Cairo reports to The United Press said that British planes of the Middle East Command took part in the raid and John Thompson, representing the combined United States press, said British fighters aided in escorting the medium bombers. No American planes were missing, although some landed on emergency fields, according to The Associated Press. About 500 planes took part, according to the London radio.]

Weeks of special training prepared the Allied airmen for attacks only on military targets. The chief of these were freight yards, through which pass thousands of tons of military matériel each day and thousands of German reinforcements intended for Axis fighters in Sardinia and Sicily, or on their way south to hold the wavering Italian people in bondage.

Extensive war industries have been built up by Premier Mussolini in and around Rome in the belief that they would never be bombed by Allied air power. Many of these were built close to churches and shrines. In some holy places the vibration of high powered generating plants that run war factories can be felt.

Leaflets Warn Population

Allied bombardiers also attacked these war industries as they flew high over the city, whose population of about 1,200,000 had been warned of the raid by leaflets dropped before the bombs were dropped. These leaflets said that Italians or Germans might bomb the center of Rome or even Vatican City in an effort to rouse Catholic opinion throughout the world against the Allies.

[The basilica of San Lorenzo fuori le Mura was "seriously damaged" and was visited by Pope Pius, according to the Vatican radio.]

The attack on Rome was the climax of months of careful planning. Once it was decided that railroad yards and industrial objectives in and around Italy's capital had to be bombed to check the flow of troops and matériel southward special bomber crews were selected for training.

A huge map of the target areas was studied by each crew. Pilots, navigators and bombardiers memorized it so well that before the start of the mission they had a clear picture not only of their targets but also of the exact location of Vatican City, holy places, architectural treasures and museums that were to be left untouched.

The briefing was done by intelligence officers who had lived in Rome before the war and who knew the locations of factories and railroad junctions, which the Italians believed were immune from bombing because of their location.

Rome a Railway Center

The Italian capital is one of five great junctions that control the Italian railroads. The others are Naples, Foggia, Milan and Bologna. Naples and Foggia have been hammered by bombers flying from this theatre.

Two main railroads from Genoa and Bologna enter Rome from the north. There is a spur line to the

Continued on Page Three

War News Summarized

TUESDAY, JULY 20, 1943

Rome, the only European capital of the great warring countries to have been spared the horrors of war, was heavily bombed by Allied airmen yesterday. Fliers of the Mediterranean Air Command from North Africa and Libya concentrated upon military targets after earlier planes had dropped leaflets warning the people of the impending attack and promising to avoid all cultural and religious centers. After the attack Rome, the military center, was devastated, but Rome, "the Eternal City" was untouched.

The three principal targets were the San Lorenzo railroad yards in southeast Rome, the Littorio yards at the northern edge of the city and the Ciampino airfield, four miles southeast of the city. Liberators of the Ninth United States Air Force were over the Littorio yards for more than an hour and dropped 350 tons of bombs. In its warning leaflets the Allied command said the yards were "of the greatest importance to the Axis war effort and in particular to the movement of German troops." [1:8; map, P. 3.]

How well the Allies respected their pledge not to harm Vatican City and other shrines was attested by a correspondent of THE NEW YORK TIMES, who was one of seven newspaper men in a Flying Fortress that was part of the last wave to attack Rome. The pilots and bombardiers had been specially trained for weeks before the raid and the sacred places were marked on their maps "must on no account be damaged." [1:4.]

The Axis immediately condemned the attack upon the center of Catholicism. Rome said the Pope planned a protest to President Roosevelt and Prime Minister Churchill. [1:7.] London accepted the raid as a military necessity [1:6-7] and Washington observers voiced general approval mixed with regret that the bombing finally had to take place. [3:1.]

In Sicily, Allied troops continued their advances. Americans captured Caltinesetta, the Canadians took Piazza Armerina, and both closed in on Enna. The British were overcoming fierce opposition on the outskirts of Catania. [1:6-7; map P. 2.] A formation of Lightning P-38s annihilated a force of fifteen Junkers-52 transport planes rushing reinforcements from Sardinia. [3:5.]

In Russia, the Red Army advanced another five miles to within twelve miles of Orel, capturing 130 inhabited places during the advance. [1:3.]

Allied forces in the South Pacific edged closer to the Japanese airfield at Munda on New Georgia Island and the enemy base at Salamaua, New Guinea. [1:5.]

More than 300 Republicans, including party leaders and office holders from northeastern States, met in this city yesterday, and served notice that unless the party dropped its "narrow isolationism" the voters would have no other choice than to vote for a fourth term. [1:1.]

Green Warns of Wage Demands Unless Food Prices Are Reduced

Special to THE NEW YORK TIMES.

DETROIT, July 19—Charging that the Government had failed to hold the line against inflation and that labor and consumers were being discriminated against by Congress, William Green, president of the American Federation of Labor, declared in an address here today that "unless prices of food are brought down to a reasonable level" organized labor will have "no other recourse but to demand wage increases."

He spoke before 700 delegates to the national convention of the Brotherhood of Maintenance of Way Employes and his speech was applauded.

Delivering what was in effect an ultimatum to Government agencies having to do with wage and price controls, he asserted that "drastic action must be taken at once to avert a breakdown of our wartime economy."

"Our domestic war economy," he said, "has not been geared to the need of protecting the workers against the hazards of inflation and its concomitant evils. This situation is becoming more and more serious each day. Profiteers and speculators are sapping the strength of the nation's army of workers."

He declared that AFL surveys showed that food prices had increased from 50 to 200 per cent since the beginning of the war and demanded "intelligent and orderly action to assure workers and their families of a decent place to live in and enough nourishing food to

Continued on Page Ten

British Press Is Solid in Support Of Bombing War Targets in Rome

By JAMES MacDONALD

By Cable to THE NEW YORK TIMES.

LONDON, Tuesday, July 20—If the British press is any guide to public opinion then that opinion is unanimous in its endorsement of yesterday's air raid against military objectives in Rome.

It is universally recognized that Rome is unique in that it embraces Vatican City and has many cultural monuments. At the same time it is emphasized that Rome also has important objectives such as freight yards and key railroad lines that are liable to legitimate attack.

The Times of London says that much unnecessary and irrelevant controversy over the Rome bombing will be averted if people bear in mind that the raid was a "military operation, pure and simple." The editorial reminds its readers that it was clearly intimated months ago by the United States and British Governments that they regarded Rome as containing objectives subject to legitimate attack.

It says terrorization by promiscuous bombing is not and never has been a factor in Allied strategy and adds:

"No Allied commander in his senses would send young airmen to risk their lives in destruction of 'cultural monuments.' The war will be won by unconditional concentration upon the ruin of the armed forces and war potential of the enemy. To that purpose our bombing policy has conformed and will continue to conform and from

Continued on Page Four

"All the News That's Fit to Print."

The New York Times.

LATE CITY EDITION
Moderately warm today, with gentle winds.
Temperatures Yesterday—Max., 85; Min., 70
Sunrise, 5:46 A. M.; Sunset, 8:19 P. M.

Copyright, 1943, by The New York Times Company.

VOL. XCII..No. 31,229. Entered as Second-Class Matter, Postoffice, New York, N. Y. NEW YORK, MONDAY, JULY 26, 1943. THREE CENTS IN NEW YORK CITY

MUSSOLINI OUSTED WITH FASCIST CABINET; BADOGLIO, HIS FOE, MADE PREMIER BY KING; SHIFT BELIEVED FIRST STEP TOWARD PEACE

PEACE INITIATIVE URGED BY WALLACE ON AMERICA NOW

For 'Common Man' He Asks Full Production, Employment and Security

WITH DEMOCRACY FOR ALL

Vice President, at Detroit, Accuses 'Fascists' of Trying to Undermine Roosevelt

The text of Mr. Wallace's address is on Page 10.

By The United Press.

DETROIT, July 25—Vice President Henry A. Wallace called upon America today to take the initiative now and plan a war-proof post-war world pledged to enlightenment of all peoples, "full production and full employment" and cooperation with other nations to enforce international justice and security.

Urging America to heed a destiny "that calls us to world leadership," he assailed "small but powerful groups which put money and power first and people last" and declared that "nothing will prevail against the common man's peace in a common man's world."

A crowd of 20,000, composed predominantly of workers, filled the center grandstand at the State fairgrounds track to hear Mr. Wallace's thirty-minute address, "America tomorrow," which was also broadcast by radio.

"Defeatists" for "Good Old Days"

The Vice President deviated from his prepared address to voice indirectly the charge he made yesterday that "certain American Fascists" had turned against the present Administration because President Roosevelt "stopped Washington from being a way station on the way to Wall Street."

He asserted that "defeatists who talk about going back to the good old days of Americanism (after the war) mean the time when there was plenty for the few and scarcity for the many."

Then, departing from his text, he raised his right arm and said:

"Or the days when Washington was only a way station in the suburbs of Wall Street."

Mr. Wallace was introduced by R. J. Thomas, president of the United Automobile Workers, CIO, as "the architect and crusader for a new world."

It was Mr. Wallace's first address since President Roosevelt abolished the Board of Economic Warfare, which Mr. Wallace had headed, to end a public quarrel between the Vice President and Secretary of Commerce Jesse Jones over war buying policies.

Roosevelt Foes Denounced

Indicating no rift in his relations with the President, Wallace assailed persons sniping at the Chief Executive while he is engaged in prosecuting the war.

He charged that powerful money-minded groups—"some call them isolationists, some reactionaries and others American Fascists"—seek to destroy Mr. Roosevelt's domestic achievements of the past ten years by capitalizing on his preoccupation with the war.

"I have known the President intimately for ten years and in the final showdown he has always put human rights first," he said. "Sooner or later the machinations of these small but powerful groups which put money and power first and people last will inevitably be exposed to the public eye."

He inveighed against those who oppose post-war planning now to hold to the realities of the past or cling to the present without thought of the future.

"Both opinions," he said, "are fighting delaying actions against our destiny in the peace—a destiny

Continued on Page Ten

Cheers Halt Games As Duce Strikes Out

The thousands of baseball spectators at parks where the Mussolini incident was announced yesterday roared and jumped up from their seats. Games were halted as happy men and women thronged the aisles and shouted the news to each other.

At the Yankee Stadium, where 36,779 had suffered with the Yankees as the New Yorkers lost the first game of a double-header to the White Sox, baseball momentarily ceased to exist when the news of the resignation came through the loudspeakers in the sixth inning of the second contest. The rest of the announcement, to the effect that King Victor Emmanuel had taken over, was lost in the tumultuous reaction.

A similar circumstance was reported in Pittsburgh, where 30,309 onlookers saw the Pirates sweep a double-header from the Brooklyn Dodgers.

NORTH JERSEY OPA DROPS DRIVING BAN

Maze of Rulings, Plus Vacation Permits, Is Too Confusing—Inspectors Tired of Abuse

Enforcement of the "pleasure driving" ban in northern New Jersey broke down completely yesterday with Office of Price Administration officials in that area frankly admitting that they were making no effort to enforce the restriction. New Jersey highways leading from bridge and tunnel exits that had been more or less deserted since initiation of the "pleasure ban" were heavily burdened yesterday with motorists blandly disregarding the ban and inspectors conspicuous by their absence.

OPA inspectors indicated that they were "throwing up the sponge" because they found themselves entangled in a maze of conflicting rulings from Washington and by local ration boards. In addition they are tired of being sneeringly referred to as "Gestapo agents, sneaks and snoopers" by drivers they stop for questioning.

No Inspectors on Roads

"It is true there were no inspectors on the highways today," Nathan L. Jacobs, chief OPA enforcement attorney in the northern New Jersey area, said. "We have discovered that ration boards have issued so many vacation permits that it is a waste of time to stop cars."

While other OPA officials refused to be quoted it was generally conceded that no effort was being made to enforce the "pleasure ban."

"We are continuing to the best of our ability to enforce the law," an inspector declared. "However, the maze of conflicting rulings

Continued on Page Thirty-two

RUSSIANS PUSH ON

Drive 2½ Miles Closer to Orel and Take 30 More Villages

NAZI STAND STIFFER

Enemy Counter-Attacks Desperately to Hold Escape Corridor

By The Associated Press.

LONDON, Monday, July 26—The great Russian counter-offensive battering upon Orel from three directions engulfed thirty more populated places and swept forward two and a half to five and a half miles yesterday, Moscow announced in a special communiqué. Complete encirclement of the great Nazi base appeared only a matter of time.

Red Army columns driving down behind Orel have cut to within seven miles or so of the Bryansk railway feeding supplies and reinforcements into the stronghold.

The Russians are steadily narrowing the fifty-mile escape corridor held open by the half-encircled Germans, for another Soviet column is pushing up from the south to the west of the city.

Beating down severe German counter-attacks, the Red Army slogged on to capture the important railroad station of Glazunovka and the populated places of Popovov, Chizhovka and Narykovo on the western bank of the Oka River northeast of Orel, said the communiqué, broadcast by Moscow and recorded by the Soviet monitor.

Other villages included among the thirty reported captured yesterday were Rybnitsa, Gremyache, Zakharovka, Lebedikha, Voronets, Verkhneye Sagino and Nizhneye Sagino.

South, in the Belgorod area, there were scouting engagements and "fighting of local importance," while scouts increased their activities in the battle areas on the Donets front still farther south, it added.

Advance on Three Sides

The regular midnight communiqué said the Red Army had advanced on the north, east and south sides of Orel, knocking out twenty-eight tanks, killing 2,840 Germans, taking prisoners and capturing an important height on the south side of the city.

Several populated places were captured east and south of Orel, the announcement added. In several places the Germans mounted strong counter-attacks.

In other sectors, the communiqué said, twenty-one more German tanks were destroyed and over 800 Germans killed.

A previous special announcement of the Soviet command had declared that the German wedge, nine by twenty-two miles, that had been driven into Russian lines at

Continued on Page Eight

LONDON IS CAUTIOUS

Evidence of Crack in the Rome-Berlin Axis Is Viewed With Joy

BADOGLIO 'WAR HERO'

Britons See Possibility of His Being 'Front' for Fascist Deal

By RAYMOND DANIELL
By Cable to THE NEW YORK TIMES.

LONDON, Monday, July 26—London's first reaction to the news that Benito Mussolini had stepped down as head of the Fascist Government of Italy was that it left the military situation unchanged.

It was seen as the first tangible evidence of a crack in the Rome-Berlin Axis. But emphasis was put on the point that, whatever internal troubles led Signor Mussolini to get out in favor of Marshal Pietro Badoglio on the eve of his sixtieth birthday after twenty years of dictatorship over Italy, King Victor Emmanuel's proclamation made it clear that for the moment at least Italy intended to carry on the fight.

The possibility that the dramatic shift in leadership by Italy might be the forerunner of an attempt to sue for a separate peace was not overlooked, however.

For a long time it has been suspected here that, when things got too tough for the Fascists or the Nazis in the Reich, they would try to save their necks by elevating someone they believed acceptable to the United Nations as front man to arrange a soft armistice.

Not Trusted by Britain

Marshal Badoglio, 73-year-old Italian Army Chief, who has been regarded as a critic of Mussolini and as a bogus friend of Britain, is one of those men. Count Dino Grandi, a former Ambassador to London, is another.

But the fact that Victor Emmanuel chose his old friend, Marshal Badoglio, who rallied Italy in World War I after the Caporetto disaster, instead of Count Grandi, is susceptible to two interpretations.

The first, taking the proclamations of the Italian King and his new Premier at their face value, is

Continued on Page Five

ONE IS OUT, THE OTHER IN

Benito Mussolini and his successor as Premier, Marshal Pietro Badoglio — Associated Press

British Eighth Army Opens New Drive to Take Catania

By DREW MIDDLETON
By Wireless to THE NEW YORK TIMES.

ALLIED HEADQUARTERS IN NORTH AFRICA, July 25—Routed in the west by the hard-hitting American Seventh Army, the battered Axis forces are retreating across the north central sector of Sicily today to the sanctuary of the Germans' new "Etna line." The southern and southwestern faces of this line are already being hammered by the British Eighth Army, which is inflicting dreadful casualties on the stubborn German defenders of the position. The Canadian forces, striking northward and northeastward on the Eighth Army's left flank, are making good progress. [The Canadians have driven a wedge well into the enemy's lines, the United Press said.]

After two weeks of smashing success unequaled by any other American Army in this war, the Seventh Army is wheeling east-

Continued on Page Three

BERLIN RADIO SEES MUSSOLINI AS 'ILL'

First Nazi Comment Arrives Five Hours Late—Official Statement Lacking

LONDON, Monday, July 26 (AP)—The Berlin radio in its first comment on the Mussolini resignation—made almost five hours after Rome's first announcement—quoted the Italian-Stefani news agency as saying that the change of Italian Government was believed to have been owing to the Premier's health. Premier Mussolini "has been ill for some time," Berlin said.

Official Comment Lacking

By Telephone to THE NEW YORK TIMES.

BERNE, Switzerland, Monday, July 26—Official quarters in Berlin were still out of telephonic touch with Berne at an early hour Monday morning, and authoritative reaction to the resignation of Signor Mussolini and his Cabinet

Continued on Page Two

ITALY SEEN MAKING FIRST PEACE STEP

Observers in Washington Look for Similar Action by Axis Satellites in Balkans

By HAROLD CALLENDER
Special to THE NEW YORK TIMES.

WASHINGTON, July 25—The transfer of power in Italy from Premier Mussolini to Marshal Pietro Badoglio was interpreted by military and diplomatic observers tonight as a first step toward an Italian appeal for peace. They thought that this would be quickly followed by similar appeals from Hungary, Rumania and Bulgaria, which might seek favorable terms by acting swiftly.

The immediate consequences, military men thought, would be an Allied occupation of Italy, especially the air bases in the north near the German border, and the surrender of the Italian Army, Navy and air fleet.

In diplomatic circles it was predicted that Marshal Badoglio would seek a negotiated peace, but it was assumed that the unconditional surrender doctrine would be applied in the qualified form given to it by the recent statement to Italians by President Roosevelt and Prime Minister Churchill. This implied generous treatment for Italy once the fascist regime had disappeared.

It has been authoritatively indicated here that the Allied Govern-

Continued on Page Six

ARRESTS REPORTED

Berne Hears the Fascist Leaders Are Being Held in Homes

'PEACE' CRY IN ROME

Nazis in Milan Said to Have Fired on Mob of Demonstrators

By DANIEL T. BRIGHAM
By Telephone to THE NEW YORK TIMES.

BERNE, Switzerland, July 25—King Victor Emmanuel announced to Italy tonight that he had accepted the "resignations" of Premier Benito Mussolini and his entire Cabinet. He ordered Marshal Pietro Badoglio to form a military government "to continue the conduct of the war."

The announcement was made in a proclamation that was broadcast to the people of Italy from Rome at 11 P. M. Rome time. The Rome radio then signed off for twenty minutes, resuming its broadcast at 11:20 to carry a proclamation by Marshal Badoglio. Before giving this, however, the announcer said:

"With the fall of Mussolini and his band, Italy has taken the first step toward peace. Finished is the shame of fascism! Long live peace! Long live the King!"

Badoglio Says He'll Fight

Marshal Badoglio's proclamation was then read. It appealed to the nation for "calm" in this hour of trial, saying:

"Italians! On the demand of His Majesty the King-Emperor, I have assumed the military government of the country with full powers. The war will continue. Italy, bruised, her provinces invaded, and her cities ruined, will retain her faith in her given word, jealous of her ancient traditions.

"We must tighten our ranks behind the King-Emperor, the living image of the country, who stands as an example for all today. The task I have been charged with is clear and precise. It will be executed scrupulously, and whoever believes he can interrupt the normal progress of events or whoever seeks to disturb internal order will be struck down without mercy.

"Long live Italy! Long live the King! PIETRO BADOGLIO."

For the first time in twenty-one years the Italian radio signed off a nation-wide program by playing only the royal march. "Giovinezza," the fascist anthem, like fascism, is dead.

[Field Marshal General Albert Kesselring, German Commander in Chief in Italy, and Hans-Georg Viktor von Mackensen, the Ger-

Continued on Page Three

War News Summarized

MONDAY, JULY 26, 1943

The Fascists surrendered their control over Italy yesterday when Premier Mussolini quit. He presented his own resignation and those of his Cabinet to King Victor Emmanuel, who immediately accepted them and named Marshal Badoglio as Prime Minister. Thus, after twenty years of complete power, Mussolini became the first Axis dictator to have run his course.

The King gave the news to the world when a proclamation signed by him was broadcast to the Italian people, saying that Marshal Badoglio would form a military government to continue the conduct of the war. The Rome radio announcer declared the development was the first step toward peace, but the Marshal said the war would go on.

The Italian people immediately demonstrated in the streets, looking for Blackshirts. A report from Milan said German troops had fired on demonstrators. [All the foregoing 1:8.]

While London welcomed the first sign of a crack in the Rome-Berlin Axis, observers were not too greatly impressed. They saw in it an effort to make the best peace terms by putting an anti-Fascist at the head of the Italian Government. They also saw an attempt by the Italian King to save his crown. [1:4.]

The Italian political upheaval served to overshadow what was one of the most active days on the military fronts. Allied troops in Sicily were pressing the Axis defenders into a small triangle, with Messina as the apex. [1:5-6; map P. 2.] Flying Fortresses flew 1,500 miles without meeting any opposition to blast the north Italian rail junction at Bologna, while other planes concentrated on southern Italian communications. [3:1.]

British and American air forces struck their heaviest blows against Germany. The RAF rocked Hamburg Saturday night with 2,500 tons of bombs. Yesterday Flying Fortresses hit that port again and pounded Kiel and other centers. The RAF's big bombers raided Germany again last night. [1:6-7.]

The Red Army captured another thirty villages, halted incessant German counter-attacks and virtually encircled the enemy base at Orel. [1:3.]

The Fourteenth United States Air Force in China beat off four waves of more than 100 planes when the Japanese attacked advanced American bases in Hunan Province. Forty-four enemy planes were destroyed or damaged; damage to the air bases was slight. [9:4.]

More than 200 Allied planes gave the beleagured Japanese base at Munda, in the Solomons, its heaviest bombing of the South Pacific war. [9:1.]

Mayor Sees Slight Hope for Meat; Warns City Will Boycott $1 Eggs

Although the meat supply for New York City looks better for the coming week, there is no assurance that the civilian population will get it, Mayor Fiorello H. La Guardia warned yesterday in his weekly radio broadcast. He said the black market would continue until there was proper identification of meat, tracing it from the slaughterhouse to the retailer.

The outlook is serious on eggs, the Mayor said, with prices at present as high as 66 cents a dozen for jumbos, 62 cents for extra large and 60 cents for large. He said the news that the price ceilings of eggs would go up about a cent a week was "disturbing" and that some persons were predicting egg prices would reach $1 a dozen before winter.

"I hope not," he declared. "Now I just want to serve notice on everybody that if eggs continue to increase in price much higher and before it arrives at the dollar a dozen, we in New York will adjust ourselves to substitutes for eggs. I hope that will not be necessary, but I am not in a position now to say that New York City will take a-dollar-a-dozen eggs without protest."

Mayor La Guardia expressed disappointment that the Office of Price Administration and the Food Distribution Administration had not yet taken final action on his proposal to cut the ration point values of pork products and eliminate some of them from rationing entirely, which, he said, would have relieved the meat situation.

"Our Government is paying millions of dollars in subsidies to

Continued on Page Thirty-two

Biggest RAF-U. S. Raids on Reich Blast Hamburg, Hit Baltic Cities

By The United Press.

LONDON, Monday, July 26—United States heavy bombers struck deep and hard into Germany by daylight yesterday, hammering aircraft factories at the Baltic port of Warnemuende and showering hundreds of high explosives into the smoking ruins of Hamburg, gutted by the British Royal Air Force's night bombers twelve hours earlier in the greatest bombing assault of the war.

At the same time, other American heavies struck in force at the great German shipyards in Kiel and raided the Baltic industrial center of Wustrow, twenty-five miles west of Rostock.

The attack marked the biggest around-the-clock aerial assaults yet made by the American-British bombing teams. The raid on Warnemuende, seaport for the big manufacturing center of Rostock, was the deepest penetration of Germany yet made by the United States Eighth Air Force.

The RAF's night bombers in fifty blazing minutes blasted Hamburg with 2,300 tons of explosive and incendiary bombs, a far greater weight of bombs than ever before had been dropped in a single operation. [The British Air Ministry gives its figures in tons of 2,240 pounds; at 2,000 pounds to the ton, the RAF blasted Hamburg with 2,576 tons of bombs.]

RAF heavy bombers returned to the assault on Germany during last night, British officials reported early today. Channel coast watchers reported that a ninety-minute procession of heavy bombers flew

Continued on Page Seven

Mayor Expects Italy To Surrender Soon

Mayor Fiorello H. La Guardia declared yesterday afternoon that in view of the dismissal of Premier Benito Mussolini he expected the complete capitulation of Italy within a few days.

His statement follows:

"I anticipate the complete capitulation of Italy within the next few days. Of course to me it's a source of great satisfaction that Mussolini has been finally discovered. He will go down in history as the betrayer of Italy.

"If there is one amusing sidelight to this whole thing, that is the cheap, gutter politicians in this country who catered to Mussolini when they thought he was going strong. I had to fight that very tendency in 1929 and 1933.

"In so far as Italy is concerned, she is out of the war.

"We must now prepare to meet the situation, as the Nazis will consolidate their lines. The Office of War Information is now free to release the appeal that I made to the King several months ago."

"All the News That's Fit to Print."

The New York Times.

LATE CITY EDITION
Warm and humid today; light w... s.
Temperatures Yesterday—Max., 85; Min., 72
Sunrise, 5:46 A. M.; Sunset, 8:18 P. M.

VOL. XCII..No. 31,230. Entered as Second-Class Matter, Postoffice, New York, N. Y. NEW YORK, TUESDAY, JULY 27, 1943. THREE CENTS IN NEW YORK CITY

ITALY PUT UNDER MARTIAL LAW BY BADOGLIO TO PREVENT CIVIL WAR; FASCIST RULE ENDED; HAMBURG BLASTED AGAIN; RUSSIANS DRIVE ON

30 MINERS INDICTED AS KEY PROMOTERS OF WILDCAT STRIKE

Grand Jury at Pittsburgh First to Act Under New Federal War Labor Disputes Law

STIFF PENALTIES LOOM

Government Charges Coal Pits It Was Operating Were Tied Up by Leaders of Walkout

By LOUIS STARK
Special to The New York Times.

WASHINGTON, July 26—Thirty leaders of the recent strike by insurgent coal miners in southwestern Pennsylvania were named in indictments returned today by a Federal grand jury at Pittsburgh, the first to be handed down on charges of violating the new Smith-Connally War Labor Disputes Law. Under the law the maximum penalty is a fine of $5,000 or imprisonment for one year, or both, on each count.

The defendants are charged with having directed strikes and to have otherwise interrupted the operations of twenty-four coal mines which were in the possession of the Government.

The indictments, which were disclosed here by Attorney General Francis Biddle, charge violations of the law beginning June 26 and continuing up to the present time. All the defendants are officers or members of local unions of the United Mine Workers of America.

The May grand jury reconvened July 14 after Charles F. Uhl, Federal attorney, had petitioned Federal Judge F. P. Schoonmaker for the grand jury's consideration of "matters of great importance to the United States."

FBI Investigates Strike

After a refusal by the insurgent leaders to obey the orders of their union officials to return to work, the grand jury investigation was begun. Agents of the Federal Bureau of Investigation spent several weeks in the coal region gathering evidence.

Large numbers of miners had refused to return to work at the end of the third coal strike called since May 1 by John L. Lewis and the United Mine Workers. Their refusal was based on the fact that their leaders had not succeeded in arranging a contract with the bituminous coal operators.

Interruption of production by the insurgents caused a temporary shutdown of steel furnaces and by-product coke plants in the California-Brownsville district of Pennsylvania.

The cases were presented to the grand jury by Henry Schweinhaut and Irving Hill, special assistants to the Attorney General, assisted by the Federal attorney, Mr. Uhl.

In one indictment against twenty-one defendants there is one count charging them with conspiring to interfere by strike and by other interruptions with production in all the Government-operated coal mines in Fayette, Greene and Washington Counties, and thus to bring about a complete work stoppage.

The other nineteen counts in this indictment charge the defendants with specific acts of interference, such as recruiting, securing, transporting and leading pickets; picketing, inducing and encouraging mine employes to strike, and the calling of local union meetings at which they endorsed, urged and counseled strikes.

21 Named in One Indictment

Defendants under this indictment include the following:

Alphonse Congello, Tower Hill, Pa. —Employed at the Isabella mine and president of the Isabella Local, UMW.

Anider Barnes, Allison, Pa.—Employed at the Isabella mine and a member of the Isabella Local, UMW.

Alvin Bindle, Brownsville, Pa. Employed at the Bridgeport mine and check-weigh man for Bridgeport Local, UMW.

Williard Biddle, Brownsville—Em-

Continued on Page Twenty-one

Wake Isle Bombed, Axis Radio Reports

A Tokyo dispatch broadcast by the Berlin radio yesterday said that eight Liberator bombers had attacked Japanese-held Wake Island early Sunday, The Associated Press reported.

Two of the raiders were declared to have been brought down, against a loss of two Japanese fighter planes, one of which was credited with purposely crashing into one of the bombers to carry it to earth. The broadcast did not touch on the damage aground.

Presumably the planes were American-manned, although the report of the raid was not confirmed in United States announcements.

8 FROM U. S. INDICTED AS AIDING THE AXIS

Ezra Pound, Jane Anderson and Other Expatriates Face Trials for Treason

Special to The New York Times.

WASHINGTON, July 26—Eight American citizens, including two women, who have been broadcasting Axis propaganda from Germany and Italy, were indicted for treason today by a District of Columbia grand jury. Whenever possible, they will be tried and on conviction can be punished by penalties ranging from death down to five years and a $1,000 fine.

Seven have been sending out their venom by radio short-wave from Germany. The eighth broadcasts from Rome. The grand jury named them as these:

Ezra Pound, 57, Idaho-born poet, at one time of New York.

Frederick Wilhelm Kaltenbach, 48, formerly of Dubuque, Iowa.

Robert Henry Best, 47, formerly of Sumter, S. C.

Douglas Chandler, 54, formerly of Baltimore.

Edward Leo Delaney, 57, formerly of Olney, Ill.

Constance Drexel, 48, a native of Germany, once employed in Philadelphia.

Jane Anderson, 50, formerly of Atlanta.

Max Oscar Otto Koischwitz, 41, formerly of New York.

Pound has been broadcasting from Rome. The others are hired by the Nazis and transmit from Berlin and other Reich points.

The action of the grand jury proves, said Attorney General Francis Biddle, that this country "will not tolerate traitors at home or abroad.

"It is our intention when we can," he added, "to apprehend these defendants and to bring them to trial before a jury of their fellow-citizens, whom they are charged with betraying.

"It should be clearly understood that these indictments are based not only on the content of the propaganda statements, the lies and falsifications which were uttered, but also on the simple fact

Continued on Page Six

FORTRESSES STRIKE

Hit Hamburg 4th Blow in Two Days—Pound Other Reich Ports

RAF BATTERS ESSEN

2,000-Ton Bombing of Ruhr City a Part of Vast Air Offensive

By The United Press.

LONDON, Tuesday, July 27—Guided by a 20,000-foot column of smoke rising from the burning city, American Flying Fortresses blasted Hamburg yesterday for the fourth pounding of the big enemy port in forty-eight hours and also hit Wilhelmshaven and Wesermuende to lay out a flaming path of destruction across Germany's northwest coast.

Still another Fortress formation swept far inland and wrecked one of Germany's biggest synthetic rubber plants at Hanover, 112 miles west of Berlin, as the Allied air offensive rose to a new pitch that saw more than 2,000 heavy bombers and many hundreds of smaller aircraft loosing their fury.

The unescorted Fortresses encountered strong enemy fighter opposition and shot down more than fifty German planes.

Since midday Saturday there has been hardly an hour of the day or night without the crash of Allied bombs on Germany and Nazi-occupied territory. Of all the targets, Hamburg had taken the worst beating.

Essen Blow Is Concentrated

Yesterday's daylight attacks followed the heaviest raid of the war on Essen in the Ruhr by Royal Air Force heavy bombers over Sunday night. British and Canadian planes dropped 2,000 tons of explosive and incendiary bombs on the No. 1 Nazi arms center and home of the great Krupp Works. Fires of gigantic proportions sent smoke four miles into the air, pilots said.

The blasting of Essen was "concentrated and effective," carried out within fifty minutes beginning at 12:25 A. M., the British Air Ministry said.

In addition, on Sunday night the RAF sent out fast Mosquito bombers that made an attack on Hamburg and raided Cologne. The Bomber Command planes shot down two Nazi fighters during the night.

Mosquito planes of the British Fighter Command flew on intruder patrol over Nazi bases in northwest Germany, the Low Countries and France, destroying three Nazi planes.

By daylight, medium bombers of the United States Eighth Air Force struck at the St. Omer airfield in north France and "good bombing results were reported on all targets," said a joint American-British communiqué.

Many squadrons of RAF and Allied Spitfire fighters and Ty-

Continued on Page Five

Mussolini's Arrest In Flight Reported

By The Associated Press.

LONDON, July 26—Stockholm and Berne dispatches reported the broken Benito Mussolini had been arrested while trying to flee to German sanctuary from the nation he brought to the brink of disaster after twenty-one years of dictatorship.

Mussolini was said in a dispatch from Berne, Switzerland, to be under heavy guard at a villa near Rome, but this was not confirmed directly from Italy.

LONDON, July 26 (UP)—The extraordinarily stern martial law regime in Italy, suspending every normal means of travel, might indicate determination by the new government that Benito Mussolini must not escape.

AMERICANS DRIVE FOR EASTERN SICILY

Seventh Army Races to Join Big Offensive on Enemy's Last Major Defenses

By DREW MIDDLETON
By Wireless to The New York Times.

ALLIED HEADQUARTERS IN NORTH AFRICA, July 26—The victorious American Seventh Army smashed eastward today to join in the general assault on the "Etna line," taking 7,000 more prisoners including six generals and an admiral. More than 70,000 prisoners are already in the Allies' hands.

The Germans rushed the Twenty-ninth Motorized Infantry Division into the Messina bridgehead, increasing the number of Axis combat troops in northeastern Sicily to about 97,000. Of these, about 52,000 are Germans.

Planes Attack Northern Port

While the ground forces concentrated for what may be the final struggle of the campaign, Allied planes attacked the north coast port of Milazzo, through which the Germans have been moving supplies and troops since Messina was made virtually useless by Allied bombs. The port was heavily bombed by Royal Air Force Bostons and Mitchells of the United

Continued on Page Two

OUR TERMS STAND

Hull Cites 'Surrender,' Calls Italy's Status a Military Question

PRESIDENT CHEERFUL

Recent U. S. Contact With Badoglio or House of Savoy Is Denied

By HAROLD CALLENDER
Special to The New York Times.

WASHINGTON, July 26—That the exit of Italy from the war was for the present a military question and that the Allies' "unconditional surrender" terms were unlikely to be modified was indicated by Secretary of State Cordell Hull and other officials here today.

President Roosevelt made no comment, but visitors reported him in a cheerful mood that they associated with the news from Rome.

Mr. Hull denied reports that this Government had been in contact with Marshal Pietro Badoglio recently. To a question regarding similar contacts with the Vatican in connection with Italy's future, he replied he had heard nothing to that effect.

As to negotiations with Italy's royal house of Savoy, Mr. Hull said he had not discussed that with the President and so far as the State Department was concerned the question had not arisen.

Fighting Is Our Present Task

While remarking that fascism carried within it the seeds of its own destruction and that the timely and appropriate end of Benito Mussolini's power seemed to him the first major step in the early and complete destruction and eradication of every vestige of fascism, nationally and internationally, Mr. Hull insisted that everything waited upon military developments.

When asked what this Government was doing meanwhile, he replied that we were fighting like the devil.

To a question whether unconditional surrender applied to Hungary, Rumania and Bulgaria as well as the major Axis countries,

Continued on Page Three

Badoglio's Cabinet Is Seen As Step to Avoid Surrender

Berne Diplomats Expect Negotiations for an 'Honorable Capitulation' While German Forces Get Time to Flee

By Telephone to The New York Times.

BERNE, Switzerland, July 26—With a celerity indicative of definite ideas of what his task would be, Premier Pietro Badoglio announced tonight the members of his "transitory military government which will operate with full powers from the King."

It contains not one new member who might not belong to an "armistice cabinet." Several might have belonged to a new "conservative fascist" government, but none belongs to the rabidly "anarchistic" group hitherto in the saddle, which was prepared to sacrifice all for survival.

The new government is expected in diplomatic quarters here to present a "solid national front" to the Allies while Premier Badoglio negotiates an "honorable capitulation" rather than an "unconditional surrender."

While peace negotiations may already be under way—such a report was semi-officially denied in Italian diplomatic circles tonight—his next greatest task will then be to present a sop to Germany, which still has strong forces in Italy, by giving German commanders more time for "preliminary" evacuation. This point, it is believed, is what caused the marshal to say last night that the war would continue.

Having successfully negotiated these first two hurdles, he would then face the problem of an "orderly and peaceful reconstruction" without revolution fomented by the long-suppressed parties with socialist leanings. His tasks are so huge that diplomatic circles reserved estimates as to the probable duration of his new cabinet.

The new chief of government's consultations were few. A bidding from him to join the cabinet appears to have been received as an order from the King. With one exception, understood to be that of

Continued on Page Five

Russians Take 70 Villages, Gain 6 Miles in Orel Drive

By The Associated Press.

LONDON, Tuesday, July 27—Russian troops captured seventy villages, gained six miles and killed 5,000 enemy soldiers yesterday in their steady semi-encirclement of the big German base at Orel, where thousands of Axis troops risk entrapment, it was announced early today in Moscow.

With the Russian troops within eight miles of the city's northeastern and eastern gates, a special communiqué said, other units have swept across the Oka River directly above the base in a wide wheeling movement threatening to cut the last supply line into Orel—the railway running northwest to Bryansk.

[The Russians have cut the Orel-Bryansk Railroad and crossed the Oka at new points in wild fighting that cost the Germans almost 9,000 men killed, The United Press reported.]

Village after village on the west bank of the Oka River fell to the Russians. One column also took Berestna, forty-five miles northwest of Orel. The vastness of the Russian drive indicated that Bryansk, as well as Orel, was an objective. Both are the keystones to the entire German south-central front in Russia.

Two thousand Germans were killed northwest of the city in a desperate effort to halt the first successful Red Army summer offensive of the war.

South of Orel, Russian troops, pushing up the railway from Kursk captured Kurakina and Yeropkino, which is only seventeen miles below Orel. The Germans lost 2,100 men before retreating in furious counter-attacks along the railway, including one stiff engagement at Glazunovskaya. The

Continued on Page Nine

GERMAN COMMENT IS STILL WITHHELD

Foreign Office Insists Ouster of Mussolini Is 'Internal' Affair of Italy Alone

By GUIDO ENDERIS
By Telephone to The New York Times.

BERNE, Switzerland, July 26—Responsible German quarters made no comment tonight on the "resignation" of Premier Mussolini.

The Foreign Office disposed of inquiries today with the remark that Mussolini's disappearance after twenty-one years' rule concerned Italian internal policy alone. The earlier explanation that his retirement had been caused by ill health was abandoned during the day.

Up to a late hour serious comment on the effect of Mussolini's ouster on the tri-partite pact, Axis relations with Japan and particularly Axis collaboration in the Balkans was still lacking. Marshal Pietro Badoglio's slogan, "The war goes on," was the one dream of hope from which official circles professed to extract comfort. It was put to the fore in all comment.

Berlin and the rest of Germany got the first news of the Roman

Continued on Page Five

ITALIANS REJOICING

Crowds in Streets Call for Peace—Mussolini's Paper Plant Burned

LEFTISTS ISSUE CALL

Five Parties Urge That Fascists Be Punished for Causing War

The text of the manifesto by Marshal Badoglio is on Page 4.

By DANIEL T. BRIGHAM
By Telephone to The New York Times.

BERNE, Switzerland, July 26—Manifestations of popular approval of the departure of Benito Mussolini began in Rome late last night and continued in all the largest cities of Italy throughout the day. Late this afternoon in Milan a mob stormed the offices of Mussolini's newspaper, Popolo d'Italia, in which fascism was created after World War I. According to a report from the Corriere della Sera of Milan, the office was destroyed.

While the spontaneity of this and other demonstrations is beyond doubt, and their widespread recurrence would appear to point to a coordinated direction, no reports received from Italy indicated the country was passing through a revolution. Aside from a free-for-all fist fight in Bologna early this afternoon, no bloodshed was reported.

Martial Law Is Proclaimed

Marshal Pietro Badoglio, the Premier, proclaimed martial law. He ordered that all armed police and militia be put under his orders and that their commanders report to local army commanders for instructions.

A dusk-to-dawn curfew was ordered, with only priests, doctors and midwives permitted on the streets. Civilians using night trains were ordered to carry identification papers.

Public places, including theatres, movies and sports halls, were ordered closed during curfew hours. Gatherings of more than three persons, including any behind locked doors, were forbidden.

Though long dormant political parties were lifting cautious heads in various political centers, Italy appeared to be waiting developments, patiently, but ready to make trouble. An indication of this came from Turin late tonight in a proclamation to the Italian workers, signed by five leftist political parties. It left no doubt as to the fate of the fascist leaders if the workers get power.

Five Parties Proclamation

As printed in the Stampa Sera of Turin, the proclamation read:

"Italians!

"The painful nightmare that has dominated our political life for the past twenty years is now ended.

Continued on Page Four

War News Summarized

TUESDAY, JULY 27, 1943

General rejoicing and celebration marked Italy's first day in more than twenty years free from the yoke of fascist rule. The fact that the Italian Empire had disappeared and that most of Sicily had been conquered did not seem to impress the people as much as the fact that Mussolini had gone.

Marshal Badoglio formed his Cabinet and immediately proclaimed martial law. He mustered the fascist militia into the King's service, imposed a dusk-to-dawn curfew and forbade the gathering of three or more persons. [All the foregoing 1:8.]

The new Italian Cabinet was considered a potential "armistice Cabinet" that would demand of the Allies "honorable capitulation" rather than "unconditional surrender." [1:6-7.]

The downfall of Mussolini was characterized by the German Foreign Office as an internal matter having no relation to the war. [1:7.] In London, the British War Cabinet met and every indication was that the peace terms remained unchanged—unconditional surrender and free use of Italy as a base against Germany. [3:6.] Although the White House withheld comment, Secretary of State Hull hailed the disappearance of Mussolini as the first step in the eradication of fascism throughout the world. He said the State Department had had no contact with Marshal Badoglio. [1:5.]

In Algiers the French Committee of National Liberation made it clear that, as Italy's closest neighbor and victim, France must be represented in any settlement with Italy. [3:1.]

Across the narrow Strait of Messina, Italy was still at war with the Allied invaders in Sicily. Canadian troops in the center of the Catania front were meeting fierce resistance, while the Americans were smashing eastward to join the assault on the Etna line. [1:4; map, P. 2.]

Combined Allied air forces continued their smashing attacks on Germany. The RAF and RCAF heavily bombed Essen, Hamburg and Cologne on Sunday night. Yesterday Flying Fortresses hit Hamburg again, as well as Hanover, Wilhelmshaven and Wesermuende, and destroyed more than fifty enemy fighters. Airfields in France and Belgium were also battered. Forty-six bombers were lost in all the attacks. [1:3, map P. 5.]

In Russia the Red Army cut the vital Bryansk-Orel railway, crossed the Oka River and captured more than seventy additional villages. More than 9,000 Germans died in yesterday's fighting around Orel. [1:6-7.]

Allied ground forces made a general advance in front of the Japanese base at Munda in the Solomons, aided by bombardment from the air and shelling from naval forces. Other enemy strongholds in the South Pacific were also heavily attacked by Allied fliers. [8:1.]

Beer Shortage Develops in City; Brewers Are Rationing Supply

A beer shortage has developed because of the inability of brewers to get corn and other grains, spokesmen for the industry agreed yesterday. It is expected to get worse as the summer wears on and reserves that were brewed a month or six weeks ago are used up, but a measure of relief is possible in the fall when the new grain crop becomes available, according to one authority.

Intensifying the shortage of beer are equipment and transportation difficulties. Some brewers are short of bottles, others of barrels, and all brewers in the Eastern gasoline shortage area are feeling the effects of delivery restrictions imposed by the Office of Defense Transportation.

As yet no industry-wide program for apportioning available supplies among retail outlets has been adopted, but each brewer is using a form of rationing of his own devising. Some are pro-rating available supplies among regular customers, others are curtailing their delivery areas, still others are concentrating on the output of either draft or bottled beer, according to an official of the United States Brewers Association.

One of the first effects of the shortage has been a marked curtailment in the flow of beer from one production area to another; brewers are apparently delivering a major part of their production to the markets in the immediate vicinity of their plants, making their biggest cuts on shipments to distant points.

In Washington, receipts of out-

Continued on Page Thirteen

OWI Broadcast to Italy Calls Ruler 'Fascist' and 'Moronic Little King'

The Office of War Information, in transmissions beamed to Italy and the rest of Europe, broadcast yesterday statements characterizing King Victor Emmanuel as "the moronic little King" and "the Fascist King." The OWI short-wave stations, which are known collectively as "The Voice of America," also assailed Marshal Pietro Badoglio as "a high-ranking Fascist."

Immediately after Premier Benito Mussolini's "resignation" was made known Sunday, the overseas division of the OWI merely broadcast that there was "no essential change" in the government of Italy. Yesterday, however, the government propaganda agency directed its fire against the two new Italian leaders personally.

In presenting "typical unofficial reaction" to the events in Italy, the OWI employed the device of quoting an imaginary "American political commentator." "John Durfee." According to "Mr. Durfee," it was announced, the United States will continue the war irrespective of whether Signor Mussolini, Marshal Badoglio or "the Fascist King himself" rules Italy.

The OWI also quoted extensively from a Sunday-night radio speech by Samuel Grafton, columnist for The New York Post. It was Mr. Grafton who described King Victor Emmanuel as "the moronic little King."

This reference was carried in the hourly English-language transmission at 2 P. M., as broadcast over the 16, 19 and 23 megacycle bands.

Continued on Page Three

Armistice Talks In Vatican Reported

By The Associated Press.

LONDON, Tuesday, July 27—A Reuter dispatch from Stockholm today said preliminary negotiations for an armistice between Italy and the Allies were begun in Vatican City last night.

The Berne correspondent of Svenska Dagbladet was the source of the report. There was no confirmation whatever.

While negotiations were going on in the Vatican, it was said, the German Ambassador to Rome, Hans Georg Viktor von Mackensen, was holding a series of talks with Marshal Badoglio. An Italian and German communiqué on the von Mackensen-Badoglio talks was expected shortly, the dispatch said.

ALGIERS, July 26 (Reuter)—Declaration of Rome as an open city is considered here as a likely step toward ultimate surrender of Italy.

"All the News That's Fit to Print."

The New York Times.

LATE CITY EDITION
Moderate temperatures today with moderate to fresh winds.
Temperatures Yesterday—Max., 76; Min., 62
Sunrise, 6:09 A. M.; Sunset, 7:50 P. M.

VOL. XCII..No. 31,253. Entered as Second-Class Matter, Postoffice, New York, N. Y. NEW YORK, THURSDAY, AUGUST 19, 1943. THREE CENTS IN NEW YORK CITY

RAF BLASTS SECRET NAZI RESEARCH AREA; ARMIES READY TO GO, SAYS EISENHOWER; ALLIES BID PEOPLES OF EUROPE PREPARE

SANCTIONS FIXED AGAINST STRIKERS IN WAR INDUSTRIES

President Orders Withdrawing of Union Funds or Contract by WLB Under New Law

DRAFT DEFERMENT TO END

Stoppage of Materials, Fuel or Transportation Authorized if Employers Defy the Board

Text of the President's letter and order appears on Page 40.

Special to THE NEW YORK TIMES.

WASHINGTON, Aug. 18—New powers by which the National War Labor Board may proceed against war industry employe as well as employer refusing to comply with its orders were bestowed by President Roosevelt in action disclosed today.

The Selective Service System was authorized to cancel draft deferments of recalcitrant individual union employes. Power was granted to withhold in escrow union dues collected under union agreements by employers in plants which have been seized by the Government because of strikes.

The law gives the Government power to seize plants of an employer refusing to comply with WLB orders. "Less drastic sanctions" were authorized, however, such as "control of war contracts, of essential materials and of transportation and fuel," if these steps could be taken without impeding the war effort. Fred M. Vinson, director of the Office of Economic Stabilization, was directed to follow this policy hereafter.

Executive Order Issued

In a letter to William H. Davis, chairman of the WLB, released by the President's office, Mr. Roosevelt revealed that an executive order had been issued under the War Labor Disputes Law (the Smith-Connally act). It appeared necessary, he said, "for bringing about compliance in the relatively few cases in which executive action may become necessary."

The order was described by a WLB official as "putting a lower set of teeth" in the powers of that agency.

This official noted that there had been widespread criticism of the fact that the only penalties heretofore imposed for strikes in war industries had been seizure of the employer's plant, even though the employer was innocent.

"This gives the board teeth with which to bite the employes as well as the employers in case of noncompliance with board directives," he said.

The directive was seen here as strengthening the hand of the WLB in the still unsettled coal mine dispute. Under it miners' dues here going to John L. Lewis' United Mine Workers could be withheld if the union refused to sign a new contract with the operators.

Action Up to Union Leaders

The essential effect of the order regarding unions was described by Mr. Roosevelt as follows in his letter:

"When a local union refuses to comply, by directing or advising workers not to work under the terms and conditions prescribed by the board, action by the responsible national or international officers has thus far, in all but one or two cases, sufficed to bring about compliance.

"If such action should prove ineffective, or if a national or international union should itself be the offender, the plant will be taken over under the War Labor Disputes Act and operated by the Government, if this is necessary to prevent interference with production and to protect the workers who wish to work."

The letter said that when the Government had to take over plants or industries because of labor noncompliance, "Government operation will be conducted with the least possible interference with existing management."

The letter also noted that as to "certain types of interference with production by individuals, the law provides penalties enforceable by the Attorney General."

The board was praised for its "remarkable record" in the last eighteen months of disposing of more than 1,000 disputes and of having had to refer only seven to the President "because of persistent non-compliance."

The industry, labor and public members of the board had each played an effective part in making

Continued on Page Forty

Eisenhower Praises Land, Sea, Air Aides

By The Associated Press.

ALLIED HEADQUARTERS IN NORTH AFRICA, Aug. 18—Gen. Dwight D. Eisenhower, commander of Allied Forces in North Africa, sent congratulations today to his land, air and naval chiefs—Gen. Sir Harold Alexander, Air Chief Marshal Sir Arthur Tedder and Admiral Sir Andrew Browne Cunningham—asking each to extend appreciation to the officers and men for the successes they have achieved.

The message to General Alexander said:

"With the Sicilian campaign at an end, I have the happy opportunity once again to express to you my appreciation of the outstanding services you continue to render the Allied cause and assure you of my personal thanks for always making my own task easier.

"I hope you extend to Generals Montgomery and Patton and to the magnificent troops serving under them my commendations and congratulations for their energy, determination and aggressiveness in driving the enemy out of Sicily. With such soldiers as these we can look forward with confidence to the future."

COAL PAY CASE GOES TO THE WLB AGAIN

Operators Get Board to Take It After They and Union Fail to Agree on Wage

Special to THE NEW YORK TIMES.

WASHINGTON, Aug. 18—At the request of the Anthracite Coal Operators Association, the National War Labor Board announced today that it would resume jurisdiction over the four-and-one-half-month-old wage dispute between the operators and the United Mine Workers of America and set a public hearing on the issue here for Monday morning.

The WLB announcement said the action was taken after counsel for the operators sent word that they had not been able to reach an agreement with the union despite long negotiations.

The board sent telegrams to Walter Gordon Merritt, operators' counsel, and John L. Lewis and Thomas Kennedy, respectively president and secretary treasurer of the UMW, stating that "you and your associates are invited to attend" the hearing.

May Await Private Custody

"Unless an application under the provisions of Section 5 of the War Labor Disputes Act is made for a change in wages and other terms and conditions of employment in the manner specified in said section," the telegram stated, "any order which the board might make changing the wages or other terms and conditions of employment existing in any particular mine would become effective together with any retroactive provisions upon return of such mine to private operation and not during the period of Government operation."

Section 5 of this act (the Smith-Connally law) provides that the WLB may order changes in wages and working conditions of a seized war facility if either party applies for such a change.

The anthracite wage negotiations, affecting about 80,000 miners, began on March 31, when the miners' union presented twenty-one demands which the operators said would necessitate an increase

Continued on Page Seventeen

GENERAL HAILS MEN

Solid Victory Won in Real Combined Operation, Eisenhower Says

FOE'S CASUALTIES 167,000

1,691 Enemy Planes Destroyed or Taken—25,000 of Our Troops, 274 Aircraft Lost

By MILTON BRACKER

By Wireless to THE NEW YORK TIMES.

ALLIED HEADQUARTERS IN NORTH AFRICA, Aug. 18—With the battle of Sicily over ahead of schedule, although an artillery combat raged across the Strait of Messina, Gen. Dwight D. Eisenhower sat down in a map-walled room today and hailed the American soldiers for having achieved a solid victory that was a combined operation in the most literal sense.

"It was a real victory and our troops have done everything that the best troops in the world could have done—and that includes the three services," the Allied Commander in Chief in this theatre declared. The cooperation between the American Seventh Army and the British Eighth Army, he added, could be described as a "one-two punch" that Gen. Sir Harold R. L. G. Alexander could bring into action whenever he desired.

Losses 167,000 to 25,000

General Eisenhower's staff issued a statistical summary of the campaign showing that, up to Aug. 10, German and Italian prisoners taken had exceeded 135,000, while the enemy's losses in killed and wounded were not fewer than 32,000. It was estimated that the total of prisoners alone might eventually reach 200,000. General Eisenhower indicated that the total Allied casualties, on the basis of incomplete figures, stood at about 25,000. The casualties suffered by the Seventh Army were known to have been relatively severe in the fighting around Troina.

The first month of the thirty-eight-day struggle cost the Axis 260 tanks and 502 guns. Through Aug. 17, 1,691 enemy aircraft were shot down or captured, against the Allies' loss of 274.

The great majority of the planes lost by the enemy were captured on deserted airfields. Many of them have already been reconditioned and put to use. Moreover, many thousands of military vehicles of all types fell into our hands and quantities of stores are still being collected all over the island.

General Glad It's Over

General Eisenhower sat at the head of a table, surrounded, at both chair and floor level, by correspondents. He wore ribbons symbolizing only two decorations—the Knight Commander of the Bath, recently awarded by King George VI, and a French medal presented by Gen. Henri-Honoré Giraud.

General Eisenhower made it plain that he was glad that the job had been done and that he was particularly satisfied at new evidence of coordination among the Allies and

Continued on Page Four

AT QUEBEC: THE MEN WHO WILL DETERMINE NEXT PHASES OF THE WAR

Principals at the conference: With President Roosevelt in the front row are Prime Ministers Churchill (right) and King; in the rear row, left to right, are Gen. Henry H. Arnold, Air Marshal Sir Charles Portal, Gen. Sir Alan Brooke, Admiral Ernest J. King, Field Marshal Sir John Dill, Gen. George C. Marshall, Admiral Sir Dudley Pound and Admiral William D. Leahy.

Associated Press Wirephoto

GERMANS QUITTING CALABRIA FOOTHOLD

Flee by Land and Sea Under Bombardment by Allies' Artillery and Planes

By The United Press.

ALLIED HEADQUARTERS IN NORTH AFRICA, Aug. 18—The Germans have begun evacuating the Reggio Calabria area of southern Italy opposite Messina, it was reported today.

As their overland escape route by southern Italy continued to suffer heavy aerial bombardment, the Germans were reported to be taking to boats to run through the Strait of Messina around to the port of Palmi, twenty miles north of Reggio Calabria on the Gulf of Gioia. The battle of Italy had apparently begun.

Allied planes roared back and forth across the strait, battering railroads and highways and pouncing on Axis escape boats sailing along under the protection of anti-aircraft guns but with virtually no air cover.

Allied and Axis artillery traded

Continued on Page Three

Eden Joins Quebec Parley; Political Phase Is Reached

By JOHN H. CRIDER

Special to THE NEW YORK TIMES.

QUEBEC, Aug. 18—The momentous conference at which President Roosevelt and Prime Minister Churchill are planning the military strategy to end the war took a definitely political turn today with the arrival of Anthony Eden, Britain's much-traveled Foreign Secretary.

Joining the conferees any day now, perhaps tomorrow, will be Cordell Hull, Secretary of State, to round out the foursome who will decide such pressing problems as how to deal with Italy and Germany on their surrender, recognition of the French Committee of National Liberation, greater political and military collaboration with Soviet Russia, and the parts that the military forces of each United Nation, including the exiled governments, will have in the impending invasion of continental Europe.

It was significant that no observers from any of the United Nations other than the United States, Great Britain and Canada were in attendance here, according to an authorized spokesman.

Meanwhile, as President Roosevelt proceeded speedily into conferences with Mr. Churchill and military advisers after his arrival

Continued on Page Five

RUSSIANS RESUME KHARKOV ADVANCE

Capture Key Town in Smash Across Donets—New Gains Deepen Other Fronts

By The United Press.

LONDON, Thursday, Aug. 19—The Russian Army, resuming a general advance after crushing counter-attacks into which the German command had thrown its reserves, made important gains yesterday in all three areas of the Kharkov front—southeast, northwest and west of the city.

Zmiyev, a key town twenty-one miles southeast of Kharkov, was captured after a new break across the Donets River. Three towns nine miles south and southeast of the big German base of Sumy were taken northwest of Kharkov. On the west, the Red Army captured Oposhnya, twenty-four miles north of the rail and agricultural center of Poltava and seventy miles west of Kharkov, on the way to the Dnieper River.

In all, more than fifty towns and villages were taken on the Kharkov front in gains of more than six miles, made in the face of continued counter-attacks.

The Russian midnight communi-

Continued on Page Nine

ALLIES' RADIO HINTS AT EARLY INVASION

Occupied Countries Told to Get Ready—Signal for Blow to Come at Last Minute

By The Associated Press.

LONDON, Aug. 18—The United Nations radio in Algiers told the people of occupied Europe tonight to perfect their preparations "for the day when you will hear the call of the Allied High Command" on the eve of the invasion of the Continent.

The broadcast said that, although "we are obviously not going to reveal where the next blow will fall," the people of "the occupied country that is to be the first to welcome the armies of liberation will be notified at the last minute." It added that the time might be near at hand.

Although the broadcast especially mentioned metropolitan France, in effect all those awaiting freedom from Greece to Norway were told to make their preparations for "the new phase, the liberation of the occupied countries," which, it said, has already begun. The announcer concluded the broadcast by saying that the message was from the "Allied High Command."

[The heavy American assaults on French airfields are viewed by the Germans as the prelude to the invasion of France, The Associated Press said on the basis of German dispatches to Stockholm.]

Gen. Dwight D. Eisenhower broadcast the first warning to occupied countries to prepare for the battle of Europe on July 10, when the invasion of Sicily began. Speak-

Continued on Page Five

War News Summarized

THURSDAY, AUGUST 19, 1943

British, American and Canadian bombers yesterday ripped Germany in widespread night and day raids in a record twenty-four-hour assault by nearly 3,000 planes. The chief target was Peenemuende, site of a secret Nazi research and development factory on the Baltic coast. Forty-one British heavy bombers were lost. [1:8, map, P. 10.]

The people of occupied Europe were told by the Allied-controlled radio in Algiers to "perfect preparations" for their part in the imminent invasion of the Continent. "The new phase, the liberation of occupied countries, has begun," the message declared. [1:7.]

In preparation for the assault on Hitler's fortress, President Roosevelt and Prime Minister Churchill worked with military leaders in Quebec over a detailed master plan for forcing and taking the Nazi bastion. British Foreign Secretary Anthony Eden arrived in the Canadian city. At the close of the conference President Roosevelt is to visit Ottawa, where he may address a special session of the Canadian Parliament. [1:5-6.]

On the Russian front the titanic struggle continued, with the Red Army surging ahead in a general advance on the Kharkov line after encountering bitter counter-attacks into which the Germans had thrown huge reserves. The Russians captured Zmiyev, twenty miles south of Kharkov, and more than fifty smaller places. On the Bryansk front the Soviet forces took forty villages in an advance of four to six miles. [1:6; map, P. 9.]

With the Sicilian campaign over, Allied forces gave the enemy no rest as beaches, roads and communications in southern Italy came under air and artillery attack. Every effort was being made to disrupt Axis efforts to reorganize the forces that had fled across the Strait of Messina. [1:4; map, P. 2.]

General Eisenhower disclosed at a press conference at Allied Headquarters in North Africa that Axis losses in the thirty-eight-day battle for Sicily were 135,000 captured and 32,000 killed and wounded against our 25,000 casualties, with tremendous losses to the enemy in matériel yet to be estimated. [1:3.]

Marshal Badoglio and former Premier Orlando addressed the Italian nation by radio and bemoaned the loss of Sicily. [4:2.]

Allied planes in the southwest Pacific returned to blasted Wewak in New Guinea to finish off all but ten of 225 enemy planes there. An Allied sea victory was reported in Vella Gulf in the Solomons. [12:2.]

Americans' Way Lit by Full Moon On Last Night of Battle for Messina

By HERBERT L. MATTHEWS

By Wireless to THE NEW YORK TIMES.

MESSINA, Sicily, Aug. 17 (Delayed)—The Sicilian campaign ended at dawn today when patrols of the American Third Division entered Messina, to find it deserted by the Germans.

Only a few snipers remained. Three hours later the British patrols, followed by tanks that had been held back by demolitions, entered Messina from the south.

The Germans deserve credit for having fought skillfully and tenaciously throughout. They left a minimum of material and men to be captured. However, their divisions had been severely mauled, particularly at Troina, so it is doubtful whether they got away with most of their strength.

The end came suddenly and almost tamely. It had been foreseen, but it was always possible for the Germans to make a final delaying stand.

Contact with them had been lost at dusk last night and units of our Third Division began pressing up the road that goes across the ridge straight to Messina, as well as the coastal road that makes a great loop. Meanwhile, Rangers had reached a secondary road running north and south along the ridge.

Such good progress had been made before midnight that it was obvious that Messina would fall very soon. The all but full moon was an extraordinary blessing for everybody but the Germans. It gave a character of unreality to

Continued on Page Three

RECORD DAY IN AIR

3,000 Planes Smash 16 Targets in Non-Stop Attrition Drive

BERLIN RAIDED 71ST TIME

Other Blows Range From Baltic to France—New Night Raids in Europe Indicated

By The United Press.

LONDON, Thursday, Aug. 19—Royal Air Force and Canadian bombers attacked targets in Germany Tuesday night, singling out a secret German research and development plant on the Baltic coast for a 1,500-ton attack, and coast observers reported new streams of bombers beating steadily toward Europe last night on routes usually taken to Germany.

Mosquito bombers gave Berlin its seventy-first raid of the war Tuesday night, topping off a twenty-four-hour non-stop attack that probably set a record in air war history.

The German mystery plant, hidden in a four-and-a-half-square-mile patch of woods at Peenemuende, in northeastern Germany, was ripped open by more than 1,500 tons of high explosives and incendiaries showered down by the RAF and RCAF bombers from a low level.

Nearly 3,000 British, American and Canadian planes carried out sixteen separate operations, closely coordinated, in the twenty-four-hour period at a price of thirty-six American and forty-one RAF heavy bombers in two major operations alone.

Northern Airdromes Attacked

Today American Marauder medium bombers, under an escort of British, Canadian and other Allied Spitfire fighters, maintained the attack by raiding German airdromes at Woensdrecht, the Netherlands, and Lille, France.

The raids were a complex pattern in Allied plans to cripple German industry from the first manufacturing processes to the finished products, to soften the path for the opening of a new front in western Europe and to drain the blood from the German fighter air force.

[Government monitors reported that the Allouis and Paris radio stations shut down last night, indicating that Allied bombers might be raiding the Continent for the fifth straight night. An air alert in Switzerland indicated raids in the Lake Constance area of Germany, according to a Rome broadcast heard by the Columbia Broadcasting System. A large force of Allied bombers passed over Hungary from south to west, evidently bound for Austria, Reuter reported.]

The great four-motored bombers of the RAF, in their night raid, attacked heavily in bright moonlight the research factory at Peenemuende, sixty miles northwest of Stettin on the Bay of Pomerania at the estuary of the Peene River. The town, never before attacked, is the site of the biggest German research and development station, specializing in scientific work on aircraft radio-location and armament.

Loss of Bombers Heavy

Enemy fighters battled the raiders along a great part of their 1,200-mile round trip flight, and the forty-one bombers reported missing represented the greatest RAF loss since the heavy raid on Krefeld on June 21, when forty-four planes were lost.

An undisclosed number of German night fighters were shot down by the raiding force and RAF quarters indicated that the importance of the targets at Peenemuende justified the heavy losses sustained.

Supporting the main attack, speedy Mosquito bombers raided Berlin for the fourth time in the last five nights and RAF intruder planes stabbed at airfields and railway targets in France, the Low

Continued on Page Ten

U. S. Ruling on Austria's Status Asked by Court on Alien's Plea

The State Department will be asked to take a definite stand on the question of the incorporation of Austria into the German Reich under one of three decisions bearing on the status of aliens of Austrian origin, handed down yesterday by the United States Circuit Court of Appeals.

The court held, in one case that Frederic Walker D'Esquiva was not a "citizen" of Germany, whether or not this country recognizes the disappearance of Austria into Germany. But if the State Department has recognized the factual absorption of D'Esquiva's native land, he may be considered a "native" of Germany. D'Esquiva is in custody as a "dangerous alien enemy." The Department will be asked to settle the question of recognition, before his status under the Alien Enemy Law is settled.

The court also ruled that, regardless of the attitude of the State Department, Germany had no right to force German citizenship upon Austrians not living in their own country, without either their tacit or express consent.

With this ruling it reversed a District Court decision that Dr. Paul Schwarzkopf was a citizen of Germany. The lower court was directed to sustain a writ of habeas corpus obtained by Dr. Schwarzkopf and discharge him from custody. This procedure would usually take about two weeks, unless the Government should win a stay pending appeal of the decision to the Supreme Court.

The third case was that of Ivan

Continued on Page Six

"All the News That's Fit to Print."

The New York Times.

LATE CITY EDITION
Little change in temperature; showers and cooler in evening.
Temperatures Yesterday—Max.,89; Min.,71
Sunrise, 6:16 A. M.; Sunset, 7:40 P. M.

Copyright, 1943, by The New York Times Company.

VOL. XCII...No. 31,260. Entered as Second-Class Matter, Postoffice, New York, N. Y. NEW YORK, THURSDAY, AUGUST 26, 1943. THREE CENTS IN NEW YORK CITY

ROOSEVELT WARNS HITLER TO SURRENDER NOW; SAYS ALLIES WILL END 'GANGSTERISM' IN WORLD; MOUNTBATTEN TO COMMAND IN SOUTHEAST ASIA

VAST WAR EXPORTS DELAYED BY LACK OF RAIL LABOR HERE

Scarcity of Freight Handlers Holds Up Thousands of Cars Along Seaboard

URGENT PLEA TO WORKERS

Roads Combing Inland Points to Recruit Own Employes to Help Meet Crisis

An acute railroad manpower shortage is threatening the movement of huge quantities of military and lend-lease exports in the New York area and elsewhere along the Atlantic seaboard, it was disclosed yesterday.

With insufficient labor to unload freight cars as they come in to the yards along the New Jersey shore, thousands of cars have been delayed in recent weeks, and it was reported that 8,000 cars were waiting for freight handlers yesterday. At a more acute period within the last few weeks there were 10,000 cars in the backlog.

An appeal for the mobilization of hundreds of workers has been made to the Railroad Retirement Board at its regional headquarters in New York, and the railroad companies themselves are conducting enlistment campaigns among their own employes at inland points, where trackmen, office employes and others who can be spared are being recruited and sent to seaboard points.

According to spokesmen for the board and the railroads, at least 3,200 men are needed at once in the New York area alone, and Robert Ware, Retirement Board official at the 58 Hudson Street office, said the various railroad lines involved in the shortage had reported 7,000 vacancies among their staffs in New York and the immediate New Jersey shore area.

New Tactic Is Taken On

The Retirement Board, charged by law with the administration of the Railroad Unemployment Insurance Act, promotes employment stabilization within the industry. During the war it has taken on the task of keeping the roads supplied with sufficient men for adequate operation.

In the last seven weeks the board has furnished 3,000 workers in the New York district alone, and 10,000 in the entire region extending from Manhattan to and including Maryland and the District of Columbia.

Appeals for men are constantly made through advertisements in newspapers, through public appeals in municipalities and with the aid of civic and veterans' groups. The urgency of getting war materials unloaded for arriving convoys is stressed.

A spokesman for the affected railroads, which include the New York Central, Baltimore & Ohio, Jersey Central, Lackawanna, Lehigh Valley, Erie, Pennsylvania and the West Shore Division of the New York Central, said that while a very acute tie-up some days ago had been relieved through the joint efforts, the situation was still critical and will continue to develop.

Port Itself Is Threatened

"It not only menaces the war effort and the movement of supplies but it is threatening the position of the Port of New York," he said. "We ought to have another 1,600 men every day at the very minimum. We have had such heavy business in recent weeks that there simply hasn't been enough men to handle the cargo. The number of freight cars entering the area with goods is greater by far than at any time in the history of the port."

The shortage was attributed to the "raiding" of railroad manpower by other industries that pay higher wages, to the draft and to the failure of rail workers to obtain a wage increase.

The local War Manpower Commission offices in Newark communicated the appeal for men to the regional Railroad Retirement

Continued on Page Thirteen

SUPREME COMMANDER IN SOUTHEAST ASIA

Lord Louis Mountbatten
Associated Press, 1943

Jersey OPA Secretly Allots 'Gas' to Party Fishing Boats

While some of the Long Island gasoline stations reserved for use of war workers because of the Eastern petroleum drought ran dry yesterday before noon, it developed that the Office of Price Administration had secretly granted special gasoline allotments for party fishing boats in Atlantic City and other New Jersey coastal resorts.

A spokesman for the Atlantic City rationing board said that the special allotments—which enabled several boatloads of amateur fishermen to put out last Saturday and Sunday—had been authorized by the OPA district office at Camden. He said the Camden OPA had instructed local boards to "keep quiet" about the grants lest "hordes of fishermen" descend on the piers and quays.

The plan of secrecy went awry when Atlantic City's municipal press agent, not bound by any promises to OPA, let the cat out of the fishbag with a rosy announcement of the catches in store for anglers who took advantage of the rationing board's liberality.

"Coast Guard regulations still bar the boats from going to sea, but big schools of weakfish, kingfish, croakers and flounders are back in the bays, waiting to be caught," read the blurb that Mall Dodson, the municipal barker, sent to the fish-and-game editors of newspapers.

OPA Here Taken by Surprise

The situation took OPA officials in New York by surprise. At the district office, which has jurisdiction over Sheepshead Bay and the Long Island resorts whose party fishing boats have been idle since the ban against pleasure-driving was held to include such craft, it was said that no rations had been issued here for such boating and

Continued on Page Twenty-five

KELLAND DEMANDS 'IMPREGNABLE' U. S.

Defense System From Dakar to Far Pacific Suggested to Supplement Alliances

A program of American imperialism in the post-war world, as opposed to American participation in any "Utopian super-state," will be presented to the Republican Post-War Policy Committee meeting to be held at the call of Republican National Chairman Harrison Spangler at Mackinac Island in early September.

Its author, Clarence Budington Kelland, a member of the Spangler committee, National Committeeman from Arizona and former executive director of the Republican National Committee, outlined the plan here yesterday and asserted that it had considerable support within the Spangler group, which was set up to counteract the unofficial Republican Post-War Policy Association, inspired by Wendell Willkie.

Mr. Kelland advocated a "five-ocean" navy, making the Pacific an American lake by holding all necessary islands; the taking "by treaty or by occupation" of bases in Iceland, Greenland, Dakar and

Continued on Page Thirty-eight

WLB Voids Lewis' Illinois Deal, Calling It Hidden Mine Pay Rise

By LOUIS STARK
Special to THE NEW YORK TIMES.

WASHINGTON, Aug. 25—The War Labor Board, by a vote of eight to four, with the labor members dissenting, has rejected the agreement negotiated by John L. Lewis, president of the United Mine Workers, with the Illinois Coal Operators Association, providing for the payment of $1.25 a day to cover travel time from portal to portal, according to an announcement today by William H. Davis, chairman of the WLB.

Mr. Davis, who is preparing the majority opinion and the formal directive, said that the public and industry majority of the board had been unable to approve the settlement made on behalf of 3,500 Illinois miners because it was not related to what the union might have recovered under the Fair Labor Standards Act and did not constitute a "genuine settlement of claims arising under the act" as directed by the board on May 25.

In effect, the board held that the $1.25 a day was a hidden wage increase.

Matthew Woll, vice president of the American Federation of Labor, fought all day yesterday to win the board's acceptance of the Illinois agreement, which was made public on July 21 by the miners' union and the operators and submitted to the board for approval.

A labor member of the WLB, Mr. Woll read correspondence between himself and Mr. Lewis covering various objections previously raised by board members. It is

Continued on Page Thirteen

BURMA DRIVE SEEN

Lord Louis Is Named at Ottawa as Result of Allied Parleys

LIKELY TO ACT SOON

As Head of Combined Operations Admiral Led Commandos

By JOHN H. CRIDER
Special to THE NEW YORK TIMES.

OTTAWA, Aug. 25—The creation of a separate Allied Southeast Asia Command and the appointment of Lord Louis Mountbatten, an acting vice admiral, as its commander were announced today from the Citadel in Quebec, where President Roosevelt and Prime Minister Churchill mapped their war strategy in the historic conference that ended yesterday. The announcement was made by British spokesmen who accompanied the President here.

Thus, within a day of the conclusion of the sixth war conference of the President and Mr. Churchill, the pattern of new events in the Pacific began to unfold. In their statement at the conclusion of their conference the leaders emphasized that the greater part of their Quebec talks were devoted to Pacific strategy.

Of equal importance to the appointment of the colorful Chief of Combined Operations, which includes the Commandos, to head the new Southeast Asia Command, was the fact that such a command has now been created. Lord Louis is a second cousin of King George.

Announcement of Shift

"It has been decided," the brief announcement said, "to set up a separate Southeast Asia Command for the conduct of operations based on India and Ceylon against Japan. It will be an Allied command similar to that set up in North Africa.

"The King has been pleased to approve the appointment of Acting Vice Admiral the Lord Louis Mountbatten, G. C. V. O., D. S. O., A. D. C., to be Supreme Allied Commander, Southeast Asia."

The announcement carried three important implications:

1. That President Roosevelt and Mr. Churchill meant not only ac-

Continued on Page Four

RAF GOES OUT AGAIN

New Blows in Germany Indicated—French Air Bases Pounded

BERLIN BOMBED ANEW

Mosquitos Add to Havoc —Big Plants Wrecked, Human Toll Heavy

By The United Press.

LONDON, Thursday, Aug. 26—Powerful forces of British heavy bombers swarmed last night toward the Continent, where large areas of Berlin have been devastated in two nights of "Hamburg pattern" bombing.

The four-motored bombers thundered across the Channel in an hour-long procession that coastal observers said was as great as the armada that blasted the German capital Monday night.

As they streamed out in a southeasterly direction Axis radio stations in Germany and the occupied countries fell silent one by one, from Paris to Munich. British radio monitors reported that the radio silence blanketing the Continent was more complete than at any time in their memory.

In the midst of the unprecedented radio blackout a radio "ghost voice" crashed in powerfully on continental wave lengths with an ominous warning to the German people that Adolf Hitler "is sending you to your deaths."

Mosquitos Return to Berlin

Tuesday night the RAF's fast Mosquito bombers, following the pattern that virtually destroyed Hamburg last month, opened the second round of the Battle of Berlin by heaping their bombs on the fires still blazing in the battered German capital from Monday's record raid.

American and British medium bombers swarmed over France, striking hard at the enemy's network of coastal airfields without loss.

B-26 Marauders of the Eighth United States Air Force attacked the airdrome at Tricqueville, northeast of Caen, and blasted a power station near Rouen. RAF Mitchells bombed the St. Martin airfield at

Continued on Page Nine

War News Summarized

THURSDAY, AUGUST 26, 1943

Speaking to 30,000 Canadians, on Parliament Hill in Ottawa yesterday, President Roosevelt gave the Nazis stern warning that "surrender would pay them better now than later." He added that at the Quebec Conference he, Prime Minister Churchill and their military leaders had "talked constructively of our common purpose in this war." That purpose is "a determination to achieve victory in the shortest possible time." Revealing no actual decisions of the historic meeting, Mr. Roosevelt said: "We are going to be rid of outlaws this time." [1:8.]

The people of Canada's capital city gave Mr. Roosevelt, first United States President to visit Ottawa, an ovation on his arrival. [3:2-3.]

From the Citadel in Quebec came the announcement that Lord Louis Mountbatten, cousin of King George VI and British Chief of Combined Operations, has been named Supreme Allied Commander in Southeast Asia. In a post similar to the North African Command of General Eisenhower and the Southwest Pacific Command of General MacArthur, Lord Louis will direct the attack against Japan from India and Ceylon. [1:4, map P. 4.] In London the announcement was interpreted as presaging the near completion of plans for an all-out offensive against Japan. [4:2.] Visiting the Allied Headquarters in the Southwest Pacific, Under-Secretary of War Patterson predicted blows of increasing strength against Japan. [5:1.]

In the European theatre, Berliners found no rest from the continuing air assaults on their city. British Mosquito bombers knifed through the smoke of fires set in Monday night's 700-plane raid to wreak fresh destruction. Last night a strong force of Allied heavy bombers was reported sweeping out across the English Channel. [1:5.]

Maj. Gen. Harold L. George, Chief of the United States Transport Command, predicted economic collapse for Germany by the end of the year if the air offensive could be continued with a reasonable rise in tempo. [9:1.]

Allied raids on Italian communications and transport facilities continued. Rail lines south of Naples were torn by British Wellington bombers, and a lone American fighter-bomber blew the stern off an Italian cruiser, leaving the vessel sinking. Enemy air opposition was nonexistent [6:4.]

The Russian Army continued to plunge deep into the Ukraine, capturing Zenkov, eighty-five miles northwest of Kharkov, and sixty other places. In the Donets Basin far to the southeast other units captured several towns and considerably improved their positions. The Nazis resisted feverishly the enveloping Soviet drives. [1:7; map, P. 10.]

PRESIDENT ADDRESSING CANADIANS

Franklin D. Roosevelt at Ottawa yesterday
Associated Press Wirephoto

President Says Surrender Will Free Axis Peoples

Special to THE NEW YORK TIMES.

WASHINGTON, Aug. 25—Except for the "responsible fascist leaders," the peoples of the Axis need not fear unconditional surrender to the United Nations, President Roosevelt declared today in a letter transmitting to Congress a report which showed that lend-lease assistance to our Allies had reached the total of $13,973,339,000 on July 31.

For the first time, the report showed, monthly lend-lease aid exceeded a billion dollars in June. The total in July exceeded the June figure by $20,000,000. Aid to Russia reached a peak in April, but dropped off sharply in May and June, while aid to Great Britain continued a steady rise.

Mr. Roosevelt, in his letter of transmittal, assured the Axis peoples that the unconditional-surrender proclamation of his Casablanca conference with Prime Minister Winston Churchill did not mean they must trade "Axis despotism for ruin under the United Nations," but that the Allies' goal was "to permit liberated peoples to create a free political life of their own choosing and to attain economic security."

He also brought out that the might of the United States and its Allies was being felt in the Axis satellite nations of the Balkans and middle Europe as well as in Nazi Germany.

"Crushing Force" Widespread

"From Hamburg on the North Sea to Ploesti in Rumania," the President declared, "the people know from first-hand experience with what crushing force the United Nations can strike."

The subjugated peoples of Nazi Europe are now aware that the European fortress is not impregnable, he stated.

"The great offensives of the So-

Continued on Page Eleven

RED ARMY EXTENDS WEDGE IN UKRAINE

Zenkov and 60 Other Places Fall in Renewed Drive—Donbas Threat Grows

By The United Press.

LONDON, Thursday, Aug. 26—Driving ahead after smashing strong German resistance, the Russian Army yesterday captured more than sixty towns and villages northwest of Kharkov, including the flour milling center of Zenkov, to reach a new farthest west point in their offensive.

Zenkov, a town of 11,000 persons, is eighty-five miles northwest of Kharkov and 101 miles southwest of Belgorod, where the Red Army started its great summer attack.

Desperate fighting raged over the whole Kharkov and Donets Basin fronts and a Russian operational bulletin revealed that the big base of Akhtyrka, twenty-three miles northeast of Zenkov, had changed hands several times since its capture Aug. 11, until it was finally won by storm. The Germans had claimed that they had surrounded the Russians at Akhtyrka.

West and south of Kharkov the Russians continued their advance.

Continued on Page Ten

Coordinator of Post-War Planning Is Reported Chosen by Roosevelt

By JOHN MacCORMAC
Special to THE NEW YORK TIMES.

WASHINGTON, Aug. 25—Appointment of a coordinator of the plans which are being made by over a dozen different Government departments and agencies for the reconversion of American agriculture and industry to peace will be announced early next week by President Roosevelt, it is understood. It will be a corollary to the plans made at Quebec.

Who is to be the President's choice for the post, which is likely to prove as difficult as it is important, is not yet known. The names of Secretary of Commerce Jesse H. Jones, Chairman Donald M. Nelson of the War Production Board and Leo T. Crowley, Alien Property Custodian and head of the Office of Economic Warfare, were being mentioned today, but all three were said to have denied to friends that they were seeking or would get the appointment. Lewis W. Douglas, deputy administrator of war shipping, was believed to be another possibility.

Whoever proves to be the appointee, the heads of four of the Government branches which would have to participate in the making of post-war plans admitted that they thought the time ripe for an announcement by the Government that arrangements were being made to allow industry, when the time comes, to be reconverted without dislocation or undue delay to the manufacture of civilian goods.

They said this would have a salutary effect on war production,

Continued on Page Thirteen

PRESIDENT IS GRIM

Only Long Peace Could Justify Sacrifices, He Declares in Ottawa

POST-WAR AIMS SET

Chief Executive Shows Scope at Quebec Was Wider Than Reported

The text of the President's address is printed on Page 2.

By P. J. PHILIP
Special to THE NEW YORK TIMES.

OTTAWA, Aug. 25—As a sequel to the Quebec conference President Roosevelt in Ottawa today summoned Adolf Hitler and his generals to surrender now before it is too late.

Standing in the Gothic archway of the great Peace Tower that forms the principal entrance to the Canadian Parliament, he gave Hitler this warning:

"If he and his generals had known our plans they would have realized that discretion is still the better part of valor and that surrender would pay them better now than later."

What these plans are, he added, would be communicated in due time to Germany, Italy and Japan "in the only language their twisted minds seem capable of understanding."

Thirty thousand persons had gathered on the lawns in front of the building to welcome the President and to hear him speak and their cheers rolled up in a storm when he uttered that warning.

They cheered again with hope when he declared that "during the past few days in Quebec we have talked constructively of our common purposes in this war—of our determination to achieve victory in the shortest possible time—of our essential cooperation with our great and brave fighting Allies. And we have arrived harmoniously at certain definite conclusions. * * * We are making sure—absolutely, irrevocably sure—that this time the lesson is driven home to them once and for all. Yes, we are going to be rid of outlaws this time."

Much Post-War Discussion

But the Quebec conference, he said, was not concerned only with winning the war. There was much talk, he said, of the post-war world—a discussion doubtless duplicated simultaneously in dozens of nations in hundreds of cities and among millions of people.

"There is a longing in the air," he said and the road to its realization lies first in absolute victory, which will prove what concerted action can accomplish. He said that by such concerted action greater freedom from want could be assured than the world had ever known while "by unanimous action in driving out the outlaws and keeping them under heel forever we can attain freedom from fear of violence."

The President's visit to Ottawa was a fitting culmination to the Quebec conference. It gave the capital and the Canadian people a long-awaited opportunity of expressing the depth of their feeling toward the people of the United States and their personal regard for the President.

To the enthusiasm of their cheering the recent successes in Sicily and Kiska gave a joyous note. A gust of laughter swept the great crowd when the President, referring to the Japanese withdrawal from the Aleutians, said:

"We have been told that Japs never surrender; their headlong retreat satisfies us just as well."

Flays Band of Gangsters

But there was also fierce approval in the handclapping that broke out after such a sentence as this:

"We spend our energies and our resources and the very lives of our sons and daughters because a band

Continued on Page Three

"All the News That's Fit to Print."

The New York Times.

LATE CITY EDITION
Moderately cool with gentle winds today.
Temperatures Yesterday—Max., 80; Min., 73
Sunrise, 6:23 A. M.; Sunset, 7:27 P. M.

Copyright, 1943, by The New York Times Company.

VOL. XCII..No. 31,268. Entered as Second-Class Matter, Postoffice, New York, N. Y. NEW YORK, FRIDAY, SEPTEMBER 3, 1943. THREE CENTS NEW YORK CITY

ALLIES LAND IN ITALY OPPOSITE MESSINA; 8TH ARMY LEADS, WITH AIR-NAVAL COVER; RUSSIANS DRIVE AHEAD, CAPTURING SUMY

HULL TO TAKE REINS OVER ALL AGENCIES IN ECONOMIC FIELD

Coordination of OEW, OFRRO and Lend-Lease Under State Department Is Due Soon

NOT ALL FRICTION ENDED

WFA and OEW at Odds—Capital Speculates on What Course Lehman Will Pursue

By JOHN MacCORMAC
Special to THE NEW YORK TIMES.

WASHINGTON, Sept. 2—The coordination of the Office of Economic Warfare, the Office of Lend-Lease Administration and the Office of Foreign Relief and Rehabilitation Operations by the State Department in a way which will give the department complete control over their activities and leave them as instruments executing its policies has been planned and will shortly be put in effect, it was learned today.

Part of the plan is the formulation of a definite and coordinated policy with regard to the international economic activities of the Government. Hitherto there has been a general understanding in theory, but in practice some of the agencies which were supposed to execute economic policy have worked at cross-purposes.

The conflict between the foreign activities of some of the Reconstruction Finance Corporation subsidiaries and those of the Board of Economic Warfare exploded recently in the row between Vice President Wallace and Secretary Jones, which led to the coordination of these activities by the OEW under Leo T. Crowley as its new head.

Some Friction Still Exists

But there is still uncertainty regarding the representative spheres of OEW, Lend-Lease and OFRRO and, for that matter, friction between OEW and the War Food Administration as regards foreign food purchases. The plan, therefore, is to have the State Department effect a final coordination of their efforts, and there is a possibility that some or all of them might be absorbed in the process.

This is not only believed to be the policy of the President and Secretary Hull, but it is understood to be approved by Mr. Crowley and Edward Stettinius Jr., lend-lease administrator. There is some doubt, however, whether ex-Gov. Herbert H. Lehman is willing to subordinate OFRRO to the State Department to the extent desired.

From a spokesman for Mr. Crowley it was learned that close collaboration with the State Department has from the first been one of his objectives. Mr. Crowley has indicated that as soon as the coordination is made and the administrative facilities have been set up, the time will have arrived for a substantial simplification of the Government's foreign economic set-up.

OEW Changes Held Temporary

It was because of these views that the reorganization of OEW announced Tuesday was regarded as of a transitory rather than permanent character.

For instance, James L. McCamy, who was appointed assistant to the director, will soon leave again to join the Bureau of the Budget. Hugh B. Cox, who will act as general counsel, will work only part time with OEW, and the rest of the time as assistant attorney general of the United States. No executive director was named, and Lauchlin Currie, who will act as executive officer, is on "loan" from the President's office.

Before OEW and lend-lease are placed under the State Department, however, the details of foreign economic policy will have been worked out and men of the requisite business ability will have been added

Continued on Page Seven

Meat Ration Points Are Cut But Butter Will Need More

Thirty-five Meat Items Are Reduced 1 to 2 Points on Report of Larger Supplies—Changes Take Effect Sunday

Special to THE NEW YORK TIMES.

WASHINGTON, Sept. 2—Point values of most meats were lowered today by the Office of Price Administration, effective Sunday through September. An exception is the increased purchasing power of red stamps was creamery butter. It will call for twelve instead of ten points a pound. The buying power of blue stamps was reduced by an increase in the point values of many processed fruits and vegetables.

The changes in red stamp values were based on the belief that more meat would be available to civilians for the rest of this month. The ration costs of most lamb and bacon cuts were reduced one to two points a pound. Lower values were fixed for sirloin steak, roasts of beef and several variety meats.

The increase in the point value of creamery butter is not likely to be noticed in most urban areas, where dealers, because of acute shortages, have been restricting customers to a quarter pound at a time and getting three points for the quarter pound, or twelve points a pound.

Farm or country butter was listed separately for the first time in the new point value schedules. To it a point value of six points a pound was assigned. Previously country butter had the same point value as creamery butter. The reduction was intended to spur the movement of farm-churned butter to urban markets to relieve the shortage of creamery butter.

"The further increase in the point value of creamery butter is necessary because purchases near butter-producing areas have been so large at a ten-point value that shortages developed in other parts of the country," the OPA said. "In addition butter production during

Continued on Page Eight

CONGRESS TAX MOVE IRKS MORGENTHAU

Joint Committee Plans to Subpoena Data Direct From Internal Revenue Body

Special to THE NEW YORK TIMES.

WASHINGTON, Sept. 2—A conflict has arisen between the joint committee of Congress on internal revenue taxation and the Treasury over the committee's power to obtain tax data direct from officials of any Government department or agency and this may lead to a test in the courts of the committee's authority.

The 1942 revenue act empowered the committee to obtain such data from officials of the Bureau of Internal Revenue or any other department without sending its requests through departmental heads.

The committee, jointly set up by the Senate Finance and House Ways and Means Committees, has seldom agreed with the Treasury on tax matters in recent years. Of late it has been paying less and less attention to the Treasury's views and insisting on writing its own tax bills.

It was to give Colin F. Stam, the committee's chief of tax experts, opportunity to make use of the fiscal and economic experience to be found in Government departments and particularly in the Internal Revenue Bureau that Congress was asked to authorize it to go over the head of Secretary Morgenthau to his subordinates and to deal similarly with other divisions.

Although neither the Treasury nor Mr. Stam would comment on

Continued on Page Ten

1,330 JAPANESE SAIL ON EXCHANGE LINER

Gripsholm Leaves on Second Trip—Teia Maru to Bring Americans Back Home

The exchange liner Gripsholm, painted white and carrying in huge letters on her side the word "Diplomat," sailed from her anchorage in New York Harbor early yesterday on her second mission to exchange Japanese civilians for Americans who have been interned in the Orient since December, 1941.

Gaily painted like the cruise ship she was before the United States Government chartered her in the spring of 1942 from the Swedish-American Line, the big vessel carried the gold and blue marks of Sweden, painted flags and brilliant lighting arrangements to identify her through submarine-infested waters.

In her cabins there were, according to announcements of the War and State Departments in Washington, 1,330 Japanese civilians who will be exchanged for Americans and nationals of other Western Hemisphere nations in the port of Mormugao, Portuguese India, on or about Oct. 15.

The Americans and their fellow internees—1,500 of them, including 1,250 citizens of the United States—are to travel from the Orient on the Japanese-flag liner Teia Maru.

The Washington announcements said that the Teia Maru was scheduled to leave Japan on Sept. 15, touching at ports in China, the Philippines and Indo-China to take on additional passengers, and calling at Singapore for fuel and wa-

Continued on Page Five

Browder Charges 'Bad Faith' Delays Opening a Second Front

Earl Browder, general secretary of the Communist party of the United States, asserted at a party meeting last night in Manhattan Center, 311 West Thirty-fourth Street, that Anglo-American relations with Soviet Russia would "deteriorate sharply" unless a second front in Western Europe was opened before the end of summer.

The meeting was a special one called to hear Mr. Browder discuss the present situation. About 3,000 persons were in the hall.

Mr. Browder argued that we should not wait until next spring in the hope that victory can then be "bought much more cheaply," but should land in full force now in an effort to win a quick victory and take some of the burden of land fighting off the Red Army. He held that military occupation by "fighting armies" was the only way nazism could be ended.

Mr. Browder, who is not a military expert, vigorously expressed the opinion that our troops were overwhelmingly able to open a second front whenever their leaders gave the word. But the British and American general staffs, he charged, have acted in the role of "politicians subject to reactionary influence," and have overruled themselves as military leaders, in which capacity, he said, they realize the need for a second front. Counting out "weakness" as a reason for not opening a second front, he said the only alternative was "bad faith."

Mr. Browder charged that "dark and sinister forces" in this country were accusing the Soviet Union of

Continued on Page Four

AIR BLOWS PRESSED

French Fields Pounded as Fortresses Join British in Sweeps

POWER PLANT IS HIT

Canal Locks Smashed on Key Dutch Route Serving Antwerp

New, Heavy Air Raids As Allies Land in Italy

By The United Press.

LONDON, Friday, Sept. 3—Powerful forces of Allied bombers ranged over the northern flank of the European continent early today, almost simultaneously with the invasion of Italy.

A long procession of bombers streamed out over the British coast, flying so high they could not be seen from the ground, although the roar of their motors was audible.

By The United Press.

LONDON, Friday, Sept. 3—American Flying Fortresses, culminating an evening of widespread activity that saw Royal Air Force Fighter Command planes in their biggest operation of the year, blasted enemy airfields at Mardyck and Denain in northern France late yesterday, a joint British-American communiqué reported today.

Squadrons of British Spitfires and Typhoons escorted medium B-26 Marauder bombers of the Eighth United States Air Force and RAF Boston, Mitchell and Ventura bombers in attacks on targets in Pas de Calais Department.

Fast and deadly P-49 Thunderbolts covered the Fortresses in their hard-hitting foray against the northern French airfields. "Good bombing results were observed on all targets," the joint communiqué said, adding that four enemy aircraft were destroyed—one by the Fortresses and three by Spitfires. One medium and one light bomber and two fighters were lost in the heavy operation.

The B-26 Marauder medium bombers of the Eighth United States Air Force attacked the power station at Mazingarbe, near Bethune, France, "with good results," the fighter pilots reported.

Continued on Page Six

RED ARMY ROLLING

Storms Ukraine Citadel and Seizes Towns on Kiev Rail Line

DONBAS KEYS TAKEN

Nazis Retreat Toward Dnieper—550 Places Fall in Two Days

By The Associated Press.

LONDON, Friday, Sept. 3—Moscow announced early today that five Red armies plunging westward had cut the Bryansk-Kiev railway 150 miles from Kiev, smashed German reinforcements in a six-mile gain on Smolensk and rolled up Axis lines in a new forty-five-mile-wide spurt in the Donets Basin.

Premier Joseph Stalin, in an order of the day, announced late yesterday that the Ukraine citadel of Sumy, ninety miles northwest of Kharkov, had fallen to Gen. Nikolai Vatutin's army, and a communiqué announced the capture of Krolevets and Yampol, two points on the vital Bryansk-Kiev railway linking the enemy's central and southern fronts.

Lisichansk, Voroshilovsk, Slavyanoserbsk and other cities were seized in the Donets Basin, while Budennovka, twenty miles from Mariupol, was taken in the push along the rim of the Sea of Azov, said the communiqué, recorded by the Soviet monitor.

250 More Places Overrun

The swiftness of the Russian advances and the tone of the communiqué indicated that the Germans were engaged in a large-scale retreat toward the Dnieper River, particularly in the huge Donets Basin. The bulletin, however, emphasized that the Germans were fighting stubbornly all along the 600-mile front.

More than 9,000 Germans were killed yesterday as the Red Armies overran nearly 250 cities and villages, many of them strategic prizes, for a two-day bag of nearly 550 localities.

Germany's 1941 invasion lines now have been cracked by the Russians in a 1943 offensive that has carried the Red Army more than half way along the comeback trail

Continued on Page Four

ACROSS NARROW WATERS TO EUROPE

Sept. 3, 1943

Allied forces spanned the Strait of Messina this morning to land on the toe of Italy. This map, a perspective view looking eastward, gives an idea how the mainland appeared to the invaders.

Other Invasions This Year Anticipated in Washington

By ROBERT F. WHITNEY
Special to THE NEW YORK TIMES.

WASHINGTON, Friday, Sept. 3—While Washington slept, its somnolent thousands secure in the knowledge that plans laid at Quebec last week would be efficiently carried out, the word was flashed to the capital that the invasion of the Italian mainland had begun. It was the first penetration by the Allies of Fortress Europe and thus a historic event which defied the pledge of Adolf Hitler that his Reich, by its aggressions, would secure its future for a "thousand years."

Unlike the invasion of North Africa by American troops nearly a year ago and the opening of the Sicilian campaign about two months ago, the invasion was not announced in Washington. The first news to the public came in flashes from North Africa.

The announcement, as received here, told of Allied troops swarming across the Strait of Messina. Only on Tuesday Prime Minister Churchill, in his Canadian speech, had stated that the Germans had augmented their forces in Italy and intended to make a battleground of that country.

The Allied invasion was seen here as an answer both to that challenge by the Germans and to the demands that a second front be opened in Europe this year.

When the news came, it is probable that the President and Mr. Churchill, the pair who are directing the strategy of the two English-speaking nations of the United Nations, were awaiting the news of a successful landing together in the White House study, as it is known that when they meet neither one retires early.

It was hoped here in semi-official quarters that the invasion of Italy would answer the prayers of Russia that her Allies in the west would lift some of the load off her shoulders by an attack on the European Continent.

While it was confidently expected that the invasion of Italy

Continued on Page Three

PLANE OUTPUT 7,700 FOR AUGUST, A JUMP

Production This Month May Reach 8,000, WPB Says—Rise Despite New Designs

Special to THE NEW YORK TIMES.

WASHINGTON, Sept. 2—Aircraft production last month totaled 7,700 planes, compared with 7,373 in July, the WPB reported today in tones of elation.

On the basis of the August figure, airplane production in September will top 8,000, it was said.

The rise in output last month as compared with July was at the rate called for in the production schedule. Both July and August production were below the original schedule, WPB officials said. But they maintain that the schedules are "unrealistic" in that they do not take into consideration the shifts in production occasioned by design changes and by many other factors.

Schedules have been adjusted three times so far this year, one official said, and are likely to be changed again. He added that "I'd rather make 6,500 planes of the type we needed than to meet the schedules which include many of the types we don't need and would rather not have."

He contended that "we got the planes we wanted. Those we didn't want we didn't get."

The discrepancy between the

Continued on Page Seven

War News Summarized

FRIDAY, SEPTEMBER 3, 1943

Allied forces crossed the Strait of Messina from Sicily and landed in southern Italy early this morning to start the long-awaited invasion of Europe, according to a communiqué issued by the Allied Headquarters in North Africa. The landing was the culmination of a series of devastating air blows. [1:8, maps pages 1, 2 and 3.]

The Russian war machine rolled relentlessly on yesterday. The important Ukrainian town of Sumy was captured, the Bryansk-Kiev railway was severed and a wide advance was made in the Donets Basin, with every indication that a German retreat to the Dnieper River was in full swing. [1:5, map P. 4.]

Continuing the softening-up process on the Continent, Allied fighters and bombers hit airfields in Northern France shortly after RAF fighters had returned from the Netherlands, where they struck at some of the most vital water communications controlled by the Germans. The bomb racks were unloaded on the strategic Hansweert Canal, where three locks were hit. The RAF reported that 107,520 American tons of bombs had been dropped on Germany in the first eight months of 1943. [1:4, map p. 6.]

The Navy Department in Washington still withheld details of Tuesday's raid on the Marcus Islands, but some of the mystery was dispelled by the Japanese, who acknowledged damage to the strategic air and observation base and estimated the American task force at 160 fighter and bomber planes from two carriers. Military observers at Pearl Harbor believe that the Marcus raid was just a feint and that a major blow against Japan's outer defenses is near. [5:1.]

Allied bombers dropped a record of 206 tons of bombs on the Japanese bases at Madang, New Guinea, General MacArthur reported. Ground troops also were strafed at Salamaua. [5:5, with map.]

The Pacific phase of the war is believed to be one of the principal subjects being discussed by Prime Minister Churchill and President Roosevelt in Washington. They have been holding day and night sessions. The Prime Minister also has conferred with high military and supply mission heads. [4:4.]

Another indication of the stepped-up pace to launch a second or a third front was the report from Washington of an August output of 7,700 planes as against 7,373 for July and indications that the figure might top 8,000 in September. [1:7.]

Portugal Weighs Idea of Fighting; Premier Tells People to Prepare

Neutral diplomatic quarters in London reported yesterday that Portugal was contemplating a declaration of war against Japan and might follow it with declarations against other Axis powers, according to The United Press.

The Portuguese action is said to arise from the fact that the Japanese established military control over Macao, in China near Hong Kong, as well as from Japanese occupation of Timor, in the southwest Pacific north of Australia.

Portuguese naval reservists have been called up during the past ten days. It was understood reliably that 10,000 reservists were being called to the Army. It was suggested that Portugal was now prepared to send expeditionary forces to free Macao and Timor.

The Government of Portugal on Wednesday night issued a formal statement "following fantastic rumors" and this statement gave the impression Portugal was on the eve of some important action.

LISBON, Sept. 2 (UP)—Premier Antonio de Oliveira Salazar stated today that Portugal's stepped-up military preparations were defensive but "in the unfortunate times in which we are living may have to be used against foreign enemies as much as against internal elements of national disintegration."

Clamping a tight censorship on speculation regarding the military preparations, Dr. Salazar cautioned against expecting any change in the country's foreign policy.

[The London Evening Standard interpreted the "mobiliza-

Continued on Page Five

DAWN IS ZERO HOUR

British and Canadians Storm Over Narrow Strait of Messina

ROME SAYS NOTHING

Allies Invade on Fourth Anniversary of Their War Declaration

By MILTON BRACKER
By Wireless to THE NEW YORK TIMES.

ALLIED HEADQUARTERS IN NORTH AFRICA, Friday, Sept. 3—The Allies have breached the "Fortress of Europe." On the fourth anniversary of the British and French declaration of war against Germany, Allied troops are striving to establish a bridgehead on the Italian side of the Strait of Messina.

Under the thunderous support of Allied sea and air power, British and Canadian forces of the British Eighth Army crossed the narrow strip of water to bring the war at long last to the mainland of the Continent that Germany has enslaved.

Preceded by a pounding artillery barrage across the strait and by a number of reconnaissance landings, the main party set foot on the tip of the Calabrian Peninsula, opposite Messina, at 4:30 A. M. today [10:30 P. M. Thursday, Eastern War Time].

No details were available on either this morning's historic assault or the previous reconnaissance missions. The latter were, plainly, those referred to in German broadcasts as landing attempts beginning on Aug. 29, which the Germans said had been repulsed with heavy losses.

[A Mutual Broadcasting System commentator, speaking from Algiers, quoted an official Allied spokesman today as saying that the Allies were "apparently engaged in heavy fighting." The Associated Press reported from London.]

A special communiqué issued here at 7:20 A. M. said merely: "Allied forces under General Eisenhower continued their advance. British and Canadian troops of the Eighth Army, supported by Allied sea and air power, attacked across the Strait of Messina early today and landed on the mainland of Italy."

Field Guns Pave Way

ALLIED HEAQUARTERS IN NORTH AFRICA, Sept. 3 (UP)—British, Canadian and other troops of the British Eighth Army spearheaded the invasion armies, swarming across the Strait of Messina from Sicily under cover of Allied aircraft and the big guns of British and American warships. The Eighth Army's field guns helped to pave the way for the invasion troops with a thunderous barrage that silenced several of the

Continued on Page Two

Arnold in Britain To Meet Air Chiefs

By The Associated Press.

LONDON, Sept. 2—Lieut. Gen. Henry H. Arnold, chief of the United States Army Air Forces, and Maj. Gen. William C. Lee, commander of an air-borne division, who is known as the father of American parachute troops, arrived in Britain today from the United States. They plunged immediately into a study of the military set-up and recent operations by the Eighth United States Air Force.

General Arnold is here for conferences with Air Chief Marshal Sir Charles Portal, Lieut. Gen. Jacob L. Devers, commanding all United States forces in the European theatre; Maj. Gen. Ira C. Eaker, commander of the Eighth Air Force, and other British and American officers.

"All the News That's Fit to Print."

The New York Times.

LATE CITY EDITION
Continued moderately cool today; moderate winds.
Temperatures Yesterday—Max., 74; Min., 67
Sunrise, 6:29 A. M.; Sunset, 7:17 P. M.

VOL. XCII..No. 31,274. Entered as Second-Class Matter, Postoffice, New York, N. Y. NEW YORK, THURSDAY, SEPTEMBER 9, 1943. THREE CENTS IN NEW YORK CITY

ITALY SURRENDERS, WILL RESIST GERMANS; ALLIED FORCES LAND IN THE NAPLES AREA; RUSSIANS IN STALINO, CLEAR DONETS BASIN

SOVIET TIDE RISES

Swift Red Army Blows Capture Key City, Free Rich Region

DRIVE NEARS DNIEPER

More Rail Hubs Fall—Thrust Toward Kiev Also Extended

By The United Press.

LONDON, Thursday, Sept. 9—The Red Army recaptured Stalino, Russia's twelfth city, yesterday and freed the Donets Basin, which before the war produced more steel than Japan and Italy combined, in a great surge that took it to Grishino, ninety miles east of Dniepropetrovsk on the lower Dnieper River.

While the armies of Gen. Rodion Y. Malinovsky and Gen. Fedor Tolbukhin drove the enemy from the rich Donets Basin, crowded with coal mines and factories, the army of Gen. Konstantin Rokossovsky drove to a point ninety-six miles northeast of Kiev by capturing Borzna, twenty-three miles west of Bakhmach.

Bakhmach and Romni, forty-two miles to the southeast, were surrounded on three sides, a Moscow radio bulletin reported, and thus the Bakhmach-Kremenchug railroad was cut. The roads leading from Bakhmach to Kursk and Gomel had been cut previously and only the lines to Kiev and Odessa remained open.

Picked Troops Take Stalino

Red Army shock troops, picked from the sixteen infantry divisions that had driven the Germans through city after city in six days of tireless fighting, took Stalino by storm.

The Russian communiqué said the Red Army troops drove in on Stalino throughout Tuesday night and yesterday morning. They fought through the suburbs and then stormed the city from north and south, routing the enemy in a street-by-street fight and capturing a great store of spoils.

Twenty-five miles northwest of Stalino the Russians took Krasnoarmeiskoye, a big railroad junction controlling two of four rail roads leading west from the basin.

In all the Russians took, in addition to Stalino, a city of 462,000 persons, more than 150 towns in the Donbas alone, twenty of them important, in gains of up to twelve and a half miles. During their Donbas offensive the Russians took twelve towns of more than 50,000 persons each.

The Germans at Krasnoarmeiskoye were so swiftly beaten that the Russians took nineteen planes and several loaded railroad trains.

March on Kiev Gains

On the Kiev front, the Russians took more than sixty towns in advances of up to twelve and a half miles. Their capture of Borzna in that area meant that the battle for the Dnieper River line had started. An advance of twenty-three miles to Nezhin would cut the only remaining German supply line east of the river. The Russians had already advanced 101 miles in nine days from Rylsk, half the distance to Kiev.

More than 1,000 Germans were killed at Borzna, and 1,000 were killed in another sector.

South of Bryansk the Russians advanced up to six miles to take several villages. They were reported only twenty miles south of Bryansk. The Soviet communiqué, recorded from the Moscow radio, reported that the Russians were advancing west of the Navlya railroad junction in this area, driving the Germans through dense forests.

West and southwest of Kharkov nearly four miles were gained in some sectors and about 1,200 Germans were killed.

The Germans were first to ad-

Continued on Page Twenty-two

New Fascist Regime Set Up, Nazis Report

By Cable to THE NEW YORK TIMES.

LONDON, Thursday, Sept. 9—The German radio announced early today that a "National Fascist government has been set up in Italy and functions in the name of Benito Mussolini."

The announcement, called a "proclamation by the National Fascist Government of Italy," said "this Badoglio betrayal will not be perpetrated. The National Fascist Government will punish traitors pitilessly."

The broadcast, in Italian, said nothing about the whereabouts of Mussolini, who has been reported under arrest. It was preceded by the playing of "Giovinezza," the Fascist anthem.

FOE'S MARCUS LOSS 80%, NIMITZ SAYS

U. S. Carrier Planes Alone Hit at Japanese Isle—Hell Cat Fighter Excels in Test

By ROBERT TRUMBULL

By Telephone to THE NEW YORK TIMES.

PEARL HARBOR, Sept. 8—Admiral Chester W. Nimitz, Commander in Chief of the Pacific Fleet, issued today a communiqué that gave the first details of the raid on Marcus Island Sept. 1. Coincidentally three naval air officers who participated in the action gave an interview covering all phases of the raid, which they said destroyed a surprisingly well-fortified Japanese air base.

Action Consisted of Bombing

Admiral Nimitz's communiqué said that a United States Pacific Fleet task force under command of Rear Admiral Charles A. Pownall attacked the little island, 1,185 miles southeast of Tokyo, at dawn Sept. 1. The air officers revealed that the action consisted entirely of bombing and strafing by carrier-borne aircraft.

They said that the new Grumman F6F Hellcat fighter was employed in combat for the first time in the

Continued on Page Twenty-two

IN HEART OF ITALY

American 7th Army Is Reported in Van of Naples Operation

MORE POINTS NAMED

Landings Rumored at Genoa, Pizzo, Gaeta and Leghorn

By Wireless to THE NEW YORK TIMES.

ALLIED HEADQUARTERS IN NORTH AFRICA, Thursday, Sept. 9—The Allies have carried the land campaign against the Nazis in Italy to the vicinity of Naples in new operations announced within twelve hours of the disclosure by Gen. Dwight D. Eisenhower that the Italian armed forces had unconditionally surrendered.

The news was announced here a few minutes past 6:30 A. M. in the following thirteen words:

"Further operations have started on the Italian mainland in the vicinity of Naples."

In the absence of the slightest expansion of the communiqué, no details are available as to the forces participating. The single fact remained that the attack had been pressed near Italy's southern metropolis and port, second only to Genoa, in what obviously was a major amphibious thrust.

Naples is a city of more than 700,000 population—nearer 1,000,000 if the suburbs are included. The assault was launched eighty-three years and two days after Garibaldi entered the city alone in a dramatic liberation gesture, which culminated in the unification of the country ten years later.

Although there is no indication just how near the city itself the landing or landings were carried out, it is plain that Naples is the objective of the sea-borne invaders.

[This dispatch did not indicate the make-up of the landing parties. A Tunis radio broadcast

Continued on Page Four

War News Summarized

THURSDAY, SEPTEMBER 9, 1943

Italy has surrendered unconditionally, and all hostilities between that country and the United Nations ceased yesterday. An armistice was signed last Friday, the same day that Italy was invaded, but the victors reserved the right to withhold announcement until the most favorable moment for the Allies. The armistice terms had been approved by the United States, Britain and Russia.

General Eisenhower, announcing the surrender, promised support to all Italians who helped fight the Germans. Marshal Badoglio issued a proclamation ordering all fighting against the "Anglo-American forces" to cease and commanding resistance to "attacks from any other quarter."

Allied radios and planes carried messages urging the Italians to take vengeance on their "German oppressors" and to prevent trains, ships and trucks from carrying German troops or supplies. [All the foregoing, 1:8; map, P.3.]

Landings in the Naples area followed only a few hours after the surrender announcement and it was believed the Allies were attempting to cut off German troops in southern Italy. The American Seventh Army was reported among the invading forces. [1:3; map, P. 4.] Earlier, the Italian Navy and merchant marine had been urged to take their ships to designated points and to scuttle the vessels as a last resort to keep them from the Germans. [7:4.]

Wild demonstrations of joy were reported from all over Italy, but in the north they gave way to sober realization of continued danger when the Germans occupied Milan and other cities and imposed martial law. [3:1.] No official comment came from Berlin, but the German radio, after withholding the news for hours, was furious at the "treachery." [1:5-6.]

Germany's Balkan satellites were so shaken by the Italian surrender that Bulgaria, Rumania and Hungary were reported ready to follow Italy out of the war. [10:3.]

President Roosevelt, in a radio address last night, termed the surrender a great victory for the Italian people as well as for the United Nations. But he warned: "The time for celebration is not yet. Our ultimate objectives in this war continue to be Berlin and Tokyo." [1:5-6.]

The actual fighting in Italy was of a minor nature. Land forces advanced on both coasts. [3:6.] Airfields were hit by Allied bombers and the Rome radio reported heavy raids on suburbs of the city. [4:1.]

With one Axis partner out of the war, the two others continued to be hit hard. The Red Army captured Stalino and cleared the Germans out of the Donets Basin. [1:1; map, P. 22.] Allied bombers from Britain struck enemy airfields in France and Belgium [23:2], while down in New Guinea Japanese troops were providing weak opposition as the Allies closed in on Lae. [22:1.]

The naval task force that raided Marcus Island Sept. 1 destroyed 80 per cent of the Japanese military installations. We lost three planes. [1:2.]

U. S. SOLDIERS IN LONDON CHEER THE NEWS

Americans in front of the Red Cross Washington Club in the British capital when the news of Italy's surrender was announced.

Associated Press Radiophoto, passed yesterday by censor

Announcements of the Surrender

By Broadcast to THE NEW YORK TIMES.

ALLIED HEADQUARTERS IN NORTH AFRICA, Sept. 8—The texts of the proclamations by Gen. Dwight D. Eisenhower and Premier Pietro Badoglio follow:

By GENERAL EISENHOWER

This is Gen. Dwight D. Eisenhower, Commander in Chief of the Allied Forces.

The Italian Government has surrendered its armed forces unconditionally. As Allied Commander in Chief, I have granted a military armistice, the terms of which have been approved by the Governments of the United Kingdom, the United States and the Union of Soviet Socialist Republics. Thus I am acting in the interest of the United Nations.

The Italian Government has bound itself to abide by these terms without reservation. The armistice was signed by my representative and the representative of Marshal Badoglio and it becomes effective this instant.

Hostilities between the armed forces of the United Nations and those of Italy terminate at once. All Italians who now act to help eject the German aggressor from Italian soil will have the assistance and the support of the United Nations.

By PREMIER BADOGLIO

The Italian Government, recognizing the impossibility of continuing the unequal struggle against the overwhelming power of the enemy, with the object of avoiding further and more grievous harm to the nation, has requested an armistice from General Eisenhower, Commander in Chief of the Anglo-American Allied forces. This request has been granted. The Italian forces will therefore cease all acts of hostility against the Anglo-American forces wherever they may be met. They will, however, oppose attack from any other quarter.

CITY 'JUMPS GUN' IN WAR BOND DRIVE

Rallies, Sales Begin on Vast Scale—State Savings Banks Will Invest $600,000,000

As President Roosevelt and Secretary of the Treasury Henry J. Morgenthau Jr. opened the Third War Loan Drive for $15,000,000,000 last night over the radio, it was announced here that in the campaign to raise the State's quota of $4,709,000,000 the mutual savings banks in the State would buy $600,000,000 in Government bonds. The United States Steel Corporation and its subsidiaries will buy $100,000,000 in Government securities, with parts of the total allocated to districts where the corporation operates.

Restive to get its drive under way, New York City held preliminary rallies yesterday as Army convoys took into the five boroughs Navy gunners who had been rescued at sea. The largest meetings were held in Times Square and on the steps of the Sub-Treasury Building at Wall and Broad Streets.

Burgess Hails Italy's Surrender

The thousands assembled in the streets for these two gatherings cheered wildly as speakers announced the capitulation of Italy. Ticker tape, confetti and torn paper were thrown from the windows of buildings where workers in the financial community were listening to the rally.

The unconditional surrender of Italy is "bullish news" and will be a great help in the bond drive, W. Randolph Burgess, chairman of the War Finance Committee for New York State, said later in the

Continued on Page Sixteen

President Hails Victory But Warns of Real Foes

By JOHN H. CRIDER

Special to THE NEW YORK TIMES.

WASHINGTON, Sept. 8—President Roosevelt hailed the surrender of Italy tonight as "a great victory for the United Nations" and also "a great victory for the Italian people" against "their real enemies, the Nazis," but cautioned against over-optimism. Addressing the nation on the opening of the Third War Bond drive, the President said "the time for celebration is not yet" and added that "our ultimate objectives in this war continue to be Berlin and Tokyo."

Toward the middle of his speech the President interpolated three words which gave basis to reports that Allied armies already were on the move again in the Mediterranean when he spoke of troops in landing barges moving up to enemy coasts "at this moment."

"This war does not and must not stop for one single instant," he declared. "Your fighting men know that. Those of them who are moving forward through jungles against lurking Japs—those who are landing at this moment in barges moving through the dawn up the strange enemy coasts—those who are diving their bombs down on the target at roof-top level at this moment—every one of these men knows that this war is a full-time job and that it will

Continued on Page Seventeen

Germans Charge Betrayal by Italy In Plot With Russian Government

By GEORGE AXELSSON

By Wireless to THE NEW YORK TIMES.

STOCKHOLM, Sweden, Sept. 8—Berlin's newspapers branded Italy's capitulation as cowardly treachery last night. The German press abounds in scatching denunciation of Premier Pietro Badoglio and King Victor Emmanuel, as well as the Italian people.

"Mussolini was too great a person for a nation like that," a German official said. This is the second time that Victor Emmanuel has broken his word, the newspapers say, because the King "left Germany in the lurch" in 1915 when he joined the Allies.

Forgetting its praise of the Italians during the heyday of their pact, Berlin now condemns the Italians as third-rate individuals. "The cowardly perfidy of Badoglio caps the crime," one paper said, "by being committed in collusion with the Soviet Government, which is treason not only against Italy and Germany but also against all Europe."

Berlin added that the Germans had no intention of giving up their entrenchments in Italy, where they hoped to offer efficient resistance. Italy, since last night, is German-occupied territory to the extent that the Germans have been able to gain a firm footing there. In the Italian provinces occupied by the Germans, Berlin boasts fascism will be revived even if "we leave it to the Italians in those provinces to organize themselves along fascist lines.

Official circles are reviving accusations of broken words of honor

Continued on Page Nine

GEN. EISENHOWER ANNOUNCES ARMISTICE

Capitulation Acceptable to U. S., Britain and Russia Is Confirmed in Speech by Badoglio

TERMS SIGNED ON DAY OF INVASION

Disclosure Withheld by Both Sides Until Moment Most Favorable for the Allies—Italians Exhorted to Aid United Nations

By MILTON BRACKER

By Wireless to THE NEW YORK TIMES.

ALLIED HEADQUARTERS IN NORTH AFRICA, Sept. 8—Italy has surrendered her armed forces unconditionally and all hostilities between the soldiers of the United Nations and those of the weakest of the three Axis partners ceased as of 16:30 Greenwich Mean Time today [12:30 P. M., Eastern War Time].

At that time, Gen. Dwight D. Eisenhower announced here over the United Nations radio that a secret military armistice had been signed in Sicily on the afternoon of Friday, Sept. 3, by his representative and one sent by Premier Pietro Badoglio. That was the day when, at 4:50 A. M., British and Canadian troops crossed the Strait of Messina and landed on the Italian mainland to open a campaign in which, up to yesterday, they had occupied about sixty miles of the Calabrian coast from the Petrace River in the north to Bova Marina in the south.

The complete collapse of Italian military resistance in no way suggested that the Germans would not defend Italy with all the strength at their command. But the capitulation, in undisclosed terms that were acceptable to the United States, the United Kingdom and the Union of Soviet Socialist Republics, came exactly forty days after the downfall of Benito Mussolini, the dictator who, by playing jackal to Adolf Hitler, led his country to the catastrophic mistake of declaring war on France three years and three months ago this Friday.

Negotiations Begun Several Weeks Ago

The negotiations leading to the armistice were opened by the war-weary and bomb-battered nation a few weeks ago, it was revealed today, and a preliminary meeting was arranged and held in an unnamed neutral country.

The Italians who had approached the British and American authorities were bluntly told that the terms remained what they had been: unconditional surrender. They agreed, and the document was signed five days ago. But it was agreed to hold back the announcement and its effective date until the moment most favorable to the Allies.

That moment came today, when the Allied Commander in Chief, in a historic broadcast, announced the armistice. He concluded with the reminder that all Italians who aided in the ejection of the Germans from Italy would have the support and assistance of the United Nations.

One hour and fifteen minutes after the General's voice had gone out over the air, Marshal Badoglio faced a microphone in Rome and confirmed the armistice. He concluded with the promise that the Italian forces would oppose attacks "from any other quarter," although they were laying down the arms that they had taken up against the Anglo-American armies.

Military Aspect Emphasized

Although it was emphasized that the armistice was a strictly military instrument, "signed by soldiers," it was disclosed that it contained a clause binding Italy to comply with political, economic and financial conditions to be imposed at the Allies' discretion.

[It was believed that the armistice conditions were substantially the same as those imposed on France in 1940, which allowed the Germans to use all strategic French ports and military bases to wage war against Britain, The United Press reported.]

Immediately after the announcement of the armistice, the Allies made two appeals—one to the Italian people and one to the Italian Fleet—urging them to rally to a cause that was, in effect, the liberation of their own country. The appeal to the people was disseminated by radio and air-borne leaflet, while that to the Navy was broadcast by Admiral Sir Andrew Browne Cunningham, the Allies' Mediterranean naval commander.

The Italian people, particularly transport, railroad and dock workers, were asked not to give the slightest aid to the Germans. The men who man Italian ships received specific instructions how to bring their vessels into the protection of the United Nations.

Although the fear was proved unjustified by Marshal Badoglio's broadcast, the Allies had taken no chances of a German move to forestall his giving the news to the people. As a safeguard, they had obtained from the Italians an agreement to leave one senior military representative behind when the others returned to Rome. This man is now in Sicily and presumably, had Marshal Badoglio not gone on the air, his representative would have broadcast the decision to the Italian public.

As a further earnest of good faith, Marshal Badoglio had arranged to send the text of the proclamation that he made this evening to Allied Headquarters here. He kept his word.

1,181 Days at War and Losses

Italy quit the war after 1,181 days, during which she steadily lost territory and prestige. Last May 7, with the fall of Tunis and Bizerte, the last Italian soldier in North Africa was doomed. Since then, Sicily, part of Metropolitan Italy, was occupied in thirty-eight days.

The Italians endured two raids on military targets in Rome

Continued on Page Three

"All the News That's Fit to Print."

The New York Times.

LATE CITY EDITION
Slightly warmer today with moderate to fresh winds.
Temperatures Yesterday—Max., 69; Min., 46
Sunrise, 7:04 A. M.; Sunset, 6:30 P. M.

Copyright, 1943, by The New York Times Company.

VOL. XCIII..No. 31,308. Entered as Second Class Matter, Postoffice, New York, N. Y. NEW YORK, WEDNESDAY, OCTOBER 13, 1943. THREE CENTS IN NEW YORK CITY

ITALY WILL DECLARE WAR ON GERMANY TODAY; 3 POWERS TO GIVE HER COBELLIGERENT STATUS; PORTUGAL GRANTS ALLIES USE OF AZORES BASES

PRESIDENT REPLIES TO SENATE CRITICS OF WAR AND ALLIES

Does Not Know if Russia Is Ready to Tackle Japan Too, He Remarks on Lodge

THEN HE CITES SOME FACTS

Senate Debates Reports in an Open Session as Ellender Is Denounced by Hatch

By JOHN H. CRIDER

Special to THE NEW YORK TIMES.

WASHINGTON, Oct. 12—President Roosevelt, commenting on the report of Senator Henry Cabot Lodge Jr. that a million American lives could be saved if Russia would make Pacific bases available to the United States, declared this afternoon that he did not know enough about the facts to say whether Russia was ready to declare war on Japan.

Certainly, the President said, Russia is busy on her western front, and, having knocked down the Nazis several times, maybe they'll stay down next time.

This was one of several contentions of the five Senators recently returned from battlefronts, which President Roosevelt contradicted at his press conference this afternoon; but although he admitted that the performance of the Senators had, on the other hand, caused some embitterment abroad—he referred specifically to England—on the other hand the debate which followed their statements did lead to a more sound public opinion. He was, he said, of two minds on the question whether the whole thing was good or bad.

Senate Debates the Reports

The President was not alone in commenting on the situation created by the reports of the committee members, for the Senate itself spent most of the day in a public debate on the question which rivaled in intensity the meetings held behind closed doors last week at which the five "fellow-travelers," as the President called them, made their secret reports.

The President was told of "a serious article" in THE NEW YORK TIMES reporting from London the feeling in Britain that the Senate development was an unfortunate thing, and he was asked if he felt that way.

You've always got to remember, the President said, that when members of a legislature get up on their feet and say things, the effect of which is not well thought out, it may create bitterness. He then pointed to some quotations on his desk from the British press, commenting that editorials in the British press certainly showed that this incident had created sor. bitterness.

But, he added, The Daily Telegraph of London declared that the so-called "secrets" were "childish nonsense" and perhaps it would be a good thing for Anglo-American relations if the whole thing was subjected to public debate.

That's why he was of two minds on the question, Mr. Roosevelt continued. It takes a certain amount of time to dig up this stuff like he had been talking about today (the factual denials of some of the Senators' reports) and last week (a reference to the facts he gave the press last week on arrangements with Britain on the use of petroleum resources).

One Effect of the Discussion

Getting the information to refute such contentions is time consuming, President Roosevelt said, but it does lead to a more sound public opinion. It gets the public interested, teaches geography, teaches problems of supply and of moving men overseas, the need for more ships, the need for more planes—more than everything else.

So in one sense, he declared, it's a damned nuisance, and in the other sense probably it's a good thing.

Mr. Roosevelt added that it made for publicity and discussion, and he had never deliberately dodged that.

The President was asked if

Continued on Page Nine

Motorists' Requests For Ration Books Lag

The New York District Office of Price Administration, Empire State Building, disclosed yesterday that local rationing boards and automobile dealers throughout the city had reported that only a handful of gasoline ration book holders had asked for their application renewal blanks.

Oct. 21 is the deadline for motorists to present their ration renewal blanks, according to a warning by William H. McKenna, chief District OPA Rationing Officer. Those failing to do so face a three-week delay between Nov. 8, when the present books expire, and Dec. 1, when they may apply again.

OPA representatives cautioned also that motorists should fill out their applications before they go to public schools next Tuesday, Wednesday and Thursday afternoons, Oct. 19, 20 and 21, from 3 to 7 o'clock, to obtain their new A books.

POPE SAID TO SPURN 'HAVEN' IN GERMANY

Pontiff Refuses Request to Seek Safety in Liechtenstein or Reich, Neutrals Say

By The United Press.

LONDON, Oct. 12—The Germans have advised Pope Pius XII to leave Rome because they cannot guarantee the Vatican's safety if the city becomes a battleground, and they have "offered" to move him to the neutral Principality of Liechtenstein or to Germany, dispatches from neutral capitals said today.

The Pope refused the "offer" and said that he would not leave the Vatican while he was alive, the dispatches said.

[A German broadcast, apparently designed deliberately to give the impression that the Vatican anticipated military action or at least demolitions in the Rome area, said that Vatican City had "started building some great water reservoirs" as a "precautionary measure in connection with war circumstances," according to the Federal Communications Commission.]

An Algiers dispatch to the Stockholm Social Demokraten said that the German envoy in Rome had advised the Pope to seek refuge in Liechtenstein, a predominantly Catholic State nestled along the eastern border of Switzerland.

These reports were not verified in any official quarters.

Germany announced on Sept. 10 that her troops had assumed the "protection" of the Vatican, policing St. Peter's Square in place of Italian carabinieri formerly ported there to protect the Vatican against "irresponsible elements." Since that time German broadcasts have maintained that relations with the Vatican were "normal."

Not long after German troops had moved into Rome, however, the Berlin radio broadcast a statement by Benito Mussolini's National Fascist Republican Government assailing the Vatican for alleged anti-fascist attitudes.

1373 PACT INVOKED

British Land Troops—Blow to U-Boats and Aid to Invasion Seen

REPRISALS DOUBTED

Churchill Gives Lisbon Assurance, However, of Aid in 'Emergency'

The text of Mr. Churchill's statement is on Page 8.

By JAMES B. RESTON

By Cable to THE NEW YORK TIMES.

LONDON, Oct. 12—Portugal has agreed, at the request of the British Government, to permit the United Nations to use the Azores, her watchtower archipelago in the mid-Atlantic for the protection of the great convoys that must in the next few months bring the invasion armies of the United States to Britain and North Africa.

This was announced today by Dr. Antonio de Oliveira Salazar, Portuguese Premier, and by Prime Minister Churchill, who emphasized that this concession was in accord with an Anglo-Portuguese treaty of 1373 and did not alter the desire of both countries to keep Portugal out of the war.

British forces have already landed on the nine islands of the Azores, which lie along main Atlantic shipping lanes 1,000 miles from Lisbon, 900 from Africa and 1,400 from Newfoundland. So far as can be discovered, no United States troops took part in the operation; but United States warships and aircraft will use the naval and air bases in the islands whenever they like.

The arrangement is for the duration of the war and includes provision for British assistance in furnishing material and supplies to Portuguese armed forces. It does not, Mr. Churchill told the House of Commons, prejudice Portuguese sovereignty in any way, and in the British view it is not incompatible with Portugal's neutrality.

Nazi Reprisal Doubted

At a late hour blacked-out Lisbon was peaceful and the general feeling in London was that the Nazis are too busy in Russia and Italy and on the home front to risk any punitive expedition across the Pyrenees.

The acquisition of bases in the Azores must be considered in relation to the invasion of the Continent, which President Roosevelt and Prime Minister Churchill have promised will come "at the right moment."

The Azores lie alongside not only the southern route from the United States to Britain but directly on the route between Venezuela, which Britain gets a lot of her oil, and the United Kingdom.

They will also serve as a supply base for planes and ships protecting convoys into the Mediterranean and be of great assistance as a center of meteorological information.

Considerable engineering works

Continued on Page Eight

OPENING OF NEW BASE TO THE ALLIES BRIDGES GAP IN THE ATLANTIC

CANADA
LABRADOR
Quebec
Montreal
NEWFOUNDLAND
St. Johns
Halifax
Boston
New York
WASHINGTON
UNITED STATES
Charleston
BERMUDA
BAHAMA IS.
CUBA
WEST INDIES
HAITI
DOMINICAN REP.
PUERTO RICO
ANTIGUA
MARTINIQUE
ST. LUCIA
Caribbean Sea
CURACAO
TRINIDAD
S. AMERICA
ATLANTIC OCEAN
AZORES (PORTUGAL)
GREENLAND
EIRE
ENGLAND
Brest
PARIS
St. Nazaire
FRANCE
Bordeaux
PORTUGAL
LISBON
SPAIN
Gibraltar
Casablanca
MOROCCO
MADEIRA (PORTUGAL)
ALGERIA
CANARY IS. (SPAIN)
RIO DE ORO
FRENCH WEST AFRICA
CAPE VERDE IS. (PORTUGAL)
Dakar
GAMBIA
PORT. GUINEA
SIERRA LEONE
1000 MILES
500 MI.
800 MI.
900 MI.
Oct. 13, 1943

Portugal has agreed to allow Britain and the United States to use the Azores in the war against U-boats, and the British have already landed there. The mid-Atlantic area bounded by the arcs on the map is the zone that it has not been possible to patrol with land-based planes. With the Azores as a base the area within the large circle will be brought within bomber range and so a substantial and important section of the "open" area will be removed. Thus the routes from the United States to the British Isles and the Mediterranean, as well as from South America to Britain, will now be better protected against submarine attacks.

U.S. TO USE AZORES, PRESIDENT AFFIRMS

He Stresses Joint Action With British to Guard American Lives and Shipping

By BERTRAM D. HULEN

Special to THE NEW YORK TIMES.

WASHINGTON, Oct. 12—President Roosevelt indicated definitely at his press conference today that the United States would use the Azores along with the British.

What could be said at present, he explained, was that the British and we are allies, that we are trying to win the war, and that we conduct joint operations. While we have no agreement with Portugal,

Continued on Page Five

Russians Deepen Thrusts Over Dnieper, Flank Kiev

By The Associated Press.

LONDON, Wednesday, Oct. 13—Soviet forces widened their areas of penetration on the west bank of the Dnieper in close-quarter fighting yesterday after battering down German counter-attacks, and the Berlin radio said the Red Army had opened a new drive "north of Kiev." The Russian operational bulletin and midnight supplement, broadcast from Moscow and recorded by the Soviet monitor, disclosed today that Red Army troops had edged closer to the White Russian citadel of Vitebsk in the north in the face of stern enemy opposition.

[Moscow heard reports that German demolition squads had begun a systematic destruction of Kiev preparatory to evacuat-

Continued on Page Ten

INVADERS OF ITALY CONSOLIDATE GAINS

Artillery Takes Larger Role as Battle Northwest of Capua Is Reported by Cairo

By Wireless to THE NEW YORK TIMES.

ALGIERS, Oct. 12—Both Allied armies in Italy have come to a virtual standstill, it was officially announced yesterday. Aside from continued artillery exchanges on the central front and patrol activity up and down the line, the campaign has reached its greatest lull since Lieut. Gen. Mark W. Clark's Fifth Army landed below Salerno on Sept. 9.

[A thundering artillery exchange blazed across the Volturno Valley as Allied troops prepared to storm the river barrier, The United Press reported. It quoted a Cairo radio report that a heavy battle was in progress northwest of Capua, on the far side of the Volturno.

[German broadcasts admitted that British and Canadian troops in the middle of the line had thrust to the area of Jelsi in a new ten-mile advance putting them twenty-three miles north of Benevento and only eight miles southeast of Campobasso.]

Both the Fifth and the British Eighth Armies had plenty to do in bringing up supplies and consolidating positions. But their distance from Rome remained the

Continued on Page Three

U. S. ASKS ITALIANS TO BACK BADOGLIO

Berle Brings Roosevelt Pledge to Labor Group Here That No Regime Will Be 'Imposed'

Quoting an authorized statement by President Roosevelt to give point to his utterances, Adolf A. Berle Jr., Assistant Secretary of State, asked Italian-American anti-Fascists in a Columbus Day address here last night to halt present criticism of the government of Marshal Pietro Badoglio and to cooperate with it for the reconquest of Italy.

Revealing also, in what amounted to an official statement, that the State Department will support an immediate move by organized labor to re-establish free trade unions in Italy, Mr. Berle spoke before 1,200 persons at a dinner held in the Hotel Roosevelt under the auspices of the Italian-American Labor Council.

Mr. Berle also declared that the

Continued on Page Four

TO JOIN THE ALLIES

Badoglio Regime's Move to Have Backing of the U. S., Britain, Russia

FLEET ACTION IS SEEN

Operation of Warships by Italians Is Hinted At by Churchill

Italy formally will declare war on Germany today and will be recognized as a cobelligerent against her former Axis partner, according to private advices reaching THE NEW YORK TIMES last night.

The action, it was understood, will be taken with the approval of the United States, Britain and Russia, which have agreed to grant Italy cobelligerent status, according to the report. Such recognition would not include Italy among the United Nations, although presumably the Allies would be compelled to equip with lend-lease material any large Italian forces put into the field.

The declaration of war, to be made, apparently, by the Badoglio Government as at present constituted, would, however, regularize the position in which Italy has found herself since the fall of Mussolini last July 25 and the surrender negotiated by King Victor Emmanuel and Marshal Pietro Badoglio.

Already Acts With Allies

For although technically in a condition of occupation by victorious armies, Italy through her military leaders has already been acting with British and American commanders on Italian soil in regard to "military operations of mutual interest." That was the phrase used in the official communiqué to describe the topics discussed Sept. 30, when Marshal Badoglio and his military aides met Gen. Dwight D. Eisenhower, Admiral Sir Andrew Browne Cunningham and other Allied leaders aboard a warship at Malta.

Also, it was recalled, Marshal Badoglio, although the head of a surrendered and therefore presumably nonbelligerent government, early called on all Italians to consider the Germans as enemies. Meanwhile, at least skeleton Italian forces have remained in being behind the Allied lines in Italy, and Italian regular troops have been reported carrying on guerrilla war against the Germans in the north.

The report of Italy's forthcoming action and her recognition as a cobelligerent by the three large Allied nations came at a time when representatives of those powers already were setting up a joint military-political commission for the Mediterranean area at Algiers. One of the principal aims of the body, named the Politico-Military Commission, is cooperative action in establishing the broad plan of operations in the Italian sphere.

The recognition of Italy as a cobelligerent by the three great powers fighting the Axis in Europe may serve as a counter to whatever Italian strength has been mustered behind the puppet government set up by the Germans in the north under the purported leadership of Mussolini.

Suggest Hint by Churchill

What forces a cobelligerent Italy might be able to send to war against Germany currently probably is obscure to all except the Allied High Command, but some saw a hint last night in a statement of Prime Minister Winston Churchill that the Italian Fleet might fight under its own commanders on the United Nations side.

The British Prime Minister in a reply to a House of Commons questioner yesterday revealed not only that more than 100 Italian warships were in Allied hands but that their employment still was under advisement. He added, according to The Associated Press, that the

Continued on Page Four

War News Summarized

WEDNESDAY, OCTOBER 13, 1943

Important developments have been quick to follow Allied successes in the Mediterranean. Private advices reaching THE NEW YORK TIMES said that Italy, with the consent of the United States, Great Britain and Russia, would declare war on Germany today and become a cobelligerent. [1:8.]

Portugal effectively threw in her lot with the United Nations by granting Great Britain's request for the use of the Azores as an Allied naval and air base. The islands, which lie at the apex of a triangle approximately 1,000 miles from Newfoundland and England, will provide added protection for the large convoys for the invasion of Europe. The British, who were already on the new bases, assured Portugal that her sovereignty was unaffected and that all forces would be withdrawn after the war. [1:3.]

The United States will also use the base, President Roosevelt indicated. He also indicated that the Cape Verde Islands, between Africa and South America, would become available. [1:4.]

In Lisbon Premier Salazar declared that Portugal had not altered her determination to remain neutral [8:1.], and Spain saw nothing in the developments to change her attitude. [6:1.] The Axis was apparently caught by surprise. Berlin had no official comment. [7:1.]

Another diplomatic setback for the Axis was seen in the report that Brazil's Foreign Minister Aranha had indicated the likelihood of an Argentine break with Germany and Japan. [1:6-7.]

In the fighting in Russia the Red Army widened its bridgeheads across the Dnieper in moves to flank Kiev. Moscow heard the Germans were preparing to abandon that city. [1:5-6.]

Bad weather over the Italian front continued to hold up ground action, which was limited to patrol activity and artillery exchanges. [1:7; map P. 2.] Yugoslav Partisans reported additional gains. [3:1-2.]

Four Thunderbolts fought it out with thirty-two Japanese planes over Wewak, New Guinea, and shot down eight and probably ten of the enemy without loss. [15:1.] President Roosevelt told his press conference that our Navy, mainly with submarines, in the last six months had sunk Japanese ships at the rate of 130,000 tons a month. He said that 855 United States planes had participated in last Friday's raid on Bremen. [13:1.]

Mr. Roosevelt took issue with many of the criticisms voiced by Senators recently returned from a world tour. He said Russia was too busy knocking down Hitler to protect any Siberian bases she might let us use if Japan should declare war against her. [1:1.]

Navy Secretary Knox said the British midget submarines that damaged the Tirpitz were two-man craft, and added that our Navy was taking over a British airfield as a bomber base. [10:3.]

In an effort to halt coal strikes and assure fuel for all purposes Great Britain plans to conscript coal miners on the same basis as soldiers. [16:2.]

Ickes Turns Back Last Coal Mines, Terminates Government Operation

Special to THE NEW YORK TIMES.

WASHINGTON, Oct. 12—Government possession of coal mines ended today when Secretary Ickes, as Coal Administrator, turned back to private owners the 1,700 coal mines remaining under Government control.

With the announcement that "we are now out of the coal mining business," Mr. Ickes said the Coal Mines Administration will be liquidated immediately. The agency was established last July to operate the 3,300 mines taken over by the Government on May 1 when failure of miners and operators to agree on a new wage contract had stopped production.

About 1,600 mines had been turned back to private ownership previously, the first group having been restored to the control of their owners on Aug. 30. Most of the miners still have no contract.

"We are grateful that sufficient progress has been made in restoring the mines as nearly as possible to normal productive efficiency, all things considered, thus allowing us to terminate this emergency function and wind up the affairs of the Coal Mines Administration," Mr. Ickes said.

The Administrator praised the work of Carl E. Newton, deputy coal administrator, and members of his staff who are resigning.

"I want to express my thanks to Mr. Newton for having left his important post as president of the Chesapeake & Ohio Railroad in Cleveland to come here in this emergency to share an extremely heavy load," Mr. Ickes said. "To him and to his hard-working staff, who are resigning with him, I say,

Continued on Page Sixteen

Argentine Break With Axis Near, Brazil Report to Hull Indicates

By The United Press.

RIO DE JANEIRO, Brazil, Oct. 12—Preliminary moves for an Argentine break with the Axis have been completed and an announcement is expected within two weeks, an unimpeachable diplomatic source said tonight.

The return to Buenos Aires of Norman Armour, United States Ambassador to Argentina, and the appointment of Adrian Escobar as Argentine envoy to Washington were direct consequences of the moves preliminary to a break, the informant said.

Secretary of State Cordell Hull, at Natal on his way by plane to attend the American-British-Russian diplomatic conference, conferred there with Brazilian Foreign Minister Oswaldo Aranha and Jefferson Caffery, our Ambassador to Brazil. Dr. Aranha and Mr. Caffery gave Mr. Hull first-hand information on the prospective Argentina-Axis break, it was believed.

[Reuter reported from Montevideo, Uruguay, last night a Cabinet shake-up in Argentina in which the Ministers of Finance, Public Works and Justice and Public Instruction had resigned.]

One consequence of the expected break, the informant said, probably would be United States financial aid to Argentina in some form.

The informant understood that Argentina's basis for a break would be simply compliance with the terms of the Pan-American agreements, to which Argentina is a signatory.

Brazil was understood to be playing a leading role in negotiations

Continued on Page Six

"All the News That's Fit to Print."

The New York Times.

LATE CITY EDITION
Showers and cooler this afternoon; partly cloudy tonight.
Temperatures Yesterday—Max., 56; Min., 43
Sunrise, 7:31 A. M.; Sunset, 5:18 P. M.

VOL. XCIII..No. 31,332. Entered as Second-Class Matter. Postoffice, New York, N. Y. NEW YORK, SATURDAY, NOVEMBER 6, 1943. THREE CENTS IN NEW YORK CITY

SENATE VOTES 85 TO 5 TO COOPERATE IN PEACE; ALLIES GAIN IN ITALY, RUSSIANS DRIVE ON KIEV; 500 U. S. BOMBERS SMASH AT TWO BIG NAZI CITIES

MINE PAY INCREASE APPROVED BY WLB IN VOTE OF 11 TO 1

Board Sanctions Lewis-Ickes Pact With Some Qualifications as Morse Dissents

HE HITS 'ECONOMIC FORCE'

Davis Upholds the Award as Meeting Stabilization Policy—Union Speeds Return

By LOUIS STARK
Special to THE NEW YORK TIMES.

WASHINGTON, Nov. 5—The National War Labor Board, by a vote of 11 to 1, approved tonight the contract arranged between Secretary Ickes and the United Mine Workers of America, subject to clarification and resubmission of some details to the board. Wayne Lyman Morse, public member, filed a sharp dissent.

The vote was taken at 10:45 o'clock tonight at the conclusion of the second day's discussion, during which the board considered the contract submitted to it forty-eight hours ago.

Following the board's announcement, John L. Lewis and members of the union's policy committee met and decided to seek clarification from Secretary Ickes of the questions raised in the decision, such as that over piecework. Mr. Lewis then sent the members to the coal fields to press for the early return of all of the 530,000 miners. It was estimated that 15 to 20 per cent were back at work today and that production would be fully resumed Monday.

The WLB chairman, William H. Davis, in a separate statement, pointed out that the Ickes-Lewis contract would pay the day-rate men $1.50 an hour for an extra full hour of work.

Increases totaling 70 cents a day, in addition to allowances for tools and vacation payments, were approved for the anthracite field.

Statement by Davis

The text of the statement by Mr. Davis follows:

"The contract signed by Secretary Ickes and the president of the United Mine Workers pays the day-rate mine workers one dollar and a half for an extra full hour of work each day. This is what they would get under the present contract. When corrected for tonnage workers it will be within the limits of the national wage stabilization policy, because the increased daily earnings will then all be in payment for increased production of coal.

"Four stoppages of work have occurred in this basic industry since the president of the UMW announced to the country that he was going to obtain for no more work a $2-a-day wage increase, no more, no less, regardless of the wage stabilization policies of this board. Under the contract with the Government the extra pay is for extra work paid for at the old rate or for overtime pay required by the Fair Labor Standards Act."

Morse Assails the Action

In his dissenting opinion Mr. Morse, dean of the University of Oregon Law School, opposed approval on the ground that the contract was "the product of the use of economic action against the Government and the nation and, therefore, should be disapproved as being against sound policy."

Charging that the acceptance of the agreement by the board violated the Government's policy that strikers must first return to work, Mr. Morse declared that the example set by the procedure in this case "is likely to cause serious interruption of production in any other industry in which there may be irresponsible union officials who are not loyal to their no-strike pledge."

In a letter to Secretary Ickes Chairman Davis said that while the proposed contract applied to employes working on a day-wage basis who were paid for portal-to-portal time under the Fair Labor Standards Act for time worked after forty hours weekly, "the provisions as to tonnage workers do

Continued on Page Nine

President Names 5 of WLB For Cost of Living Inquiry

Order to Report in 60 Days Is Interpreted as 'a Delaying Action' to Counter Move to Scrap Wage Formula

By ROBERT F. WHITNEY
Special to THE NEW YORK TIMES.

WASHINGTON, Nov. 5—President Roosevelt named a five-man committee of War Labor Board members today to investigate the cost of living and to report within sixty days. This move, coinciding with the decision of the Congress of Industrial Organizations to scrap the "Little Steel" formula, was interpreted as "a delaying action," which insured retention of that wage program for at least two months.

At the same time WLB personnel, in unofficial comment on the CIO decision, expressed the opinion that scrapping the "Little Steel" formula would open the door to inflation, as it would require an all-round wage adjustment for the country's wage-earning classes as well as for revision of farm costs.

Just how much of a revision in the "Little Steel" formula and in the present wages in the steel industry would satisfy the CIO was not indicated today. In labor circles it was believed that while the American Federation of Labor and CIO might come out for a 10 per cent upward adjustment, a compromise of 6 or 7 per cent would be acceptable.

Applied to a national wage bill of at least seventy-five billion dollars, it was estimated that such an adjustment would add between $4,500,000,000 and $5,000,000,000 to the annual income of the 54,000,000 employed.

Coming on the heels of the agreement made by Secretary Ickes and John L. Lewis in the coal crisis, the CIO abandonment

Continued on Page Nine

CIO TO OPEN FIGHT ON PAY RISE CURB

Wage Demand for 900,000 Steel Workers to Begin Drive —Murray Is Re-elected

By WALTER W. RUCH
Special to THE NEW YORK TIMES.

PHILADELPHIA, Nov. 5—A flat increase of at least 15 cents an hour for 900,000 steel workers will be the opening demand in the campaign of the Congress of Industrial Organizations for wage increases greater than those allowed by the "Little Steel" formula, it was learned tonight.

The demand, having the effect of increasing the basic hourly wage rate for common labor in the steel industry from 78 cents to 93 cents, will presage many similar requests from thousands of CIO locals throughout the country, it can be stated.

The CIO views the agreement between John L. Lewis and Secretary Harold L. Ickes, as Solid Fuels Administrator, to give to soft and hard coal miners a wage increase of $1.50 a day not as the cause for their action but as the coup de grace to a series of blows violating the "Little Steel" formula, it was said.

The CIO campaign will begin on Monday when the executive board of the United Steel Workers of America, whose president, Philip Murray, also is president of the CIO, meets here to lay the groundwork for a drive to raise wages for 900,000 in that industry, covered by 1,300 individual contracts.

Other unions in the CIO, which embraces 5,285,000 members, will take their cue from the action by the steel workers, it was learned. More than 9,000 contracts cover CIO war workers.

These things were learned tonight as the CIO national conven-

Continued on Page Nine

U. S. COLLEGES SET OWN 'LEND-LEASE'

Plan to Train Large Number of Foreign Students to Rebuild Occupied Lands

By BENJAMIN FINE

Plans for the immediate training in American colleges, universities and technical schools of a considerable number of persons from the occupied countries, to prepare them to work in specific fields of reconstruction and rehabilitation in their own lands, have been approved by educational leaders of the United States and representatives of foreign nations, it was revealed yesterday.

A sixteen-point program of action, setting up standards for the most extensive system of scholarships ever attempted in this country, has been adopted. This action is the culmination of nearly two years of conferences and discussions between educators here and abroad. Final details still are to be worked out, but the broad outlines of the project have been determined.

Greece, Poland, Czechoslovakia and Norway already have agreed in principle to the program of scholarship exchange, Dr. Stephen Duggan, director of the Institute of International Education, who has just returned from London, where he studied the problem, reported. Other nations are expected to become part of the general program soon.

Educators from this country and representatives of many of the occupied nations of Europe attended an Institute on International Exchanges and Scholarships at New York University yesterday afternoon under the auspices of the United States Committee on Educational Reconstruction. Dr.

Continued on Page Eight

Curran in 2A on Hershey Order; Future Induction Is Not Likely

Joseph Curran, 37-year-old president of the National Maritime Union, once again had his draft classification changed yesterday from 1-A to 2-A—and this time his deferment as an essential union leader, by order of Maj. Gen. Lewis B. Hershey, national director of Selective Service, should finally and safely remove any possibility of his induction into the armed forces because he will reach his thirty-eighth birthday before this reclassification for six months expires.

Mr. Curran was placed in 1-A on Sept. 17 by Selective Service Appeal Board No. 4 of this city, which held that he was "not necessary" in either the operation of his union or American ships and therefore not entitled to deferment in Class 2-A, which is reserved for a man necessary in his civilian activity. Col. Arthur V. McDermott, New York City Director of Selective Service, had appealed Mr. Curran's 2-A classification by Local Board 18 at 1133 Broadway.

Announcement of the reclassification order from General Hershey, contradictorily designating Mr. Curran, who is married but has no children, as "essential to civilian activity," was made by the Rev. Francis K. Shepherd, chairman of Local Board 18 and also pastor of the North Baptist Church at 232 West Eleventh Street. The reversal of Appeal Board No. 4 here, Mr. Shepherd said, resulted from an appeal to the President by officials of the National Maritime Union.

The President has authority to delegate his rights and prerogatives in Selective Service matters

Continued on Page Nine

5TH ARMY STRIDES

Reaches the Garigliano River, a Little Over 75 Miles From Rome

8TH WINS SAN SALVO

Drives On Toward Nazis' Adriatic Anchor as Foe Yields Along Line

By MILTON BRACKER
By Wireless to THE NEW YORK TIMES.

ALGIERS, Nov. 5—With the German line snapped in two at Isernia and the retreating Nazis flooding some western coastal sectors in the path of the advancing Allies, both the Fifth and Eighth Armies in Italy drove ahead faster yesterday.

Gen. Sir Bernard L. Montgomery's British and Canadians finally wrested San Salvo on the Adriatic front from the enemy while Lieut. Gen. Mark W. Clark's Americans and British swept up the Tyrrhenian coast to the south bank of the Garigliano River just over seventy-five miles from Rome.

The Germans were expected to repeat their tactics of digging in on high ground across the Garigliano in the hope of slowing the Allied advance, once the two armies, and the Fifth in particular, complete the literally downhill battle made possible by the cracking of the Massico-Isernia line.

Eighth Army Nears Vasto

On the Eighth Army front the capture of San Salvo along with the establishment of several more bridgeheads around Montemitro despite stubborn counter-blows powered by German tanks, put General Montgomery's veterans within four miles of Vasto, which is the northern anchor of the enemy's transpeninsular front. The capture of Vasto will mean that the first stage of the battle for Rome has definitely ended.

The fall of Isernia brought swift Allied envelopment of a number of other towns, as has been foreshadowed in the past few days. The Eighth Army took Carpinone, five miles east of Isernia on a secondary road loop, while the Fifth seized San Agapito, four miles south of Isernia and two miles behind the new Isernia-Vallecupa line.

Vallecupa, also on the American

Continued on Page Five

ALLIES CONTINUE TO ADVANCE SWIFTLY IN ITALY

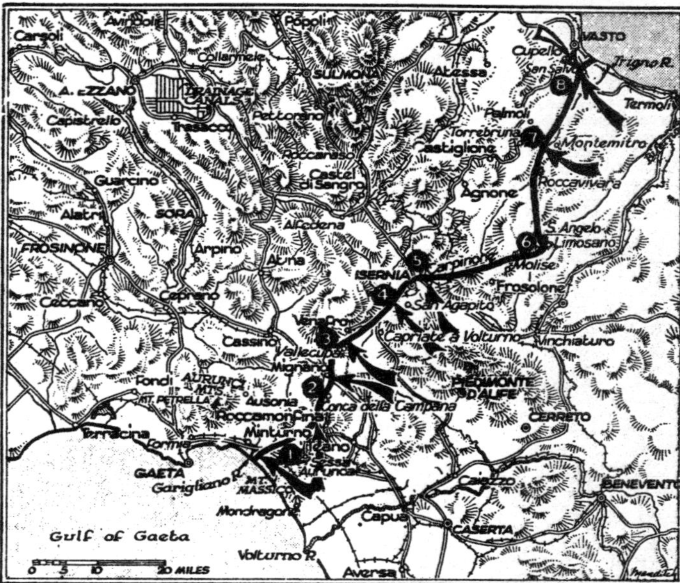

The Fifth Army, reaching the south bank of the Garigliano, overran a score of villages between the coast and Roccamonfina (1). It pushed ahead to within a mile of Mignano (2), captured Vallecupa (3) and reached the outskirts of Venafro. San Agapito (4) and Carpinone (5) also fell to General Clark's men. A rectification of the Eighth Army's line showed it holding San Angelo and Limosano (6) rather than advance points previously claimed. It gained more bridgeheads near Montemitro (7) and seized San Salvo (8) despite counter-attacks.

GELSENKIRCHEN HIT IN DAYLIGHT BLOWS

Big Planes With Fighter Cover All Way Batter Ruhr City, Muenster—Bag 38 Nazis

By DREW MIDDLETON
By Cable to THE NEW YORK TIMES.

LONDON, Saturday, Nov. 6—In the heaviest American daylight attack on the Reich, close to 500 Flying Fortresses and Liberators flew through an unprecedented barrage of Nazi anti-aircraft fire yesterday to blow the heart out of the great oil manufacturing center of Gelsenkirchen in the Ruhr and shatter the railroad yards at Muenster to the northeast.

The assault by the United States Eighth Air Force's heavies was the most telling strike in a day of widespread operations. American

Continued on Page Six

Red Army in Kiev Suburbs; Dnieper Delta Freed of Nazis

By The Associated Press.

LONDON, Saturday, Nov. 6—Soviet forces swarmed down from the north into the northern and western suburbs of Kiev to outflank that historic cathedral city and surround it on three sides in a major new Russian drive that broke through two German defense lines, Moscow announced today.

Entrenched for more than a month on a Dnieper River island a few hundred yards from the eastern cliffs of Kiev, the Russians suddenly pounced down on the city from their bridgehead in the north and in a sixteen-mile advance in twenty-four hours broke the German defense lines one after the other.

A number of strongly fortified settlements fell to the victorious Russians as large German forces fled, a midnight bulletin said.

The Russians captured Priorka, three miles north of Kiev, and then smashed into Svyatoshino, four miles to the west, cutting first the railway to Korosten, eighty-two miles to the northwest, then the highway to Zhitomir, eighty miles to the west.

"Large enemy forces were routed," said the Moscow midnight communiqué supplement recorded by the Soviet monitor.

"The enemy is desperately trying to halt the advance of the Soviet troops. He is hastily bringing up reserves of infantry and tanks and throwing them into the battle from the march.

"Eleven Hitlerite counter-attacks were repulsed with heavy losses to them. About 3,000 German officers and men were wiped out."

The Russians said their troops

Continued on Page Three

JAPAN'S WARSHIPS RUSHING TO RABAUL

Convoys With Cruisers and Destroyers on Way From Truk—One Attacked

By The Associated Press.

ALLIED HEADQUARTERS IN THE SOUTHWEST PACIFIC, Saturday, Nov. 6—Presaging heavy naval and air battles to come, Japan is rushing both heavy and light cruisers and destroyers down from Truk to Rabaul in a frantic effort to halt the Allied drive up the Solomons, headquarters disclosed today.

It appeared likely that at least five such convoys now are southbound over the 800 miles from Truk toward Kavieng, New Ireland, and Rabaul, New Britain.

The largest convoy spotted by Allied reconnaissance planes included five heavy cruisers, three light cruisers, five destroyers, two corvettes, a whaling ship and three freighters, of which one probably is a transport.

General MacArthur said the Japanese were trying to "retrieve the

Continued on Page Six

War News Summarized

SATURDAY, NOVEMBER 6, 1943

Having smashed through the center of the German line in Italy at Isernia, the Allied armies struck yesterday toward both anchors, taking San Salvo on the Adriatic front and moving ahead to the Garigliano River on the Tyrrhenian end. The Germans flooded the coastal areas in the path of the Fifth Army advance. [1:4.]

Making the second record daylight assault in three days, 500 United States bombers blasted war industries at Gelsenkirchen and railway yards at Muenster in western Germany while American and British medium bombers attacked targets in northern France. [1:5.]

Kiev, third largest city in Russia, was flanked on the west by Russian forces that plunged sixteen miles south and cut the main Zhitomir highway. The city is now hemmed in on three sides. In the south thirty places were captured between the Dnieper and the Black Sea. [1:6-7, map P. 2.]

Washington reported that Russia and Czechoslovakia would sign a twenty-year defensive alliance against Germany [3:2.], while in Stockholm it was indicated that Finland and Russia would get together on peace talks within the next few days. [3:8.] Despite the success of the Moscow conference, which some observers thought would obviate the much-heralded Roosevelt-Churchill-Stalin meeting, President Roosevelt said in Washington that he was very anxious to meet Premier Stalin. [3:6.]

Although conceding that the Moscow conference was a step along the right road toward Axis defeat, the French Committee of National Liberation was outspokenly piqued for having been excluded from the talks. It announced in Algiers that France would not be bound by decisions in which she had not participated. [3:1.]

In the Balkans, Tito's Partisans reported victories over the Germans in Montenegro and claimed that the important Spalato-Sinj railway in Dalmatia had been "destroyed." [4:1.]

General MacArthur announced that the Japanese were heavily reinforcing Rabaul, New Britain, their principal remaining base in that area, and probably would fight hard to keep it. He said five convoys with warships were on their way to replace losses inflicted by United States bombers there. [1:7.]

Complete agreement on the prosecution of the continental campaign in the Far East has been reached after a five-day conference between Generalissimo Chiang Kai-shek and British-American military leaders in Chungking, President Roosevelt announced. [1:6-7.]

Reversing a position taken twenty-four years ago when the League of Nations was snubbed, the Senate voted, 85 to 5, to approve United States participation in a general international organization to keep the peace. [1:8.]

Roosevelt Says Land Offensive Against Japan Is All Mapped Now

By JOHN H. CRIDER

WASHINGTON, Nov. 5—President Roosevelt announced today the successful conclusion of a five-day British and American military conference with Generalissimo Chiang Kai-shek on plans for a continental offensive against Japan. It means bad news for the Japanese, he said.

The conference was seen as bringing nearer the stepped-up Pacific war program agreed upon by the President and Prime Minister Churchill at the Quebec conference, which was immediately followed by the appointment of Admiral the Lord Louis Mountbatten as supreme commander for Southeast Asia.

Admiral Mountbatten, the President said, was one of the participants in the Chungking conference. Others were Lieut. Gen. Joseph W. Stilwell, American commander of operations in China; Maj. Gen. Claire L. Chennault, our air commander in that theatre, and Lieut. Gen. Brehon B. Somervell, chief of the Services of Supply.

Shortly after the President's press conference General Somervell called on the Chief Executive to report on the Chungking conference, carrying with him as souvenirs a stone battle axe of New Guinea tribesmen and a bow and cluster of arrows used by the head-hunting natives of the Naga Naga Hills, in Burma.

The President declared General Somervell's presence in China obviously was concerned

Continued on Page Seven

WORLD STAND MADE

Moscow Pact Is Backed in Adopting Post-War Organization Policy

ALL CHANGES LOSE

President Expresses His Satisfaction—Johnson Again in Minority

By C. P. TRUSSELL
Special to THE NEW YORK TIMES.

WASHINGTON, Nov. 5—The Senate, by a record vote of 85 to 5 with announced positions of absentees carrying the margin to 90 to 6 to represent its entire membership, declared late today for post-war collaboration to secure and maintain peace for the world and for the establishment of a general international organization that might become a new League of Nations.

Voting against the recently revised Connally resolution containing the declaration were two Democrats, Senators Burton K. Wheeler of Montana and Robert E. Reynolds of North Carolina, chairman of the Committee on Military Affairs, and three Republicans, Senators Hiram Johnson of California, William Langer of North Dakota and Henrik Shipstead of Minnesota.

Senator Johnson voted against the Treaty of Versailles of World War I. Senator Robert M. La Follette Jr., Progressive of Wisconsin, whose father joined Mr. Johnson in opposing that treaty, was announced, in his absence, as desiring to vote against the resolution adopted today.

Voting for the resolution were fifty-one Democrats and thirty-four Republicans. Four absent Democrats, Senators Carter Glass of Virginia, Josiah W. Bailey of North Carolina, Homer T. Bone of Washington and Pat McCarran of Nevada, and one Republican, Senator Styles Bridges of New Hampshire, were announced as desiring to vote for the measure.

Copy Sent to White House

Before making its decision, which was hailed promptly by participants as a great stride toward establishing the international policy of the United States, the nation's treaty-ratifying body voted down, viva voce and in rapid succession, five amendments or substitutes for the draft upon which the Senate divided for a time following the American-British-Russian-Chinese declaration of Moscow.

As adopted, the measure remained unchanged.

Although the resolution does not require White House approval or disapproval, the Senate decided unanimously to send an engrossed copy of it to President Roosevelt as an expression of its sentiment on post-war policy.

Senator Alben W. Barkley, majority leader, who proposed this action, at first suggested that the copy be sent to the Chief Executive "for his advice." He withdrew this when Senator Robert A. Taft, Republican, of Ohio, objected, asserting that advice to the President in the constitutional sense could be forwarded only by a two-thirds vote of the Senate.

President Voices Satisfaction

The resolution is one which apparently will please Mr. Roosevelt. At his press-radio conference this morning he viewed as a grand idea the incorporation in the Connally resolution of Article 4 of the Moscow Agreement, in which recognition is given to a necessity for a general international organization, open to all peace-loving nations, for maintenance of future world security.

At the same time the President gave to the press his answer to apprehension which had arisen in some Senate quarters that the Moscow declaration might have by-passed the requirement for Senate ratification of any treaty affecting American participation in the proposed international organization or to carry out other phases of the declaration

Continued on Page Two

"All the News That's Fit to Print."

The New York Times.

LATE CITY EDITION

Fair and cold today; not so windy.

Temperatures Yesterday—Max.,39; Min.,29

Sunrise, 7:28 A. M.; Sunset, 6:28 P. M.

Copyright, 1943, by The New York Times Company.

VOL. XCIII..No. 31,350. Entered as Second-Class Matter, Postoffice, New York, N. Y. NEW YORK, WEDNESDAY, NOVEMBER 24, 1943. THREE CENTS NEW YORK CITY

RAF BOMBERS RETURN TO DEVASTATED BERLIN AFTER 2,300-TON ATTACK, GREATEST IN HISTORY; U. S. FORCES CAPTURE MAKIN, GAIN ON TARAWA

SUBSIDIES BEATEN IN HOUSE, 278 TO 117; SENATE ACTS NEXT

Vote Against Administration on Food Prices Great Enough to Override a Veto

COMPROMISE MOWED DOWN

98 Democrats, 178 Republicans Join in Final Roll-Call on Adopting Measure

By SAMUEL B. BLEDSOE

Special to THE NEW YORK TIMES.

WASHINGTON, Nov. 23—The House late today adopted and sent to the Senate the Commodity Credit Corporation Bill, which would end food subsidies after Dec. 31. The vote was 278 to 117.

The majority for the anti-subsidy measure was more than the two-thirds necessary to over ride a Presidential veto, but the issue was not clear-cut on final passage, since some subsidy supporters, including Representative Wright Patman of Texas, voted for the bill. In addition to the ban on the use of food subsidies to hold down the cost of living, the measure would extend the life of the Commodity Credit Corporation, the $3,000,000,000 agency which finances many agricultural programs, from Dec. 31 until July 1, 1945.

A coalition of Republicans and Democrats defeated the Administration on the highly controversial issue, as on a similar occasion last summer during the consideration of a Commodity Credit Corporation bill. This measure reached the White House, was vetoed and the House sustained the President. During debate today Representative John W. McCormack of Massachusetts, the House majority leader, predicted another veto if the pending bill reaches the White House. Subsidy opponents said tonight that they were confident that the Senate would vote against the Administration.

How the Parties Lined Up

On the vote on final passage 178 Republicans, 98 Democrats and two minor party members voted for the measure and 100 Democrats, 15 Republicans and two minor party members against it.

The result had been a foregone conclusion, since the House, by a teller vote, rejected, 154 to 120, an amendment by Representative A. S. Mike Monroney, Democrat, of Oklahoma, which would have provided $750,000,000 for a continuation of the food subsidy program until Oct. 1, 1944, but would have tied the continuation of subsidies to the "Little Steel" wage formula.

In the event of a general wage increase, the subsidy program would have been discontinued under Mr. Monroney's amendment.

Continued on Page Twelve

Up-State Snow Cuts City's Milk Supply

A warning that New York City's supply of milk would be "exceedingly short" today as a result of the heavy snowstorm in Eastern New York and New England was released from Mayor La Guardia's office last night.

"Consumers not having children in the family are requested not to buy milk in order that it will be available for children first," the announcement added. "This particularly applies to restaurants and places of public eating. The supply will be normal as soon as weather conditions permit."

Spokesmen for the major milk distributors explained that the storm had "played havoc" with truck and rail transportation, particularly in the Champlain Valley, where the snowfall was twenty inches. Describing the snow, as "the toughest first storm of the season in years," the milk company representatives estimated that supplies here today would be cut at least 20 per cent.

LIMIT ON SLAUGHTER OF CATTLE IS LIFTED

Quotas for Civilian Supplies Dropped Until Further Notice —Point Values May Be Cut

In an effort to move the nation's record surplus of 17,000,000 head of cattle, the War Food Administration announced yesterday suspension of quota limitations on slaughter of livestock. The new order permits packers and butchers holding Government slaughter licenses to kill livestock for civilians without quota limitations until further notice.

"This action was taken to facilitate the marketing and slaughter of record numbers of livestock produced by the nation's farmers in answer to the call for more food," according to a WFA statement released here by the local offices of the Food Distribution Administration, 150 Broadway.

"The original suspension order lifted limitations of slaughter for civilian consumption through September and October. This period was subsequently extended to Dec. 1."

Ration-Point Revision Seen

At the same time word came from Washington that heavy current slaughtering might bring an early reduction in the number of ration points required for meats next month. Formal announcement of the new point values is expected on Dec. 3, and reports in the capital indicate that OPA is giving serious consideration to lower point values because supplies of meats for civilians have improved in recent weeks.

Meanwhile, over the telephone from Washington, former Judge Joe C. Montague, counsel for the Texas and Southwestern Cattle Raisers Association, declared that the suspension of quota limitations on slaughter for civilians would not help the civilians until meat-

Continued on Page Twelve

SUCCESS IN PACIFIC

Our Troops Mop Up Foe on Makin, Dig In on Tarawa, Gain on Betio

ABEMAMA IS IN HAND

Army and Navy Planes Blast Nauru—Tokyo Forecasts Fleet Fight

By GEORGE F. HORNE

By Telephone to THE NEW YORK TIMES.

PEARL HARBOR, Nov. 23—Makin atoll in the northern Gilbert Islands has been captured and our invasion of other islands is progressing well.

Admiral Chester W. Nimitz, Commander in Chief of the Pacific Fleet, announced today the capture of Makin. He said that on Tarawa the United States Marines were consolidating their positions and that they were making progress against enemy concentrations on the eastern end of Betio Island, an important isle in Tarawa atoll and the one on which desirable air strips are our main objectives.

On Abemama, which we invaded in a second attack following the initial assault on Tarawa and Makin, the situation is "well in hand," the admiral's communiqué reported. Everywhere in the central Pacific offensive, which is initiating a new and brilliant phase of this important year's operations against the Eastern enemy, we are surging ahead, and details made available today make it clear that the surging was against considerable resistance, at least on Betio, where the Japanese garrison put up a terrific fight to hold their land air base.

Our Men Shove Foe Back

It has been in vain, for the Second Marines, including veterans of Guadalcanal and other fighting in the Pacific, have pushed the enemy back to Betio's eastern end, indicating that we landed on the western approaches when the action began last Saturday morning.

Today's communiqué, issued at 11:30 A. M. Hawaiian time, reads as follows:

"Our forces have captured Makin. On Tarawa the marines have consolidated their positions and are making good progress against enemy concentrations on the eastern end of Betio Island, with capture assured. The situation on Abemama is well in hand.

"Raids are being continued against the Marshalls by carrier aircraft and Army Seventh Air Force Liberators."

Spokesmen revealed that the Marshall carrier plane blow was on Mili atoll and that it took place yesterday. Enemy air activity was limited. The bases attacked by Maj. Gen. Willis H. Hale's Seventh United States Army Air Force were not identified.

As to the mopping up phase of Makin, it was stressed that the Makin atoll was entirely in our hands and that the mopping up consisted of cleaning out snipers. The mopping up, it is said, is now being completed and the termina-

Continued on Page Three

SCENE OF WORLD'S MOST DESTRUCTIVE AERIAL BOMBARDMENT

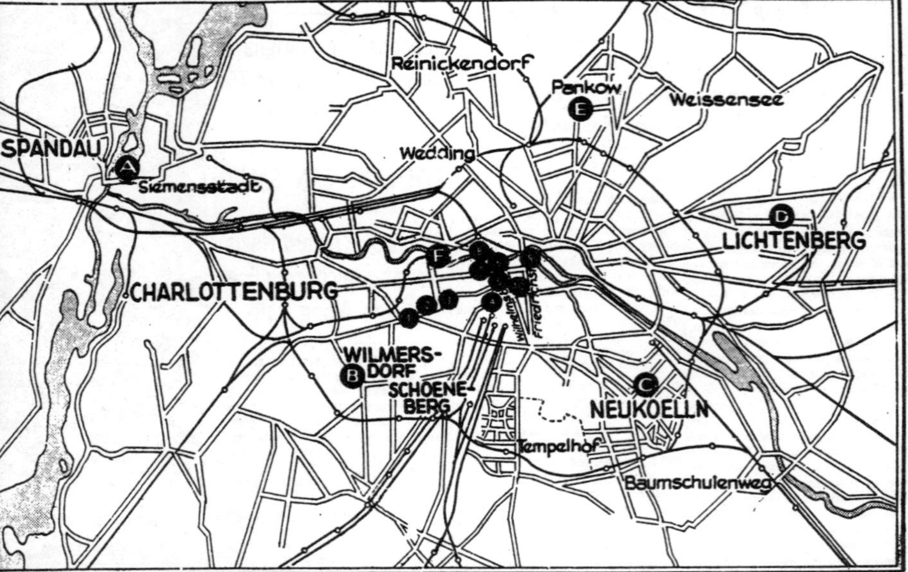

Royal Air Force planes showered 2,300 tons of bombs on Berlin and its industrial suburbs Monday night. The suburbs hit included Spandau and Siemensstadt (A), Wilmersdorf (B), Neukoelln (C), Lichtenberg (D), and Pankow (E). In the heart of the city (F) the Kaiser Wilhelm Gedaechtniskirche (1) was reported damaged, as were the Hungarian Legation (2) and the Swedish Legation (3). The Potsdam railroad station (4) was said to have been destroyed and the British Embassy (5) and the French Embassy (6) were declared to have been razed. Other places reported damaged were the Finnish Legation (7), the Danish Legation (8), the State University (9) and the Foreign Office (10). Vast fires were set and casualties were estimated at 10,000 killed and wounded.

NIMITZ SEES CHINA AS JAPAN'S NEMESIS

Says Final Defeat of Foe Will Come From Chungking's Area —Cites Men, Airfields

By Telephone to THE NEW YORK TIMES.

PEARL HARBOR, Nov. 23—The final defeat of Japan will come from China, in the opinion of Admiral Chester W. Nimitz, Commander in Chief of the United States Pacific Fleet.

In a press conference this afternoon, his first in nearly a year, he said that "my opinion is that Japan will be defeated from China." "China, with her reservoir of personnel and the possibility of airfields in easy striking distance of Japan, is one of the steps along the road," he remarked.

Seated behind his table with his schnauzer puppy at his feet and more than a score of reporters and

Continued on Page Four

Patton Struck Ailing Soldier, Apologized to Him and Army

By MILTON BRACKER

By Wireless to THE NEW YORK TIMES.

ALGIERS, Nov. 23—Lieut. Gen. George S. Patton Jr. struck and insulted a shell-shocked American soldier in an evacuation hospital in Sicily last August and ordered the patient to return to the front lines, it was officially revealed today. Gen. Dwight D. Eisenhower denounced the conduct of the commander of the American Seventh Army as "despicable" and threatened to break him unless he made amends at once. General Patton thereupon apologized to the soldier, to the officers and patients who had witnessed the incident and to the Seventh Army.

Although there were at least fifteen witnesses to the incident, none was a professional reporter. The first two reporters to check on the episode arrived at the hospital about twenty-four hours later. One of them was Merrill Mueller of the National Broadcasting Company, who gave his version today in the

Continued on Page Six

'DOOMSDAY' SCENE IN BERLIN PAINTED

Swedish Traveler Reports Fires Created Almost a Summer Temperature

By GEORGE AXELSSON

By Cable to THE NEW YORK TIMES.

STOCKHOLM, Sweden, Nov. 23—An eyewitness from Berlin of the British bombing attack last night told the writer here today that the French Embassy on the Pariser Platz and the British Embassy on Wilhelmstrasse were razed by explosives and incendiaries.

Reich Foreign Minister Joachim von Ribbentrop's official residence on Wilhelmstrasse was destroyed. The top stories of the Foreign Office building and of Adolf Hitler's Wilhelmstrasse residence were burned out. Dr. Joseph Goebbels' Propaganda Ministry building across the street from Hitler's residence was undamaged. [Other persons reaching Stockholm said the Hitler residence was destroyed, Reuter reported.]

The big Potsdam railroad station was wiped out, as were the Haus Vaterland and the Potsdamer Platz restaurant near by.

At the Anhalter station the tracks were torn up and no trains were able to arrive or leave there today. The Stettin station was badly damaged and tracks at the Lehrter station were torn up. The Friedrichstrasse station was not hit, but the district immediately north of it was battered.

On the north side of the Pariser

Continued on Page Five

War News Summarized

WEDNESDAY, NOVEMBER 24, 1943

The RAF returned to Berlin last night to carry on the work of destruction begun Monday, when 775 bombers gave the German capital the worst pounding ever administered to any city from the air. In that attack more than 2,300 tons of explosives fell on the target at the rate of seventy-seven tons a minute. The center of the city and the suburbs were left a "sea of flames." Twenty-six planes, four Canadian, were lost. [1:8.]

A Swedish traveler who returned to Stockholm yesterday reported that Berlin had suffered an "all-time major catastrophe." When he left in the afternoon the city was still ablaze and the acrid smoke was so thick in places one could not see at arm's length. Embassies and Government buildings were razed, he said, and he estimated the dead and homeless in tens of thousands. [1:7.]

The Pacific end of Hitler's Axis also suffered severe blows. Makin atoll in the Gilberts was captured by American troops and neighboring Tarawa was about to fall to the marines, who had herded the Japanese into the eastern end of Betio Island. [1:3; map, P. 2.] In the South Pacific, Allied planes heavily bombed Gasmata on New Britain for the third consecutive day. [3:3-4.]

Admiral Nimitz told reporters at Pearl Harbor that the Gilberts were securely in our hands but that the final defeat of Japan would come from China. Sooner or later the enemy fleet must join battle with us, he said. [1:4.] In Washington, Navy Secretary Knox said the attack on the Gilberts was the beginning of a new campaign "on a much more direct route to Japan." [3:1.]

In the European land fighting the Russian armies scored important advances on most fronts, but admitted withdrawing from several more inhabited places in the Chernyakhov-Brusilov area, indicating that the Germans had pushed part way back to Kiev from Zhitomir. [1:6; map, P. 8.]

Mud virtually halted ground activities in Italy. Allied fliers were busy, particularly in the area from Pescara to Ancona on the Adriatic coast and inland to Foligno. [4:3.] The British announced the evacuation of the Aegean Island of Samos. [4:7.]

General Eisenhower disclosed that Major General Patton had slapped and cursed a shell-shocked soldier in Sicily last August and had ordered the private out of the hospital. General Patton was told to apologize to all concerned and he did so, even apologizing to as many soldiers as could be assembled at all Seventh Army divisional headquarters. [1:5-6.]

RUSSIANS RETREAT TOWARD KIEV AGAIN

Germans Win Several Towns at High Cost, but Red Army Gains on Other Fronts

By The United Press.

LONDON, Wednesday, Nov. 24—German forces, driving back toward Kiev and the Dnieper line without regard for prodigious losses, yesterday reached the vicinity of Brusilov, less than fifty miles from the Ukraine capital, Moscow acknowledged today.

The Soviet operational and supplementary communiqués reported that the Red Army had abandoned several towns and villages north of Zhitomir, in the area of Chernyakhov, and east of the rail junction recaptured Saturday by the Nazis, around Brusilov.

On other fronts the bitter and long-continued battle for the Dnieper favored the Russians.

At the northern end of the active front Moscow reported slow prog-

Continued on Page Eight

BIG BLOWS PRESSED

Reich Capital Set Afire, City's Heart Blasted by 775 Planes

CLOUDS PROVE AN AID

British Lose 26 Craft—Nazis Claim a Greater Toll in New Assault

Heavy bombers of the Royal Air Force rained fresh destruction on Berlin last night as the German capital lay smoking and devastated from a record British assault twenty-four hours earlier, London officials stated early today, according to The Associated Press.

The new attack apparently was carried out in great force.

The preliminary British announcement gave no details, but it confirmed the fact of the new blow, of which first word came in a German broadcast reported by the Federal Communications Commission.

New Blow Expected, Nazis Say

"The attack was expected and special defense precautions were taken," the German broadcast said, asserting that "a considerable number" of attacking planes were shot down.

"The weather favored the defense more than the previous night," the German-language broadcast added. It characterized the attack with the customary Nazi propaganda designation for a heavy assault—"terror raid."

A later Nazi broadcast early today, reported by The Associated Press from London, said that new devastation had been wrought by the attackers in several sections of the smoldering capital.

This broadcast said that the British planes had been attacked by Nazi fighters before they reached the coast of Europe.

Aim Is End of Berlin

By DREW MIDDLETON

By Cable to THE NEW YORK TIMES.

LONDON, Wednesday, Nov. 24—A great armada of British bombers won one of the war's most significant victories Monday night when in the heaviest air assault of history it blew the heart out of Berlin with more than 2,300 long tons of high explosive and incendiary bombs and repaid the debt of London.

The force, which this writer estimates at about 775 four-motored bombers, dropped its missiles at a rate of seventy-seven tons a minute in a half hour's time. It left the German capital ablaze with scores of huge fires and shattered by explosions.

All accounts by the returning airmen and reports from the Continent agreed that Berlin suffered its severest blow as Air Chief Marshal Sir Arthur T. Harris and his Royal Air Force Bomber Command continued the Allies' inexorable campaign to knock the city and Germany out of the war.

Soon after dark last night more strong forces of British heavy bombers streamed out toward Europe. For about three-quarters of an hour an unbroken procession of planes swept across the Strait of Dover.

Victory at a Low Price

The destruction of the center of Berlin and of part of the city's important industrial suburbs was only a portion of the RAF's signal triumph Monday night.

The attack was made through heavy clouds that kept the Nazi night fighter interference at a minimum and enemy anti-aircraft fire, although heavy, was wild.

The British lost twenty-two heavy bombers and the Royal Canadian Air Force reported four missing.

For this proportionately low price of twenty-six planes the RAF bought victory. The cascade of bombs, which included hundreds of two and four ton block busters, wrecked the center of Berlin.

The reports from the Continent spoke of widespread devastation

Continued on Page Five

Says Army Will Run Bay State Plants

By The United Press.

BOSTON, Nov. 23—State Labor Commissioner James T. Moriarty said tonight that the Army would take over thirty-two Salem and Peabody leather plants now tied up by a strike of 2,500 workers.

Picketing around the plants continued today, despite orders by the regional and National War Labor Boards and President Roosevelt that the strikers return to work. The three-week-old strike is the result of a jurisdictional dispute between the International Fur and Leather Workers Union (CIO) and the Independent National Leather Workers Association.

Special to THE NEW YORK TIMES.

WASHINGTON, Nov. 23—The only word available at the War Department tonight concerning the leather strike in Massachusetts was that it had as yet received no directive to take over operation of plants there.

The WLB recently referred the matter to the White House, and it was said that since then Army officers had been on the scene looking over the situation.

U. S. Cracks Down on Bootleg Ring; 44 Seized in 36 Liquor Raids Here

Fanning out in a three-pronged drive, Federal agents swept yesterday through Manhattan, Brooklyn and the Bronx and, in a smashing blow against the revived bootleg industry in New York City, conducted thirty-six liquor raids in which forty-four persons, including an alleged ringleader, were arrested.

Reinforced by thirty city policemen, seventy Federal men under W. E. Dunigan, assistant district supervisor of the Alcohol Tax Unit of the Treasury Department, seized vast quantities of illicit liquor in simultaneous descents upon taverns, grocery stores, a wholesale butcher, a newsstand dealer, and other places on the calling list of the bootleg mob.

Jacob Kessler, described by Mr. Dunigan as the head of the ring operating here, was arrested in his office at 1123 Broadway with three other alleged members of the ring. These three were identified as Jack Schiff, Isadore Schimmel and Isadore Jaffe. According to Mr. Dunigan, Kessler, who lives at the Windermere Hotel, 666 West End Avenue, is a familiar figure in bootlegging circles, having been head of a gang in prohibition days, maintaining offices then as now in the same Broadway building where he was seized yesterday.

What was termed by the agents as the "cutting" plant of the ring was found in the home of Vincent and Jennie Luciano at 1458 West Eightieth Street, Brooklyn, where Mrs. Luciano was arrested. Agents said they found sixty-five five-gallon cans of alcohol, a number of

Continued on Page Thirteen

Washington Censorship Blocks Carol's Radio Talk From Mexico

The radio address that was to have been delivered last night from Mexico City by former King Carol of Rumania over the Columbia Broadcasting System was canceled a few hours before the exiled monarch was to have gone on the air. An order of the Office of Censorship in Washington rescinded its previous approval of the broadcast.

The Office of Censorship issued the following statement to CBS, which was made public from the CBS offices here:

"Owing to considerations that we are not at liberty to disclose, we find it necessary to cancel the previously authorized use of the lines from Mexico City for the scheduled broadcast tonight by former King Carol of Rumania."

Copies of the scheduled address had been given out by Russell Bird-well of 30 Rockefeller Plaza, the former King's press representative in this country, before news of cancellation of the broadcast arrived.

In disclosing the order of the Office of Censorship forbidding the broadcast, Columbia made public the following statement:

"The text of Carol's proposed broadcast was submitted to censorship by CBS last Saturday. It was cleared, and leaders of anti-Carol movements in the United States were asked to nominate a spokesman to speak on the same program after Carol had finished reading his statement from Mexico City.

"The former King of Rumania had frequently been quoted in the press, but since his exile he has never before been scheduled to talk

Continued on Page Seven

"All the News That's Fit to Print."

The New York Times.

LATE CITY EDITION
Fair, not quite so cold in morning; cloudy, warmer later.
Temperatures Yesterday—Max., 46; Min., 36
Sunrise, 8:01 A. M.; Sunset, 5:30 P. M.

VOL. XCIII. No. 31,358. Entered as Second-Class Matter, Postoffice, New York, N. Y. NEW YORK, THURSDAY, DECEMBER 2, 1943. THREE CENTS IN NEW YORK CITY

CRUSHING OF JAPAN MAPPED AT CAIRO PARLEY; EMPIRE WILL BE STRIPPED TO PRE-1895 STATUS; 8TH ARMY DRIVES ON; U. S. FLIERS AGAIN HIT REICH

1,440 ON GRIPSHOLM WILDLY HAPPY HERE; RETICENT ON TRIALS

Civilians Freed by Japanese Burst Into Song at Sight of Statue of Liberty

FBI CHECKS ON ARRIVALS

Overcrowding and Poor Food in Camps Described but Most Are Healthy After Voyage

Sun-tanned, healthy and ecstatically happy, but exceedingly reticent about many of their experiences, more than 1,000 of the 1,440 passengers—1,222 Americans and 217 Canadians—aboard the diplomatic exchange liner Gripsholm debarked yesterday after the 18,353-ton Swedish ship docked at Pier F, Jersey City.

Two hundred of the passengers were still on the ship late last night, awaiting the same exhaustive examination that agents of the Federal Bureau of Investigation and officers of Army and Navy Intelligence already had given their companions. Navy press relations officers expressed hope they would all be cleared by midnight, but said that many of the passengers, including some already cleared, would voluntarily remain on the Gripsholm until this morning.

An undisclosed number of those aboard were removed by the FBI to Ellis Island for further investigation. The officials in charge of the search were reluctant to discuss this aspect of the arrival, but it was recalled that when the exchange ship Drottningholm docked last June they found among the expatriates a man named Herbert Karl Friedrich Barr, who subsequently was convicted of espionage.

Canadians Take Sealed Train

The Canadians on the Gripsholm were among the first to land. By an agreement between the Canadian and the United States Governments they were escorted to buses which took them to a special train, which was sealed and guarded en route to prevent anyone from having access to them as they were speeding north to Montreal.

Joy at their safe arrival in this country and concern lest some careless remark might be carried back to their former jailers and infuriate the Japanese against the 6,800 Americans still remaining in the internment camps seemed to be the emotions most strongly felt by the hundreds who passed the gantlet of questioning and were permitted to land.

Their delight at their return, which prompted those on deck when the big liner passed the Statue of Liberty to burst spontaneously into "God Bless America," was visible in every countenance, from those of children of 3 or 4 to those of gray-haired missionaries who were back home after thirty, forty or more years in the East.

Others Remain Prisoners

But even though they were bubbling over with the sheer happiness born of freedom, it was evident that not for a minute did they forget their unfortunate former companions who are still at the mercy of the Japanese. As 9-year-old Suzanne Hazard of San Francisco put it when reporters and photographers clustered about her and her 6-year-old sister Joan:

"We can't tell you all of the things about the camp."

Before they were permitted to leave at least one of the internment camps, it was learned, some of those who arrived yesterday were sternly warned by Japanese officials not to criticize conditions upon their arrival here. This warning was reinforced by the injunctions of State Department officials on the Gripsholm, who are even now hoping to arrange another exchange and wish to avoid antagonizing Japanese officialdom.

Those who would tell about the camps at all gave almost unanimous testimony to the terrific overcrowding and the entire lack

Continued on Page Eighteen

Colombians Urged To Give Their Blood

By Cable to THE NEW YORK TIMES.

BOGOTA, Colombia, Dec. 1—Colombia is not likely to send troops to battle fronts, but Colombian blood will be shed for the United Nations here as the result of a decree, issued today, calling for blood plasma.

Following unanimous approval by the House of Representatives of a state of belligerency against Germany it is expected the Conservatives will support the Government despite the vote of thirteen Conservative Senators against the belligerency resolution and the charge by Conservative Senator Guillermor Leon Valencia that American submarines sank the Colombian schooner Ruby. The sinking caused the action against Germany.

BEEF AND 15 FOODS GET CUT IN POINTS

Citrus Fruit Juices and Most Soup on Ration-Free List—Higher Values on Cheese

By CHARLES E. EGAN
Special to THE NEW YORK TIMES.

WASHINGTON, Dec. 1—Ration point values on meats and on fifteen types of processed foods were reduced by the Office of Price Administration today in establishing a scale which will apply beginning Sunday through December. The reductions reflected a seasonally easier supply situation in meats, and improvement in available stocks of a variety of processed foods, OPA officials said.

The average point value of all meats was brought to slightly less than five a pound, lowest since rationing began. Changes were confined almost entirely to beef cuts, where point slashes averaged two to three points.

Veal steaks and chops were lowered two points and veal leg roasts were lowered one point, but other veal cuts, as well as all lamb and mutton, which were reduced substantially for November, were not changed.

Reductions made on many pork cuts in mid-November, when point values were brought down an average of more than 25 per cent, were left in force except on all hams and most bacon cuts, which were increased one point.

Grapefruit juice and other citrus juices, ready-to-serve soups (except tomato), and canned sauerkraut were made ration-free for this month. Reductions of one to ten points were made on fifteen items of processed food, the largest number of slashes made at any one time since rationing began.

Tomato Products Raised

Other reductions in point values included green and wax beans, soy beans, all varieties of canned dry beans, including pork and beans, carrots, spinach and dry frozen beans and some other frozen fruits and vegetables.

Three items, tomato soup and two varieties of tomato sauces, were raised one to three points.

The adjustments on processed

Continued on Page Twenty-three

GERMANS HOLD ON

Fiercest Air Support of Mediterranean War Resisted in Italy

COUNTER-BLOW SEEN

Capture of Three More Towns Is Reported—Fifth Army Gains

By MILTON BRACKER
By Wireless to THE NEW YORK TIMES.

ALGIERS, Dec. 1—The smashing British Eighth Army offensive that has now brought the Allies complete control of the ridge dominating the Sangro Valley in the coastal sector surged ahead yesterday against fiercely resisting Germans.

The enemy suffered the heaviest tactical strafing and bombing ever provided by any air force in the entire Mediterranean campaign. But even wave after wave of bombers and fighter-bombers could not rout the Germans, who, it is believed, still cling to the immediately threatened points of Lanciano and Castelfrentano and have yet to throw in a major counter-attack.

The capture of Lanciano, Castelfrentano and Casoli was announced tonight by the Algiers radio, but the broadcast could not be confirmed through regular channels. If true, this would mean that the Eighth Army had surged over at least two-thirds of the inland road loop from San Vito Chietino, on the coast, to Casoli and that, at Castelfrentano, it was within fifteen miles of Chieti, the capital of Abruzzi, just below the Pescara-Rome transverse road.

Germans' Losses Heavy

The Germans have suffered heavy losses in violent hand-to-hand infantry fighting since the British, Indian and New Zealand troops crossed the flood-swollen Sangro River. The enemy has lost killed, wounded and prisoners in a series of stubborn but futile counter-jabs. But, despite the unbalancing of the entire Adriatic defense line by the loss of the ridge below Foccacesia, the Germans show every tendency to keep fighting and there is no indication of an untroubled Allied procession northward to the Pescara-Rome road.

On the Fifth Army's front the situation remains largely unchanged, but Gen. Mark W. Clark's forces made slight gains north of Venafro and generally straightened and consolidated their positions.

The Fifth Army encountered large quantities of barbed wire, which had not been used in this campaign before. It has added to the more modern hazards of mines, demolitions and booby traps.

Artillery exchanges continued all along the front. Our positions at Galluccio, behind the line between Calabritto and Mignano, suffered particularly from violent shelling.

The height of the day's action occurred just before the broad Sangro bridgehead, where nine separate waves of light bombers,

Continued on Page Thirteen

PRINCIPALS IN THE WAR CONFERENCE HELD AT CAIRO

Generalissimo Chiang Kai-shek, President Roosevelt, Prime Minister Churchill and Mme. Chiang Kai-shek.
The New York Times (OWI Radiophoto)

FORTRESSES STRIKE AT SOLINGEN AGAIN

Deal Second Heavy Blow in 24 Hours at Cost of 27 Planes—Coast Airdromes Strafed

By DREW MIDDLETON
By Cable to THE NEW YORK TIMES.

LONDON, Dec. 1—Strong formations of Flying Fortresses and Liberators battled their way through clouds of German fighters to hammer the important industrial city of Solingen, north of Cologne, in the Rhineland, today, in a most important series of punishing attacks by Allied bombers on German targets in northern Europe. It was the second attack on Solingen in two days.

Bombs cascaded onto Solingen through heavy overcast in another United States Eighth Air Force

Continued on Page Fourteen

Bid to Soviet Is Discerned In Some of 'Stripping' Terms

By JOHN H. CRIDER
Special to THE NEW YORK TIMES.

WASHINGTON, Dec. 1—The dramatic meeting of the Pacific Big Three was hailed in Washington today as a turning point in the war which timed intensification of the drive against Japan with the faster ticking of Germany's clock of doom.

Aside from the tremendous importance to the conduct of the war and to post-war international collaboration attached to President Roosevelt's first meeting with Generalissimo Chiang Kai-shek and his seventh war conference with Prime Minister Churchill, the following points were noted here as of special significance rising out of their joint communiqué:

1. Agreement to strip Japan's empire down to its original basis before the Sino-Japanese War of 1895, is a statement of war aims in the Pacific going beyond "unconditional surrender"—it is unconditional surrender, plus.

2. This stripping of the Japa-

Continued on Page Four

RED ARMY SLOWED BY GERMAN BLOWS

Only Minor Gains Made as Foe Throws Fresh Forces Into Fierce, Spreading Battles

By The Associated Press.

LONDON, Thursday, Dec. 2—The Germans have struck out with new vigor in every sector of the Russian front in a major bid to stem the Russian offensive, counter-attacking yesterday as many as fifteen times in one area and slowing the Red Army to minor gains along the 600-mile front.

The intensity of the fighting was undiminished, equal perhaps to the heaviest of the war, but Moscow reported only a dozen populated places taken—a slowdown after four months of steady progress. All of them were in three areas—north of Gomel, along the Pripet River and in the Dnieper River bend.

There was fighting in other sectors but it won no mention in either the operational bulletin or the midnight supplement recorded

Continued on Page Twelve

SCENE OF PARLEY LIKE ARMED CAMP

Each Delegate's Villa and Hotel Where Sessions Were Held Under Heavy Guard

By Cable to THE NEW YORK TIMES.

CAIRO, Egypt, Dec. 1—Not since the days of the Ptolemys has Egypt been such a cynosure of attention from the civilized world.

The fact that something big was about to happen was a wide-open secret in the rumor-ridden cities of the African periphery for weeks. Finally, after a flood of rumors, it was blandly announced on the morning of Nov. 22 that Prime Minister Churchill, President Roosevelt and Generalissimo Chiang Kai-shek, accompanied by their principal military advisers, had arrived here.

Chiang Flies in American Plane

Dr. Hollington Tong, the Chinese Vice Minister of Information, then told about the Generalissimo's first visit thus far west except for his trip to Moscow several years ago. The Chinese party came in two four-engined American planes with American crews. General Chiang's plane arrived at 7 P. M. on Nov. 21. Mme. Chiang was not in good health but felt that her presence was needed. Only two long stops were made on the four-day journey, General Chiang's first from China since his trip to India in 1942.

Major George Durno, a former White House correspondent who is handling Mr. Roosevelt's press relations, then spoke of the Presi-

Continued on Page Four

ALL-OUT WAR SET

Allies Plan to Retake Manchuria, Formosa and Seized Islands

PLEDGE FREE KOREA

Will Relinquish Own Claims and Help Rebuild China

By C. L. SULZBERGER
By Cable to THE NEW YORK TIMES.

CAIRO, Egypt, Dec. 1—What might be termed a Pacific Charter, outlining a specific program for obtaining the unconditional surrender of Japan and her reduction to her frontiers before 1895 with the ensuing liberation of her vast Asiatic mainland and Pacific island empire, was published tonight following a sensational five-day series of conferences among President Roosevelt, Prime Minister Churchill and Generalissimo Chiang Kai-shek and their principal military and political staffs.

The meetings took place somewhere in Africa from Nov. 22 through Nov. 26. All Allied principals departed for unannounced destinations before the disclosure of a historic communiqué outlining crystallized Allied pledges, dated Cairo, Dec. 1.

In brief this document promised full agreement on the strategy of future military operations against Japan that the three great powers discussed.

It resolved:

1. To press unrelentingly the war against their brutal enemies by sea, land and air and stated that pressure is already rising.
2. To renounce all territorial gains for themselves and to strip the Japanese of all Pacific islands seized since 1914.
3. To restore to China the lost lands of Manchuria, Formosa and the Pescadores.
4. To expel Japan from all other territories she has taken by violence and greed.
5. To guarantee the future independence of enslaved Korea.
6. To persevere in the serious and prolonged operations necessary to procure the unconditional surrender of Japan.

Confer Day and Night

These grimly determined pledges to reduce the Japanese Empire to the non-menacing status of those days prior to the date when, by seizing Formosa in 1895, later expanding at the expense of Russia, Korea and China and finally climbing on the Allied bandwagon in the last war, she seized strategic German island positions and has never ceased expanding, were formulated at a series of day and night staff talks in which virtually every military luminary of the three powers except Gen. Douglas MacArthur as well as numerous political leaders participated. General MacArthur was represented by his Chief of Staff, Major Gen. Richard K. Sutherland.

It is obvious both from the type of strategic talks held, whose specific results obviously are the most secret, and the political pledges from the chiefs of state that any criticism to the effect that the Asiatic war will be considered a "second class" affray must now be ended.

China's position as a great power ally, already boosted as a result of the Moscow conference, now unquestionably is established on terms of full equality, and it is equally certain that the Anglo-American delegates considered the war in Europe now advanced far enough toward victory so that increased attention could be directed toward Asia.

It was the first face-to-face meeting for Generalissimo Chiang with either President Roosevelt or Prime Minister Churchill. The chiefs of state were in constant consultation throughout the parleys, which were held in their residences with the Generalissimo's wife, who accompanied Generalissimo Chiang's delegation as an interpreter. The purely strategic

Continued on Page Three

War News Summarized

THURSDAY, DECEMBER 2, 1943

Japan's "East Asia Co-Prosperity" dream has been shattered in Cairo, where President Roosevelt, Prime Minister Churchill and Generalissimo Chiang Kai-shek drew up a Pacific Charter stripping Japan of all her possessions gained since 1895. The highest military leaders of the three United Nations simultaneously perfected plans to make the declaration effective.

The conferences lasted five days, from Nov. 22 to 26. A communiqué issued yesterday declared that the "three great Allies" sought no gain or territory but were pledged to "punish the aggression of Japan" by:

1. Stripping Japan of all her Pacific islands;

2. Returning to China all territory wrested from her, including Manchuria;

3. Granting independence to Korea, and

4. Expelling Japan from all other territory acquired "by violence and greed."

Among the military chiefs in the Cairo talks were Generals Marshall, Eisenhower and Stilwell, and General MacArthur's Chief of Staff, Admirals King and Leahy, Admiral Mountbatten, Air Marshal Tedder and Generals Dill and Alexander. [All the foregoing, 1:8; map P. 5.]

Washington observers believed that the Cairo decision, since it might result in restoring to Russia territory she lost in the Russo-Japanese War, could be viewed as a bid for Soviet military action against Japan. [1:5-6.] London authorities considered Cairo an excellent prelude to a conference with Premier Stalin [3:1], while Axis propagandists sought to belittle the sessions as a sign of Allied weakness. [5:3-4.]

Yesterday saw the return of nearly 1,500 Americans and Canadians from Japanese prison camps. They reached New York on the Gripsholm, but would not talk for fear of reprisals against those still held prisoner. [1:1.]

In the war against Japan Allied warships shelled Madang on New Guinea and Gasmata on New Britain. [1:6-7; map, P. 7.] The Chinese regained full possession of Changteh and recaptured several other cities [11:2], and in Burma Allied fliers battered enemy positions in wide attacks. [8:1.] The Navy announced that our losses on Tarawa were 1,026 killed and 2,557 wounded; on Makin and Abemama sixty-six killed, 123 wounded. [19:1.]

The Eighth Army in Italy pushed ahead against bitter German resistance [1:3] and in Russia Hitler's generals launched numerous counter-attacks in an effort to bring the Red Army advance to a halt. [1:6.] Flying Fortresses attacked Solingen in the Ruhr for the second consecutive day, meeting strong fighter and rocket opposition. We lost twenty-seven bombers. [1:4.]

Sweden lodged a "most urgent request" with Germany, "in the interest of future Swedish-German relations," to cancel the arrest and deportation of 1,200 Norwegian students and professors seized at Oslo. [17:3.]

Only 197 of 3,000 Quit in Schools; No Disturbance as AFL Fills Jobs

The strike called yesterday by John L. Lewis' School Custodial Workers Union, Local 112, an affiliate of the United Construction Workers of the United Mine Workers of America, was an almost complete failure.

An official tabulation made public last night by the Bureau of Operations at Police Headquarters showed that only 197 of the 3,000 workers at forty-three of the city's 767 elementary and high schools responded to the strike call issued by Leon Zwicker, regional director of the United Construction Workers, and officials of Local 112. The strikers' places were filled by AFL unions holding jurisdiction over the school custodians and their employes. Not a single school was closed and not a classroom suffered any inconvenience. Mr. Zwicker's boast that at least 2,300 of the 3,000 employes would join the walkout proved to be unfounded.

The police tabulation showed the effects of the strike by boroughs as follows: Manhattan, six schools affected, thirty-four employes absent; Bronx, twenty-one schools, seventy-two absent; Brooklyn, seven schools, forty-three absent; Queens, eight schools, forty-seven absent: Richmond, one school, one absent.

Although Mr. Zwicker had promised that there would be no picketing, a group of pickets appeared at 3 o'clock at the Thomas Jefferson High School in Brooklyn as classes were being dismissed. The pickets did not molest anyone. The police, who kept close watch on the situation, reported no picketing

Continued on Page Twenty-two

Warships Push Into New Areas To Shell Foe in Southwest Pacific

By The Associated Press.

ALLIED HEADQUARTERS IN THE SOUTHWEST PACIFIC, Thursday, Dec. 2—American light naval craft shelled Gasmata, New Britain, and Madang, New Guinea, during the night and dawn hours of Nov. 29 and 30. It was the first sea bombardment of these enemy strongholds.

The naval vessels—probably destroyers—sought to blast out Japanese shore installations at Gasmata, and aerial spotters, a headquarters spokesman said, termed their marksmanship "effective."

The attack on Madang, strong enemy aerial and barge point on Astrolabe Harbor, northeast New Guinea, was a foray deep into Japanese territory. Shells were hurled into shore installations, and a small, unidentified enemy vessel was sunk in Dallman Passage.

These bold naval strokes not only accelerated the action against the enemy in the New Guinea-New Britain area, which has been pounded heavily by Allied aircraft of late, but also gave some indication of the policies of Vice Admiral Thomas C. Kinkaid, who recently was made chief of naval forces in the Southwest Pacific. It was Admiral Kinkaid who commanded naval forces in the Aleutians when Americans won back Attu and reoccupied Kiska.

In another phase of the concentrated attacks on the enemy's bases in the Southwest Pacific, Allied bombers again hit the Japanese air strips at Cape Gloucester, on the western tip of New Britain,

Continued on Page Seven

"All the News That's Fit to Print."

The New York Times.

LATE CITY EDITION
Cloudy, little change in temperature today; moderate winds.
Temperatures Yesterday—Max., 52; Min., 45
Sunrise, 8:08 A. M.; Sunset, 5:28 P. M.

Copyright, 1943, by The New York Times Company.

VOL. XCIII..No. 31,360. Entered as Second-Class Matter, Postoffice, New York, N. Y. NEW YORK, SATURDAY, DECEMBER 4, 1943. THREE CENTS IN NEW YORK CITY

ROOSEVELT, STALIN, CHURCHILL AGREE ON PLANS FOR WAR ON GERMANY IN TALKS AT TEHERAN; 1,500 MORE TONS OF BOMBS DROPPED ON BERLIN

SOLDIER-VOTE BILL SHIFTED BY SENATE TO LET STATES RULE

Republicans Join With Southern Democrats in Scrapping the Plan for Federal Control

CONGRESS ONLY TO ADVISE

Opponents Charge Substitute Will Make Balloting Impossible for Forces Abroad

By C. P. TRUSSELL
Special to THE NEW YORK TIMES.

WASHINGTON, Dec. 3—After spending six days in rewriting the Green-Lucas Service Men's Absentee Voting Bill, the Senate threw that measure aside today and passed instead, by a vote of 42 to 37, a substitute sponsored by three Southern Democrats which would put the balloting program for the armed forces back into the hands of State election officials and under State laws.

The substitute now goes to the House, where key men predicted tonight that it would be adopted there in principle if not with the same text.

The Senate's shift from its extensive patchwork on the program of the coalition which chose the substitute measure came quickly. Senators who had been successful in getting amendments into the original measure, seeing what was coming, moved to transfer their proposals to the State law program before it was brought to its showdown vote.

Sponsored by Senators James O. Eastland of Mississippi, John L. McClellan of Arkansas and Kenneth McKellar of Tennessee, the substitute won the votes of twenty-four Democrats, including all thirteen representatives of poll tax States who were present (Alabama, Arkansas, Georgia, Mississippi, South Carolina, Tennessee, Texas and Virginia) and of eighteen Republicans. Twenty-five Democrats and twelve Republicans opposed it. The much amended Green-Lucas bill, brought in by the Committee on Privileges and Elections was thus not permitted to come to a vote.

Some Easterners for Change

Among the Democratic Senators voting for the substitute were Gerry of Rhode Island, Walsh of Massachusetts and Walsh of New Jersey. The Republican group favoring the substitute included Buck of Delaware, Danaher of Connecticut, Hawkes of New Jersey, Tobey of New Hampshire and White of Maine.

Senator Scott W. Lucas, Democrat, of Illinois, co-author of the Green-Lucas bill, declared today's action "the hardest blow that was ever struck at the political rights of a soldier in time of war."

"Those who favored the passage of this amendment will have to accept the responsibility to the soldiers, their fathers, mothers, wives and friends," he said.

Supporters of the Green-Lucas bill, who insisted that the measure would permit service men and women throughout the world to take part by millions in the election of the President, Vice President and Seventy-ninth Congress next year, contended that the Eastland-McClellan-McKellar substitute would make it "impossible," because of restrictions in State election laws, for those serving overseas to vote.

Those supporting the substitute contended that it would "make the service absentee voting program constitutional" and put the responsibility for getting out the vote of their citizens upon the States themselves. They said that they did not share the disbelief expressed by supporters of the Green-Lucas bill that Legislatures would get busy and amend their election laws so as to make possible absentee voting by those in the armed forces from their States, here and abroad.

Power Only to Recommend

By the terms of the substitute, Congress instead of setting up a Federal War Ballot Commission to administer the absentee-voting program and prescribing the system of balloting, would express itself as favoring and recommending to the States that they enact legis-

Continued on Page Eight

British Reveal Cost of Fields Lent to Us

By Cable to THE NEW YORK TIMES.

LONDON, Dec. 3—Britain is spending more than the equivalent of $4,000,000 for each airfield being used by the United States Air Forces in this country, the Committee of Public Accounts made known today. This is written down as reciprocal aid.

The question of reconverting the land to its original use will be one for Parliament to settle, since the cost of ripping up the concrete runways and removing buildings will be high, far more than the cost of buying the land.

OLIVE OIL IMPORTS ARE BANNED BY U. S.

Importers Here Say Bumper Crop in Mediterranean Area May Go Begging

By JEFFERSON G. BELL

New York importers disclosed yesterday that the Mediterranean area's bumper crop of olive oil this year may go begging. They revealed that to date they had failed to win the State Department's permission to bring in some 3,000,000 gallons to ease the domestic shortage.

As the nation's relief program contemplates the shipment of some 2,000,000,000 pounds of fats and oils abroad, the olive oil importers were not impressed by the State Department's reasons for not issuing a permit for importation.

Nine European occupied countries exclusive of Soviet Russia have reported to the United Nations Relief and Rehabilitation Administration that in the first six months following the cessation of hostilities their aggregate needs of oilseeds, oils and fats requiring shipping space will be approximately 1,076,000 metric tons.

The Olive Oil Association of America, Inc., 52 Stone Street, disclosed that its usual sources had reported that not only Spain and Portugal but even war-torn Tunisia were harvesting a record-breaking crop of olive oil.

Members said that there was virtually no demand for the surplus among southern Europeans. They added that Norway, which normally used substantial quantities for its sardine packing, had been entirely cut off from the market since German occupation.

Bumper Crop in Spain Seen

"Reliable reports indicate that Spain will have a bumper crop of olive oil this year," declared the Olive Oil Association of America, Inc. "The figure is said to exceed 425,000 tons—about 123,250,000 gallons. This constitutes one of the best productions of olive oil in the history of Spain and, for the first time in many years, leaves a sizable export surplus. The domestic consumption in Spain is about 300,000 tons, thus, there should be available for export and stockpiling 125,000 tons.

"Due, no doubt, to the insistence of the olive oil importers and packers in the United States, under leadership of the Olive Oil Association of America, Inc., an associa-

Continued on Page Fourteen

1,000 BIG BOMBERS, 7,789 OTHER PLANES BUILT IN NOVEMBER

Record Productions Achieved at Pace of One Every Five Minutes Around Clock

NEW PEAKS IN NAVY YARDS

250,000-Ton Output Is Largely of Combat Ships, Among Them Many Aircraft Carriers

Special to THE NEW YORK TIMES.

WASHINGTON, Dec. 3—More than 1,000 four-engined bombers were among 8,789 planes turned out by aircraft factories in November, and about a dozen aircraft carriers were included in more than 250,000 standard displacement tons of naval craft completed in shipyards during the month, which set new records in war production.

Announcements of the production achievements were made today by Donald M. Nelson, chairman of the War Production Board; Frank Knox, Secretary of the Navy, and James Forrestal, Under-Secretary in charge of the Navy's program.

November airplane production was 97 per cent of the month's goal and brought the total of planes produced this year to 76,000. A plane goal for 1943 of 125,000 was announced by President Roosevelt on Jan. 6, 1942, but this figure was revised downward as average plane weights were revised upward.

Airplanes rolled off the production lines continuously day and night at a rate faster than one every five minutes, exceeded the October output by 427 planes, notwithstanding the shorter month, and exceeded the total weight of October's output by 7 per cent, Mr. Nelson reported.

2,000 Planes for the Navy

The Navy's war contractors turned out well over 2,000 planes, of which nearly 2,000 were fighters and bombers, Mr. Knox said. He declared he was particularly gratified by the excellent fighter plane production record, since the Navy had set "extremely steep" schedules to make up for delays caused by the introduction of two new types, the Corsair and the Hellcat.

"By far the largest percentage" of the more than 250,000 tons of ships produced were combat vessels, but the Secretary said he was unable to reveal the exact number of carriers completed. Eight were escort carriers, however. The Wasp, of 27,000 tons, was completed Nov. 24, it had been previously announced.

Under-Secretary Forrestal said that the Navy should be able to turn out at least eight aircraft carriers each month now, including the converted merchantman "Baby Flat-top" type. Several admirals in charge of war output bureaus reported that, for the most part, production bottlenecks had been "licked."

This week-end President Roosevelt's 1943 goal of 260 destroyer

Continued on Page Four

Heavy 'Retaliation' Threatened by Nazis

By The Associated Press.

LONDON, Dec. 3 — Again threatening retaliation for the air war upon Germany, the Berlin radio said today that the German High Command "intends by one fell, drastic stroke to end the unbridled mass murder," and added that "mankind is not far from the point where it can at will blow up half the globe."

The broadcast quoted the periodical Reich as saying that "the commencement of retaliation no longer depends on technical matters, but solely on the object which is to be attained by it."

"The retaliation," it continues, "will be so powerful and will be started at such a psychologically opportune moment as to influence the development of the war. It would be superfluous to retaliate for ruins with ruins. The sense of retaliation will find quite a different and surprising expression spiritually as well as politically."

WALKER OPPOSES POSTAL RATE RISES

Tells Senators Department Is Studying Issue — Swope Fights Racing Levy

Special to THE NEW YORK TIMES.

WASHINGTON, Dec. 3—Postmaster General Frank C. Walker opposed before the Senate Finance Committee today the increase in postal rates carried in the $2,140,000,000 tax bill passed by the House.

Other witnesses opposed the increase in the fur tax carried in the House bill; the proposed 5 per cent pari-mutuel tax and a proposal to place a graduated tax on distilled spirits held in a bonded warehouse longer than four years. The witnesses who appeared in opposition to the liquor and pari-mutuel increases were questioned by Senator Alben W. Barkley of Kentucky, majority leader, apparently indicating sympathy with their position.

Drew Pearson, newspaper columnist, was scheduled to appear for questioning regarding published statements made by him that Ellsworth C. Alvord, Wash-

Continued on Page Eight

AIR BATTLES SHARP

Nazi Fighters and Guns Down 41 of RAF's Attacking Planes

SOUTH BERLIN HIT

New Factory Area the Target in Fifth Heavy Blow in 15 Nights

By DREW MIDDLETON
By Cable to THE NEW YORK TIMES.

LONDON, Dec. 3—More than 500 Lancaster and Halifax bombers of the Royal Air Force cracked the strongest defense the Germans had yet been able to organize and hammered Berlin last night with more than 1,500 long tons of bombs in a signal victory.

Great fires raging in the south and southeastern sections of the Reich capital were visible 200 miles from the target as the British and Canadian formations flew homeward.

What was believed to be the largest night engagement of the air war was fought along the approaches to Berlin and over the city during the fifth major assault on Berlin in fifteen nights. More than 500 Nazi fighters, favored by every advantage the weather could give, hacked at the RAF planes.

Forty-one bombers, one of them a Canadian craft, were missing as a result of the enemy's interception and very heavy anti-aircraft fire.

[London officials said early today that British bombers during the night again attacked Germany. The announcement followed reports that RAF formations had flown out toward the Continent after midnight, a change in timing from the evening operations of previous big blows in the current aerial offensive.]

Despite the well-planned defense, including an "avenue of flares" starting fifty miles from Berlin, returning British fliers said, the big bombers penetrated to the areas marked out by pathfinder planes and bombed their targets heavily. They shot down three Nazi fighters during the attack, which began just after 8 o'clock

Continued on Page Four

8th Army Drives 6 Miles Up Coast Toward San Vito

Town 15 Miles From Key to Road to Rome Is Reported Taken — Inland, Montgomery Wins Castelfrentano—5th Army Gains

By MILTON BRACKER
By Wireless to THE NEW YORK TIMES.

ALGIERS, Dec. 3—The Eighth Army has captured Castelfrentano and moved up the coastal road from Fossacesia toward San Vito. [The coastal advance covered six miles, The Associated Press said.]

The Allied air offensive continued with increasing violence in front of the Fifth Army, notably at points around Cassino, and Royal Air Force Spitfire pilots reported fierce fighting between the Germans and Lieut. Gen. Mark W. Clark's American and British forces.

The progress of Gen. Sir Bernard L. Montgomery's British, New Zealand and Indian troops on the Adriatic front was somewhat slower than the day before. The enemy repeatedly counter-attacked at Castelfrentano after the Allies had seized the town and a furious battle was going on for Lanciano, three miles nearer the coast than Castelfrentano along the inland road loop. Mines and demolitions continued to impede the advance.

[The Algiers radio reported that the Eighth Army had captured San Vito, which is fifteen miles from its objective, Pescara, and a DNB broadcast from Berlin said that the Germans had evacuated Lanciano.]

No details were available here regarding the bitter fighting on the Fifth Army front observed by British airmen, but it was officially announced that General Clark's men had managed to make short

Continued on Page Five

Red Army Tightens Noose On Rail Junction of Zhlobin

By The Associated Press.

LONDON, Saturday, Dec. 4—Mud-spattered Red Army troops bit into the important German railway network northwest of Gomel in two directions yesterday, stood firm against repeated Nazi counter-attacks in the hotly contested Cherkassy area and expanded their Dnieper River bridgehead below Kremenchug to twenty miles west of the city through powerfully defended territory, Moscow announced early today.

German troops recoiling before the Russian attacks northwest of Gomel suffered heavy losses, the Soviet midnight bulletin said, as the Russians swept up more than 100 villages and hamlets. Key points taken in this drive—carried out through blizzards, howling winds and rain—were Sverzhin and Dovsk, twelve miles and eighteen miles east of Rogachev, respectively, and Soltanovka, twelve miles southeast of Zhlobin on the Gomel railroad.

[An additional thrust beyond Soltanovka carried the Red Army to the village of Staraya Rudnya, nine miles southeast of Zhlobin.]

The towns captured yesterday screen the approaches to the hubs of the German rail network in that region — Zhlobin and Rogachev. Seven hundred Germans were killed alone in one sector of the fighting in that area.

Determined Soviet troops, blasting their way forward through complex German trench systems and dug-outs protected by mine fields and barbed wire entanglements, took Novogeorgiyevsk, a district center of the Kirovograd region, and killed hundreds of Germans, the communiqué said.

[The Russians also announced the capture of Klochkovo, twenty miles west of Kremenchug along the right bank of the Dnieper.]

With their westward thrust into the Dnieper sack below Kremenchug the Russians moved to relieve the pressure on their com-

Continued on Page Six

AUSTRALIANS PERIL ANOTHER HUON BASE

Close In on Wareo, Japanese Stronghold in New Guinea—New Britain Is Battered

By The Associated Press.

ALLIED HEADQUARTERS IN THE SOUTHWEST PACIFIC, Saturday, Dec. 4—Australian jungle troops supported by artillery, are closing in on Wareo, a Japanese stronghold on the Huon Peninsula of northeastern New Guinea.

Wareo is inland about eleven miles northwest of coastal Finschhafen, the base which the Allies captured Oct. 2.

Gen. Douglas MacArthur's headquarters, announcing the latest progress today, said that the Australians were mopping up on enemy strong points along the track that leads from Allied-won Bonga on the coast north of Finschhafen westward to Wareo.

To the east, just across narrow waters from the peninsula, General MacArthur's bombers continued to hit at targets on New Britain in an area of that important enemy island that is most vulnerable to invasion.

For the second straight day Borgen Bay's dumps and supply barges were the targets. Sixty-three tons of explosives were dropped by Mitchell medium bomb-

Continued on Page Three

DECISIONS VARIED

Moscow Radio Asserts Political Problems Were Settled

PARLEY NOW IS OVER

Axis Reports Predict an Appeal to Germans to Quit Hitler

By JAMES B. RESTON
By Cable to THE NEW YORK TIMES.

LONDON, Saturday, Dec. 4—The Moscow radio announced early this morning that President Roosevelt, Prime Minister Churchill and Premier Stalin had met in Teheran, Iran, "a few days ago" to discuss questions relating to the war and the post-war period.

"A few days ago," the Moscow radio said shortly after midnight, "a conference of the leaders of the three Allied nations — President Roosevelt, Prime Minister Churchill and Premier Stalin—took place at Teheran.

"Military and diplomatic representatives also took part. The questions discussed at the conference related to the war against Germany and also to a range of political questions. Decisions were taken which will be published later."

[An Associated Press dispatch from London quoted the Soviet monitor as saying that full details of the conference might be announced between noon and 2 P. M., Eastern war time today, basing this prediction on the usual routine of the Moscow radio when announcing future broadcasts.]

The radio announcement, which came as a surprise to official quarters in London, said nothing about the present location of Mr. Roosevelt and Mr. Churchill, who held a five-day meeting with Generalissimo Chiang Kai-shek last week and made plans for the defeat of the Japanese and the dismemberment of their empire.

Details Are Awaited

Early this morning the Moscow radio had not indicated the nature of political and military discussions that took place in the Iranian capital, but it was generally assumed they dealt with the coordination of military plans for the final assault on Hitlerite Germany and with the unification of political plans for making peace with Germany on the basis of "unconditional surrender."

Official information that has come back to London since the Prime Minister left the capital has been extremely limited and indeed until the Moscow radio made its announcement the German radio was the main source of reports on the movements of the three leaders. It was, however, generally expected in London that the three leaders would in the course of their discussions decide to appeal to the German people over the heads of their Government to surrender or take the consequences of the air war in the west and an invasion of Russian armies from the east.

Stalin Crosses Own Border

While Mr. Churchill and Mr. Roosevelt had had seven previous conferences on the war, this was the first among the three leaders, and so far as is known it marked the first time that Mr. Stalin had left the Soviet Union since the revolution in 1917. The meeting was foreshadowed after the Quebec conference when Mr. Churchill told the House of Commons he "hoped" to meet with Mr. Roosevelt and Mr. Stalin before the first of the year.

The Prime Minister had met Premier Stalin once before in the autumn of 1942, when he journeyed to Moscow to explain to him why it was impossible for the United States and Britain to invade the continent of Europe from the west that year.

Previous to that conference the United States and Britain had undertaken to concern themselves with the "urgent tasks" of creating a second front in 1942, and it is now known that the first Stalin-

Continued on Page Two

Longo, Hague Foe, Is Imprisoned; Edison Joins U. S. Inquiry Plea

Special to THE NEW YORK TIMES.

JERSEY CITY, N. J., Dec. 3—John R. Longo, former deputy Hudson County clerk and long a political foe of Mayor Frank Hague of this city, was sentenced today by Judge Thomas H. Brown to a prison term of eighteen months to three years on a charge of "fraudulently altering" his voting record.

The sentencing of Longo came only a few hours after Gov. Charles Edison declared it was "not only the right but the imperative duty" of the Department of Justice to investigate alleged suppression of civil rights in Hudson County. The investigation was demanded in a petition filed yesterday by the City Affairs Committee of Jersey City with United States Attorney General Francis J. Biddle. The Longo case was one of several cited as emphasizing a need for the inquiry.

Governor Edison said that under the "ineffective 99-year-old State Constitution few powers are granted to a Governor of New Jersey and among the powers he lacks is that of protecting the civil liberties of the people of his State." The Governor added that he "deeply regretted the existence of the situation complained of in Jersey City."

Longo, convicted Nov. 15 by a jury before Judge Brown, was denied a certificate of reasonable doubt by Judge Brown today after Raymond Chasan, his counsel, presented a writ of error, issued by the New Jersey Supreme Court, to the judge. In denying the certifi-

Continued on Page Twenty-six

War News Summarized

SATURDAY, DECEMBER 4, 1943

The Moscow radio announced last night that the historic conference of President Roosevelt, Prime Minister Churchill and Marshal Stalin was held "a few days ago" in Teheran, Iran, and that plans were laid to knock Germany out of the war. Political as well as military questions were discussed by diplomatic and military representatives, with the decisions to be given to the public later. [1:8.]

Meeting the stiffest resistance to date, 500 Lancaster and Halifax bombers dropped more than 1,500 tons of bombs on Berlin in Thursday night's attack, the fifth heavy blow there in fifteen nights. Huge fires in Berlin's southern and southeastern industrial sections were visible 200 miles away, but the RAF lost forty-one bombers at the hands of 500 German night fighters. [1:5.] In November more than 13,000 tons of British bombs hit Germany in ten major attacks. [1:6-7.]

In the Mediterranean area, the assault on the Marseille submarine pens also unleashed fierce air fighting, twenty-five German pursuit planes attacking the American Fortresses. All the bombers returned and eleven Germans were downed. Three Lightnings and four enemy fighters were lost yesterday in renewed attacks on Bolzano. [5:1.]

Throwing back repeated counter-attacks in Italy the Eighth Army captured Castelfrentano and moved north along the Adriatic coastal road toward San Vito. The Fifth Army, under increasing air cover, advanced locally near Calabritto. [1:6-7; map, P. 5.] General Clark himself was under fire, but was unhurt. [5:2-3.]

Soviet armies, moving south along the Dnieper River to outflank the railroad junction of Zhlobin, took the highway center of Dovsk, while other troops occupied Soltanovka, twelve miles southeast of the town. The Russians fought off attacks on their Cherkassy bridgehead and took Novogeorgiyevsk, four miles west of Kremenchug. [1:6-7; map, P. 6.]

Evidently fearing a Balkan invasion following the Teheran conference, the Germans were reported sending thousands of reinforcements to Yugoslavia. Troops were massing at Metkovic, in northern Dalmatia, Partisan reports said. [6:2.]

Washington believed President Benes of Czechoslovakia attended the Allied conference, acting as mediator in the Russo-Polish dispute. [2:8.]

Answering critics of heavy marine losses at Tarawa, Secretary of the Navy Knox told a press conference the island was struck by 2,900 tons of bombs and shells before the landing—more than fell on Berlin in the heaviest air attack. [3:1.]

In the southwest Pacific, Australian troops with artillery support closed in on the Japanese stronghold of Wareo, eleven miles from Finschhafen on New Guinea's Huon peninsula. Bombers hit Borgen Bay, New Britain, and the Kara and Ballale airdromes in the Bougainville sector. [1:7.]

RAF's Twin-Target Tactics Show Power in Month's Blows at Reich

By Cable to THE NEW YORK TIMES.

LONDON, Dec. 3—The British Air Ministry, outlining today the triumphs of the Anglo-American bombers in this theatre during November, when the Allies dropped 22,170 tons of bombs on Germany and Nazi-occupied territory — a figure that is believed to represent a record—stressed the importance of the twin-target type of attack in the winter air war tactics.

Three of the four heaviest Royal Air Force assaults on Germany last month were of this type, with two high-priority targets bombed simultaneously, thus splitting the Luftwaffe's interceptor forces and preventing the concentration of Nazi mobile anti-aircraft artillery around one target, such as Berlin.

The three twin-target assaults that featured the RAF's November operations were in "very great strength" — the Air Ministry's highest category of attacks. Others are in "great strength," such as last night's assault on Berlin, and "medium" and "moderate" attacks.

The writer estimates that "very great strength" means 750 to 1,000 bombers employed and "great strength" represents the use of 500 to 750 planes.

The twin-target attacks were the nights of Nov. 3, on Duesseldorf and Cologne; Nov. 18, Berlin and Ludwigshafen, and Nov. 26, Berlin and Stuttgart.

These blows and the concentrated attack on Berlin the night of Nov. 22 were the heaviest in a month in which 13,000 tons of British bombs fell on Germany and another 1,500 tons on occupied ter-

Continued on Page Four

"All the News That's Fit to Print."

The New York Times.

LATE CITY EDITION
Showers in forenoon; clear in afternoon; fair at night.
Temperatures Yesterday—Max., 50; Min., 35
Sunrise, 8:06 A. M.; Sunset, 8:29 P. M.

Copyright, 1943, by The New York Times Company.

VOL. XCIII...No. 31,363. Entered as Second-Class Matter, Postoffice, New York, N. Y. NEW YORK, TUESDAY, DECEMBER 7, 1943. THREE CENTS IN NEW YORK CITY

'BIG 3' CHARTS TRIPLE BLOWS TO HUMBLE REICH AND AGREES ON A PEACE TO ELIMINATE TYRANNY; CARRIERS ATTACK MARSHALLS; 5TH ARMY GAINS

MAYOR PORTRAYED AS SCHOOL RULER BY OUSTED OFFICIAL

Kuper, Former Law Adviser to Board, Tells NEA Inquiry Appointments Were Blocked

SEES MORALE IMPAIRED

Fear of Having Funds Held Up Kept the Members From Asserting Rights, He Says

Charges that Mayor La Guardia has interfered with the city school system, causing educational officials to bow to his will and robbing the Board of Education of its independence by threatening to withhold funds, were made at the National Education Association school inquiry, which began public hearings here yesterday.

A behind-the-scenes version of how the board operates, and of the role of the Mayor in deciding matters of school policy, was presented by Theodore Fred Kuper, law secretary of the board for eleven years until he was dismissed recently by order of the Mayor. Mr. Kuper took the witness stand at 10 A. M. and did not complete his testimony until the hearing adjourned late in the afternoon.

Hearing in Bar Building

Held in the trial room of the Bar Association Building, 42 West Forty-fourth Street, the open sessions are the culmination of three months of investigation and study by the National Education Association's panel of educators appointed to determine the charges of City Hall interference with school issues.

Dr. Ernest E. Cole, former New York State Commissioner of Education, who is acting as counsel for the inquiry, is conducting the hearings. Members of the panel include Dr. Orville C. Pratt, past president of the NEA and superintendent emeritus of schools at Spokane, Wash.; Dr. Ernest O. Melby, chancellor of the University of Montana; Miss Mabel Studebaker, president of the NEA's department of classroom teachers, and Dr. Donald DuShane, past president of the NEA and secretary of its commission for the defense of democracy through education.

Representatives of various school, civic and parents' groups appeared at the opening session. The investigation was requested by the New York High School Teachers Association and the Kindergarten-6B Teachers Association, two of the city's largest educational bodies. Mrs. Johanna M. Lindlof, president of the kindergarten group and former Board of Education member, sat through the entire session; she is to take the stand this morning.

Testimony by Kuper

Mr. Kuper marshaled a parade of statements and figures to support his contention that Mayor La Guardia interfered with local school independence and "frightened" board officials into submission. He cited incidents to illustrate the many points he raised. Members of the panel or Dr. Cole interrupted frequently to ask questions.

As a result of the Mayor's control over the school board 100 appointments to clerical and administrative positions, for which funds were provided in the budget, have been blocked, Mr. Kuper declared. This has resulted in decreased efficiency as well as a lowering of morale among the employes, he testified.

Important administrative positions, which the board sought to fill and for which money was present in the budget, remain vacant because the city Budget Director does not give the necessary certificates, it was brought out. One instance was cited in which the Superintendent of Plant Operation and Maintenance requested a supervising custodian; the position was approved by the Board of Education, but it took 404 days before the Mayor gave his consent.

"Bear in mind that the Board of Education has the inherent legal power and, in my opinion, the duty to fill these positions," Mr. Kuper

Continued on Page Twenty

Stalin Says U. S. Aid Saved the Allies

By Cable to THE NEW YORK TIMES.

CAIRO, Egypt, Dec. 6—The greatest tribute possibly ever paid American industrial production came from Premier Stalin during the Teheran talks.

In a toast at a dinner party the Soviet Premier said:

"Without American machines the United Nations never could have won the war."

He should know.

It is understood Premier Stalin said Russia was manufacturing 3,000 planes monthly against 3,500 British and 10,000 American.

FROZEN FOOD SPACE IS TO BE EXPANDED

Warehouses Here Are to Add Million Cubic Feet—Row Brews Over U. S. Hoards

By JEFFERSON G. BELL

Major warehouse interests of New York City disclosed yesterday that they already had taken steps to expand freezer capacity at least 1,000,000 cubic feet. This move is part of a program to ease storage, transportation and other problems caused by the Federal Government's vast hoard of food.

The Government stockpiles have so taxed the capacity of warehouses, notably freezer space, that the Office of Defense Transportation last week appealed for help to the War Food Administration and the Office of Price Administration.

The refrigeration expansion program was revealed by local WFA and warehouse spokesmen as chilly relations between national WFA and OPA on one side and ODT on the other threatened to develop into an interdepartmental row over charges that foods needed by civilians are being allowed to deteriorate or spoil because of improper warehousing.

Release of Supplies Suggested

In view of the explanation by warehouse interests here that they could not increase their freezer capacity sooner than sixty to ninety days, food-trade circles were unable to see what would be the solution of warehouse congestion unless supplies were released.

When Joseph B. Eastman, director of the Office of Defense Transportation, confirmed last week reports that he had asked WFA and OPA to take steps to ease the congestion of freezer facilities, he disclosed that he had received a letter promising "immediate" action. Neither Mr. Eastman nor any member of the ODT staff was reached yesterday for comment on the disclosure that plans for freezer expansion here held no promise of relief for another two or three months.

The local office of the Food Distribution Administration, WFA, 150 Broadway, disclosed that a survey of storage facilities here had showed that New York City warehouses are operating at 89 per cent of capacity.

"When we are operating at 90 to 93 per cent of capacity," explained

Continued on Page Twenty-three

BATTLING IN ITALY

3 More Camino Peaks Are Taken Despite Fierce Resistance

COUNTER-BLOW FAILS

Germans Beaten Back at Venafro—Eighth Army at Moro River

By MILTON BRACKER

By Wireless to THE NEW YORK TIMES.

ALGIERS, Dec. 6—The battle of the mountains continued yesterday in Italy as Lieut. Gen. Mark W. Clark's Fifth Army wrested three more peaks of the Mount Camino group from the Germans, who are putting up a fanatic battle for every inch of the rocky ground.

The slow and tortuous envelopment of the numberless ridges and peaks proceeded in an epic of difficult fighting in which the individual soldier had to combine the technique of the jungle fighter with that of the mountain goat. More rain tended to retard the four-day-old offensive as German gunfire swept the slopes and crevices from deeply dug-in positions. But the British and American infantry ground steadily forward and mopped up the isolated resistance strong points by-passed by the Allies' spearheads.

There is at least one ridge that our forces have pressed beyond and flanked without being able to silence the German fire from its crest. The entire tone of the struggle is one of a fierce will to resist. Despite severe losses, the German Tenth Army is setting a standard of savage defensive fighting that its opponents will never forget.

[American artillery has begun shelling Cassino, The United Press reported.]

Counter-Attack Repulsed

In the Venafro sector of the Fifth Army's front, above the Via Casilina, the Germans flung in another sharp counter-attack against American units. As they have done several times before, the Americans buried back the attack, leaving the positions in this sector about the same.

On the British Eighth Army's front, too, the weather was bad. The Germans poured in reinforcements as the battles for Orsogna and Guardiagrele raged unabated. Both points remained in the enemy's hands.

The Eighth Army has, in general, pressed nearer to the Moro River from San Vito Chietino, however, and, at Casone, some four miles inland, three miles above Lanciano and 1,000 yards from the Moro's south bank, the Allies' infantry and tanks crushed several advanced German machine-gun posts in their drive to the bank.

The Eighth Army captured at least one German tank that proved to be without question a flame-thrower. This settled the dispute that began here on Nov. 29, when a flame-throwing tank was first

Continued on Page Sixteen

THE LEADERS OF THE 'BIG THREE' MEET IN TEHERAN

Marshal Stalin, President Roosevelt and Prime Minister Churchill on the porch of the Russian Embassy

The New York Times (U. S. Twelfth Air Force)

HEAVY TASK FORCES STRIKE IN PACIFIC

Blow at the Marshall Islands Comes as Allies Step Up Air Drive Against New Britain

By GEORGE F. HORNE

By Telephone to THE NEW YORK TIMES.

PEARL HARBOR, Dec. 6—Strong carrier task forces and heavy Navy bombers have attacked a number of bases in the Japanese-held Marshall Islands in the last few days, indicating a new development in the central Pacific offensive, which was touched off by our invasion of the Gilbert Islands.

[In the southwest Pacific, Allied fliers struck with increasing violence against invasion-menaced New Britain land, on which lies Rabaul, main Japanese base in that war theatre. Our airmen poured 155

Continued on Page Seventeen

New Cairo Talks Reported To Get Turkey to Join War

By JAMES B. RESTON

By Wireless to THE NEW YORK TIMES.

LONDON, Dec. 6—The conversations that Prime Minister Churchill and, presumably, President Roosevelt had with President Ismet Inonu of Turkey in Cairo after the Teheran parleys have led to considerable speculation about the possibility of Turkey's entering the war. The background of these conversations would seem to justify this speculation. The question for Turkey, as an ally of Britain, now seems to be not whether but when and how she will help the Allies. This, it is presumed, is the question being discussed by Messrs. Churchill and Inonu.

[Reports that Messrs. Churchill, Roosevelt and Inonu were conferring in Africa have come from enemy and neutral sources.]

The basis of these conversations is the Anglo-French-Turkish treaty of alliance of Oct. 19, 1939. Article II stated: "In the event of an act of aggression by a European power

Continued on Page Seven

UKRAINE RAILWAY IS CUT BY RUSSIANS

Huge German Forces Are Split —Red Army Is Only 23 Miles From Kirovograd

By The Associated Press.

LONDON, Tuesday, Dec. 7—Russian troops smashed the enemy's Smela-Znamenka line in the central Ukraine yesterday, splitting huge German forces guarding those vital junctions on railways leading to Rumania and putting the Red Army within twenty-three miles of the Axis bastion of Kirovograd.

A Moscow communiqué and a midnight supplement announced the capture of Tsybulevo, eight miles northwest of Znamenka on the double-track railway leading to Smela, and the fall of Alexsandriya, twenty miles east of Znamenka. Twenty other towns and villages were swept up, said the bulletin, recorded by the Soviet monitor from a Moscow broadcast.

[The crossing of the Znamenka-Smela line probably took place in the Krasnoselye-Tsybulevo sector. Each village is two miles from the railroad line and represents the farthest penetration in yesterday's advance.

Continued on Page Twelve

WASHINGTON HAILS UNITY AT TEHERAN

Hull Stresses 'Concerting' of Plans to Crush Axis Forces—Congress Leaders Pleased

By BERTRAM D. HULEN

Special to THE NEW YORK TIMES.

WASHINGTON, Dec. 6—Opinion in the executive branch of the Government concerning both the Teheran and the Cairo conferences was set forth by Secretary of State Cordell Hull today in a statement declaring that the concerted plans adopted "will undoubtedly result in making effective to the fullest extent the fighting strength of all of the United Nations."

Opinion in general in the capital was that the communiqué issued on the Teheran conference showed that the three Chiefs of Government, President Roosevelt, Prime Minister Churchill and Premier Stalin, had had a meeting of minds and had reached detailed decisions for destroying the German Army, even though the declaration, perhaps significantly, did not use the phrase "unconditional surrender."

All in all, the announcement gave grounds for encouragement at a time when America is entering the third year of the war.

Way Open for Small Nations

It was of first importance that the three leaders had met, it was felt. And in meeting they had agreed to cooperate in the war and in the peace, and to invite the collaboration of small nations.

There were conjectures as to whether this collaboration might include the German people, if they sought it as a chastened people free of nazism and militarism.

Military details, obviously, could not be revealed, it was realized, but

Continued on Page Eleven

ATTACK PLANS SET

Dates Fixed for Land Drives From the East, West and South

IRAN TO BE FREED

Allied Leaders Say 'No Power on Earth' Can Balk Our Victory

The texts of the three-power declarations appear on Page 4.

By C. L. SULZBERGER

By Cable to THE NEW YORK TIMES.

CAIRO, Egypt, Dec. 6—Final concord on a campaign to destroy the German military power by land, sea and air and to erect an enduring peace in which all nations, both great and small, shall participate, was agreed upon in the momentous Teheran meeting between President Roosevelt, Premier Stalin and Prime Minister Churchill.

Simultaneously, the three leaders, as a sign of their faith in each other and as proof of the validity of their intentions toward little nations, guaranteed the post-war independence, sovereignty and territorial integrity of Iran.

These Allied agreements were announced to the world today in two joint declarations signed in order by President Roosevelt [the only titular Chief of State among the three], Premier Stalin and Prime Minister Churchill. They were issued in Teheran Dec. 1 after a long final sitting of the leaders and their innermost circles of advisers in the magnificent Soviet Embassy where President Roosevelt lived as a guest.

3-Pronged Attack Pledged

Their military promises can be summed up accordingly: the three powers will work together throughout the war; their military staffs have concerted plans for the destruction of German forces; these staffs have reached a "complete agreement as to the scope and timing of operations which will be undertaken from the east, west and south."

Guarantees satisfactory to the three chiefs now exist that the final victory will rest with the United Nations. "No power on earth can prevent our destroying the German armies by land, their U-boats by sea and their war plants from the air," says one of the joint declarations. "Our attacks will be relentless and increasing."

Seal Doom of Hitler

Thus in four days of deliberation in the romantic Iranian capital the "Big Three" laid the second half of the plans for ending the global war and establishing lasting peace for the benefit of all in its ruins. The Asiatic talks in North Africa between Mr. Roosevelt, Mr. Churchill and Generalissimo Chiang Kai-shek already had laid the program for accelerating the defeat of Japan and for building up a new Asia.

Now European talks of exactly the same length have rounded off the final plans for smashing Hitler which obviously must precede the destruction of Japan in the over-all scheme of the Allied grand strategy planners. Britain and America have clearly coordinated their ultimate schedule for the invasion of Europe from several points from the west and south with a program for new Russian offensives against the Reich.

It may be assumed that once the fulfillment of these plans comes about and Moscow's long pleas for a second front are entirely answered that the Soviet Union might conceivably alter its present neutral attitude toward Japan. This certainly was discussed at Teheran but the outcome of these discussions is not known.

It would seem a fair assumption from a complete survey of both the present wartime and future post-war problems indicated in the latest declarations that the three powers must now have agreed on

Continued on Page Four

War News Summarized

TUESDAY, DECEMBER 7, 1943

President Roosevelt, Premier Stalin and Prime Minister Churchill announced to the world yesterday that "no power on earth can prevent our destroying the German armies by land, their U-boats by sea and their war plants from the air."

The three leaders, in a declaration dated Teheran, Dec. 1, said they had "reached complete agreement as to the scope and timing of operations which will be undertaken from the east, west and south."

"We came here with hope and determination," the three men said. "We leave here friends in fact, in spirit and in purpose." One of the purposes is to "work together in the peace" that will follow the war. All countries, large and small, were invited into "a world family of democratic nations" pledged to eliminate tyranny, oppression and intolerance and to "banish the scourge and terror of war for many generations."

In a second declaration the conferees pledged the independence and territorial integrity of Iran as a token of their determination to protect small nations. [All the foregoing 1:8; map P. 5.]

The meetings were held in the Soviet Embassy at Teheran about a round table ten feet in diameter. It was the first time Mr. Roosevelt had ever met Premier Stalin and the first time the latter had left his country since 1909. [3:1.]

A third international meeting was reported to have followed in North Africa, where, it was said, Mr. Roosevelt and Mr. Churchill conferred with President Inonu of Turkey regarding his country's entrance into the war. [1:5-6.]

The military plans laid at Teheran were expected to be in full effect by March or April of next year, when invasion from Britain would follow the Russian winter drive and an all-out aerial offensive against Germany. [1:6-7.]

Secretary of State Hull declared that the fighting strength of the United Nations could now become fully effective [1:7] and London opinion held that the Teheran announcement was designed to conceal more than was revealed. [9:2.] The people of Moscow were delighted that agreement on timing all blows against Germany had ended the "second-front" issue. [10:1.]

Allied troops continued to make progress on all fronts. Both the Eighth and Fifth Armies in Italy pushed forward against bitter opposition, reaching the Moro River and bringing Cassino under artillery fire. [1:3; map, P. 16.] The Red Army, smashing southwest of Kremenchug, was only four miles from Znamenka as it cut the Smela-Znamenka rail line. [1:6; map, P. 12.]

In the Pacific 155 tons of bombs were showered on Cape Gloucester as the assault on the western end of New Britain was maintained. [17:2-3.] A strong American carrier force attacked Japanese positions in the Marshall Islands [1:4] and United States submarines sent eleven more enemy ships to the bottom. [16:6.]

2d Brooklyn Jury Scores Mayor For Failing to Hire Enough Police

Already under censure by the August grand jury in Kings County for alleged failure to suppress crime in the Bedford-Stuyvesant section of Brooklyn, the administration of Mayor La Guardia was accused yesterday by the holdover July grand jury of inadequately policing the entire borough.

"We charge," the July panel declared in a presentment to County Judge Franklin Taylor, "that the present administration over a long period of years has utterly failed to take adequate measures to promptly fill the vacancies regularly occurring in the department, and also to provide additional patrolmen during this time."

At the same time County Judge Nathan R. Sobel was charging the December grand jury and pointing out, for the guidance of the August panel, that its presentment was faulty in that it had the effect of "indicting" an entire people for the crimes of a very few and "stirring up resentment, hatred and fear."

The August panel reconvened yesterday, continuing its inquiry into what it declares to be widespread and unchecked lawlessness in Brooklyn's "Little Harlem." It heard the testimony of several witnesses, then adjourned without disclosing when it would meet again.

In its presentment the July grand jury, whose term had been extended to permit it to investigate police protection in the city's most populous borough, attributed the critical police situation to the "short-sighted, improvident policies of this administration," which it said "have in large part contributed to the development of a situ-

Continued on Page Twenty

First Quarter of 1944 Likely to See Fruition of the Teheran Strategy

By DREW MIDDLETON

By Cable to THE NEW YORK TIMES.

LONDON, Dec. 6—Military plans for the defeat of the Wehrmacht drawn at Teheran, Iran, by President Roosevelt, Prime Minister Churchill and Premier Stalin, will probably be fully activated in the first three months of 1944.

During that period the strategic aerial offensive against Germany will assume its maximum proportions, the winter offensive of the Red Army should have brought it to the Dniester in the south and into Poland in the north and the Anglo-American invasion of northern Europe from Britain will be ready to start, with the tactical air forces already operating against the defenses in Western Europe and the lateral communications on which those defenses rely.

One of the first tangible results of the Teheran conference should be the arrival of Gen. George C. Marshall, United States Army Chief of Staff, in Britain to take up his position as Commander in Chief of all Allied invasion forces.

Once the invasion leader is settled into his job it is considered likely that the long-awaited announcement of the formation of an Allied Tactical Air Force and the names of its commanders and the appointment of American and British commanders to lead Allied Army groups involved in the invasion, will follow.

It may well be that the southern Europe front now represented by a slow, painful advance in Italy may

Continued on Page Five

"All the News That's Fit to Print."

The New York Times.

LATE CITY EDITION
Cloudy and warmer today; fresh winds.
Temperatures Yesterday—Max., 30; Min., 9
Sunrise, 8:18 A. M.; Sunset, 5:34 P. M.

VOL. XCIII. No. 31,381. Entered as Second-Class Matter, Postoffice, New York, N. Y. NEW YORK, SATURDAY, DECEMBER 25, 1943. THREE CENTS IN NEW YORK CITY

EISENHOWER NAMED COMMANDER FOR INVASION; 3,000 PLANES SMASH FRENCH COAST; BERLIN HIT; ROOSEVELT PROMISES NATION A DURABLE PEACE

STRIKE CALLED OFF BY 230,000 IN TRAIN AND ENGINE UNIONS

But Non-Operating Men Meet Carriers and Reject Offer Made for Overtime Pay

GIVE BYRNES NO ANSWER

He Says Agreement Must Meet Requirements Set Forth in the Stabilization Program

By LOUIS STARK
Special to THE NEW YORK TIMES.

WASHINGTON, Dec. 24—The Brotherhood of Locomotive Engineers and the Brotherhood of Railroad Trainmen today canceled notices for a strike of their 230,000 members on Dec. 30 in view of President Roosevelt's offer and their acceptance of arbitration by the Chief Executive.

The conductors, firemen and switchmen's unions, also members of the "Big Five" operating and transportation brotherhoods, representing more than 120,000 employes, have rejected arbitration by the President and have not called off the strike of their members set for Dec. 30.

The other major development today in the railroad wage situation was a three-hour conference in the office of James F. Byrnes, chief of the Office of War Mobilization, participated in by committees of the railroads and of spokesmen for the fifteen non-operating unions, whose 1,100,000 members are scheduled to strike on Dec. 30.

At this meeting it was reported that the non-operating unions asked for a wage increase of 6 cents an hour as compensation for overtime after forty hours. These employes receive overtime after forty-eight hours of service. The carriers are reported to have offered 4 cents an hour for overtime, but it is understood that this was rejected by the unions.

Insists on Negotiations

B. M. Jewell, chief negotiator for the unions, is said to have been pressed by Mr. Byrnes for a reply to the President's demand that the non-operating employes permit him to act as sole and final arbiter in their dispute with the carriers.

The union leader is said to have replied with some asperity that the President last night gave the unions until Monday to reply to the arbitration proposal, and that in the meantime they had obtained from the President authority to proceed and seek an agreement with the carriers, whose committees were headed by Jacob Aronson, vice president of the New York Central Railroad.

The offer of 4 cents an hour for overtime was understood to be above the 4 to 10 cents an hour sliding scale wage increase recommended in the non-operating unions' case by an emergency board, convened after Frank M. Vinson, the Economic Stabilization Director, had rejected the 8 cents an hour proposal of a previous emergency board.

Byrnes' Statement

The conference in Mr. Byrnes' office, which was attended for a short time by Mr. Vinson, ended at 5:30 P. M. and the following statement was issued on Mr. Byrnes' behalf:

"The representatives of the carriers and the non-operating brotherhoods met in the conference room of the Office of War Mobilization.

"The representatives of the carriers were not present at the conference the President held with the representatives of the brotherhoods yesterday afternoon. Justice Byrnes advised the carriers' representatives that the President desired to know whether they would object to his arbitrating the differences between the carriers and the non-operating brotherhoods.

"The representatives of the carriers stated that they were entirely willing to agree that the President should arbitrate the differences just as they had agreed in

Continued on Page Twenty-six

17 Perish as Fire Sweeps 42d Street Lodging House

Scores Hurt in 'Bowery-Type' Building Disaster, Worst of Its Kind Here in Years—Many Trapped Asleep

Sixteen bodies had been removed last night from a five-story brick structure at 437-439 West Forty-second Street, between Ninth and Tenth Avenues, the four upper floors of which were occupied by a "Bowery-type" lodging house, after one of the city's worst fires in years virtually had consumed the entire interior.

A seventeenth victim died at 7:15 P. M. in Roosevelt Hospital, to which most of the score of injured were removed.

The actual loss of life probably never will be known. With most of the victims burned beyond recognition and in many cases nothing remaining but bones, the task of counting the dead and identifying them was proving almost impossible. Authorities, after checking for hours, could not even determine how many persons were in the building at the time of the fire. They were faced with the fact that the lodging house had beds in three-foot by six cubicles, separated by flimsy plywood partitions, and in hall-like dormitories "accommodating" 248 persons. It was said the beds were well filled with restaurant and other night workers.

The fire believed to have smoldered for three hours, started at 2 P. M. as if set by a hundred torches. Trapped in their sleep many were burned to death in their "cells," rooms so tiny that a lodger had literally to crawl into bed through a special door on a central vertical hinge that folded to permit entry.

The victims groped through con-

Continued on Page Twenty-six

WLB PEACE OFFER WIRED STEEL UNION

Davis Tells Murray Retroactivity Can Be Reconsidered Within Wage Formula

Special to THE NEW YORK TIMES.

WASHINGTON, Dec 24—William H. Davis, chairman of the War Labor Board, telegraphed today to Philip Murray, president of the CIO United Steel Workers, that if labor members of the board desired to reconsider their vote on the retroactive pay issue "the public members will favor such reconsideration."

But, while he indicated that a retroactive basis might be approved within the framework of the present ("Little Steel") wage stabilization formula, Mr. Davis stated in his message that the public members could not now determine "any question of retroactivity that might come up in any future change in the wage stabilization policy."

Presuming that any such future change would be applied to "all wage-earners," he wrote that retroactivity in general or in particular ought to be decided when and if the change is made.

[A production stoppage was reported early this morning by The Associated Press with the expiration of contracts at midnight covering 35,000 employes at the Republic Steel Corporation and Youngstown Sheet and Tube Company. At these plants in Youngstown and in Cleveland picketing began.]

"Misunderstanding" Deplored

Mr. Davis' telegram said:

"You are quoted as saying that the proposal of the public members of the War Labor Board as to retroactivity in the steel negotiations violates principles enunciated by the board in the recent cases affecting hundreds of thousands of workers, that the proposal of the

Continued on Page Twenty-six

CITY AN OPEN HOUSE FOR WARTIME YULE

Heart-Warming Parties for Service Men and Women Are Chief Among Festivities

New York was far from a big, cold, gray city as it ushered in its third wartime Christmas last night with heart-warming church services, gay parties, gifts for the ill and unfortunate, and messages of good-will that brought cheer to its teeming millions and to the men and women visitors in the services.

It will not be a white Christmas, according to the weather man, but it will be cold.

Tens of thousands of visitors, many of them members of the families of service men, were in the city for the week-end. Railroads, doing a peak business, were handicapped by the bitter cold in the surrounding country. Virtually every train to and from the city was loaded to capacity, with standees in the aisles. Because of the cold, many trains were late.

Grand Central Terminal and the Pennsylvania Station were packed. Policemen kept the crowds moving. Buses and bus terminals throughout the city did a land-office business, too.

Stores Experience Let-Up

Only in the stores did Christmas Eve bring a let-up. While business was brisk, the real crush had subsided and only last-minute shoppers were on hand.

The churches of all faiths welcomed the Holy Day with midnight services, offering prayers for a victorious peace. There were many men in uniform at masses, carol services and communion.

Virtually every Roman Catholic church celebrated a midnight mass by permission of Archbishop Francis J. Spellman. Episcopal churches celebrated communion, while many churches of other faiths held can-

Continued on Page Nine

Biggest of War Plants Will Make Army Bomber Engines at Chicago

By The United Press.

CHICAGO, Dec. 24—The country's largest war plant, a series of structures sprawling over 500 acres of land, was ready today to turn out an unending stream of engines for Army bombing planes.

The giant inland plant on Chicago's South Side was built by the Dodge division of the Chrysler Corporation. Willow Run could be set down in the main building with enough room left to lay out twenty baseball diamonds.

There are nineteen buildings in the plant, all ready for production. The main building, the machining-assembly unit, covers eighty-two acres.

The plant has fourteen cafeterias and kitchens, butcher shops and bakeries to feed employes.

A parking lot a mile and a quarter long will accommodate 14,000 automobiles. The interplant communication system has 500 miles of telephone lines. Utility services are sufficient for a city of 75,000 population.

Officials revealed that the machine shops had been turning out parts for 2,200-horsepower, eighteen-cylinder Wright engines.

The plant, already called "Hitler's headache," will employ more than 25,000 persons when it enters mass production.

Prior to the completion of the Chicago plant, the bomber factory owned by the Government and operated by Henry Ford at Willow Run, twenty-five miles from Detroit, was called the largest war production unit in the world. It covers two square miles.

RECORD AIR BLOW

'Forts,' Liberators and Medium Bombers Rock 'Special' Targets

ALL CRAFT RETURN

RAF Pounds the German Capital With 1,120 Tons Before Dawn

By DAVID ANDERSON
By Cable to THE NEW YORK TIMES.

LONDON, Dec. 24—The greatest number of American heavy bombers ever to take off from Britain attacked "special military installations" of the Germans along the coast of northern France today as part of record operations of probably 3,000 Allied warplanes across the Channel.

Before dawn hundreds of the most powerful bombers of the Royal Air Force struck Berlin again with more than 1,120 tons of high explosives and fire missiles.

Several features of this two-fisted battering by the Allied air forces on the eve of Christmas made the day a memorable one for the enemy, even taking into account the Anglo-American achievements of recent weeks.

Headquarters of the United States Eighth Air Force announced that 1,300 planes handled by American crews took part in the daylight missions.

An even greater number of RAF, Dominion and Allied planes were out. Every one of the bombers and fighters of the joint forces returned to its base, according to a communiqué issued by headquarters of the United States Army here and the British Air Ministry.

Included in the American force were the largest formations of Flying Fortresses and Liberators ever sent into the air. Since an estimated 750 United States "heavies" at one time have attacked targets in western Germany within the past month, the day's operations entailed the use of close to, if not exceeding, 800 four-motored bombers.

The most concentrated attacks were carried out in the Pas-de-Ca-

Continued on Page Three

TO KEEP IT BY ARMS

President Says 4 Nations Agree on This for as Long as Necessary

'COST MAY BE HIGH'

German Might Must End, He Says on Air, Warning 'Japs' of Bad News

The text of the President's address appears on Page 8.

By JOHN H. CRIDER
Special to THE NEW YORK TIMES.

HYDE PARK, N. Y., Dec. 24—President Roosevelt promised the country and the world this Christmas Eve that they could look for insured peace with "certainty," even though "the cost may be high and the time long," and said that the United States, Great Britain, Soviet Russia and China were agreed to use force to maintain that peace "for as long as it may be necessary."

Speaking from the study in the Franklin D. Roosevelt Library, one of his favorite rendezvous, with his family gathered informally around him, the President gave his first comprehensive report on his recent conferences in the Middle East over the most extensive broadcast facilities ever set up in this country.

For the first time the President tempered his "unconditional surrender" ultimatum of Casablanca by stating that the United Nations did not want to enslave the German people but wanted them to have "a normal chance to develop in peace as useful and respectable members of the European family."

Here appeared to be one of the great achievements of the conference at Teheran—a united view by the Allies in Europe on what kind of a post-war Germany they would look for, which closes the gulf which appeared to exist between the Anglo-American "unconditional surrender" demand, and the more hopeful outlook for the future which the Russians have been

Continued on Page Eight

War News Summarized

SATURDAY, DECEMBER 25, 1943

President Roosevelt proudly announced to the world yesterday the appointment of General Dwight D. Eisenhower as supreme commander of the Anglo-American invasion forces—a selection, he said, that was made at the Teheran conference, where every point concerning the impending east-west-south attack on Germany had been decided.

It was announced from London that General Wilson would succeed General Eisenhower as commander of the Allied forces in the Mediterranean theatre; that General Montgomery would be chief of British Army units under General Eisenhower; that General Alexander would head the Allied forces in Italy, and that General Spaatz would be American Air Force commander against Germany. [All the foregoing, 1:8.]

Peace is certain, but the cost of bringing it about will be high and the realization may be distant, President Roosevelt declared during the Christmas Eve broadcast from his Hyde Park home. He said the United Nations had no desire to enslave the German people but wanted them to develop as respectable members of the European family. As for Japan, he said that empire is being enveloped in a band of steel and there is plenty of bad news for the Japanese in the offing. [1:5.]

Speaking from the German-surrounded Vatican, Pope Pius XII made a plea for a just peace and declared that a normal measure of power and the employment of force were needed to achieve it, but he decried any harsh imposition supported by arms alone. [1:6-7.]

An estimated 3,000 American and British planes of virtually all types—the greatest concentration in air history—bombed the Pas-de-Calais area of France, where, it is believed, the Germans have implanted rocket guns. In this, the fifth straight assault on these targets, the American Eighth Air Force sent 1,300 planes, a record number for any single operation. All Allied planes returned. The attack followed a Royal Air Force blow at Berlin, reportedly hitting the southeast industrial area near Tempelhof. [1:4, map P. 3.]

The fortified town of Gorodok, seventeen miles from Vitebsk and on the Vitebsk-Nevel railroad, was successfully stormed by the Russian Army, which drove ahead to capture sixty other places. Southwest of Zhlobin, in southern White Russia, large German tank and infantry attacks were beaten back. [1:7, map, P. 5.]

The British Eighth Army captured Vezzani, three miles southwest of the Adriatic port of Ortona, where fighting continued in the streets. There was little activity except for patrol thrusts on the Fifth Army front, because of deep mud. Medium Allied bombers struck at the Riviera coast, hitting bridges, railroads and viaducts. [1:6-7.]

Cape Gloucester, which seems to be shaping up as another possible invasion point on New Britain Island, was hit by 300 more tons of Allied aerial bombs, bringing the total tonnage dropped since Dec. 1 to 2,500. [6:1.]

The Navy announced that the United States submarine Grayling was presumably lost with her complement of sixty-five men. [6:2.]

NEW INVASION COMMANDER IN CHIEF

Gen. Dwight D. Eisenhower

The New York Times, 1943

Pope Prays for Just Peace Kept by Wise Use of Force

By The Associated Press.

LONDON, Dec. 24—Praying that this may be the last war Christmas and that a truly Christian peace may be celebrated in the coming year, Pope Pius XII today called for the world's responsible leaders to check the instincts of hate and vengeance and give rise to "the resplendent dawn of a new spirit of world union."

The text of the Pope's address appears on Page 10.

Raising his voice to a vibrant ring in outlining "the principles for a peace program," the Pontiff called for a "normal measure of power," sanctions and "the employment of force" to achieve and maintain peace, but warned that true peace "can never be a harsh imposition supported by arms" alone.

"An hour like the present—so full of possibilities for vast beneficent progress no less than for fatal defects and blunders—has perhaps never been seen in the history of mankind," said the Holy Father, who spoke on Christmas Eve from the bayonet-circled Vatican, where he has been isolated except by radio since the Germans occupied Rome in September.

The 35-minute address was delivered on the radio in Italian, but an official English language translation later was made available.

Juridical Basis for Peace

"A true peace is not the mathematical result of a proportion of forces, but in its last and deepest meaning is a moral and juridical process," said the Pope, speaking from what he called the "abysmal ruins of this terrible war."

"It (peace) is not, in fact, achieved without the employment of force, and its very existence

Continued on Page Ten

RED ARMY TAKES KEY TO VITEBSK

Gorodok, 17 Miles From Goal, Falls After Russian Feint Outwits Nazi Defense

By The Associated Press.

LONDON, Saturday, Dec. 25—The Russian Baltic Army cracked a model German defense-in-depth line and captured the heavily fortified lake town of Gorodok, seventeen miles north of Vitebsk yesterday, sweeping on over 2,000 German dead in a continuing offensive to take sixty more towns and hamlets, Moscow announced early today.

Resuming their drive after a two-day slow-down, the Russians swept to within fifteen miles of the Vitebsk-Polotsk rail line, an important east-west supply artery for the Germans, as they advanced southward along the Nevel-Vitebsk railroad.

In another fighting area to the south—southwest of Zhlobin—the

Continued on Page Five

8th Army Wins Town Near Ortona; Americans Take a Hill, Lose One

By MILTON BRACKER
By Wireless to THE NEW YORK TIMES.

ALGIERS, Dec. 24—The Allied armies in Italy kept up pressure all along the line yesterday despite the imminence of Christmas, but were unable quite to complete the capture of Ortona or accomplish substantial gains on the Tyrrhenian half of the front.

Although Canadian units of Gen. Sir Bernard L. Montgomery's Eighth Army had driven back the last German defenders of Ortona to the northwest corner of the shell-blasted and tank-razed town, the defenders kept returning fire and apparently intended to deprive the Allies of the full use of the most important port immediately below Pescara as long as possible.

Evidence of the toll the Germans have been paying for their desperate defense of the area was the discovery of a new cemetery at the crossroads just southwest of Ortona with at least 100 German graves.

The Eighth Army did manage to wrest from the enemy another village three miles southwest of Ortona and a mile beyond the Ortona-Orsogna road. It was Vezzani, which is three and a half miles from the coast and, like Ortona, just about twelve from Pescara. Other units of General Montgomery's veteran army have also penetrated to the outskirts of Villa Grande, a mile northeast of Vezzani on a secondary road paralleling the coast.

On the Fifth Army front the

Continued on Page Three

GENERAL IS SHIFTED

Choice of 'Big 3' Parley, He Has Montgomery as British Field Leader

WILSON IS SUCCESSOR

Mid-East Head Honored —Spaatz to Direct U. S. Air Strategy

Special to THE NEW YORK TIMES.

HYDE PARK, N. Y., Dec. 24—President Roosevelt announced today the appointment of Gen. Dwight D. Eisenhower to lead the invasion of Europe from the north and west, and from London came word that Gen. Sir Bernard L. Montgomery of North African fame would head the British troops under General Eisenhower to form a proved and hard-hitting team to lead the assault on Adolf Hitler's "Fortress Europe."

The President's announcement of General Eisenhower's selection at the recent Teheran conference to lead the main attack against Germany also set to rest the old rumors regarding the probable appointment of Gen. George C. Marshall, Army Chief of Staff, to that post.

The President, in his radio report today on the recent conferences at Teheran and Cairo, also named Lieut. Gen. Carl A. Spaatz as commander of "the entire American strategic bombing force operating against Germany."

This was taken to mean that while General Eisenhower will confine his command to the mass attack on Europe from the north and west, General Spaatz' command over all American strategic bombardment of Germany extends to operations against Germany from all neighboring bases.

Quashes Marshall Rumors

The President gave a vivid picture in his radio report of complete agreement between Prime Minister Churchill, Premier Stalin and himself regarding a detailed program for the annihilation of Germany by land and air from all directions.

He also paid high tribute to General Marshall, presumably to set old rumors at rest. Some persons have argued that the position to be occupied by General Eisenhower is of greatest importance, but the official decision now revealed seems to give credence to the opinion that the most important position in the Army is that of Chief of Staff, just as Washington is the only place from which the whole global operation can be commanded.

"To the members of our armed forces, to their wives, mothers and fathers, I want to affirm the great faith and confidence that we have in General Marshall and Admiral King (Chief of Naval Operations), who direct all of our armed might throughout the world," the President declared.

Their Military Genius Stressed

"Upon them," he said, "falls the responsibility of planning the strategy; of determining where and when to fight. Both of these men have already gained high places in American history; places which will record in that history many evidences of their military genius that cannot be published today."

The announcement from London told not only of General Montgomery's appointment to head the British invasion forces under General Eisenhower but also of Gen. Sir Henry Maitland Wilson's appointment to replace General Eisenhower as commander of the Mediterranean Theatre and Gen. Sir Harold R. L. G. Alexander's appointment to command all Allied forces in Italy.

The Teheran military decision announced by the President proved as much as anything else that the American handling of the invasion of North Africa and of Italy had deeply impressed the United States allies. Those invasions may now be regarded as the testing phase of the main European invasion, since the American officers identi-

Continued on Page Two

"All the News That's Fit to Print."

The New York Times.

LATE CITY EDITION
Cloudy, moderate temperature; partly cloudy and warmer tonight.
Temperatures Yesterday—Max., 35; Min., 16
Sunrise, 8:20 A. M.; Sunset, 5:38 P. M.

Copyright, 1943, by The New York Times Company.

VOL. XCIII..No. 31,387. Entered as Second-Class Matter, Postoffice, New York, N. Y. NEW YORK, FRIDAY, DECEMBER 31, 1943. THREE CENTS IN NEW YORK CITY

RUSSIANS BREACH LINE, ROUT 22 DIVISIONS; BIGGEST U. S. AIR ARMADA SMASHES REICH; MARINES WIN CAPE GLOUCESTER AIRFIELD

ICKES BARS WEST FROM ANTHRACITE TO AID EAST COAST

Puts 3-Month Embargo on All Shipments to West of Ohio-Pennsylvania Line

100,000 TONS A MONTH GAIN

New York to Get 4,000 More Tons of Bituminous a Day—8,000 of Anthracite 'Frozen'

By WINIFRED MALLON
Special to THE NEW YORK TIMES.

WASHINGTON, Dec. 30—To make up the coal shortages which are assuming crisis proportions along the Eastern seaboard, Secretary Ickes said today that from New Year's Day until April 1 shipments of anthracite to points west of the Pennsylvania-Ohio line will be prohibited.

These supplies, amounting to 100,000 tons a month, will be diverted to the East Coast region. By this means, Mr. Ickes said, it is hoped that allocations already made may be filled, despite the falling off in anthracite production.

Meanwhile, to meet the present and prospective shortage in the New York metropolitan area, additional daily supplies of 4,000 tons of fine run, low volatile (smokeless) bituminous coal will be made available.

To provide for householders who cannot under any circumstances use even the best soft coal, an order has been issued "freezing" for distribution to such consumers only, 8,000 tons of anthracite now on hand or in transit to New York.

The "freeze" order, Mr. Ickes said, refers only to anthracite within the limits already allocated to New York, the total amount of which cannot be increased, and must be used in full recognition of that fact.

Says Those Who Can Must Use It

"There just isn't anthracite enough to go around, and anyone who can use bituminous must do so," Mr. Ickes said.

"Much of the trouble in New York, Jersey City and Atlantic City has been due to the refusal of dealers to accept bituminous coal, of which there is plenty. They wait for anthracite shipments that will not and cannot be forthcoming.

"People will have to be realistic about these things and know that whether they have ever used soft coal before or not, they will have to do it now, as nearly all of them can, and as we intend to see they have an opportunity to do. If the dealers will not accept it, we will ship it in anyhow, and see that it is made available to those who need and will be glad to use it."

Says Some Soft Coal Is Rejected

One company in New York, for instance, Mr. Ickes said, refused last week to take 6,500 tons of bituminous coal which it might have had. Dealers in Atlantic City also were refusing coal available to them, he added, and were insisting on specifically better grades.

"They want to know even what mines the coal is from," Mr. Ickes said. "And still other dealers, who have been supplying only anthracite, are refusing to take any bituminous of whatever grade.

"Such an attitude, in times like these, is unreasonable and inexcusable, and cannot be allowed to keep from consumers coal they need and could have."

According to officials here, there is very little difference between the low volatile bituminous coal and the hard coal which many consumers have been using. Smokeless bituminous can be substituted for anthracite in many home furnaces, Mr. Ickes said, and for those who cannot by any possibility use it, allocations will be made from the 8,000 tons of anthracite reserved for their special needs.

"But I am not God," Mr. Ickes said. "I can't make anthracite available if there just isn't any to be had."

Says Miners Are Drawn Away

All coal production fell off last week, the Secretary went on, but production of anthracite has been decreasing steadily for the last five weeks, largely because miners were taking jobs in near-by war plants.

To "a considerable extent, and increasingly so," he declared, the coal shortage was a manpower crisis. He took issue here with the view expressed yesterday by Lawrence A. Appley, executive director of the War Manpower Commission, who attributed the coal shortage to miners' strikes and the

Continued on Page Thirty

Traffic Lights Go On Throughout the City

Announcing that the traffic lights would go on again all over the city on New Year's Day, Chief Magistrate Henry H. Curran said yesterday that uniform fines would be imposed for passing red lights. The night fine, he said, would be reduced from $10 to $5, and the day fine increased from $2 to $5.

The disks that have covered traffic lights will have been removed from all signals by tomorrow, he said, and "they will be as they were before the war, the old friendly green and the forbidding red shining out again."

ARMY SAYS UNIONS BALK RAIL RETURN

Two of Them Only 'Postpone' Strike, It States—Case Mishandled, Say 3 Chiefs

By LOUIS STARK
Special to THE NEW YORK TIMES.

WASHINGTON, Dec. 30—Government operation of the railroads for an indefinite period seemed likely tonight as President Roosevelt and eighteen railway unions prepared for a show-down fight on wages.

The War Department announced that so long as the wage issues were not settled it would be unable to return the roads to their owners. In a statement the War Department virtually accused two of the three operating unions which called off the strike last night as having acted in bad faith, since the department had been led to understand that the strike order would be canceled rather than that it would be postponed.

The War Department's statement, issued by its Bureau of Public Relations, said:

"The War Department made public today that the orders issued by certain of the railway brotherhoods do not cancel the strike order, as it had been given to understand, but merely postpone it. Mr. [D. B.] Robertson's order to the Brotherhood of Locomotive Firemen and Engine men reads: 'Due to Federal control of railroads strike postponed.'

"A general chairman of Mr. [H. W.] Fraser's organization of the Order of Railway Conductors, issued orders reading: 'Due to Federal control of railroads, strike by members of the O. R. C. and others of our craft, which has been called for 6 A. M., Dec. 30, has been postponed. Please consider this bulletin not to leave the service Dec. 30.'

"The wording of the order issued to the Switchmen is not known to the War Department.

"However, as long as this condition persists the War Department will not be able to gratify its desire to return the railroads to private ownership, as the orders merely relate to the temporary situation during Government control."

In reply to this statement, spokesmen for the firemen, conductors and switchmen's brotherhoods declared that, under their laws, once a strike vote were taken it remained "alive" until the issues which called it forth were settled. The unions, as observers see it, thus have reserved the right to strike at any time, not against the Government but against the owners, when and if the roads are returned to private hands, provided the dispute is still unsettled.

Later tonight, the chiefs of the firemen, conductors and switchmen, in a joint statement, charged the Administration with delays and accused it of mishandling the wage dispute.

One major aspect of the dispute which has led the Administration into serious conflict with the rail-

Continued on Page Eight

JAPANESE CRUSHED

Americans Capture Key New Britain Airdrome After 4-Day Battle

MANY OF ENEMY KILLED

Marines Take Strong Points With Flame Throwers—Our Casualties Are Light

By FRANK L. KLUCKHOHN
By Wireless to THE NEW YORK TIMES.

ADVANCED ALLIED HEADQUARTERS IN NEW GUINEA, Friday, Dec. 31—United States marines have captured the Cape Gloucester airdrome, their objective, just four days after their landing on the northwestern tip of New Britain.

One of the airdrome's two strips was won late Wednesday night after a severe aerial bombing and artillery pounding. Then, on Thursday, following a devastating air attack and artillery preparation, the final land assault was begun on the second strip, the more easterly of the two. By noon it was taken, completing the conquest of the airdrome.

The speed with which the Cape Gloucester air base was captured contrasted with the period of more than a month taken last summer to reduce the Munda airfield on New Georgia Island in the Solomons. Possession of the newly won airdrome increases the threat to Rabaul, main southwest Pacific bastion of the Japanese, and brings Kavieng, New Ireland, and the Admiralty Islands within easy range of Allied bombers. Domination of the Dampier and Vitiaz Straits, enemy supply routes to New Guinea, is also insured.

Snipers Cleaned Out

The Marines advanced four to six miles from their landing points through a tangle of trees and undergrowth to reach the Cape Gloucester airdome. "Alligators" played a major role, their six-man crews driving them straight into deep-rooted trees while enemy snipers were cleaned out by Americans who knew more tricks than the Japanese in this type of fighting.

Meanwhile heavy attacks from the Borgen Bay area, where the marines set up their main bridgehead, were repulsed with heavy enemy losses. The marines cut down the attackers in large numbers from entrenched positions that the Japanese were unable to dent.

Fighters based on the airfield in the American Bougainville bridgehead made another attack on Rabaul. They shot down eighteen enemy fighters and probably seven more for a loss of three fighters. Fifty Japanese Zeros and a smaller number of American planes took part in the battle.

United States Army troops at Empress Augusta Bay on Bougainville Island smashed an enemy strong point east of the Torokina River's mouth on Tuesday.

Softened by Air Assaults

ADVANCED ALLIED HEADQUARTERS IN NEW GUINEA, Friday, Dec. 31 (AP)—Details of the final hours of the battle for the

Continued on Page Two

1,300 CRAFT STRIKE

Hit Southwest Targets —34 Machines Lost to Enemy's 23

2,240 TONS ROCK BERLIN

20 of 750 Bombers Missing in Night Attack—24-Hour Offensive Sets Record

By DREW MIDDLETON
By Cable to THE NEW YORK TIMES.

LONDON, Friday, Dec. 31—More than thirteen hundred American heavy bombers and fighters, the largest force ever dispatched by the United States Army Air Forces in any theatre, blasted targets in southwest Germany yesterday to bring to a climax an offensive that involved more than 2,000 Allied planes, including strong formations of American and British medium bombers and hundreds of fighters.

[The American targets in southwestern Germany were not immediately identified by the United States Eighth Air Force, but British press reports from Switzerland said the main target had been the I. G. Farbenindustrie's poison gas plant at Ludwigshafen, 450 miles from Britain and one of the Reich's biggest chemical centers, The United Press reported.]

This great onslaught followed the smashing British victory in the Berlin offensive Wednesday night in which between 750 and 1,000 four-engined bombers, piloted by Britons, Canadians and Australians, pounded the German capital with more than 2,240 tons of bombs, starting vast fires that were visible for 200 miles and raising a funeral plume of smoke 16,000 feet high over the stricken city.

The RAF Bomber Command apparently continued the offensive last night. Bombers roared out over one southeast coast district toward France for half an hour just after nightfall. Two hours later a number of bombers were heard returning from the Continent.

Allied Losses Light

It was considered likely that 3,000 aircraft were employed by the Allies in the twenty-four hour period in a demonstration of overwhelming Allied air power in this theatre. This power, dwarfing any exerted heretofore, is being employed to paralyze industrial Germany and to disrupt and weaken the outer defenses of Festung Europa for the Allied invasion.

Twenty-three enemy fighters

Continued on Page Two

GERMAN ARMIES ARE SENT REELING WESTWARD

Moscow reported continued gains in the Vitebsk area (1), where the Soviet drives threaten to unhinge the entire German line northward. In the sectors west of Kiev, according to Moscow, twenty-two enemy divisions have been routed and deep gains made along a 186-mile front (shaded area) in six days of the offensive there. The Russians have reached Luginy (2), forty-two miles from the pre-war Polish border, and Chervonnoarmeisk (3), forty-six miles from it. In addition they have captured the junction of Kazatin (4) in their menacing southwestward slant. Near Zaporozhye the Red Army occupied Tomakovka and Belenkoye (5).

WORLD EDGE IN AIR IS WON BY ALLIES

RAF Reports More U-Boats Sunk by Planes in 1943 Than in 3 Prior Years Combined

By The Associated Press.

LONDON, Dec. 30—The Allies have achieved air superiority in every theatre of the war and sent planes on the offensive all around the world, the Royal Air Force announced today.

In a triumphant review of the aerial war of 1943 Britain's air arm said the year's fighting produced these victories and accomplishments in various fields of operation:

1. Nine of Germany's twenty-one industrial cities with populations of more than 250,000 each have been "so seriously devastated that in all probability they have been forced for some time to consume more than they produce."

2. Many more U-boats have been

Continued on Page Three

Admiral King Plans to Hit Japan Before Nazi Defeat

By The Associated Press.

WASHINGTON, Dec. 30—A tremendous offensive against Japan in 1944 is planned, it was made clear today by Admiral Ernest J. King, who said the United Nations would begin shifting their power from the Atlantic to the Pacific theatre before the final defeat of Germany. The naval Commander in Chief stood before a chart in his office, using a cigarette holder as a pointer, to give in an interview the frankest discussion of the Pacific war by a high naval figure. These were his main points:

1. He agrees with Gen. Dwight D. Eisenhower that defeat of Germany next year may be expected and, meantime, "unremitting pressure on Japan will be continued and increased."

2. Strategy for the defeat of Japan and the "main lines of attack" have been determined. The means for carrying out this strategy will be available with the transfer of power from the European theatre. "Studies have been under way for several months," he said, "looking to a shift of power from the European theatre to the Pacific theatre not only when Germany is defeated but as her defeat seems near at hand."

3. He discounted the possibility that the Japanese can, as they have threatened, launch offensive operations in 1944. "I don't quite see how they are going on the offensive where they are in contact in the Pacific," he said. "What they may do in China, Manchuria or even Burma is something else." A restraining factor against a Japanese offensive is the enemy's shortage of shipping, he said, add-

Continued on Page Four

8TH ARMY PUSHES TOWARD PESCARA

Fifth Army Storms Mountain —DNB Tells of Allied Landing Above Garigliano's Mouth

By MILTON BRACKER
By Wireless to THE NEW YORK TIMES.

ALGIERS, Dec. 30—The British Eighth Army has pushed a mile beyond Ortona along the direct coastal route to Pescara and is now barely eleven miles from the Adriatic terminus of the trans-peninsular road to Rome

Farther inland Gen. Sir Bernard L. Montgomery's troops occupied a dominating position a half mile north of Villa Grande. Eighth Army troops are just over nine miles from Chieti, capital of Abruzzi, eight miles inland from Pescara.

The Canadian captors of Ortona found the area seeded with booby traps and time-bombs that hampered their progress out of the town toward Francavilla and Pescara. The weather was cloudy and cold.

[The German news agency

Continued on Page Four

NAZI ARMIES FLEE

6-Day Russian Push Rips 186-Mile Gap Through Zhitomir Defenses

KAZATIN JUNCTION FALLS

Germans in Dnieper Bend Face Loss of Supply Route —Vitebsk Front Aflame

By RALPH PARKER
By Wireless to THE NEW YORK TIMES.

MOSCOW, Friday, Dec. 31—Premier Joseph Stalin revealed yesterday in an order of the day that the seven-day-old counter-offensive of Gen. Nikolai F. Vatutin had sent twenty-two of Hitler's divisions reeling in flight along a 186-mile front north, west and south of Zhitomir. In the first six days of the Red Army offensive more than 1,000 towns and villages have been recaptured from the Germans.

The Zhitomir-front offensive has restored most of the original gains made in the Russian drive last month, and has added much additional territory to the south that Soviet forces had not yet overrun before beginning their retreat under Field Marshal Gen. Fritz von Mannstein's abortive campaign to recapture Kiev.

Conspicuous among the new positions gained during the new week-long Soviet offensive was the capture of Kazatin, important railway junction seventeen miles southeast of Berdichev.

General Vatutin's offensive is striking southwestward at a pace that threatens the enemy with a disaster as overwhelming as that which overtook the armies of Field Marshal Gen. Friedrich von Paulus at Stalingrad almost a year ago. Inexorably, the powerful German forces in the Dnieper bend are having their escape route narrowed to lines that lead toward the Balkans and away from the Polish frontier. At their closest point, Luginy, the Russians are now forty-two miles from the old Polish border.

Premier Stalin announced that in the six days for which he gave an accounting eight German tank divisions and fourteen infantry divisions had been routed. Advances of from thirty to sixty-two miles had been made, he said.

Zaporozhye Drive Gains

LONDON, Friday, Dec. 31 (UP)—The tremendous break-through along a 186-mile front found the Germans throwing away their arms in their haste to escape as General Vatutin's First Ukranian Army swept into Kazatin, one of the two key junctions on the Nazi's last double-tracked railroad leading out of the Dnieper bend.

Important gains also were scored west of Zaporozhye, where Gen. Rodion Y. Malinovsky's Third Ukrainian Army drove nineteen miles and captured Chumaki, twenty-eight miles beyond the Dnieper dam city in the second day of a new offensive. The entire Ger-

Continued on Page Two

'Emergency' in Fire Department Gives Men 8 Extra Payless Hours

A "state of emergency" for the Fire Department of this city was declared last night by Fire Commissioner Patrick Walsh after a brief conference with Mayor La Guardia at 4:30 P. M.

In the emergency, Mr. Walsh said, the 6,590 firemen and officers would be required to work one extra eight-hour tour of duty a week without the $420 bonus that was canceled by the Mayor after the men rejected it.

"I don't know how long it's going to last. I might have to change it, but I have to have men to man the apparatus," the Commissioner declared as he left the Mayor's office at City Hall.

Commissioner Walsh said the special departmental order would be read to all tours of duty today and tomorrow. Effective at 12:01 A. M., Saturday, every man in his department is to serve three eight-hour tours of extra duty during the cycle of three six-day tours. The extra duty will occur at the end of the tour of the third working day in the fireman's work week.

Shortly after Mr. Walsh's announcement Vincent J. Kane, president of the Uniformed Firemen's Association, said this plan was virtually the same as that submitted by the membership of his organization a little more than a week ago. The plan was rejected.

Mr. Kane said the next meeting of the U. F. A. was scheduled for Jan. 18, but that a special meeting would be held if the members petitioned for it.

A meeting of representatives of the four line organizations of the Fire Department—chiefs, captains,

Continued on Page Eight

War News Summarized

FRIDAY, DECEMBER 31, 1943

The Nazi defense wall west of Kiev has cracked wide open on a 186-mile front. Russian troops surged through the breaks yesterday and advanced up to sixty-two miles, capturing 300 places, including Kazatin, on the vital Kiev-Vinnitsa railway. This junction is fifteen miles southeast of Berdichev, which, with Zhitomir, is one of the immediate Soviet objectives. The fall of Kazatin put the Russians within 100 miles of Rumania and forty-two miles from the old Polish border. It was estimated that twenty-two Nazi divisions of about 300,000 men were in the reported rout. [1:8.]

Targets in southwest Germany were blasted by the largest American bomber and fighter force ever sent into enemy territory. After Berlin had received a terrific pounding by 2,240 tons of explosives dropped by the Royal Air Force Wednesday night. The operations involved more than 2,000 planes, of which 1,300 were American. Fires left in the Reich capital sent plumes of smoke 16,000 feet into the air and could be seen for 200 miles. The "rocket-gun coast" of France also was hit heavily by the Eighth Air Force. [1:4.]

As the year neared its end the Royal Air Force reviewed Allied achievements and was able to announce air superiority in every theatre of war. [1:5.]

The British Eighth Army advanced one mile beyond Ortona—bomb-shattered and full of booby traps—to within eleven miles of the Adriatic port of Pescara, from where one of Italy's main arteries leads westward to Rome. Heights just north of Villa Grande also were taken. A German report said there had been an Allied landing at the western end of the line. [1:7.]

In Washington Admiral King disclosed that, in preparation for a great offensive against Japan in the coming year, the Allies would start shifting their weight from the Atlantic to the Pacific even before the defeat of Germany, which he forecast for 1944. [1:6-7.]

Speaking in London, General Devers pictured 1944 as the year of deliverance with significance unparalleled in history. [4:1.]

Reich Propaganda Minister Goebbels wrote that 1944 would be "a dangerous year," but insisted that German morale was strong and victory certain. [4:5.]

Using flame-throwers and artillery against Japanese pillboxes, the United States Marines have captured the important airdrome on Cape Gloucester, New Britain, four days after their landing. Eighteen enemy fighters were downed while challenging a bombing of Rabaul, air and supply base on the northeast tip of the island. [1:3; map, P. 2.]

Mail Rights Denied to Esquire; Magazine to Fight Order in Court

By The Associated Press.

WASHINGTON, Dec. 30—Esquire Magazine, in which the Varga girl drawings and other material offended the Postoffice Department's sense of modesty, was ordered deprived of its second-class mailing privileges tonight.

Without ruling directly on the question whether the magazine was obscene, a question much debated during long hearings, Postmaster General Frank C. Walker ordered the mail privileges revoked effective Feb. 28.

The action was taken on the ground that the magazine failed to meet the requirements of being "originated and published for the dissemination of information of a public character or devoted to literature, the sciences, arts, or some special industry."

During the long hearings Postoffice Department lawyers sought to show that the magazine was not only obscene but lewd and lascivious. In turn the publication marshaled a long list of witnesses, including Henry L. Mencken, who defended the use of such words as "backside" and "bawdy house"; and a neuropsychologist who called the lightly clad Varga girls "good, clean pictures, a tribute to American womanhood."

Describing the language of the second-class mailing act as "plain and specific," Postmaster General Walker said:

"Whatever the featured and dominant pictures, prose and verse of this publication may be, they are not 'information of a public character' or 'literature, the sciences, arts or some special industry,' contributing to the public wel-

Continued on Page Thirteen

Higher Rank Is Seen For Marshall, King

By The Associated Press.

WASHINGTON, Dec. 30—The Army and Navy Journal expressed belief today that President Roosevelt intends some new and special rank for Gen. George C. Marshall, Army Chief of Staff, and Admiral Ernest J. King, Commander in Chief of the Navy.

The unofficial service publication said there had been sentiment in the past for making General Marshall a field marshal and designating Admiral King as admiral of the fleet.

It recalled President Roosevelt's praise of the two men in his recent radio address and said, "there is likelihood the President may reinstate the movement to give them higher rank."

The publication also said:

"There is some talk that General Marshall may visit England for inspections and conferences prior to the invasion, but it is not believed that he would stay there long."

"All the News That's Fit to Print."

The New York Times.

LATE CITY EDITION
Mostly cloudy and continued mild with moderate winds today.
Temperatures Yesterday—Max., 44; Min., 32
Sunrise, 8:15 A. M.; Sunset, 6:01 P. M.

Section 1

NEWS INDEX, PAGE 39, THIS SECTION

VOL. XCIII..No. 31,410. Entered as Second-Class Matter, Postoffice, New York, N. Y. NEW YORK, SUNDAY, JANUARY 23, 1944. Including Magazine and Book Sections. TEN CENTS New York City and Suburban Area (15c Elsewhere)

ALLIED UNITS LAND BEHIND NAZIS IN ITALY, 16 MILES FROM ROME; LITTLE OPPOSITION; 2,240 TONS OF RAF BOMBS SMASH MAGDEBURG

PARTY CHIEFS ASK ROOSEVELT TO STAY AS WORLD LEADER

National Committee Declares History Has Drawn Issues and We Cannot Go Backward

DINERS ALSO CHEER CALL

Democrats Offer No 'Imitation Liberal,' Rayburn Says—Hannegan Made Chairman

Text of the resolution paying tribute to Roosevelt, Page. 32.

By CHARLES HURD
Special to THE NEW YORK TIMES.

WASHINGTON, Jan. 22—Conclusive demonstrations that Democratic leaders consider President Roosevelt the only possible nominee for this year's Presidential race were given here at today's meeting of the National Committee and at tonight's Jackson Day dinner.

At the committee meeting Robert E. Hannegan of Missouri was elected chairman to succeed Postmaster General Frank C. Walker and Chicago was selected as the site of the National Convention. Mr. Hannegan will specify the date later, but it is expected to fall around July 24. The new chairman resigned immediately as Collector of Internal Revenue.

The National Committee members stood and cheered in adopting unanimously a resolution of tribute to Mr. Roosevelt's leadership, which stated that the members "do now earnestly solicit him to continue as the great world leader."

The committee declaration ended as follows:

"We believe that history has drawn our issues. We are ready to set the twelve years of Franklin D. Roosevelt against the preceding twelve years of Republican 'normalcy,' when America retreated into feudal isolation, when America sped into wild inflation and made the depression inevitable, when America sunk its Navy and corruptly sold its Navy's oil reserve.

No Backward Step, It Says

"We do not believe the American people are ready to take a backward step. Therefore, it is with full confidence in the people's intuitive ability to distinguish truth from falsehood, to mark out accomplishment from misrepresentation, that we resolve:

"That the National Committee of the Democratic party, representing the millions of sincere and devoted people who have three times elected Franklin D. Roosevelt to be their President, does hereby gladly and proudly express its full and unflinching confidence in and admiration for that leadership both at home and abroad, and it further pledges its every energy and every purpose to the erection of a lasting and enduring peace in which an America free from unemployment and poverty will take its rightful place in a world free of the threat of war; and it does further express its deep conviction that the liberal spirit and farsighted practical idealism of this nation, exemplified to the world by Franklin D. Roosevelt, must be imprinted in the peace which follows victory, so that no man who dies in this war shall indeed have died in vain.

"We, assembled here, realizing his world leadership and knowing that our Allies are praying with us for the continuation of his services both in war and peace, do now earnestly solicit him to continue as the great world humanitarian leader."

In the larger audience at the $100-a-plate fund-raising dinner tonight there were more vociferous demonstrations at mention of the President's name. He was not present, but Mrs. Roosevelt sat at the speakers' table.

No Other Names Proposed

Equally significant was the fact that among the experienced, practical politicians who gathered in Washington, ranging from original "New Dealers" to sectional leaders such as Edward J. Flynn of the Bronx, former party chairman; Mayor Frank Hague of Jersey City, and Mayor Edward J. Kelly of Chicago, there was not even cursory discussion of an alternative candidate.

At the same time a sharp contest seemed developing over the nomination of a running-mate for Mr. Roosevelt —if he accepts the nomination—with speculation centering on Vice President Wallace and

Continued on Page Thirty-two

Woolley Loses Plea; Must Use Old Car

Daniel P. Woolley, regional administrator of the Office of Price Administration, disclosed yesterday that he had failed to get official approval of an application to buy a new, or 1942 model, automobile. The Midtown War Price and Rationing Board at 1775 Broadway has denied the application of the highest OPA official in the five-State region.

In announcing his failure to pass OPA's rigid tests Mr. Woolley explained that in the interest of saving gasoline he had wished to trade in a large car and get a smaller one. The board held that since his car was usable he was not eligible for a certificate to buy another car.

"The board was absolutely right," Mr. Woolley conceded. "The regulations must apply to all applicants."

CONDITIONS AT SPCC FOUND 'WRETCHED'

Jurists and Herlands Charge 'Incalculable Harm' to Children at Shelter

Commissioner of Investigation William B. Herlands made public yesterday an official report denouncing as "wretched" the conditions prevailing at the children's center maintained at 2 East 105th Street by the New York Society for the Prevention of Cruelty to Children.

The report prepared by Mr. Herlands and a Domestic Relations Court committee consisting of Justices Joseph E. Maguire, Hubert T. Delany, Justine Wise Polier and W. Bruce Cobb charged that "the society has failed in its obligations to the children in every aspect of its shelter operation" and "has wrought incalculable harm to thousands of children entrusted to it for care."

Inquiry Started After Riot

Mr. Herlands and the four jurists began their investigation last fall after a riot at the shelter focused public attention on the institution. The joint report, on the basis of which Mayor La Guardia is expected to take early remedial action, is a document of 150 pages, covering every aspect of life at the shelter, toward whose maintenance the city makes a substantial contribution each year. Findings in the report were based upon testimony taken by the four justices and the observation of investigators representing the Department of Investigation and directed by Miss Sophie Van S. Theis of the State Charities Aid Association.

No comment on the report was obtained from officers or directors of the society. What action Mayor La Guardia plans to take was still an official secret, but those close to the situation believe that there will be a withdrawal of the city's financial support and an effort to find other accommodations for children now sent to the shelter.

Management Is Condemned

Responsibility for conditions at the shelter was placed by the report on the society's management, which the investigators found was "for the most part—still living in the 'days of Commodore Perry' * * * and which displayed a woeful ignorance of conditions." The report declared that members of the "ladies committee" charged with supervision of the institution were "uninformed not only as to essential standards of child care but as to actual conditions in the shelter."

The shelter, according to the report, serves as principal temporary detention home for delinquent, dependent and neglected children

Continued on Page Thirty-three

RUSSIANS CLOSE IN

Push to Within 5 Miles of Krasnogvardeisk, Hub on Leningrad Front

A LINE TO MOSCOW FREED

Red Army Fanning Out From Novgorod After Destroying Isolated Nazi Remnants

By RALPH PARKER
By Cable to THE NEW YORK TIMES.

MOSCOW, Sunday, Jan. 23—The Red Army made further important progress in north Russia yesterday, capturing more than seventy additional places in the Leningrad area, the Soviet Command announced late last night.

The Leningrad-Mga-Kirishi railroad, which runs through to the Moscow network, is now completely in Russian hands, it was announced.

The German group surrounded in the forest west of Novgorod has been fully liquidated.

Advances on the sectors southwest and south of Krasnoye Selo, to the southwest of Leningrad, where more than forty places were taken, brought Gen. Leonid A. Govoroff's men deep into high ground at Nizkovitsy, ten miles southwest of Ropsha and but nine miles from the main railway to Narva, Estonia. Exploiting other successes in this sector in a drive southward from Dudergof, some of General Govoroff's troops captured Novopudost, about five miles from Krasnogvardeisk on the railway, one of the principal advance Nazi bases. The southwest advance in this sector reached to Bolshoye Ondrovo.

Push From East Progresses

In sectors described as north and northeast of Tosno, the Russians took thirty places, including Otradnoye, seven miles west of Mga; Voitovalo, four miles south of Mga; Lezye, Maluska and Shapki, all on the eastern facet of the German salient, the head of which was smashed by the Red Army in capturing Mga on Friday.

The capture of Shapki placed the Russians under Gen. Kirill A. Meretskoff at the end of a small spur line running seventeen miles to Tosno on the main Leningrad-Moscow railroad.

The Red Army's gains on the front around Novgorod, ninety miles southeast of Leningrad, extended ten miles southwestward to Dubnya and Sutoki and fourteen miles northwestward to the station of Tatino on the Leningrad-Novgorod railroad.

These advances compressed the Germans on the whole northern front within a rough arc sixty-five miles across from Krasnogvardeisk to Tatino.

In the Kalinkovichi sector of the Pripet front, 550 miles south of Leningrad, the White Russian Army captured a number of villages and settlements on high ground around Ozerichi, whose fall was announced Friday night.

The push northwest of Kalinkovichi, under Gen. Konstantin Rokossovsky, had advanced at least fifteen miles and was carrying the Red Army toward the Nazi-held

Continued on Page Eighteen

13 Michigan Legislators Named With 13 Others for Bill Bribery

Special to THE NEW YORK TIMES.

LANSING, Mich., Jan. 22—Arrest of twenty present and former Michigan legislators and six automobile finance company officials was ordered today in a warrant issued by a one-man grand jury after an investigation which began in August.

Those indicted are charged with conspiracy to obtain the enactment of three bills in the 1939 Legislature through bribery. Kim Sigler, special prosecutor for Circuit Judge Leland W. Carr's grand jury, said that $25,000 changed hands during the conspiracy and that more warrants would be forthcoming. The blanket warrant did not give details of the conspiracy charged.

Those indicted include thirteen present and seven former members of the Legislature. Of the twenty indicted, eighteen are Democrats and two Republicans. Fifteen are from Detroit or Wayne County, and five from out-State. They are:

Senators Charles C. Diggs, Leo J. Wilkowski and former Senators William F. Bradley, Detroit Democrats; Jerry T. Logie, Bay City Republican, and former Senators D. Stephen Benzie of Norway and Henry F. Shea of Laurium, Democrats.

Also Representatives William G. Buckley, Adam W. Sumeracki, Walter N. Stockfish, Stanley Dombrowski, Martin A. Kronk, Joseph J. Kowalski, Francis J. Nowak, Earl C. Gallagher, Edward J. Walsh, Detroit Democrats; Miles M. Callaghan, Reed City Republican.

Continued on Page Thirty-three

Air Attacks Seen As Invasion Prelude

By Telephone to THE NEW YORK TIMES.

BERNE, Switzerland, Jan. 22—Almost daily bombing of the Channel coast approximately between Dunkerque and Boulogne is producing symptomatic reactions among both the French and Germans.

The quantity of bombs dropped by Allied planes is such that analogy with the Eastern Front is unavoidable. Even German military commentators stress that Russian progress is invariably prepared now by unprecedented masses of artillery. So it is on the French coast, except that in this case the preparation comes from the air.

Evacuation of the French population in the threatened areas is proceeding. Refugees report the destruction of everything above ground. The intensity of the bombing is such that refugees are sure that nothing can possibly withstand them.

CONVOY BEATS OFF AIR-U-BOAT ATTACK

Even German Glider Bombs Fail in Four-Day Battle From Azores to Britain

By DAVID ANDERSON
By Cable to THE NEW YORK TIMES.

LONDON, Jan. 22—For the first time in the Battle of the Atlantic the Germans have delivered a concentrated attack both by submarine and heavy bombers in a desperate attempt to halt a convoy steaming on its course between the Azores and the coast of Europe. The Air Ministry and Admiralty in a joint communiqué reported the enemy repulsed, despite recourse to numerous radio-controlled glider bombs.

The action, which was said to have occurred "several weeks ago," continued intermittently over a period of four days and three nights. In the early stage of the engagement the Nazis pressed home their attack with a pack of at least ten U-boats, one of which was destroyed, another probably sent to the bottom and several believed seriously damaged by surface escort craft of the Royal Navy.

The later phases of the encounter were marked almost entirely by air

Continued on Page Nineteen

1,000 BOMBERS OUT

Main Attack Saturates War-Plant City of Central Germany

SOME PLANES HIT BERLIN

Nazis' Biggest Night Action in Year Sends 90 Craft Over England—10 Destroyed

By JAMES MacDONALD
By Cable to THE NEW YORK TIMES.

LONDON, Jan. 22—Soaring far and wide over Germany and German-occupied territory, more than 1,000 British bombers blasted Magdeburg, one of the most important industrial cities of north central Germany, gave Berlin a minor hammering, dropped bombs in northern France and laid mines in enemy waters last night.

Royal Air Force fighters on additional intruder operations over enemy airfields in western Europe destroyed one Nazi plane during the night.

The RAF dropped more than 2,240 tons of high-explosive and incendiary bombs on Magdeburg, which has a population of about 320,000 and is the site of two armament factories, including a Krupp tank branch, a Junkers airplane engine plant and synthetic oil works, all of which were on the Allies' bombing schedule for attention.

Reports from the bomber crews indicated that the smashing attack, carried out in thirty-four minutes, virtually wiped the city off the list of centers of the German war effort.

Berlin Blow Dupes Luftwaffe

Magdeburg, about eighty miles southwest of Berlin and fifty miles southeast of Brunswick, is near Oschersleben, which, like Brunswick, was attacked during daylight in the great United States Eighth Air Force attack of Jan. 11.

While the main bomber force was making its saturation attack on Magdeburg, ancient capital of Saxony, fast-flying, four-motored Lancasters and smaller plywood Mosquitos carried out a diversionary action against Berlin, thereby distracting the Luftwaffe's night defense.

Apparently thinking that Berlin was to be heavily attacked, the

Continued on Page Nine

War News Summarized

SUNDAY, JANUARY 23, 1944

The Allies took the Germans by surprise early yesterday and landed British and American troops on the Italian shore only a short distance south of Rome. Under the cover of guns from warships of five of the United Nations, troops went ashore behind the German lines, probably between the mouth of the Tiber and the port of Nettuno. British Commandos and American Rangers were among those who "hit the beach" along a thirty-mile front at 2 A. M. A German report said the Allies were only sixteen miles from Rome and that the port of Nettuno had been captured. [1:8.]

The bold flanking attack caught the Germans so unprepared, according to an eye-witness, that our troops just landed and stood around waiting. There was virtually no enemy opposition, although heavy counter-attacks were expected. [1:6-7.]

The new amphibious attack may compel the Germans so to weaken their defenses along their vaunted Gustav and Adolf Hitler lines that Fifth Army units will be able to drive quickly up the Liri Valley and join their comrades below Rome. [5:7.]

Allied heavy bombers hit a road defile at Terracina, a key point between the two Fifth Army groups. Other planes, having isolated Rome and neutralized all but one of its airfields, shifted the attack to the Marseille area, where radio-controlled German glider planes are based. [8:1.]

More than 1,000 British bombers struck Germany Friday night, concentrating particularly on Magdeburg, which was buried under 2,240 tons of explosives. The enemy retaliated with the heaviest raid on England in more than a year, sending over ninety planes, which dropped only ninety tons. Ten of the raiders were destroyed. [1:5.]

Lieut. Gen. Spaatz said that, with favorable weather, the German Air Force was likely to be knocked out during the summer. He said shuttle bombing between Britain and Italy would play a part in the coming invasion campaign. [9:1.]

Packs of U-boats and German planes with glider bombs fruitlessly attacked an important convoy on the way to England for four days and three nights. Aided by planes from Gibraltar, the Azores and Britain, the escort saved the convoy, destroyed or damaged several U-boats and shot down a number of enemy planes. [1:4.]

Russian armies continued their gains in the Leningrad area, capturing more than seventy new places and cutting down the rail communications so vital to the Germans. [1:3; map P. 18.]

Australian troops in New Guinea were closing in on the Japanese bases of Bogadjim and Madang. [29:4]. Far to the north two groups of Navy planes raked both ends of Paramushiru Island in the Kuriles. [29:1.]

Anthony J. Drexel Biddle Jr. has resigned as Ambassador-Minister to the exile governments in London to become a lieutenant colonel on General Eisenhower's staff. He will serve as liaison officer between military and civil chiefs and probably coordinate underground activity. [1:6-7.]

ROME IS OBJECTIVE BEHIND BEACHES

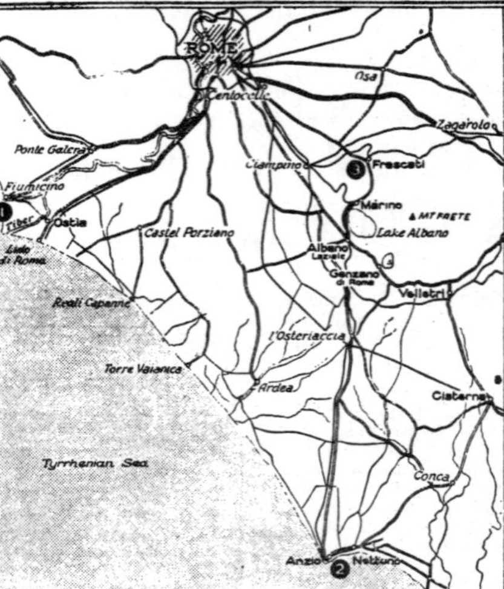

Somewhere between the mouth of the Tiber River (1) and Nettuno (2) American and British troops made surprise landings and pushed inland toward Rome. In a day of heavy and widespread strategical and tactical bombing, Allier fliers smashed a German Air Force headquarters near Frascati (3).

Allies 'Just Walked' Ashore On Empty Italian Beaches

By DON WHITEHEAD
Associated Press Correspondent Representing the Combined United States Press

WITH THE FIFTH ARMY'S AMPHIBIOUS FORCES, South of Rome, Jan. 22—We walked in behind the German lines today with hardly a shot fired in a most sensational amphibious operation. It was so easy and simply done and caught the Germans so completely by surprise that, as I write this dispatch six hours after the landing, American troops are standing with their mouths open and shaking their heads in utter amazement.

"Maybe," Lieut. Col. Edgar C. Doleman said, "the war is over and we don't know it." "I still don't believe it," said a Fifth Army infantryman who had made other amphibious landings.

The infantry swarmed ashore at 2 A. M., expecting to have to fight its way in over the beach through barbed wire and minefields. I landed with the second wave at 2:10 A. M. Then we began walking, expecting each moment that the enemy would open with a blinding flash of fire. But we just walked. Nothing happened in my sector. There were only a few scattered shots fired and most of them came from our own tense troops.

To our north, there was a sound of gunfire, but it was very light and at this early stage there was every indication that Lieut. Gen. Mark W. Clark's Fifth Army had pulled a brilliant maneuver to hit the enemy from the side and open the road to Rome. The next few hours will decide that, if the expected German counter-attack develops.

[General Clark visited the new landing area and said that he was delighted with the progress being made, another dispatch said.]

Moving swiftly in from the beach, troops in this sector reached

Continued on Page Four

ENEMY POST RAZED NEAR POPE'S VILLA

German Air Headquarters at Frascati Destroyed by Our Fighter-Bombers

By The Associated Press.

AN ADVANCED AIR BASE, in Italy, Jan. 21 (Delayed)—A German front-line air corps headquarters, carefully hidden in what was previously considered "neutral" territory because of its proximity to the summer residence of Pope Pius XII, was reported to have been destroyed today by dive-bombing Invaders from the Twelfth United States Air Support Command.

Returning pilots, who had been painstakingly briefed for the special mission, said that the Pope's summer home and surrounding areas of Castel Gandolfo, south of Rome, had "never felt a thing."

The German Flieger Corps headquarters was housed in a villa near Frascati, south of Rome and only about five miles from Castel Gandolfo. The entire area had been voluntarily restricted by the Allies and our planes had been forbidden to fly over it. Apparently the Germans learned of the restric-

Continued on Page Six

Biddle Resigns as Envoy to Exiles To Take Post With Invasion Army

Special to THE NEW YORK TIMES.

WASHINGTON, Jan. 22—President Roosevelt announced today the resignation of Anthony J. Drexel Biddle Jr. as Ambassador-Minister to the Exile Governments in London to become a lieutenant colonel on the staff of Gen. Dwight D. Eisenhower.

The President made it clear in his letter accepting Mr. Biddle's resignation that the Ambassador would carry on work under General Eisenhower similar to that he has been doing, except that it would be in a military context.

His position under General Eisenhower will be that of liaison officer on the staff of the Supreme Allied Commander for Relationships with the Allied Governments in London. The change of positions for Mr. Biddle appeared to be one of the preparations for the invasion of Europe.

Mr. Biddle's work as Ambassador-Minister will be carried on by the chargé d'affaires while he is in the Army and no replacement is contemplated, the White House said.

President Roosevelt said he accepted the Ambassador's resignation "with mixed feelings," and he highly praised Mr. Biddle's work in his present position, which the President described as "unique in all history," no one having before represented a country to so many Governments at one time.

"In view of the fact that we are, I hope, approaching the period

Continued on Page Nineteen

HARBOR CAPTURED

Nettuno Taken by British and American Units, Germans Admit

BEACHHEAD RUNS 30 MILES

Coordinated Advance on Whole Fifth Army Front in South Accompanies Landings

By MILTON BRACKER
By Wireless to THE NEW YORK TIMES.

ALGIERS, Jan. 22—In the most stunning and potentially hazardous operation of the Italian campaign so far, British and American troops of the Fifth Army waded ashore on the west coast of Italy south of Rome at 2 A. M. today.

They have established a beachhead of several miles in the virtual absence of resistance by the Germans, who were apparently completely surprised. While enemy broadcasts say that the exact area of the amphibious attack was between the Tiber Estuary and the historic bathing beach of Nettuno, thirty miles south and slightly east of Rome, Allied Headquarters here declined to be more specific. But the fact that the phrase "south of Rome" was officially authorized would indicate that the landing was nearer the Anzio-Nettuno strip than the mouth of the Tiber, twenty-eight miles farther up the coast.

[The landings were made along a thirty-mile front and, according to German broadcasts, the Allies were at one point only sixteen miles from Rome, The United Press reported. It added that the Allies had confirmed the German reports of the landing points.]

Germans Report Loss of Nettuno

The German broadcasts declared that the Allies had taken Nettuno and had also begun a sea and air assault farther south in the Gulf of Gaeta and around Terracina. There, it was said, a naval force including at least six cruisers had opened up on the coast below the Pontine Marshes. No confirmation was available here.

The Allied command described the assault as being deep behind the enemy's line through Cassino and as making "satisfactory progress." It not only underlines dramatically the recent assertion by Lieut. Gen. Sir Henry Maitland Wilson that Rome was the "ultimate objective" of the Italian campaign but plainly holds a potential threat to all communication lines between the German forces north of the invasion point and the five divisions holding the Garigliano River-Gustav Line some eighty miles below Rome.

Old Front More Active

It was officially asserted that heavy naval and air support and a smashing coordinated attack by British, American and French units of the Fifth Army along the Garigliano-Cassino front had accompanied the daring thrust below Rome. In that area British Commandos and American Rangers were among the troops cutting their way inland against an utter lack of resistance of the type made familiar by the Germans. But the menace of a thunderous counter-attack was ever present and the Germans were expected to throw in a heavy blow when the moment seemed best, for the beachhead is

Continued on Page Three

Five Nations' Navies Back New Landing

By The Associated Press.

ALGIERS, Jan. 22—American, British and Greek naval units carried out the "successful landing of British and American troops" on the west coast of Italy today.

French and Netherland vessels joined in providing support for the troops.

The naval forces were under the command of an American, Admiral Frank Jacob Lowry. A Briton, Admiral Thomas Hope Troubridge, was in charge of the ships landing British troops.

"All the News That's Fit to Print."

The New York Times.

LATE CITY EDITION
Fair and moderately cold today; light winds.
Temperatures Yesterday—Max., 43; Min., 27
Sunrise, 8:14 A. M.; Sunset, 6:08 P. M.

VOL. XCIII..No. 31,412. Entered as Second-Class Matter. Postoffice, New York, N. Y. NEW YORK, TUESDAY, JANUARY 25, 1944. THREE CENTS IN NEW YORK CITY

ALLIED GUNS SHELL APPIAN WAY; FOE HITS BACK ON CASSINO FRONT; RUSSIANS CUT RAILWAY TO ESTONIA

SENATE FOES FIGHT COMPROMISE PLAN ON SOLDIER VOTING

Bill to Displace 'State' Program Threatened by Some Southerners and Republicans

TAFT HITS STIMSON, KNOX

He Alleges Secretaries Seek a 'Fourth Term'—Sponsors Weigh New Concessions

By C. P. TRUSSELL
Special to THE NEW YORK TIMES.

WASHINGTON, Jan. 24—The Senate's new Service Men's Voting Bill, supposedly bearing compromises suitable to all factions, received a far from harmonious reception as it reached the floor today. By nightfall its position was admittedly uncertain, with sponsors studying further concessions in the hope of getting it through.

Throughout the day the measure, designed to displace the "States' Rights" Bill which the Senate passed on Dec. 3, was under attack by Southern Democrats as failing to give adequate guarantees of State sovereignty in elections, and by Republicans as discriminating in favor of a Federal ballot and against State tickets.

The War and Navy Departments were accused of contributing to discrimination against State ballots in saying what they could and could not do in the distribution and collection of service ballots.

"In my opinion," said Senator Robert A. Taft, Republican, of Ohio, at one period in a day-long debate, "Secretaries Knox and Stimson are today running for a fourth term. I say that in the most kindly spirit. It is only natural that men who have the responsibility which they have are convinced that their continuance in office is essential to the welfare of the world and of this country."

Barkley Strikes Out at Taft

Senator Alben W. Barkley, the majority leader, obviously surprised at the fourth-term charge against the only Republican members of President Roosevelt's Cabinet, interjected:

"Is the Senator going to try to convince the people of Ohio that his presence here is equally indispensable?"

Ignoring this, Mr. Taft went on: "I only say that they have assumed a partisan position in connection with this bill and I do not believe what they say regarding the inability of the War and Navy Departments to transmit the (State) ballots to soldiers throughout the world."

The departmental assertion that no guarantees could be given as to delivery and collection of State ballots, averaging two ounces in weight, as compared with Federal ballots weighing eight-tenths of an ounce, had caused the first suspicious glances at the new Green-Lucas bill. Senator Arthur H. Vandenberg, Republican, of Michigan, noted that the bill itself gave transmission priority to Federal ballots over all unofficial communications and over many official ones, while State ballots would be sent out and collected when they did not interfere with other communications.

Asking what good it would do for State legislators to convene in special sessions to enact uniform absentee voting laws under such handling of State ballots, Mr. Vandenberg pronounced the section of the bill dealing with State elections "mere window dressing."

Overton Asks New Guarantee

Whereas the Senate Committee on Privileges and Elections had voted to leave the determination of the validity of ballots entirely with State election officials, thus putting the counting of the votes on a States' rights basis, Senator John H. Overton, Democrat, of Louisiana, called for a further guarantee. He proposed an amendment specifically to direct State election officials to follow State law in determining the validity of ballots.

Under this system, the election officials of States which had not voluntarily waived personal registration, the poll tax and other requirements would be directed, in effect, by Congress to ignore the waivers written into the Federal Soldier Voting Bill of 1942.

Going further, a group of eight Southern Senators put their names to another amendment, headed "States' Rights Not Affected," which, to supplement the provisions of the Overton proposal, would specify that nothing in the act "does in fact or shall be construed to violate, repeal, abrogate, nullify or change in any form or manner" the election laws, rules and regula-

Continued on Page Twelve

Pope Refuses to Go To Reich, Say Swiss

By The Associated Press.

STOCKHOLM, Sweden, Jan. 24—The newspaper Aftontidningen said in a dispatch from Zurich, Switzerland, today that Pope Pius XII had declined renewed German proposals since the Allied landing south of Rome that he go to some city in Germany.

The German-controlled Scandinavian Telegraph Bureau said in a Rome dispatch that the Pope's guard has been strengthened since the landing, and that Vatican City's defenses have been put in a state of "great preparedness."

GOV. EDGE SUBMITS NEW CONSTITUTION

Legislative Committees Will Open Hearings on Tentative Draft Next Week

Special to THE NEW YORK TIMES.

TRENTON, Jan. 24—The Legislature received today from Gov. Walter E. Edge the tentative draft of a proposed new State Constitution designed to replace the one under which the State Government has operated for ninety-nine years. The new Constitution would completely reorganize the judiciary, consolidate the scores of departments, boards, commissions and agencies into not more than twenty principal divisions, greatly increase the executive authority and curb some of the powers now exercised by the Legislature.

By an overwhelming vote in November the people directed the 1944 Legislature to rewrite the basic law and submit the new draft to them next November for adoption or rejection. Governor Edge, who was elected in November, at once named three committees of legislators to start work on the task. In submitting the draft today, he sent to the Senate and Assembly this message:

"I trust this mandate from the citizens of New Jersey will constitute your first order of business and after that, after careful study, a final draft embodying these principles will be adopted promptly for submission to the voters. I consider affirmative action your most urgent responsibility."

To Hear Objections First

The committees sitting separately will begin a series of public hearings on Tuesday, Wednesday and Thursday of next week. It is their plan first to hear objections to the provisions of the tentative draft and then to call for suggestions by revision advocates.

Under the draft now before the Legislature, which follows for the most part the recommendations of a commission appointed by Mr. Edge's predecessor, Charles Edison, the term of the Governor would be extended from three to four years, beginning with the successor to Mr. Edge. The existing prohibition against an immediate second term would be continued. Four-year terms also are proposed for State Senators (now three) and two years for members of the Assembly (now one).

Salaries of the members of both branches would be increased to $2,000 a year, with an added $1,000 for the Senate President and House speaker. The Legislature would meet annually, as now, but the session would be limited to ninety calendar days.

The existing taxation provision is revised by substitution of "fixed standards of value" for "true value" as the basis of assessment. This would remove the principal argument on which the method of railroad taxation approved by the

Continued on Page Twelve

TIE WITH BOLIVIA REJECTED BY U. S.; HOSTILE LINK SEEN

Economic Steps May Be Taken Against Regime That Seized Power—Envoy Recalled

FIVE MORE NATIONS ACT

Brazil Among Them—Britain May Join In—Washington Note Omits Argentina

By BERTRAM D. HULEN
Special to THE NEW YORK TIMES.

WASHINGTON, Jan. 24—The State Department announced today that the United States would not recognize the revolutionary regime in Bolivia.

The decision was based upon investigations conducted by this and eighteen other American Governments showing that the revolution was linked with subversive groups hostile to the Allied cause.

[Seven Latin-American countries have to date announced refusals to recognize the Bolivian regime. Brazil, Costa Rica, Guatemala, Peru and Venezuela acted on Monday and Cuba and Uruguay previously. It was reliably reported Britain would deny recognition to the La Paz Government, which has been accepted only by Argentina thus far.]

Pierre de L. Boal, American Ambassador in La Paz, was ordered to return home. The embassy will continue to function under a chargé d'affaires.

In addition, economic action may be taken against Bolivia, such as freezing her credits in this country and banning shipments of supplies to her from the United States.

Subversive Moves Scored

There was no mention of Argentina, an omission that caused surprise in view of expectations that she would be named as a source of the revolutionary plot.

In a brief statement announcing the decision, the State Department said the revolution represented "one act committed by a general subversive movement having for its purpose steadily expanding activities on this continent."

The statement ended on a conciliatory note assuring the people of Bolivia and of the other American republics of the good-will of the United States and explaining that the action had been taken in the interests of hemispheric defense.

All the other republics of this continent except Argentina, which did not participate in the investigation, are expected to take similar action.

TEXT OF STATEMENT

The text of the announcement follows:

This Government has been aware that subversive groups hostile to the Allied cause have been plotting disturbances against the American Governments operating in defense of the hemisphere against Axis aggression.

On Dec. 20, 1943, the Bolivian Government was overthrown by force under circumstances linking this action with the subversive groups above mentioned.

The most important and urgent question arising from this development in Bolivia is the fact that this is but one act committed by a general, subversive movement having for its purpose steadily expanding activities on the continent. These developments, viewed in the light of the information the American republics have been exchanging among themselves, dispose negatively of the matter of this Government's recognizing

Continued on Page Eleven

RED ARMY ROLLS ON

Russians Bar Escape of Germans on Major Line to the West

2 HISTORIC TOWNS TAKEN

Soviet Troops Gain in Novgorod Area—Vinnitsa Battle Still Rages on Big Scale

By W. H. LAWRENCE
By Cable to THE NEW YORK TIMES.

MOSCOW, Tuesday, Jan. 25—Moscow's victory guns boomed again last night and red, green, blue and white flares from 124 guns lighted the sky in a salute to the advancing troops on the Leningrad front who had captured the important enemy centers of Pushkin, Pavlovsk and Ulyanovka while severing the railway line between Gatchina and Narva, one of the few major roads available for German troops in their retreat westward.

A special order of the day by Premier Stalin announced the capture of Pushkin, which formerly was Tsarskoye Selo, and Pavlovsk, which formerly was Slutsk, and directed that tribute be paid to the victorious fighting men in the form of twelve salvos from 124 guns.

Of equal importance was the latter announcement of the capture of Ulyanovka, which the Soviet High Command said had been built by the enemy into a strong defense point. Troops in this sector also captured the railway junction of Sablino on the main railway line between Leningrad and Moscow and it was indicated that most of the twenty-four miles of this important line between Sablino and Leningrad was in Soviet hands.

Another Railway Cut

To the south and west of Ulyanovka other Red Army men cut through the railway line leading from Gatchina to Narva.

[The Narva-Gatchina railway was cut near the village of Smolkovo, fifteen miles west of Gatchina between the stations of Yelizavetino and Kikerovo in a six-mile drive southward from the Oznakovo area. Gatchina is the important junction near the town of Krasnogvardeisk, which was formerly called Gatchina.]

The High Command's announce-

Continued on Page Eight

A PRECAUTION AS WAR MOVES CLOSER TO ROME

Vanloads of art treasures from the Monte Cassino Monastery arrive at the Vatican for safekeeping. In the background is the dome of St. Peter's. Picture was made available in London.

Associated Press Radiophoto, passed by British censor

ALLIES PUSH INLAND

Rome Admits Capture of Town—Enemy Tanks Offer Resistance

RAPIDO BRIDGEHEAD LOST

Americans Thrown Back Over River—British and French Beat Off Counter-Blows

By MILTON BRACKER
By Wireless to THE NEW YORK TIMES.

ALGIERS, Jan. 24—Apparently still ignoring the Allies' amphibious forces that drove inland from the expanding Nettuno beachhead south of Rome to a point within seven or eight miles of the Appian Way, the German Army in Italy has replied to the over-all threat of the Fifth Army with a series of whip-like counter-blows along the Garigliano River-Gustav Line that hurled the Americans back across the Rapido River after a last-ditch clash of bayonets, it was officially announced today.

While the invasion forces fanned out from the Nettuno-Anzio area and were assumed to have occupied Anzio as well as Nettuno, the Germans some sixty miles below plunged ahead along virtually the whole distance from the mouth of the Garigliano to the Colli-Atina road and unleashed a general attack believed to have been planned before the Allies landed far up the coast.

[A Swiss broadcast recorded by the Columbia Broadcasting System quoted a Rome report that the Allies had captured Littoria, twelve miles east of Nettuno.

[The Berlin radio reported a German broadcast telling of a clash in the village of Aprilia, ten miles northwest of Nettuno, according to The United Press. According to the Germans, Allied scouting parties were driven from the village. Stiffened resistance, aided by tanks, was reported in front dispatches.

[A British broadcast heard by the Columbia Broadcasting System said that the Allies were shelling the Appian Way with naval guns and with coastal batteries captured intact from the Germans and turned inland.]

Shift of Forces Held Aim

The savage German offensive is plainly intended now to keep the two Allied forces as far apart as possible. It is also believed to be calculated to permit some of the nine divisions in the central sector—which are being hammered from the air and face the slashing of their supply lines by the British and Americans in the north—to shift and come to grips with the rapidly enlarging and advancing invasion party.

In the largely confused picture of developments, the allocation of German units in and above Rome remained the primary question. Since the Allies' bombs have at least temporarily severed the capital's rail connections with the north, the problem of moving an assault force through the Rome area and against the left flank of the invaders would be difficult.

Peril to Germans Grows

Nevertheless, the actual menace to the German lines in the south increased with every minute as the virtually unopposed sea-borne troops swept farther inland along the beachhead of several miles around Cape d'Anzio. This is a small promontory thirty miles below Rome, tipped by the pleasant bathing resort of Anzio.

Nettuno is only one and three-quarters miles farther on along the south side of the cape. Its capture by the Allies was confirmed here today. The assumption that Anzio, too, was in our hands was based on the known depth of the beachhead and the fact that, for practical purposes, the Anzio-Nettuno strip was one objective.

The Allies' penetration was officially estimated at a minimum of four miles, but this is taken as a minimum in view of the collateral announcement that the Appian Way was within seven to eight miles—easy artillery range—of the spearheads. From the easternmost fringe of Nettuno, the vital junc-

Continued on Page Two

WIDE AIR ATTACKS BLAST MARSHALLS

U. S. Bombers Strike at Six Atolls, Batter Installations, Hit 5 Ships, Down 6 Planes

By GEORGE F. HORNE
By Telephone to THE NEW YORK TIMES.

PEARL HARBOR, Jan. 24—Army and Navy planes have unleashed a powerful assault on atolls of the Marshall Islands in the last two days, striking eight objectives in six separate atolls, knocking down Japanese planes, bombing ships and strafing and raiding shore installations.

Around the clock over Saturday and Sunday (West Longitude dates) Mitchell Liberators and Venturas of the Seventh Army Air Force and the Navy's Fleet Air Wing 2 roared over the islands in one of the most persistent and

Continued on Page Seven

U. S. Bombers Hit at Reich; Pounding of Coast Goes On

By HAROLD DENNY
By Cable to THE NEW YORK TIMES.

LONDON, Tuesday, Jan. 25—United States heavy and medium bombers struck in force yesterday at industrial targets in western Germany and Nazi defensive installations along and behind the coast of western Europe, especially the Pas-de-Calais area of France. It was the seventh attack this month against these targets.

Our bombers streamed out over the Channel in two great waves beginning at dawn, hot on the heels of British-American air attacks Sunday that had pounded and harassed the Germans throughout the areas.

[The Berlin radio said "Anglo-American planes" were over Berlin early Tuesday, The United Press reported from London.

[Switzerland had air-raid alarms Monday night. A Berlin broadcast reported by The Associated Press told of Allied bombing in "southwestern Danubia" and Hungarian reports by way of Sweden said an armament center, apparently in Austria, was attacked.

[The Bulgarian capital of Sofia was bombed again Monday noon by American planes, said an earlier German broadcast.]

The daylight attacks provoked spirited defense by German interceptors and a series of running battles was fought over Germany, France, Belgium and the Netherlands by Flying Fortresses, Liberators, Marauders and their escort fighters and by Royal Air Force bomber and fighter formations.

Twenty-one Nazi fighters were destroyed in the United States Eighth Air Force's heavy bombing attack over Germany—two by the big bombers and nineteen by escort fighters.

Three other Nazis were shot

Continued on Page Four

CONFEREES AGREE ON DISCHARGE PAY

Senate and House Group Set $100 to $300 as Mustering-Out Grant for Veterans

Special to THE NEW YORK TIMES.

WASHINGTON, Jan. 24—A compromise that would give veterans of this war payments from $100 to $300 when mustered out was agreed upon by House and Senate conferees today.

The conferees were confident that the bill as rewritten would receive early favorable action from both houses of Congress. This action may be completed by the House tomorrow. If adopted, it will be ready for introduction in the Senate tomorrow or Wednesday.

Taking into account both length and place of service, the compromise provides $300 for each man or woman who served overseas. A payment of $200 would be made to those who have served in the continental United States for more than sixty days and $100 to those who serve in the United States for less than sixty days.

Senator Johnson, Democrat of Colorado, one of the conferees, esti-

Continued on Page Twelve

War News Summarized

TUESDAY, JANUARY 25, 1944

German infantry, tanks and artillery began to strike back in a small way at several advanced points of the Fifth Army's beachhead below Rome. Early reports gave no indication whether the clashes were the start of a real counter-offensive or merely isolated actions, but there was nothing equivocal about furious drives launched against Allied positions on the main battle line from Minturno to beyond Cassino. The enemy struck with all his strength.

Supplies and reinforcements were being rushed into the ever-growing beachhead around Nettuno. The Appian Way was within range of our artillery and Littoria was said to have been captured. [All the foregoing 1:8; map P. 2.]

The German counter-attack in the main battle line, if successful, could prove to be an answer to the Nettuno landings. The fighting was sanguinary and the casualties were heavy among American troops forced to give up their Rapido River bridgehead. [1:6-7.] General Sir Maitland Wilson declared that his men on the beaches were prepared to repel German onslaughts equal in violence to those encountered at Salerno. [3:5.]

United States heavy bombers, after a lay-off of nearly two weeks, returned to western Germany and smashed industrial targets. Other planes struck northern France. Twenty-four enemy fighters were shot down; we lost ten fighters and three bombers. [1:6-7.]

The Russians cut the railroad line to Narva, Estonia, near Smolkovo in advances below Leningrad that liberated more than forty places, including Pushkin, the old Tsarskoye Selo, where the Czars had had their summer palace, and Pavlovsk. In the Novgorod sector other Red Army forces captured Stekhovo, sixteen miles from the Leningrad-Dno railroad, one of the two remaining routes left to the Germans. [1:4; map, P. 8.]

Allied planes struck hard at Japanese bases in the Pacific. Eighteen enemy fighters were shot down and two more probably destroyed at Rabaul, New Britain, while over Wewak, New Guinea, thirty-three enemy aircraft were destroyed, with twelve more probables. We lost a total of eleven planes. [7:1.] Army and Navy bombers struck eight objectives in two days in the Marshall Islands. Japanese installations, shipping and fighter defenses suffered heavily. [1:5.]

Viscount Halifax told the Toronto Board of Trade that the United Kingdom, alone, could not claim equal partnership with the United States, Russia and China. The whole British Commonwealth and Empire, he said, must form a fourth great power to help the three others keep peace. [5:1.]

The United States will not recognize Bolivia's revolutionary regime because investigation linked the coup to a subversive movement hostile to the United Nations. Other American countries were quick to follow Washington's lead and London reported that Great Britain would also refuse to recognize the new government. [1:3.]

City Bond Total 15.3% of Quota; 'Lend to the Limit,' Dewey Pleads

With sales of bonds in the Fourth War Loan Drive mounting in city, State and nation, a thousand volunteer salesmen in this area gathered last night at a dinner in the Commodore Hotel to hear first-hand reports of how the dollars they raise are fighting on battlefronts all over the world.

From Maj. Gen. Alvin C. Gillem, commander of the Thirteenth Corps, they heard a report from the Mediterranean fighting front; John Goette, war correspondent for International News Service, told of action in the Pacific; Henry J. Taylor, war correspondent for United Press and the Scripps-Howard newspapers, gave a report from the Atlantic, while Lieut. (j. g.) Edward A. Heinberger of the Navy, who was Eddie Albert of the films, told of the bitter struggle on Tarawa.

This first report dinner, one of many held throughout the nation, heard also speakers from the home front, including Governor Dewey and Mayor La Guardia, emphasize the urgent need for the purchase of more and still more war bonds to provide the tools of war for our fighting men.

Governor Dewey, speaking from the executive mansion in Albany in a program scheduled to last until the early hours of the morning, declared the Fourth War Loan drive was destined to be the most important of all to date. He took as his theme "Lending to the Limit."

"As we approach the supreme effort," the Governor said, "we know that the outcome depends upon the determination of Ameri-

Continued on Page Ten

Americans Swim Rapido River To Escape Crossfire of Germans

By C. L. SULZBERGER
By Wireless to THE NEW YORK TIMES.

WITH THE FIFTH ARMY ON THE RAPIDO RIVER, Jan. 23 (Delayed)—After a terrific drubbing from the Germans' powerful prepared positions, the remnants of the American force that had staged a series of heroic frontal attacks across the savagely cannonaded Rapido River through minefields and into a trap of machine-gun crossfire withdrew yesterday afternoon by swimming through the raging, icy water.

The Allies could not call in their artillery against the enemy's machine guns because the Allies' troops were scattered about in small units all over. They stuck there, tossing their grenades and getting blown out of one hole after another. One unit was cut off and simply stayed, fighting to the last man.

There were so many casualties that a sergeant of one company had to go back for first aid, recrossing the river by swimming past a blown-up bridge. There was no one left in that area but enlisted men.

Last night twelve Medical Corps men volunteered to cross the river and bring back many of the wounded. They managed to evacuate several. All the time the Germans were shouting: "Give up!"

As they attacked and attacked again, more men slumped through the field, hunched under the weight of their boats suddenly cascading upward as mines exploded. They

Continued on Page Three

"All the News That's Fit to Print."

The New York Times.

LATE CITY EDITION
Cloudy and warmer today with moderate winds.
Temperatures Yesterday—Max., 46; Min., 29
Sunrise, 8:18 A. M.; Sunset, 4:06 P. M.

Copyright, 1944, by The New York Times Company.

VOL. XCIII..No. 31,413. Entered as Second-Class Matter, Postoffice, New York, N. Y. NEW YORK, WEDNESDAY, JANUARY 26, 1944. THREE CENTS NEW YORK CITY

NAZIS BELIEVED QUITTING CASSINO AS ALLIES DRIVE TO APPIAN WAY; ARGENTINA TO CURB GERMAN SPIES

'WHITE COLLAR' PAY MUST BE INCREASED, SAY LABOR LEADERS

Murray Tells Senate Group Steel Workers Have Had 50% Living Cost Rise Since 1941

DISPUTES BUREAU INDEX

Hinrichs Defends 23% Figure —Truck Driver 'Steals Show' in City Workers' Plea

By FREDERICK R. BARKLEY
Special to THE NEW YORK TIMES.

WASHINGTON, Jan. 25—The plight of an estimated 15,000,000 "white collar" persons and others who must live on largely fixed incomes in the face of increasing costs was laid before a Senate group today by six witnesses in the first day's hearings on this problem.

Although the subcommittee of the Senate Education and Labor Committee has no bill before it and apparently has not approached any answer to the problem, the three members present appeared today sympathetic with the complaints.

These came chiefly from Philip Murray, president of the Congress of Industrial Organizations, who said steel workers' living costs had increased 50 per cent since 1941; and Abram Flaxer, president of the CIO's State, County and Municipal Workers Union, who held that such workers needed at least a 25 per cent pay increase to raise them above the level of barest subsistence.

Truck Driver "Steals Show"

While these two witnesses presented detailed figures to back their points, the day's "show" was stolen by John Alessi, a 43-year-old truck driver for the New York City Department of Sanitation, who presented a graphic picture of the difficulties of supporting a family of five in New York on a salary of $2,236 a year.

Mr. Alessi's story of what happened to his family finances when his twins were born, when the bed broke down, when his wages were garnisheed and what happened these days when his wife tried to get up a week-end macaroni dinner, brought compliments from committee members on its documentation and its presentation.

Mr. Alessi, who pictured his hours of work as long and municipal truck driving as hazardous, particularly during a snow-clearing operation, was one of several municipal employes presented by Mr. Flaxer to corroborate his arguments.

The only differences of opinion which arose in the day's testimony came between Mr. Murray and A. F. Hinrichs, acting commissioner of the Bureau of Labor Statistics, over how much living costs had increased.

The bureau's figure of 23.5 per cent since January, 1941, might well be subject to some questioning, Mr. Hinrichs admitted, but he held that Mr. Murray's 50 per cent estimate for a "typical" steel worker was a "very daring" one for anyone to present as typical. The committee asked Mr. Hinrichs to come back later in the week after making a detailed study of Mr. Murray's figures.

Murray Offers Budgets

Mr. Murray, speaking extemporaneously, submitted budgets of what he called two "typical" steel workers in his CIO union to make his point about the 50 per cent increase in living costs. The two examples, he said, were selected from a scientific study of 1,500 steel workers chosen at random in accordance with instructions from the Bureau of Labor Statistics on how to do the job.

He asked that the subcommittee investigate whether the bureau's index really reflected the rise in food prices, quality deterioration and upgrading, disappearance of cheaper goods, rent increases and price increases and black market operations.

Mr. Hinrichs testified that the CIO steel workers' study "ably demonstrates that even at a wage level of $50 a week families have to live very narrowly, and with no access to luxury goods."

"But his data do not help us in creating our own cost-of-living index," he added. "We know that that index has been violently criticized, but within the appropriations Congress has seen fit to grant us we have done the best we can to make it more comprehensive and to check it against these criticisms."

He said the American Statistical

Continued on Page Thirty-eight

Best Enemy Fliers Back Over Rabaul

By The Associated Press.

ADVANCE SOUTH PACIFIC AIR BASE, Jan. 18 (Delayed)—Crack Japanese fighter pilots are flying in defense of Rabaul, Lieut. Comdr. Hawley (Monk) Russell of Scituate, Mass., warned American pilots attacking that New Britain base.

"They may have had the second team in there against us at Bougainville, but they've run the first team back in at Rabaul," the 30-year-old commander said at the end of his naval air squadron's third tour of duty in the northern Solomons.

The squadron, first to fly the Grumman Hellcat from a land base, has retired temporarily from combat, as is customary after three tours. The pilots who flew these stub-winged fighters brought down seventy-six Japanese planes at a loss of eleven of their own men.

SPCC CALLS CRITICS OF SHELTER UNFAIR

Statement Attacks Methods of Children's Court Judges and Hints at Politics

The New York Society for the Prevention of Cruelty to Children, criticized a few days ago for alleged "wretched" treatment of its wards and for alleged archaic conduct of the institution, sharply rebuked its critics yesterday.

It attacked the investigators, Commissioner of Investigation William B. Herlands and a judicial Domestic Relations Court Committee, for "utter disregard of the most fundamental principles of fair play," spoke of "totalitarian methods" used by investigators, and indirectly attributed the committee's report to politics.

The society in a statement held that extra strain had been placed on the institution by Children's Court judges who had crowded the shelter with "vicious and dangerous young thugs, some bigger and stronger than the average adult."

The society promised to meet all the charges in the committee report, which it labeled as "one-sided" and "prejudiced."

TEXT OF STATEMENT

The attack made upon the New York Society for the Prevention of Cruelty to Children is characterized by carelessness with the truth and an utter disregard of the most fundamental principles of fair play. We are confident that the people of New York County, whom we have served for seventy years, will withhold judgment until they get the facts, especially when they realize that the so-called investigations made by Mr. Herlands, the Commissioner of Accounts [former title of the Commissioner of Investigation] and by three Children's Court Judges were conducted without giving us any opportunity to confront or cross-examine our accusers and that the report of these investigations was not delivered to or even shown to us until long after it had been delivered to the newspapers of this city. After publication in the press on Jan. 23 of the attacks upon our society we were given a copy for the first time on Jan. 24. This 125-page report and schedules which we have just received will be analyzed and met by us.

Our society, from its inception, has refused to be dictated to by politicians and has frequently incurred the enmity of officeholders in the past. However, no political machine heretofore has been so contemptuous of the American spirit of fair play as to

Continued on Page Twelve

$664,900,000 RISE IN INCOME TAX WINS CONFEREES' ACCORD

House Group Yields to Senators, Bringing Agreement Near on Revenue Measure

VICTORY LEVY IS RETAINED

Flat 3 Per Cent Is Provided—Earned-Income Credit and U. S. Excise Cuts Dropped

By SAMUEL B. BLEDSOE
Special to THE NEW YORK TIMES.

WASHINGTON, Jan. 25—House and Senate tax bill conferees rejected today House individual income tax proposals in favor of the Senate provision, leaving most taxpayers with the prospect of somewhat higher payments for 1944 than they made for 1943. The total annual increase in individual income taxes is estimated at $664,900,000. Thus a substantial step was taken toward agreement by the joint conference on the $2,275,600,000 revenue measure.

Net results to the taxpayer indicated that he might expect another year with very little change in individual income tax.

The Senate bill leaves the individual income tax provisions about as they were. The House bill would have repealed the Victory tax, increased the normal tax from 6 to 10 per cent and would have substituted a special 3 per cent levy on lower income groups.

In the Senate bill the Victory tax is made a flat 3 per cent instead of 5 per cent, with credit for dependents, life insurance and other items. The Senate and House bills repeal the credit on earned income for individual income taxpayers and also repeal provisions which allow deductions for certain Federal excise taxes paid.

Rise in Tax Is Predicted

These provisions, it has been estimated, will cost taxpayers a total of $664,900,000 more.

The House gave way on almost its entire individual income tax schedule. The conferees approved House language in the section which provides that the status of the taxpayer, so far as personal exemption and credit for dependents are concerned, will be determined by his status as of July 1.

For example, if a taxpayer were married and had two dependents on July 1, 1944, he would get the exemptions which go with such a status, even if his situation with regard to dependents and marital status changed during the year.

With one exception, the House conferees, headed by Representative Robert L. Doughton, chairman of the Ways and Means Committee, went along with the Senators on every section in the tax bill on which there was agreement today, although one or two provisions which were taken up were passed over. The Senate gave way only on its provision which would have given corporations exemptions for tax purposes on contributions to veterans' organizations.

Mustering-Out Pay Is Exempted

The House accepted the Senate amendment which would exempt mustering-out pay of members of the armed forces from income tax. It accepted the Senate version of the so-called last-in, first-out inventory, which is designed to help the taxpayer in certain circumstances where inventory values and replacement costs have risen.

The conferees accepted the Senate version of the section which would require labor organizations, farm cooperatives and other tax-exempt non-profit organizations to file financial returns with the

Continued on Page Ten

Briggs Is Indicted as the Forger Of Letter Attributed to Hopkins

By LEWIS WOOD
Special to THE NEW YORK TIMES.

WASHINGTON, Jan. 25—George N. Briggs, suspended assistant to Secretary Ickes, was indicted by a Federal grand jury today on a charge of forging the celebrated "Harry Hopkins" letter, heart of the mystery which has stirred Washington.

In three indictments he was accused of forgery, of using the mails to defraud and of obtaining money under false pretenses in connection with the document. He is due to appear in Federal court tomorrow to give bond pending an arraignment either Friday or early next week.

The indictments completed the grand jury investigation started two weeks ago into the origin of the letter purported to have been written by Mr. Hopkins, Special Assistant to President Roosevelt, to Dr. Umphrey Lee of Dallas, and made public by C. Nelson Sparks of Akron in the book "One Man—Wendell Willkie."

If convicted on every allegation made against him, Briggs could be sentenced to a maximum of fifty-three years in prison and an $8,000 fine, but Department of Justice officials said this total penalty was hardly likely.

Briggs, the grand jury stated, "unlawfully, willfully, feloniously and falsely made and forged" the Hopkins letter, "and in truth and fact there never had been in existence any such genuine letter from

Continued on Page Twelve

BUENOS AIRES ACTS

Decision on Severe Step Against Nazis to Be Announced Today

MONTEVIDEO SEES BREAK

Says Diplomats Were Told of Rupture — Newspapers Blazon Betrayal by Reich

By ARNALDO CORTESI
By Cable to THE NEW YORK TIMES.

BUENOS AIRES, Jan. 25—Foreign Minister Alberto Gilbert, speaking to the press, tonight announced the Argentine Government would take severe measures against German espionage. The case against the Germans, he said, has been fully proved and the Government is determined to end such activities once and for all because they injure Argentina's good name and national honor. He said the Government's decisions would be announced tomorrow.

[A Reuter dispatch from Montevideo, Uruguay, said General Gilbert had issued a statement to foreign diplomats saying his Government had officially decided to break with the Axis.

[The Argentine Cabinet and high military officers met last night, The Associated Press reported. Otto Meynen, German chargé d'affaires, vainly tried for the second time within a few hours to see General Gilbert, The United Press said.]

President Pedro Ramirez made an address to the nation by radio tonight, but did not refer to international problems. Most of his speech was devoted to the San Juan earthquake, but he also spoke severe words against Communists and "professional politicians."

This afternoon's papers unanimously saw a connection between the turn events have taken in the last twenty-four hours and the announcement last Friday that the Government had taken energetic measures to investigate German espionage in Argentina when it learned of the arrest by British authorities in Trinidad of the Argentine consul Osmar Albert Hellmuth on the grounds that he was "an enemy agent."

Arrested Last October

Hellmuth was arrested last October and the government, therefore, had three months to investigate the charge that a widespread spy ring operated out of Argentina. That the investigations were not fruitless was shown by the fact that the government announced that several persons had been arrested. The press today takes the view that the Axis violated

Continued on Page Five

EXPANDING BEACHHEAD DIVERTS GERMAN FORCES

Jan. 26, 1944

An Allied patrol broke into Cassino (A on inset) and found the stronghold largely deserted. This suggested the enemy was shifting troops to meet the new invasion. The landing parties had driven more than twelve miles inland. One report had Littoria (1) taken and it was established that Allied troops had crossed the Mussolini Canal (2). Field dispatches said the Americans had reached the Appian Way near Cisterna (3), then fanned out. A Berlin report suggested they had advanced to Velletri (4). Still another report told of the capture of the town of Aprilia (5).

HOPE FOR SUPPORT OF RUSSIA ON GOLD

Our Experts Look to Monetary Leader in Soviet for Aid in Currency Stabilization

By JOHN H. CRIDER
Special to THE NEW YORK TIMES.

WASHINGTON, Jan. 25—A possibility that Soviet Russia will side with United States experts to break the deadlock with British monetary negotiators on the question of post-war currency stabilization is being hopefully considered in some official quarters. Mr. Chechulin, deputy president of the State Bank of Russia and chairman of the Soviet Monetary Delegation, is expected to arrive in Washington soon for talks with our experts.

The basis for speculation that the Russians will be more agree-

Continued on Page Four

War News Summarized

WEDNESDAY, JANUARY 26, 1944

The Fifth Army retained the upper hand at all points in Italy yesterday. Anzio, on the coast below Rome, was captured, and Allied troops pushed twelve miles inland without meeting real opposition. Berlin implied that the Germans had abandoned Velletri, about twenty miles from Anzio and the same distance below Rome. Enemy counter-attacks on the Cassino-Minturno main battle line were repelled and there were indications that the Germans had pulled out of Cassino. [1:8.]

Advance United States troops battled throughout the night for possession of bridges over the Mussolini Canal. When daylight came the positions were in American hands despite tanks used by the Germans. [3:2-3.]

The Red Army continued to sweep forward in the northern sectors and to halt German counter-attacks in the center of the long front. The Russians loosened the enemy's grip on the few rail lines at his disposal around Pushkin, Kirishi and Novgorod. [1:6-7; map P. 2.]

Air Marshal Sir Arthur Coningham, who headed the Allied tactical force in the Mediterranean, was put in command of the RAF No. 2 Tactical Air Force for the invasion of western Europe. [6:1.] American Thunderbolts without loss hit airfields and other targets in the Netherlands. [7:1.]

Allied fliers in the Southwest Pacific destroyed or damaged at least eighty-three Japanese planes, numerous ships and gun positions in continuing attacks upon the Admiralty Islands, New Britain and New Guinea. [8:2.]

Argentina, apparently finally stung by United Nations' resentment against Axis espionage and plotting within her borders, announced she would take energetic action to end such German activities. There were also indications that she might break with the Axis. [1:4.]

Secretary of War Stimson said a National Service act was necessary because trouble had broken out on the home front at the moment our troops were preparing for decisive action. He declared there were twenty-two strikes last week that had caused the loss of 135,000 man-days of war production. [1:6-7.] Chairman Nelson of the WPB said the major problems of mass production of munitions had been solved. No expansions were planned for the next year and the emphasis would be on shifts in production, he added. [10:2.]

Russians Storm Rail Key; Sever Foe's Escape Routes

By W. H. LAWRENCE
By Cable to THE NEW YORK TIMES.

MOSCOW, Wednesday, Jan. 26—The Red Army was reported officially last night to have smashed forward another eleven miles in the center of the highly fortified German defense line south of Leningrad, while other troops on that front drove to the suburbs of Krasnogvardeisk, where they engaged the Germans in fierce battle for control of that terminus of the Gatchina-Narva-Talinn railway.

An advance by Gen. Kyrill A. Meretskoff's forces west and southwest of Kirishi was the most important Red Army gain recorded in the day's Soviet High Command communiqués. It was achieved in the face of strong resistance, bulwarked by a system of engineering fortifications on difficult forest roads, and the new successes brought the Soviet forces "right up to the Chudovo-Tosno railway line" at several places.

That line is virtually all of the main Moscow-Leningrad railway that still remains in German hands and the communiqués indicated it soon would be cleared up.

Two days ago the drive against the center of the German line had proceeded only fourteen miles from Kirishi, but the communiqué's declaration that Soviet troops were right up to several points on the Moscow-Leningrad main trunk line

Continued on Page Two

3 HOSPITAL SHIPS BOMBED OFF ITALY

One Sunk in Heavy German Air Attack—All 'Lighted Up Like Christmas Trees'

Three Allied hospital ships lying off the Italian beach at Anzio were bombed by German planes and one was sunk despite the fact that all were "lighted up like Christmas trees," a CBS correspondent reported yesterday.

The attack occurred late on Monday afternoon, according to the correspondent, John Daly. His broadcast account of the bombing follows:

"I was in an American destroyer just off the beach when the first wave of enemy planes attacked at 4:44 P. M. Few details of that raid,

Continued on Page Three

Stimson Says Strikes Cost Army 135,000 Man-Days' Output in Week

Special to THE NEW YORK TIMES.

WASHINGTON, Jan. 25—Even while the great battles of the war still lie ahead and the situation is critical, strikes have become so common on the home front that newspapers no longer notice them as feature news, Secretary Stimson said tonight in a radio address in which he pleaded for a National Service Act.

No less than twenty-two strikes took place in the week ending last night, Mr. Stimson stated, and these disputes, he said, meant a loss of 135,000 man-days in the output of vital material for the men on the fighting fronts, or the "equivalent of nine divisions gone A. W. O. L. for one day."

Strikes, he went on, are not "unfelt" in the fighting forces, where the men are puzzled because they see their country divided into two classes. On the one hand are the fighting men, inducted into uniform by the Selective Service law. On the other hand the soldiers see that the Government imposes no corresponding duty on the other men and "even permits them to leave the most important war jobs without regard to the needs of their country."

The Secretary of War, who spoke on a National Broadcasting Company network, scouted the suggestion that a National Service act was needless, and that to penalize strikes was enough to do. This, he asserted, was merely a diagnosis which "treats a symptom and not the cause."

"The cause of the present situa-

Continued on Page Thirty-eight

U. S. PATROL ENTERS

Americans Find Town Almost Empty—Guns in Hills Rout Them

INVADERS PUSH 12 MILES

Appian Way, Coast Railroad Reported Cut as Allies' Formations Fan Out

By The United Press.

AN ADVANCE COMMAND POST, Overlooking Cassino, Jan. 25—An American patrol of fourteen men, led by Second Lieut. Filbert Munoz, 22 years old, of Kansas City, Kan., entered the outskirts of Cassino today and penetrated to a point within 400 yards of the heart of the city. A solitary German sentry walking along a street was the only sign of life.

The Americans had forced the Rapido River, north of the town, against surprisingly light opposition after a previous foothold had been wiped out in German counter-attacks. Heavy anti-personnel mines were encountered, but there were few enemy troops and only light artillery fire. This supported the suspicion that the Germans were withdrawing to the new invasion area around Nettuno.

"We advanced almost to the heart of the town before the Germans opened up on us with mortars and machine-guns," Lieutenant Munoz said. "We crawled on our bellies to an irrigation ditch and kept out of the range of the machine-guns as we sank six inches into the mud.

"Mortars rained shells from Hill 175, to the northwest of Cassino, and wounded some of my men, but the Germans made no action from Cassino itself."

Landing Forces 12 Miles Inland

By MILTON BRACKER
By Wireless to THE NEW YORK TIMES.

ALGIERS, Jan. 25—The Allies' invasion forces, fanning out through the minefields surrounding the captured ports of Anzio and Nettuno, thirty miles south of Rome, have thrust inland twelve miles and are within a mile or two of both the principal coastal railway and the Appian Way, it was officially announced today. These intersect at Cisterna, which is less than fifteen miles northeast of Anzio and barely thirteen miles beyond Nettuno.

Patrols were already probing beyond the rim of the general penetration and may already be astride the vital communications lines. No major German resistance had yet developed and the terrible sting of the German counter-offensive along the Garigliano River-Gustav Line, sixty miles below Anzio, seemed to have lessened.

[The Allies have cut both the Appian Way and the coastal railroad at a point about twenty-five miles south of Rome and are striking toward the Via Casilina, The United Press reported.

[A Swiss broadcast recorded by The Associated Press quoted a Bari radio report that Allied troops had captured Littoria and Aprilia.

[A German broadcast recorded by The Associated Press said that Allied bombers had destroyed Velletri, on the Appian Way, twenty-four miles south of Rome, and implied that the Allies had captured the town. Tuesday's German communiqué indicated that throughout Italy the Allies were on the offensive and the Germans had abandoned counter-attacks to fight purely defensive actions.]

Withdrawal From South Begun

It was indicated that the Germans had definitely begun withdrawing some troops from the southern front to meet the threat in their rear, where so far the Allies have encountered only hastily formed battle groups. Poor flying weather prevented large-scale bombing and strafing of this withdrawal.

While the fury of the fighting on the southern front was evidenced by the testimony of one eyewitness that the German dead around Minturno had made him think of the carnage of the Somme

Continued on Page Four

"All the News That's Fit to Print."

The New York Times.

LATE CITY EDITION
Fair and continued cold today; winds slowly diminishing.
Temperatures Yesterday—Max., 37; Min., 17
Sunrise, 6:07 A. M.; Sunset, 6:18 P. M.

VOL. XCIII..No. 31,420. Entered as Second-Class Matter, Postoffice, New York, N. Y. NEW YORK, WEDNESDAY, FEBRUARY 2, 1944. THREE CENTS IN NEW YORK CITY

U. S. FORCE WINS BEACHES ON MARSHALLS ATOLL; BATTLES RAGE ON FIRST JAPANESE SOIL INVADED; ALLIES ATTACK BELOW ROME; RUSSIANS ADVANCE

ROLL-CALL RECORD ON SOLDIERS' VOTE REFUSED BY HOUSE

180 Republicans, 52 Democrats Opposed—146 Democrats, 11 Republicans for It

A 'STATE RIGHTS' VICTORY

President Says People Need to Know How Members Stand—Senate Test Likely Today

By C. P. TRUSSELL
Special to THE NEW YORK TIMES.

WASHINGTON, Feb. 1—The House by a vote of 233 to 160 refused today to subject itself to the "stand-up-and-be-counted" showdown between Federal and State ballot plans for the armed forces as President Roosevelt urged in his recent message to Congress.

On the question of forcing a roll-call test on the Worley Federal ballot bill, endorsed by the Administration, in direct competition with the "States' rights" (Eastland-Rankin) measure, the House divided as follows:

For a roll-call test: 146 Democrats, 11 Republicans, 2 Progressives and 1 American-Laborite.

Against a roll-call test: 180 Republicans, 52 Democrats and 1 Farmer-Laborite.

Vote Is on Committee Rule

While the vote was construed as an expression of attitude on the Worley bill, as against the Eastland-Rankin bill, the question upon which the issue was joined was a parliamentary one.

The Eastland-Rankin bill had been taken to the floor under a rule of the Rules Committee which did not assure a record vote on the Worley bill. To amend this rule the House was required to defeat a motion to close consideration and debate at the end of an hour's debate. Instead the motion carried and the rule was adopted. Thus the roll-call was blocked.

Fifty of the fifty-two Democrats who helped block the roll-call were from Southern States. Five were from Alabama, three from Arkansas, nine from Georgia, one from Kentucky, six from Louisiana, seven from Mississippi, the solid vote of the delegation; two from North Carolina, one from Oklahoma, three from South Carolina, one from Tennessee, eight from Texas and four from Virginia. The others were Representatives Slaughter of Missouri and Jellicott of California.

The eleven Republicans voting to assure the roll-call vote were Representatives Andrews, Kearney, Mruk and Taylor of New York; Anderson and Welsh of California, Bender of Ohio, Burdick of North Dakota, Gale of Minnesota, La Follette of Indiana and Wolverton of New Jersey.

President's Remark on Test

President Roosevelt, when told of the House's action at his press conference soon after the vote was taken, observed that roll-calls were a part of representative government, and said that he could not cast an intelligent vote in an election without knowing how his Congressman voted.

The House having made the first voting decision in the controversy, the Senate, after six hours of heated debate over constitutional phases of the issue and the President's charge that the "States' rights" bill passed by the Senate was a "fraud," as well as the delay in test voting in Congress, agreed to vote not later than noon tomorrow on the Overton amendment to the Green-Lucas Federal ballot bill.

This amendment would prescribe that while the Federal ballot might be used, State and local election officials would determine the validity of the votes cast in accordance with State law. The principal effect would be to repeal provisions of the existing soldier voting law which suspend requirements for personal registration and payment of poll taxes and, to an undetermined extent, invalidate the Federal ballot.

Members of the "States' rights"

Continued on Page Twelve

Public Told to Delay '44 Tax Estimates

Taxpayers are being advised not to file their estimates of 1944 income with their tax returns for 1943, because Washington legislation is expected to affect the rates on 1944 income. Internal revenue officials in New York City believe Congress will authorize a delay of at least thirty days for the declarations.

"We are trying to discourage taxpayers from filing their declarations of estimated 1944 income until we get the new forms," one internal revenue official said. He indicated that the new legislation could not be made effective before March 1 and that April 15 was regarded as a logical date for the necessary extension.

RISE IN CITY RENTS FOUGHT BY MAYOR

He Urges OPA 'Unqualifiedly' to Reject Landlords' Plea for 10% Blanket Increase

By LEE E. COOPER

Mayor La Guardia has asked the Office of Price Administration to reject "unqualifiedly" the petition of New York City landlords for a blanket increase of at least 10 per cent in housing rents, it became known last night.

In a 10,000-word memorandum filed with the OPA "as Mayor and on behalf of the tenants residing in the City of New York," Mr. La Guardia replied in detail to each of the objections to the rent ceiling regulations voiced by property owners in their plea for an increase, and called an upward adjustment of charges for living quarters here "unjustified and unwarranted."

He charged that the petitioners had "only one real aim—to impair the successful administration of rent control in New York."

The Mayor's brief challenges as "false and fantastic" the estimates of the petitioning groups that there were upward of 79,000 habitable apartment units available for rent in the five boroughs on Oct. 8, 1943.

He cited figures and surveys, including many by the Real Estate Board of New York, to support his contention that New York owners have been enjoying the "best rental market in almost two decades," disputed the argument that there had been a general increase in realty taxes and in scathing tone answered the statistics regarding foreclosures and depressed conditions in the realty market.

The Mayor's memorandum was tinged with sarcasm also in his answer to the plea that higher operating costs of buildings justified a rent rise. He expressed the view that the increase in apartment occupancy alone had "entirely or at least substantially offset any increase in building maintenance costs," while many building owners at the same time, he charged, were employing fewer workers and curtailing service. Although there has been a rise in fuel costs, he added, "thousands of tenants have

Continued on Page Fifteen

TWIN GAINS IN ITALY

British 16 Miles Below Rome After Cutting Coastal Railway

CISTERNA IS MENACED

Americans Half Mile From Town—Allies on Lower Front Gain

By MILTON BRACKER
By Wireless to THE NEW YORK TIMES.

ALGIERS, Feb. 1—Smashing ahead against furious resistance, American troops have driven into the suburbs of Cisterna, the most vital choke-point in the German supply system below Rome.

There the Appian Way and the main coastal railway intersect. Through the town enormous quantities of supplies have passed to the German forces on the lower front.

[The Americans were only a half-mile from Cisterna proper, according to The United Press.]

British units farther west have eased the Americans' task by driving three miles beyond Aprilia along the road from Anzio, cutting the railroad at the Campoleone station ten miles above Cisterna and hammering into the outskirts of Campoleone proper, one mile beyond.

But, while the Allies appear to be about to sever the electrified trackage at two points and the historic highway at one, the Germans have finally brought down reinforcements from north of Rome. Thus, although the British and American penetrations threaten the flank of the German defense line along five miles of the railway between the Campoleone station and Cisterna, the Allies must be prepared to meet a thrust from the north on their own exposed left flank.

No Factor of Surprise

The probability of new German pressure from the north has long been expected and in no way gives the Germans the advantage of surprise. But how large a force the enemy has been able to divert to the south and whether he can build it up to constitute a grave menace are not known.

Offsetting factors are the continuing Allied air offensive against all the supply routes leading to Rome, which militates against further troop movement, and the fine weather around the beachheads, which is permitting the Allies to expand on an even more solid foundation.

The battlefield is still wedge-shaped. Its point is at the Anzio-Nettuno area and its rim extends between Campoleone and Cisterna. At the outskirts of the former village the British are barely sixteen miles from Rome, while the Americans clamping down on Cisterna are twenty-six miles from the capital. The ten-mile stretch between, along which the Germans have built their defenses, is within easy range of light artillery. Continued naval bombardments between the beachhead and Formia throttled

Continued on Page Eight

$103,889,600 in War Bonds Sold At Rally on Stock Exchange Floor

After being "sold" by the marines—specifically Lieut. Gen. Alexander A. Vandegrift, commandant of the Marine Corps—Wall Street yesterday "told" it to Hitler and Hirohito by subscribing for $103,889,600 in bonds of the Fourth War Loan.

General Vandegrift, addressing 2,000 brokers and employes at a rally on the floor of the New York Stock Exchange, Wall and Broad Streets, declared the quick success of the drive would be "equal to a major victory on the battlefield—and it will not cost a single drop of blood."

Emil Schram, president of the Exchange, announced the day's total, which brought the aggregate of both purchases and sales made by members of the Exchange in 322 cities and forty-six States to $501,000,000 in the current drive.

Another large subscription announced yesterday was $55,000,000 by the Mutual Life Insurance Company of New York. Lewis W. Douglas, president, said it was the company's way of celebrating its 101st birthday. The Mutual Life's Government bond holdings have increased by $310,344,000 since Pearl Harbor, he said.

Huge sales were recorded in city, State and nation yesterday, the first day on which the books were opened in the drive for corporate subscriptions. At the same time sales of E-bonds, the type favored by the small investor, continued to soar as they have since

Continued on Page Fourteen

MARSHALL ISLANDS BASE WHERE WE HAVE ESTABLISHED BEACHHEADS

The Japanese airfield on Roi (left). Coral strip connects it with Namur (right), on which the enemy has a roadway.

Associated Press Wirephoto (U. S. Navy)

BERLIN'S BLOT-OUT PUT NEARER BY RAF

10,000 Tons of Bombs Loosed in January on City—Sunday's Blow Fired Plant Areas

By DREW MIDDLETON
By Cable to THE NEW YORK TIMES.

LONDON, Feb. 1—The city of Berlin, until lately the heart of Hitler's great military empire, is dying under the British bombing assault, which in January devoted about 10,000 tons of missiles to the destruction of the Reich capital in six great assaults.

[During daylight RAF Coastal Command planes attacked German shipping off Norway, sinking a mine-sweeper, setting a cargo ship afire and shooting up an escort vessel.

[Telephone contact between Stockholm and Berlin was broken early Tuesday night, but was re-established at 11:45 P. M. and Swedish correspondents in the Reich capital gave no indication that there had been a new at-

Continued on Page Seven

Soviet Republics Get Right To Own Armies and Envoys

By W. H. LAWRENCE
By Wireless to THE NEW YORK TIMES

MOSCOW, Feb. 1—The Supreme Soviet late tonight unanimously approved a proposal by Foreign Commissar Vyacheslaff M. Molotoff for major changes in the Soviet constitutional system under which each of the sixteen constituent republics will form its own army formations and have separate diplomatic representation abroad.

[The text of Mr. Molotoff's statement appears on page 10.]

In less than four hours of debate, including the forty-three-minute opening address by Mr. Molotoff, both chambers approved the constitutional changes by a show of hands without having the full text read to them. They had copies of the proposal in their desks but they waived the reading of it.

On the motion of President Mikhail I. Kalinin, the Supreme Soviet also elected Nikolai Shevrnik as first Vice President of the Presidium of the U.S.S.R. and then adjourned sine die.

While Premier Joseph Stalin looked on from a back-row seat on the platform, Mr. Molotoff gave a general outline of the Government's new plan which, he said, resulted

Continued on Page Ten

KINGISEPP IS TAKEN IN RED ARMY SWEEP

Entry of Estonia Is Indicated as Three-Way Drive Squeezes the Germans in Pocket

By The United Press.

LONDON, Wednesday, Feb. 2—Gen. Leonid A. Govoroff's Leningrad army captured the German stronghold of Kingisepp yesterday after brief street battles, while his advanced spearheads pushed on toward Estonia along a ten-mile front, reaching to within less than a mile of the border at the town of Keikino. [The western edge of Keikino is only 300 yards from the border.]

The Red Army was nearing the border on a front northwest of Kingisepp and it was probable that some units might have crossed into the Baltic State.

More than fifty towns and settlements were captured yesterday—the eve of the first anniversary of the German defeat at Stalingrad—by General Govoroff's army, which concentrated its over-all offensive in three directions along a sixty-five-mile front curving down from the Gulf of Finland to within thirty-three miles north-

Continued on Page Eleven

FLEET CONFIDENT ON WAY TO ATOLL

Fight Tougher Than Tarawa Seen but Men Were Sure Marshalls Would Fall

By ROBERT TRUMBULL
By Wireless to THE NEW YORK TIMES.

ABOARD A FLAGSHIP APPROACHING KWAJALEIN ATOLL, Jan. 30 (Delayed)—A large part of the American Navy, constituting the most powerful sea force ever assembled, is converging from north and south today on Kwajalein Atoll in the Japanese mandated Marshall Islands. We have already attacked with planes and naval gunfire, and tomorrow we land our troops.

Today a number of battleships, including our newest and largest, opened fire on Kwajalein's principal shore installations.

For the first time we are invading a part of the Japanese empire and in so doing we are exposing ourselves to possible strong aerial and submarine opposition and natural hazards of which we have little knowledge. We are in waters now that have been the cruising area of the Japanese fleet exclusively for many years. We would like very much to meet that fleet here and now.

Tomorrow the Fourth Marine Division and the Seventh Army Division comprising an amphibious force under command of Rear Admiral Richmond Kelly Turner will make the most audacious attack attempted by the United States in this war.

We expect Kwajalein to be tougher than Tarawa. We know we will lose many men on the beaches. We expect Japanese dive bombers and submarines to sink

Continued on Page Four

War News Summarized

WEDNESDAY, FEBRUARY 2, 1944

American marines and soldiers set foot for the first time in this war on Japanese territory and established beachheads near Roi and Kwajalein Islands in the Marshalls. Under the cover of hundreds of planes and the guns of battleships, cruisers and smaller craft, the American forces were beating down strong opposition with apparently moderate casualties.

The Seventh Infantry Division landed near Kwajalein and the Fourth Marine Division near Roi, both in the Kwajalein Atoll. The combined air forces pounded Maloelap, Wotje, Mili, Jaluit and Eniwetok and Wake Island in addition to Kwajalein. [All the foregoing 1:8, map P. 2.]

A large part of our Navy sailed confidently into a ring of Japanese air and submarine bases to hammer the Marshalls and protect the landing forces. [1:7.] Tokyo papers said an American victory there would be a "regrettable loss." [3:5.]

In the Southwest Pacific and in Burma the Japanese were also under heavy attack. At Rabaul, New Britain, they lost at least twenty-three planes and it was revealed that an Allied post had been established within Netherland New Guinea. [3:1, with map.] American-trained Chinese troops advanced five miles in two days in the Hukawng Valley in Burma. [7:5.]

President Roosevelt answered Japanese propaganda by saying our troops were in India not for political but for military purposes—"to assure the defeat of Japan." [4:2.] He repeated assurance that the individuals responsible for atrocities against prisoners would be tracked down and brought to justice. [5:5.]

The Fifth Army fighting on the beachhead below Rome had reached the outskirts of Campoleone and Cisterna, threatening to close a pincers around the Germans, who were said to be rushing reinforcements from northern Italy. [1:3; map P. 8.] American fliers hit the enemy's refueling airfields at Klagenfurt, Austria, and Aviano and Udine; the RAF struck Trieste. [8:1.]

Russian troops captured Kingisepp and moved to within a few hundred yards of the Estonian border. More than ninety places were recaptured in gains on many fronts. [1:6; map P. 11.]

Moscow presented a sudden, new development when the Supreme Soviet unanimously approved proposals of Foreign Commissar Molotoff changing the constitutional system whereby the sixteen constituent republics would have their own army formations and their own diplomatic corps. This would tend to give Russia sixteen votes at the peace conference. [1:5-6.] A writer in the Soviet newspaper Izvestia said the Vatican's policy was "pro-fascist in character." [1:6-7.]

Izvestia Calls Pope Pro-Fascist; Says Catholics Are Disillusioned

By The United Press.

MOSCOW, Feb. 1—The Government newspaper Izvestia asserted today that Vatican foreign policy had disillusioned Catholics throughout the world and "earned the hatred and contempt of the Italian masses for supporting fascism."

Endorsing a report issued on Jan. 15 by the Foreign Policy Association, New York, which said that a rising tide of anti-clericalism might be expected in Italy, the Soviet organ said the Vatican pledged its support to Italian fascism following conclusion of the Lateran treaty in February, 1929, "but the Vatican's support for fascism wasn't limited solely to Italy. It approved many acts of aggression by fascism although the true meaning of these aggressions was no secret.

"The Vatican is now suffering the consequences of its endorsement of the Italian conquest of Abyssinia and is now reaping the fruits of the débâcle of the Italian African empire."

Reviewing Vatican foreign policy before and during the present war, Izvestia said "the disgraceful role the Vatican played in Hitler's and Mussolini's Spanish adventure is widely known. The Vatican emerged in the role of a supporter of armed intervention."

It said Generalissimo Francisco Franco of totalitarian Spain was a "Vatican pet" and that Generalissimo Franco's Spain was the "image of the clerical States of post-war Europe" which the Vati-

Continued on Page Eleven

GRIP ON KWAJALEIN

Marine and Infantry Units Strike, Shielded by Record Armada

LOSSES ARE MODERATE

Our Forces as Close to Japan as Foe Was to U. S. at Pearl Harbor

By GEORGE F. HORNE
By Telephone to THE NEW YORK TIMES.

PEARL HARBOR, Feb. 1—Tremendous American amphibious forces have invaded the Marshall Islands and established beachheads in bitter fighting on islands of the Kwajalein Atoll.

Admiral Chester W. Nimitz, Commander in Chief of the Pacific Fleet and of the Pacific Ocean Areas, announced this morning what most of the world had surmised: that United States fighting strength was being pitted on Japanese soil for the first time in what must be considered a decisive battle in the war of the Pacific.

Protected by fire power overshadowing anything we had concentrated against the fierce warriors who dreamt of dictating peace terms in the White House, well-trained forces, both marines and Army infantrymen now skilled in amphibious operations, stormed ashore yesterday morning in daylight.

As they went in at fighting pitch and armed with the best weapons ingenuity can provide, carrier aircraft and surface forces bombarded and raked near-by atolls to blanket the enemy.

The assault forces landed on unidentified islands in the vicinity of Roi and Kwajalein, both in the Kwajalein Atoll.

Strong opposition has been encountered, but first reports from the area, necessarily meager, are in an optimistic tone. The first stages of the operation appear to have opened successfully.

[Besides Kwajalein and Roi, the landing forces had as an objective a third Japanese base, Namur Island.

[A Japanese Imperial Headquarters announcement recorded from the Tokyo radio by CBS said Army and Navy garrisons had counter-attacked and that "furious fighting is now in progress."]

Admiral Nimitz's communiqué stated that "initial information indicates that our casualties are moderate."

Spruance Again in Command

Vice Admiral Raymond A. Spruance, who directed the successful Gilberts invasion only ten weeks ago, again is in command.

Roi Island is in the northern

Continued on Page Three

We Lose 22 Planes, Save All but 6 Men

By The United Press.

WASHINGTON, Feb. 1—The Navy revealed tonight that twenty-two Corsair fighter planes from a twenty-three-plane marine squadron were lost in a severe storm last Friday while on a "routine flight" between the American-held Gilbert and Ellice Islands.

All but six of the pilots have been rescued. The body of one was also recovered.

One of the twenty-two planes made a crash landing in the Ellice Islands, but the other twenty-one, so far as is known, were forced down at sea.

The Navy said search operations were started immediately after the one plane had arrived safely at the Ellice Island base.

The next of kin of the dead pilot and the five still missing have been notified.

Loss of the planes was revealed in a Pacific Fleet headquarters announcement released here and at Pearl Harbor.

"All the News That's Fit to Print."

The New York Times.

LATE CITY EDITION
Cloudy and windy with showers this afternoon; colder tonight.
Temperatures Yesterday—Max., 45; Min., 28
Sunrise, 5:08 A. M.; Sunset, 5:16 P. M.

Section 1

NEWS INDEX, PAGE 43, THIS SECTION

VOL. XCIII..No. 31,424. Entered as Second-Class Matter, Postoffice, New York, N. Y. NEW YORK, SUNDAY, FEBRUARY 6, 1944. Including Magazine and Book Sections. TEN CENTS New York City and Suburban Area (15c Elsewhere)

BRITISH REPEL NAZI TANK ATTACKS; RUSSIANS TAKE LUTSK AND ROVNO; KWAJALEIN ISLAND IS CAPTURED

FEDERAL VOTE FOES BALKED IN SENATE ON POINT OF QUORUM

Barkley Brings Quick End to Saturday Sitting as His Side Is Outnumbered

MEMBERS STILL ARRIVING

Only 44 on Hand When Count Is Made, With at Least 24 Listed for State Plan

By C. P. TRUSSELL

Special to The New York Times.

WASHINGTON, Feb. 5—Quick action by Administration forces brought an extraordinary Saturday session of the Senate to an abrupt halt without the transaction of any business today when it appeared that the Green-Lucas bill for the service men's ballot under Federal auspices was heading into new difficulties.

Senator Alben W. Barkley, the majority leader, moved for adjournment after only forty-four members had responded to the quorum calls. He acted so unexpectedly that opponents of the Green-Lucas measure were caught off guard. Senators arriving in the chamber a little later were surprised to find the session ended.

Twenty-six of those present when the adjournment motion came had supported the motion of Senator John H. Overton of Louisiana yesterday to lay aside the Green-Lucas bill and take up amendments to the House-adopted Eastland-Rankin "States' Rights" bill, a motion which lost by a tie vote of 42 to 42. Only seventeen of those who had opposed the Overton motion, which was scheduled to be renewed today, had made their appearance.

Alignment of Absentees

Among the absentees were twenty-four who were opposed to taking up the House amendments before completing action on the Green-Lucas bill and only sixteen who voted yesterday for adoption of the Overton motion.

A checking of the quorum roll call showed further that twenty-four supporters of the Senate "States' Rights" substitute for the Green-Lucas bill, which was defeated yesterday by a vote of 46 to 42, but provisions of which are scheduled for further tests, were present, while only twenty Green-Lucas bill backers were on hand.

The absentees included twenty-six Senators who had helped defeat the "States' Rights" substitute yesterday and eighteen of its supporters.

The Overton motion had the status of being not only renewable, but privileged, and could have taken preference over the issue now pending before the Senate. This issue is an amendment by Senator John A. Danaher, Republican, of Connecticut, to provide that the proposed Federal ballot, which would be issued in blank form automatically to all eligible voters in the armed forces, would be valid only if received by the appropriate election officials of the district, county or other voting unit of the State of residence of the voter not later than 12 o'clock noon on the date of the election.

1942 Arrest Motion Cited

Some States permit the counting of absentee ballots which arrive nearly a week after election day, while some require that they arrive twenty-four hours before the election.

In the light of Senator Barkley's maneuver today it was recalled that during the Saturday session of Nov. 14, 1942, he offered a motion for the arrest of absentee Senators. That was when the poll tax bill filibuster was on.

Whereas forty-three Senators were reported to be out of town on that day, Senator Barkley spoke of only three as being out of town today and one ill. All four opposed both the Overton motion and the "States' Rights" substitute yesterday. Their absence, Senator Barkley said, was a factor in his decision to move adjournment.

Postponement of further action in the Senate until Monday brought with it an indication that the soldier voting issue will remain on the floor well into next week, despite the asserted urgency of action on the legislation providing for continuance of the Commodity Credit Corporation, which is handling much of the consumer price subsidy program, beyond Feb. 17, to which it was extended when

Continued on Page Thirty-four

£20,000 to Churchill By Strakosch Will

By Cable to The New York Times.

LONDON, Feb. 5—Winston Churchill, Field Marshal Jan Christiaan Smuts, Viscount Simon, Minister of Information Brendan Bracken and Sir Otto Niemeyer and Sir Findlater Stewart, financial experts, are included among a number of prominent people mentioned as legatees in the will of Sir Henry Strakosch, banker and economist, which was made public today.

Sir Henry, who died last Oct. 30, bequeathed £20,000 to Mr. Churchill "as a token of friendship and gratitude for his and his wife's great kindness and hospitality." Marshal Smuts, with whom Sir Henry had a long association, receives £10,000, Lord Simon £5,000 and Mr. Bracken, Sir Otto and Sir Findlater £2,500 each.

Sir Henry left more than £2,454,500 gross in the largest individual fortune to be probated since that of Walter Melville Wills, British tobacco magnate, who died in January, 1941, leaving a fortune of more than £4,371,300.

E-BOND BUYERS SET CITY RECORD IN DAY

Individuals' Purchases Now 53% of Quota—Over-All Total Here at 86%

New York City's growing army of small investors rang up their biggest single day in the Fourth War Loan drive on Friday when they bought $8,772,000 worth of E bonds, according to figures released yesterday by the War Finance Committee of New York. Manhattan accounted for $5,357,600 worth.

For the entire city total sales of all issues to individual investors have reached $373,406,800, or 53.5 per cent of the city's quota for individuals. Subscriptions by all classifications of buyers are now within 14 per cent of the over-all drive quota of $3,683,311,000. This is made up largely of "big money" purchases of the market issues.

In Washington, the Treasury reported that sales in the fourth war loan drive totaled $10,752,000,000 through today, or 77 per cent of the $14,000,000,000 goal, according to The Associated Press. Sales to individuals totaled $2,837,000,000 and to corporations $8,115,000,000.

In a nation-wide radio program yesterday afternoon Under-Secretary of the Treasury Daniel W. Bell accredited 1,500,000 Boy Scouts as war bond aides for Boy Scout Week, which begins Tuesday. They will make a door-to-door canvass throughout the country.

Addressing 400 Scouts at the National Broadcasting Company studio here, Capt. Eddie Rickenbacker, a member of the national executive board of the Boy Scouts of America, emphasized the need for greater effort on the home front. He reminded the Scouts that they were now "tackling the biggest, the most important, mission in Scout history." He said that if each Scout sold ten bonds it "might help tip the balance and bring victory closer."

Dr. Elbert K. Fretwell, Chief Scout Executive, recalled that in the last war the Scouts, with a membership of less than 400,000, sold $2,300,000 worth of Liberty Bonds, or more than five bonds apiece. With a present membership of four times that of World War I, he suggested, the Scouts

Continued on Page Seventeen

HOSPITALS TO GET 100% MORE BUTTER FROM U. S. STOCKS

Prices Tumble in Black Market as Many Consumers Shift to Use of Oleomargarine

STORES' SUPPLIES RISING

But Government Sounds Note of Caution—City Patients Due to Get Chicken

By JEFFERSON G. BELL

The Federal Government is doubling the allotment of butter recently made to hospitals from its huge hoard of 130,000,000 pounds. At the same time the black market is offering stocks at reductions of as much as 11 cents a pound.

Those and other surprises in a rapid succession yesterday found the trade agog along the butter front. Not the least speculation centered around another big shipment of butter reported en route from Argentina.

Stocks of butter in the hands of local retailers gradually are increasing. Improved supplies are attributed not only to increased national production but to larger production in the New York milkshed as handlers find they must churn large quantities of heavy cream that cannot compete with Western cream, about $5 a tin cheaper, in the manufacture of ice cream and sour cream.

Butter Consumption Lower

Moreover, the trade reports a huge drop in butter consumption may be attributed in part to butterless luncheons begun by restaurants and hotels in response to proclamations by Mayor La Guardia.

Cottage cheese, marmalade and, above all, oleomargarine have taken the place of butter on luncheon menus. There is much speculation on the extent to which these substitutes permanently may supplant butter. This speculation is based in part on Government statistics showing that the nation's production of oleomargarine jumped to 610,131,000 pounds in 1943, from 423,277,000 in 1942 and 365,209,000 in 1941. As production of margarine goes up production of butter goes down.

The nation's production of creamery butter totaled 1,685,825,000 pounds in 1943, representing a drop of 4 per cent in 1942 production and 3 per cent in the ten-year average from 1931 to 1942.

The improvement in local supplies of butter in retailers' hands was estimated last week at 30 per cent above the preceding week by City Markets Commissioner Henry M. Brundage. The increase was sufficient to restore confidence among some shopkeepers who began to paste signs in their windows, reading:

"Yes, we have butter; come in and get it."

A Note of Caution Sounded

Government representatives are prompt to sound a note of caution against overoptimism based on what they characterize as only a very slight improvement in butter supplies. They point out that huge quantities still are required for the armed forces, lend-lease and other priority groups. They explain that the release of additional supplies to hospitals has been made possible by a number of other factors than by increased January production.

Last November the War Food Administration released some 5,000,000 pounds of butter from excess stocks to hospitals throughout the country. Stocks were sufficient to allow each patient three-

Continued on Page Thirty-six

Nazis Say Norway Fears Russian Blow

DNB broadcast a report from Oslo yesterday saying that Norwegians feared a Russian attempt to launch an invasion on the northern tip of Norway. The broadcast, recorded by The United Press, quoted the newspaper Aftenposten as saying:

"The fact that Soviet landing barges were sailing in a convoy that was recently attacked by U-boats off Murmansk has caused wide anxiety in Norway. What do the Soviets intend to do with these landing barges? It is evident that they could be used only against Norway."

NEW ALLIED POLICY ON FRENCH IS SEEN

Algiers Committee Now Viewed as an Asset—Dropping of Italian King Held Likely

By JOHN MacCORMAC

Special to The New York Times.

WASHINGTON, Feb. 5—A reorientation of Anglo-American foreign policies that will entail closer cooperation with the French Committee of National Liberation, recognition of the hopeless unpopularity of King Victor Emmanuel of Italy and his son, Crown Prince Humbert, and continued pressure on Spain to drop all connection with the Axis is believed to be imminent.

The lack of definiteness in Anglo-American policy in regard to political situations in Europe, for which Washington and London have been criticized, has been largely caused, it is said, by military exigency. In French North Africa, in Italy and in Spain military considerations were recognized as paramount and, as a result, political action has been subject to the continuing vetos of the Combined Chiefs of Staff and the military commanders in the field.

In Italy, for instance, all political activity was prohibited until a few weeks ago by a Combined Staff directive. Since then, another directive has been issued giving the commanding general discretion to allow political meetings.

Relations with Spain have also

Continued on Page Seven

3 MORE ISLES WON

Southern Tip of Giant Kwajalein Atoll Taken After 4-Day Battle

WAKE ISLAND IS HIT AGAIN

U. S. Bombers Also Strike at Eniwetok, Jaluit and Mili in Marshalls Campaign

By GEORGE F. HORNE

By Telephone to The New York Times.

PEARL HARBOR, Feb. 5—Seventh Division Army troops have captured Kwajalein Island and two other important isles of the Kwajalein Atoll, Pacific Fleet headquarters announced today, and the most successful naval and military operation in the central Pacific campaign is nearing its final phase.

Kwajalein's defenses collapsed under the unrelenting pressure of the veterans of Attu, the amphibious troops of Maj. Gen. Charles H. Corlett's infantry division. It was struck by our fighting men last Tuesday and they have fought their way doggedly across the reef-fringed island, about two and one-half miles long, against bitter resistance.

In the first stages of the battle the enemy dead reached more than 1,000, and as the garrison was estimated to have numbered only 2,000 men, the extension of the battle through four days is a clear indication that the enemy still fights to the end when cornered.

Our Losses Are Light

Our losses continued to be moderate, it was indicated.

Ebeye and Loi were the two other islands that fell to the Americans, Admiral Chester W. Nimitz said.

[An attack by landing troops on strongly fortified Gugegwe Island, four and one-half miles north of Loi, was under way and its fall was expected soon.

[Ebeye Island is a seaplane base equipped with hangars, shops and a radio station.]

The speed with which the invasion was accomplished has surprised everyone, including the enemy, and the moderate American losses in both the Seventh Infantry

Continued on Page Twenty

GERMANS PUNCH AT OUR LINE IN ITALY

The enemy lunged fiercely at British forces on the Anzio-Nettuno beachhead, possibly between Aprilia and Campoleone or south of the German defense line between Campoleone and Cisterna. The Germans continued to say they had trapped Allied "battalions" north of Aprilia and beaten off relief tank attacks.

NEW BLOW AWAITED

Heavy Losses Inflicted on Germans Striking Back Near Rome

FOE CLINGS TO CASSINO

Americans Flank Stronghold on South—Berlin Reports Half of Town Lost

By MILTON BRACKER

By Wireless to The New York Times.

ALGIERS, Feb. 5—Like louder rumbles before the storm, the Germans continued their counter-attacks in the Allies' wedge below Rome yesterday while, sixty miles to the south, other German troops clung to Cassino despite a see-saw battle in the northeast corner, where streets and buildings changed hands many times.

[Each side holds half the town, according to a Berlin broadcast recorded by The Associated Press.

[American troops slashed southward through the mountains behind Cassino on Saturday, leaving the town three-fourths encircled, The United Press reported from the front.]

The latest German blows on the upper front were aided by tanks. But this was not believed to be the main counter-offensive, which is expected at any time and is regarded as having serious possibilities. But the British and Americans have so far proved equal to the situation.

Yesterday British troops threw back the defenders with heavy losses. Ninety more German prisoners were taken, to raise the total in this sector since the landing to 1,500 and the grand total for the campaign to more than 10,000.

Blow Struck Near Aprilia

The latest German punch was put in north of Aprilia, ten miles due north of Anzio on the main road connecting with the Appian Way. As in the previous counter-attacks north of Padiglione and near Cisterna, the exact site of the battlefield was not specified.

This was particularly puzzling today because it was known that several days ago, British spearheads had thrust four miles beyond Aprilia to cross the coastal railway at the Campoleone station and push on to Campoleone proper. The possibility was noted, therefore, that the latest German assault had been made across the road between Aprilia and Campoleone and had thus threatened to cut off the northernmost British forces.

It seemed more likely that the attack had been made somewhat east of the road and had been based on the known German defense line along the coastal electrified trackage linking the Campoleone station and Cisterna, ten miles below. This would also be northwest of Padiglione, and the theory would tend to confirm yesterday's suggestion that the present German striking forces were somewhere between the railway defenses and Padiglione.

Some of the latest prisoners in this area were identified as belonging to the German Twenty-sixth Armored Division. This made at least the third German division identified on this front. It indicates how, despite the ceaseless Allied air and naval support, the Germans have been able to provide reinforcements for the region. The Allies' air offensive, which was greatly curtailed yesterday by the weather, has recently hammered at Popoli and Avezzano, on the Pescara-Rome road along which, conceivably, the Germans would travel from the Adriatic to the Rome area.

Cassino Position Unchanged

The general picture around Cassino yesterday duplicated that of the previous day. The Americans, who have tortuously hooked their way to the back door of the town via the Gustav Line and the mountains to the north, drove ceaselessly downhill from Mount Majola to the northeastern rim of their objective.

Tanks were brought up with

Continued on Page Four

Russians Take 200 Places In 50-Mile Thrust in Poland

By RALPH PARKER

By Wireless to The New York Times.

MOSCOW, Sunday, Feb. 6—The Russians last night announced the capture of Rovno, Lutsk and Zdolbunovo, as well as 200 other places deep in Poland. At the same time, it was announced that 2,000 prisoners had been taken so far in the resumed offensive of Gen. Nikolai F. Vatutin and that remnants of the Eighteenth and Nineteenth Hungarian Divisions had been routed in battle.

[The Russians are now eighty-five miles inside Poland on an east-west line, The Associated Press announced. A fifty-mile gain from the last reported positions held by the First Ukrainian Front armies was thereby indicated.]

The Soviet announcement also stated that strong German tank attacks launched south of Shpola and west of Zvenigorod in an attempt to break out of the middle Dnieper trap had failed. It was reported that, instead, the ring had tightened on the enemy.

[Two Russian columns, following the Dnieper River and advancing toward each other from the Kanev and Cherkassy areas, effected a junction near Kreshchatik, at the northeastern section of the ring containing the trapped Nazis. The Germans hugging the Dnieper thereby lost their last foothold on the river.]

On the Leningrad front Soviet forces were clearing the eastern bank of the Narva River and advancing along Lake Peipus. Further advances on Luga from the north also were announced.

Earlier last evening Premier Joseph Stalin had announced the spectacular Red Army gains in Poland. In an order of the day the fall of Rovno, Lutsk and Zdolbunovo Junction were announced, and

Continued on Page Twelve

BIG U. S. PLANES HIT FRENCH AIRFIELDS

1,600-Ton Blow at Nazi Bases Beyond Paris Paces Attack by 2,000 Allied Craft

By JAMES MacDONALD

By Cable to The New York Times.

LONDON, Feb. 5—Powerful formations of American Flying Fortresses and Liberators escorted by large numbers of fighters—an estimated 1,200 Allied warplanes were on the mission—penetrated deep into France today. The "heavies" blasted six Nazi air bases around and beyond Paris.

This was one of the deadliest air onslaughts of the war, designed to weaken the Germans' waning power to attack.

United States Army headquarters here said among the targets hit were three bomber fields, on which were based the Heinkel 177's that launch the robot glider-bombs used recently in Nazi forays on Allied convoys. Others were fighter training bases and the big Luftwaffe repair depot at Villacoublay.

Tonight indications were that the Royal Air Force was attacking Germany—perhaps Berlin again.

Continued on Page Eleven

War News Summarized

SUNDAY, FEBRUARY 6, 1944

The German Twenty-sixth Armored Division continued to probe the perimeter of the Allied bridgehead below Rome yesterday in what Algiers believed was only the preliminary to a full-scale assault. Allied headquarters said British elements had contained the German attacks. [1:8.]

Moscow announced with a full salute of guns the capture of Rovno and Lutsk in Poland. Berlin had announced "evacuation" of the two centers two days before. The Russians said the advance was on a sixty-five-mile front and that they had liberated 200 towns and captured 2,000 Hungarian soldiers during the drive. The expanding salient put the Red armies eighty miles inside Poland and within 290 miles of the pre-war German border. To the southeast other Soviet forces continued to attack the ten German divisions caught in the middle Dnieper River pocket. The Red Air Force shot down twenty-two more Junkers transport planes, bringing the two-day bag to 106 planes. [1:6-7; map, P. 12.]

American heavy bombers based on Britain shifted their target for the day from German factories to German airfields and heavily attacked six airdromes in the vicinity of Paris. The Luftwaffe declined the issue. Only two bombers were lost. Headquarters said that three of the airfields hit were those from which German glider-launching bombers had been taking off for raids on Atlantic convoys. At least 700 of our bombers and 500 fighters were believed to have participated. While the "heavies" were hitting the Paris airfields medium bombers were ranging fighter strips and other enemy defenses along the Channel coast. [1:7.]

Other American heavy bombers, based in the Mediterranean, attacked the former French naval base at Toulon for the first time since Nov. 24. The Vichy radio said they had hit and left burning the 26,500-ton battleship Dunkerque, which the French Navy scuttled and which the Germans were reported attempting to salvage. [8:1.]

Halfway around the world, in the Marshall Islands of the central Pacific, United States combined operations cleaned out remaining Japanese resistance on three islands of Kwajalein Atoll, cutting all but eleven of the thirty coral spits in full American control. Admiral Nimitz announced at the same time that during the last three days Army and Navy planes had raided Jaluit, Mili, Eniwetok and Wake to keep immobilized any possible air retaliation from those Japanese bases against the Kwajalein operation. [1:5; map, P. 20.]

That the Japanese were becoming daily more concerned was indicated in a broadcast by Premier Tojo. He told his people the war was "increasing in ferocity" and that the nation must be even more completely mobilized than it is now "to win the decisive victory." [19:3.]

On the diplomatic front, Washington observers saw in the offing a reorientation of British-American foreign policies involving closer cooperation with the French Committee of National Liberation, a recognition of the unpopularity of the throne in Italian political circles and continued pressure on Spain to sever all Axis ties. [1:4.]

50 Shells From Freighter's Gun Fall in 2 Staten Island Villages

The quiet of the old residential villages of Grymes Hill and Ward Hill on Staten Island was shattered early yesterday afternoon by exploding shells, accidentally fired from a 20-millimeter rapid-fire anti-aircraft gun mounted on a freighter anchored in Upper New York Bay, between Tompkinsville and Stapleton.

Within two minutes more than fifty shells, unexploded and exploded, crashed into streets and yards, shattering a garage door, blasting a tree and wrecking the rear of a parked automobile. There was great excitement among the 800 residents of the villages, but the police reported that no one had been injured.

Residents said that the whine of the shells in flight and the resultant explosions resembled a miniature battle. The ship is anchored about two miles from the two villages, which are on high elevations. It was reported that fifty-six shell cases, automatically ejected after firing from the gun's mechanism, were found on the deck of the vessel. The police said they had been informed that a gunner on the vessel was removing a canvas storm cover from the gun when it was inadvertently set into action.

Several shells landed in the street near the home of Mr. and Mrs. Louis Marchi, who were at home with their two sons, Ensign John Marchi, 22 years old, and Ferdinand Marchi, 19, who soon will enter the armed forces. Mr. Marchi was ill.

"The shells as they came over

Continued on Page Twenty-seven

U. S. to Lay Oil Line in Near East; 1,200-Mile Pipe to Aid Our Forces

By JOHN H. CRIDER

Special to The New York Times.

WASHINGTON, Feb. 5—By building a pipeline about 1,200 miles across Saudi Arabia from Persian Gulf refineries to the Mediterranean at a cost of $130,000,000 to $165,000,000 the United States is going to obtain a minimum reserve of 1,000,000,000 barrels of petroleum to meet military and naval needs.

Announcement of the pipeline project was made tonight by Secretary Ickes in his capacity of President of the Petroleum Reserves Corporation.

The announcement marked the end of long negotiations between Mr. Ickes and three American oil companies which have interests in the Persian Gulf region, in which the Secretary lost out on proposals which oil company sources indicated would have carried the Government's participation in development of Arabian oil resources into the area of part ownership or control.

Under the agreement announced by Secretary Ickes between the Government and the Arabian-American Oil Company (owned by Standard Oil of California and the Texas Company) and Gulf Exploration Company (owned by the Gulf Oil Corporation), the Government undertakes to construct the pipeline.

More than the fact that this is

Continued on Page Seventeen

"All the News That's Fit to Print."

The New York Times.

LATE CITY EDITION
Rain and warmer, with fresh to strong winds.
Temperatures Yesterday—Max., 40; Min., 22
Sunrise, 7:21 A. M.; Sunset, 6:54 P. M.

Copyright, 1944, by The New York Times Company.

VOL. XCIII..No. 31,454. Entered as Second-Class Matter. Postoffice, New York, N. Y. NEW YORK, TUESDAY, MARCH 7, 1944. THREE CENTS NEW YORK CITY

800 U. S. BOMBERS SMASH AT BERLIN BY DAY; 68 LOST IN BATTLES, 123 OF FOE SHOT DOWN; SOVIET DRIVE SLASHES ODESSA-LWOW LINE

ROOSEVELT CALLS ON AFL TO ALLOW CIO A VOICE IN ILO

Green Is Told That Rival Group Must Have Delegate at Philadelphia April 20

MURRAY'S DEMAND HEEDED

President Said to Have Asked for Solution by a Method to Share Representation

By LOUIS STARK
Special to THE NEW YORK TIMES.

WASHINGTON, March 6—President Roosevelt is reported to have informed William Green, president of the American Federation of Labor, today that the Congress of Industrial Organizations will have to be represented in the top delegation at the meeting of the International Labor Office in Philadelphia on April 20.

The President took a hand to settle a question that has been a thorny one for the Administration since 1936 when the CIO, through John L. Lewis, first made a demand that it have an official workers-delegate representative at the ILO rather than be limited to a certain number of labor advisers.

The AFL view has been that the constitution of the ILO provides that the workers-delegate and the industry-delegate shall be chosen from nominations made by the "most representative" labor and industry organizations. Thus far it has been held that these organizations in the United States are respectively the AFL and the Chamber of Commerce of the United States.

AFL Asked to Change Position

Mr. Green is said to have informed Mr. Roosevelt of the federation's objection to sharing the top workers' delegation with the CIO, which it regards as a "rival, rebel organization."

In the presence of Secretary of Labor Perkins who has usually been the Administration's go-between in matters dealing with delegates to the ILO, the President is understood to have indicated to Mr. Green that a way would have to be worked out to give the CIO adequate top recognition at the ILO conference.

How definite a reply Mr. Green made to the President was not ascertained. But it was later reported that Mr. Green would probably canvass opinions of members of the federation's executive council.

In this situation the Administration is reported to be between two fires because the CIO has become strong enough to challenge the position of the AFL and to threaten retaliation by a policy of "non-cooperation" in certain labor projects of the Administration.

Demand for 'Realistic' Policy

Several months ago a State Department committee on labor standards and social security, on which the AFL and CIO were represented, drew up a report which bore upon the work of the ILO.

Philip Murray, president of the CIO, refused to sign the report, contending that if the ILO was to handle such problems in "realistic" fashion it should be sufficiently "realistic" to include a CIO delegate in its top labor group at next month's meeting.

A memorandum to that effect was formulated by J. Raymond Walsh, CIO research chief, and served on Secretary Perkins. Since then the matter of a CIO delegate had been held in abeyance.

A Western Hemisphere meeting, fostered by the ILO in Havana in 1939 had two workers-delegates from the United States, George M. Harrison of the AFL Railway Clerks and James B. Carey of the CIO.

The AFL at that time asserted that Mr. Carey's appointment had not been made in consonance with an agreement which the federation had with Secretary Perkins. She is understood to have promised that "it will not happen again."

This incident was put in the "unofficial" category, since the Havana meeting was termed an "unofficial" and not "regular" meeting of the ILO.

However, now that President Roosevelt insists on CIO recognition, the AFL may have to decide on its formula for such representation. At Havana Mr. Harrison and Mr. Carey each had a half vote. Some such method may be the present solution.

The workers-delegate from the United States on the governing body of ILO since 1936 has been Robert J. Watt. He has also been the workers-delegate at the regular ILO meetings.

May 21 Designated As New Citizens Day

Special to THE NEW YORK TIMES.

WASHINGTON, March 6—President Roosevelt, acting under authority of a Congressional resolution, issued today a proclamation designating Sunday, May 21, as "I Am an American Day," a public occasion for giving special recognition to all of our citizens who have attained their majority or have been naturalized during the past year."

The proclamation urged that exercises be held throughout the nation "to assist our citizens, both native-born and naturalized, to understand more fully the great privileges and responsibilities of citizenship in our democracy."

"Our nation," it said, "has been enriched, both spiritually and materially, by the naturalization of many thousands of foreign-born men and women and by the coming of age of great numbers of our youth, who have thereby achieved the full status of citizenship, and these citizens have strengthened our country by their services at home and on the battlefield."

SOLDIER VOTE BILL IS REVAMPED AGAIN

Conferees' Move to Allow Some Use of Federal Ballot Here Stirs Mixed Opposition

By C. P. TRUSSELL
Special to THE NEW YORK TIMES.

WASHINGTON, March 6—The long contested service men's voting legislation ran into new troubles today when Senate and House conferees, meeting to give final approval to the "States' Rights" course adopted last week, decided instead to permit use of the Administration-endorsed Federal short) ballot in the United States under some circumstances.

By an undisclosed vote, the conferees adopted a provision under which service personnel from States having no absentee balloting laws, whether stationed in this country or overseas, could use the short ballot, provided the Governors of the States made two certifications by July 15.

First, the Governors would be required to certify that their States had made no provision for absentee balloting, and then that the use of the Federal ballot had been authorized by State law.

Previously the conferees had voted to prohibit the use of the short ballot by service personnel stationed in continental United States. Today's action was taken in the interest of citizens of Kentucky and New Mexico, and of South Carolina if its Legislature, now in session, fails to provide an absentee voting measure.

Mixed Opposition Encountered

The proposed relaxation of Federal ballot bans, the first since the conferees began tightening up the legislation, provoked adverse reactions, not only among the conferees themselves, but in the House, where the Eastland-Rankin bill, providing only for the use of State ballots, was adopted last month by the "stand-up-and-be-counted" vote for which President Roosevelt had asked.

Complaints were registered by backers of the Federal ballot as well as by those who wanted no relaxation at all. Representative Eugene Worley of Texas, head of the House conferees and himself the author of a Federal ballot plan, joined the dissenters.

Contending that the move on behalf of Kentucky and New Mexico was discriminatory, Mr. Worley in-

Continued on Page Thirty-four

Rebuilt U. S. Tanker Yugoslav Flagship

By The Associated Press.

MALTA, March 6—The American tanker Ohio was taken over today by the Yugoslav Navy as headquarters ship after a thorough overhauling.

The Ohio's battered hulk arrived in Malta in August, 1942, her cargo of oil intact, after being heavily attacked while crossing the Mediterranean in a convoy.

[The Ohio was built in 1940 at Chester, Pa., for the Texas Oil Company. The 9,624-ton vessel is 488 feet long and carried a crew of forty-three.]

CAIRO, Egypt, March 6 (Reuter)—Two Ministers of the Royal Yugoslav Government have been sent to London. This is regarded in the Middle East as the first move in important developments with regard to the Yugoslav émigré Government.

CAPITAL HOPEFUL OF AMERICAS' UNITY

Resolution Opposing Recognition of Argentine Regime Voted by Uruguay Chamber

Special to THE NEW YORK TIMES.

WASHINGTON, March 6—Hopes are held here that Uruguay and Paraguay will withhold recognition from the Farrell government in Argentina and that Chile will be found to have been the only Government to break the inter-American bloc by extending recognition in the present status of affairs.

Both countries were still watched closely today for signs indicating the course they would follow. Eyes also were focused on Brazil, not because of any special reports but apparently in the feeling that, if she extended recognition in the face of the refusal of the United States to do so, American solidarity would definitely be cracked.

[The Uruguayan Chamber of Deputies on Monday approved a motion suggesting that Uruguay not recognize the present Argentine Government. The United Press reported from Montevideo. The resolution termed the Farrell regime pro-fascist.]

Chile's Ties Understood

There is understanding here why Chile took her step, in view of her close relations with Argentina. But if the movement spread to other countries the diplomatic situation in this hemisphere would be altered. There were informal predictions that in this event the efficacy of the good-neighbor policy might be called into question.

There were hopes not only that Chile would be the only American Government, apart from the revolutionary junta in Bolivia, to recognize Argentina as matters stand but that the effect of her action might be softened by her using her influence in Buenos Aires to have Argentina carry out the measures urged by the United States.

It was apparent that hopes were being maintained that Argentina would straighten affairs satisfactorily to us. It was felt the Government might do so voluntarily. If it is not disposed to do so, there are elements in Argentina that

Continued on Page Eleven

ENEMY IS ISOLATED

20-Mile Breach Severs Foe's Direct Supply Route to Ukraine

TARNOPOL HUB MENACED

Red Army 11 Miles From Goal —Additional Soviet Attack Reported Farther East

By W. H. LAWRENCE
By Wireless to THE NEW YORK TIMES.

MOSCOW, Tuesday, March 7—The Soviet High Command announced last night that Marshal Gregory K. Zhukoff's troops of the First Ukrainian Front had smashed across the vital Odessa-Lwow railway and occupied a twenty-mile stretch of it between Proskurov and Tarnopol. The Russian communiqué said that preliminary reports of the first two days of this offensive had resulted in the death of more than 15,000 German officers and soldiers and the destruction or capture of large amounts of enemy material.

The most important news contained in the communiqué was that of the Red Army's severance of the Nazis double-track supply line by the capture of Volochisk. Voltovtsy, fifteen miles east of Volochisk, and Narkevichi, eighteen miles west of Proskurov, also were captured.

The loss of this railroad on such a wide front presents a grave danger for the German troops remaining in the southern and western Ukraine, for it was the main line connecting them directly with Poland and Germany—and it was on that railroad that they had relied in large part for their supplies.

Because of their disaster they must fall back on lesser and indirect railroads that lead across the southern Ukraine into Bessarabia. They could, of course, be supplied or leave Russia by highway, but by any military standard such a method is inferior to the use of a good main-line railroad.

Red Army men moving on Tarnopol, well inside the western Ukraine and seventy-five miles east of Lwow, were doing their part to dismember the German communications system. The capture of Zbarazh, eleven miles northeast of Tarnopol, reveals that they have cleared the Shepetovka-

Continued on Page Eight

BACK FROM OUR FIRST ATTACK ON BERLIN

Pilots of Mustang fighters discussing their experiences after returning to their base in England on Saturday. Left to right: Lieuts. Carl G. Bickel, Alhambra, Calif.; Charles Koenig, Oakland, Calif.; Felix W. Rogers, West Newton, Mass., and James P. Keane, Penllyn, Pa.

The New York Times (U. S. Signal Corps Radiotelephoto)

ITALIAN CAMPAIGN SAPS FOE IN WEST

Germans Forced to Use Crack Anti-Invasion Troops and Drain Reserve Pool

By C. L. SULZBERGER
By Wireless to THE NEW YORK TIMES.

WITH THE FIFTH ARMY, in Italy, March 6—Although the Allies' campaign in Italy has clearly been disappointing and negative in its results, from the short-range viewpoint, in the effort to expand the Anzio beachhead, and simultaneously to penetrate the Liri Valley, effecting an eventual junction, it is necessary to view certain positive accomplishments in terms of the broad strategic picture.

This secondary front is indubitably aiding both the Russian advances and the western invasion preparations by forcing the Germans to commit some of their best divisions and drain their shrunken reserves on the virtual eve of a climactic spring. Thus, as the Germans are devoting perhaps 50 per cent of their war production efforts to the imminent invasion and have left only perhaps 18 per

Continued on Page Six

U. S. Troops Go Into Action In Burma, Trap 2,000 of Foe

By The Associated Press.

NEW DELHI, India, March 6—American infantry units, in action for the first time on the Asiatic continent, have opened an attack in northern Burma under the direction of Lieut. Gen. Joseph W. Stilwell, who swore he would get even with the Japanese for the "hell of a beating" they gave him two years ago.

Veterans of the jungles of Guadalcanal and the southwest Pacific, scoring their first success in the drive to open a short-cut to China's Burma Road, have marched 200 miles through the thick bush and struck the enemy a surprise blow from the rear, a communiqué from General Stilwell's headquarters announced.

Using an American adaptation of the roadblock—a tactic used by the Japanese in Burma two years ago and a trick that General Stilwell never forgot—the Americans planted themselves squarely across the Japanese line of retreat from Maingkwan, chief village of the Hukawng Valley.

Chinese Press From North

About 2,000 of the enemy were believed cut off by the American column that marched 117 miles from their railhead in northeast India, then struck eastward, then southward and eastward again and came out on the Walawbum Trail.

General Stilwell's Chinese troops, who have been pushing the Japanese back steadily for nearly two months in the Hukawng Valley, pressed in from the north, taking Maingkwan, while the Americans took Walawbum, ten miles southeast of Maingkwan.

Another strong force of Chinese moved to within ten miles of closing the encirclement by capturing a point to the northeast of Maingkwan, completing mopping-up operations at Wagahtawng, surrounding an enemy force at Lashu Ga and advancing southward.

The Americans were about seventy miles northwest of Myitkytina, the northern end of the railroad from Mandalay and 110 miles west of the Salween River, which in gen-

Continued on Page Two

AMERICANS JUMP NEARER TO MADANG

Amphibious Force Lands 30 Miles Above Saidor—Our Troops Gain in Admiralties

By FRANK L. KLUCKHOHN
By Wireless to THE NEW YORK TIMES.

ALLIED HEADQUARTERS IN THE SOUTHWEST PACIFIC, Tuesday, March 7—Troops of the dismounted First Cavalry Division pushed northward on the narrow peninsula of Los Negros Island in the Admiralties under Japanese artillery fire, and a small American amphibious force landed behind the enemy lines at Yaula Plantation, thirty miles northwest of Saidor on the New Guinea coast, Gen. Douglas MacArthur stated today.

Motor torpedo boats, instead of destroyers, along with bombers paved the way for the United States forces that leap-frogged the Japanese above Saidor in the Allied drive toward Madang. American patrols had already reached Herwarth Point, twenty miles above Saidor.

The landing at Yaula Plantation was a replica of the preceding larger landings in every sense. Royal Australian Air Force Kittyhawks and Bostons unloaded their explosives, while the PT boats kept up a constant fire as the infantrymen hit the beaches, following a preliminary shelling of enemy shore artillery. The Americans stormed ashore Sunday morning.

On Los Negros, in the Admiral-

Continued on Page Two

AIR WAR AT PEAK

Fortresses, Liberators Loose 2,000 Tons on German Capital

FIGHTERS SWARM ON NAZIS

Three-Hour Combat Over the Reich Gives Major Victory Against Luftwaffe

By DREW MIDDLETON
By Cable to THE NEW YORK TIMES.

LONDON, Tuesday, March 7—The war in the air reached a new and perhaps decisive phase yesterday when about 800 American heavy bombers fought their way through the massed strength of the Germans' metropolitan air force to blast factories, airfields and other military installations in the Berlin area.

The air battles that raged around and within the tight, wedge-shaped formations of Flying Fortresses and Liberators were the greatest in history, with American fighters, hundreds of which accompanied the bombers, and the "heavies" engaged throughout the mission.

Preliminary reports on the American victories said that eighty-three Nazi fighters were knocked down by the Mustangs, Thunderbolts and Lightnings of the United States Eighth and Ninth Air Forces and Royal Air Force that escorted and supported the big bombers.

The total of enemy fighters destroyed by the bombers had not yet been tabulated, but the gunners of one division alone of our "heavies" destroyed at least forty Nazi planes, boosting the minimum number of enemy aircraft shot down to 123.

Bombing Is Effective

In addition to these heavy losses to the Nazi fighter force, already suffering from the effects of two weeks of the Allies' heavy day and night attacks over the Reich, returning pilots reported "first rate" bombing results in the Berlin district.

[Probably more than 2,000 tons of bombs were dropped on Berlin's vital industrial and military targets, The Associated Press reported.]

American losses in the big blow at the Nazi capital were serious. Sixty-eight heavy bombers and eleven fighters were missing—representing a loss of nearly 700 trained airmen—Lieut. Gen. Carl A. Spaatz's Strategic Air Forces headquarters here reported.

The German radio claimed that 129 American planes had been shot down.

Last night RAF bombers continued the offensive. The British Air Ministry said in a first report only that the planes, which flew out soon after dusk, had struck in enemy-occupied territory.

The Nazi radio station at Frankfort on the Main, carrying out the new German warning system, said during the evening that "enemy planes are circling over our town." About the same time Hanover was heard saying that "enemy aircraft are on their flight back."

Stockholm reported telephone service to and through Berlin cut off, possibly by a direct American bomb hit on the Berlin exchange.

Berlin Vulnerable Day and Night

Talks with high American officers here last night made it clear that the air war had entered a new stage, one in which Berlin is vulnerable to day as well as night attacks—and in which those German factories that the RAF's mass bombing by night has missed will be attacked repeatedly by daylight precision bombing until they too are eliminated from the enemy's war industry.

The attack, which was not the biggest daylight air operation of the war, was by far the heaviest daylight attack on Berlin. The hundreds of tons of bombs loosed by the United States planes started pillars of smoke climbing skyward.

"Bombs were seen to fall on assigned targets," said General Spaatz's communiqué; but many of the missiles were loosed through a heavy overcast.

The air battles began as soon as

Continued on Page Four

War News Summarized

TUESDAY, MARCH 7, 1944

The United States Army Air Forces went all out against Berlin for the first time yesterday. Some 800 Flying Fortresses and Liberators, escorted by hundreds of fighters, fought their way through massed enemy air defenses to the Reich's capital for the heaviest daylight attack Berlin had ever suffered. First-rate results were reported by the bombardiers who had aimed at factories and other military targets.

The bombing attack involved fighting the greatest air battle in history almost from the coastline to Berlin and back. The enemy charged into our tight formations, losing eighty-three planes verified, at least thirty-five probably destroyed and seventeen damaged. These losses were inflicted by our fighters alone. The bombers' score was not completed, but one division reported having knocked out at least forty enemy fighters. Sixty-eight of our bombers and eleven fighters failed to return. [All the foregoing 1:8.]

Yesterday's attack was believed to mark the start of literal round-the-clock bombing of Berlin and the rest of the Reich. The Allies have set out to destroy the German Air Force in the shortest possible time, shooting down planes already built and blasting factories to prevent their replacement. [4:1.] Strategic bombing, having now reached its height, can be expected to demonstrate in the near future whether air power alone is more effective than when used in tactical cooperation with ground forces. [4:4.]

The Nazis continued to take a terrific beating on the Russian front also. The Odessa-Lwow railroad was cut along a twenty-mile stretch, imperiling a vast German force in the lower Ukraine now dependent upon inadequate communications for supplies and for retreat. More than 200 places were captured by the Russians. [1:4; maps, P. 8.]

Finland was warned by the Communist newspaper Pravda that if she mistook the "generosity" of Moscow's peace proposal for weakness she would be "bitterly disillusioned." Delay in replying to the offer was creating doubt of Finland's good faith, Pravda said. [8:1.]

The slow pace of Allied progress in Italy was reported compensated by the long-range gain in tying up so many of Hitler's best divisions. [1:5.] Rain put a virtual halt to military operations, but it was revealed that it had cost the Germans 24,000 casualties to try vainly to crack the Anzio beachhead. [7:1.]

The United States Army went into action for the first time on the Continent of Asia when it captured Walawbum, southeast of Maingkwan, in an encircling movement in Burma's Hukawng Valley. With American-trained Chinese troops they were closing a trap around 2,000 Japanese in that area. [1:6-7; map P. 2.]

General MacArthur "leap-frogged" a small force up the New Guinea coast to seize Yaula Plantation, behind the Japanese lines near Madang. Progress was being made in the Admiralties against shelling from four-inch naval guns on six neighboring islands. [1:7.]

County Chiefs Shun Transit Issue; Windels Makes Pleas for Action

The proposed 10-cent fare on the city-owned transit lines remained a political orphan yesterday, despite Mayor La Guardia's best efforts in his Sunday broadcast to have it adopted by the four county leaders, who, he said, "control the two major parties."

Edward J. Flynn, Democratic leader in the Bronx, commenting on the Mayor's assertion that the Legislature in Albany and the City Council would "take the nod" from the four leaders, would say only:

"As far as I know, I'm neither a member of the Legislature nor of the City Council."

Thomas J. Curran, Republican leader of Manhattan, said tersely: "I have no comment."

John E. Crews, Republican leader of Brooklyn, recalled that he had voted against higher-fare legislation back in 1921 and indicated he intended to be consistent.

Frank V. Kelly, Democratic leader of Brooklyn, the fourth named by the Mayor, is on his way home from the South.

But an appeal was made to the four leaders to declare a political armistice and meet the controversial issue on its merits. In making this plea in an open letter to the leaders, Paul Windels, chairman of the newly created Citizens Transit Committee, pictured the Mayor as being unwilling to take a forthright stand on the higher fare without the support of the other political leaders. Mr. Windels also heads the Committee of Fifteen that sponsored the bill now pending in the Legislature for a Transit Authority in the city under mandate to collect a self-sustaining fare not to exceed ten cents. His letter follows:

"I am writing to you as the re-

Continued on Page Thirty-four

U. S. Sent 28,000 Planes to Allies And Kept 122,000 in Three Years

Special to THE NEW YORK TIMES.

WASHINGTON, March 6—The United States has sent almost 28,000 airplanes to the growing air forces of its Allies, together with $1,600,000,000 worth of aircraft engines and parts, since lend-lease began three years ago, Leo T. Crowley, Foreign Economic Administrator, disclosed today.

The country has done this, he said, while creating the greatest army and naval air forces for itself. Since March, 1941, the United States has produced 150,000 aircraft, of which 122,000 have been retained for its own use. This is a production achievement, Mr. Crowley commented, that will not "be of any aid or comfort to our enemies."

The administrator explained that 21,000 of the planes shipped or ferried abroad were sent under lend-lease provisions. The other 7,000 were paid for in cash, principally by the British.

A total of 7,800 planes went to the Soviet Union, 4,000 to Allied forces in the Pacific and Far East theatres, and more than 16,000 to all other combat and training areas abroad.

Three-fourths of the planes have been combat types, and one-fourth trainer and transport planes. There have been 9,800 four-engine, two-engine and single-engine bombers sent across, and 10,700 single-engine and two-engine fighter planes. Four thousand of the aircraft have been naval planes.

"The British and the Russians produce, themselves, most of the planes they are using in this war," said Mr. Crowley. "But American lend-lease planes, with British,

Continued on Page Five

"All the News That's Fit to Print."

The New York Times.

LATE CITY EDITION
Fair and warmer; cloudy late in day.
Temperatures Yesterday—Max., 33; Min., 20
Sunrise, 7:15 A. M.; Sunset, 6:58 P. M.

Copyright, 1944, by The New York Times Company.

VOL. XCIII. No. 31,458. Entered as Second-Class Matter, Postoffice, New York, N. Y. NEW YORK, SATURDAY, MARCH 11, 1944. THREE CENTS NEW YORK CITY

IRISH REFUSE TO OUST AXIS ENVOYS, DENYING THEY SPY ON OUR TROOPS; RUSSIANS BREAK 110-MILE FRONT

PROGRESSIVE GROUP IN EDUCATION TAKES NEW NAME, POLICY

Now the American Education Fellowship, It Will Center on Community, Not Child

SEEKS WIDER MEMBERSHIP

Opposition Leader Describes Shift as 'Surrender' to Traditional Teaching

By BENJAMIN FINE

By a membership vote of nearly ten to one, the Progressive Education Association, for the last twenty-five years the spearhead for the progressive movement in the American school field, has adopted a new program and changed its name to the American Education Fellowship, it was learned yesterday.

At the same time, the association has dropped its monthly publication, Frontiers of Democracy, edited by Dr. Harold Rugg of Teachers College, and is now considering a substitute name for its official journal, the magazine Progressive Education. Later this month the board of directors of the fellowship will meet to decide on a substitute name for this publication, although it is known that some members wish to retain the present title.

In a statement of policy sent to all members, the association outlined "a new program for new times." The base of the organization has now been broadened, and parents, interested lay citizens and youths from 17 to 22 will be admitted to membership.

Board to Be Reconstituted

Under the plan of reorganization, the association will pay greater attention to the community and less to the child itself. The board of directors is to be reconstituted and at least four vacancies are to be filled at once by representative leaders of the community—such as a parent, business man, farmer and a member of organized labor. The aim will be to build a board "as cross-sectional of American interests as possible," but with teachers and other educators strongly represented.

"Whereas the earlier period of progressive education was marked by strong concern for the interests and capacities of the individual child, and with group activities largely within the school itself," the new program explained, "the period which we are now entering should be marked by a more intimate and fruitful relationship with parents, interested groups, adult education—in short, with all aspects of the community which surround the child and curriculum, and which largely determine whether the schools are or are not to function as people's schools."

Credited With Strong Influence

Founded in 1919, the Progressive Education Association, through its regional and national conferences, its publications and studies, has been in the forefront in trying to get "progressive" principles adopted in the classrooms of this country. Its journal has served as a sounding board for many ideas and deliberations in this area. The organization, in a sense, built its philosophy around the doctrines of John Dewey, its honorary president.

Frequently attacked, the association has been credited with exerting a strong influence on American schools despite its rather small roll of active members. It has numbered around 10,000, although since the war began the membership has dropped to 7,000.

Continued on Page Sixteen

Tax Form Baffles Even Prof. Einstein

By The Associated Press.

PRINCETON, N. J., March 10—Prof. Albert Einstein, world famous mathematician and wizard of the fourth dimension, said tonight that he like millions of ordinary Americans who are mulling through complex income tax forms, had to call in a tax expert to help him prepare for the March 15 deadline.

Asked what his reaction was to the maze of income tax questions, Professor Einstein, whose theory of relativity is supposedly understood by only seven persons in the world, replied:

"This is a question too difficult for a mathematician. It should be asked of a philosopher."

WPB STEMS INFLOW OF CANE BEVERAGES

Issues Quota Order to Obtain More Molasses for War Alcohol—Protests Arise

Special to The New York Times.

WASHINGTON, March 10—All imports of alcoholic beverages derived from cane sugar will be reduced by an order issued today by the War Production Board putting them under strict quotas beginning March 15.

The order, designed to "prevent further excessive diversion to beverages of molasses vital to war-essential alcohol production," affects imports from Mexico, Cuba and other Latin countries as well as from Puerto Rico and the Virgin Islands.

After obtaining data from the trade on imports for each calendar quarter from 1940 to date, the WPB will assign the quotas under the order which, it said, "follows directly upon the recently concluded negotiations with Cuba." It added:

"However, the Cuban agreement permits the island's exports of beverage liquor to the United States to equal the high record figure of 14,300,000 proof gallons exported to the United States in 1943 and it is anticipated that quotas assigned to other foreign countries will be worked out on much the same basis."

Hearing Set by House Group

With this basis indicated by an expected reduction of cane beverage imports from Cuba exceeding 50 per cent, the order had immediate repercussions in the trade and in Congress.

Importers asserted that the WPB had exceeded its authority by interfering with treaties and talked of a court test. In reply, spokesmen for the WPB maintained that it had ample authority and disclosed that before acting it had consulted the State Department and the Foreign Economic Administration.

An insular affairs subcommittee of the House set Monday to hear representatives of the WPB, the Foreign Economic Administration and the State Department on the matter.

The committee was said to be particularly interested in the molasses and industrial alcohol agreement with Cuba recently negotiated by a committee headed by Sidney Scheuer, representing the FEA.

Mr. Scheuer was understood to have told the Cubans that in exchange for limiting Cuba beverage alcohol imports into the United States to 14,300,000 proof gallons for 1944, this Government would undertake to limit shipments from Puerto Rico, the Virgin Islands and Mexico to 1943 levels this year.

Producers in Puerto Rico have complained to the committee that the order of the WPB was issued to make good on Mr. Scheuer's promises to the Cubans. They

Continued on Page Twenty-eight

M'ARTHUR, STASSEN CAN BE NOMINATED UNDER NEW RULING

But a Regular Officer Must Not Himself Seek to Be Picked by a Party, Army and Navy Say

ROOSEVELT TELLS OF PACT

Reserves Can File as Candidates but All in Service Are Barred From Campaigning

By CHARLES HURD

Special to The New York Times.

WASHINGTON, March 10—Regular officers of the armed services can accept such nominations for political office as come to them without solicitation by themselves, according to an interpretation of regulations announced today by President Roosevelt. This means that Gen. Douglas MacArthur would be eligible to run for the Presidency if selected by a convention, but would not be able to authorize the use of his name on primary ballots or in any pre-convention activity.

In contrast to this ruling on regular officers, reserve officers will be permitted to file as candidates in the pre-convention period. Lieut. Comdr. Harold Stassen, former Governor of Minnesota and also prominently mentioned for a Presidential nomination, is General MacArthur's counterpart in this category.

The interpretations were made public by the President in a statement embodying a joint Army and Navy agreement signed by Secretary Stimson and Secretary Knox.

In actual practice political observers here believe that the distinction between regular and reserve officers is without much importance.

Restrictions on Campaigning

General MacArthur's sponsors have been championing his candidacy without public word from the general and Commander Stassen has consistently refused to take an active part on his own behalf.

Otherwise these two possible candidates for the Presidency, and any other officers who might be named for similar or subsidiary positions, are under the same restrictions. None may take time out from military duties to devote to politics and none may perform duties to which he may be elected while he remains on active service. Neither can the officers make speeches or conduct election campaigns while on active duty.

If elected to office, national or State, any officer will be retired or honorably discharged, according to the type and length of his service.

The position of regular officers is set by a law which specifically prohibits any such officer from holding any type of elective or appointive public office in civilian life while performing military duties. The Army-Navy agreement added:

"A member of the regular components of the land or naval forces, while on active duty, may accept a nomination for public office, provided such nomination is tendered without direct or indirect activity or solicitation on his part. He may then file such evidence of his candidacy as is required by local law."

This was taken to mean that if the Republican National Convention should nominate General MacArthur he could then comply with formalities necessary to put his name on State ballots.

Since reserve officers have essentially a civilian status, it was ruled that these, "while on active duty may become candidates for

Continued on Page Nine

THIRD DRIVE OPENS

Red Army Wins Major Stronghold of Uman in 44-Mile Advance

HUGE NAZI FORCE ROUTED

20,000 Germans Die and 300 Villages Fall—Two Other Ukraine Pushes Gain

By W. H. LAWRENCE

By Wireless to The New York Times.

MOSCOW, Saturday, March 11—The Soviet High Command last night announced a smashing new offensive on the Second Ukranian front, where Marshal Ivan S. Koneff's men in a five-day battle were reported to have inflicted a heavy defeat on fourteen German divisions, killing 20,000 Germans, capturing 2,500 prisoners and seizing large amounts of material while advancing twenty-five to forty-four miles on a 110-mile front.

Marshal Koneff's army, which had paused only briefly to regroup forces after completing the liquidation of the ten encircled German divisions in the Dnieper bend, drew a salute of twenty salvos from 244 Moscow guns tonight in celebrating its capture of the important towns of Uman and Khristinovka, as well as more than 300 inhabited points.

With the Second Army again on the move, the Germans' hard-pressed forces remaining in the southern Ukraine are being smashed back toward the Black Sea and Rumania by three Russian separate armies, all of which are reported to be making remarkable progress despite an early spring thaw that is producing deep mud on the flat steppes.

Tarnopol Fighting Continues

Marshal Gregory Zhukoff's First Ukrainian Army was reported last night to be continuing its street fighting in Tarnopol, as well as moving on Proskorov and smashing German communications centers north of Vinnitsa.

Gen. Rodion Y. Malinovsky's Third Ukrainian Army, whose offensive was announced Thursday night, continued to advance today, taking Novgorodka and Bashtanka, as well as more than 150 other inhabited points, inflicting large losses of men and material upon the retreating Germans.

The biggest news, of course, was the resumption of Marshal Koneff's

Continued on Page Five

A NEW RUSSIAN BREAK-THROUGH IN THE SOUTH

The Red Army advanced nine miles closer to Nikolayev by capturing Dobroye (1) and also took Baratovka (2). In a smashing new drive along a 110-mile front extending from Kapustino (3) to Monastyrishche (5) it overran an area (shown by striping) reaching as far south as Kamenechye and Kocherzhintsy (4) and captured the important bases of Uman and Khristinovka. In the drive toward Vinnitsa the Russians seized Yanov and Khmelnik (6). In the Proskurov area Gorbasov and Krasilov (7) were taken. Street fighting continued inside Tarnopol (8).

FOE REPORTS ALLIES ON DALMATIAN ISLE

1,500 British, U. S. Commandos Under 'Gen. Churchill' Struck at Lissa, Berlin Says

By The Associated Press.

LONDON, March 10—The Berlin radio said today that 1,500 British and American "commandos"—"under the command of General Churchill"—had landed on the tiny Adriatic island of Lissa and that other raids on the Dalmatian coast and near-by islands might be expected.

The German reference to a "British general with the name of Churchill" suggested it might be Capt. Randolph Churchill, 32-year-old son of Prime Minister Churchill, who was recently reported to have parachuted into Yugoslavia to confer with Marshal Tito (Josip Broz).

British sources said they had no information about the reported landing or whether the raiders were led by Captain Churchill. There has been no official an-

Continued on Page Seven

Talasea Airfield Captured By Marines in New Britain

By The Associated Press.

ALLIED HEADQUARTERS IN THE SOUTHWEST PACIFIC, Saturday, March 11—United States marines captured Talasea airdrome Wednesday and then wheeled north to occupy the township the following day, thus cutting in two the Willaumez Peninsula of north New Britain, which they invaded only last Monday.

Headquarters reported the victories today. The successes firmly implanted Gen. Douglas MacArthur's forces more than 100 miles east of their Cape Gloucester holdings and within 170 miles of bomb-ravaged Rabaul.

No details were available concerning the final fight for the airstrip and town, but a spokesman said enemy reaction, which had developed several hours after units of the First Marine Division gained its beachhead Monday, reached its peak of intensity Tuesday.

The leathernecks, who landed on the peninsula's west coast opposite Talasea, cleared a path through land mines and pushed across the five-mile-wide peninsula.

Trap Set Up on Peninsula

The occupation of Talasea trapped any Japanese caught on the northern tip of the narrow land strip, which sticks up like a thumb from the northern coast.

[Japanese troops broke through American barbed-wire entanglements on the northern perimeter of our positions on Bougainville and captured several pillboxes. Their artillery shelled two American air strips, but the air strips were still in use, according to word from the area.]

In the invaded Admiralty Islands to the north of the New Britain action, troops of the dismounted First Cavalry Division have pushed their steadily expanding lines three and a half miles northwest of captured Momote airdrome on Los Negros. Japanese planes strafed the sector without effect.

In still another action on the borders of the Bismarck Sea, Amer-

Continued on Page Three

DUBLIN MOBILIZES, SEEING ULTIMATUM

Border, Ports, Airfields Are Guarded—Politics Suspected in de Valera's Reaction

By JAMES B. RESTON

By Cable to The New York Times.

LONDON, March 10—The Irish Government not only rejected the United States request that German and Japanese diplomatic missions be closed but chose to interpret the State Department's note as an ultimatum and immediately took military precautions against an Anglo-American invasion of southern Ireland.

All leaves in the Irish Army were canceled immediately after David Gray, United States Minister in Dublin, presented the State Department's protest, special guards were placed over airfields, ports and other strategic positions; bridges leading from Ulster into southern Ireland were mined and the Irish local defense volunteers were mobilized and armed.

It is understood that despite Mr. Gray's statements the State Department's note meant just what it said and did not imply a threat to take over the Irish ports or to "invade" the country, Mr. de Valera took all precautions and cabled immediately to his Minister in Washington for reassurances that the note was not an

Continued on Page Four

U. S. DEMANDS BAN

Charges Eire Is a Base for Espionage That Imperils Our Army

NOTE BACKED BY BRITAIN

De Valera Replies That Close Watch Is Kept—Use of Nazi Radio Denied

Our note and the Irish Government's reply are on Page 4.

By BERTRAM D. HULEN

Special to The New York Times.

WASHINGTON, March 10—An appeal by the United States for the Irish Government to remove German and Japanese consular and diplomatic representatives from the country because of their espionage activities, coupled with a hope that this would be followed by Ireland's severing diplomatic relations with the Axis, has been rejected by Prime Minister Eamon de Valera.

The American request was based on the contention that there were espionage activities that constituted a danger to the lives of American soldiers and to the success of the Allied military operations.

Mr. de Valera replied at once orally and later formally that it was "impossible" to comply with the request. To do so, he declared, would mean the first step toward war and a betrayal of Ireland and her neutrality. There was no basis to the charges, he declared.

Britain Supports Our Action

Britain supported the American action which was in the form of a note delivered by David Gray, the American Minister in Dublin, on Feb. 21. We stressed that the Axis representatives through their official position had been able to gather important military information and transmit it by radio to Germany.

The note was made public by the State Department tonight, and the Irish Legation then gave out the reply of Prime Minister de Valera, which was dated March 7.

Mr. de Valera contended that the American charges were "out of harmony" with the facts and that his Government was doing everything possible to prevent espionage.

[An official spokesman in Dublin said early Saturday morning that neither the German nor Japanese envoys here has a diplomatic mail pouch and that neither has a way of communicating with his country except by cable, which passes through London.]

"Should American lives be lost," he said, "it will not be through any indifference or neglect of its duty on the part of this State."

He promised that Ireland would continue to safeguard the interests of the United States.

Objects to "Grave" Note

Pleading for friendship, he nevertheless considered our note of "so grave" a character that it should never have been sent.

What action the United States and Britain will now consider taking to impress upon Eire the seriousness of the situation was not indicated here.

President Roosevelt was asked at his press conference what could be done by Ireland to help the United Nations.

"What an if question!" he exclaimed, and dismissed the subject.

However, Mr. de Valera in his note referred to a personal message he had received from Mr. Roosevelt on Feb. 26, 1942, to the effect that we would never invade Ireland and said Mr. Gray had now repeated it to him. This was reinforced by renewed assurances on Feb. 29 that no military or other measures were being contemplated because of his refusal to comply with our request.

Axis Spying Is Stressed

The note delivered by Mr. Gray declared flatly that it had been demonstrated "over and over again" that Axis representatives in neutral countries had used their

Continued on Page Four

War News Summarized

SATURDAY, MARCH 11, 1944

The New York-born Prime Minister of Eire, Eamon de Valera, has categorically refused the United States Government's request that he close the German and Japanese Ministries in Dublin, it was announced in Washington yesterday. In a written confirmation of a verbal "no" given when the request was made on Feb. 21, Mr. de Valera denied Axis officials were successfully transmitting military intelligence on Allied ship and troop movements, and declared the Eire Government was well able to keep espionage under control and was determined to maintain its present neutral status. [1:8.]

When the American note was delivered, it was reported in London, the Irish interpreted it as an ultimatum and took military steps to contest any violation of their sovereignty by United States or British forces, increasing the border guard and placing special details at all airports and seaports. [1:7.]

Against this diplomatic setback, the day brought news of a new Russian drive in the Ukraine that portended a climactic battle in the Russian-German war. The new drive of the Red armies, under way for five days, Moscow announced, is in the center of what now is a 500-mile-long battleline. To the northwest the troops of Marshal Zhukoff were still fighting in the streets of Tarnopol. To the southeast the armies of General Malinovsky were pressing on in the Dnieper Bend toward the Black Sea ports of Nikolayev and Kherson. The action in the center, under Marshal Koneff, had for its first major prize the Nazi stronghold of Uman. [1:4.]

With the United States Air Force in Britain earthbound and a night attack by RAF heavy bombers on an airplane plant near Marseille the only major air activity of the last twenty-four hours [6:1], the Mediterranean arm of Allied air might swung into action with another attack on the railroad yards of Rome. On land, in Italy, two sharp but small-scale attacks on the Anzio beachhead were hurled back. [1:6-7.]

On the eastern side of the Adriatic, the sea separating Italy from the Balkans, a combined British-American force landed on the island of Lissa, twenty-five miles below the Yugoslav port of Spalato, the Berlin radio announced. The Germans said the troops were under the command of "General Churchill." [1:5, map, P. 7.]

The marines who landed Monday on the Willaumez Peninsula of New Britain took the Talasea airport Wednesday and the town Thursday, General MacArthur announced, giving the Allied forces in the southwest Pacific a second air base within 150 miles of the Japanese base at Rabaul. [1:6-7; map, P. 3.]

Lieut. Gen. Joseph Stilwell's Chinese - American forces in Burma continued to make progress in their campaign to oust the Japanese from the Hukawng Valley on the flank of the Ledo Road to China. [3:1.]

Our Bombs Rip Rome Rail Yards, Blow Up Warehouses and Cars

By The Associated Press.

ALLIED HEADQUARTERS, Naples, March 10—Fighter-escorted American medium bombers attacked railroad yards in Rome again today, and heavy damage was reported. On the Anzio beachhead the Germans made two localized attacks yesterday.

[The Nazi-controlled Rome radio, telling of Friday's bombing, said "a large number of houses were hit, and it is feared casualties are high." The broadcast made the claim, unsupported in Allied announcements, that two of the raiders crashed in flames near the outskirts of the city. The Swiss radio, meanwhile, quoted the German commander of Rome as saying that Rome was considered an open city and had no anti-aircraft guns.

[Thursday night Royal Air Force bombers based in Britain bombed a factory at Marignane, near Marseille, that has been constructing six-engined flying boats and converting French planes into troop carriers.]

The Tiburtina yards in Rome's eastern suburbs were hit by Marauders escorted by American-piloted Spitfires, and rolling stock and warehouses were declared blown up.

Thunderbolt-escorted Mitchells struck the Littorio yards on the northern limits of the city, which were bombed last Tuesday.

Photographs indicated that the main rail line from Rome to Florence, down which the Germans have been sending supplies to

Continued on Page Seven

First Lady Guessing On Fourth Term, Too

By Wireless to The New York Times.

SAN JUAN, P. R., March 10—Asked at a press conference today whether the President would run for a fourth term, Mrs. Franklin D. Roosevelt said:

"It's something I know nothing about, although no one ever believes it. I've never asked the President. I believe a man's family has no right to influence such a decision. Circumstances at the time control the decision, and probably the President himself does not know what he is going to do."

She held the press conference after a day in which she visited Army and Navy bases and inspected several stations for the distribution of milk for children.

20 School Annexes to Be Closed By La Guardia to Save $1,345,000

Mayor La Guardia announced yesterday that he would close the twenty annexes in the academic high schools termed "unnecessary" in a survey earlier this week prepared by Manhattan Councilman Stanley M. Isaacs and Theodore Fred Kuper, former law secretary of the Board of Education. By closing the annexes, the Mayor said, the city would need 31 fewer teachers at a saving of $1,345,000.

In discussing the Legislature's failure to take a definite stand thus far on restoring the cut in State aid, amounting to $4,500,000 for this city, the Mayor declared that closing of the annexes would go a "long way" toward making up the deficiency in school funds. He also indicated that some of the vocational annexes would be closed, but did not know the number until the board's report on the subject was completed.

The question of whether the twenty academic and twenty-four vocational annexes could be closed was raised in the Isaacs-Kuper study. Figures were cited showing that most of the annexes, especially in the academic division, could be discontinued with a saving in maintenance costs and an improvement in facilities.

"Have you anything to say on the Legislature's apparent decision not to increase State aid to schools?" Mayor La Guardia was asked.

"The problem is solved for us," the Mayor answered. "We don't have to worry about this any more. I'm taking the recommendation of the National Education Associa-

Continued on Page Twenty-eight

"All the News That's Fit to Print."

The New York Times.

LATE CITY EDITION
Increasing cloudiness, and somewhat warmer.
Temperatures Yesterday—Max., 43; Min., 25
Sunrise, 6:57 A. M.; Sunset, 7:10 P. M.

Copyright, 1944, by The New York Times Company.

VOL. XCIII...No. 31,469. Entered as Second-Class Matter, Postoffice, New York, N. Y. NEW YORK, WEDNESDAY, MARCH 22, 1944. THREE CENTS NEW YORK CITY

MARINES ON ISLE 600 MILES FROM TRUK; RUSSIANS 28 MILES FROM THE PRUT RIVER; NAZIS SHIFT TROOPS TO DOMINATE HUNGARY

SAYS WHITE HOUSE SILENCED REDMAN ON FCC 'BUNGLING'

Rep. L. E. Miller Asserts Rear Admiral Drew Fire for His Data to House Group

PERIL TO NAVY FORCE TOLD

Missourian Declares Threat of Demotion Was Used—Fly Charges 'Innuendoes'

Special to The New York Times.

WASHINGTON, March 21—Representative Louis E. Miller, Republican, of Missouri, declared today that because of "bungling" by the Federal Communications Commission a Navy task force in Alaskan waters was ordered out on a fruitless mission, in the course of which a man was disabled, and that for disclosing the fact to the Special House Committee investigating the FCC demotion was recommended of Rear Admiral Joseph R. Redman, director of naval communications, and representative of the Navy Department on the Board of War Communications.

Mr. Miller's statement, made at today's hearing by the committee, identified, for the first time, Admiral Redman as one of the naval officers upon whom, together with Rear Admiral Stanford C. Hooper, now retired, T. A. M. Craven, FCC Commissioner, testified last December that "reprisals" were visited for opposition to the policies of James Fly, chairman of the commission, and of the War Communications Board.

That Admiral Hooper was one of the two officers referred to by Commissioner Craven, who gave the names to the committee in executive session, was revealed last Dec. 10 by Representative Clinton Anderson, Democrat, of New Mexico.

"Disciplinary Action" Was Urged

It was reported at the time, but not officially confirmed, that "disciplinary action" had been recommended but not taken, in the case of Admiral Redman for supplying information to the committee, as had Admiral Hooper, before the Presidential order forbidding cooperation with it by officers of the Army and Navy.

The matter was brought up at today's hearing of Charles Denny, FCC counsel, when the witness was asked by Representative Miller to "furnish a copy of the letter written by an Under-Secretary of the Navy in reference to the demotion of Admiral Redman."

Mr. Denny said that he had no knowledge of such a letter, and Mr. Miller outlined its "factual background" as follows:

"Admiral Redman had testified before the staff of this committee. He had given certain testimony regarding Pearl Harbor and regarding an accident that had occurred to the task force operating in Alaskan waters. After this testimony was given by Admiral Redman, a copy of his statement was requested by the White House. After the contents had been learned, Mr. Fly read, in the presence of Commissioner Craven, a letter presumably from the White House in which it was stated that certain things might happen to Commissioner Craven and others who testified in secret before the committee investigating the FCC. A copy of this alleged letter or note from the White House was shown to Commissioner Craven."

Would Produce a Letter

Mr. Miller added that if the Navy Department would relax its rules and permit him to do so he would produce the letter, and Mr. Denny replied that he wished he would, because he would "love to know the date when this task force is supposed to have gotten into difficulties because of information given by the FCC."

Mr. Miller suggested that he get in touch with Admiral Hooper, who could tell him "what task force it was, where it was, and what happened as a result of the bungling of the FCC."

Mr. Denny protested that the charge was a "terribly serious" one, of which there "is no evidence whatever," to which Representative Miller retorted sharply:

"Of course there is no evidence, because Admiral Hooper has been silenced by executive order. You know that and I know that and everybody here knows that."

Mr. Denny entered a 'categorical denial' of the incident, declaring that when he was informed as to "when it is supposed to have happened" it would be "affirmatively disproved."

"You mean you propose to af-

Continued on Page Thirteen

President Kept In By Another Cold

Special to The New York Times.

WASHINGTON, March 21—President Roosevelt was confined to his quarters today with a head cold, but was reported to have no fever.

The President was sneezing and restless during the night, according to Stephen T. Early, his press secretary. Mr. Early said that Vice Admiral Ross T. McIntire, the President's physician, treated him for a head cold and ordered all appointments canceled for the day. Thus the usual Tuesday press conference was not held. Admiral McIntire later described Mr. Roosevelt's condition as definitely improved.

The President earlier this year had grippe, from which he was reported slow to recover. He lost ten pounds from that illness, it was said.

WILLKIE CONDEMNS ISOLATIONIST VIEWS

He Tells Wisconsin Voters That if Republicans Campaign on Them Roosevelt Will Win

By JAMES A. HAGERTY
Special to The New York Times.

GREEN BAY, Wis., March 21—With more vehemence than he had previously shown in his Wisconsin campaign, Wendell L. Willkie hit today at his rivals for the Republican Presidential nomination. He charged avoiding discussion of issues, denounced a campaign of defamation against him, stuck firmly to his position for cooperation of the United States with other nations to maintain peace after the war, and declared that, if isolationists of the school of thought represented by The Chicago Tribune prevailed at the national convention and adopted a platform and named the candidate, Franklin D. Roosevelt would continue to be President for at least another four years.

Emphasizing the importance of the election of delegates pledged to him in the Wisconsin primary, Mr. Willkie struck directly at his rivals in this primary, Governor Thomas E. Dewey of New York, Lieut. Comdr. Harold E. Stassen of Minnesota, and Gen. Douglas MacArthur. Informed of Commander Stassen's message to Secretary Knox, that he was not an active candidate for the Presidential nomination but would accept if nominated, Mr. Willkie said:

"It is difficult to know from the announcement whether Governor Stassen is a candidate or not. As I have emphasized in this campaign in Wisconsin, the only way our system can function is through public discussion. The primary in Wisconsin is for the purpose of providing the people of Wisconsin with a method of making a choice after they have heard a discussion of the issues.

Discussion or Withdrawal

"Obviously those who seek the preference of the voters of Wisconsin should discuss the issues with them or, if they have rendered themselves unable to do so, then it occurs to me that they should decisively, not ambiguously, withdraw from the contest.

"All the men for whom delegates are running in Wisconsin can say in very simple and unambiguous language that they do or do not desire the voters of Wisconsin to vote for the delegates pledged to their respective candidacies."

Before his comment on the Stassen message, which in effect called upon Messrs. Dewey, Stassen and MacArthur to tell the Wisconsin voters how they stood on issues or withdraw, Mr. Willkie in a speech to the students and Navy trainees of Lawrence College in the college

Continued on Page Thirty-six

BALKAN UNITS MOVE

3 Divisions From Serbia Sent to Crush Forces Resisting in Hungary

SOUTH GRIPPED BY CHAOS

Liberation Units Seen Merging —March on Rumania and Action in Sofia Reported

By DANIEL T. BRIGHAM
By Telephone to The New York Times.

BERNE, Switzerland, March 21—Overwhelmed by developments for thirty-six hours in which German forces seized most of the key objectives in the occupation of Hungary, internal resistance in that country since early this morning has coalesced into what may develop into an "Army of Liberation," information from the Balkans indicated tonight.

[German troops were reported Wednesday to have taken over vital communication facilities in Sofia and Nazi armored columns were said to be moving swiftly on Bucharest, indicating that both Bulgaria and Rumania might soon share the fate of Hungary, The Associated Press said.

[The United Nations radio in Algiers said Tuesday that the Budapest radio had gone off the air after announcing an air raid.

[Broadcasting from the Hungarian capital was interrupted a second time some time later, United States Government monitors reported.]

Bucharest Lines Restored

With Budapest communications still severed, most of the information received in Berne tonight came via Bucharest, with which communications were re-established this morning.

Eyewitnesses who had eluded German patrols along the Transylvanian frontier told of "complete chaos" throughout southern Hungary, where isolated forces appear to have refused to accept orders from the regime supposedly set up by the pro-Nazi Bela Imredy, and in at least two large garrison towns they have successfully resisted all German efforts to disarm them.

So serious does the potential military reaction appear that this afternoon the command of all German occupation operations was given to Field Marshal Baron Maximilian von Weichs, who is reported proceeding toward Budapest with at least three Elite divisions of Balkan fighters from northeastern Serbia, where they had been re-formed after a fierce encounter with the forces of Marshal Tito [Josip Broz] about a fortnight ago.

Their progress is expected to be slow, since railway communications have been attacked by sapper units of the regular Hungarian Army.

Field Marshal Franz Szombathelyi, Hungarian Chief of Staff, erroneously reported as arrested by the Germans, is now known to have accepted responsibility for the defense of the Carpathian region, whither he had proceeded as early as March 13 to take charge of what is believed to be nearly an

Continued on Page Twelve

NAZI RAIL LINK CUT

Red Army Drives Wedge Into Retreat Route Near Rumania

HOLD ON DNIESTER GROWS

310 Places Fall in 6 Sectors— Two More Strong Points Imperiled by Advance

By W. H. LAWRENCE
By Wireless to The New York Times.

MOSCOW, Wednesday, March 22—The Red Army, capturing more than 310 inhabited points in its sustained advance in six sectors on the southern Soviet-German front, was reported last night to have cut the Beltsy-Cernauti railway, fifteen miles beyond the Dniester at its Mogilev-Podolski crossing and the only rail line leading directly to Germany from central Bessarabia.

[The point at which the rail line was cut, in the vicinity of Drokiya, is only twenty-eight miles from the Prut River border of Rumania, where German and Rumanian forces launched the southern wing of the invasion of Russia in June, 1941.]

While the western thrust for Lwow and parallel drives for the Black Sea ports from Novoukrainka and Bobrinets continued to make progress, the most important news was that Soviet forces had made another successful crossing of the Dniester in the region of Mogilev-Podolski, which was taken two days ago, and had widened their bridgehead on the right bank until the forces cut across the railway.

Germans Forced to Detour

Loss of this railway severely hampers the Germans. It forces an important detour for railmoved supplies and reinforcements from Germany and the satellite states destined for the southern Ukrainian troops. They now must be diverted through Jassy, which is inside Rumania.

In the Bessarabian area, despite increasing German resistance, including greater use of the Luftwaffe, the Russians said, their troops took the district center of Ataki and more than forty other inhabited points.

The drive for Lwow southwestward from Dubno netted fifty pop-

Continued on Page Eleven

ALLIED RING FORGED IN BISMARCK ARCHIPELAGO

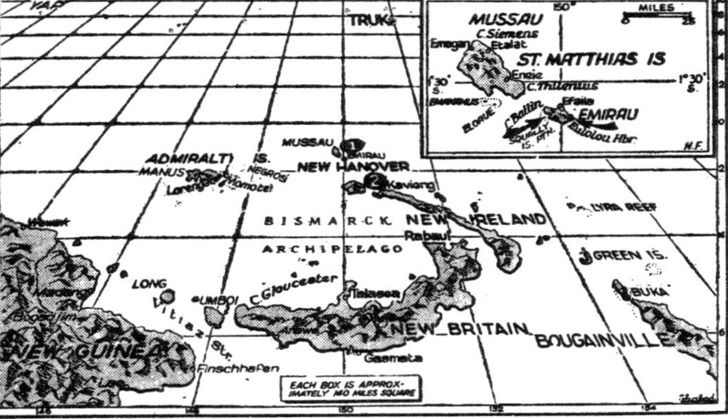

United States marines have landed on Emirau Island (1), a favorable site for air and naval bases, and have thus effectively cut off Japanese troops to the south and placed our forces within 600 miles of Truk (top of map). The marines went ashore at the east end of the island and over reefs at the southwestern corner (inset). At the same time the enemy base at Kavieng (2) was in part leveled by a three-and-a-half-hour bombardment by our battleships.

BY-PASS KAVIENG

U. S. Forces Meet Feeble Opposition in Moving on Emirau Isle

BATTLESHIPS IN ACTION

Pour 1,000 Tons of Shells Into Kavieng, Japanese Base on New Ireland

By FRANK L. KLUCKHOHN
By Wireless to The New York Times.

ALLIED HEADQUARTERS IN THE SOUTHWEST PACIFIC, Wednesday, March 22—With planes strafing the beaches before them, United States Marines landed on Emirau Island, potential air and sea base less than 600 miles from Truk, and quickly overran the Japanese scattered, supportive opposition. Eiomusso, an islet half mile offshore, was also occupied.

Coincidentally, American battleships leveled parts of the enemy's New Ireland stronghold at Kavieng, seventy-five miles to the southeast, with a terrific three-and-one-half-hour bombardment. The battleships hurled 1,000 tons of shells into Kavieng in perhaps the heaviest shelling of the war on a point at which we did not intend to land. The enemy's shore batteries started to bark as the "battlewagons" moved close inshore, but our big guns quickly silenced them.

The twofold operation was carried out early Monday under Gen. Douglas MacArthur's strategic direction by Admiral William F. Halsey Jr. with important elements of the United States Fleet, including cruisers and destroyers as well as battleships.

Entrapment of Japanese forces remaining in the Bismarcks and the Solomons is now complete. We hold the Admiralties to the east of the blockaded enemy on New Guinea and northwest of New Britain, the Solomons to the south, the Green Islands to the southeast and the seizure of Emirau puts a stopper in the northern end.

Marines Land Easily

This correspondent watched the mighty armada from the air as it stretched out over the sea on its way to deal the Japanese another heavy blow. Once again our forces landed where the Japanese were not present in force, the marines going in easily on the beach at the eastern end of the eight-miles-by-five island and in amphibious tracked landing craft over the reef at the southwest end of Emirau.

Kavieng, where the enemy has a considerable force, as well as Rabaul, even farther south, were bypassed, a result of their virtual isolation even before this move by General MacArthur's surprise capture of the Admiralties. However, the sixteen-inch guns of the big gray battleships, pounding hour after hour, eliminated the so-called "Chinese quarter" of Kavieng and further advanced the destruction of gun emplacements, ammunition dumps and other installations already severely punished by the South Pacific Air Force. Our ships suffered no losses.

When the marines dashed through the surf surrounding the green, dagger-shaped island housing a Japanese radio station they knew they were closer to the enemy's central Pacific base of Truk than any other Americans. While Emirau is probably too far from Truk for bombers to hit with fighter escort, its seizure tightens the net around the bastion and permits two-way bombing as we already hold Eniwetok to the east.

Solomons Heroes Participate

Among the landing troops were raider battalions which had already made history in retaking the Solomons. They were commanded by Brig. Gen. Alfred H. Noble of the Marine Corps. Commodore Lawrence F. Reifsneider commanded the amphibious task force.

Just north of Emirau lies Mussau Island, the largest of the St. Matthias group. Schadel Bay there has been consistently used by Japanese float planes and was employed by German South Seas raiders in the last war.

In the landing party were picked

Continued on Page Two

Finland Rejects Armistice; Russia Warns of Dire Fate

By The Associated Press.

LONDON, March 21—Finland announced the rejection of the Russian armistice terms today and a few hours later an official Soviet statement broadcast from Moscow declared that the refusal placed full responsibility for the consequences on the Finnish Government. Together the two declarations indicated a complete and final breakdown in peace negotiations.

[The texts of the Finnish and Russian statements are on Page 10.]

The Moscow statement was brief, outlining tersely the order and substance of the notes exchanged by the two Governments leading up to Finland's rejection of Russia's six-point proposal.

"By this action it [the regime of Premier Edwin Linkomies] has taken upon itself full responsibility for what will follow," said the statement, recorded by the Soviet monitor.

The statement was signed by the Information Bureau of the People's Commissariat for Foreign Affairs of the U.S.S.R.

It pointed out that Finland's first answer to the offer of peace, made public March 1, had been a reply that the Soviet terms were difficult to accept.

The Soviet Government informed

Continued on Page Ten

ALLIES' BIG ATTACK IN CASSINO BOGGED

Momentum of Assault Cracks as Germans Reoccupy Wreckage of Hotel

By C. L. SULZBERGER
By Wireless to The New York Times.

WITH THE FIFTH ARMY AT CASSINO, March 21—The Allies' third major attack on Cassino appeared today to have bogged down temporarily after seven days of sharp and continuous fighting.

The initial momentum gained by New Zealand and Indian troops after the unprecedented aerial bombing and the terrific artillery barrage of March 15 that enabled them to occupy virtually all the leveled town has ground to an apparent standstill for the moment. New German reserves, including armored grenadiers, have moved into the line supporting the First Parachute Division and the Germans probably have about nine combat battalions well dug in in strong points around the town and south of it, as well as on the rugged hill topped by the battered Abbey of Mount Cassino.

During the past forty-eight hours the positions have been relatively static. There has been reshuffling on both sides, although a considerable exchange of fire by all arms continues by night and day.

Last night and today the initiative appeared to have been fairly evenly distributed. It is evident that the Allies will have to put their shoulders to the wheel once again and dislodge the enemy from

Continued on Page Thirteen

WORLD UNITY URGED BY HULL AS OUR AIM

He Says Our Foreign Policy Requires Cooperation of All Under Atlantic Charter

The text of Secretary Hull's statement is on Page 12.

By BERTRAM D. HULEN
Special to The New York Times.

WASHINGTON, March 21—The foreign policy of the United States was defined by Secretary of State Cordell Hull tonight in terms of our fundamental national interests and our responsibility for cooperating with other nations in a statement issued through the State Department.

The announcement was in the form of a summarization of basic points of the policy as defined by Mr. Hull in public addresses and pronouncements over the past two years. It amounted to a restatement of policy.

It was preliminary to a radio address further developing the subject, which Mr. Hull said he was now preparing with the view of delivering it soon. He was not able, however, as yet to set the date for his radio address.

In all this he explained that he was taking notice of the growing interest in foreign policy manifested in the United States and an increasing number of requests for information on the subject.

Congress' Interest Increases

That interest has also been manifested in a growing demand in Congress for a more definite exposition of our foreign policy by the Administration, including requests for enlightenment from Republican members who have supported the Administration's foreign policy in the past.

Mr. Hull indicated that he would deal with the Atlantic Charter in his address. Asked at his press conference whether the principles of the charter still prevailed and whether they could be reconciled with the realities of a world or

Continued on Page Twelve

War News Summarized

WEDNESDAY, MARCH 22, 1944

United States Marines landed early Monday (Australian time) on Emirau Island in the St. Matthias group, eighty-four miles northwest of the major Japanese base of Kavieng, on New Ireland, and less than 600 miles from Truk, General MacArthur's headquarters announced. Little opposition was met. In a diversionary action, battleships of the Pacific Fleet pounded Kavieng with 1,000 tons of shells. [1:8.]

One of the explanations for the American advances in the Pacific was given in an announcement in Washington that United States submarines had sunk fifteen more Japanese vessels, one of them a large transport, and a communiqué from London that British submarines had sunk seven more. [3:1.]

In Burma the Japanese still were advancing "in force" toward the Indian frontier through the Kabaw Valley. Part of the enemy force was the so-called Indian National Army recruited by the Indian renegade Subhas Chandra Bose. [2:2; map, P. 2.]

The Russian armies drove on across Bessarabia to cut the last north-south railway in German hands. They stood yesterday, Moscow said, within twenty-eight miles of the Prut River, pre-war boundary of Rumania. "The battle of the south has been won," declared the official army organ, Red Star. [1:4; map, 11.]

The news from Hungary was still somewhat confused and came via Rumania and other sources. What was certain was that the Germans had marched in, perhaps as many as 100,000 of them. The Hungarian Commander in Chief, Marshal Szombathelyi, was said to have taken a stand in the mountains with loyal troops and to be resisting, or preparing to resist. [1:3.]

The developments in Hungary were said to have created a great impression in Finland, but they did not change the position of the Government, which officially announced it had rejected the Russian armistice terms. A Moscow statement warned the Finns they now must take the consequences. [1:5-6.]

The Battle of Cassino settled down to a stalemate with the Germans infiltrating back around the town and still firmly holding the approaches to the Liri Valley gateway to Rome. [1:6.]

Germany had a respite from air attack during the day, but her army did not as Liberators bombed the Pas-de-Calais area and Mustang fighters made a 450-mile sweep across Nazi airdromes in France. Seven fighters but no bombers were lost. [6:1.]

Secretary Hull announced in Washington that he was working on a speech that would clarify the United States foreign policy which, he said in his statement, basically, was a protection of national interests and international cooperation. [1:7.]

The Army announced that General Patton, who had slapped a shell-shocked soldier during the Sicilian campaign, had been replaced as head of the Seventh Army by Maj. Gen. A. M. Patch, from the South Pacific, but had received another command. [1:6-7.]

Eric Johnston Accepts Stalin Bid To Visit and Study Soviet Russia

By JOHN H. CRIDER
Special to The New York Times.

WASHINGTON, March 21—Eric A. Johnston, president of the Chamber of Commerce of the United States, has accepted an invitation from Premier Stalin to visit Soviet Russia. Tentative plans call for his leaving about May 12 and returning to the United States June 20.

Mr. Johnston, an outspoken proponent of the American free enterprise system, accepted the invitation so he could have a look at how the Soviet system operates from the point of view of an American business man.

It can be taken for granted, according to persons close to the chamber president, that he will be as blunt in his statements to the Soviet people as he was in talking to the British when he visited England last summer.

Mr. Johnston's view regarding Soviet Russia has been that Americans must recognize that it has a different economic system but American business men welcome the competition of any other systems and are confident theirs can out-produce them. He also has stated that while we underestimated Russia's economic and military strength before the war we must not underestimate it after the war.

Characteristic of Mr. Johnston's outspoken approach to the prob-

Continued on Page Ten

Patton Shifted to New Command As Patch Heads the Seventh Army

By The Associated Press.

NAPLES, March 21—Lieut. Gen. George S. Patton Jr., known in the field as "Old Blood and Guts," has been replaced by Maj. Gen. Alexander M. Patch, a veteran of the Pacific fighting, as commander of the American Seventh Army, headquarters announced today.

[In Washington the War Department announced that General Patton had been put in command of "another army," but Army officials declined to identify the unit or reveal his present whereabouts. It was assumed that his new assignment was connected with plans for the invasion of western Europe.]

While several units formerly with the Seventh Army have been assigned to the Fifth Army in Italy, the whereabouts of the Seventh Army has not been disclosed. It has been the subject of considerable guesswork by the Germans, who at one time reported that it had gone to sea.

General Patton led the Seventh Army to victory in Sicily. His forces took Messina, the last Sicilian city captured. Later he received wide publicity over an incident involving the slapping of an American soldier in a field hospital near Palermo.

He was rebuked by Gen. Dwight D. Eisenhower, and he apologized to the officers and men of the Seventh Army. His nickname is derived from his explosive temperament, which finds him contemptuous of his personal safety in the heat of battle. He is also known

Continued on Page Thirteen

"All the News That's Fit to Print."

The New York Times.

LATE CITY EDITION
Partly cloudy and warmer today; gentle to moderate winds.
Temperatures Yesterday—Max., 56; Min., 41
Sunrise, 6:52 A. M.; Sunset, 7:13 P. M.

VOL. XCIII..No. 31,472. Entered as Second-Class Matter, Postoffice, New York, N. Y. NEW YORK, SATURDAY, MARCH 25, 1944. THREE CENTS NEW YORK CITY

RUSSIANS REACH BUKOVINA BORDER; REICH CITIES AND LONDON BOMBED; CHURCHILL PLEDGES INVASION SOON

NEWS SUPPRESSION BY ADMINISTRATION CHARGED BY DEWEY

Governor Says Capital Seems Embarked on a 'Deliberate and Dangerous' Policy

PARATROOP LOSS IS CITED

Effort to 'Discredit' Congress Seen in Attacks on Its Attitude Toward Peace

The text of Governor Dewey's address is on Page 10.

Asserting that much important news from abroad has been released only after it leaked out and became the subject of widespread gossip, Governor Dewey charged last night that the Roosevelt Administration seemed to have embarked on "a deliberate and dangerous policy of suppression of news at home."

Citing the loss of twenty-three transport planes and 410 American paratroopers in Sicily, which became known eight months after it occurred, and the limited extent to which the public was informed of what happened at Teheran, the Governor declared:

"One such incident might be charged to blunder; two such incidents begin to lay the unpleasant suspicion of Administration policy."

Governor Dewey, widely mentioned for the Republican Presidential nomination, though he disavows such ambition, delivered his sharpest thrust at Administration policy in a s..ks as he awarded prizes at the ninth annual exhibit of the Press Photographers Association of New York at the Museum of Science and Industry in Rockefeller Center.

Signs of Curbs on News

In the speech, which ran for fifteen minutes and was broadcast over a nation-wide hook-up from Station WEAF, the Governor declared a free press had kept Americans "the best informed people in the world," but he said there have been "increasing signs of late that our newspapers are being denied the right to print all the news."

"Only now do we learn, because it leaked out," he said, "of the shooting down of twenty-three transport planes and the killing of 410 American paratroopers in Sicily eight months ago. Even after a Presidential broadcast we still know precisely nothing of what really happened at the much-heralded conference in Teheran. We only know of the disquieting evidences of disunity which have since occurred, in the Pravda attacks on the British and the Vatican, followed by the startling repercussions brought out by the President's announcement of the three-way division of the Italian fleet."

Admitting the need for military censorship to keep such news as troop movements from the enemy, Governor Dewey said the events of which he spoke "have not been suppressed to keep information from the enemy so much as to keep them from our own people."

"When we find the State Department requesting the British censor to suppress political news sent to American papers by American correspondents abroad, it begins to amount to a deliberate policy of suppression of the news at home," he said.

"Being Constantly Surprised"

"Despite millions of dollars spent on War Information Service, we are constantly being surprised. Often we learn of important events through the pronouncements of foreign statesmen or by reading dispatches cabled back to this country from foreign papers. After making all due allowances for wartime conditions, it still remains that we know far too little about our own foreign policies and practically nothing about our diplomatic commitments."

Hailing the cooperation of the American press in accepting "voluntary censorship," Governor Dewey asserted that the "stakes in this war are too high for it to be fought in the dark."

"There seems to be too little recognition," he said, "of the fact that free people cannot fight a war with blinders on their eyes. Knowing the present dangers and the hardships ahead, they will brace themselves to any task. They will sacrifice as deeply as the welfare of the nation demands. They can do neither if they are not told where they are going and why. Our people can take the bad news with the good, but they have a right to know the facts. We need a free,

Continued on Page Ten

Soldier Vote Action Is Set for Midweek

Special to The New York Times.

WASHINGTON, March 24—President Roosevelt said today that he would wait until the middle of next week to act on the Soldier Vote Bill. He has until midnight of next Friday to approve it, veto it or let it become law without his signature.

When he said that there would probably be something on the bill by midweek, a reporter asked whether it would be a message. The President replied, hesitating, that perhaps it ought to be called a statement.

Some observers construed this to mean that he might let the bill become law with an explanatory statement, because if it were to be vetoed there would be a message.

Only a veto message would be expected just before the deadline for action. In any event, the President's remark at his press conference appeared to be offhand.

RULING BY WALLACE ANGERS SENATORS

McKellar Denounces 'Legislative Trick' Phrase—TVA Curbed, Agencies Doomed

By C. P. TRUSSELL
Special to The New York Times.

WASHINGTON, March 24—The Senate, after a week's controversy, passed the $8,000,000,000 Independent Offices Appropriations bill this evening and sent it back to the House loaded with provisions forced into it in one of this year's bitterest political floor fights.

The clashes over the bill reached a climax this afternoon with a row centering about Vice President Wallace's ruling against a proposal from the floor which he suggested would amount to "a legislative trick."

His phrase angered Senator Kenneth McKellar of Tennessee, who denounced the statement as "damnable," it being made during consideration of the admissibility of Mr. McKellar's amendment to put the Tennessee Valley Authority under tight Congressional control.

Senator Bennett C. Clark of Missouri backed the Tennessean, asking whether the Vice President could "flagrantly and brazenly" disregard the rules of the Senate by so ruling.

Ruling Is Overridden

The Vice President, asserting that he meant no reflection on the Tennessee Senator, said that he would be "happy" to withdraw his statement. Then, by a vote of 46 to 17, the Senate overrode Mr. Wallace's ruling.

With attention focused on the President's Fair Employment Practices Committee, the Senate voted for the abolition of all Presidentially created agencies which have functioned for a year unless Congress makes specific appropriations to maintain them.

This was done after a Republican-sponsored amendment, exempting the FEPC from the restrictions of the amendment offered by Senator Richard B. Russell of Georgia had been adopted, reconsidered and then killed.

Victories for McKellar

Without debate, the Senate approved the amendment of Senator McKellar under which all officials and employes of the Government in executive departments and agencies who receive $4,500 or more a year would have to be confirmed by the Senate.

A Republican-sponsored motion to reconsider this action was voted down, 31 to 23.

By a vote of 39 to 26, the Senate

Continued on Page Nine

NEW DRAFT ORDERS SPEED CALL TO MEN WHO ARE NOT YET 26

Status of Older Registrants Will Not Be Changed Until the Younger Are Screened

WMC ACTS ON VITAL SKILLS

War Agency Committee Headed by McNutt to Apportion All Deferments of Experts

By CHARLES E. EGAN
Special to The New York Times.

WASHINGTON, March 24—Five major rules which must be followed by State Directors of Selective Service in inducting men in the age group under 26 were sent out ton.ht by Gen. Lewis B. Hershey, Director of Selective Service.

The regulations, which followed conferences among war agency heads, the Army, Navy and Selective Service, represent their solution of the difficult problem presented by the necessity of filling the forces' needs for young men without disrupting war activities. The services intend to build their strength to 11,300,000 by July 1. The total now is at 10,600,000.

Earlier in the day the War Manpower Commission set up a special committee under the chairmanship of Paul V. McNutt, chairman of the WMC, which will screen and submit to Selective Service recommendations for special deferments of irreplaceable men in approved war activities and plants.

The "claimant agencies" which will be represented on the new committee include the production executive committee of the War Production Board, spokesman for war-production activities; the Petroleum Administrator for War, Solid Fuels Administration, the Rubber Director, Office of Defense Transportation, the War Food Administration, Maritime Commission, the War Shipping Administration and the armed services.

Agencies Will Submit Requests

The requests of these agencies for deferments must be in the committee's hands by Monday and, after screening by the committee, will be sent to Selective Service directors in the various States in the form of quotas. Decisions on deferments for individuals are to be made in the States within the quotas assigned.

The five provisions outlined by General Hershey included instructions to give first attention to those up to 26 in reviews and reconsideration of draft deferments before taking up cases of registrants in the age group of 26 to 37 years.

The detailed instructions were as follows:

(1) The War Department, Navy Department, the Maritime Commission, War Production Board, Office of Defense Transportation, War Food Administration, War Shipping Administration, Petroleum Administrator for War, Solid Fuels Administration, and the Office of the Rubber Director are authorized to designate representatives in each State to endorse special requests for deferment of key registrants under the age of 26 in war activities other than agriculture, and employed in establishments coming within their jurisdiction.

(2) State Directors of Selective Service are directed to issue orders to report for pre-induction physical examination by the armed forces to all registrants under the age of 26 who are occupationally deferred in Class 2-A, that is, those deferred for work in support of the war effort; and in 2-B those

Continued on Page Eight

Drinks Go Up 2 to 4 Cents April 1; Tax Adds Cent for Glass of Beer

Special to The New York Times.

WASHINGTON, March 24—Higher excise taxes effective April 1 will add 2 to 4 cents to the price of liquor or sparkling wine and 1 cent to the cost of an eight-ounce glass of beer, ale, porter or stout, the Office of Price Administration stated today.

Allowable increases for straight or mixed drinks as made public by the OPA are:

Drinks containing not less than half an ounce and not more than an ounce of distilled spirits of 80 proof or more, 2 cents; more than an ounce but less than 1¾ ounces, 3 cents; 1¾ ounces or more, 4 cents.

Drinks containing one ounce or more of distilled spirits of less than 80 proof, 2 cents.

Drinks of 2½ ounces or more of still wines containing more than 14 per cent but not over 21 per cent of alcohol, 1 cent.

Drinks of 3 ounces or more of champagne, sparkling wine, carbonated wines or wine-based cordials, 3 cents.

The new excise rates increase the tax on distilled spirits from $6 to $9 a gallon while the tax on beer jumps from $7 to $8 a barrel.

Wine with less than 14 per cent of alcohol will be taxed 15 cents per gallon under the new law, compared to 10 cents now. Wine containing from 14 to 21 per cent of alcohol is to be taxed 60 cents per gallon as against the old rate of 40 cents.

Sparkling wine, now taxed at 10 cents a half pint, will be taxed at 15 cents a half pint and all other wines at 10 cents a half pint, double the prevailing scale.

BERLIN IS HIT AGAIN

RAF Blow Follows U. S. Attack on Frankfort and Schweinfurt

FRENCH AIRFIELDS BOMBED

Few Enemy Fighters Are Seen on Day After Americans Felled 61 Nazi Planes

By GENE CURRIVAN
By Wireless to The New York Times.

LONDON, Saturday, March 25—Establishing a new United States Air Force record for attacks against Hitler's Continental fortress, Flying Fortresses and Liberators blasted away yesterday at the Reich and other European points for the nineteenth time this month.

The Royal Air Force followed up the American attack with a heavy blow on Berlin last night, a British communiqué announced. A force that required an hour to pass an East Coast town went over the Reich, with the capital as the principal objective.

[A broadcast of the German news agency DNB said Leipzig, transport and heavy industry center, ninety-three miles southsouthwest of Berlin, and Weimar, 145 miles southwest of Berlin, also had been bombed, The United Press reported.]

[Describing the attack on the Reich capital, the Berlin radio said high explosives and fire bombs blanketed all Berlin.]

While the RAF was over Berlin, a sizable number of German bombers rained high explosives and incendiary bombs on London for more than an hour.

A number of fires were burning in the British capital long after the "all-clear" signal.

American targets in Germany yesterday were Schweinfurt, where the much-damaged ball bearing plant was pounded again and Frankfort on the Main aircraft and distribution center, still burning after Wednesday's 3,360-ton bombardment.

German Air Base Hit

At the same time the Liberators swept through heavy flak but little other opposition to bomb fighter bases at Nancy and St. Dizier in northeast France. In another branch of this general operation 100 Thunderbolts strafed and attacked the airfield at Bernay St. Martin thirty-five miles from Havre. Machine-gun fire and

Continued on Page Five

ALLIED LEADERS INSPECT U. S. SOLDIERS IN ENGLAND

Prime Minister Churchill and General Dwight D. Eisenhower reviewing paratroopers
Associated Press Radiophoto, passed yesterday by censor

ROOSEVELT WARNS GERMANS ON JEWS

Says All Guilty Must Pay for Atrocities and Asks People to Assist Refugees

The President's statement on aid to refugees, Page 4.

By JOHN H. CRIDER
Special to The New York Times.

WASHINGTON, March 24—President Roosevelt took the unusual step today of appealing to the German people, as well as the peoples of all subjugated Europe, to do all in their power to assist the escape of Jews and other victims of Nazi persecution. With particular reference to the Jews who escaped to Hungary and the Balkans from Germany, he declared it would be a "major tragedy" if they should "perish on the very eve of triumph over the barbarism which their persecution symbolizes."

[Secretary of State Cordell Hull, on Friday, called upon Hungary to rise against the Nazis. He declared that resistance to the German invader was the only way for the Hungarians to regain the respect and friendship of the free nations of the world.]

The President said his statement

Continued on Page Four

War News Summarized

SATURDAY, MARCH 25, 1944

A new catastrophe appeared to be in the making for the German Armies in the Tarnopol-Proskurov region at the northwestern end of the Ukrainian front yesterday as the Red Armies that had broken through the Nazi lines above and below Tarnopol drove on to the Dniester on the south and across the Sereth River to the north to sever most of the escape routes. Far to the south and east other Russian forces took the Bug River strong point of Voznesensk. [1:8; map, P. 2.]

Hitler continued to pour reserves into the Balkans in an apparent effort to set up a defense line at the Carpathians. Nazi troops marched into Slovakia and probably also into Rumania. The status of the latter country was somewhat clouded. The Rumanian legation in Turkey was reported as saying the Germans had "occupied" the country, but this was contradicted from sources in Switzerland. [4:1.]

President Roosevelt issued an appeal to those Germans who do not approve Hitler's campaign of terror against the Jews and to all men of good-will everywhere in Europe to hide refugees and help them escape. He said it would be a tragedy if the Jews who had fled to the Balkans should be caught now so near the hour of deliverance. [1:5.]

The American air force carried the round-the-clock attack on the Germans through its third day with virtually unopposed assaults on the industrial cities of Frankfort and Schweinfurt and fighter fields at Nancy and St. Dizier. Three bombers and five fighters were lost. It was the nineteenth American operation in March for a new record and followed RAF night attacks on the Lyon area and the railway yards at Laon. The RAF attacked Berlin last night. [1:4; map, P. 5.] The Germans struck back at London in what was reported as an unusually heavy fire raid. It was the fourth straight night the sirens had sounded. [5:4.]

Two statements by British leaders were interpreted as indicating preparations for invasion were near an end. Prime Minister Churchill told American troops Thursday they "soon will have the opportunity" to strike a blow for freedom. General Montgomery, addressing a London luncheon, gave the invasion watchword as "Let God arise and let His enemies be scattered." [1:6-7.]

As the New Zealanders in Cassino started a drive from the east toward Abbey Hill, the stubbornly fighting Germans were reported to have continued their infiltration of the ruins and to hold now several new strong points embracing at least a quarter of the town. [1:7.]

Allied headquarters in India reported that the Japanese columns converging on Imphal were being heavily engaged and that successes had been scored at several points. [1:6-7.]

Fight for a Better World, Premier Tells U. S. Troops

By DREW MIDDLETON
By Cable to The New York Times.

LONDON, March 24—Prime Minister Churchill has reviewed thousands of American air-borne troops and told them yesterday of the great part they will play "soon" in the invasion of Europe. Mr. Churchill, with Gen. Dwight D. Eisenhower, Allied Commander in Chief, and Lieut. Gen. Omar N. Bradley, senior United States ground commander in Britain, inspected what the Prime Minister called "the most modern expression of war"—air-borne soldiers. His review helped heighten the impression here that the invasion force was now completing its training for the great operation.

[The text of Mr. Churchill's remarks is on page 3.]

It seems clear that organization has progressed so swiftly that the opening of Anglo-American operations now depends on other factors, such as the Russian advance and the conclusion of the campaign to break the Luftwaffe, rather than on the readiness of the vast number of troops concentrated in these islands.

Gen. Sir Bernard L. Montgomery, who will command some of the finest divisions ever raised in the British Army, outfits schooled on the battlefields from Belgium to the Nile, gave his countrymen the invasion watchword in a speech at a "Salute the Soldier" luncheon at the Mansion House today.

It was "Let God arise and let His enemies be scattered," a war cry that reflects the grim Cromwellian character of the commander of the British group of armies.

[Terming the approaching test the "biggest tug-of-war the world has ever seen," General Montgomery said it might last a year or longer, The United Press reported. "It will be a magnificent party and we shall win," he added.]

General Montgomery also appealed for a national reawakening to the tasks that face the invasion troops and asked the nation to help

Continued on Page Three

GERMANS RETAKE FOURTH OF CASSINO

Using Underground Passages, They Infiltrate Allied Lines—Hold 6 Strong Points

By The United Press.

NAPLES, March 24—Stubbornly fighting Germans, infiltrating the ruins of Cassino by subterranean passages and hidden gullies, have recaptured one-fourth of the town after winning possession of six strong points, front dispatches disclosed tonight.

The Germans now hold a belt of territory along the western side of the town running from the southern extremities of Cassino past Highway Six into the northern section.

The Germans' northern toe-hold in the ruin of the town is anchored within 250 yards of the most advanced point reached by the Allies before the deluge of bombs that preceded the present battle, James E. Roper, United Press correspondent with the Fifth Army forces fighting for the town, reported.

Three Enemy Tanks in Hotel

German "Green Devil" parachutists seized this bit of ruined buildings in fierce street fighting, Roper's dispatch said.

Three German tanks have been sneaked into the Hotel Continental, one of the six key positions in the embattled city, where their cannon fire now is added to the German

Continued on Page Three

British Drive the Japanese Back On One Invasion Route to India

By The United Press.

NEW DELHI, India, March 24—British Imperial troops have driven the Japanese from three positions covering the Tiddim-Imphal invasion road into India and smashed enemy attacks in the Kabaw Valley border sector, inflicting heavy casualties, Admiral Lord Louis Mountbatten's headquarters announced today.

Japanese columns were scattered over a 180-mile "front," from the Chin Hills, south of Manipur State, to the Somra Hills tract, and some enemy units still were within twenty-five miles of Imphal, but a spokesman said none of the invaders had reached the Imphal Valley.

Superior British forces were closing in from the north and south on a Japanese road block seventeen miles north of Tiddim after inflicting considerable losses on the counter-attacking enemy. The Japanese also suffered heavy casualties when they were thrown out of a newly occupied vantage point in the Chin Hills.

On the central sector of the border front the Japanese advanced into the hills north of Tamu, seventy miles northeast of Tiddim, but failed in attempts to gain a foothold on the Tamu-Palel road, which links Imphal with the Kabaw Valley. One enemy detachment approaching the important link was dispersed Tuesday, the communiqué said, and another was thrown back when it attacked a British administrative unit on the road.

Imperial troops ambushed a

Continued on Page Six

VITAL RAIL LINE CUT

Red Army in Outskirts of Beltsy as Other Unit Chokes Off Supplies

VOZNESENSK IS CAPTURED

Zhukoff's Offensive Plunges 30 Miles in 24 Hours to Gateway of the Balkan States

By RALPH PARKER
By Wireless to The New York Times.

MOSCOW, Saturday, March 25—Spearing southward between Tarnopol and Proskurov, the Red Army yesterday made a spectacular thirty-mile gain to reach the Dniester River at the town of Zaleshchiki, twenty-five miles from Cernauti. In taking Zaleshchiki, the troops of Marshal Gregory K. Zhukoff took possession of the "gateway to the Balkans," situated on the border of Bukovina, former northern frontier province of Rumania.

The Second Ukrainian Army, led by Marshal Ivan S. Koneff, continued its race across Bessarabia by pushing to the outskirts of the large railroad junction city of Beltsy. By capturing Floreshty, eighteen miles east of Beltsy, the Russians severed the Beltsy-Slobodka railroad, the next to last east-west rail route supplying the Germans in the Nikolayev-Odessa section of the lower Ukraine. Reports indicated that Red Army troops already were fighting in the outskirts of Beltsy. Peleniya Station, three miles northwest of the junction, was among the fifty localities taken in the Bessarabian drive.

Bug River Citadel Falls

Gen. Rodion Y. Malinovsky's Third Ukrainian Army, meanwhile, captured the lower Bug River citadel of Voznesensk, giving the Russians control of the river as far as the outer defenses of Nikolayev, which itself is about two-thirds encircled.

[While the Russians were scoring their victories in the Ukraine, the Germans reportedly staged a coup in the far north. According to London diplomatic sources Friday, the Nazis have landed troops on the Finnish Aaland Islands, commanding the entrance to the Gulf of Bothnia. Dispatches from Stockholm on Saturday, however, quoted competent sources in Helsinki as denying the truth of the report.]

The advance of Marshal Zhukoff to the junction of Zaleschiki, which is about sixty miles from the boundary of pre-war Czechoslovakia, places the Red Army within a like distance of Jasina Pass in the Carpathians. The Jasina Pass route was followed by the Imperial Russian Army ninety-five years ago when it moved into Hungary.

Drive Is Four Days Old

Premier Stalin's order of the day to Marshal Zhukoff announced the news yesterday of the swift advance to Bukovina. The order also named the important towns of Chortkov and Gusyatin as among the 400 places captured in the drive southward. Marshal Zhukoff's renewed offensive, opened four days ago with a surprise attack, has covered some sixty-five miles and drawn an iron screen across the westward retreat route of all German forces north of the Dniester and west of Marshal Koneff's salient.

The German forces, believed to be substantial, are now confined to the railway running southward to Kamenets-Podolsk, beyond which, according to official British maps, the line does not go. A rough road runs from there across the Dniester to Cernauti and other Bukovina towns.

The fact that many of Marshal Zhukoff's most celebrated generals were listed in Premier Stalin's order means that very powerful forces are involved in the new offensive toward the Carpathians.

Besides capturing 400 places in the four-day drive, Marshal Zhukoff's armies killed more than 20,000 Germans and captured 3,500. In addition, large quantities of war

Continued on Page Two

"All the News That's Fit to Print"

The New York Times.

LATE CITY EDITION
Fair and continued cool today; moderate winds.
Temperatures Yesterday—Max., 54; Min., 38
Sunrise, 6:12 A. M.; Sunset, 7:38 P. M.

Copyright, 1944, by The New York Times Company.

VOL. XCIII..No. 31,496. Entered as Second-Class Matter, Postoffice, New York, N. Y. NEW YORK, TUESDAY, APRIL 18, 1944. THREE CENTS NEW YORK CITY

BRITISH BAN ENVOYS' TRAVEL AND CODE USE IN MOVE TO PROTECT INVASION SECRETS; RED ARMY HEMS IN BATTERED SEVASTOPOL

AIRLINER CROSSES COUNTRY IN 7 HOURS, SETTING A RECORD

TWA-Lockheed Transport Clips 30 Minutes Off Time From Coast to Coast

SPEED 355 MILES AN HOUR

Howard Hughes at Controls of Giant Plane Capable of Carrying 100 Troops

By The Associated Press.

WASHINGTON, April 17—A new giant of the air paths, the Lockheed Constellation, crossed the continent today in 6 hours 58 minutes, an average speed of about 355 miles an hour, a speed well beyond anything flown previously for a similar distance.

The big triple-rudderd ship with a shark's body contour flew east from Burbank, Calif., in the colors of Transcontinental & Western Air, Inc., which sponsored its development, but it is being turned over to the Army for use in war transport work.

Compared with the Constellation's time for the non-stop flight is the previous fastest cross-country trip of 7 hours 28 minutes flown in a specially designed plane by Howard Hughes on Jan. 19, 1937. Hughes flew from Burbank to Newark, N. J., on a 2,445-mile route at an average speed of 327 miles an hour.

In contrast with his lone trip, however, the Constellation carried seventeen persons, and there was room in its cabin for forty more passengers with luxury accommodations. As a troop transport it could carry 100 soldiers with full equipment.

The fastest transport crossing previously flown was 10 hours 22 minutes by Leland S Andrews and H. B. Snead in a two-engine Vultee from Los Angeles to Washington on Feb. 20, 1935, at an average speed of 221.6 miles an hour.

Hughes at the Controls

Hughes, an outstanding figure in aviation as well as a motion-picture producer, shared the controls of the Constellation with Jack Frye, president of the TWA. They flew between 15,000 and 19,000 feet, with some help from tailwinds. Despite the record, it was understood that the plane was slightly behind schedule.

Army officers declined to permit publication of any official figures on the flight, but did permit Frye and Hughes to say that the flight was a record.

"It is a perfectly marvelous ship," Mr Frye said. "It is simply great. It flies and handles like a pursuit [meaning a fighter plane]. I guess the thing to say is that it flies like a dream."

Greeting Guy W. Vaughan, president of Wright Aeronautical Corporation, which builds the 2,200-horsepower Whirlwind engines used in the Constellation, Mr. Frye said the power plants "purred like kittens all the way."

The plane left Burbank at 3:56 A. M. Pacific War Time and was over the Washington National Airport at 1:54 P. M. Eastern War Time. It made a perfect landing four minutes later after circling once. The time is figured from the moment the wheels begin rolling at the take-off until the finish line is crossed in flight.

Payload of 14 Tons

The Constellation has a gross weight of around forty tons and also has a payload of more than fourteen tons. Its wingspread is 123 feet, slightly longer than the flight of the Wright brothers at Kittyhawk, and thirteen feet longer than the span of a B-24 Liberator.

The airline distance between Los Angeles and Washington is 2,663 miles. The great circle distance, which the Constellation probably attempted, is 2,292 miles. Its actual distance probably was somewhere between the two figures.

In addition to Hughes and Frye as pilots, the crew comprised Howard Bolton, navigator; R. I. Proctor, flight engineer, and C. E. Glover, radio operator.

The passengers were L. J. Chiappino, Leo Baron, Robert L. Loomis, E. J. Minser, Orville R. Olson, Lee Spruill and Richard De Compo of TWA; Richard Stanton, R. L. Thoren and Thomas Watkins of Lockheed; S. J. Solomon, chairman of the airlines' committee on post-war aviation policy, and Lieut. Col. C. A. Shoop of the Army Air Forces.

CHICAGO, April 17 (UP)—Designed for civilian "super luxury" but drafted into wartime duty, that's the story told today by the men behind the Constellation.

Built for TWA by Lockheed, the

Continued on Page 8

Hull to Put Policy Before 6 Senators

By The Associated Press.

WASHINGTON, April 17—Secretary Hull is scheduled to begin discussions this week with a bi-partisan Senate committee in an apparent effort to keep the main lines of American foreign policy out of the channels of political controversy.

Mr. Hull's expressed hope is to obtain from the committee, which consists of three Republicans and three Democrats, such advice and guidance on post-war issues, including a world organization to maintain peace, that it will be possible eventually to go to foreign governments with American plans which are assured of national and Congressional support.

The proposition was discussed by the Secretary and Chairman Connally of the Senate Foreign Relations Committee at Mr. Hull's office today.

The Secretary then told a press conference that the coming meeting was a result of his invitation expressed in a recent speech.

35 YEARS TO LIFE GIVEN TO LONERGAN

Wife Slayer Rushed to Prison After One Minute in Court—Broderick Plans Appeal

With the same apparent indifference that characterized his conduct during both his trials, Wayne Thomas Lonergan heard General Sessions Judge James G. Wallace sentence him yesterday to "thirty-five years to imprisonment for the rest of your natural life" for the slaying of his wife, Patricia.

The proceedings before Judge Wallace took less than a minute, one of the briefest in a murder sentence, and included denial of a motion by Edward V. Broderick, Lonergan's lawyer, to set aside the verdict of the blue-ribbon panel that convicted the former Royal Canadian Air Force aircraftman on March 31 of second-degree murder. Mr. Broderick said he would appeal.

Soon after 2 P. M. Lonergan arrived at Sing Sing prison and gave Mr. Broderick as his "only friend." When asked if he had any money or other valuables, he said. "I have nothing."

After the brief court session Mr. Broderick announced his intention to appeal, saying: "Last week District Attorney Frank S. Hogan received a major setback when the Court of Appeals reversed another murder conviction obtained by his office. I expect my appeal will add to the list of Mr. Hogan's setbacks." Court attachés said the cases had little in common.

Contempt Case Up Friday

Mr. Broderick and Mr. Hogan will be adversaries again Friday when the defense lawyer must answer a contempt of court citation issued by General Sessions Judge John J. Freschi as an outgrowth of Mr. Broderick's conduct in the abortive attempt last February to obtain a jury in the first Lonergan trial. After four days of turmoil a mistrial was declared without a juror having been chosen. Mr. Hogan will represent the State at the contempt hearing.

Evidently surprised at the severity of the sentence, since any term of twenty years or more is discretionary with the court, Lonergan, after a startled glance at Mr. Broderick, promptly and quietly accompanied court attendants to his Tombs prison cell to await transfer to Sing Sing Prison. He is eligible to ask for parole after twenty-three years and four months.

Soon after 1 P. M. Lonergan was

Continued on Page 13

RAIL HUBS BOMBED

U. S. Planes Rock Sofia and Belgrade—Hit Air Plants and Field

RAF STRIKES AT BUDAPEST

Russian and American Fliers Attack Rumania—Blow at Pas-de-Calais in West

By Wireless to THE NEW YORK TIMES.

NAPLES, April 17—The Allied aerial offensive against rail centers and Nazi aircraft production centers in the Balkan-Danubian region continued in full swing today, with the heavy bombers of the United States Fifteenth Air Force attacking the Sofia and Belgrade rail yards and two plane plants at Belgrade in full strength.

British Wellingtons and Liberators made a new smashing attack on the Budapest rail yards last night.

Our Flying Fortresses and Liberators paid their first visit of the war to the enemy-held Yugoslav capital, although yesterday's program of the Mediterranean Allied Air Forces included blows by the "heavies" at the Zemun airfield and an adjacent factory on the outskirts of Belgrade, which the Luftwaffe ravaged three years ago this month.

Double Blows at Rumanian Town

During a 1,800-sortie day yesterday American four-motored giants also bombed the rail yards at Brasov, Rumania, on the northern slope of the Transylvanian Alps, and at Turnu Severin in western Rumania.

[Soviet bombers Sunday night attacked the Rumanian port of Galati on the lower Danube, key point behind the southeastern end of the Nazi line facing the Red Army.

[Britain-based American Liberators on Monday resumed the air assault on western Europe with a 250-plane bombing of the German anti-invasion targets in the Pas-de-Calais area of France. German radio warnings Monday night reported Allied planes over the Reich.]

Turnu Severin had undergone bombardment Saturday night by the Royal Air Force's Wellingtons from Italy, roaring over the historic Iron Gate of the Danube.

Thus the offensive against sources of the strength and the movement of German troops facing the Russians in southeastern Europe has become literally a day-and-night affair, with the Fifteenth Air Force's "Forts" and Liberators and the RAF's Liberators and two-motored Wellingtons virtually overlapping in assaults on targets, most of which had not been hit prior to this month.

The Bulgarian capital of Sofia, which was last bombed for the eighth time, March 30, is the virtual hub of all Balkan rail lines. Belgrade, where early reports indicated today's bombing was successful, is also on the Zagreb-Bucharest line, which is the major Nazi feeder route to the Eastern Front from Austria and Yugoslavia.

Besides the rail yards the targets at the Yugoslav capital, which

Continued on Page 2

FOE FIGHTS HARDER

Russians Force Siege Lines Closer to Port From South and East

KEY TO BALAKLAVA TAKEN

Varnutka Junction Falls—Nazis Herded Into Corner—Kishinev Battle Raging

By The United Press.

LONDON, Tuesday, April 18—A Red Army flanking column swept twelve miles down the southern Crimean coast yesterday to capture the key highway junction of Varnutka, eleven miles southeast of Sevastopol, while other Soviet forces driving in from the north and east were meeting stiffened resistance from enemy troops fighting in fortifications built by the Russians during the 1941-42 siege.

The Moscow midnight war communiqué announced that troops of Gen. Andrei I. Yeremenko's Independent Maritime Army advancing toward Sevastopol from the southeast through the Baidary Valley were in hot pursuit of the enemy, who were abandoning arms and equipment in retreat.

Gen. Feodor I. Tolbukhin's Fourth Ukrainian Army, however, was meeting "strong resistance" as it reached the approaches of a powerful ring of German fortifications anchored on the heights east and northeast of the city. In yesterday's fighting the Fourth Army captured Mekenziyev, four miles northeast of Sevastopol across Sevastopol Bay, and Cherkez-Kermen, eight miles east of the city.

Kishinev Fighting Is Severe

The Moscow communiqués told of fighting on only one other sector of the long southern front, that in the Kishinev area of Bessarabia, where troops of Gen. Rodion Y. Malinovsky's Third Ukrainian Army captured bridgeheads on the west bank of the Dniester River Monday. Moscow said the Russians had fought yesterday to widen the bridgehead, and that one Soviet mobile detachment broke into the enemy's rear and wiped out nearly a battalion of 1,000 men.

Moscow dispatches said furious fighting was in progress east of Kishinev, where the Germans were holding strong positions anchored in the marshy terrain. The Berlin communiqué reported strong Soviet attacks in that area. It also told of

Continued on Page 2

ODESSA HAILS ITS LIBERATORS

Residents cheering Russian soldiers as they entered the city
The New York Times (Sovfoto Radiophoto)

ALLIES CUT BLOCK ISOLATING KOHIMA

Vital Gain Against Burma Foe Insures Dimapur Supply Link—Imphal Front Improves

By The Associated Press.

NEW DELHI, India, April 17—Tanks and infantry have cleared Japanese road blocks four miles north of Kohima on the road to Dimapur in heavy fighting in which Rajputs, Punjabis and British were involved, a front-line account from an Indian eyewitness said today.

Enemy artillery in the area was outgunned five to one, it was said.

"Everyone in Dimapur"—important operating center or the Bengal-Assam supply railroad—"now has an operational role" in patrolling and guarding the vital line of communications and making reconnaissances in the hills, it was said. Important installations were reported under guard.

The Dimapur personnel includes many American soldiers who as transport troops took over operation of the railway several months ago.

Enemy Losses Heavy

KANDY, Ceylon, April 17 (UP)—Japanese invasion forces that cut the important Allied supply road between Kohima and Dimapur in eastern India last week have been thrown from important positions and have suffered "very heavy"

Continued on Page 12

Badoglio Cabinet Resigns; Coalition to Govern Italy

By MILTON BRACKER
By Wireless to THE NEW YORK TIMES.

NAPLES, Italy, April 17—The short-lived government of Premier Pietro Badoglio fell today. But it fell easily; and, as expected, King Victor Emmanuel accepted the resignation with the request that the marshal, who gave the Allies the armistice last September, form a new Cabinet on "a broad foundation" taking account of the wishes of "all the parties."

Thus the first post-armistice phase of Italian politics ended along lines that had been plainly marked since the King announced his willingness to retire in favor of Crown Prince Humbert when Rome is liberated.

A statement of less than fifty words, at first issued unofficially, but subsequently labeled "official," wound up the government. It read:

Today Marshal Badoglio presented to the King the resignation of the Ministry presided over by him.

The King took note of the resignation and has asked Marshal Badoglio to form a new Ministry with a broad foundation taking account of the wishes expressed by all the parties.

A series of conferences began today between Marshal Badoglio and representatives of the six parties that make up the executive junta of the opposition. It was interesting, if not significant, that the first to call at the seat of government was Palmiro Togliatti [M. Ercoli], Communist leader. Tomorrow the Socialists will present a list of potential Cabinet members, and so on until each of the groups that on Saturday agreed in lukewarm fashion to share in a new Government has had a chance to bid for places.

A source high in Allied political circles expressed the belief tonight that it would be a matter of only a few days before a new Cabinet was established. In no informed quarter was there a suggestion that Marshal Badoglio might be unable to form a Cabinet.

The question thus came down to who would make up the new Cabinet, which will be entrusted with the job of putting Italy more fully and efficiently behind the work of driving the Nazis out. Some of the former Cabinet members will

Continued on Page 6

5,000 NEW PLANES LOST BY GERMANS

Result of 6 Months of USAAF Blows at Luftwaffe Supply Centers an Invasion Factor

By DREW MIDDLETON
By Cable to THE NEW YORK TIMES.

LONDON, April 17—The Luftwaffe has suffered its most serious defeat of the war in the past six months, according to a reliable source here today.

The United States Army Air Forces have drawn the fangs of the German Fighter Command, according to figures supplied by this source, and that command, although it will undoubtedly be a factor in the enemy's anti-invasion effort, will be far below its planned strength for that operation.

Here are the latest figures of Nazi air losses, figures that, according to the source, are the product of the most exhaustive research and careful checking.

Nearly 5,000 single and twin-engined fighters have been denied the Luftwaffe since early last November by damage done to its basic factories, assembly plants and replacement areas by the heavy bombers of the United States Eighth Air Force from Britain and the Fifteenth Air Force from Italy. That is, German production was cut by this amount as a result of our bombings.

In actual combat since the first of this year, 3,560 German fighters have been destroyed by the heavy bombers of the Eighth Air Force and their fighter escorts and by the medium bombers and fighters of the Ninth Air Force, all flying from Britain.

Probably 1,700 more Nazi inter-

Continued on Page 3

U. S., SOVIET EXEMPT

Sealed Mail Pouches of Diplomats Also Are Prohibited

ACTION IS UNPRECEDENTED

Britain Will Send Messages for Others in Own Diplomatic Code if Necessary

By RAYMOND DANIELL
By Wireless to THE NEW YORK TIMES.

LONDON, April 17—Britain took an action, unprecedented in international law, tonight to safeguard the lives of Allied troops who will soon be hurled against the battlements of Adolf Hitler's Festung Europa.

Without prior warning an edict was handed down by the Government that wrote a wartime finis to anything resembling diplomatic immunity both for Allied and neutral envoys with those of Russia and the United States as the sole exceptions.

Henceforth the rule is that no foreign diplomats or members of their staffs can go home. Nor can they send or receive telegrams in code. They are forbidden even uncensored use of diplomatic pouches, a privilege accorded to foreign legations in every capital under the sun for generations.

Other Measures Taken

This trail-blazing diplomatic precedent was undertaken by the British Government in the interest of security as part of a general campaign to isolate the happenings on this island until it is too late for the enemy to profit by the knowledge of what kinds of arms they bear and where they are planning to strike. It is but one of many measures that have been taken and that are contemplated to safeguard secrets of military importance and thus give the Anglo-American assault force that essential element of strategic surprise when "D-day" comes.

Some steps in this direction have been taken already. Telephone and telegraph communication with Eire has been cut off and travel has been made difficult between this country and that part of the British Commonwealth of Nations that chose to remain neutral. Ships of the Royal Navy are doubtless guarding Ireland's coast not only against incursions by the Germans but to make certain that there will be no surreptitious landings of submarines there to circumvent Britain's interest in strict neutrality.

Britain's unprecedented act in ending diplomatic privileges for all missions resident in London, whether neutral or Allied, was part and parcel of the present attempt to make this island impregnable to espionage. There has been some reason to suspect that indirectly at least the Germans have had several spyglasses focused from London on the invasion front.

British Inform Diplomats

Some neutrals have made it perfectly plain that their sympathies lay with the enemy. Others, who have enjoyed the privileges of diplomatic immunity in London, have been a fence for Hitler. With military operations of decisive nature impending it would be foolhardy under the circumstances for the British to maintain the pretense of observing the Marquess of Queensberry rules in a fight that long since has become a knock down and drag out affair in which Hitler himself has said that only one side can survive.

And so tonight the heads of all diplomatic missions here were informed that from midnight on they would have no privileges of communication with their governments and no facilities of travel other than any other foreign resident or subject of the King enjoyed. As one diplomat phrased it, Britain has taken steps that are sure to bring criticism even from her friends, but it is "nothing to what would be said of her if she had overlooked a leak that would have enabled the enemy to concentrate a sufficient force to beat off an invasion at any given time or place; Britain is

Continued on Page 5

War News Summarized

TUESDAY, APRIL 18, 1944

Great Britain last night stripped all foreign diplomats, except those from the United States and Soviet Russia, of privileges hitherto customary in international relations. The unprecedented move, designed to seal every possible leak in connection with invasion plans, forbade any foreign representative, neutral or Allied, to leave Great Britain, to send or receive code messages, or to use the sacrosanct "diplomatic pouch." It is believed that the new embargo, by safeguarding the element of strategic surprise, will save many lives during the invasion of Western Europe. [1:8.]

Germany, giving every indication of her conviction that the Allies would strike sooner than had been expected, was reported to have laid a mine belt three miles wide off Jutland in Denmark. Increased protection for defending troops against air blows was being rushed. [1:6-7.]

The power of the Luftwaffe to counter the invasion has been drastically reduced by the air war waged from Britain and Italy, an American authority reported. He said Germany had lost at least 5,000 fighter planes through damage to aircraft factories in the past six months and that since Jan. 1 United States fliers from Britain had shot down in combat 3,560 enemy interceptors, while fliers from Italy had shot down 1,700 more. [1:7.]

The Allied aerial pincers were closing as tightly around the Balkans as around Germany. Russian bombers blasted the rail junction and Danube inland port of Galati, Rumania, setting great fires and many explosions. Galati is only 115 miles from Brasov, Rumania, hit Sunday by American planes from Italy. Yesterday Sofia, capital of Bulgaria, and Belgrade, capital of Yugoslavia, were daylight targets following a Sunday night attack on the Hungarian capital of Budapest. British-based American planes struck the Pas-de-Calais area of France. [1:3; map, P. 2.]

The Red Army was battling its way through artificial barriers and the Crimean mountains toward the outskirts of Sevastopol, the Germans' last remaining foothold. Other Russian forces were exploiting their bridgeheads over the Dniester in the Kishinev area. [1:4; map P. 2.]

For the second day in a row an American patrol made a raid two miles deep into German lines behind the Anzio beachhead in Italy, blowing up an ammunition dump. [8:1.] Marshal Badoglio and his Ministers resigned yesterday. King Victor Emmanuel immediately asked the marshal to form a new Ministry "with a broad foundation taking into account the wishes expressed by all parties." [1:6-7.]

Allied forces in India and Burma continued to improve their positions. [1:5.] In the Pacific American fliers ranged over wide areas from Kavieng, New Ireland, to Timor, with the heaviest blows struck at Wakde Island, off New Guinea, and also at Truk and the Marshall Islands. [12:5.]

German Invasion Alarm Growing; Jutland Coast Is Reported Mined

By Cable to THE NEW YORK TIMES.

LONDON, April 17—The Germans have completed a mine belt three miles wide along the west coast of Jutland in Denmark as part of their invasion defenses, and preparations to meet the Anglo-American onslaught from the west have been reviewed in Berlin where Adolf Hitler and Field Marshal Gen. Wilhelm Keitel, chief of staff to the Supreme Command, met Field Marshal Gen. Karl von Rundstedt, commander of the Wehrmacht in France.

These developments, reported from Stockholm today, appear to be part of a general program forced on the enemy by recent events. The extension of Allied fighter range through introduction of long-range fighters such as the Mustang and Thunderbolt has made it necessary to prepare defenses for coasts that two years ago would have been considered "safe" from invasion because they were outside fighter range.

Lately, also, German newspaper and radio reports have indicated that the High Command now believes the invasion will come much earlier than originally expected. According to the Berlin correspondent of the Swedish newspaper Aftonbladet, the second half of May is judged in Berlin as the period that will be "most critical."

Through all reports that are relayed from Germany by Stockholm and other neutral news centers runs a thin vein of truth or at least plausible supposition.

It is not probable that the enemy is blasting "huge caves in the cliffs of the Channel coast," as

Continued on Page 8

New Chemical Magic Transmutes Soft Woods Into Best of Timber

By WILLIAM L. LAURENCE

A new chemical process that transmutes all types of soft wood into wood of any desired hardness, thus providing a chemical magic wand with which hundreds of millions of acres of American forests of pine and other soft woods can be transformed into woodlands yielding the best of timber, was announced yesterday by E. I. du Pont de Nemours & Co.

With the new process, it was announced, "poplar becomes harder than hard maple, which in turn can be made harder than ebony." The compressive strength of wood is so increased and other properties imparted by the process to such an extent, it was added, "that the result is actually no longer natural wood, but a new material that may be termed transmuted wood."

The chemicals used in the process are derived from coal, air and water. The first step is to use these three for synthesizing ammonia, carbon dioxide and methanol (synthetic wood alcohol). The carbon dioxide and ammonia react to form urea, a substance widely used as a fertilizer. The methanol yields formaldehyde, which condenses with urea to form a substance named di-methyl-urea. When the latter is mixed, in water, with urea, compounds are formed that are known as methylol-urea. These chemicals are the magic wands that can transform soft woods in a few hours into hard woods that take nature a hundred years to grow.

Both urea and di-methyl-urea, it was explained, are commercially

Continued on Page 38

"All the News That's Fit to Print"

The New York Times.

LATE CITY EDITION
Cloudy and warmer with showers; probably thunderstorms today.
Temperatures Yesterday—Max., 68; Min., 41
Sunrise, 6:05 A. M.; Sunset, 7:44 P. M.

VOL. XCIII..No. 31,502. Entered as Second-Class Matter, Postoffice, New York, N. Y. NEW YORK, MONDAY, APRIL 24, 1944. THREE CENTS IN NEW YORK CITY

AMERICANS LAND ON NORTH NEW GUINEA COAST; ADMIRAL KING SEES PACIFIC VICTORY ROAD OPEN; 2-WAY BLOWS MARK 7TH DAY OF AIR OFFENSIVE

ROOSEVELT ORDERS WARD STRIKE END PENDING NLRB POLL

Deadline Set at Tomorrow Noon, With Company Under Command to Obey WLB

NEW ACTION THREATENED

Any Defiance to Be Met With Step in Nation's 'Interests'—Union Wires Compliance

By WALTER H. WAGGONER
Special to THE NEW YORK TIMES.

WASHINGTON, April 23—President Roosevelt today set Tuesday noon as the deadline by which Montgomery Ward & Co., which has refused to comply with an order by the National War Labor Board, and the company's union employes, who are on strike, must take initial steps which he laid down for the settlement of their dispute.

He directed the union to end its strike, which has been in progress since April 12, and the company, to obey the WLB order, both to take these actions "forthwith," and warned:

"Unless, before noon Tuesday, April 25, I am informed by each of you that the steps to be taken by the company and the union, as herein outlined, have been initiated, I shall take such further action as the interests of the nation require."

Duplicate Telegram Sent

The orders were contained in a telegram sent simultaneously to Sewell Avery president of the mail-order house, and Samuel Wolchok, national head of the United Retail, Wholesale and Department Store Employes of America, a CIO union.

[Mr. Wolchok wired from New York yesterday, according to The Associated Press, that he would order the strikers to return to work in compliance with President Roosevelt's order.]

In the telegram the Chief Executive sternly ordered both parties also to cooperate in a National Labor Relations Board election to determine whether the union should be the bargaining agent for the company's employes.

A union contract with the company expired in December and Mr. Avery, questioning whether the union still represented a majority of the employes, refused to continue it.

By inference, the President's message refuted the contention in arguments by the company that the mail-order house was not engaged in war work and was therefore immune from Government seizure.

The President said that he was "informed" that the dispute involved several thousand workers and was holding up delivery of farm equipment and machinery, repair parts, electrical appliances, automobile tires "and other goods essential for the economy in wartime."

"Danger" of Strike Spread

He asserted that he had also been told that the strike was being supported by other unions and that there was "grave danger" it would spread to other industries.

"These conditions cannot be permitted to continue in a nation at war," he declared.

More than half of the telegram consisted of a summary of the background of the deadlock which the President has been asked, by all members of the WLB, to adjudicate.

Extensive speculation during the past week over the action the Government might take brought the report that Jesse Jones, Secretary of Commerce and Director of the Reconstruction Finance Corporation, might take over for the Government, an action which would be without precedent.

This possibility was not ruled out by the President's wire. The phrase "further action" was generally interpreted to mean seizure of the company. Seizure has been a solution, in most cases temporary, for

Continued on Page 12

Western Union Asks To Send Greetings

By The Associated Press.

WASHINGTON, April 23—The American Communications Association (CIO), union of telegraph workers, today made public a protest to the Board of War Communications against a request of the Western Union Telegraph Company for permission to resume transmission of congratulatory telegrams.

The protest was echoed in a letter by Representative Marcantonio of New York to James L. Fly, board chairman.

Joseph P. Selly, president of the union, said the telegraph company's wartime service would be impeded if the request, pending before the Federal Commission, was granted.

Western Union, with the permission of the FCC, on Sept. 18, 1942, eliminated singing telegrams and fixed-text holiday and social greetings, and three months later stopped accepting congratulatory and holiday messages except to soldiers and sailors in expeditionary forces.

PUBLISHERS REPORT UNITY FOR VICTORY

Gathering Here for Meetings Starting Today, They See War Overshadowing Politics

By FRANK S. ADAMS

Americans in all sections of the country are grimly intent on winning the war, and are determined to let nothing stand in the way of attaining victory as speedily as possible, according to publishers who are in New York for the annual meeting of The Associated Press today and the fifty-eighth annual convention of the American Newspaper Publishers Association on the three succeeding days.

Although some concern was expressed over the slow progress of Allied armies in Italy, the concensus of those interviewed was that on the whole the military situation was developing favorably. They reported that the coming invasion of western Europe by the American and British forces under Gen. Dwight D. Eisenhower was of course being tensely awaited by residents of every part of the United States.

Manpower Still a Problem

Manpower shortages are still causing pinches in many areas, but nevertheless production records in both the agricultural and the industrial fields are being maintained at astonishingly high records, the publishers declared. They expressed less concern over problems of re-conversion than spokesmen for some other business groups who have gathered here recently.

Several of those interviewed expressed their belief that Governor Dewey would be the Republican nominee for the Presidency. On the whole the feeling seemed to be, however, that the political situa-

Continued on Page 17

NAVY IS CONFIDENT

Chief Says in Report We Are Ready to 'Travel Far and Fast'

CITES RISING MIGHT

Japan Muffed Chance Off Savo, He States—Lauds Team-Work

By SIDNEY SHALETT
Special to THE NEW YORK TIMES.

WASHINGTON, April 23—Emphasizing the enormous strategic and material gains made by the United States Navy since the beginning of the war, when, he frankly admitted, it was powerless to launch an offensive, Admiral Ernest J. King declared in an unprecedented report, made public tonight, that the future is "as dark and threatening to Japan as it is full of promise to us" and that "the encirclement of Germany is in sight."

Admiral King, Commander in Chief of the United States Fleet and Chief of Naval Operations, said that Japan's position was even worse than the war maps indicated, for her losses at sea and her dwindling recuperative powers, countered by our growing might, represented strategic defeats that must be added to the actual territory she has lost

In the first report of its type he has submitted to Secretary of the Navy Frank Knox, Admiral King gave a sweeping and revealing picture of progress in combat, production and training, and held forth extremely confident hopes for the future. He did not hesitate to give some of the unfavorable aspects of naval operations, revealing, for instance, with perhaps more frankness than any high Navy official previously has shown, what a severe defeat we suffered through inexperience and bad planning at Savo Island in August, 1942.

High Points of Report

The high points of the admiral's 50,000-word report were:

1. Though long roads still lie ahead both in Europe and in the Pacific, we now are prepared to "travel far and fast to victory."
2. Even without the losses sustained at Pearl Harbor, the Navy could not have carried the war to the enemy, as neither the Army nor the Navy was sufficiently expanded. Nor could our fleet have saved Manila, even if the Pearl Harbor disaster had not occurred.
3. The Japanese muffed an opportunity to strike a disastrous blow against our weakened Pacific Fleet after our Savo Island defeat and subsequent loss of two carriers, just as the Germans made a serious mistake by delaying for more than a month in fully opening their U-boat campaign after the declaration of war.
4. Nazi submarines in the Atlantic

Continued on Page 10

NAZI BASES RIPPED

Bombers, Fighters From Britain Hit All Day in France, Belgium

RAF HAMMERS REICH

Duesseldorf a Target—U. S. Planes From Italy Rock Austrian Plants

By GENE CURRIVAN
By Cable to THE NEW YORK TIMES.

LONDON, Monday, April 24—On the seventh day of the greatest sustained air offensive the world has even known, seemingly unending streams of Allied planes shuttled back and forth yesterday between Britain and the Continent, blasting the military installations and traffic centers of western Europe that are the backbone of Hitler's defenses against impending invasion.

Daylight attacks on Nazi airfields and other vital enemy objectives in northern France and Belgium followed with little respite a four-pronged assault by the Royal Air Force over Saturday night on three Reich cities and a locomotive depot at Laon, France.

More than 1,000 British and Canadian planes participated in the night bombings of Duesseldorf, Brunswick and Mannheim, Germany, and Laon. An estimate of 1,500 would be conservative for the number of American, British and Allied aircraft out by day.

Last night great formations of RAF bombers flew out again over the familiar sky lanes toward the Continent.

[From Italy on Sunday about 500 American heavy bombers attacked Nazi plane production centers at Wiener Neustadt and two other places in Austria.

[Sunday night, according to Axis radio reports, Budapest and Békés, a rail town in eastern Hungary, were attacked by Allied planes. Berlin said Allied aircraft were over Germany.

[German raiders caused alerts along the south coast of England early Monday and bombs were dropped at several points, The Associated Press reported.]

All day observers on the south-

Continued on Page 3

AMERICANS LEAP-FROG UP THE NEW GUINEA COAST

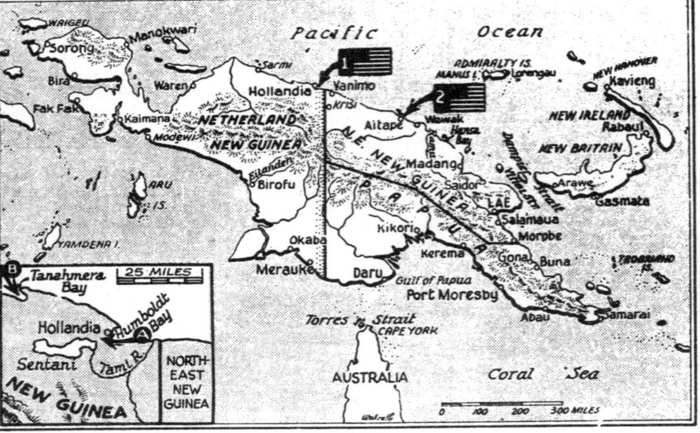

April 24, 1944

In the greatest amphibious operation of the southwest Pacific, American troops, covered by strong naval forces, landed at Hollandia (1) and Aitape (2), isolating 60,000 Japanese to the east. At Aitape the airdrome is already in our hands. Around Hollandia the landings were made at Humboldt Bay (A on inset) and Tanahmera Bay (B). The troops' objectives there are three airfields: two of them west of Hollandia and the third at Lake Sentani. General map on Page 9.

Allies Assert Death Blow For Luftwaffe Is in Sight

By HAROLD DENNY
By Cable to THE NEW YORK TIMES.

LONDON, April 23—American and British air forces have at last turned the corner of their long and desperate battle to knock the Luftwaffe out of the skies and are within sight of victory. The Germans, who converted their aircraft construction from bombers to fighters in a confidence bred of their own defeat in the Battle of Britain that fighters were the answer to the Allied bombing, are losing another gamble. They have not stopped the Allied bombing nor prevented it from growing in intensity and effectiveness. And now for the first time the Luftwaffe is losing more fighter planes than the Reich can produce.

The authorities for these happy conclusions are the British Air Ministry and the United States Strategic Air Forces in Europe.

[The text of their statement appears on Page 4.]

These authorities recently have been exercising unusual conservatism in estimating the effects of Allied air activity. Appropriately they chose today—St. George's Day devoted to England's patron saint who slew the dragon—to is-

Continued on Page 4

REVOLT ON 3 SHIPS CRUSHED BY GREEKS

Clash Bares Demand, Laid to Officers and Leftists, for Ouster of Late Regime

By C. L. SULZBERGER
By Wireless to THE NEW YORK TIMES.

CAIRO, Egypt, April 23—A mutiny in the Greek fleet which, according to an official British naval communiqué, had lasted three weeks, was partly quelled last night when Greek officers and men, acting under orders from their Commander in Chief, Vice Admiral Petros Voulgaris, boarded three warships and, after some fighting, assumed control.

[An Associated Press dispatch from Alexandria ascribed the revolt to the arrest of Army, Navy and Air Force officers who had demanded the ouster of the Cabinet of Emmanuel Tsouderos, who later resigned as Premier. The United Press in a Cairo dispatch said left-wing elements had mutinied.]

Machine-gun and rifle shots inflicted casualties. There was no official mention of any use of heavier weapons.

The vessels stormed were the destroyer Ierax and the corvettes Apostolis and Sachtouris of the

Continued on Page 5

JADE CENTER WON BY BURMA ALLIES

Air-Borne Chindits in Lonkin—Japanese Fall Back From Besieged Kohima

By The United Press.

SOUTHEAST ASIA HEADQUARTERS, Kandy, Ceylon, April 23—Air-borne troops have captured the jade center of Lonkin in the course of their attacks on Japanese communications in North Burma while in eastern India the defeated besiegers of Kohima have fallen back to regroup, it was disclosed tonight.

The air-borne troops, known as Chindits, were trained in behind-the-line warfare by the late Maj. Gen. Orde Charles Wingate and are now commanded by Maj. Gen. W. D. A. Lentaigne. They took Lonkin at an unspecified date. Lonkin is forty miles northwest of the rail town of Mogaung, which is being approached from the north by Chinese under Lieut. Gen. Joseph W. Stilwell.

The Lonkin mines produce the finest jade in the world and before Burma fell all exports were bought by China for the extensive jade-carving trade.

Allies Firm in Kohima

British Imperial troops are consolidating their successes in and around Kohima, the greater part of which was in Japanese hands for twelve days while a Home Counties regiment stood off attacks until relieved.

The British are consolidating gains northeast of Imphal but eighteen miles southwest of that Manipur capital hard fighting is under way in the area of Bishenpur, terminus of a secondary road leading to the Assam-Bengal railroad, where "the enemy advance is

Continued on Page 11

GREAT PACIFIC LEAP

MacArthur and Nimitz Join in 500-Mile Jump to Hollandia Base

AITAPE ALSO INVADED

General Directs Attack as Troops Pour Ashore and Win First Goals

By FRANK L. KLUCKHOHN
By Wireless to THE NEW YORK TIMES.

ALLIED HEADQUARTERS IN NEW GUINEA, Monday, April 24—With many warships of the mighty United States Fleet protecting the landing by pouring shells on the beaches, Gen. Douglas MacArthur hurled large forces ashore along a 150-mile stretch of northern New Guinea early on Saturday, cutting off the Japanese Eighteenth Army, estimated to number 60,000 men.

General MacArthur, personally directing his troops from a cruiser, again surprised the enemy, who concentrated his forces farther east. The American forces poured ashore virtually unopposed at Hollandia and Tanahmera Bay, Netherland New Guinea, and at Aitape, within Australian New Guinea, and quickly attained initial objectives against light enemy opposition.

With the support of a large part of the Pacific Fleet operating under Admiral Chester W. Nimitz, the American forces thus jumped about 500 statute miles up the coast from Saidor on the route to the Philippines and Japan. This is perhaps the Pacific equivalent of the opening of the "second front," since the major United States Navy, Army and Air Forces in the Pacific have joined in an offensive.

Good Harbor Is Captured

Excellent harborage in Humboldt Bay has already been won. Important Japanese air fields near Hollandia are expected soon to be in our hands for further advances toward the heart of the Japanese empire. These are only 1,100 miles southeast of Davao in the Philippines. It is the first Netherland territory recaptured so far in the war.

Three big forces of cruisers and destroyers raked each landing beach for an hour with roaring, smothering fire. When the dizzy crisscross of their streaking tracers and the throaty boom of exploding shells ceased, dive-bombers and trim fighters from many carriers screamed down to bomb and strafe gun positions, installations and finally the beach itself, making the shore a mass of billowing black smoke. Then, with rocket boats making the immediate objective a hell of red fire, every type of landing craft gathered from the entire Pacific carried the first waves of infantry ashore from transports, dock slips and destroyer transports.

Japanese Are Tricked

One reason for the surprise was that vessels making up the three task forces involved steamed in the direction of Palau from a rendezvous point north of the Admiralties. Destroyers and heavy light cruisers swept the seas ahead, while escort carriers were providing protection astern. The carrier force, with its own screen, and other units, acted as separate forces.

At the last moment the giant convoy, which traveled about 900 miles from the embarkation point, swung south. This was on Friday at 7 P. M. At 5 A. M. Saturday the three task forces stood off the various landing beaches. So great was the surprise that abandoned Japanese breakfasts were found on one beach.

The first troops ashore hit the easternmost beach at Aitape at 6:45 A. M. after Japanese positions on two offshore islands had been bombarded. Following scattered fighting in swamps in which at least fifteen Japanese were killed

Continued on Page 9

65 Feared Lost as Liberty Ship Breaks in Half on Alaskan Run

By The Associated Press.

SEATTLE, April 23—The Liberty ship John Straub, laden with explosives for the Alaska war theatre, broke its back and sank with a presumed loss of sixty-five of the eighty men aboard, E. M. Murphy, superintendent of the Alaska Steamship Company, announced today.

Master of the Straub, a new vessel making its third voyage, was Capt. A. W. Westerholm of Seattle, a veteran of twenty-six years with the Alaska Steamship Company.

All ship's officers, forty merchant seamen, fourteen Navy men and the cargo security officer were reported lost.

The wreck occurred twenty-one miles off Sanak Island, a small island south of the pass between Unimak Island and the Alaska Peninsula, which extends westward to the beginning of the Aleutian chain.

First reports mentioned a fire and explosions, but a party of Coast Guardsmen which boarded the after part of the wreck found no evidence of fire, Mr. Murphy said.

All but one of the lifeboats on the Straub had been accounted for, Mr. Murphy said, leaving but scant hope that more survivors of the wreck would be found.

The accident occurred at 5:30 A. M. Wednesday. The Straub, north bound, was reported by the boarding party to have parted aft the engine bulkhead. The forward section sank immediately.

The Coast Guardsmen reported no evidence of life on the after part, which sank fourteen hours after the break-up.

The fifteen survivors were taken to the Army Hospital at Cold Bay, Alaska, where only the names of

Continued on Page 22

War News Summarized

MONDAY, APRIL 24, 1944

The greatest American offensive in the Southwest Pacific fell suddenly upon surprised Japanese along a 150-mile front on New Guinea Saturday morning and made good two landings: at Hollandia and at Aitape. Some 60,000 enemy troops were encircled by the latest move and, in the words of General MacArthur's communiqué issued last night: "Their situation reverses Bataan."

Great bodies of American soldiers poured ashore after a terrific air and sea bombardment. Tadji airfield at Aitape was promptly seized, and after beachheads had been made secure on Humboldt Bay forces were rushed inland to capture Hollandia's cluster of three airfields. At Hollandia the Allies recovered the first Netherland territory from the Japanese.

General MacArthur watched the operations from a cruiser—operations that brought the Philippines within range of land-based bombers. American losses were slight. [All the foregoing 1:8; maps Pages 1 and 9.]

The news from the Southwest Pacific served to emphasize the assertion of Admiral Ernest J. King, Commander in Chief of the United States Fleet, that the future for Japan is "as dark and threatening as it is full of promise for us." In a frank "Report of Progress" Admiral King traced the growth of our naval might from its weak defensive Pearl Harbor days to its offensive strength today. In the Atlantic, he said, U-boats have been "reduced from a menace to a problem." [1:3; related stories and charts P.10.]

The air war against Germany continued without pause. An estimated 1,500 American and British planes battered at least seven widely separated enemy air bases in northern France and Belgium yesterday. Saturday night the RAF heavily attacked Duesseldorf, Brunswick, Mannheim and the French railroad center of Laon. [1:4; map P. 2.] The British and American Air Forces, in a joint statement, said Germany was losing more fighters than she could produce. As the air battle neared a climax enemy plane reserves were called a "mere trickle in the pipeline between factory and operating units." [1:5-6.]

American bombers from Italy added their weight to the destruction of German fighter production with a heavy assault on the main Messerschmitt plant at Wiener Neustadt and other targets in Vienna's suburbs. [3:1.]

Fighting on the European land fronts was desultory. American troops at Cisterna, on the Anzio beachhead, made some slight gains [8:2.] while Moscow reported that "no important changes took place on the fronts." [5:1.]

Chinese troops in Burma captured Lonkin, threatening Mogaung and the Burma railroad. The situation at Imphal and Kohima was reported well in hand. [1:7.] The Japanese were making progress in heavy fighting around Chengchow in China. [9:1.]

British Rehearse for Air Invasion; Enemy Threatens Surprise Blow

By The United Press.

LONDON, April 23—Thousands of British glider and parachute troops have completed one of the biggest and most dramatic maneuvers yet held in cooperation with the Royal Air Force and the American troops, who, like them, are poised for the invasion of western Europe, it was disclosed tonight.

Air Chief Marshal Sir Arthur Tedder, deputy to Gen. Dwight D. Eisenhower, the Allies' Commander in Chief, and other high British and American officers watched the operation, held yesterday somewhere in England while the Germans nervously speculated on the time set for D-Day. Gliders, towed by twin-motored Albemarle bombers, and special twin-motored planes of other types were used in the exercise, a grimly realistic simulation of a landing in the heart of enemy territory to seize high ground near a canal so that a British infantry division could attack the enemy in the flank.

From the landing area to the horizon, the lines of gliders and their towing planes dotted the sky. One thousand men or more landed from each wave of planes. It took twenty minutes for the gliders, swooping down at intervals of only a few seconds, to land their men.

The parachutists, wearing American-style steel helmets, were dropped at a near-by airdrome, along with doctors, stretcher-bearers, a chaplain and, attached to special parachutes, an arsenal of weapons in addition to folding bicycles, radio sets and rations. So accurate was the timing that only a few parachutists failed to land on the airdrome itself. Within a few minutes, all the parachutists had collected their arms and taken cover. As they did so, a

Continued on Page 2

"All the News That's Fit to Print"

The New York Times.

LATE CITY EDITION
Partly cloudy, slightly warmer today; gentle to moderate [illegible]
Temperatures Yesterday—Max., 63; Min., 55
Sunrise, 5:26 A. M.; Sunset, 8:23 P. M.

VOL. XCIII.No. 31,544. Entered as Second-Class Matter, Postoffice, New York, N. Y. NEW YORK, MONDAY, JUNE 5, 1944. THREE CENTS IN NEW YORK CITY

ROME CAPTURED INTACT BY THE 5TH ARMY AFTER FIERCE BATTLE THROUGH SUBURBS; NAZIS MOVE NORTHWEST; AIR WAR RAGES ON

TRANSIT MEN BALK AT MAYOR'S INQUIRY INTO OUTSIDE JOBS

Demand for Sworn Statements Covering Family Earnings Evokes Union Protest

RESENTMENT WIDESPREAD

Many Department Heads Cold Toward Policy and Some Authorize Dual Work

By PAUL CROWELL

Widespread resentment among city employes against Mayor La Guardia's crusade to keep them from holding outside jobs on their own time was intensified yesterday. It became known that Investigation Commissioner Edgar Bromberger, by direction of the Mayor, had asked the 35,000 employes of the unified transit system to make sworn answers to forty questions concerning their own employment and that of all working members of their families.

The Transport Workers Union and other organizations representing city transit workers already have registered informal protests and are considering formal action. It was reported that the TWU was prepared to ask its members receiving such questionnaires from Commissioner Bromberger's office to turn them over to the union.

The questionnaire, of a type said to have been sent to employes of other city agencies, asks the transit worker to give full details about his own job, any job he may have outside, any job his wife may hold, any jobs his children may be filling. Full details concerning pay rates on all such jobs are demanded. The workers are asked also how they obtained outside jobs, whether they paid anyone to get them and whether they are making payments to anyone in connection with outside jobs.

Board Members Dislike Policy

The regulations of the Board of Transportation do not forbid the holding of outside jobs and individual members of the board were known to feel that so long as employes were punctual and efficient in their tasks their outside activities were their own affair. Despite this feeling, however, the board is prepared to carry out the policy laid down by the Mayor. An informal survey of other city agencies conducted last week indicated that most of their heads held about the same attitude, but felt that the Mayor's policy must be carried out if he insisted upon it.

The Mayor's insistence that city employes, regardless of departmental rules forego such activities, led him recently to demand that charges be brought against an electrical engineer employed by the Board of Transportation who was teaching one night a week at City College, receiving $12 for each night's work. An exchange of views between the Mayor and the Board of Transportation resulted in a decision to let the employe continue teaching until the end of the current term, with the understanding that he would not resume teaching in the fall.

The electrical engineer, who is a graduate of one of the country's leading technical schools, was certified by the Board of Transportation, after investigation, to be efficient, painstaking and punctual, and the Mayor was told that his outside work made him a better city servant, while the small additional income was a welcome addition to his modest salary. It was also pointed out to the Mayor that there was nothing in the board's rules or the law to bar the outside work. The Mayor is reported to have replied that the man must keep one job or the other, but could not hold both.

Outside work by employes is a live issue in the Board of Transportation, where it is estimated that at least 10 per cent of the 35,000 transit workers have extra work to increase family income.

Resentment against the Mayor's

Continued on Page 11

Laval Tries to Shift Funds to Argentina

Pierre Laval, chief of the Vichy government, recently tried to transfer $50,000 from Spain to Argentina, the Brazzaville radio said yesterday in a broadcast recorded at the Columbia Broadcasting System's short-wave listening station.

"A Madrid bank revealed to the Spanish authorities that a deposit of $50,000 had been made with them for transfer to an Argentinian bank," the French radio said. "An inquiry was opened, and the person behind the depositor was discovered: He is Pierre Laval."

The same broadcast reported: "Germans in France have been buying gold at very high prices. Among the German agents arrested by French police for illegal traffic in gold was one who identified himself in order to be freed. He told the police commissioner that he was the director of a bank in a small German town. Because of his age, he had not been drafted into active military service, but his competence in financial matters made possible his being used in this work, in which he had been engaged since 1940."

JOHNSTON IN RUSSIA SCOFFS AT U. S. REDS

Business Leader Also Praises Soviet 'Capitalism'—Calls Ideologies Bridgeable

By The United Press.

MOSCOW, June 4—With straight-from-the-shoulder frankness, Eric Johnston, president of the United States Chamber of Commerce, told 100 Soviet trade leaders yesterday that a gulf separated the economies of the United States and Russia, but that bridges of practical cooperation could be thrown across that gulf.

Mr. Johnston advocated extensive post-war trade and visits between American business and "Soviet capitalists" as one bridge, but said that "each of our countries should be allowed to pursue its own unique economic experiment unimpeded by the other."

Bluntly, he told the Russians that Americans "were most private-minded and most individual-minded and, make no mistake, we are determined to remain so and even become more so."

Mr. Johnston, who arrived in Russia last week, was luncheon guest of A. I. Mikoyan, Soviet Foreign Trade Commissar, at Spiridonovka House. At the table sat Soviet trade experts, members of the Soviet Foreign Office, United States Ambassador W. Averell Harriman and Soviet military men.

At first the Russians appeared nonplussed by Mr. Johnston's bluntness, but later they burst into gales of mirth at his sallies at American Communists and Marxians.

"I shall try to show you my admiration for your heroic deeds and

Continued on Page 6

FOE 'EXPLAINS' STEP

Hitler Ordered Troops Out to Save Rome, Germans Assert

ENEMY PLEA BARED

Kesselring Made Last-Minute Renewal of Open-City Offer

By The Associated Press.

LONDON, June 4—The Germans announced tonight in a special communiqué—broadcast after the Allies had liberated Rome—the withdrawal of German troops to the northwest of the city and said that the Allies had received a plan whereby Rome would have been regarded as an "open city."

The open-city proposals were said to have been advanced at 11 P. M. on Saturday, less than twenty-four hours before Rome changed hands. The first word from Adolf Hitler's headquarters in several days asserted that the fight in Italy would continue and that measures were being taken "to force final victory for Germany and her allies." The communiqué said:

"As the front line, in the course of the present fighting in Italy, was gradually approaching nearer and nearer to the city of Rome, there was danger that Rome, one of the oldest cultural centers of the world, would be directly involved in the present fighting. Hitler has ordered the withdrawal of German troops to the northwest of Rome to prevent the destruction of Rome.

"The struggle in Italy will be continued with unshakable determination to break the enemy attacks and to force final victory for Germany and her allies. The necessary measures for an eventual German victory are being taken in close collaboration with fascist Italy and other allied powers.

"The year of invasion will bring Germany's enemies an anninilating defeat at the most decisive moment."

Kesselring's Proposals Listed

Field Marshal Gen. Albert Kesselring, the German commander in Italy, sent the Allies proposals that Rome be regarded as an open city, a special announcement from Hitler's headquarters said. The statement was broadcast by the German radio and was received only after a dispatch filed from Rome had announced the crushing of the last German resistance units within the city. The broadcast said:

"The German High Command announced that the supreme commander of German troops in Italy, Field Marshal Kesselring, had submitted proposals to the Vatican with the request that they should be conveyed to the Anglo-American High Command. The proposals confirmed the recognition of Rome

Continued on Page 4

Enraged Bull Kills 2 Brothers, Gores Neighbor on Long Island

Special to THE NEW YORK TIMES.

BABYLON, L. I., June 4 — Two dairy farmers, brothers, were found this morning gored and trampled to death on the Ames Farm in North Babylon, victims of their Guernsey bull, which had run wild and scattered their herd of thirty cows over near-by roads. A neighbor, trying to round up the scattered herd, was gored in the groin by the infuriated animal.

State troopers were forced to shoot and kill the belligerent bull.

The victims were George W. Ames, 41 years old, and his brother, James Hawley Ames, 35, who operated the Ames Farm on Phelps Lane, North Babylon. So far as is known no one saw the unequal encounter that cost them their lives. Their bodies were discovered, lying about 100 feet apart, several hundred yards from the cow barn.

The first intimation that anything was amiss came with complaints to the State Police in North Babylon that the Ames cows were wandering off the pasture and on the near-by Phelps Lane and Belmont Road. Two State troopers were sent to the farm and succeeded in getting most of the cows back into the pasture along with the bull. They put in a call for two additional troopers to round up the remainder of the herd.

Their suspicions aroused by the fact that the milk delivery truck, fully loaded, was standing in its place although it usually left on its rural route at 8 A. M., the troopers made their way to the farmhouse. There they found Mrs. Kathleen Ames, mother of the two men, and her daughter, Jane L. Ames, a school teacher.

A search of the farm was begun and Trooper Anthony Cherry came

Continued on Page 20

THE FIRST OF EUROPE'S WAR CAPITALS TO FALL TO THE ALLIES

The sign tells the troops they have entered Rome. The New York Times (U. S. Signal Corps Radiotelephoto)

U. S. 'HEAVIES' BOMB IN FRANCE ALL DAY

Attack Boulogne Area Twice, Rip Rail, Air Targets Near Paris—Genoa Blasted

By JAMES MacDONALD
By Cable to THE NEW YORK TIMES.

LONDON, Monday, June 5—Continuing to pave the way for the Allied invasion of the Continent hundreds of Allied bombers and fighters from Britain scorched a 200-mile stretch of the French coast yesterday and penetrated inland.

Three separate missions were carried out by the Flying Fortresses and Liberators of the United States Eighth Air Force with fighter escort over northwestern France. They met little Luftwaffe opposition; the enemy flak ranged from moderate to heavy.

In the morning and again in the afternoon strong formations of the

Continued on Page 5

Road to Rome Hard Fought, Yet Crowded With Civilians

By MILTON BRACKER
By Wireless to THE NEW YORK TIMES.

IN THE OUTSKIRTS OF ROME, June 4—The Fifth Army's entry into the suburbs of Rome was made along Highway 6—the Via Casilina—which runs into Rome at Centocelle, a suburb test known for its airport. But the advance did not mean a simple triumphal procession into the heart of Rome. It meant going in in careful infantry columns along the sides of the road. Most of the men had their bayonets fixed and they wore deadly earnest expressions because two wrecked Sherman tanks along the approaches told what had happened to other Americans earlier today.

Just before 4 P. M., a huge column of smoke billowed up from the southwest corner of the city, indicating a demolition. At the same time, a mine went off with a terrible burst beyond the farthest of the two tanks, and it tore an Italian woman to pieces. As the afternoon wore on, the sniping

Continued on Page 4

War News Summarized

MONDAY, JUNE 5, 1944

Rome was liberated from the Nazi-Fascist aggressors last night. The first European capital to be wrested from the enemy came under full Allied control when a force that had fought its way up from the old Anzio beachhead knocked out a German scout car in the center of the city. There was fierce fighting with enemy rear-guard detachments at the outskirts of Rome before the city was liberated.

Fifth Army units and the vanguard of the Eighth Army, which entered the Eternal City later, were sent in hot pursuit of the fleeing Germans. Rome was found to be 95 per cent intact, with destruction centered in the railroad yards. [All the foregoing 1:8; maps P. 2.]

German artillery and snipers held off the Allied advance between the airport at Centocello and the city limits. Civilians, obviously happy over the departure of the Nazis, remained calm as United Nations troops moved in. [1:5-6.]

Hitler's headquarters announced after the Fifth Army had entered the city that the Germans had withdrawn to new lines northwest of Rome. Shortly before the city fell they dispatched a proposal that Rome be declared an open city. [1:3.]

Capture of Rome, according to military observers in London, made it much more likely that the main objective of the offensive—destruction of the German Tenth and Fourteenth armies—would be accomplished, with possible enemy losses reaching up to 100,000. [3:1.]

The AMG, following closely upon the victorious Allied forces, was fully prepared to undertake the gigantic task of feeding some 2,000,000 civilians. Vast stocks of food have been accumulated for distribution. [1:6-7.]

Washington withheld official comment until President Roosevelt's radio address tonight, but the capital was interested in how soon King Victor Emmanuel would fulfill his promise to retire when Rome had fallen to the Allies. [1:7.]

American heavy bombers from Britain smashed three times at enemy installations in France yesterday as the air invasion continued unabated against little enemy opposition. Italian-based aircraft struck rail lines on the French-Italian border. [1:4.]

United States troops resumed the offensive against the three airfields on Biak Island, off New Guinea. Thirty Japanese planes were shot down in widespread fights from Biak to Truk. [8:2.] Continued improvement in Allied positions was reported from Burma [8:3] although in China the Japanese made some gains toward Changsha while losing ground in other sectors. [8:4-5.]

Eric Johnston, president of the United States Chamber of Commerce, told 100 Soviet trade leaders at a Moscow luncheon that the way to bridge the economic gulf separating American and Russian economies lay in closer knowledge and greater mutual respect. [1:2.]

CONQUERORS' GOAL REACHED BY ALLIES

Fifth and Eighth Armies Drive Up From South on Rome in a Historic Campaign

By HERBERT L. MATTHEWS
By Wireless to THE NEW YORK TIMES.

ROME, June 4—The Allies' troops fought their way into Rome this morning and at nightfall they were still fighting on the outer edges, which the Germans were defending despite all their protestations about considering Rome an open city. Other large German units faced entrapment south of Highway 6 unless they could be pulled back across the Tiber or through Rome.

But Rome has been reached—the goal of conquerors throughout the ages, though none was ever before able to make the almost impossible south-north campaign. What Hannibal did not dare to do, the Allies' generals accomplished, but at such a cost in blood, matériel and time that it will probably never again be attempted.

All roads from all over the world led to Rome today as a United

Continued on Page 3

CITY'S FALL FOCUSES POLITICAL CHANGES

Victor Emmanuel's Promise to Retire Recalled—Badoglio Cabinet May Step Down

Special to THE NEW YORK TIMES.

WASHINGTON, June 4 — Pending receipt of final details of the fall of Rome, most Government leaders tonight refrained from direct comment. It was felt that the first official reaction to the Allied victory would come from President Roosevelt in the radio address that the White House announced he would make tomorrow night.

Interest in the news of the capture of the Italian capital centered not so much in the military victory as in the probable political consequences, particularly those stemming from King Victor Emmanuel's recent statement that he planned to retire as Italy's ruler as soon as Rome fell to the Allies.

The King announced April 12 that he intended to turn Italy's affairs over to Crown Prince Humbert, and said the transfer of power would take place "on the day on which the Allied troops entered Rome."

Even more important than this move are the effects the change may have on the future of the Italian Government now headed by Marshal Pietro Badoglio. Developments, it was said, will be watched closely not only as to other high appointments to be made after Prince Humbert takes over control but also as to any alterations in the structure of the Italian Government.

While the diplomatic and politi-

Continued on Page 4

AMG Will Rush Food for Rome, Teeming With 750,000 Refugees

By HAROLD CALLENDER
By Wireless to THE NEW YORK TIMES.

ALGIERS, June 4—The fall of Rome will add about 2,000,000 persons to those whom the Allies have assumed responsibility of feeding Allied authorities estimated today. But the Allied Military Government, now operating under the Allied Control Commission, has long prepared for the task and is believed to be ready.

The normal population of the Italian capital is estimated to have been swollen by 750,000 refugees from Naples and other places.

Allied authorities have stocks of wheat, canned milk and dehydrated vegetables ready to send to Rome quickly with the cooperation of the Fifth and Eighth Armies regarding transport by trucks.

At Anzio landing facilities have been built since the establishment of the bridgehead, and ships can be unloaded at Gaeta.

In the plans already made Rome has been divided into regions for the distribution of foodstuffs by Italian and Allied personnel under the authority of the commission. An emergency system has been prepared to provide strict control over the black market, which otherwise might absorb the local produce destined to go into the Allied pool for distribution on a ration basis to the masses who cannot afford the black market.

Capt. Matthias F. Correa, former United States Attorney for the Southern District of New York, has a staff of investigators, including 150 Guardia di Finanza, ready to combat the black market

Continued on Page 4

AMERICANS IN FIRST

U. S. Armor Spearheads Thrust Through Last Defenses of Rome

FINAL BATTLE BITTER

Fifth and Eighth Armies Rush On Beyond City in Pursuit of Foe

By The United Press.

NAPLES, June 4—The Fifth Army captured Rome tonight, liberating for the first time a German-enslaved European capital. German rear guards were fleeing in disorganized retreat to the northwest.

Except for the railway yards, smashed by the Allies' bombs, the city is 95 per cent intact United Press correspondents reported, after their arrival in the city.

Late tonight, the British Eighth Army, rushing into Rome from the southeast along the Via Casilina, was reported to be joining the Fifth Army in close pursuit of the hard-pressed enemy remnants, under orders to destroy them to a man if possible. Only enough troops to maintain order and ferret out any German snipers or suicide nests were to be left in Rome as the Allies' main armies pounded on without pausing to celebrate their greatest triumph, coming 270 days after the start of the Italian campaign.

[The Allies battled German rear guards to the edge of the ancient Forum, The Associated Press reported. A force from the old Anzio beachhead completed the mopping up of German forces at 9:15 P. M. by knocking out an enemy scout car in front of the Bank of Italy, almost within the shadow of Trajan's Column.]

Final Stand at Rome's Gates

At the very gates of Rome, the Germans had made a final stand but Lieut. Gen. Mark W. Clark, after having waited three hours for the enemy troops to withdraw in accordance with their own declaration of Rome as an open city, ordered a violent anti-tank barrage. Then masses of Fifth Army men and weapons crashed into the city and began mopping up enemy snipers and a few tanks and mobile guns trying to cover the retreat.

More of the enemy survivors of the Allies' whirlwind offensive were streaming in congested retreat to the northwest at the mercy of the Allies' planes, which, during the day, destroyed or damaged 600 enemy trucks and other vehicles. The Germans' jammed traffic columns stretched fifty-five miles to Lake Bolsena.

Direct radio contact with American correspondents in Rome was established tonight. A United Press reporter said that the main entry into the city had been made along the Via Casilina, which passes through the Porta Maggiore at the southeastern edge of the city. Other Allied troops were reported to have fought their way through the Ostiense freight yards, just south of St. Paul Gate, the main entrance to the city from due south and only one and one-quarter miles from the Venice Palace.

The entry into Rome came with dramatic suddenness after the Al-

Continued on Page 3

President to Talk On Rome Tonight

By The United Press.

WASHINGTON, June 4—A fifteen-minute radio address will be made by President Roosevelt to the nation tomorrow night on the liberation of Rome, the White House announced tonight.

Mr. Roosevelt will speak from 8:30 to 8:45 P. M.

The President's message will be broadcast over all major networks.

"All the News That's Fit to Print"

The New York Times.

Copyright, 1944, by The New York Times Company.

6 A. M. EXTRA

Partly cloudy and warmer today; moderate to fresh winds.

Temperatures Yesterday—Max., 67; Min., 51
Sunrise, 5:25 A. M.; Sunset, 8:26 P. M.

VOL. XCIII . No. 31,545. Entered as Second-Class Matter, Postoffice, New York, N. Y. NEW YORK, TUESDAY, JUNE 6, 1944. THREE CENTS NEW YORK CITY

ALLIED ARMIES LAND IN FRANCE IN THE HAVRE-CHERBOURG AREA; GREAT INVASION IS UNDER WAY

ROOSEVELT SPEAKS

Says Rome's Fall Marks 'One Up and Two to Go' Among Axis Capitals

WARNS WAY IS HARD

Asks World to Give the Italians a Chance for Recovery

The text of President Roosevelt's address is on Page 5.

By CHARLES HURD

Special to THE NEW YORK TIMES.

WASHINGTON, June 5—President Roosevelt hailed tonight the capture of Rome, first of the three major Axis capitals to fall, as a great achievement on the road toward total conquest of the Axis. Rome, he said, marked "one up and two to go."

The President spoke for a quarter-hour on the radio, as had been announced yesterday, but his speech was notable for its lack of heroics. It was in no sense a speech of triumph, but rather a tribute to the United Nations forces and leadership that drove the Germans from Rome.

With this tribute he combined a solemn warning that much greater fighting lies ahead before the Axis is defeated, as well as high tributes to the Italian people, whom he again welcomed as a people into the family of nations opposed to the Axis.

"Italy should go on," Mr. Roosevelt said, "as a great mother nation, contributing to the culture and the progress and the good-will of mankind, developing her special talents in the arts, crafts, and sciences, and preserving her historic and cultural heritage for the benefit of all peoples.

"We want and expect the help of the future Italy toward lasting peace. All the other nations opposed to fascism and nazism ought to help to give Italy a chance."

Shrines Should Live, He Says

President Roosevelt saw considerable significance in the fact that Rome should be the first Axis capital to fall. He remarked its shrines, "visible symbols of the faith and determination of the early saints and martyrs that Christianity should live and become universal," and added that "it will be a source of deep satisfaction that the freedom of the Pope and of Vatican City is assured by the armies of the United Nations."

There is significance, too, he added, in the fact that Rome was liberated by a composite force of soldiers from many nations.

Reviewing the military picture, the President pointed out that "it would be unwise to inflate in our own minds the military importance of the capture of Rome." He cautioned his auditors that while the Germans have retreated "thousands of miles" across Africa and back through Italy "they have suffered heavy losses, but not great enough yet to cause collapse."

"Therefore," he added, "the victory still lies some distance ahead. That distance will be covered in due time—have no fear of that. But it will be tough and it will be costly."

Turning to the relief problem in the newly liberated portion of Italy, Mr. Roosevelt noted that some persons thought of the financial cost, but he maintained that the work would pay dividends "by eliminating fascism" and any future desire by Italians to "start another war of aggression." Relief has been planned, he added, but transport demands are so great that "improvement must be gradual."

He warned Italy that it "cannot grow in stature by seeking to build up a great militaristic empire,"

Continued on Page 5

Conferees Accept Cabaret Tax Cut

By The Associated Press.

WASHINGTON, June 5—A House-Senate conference committee agreed today to cut back the cabaret tax from 30 to 20 per cent, but eliminated a provision exempting service men and women from the levy.

The group decided to put the national debt limit at $260,000,000,000 as originally requested by the Administration.

The action is subject to House and Senate votes. The conferees met informally today, but members said that the decisions probably would stand as their final recommendation.

The House, at the insistence of a group of Republicans, passed a bill raising the debt ceiling only from $210,000,000,000 to $240,000,000,000. The Senate then put the figure at $260,000,000,000 and attached a rider reducing the cabaret tax from 30 to 20 per cent and exempting men and women in uniform from paying the tax on their checks.

Some tax experts argued that this exemption would make administration of the excise on night clubs impossible.

FEDERAL LAW HELD RULING INSURANCE

Supreme Court, 4-3, Decides Business Is Interstate and Subject to Trust Act

Special to THE NEW YORK TIMES.

WASHINGTON, June 5—The Supreme Court, by a four-to-three decision today, held that the insurance companies of the country, with assets of $37,000,000,000 and annual premium collections in excess of $6,000,000,000, are in interstate commerce and thus subject to the Sherman Anti-Trust Law.

The decision upset precedents which began with a contrary decision by the court more than seventy-five years ago and have been reaffirmed repeatedly since the adoption of the anti-trust law in 1890.

The majority decision, written

Continued on Page 13

PURSUIT ON IN ITALY

Allies Pass Rome, Cross Tiber as Foe Quits Bank Below City

PLANES JOIN IN CHASE

1,200 Vehicles Wrecked —Eighth Army Battles Into More Towns

By The Associated Press.

ROME, June 5—The Allies' armor and motorized infantry roared through Rome today without pausing, crossed the Tiber River and proceeded with the grim task of destroying two battered German armies fleeing to the north.

Fighter-bombers spearheaded the pursuit, jamming the escape highways with burning enemy transport and littering the fields with dead and wounded Germans. The enemy was tired, disorganized and bewildered by the slashing assault, which in twenty-five days had inflicted a major catastrophe on the Germans and liberated Rome almost without damage.

Railway Yards Bombed

Five hundred American heavy bombers blasted railway yards at five points in northern Italy between Venice and Rimini along which the Germas might attempt to move reinforcements and equipment to bolster their beaten armies. Hour after hour, the Allies' planes swept down on highways leading northward and tore the fleeing enemy apart. Twelve hundred combat vehicles were destroyed from dawn to dark yesterday, and hundreds more today. Farther north, medium bombers smashed bridges and rail facilities.

[The Germans have abandoned the entire left bank of the Tiber from Ostia, at its mouth, to Rome, according to a Vichy broadcast quoted by The Associated Press.

[The Germans are already entrenched in mountain positions

Continued on Page 2

War News Summarized

TUESDAY, JUNE 6, 1944

The invasion of western Europe began this morning.

General Eisenhower, in his first communiqué from Supreme Headquarters, Allied Expeditionary Force, issued at 3:30 A. M., said that "Allied naval forces supported by strong air forces began landing Allied armies this morning on the northern coast of France."

The assault was made by British, American and Canadian troops who, under command of Gen. Sir Bernard L. Montgomery, landed in Normandy. London gave no further details but earlier Berlin had broadcast that parachute troops had landed on the Normandy Peninsula near Cherbourg and that invasion forces were pouring from landing craft under cover of warships near Havre. Dunkerque and Calais were being heavily bombed, the Germans said.

Later announcements from Berlin said that there was fighting between Caen and Trouville and that shock troops had swung into action to halt the invasion. [All the foregoing, 1:8.]

General Eisenhower, in an order of the day to each member of the "great crusade," told his men the enemy would fight savagely and added: "We will accept nothing less than full victory. Good luck." In a broadcast to the "Peoples of Western Europe," he said the day would come when he would need their full help. A special word to France added that Frenchmen would rule the country. [1:6-7.] Almost simultaneously it was announced that General de Gaulle had arrived in London. [6:2.]

The liberation of Rome in no way slowed the Allied pursuit of the tired and disorganized German armies in Italy yesterday. Armored and motorized units sped across the Tiber River to press hard upon the retreating enemy's heels. Five hundred heavy bombers joined with lighter aircraft to smash rail and road routes leading to northern Italy and to add to the foe's demoralization. The Eighth Army, despite heavy opposition, especially northeast of Valmontone, captured a number of strategic towns. [1:3; map P. 2.]

General Clark said that parts of the two German armies had been smashed. He doubted the ability of the German Fourteenth to put up effective opposition and declared that the Tenth had taken a bad beating. [3:1.]

King Victor Emmanuel fulfilled his promise and turned over all authority to his son, Crown Prince Humbert. [1:5-6.]

President Roosevelt warned the people of the United States in a radio talk last night not to over-emphasize the military significance of the liberation of Rome. "Germany has not yet been driven to surrender," he said. "Victory still lies some distance ahead. * * * It will be tough and it will be costly." The President appealed to the world to give Italy a chance to contribute her share to a lasting peace. [1:1.]

In the Pacific theatre Americans were converging on the Biak airfields. Allied planes sank one and damaged two Japanese destroyers and shot down at least eighteen aircraft. [8:1.]

FIRST ALLIED LANDING MADE ON SHORES OF WESTERN EUROPE

June 6, 1944

General Eisenhower's armies invaded northern France this morning. While the landing points were not specified, the Germans said that troops had gone ashore near Havre and that fighting raged at Caen (1). The enemy also said that parachutists had descended at the northern tip of the Normandy Peninsula (2) and heavy bombing had been visited on Calais and Dunkerque (3).

POPE GIVES THANKS ROME WAS SPARED

Voices Appreciation to Both Belligerents in Message to Throng at St. Peter's

By Wireless to THE NEW YORK TIMES.

VATICAN CITY, June 5—Pope Pius XII appeared on the balcony of St. Peter's at 6 P. M. today to thank God that Rome had been spared from the ravages of war while before him in the densely packed square of St. Peter's and the new broad Via Della Conciliazione tens of thousands of Romans cheered themselves hoarse.

It was the third time today that the Pontiff had showed himself to cheering crowds, as he had appeared twice at a window of his office this morning. But this was a solemn, sacred occasion and no one knowing anything about Pius XII can doubt the fervor of his thankfulness that Rome had been saved.

The Pontiff seemed strong and well and his voice carried far, though it was difficult to hear every word he said because of the crowd.

"We must give thanks to God for the favors we have received," said the Pope. "Rome has been spared. This day will go down in the annals of Rome."

He went on to say he hoped that Italians would be worthy of the grace shown them and put aside hatred and all personal vendettas. He then thanked both belligerents—the Allies and Germany—for having left Rome intact.

After a prayer of thankfulness to the Blessed Virgin and Saints Peter and Paul, guardians of Rome, the Pontiff gave his blessing, "urbe et orbis," as the immense crowd knelt before him.

[The Associated Press estimated the crowd was between 250,000 and 500,000.]

The world has changed for Rome but the Vatican goes on imperturbably as it has through so many other conquests in centuries gone by. It is neutral in fact and spirit. The Pope and all high officials went about their daily routine today as in the past. Except for the tanks and armored cars running along the street in front of St. Peter's one could never know what had happened today.

Continued on Page 5

Italy's Monarch Yields Rule To Son, but Retains Throne

By The Associated Press.

NAPLES, June 5—Victor Emmanuel III stepped aside as King of Italy today, as he previously had said he would do upon the liberation of Rome, and handed to his 39-year-old son, Crown Prince Humbert, all "royal prerogatives." Italian political pressure had been brought to bear against him since the occupation of Naples.

In a decree signed by himself and countersigned by Premier Pietro Badoglio, head of the Italian Liberation Government, the King named his son Lieutenant General of the Realm. The monarch, however, retained his title as head of the House of Savoy and remains as King without power.

[The first act of the Council of Ministers after the transfer of royal powers was a formal denunciation of the 1940 armistice treaty inflicted on France, The United Press said.]

Victor Emmanuel, who became King July 29, 1900, had announced last April 12 his "irrevocable" decision to withdraw from public life "on the day on which Allied troops enter Rome."

Little more than a figurehead since Benito Mussolini assumed the dictatorship of Italy, Victor Emmanuel had won a reputation in the first years of his reign as a sympathetic monarch, interested in his people and their problems.

Prince Humbert, tall and erect, opposed fascism in Italy at the start, but later made a truce with Mussolini. In effect, Humbert becomes the King's regent.

TEXT OF ROYAL DECREE

The King's withdrawal decree:

I, Victor Emmanuel III, by the grace of God and by the will of the nation King of Italy, in collaboration with the President of the Council of Ministers and with the agreement of the Council, have ordered and order as follows:

My beloved son, Humbert of Savoy, Prince of Piedmont, is nominated our Lieutenant General. In collaboration with responsible Ministers he will in our name superintend all matters of administration and exercise all royal prerogatives without exception, signing royal decrees which will be countersigned and authenticated in the usual way.

We order all concerned to observe this decree and to see that it is observed as the law of the State.

Given at Ravello June 5, 1944.

VICTOR EMMANUEL.

(Countersigned) PIETRO BADOGLIO.

The withdrawal was presented to

Continued on Page 4

ALLIED WARNING FLASHED TO COAST

People Told to Clear Area 22 Miles Inland as Soon as Instructions Are Given

By Cable to THE NEW YORK TIMES.

LONDON, Tuesday, June 6—The British Broadcasting Corporation began its 8 A. M. news bulletin this morning with quotations from a Supreme Headquarters' "urgent warning" to inhabitants of the enemy-occupied countries living near the coast.

Gen. Dwight D. Eisenhower has directed that whenever possible in France a warning shall be given to towns in which certain targets will be intensively bombed.

This warning, the broadcast said,

Continued on Page B

PARADE OF PLANES CARRIES INVADERS

Witness Says First 'Chutists Met Only Light Fire When They Landed in France

The first eyewitness account of the Allies' invasion of Europe was given in a pool broadcast from London this morning by Wright Bryan of the National Broadcasting Company, who accompanied the airborne troops in their landings.

His account said the first spearhead of Allied forces landed by parachute in northern France in the first hour of D-day.

"In the navigator's dome in the flight deck of a C-47, I rode across the English Channel with the first group of planes from the United States Ninth Air Force Troop Carrier Command to take our fighting men into Europe," Mr. Brvan said.

He added that just before he left French soil for the return trip he saw seventeen American paratroopers, led by a lieutenant colonel, jump with their arms, ammunition and equipment into German-occupied France."

He declared that his group at the head of the leading wing was met with "only scattering small

Continued on Page B

Eisenhower Instructs Europeans; Gives Battle Order to His Armies

Following are the texts of a statement by Gen. Dwight D. Eisenhower broadcast to the people of western Europe and his Order of the Day to the Allied Expeditionary Force as recorded by The New York Times and the Columbia Broadcasting System:

People of western Europe! A landing was made this morning on the coast of France by troops of the Allied Expeditionary Force. This landing is part of the concerted United Nations plan for the liberation of Europe, made in conjunction with our great Russian Allies. I have this message for all of you. Although the initial assault may not have been made in your own country, the hour of your liberation is approaching.

All patriots, men and women, young and old, have a part to play in the achievement of final victory. To members of resistance movements, whether led by national or outside leaders, I say: "Follow the instructions you have received." To patriots who are not members of organized resistance groups I say, "continue your passive resistance, but do not needlessly endanger your lives until I give you the signal to rise and strike the enemy. The day will come when I shall need your united strength. Until that day, I call on you for the hard task of discipline and restraint."

Citizens of France! I am proud to have again under my command the gallant forces of France. Fighting beside their Allies, they will play a worthy part in the liberation of their

Continued on Page 3

EISENHOWER ACTS

U. S., British, Canadian Troops Backed by Sea, Air Forces

MONTGOMERY LEADS

Nazis Say Their Shock Units Are Battling Our Parachutists

Communique No. 1 On Allied Invasion

By Broadcast to THE NEW YORK TIMES.

LONDON, Tuesday, June 6—The Supreme Headquarters of the Allied Expeditionary Force issued this communiqué this morning:

"Under the command of General Eisenhower, Allied naval forces, supported by strong air forces, began landing Allied armies this morning on the northern coast of France."

By RAYMOND DANIELL

By Cable to THE NEW YORK TIMES.

SUPREME HEADQUARTERS ALLIED EXPEDITIONARY FORCES, Tuesday, June 6—The invasion of Europe from the west has begun.

In the gray light of a summer dawn Gen. Dwight D. Eisenhower threw his great Anglo-American force into action today for the liberation of the Continent. The spearhead of attack was an Army group commanded by Gen. Sir Bernard L. Montgomery and comprising troops of the United States, Britain and Canada.

General Eisenhower's first communiqué was terse and calculated to give little information to the enemy. It said merely that "Allied naval forces supported by strong air forces began landing Allied armies this morning on the northern coast of France."

After the first communiqué was released it was announced that the Allied landing was in Normandy.

Caen Battle Reported

German broadcasts, beginning at 6:30 A. M., London time, [12:30 A. M. Eastern war time] gave first word of the assault. [The Associated Press said General Eisenhower, for the sake of surprise, deliberately let the Germans have the "first word."]

The German DNB agency said the Allied invasion operations began with the landing of airborne troops in the area of the mouth of the Seine River.

[Berlin said the "center of gravity" of the fierce fighting was at Caen, thirty miles southwest of Havre and sixty-five miles southeast of Cherbourg, The Associated Press reported. Caen is ten miles inland from the sea, at the base of the seventy-five-mile-wide Normandy Peninsula, and fighting there might indicate the Allies' seizing of a beachhead.

[DNB said in a broadcast just before 10 A. M. (4 A. M. Eastern war time) that the Anglo-American troops had been reinforced at dawn at the mouth of the Seine River in the Havre area.]

[An Allied correspondent broadcasting from Supreme Headquarters, according to the Columbia Broadcasting System, said this morning that "German tanks are moving up

Continued on Page A Following Page 3

"All the News That's Fit to Print"

The New York Times.

LATE CITY EDITION
POSTSCRIPT
Sunny and moderately warmer.
Temperatures Yesterday—Max., 77; Min., 59
Sunrise, 5:25 A. M.; Sunset, 8:25 P. M.

VOL. XCIII No. 31,546. Entered as Second-Class Matter, Postoffice, New York, N. Y. NEW YORK, WEDNESDAY, JUNE 7, 1944. P THREE CENTS NEW YORK CITY

HITLER'S SEA WALL IS BREACHED, INVADERS FIGHTING WAY INLAND; NEW ALLIED LANDINGS ARE MADE

COUNTRY IN PRAYER

President on Radio Leads in Petition He Framed for Allied Cause

LIBERTY BELL RINGS

Lexington and Boston's Old North Church Hold Services

By LAWRENCE RESNER

Led by President Roosevelt, the entire country joined in solemn prayer yesterday for the success of the United Nations armies of liberation.

Over the radio networks at 10 P. M. the President read the prayer which he had composed in the early invasion hours yesterday morning, the text of which had already been heard in both houses of Congress.

The prayer had been sent out throughout the country and printed in newspapers so that the millions who listened to the broadcast could recite the words with the President as he spoke.

The President's prayer that the Allied forces be led "straight and true" in the struggle to liberate the suffering humanity of Europe was the climax of a day marked both by the solemn appreciation of the human values involved and exhilaration over the fact that the great battle had been joined.

His expression of faith that with the Grace of God, "and by the righteousness of our cause, our sons will triumph," was echoed in the hearts of his countrymen, in special prayers offered in great cathedrals and small parishes, and in the ordinary conversation of Americans everyhere.

"Heartbreaking Days Ahead"

In Congress, after the prayer was read, Joseph W. Martin of Massachusetts, House minority leader, warned that "many heartbreaking days lie ahead," and Senator Alben W. Barkley of Kentucky, the majority leader, said that "all we need or ought to do or can do is pray fervently and devoutly for the success of our troops and those of our allies."

At Albany, Governor Dewey, accompanied by Mrs. Dewey, attended St. Peter's Episcopal Church for a few brief moments of prayer, while here in New York City an estimated 50,000 persons who gathered at Madison Square were led in prayer by Mayor La Guardia.

The observance at Madison Square was typical of smaller gatherings called in many American cities and attended by persons of all faiths and creeds.

In Columbus, Ohio, Governor John W. Bricker called the landings in France "the beginning of the end of the forces of evil and destruction," and in Chicago Bishop Henry St. George Tucker, president of the Federal Council of the Churches of Christ in America, suggested the words for a D-day prayer.

In many communities the news of Gen. Dwight D. Eisenhower's first invasion communiqué was greeted with sirens or whistles.

The Liberty Bell in Philadelphia, which heralded the nation's independence, was rung six times to mark the landings. In Boston and Lexington services were held in historic churches.

Both The Associated Press and The United Press reported a generally undemonstrative reception of the news. Groups gathered at newsstands, or stood before radio loudspeakers, eager to learn the fullest details of the actual military events, but, with very few exceptions the thousands of war workers in the principal industrial areas were credited with receiving with solemn intentness the confirmation of the Allied invasion, and in many instances were said to have worked with extra zeal thereafter.

The news was brought to workers on night shifts over plant loud-

Continued on Page 3

"Let Our Hearts Be Stout"

A Prayer by the President of the United States

This is the invasion prayer that President Roosevelt wrote while Allied troops were landing on the coast of France and which he read to the nation with his introductory words on the radio last night, as recorded and transcribed by THE NEW YORK TIMES:

My Fellow-Americans:

Last night when I spoke with you about the fall of Rome I knew at that moment that troops of the United States and our Allies were crossing the Channel in another and greater operation. It has come to pass to success thus far.

And so in this poignant hour, I ask you to join with me in prayer:

Almighty God: Our sons, pride of our nation, this day have set upon a mighty endeavor, a struggle to preserve our Republic, our religion and our civilization, and to set free a suffering humanity.

Lead them straight and true; give strength to their arms, stoutness to their hearts, steadfastness in their faith.

They will need Thy blessings. Their road will be long and hard. For the enemy is strong. He may hurl back our forces. Success may not come with rushing speed, but we shall return again and again; and we know that by Thy grace, and by the righteousness of our cause, our sons will triumph.

They will be sore tried, by night and by day, without rest—until the victory is won. The darkness will be rent by noise and flame. Men's souls will be shaken with the violences of war.

For these men are lately drawn from the ways of peace. They fight not for the lust of conquest. They fight to end conquest. They fight to liberate. They fight to let justice arise, and tolerance and good-will among all Thy people. They yearn but for the end of battle, for their return to the haven of home.

Some will never return. Embrace these, Father, and receive them, Thy heroic servants, into Thy kingdom.

And for us at home—fathers, mothers, children, wives, sisters and brothers of brave men overseas, whose thoughts and prayers are ever with them—help us, Almighty God, to rededicate ourselves in renewed faith in Thee in this hour of great sacrifice.

Many people have urged that I call the nation into a single day of special prayer. But because the road is long and the desire is great, I ask that our people devote themselves in a continuance of prayer. As we rise to each new day, and again when each day is spent, let words of prayer be on our lips, invoking Thy help to our efforts.

Give us strength, too—strength in our daily tasks, to redouble the contributions we make in the physical and the material support of our armed forces.

And let our hearts be stout, to wait out the long travail, to bear sorrows that may come, to impart our courage unto our sons wheresoever they may be.

And, O Lord, give us faith. Give us faith in Thee; faith in our sons; faith in each other; faith in our united crusade. Let not the keenness of our spirit ever be dulled. Let not the impacts of temporary events, of temporal matters of but fleeting moment—let not these deter us in our unconquerable purpose.

With Thy blessing, we shall prevail over the unholy forces of our enemy. Help us to conquer the apostles of greed and racial arrogances. Lead us to the saving of our country, and with our sister nations into a world unity that will spell a sure peace—a peace invulnerable to the schemings of unworthy men. And a peace that will let all men live in freedom, reaping the just rewards of their honest toil.

Thy will be done, Almighty God.

Amen.

EISENHOWER VISITS PARATROOPERS BEFORE TAKE-OFF FOR THE INVASION

The Supreme Commander in an intimate chat with some of his men in England prior to their boarding planes for the first assault on France.

The New York Times (U. S. Signal Corps Radiotelephoto)

ALL LANDINGS WIN

Our Men Are Reported in Caen and at Points on Cherbourg Peninsula

BIG AIR ARMADA AIDS

10,000 Tons of Bombs Clear the Way—Poor Weather a Worry

Latest Communique

By The Associated Press.

SUPREME HEADQUARTERS, Allied Expeditionary Force, Wednesday, June 7—Allied forces continued landings on the northern French coast throughout yesterday and "satisfactory progress was made," headquarters announced today.

United States Rangers and British Commandos formed part of the assault forces, the third invasion bulletin said.

"No further attempt at interference with our sea-borne landing was made by enemy naval forces," it continued.

"Those coastal batteries still in action are being bombarded by Allied warships," the bulletin said.

"At twilight yesterday and for the fourth time during the day Allied heavy bombers attacked rail communications and bridges in the general battle area, and "there was increased air opposition," the announcement added.

By DREW MIDDLETON
By Cable to THE NEW YORK TIMES.

SUPREME HEADQUARTERS, Allied Expeditionary Force, Wednesday, June 7—The German Atlantic Wall has been breached.

Thousands of American, Canadian and British soldiers, under cover of the greatest air and sea bombardment of history, have broken through the "impregnable" perimeter of Germany's "European fortress" in the first phase of the invasion and liberation of the Continent.

Communiqué 2, issued at the Supreme Headquarters, Allied Expeditionary Force, before last midnight, reported that all initial landings, which had earlier been located on the coast of Normandy, in northern France, had "succeeded." The Germans told of heavy fighting with Allied air-borne troops in Caen, road and railroad junction eight and one-half miles inland from the Seine Bay coast, and the enemy said

Continued on Page 2

ITALIAN DRIVE GAINS ON 70-MILE FRONT

2,000 Germans Captured Near Mouth of Tiber—French Take Tivoli Junction

By The United Press.

ROME, June 6—The Allies swept ahead on a seventy-mile front today to speed the destruction of the German armies routed from Rome.

American troops smashed five miles beyond the Tiber while French troops, now in the thick of the pursuit, captured the Tivoli junction, sixteen miles east of Rome. Near the mouth of the Tiber, British troops captured 2,000 Germans who became stranded when the Allies' bombers detroyed their escape bridges. On all sectors prisoners were being collected in batches as the bomb-hounded enemy withdrawal became more and more demoralized.

[A United Nations broadcast from Algiers, reported by the

Continued on Page 11

Roosevelt and Churchill Pleased by Invasion Gains

Special to THE NEW YORK TIMES.

WASHINGTON, June 6—President Roosevelt told a news conference, held thirteen hours after the initial announcement of the invasion of France, that the operation was proceeding according to schedule. He made this statement in a calm, rather low voice, but, with obvious satisfaction that his composure did not entirely hide.

"How do you feel about the progress of the invasion?" a reporter asked.

"It's up to schedule," Mr. Roosevelt replied, then smiled.

This was the summation of all of today's dispatches as they were analyzed by the Constitutional Commander in Chief of the Armed Forces of the United States, who, since being awakened early with news that the invasion had started, had read reports and conferred with top-ranking officers.

Small Losses Are Reported

The President added that, as of noon today, General Eisenhower had reported the loss of only two American destroyers and one LST (landing ship, tank), a heavy type of invasion barge. Losses of our air forces in the same period, Mr. Roosevelt added, were about 1 per cent of the airplanes involved. There was no figure on personnel casualties.

Other salient points emphasized by the press conference included the following:

1. Tentative dates for the invasion were set last December at the Teheran conferences, slated in May or early this month, according to the weather.
2. General Eisenhower alone decided the actual date and place.
3. Marshal Joseph Stalin has known of the plan since Teheran and has been entirely satisfied with it.
4. A "second front" a year ago would have been impossible because of lack of available men and equipment.
5. The war is not over by any means; this operation is not even over, and this is no time for overconfidence.

The President's press conference, a regularly scheduled one, was attended by 181 reporters, who filled the Executive Office almost to capacity. They found Mr. Roosevelt looking tired around the eyes but smiling. He sat at his desk in shirtsleeves, wearing a dark bow tie. He smoked a cigarette stuck into a yellow amber holder.

Mr. Roosevelt said that relatively few persons in the United States knew the tentative date for the invasion and that very few knew the actual date. He added that the ac-

Continued on Page 7

By The United Press.

LONDON, June 6—The Allied grand offensive in the west is proceeding much better than expected and "there already are hopes that an actual tactical surprise has been attained" over the German forces in France, a supremely confident Prime Minister Churchill reported today in two D-day appearances before a cheering House of Commons.

[*The text of Prime Minister Churchill's speech is on Page 4.*]

Responding to Parliament's eagerness to hear news of the latest developments across the Channel, Mr. Churchill, after announcing at noon that more than 4,000 ships and 11,000 first-line planes were behind the unprecedented assault, returned to the Commons at 6:30 P. M. with word that the "operation is proceeding in a satisfactory manner."

[Mr. Churchill promised a new statement in the Commons Wednesday on overnight developments in the invasion, The Associated Press said. Between his two statements Tuesday, it was disclosed, the Prime Minister flew to the motor caravan somewhere in rural England from which General Eisenhower is directing the invasion.]

The Prime Minister, obviously enjoying his old role of war reporter, painted a glowing picture of the initial Allied successes, which he said were accomplished with "extremely little loss," although he

Continued on Page 4

LANDING PUTS END TO 4-YEAR HIATUS

Fiery Renewal of Battle for France—Britain Recalls Grimness of Dunkerque

By RAYMOND DANIELL
By Cable to THE NEW YORK TIMES.

LONDON, June 6—This was D-day and it has gone well.

At daybreak Anglo-American forces dropped from the skies in Normandy, swarmed up on the beaches from thousands of landing craft and renewed the battle for France and for Europe, broken off four years ago at Dunkerque.

And when darkness fell, on the word of no less than Winston Churchill, the King's First Minister, who is still this country's best reporter, they had toeholds on a broad front and were fighting as far back from the coast as Caen, which is eight and a half miles behind the Channel beaches and 149 miles from Paris.

At the time he spoke the Prime Minister said that the battle which was just beginning was progressing in "a thoroughly satisfactory manner." But even he, like most people in this island, had his fingers crossed.

The Germans' resistance until now has been surprisingly, perhaps ominously, slight. Several obstacles to any amphibious operation have been surmounted. The concentration of ships has escaped serious

Continued on Page 4

Invasion and Other War News Summarized

WEDNESDAY, JUNE 7, 1944

The invasion of western Europe rounded out its first day with all initial landings successfully completed. The battle was proceeding in a 100-mile area centered at Caen, between Havre and Cherbourg, and ten miles from the Channel coast. Fighting was going on in the streets of Caen.

Elaborate defensive under-water and beach obstacles, some of which extended 1,000 yards inland, were quickly breached and Allied troops poured into enemy-held territory. According to the Germans, the invasion forces held a firm grip on the Caen-Cherbourg road and bridgeheads on the Orne estuary. Further landings and progress were reported in today's communiqué. [All the foregoing 1:8; map P. 2.]

The greatest air-borne force in the history of war was landed with surprisingly low losses and under adverse weather conditions. [5:1.]

More than 1,000 RAF heavy bombers blasted a pathway for the soldiers from midnight to dawn, when 1,300 Fortresses and Liberators took over. In eight hours the combined forces flew 7,500 sorties and dropped more than 10,000 tons of bombs on coastal defenses and enemy concentrations. Fighters attacked bridges and communications lines and even battled tanks. [3:1.] Guns of more than 600 ships poured shells into the German "Atlantic Wall" to help flatten coastal batteries. [5:3.]

Prime Minister Churchill told the House of Commons that tactical surprise had apparently been achieved in the first of a series of landings "to grow constantly in scale and intensity for weeks to come." He disclosed that more than 4,000 ships, exclusive of smaller landing craft, had participated in the landings and that the Allies had 11,000 first-line planes to throw into the battle. Mr. Churchill rejoiced over the low losses thus far incurred, but warned of heavy fighting to come. [1:5-6.]

President Roosevelt said that the invasion was "up to schedule" and that up to noon yesterday naval losses had been two destroyers and one heavy invasion barge sunk; plane losses were 1 per cent. [1:5-6.] Last night the President led the nation in prayer over the radio. [1:2-3.]

Weather over the invasion area grew steadily worse but the Allies continued to land more men and material. [5:4-5.] One reason for this was that Gen. Sir Bernard L. Montgomery expected Field Marshal Rommel to try to break the invasion by prompt counter-attacks. [6:2.]

Leaders of occupied countries broadcast messages to their countrymen to remain calm and to comply strictly with all Allied orders. General de Gaulle further urged Frenchmen to fight and to avoid capture. [6:1.]

The Berlin radio predicted more landings in France and suggested that the Allies might strike quickly for Paris. [5:7.]

London military observers predicted that the Russian army would launch a coordinated blow from the east before this week was out. [1:6-7.] Flying Fortresses made their first attack from Soviet bases when they smashed the German airfield at Galati, Rumanian Danube port. [8:4.]

Allied troops in Italy were pursuing the Germans, who were falling back in disorder. The Fifth Army was reported five to nine miles past the Tiber River. [1:4; map P. 11.]

The Axis received another blow when Portugal agreed to close down her wolfram mines and end shipments to Germany immediately. [8:8.]

In the Pacific, American troops advanced to within a mile and a half of the Mokmer airfield on Biak Island. [11:6.] The Japanese broke into the outer defenses of Changsha and were only twenty-two miles from that Chinese city. [11:7.]

Russians Poised to Attack in East; Moscow Joyous on 'Second Front'

By The United Press.

LONDON, Wednesday, June 7—Probably within twenty-four to forty-eight hours—and almost certainly before the end of the week—Soviet armies will swing their vast power into a synchronized offensive with the British-American western front forces under the master plan of Teheran envisaging the destruction of Germany this year, military observers here believe.

The Soviet operational bulletin, broadcast last night by the Moscow radio, reported that the fighting north and northwest of Jassy, Rumania, had entered its second week with Red Army forces again repulsing all attacks by large forces of enemy tanks and infantry.

Moscow announced that in Monday's fighting the Russians destroyed or disabled forty-nine enemy tanks and shot down forty-two planes. That made a total of 333 tanks wrecked, 355 planes downed and 7,300 Germans killed in the first week of the battle.

There were no changes in other sectors. In all Monday's fighting the Russians shot down forty-eight planes.

Monday night Soviet long-range planes mass-raided Jassy, setting about ninety fires, accompanied by strong explosions, among military trains, buildings and military dumps. The fires were visible more than sixty miles. All the Soviet planes returned.

The Soviet midnight supplementary bulletin reported that the Germans, having suffered heavy

Continued on Page 9

Turks Hear Report Of Landing in Greece

By Cable to THE NEW YORK TIMES.

LONDON, June 6—The Reuter agency is distributing a Turkish radio report quoting a Berlin radio report that Allied motorized troops landed at Patras in Greece and that "very great" Allied air activity over Greece had been reported from Bulgarian sources.

This was not heard direct from any German station nor was it confirmed from any other source.

ANKARA, Turkey, June 6 (AP)—Ankara buzzed tonight with reports of an Allied landing in the Peloponnesus in Greece and, although there was no official confirmation, responsible quarters said it could be true now or shortly.

A high source said that an Allied landing there would not change Turkey's neutrality.

"All the News That's Fit to Print"

The New York Times.

LATE CITY EDITION
POSTSCRIPT
Sunny and moderately warmer.
Temperatures Yesterday—Max.,74; Min.,63
Sunrise, 5:23 A. M.; Sunset, 8:25 P. M.

Copyright, 1944, by The New York Times Company.

VOL. XCIII..No. 31,547. Entered as Second-Class Matter, Postoffice, New York, N. Y. NEW YORK, THURSDAY, JUNE 8, 1944. THREE CENTS NEW YORK CITY

ALLIES CAPTURE BAYEUX, CLEAR BEACHES, AS NAZI RESISTANCE STIFFENS STEADILY; BOTH SIDES RUSHING IN AIRBORNE TROOPS

FOE FLEES IN ITALY

Allies' 40-Mile Advance Above Rome Takes Civitavecchia

RESISTANCE IS WEAK

Alexander Urges Italian Patriots to Hamper German Retreat

By The Associated Press.

ROME, Thursday, June 8—Fifth Army troops have captured the port of Civitavecchia, forty miles northwest of Rome on the Italian west coast, after a rapid advance from the Eternal City, Allied headquarters announced today.

Advance elements of the Fifth Army also reached Bracchiano, about fifteen miles north of Rome, a communiqué said.

At the same time the Eighth Army seized Subiaco, about eight miles south of the main highway running across the Italian Peninsula from Rome to the Adriatic.

Allied airmen, meanwhile, ranged far ahead of the advancing armies, blasting Nazi communications and supply centers.

The Fifth Army smashed ahead north and west of Rome last night in a drive so rapid and powerful that the Germans themselves described it officially as a "major break" through their lines.

Gen. Sir Harold R. L. G. Alexander, the Commander in Chief in Italy, proclaimed that "the strength of the German armies has been broken."

The Allied Command described the German resistance as "only light." It had dwindled to disorganized activity by delaying infantry units and self-propelled guns.

Important Peaks Reached

The advance was made along all main highways west and northwest of the city. The Allies reached yesterday within five miles of Lake Bracchiano. The march also reached the important peaks of Mount Grossara, Mount Agujro and Mount Forno, commanding the Bracchiano route for two miles.

The disorganized resistance that the Allies were encountering came from small battle groups made up of elements of various beaten units. Already more than 18,000 prisoners had been taken by the Fifth Army alone, and the total was growing.

More thousands were captured by the British Eighth Army, which was still meeting strong enemy defenses northeast of Rome as the Germans threw heavy demolitions and mine fields into the path of the advance. The Germans played for time to retreat from the mouth of a net closing in the hills above Rome.

"The hardest fighting is now centered northeast of Rome," yesterday's communiqué said. "The Germans were described as "offering strong resistance" in this area.

On the front fifty miles east of Rome New Zealanders slashed forward from Sora and captured Balsorano, seven miles to the north.

Alexander Appeals to Patriots

As the battered German Tenth and Fourteenth Armies fell back, General Alexander broadcast to Italian patriots urging them to do all that they could to upset the retreat.

["Do all in your power to impede the enemy movement," General Alexander urged, according to The United Press. "Add to the enemy's confusion in his rear and give shelter to those German nationals who will lag behind to free themselves, as you do, from the German yoke."

[The Allies are furnishing arms, explosives, food, clothing and money to Italian resistance leaders in the north to implement their help, George Hall, Parliamentary Under-Secretary of the Foreign Office, declared in London, The United Press said.]

It was apparent last night that

Continued on Page 11

Churchill Planned To Join the Invasion

By The Associated Press.

LONDON, June 7—It took a lot of persuading to keep Prime Minister Churchill from accompanying the invasion forces when they stormed the beaches of France, it was disclosed today.

Admiral Sir Bertram Ramsay, Allied naval commander, told a correspondent that he had convinced the Prime Minister "only with much difficulty" not to go along.

Admiral Ramsay said he pointed out to Mr. Churchill that the extra work involved in safeguarding him would be very great, and the Prime Minister finally relented.

HOUSE OVERRIDES RULES COMMITTEE

In First Repudiation in Years It Refuses to Admit Labor Curbs to Price Measure

By C. P. TRUSSELL
Special to The New York Times.

WASHINGTON, June 7—The House revolted today against its Rules Committee which, it was asserted, had become enabled through a coalition of Republicans and Southern Democrats to override the prerogatives of legislative committees and dictate what legislation could or could not go to the floor for consideration and vote.

At issue was labor control legislation, sponsored by Representative Howard W. Smith of Virginia, which the Rules body had decreed to be admissible as amendments to the measure to extend wartime controls over prices, wages and rents. After an hour of almost incessant oral chastisement of the committee the House repudiated with votes its latest decision and administered to it the most decisive defeat the committee has suffered in many years.

By one standing vote of 153 to 64 the House opened this decision up to alteration by defeating a motion to close debate, and by another, 170 to 44, subjected to points of order all the proposed Smith

Continued on Page 38

ALLIES REINFORCED

Sky Train 50 Miles Long Lands Men and Gear at Vital Points

LOSSES STILL SMALL

Second Airborne Phase Carried Out Despite Strong Defenses

By FREDERICK GRAHAM
By Cable to The New York Times.

LONDON, June 7—The second phase of the Allies' gigantic airborne invasion of Europe was successfully carried out late last night and early today when a fifty-mile-long train of transport planes and gliders crossed the Channel to reinforce and resupply the troops put down in the Cherbourg peninsula area early in the morning of D-day.

The thousands of United States and British paratroopers and glider-borne infantrymen who were landed in the Cherbourg area by more than 900 tow planes and gliders of the Ninth Air Force Troop Carrier Command before and after the Allied assault troops hit the beaches not only have been reinforced by new troops but have received new supplies and equipment as a result of the latest air-borne operations.

Flying in at least four separate waves—all of considerable size—the Ninth Air Force Troop Carrier Command and the Transport Command of the Allied Expeditionary Air Forces carried out the operation with small losses. Twelve tow planes and a like number of gliders were lost by the Americans and, although the exact British losses were not given, it was understood that they were low.

Varied Supplies Delivered

The first of three American waves, made up entirely of gliders towed by C-47 Douglas transports, went deep into the Cherbourg peninsula late last night to drop airborne engineers and their equipment.

The second wave, consisting of

Continued on Page 4

War News Summarized

THURSDAY, JUNE 8, 1944

The Allied Expeditionary Force captured its first important French town yesterday when it stormed into Bayeux and cut the highway to Caen. Bayeux is a fortified community at the junction of several roads about midway between Cherbourg and Havre.

The invading forces seemed to have gained their second wind and pushed steadily forward against increasing enemy resistance. All beachheads had been cleared of enemy fire and in some cases consolidated with others. German coastal batteries were silenced by naval shells and aerial pounding. More troops and supplies were pouring in a steady stream onto the beachheads despite bad weather and heavy seas.

The first enemy tank attack was beaten off in the Caen area. Today's 5 A. M. communiqué said that Allied seaborne troops had joined their airborne comrades. [All the foregoing 1:8; map P. 2.]

A fifty-mile train of transport planes and gliders ferried reinforcements to the Cherbourg Peninsula throughout Tuesday night. Artillery and jeeps were among the supplies while engineers and medical men were among the troops. [1:3.]

Allied planes maintained a protective curtain of fire along an arc extending fifty miles inland from the beaches. Roads, bridges, convoys and troop concentrations were battered by bombers and fighters to prevent the Germans from getting a counter-offensive started. The Luftwaffe began to show signs of life, but accomplished little. [1:4.]

RAF Beaufighters crippled three German destroyers on the way out of the Bay of Biscay and light Allied naval craft sent a superior enemy force scurrying through the English Channel with its casualties. [3:4.]

General Eisenhower cruised off the invasion beaches on a British warship and conferred with his operational commanders. [1:6-7.] Earlier he had announced that an agreement had been reached on military matters with General de Gaulle, and from Washington came word that President Roosevelt would name a new representative to the French Committee of National Liberation. [1:7.]

Hitler's forces suffered a reversal on the eastern front, where, according to Moscow, 10,000 men, 451 planes and hundreds of guns have been lost by them in a futile eight-day attack on Soviet lines near Jassy. [7:7.]

The Fifth Army in Italy pushed steadily beyond Rome against light resistance to take Civitavecchia. Berlin conceded a major break-through north of Rome and a split of the German lines to the west. The Eighth Army scored advances despite demolitions and minefields. [1:1.]

American troops on Biak Island off New Guinea captured the Mokmer airfield in a wide sweep that closed in on the strip from the rear. Mokmer is within bomber range of the Philippines and strategic Japanese island bases. [1:5-6; map P. 15.] Chinese troops cut the Burma Road so that it is no longer available to the Japanese, isolated Lungling and captured Lameng. The enemy was withdrawing rapidly from the Kohima area on the Burma-India border. [1:5; map P. 14.]

Only in China were the Japanese successful. They pushed to within ten miles of Changsha in Hunan Province. [14:2.]

AMERICANS ESTABLISHING BEACHHEAD ON THE COAST OF FRANCE

Assault troops moving in from landing craft as other units push over near-by hills

The New York Times (U. S. Signal Corps Radiotelephoto)

BOMBINGS CURTAIN OUR GROUND FRONT

Air Forces Batter Germans on 50-Mile Arc Beyond Troops —Luftwaffe Loses 75

By HAROLD DENNY
By Cable to The New York Times.

LONDON, Thursday, June 8—Allied air forces laid down a steady curtain of fire yesterday in a great arc extending an average of fifty miles inland from the zones where our troops are battling in France, in an all-out aerial offensive to block German attempts to counterattack in strength.

With the beachheads established and reinforcements flowing to them unhampered at sea, the United States Army Air Forces and the Royal Air Force were able to concentrate almost their entire effort on a new phase of battle.

That was by assaults on the Nazis' communication lines and troop and supply columns and trains to screen the areas we are occupying against the efforts of the Germans to throw in their operational reserves.

[The Allied air forces maintained a constant cloud of 2,000 fighters over our invasion troops Wednesday and early Thursday, a United Press dispatch said.]

Last night RAF bombers were over France in strength, striking in support of our invasion forces. [Nazi broadcasts said Breton ports and the Paris area were bombed Wednesday night.]

Full Air Cover Extended

From the first light today Allied bombers and fighters in wave after wave were seen flying out toward Pas-de-Calais, and the weather in the Strait of Dover was improving. Soon afterward bombers began to return, and outgoing and incoming formations passed in the sky.

Allied reconnaissance pilots yesterday brought back reports of increased enemy road movements ahead of our foremost lines and photographs of Nazi tanks and trucks hurrying up to battle.

Bombers and fighters of all types went in with the answer to the foe's attempted counter-blows, bombing and machine-gunning sometimes from roof-top height.

For the second day of the invasion they accomplished their missions and at the same time maintained an air cover of 600 square miles over our ground operations from Cherbourg to Havre with little interference. Our air forces had a superiority of 200 to 1.

The Luftwaffe showed more signs of life, however, and tangled with our planes in dogfights.

Incomplete reports gave a tally

Continued on Page 4

Americans Win Biak Airfield Within Range of Philippines

By The United Press.

ALLIED HEADQUARTERS IN THE SOUTHWEST PACIFIC, Thursday, June 8—American invasion forces captured the Mokmer airdrome on Biak Island yesterday, eleven days after their landing on the Japanese stronghold in Netherland New Guinea, to give the Allies an airfield within easy bombing distance of the southern Philippine Islands, less than 900 miles away, it was announced today.

The Allies' communiqué announced that the capture had been effected by troops who drove inland through the mountains and, attacking from the rear, wiped out enemy positions that for more than a week had held up American forces advancing on the airfield along a coastal road from the east. A headquarters spokesman said that the American forces were now nearing the Boroku airdrome, a little beyond the Mokmer field.

In the final rout of the Japanese around Mokmer, the communiqué said, our losses were light. Air and naval forces closely supported the closing drive, shelling and bombing enemy positions.

The Americans cleared the entire area of Japanese. As the coastal forces applied frontal pressure to the enemy, other American columns working inland through precipitous hills and palisades forced the Japanese to withdraw to Boroku.

The American forces landed on the island on May 27, capturing the village of Bosnek and advancing rapidly west toward the Mokmer field, the most important of three Japanese airstrips on Biak. But enemy snipers and machine

Continued on Page 15

BURMA ROAD CUT, ISOLATING ENEMY

Shattered Japanese Forces in General Retreat From Kohima in India

By BROOKS ATKINSON
By Wireless to The New York Times.

CHINESE EXPEDITIONARY FORCE HEADQUARTERS, June 7—All sections of the Burma Road hitherto available to Japanese transportation are now cut. Encountering little opposition and maintaining remarkable speed, the Chinese troops who crossed the Salween River a week ago arrived within two miles of Lungling yesterday and cut the road to the north and south.

The road between Lungling and Tengyueh also was cut. At present the only road to the south available for Japanese transportation is between Tengyueh and Bhamo. It is not known here whether that road can be used by motor vehicles all the way.

[The Japanese are in a general retreat east of Kohima in India, the Southeast Asia Command announced, according to The Associated Press.]

There is very little Japanese response to Chinese artillery fire in the Lameng sector overlooking the Burma Road crossing of the Salween River. The Japanese are unable or unwilling to continue the artillery duel, but fighting is serious in the fortified hills around Lameng.

Lameng, which controls the Burma Road crossing of the Salween River, fell to the Chinese after artillery fire and bombing by the United States Fourteenth Air Force. For two years the Japanese had heavily fortified the strategic crossing.

As a consequence of aggressive action by Gen. Sung Hsi-lien's troops, the Japanese no longer are able to move vital reinforcements and supplies between Lungling and the Salween. Although it is not certain the Chinese have permanently cut the road between Lungling and Tengyueh, the Japanese are unable to transport troops and supplies in either direction between two of their most important bases.

Meanwhile, another Chinese unit

Continued on Page 14

EISENHOWER HAILS FRENCH AGREEMENT

He and Committee in Full Accord on Military Problems—Visited by de Gaulle

By RAYMOND DANIELL
By Cable to The New York Times.

LONDON, June 7—On Monday evening, just before the signal for the start of the invasion was given, Gen. Dwight D. Eisenhower told correspondents at advanced headquarters that there was complete agreement between him and the French Committee of National Liberation on the military level. He made this statement after a conference on Sunday with Gen. Charles de Gaulle, Prime Minister Churchill, Foreign Secretary Anthony Eden, Field Marshal Jan Christiaan Smuts and others.

This information, which was released for the first time tonight, was taken as an indication that General Eisenhower and General de Gaulle had been able to separate the military from the political problems connected with the liberation of France. That in turn is taken to mean that, while the political status of the Committee is left to statesmen in Washington and London, General de Gaulle has offered to give what help he can to the Allies and the offer has been accepted.

It is believed that, beyond that broad basis of agreement, some details are still open for further discussion. At any rate, General de Gaulle has had several conferences with General Eisenhower since

Continued on Page 5

Eisenhower Holds War Council On Battleship Near Beachhead

By STANLEY BURCH
Reuter Correspondent
For the Combined Allied Press

ON BOARD A BRITISH WARSHIP, Off the French Invasion Beaches, June 7—For four and a half hours this afternoon Gen. Dwight D. Eisenhower, with Admiral Sir Bertram Home Ramsay, Allied naval commander, cruised to and fro off the invasion beaches and held a series of conferences with his operational commanders.

Since we arrived off the Cherbourg Peninsula, just before midday, Gen. Sir Bernard L. Montgomery, commander of the invasion ground forces; Rear Admiral Alan G. Kirk, United States naval commander, field commanders whose names are still secret, and the commanders of the "task forces" who launched the invasion, have climbed aboard this warship and gone into immediate conference with General Eisenhower in the captain's cabin.

In this tremendous setting, surrounded by the anchored armada of thousands of ships, the Supreme Commander has secured the most up-to-date and exhaustive information of the battlefront situation within thirty hours of "H-hour."

He undertook this audacious unescorted trip, which at one point took him within five miles of the enemy, because he knew he could get infinitely more valuable information of the progress of the battle by personal meetings than by reliance on cross-Channel signals. The cruise fully justified his hope.

When General Montgomery, in

Continued on Page 4

VITAL ROAD IS CUT

Cherbourg's Link to East Severed—Our Position Now Firm

FOE'S TANKS BEATEN

First Big Counter-Blow by Enemy Launched in Night at Caen

Late Communique

By The Associated Press.

SUPREME HEADQUARTERS, Allied Expeditionary Force, Thursday, June 8—Supreme Headquarters announced today that "progress continues" after the capture of the French town of Bayeux and a crossing of the Bayeux-Caen road at several points.

"Contact has been established between our sea-borne and air-borne troops," the communiqué added.

"A steady build-up of our force has continued. During the night forces of E-boats made unsuccessful attempts to interfere with the continual arrival of supplies."

By DREW MIDDLETON
By Cable to The New York Times.

SUPREME HEADQUARTERS, Allied Expeditionary Forces, Thursday, June 8—The town of Bayeux, on the main highway and railroad from the Cherbourg Peninsula to Paris, has been stormed and captured by Gen. Sir Bernard L. Montgomery's infantry and tanks, and the highway through it, the enemy's principal lateral road in Normandy, has been crossed and severed at several points, according to a special announcement made by Allied Headquarters early today.

The Allied beachhead was steadily expanding under the impact of heavy attacks in the face of bitter German resistance. The deepest penetrations had been made at Bayeux and Caen, about five and ten miles, respectively, from the coast. If the forces at those towns have joined up, as seems likely from earlier reports of "linked" beachheads, it is probable that the Allies now hold a twenty-mile front along the Bayeux-Caen road.

Armored Blow Repulsed

Field Marshal Gen. Erwin Rommel hurled armored units of the Seventh and Fifteenth German Armies into a violent counter-blow on the night of Tuesday-Wednesday, the first important enemy counter-attack of the campaign. It faltered and broke under Allied fire, and all day Wednesday reinforcements streamed into the beachheads by sea and air under cover of another thunderous bombardment by the Allied Expeditionary Air Force and long-range fire from Allied warships, which silenced what few enemy coastal defense guns were still holding up the progress of the Americans, British and Canadians.

The capture of Bayeux may be an important step toward isolation of the Cherbourg Peninsula. Cherbourg's best links with the Seine

Continued on Page 2

Allied Fleet Said To Be Near Genoa

By The United Press.

ZURICH, Switzerland, June 7—Unconfirmed reports from German-occupied Milan said today that a large Allied fleet has been sighted off Genoa and that a landing on the Ligurian coast of northwestern Italy was expected hourly.

LONDON, June 7 (AP)—A report to the London press through Switzerland said today that an Allied landing was expected near Genoa or on southern France.

"All the News That's Fit to Print"

The New York Times.

LATE CITY EDITION
POSTSCRIPT
Partly cloudy and warmer today.
Temperatures Yesterday—Max., 72; Min., 51
Sunrise, 5:24 A. M.; Sunset, 8:26 P. M.

VOL. XCIII..No. 31,548. Entered as Second-Class Matter, Postoffice, New York, N. Y. NEW YORK, FRIDAY, JUNE 9, 1944. THREE CENTS IN NEW YORK CITY

ALLIES EXPAND BEACHHEADS IN NORMANDY; AMERICANS BATTLE FOR CHERBOURG ROAD; GERMANS PURSUED 38 MILES BEYOND ROME

FARLEY STEPS OUT AS STATE CHAIRMAN FOR LACK OF TIME

Pressure of Private Business Makes It Impossible for Him to Continue, He Declares

GIVES NO OTHER REASON

But His Opposition to Fourth Term Is Known—Successor to Be Chosen July 11

By JAMES A. HAGERTY

Saying the pressure of private business made it impossible for him to continue, James A. Farley announced yesterday his resignation as chairman of the Democratic State Committee to take effect on July 11, when a meeting of the committee will be held to elect his successor.

Mr. Farley, who has been chairman of the committee since 1930 and was last re-elected on April 12, will leave today on a business trip to the Southwest and Mexico and will return the first week in July in time to attend the meeting. He is chairman of the board of the Coca-Cola Export Corporation and the Coca-Cola Export Sales Corporation and president of the Boston Coca-Cola Bottling Corporation.

Mr. Farley declined to answer at this time questions about political implications that might be drawn from his resignation, saying he wished to stand on the statement announcing his resignation.

Won't Lose Interest in Politics

Asked if he would continue to be interested in politics, he replied:

"It would be only natural for a fellow who has always been a Democrat to be interested in the success of the Democratic party."

He added that he would attend the Democratic National Convention as a delegate.

"Will you be a candidate?" he was asked, the question referring to the possibility of presentation of his name as a candidate for the Presidential nomination.

"No comment," he replied with a smile.

It is known definitely, however, that Mr. Farley is even more strongly opposed to a fourth term for a President than he was opposed to a third term. It is regarded as virtually certain that his name will be presented to the convention as a candidate for the Presidential nomination if such action is necessary to permit delegates to record their opposition to the renomination of President Roosevelt.

Recent developments in southern States, particularly in Texas, Mississippi and South Carolina, indicate an increasing opposition to the renomination of President Roosevelt within his party. While this is not expected to be strong enough to prevent his renomination, it is expected that a sufficient number of delegates will oppose it to register a significant protest.

There is no doubt that Mr. Farley will be an active factor in promoting this opposition, and that he will express his opposition to a fourth term at the time of the convention. What he will do in the campaign for election, in the expected event of President Roosevelt's renomination, is known only to himself.

Announcement by Farley

Mr. Farley indicated that he would not attempt to influence the committee in the choice of his successor. With very few of the party leaders having had advance notice of Mr. Farley's intention to resign, there has been so far no agreement on a new State chairman. Vincent Dailey, Mr. Farley's aide, is known to be a candidate for the place.

Mr. Farley's formal statement announcing his resignation, issued by him at State headquarters in the Hotel Biltmore, follows:

In 1928 I was elected secretary of the Democratic State Committee. In 1930 I was elected chairman, and I have served continuously in that office.

During all the years I have

Continued on Page 11

Industry Is Able to Finance Post-War Job, SEC Asserts

Study Shows Net Working Capital at Peak, Making Reconversion Possible and Some Expansion Without Any Aid

By WALTER W. RUCH
Special to THE NEW YORK TIMES.

PHILADELPHIA, June 8—American industry as a whole will be able to handle the stupendous task of reconversion to peacetime production and even undertake considerable expansion without asking for any financial assistance, the Securities and Exchange Commission declared today, basing its statements on an analysis of the current assets and liabilities of all corporations other than banks and insurance companies.

The study, first of its kind made by the commission and unique in its scope, included figures for about 450,000 corporations. Care was taken, however, to avoid duplications in the cases of subsidiaries and their parents by taking the aggregate figures of the latter to cover the former.

The commission's findings, which appeared to be at variance with fears frequently expressed by industrial and other Government officials, said that at the close of last year American corporations were in as favorable a financial position as ever in their history.

"Their net working capital (current assets less all current liabilities, including provisions for renegotiation)," the SEC said, "which was at an unprecedented level, was in extremely liquid form, with cash accounting for a very substantial proportion of the total."

The commission estimated that the increase in working capital during the four-year period from the end of 1939 to the end of 1943 amounted to $17,000,000,000, a rise of nearly 70 per cent. Whereas in 1939 working capital aggregated $24,600,000,000, it increased to $27,-

Continued on Page 25

NEW DEAL FOES MAP DIXIE-WIDE REVOLT

Meet in Shreveport, La., Today to Expand Movement Led by Texas and Mississippi

Special to THE NEW YORK TIMES.

SHREVEPORT, La., June 8—Anti-fourth term Democrats from Mississippi, Arkansas and Texas will meet in Shreveport tomorrow to discuss with Louisiana Democrats action to be taken in the presidential election.

E. Wayles Browne of Shreveport, chairman of the Caddo Parish Democratic executive committee, and vice-chairman of the State central committee, disclosed that the meeting would be held but that no details would be available beforehand. Neither is it known who will represent other States at the meeting.

Texas and Mississippi have already held their Democratic conventions, and both refused to bind their presidential electors to a party vote. Reports have been current that North and South Carolina would have representatives at the conference, along with possibly some other States.

Mr. Browne took part in the Chicago conference of Democrats called several months ago by Harry Woodring of Kansas, who since has announced that he was withdrawing his leadership of the anti-Roosevelt movement.

General Plan Disclosed

By TURNER CATLEDGE
Special to THE NEW YORK TIMES.

JACKSON, Miss., June 8—The action of the Mississippi State Democratic convention yesterday in naming an uninstructed delegation to the Chicago convention and a footloose slate of electors to cast the State's electoral vote following November's election, was said here today to have been part of a region-wide plan intended to restore the voice of the South in national Democratic party councils.

This was the assertion of several party leaders who participated in what observers termed the best organized political meeting the Magnolia State had seen in a generation. It was the statement, furthermore, of officials of the Draft-Byrd-for-President Committee who came from New Orleans to observe the proceedings.

"The Mississippi action "was merely the result of deliberate planning," John U. Barr, national chairman of the group backing Senator Harry F. Byrd of Virginia for President, said in an interview in a local newspaper.

"The Democrats of Mississippi knew what they wanted and set out to get it the quickest way," he added.

J. J. Kramer, national executive secretary of the Byrd committee,

Continued on Page 11

BONOMI IS CHOSEN AS ITALIAN PREMIER

Pre-Fascist Prime Minister Is Asked to Form Cabinet After Badoglio Meets Impasse

By HERBERT L. MATTHEWS
By Wireless to THE NEW YORK TIMES.

ROME, Friday, June 9—Former Premier Ivanoe Bonomi was chosen by all parties of both Naples and Rome as candidate for next Premier of Italy, it was learned this morning. His selection followed a day of meetings after the arrival here from Naples of Prince Humbert, former Premier Pietro Badoglio and six leaders of the Committee of National Liberation.

Signor Bonomi headed that committee during the underground movement here. Marshal Badoglio withdrew gracefully when faced with a unanimous demand. Count

Continued on Page 9

DEBACLE IN ITALY

Deep-Water Port Won at Civitavecchia as Allies Rush On in 5 Columns

ENEMY UNITS CUT UP

Fifth Army Takes Rail Center Above Rome—8th Seizes Key Towns

By The Associated Press.

ROME, June 8—In lightning drives of as much as twenty-six miles in twenty-four hours, the Allied Fifth Army today captured Civita Castellana, thirty-two miles north of Rome, after other swift armored units had pounded through Civitavecchia, important seaport thirty-eight miles northwest of the Italian capital.

Only the slightest resistance was being encountered by Lieut. Gen. Mark W. Clark's troops as they pressed after the reeling German Fourteenth army, which an Allied spokesman declared had been reduced to "battered remnants." There yet was no indication where the disorganized enemy would attempt to halt the Allied steamroller.

Civita Castellana is the junction of three main highways and two electric railways. Light reconnaissance units entered the town early in the evening. Civitavecchia is a city of 36,000 population, with docks that will be of value to the pursuing Allied forces.

Third Column Enters Bracciano

A third Fifth Army column drove into Bracciano, ancient iron smelting center nineteen miles northwest of Rome near Lake Bracciano, and also threw an arm around the eastern side of the lake. Captured in the swift thrust northward was the former headquarters of the Nazi commander, Field Marshal Gen. Albert Kesselring. The "elaborate, tunneled underground stronghold" was situated about three miles southeast of Civita Castellana.

An Allied spokesman declared that "the battered remnants of the

Continued on Page 9

War News Summarized

FRIDAY, JUNE 9, 1944

The situation along the Allied beachhead in France showed improvement yesterday following the arrival of vital supplies that had been delayed twenty-four hours by bad weather. Bitter fighting was raging along the entire front, particularly at Caen and for control of the main coastal road on the eastern side of the Cherbourg Peninsula near Ste. Mere-Eglise.

The disposition of General Montgomery's Twenty-first Army Group was disclosed sufficiently to show that British and Canadians held the left of the line, with the Sixth Airborne Division at the extreme left, and that American beachheads were at the right. Among the United States units was the "Fighting First" Infantry Division.

Huge convoys, both sea and air, piled needed reinforcements of men and equipment on the beaches. Warships and planes abruptly halted every enemy attempt to interfere. The Allies expected to complete consolidation of the beachheads before the main German counter-offensive was launched. Today's 5 A. M. communiqué reported continued landings and reduction of by-passed enemy strong points. Progress was made in all sectors. (All the foregoing 1:8; map P. 4.)

More than 27,000 sorties were flown by Allied planes in the thirty hours up to yesterday noon. Ships and men were kept ceaselessly covered while bombers blasted bridges, junctions, airfields and railway yards in an arc extending 150 miles from the beachhead. The Luftwaffe began to show more of a disposition to fight. Enemy losses were set at 176 planes; 289 of our aircraft were missing. [1:5.]

General Eisenhower declared that his faith in his men had been justified and General Montgomery remarked, "Everything is going excellently." [3:1.] However, Secretary of War Stimson warned that "we must look for the full fury of savage counter-attacks at an early moment" [3:4] and Prime Minister Churchill cautioned that "great dangers lie behind but enormous exertions lie before us." [3:8.]

The citizens of Bayeux, the first community to be liberated, greeted Allied troops with shouts of "On to Paris!" [1:7.] The French underground was actively at work sabotaging enemy positions, and Europeans from France to Norway were warned by the Allies not to fish in coastal waters for a week from last midnight. [1:6-7.]

German troops were retreating quickly and offering little resistance in Italy. The Fifth Army, advancing twenty-six miles in a day, captured Civita Castellana and Civitavecchia. The Eighth Army took Monterotondo. [1:4; map P. 9.] The Red Army seized an important position near Jassy after having stopped all German counter-attacks. [8:1.]

A Japanese cruiser was hit with two bombs off Waigeu Island, west of New Guinea. On Biak, artillery and naval fire were helping tanks blast the enemy from the caves and cliffs east of captured Mokmer airfield. [10:3.] Chinese troops driving down the Burma Road captured part of Lungling [10:1] but within China the Japanese edged closer to Changsha in Hunan Province. [10:2.]

DEFENDERS OF FORTRESS EUROPE CAPTURED

Germans from beach fortifications taken by Canadian assault troops stand with hands upraised
Associated Press Wirephoto (U. S. Signal Corps Radiophoto)

ALLIES RAIN BOMBS OVER 150-MILE ARC

Sorties Since D-Day Increase to 27,000—Germans Offer More Resistance in Air

By HAROLD DENNY
By Cable to THE NEW YORK TIMES.

LONDON, Friday, June 9—The Allied air assault on enemy rear positions in France reached a new intensity yesterday and drove still deeper into the Nazis' transportation network.

The offensive was on a much broader pattern. While medium bombers and fighters continued to lay down a creeping aerial barrage ahead of our advancing ground troops and check every attempt of the enemy to interfere with our convoys or attack our men on the beaches, both American and British heavy bombers carried destruction as far east as Paris and as far south as the Loire Valley.

This aerial zone of the liberation battlefield was roughly in the form of a triangle, its base stretching 300 miles from Pas-de-Calais to Nantes just inland from the Bay of Biscay with its apex at the French capital, 125 miles to the rear of the present ground fighting around Caen.

Bombers Lash Area

In the invasion zone itself very strong forces of Flying Fortresses and Liberators bombed bridges, railroad junctions, enemy airdromes and railway yards within a wide arc, 100 to 150 miles south, southeast and southwest of the beachhead on the coast of Normandy.

[An announcement early Friday said the United States Eighth and Ninth Air Forces had shot down a total of thirty-two planes in air combat Thursday and that the Eighth had destroyed twenty-one more on the ground, The Associated Press reported.

[Four American bombers and twenty-four fighters were lost.]

Consolidated figures issued last night by Supreme Allied Headquarters showed that from dawn of D-day to midday yesterday Allied aircraft had flown the amazing total of 27,000 sorties. In this period 176 enemy aircraft were destroyed while the Allies lost 289 aircraft.

Within this general pattern air attacks now are being concentrated in three fields. The first is the area between the Bay of Biscay and the Seine. The second runs from Tours to Nantes. The third lies between these two zones. These, of course, are in addition to the missions immediately in front of the advancing troops and over

Continued on Page 4

Fishermen Warned Off Sea From Norway to France

By The Associated Press.

LONDON, June 8—Allied High Command broadcasts warned Atlantic shore peoples from France to Norway tonight not to fish in their coastal waters for one week beginning tonight, so they will "not hinder the operations of the Allied forces." These instructions went out from London and North African stations as the German commentator, Martin von Hallensleben, wrote that the Germans were on the alert for invasions on northern coasts. Hallensleben said German reconnaissance had observed "great concentrations of shipping in English ports farther north, including the Bristol channel, the Irish Sea and Scotland."

The text of the broadcasts read:

"A warning addressed to fishermen who use Atlantic coastal waters of Norway, Denmark, Holland, Belgium and France:

"The Supreme Allied Commander requires that all fishing should cease in these waters for a period of seven days beginning at 9 P. M. Thursday, June 8 (3 P. M., Eastern War Time) and extending until 9 P. M., Thursday, June 15. Therefore fishermen now in port must remain there. Those at sea must return to port immediately. Follow this order strictly and quickly. Failure to do so may be fatal to yourselves and will hinder the operations of the Allied forces."

LONDON, June 8 (U.P.)—The French underground patriot army and Vichy's pro-Nazi mercenaries began a fratricidal war to the

Continued on Page 6

BAYEUX ECSTATIC AS ALLIES ARRIVE

'We Knew You'd Come,' French Cry as They Shower Flowers on Liberating Troops

By RICHARD D. McMILLAN
United Press Correspondent

BAYEUX, Allied Front Line, Normandy, June 7 (Delayed)—Allied troops streamed into this historic town at noon today, the first community of France to be freed from the Germans, and its people went wild with joy, crying "On to Paris!"

I entered Bayeux with the Allied vanguard after touring the front, where British and German dead lay in the sunlight beside the roads while the peasants of Normandy, only a few hundred yards away, tended their sheep and cattle in the poppy-speckled fields.

Only recently, a French woman said, Field Marshal Gen. Erwin Rommel, commander of the Nazi anti-invasion forces in the west, visited Bayeux and pronounced

Continued on Page 7

Allied Ships Defy Coastal Batteries, Fire on Foe at Point-Blank Range

By HANSON W. BALDWIN
By Wireless to THE NEW YORK TIMES.

ABOARD ADMIRAL KIRK'S FLAGSHIP, Off the French Coast, June 6 (Delayed)—Allied troops landed from the sea and the air on a wide front near the eastern base of the Cherbourg Peninsula early today. Probably more than 8,000 planes gave direct or indirect support to the landings, and some 800 fighting craft ranging from trawlers and motor torpedo boats to sixteen-inch-gunned battleships escorted and supported an invasion fleet of more than 3,300 transports and landing craft.

Parachute troops were the first to land on French soil. They leaped into blackness in the middle of the short western European night and were followed later by glider-borne infantry, thirteen fully equipped soldiers to each glider.

The landings from the sea were made shortly after dawn and were prefaced by brief but sharp bombardments from planes, warships and landing craft. Some 2,000 tons of shells, it was estimated, were fired by supporting Allied warships against enemy beach positions and coastal batteries in the first ten to twenty minutes. The beaches where American troops landed were bombed and strafed by scores of planes, which dropped some 800 tons of explosives on each beach to soften up the enemy's resistance.

Despite these preparations, the battle is expected to be very severe. The Germans are known to have considerable forces in the vicinity of the landings and can bring in additional divisions quickly.

The invasion may hang in the

Continued on Page 6

NAZI RESERVES FAIL

Local Counter-Attacks Repulsed—Caen Is Within Allied Grasp

OUR SUPPLIES GAIN

Americans Widen Grip on Cherbourg Peninsula During Reinforcing

5 A. M. Communique

By The Associated Press.

SUPREME HEADQUARTERS, Allied Expeditionary Force, Friday, June 9—Allied troops on the Normandy beachhead have continued to make progress in all sections despite further German tank reinforcements, it was announced today.

Communiqué No. 7 from Gen. Dwight D. Eisenhower's Headquarters said landings have continued on all beaches and by-passed enemy strong points are being steadily reduced.

Some Nazi coastal batteries again broke out yesterday with desultory firing, but they were silenced by shells from Allied warships.

By DREW MIDDLETON
By Cable to THE NEW YORK TIMES.

SUPREME HEADQUARTERS, Allied Expeditionary Force, Friday, June 9—British and Canadian infantrymen, supported by strong armored formations, are hacking their way forward on the left of the Allied line in Normandy, while on the right, or west, American forces, including the famous "Fighting First" Infantry Division, are gradually enlarging their beachheads.

Doughboys are fighting veterans of Field Marshal Gen. Erwin Rommel's armored infantry divisions for control of the main lateral road running along the east side of Cherbourg Peninsula, southeastward of Ste. Mere Eglise, where the enemy reported heavy fighting. Ten German divisions have now been identified in the battle areas. All German counter-attacks, in which Marshal Rommel was using his local reserves, had been checked by the Allies, and the position on the front of the British Sixth Airborne Division to the left of the British sector and in the Caen-Bayeux area was regarded here as "satisfactory."

Generally the position of Gen. Sir Bernard L. Montgomery's Twenty-First Army Group shows considerable improvement over that of the night of Tuesday-Wednesday. After a delay in unloading, because of bad weather, supplies are now moving ashore steadily. Last night's communiqué, issued here, reported the arrival of convoys of merchant ships, which were being unloaded. The airborne divisions' ammunition and food were successfully replenished Thursday morning in another large-scale operation by transport aircraft gliders.

Reinforcing Proceeds

Improvement in the weather was one of the most significant factors in the situation, for Wednesday's high seas imposed an almost twenty-four delay on the unloading program. With reinforcement again proceeding steadily, opinion here was that the second phase of the operation, consolidation of the beachhead, could be accomplished before the main enemy counter-offensive was launched.

The improved position was reflected in statements made by Gen. Dwight D. Eisenhower and General Montgomery Thursday. The supreme commander declared that his confidence in the Allied forces had been "completely justified" by operations in the first fifty-four hours of the campaign, and he declared that General Montgomery's Twenty-first Army Group, which includes Americans,

Continued on Page 4

"All the News That's Fit to Print"

The New York Times.

LATE CITY EDITION
POSTSCRIPT
Cloudy with moderate winds today
Temperatures Yesterday—Max., 78; Min., 57
Sunrise, 5:24 A. M.; Sunset, 8:27 P. M.

VOL. XCIII—No. 31,549. Entered as Second-Class Matter, Postoffice, New York, N. Y. NEW YORK, SATURDAY, JUNE 10, 1944. THREE CENTS IN NEW YORK CITY

ALLIES CUT GERMAN LINKS TO CHERBOURG; ROUT NAVAL ATTACK, HIT 4 DESTROYERS; DE GAULLE INVITED TO MEET PRESIDENT

COTTON PRICE RISE IS VOTED BY SENATE IN EXTENDING OPA

Bowles' Warning of $250,000,000 Rise in Clothing Bill of People Is Swept Aside

AMENDMENT WINS 39 TO 35

20 Democrats, 19 Republicans for It—Veto Is Forecast if House Accepts Measure

By CHARLES E. EGAN
Special to The New York Times.

WASHINGTON, June 9—Legislation to extend price, wage and rent controls for eighteen months beyond June 30 was adopted by the Senate today with the cotton amendments, which the Office of Price Administration has said will add at least $250,000,000 to the country's annual clothing bill.

Persons close to the White House have predicted that if the cotton amendments, which were sponsored by Senator Bankhead of Alabama, were in the bill finally adopted by Congress, President Roosevelt would veto the measure.

While the Senate was voting 39 to 35 to accept the cotton amendments, which would tie the prices of finished cotton goods to the prices paid by mills for raw cotton, the House rejected an even more sweeping proposal for profit guarantees on all agricultural commodities by a vote of 127 to 91. The House version of the Bankhead amendment, however, still faces a test in that chamber.

The Senate rejected an amendment by Senator Thomas of Oklahoma which would raise crude petroleum prices by adoption of a parity formula similar to that used in setting prices on tobacco. OPA officials had said the Thomas proposal would increase consumers' costs for petroleum products $1,000,000,000 a year. The amendment lost by a vote of 42 to 25 when Midwest Republicans and several Southern Democrats who had been ready to support the measure voted against it.

White-Collar Pay Plan Voted

An amendment offered by Senator Wiley, Republican, of Wisconsin, which would allow increases in wages and salaries to $37.50 a week without application to any Government agency was adopted by the Senate by a voice vote. Senator Wiley said that there are 20,000,000 white-collar workers not engaged in war work whose incomes have not increased in proportion to the rise in living costs.

Meanwhile the House tentatively adopted a proposal by Representative Ed V. Izac, Democrat, of California, providing for rent increases for apartment houses, single family houses and other dwellings. Under the amendment, OPA would be forced to approve increases in rent ceilings sufficient to reflect advances in taxes and operating costs.

Passage of the Senate bill came soon after the Bankhead amendment, which has been under debate for two and a half days, and the Thomas amendment were disposed of.

Cotton Amendment Modified

The House will go back to work on its bill tomorrow at 11 A. M. in the hope of passing it by nightfall although a score of amendments are awaiting debate. Both houses are eager to send their bills to conference as soon as possible so final enactment can be effected at least ten days in advance of the convention-campaign recess. Thus the members would be here to act in case of a veto.

The Bankhead amendment was modified from the version which the Alabaman had succeeded in having included in the bill offered to the Senate by the Banking and Currency Committee.

As adopted, the amendment provided that OPA base its prices on cotton textile items on the parity price of raw cotton; a generally fair and equitable allowance for the total current cost of the manufac-

Continued on Page 10

1,000 Refugees Will Enter, To Be Housed at Fort Ontario

President Tells of Orders to Ambassador Murphy at Algiers and Agencies Here—Says Group Is All That Is Coming

Special to The New York Times.

WASHINGTON, June 9—The United States will accept 1,000 refugees from Italy and give them temporary sanctuary at Fort Ontario, N. Y., President Roosevelt announced today. He added that this was the total number of refugees who would be brought to the United States.

He made his statement at a news conference while Congress continued to study legislation to authorize the establishment of "free ports" in this country, where temporary asylum could be granted to refugees from the European war theatre. The President did not term Fort Ontario a "free port" but referred to it as an emergency refugee shelter.

Coincident with his statement he made public a message of instructions regarding the refugees which has been cabled to Ambassador Murphy at Algiers.

Mr. Roosevelt told of the refugee program before the question period began. He said that these refugees were coming in large numbers into Italy and that more than 1,000 arrived last week from Yugoslavia alone, and were creating an increasing problem for the Allied military authorities.

They are being moved from Italy into many centers, located, among other places, in Tripolitania, Cyprus, Sicily and Cyrenaica, Mr. Roosevelt said. He revealed that there was a large settlement in Casablanca to accommodate refugees from Spain, most of whom, he said, were Frenchmen or persons

Continued on Page 9

SWIFT ALLIED GAINS CONTINUING IN ITALY

Tarquinia, 55 Miles Northwest of Rome, and Viterbo Fall—Nazis Begin Adriatic Retreat

By The Associated Press.

ROME, June 9—Pursuing the shattered German Fourteenth Army at continued breakneck pace northwest of Rome, Lieut. Gen. Mark W. Clark's Fifth Army forces swept through the communication centers of Viterbo, Vetralla and Tarquinia today as Nazi troops in the Adriatic sector joined the general enemy flight up the Italian peninsula.

Viterbo, a vital highway and rail junction forty miles from Rome, fell before a swift seven-mile thrust from the area of Lake Vico. Tarquinia, on the main coastal highway fifty-five miles northwest of the capital, was seized in a ten-mile stab by Allied troops driving on from the captured port of Civitavecchia. Vetralla is on a lateral highway connecting Viterbo and Tarquinia.

There yet was no sign that Field Marshal Gen. Albert Kesselring had been able to rally his fleeing remnants, and it was doubted here that he would attempt to make another serious stand short of a line beyond Florence, some 150 miles from Rome. Although General Clark's forces were averaging roughly fifteen miles a day in their grim chase, they found it difficult to keep within shooting distance of the Nazis.

Fifth Army vanguards were more than 130 airline miles from the starting points of the big offensive launched less than a month ago.

A five-month deadlock was broken in the Adriatic sector when

Continued on Page 6

ITALIAN PREMIER SELECTS CABINET

Bonomi Picks Ministers With Anti-Fascist Records—Badoglio Not Included

By HERBERT L. MATTHEWS
By Wireless to The New York Times.

ROME, June 9—The new Italian Government, which it is hoped will head the country until the Germans are hurled out, was formed tonight after a last-minute crisis that threatened to upset previous hopes.

Premier Ivanoe Bonomi also holds the portfolio of Minister of the Interior and the interim portfolio of Minister of Foreign Affairs. Six others, representing the Italian Committee of Liberation parties, have been named Ministers Without Portfolio.

The Ministers Without Portfolio are: Palmiro Togliatti [Ercole], Communist; Count Carlo Sforza, Independent; Alcide Degaspari, Christian Democrat; Meuccio Ruini, Democrat-Labor; Alberto Cianca, Actionist, and Signor Saragat, Socialist.

The nine other portfolios were split among the six parties. The Liberals got two ministerial posts. The only military figure to remain in the Cabinet was Raffaele de Courten, who has the portfolios of war and of air.

It was a day of great argumentation, which was resolved only because all concerned were determined to form a Cabinet quickly. The snag came over the insistence of the younger men that no man who had ever been a member of the Fascist party could become a Minister.

The Government, it is understood, has been promised that it can soon begin functioning in Rome, perhaps in a week or two.

Continued on Page 6

Two Congress Republicans to Get Places in Monetary Delegation

Special to The New York Times.

WASHINGTON, June 9—The American delegation to the United Nations Monetary and Financial Conference opening July 1 at Bretton Woods, N. H., the composition of which became known here today, will include Edward F. Brown of the First National Bank of Chicago, who is president of the Federal Advisory Council of the Federal Reserve System, and two Republican members of Congress.

President Roosevelt said at his news conference this morning that he was unable to announce the delegates because one of the Congressional delegates had not yet been agreed upon. It was learned tonight that this choice would probably be Senator Robert A. Taft of Ohio, third ranking minority member of the Banking and Currency Committee.

Senator Robert F. Wagner of New York, chairman of the committee, will be in the delegation, as will Brent Spence of Kentucky, chairman of the House Banking and Currency Committee, and Jesse P. Wolcott of Michigan, ranking minority member of that committee.

Although no explanation for the Republican selection on the Senate side was immediately available, some discussion may have arisen over the question of adhering to the seniority basis.

The ranking minority member of the Banking and Currency Committee is Senator Charles W. Tobey of New Hampshire. However, Senator John A. Danaher of Connecticut, second ranking minor-

Continued on Page 8

ROOSEVELT AGREES

Proposes Dates for Visit of French Leader in June or July

INFORMAL TALK SEEN

French to Administer Own Civil Affairs, Eisenhower Says

By CHARLES HURD
Special to The New York Times.

WASHINGTON, June 9—President Roosevelt has granted a request by Gen. Charles de Gaulle that the Chief Executive receive him here, and has indicated dates either late this month or early in July when he will have time for conversations with the leader of the self-styled Provisional Government of the French Republic at Algiers.

The President notified General de Gaulle that he would be glad to see him either between June 22 and 30, or between July 6 and 14.

[A reporter asked why those dates, and Mr. Roosevelt said they were the only times available, The Associated Press said.

[The reporter commented that there was a national convention coming along in there.

[Oh, yes, Mr. Roosevelt replied, and there is an election in the fall and Christmas is coming, too.]

The President's message was transmitted to General de Gaulle by Vice Admiral Raymond A. Fenard, senior officer of the French Navy and chief of the French Military Mission in the United States since the African invasion.

[In London Gen. Dwight D. Eisenhower said in a proclamation to the people of France that it was for them to provide their own civil administration and to safeguard Allied troops by the effective maintenance of law and order. "Members of the French military mission attached to me will furnish assistance to this end," the commander revealed.]

Mr. Roosevelt told reporters at a news conference this morning that Admiral Fenard had arrived

Continued on Page 5

AMERICAN PARATROOPERS MOVING ON ENEMY

Assembling after landing near a French churchyard, they advance under cover of a stone wall.
The New York Times (U. S. Signal Corps Radiotelephoto)

U. S. PACIFIC FLIERS SINK 4 DESTROYERS

Fifth Is Damaged in Attack on Japanese Trying to Carry Reinforcements to Biak

By The Associated Press.

ALLIED HEADQUARTERS IN NEW GUINEA, Saturday, June 10—Gen. Douglas MacArthur's Mitchell bombers sank four Japanese destroyers off Manokwari, Netherland New Guinea, it was announced today.

Headquarters reported a fifth destroyer was damaged. A cruiser and a sixth destroyer fled.

Ten Mitchells were credited with blocking the enemy attempt to reinforce its Biak garrison Thursday.

The attack upon the cruiser and six destroyers took place in Geelvink Bay, the entrance to which is

Continued on Page 8

2 Enemy Warships Wrecked, British Craft Hit Off Ushant

By GENE CURRIVAN
By Cable to The New York Times.

SUPREME HEADQUARTERS, Allied Expeditionary Force, June 9—In the first naval engagement of any moment since invasion day, a force of British, Canadian and Polish warships intercepted four German destroyers about ten miles southwest of Ushant, off the Brittany peninsula, early this morning, and when the smoke of battle cleared, one enemy craft had been blown apart, another left in flames on the beach and the other two escaped after receiving damaging hits.

Later several German E-boats attempted to enter the assault area but were driven off by light coastal forces.

Ushant is in the Brest area. During the Napoleonic Wars a formidable British blockade was established directly off that point.

[Eight Allied ships took part in the action. Allied naval guns continued battering the invasion coast, smashing at forty-six shore targets in the twenty-four hours ending at 8 A. M. Friday.]

The German destroyers, the first to show themselves since Tuesday when three attempted to leave the Bay of Biscay but were driven back by coastal Beaufighter planes, were spotted shortly after midnight by an aircraft patrol. Word was flashed to the Allied force, and within a short time contact was made.

As they met, the opposing forces were steaming in opposite directions. Four of the Allied ships turned north to bring all their guns to bear. At the same time the German force swung in the same direction, running a parallel course and firing torpedoes.

Forced to alter course to avoid the torpedoes, the division, led by H. M. S. Tartar, turned directly

Continued on Page 3

MARSHALL, ARNOLD AND KING IN LONDON

Arrive for Joint Talk With British Chiefs, May Visit Normandy Beachhead

Special to The New York Times.

WASHINGTON, June 9 — The United States Joint Chiefs of Staff—top commanders of the land, sea and air forces—arrived in Great Britain today, the White House announced tonight. The commuting commanders are Gen. George C. Marshall, Army Chief of Staff; Admiral Ernest J. King, Chief of Naval Operations, and Gen. Henry H. Arnold, Commanding General of the Army Air Forces.

Safe arrival of the three men who welded into being the vast American services now fighting around the world was announced on behalf of President Roosevelt by Stephen T. Early of the President's secretariat.

"The President is happy to announce," Mr. Early said, "that the Joint Chiefs of Staff, General Marshall, Admiral King and General Arnold, have arrived safely in London. They went to London to attend a previously scheduled conference of the Combined Chiefs of Staff there, which was planned to

Continued on Page 2

War News Summarized

SATURDAY, JUNE 10, 1944

Allied capture of Ste.-Mere-Eglise, eighteen miles south of Cherbourg, and the cutting of main enemy communication lines yesterday increased the threat to that great French port, seizure of which would provide a precious funnel through which to pour men and supplies into the invasion area. Formigny, three miles inland on the road between Bayeux and Isigny, was reported taken also. A fierce battle raged at Caen. [1:8; map P. 2.] An enemy naval force thrust at the invasion sea line, but was driven off. One German destroyer was sunk, another driven ashore and destroyed. [1:6-7.]

Because of bad weather, our troops did not have their usual air support until later in the day. Allied bombers hit enemy supply and communication lines in France, while more than 750 Italy-based planes blasted Munich. [4:1.]

American parachute troops, who surprised the Germans south of Cherbourg Tuesday, brilliantly carried out a vital part of the most successful airborne operation in history, the Allied Command disclosed. The official report ridiculed German claims of heavy casualties and pointed out that losses were about 2 per cent of the more than 1,000 planes used. [1:6-7.]

The American joint chiefs of staff, General Marshall, Admiral King and General Arnold, arrived in London. [1:7.]

General Eisenhower told the French people that the French military mission would help them in providing their own civil administration. He promised free, democratic elections when victory is won. [5:1.]

Meanwhile, French patriots for the most part were biding their time, with their self-control under tremendous pressure. [4:5.]

President Roosevelt announced that he had granted a request from General de Gaulle for a conference with him in Washington and had set the dates for such a meeting between June 22 and 30 or between July 6 and 14. [1:4.]

Battered German troops continued their rapid retreat northwest of Rome. Viterbo, a highway and rail junction forty miles from Rome, Vetralla and Tarquinia fell to Allied troops. It appeared unlikely that the enemy would attempt a stand short of a line beyond Florence, about 150 miles from the Italian capital. [1:2; map P. 6.]

Ivanoe Bonomi, who succeeded Marshal Badoglio, formed a new Cabinet in which he holds the portfolios of Minister of Foreign Affairs and Interior. [1:3.]

The expected Russian offensive may not start until Allied operations in western Europe have developed fully, in the opinion of military observers in London. Moscow reported no important changes on the Eastern Front. [8:6.]

Japanese troops in China stormed across the Laotao River and were approaching Changsha. [8:4-5.] In Burma, however, Allied forces punched forward in all major sectors. [8:2.] Allied fliers sank four Japanese destroyers off Manokwari, Netherlands New Guinea. [1:5.]

Allied Parachutists Far Excelled Germans' Feat in Attack on Crete

By The Associated Press.

SUPREME HEADQUARTERS, Allied Expeditionary Force, June 9—The High Command in its first detailed story disclosed today that United States parachute troops descending on the Ste.-Mère-Eglise sector below Cherbourg Tuesday brilliantly carried out a vital part of history's most successful airborne operation—a vertical attack far excelling the German sky assault on Crete.

The official report said losses approximated about 2 per cent of the more than 1,000 United States and Royal Air Force planes used, and a high staff officer who accompanied the Americans, in ridiculing German claims of inflicting heavy casualties on the parachutists, said:

"You need not worry about American paratroopers. They can take care of themselves and they are tough as hell."

New secret devices enabled the Americans to land in designated spots despite layers of clouds, and two hours after the landing some parachutists were utilizing captured German transport equipment.

Glider drops were made on a much bigger scale than even contemplated by the Germans in the Crete operation of three years ago. Both the Americans and British used gliders in daylight on D-day with small losses, whereas the Germans gave up the use of gliders in Crete after suffering severe losses.

Some of the highlights of the operation were:

One glider landed on top of a

Continued on Page 3

TAKE KEY TO ROAD

Americans Push Deeper Into Peninsula—Nazis See Threat to Port

CAEN BATTLE RAGES

British and Canadians Repulse All Attacks—Captives Total 4,000

5 A. M. Communique

By The Associated Press.

SUPREME HEADQUARTERS ALLIED EXPEDITIONARY FORCE, June 10—American troops have captured Isigny, an Allied communiqué said today.

"Despite unfavorable weather conditions, disembarkation of further men and material was uninterrupted," the communiqué continued.

Canadian troops are standing firm in the Caen area despite heavy enemy attacks and Allied troops have made contact with strong enemy forces in Condé-sur-Seulles, the war bulletin said.

American troops are attacking both north and south of captured Ste. Mere Eglise.

Isigny is seven miles east of Carentan on the main highway leading to Bayeux.

By DREW MIDDLETON
By Cable to The New York Times.

SUPREME HEADQUARTERS, Allied Expeditionary Force, Saturday, June 10—The American wing of the Allied front in Normandy has cut the main highway and railway from Carentan to Cherbourg and is pushing German tactical reserves out of the coastal zone.

Lieut. Gen. Omar N. Bradley's veteran "doughboys" captured Ste.-Mère-Eglise yesterday and entered the outskirts of Carentan. There also is heavy fighting in Formigny on the Bayeux-Carentan road. [The Associated Press reported that Formigny had been captured by American troops.]

The British and Canadian troops are methodically smashing German defensive positions in the Caen area, where both sides are massing armored formations and the enemy is staging his heaviest counter-attacks.

The British Sixth Airborne Division, fighting in the area northeast of Caen, is using light tanks, some of which have been carried into the beachhead by gliders. These tanks have sifted around behind the main concentration of German armor and are striking at transport columns supplying the Panzers.

[An Allied communiqué said that numerous enemy strong points, by-passed during the early stages of the invasion, had been wiped out, The United Press reported.]

Thus far, more than 1,900 prisoners have checked through Allied bases and it is unofficially estimated that the total number is now between 4,000 and 5,000. A number of Russians and Poles and one Japanese have been captured.

Nazis in Cherbourg Imperiled

The American advance yesterday imperils the position held by German troops around Cherbourg. In addition to the Americans' cutting of the main highway and railroad another danger spot for the enemy is in the area west and southwest of Bayeux, where the Germans report the success of an Allied push toward Saint Lo.

The beachhead has been increased to forty miles as a result of the fighting in the twenty-four hours ended at midnight last night, according to the enemy.

Air power played little part in early yesterday's operations because of bad weather, according to last night's communiqué. Heavy

Continued on Page 2

"All the News That's Fit to Print"

The New York Times.

LATE CITY EDITION
POSTSCRIPT
Rain ending early this morning
Temperature Yesterday—Max., 65; Min., 60
Sunrise, 5:24 A. M.; Sunset, 8:27 P. M.

Section 1

NEWS INDEX, PAGE 47, THIS SECTION

Copyright, 1944, by The New York Times Company.

VOL. XCIII..No. 31,550. Entered as Second-Class Matter, Postoffice, New York, N. Y. NEW YORK, SUNDAY, JUNE 11, 1944. Including Magazine and Book Sections. TEN CENTS New York City and Suburban Area (15c Elsewhere)

ALLIES GAIN ON WHOLE NORMANDY FRONT; AIR BASES NOW IN FRANCE, AID INTENSIFIED; FLEEING GERMANS TURN TO FIGHT IN ITALY

REALTY TAX ROLLS AT $15,845,991,014, LOWEST SINCE 1928

Bulk of Reductions Granted in Manhattan, With Total of $126,803,200 for Next Year

ONLY QUEENS SHOWS RISE

Utility Real Estate Lowered $11,094,820—Franchises Increased $6,211,603

For the first time since 1928 the assessed valuation of taxable real estate and special franchises in New York City has dropped below $16,000,000,000.

William Wirt Mills, president of the Tax Commission, reported to Mayor La Guardia yesterday that the final assessment figure for the five boroughs for the fiscal year starting on July 1, 1944, had been fixed at $15,845,991,014, or $165,233,042 less than the final total of $16,011,224,056 for 1943-44.

A study of the elaborate tables prepared by the tax officials showed that by far the greater part of the reduction was effected on Manhattan holdings. The report also indicated a continuance of the effort to bring down the inflated valuations fixed in boom years, and emphasized the wartime stagnation of private construction work here.

Year's Building Only $8,809,945

With civilian building virtually at a standstill and no new towering edifices added to the Manhattan skyline, only 574 structures, mostly of a minor character, were placed on the assessment rolls to boost the assessment figure by only $8,809,945 for the year, in contrast to 2,511 new buildings that represented an increment of $75,212,045 in tax valuations for 1943-44, which had been considered an unusually lean year.

With more than 40,000 hearings held between March 1 and May 25 on pleas for reductions in this year's tentative valuations, the Tax Commission during this period granted cuts amounting to $66,968,420 on "ordinary" realty, Mr. Mills announced. It granted $1,858,900 in reductions and an exemption of $57,000 on properties of utilities, but increased the assessment on special franchises by $6,211,603 over the tentative figure given earlier in the year.

The reduced valuations and the prospect of a cut of about fifteen points in the tax rate offered some measure of relief for property owners, but some of them yesterday cited recent sales statistics prepared by the Real Estate Board of New York to support their argument that market prices justified a much sharper decrease.

Net Realty Cut $160,349,825

The total reductions for the coming year on ordinary realty, including the $66,968,420 granted on pleas by owners, amounted to $160,349,825. Gross reductions of $187,345,656 made by field assessors on some properties were offset in part by increases on others aggregating $93,964,251.

Manhattan owners, who contend that their market has been laboring under more burdens than those of the adjoining boroughs, will get the benefit of the bulk of the reductions this year. This borough got a cut of $126,803,200 on ordinary realty for the coming fiscal year and a reduction of $17,342,960 on properties of utilities.

Brooklyn's ordinary realty was reduced by $24,920,130 and the Bronx by $9,195,590. Queens was the only borough to register a gain in aggregate assessments on regular real estate, rising $1,811,200 for a total valuation of all taxable realty, special franchises and utility property of $2,450,316,118. The aggregate figure for each of the other boroughs was Manhattan, $7,403,742,150; the Bronx, $1,990,734,057; Brooklyn, $3,698,243,145, and Richmond, $302,955,544.

The valuation of special fran-

Continued on Page 47

Major Sports Results

HORSE RACING

American racing history was made at Aqueduct yesterday when Bossuet, Wait a Bit and Brownie finished in a triple dead heat for first place in the Carter Handicap before 25,386 spectators. The day's proceeds of approximately $100,000 were earmarked for war relief. Mouse Hole and Kaytee won the two divisions of the Kent Stakes at Delaware Park.

TRACK AND FIELD

Bill Hulse led the New York A. C. to another metropolitan A. A. U. title by taking the half-mile and mile races at Randalls Island. Illinois captured N. C. A. A. honors at Milwaukee.

BASEBALL

The Cardinals crushed the Reds, 18—0, at Cincinnati for the most decisive shut-out victory in the National League since 1906. The Giants, Dodgers and Yankees were kept idle by rain.

(Full details in Section 3)

PRICE CEILINGS PUT ON ALL USED CARS

OPA Order for July 10 Issued by Bowles in Face of Sharp Rise, Hoarding, Hardship

Special to THE NEW YORK TIMES.

WASHINGTON, June 10—The prices of all used passenger automobiles will be brought under Government control starting July 10 in an effort to stop the rise of prices which have gone up 30 per cent in thirty months, Price Administrator Chester Bowles stated today.

Because the Government recognized the danger of creating a black market through controlling the prices of used cars, he said, it had hesitated to issue the order, but he pointed out that the used car market represented a $2,000,000,000 annual turnover which was affecting the cost of living through the hoarding of cars and the charging of exorbitant prices.

Under the order of the Office of Price Administration, specific dollars-and-cents prices at the levels prevailing in January, 1944, will be established by body and model type for twenty-three makes and about 6,000 models, manufactured between 1937 and 1942.

Price Categories and Areas

Two prices will be permitted, one for unguaranteed cars, to be known as the "as is" price, and a warranted price for cars guaranteed for 1,000 miles or thirty days.

The ceiling prices will differ in three areas of the country, the "A" area covering all States to the east of the Mississippi River, where the lowest prices will prevail, the "C" area, including Oregon, Washington, California, Nevada and Arizona, where the highest prices will be allowed, and the "B" area, comprising all the other States, where the prices will be

Continued on Page 46

TUSCANIA IS TAKEN

Fifth Army Slows as Foe Makes Stand in Area Beyond Viterbo

ORSOGNA OURS AGAIN

Eighth Army Occupies 6 Other Towns in East, Central Sectors

By The Associated Press.

ALLIED HEADQUARTERS, in Italy, June 10—The German forces in Italy, fleeing northward in a rout that, the Allies' Command declared, has become a "catastrophe," turned to make a stand of stubborn but not fully disclosed proprotions late today around a village some miles northeast of Viterbo, which is forty miles above Rome.

An Associated Press correspondent with the Fifth Army in the field wrote, in a dispatch timed at 9:30 P. M., that the previously almost unopposed race of the Allies to overtake the retreating Germans had slowed perceptibly when they ran into a maze of German 88-mm. and anti-tank guns in and around the village. The Allies brought up tanks, infantry and artillery and the fighting "quickly assumed the character of a sizable action," the dispatch said.

The Fifth Army, which has advanced at a speed of about fifteen miles a day since the fall of Rome last Sunday, has apparently succeeded in its racing efforts to overtake and engage some important units of the German Fourteenth Army. Capturing the ancient town of Tuscania, thirteen miles northeast of Tarquinia, which fell yesterday, the Fifth Army had fanned out with just such an overtaking battle intended.

Earlier today a headquarters spokesman had described the German Army as "retreating in a completely disorganized fashion" and the Fifth Army as "unable to catch up with any important element of it," despite the speed of the pursuit. The front dispatch said tonight that the Germans were beaten "but by no means disorganized."

Orsogna Recaptured

The German withdrawal before the British Eighth Army on the Adriatic front, first announced yesterday, continued. The Allies advanced more than five miles, captured the wrecked towns of Orsogna, Guardiagrele, Giuliano, Miglianico and Filetto, and crossed the Foro River.

The Eighth Army's front east of Rome was also advanced. The troops, fighting their way through demolitions and minefields in the rough country, captured Moricone, eleven miles north of Tivoli, and Arsoli, nine miles northwest of Subiaco.

The cutting up of the Fourteenth

Continued on Page 28

BIG AERIAL SUPPORT

Hundreds of Planes Hit Nazi Line and Rear in Caen Battle

U. S. 'HEAVIES' STRIKE

Our Fighters Fly 2,000 Sorties Over Normandy —RAF Stabs at Berlin

By The Associated Press.

SUPREME HEADQUARTERS, Allied Expeditionary Force, Sunday, June 11—The Allied air forces, establishing their first bases on the beachheads in France, hammered German concentrations of troops and tanks, big gun positions and airdromes with hundreds of planes of all types yesterday after the weather had cleared and enabled heavy bombers to resume their support of the invasion.

Bombs, rockets and a hail of bullets were poured down upon the Germans as the Allied airmen put a protective roof over the embattled infantrymen aground and blasted positions in and behind the German lines.

Berlin was bombed last night for the second night in a row by Royal Air Force bombers, which also blasted targets behind the Germans' invasion battle lines. Mosquitos hit the Reich capital, while RAF "heavies" kept up the air assault in support of our ground forces in France.

[The greatest air support ever concentrated in a single area, barring perhaps only Cassino, was thrown Saturday against the embattled Caen region by Allied medium and fighter bombers in an attempt to seal off the Germans' effort to reinforce their divisions there, said a United Press dispatch.

[The greater part of about 7,000 sorties flown by Allied bombers and fighters in support of invasion troops in the twenty-

Continued on Page 37

AMERICANS ADVANCING THROUGH FLOODED FIELDS

Troopers march through an area in France inundated by the Germans to prevent glider landings.

The New York Times (U. S. Signal Corps Radiotelephoto)

U. S. FIGHTERS RIP PLOESTI REFINERY

Last Major Plant Bombed by Lightnings—Oil Installations in North Italy Blasted

By The Associated Press.

FIFTEENTH AIR FORCE HEADQUARTERS, Italy, June 10—Squadrons of Lightnings, in the longest fighter-bomber mission ever flown in this theatre, attacked the last major refinery still producing in the Ploesti oil fields today and left the target enveloped in smoke.

Then, as the fast fighters turned for the 500-mile flight back to base, they blasted out of the sky a number of the almost 100 Messerschmitts and Focke-Wulfs that swarmed up to meet them. All the

Continued on Page 39

War News Summarized

SUNDAY, JUNE 11, 1944

American invasion troops smashed a third of the way across the Cherbourg peninsula yesterday and the enemy admitted that our forces were attacking his "shortened" defense lines only fifteen miles southeast of the great port of Cherbourg. British and Canadian forces on the left flank continued to battle the desperately resisting Germans at Caen, old Gothic city near the mouth of the Orne River. [1:8; map P. 33.]

The ground forces in France were receiving effective support from the Allies' aerial armadas. Striking from their first bases on the beachheads, air battalions put a protective umbrella over our own men while punching German concentrations of troops and tanks and blasting enemy gun positions and airfields. [1:4.] At sea, men of the Allied navies hunted enemy craft that might try to interfere with the invasion line. They ferreted out two groups of Nazi vessels and got four out of seven. [35:5:]

The Vichy radio asserted Allied warships were shelling Toulon, south French naval base, soon after Swiss reports said the Germans expected an invasion of southern France. [1:7.]

The French underground became increasingly active, and Frenchmen in liberated areas praised General de Gaulle as "the only leader for us." [38:1.] General de Gaulle said in London that General Eisenhower's plans for administration of liberated territory were "unacceptable." He said he would be "honored" to visit President Roosevelt. [1:6-7.]

In Italy, the disorganized enemy, who had retreated so fast that American troops could not catch up, turned to fight northeast of Viterbo. The Allied command described the German defeat as a "catastrophe." Allied troops, advancing fifteen miles a day since the fall of Rome, captured the ancient town of Tuscania, thirteen miles northeast of Tarquinia. [1:3; map P. 28.]

The last major refinery still producing in Rumania's Ploesti oil fields was blasted and left enveloped in smoke by Italy-based fighter-bombers. About 500 heavy bombers hit another blow at Germany's oil sources by attacking the Aquila refinery at Trieste, one of the largest available to the enemy outside Rumania. [1:5.]

The Chinese announced that "grim fighting" was continuing in the outer defenses of Changsha. [30:1.] To the southwest, Chinese forces advancing toward Burma threw a strong road block across the Burma Road south of Mangshih and stormed the northern and eastern gates of Lungling. [30:3.] Another attempt by the Japanese to reinforce their troops on Biak was frustrated by our destroyers. [31:1.]

The New York Times regrets that in the past week it has been unable to accommodate 310 columns of display advertising. Space for classified advertising also has been sharply reduced and numerous other economies have been effected to maintain the quality of Times news presentation and still conform to newsprint restrictions.

House Strikes OPA in 3 Test Votes; Oil Rise Favored, Retail Curb Hit

By CHARLES E. EGAN

Special to THE NEW YORK TIMES.

WASHINGTON, June 10—Administration forces working for re-enactment of price, wage and rent control laws in their present form, were mauled in the House today where test votes carried by overwhelming majorities three proposed amendments which are opposed by the Office of Price Administration.

Discussions over the amendments, the first eliminating the existing "highest price-line limitation" regulation applied to apparel stores by OPA, the second providing for an advance of 35 cents a barrel in crude petroleum prices, and a third to exempt property sold by court order from price ceilings, slowed up action to such an extent that there was doubt that the legislation could be voted out in final form before Tuesday night. Leaders had hoped to get a final vote on the bill today.

Today's setbacks, coming as the body sat in Committee of the Whole, followed the defeat of the Administration yesterday in the Senate when that body approved the cotton amendments sponsored by Senator Bankhead of Alabama.

An amendment identical with that of the Senate cotton measure has been prepared by Representative Brown of Georgia, and was to have been presented in the House today. Because of the long debate on other amendments Representative Brown did not get a chance to offer his measure, but is expected to do so on Monday.

There was no conference among

Continued on Page 46

De Gaulle Hits Allies' Plans; 'Honored' by Roosevelt Bid

By RAYMOND DANIELL

By Wireless to THE NEW YORK TIMES.

LONDON, June 10—Gen. Charles de Gaulle expressed dissatisfaction today with Gen. Dwight D. Eisenhower's preparations for the administration of liberated French territory. He protested, too, against the Allies' issuance of French currency.

It was the first time that the chairman of the French Committee of National Liberation, which prefers to be known as the Provisional Government of France, had publicly expressed his attitude since his arrival here.

He has issued no statements except the formal speech that he made to the people of France on D-day and has refused all requests by representatives of the American and British press for interviews. But today the Agence Française Indépendante published the text of an interview in question-and-answer form.

"Honored" by Invitation

Declaring that he would be "honored" to go to the United States to talk over French problems with President Roosevelt, General de Gaulle expressed satisfaction with the present military situation in Normandy. France, he said, is ready to bear her share of the burden of liberation, but it is "obviously in full sovereignty that she intends to wage war today and tomorrow to make peace."

"At present there is unfortunately no agreement between the French Government and the Allies' Governments concerning the cooperation of the French administration with the Allies' armies in liberated French metropolitan territory," he said. "Furthermore, the proclamation addressed to the French people on June 6 and the

Continued on Page 38

TOULON REPORTED UNDER ALLIED FIRE

Vichy Tells of a Naval Blow at Base—Germans Expect South France Landings

By The United Press.

LONDON, Sunday, June 11—The Nazi-controlled Vichy radio was heard broadcasting an announcement that Allied warships were bombarding the Mediterranean naval base of Toulon early today, soon after Swiss press dispatches reported that Berlin believed an Allied invasion of southern France was imminent.

British Broadcasting Corporation monitors reported the Vichy broadcast, which gave no details.

[In its first Sunday news broadcast the British radio did not mention the Vichy report. The Berlin radio said "good night" at 11:15 A. M., Sunday morning, without mentioning the reported shelling, according to the Columbia Broadcasting System. The International Information Bureau, German news agency, had broadcast that "early on the morning of June 9 a German patrol vessel had a

Continued on Page 36

Allies Landed Men Months Ago To Dig Sample of Normandy Soil

By Cable to THE NEW YORK TIMES.

SUPREME HEADQUARTERS, Allied Expeditionary Force, June 10—A "commando" raid by a group of civilian scientists, a search through obscure seventeenth-eighteenth-century French manuscripts, months of study of geological reports, experiments with model beaches—all these were a part of the Allied preparations for the invasion of Normandy that is one of the most remarkable stories of the war.

Months before the invasion parties of civilian scientists, not all of them young or signally muscled, landed on the beaches up which the Allied infantry were to scramble last Tuesday. Wriggling along on their bellies, within range of German guns, they obtained samples of sand soil so when the tanks and trucks bustled ashore the drivers would be prepared for the terrain and equipment would be on hand to bridge the worst spots.

The dramatic story of the preparations, which began in musty libraries, shifted to laboratories and ended on the shell-swept beaches, was told today by a mild-mannered professor in baggy clothes.

When the invasion was planned he was consulted by the Allied staff on the character of the beaches. He referred the officers to the old manuscripts, which, he said, stunned the staff officers. "But I convinced them they were worth studying so we went to work," he said.

"The geologists expected trouble because the area had been an Ice Age forest," the scientist added. "But the military people did not like all this book talk. So the only thing to do was to go and see."

Photographs and pre-war re-

Continued on Page 36

AMERICANS PUSH ON

Berlin Reports Forces of Bradley 15 Miles From Cherbourg

NAZIS FLOOD FIELDS

Battles Rage Near Caen and Carentan as Foe Counter-Attacks

5 A. M. Communique

By The Associated Press.

SUPREME HEADQUARTERS, Allied Expeditionary Force, Sunday, June 11—British armored thrusts have reached Tilly-sur-Seulles, headquarters communiqué No. 11 announced today.

American troops were declared to have captured high ground between Isigny and Carentan and are "everywhere south of the flooded areas in the lower Aure valley."

In the vicinity of Caen the Germans made no progress against Allied positions despite continuous and vigorous attacks.

Driving northwest of Carentan Allied troops crossed the Merderet River and overcoming enemy resistance have made further progress, the war bulletin said.

By DREW MIDDLETON

By Cable to THE NEW YORK TIMES.

SUPREME HEADQUARTERS, Allied Expeditionary Force, Sunday, June 11—Two fierce tank and infantry battles are now raging around Carentan and Caen, focal towns at the extremities of Allied invasion bridgehead in Normandy, although the Allies continued to gain on the whole Normandy front according to last night's official Allied communiqué.

Lieut. Gen. Omar N. Bradley's American Army, which in the previous twenty-four hours had captured the small but tactically important towns of Trevieres and Isigny, is striking for Carentan, key to the approaches to the Cherbourg peninsula, through areas flooded by the Nazis.

British and Canadian tank and infantry units meanwhile are hammering at enemy armor that Field Marshal Gen. Erwin Rommel has thrown into a major counter-attack in the Caen area.

Americans Push West

The latest report from the front is that American patrols, filtering across the main highway from Valognes to Ste. Mere-Eglise, are now west of the main railway running south from Cherbourg.

[Varying reports placed the advance units at one-third to one-half the way across the peninsula in that region, The United Press said, while The Associated Press quoted a German report that the Americans had advanced close to Montebourg, only fifteen miles south-

Continued on Page 33

Algiers Shuts Gate To Spanish Morocco

By Wireless to THE NEW YORK TIMES.

ALGIERS, Sunday, June 11—The French Committee of National Liberation closed the frontier between French and Spanish Morocco at midnight "for reasons of security," it was announced today.

At the same time the committee prohibited all communications in code between neutral governments and their representatives in French North Africa.

The closing of the frontier does not apply to diplomatic or consular officers of the United States, Britain, the Soviet Union and France.

"All the News That's Fit to Print"

The New York Times.

LATE CITY EDITION
POSTSCRIPT
Fair and somewhat warmer today.
Temperatures Yesterday—Max., 77; Min., 57
Sunrise, 5:24 A. M.; Sunset, 8:28 P. M.

VOL. XCIII..No. 31,551. Entered as Second-Class Matter. Postoffice, New York, N. Y. NEW YORK, MONDAY, JUNE 12, 1944. THREE CENTS IN NEW YORK CITY

AMERICANS DRIVE INLAND TOWARD KEY JUNCTION AND BATTLE FOR TOWN ON ROAD TO CHERBOURG; LINE IN ITALY ROLLS ON; SMASH AT FINNS GAINS

LEPKE 'SUCCESSOR' SEIZED AS SLAYER IN NEW GANG WAR

Louis (Babe) Silvers Held After Bookmaker Is Found Shot Dead in Brooklyn Street

SET UP AS NEW OVERLORD

Preyed on Gamblers, but the Victim, Jake (the Ox) Finkel, Wouldn't Pay, Police Believe

Jake (the Ox) Finkel was shot dead yesterday morning in the first fatal flare-up of gang warfare in Brooklyn since Louis (Lepke) Buchalter went to the electric chair early in March.

Held in the killing was Louis (Babe) Silvers, who had proclaimed himself gang overlord of the Brownsville precincts that formed part of the domain of the Brooklyn murder ring before the law liquidated its members and closed its books.

Finkel was not called the Ox for nothing. He used his ham-like fists to advantage before a bullet drilled him through the head and he pitched forward in the gutter in front of the Embassy Club, a cabaret, at 1650 Flatbush Avenue, in the Flatlands section of Brooklyn.

Under his body were four discharged cartridges from a .32 automatic pistol, thought to have been the murder weapon, and a fully loaded .38 revolver, believed to have been the dead man's.

Suspect Went to Hospital

That was at 3 A. M. A short distance away, in Beth-El Hospital, Rockaway Parkway and Avenue A, Silvers was waiting in the emergency ward a few minutes later to be treated for a scalp wound and two black eyes. He seemed nervous and upset and kept asking the nurse "Do you think I'm shot?"

She notified police and he was picked up along with a girl who said she was Lila Harris, 20 years old, of 276 Troy Avenue, Brooklyn.

She told police she had a date with Silvers for 2:30 A. M. at East New York Avenue and Saratoga Avenue and that when she met him he said he had been beaten up by two men.

The police knew that Silvers' car, registered in the name of his wife, Mrs. Florence Silvers, was parked across the street from the Embassy Club at the time of the killing, and in Miss Harris' handbag they found the car's keys.

At 9 o'clock last night Silvers was formally "booked" on a homicide charge at the Vanderveer Park police station in Brooklyn. He is due to appear in the line-up this morning, after which he will be arraigned in Brooklyn Felony Court. The police said they would request the District Attorney's office to detain Miss Harris as a material witness.

Police Reconstruct Slaying

As police reconstructed events preceding the slaying, three men and a woman were in a party in the Embassy Club drinking shortly before closing time. Finkel came in and had words with one of the men. He left, was followed by the others and almost in the next instant there were four shots. Finkel's body was found in the street.

The case histories of Silvers and Finkel convinced police this was no ordinary shooting resulting from a barroom quarrel. Silvers, they said, decided last fall to "take over" the Brownsville territory of the old Lepke gang. He surrounded himself with a number of thugs, including several discharged from the Army as unfit. He was ready to move, but Lepke, even while under sentence of death, acted as a deterrent.

But, according to police, he went out at once to assert his supremacy in the neighborhood. In a convincing demonstration, they suspect, he shot down on Sept. 25, 1943, Harry Davidoff (Little Gangie) and his brother, William (Big Gangie), while they stood at a bar at 621 Chester Street, near Dumont Avenue. The Davidoffs,

Continued on Page 13

550,000 Cheer War Parade 'Jumping Gun' in Bond Drive

Veterans From Italy Among Those Who March as City Starts Early—Nation's Campaign for 16 Billion On Today

By FRANK S. ADAMS

Stalwart American infantrymen—many of them recent veterans of the fighting in Italy—swung up Fifth Avenue yesterday between massed crowds of men, women and children estimated by the police to number 550,000, as New York City "jumped the gun" by one day on the rest of the nation in launching the Fifth War Loan drive.

An awe-inspiring display of the kind of tools of destruction now being wielded by the Americans invading France was opened by the Army at the close of the parade to give New Yorkers visual evidence of the equipment paid for by their war bond purchases. It occupies a twelve and one-half acre site in Central Park, running from Seventy-ninth to Eighty-sixth Streets.

The national drive will get under way with an hour-long radio broadcast over the four major networks starting at 10 P. M., Eastern War time, in the course of which President Roosevelt will address the nation. Henry Morgenthau Jr., Secretary of the Treasury, and the Governors of five States as well as many prominent stars of the radio, stage and screen will be heard on the program, broadcasting from Texarkana, on the Texas-Arkansas line.

More than 300,000 persons were on hand for the opening of "Weapons of War," as the display is known, and additional crowds thronged through the reservation in such great numbers that officials estimated the total might reach 1,000,000 by midnight. The exhibition, which is free, will remain open daily from 11 A. M. to midnight for two weeks.

Gigantic American tanks and

Continued on Page 21

TROOPS SEARCH CITY FOR NAZI PRISONER

Coast Guard and Police With Bloodhounds Join Hunt for Staten Island Fugitive

A German prisoner of war escaped early yesterday morning from Halloran General Hospital on Staten Island and became the quarry in one of the most intensive manhunts ever conducted in the New York metropolitan area.

Within a few hours, machine guns manned by soldiers had been set up at all the bridge and ferry exits from the island; the police were stopping trucks and wagons, while Coast Guard cutters and police launches churned the waters separating Staten Island from the New York and New Jersey mainland and from Long Island.

Two bloodhounds, brought by truck from the State Police barracks at Hawthorne, N. Y., joined the search in the afternoon.

Posses Search the Island

As word of the escape got about, hundreds of Staten Island residents formed posses to beat through the thousands of acres of woodland in the island's fifty-seven square miles. Last night the search continued under the glare of searchlights mounted on Army trucks and those of a police emergency truck.

The escape alarm, first made public by the Federal Bureau of Investigation and later put on the nine-State teletype circuit by the police, was the first public announcement that enemy prisoners of war have been stationed within the city limits. It was learned later that both German and Italian prisoners have been used for some time for general labor tasks at the Army hospital situated on a 383-acre wooded estate in the Willow Brook Park section.

Authorities believed last night that the fugitive was still on the island. His absence from a two-story brick detention barracks, one of about forty buildings in the hospital cluster, was noticed shortly before 7 P. M. Shortly after 1 P. M. the police received a call from a Department of Parks employe who said he had just seen a man in a dark suit, which resembled a uniform, in La Tou-

Continued on Page 34

BURMA ROAD DRIVE REGAINS LUNGLING

Japanese Also Defeated in India and In and Around Their Myitkyina Base

By The Associated Press.

CHUNGKING, China, June 11—The complete occupation of Lungling, the second most important Japanese base in Yunnan Province, was announced tonight by the Chinese communiqué, which called it "the greatest success to date for our troops in the Salween offensive."

Personally led by Maj. Gen. Sung Hsi-lien, troops of an Eleventh Army group, who stormed through the city yesterday, were mopping up trapped remnants of the Japanese garrison, the communiqué said. They also were pressing attacks of extermination outside Lungling.

The fall of Lungling, field dispatches have indicated, would cut off large concentrations of Japanese at the main enemy base of Tengyueh, forty miles to the northwest.

"Only one small group of less than fifty men remains in the city, trapped near the west gate, where they now are being annihilated," the communiqué said. "Another group estimated at approximately fifty Japanese is surrounded on the airfield outside the city, where attacks of extermination were being pressed by us last night.

"Not more than 300 Japanese were able to escape from the west gate of the city, from which they were pursued more than nine miles to the west. Many were destroyed."

This remarkable Chinese drive west of the Salween River, accomplished in spite of monsoon rains and formidable supply problems, may ease the supply problem. General Sung has said that within a short time engineers could put to use the part of the Burma Road seized in the offensive and step up the flow of supplies, which up to now have been carried forward by soldier-coolies, thousands of Chinese civilians behind the lines and endless slow-moving pack trains.

The drive at the same time has been of benefit to the north Burma front at Myitkyina, 100 miles to the west, where Lieut. Gen. Joseph

Continued on Page 10

AVEZZANO IS TAKEN

Eighth Army Drives Into Pescara, Chieti and Sulmona in East

FIFTH ARMY GAINING

Overruns Towns Beyond Viterbo, Crushing German Barrier

By The United Press.

ROME, June 11—The German rout in Italy spread to all sectors of the front today as the British Eighth Army captured the road junction of Avezzano, forty-eight miles east of Rome, in a drive that threatened the avenues of retreat for German forces fleeing from the Adriatic sector after having abandoned the strongholds of Pescara, Chieti and Sulmona.

American troops of the Fifth Army, racing to bring the shattered remnants of the German Fourteenth Army under their gunsights once again, pounded fifteen miles north from Viterbo to the northeastern corner of Lake Bolsena in a drive that carried two-thirds of the way up the Italian peninsula and within eighty-eight miles of Florence. Other Fifth Army forces smashed twelve miles up the Tyrrhenian coastal highway and occupied the town of Montalto di Castro, seventy road miles northwest of Rome.

The Allies' minesweepers, however, have made the deepest penetration thus far beyond Rome. They occupied the island of San Stefano, eighty miles from the capital and forty miles southeast of the island of Elba, on Friday.

Avezzano, on Highway 5 leading from Rome to Pescara, was taken by an eastward thrust along the road. Headquarters announced that all enemy forces in the area had retreated into the hills north of the highway. Its capture increased the possibility that the Eighth Army would cut laterally across the Apennine Mountains and endanger roads of retreat for the Germans in the Adriatic sector.

At Avezzano the Eighth Army

Continued on Page 6

OUR PARATROOPERS ON ALERT IN A FRENCH VILLAGE

Watching for German snipers as they advance through Ste. Mere-Eglise

Associated Press Wirephoto (U. S. Signal Corps Radiophoto)

MARIANAS STRUCK BY U.S. TASK FORCE

Carrier Fliers Batter Saipan, Tinian and Guam—Liberators Smash 22 Planes at Palau

By GEORGE F. HORNE

By Telephone to The New York Times.

PEARL HARBOR, June 11—Japan's three heavily defended bases in the Marianas Islands, Saipan, Tinian and Guam, were attacked yesterday by a powerful Pacific Fleet task force, Admiral Chester W. Nimitz reported today.

No details are available and it is not known whether the attack went into its second day as did the one late in February when a similar force consisting of carriers supported by strong forces of heavy craft, cruisers and destroyers, laid waste much of Saipan's defense installations and destroyed many

Continued on Page 12

Russians Advance 15 Miles, Take 80 Villages in Karelia

By W. H. LAWRENCE

By Wireless to The New York Times.

MOSCOW, Monday, June 12—The Soviet High Command, through Premier Stalin, announced last night the opening of a new offensive against German and Finnish troops on the Karelian Isthmus, breaking through fortifications on a twenty-five-mile-wide front and driving forward fifteen miles.

More than eighty inhabited points were taken, including Terijoki, six miles west of the 1938 Russo-Finnish border.

Moscow greeted Premier Stalin's announcement of the new offensive against the Finns with a salute of twenty salvos from 224 guns. Myriad red and green flares illuminated the sky, which was filled with hundreds of barrage balloons, and brought thousands of persons into the streets to share in the first victory celebration since Sevastopol fell on May 10.

For the Finns there was an ominous final sentence in Mr. Stalin's special order of the day. He ended with the declaration: "Death to the German and Finnish invaders!" Previous orders of the day had named only German invaders.

U. S.-Soviet Pact Celebrated

Finland several weeks ago turned down Soviet peace proposals despite pleas from President Roosevelt, the King of Sweden and many others who thought the Russian proposals were generous.

The first official news of the offensive against the Finns was given yesterday by the Foreign Commissar, Vyacheslaff M. Molotoff, at a luncheon celebrating the second anniversary of the mutual assistance pact between the Soviet Union and the United States, and was made public last night.

The Karelian campaign, which is being directed by the commander of the Leningrad army, Leonid A. Govoroff, was the first mention of

Continued on Page 8

U. S. 'HEAVIES' BOMB CLOSE TO OUR LINES

8th Air Force Also Pounds Nazi Pas-de-Calais Defenses—Planes Fight Foe's Tanks

By FREDERICK GRAHAM

By Cable to The New York Times.

LONDON, Monday, June 12—The non-stop aerial support of the Allied armies in France continued through Saturday night and yesterday along the lines of the three-phase operations developed by American and British air power—heavy bombing of main Nazi traffic centers and vital defense points, tactical bombings closer to the battle area and far-ranging fighter and fighter-bomber cover.

[The weather in the Channel area turned clear and warm Monday morn, with good visibility.

[Nearly 7,000 Allied planes flew over France Sunday in operations that included running battles with Nazi tanks, press service dispatches said.

[Reports up to Sunday midnight, The United Press stated, showed that twenty-five German planes had been shot down in the twenty-four hours to then, while the Allies lost forty-one planes,

Continued on Page 6

War News Summarized

MONDAY, JUNE 12, 1944

Important advances scored yesterday on the Normandy front expanded the Allied beachhead to nearly 600 square miles with a maximum depth of fifteen miles at two points. This area was won during the first week of the invasion was believed to make the foothold secure.

American troops, after having forded the flooded lower Aure Valley, liberated Lison and reached the Foret de Cerisy, thus threatening St. Lô, communications center for the entire Cherbourg Peninsula.

British soldiers captured Tilly-sur-Seulles after heavy fighting with German armored units. [All the foregoing 1:8; map P. 4.]

Thousands of planes continued to give the invading troops constant cover, carrying their operations from the beachhead to the Paris area. Large forces of Flying Fortresses and Liberators, well escorted, blasted nine German airfields, eight bridges and an army headquarters, in addition to pounding enemy communications and troop concentrations. [1:7.]

It was disclosed that the Allied Expeditionary Force had sent its civil affairs unit over with the first glider detachments to fight its way into French villages, then organize local civilian life and see that the roads were kept clear for military movements. [5:2.] Reports from southern France indicated that patriots had started to fight and shoot Vichyites, particularly in Toulouse, Limoges and Tarbes. [1:6-7.]

Allied air activity was not confined to the French coast. RAF Mosquitos from Britain struck Berlin, and 1,000 American planes from Russia and Italy bombed targets throughout the Balkans. The first shuttle group to reach Soviet bases returned to Italy, with Lieut. Gen. Ira C. Eaker in one plane, and bombed Nazi airfields in Rumania. The Black Sea port of Constanta was also blasted. [8:1.]

Allied progress in Italy continued unchecked. The Eighth Army captured Avezzano and also seized Pescara and Chieti, posing another encirclement threat for the retreating Germans. Sulmona was evacuated by the enemy. The Fifth Army maintained its fast drive north of Rome, and minesweepers occupied the island port of San Stefano, eighty miles above the capital. [1:4, map P. 6.] Allied amphibious forces, aided by Partisans, made a five-day raid on the island of Brac, off Yugoslavia, wiping out the German garrison at Bol. [6:1.]

Hitler's northern partner, Finland, felt the might of the Red Army when the Russians launched a full offensive on the Karelian Isthmus. In two days of fighting advances up to fifteen miles on a twenty-five-mile front were scored, more than eighty places were captured and the Finns' defense line was breached. [1:6-7; map P. 8.]

A powerful American carrier task force has pounded the vital Japanese islands of Saipan, Tinian and Guam in the Marianas, and bombers from the southwest Pacific hit Truk and Palau. [1:5; map P. 12.] Chinese troops along the Salween on the Burma front captured Lungling. [1:3; map P. 10.] The Japanese, stalled before Changsha in China's Hunan Province, started a drive north from Canton. [2:3-4; with map.]

Three Cities Reported Attacked By Patriots in Southern France

By The Associated Press.

IRUN, Spain, June 11—French patriots have occupied strategic centers in the cities of Toulouse, Limoges and Tarbes in southern France and have shot the prefects of police, Mayors and other collaborationist authorities in all three cities, direct dispatches reaching here said today.

The dispatches did not make clear whether the actions constituted a general uprising, saying only that important points in the three cities, as well as in the regions surrounding them, had been occupied by the patriots.

[Officials of the French Commissariat of the Interior in Algiers denied the reports that patriots had seized strategic points in Toulouse, Limoges and Tarbes, The United Press reported.

[A major uprising, extending from Metz to Avignon—almost the entire length of eastern France—and including a "major coup" at Bellegarde, near the Swiss border, was described in Swiss and Swedish newspaper accounts, the Office of War Information reported. About 100 French patriots were said to have seized the Bellegarde railway station, the site of a German headquarters, and to have "proceeded systematically to sabotage all the installations." About a mile away, the reports said, forty-eight Germans were killed and 150 were captured in a "violent clash" between Germans and patriots last Thursday.

[Reports up to Sunday midnight...

[The Berne radio, quoting a dispatch from the French frontier, said that a battle had been joined "in the regions of Oyon-

Continued on Page 7

ST. LO THREATENED

U.S. Troops Push 8 Miles in Drive for Highway Center of Peninsula

BRITISH ALSO GAIN

Take Seulles River Town in Air-Land-Sea Battle —Beachhead 'Secure'

5 A. M. Communique

By The United Press.

SUPREME HEADQUARTERS, Allied Expeditionary Force, Monday, June 12—The American advance east of the Vire River has continued into the Forest of Cerisy, the Allied communiqué said today.

Some further progress has been made west of the inundated valley of the Merderet River.

The Americans who advanced into the Cerisy Forest were developing their capture of Lison.

The Allies have gained a "firm, secure foothold on the bridgehead," it was stated officially. Allied warships kept up fire on enemy mobile batteries.

British forces are continuing intense fighting against German armor in the area of Tilly-sur-Seulles.

By DREW MIDDLETON

By Cable to The New York Times.

SUPREME HEADQUARTERS, Allied Expeditionary Force, Monday, June 12—Two American divisions have captured the tiny town of Lison, five miles southeast of Isigny, and have fought their way across the flooded country another six miles to the edge of Foret de Cerisy, where, after a general advance of almost eight miles, they threatened the Germans' hold on St. Lô, chief enemy communications center for the Cherbourg Peninsula south of Carentan.

This signal success, which started from positions in the Isigny-Trevieres line, was accompanied by a hard-hitting attack on the extreme right wing of Lieut. Gen. Omar N. Bradley's army. The doughboys are fighting to the north and south of Montebourg, sixteen miles southeast of Cherbourg, and are across the Merderet River, northwest of Carentan, as General Bradley extends his flank along the coast.

Hold 600 Square Miles

These American advances were matched yesterday morning by the British capture of Tilly-sur-Seulles, after a short and fierce battle in which the fire of two British cruisers, the Argonaut and the Orion, at 20,000 yards, helped to crumble up German armor and knock out a blockhouse. Yesterday afternoon the enemy was counter-attacking heavily along the Seulles River but British infantry and guns were breaking attack after attack.

These advances on the right-center of the Allied front have expanded the beachhead to approximately 600 square miles, enough elbow room to mount a major Allied attack and gain a strategic initiative. The two deepest penetrations in the beachhead are south-east of Lison, on the edge of Foret de Cerisy and Tilly-sur-Seulles, each about thirteen miles from the coast. At present the Germans are clinging to Caen and Carentan, two positions that must be taken before a major offensive can be launched.

[Allied forces have widened the beachhead to a distance of eighty miles along the coast, the London radio said early Monday in a broadcast heard by National Broadcasting Company.]

Carentan Barrier to Bradley

The principal American objective at present, the cutting off of the Cherbourg Peninsula, cannot be accomplished as long as Carentan holds out. General Bradley is moving along the east coast of the peninsula toward the port at its tip. Since Cherbourg is shielded from an attack from the south by

Continued on Page 4

"All the News That's Fit to Print"

The New York Times.

LATE CITY EDITION
POSTSCRIPT
Partly cloudy; cooler tonight.
Temperatures Yesterday—Max., 83; Min., 65
Sunrise, 5:24 A. M.; Sunset, 8:28 P. M.

Copyright, 1944, by The New York Times Company.

VOL. XCIII..No. 31,552. Entered as Second-Class Matter, Postoffice, New York, N. Y. NEW YORK, TUESDAY, JUNE 13, 1944. THREE CENTS IN NEW YORK CITY

AMERICANS WIN CARENTAN, A KEY TO CHERBOURG; CAPTURE FOREST 7 MILES FROM ST. LO JUNCTION; PRESIDENT SAYS INVASION SPEEDS PACIFIC WAR

HIS TONE CONFIDENT

Roosevelt Says Our Men Are Ready to Defeat Nazi Counter-Attack

OPENS BOND DRIVE

Nation Urged Over Radio to Continue to Forge Weapons of Victory

Roosevelt's address opening Fifth War Loan drive, Page 14.

By CHARLES W. HURD
Special to THE NEW YORK TIMES.

WASHINGTON, June 12—Reporting that "we have firm footholds in France with losses lower than expected," President Roosevelt asserted tonight that our policy of smashing Germany first would make it possible to "force the Japanese to unconditional surrender or to national suicide much more rapidly than has been thought possible." Our invasion forces, he added, "are now ready to meet the inevitable counter-attack of the Germans with power and confidence."

The President spoke over a national radio program starting the Fifth War Loan with a goal of $16,000,000,000, and in addition to giving firm assurance of initial success on the Normandy beachhead he took this opportunity to give an up-to-the-minute report on the war, which he said now is marked by Allied offensives around the world.

There is much more war being fought, Mr. Roosevelt remarked, than the contest on the English Channel that currently engages the greatest attention.

As for Germany, "our enemy first on the list," the President said that country has its back against "three walls at once." These he listed as Italy, where the Germans are retreating from the center of the peninsula, the Russian front and the Western front.

"On the East," he said, "our gallant Soviet allies have driven the enemy back from the lands which were invaded three years ago. Great Soviet armies are now initiating crushing blows."

Says Impossible Was Achieved

In France, he went on, "millions of tons of weapons and supplies, and hundreds of thousands of men assembled in England are now being poured into the great battle in Europe."

"From the standpoint of the enemy," Mr. Roosevelt said, "we have achieved the impossible. We have broken through their supposedly impregnable wall in Northern France. The assault has been costly in men and materials. Some of our landings were desperate adventures; but from the advices received so far, the losses were lower than our commanders had estimated would occur.

"We have established a firm foot-hold; and are now prepared to meet the inevitable counter-attacks of the Germans—with power and confidence. We all pray that we will have far more than a firm foot-hold."

While detailing these gains, the President voiced the cautioning note that "no one front can be considered alone without its proper relation to all."

Gains Over Japan Reviewed

In the Pacific, he said, "we have deprived the Japs of the power to check the momentum of our ever-growing and ever-advancing military forces."

"We have reduced their shipping," President Roosevelt reported, "by more than 3,000,000 tons. We have overcome their original advantage in the air. We have cut off from a return to the homeland tens of thousands of beleaguered Japanese troops, who now face starvation or surrender. We have cut down their naval strength so that for many months they have avoided all risk of encounter with our naval forces.

"True, we still have a long way to Tokyo. But, carrying out our

Continued on Page 14

Americans Escort Japanese to Vatican

By The United Press.

VATICAN CITY, June 12—American soldiers in two jeeps and on six motorcycles escorted Ken Harada, Japanese Ambassador to the Vatican, from Rome into Vatican City today to see Vatican authorities, and shepherded him back into Rome where he and other Axis diplomats are living under Allied protection.

During his two-hour visit Mr. Harada arranged to move into neutral Vatican City.

It is expected that the Japanese, German, Hungarian, Rumanian and Slovak delegations to the Vatican will move into the Vatican City apartments vacated by Harold Tittman, President Roosevelt's Vatican representative, and the British, French, Belgian and other Allied envoys, who can now live in Rome.

16 POST-WAR STEPS URGED ON CONGRESS

Senate Committee and Byrnes Call for Immediate Action to Assure Employment

By C. P. TRUSSELL
Special to THE NEW YORK TIMES.

WASHINGTON, June 12—The Senate received from its special Post-War Economic Policy and Planning Committee today a budget of sixteen legislative obligations for Congress to meet without delay in preparing for the impacts of unemployment and readjustment when war production ceases. No extended Congressional recess, the committee contended, should even be considered pending action on the problems.

Referring to Bernard M. Baruch's recommendations, the committee, which is headed by Senator Walter F. George of Georgia, said that if Congress discharges its obligations, "we can well have what Mr. Baruch called an adventure in prosperity."

"If it does not survey these fields and reach wise decisions in them," the committee said, "we can have economic chaos."

As the report awaited formal presentation to the Senate, James F. Byrnes, Director of War Mobilization, appeared before the Senate Military Affairs War Contracts Subcommittee on behalf of the George-Murray bill, which is being drafted around the Baruch-Hancock post-war readjustment report issued last February.

Says Cut-Backs Are Likely

Mr. Byrnes urged a general speeding up of Congressional action on post-war legislation, and warned that the program for termination of war contracts "can only limp along" until the House passes the legislation adopted by the Senate providing for a uniform system of such operations. He presented eight specific recommendations.

"Assuming that Germany is still at war with us when we reach the fourth quarter of this year," Mr.

Continued on Page 36

ALL-OUT AIR COVER

1,400 U. S. 'Heavies' in Record Strike Bomb 16 Luftwaffe Fields

NAZI PLANES FIGHT

Allies in 10,000 Sorties Down 53 of the Foe—RAF Hits Rail Points

By E. C. DANIEL
By Cable to THE NEW YORK TIMES.

LONDON, Tuesday, June 13—The first really good flying weather since the Allied invasion of western Europe began a week ago released 1,400 United States heavy bombers—the largest number ever dispatched on a single mission—for attack yesterday on sixteen Nazi air bases and other targets in France, all within a few minutes' flying time of our Normandy beachhead.

The Nazi Air Force took up the mighty Allied challenge to its dwindling strength in greater force than at any time since D-day.

"If anybody asks you where the Luftwaffe is, we saw 'em this morning," said First Lieut. William J. Weaver of Webster, N. D., a fighter-bomber pilot.

But not one of the Eighth Air Force's Flying Fortresses and Liberators, which also attacked six vital bridges, fell to enemy fighters, although seven failed to return as a result of flak or other damage. The strong escorting forces of Mustangs, Lightnings and Thunderbolts diverted the enemy from our big bombers, losing fourteen fighters to seventeen of the Luftwaffe they shot down.

RAF Again Out in Strength

The clearing skies also meant resumption of around-the-clock bombing on a grand scale. The Royal Air Force's "heavies," which blasted four more of the enemy's key rail points in France Sunday night, were out again last night in greater numbers than usual. Some headed southward from the English coast before dark.

Targets in the new night bombings were in both France and Germany, said a brief British announcement early today. A Nazi DNB broadcast about 1:30 A. M. said Cologne, a major Rhineland rail point for the movement of enemy reserves, had been hit by British bombers.

Latest reports on yesterday's vast Allied air operations over France gave fifty-three Luftwaffe planes shot down, plus seventeen destroyed on the ground.

The Allies' total losses for the day were thirty-nine planes, including the seven American heavy bombers, thirty-one fighters and one medium bomber.

[At least 10,000 Allied sorties were flown Monday, probably 7,000 up to noon, The Associated Press estimated.]

One whole sky train of American cargo planes that delivered 23,000 pounds of supplies to American units on the Cherbourg Penin-

Continued on Page 4

CONGRATULATIONS ARE IN ORDER ON THE INVASION BEACHHEAD

Lieut. Gen. Omar N. Bradley (left), commander of our ground forces in France, is greeted by Gen. George C. Marshall, Chief of Staff of the United States Army. Looking on is Gen. H. H. Arnold, chief of the United States Army Air Forces.
The New York Times (U. S. Signal Corps Radiotelephoto)

NAZIS FIGHT HARD

U. S. Battleships Forced to Batter Carentan to Aid Infantry

PATROLS NEAR PORT

British Battle Fiercely for Caen—Captives Rise to 10,000

5 A. M. Communique

By The United Press.

SUPREME HEADQUARTERS, Allied Expeditionary Force, Tuesday, June 13—Steady progress has been made on sectors of the Allied front in France but no marked advances have been recorded, the Allied communiqué said today.

Strong enemy resistance continues in the Tilly-sur-Seulles sector west of Caen.

The capture of Carentan "materially strengthens the link established between our two major bridgeheads," the communiqué said, and the build-up of positions "is progressing satisfactorily."

Allied planes attacked enemy troops, railroad targets and vehicles in great strength throughout Monday afternoon and evening, and bombed French railway junctions during the night. Our planes also bombed a tank concentration in the Grimbosq Forest, southwest of Caen, and blew up an enemy ammunition dump.

By DREW MIDDLETON
By Cable to THE NEW YORK TIMES.

SUPREME HEADQUARTERS, Allied Expeditionary Force, Tuesday, June 13 — Allied forces extended their hold yesterday on that slender strip of Europe reclaimed from the Nazis after four years of blood and sweat and toil and tears.

Almost four years since he made his bootless appeal to France to carry on as Britain's ally Prime Minister Churchill returned to France to see for himself how the fighting was going.

It was going well when the Prime Minister and an assortment of political and military big-wigs toured beachheads, indicating by their presence that the ground so hardly won was held securely.

Carentan had fallen to the American infantry. Elsewhere on the perimeter of that sixty-mile front, patrols had penetrated to within fourteen miles of Cherbourg's defenses and had fought their way to a point seven miles from St. Lô.

Drive to Cut Off Peninsula

Lieut. Gen. Omar N. Bradley's forces on the right wing of Gen. Sir Bernard L. Montgomery's Twenty-first Army Group rolled forward in a drive to isolate the Cherbourg peninsula.

North and northwest of Carenta the Americans fanned out, crossing

Continued on Page 3

RUSSIANS ADVANCE, BUT FINNS STIFFEN

Red Army Batters Out Gains of 4 to 6 Miles as Foe Pours In Strong Reserves

By W. H. LAWRENCE
By Cable to THE NEW YORK TIMES.

MOSCOW, Tuesday, June 13—The Red Army drove forward yesterday along the tortuous forest roads between lakes and swamps in the face of strong defensive fortifications to capture the rail station of Raivola, forty miles below Viborg, as well as thirty other inhabited points on the Karelian Isthmus, the Soviet High Command announced last night. Gains of four to six miles were punched through the Finnish lines in the day's fighting.

The Soviet communiqué, which contained few details, indicated that a strong force of infantry,

Continued on Page 4

Periled Americans Saved Beach, Says Montgomery

By The Associated Press.

WITH ALLIED TROOPS IN FRANCE, June 11 (Delayed)—High praise was given by Gen. Sir Bernard L. Montgomery to American troops at a press conference tonight, when he revealed that prisoners had included some Japanese and that snipers in action in France included women who had been killed while shooting at Allied soldiers.

"A great many of the enemy have been killed," General Montgomery said.

The Japanese—regular soldiers, not merely observers—were fighting alongside their Axis partners, General Montgomery said, and small numbers of them have already been taken prisoner and others killed.

Outspokenly pleased with the feats of American troops, General Montgomery said:

"The beach where the landing of the Americans took place east of the Carentan estuary was found being defended by a German division which was not a coastal divi-

Continued on Page 5

VICHY'S AUTHORITY VANISHING RAPIDLY

Germans Take Over in Capital as Petainists Gather in Madrid Around Envoy

By JOHN MacCORMAC
By Wireless to THE NEW YORK TIMES.

LONDON, June 12—So strong is French patriots' resistance that the extension of German control over a large part of central France, including Vichy, was announced today by the Vichy radio.

Armed uprisings by patriots have reached such proportions that it has apparently been found necessary to supplant or reinforce Chief of Government Pierre Laval's authority in a territory within which he had sought so long and faithfully to serve German interests. That this did not mean the end of collaboration, however, was indicated by the Paris radio announcement that the mobilization of the militia would be hastened to cope with the situation.

Other measures demonstrating that French resistance was beginning to complicate German defense plans included the extension of the 9 P. M.-7 A. M. curfew to all inhabitants of Limoges, said to be one of the chief centers of revolt, and the suspension of all motor traffic except movements of doctors and food trucks in the Allier, Haute-Loire and Puy-de-Dôme departments.

[The Brazzaville radio, heard by The United Press, said that, while France might be considered to be in a state of latent insurrection, the underground, in com-

Continued on Page 6

GERMAN 14TH ARMY DISPERSED IN ITALY

10th Army Fleeing in Broken Units—Allies Pound Ahead Across Peninsula

By The Associated Press.

ROME, June 12—The German Fourteenth Army has been "dispersed to the four winds," Allied headquarters declared today as the Fifth Army, pursuing the disorganized Germans up the Italian west coast, approached Orbetello, seventy-one miles northwest of Rome.

As depleted enemy units fell back toward the Florence area with the greater part of their equipment lost, the German High Command faced the immediate necessity of sending heavy reinforcements from France or elsewhere in Europe if any real attempt were to be made to hold northern Italy.

"It is now quite clear," the Allies' announcement said, "that the original Fourteenth Army * * * has been dispersed to the four winds. All that remains is a few scattered remnants who mainly are engaged in stealing one an-

Continued on Page 7

War News Summarized

TUESDAY, JUNE 13, 1944

Carentan has fallen to the Americans, who now hold a sixty-mile strip along the French coast. The day's advances carried American troops to within fourteen miles of Cherbourg and seven miles of St. Lô. The Forest of Cerisy was cleared of Germans. Marshal Rommel has thrown three motorized divisions into the battle at Caen, and the enemy was estimated to have 240,000 men along the fighting front. More than 10,000 prisoners have been taken. [1:8; map P. 2.]

Among the prisoners were some Japanese troops fighting alongside their Axis partner, General Montgomery said. The Germans were also using women snipers, he added. The Allied ground leader gave high praise to United States troops who were compelled to beat down a German field division before gaining 100 yards on the beach. [1:5-6.]

Every type of Allied plane struck every kind of military target along a 400-mile arc from St. Nazaire to Lille in the best flying weather since the invasion. The Eighth Air Force sent out more than 1,400 bombers in its greatest single operation of the war to hit sixteen airfields and six bridges. The Luftwaffe put up its heaviest opposition, and at the end of the day seventy enemy planes had been destroyed; thirty-nine Allied aircraft were missing. [1:3.]

Prime Minister Churchill and General Eisenhower led two separate groups of high ranking leaders on a five-hour visit to the battlefields. [1:6-7.]

Vichy authorities in southern France was reported to be disintegrating in the face of patriot sabotage. [1:7.] The German radio estimated Allied troops in the beachhead at 500,000 as the Reich propaganda tone shifted from boastful to cautious. [4:1.]

Allied troops continued to sweep forward along the entire Italian line, and Allied Headquarters declared that the German Fourteenth Army had been dispersed as a fighting unit. [1:6; map P 7.] The Red Army, smashing through Finnish defenses, captured more than thirty towns on the Karelian Isthmus, including Raivola on the main railroad to Viborg. [1:4; map P. 4.]

A United States carrier task force struck at the Marianas Sunday for the second day in a row, hitting Guam, Tinian, Saipan and Rota. [12:2.] Fourteenth Air Force fliers were raising havoc with Japanese troops in the Changsha area of China, one mission killing or drowning 1,000 of the enemy. [12:7.] In Burma the Chinese captured the jade center of Lonkin. [12:3.]

President Roosevelt, opening the Fifth War Loan drive last night, said "we can force the Japanese to unconditional surrender or to national suicide much more rapidly than had been thought possible" as a result of the strategy of concentrating first upon Hitler. The Allied beachhead in France is now strong enough to meet the inevitable German counter-attacks, he declared. [1:1.]

President Predicts Murder Orgy By Nazis to Wipe Out Minorities

Special to THE NEW YORK TIMES.

WASHINGTON, June 12—President Roosevelt, notifying Congress formally today of his action last week in setting up a camp for 1,000 war refugees at Fort Ontario, Oswego, N. Y., declared that the Nazis, with defeat in the war approaching, were determined to complete their plans to exterminate minorities in Europe.

"As the hour of the final defeat of the Hitlerite forces draws closer," he said in a special message to Congress, "the fury of their insane desire to wipe out the Jewish race in Europe continues undiminished. This is but one example; many Christian groups also are being murdered. Knowing that they have lost the war, the Nazis are determined to complete their program of mass extermination.

This program is but one manifestation of Hitler's aim to salvage from military defeat victory for Nazi principles—the very principles which this war must destroy unless we have fought in vain."

Recalling that in January he had established the War Refugee Board, the President said that the board "was entrusted with the solemn duty of translating this Government's humanitarian policy into prompt action."

Such action, he asserted, "has brought new hope to the oppressed peoples of Europe."

"From various sources," he went on, "I have received word that thousands of people, wearied by their years of resistance to Hitler and by their sufferings to the point

Continued on Page 8

Text of President's message on refugees, Page 9.

Churchill Inspects the Beachhead; Our Top Military Men Also There

By The Associated Press.

SUPREME HEADQUARTERS, Allied Expeditionary Force, June 12—Prime Minister Churchill set foot on French soil today for the first time since 1940, while General Eisenhower, commander of the Allied invasion forces, led a party of top United States military and naval commanders on a tour of the American-held section of the Normandy battlefront.

Great Britain's Prime Minister was accompanied by Field Marshal Jan Christiaan Smuts, Premier of South Africa, and Gen. Sir Alan Brooke, Chief of the Imperial General Staff.

In General Eisenhower's party were Gen. George C. Marshall, United States Army Chief of Staff; Gen. Henry H. Arnold, American Air Chief; Admiral Ernest King, Commander in Chief of the United States Fleet; Lieut. Gen. Omar N. Bradley, commander of American ground forces in France, and Rear Admirals Alan G. Kirk and John Leslie Hall, commanders of naval task forces in the invasion.

Mr. Churchill and his companions crossed the Channel today on the British destroyer Kelvin, and while they were aboard the ship it took part in bombarding a German position on the northeastern Normandy flank.

Arriving on the beaches shortly before noon, they spent three hours ashore; lunched with Gen. Sir Bernard L. Montgomery, commander of Allied ground forces in France; visited Army Headquarters; watched the landing of troops and supplies, and then steamed through the battle fleet that was bombarding the shore.

During the day Mr. Churchill

Continued on Page 5

London Has 2 Alerts, First Since April 27

By The Associated Press.

LONDON, Tuesday, June 13—The Luftwaffe sent a small number of raiders over Britain early today, apparently in an effort to divert attention at home from the weakness of Nazi air support in the battle for Normandy, giving London its first alert since April 27.

A few casualties were caused when some persons were trapped in a building hit by a high explosive bomb.

Downtown London had two alerts within an hour, and outlying sections heard three warnings. At least one enemy plane was shot down, crashing into East London houses.

Raiders were also over East Anglia and southern England.

"All the News That's Fit to Print"

The New York Times.

LATE CITY EDITION
POSTSCRIPT
Rain and cool today.
Temperatures Yesterday—Max.,71; Min.,58
Sunrise, 5:13 A. M.; Sunset, 8:29 P. M.

VOL. XCIII..No. 31,554. Entered as Second-Class Matter, Postoffice, New York, N. Y. NEW YORK, THURSDAY, JUNE 15, 1944. THREE CENTS IN NEW YORK CITY

NAZIS SEND 4 TANK DIVISIONS AGAINST ALLIES; WIN SOME GROUND; U. S. UNITS GAIN AT CARENTAN; RECORD AMERICAN BOMBER BLOWS AID TROOPS

FIRST DAY OF LOAN DOUBLES MARK SET IN 4TH CAMPAIGN

Monday's Sales in City Total $5,096,179—6.1% of Quota Raised Before the Drive

BONDS' BUYING POWER UP

Army Gets 2 Big Bombers for $500,000 to 1 Last Year—Other Costs Are Slashed

Tangible proof that the Fifth War Loan drive has got away to a flying start was provided yesterday by Nevil Ford, chairman of the War Finance Committee for New York State, who made public the first tabulations of sales. They showed that the opening day's sale of E bonds more than doubled those of the first day of the Fourth War Loan.

New York City purchases of E bonds, the savings bonds the Treasury is particularly anxious to place in the hands of small investors, aggregated $5,096,179 on Monday, against $2,205,700 on Jan. 18, opening day of the last campaign. In New York State as a whole Monday's sales of E bonds were $7,600,000, compared with $3,300,000 in the Fourth Loan.

Sales of all issues of war bonds to individual purchasers through the close of business Tuesday night amounted to $33,357,544 in New York City and $53,600,000 in New York State, Mr. Ford announced. He explained that the Treasury had ordered that only sales to individuals would be reported through June 26, although subscriptions from all investors are being received. The over-all totals will be made public beginning June 27.

Early Sales Credited to Drive

As in previous drives, Mr. Ford explained, the figures for all savings issues—E, F and G bonds and Series C Savings Notes—include all sales made since the first of the month in which the drive started. Eventually all sales of these issues made throughout July also will be credited to the Fifth War Loan, he explained, although the period of the drive is from June 12 to July 8.

Total E bond sales from June 1 through Monday night in New York City amounted to $13,767,419, or 6.1 per cent of the city's quota of $227,526,600 for this class of investment. The total sales of E bonds in New York State for the same period amounted to $30,200,000, or 8.2 per cent of its $367,000,000 goal. The over-all goals of the State and City for all investors are $4,801,000,000 and $4,167,028,000, respectively.

The following table, compiled by the Division of Research and Statistics of the War Finance Committee, shows the break-down of sales of E bonds in the various boroughs of the city through Monday night:

Counties.	Cumulative Sales to Individuals. Series E.	Ttl. All Issues.	% of E Quota Sold to Date.
Manhattan.	$9,026,706	$25,994,612	6.2
Bronx	621,075	1,405,720	5.1
Kings	2,838,113	4,294,855	5.9
Queens ...	1,153,669	1,517,301	6.2
Richmond..	127,856	145,056	4.7
N. Y. City Total	$13,767,419	$33,357,544	6.1

Bonds Buy More Now

War bond sales to individuals throughout the nation in the first two days of the drive totaled $484,000,000, the Treasury Department announced in Washington, according to The United Press. A spokesman of the Treasury pointed out that bonds now purchase more fighting equipment than they did a year ago, because costs have dropped.

The cost of a heavy bomber has been reduced from $500,000 to $250,000 in that period, according to figures furnished by the War Department, and a fighter plane that cost $150,000 a year ago now costs only $50,000. Bofors anti-aircraft guns have been cut from

Continued on Page 11

Price Bill Voted by House; Cotton Amendment Beaten

Measure Sent to Conference Would Allow Courts to Enjoin OPA—Parity for All Farm Crops Is Called For

By CHARLES E. EGAN
Special to THE NEW YORK TIMES.

WASHINGTON, June 14—The House by a voice vote adopted the bill to continue price, rent and wage controls for a year beyond June 30, after defeating the "cotton amendments" but accepting the Dirksen amendment giving Federal district courts jurisdiction over Office of Price Administration regulations with power to enjoin enforcement.

The measure will go to conference in an attempt to iron out differences with the Senate bill. The latter contains the cotton amendment, which leaders of both sides of the House characterized as inflationary.

OPA officials, as well as spokesmen for the House Banking and Currency Committee, termed the amendment sponsored by Representative Everett M. Dirksen, Republican, of Illinois, the most serious threat to effective price control and enforcement offered since the stabilization bill came up in Congress three weeks ago. The amendment was approved on a roll-call vote, 206 to 181, with anti-New Deal Southerners voting with a majority of the Republicans.

On a previous roll-call vote Administration forces won in a fight against the proposal of Representative Wesley E. Disney, Democrat, of Oklahoma, to make mandatory an increase of 35 cents a barrel for crude petroleum. The amendment was voted into the bill tentatively Saturday while the House was sitting as Committee of the Whole. In its vote today that decision was reversed, 204 to 178.

Other amendments rejected by the House after being approved in

Continued on Page 26

PEARL HARBOR LAG BLAMED ON OFFICER

House Group Lays Misconduct to Col. Wyman for Delays in Air Warning System

By KATHLEEN McLAUGHLIN
Special to THE NEW YORK TIMES.

WASHINGTON, June 14—More than a hundred pages of testimony comprise a report submitted today by the Military Affairs Committee of the House, alleging flagrant misconduct and malfeasance in office of an Army officer whose alleged negligence, it was indicated, might have figured largely in the success of the Japanese attack at Pearl Harbor.

In passing the report mentions the award of the Distinguished Service Medal, months after that tragedy, to Col. Theodore Wyman Jr., a focal figure in the investigation, who is said to be serving now overseas.

Accounts of many witnesses add up to a heavy total of charges against Colonel Wyman, although so far, the committee noted, no disciplinary move had been made in his direction by the War Department. Further action by the Military Affairs Committee awaited the response of the military authorities, Chairman Andrew J. May of Kentucky said this afternoon.

Major Items in the Charges

Major items in the accusations are that Colonel Wyman, as Division Engineer in Hawaii, was responsible among other things for the construction of aircraft warning stations for which the completion date was stipulated in the contract as June, 1941, but that the work was less than 37 per cent

Continued on Page 10

MAYOR PROPOSES RECONVERSION PLAN

Tells Senators of His 7-Point Program—Indorses Kilgore Bill, Which Patterson Hits

By C. P. TRUSSELL
Special to THE NEW YORK TIMES.

WASHINGTON, June 14—Mayor La Guardia proposed to the Senate Military Affairs Committee today a seven-point program for handling the unemployment and other problems developing from industry's reconversion to peacetime production.

His testimony laid the groundwork for a concerted drive by spokesmen for CIO unions, largely representing New York City workers, to have the committee approve the Kilgore Office of War Mobilization and Adjustment Bill, which would empower a single director to unify all Government production and cutback activities and issue directives on program, policy and operations to the Federal agencies involved.

At almost the same time, however, Robert P. Patterson, Under-Secretary of War, in a communication to the Military Affairs Committee's subcommittee on war contracts, endorsed in general terms the latest draft of the George-Murray bill, under which the Director of War Mobilization and Adjustment would coordinate the reconversion activities of other executive agencies but not have veto power over them, and pronounced the Kilgore measure "unwise and unworkable."

The Kilgore bill, Mr. Patterson said, would set up a demobilization establishment that would be "complex," "unduly large," would over-

Continued on Page 10

27 Died, 100 Missing, 380 Hurt In Pearl Harbor Blast on May 21

By The Associated Press.

WASHINGTON, June 14—The Navy announced tonight that twenty-seven men were killed, 100 are missing and 380 were wounded in the explosion which destroyed several small landing craft in Pearl Harbor May 21.

At the same time it reported that a magazine at the ammunition depot on Oahu Island, T. H., blew up last Sunday, killing three men. Seven others are missing as a result of this accident.

The explosion among landing craft in Pearl Harbor was reported previously by Admiral Chester W. Nimitz, Commander in Chief of the Pacific Fleet, who said that it occurred while ammunition was being unloaded from one of the small craft.

Casualties caused by the explosion and subsequent fire were: Dead—Army, eight; Navy, nine; Marine Corps, ten. Missing—Army, fifty-three; Navy, twenty-one; Coast Guard, twenty-six. Injured—Army, fifty-six; Navy, 143; Coast Guard, three; Marine Corps, 159, and civilians, nineteen.

In the explosion last Sunday, Pacific Fleet Headquarters said, several torpedo warheads being transferred from a truck to a platform were detonated. Damage was caused in the general magazine area and minor damage was done to power lines and railroad tracks. Names of the three men killed and the seven missing are being withheld pending notification of their next-of-kin.

The text of the press release was as follows:

"No. 443. The Commander in

Continued on Page 10

1,500 'HEAVIES' FLY

Seven Nazi Airfields, Oil Center on Rhine, Are Blasted in Attack

BATTLE COVER VAST

RAF Wipes Out Enemy Unit When It Pushes Allies From Village

By DAVID ANDERSON
By Cable to THE NEW YORK TIMES.

SUPREME HEADQUARTERS, Allied Expeditionary Force, Thursday, June 15—The United States Eighth Air Force put more than 1,500 heavy bombers into an assault on the Nazis from France to the upper Rhineland yesterday—a number exceeding by at least 100 the previous high mark for "heavies" dispatched in a single operation.

The waves of Flying Fortresses and Liberators struck at seven enemy airfields and at rail bridges in France, Belgium and the Netherlands and at a big oil refinery at Emmerich, northwest Germany.

Their contribution to the battle in Normandy was furthered by the fighter escort, numbering at least 790, which scoured the countryside of western Europe shooting up Nazi transport, aircraft and military installations. Fifteen bombers and eight fighters failed to return.

Two-Way Attacks Mounted

Great though it was, that mission was a relatively small part of Allied activity in the air by daylight. From Britain and from bases in Italy up to 12,000 sorties were flown by the United States Army Air Forces and the Royal Air Force.

Five Nazi fighters were shot down over France. Allied losses in this theatre, besides those of the Eighth Air Force, were three medium bombers and seven fighters.

As the vast aerial support continued last night, heavy bombers of the RAF in very great strength went out from British east coast

Continued on Page 5

GENERAL DE GAULLE ON INVASION BEACHHEAD

The French leader talking with Allied officers in Normandy
Associated Press Wirephoto (British official via U. S. Signal Corps Radiophoto)

NAVY GUNS BATTER MARIANAS, KURILES

Battleships Bombard Saipan and Tinian as Nimitz Draws Pacific Arc Nearer Japan

By GEORGE F. HORNE
By Telephone to THE NEW YORK TIMES.

PEARL HARBOR, June 14—Action against the Japanese in the last few days flamed across thousands of miles in the Pacific from the lower Marianas to the Kuriles, the latter within 600 miles of the home island of Hokkaido, it was disclosed here today.

[Army and Navy heavy bombers struck at Japanese-held Truk in the Carolines Monday, damaging air fields and setting several fires, the Navy reported Thursday night, in an Associated Press dispatch.]

Heavy bombardment of enemy positions in the Marianas has begun and another powerful task

Continued on Page 12

War News Summarized

THURSDAY, JUNE 15, 1944

A fierce tank battle was being waged in the central sector of the Normandy beachhead as the Germans launched powerful counter-attacks at the most advanced Allied holdings. Towns were changing hands frequently, and at latest reports the enemy had recaptured Montebourg, Caumont, Tilly-sur-Seulles and Troarn. Massed artillery fire prevented the Germans from scoring any break-through. From Carentan our forces advanced two miles after having beaten off attacks. [1:8; maps Pages 2 and 4.]

The supporting air assault reached a new peak of intensity yesterday. More than 1,500 Fortresses and Liberators smashed an oil refinery in Germany and enemy airfields in Belgium, the Netherlands and France. Ground targets were kept under constant punishing fire. From Italy other planes hit the Munich area for the third time in four days and raked oil targets in the Balkans. During the first week of the invasion Allied aircraft from Britain flew 56,000 sorties and dropped 44,000 tons of bombs. [1:4.]

Secretary of the Navy Forrestal disclosed that there were 1,300 United States ships among the 4,000 vessels participating in the invasion. [5:1.]

The darkest international cloud was the deterioration in relations with General de Gaulle. Washington reported that at the last moment he had denied several hundred specially trained French liaison officers permission to accompany the invasion forces to France [7:1] and the French Committee's agencies in Algiers grew more outspoken in their denunciations of President Roosevelt and the United States. [7:5.] General de Gaulle, however, was permitted to visit the Normandy battlefield yesterday. Prime Minister Churchill told the Commons that any discussion of the relations with the French Committee could only give comfort to the enemy. [1:6-7.]

In Italy the Allies smashed through the latest German defense line at three points. Orbetello and Bagnoregio were captured; Terni was being encircled. [1:7.] The Red Army widened its Karelian front to twenty-eight miles and was reported thirty-seven miles from the Finnish city of Viborg. [8:1, with map.]

Japan's outer defenses were pounded from the north and the south by the Pacific Fleet. Battleships, cruisers and destroyers heavily shelled Tinian and Saipan in the Marianas and carrier aircraft carried the assault north to Pagan Island. At the same time another task force shelled Matsuwa, 600 miles from Japan, and aircraft hit Shimushu and Paramushiru, all in the Kuriles. [1:5; map P. 12.]

Planes from the Southwest Pacific maintained the bombing of the Carolines, destroying twenty of fifty intercepting Japanese aircraft over Palau and many more on the ground. [12:6.] Chinese troops driving on Burma captured Hsiangta and other towns opening the way to the Shweli Valley. [12:1.]

Vice President Wallace declared in an article that this country's self-interest demanded eventual economic and political freedom for India and other colonial countries, as well as a helping hand to a peaceful Japan in a "free Asia." [1:6-7.]

De Gaulle Visits Normandy; Churchill Puts Off Debate

By RAYMOND DANIELL
By Wireless to THE NEW YORK TIMES.

LONDON, June 14—Only a few days less than four years since he raised the standard of French resistance to the enemy, Gen. Charles de Gaulle visited today that strip of France that the Allies have reclaimed from German domination. He crossed the Channel aboard the French destroyer Combattante, flying the French colors. It was a sentimental visit rather than a return to his native land for the man whom Vichy declared a traitor and sentenced to death in August, 1940, for defying orders to return to a France under the German heel.

[After enthusiastic welcomes in French towns, General de Gaulle re-embarked for England, The United Press reported.]

But for the head of the French Committee of National Liberation, who is seeking recognition for it as the Provisional Government of France, even to set foot on the beachhead required the assent of Gen. Dwight D. Eisenhower as Commander in Chief of the Allies' forces and the approval of President Roosevelt and Mr. Churchill. For that reason his visit helped to allay some of the anxiety caused here by the failure of the United States and Britain to devise a formula of cooperation and by Mr. Churchill's urgent appeal to the House of Commons today to spare the Government for the present from justifying its course in that direction, on the ground that to do so now could only comfort the enemy.

[French headquarters in London indignantly denied Washington reports that, at the last minute, General de Gaulle had canceled orders that would have sent several hundred French officers into France with the

Continued on Page 7

NEW GERMAN LINE IN ITALY IS PIERCED

Impromptu Defense Arc Cut at 3 Points—Allies Drive On Grosseto and Terni

By The United Press.

ROME, June 14—The Allies, in hard fighting, have broken through a hastily established German defense arc above Rome at three vital points and are nearing the important highway hubs of Grosseto, 114 road miles northwest of the capital, and Terni, sixty-two road miles north of it, it was announced today.

The attempted German stand from the Tyrrhenian coast around the top of Lake Bolsena was of brief duration, shattered by attacks by Allied armor and infantry. Nor could the enemy hold in the Tiber Valley, the central sector or the Adriatic sector, and front dispatches reported Allied advances all along the 200-mile front.

One break-through was made on the Tyrrhenian coast by American forces. Another, at the northwest corner of Lake Bolsena, was made by British and American units, and the third, southwest of Terni, was made by British troops.

British Eighth Army forces continued their advance on the Adri-

Continued on Page 9

Wallace Urges Freedom for India, Dutch Indies and Other Peoples

Special to THE NEW YORK TIMES.

WASHINGTON, June 14—The United States should, in its own interest, promote the economic and political freedom of India, the Netherlands Indies and other colonial areas in the Pacific and should help bring a defeated Japan into the ranks of a "free Asia" after the war, Vice President Henry A. Wallace suggests in a pamphlet issued today by the American Council of the Institute of Pacific Relations.

It is not the mission of the United States either to write declarations of independence for the colonies of other powers or to underwrite "other people's declarations of continuing empire," Mr. Wallace says, but, he adds, "it is to our interest to approve and cooperate with all trends which lead toward our own standard of government of the people, by the people and for the people."

The Vice President does not suggest how the British are to solve the political and religious problems involved in giving India her independence, but he proposes that the British and other colonial powers should take steps to prepare a definite system of training and preparation for self-government and he suggests that they announce a specific date on which they will terminate their "trusteeship" over the colonial areas of the Pacific.

"While the British and Dutch Governments and the French Committee of National Liberation have given evidence that they recognize the need of revising their colonial policies in the direction of a larger

Continued on Page 18

BIG BATTLE JOINED

Enemy Hurls Strength in Night Attacks in Move to Turn Tide

ALLIED LINES FLUID

Caumont, Villers-Bocage and Troarn Change Hands in Fighting

5 A. M. Communique

By The Associated Press.

SUPREME HEADQUARTERS, Allied Expeditionary Force, Thursday, July 15—British forces have been pushed out of Troarn, east of Caen, by a German counter-attack, it was announced today.

Americans, attacking on a nine-mile front, have driven six miles west of Carentan, itself six miles inland from the sea.

This advance placed the Yankee troops within seven miles of high ground controlling the last remaining German traffic artery to Cherbourg to the north, and violent German reaction was expected.

Communiqué No. 19 said that "on all parts of the front Allied forces continue to carry the fight to the enemy."

Americans and Germans still are fighting in the streets of Montebourg, fourteen miles southeast of Cherbourg, it announced.

The heaviest fighting was reported in the Carentan, Montebourg and Caen areas.

By DREW MIDDLETON
By Cable to THE NEW YORK TIMES.

SUPREME HEADQUARTERS, Allied Expeditionary Force, Thursday, June 15—Tanks and infantry of four German armored divisions yesterday launched a series of heavy counter-attacks on the two salients that British tanks and American infantry had driven through enemy positions south of Bayeux, Allied Supreme Headquarters revealed last night. The largest armored battle of the war in western Europe was raging last night in the quadrilateral whose four points are Caumont, Villers-Bocage, Tilly-sur-Seulles and Balleroy.

German Panzer grenadiers and regular infantry also counter-attacked sharply on the extreme right of the Allied line, and the Americans had given up Montebourg. The Germans were also attacking British divisions holding a bridgehead on the Dives River east of Troarn on the left flank of the front.

The fighting in all areas was fluid. Towns and villages were lost and recaptured and lost again by both sides in the savage, bitter actions swirling over the thickly wooded hills and tiny fields of Normandy.

Foe Retakes Tilly-sur-Seulles

Although the Allies gave ground in several areas, as around Tilly-sur-Seulles, where the town is in German hands, generally the German counter-blows were held. The enemy is far from exhausted, however, and further assaults can be expected. In most areas the Allies retain the initiative and are concentrating for further thrusts.

The German threat, however, is the most serious one of the campaign. In the present German establishment four tank divisions are equal to 800 tanks if all divisions are up to strength. Two of the divisions fighting in the quadrilateral, the Second and Twenty-first, are first-class formations. The Twelfth SS, a Hitler Elite Guard youth division, is not up to them in matériel but is composed of fanatical youngsters. The Fourth Division is composed of a curious mixture of new and outmoded tanks. Both the Twenty-first and Twelfth have been badly mauled in recent fighting.

With elements of all four of these

Continued on Page 8

"All the News That's Fit to Print"

The New York Times.

LATE CITY EDITION
POSTSCRIPT
Partly cloudy and warmer today
Temperatures Yesterday—Max., 67; Min., 57
Sunrise, 5:23 A. M.; Sunset 7:29 P. M.

VOL. XCIII—No. 31,555. Entered as Second-Class Matter, Postoffice, New York, N. Y. NEW YORK, FRIDAY, JUNE 16, 1944. THREE CENTS IN NEW YORK CITY

OUR SUPERFORTS BOMB CITIES IN JAPAN; AMERICAN FORCES LANDING IN MARIANAS; ALLIES GAIN ON CHERBOURG PENINSULA

NAZI ROADS IN PERIL

Americans Are Nearing Two Vital Points on Cherbourg Neck

GERMAN TANKS LOSE

British Gain in Caen Sector—Battleship Shells Le Havre

5 A. M. Communique

By The United Press.

SUPREME HEADQUARTERS, Allied Expeditionary Force, Friday, June 16—Allied forces on the Cherbourg peninsula have made further progress west of Pont l'Abbé, seventeen miles from the west coast, a communiqué said today.

No major change has been made in any sector, the communiqué 21 said.

All attempts by the Germans to seize the initiative have been frustrated and their counter-attacks have been repelled.

At midnight Thursday, it was learned American troops were six miles from La Haye du Puits, where western communications along the peninsula narrow to a junction before running on southward.

By DREW MIDDLETON

By Cable to THE NEW YORK TIMES.

SUPREME HEADQUARTERS, Allied Expeditionary Force, Friday, June 16—Americans, supported by tanks, are advancing on a front of ten miles across the neck of the Cherbourg Peninsula, threatening La Haye du Puits and St. Sauveur-Le Vicomte, two of the most important links in the enemy's chain of communications with Cherbourg.

Late yesterday Allied patrols were reported fighting in Pretot, four miles northeast of La Haye, and at Reigneville, only three miles northeast of St. Sauveur-Le Vicomte, after the occupation of Baupte, nine and a half miles east of La Haye and five miles west of Carentan. Baupte was occupied yesterday morning as the Allied American offensive to cut off the great Norman port developed swiftly.

The Allied line in this area is now only about seven miles from the main enemy supply network on the western side of the peninsula.

Quinéville, on the east coast of the peninsula, four and a half miles northeast of Montebourg, has also been captured and the American right now is firmly anchored on the sea.

No Major Fight in Quadrilateral

Although there were still a number of sharp skirmishes in the quadrilateral of Balleroy, Tilly-sur-Seulles, Villers-Bocage and Caumont, neither side launched a major attack yesterday. German armored divisions suffered "substantial" tank casualties in Wednesday's fighting, which culminated in a "very heavy" assault in the Villers-Bocage area in which eight Panther and nine Tiger tanks were destroyed by British tanks and anti-tank guns. British veterans, including men of a once famous division in the Troarn area, were slowly pushing forward southwest of Troarn in the face of bitter enemy resistance.

Hundreds of airplane engines sounded reveille over the front at dawn yesterday as the United States Ninth Air Force and the British Second Tactical Air Force launched large-scale operations in support of the ground forces. Fighter-bombers and fighters skimmed over Allied tanks and troops to harry German troop concentrations, tanks, convoys and supply dumps in the battle area.

The flow of enemy reinforcements to the fighting zone was seriously hampered by Marauders and Havocs, which bombed bridges at Conde-sur-Noireau, St. Lô, Lessay, Chartres, Coltainville and a road junction at Argentan.

The Navy's part in the cam-

Continued on Page 6

President Outlines U. S. Plan For World Security Union

Four Major Powers Would Have Permanent Place in Elected Council—All Would Keep Forces to Halt War

By CHARLES HURD

Special to THE NEW YORK TIMES.

WASHINGTON, June 15—President Roosevelt advanced a plan today for post-war international security calling for the formation of "a fully representative organization" of peace-loving countries. It would elect a smaller council on which the four major United Nations would be constantly represented with a "suitable" number of smaller countries. An international court of justice would be set up.

"The purpose of the organization," the President's statement said, "would be to maintain peace and security and to assist the creation, through international cooperations of conditions of stability and well-being necessary for peaceful and friendly relations among nations."

Of course, he said, the plan will become possible only when our present enemies are defeated "and effective arrangements are made to prevent them from making war again."

Mr. Roosevelt suggested no formal name for the proposed organization and made no recommendations as to the details of establishing it. He said, however, that "we are not thinking" of a super-state with its own armies and police forces. Instead "we are seeking" effective arrangements through which the nations would maintain adequate forces to prevent war and make impossible deliberate preparations for war and, when necessary, to have such forces available for joint action.

At first glance the plan, in the skeleton outline by the President, rested on about the same basis as the League of Nations; that is, an

Continued on Page 12

SAIPAN IS STORMED

Americans Fight Way Inland on Base Vital to Japan's Defense

BATTLING IN TOWN

Navy's Fire Covers Leap to Marianas, 1,465 Miles From Tokyo

By GEORGE F. HORNE

By Telephone to THE NEW YORK TIMES.

PACIFIC FLEET HEADQUARTERS, June 15—American troops who fought their way ashore on Saipan Island in the Marianas Islands on Wednesday have firmly established their beachheads and are making good progress in an advance inland against heavy opposition, Admiral Chester W. Nimitz said in a communiqué tonight.

The enemy is fighting bitterly and has attempted several counter-attacks with tanks, but they have been broken up by our troops with the support of aircraft and warships lying offshore. Thus the most important battle fought so far in the Pacific offensive, now reaching to within 1,465 statute miles of Tokyo and a threat to the Japanese homeland itself, was going well for the invaders.

Tonight's communiqué was the second of the day issued by Admiral Nimitz. The first confirmed previous Japanese reports that Saipan was being invaded.

Defenses Well Organized

Tonight the Commander in Chief of the Pacific Fleet told of the advance inland. He said that in general the fighting was heavy and the defenses well organized.

We have captured Agingan Point, on the southwestern extremity of the big island, he said, and troops have forced their way into the town of Charan-Kanoa, where brisk fighting was still going on. Charan-Kanoa is the center of Saipan's big sugar refining industry and has a number of mills.

Between Charan-Kanoa, the first Japanese community to witness an engagement between land forces of the United States and Japan, and Agingan Point, a distance of about two miles, stretches a flat beachland and trees. Outside is a reef.

Our control of the air over Saipan and possibly over other Mari-

Continued on Page 3

STUNNING BLOWS STRIKE FOE IN PACIFIC ARENA

June 16, 1944

Introducing a new weapon for this global war, the United States sent Superfortresses from Asiatic bases to rain explosives on Japan (1). Tokyo said several cities on the island of Kyushu had been hit (detailed map Page 2). Earlier, American amphibious forces stormed ashore on Saipan Island (2) in the Marianas group, outpost of Japan itself (detailed map Page 3). From General MacArthur's command long-range planes struck at the bases of Yap (3) and Truk (4).

B-29'S MAKE DEBUT

Tokyo Reports Assaults on Industrial Heart of Kyushu Island

20TH AAF CREATED

New Command Will Be the Air Equivalent of a Naval Task Force

Details of new Superfortress bomber plane are on Page 4.

By SIDNEY SHALETT

Special to THE NEW YORK TIMES.

WASHINGTON, June 15—The air war against the heart of the Japanese Empire has begun, the War Department announced this afternoon. B-29 Superfortresses of the new Twentieth Air Force, which is part of a new "super-air force" under the personal command of Gen. H. H. Arnold, bombed Japan today, a special communiqué revealed.

There are three epochal factors in the announcement:

First, that the monster B-29, half again as big as the Flying Fortress, is in operation.

Second, that the type of aerial attrition that reduced Germany to the stage where an invasion of Europe could be launched has commenced against Japan proper.

Third, that, in creating the Twentieth Air Force, a special organization that is not subject to the jurisdiction of any theatre commander, the Joint Chiefs of Staff have set up what virtually amounts to a separate air force.

Tokyo Road Shortened

The importance of this new phase of the Pacific war was emphasized by statements from Gen. George C. Marshall, Chief of Staff, who termed it the beginning of "a new type of offensive against our enemy"; from General Arnold, commanding general of the AAF, who declared it was "the fruition of years of planning for truly global warfare," and Secretary of War Henry L. Stimson, who asserted that the action had "shortened our road to Tokyo."

The history-making communiqué was confined to the following bare statement, personally handed out by Maj. Gen. Alexander D. Surles, War Department Director of Public Relations, at 1:39 o'clock this afternoon:

"B-29 Superfortresses of the United States Army Air Forces Twentieth Bomber Command bombed Japan today."

No details of where we struck the enemy, or how hard we hit, were revealed, although it was understood that the War Department would release this information as quickly as it felt the story might be told without imperiling security.

Representative Joe Starnes of Alabama, member of the Military Subcommittee of the Appropriations Committee, told the House that Tokyo was the target, and that a "heavy task force" of B-29's had "successfully" bombed

Continued on Page 4

DE GAULLE NAMES NORMANDY AGENT

Appointing of Commissioner While on Beachhead Visit Presents Poser to Allies

By E. C. DANIEL

By Wireless to THE NEW YORK TIMES.

LONDON, June 15—Without waiting for an agreement with the United States and Great Britain on the civil administration of France, Gen. Charles de Gaulle has already installed a Commissioner for Civil Affairs in Normandy.

This action, which became known today upon the general's return from his visit to France, apparently was taken without consulting Allied military or political authorities.

At first glance the functions of this Commissioner would seem to duplicate those of the civil affairs section which the Allied Supreme Command has organized to administer liberated areas in the rear of the advancing armies.

However, if the United States and Britain do not take umbrage at General de Gaulle's haste in in-

Continued on Page 7

ALLIED TIDE IN ITALY ENGULFS ORVIETO

8th and 5th Armies Break New German Line, Win Narni, Aquila, Many Other Places

By The Associated Press.

ROME, June 15 — Bursting through another line of defenses hastily thrown up by the retreating Germans beyond Rome, Allied forces have captured the large Italian towns of Orvieto, Aquila and Narni in a general advance and were fighting tonight in the outskirts of the important industrial and communications center of Terni, forty-five miles north of the capital.

American troops shoving up the Tyrrhenian coast captured Magliano and threatened Bengodi, only fourteen miles from Grosseto, after having seized vast quantities of Nazi food supplies at Orbetello. They had entirely cleared lateral highway 74, running inland from the coast past the northern shore of Lake Bolsena.

Eighth Army columns, now carrying the brunt of the inland advance, fought their way into Orvi-

Continued on Page 9

PETRILLO IS ORDERED TO END RECORDS BAN

WLB Tells Union, Companies to Agree on Royalty Plan—Musicians' Head Defiant

By LOUIS STARK

Special to THE NEW YORK TIMES.

WASHINGTON, June 15—The War Labor Board ordered the American Federation of Musicians today to end the ban which it put on production of phonograph recordings on Aug. 1, 1942.

In its directive, the board also provided that the transcription companies should set up machinery for the payment of royalties on records, reversing a panel recommendation which opposed payments.

Although the board did not specifically order the payment of royalties into the union unemployment fund, as had been requested, it provided that the money be held in escrow. The board did not fix the amount of these payments but proposed that the parties agree on this detail by direct conference. Failure to agree, the board stated, would result in arbitration by the board itself.

The industry members who, with the public members, made up the eight-man majority, favored the seven-point program proposed by the public spokesmen reluctantly lest a worse compromise be the alternative, it was stated.

The four labor members dissented. They did not state their reasons but it was reported that they sided with Mr. Petrillo, who had asserted that the ban was not really a strike, that the WLB had no jurisdiction of the case and that the dispute did not affect war production.

The companies involved in the case were the National Broadcasting Company, radio recording division; the Columbia Recording Corporation, and the RCA Victor division of the Radio Corporation of America.

The board held that contracts for royalty payments to the union made by a group of companies led by Decca Recordings did not require board approval since the funds set up did not involve a wage increase and thus did not require board approval under the wage stabilization program.

The union announced that it had signed agreements with more than eighty companies and it withdrew

Continued on Page 20

Tokyo Tries to Belittle Raid; Claims Two Superfortresses

By The United Press.

SAN FRANCISCO, June 15—The official Japanese radio announced today that American warplanes, including B-29 Superfortresses, had bombed Yawata, home of the great Imperial Steel Works; Moji, a communications center, and Kokura in northern Kyushu Island of the Japanese homeland Friday morning, June 16 (Japanese time).

The broadcast, recorded by United Press, admitted the attacking planes had started "two or three fires," but claimed they were "extinguished immediately."

Late news broadcasts from Tokyo continued to minimize the effects of the raid, claiming that damage was "limited" to "two or three light industrial shops."

The attacking force took off from a China air base and flew "by way of Antung, situated on the Manchukuo-Chosen border," Tokyo claimed, adding that the presence of the B-29's "came as no surprise."

The Japanese claimed their intercepting planes had shot down six of the attacking American aircraft. Two of these, said the Japanese announcement, were B-29 Superfortresses.

The Tokyo radio also reported that the railway line between Orio and Hasaka had been "slightly damaged" in the raid. The Japanese broadcast said the rail line "was repaired at once * * * and traffic service has been resumed without any hitch."

Moji is the site of the Mitsui

Continued on Page 2

RED ARMY EXPANDS WEDGE IN FINLAND

Breach Widened to 46 Miles With Spearhead Thrusting Closer to Viborg

By The United Press.

LONDON, Friday, June 16—Red Army forces have widened their breach in the Finnish lines across the Karelian Isthmus to more than forty-six miles and have pushed to within thirty-three miles of Viborg by capturing the heavily fortified town of Kanneljaervi, near the Leningrad-Helsinki Railroad, Moscow announced last night.

The Moscow bulletin announced that Gen. Leonid A. Govoroff's Leningrad Army, in the six days it has been on the offensive, had smashed through two powerful Finnish defense belts, advanced a total of almost twenty-five miles and widened its break-through to

Continued on Page 8

Invasion and Other War News Summarized

FRIDAY, JUNE 16, 1944

Japan felt the force of two mighty American blows, while her Axis partner was being steadily pushed back on the fields of Normandy.

The new B-29 Superfortresses made their initial major bow with a sudden heavy assault on the island of Kyushu, part of the Japanese home territory. It was the first time bombs had fallen on Japan itself since General Doolittle's Shangri-la sweep more than two years ago. The only details disclosed by Washington were that the B-29's had "probably" operated from bases in China and were from a new Twentieth Air Force.

This force, under direct command of General Arnold and supervision of the Joint Chiefs of Staffs, will be used as an aerial battle fleet, or major task force, in future operations. [All the foregoing 1:8.]

Tokyo's version of the attack said that Yawata, site of the Imperial Steel Works, the communications center of Moji and the suburbs of Kokura, all near Shimonoseki, had been hit. The Japanese asserted two Superfortresses and five other American planes had been shot down. [1:6-7; map P. 2.]

The B-29 flies so high and so fast that it appears to ground defenders as a small gnat with a vapor trail. It carries the heaviest bomb load of any plane in the world. [4:2-8.]

While Japan was bearing this blow at home it was announced that American amphibious forces had stormed ashore on the strategic island of Saipan in the Marianas. A four-day battering by ships and planes preceded the first assault on Wednesday. Strong forces have landed and are battling fierce enemy opposition. A late communiqué said beachheads had been secured and our troops were advancing inland. [1:4; map P. 3.]

Tokyo reported early today that an American task force had attacked the Bonin Islands, midway between Japan and Saipan, and that hostile planes had attacked Korea. [Box 1:8.]

Southwest Pacific planes kept the enemy occupied by dumping 180 tons of bombs on Truk in the heaviest attack yet made on that island by General MacArthur's fliers. Yap and other neighboring places were also hit. [3:8.]

In Burma airborne Chindits launched a sudden attack on Mogaung, supporting base for Myitkyina, but along the Shweli River the Japanese recaptured Hsiangta and threatened to win back Lungling. [4:1.]

The invasion of Normandy showed steady progress yesterday. Americans advancing on a ten-mile front across the neck of the Cherbourg Peninsula menaced La Haye. Baupte and Quineville were captured and the Germans suffered heavy tank losses in strong counter-attacks in the Caumont-Tilly sector. Battleships and cruisers poured shells into enemy positions and Le Havre. [1:1; map P. 6.]

More than 7,000 Allied aircraft gave close support to the ground troops. The E-boat base at Le Havre was heavily bombed, and on Wednesday night the RAF struck again at the German synthetic oil center of Gelsenkirchen in the Ruhr. [5:1.]

General de Gaulle, described by his headquarters as "President of the Provisional Government of the French Republic," before returning from the beachhead installed a Commissioner for Civil Affairs without consulting Allied military or political leaders. [1:2.]

In Italy, too, the Germans were being pushed back. The Allies smashed through another defense line to take Orvieto, Aquila and Narni, and to come within eighty miles of Florence. [1:3; map P. 9.] The Red Army continued to beat down strong Finnish resistance and was only thirty-three miles from Viborg and twenty-six from Koivisto. [1:7; map P 8.]

President Roosevelt made public an outline of his plan for post-war security. He suggested an organization of all peace-loving countries, a smaller council on which the four major powers and small nations would be represented and an international court of justice. "We are not thinking of a super-state with its own police forces," he said, but of peace by agreement. [1:2-3.]

Bond Purchases by Armed Forces Help City to Raise 8.7% of E Quota

New York City fighting men purchased war bonds aggregating $4,641,751 in value between June 1 and June 10, it was announced yesterday by Nevil Ford, chairman of the War Finance Committee for New York, who said that their action has helped to lift the city's total sale of E bonds in the Fifth War Loan drive to $19,785,345, or 8.7 per cent of its E bond quota of $227,526,600.

"This striking evidence of double-action patriotism by our men and women in the armed forces should give every citizen something to think about," Mr. Ford declared. "Not only are they offering their lives—something that we are not asked to do—but they are also allotting large sums from their service pay to help speed the day of victory.

"If anyone, after reading today's headlines, still needs to be prodded in order to do his full share in raising the largest War Loan quotas ever asked of our city and State, let him think this over."

Sales of all types of issues to individual purchasers in New York City soared to a total of $48,984,276 through the close of business on Wednesday, according to Mr. Ford. Single day sales totaling $15,400,[illegible] on Wednesday to individual purchases in New York State brought the Fifth War Loan total for the State to $69,000,000.

The State-wide total sales of E bonds have risen to $33,500,000, or 9.1 per cent of the State's quota of $367,000,000 in this category. It was explained that the daily totals of E bond sales for both the city and State are one day behind those of the sales of other types to individual investors, because of the amount of work involved in processing sales from the great num-

Continued on Page 10

Air Attack on Korea Reported by Tokyo

By The Associated Press.

The Japanese Domei agency said early today in a broadcast reported by Federal Communications Commission monitors that several "enemy" planes had raided Korea, Asiatic mainland area immediately opposite Japan.

The broadcast, transmitted to occupied East Asia areas, said the planes had hit in southern Korea. It quoted an announcement issued by the Japanese Army in Keijo (Seoul) that "we suffered no losses."

A Tokyo broadcast said later an "enemy task force" had attacked the Bonin Islands southeast of the Japanese mainland Thursday afternoon. This group stands midway between Japan and the Marianas, where American forces have effected a landing.

"All the News That's Fit to Print"

The New York Times.

LATE CITY EDITION
POSTSCRIPT
Cloudy and cooler today.
Temperatures Yesterday—Max., 80; Min., 63
Sunrise, 5:24 A. M.; Sunset, 8:31 P. M.

VOL. XCIII..No. 31,559. Entered as Second-Class Matter, Postoffice, New York, N. Y. NEW YORK, TUESDAY, JUNE 20, 1944. THREE CENTS NEW YORK CITY

JAPANESE LOSE 300 PLANES IN SAIPAN BATTLE, BIGGEST SINCE MIDWAY; ISLAND AIRFIELD TAKEN; U. S. UNITS 8 MILES FROM CHERBOURG; ELBA WON

DEWEY WILL VISIT CHICAGO TO ACCEPT, SPRAGUE DECLARES

Otherwise 'Do You Think We Would Be Here to Draft Him?' Asks Campaign Chief

POINTS TO POPULAR POLLS

Convention Headquarters to Be Opened Today—Warren Pushed for the Ticket

By JAMES A. HAGERTY
Special to The New York Times.

CHICAGO, June 19—J. Russel Sprague, national committeeman from New York, announced at a press conference today that he, Edwin F. Jaeckle, State chairman, and Herbert Brownell Jr., chairman of the law committee of the Republican State Committee, representing the Republican voters and the Republican organization of New York State, had come to Chicago to get the Republican National Convention to draft Gov. Thomas E. Dewey for the nomination for President.

Mr. Sprague added that in his opinion Governor Dewey would come to Chicago to accept the nomination and would be elected in November.

He also announced that headquarters of the New York Republican organization to work for the nomination of Governor Dewey would be opened tomorrow on the twenty-fifth floor of the Hotel Stevens.

He predicted Governor Dewey's nomination without qualification, but would not say that it would be on the first ballot.

Despite the recent statement of Gov. Earl Warren that he was not a candidate for the Vice Presidential nomination and knowledge that he does not want it, the California Governor continued to be the first choice of the Dewey supporters for second place on the ticket.

"Double Draft" Is Pressed

Although there is ample precedent for refusing to run for Vice President—Senator Hiram Johnson missed a chance for the Presidency by declining to consider a second place nomination in 1920 and Frank O. Lowden refused such a nomination after it had been made in 1924—supporters of Governor Dewey still hope to have Governor Warren as Governor Dewey's running mate in a "double-draft" movement.

Although Mr. Sprague would give no detailed figures on the number of delegates counted as certain to vote for the nomination of Governor Dewey, except to declare the support of ninety-two of the ninety-three delegates from New York, in other sources the Dewey strength in the convention was estimated at 750 to 800 votes, or 200 to 250 more than the number needed to nominate.

About thirty reporters were at Mr. Sprague's press conference in Room 1205-A of the Stevens Hotel. Mr. Sprague apologized for the smallness of the room and said that tomorrow the State committee would have adequate headquarters.

"To identify myself, I will say that I am Republican National Committeeman and delegate-at-large from New York," Mr. Sprague said. "With me are Ed Jaeckle, State chairman, and Herbert Brownell, chairman of our law committee. We are here representing the Republicans of New York State and its Republican organization.

Cites Votes of 1942 and 1943

"There will be ninety-three delegates from New York State and ninety-two of them are unanimous for drafting Governor Dewey for the nomination for President. Governor Dewey carried New York in 1942 by a plurality of 647,000 and is the one Republican to be elected Governor of New York in more than twenty years. A Republican Lieutenant-Governor was elected in New York last year by

Continued on Page 12

Asks Senate Seats For Ex-Presidents

By The Associated Press.

WASHINGTON, June 19—Representative Gordon Canfield, Republican, of New Jersey, introduced a bill today to make former Presidents voteless members-at-large of the Senate for life.

Their pay and allowances would be the same as for an elected member.

Presidents are "outstanding leaders of public opinion," Mr. Canfield said. "They rate high in their ability to voice with force and accuracy the views and aspirations of a great number of their fellow-citizens. Congress is itself the nation's sounding board of public opinion.

"Except for William H. Harrison, Polk, Taylor, Lincoln, Garfield, Arthur, McKinley, Wilson and Harding, every President has survived his term long enough to have to face the problem of 'and now what?'—and without help from the people."

Governor Dewey had expressed himself as favorable to the idea, Mr. Canfield said.

BOND SALES IN U. S. TOTAL $854,000,000

14% of Individual Quota of $6,000,000,000 Raised—City Figure $85,631,918

War bond sales to individuals in the Fifth War Loan drive totaled $854,000,000 at the close of the first week of the campaign, which began June 12 and is scheduled to continue through July 8, it was announced yesterday by the Treasury Department in Washington. This represents 14 per cent of the $6,000,000,000 quota for individuals in the over-all drive for $16,000,000,000.

Sales to individual investors in New York City stood at $85,631,918 as of the close of business Saturday night, it was announced here by Nevil Ford, State chairman of the War Finance Committee of New York, while in New York State sales of all issues to individuals aggregated $117,600,000 at the close of the first week of the drive.

New York City, with total E bond purchases of $27,900,765, has attained 12.3 per cent of its goal in this category, according to Mr. Ford. The city's E bond sales objective in the drive is $227,526,600. Friday's sales of this issue, which the Treasury is particularly anxious to place in the hands of investors of small and moderate means, were 49 per cent higher than those of Thursday.

Bronx Retains Its Lead

The Bronx retained its leadership among the five boroughs, with 18.3 per cent of its E bond quota attained. Queens, with 15.8 per cent, passed Richmond and moved into second place by the narrow margin of 0.5 per cent.

A table showing the sales of E bonds, and of all other issues, to

Continued on Page 17

U.S. NOT TO BE BOUND BY MONEY PARLEY, MORGENTHAU SAYS

Any Compact on World Bank or Stabilizing of Currency Would Be Up to Congress

TAX REVISION IS UNLIKELY

Early Change Doubtful in View of Public Debt, He Says—Bond Drive Not Aided by War

Special to The New York Times.

CHICAGO, June 19—Secretary of the Treasury Henry Morgenthau Jr. said today that no commitments binding on the United States could be made at the world monetary conference which would meet July 1 at Bretton Woods, N. H.

Whatever agreements are made for stabilizing currencies and establishing a world bank will be subject to Congressional approval as far as this country is concerned, he said.

"The results of the conference will be referred to President Roosevelt, who in turn will submit the matter to Congress," the Secretary said.

American Delegates Chosen

The personnel of the American delegation has been completed and will be announced in a day or so, Mr. Morgenthau disclosed.

Mr. Morgenthau spent the day in Chicago in connection with the promotion of the Treasury's Fifth War Loan drive. He touched on a number of subjects during a forty-minute press interview.

In reply to questions, Mr. Morgenthau said that he foresaw little likelihood of a major revision in the Federal tax system in the early post-war years. Specifically he was doubtful that the present dual taxation of corporation profits, which are levied when earned and again later when paid out in dividends, would be eliminated.

"After all, we have a big public debt that must be paid off and the quicker we do that the better," he said. "It is sound fiscal policy to retire the war debt as rapidly as possible. As long as I remain in the Treasury I will stand by that policy, but of course I cannot forecast with certainty what future tax policies will be."

Denies Stifling of Incentive

Mr. Morgenthau said that business had no reason to fear that the post-war tax structure would stifle the incentive to take ventures in an attempt to make money.

"This reasoning is not sound, because if business and, in turn, workers, failed to make money, the Government would be unable to retire the national debt," he said.

One reporter asked if taxes would continue to climb between now and the end of the war. The Secretary smiled and said:

"Thank you, gentlemen, for coming. I'm afraid I'll have to be moving along now."

Mr. Morgenthau referred to the Congressional action raising the

Continued on Page 34

KEY PORT SHELLED

American Forces Drive Close to the Last Hills Outside Nazi Bastion

BY-PASS VALOGNES

British Fight Their Way Into Tilly—Allies Put New Troops in Lines

5 A. M. Communique

By The Associated Press.

SUPREME HEADQUARTERS, Allied Expeditionary Force, Tuesday, June 20—American forces making coordinated attacks northward toward the port of Cherbourg have made further advances, Supreme Headquarters announced today.

One of the advances was made east of Valognes, ten miles southeast of the port, communiqué No. 29 said. This drive carried to within two miles of this town. Westward the road from Valognes to captured Bricquebec was cut.

Lieut. Gen. Bradley's troops in their drive for Cherbourg penetrated to the outskirts of Rauville-La Bigot, eight miles southwest of the port on the road from Bricquebec.

The British recaptured Tilly-sur-Suelles on their sector of the beachhead front to ward the east.

By DREW MIDDLETON
By Cable to The New York Times.

SUPREME HEADQUARTERS, Allied Expeditionary Force, Tuesday, June 20—The American assault on Cherbourg has started with remarkable speed and success.

Advancing more than ten miles in twenty-four hours, Lieut. Gen. Omar N. Bradley's veteran divisions have smashed their way to a point within eight miles of the port and are shelling it.

Bricquebec, eleven and a half miles south of Cherbourg, fell yesterday and it is probable that

Continued on Page 3

THE SIGN POINTS TO THEIR OBJECTIVE

Americans rest beside a marker showing the way to Cherbourg and telling that the speed limit is thirty kilometers an hour. Associated Press Wirephoto (U. S. Signal Corps Radiophoto)

Americans Rush On in Rain As Speed Bewilders Nazis

By HAROLD DENNY
By Wireless to The New York Times.

WITH THE AMERICAN FORCES IN FRANCE, June 19—United States troops, advancing with unexpected rapidity, got to a point eight miles from Cherbourg today. Artillery followed in close behind the infantry and this afternoon 155-mm. rifles—'Long Toms'—began to shell that important port.

Today a cold slanting rain drenched our men and turned the roads into quagmires. Nevertheless, for all the weariness of many days of constant fighting and unbelievably rapid advances, our troops lunged at the Germans again with as much spirit as ever.

This morning's main attack was northward and met little opposition, indicating the Germans had been thrown off balance by our recent swift progress. We took Bricquebec, an important road junction, almost unopposed. Montebourg, which had been taken and lost and had caused us much trouble, was by-passed. It is held by German troops, but they will be mopped up in due course.

We also by-passed Valognes, an

Continued on Page 4

ELBA SURRENDERS TO FRENCH TROOPS

German Resistance Ends With Loss of Porto Longone—1,800 Prisoners Taken

By A. C. SEDGWICK
By Wireless to The New York Times.

ELBA, June 19—The white flag was hoisted this morning at Porto Longone to signify the German surrender of this island to French Colonial troops.

French artillery had been pounding this site of the enemy's last stand throughout the night. It was a powerful bombardment, made possible by a mass of artillery lodged in gullies.

[In Italy the British Eighth Army took Assisi and drove within three miles of Perugia, which, according to the German radio, has been evacuated. The Fifth Army gained against increasing resistance north of Grosseto.]

Constant patrols by the Allies' fighters and fighter-bombers had destroyed almost all the enemy's transport on the island. The air force and naval vessels had destroyed almost every craft from rowboats to caiques that the enemy might have used to escape. It is believed unlikely that any of the enemy attempted to get away and the check of prisoners now going on may uncover several high German officers.

All the enemy's equipment has

Continued on Page 5

NEW ROBOT SPEEDS 600 MILES AN HOUR

Spitfires Fade Like Gliders in Pursuit of Latest German Missile Passing Over Ship

By GENE CURRIVAN
By Cable to The New York Times.

ABOARD THE JOHN E. WARD, Off England, June 19—Adolf Hitler's newest terrifying weapon, a jet-propelled bomb larger and faster than anything heretofore revealed, passed over this ship last night among twenty-seven similar but smaller pilotless planes that streaked through the skies toward the English coast. Its speed is such as to make pursuing Spitfires appear as gliders.

It was the first of a procession of robot planes that started at 6:30 P. M. and continued until 4 o'clock this morning. The last, which appeared as a ball of fire directly over this ship, was less than 1,000 feet over the stack.

[The flying torpedoes hurtled over England early Tuesday for the sixth consecutive day, The United Press reported. It was disclosed that a United States anti-aircraft battery shot down the first enemy projectile the night of June 15.]

The "super-robot" came in at 1,000 to 2,000 feet. It shot on a straight line, apparently from the Calais area toward a port on the southeast coast not far from our position. At a distance the robot bomb's sound is like that of an approaching E-boat or motor torpedo boat.

The missile suddenly appeared off the ship's bow, cutting in front of four Spitfires headed for France. As it shot by them, slightly below their line of flight, the pilots realized it was an enemy craft, and one by one they peeled off and darted after it. As it passed our

Continued on Page 4

FLEET IS ATTACKED

Our Carrier Task Force Beats Off Swarms of Japanese for Hours

ONE U. S. SHIP IS HIT

But Damage Is Minor—We Cut Enemy Forces in Two on Saipan

By GEORGE F. HORNE
By Telephone to The New York Times.

PACIFIC FLEET HEADQUARTERS, Pearl Harbor, June 19—The greatest air-sea battle since Midway was fought off the Marianas yesterday, when the American carrier task force supporting the ground attack on Saipan shot down more than 300 out of swarms of Japanese planes, a number of which apparently came from Japanese carriers.

American fliers and ship gunners so successfully fought off the severe attack, lasting for hours, that, according to present information, only one of our ships was damaged, and this damage was minor. Our plane losses were not yet determined.

Meanwhile, on Saipan American marines and Army troops captured the Aslito airdrome, 1,465 miles from Tokyo and 1,470 from Davao in the Philippines, and Seabees are already putting the airfield's excellent 3,600-foot strips in condition.

Garrison Cut in Two

Coupled with this, our ground forces have cut off a number of enemy troops by fighting across the island to Magicienne Bay. We hold the western shore of the bay now and are gradually moving up the island although the enemy continues to counter-attack fiercely.

There is no indication that we have found the Japanese carriers that sent planes in support of embattled Saipan and there is no information here on the strength of their force.

Admiral Chester W. Nimitz's communiqué does not state that the enemy planes came from carriers but that "it is believed a portion of the enemy planes were carrier based and used near-by shore bases as shuttle points."

Somewhere north or west of Saipan the enemy carrier force may have come within range of land and sent off the planes to land staging points.

"However," the communiqué said, "the effectiveness of this procedure was sharply limited by our systematic bombing and strafing of the airfields at Guam and Rota."

It is altogether possible for the enemy to stage planes from the Philippines via Palau and Yap or from Truk to the southeast. It is 516 nautical miles from Davao to Palau, 830 from Palau to Saipan. From Truk to Guam it is 559 and another 111 to Saipan. It is 474 miles from Woleai to Saipan.

Ninth Day in the Marianas

All the bases have air facilities but they are being closely watched by our forces and are kept busy with bombings and strafings.

For some gun crews the battle with the Japanese planes was the first major action in which they had participated and it was something for which they had been intensively trained.

Yesterday was the ninth day of action in the Marianas. It began on June 10 when our carrier forces opened a two-day assault on Saipan and other Marianas Islands, followed by surface craft bombardment and the landing of troops on June 14.

The Seabees were working feverishly on the Aslito airfield. This is work to which they are accustomed and it should not take long. Our own airfield on Saipan will make it possible to give closer support to ground troops and keep watch over other enemy islands.

We now hold between one-fourth and one-third of Saipan with the exception of enemy pockets.

There are two pockets of enemy

Continued on Page 10

War News Summarized

TUESDAY, JUNE 20, 1944

More than 300 Japanese planes were shot down in a furious battle off the Marianas when the enemy attacked the Pacific Fleet task force covering the landings on Saipan. It was the biggest carrier engagement since the Battle of Midway. Our air losses had not been tabulated when Admiral Nimitz announced the fight, but only one of our ships was hit and damage was minor.

American soldiers and marines on Saipan captured the Aslito airstrip, and Seabees immediately set to work to repair it. The drive carried to Magicienne Bay, the west shore of which is in our possession. A large body of enemy troops was cut off and nearly one-third of the island had been captured. [All the foregoing 1:5; maps P. 10.]

The Chinese driving on Burma evacuated Lungling to avoid encirclement, but farther north pushed their gains along the Shweli River. [8:1, with map.] The Japanese were only fifty miles from the Chinese railroad city of Hengyang, south of Changsha, and civilian evacuation was said to have been ordered. Changsha still fought off the invaders. [10:2.]

The United States Ninth Division in Normandy pushed ahead ten miles in twenty-four hours to bring the port of Cherbourg within artillery range, and shells from "Long Toms" began to fall on that German stronghold yesterday. Bricquebec was captured as the Americans by-passed Montebourg and Valognes. At the other end of the line the British beat off furious enemy counter-attacks and fought their way into Tilly-sur-Seulles, recapturing the town. Allied warships continued to pour shells into German tank groups near Caen. [1:4; map P. 2.]

The Ninth Division, despite rain and fatigue, pursued the beaten Germans so relentlessly that the enemy never had a chance to regain his balance. Advance elements were eight miles from Cherbourg. [1:5-6.]

The British disclosed that Hitler's latest weapon, the robot bomber, was a jet-propelled machine launched from a ramp and controlled by a gyroscope. It has a 150-mile range, a speed of 350 miles an hour and carries a ton of explosives. [4:5.] A NEW YORK TIMES correspondent on a ship in the English Channel saw a "super-robot" streak by at an estimated speed of 600 miles an hour. [1:7.]

The Germans on Elba surrendered when the French invasion forces captured Porto Longone. More than 1,800 prisoners and vast stores of matériel were taken. [1:6; map, P. 5.] The Allied advance in Italy continued with the capture of Assisi. Fighting was reported in the outskirts of Perugia. [5:5.] The Allies recognized the Bonomi Government and it was expected Marshal Badoglio would find a place in the Cabinet. [6:5.]

The Russian Army widened the breach in the Mannerheim Line to about thirty miles between Muolaa and the Gulf of Finland and was ten miles from Viborg. [7:4-5, with map.]

Prime Minister Churchill said that Allied victories this summer might lead to "full success" and relieve the world "of the curse which has been laid upon us by the Germans." He looked forward to international cooperation, in which "the rights of small nations will be upheld and protected." [1:6-7.]

Auto Use Tax Assailed as Unfair To 'A' Driver in Plea for Repeal

Immediate Congressional repeal or revision of the $5 Federal automobile "use tax" on the ground that it is unfair to auto owners who are limited to A gasoline rations, was urged yesterday by the Automobile Club of New York. The new stamps must be pasted on car windshields by July 1.

In telegrams to Senator Walter F. George, chairman of the Senate Finance Committee; Representative Robert L. Doughton, chairman of the House Ways and Means Committee, and to Senators and Representatives from the metropolitan area, it was asserted that the tax was both "unsound in theory and inequitable in practice."

William A. Gottlieb, president of the Automobile Club, contended in the telegram that it was unfair to collect the same sum from the A card driver, who at best gets gasoline for 1,440 miles annually, as is asked of the C card holder, with no maximum mileage, and the taxi man, whose cab may operate 49,200 miles.

He compared the 1,440 miles with the 3,900 miles allowed to B ration holders in the East; the 4,800 miles for B card drivers in the West and the 5,700 miles allowed on B cards in the Midwest, pointing out further that trucks and buses with TT rations running up "huge mileages" are taxed no more than the A driver.

"Gross inequities in the present method of taxing are apparent, with all classes of users paying the same amount of tax though legal use permitted shows tremendous differences," Mr. Gottlieb said.

"A rationed users are obviously taxed way out of proportion when based on the Government's established measures of use. B rationed

Continued on Page 17

Churchill Sees Victory in Summer As Possible Fruit of Teheran Plan

By JOHN MacCORMAC
By Wireless to The New York Times.

LONDON, June 19—The plan of campaign adopted in the accord with Russia at Teheran is being steadily unrolled and may bring victory this summer, Prime Minister Churchill said Thursday in a speech to diplomats, the text of which was released today.

In his address, delivered at a luncheon given by the Mexican Ambassador, the Prime Minister said that the longer the struggle continued, the more terrible would it be in the end for Germany.

"It may be," he said, "that events will occur in the next few months which will show us whether we are soon to be relieved of the curse which was laid upon us by the Germans. Whether it be this year or next, the British and American peoples will never falter or withdraw their hands from the task they have undertaken."

[Perhaps a million men are now embroiled in the fighting in France, the Prime Minister said, according to The Associated Press.]

Mr. Churchill regretted the inconvenience suffered by the diplomatic corps through the pre-invasion curb on communications but justified it by noting that though many thousands knew the secrets of the invasion, they had been well kept. He continued:

"Of course, we have not embarked on this great adventure without being in full accord with our Russian allies and the decisions taken in Teheran, and although the execution of the plans

"All the News That's Fit to Print"

The New York Times.

LATE CITY EDITION
POSTSCRIPT
Partly cloudy and warm today
Temperatures Yesterday—Max., 84; Min., 64
Sunrise, 5:26 A. M.; Sunset, 8:32 P. M.

VOL. XCIII..No. 31,566. Entered as Second-Class Matter, Postoffice, New York, N. Y. NEW YORK, TUESDAY, JUNE 27, 1944. THREE CENTS IN NEW YORK CITY

CHERBOURG FALLS TO AMERICAN TROOPS; ENEMY LEADERS AMONG 30,000 PRISONERS; RUSSIANS CAPTURE VITEBSK AND ZHLOBIN

REPUBLICANS MAKE QUICK END TO WAR THEIR BATTLE CRY

Warren, Keynoter, Says Party Will Bring Victorious Boys Home With All Speed

DISPUTES OVER PLATFORM

Dewey Avalanche Piles Up, With Californian Unchallenged as His Running Mate

Governor Warren's keynote address is printed on Page 10.

By TURNER CATLEDGE

Special to THE NEW YORK TIMES.

CHICAGO, Tuesday, June 27—A triple pledge to bring the boys back home quickly and "victorious," to reopen the doors of opportunity to "all Americans," and to guard the peace in the future, was sounded yesterday as the Republican battle-cry at the opening of the party's twenty-third national convention.

While it was being uttered by Gov. Earl Warren of California, temporary chairman, in his keynote address to a cheering throng in the Chicago Stadium, THE NEW YORK TIMES gained access to a plank which policy writers had evolved Saturday, pledging the party to a post-war cooperative organization "among sovereign nations," to prevent military aggression and attain permanent peace in the future.

Word had come meanwhile from Wendell L. Willkie, the nominee of 1940, that he considered the foreign policy plank, as he understood it, ambiguous, and therefore was disappointed in it.

Willkie's Backers Upset

This note of controversy came as a distinct shock to a group of former backers of Mr. Willkie who have been attempting these last few days to bring him in line with the platform, and with a ticket of Thomas E. Dewey of New York for President and Governor Warren for Vice President, which is considered certain of nomination by tomorrow night.

Meanwhile, another complication appeared in the hitherto placid convention picture when the seventeen Governors who are delegates demanded opportunity to examine and possibly suggest changes in the platform before it is submitted to the convention, probably tonight, for ratification.

The Governors did not protest any particular item in the platform as it was agreed to in principle last night. They did protest the fact, however, that, as one of them put it, an "oligarchy" of Senators, members of the House and other party leaders, had assumed the prerogative of speaking for the party.

The Governors feel, as Governor Warren reflected in his keynote address, that they have been the spearhead, more than members of Congress, for the resurgence of Republicanism during the last three years. What happened here when the Governors demanded and obtained permission to appear before the resolutions committee was another chapter in a protest which first came to light at the Mackinac Island conference in September.

Led by New Englanders

The action was led, as was the move at Mackinac, largely by a New England group, in which Gov. Raymond E. Baldwin of Connecticut and Gov. Sumner Sewall of Maine were active.

These new possibilities of trouble ahead did not divert the main line of appeal upon which the party was centering—an appeal to the soldier vote, to those Americans who are weary of the New Deal, and, above all, to those wanting to avoid the tragedy of war in the future.

It was the note on which Gov. Dwight Green of Illinois opened the meeting with a welcoming ad-

Continued on Page 9

Convention Events Listed for Today

Special to THE NEW YORK TIMES.

CHICAGO, June 26—The official program for tomorrow's sessions of the Republican National Convention is as follows:

Tuesday, June 27, 10:15 A. M.
(Central War Time)

Convention called to order by the temporary chairman.

National Anthem: Miss Mildred Maule of East St. Louis, Ill.

Prayer: The Rev. Joseph Simonson, pastor of Christ Lutheran Church, St. Paul.

Report of Committee on Credentials.

Report of Committee on Permanent Organization.

Election of permanent chairman and permanent officers.

Address by permanent chairman.

Report of Committee on Rules and Order of Business.

Election of National Committee.

Report of Resolutions Committee.

Recess until 8:15 P. M.

Tuesday, June 27, 8:15 P. M.

Convention called to order by the permanent chairman, Representative Joseph W. Martin Jr.

National Anthem: Miss Mona Bradford of the Chicago Civic Opera Company.

Prayer: Rabbi Abba Hillel Silver of The Temple, Cleveland.

Music.

Address: Herbert Hoover.

Address: Representative Clare Boothe Luce of Connecticut.

Adjourn until Wednesday.

WILLKIE CONDEMNS PEACE-POLICY PLAN

Republican Draft on Foreign Relations Could Be Used to Balk Cooperation, He Says

A few hours after Wendell Willkie had received the text of the proposed Republican foreign-policy plank, the 1940 Presidential candidate issued a statement denouncing the plan as ambiguous, subject to opposing interpretations and capable of being used to throttle effective collaboration by the United States with other countries to maintain peace.

Mr. Willkie's views on the platform committee's suggestions were presented to reporters who had been invited to visit his offices at 15 Broad Street. He explained that he chose this form of making them public because he was not a delegate to the convention.

Likening the language proposed for this year's platform to that employed in 1920, Mr. Willkie recalled that thirty-one leading Republicans had assured the country that the 1920 formula "was the surest road to an effective international organization," but that President Harding, immediately after the election, "announced that the League of Nations was dead."

"A Republican President elected under the proposed platform of

Continued on Page 13

ACCORD OF NATIONS FAVORED IN PLANK ON FOREIGN POLICY

'Participation in Cooperative Organization' Provided 'to Attain Permanent Peace'

TAFT PREDICTS ADOPTION

Declaration Calls for Seeking 'Economic Stability,' Pledges Constitutional Procedure

By JAMES B. RESTON

Special to THE NEW YORK TIMES.

CHICAGO, Tuesday, June 27—The Republican party platform will favor "participation by the United States in post-war cooperative organization among sovereign nations to prevent military aggression and to attain permanent peace."

The party's Foreign Affairs Committee, headed by Senator Warren Austin of Vermont, has approved unanimously a plank which calls on the future world peace organization "to develop effective cooperative means to direct peace forces to prevent or repel military aggression."

Pending the formation of this world peace organization, the plank recommends that the United States should "pledge continuing collaboration with the United Nations."

Senator Robert A. Taft, chairman of the party's Resolutions Committee, to which the platform will be submitted later this morning, said he was certain that the foreign affairs plank as recommended by Senator Austin's committee would be adopted.

Objectives of Peace Treaties

After stating that the party favored "prosecution of the war to total victory against all our enemies in full cooperation with the United Nations and the speedy return of our armed forces," the plank emphasized that justice in the writing of the peace was the essence of realism.

"We believe that peace and security do not depend upon the sanction of force alone, but should prevail by virtue of reciprocal interests and spiritual values recognized in these security agreements," the Foreign Affairs Committee said.

"The treaties of peace should be just; the nations which are the victims of Axis aggression should be restored to sovereignty and self-government, and the organized cooperation of the nations should concern itself with basic causes of world disorder."

Elaborating on "cooperation," the committee continued:

"We shall seek, in our relations with other nations, conditions calculated to promote world-wide economic stability, not only for the sake of the world, but also the end that our own people may enjoy a high level of employment in an increasingly prosperous world. We

Continued on Page 14

ALLIED WARSHIPS SHELLING GERMAN POSITIONS IN CHERBOURG

The U. S. S. Quincy (left) and H. M. S. Glasgow bombarding the port

The New York Times (British Admiralty via U. S. Signal Corps Radiotelephoto)

U. S. TROOPS SCALE LOFTY SAIPAN PEAK

Tapotchau, Dominating Island, Is Reported Won — Carrier Planes Batter Guam and Rota

By GEORGE F. HORNE

By Telephone to THE NEW YORK TIMES.

PACIFIC FLEET HEADQUARTERS, Pearl Harbor, June 26—Mount Tapotchau on Saipan Island has been scaled by United States Marines who are now established in positions near the summit. Marines and Army troops have made substantial gains on both the eastern and western shores of the island.

[A front dispatch said that Tapotchau which dominated the island and has been the goal of our men ever since they landed on Saipan, had been captured by troops who held it against a before-dawn Japanese counter-attack Sunday.]

Admiral Chester W. Nimitz stated that the Kagman Peninsula, forming the upper arm of Magicienne Bay, was now entirely in our hands and that troops had

Continued on Page 7

Russians Begin Encircling Mogilev and Orsha Citadels

By The United Press.

LONDON, Tuesday, June 27—The Red Army, tearing out the northern and southern anchors of the German defense line in White Russia, captured the fortress cities of Vitebsk and Zhlobin yesterday and seized more than 1,700 towns and settlements, while the vanguard of their victorious forces advanced more than twenty-two miles toward Minsk for a great pincer assault on that city.

Striking with unprecedented power and speed, four Soviet armies sprinting along a 285-mile front raced to within eighty-four miles of Minsk, approached to within thirty-five miles of the Polish border, outflanked Orsha and drove to within six miles of Mogilev.

Vitebsk, the most powerful Nazi stronghold on the route to East Prussia, and Zhlobin, 157 miles to the south, fell on the fourth day of the Red Army's summer offensive—four days in which Russian troops advanced as much as fifty-six miles, seized 3,040 towns and settlements and killed more than 31,500 Germans.

More than 6,000 of the German garrison of five infantry divisions

Continued on Page 6

VIENNA WAR PLANTS GET HEAVY BOMBING

Italy-Based Planes Pound Oil, Aircraft Works—Weather Cuts Invasion Support

By The Associated Press.

SUPREME HEADQUARTERS, Allied Expeditionary Force, Tuesday, June 27—United States Flying Fortresses and Liberators 500 to 750 strong roared from Italian bases to the Vienna area yesterday through the heaviest Luftwaffe opposition in recent weeks and attacked oil refineries, rail yards and a Nazi aircraft plant.

Poor weather over western Europe halted for the day the pounding from Allied air bases in Britain and Normandy of German supply and communication lines behind the French front.

Indications of renewed Allied aerial activity came last night as the German radio interrupted programs to say an alert had been sounded in all parts of southwestern Germany. In Hungary, where British bombers of the Mediterranean Allied Air Forces attacked oil works Sunday night, the Budapest radio went off the air again at 10 P. M.

The Flying Fortresses and Liberators and their escorting Mustangs, Lightnings and Thunderbolts of the United States Fifteenth Air Force shot down large numbers of enemy planes on the route to the Vienna area, headquarters announced.

They struck refineries at Schwechat, ten miles southeast of

Continued on Page 5

14 WARSHIPS SHELL CHERBOURG AT ONCE

British Newsman Describes Destruction of Batteries Defending Harbor

By DESMOND TIGHE

Reuter Correspondent

ABOARD H.M.S. GLASGOW, off Cherbourg Harbor, June 25 (Delayed)—American battleships and heavy cruisers, supported by two British cruisers and seven destroyers, are firing broadside after broadside into German shore batteries at vital key points on the fringes of Cherbourg harbor in support of the Army.

The bombardment started at exactly eleven minutes past 12 this morning and has lasted for more than three hours with German long-range 450-mm. shore batteries returning the fire vigorously.

As I watched this bombardment from the bridge of H.M.S. Glasgow, victor of the recent Bay of Biscay battle, we are steaming steadily some 15,000 yards off the breakwater of Cherbourg harbor.

Air Resounds With Crashes

Our six-inch guns are blazing away as shells scream into a German fort. The air resounds with the crash of broadsides from the battleships, cruisers and destroyers. The Channel sea is whipped with wicked looking grey-black splashes as we are straddled time and time by German shore batteries.

The German gunnery is good and although we are plastering their concrete gun emplacements with tons of high explosives some of them keep on firing.

The United States bombardment task force is commanded by Rear Admiral Morton L. Deyo, United States Navy. Admiral Deyo is flying his flag in the heavy cruiser Tuscaloosa. Among the warships in his battle squadron are the battleships Texas, Nevada, Arkansas; the American cruiser Quincy, and the two British cruisers, Glasgow and Enterprise. We are escorted by a

Continued on Page 4

VICTORY IN FRANCE

Capture of Port Seals First Phase of Allied Liberation of Europe

FIGHT SHARP TO END

British Reported Near Main Enemy Highway at Base of Peninsula

5 A. M. Communique

By The Associated Press.

SUPREME HEADQUARTERS, Allied Expeditionary Force, Tuesday, June 27—The capture of Lieut. Gen. Carl Wilhelm von Schlieben, commander of the Cherbourg garrison, and Rear Admiral Hennecke, Nazi sea defense commander of Normandy, was announced today in Allied communiqué No. 43 confirming the fall of Cherbourg.

"Cherbourg's liberation came after a final day of fierce fighting in the northwestern part of the city," the communiqué said.

"In the battle the enemy has lost the greater part of four infantry divisions, numerous naval and marine units and line of communication troops."

Of the British gains on the east side of the beachhead, it said:

"A strong attack toward the Villers-Bocage-Caen main road has secured Cheux and Fontenay, and has advanced several miles in the face of heavy German armor and infantry. Progress continues."

By DREW MIDDLETON

By Cable to THE NEW YORK TIMES.

SUPREME HEADQUARTERS, Allied Expeditionary Force, Tuesday, June 27—Cherbourg, France's third greatest port, has fallen to the American troops in the first outstanding victory of the Allied campaign to liberate France.

The fall of Cherbourg, after a siege that lasted a week from the moment the first shells from American field guns began to pound its defenses, was officially announced here this morning just after 7 o'clock double British summer time [1 A. M. in New York.]

With the taking of the city the first phase of the campaign in which the Allies were forced to build up their armies without the use of a large port came to an end. It was estimated here recently that supplies for two divisions could be moved through Cherbourg within forty-eight hours after its fall.

Captives May Total 30,000

Last night American patrols mopped up the remaining German resistance in the vicinity of the naval base and arsenal and cleaned out snipers from buildings along the waterfront, where individual Germans held out until the last.

Although there has been no official estimate of the number of prisoners yet, it is probable the city's fall will bring more than 30,000 German soldiers and sailors into the Allied cages.

Cherbourg was the second French port and naval base to fall to Lieut. Gen. Omar N. Bradley. Bizerte in Tunisia was taken by the United States Second Army Corps under his command on May 7, 1943.

The struggle for Cherbourg drew to its victorious close yesterday when in the rain and chill wind doughboys mopped up the port. By nightfall more than one-third of the port had been occupied and by midnight two-thirds of the city was in Allied hands.

At dawn Monday 3,400 German prisoners had been taken and it is probable that twice that number was captured in the mopping up operations yesterday.

The Germans were driven from five remaining strongholds during the early evening by grenade, bay-

Continued on Page 3

War News Summarized

TUESDAY, JUNE 27, 1944

Cherbourg fell to the Americans this morning after General Bradley's troops had fought the desperate German defenders from dock to dock along the ruined waterfront. The enemy held out in four or five strong points, principally around the naval base, until each fortified nucleus had been overrun. Lieut. Gen. von Schlieben, Cherbourg garrison commander, and Admiral Hennecke, head of the German sea force off Normandy, were captured. The total of prisoners may reach 30,000.

At the eastern end of the Normandy line the British opened a new drive from Tilly-sur-Seulles and gained as much as four miles, threatening to cut the Caen-Avranches highway at the base of the Cotentin Peninsula. Since the initial landings three weeks ago the Allies have liberated more than 1,000 square miles of France, have taken more than 50,000 prisoners and have destroyed four German divisions. [All the foregoing 1:8; map, P. 2.]

Three United States battleships headed a force of fourteen Allied vessels that pounded Cherbourg's main fortifications into rubble shortly after noon Sunday. The massed naval rifles poured shells into the targets for more than three hours, clearing the way for the troops. [1:7.]

A British naval intelligence officer said in this city that the Germans had been so skillfully outmaneuvered that they massed their air defenses to counter a feint invasion aimed at Calais and Boulogne, leaving Normandy without protection. [5:1.]

Dense fog halted air operations from Britain, but a heavy force of American bombers from Italy smashed oil refineries, rail yards and an airplane plant in the Vienna area. The Luftwaffe offered the heaviest opposition in weeks. [1:6.]

Another vaunted German line crumbled when the Red Army captured Vitebsk and Zhlobin, anchors of the "Fatherland Line." More than 45,000 enemy troops were trapped at Vitebsk, and at one point the Russians were thirty-four miles from the old Polish frontier. A record number of 1,700 places was liberated in the general advance. Gains were also reported from the Karelian Isthmus on the Finnish front. [1:5-6; map P. 6]

The Fifth Army in Italy entered the port of Piombino without a fight and, inland, advanced to within fifteen miles of Siena and forty-five of Florence. The Eighth Army crossed the Chienti River northeast of Foligno in hard fighting. [6:1.]

Marines on Saipan, in the Marianas, have scaled Mount Tapotchau and dug in at the summit. The southern part of Garapan, on the west, was in American hands, and the Japanese have been cleared from Kagman Peninsula on the east. Carrier planes did widespread damage to shipping, installations and grounded enemy aircraft at enemy bases on Guam and Rota. [1:4; maps P. 7.]

Allied forces have captured Mogaung in Burma and gained on all fronts from the Indian border to China, where Hsiangtan was recaptured. [7:5.] The Japanese, after seizing Hengshan and Yuhsien, were unable to push closer to Hengyang in China's Hunan Province. [7:4.]

3-Cornered Baseball Game Yields $56,500,000 in Fifth Bond Drive

A crowd of 50,000 baseball fans, all of whom paid their way into the park by buying war bonds, turned out last night at the Polo Grounds to witness a bizarre contest in which the Yankees, Giants and Dodgers participated in a nine-inning contest. The Brooklyn nine won the game, tallying five runs; the Yankees scored one and the Giants nothing.

The program, as arranged by the Fifth War Loan Sports Committee, helped to swell New York's quota in the current bond drive by $56,500,000. Fifty million dollars of this sum came, according to an announcement by Mayor La Guardia, from the coffers of the City of New York. The remainder was contributed by the crowd as "admission fees," plus a one-million-dollar bond purchase of an autographed score card by the Bond Clothing Stores.

During the day the drive moved into high gear with the announcement of many large subscriptions here totalling around $1,000,000,000 and the disclosure that purchases throughout the nation had reached $4,591,000,000, or 29 per cent of the quota for the campaign.

Devised and conceived by Stanley Oshan of the War Finance Committee, the baseball game was followed closely by the huge throng that was seeing three major league teams tangle with each other on the same field for the first time. While Mr. Oshan was the originator of the idea it required a Columbia University professor of mathematics, Paul A. Smith, to produce a method of scoring it.

Professor Smith's assistance proved helpful, indeed, for the

Continued on Page 20

Pockets of Nazis Kept on Sniping As Americans Overran Cherbourg

By HAROLD DENNY

By Wireless to THE NEW YORK TIMES.

WITH THE AMERICAN FORCES at Cherbourg, June 26—The Germans fought a last-ditch defense in Cherbourg this evening, though the outcome was inescapable. Substantial elements of the American forces got into the city from the south only after a piece-by-piece conquest of succeeding strong points and the Germans were still firing on them in the city and from two pillboxes remaining on Fort du Roule with 88-mm. field-pieces and machine guns. The city has been considerably damaged but less than one would have thought. As a whole it is intact, though many individual buildings have been smashed.

Dominating all was the arsenal, where the last important holdout group was still firing rifles while large portions of the structure were burning with a red glow and towering black smoke.

Holding out about equally with the arsenal was one last desperate little group of cannoniers at Fort du Roule.

It stands like Gibraltar and should have been impregnable. Its fortifications of reinforced concrete, several stories deep and tunneled into solid rock, remind one of the Maginot Line fortresses, which I visited the first winter of this war. They include an electric light plant, underground barracks, an underground hospital and abundant stores of everything conceiv-

Continued on Page 4

"All the News That's Fit to Print"

The New York Times.

LATE CITY EDITION
POSTSCRIPT
Partly cloudy and warm today.
Temperatures Yesterday—Max., 80; Min., 66
Sunrise, 5:29 A. M.; Sunset, 8:31 P. M.

VOL. XCIII...No. 31,573. Entered as Second-Class Matter, Postoffice, New York, N. Y. NEW YORK, TUESDAY, JULY 4, 1944. THREE CENTS IN NEW YORK CITY

RUSSIANS CAPTURE MINSK ON 11TH DAY OF PUSH; AMERICANS OPEN NEW OFFENSIVE IN NORMANDY; NEW U. S. LANDING MADE IN SOUTHWEST PACIFIC

COMMUTERS DEFY MAYOR TO TAX THEM FOR SUBWAY COSTS

Westchester, Jersey City and Nassau Ready to Fight Levy on Those Who Work Here

LEGALITY IS QUESTIONED

Councilman Cohen Warns of Retaliation—City Leaders Still Studying Rent Tax Plan

Mayor La Guardia's proposal to tax commuters forty cents a week, as part of a transportation tax to cover the cost of subway deficits and transit improvements, met instant opposition in suburban areas yesterday. In the city, leaders of business, taxpayer, civic and real estate organizations refrained from comment on the Mayor's tax plan until they could study it further.

The Mayor, in his Sunday broadcast, offered the transportation tax, comprising six different levies, to raise $51,700,000, to be submitted with an alternative proposal of a 10-cent fare to the voters at a special referendum election before July 1, 1945. The defeat of both would retain the 5-cent fare, with the mounting subway deficit —now $41,118,808—carried by the real estate tax as at present.

Mayor's Estimates of Revenue

The tax on commuters working in the city but not living here was estimated by the Mayor to yield $5,200,000. A total of $44,500,000 would be raised through a 2 per cent tax on rents of residential properties, to be paid by tenants, a 2 per cent tax on charges for rooms in hotels and lodging houses, and a 2½ per cent tax on rents of non-residential properties. In addition there would be a 1 per cent tax on interest on mortgages, to yield $2,000,000, to be paid by the person or institution receiving the interest. The Mayor's alternative proposal of a 10-cent fare would raise an estimated $125,000,000.

In Mineola, L. I., County Executive J. Russel Sprague announced that "Nassau County would oppose any attempt of New York City to tax Nassau County commuters for the support of New York City's subway system." As a Republican national committeeman and a leader of the State Republican party, Mr. Sprague's influence would be felt in the Legislature, from which the city would have to get authorization for the new tax and its component parts. Marcus G. Christ, county attorney, concurring in Mr. Sprague's opposition, said he would study the Mayor's plan closely.

Westchester Starts Inquiry

In White Plains the Westchester County Board of Supervisors directed County Attorney William A. Davidson and its committee on miscellaneous affairs to investigate the commuter tax proposal after Supervisor Francis T. Leonard of New Rochelle had characterized the proposed tax as "unfair to residents of suburban areas such as Westchester County." Mr. Leonard, a lawyer who commutes daily to New York, said thousands of Westchester commuters would be affected. He also doubted the legality of the commuter tax.

Gustavus T. Kirby, chairman of the Westchester County Planning Commission, called the tax "asinine and ruinous." He said that increasing the subway fare would be far better, "but the whole thing is that La Guardia is afraid an increase would kill him politically."

County Executive Herbert C. Gerlach said the tax was too controversial for him to comment on at this time. Mayor Stanley W. Church of New Rochelle said that "offhand" he was opposed to it, but wanted to study it before reaching a final conclusion.

In Jersey City Mayor Frank Hague announced through a spokesman that he would fight the proposed levy on salaries of workers who commute to New York. The spokesman said:

"Mayor Hague will offer vigorous opposition to this or any new

Continued on Page 33

Flag of U. S. Capitol Flies in Rome Today

By The United Press

ROME, July 3—The American flag that flew over the Capitol in Washington on Dec. 8, 1941, when Congress declared the existence of a state of war with Japan, and three days later, when war was declared on Italy and Germany, will be flown from the first captured enemy capital on July 4, it was announced today.

President Roosevelt originally suggested that the Stars and Stripes be unfurled over Rome on Independence Day. It will be flown from a special flagpole now being erected on the Piazza Venezia, the scene of many of Benito Mussolini's bombastic speeches.

Reveille and retreat ceremonies will be arranged by the Rome area Allied command. American military bands and the Fifth Army color guard of honor will take part.

WORLD BANK URGED BY KEYNES AS VITAL

He Says It Would Cut U. S. Risks on Loans, Promote 'Expansion,' Not 'Inflation'

By RUSSELL PORTER

Special to The New York Times.

BRETTON WOODS, N. H., July 3—Lord Keynes, chairman of the British delegation to the United Nations Monetary and Financial Conference, described for the first time today the broad outlines of the plan for setting up of a $10,-000,000,000 international bank for reconstruction and development to "guarantee" international loans somewhat after the fashion of the Reconstruction Finance Corporation in domestic loans.

Speaking at an afternoon meeting of the bank commission, which will draw up proposals for approval by the conference as a whole, Lord Keynes, who is economic adviser to the British Treasury, said that the plan originated in the United States Treasury.

He called it a sound, fundamental contribution to the post-war task of rebuilding the world for a new age of peace and progress and declared that it would promote "expansion" and not "inflation."

Asks Speeding of Bank Work

The World Bank program is entirely separate from the currency stabilization goals of the proposals for an international monetary fund, also being considered here, but both plans are closely related, not only to one another, but also to the whole broad United Nations program of international cooperation to lay the economic foundation for the post-war world. The bank and the fund are intended to be permanent institutions.

Lord Keynes urged the delegates and their technical advisers, who had not given as much attention to the bank as to the fund, since they have considered the fund to be the more urgent problem, to speed their consideration of the bank proposals.

He asserted that the bank should be ready by the end of the war,

Continued on Page 15

DRIVE ON LA HAYE

Bradley's Troops Seize Hills North of Town and Village to East

GUNS POMMEL FOE

British Widen Salient Again—Attack by U. S. Surprises Germans

5 A. M. Communique

By The Associated Press.

SUPREME HEADQUARTERS, Allied Expeditionary Force, Tuesday, July 4—Allied troops in the neck of the Cherbourg Peninsula made gains up to two and one-half miles yesterday despite heavy rain that restricted air support, communiqué No. 57 announced today.

American troops pressed their offensive toward La Haye du Puits and at their most advanced point stood within about two and one-half miles of this key road junction.

The Germans made more counter-attacks against the British in the Odon River bridgehead in the Caen sector, but all were beaten off.

"The weather improved somewhat yesterday evening and defended localities, gun positions and a fuel dump in the Lessay area were effectively attacked by fighter bombers," the communiqué said.

By DREW MIDDLETON

By Cable to The New York Times.

SUPREME HEADQUARTERS, Allied Expeditionary Force, Tuesday, July 4—The American First Army has launched an offensive southward from the base of the Cherbourg peninsula toward La Haye du Puits. The assault, which smashed forward on a thirty-mile front in a driving rain, began yesterday morning at 5:30 o'clock after days of hammering at German positions by massed artillery, and by late last night it had swept forward from a mile to three miles along the entire front.

While the American line sprang forward in the First Army's second large-scale attack of the campaign, the British Second Army to the east, after four days of beating off savage counter-attacks by Field Marshal Gen. Erwin Rommel's armored divisions, captured the village of Brettevillette on the west of the salient and broke up a small enemy counter-blow early in the morning.

Rain Soaks British Sector

Operations were slowed down throughout the British sector by torrential rains that turned roads into swamps, hindering artillery as well as aerial bombardment.

Four weeks after the opening of the invasion the Allies are driving forward to the west and have retained their grip of the salient southwest of Caen to the east. Most of this has been accomplished

Continued on Page 3

DANISH PATRIOTS IN DEMONSTRATION AGAINST NAZI RULE

The caption for this picture, received here yesterday from Stockholm, says it shows citizens around a street barricade in a workers' district of Copenhagen.

Associated Press Radiophoto

ARNOLD SAYS REICH RATIONS AIR FUEL

Doubts Luftwaffe Will Fight Effectively Again—Predicts Similar Blows at Japan

By SIDNEY SHALETT

Special to The New York Times.

WASHINGTON, July 3—The United States Army Air Forces have definite information that, because of its blows against German oil centers, which have reduced the enemy's fuel supply to an estimated 30 per cent of normal, the Luftwaffe and the rest of Germany's mechanized forces are being "rationed," Gen. H. H. Arnold revealed today. It is at least a possibility, he indicated, that the

Continued on Page 6

Doughboys Land on Numfor, Swiftly Win Main Airfield

By FRANK L. KLUCKHOHN

By Wireless to The New York Times.

ALLIED HEADQUARTERS, in New Guinea, Tuesday, July 4—American troops have landed on Numfor Island, roughly 100 miles west of Biak Island and 800 miles southeast of the Philippines, as Gen. Douglas MacArthur resumed his advance toward his announced goal.

General MacArthur again fooled the Japanese, throwing his infantry ashore at an unexpected point on the west side of the island near the key Kamiri airdrome at 8 o'clock Sunday morning without opposition except from scattered shore guns, which American and Australian cruisers, destroyers and bombers quickly silenced. Less than two hours later at 9:51 A. M. the Kamiri airdrome, best of Numfor's three airfields, was captured.

Moving southward, our troops

Continued on Page 12

ALLIES TAKE SIENA, ART TREASURE CITY

Americans and French Find It Undamaged—5th, 8th Armies Drive Toward Gothic Line

By The Associated Press.

ROME, July 3—American and French forces occupied the medieval city of Siena, thirty-one airline miles from Florence, early today without damage to its famous art and architectural treasures, while American troops on the west coast who had evicted the Germans from Cecina in bitter house-to-house fighting thrust on within fifteen miles of the prize port of Leghorn.

The quick and virtually uncontested capture of Siena by French infantry and American artillery and tank units followed weeks of hard fighting on its mountainous approaches. A special announcement of the city's fall came immediately after a communiqué said the French had fought to within two miles of its ancient walls.

[Monday's German High Command communiqué said Nazi troops were withdrawn north of Siena without pressure to spare

Continued on Page 8

DANES PUSH STRIKE, DEFY BOMB THREAT

Copenhagen Halt Spreads to Provinces—Nazis Said to Agree to Oust Quislings

By The United Press.

STOCKHOLM, Sweden, July 3—Copenhagen remained under a state of siege today and a general strike spread to the Danish mainland despite appeals of municipal authorities and labor leaders for an end of demonstrations which had caused the Germans to threaten to starve the capital and, if necessary, to bomb it.

The situation was not clear, but reports that the strike had ended were premature. There were new clashes during the night in Copenhagen, according to advices. Many failed to return to work today and the strike spread to about twenty provincial towns, including Aarhus on the mainland. Many dairy farms were idle.

[Declaring that the "Copenhagen clique" had "run riot," the German Foreign Office's NPD agency said in a dispatch monitored by the Federal Communications Commission that the Danish capital would "remain cut off from all provisions" until the general strike was ended and order restored.]

Though water, gas and electric services had been restored by the Germans in Copenhagen, most factories remained closed. It was reported that the Germans resumed essential services in fear that passive resistance would become active. The Danish patriot press service here said that a German economic delegate in Copenhagen had insisted, in an angry dispute

Continued on Page 7

BASTION TOPPLES

Fate of Minsk Garrison in Doubt as Nazis Flee on Bottleneck Roads

FIGHTING IN POLOTSK

Street Battles Rage in Junction—Drive for the Baltic States Looms

By The United Press.

LONDON, Tuesday, July 4—Red Army forces yesterday captured the ancient White Russian capital of Minsk, last major enemy bastion in pre-war Russia on the road to Warsaw, while troops of the Soviet northern wing moving toward Latvia and Lithuania pushed into the streets of Polotsk, where vicious fighting was reported.

Minsk was captured on the eleventh day of a whirlwind Soviet offensive that has driven the Nazis 165 miles back across White Russia and Poland and cost them more than 213,000 men killed or captured.

The city of 238,000 was captured by the combined forces of Gen. Ivan D. Chernyakhovsky's Third White Russian Army and Marshal Konstantin K. Rokossovsky's First White Russian Army, which outflanked Minsk and then took it by storm, Premier Stalin announced in an order of the day.

While Minsk was falling, other Soviet forces smashed through powerful defense belts to open a street battle with the Germans in Polotsk, five-point rail junction 122 miles northeast of Minsk.

Red Army Near Molodechno

Forty miles northwest of Minsk the Russians smashed into the outskirts of Molodechno in what appeared to be the beginning of a drive against Vilna, sixty-five miles to the northwest on the Minsk-Molodechno-Koenigsberg railroad. On the southern end of the 400-mile front the Russians cleared a thirty-mile stretch of the Sluch River, pre-1939 frontier of Poland and Russia.

A dispatch from Moscow, filed after 324 Moscow guns had fired twenty-four salvos to salute the triumph, said:

"The fall of Minsk marked the collapse of the entire German position in White Russia and is regarded here as one of the decisive battles of the war. The Germans are now retreating in disorder under the threat of encirclement."

The Germans still had open a fifty-six-mile-wide escape gap leading westward from Minsk across country devoid of first-class roads.

The Germans now hold only about 8,000 square miles of prewar Soviet territory — approxi-

Continued on Page 5

Stimson in Italy To Inspect Front

By Wireless to The New York Times.

ROME, July 3—Henry L. Stimson, United States Secretary of War, arrived today at an airfield in Italy for a brief tour of this theatre of war. He plans to visit the front line and inspect troops and hospitals as well as to hold conferences with important figures.

Mr. Stimson was accompanied on the trip from the United States by Harvey H. Bundy, special assistant to the Secretary; Maj. Gen. Alexander D. Surles, director of public relations for the War Department; Maj. Gen. Norman T. Kirk, War Department Surgeon General; Lieut. Col. William H. Kyle, aide to Mr. Stimson; Col. T. E. Kreps, the Secretary's pilot; Capt. William T. Hodge and an enlisted stenographer.

Somewhere in Africa the Secretary's party was joined by Maj. Gen. I. H. Edwards and Lieut. Col. E. Shumaker, aide to Lieut. Gen. Jacob L. Devers, deputy supreme commander of the Mediterranean theatre.

War News Summarized

TUESDAY, JULY 4, 1944

The First and Third White Russian Armies swung suddenly together from two sides of Minsk yesterday and captured the German-held citadel in a climax of their present offensive. Elsewhere along the battle line the Red Army carried the fighting into the streets of Polotsk and the outskirts of Molodechno and also drove closer to Baranovichi. More than 1,000 towns were liberated and almost 75,000 Germans, including two divisional commanders, were captured. The campaign in Finland also progressed. [1:8; map, P. 5.]

The United States First Army launched a new offensive south toward La Haye du Puits in an evident attempt to isolate the Cotentin Peninsula from the rest of France. A day-long artillery barrage preceded the assault, which was carried forward from one to three miles along a thirty-mile front. Heavy rains did not halt the American troops, who routed German machine-gun nests while wading chest-deep across flooded mine fields. Although the mud held down the use of tanks, British forces in the Caen sector scored several gains. [1:3; map, P. 2.]

On the third European front, the Fifth Army in Italy captured Siena, thirty-one miles below Florence, and on the western coast was only fifteen miles from Leghorn. German delaying positions around Lake Trasimeno in the center were broken and the Eighth Army moved to within fifteen miles of Arezzo. Ancona, on the Adriatic coast, lay less than nine miles from the Allies' positions. [1:6; map, P. 8.]

Throughout German-occupied Europe the enemy was also in trouble, disorders on a mounting scale being reported from many countries. [7:1.] The threat of starvation, instead of halting the Copenhagen general strike, was reported to have resulted in spreading resistance. [1:7.]

Some 750 Fortresses and Liberators from Italy smashed enemy oil facilities in the Balkan countries for the second consecutive day. [4:1.]

The Allies' bombing of Germany's oil resources has resulted in rationing for the Luftwaffe and motorized divisions, General Arnold said. The enemy's fuel supply has been cut to 30 per cent of normal and aircraft production has been reduced by 70 per cent, he declared, adding that the same fate was in store for Japan. [1:4.]

General MacArthur launched his Philippine-bound forces 100 miles nearer their goal in a swift amphibious operation against Numfor Island, west of Biak. Opposition was slight and Kamiri airfield was seized within two hours. [1:5-6, map, P. 12.] On Saipan, in the Marianas, Americans were advancing through the ruins of Carapan, the capital city, and a final battle was expected in the narrow northern end of the island. [12:1.]

The Japanese, slowed down at Hengyang in China, were reported using poison gas again. They by-passed the city and cut in from Anjen to below Leiyang, nearly fifty miles south of Hengyang and that much closer to Canton. [12:4.]

Ambassador Armour, recalled from Argentina, is expected in Washington today. [1:6-7.] He probably will clarify the assertion of the Argentine War Minister that the State Department's summary of his "expansionist" speech was so altered and mutilated as to change its meaning completely. [13:1.]

Nation's E Bond Total Lags at 60% With 92% of Over-All Quota Sold

Sales of Series E bonds—the issue of lower denominations designed for purchase by the man in the street—lagged sadly last night as the city, State and nation rapidly approached over-all quotas in the Fifth War Loan Drive ending Saturday.

The nation, with $14,885,000,000 in hand, had attained 92 per cent of its $16,000,000,000 quota already in hand, had attained 92 per cent of its goal. The State had raised 84.7 per cent of its $4,801,000,000 quota, with sales totaling $4,067,600,000. New York City's sales, totaling $3,632,140,972 was 87.2 per cent of its $4,167,023,000 goal.

These were over-all sales, however, including issues designed for large individual investors, banks, corporations and other groups not eligible for the Series E bond. In the E bond category the nation had reached only 60 per cent of its quota, the State 36.2 per cent and the city 35.6 per cent.

In point of actual sales in bonds of this category, the national figure was $3,607,000,000, as against its $6,000,000,000 goal; the State figure $133,000,000, as against $367,-000,000; and the city figure $81,-075,131, as against $227,526,600.

A heartening note, because of the stress that has been placed on E bond sales in this drive, was the fact that all the figures on E sales were forty-eight hours old. Because of the volume of business, the Treasury Department was unable to tabulate Sunday and Monday sales. It was hoped that such a tabulation would reveal a sizable

Continued on Page 32

Increased Pressure on Argentina Is Possible After Hull Sees Armour

By BERTRAM D. HULEN

Special to The New York Times.

WASHINGTON, July 3 — The Argentine situation will be taken up for intensive study upon the arrival here tomorrow of Norman Armour, who was recalled from his post as United States Ambassador in Buenos Aires, for consultation.

If Mr. Armour holds views similar to those said to be held by a number of our diplomatic staffs in the field and of some Latin-American diplomats here, there may be no further rupture in the situation.

Until he arrives, however, and outlines his views at some length, nothing can be taken for granted in this respect.

It was said today that the State Department would not confront Mr. Armour with a set program and that the conversations would be fluid. At the same time there were indications that Secretary of State Cordell Hull might make a statement on the situation in a few days. This might lead to economic sanctions or only to continuing the present avoidance of ambassadorial relations and the diplomatic isolation that this entails.

On the other hand, some constructive measures can be envisaged; the present breach may be subjected to a healing process.

If economic sanctions should be applied, it is assumed that some measures would have to be devised to find substitute sources for essential war products now obtained from Argentina. She supplies meat to Great Britain and through that channel to our soldiers serving in

Continued on Page 13

"All the News That's Fit to Print"

The New York Times.

LATE CITY EDITION
Partly cloudy with moderate winds today.
Temperatures Yesterday—Max.,80; Min.,68
Sunrise, 5:42 A. M.; Sunset, 8:22 P. M.

Copyright, 1944, by The New York Times Company.

VOL. XCIII..No. 31,590. Entered as Second-Class Matter. Postoffice, New York, N. Y. NEW YORK, FRIDAY, JULY 21, 1944. THREE CENTS NEW YORK CITY

ROOSEVELT NOMINATED FOR FOURTH TERM; HITLER ESCAPES BOMB, PURGES GENERALS; CAEN DRIVE GAINS; RUSSIA OPENS NEW PUSH

FUEHRER 'BRUISED'

Bomb Wounds 13 Staff Officers, One Fatally—Assassin Is Dead

'USURPERS' BLAMED

Hitler Names New Chief of Staff—Himmler to Rule Home Front

Texts of Hitler, Doenitz and Goering speeches, Page 3.

By JOSEPH SHAPLEN

Adolf Hitler had a narrow escape from death by assassination at his secret headquarters, the Berlin radio reported yesterday, and a few hours later in a radio broadcast to the German people he blamed an "officers' clique" for the attempt to kill him. His address disclosed a movement in the armed forces to overthrow him and his regime. He announced that a purge of the conspirators was under way.

Thirteen members of his military staff were injured, one fatally and two seriously, by a bomb set off at an undisclosed place while many of his highest advisers were assembled around him. The man who played the role of assassin, Hitler said, was Colonel Count von Stauffenberg, one of his collaborators, who stood only six feet away from him as he hurled the bomb. Von Stauffenberg is dead, Hitler announced.

Waiting to see Hitler before the assassination attempt was Benito Mussolini. Reich Marshal Hermann Goering, who rushed to Hitler's side, was in the immediate vicinity. Hitler escaped with singes and bruises.

Army Clique Blamed

While Dr. Joseph Goebbels and Nazi radio propagandists at first tried to put the blame for the attempt to kill the Fuehrer upon the Allies, Hitler himself exploded the bombshell by announcing that the culprits were a group of German Army officers. He thus confirmed reports of a serious rift between the Nazi High Command and German military elements.

In his broadcast, recorded by the Federal Communications Commission, Hitler told the German people: "If I address you today I am doing so for two reasons: first, so that you shall hear my voice and know that I personally am unhurt and well, and, second, so that you shall hear the details about a crime that has no equal in German history.

"An extremely small clique of ambitious, unscrupulous and at the same time foolish, criminally stupid officers hatched a plot to re-

Continued on Page 3

Nazi-Army Rift Is Revealed In Gravest Reich War Crisis

'Usurpers' Who Hatched Plot Not Named—Accused of Being Officer Group Wanting to Repeat the 1918 'Stab in the Back'

By RAYMOND DANIELL
By Cable to THE NEW YORK TIMES.

LONDON, July 20—Broadcasting so that the German people could hear his voice and know that he was unhurt after the attempt to assassinate him, Chancellor Adolf Hitler confirmed tonight all rumors and suspicions of disaffection and unrest in the Reich.

Heinrich Himmler, the Fuehrer said, has been made commander in chief of the home army to "create order once and for all." Hitler also ordered that no "military authority, no leader of any unit, no private in the field" was to obey any orders emanating from "usurpers" who were seeking peace.

He left the identity of those usurpers something of a mystery, for he referred to them as "a small group that emerged in Germany, just as in Italy, in the belief that they could repeat the 1918 stab in the back." Later he said they had "no bond with or nothing in common with the Wehrmacht, and, above all, none with the German people."

It is clear that a real crisis has arisen in the Reich and it remains to be seen whether the Nazis have chosen the wisest way to deal with it. A purge is as likely to widen the schism as not, and the German people, with their traditional respect for their officer class, may feel that if the Nazis choose war, and the old officers favor peace, the time may have come to question the infallibility of the Fuehrer.

The announcement left open to speculation the question of not only who was behind the assassination attempt but, even more interesting, the question of who in Germany was in position to make the attempt.

That Germany is going through

Continued on Page 5

Admiral and General Told To Form New Tokyo Regime

Gen. Kuniaki Koiso, a member of the same Kwantung Army group to which former Premier Gen. Hideki Tojo belongs, arrived in Tokyo from Korea yesterday to participate with Admiral Mitsumasa Yonai in the formation of a new "critical decisive wartime" Cabinet by "command" of Emperor Hirohito, it was disclosed in Japanese broadcasts and press dispatches reported to the Office of War Information by the Federal Communications Commission.

General Koiso, Governor General of Korea, and Admiral Yonai, a former Premier and member of the Supreme War Council, were summoned as "senior leaders of the army and navy," the Japanese Domei agency said. Each is 64 years old.

Meanwhile, the Domei agency, in a wireless dispatch to the controlled East Asia press, warned its bureaus to be "on the alert" for new developments, presumably regarding an announcement of the new Cabinet's membership.

"Competent political observers expect that the new Cabinet will be formed swiftly," Domei said. Another Japanese account predicted that the new Government would be formed by "Friday morning at the latest."

Co-Premiership Doubted

Koiso and Yonai were designated to form a new Government after Emperor Hirohito had called in Marquis Koichi Kido, Lord Keeper of the Privy Seal, to sound out Japan's "elder statesmen" for candidates to serve as the nucleus for what Domei termed a "more powerful Cabinet."

In a continuation of the "elder statesman" system of choosing Cabinet leaders, Kido then called a caucus of former Premiers. After this meeting, the following an-

Continued on Page 3

ALLIES STORM ARNO ON A 25-MILE FRONT

Americans, in Hot Pursuit of Bewildered Germans, Plunge to Town 12 Miles From Pisa

By The Associated Press.

ROME, July 20—American troops battered their way across the Arno River Valley on a 25-mile front between Pisa and Florence today as German forces, bewildered by the sudden breakthrough, retreated across the Arno into the mountain defenses of their Gothic Line.

Lieut. Gen. Mark W. Clark's doughboys held complete control of hill masses overlooking the Arno from the south, and American artillery raked the entire valley in search of German rear-guard units protecting the withdrawal of the main body of enemy forces to the north of the stream.

German resistance was confined almost entirely to these small groups armed with automatic weapons—tactics similar to those that delayed the entry of General Clark's troops into Rome an entire day. One American column was firmly established on the south bank of the Arno at Pontedera, twelve miles inland from Pisa.

An Allied spokesman said Ger-

Continued on Page 5

Nazi Party Clashes With Army Reported

BERNE, Switzerland, July 20 (U.P.)—Skirmishes took place in various parts of Germany today between Nazi party members, led by SS [Elite Guard] Troopers, and groups of the regular army, according to unconfirmed reports reaching here tonight.

Conferences of the Nazi party organization were held in all principal cities of the Reich this evening, and members were asked to reaffirm their loyalty to the party and to Adolf Hitler, according to reliable information. Zurich reported that responsible quarters there had information that a subversive movement was under way in various parts of the Reich.

By Wireless to THE NEW YORK TIMES.

BERNE, Friday, July 21—There were unconfirmed reports at the Swiss-German frontier shortly after 1 o'clock this morning that some shooting had occurred on the other side of the line, but whether or not it indicated mutiny could not yet be ascertained.

Allies Report Belgian Uprising Comparable to French Sabotage

By Wireless to THE NEW YORK TIMES.

SUPREME HEADQUARTERS, Allied Expeditionary Force, July 20—Belgium's extensive and complicated network of rail and road communications was reported in a special Allied communiqué today to have been "largely disrupted" as the result of the "highly satisfactory" operations of the Belgian underground. The communiqué was the first from Supreme Headquarters to mention the Belgian resistance movement that has been declared by Belgian authorities to be a formal military organization the same as the French Forces of the Interior.

Reporting that Belgian operations "throughout the entire country" had "contributed substantially to the delaying movement of enemy reinforcements to the battle area," the communiqué also said that French forces had detained a Panzer division moving toward Normandy for thirty hours and had wrecked twenty-six strategic bridges between June 24 and July 6.

Eighty Germans were killed and 300 wounded in the attack on the Panzer division, said the communiqué, which also confirmed an earlier French report that patriots had destroyed a train carrying flying bombs in eastern France.

From July 4 to 15, the communiqué said, the French forces continued operations "in face of violent German attacks," defeating or eluding the Germans in every case.

In addition, the French slowed traffic on the "whole railway sys-

Continued on Page 4

BRITISH PUSH SOUTH

Take Troarn Rail Depot While Second Column Captures Bourguebus

ENEMY SLOWS DRIVE

Strong Anti-Tank Belt Checks Smash Toward Plains Before Paris

By DREW MIDDLETON
By Cable to THE NEW YORK TIMES.

SUPREME HEADQUARTERS, Allied Expeditionary Force, Friday, July 21—Tanks and infantry of the British Second Army, battling stubborn German rearguards at Troarn and St. André-sur-Orne, yesterday, widened the eleven-mile front south and east of Caen that Lieut. Gen. Miles C. Dempsey's troops have punched out in three days of audacious and arduous fighting.

Strong German anti-tank positions northwest of Vimont slowed down the advance to the southeast toward Vimont, momentarily at least. However, British artillery and infantry were assaulting these positions last night as the second stage of the great trial of strength with the Seventh German Army opened.

British Positions Solid

Bourguebus, five and a quarter miles southeast of Caen, was the most important of a dozen towns and villages taken by the British in the twenty-four hours ended at midnight last night. It is almost in the center of an arc extending from the Orne west of St. André to the railroad station at Caen, which marks the area in which the Second Army is solidly established.

Farther to the south, southeast and east, in front of the main positions, British tanks were operating against the German lines, seek-

Continued on Page 4

LWOW IS MENACED

Red Army Near Polish City—New Wedge Is Driven From Kovel

GRIP ON BUG WIDENS

Foe's Supply Lines Cut—Dvinsk Rail Link Slashed on West

By W. H. LAWRENCE
By Wireless to THE NEW YORK TIMES.

MOSCOW, Friday, July 21—Revealing another terrific Red Army offensive, Marshal Joseph Stalin announced last night that forces led by Marshal Konstantin K. Rokossovsky, after three days' fighting in the Kovel sector, had driven a wedge thirty-one miles deep on a 123-mile front, pushing the Germans back to the western Bug River.

He disclosed, also, that Marshal Ivan S. Koneff's First Ukrainian Army had captured Rawa Ruska, an important rail junction, severing the most direct supply and retreat route for the Germans' outflanked Lwow garrison.

These new triumphs over the battered, reeling German Army at the southern end of the eastern front were celebrated in Moscow at 10 and 11 P. M. by two salutes of twenty salvos each from 224 guns—demonstrations that brought hundreds of thousands of Muscovites into the streets.

The first salute was directed to Marshal Rokossovsky in tribute to the drive of his forces from Kovel through the strongly fortified German defense line, which culminated in reaching the western Bug at Opalin and in the capture of more than 400 inhabited points. Opalin, on the eastern side of the Bug, is less than fifteen miles from Chelm on the road to Lublin.

Other forces under Marshal Kon-

Continued on Page 6

War News Summarized

FRIDAY, JULY 21, 1944

An almost successful attempt on Hitler's life and Emperor Hirohito's command to two jingo war lords to form a new Japanese Cabinet pushed actual battlefield developments into the background yesterday.

Hitler was conferring at his secret headquarters with the staff of the German High Command, Berlin said, when Col. Count von Stauffenberg, one of his collaborators, threw a bomb at the Fuehrer. Although the assassin was only six feet away Hitler escaped with bruises and burns. One of the thirteen staff officers was killed and two others were seriously injured.

Shortly after the explosion Hitler informed the German people of what had happened, blaming an "officers' clique" that wished to bring about a revolt. He immediately placed Gestapo Chief Himmler in absolute command within the Reich, said the "criminal elements" would be ruthlessly exterminated and indicated grave concern by warning all soldiers and civilians not to obey orders unless they had been confirmed. He also named Col. Gen. Guderian Chief of Staff, replacing Field Marshal Gen. Keitel. [All the foregoing 1:1.]

In Japan, Admiral Mitsumasa Yonai, Premier during the tense days of early 1940, and his then Overseas Minister and later Governor General of Korea, Gen. Kuniaki Koiso, were commissioned to form a "critical decisive wartime" Cabinet. Both men are militarists and expansionists of the Tojo type. [1:2-3.]

Allied statesmen saw in both developments evidence of crisis in the enemy camps. London observers believed that Hitler's order for a new purge indicated clearly that unrest within Germany was general [1:2-3], while former Ambassador Grew and Secretary of State Hull in Washington expressed the prevalent opinion that Tokyo had at last admitted the gravity of the military situation. They warned, however, against expecting a Japanese collapse. [3:6.]

On the actual war fronts Allied gains were reported everywhere. The British Second Army in France was widening its eleven-mile bulge south and east of Caen and trying to force Field Marshal Rommel into a decisive tank battle. Americans advanced in the St. Lô area and crossed the River Ay to a depth of 300 yards in the Lessay sector. [1:4, map P. 2.] The resistance movement that has proved so effective in France has spread into Belgium. [1:2-3.]

Although torrential rains slowed Allied progress in Italy the Fifth Army reached the Arno River along a twenty-five-mile front above Leghorn and was close to Pisa. [1:3.]

Overhead some 2,000 planes from Britain and nearly 1,000 from Italy teamed in a coordinated attack on aircraft plants, ball-bearing factories, airfields and other targets in southeast Germany. It was one of the war's most concentrated blows. [5:1.]

The Russians scored the most impressive gains in a new offensive in the Kovel area. The Red Army reached the western Bug River on a wide front after driving as deep as thirty-one miles on a 123-mile line in three days. Another advance brought Soviet troops to within five miles of Lwow and a flanking thrust cut the main German supply and escape railroad. [1:5; map P. 6.]

Action in the Pacific was on a lesser scale. American planes blasted Guam with 721 tons of bombs in two days. [7:5.] Chinese troops were attacking the Japanese from within Hengyang and from outside the Hunan city [7:1] while along the Burma front other Chinese routed an enemy relief force trying to reach Pingka. [6:6.]

AGAIN NAMED FOR PRESIDENCY

Franklin Delano Roosevelt
Associated Press, 1944

Roosevelt's Acceptance

Following is the text of President Roosevelt's acceptance speech from a Pacific Coast naval base, as recorded and transcribed by THE NEW YORK TIMES:

Mr. Chairman, ladies and gentlemen of the convention, my friends:

I have already indicated to you why I accept the nomination that you have offered me, in spite of my desire to retire to the quiet of private life.

You in this convention are aware of what I have sought to gain for the nation, and you have asked me to continue.

It seems wholly likely that within the next four years our armed forces, and those of our Allies, will have gained a complete victory over Germany and Japan, sooner or later, and that the world once more will be at peace, under a system, we hope, that will prevent a new world war. In any event, whenever that time comes new hands will then have full opportunity to realize the ideals which we seek.

In the last three elections the people of the United States have transcended party affiliation. Not only Democrats but also forward-looking Republicans and millions of

Continued on Page 8

PRESIDENT FAVORS TRUMAN, DOUGLAS

Would Take Either as Running Mate, Letter to Hannegan Says—Battle Gets Hotter

By JAMES A. HAGERTY
Special to THE NEW YORK TIMES.

CHICAGO, July 20—In an attempt to bolster the waning strength of Senator Harry S. Truman of Missouri for the nomination for Vice President, Robert E. Hannegan, Democratic national chairman, made public tonight the letter written to him by President Roosevelt, saying that either Senator Truman or William O. Douglas, justice of the United States Supreme Court, would be satisfactory to him as a running mate and would add strength to the ticket.

Mr. Hannegan said he had not made the letter public earlier because he considered it necessary to obtain the consent of the sender before releasing a personal letter for publication. He said he had talked today with President Roosevelt by telephone and had received such consent.

The letter, which was written on White House stationery and dated July 19, 1944, was as follows:

"Dear Bob:

"You have written me about Harry Truman and Bill Douglas. I should, of course, be very glad to run with either of them and believe that either one of them would bring real strength to the ticket.

"Always sincerely,

"FRANKLIN D. ROOSEVELT."

The letter was addressed to

Continued on Page 10

ARMS USE TO KEEP PEACE IS PLEDGED

Platform Backs World Role on Sovereignty Basis—Opposes Racial Vote Ban

Text of the Democratic platform is on Page 12.

By CHARLES E. EGAN

CHICAGO, July 20—A platform calling for the participation of this country with the United Nations in a world organization, empowered to use armed force when necessary to preserve international peace, was adopted by the Democratic convention tonight.

It committed the party to support a program to have the United States join in "the establishment of an international organization based on the principle of the sovereign equality of all peace-loving states, open to membership by all such states, large and small, for the prevention of aggression and the maintenance of international peace and security."

Embodied also in the platform was a plank stating that racial and religious minorities "have the right to live, develop and vote equally with all citizens and share the rights that are guaranteed by our Constitution."

The platform, of 1,500 words, carried expressions in favor of the opening of Palestine to unrestricted Jewish immigration and

Continued on Page 12

VOTE IS 1,086 TO 90

Byrd Gets 89, Farley One—President on Radio Accepts

STANDS ON RECORD

Says 'Experience,' Not 'Immaturity,' Will Win War, Peace and Jobs

Wallace and Barkley texts, Page 10; Jackson's, Page 11.

By TURNER CATLEDGE
Special to THE NEW YORK TIMES.

CHICAGO, July 20—Franklin Delano Roosevelt of New York was nominated today for a fourth term as President of the United States by a noisy, irritable Democratic convention, meeting in the same hall where he was chosen for his first term in 1932 and for a third in 1940.

A few hours later, speaking to the convention directly by radio from his train at a Pacific Coast naval base, he accepted the nomination and opened his re-election bid on the note of "experience" versus "immaturity."

Mr. Roosevelt asserted that he considered the convention's action as a call upon him to serve. He said it was up to the American people in the November election to decide whether plans already made and men already serving to achieve victory and make America and the world a better place in which to live were to be continued or supplanted by an administration with no program but to oppose.

His Three-Point Program

He presented a three-point program—to win the war, to secure the peace with force if necessary, and to build an economy with full employment and a high standard of living—as a promise of himself and the party which had called him again to lead.

In this election, he said, the people would not consider "glowing words or platform pledges," but would decide on the record made in the war and in "domestic achievements."

The President said he was too busy, and the emergency too serious, to permit him to engage in an active campaign for re-election.

But he added that he should "feel free" to report to the American people from time to time on the progress of their efforts and to "correct misstatements of fact" which might be made by the Republican opposition.

He disclosed that he was on the West Coast now in pursuance of his "constitutional duties" in connection with the war.

Roar of Cheering for Speech

The President's words came strong and magic-like through the loud speaker system—just as it did in his acceptance speech at his third-term nomination in this hall four years ago.

At the end the crowd in the arena and galleries broke into uproarious cheering. People were still shouting in a deafening roar when adjournment was moved. They attempted to shout down the motion.

The motion was carried, however, and the convention recessed at 10:55 o'clock until 11:30 tomorrow morning when it will reassemble to settle the Vice Presidential nomination.

The renomination of the President went through swiftly.

Mr. Roosevelt received 1,086 votes on the first roll call. Senator Harry F. Byrd, who was not a candidate, received 89, and James A. Farley, former chairman of the Democratic National Committee, who would not let his name go before the convention, received one from his home State of New York.

A telegram notifying the President of his nomination was dispatched to him immediately by Senator Samuel D. Jackson, Per-

Continued on Page 9

"All the News That's Fit to Print"

The New York Times.

LATE CITY EDITION
Clear with light to moderate winds today.
Temperatures Yesterday—Max., 76; Min., 66
Sunrise, 5:43 A. M.; Sunset, 8:21 P. M.

VOL. XCIII..No. 31,591. Entered as Second-Class Matter, Postoffice, New York, N. Y. NEW YORK, SATURDAY, JULY 22, 1944. THREE CENTS IN NEW YORK CITY

NAZIS BLOCK PLOT TO SEIZE GOVERNMENT; AMERICANS LAND ON GUAM, PUSH INLAND; TRUMAN NOMINATED FOR VICE PRESIDENCY

2D BALLOT DECIDES

Wallace, Leading 429½ to 319½ on First, Is Crushed 1,100 to 66

BREAK BY MARYLAND

Real Fight Ends With Big Shift by Illinois—Ready, Says Senator

By TURNER CATLEDGE
Special to The New York Times.

CHICAGO, July 21—Senator Harry S. Truman of Missouri was nominated tonight as the Democratic candidate for Vice President in the fifth and final session of the twenty-eighth national convention of the party.

He appeared immediately before the cheering delegates massed in the arena of the great hall to accept his "responsibility" as a running mate in President Roosevelt's bid for a fourth term in the White House.

Directly following the nomination, support of the ticket was pledged by Vice President Henry A. Wallace, James A. Farley, former National Chairman, and Sidney Hillman, head of the CIO Political Action Committee, which had supported Mr. Wallace.

Mr. Truman's victory, which was also an overwhelming defeat for the renomination hopes of Vice President Wallace, came on the second ballot. The official announcement of the tally clerks gave the Missouri Senator 1,100 votes to 66 for Mr. Wallace and 4 for Associate Justice William O. Douglas.

[A tabulation of this ballot by The Associated Press from official records of the convention gave: Truman 1,031, Wallace 105. Other votes in the compilation: Governor Cooper of Tennessee, 26; Senator Barkley of Kentucky, 6; Justice Douglas, 4 and Paul V. McNutt, 1.]

Truman Speaks to Throng

Mr. Truman, who rose from comparative political obscurity in Kansas City to win the second highest honor of his party, was sitting on the platform eating a sandwich when the result was announced.

Pulled up to the microphone by Senator Samuel D. Jackson of Indiana, permanent chairman of the convention, Senator Truman responded to the demands from the crowd for a word.

"You don't know how very much I appreciate the very great honor which has come to the State of Missouri," he said in a halting, shy manner. "It is also a great responsibility which I am perfectly willing to assume.

"Nine years and five months ago I came to the Senate. I expect to continue the efforts I have made there to help shorten the war and to win the peace under the great leader, Franklin D. Roosevelt.

"I don't know what else I can say, except that I accept this great honor with all humility. I thank you."

It was the shortest speech of the day and was appreciatively applauded by a crowd that literally had become surfeited with oratory. A moment later the convention passed into history on a motion by Governor Herbert O'Conor of Maryland to adjourn sine die.

"This convention has completed the business for which it was assembled, to nominate the next President and Vice President of the United States," he said.

Swing Led by Maryland

Senator Truman, President Roosevelt's second choice for place, ran through to win the nomination after having trailed Vice President Wallace on the first ballot by 110 votes.

On the opening roll-call Mr. Wallace received 429½ ballots and Mr. Truman 319½, with the remainder scattered among fourteen other candidates who had been named in nominating speeches or

Continued on Page 8

ROOSEVELT'S RUNNING MATE

Harry S. Truman Blackstone, 1944

Monetary Parley Agrees On Terms of World Bank

By RUSSELL PORTER
Special to The New York Times.

BRETTON WOODS, N. H., July 21—The United Nations Monetary and Financial Conference reached an agreement today on a plan for an $8,800,000,000 International Bank of Reconstruction and Development to guarantee post-war international investments. The total capital of the world bank is the same as the aggregate of the international monetary fund to stabilize currencies which was accepted last week. Thus two vital parts of the post-war program to try to insure world peace and prosperity have been accepted, with some reservations, by all the forty-four United and Associated Nations participating in the conference, subject to the approval of the Congress of the United States and the executive and legislative branches of other Governments.

In order to reach an agreement, the United States delegation had to abandon its position that the subscriptions to the bank, which represent each country's risks in guaranteeing international loans, should be the same as the quotas in the fund, which represent a country's rights to acquire foreign exchange with which to buy goods in the world market.

However, it is the opinion of the United States delegation, after receiving the advice of its four members of Congress, two Republicans and two Democrats, and its one banker member, Edward E. Brown, president of the First National Bank of Chicago, that the fund and bank agreements have been

Continued on Page 28

BIG CITY BOSSES WON OVER HILLMAN

Two Presidential Letters Had Important Influence on Convention Strategy

By JAMES A. HAGERTY
Special to The New York Times.

CHICAGO, July 21—Somewhat belatedly, leaders of the Democratic organizations in a score and a half of States, headed by big city bosses, Edward J. Flynn and Frank V. Kelly of New York, Mayor Edward J. Kelly of Chicago, Mayor Frank Hague of Jersey City and Robert E. Hannegan, national chairman, of St. Louis, brought about the nomination of Senator Harry S. Truman of Missouri for Vice President by the Democratic National Convention.

By the nomination the Democratic politicians won a victory over Sidney Hillman, chairman of the Congress of Industrial Organizations Political Action Committee, who stuck to Vice President Henry A. Wallace to the last and whose influence had been suffi-

Continued on Page 10

Farley Pledges Roosevelt Backing, Accepting Decision of Convention

Special to The New York Times.

CHICAGO, July 21—James A. Farley, former Democratic national chairman and former Postmaster General, announced tonight that he would support President Roosevelt for re-election despite his opposition to a fourth term.

"I have been opposed on principle to a third or fourth Presidential term," Mr. Farley said in a statement, which he released just after the nomination of Senator Truman for Vice President. "For that reason, I voted for the nomination of Senator Harry F. Byrd of Virginia for President.

"Having participated in the proceedings of the convention, I accept its decision and will support the party nominees."

Mr. Farley declined to amplify his statement. He resigned recently as chairman of the New York State Democratic Committee and is not expected to take an active part in the campaign.

Mr. Farley, who was of great help to Mr. Roosevelt in the latter's first nomination for President and in his first and second campaigns for election, broke with the Chief Executive during the latter part of Mr. Roosevelt's second term.

Secretary of the New York State Democratic Committee in 1928, when Mr. Roosevelt was first elected Governor of New York, Mr. Farley was promoted to State chairman and managed Mr. Roosevelt's campaign for re-election as Governor in 1930. Mr. Roosevelt's plurality of 730,000 at that elec-

Continued on Page 9

RUSSIANS RACE ON

Bug River Is Crossed Again on Wide Front Due East of Lublin

LWOW BATTLE BEGUN

Brest-Litovsk Railway to Chelm Cut—Ostrov Is Captured in North

By W. H. LAWRENCE
By Cable to The New York Times.

MOSCOW, Saturday, July 22—The Soviet battle for the liberation of Poland began in earnest yesterday as the Red Army smashed across the Bug River from Lyuboml on a thirty-seven-mile front and advanced up to nine miles beyond the west bank. In that operation the railroad between Chelm and Brest-Litovsk was severed.

Other Red Army forces moved closer to Lwow and to Brest-Litovsk, and the Soviet High Command announced that Soviet troops had captured 570 inhabited points on both the northernmost and the southernmost sections of the front.

At the northern end of the front, troops of the Third Baltic Front executed an outflanking maneuver and captured the important enemy stronghold and communications hub of Ostrov—a victory that Moscow celebrated with a salute of twelve salvos from 124 guns.

Although the capture of Ostrov won the salute, from a military and strategic point of view the biggest news was the crossing of the Bug west of Lyuboml by Marshal Konstantin K. Rokossovsky's First White Russian Army and the nine-mile advance beyond it, which sent his troops streaming toward Lublin and Warsaw.

In the sector southwest of Brody, where four or five German divisions are encircled, Marshal Ivan S. Koneff's First Ukrainian Army continued the process of extermination, capturing 2,000 more prisoners and 200 artillery pieces. The

Continued on Page 5

BEACHHEADS SET UP

Americans Invade Guam After Mighty U.S. Blow From Sea and Air

OPPOSITION IS LIGHT

Resistance Increases as Japanese Are Pushed Toward Inland Hills

By GEORGE F. HORNE
By Telephone to The New York Times.

PEARL HARBOR, July 21—United States assault troops and sea forces began yesterday the long awaited invasion of the big island of Guam and have established good beachheads against light opposition, although resistance increased in some sectors as the Americans drove inland.

[Front dispatches reported that the landings were made on either side of Port Apra, The Associated Press said. From the shore areas, where Japanese defenses had been blown to pieces, the invaders drove swiftly toward a range of hills in the interior.]

They stormed ashore after enemy defenses received their seventeenth straight day of heavy attack from the air. All this week, up to the time of the landings, surface units of the Fifth Fleet had battered the island with tons of steel. They continued yesterday, covering the marines and Army assault troops making the invasion. A terrific rain of 627 tons of bombs and 147 rockets was unloosed by our planes in the day preceding the landings.

Admiral Chester W. Nimitz, Commander in Chief of the Pacific Fleet and Pacific Ocean areas, announced the landings at 1:30 o'clock this morning.

Japanese Are Weakened

With Saipan securely in our hands, the tremendous Pacific forces have turned, as was expected, to carry retribution to the Japanese where their strongly armed and confident forces poured ashore

Continued on Page 7

War News Summarized

SATURDAY, JULY 22, 1944

The few facts seeping through the tight German censorship yesterday indicated that the anti-Hitler revolt was still alive and that a purge of anti-Nazi leaders was still under way. German army officers who attempted to take Hitler's life simultaneously tried to take over the government offices in Berlin, the German radio said. The same source declared the revolt had been mercilessly suppressed and that Propaganda Minister Goebbels had frustrated the attempt to seize the Government offices. A Stockholm report said two German divisions had revolted Wednesday in East Prussia, while another dispatch from Switzerland relayed unconfirmed reports of a revolt among German naval units at Kiel and Stettin. [1:8.]

Secretary of State Hull attributed the unrest in Germany and the attack on Hitler to a spreading realization in the Reich of impending defeat. He cautioned, however, against overoptimism on an early end of the war in Europe. [3:2-3.]

Red Army forces blasted a thirty-seven-mile-wide hole in Hitler's much-publicized "East Wall" defenses along the Bug River and are threatening to crumble the whole German defense structure guarding Warsaw, now only eighty-two miles away. Other Russian troops seized Ostrov, the last Nazi fortress before the Latvian border on the direct route to Riga. The Red Army was increasing its threat to the imperiled strongholds of Lwow, Brest-Litovsk, Kaunas and Dvinsk by the hour, as beaten German armies fell back everywhere along an almost continuous 800-mile front from Finland to the Carpathian foothills. [1:4; map P. 5.]

Allied troops in Normandy slugged through rain and mud to cement positions below Caen to a depth of five miles. Canadians seized St. André-sur-Orne and St. Martin-de-Fontenay near Caen as the enemy gave ground slowly. American forces increased their pressure on Périers after winning a foothold on the road from St. Lô to Périers. [1:6-7; map P. 3.]

The two-way aerial offensive from Britain and Italy continued for the fourth consecutive day as nearly 3,000 American bombers and fighters pounded a dozen German targets. [4:1.] Ground troops in Italy pierced strong German Arno River defenses, forcing the water barrier into the mountain fringes of the "Gothic Line" in at least one place. [1:7.]

Striking at Japan's inner defense zone, American assault troops landed on Guam Island, first American territory seized by the Japanese, early Thursday and have established good beachheads. Admiral Nimitz reported that additional troops were landing against light initial Japanese resistance, and that casualties were moderate. A terrific naval and aerial bombardment of the strategic island, 1,565 miles southeast of Tokyo, softened up the enemy defense before our landings. As our troops moved inland the Japanese put up stiffened resistance in some sectors. [1:5; map P. 7.]

In China fierce fighting raged around Hengyang for the twenty-sixth day as relief forces attacking Japanese troops who have besieged that major junction on the Canton-Hankow railroad drove deeper into the enemy lines. [6:1.]

Drive South of Caen Stalls As Rain Floods Battle Area

British Forced to Withdraw Armored Units—Canadians Beat Off Fierce German Counter-Attacks in Mud and Mists

By DREW MIDDLETON
By Cable to The New York Times.

SUPREME HEADQUARTERS, Allied Expeditionary Force, Saturday, July 22—British and Canadian infantrymen, their uniforms muddy and sodden after thirty-six hours of heavy rains, were fighting a grim, bloody battle for Verrières and St. Martin-de-Fontenay on the British Second Army sector south of Caen last night, but the remainder of the Allied front in Normandy was quiet save for the measured pounding of cannon and mortars.

The offensive launched by the Second Army Tuesday morning with such high hopes had stalled, frustrated as much by the thick doughlike mud that covered the roads and fields as by the lethal fire of German anti-tank positions around Vimont. These positions now must be rooted out by infantry and artillery, under adverse conditions for the attackers, while British armored divisions follow the example of German Panzer units and retire from the battlefield until the stage has been set for a great armored battle for the road to Paris.

The gains registered yesterday were all on the western flank of the Second Army's salient along the east bank of the Orne River. Canadians were fighting German infantrymen for Etavaux and St. André-sur-Orne in conditions reminiscent of World War I.

At St. Martin-de-Fontenay, half a mile south of St. André-sur-Orne, the Canadians took the village and then stood off a heavy German counter-attack supported by tanks. When the counter-attack was over the Canadians went forward to find German dead lying thick on the muddy ground. The enemy casualties were "satisfactory," a report from the front said.

There was mud and mist everywhere and little knots of men were fighting silently with bayonets in a dank, dripping world where gun flashes were the only light.

The weather, which has favored the enemy since D-day, has imposed a stalemate on the operations in this sector, although farther west British infantrymen

Continued on Page 3

British Label Hitler Attack Rivals' Bid for False Peace

By Cable to The New York Times.

LONDON, July 21—Although the news from Germany is taken as an indication of a grave crisis within the Reich, there is no disposition here to regard it as a ground for hoping for an early termination of hostilities. As The Times of London will say tomorrow, when the enemy "wavers," that is the time for throwing in reserves, not for relaxing.

It is strongly felt here that Adolf Hitler's rivals, far from being converts to the Allied cause, are merely another brand of champions of militarism who merely believe themselves better able to rescue the Reich from disaster than the present Nazi leaders.

Their game, it was said, is to supplant Hitler so as to try to make peace on terms that would preserve the Wehrmacht for another war under more favorable conditions. Therefore, it is recognized by the people as well as officials that even had the officers' coup succeeded, peace would still be a long way off.

Generals Reach Conclusion

"Unconditional surrender" is still an Allied condition of an armistice, and there is little conviction here that even the generals who would like to rid their country of Hitler would accept that without continuing the struggle in the hope of getting better terms later.

However, this evidence of a rift in the façade of German unity is recognized as important evidence that at least some German military leaders have reached the conclusion that the Nazi direction of the war has brought Germany to a

Continued on Page 3

U. S. PATROLS STAB ACROSS ARNO RIVER

Pierce Mountain Fringes of Gothic Line While British Thrust Nearer Florence

By The United Press.

ROME, July 21—American Fifth Army combat patrols pierced strong German Arno River defenses today, forcing the river into the mountain fringes of the Gothic Line in at least one point, while artillery blasted German installations north of the river from captured high points on the south bank.

The Americans took advantage of improved weather to roll up scattered German resistance groups south of the river, while on the coast German guns of all calibers hammered the battered port of Leghorn from advantageous positions on Mount Pisano, northeast of Pisa.

This height, on which the Germans have installed many field guns, anti-aircraft batteries, machine guns and pillboxes, affords

Continued on Page 5

Invaders Find Defenses of Guam Blown to Shreds by Our Attacks

By JOHN R. HENRY
Of International News Service
For the Combined Allied Press

ABOARD A FLAGSHIP AT GUAM, July 21 (Guam Time)—A liberation force of Third Amphibious Corps marines and Army troops thundered ashore at Guam today with the destructive blast of a Pacific typhoon.

The Leathernecks spearheaded two separate beachhead assaults, storming across coral-studded shorelines in the wake of a 17-day sea and air bombardment that reached a stupefying crescendo as landing craft churned into remnants of the Japanese coast defenses.

Casualties were described as "light" for United States forces. The Japanese dead were uncounted.

At nightfall Maj. Gen. Roy Geiger's Third Amphibious Corps troops dug in on perimeters between Adlup and Asan, a point north of Orote Peninsula, and from the shattered town of Agat to Bangi Point, south of the rocky finger of land.

The northern beachhead, where the terrain was most rugged, stretched in an arc several thousand yards. The southern force shoved inland and established its own substantial beachhead. General Geiger is a marine aviator and veteran South Pacific commander.

So effective had been the preparatory barrages that troops flowed ashore with negligible initial resistance and in record time.

Despite sprinkling enemy fire

Continued on Page 7

HITLER HUNTS FOES

Thousands of Officers Reported Arrested in Purge of Army

MUTINY IS RUMORED

Sailors at Kiel, Stettin and Troops in East Said to Revolt

By RAYMOND DANIELL
By Cable to The New York Times.

LONDON, Saturday, July 22—Although reports from Berlin insist that the plot of army officers to overthrow the Nazi regime and seize power themselves has been suppressed and its instigators liquidated, the isolation of the Reich from the rest of the world continues and it is apparent that counter-measures are being pressed.

[A Swiss report to The United Press said it was understood that German naval units had revolted at Kiel and Stettin. Stockholm dispatches said 5,500 German officers had been arrested throughout Germany and that there had been disorders in eastern Germany and East Prussia.]

Everything suggests that the plot that had its climax in the attempt to assassinate Adolf Hitler was deep and well laid, with far-reaching ramifications. On evidence supplied by the highest Nazi authorities it is known that the plotters, who included Col. Gen. Ludwig Beck, who was dismissed as Chief of Staff by Hitler in November, 1938, attempted to kill Hitler and bring off a coup d'état.

The scheme apparently succeeded to the point where the conspirators were able to issue orders in conflict with the plans of Hitler and other Nazi leaders.

Leaders Revealed Troubled

The extent of the disaffection seemingly caused such consternation in the Nazi camp that Hitler, Reichsmarshal Hermann Goering and Grand Admiral Karl Doenitz felt impelled in the small hours yesterday morning to try to set things straight by urgent appeals, even though their action involved disclosure to a hostile world that a rift had developed between some high army officers and the Nazi party on the best way to save Germany from destruction.

There is no evidence to show that the challenge to Hitler's leadership and domination of the Nazi party has spread to the civilian population but Transocean, German news agency, revealed that certain "precautionary measures" had been taken in the center of Berlin.

Alfred Rosenberg, Nazi party "philosopher," writing in a special edition of the Voelkischer Beobachter yesterday morning, called the attempt on Hitler's life the opening of hostilities on a "fifth front."

Some additional light on what happened in the Reich in those crucial hours preceding Hitler's broadcast was provided last night from Berlin. According to the official story, provided for soldiers in the field, a clique that was connected with "an enemy power" had obtained control of "certain means of communications" through a subordinate officer.

Major Informed Goebbels

Through these channels, it was said, orders were sent to Major Remer, commandant of a battalion of the Berlin guard, telling him Hitler was dead, that disorders had been reported in the Reich and that the Wehrmacht had taken over the government. Major Remer was directed to occupy with his force the administrative headquarters at Berlin, which he did.

But then, according to this account, Major Remer immediately communicated with Propaganda Minister Joseph Goebbels, head of the Berlin municipal administration, who convinced him that he had been obeying faked orders. The fact that "traitors" had laid hands on certain communications systems brought about yesterday

Continued on Page 2

"All the News That's Fit to Print"

The New York Times.

LATE CITY EDITION
Fair and continued warm today but less humid.
Temperatures Yesterday—Max., 88; Min., 75
Sunrise, 5:37 A. M.; Sunset, 8:06 P. M.

VOL. XCIII—No. 31,607. Entered as Second-Class Matter, Postoffice, New York, N. Y. NEW YORK, MONDAY, AUGUST 7, 1944. THREE CENTS IN NEW YORK CITY

FOUR U. S. COLUMNS ARE DRIVING TOWARD PARIS; ALLIES TURN WHOLE GERMAN LINE BELOW CAEN; 46 JAPANESE SHIPS SUNK OR DAMAGED IN BONINS

STRIKERS GO BACK IN PHILADELPHIA; SOLDIERS ON CARS

Six-Day Transit Tie-Up Ends in Rush to Comply With Army's Work Deadline

LEADERS ARE OUT ON BAIL

Grand Jury to Start Inquiry Wednesday Into Possible Plot to Cause Walkout

By WALTER W. RUCH
Special to THE NEW YORK TIMES.

PHILADELPHIA, Monday, Aug. 7—Virtually complete service was restored to the lines of the Philadelphia Transportation Company early today as hundreds of striking workers, returning to their posts in a steadily increasing stream, broke the back of the six-day, unauthorized walkout.

Officials of the company, making a survey under supervision of Army officers, said that at midnight service over the various subway, elevated, bus and trolley lines was about 90 per cent of normal for a Sunday night. They reported, too, that 95 per cent of all the striking employes had signed cards indicating their intention of being on the job today.

The strike was broken as steel-helmeted soldiers in full battle dress rode each vehicle throughout yesterday and last night to protect the driver and passengers.

Discrimination Disproved

There was no violence. The only untoward incident reported came last evening when a Negro, mistaking a soldier's command to move to the rear of a bus as an attempt to enforce a Jim Crow custom prevailing in the South, left the bus at the next intersection to spread word through the Negro neighborhood that the soldiers were discriminating against Negroes.

Investigation disclosed that the soldiers, to keep bus aisles clear, were directing everyone, white and Negro alike, to the rear when seats were available there.

Additional police protection was sent into the area of the incident and police cars began to escort buses on the line.

No statement was issued from the headquarters of Maj. Gen. Philip Hayes, War Department representative handling the operation of the transit system, but the Army made no secret of its satisfaction with developments.

The strike, which began at 4 A. M. Tuesday in protest against the employment of Negroes as operators of passenger-carrying equipment, ended with the same conditions prevailing as provoked the walkout. By Army order, all employes are to go back to their same positions and this would mean that the eight Negroes who on Tuesday were undergoing training to operate vehicles would take it up again this morning if they desired.

Some Yield Grumblingly

The back-to-work movement began early yesterday in response to the swift series of developments Saturday night when, in rapid succession, General Hayes issued his uncompromising ultimatum to the strikers, four of the strike leaders were arrested on Federal warrants charging violation of the Smith-Connally anti-strike law, more than 5,000 fully armed troops poured into the city and a Federal grand jury investigation of the strike was ordered.

In his ultimatum General Hayes said that strikers who disobeyed his deadline would lose their jobs, be barred from other work during the war and, if between the ages of 17 and 37, be sent into the armed services.

Counseled by their leaders not to remain out any longer, the strikers started to yield, some grumblingly, before dawn yesterday. At every car barn the spirit of resistance began rapidly to melt away.

With the back-to-work movement under way, scores of agents

Continued on Page 24

Term Black Widow Deadliest Plane

By The Associated Press.

HAWTHORNE, Calif., Aug. 6—The Northrop Aircraft, Inc., announced today that the War Department had approved the release of heretofore carefully guarded details of the P-61 Black Widow night fighter, termed the world's largest and most powerful pursuit plane.

The company gave this picture:

Black Widow crews and ammunition boxes are protected from .30 and .50 caliber enemy machine gun fire by specially designed armor plate, bullet resistant glass and deflector plates.

Incorporated into the ship is the first full-span landing flap, for low landing speed, combined with a new-type aileron which retracts into the upper section of the wing, giving the Black Widow unusual maneuverability.

OIL TERMS REACHED BY U. S. AND BRITAIN

Creation of an International Commission Is Expected to Be Announced This Week

By JAMES B. RESTON
Special to THE NEW YORK TIMES.

WASHINGTON, Aug. 6—The United States and Great Britain will create, probably this week, an International Oil Commission designed to regulate the development and distribution of world petroleum supplies.

This commission, which was arranged during the negotiations between Richard Law, British Minister of State; Lord Beaverbrook, British Lord Privy Seal; Secretary of State Cordell Hull and Secretary of the Interior Harold Ickes, will be opened to all the other oil countries of the world and both British and American officials will seek to have other nations join the commission and do their business through it.

The agreement, negotiated in Washington during the last fortnight, takes note of Great Britain's need to acquire dollars from the sale of oil in the Middle East, and the right of Great Britain to raise the difficult question of her dwindling dollar reserves has been protected in the agreement.

Some Progress Toward Peace

The oil agreement is regarded as evidence that the Administration is making some progress from war to peace, but in the international as in the national field most observers here believe that military events are running ahead of the Government's plans.

As a result of past international conferences certain agreements have been made with the other United Nations on policies to govern the control of relief and rehabilitation, food, international currency and civil affairs in the countries now in the process of liberation.

In other fields at least tentative

Continued on Page 7

FLEET HITS CONVOY

Task Force Sinks 17 Ships, Including Five Japanese Warships

CRUISER LEFT AFIRE

U. S. Surface and Air Forces Strike Bonin, Volcano Islands

By GEORGE HORNE
By Telephone to THE NEW YORK TIMES.

PEARL HARBOR, Aug. 6—Forty-six Japanese ships and small craft were sunk or damaged on Thursday and Friday when a fast United States carrier task force caught a large convoy in the Bonin and Volcano Islands area, and slashed away at it in a continuing action for the two full days, Admiral Chester W. Nimitz announced today.

Along with these successes Admiral Nimitz told of a widespread attack by the task force the same two days on the Bonin and Volcano Islands, near Japan's front door.

Of the convoy craft at least five warships of destroyer or destroyer-escort class were sunk and several others damaged. Seventeen ships are listed as definitely sunk, six possibly sunk and more than twenty-three craft were damaged, including a number of barges, two of which were carrying troops. The convoy included cargo vessels, oilers and landing craft.

Convoy Virtually Destroyed

Admiral Nimitz said that the convoy was virtually wiped out by air and surface units of the task group. On Thursday, the 3d, planes sank four cargo ships of about 4,000 tons each, three escorting destroyers or destroyer-escorts and four barges. One cargo vessel and the balance of the escorting war craft, not identified as to type, were damaged.

That day another large destroyer, a cargo ship, one small oiler and several barges were sunk by our surface vessels. One damaged escort vessel escaped.

The next day the American sea force "continued the sweep," the admiral said. Carrier planes sank one escort vessel and two other small craft and damaged five barges including the two troop carriers, a landing craft and three smaller vessels.

One light cruiser and five small vessels were left burning and listed as possibly sunk. In addition damage was inflicted on ten small craft and a destroyer escort. A large cargo vessel which had been hit in one of the earlier attacks was struck again and two landing ships were damaged.

The carrier task force attacked enemy bases throughout the Bonin and Volcano Islands, shelling shipping and shore installations at Chichi Island and destroying Omura, a town on that island. On

Continued on Page 8

THE AMERICAN FORCES MOVE INTO THE KEY CITY OF RENNES

Vehicles passing through a narrow path left in a street by cheering citizens of the Brittany capital
Associated Press Wirephoto (U. S. Signal Corps Radiophoto)

8TH ARMY FIGHTING INSIDE OF FLORENCE

Troops Surge Over Arno Span as German Guns Shell South Part of City, Periling Art

By The United Press.

ROME, Aug. 6—Eighth Army troops crossed the Arno River on debris-littered Ponte Vecchio into the heart of Florence today and engaged enemy troops in sharp street fighting as the Germans, despite repeated assurance that Florence would be an open city, opened fire with 170-mm. guns—largest German guns in Italy—against Allied-held sectors of the great cultural center south of the river.

[The London radio, reported by the Columbia Broadcasting System, said Sunday that "Florence is virtually in our hands," but cautioned that a British Broadcasting Corporation reporter described it as "still something of a No Man's Land."

[The BBC reporter said that South African troops had thrown pontoon bridges across the river

Continued on Page 6

Urge Lend-Lease to Britain Continue After Reich Falls

By LANSING WARREN
Special to THE NEW YORK TIMES.

WASHINGTON, Aug. 6—Continuation of lend-lease aid to Britain after Germany's defeat and at least until Japan surrenders is under discussion in high Administration circles, according to a statement in The NAM News, weekly publication of the National Association of Manufacturers, appearing today.

British officials, the statement says, have told our leaders that such action is absolutely necessary to stave off a serious economic situation in England and is essential if Britain is to play the part expected of her in the Pacific war.

The proposal, it was said, would cost the United States $2,500,000,000 and up a year above war costs, and would be a wide departure from the present lend-lease program, which is primarily devoted to prosecution of the war.

What worries those in favor of the project most is how to obtain the support of Congress and also how to avoid similar claims from Russia, France, Belgium, Holland and other countries.

United States officials supporting the proposal, according to the manufacturers' publication, have

Continued on Page 16

FIGHT TO A FINISH PLEDGED BY HITLER

Nazi Party Leaders Informed at Meeting Germany Needs Man Who Won't Capitulate

Adolf Hitler told his party leaders in a meeting at his headquarters that the "criminal clique" that made the bombing attempt on his life on July 20 was "limited in numbers but important in influence," DNB, German news agency, said yesterday.

Quoting the National Socialist party organ, the Nationalsozialistische Parteikorrespondenz, DNB said Hitler told the assembled officials that "one day they would realize that this deed, which at the moment was so shameful, had perhaps been most beneficial for the whole German future," since it had made it possible to eliminate the "criminal clique" which up to then had not been uncovered.

Hitler said that since July 20 he had "gained a confidence" he had never had before and that he was now able to "carry on the struggle" better than anyone else who might lead the German people.

"Necessary to the Nation"

"I believe that I am necessary to the nation, that it needs a man who will under no circumstances capitulate," Hitler was quoted.

The meeting with the Nazi party leaders was held Friday at Hitler's headquarters, said the DNB dispatch, which was reported by the Federal Communications Commission.

Reichsleiter General Ritter von

Continued on Page 7

RUSSIANS CAPTURE HUGE OIL REFINERY

Drogobych in Galicia Yields 700,000 Tons a Year—Fight Is Severe at Warsaw

By The United Press.

LONDON, Monday, Aug. 7—Russian troops yesterday captured the great Polish oil center of Drogobych, wiping out the next to last major source of fuel for Hitler's war machine, while other Soviet forces extended their control of the Vistula River's east bank to more than 200 miles.

Drogobych, a city of 32,600 population in the Carpathian foothills forty-four miles southeast of Przemysl, was seized by troops of the Fourth Ukrainian Army, apparently under a new commander, Col. Gen. I. Y. Petroff, a hero of Novorossiisk and the Kuban bridgehead.

Its capture was announced in an order of the day issued by Premier Stalin, and it was the first time that the Fourth Ukrainian Army, last reported commanded by Gen. Feodor N. Tolbukhin, had been re-

Continued on Page 6

LE MANS NOW GOAL

One Spearhead Near Key Rail and Road Center on Way to Paris

ROUTE IS WIDE OPEN

Little Opposition Met—13 German Divisions Declared Eliminated

By E. C. DANIEL
By Cable to THE NEW YORK TIMES.

SUPREME HEADQUARTERS, Allied Expeditionary Force, Monday, Aug. 7—The American Army that overran the length and breadth of Brittany in four days has whipped its left flank eastward on two main roads directly toward Paris, shoving out one armored spearhead toward Le Mans, which dominates the rail network southwest of the French capital.

Without waiting for the completion of the conquest of Brittany, which has set a 1944 style in blitzkrieg for western Europe, Lieut. Gen. Omar N. Bradley has driven four spearheads to points as near Paris as is Caen at the northern end of the Allied battle line. The advance is being made on a forty-mile front, extending from Ambrieres la Grande, fifty-three miles northeast of Rennes, and southward through Mayenne, Laval and Château-Gontier, all of which have been occupied.

[A United Press report from the front said the Germans were retreating before the advancing American columns in "complete and utter confusion."]

Fighting in Brest

Meanwhile other American units were fighting in Brest, at and near St. Malo, had captured Vannes, between Lorient and St. Nazaire, and were pressing forward toward both those ports.

A report from the field said one American column had pressed twenty miles beyond Mayenne, while a second from Château-Gontier was said to be advancing on Le Mans, forty-two miles to the east and 110 miles from Paris. Roads from all these places converge on Le Mans, the hub of five main line railways, three of which lead to Paris.

Ahead of this drive no coordinated German defense line has yet taken shape. Behind it enough Allied infantry already has been poured into the Breton Peninsula from Normandy to hold all positions overrun by the armored columns. And the Americans are fanning out everywhere from St. Pois, in Normandy, to the mouth of the Loire River, on the southern side of Brittany, to build a firm base for their unflagging offensive.

German Position Critical

Alarmed Germans reported yesterday that Americans had driven up to Laval with "several" tank and infantry divisions "and were being constantly reinforced." In this area the Germans, faced with two evils—whether to concentrate on the Caen sector nearer Paris or on the more remote American threat in the west—apparently had been hoodwinked into making the wrong choice. A different choice might still have produced the same result in the end.

The Germans even began to inch back yesterday from those costly and assiduously dug-in positions south of Caen that they valued so highly. The Canadians, who have skillfully kept the Germans occupied southeast of Caen while the Americans were rampaging out to the west and the British were cleaning up the central sector, seized three villages yesterday.

The quick American hook toward Paris threatens to make all those positions around Caen useless to the Germans.

There seemed to be an air of expectancy here last night.

There was no doubt General Bradley was playing a fancy game for high stakes—stakes much higher than the conquest of Brittany. Every one is keeping his fingers crossed.

"My view," said a high British staff officer in Normandy last

Continued on Page 3

War News Summarized

MONDAY, AUGUST 7, 1944

Paris was the objective of four American armored spearheads that had passed a point fifty-three miles northeast of Rennes and were within 140 miles of the French capital at the nearest point after roaring through the towns of Mayenne, Laval and Chateau-Gontier yesterday. Other American troops, having overrun Brittany, were fighting in Brest and near Lorient, St. Nazaire and Nantes, all prize ports. [1:8, map P. 3.] All seven ships of a convoy thought to be evacuating German troops from St. Nazaire were sunk; another convoy was shelled back into port. [1:6-7.]

Almost 2,000 planes took off in continuing good weather from Britain and Italy to smash military installations in Germany and in the Rhône valley of France. Berlin, Hamburg and Kiel inside Germany and the submarine base at Toulon in southern France were among the targets. [4:1.]

In Italy Allied troops stormed across the Arno River into the heart of historic Florence and were engaged in street fighting with the enemy, who was bombarding Allied-held sectors of the great cultural center. [1:4.]

The Red Army seized Drogobych, a large oil refinery center in southern Poland. Other Soviet forces were battling fiercely resisting Germans east of the curving Vistula River near Warsaw. Before East Prussia the Red Army continued to move forward, but its pace was slowed by fresh German reinforcements. Berlin reports told of a German withdrawal on a wide front around Lake Peipus in Estonia. [1:6; map P. 6.]

The leaders of the Polish government in exile and the new Polish Committee of National Liberation met in Moscow for the first time to try to work out a solution for their differences over Poland's internal problems and her relations with Soviet Russia. [6:2.]

Adolf Hitler told a meeting of Nazi party leaders last Friday that Germany needed a leader who would "under no circumstances capitulate" and that he was that man. [1:7.]

The American Navy scored one of its greatest triumphs in a daring two-day assault on the Bonin and Volcano Islands on Thursday and Friday during which our planes and warships sank or damaged forty-six Japanese vessels. An entire enemy convoy was "virtually wiped out" and shore installations on the islands, which are less than 600 miles from Tokyo, were also blasted. [1:3.]

In China, Japanese forces smashed into the heart of Hengyang. In southwestern Kwangtung Province, the invaders are threatening Limkong at the base of the Hoihong Peninsula. [8:6.] The Japanese base of Tamu, forty-seven miles southeast of Imphal, fell to the Allied offensive in Burma. [8:1; map P. 8.]

High of 88° Is Recorded for Day; Millions Seek Relief at Beaches

The current heat wave tapered off slightly yesterday, with temperatures in the city ranging from one to twelve degrees below those of the previous forty-eight hours, when three local Weather Bureau records were established.

In addition light breezes and low-hanging, moisture-laden clouds that hid the sun throughout most of the day made pedestrians a bit more comfortable. The high for the day was reached at 2 P. M., when the official reading atop the Whitehall Building at 17 Battery Place was 88 degrees. At that time the reading at La Guardia Field was 85.2, the day's high there.

The Weather Bureau said that there was little likelihood that the heat wave would break in the next seventy-two hours, the extent of publishable predictions, but announced that today would continue warm and there would be a sharp drop in the amount of humidity.

The five city-operated beaches reported near-capacity crowds, but parks were virtually empty except for the lake areas of Central and Prospect Parks, where hundreds braved the heat to wait in line for boats. The Rockaways reported 1,325,000 visitors and Coney Island more than a million. Jones Beach was host to 55,000 persons, one of its largest assemblages since the war.

Although the normal for Aug. 6 is 76 degrees and the record high is 93.3, set in 1918, the mercury stood at 79 at midnight, dropped to a low of 75 at 5 A. M. and then moved slowly upward. At noon it had climbed to 85. The day's high was seven degrees less than the top for Saturday.

After 2 P. M. the temperature dropped steadily and at 10 o'clock last night was a fairly livable 77. However, the humidity, which was only 49 per cent when the high

Continued on Page 24

Seven Fleeing German Ships Sunk, Others Turn Back to St. Nazaire

By The United Press.

LONDON, Aug. 6—An entire German convoy of seven ships, possibly evacuating German troops from Brittany, was sent to the bottom early today off the Breton Peninsula by a British and Canadian cruiser and destroyer flotilla, the Admiralty announced tonight.

The convoy was steaming south from St. Nazaire, menaced by flying American armored columns, when it was surprised and brought under the guns of the British cruiser Bellona and the destroyers HMS Tartar, HMS Ashanti, HMCS Iroquois and HMCS Haida. In the ensuing action all German vessels, including the escort craft, were destroyed.

Later today another German convoy was spotted off St. Nazaire, but it hurried back into port. It was believed that the British and Canadian ships that stalked the second convoy had caused some damage the extent of which was not known.

A broadcast by DNB, German news agency, apparently referring to the first engagement, claimed that Allied bombers supported the British warships in the attack, which occurred between 3 A. M. and 5 A. M. Although the German report claimed the German vessels suffered little damage, it admitted that a number were "killed and wounded" aboard the ships.

The German broadcast said that several hits were scored on the attacking British destroyers, and the Admiralty acknowledged that "we suffered a small number of casualties."

In still another sea and air action off the French coast DNB claimed that a Nazi torpedo plane formation sank three Anglo-American destroyers in the Seine Bay, damaged two light cruisers or destroyers and scored a hit on a 14,000-ton transport.

"All the News That's Fit to Print"

The New York Times.

LATE CITY EDITION
Showers, ending before noon; clearing, cooler later today.
Temperatures Yesterday—Max., 86; Min., 69
Sunrise, 6:14 A. M.; Sunset, 7:41 P. M.

VOL. XCIII..No. 31,624. Entered as Second-Class Matter, Postoffice, New York, N. Y. NEW YORK, THURSDAY, AUGUST 24, 1944. THREE CENTS IN NEW YORK CITY

PARIS IS FREED; RUMANIA QUITS; MARSEILLE AND GRENOBLE WON; GERMAN FLIGHT NEARS A ROUT

BREAK IN BALKANS

King Proclaims Nation's Surrender and Wish to Help Allies

NAZIS IN AREA FIGHT

New Bucharest Regime Asks United Nations Aid Against Hungary

By DANIEL T. BRIGHAM
By Telephone to THE NEW YORK TIMES.

BERNE, Switzerland, Aug. 23—In a brief proclamation to the Rumanian people broadcast from Bucharest at 9:25 o'clock this evening, King Michael of Rumania ordered his armed forces to cease fire against the forces of the Allies, saying he had accepted their terms of unconditional surrender in the name of the nation.

The youthful King called on the nation to take up the fight immediately by the side of the Soviet forces on Rumanian soil against their common enemy, Germany.

Dramatic and apparently sudden as was the entire announcement the Germans were obviously forewarned, for when the home broadcast service at Bucharest interrupted its regular transmission at 9:24 P. M., within thirty seconds the two powerful Bucharest transmitters were shrouded by interference from a battery of German jammers of all varieties.

[Moscow, which broadcast the Rumanian surrender—beaming it especially to Germany—soon after the Bucharest announcement, reported later in the night that German troops were fighting Rumanian forces that were withdrawing from the Red Army front.

Bulgaria Expected to Quit

[Bulgaria's withdrawal from the war was believed to be imminent, according to reports from Cairo, which said the Allies were insisting on the return of territory seized in the war.]

King Michael, who had until recently been virtually a prisoner of the Gestapo, has overthrown the pro-Nazi dictatorship, ousting the Premier and Commander in Chief, Marshal Ion Antonescu. [The Berne radio, heard by Columbia Broadcasting System, said early Thursday that Antonescu had fled to Germany.]

He named as Chief of Government and Marshal of Rumania the master of his military household, Gen. Constantin Sanatescu. He announced a new Cabinet that constituted a Government of national union.

The new Cabinet includes Peasant party leader Juliu Maniu, as Minister of State Without Portfolio, and the leader of the Liberal party, Dinu Bratianu, in a similar post.

[Lucretiu Patrascanu, a Rumanian Communist party leader, and Constantin Petrescu, a Socialist leader, were also named Ministers of State, said a Bucharest broadcast recorded by the Federal Communications Commission.]

War With Hungary Evident

The new Rumanian Government is made up of a wide grouping of forces from the liberal, independent center to the extreme left.

King Michael's proclamation announced the denunciation by Rumania of the Treaty of Vienna of Aug. 30, 1940, by which the Nazis gave Transylvania to Hungary. It made it plain that Rumania is now at war with Hungary to recover Transylvania and seeks Allied backing in that effort.

A new Rumanian General Staff, as well as the country's political leaders, met at the King's palace,

Continued on Page 11

President Tells Delegates 'Four of Us' Can Keep Peace

Staying Friends and Meeting Often May Mean Generations Without War, He Says —Washington Studies U. S. Plan

By JAMES B. RESTON
Special to THE NEW YORK TIMES.

WASHINGTON, Aug. 23—President Roosevelt told delegates to the Washington Conversations on International Organization today that if the United States, Soviet Russia and Great Britain could maintain their new and close friendship and spread that friendship around the world "we may have a peaceful period for our grandchildren to grow up in."

Speaking informally to the delegates at the White House during a recess in their labors to draft an effective security league, Mr. Roosevelt seemed to emphasize the special responsibility of the great powers in maintaining peace, by the use of force if necessary.

"We have got to make not merely a peace but a peace that will last," the President said, "and a peace in which the larger nations will work absolutely in unison in preventing war by force. But the four of us have to be friends, conferring all the time on the basis of getting to know each other."

Although no representative of China was present, the President's reference to "the four of us" was interpreted as an indication that when Mr. Roosevelt thinks of "the great powers" he counts China as one of those nations.

It was a remarkable fact, Mr. Roosevelt said, that the great powers had attained such unanimity during the war, and he added that the hope of the future lay in the ability of the nations to perpetuate that unity for a long time to come.

"The prisoners of 17, 18, 20 that

Continued on Page 13

The text of the President's remarks is on Page 13.

FRENCH TAKE PORT

Pockets of Resistance Are Being Cleared Up in Marseille

ARMY JUNCTION SEEN

American Dash Inland Said to Have Carried to Annecy, Near Border

By The Associated Press.

ROME, Aug. 23—Marseille, France's second city and greatest seaport, fell to the swift onslaught of French infantry and armor today as American forces swept 140 miles inland from the Mediterranean and were within less than 240 miles of a junction with Gen. Dwight D. Eisenhower's legions below liberated Paris.

Only eight days after the landings in southern France the inspired Poilus battered their way into the heart of Marseille against slight resistance and tonight were cleaning out pockets of last-ditch defenders.

The unexpectedly easy capture of the great port assures the Seventh Army an adequate flow of supplies and reinforcements for speedy continuation of the thrust toward northern France. Prior to the city's fall, other French troops had cut the last escape route for the German garrison along the coast to the west.

Toulon Still Holding Out

The encircled and doomed German force in Toulon, big naval base twenty-seven miles east of Marseille, still was holding out tonight, but French troops had fought their way within a few hundred yards of the docks.

[Confirmed reports in Berne said American troops had entered Annecy, less than eighteen miles from the Swiss frontier. Radio France at Algiers said Allied patrols had reached Avig-

Continued on Page 6

HAILING THE LIBERATION OF PARIS

Lily Pons leads the gathering in Rockefeller Plaza in singing "The Marseillaise"
The New York Times

PARISIANS ROUT FOE

50,000 FFI Troops With Civilians' Aid Battle Germans 4 Days

POLICE HELP REBELS

Turn Ile de la Cite Into Fortress—Casualties Among People High

By RAYMOND DANIELL
By Cable to THE NEW YORK TIMES.

LONDON, Aug. 23—Paris is free again and, because of that, the rest of the world can breathe a little more freely. In a manner befitting a capital with the history and tradition of Paris, its own citizens rose and threw off the tyrant's yoke as soon as their own troops and the Allies' armies of liberation had given them the opportunity to challenge their conquerors on equal terms.

In leaving it to the French themselves to announce that the swastika had been lowered and the Tricolor had been raised over their own gracious and lovely capital, the Allies were following a policy that was both strategically and politically sound.

Gen. Dwight D. Eisenhower's columns were able to continue their eastward sweep unimpeded by the need for pausing to mop up, and France, which was knocked out of the war more than four years ago, was able to stand before the world on her own feet again.

Armored Division Enters

The French Second Armored Division, which fought its way across the African desert under Maj. Gen. Jacques LeClerc, seems to have been the first Allied force to enter Paris. It went in after the local leader of the FFI had concluded an armistice with the Germans, it was said here.

But before many more hours have passed, the Arc de Triomphe at the head of Champs-Elysées will be the scene of yet another pageant in the panoply of history, when the tread of victorious armies will mark the close of more than four years in which the City of Light had been the outpost of the jack-booted forces of darkness.

Paris, which began to weep but not to cringe on June 14, 1940, when the German heel first echoed in the boulevards, will laugh and sing again to welcome an army of repatriates and of allies who come not to conquer but to insure the newly won freedom.

Koenig Announces Liberation

Maj. Gen. Joseph Pierre Koenig, commander of the French Forces of the Interior, informed the world that the French people had at last chased the Germans out of their beloved capital. He gave some of the details. But the full story of what happened in Paris between Aug. 19 and today is a saga that will have to be written by many men over a long period before the whole story is told.

Tonight, however—seventy-seven days after D-Day—the world can rejoice without asking the whys and wherefores, for Paris is free again. "The Marseillaise" again is sung there, the Tricolor flies there again and the German tide is on the ebb in western Europe.

Until the newspaper correspondents now in Paris or waiting on the outskirts to get there can write their stories and transmit them, General Koenig's terse official statement will have to suffice.

A general insurrection, he said, began four days ago, when, in response to the orders of the underground leaders and the self-styled Provisional Government of France for a general uprising against the Germans, 50,000 members of the FFI armed and supported by "several hundred thousand unarmed

Continued on Page 3

RED ARMY SPEEDS DEEP INTO RUMANIA

Bendery and Akkerman Taken —Polish Plane Center Falls —Russians Near Tartu

By The Associated Press.

LONDON, Thursday, Aug. 24—The two-fisted Soviet offensive that knocked Rumania out of the war roared through its fourth day yesterday, capturing Vaslui, 140 miles northeast of the Ploesti oil center, and toppling the two big Bessarabian bastions of Bendery and Akkerman on the west bank of the Dniester, besides more than 400 other towns.

Disregarding developments on the political front, at least for the present, the Second and Third Ukrainian Armies deepened to as much as sixty miles the holes they have ripped in the German-Rumanian defenses and advanced within 167 miles of the capital city of Bucharest.

Rumania still was garrisoned with thousands of German troops, and the Russians were likely to continue their lightning campaign to drive the Nazis entirely out of the country, regardless of what the Rumanian troops chose to do.

While this campaign was bearing its first great fruits in Rumanian surrender, the First Ukrainian Army of Marshal Ivan S. Koneff in southern Poland lashed out westward and seized the city of Debica, a large aircraft industry center and communications point sixty-four miles east of Cracow and nineteen miles east of Tarnow, next

Continued on Page 10

47 RAILROADS SUED AS WESTERN TRUST

J. P. Morgan & Co., Kuhn-Loeb and Two Associations Accused of Conspiracy

By LEWIS WOOD
Special to THE NEW YORK TIMES.

WASHINGTON, Aug. 23—In a civil suit filed at Lincoln, Neb., today major railroad interests of the United States were accused by the Federal Government of violating the Sherman Anti-Trust Act by collusive rate-fixing and discouraging improvements in service and equipment in the western part of the country.

The Department of Justice made these charges against the American Association of Railroads, its officers and directors; the Western Association of Railway Executives; J. P. Morgan & Co., Inc.; Kuhn, Loeb & Co.; forty-seven railroads and their chief executives, and thirty-one other individuals.

Attorney General Francis Biddle, now on the Pacific Coast, announced the action here through Wendell Berge, assistant Attorney General, in charge of anti-trust prosecutions.

In a forty-page complaint, the Government charged that a "combination of private financial, industrial and railroad interests have acted collusively to maintain noncompetitive rates for transportation and to prevent and retard improvements in the services and facilities of railroads for the western part of the United States. (They) have retarded and suppressed the development and growth of the

Continued on Page 20

GRIMNESS TINGES JOY OF FRENCH HERE

Concern for Kin and Thoughts of Tasks Ahead Mingle With Jubilation Over Paris

By MEYER BERGER

The French in New York City celebrated the liberation of Paris yesterday with impressive restraint. They sang "La Marseillaise" while ticker tape and handmade confetti danced above them in the sun, but hearts were still weighed down by worry over kin from whom they have not heard for years.

A few left the streets for quiet French churches to thank God for

Continued on Page 5

French Armored Division Sent Into Paris by Bradley

The following dispatch by a representative of the Columbia Broadcasting System, the first American correspondent to enter Paris, was cabled to London and broadcast from there.

By CHARLES COLLINGWOOD

PARIS, Aug. 23—The French Second Armored Division entered Paris today after the Parisians had risen as one man to beat down the German troops who had garrisoned the city.

It was the people of Paris who really won back their city. It all happened with fantastic suddenness.

The American Army was occupied with the drive through Evreux to the mouth of the Seine, after which it planned to invest Paris. But yesterday a Frenchman burst into Lieut. Gen. Omar N. Bradley's headquarters. He was the chief of the French Forces of the Interior in Paris and he had a staggering, incredible story to tell.

He said that he had concluded an armistice with the German forces in Paris. The people of Paris had risen and had so hounded the Germans that the German commander had requested an armistice. He wanted to withdraw troops from the road blocks west and south of Paris, where they had been facing the Americans, and pass them through the city.

The armistice was to expire at noon today.

This news caused a sensation in General Bradley's headquarters because, although we had known that rioting had been going on in Paris since Saturday, we had not known that things had gone so far that obviously the French had given the Germans a terrific beating.

The whole operation was geared to the complete encirclement of the

Continued on Page 5

ENEMY FLEES 'KILL' BY ALLIES AT SEINE

Americans Drive North, British Near Le Havre—3d Army Rolls Toward Troyes

By DREW MIDDLETON

SUPREME HEADQUARTERS, Allied Expeditionary Force, Thursday, Aug. 24—The last German army south of the Seine River and west of Paris is being destroyed.

The American forces thrusting along the south bank of the Seine have taken Evreux and smashed on more than seven miles, while the British and Canadian troops on the left and center of the Allies' line are hammering the Germans back into a pocket south of Le Havre and Rouen. Two hundred miles to the east, the American column at the nose of the Third Army's salient is rolling eastward toward Troyes, on the road to Germany, in a bold operation that threatens to cut off all southern France from reinforcement from Germany.

It is estimated that almost 90,-

Continued on Page 4

War News Summarized

THURSDAY, AUGUST 24, 1944

Germany sustained a double blow yesterday when the citizens of Paris threw out the invaders and Rumania deserted the Axis to join with the United Nations.

The liberation of the French capital came after four days of hard fighting. Some 50,000 French resistance troops, supported by large bodies of unarmed civilians, had risen on signal from underground leaders. The Paris police, who had previously gone on strike, seized strategic centers. Generals Eisenhower and Patton kept their men from entering the city while the French people went about the job of creating another Bastille Day. [1:8; map, P. 2.]

King Michael proclaimed the immediate end of the war for Rumania as an Axis satellite and the joining of his country with the Allies against Germany. He ousted the Antonescu dictatorship, said armistice terms had been accepted and formed a new Government to conclude peace with the United Nations immediately. [1:1.]

Bulgaria was expected soon to follow Rumania out of the war. The Allies were reported to have demanded Bulgaria's evacuation of all territory seized in Yugoslavia and Greece and withdrawal to pre-war boundaries. [10:1.] Prime Minister Churchill planned with officials of the Greek Government in Exile that country's future military activities. [10:5.] Nothing was heard from Hungary or Finland.

Meanwhile Allied armies continued to roll through France. Marseille and Grenoble were liberated, most of Toulon had been taken, Lyon was threatened and American troops were reported in Annecy, less than twenty miles from the Swiss frontier. [1:4; map P. 6.] In northern France the Germans south of the Seine were being rapidly destroyed and herded into a pocket south of Le Havre and Rouen. The American Third Army was nearing Troyes. [1:7; map P. 4.]

Italian-based Allied planes smashed the Vienna area for the second straight day, meeting heavy opposition. Medium bombers flew deep into France to attack targets around Lyon. [8:4.]

Russian successes were reported from all fronts. The Red Army was only four miles from Tartu and eight miles from Lomzha. In the Rumanian sector they brought both points of a great pincers to within thirty-five miles of closing. [1:2, map P. 10.] The only victory Berlin could announce was the heaviest dawn barrage of flying bombs yet to strike England. [9:1.]

Allied bombers in the Pacific virtually wiped out a Japanese convoy off the Bonins and struck Davao, in the Philippines. [1:6-7.] The Japanese Premier warned his people that the United States was planning an invasion of the home islands. [11:1.]

President Roosevelt told delegates to the Dumbarton Oaks conference that "we have got to make a peace that will last" so that "we may have a peaceful period for our grandchildren to grow up in." [1:2-3.] Wendell Willkie has urged Republicans to support the State Department's proposal to permit the use of American military forces without prior approval of Congress and to approve a security organization at once, apart from the peace treaties. [1:2-3.]

Willkie Would Empower President To Use U. S. Forces to Keep Peace

By LEO EGAN

In a series of talks in the last week and a half with Republican Senators and Representatives who have sought his views with respect to the international conference at Dumbarton Oaks, Wendell L. Willkie, it was learned yesterday, has been urging Republican support for the proposal to give the President power to use the military forces of the United States, without the prior approval of Congress, in fulfillment of American obligations to any international organization set up to preserve peace.

Mr. Willkie's advice on this score has been coupled with two other suggestions as to Republican policy: 1. That the party insist that the organic structure of an international security organization be established and American participation therein approved at once, without waiting for the treaties formally ending the present conflict; and, 2, that it insist upon the fullest possible information and discussion of all proposals considered at the Dumbarton Oaks Conference and that it take the lead in developing a body of public opinion within the United States favorable to American participation in international peace machinery.

As to the form that an international security organization should take, Mr. Willkie's views, as con-

Continued on Page 13

U. S. Bombers Set Davao Aflame In Stepped-Up Philippines Blow

By The Associated Press.

GENERAL HEADQUARTERS, Southwest Pacific, Thursday, Aug. 24—Striking into the southern Philippines for the tenth time in two weeks United States Navy Liberators touched off towering fires at Davao and sank a small Japanese freighter northeast of Mindanao, headquarters reported today.

Five other enemy vessels, one a destroyer tender, were hit in raids ranging from Celebes, south of Mindanao, to Palau in the Caroline Islands north of New Guinea.

[On Wednesday Pearl Harbor reported the sinking of two Japanese cargo ships caught in a convoy by Navy bombers near Chichi, in the Bonin Islands.]

Air patrols bombed Palau Monday night, setting fires and explosions, and returned Tuesday to attack the destroyer tender and leave it dead in the water. Two enemy fighters ineffectively attempted interception, the only aerial interference reported in the raids listed today.

Near Celebes, patrol planes sank or badly damaged a small freighter and three coastal vessels on Tuesday.

In the ten raids in the southern Philippines announced since Aug. 7, the planes have bombed Davao airdromes and waterfront four times and have sunk three ships and damaged five.

Continuing aerial assaults

Continued on Page 11

"All the News That's Fit to Print"

The New York Times.

LATE CITY EDITION
Fair today and tomorrow with mild afternoons and cool nights.
Temperatures Yesterday—Max., 75; Min., 55
Sunrise, 6:16 A. M.; Sunset, 7:38 P. M.

VOL. XCIII..No. 31,626. Entered as Second-Class Matter, Postoffice, New York, N. Y. NEW YORK, SATURDAY, AUGUST 26, 1944. THREE CENTS IN NEW YORK CITY

ALLIES SWEEP TO TROYES, NAZI ROUT GROWS; GERMAN COMMANDER SURRENDERS IN PARIS; RUMANIA DECLARES WAR, BULGARIA TO QUIT

NELSON UNDER FIRE OF BRADLEY DEWEY; WPB POST IN DOUBT

Former Head of Rubber Agency Defends Program, Accuses Nelson of 'Sniping'

ISSUE PUT TO PRESIDENT

Question of Production Chief's Future Is 'Iffy,' He Says —Krug Takes Firm Hold

By CHARLES E. EGAN
Special to THE NEW YORK TIMES.

WASHINGTON, Aug. 25—The question whether Donald M. Nelson will resume his chairmanship of the War Production Board on his return from a special mission to China for President Roosevelt was raised today when the President told his press conference that he did not know whether Mr. Nelson would resume his duties at that time.

The President's statement came soon after Mr. Nelson departed on the first leg of his China journey and the day after the chairman had apparently won a fight with his executive vice chairman, Charles E. Wilson, who resigned yesterday after charging that his usefulness was being impaired by attacks from Mr. Nelson's staff. It supplied another surprising development in the explosive situation which had developed in the WPB over reconversion.

While official Washington speculated whether the President had a more important job than WPB head in prospect for Mr. Nelson or whether the war agency chairman was to be "let out" along with his first assistant, Mr. Nelson came under fire from another quarter when Col. Bradley Dewey, retiring rubber director, accused him of engaging "in typical Washington sniping" at the rubber director's office.

Dewey Takes Issue on Rubber

Colonel Dewey referred to the testimony given by Mr. Nelson before a closed session of the Senate's committee investigating national defense as the type "that has made many good Americans unwilling to give services that otherwise would be of value to the country and to the conduct of the war."

Mr. Nelson had testified that the rubber program was completed, "all but getting the tires." Questioned about Colonel Dewey's then-recent resignation, Mr. Nelson said that to call the rubber program completed would be "like the Army saying they are completed except for the shooting."

Colonel Dewey told reporters that he had never said the task of providing tires was completed, but rather that the synthetic rubber plants were turning out rubber in surplus.

The problem of providing manpower and tire cords no longer required the special powers which were reposed in the Office of Defense Rubber, Colonel Dewey added.

Krug Demands End of Sniping

"These powers are of no value to the problem of manning the plants and providing the much-needed tires," he concluded. "By Presidential directive these were and are the responsibilities of the WPB and of the War Manpower Commission."

J. A. Krug, who was named yesterday by President Roosevelt as acting chairman of the WPB in the absence of Mr. Nelson, took over the reins today. He called the vice chairmen of the agency into conference this afternoon, and, according to reports, told them that he received a clear grant of authority to run the WPB and "get it back on the track."

He warned the officials that he intended that fights within WPB should end and that he would "fire" anyone who engaged in the future in internal disputes.

Mr. Krug told reporters later

Continued on Page 24

Must Post Ceilings For Diners Monday

The Regional Office of Price Administration reminded restaurant managements yesterday that they have until Monday to file a list of forty food items and the ceiling prices they are required to post on their premises. The list in triplicate must be filed with local war price and rationing boards.

The new OPA national restaurant regulations require the posting of the forty food items and the ceiling prices. Restaurants violating the provisions of the regulation face enforcement action, OPA attachés pointed out. Each list filed by a restaurant will be compared with menus of May, 1943, and, upon approval, a copy of the list, bearing an official stamp to show approval, will be returned to the restaurant owner.

OWN MEN AT FRONT APPEAL TO LABOR

AFL and CIO Leaders in France Link War Supply Shortages to 'Our Quarrels at Home'

By SIDNEY SHALETT
Special to THE NEW YORK TIMES.

WASHINGTON, Aug. 25—"We cannot let the men whose lives depend on this equipment pay the price for our quarrels at home," six American labor leaders who are visiting the French battlefields under War Department sponsorship have declared in a message sent back here to their unions.

The message was transmitted through the War Department to William Green, president of the American Federation of Labor, and Philip Murray, head of the Congress of Industrial Organizations.

"Consciousness of the partnership that exists between the fighting fronts and the factory," it read, "the War Department has made it possible for us to travel through the battle areas and see at first hand how our soldiers are using the weapons and equipment made by American labor.

Need of Supplies to Save Lives

"As we travel along roads lined with the wreckage of American and German equipment and pass through shattered French cities and, above all, as we pause at military cemeteries and hospitals that are all too plentiful here, we are struck more forcibly than ever before with the horrible destructiveness of modern war and the importance of superior supplies in cutting down the toll of our dead and wounded.

"We are filled with pride for our Army. Its combat efficiency and morale are high. It is well-staffed and well-manned—an Army representative in the highest sense of our great American democracy.

"Everybody knows his job—from generals to privates—and we are determined to get ourselves to the job of finishing this war with the same single-minded determination as the men at the front.

"We do not know whether the war will last a short time or a long

Continued on Page 24

RED ARMY RACES ON

Russians Attack Galati Gap and Encircle 12 German Divisions

REACH DANUBE DELTA

205,000 Enemy Troops Killed or Taken in Six Days—Tartu Seized

By The Associated Press.

LONDON, Saturday, Aug. 26—Two Russian armies racing toward the heart of Rumania at a better than a mile-an-hour clip yesterday reached the Galati Gap defenses at Tecuci and also drove a spearhead down to the Danube River delta at Kiliya in a six-day whirlwind offensive that Moscow announced had cost the enemy nearly 205,000 in killed or captured.

In perhaps the greatest defeat yet inflicted on the Axis in a comparable period, the Russians also announced they had encircled twelve German divisions of upward of 60,000 men southwest of fallen Kishinev, provincial capital of Bessarabia. Thirteen thousand Germans already have surrendered in two days, and the remainder are being annihilated, said the Moscow broadcast bulletin.

Thousands of Rumanians were abandoning the struggle against the Russians and turning to fight the Germans, dispatches said, as the Second and Third Ukrainian Armies under General Rodion Y. Malinovsky and Feodor I. Tolbukhin linked up for a quick drive on Bucharest, within 113 miles of Soviet columns that seized Tecuci on the Barlad River.

Danube Delta Reached

A total of 550 towns and villages were swept up by the two armies, and the capture of Tecuci found the Russians within ninety miles northeast of the Ploesti oil wells. General Malinovsky's troops now were at the Galati Gap, a forty-five-mile stretch of defenses prepared along the Putna, Siret and Barlad Rivers just above where those streams empty into the Danube.

To the southeast, a Soviet communiqué said, the Russians had captured Kiliya on the Danube, fifteen miles west of the Black Sea port of Vilkov at the mouth of the delta, and twenty-two miles east of the port of Ismail. General Tolbukhin's Third Army seized that point. To the northwest his troops reached the Prut River on a seventy-mile front between captured Leusheny and Kagul, the latter being thirty miles northeast of the river's confluence and rail junction of Galati. The capture of Gasanbatyr put the Russians thirty miles from the port of Ismail on the northeast.

Soviet aircraft added to the slaughter by attacking Axis military trains at Galati, the supplementary communiqué said.

In six days the Russians have captured nearly all of lower Bessa-

Continued on Page 6

ALLY FIGHTS REICH

Nazis' Bombers Attack Bucharest—City Held Cleared of Germans

FIGHTING CONTINUES

Bulgaria Called Willing to Surrender to Allies Unconditionally

By SIDNEY GRUSON
By Cable to THE NEW YORK TIMES.

LONDON, Aug. 25—The new Rumanian Government, after having denounced German perfidy tonight, openly declared war on the Reich, thereby fulfilling a Russian prerequisite for acceptance of the Rumanian offer to change to the Allied side.

The United States and Great Britain, moreover, have received word from Bulgaria that she is ready to accept unconditional surrender terms. The western allies, it was learned tonight, are now filling in details of the terms. The Rumanian declaration of war came after the Nazis, according to a proclamation broadcast by the Bucharest radio, had bombed the capital heavily and German units had attacked Rumanian forces and machine-gunned civilians of Bucharest and of other places.

Nazis' Plight Called Hopeless

"By these acts of aggression, which occurred simultaneously in various parts of the country, Germany has placed herself in a state of war with Rumania," the proclamation declared. "The Government therefore orders the Rumanian Army to begin the struggle against all German military forces on Rumanian territory for the liberation of the country from German usurpation."

The Germans themselves have acknowledged their position in Rumania as being hopeless. The Nazi-controlled Scandinavian News Service said that encircled German units were trying to break through the Russian lines toward the Carpathians and Transylvania to fight their way to Hungary.

The German "Danube" radio station appealed to the Rumanian Army tonight to "refuse to fight against your former allies." But the appeal was falling on deaf ears, for the Bucharest radio shortly before had declared that the capital had been completely

Continued on Page 3

PARISIANS CELEBRATE ARRIVAL OF ALLIES

Patriots crowding around a jeep after its arrival in the French capital yesterday. This picture, one of the first to be taken inside the city, was sent from the new transmitting station set up in Cherbourg.

The New York Times (U. S. Signal Corps Radiotelephoto)

JAPANESE CRUISER FIRED BY U.S. FLIERS

Mast-Head Strike at Manado Also Smashes 7 Freighters —40 Barges Riddled

By FRANK L. KLUCKHOHN
By Cable to THE NEW YORK TIMES.

ALLIED HEADQUARTERS IN AUSTRALIA, Aug. 25—A Japanese cruiser and seven Japanese freighters were sunk or severely damaged and forty barges and luggers were shot up as a force of fewer than twenty-five of Gen. Douglas MacArthur's Liberators made a surprise low-level attack yesterday on Manado, in Netherland Celebes, which is the enemy supply point for Halmahera.

The Mitchells braved heavy ack-

Continued on Page 6

Allied Forces Help French To Rid Capital of Nazis

By The Associated Press.

SUPREME HEADQUARTERS, Allied Expeditionary Force, Aug. 25—The Paris radio announced late tonight that the French capital had been liberated and that the German commander had signed a document ordering his troops to cease fire immediately.

The announcement followed entry of American and French troops into the capital during the day. There was no immediate confirmation here.

The latest word at headquarters was that American and French troops had joined Fighting French patriots on the Ile de la Cité in the heart of the capital after bitter fighting with Germans and French collaborationist militiamen.

Gen. Charles de Gaulle, President of the French Committee of National Liberation, said in a speech broadcast from Paris:

"France will take her place among the great nations which will organize the peace. We will not rest until we march, as we must, into enemy territory as conquerors."

The commander of the Paris region for the French Forces of the Interior, Colonel Raoul, issued this proclamation to his forces, the radio said:

"FFI of the Ile de France (the Paris region), you have unleashed a rising that has liberated Paris. You have improvised your tactics, animated by the strong desire to win, and you have won."

In another broadcast the Paris radio said that the German com-

Continued on Page 5

AMERICANS SEIZE CANNES, PUSH EAST

Drive to 20 Miles From Italy, Spear Along Rhone—Lyon Is Reported in Patriots' Hands

By The Associated Press.

ROME, Aug. 25—American troops lunging suddenly eastward from their Riviera beachhead, in southern France, have captured the famous resort towns of Cannes and Antibes and tonight were fighting forward less than twenty miles from the Italian frontier.

Nice, within short artillery range of the advancing Americans, was expected to fall at any hour.

Other swift Allied columns drove methodically toward the heart of France and a junction with Gen. Dwight D. Eisenhower's armies in the north. Tonight's communiqué said forces probing into the delta of the Rhône valley were close to

Continued on Page 3

War News Summarized

SATURDAY, AUGUST 26, 1944

American forces in northern France entered Troyes, 130 miles from the German frontier, as Allied armies continued yesterday to move forward along a 200-mile front. Our bridgeheads across the Seine south of Paris were widened. The enemy was driven from Montereau, ten miles east of Fontainebleau and was in hurried retreat from the area northeast of Montargis. Far to the northwest, the remnants of the German Seventh Army, trapped with their backs to the Seine, were being driven into the river. [1:8; map P. 4.]

As the famous spire of the Eiffel Tower pierced an early morning fog, French and American forces smashed through to the heart of Paris amid a tumultuous welcome. The Free Paris radio reported that the German commander of the city had surrendered. [1:6-7; map P. 5.]

In southern France, Allied troops captured Cannes and Antibes and stood less than twenty miles from the Italian frontier. Other Allied columns were reported closing in on Lyon, Rhône Valley industrial center 170 miles inland from the Mediterranean, and French patriots were said to be in control of the city. [1:7; map P. 2.]

General de Gaulle—who is in Paris—and his committee will have a greater part in the administration of civil affairs in France by new agreements. [5:1.]

More than 3,000 planes from Britain and Italy ranged over Czechoslovakia and Germany, pounding aircraft plants, airfields and experimental and research centers for Hitler's flying bombs and other new weapons of destruction. [4:6.]

The Red Army has reached the Galati Gap, a forty-five-mile path between the Danube delta and the mountains to the west, and seized Tecuci, a railway junction within that gateway to the Balkan plains. Twelve enemy divisions have been encircled southwest of Kishinev. Moscow also reported the capture of the key city of Tartu on the Riga-Tallinn railroad in Estonia in the Russian drive to wipe out two German Baltic armies. [1:3; map, P. 6.]

Chaos mounted in the Balkans. After German planes had bombed the Rumanian capital, Bucharest radio went on the air to proclaim that King Michael's new pro-Ally Government was at war with Germany. Rumanians were battling Hungarians as well as Germans. [1:4.] The Russian sweep led Bulgaria to send word to the Allies that she was ready for unconditional surrender. [6:1.]

Allied planes set a Japanese cruiser ablaze and sank or damaged seven enemy freighters near Celebes, an important Japanese supply center for Halmahera Island. [1:5.]

Army Rules Roosevelt Address Was Political, Then Denies It

Special to THE NEW YORK TIMES.

WASHINGTON, Aug. 25—The War Department changed its mind today on whether President Roosevelt's speech at Bremerton, Wash., on Aug. 12 was "political," holding first that it was and several hours later reversing itself to hold that it was "not political."

The issue was raised by the Socialist party, which applied to the War Department for equal radio time to address fighting men overseas on the grounds that the President's Bremerton speech, in which he mainly reviewed his trip to Hawaii and the Aleutians, was "political."

Under Title 5 of the Service Men's Voting Law, the Socialists contended, they were entitled to equal time on the air. Earlier this week the War Department had announced that, under an interpretation of the statute, the Democratic, Republican, Socialist and Prohibition parties would have equal recognition for any political radio time.

Under the first ruling by the War Department today the Socialist party was granted equal time to that of the President to address the men overseas.

"The War Department," said a memorandum issued in reply to press inquiries, "has indicated to the Socialist party that, under the statute, it will accede to this request. The other major political parties have asked for and have been furnished copies of the correspondence between the War De-

Continued on Page 9

Dulles Indicates Republican Idea Is to Cooperate, Yet Criticize

By JAMES B. RESTON
Special to THE NEW YORK TIMES.

WASHINGTON, Aug. 25—Apparently the Republican party will try to lift the specific question of American participation in a world security organization out of party politics in the Presidential campaign, but there will be no moratorium on discussion of the Administration's conduct of foreign policy as a whole.

This seemed clear today at the close of the first phase of the discussion between Secretary Hull and John Foster Dulles, Governor Dewey's representative on foreign affairs, who issued a joint statement which indicated that they had not reached complete agreement on the subject of how to discuss foreign policy during the campaign nor complete agreement on the American security plan now before the Dumbarton Oaks Security Conference.

Mr. Dulles told reporters that he hoped the two major parties could reach an agreement on the American security plan now being discussed at the Dumbarton Oaks conversations and he added that he would see Mr. Hull again to that end, but he indicated that no complete agreement had been reached as yet and emphasized that the Republicans would retain their right to criticize freely the Administration's past conduct of foreign relations.

The joint statement by Secre-

Continued on Page 24

THIRD NEAR MARNE

Berlin Says Americans Have Driven to Reims, 80 Miles Above Paris

SEINE FOE CRUSHED

River Becomes a Scene of Carnage as Bombs Rain on Germans

By DREW MIDDLETON
By Cable to THE NEW YORK TIMES.

SUPREME HEADQUARTERS, Allied Expeditionary Force, Saturday, Aug. 26—Three resounding victories were won along the 200-mile-long front in northern France yesterday.

Armored patrols of the United States Third Army rumbled into Troyes, a great road and railroad center 130 miles from the German frontier as the thrust eastward on the extreme right flank of the Allies' line broke through German offensive positions in front of Troyes, thirty-seven miles from the Marne River.

Bridgeheads across the Seine south of Paris were widened, and the enemy was driven from Montereau, ten miles east of Fontainebleau, and was retreating hurriedly from the area northeast of Montargis, taken by other American forces late Thursday.

Report Reims Reached

An unconfirmed report, published in The London Chronicle, said the Germans declared that American troops had reached Reims, eighty miles northeast of Paris.

French and American troops penetrated into the center of Paris yesterday.

Aside from its tremendous effect on French morale, the Allies' occupation of Paris, the most important communications center in France, is a military triumph of first magnitude.

Finally, far to the west, British, American and Canadian forces were driving the remnants of the German Seventh Army pell-mell into the Seine. The Elbeuf pocket replaced Falaise as a graveyard. Enemy forces are now contained in an area less than 300 miles square, with the Seine to the east and north and the Risle to the west and the steadily advancing Allied line to the south.

Planes Batter Fleeing Foe

While field guns and tanks searched the forests for fleeing Germans, hundreds of medium and light fighter bombers scourged the Germans seeking to escape across the Seine.

The battle has become a race for Seine crossings, with Allied forces confident they will have killed, wounded or captured at least 40,000 of the Germans before they reach the Seine.

As ground forces drove the Germans to the Seine, American and British light naval craft, attacking German ships leaving Le Havre, blew up an escort vessel, an armed trawler and a German E-boat and damaged at least five other craft.

Between 3 and 4 o'clock yester-

Continued on Page 4

Von Kluge Killed, Stockholm Hears

By The Associated Press.

STOCKHOLM, Saturday, Aug. 26—Field Marshal Gen. Guenther von Kluge has been killed, the newspaper Dagens Nyheter said today on the basis of information received from Germany.

Circumstances of his reported death were not known here and the newspaper had no additional details.

[There was no immediate confirmation of this report in either Axis or Allied official quarters.]

Von Kluge, 61 years old, had held command of the German armies on the western front since July 6, when he succeeded Field Marshal Gen. Karl von Rundstedt.

"All the News That's Fit to Print"

The New York Times.

LATE CITY EDITION
Clear in morning, becoming partly cloudy and rath.r warm later.
Temperatures Yesterday—Max., 80; Min., 67
Sunrise, 6:38 A. M.; Sunset, 7:02 P. M.

Section 1

NEWS INDEX, PAGE 43, THIS SECTION

Copyright, 1944, by The New York Times Company.

VOL. XCIII...No. 31,648. Entered as Second-Class Matter, Postoffice, New York, N. Y. NEW YORK, SUNDAY, SEPTEMBER 17, 1944. Including Magazine and Book Sections. TEN CENTS New York City and Suburban Area (15c Elsewhere)

ROOSEVELT AND CHURCHILL PLEDGE QUICK SHIFT OF FORCES TO CRUSH 'BARBARIANS OF PACIFIC'; AMERICANS WIDEN BREACH IN THE SIEGFRIED LINE

U.S. BUILDING CURBS EASED TO RELIEVE HOUSING SHORTAGE

New WPB Order Permits Wide Apartment Remodeling in All Areas Lacking Homes

CITY TO BE SO CLASSIFIED

Thousands of New Suites in a Few Months Seen as Builders Prepare to Rush Work

By LEE E. COOPER

Federal officials opened the way yesterday for widespread remodeling of large apartments and outmoded tenements under a liberalized wartime program that is expected to help materially in relieving the critical housing shortage in New York.

The New York Regional Office of the War Production Board reported that it had received word from Washington of a joint announcement by the WPB and the National Housing Agency designed to provide housing relief in congested areas.

Under this revised plan the WPB will cooperate by granting priorities for conversion work in communities where the NHA decrees that "an extreme housing shortage" exists. For this purpose the H-3 program has been amended to permit an almost unlimited amount of housing conversions and remodeling, and without any cost limitation on an individual project. H-3 authorizations heretofore have been limited strictly to extreme hardship or emergency cases, such as where a man's house was badly damaged by fire or storm.

Order Expected Today

No work can be carried out under the amended policy unless a district is specified as a critical area. It was learned from an authoritative source that Charles S. Ascher, head of the NHA for the New York region, would act at once to put New York in this category. He is known to have favored the revised procedure to provide additional housing units quickly in this city, and an order to that effect is expected from him today.

A wave of housing improvements here is predicted by builders and realty men as a result of the liberalized program. Realty boards, the Building Trades Employers Association, building trades unions and other groups have joined in pleas to the WPB, the NHA and the Federal Housing Administration for permission to carry out remodeling work to meet the need for additional living quarters here. The petitions have declared that thousands of new suites would be created within a matter of months if the wartime restrictions were relaxed.

Most of these groups had suggested liberalization of the L-41 order, which limits structural changes in an apartment building to $1,000 annually, or in a private home to $200, unless an authorization for additional work is given by the Federal agencies. Virtually no such authorizations were being issued here and civilian residential construction activity has been at a standstill while a considerable amount of work in store and loft buildings has been going forward under a separate category with "industrial" authorizations.

Must Provide More Homes

The WPB made it clear that these limits on residential building changes still apply through L-41, as do former provisions for maintenance and repairs. The change involves only the H-3 order under which conversion work and renovations to provide additional home units are permitted. FHA approval is mandatory for this type of construction and applications must be filed with that agency, which is a unit of the

Continued on Page 34

Priorities Offered For Storm Repairs

Special to The New York Times.

WASHINGTON, Sept. 16—Every effort to make available lumber and all other building materials needed to repair damage caused by this week's hurricane will be made by War Production Board officials, it was stated here today.

The Facilities Bureau of WPB, which passes on applications for materials made by the Federal Housing Administration and by the War Food Administration (which handles applications from farmers) is prepared to give special priorities to those Atlantic Coast residents whose homes or farm buildings were wrecked or damaged by the high winds.

Jesse Jones, Secretary of Commerce, today announced that the Reconstruction Finance Corporation loan agencies at Charlotte, Richmond, Philadelphia, New York and Boston, have been instructed to give particular attention to disaster loans in those areas.

DEWEY CABINET JOB PLEDGED FAR-WEST

Governor Says New Deal Has Neglected Area and That His Party Will Aid Vast Growth

By WARREN MOSCOW
Special to The New York Times.

SPOKANE, Wash., Sept. 16 — Governor Dewey came to the Pacific Northwest today, to promise its people special consideration of its problems and a post in the national Cabinet, and to express his own faith in the frontiers of the country which he asserts the New Deal has disowned.

At the same time, in a press conference on his arrival here, he discussed the power distribution problem of the Pacific Northwest in such a way as to indicate that he was against straight Federal distribution of power produced at the great dams of Bonneville, Grand Coulee and their future rivals, but favored local option on the subject.

"I have always believed," said Mr. Dewey, "that the great natural resources must be developed by the Federal Government for the benefit of the people. I have always felt that way about the Niagara and the St. Lawrence, and have been enthusiastic about Bonneville."

He was asked his views on power distribution, the big political problem of the area. Mr. Dewey's answer was:

"That is a matter up to the local community. The Federal Government should distribute it at the bus bar in accordance with the wishes of the local community, so that the greatest advantage would be obtained from it in accordance with the desires of the people."

"You mean no Federal distribution?" he was asked.

"My answer speaks for itself," said the candidate.

The press conference was the

Continued on Page 40

FOE IS NEAR PANIC

German Civilians Flee, With First Army 28 Miles From Cologne

PATTON SMASHES ON

British, Canadians Also Drive Forward—Patch Pushes Near Belfort

By DREW MIDDLETON
By Cable to The New York Times.

SUPREME HEADQUARTERS, Allied Expeditionary Force, Sunday, Sept. 17—German civilians were streaming eastward across the Rhine yesterday as the American breach in the Siegfried Line was widened and extended by veteran armored divisions of Lieut. Gen. Courtney H. Hodges' American First Army. The whole Allied front from the North Sea to Switzerland was rolling forward. Lieut. Gen. George S. Patton's Third Army was smashing toward Germany east of Metz and Nancy after having won half a dozen grim battles, and the Canadian First and British Second Armies were pushing northward over the Netherland border, driving stubborn German rear guards before them.

Defenses Breaking Up

The German organization for the defense of the Siegfried Line was breaking under the test imposed upon it by Lieut. Gen. Omar N. Bradley. Confused by American attacks in a half dozen places the enemy has not been able to husband enough men to check the main drive east of Aachen. The elastic defense that depends on extreme mobility for defenders is impossible to the numerically inferior German units fighting gamely but vainly in the outmoded fortifications of the Siegfried Line.

Two new forces arrived on the German frontier yesterday and are probably across it by now. The Germans reported that an American armored column had crossed to the eastern bank of the Sauer River on the Luxembourg-German frontier north of Echternacht, which is approximately seven and a half miles northwest of Trier in Germany, where another American column was already operating.

Latest reports from the front said these troops were only 500 yards from the German frontier and were driving through trenches dug only five days ago. The last village west of the German frontier in this area was stormed by the onrushing Americans.

North of the main penetration east of Aachen front line reports said a First Army column had crossed the Meuse-Schelde Canal north of Mechelen and was approaching the Roer River.

Shells Pummel Aachen

There was heavy fighting in Aachen, where German soldiers were fighting a desperate rear-guard action from house to house,

Continued on Page 12

AFTER REACHING DECISIONS ON THE WAR IN EUROPE AND THE PACIFIC

Allied leaders in Quebec yesterday at the conclusion of their talks. Front, left to right: Gen. George C. Marshall, Chief of Staff of the United States Army; Admiral William D. Leahy, Chief of Staff to the President; President Roosevelt; Prime Minister Churchill; British Field Marshal Sir Alan Brooke and British Field Marshal Sir John Dill. Rear, left to right: British Maj. Gen. Hollis, British Lieut. Gen. Sir Hastings Ismay, Admiral Ernest J. King, Commander in Chief, United States Fleet; British Air Marshal Sir Charles Portal, Gen. H. H. Arnold, Chief of the United States Army Air Forces, and British Admiral Sir Andrew B. Cunningham.

Associated Press Wirephoto

MAGINOT LINE GUNS FIRED AT GERMANS

Americans Solve Technical Problems and Then Batter Enemy Across Moselle

By FREDERICK GRAHAM
By Wireless to The New York Times.

ALONG THE MOSELLE RIVER, in France, Sept. 16—Fed up with taking shelling by German artillery, a cannon company of a famous infantry division manned German guns installed in a Maginot Line fort on the west bank of the Moselle facing Thionville today and gave both the German gun positions and the dug-in soldiers

Continued on Page 14

Red Army in Bulgar Capital, Widens Gains Near Warsaw

By The Associated Press.

LONDON, Sunday, Sept. 17—Red Army troops yesterday pushed through the capitulated Bulgarian capital of Sofia in their drive toward Yugoslavia, only thirty miles beyond, while other Soviet forces shelled burning Warsaw and began laying pontoon assault bridges across the Vistula River from the captured suburban area of Praga.

Berlin broadcasts reported without Soviet confirmation that three Soviet armies, using upward of 400,000 men in a big new offensive in the north, had begun a drive on Riga and that one spearhead in an eighteen-mile advance was twenty miles south of the Latvian capital on the Baltic Sea.

A late dispatch said the Russians had begun stringing pontoons

Continued on Page 28

GERMANS DEFIANT ON OUSTER BY FINNS

Profess Difficulty of Moving Troops—Clashes Reported as War Declaration Looms

By The Associated Press.

LONDON, Sept. 16 — Finnish troops tonight were waging an undeclared war against their former German allies. Vehicles began streaming across the northern borders as war-weary Finns tried to escape to Sweden in view of an open declaration of hostilities this week-end.

The German Army in Russia will henceforth be guided "by the viewpoint of its own security against any aggressors," a German High Command statement said.

Trying to explain why several German divisions remained in Finland, a communiqué broadcast from Berlin said:

"German divisions that so far

Continued on Page 29

MARINES CAPTURE PELELIU AIRDROME

Kill 1,400 Japanese Seizing Prized Field — Tokyo Says Davao Has Been Evacuated

By ROBERT TRUMBULL
By Telephone to The New York Times.

PEARL HARBOR, Sept. 16—The Peleliu airfield, primary objective in the assault on that small island in the Palau group, was captured by the First Marine Division yesterday, with American artillery, tanks, naval gunfire and carrier-based bombers supporting the marines' determined drive through well-organized Japanese defenses.

Today's communiqué from the headquarters of Admiral Chester W. Nimitz, Commander in Chief of the Pacific Fleet, made it plain that the fighting on Peleliu had been of the severest intensity and said that it was continuing.

Fourteen hundred Japanese dead were counted by our troops by nightfall yesterday, about thirty hours after the landing. There was no mention of the marine casualties, although yesterday's communiqué said our losses on the first day were light.

[On Morotai Island, 300 miles from Mindanao in the Philippines, army troops pushed the rebuilding of the Pitu airdrome and consolidated positions with-

Continued on Page 5

War News Summarized

SUNDAY, SEPTEMBER 17, 1944

President Roosevelt and Prime Minister Churchill brought their war talks in Quebec to a close yesterday with a pledge to launch a devastating assault on Japan with all the resources of the British Empire and the United States as soon as Europe is freed from "the corroding heel of Nazism." The two leaders said they had reached quick and complete unanimity on plans for prosecuting the war against "the barbarians of the Pacific." [1:8.]

Seasoned marines who conquered Guadalcanal appeared to be well on their way toward hitting the Japanese with the same sort of lightning again. A little more than a day after their invasion of Peleliu island in the Palau group, 610 miles east of Davao in the Philippines, the battle-scarred veterans had fought through strong enemy tank and artillery fire and had conquered the island's airfield. Meanwhile, General MacArthur's Army troops, fashioning the southern claw of a pincers aimed at the Philippines, were putting the captured airfield on Morotai into shape. Alarmed Tokyo had no doubt as to the why of the two American invasions and ordered evacuation of Davao in the southern Philippines. [1:7.]

Allied forces all along the western front from the North Sea to Switzerland moved forward. The spotlight continued to blaze on the American First Army, which was widening and extending its breach of the Siegfried Line east of Aachen. This drive toward the Rhine continued unchecked, and German organization for defense of the Siegfried Line was breaking down under the impact of American hammer blows at half a dozen places at the same time. General Patton's Third Army was winning the battle of the Moselle River and was reaching for the German frontier east of the great fortress city of Metz. Canadian and British troops rolled northward over the Dutch border after overcoming stubborn German resistance. [1:3; map, P. 12.]

The Red Army entered Sofia, capital of Bulgaria, which capitulated shortly after the Russians crossed the frontier on Sept. 8, and were within sixty miles of the main German escape route from Greece. Soviet patrols were crossing the Vistula River to scout enemy positions in Warsaw, which was under terrific artillery bombardment. Berlin reports said a massive new Russian offensive in the Baltics had put the Russians within twenty miles of Riga, capital of Latvia. [1:5-6; map, P. 28.]

Finns and Germans continued to fight each other as Hitler maintained that German troops had been unable to leave Finland by Sept. 15 and would continue "to protect their security" against any attackers. Finland, which has not yet formally concluded peace with Soviet Russia, was reported moving toward a declaration of war on Germany. [1:6.]

In Italy, a great tank battle was raging within three miles of Rimini. [26:4.]

Harlem Gets Big New Playground Reclaimed From 6½ Acres of Slum

On a six-and-a-half-acre site that seven months ago was cluttered with dilapidated garages, small commercial buildings and tenements, one of the largest playgrounds in the city was opened yesterday in Harlem at Lenox Avenue between 143d and 145th Streets, with only coal bunkers between it and the Harlem River.

Two thousand fathers, mothers, youths and children from the congested neighborhood came for the opening, watched with sparkling eyes a parade, applauded when city officials and Negro leaders spoke of other improvements to come and the social importance of the playground, and remained to play ball on its new asphalt surface, to use its swings, chutes and teeter boards and to toss basketballs.

The playground, named in honor of Col. Charles Young, a Negro officer who was graduated from West Point, served in the Spanish-American War, the Philippine Insurrection and the World War and was buried in Arlington National Cemetery, was built now because Mayor La Guardia and Park Commissioner Robert Moses were able to obtain priorities for sufficient materials. Fencing is lacking for the large playfield within the playground and construction of a recreation house with bandstand will have to wait until after the war. But meanwhile there is a large area for supervised and safe play where none existed before in a heavily populated district.

Commissioner Moses, as chairman of the ceremonies, said the

Continued on Page 40

Henry Ford Will Increase Wages 'As Soon as Government Permits'

Special to The New York Times.

WASHINGTON, Sept. 16 — Henry Ford, in a statement released today by his representatives here, said:

"I have been thinking about raising wages for some time and I am going to do it as soon as the Government will permit me."

The statement marked the third time in the forty-year history of the Ford Motor Company that Mr. Ford has announced a decision to raise wages above the general standard of the country.

In 1914 Mr. Ford set a $5-a-day minimum wage when the average daily wage was much lower and in 1929 he increased the Ford minimum to $7 a day.

"I would like to raise the pay of all Ford workers despite the fact that their wages are already higher than those of the rest of the industry," he declared in today's statement.

"As long as I live I want to pay the highest wages in the automobile business. If the men in our plants will give a full day's work for a full day's pay, there is no reason why we can't always do it.

"Every man should make enough money to own a home, a piece of land and a car."

The statement came soon after indications here that the National War Labor Board's Little Steel formula limiting wage increases to

Continued on Page 35

UNITY IS STRESSED

Churchill Asserts Britain Asked a Bigger Part in War on Japan

NAZIS SEEN NEAR END

Roosevelt Says Pacific Is Too Big to Have One Commander

By JOHN H. CRIDER
By Telephone to The New York Times.

QUEBEC, Sept. 16—President Roosevelt and Prime Minister Churchill promised today the earliest possible shift of the full weight of British and American arms from Europe for the "destruction of the barbarians of the Pacific" but were unprepared to specify when the war in Europe would end.

Addressing correspondents as they did thirteen months ago on the deck of the Citadel's historic ramparts 300 feet above the broad St. Lawrence, the leaders of the two countries commanding the greatest combined military and naval strength in the world pledged that the doom of Japan would be written in the months to come, just as Germany's collapse is "now approaching its final stages" as the result of similar decisions reached here last year. They spoke as prophets with a record of fulfillment.

Their Joint Statement

The main points of their half-hour press conference, which concluded the second Quebec conference, were summarized in a joint statement as follows:

> The President and the Prime Minister and the Combined Chiefs of Staff held a series of meetings, during which they discussed all aspects of the war against Germany and Japan. In a very short space of time they reached decisions on all points both with regard to the completion of the war in Europe, now approaching its final stages, and the destruction of the barbarians of the Pacific.
>
> The most serious difficulty with which the Quebec conference has been confronted has been to find room and opportunity for marshaling against Japan the massive forces which each and all of the nations concerned are ardent to engage against the enemy.

The two great men of the Anglo-American nations faced 160 correspondents and photographers, looking just as grim and determined as they did a year ago, but they had aged perceptibly. The Prime Minister, with his big cigar, was less florid of complexion as he

Continued on Page 4

German Peace Plea To Russia Reported

By Reuter.

STOCKHOLM, Sweden, Sept. 16—The Berne correspondent of the Swedish newspaper Morgentidningen, citing a "reliable German source," said today that Adolf Hitler had asked an intermediary to ask Russia for peace.

Germany offered to evacuate Finland and the Balkans, retaining her economic connections with the latter, and to accept the Polish demarcation line fixed by Germany and Russia in 1939, the report said. The same German source, the correspondent added, heard strong rumors that the Japanese at the same time had asked Russia to make contact with the Americans and British for peace terms.

The intermediary used by Hitler is said to be Hiroshi Oshima, Japanese Ambassador in Berlin.

"All the News That's Fit to Print"

The New York Times.

LATE CITY EDITION
Cloudy with fresh to strong winds; rain tonight.
Temperatures Yesterday—Max.,67; Min.,53
Sunrise, 7:18 A. M.; Sunset, 6:10 P. M.

Copyright, 1944, by The New York Times Company.

VOL. XCIV..No. 31,681. Entered as Second-Class Matter, Postoffice, New York, N. Y. NEW YORK, FRIDAY, OCTOBER 20, 1944. THREE CENTS IN NEW YORK CITY

M'ARTHUR INVADES CENTRAL PHILIPPINES; FOOTHOLD TO SPLIT ISLANDS FIRMLY HELD; ROOSEVELT PROMISES JAPAN A LESSON NOW

10,000 POLICE READY TO GUARD ITINERARY OF PRESIDENT HERE

He Will Arrive in Brooklyn, Then in an Open Car Tour Three Other Boroughs

TO ATTEND WAGNER RALLY

Trip Will Be Made Tomorrow Preceding Foreign Policy Talk, Rain or Shine

Police Commissioner Lewis J. Valentine yesterday canceled all police leaves for Saturday and recalled all officers of the rank of captain or higher from vacations for that day to provide a police guard for President Roosevelt's campaign tour of the city that will be adequate for all emergencies. It was estimated that the Commissioner's actions will make a force of 10,000 policemen, including detectives, available for the President's protection during his stay in the city.

Robert E. Hannegan, Democratic National Chairman, released yesterday the itinerary for the President's trip and said that the tour will be made rain or shine. The President is planning to make the tour in an open car, he added.

Laughing aside a question as to whether Mayor La Guardia was taking over direction of the campaign, that had been prompted by the Mayor's supervision of the arrangements for the President's tour, Mr. Hannegan said that Mr. La Guardia "has been cooperating with us in arranging plans for visits here to this city of which he is the Mayor."

Not Solely a Health Tour

The Democratic chairman denied that the tour was arranged to prove that the President's health was good, but he conceded that it might serve that purpose.

"After the people have seen him they can make up their own minds as to his vigor and health," he explained. "The people will have a chance to see him as the correspondents do twice a week."

The President's itinerary, as released by Mr. Hannegan, provides for his arrival at the Brooklyn Army Base Terminal in the Bay Ridge section of Brooklyn. From there the President will go to the New York Navy Yard in Brooklyn via Fifty-eighth Street, Fourth Avenue, Ashland Place, Navy Street and Flushing Avenue, entering the yard through the Cumberland Street gate.

Upon leaving the Navy Yard the White House party will drive along Cumberland Street, Park Avenue, Tillary Street, Washington Street, Fulton Street and Bedford Avenue to Ebbets Field, where the President is scheduled to greet Senator Robert F. Wagner at about 10:30 A. M. This is the only time announced for a stop on the entire tour.

Wagner to Join Party

Senator Wagner is joining the Presidential party at Ebbets Field and will ride with the President for the rest of the trip. Leaving the ball park, the President will go to the United States Naval Training School, Women's Reserve (Hunter College), the Bronx, via Bedford Avenue, Empire Boulevard, Washington Avenue, Classon Avenue, Eastern Parkway, Pitkin Avenue and Interboro Parkway to Queens.

Leaving the Interboro Parkway at Metropolitan Avenue, the President and his group will cross Queens by way of Union Turnpike, Queens Boulevard, Thirty-ninth Street, Steinway Street and Astoria Boulevard north to the Triborough Bridge.

Arriving in the Bronx on the Triborough Bridge, the President will follow Bruckner Boulevard, 138th Street, St. Ann's Avenue, 149th Street, Prospect Avenue, Boston Road, Southern Boulevard, East Tremont Avenue, Washington Avenue, Fordham Road, University Avenue, Kingsbridge Road, Reservoir Avenue and Goulden Avenue

Continued on Page 12, Column 5

Moscow Is Paying For Petsamo Mines

Special to The New York Times.

OTTAWA, Oct. 19—The Government of the Soviet Union has agreed to pay 20,000,000 United States dollars to the Government of Canada for the interests in the nickel mines in the Petsamo district of Finland, owned by the International Nickel Company of Canada and its subsidiary, the Mond Nickel Company of the United Kingdom.

Announcement of the agreement, which was signed in Moscow by the British and Canadian Ambassadors, was made this evening by Prime Minister W. L. Mackenzie King. The Petsamo district was ceded to the Soviet Union by Finland under the armistice agreement of Sept. 19.

Payment will be made during six years in equal installments.

HURRICANE LASHES CAROLINA COASTS

Charleston Is Dark as Storm Roars Northward — Florida Citrus Growers Lose Millions

By The United Press.

CHARLESTON, S. C., Oct. 19—A tropical hurricane which caused damage to Florida's rich citrus crop estimated in the millions, and at least twenty-five deaths since boiling up in the Caribbean more than a week ago, lashed at this shipbuilding and naval center tonight, plunging the city into darkness through power failure.

At 8:30 P. M., the Weather Bureau said the center of the disturbance was in the Atlantic off Parris Island, site of the big marine boot training camp, but already gale winds of 55 to 60 miles an hour were sweeping this city.

Waves were pounding over the seawall at the Battery, and low parts of the old city were expected to be flooded.

[Little damage and no casualties were reported by The Associated Press from the hurricane's progress over the Carolines. Power was restored at Charleston at 1 A. M. High water caused slight damage at the Battery. Florence, S. C., and Southport, N. C., had forty to sixty-five-mile winds.]

Because of the power failure, The News and Courier was unable to publish tomorrow's editions.

Florida Citrus Crop Is Hard Hit

JACKSONVILLE, Fla., Oct. 19 (AP)—The hurricane swept northward tonight along the South Atlantic Coast after crossing Florida, causing two deaths in Miami and estimated damage of $20,000,000 to the citrus crop.

The Weather Bureau said the storm probably would reach a point off Cape Hatteras, N. C., early Friday and pass out to sea.

Relatively little damage occurred at Jacksonville, which had its worst blow since 1928, but nearly fifty beach houses were destroyed by wind and tides at Fer-

Continued on Page 32, Column 2

ALLIES NEAR VENLO

British Troops, Our Tanks Push Foe Back Upon Meuse in Holland

AACHEN MOSTLY WON

Canadians Speed Drive to Chase the Germans From Antwerp Area

By CLIFTON DANIEL

By Wireless to The New York Times.

SUPREME HEADQUARTERS, Allied Expeditionary Force, Oct. 19—Parallel columns of British and American tanks, driving through incessant rain and soggy Netherland fields, closed in today toward Venlo, on the great bend of the Meuse River thirty miles east of Eindhoven, and major junction of the main railway from the Ruhr and Rhineland industrial areas to Eindhoven. At the nearest point the Allied forces fighting under Lieut. Gen. Sir Miles C. Dempsey's command were within eleven miles of Venlo in a drive south and east of Venray.

The gains here, as elsewhere on the Western Front, were limited by persistently unfavorable weather. Canadian Army troops, pressing west against the shrinking perimeter of the German pocket on the south shore of the Scheldt estuary, approached to within 2,000 yards today of the center of the pocket at Oostburg [near Waterlandkerkje, The Canadian Press reported]. British tactical aircraft gave close support to the advance.

American First Army troops were working in the streets of Aachen. Outside Aachen today the Germans were thrown out of pillboxes that they had occupied during the night in the Haaren area, northeast of the city. A German counter-attack there gained ground this afternoon, but Americans struck back and recaptured the lost yardage.

German Armor Attacked

Generally bad weather curtailed air operations, but American Thunderbolts, operating beyond Lieut. Gen. George S. Patton's Third Army front, hit railway rolling stock at Kaiserslautern and made an accurate attack on a concentration of German tanks east of Luneville, fifteen miles southeast of Nancy.

A German counter-blow against the British Second Army advance toward the Meuse was made today from the vicinity of the village of Overbroek, just southeast of Venray. It was contained, and the Allied forces now hold a line roughly along a secondary road from Overbroek to the southwest. The American part of this Allied force was working through swamp lands south of Venray along the railway from Eindhoven and Deurne to Venlo. About 750 prisoners were taken in this area yesterday, 150 of them by the Americans.

Fighting against the French

Continued on Page 3, Column 3

EAST PRUSSIA IS HIT

Huge Red Army Blow Takes German Town, Berlin Reports

DANZIG SECOND GOAL

Soviet Pincers Feared—Debrecen's Defenses Crack in Hungary

By The United Press.

LONDON, Friday, Oct. 20—The Red Army has invaded East Prussia, capturing at least one German town in "one of the war's bloodiest struggles," Berlin said last night, while Moscow reported that other Soviet forces had cracked the German defense line south of Debrecen, Hungary's third city, and seized more than 11,000 prisoners.

Using more than 500 tanks to spearhead single thrusts, Russian troops captured the German frontier station of Eydtkau, half a mile inside the eastern border of the Junkers stronghold, and pushed across German soil toward the great East Prussian rail hub of Insterburg, thirty-eight miles to the west, Berlin said.

German broadcasts, stressing the gravity of the "mammoth" Russian offensive and speaking of a "grand assault" by "monstrous" Soviet forces, said the deepest penetration of German soil was made west of Eydtkau as the Russians drove past the town to within striking distance of the strategic rail junction of Stallupoenen.

Moscow Remains Silent

While the German radio gave a day-long picture of German troops fighting desperately against an avalanche of men and material and yielding only blood-stained ground, Moscow remained silent on the battle that reportedly has been raging for three days.

At the same time German commentators told of a grandiose Soviet plan apparently aimed at throwing a steel ring around East Prussia's 14,000 square miles. While Red Army forces attacked East Prussia's eastern borders on a fifty-mile front between the frontier station of Schirwindt and the former Polish city of Suwalki, annexed to Adolf Hitler's Greater Reich, Berlin said Soviet forces

Continued on Page 6, Column 4

GENERAL M'ARTHUR FULFILLS A GALLANT VOW

China Sea
Sulu Sea
LUZON
Philippine Sea
MINDANAO
Zamboanga
SULUAN I.
SCALE OF MILES
Oct. 20, 1944

The return to the Philippines began at Leyte Gulf (1). Tokyo said the Americans had first invaded Suluan Island (shown in detail on inset). General MacArthur announced the capture of Tacloban in northern Leyte Island, a landing near Cabalian at the southern tip and occupation of the whole eastern side of the island. Bombings were reported at Davao (2), Cotabato (3), Zamboanga (4), Cebu (5), the much-bombed area of Clark Field and Manila (6) and Aparri (7).

BEACHHEADS WON

Americans Seize East Coast of Leyte Isle, Are Widening Hold

TACLOBAN CAPTURED

Casualties Are Reported Small in Mighty Blow by Air and Sea

By The Associated Press.

GENERAL MACARTHUR'S HEADQUARTERS in the Philippines, Friday, Oct. 20 (Army radio pool broadcast)—American invasion of the Philippines was officially proclaimed today by Gen. Douglas MacArthur.

Two years and six months after he took sad leave of the islands and relinquished them to Japanese invaders, vowing "I shall return," he announced that his Navy and air-covered ground forces had landed in the archipelago.

[Japanese broadcasts, beginning some twenty-four hours previously, had listed at least three landings, all in the central sector where the invaders would be in position to split the archipelago's 150,000 defenders in half.]

General MacArthur, aboard a warship, went along with the huge convoy from New Guinea, and within four hours after his forces landed began making plans to go ashore.

East Coast Seized

The special communiqué text, in part, follows:

"In a major amphibious operation we have seized the eastern coast of Leyte Island in the Philippines, 600 miles north of Morotai and 2,500 miles from Milne Bay from whence our offensive started nearly sixteen months ago.

"The landing in the Visayas is midway between Luzon and Mindanao and at one stroke splits into two Japanese forces in the Philippines. The enemy expected the attack on Mindanao.

"Tacloban was secured with small casualties. The landing was preceded by heavy air and naval bombardment which was devastating in effect. Our grounds troops are already extending their hold."

General MacArthur said supplies were rolling ashore.

225,000 of Foe in Isles

Among participants in the action were the Sixth United States Army, Navy forces of the Seventh United States Fleet, the Third United States Fleet and the Far Eastern Air Force.

The landings pitted the invaders against Japanese Philippine defenders, estimated at 225,000 under command of Field Marshal Juichi Terauchi.

[The Japanese exulted exactly four days ago that their alleged naval-air victories off Formosa had set back "the impending invasion of the Philippines by at least two months." It turned out that they didn't score any naval-air victories either.]

Eyewitness accounts from the scene reported the American Navy and air force were on hand in such mammoth strength that the Japanese Navy was nowhere in sight and the Japanese air force, knocked out at all airfields in the Philip-

Continued on Page 10, Column 1

2 POLISH FACTIONS NEARER TO ACCORD

Parley Suspends Temporarily, but London Spokesman Is Frankly Optimistic

By The Associated Press.

MOSCOW, Oct. 19—Leaders of the Soviet-sponsored Polish Committee of National Liberation have reached a tentative understanding with Premier Stanislaw Mikolajczyk of the London Government in Exile, and a spokesman for M. Mikolajczyk's delegation said:

"We expect it will be only a matter of weeks before both Polish

Continued on Page 6, Column 2

'We'll Strangle' War Lords, Roosevelt Statement Says

Special to The New York Times.

WASHINGTON, Friday, Oct. 20—The White House declared in a statement early today that American troops had landed in the Philippines to redeem the pledge made for our return on the surrender of Corregidor and that we would press on to bring about the utter defeat of Japan. Coincident with this announcement President Roosevelt sent a message of congratulations to Gen. Douglas MacArthur, telling him that the whole American nation exulted that the day had come when he had returned to the Philippines and said:

"You have the nation's gratitude and the nation's prayers for success as you and your men fight your way back to Bataan."

[The texts of the President's statement and messages are on Page 11.]

In another message to Admiral Chester W. Nimitz and Admiral William F. Halsey, the President told of the pride with which "the magnificent sweep" of the fleet into enemy waters had been observed and praised them for their "fine cooperation" with General MacArthur.

In still another message President Roosevelt informed President Osmena of the Philippine Government that when the Japanese had

Continued on Page 11, Column 5

OUR PACIFIC FORCES KEYED FOR BIG TASK

Marvels of Land-Sea Warfare Performed by Hard-Hitting Precision Machine

By LINDESAY PARROTT

By Wireless to The New York Times.

ADVANCED HEADQUARTERS IN THE SOUTHWEST PACIFIC, Oct. 19—What has at last become one of the most elaborate and best trained military precision machines in the world and one that is perhaps unique in the history of warfare was built up for the long, hard push into the philippines under the leadership of Gen. Douglas MacArthur.

Veterans of the early fighting

Continued on Page 10, Column 5

War News Summarized

FRIDAY, OCTOBER 20, 1944

General MacArthur, at the head of the United States Sixth Army and Australian units, has landed in the Philippines.

The east shore of Leyte Island has been seized and supplies and heavy equipment are pouring onto the beachheads, he reported today. The landings were made under the guns of the United States Third and Fifth Fleets, an Australian squadron and an umbrella of carrier planes, the AF and the Far Eastern Air Forces.

The Leyte area is the hardest part of the Philippines to defend; guerrillas there have continually harassed the Japanese occupation troops. It is about 450 miles from Manila, but represents an advance of 600 miles from Morotai and 2,500 miles from Milne Bay, from which General MacArthur started the drive back up the Pacific sixteen months ago.

Meanwhile, Admiral Halsey sent some of his carrier planes over the Manila area to pin down the enemy and wreck more than 100 aircraft. [All the foregoing 1:8; maps, Pages 1 and 10.]

President Roosevelt, calling the landing just a stepping-stone to Japan, radioed General MacArthur: "The whole American nation today exults at the news that the gallant men under your command have landed on Philippine soil." [1:6-7.]

During the past year a task force of unprecedented power has been built up in the Pacific for the reconquest of the Philippines. [1:7.]

Far to the west Allied carrier planes and naval guns battered the Nicobar Islands in the Indian Ocean, Tokyo said [9:5.] and in Burma Tiddim was recaptured by the British. [11:1.]

Foul weather hampered activity on Europe's Western Front. Nevertheless, British and American armor closed in on Venlo, rail junction for the Ruhr and Rhineland, and the Netherland town of Breskens on the Scheldt estuary seemed about to fall to the Canadians. [1:3; map, P. 2.] The battle for Aachen was rapidly drawing to a close against diminishing resistance. [3:1.]

In Italy the Eighth Army bridged the Pisciatello River and captured two towns near Cesena. The Fifth Army took important heights near Bologna and on the west coast. [5:2-3.]

The Red Army, according to Berlin, has invaded East Prussia, capturing the frontier station of Eidtkau and pushing on six miles to threaten Stallupoenen. Moscow was silent on this front, reporting successes only in Latvia, Transylvania and near Debrecen, Hungary, now nearly encircled. [1:4; map, P. 6.]

A tentative understanding was reported reached in Moscow between the contending Polish factions. Premier Mikolajczyk will return to London to obtain his Cabinet's approval. The Lublin Committee was optimistic. [1:5.]

Dewey Backs State Department In Warning Nazis Over Murder

By WARREN MOSCOW

Special to The New York Times.

ALBANY, Oct. 19—Before leaving tonight for a major address in Pittsburgh tomorrow, Governor Dewey issued a statement approving the State Department's warning to Germany against acts of terrorism and extermination of victims of Nazi aggression still held in German concentration camps.

Mr. Dewey declared that the information that the Nazis were making threats to exterminate victims still alive in occupied countries came to this country "from unquestionably reliable sources."

His statement read:

"Information comes to this country from unquestionably reliable sources that the Nazis, trapped and knowing that they are faced with inevitable defeat, are now resorting to the known gangster terror device of threatening to exterminate their very victims—Poles, Jews and other non-German nationals—now imprisoned by them in their horrible concentration camps in parts of Poland and other countries still occupied by the Nazis.

"The civilized world is now in a position in unmistakable terms to warn the Nazis—military commanders, members of the German Government, their aiders, abettors and supporters—that certain and inevitable justice awaits them for these brutal and wanton murders if their schemes should be carried out.

"I am happy to note that our State Department has issued a

Continued on Page 13, Column 4

Kaiser Presents to the President 'Specific Pattern' for Reconversion

By C. P. TRUSSELL

Special to The New York Times.

WASHINGTON, Oct. 19—Henry J. Kaiser, industrialist, put before President Roosevelt today "an immediate specific pattern" for industrial reconversion to peacetime production which he and other manufacturers could begin to carry into operation "right away."

On leaving the White House, Mr. Kaiser reported that the President was "tremendously impressed," adding: "I am convinced that he believes that this pattern of aiding industry is an important step to assure now the transition to full employment in peacetime."

Under the pattern, Mr. Kaiser and other manufacturers, whom he declined to identify, would begin at once to take over war plants which have completed their contracts and are going out of business. The Kaiser group would then transfer to these plants the contracts and machine tools which are preventing reconversion to civilian production in other plants by using floor space required for peacetime production machinery.

Some manufacturers, Mr. Kaiser said, are willing to remain in war production and to take over the partly completed contracts and the machinery which handicaps the transition sought by those desiring to return to civilian manufacture as soon as possible without interfering with the war program.

To insure full-scale production for war, Mr. Kaiser emphasized, the projected reconversion pattern would have to operate gradually. However, he added, the important

Continued on Page 27, Column 1

Fleeing Toward Foe, Halsey Tells Nimitz

By The United Press.

PEARL HARBOR, Oct. 19—Admiral Chester W. Nimitz, Commander in Chief of the Pacific Fleet, said today:

"I have received from Admiral Halsey the comforting assurance that he is now retiring toward the enemy following the salvage of all the Third Fleet ships recently reported sunk by radio Tokyo."

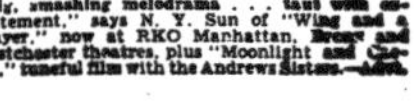

"All the News That's Fit to Print"

The New York Times.

LATE CITY EDITION
Partly cloudy and mild today with moderate to fresh winds.
Temperatures Yesterday—Max., 65; Min., 45
Sunrise, 7:18 A. M.; Sunset, 6:02 P. M.

VOL. XCIV..No. 31,686. Entered as Second-Class Matter. Postoffice, New York, N. Y. NEW YORK, WEDNESDAY, OCTOBER 25, 1944. THREE CENTS IN NEW YORK CITY

U.S. PLANES ATTACK 2 BIG JAPANESE FLEETS; SHOWDOWN BATTLE LIKELY IN PHILIPPINES; BRITISH ENTER KEY JUNCTION IN HOLLAND

SECURITY DELEGATE MUST HAVE POWER TO ACT, DEWEY SAYS

But Declares Congress Alone Should Rule What Agent's Authority Would Be

SEES DISUNITY APPEAL

Scores President's Speech—He Quotes Republican Pledges to Support Him

The text of Governor Dewey's address is on Page 14.

From a Staff Correspondent

MINNEAPOLIS, Oct. 24—Governor Dewey declared hère tonight before an audience of 18,000 persons that the American delegate on the proposed United Nations Security Council should not be required "to return to Congress for authority every time he had to make a decision."

The Governor stipulated, however, that "Congress, and only Congress, has the constitutional power to determine what quota of force it will make available and what discretion it will give our representative to use that force."

Declaring that President Roosevelt had shown that "he cannot work with a Congress of his own party," Mr. Dewey said in his broadcast speech that he held in his hand telegrams from Republican leaders of Congress, pledging their support of American leadership in organizing a world peace league. The legislators were Senators Vandenberg of Michigan, Wherry of Nebraska, Taft of Ohio, White of Maine, and Austin of Vermont, and Representative Martin of Massachusetts.

Promises to "Fill in Gaps"

The Governor, who had said earlier that his speech would "fill in the gaps" of Mr. Roosevelt's foreign policy address Saturday night, declared:

"I have not the slightest doubt that a Congress which is working in partnership with the President will achieve the result we all consider essential and grant adequate power for swift action to the American representative.

"But those who would attempt to ride roughshod over Congress and to dictate the course it should follow before it has even been acquainted with the facts are trifling with the hope of the world. They are deliberately, in my judgment, seeking to precipitate a hardening of minds. If this stubborn course is pursued, it can only result once again, as in 1919, in a disastrous conflict between the President and the Congress. To that I will never be a party."

"From the beginning of this campaign," Mr. Dewey said, "I have insisted that organization for world peace can and must be a bi-partisan effort. I shall continue to insist on that approach. The avoidance of future wars is too important to be in the sole custody of any one man, of any one group or of any one party. It is too important to hang by the slender thread of one man's continuity in office."

The nominee asserted that Mr. Roosevelt in his speech Saturday night "once again sowed among us the seeds of disunity" and thereby brought the subject back to partisan debate.

Says President "Dreamed"

Instead of informing the people of the Administration's policies regarding Poland, Italy and the Scandinavian countries, Mr. Dewey said Mr. Roosevelt "sat by the fireside and dreamed of yesterday. He paraded before the American people the ghosts of the dead past."

As against these "isolated bits of history," the Governor added that he would fill in the "vital events" that composed the whole story.

Answering Mr. Roosevelt's charge that isolationism governed

Continued on Page 14, Column 2

Street Lights Shine In German Cities

By Wireless to THE NEW YORK TIMES.

SUPREME HEADQUARTERS, Allied Expeditionary Force, France, Oct. 24—The lights have gone up again in parts of Germany. While London is still thoroughly blacked out and most other British cities still require a considerable dimout, two major German cities have turned on their street lights for at least two nights recently.

Despite the constant peril of bombing, lights shone on the nights of Oct. 18 and 19 in Duesseldorf and Cologne, within forty miles of the American First Army front.

The reasons for this display, reported for publication here tonight, are unknown. It is surmised that the Germans may have decided, for the purpose of expediting work and transport, that the advantages of having light outweigh the dangers of air attacks, which come none the less.

MORE VOTING TIME DENIED IN JERSEY

Dewey Is Expected to Decide Tomorrow or Friday on Longer Hours Here

While the question of extending polling hours in New York State remained in abeyance, following a discussion between counsel for Governor Dewey and the New York City Board of Elections, New Jersey acted definitely yesterday against any lengthening of voting hours at the national election on Nov. 7.

In New York State the Board of Elections of Nassau County joined the proponents of longer hours, announcing that because of a record registration the board favored a two-hour extension of balloting. The same two-hour span had been requested in New Jersey and in New York City.

The New Jersey action was made known in a decision of Gov. Walter E. Edge not to call a special session of the Legislature to consider spreading the New Jersey polling time, now set at 7 A. M. to 8 P. M. In a letter signed by his secretary, Edward W. Gilroy, Governor Edge rejected a request for extension put forward by Carl Holderman, chairman of the CIO Political Action Committee, who termed these hours insufficient.

Dewey Counsel Studies Case

Governor Dewey took no direct part in the New York State discussions, leaving the matter for the present in the hands of his counsel, Charles D. Breitel. It will be tomorrow or Friday before the Governor acts on the New York request for an extension, it was made known in dispatches from Albany. The request for lengthened hours here was put forward by leaders of the Democratic party and the Political Action Committee, with Mayor La Guardia joining in urging a special session on

Continued on Page 38, Column 1

PRESIDENT DEFENDS PHILADELPHIA TOUR AS KEEPING PLEDGE

Chides Some Newspapers as Quoting 'Half Sentence' in Regard to His Campaigning

CALLS CHICAGO QUERY IFFY

But Hannegan Says Speech Will Be Given Saturday—Visit to Camden, N. J., Likely

By C. P. TRUSSELL

Special to THE NEW YORK TIMES.

WASHINGTON, Oct. 24—President Roosevelt told his news conference today that an amazing number of newspapers which regard themselves as reputable had fallen into the awful habit of quoting only half a sentence in implying that he had departed, in making speaking trips, from his declaration in accepting the fourth-term nomination that he would not campaign in the usual sense. At the same time, he discussed his prospective speaking trip.

These newspapers, he said, had not brought out that he had asserted that he would not campaign in the normal sense except to answer things that were misrepresentations.

The accusation, closely paralleling charges which the President has made that his opponent, Governor Dewey, lifted matter from full context in an effort to score campaign points, came as questions poured in upon him as to future speaking engagements.

Mr. Roosevelt spoke of his Philadelphia speech Friday and also of going to Chicago, but he declined to confirm officially that he was going from Philadelphia to the rally scheduled for Soldiers Field, Chicago, on Saturday evening.

Wilmington Stop Is Predicted

Unofficial reports were that the President would stop briefly at Wilmington, Del., in connection with his Philadelphia trip and after leaving Chicago he would make a platform appearance at Fort Wayne, while on the way to an undisclosed point. Other reports have indicated stops or speeches in Cleveland and Detroit, besides his visit to Boston on Nov. 4.

Asked about future speaking dates, Mr. Roosevelt, who opened the news conference by announcing that he had not even suffered the sniffles from his four-hour tour through the rain in an open car in New York Saturday, said that he hesitated to answer for fear he would cross wires.

When it was suggested that the date for his appearance in Chicago had been set for Oct. 28, he asked what day of the week that would be. Informed that it would be Saturday, he smiled and said he would have to say D V, or Deo Volente (God Willing) on that. But he would not classify this as a confirmation, he added, because he had answered the question in an iffy way.

Asked whether there was any

Continued on Page 18, Column 2

TRAP ON FOE FORMS

's Hertogenbosch Scene of Street Fighting in Netherland Pincers

BRESKENS NOT LOST

Canadians Push Into Zuid Beveland, Lunge North of Antwerp

By CLIFTON DANIEL

By Wireless to THE NEW YORK TIMES.

SUPREME HEADQUARTERS, Allied Expeditionary Force, Oct. 24—Anchor towns at both ends of the yielding German line between the Nijmegen salient and the North Sea in the Netherlands came within range of Allied field guns today.

On the eastern end British forces closed in upon 's Hertogenbosch. On the western end Canadian First Army troops, linking up in an eight-mile front between Woensdrecht and the Belgian-Netherland border, were reported from the field to have driven within firing distance of Bergen op Zoom. These towns are at the opposite ends of railroad and road systems supporting the German positions.

[A dispatch to THE NEW YORK TIMES said the British troops were fighting in the streets of 's Hertogenbosch.]

'S Hertogenbosch was further menaced from the south today by extension of the British offensive, which crossed around the town to the south and cut its highway outlet there. There is as yet no sign of firmness in the Germans' defense of 's Hertogenbosch, and at the western end of the line field observers reported an unexpected softening of the German front.

Regain Beveland Causeway

Canadian Army forces were enabled thereby to take a firm grip again on the causeway leading from the mainland to Zuid Beveland, on the north shore of the Schelde estuary, where the Germans are holding sway over the water route to Antwerp. These forces have joined with other Canadian Army units pressing across the border toward Roosendaal, to

Continued on Page 8, Column 1

DECISIVE BATTLE LOOMS IN FAR EAST WATERS

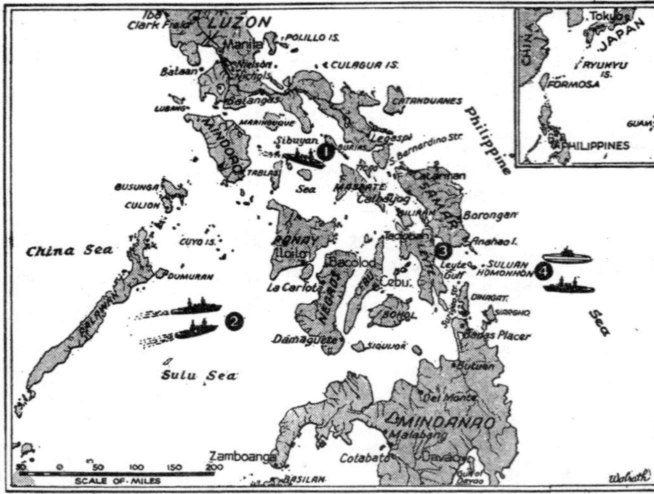

Oct. 25, 1944

Two Japanese sea forces, including battleships and cruisers—one moving eastward in the Sibuyan Sea (1), the other moving eastward in the Sulu Sea (2)—have been sighted and attacked by planes from carriers of Admiral Halsey's fleet operating just east of the Philippines (4). The enemy's objective unquestionably is Leyte Island (3), where our forces are gaining (map, Page 2).

HALSEY MEETS FOE

Airmen Leap to Strike Columns of Ships Seen Lured to Leyte

CRISIS MAY BE NEAR

Nimitz Aide Hints at Epic Moment—Fleets Clash, Tokyo Says

By GEORGE HORNE

By Telephone to THE NEW YORK TIMES.

PEARL HARBOR, Oct. 24—Japanese Navy forces have been sighted and attacked by carrier planes of the Third Fleet in the Philippines.

The enemy forces, apparently in strength, were moving eastward yesterday through the Sibuyan Sea and the Sulu Sea, apparently bearing on the east central Philippines area around Leyte, where American amphibious forces are operating.

They appear to be in two groups, judging from the wording of Admiral Chester W. Nimitz's communiqué, issued at 1 P. M. (6:30 P. M., New York time). The admiral said the enemy forces were attacked by Third Fleet aircraft, but that no further details were now available.

Historic Test Shaping

The "big" battle may already be in progress. If so, it will be the most important test of naval strength since the war began.

Vice Admiral John H. Towers, in a Rotary Club speech today in advance of Navy Day, said the fleet "right now" might be at grips with the enemy in a battle of major importance somewhere in the Philippines. [The deputy Commander in Chief of the Pacific fleet was quoted by The United Press as having said, "We have every reason to believe" that "the critical moment in our history is this moment."]

[Japanese headquarters issued a communiqué early Wednesday announcing that Japanese and American warships had clashed "east of the Philippines." It claimed eleven American ships had been sunk and two damaged, but admitted two Japanese cruisers and one destroyer had been sunk. The communiqué was recorded by the Federal Communications Commission.

[Among United States ships claimed sunk in the communiqué were four aircraft carriers, two cruisers, one destroyer and "more than four" transports.]

Again strong carrier and surface forces, this time under the command of Admiral William F. Halsey, are within striking distance of powerful enemy forces. Once more

Continued on Page 4, Column 6

'S HERTOGENBOSCH IS 50% OCCUPIED

Nazis, However, Delay British Push by Wrecking Bridges Over Strategic Canal

By JAMES MacDONALD

By Wireless to THE NEW YORK TIMES.

WITH THE BRITISH SECOND ARMY at 's Hertogenbosch, the Netherlands, Oct. 24—British forces captured about half of 's Hertogenbosch today in unspectacular fighting that followed an almost night-long barrage in which British light, medium and heavy guns blew the Germans from the surburban village of Hintham and the northeastern outskirts of the city.

Complete liberation of 's Hertogenbosch, manufacturing city with a peacetime population of about 50,000, met a setback shortly after noon, however, when the enemy began demolishing the bridges over the Zuid Willemsvaart canal which

Continued on Page 8, Column 5

25-Mile Leyte Line Gains; Step North Reported Taken

By The United Press.

ADVANCED HEADQUARTERS, on Leyte, Wednesday, Oct. 25—Gen. Douglas MacArthur's invasion troops, killing more than 3,000 Japanese, have captured at least twelve Leyte towns and villages on an expanding twenty-five-mile front and have fought their way into the outskirts of San Pablo, only seventeen and a half miles from the west coast of the island, it was disclosed today.

[The San Pablo air strip was captured, according to The Associated Press. Front dispatches broadcast by the British Broadcasting Corporation said that amphibious tanks had crossed the one-mile San Juanico Strait in the Tacloban sector in northeastern Leyte to land on important Samar, facing the open Pacific north of Leyte Gulf. Possession of the southern part of Samar would give General MacArthur's forces full control of the entrance of the gulf.]

Cooperating with Filipino guerrillas who are trickling steadily into the American lines in organized bodies under their own officers, the United States forces made rapid progress all along the front.

Southern Forces Advance

From Dulag, southern anchor of the front, the troops of the Twenty-fourth Corps under Maj. Gen. John R. Hodge of Carbondale, Ill., fanned north on the coast to take little San Jose and south to take Dao.

Moving directly inland toward the Burauen road junction and the west coast of the island, threatening to cut it in two above its waist, tanks and infantrymen of the Seventh Division and Ninety-sixth Division fought through rain, mud-

Continued on Page 3, Column 2

RED ARMY WIDENS EAST PRUSSIA GRIP

Smashes Closer to Gumbinnen Against Growing Resistance —Augustov Is Captured

By The Associated Press.

LONDON, Wednesday, Oct. 25—The Red Army, battering ahead against a desperate defense bolstered by four fresh German tank divisions, dug deeper through the East Prussian forests yesterday, conquering at least fourteen heavily fortified strong points on an expanding front more than thirty-five miles wide and pressing within six miles of the big rail and road hub of Gumbinnen.

The Soviet communiqué, in announcing these hard-won gains of as much as ten miles by Gen. Ivan D. Chernyakhovsky's Third White Russian Army, disclosed that a new thrust threatening East Prussia from farther southeast had captured the Polish-border bastion of Augustov and fifty other population centers on a twenty-mile front from Augustov to Suwalki.

The Russian announcement indicated that the first great rush of General Chernyakhovsky's men, which carried them more than

Continued on Page 10, Column 2

War News Summarized

WEDNESDAY, OCTOBER 25, 1944

Japanese naval forces spotted steaming east through the Sibuyan and Sulu Seas toward Leyte were under attack by carrier planes of the Third Pacific Fleet, and a gigantic sea-air battle was believed to be in progress. There were battleships and cruisers in at least two forces reported by Admiral Nimitz. No mention was made of Japanese carriers, but they may appear later or the enemy may be counting on support from those land-based planes in the Philippines that escaped the aerial poundings of the past weeks. Early today Tokyo said two Japanese cruisers and a destroyer had been sunk in a fierce battle east of the Philippines and that at least eleven American ships, including four carriers, had been sunk. [1:8.]

More than 3,000 Japanese troops have been killed on Leyte during the fighting that has liberated at least a dozen towns. American advances were made along the entire twenty-five mile front and the San Pablo airstrip was captured. Unconfirmed reports said landings had been made on the large island of Samar a half-mile from Leyte. [1:6-7; map P. 2.]

Some 4,000 Filipino guerrillas killed 3,800 Japanese and collected vital information during the weeks preceding the invasion. [1:6-7.]

In western Europe the British fought their way into 's Hertogenbosch and the Canadians drove on Bergen op Zoom to bring both ends of the vital salient under heavy fire. Advances were also made into Zuid Beveland and the causeway was in Allied hands. Little change was reported from other sectors. [1:4; map P. 8.] Half of 's Hertogenbosch was captured after a night-long artillery barrage. [1:5.]

American fighters, some loaded with bombs, strafed and tore up transportation facilities in Germany, hitting the Hanover-Kassel line with particular force. Eighteen planes were missing. [6:3.] Germany retorted by sending flying bombs into Belgium. [6:2.]

Russian troops, in bitter fighting, drove deeper into East Prussia and extended the front facing that area south along the Polish border below Suwalki. Chust, the first important town in Czechoslovakia to be liberated, was captured. In Transylvania the fighting had been carried into the streets of Satu-Mare. [1:7; map P. 10.]

Bologna was threatened with being outflanked from the east in a thrust by Americans of the Fifth Army in Italy. The British of the Eighth Army pushed closer to that city along the highway from Rimini and Canadians turned back German counter-attacks. [7:3.]

Under-Secretary of State Stettinius indicated that the United States would soon release to the de Gaulle government a large part of the estimated $1,000,000,000 in gold and other assets frozen in this country. [7:5.] He also forecast a security conference of all the United Nations during the winter. [11:2-3.]

Fuel Oil Freed to Former Users; War Aid by Furnace Shifts Hailed

Special to THE NEW YORK TIMES.

WASHINGTON, Oct. 24—The Office of Price Administration announced today that those on the East coast and in the Middle West who converted their heating equipment from fuel oil to coal or wood could have fuel oil if the equipment were changed back to use it.

Consumers cooperated widely in the Government's drive for converting equipment from fuel oil in 1942 when oil supplies were critically short. If they want to use oil again they are eligible for rations to meet their needs when the heating season gets under way about Nov. 1.

In a separate announcement, the Petroleum Administration for War said that the OPA action was based on "the improved fuel oil stock position." Secretary Ickes, as PAW Administrator, warned, however, that the supply was not large enough to warrant an increase in current rations.

In recommending the OPA action, Mr. Ickes told Chester Bowles, Price Administrator, that the conversions of heating equipment "were extremely helpful to us and were a big factor in enabling us to get through a very critical period."

"It has always been our feeling," he said, "that these people were entitled to first consideration as soon as the supply situation improved."

Another OPA change applying

Continued on Page 38, Column 7

Filipino Guerrillas Led the Way For Our Forces in Leyte Landing

By The United Press.

ADVANCED HEADQUARTERS, on Leyte, Oct. 23 (Delayed)—Filipino forces, armed with captured Japanese weapons, deadly bolos and ancient rifles, paved the way for the American invasion of Leyte by gathering detailed information on enemy troop dispositions and killing 3,800 Japanese, it was disclosed today.

The guerrilla army of 4,000, which will join forces with the Americans, was led by 55-year-old Col. Ruperto Kangelon, who had served in the Filipino Constabulary and Army for twenty-eight years, and his second in command was a former United States Navy PT-boat skipper.

[The dispatch did not give the PT-boat skipper's name.]

The guerrillas collected detailed information about Japanese strength and transmitted it by secret means to American headquarters. The guerrillas received a schedule of American operations in advance of the landings to permit them to evacuate civilians from threatened areas and to warn them when to go into action.

Several days before the invasion two American Army officers went ashore on Leyte to perfect final arrangements with the guerrillas. The officers were Lieut. Col. Frank Rawolle of Greenwich, Conn., and Lieut. James Johnson of Spencer, Iowa.

Colonel Kangelon and three Fili-

Continued on Page 3, Column 5

B-29's Bomb Japan; Hit Kyushu Again

By The Associated Press.

WASHINGTON, Wednesday, Oct. 25—Strategic targets on the Japanese island of Kyushu were attacked today by a task force of B-29 Superfortresses of the Twentieth Air Force, Gen. H. H. Arnold, in his capacity as commanding general of the Twentieth, announced early today.

Kyushu, at the southern end of the Japanese homeland archipelago is the site of steel centers and naval bases.

The attack was the fourth by the B-29's on Kyushu targets. The last was staged Aug. 20-21 in a coordinated day and night assault.

The Tokyo radio, heard by the Federal Communications Commission, said 100 bombers hit Kyushu and also Saishu Island, off Korea.

"All the News That's Fit to Print"

The New York Times.

LATE CITY EDITION
Sunny, cool and windy; fair and becoming cooler tonight.
Temperatures Yesterday—Max., 69; Min., 51
Sunrise, 7:19 A. M.; Sunset, 6:01 P. M.

Copyright, 1944, by The New York Times Company.

VOL. XCIV..No. 31,687. Entered as Second-Class Matter, Postoffice, New York, N. Y. NEW YORK, THURSDAY, OCTOBER 26, 1944. THREE CENTS NEW YORK CITY

U. S. DEFEATS JAPANESE NAVY; ALL FOE'S SHIPS IN ONE FLEET HIT; MANY SUNK; BATTLE CONTINUES

SPECIAL PRIVILEGE SOLD BY NEW DEAL, DEWEY CHARGES

Says Roosevelt Backs Plan for 1,000 to Put '$1,000 on the Line' to Aid Campaign

PARTY LETTER IS QUOTED

Governor Declares in Chicago Administration Lacks 'Honesty' to Solve Post-War Problems

The text of Mr. Dewey's speech will be found on Page 13.

By ALEXANDER FEINBERG
Special to The New York Times.

CHICAGO, Oct. 25—Governor Dewey declared tonight that "for $1,000 laid on the line to finance the fourth-term drive, this Administration boldly offers for sale 'special privilege,'" which includes the "assisting in the formulation of Administration policies."

Attacking the "rudimentary honesty" of the New Deal, Mr. Dewey, in a major campaign address preceding the appearance of President Roosevelt here Saturday, charged that the Chief Executive himself was the sponsor of the fund raising idea.

The Chicago Stadium, which accommodates 25,000 persons, was packed to capacity, with several thousand others clamoring to obtain admittance. Gov. Dwight H. Green of Illinois presented Mr. Dewey, who was received with tumultuous acclaim. He kept pointing to the microphone to still the demonstration, but it was just short of five minutes before he could begin his speech.

Governor Dewey said that the fund raising plan was disclosed in a letter signed by H. L. McAlister and Sam J. Watkins, State finance chairman, and written on the letterhead of the National Democratic Campaign Headquarters, Little Rock, Ark.

Dewey Quotes Letter

Mr. Dewey quoted the letter as follows:

"This is an invitation to you to join the One Thousand Club.

"The idea of such a club originated at a recent conference at the White House between the President, Robert E. Hannegan, chairman of the Democratic National Committee, and Edwin W. Pauley, treasurer of the committee. At this meeting the President commented:

"'I think it would be a good idea to have a list of one thousand persons banded together from all over the United States to act as a liaison to see that facts relating to the public interest are presented factually to the President and members of Congress.'

"Members of this organization undoubtedly will be granted special privilege by party leaders. These members will be called into conference from time to time to discuss matters of national importance and to assist in the formulation of Administration policies.

"To be eligible for membership in the One Thousand Club will require a contribution of $1,000 to the National Democratic campaign fund."

Mr. Dewey declared that "there in crude, unblushing words is the ultimate expression of New Deal policies," adding:

"And the sponsor of this idea is frankly stated in that letter to be the President himself. The man who holds the highest office within the gift of the American people at a conference in the White House sponsors an idea to sell 'special privilege' and a voice 'in the formulation of Administration policies' for one thousand dollars on the barrelhead."

The Governor said that New

Continued on Page 13, Column 1

No Extra Gasoline For Trip to Polls

By The Associated Press.

WASHINGTON, Oct. 25—Chester Bowles, OPA head, in a letter to Senator Davis, Republican, of Pennsylvania, today stated that the OPA could not allow extra gasoline rations for private automobiles to take voters to the polls if other means of transportation are available.

Pennsylvania has no absentee voting law and Senator Davis contended that many persons from his State working elsewhere would be unable to return to cast their ballots unless they received extra gas rations.

"A special ration may be granted to carry persons to and from the polls for the purpose of voting in public elections (including primary elections), provided reasonably adequate alternative means of transportation are not available," Mr. Bowles wrote.

Where no other form of transportation is available those wishing to use cars for voting may apply to their local ration boards on special forms which the boards have available.

WAGNER ACCLAIMS PARTY FARM POLICY

He Says That Dewey Is Vague on Agriculture—Calls His Platform 'Double Talk'

By CLAYTON P. KNOWLES
Special to The New York Times.

SYRACUSE, N. Y., Oct. 25—The farm plank in the Republican platform offers nothing but "double talk" and Governor Dewey, rather than clarifying the issue, puts forward proposals "as vague and airy as a wisp of smoke," Senator Robert F. Wagner declared tonight as he carried his campaign for re-election into this city in the heart of the farm area.

"Mr. Dewey ridicules the so-called alphabetical agencies," he declared. "But how could low-interest loans have been provided without the Farm Mortgage Corporation? How could farm prices have been supported without the Agricultural Adjustment Administration? How could the number of farms with central electric service have been multiplied three times without the Rural Electrification Administration?

"These programs are not perfect. They need to be improved, but they are solid, they can be seen, they can be felt. When Mr. Dewey talks about the farmer, what he proposes is as vague and airy as a wisp of smoke."

Mr. Wagner's address, broadcast over a State-wide hook-up by the Columbia Broadcasting System, said that Governor Dewey's Commissioner of Agriculture last spring set minimum milk prices "far above

Continued on Page 12, Column 4

PRESIDENT ELATED

Gives News From Halsey That Foe Is 'Defeated, Damaged, Routed'

TEST IS ON, KING SAYS

Practically All Japanese Fleet in the Battle, Admiral Believes

By LEWIS WOOD
Special to The New York Times.

WASHINGTON, Oct. 25—President Roosevelt exultantly announced late today the receipt of a report from Admiral William F. Halsey saying that the Japanese Navy in the Philippine area had been "defeated, seriously damaged and routed" by our forces.

Two hours earlier Admiral Ernest J. King, Commander in Chief of the United States Fleet and Chief of Naval Operations, had disclosed that virtually all of the long elusive Japanese Fleet had been engaged at last in the furious sea battle of the Philippines.

These two startling revelations, exciting Washington as nothing has done since the European invasions, were taken here to mean that the vaunted Japanese naval power had been seriously crippled and the road to Tokyo made much easier. At last, it was presumed, the principal part of Japanese naval strength had been nettled out of hiding and then decisively beaten.

Announcement Is Dramatic

The circumstances of the President's statement were thrilling. When only a half dozen newsmen remained in the White House press room at 5:20 P. M., Press Secretary Stephen T. Early appeared at the door.

"Come quick," he cried, slapping his palms together for emphasis.

Rushing to the President's oval-shaped office, the reporters found him seated at his desk, smiling broadly. Obviously he had been interrupted in his late afternoon dictation. Before him lay scattered papers, but directly in front of him was a single sheet of paper, inscribed apparently with his own handwriting.

He had, said the President beamingly, a "real flash," just telephoned to him by Admiral William D. Leahy, Chief of Staff to the President as Commander in Chief of the Army and Navy. Picking up the paper, Mr. Roosevelt slowly and distinctly read:

"The President received today a report from Admiral Halsey that the Japanese Navy in the Philippine area has been defeated, seriously damaged and routed by the United States Navy in that area."

For a moment there was a pause. No one said a word. Then

Continued on Page 3, Column 3

SEA POWER OF LAND OF THE RISING SUN SHATTERED IN BATTLE

Piecing together the statements of Admiral Nimitz and General MacArthur gives this picture of the battle around the Philippines: One Japanese force, including four battleships, ten cruisers and thirteen destroyers, first sighted south of Mindoro (1) steamed east, across the Sibuyan Sea, through San Bernardino Strait and down the coast of Samar (2), where Admiral Kinkaid's combined force (5) attacked it and forced it to retire northward with perhaps ten ships damaged. It was apparently in this action that the American light carrier Princeton was sunk. A second enemy force, first sighted southwest of Negros (3), included two battleships, one or two cruisers and four destroyers. It moved east across the Sulu Sea and through Surigao Strait (4). Admiral Kinkaid attacked this group and it lost one battleship and several cruisers and destroyers; the rest of the force retreated west through the strait. This whole battle scene is at (A) on the inset. A third Japanese force was engaged southeast of Formosa (B).

ALLIES CUT UP FOE IN WEST HOLLAND

British Hammer Germans in One Area of 's Hertogenbosch—Canadians Tighten Traps

By CLIFTON DANIEL
By Wireless to The New York Times.

SUPREME HEADQUARTERS, Allied Expeditionary Force, Oct. 25—The Germans were rapidly losing their grip tonight on their strongholds between the North Sea and the British Second Army's salient in the Netherlands.

British forces converging from three sides drove them out of all

Continued on Page 7, Column 2

'17 Hours of Hell' Raised In Sea Battle Off Leyte

By RALPH TEATSORTH
United Press Correspondent

ABOARD ADMIRAL KINKAID'S FLAGSHIP, off the Philippines, Thursday, Oct. 26—The Tokyo Express rammed into the American Navy Limited today. The pride of Japan was wrecked so badly it may never make another long run. It was the day our Navy had dreamed about for considerably more than a year.

It was seventeen hours of concentrated hell and the most amazing thing about the battle was that our Pacific Flight Carrier Force—which nobody thought could deliver such a terrific punch—held off the bulk of the Japanese fleet all day and had it on the run all afternoon.

When evening came and most of

Continued on Page 4, Column 7

AIR PLANT IN JAPAN SMASHED BY B-29'S

Omura Target Is 'Perfectly Patterned,' Pilots Say—Foe Lists 100 Planes in Attack

Special to The New York Times.

WASHINGTON, Oct. 25—While the remnants of the demoralized Japanese Fleet were fleeing from Admiral William F. Halsey's forces in Philippine waters, United States Army Superfortresses today were carrying the war another step closer to the heart of Japan by carrying out a successful mission against the key aircraft assembly plant at Omura on the island of Kyushu.

Twentieth Air Force Headquarters here announced that a medium-sized task force of the mammoth bombers, operating from Twen-

Continued on Page 4, Column 4

AMERICANS MAKE BIG LEYTE JUMPS

Troops Push Westward on Isle—Southern Coast of Samar to the North Now Held

By The United Press.

ADVANCED HEADQUARTERS ON LEYTE, Thursday, Oct. 26—American dismounted cavalry troops have invaded Samar, third largest of the Philippines and last island barrier on the road to Luzon and Manila, while forces fighting on Leyte have punched nine miles inland to seize the key road junction of Burauen.

Gen. Douglas MacArthur also announced in a special communiqué that Field Marshal Count Juichi Terauchi's Japanese defenders of the northern Leyte front were "disintegrating" under the American hammer blows.

The three-mile American advance that occupied Burauen, southern terminus of an inland highway, split the Japanese lines in northern Leyte and threw the enemy back toward the hills, where Filipino guerrillas were reported in action.

The new American triumphs pushed our lines nine miles inland and raised to thirty-one the number of towns and villages captured. Six airfields also have been seized.

The invasion of Samar, with an

Continued on Page 4, Column 5

BATTLESHIP IS SUNK

Seventh Fleet Smashes Two Japanese Forces Converging on Leyte

REMNANTS IN FLIGHT

They Are Hotly Pursued—Third Enemy Force Is Hit Off Formosa

The Imperial Japanese Fleet has been brought to battle. It is suffering a crushing defeat. Two of its divisions have been routed. One has been almost destroyed. Contact has been made with the main force southeast of Formosa by Admiral William F. Halsey's Third Fleet. That engagement is continuing, said the last communiqué.

Two strong Japanese naval forces converged on Leyte Gulf through the San Bernardino Strait in the Philippines to the north and the Surigao Strait to the south. Vice Admiral Thomas C. Kinkaid's Seventh Fleet smashed these two forces and put the remnants to flight after sinking or heavily damaging every ship in the southern enemy force.

One big Japanese carrier has been sunk. Two more have been heavily damaged and undoubtedly are out of action. One Japanese battleship of the Yamasiro class has been sunk. At least four others have been heavily damaged. Several enemy cruisers and destroyers have been sunk. Many others have been hit, both by bombs and torpedoes.

Enemy Defeated and Routed

The only announced American loss is the converted cruiser-carrier Princeton sunk. Other escort carriers were damaged by fire from one of the enemy battleship forces.

Gen. Douglas MacArthur reported triumphantly that "the Japanese Navy has suffered its most crushing defeat of the war." Admiral Ernest J. King, in Washington, said that "practically all" of the Japanese fleet was engaged and that he was confident of the outcome. President Roosevelt called a special press conference to announce receipt of a message from Admiral William F. Halsey reporting that the enemy has been "defeated, seriously damaged and routed."

Pending official word from Pearl Harbor, it appeared the greatest surface and naval air action in the history of naval warfare was being fought and won by the Pacific Fleet, the greatest naval force that ever went down to the sea.

Fate of Leyte Decided

SEVENTH FLEET HEADQUARTERS, Philippines, Thursday, Oct. 26 (UP)—Japan lost the first, and possibly the decisive, round in an all-out battle to halt on the Philippines line the American advance toward her home islands.

This occurred early yesterday morning when Admiral Kinkaid's outnumbered fleet battered and put to rout Japanese battle forces converging on Leyte Gulf.

Complete results are lacking as the action is continuing, with planes from Admiral Kinkaid's hurt but still fighting carrier force hitting the surviving enemy warships as they are retiring. [General MacArthur said the Japanese force that came through Surigao Strait fled back through it to the west and the other was in flight in a northerly direction.]

[Gordon Walker in a Mutual broadcast from the Philippines said "a Navy spokesman here claimed that practically every

Continued on Page 3, Column 3

War News Summarized

THURSDAY, OCTOBER 26, 1944

The Japanese Navy came out to fight in the waters off the Philippines and was severely mauled. One force of four battleships, ten cruisers and thirteen destroyers moved up south of Mindoro into the Sibuyan Sea. Every battleship and at least one cruiser was hit. This flotilla rounded Samar and fled north. We lost an escort carrier.

A second force of two battleships, two cruisers and four destroyers came into the Sulu Sea from southwest of Negros Island. After all the ships had been hit it turned tail and retreated.

A third force, this one with carriers, came down from home waters and the battle was still going on. Most of the engagements were fought from the air and the enemy suffered heavily in plane losses. Our light carrier Princeton was hit and its magazine subsequently exploded. Most of the crew were saved. The Third Pacific Fleet took on the enemy carrier force and the Seventh turned back the two others. [All the foregoing 1:8.]

President Roosevelt, in an impromptu press conference, said that Admiral Halsey, commanding the Third Fleet, had just reported that the Japanese Navy had been "defeated, seriously damaged and routed." Earlier Admiral King had said that almost the entire enemy naval strength was involved in the Philippines battle. Fighting covered an area 600 miles north and south and 250 east and west. Navy officials were elated and felt the whole course of the war might be speeded. [1:3.]

On Leyte American troops had pushed twenty miles north of Tacloban and nine miles inland from Dulag. Additional landings on the northern part of Leyte and the southern part of Samar won control of San Juanico Strait, which separates them. [1:7; map P. 2.]

Superfortresses delivered a smashing assault on Japan's key aircraft plant at Omura on the island of Kyushu. One B-29 was missing. [1:6.]

German positions in the Belgium-Netherland pocket were becoming increasingly untenable as Canadian and British troops drew closer and menaced the enemy retreat line. [1:4; map P. 7.] More than 2,200 American and British bombers lashed rail and oil targets in the Reich. Six bombers and one of a great fighter escort were missing. [9:1.]

Russian forces captured the German port and U-boat base of Kirkenes in Norway and thirty other Norwegian villages. [1:6-7; map P. 11.] To the south the Red Army renewed its drive on Warsaw, gained more ground in East Prussia and liberated all of Transylvania by capturing Satu-Mare and Carei. [12:1, with map.]

Mount Belmonte, guarding the southern approaches to Bologna, was captured by Americans of the Fifth Army in Italy. The British Eighth Army gained three miles in the Adriatic sector. A German withdrawal was indicated. [10:7.]

The United Nations have resumed diplomatic relations with Italy, the first former enemy state to receive recognition. [1:2-3.]

U. S. and Britain Recognize Italy; Action Is First With an Ex-Enemy

By BERTRAM D. HULEN
Special to The New York Times.

WASHINGTON, Oct. 25—Diplomatic relations with Italy were resumed by the Allies tonight.

Recognition is being accorded by the United States, the other American republics in the United Nations and Britain. The Soviet Union had previously extended recognition to the Government of Premier Ivanoe Bonomi.

Our action was announced by Edward R. Stettinius Jr., acting Secretary of State, who said that Alexander C. Kirk, who has been serving as our diplomatic representative in Rome with the personal rank of Ambassador, would now be accredited to the Italian Government with the rank of Ambassador.

It is expected that Italy will now send an Ambassador here. The appointment of Count Carlos Sforza, long a friend of the United States, to the post, has been forecast since it became evident that recognition would not long be delayed.

Announcement of the recognition has been made at London and is expected at the Latin-American capitals, except for Buenos Aires. Argentina never severed relations with Italy, although she did with Germany and Japan.

The announcement by Mr. Stettinius follows:

"After consultation with the other American republics, as provided in the Resolutions of Rio de

Continued on Page 10, Column 5

Russians Invade North Norway; Take Kirkenes in Wide Advance

By W. H. LAWRENCE
By Wireless to The New York Times.

MOSCOW, Oct. 25—Entering their ninth country in less than seven months, Red Army forces smashed across the Norwegian frontier today and liberated the Barents Sea port of Kirkenes and thirty other Norwegian villages just fifty-four months and twenty-one days after the beginning of Adolf Hitler's treacherous invasion of the Scandinavian country.

This new expedition of Russian troops outside the Soviet Union was announced by Premier Joseph Stalin in a special order of the day and was saluted by Moscow's massed guns and highlighted in tonight's communiqué.

The Soviet Union's Norwegian campaign brings Allied armies back on the soil of that restless country for the first time since June 15, 1941, when the British had to withdraw their poorly equipped forces in the face of numerically superior German forces.

[On its European front the Red Army reopened the battle for Warsaw by outflanking the Polish capital on the north, drove farther into East Prussia against desperate resistance and completed the liberation of Transylvania.]

It would be wrong to assume from this dash across the Norwegian frontier at its northernmost point that the liberation of

Continued on Page 11, Column 6

"All the News That's Fit to Print"

The New York Times.

LATE CITY EDITION
Cloudy and continued cold today with fresh winds.
Temperatures Yesterday—Max., 39; Min., 31
Sunrise, 7:15 A. M.; Sunset, 4:31 P. M.

Copyright, 1944, by The New York Times Company.

VOL. XCIV..No. 31,741. Entered as Second-Class Matter, Postoffice, New York, N. Y. NEW YORK, TUESDAY, DECEMBER 19, 1944. THREE CENTS IN NEW YORK CITY

GERMANS DRIVE 20 MILES INTO BELGIUM; ALLIED FLIERS POUND TANK SPEARHEADS; 742 JAPANESE PLANES SMASHED IN WEEK

SENATORS DEBATE GREECE, BALKANS, DEMAND POLICY KEY

Sidetrack Discussion of Six State Department Nominees for Foreign Affairs

POLISH ISSUE ALSO RAISED

Four New Dealers Lead Fight on Stettinius 'Team,' While Republicans Uphold Them

By KATHLEEN McLAUGHLIN
Special to THE NEW YORK TIMES.

WASHINGTON, Dec. 18—President Roosevelt's foreign policy and its relation to current political events in Europe had the spotlight in Senate debate today on the half dozen nominees for whom the President has asked for confirmation as "a team" for Secretary of State Edward R. Stettinius.

Throughout hours of debate, these six men and their backgrounds and foregrounds were subordinated to the anxieties expressed by the Senators over the Greek and Polish issues and their impact on our relations with other countries. From conservatives and liberals came demands that President Roosevelt himself define his foreign policy in the light of these events.

The debate made little progress toward the adjournment sine die of Congress for which the Senate is striving and which the House, its business completed, awaits. Many Representatives, including Speaker Sam Rayburn, are already on the way home.

Early Session Planned Today

It is planned to bring the State Department nominations to a vote tomorrow, which if accomplished will be the signal for adjournment. The Senate will meet at 11 A. M. instead of noon and continue in session into the night if necessary to decide on the nominees.

Only in a minor sense was the discussion confined to the qualifications of the individual members of "the team," Joseph C. Grew, named to be Under-Secretary of State, and William L. Clayton, Nelson A. Rockefeller, Archibald MacLeish, Brig. Gen. Julius C. Holmes and James Clement Dunn, as assistant secretaries.

The major issue was the British policy in Greece and Italy and the Russian policy in Poland, as it would affect smaller countries and the future of the world, and the responsibility of the United States in this crisis.

The protest against confirmation was led by four of the Administration's adherents—Senators Claude Pepper of Florida, Joseph F. Guffey of Pennsylvania, James E. Murray of Montana, Democrats, and Robert M. La Follette Jr. of Wisconsin, while Republicans, notably Senators Owen Brewster and Wallace White, acting minority leader, both of Maine, supported the President's list.

Postponing to Be Considered

Individual Senators have individual objections to each of the six men named, but almost invariably uphold others.

In this situation the first order of business tomorrow will be the resolution to postpone consideration of the issue until Jan. 3, when the Seventy-ninth Congress convenes, as proposed by the three Democrats and one Progressive. It is at present tabled.

Senator Pepper, in "a preliminary discussion" of the resolution, which took four hours, asserted that the names submitted did not originate with the President and were not characteristic of his foreign policy, therefore, he hoped that they could be "reconsidered" in the holiday recess and resubmitted to the new Congress.

One of his arguments turned on a passage from "Time for Decision," by former Under-Secretary of State Sumner Welles, relating that the Senate had been prevailed upon to pass the Neutrality Law, which prevented United States intervention later in Spain, in the absence of President Roosevelt and of Secretary Hull, neither of whom would have approved the action had they been available. The Senate derived its erroneous impression, Senator Pepper indicated, from Mr. Dunn, one of the men now under consideration for promotion.

While it has been said that the President formulates his own foreign policy and is responsible for administering it, Senator Pepper added, it is not possible for him to be closely informed and wisely advised on all occasions, unless his

Continued on Page 9, Column 2

U. S. Scientists Aid Allies in Air War

By The Associated Press.

LONDON, Dec. 18—A group of American scientists, including a Nobel prize winner, who were flown overseas to help solve the problem of the rocket bombs, has contributed to the Allies' domination of the skies over Europe, it was disclosed today.

The scientists, brought from the United States at the request of Maj. Gen. Hugh J. Knerr, commanding the Strategic Air Service Command, were credited with vital assistance in developing the accuracy of strategic bombing.

They include Dr. John L. Synge of Ohio State University, Dr. Howard M. Jenkins of Swarthmore, Dr. Oswald Veblen of Princeton, Dr. H. H. Germand of the University of Florida, and Dr. D. L. Webster of Stanford.

Dr. Carl Anderson, Professor of Physics at the California Institute of Technology and holder of the Nobel Prize, is here on a special mission in connection with rocket bombs.

15 AT ARMY BASE SEIZED IN 'KICKBACK'

Rival Gangs Are Charged With Beating Workers at Port of Embarkation, Brooklyn

The arrest of fifteen men at the Brooklyn base of the United States Army Port of Embarkation yesterday brought to light a Federal Bureau of Investigation inquiry into alleged "kickback" rackets in the carpenter department and marine repair shop there.

E. E. Conroy, local FBI chief, called the situation one of the most extensive of the war, estimated the amount of bribes taken over a two-year period at $150,000 or more, and said the profits had spurred rival gangs into "open warfare." Luigi (Lou) Salica, former bantamweight boxing champion, was among the suspects.

Two of those picked up were described as leaders of rival factions, and most of the others were said to be their henchmen. A typical practice, according to the FBI, was the collection of $3 from each victim of the racket, at each bi-weekly payday. This collection was said to be "viciously enforced," with occasional trouncings for any who seemed reluctant to pay. It covered "insurance" against periodic lay-offs.

Rival Leaders Identified

The rival leaders were identified by Mr. Conroy as Robert White, 55 years old, assistant superintendent of carpenters at the base, and Arturo Emanuel Amedo Valerio, 43, a dock boss of carpenters. White was said to be much the more active of the two.

According to the FBI, White was a "contact man between certain officials at the base and the foremen of various groups of carpenters." In this position, according to the charges, he found it possible to collect money from workmen as protection against lay-offs and for transfers from other bases to the one where he held forth and for obtaining work at the base. Also, it was made possible for two of those arrested yesterday to report for work in the morning, leave the base and report again at night as though they had done a day's work—sometimes they reported late and received overtime pay, Mr. Conroy remarked. Special fees were exacted at times and ranged from $20 to $200.

White lives at 1361 Nostrand Avenue, Brooklyn, and was em-

Continued on Page 16, Column 3

U. S. VIEW ON POLES

Stettinius Says We Will Accept Settlement on Border if Mutual

BACKS NATION'S FREEDOM

Secretary Explains Exception to Policy of Deferring Any Disputes on Boundaries

By LANSING WARREN
Special to THE NEW YORK TIMES.

WASHINGTON, Dec. 18—Secretary of State Edward R. Stettinius Jr., in a statement today giving the United States Government's stand on the Polish problem, reiterated our position in favor of deferring border settlements until after the war but said that if a mutual agreement were reached by the United Nations directly concerned this Government would raise no objections.

In defining the "basic principles of our foreign policy" as they affect the Polish dispute, the Secretary proclaimed that the United States stood "unequivocally for a strong, free and independent" Poland and the right of the Polish people to order their internal existence, but he added that the United States adhered to the policy of declining to give territorial guarantees.

The statement, which had previously been communicated to all interested governments, would therefore appear to express opposition to any settlement imposed on Poland such as seemed to be foreshadowed in Prime Minister Churchill's recent speech, but to withhold from the Polish Government in London any hope of active support for its resistance in the boundary controversy.

Pledges Aid in Transfer

Secretary Stettinius expressed sympathy for the interests of the Polish people and assurances of American assistance in the event that an agreement should make necessary a transfer of populations in the present territory of Poland. He asserted that, "subject to Congressional authority," it was the aim of the United States to aid in reconstruction and in bringing the liberated peoples to full partnership in the future world organization.

The position of the United States, as thus defined, would appear to disassociate the United States from any attempt to force a territorial settlement on Poland. It could conceivably give rise to divergences with the other great powers on the following points:

The declaration that the United States supports a free and independent Poland could possibly conflict with the policy that Russia is understood to maintain regarding the setting up of friendly democratic governments in neighboring states.

It also indirectly expresses opposition to the recently observed tendency in Europe for negotiated bilateral alliances and treaties, as instanced in the phrase underlining the fact that the United States is working instead for the establishment of a world security organiza-

Continued on Page 8, Column 4

28 SHIPS ALSO SUNK

Invasion of Mindoro Is Progressing at Faster Rate Than Expected

RESISTANCE ALMOST NIL

MacArthur States Our Losses Continue Low—New Gains Are Scored on Leyte

By FRANK L. KLUCKHOHN
By Wireless to THE NEW YORK TIMES.

ADVANCED HEADQUARTERS, in the Philippines, Tuesday, Dec. 19—Enemy planes numbering 742 were destroyed or seriously damaged during the week ended Sunday night in the battle for the Philippines, Gen. Douglas MacArthur announced last night.

Of these, 369 were destroyed by forces, including carriers, under General MacArthur's command and 373 by Admiral William F. Halsey's fast carriers operating off Luzon. From Thursday through Saturday, escort carrier planes under General MacArthur claimed sixty enemy planes destroyed and twenty-seven probables, bringing the total number of planes accounted for by those Navy planes to 460. Ground ack-ack fire, PT-boats and Army aircraft were responsible for 282 more.

[Admiral Nimitz revealed Monday night that twenty-eight ships and small craft had been sunk and sixty-six damaged in a three-day aerial strike in the Philippine area, principally off Luzon.]

These losses are serious for Japan's air force and, momentarily at least, appear to have smashed the background of enemy air power in the Philippine area. Current attacks on our Mindoro beachhead, for instance, are being made largely by single planes.

Mindoro Called "Easy" Task

American construction work on airfields in that island, 155 miles south of Manila, is officially described as "very satisfactory."

[An Associated Press correspondent, writing from Mindoro, indicated that the invasion has been the easiest major task of the Pacific war. He said: "The Japanese have offered not the slightest resistance as yet, aside from harassing air attacks by a few planes." He added that the invasion had been moving "swifter than had been hoped."]

The bristling guns of PT-boats accounted for six of the enemy planes General MacArthur's forces

Continued on Page 11, Column 4

AMERICANS BATTLE TO STEM ADVANCE OF THE ENEMY

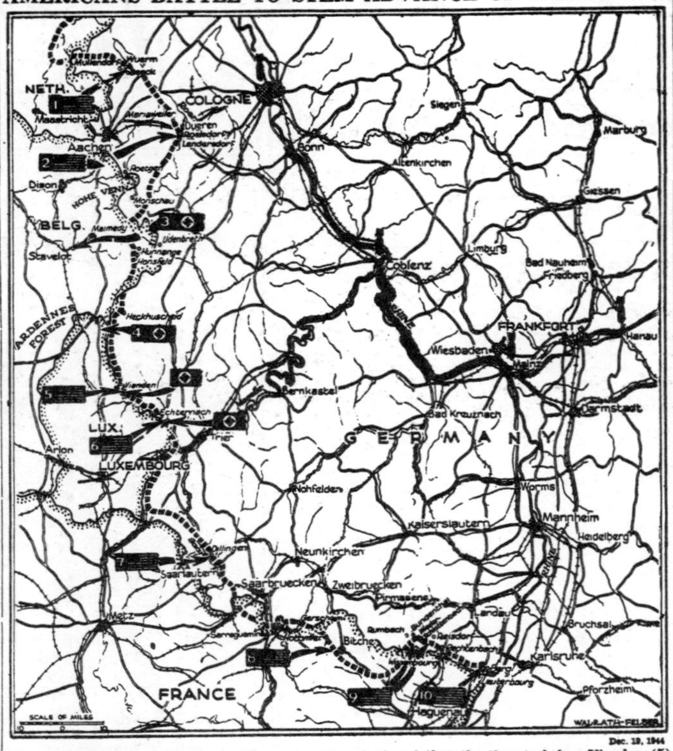

Dec. 19, 1944

On the Ninth Army front our troops cleared Wuerm, Mullendorf and Beeck (1) and before Dueren they entered Roelsdorf and Lendersdorf (2). Although there was a blackout on news of the German offensive, it was indicated that the foe was beyond Stavelot in Belgium (3), that the push at the northern tip of Luxembourg (4) had gained and that the thrusts below Vianden (5) and Echternach (6) had been stalled. The Third Army pushed to the eastern edge of Dillingen (7). The Seventh battered Maginot Line defenses near Bitche (8), entered Nieder Schlettenbach (9), west of which it gained, and passed Berg (10). Bombs show rail centers blasted.

NAZIS STILL MOVING

Fliers Attack German Armored Column West of Malmedy, Belgium

3D AND 7TH SMASH ON

Maginot Line Fortresses in the Vosges Begin to Crack Under American Guns

By Wireless to THE NEW YORK TIMES.

SUPREME HEADQUARTERS, Allied Expeditionary Force, Paris, Dec. 18—The American Ninth Air Force and the British Second Tactical Air Force dived through sleet and fog today to hammer the tank-tipped German columns pressing deeper into Belgium and Luxembourg as Field Marshal Gen. Karl von Rundstedt's counter-offensive continued to move westward for the third day.

The greatest enemy penetration revealed by the Allies was in the area west of Stavelot, which is eight miles southwest of Malmedy and twenty miles from the German frontier from which the northern arm of the offensive was launched. There, rocket-firing Typhoons of the British Second Tactical Air Force fell on a column of twenty German half-tracks, destroying three of them.

Allied Planes Batter Foe

The Allies' ground forces continued their news blackout today, but it is obvious from the reports of air battles, which involved three American tactical commands and two British fighter bomber groups, that the German counter-offensive was monopolizing the Allies' attention.

The air battles raged over this battle front, with American pilots destroying forty-five German planes and the British one. The Ninth Air Force, whose fighter bombers operated against enemy columns, claimed the destruction of ninety-five German tanks and other armored vehicles, 265 trucks and sixty railroad cars, while Marauders, Havocs and Invaders dropped more than 290 tons of bombs on five towns in the Schleiden area, well to the east of the German spearheads.

The Ninth Air Force also claimed that twenty-six tanks and other armored vehicles, sixty-five trucks and nineteen railroad cars had been damaged and that twenty fortified buildings had been destroyed and twenty gun positions silenced during the attacks today. German railroads were cut in three places.

Bombers Hit Rail Centers

In a direct blow at the supply lines of the attacking German Armies, 1,800 American and British heavy bombers attacked major German railway centers including Cologne, Coblenz and Mainz last night and today.

[Press services said that the Germans had launched a new V weapon on both the American Ninth and First Army fronts. They also reported that south of Dueren, northeast of the area under attack by the Germans, American First Army units entered Roelsdorf and Lendersdorf, about one mile from Dueren.]

The German thrust to the vicinity of Stavelot placed the northern arm of Marshal von Rundstedt's offensive in an area twenty-two miles southeast of Liége. There were no reports available here of the progress of the enemy drives into Luxembourg through Vianden and Echternach. The speed and depth of the penetration in the north, however, were disquieting.

[Press service reports from the front said the German drives around Vianden and Echternach had been stalled. At the same time the Berlin radio said German troops had crossed the northern tip of Luxembourg and were advancing toward the Belgian-Luxembourg border.]

The nature of all Allied measures taken to halt the enemy thrust cannot be revealed, but it is obvious that the two days of extensive air activity have failed to check the German offensive in the north at least. It is probable, however, that American divisions already are at-

Continued on Page 4, Column 6

SUBMARINES ERASE 33 SHIPS, A RECORD

12 Japanese Warcraft Sunk in New Pacific-Far East Toll by Our Undersea Raiders

Special to THE NEW YORK TIMES.

WASHINGTON, Dec. 18—United States submarines were credited today with their greatest single reported bag of Japanese vessels when the Navy Department reported that twelve enemy warships—the largest number ever listed in a regular communiqué—

Continued on Page 10, Column 4

War's Length Said to Hang On German Drive's Outcome

By DREW MIDDLETON
By Wireless to THE NEW YORK TIMES.

SUPREME HEADQUARTERS, Allied Expeditionary Force, Paris, Dec. 18—The German counter-offensive against the American First Army has changed the tactical situation on the northern and central sectors of the Western Front. The strength of Field Marshal Gen. Karl von Rundstedt's blow has increased, rather than lessened, in the last twenty-four hours and the Twelfth Army Group is now faced with a large-scale enemy attempt to split its front.

This correspondent believes that if the enemy can push forward for another three days in Belgium and Luxembourg, he will certainly delay the continuation of the winter offensive in the north.

Marshal von Rundstedt hopes to dislocate the American offensive in the north and possibly in the Saar Basin and, through this dislocation, perhaps force their abandonment.

Just seventy-two hours ago five Allied armies were fighting in the Reich. Today they are faced with the problem of checking and then breaking a surprisingly large German force that has already moved well to the west of the American positions on the Cologne Plain and in the Saar Basin's eastern fringe.

Such an offensive must inevita-

Continued on Page 3, Column 3

BRITISH PRY ELAS FROM ATHENS GATE

Planes Aid in Gains as All-Out Push Begins—Jail Stormed, Falls to Leftists

By A. C. SEDGWICK
By Wireless to THE NEW YORK TIMES.

ATHENS, Dec. 18—Now in a position to make their force the deciding factor in the battle of Athens, British troops swept up from Phaliron Bay last night and by morning had cleared Syngrou Boulevard and areas 200 to 300 yards deep on each side of this principal line of communications.

The defeat of the Leftists in a few days is indicated.

Thus the siege of the city has

Continued on Page 6, Column 3

Supreme Court Upholds Return Of Loyal Japanese to West Coast

By LEWIS WOOD
Special to THE NEW YORK TIMES.

WASHINGTON, Dec. 18—The constitutionality of the wartime regulations under which American citizens of Japanese ancestry were evacuated from Pacific Coast areas in 1942 was upheld by a vote of 6 to 3 in the Supreme Court today, but in another decision the court ruled unanimously that Japanese-Americans of unquestioned loyalty to the United States could not be detained in war relocation centers.

The Supreme Court rulings came only twenty-four hours after the Army announcement that exclusion of Japanese-Americans from the West Coast would be ended Jan. 2. They came also at about the time Secretary Ickes declared in a statement that he did not foresee a "hasty mass movement" of evacuees back to the West Coast.

Justice Hugo L. Black wrote the majority opinion on the evacuation question, which involved the 1942 order of Maj. Gen. John L. De Witt as applied to Fred Toyosaburo Korematsu.

Upholding the order as "of the time it was made and when (Korematsu) violated it," he deplored compulsory exclusion, but said that Korematsu was excluded because we were at war with Japan, adding:

"When under conditions of modern warfare our shores are threatened by hostile forces, the power to protect must be commensurate with the threatened danger.

"We are unable to conclude that it was beyond the war powers of

Continued on Page 14, Column 4

War News Summarized

TUESDAY, DECEMBER 19, 1944

Germany's counter-offensive against the United States First Army went through its third day under a blanket of censorship. It was disclosed, however, that Field Marshal von Rundstedt's northern flank had advanced a total of twenty miles to eight miles southwest of Malmedy. Allied fliers rained destruction through sleet and fog, smashing at least ninety-five enemy tanks and other armored vehicles and 265 trucks and shooting down forty-six German planes at a cost of eleven of our own aircraft.

The United States Ninth Army, north of the German push, gained up to two miles north of Geilenkirchen. The Third Army drove to the eastern outskirts of Dillingen and reported heavy enemy concentrations that might indicate a counter-offensive there. The Seventh Army battered down increasing enemy opposition to advance along a fourteen-mile front into the Siegfried Line defending the Palatinate. [All the foregoing 1:8.]

Much depends upon the outcome of the fighting during the next few days. If the Twelfth Army Corps can prevent von Rundstedt's troops from splitting its front and delaying Allied offensives, the Germans stand to suffer a military and moral blow. [1:6-7.] Washington was not disturbed by the enemy drive. [3:6.]

Eighth Air Force bombers smashed railyards in the Rhineland without interception, while the RAF, after having lashed out during Sunday night at Ulm, Munich, Duisburg and other targets, flew last night to Gdynia, on the Baltic, to attack German fleet units. [3:1.]

There was little change in position in the Italian fighting [5:5] but the Russians cleared the Germans out of northeast Hungary and drove into Czechoslovakia. [7:1.]

British troops have lifted the siege of Athens and have opened a campaign to wrest the capital area from Elas fighters. [1:7; map P. 6.]

Secretary of State Stettinius reiterated this country's stand against territorial changes during the war and "for a strong, free and independent Polish State with the untrammeled right" of the Poles to settle their internal affairs. However, this country will raise no objection to an agreement reached by the interested parties, he said. [1:3.]

During the past week, 742 Japanese planes have been destroyed or damaged in the Philippines. Americans on Mindoro were meeting no ground resistance, and on Leyte they reached the Valencia airfield. [1:4.] United States submarines have sunk thirty-three more Japanese ships, including a light cruiser, three destroyers and eight other combat vessels. [1:5.] Nearly 200 B-29's obtained good results in Sunday's attacks on Hankow, China, and Nagoya, Japan, without losing a plane. Today the Superforts hit Kyushu. [10:6.]

Army Orders 40,000 Draft Rise In January, February as a Need

Special to THE NEW YORK TIMES.

WASHINGTON, Dec. 18—The War Department declared tonight that circumstances were forcing it to increase its January and February calls on Selective Service from 60,000 to 80,000 men for each month.

"Whether or not it will be necessary to continue the 80,000 rate in March and April will be determined later," the War Department said in this latest announcement reflecting the increased tightness in manpower, both on the military and war industry fronts.

The Army statement went into considerable detail to explain how it had sought to avoid increasing the draft call by combing its own ranks for tough, young infantry replacements, and concluded:

"The Army has thus done its share in producing the required infantrymen before it has called upon the nation for its necessary additional quota."

Since last July, it related, the Army actually had been asking Selective Service for smaller numbers of men than "the estimated requirements."

It had been able to get by in this manner by combing its own ranks to eliminate organizations which the changed strategic situation had made no longer necessary. It took young men "physically suitable for arduous field service" out of such units and sent them into the infantry or armored groups.

Through this "liquidation" procedure 100 anti-aircraft battalions had been retrained as infantry groups and other anti-aircraft men

Continued on Page 17, Column 2

"All the News That's Fit to Print"

The New York Times.

LATE CITY EDITION
Fair and somewhat warmer today with moderate winds.
Temperatures Yesterday—Max., 26; Min., 17
Sunrise, 8:16 A. M.; Sunset, 8:32 P. M.

Copyright, 1944, by The New York Times Company.

VOL. XCIV..No. 31,742. Entered as Second-Class Matter, Postoffice, New York, N. Y. NEW YORK, WEDNESDAY, DECEMBER 20, 1944. THREE CENTS NEW YORK CITY

NAZIS GAIN IN BELGIUM IN GREAT BATTLE; FORTRESSES CALLED UPON TO STEM PUSH; B-29'S BOMB JAPAN AND CHINA CENTERS

PLOT TO RESTRICT BOMBSIGHT OUTPUT LAID TO NORDEN, INC.

2 Corporation Officials, Navy Commander and Associate Named in Indictments

INVENTOR NOT INVOLVED

Steps to Prevent Production in Outside Plant Charged—$109,000 in Fees Assailed

Carl L. Norden, Inc., Theodore H. Barth and Ward B. Marvelle, officials of the corporation, and Comdr. John D. Corrigan, USNR, were indicted yesterday charged with conspiring to defraud the Government by restricting to the Norden concern production of the famous Norden bombsight.

A second true bill handed up by a Federal grand jury here charged that Corrigan, who was suspended by the Navy last June, had taken part in another conspiracy with the industrial engineering firm of Corrigan, Osburne & Wells, Inc., and Robert H. Wells, president, to defraud the Government of Corrigan's own impartial services to the Navy. Ostensibly serving as one who had severed private business connections with the firm, Corrigan used his position as a sort of "trouble shooter" to swing to it contracts on which he gained $109,000, this indictment alleged.

Attorney General Francis Biddle asserted that Carl L. Norden, inventor of the bombsight, was in no way involved in the allegations. The corporation and Wells issued statements denying the charges completely.

Fight Against Expansion Alleged

In the first indictment, it was set forth that the War and Navy Departments had sought to increase the production of the bombsights soon after the attack on Pearl Harbor. With this in view, they contracted to have Remington Rand, Inc., turn out 8,500 of the complicated assembly known as the "football unit" for the sight at a plant in Elmira, N. Y. On April 22, 1942, the Norden concern agreed to supply to Remington Rand necessary data, drawings, specifications, and technical advice and assistance.

But, it was alleged, while entering into this agreement, the corporation and Barth and Marvelle formulated a "plan to retain in defendant Norden [corporation] control of the production and source and means of supply of Norden bombsights, and the component parts thereof." To effectuate this plan, the indictment asserted, the corporation and Barth, president, and Marvelle, vice president, did the following:

1. "Failed and neglected" to supply to Remington Rand the necessary engineering assistance.

2. Furnished "incomplete and inaccurate" specifications for the construction of the "football unit."

3. Failed to advise Remington Rand of allowable deviations from specifications, without which it was "difficult if not impossible to produce" the units.

4. Caused Remington Rand "football units" to be rejected in reinspections in New York after they had been inspected and approved at the Elmira plant by the resident Naval inspector.

5. Used such rejection "as a means and method of discrediting" units manufactured by Remington Rand and of preventing delivery of such units to the Bureau of Ordnance of the Navy.

Charges Termed "Fantastic"

In its statement the Norden corporation said:

"Charges made against Carl L. Norden, Inc., and its officials in the indictment handed down today are as utterly fantastic as they are untrue.

"Carl L. Norden, Inc., takes justifiable pride in its contribution to the war effort. This corporation developed the Norden bombsight, turned the patents over to the Navy, and has not only met but has exceeded every production schedule set up by the Navy.

"It would appear that the grand jury was not acquainted with all the true facts concerning the Government seizure of the Remington Rand plant in Elmira, N. Y. The work of Remington Rand was so fatally defective that not a single bombsight produced or manufactured by Remington Rand itself at Elmira was ever accepted by the Navy Department or considered acceptable when examined by them."

The statement went on with the assertion that there was much evidence that the corporation had

Continued on Page 36, Column 2

Congress Expires With Few on Hand

Special to THE NEW YORK TIMES.

WASHINGTON, Dec. 19—The Seventy-eighth Congress expired at 8:22 o'clock this evening with the adjournment sine die of the Senate, only thirty-eight members answering to a final quorum call.

The House, which had lacked a quorum for the last few days, formally quit at 6:59 o'clock with only twenty-two Representatives on hand.

In the final hours the Rivers and Harbors Bill died through inability of the Senate to muster a vote to approve the conference report on the legislation.

The bill providing the first rise in pay for postal employes in twenty-five years was also killed when Senator Bailey of North Carolina objected to consideration. His contention was that the bill was the first move in an attempt to break "the Little Steel formula."

SENATE CONFIRMS 6 STETTINIUS AIDES

'Filibuster' Collapses as Roosevelt Warns He Will Resubmit Nominees to New Congress

By KATHLEEN McLAUGHLIN

Special to THE NEW YORK TIMES.

WASHINGTON, Dec. 19—The Senate confirmed this afternoon all six of President Roosevelt's nominees as aides to Secretary Stettinius. The settlement providing a climax to the final legislative day of the year on Capitol Hill.

An apparent filibuster to prevent action on the appointments collapsed early in the session when Senator Claude Pepper of Florida, who was directing the opposition, announced that he had been told by the President by telephone that if postponement were taken until Jan. 3, as provided in a resolution presented by Senators Pepper, Murray of Montana, Guffey of Pennsylvania and La Follette of Wisconsin, the identical names would be resubmitted by him at that time.

The Floridian said, therefore, that he and the other three Senators would no longer prolong the debate, while reserving their protests.

The six nominees, Joseph C. Grew, to be Under-Secretary of State, and William L. Clayton, Nelson A. Rockefeller, Archibald MacLeish, James C. Dunn and Brig. Gen. Julius C. Holmes as Assistant Secretaries, were approved by a safe margin.

The roll-calls were: Mr. Grew, 66-7; Mr. Rockefeller, 62-9; Mr. Clayton, 52-19; Mr. Dunn 62-10; General Holmes, 61-9, and Mr. MacLeish, 43-25.

Clark Votes for MacLeish

There were changes in alignment in the roll-calls, and Senator Bennett Champ Clark, Democrat, of Missouri, who sharply questioned Mr. MacLeish during committee hearings, astonished the gallery by voting for him today.

The four Senators who sponsored the postponement resolution broke ranks on the final votes, with Senator La Follette alone holding firm against the list. Senators Pepper, Guffey and Murray voted "no" on all of the nominees except Mr. Clayton, on whom Senator Murray withheld his vote, but all three switched to "aye" for Mr. MacLeish.

Mr. Pepper, in telling the Senate of Mr. Roosevelt's opposition to the postponement resolution sponsored by the four Senators, declared:

"The President told us that he needed men of experience in the Department of State, and he felt that these men would conscien-

Continued on Page 16, Column 2

KYUSHU HIT AGAIN

Omura Aircraft Factory Raked—Shanghai and Nanking Also Seared

HANKOW BLOW A RECORD

250 Planes Loose 1,000 Tons, Setting Huge Fires—Direct Strikes Scored at Nagoya

By The Associated Press.

WASHINGTON, Dec. 19—The big Omura aircraft factory on the Japanese home island of Kyushu came in for another blasting from American Superfortresses today while other B-29's hit targets at enemy-held Shanghai and Nanking on the Chinese mainland.

Those new blows in the stepped-up air war aimed to knock out Japanese sources of airpower and supply lines for the enemy forces in China were reported in a War Department communiqué.

China-based B-29's in "medium force"—an expression that usually means about forty planes—bombed Omura through an overcast with precision instruments. It was the fifth time that Omura, which has a huge aircraft assembly works, has been hit since last July.

"Good to excellent" results were reported for the attacks on docks and engineering works at Shanghai and Nanking. The B-29's shot down five enemy fighters, probably bagged three others and damaged an additional nine, although a communiqué said little opposition was encountered.

Meantime checks of air photographs showed that heavy damage was inflicted by strikes twenty-four hours earlier at Nagoya, Japan's third city, and Hankow, China.

Black smoke rolled up to 1,000 feet above a big airplane plant at Nagoya, a communiqué said, while it was disclosed that more than 250 planes—the largest force ever sent into the air over China—participated in the attack on Hankow.

Heaviest Blow on Hankow

Walter Rundle, representing the Combined American Press, who flew with China-based forces in the raid on Hankow, reported the striking force was made up of B-29's, smaller bombers and fighters.

It dropped the heaviest bomb-load, more than 1,000 tons, ever dropped on the Asiatic mainland. Docks and rail yards of this principal supply port for the Japanese forces in south-central China were plastered, as was the Hankow airport, the most important Japanese airfield in China.

Huge fires were left blazing along almost the entire length of Hankow's three-mile-long Yangtze River waterfront, said a dispatch sent by Associated Press Correspondent Charles A. Grumich from a Superfortress base in Szechwan Province, China. Many of the B-29's which participated in this raid carried their maximum load of substantially more than eight tons each. Hundreds of tons of incendiaries were dropped.

Details of the damage done at Nagoya, on the main Japanese island of Honshu, were given in a

Continued on Page 14, Column 2

FOE IN LEYTE TRAP

Americans Cut Ormoc Corridor in 2 Places, Take Stronghold

ENEMY CASUALTIES LEAP

Japanese Offer No Ground Resistance on Mindoro—12 Planes Downed

By FRANK L. KLUCKHOHN

By Wireless to THE NEW YORK TIMES.

ADVANCED HEADQUARTERS, on Leyte, Wednesday, Dec. 20—American troops, smashing north and south, have cut the main highway running north and south through western Leyte's Ormoc corridor at two points, dividing the Japanese troops in the corridor into three segments.

The Seventy-seventh Division, with a preponderance of men from New York, New Jersey and Connecticut, smashed into the town of Valencia, two and a half miles south of Libongao. From Libongao a road leads west toward Palompon, on the northwest peninsula of Leyte, which the Japanese have been using as their supply port since Ormoc fell.

Meanwhile the crack First Cavalry, driving southwest out of hills that had long slowed their advance, cut the main road three miles north of the junction by capturing the town of Lonoy.

For the first time in the weeks of heavy fighting the Japanese positions in the corridor appeared to be crumbling. They might be forced to withdraw into the hills of the northwest peninsula where they would be ineffective.

These developments occurred Monday.

The Japanese trapped southwest of Valencia are being eliminated. Some are retreating rapidly, trying to escape the trap. Most of the 1,484 Japanese dead counted Monday were in this sector.

Except for escape over the hills a big bitterly fighting Japanese force is cut off between the First Cavalry and the Thirty-second Division, which is still plugging southward over the toughest country in all Leyte.

Only six miles of highway now separate the First Cavalry to the

Continued on Page 13, Column 4

ATTEMPTED LANDING BEHIND OUR LINES FAILS

Soldiers of the Ninth Army inspecting a transport plane that was shot down while carrying paratroopers to participate in the present German counter-offensive.

The New York Times (U. S. Signal Corps Radiotelephoto)

NAZI TANKS HALTED BY EPIC U. S. STAND

Veterans, Refusing to Retreat, Are Crushed in Trenches—Lost Hospital Recaptured

By WES GALLAGHER

Associated Press Correspondent

IN BELGIUM, South of Monschau, Dec. 19—Veteran American doughboys, flung into one of the war's weirdest battles on a moment's notice, brought the German attack on the northern flank near here to a bloody halt today in a welter of wrecked tanks and dead men.

At least six German counter-attacks were smashed.

Farther to the south the situation remained fluid and obscure, with deep German penetrations reported, but in this mountainous pine-covered area, where millions of snow-covered evergreens stand like Christmas trees, the Germans' Elite Guard tank columns have

Continued on Page 4, Column 3

Atlantic Charter Unsigned But Intact, Roosevelt Says

By C. P. TRUSSELL

Special to THE NEW YORK TIMES.

WASHINGTON, Dec. 19—President Roosevelt, tanned and looking much rested after a three-week vacation interspersed with work at "the Little White House" in Warm Springs, Ga., returned to Washington today and held his first news conference since he left for the South on Nov. 27.

Under a barrage of questions that awaited his signal, Mr. Roosevelt disclosed that the date for his next meeting with Prime Minister Churchill and Premier Stalin had not yet been set, answered recent demands by Administration supporters in the Senate for a restatement of the foreign policy of the United States by declaring that it was already on the record, and said that there was not and never had been a formal, complete Atlantic Charter signed by him and Mr. Churchill.

Asked whether he was moving "to the left," as some observers contended during his absence, or "to the right," as others had concluded from his recent appointments to ranking posts in the reorganized State Department, the President said that he was going down the old line a little left of center. He had said that eleven and one-half years ago, he added, and it still goes.

He parried other foreign-policy questions, including one concerning the recent assertion by Ernest Bevin, British Minister of Labor, that Mr. Roosevelt had initialed at the latest Quebec conference a British plan for "stabilization" in Greece. It was contentious, he said, and he suggested that it not be brought up again.

An inquiry on the "generalship" of Mayor La Guardia, who long has been reported to be slated for a high military post in Italy, caused the President to smile and pause. Then he said that that matter was, to employ a French phrase, en train. If that meant anything to the interrogator, he chuckled, that was grand.

The Atlantic Charter entered the questioning with a query whether

Continued on Page 15, Column 4

JOY BECOMES GLOOM IN A BELGIAN TOWN

People Take American Flags Down—'You'll Be Back,' Woman Innkeeper Says

By HAROLD DENNY

By Wireless to THE NEW YORK TIMES.

WITH THE UNITED STATES FIRST ARMY, Dec. 19—For months now some of us have been living in a pleasant, friendly Belgian city, and it had become home to us. It is near the German border and is one of those towns that our troops liberated on their march into the Siegfried Line last September.

Now, by the fortunes of war we have had to leave it suddenly. The Germans in a powerful counter-offensive have lunged back from behind their Westwall at points where we had penetrated it. The battle has roared over some of these places, including this little city of ours.

There is so much that correspondents are prevented by the military situation from writing. And it is difficult to write about it because having to give ground in such circumstances is both bewildering and saddening.

You wonder what is going to happen to your recently freed friends when the Germans come back.

Our move was decided upon and carried out suddenly yesterday

Continued on Page 5, Column 1

OUR MEN CONFIDENT

Americans Fight Their Biggest Battle to Check Foe's Drive

WE HIT WITH BIG BOMBERS

Strategic Fortresses Used for Tactical Blows at Supply Points—News Curb Severe

By HAROLD DENNY

By Cable to THE NEW YORK TIMES.

WITH UNITED STATES FIRST ARMY, Dec. 19—Powerful German columns pushed farther into Belgium today in what has become by far the greatest battle in American history.

The most threatening are two thrusts south of Monschau, which are running approximately parallel.

The drive into Luxembourg from the direction of Echternach is continuing, but against furious opposition, and it is believed now to be well in hand. Our forces fighting the German columns moving from south of Monschau have blocked them at some places and are building new defensive lines back of where a heroic defense was made against a tremendous assault.

In the general area south of Monschau troops that received the brunt of the Germans' first attack there Saturday had repulsed the German attacks, which were supported by tanks and had improved their position.

Germans' Bid for Victory

There is complete realization here that this German attack "is it." There is no longer any temptation for anyone to regard it as anything less than the Germans' last bid for victory—and a very competent one at that. This German operation may be considered final proof that the German Army is no longer under Hitler's intuition or the Nazi party's inspiration, but is being run now by its own generals.

Field Marshal Gen. Karl von Rundstedt is at the top, and conducting this specific operation is Field Marshal Gen. Walther von Model. Both are formidable adversaries for any general.

These generals have thrown the cream of what remains of Germany's still formidable army into this fight, including crack panzer and infantry divisions that the enemy has been saving for his last throw of the dice. In making that throw now he undoubtedly hopes for victory. And at worst he has moved a considerable portion of the battlefield off his own soil, so that now it is the towns and villages of our friends that will be fought over in place of his own.

As the Germans have thrown increasing weight into their attack our commanders also have been conducting counter-measures. It is no exaggeration to call the present situation on the First Army's front serious. Yet there is confidence among our leaders that this counter-offensive will in time be stemmed. And then how much will Germany have left?

[News from Supreme Headquarters, Allied Expeditionary Force, said that more than 300 Flying Fortresses bombed tactical supply targets just behind the enemy lines Tuesday—the first time the Allies had used strategic bombers against tactical targets since the Battle of Normandy.]

No Minefields Delay Foe

In these opening stages of the German offensive the enemy has several advantages, plus the fact that he is attacking over the ground where he made his blitz in 1940. One is that as our forces were in an attacking attitude we had no minefields or roadblocks out in front, such as the Germans have used so extensively in combating our advances.

[According to a radio report heard Tuesday night civilian evacuation of the Belgian town of Liege, twenty-two miles northwest of Stavelot, where the Germans were last reported, has been ordered. This information

Continued on Page 3, Column 2

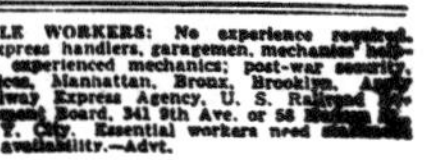

City's Muddled Meat Situation Agitated by Rumor of Price Rise

The city's meat muddle was further complicated yesterday by the question whether establishment of livestock price ceilings—which has been urged by the retail and wholesale trade, the Office of Price Administration, Mayor La Guardia and consumer groups—might entail an increase in the retail ceiling price of some meats.

In the face of reports from Washington that a possible price increase to consumers had been mentioned at the meetings held Monday in the capital between Mayor La Guardia and the heads of Federal agencies, Daniel P. Woolley, regional head of the OPA, said last night that he would fight any proposal to make the consumer pay more.

Mayor La Guardia refused to say what proposals had been discussed by him with national OPA Director Chester Bowles, Director of Economic Stabilization Fred M. Vinson, and Marvin Jones, head of the War Food Administration.

Asked directly whether he had offered a plan that would increase the cost to the consumer of choice beef, the Mayor said: "I am not confirming or denying anything that is not said by Mr. Bowles, Mr. Vinson or Mr. Jones."

The Mayor, reached at his home, was asked first if it was true that he had suggested an increase of 2 cents a pound for choice beef at the retail level. He said that was not so. He was told then that the Washington report was to the effect that he had favored an in-

Continued on Page 19, Column 1

War News Summarized

WEDNESDAY, DECEMBER 20, 1944

German troops pushed deeper into Belgium yesterday, but were being held along the Luxembourg line. The situation, while admittedly serious, was reported to have improved from an Allied standpoint. The United States First Army held at some places and rushed new defense lines at others in the path of the enemy's two parallel thrusts south of Monschau. The bitterness and significance of the fighting in this great battle now raging were likened to the situation at Kasserine Pass almost two years ago when the fate of the Tunisian campaign hung in the balance.

General Eisenhower yesterday, as then, called on strategic heavy bombers to support the sorely pressed troops. Bad weather virtually grounded tactical planes, but British and American heavies blasted a fifty-mile swath across road and rail arteries feeding the German spearheads.

The First Army was reported to have pushed troops across the Roer River near Dueren, with patrols entering the town. This could be the beginning of an Allied drive to cut the enemy's communications. Elsewhere along the front the Germans were holding firm and only slight gains were reported from the Third and Seventh Army fronts. [All the foregoing 1:8; map P. 2.]

The speed of the German advance forced correspondents and other noncombatants to evacuate a border Belgian city hurriedly. [1:7.]

In Italy, also, the enemy counter-attacked, compelling the Eighth Army to fall back to the northern edge of Faenza, but the Allies were developing flanking movements. [8:6.]

A new trap was being fashioned by the Red Army in Hungary around a sizable German force north of the Matra Mountains, and in Czechoslovakia the Russians were closing an arc about Kosice. [6:1, with map.]

British troops in Greece strengthened their hold on Athens except at Averof Prison, held by the Elas, and RAF air headquarters, under Leftist attack. King George was reported cool to Premier Papandreou's recommendations to accept the regency of Archbishop Damaskinos. [8:1.] UNRRA Administrator Lehman said most relief missions had been withdrawn from Greece on military orders [8:4] and British Laborites forced a new debate in the Commons on Greece. [9:5.]

B-29's, in yesterday's attack on Kyushu, hit the Japanese city of Omura through clouds, while other Superfortresses obtained fine results at Nanking and Shanghai. Seventeen enemy planes were destroyed or damaged. More than 200 B-25's of the Fourteenth Air Force immediately followed up Monday's B-29 attack on Hankow to find huge fires in the city, to pound the airfields themselves and to destroy or damage thirty-five planes. [1:3; maps, P. 14.]

Japanese positions on Leyte deteriorated further when the Ormoc corridor road was cut in two places, splitting the enemy into three segments. Valencia was captured and one of its airfields, found undamaged, was being used by American planes. There was no ground action on Mindoro. [1:4; map, P. 13.]

In Washington the Senate confirmed the nomination of Under-Secretary of State Grew and all five Assistant Secretaries of State. [1:2.]

European Supply Strain on Allies Laid to Quebec Pacific War Plan

By JOHN H. CRIDER

Special to THE NEW YORK TIMES.

WASHINGTON, Dec. 19—High ranking officials are telling inquirers that the liberated peoples of Europe are not getting the adequate relief supplies that were promised because of an acute strain on Allied shipping resulting from the prolongation of the war in Europe beyond the time contemplated by President Roosevelt and Prime Minister Churchill when they met in Quebec early in September.

Some officials also point to the same circumstance as bearing upon shortages in some categories of military supplies in the European theatre. Whatever the facts may be, several high ranking officials have within the last few days stated their belief that the President and Mr. Churchill predicated their decision to step up the pace of the Pacific war on the assumption that the war with Germany would be over before this time.

The shipping shortage is a major paradox of the war, because never in the history of the world has a group of nations mustered such tremendous tonnage of merchant shipping to supply fighting forces as have the Allies in this war. According to a report of the Office of War Information on Nov. 3, the United States alone was providing 37,000,000 deadweight tons of shipping for this purpose in mid-1944. The American tonnage contribution was about equal to the combined tonnage of the British and

Continued on Page 15, Column 7

"All the News That's Fit to Print"

The New York Times.

LATE CITY EDITION

Increasing cloudiness followed by light snow today.

Temperatures Yesterday—Max., 27; Min., 12

Sunrise, 8:17 A. M.; Sunset, 5:33 P. M.

VOL. XCIV...No. 31,745. Entered as Second-Class Matter, Postoffice, New York, N. Y. NEW YORK, SATURDAY, DECEMBER 23, 1944. THREE CENTS IN NEW YORK CITY

GERMANS SWEEP WEST THROUGH LUXEMBOURG; REPORT PATTON ATTACKING ON SOUTH FLANK; EISENHOWER URGES GREATEST ALLIED EFFORT

MAYOR DEMANDS U.S. ACT AT ONCE ON MEAT CRISIS

Calls for at Least a Temporary Plan So That Shops That Obey Law Can Stay Open

BREAD, PIE MAKERS CLOSE

Shut for Christmas Week-End in Labor Row—Hotels and Restaurants Affected

Mayor La Guardia joined hands yesterday with the city's retail butchers in demanding that the Federal Government step in immediately with some workable plan for averting a "meat holiday" here. With retailers threatening to stop sales beginning on Christmas, the Mayor said: "Washington cannot remain idly by in a situation where dealers want to comply with the law."

The city was threatened with a shortage in another food field when major producers of pies and bread decided to abandon all operations over the Christmas week-end because of an impending strike of bakery wagon drivers over wage demands. The pie shortage was expected to affect hotels and restaurants principally and the bread curtailment the delicatessen shops and restaurants that use rye and pumpernickel varieties. Spokesmen for the bakeries said the bread loss would amount to 100,000 pounds daily, and the pie manufacturers said they provided 75 per cent of that pastry consumed in the city's eating places.

Mayor Asks Urgent Action

In the meat crisis the Mayor sent messages to Marvin Jones, head of the War Food Administration; Fred M. Vinson, director of the Office of Economic Stabilization, and Chester Bowles, administrator of the Office of Price Administration, making clear the city's position in protecting consumers and dealers desirous of operating within the law.

He said there was need for at least an immediate temporary plan, adding that he had the assurances of all retailers' associations that they would keep open provided they could buy meat from their wholesalers at "lawful ceiling prices."

"If there is no meat available, then the closing of stores is justified," he advised the Federal officials. "I cannot and neither can the United States Government compel anyone to do business by violating the law and paying more than ceiling prices and compel him to obey the law in retailing at ceiling prices.

"Therefore, I specifically recommend, first, immediate order of proper allocation of meat supply to the metropolitan area; second, proper supervision of sales to retailers under existing regulations at lawful ceiling prices and, third, such modification and amendment of existing regulations as will assure continued flow of meat in accordance with proper proportion of supply to this area based on population. Any plan which will effectuate this result will be welcome and I can assure you of our complete cooperation."

Butchers Give Assurances

Following a meeting with retailers' and union representatives at City Hall yesterday, the Mayor said he had received their assurances that their members would buy all meat available at ceiling prices and retail it at lawful ceiling prices.

He said he assured the dealers that the entire force of the Department of Markets would aid in supervision of meat sales. The Mayor said the city would offer to buy the meat of any wholesaler who refused to sell to the retailer at OPA ceilings and if he persisted in his refusal to sell "appropriate action will be taken by the city."

The wholesalers insist that they cannot buy at ceiling levels themselves and it is generally agreed all along the line that the answer lies in a ceiling for cattle "on the hoof." This point was pounded home by a committee representing retailers, consumers and labor in Washing-

Continued on Page 18, Column 3

President Accepts Just One Columnist

Special to THE NEW YORK TIMES.

WASHINGTON, Dec. 22—President Roosevelt called columnists today an unnecessary excrescence on our civilization.

Asked to comment on reports of proposals for the establishment of an international board to function on political and economic matters similar to the Joint Chiefs of Staff in the military field, Mr. Roosevelt turned the question aside by saying they were written by a columnist.

"But, Mr. President," said Mrs. Elisabeth May Craig, correspondent for Maine newspapers, "you've got one in the family!"

That was true, Mr. Roosevelt said, amid the roars of laughter, but this column was different in most ways, as it was a diary.

The reference was to Mrs. Roosevelt and her daily syndicated column, "My Day."

CITY BUDGET SUIT UPHELD ON APPEAL

La Guardia Criticized by Court for Inclusion of Lump Sum Item of $3,000,000

Mayor La Guardia's inclusion of a $3,500,000 lump sum appropriation in his executive budget for 1944-45 was criticized yesterday by the Appellate Division in a unanimous decision reversing the action of Supreme Court Justice Benjamin F. Schreiber in dismissing a taxpayer's suit sponsored by the Citizens Budget Commission. The suit, brought by Lucius Wilmerding, a trustee of the commission, charged that the appropriation was illegal, and asked for both temporary and permanent injunctions.

Declaring that the suit stated a valid cause of action and that its dismissal was improper, the Appellate Division upheld, nevertheless, Justice Schreiber's denial of the request for a temporary injunction. The denial, the Appellate Division said, was within the lower court's discretion. The effect of the higher court's ruling is to require a trial of the taxpayer's suit on its merits.

"Sundry Expenses" Lumped

The $3,500,000 item in the budget submitted by the Mayor to the Board of Estimate on April 1 covered "motor vehicle equipment, repair parts, special machinery, unforeseen expenditures and sundry expenses." It was approved on April 28 by the Board of Estimate, but was stricken from the budget by the City Council on May 20. The Council's action was vetoed by Mayor La Guardia on June 2, and on June 9 the Council failed to override the veto. The taxpayer's action then was filed.

Soon after the final adoption of the budget, the Board of Estimate transferred $3,000,000 of the lump sum appropriation to the Fire Department, earmarked for payment of cost-of-living bonuses to firemen. The bonus payments since July 1 presumably have been made out of the transferred funds and a final court victory for the taxpayer

Continued on Page 11, Column 6

ROOSEVELT URGES HOMEFOLKS TO BACK SOLDIERS AT FRONT

Calls the Carrying Out of Tasks the Best Christmas Gift to Troops

'FULL WAR' BUDGET DUE

President Says Principles of Atlantic Charter Are as Valid Today as in 1941

By C. P. TRUSSELL

Special to THE NEW YORK TIMES.

WASHINGTON, Dec. 22—President Roosevelt appealed to the people on the home front today to back up the fighting forces with a sustained concentration on efforts which will help win the war as quickly as possible.

"We can best help the Christmas season of our fighting men," he said at his news conference, permitting himself to be quoted, "if we carry on our respective tasks, doing those things which will contribute to winning the war at the earliest possible moment.

"Therefore, I urge that each of us resolve to keep on the job and maintain the steady output of supplies needed by our men on the fighting fronts."

Several persons, Mr. Roosevelt said, had asked him to say something about Christmas. This was his message to those at home.

He was asked whether there was something he could say, beyond the communiqués, about the present situation in Europe.

He did not think so, the President replied. If he did, he remarked, it would be only an expression of an individual who did not know much more about it than the press did.

There were some dispatches that came to him, he explained, but he added that those he had received from the Belgian-Luxembourg area were not up to date, covering the situation as of Tuesday or Wednesday.

Is Questioned on Budget

When questioned about the budget for the next fiscal year, the President said that he had talked with Harold D. Smith, the budget director, only by telephone. He declared, however, that the budget would be based on the determination that the war must continue full force until Germany was licked, rather than on assumptions that this or that phase, or the whole war would end.

That declaration appeared to a questioner to be the President's answer to reports that the budget was being constructed along several patterns, one that Germany would be defeated during the next fiscal year, one that Japan would be, and another that war would continue against both enemies.

In time of war, Mr. Roosevelt said, a budget could be made up in many ways and on various assumptions, but assumptions as to victory dates were impossible. He was not assuming now any more than he had before, he declared, adding that he appeared to be just

Continued on Page 10, Column 3

Belgium Regains $223,292,000 In Gold, Given to Nazis by Vichy

The Federal Reserve Bank of New York yesterday transferred $223,292,833 in fine gold from the account of the Bank of France to the account of the National Bank of Belgium, thus terminating litigation begun in New York courts in February, 1941, arising out of the delivery of that amount of gold by the Vichy Government of France to Nazi occupation authorities in that year.

Announcement of the transfer of the gold, and of a formal settlement between the two banks on Oct. 19, 1944, was made by John Foster Dulles of the law firm of Sullivan & Cromwell, which represented the Belgian Bank in the proceedings. Mr. Dulles was an adviser on foreign affairs to Gov. Thomas E. Dewey in the Presidential campaign.

Coudert Brothers, New York law firm which represented the Bank of France in the litigation, declared yesterday that, throughout the years of court action here, the Bank of France had engaged in settlement negotiations with the National Bank of Belgium, offering to guarantee the return of its gold as soon as hostilities ceased.

The gold transferred amounts to some 198 metric tons. In detail, the agreement called for the restoration to the Bank of Belgium of 198,433 kilograms, 841 grams, 69 milligrams of gold.

Mr. Dulles said that after the liberation of France, prompt steps were taken by the Bank of France to assure that the relations between the two central banks "would be on that basis of mutual

Continued on Page 5, Column 3

GERMAN TOWN REDUCED TO RUBBLE AFTER SHELLING BY BOTH SIDES

Not much remains of the buildings in Pier, about five miles northeast of Eschweiler, after being fired upon by the United States 104th Division and the Nazis in positions across the Roer River.

The New York Times (U. S. Signal Corps)

NEW RUSSIAN DRIVE IN BALTIC REPORTED

Offensive Directed at Libau in Latvia, Foe Says—Enemy Squeezed in Hungary

By The United Press.

LONDON, Saturday, Dec. 23 — Berlin said last night that the Red Army had opened its winter offensive, hurling about 270,000 men into battle in Latvia, while Moscow announced Soviet advances in Czechoslovakia to within nine miles of the menaced rail city of Lucenec.

Berlin said that fighting in northeastern Europe already was spreading to East Prussia. In Hungary, the Germans said that Soviet forces had driven to within two miles of Szekesfehervar, keystone of Budapest's southwestern defenses.

Although these reports were not directly confirmed by Moscow, the Soviet High Command announced that 101 German tanks and sixty-eight German planes had been destroyed on the eastern front

Continued on Page 6, Column 3

Commander in Chief Hails Chance to Destroy Enemy

By Wireless to THE NEW YORK TIMES.

SUPREME HEADQUARTERS, Allied Expeditionary Force, Dec. 22—As German forces continued to expand their penetration in Belgium and Luxembourg and their offensive neared its second week, Gen. Dwight D. Eisenhower issued a dramatic Order of the Day to every member of the Allied Expeditionary Force calling on soldiers and airmen to turn the enemy's "great gamble into his worst defeat" and urging them "to destroy the enemy on the ground, in the air, everywhere—destroy him!"

Here is the text of the Allied Commander in Chief's order:

To every member of the Allied Expeditionary Force:

The enemy is making his supreme effort to break out of the desperate plight into which you forced him by your brilliant victories of the summer and fall.

He is fighting savagely to take back all that you have won and is using every treacherous trick to deceive and kill you. He is gambling everything, but already in this battle your gallantry has done much to foil his

Continued on Page 3, Column 1

CHECK BY 3D ARMY ADMITTED BY NAZIS

Fierce Blows Halt Offensive in South—Fall of St. Vith and Garrison Claimed

By JOHN MacCORMAC

By Wireless to THE NEW YORK TIMES.

LONDON, Dec. 22—The German Transocean news agency interrupted an Eastern Front broadcast tonight to flash a statement that Field Marshal Gen. Karl von Rundstedt's offensive in the west had been halted by "increasingly furious counter-attacks by several divisions of the United States Third Army," to the south of the First Army front.

[The situation on the southern flank was still critical, however, according to a United States First Army staff officer quoted by press services.]

The most important gain claimed by the Germans tonight for their western offensive was the establishment of bridgeheads over the Ourthe River and the capture of St. Vith with its American garrison. Twenty-four hours ago Marshal von Rundstedt had announced the cutting of the Liége-Arlon road. The Ourthe crosses this road at Houffalize and then runs northwest to a point eleven miles west of it before rejoining it again at Liége and flowing into the Meuse.

If the German claim is true, Ger-

Continued on Page 4, Column 5

FOG AT FRONT LIFTS ON A SCENE OF RUIN

28 German Tanks Lie Twisted in One Area—Our Men Hurl Gasoline on Foe's Machines

By HAROLD DENNY

By Wireless to THE NEW YORK TIMES.

WITH THE UNITED STATES FIRST ARMY, Dec. 22—The fog that had shrouded the battlefield for two days turned to snow last night. It hid the mud and enhanced the beauty of the fir groves through which our men are fighting, but increased their discomfort. So it will be a white Christmas here in the Eifel Range—but what a Christmas!

The air was still too thick to let an airplane off the ground until midafternoon, when it suddenly cleared and we got cub planes up to spot for our artillery. It was too late, though, for our fighter-bombers to get into action against the German tanks, transport and troops.

A blackout has now been placed by high military authority on news of the current military operations here to insure that the Germans learn nothing. Today's operations in this greatest battle of the war therefore cannot be told.

The lifting of the fog over the battlefront, however, revealed some of the destruction inflicted on the enemy in recent days. In places it was appalling. In one sector in front of the lines where our troops had been hard pressed throughout this battle, the hulks of twenty-eight wrecked enemy tanks were found this morning. In another sector our men have accounted for sixty to seventy tanks. These were recovered by the enemy, however, when he rolled those men back. Many of them can be repaired and will fight us again.

Faced with attacks of such weight and fury as have been

Continued on Page 2, Column 2

War News Summarized

SATURDAY, DECEMBER 23, 1944

The German offensive, unchecked, moved westward through Belgium for its seventh consecutive day. Reports indicated that the enemy, up to late Wednesday, had swept through Luxembourg, isolated the important rail junction of Bastogne, in Belgium, and then advanced another thirteen and a half miles northwest to La Roche for a total gain of thirty-five miles. Another German column swung westward from Bastogne for a gain of fifteen miles to reach St. Hubert. The enemy claimed to have crossed the Ourthe River [1:8; map P. 3.] Clearing skies late yesterday gave promise that our hard-pressed ground troops might at last receive the aid of our bitterly impatient flying forces. [1:7.]

German radio reports said the southern flank of the German drive had been slowed down by counter-attacking divisions of General Patton's Third Army. The enemy also admitted heavy fighting on his northern flank, but claimed the destruction of seven American divisions and the capture of 25,000 prisoners. [1:6.]

General Eisenhower told his troops that the German offensive was born of desperation and predicted that it would "completely fail." The Allied Commander in Chief urged his men to "turn the enemy's great gamble into his worst defeat" and to go forward "to our greatest victory." [1:5-6.] War Secretary Stimson said there was no need to become panicky over the German offensive. [5:1.]

As a further indication of the dwindling hopes for an early peace, the British Government announced it would soon provide 250,000 additional front-line troops through a new draft of civilians and reclassification of men already in uniform. [1:6-7.]

The Red Army has opened a new drive to crush a German pocket in Latvia, where about thirty enemy divisions are pinned against the Baltic Sea, according to Berlin. The Russians continued to gain in their drive to surround a big German force north of the Matra Mountains in Hungary. [1:4; map P. 6.]

Japan's big aircraft-producing center at Nagoya on Honshu Island was attacked for the third time within nine days by a fleet of Superfortresses. The sky mammoths—estimated to number 100 by the enemy—took off from Saipan to hit the target shortly after noon. Moderate fighter and anti-aircraft opposition was encountered. [7:3.]

The Japanese defeat on Leyte in the Philippines became a rout as our troops punched three miles closer to Palompon, the last escape port of any consequence left to the enemy. American artillery was shelling the port and exacting a heavy toll from the fleeing foe. [7:1.]

General de Gaulle is expected to sit with the heads of the Soviet Union, Britain and the United States at an early meeting and France soon will formally join the other United Nations by signing a joint declaration of policy, it was reported from Paris. [5:6.]

Britain to Call Up 250,000 Men, In Excess of Plans, to Fight in '45

By CLIFTON DANIEL

By Wireless to THE NEW YORK TIMES.

LONDON, Dec. 22—Britain's opinion of what the present war situation demands was made plain tonight by an announcement from Prime Minister Churchill's office that 250,000 more fighting men would be found for the United Kingdom's armies in 1945.

Although Britain already has the highest rate of manpower mobilization among the United Nations, the announcement said that a "large part" of these new soldiers would be obtained by a new call-up from civilian life. The remainder will be transferred from the Navy and the Royal Air Force and from static jobs in the Army itself.

The revelation that the British Army, after five weary years of war, still needs more fighting men came three days before what the British hope will be their last Christmas of war in Europe. It had an immediate sobering effect.

It was authoritatively stated, however, that the new call-up was not caused by the recent worsening of the Allied position on the Western Front. The demand for additional men was interpreted rather as further evidence of this country's intention to prosecute the war to the absolute limit of its abilities in the Far East as well as in the West.

The additional call-up is such a far-reaching, long-term proposition that it must have been conceived before German Field Marshal Gen. Karl von Rundstedt's attack in Belgium. But one suspects

Continued on Page 2, Column 4

RAIL HUB ISOLATED

Panzers Smash 15 Miles Past Bastogne—Enemy Slowed on Flanks

NEAR FRENCH BORDER

Americans Recapture 2 Towns—Reports Still 48 Hours Late

By DREW MIDDLETON

By Wireless to THE NEW YORK TIMES.

SUPREME HEADQUARTERS, Allied Expeditionary Force, Dec. 22—The great German winter offensive smashed westward through Belgium unchecked today for the seventh consecutive day.

Although American infantry and tanks have managed to hold positions along the sides of the flood tide of enemy soldiery, the advance in the center shows no signs of slowing down.

By late Wednesday panzer units had swept through the duchy of Luxembourg, isolated the great railroad communications center of Bastogne in Belgium and then pushed on thirteen and a half miles northwest to the vicinity of La Roche.

Front-line reports said that another German column advancing from Bastogne had rolled fifteen miles west through a pine forest and snow-covered fields to reach the vicinity of St. Hubert. The German communiqué reported today that the enemy had crossed the Ourthe River, probably in the La Roche area.

Malmedy and Stavelot Retaken

American counter-measures on the flanks had by Wednesday night retaken Malmedy as well as Stavelot in the north, and in the south had checked the German onslaught in the vicinity of Echternach and at Dickweiler, Osweiler and Berdorf, small villages two and a half miles south southwest of Echternach. Moreover, the German push through Consdorf toward the city of Luxembourg, twelve miles away, had by that time been checked.

These reports are forty-eight hours old, however. When they were made the Germans were concentrating armor in the Stavelot-Malmedy-St. Vith triangle and it is probable that they planned a resumption of the drive, which on Tuesday had sent armored reconnaissance elements into Habiemont, thirty miles west of the German frontier.

[An Associated Press field dispatch reported that the fighting had spread far south through Belgium to the area of Arlon, ten miles from the French border and forty miles due east of historic Sedan.]

300 RAF Planes Help

For the fourth consecutive day low clouds kept the Ninth Air Force's bombers and fighter-bombers pinned to their airfields. The weather cleared a bit in the north, however, and the British Second Tactical Air Force sent 300 bombers and fighters down to give what aid was possible to the hard-pressed doughboys.

Mitchells bombed a German supply dump supporting Field Marshal Gen. Karl von Rundstedt's columns, but a thick overcast prevented ob-

Continued on Page 3, Column 2

Nazi 'V-1½' Weapon Called Flying Shell

By The Associated Press.

LONDON, Dec. 22—The Germans' new secret weapon in use on the Western Front was described here today as "not V-3 or V-4, but V-1½."

Apparently a barrage weapon, it takes the form of a self-propelled shell, it was said. It has been described in front dispatches as a small V-2 rocket.

Classifying it as V-1½ might indicate that it has some features of both V-1, the flying bomb, and V-2, the long-range rocket.

"All the News That's Fit to Print"

The New York Times.

LATE CITY EDITION
Cloudy and colder today. Cloudy, cold with snow or rain tomorrow.
Temperatures Yesterday—Max.,35; Min.,12
Sunrise, 8:20 A. M.; Sunset, 5:42 P. M.

Copyright, 1945, by The New York Times Company.

VOL. XCIV...No. 31,757. Entered as Second-Class Matter. Postoffice, New York, N. Y. NEW YORK, THURSDAY, JANUARY 4, 1945. THREE CENTS IN NEW YORK CITY

1ST ARMY OPENS DRIVE AT TOP OF BELGIAN BULGE; 3D GAINS BEYOND BASTOGNE, 7TH FORCED BACK; U. S. FLIERS BOMB LUZON, FORMOSA AND JAPAN

DEWEY ASKS STATE TO SPEND BILLION IN POST-WAR AIDS

Urges More Social Welfare, $6,500,000 Pay Rise in Reading Message to Legislature

FOR NEW SURPLUS FREEZE

Advises Present Commercial Rents, More Housing Here and Present Tax Rate

The text of the Governor's message appears on Page 12.

By LEO EGAN
Special to THE NEW YORK TIMES.

ALBANY, Jan. 3—Addressing the opening session of the State Legislature of 1945 today, Governor Dewey outlined a huge program of State public works, to be undertaken in the post-war period at a cost that might exceed $1,000,000,000. He recommended an immediate start toward expanding the State's social welfare laws and advocated "locking up" an expected Treasury surplus of $150,000,000 with the $163,000,000 put aside from last year.

Delivering his message in person at a joint meeting of the Senate and the Assembly and speaking for an hour, the Governor also advised a program of pay increases for State employes, including members of the Legislature, that will increase payrolls by about $6,500,000 a year; reforms to meet the problems of juvenile delinquency and the rehabilitation of criminals; changes in the methods of selecting judges and more State aid for education.

High Points Broadcast

A condensed version of the message was delivered by the Governor in a State-wide broadcast from 6:15 to 6:40 o'clock in the evening. In the broadcast, as in the message, he declared that the overriding task for all in the country was still the winning of the war, and so far as that job was concerned, the most trying months were still ahead.

But, as a result of measures that had been adopted in New York, the State was today better able to meet the demands of the future than at any time in its history. As the result of the establishment of a post-war reconstruction fund the State would be able to plan a construction program as a unit. This would serve the twofold purpose of taking up the slack in employment caused by the cessation of war industries and meet the needs of the people of the State.

Political Angle Seen

It was the Governor's first major public appearance since his defeat for the Presidency and there were some among his listeners who saw political significance in his suggestions for expanding social welfare laws. The expansions, in general, aim to put into effect for the State the change he advocated on a national scale in his San Francisco and Los Angeles speeches in the Presidential campaign.

Without specifically endorsing the adoption of a merit rating system for levying unemployment insurance taxes, the Governor presented the major arguments in favor of such a change and recommended that a decision on the subject be reached at the current session.

Of particular interest to New York City were recommendations that the Legislature approve measures for freezing commercial rents within the city; enact laws designed to curb and eliminate racial and religious discrimination, and allocate an additional $35,000,000 of the State Housing bond issue of $300,000,000 for low cost housing for New York City.

At the outset of his address, the Governor disclosed that the State's budgetary surplus this year would be about $150,000,000, roughly $20,000,000 higher than unofficial estimates made as recently as a week ago. He recommended that this surplus be locked up in a post-war reconstruction fund as was the

Continued on Page 12, Column 6

Mayor Forecasts Increase In Realty Valuations Here

Says No One Can Tell Tax Rate for Next Year — Wants Sales and Other Emergency Levies Made 'Permanent'

By PAUL CROWELL

Whether the basic real estate tax rate for 1945-46 is higher or lower than the current rate of $2.74 for each hundred dollars of assessed valuation, there will be substantial increases in realty valuations for the coming fiscal year, Mayor La Guardia indicated yesterday in his annual message to the City Council.

At the same time, in a review of the city's wartime fiscal problems, he gave notice that the Legislature would be asked to make "permanent" the existing emergency taxes, chief of which is the 1 per cent sales tax, and also restore to the city the public utility and stock transfer taxes collected in the city.

The Mayor's remarks on taxes and valuations gave point to a ninety-five-minute talk to the Council, in which he painted the city as a solvent organization and described its huge post-war capital outlay program and the need for funds to maintain essential city services.

The message, delivered by the Mayor in person, told the Council that the 1945-46 real estate rate was unpredictable at this time, but that he wanted to say "with all its significance" that property values throughout the city had increased during the past year. As he was leaving City Hall the Mayor was asked whether the quoted words indicated that increased valuations were in the offing.

"Atta boy! You've guessed it!" he replied.

"At this moment," the Mayor declared, in his message to the Council, "I do not believe there is anyone in the City of New York who can predict whether we will have a higher or a lower tax rate. It all depends on local, State and national conditions. We have a

Continued on Page 20, Column 2

18-25 Farm Labor in Draft; Hershey Acts on Byrnes Plea

By JOHN H. CRIDER
Special to THE NEW YORK TIMES.

WASHINGTON, Jan. 3—Maj. Gen. Lewis B. Hershey, Director of Selective Service, telegraphed to State directors this afternoon directions to re-examine all deferred farm workers of 18 through 25 years of age for possible induction. His action followed receipt of a letter from James F. Byrnes, Director of War Mobilization and Reconversion, asking him in behalf of President Roosevelt and himself to look into the draft status of the 364,000 men in the 18-25 group deferred in agricultural employment.

Only two days ago, in his report to Congress, Mr. Byrnes urged legislation to permit the Government to compel men classified as 4-F to work in war jobs or join the armed services.

Both actions reflected the critical manpower situation resulting from demands of the War and Navy Departments for more young fighting men which, Mr. Byrnes said in a letter to General Hershey, will exhaust "the eligibles in the 18 through 25 year age group at an early date."

General Hershey's telegrams to State directors contained the text of the Byrnes letter and requested them to forward the letter to local and appeal boards and to direct local boards to review promptly "the cases of all registrants ages 18 through 25 deferred in Class II-C, excluding those identified by the letters 'F' or 'L'."

The letters "F" and "L," Selective Service officials explained, apply to some 800,000 men either rejected or approved for limited service last spring, who were permitted to retain their occupational deferments if they continued working at their essential jobs.

The telegrams also asked directors to direct local boards "to issue orders for pre-induction physical examination" to all of the same category of registrants "in accord-

Continued on Page 11, Column 3

WALLACE IS ASKING FOR COMMERCE POST

Preference for Secretaryship Is Said to Have Been Stated in Letter to President

By LEWIS WOOD
Special to THE NEW YORK TIMES.

WASHINGTON, Jan. 3 — Vice President Henry Wallace has written to President Roosevelt, expressing his preference to become Secretary of Commerce, if that post should be open, it was stated in Administration circles today. The President, it was added, has not replied unless he did so recently.

It has been variously reported that Mr. Wallace would like to head the Commerce establishment, but this, it is said, is the first disclosure that he conveyed his desire to the President in a letter rather than in person. On the other hand, it was said that Mr. Wallace had scrupulously refrained from any conversation with Mr. Roosevelt on the subject, holding that this might embarrass his chief. The Vice President has also refused at least one offer of personal intervention.

From the same source it was ascertained that Mr. Wallace's ambition to become Secretary of Commerce is based on a belief that he might be able to use some Government funds for the benefit of the small business man, instead of

Continued on Page 36, Column 2

DIES GROUP IS PUT ON PERMANENT BASIS BY HOUSE, 207 TO 186

70 Democrats Join in Surprise Move as Congress Meets on Note of Win the War Quickly

RAYBURN CALLS FOR UNITY

Warns Against Over-Optimism and Urges 'Total Duty'—600 Bills Are Offered

By C. P. TRUSSELL
Special to THE NEW YORK TIMES.

WASHINGTON, Jan. 3—The Seventy-ninth Congress convened today in an atmosphere denoting determination to see the war through as quickly as possible, but marked by expressions of uncertainty as to the courses its legislative programs will take. Caution on war and peace plans was the watchword, while the members awaited President Roosevelt's message on the state of the Union, which will be read Saturday.

The House, however, departed unexpectedly from routine business to vote, 207 to 186, to make permanent the special Committee on Un-American Activities, a group which the Administration has opposed since its creation in 1938.

This action was viewed on Capitol Hill as a confirmation of predictions that, despite the Democratic gains in November, the President would still have to deal with coalitions in Congress, on home-front issues at least. Seventy Democrats, sixty-three of them from Southern States, voted in favor of the committee.

Senate Accepts Bust of Hull

The Senate, meanwhile, barred legislative business, inducted its newly elected and re-elected members, departed from its routine only to permit the presentation of a bust of former Secretary of State Hull and adjourned until Saturday.

In cloakroom and corridors, members viewed seriously the news of setbacks on the Western Front and spoke apprehensively, though with frank admission that first-hand knowledge was lacking, of political and other developments abroad. Some legislators reported that their constituents were press-

Continued on Page 36, Column 4

96,369 Planes Produced in 1944, Frame Weight Is 50% Above 1943

Special to THE NEW YORK TIMES.

WASHINGTON, Jan. 3—In a production effort corresponding to the record-breaking achievements of other war industries last year, the country's aircraft plants turned out 96,369 planes of all types in 1944, with a total air-frame weight of 1,112,000,000 pounds, J. A. Krug, chairman of the War Production Board, announced in a year-end report today.

Even with planned reductions in aircraft production undertaken as early as last summer, when the first cutbacks were announced, the output in 1944 was substantially greater than the previous record of 85,946 planes delivered in 1943.

Nevertheless, in air-frame weight, the achievement was even more impressive, since total weight of all planes last year exceeded by about 50 per cent their total air-frame weight in 1943. This rise indicated the degree by which war planners were shifting from the light planes, such as trainers, to the heavy combat bomber.

Production in December alone, Mr. Krug said, was "a good accomplishment" only when the short month and Christmas holidays were taken into consideration. Overall output of 6,697 planes fell

First-of-the-year plans, however, called for 109,000 planes in 1944.

Continued on Page 23, Column 6

ENEMY HIT HARD THROUGHOUT FAR EAST THEATRE

As neutralizing attacks against Japanese bases on Iwo and Haha Islands (1) were pressed by Army bombers, B-29's, directed from a new headquarters on Guam, hammered Nagoya, on Honshu (2). Carrier-based planes struck at Okinawa in the Ryukyu Islands (3) and at Formosa (4). These carrier blows were probably preparatory to important future operations focusing on Luzon (5). The southeastern tail of that island was raked by Allied planes, which also sank or fired twenty-five enemy ships off the west coast. In Burma the Chinese captured Wanting (6) and with a column below Bhamo (7) clamped a pincers on Namhkam. The British took Ye-u (8).

25 Ships Sunk or Set Afire Off Luzon; Carriers Strike Formosa and Okinawa

MacArthur's Fliers Cause Much Luzon Damage—New Landings Made on Mindoro—Leyte Casualties Go Up to 121,064

By The Associated Press.

ADVANCED HEADQUARTERS, on Leyte, Thursday, Jan. 4—American forces, putting increasing pressure on the northern Philippines, sank or set afire twenty-five Japanese ships along the west coast of Luzon New Year's Day while American troops made two additional unopposed landings on the east and west coasts of Mindoro.

The heavy blows against enemy shipping ranged virtually the full

Continued on Page 10, Column 4

Japanese Record Sounds Made by Superfortresses

Domei said yesterday that the Japanese Broadcasting Association had recorded the sound of the engines of the Superfortresses and that the recordings would be broadcast "to familiarize the public with the sound." The dispatch was reported by the Federal Communications Commission.

BURMA ROAD POINT IS WON BY CHINESE

Wanting Is Regained—British Occupy Ye-u in the Drive Toward Mandalay

By The Associated Press.

CHUNGKING, China, Thursday, Jan. 4—The Chinese High Command announced today the recapture of Wanting, Burma Road town on the Chinese-Burma border, in a smashing climax to China's first real offensive of the war.

A communiqué said that the town, which was captured by the Japanese in May, 1942, fell at 4 P. M. yesterday and that "enemy dead and war trophies were being counted, while enemy remnants were fleeing southward, with our troops in pursuit."

[The Chinese at Wanting also

Continued on Page 10, Column 4

Navy Fliers Attack Foe's Base Only 310 Miles From Japan—Iwo Gets Its 26th Bombing—Army Planes Bomb in Bonins

By ROBERT TRUMBULL
By Telephone to THE NEW YORK TIMES.

PEARL HARBOR, Jan. 3—Pacific Fleet carrier planes made simultaneous strikes yesterday at Formosa and Okinawa. The latter base is in the Ryukyu Islands, only 310 nautical miles from the southern tip of Japan proper.

The attacks, announced by Fleet Admiral Chester W. Nimitz this morning, were the second seaborne operation of the war against both of these extremely important air bases, deep within the enemy's inner defensive zone.

No details of the strikes were available here today. The ships participating, believed to be composed of fast carrier task forces from Admiral William F. Halsey's Third Fleet, under immediate command of Vice Admiral J. S. McCain, presumably are not yet in a position to break radio silence. It is possible that the attacks are continuing, although the communiqué gave no such indication.

The blow at Formosa followed the first Philippine base air attack of the war on this island Sunday by Navy Liberators, presumably from Mindoro. Formosa had previously been hit by B-29's from airdromes in Asia.

Fleet Admiral Nimitz also announced today the twenty-sixth consecutive bombing of Iwo in the Volcano Islands and an attack on the town of Okimura on Haha in

Continued on Page 9, Column 5

War News Summarized

THURSDAY, JANUARY 4, 1945

The United States First Army went over to the offensive on the northern flank of the German salient in Belgium, complementing the Third Army's smash in the south fanning out from Bastogne. No details were available on the progress of the new American assault, but General Patton's men were punching out small gains against heavy resistance.

In the Saar the enemy was attacking along a thirty-nine-mile front in an effort to drive the Americans in that area from Reich soil. The Seventh Army, although holding or slowing the Germans, was reported to have withdrawn to a line behind the Lauter River, in the east. [All the foregoing 1:8; maps P. 4.]

The Eighth Air Force established a new winter record of twelve consecutive days of bombing yesterday when it showered 3,000 tons on more than a dozen communications centers in western Germany. The RAF again struck benzol plants, this time near Dortmund. [3:1.]

Germans trying to relieve their trapped garrison in Budapest drove through Russian lines southeast of Komarno, thirty miles from the Hungarian capital. In Czechoslovakia the Red Army drew closer to Lucenec. [1:6-7; map P. 2.] Fifth Army patrols in Italy pushed toward Massa, the strongest German position on the Tyrrhenian. [5:7.]

General Plastiras has formed a new Greek Government described as liberal but not radical. In addition to the Premiership he took over the War, Navy, Air and Merchant Marine posts. [8:3.]

Japan was hit heavy blows from several directions in coordinated attacks participated in by Superfortresses, carrier planes and land-based aircraft. Pacific Fleet bombers struck Formosa and Okinawa, largest of the Ryukyu Islands, 310 miles southwest of Japan. Installations on the Bonin Islands were hit by other planes and Iwo Island, in the Volcanos, was smashed for the twenty-sixth straight day. [1:7.]

B-29's carried the war to industrial targets on the main home island of Honshu. Tokyo said ninety Superfortresses had bombed Nagoya, Osaka and Hamamatsu. One big bomber was lost. [10:1.]

General MacArthur sent his aircraft against Luzon, sinking or setting afire twenty-five ships on a sweep of the island's west coast, smashing installations and barracks from Legaspi to Batangas in the south and destroying at least eleven planes in an attack on Manila's Clark Field. American troops made new unopposed landings on both the east and west coasts of Mindoro. [1:5.]

Wanting, on the Burma Road, was captured by Chinese troops who pushed on to Kiuko, leaving only fifteen miles of the Ledo-Burma supply route to be cleared. In central Burma the British occupied Ye-u. [1:6.]

Turkey, in response to American and British requests, will break diplomatic and economic relations with Japan on Saturday. [9:1.]

Nazis Push Back Toward Budapest; Take Danube Towns From Russians

By The Associated Press.

LONDON, Thursday, Jan. 4—Strong German counter-attacks northwest of Budapest, which the Russians said were aimed at relieving the trapped Nazi garrison in the embattled Hungarian capital, have overrun several towns on the south bank of the Danube, Moscow announced last night.

The broadcast Soviet communiqué declared enemy blows southeast of Komarno, on the Danube, almost forty-five miles northwest of Budapest, had been repulsed, then added:

"At the cost of heavy losses in men and matériel, the enemy was able to capture several populated places on the southern bank of the Danube."

The names and locations were not reported, but the communiqué referred to "large enemy forces of infantry and tanks." An early morning report from Moscow said more than forty German tanks were destroyed and "several thousand" Germans killed in that area.

The Soviet communiqué also announced that troops of Marshal Rodion Y. Malinovsky, driving on Lucenec, communications center in southern Slovakia near the Hungarian border northeast of Budapest, had captured Sacher, a town

Continued on Page 2, Column 3

U. S. MOVE IS VEILED

Point of Drive Against Salient Not Disclosed—Patton Widens Breach

SNOW CURBS FLIERS

7th Army Burns Bridges in Withdrawal—Foe Still Seeks Weak Spot

By DREW MIDDLETON
By Wireless to THE NEW YORK TIMES.

SUPREME HEADQUARTERS, Allied Expeditionary Force, Jan. 3—Gen. Dwight D. Eisenhower dealt the shrewdest blow of his counter-offensive today, when, with Lieut. Gen. George S. Patton's tanks and infantry fanning out east, west and north of Bastogne on the south, he launched the American First Army against the northern flank of the German salient in Belgium.

The attack opened at a grave moment for the Allies. The Germans are pressing their southern attacks along the thirty-nine-mile front from Shaffhausen, in the Saar, to Phillipsbourg in the Eastern Vosges, and, although the American resistance in that area is stiffening, the Germans are still on the move, threatening to drive the Allies out of the Saar on the west and menacing control of the Alsace plain on the east.

From the area south of Liége, on the north, to Wissembourg gap on the south Allied and German armies were locked in a great battle. The American Third and First Armies were assaulting the flanks of Field Marshal von Rundstedt's offensive in the north, but to the south the initiative lies with the enemy, who is hammering boldly and successfully at American positions.

Little Tactical Air Support

For the first time in nine days American armies fought without extensive support from tactical air forces. With fighter-bombers and medium bombers of the Ninth Air Force pinned on their airfields by weather and the Second Tactical Air Command restricted to a few sorties by Mitchells and Bostons against Houffalize, north of Bastogne, it was once again left to the Eighth Air Force to deliver the heaviest Allied attacks.

More than 1,100 Flying Fortresses and Liberators hammered rail and road centers northwest of Karlsruhe in the area behind the German attacks in northern Alsace and near Belgian-German frontier, among other targets.

The First Army's assault in the north has placed von Rundstedt in a defensive position for the first time since he opened his offensive Dec. 16. With eight divisions in line, four of them armored, he has managed to hold the attack by General Patton's Third Army on the southern flank in check so long as there has been no important Allied attack against the northern flank of his position.

Halts German Offensive

Little is known here of the assault from the north save that it has begun. However, since Lieut. Gen. Courtney H. Hodges — who, according to last reports here, is still in command of the First Army —has had more than two weeks to collect his forces, the attack is believed to be on a considerable scale. Its start certainly relieves the Allies of any concern about serious continuation of the German offensive westward in this area.

Moreover, it is now clear that von Rundstedt has committed a considerable proportion of his Panzer and Panzer Grenadier divisions to the defense of the Ardennes salient. It may prove impossible to cut off these divisions, but with the start of the First Army's attack it is clear that they will be brought to battle and perhaps destroyed.

The moment that the American First Army began today is not part of a pincers operation. It is the opening on the north of an Allied counter-offensive against a

Continued on Page 4, Column 3

"All the News That's Fit to Print"

The New York Times.

LATE CITY EDITION
Fair and cold today. Cloudy and slightly warmer tomorrow.
Temperatures Yesterday—Max., 33; Min., 19
Sunrise, 8:17 A. M.; Sunset, 5:06 P. M.

Copyright, 1945, by The New York Times Company.

VOL. XCIV...No. 31,771. Entered as Second-Class Matter, Postoffice, New York, N. Y. NEW YORK, THURSDAY, JANUARY 18, 1945. THREE CENTS IN NEW YORK CITY

RUSSIANS TAKE WARSAW, REPORTED IN CRACOW; WIN A CITY 14 MILES FROM REICH IN 24-MILE GAIN; BRITISH ADVANCE, AMERICANS CLOSE ON ST. VITH

ROOSEVELT URGES WORK-OR-FIGHT BILL TO BACK OFFENSIVES

Letter to May Calls for Prompt Action on 18-to-45 Measure—King, Marshall Tell of Needs

RECENT LOSSES ARE HEAVY

House Group Abruptly Ends Hearings—Approval of Legislation Expected by Tonight

Appeals by the President, Gen. Marshall, Adm. King, Page 13.

By C. P. TRUSSELL
Special to THE NEW YORK TIMES.

WASHINGTON, Jan. 17—President Roosevelt called on Congress today for prompt action on a work-or-fight bill for men between 18 and 45, since it was vital that the Allied "total offense should not slacken because of any less than total utilization of our manpower on the home front."

In support of his appeal, which was addressed to Chairman Andrew J. May of the House Military Affairs Committee, the President attached a copy of a joint letter sent to him by General Marshall and Admiral King.

Replacements Needed

As "the agents directly responsible" for the conduct of military operations, they also urged "immediate action" on the home front to meet requirements for young and vigorous replacements in battle zones and to provide the necessary manpower to multiply production of critical munitions, build new ships and repair those damaged in combat.

Mr. Roosevelt said that the need for statutory controls to channel 4-F's to essential war work was more urgent now than it was eleven days ago when he asked for it as a stop gap, pending enactment of a national service law, and urged action "without delay" on the May-Bailey bill providing for "limited national service" and covering all 18 to 45 deferred registrants.

Hearings on the May-Bailey bill were ended abruptly, and Mr. May called an executive session of the committee tomorrow. He predicted that the measure, in some form, would be approved by nightfall.

"Time to Act," May Says

"We've discussed this matter long enough," Mr. May said. "It's now time to act."

Committeemen joined their chairman in expected approval of the bill, but they predicted that changes would be made, warned that much care must be exercised in revising the measure, and looked for a "tough" fight when it reached the House floor.

Earlier, the National Association of Manufacturers joined organized labor in opposing the bill, as well as national service generally, before the committee.

Frederick C. Crawford, chairman of the NAM executive committee, testified that if legislation were to be written, it should only put teeth into the controls of existing machinery and programs. He said that intensified cooperation between Government, management and labor could supply the manpower demands for the armed service and war production replacements now and in the next six months, when an estimated 1,600,000 men will be required. Recent employment gains were cited.

The President in his letter to Mr. May said that it was true that there had been a trend toward increased placement of manpower in the last fortnight, but he added that there was danger that this trend, accelerated by belief that Congress was about to act on work-or-fight measures, would be reversed by indications that such action was likely to be delayed.

Although the May-Bailey bill is not a complete national service measure, Mr. Roosevelt said, it would "go far" to effect essential

Continued on Page 13, Column 2

Russian Super-Tank Reported by Nazis

By The Associated Press.

LONDON, Jan. 17—A German reporter, speaking on the Berlin radio from the Kielce sector of Poland tonight, paid high tribute to the power of a new Red Army heavy tank, called the Joseph Stalin.

"The Russians are using their new Joseph Stalin super-tank on an ever-increasing scale," the Nazi reporter, Heinz Megerlein, said. "This most powerfully gunned and armored vehicle in the world is more than a match for our best tank, the Royal Tiger."

The German broadcaster said the Russian super-tank carried a 122-mm. [4.8-inch] gun.

The German Royal Tiger tank has been reported to mount a new version of the famous 88-mm. gun.

U.S. POLICY ON ROWS IS FIRM, GREW SAYS

Position, Stated Vigorously, Is Not to Allow Differences to Mar Unity, He Asserts

Joseph C. Grew, Under Secretary of State, declared last night that our State Department has vigorously stated, and would continue to state to its allies, the American position on issues in dispute, but that it was the policy of this Government not to allow these differences to interfere with the unity of action essential to winning the war, or to disrupt that unity after the war.

He made this reply to recent critics of our foreign policy at a meeting in The New York Times Hall, 240 West Forty-fourth Street, at which Senator Warren R. Austin of Vermont called for the earliest practicable meeting to establish the Dumbarton Oaks Organization, and Senator J. William Fulbright of Arkansas assailed our handling of foreign affairs as hesitant, timid, and lacking in forthrightness.

Nicholas Roosevelt was moderator of the meeting, which was arranged by THE NEW YORK TIMES on the topic, "America's Place in World Affairs." The prepared addresses of the three speakers were broadcast over radio stations WQXR and WQXQ. Senators Austin and Fulbright then took part in a discussion and question-and-answer period that followed, for which Mr. Grew was unable to remain.

Fulbright Assails Delay

Senator Fulbright said that our failure to take part in formulating decisions in such pressing matters as the situations in Greece, Italy and Poland was forcing Great Britain and Russia to make their own decisions. He declared that our failure to assume a share of the responsibility for the decisions in the case of Greece had had the effect of making one of our Allies, Great Britain, "the undeserved goat" and had stirred up feeling

Continued on Page 12, Column 2

FOE STIFF IN WEST

Fog and Tanks Help the Germans Slow British and U. S. at Front

OUR AIR ARM BARRED

Montgomery Push Gains Town—Americans Lift Threat to Strasbourg

By CLIFTON DANIEL
By Wireless to THE NEW YORK TIMES.

SUPREME HEADQUARTERS, Allied Expeditionary Force, Jan. 17—While the drive to beat back the German salient continued despite thick, freezing weather and repeated German counter-attacks, which cost the Germans at least twenty-four tanks today, British forces northeast of Aachen also made painful progress into the flank of the Maeseyck bulge.

Beating their way with a flail of tanks through mine fields, dense fog and stinging sleet, they advanced 2,000-odd yards in the first twenty-four hours. Their progress was marked on the map by two river crossings and a village captured—Dieteren. The attack seemed less ambitious than originally appeared, but it still held symbolic value as representing a resumption of the Allied initiative.

The American threat to St. Vith, the last important road junction on the Germans' retreat route from the Ardennes, grew serious today as the battle-wise Old Hickory Division pressed down on the devastated town through knee-deep snow, thick woods and treacherous hills, reaching within five miles of St. Vith's outskirts. A forest belt of two and a half miles and a maze of knobby hills still stand between the town and the attacking Americans, however.

Americans Gain in Alsace

In Alsace American forces attacking the perimeter of the German bridgehead over the Rhine north of Strasbourg not only redressed the setback inflicted by the Germans last night but pushed their way into the western stronghold of the German pocket at Herrlisheim. This advance, though local and limited, will be regarded with satisfaction, particularly by the French, who have been viewing the bridgehead and its threat to Strasbourg with apprehension for many days.

Militarily, Strasbourg does not seem more important than any other city, but politically it is a far greater prize for either the Germans or the French. As the capital of the lost and regained province of Alsace and the "second city of France," it is a major symbol for France, and its loss might have a painful effect on French morale, already at a low ebb because of the unduly severe winter.

However, French forces holding the city are regarded as sufficient at the moment to counter any

Continued on Page 9, Column 1

RED ARMY TEARS GERMANS' DEFENSES IN POLAND ASUNDER

Jan. 18, 1945

Breaking from their Narew River positions, the Russians punched out a salient between Ciechanow and Pomiechowek (1). In an encircling operation they finally toppled Warsaw and some units sped westward to Leszno (2). South of the Polish capital the Warsaw-Lodz railroad was cut with the capture of Zyrardow (3). The rail junction of Skarzysko-Kamienna was being encircled as Soviet forces moved into Szydlowiec and Konskie (4). The Red Army's closest approach to Germany was at the important Polish city of Czestochowa, fourteen miles from the Silesian border (5). Although the Lublin radio reported the fall of Cracow, Moscow merely said that Sadowie (6), eight miles away, had been taken, but the city's capture was obviously at least imminent.

U. S. MEN USE TNT TO SLIT ICY GROUND

Fight Polar Weather in Hills of Ardennes as Well as Atrocity-Bent Germans

By Wireless to THE NEW YORK TIMES.

SUPREME HEADQUARTERS, Allied Expeditionary Force, Jan. 17—Up in the Ardennes hills, where the United States First Army is attacking toward St. Vith, the ground is so hard that the troops have to use dynamite and mortar shells to dig slit trenches.

The hills are so steep and slippery with snow that tanks sometimes slide down them like sleds. When pinned down by enemy fire or while waiting to attack Ameri-

Continued on Page 8, Column 2

MacArthur Protects Flank By 17-Mile Dash Along Gulf

By LINDESAY PARROTT
By Wireless to THE NEW YORK TIMES.

ALLIED HEADQUARTERS, on Leyte, Thursday, Jan. 18—The pace of the American advance on Luzon in the Philippines has been fastest in the extreme northwest where Gen. Douglas MacArthur's infantrymen have been feeling their way into Bolinao Peninsula, which forms the western shore of Lingayen Gulf. Here, in a sprint of seventeen miles from captured Alaminos, Sixth Army men reached Bolinao, a town on the extreme point of the peninsula.

Other detachments are moving southwestward toward Dasol Bay and the highway that leads west of the Zambales Mountains toward Bataan, a communiqué announced today.

[The capture of Bolinao sealed

Continued on Page 3, Column 3

OUR CHINA STRIKE IN 4TH DAY, FOE SAYS

Tokyo Cites 300-Plane Blow at Coast Ports—B-29's Join in Attack on Formosa Base

By The United Press.

PEARL HARBOR, Jan. 17—Tokyo reported today that more than 300 American carrier planes hit the China coast for the fourth successive day, battering Hong Kong, Canton and Hainan Island.

B-29 Superfortresses joined the mounting two-way offensive with new blows against Formosa.

[A new attack on Formosa Wednesday night was reported by General Douglas MacArthur's headquarters on Luzon. The report stated that long-range patrol planes harassed the Okayama airdrome.]

There was no immediate confirmation that Admiral William F. Halsey's Third Fleet planes had

Continued on Page 3, Column 5

ACCORD ON POLAND AT ONCE HELD VITAL

Red Armies' Sweep to West Seen Spurring Need for 'Big 3' Agreement

By RAYMOND DANIELL
By Cable to THE NEW YORK TIMES.

LONDON, Jan. 17—The fall of Warsaw and the swift advance of the Red Armies across western Poland toward the old frontiers of Germany have made it imperative that President Roosevelt and Prime Minister Churchill reach a final agreement with Premier Stalin on Poland's territorial and political future at their next meeting, it is believed here.

There are signs that the exiled Polish Government under Premier Tomasz Arciszewski is approaching the problems of its relations with Russia with a new sense of urgency but without much outward evidence to support an optimistic view of the outcome.

Mr. Arciszewski, in a statement on the liberation of Warsaw, cited the words of Lieut. Gen. Tadeusz Komorowski [General Bor], just before he and his underground army defending Warsaw yielded to the Germans after a heroic sixty-three-day struggle: "We are fighting for freedom, we are fighting for the right to be free!" Mr. Arciszewski commented: "At this moment these words embody, as

Continued on Page 6, Column 2

RIPS LINE IN POLAND

Red Army Races West After Storming Into Vistula Citadel

KONEFF NEAR SILESIA

Capture of Czestochowa Threatens Heart of Reich's Industries

By The United Press.

LONDON, Thursday, Jan. 18—Russian and Polish troops yesterday captured devastated Warsaw to free its last survivors of five years of Nazi tyranny as the Red Army's greatest offensive surged twenty-four miles across western Poland, taking Czestochowa and reaching within fourteen miles of the German border.

At the same time the Red Army launched another offensive north of Warsaw that carried within 130 miles of Danzig and twenty-two miles south of the East Prussian border. Cracow, the fourth city of Poland, also was reported to have been liberated, but Moscow said only that Russian armored spearheads were eight miles northeast of the city at Sadowie.

Shoulder to shoulder, three crack Soviet armies were driving westward across Poland along a twisting 450-mile front. They were headed straight for Germany and were 260 to 288 miles from Berlin.

Racing Toward Lodz

With Warsaw, the first European capital to be overrun by Adolf Hitler's victory-flushed troops, behind them, the Russians were racing westward toward Lodz, second city of Poland, and Russian spearheads already were at Babsk, thirty-six miles east of Lodz on the main Warsaw-Berlin highway.

German troops were retreating hastily toward the borders of the Reich and Berlin reports indicated that the Nazis might be pulling out of Poland entirely, writing off their 1939 conquest of the country. German newspapers reaching Stockholm said the German High Command had moved the puppet Government General of Poland from Cracow to Central Germany.

The Russians were striking with blitzkrieg speed that paled Germany's lightning marches through Poland in 1939 and France in 1940, and though Berlin protested that its troops were fighting far behind advance Soviet lines, the German Army appeared to be in full rout.

More than 2,000,000 Soviet soldiers were committed to the huge offensive and Moscow dispatches said savagery unparalleled in four winters of war raged on the Eastern Front as the Russians tore gaps in the German lines and split and resplit enemy groups falling back toward the Oder River—the Rhine of the east.

Silesian Center Outflanked

Thousands of German troops were killed yesterday as Soviet troops, advancing at a mile-an-hour clip, outflanked the rich coal and steel region of upper Silesia and split its defenders from the main German armies in the Lodz area. Capturing Slawniow, the Russians were only twenty-four miles northeast of Dabrowa, easternmost industrial center of Silesia.

Premier Joseph Stalin announced the capture of Warsaw, "the capital of our ally, Poland," just five years, three months and twenty days after Hitler's troops marched into the bombed city, and the free Warsaw radio broadcast to the world: "The city is razed, but we live on."

Marshal Stalin announced the victory in an order of the day. In Moscow victory guns fired without interruption for three hours to mark it and two subsequent orders of the day from the Red Army's Commander in Chief.

The second told of the new offensive north of Warsaw by the Second White Russian Army under the command of Marshal Konstantin K. Rokossovsky, which had ad-

Continued on Page 6, Column 3

War News Summarized

THURSDAY, JANUARY 18, 1945

Warsaw, the first European capital to fall to Hitler's blitzkrieg five years and four months ago, was liberated by Russian and Polish troops yesterday. The First White Russian Army captured the city after a wide encircling dash that swept up more than 800 other places.

The Red Army steamroller, which at its closest point was 260 miles from Berlin, moved north of the Polish capital when the Second White Russian Army, from its two bridgeheads across the Narew River, advanced twenty-four miles on a sixty-two-mile front, freeing Makow, Pultusk, Ciechanow and 500 other communities.

At the southern end of the long surging line the First Ukrainian Army liberated Czestochowa, Radomsko and 700 more inhabited places, and Lublin reported that Cracow had also fallen. This Russian army was only fourteen miles from the Reich. [All the foregoing 1:8.]

Gloom hung heavy over Germany. The enemy press and radio prepared the people for retreat on the Eastern front as the "final onslaught against Germany planned at Teheran" got under way. [6:1.]

The Warsaw victory brought to a climax the diplomatic impasse over recognition of a single Polish Government by all the Allies. The Polish Government in London indicated it would seek an early return to Warsaw and the Moscow-fostered Lublin regime was expected to move into the capital immediately. [1:7.]

Reverses in the east did not prevent the Germans from stiffening against the new British Second Army drive north of Aachen. The British advanced 2,000 yards, crossed the Roode River in two places and captured two villages, one of which was Dieteren. To the south, Americans took Vielsam and were five miles from St. Vith. The Third Army trapped a German force in the woods southeast of Tettingen. Inconclusive small battles were fought in the Alsace area. [1:3; map, P. 9.]

Some 700 American heavy bombers and 350 fighters carried the air war to oil and submarine plants in the Hamburg-Harburg area and rail targets in northwest Germany. [8:5-4.]

Americans on Luzon speared seventeen miles from Alaminos on the extreme right of the line to capture Bolinao, at the southwest tip of Lingayen Gulf. They also cut across the peninsula toward Dasol Bay, on the China Sea. At the other end of the line patrols entered Pozorrubio while main forces were half a mile from Rosario. Allied planes, in their best day, destroyed sixty-two enemy aircraft, all but one of which were caught on the ground. [1:5-6; map P. 2.]

Tokyo said that Pacific Fleet carrier planes had hit China for the fourth day, 300 of the Navy's aircraft striking Hong Kong, Canton and Hainan Island. A sizable force of B-29's—Tokyo said eighty—hit air installations at Shinchiku, on Formosa's northwest coast, with good effect, and General MacArthur's fliers again struck Okayama, on the southwest coast. [1:6.]

Continued on Page 34, Column 3

Douds Receives Formal Charges Aimed at Removal From NLRB

Formal charges aimed at forcing his resignation as regional director of the National Labor Relations Board were received yesterday by Charles T. Douds. The document was signed by Lester A. Asher, associate administrative examiner of the board in Washington.

Filing of the charges was announced in a statement on Tuesday by Harry A. Millis, chairman of the board, who said that Mr. Douds' removal was being sought "to promote the efficiency of the service" and on grounds of a "lack of fitness and capacity to supervise and direct the work of the staff" of the New York office. In making known that removal proceedings had been instituted against Mr. Douds, Dr. Millis voiced an implied reprimand to Mr. Douds for carrying the controversy between himself and the board into the press.

Mr. Douds, who had refused to comply with the board's previous request that he resign, demanding that formal charges be filed against him so that he might answer them in accordance with prescribed procedure, confirmed receipt of the charges yesterday but declined to discuss them. He made the following statement:

"This afternoon I received formal charges from the board. I first learned of the transmission of these charges from the papers this morning. I will answer these charges to the board and not through the newspapers.

"Dr. Millis implied in his statement this morning that the information already made public on this matter emanated directly or indi-

Continued on Page 34, Column 3

McGuire, Pacific Air Ace, Killed; He Downed 38 Japanese Planes

By The Associated Press.

SAN ANTONIO, Tex., Jan. 17—Major Thomas B. McGuire Jr. of San Antonio and Ridgewood, N. J., the leading American active ace with thirty-eight Japanese planes to his credit, was shot down and killed in the Philippines Jan. 7, Lieut. Gen. George C. Kenney, commanding the Allied Air Forces in the Pacific, informed Mrs. McGuire in a letter dated Jan. 8.

Mrs. McGuire received General Kenney's letter today. The Allied air chief said that the word Major McGuire had been shot down brought him the worst of a number of bad moments he had had to face since the war began.

"I felt that he would make a name for command as well as for leadership and for great personal courage," the letter stated.

"The accident, which left him vulnerable on Jan. 7 and in which he met his death, was sheer chance as Major McGuire was one of the most capable fighter pilots I have ever known."

"Your husband was one of the men the Air Forces can never forget. We will find it more difficult to carry on without him," General Kenney added.

The letter indicated that Major McGuire's plane was in some way disabled in the air, making him an easy prey to defending enemy fighters. Mrs. McGuire said she had received no official notification of her husband's death from the War Department.

Major McGuire became the leading ace when Maj. Richard I. Bong of Poplar, Wis., returned to the United States on leave. Major

Continued on Page 5, Column 3

"All the News That's Fit to Print"

The New York Times.

LATE CITY EDITION
Sunny and moderately cold today; moderate winds.
Temperatures Yesterday—Max., 40; Min., 29
Sunrise today, 6:56 A. M.; Sunset, 6:19 P. M.

VOL. XCIV..No. 31,790. Entered as Second-Class Matter, Postoffice, New York, N. Y. NEW YORK, TUESDAY, FEBRUARY 6, 1945. THREE CENTS NEW YORK CITY

MANILA FALLS, 1,350 FREED FROM SECOND PRISON; RUSSIANS ARRAYED AT ODER ON 75-MILE FRONT; PATTON CLEARS WESTWALL; COLMAR TRAP SET

RESTAURANTS BALK AT SAVING ON MEAT THREE DAYS A WEEK

Many Ignore Mayor's Plea for 'Conservation Monday,' Serving Steaks and Roasts

THOSE WHO HEED IT IRKED

Spokesman Says Observance Must Be General or Plan Should Be Discarded

Many restaurants, after a punctilious observance of meatless Tuesday and Friday last week, balked yesterday at Conservation Monday, the third of Mayor La Guardia's devices for reducing the use of meat in public eating places.

The result was that New Yorkers who felt like ordering steaks, roasts or chops had a wide choice of luncheon or dinner places, although for some it meant switching from their favorite restaurant to another that boldly advertised its meat dishes in the window.

Restaurateurs who had heeded the Mayor's call for voluntary participation in Conservation Monday were frankly upset by yesterday's experience and decided to send a committee to City Hall for a showdown unless some uniformity of observance was brought about by next Monday.

Paul Henkel Gives Views

Asserting that the first test of Conservation Monday has caused "unfair competition" among restaurants, Paul Henkel, president of the Society of Restaurateurs, said:

"All of our members adhered to the Mayor's suggestion to serve no steaks, roasts or chops and to use meat in 'stretch-out' dishes, such as hash, and to serve such specialty meats as are available. Many other restaurants, however, used meat freely. That looks like a breakdown of the plan."

Mr. Henkel said he was willing to believe that some restaurants might have misunderstood what Conservation Monday meant "because the Mayor did not emphasize the Mondays as strongly as the Tuesdays and Fridays." For that reason, he said, he was inclined to "give it another try" next Monday.

"But if it's not done on a uniform basis then, we'll send a committee to visit the Mayor," Mr. Henkel added. "He'll have to see that it's observed or else let up on the Monday part of his program."

Meat signs were easy to spot on restaurants all over town yesterday. A Times Square luncheon had a single message spelled out on its window board in the movable characters that are changed daily. It read: "Sirloin steak, potatoes, vegetables, 65c."

A restaurant just off Fifth Avenue had a paper strip with two words in its window—"Pork Chops." A crowded eating place near the Pennsylvania Station was serving braised breast of lamb, chopped steak, London broil and pork chops. These were not isolated cases.

That some restaurant men had confused Conservation Monday with Left-Over Monday, another La Guardia device that made its debut yesterday, was indicated by the explanations of some of those who served meat. Others said plainly: "Two days in one week is enough conservation."

Left-Over Idea Only for Homes

Left-Over Monday was meant by the Mayor to be observed in the homes, not in restaurants. With virtually all the non-kosher butcher shops closed on Mondays, starting yesterday, the Mayor had called on housewives to prepare their Monday dinners from left-over meats of the last few days. More than one restaurateur said yesterday that he was serving chops or roasts because he "had no left-over meats."

A spokesman for the Childs restaurants, which offered hot baked ham on toast and braised beef

Continued on Page 24, Column 3

UAW Wants Million For WPB 'Mix-Up'

By The United Press.

DETROIT, Feb. 5 — Early morning shifts reported at nearly a dozen war plants today, ending a week-end "holiday" resulting from muddled Government orders by which 30,000 war workers were idle.

United Automobile Workers, CIO, officials said that they would seek to recover an estimated $1,000,000 in lost wages from the Government.

Confused War Production Board orders intended to curtail use of industrial gas because of reported shortages started the "holiday" Friday.

The orders were promptly countermanded, but confusion was so general that 30,000 workers remained off the job over the week-end. UAW leaders said that they would demand investigations of the mix-up.

17 DEAD, 23 MISSING IN SHIP BLAST HERE

113 Others Injured as Loaded Tanker Explodes and Burns After Collision

Seventeen men died, about twenty-three are missing and 113 were injured, six gravely, in a tanker explosion in Upper New York Bay, between Stapleton, S. I., and lower Bay Ridge in Brooklyn, at 8:57 A. M. yesterday.

Eight of the bodies taken from the ice-filled waters were those of Navy personnel—gun-crew men, chiefly—and nine were men of the Merchant Marine.

The Navy is withholding the names of its dead until next-of-kin have been notified. The bodies of only five of the merchant seamen have been identified. These were:

Clyde Henry Crawford, 39 years old, 9605 Yeakel Avenue, Cleveland, Ohio; John Priess, 27 years old, Ogden Street, Philadelphia; George Baker, 26; Jakob Kristian Jakobsen, 35; Amund Amundsen, 50. The authorities had no addresses for the last three on this list, except that Jakobsen and Amundsen were from Norway. Most of the dead merchant seamen were oilers or firemen.

The police estimated that 70 per cent, or more, of the dead, the missing and the injured were from the American tanker Springhill, a 17,000-ton vessel, on which the explosion occurred. All the injured are in the Marine Hospital in Stapleton, some burned, some suffering from submersion, some from body bruises.

The tanker Springhill, the ship burned after the explosion, was only a steel shell when the fire was completely out in late afternoon. Fire crews searched the ruin for bodies.

The Norwegian tanker Vivi, spattered by burning oil after the explosion, pulled clear and escaped with comparatively minor damage. The Pan-Clio, which rammed the Springhill and touched off the explosion on the Springhill, accord-

Continued on Page 21, Column 5

RED ARMY LINED UP

Springboard on River, 33 Miles From Berlin, Captured at Zellin

FRANKFORT FLANKED

Nazi Groups Isolated—Foe Claims Drive on Stettin Is in Check

By The United Press.

LONDON, Tuesday, Feb. 6—The First White Russian Army reached the Oder River east of Berlin on a seventy-five-mile front yesterday, pushing to within thirty-three miles of the German capital with the capture of Zellin. The fortress of Kuestrin has been outflanked on the north and south.

Berlin reported that the Russians had crossed the Oder northwest of Kuestrin, last bastion on the shortest road to Berlin; had opened a new offensive that breached the upper Oder below Breslau, and were trying to strike northward across Pomerania toward the Baltic port of Stettin.

After having gained up to eight miles and seizing 100 communities in the Berlin home province of Brandenburg, the Russians drove close to nine rail and highway bridges crossing the winding Oder. They pushed a wedge between the twin fortresses of Kuestrin, on the east bank, and Frankfort on the Oder, which straddles the river sixteen miles to the south.

Foe Reports a Victory

The drive to the Oder, accomplished in a 280-mile advance that Marshal Gregory K. Zhukoff's First White Russian Army began twenty-three days ago from the Warsaw suburb of Praga, has split German lines east of the river. It has left to enemy forces holding east-bank positions in Pomerania and Silesia along the remainder of the Oder the alternatives of evacuation or entrapment.

Elsewhere on the Eastern Front, Moscow reported new gains by Gen. Ivan D. Chernyakhovsky's Third White Russian Army on the Samland Peninsula west of the encircled East Prussian capital of Koenigsberg; the recapture of five towns in the Szekesfehervar area of Hungary, where the Germans had sought to break through and relieve besieged Budapest, and the capture of an armaments factory in the encircled Polish city of Posen, 100 miles behind the Oder front.

The drive to the Oder carried the Russians to points thirty-three miles northeast of Berlin, thirty-six miles to the east and thirty-eight miles to the southeast. Berlin said the Russians also had struck northward but had been repelled south of the big Pomeranian communications center of Stargard, twenty miles southeast of Stettin, and near Pyritz, twenty-three miles southeast of the Baltic port.

Moscow identified ten towns seized in a seventy-five-mile

Continued on Page 11, Column 3

OUR RETURN TO MANILA HAS BROUGHT THEM LIBERTY

American and British civilian internees stand with their baggage on the grounds of the Santo Tomas internment camp in the Philippine capital. This photo, found in a Japanese barracks after the capture of Tacloban, Leyte, obviously was taken during January, 1942, in the early days of the camp.

The New York Times (U. S. Navy)

JAPANESE CUT OFF

MacArthur Declares City Won as Troops Close In From Three Sides

11TH DASHES 35 MILES

Airborne Troops Seal Foe From the South—37th Takes Bilibid Prison

By LINDESAY PARROTT
By Wireless to THE NEW YORK TIMES.

ADVANCED HEADQUARTERS on Luzon, Tuesday, Feb. 6—Gen. Douglas MacArthur formally announced the fall of Manila at 6:30 this morning and the liberation of about 5,000 prisoners of war and civilian internees.

The liberated prisoners included about 4,000 Americans as well as British and other members of the United Nations. More than 800 were war prisoners liberated from Bilibid Prison in the heart of Manila as troops of the Thirty-seventh Infantry stormed its gates in a burst of small arms fire.

General MacArthur in his official announcement of the fall of the city that in turn has been the seat of Spanish and American governments, and latterly the Japanese puppet regime, gave promise of future strokes against the enemy's conquered empire. "Japan itself is our final goal," he said.

Two Bridges Destroyed

The general's statement was issued as columns of American troops of the Sixth and Eighth Armies were rapidly pouring into the city from three directions, overwhelming sporadic enemy resistance in streets, assuring us a solid grip on all sections north of the Pasig River and menacing from the south the Japanese positions beyond that line.

American soldiers still could see fires and hear explosions as the Japanese continued demolitions. These included two of the four main bridges across the deep Pasig—the Quezon and Ayala spans. The two others remained standing, however, offering possible ingress from the north to the area of the city still in enemy hands.

General MacArthur summed up the situation, declaring that the Japanese defenders of Manila were surrounded and "their complete destruction is imminent."

Perhaps the most sensational incident in the capture of Manila came as the National Guardsmen of the Thirty-seventh Division stormed Bilibid Prison—effecting the second rescue in two days of prisoners taken by the Japanese when the city fell in 1942. Besides about 800 prisoners of war, 550 civilian internees—women and children included—were freed by the Americans, who fought small scale but desperate enemy resist-

Continued on Page 4, Column 4

CANADIAN VOTERS SPURN M'NAUGHTON

Defense Chief Is Defeated by Oppositionist in Grey North—Setback on Draft Policy

By P. J. PHILIP
Special to THE NEW YORK TIMES.

OTTAWA, Feb. 5—Prime Minister W. L. Mackenzie King's Government and policy received a severe setback today by the election in Grey North of the Progressive Conservative candidate, Garfield Case, opposing Defense Minister General A. G. L. McNaughton.

The election campaign was conducted by the opposition parties as implying a vote of censure of the Government for its manpower policy and its long refusal to apply full conscription for overseas service.

Although a Liberal member resigned at Grey North to make a place for General McNaughton in Parliament, the Conservatives de-

Continued on Page 9, Column 1

3d Army Wins Key Junction; Big Push in West Seen Near

By The Associated Press.

SUPREME HEADQUARTERS, Allied Expeditionary Force, Feb. 5—The American Third Army smashed clear through the Siegfried Line today, knocked out a key communications center before Pruem, and struck to within three and a half miles of that western German mountain stronghold against an astounding lack of resistance.

The battle of western Germany was taking a more ominous turn for the enemy, as the American First Army to the north—which by one front account yesterday breached the Westwall where it divides into two defense belts—seized control of two vital Roer River dams.

As the whole front stirred restlessly, American tanks and French colonial infantry slammed the door of escape on German forces in southern Alsace.

Supreme Headquarters confirmed that Lieut. Gen. Omar N. Bradley once more was in command of these operations, with the First

Continued on Page 6, Column 2

DE GAULLE LISTS DEMANDS IN PEACE

Entire Rhineland First—U. S. Seen as Security Leader—Big 3 Exclusion Hit

The text of General de Gaulle's address is on Page 10.

By HAROLD CALLENDER
By Wireless to THE NEW YORK TIMES.

PARIS, Feb. 5—Gen. Charles de Gaulle in effect notified the Big Three tonight that their decisions would not be binding on France until she had so decided after having had an opportunity to discuss them with the major Allies on an equal basis.

He then formulated what he called the French peace plan involving the minimum French terms for both western and eastern Europe. He said that he hoped—but he indicated that he was not sure—that the Allies would accept them. He made this declaration in a broadcast couched in emphatic terms and addressed to both the Big Three and the French people.

He described "the conditions that France considers essential" for peace as "the definite presence of French forces from one end of the Rhine to the other, the separation of the territories on the left bank

Continued on Page 10, Column 6

INTERNEES IN TEARS AS OLD GLORY RISES

Americans in Manila Sing Anthems When Sight of Flag Crowns Liberation

The following dispatch is by the Manila correspondent of THE NEW YORK TIMES, *who has just been liberated from the Santo Tomas internment camp. He had been ill just before the Japanese captured Manila in January, 1942, and was unable to leave the city.*

By FORD WILKINS
By Wireless to THE NEW YORK TIMES.

SANTO TOMAS CAMP, Manila, Feb. 5—Two hundred civilian hostages were released by the Japanese after the long siege of a barricaded camp building in an exchange. Between long lines of heavily armed American soldiers, the Japanese commandant, his staff and guards filed from this internment camp through the city to a Japanese stronghold on Lepanto Street, a mile and a half away.

There, in a stiffly formal ceremony, the Japanese were released without incident to join their forces in accordance with an agreement reached after long negotiations. Brig. Gen. William C. Chase reluctantly consented to the terms imposed by the commandant, Lieut. Col. Hayashi, who threatened to shoot it out with the American soldiers, knowing that it would mean death and injury to innocent civilians.

The released civilians, who had been crowded for two nights into cramped quarters on the third floor of one of the large residence buildings of the camp, part of the time without food or beds and constantly under the threat of guns, were warned not to attempt to escape at the end of their three

Continued on Page 4, Column 3

Vandenberg Links Treaty to Keep Axis Disarmed With Oaks Plan

Special to THE NEW YORK TIMES.

DETROIT, Feb. 5—Senator Arthur H. Vandenberg, Republican, of Michigan, declared here tonight that his proposal for permanent demilitarization of Germany and Japan through a "hard and fast" treaty signed by the major Allies would not be a substitute for the Dumbarton Oaks plan, but the latter would be an "indispensable sequel to the former."

Calling for a "fraternity for peace" in a broadcast speech before the Variety Club, the Senator said that his Axis demilitarization plan, on which he urged immediate action, would also render "academic" the controversial question whether the President should have the power without reference to Congress, to join American armed forces with those of the peace league to stop aggression, because, he added:

"If we first deal with our enemies through unequivocal post-war restraints upon them, we have remaining only our friends to consider in charting the organization of our post-war peace league."

"Remember," he continued, "that we are talking about the future use of force against one of our present Allies who subsequently becomes a military aggressor to threaten the peace of the world. Obviously it can only be one of our present major allies. It will have to be a present major ally who has broken a solemn pledge to abandon force as an instrumentality of foreign policy. It will have to be a major ally who has successively defied all of the intervening machinery for the pacific

Continued on Page 13, Column 3

War News Summarized

TUESDAY, FEBRUARY 6, 1945

Liberation of Manila was announced by General MacArthur, although the Japanese still held parts of the city, after the Eleventh Airborne Division, in a thirty-five-mile overnight march, had entered from the south and the Thirty-seventh Infantry had gone in from the north. The dismounted First Cavalry was cleaning out snipers from occupied areas.

Thirteen hundred fifty internees were freed when Bilibid Prison was captured, raising the total of Allied citizens released to 5,000, of whom 4,000 are Americans. Elsewhere on Luzon United States forces continued to make good progress and bombers smashed enemy strong points. [All the foregoing 1:8; maps P. 2.]

Brig. Gen. William C. Chase, to save the lives of 221 civilian hostages, reluctantly granted safe conduct to the Japanese commander and sixty-five of his men holding out in the last building of Santo Tomas camp. [1:7.] A regime of slow starvation was instituted there when the Japanese Army took over control a year ago. [4:5.] All sixty-nine nurses, "Angels of Bataan and Corregidor," were among those freed. They celebrated by caring for persons wounded in the fighting. [3:1.]

Four of Britain's newest and most powerful carriers, escorted by the battleship King George V, three cruisers and three destroyers, delivered two smashing blows to Japan's oil resources at Palembang, Sumatra. It was estimated that 75 per cent of the military gasoline supply was knocked out. Ninety-three enemy planes were destroyed or damaged, against a British loss of fifteen. The Japanese lost six more planes in a harmless attack on the ships. [1:6-7; map P. 5.]

In Europe the United States Third Army cleared the Siegfried Line and pushed to within three and one-half miles of Pruem. The First Army seized two Roer River dams in a good advance. A new American army was reported about to enter the conflict. French and American troops in the south split the Colmar pocket and cut the German escape route from southern Alsace. [1:5-6; maps, P. 6.]

The First Army has been restored to General Bradley's Twelfth Army group. [6:1.]

The Red Army extended its front along the Oder River to seventy-five miles and reached Zellin, thirty-three miles from Berlin. Arcs around Kuestrin and Frankfort were extended. [1:3; map, P. 11.]

The Lublin regime has begun to incorporate parts of German Silesia into Poland and will go into East Prussia when the military situation permits. This is in line with the plan to compensate Poland for territory ceded to Russia. [11:1.]

General de Gaulle, in a radio address, reiterated his demands for French troops on the Rhine and separation of the Rhineland and Ruhr areas from Germany. He asked independence for Poland, Czechoslovakia and the Balkan nations. France, he said, would not be bound by decisions of the Big Three made in her absence. [1:6.]

The Government of Prime Minister King in Canada received a setback when the Progressive Conservative candidate opposing Defense Minister McNaughton's program was elected in Grey North. [1:4.]

British Carrier Blow at Sumatra Costs Japan 75% of Aviation Fuel

By Wireless to THE NEW YORK TIMES.

LONDON, Feb. 5—Seventy-five per cent of all the aviation gasoline used by the Japanese army and navy is estimated to have been destroyed by carrier-borne aircraft of a powerful British naval force in two strong attacks on enemy oil refineries in Palembang, Sumatra, according to a statement issued here tonight.

It was announced that the 23,000-ton four-screw Indefatigable, Britain's newest, fastest and most modern aircraft carrier, took part in the attack, this being the first intimation that she was in commission.

The first attack against the Paldpu refinery occurred on Jan. 24. Avenger aircraft from the decks of the Indefatigable and the carriers Indomitable, Illustrious and Victorious dive bombed through barrage balloons and heavy flak after a long flight over occupied territory during which escorting Firefly fighters shot down thirteen enemy fighters, probably destroyed six others and destroyed thirty-four and damaged twenty-five aircraft on the ground.

The second attack was pressed home on Jan. 29 when eight enemy aircraft were shot down over the target area and three more were probably shot down. Four were destroyed on the ground and six more were shot down while attacking the Fleet.

Photographs showed that many of the principal installations received direct hits and were afterward burned by oil fires spreading from near-by reservoirs. During

Continued on Page 5, Column 2

MacArthur's Slogan Now Is 'On to Tokyo'

By The Associated Press.

ADVANCED HEADQUARTERS, on Luzon, Tuesday, Feb. 6—Gen. Douglas MacArthur, hailing the "fall of Manila," said in a statement today:

"The fall of Manila was the end of one great phase of the Pacific struggle and set the stage for another.

"We shall not rest until our enemy is completely overthrown.

"We do not count anything done as long as anything remains to be done.

"We are well on the way, but Japan itself is our final goal.

"With Australia saved, the Philippines liberated and the ultimate redemption of the East Indies and Malaya thereby made a certainty, our motto becomes: 'On to Tokyo!'

"We are ready in this veteran and proven command when called upon.

"May God speed the day!"

"All the News That's Fit to Print"

The New York Times.

LATE CITY EDITION

Intermittent light rain and windy today.

Temperatures Yesterday—Max., 42; Min., 26
Sunrise today, 7:59 A. M.; Sunset, 6:22 P. M.

VOL. XCIV..No. 31,792. Entered as Second-Class Matter, Postoffice, New York, N. Y. NEW YORK, THURSDAY, FEBRUARY 8, 1945. THREE CENTS IN NEW YORK CITY

BIG 3 SET FINAL STEPS TO CRUSH GERMANY, TURN TO PEACE ISSUES IN BLACK SEA TALK; U. S. 3D ARMY INVADES REICH AT 10 POINTS

NAVAL CHIEFS URGE JOB DRAFT TO BEAT JAPANESE QUICKLY

Forrestal, Bard Say May Bill Will Insure Rapid Repair of Damaged Vessels

SHIPBUILDING LAG BARED

McNutt Supports Measure, but Urges That WMC Have Control of Program

By C. P. TRUSSELL
Special to THE NEW YORK TIMES.

WASHINGTON, Feb. 7—Secretary James Forrestal and Ralph A. Bard, Under-Secretary of the Navy, called on Congress today to provide "insurance" that as battle damage to ships mounted with increased pressure on the enemy in the Pacific, adequate repair forces, constantly alerted, would be available to get the vessels back into action at the earliest possible moment. This "insurance," they said, was in the May-Bailey bill for limited national service, adding that speed in its enactment was vital.

As they appeared before a closed session of the Senate Military Affairs Committee, other sources disclosed that the Navy views the labor turnover at critical war production points as having become "uncontrollable"; that it has found its ship-construction program "in an alarming state of slippage," and that the repairs situation, accentuated by extensive damages to naval vessels aiding in the Philippines liberation, is "increasingly grave."

Paul V. McNutt, chairman of the War Manpower Commission, also testified before the committee and urged that the pending 18-to-45 labor-draft bill be "favorably considered by Congress."

"That recommendation was not based upon any conclusion that our manpower program has failed," Mr. McNutt asserted, "but upon a recognition of the fact that at this crucial period of the war we must be sure that there will be no failure in our ability to man urgent plants promptly."

McNutt Urges Amendments

Mr. McNutt asked, however, that t[illegible] committee adopt again the a[illegible]ments it voted last week, the[illegible]ubbed its slate clean pending the hearings. These proposals would take from Selective Service much of the authorities granted it by the May-Bailey bill and put the WMC largely in charge of the operations of the program.

The accumulated experience, understanding and acceptance by workers, employers and affected Government agencies, Mr. McNutt argued during his three hours' testimony, would be "destroyed" if the House version of the legislation was enacted.

The committee appeared to be still widely divided on the issue of limited national service after hearing the naval and manpower chiefs for five hours.

Senator Elbert D. Thomas, chairman, expressed the opinion that while the testimony had developed that, as of Jan. 1, the manpower situation as a whole was better than at any other time in the country's history, there remained the question: Should the bill be enacted in the interest of its effect on the morale of the fighting men and because of the uncertainty as to the future requirements of warfare?

Senator Albert B. Chandler of Kentucky said that he had not been convinced of a need for the application of limited national service to draft registrants at this time, adding that he did not believe Mr. McNutt was "so strong for it."

Senator Joseph C. O'Mahoney of Wyoming asserted that the fears voiced by the Navy spokesmen that war workers, believing the

Continued on Page 13, Column 2

MacArthur Enters Manila; Hailed by Freed Prisoners

'I'm a Little Late, but We Finally Came,' General Says—Women Embrace Him at Santo Tomas Camp

By FORD WILKINS
By Broadcast to THE NEW YORK TIMES.

SANTO TOMAS CAMP, Manila, Feb. 7—Gen. Douglas MacArthur has returned to the Philippine capital, fulfilling the promise made when he departed in December, 1941, for Bataan, making Manila an open city.

Accompanied by a small staff he first visited the Santo Tomas Camp, handshaking his way through cheering crowds of old Manila friends, whose rescue was a high point of his army's step by step progress northward from Australia. The visit was informal, more like a return home than a triumphal entry.

The general left the camp within half an hour. He made no public address, simply passing through the lobby of the main building, which was jammed with men and women. He went through a side door to the children's hospital and then went to the second floor of the main building to study conditions there.

When General MacArthur entered the building the American flag was raised overhead. Guards saluted and music was played, officially signifying that the 3,700 persons who had endured Japanese regimentation for three years were once more free citizens under the Stars and Stripes.

The city of Manila, which General MacArthur had left intact, presented a picture of widespread destruction today. Smoke spread from the still burning areas around the camp. Mopping up operations progressed as fast as possible.

Three years of methodical stripping operations by the Japanese military alien property division had removed to Japan all convertible property of Americans and others. All vehicles were removed from the city. All supplies of food, medicines and machinery left be-

Continued on Page 3, Column 2

PIERLOT PREVENTS VOTE BY RESIGNING

Interrupts Belgian Deputies' Debate—Regent Summons Possible Successors

By DAVID ANDERSON
By Wireless to THE NEW YORK TIMES.

BRUSSELS, Feb. 7—Premier Hubert Pierlot handed his own and his Cabinet's resignations to Prince Regent Charles today. The Regent accepted the resignations and immediately called the first of a long series of conferences to determine who could be charged with forming a new Government.

Even after the lengthy fight against M. Pierlot, the end surprised everyone in the Chamber. There was no vote on the debate over the efficiency of the Government. M. Pierlot simply walked to the rostrum soon after noon and told the Chamber of Deputies that he was satisfied that there was no confidence in his Administration and that he was finished.

No one moved or said a word while the Premier retraced his steps. Frans van Cauwelaert, the President of the Chamber, broke the spell by saying: "The statement that you have just heard from the Premier in the name of the Government evidently brings the debate to an end. I declare the session closed."

M. Pierlot's action was not without political significance. By avoiding a vote, he deprived the Socialists of a chance to sweep into succession on a wave of emotion. He left the parties opposing him uncertain where they stood and he

Continued on Page 6, Column 2

U. S. FORCES CLEAR NORTHERN MANILA

Drive Delayed by Destruction of All Bridges but Troops to South Tighten Trap

By LINDESAY PARROTT
By Wireless to THE NEW YORK TIMES.

ADVANCED HEADQUARTERS, on Luzon, Thursday, Feb. 8—Gen. Douglas MacArthur announced today that the northern part of Manila and Quezon City had been cleared by troops of the Thirty-seventh Division and the First Cavalry Division, who first entered the city last week.

All bridges across the Pasig River, which runs through the center of Manila, were destroyed by the Japanese in their retreat southward, offering a serious obstacle to further American penetration from the north. It had been announced previously that the Quezon and Ayala bridges had been destroyed, while the fate of the other bridges had been in doubt.

The Japanese positions south of the river became increasingly doubtful today when the Eleventh Airborne Division, which marched into the city from the beachhead in Batangas Province, reached the vicinity of Nichols Field on the shore of Manila Bay. Mopping up operations are continuing there. The communiqué stated there was a short gap between the American northern and southern forces in the capital.

With the American forces solidly in Manila four weeks after the landing on the beach of Lingayen Gulf, 110 miles to the north, Gen-

Continued on Page 3, Column 4

Petrillo Charged With Seeking Control Over Music Teachers

Special to THE NEW YORK TIMES.

ANN ARBOR, Mich., Feb. 7—James C. Petrillo, president of the American Federation of Musicians, is making his "first attempt to control the field of music teaching" by putting the National Music Camp at Interlochen on the union's "unfair list," it was charged here today by Dr. Joseph E. Maddy, director of the camp.

Dr. Maddy, who is Professor of Music at the University of Michigan, said that the camp expected to fight the union's action in the courts and insisted that the school would continue next Summer, even if it were necessary to employ non-union instructors.

Disclosure of the union's listing of Interlochen as "unfair" was made yesterday in New York. The effect of the move, it was said, would be to prevent many teachers, should they continue working at the school, from accepting [illegible] commercial engagements which ordinarily constituted their major source of income. Radio stations carrying an Interlochen concert would face the loss of musicians on all programs.

The dispute between the union and school started in July, 1942, when the federation forced the Interlochen High School Orchestra off the air.

Dr. Maddy asserted that the "unfair" listing represented a departure from Mr. Petrillo's pre-

Continued on Page 14, Column 2

RUSSIANS SMASH ON

Zhukoff, 31 Miles From Berlin, Is Reported Across the Oder

FRANKFORT MENACED

Near-by Kunersdorf Won—Tanks Stab Kuestrin—Koneff Gains

By The United Press.

LONDON, Thursday, Feb. 8—Soviet troops expanded their hold on the Oder River's east bank northeast of Berlin yesterday in a seven-mile advance that carried them within thirty-one miles of the German capital, and Berlin said the Russians had won a fourth bridgehead across the water barrier on the shortest road to the threatened city.

The key citadels of Kuestrin and Frankfort on the Oder, guarding the approaches to Berlin, were gravely menaced. Soviet troops drove to within a mile and a half of Kuestrin, capturing the northwestern suburb of Alt-Drewitz. Three miles before Frankfort they won the historic battlefield of Kunersdorf.

These gains were revealed in the Russians' guarded communiqués as Berlin and Moscow reports indicated that a decisive battle for the gates to the capital had been joined and that the Red Army already was ripping up the city's outer defenses.

Oder Citadels Shelled

Enemy reports acknowledged that each of four bridgeheads on the Oder's west bank within a few minutes flying time from Berlin was being widened in tank and artillery battles that presaged the encirclement of Kuestrin and Frankfort. Both cities were under artillery fire and Soviet tanks broke into Kuestrin's center.

The German reports indicated that Soviet assault troops were across the Oder defense line in great strength thirty-three to

Continued on Page 2, Column 3

PATTON OVER RIVER

Four Divisions Cross Our and Sauer at Night to Hack Westwall

WIDE FRONT ABLAZE

1st Army Is Nearer Dam Control—2 Complete Siegfried Line Cuts

By CLIFTON DANIEL
By Wireless to THE NEW YORK TIMES.

SUPREME HEADQUARTERS, Allied Expeditionary Force, Feb. 7—The coordinated attack by two American Armies against the Siegfried Line broadened to a front of seventy miles today when four divisions of Lieut. Gen. George S. Patton's Third Army renewed their eastward thrust and burst over the German border at ten places beyond the Luxembourg frontier.

American infantrymen, who had already been thrusting into the Siegfried Line to the north, meanwhile drove clean through the main permanent defenses of the last remaining zone of the Siegfried Line in two places, one on the Olef River southwest of Schleiden, the other only three miles from Pruem, vital road junction in Germany southeast of St. Vith.

Allied advances had left a fat salient bulging as much as fourteen miles into our lines along the Luxembourg frontier, and the Third Army forces struck a series of determined blows today to flatten that bulge. Striking across the distended Sauer and Our Rivers, which mark the German border, they pushed into Germany as much as a mile in one place and an average of a half mile elsewhere.

Broadening of the offensive brought a total of at least twelve divisions into the attack on the Siegfried zone between Echternach in the south and Schmidt in the north, a distance of seventy miles. Beyond Schmidt and around Aachen the Westwall has already been effectively reduced, and the

Continued on Page 10, Column 4

War News Summarized

THURSDAY, FEBRUARY 8, 1945

"Complete agreement" has been reached "for joint military operations in the final phase of the war against Germany," President Roosevelt, Prime Minister Churchill and Premier Stalin announced in communiqués issued simultaneously in Washington, London and Moscow. This was the first official announcement that the Big Three conference was under way. It is taking place "in the Black Sea area."

Having settled the military problems, the three leaders said they were discussing "joint plans for the occupation and control of Germany," political and economic problems of liberated Europe and "the earliest possible establishment of a permanent international organization to maintain peace." Acting Secretary of State Grew, in Washington, indicated that France would have a part in fixing Europe's post-war boundaries. [All the foregoing 1:8; map P. 4.]

Richard Law, British Minister of State, told the Commons "all powers together" must decide the boundary question. London observers expected decisive blows against Germany to follow quickly upon the conference. [4:5.] The Netherlands Government presented a memorandum to the three leaders, urging greater power for the smaller nations under the Dumbarton Oaks plan. [1:7.]

The United States Third Army broke into Germany at ten points along a twenty-four-mile front from Echternach north, and with the First Army smashed through the Siegfried Line in at least two places. One was northwest of Pruem, the other on the Olef River southwest of Schleiden. [1:5.]

Cleve and Goch, lying directly ahead of the British Second Army's long dormant sector in the Netherlands, were heavily attacked in a sudden assault by RAF bombers. [11:1.]

The first aggressive action by the Fifth Army in Italy in several weeks resulted in gains against the defenses of Bologna, despite strong German resistance. [6:7.]

Russian tanks were reported in the center of Kuestrin following capture of the suburb of Alt-Drewitz. The Red Army, clearing the Germans from the east bank of the Oder River, extended its front toward Stettin. The bridgehead southeast of Breslau was widened. [1:4; map, P. 2.]

Quezon City and the northern part of Manila have been cleared of the Japanese. The Eleventh Airborne Division was mopping up the southern section. The enemy destroyed all bridges over the Pasig River. Japanese casualties on Luzon were estimated at 48,000; ours were 7,067, of which 1,600 were killed. [1:3.] General MacArthur returned to Manila, as he had promised more than three years ago, and found large areas destroyed. [1:2-3.]

Two separate forces of B-29's from India struck military installations at Saigon, French Indo-China, and bridges and other communications in the Bangkok area of Thailand. [4:1.]

Political developments included the resignation of Belgian Premier Pierlot and his Cabinet [1:2] and a personal appeal by General Mikhailovitch to President Roosevelt, Prime Minister Churchill and Premier Stalin to assure a democratic government for Yugoslavia. [6:4.]

PATTON MOVES HIS LINE FORWARD

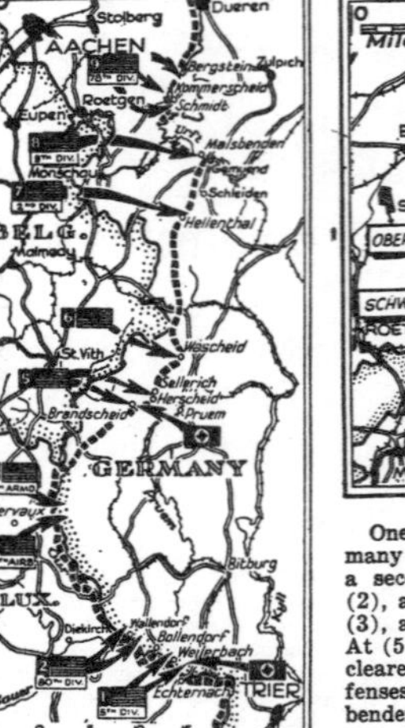

Feb. 8, 1945

One division invaded Germany above Echternach (1), a second around Wallendorf (2), a third east of Clervaux (3), a fourth just north (4). At (5) and (6) and at (7) we cleared the main Westwall defenses. Patrols entered Malsbenden (8). Three columns neared Schmidt (9). Roer dams shown on map at right.

Americans in Assault Boats Beat Torrents and Nazi Fire

By GENE CURRIVAN
By Wireless to THE NEW YORK TIMES.

WITH UNITED STATES THIRD ARMY, Feb. 7—Long before dawn, when heavy fog shrouded their movements, troops of the Third Army crossed the Our and Sauer Rivers into Germany at ten places. They fought bitterly to make crossings under the guns of the Siegfried Line—and held them.

The crossings were made along a twenty-four-mile front from the vicinity of Echternach northward, while other advances were made for an additional ten miles along the front. Four of the crossings were made on the Sauer River, between Echternach and Wallendorf to the north, where the Sauer and Our join, while the remaining six were above Wallendorf on the Our.

In all cases progress was comparatively slow against a combination of deterring elements. There was in the first place the weather with its fog, which had its virtues and its drawbacks. Then there were the swollen rivers, submerged barbed wire on the east banks and the formidable Siegfried Line.

The River Our, which is some nine feet above its normal level, had been covered with barbed wire meant for beach obstacles, while the velocity of the current was an additional hazard. But with all this, including grazing machine-gun fire at water level, the crossings were accomplished, and in one case a command post was established right in the middle of the Siegfried Line.

This was done by Maj. Arthur H. Clark of Buffalo, of the Eightieth Division. He is "comfortably situated" in a former German pillbox, but at this writing he is having few visitors.

This tenfold crossing into the Reich was the result of concerted action by four outstanding divisions of Lieut. Gen. George S. Patton's Army—an Army that Nazi radio announcers worried about only last week when they asked, "Where is 'Bloody' Patton?" To-

Continued on Page 11, Column 4

DUTCH OPPOSE IDEA OF OAKS BIG 5 VETO

Plea to Roosevelt, Churchill and Stalin Asks Wider Small Nations' Role in Security

By JAMES B. RESTON
Special to THE NEW YORK TIMES.

WASHINGTON, Feb. 7—The Netherland Government transmitted to President Roosevelt, Prime Minister Churchill and Marshal Stalin, just before the Big Three meeting, a seventeen-page document containing "suggestions" for the improvement of the Dumbarton Oaks world security plan.

These suggestions, it was learned today, include proposals for strengthening the position of the smaller powers on the proposed World Security Council, and they argue specifically against the right of the United States, Britain, Soviet Russia, China and France to judge all charges against themselves.

The Netherland note, which was handed to our Government by Ambassador Alexander Loudon before Mr. Roosevelt went to confer with Mr. Churchill and Marshal Stalin, is open to several interpretations, one of which is that unless the position of the smaller powers is strengthened the Netherland people might not enter the security organization with satisfaction, but in general it seems to stress two points:

(1) It concedes that the powers

Continued on Page 4, Column 5

Captured Fuehrers' College Bares Nazi System for Leaders' Clique

By HAROLD DENNY
By Wireless to THE NEW YORK TIMES.

WITH THE UNITED STATES FIRST ARMY, Feb. 7—The capture of Ordensburg-Vogelsang—one of Adolf Hitler's first schools for fuehrers—by our Ninth Infantry Division last Sunday was, from a military standpoint, a minor incident in a great campaign. The more one learns, however, of what went on within those rugged walls, the more that capture looms as a symbolic victory of the first magnitude.

This institution, where Yankee soldiers now nap and heat up C rations while spiteful shells from German guns across the Urftstausee crash harmlessly overhead, was a very nursery for spreading and perpetuating every ugly impulse in the Nazi "philosophy," the core of Hitler's scheme to supplant reason and tolerance with hate and force for 1,000 years.

This school, and five more like it, were seminaries of arrogance, racial prejudice and the technique of tyranny, with lessons in horsemanship and drawing-room procedure thrown in. The horsemanship was for the purpose of teaching students "how to ride a horse, to rule the living animal with their iron will."

We learn these facts about this

Continued on Page 11, Column 2

STAFF CHIEFS MEET

3 Nations' Top Military Men With Heads of State at Parley

EXACT SITE IS SECRET

Europe's Future Studied by Allies' Leaders in 'Black Sea Area'

By BERTRAM D. HULEN
Special to THE NEW YORK TIMES.

WASHINGTON, Feb. 7—President Roosevelt, Premier Stalin and Prime Minister Churchill are meeting in the "Black Sea area," have already reached an agreement "for joint military operations in the final phase of the war against Nazi Germany" and are now proceeding to consider the problems of a secure peace.

This was announced this afternoon in a communiqué issued simultaneously in Washington, Moscow and London. The communiqué was given out here from the White House without comment. It was the first official announcement that the conference had convened. While it was issued as the Russian armies were advancing close to Berlin and more Americans were pouring into Germany, presumably it had been withheld until the first phase of the meeting, that concerning military questions, had been concluded.

The communiqué given out today did not specify the place of the meeting, but it said that the three heads of government were accompanied by their Chiefs of Staff, their Foreign Secretaries and other advisers. The leaders, it was announced, were conferring "to concert plans for completing the defeat of the common enemy and for building, with their Allies, firm foundations for a lasting peace." This declaration of aims, coupled with such few details as were given, was considered a warrant for regarding it as a very broad conference.

Discussion of Japan Doubted

However, the fact that the military plans were described as aimed at defeating the "common enemy" was looked on as indicating that the military discussions had not covered plans for the defeat of Japan, since Russia has not been at war with that country. A possibility that Premier Stalin might have now decided to enter the war against Japan was ruled out in opinion here, inasmuch as the communiqué said that, in the military discussions, "the present situation on all the European fronts" had been reviewed and announced complete agreement for joint military operations against Germany.

The military discussions had first place on the agenda. Now, as peace problems are being discussed, detailed plans for the operations are being worked out by the military staffs of the three Governments. For that purpose President Roosevelt is said to have with him Admiral William D. Leahy, his personal Chief of Staff; Admiral Ernest J. King, Commander in Chief of the United States Fleet and Chief of Naval Operations, and Gen. George C. Marshall, Chief of Staff of the Army.

The problems involved in establishing a secure peace, the communiqué said, will cover "joint plans for the occupation and control of Germany, the political and economic problems of liberated Europe and proposals for the earliest possible establishment of a permanent international organization to maintain peace." Plans for the occupation and control of Germany were worked out months ago for the armistice period by the European Advisory Commission, but they are expected to be reviewed in detail at the Big Three conference and will probably be amended.

Continued on Page 4, Column 3

"All the News That's Fit to Print"

The New York Times.

LATE CITY EDITION
Cloudy, becoming clear this afternoon; fresh to strong winds.
Temperatures Yesterday—Max., 40; Min., 30
Sunrise today, 7:03 A. M.; Sunset, 6:30 P. M.

VOL. XCIV...No. 31,798. Entered as Second-Class Matter, Postoffice, New York, N. Y. NEW YORK, WEDNESDAY, FEBRUARY 14, 1945. THREE CENTS IN NEW YORK CITY

BUDAPEST IS TAKEN AT COST OF 159,000 TO FOE; BRITISH CLEAR REICHSWALD, PATTON PUSHES ON; CAVITE WON, END OF MANILA CAMPAIGN 'IN SIGHT'

HEARING IS VOTED ON IVES-QUINN BILL IN SENATE REVOLT

Coudert Prompts Step in the Committee on Petition of State Industry Leaders

'FAIR PLAY' IS EMPHASIZED

Lack of Due Consideration of Controversial Plan Alleged—Assembly May Follow Suit

Texts of statements on the discrimination bill, Page 15.

By LEO EGAN
Special to THE NEW YORK TIMES.

ALBANY, Feb. 13 — A large-scale revolt against demands of Republican legislative leaders for enactment of the Ives-Quinn anti-discrimination bill got under way today. Its first definite accomplishment was to cause the Senate Finance Committee to agree to a public hearing on the bill before it is called up for action in that chamber.

Spreading rapidly to the Assembly, the revolt appeared strong enough to force the leaders there to agree also to a public hearing before a final vote was taken, even if it involved a complete revision of the Assembly's schedule.

When the measure was reported last week from the Ways and Means Committee, the Assembly leaders decided to call it up for a vote next Tuesday. If a public hearing is granted, the final vote faces a delay of at least a week and probably two.

Such a delay might cause a shift in present plans to adjourn on March 22.

Some advocates of the discrimination bill were expressing serious doubts that they would be able to muster enough votes to put it through the two branches of the Legislature in view of the extent and mounting intensity of the opposition.

CIO Pressure a Factor

Whip-cracking tactics and pressure from Congress of Industrial Organization unions appeared to be alienating some up-State Republican support of the measure. Democratic leaders, who have been subjected to opposition pressure along with Republicans, are still confident that they can hold their ranks in favor of the legislation, with only one or two defections.

As yet Governor Dewey has taken no part in the efforts of Republican legislative leaders to round up enough votes to pass the measure. Even if he were to apply pressure, legislators doubt that many votes could be changed.

The opposition is drawing its greatest strength from the belief that the bill, if enacted, would do more to arouse racial and religious feeling than to allay it. This view has been expressed by business and industry representatives and by spokesmen for the railroad brotherhoods.

As proposed, the bill sets up a five-man commission and empowers it to compel employers, unions and employment agencies to cease job discrimination on racial or religious grounds. The orders of the commission would be enforceable through the courts in the same fashion as orders of the State Labor Relations Board and, in addition, anyone interfering with the commission's work or failing to obey its mandates would be subject to fines up to $500 and imprisonment for one year or both.

Coudert Touches Off Revolt

The revolt, which had been gathering strength for some days, was touched off when Senator Frederic R. Coudert Jr., Republican, of Manhattan, moved in the Senate Finance Committee to hold a public hearing on the proposal before the committee reported it to the Senate. Seventeen of the twenty-five committee members were present. The vote in favor of holding the hearing was 15 to 2. Senator James J. Crawford, Democrat, of

Continued on Page 15, Column 1

Stalin Accepts Majority Vote On Non-Punitive Peace Issues

Russia Wins Point on Unanimity Among Great Powers in Cases Entailing Economic or Military Action

By JAMES B. RESTON
Special to THE NEW YORK TIMES.

WASHINGTON, Feb. 13—It may now be stated with certainty that Premier Stalin agreed at the Crimea Conference to the following compromise on the voting procedure in the proposed United Nations security council:

(1) In all cases not involving punitive measures, decisions would be taken by a simple majority of the eleven-nation security council.

(2) In all such cases (not involving punitive action), no parties to a dispute would have the right to vote on their own cases.

(3) In cases involving punitive action (such as economic or military sanctions) against a nation charged with aggressive intentions or actions, however, decisions would be taken only when a majority of the security council, including the United States, Russia, Britain, France and China, voted affirmatively.

(4) In these cases (involving punitive action), Russia and the other permanent members of the council would thus retain their veto power.

The delegates at Dumbarton Oaks discussed the veto-power question for more than a month in the hope of getting the Russian delegates to depart from the position that the permanent members of the security council should have the right to veto all decisions before the council and even to veto any proposals to bring any given subject before the security council.

At Yalta, however, when President Roosevelt raised the question, it is understood, Premier Stalin

Continued on Page 8, Column 6

ROOSEVELT SHAPED 2 YALTA SOLUTIONS

Byrnes, Home, Says President Initiated Plan for Poland, Security Vote Formula

By BERTRAM D. HULEN
Special to THE NEW YORK TIMES.

WASHINGTON, Feb. 13 — The solution of the Polish question and the formula on voting procedure in the council of the projected world organization for security and peace—two of the thorniest problems resolved by the Crimea Conference—were proposed by President Roosevelt, James F. Byrnes, Director of War Mobilization and Reconversion, disclosed today on his return from the meeting.

He returned with Admiral Ernest J. King, Commander in Chief of the United States Fleet and Chief of Naval Operations. They were the first to get back in the capital from the historic meeting.

At an hour's news conference in the White House Mr. Byrnes stressed the importance of the decisions reached. He warned that the war in Europe was far from over.

While he did not reveal the voting formula, pending its present consideration by the three powers with France and China, he disclosed that through no formal vote, but by the ready consent of Prime Minister Churchill and Premier Stalin, President Roosevelt presided at the meetings.

President Roosevelt brought the proposal concerning liberated areas to the conference, Mr. Byrnes said, because of a feeling in this country that recent unilateral actions were leading to spheres of influence. Now, under the declaration, the United States assumes a share of the responsibility for conditions in such countries as Poland, Yugoslavia, Greece, Rumania and Bulgaria. The status of the Baltic

Continued on Page 10, Column 5

ACCORD REJECTED BY LONDON POLES

Exile Government Denounces 'Fifth Partition' of Nation—End of Regime Is Seen

The statements by the Polish Government in Exile, Page 12.

By RAYMOND DANIELL
By Wireless to THE NEW YORK TIMES.

LONDON, Feb. 13—In a statement so blistering that it is bound to strain the patience of the British and American Governments, the Polish Government in London denounced tonight all the decisions regarding its country's future reached by President Roosevelt, Prime Minister Churchill and Premier Stalin in Yalta.

After a long Cabinet meeting Premier Tomasz Arciszewski's Government, which former Premier Stanislaw Mikolajczyk and his Peasant party followers refused to join, denounced the proposed frontier revisions as the "fifth partition of Poland," this time accomplished by "her Allies," and declared that it could not be bound by ex parte decisions regarding Poland's future Government.

British circles said that the exile Government, by refusing to cooperate in a settlement of the long-standing quarrel with the Soviet Union along the lines of the tripartite agreement, was merely hastening its demise. In any case, British and American recognition of the Arciszewski Government will be withdrawn after the new Government, made up of Lublin Committee of National Liberation members, resistance leaders in Poland and other Poles abroad, has been established.

There are understood to be some supporters of Premier Arciszewski, however, who feel that a mistake was made in not accepting the in-

Continued on Page 12, Column 2

French Plan Big Base at Dakar For Empire and World Security

By HAROLD CALLENDER
By Wireless to THE NEW YORK TIMES.

PARIS, Feb. 13—The French Cabinet announced today that it had decided to create a "large land, air and naval base" at Dakar, which, some feared, might slip out of France's control as a result of the American occupation of it during the war.

On Thursday, Gen. Charles de Gaulle will make a speech about French Indo-China, whose return to French control no Allied communiqué has promised. These incidents illustrate France's jealousy of her sovereignty and her right to "greatness" at this moment of the seeming formation of two oddly different peace systems that have been shaped by others while France looked on.

It is believed here that Russia had her way on the Dumbarton Oaks scheme and largely on Poland, while the Allies in return gained her acceptance of an inter-Allied regime for Germany, which rules out puppet governments under Field Marshal Gen. Friedrich von Paulus of the Free German National Committee or anyone else. The French believe that the Russians held strong cards regarding Germany and Poland but were influenced by their need of American machinery for the reconstruction of Russia.

The French Cabinet "took cognizance" of the Big Three's communiqué today, an official statement said, but showed no tendency to unrestrained rejoicing over the dip-

Continued on Page 13, Column 2

NAVAL BASE SEIZED

Nichols Field Also Won as Trap Narrows on Besieged Garrison

BAY FRONT REACHED

Dash Across City Perils Enemy Flank—New Atrocities Reported

By The United Press.

MANILA, Wednesday, Feb. 14—United States troops have seized the big Cavite naval base southwest of Manila and the end of the fierce battle of Manila is in sight, Gen. Douglas MacArthur announced today.

Cavite is on a point of land eight miles southwest of Manila and was the former United States naval headquarters in the Philippines. The Japanese heavily bombed the base in an attack shortly after the start of the Pacific war.

The base was captured by troops of the Eleventh Airborne Division, who also cleared the Japanese from stubbornly defended Nichols Field south of the capital. Ten Japanese seaplanes and a battery of 3-inch guns were captured intact at Cavite.

The capture of Cavite left the Japanese still in control of Manila Bay, however, from the island fortress of Corregidor and the southern tip of Bataan. General MacArthur disclosed that Liberator heavy bombers, continuing to soften up Corregidor, dropped 150 tons of bombs on its coastal defenses, hitting four heavy gun batteries.

A Small-Scale Stalingrad

On the twelfth day of the battle of Manila, which military observers said was the fiercest street battle since Stalingrad, although on a smaller scale, General MacArthur announced:

"The end of the enemy's trapped garrison is in sight."

He also disclosed that for the first five weeks of the Luzon campaign, which started Jan. 9, Japanese casualties now exceed 68,000. American casualties are 2,102

Continued on Page 6, Column 4

THE BRITISH MASSING FOR ASSAULT IN GERMANY

Infantrymen crowd tanks and other vehicles before moving into Reich Forest in Cleve area
Associated Press Wirephoto (U. S. Signal Corps Radiotelephoto)

JOB DRAFT URGENCY RISES, BYRNES SAYS

Men in Combat, Whose Total Will Set a Record in March, Must Be Supplied

By C. P. TRUSSELL
Special to THE NEW YORK TIMES.

WASHINGTON, Feb. 13—James F. Byrnes, Director of War Mobilization and Reconversion, renewed his call today for enactment of a limited national service law to assure a full measure of ammunition and supplies on the front lines.

Mr. Byrnes said that nothing had occurred during his absence at the Crimea conference to change his support of the May-Bailey bill, which is now in its second week of consideration by the Senate Military Affairs Committee after passage by the House.

"On the contrary," he told a news conference, "there is even more need for the May-Bailey bill

Continued on Page 17, Column 1

Canadians Gain Near Cleve; 3d Army Links Bridgeheads

By CLIFTON DANIEL

SUPREME HEADQUARTERS, Allied Expeditionary Force, Feb. 13—The Allied attack through the northern wing of the Westwall at Cleve developed into a slugging match between major forces today as British infantry broke into open ground beyond the Reichswald and Cleve today in a drive toward Goch, second of the two major road centers and Siegfried fortress towns in the battle area. The Germans have now thrown elements of seven divisions into the path of Gen. H. D. G. Crerar's unwavering advance, which is less than three miles from Goch.

Both at Goch and near Echternach on the American Third Army front the Germans concentrated field guns to beat back the Allies. But Lieut. Gen. George S. Patton's forces also rolled steadily forward, creating a solid ten-mile bridgehead across the Our and Sauer Rivers near Echternach. Three divisions are now grouped on that front, and two of them have already opened avenues through the main line of Westwall pillboxes.

Brighter weather put considerably more than 2,500 Allied tactical aircraft out ahead of the ground armies today to beat up the opposing German forces and continue the program of isolating the battlefield that in time may create a major disaster for Field Marshal Gen. Karl von Rundstedt.

United States Ninth Air Force fighter bombers swept the area east of Vianden and among other places attacked the three troop-filled towns of Chanweiler, Meckel and Wolsfeld, just north of General Patton's bridgehead and six to eight miles south of Bitburg.

British medium bombers unloaded high explosives over the villages of Weeze, Uden, Exanter and Kevelaer, behind the German lines on the Canadian First Army front, and fighters and bombers repeatedly strafed the Cleve City Forest just east of the Reichswald and

Continued on Page 2, Column 2

HULL WILL ATTEND SECURITY PARLEY

May Head the United Nations Session in San Francisco—Vandenberg a Delegate

Special to THE NEW YORK TIMES.

WASHINGTON, Feb. 13—Secretary Stettinius will be chairman of the United States delegation to the United Nations conference on drafting a world security plan on the basis of the Dumbarton Oaks proposals, which will convene at San Francisco on April 25.

The delegation will include Cordell Hull, former Secretary of State, who will serve as its senior adviser; four members of Congress, and two others. The latter six are:

Senator Tom Connally, Democrat, of Texas, chairman of the Committee on Foreign Relations; Senator Arthur H. Vandenberg, Republican, of Michigan, author of the resolution proposing an immediate agreement by the Allies for keeping Germany and Japan permanently demilitarized; Representative Sol Bloom, Democrat, of New York, chairman of the House Committee on Foreign Affairs; Representative Charles A. Eaton, Republican, of New Jersey, ranking minority member of the House Committee; Commander Harold Stassen, former Governor of Minnesota and a strong advocate of international

Continued on Page 8, Column 2

War News Summarized

WEDNESDAY, FEBRUARY 14, 1945

Budapest fell to the Red Army after a fifty-day siege during which the Germans lost 110,000 prisoners and 49,000 killed. The road to Vienna has been opened, Moscow said. Other Russian troops crossed the Bober River and reached the Queis in a drive that carried to Klitschdorf, seventy miles from Dresden, captured Beuthen and encircled Glogau. The advance through the Polish Corridor was within six miles of Chojnice, on the Stettin-Danzig railroad. [1:8; map P. 4.]

Germany massed field guns in attempts to stop the Canadian First and United States Third Armies on the western front. The former reached open ground beyond Cleve and the Reichswald and was three miles from the road center and fortress of Goch. Seven enemy divisions were thrown into the battle. The Third Army merged its two bridgeheads over the Sauer and Our Rivers into a solid stretch more than ten miles long and two deep. [1:6-7; maps P. 2.]

The end of Japanese resistance in Manila was in sight, General MacArthur reported. The Cavite naval base was captured, Nichols and Nielson airfields were cleared and Manila Bay was reached in the Pasay district. Infantry was closing in on the dock area of Intramuros, where the enemy was making his last stand. To the north Baler and its airfield on the east coast were captured. [1:4; maps P. 6.]

The escort carrier Ommaney Bay, which during her six months at sea sank or damaged the equivalent of a Japanese task force, has been sunk. [7:1.]

Superfortress attacks on Japan have been so effective that Tokyo announced removal of airplane and other vital war industries to Manchuria. [6:3.]

President Roosevelt presided over the Big Three Conference and proposed the "Declaration of Liberated Europe" with its Polish formula and also the voting procedure in the United Nations Council. In disclosing these facts War Mobilization Director Byrnes conceded that the decision on Poland was a compromise. [1:2.] The Polish Government in London denounced the Crimea formula and refused to be bound by it. [1:3.]

It was learned in Washington that President Roosevelt's proposal for procedure in the United Nations council forbade an interested power to vote on matters that did not involve punitive measures, but in punitive cases all the big powers would have to vote affirmatively. [1:2-3.]

Acting Secretary of State Grew called the decisions reached at Yalta a great step toward victory and enduring peace. [10:1.] Congressional opinion was varied, but the great majority approved what the three leaders had done. [11:1.] Berlin described the decisions as a "mass murder plan" and said Germany, now released of all moral obligations, would henceforth conduct the war as she saw fit. [9:1.]

The French Government announced it would establish a sea, air and land base at Dakar for empire and world security. [1:2-3.]

Former Secretary of State Hull, Comdr. Harold Stassen, Dean Virginia Gildersleeve and four Congressmen will represent the United States at the United Nations Conference in San Francisco. Secretary of State Stettinius will head the group. [1:7.]

Forces to Get More Cigarettes, Cutting Supplies for Civilians

Special to THE NEW YORK TIMES.

WASHINGTON, Feb. 13—The shortage of cigarettes in the civilian market is "directly traceable" to the volume moving to the armed services and to allies, and increased military demands this year are likely to reduce the domestic supply further, the Federal Trade Commission reported today.

The report, based on an investigation by the commission at the request of Senator Wheeler of Montana, chairman of the Interstate Commerce Committee, added that the shortage caused by the movement of cigarettes abroad had been "magnified" by the increased demand at home. Factors contributing to the greater consumption by civilians were described by the FTC as "prosperity," which has enabled many who could not afford manufactured cigarettes to buy them now; a general increase in the number of smokers, "overbuying" by smokers fearful of being caught short and the "huge volume" sent to the armed forces overseas.

In addition to finding "small prospect of much increase in production" this year, the commission pointed to plans by the Army to purchase at least 77,000,000,000 cigarettes in 1945, in contrast to the 68,000,000,000 last year, as evidence of prospective further curtailment in the domestic market.

The only means of alleviating

Continued on Page 17, Column 4

AXIS CENTER FALLS

Russians' 50-Day Siege of Hungarian Capital a New 'Stalingrad'

KONEFF PASSES RIVER

Bober Line Is Shattered in Push to Within 70 Miles of Dresden

By The United Press.

LONDON, Wednesday, Feb. 14—The Red Army yesterday completed its conquest of Budapest, ending a fifty-day siege of the battle-scarred capital of Axis Hungary. In German Silesia, Russian forces shattered the enemy's Bober River defense line before Dresden and advanced nine and a half miles toward the capital of Saxony.

The Germans and their Hungarian satellites, ordered by Adolf Hitler to make Budapest a "Hungarian Stalingrad," lost more than 159,000 troops killed or captured, Moscow reported. It was the greatest enemy loss in a single operation since the Nazi catastrophe at the historic Volga River city little more than two years ago.

In a powerful westward drive across Lower Silesia that ultimately may outflank Berlin, Soviet troops forced the Bober River some 100 miles southeast of the German capital and reached the east bank of the Queis River, the first of three remaining water barriers before Dresden, on a nine-mile front.

Glogau Fortress Encircled

They drove to within seventy miles northeast of Dresden by capturing Klitschdorf, twenty-one miles from the Neisse River stronghold of Goerlitz.

North of these forces Red Army tanks thrust to within seven miles of Sagan, site of three big American and British prisoner of war camps. Behind them the Oder River fortress of Glogau, fifty-two miles northwest of besieged Breslau, was encircled.

Simultaneously, Soviet troops, increasing the threat to the Baltic ports of Danzig and Gdynia, smashed to within six miles of the Danzig-Stettin-Berlin railroad, key enemy defense line of German troops holding a deep salient north of the Red Army's wedge on the approaches to Berlin.

Before the German capital, according to enemy broadcasts, the Russians were fighting in the streets of Lebus, on the west bank of the Oder thirty-three miles east of Berlin.

The capture of Budapest released two Soviet armies and troops under seventy-three generals for a drive toward the Austrian capital of Vienna, guarding the approaches to the Alps, where Nazi leaders may attempt to make their last stand. It cleared the way for Soviet offensives to the puppet Slovak capital of Bratislava and the rich industrial regions of Bohemia.

Seventeenth Capital Liberated

The fall of Budapest, after street fighting that leveled large areas of one of the world's most beautiful capitals, was announced by Premier Joseph Stalin. It was the eighth capital to be entered by the Red Army and the seventeenth to be liberated by the Allies.

More than 49,000 Germans and Hungarians were killed in the prolonged battle for the city and more than 110,000 troops were captured.

"German officers used to shoot soldiers who said the position of the Budapest garrison was hopeless," Moscow said. "But all these savage measures did not save the enemy from defeat."

In an underground sewer the Russians captured the commander of the Budapest defenders, Col. Gen. Pfeffer-Wildenbruch, and his staff.

Tens of thousands of mines, trenches, barricades and blown-up buildings that the Russians encountered in Budapest forecast the grim struggle that lies ahead for the Allies in Berlin. In all, it took the Red Army fourteen weeks to

Continued on Page 4, Column 2

"All the News That's Fit to Print"

The New York Times.

LATE CITY EDITION
Partly cloudy, moderately warm and windy today.
Temperatures Yesterday—Max., 43; Min., 29
Sunrise today, 7:00 A. M.; Sunset, 6:21 P. M.

Copyright, 1945, by The New York Times Company.

VOL. XCIV..No. 31,800. Entered as Second-Class Matter, Postoffice, New York, N. Y. NEW YORK, FRIDAY, FEBRUARY 16, 1945. THREE CENTS IN NEW YORK CITY

1,200 PLANES OF U. S. FLEET ATTACK TOKYO AS SHIPS AND FLIERS BOMBARD IWO ISLE; RUSSIANS NEARING COTTBUS, WE BOMB IT

WORLD FUND BILL OFFERS SURPRISES AS GIVEN CONGRESS

New Appropriations Would Be Avoided Under the Plan by Use of Stabilization Fund

AND I. O. U.'S OF TREASURY

Power Over Gold Would Be Reserved to Congress in 'Nonpartisan' Program

Special to THE NEW YORK TIMES.

WASHINGTON, Feb. 15—Approval of the monetary and financial agreements tentatively approved by representatives of forty-four nations at Bretton Woods in July was asked of Congress today in a bill introduced in both Houses. The measure treats the matter as an executive agreement rather than a treaty.

The bill, introduced jointly in the Senate by Senator Wagner, chairman of the Banking and Currency Committee, and Senator Tobey of New Hampshire, ranking minority member of the committee, and in the House by Representative Spence, chairman of the Banking and Currency Committee, contained several surprises:

1. It requires not one cent of appropriation for the United States contributions of $2,750,000,000 to the proposed monetary fund and $3,175,000,000 to the proposed Bank for Reconstruction and Development, this total subscription of $5,925,000,000 to be financed under the bill by a transfer of the $1,800,000,000 of the United States stabilization fund, which has never been used, to the International Monetary Fund, with the balance to be financed through advances of non-interest bearing Treasury notes, or I.O.U.'s, which would be deposited with the international bodies and replaced by actual dollars only as needed by these institutions.

Part Repeal of Act Sought

2. It provides a repeal in part of the Johnson Act, which prohibits private commercial loans to countries defaulting on debts to the United States resulting from the first World War. Under the bill the act would be repealed in favor of any of the affected countries which would become members of the proposed international institutions, so that an additional inducement would be provided for their participation.

3. It reserves to Congress by specific language such powers as changing the value of the dollar in terms of gold, making any loans to the fund or the bank, or changing the United States quota in the fund.

4. It continues indefinitely the United States Treasury stabilization fund which would expire under present law as of June 30, 1945. With the transfer of the $1,800,000,000 to the monetary fund, the stabilization fund would have a balance remaining of about $280,000,000.

All three sponsors of the bill in Congress were members of the United States delegation to the Bretton Woods conference. A fourth Congressional member, Representative Wolcott, ranking minority member of the Banking and Currency Committee, has not committed himself regarding the proposal. However, House rules forbid joint introduction of bills in that chamber.

Four Joined in Drafting Bill

Representative Spence told the House that the measure was the "fruit of nonpartisan cooperation." He said that Representative Wolcott collaborated with Senators Wagner and Tobey and himself in drafting the legislation.

The chairman of the House Banking and Currency Committee described the legislation as "a bill to insure the economic side of world peace."

"The first action by any of the forty-four participating nations to confirm the proposals made at the Bretton Woods Monetary Confer-

Continued on Page 12, Column 5

Roosevelt Hopeful In Note to Stalin

By The Associated Press.

LONDON, Feb. 15—President Roosevelt's farewell message to Premier Stalin at the conclusion of the Crimea conference predicted that the people of the world would see the results of the meeting "as a real guarantee that our three great nations can work in the peace just as well as in the war."

The text of the message as broadcast from Moscow tonight said:

"On leaving the hospitable shores of the Soviet Union I wish to tell you how deeply grateful I am to you for all the kindness you have shown me while I was your guest in the Crimea.

"I am departing much encouraged by the results of the conference between you, the Prime Minister and myself.

"The peoples of the world, I am sure, will see the achievements of this conference as a real guarantee that our three great nations can work in the peace as well as in the war."

GEORGE BILL PASSES FIRST TEST IN HOUSE

Two Wolcott Amendments Killed, 202-192, but Fate of Measure Is Undecided

By JOHN H. CRIDER

Special to THE NEW YORK TIMES.

WASHINGTON, Feb. 15—Administration forces saved the George bill from Republican amendments in the House today by the narrow margin of 192 to 202 to pave the way for a decisive vote tomorrow on a motion to recommit, which if successful, would make doubtful Senate confirmation of Henry A. Wallace as Secretary of Commerce.

The George bill, already passed by the Senate, which delayed action on the Wallace confirmation until March 1 to give the House time to act on the measure, provides for divorce of the lending agencies from the Commerce Department. Administration leaders in Congress regard its passage as essential to assure confirmation of Mr. Wallace.

House Republicans presented a solid front on the one vote today, which was on the question whether to retain the rule reported by the Rules Committee denying the minority an opportunity to present two amendments. One of the proposals would have made the Export-Import Bank an independent agency, have cut its board from eleven to five and barred the Secretary of Commerce from its board. The other would have repealed the war powers under which the President might transfer additional agencies to the Commerce Department.

The 173 Republicans who voted against the rule were joined by nineteen Democrats. Voting for the rule were 200 Democrats, an American Laborite and a Progressive.

The nineteen Democrats were Abernethy of Mississippi, Andrews of Alabama, Bell of Missouri, Boykin of Alabama, Cox of Georgia,

Continued on Page 15, Column 1

NEW SOVIET THREAT

Koneff Smashes Toward Twin Bastions Guarding Berlin on South

KEY RAIL POINTS FALL

Junction With Zhukoff Reported—Drive for Danzig Also Gains

By The United Press.

LONDON, Friday, Feb. 16—Red Army forces posed a new threat to Berlin from the southeast yesterday, smashing across the Brandenburg border from Silesia and driving to within sixty-six miles of the Nazi capital in swift advances that threatened Guben and Cottbus, twin citadels guarding Berlin's southern approaches.

In a two-day, twenty-five-mile advance, Marshal Ivan S. Koneff's First Ukrainian Army fought to within fourteen miles of Guben and twenty-five miles east of bomb-ravaged Cottbus, attacked yesterday by American heavy bombers.

Premier Joseph Stalin revealed the new gains that threatened to drive a wedge between Berlin and Dresden. Enemy broadcasts, however, said Marshal Koneff's spearheads had outflanked Guben on the south and had driven to Forst, fifty-seven miles southeast of Berlin and twelve miles east of Cottbus.

Koneff Reaches the Neisse

Moscow reports said Marshal Koneff's tanks and infantry had reached the Neisse River, the last natural barrier before Dresden, and were threatening Goerlitz, forty-eight miles east of the Saxon capital. The Soviet High Command reported only that Marshal Koneff's troops had forced the Queis River on the approaches to the Neisse.

In West Prussia, Soviet forces toppled the fortress cities of Chojnice and Tuchola, sixty and fifty-nine miles southwest of Danzig, and shattered the enemy's Pomeranian defense line based on the Danzig-Stettin-Berlin trunk railroad.

In western Poland Red Army troops captured the greater part of the encircled fortress of Posen. The fall of the city would give the Red Army a direct railroad supply route from Warsaw to the Frankfort-Kuestrin sector east of the Nazi capital.

Into bridgeheads on the west bank of the Oder River thirty-one to forty-three miles east of Berlin, Marshal Gregory K. Zhukoff's First White Russian Army was reported pouring men and material in preparation for a possible frontal assault or outflanking maneuver from the northeast.

Almost due south of this front Marshal Koneff's army rapidly was drawing up level with Marshal Zhukoff's army, approaching, if not reaching, the line of the Neisse River, which joins the Oder twenty miles south of besieged Frankfort.

Continued on Page 6, Column 6

RAIL CITY BLASTED

500 U.S. 'Heavies' Bomb Town in the Direct Path of Red Army Troops

DRESDEN NEARS RUIN

RAF Rips Berlin, Mainz, Chemnitz, Nuremberg, Duisburg, Dessau

By GLADWIN HILL

By Wireless to THE NEW YORK TIMES.

LONDON, Feb. 15—The Allies' great air offensive in support of the Russian front, the first major military development to follow the Crimea Conference, surged into its third day today.

The night-and-day bombing pattern, started off by the Royal Air Force and the United States Army Air Forces Tuesday and Wednesday, was repeated. Berlin and its network of key satellite cities in the path of the Russian onslaught underwent a second series of trip-hammer blows.

The great city of Dresden, now only about fifty miles from the Russian front, received its fourth attack in less than forty-eight hours, jeopardizing the architectural if not the artistic treasures that made it "the German Florence."

An even closer supporting blow was struck by the United States Eighth Air Force at Cottbus, a rail center that the Germans said was only twelve miles ahead of the Russian troops.

Targets Closely Dovetailed

The targets were dovetailed closely, the RAF having sent 800 bombers in two attacks last night against Chemnitz, hit a few hours before by 450 American bombers, and having taken their second crack at Nuremberg, reported German emergency capital; while the Eighth Air Force's daylight bomber attacks were on Dresden and Magdeburg.

Gasoline—the Germans' critical resource that American and British air officials announced tonight had been cut 80 per cent in production

Continued on Page 6, Column 2

AMERICAN SEA FORCES CARRY FIGHT TO JAPAN

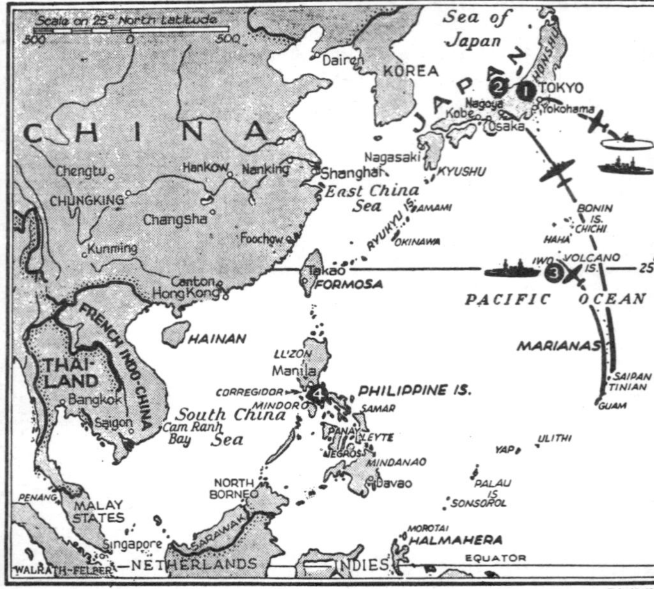

A powerful navy task force launched carrier planes against targets in and around Tokyo (1). The fact that aircraft and airbases were hard hit suggested an effort to fetter the enemy's air arm while operations were carried on elsewhere. A warship shelling and aerial bombardment of Iwo (3) further suggested that the operations would focus on this island (detailed map of Iwo Page 4). Superfortresses flying from Saipan and Tinian again pounded Nagoya (2). The Japanese reported that American warships had shelled Corregidor (4) at the entrance to Manila Bay.

FIRST GREAT BLOW

Powerful Carrier Force Smashes at Air Bases In and Near Tokyo

FIERCE SKY FIGHTS ON

Fastest U. S. Battleships With 200-Mile Armada Off Honshu Coast

By WARREN MOSCOW

By Wireless to THE NEW YORK TIMES.

ADVANCED HEADQUARTERS, Guam, Friday, Feb. 16—American carrier planes are conducting a full-scale attack on Tokyo from a powerful task force close to the Japanese mainland. They are taking the war home to the eight million inhabitants of the Tokyo area in a way they have never seen it before.

In place of the "Thirty Seconds Over Tokyo" of sixteen Mitchell bombers in the early days of the war, or the high-flying B-29's that have been bombing the city since last November, there are swarms of planes striking at tree-top level, hitting airfields, aircraft and other military targets around the city in strafing attacks. More than 1,200 planes of various types are taking part in the attack, it is estimated.

A Full-Scale Attack

This is a full-scale long-planned offensive. United States warships simultaneously, 700 miles to the south, are bombarding Iwo Island in the Volcanos. Iwo also was under attack from the air along with the Bonin Islands.

The Tokyo area contains several dozen operational air fields, air depots and storage bases as well as several aviation training centers. Military airfields are scattered all over Honshu, the main Japanese island, but the principal fields are in the vicinity of large centers of war industry and commerce like Tokyo. In addition, there is the Yokosuka Navy Yard, headquarters of the Japanese Navy, with army headquarters elsewhere in the city.

Admiral Chester W. Nimitz in his communiqué announced that Vice Admiral Marc A. Mitscher is in command of the task force, while Admiral Raymond A. Spruance is in tactical command. This means that the attack on Tokyo is being carried on by the Fifth Fleet.

The task force is estimated to include fifteen to twenty of the largest and fastest carriers, protected on this extremely hazardous mission by the fastest battleships, a covering screen of destroyers, cruisers, submarines and mine-sweepers. [An Associated Press correspondent said that the United States warships standing off Honshu, Japan, would form a line 200 miles long up and down the coast.]

There was no indication that the Japanese Fleet was coming out to meet the American forces, though the American command would welcome such a move. The first announcement of the Tokyo attack came after the Tokyo radio went off the air at 7 A. M., Friday, Tokyo time, and then in a news broadcast an hour and twenty minutes later said that the air-raid alarm sounded at 7:15 A. M. due to an attack on Tokyo airstrips by "small enemy planes." Tokyo also said that American surface units had been observed the past few days off the coast of Japan.

TEXT OF COMMUNIQUE

The text of Admiral Nimitz's communiqué follows:

"Vice Admiral Marc A. Mitscher is in command of a powerful task force of the Pacific Fleet which is now attacking enemy aircraft, air bases and other military targets in and around Tokyo.

"This operation has long been planned and the opportunity to accomplish it fulfills the deeply cherished desire of every officer and man of the Pacific Fleet.

"Surface units of the Pacific Fleet are bombarding Iwo Jima

Continued on Page 4, Column 4

Canadian Rhine Hold Wider; U. S. 3d and 7th Push Foe

By CLIFTON DANIEL

By Wireless to THE NEW YORK TIMES.

SUPREME HEADQUARTERS, Allied Expeditionary Force, Feb. 15—Impeded by a morass of mud, showered with shellfire by reinforced German units and robbed of air support by weather again, United Kingdom troops under Canadian command still pressed on today toward the bristling defenses of Siegfried Line hedgehog positions around Goch.

Heavy blasts of enemy fire pinned down British forces sweeping around to the east of the pill-box cluster at Goch, but Scottish troops bearing down on the town from the west have pushed the

Continued on Page 7, Column 2

ONLY 4 OIL PLANTS OPERATING IN REICH

German Output Cut 80% by Allies' Air Offensive and Ground Advances

By Wireless to THE NEW YORK TIMES.

SUPREME HEADQUARTERS, Allied Expeditionary Force, Feb. 15—The Allies' strategic air forces' offensive against German gasoline production, which has been reduced to 20 per cent of its April, 1944, level, has now come very near to being decisive, according to information available here.

At the moment all Germany's crude oil refineries are inoperative. Only four of her synthetic oil plants are producing and one of these was bombed twice this week.

It has been definitely ascertained by Allied intelligence that the Germans in fact are producing only 103,000 tons of gasoline a month, compared with 500,000 tons a month early last year.

A steady improvement of the

Continued on Page 6, Column 1

NAGOYA FIRES SET IN BIG B-29 STRIKE

'Superforts' Fly From New Tinian Base and Saipan—Foe Lists 60 Attackers

By The Associated Press.

HEADQUARTERS OF 21ST BOMBER COMMAND, on Guam, Feb. 15—B-29 Superfortresses, operating from a new base in the Marianas, joined in a large-scale attack today on the industrial area of Nagoya, Japan.

The big force of bombers flew from Saipan and from the new base on near-by Tinian, the Twenty-first Bomber Command announced. [A Tokyo broadcast estimated the number of attackers at sixty.]

Weather reports indicated the targets were covered by clouds. No details were announced.

[In Washington the War Department announced that the principal Nagoya target had been the Mitsubishi aircraft factory, The United Press said. The report said that opposition was moderate and no planes were lost to enemy action. At the same time the Tokyo radio said that a small force of B-29's had also attacked Yokohama.]

The Tokyo radio reported in a communiqué and the Domei News Agency broadcast that the Superfortresses had centered their attacks on the Nagoya industrial area, and also had caused some damage in the city proper. [The broadcast acknowledged that fires had been started in the factory

Continued on Page 5, Column 6

B-29 Plunges Into Flushing Bay; Five of Crew Rescued, Five Lost

Splitting into two flaming sections, a B-29 Superfortress on an undisclosed mission crashed into Flushing Bay, one-half mile east of the Administration Building at La Guardia Field, at 3:50 P. M. yesterday when it overshot a runway while coming in for an emergency landing.

Five of its crew of ten were rescued by a police launch that managed to affix hooks to their parachute slings. The others apparently were trapped in the forward wreckage, which sank in twenty minutes in a pool of blazing oil. Last night Coast Guard craft were trying to locate the wreck and the missing crewmen.

In accordance with Army procedure the names of the airmen were withheld pending notification of the next of kin. Of the survivors, all taken to Fort Totten Hospital at the Army post at Bayside, Queens, four were reported in "good shape," but the condition of one was listed as critical.

It was the worst crash at the airport since it was opened in 1939 and the second in which lives were lost.

The big bomber had called briefly at Mitchel Field, according to Army Transport Command officials, who took charge of the investigation, and was winging its way over La Guardia Field when the pilot radioed that the left out-

Continued on Page 36, Column 6

War News Summarized

FRIDAY, FEBRUARY 16, 1945

Tokyo has been brought under attack of a powerful United States task force, "fulfilling," in the words of Admiral Nimitz' communiqué, "the deeply cherished desire of every officer and man of the Pacific Fleet."

In a long-planned action, at least 1,200 carrier planes from the force commanded by Admiral Mitscher smashed air bases and other targets in the Tokyo area. At the same time Admiral Spruance's Fifth Fleet stood off Iwo Island in the Volcanos and bombarded that Japanese base. Land-based bombers also attacked Iwo and adjacent islands in the Bonins.

No details of the actions, which were continuing when Admiral Nimitz issued his communiqué from Guam, were available. [All the foregoing, 1:8; maps, Pages 1 and 4.]

B-29's, operating from a new base on Tinian as well as from Saipan in the Marianas, showered explosives through clouds on the Mitsubishi airplane plant at Nagoya, Japan. [1:7.]

Further progress was reported from the Philippines in clearing the enemy from south Manila. Americans have pushed their advance south on Bataan, and Corregidor was kept under aerial pounding. [1:6-7.]

Japan's position on the Asiatic continent was deteriorating rapidly, General Wedemeyer said. Chinese in Burma captured Kutkai, forty-eight miles from Lashio, and Chungking announced conscription of 500,000 new troops for an offensive to be synchronized with expected American landings on the China coast. [5:5.]

Paris heard that it had been decided at Yalta to place all mandated Pacific islands formerly under Japan in American control after the war and have France take military control of most of southwest Germany, including the Rhineland. [10:5.]

Russian armies narrowed the German pocket in East Prussia, and in Poland captured Chojnice on the Stettin-Danzig railroad. In Silesia and Brandenburg they broke through toward Berlin and, according to the enemy, reached Forst, twelve miles from Cottbus, which was a major target for American bombers from Britain. [1:3.]

The Eighth Air Force sent out 1,100 bombers yesterday, which, in addition to hitting Cottbus, struck burning Dresden again and a synthetic oil plant at Madgeburg. Chemnitz, also in the path of the Red Army, was ablaze from two night RAF attacks. [1:4, map P. 6.] The aerial pounding Germany has received has cut her gasoline production to 20 per cent of last April's output, and may prove decisive. [1:6.]

Mud and stiffened resistance slowed the British advance on Goch, but Scottish troops pushed the Germans from a five-mile stretch of the Niers River's south bank and cleared Kessel. North of Cleve the Rhine was reached opposite Emmerich. The Roer was receding in front of the United States First Army, the Third Army gained north of Echternach and the Seventh advanced east of Sarreguemines. [1:5-6; map P. 7.]

General Clark and the Italian General Staff urged patriots in northern Italy to increase their sabotage and prepare, for the "moment of the final attack is approaching." [8:5.]

Our Guns in Range of Corregidor; Tokyo Reports U. S. Ships Off Bay

By GEORGE E. JONES

By Wireless to THE NEW YORK TIMES.

MANILA, Friday, Feb. 16—The southward drive along the east coast of Bataan by American infantrymen has secured the Balanga-Pilar area, within artillery range of Corregidor, Gen. Douglas MacArthur announced today.

The fighting of the past few days has put the Eleventh Corps forces in positions that it took months for Japan's best troops to occupy in 1942, and the enemy grip on the historic peninsula now seems lost.

[An American naval force led by two battleships bombarded Corregidor Tuesday, while twenty minesweepers swept an entrance to Manila Bay preparatory to a seaborne thrust at Manila, the Japanese Domei agency said Thursday. "Some ten transports" were believed to be following the American naval force, Domei said.]

Those who served with General MacArthur and Lieut. Gen. Jonathan M. Wainwright three years ago point out that it was not until the Japanese could drive to the stretch of the eastern peninsula coast between Abucay and Mariveles that our position on Bataan and Corregidor became untenable.

Yesterday's communiqué announced that American troops had occupied Abucay, the eastern an-

Continued on Page 5, Column 2

"All the News That's Fit to Print"

NEWS INDEX, PAGE 35, THIS SECTION

The New York Times.

LATE CITY EDITION

Partly cloudy with fresh to moderate winds today.

Temperatures Yesterday—Max., 39; Min., 33

Sunrise today, 7:47 A. M.; Sunset, 6:34 P. M.

Section 1

VOL. XCIV..No. 31,802. Entered as Second-Class Matter, Postoffice, New York, N. Y. NEW YORK, SUNDAY, FEBRUARY 18, 1945. Including Magazine and Book Sections. TEN CENTS New York City and Suburban Area (15c Elsewhere)

M'ARTHUR'S TROOPS LAND ON CORREGIDOR; IWO SHELLED AGAIN, FOE REPORTS INVASION; BRITISH SPLIT NAZI DEFENSES NEAR GOCH

DEFERMENT OF MEN UNDER 30 ALLOWED IN NEW PROGRAM

15 Agencies Are Authorized to Make Requests for Selections in Key Jobs

DRAFT BOARD RULE FINAL

Krug Demands That Congress Act to Insure Full Utilization of Country's Manpower

By JAY WALZ

Special to THE NEW YORK TIMES.

WASHINGTON, Feb. 17—Fifteen Government procurement agencies are authorized to make requests for deferment of men under 30, who hold key jobs in war factories under a plan approved today by James F. Byrnes, Director of War Mobilization and Reconversion.

While local draft boards will retain the right of final decision, operation of the plan, it is hoped, will protect vital war production from the loss of irreplaceable men. The fifteen agencies may certify to local draft boards the names of men, 18 through 29, who they believe should be given consideration for deferment in the interests of the war program or public health and safety.

All of the agencies are responsible for procurement and production of war goods, and for the maintenance of essential services.

The plan will not interfere with the regular draft board procedure to defer registrants, whether they are certified or not, who are judged "necessary to and regularly engaged in" war production or a war supporting activity, it was said.

The final decision as to whether a man will be deferred or not will rest solely with the local board.

Called Best Plan at This Time

Paul V. McNutt, chairman of the War Manpower Commission, who was joined by Gen. Lewis B. Hershey, Director of Selective Service, in announcing the new plan, said it "constitutes the best reconciliation of the competing needs for manpower that can be worked out at this time."

The committee, which worked out the procedure, was appointed on Jan. 17 by Justice Byrnes to protect the "vital core" of workers in the 26 through 29 age group. The group included, in addition to General Hershey and Mr. McNutt, J. D. Small, executive officer of the War Production Board; Howard Bruce, acting director of matériel of the War Department, and Real Admiral F. G. Crisp, director of the division of shore establishments and civilian personnel of the Navy Department.

The agencies that may certify names of workers under the new program are the Army Service Forces, the Navy, the Army Air Forces, War Production Board, United States Maritime Commission, Petroleum Administration for War, Office of Defense Transportation, War Food Administration, Coordinator of Fisheries, Rubber Reserve, Solid Fuels Administration for War, Review Committee on Deferment of Government Employes, National Roster of Scientific and Specialized Personnel (for the committee on research and scientific personnel), Office of Scientific Research and Development and Procurement and Assignment Service.

For Very Limited Number

WASHINGTON, Feb. 17 (AP)—The Government set up machinery today for deferring a "very limited number" of draft registrants under 30 in war jobs.

In the first slight easing of plans to draw heavily from this age group to meet mounting military needs, Selective Service and the War Manpower Commission announced that the new procedure will apply to otherwise qualified

Continued on Page 28, Column 4

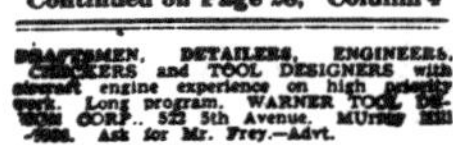

Air Traffic Control To Aid Pacific War

WASHINGTON, Feb. 17—So firmly are American bases established in the western Pacific and so intensively are they being used in the attack on Japan that the Civil Aeronautics Administration has been asked by the Army to install air traffic control centers at Johnston Island, Kwajalein, Guam and one other point yet to be named.

Recruited from the domestic airways, traffic controllers have long been handling the heavy air traffic between Hawaii and the mainland, providing radio beams, weather information and flight instructions on an overocean airway as congested as all except a few in the United States.

With hundreds of bombers and fighters daily in the air in the combat areas, these experts have now been asked to regulate the base traffic, apparently with no fear that any Japanese planes will find a chance to take advantage of the aids.

U. S. FOR A LEAGUE, WAGNER DECLARES

Senate Will Not Repeat the Blunder of World War I, He Tells Victory Dinner

The United States Senate, which blocked the United States from joining the League of Nations after the first World War, will not repeat that blunder but will support an international organization to maintain peace as agreed upon by President Roosevelt, Marshal Stalin and Prime Minister Churchill at their recent conference at Yalta on the Black Sea.

This was the declaration made last night by Senator Robert F. Wagner at the Roosevelt-Truman-Wagner Victory Dinner of the Democratic County Committee of New York County, better known as Tammany, in the Grand Ball Room of the Commodore Hotel. About 2,000 persons attended.

"There is no member of the present Senate who is going to wear the mantle of Henry Cabot Lodge," Senator Wagner said. "The greatest deliberative body in the world is committed beyond retreat to a strong, permanent peace organization. This will benefit the whole American people. It will be a blessing to the whole world. Instead of Hitler's thousand years of his New Order of slavery we must have a thousand years of peace and freedom."

Tells of Chat With President

Senator Wagner told a chat he had with President Roosevelt, whom he described as in excellent health, buoyant and confident.

"He knows that his superb efforts as Commander in Chief are to be crowned with glorious victory on all fronts," he said of the President. "He feels sure that America will never again repeat the blunders of the 1920's, when

Continued on Page 19, Column 4

Wife Paid Foe $100,000 Blackmail To Bar Seizure of Frank Jay Gould

By The Associated Press.

PARIS, Feb. 17—Mrs. Frank Jay Gould said today that she had invested more than $100,000 in a Monte Carlo bank last July to keep the Germans from taking her millionaire husband to Germany.

It was a sort of blackmail payment, the business manager for the former Florence Lacaze asserted. French authorities say that the Riviera bank mentioned by Mrs. Gould was controlled by the Germans when they occupied France.

Mrs. Gould said that she undoubtedly was "the wife of a very prominent American" mentioned by Secretary of the Treasury Henry Morgenthau Jr. as being under investigation by the French authorities. He said on Tuesday that the United States had told the French Government that it would assist in a French investigation of a "very famous" American couple suspected of collaboration with the Germans.

Mrs. Gould is a former Parisian actress and the third wife of Mr. Gould, who has lived in France for thirty-six years. The youngest son of Jay Gould, he inherited an estate estimated at $10,000,000 from his father's $83,000,000 fortune.

"I haven't the slightest fear of this investigation," Mrs. Gould added. "Not half the story has yet been told. Mr. Morgenthau should have known the full details before he spoke.

"Yes, it is true that I invested some of my own money in this banking concern—5,000,000 francs

Continued on Page 16, Column 5

TOMMIES CUT ROAD

Two-Mile Lunge Slashes Goch-Calcar Highway, Flanks Key Town

OTHER UNITS CLOSE IN

3d Army Again Pierces Westwall by Seizing Rohrbach in Reich

By The Associated Press.

SUPREME HEADQUARTERS, Allied Expeditionary Force, Feb. 17—British troops of the Canadian First Army split the German defense line sixteen miles from the vital Ruhr valley today in a two-and-a-half-mile lunge that was toppling the stronghold of Goch and was less than three miles from the rear communications base at Uedem.

This charge by infantry—described in a dispatch from the front as a near break-through—severed the Goch-Calcar highway, cutting off the garrisons of the twin strongholds from direct communication. The British fought clear of rear Westwall fortifications that had ensnarled them.

At the same time the American Third Army drove a new breach into the Westwall by the capture of Rohrbach in the Echternach sector.

[About 500 Flying Fortresses and escort fighters of the United States Eighth Air Force bombed rail yards at Frankfort-on-the-Main and Giessen through thick weather and shot up German rail traffic from the Rhineland to Munich.]

In hard fighting on their twenty-five-mile front Field Marshal Sir Bernard L. Montgomery's troops fought to within a mile of Goch, a mile and a half of Calcar—seven miles to the northeast—and battered both with artillery and mortars.

British Outflank Goch

Goch was being outflanked on the east by the British moving on Uedem and by Scotch and British on the west, who seized Asperden, a mile and a half to the northwest, and were battling through Hassum, three miles west. [Muell was captured by these troops, The United Press said.]

More than 1,300 prisoners plodded back to the Allies' prison cages, the biggest single day's bag since the opening of the offensive ten days ago.

On the south flank, Scotch infantry with flamethrowers drove a mile up the Meuse (Maas) River and into Afferden, five miles south of where the Germans made their first strong stand at Gennep.

Here they were sixteen miles north of the Meuse River strongpoint of Venlo, and were gradually rolling up the eastern German defense line that has held back a British-Canadian eastward drive to the Rhine. Floods kept the north

Continued on Page 17, Column 4

IWO BATTLE GROWS

Tokyo Says Americans Made 2 Landings but Were Driven Off

U. S. SHIP DAMAGED

Hit by Shore Guns as Our Planes Meet Heavy Fire —Nimitz Silent on Japan

By WARREN MOSCOW

By Wireless to THE NEW YORK TIMES.

ADVANCED HEADQUARTERS, Guam, Sunday, Feb. 18—A heavy engagement is raging in the Volcano Islands off Iwo, Japanese air base 750 miles from Tokyo, Admiral Chester W. Nimitz reported this morning.

His communiqué made no mention of landings on Iwo, which the Japanese radio said took place Saturday morning on two beaches, only to be repulsed, and there was no comment here on the Japanese reports.

[The Tokyo radio said Saturday night that the situation on Iwo "warrants us no optimism" but asserted that "not a single enemy has been permitted to land on Iwo yet."]

At Iwo our battleships, cruisers and carrier aircraft were continuing the duel with the Japanese shore batteries and anti-aircraft guns, Admiral Nimitz's communiqué said. One of our ships was damaged by shore gunfire, which was described as intense.

The Tokyo radio has estimated the American naval force off Iwo at thirty ships.

Anti-Aircraft Fire Is Heavy

Carrier aircraft, presumably working from escort carriers, and Army Liberators of the Seventh Air Force were meeting heavy anti-aircraft fire in the attack on Iwo.

The Nimitz communiqué said that further reports on the Friday and Saturday (Japanese time) attacks on the Tokyo area by carrier

Continued on Page 4, Column 1

IWO: JAPANESE PACIFIC BASE NOW UNDER ATTACK

A Liberator bombing the enemy stronghold previous to the present action

The New York Times (U. S. Army Air Forces)

RED ARMY CROSSES DRESDEN BARRIER

Spans Queis River as Russian Planes Pound Berlin's Gates —Foe Reports Sagan's Fall

By The United Press.

LONDON, Sunday, Feb. 18—Russian troops, smashing across the Germans' Queis River defense line, drove yesterday to within sixty miles of Dresden, capital of Saxony. Berlin reported that the medieval fortress town of Sagan, southeast of Berlin, had fallen.

While Moscow reported that fleets of Russian planes, flying 10,000 sorties a day, were lashing the outskirts of Berlin ahead of Soviet spearheads, the Red Army

Continued on Page 12, Column 3

War News Summarized

SUNDAY, FEBRUARY 18, 1945

General MacArthur announced that American forces in the Philippines had landed on Corregidor, the strategic isle at the entrance to Manila Bay that we were forced to yield to the Japanese on May 6, 1942, and had seized its "decisive points," assuring its "complete capture." Paratroopers surprised the enemy by landing in the rear of his defenses and were followed closely by sea-borne infantrymen, who stormed ashore on the southern end of the rocky fortress after crossing from Bataan and then penetrated inland to join forces with the paratroopers [1:8; map P. 2.]

Iwo, strategic island of the Volcano group about 750 miles from Tokyo, is still under heavy shelling from the big guns of the American Navy, a terse communiqué by Admiral Nimitz reported. The Japanese, however, declared our amphibious troops had invaded the enemy base, whose conquest would enable our heavy bombers to attack the Japanese capital with fighter escort. [1:4; map P. 4.]

The Canadian First Army hammered out a two-and-a-half-mile gain to split the enemy defenses sixteen miles from the Ruhr, one of the main sources of the lifeblood of Germany's military might. The advance severed the highway linking Goch and Calcar, two key road junctions, and put Allied forces three miles from Uedem, another enemy stronghold. [1:3; map P. 17.]

The Allied aerial offensive went into its fourth straight day, although at a much lower tempo because of bad weather. About 350 Fortresses hurled 1,000 tons of bombs into the rail yards of Frankfort on the Main and Giessen to disrupt German movements. [17:1.]

The lull on the Italian front may be broken soon by efforts of the enemy, under heavy pressure on the Eastern and the Western fronts, to pull out his troops from the northern end of the peninsula. General Clark, stressing the increasing likelihood of such a move, said the full might of Allied air forces would be used to make it as costly as possible. [7:1.]

The Red Army scored important new gains all along its active front, from East Prussia, where two fortress towns were captured, to Silesia, where Rauscha, sixty miles northeast of Dresden, was seized. The ring around Breslau, besieged Silesian capital, was tightened and in Poland the fall of Posen, encircled since Jan. 27, appeared imminent. The enemy reported the Russian capture of Sagan, eighty-five miles southeast of Berlin. [1:5; map P. 12.]

President Roosevelt's invitation to General de Gaulle to a meeting in southern France shortly after the close of the Crimea Conference reportedly was rejected by the head of the French Government, who was said to be dissatisfied because he had not been invited to meet with the Big Three at Yalta. [1:6-7.]

Argentina took a step toward war against Germany when she warned that country that a "threat" to deny safe conduct to Argentine diplomats would be considered a hostile act. [1:7.]

Secretary of State Stettinius, on his way back from Russia, arrived in Rio de Janeiro to confer with President Vargas. He was to proceed to Mexico City for the Inter-American Conference opening on Feb. 21. [1:6-7.]

De Gaulle Is Said to Refuse Invitation to Meet Roosevelt

By HAROLD CALLENDER

By Wireless to THE NEW YORK TIMES.

PARIS, Feb. 17—Gen. Charles de Gaulle declined an invitation from President Roosevelt to visit him somewhere in the Mediterranean just after the Big Three conference, reliable authorities confirmed tonight. General de Gaulle delayed his answer to the invitation for approximately two days while he discussed it with his Cabinet. It had been transmitted to him through the American Ambassador in Paris on Monday night and the refusal was sent on Wednesday.

The reason for General de Gaulle's attitude was understood to be that he felt that, as the official head of the French State, he should have been asked to the Big Three meeting itself and not to lesser gatherings afterward, where his presence would indicate that France was on a less than equal footing with the other powers. Regardless whether it formed part of his motive in this case, the fact is that General de Gaulle holds the President chiefly responsible for his absence from the Big Three conference.

Opinion Sharply Divided

In the limited diplomatic circles that were aware of it and within the French Cabinet General de Gaulle's refusal to confer with the President this week caused considerable dismay and a sharp division of opinion. Some of those who think that his attitude on France's claims is correct nevertheless regret his "sulking" manner of defending that attitude.

How far this fact may have played a part in General de Gaulle's decision is not clear, but it was learned today that the Big Three had decided that action taken under regional agreements should re-

Continued on Page 20, Column 4

ARGENTINA TAKES FIRST STEP TO WAR

Warns Germany That She Will Act if 'Threat' to Diplomats Is Not Ended at Once

By ARNALDO CORTESI

By Wireless to THE NEW YORK TIMES.

BUENOS AIRES, Feb. 17—The first step toward a declaration of war against Germany and toward preparing Argentine public opinion for entering the war was taken today when the Foreign Ministry published the text of a note addressed to the German Foreign Office through the Swiss Legation.

The Argentine Government's note protested energetically against the German "threat" to deny safe conduct to some of the Argentine diplomats awaiting exchange in Goeteborg, Sweden. It warned the German Government that, if this threat were insisted on, Argentina would consider it an "act of hostility," and "reserves from this moment full freedom of action to adopt whatever measures she may consider necessary in defense of her sovereignty and of her citizens."

The text of the note was accom-

Continued on Page 10, Column 2

Stettinius Arrives in Brazil on Way From Crimea to Mexico City Talks

By Wireless to THE NEW YORK TIMES.

RIO DE JANEIRO, Feb. 17—Secretary of State Edward R. Stettinius Jr. arrived today on his way to the inter-American conference in Mexico City. The American diplomat flew from the Crimea, where he had taken part in the Big Three conference.

Mr. Stettinius was welcomed by Foreign Minister Pedro Leão Velloso Netto, Paul Daniels, American Chargé d'Affaires, and leading Brazilian officials. He went directly to the American Embassy.

The Secretary of State conferred for an hour and a quarter with President Getulio Vargas and Senhor Velloso Netto at the summer residence of the Governor of Rio de Janeiro. Later the following statement was issued:

"The President of Brazil and the Secretary of State met in friendly discussion, and as a result of this discussion made the following joint statement:

"We have had a full and friendly discussion of all phases of Brazilian-United States relations and of avrious aspects of the world situation.

"We discussed particularly the wartime collaboration of Brazil and the United States and means by which the two countries could continue this collaboration after the war to their mutual benefit.

"We reviewed the achievements

Continued on Page 21, Column 1

MANILA BAY OPENS

Paratroops and Forces From Bataan Win Fort at Harbor Entrance

ENEMY IS SURPRISED

Attacks on Intramuros Renewed—Japanese Ignore Ultimatum

By LINDESAY PARROTT

By Wireless to THE NEW YORK TIMES.

CORREGIDOR, Feb. 16 (Delayed)—The American flag was planted again today on Corregidor, rocky island fortress in the mouth of Manila Bay, where American arms suffered their bitterest defeat in this war nearly three years ago.

[Gen. Douglas MacArthur's communiqué said "decisive points" of Corregidor had been seized and that "its complete capture is now assured.

[General MacArthur watched the assault on Corregidor from a point on the Bataan shore, an Associated Press dispatch said.]

At 8:30 this morning waves of parachute troopers of the 503d Airborne Regiment dropped on the rugged crest of the island from a fleet of transport planes which flew through plumes of smoke that were still rising from the hour of tremendous aerial bombardment that preceded their landing.

Meanwhile a flotilla of landing craft, led by destroyers, rocket craft and gunboats, dashed out of Mariveles harbor, captured yesterday in an amphibious landing by Maj. Gen. Charles P. Hall's Eleventh Corps, swung in long rows around Cape Corregidor and hit the sandy beach on the south side of Corregidor near the wrecked south dock.

Enemy Resistance Light

Two hours and forty minutes after the first paratrooper had hit the ground the airborne infantry had already taken control of the island's rocky plateau, where the old American barracks and gun emplacements stood. They met only sporadic resistance from small groups of Japanese who had been stunned by the long air bombings and naval shellings.

Meanwhile our landing troops, swarming ashore near the south dock, pushed across the narrow 500-yard neck of the island and crawled to the top of Malinta Hill. Scattered fire of mortars, machine guns and small arms met them as they came ashore. One enemy gun, apparently a five-incher, threw a few rounds at American gunboats and rocket ships that were lying close inshore.

The enemy gunfire was silenced as tons of shells and rockets swept the ravines above the beach ahead of the advancing troops. Brig. Gen. William C. Chase, who led the first American troops into Manila and commanded the amphibious landing, later received a report as he stood aboard the flagship of Rear Admiral Arthur D. Struble that resistance was slight.

Bombers Attack at Dawn

The Corregidor operation began at dawn this morning with a renewed aerial attack, supplementing the 485 tons of explosive dropped on the island yesterday. Four-motored Liberators of the Far Eastern Air Force, which has operated under General MacArthur's command since its formation, dropped their loads with a thunderous crash just as the sun came up.

Then, for an hour, attack bombers singly and in groups swept low over the rugged plateau at the western end of the island, bombing and strafing points where the Japanese are believed to be still dug in. At last came the paratroopers, dropping from a line of transport planes which stretched away to the western horizon.

Smoke was still rising from fires

Continued on Page 3, Column 1

"All the News That's Fit to Print"

The New York Times.

LATE CITY EDITION
Clear and continued cold with moderate winds today.
Temperatures Yesterday—Max.,33; Min.,23
Sunrise today, 7:46 A. M.; Sunset, 6:35 P. M.

VOL. XCIV No. 31,803. Entered as Second-Class Matter, Postoffice, New York, N. Y. NEW YORK, MONDAY, FEBRUARY 19, 1945. THREE CENTS IN NEW YORK CITY

U. S. MARINES STORM ASHORE ON IWO ISLAND; 509 PLANES, 36 SHIPS SMASHED IN TOKYO BLOW; BRITISH AT EDGE OF GOCH; PATTON STRIKES AGAIN

STIMSON ASSAILS DELAY ON JOB BILL AS COSTLY IN LIVES

Using 'Plain' Words as 'Duty,' He Says Senate Committee Listens to 'Trivial' Pleas

'DEADLY SHORTAGES' LOOM

Secretary Calls It 'Failure' of Our Democracy Not to Compel Full War Output

Secretary Stimson's address is printed in full on Page 11.

Special to THE NEW YORK TIMES.

WASHINGTON, Feb. 18—Secretary of War Stimson denounced tonight Senate delay in acting on the National Service Bill and called absence of legislation to keep men at their wartime jobs a "failure of American democracy."

In a speech over the Blue Network, he addressed himself "to all Americans, but primarily to those who have sons or husbands or other dear ones at the front" and declared that it was his "duty to speak plainly."

He asserted that we had "reached a crisis in this war" and that "we dare not delay longer" in providing the legislation to give to our fighting men the full support of "our strength." Delay, he warned, meant prolonging of the war and waste of American lives.

He praised the House for having "risen to the occasion" and passed the National Service Bill, but said that the Senate Military Affairs Committee, listening to voices speaking for "special interests" and, by comparison with the national interest, "trivial interests," had kept the bill suffocated for nearly three weeks until "enemies of the measure are beginning to boast today in the streets of Washington that they have killed it."

Roosevelt Plea Possible

It was reported in Senate circles tonight that one of the first acts of President Roosevelt on his return from the Crimea Conference would be to call again for action on the bill.

Some Senators predicted tonight that "some sort of a bill" would be reported by the committee during the week. A group of conservative Republicans and several Democrats were reported to favor a substitute which would give statutory authority to the War Manpower Commission and order a survey of war plants to root out any hoarded labor. Other compromises were also being discussed.

Secretary Stimson was emphatic in his speech about the gravity of the situation. He declared that "ever since the beginning of the war" there had been "an alarming turnover of workers in war industries."

"Every responsible leader of the military and naval forces" from the President down, he said, agreed on the need for adoption of national service legislation to keep workers at their wartime tasks.

"The inevitable result of this failure of American democracy," he went on, "is now becoming apparent at this crisis of the war.

Warns of "Deadly Shortages"

"Shortages, deadly shortages, are now looming up before us at a moment when every ounce of power should be thrown into the combat. I mean both shortages of weapons and shortages of manpower caused by the misplacement of our men."

He pointed out that the United States alone among the Allies had no service law and that Britain and Russia had been working under such laws "since the very beginning of the war."

Our enemies, of course, he added, have been so organized from the start.

"We alone," he proceeded, "are depending upon voluntary and therefore ineffective methods of organization among the workers who

Continued on Page 11, Column 4

Battle in Skagerrak Reported by Swedes

By The United Press.

LONDON, Feb. 18—The Swedish radio said today that a "very large-scale" battle involving a southbound German convoy had been fought yesterday off the Swedish Skagerrak coast.

The battle was reported to have lasted four hours. The broadcast said that Allied naval and air units had probably participated. "Observers say they have never before heard anything like it and are of the opinion that direct hits must have been made on ships," the broadcast asserted.

ORDERS PRICE TAGS ON COTTON CLOTHES

OPA Demands Exact Ceiling Be Shown on Most Such Apparel to Avert Rises

Special to THE NEW YORK TIMES.

WASHINGTON, Feb. 18—Consumers, beginning on March 5, will find most cotton garments, from infants' rompers to women's dresses, tagged with a manufacturer's ticket showing the exact OPA ceiling price permitted on each separate article, Chester Bowles, OPA Administrator, said today in outlining the first step in a broad program to check clothing prices.

The action, the administrator said, would also have the effect of bringing back more of the essential articles of apparel to the low and medium price range. However, the benefits of this part of the program might not be noticeable before early summer, he warned.

Practically all infants' and children's cotton apparel and "a very large part" of the output of men's and women's cotton garments will carry the tags, according to Mr. Bowles.

Eventually from 65 to 90 per cent of all civilian woven cotton apparel will be subject to the program's controls, which, it was explained, would tie in with a recent War Production Board order channeling most of the cotton fabrics available for civilian use into popular and medium priced garments.

The Ticket for Each Garment

The plan, which Mr. Bowles described as one "easy" for both retailers and the buying public to understand, begins with the manufacturer pinning to each piece of clothing affected by the order a ticket which will read as follows:

"OPA Ceiling Price $0.00.

"Lot Number —— (or brand name).

"WPB 385 or WPB 328-B."

The WPB figures refer to War Production Orders through which the maker obtained the material in a piece of clothing.

The prices fixed by the manufacturer would be based on OPA regulations, which provided, Mr. Bowles said, for slight variations that had always been allowed in ceiling prices for similar garments in different retail stores. Such variations take into account differences in cost to the retailer, depending on whether he buys di-

Continued on Page 30, Column 5

NAZI BASE DOOMED

British Artillery Pounds Goch to Aid Infantry 1,000 Yards Away

CALCAR FIGHT RAGES

3d Army Enters Reich Above Vianden—7th Also Crosses Line

By CLIFTON DANIEL

By Wireless to THE NEW YORK TIMES.

SUPREME HEADQUARTERS, Allied Expeditionary Force, Feb. 18—From low hills overlooking Goch British gunners picked off targets inside the town today and under a canopy of artillery fire Gen. H. D. G. Crerar's infantrymen assaulted the anti-tank ditches on the eastern defense perimeter of the town, which now looks as if it were doomed.

At the same time the American Third Army again expanded its bridgehead over the Our and Sauer Rivers north of Echternach, spreading it out today to a width of almost five miles. [The United Press said that a new division, not yet identified, had invaded Germany at a new point north of Vianden, Luxembourg.]

[Press services also reported that the American Seventh Army had re-entered Germany in the Saarbruecken area.]

The Canadian First Army, with its Canadian and United Kingdom troops, still carried the burden of the Western Front fighting today, however. Goch, with its reinforced and fortified houses, was one of two strong bastions of the line that the Germans held when the Canadian First Army attacked the northern end of the Westwall ten days ago, but patrols prodding its outskirts today found that opposition was light, the town having been outflanked and all but surrounded.

German Defense Loose

The Germans began to lose coordination in their defense yesterday and it now looks as if they would give up another important stretch of ground, but meanwhile they are fighting fiercely to hold flanks of General Crerar's advance along the Meuse (Maas) on one side and the Rhine on the other. Having lost their firm grip on Goch, the Germans are struggling to retain Calcar, the second most important front-line supply center left to them in the battle area. On the opposite side of the front they are likewise trying to halt the United Kingdom forces creeping down along the Meuse beyond Afferden toward Venlo.

The suddenness of the break in the coordination of German defense was illustrated by the fact that in driving across the road from Goch to Calcar the British made a surprise move and captured more than 900 prisoners in one day. The total number of Germans now captured since the beginning of General Crerar's offensive is more than 8,000. In an effort to minimize the reinforcement and supply of the remnants

Continued on Page 6, Column 2

AMERICAN TANK RUNNING A GANTLET OF STEEL IN MANILA

An amphibious vehicle crossing the Pasig River under Japanese machine gun fire while shells from a protecting barrage laid down by our artillery burst on the far shore.

Associated Press (U. S. Signal Corps)

FINAL ROUND IS ON, MONTGOMERY SAYS

Marshal Calls on His Soldiers to Help Strike Knockout Blow at German Army

By The Associated Press.

THE TWENTY-FIRST ARMY GROUP HEADQUARTERS, in Europe, Feb. 18—Field Marshal Sir Bernard L. Montgomery in a personal message to troops under his command declared today: "We now have come to the last and final round, and we want and will go for the knockout blow."

The text of his order follows:

The operations of the Allies on all fronts have now brought the German war to its final stage. There was a time some years ago when it did not seem possible that we could win this war. The present situation is that we can-

Continued on Page 6, Column 5

Americans Seize Hospital In Manila and Free 7,000

By LINDESAY PARROTT

By Wireless to THE NEW YORK TIMES.

ADVANCED HEADQUARTERS, on Luzon, Monday, Feb. 19—Seven thousand persons, including patients, internees and civilians, both American and Filipino, were freed as American troops seized the Philippine General Hospital on Taft Avenue in the Ermita section of Manila, where fanatically resisting Japanese fought back against an ever-tightening ring that was steadily pushing them into Manila Bay.

The hospital was captured after advancing Americans shelled the walls and north and east gates of the hospital grounds, adjoining the campus of the University of Philippines. Gen. Douglas MacArthur's communiqué stated that those released, including 100 Americans, had been evacuated to safety.

Last night the grounds of the hospital, extending to within four blocks of Dewey Boulevard and the

Continued on Page 3, Column 1

RED ARMY NEARING BORDER OF SAXONY

German Resistance Stiffens—Russians Capture Sagan and Break Into Grudziadz

By The United Press.

LONDON, Monday, Feb. 19—Red Army forces in German Silesia yesterday fought through stiff enemy resistance to within nineteen miles of the Saxon border and sixteen miles east of Goerlitz, key industrial city guarding the road to Dresden.

In its tenth major encirclement of the winter offensive the Red Army also surrounded and broke into the outskirts of the Vistula River fortress of Grudziadz in Poland, fifty-seven miles south of Danzig. Two additional pockets of enemy troops were wiped out in Pomerania and in Brandenburg.

In three other actions Russian troops hammered deeper into the streets of the Silesian capital of Breslau, virtually completed the mop-up of the Polish city of Posen, and tightened the ring around enemy troops in East Prussia, where Gen. Ivan D. Chernyakhovsky, 37, commander of the Third White Russian Army, was killed in action.

The new Soviet successes were carried out as six great battles

Continued on Page 8, Column 3

AIR BLOW AT TOKYO 'DECISIVE VICTORY'

Nimitz Says Fifth Fleet Scored 'Complete Tactical Surprise' in Two-Day Attack

By The Associated Press.

ADVANCED HEADQUARTERS, Guam, Monday, Feb. 19—American carrier planes scored a "decisive" victory over the Japanese in the mighty 1,500-plane attacks on the Tokyo-Yokohama area of the Japanese homeland Friday and Saturday, Admiral Chester W. Nimitz announced today.

Admiral Nimitz announced the Americans, scoring a "complete tactical surprise," destroyed 332 Japanese aircraft in the air and 177 on the ground. At least 150 more Japanese planes were probably destroyed or damaged on the first day and an unknown number were damaged on the second day.

He said one Japanese escort carrier was bombed and set afire, nine coastal vessels were sunk, one destroyer was sunk, two escort destroyers sunk, one cargo ship sunk and twenty two enemy coastal ships damaged, besides various Japanese picket vessels destroyed.

Forty-nine American planes were lost in the two days of destructive raids, Admiral Nimitz said. Thirty to forty Yank fliers were lost.

"None of our ships suffered damage from enemy action," the special communiqué reported.

The Fifth Fleet force under Admiral R. A. Spruance, one of the greatest ever assembled, "achieved a decisive victory over the enemy in attacks on Tokyo, Feb. 16 and 17 (east longitude date)," Admiral Nimitz announced.

He said a "complete tactical surprise" was accomplished under a cover of weather so adverse it also hampered enemy operations.

Admiral Nimitz congratulated

Continued on Page 4, Column 6

LANDING EFFECTED

Nimitz Reports Invasion of Volcano Isle 750 Miles From Tokyo

FIERCE FIGHTING IS ON

Japanese Report Battle at Futatsune Beach on Southwest Coast

By The Associated Press.

ADVANCED HEADQUARTERS, Guam, Monday, Feb. 19—American Marines, their path cleared by the most intensive neutralization campaign of the Pacific war, have landed on strategic little Iwo Island, one of the Volcano group, 750 statute miles south of Tokyo.

The landing was made this (Monday) morning. The Fourth and Fifth Marine Divisions made this first Marine operation since the Palaus were invaded last September. [Lieut. Gen. Holland M. Smith, victor over the Japanese on Saipan, was in command of the Marines, The United Press said.]

Admiral Chester W. Nimitz announced in a special communiqué today the momentous development in the fast-moving Pacific war which put American troops on the logical ocean stepping-stone to Tokyo.

Iwo is so close to Tokyo that it is administered by Tokyo prefecture.

American fighters and medium bombers based on Iwo's large airdrome would be within land-based striking range of Tokyo for the first time.

Japanese Tell of Invasion

American troops going ashore in 100 landing boats made a successful landing on Iwo at 8 A. M. Monday (Japanese time), the Tokyo radio announced late last night.

A broadcast, recorded by The United Press in San Francisco, said "part of the enemy forces have landed."

It was the first indication from the enemy radio that a successful landing had been made. Previously Tokyo had reported four "attempted landings" were made on the island Saturday but had been "repulsed."

The text of the enemy broadcast:

"Following a series of abortive landing attempts a part of the enemy forces have finally started landings on Iwo Jima since 8 o'clock this Monday morning.

Heavy Fighting Reported

"The landing is being made on the southeast coast of the island. The Japanese garrison immediately pushing the enemy invaders back to the shore is now engaged in fierce counter-attack against the enemy.

"The landing was preceded by persistent naval and air attacks since early last Wednesday morning."

The Japanese Domei agency reported that "heavy fighting" was in progress between the Japanese garrison and American forces that landed on the island with "about 100 landing vessels."

The Japanese Domei agency declared that the landing forces had hit Futatsune beach, on the southwestern sector of the island.

In an English-language dispatch recorded by the Federal Communications Commission, Domei

Continued on Page 3, Column 5

War News Summarized

MONDAY, FEBRUARY 19, 1945

United States Marines of the Fifth Amphibious Corps went ashore on Iwo Island in the Volcano group, establishing two beachheads. Tokyo reported bitter fighting on the island, 750 miles from the Japanese capital. The landings followed a fierce bombardment by naval craft, including battleships, and land-based planes. Other bombers hit Truk and targets in the Palaus, while carrier aircraft struck Chichi Island in the Bonins, nearer Japan than Iwo. [1:8; map P. 3.]

Five hundred and nine Japanese planes were destroyed, an escort carrier, three other warships and ten more ships were sunk, and heavy damage was done to airfields and factories in last week's 1,500-plane carrier attack on the Tokyo-Yokohama area, Admiral Nimitz announced today. An additional 150 enemy planes were probably destroyed. We lost forty-nine aircraft. [1:7.]

The blows now being struck at Japan were made possible by the heroic stand of the "Dead Army" of Bataan in 1942, General MacArthur said. He reported further gains on Corregidor and Bataan and in the Manila mop-up. [1:5-6.]

British troops in Burma crossed the Irrawaddy in captured Japanese boats thirty miles west of Mandalay, threatening to outflank that city. Another landing was made on the west coast at Ru-ywa, sixty-five miles southeast of Akyab, cutting the enemy's coastal escape road. [5:1.] In China the Japanese recaptured Pingshek and moved on Ichang in an effort to regain twenty-five miles of the Canton-Hankow railway. [3:1.]

Patrols of the Canadian First Army fought their way into the outskirts of Goch amid mounting signs of disintegration in the German defense. The United States Third Army crossed into the Reich near Vianden, and the Seventh reinvaded the Saar Basin southwest of Saarbruecken. [1:3; maps, P. 6.]

Field Marshal Montgomery told his troops they were in the "last and final round." It "may be long and difficult," he said, but a somewhat different "knockout blow" will be "delivered from more than one direction." [1:4.]

RAF planes hit Berlin and Mannheim last night after Wesel, sixteen miles from the Canadian First Army front, had been attacked. Allied bombers were reported over Germany later in the night. Americans from Italy blasted rail targets at Linz, Austria. [7:2.]

The Red Army advanced in most sectors, encircling and fighting into the outskirts of Grudziadz in the "Polish Corridor" and capturing the river strongholds of Sagan and Naumburg in Silesia. [1:6; map P 8.]

It was said in Paris that General de Gaulle had coupled his refusal to meet President Roosevelt in Algiers with an invitation to visit Paris. [9:2.]

Senator Bridges received from Geneva alleged Allied armistice terms to Italy that stripped that country of all military power and considerable territory and placed her economy under Anglo-Saxon control. Some 2,000,000 Italians would help reconstruct ravaged Europe. [7:5.]

Diplomats reaching Mexico City for the Inter-American Conference favored greater power for small nations in post-war plans and, while doubtful of Argentina's intentions, hoped for friendly relations. [1:6-7.]

City-Wide Produce Tie-Up Looms As Drivers Halt Bronx Deliveries

A strike of truckmen affiliated with Local 202, International Brotherhood of Teamsters, was called early today at the Bronx Terminal Market, tying up all produce deliveries in that borough and was threatening to spread city-wide.

However, the full effects will not be felt in the other boroughs until the end of the week, as the contracts in Manhattan and Brooklyn do not expire until Friday.

Meanwhile, carloads of produce were piling up at piers and freight terminals, and Washington wholesale market was crowded with fruits and vegetables as union delegates warned their men not to handle any foodstuffs for sale or delivery to Bronx dealers. Then they added, "tonight the Bronx, next week Brooklyn and Manhattan."

At 1 A. M. when 300 trucks normally would start toward Washington Market to pick up produce for the Bronx Terminal for ultimate distribution through jobbers to retail outlets "not a wheel was turning." Two hundred platform men and 300 chauffeurs, meanwhile, were idling about with instructions from union delegates not to work as a contract that expired Friday had not been signed.

The proposed contract, union representatives said, called for a

Continued on Page 18, Column 3

Mexico Talks Designed to Link Hemisphere to Dumbarton Oaks

By JAMES B. RESTON

Special to THE NEW YORK TIMES

MEXICO CITY, Feb. 18—The Inter-American Conference on Problems of War and Peace will not open until Wednesday but most of the delegates are here and many of the decisions that will be announced in the next few days are now being taken in a series of conferences in the capital.

In this respect the forthcoming conference is not unlike a political convention at home. Preparation is at least two-thirds of the battle and what important decisions have not already been made are likely to be made within the next few days.

The two main political questions before the conference, for example, are what policy the American nations are to take regarding the proposed Dumbarton Oaks international security organization and what they are to do about the Argentine Government whose undemocratic actions at home and defiance of the United States abroad have virtually isolated her from the American community of nations.

There will be many different opinions expressed here about these two questions in the next fortnight and Ezequiel Padilla, Mexican Foreign Secretary, will undoubtedly seize the opportunity to champion greater rights for the small na-

Continued on Page 4, Column 3

Fleet in Manila Bay, U. S. Radio Reports

The American Broadcasting Station in Europe declared last night that United States Seventh Fleet warships "have steamed into Manila Harbor without incident."

Quoting "a dispatch from Luzon," the broadcast said: "Manila Bay is described as now open to American naval vessels." The broadcast was recorded by the Columbia Broadcasting System.

"All the News That's Fit to Print"

The New York Times.

LATE CITY EDITION
Rain or drizzle with moderate winds today
Temperatures Yesterday—Max., 35; Min., 19
Sunrise today, 7:43 A. M.; Sunset, 6:37 P. M.

VOL. XCIV..No. 31,805. Entered as Second-Class Matter. Postoffice, New York, N. Y. NEW YORK, WEDNESDAY, FEBRUARY 21, 1945. THREE CENTS IN NEW YORK CITY

MARINES CONQUER AIRFIELD, HOLD THIRD OF IWO; ROOSEVELT GETS NEW CHURCHILL VOW ON JAPAN; PATTON SPEEDS UP ADVANCE ON 50-MILE FRONT

SENATORS CONSIDER NEW JOB MEASURE; IGNORE ROOSEVELT

Group Shunts May Bill Aside After Getting President's Note Urging Enactment

'LABOR DRAFT' IS OMITTED

Substitute Aimed at Employers and Would Strengthen WMC's Program

By C. P. TRUSSELL
Special to THE NEW YORK TIMES.

WASHINGTON, Feb. 20—The Senate Military Affairs Committee shunted aside the May-Bailey bill for "limited national service," on which it had been working since Feb. 2, and voted, 12 to 6, today to consider a substitute which would continue the War Manpower Commission programs, supplemented by statutory controls, and keep all "labor draft" aspects out of worker mobilization and placement.

This action was taken a few hours after the committee had received from President Roosevelt a memorandum, signed "F. D. R." which said:

"I hope that legislation embracing the principle of the May bill can be speedily enacted. It will assure the armed services they can rely on the flow of necessary supplies and greatly contribute to the success of our arms."

Comment of committee members indicated that the memorandum, addressed to Senator Alben W. Barkley, majority leader, and dated Feb. 11, received scant consideration.

While the President has been away for some time, things have happened at home to change or solidify views on manpower control matters, some members asserted, adding that the committee would present a better bill than the one providing "limited national service" principles which Mr. Roosevelt seeks to preserve.

Votes to Report "a Bill"

Partly in answer to Secretary of War Stimson, who denounced delay in action in a Sunday night broadcast, the committee voted unanimously to report out "a bill" as promptly as it could. This, it was asserted, had been the committee's attitude throughout.

Chairman Elbert D. Thomas expressed the belief that "a bill," probably the one now at hand, would be reported to the Senate not later than Thursday. He did not expect debate to begin before next Monday.

While today's action was viewed as tantamount to committee rejection of the May-Bailey bill, even as it was amended tentatively by the same group at one time to transfer proposed labor placement controls from the Selective Service system to the WMC, the substitute still must win committee approval.

Sponsored by a bipartisan group of six Senators, the new measure won the tentative support today of seven committee Democrats and five Republicans, while four Democrats and two Republicans voted to continue consideration of the May-Bailey bill.

Voting for taking up the substitute were Senators Johnson of Colorado, Downey of California, Chandler of Kentucky, Kilgore of West Virginia, Murray of Montana, O'Mahoney of Wyoming and Wagner of New York, Democrats; and Burton of Ohio, Thomas of Idaho, Wilson of Iowa, Revercomb of West Virginia and Bridges of New Hampshire, Republicans.

Chairman Backs May Bill

Those who supported the May-Bailey bill were Senators Thomas of Utah, Hill of Alabama, Maybank of South Carolina and Stewart of Tennessee, Democrats; and Austin of Vermont and Gurney of South Dakota, Republicans.

It was indicated that even though the committee should report out the substitute, the May-Bailey measure, which has been approved

Continued on Page 12, Column 3

Bars and Night Clubs Act To Comply With Curfew

Many Places to Open Earlier—Enforcement Plans to Be Worked Out in Washington Today—Mayor to Consult Byrnes

New York, and to a lesser extent the rest of the nation, began taking steps yesterday to move ahead its after-dinner pleasures by an hour or more to crowd in as much fun as possible before midnight, the hour of the curfew on all places of amusement that will start Monday.

Many of the night clubs announced they would open earlier than usual, to be able to present two floor shows before the 12 o'clock closing, and bowling alleys moved their scheduled team play, including that of war-plant leagues, closer to the dinner hour.

The time changes evidenced the willingness of most entertainment managements to back the pledges wired to War Mobilization Director James F. Byrnes by such trade bodies as the National Tavern Association and the Cafe Owners Guild that they would comply exactly with the curfew, the main purpose of which is said to be to conserve fuel.

For places that balk at the curfew or seek to circumvent it, enforcement details and the imposition of sanctions by at least four Federal agencies were to be worked out today. Mayor La Guardia said he would go to Washington today to discuss details with Mr. Byrnes.

"I spoke to Mr. Byrnes today," the Mayor said. "I'll know more about it tomorrow."

Police Commissioner Lewis J. Valentine disclosed that heads of several Federal agencies would confer on enforcement problems. His reply to all questions about police enforcement of the curfew was: "No comment, pending conference with officials of the War Production Board and other governmental agencies concerned."

A survey yesterday indicated that reprisals against places failing to heed the Byrnes "request" might include, in addition to those previously mentioned, reduction or revocation by the Office of Price

Continued on Page 12, Column 2

BIAS BILL BATTLE WAGED AT HEARING

Spokesmen for Churches, Labor and Racial Groups Throng the Assembly Chamber

By LEO EGAN
Special to THE NEW YORK TIMES.

ALBANY, Feb. 20—The public hearing on the Ives-Quinn anti-discrimination bill that opponents of the measure had forced in the hope of killing the proposal or obtaining drastic modifications of it appeared tonight to have backfired against them. In the opinion of leading advocates and adversaries of the bill, after the hearing had been under way for about four hours, the chances for passage of the measure are now greater than they were before.

"It looks as though we are banging our heads against a stone wall," one of the leading Senatorial opponents of the measure remarked after listening to representatives of the three major religious faiths of the country join with spokesmen for labor and Negro organizations in asking its passage. The Senator added that he might withhold an amendment he had intended to offer.

About 400 persons attended the hearing in the Assembly Chamber. They filled all the seats on the floor and in the galleries and lined up against the walls two and three deep in places. Two to three dozen members of the Legislature were in attendance most of the time.

Opposition came chiefly from employer groups, representing commerce and industry in all parts of the State. They contended that the Ives-Quinn bill, if enacted, would increase racial tension, re-

Continued on Page 15, Column 1

STASSEN ACCEPTS SECURITY DUTIES

Will Be Relieved by Navy for Conference—Calls Task a Political Liability

By SIDNEY SHALETT
Special to THE NEW YORK TIMES.

WASHINGTON, Feb. 20—Comdr. Harold E. Stassen asserted today that, although he considers his appointment by President Roosevelt as a delegate to the United Nations Security Conference a personal political liability, he has accepted because, he said:

"I feel it as much my duty to take an assignment to work for a successful peace as to work for a successful war."

The former Governor of Minnesota, often mentioned as Republican Presidential timber, now flag secretary and assistant chief of staff for administration to Admiral William F. Halsey Jr., in the Western Pacific, revealed that he will step out of the Navy temporarily in order to be free to speak and act as he sees fit at the San Francisco conference.

Admiral Halsey has promised to send him at the proper time to San Francisco, where the commander, going on inactive duty, will participate in the conference as a civilian. After the conference he will return to active duty with Admiral Halsey.

Commander Stassen is in Washington with his chief for Navy Department conferences.

He will return to the Pacific with Admiral Halsey before the San Francisco conference.

Commander Stassen said he had dismissed the "political liability" aspect of the appointment because

Continued on Page 5, Column 1

WLB Orders 55c Textile Pay Base And Bargaining for Meat Packers

By JOSEPH A. LOFTUS
Special to THE NEW YORK TIMES.

WASHINGTON, Feb. 20—The War Labor Board today ordered a minimum wage of 55 cents an hour for 50,000 Northern and Southern textile workers under its authority to correct substandard wage rates. The order provides for an increase of at least 5 cents an hour for all the workers affected.

In making these and other awards to the textile workers, as well as certain concessions to 144,000 meat-packing employes, the WLB stayed the actual financial effectuation of its decisions until a further order, which it promised to issue as soon as policy problems between it and Fred M. Vinson, Director of Economic Stabilization, have been resolved.

The WLB's action in releasing the textile and meat-packing decisions which had virtually been reached two months ago, is expected to have the effect of shifting most of the pressures which have been at work to Mr. Vinson's office.

The 55-cent minimum wage award is expected, eventually, to become a national WLB policy. The board had gradually evolved the policy of a 50-cent minimum which employers could place in effect without specific permission. In some disputes cases the board had ordered a 50-cent minimum.

In the meat-packing case the board ordered, in principle, that

Continued on Page 32, Column 3

SECOND TALK HELD

Prime Minister Pledges Full Effort in Parley at Egyptian Port

EASTERN KINGS CALL

Farouk, Haile Selassie and Ibn Saud Visit Western Leaders

The announcement by the White House is on Page 8.

By BERTRAM D. HULEN
Special to THE NEW YORK TIMES.

WASHINGTON, Feb. 20—President Roosevelt and Prime Minister Churchill conferred in Alexandria, Egypt, after the Crimea Conference, on the war against Japan and other questions, the White House announced today, and the Prime Minister gave assurance of active British aid in the Pacific.

During the conference of less than four hours, it was said, Mr. Churchill "told the President in blunt words that his Government was determined to throw everything it had at the Japanese as soon as Germany has been defeated and, meanwhile, would do all it could to strengthen its forces already engaged in that conflict."

The White House announcement was in the form of a series of dispatches, undisclosed as to time and place, except that it covered events through the President's departure from Algiers, his last scheduled stop, before reaching home. It was in the form of a travelogue covering the high points of his journey, which, when completed, will encompass some 14,000 miles.

It disclosed that President Roosevelt had received three Middle Eastern rulers when on an American war vessel anchored in Great Bitter Lake, through which the Suez Canal passes. They were King Farouk of Egypt, Emperor Haile Selassie of Ethiopia and King Ibn Saud of Saudi Arabia.

President Roosevelt, through the announcement, expressed deep re-

Continued on Page 8, Column 3

MARINES CHARGE OVER A CREST ON IWO ISLAND

Leathernecks of the Fourth Division dash up a rise from the beach
Associated Press Wirephoto (Navy radio from Guam)

RUSSIANS ADVANCE IN COTTBUS SECTOR

Koneff 8 Miles From Guben After Forcing the Bober—Drive for Danzig Gains

By The United Press.

LONDON, Wednesday, Feb. 21—The Red Army battled across a twenty-mile stretch of the Bober River defense line southeast of Berlin yesterday to within eight miles of industrial Guben, an outer fortress of the Nazi capital. Other Soviet forces hammered to within forty miles of Danzig.

Guben, a twelve-way communications center fifty-one miles southeast of Berlin, was threatened by troops of Marshal Ivan S. Koneff's First Ukrainian Army that

Continued on Page 6, Column 2

War News Summarized

WEDNESDAY, FEBRUARY 21, 1945

United States Marines have driven across Iwo Island, isolating Mount Suribachi, have occupied 2,000 yards of the west beach and have captured the south airfield. The Japanese are fighting fiercely, especially on the flanks, and it has been impossible as yet to estimate our casualties. Night counter-attacks and minor enemy air raids have been beaten off as artillery and supplies continued to land on the beachheads. The Fifth Fleet has sent more than 8,000 tons of shells crashing against rocky strong points. [1:8; map P. 2.]

Fighting in the Philippines was on a reduced scale. The Japanese have been compressed into an area 1,200 by 800 yards in south Manila. During the six-week campaign on Luzon Japanese casualties have been 92,000; ours 12,929, of whom 2,676 were killed. [4:7.]

In Europe the United States Third Army, advancing along a fifty-mile front in the west, gained up to two and a half miles, capturing eleven villages and entering five others between Pruem and Merzig. General Patton's men have been taking 1,500 prisoners a day. The Canadian First Army was locked in hard battles near Calcar. [1:6-7; map P. 10.]

Nuremberg's railroad station, freight yards and repair shops were hit by 900 Flying Fortresses from Britain. More than 700 Mustangs and Lightnings shot up airfields and rail lines, destroying fifty-three German planes and hundreds of locomotives and cars. Last night more than 1,200 RAF planes hit Dortmund and Berlin. [10:4.]

The Russians tightened their grip on East Prussia and threw back Germans trying to escape from the Koenigsberg area toward Pillau. Other Red Army forces moved closer to Danzig, and in Brandenburg crossed the Bober River near its confluence with the Oder. [1:5; map P. 6.]

President Roosevelt, on his way home from the Crimea, saw Prime Minister Churchill at Alexandria and three Middle East rulers in the Suez region. The British leader told the President Britain would "throw everything it had at the Japs" as soon as the European war ended. A "travelogue" on Mr. Roosevelt's 14,000-mile trip, issued in Washington, expressed the President's disappointment over failure to meet General de Gaulle at Algiers. [1:4; map Page 8.]

Tangled Middle East problems were believed to have been discussed when Mr. Roosevelt met King Farouk of Egypt, Emperor Haile Selassie of Ethiopia and King Ibn Saud of Saudi Arabia in Suez waters. [8:1.]

Mr. Churchill told the Commons things looked "smoother" but would not discuss the Big Three meeting. He and Foreign Secretary Eden had earlier seen King George. [9:1.]

Trouble appeared to be returning to Greece, where Interior Minister Rhallis resigned as opposition to Premier Plastiras' firm treatment of the Left Wing rose. [7:2-3.]

Secretary of State Stettinius arrived in Mexico City to attend the Inter-American Conference, which opens today. The Argentine situation may be fully discussed by the delegates. [11:1.] Argentina placed an embargo on German credits to assure payment of damages she charges against the Reich. [11:6.]

U. S. Third Takes 11 Places; Foe Hits Canadians in North

By CLIFTON DANIEL
By Wireless to THE NEW YORK TIMES.

SUPREME HEADQUARTERS, Allied Expeditionary Force, Feb. 20—Stepping up the daily pace of their advance to two and a half miles in some places along a fifty-mile front, American Third Army troops captured eleven hamlets between Pruem and Merzig today and entered five more in a drive that has been corralling German prisoners at the rate of more than 1,500 per day.

Although yielding ground before Lieut. Gen. George S. Patton's pounding, the German forces stiffened their lines in the north to defend more vital objectives under attack from Gen. H. D. G. Crerar's Canadian First Army. Col. Gen. Kurt Student's resourceful German parachute army, again reinforced, snatched back a few patches of ground from the United Kingdom and Canadian troops in a fierce battle for Calcar beyond the northern end of the Westwall today, while Scots and Welshmen almost completed occupation of the more formidable fortress of Goch, seven miles to the southwest of Calcar.

Although the lines on the map move slowly, both General Crerar's forces and General Patton's Third Army are imposing a remarkably high rate of attrition on weakened German armies in slugging matches preceding what Field Marshal Sir Bernard L. Montgomery has called the coming "final round" of the offensive against Germany. The Canadian First Army has penned more than 9,500 prisoners in less than two weeks of its offensive between the Meuse (Maas) and the Rhine.

Four of the many divisions in General Patton's command have captured more than 4,600 prisoners in the past three days, which is

Continued on Page 10, Column 2

AMERICANS STRIKE FROM IWO FOXHOLES

Marines Edge Ahead on Wings, Then Beat Off Japanese Night Counter-Attack

By ROBERT TRUMBULL
By Wireless to THE NEW YORK TIMES.

IWO, Volcano Islands, Feb. 20 (11 A. M.)—The battle that may shorten the Iwo campaign began today when the Fourth and Fifth Marine Divisions came out of their brittle volcanic ash, and attacked on both flanks in the face of heavy artillery and mortar fire.

The marines, who were in the narrow neck of Iwo yesterday, pushed south to envelop Mount Suribachi, grim, 511-foot volcanic cone whence enemy emplacements in caves and brown rock continue to pepper our beachhead despite fierce bombing and strafing. The leathernecks now hold the southern airfield and are attempting to move northward into the boulder-strewn badlands and Airfield No. 2.

The Japanese still hold the highest ground. Their commander has relied on his artillery and avoided commitment of his tanks and manpower.

The Japanese suffered minimum

Continued on Page 3, Column 2

U. S. Warship Becomes Arab Court In Miniature for Ibn Saud's Voyage

By Wireless to THE NEW YORK TIMES.

CAIRO, Egypt, Feb. 20—When King Abdul Aziz Ibn Saud, 65-year-old monarch of Arabia Deserta, left his country for the first time to visit President Roosevelt his voyage was a fantastic potpourri of contrasting scenes of the modern world with an ancient westward journey by the Three Wise Kings of the Orient.

From his huge palace at Ryadh, which includes both the traditional harems of Islam and the only electric elevators in Saudi Arabia, he traveled southward to Jidda—where pilgrims debark on their holy trip to Mecca—by motor convoy. In this steaming Red Sea port a destroyer was waiting—the first American warship to enter that harbor, to which it had been piloted by a barefooted Arab.

Special arrangements, probably without precedent in American naval annals, had been made to make the King comfortable. Dozens of thick carpets were spread on the foredeck and a royal tent was set up in front of the forward gun turret for the King to sleep in.

A sheep pen was built on the fantail. King Ibn Saud had offered to send enough sheep aboard to feed the whole crew, but the accommodations permitted only enough to feed the royal party.

On the first night out the King invited the entire officer complement of the vessel to a banquet held in approved Arab fashion, squatting on the deck and eating

Continued on Page 9, Column 3

WEST SHORE GAINED

Invaders Cut Across Iwo in Bloody Fighting—Enemy Fire Heavy

VOLCANO IS CUT OFF

Our Ships and Planes Keep Shelling Isle—Supplies Pour In

By WARREN MOSCOW
By Wireless to THE NEW YORK TIMES.

ADVANCED HEADQUARTERS, Guam, Wednesday, Feb. 21—Fighting as bitter as any seen in the Pacific has raged for two days on the tiny island of Iwo. A large Japanese garrison equipped with rockets and heavy artillery has been shelling and killing our marines, who are seeking to overrun the key spot on the road to Tokyo.

In a communiqué issued at 7:30 A. M. today, Admiral Chester W. Nimitz revealed that in the last six hours covered by the communiqué the Fourth and Fifth Marine Divisions had gained only 100 yards more in the drive north, but that in gaining this they had driven the enemy clear off the first airplane strip on the island, the major objective of the first two days' attack and one achieved on time.

[The marines hold the southern third of Iwo, press services noted. Having captured the No. 1 airfield, they pushed on 200 yards toward the island's central airdrome.

[Viewing the action from a warship just off the beachhead, Lieut. Gen. Holland M. Smith, Commander of Pacific Marines, said: "The fighting is the toughest we've run across in 168 years."]

West Toehold 2,000 Yards

That the Iwo airfield had been overrun and the marines had cut across the island from the east beaches, where the landing was made Monday morning at 9 A. M., (Guam time) was announced last midnight. Our beachhead ran 4,500 yards on one side of the island and about 2,000 yards on the west side.

This cut off Surabachi, volcanic cone at the southern end of the island, but from its slopes the Japanese continued to pour mortar and small-arms fire on marines trying to inch up its slopes.

At the northern end of the American line the enemy was giving the Americans everything he had in the way of heavy artillery and mortar fire. The marines were hitting back with flame throwers and artillery, ashore in quantity for the first time. The old unsinkables of the Pacific Fleet—six of our oldest battleships—supported by cruisers and destroyers, poured in part of the 8,000 tons of ammunition to which Iwo has been subjected.

Enemy Planes Turned Back

Last midnight's communiqué reported that our night carrier fighters had beaten off small units of enemy air raiders which failed to reach the island. This presumably means that the Japanese airfields in the near-by Bonins have not yet been neutralized.

[General Douglas MacArthur announced early Wednesday that Japanese casualties on Luzon, in the Philippines, had reached 92,000 and that American losses were 2,676 killed, 10,008 wounded and 245 missing. Fighting continued in Manila and on Corregidor.]

Iwo is half way between our big bases in the Marianas and Tokyo, and the Japanese are not giving up. For them to come out of their caves, where they are safe from anything but a direct artillery hit or from the flame throwers we have been using, means that they have orders to clear us off the island at all cost rather than to inflict losses on us.

They are not, however, clearing us off, and our troops, probably the largest concentration per

Continued on Page 3, Column 5

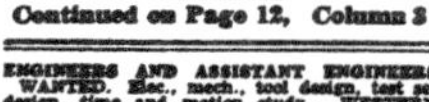

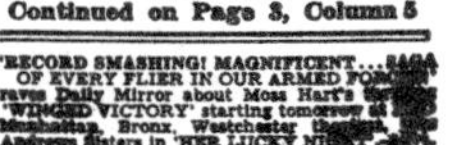

"All the News That's Fit to Print"

The New York Times.

LATE CITY EDITION
Fair with moderate temperature today and tomorrow.
Temperatures Yesterday—Max., 50; Min., 38
Sunrise today, 7:20 A. M.; Sunset, 6:01 P. M.

VOL. XCIV..No. 31,808. Entered as Second-Class Matter, Postoffice, New York, N. Y. NEW YORK, SATURDAY, FEBRUARY 24, 1945. THREE CENTS IN NEW YORK CITY

EISENHOWER OPENS WIDE ROER OFFENSIVE, 1ST AND 9TH ARMIES DRIVE TOWARD RHINE; MARINES GAIN SLOWLY IN CENTER OF IWO

CURFEW IS STAYED UNTIL MAYOR ACTS; CAFES SEE REPRIEVE

La Guardia Promises to Give 'Ample Notice' After Reading Clarification, Due Today

CLUBS, MUSICIANS CONFER

Former Feel Free to Drop Bands, but Union Defers Reply to Plan

Mayor La Guardia announced yesterday that night clubs and other places of amusement would be permitted to continue under their present closing schedules, 4 A. M. on weekdays and 3 A. M. on Sundays, pending announcement from him.

"All the people operating may continue the status quo until I make an official announcement in New York City," he said at City Hall.

Mr. La Guardia made it clear that after he has studied the order "ample notice" will be given to amusement places concerned.

"We feel that this is a reprieve and we will remain open until present closing hours pending word from the Mayor," Noah L. Braunstein, attorney for the Cafe Owners Guild, Inc., said.

The Mayor announced that he expected to confer today with Mrs. Anna M. Rosenberg, regional director of the War Manpower Commission, which will enforce the early closing hour with the aid of municipal enforcement agencies.

Denies Asking Extension

Reports that the WMC was extending the midnight "curfew" until 1 A. M. at his request were denied by Mayor La Guardia and a WMC spokesman in Washington. This spokesman added that enforcement rules are still in the discussion stage and nothing yet has been decided.

"I have made no statement to anyone at any place," the Mayor said. "Any announcement purporting to come from me is not correct. Nothing has been received from Washington."

Any order he issues, the Mayor said, will be forthcoming only after he receives definite instructions from Washington with respect to the midnight curfew "requested" by War Mobilization Director James F. Byrnes. The nationwide midnight closing of all places of amusement is set for Monday.

At 7 o'clock last night WNYC, the city-owned radio station, broadcast that the Mayor had asked the station to inform the public that Washington had just notified him the definitive order he requested would be in his hands either late last night or today. The Mayor will study the order as it affects New York City and later will make his official announcement.

The Mayor had spent two days in Washington seeking a clarification of the Byrnes mandate as it affects municipalities such as New York City, where millions of dollars are invested and labor and contractual obligations are involved.

Hopes for Two-Week Notice

"I expect to confer with Mrs. Rosenberg tomorrow. In the meantime, everyone concerned is urged not to get excited. Insofar as I am concerned, nothing will be expected on a few hours' notice. If anything definite comes through Saturday, I will see how much is involved and ample notice will be given.

"Let me repeat, no one in Washington; no one in City Hall or no one authorized has made any announcement of any plan or method of operation whatsoever."

Speaking for cafe owners, Mr. Braunstein said the Mayor's action would provide an opportunity for night club owners to "get their

Continued on Page 16, Column 6

1,000-Pound Rocket Fired by Iwo Foe

By The Associated Press.

ABOARD ADMIRAL TURNER'S FLAGSHIP, Off Iwo, Feb. 23—The Japanese are using a new weapon, 1,000-pound rockets, in their fight for Iwo.

The shell is described as having a nose fuse and a rocket motor. Gunnery experts said the rockets probably were launched by jet propulsion, carried through the air by rocket power and then detonated at their destination by their nose fuses.

The enemy also used regular rockets, artillery, dual-purpose anti-aircraft guns, mortars and automatic weapons.

Another example of the Japanese strength developed today when several hits by rocket firing planes were necessary to destroy an enemy pillbox. The pillboxes are of concrete, covered with sand.

17 DEAD, 5 INJURED IN AIRLINER CRASH

Continental Plane Runs Into Rain in Virginia and Hits Mountain in Blue Ridge

By The United Press.

MARION, Va., Feb. 23—An American Airlines plane, flying from New York to Los Angeles, crashed into a mountainside near Cedar Springs, Va., early today, killing seventeen of the twenty-two persons on it.

The five survivors were brought here to the Lee Memorial Hospital from the almost inaccessible mountainside in the Blue Ridge where the airliner crashed at 3:30 A. M.

The survivors were:

Mrs. John B. Padgett, 25 years old, of Nashville, Tenn., the plane's stewardess, broken collar bone, scalp and brow injuries, and possibly injury to spinal cord.

Ensign Fred Middaugh of 636 South Harding Avenue; Los Angeles, described as the most seriously injured, with a crushed shoulder, fracture of left thigh and brain concussion.

Marine Lieut. Irving W. Schwartz of 153 Milner Avenue, Syracuse, N. Y.; scalp and brow cuts and left hip injury.

Marine Lieut. Leonard Joseph Ricci of Mountain View Lodge, Southington Road, Meriden, Conn.; right hip injury, cuts and abrasions.

Mrs. Viola Ulen of 4000 Cathedral Avenue, N. W., Washington, D. C.; slight injuries and scratches.

Dr. George Wright of the hospital quoted one of the patients as saying that the plane ran into a severe rain storm and that its engines began to give trouble. He said that the patient could not give a clearer picture of what happened because of his condition.

The dead among the passengers included Carlo Audifred of Mexico City and Clyde J. Pinney of Philadelphia, a representative of the Baldwin Locomotive Works.

Crew members killed were Capt.

Continued on Page 26, Column 2

AIRFIELD EDGE WON

Third Marine Division Fights Way to Fighter Strip on Iwo Isle

4TH GAINS, 5TH HELD

All Three Side by Side in Fierce Battle—Suribachi Captors Kill 717

By WARREN MOSCOW

By Wireless to The New York Times.

ADVANCED HEADQUARTERS, Guam, Saturday, Feb. 24—United States marines fighting their way northward on Iwo Island won the southern edge of the central airfield, a fighter strip, Admiral Chester W. Nimitz announced in a communiqué at 10 A. M. today, reporting on the fighting up to 6 P. M. Friday night.

The right flank of the marines pushed a maximum of 300 yards northward. Gains in the center where the air strip is situated were slight but sufficient to put the marines there on the south edge of the field.

[The Third Marine Division, recently landed on Iwo, reached the fighter airfield while on its left flank the Fifth Division was held to no gains, Admiral Nimitz's communiqué said. On the Third's right flank, the Fourth Marines made the 300-yard advance.]

717 of Foe Killed on Volcano

On Mount Suribachi, the marines who reached the summit and planted the American flag there yesterday continued mopping up the entrenchments and caves on the volcano during the day. Blockhouses and pillboxes inside and outside the crater were worked on with flame-throwers and grenades. A total of 717 Japanese dead were counted in the Suribachi sector.

Kangoku Rock, 2,000 yards off the west shore of Iwo, has been hitting our positions with mortar fire, it was disclosed. A destroyer sailed up and silenced the fire and presumably eliminated the defenders. Several landing craft at the Rock were destroyed. General support of the land operations by the fleet's guns and carrier aircraft was continued.

In a communiqué issued at 10:45 last night, Admiral Nimitz told of roads that had been constructed over volcanic ash terraces on Iwo by construction crews and engineers working under shell and mortar fire. The roads improved a hitherto crippling transportation problem so that supplies for the front lines could be moved.

The marines surmounted the Suribachi volcano against Japanese pouring down a hail of fire on many American troops within range. The first communiqué telling of the scaling of Suribachi was issued yesterday afternoon, when Admiral Nimitz announced the planting of the flag on its top by

Continued on Page 5, Column 3

POSEN CAPITULATES

Russians Topple Citadel After Month's Siege Costing Foe 48,000

ARNSWALDE GIVES UP

Koneff Stabs Deeper in Breslau — Berlin Forts Pierced, Germans Say

By The United Press.

LONDON, Saturday, Feb. 24—Russian troops completed the conquest of the Polish fortress city of Posen yesterday, ending a month-long siege in which 48,000 Germans were killed or captured. They also seized the Pomeranian rail hub of Arnswalde.

Battling to clear centers where suicide forces were delaying the drives on Berlin, Stettin and Dresden, the Red Army also intensified the struggle for Breslau, encircled Lower Silesian capital, and tightened the arc around trapped German forces in East Prussia.

Sudeten Hills Menaced

German reports said that Soviet troops had broken into the twin Neisse River strongholds of Guben and Forst, fifty-one and fifty-seven miles southeast of Berlin, added that the Russians had won bridgeheads across the Neisse and reported a Red Army breakthrough to the Sudeten Mountains southwest of Liegnitz in Silesia.

[A Rumanian communiqué, recorded by the Federal Communications Commission, said that Russian and Rumanian troops in the Lower Tatra Mountains of Czechoslovakia were attacking German-Hungarian forces defending the Hermann Goering iron works at Podbrezova in the Hron River valley eighteen miles west of Banska Bystrica.]

In an order of the day Marshal Stalin announced that Marshal Gregory K. Zhukoff's First White Russian Army had cleared the biggest bottleneck behind the Oder River front, thirty-one to forty-eight miles east of Berlin, by clearing the last enemy remnants from Posen, Poland's fourth largest city.

Since Posen, which had a prewar population of 272,000, was en-

Continued on Page 4, Column 6

THE BIG PUSH TOWARD COLOGNE IS BEGUN

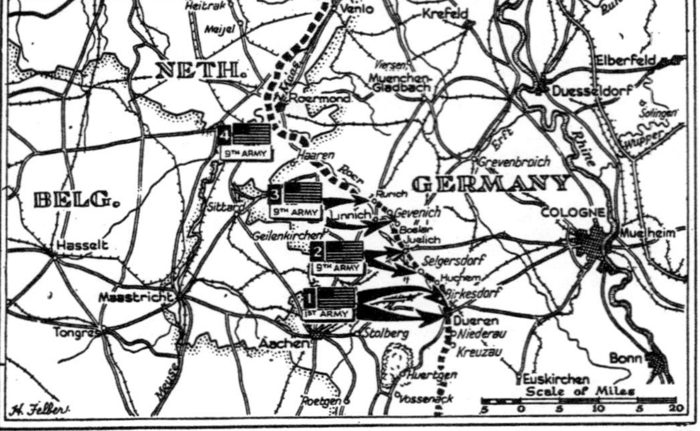

The First Army smashed directly across the Roer into Dueren and also entered its northern suburbs, capturing Huchem and Birkesdorf (1). The Ninth Army, spanning the river at many points, took Selgersdorf and all of Juelich but its citadel (2). It also seized Boslar, Gevenich and Rurich (3). The Germans reported that our offensive extended as far north as Roermond (4).

JUELICH CAPTURED

Dueren Also Is Stormed as Two Armies Gain One to Two Miles

8 TOWNS ARE WON

3d Narrows Pruem Gap, Crosses Saar Again—7th Nears Saarbruecken

By CLIFTON DANIEL

By Wireless to The New York Times.

SUPREME HEADQUARTERS, Allied Expeditionary Force, Feb. 23—The expected great attack toward the Rhine was opened by two American armies across the Roer River beyond Aachen today and its first overwhelming surge swept a mile or two beyond the tumbling, flooded stream, burst into the river fortress town of Juelich and reached commanding heights on a ridge along the east side of the Roer.

While assault troops of the American Ninth Army were routing the Germans out of all of Juelich except its forbidding walled citadel, forces of Lieut. Gen. Courtney H. Hodges' American First Army burst across the river into the midst of the stunned and startled defenders farther south, in the neighborhood of Dueren. [A late dispatch from the front said First Army troops were fighting in Dueren and in Birkesdorf, its northern suburb.]

Fight Into Rhineland Plain

Both armies, after having spanned the angry, booby-trapped Roer, were fighting out into the clear on the Rhineland Plain in area only twenty miles from Cologne, twenty-five from Duesseldorf and forty miles southwest of the Ruhr industrial basin, primary source of Germany's war-making power.

Preceded by an artillery and air bombardment that obliterated one German village after another, Lieut. Gen. William H. Simpson's fresh and fit Ninth Army infantrymen plunged straight through Juelich to the towering walls of the citadel in the northern end of the town.

This moated fortress, which probably is garrisoned by Germans and which had been raked by American aircraft twice this week, is surrounded by a wall about 2,000 yards long, fourteen feet thick and forty-five feet high. Outside the wall is a moat twenty feet deep and seventy to 100 feet wide—broader than the Roer, itself, normally is.

Juelich and Dueren are the two principal towns on the Roer in the battle sector, which appeared from incomplete reports to stretch twenty-two miles along fronts of the two armies.

Ninth Captured Five Towns

On both sides of Juelich and beyond it, General Simpson's forces quickly captured a string of five small towns, including Selgersdorf, two and a quarter miles southeast of Juelich; and Rurich, two miles north of Linnich. [A report from the front said Glimbach, Boslar and Gevenich also were captured.] Linnich itself is on the west side of the River.

Gains of one to two miles were made along the whole Ninth Army front in the first stage of the offensive and these advances placed General Simpson's troops well across the road between Linnich and Juelich and on top of some of the highest points in the ridge dominating the river. Although these reports cover only the first few hours or less of the attack, Ninth Army forces certainly had not reached the first main line of field defenses guarding Cologne nor the bulk of the forces that will man those defenses.

Faced with challenge that he must take the offensive unless he wants to see Gen. Dwight D. Eisenhower's armies on the Rhine, Field Marshal Gen. Karl von Rundstedt was reported by American fighter

Continued on Page 2, Column 2

HEMISPHERE PEACE SOUGHT AT PARLEY

Colombia Proposes That States Guarantee Boundaries, No Matter by Whom Violated

United States' proposal on Pan-American policy, Page 7.

By JAMES B. RESTON

Special to The New York Times.

MEXICO CITY, Feb. 23—The United States today introduced at the Chapultepec Conference a resolution calling on the American Foreign Ministers to meet annually to study situations that might disturb the peace. It also indicated its support of another resolution proposing a general guarantee of all American boundaries against any aggressor within or without the hemisphere.

This was "resolutions day" on "Grasshopper Hill," where the Inter-American Conference on Problems of War and Peace is being held, and the proposals covered everything from the rights of man to the abolition of censorship in this hemisphere. But Colombia's

Continued on Page 7, Column 2

Massive Barrages Precede 1st and 9th Army Attacks

By HAROLD DENNY

By Wireless to The New York Times.

WITH AMERICAN FIRST ARMY, on the Roer, Feb. 23—The battle for the Cologne Plain appears to have begun.

Assault troops of the American First Army, in conjunction with troops of the American Ninth Army, drove across the Roer River early today and by nightfall had made gains of one to two miles east of the river.

Sweeping over the river in assault boats, some infantrymen of the First Army drove directly into Dueren and tonight were reported fighting inside that city. To the north other troops crossed the river and fought into Birkesdorf, northern suburb of Dueren. The twin towns of Huchem and Stammeln also fell in the attack.

In the pitch darkness at 3:30 A. M., after a terrific forty-five-minute artillery barrage, elements of the First Army plunged across the swollen river that so long had held them up.

In a way it was a second D-day. It was a water crossing by means of assault boats against a defended shore and it had the most spectacular beginning of any American operation since our troops first splashed ashore in Normandy. The barrage itself was breath-taking. Some 2,000 of our guns fired many thousands of rounds of every sort of ammunition before and in the early stages of the infantry attack. There have been longer and heavier barrages in other battles, but none has ever surpassed the scenic effect as these vari-colored bursts lit up the churning landscape. After daylight our aircraft dashed into the battle. Ground defenses shot down seven German planes, six of them jet-propelled.

The enemy resisted all along the line, according to reports from many parts of the front, but his opposition was less than had been

Continued on Page 3, Column 2

By SYDNEY GRUSON

By Wireless to The New York Times.

WITH THE AMERICAN NINTH ARMY on the Roer, Feb. 23—The American Ninth Army offensive toward the Rhine has begun with gains up to two miles in an offensive launched across the Roer River.

Juelich, a strongly fortified town on the east bank of the Roer, has been cleared, with the exception of a citadel in the northern section of the town, and five towns have been captured—Selgersdorf, Glimbach, Gevenich, Rurich and Boslar—all lying from three-quarters of a mile to two miles from the Roer. The river was crossed in the bright moonlight by assault battalions of the Ninth Army.

Assault platoons jumped off from the west bank of the river at 3:30 A. M. after a forty-five-minute artillery barrage from hundreds of big guns ranged along the entire front. It was one of the heaviest artillery preparations for any major American offensive of the war.

Rubber and wooden assault craft and alligators carried the opening infantry waves over the receding flood waters of the Roer. Alerted by the artillery barrage, the Germans reacted vigorously with artillery, mortar and small arms fire. They have concentrated their fire almost entirely on our crossing sites and bridges, which are still receiving artillery and mortar shells tonight.

Several of the bridges were thrown across the last major river barrier to the Rhine in the morning still.

Our casualties were said officially to be very light.

The weather has turned in our favor. Cloudless skies enabled the Twenty-ninth Tactical Air Command to bomb everything moving in the enemy's rear areas yesterday and today and the fighters

Continued on Page 3, Column 5

War News Summarized

SATURDAY, FEBRUARY 24, 1945

In a great offensive to put the Allied forces on the Rhine, the American First and Ninth Armies launched a powerful attack early yesterday in the area east of Aachen and twenty miles west of Cologne. After a massive barrage—the Germans said a torrent of 60,000 to 100,000 shells fell on their defending troops—our men stormed across the swollen Roer River, guarding the approaches to the rolling country before the Rhine. Most of the fortress of Juelich was won and seven other towns were captured in the first few hours of the big drive. [1:8; maps pages 1 and 2.]

The crossing of the racing water barrier, made with the aid of assault boats and crocodile tanks, was described as the most spectacular beginning of any American operation since the invasion of Normandy. Casualties so far have been light [1:6.]

The aerial offensive to paralyze the enemy's transport and his power to resist our ground forces continued in its eleventh day as more than 6,000 Allied planes struck at Germany's rail sinews. In the last two days 20,000 tons of explosives have been dropped on Germany's battered transportation system. [4:1, with map.]

In Italy, American troops seized the southern slopes of Mount della Torraccia in the Belvedere area west of the Bologna-Pistoia road. [6:5.]

The Red Army completed its conquest of the strongly fortified highway and rail junction of Posen in western Poland, ending a month-long siege and erasing a bottleneck that was hampering communications between Marshal Zhukoff's men before Berlin and their supply sources. The surrounded Pomeranian rail hub of Arnswalde also fell. [1:4.]

The battle for Iwo was still a savage one for the American marines who fought across a battlefield strewn with Japanese dead to occupy one end of the airfield in the center of the island. A gain of 300 yards was the largest that was scored. Carrier planes and naval guns blasted the enemy, who continued to resist grimly from elaborate defenses. [1:3, map P. 5.]

In the Philippines, American troops were mopping up the last enemy remnants trapped in southern Manila after smashing into the ancient walled city of Intramuros, the last Japanese stronghold in the capital. [5:8.]

A United States resolution asking the Foreign Ministers of the American republics to meet annually to study any situation that might threaten the peace of the hemisphere was introduced at the Inter-American conference in Mexico City. Colombia proposed a guarantee of present hemisphere boundaries against any aggressor. [1:5.]

Turkey, which for six years has been walking the tightrope of neutrality, decided to declare war on Germany and Japan to win a seat at the United Nations conference table. [1:6-7.]

3 Named as Gambling Overlords At Sports Events by Valentine

Police Commissioner Lewis J. Valentine told Kings County Judge Samuel S. Leibowitz in Brooklyn yesterday that even if college basketball games went back to their campus gymnasiums gambling could not be stopped. The jurist, sitting as a committing magistrate, was told that such a move, however, might aid in the drive to end corruption.

Mr. Valentine named Frank Costello, alleged slot-machine czar; Frank Erickson, race-track gambler, and Joe Adonis, alleged Brooklyn underground boss, as those who controlled big-time gambling in New York City. He characterized them as "those with the big money."

It was the third of a series of hearings before Judge Leibowitz as a result of the confession of five Brooklyn College basketball players that they had taken money to "throw" a game scheduled with Akron University in Boston. The game was called off.

Questioning by Assistant District Attorney Charles N. Cohen brought out that Mr. Valentine had conferred with Ned Irish, acting president of the Madison Square Garden Corporation, in the hope the gambling evil could be curbed, especially at intercollegiate basketball games. The Commissioner said Mr. Irish had been cooperative.

Mr. Valentine made public the names of about fifty individuals who were on the Garden "blacklist." Among them was Martin Krompier, who was alleged to have been a member of the Arthur (Dutch Schultz) Flegenheimer gang.

Before the hearing was ad-

Continued on Page 26, Column 4

Turkey Declares War on the Axis To Get San Francisco Parley Seat

By JOSEPH M. LEVY

By Wireless to The New York Times.

ANKARA, Turkey, Feb. 23—Turkey declared war on Germany and Japan today. The Grand National Assembly voted for war unanimously after hearing a request from Foreign Secretary Hasan Saka.

Mr. Saka said that Allied diplomats had informed the Turkish Government Tuesday of the Yalta decision that only nations actively at war with the Reich by March 1 will participate in the San Francisco World Security Conference. Prime Minister Shukru Saracoglu addressed a two-hour Assembly session, urging affirmative action.

Full implications of the move, especially the military possibilities, were not disclosed.

The Assembly debate preceding the vote emphasized the friendly Turkish-Russian relations and Turkey's record of friendliness to the Allied cause. Assembly Vice President Gunaltay said: "In the earliest days of the Turkish struggle for independence Soviet Russia was a staunch friend." He stressed that Turkey's war declaration coincided with the anniversary of the Red Army and lauded the Soviet troops.

Foreign Minister Saka revealed that he had received a written memorandum following the Yalta conference that said that the nations that declared war against the Axis before March 1 would participate in the San Francisco conference. The note was delivered to the Turkish Government by Sir

Continued on Page 6, Column 3

"All the News That's Fit to Print"

NEWS INDEX, PAGE 39, THIS SECTION

The New York Times.

LATE CITY EDITION
S..nny with moderate winds.
Temperatures Yesterday—Max., 44; Min., 34
Sunrise today, 7:39 A. M.; Sunset, 6:41 P. M.

Section 1

VOL. XCIV..No. 31,809. Entered as Second-Class Matter, Postoffice, New York, N. Y. NEW YORK, SUNDAY, FEBRUARY 25, 1945. Including Magazine and Book Sections. TEN CENTS New York City and Suburban Area (15c Elsewhere)

AMERICANS DRIVE FOUR MILES BEYOND THE ROER; OUR CARRIER AIRCRAFT SLASH AT TOKYO AGAIN; MARINES WIN HALF OF IWO'S CENTRAL AIRFIELD

WMC DASHES HOPES OF EASED CURFEW; MAYOR ACTS TODAY

He Is Expected to Announce Order to Guide Cafes—Latter to Drop 25,000

LICENSE REFUND PLEA SET

Clubs Packed by Many Having Last Fling and Big Crowds Are Due Tonight

Hopes fostered by operators of night clubs and other amusement places that tomorrow night's midnight "curfew" might be eased to 1 A. M. received a jolt yesterday when the War Manpower Commission, in Washington, decreed that the "request" for midnight closing as originally announced by War Mobilization Director James F. Byrnes would not be altered.

Meanwhile, as night spots were packed and prepared for larger crowds tonight for last-minute flings, Mayor La Guardia stood his ground on the position he took Friday that the closing time for New York City places would remain the same until he had an opportunity to study the WMC edict.

The Mayor will confer with Mrs. Anna M. Rosenberg, regional director of the WMC, at 11 o'clock this morning in City Hall and is expected to make some definite announcement in his weekly broadcast over WNYC, city-owned station.

A survey of midtown night clubs, both in the Broadway area and on the East Side, showed they were doing a capacity business, but the managers were unanimous in declaring that capacity business had been the rule on Saturday night for some time past. All said, however, that reservations and telephone queries indicated larger crowds than usual tonight.

Tavern Owners Accuse Drys

Tavern owners throughout the city lined up with Billy Rose, owner of the Diamond Horseshoe, who had charged that the "curfew" was an "insidious move on the part of the drys to force prohibition back on the country."

Joseph Maguire, president of the United Liquor Dealers of Manhattan, tavern owners' group, said last night that at least 25,000 persons employed in the city's 7,500 taverns will get "pink slips" tonight.

After a meeting of his organization and the Bronx Tavern Owners Association, headed by John Kyle, at 257 Broadway, Mr. Maguire said a resolution was adopted characterizing the Byrnes order as "discriminatory" and declaring that "no increased war effort will be justifiably accomplished through its operation."

Tavern owners in New York City, he said, will send a committee to call upon the New York State Liquor Authority tomorrow morning to "demand a refund" on the $1,200 license fee they pay for operating until 4 A. M. six days a week and 3 A. M. on Sundays.

Says Men Can't Do War Work

"The men who will be thrown out of work as a result of this order are definitely unsuitable for any important part in the war effort," Mr. Maguire said. "Our industry has been gone over with a fine toothcomb by the Army and those now employed would be of little use in any war plant.

"Speaking for the tavern owners in this city and throughout the country, we cannot make too emphatic our feeling that this is just another move on the part of the million-dollar dry lobby in Washington to use the war as an instrument for forcing prohibition back on us."

Mr. Maguire said that his organization was sending a letter to Governor Dewey demanding that he "declare himself in keeping State rights intact." The Byrnes order, he asserted, is a direct violation of State rights in that it

Continued on Page 36, Column 2

Germans Are Gloomy About U.S. Offensive

By The Associated Press.

LONDON, Feb. 24—Amid unconfirmed reports that the Russians were crossing the final German defense lines before Berlin, German commentators said today that the "greatest mass of men and material ever assembled since the Normandy invasion" was forcing open the historic gate between the Maas [Meuse] River and the Eifel Mountains.

The German commentator, Capt. Ludwig Sertorius, declared that the Allies had hurled at least forty divisions at the Maas-Eifel sector alone and he predicted still greater blows to the south. Cologne was reported to be aflame after an aerial hammering and Berlin admitted that "many" bridgeheads had been merged across the Roer River between Linnich and Dueren in the past twenty-four hours as the Americans wedged deeper into the German defenses.

JOINT ARMS BOARD SHAPED IN MEXICO

Inter-American Parley Likely to Set Up Defense Council—U. S. Backs Proposal

By CAMILLE M. CIANFARRA
Special to The New York Times.

MEXICO CITY, Feb. 24—The Inter-American Conference on Problems of War and Peace is expected to create a permanent military board to draft and develop joint plans for the defense of this hemisphere, it was learned today.

This step, which is supported on the whole by the United States, is proposed in a resolution that Mexico will submit next week. It will call for the creation of a body composed of representatives of the general staffs of all the American nations represented at the Chapultepec conference.

Its aim is to build machinery for unified military action against any power outside or on this continent that attacks an American nation. One objective will be the standardization of military equipment and training methods throughout the hemisphere.

Latin-American delegates said that, if approved, Mexico's suggestion would represent a highly important development in the evolution of inter-American collaboration. Fundamentally it is designed to implement and strengthen the plans submitted by many nations here, including the United States, Colombia and Uruguay, for a regional security system within the framework of the Dumbarton Oaks proposals.

Some of these plans advocate the use of force in the event of aggression against an American nation, and the Mexican resolution would provide for machinery to implement that principle. The view of the Mexican delegation is that its suggestion would be not only in harmony with the Dumbarton Oaks plan for dealing with threats to the peace or acts of aggression, but also a valuable addi-

Continued on Page 17, Column 4

BIG FORCE STRIKES

Tokyo Indicates 1,600 Planes Hit in Waves—Sky Fights Swirl

5TH FLEET OFF COAST

Military, Naval and Air Bases Are Targets, Nimitz Announces

By Wireless to The New York Times.

ADVANCED HEADQUARTERS, Guam, Sunday, Feb. 25—Our fleet is at it again. A great force of carriers and battleships is steaming along close to Japan's shore while hundreds of carrier aircraft, perhaps as big a force as that which hit the same territory nine days ago, are striking again at the same target, the industrial center of Tokyo.

[Tokyo broadcasts estimated that the attacking force numbered as many as 1,600 planes, about 400 more than were believed to have taken part in the previous smash at the Japanese capital on Feb. 16 and 17.]

Remnants of the Japanese air force, which lost 500 planes positively destroyed and 150 damaged in the previous American attack on the Japanese capital, were presumed to be rising to the defense of its homeland as our Hellcats strafed military objectives, airfields and naval installations.

[Enemy broadcasts recorded by the Federal Communications System said Japanese planes were battling the attackers over the Tokyo area.]

Spruance in Command

The attack was announced briefly in a communiqué from Admiral Chester W. Nimitz reading as follows:

"Carrier aircraft of the Fifth Fleet are attacking military, naval and air installations in and around Tokyo. Admiral Raymond A. Spruance is present in command of the Fifth Fleet and Vice Admiral Marc A. Mitscher is in tactical command of the fast carrier task force making the attack."

Admiral Mitscher's force, the famous Task Force 58, is presumed to include fifteen to twenty of the fastest carriers and swiftest battleships, protected by a screen of destroyers, cruisers and minesweepers.

When the force struck on Feb. 16 and 17 we escaped without a single Japanese plane's having hit the floating bases from which the Hellcats had come, despite the fact that the attack lasted two days. In that strike the Hellcats bore the burden the first day, hitting the airfields. Helldivers and Grumman Avengers struck aircraft factories, engine, power and electronic plants the second day. This attack may be following the same pattern, although no information on this is available here.

The Tokyo radio was off the air most of the morning. The enemy

Continued on Page 25, Column 5

JAPANESE OVERRUN

Marines Smash Through Maze of Defenses in Bloody Iwo Battle

REACH PLATEAU'S TOP

Drive to Strip's Center, Widen Beachhead, Mop Up on Volcano

By WARREN MOSCOW
By Wireless to The New York Times.

ADVANCED HEADQUARTERS, Guam, Sunday, Feb. 25—Despite bazooka-type weapons and new 1,100-pound rocket bombs used by fiercely fighting Japanese in a mass of powerful interlocking defenses, the marines on Iwo Island pushed northward 300 to 500 yards to overrun half of a fighter airstrip in the center of the island on Saturday.

In a general push they widened the beachhead on the eastern coast by 600 yards, overcoming a maze of connecting pillboxes, blockhouses and fortified caves. They passed through heavily mined areas to make the advances, the greatest in one day since the landing on Monday.

[Secretary of the Navy James V. Forrestal is at Guam for conferences with Admiral Nimitz after having gone ashore at Iwo, The Associated Press reported.]

In a single area of 400 by 600 yards on the east coast, the marines had to neutralize about 100 caves, thirty to forty feet deep, indicating clearly why the seventy-four-day aerial bombardment of the island and the three-day ship shelling prior to our landing failed to decimate the garrison or its supplies.

Supplies Pouring Ashore

The marines are benefiting from the capture of Mount Suribachi, volcano at the southern end of the island, and the advance northward. Enemy artillery fire no longer is dominating the interior area under American control. The mortar fire on the marines' landing places has been reduced and supplies are pouring ashore.

Apparently the Japanese on Iwo are using new techniques developed from lessons of previous American

Continued on Page 28, Column 4

OLD GLORY GOES UP OVER IWO

Marines of the Fifth Division hoist the American flag atop Mount Suribachi
Associated Press Wirephoto (Navy radio from Guam)

EGYPTIAN PREMIER SLAIN IN CHAMBER

Extremist Lawyer Shoots Him After Reading of Decree Putting Nation in War

By SAM POPE BREWER
By Wireless to The New York Times.

CAIRO, Egypt, Feb. 24—Premier Ahmed Maher Pasha was shot and killed in Parliament tonight after he had read a royal decree declaring war against Germany and Japan.

Critically wounded by four revolver shots, the Premier was carried to a first-aid room in the

Continued on Page 10, Column 3

Eisenhower Points New Push At Knockout Blow in West

By Wireless to The New York Times.

SUPREME HEADQUARTERS, Allied Expeditionary Force, Feb. 24—Gen. Dwight D. Eisenhower asserted today that the offensive on the western front was expected "to destroy every German" in its path west of the Rhine and that, if necessary to quell German resistance, the Allied armies would drive on into the center of the Reich to meet the Russian armies.

"Our liaison with the Russians has always been as close and as intimate as was necessary to meet the situation at a particular moment," he told a press conference here. "The Russians have furnished me with all the information I have needed to know and they have done it willingly and cheerfully."

The Supreme Commander seemed entirely satisfied with the progress so far made in the resumed advance toward the Rhine and indicated that he expected that the offensive would be carried through without unusual losses. However, he held out no hopes for a quick and final victory over Germany and, with a laugh at the sourness of his own previous prediction, declined to forecast the date of the end of the war.

For the first time, officially, he disclosed that the American Ninth Army, one of the two that attacked across the Roer River yesterday, had remained under the control of Field Marshal Sir Bernard L. Montgomery, after it had been trans-

Continued on Page 4, Column 2

SOVIET FORCES GAIN IN 'POLISH CORRIDOR'

Red Army Stabs Up to 3 Miles on Wide Front—15 Blocks Captured in Breslau

By The United Press.

LONDON, Sunday, Feb. 25—Red Army troops, advancing up to three miles on a sixty-five-mile front up the "Polish Corridor" and across eastern Pomerania, yesterday hacked to within thirty-three miles south of Danzig and sixty-four miles of the Pomeranian coast in a drive to seal off the former free city and its twin Baltic port of Gdynia.

Troops of Marshal Konstantin K. Rokossovsky's Second White Russian Army threatened the German stronghold of Preussisch Friedland in Pomerania, and in the "Polish Corridor" drove to a point nine

Continued on Page 21, Column 1

21 TOWNS ENTERED

1st Army Captures Half of Dueren as 9th Drives On East of Juelich

4,000 CAPTIVES TAKEN

Third Army Clears 21 More Places in 5-Mile Gain Along Saar

By CLIFTON DANIEL
By Wireless to The New York Times.

SUPREME HEADQUARTERS, Allied Expeditionary Force, Feb. 24—The all-out American offensive to reach the Rhine and destroy the German forces west of it has rolled four miles beyond the Roer River in its first two days, overrunning twenty-one German towns and villages, penetrating four more and bringing in more than 4,000 prisoners.

Battling the racing flood of the Roer, the American First and Ninth Armies established a bridge and ferry system last night to move a steady flow of troops across the stream and now have a series of firm and well-manned lodgments on the east side of the Roer along a twenty-two-mile front. From the river, Lieut. Gen. William H. Simpson's and Lieut. Gen. Courtney H. Hodges' troops were fanning out onto the Cologne Plain "according to schedule," which means the Allies' Supreme Command is thoroughly satisfied.

Patton Gains Five Miles

Both the Canadian First and the American Third Armies took advantage of the German fluster over the powerful Roer assault to step up gains north and south of the new attack.

British infantry and armor swept through the Scottish troops south of Goch to resume the attack on Gen. H. D. G. Crerar's front. Along the line General Crerar's forces were thrusting toward Weeze and closing in around Uedem and Calcar. In the Uedem district there was slight evidence of a German withdrawal.

With advances up to five miles today, Lieut. Gen. George S. Patton's Third Army captured twenty-one towns and squeezed the tip of the German salient along the Luxembourg border down to a space three miles long and two miles wide. The tip is expected to be sliced off momentarily. Up to this morning the Third Army had dragged more than 1,000 prisoners out of the area. Resistance was becoming disorganized.

First Wins Half of Dueren

While the Ninth Army was ripping through a series of villages around and beyond Juelich and Linnich, the American First Army, only twenty miles from Cologne, drove the enemy out of half of Dueren, the largest of the Roer River towns and the main hinge of the German line. The First Army also swept out villages on both sides of Dueren, and the Ninth Army was reported from the front to have pushed on four miles beyond the Roer in the maximum advance. Together, the armies already are well established beyond the main road paralleling the east bank of the Roer and are approaching the edges of the thick forest lands east of Juelich, which are the first great natural obstacles in their path.

The two armies—the Ninth under the operational command of Field Marshal Sir Bernard L. Montgomery's Twenty-first Army Group and the First under Lieut. Gen. Omar N. Bradley's Twelfth Army Group—were disclosed by Supreme Commander Dwight D. Eisenhower to have crossed the Roer in strength—that is, on a major scale and with the intention of a strong, steady advance. Berlin reports said that the full force of the offensive had yet to be reached and that Generals Simpson and Hodges had massed twenty divisions, in-

Continued on Page 3, Column 5

More Men, 30 to 34, to Be Drafted Unless Necessary to Industry

By JOSEPH A. LOFTUS
Special to The New York Times.

WASHINGTON, Feb. 24—Men up to the age of 34 will have to meet more rigid specifications to be eligible for occupational deferments under new regulations announced today by Selective Service headquarters.

Asserting that demands for the armed forces are rapidly depleting the younger age groups, a memorandum to local boards told them to dig deeper into the age brackets of 30 through 33. Registrants of those ages to be eligible for deferment must be "necessary to and regularly engaged in" an activity in war production or in support of the national health, safety or interest.

Previously the only requirement was that registrants in this age group, to be eligible for deferment, must be "regularly engaged in" an activity in support of the national health, safety and interest or in an activity in war production.

The memorandum also states that "if all other factors are equal, a father should be given greater consideration for occupational deferment than a non-father in this age group."

Concerning registrants of the ages thirty-four through thirty-seven, the memorandum states that "merely the determination is required that the registrant is

Continued on Page 31, Column 2

War News Summarized

SUNDAY, FEBRUARY 25, 1945

The American drive toward the Rhine smashed four miles beyond the Roer River, its first major obstacle, and engulfed at least twenty-one towns as it achieved its preliminary objectives on schedule and with light casualties. The American Ninth Army, under Marshal Montgomery, was crashing through a string of villages beyond Juelich and Linnich, while the First, under General Bradley, was fighting through Dueren, main bastion of the Germans' Roer defenses. All enemy counter-attacks were beaten off, and it was believed the American drive had yet to reach its peak. [1:8; maps P. 3.]

First Army troops battering their way through Dueren already had occupied half of that industrial town in house-to-house fighting and reinforcements and supplies were reaching them over several bridges flung across the swollen river by engineers. [5:1.] Enemy resistance along the Ninth Army front was described as moderate and some Germans captured were youths of 15, but opposition was expected to become more intense as we penetrate deeper. [4:1.]

General Eisenhower spurred on his men by telling them the goal of the offensive was the destruction of every German west of the Rhine. He termed the progress of the First and Ninth Armies "certainly satisfactory" and said the Allied forces, if necessary, would drive into central Germany to meet the Russians moving in from the east for the kill. [1:6-7.]

The most devastating aerial offensive of the war continued in its twelfth day with fleets of heavy bombers blasting submarine yards and oil refineries in northwestern Germany. [3:1.]

The Red Army rolled toward the Baltic on a sixty-five-mile front, reaching within thirty-three miles of Danzig and sixty-four of the Pomeranian coast. [1:7.]

Hitler called on the German people to fight to the bitter end, warning them that "whoever is weak must perish." [13:1.]

Admiral Mitscher's naval task force again moved into the waters off Tokyo and its carrier planes renewed their attack on the Japanese capital. [1:3.]

The marines on Iwo captured half of the island's central airfield in the face of fierce resistance. [1:4; map P. 28.]

Manila's liberation was completed after a three-week battle as the last remnant of the Japanese garrison was destroyed. [1:6-7.] American troops in the Philippines achieved another signal success when they seized the Japanese internment camp at Los Banos, thirty-five miles southeast of Manila, freeing 2,146 prisoners. [26:3, with map.]

Just after he had read a decree declaring war on the Axis, Egypt's Prime Minister was shot and killed in the Chamber of Deputies in Cairo. [1:5.]

A permanent military board to plan for the defense of this hemisphere is expected to be set up at the Inter-American conference in Mexico City. [1:2.]

Foe's Manila Garrison Wiped Out; 2,146 Civilians Freed in Camp Raid

By The Associated Press.

MANILA, Sunday, Feb. 25—The three-week-old fight for Manila ended Saturday with the complete destruction of the Japanese garrison. Already more than 12,000 enemy dead have been counted.

Skyborne troops, infantrymen and Filipino guerrillas rescued 2,146 civilians from the Japanese internment camp at Los Banos, thirty-five miles south of Manila, at dawn Friday after killing the entire Japanese guard contingent of 243.

The internees, mostly Americans, were evacuated from the camp in amphibious tractors across Laguna de Bay before an estimated 8,000 enemy troops in the district could interfere with more than patrol fire. Two internees were hurt, and two rescuers were killed and two wounded.

Gen. Douglas MacArthur announced the conclusion of the slow, bloody street-by-street fight in Manila brought to a climax by overwhelming of enemy troops in Intramuros, the old walled city. Three thousand civilians of many nationalities were liberated in the final onslaught.

"Troops of the Thirty-seventh Infantry and First Cavalry Divisions of the Fourteenth Corps overwhelmed the enemy's final positions in South Manila and completed the destruction of the trapped garrison," General MacArthur announced. "More than 12,000 enemy bodies have already

Continued on Page 23, Column 3

"All the News That's Fit to Print"

The New York Times.

LATE CITY EDITION
POSTSCRIPT
Partly cloudy today. Fair tomorrow
Temperature Yesterday—Max., 49; Min., 32
Sunrise today, 7:17 A. M.; Sunset, 6:57 P. M.

VOL. XCIV—No. 31,822. Entered as Second-Class Matter, Postoffice, New York, N. Y. NEW YORK, SATURDAY, MARCH 10, 1945. THREE CENTS IN NEW YORK CITY

1ST AND 3D ARMIES TRAP 5 NAZI DIVISIONS; RHINE BRIDGEHEAD GROWS, FOE REPELLED; 300 B-29'S FIRE 15 SQUARE MILES OF TOKYO

PRODUCTION LAGS CHARGED TO UAW; THOMAS HITS BACK

Romney Tells Senators That Stoppages and Strikes Mark Union Usurpation Plan

1,266,000 MAN-DAYS 'LOST'

Union Leader Says Industry Is Clearing Way for 'Aggression' Against Labor

DETROIT, March 9—Conflicting views on the reasons for the decline in war production by automobile plants were given today before a Senate sub-committee in testimony from leaders of the industry and of labor.

George Romney, as spokesman for the auto industry, called the CIO, of which the United Automobile Workers Union is an affiliate, "the most powerful private organization in the history of our country" and alleged that labor was reducing its production efficiency in auto plants by 25 to 50 per cent despite war needs.

On the other hand, R. J. Thomas, international president of the United Automobile Workers, told the subcommittee that automotive executives were "sacrificing war requirements to preparations for a quick grab at post-war civilian sales."

Mr. Romney charged that through the fostering by the union of disputes, stoppages and strikes, all designed as an attempt at usurpation of the functions of management, 1,266,000 man-days were lost in the industry in the first eleven months of 1944. This, he declared, was the equivalent of 4,200 regular workers.

Mr. Romney, managing director of the Automotive Council for War Production, testified at the opening hearing conducted by the Mead War Investigating Committee studying manpower needs in the Detroit area. He spoke as the representative of the entire automotive industry and of other employers throughout Michigan.

"Organized Anarchy" Charged

He cited "documented" instances of alleged interference in purely plant management affairs by the UAW union in an effort to show that "organized anarchy" existed in the industry. Most strikes and stoppages now, he charged, were being called to prevent management from discharging its "functions, as contrasted with disputes over union recognition and wages and hours before the war. Forty-three per cent of 1,045 strikes and work stoppages in 1944 were of this character, he declared.

Asserting that he based his figures on the Government's own Bureau of Labor Statistics, Mr. Romney said that there were five times as many strikes in automotive plants in 1943 as there were in 1940.

"It is a deplorable fact," he stated, "that during the first eleven months of 1944 there were more strikes and work stoppages in the automotive industry than there were in 1937, the year of the infamous sitdown strikes."

The post-war aim of the CIO, Mr. Romney charged, was to "divide and rule" through union-management Government boards. To thwart this and to correct existing abuses he urged legislation now to end the privileged status of unions and at the same time set forth a detailed "modern national labor policy."

Attacking as the "heart of the problem" the question whether union leaders were to be backed by the Government "in further usurpation of the functions, authority and responsibility of management," Mr. Romney said:

"The question in the minds of production men who built this great industry and its efficient production record is whether the

Continued on Page 12, Column 4

12 Japanese Ships Sunk by Submarines

Special to The New York Times.

WASHINGTON, March 9—Another Japanese escort aircraft carrier, a destroyer and ten merchant vessels have been sunk by United States submarines operating in Far Eastern waters, raising the total of announced sinkings by our submarines to 1,057, the Navy announced tonight.

American submarines now have definitely sunk three Japanese carriers, including one of a large type, probably sunk two others and damaged another two. Forty-seven destroyers, seventeen cruisers, three tenders and forty-two other naval vessels have been sunk.

The merchant ships reported sunk in the latest communiqué include a large cargo transport, a large tanker, two medium-sized cargo transports, five medium cargo vessels and a small cargo transport. Non-combatant ship sinkings total 945.

In addition, several hundred other ships have been probably sunk or damaged.

DAKOTA FARMER NAMED TO SENATE

M. R. Young, Republican, Will Back Roosevelt's Foreign Policy as Did Moses

By Telephone to The New York Times.

BISMARCK, N. D., March 9—State Senator Milton R. Young, a farmer and a member of the conservative wing of the Republican party who has pledged support of President Roosevelt's international policies, was named United States Senator from North Dakota today to succeed John R. Moses, Democrat, who died Saturday after a long illness.

The appointment by Gov. Fred G. Aandahl, a Republican, set at rest reports that Gerald P. Nye, former isolationist Senator from this State, who was unseated by Mr. Moses last November, might regain his place in the Senate.

Active in politics since 1933, Mr. Young, who will serve until the 1946 election, is 47 years old and operates a large farm near Berlin in LaMoure County, in the populous eastern part of the State.

Factors in the Selection

His appointment is a combination of political reward for his efforts in managing the conservative Republican faction campaigns since 1942 and also is based on "geographical" reasons.

The eastern part of the State had been without representation in the Senate for some years. Mr. Moses was from Bismarck and so is Governor Aandahl.

A towering six-footer, Mr. Young was born of farmer parents in Berlin. He is married and has three children. He entered politics in 1933 with his election to the State House of Representatives and four years later was elected to the State Senate.

He often has been referred to as

Continued on Page 11, Column 4

RECORD AIR ATTACK

B-29's Pour Over 1,000 Tons of Incendiaries on Japanese Capital

BOMBS RAIN 1½ HOURS

Tremendous Fires Leap Up in Thickly Populated Center of Big City

By BRUCE RAE

By Wireless to The New York Times.

GUAM, Saturday, March 10—A blanket of fire was thrown over an area of fifteen square miles in the heart of Tokyo early today by a fleet of 300 B-29's in the largest and most intensified raid on that city to date.

This announcement by headquarters was made after the force of Superfortresses returned to their three operating bases in the Marianas with ranks virtually intact. The raid was designed to attack an area of ten square miles, but clear weather and the fact that the bombing was visual widened the territory that could be set ablaze by 50 per cent. The airmen reported the flames so high and so bright that they read watch dials at an altitude of 20,000 feet while smoke arose 18,000 feet.

Enemy Is Surprised

More than 1,000 tons of incendiary bombs fell on the city's center in this all-out incendiary attack, and these rushed down on a section where the density of population is 100,000 to the square mile and where heavy industrial sections, residential neighborhoods and wholesale and retail districts adjoin.

[A Tokyo broadcast Saturday recorded by The United Press said, "the enemy is now attempting to make a landing on Japan proper," but the context made it doubtful that that is what the announcer intended to imply.]

At one point the fringe of the bombed area is only two miles from the Imperial Palace. The home of Emperor Hirohito was not touched, however, although block after block of buildings flamed close by.

The raiding planes operated from Guam, Saipan and Tinian. The Superfortresses, which can carry as much as ten tons of the incendiaries, took along on this attack the largest bomb load ever transported to Japan.

The B-29's sowed their loads well, the 300 ships riding in a designed pattern over Tokyo from 2 A. M. until 3:30 A. M.

"There was every indication that the Japanese were caught flat-footed," said an officer. "Although the anti-aircraft fire was heavy and concentrated, the fighter opposition, at least half-way through the raid, was meager."

The record flight was directed from headquarters here by Maj. Gen. Curtis E. LeMay, who remained at his post throughout last night.

Continued on Page 6, Column 2

Brooklyn Bridge Car Runs Wild; 54 Are Injured as It Hits Pole

A forty-year-old wooden BMT trolley car, its air brakes "gone," careened wildly down the steep grade of Brooklyn Bridge and crashed into a steel power pole at the loop leading to the Manhattan terminal at 6:05 o'clock last night.

The impact sheared the trolley's body from its undercarriage and it landed on its side across the tracks. Fifty-four of the 100 passengers, most of them workers at the Navy Yard in Brooklyn, were injured, two critically and six seriously. It was believed unlikely that trolley service over the bridge would be resumed before morning.

Herman Mann of 637 East 175th Street, the Bronx, the motorman, discovered the air-brake failure as the trolley started down the 1,000-foot grade from the center of the span, quickly realized the danger and shouted to the passengers to huddle in the rear. Many were in front of the turnstile and they frantically hurdled the barrier and climbed over one another in their haste to obey.

Mann stayed by his controls, trying to get the brake system working. When he realized it was futile, he appealed to men near him to help turn the crank-driven hand-brake, a slow process. Before it could be wound up, the trolley, gathering speed, rounded the turn, 200 feet from Park Row, and smashed into the supporting power pole.

The wooden framework sprawled grotesquely across the tracks, its turnstiles ripped from the floor, every pane of glass broken and seats torn from the bolts. Even the roof was shattered. The metal undercarriage stood firm.

The motorman's chant of "get

Continued on Page 12, Column 3

WHERE THE HISTORIC CROSSING WAS MADE OVER THE RHINE

The Ludendorff Bridge at Remagen that was captured intact by the Ninth Armored Division of the First Army. This picture was taken from the east bank of the river on Thursday, the day after the span was seized.

The New York Times (U. S. Signal Corps Radiotelephoto)

REINS IN INDO-CHINA WRESTED BY JAPAN

French Disarmed, Key Points Seized—U. S. Operates Air Base There, Tokyo Says

By The Associated Press.

LONDON, Saturday, March 10—The Japanese wiped out the last vestige of French control over the puppet state of Indo-China early today, taking over full administration of the land after charging that French officers had tried secretly to join hands with the Allies.

Moving swiftly, the Japanese Army seized all key installations and facilities from the "resisting" French and announced that they

Continued on Page 6, Column 6

Bridge Over Rhine Seized With 10 Minutes to Spare

By GLADWIN HILL

By Wireless to The New York Times.

AT THE RHINE BRIDGEHEAD, March 9—Details of the American capture of the Ludendorff railroad bridge across the Rhine at Remagen revealed today that the Americans had seized the bridge just before the Germans had planned to blow it up.

[The Associated Press said they had just ten minutes to spare.]

As the Americans reached Remagen Wednesday afternoon German prisoners told them the Germans had ordered the bridge destroyed at 4 P. M. They raced for the structure.

As the Americans approached, a German demolition worker in a tower at the west end of the bridge pulled a switch and ran across to the east bank. Some damage was caused, but before the remainder of the charges could be set off the

Continued on Page 3, Column 5

GERMAN COLLAPSE IN BONN AREA SEEN

Divisional Chief and 3,200 Men Among Prisoners Captured in Third Army's Sweep

By GENE CURRIVAN

By Wireless to The New York Times.

WITH THE UNITED STATES THIRD ARMY in Germany, March 9—The United States Third and First Armies joined forces on the Rhine tonight, giving the Americans virtually a forty-six-mile front on the last great natural barrier between them and Berlin. There are still pockets of resistance along this line, especially in the area just above Coblenz, but for all practical purposes the west side of the river from Cologne to the area just above Coblenz is in American hands.

The junction was made in the vicinity of Andernach and Brohl, two Rhine cities captured by the Eleventh Armored Division of the Third Army after it had paralleled the Fourth Armored Division spearhead across Germany on the north. Meanwhile, Third Army infantry fanned out below them, cleaning out pockets and consolidating the advances.

These multi-direction thrusts have made imminent the military collapse of the enemy north of the Moselle.

In the area above the Moselle, in a seventy-mile stretch between Trier and Coblenz, a narrow, unhealthy corridor has been formed and it is from here that the Germans are now withdrawing back

Continued on Page 3, Column 3

RUSSIANS 10 MILES FROM DANZIG PORT

Foe Intimates Soviet Force Has Entered Kuestrin—Stettin Outposts on Oder Fall

By The United Press.

LONDON, Saturday, March 10—Red Army troops have driven to the outskirts of both Stettin and Danzig, Moscow dispatches said last night, and a German report implied that the key Oder fortress of Kuestrin, thirty-eight miles east of Berlin, had fallen.

Advancing as much as eighteen miles, the Russians pushed the eastern flank of their 165-mile long Baltic front to within ten miles west of Danzig, capturing Przyjazd, and to the west compressed a siege arc on Stettin and its harbor.

Three armored columns, followed by motorized infantry, were converging in Danzig's suburbs from west, east and south, unofficial Moscow reports said. A Soviet army of twenty-five rifle divisions, four tank corps and a cavalry

Continued on Page 5, Column 4

War News Summarized

SATURDAY, MARCH 10, 1945

Both banks of the Rhine quivered under the impact of Allied blows yesterday as our forces sought to pry open the door to the interior of Germany.

The American First and Third Armies trapped five or six German divisions as they joined forces west of the river barrier between Coblenz and Remagen, while other American forces threw back a German counter-attack against their bridgehead on the east bank opposite Remagen. Meanwhile, reinforcements and supplies were pouring across the 1,300-foot Remagen bridge, captured intact in a daring maneuver, to strengthen and expand the bridgehead, which reports indicated was ten miles wide and five deep.

Capture of the university city of Bonn was completed and at the northern end of the front enemy troops still holding out on the Rhine's west bank near Wesel were being pushed slowly toward the river in hard fighting. [All the foregoing, 1:8; maps Pages 2 and 3.]

The capture of the Remagen Bridge, one of the war's great exploits, was made only ten minutes before it was to have been blown up. [1:5-6.]

A new American Army, the Fifteenth, commanded by Lieut. Gen. Leonard T. Gerow, has been added to General Bradley's forces, which means that more than 1,000,000 Americans under that veteran leader are now ready to add to the Germans' woes. [4:6-7.]

More than 1,000 American heavy bombers backed up the ground forces in smashing attacks on German industrial and communication centers, particularly facilities through which the Germans must transport vital raw materials from the Ruhr. [4:1.]

The Red Army punched out new gains as it drew closer to both Stettin and Danzig, after rolling up huge areas of Pomerania and former Polish territory. Moscow maintained silence on operations before Berlin, but enemy reports intimated that the Oder fortress of Kuestrin, thirty-eight miles east of the German capital had fallen. [1:6; map P. 5.]

In the war against Japan more than 300 Superfortresses carried out the greatest attack against Tokyo by dropping more than 1,000 tons of bombs on a ten-square-mile area near the center of the enemy capital, starting huge fires in the world's third largest city. [1:3; map P. 6.]

The bitter battle on Iwo continued, with the American marines grimly advancing yard by yard against the small northern end of the battle-scarred island still remaining in enemy hands. [7:1.] General MacArthur announced that our troops in the Philippines had broken into the enemy Shimbu defense line east of Manila, but he said nothing about a Japanese report that we handed Thursday on Mindanao. [8:2.]

In Burma, Indian troops pushed deeper into Mandalay after seizing a strategic hill in that storied metropolis. [7:5.]

Japan announced that she had imposed complete military control over Indo-China. [1:4.]

V-E Day Will Bring the Return Of Troops for Redeployment

Special to The New York Times.

WASHINGTON, March 9—A "big load" of soldiers, now fighting in Europe, will return to this country after V-E day before redeployment to the Far East, while others will be shipped directly to the Orient, Lieut. Gen. Brehon Somervell stated tonight.

"The redeployment problem is by all odds the most difficult the War Department has had to face," the commander of the Army service forces asserted in a nation-wide radio speech marking the third anniversary of the service and supply branch of the Army.

He stated that ASF had closed about one-fourth of the capacity of Army posts in the United States and was holding them in readiness for troops who would return from Europe, either for discharge or redeployment to the Pacific.

Addressing himself to the men and women of the organization, he said:

"Our job will be larger, not smaller, after V-E day. We will rejoice when Hitler is defeated, but it will be too early for celebration or relaxation."

Emphasizing some of the other difficulties, he pointed out that occupation troops in Germany must be supplied; that "millions of tons" of supplies and equipment must be divided between needs of the occupation troops and needs of the Pacific war; that new staging areas and port facilities must be provided, and that camps must be reopened and equipped for training of men for the Far Eastern war.

The war itself "will be hard and it may be long," General Somer-

Continued on Page 3, Column 4

U. S. COLUMNS JOIN

Clear Rhine West Bank From Cologne South to Coblenz Area

FOE SHELLS BRIDGE

9th Army Guns Pound Essen Area—15th Army Now on West Front

By DREW MIDDLETON

By Wireless to The New York Times.

PARIS, March 9—A series of lightning moves by the United States First and Third Armies of Lieut. Gen. Omar N. Bradley's Twelfth Army Group insured the destruction of five or six divisions of the German Seventh Army west of the Rhine while other units of the First Army extended and expanded their bridgeheads over the river.

Forces from the two American armies linked up on the Rhine between Remagen and Coblenz, trapping the German divisions to the west.

Today was one of unbroken success all along the Allies' long front. The First Infantry Division of the United States First Army completed the capture of Bonn, twelve and a quarter miles north of the First Army's bridgehead across the Rhine at Remagen.

German Attack Smashed

The Ninth Armored Division, which made the original crossing of the Rhine, repulsed a German armored counter-attack against the bridgehead today, sending the enemy reeling back with heavy losses. Reinforcements and supplies were pouring across the 1,300-foot, three-span Ludendorff bridge at Remagen as the bridgehead was being steadily expanded and strengthened.

[An Associated Press dispatch from that front early Saturday said the Germans were shelling the bridge while German columns were converging on the area. The United Press said jet-planes also were attacking the bridge.

[An earlier dispatch from the front Friday said German columns had been sighted by fliers moving toward the bridgehead area.]

According to a dispatch from the front, Erpel, near the eastern end of the Remagen Bridge, has been captured by First Army forces. One report said the bridgehead had been expanded to a depth of five miles and a width of ten miles. The German radio said tonight that Amer-

Continued on Page 2, Column 3

Young Ohio Butcher First Across Rhine

By The Associated Press.

ON THE RHINE BRIDGEHEAD, March 9—A gangling, embarrassed young butcher from Holland, Ohio, received the praise today of his commanding general for having led the heroic charge across Remagen Bridge and completed the capture of the span that gave the United States First Army the first Allied bridgehead across the Rhine.

A careful check disclosed that Sgt. Alexander A. Drabik actually was the first American to step on the east bank of the Rhine. And behind him came ten riflemen, shooting as they ran, in a wild dash that surprised the Germans before they could blow up this vital link, which right now is perhaps the most valuable bridge in the world.

This takes none of the glory from Lieut. Emmet Burrows, Jersey City officer, whose platoon was in the fight also and helped capture Remagen Bridge.

Maj. Gen. William M. Hoge of Lexington, Mo., praised Drabik's heroism as the greatest single factor in establishing the bridgehead and singled him out as the man who deserved the most individual credit.

"All the News That's Fit to Print"

The New York Times.

LATE CITY EDITION
Fair and warm today. Cloudy and warm tomorrow.
Temperatures Yesterday—Max., 50; Min., 34
Sunrise today, 6:54 A. M.; Sunset, 7:12 P. M.

VOL. XCIV..No. 31,836. Entered as Second-Class Matter, Postoffice, New York, N. Y. NEW YORK, SATURDAY, MARCH 24, 1945. THREE CENTS NEW YORK CITY

PATTON CROSSES RHINE IN A DARING DRIVE WITHOUT BARRAGE, EXPANDS BRIDGEHEAD; NAZIS SAY RUSSIANS ARE MOVING ON BERLIN

SENATE, BY 52 TO 36, REJECTS WILLIAMS AS DIRECTOR OF REA

Nineteen Democrats Join With 33 Republicans to Defeat the Former Chief of NYA

HE DENOUNCES HIS FOES

And Declares With Patton of Farmers Union That Issue Is Whether People Shall Rule

By WILLIAM S. WHITE
Special to THE NEW YORK TIMES.

WASHINGTON, March 23—The Senate rejected today, 52 to 36, President Roosevelt's nomination of Aubrey Williams to be Rural Electrification Administrator. The adverse vote came through a coalition of Republicans and Conservative Democrats. Most of the latter came from the South, and some of them had been termed "Tories" by the nominee.

Nineteen Democrats joined thirty-three Republicans in voting to deny confirmation to Mr. Williams, the first such denial of an important executive appointment since 1939. Thirty-one Democrats, four Republicans and the Senate's single member of the Progressive party, LaFollette of Wisconsin, voted for the nomination.

Immediately after the Senate vote, the National Farmers Union, of which Mr. Williams has been national director of organization, vowed political vengeance on his opponents, and said that Mrs. Franklin D. Roosevelt would address a "Victory Dinner" for Mr. Williams Wednesday night that would begin "a total war of issues."

The Southern Democrats who opposed Mr. Williams were principally those whose views on economics are radically opposed to the New Dealism of Mr. Williams.

Barkley Upholds Nominee

A last minute speaker for Mr. Williams was Senator Barkley of Kentucky, the majority leader.

"The record shows," he said, "that Williams was not connected with communism, but that he combated communism."

Mr. Williams asserted that he had been rejected by "those who stand for control by the few, fearing an economy in which everybody would share."

Then, in a joint press conference at the headquarters of the Farmers Union, both he and James G. Patton, president of the National Farmers Union, indicated that the Senate's action would be used as the starting point of an intensive national organizing and political campaign by the union to be concentrated in the Deep South.

"We'll be seeing some of those Senators out where the people live," Mr. Patton declared. Remarking that the forthcoming "Victory Dinner" had been so named because the vote in the Senate "showed us how we stand," he added:

"This is the first battle in a total war of issues in this country to decide whether the country is to be conducted for the people or for the vested interests. The Farmers Union people will become much more intense in their feelings because of Mr. Williams' rejection. We are going to take whatever steps are necessary to begin to implement our feelings more drastically."

Denies Competence an Issue

Mr. Patton and Mr. Williams have been associated, as individuals, with the CIO's Political Action Committee, although the Farmers Union as an official entity has not been so connected. What the union's precise mechanism would be in its new campaign had not been determined, Mr. Patton said, although he indicated that no consideration had been given to the question of setting up a separate political organization.

Mr. Williams declared that "such Senators" as Bushfield, Republican of South Dakota; Willis, Republican, of Indiana; McKellar, Democrat, of Tennessee; Taft, Republi-

Continued on Page 15, Column 7

Women's Jury Bill Goes to Governor

Special to THE NEW YORK TIMES.

ALBANY, March 23—With unanimous adoption by the Senate, Governor Dewey received today Assemblyman Philip Schuyler's bill making jury service for women mandatory instead of optional. The only exceptions permitted under the bill are those where a woman has children under 16 years of age or is caring for a sick or invalid person.

Enactment of the measure after several years of experience under permissive jury service follows a considerable demand from women's groups, notable among which is the League of Women Voters.

A year ago former Assemblywoman Jane H. Todd sponsored a similar bill, which passed the Assembly, but died in committee in the upper house. There has been no indication as to what Governor Dewey's views are with regard to the proposal.

RISE OF $14,000,000 IN SCHOOL AID VOTED

Legislature Moves to Adjourn Today—Assembly Passes Merit Rating Truce

By LEO EGAN
Special to THE NEW YORK TIMES.

ALBANY, March 23—By unanimous vote in both houses, the Legislature passed and sent to Governor Dewey today a bill revising the apportionment of State aid for education to increase the total by about $14,000,000 over that provided by existing law and $18,000,000 over that required by the old formula.

The Assembly rejected, 66 to 78, the Young-Demo merit rating bill after a debate lasting almost five hours and then passed unanimously the "harmonizing" merit rating proposal, which had the endorsement of Governor Dewey, the Ives Committee on Labor and Industrial Conditions, the AFL and the CIO.

A majority of the Assembly Republicans favored the Young-Demo bill and threatened for a time to revolt against their leaders, who, along with Governor Dewey, opposed it.

Bowing to Labor Charged

In private conversation and, according to some reports, at a closed party conference, the Young-Demo backers accused the leadership of bowing to organized labor. There was a great deal of private bitterness over the action of Irving M. Ives, the majority leader, and Oswald D. Heck, the Speaker, in persuading a number of Republicans favoring the Young-Demo plan to switch to the "harmonizing" bill.

The "harmonizing" bill, which in most essentials is identical with the last of the Falk-Gugino bills, will be taken up in the Senate tomorrow, with passage, in view of the Assembly action, regarded as certain.

By disposing of the education-aid and merit rating measures, which rank among the most impor-

Continued on Page 15, Column 2

HOUSE UNANIMOUS IN VOTE TO EXTEND DRAFT ACT A YEAR

Senate Leaders Seek Rapid Action on Measure Free of Civilian Job Issue

NO BREAK IN DEADLOCK

New Compromise to 'Freeze' Workers Is Considered by Conferees—Vote Set Today

By C. P. TRUSSELL
Special to THE NEW YORK TIMES.

WASHINGTON, March 23—The House quickly passed by unanimous vote and sent to the Senate today a bill to extend the Selective Service Act for one year beyond May 15.

On the Senate side leaders assumed that chamber also would act promptly on the bill, without the attachment of riders which would link the drafting of men for the armed services to the mobilization of manpower on the home front.

The question of a "labor draft" remained deadlocked, with Senate and House conferees seeking to find a compromise in the conflicting civilian manpower bills which the two branches have passed.

A new compromise, or trade, was proposed today and was scheduled for a vote tomorrow. It was suggested that if the House would abandon its "limited national service," or draft, provisions, the Senate would agree to impose penalties on workers as well as employers for violations of employment ceilings and other War Manpower Commission controls.

Workers Would Be "Frozen"

Under the proposed compromise there would be a "freezing" of essential war workers into their present jobs as long as they were needed.

An expected move to prohibit the sending of draftees into combat zones within five months after their induction into the Army failed to develop in the House.

The Military Affairs Committee, which reported the extension bill yesterday, was told by Maj. Gen. Idwal Edwards, Assistant Chief of Staff in charge of training, that such a restriction would be "very definitely harmful" to an orderly system of providing men for the fighting fronts.

While the House was acting with unanimity, conferees on the manpower bills spent hours this afternoon studying the compromise offered by Senator Austin, Republican, of Vermont, and the amendments to it which have been presented by Representative May, Democrat, of Kentucky.

As a recess was taken, the conferees had before them a proposal for the newer compromise. Concededly, it was not certain that the Senate conferees would be willing to apply penalties to employes when WMC regulations were violated, even though the House conferees should agree to abandon all "labor draft" concepts.

Among Senate conferees there

Continued on Page 14, Column 3

THE RHINE IS BRIDGED AND OUR MATERIEL ROLLS ACROSS

A strong span is stretched on pontoons, over which heavy trucks are carrying supplies to our forces on the east bank
The New York Times (U. S. Signal Corps)

ODER BRIDGEHEADS REPORTED MERGED

Foe Puts Red Army 6 Miles Past Kuestrin—Danzig and Gdynia Split—Push in South Gains

By The Associated Press.

LONDON, Saturday, March 24—Berlin said last night that the Red Army had reopened a blazing battle for the imperiled German capital, while Moscow announced that Russian forces had split the defenders of the prize Baltic ports of Danzig and Gdynia.

Waves of Russian infantry and tanks were reported by the enemy to have broken through defenses along Berlin's Oder River line and to have swept six miles beyond captured Kuestrin to within thirty-one miles east of the capital. [German reports cited by The United Press said that two Oder bridgeheads had been linked.

Continued on Page 7, Column 2

New Rhine Bridgehead Won Without Loss of Single Man

By EDWARD D. BALL
Associated Press Correspondent.

WITH THE UNITED STATES THIRD ARMY east of the Rhine, March 23—The United States Third Army stormed across the Rhine at 10:25 o'clock last night without loss of a man and without drawing a single shot from the Germans until a good twenty minutes after the crossing was made good.

By dawn today a solid bridgehead had been driven into Hitler's inner fortress against opposition that still was spotty and erratic despite some artillery and mortar fire.

Most of the enemy weapons were soon silenced.

By dawn many infantry units had gone across, and by that time the first waves of doughboys had pushed inland.

There was a minimum of noise and confusion at the bridgehead, where droves of assault boats were speeding back and forth with men and supplies.

Within eight hours Lieut. Gen.

Continued on Page 4, Column 4

AIR FLEETS FLATTEN NAZIS AROUND RUHR

U. S. 'Heavies' Strike at 12 Rail Yards, RAF Hits Bridges and Enemy Troops

By SYDNEY GRUSON
By Wireless to THE NEW YORK TIMES.

LONDON, Saturday, March 24—Allied airmen poured more thousands of tons of bombs on the Germans east of the Rhine, especially in the Ruhr area, yesterday, in the third successive day of record operations to flatten everything in the path of the American and British Armies massing for a crossing of the Rhine on the northern sector of the Western Front.

Last night, as the Ruhr's industrial towns and the great plain leading to north Germany blazed from countless fires set by thousands of heavy, medium and light bombers, more blows were struck in the aerial softening-up.

[A powerful fleet of British heavy bombers battered German troops and positions on the east bank of the Rhine during the night, London officials announced early Saturday, The Associated Press said. British planes also bombed Berlin for the thirty-second straight night.]

More than 1,250 Flying Fortresses and Liberators of the United States Eighth Air Force and three fleets of Lancasters and Halifaxes of the Royal Air Force, all of them escorted by fighters, flew by daylight through towering clouds of smoke rising from the ashes of dead cities.

In weather so clear the heavy bombers' targets could be picked up by naked eye from five miles up, the American and British crews pounded rail yards and

Continued on Page 5, Column 2

U. S. CARRIER LOST IN BATTLE OFF IWO

Bismarck Sea, Escort Craft, Is Victim of Air Blow — Fleet Strike in Ryukyus Reported

By The Associated Press.

GUAM, Saturday, March 24—Loss of the U. S. S. Bismarck Sea, an escort aircraft carrier, to enemy aerial attack off Iwo Island on Feb. 21 was announced by Admiral Chester W. Nimitz today. Most of the Bismarck Sea's company was rescued, he stated. The normal complement of an escort carrier is about 1,500 officers and men.

[Delayed dispatches from the fleet off Iwo said there were more than 300 casualties among the crew of the Bismarck Sea, including 100 who, struggling in the water, were strafed and killed by Japanese fliers.]

[The Tokyo radio said early Saturday that American carrier aircraft, which earlier in the week ravaged Japanese air and naval strength in the home islands, made attacks Friday and Saturday (today) on Okinawa Island, Japanese air and naval base in the Ryukyu group, mid-

Continued on Page 10, Column 2

War News Summarized

SATURDAY, MARCH 24, 1945

The American Third Army has stormed across the Rhine in large force and established a firm bridgehead, the second one now held by our troops. The new crossing was made at 10:25 P. M. Thursday and the bridgehead has been expanded since then. Its site was not officially disclosed, but the Germans said it was near Frankenthal, four and a half miles north of Ludwigshafen.

The mighty German armies once deployed west of the Rhine have been either destroyed or driven to the east bank almost in their entirety. American tanks crashed into Speyer, one of the last enemy strongholds west of the Rhine, while the enemy bridgehead in the Palatinate was compressed further to an area about fifteen miles from east to west with a base of less than twenty miles along the river. Tremendous aerial blows on German communications north of the Ruhr may be part of preparations for a new offensive by Marshal Montgomery. [All the foregoing 1:8; map, P. 2.]

Thousands of Allied bombers again struck in support of the ground forces, seeking to pulverize enemy installations east of the Rhine and soften the foe's power and will to resist. Countless fires were started in the industrial areas of the Ruhr as our flying artillery pounded marshaling yards. [1:7]

The Red Army has renewed its drive on Berlin after breaking through German defenses along the Oder River line, the enemy reported. The Nazis also said the Russians had smashed six miles beyond Kuestrin to within thirty-one miles of the capital, reaching Golzow on the main Kuestrin-Berlin railroad. Soviet troops on the Baltic split the enemy before Danzig and Gdynia by knifing to the Bay of Danzig midway between the two ports. [1:4; map P. 7.]

An American escort carrier, the Bismarck Sea, was lost to enemy action off Iwo Feb. 21, the Navy announced. Another naval bulletin revealed that our carrier planes had caused extensive damage at seven Japanese ports and bases on Kyushu Island during the attack by Fifth Fleet forces early this week. Further details also put at 731 the number of enemy planes destroyed or damaged. [1:6; map P. 10.] The B-29 attack on Tokyo March 9 knocked out 20 per cent of the city's productive facilities for at least three months and the punishment given the Japanese in the five recent aerial assaults against their industrial cities probably was the most severe suffered by any people in a similar period, it was emphasized by General Norstad. [9:4.]

In the Philippines American forces took Naguilian and its airfield, twelve miles northwest of Baguio, on Luzon. [10:6.]

The Japanese opened a new offensive northwest of Hankow in central China with 60,000 troops. The drive apparently had the twin aims of capturing several Allied airfields in its path and seizing the wheat crop. [9:2; with map.] The British, striking out south of Mandalay in Burma, continued to cut up the foe. [9:5.]

3D WINS FIRM HOLD

Spans the River at Night Above Ludwigshafen, Catches Foe Asleep

1ST SPEEDS UP PUSH

Palatinate Escape Gap Cut Again—Thousands More Captured

By DREW MIDDLETON
By Wireless to THE NEW YORK TIMES.

PARIS, March 23—Troops of Lieut. Gen. George S. Patton's United States Third Army have established a bridgehead over the Rhine in a bold, skillful assault.

The river was crossed at 10:25 o'clock Thursday night. The bridgehead established at that time has been steadily expanded since. [Press services said the crossing was virtually unopposed for two hours.]

The Twelfth Army Group, whose announcement was released here tonight, did not locate the bridgehead, but the German radio said that it was east of Frankenthal, four and a half miles north of the northern outskirts of Ludwigshafen.

[Earlier German broadcasts said that Third Army troops had crossed the Rhine at Oppenheim, ten miles south of Mainz, and that other American troops had attempted crossings at Duesseldorf and six miles south of Cologne, The Associated Press reported. The Germans said the crossings at Duesseldorf and in the Cologne area had been repulsed.]

Crossing Is Bold Stroke

At his headquarters, Lieut. Gen. Omar N. Bradley, Twelfth Army Group Commander, said that the Allies were in a position to cross the Rhine virtually "anywhere at any time."

The Third Army's crossing of the Rhine was an operation as daring as the character of its commander. General Patton hurled his troops across the river without preparation by artillery or air force in a surprise move that evidently caught the enemy asleep.

Since that time his troops have been striking out from the bridgehead and expanding it.

A great east-west highway runs through Frankenthal. There was a bridge under construction there in May, 1944. No recent information concerning the bridge is available here.

Frankenthal, where the Germans said the crossing was made, is six miles northwest of Mannheim on the east bank of the Rhine opposite Ludwigshafen. If the crossing was made in this area, as the enemy claimed, then General Patton has placed his troops in a fine position to attack Mannheim from the north or east. Frankenthal also is twenty-five miles southwest of the industrial city of Darmstadt.

Germans Nearly Wiped Out

Meanwhile Gen. Dwight D. Eisenhower's order to destroy the German armies west of the Rhine is almost fulfilled.

Tanks of General Patton's Third Army rumbled into Speyer, one of the last German strongholds west of the Rhine, today, while a series of savage blows by armored and infantry divisions of the Third Army and Lieut. Gen. Alexander M. Patch's Seventh Army hammered down the enemy bridgehead in the Palatinate to a rough triangle fifteen miles from east to west with a base of less than twenty miles along the west bank of the Rhine.

The tremendous aerial assault on the German Army's defense depots and communications in the area north of the Ruhr and west of the Rhine opposite the front of Field Marshal Sir Bernard L. Montgomery's Twenty-first Army group was maintained from early morning today.

Nothing more than routine pa-

Continued on Page 3, Column 2

Moses Threatens to Resign in Row Over 'Talk Out of Mayor's Office'

Park Commissioner Robert Moses, for years one of Mayor La Guardia's stanchest political and administrative supporters, told the Board of Estimate yesterday that he keenly resented "talk right out of the Mayor's office" insinuating that he favored a tree-removal appropriation of $145,000 because he "had to take care of favored contractors."

Commissioner Moses appeared at an adjourned meeting of the Board of Estimate to speak in support of a recommendation by Borough President James A. Burke of Queens that $145,000 be appropriated to make possible the removal, by a private contractor, of the 5,330 trees blown down by the hurricane last September and still cluttering city streets in Queens and Brooklyn. The hurricane left 16,730 trees to be removed from the streets. Of these 7,933 have been removed by contract and 3,467 by departmental forces of the Park Department, cooperating with employes of the Department of Sanitation and the offices of the borough presidents.

Discussion of the Burke proposal provoked a heated argument between Commissioner Moses and Deputy Mayor Rufus E. McGahen, who insisted that the proposal be referred to Budget Director Thomas J. Patterson for a report in accordance with routine procedure. Before the argument ended Commissioner Moses, pale with anger, indicated his willingness to

Continued on Page 15, Column 5

Germans Speed Arms to Mountains As Allies Map Their Destruction

By Wireless to THE NEW YORK TIMES.

PARIS, March 23—The Germans are speeding work on a great national redoubt, a defensive position based on the mountains of the southern Reich, where SS divisions, some regular soldiers and Nazi party officials hope to continue the war after the German field armies have been destroyed.

A reliable source who recently returned from Switzerland said the work on the redoubt has been rushed since the last Russian offensive and the Anglo-American victories west of the Rhine and that, according to neutrals who lately had been in the Reich, the Germans also were constructing another redoubt on the Kiel Canal in the north.

The Swiss, he said, are extremely worried, since the preparation of the redoubt in the south foreshadows heavy fighting near their borders by Russian as well as American and British armies.

According to this source a nobleman, who must remain unidentified, recently drove from his domain to Vienna and back. Both trips were exceedingly difficult because the Germans had closed many of the roads leading into the redoubt and he had to detour around the position. He reported that the Germans were pouring many hundreds of tons of supplies of all kinds into the redoubt.

The exact limits of the position where the Germans hope to retire

Continued on Page 3, Column 1

"All the News That's Fit to Print"

The New York Times.

LATE CITY EDITION

Fair and warmer today. Partly cloudy, continued mild tomorrow.

Temperatures Yesterday—Max.,57; Min.,41

Sunrise today, 6:29 A. M.; Sunset, 7:28 P. M.

Section 1

NEWS INDEX, PAGE 37, THIS SECTION

VOL. XCIV..No. 31,851. Entered as Second-Class Matter, Postoffice, New York, N. Y. NEW YORK, SUNDAY, APRIL 8, 1945. Including Magazine and Book Sections. TEN CENTS New York City and Suburban Areas (15c Elsewhere)

U. S. FLIERS SINK JAPAN'S BIGGEST WARSHIP; BRITISH NEAR BREMEN; HANOVER FLANKED; PATTON SEIZES NAZI HOARD OF GOLD AND ART

FOUR STABILIZERS ASK FIRM CONTROL BEYOND END OF WAR

Policy 'With Boldness' Is Vital to Prevent Any Runaway Inflation, They Assert

SAY 'LINE IS HELD' TO DATE

Davis, Bowles, Jones, Taylor Summarize Their Work in Report to Roosevelt

The report on price and wage control is on Page 34.

Special to THE NEW YORK TIMES.

WASHINGTON, April 7—A call for continuance of price and wage controls during the transitional period after the war to provide stabilization and guard against inflation was made to President Roosevelt today by the four officials who exercise primary responsibility in those fields. Their report told the Chief Executive that, to date, "essential stabilization has been achieved."

The report was made in a letter on the second anniversary of the President's "hold-the-line" order by William H. Davis, director of the Office of Economic Stabilization; Chester Bowles, administrator of the Office of Price Administration; Marvin Jones, administrator of the War Food Administration, and George W. Taylor, chairman of the National War Labor Board. It was given out for publication by the White House without comment.

Post-War Tasks Stressed

The joint communication stressed the difficulty of the tasks ahead, while expressing confidence that the American people "will be wary of those who will call for an abrupt ending of controls" and "insist that the problems of transition be attacked with boldness."

"There is still the gravest danger of a runaway price rise which would undo all that we have accomplished thus far, delay victory and cause untold personal suffering," the report warned. "But at the same time that we exert ourselves to prevent such a development we must prepare to deal with the deflationary tendencies which may appear in the transition period. To maintain stability in the face of the dangers ahead will require the full support of yourself, Mr. President; the Congress and the American people."

The report recalled that a year ago "we reported that the line had been held," and in stating that the line was still being held it said that the nation's cost-of-living index now stands "little more than 2 per cent above its level of two years ago."

A large number of items has been held absolutely steady, while some items, chiefly in the food group, have declined, the report pointed out. Although clothing prices have had a gradual unbroken rise during the past two years, it promised that new programs will stop the rise and added that "plans are under way to roll back prices on essential clothing items."

Wage Costs Called Stable

Average straight - time hourly earnings were estimated, in the report, to be 10 per cent above the level of two years ago, "largely as a result of promotions and increased production," but wage costs were pictured as having been kept relatively stable and not to have contributed to "any significant rises in the cost of living through pressures on production costs."

Stabilization too, was said also to have been effective for farm and industrial levels, with prices having increased only about 2 per cent in a period of record industrial and farm production.

The "slight increases" in the

Continued on Page 34, Column 3

309,258 Germans Seized in 2 Weeks

By The Associated Press.

PARIS, April 7—In one of the most dramatic fortnights of the war—since the Allies carried their offensive across the Rhine—the Germans have lost more than 309,258 troops in prisoners alone and roughly 18,000 square miles of territory east of that river.

The number of Germans captured since the Rhine crossing already exceeds the 250,000 captured in the three-week March mop-up west of the Rhine, which Gen. Dwight D. Eisenhower declared "one of the greatest victories of this or any other war."

The figure of 309,258 does not include the thousands catch of Army Group B pinned in the Ruhr or the other thousands of Army Group H caught in the western Netherlands.

PRESIDENT PRAISES RECONVERSION PLAN

Letter Hails Gardner for Idea of OWM Board to Stress Peacetime Abundance

Correspondence on post-war reconversion is on Page 30.

Special to THE NEW YORK TIMES.

WASHINGTON, April 7—President Roosevelt made public today an exchange of correspondence with O. Max Gardner, chairman of the War Mobilization and Reconversion Advisory Board, in which he applauded Mr. Gardner's demand for post-war full employment to be obtained "under our system of competitive free enterprise" and without "any compromise with traditional American institutions."

"America is fortunate to have such a reaffirmation of the uninterrupted tradition of an advancing America enunciated by men who represent great organizations of labor, industry and agriculture working together with others who represent the public," the President declared.

The President virtually reiterated the words of Mr. Gardner when he called for "a peacetime economy far more abundant and productive than we have ever had before." But, he added:

"Victory without the use of abundance of the powers we have developed in production for war would be, indeed, a hollow victory. We must plan security and abundance together. Such a strong American economy will be essential to carry out the responsibilities that lie in plans made at Bretton Woods, Hot Springs and Dumbarton Oaks. Similarly, abundance at home depends upon organization for order and security in the world."

In view of the board's recently expressed desire to be consulted, the following passage of Mr. Gardner's letter suggested that he might have taken this occasion to express the board's hope that the

Continued on Page 30, Column 3

VIENNA ARC WIDENS

Capital Is Three-fourths Ringed—Russians at Danube to North

ESCAPE GAP SHRINKS

Munich-Linz Trunkline Slashed—Red Army 12 Miles From Teschen

By The Associated Press.

LONDON, Sunday, April 8—Red Army tank columns, in a fourteen-mile sweep around western Vienna, three-fourths encircled the Austrian capital yesterday, leaving to the enemy garrison a twenty-four-and-a-half-mile escape gap, as other shock troops gained in a frontal assault through the city's streets.

By reaching the Danube River northwest of the city, Russian troops sliced across six of Vienna's escape routes and left the imperiled capital with only seven of an original twenty-two major railroads and highways.

Berlin reports said that the escape gap to the north already had been narrowed. Soviet cavalrymen were said to have forded the Morava River northeast of Vienna and to have established bridgeheads that threatened to close the enemy's last retreat roads.

At the same time, Berlin reported that Soviet tank spearheads had broken twenty-three miles through the Vienna Woods west of the capital.

While Moscow officially confirmed that Soviet forces had broken across Vienna's southern city limits and were battling toward its heart, Soviet troops elsewhere on the Eastern Front carved out new gains.

12 Miles from Teschen

Cleaning out southwestern Poland, the Russians moved within twelve miles of Teschen [Cieszyn], and in Czechoslovakia gained up to ten miles on an eighty-mile front. In Yugoslavia, other Russian units battered to within 100 miles of Italy at a point forty-two miles northeast of the Croatian capital of Zagreb.

As the Germans proclaimed that Vienna "will be defended to the last sewer," two Soviet armies extended the siege arc around Vienna to 112 miles on the west, south and east. Moscow reports said high German officials already were fleeing over the last crowded roads out of the city.

The greater part of the city was encircled when Marshal Fedor I. Tolbukhin's Third Ukrainian Army tankmen battered fourteen miles through the Vienna Woods in a two-day advance, sweeping through the town of Pressbaum, seven miles west of the city, to reach the Danube at Klosterneuburg, one mile from Vienna's northwestern limits.

The swift surge that isolated

Continued on Page 25, Column 1

ALLIES RACE AHEAD

British 13 Miles From Bremen While Ninth Heads for Brunswick

1ST CROSSES WESER

Third Smashes Strong German Attack—7th Gains 36 Miles

By DREW MIDDLETON

By Wireless to THE NEW YORK TIMES.

PARIS, April 7—American and British armored forces broke out from their bridgeheads east of the Weser River today and raced across the province of Hanover, while on the left flank of the advance the British Seventh Armored Division struck northward to positions that field reports say were only thirteen miles from Bremen early this afternoon.

Battered by the sledge-hammer blows of the armored columns and harried by clouds of fighter-bombers, Germany is falling apart in the north. Pilots of the Royal Air Force, flying over the front of the British Second Army today, reported no coherent resistance anywhere in the British sector.

The United States First and Third Armies in the center of the Allies' battleline were relatively inactive today according to the scanty reports available here. [Press service reports from the front, however, said the Third Army had smashed a heavy German counter-attack northwest of Muelhausen and had destroyed forty German tanks.]

[Other press service reports said the First Army had crossed the Weser River at numerous points and was now engaged in a raging battle with German troops held in their battle positions by officers with pistols.

[A United Press dispatch from the Seventh Army front late Saturday declared that the Tenth Armored Division had broken through for a thirty-six-mile gain and had captured the town of Crailsheim, ninety-four miles northwest of Munich and forty-

Continued on Page 12, Column 1

JAPANESE FLEET REMNANTS BATTERED ANEW

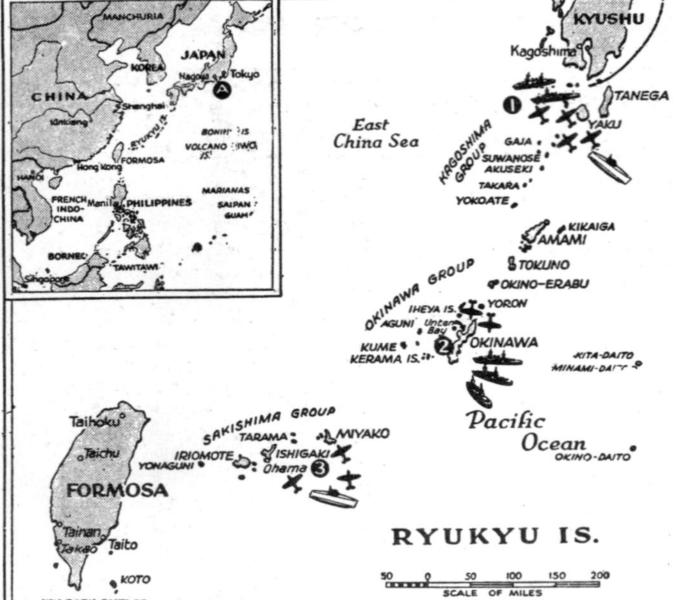

An enemy flotilla that had steamed around the southern tip of Kyushu into the East China Sea was caught fifty miles southwest of that Japanese home island (1) by our carrier planes, which sank the foe's most powerful battleship, two cruisers and three destroyers. Previously 116 enemy aircraft had been downed in an attack on our invasion flotilla off Okinawa (2). A British carrier force smashed airfields and other targets on Miyako and Ishigaki in the Sakishima group (3). It was disclosed that plane plants in Tokyo and Nagoya (A on inset) had been hit by more than 300 Superfortresses escorted by Mustang fighters from our new airfields on Iwo Island.

VICTORY IN PACIFIC

Carrier Planes Sink the Battleship Yamato and 5 Other Warships

BATTLE OFF KYUSHU

Foe Loses 417 Planes, Bulk of Them in Blow at Fleet Off Okinawa

By BRUCE RAE

By Wireless to THE NEW YORK TIMES.

GUAM, Sunday, April 8—The United States Fifth Fleet, after shattering an all-out Japanese aerial attack off Okinawa, on Friday (East Longitude time) launched a counter-offensive in the sky Saturday and delivered a smashing blow to the remnants of the Imperial Navy—sinking six warships, including the most powerful remaining unit, the battleship Yamato. The sinkings were in the East China Sea about fifty miles southwest of Kyushu, southernmost island of the Japanese homeland.

[In Washington an official Navy spokesman said "a good 25 per cent of the remaining Japanese major combat force" was lost or put out of action in the engagement.]

Admiral Chester W. Nimitz announced the victories last night as the Navy clocks neared midnight and this morning he supplemented his statement.

Four hundred and seventeen Japanese planes were shot down, most of them in the Okinawa area of the Ryukyus during the Japanese aerial assault, which was resumed in a minor way Saturday and again crushed.

Score of Two-Day Battle

The score:

Japanese ship losses—ships sunk, one battleship, the Yamato, 45,000 tonner; one light cruiser of the Agano class, about 5,000 tons; one smaller light cruiser or large destroyer and three destroyers. In addition, three Japanese destroyers were left burning. About three enemy destroyers escaped. Further, four small cargo ships and many smaller craft were sunk off the Ryukyus.

United States ship losses—three destroyers sunk in the Japanese air attack. One heavy unit and several destroyers and smaller craft were damaged by the Japanese planes. The heavy unit, presumably a battleship or carrier, remained in operation. Seven United States aircraft were lost in the carrier plane attack on the Yamato and other enemy warships.

Early Saturday morning search aircraft of Fleet Air Wing One cruising on the watch for enemy planes or ships sighted a large group of Japanese ships. The enemy fleet was moving southward from Kyushu, presumably making an effort to reach sorely pressed Okinawa. The enemy ships had steamed out of the quiet, sunlit waters of the Inland Sea and had turned into the reaches of the East China Sea.

Task Force Gets the Word

The search planes flashed the discovery over the intervening miles back to the fast task force of Vice Admiral Marc A. Mitscher. The task force, as usual, was prowling around hopefully, hoping that an honest-to-goodness Japanese warship or two would turn up. The word that went to the delighted vice admiral, his staff and his boat loads of eager fliers was that the Yamato, the Agano class cruiser and the other warships were within reach.

Admiral Mitscher's men and his ships went into high gear. The sea foamed from the bows of the fast carriers, and the engine rooms hummed. At high speed the task force went for the enemy, and as noon drew near put the enemy under air attack.

Plane after plane from carrier

Continued on Page 3, Column 2

100 Tons of Gold and Cash Found in German Salt Mine

By The United Press.

WITH THE NINETIETH INFANTRY DIVISION, Merkers, Germany April 7—American soldiers found a vast treasure trove, said to include the entire German gold reserve, in a salt mine today. Dr. Fritz Vieck, a Reichsbank official, was on guard. He said that the subterranean vaults contained approximately 100 tons of gold bullion; $2,000,000 in American currency, 1,000,000 francs in French currency, £110,000 in British currency, 4,000,000 Norwegian crowns and lesser amounts in other currencies. The salt mine also sheltered

Continued on Page 16, Column 3

ALLIES ERASE ARMY OF 50,000 IN BURMA

Enemy in Mandalay-Meiktila Pocket Crushed—5,000 of Foe Killed in China Battle

By The Associated Press.

CALCUTTA, India, April 7—The shattered Japanese Fifteenth Army in central Burma, officially estimated three weeks ago at 50,000 men, "no longer exists as an effective fighting force," a Southeast Asia communiqué announced today. A headquarters spokesman said that two other enemy armies, the Thirty-third and Twenty-eighth, had been badly mauled in attempts to rush relief.

"There are no organized Japanese forces" left inside the Mandalay-Meiktila pocket, the announcement said.

The communiqué, stating that

Continued on Page 9, Column 1

TWIN B-29 ATTACKS BLAST 173 PLANES

'Superforts' Have Their Biggest Fight in Escorted Blow at Tokyo and Nagoya Plants

By Wireless to THE NEW YORK TIMES.

GUAM, Sunday, April 8—The deadly Superfortresses have written another bad chapter for the Japanese—this time with the aid of Mustang escorting fighters, it was made known today by the Twenty-First Bomber Command. It was the first time the B-29's had fighter protection on the long jaunt to Japan.

[On Sunday, Japanese time, a "substantial force" of B-29's from the Marianas hit Japan again, bombing military targets in the Kanoya area on the southern tip of Kyushu Island, Twentieth Air Force headquarters reported.]

The twin attack yesterday was directed at the Mitsubishi engine plant at Nagoya and at the Musashino-Nakajima factory in the suburbs of Tokyo. Both targets were hit squarely by 500-pound demolition bombs. The Superfortresses shot down or damaged 136 Japanese planes, while the Mustangs accounted for thirty-seven, for a total of 173.

Another "first" on the double attack was the fact that it led to

Continued on Page 5, Column 5

War News Summarized

SUNDAY, APRIL 8, 1945

An important segment of the Japanese Fleet ventured out of hiding and quickly regretted its boldness. The American Fifth Fleet, waiting for just such a move, sent carrier planes against the enemy force, sinking six Japanese warships, including the 45,000-ton battleship Yamato, two light cruisers and three destroyers, in an action fifty miles southwest of Kyushu. We lost seven planes. Three of our destroyers were sunk by enemy planes off Okinawa but we destroyed 417 Japanese aircraft.

In the ground fighting on Okinawa our Marines continued to push forward to the north with little resistance to reach the vicinity of Nago on the west coast and Ora Bay on the east coast. The drive to the south toward Naha, the capital, faced stubborn opposition from the enemy entrenched in strongly prepared positions. [All the foregoing, 1:8, maps P. 1 and 4.]

A Navy spokesman in Washington said the sea action had put one-fourth of the Japanese Navy's remaining major combat force out of action, leaving only such enemy strength as "could be handled easily." [3:1.]

A shake-up of the military and air commands accompanied the formation of a new Japanese Cabinet headed by Baron Suzuki. The 77-year-old Premier, who took office in the presence of Emperor Hirohito, told his countrymen that the war had reached a "crucial state" and that "the very basis of our Empire's existence" was threatened. [6:1.]

At least 173 Japanese planes were destroyed or damaged by 300 Superfortresses and Iwo-based fighter escorts that attacked plane plants in Tokyo and Nagoya. B-29's bombed Japan again today. [1:7.]

In Burma, too, the Japanese were suffering reverses. The Japanese Fifteenth Army, estimated to number 50,000, has been destroyed. [1:6.]

American troops in the Philippines made new gains. Netherlands Indies fliers struck a Japanese cruiser. [7:3.]

German armies on the northern end of the Western Front were disintegrating as Allied forces smashed from bridgeheads east of the Weser toward Hanover. British troops were only thirteen miles from Bremen. However, the enemy force of 100,000 or more encircled in the Ruhr pocket offered bitter resistance. [1:4; map P. 12.]

The United States Third Army seized a gold cache valued at more than $100,000,000 in a hidden salt mine 140 miles southeast of Berlin. [1:5-6.]

At least eighty-seven of a fleet of German planes that sought to intercept a force of 1,300 American heavy bombers and 850 fighters, which hit in the Kiel-Hamburg-Bremen area, were shot down in a big air battle. Our losses were twenty-two bombers and three fighters. [15:1.]

The Red Army swept around western Vienna and had more than two-thirds of the Austrian capital encircled. Soviet shock troops drew closer to the heart of the city. [1:3; map P. 25.]

In Italy, the American Fifth Army captured Mount Fragolito in its drive along the west coast toward La Spezia. [27:5.]

Patton's Contempt of German Army Deals Hard Blow to Enemy Morale

By GENE CURRIVAN

By Wireless to THE NEW YORK TIMES.

WITH THE UNITED STATES THIRD ARMY, in Germany, April 7—Most German commanders would rather fight almost anywhere than in front of Lieut. Gen. George S. Patton Jr. He not only worries them to death with his unorthodox moves but has now added a contemptuousness that must reduce to a minimum any remaining German morale.

When General Patton's armored columns take off in the morning on one of their now-familiar spearheading drives they seldom slow up before sundown. When cities or towns in their path become too rough they merely by-pass them and leave the enemy garrison wondering what is coming next. General Patton's armor moves out in two columns, flanking the city and keeps going while infantry following in its wake takes over the task of capturing the city. Tanks and narrow crowded streets are not militarily compatible anyway and this type of battle against a dug-in garrison is infantry work, although armored units have often tackled it successfully. This by-passing procedure is sound tactically but the added element of contempt gives that little discouraging feature that doesn't exactly bolster the enemy's spirit.

The same applies in the bridging operations, where, after the first few days of hell, the military supply train runs bumper to bumper

Continued on Page 13, Column 6

Army Day Parade Minus the Army Is Cheered by 200,000 in 5th Ave.

Under perfect spring skies, New York paid a colorful and dramatic tribute yesterday to the nation's Army, as 18,000 men, women and children marched down Fifth Avenue in the eighteenth annual observance of Army Day.

From the green-brown uniform of close-stepping marines to the gay colors of drum majors and youth organizations in gold, yellow, blue and red, the marchers presented a pageant of tribute to the men and women of the Army, a tribute which took on added dramatic quality by the absence of regular Army units in the line of march. Police estimated that between 200,000 and 250,000 spectators lined the city's traditional parade avenue from Ninetieth Street to Sixty-fourth.

Lieut. Gen. George Grunert, commanding general of the Eastern Defense Command, who reviewed the marchers at the official stand at Sixty-seventh Street, agreed with other notable guests that it was the most successful Army Day parade since the observance became official in 1928. This year, as in the past, the observance was sponsored by the Military Order of the World Wars.

It took the long line of paraders nearly two hours to pass the reviewing stand. They came in two divisions, with the youth organizations in first place, followed by the older units, including contingents of the Navy, Marine Corps, Waves, American Legion posts, the Red Cross and many women's volun-

Continued on Page 37, Column 4

"All the News That's Fit to Print"

The New York Times.

LATE CITY EDITION
Clearing and warm today.
Fair, continued warm tomorrow.
Temperatures Yesterday—Max., 74; Min., 54
Sunrise today, 6:21 A. M.; Sunset, 7:33 P. M.

VOL. XCIV...No. 31,856. Entered as Second-Class Matter, Postoffice, New York, N. Y. NEW YORK, FRIDAY, APRIL 13, 1945. THREE CENTS IN NEW YORK CITY

PRESIDENT ROOSEVELT IS DEAD; TRUMAN TO CONTINUE POLICIES; 9TH CROSSES ELBE, NEARS BERLIN

U. S. AND RED ARMIES DRIVE TO MEET

Americans Across the Elbe in Strength Race Toward Russians Who Have Opened Offensive From Oder

WEIMAR TAKEN, RUHR POCKET SLASHED

Third Army Reported 19 Miles From Czechoslovak Border—British Drive Deeper in the North, Seizing Celle—Canadians Freeing Holland

By DREW MIDDLETON
By Wireless to THE NEW YORK TIMES.

PARIS, April 12—Thousands of tanks and a half million doughboys of the United States First, Third and Ninth Armies are racing through the heart of the Reich on a front of 150 miles, threatening Berlin, Leipzig and the last citadels of the Nazi power.

The Second Armored Division of the Ninth Army has crossed the Elbe River in force and is striking eastward toward Berlin, whose outskirts lie less than sixty miles to the east, according to reports from the front. [A report quoted by The United Press placed the Americans less than fifty miles from the capital.] Beyond Berlin the First White Russian Army has crossed the Oder on a wide front and a junction between the western and eastern Allies is not far off.

[The Moscow radio reported that heavy battles were raging west of the Oder before Berlin, indicating that Marshal Gregory K. Zhukoff had launched his drive toward the Reich's capital. The Soviet communiqué announced further progress by the Red Army forces in and around Vienna.]

Paris is wild with excitement tonight. A special edition of the newspaper France-Soir carries a report by the radio station "Voice of America" that places American forces fifteen and five-eighths miles from Berlin after an airborne landing that had linked up with Lieut. Gen. William H. Simpson's forces advancing eastward from the Elbe. This would put American forces only seventy-five miles from the Red Army vanguard.

No Confirmation at Headquarters

There was no confirmation of this report at Allied Supreme Headquarters, which by its own admission was thirty-six hours behind developments on some sectors of the front.

Resistance was continuing only on the northern and southern flanks. The center had burst wide open. Weimar fell to Lieut. Gen. George S. Patton's infantry, and reports from the front said Erfurt also had been cleared. Schweinfurt and Heilbronn, two German bastions on the south, had fallen to United States Seventh Army forces, who were driving on Bamberg, while farther north Third Army forces were about thirty-five miles from the Czechoslovak frontier in the area east of Coburg.

[The German radio reported American Third Army forces at Lichtenberg, nineteen miles from the Czechoslovak border, The United Press said.]

The offensives to liberate the Netherlands and reduce the Ruhr

Continued on Page 12, Column 2

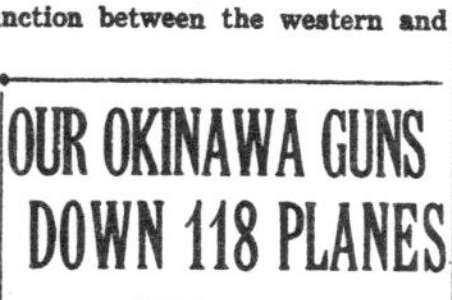

OUR OKINAWA GUNS DOWN 118 PLANES

Japanese Fliers Start 'Suicide' Attacks on Fleet, Sink a Destroyer, Hit Other Ships

By W. H. LAWRENCE
By Wireless to THE NEW YORK TIMES.

GUAM, Friday, April 13—Japanese attempting to halt the American march to Tokyo, have started "desperate, suicidal" aerial attacks upon our ships and men in the Okinawa area, losing 118 planes on Thursday alone, Fleet Admiral Chester W. Nimitz announced today.

The Japanese succeeded in sinking a destroyer and damaging several other surface units, the communiqué said. All of the damaged vessels remained in action.

It was the first time that the Navy had revealed the suicidal nature of the Japanese air missions against our ships and men. The Japanese radio has been saying that this type of assault was being carried on by a "special attack corps" known in Japanese as "kamakazi," which, translated literally, means "divine wind."

Attack at Low Levels

The Japanese fliers launched their attacks upon our ships and men at a high speed and from low levels, diving directly into a ship or troop concentration to explode their bombs as they crashed.

There was no official estimate of the total number of enemy aircraft engaged in the Okinawa area attack other than the report of the 118 enemy planes destroyed.

Admiral Nimitz reported that the attacks began early on April 12 (Eastern Longitude time) with seven enemy planes shot down during the morning in the vicinity of the Hagushi beaches.

The tempo of the attack was stepped up in the afternoon as the Japanese bore in on our ships in wave after wave. Admiral Nimitz said that ships' guns, carrier aircraft and shore-based anti-aircraft shot down 111 of the attackers.

The revelation of the suicidal Japanese air attacks was the highlight of Admiral Nimitz' regular morning communiqué, which also disclosed the identity of two Marine and two Army divisions that have gone into action on Okinawa. These included the Twenty-seventh Army Division, formed from New York National Guard units, which are seeing action for the first time since the Saipan campaign and previously had engaged in the Gilbert Islands assault. It is com-

Continued on Page 18, Column 2

Army Leaders See Reich End at Hand

By The Associated Press.

WASHINGTON, April 12—High Army officials told Senators today that the end of organized fighting in Germany probably would come within a few days.

Describing the pell-mell dash of American Armies across Germany, General Staff officers expressed the opinion to members of the Senate Military Committee that a collapse of German arms was imminent.

Those who attended said the army chiefs declared that they were so sure of the results that orders had been drawn for a drastic reduction in shipments of durable equipment to Europe.

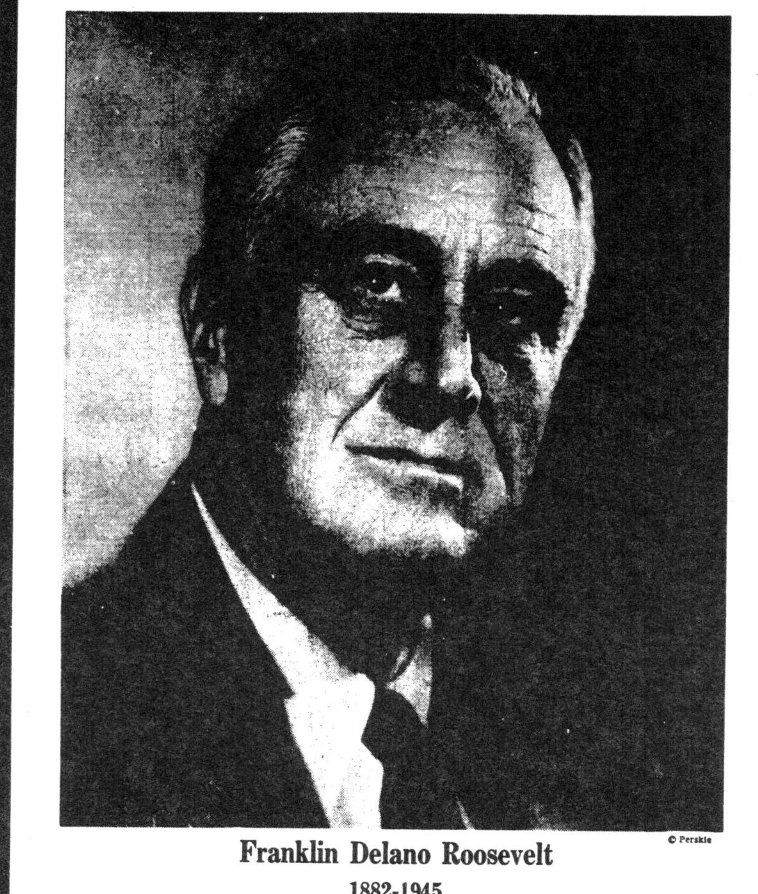

© Perskie

Franklin Delano Roosevelt
1882-1945

SECURITY PARLEY WON'T BE DELAYED

State Department Urges That World Be Shown We Plan No Changes in Policy

By JAMES B. RESTON
Special to THE NEW YORK TIMES.

WASHINGTON, April 12—The United Nations Security Conference will open in San Francisco on April 25, despite the death of President Roosevelt, Secretary of State Edward R. Stettinius Jr. announced tonight.

Mr. Stettinius said that he had been authorized by President Harry Truman to make this announcement after a meeting of the Cabinet at the White House.

Most of the overseas delegations to the San Francisco conference have either arrived in this country or are now on their way, but while this was said to have been a factor in the decision to proceed with the conference, State Department officials urged that every attempt be made to give immediate evidence to the world that President Roosevelt's foreign policy would be sustained by the new Administration.

President Roosevelt had planned to address the San Francisco conference. His interest in an international organization of nations to maintain peace and security had gone back to his service in the Wilson Administration, when he sat in the gallery of the Senate and listened to the debate that resulted in the rejection of the League of Nations Covenant. He had expressed to friends his desire to participate in the San Francisco conference and to see the United States enter the new league during his term in office.

The sudden elevation of Presi-

Continued on Page 2, Column 1

War News Summarized

FRIDAY, APRIL 13, 1945

President Roosevelt died yesterday afternoon, suddenly and unexpectedly. He was stricken with a massive cerebral hemorrhage at Warm Springs, Ga., on the eve of his greatest military and diplomatic successes—the impending fall of Berlin and the opening of the San Francisco Conference to set up a World Security Organization that would make the world free from martial and economic strife [1:7-8.]

Mr. Roosevelt had been sitting in front of the fireplace of his Little White House, having gone to Warm Springs on March 30 for a three-week rest. About 2:15 Eastern war time he said, "I have a terrific headache," lost consciousness in a few moments and died at 4:35. He was 63 years old. [1:6.]

The tragic word spread quickly around the world. Expressions of sorrow poured in from all sections. [4:5.] American soldiers and sailors refused to believe the reports until there was no longer doubt that their Commander in Chief had gone. [4:2-3.]

Harry S. Truman was sworn in as President at 7:09 o'clock last night, and a few minutes later Mrs. Roosevelt left for Warm Springs. [1:7.] The new President immediately called a Cabinet meeting and declared that Mr. Roosevelt's policies would be continued, that the war would be carried on until Germany and Japan surrendered unconditionally and that the San Francisco Conference would open April 25 as scheduled. [1:3.]

Some 500,000 American soldiers of the Third and Ninth Armies, and thousands of tanks, sped along a 150-mile front toward Berlin and Leipzig. The Ninth, surging across the Elbe, according to delayed reports was less than fifty miles from the German capital and 115 from the Russians along the Oder. The Third Army captured Weimar, home of the late German Republic, and was twenty-three miles below Leipzig, with the First closing a pincers from the north. [1:1-2; map P. 2.]

The Moscow radio reported that the Red Army was waging fierce battles east of Berlin, indicating resumption of the drive on that city. Elsewhere Russian troops scored wide gains and cut the last escape railroad from Vienna. [13:1.]

Open cities were ruled out and every German was ordered by Himmler to fight to the death, although Goebbels said "the war cannot last much longer." [12:6-7.]

The Ninth Air Force destroyed at least 117 more German planes yesterday. [11:8.]

In Italy the Eighth Army advanced along a thirty-mile front toward Bologna and the Po Valley; the Fifth Army also made good gains and was eleven miles from La Spezia. [13:8, with map.]

Japanese planes resumed their suicide attacks on American ships off Okinawa, sinking a destroyer and damaging several other vessels. One hundred and eighteen enemy planes were shot down. [1:2.] The Americal Division invaded Bohol, last of the enemy-held central Philippines. [18:6.] The B-29 attack on Koriyama, 110 miles north of Tokyo, set a new Superfortress distance record. [18:2.]

Secretary of State Stettinius and Secretary of War Stimson, denouncing Germany's "steadily increasing" mistreatment of American prisoners, said those responsible would be brought to justice. [13:6-7.]

Clashes between Right and Left wing elements in Iran were reported from Moscow. [13:2.]

LAST WORDS: 'I HAVE TERRIFIC HEADACHE'

Roosevelt Was Posing for Artist When Hemorrhage Struck —He Died in Bedroom

By The Associated Press.

WARM SPRINGS, Ga., April 12—President Franklin D. Roosevelt's last words were:

"I have a terrific headache."

He spoke them to Comdr. Howard G. Bruenn, naval physician.

Mr. Roosevelt was sitting in front of a fireplace in the Little White House here atop Pine Mountain when what was described as a massive cerebral hemorrhage struck him.

The President's Negro valet, Arthur Prettyman, and a Filipino messboy carried him to his bedroom. He was unconscious at the end. It came without pain.

Dr. Bruenn said that he saw the President this morning and he was in excellent spirits at 9:30 A. M.

"At 1 o'clock," Dr. Bruenn added, "he was sitting in a chair while sketches were being made of him by an artist. He suddenly complained of a very severe occipital headache (back of the head).

"Within a very few minutes he lost consciousness. He was seen by me at 1:30 P. M., fifteen minutes after the episode had started.

"He did not regain consciousness, and he died at 3:35 P. M. (Georgia time)."

The artist sketching Mr. Roosevelt was N. Robbins of 520 West 139th Street, New York.

Only others present in the cottage were Comdr. George Fox, White House pharmacist and long an attendant on the President; William D. Hassett, Presidential secretary; Miss Grace Tully, con-

Continued on Page 4, Column 3

END COMES SUDDENLY AT WARM SPRINGS

Even His Family Unaware of Condition as Cerebral Stroke Brings Death to Nation's Leader at 63

ALL CABINET MEMBERS TO KEEP POSTS

Funeral to Be at White House Tomorrow, With Burial at Hyde Park Home—Impact of News Tremendous

By ARTHUR KROCK
Special to THE NEW YORK TIMES.

WASHINGTON, April 12—Franklin Delano Roosevelt, War President of the United States and the only Chief Executive in history who was chosen for more than two terms, died suddenly and unexpectedly at 4:35 P. M. today at Warm Springs, Ga., and the White House announced his death at 5:48 o'clock. He was 63.

The President, stricken by a cerebral hemorrhage, passed from unconsciousness to death on the eighty-third day of his fourth term and in an hour of high triumph. The armies and fleets under his direction as Commander in Chief were at the gates of Berlin and the shores of Japan's home islands as Mr. Roosevelt died, and the cause he represented and led was nearing the conclusive phase of success.

Less than two hours after the official announcement, Harry S. Truman of Missouri, the Vice President, took the oath as the thirty-second President. The oath was administered by the Chief Justice of the United States, Harlan F. Stone, in a one-minute ceremony at the White House. Mr. Truman immediately let it be known that Mr. Roosevelt's Cabinet is remaining in office at his request, and that he had authorized Secretary of State Edward R. Stettinius Jr. to proceed with plans for the United Nations Conference on international organization at San Francisco, scheduled to begin April 25. A report was circulated that he leans somewhat to the idea of a coalition Cabinet, but this is unsubstantiated.

Funeral Tomorrow Afternoon

It was disclosed by the White House that funeral services for Mr. Roosevelt would take place at 4 P. M. (E. W. T.) Saturday in the East Room of the Executive Mansion. The Rev. Angus Dun, Episcopal Bishop of Washington; the Rev. Howard S. Wilkinson of St. Thomas's Church in Washington and the Rev. John G. McGee of St. John's in Washington will conduct the services.

The body will be interred at Hyde Park, N. Y., Sunday, with the Rev. George W. Anthony of St. James Church officiating. The time has not yet been fixed.

Jonathan Daniels, White House secretary, said Mr. Roosevelt's body would not lie in state. He added that, in view of the limited size of the East Room, which holds only about 200 persons, the list of those attending the funeral services would be limited to high Government officials, representatives of the membership of both

Continued on Page 3, Column 3

TRUMAN IS SWORN IN THE WHITE HOUSE

Members of Cabinet on Hand as Chief Justice Stone Administers the Oath

By C. P. TRUSSELL
Special to THE NEW YORK TIMES.

WASHINGTON, April 12—Vice President Harry S. Truman of Missouri, standing erect, with his sharp features taut and looking straight ahead through his large, round glasses, became the thirty-second President of the United States in a ceremony lasting not more than a minute in the Cabinet Room of the White House at 7:09 o'clock tonight.

The oath was administered by Chief Justice Harlan F. Stone two hours and thirty-four minutes after the sudden death of President Roosevelt at Warm Springs. Mr. Truman had picked up a Bible from the end of the big Cabinet conference table, held it with his left hand and placed his right hand upon the upper cover. After repeating the oath, he bowed his head, lifted the Bible to his lips and kissed it.

Even before he had taken the oath Mr. Truman had asked President Roosevelt's Cabinet to continue in service. He also authorized Edward R. Stettinius Jr., Secretary of State, to announce that the United Nations Conference for International Organization would go on as scheduled.

To the newsmen at the White House he sent this word, through Stephen Early, press secretary:

"For the time being I prefer not to hold a press conference. It will be my effort to carry on as I believe the President would have done, and to that end I have asked the Cabinet to stay on with me."

Soon after he became President, Mr. Truman left the White House for the five-room Connecticut Avenue apartment where he has resided with Mrs. Truman and their 20-year-old daughter, Mary Margaret, for four years. He said he was "going home, to bed."

It was shortly after he had finished presiding over the Senate debate on the United States-Mexican Water Treaty late this afternoon that Mr. Truman received word from the White House of President Roosevelt's death. This was at about 5:15 P. M., a half hour before the news was made public. Reaching for his hat, he dashed out of the office, calling back to his staff that he was going to the White House.

Arriving at the White House, the

Continued on Page 3, Column 6

Byrnes May Take Post With Truman

Special to THE NEW YORK TIMES.

WASHINGTON, April 12—James F. Byrnes, recently resigned as Director of War Mobilization and Reconversion, known to be one of President Truman's warmest friends in official Washington, is expected to be called to the White House for consultation, and possibly to take an important post in the Cabinet, in the immediate future.

President Truman's admiration of former Justice Byrnes is well known here. He undoubtedly would have been Mr. Truman's choice as a successor to Cordell Hull as Secretary of State.

"All the News That's Fit to Print"

The New York Times.

LATE CITY EDITION

Showers, cloudy and warmer today. Partly cloudy and warm tomorrow. Temperatures Yesterday—Max., 51; Min., 47 Sunrise today, 6:15 A. M.; Sunset, 7:37 P. M.

VOL. XCIV..No. 31,860. Entered as Second-Class Matter, Postoffice, New York, N. Y. NEW YORK, TUESDAY, APRIL 17, 1945. THREE CENTS IN NEW YORK CITY

TRUMAN ASKS WORLD UNITY TO KEEP PEACE; 7TH IN NUREMBERG; SOVIET PUSH REPORTED; NAZIS LOSE 905 PLANES, MOSTLY AGROUND

NAZI BASE ENTERED

Hitler's Shrine Stormed After Full-Scale Drive by Patch's Forces

FIRST FLANKS LEIPZIG

9th Deepens Bridgehead Over Elbe—Canadians Clear North Holland

By The Associated Press.

PARIS, Tuesday, April 17—Three American armies battled possibly seventy-five to eighty-five miles from Russian lines today, hammering five miles beyond the Elbe River, outflanking the great fortress of Leipzig and driving a steel wedge thirty miles from the enemy's eastern front base of Dresden.

The Paris radio reported without official confirmation early today that American and Russian spearheads had met in the Elbe River Valley south of Dresden.

The broadcast did not give the source of the report, which said the alleged meeting had taken place between Pirna and Tetschen.

[Tetschen is a Czechoslovak customs station, five miles inside the Czechoslovak border on the Prague-Dresden railroad, The United Press said.]

Another United States Army, the Seventh, broke into the Nazi shrine city of Nuremberg, ninety miles north of Munich.

New Elbe Crossing Reported

The United States Ninth Army was fifty-two miles southwest of Berlin, after having hacked out a foothold five miles beyond the Elbe, and unconfirmed German reports said the Americans had forced a new crossing farther north at Havelberg, forty-five miles northwest of Berlin and some eighty-five miles from Russian lines.

The United States First Army cut loose with a fourteen-mile tank dash that swept into Wurzen, twelve miles east of Leipzig, where an estimated 1,000,000 civilians faced an ordeal of fire and steel because 30,000 German troops are bent on making a Stalingrad of that refugee-swollen fifth city of the Reich. Infantry battled up four miles south of the city and artillery began to shell it.

The United States Third and First Armies were slashing into the rear area of German forces on the Eastern Front. Both were up to, if not across, the western boundary of German territory marked for Russian occupation.

Third Besieges Chemnitz

The Third Army laid siege to Chemnitz, was seven miles from the border of Czechoslovakia and pushed out a steel fist northeast of Chemnitz thirty miles from the Elbe and Dresden.

The First Army at Wurzen was eighteen miles from the Elbe—along which the Germans may make their final stand in central Germany—and was less than two miles from the river farther north as it opened an attack at the approaches to Dessau, fifty-two miles southwest of Berlin.

With the British and Canadians threatening the north German ports of Bremen, Emden and Hamburg in resumed offensives, and with the Allies squeezing enemy pockets in the western Netherlands, the Ruhr and on France's Atlantic coast, German soldiers were giving up by the thousands.

A total of 66,191 prisoners was counted Sunday, most of them from the Ruhr, where a German Panzer Lehr Division that had fought in North Africa and Normandy surrendered. Equally surprising was the abrupt capitulation of tough German marines to the Canadians at Groningen, the Netherlands' fifth largest city.

For all that, Gen. Dwight D. Eisenhower dampened any optimism that the end of the war in Europe was imminent.

He told visiting radio corre-

Continued on Page 3, Column 2

218,000 Prisoners Taken in 72 Hours

By The United Press.

WITH THE AMERICAN FIRST ARMY, in Germany, April 16—The American First, Third and Ninth Armies have taken more than 218,000 German prisoners in the past seventy-two hours in a mass roundup that at many points has lost all resemblance to war.

LONDON, April 16 (Reuter)—Gen. Dwight D. Eisenhower today announced the greatest daily haul of prisoners in this war.

His communiqué said the Allies in the west took 87,779 prisoners on Saturday alone. This is four times greater than the highest prisoner total for one day in the previous greatest Axis collapse of the war—in Tunisia two years ago.

AIRBORNE RUSSIANS SAID TO LEAP RING

Red Army Paratroops Within 18 Miles of Berlin as Drive Opens, Germans Say

By The Associated Press.

LONDON, Tuesday, April 17—The Germans reported today that Soviet parachutists had landed behind German lines in Berlin's defense ring somewhere between the city's eastern limits and positions won by the Red Army twenty-three miles to the east. German reports indicated that four Russian armies, totaling perhaps 2,000,000 men, were on the move.

The long-expected offensive burst upon the Germans at 3:50 A. M. yesterday, the German High Command announced, and drove forward along a 120-mile front at two points eighty-five miles from the American Third and Ninth Armies. Berlin conceded that a rapid link-up was possible.

The thunder of 1,000 Russian guns was heard throughout the day in Berlin, the enemy acknowledged, as Soviet assault units battled into massive reinforced fortifications under cover of hundreds of planes bombing and machine-gunning German positions on Berlin's eastern approaches.

New Footholds Reported

All along the front, Red Army engineers were speeding amphibious tanks and armored units into bridgeheads across the Oder and Neisse Rivers that were being built up hourly, according to German reports. At least two new footholds across the Oder were reported—the latest at the river's elbow east of Eberswalde, some eighteen airline miles northeast of Berlin's city limits.

Overshadowed by the reported operation, not yet officially confirmed by the Soviet High Command, were Red Army drives in Austria, Czechoslovakia and East Prussia.

In the Austrian Alps, Marshal Fedor I. Tolbukhin's Third Ukrai-

Continued on Page 4, Column 2

LUFTWAFFE IS 'OUT'

U. S. Fighters Spearhead 6,000-Sortie Assault Over All Germany

8TH HITS 40 AIRFIELDS

Big Bombers Rip Rails—Strategic Forces' Job Done, Spaatz Says

By The Associated Press.

LONDON, Tuesday, April 17—At least 845 German planes were destroyed yesterday by Allied fighters in a cataclysmic blow against the Nazi Air Force, and last night an observer commented, "The Luftwaffe has been knocked out."

[The figure for the "kill" of German planes Monday rose with additional reports from Allied air units. A United Press dispatch gave it as 905.]

Gen. Carl A. Spaatz, commander of the United States Strategic Air Forces in Europe, issued a special order of the day saying the strategic air war against Germany had ended victoriously and that hereafter United States heavy bombers would be used for tactical operations.

More than 6,000 Allied planes joined in the mighty daylight assault on the enemy. Some 2,000 fighter pilots smashed 812 Nazi planes on the ground and shot thirty-three from the skies.

RAF "Heavies" Strike by Night

Last night a big armada of Royal Air Force heavy bombers battered railway targets on both sides of the German-Czech frontier, where United States and Red Army troops are near a meeting. Other planes hit Berlin again, the British Air Ministry reported.

The United States Eighth Air Force, which sent nearly 2,100 warplanes from bases in Britain during the day, reported early today that eight of its heavy bombers and thirty-four fighters were missing.

More than forty Nazi airfields in the Pilsen-Prague area of Czechoslovakia were punished by the Eighth Air Force fighters that escorted the Eighth's heavy bombers on a mission against enemy communications targets in Bavaria. The Allies' tactical air forces based on the Continent fanned out in a series of attacks against enemy airdromes and targets over a wide area.

The Eighth's Mustangs and Thunderbolts, whose services as escorts for our heavy bombers were scarcely needed, dropped down for gunning runs and destroyed at least 647 planes on the ground. They shot down three others in combat during the Nazis' only effort at interception.

Some 1,000 Ninth Air Force fighters and fighter-bombers, at a loss of two planes, wrecked 159

Continued on Page 4, Column 5

THE THIRTY-SECOND PRESIDENT MAKING HIS FIRST SPEECH TO CONGRESS

President Truman addressing the joint session in the House chamber yesterday — Associated Press Wirephoto

ALLIES' ITALY PUSH CAPTURES VERGATO

5th Army Topples Apennine Barrier—British Eighth 1 Mile From Argenta

By MILTON BRACKER

By Wireless to The New York Times.

FIFTEENTH ARMY GROUP HEADQUARTERS, Italy, April 16—Heralded by the greatest use of air power in the history of the Mediterranean theatre, the long-awaited all-out offensive in Italy began this morning, with the American Fifth Army hammering forward through the last Apennine barriers before Bologna.

Exhorted by their commanders to strike the blows that will mean final victory, both the Fifth and the Eighth Armies scored important gains along a fiery fifty-mile

Continued on Page 6, Column 2

B-29'S WIPE OUT 50% OF TOKYO INDUSTRY

Gutted Area Tops 27.5 Square Miles—368 Japanese Craft Destroyed in Five Days

By GEORGE E. JONES

By Wireless to The New York Times.

GUAM, Tuesday, April 17—Fire-blackened and burning Tokyo is emerging today from a week-end of misery and horror visited on that crowded, inflammable metropolis by incendiary-laden Superfortresses and swarms of long-range land-based fighters. [This was the first mention of fighter planes in the latest attacks.]

[United States fliers and land and ship gunners destroyed 368 Japanese planes in five days of air warfare ranging from Oki-

Continued on Page 8, Column 4

Soviet Will Insist Lublin Act for Poland at Parley

By The United Press.

LONDON, Tuesday, April 17—The Moscow radio reported today that the Soviet Government had decided to insist on the admission of the Provisional Polish Government—the former Lublin regime—to the San Francisco Conference despite negative replies by the American and British Governments to a previous proposal.

Radio Moscow, in its 4 A. M. news broadcast, devoted its entire time to an account of President Truman's address before Congress yesterday and a reading of the Moscow communiqué on the Russian war fronts.

The Moscow radio, recalling the Soviet approach to the American, British and Chinese Governments regarding the admission of the Warsaw representatives to the United Nations' Conference, said:

"The answer of the British and American Governments has been negative. The Chinese Government answered that it so far had taken no decision on the subject, pointing out that since the Anglo-Americans had turned down the proposal, the Chinese Government's agreement or disagreement has no practical importance.

"It is reported the Soviet Government has decided to insist on its proposal to admit representatives of the Provisional Polish Warsaw Government to the San Francisco Conference."

London Poles Dissatisfied

By Wireless to The New York Times.

LONDON, April 16—Reports that Polish underground leaders are conferring with Soviet authorities on the creation of a new Polish Government have been so persistent that even the exiled Polish

Continued on Page 15, Column 4

TRUMAN SEES EDEN, AWAITS MOLOTOFF

President Gets Churchill Messages—Talks by Radio to Armed Forces Tonight

By BERTRAM D. HULEN

Special to The New York Times.

WASHINGTON, April 16—President Truman conferred today with Anthony Eden, the British Foreign Secretary, who brought to him messages from Prime Minister Churchill.

Mr. Eden arrived at the White House at 10 A. M., accompanied by the Earl of Halifax, the British Ambassador. Secretary of State Edward R. Stettinius Jr. was present during the conference, which lasted twenty minutes.

On leaving, Mr. Eden said:

"I was very pleased to have the privilege of calling on the President and very grateful that he found time to see me on this day when he has his first important speech to deliver.

"Naturally I brought him some messages from the Prime Minister telling him how gratified we are

Continued on Page 14, Column 1

War News Summarized

TUESDAY, APRIL 17, 1945

Allied Armies continued to whittle down the area of Germany still in enemy hands, with Berlin reports placing the United States Ninth Army forty-five miles from the capital. Leipzig was outflanked by the First Army. The Seventh broke into Nuremberg, and the Third laid siege to Chemnitz, while in the north the British Second Army resumed its assault on Bremen and the Canadian First Army captured Groningen in the Netherlands. [1:1; maps Pages 2 and 4.]

Despite the disintegration of German lines General Eisenhower said he did not expect the war to end until all of Germany had been occupied and that there would be no announcement of V-E Day until every important enemy pocket on the Western Front had been wiped out. [5:4.]

French troops captured Royan, at the mouth of the Gironde River, in the battle to reopen the port of Bordeaux. [4:3-4.]

There was little left of the Luftwaffe after Allied fliers swept German airfields to destroy the record number of 905 enemy planes, most of them on the ground. Strategic bombing is over for the Germans, as there are no more targets, said General Spaatz. [1:3.]

Although Moscow maintained silence on any move toward Berlin from the east, the German radio said that Russian parachutists had landed less than twenty-three miles from the city and that four Soviet armies, totaling 2,000,000 men, were on the move. [1:2.] Hitler issued an order of the day asking the Germans to drown the Russians in a sea of blood and hold Berlin at all costs. [6:5.]

The Allies have opened their spring offensive in Italy, striking along a fifty-mile arc in a determined effort to end the war. Two days of unprecedented air blows in the Mediterranean area heralded the drive. [1:4; map, P 6.]

Vast fires and explosions visible more than 100 miles away were left by B-29's in their latest attack on Tokyo. At least half the city's industry has been destroyed and the burned out area is not less than 27.5 square miles. [1:5.] Pacific Fleet planes destroyed 368 Japanese planes in raids over Kyushu, the Ryukyus, and the Okinawa area. There was little change in position on Okinawa, although Ie Island, off the west coast, was invaded. [8:1.]

Taungup, last Japanese coastal supply base in the Arakan area of Burma, was captured by British and Indian troops. [10:3, with map.]

President Truman, addressing Congress for the first time, pleaded for united public support to help him "defend those ideals which have been so eloquently proclaimed by Franklin Roosevelt." Unconditional surrender remains our war aim, he said, and there will be no change in military leadership. He pledged himself to fight for a "strong and lasting United Nations organization." [1:3.]

The Moscow radio said Russia insisted upon the presence of the Polish Provisional (Lublin) Government at the San Francisco Conference despite British and American opposition. [1:6-7.]

18,000 Vote Phone Strike Here; Delay Likely to Let Truman Act

A strike that might cripple local and long line telephone service in New York, and spread to other sections, was voted last night by an overwhelming majority of 18,000 workers affiliated with two independent unions in protest against a War Labor Board order of a $5 a week increase in pay.

There were 14,471 valid ballots cast, the National Labor Relations Board announced, and of these 94 per cent were marked in favor of a strike.

Unless a Presidential seizure order is issued, the unions involved—the Traffic Employes Association, representing 12,000 operators, and the Federation of Long Lines Telephone Workers—may possibly walk out soon after their executive boards meet in joint session at 2 P. M. today at the office of the latter union, 260 West Broadway. The local operators are employed by the New York Telephone Company and the others by the American Telephone and Telegraph Company.

Only 540 of the traffic workers voted against a strike while 9,999 were in favor, according to a representative of the NLRB who supervised the balloting that started at 7 A. M. yesterday and ended at 10 P. M.

The long distance workers did not complete their vote until after 11 P. M. and it followed the same pattern, 3,814 voting to strike while only 118 voted "no."

Both unions originally had demanded a $5 weekly pay rise. Telephone company officials had offered them $4, and had given the WLB data in support of the increase. On Saturday the board refused to reconsider the matter and

Continued on Page 24, Column 2

Roosevelt Estate Is Left in Trust To Widow and Then to 5 Children

Special to The New York Times.

POUGHKEEPSIE, N. Y., April 16—The will of Franklin D. Roosevelt, leaving his estate, after certain minor bequests, to his wife and children, was filed at 4:30 o'clock this afternoon before Frederick S. Quinterro, Surrogate of Dutchess County, by Henry T. Hackett, a Poughkeepsie attorney and personal friend of the President.

[The text of Mr. Roosevelt's will appears on Page 18.]

There was nothing in the document to indicate the value of the estate. Under the will of his mother, Mrs. Sara Delano Roosevelt, Mr. Roosevelt inherited nine-tenths of her estate. It was appraised at $1,089,872, according to a New York State transfer tax appraisal filed on April 23, 1942.

The late President directed that his residuary estate should be held in trust for Mrs. Roosevelt for her lifetime. At her death half of the principal is to be divided equally among their five children, Mrs. Anna Roosevelt Boettiger and James, Elliott, Franklin Jr. and John Roosevelt. The remaining half of the principal is to be divided into separate trusts for their benefit.

He directed that his wife should have the right to select any personal property that she desired to utilize during her lifetime and that each of the five children should have the right to select one-fifth of the rest of the personal property.

Any personal property not chosen by them is to be offered by the executors to the United States Government as a gift for

Continued on Page 18, Column 2

STATES HIS POLICY

President Pledges U. S. to Work for World Security League

TO PUSH WAR TO END

Congress Told Roosevelt Drive for Common Man Will Be Continued

The text of the President's address is printed on Page 12.

By FRANK L. KLUCKHOHN

Special to The New York Times.

WASHINGTON, April 16—President Truman pledged himself today to carry out the war and peace policies of Franklin D. Roosevelt.

The pledge was given in a speech before a joint session of Congress, attended by the Cabinet, Supreme Court justices and representatives of foreign nations, including Anthony Eden, British Foreign Secretary.

Mr. Truman appealed for united public support of a program for unconditional surrender of the enemy, as already determined by the United Nations, and to establish "a strong and lasting United Nations Organization" for world peace.

He received an ovation both when he entered the House chamber and when he departed after his appeal for national support, which was broadcast throughout the country and the world. He was applauded frequently during his address.

"I call upon all Americans to help me keep our nation united in defense of those ideals which have been so eloquently proclaimed by Franklin Roosevelt," the new President said.

Will Keep Military "Team"

He disclosed that he intended to maintain the present American High Command for waging "the fight for freedom until no vestige of resistance remains," adding:

"I appeal to every American, regardless of party, race, creed, or color, to support our efforts to build a strong and lasting United Nations Organization."

On the domestic front, he pledged that the drive begun by Mr. Roosevelt to improve the lot of the common people would be continued, but the bulk of his speech was devoted to the war and approaching peace problems.

Regretting the death of Mr. Roosevelt and remarking that "no man could possibly fill the tremendous void left by the passing of that noble soul," Mr. Truman asserted that the world was looking to America for "enlightened leadership" and emphasized that this could be offered only by a country which was itself united.

War Will Be Pushed

Germany and Japan, he continued, could both rest assured that our fight would be pressed against them until all resistance ended, adding that, although we knew "much hard fighting" lay ahead, we already had paid a high price, and "America will never become a party to any plan for partial victory."

To do otherwise, he said, would mean only a temporary breathing space, concurrently putting in jeopardy future world security.

"Our demand has been, and it remains—unconditional surrender!" Mr. Truman asserted, pounding the table before him in one of the two gestures he made during his speech.

The victors, he asserted, must be responsible for the making of the peace and, although unnecessary and unjustified suffering must be avoided, war criminals must be

Continued on Page 12, Column 1

"All the News That's Fit to Print"

The New York Times.

LATE CITY EDITION
Partly cloudy, windy, mild today. Partly cloudy, cooler tomorrow.
Temperatures Yesterday—Max., 72; Min., 51
Sunrise today, 6:14 A. M.; Sunset, 7:38 P. M.

VOL. XCIV..No. 31,861. Entered as Second-Class Matter, Postoffice, New York, N. Y. NEW YORK, WEDNESDAY, APRIL 18, 1945. THREE CENTS IN NEW YORK CITY

BRITISH ARMY 25 MILES FROM HAMBURG; U. S. THRUST TOWARD BERLIN IS AT A HALT; NAZIS REPORT 4 SOVIET DRIVES ON CAPITAL

TRUMAN FOR TALKS WITH ALLIED CHIEFS; BACKS TRADE PACTS

Endorses Bretton Woods Plan and a Continued Curfew and Ban on Racing

EXTENDS LEND-LEASE ACT

President Addresses Armed Forces Throughout World in Evening Broadcast

By BERTRAM D. HULEN
Special to THE NEW YORK TIMES.

WASHINGTON, April 17—President Truman, at his first press conference this morning, expressed his desire to confer with leaders of the United Nations, endorsed the Bretton Woods international financial agreements, declared for a continuation of the reciprocal trade policy, and said he would support the San Francisco conference of the United Nations from Washington but would not attend it personally.

In a broadcast tonight at 10 o'clock to our armed forces throughout the world, the President declared that he would not falter any more than did Franklin D. Roosevelt.

"We are depending on each and every one of you," Mr. Truman said, in praising Mr. Roosevelt as a hard-hitting Chief of the services. His cause now was ours, he said, in telling that he assumed the Presidency as a duty when the Commander had fallen, and these duties, Mr. Truman asserted, would be carried on "in keeping with our American tradition."

Service men and women would not be forgotten, the President said in mentioning his own part in the first World War.

Mr. Truman ended the broadcast by quoting from Lincoln's Second Inaugural.

[The text of President Truman's broadcast to the armed forces is printed on Page 14, column 2.]

During the day, the President signed the third extension of the lend-lease act and announced that this aid to our Allies "will be carried on until the unconditional surrender or complete defeat of Germany and Japan." Specifically, he gave another year of life to the act as from June 30.

President in Good Form

Speaking crisply and frankly to the correspondents at the White House on both foreign and domestic issues, the President also declared that the curfew and other restrictions, including the ban on horse racing, imposed by James F. Byrnes when he was director of War Mobilization, would be continued.

Mr. Truman's announcement concerning his readiness to confer with Allied leaders was made in response to a question as to whether he would like to see Marshal Stalin and Prime Minister Churchill.

He responded promptly that he would like to see not only them but others, including Generalissimo Chiang Kai-shek and General de Gaulle. He added that he had not taken the initiative in this regard himself.

A record number of correspondents—348 in all—more than even had greeted President Roosevelt and Prime Minister Churchill in their joint conferences, crowded into the oval office of the President.

His Replies Are Unequivocal

They left after a conference that lasted twelve minutes impressed with the feeling that Mr. Truman had firmly graspd the reins of office and had demonstrated his ability to meet impromptu questions with sharp and direct replies.

This was illustrated most impressively when he was asked whether he expected to see V. M. Molotoff, the Soviet Commissar for Foreign Affairs, when he is

Continued on Page 16, Column 3

Top Medal Asked For Late President

By The United Press.

WASHINGTON, April 17—A bill was introduced in the Senate today to award the country's highest decoration, the Medal of Honor, to the late President Roosevelt.

Senators Lucas, Democrat, of Illinois, and Barkley, Democrat, of Kentucky, introduced the bill, which would authorize President Truman to award the medal posthumously. No Chief Executive ever has received the decoration.

"Franklin D. Roosevelt," the Senators said in a statement, "has gallantly and unselfishly given his life in the service of this nation, as Commander in Chief of the armed forces, and was the outstanding leader of the Allied nations in the cause of world peace.

"No man in the history of the country had labored longer and worked with such patience and diligence in his battle against a form of tyranny which, if successful, would have enslaved us all."

Representative George F. Rogers, Democrat, of New York, introduced a similar bill in the House.

SEIZES A PLANT OF CITIES SERVICE

Truman Orders Action When Rent Dispute Causes Blockade at Lake Charles, La.

By The Associated Press.

WASHINGTON, April 17—President Truman tonight directed Secretary Ickes to seize the plant of the Cities Service Refining Corporation at Lake Charles, La., strike-bound because of a controversy over rental charges in a near-by housing project.

In a subsequent statement, Fred M. Vinson, War Mobilization Director, declared that the company and the union, the Lake Charles AFL Metals Trades Council, have a contract which is "mutually satisfactory," and that "neither is responsible for the stoppage of production."

The plant is one of the largest high octane gasoline producing refineries in the country.

"The production stoppage exists because of a barricade (a picket line) which prevents safe access to the plant," Mr. Vinson declared.

"This barricade is manned by a group of men dissatisfied with their rents in a near-by privately owned and privately operated housing development."

Mr. Ickes, as Petroleum Administrator for War, was authorized to take possession of and operate the plants and facilities of the corporation in and around Lake Charles.

President Truman said in his executive order that because of the interruption in the plant's activities the war effort "will be unduly impeded or delayed."

Stock Ownership Is Wide

Cities Service Company, one of the country's largest public utility holding companies, and parent

Continued on Page 15, Column 3

RUSSIANS HIDE AIM

But Foe Tells of Blows From Oder and Neisse That Pierce Lines

SEES LINK IN SOUTH

Pocket in East Prussia Reduced to a Port—Oil Center Falls

By The Associated Press.

LONDON, Wednesday, April 18—The Germans said today that Russian forces were driving hard within eighteen and twenty miles of Berlin in three drives while another Soviet force speared into the Nazis' southern escape corridor through Saxony.

Moscow maintained silence on the operations along the 150-mile front from the Bohemian border to the Oder estuary, proclaiming in its latest communiqué the liquidation of all the remaining area of the Samland Peninsula of East Prussia except the escape port of Pillau. It also announced the capture of the important Austrian oil-producing center of Zistersdorf, twenty-five miles northeast of Vienna.

The German High Command reported a Soviet jump-off from Neisse River bridgeheads along a thirty-three-mile front from Forst to Rothenburg, headed toward a junction with American forces driving into Saxony from the west. Then the German Army clamped a news blackout on place names.

"Organic Front" Destroyed

German Commentator Max Krull, discussing Allied "breakthroughs" from the east and west, declared the "organic structure of the German front has ceased to exist; the terms Western Front and Eastern Front have lost their meaning."

The Berlin radio said the Oder offensive was clutching at Berlin from the northeast, east and southeast. One column that stormed the river west of Zehden was reported sending tanks to the main Berlin-Stettin road near Eberswalde, eighteen miles from the capital.

Other forces, the announcement said, were pressing a frontal assault in the Frankfort-Kuestrin-Zellin triangle, using six divisions. Heavy fighting was reported around Wriezen and in the Seelow heights area. The Germans said Russian spearheads had cut the Seelow-Alt Friedland road less than twenty miles east of Greater Berlin and had penetrated deeply staggered defenses beyond.

A third push was reported to have reached Muellrose, twenty-eight miles southeast of the capital.

Other Russian forces were pushing up the road to Bruenn in Czechoslovakia and westward on separate fronts toward Linz and Graz. Fighting also flared in Upper Silesia, where the German High Command said a fierce conflict was raging in the area of Ratibor.

Reports from Moscow said residents there were expecting some

Continued on Page 10, Column 5

ALLIED ARMIES BATTLE FOR KEY PLACES INSIDE THE REICH

April 18, 1945

Canadian troops drove close to the Ijsselmeer at Barneveld and cleared Apeldoorn (1). They also took Harlingen and advanced to the north end of the Ijsselmeer causeway (2). The British (3), seizing Schneverdingen, pushed on to cut the Bremen-Hamburg railroad and reached a point ten miles south of Lueneburg. The American Ninth Army (4) battled inside Magdeburg, expanded its Barby bridgehead slightly and made another junction with the First Army near Bernburg east of the Harz Mountains pocket. The First (5) conquered half of Halle, drove into Leipzig's outskirts and entered Borsdorf. The Third Army (6) smashed close to Chemnitz, took Werdau and Greiz, drove through Plauen and Oelsnitz and advanced beyond Trogen. To the south the Seventh Army (7) was closing around Nuremberg and occupied Rothenburg. French troops (8) reached Nagold and took Oberweier and Allmannweier. Still unconfirmed German reports told of Soviet thrusts in three areas east of Berlin (9) and another to the south (10). In the direction of Bruenn the Russians took Sitborice and Vranovice (11) and continued to surge forward.

INFANTRY RINGS FOE ON IE, OFF OKINAWA

Americans Hold Two-thirds of Isle—Guns in Fierce Duels on Main Ryukyu Mass

By GEORGE E. JONES
By Wireless to THE NEW YORK TIMES.

GUAM, Wednesday, April 18—American infantry on Ie, small island about three miles off the western coast of Okinawa, invaded Monday, met "moderate resistance" from the Japanese defenders, Fleet Admiral Chester W. Nimitz announced today. Twenty-fourth Corps infantrymen who landed on the southern beaches and pushed to the island's northern beachline wheeled east and now occupy more

Continued on Page 3, Column 2

Nazi Death Factory Shocks Germans on a Forced Tour

By GENE CURRIVAN
By Wireless to THE NEW YORK TIMES.

BUCHENWALD, Germany, April 16 (Delayed)—German civilians—1,200 of them—were brought from the neighboring city of Weimar today to see for themselves the horror, brutality and human indecency perpetrated against their "neighbors" at the infamous Buchenwald concentration camp. They saw sights that brought tears to their eyes, and scores of them, including German nurses, just fainted away.

They saw more than 20,000 nondescript prisoners, many of them barely living, who were all that remained of the normal complement of 80,000. The Germans were able to evacuate the others before we overran the place on April 10.

There were 32,705 that the "vis-

Continued on Page 8, Column 1

ARMY BEGINS SHIFT TO PACIFIC FRONT

Some Supplies Diverted in U. S., Others Sent From Europe—War Output Still High

By SIDNEY SHALETT
Special to THE NEW YORK TIMES.

WASHINGTON, April 17—Redeployment of men and matériel from Europe to the Pacific has actually begun, a high War Department official revealed today. It is only token redeployment thus far, but it is officially viewed here as indicative of a trend which will be stepped up, even as the European war still is being fought to its end.

Two other disclosures made by

Continued on Page 4, Column 2

HALT AT THE ELBE LAID TO LOGISTICS

Tactical Unity With Red Army Believed Lacking—Russians May Enter Berlin First

By DREW MIDDLETON
By Wireless to THE NEW YORK TIMES.

PARIS, April 17—The eastern thrust of the Twelfth Army Group, Gen. Dwight D. Eisenhower's main striking force in the battle of Germany, has halted. There undoubtedly will be filling-up operations to the lines of the Elbe and Mulde rivers by United States Ninth, First and Third Armies; there may even be a drive eastward to Dresden by Lieut. Gen. George S. Patton's tanks. Generally, however, the great offensive has come to a halt.

In the opinion of this correspondent, Russian and not American formations will enter Berlin first. A junction of the Allied Expeditionary Force and the Red Army is more likely to occur when the flanks of the two forces brush each other at the beginning of the vast policing operation that must start in the near future. It is extremely unlikely that any headlong contact will be made by

Continued on Page 5, Column 3

War News Summarized

WEDNESDAY, APRIL 18, 1945

The American drive on Berlin came to a halt yesterday when General Eisenhower's forces concentrated upon clearing the Germans from more territory and reducing pockets behind the battle lines. The Canadian First Army in the Netherlands swept through Apeldoorn, forty-five miles from Amsterdam. The British Second was twenty-five miles from Hamburg. The United States Ninth smashed into Magdeburg, the First surrounded Leipzig and was reported in that city, the Third laid siege to Chemnitz and also was little more than four miles from the Czech border; the Seventh was fighting in Nuremberg. [1:8.]

Supply problems and difficulties in coordinating tactical plans with those of the Russians were believed the main reasons for the halt in the push on Berlin from the west. [1:7.]

Berlin placed the Red Army eighteen and twenty miles east of the German capital, but Moscow maintained its silence about action there. The Russians cleared the Germans out of all the Samland Peninsula except the Pillau area and also occupied the Austrian oil region. [1:3.]

The Allied offensive in Italy pushed ahead against stubborn resistance. The Eighth Army was nine to thirteen miles from Bologna and had by-passed Argenta; the Fifth conquered more mountain peaks on the west. [10:1, with map.]

Allied fliers have destroyed 4,139 German planes this month, most of them on the ground. Yesterday the Eighth Air Force hit rail and oil targets in Germany and Czechoslovakia, wiping out 282 more enemy aircraft. [1:6-7.]

Transfer of troops and supplies from Europe to the Pacific has already begun, the War Department disclosed in Washington. [1:6.]

Superfortresses went on their first tactical missions when large forces of B-29's struck airfields on Kyushu from which Japanese planes have been attacking the Okinawa invasion fleet. [3:1]. There was little change in positions on Okinawa, but two-thirds of Ie Island has been occupied. [1:4; map P. 2.]

More than 7,000 civilians, mostly Filipinos, have been freed by United States troops, who have reached the outskirts of Baguio, Philippine summer capital. [4:7.]

Churchill Eulogizes Roosevelt As Best U. S. Friend to Britain

By CLIFTON DANIEL
By Wireless to THE NEW YORK TIMES.

LONDON, April 17—Great Britain paid tribute to the late President Roosevelt today, with Prime Minister Churchill eulogizing him in the House of Commons as "the greatest American friend we have ever known," and with an earlier memorial service in St. Paul's Cathedral, attended by the royal family, the country's leading officials, as well as by ordinary persons.

Mr. Churchill, who wept at the memorial service, told Commons that the death of the "greatest champion of freedom who has ever brought comfort and help from the New World to the Old" was "a loss, indeed a bitter loss, to humanity."

"At Yalta," the Prime Minister continued, "I noticed that the President was ailing. His captivating smile, his gay, charming manner had not deserted him, but his face had a transparency, an air of purification, and often there was a far-away look in his eyes.

"When I took leave of him at Alexandria I must confess that I had an indefinable sense of fear that his strength and health were on the ebb."

Saying that Mr. Roosevelt "had raised the strength, might and

Continued on Page 18, Column 2

Fliers 'Kill' 440 More Nazi Planes; 8th Bombs Dresden-Prague Rails

By SYDNEY GRUSON
By Wireless to THE NEW YORK TIMES.

LONDON, Wednesday, April 18—Another 282 German planes were destroyed by the United States Eighth Air Force yesterday and headquarters announced that in ten days the Eighth had wiped out 1,720 park enemy aircraft—the front-line operational strength of a once-masterful Luftwaffe.

Thirteen of the Eighth's bag yesterday were destroyed in combat as 1,000 Flying Fortresses and Liberators bombed three railway yards at Dresden, five junctions in Czechoslovakia and a large underground oil storage depot at Raudnitz, twenty-two miles north of Prague. More than 850 fighters went along and got Nazi kill.

[Allied fliers striking from the west destroyed at least 440 German planes Tuesday, bringing the total kill against the Luftwaffe for April to 4,139.

[American and British tactical planes based in Europe attacked in strength by day. Tuesday night strikes by the Royal Air Force Bomber Command over Berlin and central Germany were indicated, The Associated Press reported.]

The Eighth Air Force flew a

Continued on Page 10, Column 3

HEM IN REICH PORTS

British Closing to Elbe—U. S. Troops in Leipzig, Reduce Magdeburg

DUESSELDORF IS OURS

3d Army Is Reported in Bohemia—149,000 Taken in One Day

By Wireless to THE NEW YORK TIMES.

PARIS, April 17—British armored divisions on the left flank of the Allied Expeditionary Force's main battlefront raced northward to within twenty-five miles of Hamburg today, while in the center the armies of Gen. Omar N. Bradley's Twelfth Army Group began a reduction of the principal German strongholds behind forward positions of the United States Ninth, First and Third Armies along the Elbe and Mulde Rivers.

Tanks and infantry of the Ninth Army smashed into the flaming streets of Magdeburg this afternoon. First Army infantry have surrounded Leipzig and, according to one report from the front, have already pushed into the outskirts of the city, the fifth largest city in the Reich. The German commander at Chemnitz has turned down a demand by the Third Army to surrender the city.

The Forty-fifth Division of the United States Seventh Army is fighting its way into Nuremberg.

There has been no forward movement toward Berlin. The Ninth Army is clinging to its bridgehead over the Elbe near Barby, after repulsing a savage German counter-attack that cost the Germans fifteen to twenty tanks and heavy casualties in personnel.

Four German Pockets Shrink

Four of the most important German positions behind the Allied battle line — those in the Netherlands, the Ruhr, the Harz Mountains and at the mouth of the Gironde River in France—were shrinking under heavy Allied blows.

The Canadians have captured Apeldoorn, forty-five miles from Amsterdam, in the center of the German position in the Netherlands. The Ruhr pocket has now been reduced to only 125 square miles. First and Ninth Army forces have linked up in the Harz Mountains.

[The Luxembourg radio in a broadcast heard by the Columbia Broadcasting System said that "enemy resistance in the Ruhr pocket has collapsed and Duesseldorf has surrendered."]

On the Atlantic front the Allied offensive to open Bordeaux to shipping is nearing its end, with French tanks rolling through German positions and poilus mopping up knots of German infantrymen.

The tremendous losses that the German Army has suffered in the great battles of this month were emphasized by an announcement that the AEF had captured more than 760,000 prisoners from April 1 through yesterday. The First and Ninth Armies took 266,806 prisoners from the Ruhr pocket during this period, and the three armies of General Bradley's army group alone have captured 1,489,261 Germans since the beginning of operations on this continent 316 days ago.

149,000 Prisoners in One Day

Yesterday's prisoner bag is believed to be the greatest yet taken by the AEF. More than 149,000 Germans were rounded up by the Allies in the one day. The United States First Army captured 97,118 of these, boosting its army total to 659,117.

The phase of the operations into which General Bradley's Army Group has now entered will in many ways be as difficult as the great sweep eastward from the Rhine. Infantry will have to storm the principal enemy towns, most of them strongly held, while other doughboys seek out and destroy

Continued on Page 6, Column 1

"All the News That's Fit to Print"

The New York Times.

LATE CITY EDITION
Sunny and cool today. Increasing cloudiness, warmer tomorrow.
Temperatures Yesterday—Max., 52; Min., 47

VOL. XCIV..No. 31,871. Entered as Second-Class Matter, Postoffice, New York, N. Y. NEW YORK, SATURDAY, APRIL 28, 1945. THREE CENTS NEW YORK CITY

U. S. AND RED ARMIES JOIN, SPLIT GERMANY; 3D ARMY IN AUSTRIA; RUSSIANS IN POTSDAM; PARLEY BARS LUBLIN, SOVIET GETS 3 VOTES

RUSSIAN ISSUES OUT

Plea for 4 Chairmen Won but Stettinius Will Head Vital Committees

EQUALITY CALLED AIM

Heads of 14 Delegations Are Named as Members of Executive Group

By JAMES B. RESTON

Special to THE NEW YORK TIMES.

SAN FRANCISCO, April 27—The United Nations Conference on International Organization today accepted two of the three requests put before it by Soviet Russia, and rejected the third.

First, the delegates of the forty-six nations gathered here to establish an international security organization accepted Russia's request that there should be four presidents of the conference, Edward R. Stettinius Jr., American Secretary of State; Vyacheslaff M. Molotoff, Russian Foreign Commissar; Anthony Eden, British Secretary of State for Foreign Affairs, and T. V. Soong, Chinese Foreign Minister.

They agreed, however, that while the four presidents would preside in turn over the plenary sessions of the conference, the four presidents would delegate to Mr. Stettinius the chairmanship of the Executive and Steering Committees of the conference, and allow him to preside over the meetings of the four presidents whenever they conferred.

Second, they accepted Marshal Stalin's proposal that two of the sixteen Soviet Republics, White Russia and the Ukraine, should become initial voting members of the new world security organization, after President H[illegible] S. Truman had instructed the [illegible] States delegation to fulfi[illegible] D. Roosevelt's promise [illegible] this action.

Third, they rejected Russia's request, made publicly in Moscow, and brought up privately but not pressed here, that the present Polish Provisional Government of Warsaw (classed as the Lublin regime) be allowed to attend the conference. Instead, the conference passed a resolution expressing the hope that Poland would be represented at the conference as soon as the present difficulties over the "broadening" of the Polish Government were resolved.

Reply on Poland Drafted

On this latter point there was one important development. Marshal Stalin's reply to the report he received on the conversations which took place with President Truman and the Foreign Ministers of "the Big Three" in Washington several days ago has been received and studied here. It does not, in the opinion of those members of the American and British delegations who have seen it, change the basic issue over the expansion of the Warsaw Government to include "democratic elements" from inside and outside Poland.

A reply to Marshal Stalin's note has been drafted here and has been approved by Washington and sent to London for Prime Minister Churchill's observations. It will be sent to Moscow, probably this week-end. In the meanwhile, the deadlock continues.

It is generally admitted here that Mr. Molotoff received approval on the two issue, on which he insisted. He wished to establish two principles and made this clear to the heads of the delegations:

First, he wanted to establish the principle of equality among the four sponsor powers running the conference; second, he desired to establish the principle that the Soviet Republics were independent entities with the right to sit and vote at international conferences. These two principles were accepted in this afternoon's plenary session

Continued on Page 10, Column 3

Parley Sessions Opened to Press

By The Associated Press.

SAN FRANCISCO, April 27—A United States proposal to apply the principle of free information to the United Nations Conference was adopted today by the steering committee of forty-six chiefs of delegations.

Secretary Stettinius told a news conference that plenary sessions of the conference and meetings of the four principal commissions would be held in public, open to complete reporting.

He also said that principal officers of the conference would hold regular meetings with accredited press, radio and photography representatives.

The commissions, however, were authorized to hold some closed meetings, at their own direction, and sessions of technical committees and subcommittees were made secret.

The Dumbarton Oaks Conference, at which the original proposals for a world security conference were drafted, was entirely closed.

DRAFT EXTENSION SENT TO PRESIDENT

House Adopts Senate Training Amendment After Hearing 'Declaration of Intent'

By C. P. TRUSSELL

Special to THE NEW YORK TIMES.

WASHINGTON, April 27—The House accepted unanimously today the Senate amendment to the Draft Extension Bill which bars the Army from ordering 18-year-old inductees into combat until they have had at least six months of military training.

In sending the measure to President Truman, the House went on record with an interpretation of the amendment whereby 18-year-old soldiers already on battle fronts will not be withdrawn and marines will be classified with soldiers in training requirements.

The amendment provides:

"That no man under 19 years of age who is inducted into the land or naval forces under the provisions of this (Selective Service) act shall be ordered into actual combat service until after he has been given at least six months of military training of such character and to the extent necessary to prepare such inductee for combat duty.

"This proviso shall not be construed as preventing the assignment of enlisted men of the Navy or Coast Guard and the reserve components thereof to duty for training on combat vessels of the Navy or Coast Guard and at naval bases beyond the continental limits of the United States."

Before taking the question to the floor, the House Military Affairs Committee had decided that the measure, which extends the draft for a year from May 15, should not be sent to conference because of

Continued on Page 3, Column 7

BERLIN NEAR FINISH

Spandau Arsenal and Potsdam Fall—Koneff Wins Big Airfield

¾ OF CAPITAL SEIZED

Two Columns Strike West—Russians Drive to Seal Baltic Ports

By C. L. SULZBERGER

By Wireless to THE NEW YORK TIMES.

MOSCOW, Saturday, April 28—Russian assault groups overwhelmed the southern half of Berlin yesterday, capturing four city districts, including the famous Tempelhof airdrome, and advancing to within one mile of Unter den Linden. [Three-fourths of the capital was in the Red Army's hands, The Associated Press reported.]

At the same time the Russians ground their way into martial Potsdam, where lie the remains of Frederick the Great, and seized Spandau, where since that monarch's reign the best German small-arms weapon had been manufactured in old ordnance plants.

On the western outskirts of the city it was Marshal Gregory K. Zhukoff's First White Russian Army group that battered its way through Potsdam and Spandau, last two strongly held outer bastions of Berlin's crumbling defense. In the south Marshal Ivan S. Koneff's well-schooled street fighters plunged through the rubble of Neukoelln, Steglitz, Schmargendorf and central Tempelhof, on whose airdrome Adolf Hitler's lackeys landed and from which perhaps they had hoped to fly to doubtful and impermanent havens.

[The United Press reported from Moscow that small Soviet bombers were able to land on captured Tempelhof airdrome.

[Lieut. Gen. Kurt Dittmar, German strategist, whose surrender this week to the American Ninth Army was announced Friday, added his voice to the Germans' insistence that Hitler was in the capital. He said that the war was over and that the great redoubt was largely a myth.]

Ring Being Closed Anew

Only two smoking districts separate the southwestern segment of the iron ring around Berlin from Charlottenburg and Unter den Linden—Wilmersdorf and Schoenberg.

Marshal Zhukoff's forces took 8,500 prisoners around Berlin.

It seemed early today as if the Russians had penetrated the Grunewald Forest, south of Charlottenburg. Bitter fighting continued in the northern and northeastern areas under ever-growing smoke layers.

Marshal Koneff made a sensational advance all the way from the western suburbs of Berlin to the Elbe River, capturing Wittenberg and making imminent a new

Continued on Page 5, Column 2

HANDS ACROSS THE ELBE: AMERICANS AND RUSSIANS MEET IN REICH

United States First Army infantrymen and Soviet troops on a broken bridge over the river at Torgau

Associated Press Wirephoto (U. S. Signal Corps Radiophoto)

GENOA IS ENTERED BY 5TH ARMY MEN

Partisans Seize Large Part of Italy's Greatest Port—Allies Dash Toward Milan

By VIRGINIA LEE WARREN

By Wireless to THE NEW YORK TIMES.

ADVANCED ALLIED FIELD HEADQUARTERS, Italy, April 27—Genoa, Italy's largest port, with nearly 1,000,000 inhabitants, was entered by a Fifth Army task force this morning after Italian Partisans had gained control of a large part of the city. Commanded by Maj. Gen. Edward M. Almond and operating directly under the Fifteenth Army Group, the task force was made up of the

Continued on Page 6, Column 5

First Link Made Wednesday By Four Americans on Patrol

By HAROLD DENNY

By Wireless to THE NEW YORK TIMES.

AT A RED ARMY OUTPOST, on the Elbe, April 27—The United States and Russian armies have met on the Elbe. The Western and Eastern fronts are at last linked up and Germany is cut in two. First contact was made two days ago—at 4:40 P. M., April 25, by a four-man patrol of the 273d Infantry Regiment of the Sixty-ninth Infantry Division and a Russian outpost at the sizable town of Torgau, twenty miles west of our then most advanced forces.

On the American side the honor of making this historic junction goes to Gen. Courtney H. Hodges' United States First Army, which forced the Normandy beaches last June and has advanced 700 miles through France, Belgium and Ger-

Continued on Page 4, Column 5

SURRENDER OFFERS BY NAZIS REPORTED

Group Said to By-Pass Hitler in Bid to Western Allies, Who Stand on Role by Russia

By SIDNEY SHALETT

Special to THE NEW YORK TIMES.

WASHINGTON, April 27—Reports current in Washington—reports more numerous and more authoritative than any of the sort previously heard in this capital—indicated tonight that Nazi Germany had made known a willingness to surrender unconditionally to the United States and Britain, but not to the Soviet Union, and that the Western Allies have told the enemy negotiators that they will accept "only for all."

The reports stirred belief here that a formal admission of defeat from Germany was imminent.

This information is not made

Continued on Page 2, Column 2

MEETING OF ARMIES HAILED BY TRUMAN

Says Last Hope of 'Hitler and His Gangster Government Has Been Extinguished'

Text of President's announcement of junction, Page 3.

By BERTRAM D. HULEN

Special to THE NEW YORK TIMES.

WASHINGTON, April 27—President Truman announced today that the Anglo-American armies and the Soviet forces have made their long-expected junction "where they intended to meet—in the heart of Nazi Germany."

The junction was made, the White House said, at Torgau, a town on the Elbe River, seventy-five miles south of Berlin. According to the War Department the forces met yesterday at 10 A. M., E. W. T. Patrols had made contact on Wednesday at 10:30 A. M., E. W. T.

Simultaneous announcements were made in London and Moscow.

In making the announcement, President Truman's statement declared that "the enemy has been cut in two." However, he warned that this was not the final victory in Europe, although, he said, the hour for which all "have toiled and prayed so long" was drawing near.

It means, he asserted, that "the

Continued on Page 3, Column 2

FIRM LINK FORMED

Junction of Two Armies Splits Rest of Reich Into Huge Pockets

PATTON RACES SOUTH

Crosses Austrian Border Without Opposition—New Linkup Impends

By DREW MIDDLETON

By Wireless to THE NEW YORK TIMES.

PARIS, April 27—Two armies of plain men who had marched and fought from the blood-splashed beaches of Normandy and the shattered streets of Stalingrad have met on the Elbe River in the heart of Germany, splitting the Third Reich and sealing the doom of the German Army, whose tread shook the world only three short years ago.

The junction on the Elbe River of Gen. Courtney H. Hodges' United States First Army and Marshal Ivan S. Koneff's First Ukrainian Army transcends all other developments on the Western Front, even a thrust across the Austrian border by an armored column of Gen. George S. Patton's United States Third Army, which is diving eastward toward Marshal Fedor I. Tolbukhin's Soviet forces smashing westward eighty miles away.

Junction Made Wednesday

The first official contact between the Red Army and the Allies' Expeditionary Forces was made at 4:40 P. M. on Wednesday, when a second lieutenant and three men of an intelligence and reconnaissance platoon of the 273d Regiment of the Sixty-ninth Infantry Division of the First Army met elements of the 173d Regiment of the Fifty-eighth Guards Division of the First Ukrainian Army on the girders of a demolished bridge at Torgau on the Elbe, twenty-eight miles northeast of Leipzig. Yesterday afternoon at 4 o'clock Maj. Gen. Emil F. Reinhardt, commanding the Sixty-ninth Division, conferred with the commander of the Soviet Guards Division at Torgau on the mutual exchange of liberated prisoners of war.

Tonight the meeting of the East and West is sealed and details of both armies are guarding the roads between the two fronts while senior officers of both sides pay their respects to their comrades in arms.

The German front was split after a junction that ended a drive of 1,400 miles to the west by the Red Armies starting from Stalingrad and 700 miles to the east by the First Army, whose first elements came ashore in Normandy last June.

Mop-Up Work Remains

From now on pockets and redoubts of varying sizes and strengths are the main tactical objectives of the Anglo-American and Red Armies and the advances will be to the north and south rather than to the east and west, as so long has been the case.

With the American and Red Armies now in firm contact to the north, the United States Third Army and Marshal Tolbukhin's Third Ukrainian Army are moving swiftly toward each other and another junction in Austria which would isolate the Bohemian redoubt in western Czechoslovakia. At the same time the United States Seventh Army and the French First Army have broken German defenses in the western part of the Bavarian foreland and are rolling down on the northern boundary of Hitler's Alpine redoubt.

At last reports tonight columns of both the United States Seventh and Third Armies were less than forty miles from Munich, key to the outer defenses of the redoubt, and tanks of the Tenth Armored Division on the Seventh Army's right flank were only twenty-seven miles north of the Austrian frontier at the western end of the redoubt.

The swift advances of the last

Continued on Page 3, Column 6

State Leads in Care of Veterans, Dewey Says in 'Report to People'

Special to THE NEW YORK TIMES.

ALBANY, April 27—Governor Dewey, in a radio report tonight to the people of the State, hailed "the tremendous news of the final juncture of the Allied and Russian armies in Nazi Germany" and said New York has led all other States in providing for its returning war veterans.

[The text of the Governor's address will be found on Page 9.]

The Governor, before discussing the accomplishments of the 1945 Legislature and of his administration, said the news from Europe offers occasion for reaffirmance of our determination to bring about complete defeat of our remaining enemies in Germany and Japan and rigorous punishment of war criminals. He added:

"At the same time the United Nations work earnestly at San Francisco to make the peace to come secure and lasting."

Governor Dewey's talk covered a wide range of subjects, from aid for veterans to experience rating in unemployment insurance. He asserted:

"Of one thing you may be sure. Your State Administration has given progressive and financially sound administration. The rights of our workers have been advanced and the opportunities in business and employment have been increased."

Governor Dewey will give another radio report to the people next Friday night. It was explained that the large number of new laws and administrative changes made it impossible for him to cover the entire field in a single

Continued on Page 9, Column 3

War News Summarized

SATURDAY, APRIL 28, 1945

The eagerly awaited announcement that the Allied armies that entered Europe via the beachheads of Normandy and the Red Army that turned back the Nazi tide at Stalingrad had met in the heart of Germany came simultaneously yesterday from Washington, London and Moscow. The epochal linking of the western and eastern fronts took place on Wednesday afternoon at Torgau, on the Elbe River, twenty-eight miles northeast of Leipzig. [1:8; map P. 2.]

The armies' first contact was between patrols of the Sixty-ninth Division of General Hodges' American First Army and the Fifty-eighth Guards Division of Marshal Koneff's First Ukrainian Army. The meeting was accidental and the Russians mistook the Americans at first for Germans. [1:5-6.] The splitting of the German forces is expected to speed the destruction of the enemy, for Allied armies now can turn their might toward either side, with the reduction of the redoubts in the north and south having top priority. [5:6]

With three-fourths of Berlin in Russian hands, the Red Army struck westward for a new junction with Allied forces, this time with the American Ninth Army west of the rubbled German capital. A thirteen-mile gap separated the two army forces. German resistance within Berlin was crumbling. The Russians seized Tempelhof airport and Potsdam and it appeared that few, if any, of the Nazi leaders in the capital would be able to escape. [1:3.]

Hitler is still in Berlin and intends to die there, according to General Dittmar, who surrendered to American troops. The Nazi officer, who was the radio voice of the German High Command, predicted that the war would end in a few days with the fall of Berlin. [4:1.]

In Italy, the American Fifth Army slashed into Genoa, the last German naval base on the Mediterranean, and swept closer to Turin and Milan through weak and disorganized resistance. [1:4; map P. 6.] Benito Mussolini was captured by Italian Partisans as he tried to cross the Swiss border, according to information at the frontier. [6:6.]

In the Pacific, American forces hammered through Japanese defenses on southern Okinawa to the area of Machinato, two miles from Naha, the island's capital. [1:6.] Our troops on Mindanao, in the Philippines, were within sight of Digos, on Davao Gulf, after a ten-mile eastward push. [8:6.]

The United Nations conference in San Francisco agreed to give White Russia and the Ukraine a vote each in the proposed Assembly of the new world security organization, but refused to invite the provisional Polish regime in Warsaw. The delegates accepted the Soviet request for four presidents at the conference. [1:1.]

General Gain Made on Okinawa; 27th Division Nears Key Airfield

By ROBERT TRUMBULL

By Wireless to THE NEW YORK TIMES.

GUAM, Saturday, April 28—In a day of general advances by Army troops on Okinawa, elements of the Twenty-seventh Infantry Division [former New York National Guard organization] were approaching the Machinato airstrip on the western side of the island Thursday, Fleet Admiral Chester W. Nimitz reported in a communiqué this morning.

Twenty-seventh Division troops were in the vicinity of the airfield by 6 o'clock Thursday evening. Attacks in this and other sectors on a front bisecting the narrow island were resumed yesterday morning.

American aircraft were operating from airfields previously taken.

The situation continued to be quiet in the northern section of Okinawa, held by marines of the Third Amphibious Corps under Maj. Gen. Roy S. Geiger. Activity was restricted to patrolling Thursday and Friday.

A minesweeper shot down three Japanese planes early yesterday, a great feat for such a small vessel. Very few enemy aircraft appeared over the American forces.

In the southern Ryukyus, carrier aircraft of the United States Pacific Fleet carried attacks on the Sakishima Islands into the third successive day. This group has five major airstrips on the islands of Miyako and Ishigaki, which have been pounded incessantly by American and British carrier planes throughout the past month.

Routine air operations elsewhere in the Pacific included attacks on harbor installations on Chichi Island in the Bonins by Marine

Continued on Page 8, Column 7

"All the News That's Fit to Print"

The New York Times.

LATE CITY EDITION
Cloudy and cool; showers tonight. Clearing and warmer tomorrow.
Temperatures Yesterday—Max., 54; Min., 41
Sunrise today, 5:56 A. M.; Sunset, 7:40 P. M.

Section 1

NEWS INDEX, PAGE 39, THIS SECTION

Copyright, 1945, by The New York Times Company.

VOL. XCIV. No. 31,872. Entered as Second-Class Matter, Postoffice, New York, N. Y. NEW YORK, SUNDAY, APRIL 29, 1945. Including Magazine and Book Sections. TEN CENTS

ALLIES BAR PEACE PLEA THAT OMITS RUSSIA; SURRENDER REPORT UNTRUE, TRUMAN SAYS; MUNICH REVOLTS; HITLER SAID TO BE DYING

RUSSIANS DEMAND IMMEDIATE SEATING OF TWO REPUBLICS

Latin-Americans Then Insist That Argentina Be Admitted —Settlement Is Likely

PEACE TALK STIRS PARLEY

Small Countries Find the Big 4 Striving to Speed Actions Before V-E Day Comes

By JAMES B. RESTON
Special to THE NEW YORK TIMES.

SAN FRANCISCO, April 28—The phase of political maneuvering at the San Francisco Conference is drawing to a close, but it is not quite finished.

A new controversy among the United States, Britain and Soviet Russia developed today over the insistence of the Soviet Foreign Commissar, Vyacheslaff M. Molotoff, that the representatives of White Russia and the Ukraine be seated in the conference before the working committees of the conference start their deliberations.

This controversy, referred to the Executive Committee of the conference, is further complicated by the fact that some of the Latin-American countries are insisting that, if the two Soviet republics are seated, Argentina should be invited to join the United Nations and attend.

Every effort is being made by the American and British delegations to keep these two questions from being involved with each other, while it is becoming increasingly evident that the Russians are sensitive to the voting power of the countries of the Western Hemisphere. There is, however, reason for saying that the basis for a private agreement has already been reached under which all three will be seated in the conference next week.

Small Powers Give Views

While this question was being discussed behind the scenes, the delegates gathered in the Opera House this morning and again this afternoon for two plenary sessions at which the representatives of the smaller countries expressed a general willingness to accept the Dumbarton Oaks security formula.

Reports of the German surrender, which were circulated in newspaper headlines on the floor of the opera house during this afternoon's plenary session, led to demonstrations of exultation.

The demonstrations took place while the official translator was reading an English translation of the Uruguayan Foreign Minister's address before a plenary session of the conference.

The head of the Honduran delegation, Julian R. Caceres, walked into the opera house with a copy of a San Francisco paper in his hand. It was an extra edition with a headline reading: "Nazis Quit." Mr. Caceres walked down the aisle holding the paper above his head, circled in front of the audience and held the newspaper aloft.

Delegates all over the chamber stood up and broke into applause. It was several minutes before order was restored.

It was increasingly evident today that the possibility of an imminent peace in Europe was beginning to play an important part in the deliberations of the four powers sponsoring the conference.

Russian Question Speeded

That is why the question of seating the Russian delegates was being dealt with at once.

Mr. Molotoff, it is now learned, told the Steering Committee yesterday that he wanted the two Soviet republics brought into the conference immediately. There was a tendency on the part of some members of the committee to accede to this request at once, but

Continued on Page 28, Column 1

Berlin's 'Fleet' Sails To Elbe to Surrender

By The Associated Press.

WITH THE UNITED STATES NINTH ARMY, on the Elbe River, April 28—American doughboys on this topsy-turvy front have now seen everything. The ultimate was reached last night when a German "fleet" sailed up the Elbe and surrendered. It had come from Berlin through inland waterways.

The fleet consisted of six tugboats, ten river barges, three houseboats and eleven assorted escorts loaded with wounded and marked with red crosses. The entire fleet surrendered to Lieut. Andrew Gadek of 43 Fremont Street, Woodbridge, N. J.

A German major in charge said they feared the approach of the Russians because of their "inhumanity." Gadek replied there were a few scenes of "inhumanity" near there, where the Germans had burned 1,100 prisoners to death in a barn.

An English-speaking nurse replied: "Oh, that s different."

ANTHRACITE MINES FACING SHUT-DOWN

Union Withholds Approval of Contract Extension—Lewis Sees New Pact Possible

A shut-down of Pennsylvania anthracite production Tuesday was threatened yesterday when the United Mine Workers withheld approval of the request of Secretary of the Interior Harold L. Ickes for a thirty-day extension of the coal contract, which expires at midnight tomorrow.

While anthracite operators, meeting at the Waldorf-Astoria Hotel, telegraphed Mr. Ickes of their agreement to his request, the union announced it was "continuing to give the subject consideration."

John L. Lewis, president of the UMW, insisted that an extension would lead to "prolongation of uncertainty and is in every way undesirable." He said that "we think the [anthracite coal] conference is in a position to complete the execution of a new contract before Monday night."

"We see no reason for procrastination," he asserted. "We are deferring any decision on the request for a thirty-day extension until we can determine whether or not this conference is going to finish its work."

Lewis Stand Not Challenged

Although there have been no announced compromises on the miners' demands, none of the operators challenged Mr. Lewis' statement that "the issues of the conference are boiled down and concentrated to certain specific items on which decision can easily be made by Monday night." In addition he said that "we think every moral, economic and national consideration calls for completion of

Continued on Page 31, Column 2

REICH ARMY REBELS

Uprisings Led by Revolt in the Cradle of Nazism Sweep South Germany

TROOPS DROP ARMS

Bloody Disorders Follow Abortive Coup Tuesday in City of Salzburg

By DANIEL T. BRIGHAM
By Telephone to THE NEW YORK TIMES.

BERNE, Switzerland, April 28—Led off by the city of Munich, home of the National Socialist movement, which rose to throw off the yoke of nazism at 3 o'clock this morning, the civilian population of southwestern Germany, joined by increasing numbers of German Army garrisons that are deserting en masse right up to the Swiss frontier tonight, is in the throes of one of the bloodiest revolutions in German history.

[Allied Headquarters in Paris said more than 80,000 Germans had been captured on the western front on Friday while Soviet reports declared taht 27,000 Germans had given up the fight in the Berlin area.]

Everywhere from the outskirts of the Alpine redoubt back up railway and road lines of communications to the foremost spearheads of the Allied armies marching southward come reports from neutral automobile and truck drivers, from refugees and even the military telling of pitched battles between the German Army and Nazi party with most of the engagements turning entirely in favor of the former.

From semi-official sources it also was learned tonight that a second "freedom movement" had sprung up Tuesday in Salzburg where a dissident government headed by Reichsbank President Walther Funk called on Austrians inside the redoubt to rise and "throw off your oppressors." The move is said to have failed.

Rebels Hold Half of Munich

At Munich itself the uprising, according to the latest information pieced together from official and clandestine German sources as well as neutral Swiss reports, shows that after an initial success of some nine hours the revolt turned briefly against the rebels, permitting the Nazis to recapture the Munich radio station, which at midnight tonight was still in party hands. But broadcast orders on army radios of the German Army show that the situation is rapidly turning back in favor of the insurgents, who now hold more than half of the city of Munich, from the Isar River to its northwestern outskirts at Rothkirchen.

First news of the outbreak came at 7:30 this morning, when the Munich radio station suddenly announced its program was being

Continued on Page 10, Column 1

BERLIN TOTTERING

Germans Squeezed Into 25 Square Miles of Shattered Heart

27,000 TROOPS YIELD

Soviet Forces North of Capital Strike Out for Hamburg Pocket

By C. L. SULZBERGER
By Wireless to THE NEW YORK TIMES.

MOSCOW, Sunday, April 29—The defenses of inner Berlin were cracked wide open yesterday as two giant Soviet armies captured 27,000 prisoners in wholesale surrenders and as Russian assault groups plunged deep into the shattered capital from all points of the compass.

Marshal Ivan S. Koneff's troops smashed into three more city districts in the western part of the metropolis, occupying Friedenau, Grunewald and Ruhleben, while in the woods to the southeast his First Ukrainian Army joined forces with Marshal Gregory K. Zhukoff's First White Russian Army to surround a large pocket of Germans.

In the northwestern part of the flaming citadel, meanwhile, Marshal Zhukoff thundered through Charlottenburg as far as Bismarckstrasse and occupied completely the western section of the Moabit district, which had already been largely overrun, and the eastern part of Schoenberg. Thus Marshal Zhukoff's forces have almost entirely surrounded Berlin by themselves, except for the southwestern and part of the southern segment of the steel ring compressing Berlin.

Two army groups have effected a new junction below Siemens-

Continued on Page 5, Column 7

RUSSIANS FIGHTING IN THE STREETS OF BERLIN

Red Army tanks and infantrymen advancing along Berlinerstrasse

The New York Times (Sovfoto Radiophoto)

7TH ARMY CROSSES AUSTRIAN FRONTIER

Enters at Two Points Near Innsbrueck as Gen. Patton Speeds Salzburg Drive

By DREW MIDDLETON
By Wireless to THE NEW YORK TIMES.

PARIS, April 28—Tanks and doughboys of Lieut. Gen. Alexander M. Patch's United States Seventh Army have smashed the last German defenses in the Bavarian foreland and have swept over the Austrian frontier at two points to hammer the northern gates of Hitler's Alpine redoubt after an advance that has covered 130 miles from Nuremberg in nine days.

The United States Third Army's thrust down the Danube toward

Continued on Page 7, Column 1

15th Army to Occupy Reich, With No Pampering of Foe

By The Associated Press.

PARIS, April 28—Lieut. Gen. Leonard T. Gerow's United States Fifteenth Army will take over the occupation of the United States section of Germany—and see to it that there is no pampering of the vanquished—headquarters indicated today. Its field of occupation is expected to embrace much of southern Germany.

The general's headquarters said German civilians would be allowed a maximum diet of 1,150 calories a day—only about a third as bountiful as that of American soldiers in the German theatre, and slightly more than half as great as the average for civilians in liberated countries.

How well the Germans eat will depend largely on how willing they are to help themselves by producing the foodstuffs, it was made clear, because the plans call for importation of food into Germany only if necessary to avert famine and disease.

The Germans will be expected to produce enough to feed themselves and displaced Russians, French, Belgian, Polish and other nationals awaiting transportation home, a spokesman said.

Food to Be Third of Ours

At the office of Col. Thomas J. Moroney of Dallas, Tex., assistant chief of staff of G-5 under General Gerow, an officer said the maximum diet of 1,150 calories meant lean meals, but that not all Germans received that much now.

The average American soldier in the theatre to be occupied receives 4,000 calories a day and the average civilian in liberated countries receives 2,000.

Control of the German diet by the occupying forces will be exercised through civilian provincial and local officials, it was said. Fewer than one-fourth of the 2,210,000 German prisoners taken on the western front have put to work, but in these final weeks of the war the Allies are considering a plan to make them work and

Continued on Page 9, Column 1

ESCAPE ROUTES CUT BY ALLIES IN ITALY

Fifth Army Takes Bergamo and Brescia at Foot of Alps as German Debacle Develops

By VIRGINIA LEE WARREN
By Wireless to THE NEW YORK TIMES.

ROME, April 28—Fifth Army forces, which burst out of the Apennines just nineteen days ago to sweep the Po Valley clean of the bulk of the Wehrmacht, have almost cut off the remaining German troops in northwest Italy by capturing Bergamo at the foot of the Alps thirty miles from the Swiss border, and Brescia, about thirty miles east of Bergamo.

[The Swiss radio said Saturday night that the Germans had agreed to surrender in Lombardy and Piedmont and that all fighting had ceased in those two north Italian provinces, which border on Switzerland, The Associated Press reported. The broadcast, which was unconfirmed, said that a German general and colonel had made the surrender to Gen. Rafaele Cardona, commander of Italian forces in northern Italy, and to an American and a British officer.

[Milan and Turin were freed of German troops except for isolated pockets, according to Italian Partisan radio stations, which also broadcast a report "from a non-official source" that

Continued on Page 12, Column 1

NAZIS' END NEAR

But President on Word From Eisenhower Corrects Rumor

HIMMLER IN CHARGE

He Must Capitulate for Beaten German Army to Big 3 Powers

Special to THE NEW YORK TIMES.

WASHINGTON, April 28—President Truman announced at 9:36 o'clock tonight that there was no foundation for a report that Nazi Germany had surrendered unconditionally.

The report was circulated from San Francisco, after information had been received that Heinrich Himmler had offered a German surrender to the United States and Britain. The Western Allies stood on the terms that Germany must surrender unconditionally to the three great powers, including the Soviet Union.

The fact that there was no foundation for the full-surrender rumor was established by Fleet Admiral William D. Leahy, the President's Chief of Staff, through a telephone call to General Dwight D. Eisenhower.

Truman's Direct Statement

President Truman summoned reporters to his office in the White House and stated that he had heard the rumor while working in his office this evening.

The White House permitted direct quotation of President Truman's announcement. This is it:

"Well, I was over here as you can see doing a little work, and this rumor got started.

"I had a call from San Francisco and the State Department called me.

"I just got in touch with Admiral Leahy and had him call our headquarters Commander in Chief in Europe, and there is no foundation for the rumor. That is all I have to say."

Earlier in the evening the report had been generally accredited in White House circles, and members of the secretariat and other officials returned to the Executive Offices.

Plans Made for Broadcast

In case the rumor should have been verified, President Truman started preparation of a proclamation to be read to the American people over all the radio networks to announce the fall of Germany.

[The Moscow radio said it had been "confirmed by responsible Soviet circles" that Himmler had made an offer to surrender Germany unconditionally to the United States and Britain and that the Western Allies had rejected the proposal.

[Himmler, who transmitted his offer through Sweden, is understood to have told London and Washington Adolf Hitler was dying and that he was acting as next in command, The Associated Press reported.

[A United Press dispatch from San Francisco said Allied diplomatic quarters there suggested that Himmler had put Hitler to death to give cynical evidence to the Allies of his "good faith" in offering to surrender Germany unconditionally.

[These quarters said Himmler had advised the Allies through Stockholm that Hitler "may not live another twenty-four hours." The timing of the Himmler message was such, it was believed, that Hitler may already be dead at the hands of the man who was his lieutenant in terrorism, The United Press added.]

The President told White House reporters that he had returned to his office after dinner from Blair House, his temporary residence, and it was about that time, 7:35

Continued on Page 3, Column 2

War News Summarized

SUNDAY, APRIL 29, 1945

President Truman denied last night that there was any foundation for widely circulated reports, emanating from San Francisco, that Germany had surrendered unconditionally. General Eisenhower, reached by the White House, said there was no basis for the rumors.

The denials came in the wake of widely circulated reports throughout the day that the final collapse of Germany was an hourly possibility and that the Allies had given her an ultimatum to accept their terms before Tuesday. Heinrich Himmler was said to have declared that Hitler was dying and that he, as second in command, wanted to surrender to the United States and Britain. This offer was rejected with the emphatic statement that nothing less than unconditional surrender to all three big powers would be acceptable. [1:8.]

Munich, where nazism was born and nourished into a hydra-headed menace to the world, and other areas in southwestern Germany were swept by revolts. Die-hard Nazis were reported in bloody combat with German troops. [1:3.]

Berlin was tottering, with almost all the German capital, except a twenty-five square-mile pocket in the shattered city's center, in Soviet hands. While enemy resistance was fanatical in some places, thousands were surrendering to the Russians. Meanwhile the Red Army north of Berlin gained another twenty-two miles as it slashed across the Mecklenburg plains on an expanding front toward Rostock and Hamburg. [1:4; map P. 5.]

The American Seventh Army lanced across the Austrian border at two places, after advancing 130 miles from Nuremberg in nine days, to batter at the northern gates of Hitler's mountain redoubt. The Third Army took Augsburg and was within twenty-seven miles of Munich. In the center of what had been the Western Front, held by the First Army, there was little fighting, but thousands of Germans, seeking escape from the Soviet tide around Berlin, were moving into our lines to surrender. [1:5.]

Allied troops in Italy seized Bergamo, thirty miles from the Swiss border and 125 from the Brenner Pass, and Brescia, thirty miles southeast of Bergamo, as they continued their swift dash northward. [1:7; map P. 12.] Marshal Graziani, former commander of Italian armies in north Africa, and several lesser Fascists were captured. Swiss reports said Benito Mussolini had been taken to Milan after his capture near Lake Como. [13:1.]

In the Pacific, Japanese aircraft attacked American warships off Okinawa, sinking an auxiliary surface vessel. Fifty-seven enemy planes were shot down in this and related actions. Our troops on the island increased their pressure toward Naha, the capital. [25:1.] American troops in the Philippines captured Baguio, on Luzon Island, the summer capital. [1:2-3.]

In Burma the peril to Rangoon mounted hourly as the British raced sixty-four miles toward the big port against light Japanese resistance and at last reports were fifty-four miles from the city. [24:1; with map.]

The New York Times regrets that it is obliged to omit large quantities of advertising from today's issue in order to make available adequate space for the present heavy flow of news. In doing this The New York Times is following the policy it has pursued from the beginning of newsprint rationing. This policy is based on the premise that news must be given the right of way.

Philippines' Summer Capital Falls To Americans After Long Battle

By The Associated Press.

MANILA, Sunday, April 29—Baguio, mile-high Philippine summer capital and one-time Japanese military headquarters on northern Luzon, fell to the Thirty-third and Thirty-seventh United States Infantry Divisions on Friday, after one of the longest and bitterest fights of the Philippine campaign.

Gen. Douglas MacArthur's announcement today said the important city, one of the greatest gold-mining centers of the entire archipelago, was taken by the Thirty-third Division under Maj. Gen. Percy W. Clarkson, newly augmented by the Thirty-seventh under Maj. Gen. Robert S. Beightler. The Thirty-seventh helped conquer Manila in February.

Mountainous Baguio, a prime objective of General MacArthur's men since their Jan. 9 invasion of Luzon island at Lingayen Gulf, was taken in a gradual encircling move with artillery and aircraft strongly supporting the foot soldiers.

The Japanese garrison was destroyed, General MacArthur said. American casualties were termed "amazingly light."

Twenty-fourth Division troops, meantime, completed their crossing of southern Mindanao from Moro Gulf to Davao Gulf by reaching Digos, twenty-five road miles south of Davao City, a principal port of the Philippines.

General MacArthur announced that the Thirty-first Army Division had joined the Twenty-fourth for the push to Davao, where the

Continued on Page 25, Column 3

Stuttgart Row Reported Settled; French Troops Will Stay in City

By GLADWIN HILL
By Wireless to THE NEW YORK TIMES.

PARIS, April 28—The French announced semi-officially tonight that "a satisfactory solution" had been reached in the question of the replacement of French troops by Americans in Stuttgart.

The settlement, which was attributed to "a high degree of understanding by General Eisenhower" was understood from an authoritative source to constitute a revocation, at least in principle, of the Sixth Army Group's order to the French to leave the city and authorization for the French military government to remain there in line with the French Cabinet declaration yesterday.

[The French have handed Stuttgart over to the Americans, according to a Brussels broadcast that said the information was obtained from official sources. The Exchange Telegraph Agency recorded the broadcast, according to The United Press.]

Supreme Headquarters said today the French First Army had been ordered out of Stuttgart—the first big German city occupied by the French—by the Sixth Army Group, of which it is a part, because the city's "important rail communications and supply center" had been "selected to serve the military requirements of the Seventh United States Army." The statement said that, in the absence of the Stuttgart facilities, inferior ones would have to be developed.

The immediate French reaction, however, was that they were be-

Continued on Page 8, Column 1

"All the News That's Fit to Print"

The New York Times.

LATE CITY EDITION
Partly cloudy today. Mostly clear and warmer tomorrow.
Temperatures Yesterday—Max., 63; Min., 41
Sunrise today, 5:57 A. M.; Sunset, 7:50 P. M.

VOL. XCIV..No. 31,873. Entered as Second-Class Matter, Postoffice, New York, N. Y. NEW YORK, MONDAY, APRIL 30, 1945. THREE CENTS IN NEW YORK CITY

U. S. 7TH IN MUNICH, BRITISH PUSH ON BALTIC; RUSSIANS TIGHTEN RING ON BERLIN'S HEART; MILAN AND VENICE WON; MUSSOLINI KILLED

BIG POWERS SCAN 4 OAKS CHANGES PROPOSED BY U. S.

Revising of Charter by Later Parley and Wider Scope for Assembly Are Emphasized

LEAGUE FUNCTIONS KEPT

Soviet-Latin Trade on Bids to Argentina and Lublin Reported Sought

By JAMES B. RESTON
Special to The New York Times.

SAN FRANCISCO, April 29—Delegates of the big four nations at the San Francisco Conference began exchanging views on amending of the Dumbarton Oaks proposals this weekend, but the question of bringing Argentina and Poland into the United Nations Conference on International Organization continued to hamper progress on this important subject.

There were several private meetings among various members of the sponsor nations yesterday and today. In one of these it was apparently decided that White Russia and the Ukraine should be brought into the conference this week, but when the question of inviting Argentina was raised the Russian Foreign Commissar, Vyacheslaff M. Molotoff, again proposed inviting representatives of the Polish government in Warsaw.

This suggestion, which had been defeated in the steering committee, was again opposed in the firmest manner by the American Secretary of State and the British Foreign Secretary, and it now is likely that the Russians will not insist on forcing the Polish issue to a vote, although they are clearly not yet happy about inviting Argentina.

Four Changes Offered

The United States suggested to the other sponsor powers that four changes be made in the Dumbarton Oaks proposals. These changes would provide:

First, that the charter to be written at this conference be subject to revision in a United Nations constitutional convention at a future date. The principle of writing a temporary rather than a permanent charter has been accepted by all members of the American delegation and is supported by the British, but the amendment as it now stands does not stipulate where the constitutional convention would be held and some members of the delegation think that it should. This will be discussed when the conference commissions are set up this week and the subject will be followed up in the commissions by Comdr. Harold E. Stassen.

Second, that all members obligate themselves to settle disputes in accordance with justice and fundamental human rights, and specifically to adhere to the principles of the Atlantic Charter.

Third, that the assembly have the right to recommend the revision of treaties and the removal of conditions that might lead to a breach of international peace and security.

Fourth, that the charter make provision for taking over responsibility of the functions of the old League of Nations, including responsibility for the League mandates, and also provide for a system of trusteeship over colonial areas.

Some Vandenberg Points Fail

In the final meetings here among members of the American delegation on the Dumbarton Oaks proposals, several specific proposals by various members of the delegation were rejected. Although Senator Arthur H. Vandenberg, Republican, of Michigan, put in several amendments that were accepted in the points listed above, two of his proposals dealing with the rights of the General Assembly were rejected.

One of these was that the General Assembly should—contrary to the Dumbarton Oaks proposals—be authorized to make recom-

Continued on Page 10, Column 4

Moscow Blackout Ends for May Day

By Wireless to The New York Times.

MOSCOW, April 29—Moscow's stifling blackout ends tomorrow after almost four years of war. For some weeks now, increasing numbers of street lamps have been turned on, but the obscuring of lights in homes remained rigidly enforced.

The removal of this confounded nuisance will add to the general festivities accompanying the May Day holiday and the imminent fall of Berlin and the end of the European conflict. Workmen on scaffolds have been putting light bulbs back into the huge stars on the Kremlin's towers.

CARRIER ROOSEVELT IS CHRISTENED HERE

Widow Speaks at Floating of $90,000,000 Ship—Forrestal Reveals Navy's Strength

As gray sea water lapped at her keel in building dock 5 of the New York Navy Yard in Brooklyn, a gigantic new aircraft carrier was christened the Franklin D. Roosevelt in impressive ceremonies yesterday morning. The 45,000-ton vessel, built at a cost of $90,000,000, is one of a class of three ships described by the Navy as the largest warships afloat and the biggest ships of any type ever built in this country.

At the ceremony Mrs. Franklin D. Roosevelt, clad in deepest mourning, made her first public appearance since her husband's funeral. In a brief, unscheduled address she expressed her gratitude that the Navy had given her husband's name to the new carrier, previously scheduled to be called the U. S. S. Coral Sea, and voiced a prayer that the ship would bring her officers and men home safe and victorious.

James V. Forrestal, Secretary of the Navy, who made the principal address, revealed some hitherto secret figures about the present size of the United States Fleet. He said that it now consisted of twenty-three battleships, twenty-six combat aircraft carriers, sixty-five escort carriers, sixty-seven cruisers, 386 destroyers, 368 destroyer escorts, and 240 submarines.

For Strong Naval Force

Secretary Forrestal warned those at the ceremony that the United States must retain the military ability "for swift and effective application of force" if peace is to be maintained in future years. He said that the retention of force by the United States would not conflict with her aspirations at the San Francisco Conference, but was essential for realizing the aims sought there.

Unlike the previous 45,000-ton ships built at the New York Navy Yard, the battleships Iowa and Missouri, the Franklin D. Roosevelt was not launched in the traditional fashion down greased building ways into the East River.

Continued on Page 32, Column 2

SLAIN BY PARTISANS

Italy's Former Dictator Shot After Trial—Other Fascists Executed

SEIZED AS HE FLED

Onetime Premier Begged for Life—Bodies on Display in Milan

By MILTON BRACKER
By Wireless to The New York Times.

MILAN, April 29—Benito Mussolini came back last night to the city where his fascism was born. He came back on the floor of a closed moving van, his dead body flung on the bodies of his mistress and twelve men shot with him. All were executed yesterday by Italian Partisans. The story of his final downfall, his flight, his capture and his execution is not pretty, and its epilogue in the Piazza Loretto here this morning was its ugliest part. It will go down in history as a finish to tyranny as horrible as any ever visited on a tyrant.

At 9:30 A. M. today, Mussolini's body lay on the rim of the mass of corpses, while all around surged a growing mob wild with the desire to have a last look at the man who once was a Socialist editor in this same city. The throng pushed and yelled. Partisans strove to keep them back but largely in vain. Even a series of shots in the air did not dissuade them.

Bullet Hole in Head

Mussolini had changed in death, but not enough to be any one else. His closely shaved head and his bull neck were unmistakable. His body seemed small and a little shrunken, but he was never a tall man. At least one bullet had passed through his head. It had emerged some three inches behind his right ear. There was another small hole nearer his forehead where another bullet seemed to have gone in.

As if he were not dead or dishonored enough, at least two young men in the crowd broke through and aimed kicks at his skull. One glanced off. But the other landed full on his right jaw and there was a hideous crunch that wholly disfigured the once-proud face.

Mussolini wore the uniform of a squadrist militiaman. It comprised a gray-brown jacket and gray trousers with red and black stripes down the sides. He wore black boots, badly soiled, and the left one hung half off as if his foot were broken. His small eyes were open and it was perhaps a final irony that this man who had thrust his chin forward for so many official photographs had to have his yellowing face propped up with a rifle-butt to turn it into the sun for the only two Allied cameramen on the scene.

When the butt was removed the face flopped back over to the left. Meanwhile I crouched over the body to the left in order not to

Continued on Page 7, Column 1

THE INGLORIOUS END OF A DICTATOR

Benito Mussolini in Milan's Piazza Loretto after his execution by Italian Partisans. Also seen is the body of Clara Petacci
The New York Times Radiophoto

3 DIVISIONS ENTER

Americans Roll Into Nazi Birthplace Without Meeting Opposition

ITS FALL IS REPORTED

British Cross the Elbe and Drive Northeast to Cut Off Denmark

By DREW MIDDLETON
By Wireless to The New York Times.

PARIS, April 29—American and British Armies dealt shattering blows to waning German hopes of holding out in the southern and northern redoubts today.

Troops of the United States Seventh Army crashed into Munich, birthplace of the Nazi party and the principal enemy stronghold barring the roads to the redoubt in the Austrian Tyrol while Tommies of the British Second Army smashed over the Elbe southeast of Hamburg.

Elements of the Twelfth Armored and Forty-second Infantry Divisions entered Munich at 4 o'clock this afternoon, meeting only light resistance, according to reports from the front. Later the Twentieth Armored Division rolled in.

Beer Cellar Occupied

Reports from the front line tonight said that Munich had fallen. There was no confirmation of these reports, either at Supreme Headquarters or at any Army group, but in view of the slackening resistance all over Germany and the failure of the enemy to attack the first troops entering the city, it is entirely possible that Munich has been taken.

Munich was reached after a twenty-mile advance by Seventh Army columns. According to reports from the front the Americans hold the beer cellar where Hitler planned his premature putsch of 1923 and where he addressed Nazi leaders yearly. The cellar was partly destroyed by a bomb in the autumn of 1939.

The infamous concentration camp at Dachau is believed to have been overrun in the advance to the city.

Push on Redoubt Gains

The thrust into Munich was accompanied by a general advance to the south and southeast toward the northern face of the redoubt by the United States Third and Seventh Armies, while on the right flank of the Seventh Army infantry felt its way southeastward into the redoubt, pushing toward Innsbruck and the valley of the Inn River, the most important, indeed the only communications system within the redoubt.

The thrust over the Elbe by the Fifteenth Scottish Division and the British First Commando Brigade to the north followed a bombardment in typical Montgomery fashion in which more than 400 guns were employed. It was accompanied by heavy blows on the German line west and east of the Weser and the flattening of an enemy salient northeast of Bremen.

The Ninth Army front, long dormant, awoke today when Lieut. Gen. William H. Simpson's troops suddenly attacked out of their bridgehead over the Elbe, capturing the towns of Zerbst, Jutrichau and Bias and advancing northeast and southeast of the towns. This attack was described here as a "local attack."

Four divisions, the Twelfth and Twentieth Armored and the Third and Forty-second Infantry Divisions, moved on Munich this morning. The Twentieth is a new division, fed into the battle yesterday by Lieut. Gen. Alexander M. Patch.

Between Munich and the Austrian frontier around Fuessen, other armored, cavalry and infantry units of the Seventh Army drove on toward the southeast, crossing the Lech River in force.

The Forty-fourth Infantry Division, which is moving methodically

Continued on Page 3, Column 6

5TH SEIZES MILAN, FASCISM'S CRADLE

Americans Surge On to Como—8th Army Takes Venice and Cuts Adige Line

By VIRGINIA LEE WARREN
By Wireless to The New York Times.

ADVANCED ALLIED FIELD HEADQUARTERS, Italy, April 29—United States Fifth Army troops today entered Milan, Italy's largest, wealthiest and most politically conscious city, where the history of

Continued on Page 3, Column 4

Nazis in Berlin Compressed Into 18-Square-Mile Pocket

By C. L. SULZBERGER
By Wireless to The New York Times.

MOSCOW, Monday, April 30—Determined Russian troops drove deeper into the heart of Berlin's wreckage yesterday, nearing the hastily fortified Tiergarten from two sides and edging to within a mile of the Reichstag as division after division gave itself up to the Red Army. Within the past forty-eight hours the First White Russian Army and the First Ukrainian Army have captured more than 50,000 prisoners in and around the burning capital.

Southeast of the city, in the

Continued on Page 4, Column 5

NEW NAZI PROFFER ON PEACE AWAITED

Stalin Note to Truman and Churchill Said to Spurn Himmler's Proposals

By CLIFTON DANIEL
By Wireless to The New York Times.

LONDON, Monday, April 30—London took Saturday night's "peace scare" calmly and yesterday confidently marked time in anticipation of an actual capitulation by Germany and peace in Europe within a matter of days. Amid reports about negotiations with Heinrich Himmler and a variety of rumors of the death of Adolf Hitler, official quarters here quietly awaited a Nazi reply to the British and American Governments' statement that unconditional surrender could be accepted only by all three major Allies.

Opinion was strong that Himmler's offer of surrender would be extended to the Russians—an opinion based on the belief that the Gestapo chief, now evidently ruler of the Reich, would never have made his proposal if Germany's situation had not been so desperate as to preclude further resistance.

[Reuter reported that Premier Stalin in a note to President Truman and Prime Minister Churchill has urged rejection of Himmler's proposals. Mr. Church-

Continued on Page 3, Column 2

AUSTRIA CREATES INTERIM REGIME

Moscow Announces Renner Is Premier—Britain and U. S. Not Consulted

By Wireless to The New York Times.

MOSCOW, April 29—An Austrian Provisional Government, the first independent authority in that German-speaking country since the Nazi annexation of more than seven years ago, has been created in Vienna under the leadership of Dr. Karl Renner, 74, a Social Democrat.

His Cabinet of thirteen men includes three non-party representatives, three Social Democrats, four Christian Socialists and three Communists. The Communists hold the key posts of the Interior and Education Ministries as well as one of the three seats on the political

Continued on Page 4, Column 7

Enemy Suicide Pilot Dives Plane On U. S. Hospital Ship Off Okinawa

By W. H. LAWRENCE
By Wireless to The New York Times.

ABOARD AMPHIBIOUS FLAGSHIP, off Okinawa, April 28 (Delayed)—A Japanese "suicide" pilot machine-gunned and then crashed his bomb-laden plane squarely into the well-lighted, unarmed United States naval hospital ship Comfort fully loaded with casualties from Okinawa in clear weather about sixty miles southeast of here at 8:58 o'clock tonight.

Twenty-nine were killed by the exploding airplane, which apparently struck the surgery section of the hospital ship as she was bearing wounded toward rear area hospitals.

Although first reports from the ship indicated that it would be necessary to abandon ship, it later was found that the damage was not as heavy as it seemed, and the vessel was able to continue under her own power.

Tempers ran high in naval circles at this premeditated and cold-blooded attack upon the hospital ship, which was proceeding alone with full illumination, including powerful searchlights that lighted up huge red crosses painted on the sides, superstructure and stack.

It was the first time that the Japanese had been known to attack an American hospital ship deliberately, although two other hospital ships were menaced during the Okinawa operation. Until tonight's incident, naval men had been inclined charitably to attribute these attacks to mistakes.

But there was no possibility of mistake about tonight's attack. There was a full moon and the sky was clear. The Japanese plane, one of several in the area, swept in

Continued on Page 8, Column 3

War News Summarized

MONDAY, APRIL 30, 1945

Munich, birthplace of nazism, and Milan, cradle of fascism, were entered by American troops yesterday while the world waited for further word on what Himmler was going to do about the Allied demand that Germany surrender unconditionally to Great Britain, the United States and the Soviet Union. Count Bernadotte, who carried the Nazi's proposal to give up to the western Allies only, was returning from seeing Himmler again, presumably with a reply to the Allied ultimatum. [1:7.]

It was the United States Seventh Army that smashed into Munich after a twenty-mile advance. Opposition was light, and the Americans were soon in occupation of that beer cellar from which Hitler launched his ill-fated revolt in 1923. Front reports said Munich had been captured. The Third Army was advancing on Berchtesgaden and Salzburg, while in the center the Ninth burst from its Elbe River bridgehead toward the Russians in the Wittenberg area. To the north the British Second Army crossed the Elbe southeast of Hamburg, and the Canadians progressed along the coast. The French First Army was twelve miles from Austria in the Alps. [1:8; map P. 3.]

Milan was taken by the United States Fifth Army, which also reached Como and the north end of Lake Garda. The British Eighth Army captured Venice and seized Mestre, eighty-five miles from Trieste. The Brazilian Expeditionary Force compelled a German division to surrender. The captured Marshal Graziani was arranging for the surrender of his Fascist Ligurian army. [1:4; map, P. 3.]

Mussolini's body was dumped from a moving van into a Milan square, where it received the scornful attention of the residents. He, his mistress and more than a dozen other Fascists had been executed by Partisans near Como. [1:3.]

Berlin's last-ditch defenders were squeezed into an eighteen square mile area in the center of the city, and Russian troops were within half a mile of Hitler's ruined chancellery. A German pocket southeast of the city was liquidated, while in the north two Soviet armies joined forces and swept toward Rostock and Swinemuende. [1:5-6, maps P. 4.] A wave of suicides was said to be sweeping Berlin. [4:1.]

Washington and London learned from Moscow that a provisional anti-fascist government had been set up in Austria headed by Dr. Karl Renner, former Chancellor and last president of the free Assembly. [1:6.]

A marked trend toward the Left was shown in early returns from France's first elections since 1937. Communists jumped into the lead in Paris. [1:6-7.]

A clearly marked Navy hospital ship was attacked off Okinawa by a Japanese plane, which killed twenty-nine and injured thirty-three; one man was missing. Some 200 other enemy planes kept the Pacific Fleet under prolonged attack, damaging some light units; 104 of the enemy aircraft were destroyed. On shore, troops captured the northern half of Machinato airfield in a general advance. [1:2-3.]

Americans on Mindanao seized the Padada airfield along Davao Gulf and advanced up to seventeen miles in the center. [6:5.] Japanese resistance slowed the British drive on Rangoon, in Burma. [8:7.]

Communists Take Lead in Paris As France Holds First Elections

By The Associated Press.

PARIS, April 29—Communist candidates for municipal office in Paris held a commanding lead on the basis of almost complete returns today.

Election returns from other metropolitan centers indicated that their voters, too, had supported candidates of the leftist parties in contests for municipal offices, the only ones at stake in today's voting. Only a few returns had been received from traditionally conservative country districts.

In Paris and other principal cities the Communists' lead seemed to be safe, while Socialists and Radicals ran well ahead of center parties and rightists. Political observers speculated that eleventh-hour Communist demands for the quick trial and conviction of Marshal Henri-Philippe Pétain had drawn support to the party candidates, including many voters unaffiliated with any party.

André Mornet, Attorney General, who will conduct the case against Pétain, was returned to office with a heavy plurality. Edouard Herriot, former President of the Chamber of Deputies, who has just reached Switzerland from a German prison camp, was elected to the Municipal Council of Lyon by a 4-to-1 margin. Six members of the Cabinet who ran for city offices were also elected.

Joseph Paul-Boncour, a member of the French delegation to the San Francisco Conference, was also elected by a big margin.

Not only was this the first election that France had held since her fall to the Germans but it was the first time that women were al-

Continued on Page 5, Column 6

"All the News That's Fit to Print"

The New York Times.

LATE CITY EDITION
Clearing and windy today. Clear and warmer tomorrow.
Temperatures Yesterday—Max., 58; Min., 49
Sunrise today, 5:56 A. M.; Sunset, 7:58 P. M.

VOL. XCIV No. 31,874. Entered as Second-Class Matter, Postoffice, New York, N. Y. NEW YORK, TUESDAY, MAY 1, 1945. THREE CENTS IN NEW YORK CITY

RUSSIANS FLY VICTORY FLAG ON REICHSTAG; U. S. 7TH WINS MUNICH, DRIVES FOR BRENNER; FOE BROKEN IN ITALY; TITO MEN IN TRIESTE

PARLEY, 31-4, VOTES TO SEAT ARGENTINA; MOLOTOFF BEATEN

Fight on Proposal Carried to Open Floor After Its Adoption in Two Committees

POLISH EXCLUSION STANDS

Russian Links Issues in Asking Delay on Latin Nation—White Russia and Ukraine In

By JAMES B. RESTON
Special to THE NEW YORK TIMES.

SAN FRANCISCO, April 30—The United Nations invited Argentina to attend the San Francisco Security Conference today despite sharp and repeated requests by Russia that Argentina be omitted until the Polish Government in Warsaw is invited.

The delegates brought White Russia and the Ukraine into the conference without a dissenting vote, but the Russian Foreign Commissar, Vyacheslaff M. Molotoff, fought the Argentine invitation in the executive committee, carried the fight to the steering committee and then, defeated in both places, appealed to the press and to the full plenary session of the conference, which finally rejected his motion, 31 to 4.

In a day of continued maneuvering behind the scenes by the United States, Britain and Soviet Russia, the main developments were as follows:

First, both the executive and steering committees of the conference voted unanimously to invite White Russia and the Ukraine to the conference.

Recapitulation of Votes

Second, the fourteen-nation executive committee voted, 9—3, to invite Argentina to the conference, Soviet Russia, Czechoslovakia and Yugoslavia voting against it, and China abstaining. One nation was not present. In the steering committee the vote to invite Argentina was 29 for and 6 against. In the plenary session the vote against postponing the invitation, as requested by Mr. Molotoff, was 28 to 7. The final plenary vote on the invitation was thirty-one votes for and four against.

Those who voted for postponing the question of inviting Argentina were Russia, Belgium, Czechoslovakia, Norway, Yugoslavia, New Zealand and Iran, and the four who, in the final ballot, voted against inviting Argentina were Russia, Czechoslovakia, Yugoslavia and Greece.

Third, discussions on naming the heads of the working commissions and committees of the conference continued amid authoritative reports that Mr. Molotoff would turn over discussion of the Dumbarton Oaks proposals to Andrei A. Gromyko, Soviet Ambassador to Washington, and leave for Moscow early next week, if not before.

Anthony Eden, British Foreign Secretary, is expected to leave soon after Mr. Molotoff. Despite these indications, Secretary of State Stettinius expressed confidence that the conference would continue without interruption, this to hold also in the case of the end of the war in Europe.

Molotoff Skill Praised

Today was one of sharp and cogent argument by the Russians on fundamental issues, and it is only fair to report that, while there was general opposition among the delegates to the Russian argument in favor of the Warsaw Poles, there was more than a little support for argument against Argentina and considerable admiration for the skill and persistence with which Mr. Molotoff put his case.

Manifestly believing that he saw weaknesses in the Anglo-American argument for the Farrell-Peron regime in Argentina, Mr. Molotoff proceeded to use this to attain the end he has been seeking ever since

Continued on Page 14, Column 4

54 Wounded View Parley in Action

By The Associated Press.

SAN FRANCISCO, April 30—The Navy brought fifty-four wounded sailors and marines today to see for themselves how the United Nations are trying to organize to prevent another war.

All young men, they were amputation cases. They came from the Navy Hospital at Mare Island, thirty-five miles away.

When asked how much interest they had in the conference, while they sat in the Opera House just before today's session began, they had comment such as this:

"We're interested. We want to see peace. We had a big stake in this war. We want to see what comes out of this war."

The Navy asked wounded men at Mare Island whether they wanted to view the conference in action. More said "yes" than could be taken today.

WLB ORDERS LEWIS TO KEEP MINES OPEN

Directive to Extend Anthracite Contract Comes on Eve of General Work Stoppage

The War Labor Board in Washington last night ordered John L. Lewis and his United Mine Workers to extend their contract with anthracite operators, which expired at midnight last night, until their differences in negotiations for a new wage agreement are "peacefully and finally resolved."

The board ordered Mr. Lewis and a committee of the operators to appear before it at a hearing in Washington at 2:30 P. M. today to show cause why the contract should not be extended.

Today's proceedings in Washington will not avert the general stoppage of 72,000 miners in the anthracite field of Pennsylvania, which will go into effect this morning in the absence of a new wage agreement.

The WLB order was served on Mr. Lewis by Howard T. Colvin, acting director of the United States Conciliation Service, after Frances Perkins, Secretary of Labor, had certified the dispute to the board following failure of the miners and operators to agree on a new contract.

Her Compromise Rejected

Miss Perkins had sat in with the conferees for several hours at the Hotel Waldorf-Astoria yesterday afternoon, when she offered a compromise for a settlement accepted by the miners and rejected by the operators.

Following this development Mr. Lewis again refused to accept the request made several days ago by Harold L. Ickes, Fuel Administrator, for an extension of the old agreement pending continuance of negotiations. Miss Perkins re-

Continued on Page 19, Column 3

Sugar Ration Slashed 25 Per Cent; OWI Puts Reserves at Rock Bottom

Special to THE NEW YORK TIMES.

WASHINGTON, April 30—The Government tonight cut sugar rations by 25 per cent. The announcement was made by the Office of War Information, which said sugar reserves in the United States are at "rock bottom."

OWI, which spoke for the Office of Price Administration and the War Food Administration, said that Sugar Stamp 36, good for five pounds, which becomes valid tomorrow, would be stretched over a four-month period instead of three, and that no additional stamp would be validated before Sept. 1.

In addition, local OPA boards were instructed to issue only up to 70 per cent as much sugar for home canning as they issued last year and to limit amounts per individual to fifteen pounds, compared with last year's maximum of twenty. The maximum allowed to any family, regardless of size, is now to be 120 pounds, instead of the 160 pounds announced earlier in the year, the agency said.

Sugar allotments for hotels, schools, restaurants and other institutional users also were reduced, and OPA indicated that still further cuts were in prospect on July 1 for industrial users.

The reasons for the reduction, OWI said, were a heavy decline in supplies, greatly increased requirements for liberated Europe and a rate of civilian consumption far in excess of allocations.

"Consumers this year for the first time in two decades must depend entirely on current production," OWI declared.

The agency's report stated that tentative allotments proved too great in view of a drop in production and a rise in the military demand.

CLARK SEES FINISH

Says Germans' Force Is Spent—Turin Falls to Allies, Partisans

120,000 CAPTURED

Fifth, Eighth Armies Push North—French Advance in West

By VIRGINIA LEE WARREN
By Wireless to THE NEW YORK TIMES.

ADVANCED ALLIED HEADQUARTERS, Italy, April 30—The German armies in Italy have been "virtually eliminated," Gen. Mark W. Clark, the Allies' ground commander, said today.

Turin, thirty miles from the French border and the last great city north of the Po River, is in the Allies' and the Partisans' hands tonight. At the opposite end of the battle line, units of the British Eighth Army have driven within seventy-five miles of Trieste.

The hopelessness of the German situation was summed up today when General Clark said: "The military power of Germany in Italy has practically ceased, even though scattered fighting may continue." Pointing out that this destruction had been accomplished since the offensive began on April 9, he said: "Twenty-five German divisions, some of the best in the German Army, have been torn to pieces and can no longer resist our armies; thousands of vehicles, tremendous quantities of arms and equipment and over 120,000 prisoners have been corralled."

Partisans Take Turin

Turin, like Milan, Genoa and Venice, had been taken over by the Partisans before the Fifth Army's 442d Infantry Regiment, composed of Japanese-Americans, entered it this morning. The city has a population of 700,000 and is Italy's automobile (Fiat), vermouth and chocolate production center.

The First Armored Division, which entered Milan yesterday, drove on thirty-two miles west of the city today and seized crossings over the Ticino River after having taken more than 12,000 prisoners in the past twenty-four hours. The bag included Maj. Gen. von Behr, commanding the Ninetieth Armored Grenadier Division; his staff and other high officers. Milan has been cleared of all but a few Germans.

But there is still scattered enemy resistance and American and British soldiers are still being wounded and killed. After Padua had been taken a large German column advanced on the city from the southwest and in the resultant fighting 1,000 more prisoners were bagged. At the north end of Lake Garda the American Fourth Corps repulsed fairly heavy local counter-attacks while elements of the

Continued on Page 3, Column 3

ALPS DEFENSE CUT

Three Divisions of 7th and French Push Into Western Austria

3D CROSSES THE ISAR

9th and 1st Join Soviet Forces Again—Yanks Enter Baltic Drive

By DREW MIDDLETON
By Wireless to THE NEW YORK TIMES.

PARIS, April 30—Long columns of tanks and infantry of three divisions of the United States Seventh Army are smashing down the narrow valleys of the Austrian Tyrol toward Innsbruck and the communications system along the valley of Inn River, which is the strongest and best prepared of Hitler's three largest German pockets in western Europe.

Lieut. Gen. Alexander M. Patch's drive into the Alpine redoubt set the pace for a day of highly successful Allied operations against the crumbling remains of the German military empire along the long front that the Allies hold from Austria to the North Sea.

Munich Won at 5 P. M.

Behind the Seventh Army's battle line, which at one point is only thirteen miles from Innsbruck at the northern end of the Brenner Pass, Munich, the third city of Germany, was overrun by General Patch's tanks and infantry. [A dispatch from Munich said all resistance, except for that of a suicide squad of twenty-five SS troops, ended at 5 o'clock Monday afternoon.]

Troops of the United States Ninth Army made a second junction with Red Army forces on the east bank of the Elbe River at Apolensdorf, northeast of Dessau, while United States First Army forces have made a new contact with the Russians around Wittenberg.

Field Marshal Sir Bernard L. Montgomery's drive across the

Continued on Page 4, Column 3

SUICIDE PILOT COMES CLOSE TO U. S. WARSHIP

This Japanese succeeded in accomplishing his own death, but failed in attempt to crash into the ship. The plane plunged into the sea alongside the vessel.

Associated Press Wirephoto (U. S. Navy)

27TH DIVISION WINS OKINAWA AIRFIELD

Former New York Guardsmen Take Strip Near Naha—54 Enemy Planes Downed

By ROBERT TRUMBULL
By Wireless to THE NEW YORK TIMES.

GUAM, Tuesday, May 1—Twenty-seventh Army Infantry troops have captured Machinato airfield, on the west coast of Okinawa, Fleet Admiral Chester W. Nimitz announced this morning.

The long, narrow strip, a goal of the Twenty-seventh for several days, finally fell on Sunday (Tokyo time). The Twenty-seventh, former New York National Guard organization, thus advanced

Continued on Page 10, Column 2

War News Summarized

TUESDAY, MAY 1, 1945

German propagandists told their people that the war was drawing to a close and the "end may come tomorrow." There was visual evidence on all sides as the disintegrating fronts failed to stand anywhere against final Allied thrusts. Count Bernadotte was reported to have Himmler's acceptance of the Big Three's ultimatum [1:6-7], and Stockholm heard that the Germans were negotiating a withdrawal from Denmark under supervision of a Swedish commission. [1:7.]

Two Soviet armies were cleaning up Berlin, the fall of which was imminent. The Reichstag building, which when it burned enabled Hitler to dramatize his hatred of Communists, was captured and the Russian flag was raised on the ruins. Moravska Ostrava and Zilina in Czechoslovakia were taken. To the north the Red Army compressed the Baltic pocket and drove closer to the British Second Army, along the Elbe River. [1:8, maps Pages 6 and 4.]

The United States Seventh Army captured Munich and was thirteen miles from Innsbruck. Germany's southern redoubt was being torn into several segments, with the United States Third Army moving on Salzburg and Berchtesgaden and the French First Army crossing into Austria and entering Vorarlberg. The United States Ninth Army joined the Red Army northeast of Dessau, and the First Army made a second contact near Wittenberg. [1:4; map P. 4.]

General Clark declared that the German Army no longer existed as a military force in Italy. American troops entered Turin, thirty miles from France, after the city had been liberated by Partisans. Treviso, north of Venice, was seized by South African units, and Mussolini's villa on Lake Garda was taken by Americans. Yugoslav Partisans have nearly captured Trieste. [1:3; map P. 4.] This brought an Italian demand that the Allies put out Marshal Tito and return the city to Italy. [3:8.]

The notorious Nazi extermination camp at Dachau was captured by the Seventh Army following a furious battle and 32,000 prisoners freed. [1:6-7.] American and British officials were amazed by an accusation of the head of the Soviet Repatriation Committee that liberated Russians were not "always being treated as citizens of an Allied State." [5:1.]

Acting Secretary of State Grew said the United States did not recognize a provisional Austrian Government, announcement of which had come from Moscow. Britain's attitude is similar. [8:1.]

Machinato airfield on Okinawa has been torn from the stubborn Japanese defenders. [1:5.] Americans on Mindanao advanced ten miles from Digos to seventeen miles south of Davao. Talikud Island, off that city, was captured by guerrillas. [10:6.]

Foreign Commissar Molotoff was voted down in the executive committee and steering committee and at a plenary session of the San Francisco Conference when he opposed admission of Argentina. White Russia and the Ukraine were seated without opposition. [1:1.] Mr. Molotoff held that Argentina, which had been characterized as fascist by American officials, should not be invited while Poland was excluded. [14:2-3.]

Nazi Predicts the End Soon; London Sifts Peace Prospects

By CLIFTON DANIEL
By Cable to THE NEW YORK TIMES.

LONDON, April 30—For the first time the German people were told by their own propagandists tonight what the Allied world is hoping—that the war in Europe is drawing to a close, that it might even end "tomorrow." Britain's expectation of an early peace was maintained as the War Cabinet met twice today.

Stockholm reports said negotiations between Count Folke Bernadotte of the Swedish Red Cross and Heinrich Himmler were continuing and the Gestapo chief was believed to have expanded his surrender offer to include the Soviet Union.

[The Stockholm newspaper Dagens Nyheter said Count Bernadotte had forwarded the German answer to capitulation demands to an Allied legation in Stockholm late Monday through the Swedish Foreign Office and was due back in Stockholm Tuesday.

[President Truman indicated to reporters that no news on peace developments was to be expected from the White House over Monday night, The Associated Press reported from Washington.]

After discussing the situation with reference to peace in Europe at its regular daily meeting, the British War Cabinet met again tonight, but it was understood that it had no specific proposition to consider. Whitehall did not exclude a concrete development suddenly.

Another meeting of the Cabinet is expected to be held tomorrow morning to decide whether any change is needed in the scheduled order of business for the House of

Continued on Page 8, Column 7

NAZIS IN DENMARK SEEN CAPITULATING

Withdrawal From Country Is Reported After Parleys by Bernadotte of Sweden

By GEORGE AXELSSON
By Cable to THE NEW YORK TIMES.

STOCKHOLM, Sweden, Tuesday, May 1—A surrender of the Germans in Denmark seems imminent, according to information received here at 1:30 A. M. today regarding negotiations conducted at Nazi headquarters in Copenhagen under the leadership of Count Folke Bernadotte.

[Free Danish underground sources in Malmoe on the southern coast of Sweden reported that German forces had begun moving out of Copenhagen early Tuesday with the apparent intention of abandoning Denmark, said an Associated Press dispatch from Stockholm. The newspaper Stockholms Tidningen reported a German plan to evacuate Denmark Tuesday, al-

Continued on Page 8, Column 1

Dachau Captured by Americans Who Kill Guards, Liberate 32,000

By The Associated Press.

DACHAU, Germany, April 30—Dachau, Germany's most dreaded extermination camp, has been captured and its surviving 32,000 tortured inmates have been freed by outraged American troops who killed or captured its brutal garrison in a furious battle.

Dashing to the camp atop tanks, bulldozers, self-propelled guns—anything with wheels—the Forty-second and Forty-fifth Divisions hit the notorious prison northwest of Munich soon after the lunch hour yesterday. Dozens of German guards fell under withering blasts of rifle and carbine fire as the soldiers, catching glimpses of the horrors within the camp, raged through its barracks for a quick clean-up.

The troops were joined by trusty prisoners working outside the barbed-wire enclosures. Frenchmen and Russians, grabbing weapons dropped by slain guards, acted swiftly on their own to exact full revenge from their tormentors.

The sorting of the liberated prisoners was still under way today but the Americans learned from camp officials that some of the more important captives had been transferred recently to a new hide-out, probably in the Tyrol. These were said to have included Premier Stalin's son, Jacob, who was captured in 1941; the former Austrian Chancellor, Kurt Schuschnigg, and his wife; Prince Frederick Leopold of Prussia, Prince Xavier de Bourbon de Parme and the Rev. Martin Niemoeller, the German Lutheran, who was arrested when he defied German attempts to control his preaching.

[Prisoners at another camp

Continued on Page 5, Column 2

STALIN HAILS EVENT

Interior Ministry Won—Tiergarten Region of Berlin Is Besieged

TOLL OF NAZIS SOARS

1,800,000 Captured or Killed in 4 Months—Baltic Port Seized

By The Associated Press.

LONDON, Tuesday, May 1—Red Army troops, storming the blazing administrative heart of Berlin, captured the gutted shell of the German Reichstag yesterday, running up the Russian victory flag over the Nazi monument in a sweep that threatened to split the last defenders of the German capital.

The fall of all Berlin appeared imminent. The Russians stepped up their struggle for the city to unprecedented proportions in a possible bid to win the entire city today while Moscow celebrates May Day.

Soviet troops were within a mile of tearing the capital into two isolated pockets, each less than nine square miles. They had won the Ministry of the Interior, near the Reichstag; were laying siege to Hitler's underground fortress in the Tiergarten, were at Berlin's triumphal arch, the Brandenburg Gate, and were across the Spree River from Berlin's cathedral.

Stalin Issues May Day Order

German broadcasts admitted that the ten-day battle for the devastated capital was as good as lost, while Premier Stalin, in a May Day order of the day, said that the war was approaching its end and declared: "The last assault is on."

Marshal Stalin said that 1,800,000 Germans had been killed or captured during the last three to four months of fighting on the eastern front. His announcement meant that 11,540,000 German casualties had been inflicted by the Red Army in less than four years of war.

As 9,000 more German troops surrendered in Berlin, raising to 65,500 the toll of enemy dead and captured in four days, north of the dying capital Red Army troops, rolling out mile-an-hour gains across Mecklenburg Province, seized the Baltic port of Greifswald and smashed within forty-two miles of Rostock. The port of Swinemuende was isolated.

Far to the south, Gen. Andrei I. Yeremenko's Fourth Ukrainian Army captured Moravska-Ostrava, the "Pittsburgh of Czechoslovakia," while cavalrymen of the Second Ukrainian Army plunged through the Morava River Valley toward a junction that would roll up a German salient in eastern Moravia.

The capture of the famous Reichstag building, which was

Continued on Page 6, Column 6

Invasion of Borneo By Allies Reported

By The United Press.

The Tokyo radio reported this morning that an Allied force had landed yesterday on the east coast of Borneo.

The enemy broadcast said the landing was made in the Tarakan area late at night under cover of an offshore bombardment.

As recorded by The United Press at San Francisco, the broadcast asserted that a landing attempt at noon on Monday was repulsed.

The Tokyo broadcast said:

"In the Tarakan area on the east coast of Borneo Japanese garrisons are engaged in fierce combat with an enemy force which landed late Monday night under cover of offshore bombardment. Previously, at noon Monday, a landing attempt was repulsed."

"All the News That's Fit to Print"

The New York Times.

LATE CITY EDITION
Clearing and warmer today. Cloudy with moderate winds tomorrow.
Temperatures Yesterday—Max., 51; Min., 44
Sunrise today, 5:54 A. M.; Sunset, 7:53 P. M.

VOL. XCIV..No. 31,875. Entered as Second-Class Matter, Postoffice, New York, N. Y. NEW YORK, WEDNESDAY, MAY 2, 1945. THREE CENTS IN NEW YORK CITY

HITLER DEAD IN CHANCELLERY, NAZIS SAY; DOENITZ, SUCCESSOR, ORDERS WAR TO GO ON; BERLIN ALMOST WON; U. S. ARMIES ADVANCE

MOLOTOFF EASES PARLEY TENSION; NEW MOVES BEGUN

Russian Says Country Will Cooperate in World Plan Despite Argentine Issue

4 COMMISSIONS SET UP

They Will Deal With Council, Assembly, Court and Some General Problems

By JAMES B. RESTON
Special to THE NEW YORK TIMES.

SAN FRANCISCO, May 1—The United Nations Conference on International Organization has survived its first basic crisis and after six days of political maneuvering on secondary issues, it began to move at rapid tempo today toward its primary task—the creation of a world organization which would stop what Field Marshal Jan Christiaan Smuts called "this pilgrimage of death."

The test came last night. Rebuffed by the conference on his attempts to keep Argentina out of the conference and bring the Warsaw Poles in, Soviet Foreign Commissar Vyacheslaf M. Molotoff went late last night to Secretary Stettinius' penthouse at the Fairmont Hotel. He immediately made his position clear.

He still disapproved the conference actions on the Poles and the Argentine, but he wanted the conference to succeed; he would cooperate in its labors, and while he was under urgent pressure by the events in Europe to return to Moscow, he would remain at least for a few days until the major issues on the charter were thrashed out among the four sponsor powers. Then, he said, he would have to leave, probably at the week-end or early next week.

"Friendly Meeting" Is Held

Immediately, in what the Foreign Ministers of the United States, Great Britain and China described to their colleagues as "the most friendly meeting of the conference," the big four approved the formation of the working commissions and committees of the conference, and other committees began discussing, not the personalities or procedures of the conference, but the basic questions of creating an organization which would win the support, with the power, of the great nations without violating the rights and principles of all nations.

The three main developments of the day were as follows:

First, the conference approved four commissions to deal with the security council of the proposed organization, the general assembly, the judicial agency and general problems, and established twelve committees to study specific problems under these four commissions.

The heads of the four commissions were: Trygve Lie of Norway, Security Council; Field Marshal Smuts, General Assembly; Carraciolo Parra Rez of Venezuela, judicial organization; and Paul Henri Spaak of Belgium, general provisions.

Second, Field Marshal Smuts called on the four major powers to accept the special responsibilities which flow from the special authority given them under the Dumbarton Oaks proposals and urged all the nations here to pay more attention to the spiritual and economic aspects of the new charter than they had in the past.

Third, the Russians began studying in some detail the sixteen amendments to the Dumbarton Oaks proposals which were submitted by the United States. The other delegations started circulating amendments and exchanging views on proposals already circulated.

The facts on the crisis among the Big Three over Poland, Argentina, White Russia and the Ukraine can now be put down with assur-

Continued on Page 18, Column 6

Allies Invade North Borneo; Fighting Fierce, Tokyo Says

Australia Informed of Landing by Treasury Minister—MacArthur Reports Only Air Attacks and New Gains on Luzon

By The United Press.

MANILA, Wednesday, May 2—An official Australian announcement said yesterday that Allied troops had invaded Borneo, the world's third largest island, but Gen. Douglas MacArthur's communiqué early today reported only that heavy bombers were neutralizing enemy bases and airdromes on the oil-rich island.

Tokyo also reported the landings and said they had been made on the ten-square-mile island of Tarakan on the northeast coast, a region rich in oil wells, which the Netherlanders destroyed before the Japanese captured them in 1942. The enemy broadcast said "fierce fighting" was in progress.

[A later Japanese broadcast, picked up in San Francisco, reported that Allied units had landed on Tarakan Island at 6:30 A. M., Tuesday, Tokyo time. The broadcast said "the enemy had been bombarding the island since April 27, and on Monday morning began approaching the island in their landing attempts." It reported the landing force consisted of "about 5,000 soldiers" and said Japanese forces on the island "are holding secure their positions, obstructing the enemy's advance."]

General MacArthur announced that heavy bombers in attacks on Borneo had struck Kuching, Macassar and Kendari, while medium units and fighters had attacked Japanese gun positions on Tarakan.

General MacArthur announced that on Mindano Island the Twenty-fourth Division, in another swift drive, had advanced eleven miles

Continued on Page 16, Column 2

NEW CIGARETTES FACE PRICE INQUIRY

OPA Calls on Manufacturers of 21-Cent Brands to Prove Quality Merits Charge

By JAMES E. POWERS

Manufacturers of hitherto unheard of brands of cigarettes that have appeared on the market in recent weeks and are being retailed at four or more cents a package higher than ceiling prices for scarce popular brands will be called upon by the Office of Price Administration to show that the new products are of a quality rating the prices charged, it became known yesterday.

Daniel P. Woolley, regional OPA administrator, said an investigation was in progress as a result of complaints by smokers who said they had paid 21 cents a package for cigarettes "they had previously never heard of."

The United Wholesale Tobacco and Cigarette Distributors Association, a sub-jobbers' group, in a telegram to Senator William Langer of North Dakota, who recently introduced a resolution to set up a committee to look into the "black market" in cigarettes, demanded an immediate investigation of the entire cigarette shortage.

Mr. Woolley declared that as a result of OPA prosecution of violators of price ceilings, the black-market condition largely had been corrected here. He said he was centering on the pricing of the new cigarette brands.

Mr. Woolley added that studies were being made to determine

Continued on Page 40, Column 4

HARD COAL 'HOLIDAY' BRINGS WLB BAN

New Order by Board Asserts Output Is Urgent—Seizure Action Is Postponed

By JOSEPH A. LOFTUS
Special to THE NEW YORK TIMES.

WASHINGTON, May 1—The War Labor Board issued a new order tonight to the United Mine Workers and the operators to resume the production of hard coal. To give the UMW leaders an opportunity to act on the order it decided to defer for twenty-four to forty-eight hours a recommendation to President Truman for Government seizure of the mines.

The miners went on a holiday today after expiration of their contract at midnight.

Dr. George W. Taylor, WLB chairman, in a telegram to both parties took cognizance of the miners' traditional "no contract, no work" policy.

"The board's order provides for a continuing contract," he said. "It is urgent that production should be immediately resumed."

As in acting on the soft coal dispute a month ago, the WLB provided in the new order that any legal wage adjustment agreed upon or finally ordered be retroactive to the expiration date of the old contract.

Union spokesmen told the WLB at a brief hearing that the Tri-District Scale Committee had voted to advise the miners to return to work when the operators accepted the settlement proposal made by Secretary of Labor Perkins.

Dr. Taylor, in questioning John Owens of the UMW, noted that

Continued on Page 40, Column 3

Eisenhower Halted Forces at Elbe; Ninth Had Hoped to Storm Berlin

By The Associated Press.

WITH THE UNITED STATES NINTH ARMY, in Germany, April 26 (Delayed by Censorship)—A direct order from Supreme Allied Headquarters halted the United States Ninth Army's drive to Berlin at the Elbe River at a time when the most pessimistic officers were predicting that Lieut. Gen. William H. Simpson's forces could reduce the German capital in ten days, "even if the Germans fought hard."

General Eisenhower's order said the Ninth would halt on the Elbe and await the arrival of Russian forces from the east, thereby leaving the capture of the capital to the Red Army. It also was understood that the American First and Third and British and Canadian armies received similar orders to halt at the Elbe.

It was not clear whether General Eisenhower's order was dictated by political policy agreed upon by the Great Powers or in a belief that it was a military necessity.

It was felt by high staff officers in the field, however, that the Ninth and other American forces could push on to the capital without great difficulty. While the order disappointed some staff officers, it was not altogether unexpected. It was known that the Ninth Army had pushed past the eventual British-American occupation area when it crossed the Weser River.

While the staff officers were disappointed, the American doughboys and tankmen who had to do the fighting and dying to get to Berlin expressed no regret. Almost to a man, they felt they could do with-

Continued on Page 4, Column 4

REDOUBTS ASSAILED

U. S. 3d, 7th and French 1st Armies Charging Into Alpine Hideout

NEAR BRENNER PASS

British in North Close About Hamburg—Poles Gain in Emden Area

Von Rundstedt Caught

By The Associated Press.

WITH UNITED STATES SEVENTH ARMY, Wednesday, May 2—Field Marshal Karl von Rundstedt has been captured by United States Seventh Army troops.

The Seventh Army caught the former German commander in the west in its drive into the Nazis' southeastern redoubt area.

By DREW MIDDLETON
By Wireless to THE NEW YORK TIMES.

PARIS, May 1—The last defenses of the Third Reich were crumbling as Allied tanks and infantry swept almost unopposed into the northern and southern redoubts.

Gen. George S. Patton's United States Third Army has resumed its offensive into Austria, crashing to within twenty miles of Linz, and is only fifty-four miles from Amstetten, where Marshal Fedor I. Tolbukhin's Third Ukrainian Army was last reported. According to reports from the front, radio contact has been established between tanks of the United States Eleventh Armored Division and the vanguard of the Soviet armies.

Other armored columns of the

Continued on Page 14, Column 1

NAZI CORE STORMED

Russians Drive Toward Chancellery Fortress, Narrowing Noose

BRANDENBURG TAKEN

Stralsund Port Swept Up in New Baltic Gains—Vah Valley Cleared

By C. L. SULZBERGER
By Wireless to THE NEW YORK TIMES.

MOSCOW, Wednesday, May 2—Street battles within smoldering Berlin today entered their twelfth day since the Russians first broke into the city, with Nazi die-hards still holding grimly to the central part of the town, whittled down by yesterday's fighting, in which Marshal Gregory K. Zhukoff's First White Russian Army group completely occupied Charlottenburg and Schoeneberg and more than 100 blocks in the capital's central region.

Some 14,000 prisoners were taken within the city on Monday, the Russians announced. At the same time, the remnants of a hold-out group south of Berlin, part of which had been annihilated at Wendisch Buchholtz, was split in two and the survivors are being ground to death by Marshal Zhukoff's men.

Curiously enough, the midnight communiqué does not mention Marshal Ivan S. Koneff's First Ukrainian Army group, which has been working from the southwestern sector of the city toward the desperately defended Tiergarten.

Marshal Zhukoff's forward spearheads meanwhile struck deep into Brandenburg Province, capturing the city of Brandenburg, halfway to Magdeburg from Berlin.

While Gen. Andrei I. Yeremenko proceeded apace in his lightning

Continued on Page 3, Column 3

War News Summarized

WEDNESDAY, MAY 2, 1945

Hitler is dead, according to the Hamburg radio, and on Monday, the day before he allegedly fell at his command post in the Chancellery in Berlin, he appointed Admiral Karl Doenitz to be the new Fuehrer. The head of the German Navy, who had made his mark directing the enemy's U-boats campaign, pledged continuance of the war. [1:8.]

Washington received the news, as did London, with some skepticism and a desire to see the body. Selection of Admiral Doenitz was considered logical in view of his strong Nazi feelings. [1:7.]

The new development was interpreted in London as a move to counteract Himmler's reported peace bids, but Prime Minister Churchill broadly intimated in the Commons that he might have "information of exceptional importance" to impart before Saturday. Peace will probably come before all enemy forces have surrendered, he said. [1:6-7.] Germany was reported to have begun evacuation of Denmark and to be ready to leave Norway. Count Bernadotte said in Sweden he had no new Himmler proposals, and the Nazis' Scandinavian withdrawals were related there to a prospective general capitulation. [11:1.]

Meanwhile, general Allied progress on the battlefields against slight resistance continued. The United States Third Army, on the day Hitler was declared to have died, captured Braunau, his birthplace. The drive into Austria was resumed and had reached to within twenty miles of Linz and fifty-four of the last known Russian position. The Seventh Army smashed through the Tyrol on a broad front and cleared Munich. The British Second Army, by-passing Hamburg, raced to within eighteen miles of the Baltic port of Luebeck. [1:4; map P. 14.]

General Eisenhower, it was revealed, personally ordered the halt of the Allied drive on Berlin from the west to permit the Russians to take the capital. [1:2-3.]

The Russians greatly cut down the German holding in Berlin, capturing the districts of Charlottenburg and Schoeneberg. West of the city they occupied Brandenburg and along the Baltic they seized Stralsund. [1:5; maps Pages 2 and 14.]

New Zealand troops in Italy made contact with Yugoslav Partisans at Monfalcone near Trieste and the British entered Udine. While the Eighth Army was closing a trap along the Swiss border, the Fifth neared France. [1:6-7; map P. 14.]

Mussolini and his mistress were buried in unmarked paupers' graves in Milan. [13:1.] Admiral Horthy, former Regent of Hungary, was captured. [4:3.]

Invasion of Borneo was officially disclosed in Australia, although no word of the break into the Japanese-held Netherlands East Indies had come from General MacArthur. On Mindanao in the Philippines, Americans were within six miles of the city of Davao. [1:2-3; map P.16.]

Seventh Division troops on Okinawa resumed their southward advance, entering the village of Kuhazu. [15:1.] More than 400 starved, naked Allied prisoners of war were liberated by the British as they drove on Rangoon in Burma. [15:3.]

Good progress was made at the San Francisco Conference. Foreign Commissar Molotoff, after assuring Secretary of State Stettinius of his desire that the conference succeed, announced that pressure of events would compel his return to Moscow within a few days. [1:1.]

ADOLF HITLER — The New York Times, 1938

Clark's Troops Meet Tito's In General Advance in Italy

By VIRGINIA LEE WARREN
By Wireless to THE NEW YORK TIMES.

AT ADVANCED ALLIED HEADQUARTERS, in Italy, May 1—After advancing fifty-five miles in less than a day along the coastal road rimming the Gulf of Venice, units of one division of the Fifteenth Army Group made contact this afternoon with Marshal Tito's forces at Monfalcone while other troops under Gen. Mark W. Clark continued to sweep German remnants from the valleys of north Italy and to seal off the few remaining escape routes through the Alps.

No details of the meeting at the small seaport northwest of Trieste between Marshal Tito's men, who had driven fourteen miles from Trieste, and leading elements of the Eighth Army's Second New Zealand Division were given in tonight's communiqué.

On the other side of Italy another historic meeting was imminent as Fifth Army troops, continuing their drive along the Gulf of Genoa, advanced on the Aurelian Way to within sixty miles of the French border, which has already been crossed by French troops headed this way.

General Clark announced yesterday that the military power of Germany had virtually collapsed, but there still are drives for his two armies to make and engagements still to be won. The Germans, trying to regroup for their flight across the Alps, were deprived of two key road junctions leading to mountain passes west of Brenner when Belluno and Udine were occupied this afternoon by units of the Eighth Army.

Udine, which was taken by the British Sixth Armored Division, is twenty-eight miles southwest of Caporetto, the scene of the Italian disaster in World War I. The forces that entered Belluno went on five miles to Ponte nell 'Alpi, guardian of the approach to Italy's

Continued on Page 13, Column 5

DOENITZ' ACCESSION VIEWED AS A BLIND

Capital Lays His Designation to General Ignorance of His Allegiance to Party

By The Associated Press.

WASHINGTON, May 1—If Adolf Hitler really designated Grand Admiral Karl Doenitz his successor, military men here believe, he did so for the following reasons:

1. Doenitz is a Nazi supporter who could be counted on to keep German resistance going if possible.

2. But he is not associated in the Allies' minds with German atrocities and the extreme policies of the Nazi party. Therefore, Hitler probably figured that he might be able to get better treatment from the Allies when the hour of surrender came.

3. He is immensely popular with the German people.

There was a disposition here tonight to look for continued organized resistance whose core would now be centered in the Baltic and North Sea port areas. Those places are the homes of the German Navy and especially of the U-boat fleet that Doenitz commanded from 1936 until he succeeded Grand Admiral Erich

Continued on Page 5, Column 1

Churchill Hints Peace This Week; 2-Day Celebration Is Authorized

By CLIFTON DANIEL
By Wireless to THE NEW YORK TIMES.

LONDON, May 1—The general belief that peace with Germany will be announced this week persisted in Britain today, encouraged by Prime Minister Churchill himself and by Grand Admiral Karl Doenitz's announcement of the death of Adolf Hitler.

The War Cabinet again held a session tonight but so far as was known did not have any concrete proposal to consider. The chances that Heinrich Himmler ultimately will deliver an acceptable peace are now held in some official quarters to be only "fifty-fifty."

Nevertheless the buoyant Prime Minister told the House of Commons today that he might have "information of importance" to announce before Saturday.

The public's hopes were raised still further by a long Home Office circular giving the Government's views on how Britain should observe V-E Day, which the British, it appears, will be expected to celebrate strictly according to form.

[Stockholm reported, with the return there of Count Bernadotte, the "imminent liberation" of Denmark and Norway—already taking effect locally in Denmark—as a phase of a prospective general German capitulation that must be acceptable to the Allies' military commands.]

The hurrahing will begin with the announcement of the cessation of hostilities by Mr. Churchill over a nation-wide radio network. The King will speak at 9 o'clock that evening. And throughout that day

Continued on Page 10, Column 4

ADMIRAL IN CHARGE

Proclaims Designation to Rule—Appeals to People and Army

RAISES 'RED MENACE'

Britain to Insist Germans Show Hitler's Body When War Ends

By SYDNEY GRUSON
By Cable to THE NEW YORK TIMES.

LONDON, May 1—Adolf Hitler died this afternoon, the Hamburg radio announced tonight, and Grand Admiral Karl Doenitz, proclaiming himself the new Fuehrer by Hitler's appointment, said that the war would continue.

Crowning days of rumors about Hitler's health and whereabouts, the Hamburg radio said that he had fallen in the battle of Berlin at his command post in the Chancellery just three days after Benito Mussolini, the first of the dictators, had been killed by Italian Partisans. Doenitz, a 53-year-old U-boat specialist, broadcast an address to the German people and the surviving armed forces immediately after the announcer had given the news of Hitler's death.

[The British Foreign Office said that it would demand the production of Hitler's body after the end of hostilities, The Associated Press reported.]

First addressing the German people, Doenitz said that they would continue to fight only to save themselves from the Russians but that they would oppose the western Allies as long as they helped the Russians. In an order of the day to the German forces he repeated his thinly veiled attempt to split the Allies.

Radio Prepares Germans

Early this evening the Germans were told that an important announcement was to be broadcast tonight. There was no hint of what was coming. The stand-by announcement was repeated at 9:40 P. M., followed by the playing of excerpts from Wagner's "Goetterdaemmerung."

A few minutes later the announcer said: "Achtung! Achtung! In a few moments you will hear a

Continued on Page 5, Column 4

Copenhagen Writer Again Phones Story

By Cable to THE NEW YORK TIMES.

STOCKHOLM, Sweden, May 1—For the first time in more than five years THE NEW YORK TIMES correspondent in Copenhagen, Svend Carstensen, tonight telephoned a story from the Danish capital. The Nazi-imposed censorship there has been lifted. Mr. Carstensen said:

"The Danes are overjoyed at their imminent liberation, but it is not noticeable on the Copenhagen streets.

"Anxious to avoid trouble on May Day, Copenhageners have been staying indoors. The blackout is still enforced and it is pitch dark in Copenhagen tonight. All Copenhageners are glued to radios listening to broadcasts on Hitler's death.

"We expect King Christian will resume his functions and name a new Cabinet any day now. In the meantime the strictest discipline is being observed so as not to give the Germans any excuses for starting more trouble."

On April 9, 1940, Mr. Carstensen was the first to give the world the news of the German invasion of Denmark in a wireless dispatch to THE NEW YORK TIMES. His dispatch was cleared less than an hour before the Nazis seized the radio station and was the last to be sent.

"All the News That's Fit to Print"

The New York Times.

LATE CITY EDITION
Cloudy; rain tonight. Cloudy, showers and colder tomorrow.

Copyright, 1945, by The New York Times Company.

VOL. XCIV..No. 31,876. Entered as Second-Class Matter, Postoffice, New York, N. Y. NEW YORK, THURSDAY, MAY 3, 1945. THREE CENTS IN NEW YORK CITY

BERLIN FALLS TO RUSSIANS, 70,000 GIVE UP; 1,000,000 SURRENDER IN ITALY AND AUSTRIA; DENMARK IS CUT OFF; HAMBURG GIVES UP

$7,445,000,000 CUT IN COMING BUDGET ASKED BY TRUMAN

He Tells Congress Most of It Can Be Sliced From Program for 1946 Shipping

CUTS AGENCIES $80,000,000

Studies Leading to Additional Economies Are Continuing, President Assures Press

President Truman's statement on cuts in war costs, Page 38.

By BERTRAM D. HULEN
Special to THE NEW YORK TIMES.

WASHINGTON, May 2—President Truman started an economy program today with proposals looking to the saving of more than $7,445,000,000.

The biggest cut was applied to the Maritime Commission through a recommendation in a letter to Congress for reduction of funds for ship construction of more than $7,000,000,000 in current appropriations and contract authorizations.

In another recommendation the President called for a reduction of more than $80,000,000 in the budgets of eight agencies for the fiscal year beginning July 1.

Mr. Truman also informed Congress that he was terminating the Office of Civilian Defense by June 30 and withdrawing its proposed budget of $369,000 for the next fiscal year.

The Joint Congressional Committee on Internal Revenue has been continuing tax studies for months and the leaders in Congress are hopeful that the question can be taken up actively after V-E Day.

Details at Press Conference

So far as the Maritime Commission is concerned, Vice Admiral Emory S. Land, the chairman, assured ship contractors that there would be funds for the completion of the construction program under which 12,000,000 deadweight tons of new ships are being built this year.

In addition he expects that reserves of many millions of dollars can be set up for Government agencies for the current fiscal year.

Furthermore, the President said at his press conference, the second he has held since entering the White House, that other cuts were under consideration. Studies are now being made of possible reductions in employe personnel.

Indications were that the President was hopeful that tax revision would be possible, once substantial reductions in expenditures had been accomplished and hostilities had ceased in Europe. He said he was discussing tax matters with Secretary Morgenthau.

In Line With Congress Policy

The approaching end of the European war and the favorable progress of the war in the Pacific have made the savings possible. Moreover, the President's action is in line with the policy set by Congress last year in the second Deficiency Bill requiring a continuous study of appropriations and contract authorizations and their review by the President.

It is regarded as certain that Congress will adopt the recommendations. They are taken as meaning not only immediate economies, but also as signifying that President Truman is bent upon having the Executive Branch conducted primarily through the Cabinet departments rather than through agencies and boards, many of which have been set up in recent years for emergency purposes.

The agencies affected by the recommendations today are the Office of War Information, War Production Board, Office of Censorship, Office of Defense Transportation, Petroleum Administration for War, Federal Security

Continued on Page 38, Column 2

De Valera Proffers Sympathy to Reich

By The United Press.

DUBLIN, May 2—Prime Minister Eamon de Valera made a personal call at the German Legation today to express condolences for Adolf Hitler's death.

He was accompanied by Joseph Walsh, Secretary of the Department of External Affairs, and was received by the German Minister, Dr. Eduard Hempel.

Hitler's death was widely discussed throughout neutral Eire and received wide play in newspapers.

The Portuguese Government ordered two days of mourning for Hitler and flags will be flown at half-staff on "all public buildings," the American Broadcasting Station in Europe said yesterday, according to the Office of War Information.

BRITISH GO ASHORE SOUTH OF RANGOON

Force Moves to Join the 14th Army Troops North of City in Attack—Isles Shelled

By The United Press.

CALCUTTA, India, May 2—In a daring amphibious thrust, British troops landed today on the southern tip of Burma, twenty miles south of Rangoon, and stormed northward in order to join forces with Fourteenth Army troops twenty-eight miles north of Rangoon for a two-way assault on the Japanese-held capital.

The landings were made on both sides of the wide mouth of the Rangoon River where it empties into the Gulf of Martaban. They followed a drop yesterday by parachute troops from low-flying transport planes to clear the landing beaches for the amphibious forces.

Before the landings warships of the British East Indies fleet swept the Gulf of Martaban and destroyed ten Japanese craft filled to the gunwales with enemy troops fleeing Rangoon. A Southeast Asia Command communiqué announced that the British ships suffered no damage or casualties.

Andaman Sea Isles Shelled

It was not disclosed what type of warships participated in the operations in the Gulf of Martaban, but it was officially announced that other powerful British units, including aircraft carriers and the French battleship Richelieu, had carried out a two-day strike at Japanese airfields and installations in the Nicobar and Andaman Islands, far to the southwest in the Andaman Sea.

Battleships, cruisers and destroyers, the communiqué said, bombarded airfields on Car Nicobar Island, 675 miles southwest of Rangoon, and steamed northward to shell port installations at Port Blair, 425 miles southwest of Rangoon. Carrier planes followed up both operations.

[A BBC dispatch asserted that

Continued on Page 13, Column 3

WAR IN ITALY ENDS

Last Enemy Force Gives Up Just 20 Months After Landings

DEFEAT IS COMPLETE

Unconditional Surrender Opens 'Back Door' to German Bastion

By VIRGINIA LEE WARREN
By Wireless to THE NEW YORK TIMES.

ADVANCED ALLIED HEADQUARTERS, Italy, May 2—Twenty months after the Allies' troops first set foot on Italian soil the war for Italy ended at noon today, when hostilities ceased under the unconditional surrender signed by the Germans last Sunday afternoon at Allied Headquarters in Caserta.

The terms, revealed only today, cover all land, sea and air forces, estimated at almost 1,000,000 men. They apply to all northern Italy to the Isonzo River in the northeast and to the Austrian provinces of Vorarlberg, Tyrol and Salzburg and portions of Carinthia and Styria.

The surrender of the Austrian provinces swept away most of the area that the Germans had claimed that they would use for a redoubt. It also greatly lessened the chances for any last-ditch stand on the Continent. The portion of Italy not included in the surrender lies along the Yugoslav border and takes in the Istrian Peninsula, already in the hands of Yugoslav Partisans.

Germans Must Disarm

Soon after noon today the German command's radio ordered its forces still trying frenziedly to flee into the Alps before the Fifth and Eighth Armies to lay down their arms. The unconditional-surrender terms call for the "immediate immobilization and disarmament of the enemy's ground, sea and air forces."

The Germans gave up just twenty-one days after the Eighth Army and fourteen days after the Fifth Army had begun the spring offensive that swept over every important city in northern Italy, brought in more than 160,000 prisoners and sealed off all the major Alpine passes. The surrender of Col. Gen. Heinrich von Vietinghoff-Scheel, the German Commander in Chief in the southwest and Commander in Chief of Army Group C, marked the first time in this war that Germany had formally acknowledged the loss of a country that she had dominated. Even Field Marshal Sir Harold R. L. G. Alexander, the Allies' commander in this theatre, had said that Italy might well be the last battlefield.

The instrument of surrender was signed in the former summer palace of the Neapolitan Kings in Caserta by one German represent-

Continued on Page 3, Column 1

GERMANS AND ALLIES SIGNING UNCONDITIONAL SURRENDER IN ITALY

Left: Representative of Col. Gen. Heinrich von Vietinghoff-Scheel affixing signature to the document in royal palace at Caserta as his aide looks on. Right: Lieut. Gen. W. D. Morgan, British Army, placing his name on the articles. Standing behind him are (left to right) Air Vice Marshal George Baker, Chief of Staff to the Allied Mediterranean Air Forces; Maj. Gen. A. P. Kisienko and Lieut. M. Vraevsky, both representing Russia, and Maj. Gen. Lyman L. Lemnitzer, American deputy chief of staff in the Mediterranean.

The New York Times (British Official via U. S. Signal Corps Radiotelephoto)

BIG THREE WRESTLE AGAIN OVER POLAND

Russian Arguments Persist but Hope Remains—Changes in Dumbarton Plan Weighed

By JAMES B. RESTON
Special to THE NEW YORK TIMES.

SAN FRANCISCO, May 2—The United States, Great Britain and Soviet Russia made another attempt to solve the Polish Government controversy today and, while they did not succeed, the negotiations are active again and not entirely without hope.

Two major conferences were held during the day. This morning, Vyacheslaff M. Molotoff, Foreign Commissar, went to the headquarters of the American delegation and met with W. Averell Harriman and Sir Archibald Clark-

Continued on Page 16, Column 3

Goebbels and Fuehrer Died By Own Hands, Aide Says

By Cable to THE NEW YORK TIMES.

LONDON, Thursday, May 3—A deposition by Joseph Goebbels' chief assistant that both the German propaganda chief and Adolf Hitler had committed suicide in Berlin was given to the world early today by Red Army forces after they had occupied the capital of the crumbling Reich.

Hans Fritsche, Goebbels' deputy, was quoted in the Soviet communiqué as having reported also the suicide of General Krebs, who was disclosed to have been appointed Chief of the German General Staff in place of Field Marshal Gen. Wilhelm Keitel, lately believed to have been backing Heinrich Himmler's peace bid to the Western Powers.

The statement of Fritsche, who was captured in Berlin with a large assortment of defense chiefs, added another version of the Fuehrer's demise to two already given—that he had died in battle and

Continued on Page 10, Column 1

DENMARK CUT OFF; HAMBURG YIELDS

Luebeck Also Occupied, With the Surrender of Holland Believed Imminent

By The Associated Press.

LONDON, Thursday, May 3—British forces have occupied Hamburg, a broadcast by the Hamburg radio declared today.

The broadcast announcing the fall of the big North German port was in the German language but evidently it was made by the British.

It decreed a curfew for the entire population and declared that restrictions on civilian movements depended upon "the behavior of the population."

Hamburg is Germany's second largest city. It had a pre-war population of 1,682,220.

Hamburg had earlier been declared an open city, the Hamburg

Continued on Page 6, Column 1

War News Summarized

THURSDAY, MAY 3, 1945

Berlin fell to the Russians yesterday and more than 70,000 prisoners were taken. The German pocket southeast of the capital was liquidated. The Baltic ports of Rostock and Warnemuende were won. [1:8; map P. 6.]

Unconditional surrender was accepted by Col. Gen. von Vietinghoff, commanding German forces in northern Italy and western Austria. The terms, signed Sunday, became effective yesterday; thus another enemy pocket vanished. [1:3; map P. 2.]

The end was near on the Western Front, according to front-line dispatches that told of rapidly disappearing resistance. The British seized Hamburg, Luebeck and Wismar—only thirty miles from the Russians at Rostock. The United States Ninth Army linked up with the Russians northwest of Berlin, and in the south the Bavarian pocket was being reduced. [1:6, map P. 6.]

Moscow declared that Hitler and Goebbels had committed suicide in Berlin. [1:5-6.] General Eisenhower denied that Hitler had died a hero's death, indicating he had succumbed to a cerebral hemorrhage. [10:5.]

Acting Secretary of State Grew made public a chronology of the dealings with Himmler, during which President Truman told the Germans to surrender to Allied local commanders. [12:1.] Despite reports of capitulation in Scandinavia the German commanders in Norway and Denmark ordered their men to fight on, probably in anticipation of a final U-boat thrust by Admiral Doenitz. [1:6-7.] The new Fuehrer dismissed von Ribbentrop as Foreign Minister and appointed Count Lutz Schwerin von Krosigk his successor. [4:6.]

Pierre Laval, attempting to escape from Germany, landed in Spain. When he refused to leave he was interned. [1:2.3.]

Invasion of Tarakan Island, east of Borneo, by Australians was confirmed by General MacArthur. Americans on Mindanao reached the western edge of Davao. [14:2, with map.]

British paratroops and invasion forces landed on both banks of the Rangoon River below Rangoon in Burma. [1:2; map P. 13.] Americans gained 1,400 yards on Okinawa and were a mile from Yonabaru. [13:4, with map.] United States submarines have sunk twenty-one more Japanese ships. [13:1.]

Another attempt was made at San Francisco by Great Britain, the United States and Russia to settle the Polish question. While no progress was reported the atmosphere was said to have been improved and discussions will continue. [1:4.]

Spain Detains Laval for Allies After His Flight to Barcelona

By PAUL P. KENNEDY
By Cable to THE NEW YORK TIMES.

BARCELONA, Spain, May 2—Pierre Laval, former French Premier, who arrived at the Barcelona airport this afternoon seeking refuge, tonight was in the Montjuich fortress outside Barcelona, interned for disposition by the Allied Governments.

With him in custody are fellow-passengers and the crew of an armed Junkers military plane which arrived at the airport at 12:30 P. M. The passengers included Abel Bonnard, former Vichy Minister of Education; Maurice Gabolde, former Vichy Minister of Justice; Mme. Laval, Paul Neraud, Laval's private secretary, and Eugene Bonnard, son of the former Minister.

David Key, United States Consul General here, said Laval had the choice of leaving Spain immediately or internment pending disposal of his case by the Allied powers. After two hours of debate among the party, during which the plane was refueled and made ready to depart, Laval informed the authorities they chose internment.

Laval said he did not desire to be sent to France, because he feared he would not receive a fair trial there.

The Spanish Government apparently was surprised by the plane's arrival. Barcelona's Civil Governor, Antonio Correa Verglis-

Continued on Page 7, Column 1

MOSCOW JOY MAD AS BERLIN IS WON

Stalin Announcement Starts Unprecedented Celebration in Honor of Victory

By CYRUS L. SULZBERGER
By Wireless to THE NEW YORK TIMES.

MOSCOW, Thursday, May 3—News of the fall of Berlin was received here with wild acclaim although it had been expected hourly for several days.

It was Marshal Stalin's order of the day officially announcing the capture of the Nazi capital which really set things off.

It is poetic justice that among the Soviet officers specially singled out in Marshal Stalin's order for participating in the conquest of Berlin was his son, Col. Vassily Stalin, who took part as a Red Air Force pilot in the aerial destruction of the city.

While the news electrified the already jubilant capital of the Soviet Union, which was concluding the two-day May Day holiday, it is noteworthy that no more than the usual salute given for the conquest of an enemy or the liberation of a friendly capital was ordered in the case of Berlin—324 guns firing twenty-four salvos each.

But never has this largest Soviet salute been received with more acclaim. Shouting Muscovites, usually quite restrained even with the

Continued on Page 6, Column 6

Copenhagen Certain Foe Must Go, But Nazis Deny Norse, Danish Exit

By SVEND CARSTENSEN
By Telephone to THE NEW YORK TIMES.

COPENHAGEN, Denmark, May 2—The Germans are still staying in Copenhagen, but it looks as if they are on the way out. Optimism here about their immediate departure from Denmark subsided considerably today, but it was reasoned here that if the Danes have waited five years they can afford to wait another two weeks.

Therefore the Danes are lying low in the expectation that events will force the Nazis to evacuate Denmark in the shortest order whether they mean to or not.

[Upsetting reports that the Nazis were negotiating to vacate Denmark and Norway, the German High Commands in both countries announced a fight to the death, The United Press reported. This action was linked to the possibility of a final, desperate U-boat campaign from Norway.

[At the same time Grand Admiral Karl Doenitz announced the ousting of Joachim von Ribbentrop as German Foreign Minister and his replacement by Count Lutz Schwerin von Krosigk.]

King Christian and former Premier Vilhelm Buhl conferred repeatedly today and it was generally thought that Mr. Buhl's visits to the royal castle concerned the formation of a constitutional

Continued on Page 5, Column 1

EPIC SIEGE IS OVER

Shell of German Capital Yielded to Red Army by Beaten Nazis

343,000 LOST BY FOE

Baltic Link With British Is Near as Rostock and Warnemuende Fall

By The Associated Press.

LONDON, Thursday, May 3—Berlin, greatest city of the European Continent, fell yesterday afternoon to the Russians as 70,000 German troops laid down their arms in the surrender that Adolf Hitler had said never would come.

The Soviet triumph, after twelve days of history's deadliest street fighting, was announced last night by Premier Stalin in an Order of the Day and in the Soviet communiqué broadcast from Moscow this morning.

Marshal Stalin first issued an Order of the Day announcing destruction of the German Ninth Army trapped southeast of Berlin, with the capture of 120,000 of its men and the slaughter of at least 60,000.

Rostock and Warnemuende Fall

A second Order announced the capture of Germany's big Baltic ports of Rostock and Warnemuende in a forty-four-mile drive by the Second White Russian Army.

Then Marshal Stalin proclaimed the fall of Berlin. It capitulated at 3 P. M., Moscow time, and by 9 P. M. 70,000 of its staggering defenders had been rounded up and counted by the Russians.

[The defense of Berlin cost the Germans 343,000 men killed or captured, according to Soviet casualty figures, The United Press reported.]

For the conquest of Berlin his proclamation called for the top Moscow victory salute of twenty-four salvos from 324 cannon in tribute to the armies that took Berlin, the First White Russian and the First Ukrainian.

Those armies, commanded by Marshals Gregory K. Zhukoff and Ivan S. Koneff, had jumped across the Oder River sixteen days previously and on April 21 had fought into Berlin. They encircled the sprawling city, which already had been wrecked by American and British bombers, and tore the remains to bits in some of the bitterest big-scale street fighting of all time.

End of Six-Year Empire

Thus fell the once mighty capital, which Marshal Stalin described as "the center of German imperialism and heart of German aggression" and Hitler had proclaimed as the seat of his "thousand-year Reich" empire—the empire that in less than six years died as it had been born, in blood and suffering.

The greatest city ever to fall in battle, Berlin lay a 341-square-mile monument to the death of millions and to the diseased ambition of one man, Adolf Hitler.

How many persons died there will never be known with accuracy, but before the war that greatest of continental cities had a population of 4,335,000, and only Monday night the Russians announced that the fanatical Nazi defenders were killing many of the civilians with their fire.

The fury of that defense was everything that Hitler had said it would be, and even Wednesday afternoon his dwindling cohorts had contended over the Hamburg radio that resistance in Berlin was "not yet broken," even while admitting that the garrison had been ripped into isolated pockets.

The finale came in the innermost heart of the city, in the govern-

Continued on Page 5, Column 5

"All the News That's Fit to Print"

The New York Times.

LATE CITY EDITION
Cloudy with showers today. Partly cloudy and cooler tomorrow.
Temperatures Yesterday—Max., 64; Min., 47
Sunrise today, 5:46 A. M.; Sunset, 7:59 P. M.

VOL. XCIV..No. 31,881. Entered as Second-Class Matter. Postoffice, New York, N. Y. NEW YORK, TUESDAY, MAY 8, 1945. THREE CENTS IN NEW YORK CITY

THE WAR IN EUROPE IS ENDED! SURRENDER IS UNCONDITIONAL; V-E WILL BE PROCLAIMED TODAY; OUR TROOPS ON OKINAWA GAIN

ISLAND-WIDE DRIVE

Marines Reach Village a Mile From Naha and Army Lines Advance

7 MORE SHIPS SUNK

Search Planes Again Hit Japan's Life Line—Kyushu Bombed

By WARREN MOSCOW
By Wireless to THE NEW YORK TIMES

GUAM, Tuesday, May 8—In an island-wide American advance on Okinawa yesterday the First Marine Division drove south to the edge of Dakeshi Village, about a mile from Naha, the capital, straightening out the line on our right flank. In the center the Seventy-seventh Army Division used flame-throwing tanks for considerable advances, while the Seventh Army Division moved forward on the left flank.

[Airfields on Kyushu, southern Japan, were bombed Monday and Tuesday by Superfortresses, two of which were lost in heavy air opposition.

[Allied fliers started operating from the Tarakan airfield although fighting continued on that island off Borneo, and in the Philippines American troops made advances on Mindanao and Luzon.]

Japanese Dead at 36,535

As the United States forces on Okinawa resumed their drive, Fleet Admiral Chester W. Nimitz revealed that Japanese killed on the island had mounted to 36,535 on Monday, showing that the Americans were maintaining their rate of 1,000 a day.

The Americans have not yet taken the main Japanese artillery emplacements on Okinawa, which were the principal targets of the fleet off the island. The fleet's guns continued yesterday, along with carrier aircraft, to support the ground movements.

Meanwhile search bombers of Fleet Air Wing 1 continued to give an impressive demonstration of what the tightening air blockade of Japan will mean. Attacking at mast-head height with bombs and machine guns, these long-range aircraft, based in the Okinawa area, sank four more ships in waters off Korea and damaged five others.

The ships sunk were a large cargo ship, a medium cargo ship, a medium oiler and a large fleet tanker. Two small freighters were

Continued on Page 12, Column 2

Leopold Rescued By 7th Army Troops

By The Associated Press.

WITH THE UNITED STATES SEVENTH ARMY, Tuesday, May 8—Léopold III, King of Belgium, and his wife, Princess Rethy, have been liberated by the Seventh Army, it was announced today.

They were found near Strobl, eight miles east of Salzburg. The Americans had been told of their whereabouts by civilians.

With the King and his wife were eighteen members of their staff and four children. All were in good health.

Elements of the American 106th Cavalry Group had to overpower German Elite Guards to make the rescue. Seventh Army troops are now closely guarding the royal party.

The Pulitzer Awards For 1944 Announced

The Pulitzer Prize awards announced yesterday by the trustees of Columbia University included: For a distinguished novel, to "A Bell for Adano," by John Hersey; for an original American play of the current season, to "Harvey," by Mary Chase.

Among the newspaper awards were those to Hal Boyle, Associated Press war reporter, for distinguished correspondence; to James B. Reston of THE NEW YORK TIMES for his reporting of the Dumbarton Oaks Security Conference; to Joe Rosenthal, Associated Press photographer, for his photograph of marines raising the American flag at Iwo and to The Detroit Free Press for "distinguished and meritorious public service" in its investigation of legislative corruption at Lansing, Mich.

Further details of the awards will be found on Page 16.

MOLOTOFF HAILS BASIC 'UNANIMITY'

He Stresses Five Points In World Charter, but His View on One Is Questioned

By JAMES B. RESTON
Special to THE NEW YORK TIMES.

SAN FRANCISCO, May 7—The major allies who forced Germany's unconditional surrender have reached "unanimity" on the kind of world security organization which should be created at the United Nations conference to protect their newly won victory, Vyacheslaff M. Molotoff, Russian Foreign Commissar, said today.

While the delegates at the conference celebrated the end of the European war, and three Foreign Ministers, T. V. Soong of China, Paul Henri Spaak of Belgium and Trygve Lie of Norway left the conference to deal with urgent official business elsewhere, Mr. Molotoff told the press that the Soviet Union attached the "greatest importance" to five agreements reached by the heads of the Big Four delegations.

First, he said, these leaders agreed to support the principles of justice, international law, human rights and fundamental freedom for all.

Second, he added, the Big Four agreed not to make provision in the security charter for the revision of treaties.

His statement on this point was ambiguous and led to some speculation as to the unanimity of all four on the question.

Revision Power Called Danger

A reference in the United Nations charter to the necessity of revising treaties, Mr. Molotoff stated, "would play into the hands of enemy countries, which would certainly like to undermine and emasculate these treaties." Furthermore, he declared, to give the new League of Nations authority to consider revision of treaties would be a violation of national sovereign rights, which are guaranteed in the Dumbarton Oaks Charter.

For these reasons, he concluded, "the idea of revising treaties was rejected as untenable."

Third, Mr. Molotoff said, it was agreed among the Big Four that treaties directed against Germany, such as Russia's twenty-year alliances with Britain, France, Czechoslovakia, Yugoslavia and the Warsaw Poles, "should remain in force until such time as the Government concerned felt that the international security organization was really in a position to undertake the accomplishment of the tasks of

Continued on Page 15, Column 2

GERMANY SURRENDERS: NEW YORKERS MASSED UNDER SYMBOL OF LIBERTY

Thousands filling Times Square in spontaneous celebration yesterday — The New York Times

PRAGUE SAYS FOES ACCEPT SURRENDER

Czechoslovak Radio Reports All Fighting in Bohemia Will Be Ended Today

By The Associated Press.

LONDON, Tuesday, May 8 — The Czechoslovak - controlled Prague radio announced today that the Germans in Prague and throughout Bohemia, a last major holdout pocket of German resistance, had accepted unconditional surrender.

The announcement came as the United States Third Army was reported to have advanced to the outskirts of the Czechoslovak capital, and three Russian armies hammered toward the same goal from the east and north.

"The German military plenipotentiary is negotiating with the Czechoslovak National Council on the modalities of unconditional surrender," said the broadcast, detailing what purported to be the

Continued on Page 11, Column 2

Wild Crowds Greet News In City While Others Pray

By FRANK S. ADAMS

New York City's millions reacted in two sharply contrasting ways yesterday to the news of the unconditional surrender of the German armies. A large and noisy minority greeted it with the turbulent enthusiasm of New Year's Eve and Election Night rolled into one. However, the great bulk of the city's population responded with quiet thanksgiving that the war in Europe was won, tempered by the realization that a grim and bitter struggle still was ahead in the Pacific and the fact that the nation is still in mourning for its fallen President and Commander in Chief.

Times Square, the financial section and the garment district were thronged from mid-morning on with wildly jubilant celebrators who tooted horns, staged impromptu parades and filled the canyons between the skyscrapers with fluttering scraps of paper. Elsewhere in the metropolitan area, however, war plants continued to hum, schools, offices and factories carried on their normal activities, and residential areas were calmly joyful.

One factor that helped to dampen the celebration was the bewilderment of large segments of the population at the absence of an official proclamation to back up the news contained in flaring headlines and radio bulletins. With the premature rumor of ten days ago fresh in everyone's mind, and millions still mindful of the false armistice of 1918, there was widespread skepticism over the authenticity of the news.

By mid-afternoon loudspeakers were blaring into the ears of the exulting thousands in the amusement district the news that President Truman's proclamation was being held up by the necessity of coordinating it with the announcements from London and Moscow, and that the formal celebration of the long-awaited V-E Day would be delayed until today.

This sobering note gradually

Continued on Page 7, Column 6

SHAEF BAN ON AP LIFTED IN 6 HOURS

Action Comes After Protests From Newspapers and Public —Writer Still Barred

Suspension of filing facilities of The Associated Press in the European theatre was clamped on by Supreme Headquarters, Allied Expeditionary Forces (SHAEF), yesterday in an unprecedented action and was lifted six hours and twenty minutes later.

The ban was continued, however, on all copy submitted for clearance by Edward Kennedy, chief of the press association's staff on the Western Front, who sent the momentous story announcing Germany's final surrender in a dispatch from Reims, France, which was received in New York over the AP wires at 9:35 A. M. (EWT).

It was not until seven hours and fifty-five minutes had elapsed aft-

Continued on Page 4, Column 2

Summary of News of the War and German Surrender

TUESDAY, MAY 8, 1945

The war ended in Europe yesterday after five years, eight months and six days of the bloodiest conflict in history. Grand Admiral Karl Doenitz surrendered unconditonally to the Allies in a little red schoolhouse at Reims, France. At 8:41 P. M. Sunday, New York time, Col. Gen. Gustav Jodl signed for the enemy and Lieut. Gen. Walter Bedell Smith, General Eisenhower's Chief of Staff, for the Allies. In the absence of any official announcement there was some confusion as to the compliance with the surrender. Fighting had been going on in Czechoslovakia and nothing had been heard from German pockets along the French coast. [1:7-8.]

President Truman planned a broadcast from the White House at 9 o'clock this morning. Washington, gratified that the war in Europe was over, was confused by lack of confirmation. [2:2.]

Prime Minister Churchill will also broadcast at 9 A. M. from London and Premier Stalin is expected to make a simultaneous announcement in Moscow. King George will talk over the radio six hours later. [2:8.] London will celebrate V-E Day today, but, unable to restrain its joy, staged many impromptu celebrations yesterday. [2:7.]

Most New Yorkers took the news calmly and thankfully, sobered by realization that the war in the Pacific was far from over. There were, however, noisy outbursts in such centers as Times Square and Wall Street. Scrap paper showers fluttered from roofs and windows. [1:4-5.]

German Foreign Minister Lutz Schwerin von Krosigk broke the news to his people. The future will be difficult, he warned, and then added: "We must make right the basis of our nation. In our nation justice shall be the supreme law and the guiding principle. We must also recognize law as the basis of all relations between the nations." This sudden, complete reversal in German policy was received with skepticism by the Allies. [3:1.]

Perhaps one reason for this was the announcement from Moscow that 4,000,000 men, women and children had been done to death by gas, shooting, famine, poisoning and torture in the German extermination camp at Oswiecim, Poland. [12:5.]

The actual situation in Czechoslovakia was obscure. Late last night a Patriot broadcast said the Germans were negotiating with the Czechoslovak National Council details of surrender in Prague and Bohemia. Fighting had continued throughout yesterday and German planes had bombed public buildings and hospitals. [1:3; map P. 11.].

The United States Third Army continued its general advance into Czechoslovakia and the Fifth and Seventh Armies joined again in the Alps. The British Second Army moved to Denmark and Poles entered the shattered port of Wilhelmshaven. [11:1.] Breslau fell to the Red Army after an eighty-four-day siege; 40,000 Germans were captured. [11:5.]

Japan accepted the surrender of her Axis partner with a statement that she never had expected German aid and would go on to victory without the Reich. [13:1.]

Infantry and marines on Okinawa scored another general advance after naval bombardment had pulverized Japanese strong points. Pacific Fleet planes sank or damaged thirteen more ships off Korea and Japan. [1:1; map, P. 12.] B-29's maintained their assault on Kyushu airfields. Two of the big planes were shot down. [14:3-4.]

On Tarakan Allied troops were within a mile and a half of the eastern shore. Americans gained on Mindanao and Luzon in the Philippines. [12:3-4.]

Foreign Commissar Molotoff said in San Francisco that unanimity on amendments to Dumbarton Oaks assured success of the conference. He declared that the Big Four consultations had ended. [1:2.]

GERMANS CAPITULATE ON ALL FRONTS

American, Russian and French Generals Accept Surrender in Eisenhower Headquarters, a Reims School

REICH CHIEF OF STAFF ASKS FOR MERCY

Doenitz Orders All Military Forces of Germany To Drop Arms—Troops in Norway Give Up —Churchill and Truman on Radio Today

By EDWARD KENNEDY
Associated Press Correspondent

REIMS, France, May 7—Germany surrendered unconditionally to the Western Allies and the Soviet Union at 2:41 A. M. French time today. [This was at 8:41 P. M., Eastern Wartime Sunday.]

The surrender took place at a little red schoolhouse that is the headquarters of Gen. Dwight D. Eisenhower.

The surrender, which brought the war in Europe to a formal end after five years, eight months and six days of bloodshed and destruction, was signed for Germany by Col. Gen. Gustav Jodl. General Jodl is the new Chief of Staff of the German Army.

The surrender was signed for the Supreme Allied Command by Lieut. Gen. Walter Bedell Smith, Chief of Staff for General Eisenhower.

It was also signed by Gen. Ivan Susloparoff for the Soviet Union and by Gen. Francois Sevez for France.

[The official Allied announcement will be made at 9 o'clock Tuesday morning when President Truman will broadcast a statement and Prime Minister Churchill will issue a V-E Day proclamation. Gen. Charles de Gaulle also will address the French at the same time.]

General Eisenhower was not present at the signing, but immediately afterward General Jodl and his fellow delegate, Gen. Admiral Hans Georg Friedeburg, were received by the Supreme Commander.

Germans Say They Understand Terms

They were asked sternly if they understood the surrender terms imposed upon Germany and if they would be carried out by Germany.

They answered Yes.

Germany, which began the war with a ruthless attack upon Poland, followed by successive aggressions and brutality in internment camps, surrendered with an appeal to the victors for mercy toward the German people and armed forces.

After having signed the full surrender, General Jodl said he wanted to speak and received leave to do so.

"With this signature," he said in soft-spoken German, "the German people and armed forces are for better or worse delivered into the victors' hands.

"In this war, which has lasted more than five years, both have achieved and suffered more than perhaps any other people in the world."

LONDON, May 7 (AP)—Complete victory in

Continued on Page 3, Columns 2 and 3

"All the News That's Fit to Print"

The New York Times.

LATE CITY EDITION
Sunny and mild today. Fair and mild tomorrow.
Temperatures Yesterday—Max., 61; Min., 52
Sunrise today, 5:45 A. M.; Sunset, 8:00 P. M.

VOL. XCIV..No. 31,882. Entered as Second-Class Matter, Postoffice, New York, N. Y. NEW YORK, WEDNESDAY, MAY 9, 1945. THREE CENTS IN NEW YORK CITY

FINAL SURRENDER SIGNED IN BERLIN RUINS; SOVIET JOINS IN PROCLAIMING TRIUMPH; TRUMAN WARNS VICTORY 'IS BUT HALF WON'

PROPOSE RELATING PAN-AMERICAN PLAN TO WORLD SECURITY

United States Delegates Present to Big Four Formula for League Link

MOLOTOFF LEAVES TODAY

Americans and British Agree to Support Canadians on Economic Council Change

By JAMES B. RESTON
Special to THE NEW YORK TIMES.

SAN FRANCISCO, May 8—The United States tonight offered to Great Britain, Russia, China and France a formula for relating the Pan-American security system to the proposed new League of Nations and every indication was that this difficult problem would be decided before long.

This formula, discussed this morning among Secretary Stettinius and the Foreign Ministers of eight Latin-American republics and placed before the Big Four tonight, would allow the Pan-American system to deal with disputes in this hemisphere for a limited period unless such disputes endangered the peace of other areas of the world.

Some of the Latin-American nations have urged that the Security Council be forbidden to deal with disputes in this hemisphere unless those disputes should threaten the peace of other areas. But instead of this direct approach, it has been suggested that the Security Council authorize the Pan-American system to deal with its own disputes until the new world security organization is charged by the States concerned with the primary responsibility of dealing with disputes in this hemisphere.

Acceptance Is Expected

This more polite formula, which would have the same effect as a direct prohibition on the Security Council from dealing with disputes in this hemisphere, is still opposed by some members of the United States delegation, who feel that the Security Council's authority should not be restricted any more than necessary. But the pressure from the Latin-American nations and from the United States Senate for some independence in dealing with disputes in the Western Hemisphere is expected to result in acceptance of the formula outlined above.

The Russian Foreign Commissar Vyacheslaff M. Molotoff was asked to go to Mr. Stettinius' headquarters tonight for a discussion of several changes which will undoubtedly be made in the Dumbarton Oaks charter as amended by the Big Four conversations. Mr. Molotoff is departing for Moscow tomorrow.

The United States delegation, realizing that they were under pressure from the Latin-American delegations and from the Senate on the regional issue, expressed to him the belief that they would have to amend the charter to meet the demand of the Latin-American Ministers. Delegates who were at the Big Four meeting tonight gained the impression that neither Mr. Molotoff nor Ambassador Gromyko, who will take over the Russian delegation tomorrow, would make trouble on this issue.

There were four other developments at the United Nations Conference today.

First, the United States and Great Britain agreed to support, in principle, the Canadian amendment to redraft and strengthen the Economic and Social Council of the League.

Second, a group of advisers to the United States delegation, led by Clark Eichelberger of the American Association for the United Nations, have proposed the creation of an interim United Nations Security Council and Eco-

Continued on Page 19, Column 2

All Okinawa Guns Fire V-E Day Salvo

By Wireless to THE NEW YORK TIMES.

ON SOUTHERN OKINAWA, May 8—The doomed Japanese defenders of Okinawa received today a steel notification that the Germans had surrendered unconditionally, and that their country must now stand alone against the full force of the United Nations. Every shore and ship battery trained on a Japanese target fired one shell simultaneously at precisely midnight, nine hours before the official announcement of V-E Day was made, but after the commanders here had received word of the surrender.

VICTORY COST SET AT 275 BILLIONS

Morgenthau Bares Huge Sum in Appeal to Support the Seventh War Loan

Special to THE NEW YORK TIMES.

WASHINGTON, May 8—The cost of our part in bringing Germany to her knees and waging the war so far against the Japanese has reached the huge total of $275,703,000,000, Secretary Henry Morgenthau Jr., announced today.

Urging support of the Seventh War Loan Drive, starting next Monday, the Secretary of the Treasury begged Americans to buy bonds and thus hasten the day of unconditional surrender for Japan, just as it has been forced upon the beaten Reich.

"Although V-J Day may be still far off, every bond bought will bring the final victory nearer," he said.

Greeting V-E Day as the moment "for which the great architect of victory, Franklin D. Roosevelt, lived and died," Mr. Morgenthau warned that the need for war loans had not lessened since the Allied victory in Europe. On the other hand, he pointed out, March expenditures were the highest during any month of the war, with the further likelihood of "high level" expenses for many coming months.

Contrasts Costs of Wars

Contrasting the cost of other of our wars, the Secretary could give no estimate for the Revolution but noted that $70,000,000 was paid in pensions. The war of 1812 was unofficially estimated at $133,700,000, and the Mexican War at $166,000,000. The War Between the States cost more than $15,000,000,000, with pensions included, and the War with Spain above $2,000,000,000.

World War I was listed thus: To June 30, 1921, $25,729,000,000; continuing costs (pensions, interests, etc.); since then, $16,036,000,000 (to June 30, 1934); total to that date $41,765,000,000.

Expenses of the present conflict have necessarily mounted steadily since our entrance. In the few months of our participation in 1941 $6,700,000,000 was needed. Then

Continued on Page 40, Column 2

BIDS JAPANESE QUIT

The President Calls for 'Work, Work, Work' to Finish War

SETS PRAYERS SUNDAY

White House Leaves Germany's Surrender Details Unexplained

Leaders' addresses on V-E Day, Pages 5, 6, 8, 10, 12 and 13.

By BERTRAM D. HULEN
Special to THE NEW YORK TIMES.

WASHINGTON, May 8—The final and unconditional surrender of Germany, marking the end of the war in Europe, was officially announced today at 9 A. M. by President Truman in what he called "a solemn but a glorious hour." He spoke on all national networks and issued a proclamation in which he appointed Sunday as a day of prayer.

"The flags of freedom fly over all Europe," he said.

In a separate statement which was not broadcast the President called on Japan to surrender unconditionally and urged the Japanese to do so by stating that otherwise utter destruction awaited them. He explained that unconditional surrender "does not mean the extermination or enslavement of the Japanese people."

Cautions Against Easing Up

Mr. Truman warned the American people not to relax until the last battle had been won. He urged them to "work, work, work." Giving thanks to Providence for the success of our arms in Europe, he nevertheless said soberly, "Our victory is but half won."

"The West is free," he added, "but the East is still in bondage to the treacherous tyranny of the Japanese. When the last Japanese division has surrendered unconditionally, then only will our fighting job be done."

The peace that comes after victory, he said, with his thoughts on San Francisco, must be rooted in justice and law.

The President sent congratulatory messages to Prime Minister Churchill, Marshal Stalin, Gen. Charles de Gaulle and Gen. Dwight D. Eisenhower.

The President's appeal for everyone to stay on the job until Japan had surrendered was echoed widely here.

In his pronouncements President Truman did not reveal any of the circumstances of Germany's surrender, although he remarked that we had been prepared for it since Saturday. He said nothing about peace arrangements or how Germany would be handled politically. Nor did he give any indication

Continued on Page 6, Column 2

THE UNCONDITIONAL SURRENDER THAT ENDED THE WAR IN EUROPE

Representatives of the Allies and the Germans at the conference table in the schoolhouse at Reims, France. At the left are Maj. Gen. Wilhelm Oxenius, Col. Gen. Gustaf Jodl and General Admiral Hans Georg Friedeburg. Man leaning over is unidentified. At the right side of the table are (left to right) British Lieut. Gen. Sir Frederick E. Morgan, SHAEF staff deputy; Maj. Gen. Francois Sevez of France; British Admiral Sir Harold M. Burrough, Commander in Chief, Allied naval forces; Lieut. Gen. Walter B. Smith, SHAEF Chief of Staff; Maj. Gen. Kenneth W. D. Strong, Maj. Gen. Ivan Susloparoff of Russia, and Gen. Carl A. Spaatz, United States, Deputy Chief of Staff for Air.

Associated Press Wirephoto (U. S. Signal Corps Radiophoto)

NIMITZ SETS PLAN TO INVADE JAPAN

Admiral Declares Strategy Is Mapped—He Sees Early Air Aid From Europe

By WARREN MOSCOW
By Wireless to THE NEW YORK TIMES.

GUAM, Wednesday, May 9—Plans for the actual invasion of the home islands of Japan are already being drawn up, it was revealed here today by Admiral Chester W. Nimitz in an interview in which he also promised air-power blows of such intensity as the Pacific war has not yet seen.

Answering questions frankly at one of his rare press conferences, the admiral revealed that the first

Continued on Page 16, Column 2

Churchill Hails One Victory; Pledges Crushing of Japan

By SYDNEY GRUSON
By Wireless to THE NEW YORK TIMES.

LONDON, May 8—Prime Minister Churchill formally proclaimed the end of the war in Europe today, broadcasting to the world that the "evildoers * * * are now prostrate before us." But the jubilating people of Britain heard from the Prime Minister and later from their King that after a brief rejoicing they must, in the words of King George VI, "deal with our last remaining foe"—Japan.

First over the radio, then to a joyful House of Commons and then to multitudes assembled in Whitehall, Mr. Churchill spoke the words of victory and warning—words that were echoed by the King in an evening broadcast to Britain and the British Commonwealth.

Mr. Churchill in his radio proclamation of victory in Europe spoke

Continued on Page 3, Column 2

War News Summarized

WEDNESDAY, MAY 9, 1945

Germany's unconditional surrender was formally ratified in Berlin last night, long after V-E Day had been proclaimed in London and Washington. Premier Stalin waited for the Berlin ceremony before announcing victory. The cease-fire order went to the Allied forces on the Western Front yesterday, although the surrender did not become effective until last midnight. German troops facing the Russians, Yugoslavs and other Allies on the Eastern Front continued to fight until the last minute. [1:8.]

President Truman proclaimed V-E Day in this country at 9 o'clock yesterday morning, saying "The flags of freedom fly over all Europe." He designated next Sunday as a national day of prayer. "The west is free," the President added, "but the east is still in bondage," and in a statement to the press he called upon the Japanese to follow Germany into unconditional surrender or suffer the destruction that had overwhelmed the Reich. [1:3.]

Official Washington followed Mr. Truman's theme in urging everyone to stay on the job until Japan had been defeated. "Victory in Europe is not the end of our labors," Acting Secretary of State Grew said. The Japanese, well equipped for a long, fierce struggle, are "capable of finding a mad sense of glory in fighting alone," he declared. [6:5.]

Prime Minister Churchill and King George, proclaiming to the British the defeat of Germany, marshaled their people to full support of the war against Japan. [1:5-6.]

Russian troops captured the German city of Dresden and the Czechoslovak strongpoint of Olomouc in yesterday's fighting. After a day of hard battling the Germans finally withdrew from Prague. Far to the south Yugoslav Partisans liberated Zagreb, last puppet capital of what was once Hitler's domain. [2:2.]

All German ships were ordered by the British Admiralty to report their positions and proceed to designated ports. Guerrilla warfare by some U-boat commanders is anticipated. [2:4-5.]

Germany has no government other than that of the Allied Military Commission. Admiral Doenitz's pretensions were not taken seriously by the Allies nor by Sweden, Spain and Switzerland, which severed diplomatic relations. [1:6.]

A basis for a new government was seen in the "New Democratic Germany Movement," which had been working underground in Switzerland for eight years. It issued an eleven-point manifesto to the Reich calling for immediate creation of a Federal German Republic and asking the Allies not to impede the Reich's reformation. [11:1.]

Overwhelming concentration of air power will now be directed against Japan, Admiral Nimitz said. Plans for invasion are already prepared, he added. [1:4.]

Pacific Fleet guns continued to pound Japanese positions on Okinawa, but bad weather limited ground activity. Eighteen more enemy ships were sunk off Korea and Japan. [16-3:4]. B-29's that bombed Kyushu airfields by instrument met no opposition [16:5.] The Japanese, in a sudden counter-attack on Mindanao, forced back Americans in the Davao area, cutting off one battalion. [16:6.]

National Brownout Revoked; Racing Ban May End Today

Special to THE NEW YORK TIMES.

WASHINGTON, May 8—The War Production Board today lifted the "brownout" of non-essential lighting simultaneously with President Truman's proclamation for V-E Day.

There was no action on the ban on horse and dog racing or the midnight curfew, but it is expected that both of these restrictions will be ended tomorrow when Fred M. Vinson, Director of War Mobilization and Reconversion, will outline to newspapermen the economic regimen for the country for the remainder of the war.

The brownout, which has been in effect for three months and eight days, saved more than 500,000 tons of coal during "the most critical fuel shortage of the war," according to Edward Falck, director of WPB's Office of War Utilities.

"Now that we can shift from a two-front to a one-front war," Mr. Falck said, "it is felt that a mandatory order is no longer required."

He added that "all-out" conservation of fuel would be necessary until the end of the war with Japan.

The WPB appealed to users of bituminous coal, such as utilities, industrial firms and railroads, to stock up on fuel during the summer. In a letter to 25,000 soft coal consumers, J. A. Krug, WPB chairman, wrote that the storing of coal now should be considered "low cost insurance," against shortages later on.

He predicted a deficit of 25,000,000 tons of soft coal by the end of the year.

DOENITZ HINTS BID TO RETAIN POWER

Broadcast to German People Implies His Willingness to Continue at Post

By JOHN MacCORMAC
By Wireless to THE NEW YORK TIMES.

LONDON, May 8—With the formal laying down of arms on all fronts at midnight tonight, the Germany that Adolf Hitler said would last a thousand years ceased to function as a political entity and left a vacuum that will be filled only by the Allied Military Government.

The situation differs from that after the First World War in that the legal standing of Grand Admiral Karl Doenitz, self-styled Fuehrer of the new Reich who ordered its surrender, is highly ambiguous. Doenitz told the German people in a broadcast today over the Flensburg radio:

"The foundation on which the German Empire was built is a thing of the past. The unity of State and party no longer exists.

Continued on Page 11, Column 5

MILLIONS REJOICE IN CITY CELEBRATION

Night Crowds Overrun Times Square After Orderly Day—Many War Plants Close

By FRANK S. ADAMS

Under flags still at half-staff for the Commander in Chief who did not live to see the victory, an uncounted but enormous number of New Yorkers listened yesterday morning to President Truman's radio address officially confirming the unconditional surrender of Germany and calling upon every American to stick to his post until the last battle in the Pacific has been won.

Just how many of the city's 7,677,000 residents gathered around radios in homes, offices, factories, schools and in the streets to hear the President will never be known, but it seemed probable the listeners numbered at least 6,000,000. Virtually everyone but children too young to comprehend, the very old, the critically ill and those engaged in essential services gave ear to the momentous tidings.

Many millions more of Americans, scattered across the length and breadth of the United States, heard the same solemn words. The Hooper radio poll estimated last night that the biggest radio audience in history, comprising 64.1 per cent of all adult listeners, tuned in to the proceedings. The previous record was 59.6 per cent, when President Roosevelt asked Congress to declare war on Japan.

In this city and in hundreds

Continued on Page 18, Column 3

Bitter Controversy Over Ethics Follows AP Story of Surrender

With The Associated Press story of the end-of-the-war-in-Europe confirmed yesterday by the official proclamations by heads of Allied Governments, the ethics involved in the transmission of the story itself became a subject of bitter cable exchange and controversy.

Developments yesterday and last night were:

1. Gen. Dwight D. Eisenhower, replying through War Department channels to Kent Cooper, executive director of the AP, said that the suspension of Edward Kennedy, author of the story, was "due to self-admitted deliberate violation of SHAEF (Supreme Headquarters, Allied Expeditionary Forces) regulations and breach of confidence."

2. Mr. Cooper, failing to make direct contact with Mr. Kennedy because of the ban placed on the correspondent over a period of more than thirty-six hours, called on General Eisenhower to abolish military censorship in Europe now that the war is over and to permit Mr. Kennedy to state his own case "on the twenty-four-hour beat he scored on the story of Germany's surrender."

3. Fifty-four correspondents accredited to SHAEF addressed a vigorous and bitter letter of protest to General Eisenhower assailing Mr. Kennedy's action and urged a twenty-four-hour further suspension after the formal Victory-in-Europe Day of the entire AP "file" from Paris and th theatre under SHAEF's jurisdiction.

4. The AP in its cable copy pointed out that the New York

Continued on Page 15, Column 4

PEACE BEGINS TODAY

Scattered Fighting Still Goes On as Germans Fire on Prague

V-E DAY IN MOSCOW

Troops Who Defy Order to Lay Down Arms to Be Held Outlaws

By CLIFTON DANIEL
By Cable to THE NEW YORK TIMES.

LONDON, Wednesday, May 9—Germany's surrender was formally ratified yesterday in Berlin and peace in Europe came technically at 12:01 A. M. today [6:01 P. M. on Tuesday Eastern wartime].

Moscow joined in the victory celebrations, but resistance to Russian, American, Czech and Yugoslav forces continued until the last moment and beyond. While western Europe and America celebrated the unmistakable victory, the German forces in southeastern Europe still fought desperately to escape capture by the Red Army, reluctantly yielding Prague and Zagreb. The Prague radio announced at 3:30 A. M. that the Germans had re-opened fire on Prague at 1:50 A. M.

Her armies still embattled at least until midnight, Russia did not hear a victory announcement until today. Soon after 1 A. M., the Moscow radio announced the unconditional surrender of Germany for the first time and broadcast an order of the day making Victory Day in Russia. The British and American announcements were made at 3 P. M. yesterday, London time, or 9 A. M., Eastern war time.

Stalin Awaited Ratification

Premier Stalin waited for the ratification in Berlin, where, the Moscow radio said, the surrender was signed at midnight by Field Marshal Gen. Wilhelm Keitel, Gen. Admiral Hans Georg von Friedeburg and Gen. Hans Juergen Stumpff, respectively commanders in chief of the German Army, Navy and Air Force.

Air Chief Marshal Sir Arthur William Tedder, Gen. Dwight D. Eisenhower's deputy commander; Marshal Ivan Zhukoff, commander of the First Ukrainian Army; Gen. Carl A. Spaatz, commander of the United States Strategic Air Forces, and Lieut. Gen. Jean de Lattre, commander of the French First Army, witnessed the signing for the Allies.

The fact that the final deadline for unconditional surrender was actually fixed for today and not yesterday and that the German forces took full advantage of that against the Red Army seemed to explain Premier Stalin's reluctance to hasten the victory proclamation. As of last night, Russia was still fighting.

Although the terms were the same, the Moscow radio did not mention the previous surrender signed on Monday at General Eisenhower's headquarters in Reims. After the final deadline for the unconditional surrender of all German forces on all fronts at 12:01 A. M., those enemy troops that disdained the cease-fire order became outlaws subject to attack from all quarters.

Prague Has Fighting to the End

Less than two hours before the cease-fire order, Prague announced an agreement for the capitulation of the German forces in the Czechoslovak capital. As Prime Minister Churchill and President Truman were formally proclaiming the unconditional surrender of all German forces to the four major Allied powers, German guns and aircraft were killing citizens of Prague and wrecking the city's hitherto undamaged architectural monuments.

From the east and the west the Red Army and the American Third

Continued on Page 12, Column 2

"All the News That's Fit to Print"

The New York Times.

LATE CITY EDITION
Sunny and warm today. Tomorrow fair and warm.
Temperatures Yesterday—Max., 8[illegible]; Min., 62
Sunrise today, 5:24 A. M.; Sunset, 8:[illegible] P. M.

Copyright, 1945, by The New York Times Company.

VOL. XCIV..No. 31,926. Entered as Second-Class Matter, Postoffice, New York, N. Y. NEW YORK, FRIDAY, JUNE 22, 1945. THREE CENTS IN NEW YORK CITY

OKINAWA IS OURS AFTER 82 DAYS; 45,029 U. S. CASUALTIES, FOE'S 94,401; GEN. STILWELL HEADS 10TH ARMY

HOUSE REPUBLICANS SEEK TO STRIP OPA OF FOOD CONTROLS

Leaders Act on Hoover Plan to Give Real Authority to the Secretary of Agriculture

'BUNGLING' IS CHARGED

Limitation to Six Months and Cost-Plus for Farms Are Expected to Fail

Special to The New York Times.

WASHINGTON, June 21—Republican support for a reorganization of the price control structure along the lines suggested by former President Hoover developed today as the House ended two days of general debate on the Administration bill to extend the present price control act without change.

The Democratic and Republican leaders planned, with doubtful prospects of success, to seek a final vote tomorrow.

The "Hoover Plan," made public by the former President in a letter to Representative Jenkins of Ohio, was embodied by Mr. Jenkins in an amendment which would give the Secretary of Agriculture control over production, processing, distribution and pricing of food, and leaving to the Office of Price Administration only the routine mechanism of rationing.

There was a prospect that the Republicans in general would make their greatest effort to push through this amendment, hoping to recruit Democratic dissenters, particularly because the new Secretary of Agriculture, Representative Clinton P. Anderson of New Mexico, is an Administration Democrat popular with his colleagues.

Attacks Likely to Fail

It was indicated that the two other major attacks on continued price control as the Administration wants it would not succeed. These controls include the Wherry Senate amendment to guarantee farmers and stockmen a "cost-plus" price formula, and another amendment to limit the extension of the OPA to six months rather than a year.

The Democrats were especially anxious to reach a vote tomorrow. They fear that a postponement of the decision until Saturday might weaken their position by reducing their numbers on that customarily inactive day.

The day's debate found Administration speakers attacking the Wherry "cost-plus" amendment and the effort to limit OPA's extension to six months. Republican speakers, led by Representative Martin, the minority leader, attacked the administration of the Price Control Act.

Mr. Martin, asserting that "bungling and inefficiency" in OPA had been confirmed by the Democrats themselves, insisted that OPA, "right from the beginning has been run by crackpot theorists."

"And I am not referring," he added, "to the head man."

He continued:

"I will say," without publicly mentioning just what amendments he proposed to support, "that the situation has gone far enough. Congress has permitted this agency a free hand in the adoption of its regulations. We have given it every opportunity to order its affairs and to create a stable and sane method of operation which would guarantee to our people at least a minimum of the necessities of life."

Opposes Limited Extension

Representative Monroney of Oklahoma, a member of the House Banking Committee and a leader for the Administration in the fight over the bill, protested that an extension of OPA for only six months would "demoralize" the agency.

As to Republican claims of "unfairness" and poor administration in OPA, he declared the administration had in fact been "sensible" on the whole, adding:

"The umpire can't always call the plays in favor of your team."

Of the Wherry amendment, Mr. Monroney argued that it would be impossible to reach any agreed determination as to what was the legitimate "cost of production" of the farmers of the country, and that it would actually operate against the farmer's best interests by causing him to be blamed for "the devastating rise in prices" that would result.

He submitted a statement by Chester Bowles, head of OPA, declaring that the present act had ample provisions "to afford protection to farm producers."

Round-World Flight For Civilians Is Set

The round-the-world flight on commercial passenger planes of Pan American Airways in eighty-eight hours flying time on the resumption of post-war travel was announced yesterday by the Atlantic division of that organization, with headquarters at La Guardia Field. The cost of the flight was listed as $700, or less than the present round-trip rate to Europe.

Reservations have been made by eleven passengers, including several who have become nationally known as "pioneers" on first flights to new destinations.

The route from New York will cover Lisbon, Marseille, Rome, Athens, Cairo, Basra and Karachi to Calcutta of the Atlantic division, and then return via Bangkok, Canton, Tokyo, Paramushiru, Anchorage, Seattle and San Francisco to New York.

MEAT BETTERMENT PLEDGED BY TRUMAN

President Forecasts Single Control Over Prices, Food—Praises Trade Bill Passage

By The Associated Press.

OLYMPIA, Wash., June 21—President Truman promised improvement in the meat situation and forecast a single control over prices and food at a press conference today, his first outside the White House. After the conferences he went on a salmon fishing trip.

The President wore a wool pullover sweater borrowed from Gov. Mon C. Wallgren, who, with Senator Magnuson, Democrat, of Washington, sat in on the meeting. It was knitted by the Indians over on Vancouver Island, Mr. Truman explained.

The President also told reporters that he had expected the United Nations Conference to be a success; expressed confidence that Congress would pass the Bretton Woods monetary agreements as it had done with the reciprocal trade program, and called General Eisenhower a grand gentleman who is entitled to anything he wanted, adding that the President would see that he received it.

Mr. Truman spoke reassuringly of the food situation and added that the Administration was at work on a plan for single control over prices and food, but did not disclose how it would function.

Sees Meat Shortage Easing

He said that the meat shortage would automatically be straightened out as soon as Representative Anderson, Democrat, of New Mexico, took office as his new Secretary of Agriculture and War Food Administrator. The President asserted that it would have been straightened out under the contemplated program under Marvin Jones, retiring Food Administrator, as well.

He told a questioner he had not seen a statement of former President Hoover that food controls over meat distribution had broken down. He added that Mr. Hoover had been very helpful in his recent White House talk on the subject.

Saying that the San Francisco Conference seemed to have accomplished its purpose, the President pointed out that the delays were technical, involving translations into many languages which consumed time.

He said he would address the closing session Tuesday, leaving here Monday by plane, stopping over in Portland for a brief tour of the city, and flying on to San Francisco.

"The action of the Senate in ap-

Continued on Page 32, Column 5

7TH LOAN OVER TOP AT $15,982,000,000; E-BOND SALES LAG

On 39th Day of Drive Nation Passes Its Over-All Quota by Nearly 2 Billions

INDIVIDUAL GOAL IS NEAR

Both City and State Achieve Objectives in This Class—Further Effort Stressed

With the aid of heavy corporation investments, the Seventh War Loan drive surged yesterday past its $14,000,000,000 over-all national goal by almost $2,000,000,000, but the anti-inflationary E Bond Series scored up only two-thirds of quota, The Associated Press reported in Washington. Secretary of the Treasury Henry Morgenthau Jr. warned the nation that complete success would not be achieved until the total set for individuals had been reached.

Both New York State and City surpassed their quotas for individual sales, but local War Finance Committee officials feared they might fail to meet their separate goals in E Bonds by the campaign deadline June 30.

On the thirty-ninth day since the drive opened May 14, total sales throughout the country climbed to $15,982,000,000. Of that sum corporation sales accounted for $9,782,000,000 and individual sales for $6,200,000,000. Each category had a quota of $7,000,000,000.

In contrast to that, sales of E Bonds, the popular securities for small investors, had reached a total of only $2,779,000,000 of the $4,000,000,000 goal.

Morgenthau Hails Achievement

Commenting on the progress of the drive, Secretary Morgenthau said it was "most gratifying to the Treasury" but that it meant corporations had passed their quota. A large job remained to be done, he noted, before the final accounting period ends July 7.

"Reports reaching me give me every confidence that our $7,000,000,000 goal for individuals will be met by that date," he added.

Frederick W. Gehle, New York chairman of the War Finance Committee, announced that the State had exceeded its goal of $1,134,000,000 for sales to individuals. The total—$1,139,200,000—constituted a new record in war financing for New York, he said.

But, with E Bond sales continuing in a "slump," New Yorkers faced the possibility that their purchases of that series would be insufficient to meet the city and State drive quotas, he pointed out.

"This fact," he commented, "increasingly evident during the past week, means that unless subscribers put forth greater effort than at any time during the war, the current campaign, in so far as the vitally important, anti-inflationary E Bonds are concerned, will fall short of full success. The factor that counts most is represented in E Bonds and not enough people are buying them."

67.1 Per Cent of E Bonds Sold Here

To date $192,707,215 in E Bonds has been sold in the city, which is 67.1 per cent of the $287,300,000 quota. All sales to individuals amounted to $12,695,613 on Wednesday, bringing the drive total in this group to $892,986,250, or 105.4 per cent, of the local goal of $847,430,000.

All investors purchases—including corporate and financial institutions—totaled cumulatively $2,535,049,837, or 74.2 per cent of the

Continued on Page 32, Column 7

Queen Mary Never Saw a Torpedo As She Roamed Seven Seas Alone

By GEORGE HORNE

The role of the Atlantic liner Queen Mary at war is a story of high adventure—the tale of a ship with a charmed life.

It is one that should be spun from the rich memory of Sir James Gordon Partridge Bisset, K.B.E., commodore of the Cunard White Star Line, who stood on the bridge of the towering sea giant for more than three years, coursing the seven seas across the Atlantic, and from the Clyde to Sydney, from Halifax to the storm-wracked Cape, to Singapore, Bombay and Trincomalee.

And spun it was yesterday by Sir James himself, a stocky man with a bit of a roll to his gait and a rich mingling in his speech of the original Scottish burr with the salty sea jargon that knows no nationality.

"I was born in Liverpool of a Scot family," he said, stating first things first.

"I'm half Scotch and half soda," he went on, and then quickly corrected himself, "English, I mean."

Sir James loves the Queen Mary, and well he might. She has traveled 600,000 miles in the war, delivering 500,000 American soldiers where their generals wanted them to be, and another 100,000 British troops in addition. She has carried a heavy armament of fifty or sixty guns, some of them manned by

Continued on Page 6, Column 2

Okinawa Costliest Of Pacific Battles

By The Associated Press.

GUAM, Friday, June 22—The conquest of Okinawa was the longest and costliest of all the campaigns in the central and western Pacific.

With casualty figures still incomplete, the toll of enemy and American killed, captured and wounded all but equals the grand total of casualties in six major campaigns which led up to Okinawa.

The eighty-two days it took to break all organized resistance dwarfs the twenty-six days of Iwo Island. The latter, however, is less than eight square miles in area, and Okinawa is roughly 485 square miles.

The figures for Okinawa, which include Japanese casualties through June 20 and American casualties only through June 19, compared with those of six other campaigns follow:

	Japanese Killed	Japanese Captured	American Killed	American Wounded
Okinawa	90,401	4,000	11,260	33,769
Iwo	23,244	1,038	4,630	15,308
Saipan	27,586	2,161	3,426	13,099
Guam	17,442	524	1,437	5,648
Palau	13,354	435	1,302	6,115
Tarawa	5,000	150	913	2,037
Tinian	6,939	523	314	1,515

Note: Figures for Americans killed include missing.

LONDON IS PICKED AS INTERIM SEAT

Connally and Vandenberg Will Speak in Senate Two Days After Conference Adjourns

By JOHN H. CRIDER

Special to The New York Times.

SAN FRANCISCO, June 21—The United Nations Conference selected London, the "nursery" of the League of Nations, as the site for meetings of the committee which will do the planning to put life into the new world organization, as it became known today that the effort in the Senate for ratification of the new charter would start two days after the conference adjourns on Tuesday.

Senator Tom Connally of Texas, chairman of the Foreign Relations Committee, and Senator Arthur H. Vandenberg of Michigan, the two Senate representatives of the United States delegation, will make speeches Thursday, the day after they arrive by air in Washington from this conference.

Persons close to Senator Vandenberg said they were convinced

Continued on Page 8, Column 2

War News Summarized

FRIDAY, JUNE 22, 1945

Okinawa has been conquered by infantrymen and marines of the United States Tenth Army, backed by the guns and planes of the Pacific Fleet. Fighting, except for two small pockets around Medeera and Mabuni, ended yesterday on the eighty-second day of the invasion. Through Wednesday 90,401 Japanese had been killed and 4,000 taken prisoner. Tenth Army casualties to the day before were 6,990 killed and missing, 29,598 wounded. Pacific Fleet casualties to May 24 were 4,270 killed and missing, 4,171 wounded. [1:8.]

There was no final "banzai" charge by fanatical Japanese; to the contrary, the enemy at the end surrendered in unprecedented numbers. The campaign, started on Easter Sunday, April 1, was the most bitterly fought and costliest in the Pacific war. Rapid progress has been made in converting the island into a major base for future operations. [3:1.]

General MacArthur has appointed General Stilwell to succeed the late Lieutenant General Buckner in command of the Tenth Army. General Stilwell, who was in the Pacific on an inspection tour as Commander of Ground Forces, may lead an invasion of China or head an Army group against Japan. [1:6-7.]

In China Japanese troops were chased thirty-one miles up the coast from Wenchow, with indications that the enemy was abandoning the entire coast between Canton and Ningpo. Three Chinese columns were closing in on Liuchow. [2:1.]

Australians hopped eighty miles down the Borneo coast to land unopposed at Lutong in the heart of the Seria-Miri oil refining center. [1:5; map P. 2.] Filipino guerrillas captured Tuguegarao, capital of Cagayan Province, fifty miles south of Aparri, thus splitting the enemy forces. [3:6-7.]

B-29's switched to heavy explosives yesterday; great numbers dropped heavy loads on military and industrial targets on Honshu, Japan's main island. Tokyo continued to forecast an early American invasion. [1:7.]

Senator Kilgore declared that secret documents had revealed detailed plans by German industrialists to rearm the Reich for another attempt at world conquest, and the intention to finance an underground Nazi movement. Field Marshal Montgomery, from his headquarters in Germany, said members of the German General Staff would be kept in isolated prisons outside the country until militarism was broken up and that SS troops would be imprisoned for twenty years. [1:6-7.]

Yugoslavia, submitting a detailed report on 10,000 Fascist crimes, asked for the surrender of General Mikhailovitch and protested against the lenient treatment of Italian war criminals. [4:4-5.] Crowds in Milan demonstrated for a severe purge of Fascists and demanded more food and jobs. [4:3.]

OKINAWA CONQUEST EXPANDS OUR ATTACKING RADIUS

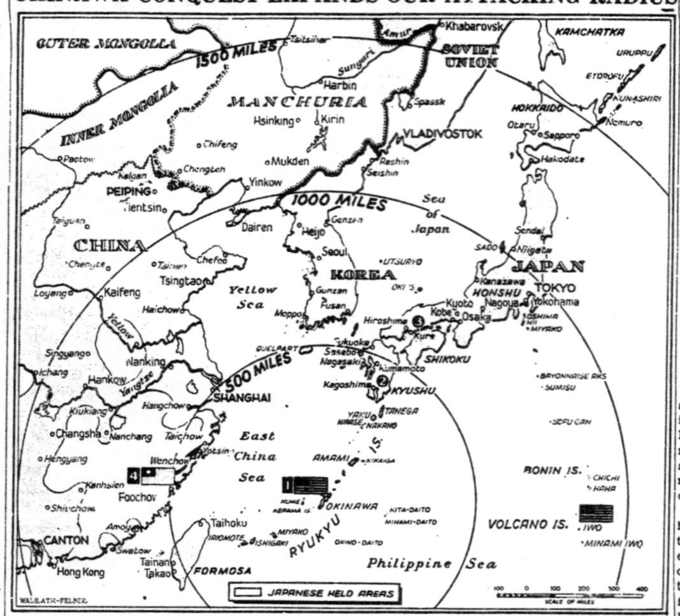

June 22, 1945

With the end of the campaign on the chief island of the Ryukyu group (1), southern Japan is brought within reach of our fighter-bombers and virtually the entire enemy empire within reach of our long-range aircraft. Already apprehensive over the next American step, the enemy reported that planes had scouted Kyushu (2) and southern Honshu (3). B-29's attacked the latter island. On the Asiatic mainland the Chinese advanced thirty-one miles beyond Wenchow(4).

AUSTRALIANS SEIZE BORNEO OIL PLANT

Make New Surprise Landing in Lutong Area, 80 Miles South of Brunei Bay

By The United Press.

MANILA, Friday, June 22—Australian Ninth Division troops have landed unopposed in Borneo's Lutong oil refinery area, eighty miles down the west coast from Brunei Bay, and dispatches from the front today said that the Australians already had captured the important refinery there—potentially the most productive in the British Empire.

Gen. Douglas MacArthur announced the new amphibious operation—this one aimed at the heart of northern Borneo's rich oil industry. A dispatch from the front said the Australians sent pa-

Continued on Page 2, Column 6

'Vinegar Joe' in Command Of Okinawa's Conquerors

By The United Press.

MANILA, Friday, June 22—Gen. Joseph W. Stilwell has been named to lead the triumphant United States Tenth Army, conquerors of Okinawa, to new battles against the Japanese, it was announced today. The disclosure was made on the very day that Fleet Admiral Chester W. Nimitz announced the complete victory on Okinawa.

General Stilwell was appointed by Army Gen. Douglas MacArthur, acting in his capacity of commander of all United States Army forces in the Pacific. He succeeds the late Lieut. Gen. Simon Bolivar Buckner, who was killed last Monday on Okinawa by a Japanese shell. The new command lifts General Stilwell out of his post as Commander of Army Ground Forces in the United States and gives him an active combat command in the field, which virtually guarantees that he will be one of the leading figures in the final destruction of Japan.

General Stilwell already is in the Pacific and has been inspecting battle conditions on northern Luzon.

The Tenth Army comprises veteran units of the Pacific fighting, including the First, Second and Sixth Marine Divisions, and the Ninety-sixth, Seventy-seventh, Twenty-seventh and Seventh Infantry Divisions.

General Stilwell is a veteran of the Burma and China fighting. He speaks several Chinese dialects. Up until last Oct. 28 he was commander of United States forces in the China-Burma-India theatre, Chief of Staff to Generalissimo Chiang Kai-shek and deputy to British Ad-

Continued on Page 2, Column 2

450 B-29'S SMASH TARGETS IN HONSHU

Kure Arsenal Is Main Site of 3,000-Ton Explosive Blow—Foe Sees Invasion Move

By Wireless to The New York Times.

GUAM, Friday, June 22—Six important industrial targets in Japan, headed by the Kure naval arsenal, one of the two most important naval arsenals in Japan, were hit today in a daylight strike by a large force of approximately 450 American "Superforts," operating from bases in the Marianas.

Earlier the Tokyo radio had linked recent air strikes to preliminary operations for an invasion of Japan.

The Kure arsenal, plus the Hiro arsenal, which was virtually destroyed in a B-29 strike on May 5, furnished the weapons and the powder for the Japanese.

There is not much of a Japanese fleet left, but what there is, we are out to deprive of supplies.

The "bombs away" signal over the six separate targets came in

Continued on Page 3, Column 3

German Staff to Be Kept in Exile; Kilgore Reports Third War Plot

By The United Press.

TWENTY-FIRST ARMY GROUP HEADQUARTERS, Germany, June 21—The Allies plan to stamp out German militarism by imprisoning the German General Staff in isolated camps outside Germany and holding all SS troops in North German camps for the next twenty years, Field Marshal Sir Bernard L. Montgomery announced today.

He did not state how long the officers of the German General Staff would be held, but he left no doubt of the Allies' determination to make sure that there was an end to Germany's ceaseless planning of wars and world conquest. The General Staff, which remained

Continued on Page 6, Column 4

Special to The New York Times.

WASHINGTON, June 21—Secret documents not presently identifiable as to source show that German industrialists last August laid plans for re-industrialization and rearming of Germany after the expected defeat, Senator Harley M. Kilgore of West Virginia asserted today.

Mr. Kilgore, who recently returned from a trip to Europe in his capacity as chairman of the war mobilization subcommittee of the Senate Military Affairs Committee, released an analysis of the documents to the press.

"Masquerading as 'neutral' business men without political allegiance," he asserted, "they [the Ger-

Continued on Page 6, Column 6

ISLE DECLARED WON

1,700 Japanese Troops Surrender Last Day of Bitter Battle

OTHERS JUMP INTO SEA

Great Base That Opens All of Japan to U.S. Attack Already in Operation

By WARREN MOSCOW

By Wireless to The New York Times.

GUAM, Friday, June 22—The battle of Okinawa is officially at an end. In a special communiqué issued at 10 o'clock last night, Fleet Admiral Chester W. Nimitz reported the end of organized resistance, and in a second one this morning he told of mopping-up operations.

Today's communiqué revealed how costly has been the price for the island for which we battled for eighty-two days. United States casualties so far disclosed amount to 45,029, and they are sufficiently far behind to indicate that the island bastion, four hundred statute miles from Japan, will have cost nearly 50,000 men in dead, missing and wounded from United States Army, Navy and Marine forces.

The cost of the Okinawa campaign was twice the toll of bloody Iwo, up to Okinawa the most costly of all our Pacific campaigns.

90,401 Japanese Killed

Through June 19 we had lost 6,990 men killed or missing in the land operations from the Army and marines and had 29,598 wounded for a total of 36,588.

The fleet losses, far higher than in any other campaign, have not been announced past May 23, almost a month ago. At that time 4,270 sailors had been killed or were missing and 4,171 wounded. This brings the Okinawa casualties to 45,029. It is likely that a month's fleet losses and the last two days of organized resistance plus what comes from mopping up will carry the total to the 50,000 mark.

The Okinawa campaign cost the Japanese around 94,401. Of these, 90,401 had been killed on Okinawa or in the Kerama Islands or on Ie Island, the three major battlegrounds of the Ryukyus campaign. About 4,000 Japanese had been captured up to last night, with the number growing rapidly. About 1,700 gave up yesterday alone.

The communiqué that announced the end of Okinawa resistance was brief and to the point. Issued at 10 P. M., Guam time, last night, it read:

"After eighty-two days of fighting, the battle of Okinawa has been won. Organized resistance ceased on June 21. Remnants of the enemy garrison in two small pockets in the southern portion of the island are being mopped up."

"Well Done," Says Nimitz

The communiqué was No. 400, issued from Pacific Fleet Headquarters. Ironically, the first communiqué, issued on June 4, 1942, told of the beginning of the Battle of Midway in the form of an announcement of a Japanese air attack on that island. Previously communiqués had been issued from Washington. That battle was the high watermark of the Japanese advance in the Pacific.

Shortly after telling of the end, Admiral Nimitz sent a "well done" to the officers and men under his command. It read as follows:

"To officers and men of all United States armed forces of the Pacific Ocean areas and of the British Pacific Fleet who have had their part in achieving this important victory, well done."

Communiqué No. 401, issued this morning at 10 o'clock, revealed that Japanese resistance ceased first in the Marine Corps sector of the island at 10:27 yesterday morning, Okinawa time. Two small pockets were still being cleaned up in the Army sector last night. All over the island's southern tip our troop movements were being hampered by the Okirawan civilians, who had been living underground

Continued on Page 3, Column 3

"All the News That's Fit to Print"

The New York Times.

LATE CITY EDITION
Sunny and warm today. Showers and warmer tomorrow.
Temperatures Yesterday—Max., 76; Min., 67
Sunrise today, 5:26 A. M.; Sunset, 8:33 P. M.

VOL. XCIV..No. 31,931. Entered as Second-Class Matter, Postoffice, New York, N. Y. NEW YORK, WEDNESDAY, JUNE 27, 1945. THREE CENTS IN NEW YORK CITY

TRUMAN CLOSES UNITED NATIONS CONFERENCE WITH PLEA TO TRANSLATE CHARTER INTO DEEDS; B-29'S KEEP UP ASSAULT ON HONSHU PLANTS

TWO BLOWS IN DAY

50 'Superforts' Batter Oil Works Few Hours After Strike by 500

TOP REFINERY IS HIT

Five Bombers Lost, 70 Reach Iwo From the Earlier Japan Mission

By The Associated Press.

GUAM, Wednesday, June 27 — Nearly fifty B-29's struck the Utsube River oil refinery on Honshu, Japan's principal producer of aviation gasoline, in a precision demolition attack before midnight last night.

The attack followed by half a day the greatest Superfortress demolition assault to date, a pinpointing of Honshu industries in which nearly 500 of the sky giants blasted ten enemy war factories with 3,000 tons of bombs.

[Twentieth Air Force headquarters in Washington reported five B-29's missing after the earlier Tuesday assault, which it said hit "the largest number of individual military and industrial targets yet attacked on a single Superfortress mission."

[Twenty-first Bomber Command crews reported "good to excellent" results in the multiple attack. They met slight Japanese fighter opposition and meager anti-aircraft fire.]

Refinery Damaged Previously

The Utsube refinery is located near Yokkaichi, eighteen miles southwest of Nagoya on Ise Bay. Since the destruction of Japanese fuel centers at Tokuyama and Otake by B-29's on May 10, the Utsube plant was the enemy's largest remaining producer of aviation gasoline.

The city of Yokkaichi was heavily damaged in an incendiary assault June 18. Some fire bombs fell into the Utsube refinery area in that attack, causing slight damage to the plant, but last night's strike was the first with the Utsube plant and storage area as the primary objective.

Ice-coated, as the result of soupy weather on their great demolition strike, more than seventy B-29's of the huge fleet in the early Tuesday attack made emergency landings on Iwo Island, the Twenty-first Bomber Command reported.

At one time Superfortresses were stacked in circles above our

Continued on Page 2, Column 6

New Invasion Attack Near South of Japan, Tokyo Says

Enemy Reports Our Convoys Moving North From Okinawa and Speculates That Upper Ryukyus May Be Goal

By The United Press.

WASHINGTON, June 26—Tokyo hinted tonight that a new United States invasion blow was impending against the northern Ryukyus, 180 miles south of Kyushu. An invasion fleet of some 200 transports, cruisers, destroyers and a battleship was moving northward along both coasts of Okinawa, Japanese broadcasts said, as recorded by the Federal Communications Commission.

[The Tokyo radio reported Tuesday night that Allied troops had landed on Kume Island, fifty miles west of Okinawa, according to The Associated Press. Later, a Japanese Domei agency broadcast said "the Japanese garrison intercepted the enemy and heavy fighting is now in progress." The broadcast, recorded by the Federal Communications Commission, referred to the Kume invasion as a "fresh landing."]

At the same time it was speculated that the Americans needed still more "stepping-stone" bases before carrying out their "certain" invasion of the home islands.

A Yomiuri Hochi newspaper dispatch quoted by Tokyo asserted that Amami and Kikai Islands, 180 miles south of Kyushu, had been chosen as the objectives of the next landing attempts. The two islands lie side by side 110 miles north of Okinawa, at the end of the Ryukyu chain.

"Apparently the enemy intends to make Okinawa the main base for the invasion of the Japanese homeland," the correspondent wrote. "Large amounts of war material are being poured into Okinawa from the Philippines and the Marianas."

However, he added, the Americans will need 500,000 to 1,000,000 men to carry out an invasion of the home islands and auxiliary bases will be needed to debark and quarter them, as well as to move

Continued on Page 3, Column 2

INDIANS IN ACCORD ON WAVELL BASIS

Viceroy's Plan for a Regime Almost Entirely Native Is Accepted by Conferees

By TILLMAN DURDIN

By Wireless to THE NEW YORK TIMES.

SIMLA, India, June 26—Today's conference between the Viceroy, Field Marshal Viscount Wavell, and Indian political leaders is authoritatively understood to have agreed to the overall acceptance of the Wavell plan for the formation of a new central government for India almost entirely Indian in composition.

This acceptance of the main principle of the Wavell proposals represents a big stride toward a successful outcome for the "little round table" sessions here and hopes are high that full accord will be reached. Difficult problems remain to be settled, however, and these may still wreck the conference.

Probably the main unsolved problem is the allocation of posts in the new government among the various political and religious groups. In accepting the Wavell proposals, the conference members agreed on parity between caste Hindus and Moslems in the new government, but it is still to be decided whether all the Moslems will be members of Mohammed Ali Jinnah's Moslem League or whether all caste Hindus will be representatives of the Congress party.

Other Problems Canvassed

After assembling at 11 o'clock this morning, the conference adjourned at 12:30 and issued a brief statement saying provisional agreement had been reached on certain main principles and that the conference had adjourned to enable the delegates to consider the remaining problems in private discussions outside the conference chamber.

It was decided to meet again tomorrow morning. This afternoon the Congress party delegates conferred with Mohandas K. Gandhi and Moslem League leaders held separate talks. Later Pandit Govind Vallabh Pant, one of the Congress party delegates, visited Mr. Jinnah in the latter's hotel room, where it is assumed the problem of apportioning posts in the new government was discussed.

In addition to accepting the Wavell plan providing for equal numbers of caste Hindus and Moslems among the Ministers of the proposed new Government, it was learned, the conference agreed on other important points, all stated outright or implied in Viscount Wavell's recent broadcast of his proposals.

It was decided that the new Government's Cabinet or Executive Council, as it is called, would

Continued on Page 4, Column 4

Generalissimo Rank For Stalin Indicated

By The Associated Press.

LONDON, June 26—The Presidium of the Supreme Soviet conferred its four highest awards today on Premier Joseph Stalin and created a new rank of generalissimo to be given "for particularly outstanding services to the motherland in the task of commanding all armed forces of the state during war," Moscow said tonight.

The broadcast did not say who would be named generalissimo, but the requirement given for this highest possible military rank seemed to indicate that Marshal Stalin might receive it.

The principal decoration conferred upon the Russian leader was the Order of Victory "for exceptional services in the organization of all the armed forces of the Soviet Union and for skillful leadership of these forces in the great patriotic war, which ended in full victory over Hitlerite Germany."

He received the Hero of the Soviet Union medal as the Marshal "who headed the Red Army in defense of our motherland and its capital, Moscow, and with exceptional courage directed the struggle against Hitlerite Germany." He also received the Order of Lenin and the Gold Star.

2 JAPANESE CHIEFS OKINAWA SUICIDES

Generals Stabbed Themselves in Formal Ceremony on Cliff —Aides Hastened Deaths

By The United Press.

OKINAWA, June 26—The bodies of Lieut. Gen. Mitsuru Ushijima, Japanese commander in chief on Okinawa, and his chief of staff, Lieut. Gen. Isama Cho, were found yesterday in shallow graves on the southern sea cliff where they had been taken after a dramatic hara-kiri ceremony.

The two generals had decided to kill themselves June 21 when their last stronghold, an elaborate system of inter-connecting caves on Mabuni ridge, had been surrendered, according to a prisoner of war.

The prisoner, who had been

Continued on Page 4, Column 3

GOLDSTEIN, O'DWYER TO BE UNOPPOSED IN THE PRIMARIES

Surpless Withdraws Despite Having More Than Enough Backing to Enter Race

MANY DEMOCRATIC FIGHTS

Six Candidacies for Public Office and 10 Leaderships in Tammany Involved

General Sessions Judge Jonah J. Goldstein of Manhattan and District Attorney William O'Dwyer of Brooklyn were assured uncontested nominations for Mayor yesterday as the deadline for filing designations was reached at 5 P. M. without the appearance of any opposition petitions. There still remained a remote possibility that opposition petitions might be placed in the mails before midnight.

The last threat of primary opposition to Judge Goldstein was removed earlier in the day when George H. Ittleman announced that Magistrate Abner C. Surpless of Brooklyn would not make a contest for the Republican nomination despite the fact that more than enough signatures had been collected to enter him in the race. Mr. Ittleman had been serving as chairman of the Surpless campaign committee.

O'Dwyer's Mates in Clear

Mr. O'Dwyer was without opposition from the start for the Democratic and American Labor nominations, and there were no last minute surprises in this respect yesterday.

An appearance of opposition to Mr. O'Dwyer's running mates on the Democratic and Labor party tickets, Vincent R. Impellitteri for President of the Council and State Senator Lazarus Joseph for Controller, was created through the filing of the Queens Democratic designating petitions bearing the names of other candidates for these offices. But the Queens candidates have already signed declinations that will be filed before the Friday deadline and Mr. Im-

Continued on Page 8, Column 2

War News Summarized

WEDNESDAY, JUNE 27, 1945

The United Nations Conference in San Francisco ended its work at 8:39 last night, completing a historic nine weeks of deliberations designed to give nations security, peoples liberty and the world peace. Adjournment came at the close of President Truman's speech, which followed signing by the fifty nations present of the Charter of the United Nations. [1:6-7.]

"You have won a victory against war itself," Mr. Truman told the conferees, and have just created "a solid structure upon which we can build a better world." But this is only a first step, he emphasized, adding: "If we fail to use it we shall betray all those who have died in order that we might meet here in freedom and safety to create it."

No nation or group can expect special privileges and all must make sacrifices for the Charter to work, Mr. Truman said. He pointed out that powerful nations have "no right to dominate the world" but must "assume the responsibility for leadership toward a world of peace," resolved that "power and strength shall be used not to wage war, but to keep the world at peace and free from the fear of war."

Fascism did not die with Mussolini nor nazism with Hitler, the President declared, and the forces of tyranny are even now trying to undermine the Allied unity that made the Charter possible. [All the foregoing 1:8.]

President Truman will personally present the Charter to the Senate on Monday and urge prompt ratification. Opposition strength was estimated at twelve to fifteen votes [1:7.]

Allied forces in the Pacific stuck to their job of defeating Japan. B-29's hit the main enemy home island of Honshu again. The city of Yokkaichi, near Nagoya, was bombed during the night only a few hours after a massive attack upon ten key factories, the largest number of such targets hit on a single B-29 mission. [1:1; map, P. 2.]

Two American columns in Luzon's Cagayan Valley were less than twenty miles from closing a trap on the Japanese between Tuguegarao and the north. [2:6.] Capture of Miri by Australians completed the reconquest of west Borneo oilfields. Allied planes concentrated on Macassar Strait targets. [4:2, with map.] Chinese forces were within 165 miles of Shanghai. [2:8, with map.]

Tokyo, still fearing invasion, declared Allied landings were imminent on Amami and Kikai, between Okinawa and the home islands. Twelve Japanese planes were shot down in a futile attack on Okinawa. [1:2-3.]

In Europe it appeared that the American plan for mass trial of war criminals by an international military tribunal would be approved by the four-power conference. [6:4.] The Big Three may discuss Russia's proposal to ease restrictions on use of the Dardanelles. [7:5-6.] The London Poles will refuse to cede authority until a new Government is chosen at free elections. [6:1.]

All factions in India were reported to have accepted in principle the new British proposals for a revised central Government, including parity of caste Hindus and Moslems. [1:2.]

PRESIDENT WITNESSES SIGNING OF SECURITY PACT

Mr. Truman looking on as Secretary of State Stettinius affixes his name to the document

100,000 HOMES HERE FACE HIGHER RENTS

U. S. Court Order on Luxury Apartments Scored by Mayor —OPA Weighs Next Step

By LEE E. COOPER

One hundred thousand families in the New York area who pay $100 or more a month in rent are subject to higher charges under the decision handed down on Monday by the United States Emergency Court of Appeals, holding rent for the so-called luxury type of living quarters to be "inadequate" under present ceilings, a study of rental records showed last night. Nearly 50,000 of these higher-rent suites are in Manhattan, and about 8 per cent of the apartments there are affected by the order.

While officials of the Office of Price Administration were considering whether they should grant an increase without further ado or try a court appeal, it was reported in authoritative circles that if the former course of action were followed the OPA order probably would not call for much more than a 5 per cent rise in the higher-priced suites.

Rentals of $99 or less are not affected by the order, and even for the "luxury" apartments and hotel suites present rentals will apply until the OPA acts. The appeals court gave the rent officials thirty days, or until July 25, to comply with its decision.

Reactions to the Decision

Mixed reactions and some uncertainty followed announcement of the decision, which applies to all of New York City, Nassau and Suffolk Counties.

Mayor La Guardia, who had opposed the appeal by the Metropolitan Fair Rent Committee and other representatives of landlords for a blanket rise of 10 per cent on rent for housing here, expressed disappointment over the court's position.

"I don't like it," he commented. "From the facts submitted, I do not believe the finding is warranted. Here we broke our backs to reduce realty taxes, and immediately the rents are raised. The court is wrong!"

Spokesmen for several realty organizations expressed gratification, but contended that the decision did not go far enough and that increases were in order also for apartments renting for less than $100, on the ground that operating costs and other charges had risen for all types of buildings. OPA executives expressed the view that the ruling was a victory for rent control because present ceilings and the general purposes of control were upheld and the order for a rise affected "only a small per-

Continued on Page 36, Column 3

Nation After Nation Sees Era Of Peace in Signing Charter

By LAWRENCE E. DAVIES

Special to THE NEW YORK TIMES.

SAN FRANCISCO, June 26—A Charter drawn to give the world a new start on the way to lasting peace was signed today by the men and women from fifty nations who had fashioned it during nine weeks of laborious effort. They sat, one at a time, at a huge round table, autographing their handiwork while newsreel and newspaper camera men recorded the event for millions, now and later, to see and hear. Great spotlights, focused on the signers and their surroundings, made the scene in the Veterans Building look like a Hollywood movie set.

To China, first of the United Nations to suffer attack by a member of the Axis, went the honor of signing first. Dr. V. K. Wellington Koo, Chungking's Ambassador to the Court of St. James, using his country's writing brush, inscribed his name at noon in two freshly printed and freshly bound volumes, one containing the text of the Charter and the statute of the New International Court of Justice and the other authority for a preparatory commission to begin at once the enormous task of getting the new league functioning.

Signing Schedule Changed

The Big Powers began the day's work, with the United States, as the host nation, listed in the official advance order as the last signer. As things worked out, however, Russia, led by Ambassador Andrei A. Gromyko, followed China, with the United Kingdom third and Argentina slipping in ahead of France.

And the delegates of the United States, instead of waiting for the

Continued on Page 11, Column 6

TRUMAN WILL HAND CHARTER TO SENATE

President Will Speak Before Chamber Monday — Plans for Ratification Pushed

By C. P. TRUSSELL

Special to THE NEW YORK TIMES.

WASHINGTON, June 26—President Truman will personally present the Charter, signed today at the United Nations Conference, to the Senate on Monday in one of the rare appearances of a Chief Executive before a single chamber of Congress.

As he presents the pledge of international collaboration to secure the peace and block future aggressions, the President will make a statement to the Senate, whose function it will be to ratify its provisions.

These plans came to light at the Capitol today as the Senate and the House, while grappling with war and administrative appropriations, followed as closely as they could the concluding proceedings at San Francisco and looked to the first-hand reports which are to be made to the Senate by its own rep-

Continued on Page 10, Column 2

Storm Skirts City and Goes to Sea, Giving Relief From the Heat Wave

After two days of mild apprehension over a tropical storm that was swinging erratically northward along the Atlantic Coast, New York City unexpectedly enjoyed its most agreeable recent weather yesterday, as the storm veered out to sea. Only cooling winds and storm warnings for small craft marked its passing in this area.

Temperatures, as a result, touched a high of only 74 degrees in midafternoon, compared with 90 on Monday. The mean temperature was 72—one degree above the normal of 71 for the date—but the humidity was in the 80's most of the day.

Benjamin Parry, meteorologist in charge of the Weather Bureau here, announced in the forenoon that the storm would skirt the city. At that time it appeared likely, however, that New York would have stiff winds and rain most of the day.

Instead, the storm center plowed steadily northeastward at about twenty miles an hour, passing some seventy miles east of Nantucket last evening. The winds here did not reach their expected maximum velocity of thirty miles an hour until just before 6 P. M. The steady rain mentioned in earlier forecasts did not materialize.

Sunny, warm weather, with the highest temperature near 80 and with moderate northerly winds was the forecast for today. For tomorrow the Weather Bureau foresaw showers and warmer weather.

NEW WORLD HOPE

President Hails 'Great Instrument of Peace,' Insists It Be Used

HISTORIC LANDMARK

Meeting Gives Standing Ovation as Executive Pictures Peace Gain

President's address, Page 10; other texts, Pages 12, 13 and 14.

By JOHN H. CRIDER

Special to THE NEW YORK TIMES.

SAN FRANCISCO, June 26—The United Nations Conference ended at 5:28 this afternoon with a demand by President Truman to translate the lofty words of the new world Charter into worthy deeds ringing in the ears of the delegates from fifty nations.

The conference had presented to the world for the second time in three decades the outlines of machinery for the maintenance of world peace — better machinery, all of the speakers at the closing session agreed, than it had ever had before. But, as President Truman admonished in his address closing the conference, "the world must now use it."

"If we fail to use it," he declared to the solemn final meeting of the delegates, "we shall betray all those who have died in order that we might meet here in freedom and safety to create it.

"If we seek to use it selfishly—for the advantage of any one nation or any small group of nations—we shall be equally guilty of that betrayal."

Fervent Interpolation

The President, speaking in the auditorium of the War Memorial Opera House, built in memory of sons of the Golden Gate city who gave their lives in the first World War, in which he himself had served, seemed to give unconscious expression to the solemn feeling of the occasion when, at the outset of his speech, he interpolated the words, half a hope, half a prayer:

"Oh, what a great day this can be in history!"

Just before the plenary session the President accompanied the eight United States delegates to the auditorium of the Veterans' Memorial Building to witness their signing of the new world security Charter.

The signing had not been completed by the time of the closing session and, for the President to witness the United States signatures, the American delegates were permitted to sign out of turn, after Nicaragua, at about 3:15. The United States was the thirty-eighth nation to sign, leaving twelve to sign. Signing was completed at 7:20.

The plenary session began at 3:50 with three bangs of the gavel by Secretary Stettinius, presiding. The President, while waiting to make the closing speech, sat, tight-lipped, reading the English versions of speeches given in seven languages which preceded his in the two-hour final session.

The President's voice had been heard once before, when he opened the conference nine weeks ago with an address delivered by wire from Washington.

Points Stressed in Speech

Points he emphasized most strongly today were:

That this Charter is only a beginning—"our thinking and all our actions must be based on the realization that it is in fact only a first step."

That the Charter is no more perfect than was our own Constitution, it must be made to live.

That the fact there is a charter, in view of the diversity of interests, "is a great wonder" for which we should give "profound thanksgiving to Almighty God."

The differences which developed at this conference, he said, were resolved in the democratic way,

Continued on Page 11, Column 2

"All the News That's Fit to Print"

The New York Times.

LATE CITY EDITION
Fair, warm and less humid today and tomorrow.
Temperatures Yesterday—Max., 85; Min., 66
Sunrise today, 5:47 A. M.; Sunset, 8:17 P. M.

VOL. XCIV..No. 31,961. Entered as Second-Class Matter, Postoffice, New York, N. Y. NEW YORK, FRIDAY, JULY 27, 1945. THREE CENTS NEW YORK CITY

CHURCHILL IS DEFEATED IN LABOR LANDSLIDE; ATTLEE PROMISES PROSECUTION OF PACIFIC WAR; ALLIES ORDER JAPAN TO QUIT OR BE DESTROYED

SUSPENDED OPA MAN ACCUSES WOOLLEY OF INTERFERENCE

Ross Alleges Chief Hampered Enforcement in the Milk and Cigarette Drives

DEMANDS PUBLIC HEARING

Makes His Counter-Charges at Last Minute in 25,000-Word Reply in Dismissal Action

By CHARLES GRUTZNER Jr.

The twice-deferred showdown over maladministration of price control in this five-State area was made public yesterday when Paul L. Ross, suspended regional enforcement executive of the Office of Price Administration, filed his defense and counter-allegations to the charges lodged against him last month by Daniel P. Woolley, regional OPA head.

Mr. Ross' reply, loaded with accusations of interference by Mr. Woolley with his own enforcement division in the carrying out of national policies, and mentioning companies said to have benefited by Mr. Woolley's action, was brought to regional OPA headquarters in the Empire State Building by a messenger from the office of Paul O'Dwyer, counsel to the suspended official, at 4:59 P. M., sixteen minutes before the deadline for making answer.

The 25,000-word reply was accompanied by a demand for a public hearing of Mr. Woolley's charges and the counter-charges by Mr. Ross before an impartial board.

Woolley Has No Comment

Mr. Woolley had left the office before the messenger arrived with the bulky document, which was accepted for Mr. Woolley by Charles Staff, regional personnel officer. A spokesman for Mr. Woolley said later that the Regional Administrator had "no comment to make at this time on the contents of the answer." He said the document had been turned over to the regional legal and civil service staffs for study and that Mr. Woolley's ouster action against Mr. Ross would be carried out in compliance with civil service procedure, which permits but does not require a public hearing in such a case.

Besides accusing Mr. Woolley of hampering the effectiveness of price control by going counter to national enforcement policy—in some cases to serve his own political ambitions, according to Mr. Ross—the reply defended Mr. Ross' record of enforcement. It said that in May court proceedings were brought in this region in some 975 price cases, 30 per cent of the national total, and that OPA "was successful in 99.4 per cent of the cases." This region covers New York, New Jersey, Delaware, Maryland, Virginia and the District of Columbia. The only region with a higher percentage of success was the New England region, with a perfect score, but that was based on only 130 cases, 4 per cent of the national total, Mr. Ross pointed out.

Charges Early Interference

The cases cited by Mr. Ross in support of his contention that Mr. Woolley had hampered enforcement ranged from one involving the Continental Food Company in December, 1943, less than a month after Mr. Woolley joined the OPA, to a cigarette drive last winter that Mr. Ross said had been engineered by Mr. Woolley, to the detriment of more important food price control work, because Mr. Woolley believed the resultant publicity would strengthen his political chances.

There were allegations also of "unwarranted interference" by the regional administrator in cases involving the Dairymen's League and the price of milk; Fan & Bill's, a well-known restaurant in Washington, and Dinty Moore's restaurant in this city. The roll of alleged interference extends to April

Continued on Page 10, Column 1

Truman Pledges Free World As He Reviews U. S. Troops

Tells Them They Fought So 'We Can Live, Think and Act as We Like'—He Says He Will Follow Roosevelt Ideas

By DREW MIDDLETON
By Wireless to THE NEW YORK TIMES.

FRANKFORT ON THE MAIN, Germany, July 26—The United States Commander in Chief saw his countrymen in arms today and they, lean young men who had fought halfway across the Continent of Europe, looked back and liked what they saw.

On a day so hot and so bright that it was like those "dog" days of the great Missouri region from which he comes, President Truman, accompanied by Secretary of State James F. Byrnes and Gen. Dwight D. Eisenhower, drove fifty miles through rigid lines of soldiers, saw the United States Army now settled into its job of occupation and told them simply how much he would have liked to have been in uniform and how soldierly they looked.

"You fought so the United States and the nations of the world can live and act and do as they like," he said. I want to implement that in following the footsteps of my predecessor, Franklin Delano Roosevelt.

At the end of the tour the President stood on an airfield outside Frankfort on the Main and pinned Distinguished Service Medals on the tunics of four officers, three British and one Canadian.

They were Gen. H. D. G. Crerar, Commander in Chief of the Canadian First Army; Maj. Gen. Sir Frederick W. De Guingand, chief of staff of the Twenty-first Army Group; Air Marshal Sir Arthur Conningham, commander of the British Second Tactical Air Force, and Air Marshal Sir James M. Robb, former Deputy Chief of Staff for Air at Supreme Allied Headquarters.

It was the first time that an American President had decorated the soldiers of an allied nation on

Continued on Page 5, Column 2

Supporters Set the Stage For Implementing Charter

By JAMES B. RESTON
Special to THE NEW YORK TIMES.

WASHINGTON, July 26—The Administration has not only assured during the present Senate debate the almost unanimous ratification of the United Nations Security Charter, according to general agreement, but has also greatly improved its chances of implementing the Charter effectively.

When the debate started on Monday there was some doubt about the way in which the Administration would assure that effective force could be put at the disposal of the League and used by it without reference in each case to Congress.

In the last four days, however, the supporters of the Charter, its opponents admit, have succeeded in establishing these two important points:

Once the treaty is ratified by the Senate on Saturday or early next week, the President, as Commander in Chief of the armed forces and particularly as the officer charged with carrying out treaty obligations, will be authorized to use the American quota of troops to "maintain international peace and security" through the World Security Council.

Cannot Bind Senate

Instead of being bound to decide on the size and type of the league force by a treaty, as it seemed obligated to do at the beginning of the debate, the administration will be free to decide this question through the device of a joint resolution of both houses of Congress, which requires a majority of both houses of Congress.

There is, of course, no way in which the administration can bind a future Senate to agree to the record which has been established in the debate, but the record now emphasizes the following three things:

The treaty obligates this country

Continued on Page 9, Column 2

MEAT RISE OF 11% IS DUE IN AUGUST

Public Will Also Gain by Cuts in Point Values—Sugar for East Increased

Special to THE NEW YORK TIMES.

WASHINGTON, July 26—About 11 per cent more meat, a little more sugar for the East and fewer canned goods appeared today to be in prospect for civilians during August.

With more meat available to civilian consumers as a result of reductions in military demand, the Office of Price Administration lowered by one and two points a pound, and in one instance by three points, the ration values of nearly all cuts of beef, lamb and veal for the rationing period beginning Sunday, July 29.

As much as 80,000,000 more pounds of sugar will be directed into the East by September as a result of a reshuffling of sugar quotas throughout the country. This resulted from an amendment to War Food Order 131.1, which allocates sugar among various consumers and refiners for the period of April through September.

The ruling, while not increasing the total amount of sugar available to civilians, is understood to

Continued on Page 20, Column 5

Federal Jobs Up 126,130 in June; Byrd Asks Reduction of 300,000

Special to THE NEW YORK TIMES.

WASHINGTON, July 26—The number of Federal civilian employes increased by 126,130 in June, and of that total 110,049 were hired by the War Department outside the United States, Senator Byrd, chairman of the Joint Committee on Reduction of Non-Essential Federal Expenditures, said today. The number of Army employes within the United States was reduced by 3,378 in the same month.

Reporting that the civilian payroll of the Government in this country had passed the three-million mark without reference to the more than a half-million War Department employes abroad, Senator Byrd said that it was his firm conviction "that at least 300,000 Federal employes could be immediately eliminated without interference with the prosecution of the war."

After the war ended, he said, "we should return to a total Federal employment of certainly less than a million employes," adding that even this figure was in excess of the Federal employment of normal times.

The increase during June, Senator Byrd stated, meant that 100 civilian employes were added to

Continued on Page 11, Column 3

TERMS LAID DOWN

U. S., Britain and China Plan Disarmament and Occupation

DOOM THE WAR LORDS

Offer Japanese People Opportunity to Gain Democratic Rule

Text of Allies' ultimatum to Japan to end war, Page 4.

By RAYMOND DANIELL
By Wireless to THE NEW YORK TIMES.

BERLIN, July 26—Against the background of the Three-Power conference in the heart of shattered Germany, President Truman and retiring Prime Minister Churchill, with the concurrence of Generalissimo Chiang Kai-shek, called on the Japanese Government and people tonight to surrender unconditionally or face "prompt and utter destruction" at the hands of the Allied land, sea and air forces "poised to strike the final blows."

The joint declaration, it was said, was drawn by Messrs. Churchill and Truman after their arrival here. Its text was transmitted to Generalissimo Chiang and released here as soon as his concurrence had been received in a personal message to Mr. Truman. At 9:30 P. M., after the President's return from Frankfort, the text of the proclamation was issued here and orders were cabled to the Office of War Information in Washington to get the message to the Japanese people by every means possible.

The joint proclamation was in the nature of an ultimatum. While it reiterated the demands for unconditional surrender, it repeated the Cairo declaration that Japan's sovereignty would be limited to her home islands, stripped of the power to wage war. It promised that the Japanese people would be neither "enslaved as a race nor destroyed as a nation."

The Japanese militarists will have to go to make way for a

Continued on Page 4, Column 3

WINNER AND LOSER IN BRITISH ELECTIONS

Clement R. Attlee Associated Press

Winston Churchill © British Combine

3 JAPANESE CITIES FIRED BY 350 B-29'S

Omuta, Chemical Center, Is Hit in 2,200-Ton Triple Blow —Shanghai Ripped Again

By W. H. LAWRENCE
By Wireless to THE NEW YORK TIMES.

GUAM, Friday, July 27—More than 2,200 tons of petroleum jelly incendiary bombs were dumped early today by a Marianas-based force of more than 350 Superfortresses on the Japanese cities of Omuta, Matsuyama and Tokuyama.

The three urban targets had a combined population of 377,000, most of engaged in war production.

[Meanwhile Gen. George C. Kenney's Far East Air Forces, returning to Shanghai in strength, blasted five major airdromes and

Continued on Page 6, Column 2

War News Summarized

FRIDAY, JULY 27, 1945

Great Britain swung to the left so completely in the recent elections that the Labor party and the Conservative party almost exactly changed their positions. Labor won 390 out of 640 seats in the Commons, compared with 163 in the outgoing Parliament, while Prime Minister Churchill's party, which had had 358, won only 195. Labor received nearly half of the popular vote. Mr. Churchill and his Foreign Secretary, Anthony Eden, were about the only survivors among Conservative Cabinet members. The Liberal and Communist parties also fared badly.

"I regret that I have not been permitted to finish the work against Japan," Mr. Churchill said after relinquishing the post he had held since May, 1940. "For this, however, all plans and preparations have been made and the results may come quicker than we have hitherto been entitled to expect." [All the foregoing 1:8.]

"We have first of all to finish the war with Japan," Clement Richard Attlee, who was advanced by the election from Deputy Prime Minister to Prime Minister, told a Labor meeting. "We want the fullest cooperation of all nations," he added. "We want a security that will banish war forever. We want a widespread prosperity among all the peoples and nations of the world." [1:6-7.]

The Big-Three conference was in recess and President Truman visited American troops along the Rhine. He told them he wanted to follow in President Roosevelt's footsteps. [1:2-3.]

Japan was ordered to surrender unconditionally quickly or face "utter devastation." Mr. Truman, Mr. Churchill and Generalissimo Chiang Kai-shek gave their answer to the enemy's pleas for softer terms in a proclamation that reaffirmed the principles of the Cairo Declaration: the end of militarism, punishment of war criminals, establishment of democracy and limitation of Japanese territory to the home islands. [1:4.]

General Devers said United States troops were being trained in "radical" new methods of warfare for a single gigantic blow against Japan. [1:6-7.]

Planes continued to carry the war to Japan and her occupied territory. B-29's set three industrial cities on Honshu, Shikoku and Kyushu afire; Iwo-based Privateers hit shipping in the Gulf of Sagami south of Tokyo; Okinawa-based planes struck Korean waters and airfields on Honshu, and 300 bombers smashed five airfields at Shanghai. [1:5; map F. 6.]

British and American carrier planes of the Third Fleet beat off the first enemy air attack since the warships went into action off Japan on July 10. Four out of ten enemy aircraft were shot down. [5:6.]

Chinese troops recaptured the seventh of eleven former American air bases lost to the Japanese when they seized Namyung, 150 miles northeast of Canton. Inconclusive fighting was raging on other fronts. [5:1, with map.]

A member of the de Gaulle Government sustained the legality of the Vichy regime in testifying against Marshal Pétain on trial for treason in Paris. The defendant was again accused of betraying France. [8:3-4.]

Attlee in First Talk Backs Harmony With U.S., Russia

By SYDNEY GRUSON
By Cable to THE NEW YORK TIMES.

LONDON, July 26—Maj. Clement R. Attlee, in his first speech as Britain's Prime Minister, pledged anew tonight this nation's determination "to finish the war with Japan" and expressed the belief that the result of the British election would give heart throughout the world to those "who believe in freedom, democracy and social justice."

Coming directly from Buckingham Palace after accepting King George VI's commission to form a new Government, Mr. Attlee addressed a wildly enthusiastic Labor party victory rally in Westminster Central Hall, not more than 100 yards from the House of Commons his party now dominates.

Seeming just the slightest bit dazed by the tumultuous day, Mr. Attlee outlined his new Government's job in a few sentences.

"We have, first of all, to finish the war against Japan," he declared. "We shall see to it that our men in the East get all the support they need.

"We want the fullest cooperation with all nations.

"We want a security that will banish war forever.

"We want a widespread prosperity among all the peoples and nations of the world.

The Tasks at Home

"Here at home we have our own great tasks. We have to bind up the wounds of war. We have to reconstruct our ruined homes—a great task in itself. We have to bring back in due course the workers who have been working on the war to be workers for peace. We have a job to build up in this country the highest standard of life that we can achieve for all."

Flanked by his chief lieutenants, Herbert Morrison and Ernest Bevin, and with the wives of all three beaming beside them, Mr. Attlee called on the crowd of 2,000

Continued on Page 3, Column 6

BRITISH BUSINESS IN GENERAL IS CALM

Coal, Power Industries Shaken by Nationalization Prospect, Rest Expect Little Change

By CHARLES E. EGAN
By Wireless to THE NEW YORK TIMES.

LONDON, July 26—Britain's business circles reacted calmly to Labor's election sweep today. Coal and power interests were shaken because the victorious party is deeply committed to nationalization in both those fields, but other industries, including cotton, iron and steel and manufacturing generally saw little immediate change in prospect.

"Leaders of the Labor party are all men with Cabinet experience accustomed to the responsibilities of government," a leading industrialist said today. "There is little danger of ill-considered radical policies sweeping the country.

"Members of my organization feel it is improbable that the party will vote to take over any of the enterprises mentioned except fuel and power. They are so deeply committed on the coal and electric power industries that it is impossible to see how they can avoid nationalizing them."

The Financial Times in its leading editorial tomorrow will say that both business and financial

Continued on Page 2, Column 4

7,000,000 Troops for Single Blow At Japan Planned, Says Devers

By SIDNEY SHALETT
Special to THE NEW YORK TIMES.

WASHINGTON, July 26—The United States Army will train and deploy its European veterans and its new troops so that, in conjunction with divisions already in the Pacific, it can hurl 7,000,000 men in a coordinated "single blow" against Japan, instead of attempting to do the job "piecemeal," Gen. Jacob L. Devers, new Commanding General of Army Ground Forces, declared today.

At his first news conference since he succeeded Gen. Joseph W. Stilwell, now in the Pacific, as head of the Ground Forces, General Devers, who commanded the Sixth Army Group in southern France, hinted at the plans for a massive blow against the enemy's homeland, and also asserted that our forces being prepared for the Pacific would be trained in "radical" new methods of warfare.

General Devers explained that he should not be taken "too literally" in his description of a 7,000,000-man blow against Japan. Obviously, he pointed out, an Army does not land that many men overnight on an enemy beachhead.

But the Army Ground Forces does intend, he asserted, to have the 7,000,000 men who will constitute

Continued on Page 7, Column 2

BRITISH TURN LEFT

War Regime Swept Out as Laborites Win 390 of 640 Seats

CHURCHILL BIDS ADIEU

Hints at Early Peace—He Stays in House, but Many Ex-Aides Lose

By HERBERT L. MATTHEWS
By Cable to THE NEW YORK TIMES.

LONDON, July 26—In one of the most stunning election surprises in the history of democracy, Great Britain swung to the Left today in a landslide that smothered the Conservatives and put Labor into power with a great majority.

Winston Churchill has resigned as Prime Minister and Clement R. Attlee has accepted the King's invitation to form a Laborite Government. The Liberals went down to an equally surprising defeat. The world, which looked to Britain for a guiding trend, has had its tremendous answer. Today and tomorrow and for months or years to come, the Left is the dominating power in global politics.

When the final result came in from the constituency of Hornchurch at 10:30 P. M., Labor had a staggering total of 390 seats out of a Parliament of 640, of which the holders of thirteen seats will not be known until early in August. In the last Parliament, Labor had only 163 and in its greatest previous triumph, in 1929, it had 288.

Conservatives Cut to 195 Seats

The Conservatives had fallen from 358 seats to 195. The Liberals, too, lost seven seats and now have only eleven members in Parliament.

Adding fourteen Liberal Nationals and one National, the former Government is down to 210 seats, whereas if the Liberals, Independent Labor with three seats, the Commonwealth with one, the Communists with two and the Independents with ten are added to Labor, one gets a total of 417.

Such a tremendous majority means that the Labor party can confidently count on a full five-year tenure of office, for it cannot be beaten on any vote of confidence. Out of nearly 25,000,000 votes, Labor alone won nearly 12,000,000. The Conservatives got a little more than 9,000,000 votes. The Labor party did not lose a single seat to the Conservatives, although it gained 130 from that party.

[The vote, according to the press services, was: Labor, 11,962,678; Conservative, 9,018,235; Liberal, 2,280,135; Independent, 545,862.]

The results were a personal, decisive repudiation of Mr. Churchill as a peacetime leader. He himself

Continued on Page 3, Column 2

Churchill Reported Ending Berlin Role

By Cable to THE NEW YORK TIMES.

LONDON, July 26—The News Chronicle will say tomorrow that Winston Churchill will not return to the Berlin conference, although the first thing Prime Minister Attlee did was to ask him to do so.

Anthony Eden, former Foreign Secretary, who has been re-elected to the Parliament, said today: "I am anxious still to do my best to help our nation hold its head high in the world as it has the right and pride to do."

Asked whether he would return to Berlin, Mr. Eden said that his services were at the country's disposal and, if he were asked to return tomorrow, as had been previously arranged, he would continue to do his best to help.

LONDON, July 26 (UP)—When Prime Minister Attlee was asked whether Mr. Churchill would return to Berlin with him, he smiled and remained silent.

"All the News That's Fit to Print"

The New York Times.

LATE CITY EDITION
Fair and less humid today. Partly cloudy and warm tomorrow.
Temperatures Yesterday—Max., 80; Min., 66
Sunrise today, 5:53 A. M.; Sunset, 8:10 P. M.

Copyright, 1945, by The New York Times Company.

VOL. XCIV..No. 31,968. Entered as Second-Class Matter, Postoffice, New York, N. Y. NEW YORK, FRIDAY, AUGUST 3, 1945. THREE CENTS IN NEW YORK CITY

GERMANY STRIPPED OF INDUSTRY BY BIG 3; 5 POWERS TO PLAN PEACE; FRANCO BARRED; BOMBERS FIRE GREAT NAGASAKI SHIPYARDS

ENEMY PORT RUINED

14 Vessels Are Smashed and 6 Planes Downed by 250 Okinawa Planes

DAY'S BAG 26 SHIPS

Kenney Fliers Wreck 12 In Coast Sweep—Toll of Carrier Blow Soars

By FRANK L. KLUCKHOHN
By Wireless to THE NEW YORK TIMES.

MANILA, Friday, Aug. 3—Nagasaki, one of the three major shipbuilding centers of Japan and ninth port of the empire, was left aflame yesterday, its dockyards smashed and its harbor littered with sunken ships by over 250 planes of Gen. George C. Kenney's Far East Air Force.

Mitchells, Liberators, Mustangs and Thunderbolts, concentrating upon this western Kyushu port, hit the Mitsubishi, Tategami and Koyagishima shipyards, plus the largest marine engine works in Japan. They left flames that were visible for twenty-five miles.

tanker and nine freighters were sunk and a submarine and three other ships were damaged.

[At least twelve other ships of varying size were sunk or damaged in widespread attacks on enemy-controlled waters from Korea southward to Borneo and the Celebes, Gen. Douglas MacArthur's communiqué said today, according to The Associated Press.]

[About one hundred American P-51 Mustang fighter planes, led by a "small number" of B-29's attacked "military targets at scattered points" in the Kanto district of central Honshu, which includes the metropolitan district of Tokyo, for one and a half hours Friday morning (Japanese time), the Japanese Domei agency reported, as recorded by the Federal Communications Commission.

[Fleet Admiral Chester W. Nimitz reported additional damage in Monday's carrier plane attacks on Japan, raising the total of enemy vessels sunk or damaged to 116, of which forty-five were warships, and of planes destroyed to 124.]

Attack at Low Level

Twenty Japanese fighters rising from the inferno . burning and exploding ships and large oil tanks at Nagasaki, were dived on by the Mustangs. Six of them were shot down, each of our fighters getting at least one Japanese plane, the rest fleeing.

Thunderbolts, flying at masthead height and carrying 1,000-pound bombs, initiated the attack that lasted for hours by sinking the tanker with seven direct hits. More Thunderbolts, arriving twenty-five minutes later, found only debris to hit among oil storage tanks and warehouses.

Penetrating the blinding weather the speedy Mustangs thereupon dive-bombed with 500-pounders, leaving a 5,000-ton freighter burning and rocked by internal explosions.

Taking the ball, a group of Mitchells hit other shipping. Heavies — Liberators — came in next, turning a 6,000-ton freighter on its side with sticks of bombs.

Before the Japanese could recover a second group of Liberators roared in, hitting a transport in the drydock and blasting storage areas.

A lone American reconnaissance plane reported that after this wave the Japanese began to creep from their shelters to fight the raging fires and attempt to rescue personnel from the flaming ships.

At that moment more Thunderbolts and Mitchells came in flat off the water, hitting oil stores, and warehouses and throwing débris, according to eye-witnesses, half a mile over the water. The

Continued on Page 2, Column 3

Army, Navy Deaths Rise to 249,264

By The Associated Press.

WASHINGTON, Aug. 2—Almost a quarter million American soldiers and sailors have died in the war—a total 249,264.

Army figures announced today by Secretary Stimson show 197,676 dead. The latest Navy count of its killed is 51,588. A week ago the dead were 196,918 for the Army and 51,219 for the Navy.

Total casualties from all causes for both services are 1,060,727, or 1,885 more than the 1,058,842 announced a week earlier.

Army wounded are 570,766, missing 34,754 and prisoners of war 117,741. Navy wounded are 72,855, missing 11,611 and prisoners 3,756.

STIMSON REFUSES SPEEDIER RELEASES

Rate to Stand for Present With Point Revisions Later, He Says —War Needs Put 'First'

Special to THE NEW YORK TIMES.

WASHINGTON, Aug. 2—Secretary Stimson declared today that the Army discharge system of eighty-five points would be revised, but not until next year, and that for the present the War Department would not increase its present rate of discharges.

Replying apparently to pressure from members of Congress and other sources for speed-ups in the release of soldiers, Mr. Stimson said:

"We shall not let any man go whose going jeopardizes the life of the men who remain to fight. The operations of the point system must be subordinate to the fighting needs of General MacArthur.

He further declared that many men with more than the required eighty-five points would not be released until replacements with similar skills had been obtained.

Since May 12, when demobilization for "high-point" men began, 235,000 have been released, the Secretary said. At present 565,000 others with eighty-five points or more were eligible for release. He reiterated the Army's pledge that 1,500,000 men would be released under the point system by June 1, 1946.

MacArthur's Needs Emphasized

In referring to General MacArthur's needs, Secretary Stimson inferentially criticized Harold L. Ickes, Secretary of the Interior, who declared recently that unless the Army released men for the coal mines civilians would be short of fuel this winter.

Stating that "our first duty is to give General MacArthur the men he needs to win the war with the least loss of men and time," Mr. Stimson interjected:

"And that's a point you want to remember when somebody says you're going to be in need of coal next winter—or some other special reasons.'

The Secretary declined, however, to reply to the attack by Sen-

Continued on Page 18, Column 2

ECONOMY MAPPED

Drain on German State Called Relatively Mild —War Curbs Severe

SOVIET NEEDS FACED

Big Powers to Supervise Small Nations' Share in the Indemnity

By JOHN H. CRIDER
Special to THE NEW YORK TIMES.

WASHINGTON, Aug. 2—The Big Three agreement on reparations was believed by officials here to reflect the view of American experts that German reparations should be of a nature and amount to provide neither the excuse for rebuilding the German industrial war potential nor a need for Allied assistance in providing for the reindustrialization that would be necessary if she were to make high cash reparation payments.

The principles laid down in the reparations section of the Potsdam agreement appeared to be mild in comparison with the exactions made of Germany after the last war, but in terms of transfer from Germany of the industrial basis for her great war-making power and the stripping of her economy down to a level merely sufficient to sustain her "peaceful needs" it was regarded as much more severe.

The reparations accord of the Big Three not only sanctioned the removal of vast amounts of Germany's industrial potential across her borders but also employed language that approves such removals as Russia has already made and will make in the immediate future.

General Principles Stated

Except for exposition of the basic "deal" between Russia, on one hand, and the United States and Britain, on the other, the Big Three confined themselves to a statement of reparation principles that will be spelled out in detail by the Allied Commission on Reparations and the Allied Control Council.

Regarded as of extreme importance was the inclusion of France as a party to the basic determination, deferred by the Big Three, which will be to decide the precise level of economic activity that should be permitted in post-war Germany and how much capital equipment she will need to sustain herself on that basis.

The Potsdam agreement continued, however, the principle that reparations shall be handled in the first instance by the great powers, with the smaller Allied nations presumably applying through them for their share of reparations and indemnity.

Specific provision is made that the Soviet Union undertakes to settle the reparation claims of Poland from its own share of reparations.

Reference to the basic determination in relation to the whole

Continued on Page 9, Column 4

THE EUROPEAN COUNTRIES AFFECTED BY BIG THREE DECISIONS

Aug. 3, 1945

The conference agreed on the principles of a coordinated policy for Germany (1) involving complete demilitarization, territorial losses and severe economic control. For Austria (2), extension of the authority of the Russian-sponsored provisional government to the whole country will be considered. Arrangement of peace treaties first with Italy (3) and then with Bulgaria (4), Rumania (5), Hungary (6) and Finland (10) was made the business of a five-power Council of Foreign Ministers, which is to meet regularly in London (11). Revision of procedure of the Allied Control Commission on reportorial freedom in southeastern Europe was furthered. The "orderly, humane" transfer of Germans from Hungary, Czechoslovakia (7) and Poland (8) was backed. Russian proposals for Poland's western boundary and Soviet acquisition of the Koenigsberg area (9, with detailed map on Page 8) were supported. The Big Three banned application for United Nations membership by the Franco Government of Spain (12).

CONFERENCE SCENE REVEALS DILEMMAS

Problem of Keeping Equality of Delegations Complicated by Layout of Palace

By TANIA LONG
By Wireless to THE NEW YORK TIMES.

BERLIN, Aug. 2—A little of the drama of the Big Three conference just ended and much of the flavor and atmosphere in which the historic meeting took place were revealed today when correspondents were allowed into the hitherto closed areas where the delegations

Continued on Page 10, Column 2

Communique Highlights

By The United Press.

WASHINGTON, Aug. 2—Highlights of the Big Three communique from Potsdam:

No mention was made of the Pacific war, nor of Russia's connection with it. But the communiqué said that the Chiefs of Staff held meetings on "military matters of common interest."

Agreement was reached on reparations from Germany. Each of the three nations will fill its own claims, largely by taking goods and equipment from its own occupation zone. In addition, Russia will get 10 per cent of removable industrial capital equipment from the western zones as a flat payment, and an additional 15 per cent for which she will pay in goods. The Western Allies retain sole claim to captured gold.

Russia will get Koenigsberg and adjacent territory in East Prussia. Poland will get a slice of Germany, including the rest of East Prussia, and the former free city of Danzig.

Germans in Poland, Czechoslovakia and Hungary shall be transferred to Germany "in an orderly and humane manner." Agreement was reached on a detailed program for the control of Germany, to strip the Reich of war-making capacity, smash huge cartels, drive out nazism and "convince the German people that they have suffered a total military defeat."

Under disarmament, all German land, naval and air forces, and all Nazi militaristic organizations will be "completely and finally abolished."

War criminal trials will begin soon. The first list of defendants will be published before Sept. 1. A Council of Foreign Ministers of the Big Five, includ-

Continued on Page 9, Column 2

War News Summarized

FRIDAY, AUGUST 3, 1945

Detailed plans for the extermination of nazism and militarism in Germany were drawn up at the Berlin Conference in terms sufficiently clear "to convince the German people that they have suffered a total military defeat and that they cannot escape responsibility for what they have brought upon themselves." Just what was accomplished by the Big Three was made public in Washington, London and Moscow yesterday.

Germany will be decentralized politically and economically at the earliest possible date.

A Council of Foreign Ministers, including those of China and France, was created to prepare tentstive peace treaties for all European Axis countries other then Germany. The first task will be a treaty with Italy.

Boundaries were generally left for the peace conference, except that Russia's request for the Baltic port of Koenigsberg was recognized and Poland's claims to a frontier along the Oder and the Neisse were tentatively approved. Full freedom in Poland and in the Balkans was promised to Allied correspondents.

So long as Spain is ruled by Franco she will not be invited to join the United Nations.

Japan was referred to only obliquely—through the inclusion of China in the Council of Foreign Secretaries; as one of the reasons for expediting peace with Italy, which has gone to war with Japan; and through the statement that "military matters of common interest" had been discussed by the American, British and Russian Chiefs of Staff. [All the foregoing 1:8; maps Pages 1 and 8.]

A large measure of agreement was reached on problems of German reparations. [1:3.]

President Truman is on his way home after having had luncheon with King George VI. He will report to the American people upon his return. [1:7.]

Pierre Laval, who wept during interrogation in Fresnes Prison, will testify at the Pétain trial today. [1:6-7.]

In the Pacific, 250 Far East Air Force planes left the port and railway terminal of Nagasaki, on Kyushu, in flames. Ten ships were sunk; three others and a submarine were damaged. One B-29 out of the 820 that dropped the record load of 6,632 tons on Honshu targets was lost. Waters between Korea and Japan were heavily mined. [1:1; map P. 2.]

Additional reports raised the havoc wrought by Third Fleet carrier planes on the Tokyo, Nagoya and Maizuru areas last Monday. Tokyo said O Island, at the mouth of Tokyo Bay, had been shelled. [2:1.]

Japanese troops pushed their floating pocket in China closer to Nanchang. Ifeng was recaptured by the Chinese and a bitter battle was reported on the outskirts of Kian. [2:8.]

PRESIDENT SAILS AFTER SEEING KING

Monarch and Truman Confer at Luncheon and Exchange Visits at Plymouth

By CHARLES E. EGAN
By Wireless to THE NEW YORK TIMES.

PLYMOUTH, England, Aug. 2—President Truman was en route home tonight aboard the cruiser Augusta after a six-hour stop-over in Britain during which he had luncheon with King George and discussed with him the results of the Big Three conference.

The informal visit took the President considerably out of his way, but it was made at his insistence as a tribute to the fighting spirit of the British people. Mr. Truman expressed regret to the King that his stay could not be longer, but explained that it was imperative that he get home and report on the conference to the American people.

Today's trip gave the President his first glimpse of Britain. As an officer in World War I, he went directly to France and returned to the United States directly from there. It also was the first time in twenty-six years that a President of the United States had visited Britain. President Wilson paid a state visit at the time of the peace conference after the last war. The

Continued on Page 10, Column 6

Laval Summoned to Testify Today; Petain's Counsel Protests Strongly

By G. H. ARCHAMBAULT
By Wireless to THE NEW YORK TIMES.

PARIS, Aug. 2—Pierre Laval must testify tomorrow in Marshal Henri-Philippe Pétain's treason trial, Judge Pierre Mongibeaux ruled today.

The decision was taken on the initiative of the jurors, who conferred for more than one hour with the three judges. As soon as the decision had been announced, Fernand Payen, the leading defense counsel, raised a point of law. He argued that, under the rules of evidence, there should be a preliminary hearing before an examining magistrate, after which Laval's testimony would be communicated to both the prosecution and the defense. He added that Laval might introduce the names of many political leaders and army commanders who would insist on being heard and thus bring the trial back to the controversial phase that the court declared yesterday to be positively ended. The court overruled the objection.

Léon Noel, Ambassador in Warsaw when the war broke out and later one of the French armistice delegates, was called by the de-

Continued on Page 6, Column 4

Vandenberg Proposes Government Call Industry-Labor Peace Parley

By LOUIS STARK
Special to THE NEW YORK TIMES.

WASHINGTON, Aug. 2—Senator Vandenberg, Republican, of Michigan, in a letter suggested today that Secretary of Labor Schwellenbach sponsor a labor-industry-Government conference so that all groups interested in industrial peace "frankly face the need for a better, a surer and wiser code for their mutual advancement in the desperately uncertain times that lie ahead in an otherwise chaotic post-war world."

Mr. Schwellenbach immediately endorsed the idea, which had originated from Mr. Vandenberg's observations at the United Nations Conference in San Francisco. The Secretary plunged at once into a series of meetings which will serve as the ground work for a plan to be submitted to President Truman on the latter's return from Europe.

In his reply to the Vandenberg letter, Mr. Schwellenbach said that he had "been thinking more and more during these last few weeks about the desirability of calling a conference of industry and labor," and he pointed to his views on the subject as set forth in an address at Superior, Wis., on July 21.

Spokesmen for labor and indus-

Continued on page 15, Column 2

NO WORD ON JAPAN

Russia Gets Majority of Reparations, Sharing in Western Zones

FRONTIERS PUT OFF

Poland Interim Ruler of Part of Reich—United Nations Bar Spain

The text of the communiqué by the Big Three is on Page 8.

By FELIX BELAIR JR.
Special to THE NEW YORK TIMES.

WASHINGTON, Aug. 2 — The broad outlines of a post-war Germany reduced to a third-rate industrial power with all its economy operating at subsistence levels, incapable of waging war and stripped of East Prussia and a large area along the Oder River were laid down in a joint communiqué today by the Big Three, reporting on the meeting in Berlin.

Bearing the signatures of J. V. Stalin, Harry S. Truman and C. R. Attlee, the document, released simultaneously at 5:30 P. M. in Washington, London and Moscow, ended any further debate whether Germany was to have a "hard" or "soft" peace. That peace, in the language of the communiqué, will be designed "to convince the German people that they have suffered a total military defeat and that they cannot escape responsibility for what they have brought upon themselves since their own ruthless warfare and the fanatical Nazi resistance have destroyed German economy and made chaos and suffering inevitable."

The document did not mention Russia's intentions on the Pacific war but it ended on the significant note that "during the conference there were meetings between the Chifs of Staff of the three Governments on military matters of common interest." If these "matters" went beyond European zones of occupation, the communiqué did not explain.

The conference warned the present Government of Spain that it need not apply for admission to the United Nations' organization. That Government, according to the communiqué, "having been founded with the support of the Axis powers, does not, in view of its orogin, its nature, its record and its close association with the aggressor states, possess the qualifications necessary to justify such

Continued on Page 8, Column 2

Big Three Prescribe Freedom of Press

By The United Press.

WASHINGTON, Aug. 2—The Big Three conference communiqué had this to say about freedom of the press in Europe:

In Poland—"The three powers note that the Polish Provisional Government * * * has agreed to the holding of free and unfettered elections * * * and that representatives of the Allied press shall enjoy full freedom to report to the world upon developments in Poland before and during the elections."

In other former Axis countries—"The three Governments have no doubt that, in view of the changed conditions resulting from the termination of the war in Europe, representatives of the Allied press will enjoy full freedom to report to the world upon developments in Rumania, Bulgaria, Hungary and Finland."

Yugoslavia was not mentioned.

In Germany—"Subject to the necessity for maintaining military security, freedom of * * * [the] press * * * shall be permitted."

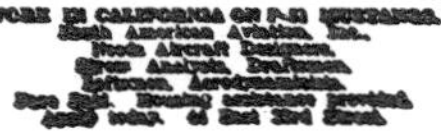

"All the News That's Fit to Print"

The New York Times.

LATE CITY EDITION
Partly cloudy, less humid today.
Cloudy and warm tomorrow.
Temperatures Yesterday—Max., 72; Min., 66
Sunrise today, 5:37 A. M.; Sunset, 8:06 P. M.

VOL. XCIV..No. 31,972. Entered as Second-Class Matter, Postoffice, New York, N. Y. NEW YORK, TUESDAY, AUGUST 7, 1945. THREE CENTS IN NEW YORK CITY

FIRST ATOMIC BOMB DROPPED ON JAPAN; MISSILE IS EQUAL TO 20,000 TONS OF TNT; TRUMAN WARNS FOE OF A 'RAIN OF RUIN'

HIRAM W. JOHNSON, REPUBLICAN DEAN IN THE SENATE, DIES

Isolationist Helped Prevent U. S. Entry Into League—Opposed World Charter

CALIFORNIA EX-GOVERNOR

Ran for Vice President With Theodore Roosevelt in '12—In Washington Since '17

Special to THE NEW YORK TIMES.

WASHINGTON, Aug. 6—Senator Hiram Warren Johnson of California lifelong isolationist who helped prevent this country's entry into the League of Nations and fought all "foreign entanglements" through a second World War, died in his sleep this morning at Bethesda Naval Hospital, nine days after, ill but consistent, he had paired his vote against ratification of the United Nations Charter. Death was caused by a thrombosis of a cerebral artery. Mrs. Johnson was with him when the end came.

When word reached the Capitol of the passing of the oldest member of the Senate in point of service, save Senator Kenneth McKellar, the President pro tempore, the mourning was deep. With great personal affection colleagues paid humble tribute to his integrity of character, his liberalism and his steadfastness to his ideals and convictions. They joined in declaring that the country had lost a great statesman.

Senator Johnson, who was serving the fourth year of his fifth term in the Senate, would have been 79 years old on Sept. 2. Although his health had been failing during the last two years and though the thundering voice which had conveyed his eloquence through innumerable stirring debates had become little more than a whisper, friends believed he planned to seek a sixth term in 1947.

He went to the hospital July 18. Five days before that he had cast the lone vote in the Foreign Relations Committee, of which he was the ranking minority member, against reporting the new World Charter to the Senate without change. He did not participate in the floor debate on this document, which won Senate approval by a vote of 82—2. However, he clashed spiritedly with colleagues while the hearings were in progress.

Funeral arrangements awaited the arrival of the Senator's son, Lieut. Col. Hiram W. Johnson Jr., who was flying here from California.

Capper Becomes the Dean

The death of Senator Johnson made Senator Arthur Capper of Kansas, who last month marked his eightieth birthday, the Republican dean of the Senate. It also elevated him to the ranking minority membership on the Foreign Relations Committee, with which Senator Johnson had been so conspicuously identified through the many years of his unshaken position on foreign policy. Mr. Capper, too, with Senators McKellar, Carter Glass of Virginia, David I. Walsh of Massachusetts and Peter G. Gerry, was in the League fight of 1919 and 1920. He supported it, with reservations.

The career of Senator Johnson, from his entrance into the Senate from the Governorship of California in March of 1917, was one distinctly lacking in compromise or reservation. In 1912 he had bolted his party with Theodore Roosevelt and had become his running mate on the Bull Moose ticket. In 1932 he again bolted to support Franklin D. Roosevelt for the Presidency but broke bitterly with the President when he ran for his third term.

In 1919 Mr. Johnson joined with Senators Lodge, Borah, Reed,

Continued on Page 23, Column 4

Jet Plane Explosion Kills Major Bong, Top U. S. Ace

Flier Who Downed 40 Japanese Craft, Sent Home to Be 'Safe,' Was Flying New 'Shooting Star' as a Test Pilot

By The United Press.

BURBANK, Calif., Aug. 6—Maj. Richard Bong, America's greatest air ace, died today in the flaming wreckage of a jet propelled fighter plane which crashed while he was testing it.

Only 24 years old, he wore twenty-six decorations including the nation's highest award, the Congressional Medal of Honor. He had survived countless air battles and shot down forty Japanese planes without a scratch.

The knowledge he gained in those battles was too valuable to risk, so he was brought home to "safe" duty. He was on that "safe" duty today when his P-80, the Shooting Star, hurtled over a clump of trees and burst like a bomb in a field.

Witnesses did not agree on the cause of the crash. One Army flier said that Major Bong overshot the Lockheed airport. Another witness, John McKinney of North Hollywood reported that he saw something fall out of the plane's tail.

"The plane started to wobble up and down, then went into a left bank and hit the ground," he stated. "It exploded and burned and scattered wreckage over about a block square."

Major Bong was trying to get out of the ship when it crashed. He had released the escape hatch and was partly clear. He had pulled the ripcord to his parachute, and the silken folds lay about the body as the flames swept over it.

With a roaring sigh, the plane, like a giant blowtorch, shot over the airport just before 3 P. M. and then lurched over the trees and nosed down into the field, a mile away.

Smoke and flame surged up and crowds rushed from the airport. By the time anyone could reach the scene the ship had been almost consumed.

The crash scene was near the intersection of Cahuenga and Oxnard Boulevards and barely out-

Continued on page 15, Column 2

MORRIS IS ACCUSED OF 'TAKING A WALK'

Fusion Official 'Sad to Part Company'—McGoldrick Sees Only Tammany Aided

The No Deal ticket, headed by Council President Newbold Morris, "can only serve the interests of Tammany Hall," Controller Joseph D. McGoldrick, candidate for reelection on the Republican-Liberal-Fusion party slate, declared yesterday in a fresh attack on the third-party ticket injected over the week-end into the city Mayoralty campaign.

A short while later Gabriel A. Wechsler, general secretary of the City Fusion party, which supported Mayor La Guardia and Mr. Morris in previous city campaigns, accused Mr. Morris of "taking a walk away from the good government forces."

To both charges Mr. Morris declared he would stand on his statement of Sunday that he was not interested in "just taking votes" away from Judge Jonah J. Goldstein, Republican-Liberal-Fusion candidate for Mayor, or from William O'Dwyer, his Democratic-American Labor party opponent.

"I have no comment," he said, "since I stand on my statement of Sunday. We are waging an affirmative campaign."

Informed that Hyman Blumberg,

Continued on Page 19, Column 6

CHINESE WIN MORE OF 'INVASION COAST'

Smash Into Port 121 Miles Southwest of Canton—Big Area Open for Landing

By The Associated Press.

CHUNGKING, China, Aug. 6—Chinese troops have broken into the South China port of Yeungkong and cleared a fifty-mile stretch of the Chinese "invasion coast" west of Hong Kong, Generalissimo Chiang Kai-shek's headquarters said today.

Swaying block-by-block street fighting is raging in the strategic coastal highway town, 121 miles southwest of Canton, a communiqué said.

By breaking into Yeungkong Chinese forces won control of a fifty-mile coastal stretch leading west to Tinpak, which lies east of Luichow Peninsula on the South China Sea. The coastal area now is open to a virtually unopposed landing should American forces choose it for a staging point for supplies to the armies of South China.

West of Luichow Peninsula another 145-mile coastal stretch extending to the Indo-China frontier is under Chinese control and observers believe the Chinese soon may launch a concerted drive from the west and east that would seal off the Japanese on the Luichow

Continued on Page 2, Column 7

Turks Talk War if Russia Presses; Prefer Vain Battle to Surrender

By SAM POPE BREWER
By Wireless to THE NEW YORK TIMES.

ANKARA, Turkey, Aug. 6—Russo-Turkish relations weigh heavy on Turkish minds these days. All leading editors commented today on various aspects of the Russian claims against Turkey.

The Potsdam conference leaves the situation virtually unchanged so far as the Turks can see, but they seem to agree that they would go to war, however hopeless such a war might be, rather than yield before the threat of force. Suggestions from London and Washington that the Russians have been asked to moderate their demands give little reassurance here.

The Potsdam communiqué created more confusion than confidence and the Turks are still trying to decide whether the fact that the conference did not deal with certain specific questions means that it was a failure.

Many point out that all the really thorny questions still are unsettled. The Turks probably do not see a relative importance among world problems of Russian demands on Turkey, but point out that the important question of principle is involved. The general and apparently official argument is that the status of the Straits cannot he modified by a bilateral agreement but must be discussed at a conference of the signatories of the Montreux Convention, with America replacing Japan. The signatories were Great Britain, France, Russia, Japan, Turkey, Greece, Rumania, Yugoslavia and Bulgaria.

The grounds for the Russian claims to Kars and Ardahan are not clear, but throughout the Near and Mideast in recent months

Continued on Page 13, Column 1

KYUSHU CITY RAZED

Kenney's Planes Blast Tarumizu in Record Blow From Okinawa

ROCKET SITE IS SEEN

125 B-29's Hit Japan's Toyokawa Naval Arsenal in Demolition Strike

By FRANK L. KLUCKHOHN
By Wireless to THE NEW YORK TIMES.

MANILA, Tuesday, Aug. 7—More than 400 fighters and bombers, speeding at chimney-top level for two hours Sunday over Tarumizu in southern Kyushu in the largest single attack launched by Gen. George C. Kenney's Far East Air Forces to date, leveled that city's munitions factories and aircraft and munitions storage depots and waterfront installations.

Rockets and demolition bombs were poured by waves of B-26 Invaders, B-25 Mitchells and Mustangs and Thunderbolts of the Fifth and Seventh Air Forces from Okinawa, supported by a few B-24 Liberators carrying big bombs.

[Tarumizu, about 350 miles from Okinawa, appeared to be a site at which the Japanese might be preparing a rocket campaign against the American base, said a United Press dispatch. FEAF pilots reported seeing in the area, which has extensive cave construction, what seemed to be Japanese robot planes and also a huge catapult-like machine, extending over the water, that might be a rocket launcher.

[About 125 B-29's hit the Toyokawa naval arsenal of Japan in a demolition bombing Tuesday noon, Strategic Air Forces headquarters at Guam reported.]

The planes over Tarumizu met scant resistance, as our fliers took their time to assure the highest

Continued on Page 11, Column 2

REPORT BY BRITAIN

'By God's Mercy' We Beat Nazis to Bomb, Churchill Says

ROOSEVELT AID CITED

Raiders Wrecked Norse Laboratory in Race for Key to Victory

The text of Mr. Churchill's statement is on Page 8.

By CLIFTON DANIEL
By Wireless to THE NEW YORK TIMES.

LONDON, Aug. 6—The hitherto secret details of the grisly race between Germany and the Allies to find a weapon so destructive that it would insure absolute victory—a race not only between scientists but also between under-cover agents—were recounted in London tonight after it had been disclosed that the first atomic bomb had been dropped on Japan.

"By God's mercy British and American science outpaced all German efforts," said a statement by former Prime Minister Churchill written before he left office and issued from 10 Downing Street by his successor, Clement R. Attlee.

"The possession of these powers by the Germans at any time might have altered the result of the war," Mr. Churchill said, "and profound anxiety was felt by those who were informed."

The British Isles, which endured the terrors of flying bombs and rockets, did hear repeated rumors that Adolf Hitler's V-3 weapon was to be an atomic bomb, but they never knew until tonight how close they came to being the first victims of its destructive power. Much less did they suspect what

Continued on Page 9, Column 1

War News Summarized

TUESDAY, AUGUST 7, 1945

One bomb hit Japan on Sunday night, but it struck with the force of 20,000 tons of TNT. Where it landed had been the city of Hiroshima; what is there now has not yet been learned.

The attack, dramatically announced by President Truman sixteen hours after the missile had struck, was with an atomic bomb, a "harnessing of the basic power of the universe," he said. "The force from which the sun draws its power has been loosed against those who brought war to the Far East. And the end is not yet."

Details of the missile are closely guarded, but the 125,000 workers who saw materials pour into their factories never saw anything go out. The bomb is the result of pooling British-American scientific knowledge begun in 1940. "We have spent two billion dollars on the greatest scientific gamble in history—and won," Mr. Truman said, and warned:

"We are now prepared to obliterate more rapidly and completely every productive enterprise the Japanese have above ground in any city. It was to spare the Japanese public from utter destruction that the ultimatum of July 26 was issued at Potsdam. If they do not now accept our terms they may expect a rain of ruin from the air."

Secretary of War Stimson detailed the story of research and production and forecast improvements to increase the effectiveness of the "atomic bomb" several times. Congress will be asked to establish a committee to control peacetime use.

Hiroshima was a major military target, a city of 318,000 persons thickly settled around a quartermaster's depot, an embarkation port, armament and airplane parts plants. [All the foregoing 1:8.]

All production was in the United States at two plants at Oak Ridge, near Knoxville, Tenn., and one at Richland, Wash. A scientific laboratory was maintained in Sante Fe, N. M. [1:6.]

Former Prime Minister Churchill told of Britain's part, including costly attacks on German "heavy water" plants and the race to outstrip the Nazis. He praised American scientific achievement and gave full credit to President Roosevelt and his advisers. [1:5.]

Tokyo made no mention of what had happened to Hiroshima but rail service in that area was canceled. [1:7.]

Okinawa sent out 400 planes that left Tarumizu, on Kyushu's Kagoshima Bay, in flaming wreckage. About 125 "Superforts" bombed Toyokawa naval arsenal by daylight. [1:4; map p. 11.]

Chinese troops have broken into the port of Yeungkong and have cleared a large stretch of the south China coast west of Hong Kong and east of the Luichow Peninsula. [1:3; map P. 2.]

Moscow, moving to implement Potsdam decisions, has resumed diplomatic relations with Finland and Rumania. [11:4.]

The Germans received an opportunity to develop democratic talents when the United States and Great Britain authorized local trade unions and political parties in their zones of occupation. [12:2.]

France is expected to ratify the United Nations Charter and then the Bretton Woods monetary plan in the near future. [13:6.] Marshal Pétain was accused of having asked Hitler for help in regaining France's colonies. [13:1.]

Argentina has lifted the state of siege in effect since Pearl Harbor. [14:6.]

Steel Tower 'Vaporized' In Trial of Mighty Bomb

Scientists Awe-Struck as Blinding Flash Lighted New Mexico Desert and Great Cloud Bore 40,000 Feet Into Sky

By LEWIS WOOD
Special to THE NEW YORK TIMES.

WASHINGTON, Aug. 6—A blinding flash many times as brilliant as the midday sun and a massive, multi-colored cloud boiling up 40,000 feet into the air accompanied the first test firing of an atomic bomb on July 16, three weeks ago today. Set in the remote desert-lands of New Mexico, the experiment was seen against a wild background where rain poured in torrents, and lightning pierced the sky up to the zero hour of the explosion at 5:30 A. M.

A steel tower from which the atomic weapon hung was vaporized. In its place was only a huge, sloping crater. At the moment of the explosion a mountain range three miles distant stood out sharply in brilliant light.

"Then," said the War Department in a description, "came a tremendous, sustained roar and a heavy pressure wave which knocked down two men outside the control tower (10,000 yards, or more than five miles, away.)"

Before the detonation scientists waited in tense expectancy. Minutes lengthened seemingly to hours. Lying face downward, with their feet toward the steel tower, the watchers waited, nearly breathless. They were "reaching into the unknown" and did not know what would happen.

On the instant that all was over these men leaped to their feet. The terrible tension ended, they shook hands, embraced each other and shouted in glee. Behind their triumph was sober consciousness of possessing the means to "insure the speedy conclusion of the war and save thousands of American lives."

The scene of the great drama was the Alamogordo Air Base, 120 miles southeast of Albuquerque. Here the scientists strove to unlock the secret upon which $2,000,000,000 had been spent.

Graphic word pictures of the

Continued on Page 5, Column 1

ATOM BOMBS MADE IN 3 HIDDEN 'CITIES'

Secrecy on Weapon So Great That Not Even Workers Knew of Their Product

By JAY WALZ
Special to THE NEW YORK TIMES.

WASHINGTON, Aug. 6—The War Department revealed today how three "hidden cities" with a total population of 100,000 inhabitants sprang into being as a result of the $2,000,000,000 atomic bomb project, how they did their work without knowing what it was all about, and how they kept the biggest secret of the war.

One of these, Oak Ridge, situated where only oak and pine trees had dotted small farms before, is today the fifth largest city in Tennessee. Its population of 75,000 persons has thirteen supermarkets, nine drug stores and seven theatres.

A second town of 7,000 was built for reasons of isolation and security on a New Mexico mesa. The third, named Richland Village, houses 17,000 men, women and children on remote banks of the Columbia River in the State of Washington.

None of the people, who came to these developments from homes all the way from Maine to California, had the slightest idea of what they were making in the gigantic Gov-

Continued on Page 3, Column 2

TRAINS CANCELED IN STRICKEN AREA

Traffic Around Hiroshima Is Disrupted — Japanese Still Sift Havoc by Split Atoms

By The United Press.

WASHINGTON, Aug. 6—The Osaka radio, without referring to the atomic bomb dropped on Hiroshima, hinted tonight at the terrific damage it must have caused by announcing that train service in the Hiroshima and other areas had been canceled.

First mention of the bomb came in a Japanese Domei agency dispatch announcing that President Truman and Prime Minister Attlee had disclosed that the new missile had been dropped on Hiroshima.

The Office of War Information began telling the Japanese today what hit them. OWI branch transmitters in San Francisco, Hawaii and Saipan beamed President Truman's statement on the atomic bomb to Japan.

Edward Barrett, director of the OWI's overseas branch, said that the President's announcement and related information on the atomic bomb will dominate the OWI's normal Japanese transmissions for the next several days.

LONDON, Tuesday, Aug. 7 (U.P.)—The Japanese Domei news agency, in a dispatch recorded by the British radio, said today that

Continued on Page 7, Column 3

Reich Exile Emerges as Heroine In Denial to Nazis of Atom's Secret

Special to THE NEW YORK TIMES.

WASHINGTON, Aug. 6—How Germany twice narrowly missed the secret of harnessing atomic energy by splitting uranium atoms and releasing the most powerful destructive force on earth was recalled today in War Department reports on the atomic bomb.

Development of the bomb after more than ten years of experimentation and research marks the first time that Prof. Albert Einstein's theory of relativity has been put to practical use outside the laboratory: the equation by which he showed the existence of a definite relationship of matter, energy and the velocity of light.

That the new bomb may be far from its maximum devastating potential was indicated by the War Department's statement that said:

"The energy we are now able to utilize in the atomic bombs, at 100 per cent efficiency, constitutes only one-tenth of 1 per cent of the total energy present in the material. But even one-hundredth of 1 per cent is still the most destructive force by far on this earth."

The principal character in the dramatic story of the long search for a method of releasing atomic energy is Dr. Lise Meitner, a woman physicist whom the Nazis expelled from Germany as a "non-Aryan." With her associates, Dr. Otto Hahn and Dr. F. Strassmann, both chemists, she had been working in the Kaiser Wilhelm Institute in Berlin, bombarding uranium atoms with neutrons and then submitting the uranium to chemical analysis.

As the War Department tells the story:

To their amazement, they found the element barium in the debris of the smashed uranium atoms.

Continued on Page 7, Column 1

NEW AGE USHERED

Day of Atomic Energy Hailed by President, Revealing Weapon

HIROSHIMA IS TARGET

'Impenetrable' Cloud of Dust Hides City After Single Bomb Strikes

Truman, Stimson statements on atomic bomb, Page 4.

By SIDNEY SHALETT
Special to THE NEW YORK TIMES.

WASHINGTON, Aug. 6—The White House and War Department announced today that an atomic bomb, possessing more power than 20,000 tons of TNT, a destructive force equal to the load of 2,000 B-29's and more than 2,000 times the blast power of what previously was the world's most devastating bomb, had been dropped on Japan.

The announcement, first given to the world in utmost solemnity by President Truman, made it plain that one of the scientific landmarks of the century had been passed, and that the "age of atomic energy," which can be a tremendous force for the advancement of civilization as well as for destruction, was at hand.

At 10:45 o'clock this morning, a statement by the President was issued at the White House that sixteen hours earlier—about the time that citizens on the Eastern seaboard were sitting down to their Sunday suppers—an American plane had dropped the single atomic bomb on the Japanese city of Hiroshima, an important army center.

Japanese Solemnly Warned

What happened at Hiroshima is not yet known. The War Department said it "as yet was unable to make an accurate report" because "an impenetrable cloud of dust and smoke" masked the target area from reconnaissance planes. The Secretary of War will release the story "as soon as accurate details of the results of the bombing become available."

But in a statement vividly describing the results of the first test of the atomic bomb in New Mexico, the War Department told how an immense steel tower had been "vaporized" by the tremendous explosion, how a 40,000-foot cloud rushed into the sky, and two observers were knocked down at a point 10,000 yards away. And President Truman solemnly warned:

"It was to spare the Japanese people from utter destruction that the ultimatum of July 26 was issued at Postdam. Their leaders promptly rejected that ultimatum. If they do not now accept our terms, they may expect a rain of ruin from the air the like of which has never been seen on this earth."

Most Closely Guarded Secret

The President referred to the joint statement issued by the heads of the American, British and Chinese Governments, in which terms of surrender were outlined to the Japanese and warning given that rejection would mean complete destruction of Japan's power to make war.

[The atomic bomb weighs about 400 pounds and is capable of utterly destroying a town, a representative of the British Ministry of Aircraft Production said in London, the United Press reported.]

What is this terrible new weapon, which the War Department also calls the "Cosmic Bomb"? It is the harnessing of the energy of the atom, which is the basic power of the universe. As President Truman said, "The force from which the sun draws its power has been loosed against those who brought war to the Far East."

"Atomic fission"—in other

Continued on Page 2, Column 2

"All the News That's Fit to Print"

The New York Times.

LATE CITY EDITION

Partly cloudy, warm, less humid today. Fair tomorrow.

Temperatures Yesterday—Max., 78; Min., 62

Sunrise today, 5:16 A. M.; Sunset, 8:04 P. M.

VOL. XCIV..No. 31,973. Entered as Second-Class Matter, Postoffice, New York, N. Y. NEW YORK, WEDNESDAY, AUGUST 8, 1945. THREE CENTS IN NEW YORK CITY

ATOMIC BOMB WIPED OUT 60% OF HIROSHIMA; SHOCK AWED FLIERS; TOKYO CABINET MEETS; CARRIER PLANES STRIKE NEAR CHINA COAST

LA GUARDIA URGES ELECTION OF MORRIS TO FOIL CITY BOSSES

No Deal Ticket Out to Win, He Says, Assailing Democratic and Republican Slates

DIG AT DEWEY IS IMPLIED

Mayor Says This Is No Time to Make Any 'Deals' for the Campaigns of '46 and '48

Text of Mayor La Guardia's address is on Page 18.

By CLAYTON KNOWLES

Mayor La Guardia pulled no punches last night as he announced his support of the No Deal party city slate, headed by Newbold Morris, in a fifteen-minute radio talk in which he promised a "real, hard, open fight against the Tammany combination as well as against the other political machine tickets."

The city's chief executive, soon to retire after twelve years as head of a fusion administration, declared the election of the independent slate provided the voters' only assurance that the city "will not be turned over to the political bosses, to big-shot racketeers, to the 'home breakers and judge-makers.'"

He ridiculed as "silly" reports that the independent slate, entered in the mayoralty campaign over the week-end, was designed "to take away votes from the Republican candidates."

"I want to have it distinctly understood that this ticket is in the field to win," he said. "That means that the ticket and its supporters will necessarily have to fight the candidates of both major parties."

Talk Eagerly Awaited

The Mayor's talk, delivered at 8:15 P. M. over station WOR, had been eagerly awaited in political circles to determine the type of campaign that would be waged. Generally understood to have fathered the third-party movement, the Mayor was thought by many to be doing it to throw aid to the Democratic-American Labor party ticket without actually endorsing it. But the blunt language of his talk last night was expected to dispel that notion in large degree.

The announcer who put the Mayor on the air told the radio audience that the time had been purchased by "one of a group of independent citizens of New York City in behalf of the No Deal candidates headed by Newbold Morris." It was later disclosed the sponsor's name was Mrs. Ella Van Cortlandt Hawkes of 1 Sutton Place.

The Mayor was in good humor after the broadcast. Asked if he had signed a No Deal petition, he exclaimed: "Indeed I have!" He then pulled out a petition and asked a reporter if he would like to sign. He put it away quickly when the reporter told him he lived in Westchester.

Mr. La Guardia charged that up until the very moment he announced he was not a candidate for re-election the Republican and Democratic city organizations were "planning and scheming to form combinations against good government."

"What was the purpose of all these conferences between Republican and Democratic bosses?" he demanded. "To oppose the kind of administration that I have been giving to the people of the City of New York for the past twelve years and to return to the old time of political control with patronage, privilege, pap, perquisites and pilfer. It was a proposed combination against good government."

With his retirement, he declared, these same leaders selected the

Continued on Page 12, Column 2

Truman Back From Europe; Holds Cabinet Conference

At White House, After Newport News Landing on Return From Potsdam, He Faces Accumulation of Problems

By The Associated Press.

WASHINGTON, Aug. 7—President Truman returned to the White House tonight from the Big Three conference at Potsdam. His special train arrived at 10:50 P. M. from Newport News, Va., where he landed from the cruiser Augusta late this afternoon.

Members of the Cabinet were at the White House and the President conferred with them until about 11:45 P. M.

John W. Snyder, director of War Mobilization and Reconversion, boarded the cruiser when it docked and accompanied Mr. Truman on the train trip.

It was announced at Newport News that the President had called a Cabinet meeting for Friday. It was also made known that the report which he will make to the country by radio on the Potsdam conference was substantially completed. Pending the address, it was stated, he would not hold a news conference.

The Augusta, bearing President Truman and his party, docked at Hampton Roads Port of Embarkation at 5:25 P. M.

Mr. Truman, looking physically fit and smiling, came down the gang plank immediately behind George Dresher, head of the Secret Service detail. Behind him came Admiral William Leahy, naval Chief of Staff to the President; Judge Samuel Rosenman, Secretary of State James F. Byrnes, and other members of the Presidential party, including Admiral Jonas H. Ingram, Commander in Chief of the Atlantic Fleet.

As the President stepped on the pier he was greeted by Rear Admiral David McD. Lebreton, commandant of the Fifth Naval District; Brig. Gen. John R. Kilpatrick, commanding general of the Hampton Roads Port of Embarkation, and Rear Admiral P. N. L. Bellinger, commander of the Air Force, Atlantic Fleet.

The President returned a snap-

Continued on Page 4, Column 4

SLOAN, KETTERING TO COMBAT CANCER

Former Makes a $4,000,000 Grant for Research Institute to Be Directed by the Latter

The first application of American industrial research techniques to cancer research was projected yesterday in an announcement by Alfred P. Sloan Jr., chairman of General Motors Corporation and sponsor of the Alfred P. Sloan Foundation, of a $4,000,000 grant for a Sloan-Kettering Institute for Cancer Research at the Memorial Cancer Center in this city.

Dr. Charles F. Kettering, vice president and director of research for General Motors, will concentrate on the organization of industrial techniques for cancer research. The financial grant will come entirely from the Sloan Foundation. It will be a personal undertaking of the two men, and will not be connected with General Motors.

Half the grant will provide for a building to be erected at an estimated cost of $2,000,000 on property now owned by Memorial Hospital adjacent to its present location at 444 East Sixty-eighth Street. In addition, the foundation will provide $200,000 a year for ten years toward operating costs, with the expectation that others interested in cancer research will make an equal annual donation.

The gift was announced in connection with the recently proposed expansion program to make Me-

Continued on Page 40, Column 2

TITO BARS RETURN OF YUGOSLAV KING

Calls Monarchy Incompatible With Democracy, Rejected by Majority of People

By The United Press.

BELGRADE, Yugoslavia, Aug. 7—Premier Tito, apparently ending any prospect for the restoration of the monarchy under King Peter II, said today that a monarchy was "incompatible with democracy in Yugoslavia."

Legislation has been drafted for immediate submission to the Avnoj, or National Assembly, to bar the king's return to the throne, it is indicated. In a fiery oration before 1,150 delegates to a National Liberation Front meeting, Premier Tito called the monarchy an "outmoded, tyrannical institution rejected by the vast majority of the people."

Not only King Peter but all "reactionary émigrés" will be barred from the new Yugoslavia, he said. He urged the creation of a liberal Republican regime.

[In London, a spokesman for King Peter said that the king was at his country home and had been informed of the speech. As yet, Peter has not expressed his attitude toward it, the spokesman said, but he may make a statement on Wednesday, when he is expected to return to London.]

Premier Tito severely criticized some western types of democracy. Under them, he said, reactionaries

Continued on page 15, Column 1

Courtroom Turns Into Arsenal At Navy Officer's Trial for Theft

By LUCY GREENBAUM

One of the strangest cases in the history of the Navy unfolded yesterday in the quiet court chamber of the New York Navy Yard in Brooklyn.

The floor of the court room became strewn with machine guns, automatic rifles and bayonets, unpacked from a wooden box as the Navy uncovered a small part of its evidence in the court-martial charges it is bringing against Lieut. Comdr. Equen B. Meader, 36 years old, of Forest Hills, Queens, for theft of Government property, violation of the customs statutes and bringing live ammunition into this country.

Officials say this case is unique in the annals of naval history in that no one individual has ever been accused of stealing so many items on so large a scale. Twelve charges with 101 specifications involving 180 stolen weapons are lodged against the defendant. The Navy has spent seven months in preparing its case, which is being prosecuted by Lieut. Comdr. Allen Blank, USNR, assisted by Lieut. Harold E. Magnuson.

In the forty-two wooden cases that Commander Meader was accused of shipping here from North Africa as personal belongings are automatic machine guns, rifles, re-

Continued on Page 8, Column 3

B-29'S HIT YAWATA

225 'Superforts' Bomb Kyushu Steel Mill Area With P-47 Escort

FEAF FLIERS STRIKE

Kenney's Planes Smash Port and Rail Center of Southern Japan

By Wireless to THE NEW YORK TIMES.

GUAM, Wednesday, Aug. 8—A fleet of more than 225 Marianas-based Superfortresses, escorted by about 140 P-47 Thunderbolt fighters from Okinawa, attacked the industrial area of Yawata late this morning, dropping about 1,500 tons of demolition bombs, Gen. Carl A. Spaatz's Strategic Air Forces communiqué said.

Bombardiers reported excellent results and huge fires raging in the target area, Japan's major steel-mill district in northwestern Kyushu, when they started back.

The attack, carried out in clear daylight against what has been one of the most heavily defended areas in the Japanese Empire, encountered surprisingly little resistance. Returning crewmen said that fighter and anti-aircraft opposition ranged from nil to moderate.

[Heavy, medium and attack bombers and fighter-bombers of Gen. George C. Kenney's Far East Air Forces from Okinawa, more than 300 strong, smashed up two southern Kyushu cities Monday. They hit the factory city and naval port of Kagoshima and the rail center of Miyakonojo.]

Yawata was one of the Japanese city areas that had been publicly warned by the Twentieth Air Force that it would be destroyed by our Superfortresses. It is called the Pittsburgh of Japan because of its steel mills and their importance in the enemy's war effort.

The B-29's target area included the towns of Yawata, Wakamatsu, Tobata, Kurosaki and Kokura, which have a combined population of more than 650,000.

This area last was hit by B-29's on Aug. 20, 1944, by China-based "Superforts" of the Twenty-first

Continued on Page 2, Column 3

THEY DROPPED FIRST ATOMIC BOMB ON JAPAN

Capt. William S. Parsons

Col. Paul W. Tibbets Jr.

Maj. Thomas W. Ferebee

Associated Press Radiophotos

CARRIERS IN SWEEP SOUTH OF SHANGHAI

Attack Tinghai Island, Base for Seaplanes—Other Flattops Bomb Wake Island

By Wireless to THE NEW YORK TIMES.

GUAM, Wednesday, Aug. 8—While the operations of Admiral William F. Halsey's Third Fleet remained in a news blackout, a carrier task force under Vice Admiral Jesse B. Oldendorf, commander of naval forces in the Ryukyus, made sweeps in the China Sea near Shanghai Saturday, Sunday and Monday, Fleet Admiral Chester W. Nimitz revealed in a communiqué this morning.

Admiral Oldendorf's planes shot down four enemy aircraft, destroyed a large barge, damaged a small coastal cargo vessel and damaged military installations on Tinghai Island, an enemy seaplane base seventy-five miles southeast of Shanghai in the China Sea.

An attack on Wake Island by other carriers and the usual extensive activities of search planes were the only other naval operations of Admiral Nimitz's command disclosed in this morning's communiqué.

Wake, where the Japanese garrison has been isolated since early in the Pacific offensive, was bombed Monday by carrier planes that destroyed or damaged small

Continued on Page 12, Column 4

War News Summarized

WEDNESDAY, AUGUST 8, 1945

Sixty per cent of Hiroshima was obliterated by the lone atomic bomb dropped on Sunday, it was announced in Guam last night. Five major industrial plants disappeared and additional damage was done beyond the wiped-out area. Only 2.8 square miles of the city's 6.9 square miles remained.

The city disappeared in a cloud of smoke, flame and dust that rose 40,000 feet. The missile struck the center of the target, a flash brighter than sunlight covered the city and several minutes later the smoke cloud reached up to the stratosphere. [All the foregoing 1:8.]

Gen. Spaatz said more B-29's were ready to follow and all would operate from the Marianas. [3:8.] Tokyo Admitted considerable damage had been done and the Cabinet held a special meeting. [1:6-7.]

The strength of the Army will be maintained at 7,000,000 men, despite the success of the new air weapon. [1:6-7.] Additional plants for the production of the atomic bomb are rising at Oak Ridge, Tenn. [6:3.]

Use of the bomb weapon "created an unfavorable impression in the Vatican," the official press office announced. [1:7.]

Carrier planes of the Pacific Fleet in the Ryukyus raked the China Sea near Shanghai for three days, damaging military installations. Other Fleet planes struck again at by-passed Wake Island. [1:5.]

Yawata was hit early today with 1,500 tons of demolition bombs dropped by 225 escorted B-29's three days after having been warned of the impending blow. Okinawa-based aircraft also struck Kyushu, 200 bombers smashing Kagoshima and 100 attacking Miyakonojo. [1:5.]

Yeungkong, south China port west of Hong Kong, has been recaptured by the Chinese. [8:2; Pacific area map, P. 2.]

King Peter has been virtually exiled and the Yugoslav monarchy liquidated by Premier Marshal Tito, who told the National Assembly that the "outmoded, tyrannical institution" was "incompatible with democracy." "Reactionary émigrés" will also be forbidden to re-enter the country. [1:3.]

Germany's inherent industrial capacity is so great that production of many items actually increased during 1944 despite Allied bombings, a Senate subcommittee warned. [15:5.]

The ten Nazi leaders to be tried at the first session of the international war crimes court at Nuremberg next month will be Goering, von Ribbentrop, von Papen, Rosenberg, Keitel, Ley, Streicher, Seyss-Inquart, Frank and Jodl. [13:5.]

Witnesses at the Pétain trial testified that the Marshal had concluded a secret agreement with Britain in 1940 through the American Embassy at Vichy promising not to yield the French fleet or colonies to Hitler. [15:1.]

Japan Keeps People in Dark On Nature of New Scourge

A report of the damage inflicted on the Japanese city of Hiroshima as a result of the atomic bomb dropped on it Monday by a B-29 was submitted to a special meeting of Japanese Government officials by Hisatsune Sekomizu, chief Cabinet secretary, this morning, according to the Domei agency.

In an English wireless dispatch directed to the United States, Domei said that the meeting, held at the official residence of Premier Kantaro Suzuki, was attended by the Cabinet Ministers, Vice Ministers and Councilors.

The dispatch said that Sekomizu had "made a report on last Monday's enemy air raid on Hiroshima" and had also reported on the "progress being made in organization" by the People's Volunteer Corps. Domei avoided describing the nature of the raid.

An earlier acknowledgment of damage was made in an Imperial headquarters communiqué, which said that the attack had been carried out by a "small number" of Superfortresses that had dropped "a new type of bomb."

The Domei agency, in a wireless transmission beamed to the United States, said that "as a result of this wanton attack, a considerable number of houses in the city were demolished while fires were caused to start at several points."

Other Japanese press and radio transmissions, both domestic and foreign, said that the bomb was dropped by parachute and exploded in the air. In none of these transmissions, recorded by the Federal Communications Commission, was there mention of "atomic bomb." The designation in all cases was "new type of bomb."

President Truman, in announcing Monday that American scientists had harnessed the basic power of the universe in developing the atomic fission missile, said that one plane dropped one bomb. It was apparent that the Japanese could not believe a single plane and a single bomb could cause so much destruction, press services noted.

The Japanese domestic radio, after broadcasting the Imperial headquarters communiqué, said

Continued on Page 7, Column 3

VATICAN DEPLORES USE OF ATOM BOMB

Official Press Office Says the Weapon Has Created an Unfavorable Impression

By The Associated Press.

ROME, Aug. 7—The Osservatore Romano, Vatican City newspaper, published today brief news reports of President Truman's announcement of the atomic bomb and in an editorial said, "this incredible destructive instrument remains a temptation for posterity."

The editorial, appended to the news stories, said that Leonardo da Vinci destroyed his plans for a submarine because he feared that man would apply it to the ruin of civilization, adding, "mankind did not think as did Leonardo."

The official Vatican Press Office allowed itself to be quoted as saying:

"The use of atomic bombs in Japan has created an unfavorable impression on the Vatican."

Other Vatican authorities declined to comment.

The brief reports of President Truman's announcement were published under a two-column headline on the first page of The Osservatore Romano. Following them was this editorial:

"Our thoughts turn to what is told of Leonardo. He planned a submarine, but he feared that man would not apply it to progress, namely to the constructive uses of civilization, but to its ruin. He destroyed that possible instrument of destruction.

"Mankind did not think as did Leonardo. Mankind thought as he

Continued on Page 6, Column 4

No Cut in the Army Is Planned As a Result of New Bomb Use

By LUTHER HUSTON

Special to THE NEW YORK TIMES.

WASHINGTON, Aug. 7—Use of the atomic bomb against Japan will not permit reduction of the size of the Army below 7,000,000 men, set as its total by the end of June, 1946, War Department sources indicated today.

Officials of the department were not prepared to talk about the new bomb, the specific results of the one that was dropped on Hiroshima, or the future of the force which was announced yesterday. It was evident from the trend of very guarded comments that what the Army has called the "cosmic bomb" was not regarded by those responsible for winning the war against Japan as the factor which, of itself, would give the war its finishing touch.

On the contrary, it was made clear that there was concern in high Army circles lest an impression become too widely accepted by the public that the atomic bomb would obviate the necessity of maintaining the Army at man-power levels already fixed. Army leaders let it be known that they believed their figures were right and could not be revised downward.

Assertions by members of Congress that the numerical strength

Continued on Page 3, Column 5

5 PLANTS VANISHED

4.1 Square Miles of City Laid Waste, Photos of Epic Blow Show

'SUPERFORT' JARRED

Smoke Seethes 40,000 Feet—Flash Is Seen 170 Miles Away

By W. H. LAWRENCE

By Wireless to THE NEW YORK TIMES.

GUAM, Wednesday, Aug. 8—The first atomic bomb wiped out 4.1 square miles of the Japanese city of Hiroshima on Monday, it was announced today. Gen. Carl A. Spaatz, commanding general of the Strategic Air Forces, made the disclosure that 60 per cent of the city had been destroyed.

Hiroshima, on the Inland Sea, had a built-up area 6.9 square miles and a pre-war population of 343,000.

General Spaatz's announcement, based on a careful study of photographs taken a few hours after the bomb had been dropped, made clear the terrific destructive power of this new secret weapon, which has harnessed the power of the universe and turned it against the Japanese.

General Spaatz said that the single bomb "completely destroyed" the area cited, including five major industrial targets. The pictures made it clear that there was other damage in the area of the city that was not completely destroyed.

Target Smashed in Seconds

It was believed that much of this terrible destruction was exacted in a split second and resulted from concussion rather than fire.

Thus, with a single bomb, we were able to destroy in a matter of seconds an area equivalent to one-eighth of Manhattan.

The bomb was dropped at 9:15 A. M. Monday from the Superfortress Enola Gay, piloted by Col. Paul W. Tibbets Jr. of Miami, Fla. The man who designed the new bomb, Capt. William S. Parsons, of Chicago, went on the mission to see how the weapon worked. The bombardier was Major Thomas W. Ferebee of Mocksville, N. C.

The missile, which crashed with the explosive power of 20,000 tons of TNT, covered the entire area of Hiroshima in two minutes with a black cloud which "looked like boiling dust" and climbed 40,000 feet.

That smoke cloud, visible as much as 160 miles at sea, still hung over the city at least four hours later.

[Crewmen of a reconnaissance Superfortress flying over Wakayama Prefecture at a point 170 miles from Hiroshima reported that they could see the flash of the bomb as well as the smoke, the United Press reported. "A tremendous flash like a ball of fire or a setting sun shone in the distance," the pilot said.]

Navy Captain Designed Bomb

That was the story told yesterday by the daring men who had charge of the first use of this tremendous agent of destruction. They were Captain Parsons, who is from Chicago and described himself as the "weaponeer"—he is a naval ordnance expert who designed the bomb in which the energy of the split atom was channelized—and Colonel Tibbets, from Miami, Fla., pilot of the Enola Gay, named for Colonel Tibbets' 57-year-old mother, also a resident of Miami.

As they told their story to assembled newsmen at headquarters of the United States Army Strategic Air Forces, they were flanked by General Spaatz and his chief of staff, Maj. Gen. Curtis E. LeMay,

Continued on Page 3, Column 1

"All the News That's Fit to Print"

The New York Times.

LATE CITY EDITION
Sunny with low humidity today. Partly cloudy, warmer tomorrow.
Temperatures Yesterday—Max., 77; Min., 66
Sunrise today, 5:59 A. M.; Sunset, 8:03 P. M.

VOL. XCIV . No. 31,974. Entered as Second-Class Matter, Postoffice, New York, N. Y. NEW YORK, THURSDAY, AUGUST 9, 1945. THREE CENTS IN NEW YORK CITY

SOVIET DECLARES WAR ON JAPAN; ATTACKS MANCHURIA, TOKYO SAYS; ATOM BOMB LOOSED ON NAGASAKI

TRUMAN TO REPORT TO PEOPLE TONIGHT ON BIG 3 AND WAR

Half-Hour Speech by Radio to Cover a Wide Range of Problems Facing the World

HE SIGNS PEACE CHARTER

And Thus Makes This Country the First to Complete All Ratification Requirements

By The Associated Press.

WASHINGTON, Aug. 8—President Truman will report to the country on the Potsdam conference over all radio networks at 10 P. M., Eastern war time, tomorrow in a thirty-minute speech.

The Presidential secretary, Charles G. Ross, said today that the speech, which probably would also be short-waved abroad, would go into greater detail than the communiqué issued by the Big Three at the close of the meeting July 26.

Mr. Truman worked on the speech today as well as on a mass of other paper work which accumulated during his month-long absence, and signed into full ratification the United Nations Charter.

He held his calling list to a minimum, including brief conferences with Senators Hatch of New Mexico and Kilgore of West Virginia, and Henry L. Stimson, Secretary of War.

The Stimson conference was devoted to further discussion of the atomic bomb.

Associates of the President indicated that his report on the Potsdam conference would probably mention the new and revolutionary bomb used for the first time against Japan.

Full Appraisal May Be Given

A full appraisal of revised conditions, including Russia's declaration of war against Japan, may come in Mr. Truman's broadcast.

Originally the speech was expected to be primarily a report on the Soviet-British-American agreements announced at the end of the Potsdam conference. These dealt mainly with Europe, keeping Germany under strict surveillance, and the writing of peace treaties.

It became known today that Mr. Truman had four or five names under consideration for the vacancy on the Supreme Court, and the decision appeared imminent.

One of the names is that of Senator Austin, Republican, of Vermont, who has been endorsed by his Democratic colleague, Senator Hatch. It was to renew his suggestion that Mr. Austin be appointed to succeed Justice Owen Roberts, who retired, that brought Mr. Hatch to the White House today.

"Of course the President made no commitments," Mr. Hatch told reporters later, "but he definitely is considering both the appointment of a Republican and Senator Austin. Of course that is only a possibility."

Justice Roberts, appointed by President Hoover in 1930, was one of two Republicans in the present makeup of the high court. Chief Justice Harlan F. Stone is the remaining member of that party.

Charter Goes to Archives

Special to THE NEW YORK TIMES.

WASHINGTON, Aug. 8—When President Truman signed today the document by which he ratified the Charter of the United Nations, the United States thereby became the first country to complete its action for bringing the Charter into force.

Several other countries have ratified or taken action with a view to ratif. on, but no instrument of ratification has yet been received from any of them by the State Department, which is the

Continued on Page 3, Column 5

Foreigners Asked To Stay at Home

Special to THE NEW YORK TIMES.

WASHINGTON, Aug. 8—Discouragement of unessential travel by foreigners to the United States was ordered by the Government today through the State Department.

"The Department of State has always traditionally done everything in its power to promote the travel of citizens of other countries of the Western Hemisphere to the United States," said the announcement. "However, the United States Government is now engaged in a gigantic military operation in deploying forces and supplies from the European theatre to the Pacific area. This tremendous task places an unprecedented burden on the transportation system."

The citizens of other countries should realize the situation, the statement said, and postpone trips to the United States unless they were directly connected with the war.

TAMMANY OUSTS LAST OF REBELS

County Committee Ratifies Executive Group's Action—Meeting Picketed

Without the slightest opposition, the New York County Democratic Committee, popularly known as Tammany, last night ratified the selection of an executive committee on which there remained no opposition to the leadership of Edward V. Loughlin or to the influence in the organization repeatedly exercised by Bert Stand, secretary, and Clarence H. Neal Jr., chairman of its elections committee.

In Brooklyn the Kings County Democratic Committee nominated United States Attorney Miles F. McDonald for District Attorney of Kings County to run for the vacancy caused by the resignation of William O'Dwyer, Democratic and American Labor party candidate for Mayor. Mr. McDonald, a graduate of Holy Cross College and Fordham Law School, in accepting the nomination, told the members of the committee that he would resign as United States Attorney.

Nearly 2,000 members, the largest number in recent years, attended the Tammany meeting in the Central Commercial High School, 214 East Forty-second Street. All resolutions presented were adopted unanimously by voice vote.

The committee ratified action taken by the executive committee in seating Robert B. Blaikie as leader of the Seventh Assembly District in place of Joseph H. Broderick and Assemblyman Patrick H. Sullivan, in spite of the claim of Mr. Broderick that he had elected a majority of county com-

Continued on Page 17, Column 2

2D BIG AERIAL BLOW

Japanese Port Is Target in Devastating New Midday Assault

RESULT CALLED GOOD

Foe Asserts Hiroshima Toll Is 'Uncountable' —Assails 'Atrocity'

By W. H. LAWRENCE

By Wireless to THE NEW YORK TIMES.

GUAM, Thursday, Aug. 9—Gen. Carl A. Spaatz announced today that a second atomic bomb had been dropped, this time on the city of Nagasaki, and that crew members reported "good results."

The second use of the new and terrifying secret weapon which wiped out more than 60 per cent of the city of Hiroshima and, according to the Japanese radio, killed nearly every resident of that town, occurred at noon today, Japanese time. The target today was an important industrial and shipping area with a population of about 253,000.

The great bomb, which harnesses the power of the universe to destroy the enemy by concussion, blast and fire, was dropped on the second enemy city about seven hours after the Japanese had received a political "roundhouse punch" in the form of a declaration of war by the Soviet Union.

Vital Transshipment Point

GUAM, Thursday, Aug. 9 (AP)—Nagasaki is vitally important as a port for transshipment of military supplies and the embarkation of troops in support of Japan's operations in China, Formosa, Southeast Asia and the Southwest Pacific. It was highly important as a major shipbuilding and repair center for both naval and merchantmen.

The city also included industrial surburbs of Inase and Akunoura on the western side of the harbor, and Urakami. The combined area is nearly double Hiroshima's.

Nagasaki, although only two-thirds as large as Hiroshima in population, is considered more important industrially. With a population now estimated at 253,000, its twelve square miles are jam-packed with the eave-to-eave buildings that won it the name of "sea of roofs."

General Spaatz' communiqué reporting the bombing did not say whether one or more than one "mighty atom" was dropped.

Hiroshima a 'City of Dead'

The Tokyo radio yesterday described Hiroshima as a city of ruins and dead "too numerous to be counted," and put forth the claim that the use of the atomic

Continued on Page 6, Column 3

RED ARMY STRIKES

Foe Reports First Blow by Soviet Forces on Asian Frontier

KEY POINTS BOMBED

Action Believed Aimed to Free Vladivostok Area of Threat

By The United Press.

SAN FRANCISCO, Aug. 8—Russia's mighty Far Eastern Army began hostilities against Japan at 12:10 A. M. Thursday [Russian time], launching a sudden attack along the eastern Soviet-Manchuria border only nine minutes after Moscow's declaration of war became effective, the enemy reported today.

A Kwantung Army headquarters communiqué issued at Changchun [Hsinking] and recorded here reported the attack and also announced that the Red Air Force already was bombing strategic points in Manchurian territory behind Japanese lines.

No details of the attack were given, but presumably the Russians would drive west from the Vladivostok area into Japanese-held territory north of the tip of Korea. Vladivostok is only about twenty miles east of the border, separated from the Japanese by fortified positions along the rugged, mountainous terrain.

The communiqué made it clear that ground forces had opened the attack—part of the Soviet Union's Far Eastern Army of more than 1,000,000 well-equipped troops, who never were called into action against Germany, but remained along the border, a constant threat to Japan.

Although the communiqué did not locate the fighting, it was believed the Russians would strike out as quickly as possible from the Vladivostok region, which is highly

Continued on Page 4, Column 6

CIRCLE OF SPEARHEADS AROUND JAPAN IS COMPLETED

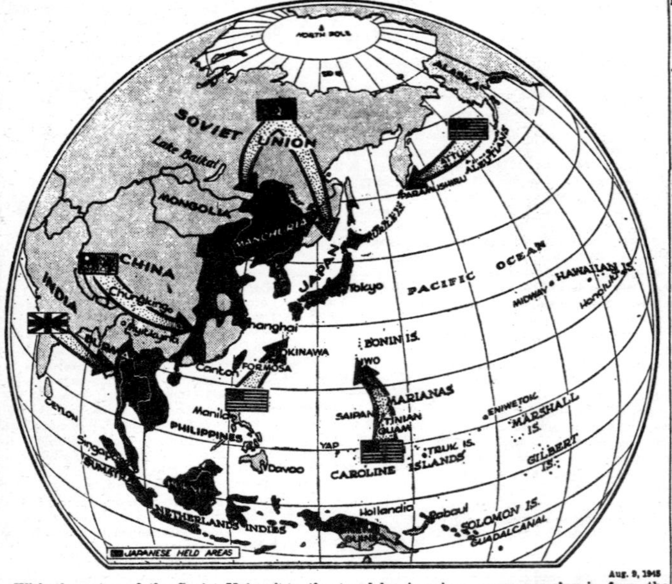

Aug. 9, 1945

With the entry of the Soviet Union into the war against Japan, the enemy is confronted with armed might from new directions—the north and northeast. Japan was already being battered by American power pressing in from the northeast and the south and by Chinese and British power from the west and southwest. The Russians are reported attacking Manchuria.

385 B-29'S SMASH 4 TARGETS IN JAPAN

Tokyo Arsenal and Aircraft Plant Are Seared—Fukuyama and Yawata Cities Ripped

By Wireless to THE NEW YORK TIMES.

GUAM, Thursday, Aug. 9—Gen. Carl A. Spaatz, armed with the confirmed knowledge that his Strategic Air Force possesses in the atomic bomb the most powerful destructive agent devised by man since gunpowder was discovered, sent four separate forces

Continued on Page 2, Column 1

U. S. Third Fleet Attacking Targets in Northern Honshu

By ROBERT TRUMBULL

By Wireless to THE NEW YORK TIMES.

GUAM, Thursday, Aug. 9—Admiral William F. Halsey's mighty Third Fleet, including British carriers, is now throwing strong air attacks at northern Honshu in the Japanese home islands, where the enemy has twenty to twenty-five airfields, Fleet Admiral Chester W. Nimitz announced this morning.

Although no specific targets were designated, the communiqué said shipping, air installations and "other military targets" were hit by strong air attacks beginning at dawn.

Today's communiqué broke nine days of silence by the Third Fleet after strikes in the Tokyo area July 30. It is possible that persistent fogs, caused by the warm Japanese Current at this time of year, forced Admiral Halsey to desist during that time from the sea-borne attacks carried out in conjunction with land-based air activity over the empire.

Northern Honshu, an area of 30,669 square miles, a little smaller than Maine and populated by 9,500,000 persons, has twenty to twenty-five airfields that are considered operational although some are small, poorly developed bases and probably are used only for the dispersal of the Japanese air force hiding out in that area.

While the northern Honshu district as geographically defined is outside the main military and industrial area of the island there is

Continued on Page 2, Column 8

TRUMAN REVEALS MOVE OF MOSCOW

Announces War Declaration Soon After Russian Action —Capital Is Startled

By FELIX BELAIR JR.

Special to THE NEW YORK TIMES.

WASHINGTON, Aug. 8—President Truman announced a few minutes after 3 P. M. today that Russia had just declared war on Japan. The dramatic statement, issued with all the casualness of a routine proclamation, came during the shortest White House press conference on record.

Flanked by Secretary of State James M. Byrnes and Admiral William D. Leahy, his Chief of Staff, the President stood before hastily summoned reporters and in steady, matter-of-fact tones declared: "I have only a simple an-

Continued on Page 3, Column 1

RUSSIA AIDS ALLIES

Joins Pacific Struggle After Spurning Foe's Mediation Plea

SEEKS EARLY PEACE

Molotoff Reveals Move Three Months After Victory in Europe

By BROOKS ATKINSON

By Wireless to THE NEW YORK TIMES.

MOSCOW, Aug. 8—Russia declared war on Japan tonight. In a dramatic press conference held at 8:30 P. M., Foreign Commissar Vyacheslaff M. Molotoff read the declaration, which was announced to the public at 10 P. M., Moscow time [3 P. M. New York time].

In view of Japan's refusal of the Allies' demand for unconditional surrender, Mr. Molotoff said, the Allies proposed that the Soviet Union "join the war against Japanese aggression and thus shorten the duration of the wa , reduce the number of victims and facilitate the speedy restoration of universal peace.

"Loyal to its Allied duty," the Foreign Commissar continued, "the Soviet Government has accepted the proposal of the Allies and has joined in the declaration of the Allied Powers of July 26. The Soviet Government considers that this policy is the only means able to bring peace nearer, free the people from further sacrifice and suffering and give the Japanese people the possibility of avoiding the dangers and destruction suffered by Germany after her refusal to capitulate unconditionally."

Closing his concise statement, Mr. Molotoff declared:

"In view of the above, the Soviet Government declares that from tomorrow, that is Aug. 9, the Soviet Union will consider itself to be at war with Japan."

The Soviet Government's declaration comes three months after the victory over Germany, supporting rumors that some months ago the Soviet Government intimated it would join in the war against Japan three months after victory was won in Europe.

For the first time Mr. Molotoff revealed that the Japanese Government had asked the Soviet Union to mediate for a cessation of hostilities about the middle of June. Japanese Ambassador Naotaka Sato delivered the message, and also a special message from

Continued on Page 3, Column 2

Allies Cut Austria Into Four Zones With Vienna Under Joint Control

By LANSING WARREN

Special to THE NEW YORK TIMES.

WASHINGTON, Aug. 8—A four-power control machinery, including France with the Big Three, has been established in Austria in accordance with an agreement between the Soviet Union, the United States, the United Kingdom and France, it was announced today.

The system resembles the military control arrangement for Germany. It divides Austria into four zones of occupation and provides that Vienna, the capital city, shall also be occupied by the forces of the four controlling powers. It creates an Allied Council, consisting of the four military commissioners, who will govern Austria as a whole. The commissioners will make the decisions for all Austria and will insure a uniformity of action in the different zones.

[The text of the statement on Austria is on Page 11.]

Under the direction of this combined Allied council each military commander will have full authority in his zone. The council will act through the commanders and through an executive committee, which will advise the council and carry out its decisions.

By this means the agreement seeks to prevent a situation that would separate too rigidly the

Continued on Page 11, Column 5

War News Summarized

THURSDAY, AUGUST 9, 1945

Russia has declared war against Japan because that country is the only great power standing in the way of peace. Foreign Commissar Molotoff so informed Ambassador Sato in Moscow yesterday. He said it was in the interests of shortening the war and bringing peace to the world that Moscow acceded to the Allied request to join the war in the Far East and subscribed to the Potsdam ultimatum of July 26. Mr. Molotoff revealed that Japan had asked the Soviet Union to mediate for peace, but that proposal "lost all foundation" when Tokyo rejected the Potsdam demands. [1:8.]

Hostilities were begun nine minutes after the war declaration went into effect at 12:01 this morning, according to Tokyo, when Soviet troops struck along Manchuria's eastern frontier with Siberia. Air attacks, it was said, quickly followed. [1:4.]

President Truman broke the news when he told a hastily called press conference: "Russia has declared war against Japan—that is all." [1:7.] Secretary of State Byrnes declared there was "still time—but little time—for the Japanese to save themselves from the destruction which threatens them." Mr. Byrnes said the President had convinced Premier Stalin that Russia must enter the war if she was to be responsible for peace. [4:2.]

Congress, jubilant and confident that Russia's aid and the atomic bomb would shorten the war materially, expected to be called back soon. [4:1.]

Japan received another blow when the second atomic bomb to fall struck Nagasaki on Kyushu. Crew members reported good results. "Practically all living things" in Hiroshima were destroyed beyond recognition by heat and pressure from the first atomic bomb, Tokyo reported. [1:3.] Fires leaped seven rivers. [6:3, with map.]

The Third Fleet, after nine days of silence, sent its carrier planes in a strong attack, still continuing at last reports, against northern Honshu and its score of airfields. [1:6-7.] B-29's hit four Japanese cities in twenty-four hours and mined home waters. [1:5; map P. 2.]

Wuhu Island, at the mouth of the Min River east of Foochow, was captured by the Chinese. [8:2, with map.]

Russia, Britain, France and the United States have signed an agreement for the occupation and administration of Austria similar to that in effect in Germany. Complete separation from Germany, restoration of the 1937 frontiers and return of democratic government were set as Allied goals. [1:2-3; maps P. 11.]

A new code of international law was adopted by the Big Four listing wars of aggression as a crime against peace. [1:6-7.]

General de Gaulle and his Cabinet, contrary to the wishes of the Consultative Assembly, will submit the questions of a new constitution and government responsibility to a referendum on Oct. 21. [13:5.]

President Truman signed the United Nations Charter yesterday. He will discuss the Potsdam Conference and the military situation in a broadcast at 10 o'clock tonight. [1:1.]

4 Powers Call Aggression Crime In Accord Covering War Trials

By CHARLES E. EGAN

By Wireless to THE NEW YORK TIMES.

LONDON, Aug. 8—A new code of international law, defining aggressive warfare as a crime against the world and providing punishment for those who provoke such wars, was announced here today.

By agreement among representatives of the United States, Great Britain, the Soviet Union and France, the legal framework necessary for the trial of the key German and Italian leaders held by the Allies was promulgated this afternoon. The document sets precedents in international law and, in the words of United States Supreme Court Justice Robert H. Jackson, the American representative, "ought to make clear to the world that those who lead their nations into aggressive war face individual accountability for such acts."

"If we can cultivate in the world the idea that aggressive war making is the way to a prisoners' dock rather than the way to honors," he said "we will have accomplished something toward making peace more secure."

[The texts of the War Crimes Committee report and Mr. Jackson's statement are on Page 10.]

The agreement, upon which the international committee has been laboring since June 26, represents

Continued on Page 11, Column 6

Tokyo 'Flashes' News 3 Hours After Event

By The Associated Press.

SAN FRANCISCO, Aug. 8—Japan's first recorded wireless reaction to Russia's war declaration was a brief factual announcement of that action by the Domei agency in an English-language transmission to Europe.

The Domei account, broadcast five hours and fifty-five minutes after the Moscow announcement, reported:

"Flash! Flash! Tokyo, Aug. 9—Tass News Agency announced late last night that Foreign Commissar Vyacheslaff M. Molotoff communicated to Naotake Sato, Japanese Ambassador to Russia, that the Soviet Union will consider itself in a state of war with Japan from Thursday, Aug. 9, according to the Moscow radio recorded here this morning."

By the time the "flash" was read, the state of war already had existed for several hours.

"All the News That's Fit to Print"

The New York Times.

LATE CITY EDITION
Sunny and warm today. Warm tomorrow, cloudy in afternoon.
Temperatures Yesterday—Max., 86; Min., 65
Sunrise today, 6:01 A. M.; Sunset, 8:01 P. M.

Copyright, 1945, by The New York Times Company.

VOL. XCIV..No. 31,976. Entered as Second-Class Matter, Postoffice, New York, N. Y. NEW YORK, SATURDAY, AUGUST 11, 1945. THREE CENTS NEW YORK CITY

JAPAN OFFERS TO SURRENDER; U. S. MAY LET EMPEROR REMAIN; MASTER RECONVERSION PLAN SET

WPB READY TO ACT

Snyder Said to Sanction Wide Program to Start as Soon as War Ends

RATION SHIFTS LOOM

Agencies Rush to Map Future Work as Many Face Liquidation

By WILLIAM S. WHITE
Special to THE NEW YORK TIMES.

WASHINGTON, Aug. 10—In the midst of a redoubling of a study by the multitude of war agencies today to speed a transformation of the country's economy from a war to a peace-time basis, it was reported that John W. Snyder, Director of the Office of War Mobilization and Reconversion, had approved a master reconversion plan to be put into effect immediately upon the end of the war with Japan.

The plan, it was declared, had been prepared by the War Production Board, which received on Thursday from President Truman the chief role in the task of switching over the country's industry to peace-time requirements.

Details of the program approved by Mr. Snyder, it was understood, would be made public Monday or sooner if the Japanese capitulation details were agreed upon before then.

Plan Classed as "Sound"

According to WPB officials who commented, the plan was "sound, simple and clear," with the purpose of "preventing a mad scramble for materials and facilities."

It is understood to include the five spurs and controls asked by Mr. Truman in his letter to J. A. Krug, WPB chairman, Thursday.

Meanwhile, in the belief that hostilities with Japan were about to end, the war agencies in Washington began working hard on plans for changing their individual programs, running from outright liquidation on the one hand to more intensive labors on the other. Staff meetings were held all over the capital.

A general survey indicated that plans for reconversion in some fields were far advanced.

In matters affecting the home, these are the prospects:

Gasoline

Rationing will end soon, probably almost immediately after Japan is out of the conflict.

Food

Some easing of the civilian supply is likely soon, although the Department of Agriculture took a restrained view, a spokesman stressing that the future demands of the Army were yet to be made known and that in a few commodities, notably sugar, fats and oils, the shortages were so pronounced and world-wide that not even universal peace would give early hope of an easing in those items. Nevertheless, it was stated that the department had long been planning for "V-J Day plus X"—that is, the time when post-victory military demands are made known—and that it would not find the department "unprepared."

Manpower Controls

The future of these was tied in with reconversion in general, which is to be carried on largely through the War Production Board, the one major civilian war agency which is likely to have a job as big as it had before in maintaining controls, especially since President Truman's order of yesterday.

Price Controls

These are certain to be carried on indefinitely if the Administration has its way, although some members of the Administration

Continued on Page 18, Column 4

Foe Curbs 'Traitors' In Kwantung Area

By The United Press.

SAN FRANCISCO, Aug. 10—The Japanese imposed martial law on the Kwantung area west of Korea Saturday afternoon, Tokyo time, for the "prevention of traitorous acts," the Tokyo radio reported tonight in a broadcast recorded here.

The Kwantung area consists of the southern tip of Liaotung Peninsula, extending southward from Manchuria. It was ceded to Japan from Russia under terms of the 1905 Treaty of Portsmouth.

Tokyo said a state of siege had been ordered at Dairen, major Japanese-held port on the peninsula, twenty miles east of Port Arthur, by the Japanese defense committee for Dairen and Port Arthur.

The enemy broadcast did not amplify the reference to "traitorous acts."

'PARTY POLITICS' LOOMS WITH PEACE

End of War Will Bring Return of Old Government System, the Capital Thinks

By CHARLES HURD
Special to THE NEW YORK TIMES.

WASHINGTON, Aug. 10—The indication of an early peace prompted questions in the capital today about the political changes that might be expected. There were signs that the wartime coalition would crumble almost as soon as Japan formally surrenders.

Some observers recognized that there would be some regrets at this reversion to "party politics," but others reflected that the democracy of the United States required this conflict, just as the British parliamentary system hinges on the existence of what is known as His Majesty's Loyal Opposition.

It may be expected that President Truman will combine his inherited role of national leader with that of leader of the Democratic party, as well as probable candidate for re-election in 1948.

These political factors involve a speed-up in Cabinet changes expected since President Truman took office and a re-shaping of Government operations to fit the pattern of political responsibility, rather than of expediency for emergencies.

This possibility is considered particularly strong in view of the cordial association between President Truman and the Democratic leaders on Capitol Hill.

It is fully expected that the President will accept soon the resignation of Secretary Stimson, head of the War Department, and replace the veteran Republican with a Democrat. No one criticizes the operations of Secretary Stimson. In fact the President has paid spe-

Continued on Page 8, Column 7

CABINET BACKS BID

Domei Says Ministers Unanimously Voted to Sue for Peace

ASKS QUICK ANSWER

Reports Emperor Issued Orders After Appeal to Soviet Failed

The text of the Tokyo Broadcast is on Page 3.

The Japanese Government's decision to sue for peace was voted unanimously by the full Cabinet, including the War and Navy Ministers, at a meeting that lasted from Thursday until dawn Friday, Domei, the Japanese news agency, reported last night.

Domei said earlier that the Japanese Government had addressed a message to the Swiss and Swedish Governments for transmission to the United States, Great Britain, China and the Soviet Union accepting the Potsdam ultimatum on the understanding that Emperor Hirohito's sovereignty was not questioned, the Federal Communications Commission reported.

Domei, quoting the message, said at 7:35 A. M. [EWT]:

"In obedience to the gracious command of His Majesty the Emperor, who, ever anxious to enhance the cause of world peace, desires earnestly to bring about an early termination of hostilities with a view of saving mankind from the calamities to be imposed upon them by further continuation of the war, the Japanese Government asked several weeks ago the Soviet Government, with which neutral relations then prevailed, to render good offices in restoring peace vis-a-vis the enemy powers.

Claims Peace Move Failed

"Unfortunately, these efforts in the interest of peace having failed, the Japanese Government, in conformity with the august wish of His Majesty to restore the general peace and desiring to put an end to the untold sufferings engendered by the war as quickly as possible, have decided upon the following:

"The Japanese Government are ready to accept the terms enumerated in the joint declaration which was issued at Potsdam on July 26, 1945, by the heads of the Governments of the United States, Great Britain and China and later subscribed to by the Soviet Government with the understanding that the said declaration does not comprise any demand which prejudices the prerogatives of His Majesty as a sovereign ruler.

"The Japanese Government hope sincerely that this * * *"

At this point the transmission

Continued on Page 3, Column 5

GI's in Pacific Go Wild With Joy; 'Let 'Em Keep Emperor,' They Say

By W. H. LAWRENCE
By Wireless to THE NEW YORK TIMES.

GUAM, Saturday, Aug. 11—There was nothing conditional today about the jubilant all-night celebration by American fighting men in the Pacific that the Japanese were willing to surrender.

In offices, barracks and tents the shouting discussion of the almost unbelievable news went on for hours and few believed that the Allies would decline the Japanese condition that the position of the Emperor must not be impaired.

Most of the men out here had known about and accepted an earlier high policy decision that the Emperor should not be bombed because he was the one single force that could be counted upon to control all Japanese troops if he decided to surrender. Only yesterday Superfortresses had dropped 3,000,000 leaflets to the Japanese people designating the Emperor as the person to whom the people should appeal to end the war so it would not be necessary for us to employ the deadly atomic bomb again against Japanese cities and people.

Men shouted and pounded each other on the backs when the first news of the Japanese surrender offer reached here by radio. Wacs cried with joy. Marines ran from tent to tent spreading the news. Bottles of whisky long hoarded suddenly appeared and were rapidly consumed.

There was no comment from any of the high officials, but most of them were smiling broadly as they

Continued on Page 4, Column 5

NEW YORK CROWDS THRILLED BY THE GREAT NEWS

Happy civilians and service men in Times Square yesterday — The New York Times

SOBER CITY AWAITS OFFICIAL V-J WORD

New York's Joy Pent Up in Contrast to Celebration in Other Countries

London, so recently delivered from V-bomb and fire, went wild in celebration yesterday over Japan's surrender offer. Chungking, remembering that China's children grew to manhood in the flames kindled by the Japanese, was beside itself for joy. Liberated Manila was hysterical. In virtually every Allied capital the world over, there were scenes of wild celebration.

In New York yesterday—and this was true of the nation as a whole—there was, except for a little release of emotional steam, only discussion, speculation, sober

Continued on Page 9, Column 2

U. S. Has List of Foe's Isles For Our Occupation at Once

By JAMES B. RESTON
Special to THE NEW YORK TIMES.

WASHINGTON, Aug. 10—The detailed terms of surrender for Japan will demand that the Suzuki Government hand over all strategic islands in the Pacific to the United Nations, but the United States will insist on the sole occupation of all Pacific islands considered essential to our future security until we agree to their final disposition at the Pacific Peace Conference.

The Administration has carefully defined what islands it wants. This list, for various reasons, cannot be disclosed at present, but it is known to include the main Japanese mandated islands from which the Japanese attacks originally were launched against the United States and also such other important strategic islands as Okinawa, which were not given to Japan by the League of Nations.

In the preliminary negotiations

Continued on Page 6, Column 6

RUSSIANS ADVANCE 105 MILES IN DAY

Speed Past Hailar From West as Four Siberian Forces Converge on Harbin

By The Associated Press.

LONDON, Aug. 10—Russian mobile columns ripped 105 miles into Japan's stolen Manchurian empire today in a spectacular sweep from the west along the Chinese Eastern Railroad, the Soviet High Command said tonight.

Four mighty Soviet forces were pouring in growing masses across the 2,000-mile Russo-Manchurian frontier from Outer Mongolia to the border area seventy-five miles northwest of the Russian port of Vladivostok, Moscow's second Japanese war communiqué said.

Tokyo said the Russians also had invaded the Japanese-conquered land of Korea and had smashed into the southern half of Sakhalin Island

Continued on Page 2, Column 3

B-29'S, NAVY HALT ATTACKS ON JAPAN

Spaatz Calls Off 'Superforts' for Day, Fleet Schedule Bare —MacArthur Presses Fight

By Wireless to THE NEW YORK TIMES.

GUAM, Saturday, Aug. 11—The United States Army Strategic Air Forces and the United States Navy announced here today they would conduct no offensive operations against the Japanese home islands during the day.

The announcements did not mean for a certainty that the war with Japan was over. Both announcements that there would be no offensive actions were confined to "today."

Gen. Carl A. Spaatz, commanding general of the USASAF, made the statement in midmorning that the Superfortresses would fly no bombing missions against Japan for the day. It was believed previously that B-29 strikes had been planned.

[Gen. Douglas MacArthur's headquarters announced Saturday that the war still is on for the forces under his command and that Far East Air Forces bombers are carrying out their scheduled missions against Japan, said an Associated Press dispatch from Manila.

[The Tokyo radio reported today a Japanese air attack on our Okinawa base at 9 P. M. Friday, Japanese time (10 A. M., EWT).

Continued on Page 4, Column 6

War News Summarized

SATURDAY, AUGUST 11, 1945

The Japanese Government has offered to surrender under an interpretation of the Potsdam ultimatum that would leave the Emperor's sovereignty unimpaired. The White House disclosed it was in communication with Britain, Russia and China, and it was reported to be willing to leave the question of the Emperor's prerogatives out of the armistice terms without, however, accepting the Japanese interpretation of the Potsdam ultimatum. [1:8.]

The Japanese peace bid was voted unanimously by the full Cabinet, including the War and Navy Ministers, after an all-night meeting, Domei reported. [1:3.]

The British Government announced that it was in communication with the Big Four powers but could make no further statement. [5:2-3.] It was believed to be prepared to follow whatever lead the United States proposes on the question of Emperor Hirohito, although British military leaders were said to feel he should be treated as a war criminal. [4:1.]

At the great American Pacific base on Guam the troops celebrated jubilantly all night. The opinion was expressed generally that the Japanese proposal that the position of the Emperor should not be impaired should be accepted. [1:2-3.]

In Chungking there was great rejoicing and enthusiasm for the Americans. [3:1.] American soldiers surged through the streets of Paris yelling. [5:1.]

Russian troops in Manchuria advanced 105 miles in a day in the Trans-Baikal sector and took Hailar on the Chinese Eastern Railway. [1:6; map, p. 2.]

Strategic Air Forces headquarters on Guam announced that no Superfortress attack would be made against Japan today. General MacArthur's forces did not halt. [1:7.]

The Third Fleet also said it would conduct no offensive operations today. It disclosed that its planes had left a trail of wreckage at northern Honshu bases Thursday and yesterday. [4:8.]

Preliminary assessment of atom-bomb damage at Nagasaki showed 30 per cent of the built-up area had been destroyed. [1:6-7.]

The Navy announced that thirteen more vessels, including a light cruiser, had been sunk by United States submarines in the Far East. A delayed dispatch disclosed that a submarine pack had made heavy inroads on shipping in the Japan Sea. [7:1.]

Chinese forces moved up to besiege Tsangwu, West River port, on the way to Canton. Three columns pushed toward Lingling. [2:8.]

The final day of the trial of Marshal Pétain went strongly in his favor with two former members of the Resistance offering testimony for him. [10:5.]

Atom Bomb Razed 1/3 of Nagasaki; Japan Protests to U. S. on Missile

By Wireless to THE NEW YORK TIMES.

GUAM, Saturday, Aug. 11—Gen. Carl A. Spaatz announced today that the atomic bombing of Nagasaki on Thursday destroyed 30 per cent of that city's sprawling industrial area, including the big Mitsubishi steel and arms works, the Mitsubishi-Urakami ordnance plant and other heavy industries that played a major role in the Japanese war.

[The Japanese Government was reported by the Domei agency to have filed a protest with the United States Government Friday "against its attack on Hiroshima with an atomic bomb" and to have sent a message through the Swiss Government, protecting power for Japanese interest, "requesting it immediately to discontinue the use of such an inhuman weapon."

[The dispatch, recorded by the Federal Communications Commission, said that news of the request was "officially revealed" in Tokyo.

[The Japanese Government also asked the Swiss Minister to explain the "objectives of the Japanese Government's protest" to the International Red Cross.]

Reconnaissance photographs taken yesterday showed that the destruction in Nagasaki was centered along both sides of the Urakami River, the most important industrial section of this city of 250,000. Nagasaki had a total built-up area of 3.3 square miles, of which .98 of a square mile was in ruins after the new and terribly destructive weapon went off Thursday.

The damage covered two miles

Continued on Page 5, Column 5

ALLIES MAP REPLY

Truman Is Said to Favor Retention of Hirohito as Spiritual Leader

END BELIEVED NEAR

Pleas Based on Potsdam and 'Understanding' Emperor Will Stay

Special to THE NEW YORK TIMES.

WASHINGTON, Aug. 10—The war with Japan was rapidly drawing to a close tonight. An offer from Japan today to accept the Potsdam surrender ultimatum and her request for clarification on the status of Emperor Hirohito was being studied by the United States, Great Britain, the Soviet Union and China.

Discussions at the White House between President Truman and his Cabinet had reached a point tonight where it can be said that this Government will not insist as an armistice condition that the Japanese rid themselves of Hirohito or that he be brought immediately to trial as a war criminal.

Armistice Terms Studied

An agreement between the four powers regarding the exact status of the Emperor in the future remained the chief obstacle to the drafting of an armistice formula after a day of continuous communication between Washington and the Allied capitals of London, Moscow and Chungking.

The only official word on the surrender offer, which came to the State Department in the middle of last night, was issued in a White House statement by President Truman's secretary, Charles G. Ross, as follows:

"Our Government, through its regular diplomatic channels, is in communication with Great Britain, Russia and China regarding the Japanese surrender offer. That is all that can be announced at this time and no further White House statement will be forthcoming today or tonight."

How long it would take the Allied powers to formulate their separate armistice terms and then draw them up in shape for presentation to the Japanese as a joint reply was a matter of conjecture, but if the feverish activity that marked the business day at the White House and the State, War and Navy Departments was any criterion, it should not take very long.

Truman Calls Cabinet

From his desk in the White House executive wing President Truman sent out hurry calls for Secretary of State James F. Byrnes, Secretary of War Henry L. Stimson and Secretary of the Navy James V. Forrestal a few minutes after he arrived at the White House at 8:30 A. M. and the three Cabinet members were on hand before 9 o'clock.

Emerging from the President's office nearly half an hour later, Mr. Byrnes said this Government had not received any official surrender offer from the Japanese Government, but it was learned that a communication containing the proposal was then on its way to his office.

Beyond this negative reply to questions, Mr. Byrnes would say only that this Government would take no action on the Japanese offer to capitulate, if and when one were received, without consultation with the other Allied Governments.

So it went throughout the day. The regular Friday Cabinet session convened and adjourned after lengthy discussion of the problems arising out of the Japanese surrender offer, but the members departed in silence. It had been

Continued on Page 3, Column 1

"All the News That's Fit to Print"

The New York Times.

LATE CITY EDITION
Cloudy, warm; showers this afternoon or evening. Showers tomorrow.
Temperatures Yesterday—Max., 88; Min., 67
Sunrise today, 6:02 A. M.; Sunset, 7:59 P. M.

Section 1

NEWS INDEX, PAGE 41, THIS SECTION

Copyright, 1945, by The New York Times Company.

VOL. XCIV No. 31,977. Entered as Second-Class Matter, Postoffice, New York, N. Y. NEW YORK, SUNDAY, AUGUST 12, 1945. Including Magazine and Book Review. TEN CENTS New York City and Suburban Areas (15c Elsewhere)

ALLIES TO LET HIROHITO REMAIN SUBJECT TO OCCUPATION CHIEF; M'ARTHUR IS SLATED FOR POST

EMPLOYERS, LABOR ASKED TO FIND JOBS MID NEW CUTBACKS

$12,000,000,000 Slash in War Contracts Is Reported—Navy Reduction Is $1,200,000,000

AGENCIES DRIVE SWIFTLY

Snyder Calls on Management and Workers for Unity to Expand Civil Industries

By JOHN H. CRIDER
Special to THE NEW YORK TIMES.

WASHINGTON, Aug. 11—Facing the gigantic task of reconversion much earlier than had been expected, the Administration called today for cooperation of management and labor to keep the problem under control, while the War and Navy Departments were ordering the first of the expected flood of contract terminations. The new terminations were estimated as approaching $4,000,000,000 in value.

[More than $12,000,000,000 in war material cutbacks, coincident with the Japanese movement toward surrender, were reported officially and unofficially today through The Associated Press. Heads of Government agencies received instructions from the White House to keep their post-war programs under wraps until President Truman gives the signal. The purpose of this, it was explained, was to allow coordination of plans of agencies and prevent disclosure before peace was an accomplished fact.]

The Navy Department announced specifically the cancellation of $1,200,000,000 of shipbuilding contracts, stopping work on ninety-five ships, including the carrier Reprisal, under construction at the New York Navy Yard, but John W. Snyder, War Mobilization and Reconversion Director, declared these Navy cutbacks were not the result of the Japanese surrender offer.

While stating that the Army would make "immediately" a sharp reduction in its buying program, Mr. Snyder stressed that the cutbacks resulted "from reviews of procurement programs held over the last few weeks."

It was evident all over the capital city that officials were working feverishly to meet the problem which came to them so much earlier than had been expected and were striving to prove untrue the prediction made ten days ago by the Senate's Mead War Investigating Committee that "should the war with Japan end at an early date we will be in a sorry state economically."

Aim to Avoid Undue Idleness

The problem was to cut down war production gradually so as not to cause undue unemployment, yet rapidly enough to speed the reconversion of the war plants which can shift into civilian production and hire those workers displaced from war jobs. The national economy is now running at an annual production rate of about $200,000,000,000, of which almost half is accounted for by Government war purchases.

A Budget Bureau official estimated that an early surrender by Japan would require a $30,000,000,000 slash in the budget for the current fiscal year.

Mr. Snyder, in a statement, called upon industry and management to "cooperate in this difficult reconversion period." He asked for cooperation in the following ways:

1. Workers displaced by contract cancellations should register themselves immediately with the nearest office of the United States Employment Service.

2. Employers having job oppor-

Continued on Page 38, Column 2

Congress to Return Sept. 4; Recess Cut on Truman Plea

Barkley, After 90-Minute White House Visit, Tells Plan for Call—Lists Five Measures for Preparatory Committee Action

Special to THE NEW YORK TIMES.

WASHINGTON, Aug. 11 — At the request of President Truman, Congress will be called back Sept. 4, about a month earlier than the scheduled Oct. 8 end of the recess. Senator Barkley, majority leader, made this announcement on leaving the White House today after a ninety-minute visit with the President.

In preparation for the reconvening committees will work to make ready for floor action legislation which is regarded as urgent.

Most House members have been away since about July 21, but the Senate did not finish its business until July 28.

The House would be called back into session by its majority leader, Representative McCormack of Massachusetts, Senator Barkley stated.

"The President feels that Congress should reconvene as soon as possible," he declared, "but he realizes there would be no point in bringing the members back if there is no legislation ready to be handled.

"So I am going out now to talk with the committees of the Senate to see what can be done about getting this emergency legislation ready. I think it can be ready by Sept. 4, but I am not prepared to say that definitely."

He listed five measures which he regarded as "emergency legislation" in view of the imminent end of the war with Japan:

1. Amendment of the Social Security laws to raise the unemployment compensation payment to $25 a week for twenty-six weeks. Recommended by President Roosevelt, this is regarded as an essential relief measure for the tem-

Continued on Page 27, Column 4

5,000,000 EXPECTED TO LOSE ARMS JOBS

U. S. Officials Predict Great Unemployment 60 Days After Japanese Surrender

By The Associated Press.

WASHINGTON, Aug. 11—Government officials estimated today that perhaps 5,000,000 munitions workers will lose their jobs within sixty days after Japan surrenders.

This news as peace negotiations continued was in sharp contrast with another home-front prospect —the end of gasoline rationing two or three weeks after V-J Day and elimination of travel restrictions a few months later.

The estimate of the cut in munitions employment, made by qualified officials who asked anonymity, would trim by about 63 per cent the total of around 8,000,000 workers now engaged in war production.

Of the 5,000,000 slated for release, it was said that a great number — perhaps half — would leave the labor market and would not be classed as jobless.

The others would be added to the current unemployment roll to swell the total to around 4,000,000 persons.

How long it will take for the majority of these to be absorbed in civilian production is anybody's guess, the officials said, although they look for openings quickly in peacetime industries.

They said also that no doubt the War Manpower Commission would be called upon for a vigorous pro-

Continued on Page 14, Column 1

RESIST COMMUNISM, HOOVER DEMANDS

In Speech on 71st Birthday He Asks America to Voice Faith in System of Freedom

Special to THE NEW YORK TIMES.

LONG BEACH, Calif., Aug. 11—Asserting that communism was sweeping over Europe and that a form of collectivism was already in evidence here, Herbert Hoover declared today that the time had come for America to reaffirm the heritage of its system of freedom.

"America should again proclaim our faith," he said. "We should proclaim our resolution to hold it. We should cease to apologize for it. Our first post-war purpose should be to restore it."

The former President spoke at the annual picnic of the Iowa Association of Southern California, which honored the seventy-first anniversary of his birth in Iowa, where he lived until he was 10 years old.

Mr. Hoover discussed "a great decision" confronting the people of the Western Hemisphere, "which is fast becoming the last hope of free men."

"Today communism or creeping socialism are sweeping over Europe," he said. "They are beginning in Asia. The causes lie deep in the holocaust of misery from the war, from power politics, from the impulse for any change from the bitter years which have passed, and from the years of propaganda of a new Utopia.

"A score of fascist nations have

Continued on Page 34, Column 5

Study of Baseball 'Color Line' To Be Made by Mayor's Group

Mayor La Guardia announced yesterday that he had mailed letters to ten prominent citizens, including Larry S. MacPhail, president of the New York Yankees, and Branch Rickey, president of the Brooklyn Dodgers, asking them to serve as a committee to make a thorough study of the question of racial discrimination or, as he termed it, "color line" in organized baseball and submit specific recommendations directly to the proper officials of the National and American Baseball Leagues.

In making public the text of his letter to Mr. MacPhail, the Mayor disclosed he was appointing the committee at the request of the Mayor's Committee on Unity, of which Charles E. Hughes Jr. is chairman. This committee was named by the Mayor several years ago as a means of promoting better inter-racial relations.

Others invited by the Mayor to serve on the committee are former Supreme Court Justice Jeremiah T. Mahoney, Daniel E. Higgins of the Board of Education, Edward Lazansky, former presiding justice of the Appellate Division in Brooklyn; Dr. John H. Johnson of the advisory board of the Department of Welfare, Arthur Daley, sports columnist of THE NEW YORK TIMES; Supreme Court Justice Charles S. Colden of Queens, Prof.

Continued on Page 41, Column 1

RUSSIANS DRIVE ON

Add 50 Miles to Gains as Spearheads Smash Closer to Harbin

VASILEVSKY AT HEAD

Veterans Lead 3 Armies in Sweep, Ignoring Surrender Talk

By The Associated Press.

LONDON, Aug. 11—Russian armored spearheads, in lightning fifty-mile advances, burst across the Great Hingan Mountain range in western Manchuria today and broke into the river-cut valleys leading down to the Japanese war arsenal city of Harbin, Moscow announced.

The pile-driving Soviet smashes, which have covered 155 miles in two days, tore through natural Japanese defenses in western Manchuria in disregard of the exchange of peace notes between Japan and the Allied nations.

Moscow's third Japanese war bulletin revealed that three Soviet Far Eastern armies had been thrown into the battle for Manchuria. Veteran commanders of the European Eastern Front led the assault under supreme command of Marshal Alexander M. Vasilevsky, former Red Army Chief of Staff.

Three Armies Bore Deeper

The three tank-tipped armies, breaking into Manchuria at least at five points along the mountainous 2,000-mile frontier, were converging on Harbin from the west, north and east in drives that threatened to cut off Japanese armies in northern Manchuria.

The Soviet advances brought hope of quick liberation to many American prisoner-of-war camps in Manchuria. The Khabarovsk radio called on Red Army men to fight with determination, demanding the "merciless destruction of the enemy."

Japanese resistance varied. In the west, Russian armored columns tore through the Japanese lines without much opposition, but in the heavily wooded, hilly terrain 100 miles northwest of Vladivostok fanatic enemy defenders of the Kwangtung Army held the Rus-

Continued on Page 13, Column 1

JAPANESE GET HINT

Press Points to Gravity of Situation—Bars National Suicide

NEED OF UNITY CITED

Papers and Broadcasts Still Fail to Mention Peace Bid, However

As if to prepare the Japanese people for surrender, the Tokyo newspaper, The Yomiuri Hochi, printed an editorial yesterday saying that "a nation does not have the right to commit suicide" and that "the highest duty of a nation is to continue her existence."

The Tokyo newspaper, the Asahi, also called on all Japanese in an article in its Sunday edition "to do his or her part as His Majesty's subjects in fullest obedience of the august wish of His Majesty" and to maintain national unity "if worst comes to worst," Domei, the Japanese news agency, reported in a broadcast recorded by the Federal Communications Commission.

The Yomiuri Hochi editorial, also quoted by Domei, added:

"There is an ebb and a flow in the tides of the affairs of every nation. Statesmen require the greatest courage when they think not of themselves but of the nation. Individuals must have the courage of self-immolation, but it may be said that a nation does not have the right to commit suicide. Therefore there are times when statesmen must have the courage to save the nation at the cost of their own lives. However, in such cases, political and military farsightedness are necessary."

Japanese Quote Confucius

The editorial recalled the story of the wars between the ancient States of Wu and Yueh 2,500 years ago, in which the leader of Yueh, after having suffered a humiliating defeat, lived a life of hardship and self-deprivation for twenty years and then came back to win a great victory.

The editorial then added: "Confucius said that it is the maintaining of victory and not the winning of it which is difficult."

All Japanese metropolitan newspapers joined editorially in "admit-

Continued on Page 9, Column 1

War News Summarized

SUNDAY, AUGUST 12, 1945

The Allied powers have agreed to the Japanese proposal to surrender on the basis of the Potsdam ultimatum, but on the condition that the Japanese Emperor come under the authority of the Allied Commander in Chief to act as his agent to assure the full accomplishment of the armistice terms. President Truman, in the name of the Allied powers, informed the Japanese that the Emperor's future status must be determined in a free election and that Allied troops would remain in Japan long enough to see that the democratic purposes of the Potsdam ultimatum were accomplished. [1:8.]

General MacArthur was reported designated the Allied Supreme Commander to accept the surrender of Japan. [1:6-7.]

Tokyo newspapers were preparing the people for capitulation, emphasizing the theme that it was the duty of a nation not to commit suicide. [1:5.]

Moscow reported sweeping gains all along the Manchurian front and revealed that Marshal Vasilevsky was in supreme command of the Far Eastern theatre. On the Trans-Baikal front an advance of 155 miles has been made in two days. [1:4; map P. 13.]

Generalissimo Chiang Kai-shek ordered his armies to keep on fighting until the order to cease fire is received. Chinese troops occupied Tsangwu on the road to Canton. [10:3.]

Admiral Nimitz in a communiqué issued Sunday morning Guam time made no mention of further attacks on Japan. He had previously issued orders to all forces under his command to continue attacking the enemy. Five hundred Far East Air Force planes on Friday smashed at the city of Kumamoto on Kyushu, a military supply center. [1:7.]

It was officially revealed that the atomic bomb that erased a third of Nagasaki had a revised destructive function that made the first one, which was used on Hiroshima, obsolete. [28:1.]

The record to date shows that Japanese Kamikaze fliers have sunk twenty United States warships and damaged at least thirty more. [1:6-7.]

General de Gaulle and Foreign Minister Bidault are to come to the United States the last week of this month on invitation from the White House, it was disclosed in Paris. [21:1.]

Prosecutor André Mornet, summing up the State's case against Marshal Pétain, demanded the death penalty. [20:1.]

REPORTED CHOSEN SUPREME COMMANDER

General of the Army Douglas MacArthur

Allied Commander Choice Recognizes U.S. Leadership

By WILLIAM S. WHITE
Special to THE NEW YORK TIMES.

WASHINGTON, Aug. 11—General of the Army Douglas MacArthur, Commander in Chief of United States Army forces in the Pacific, has been designated the Allied Supreme Commander to accept Japan's capitulation when it comes, it was authoritatively indicated today.

The White House announced simply that the representative of the United States and her Allies in this assignment of historic triumph would be "an American" but in other quarters this was expanded with the addition of the general's name.

General MacArthur, it was pointed out, is the senior officer in the Orient, both as to American and Allied forces; he has the longest acquaintance with the Orient among the top commanders and of them all has been engaging the Japanese enemy the longest.

His appointment to act for all the Allies in the surrender as the Supreme Commander suggested that command of the occupying forces probably would be offered to him. He thus would hold in the post-war cleanup period the highest exclusive responsibility granted to an American officer overseas.

The War Department declared itself without official knowledge of the arrangement, which underscored the unquestioned leader-

Continued on Page 4, Column 1

FLEET IS PREPARED TO AID SURRENDER

On War Basis Pending Notice—Heavy Attack on Kyushu Made Friday by FEAF

By ROBERT TRUMBULL
By Wireless to THE NEW YORK TIMES.

GUAM, Sunday, Aug. 12 — In what may have been the final great naval blow at Japan in this war, struck on Thursday and Friday, American and British carrier task forces destroyed or damaged 711 planes on fields of northern Honshu and sunk or damaged ninety-four ships.

Fleet Admiral Chester W. Nimitz, giving revised figures on the two-day strike in his communiqué this morning, made no mention of further action by Admiral William F. Halsey's Third Fleet, which in-

Continued on Page 11, Column 1

50 Ships Smashed by Kamikazes; Craft Once Glutted Repair Yards

By HANSON W. BALDWIN

Japanese suicide weapons in the last months of the war sank at least twenty naval vessels and damaged at least thirty and possibly scores of others. The Kamikazes caused more loss, damage and personnel casualties to the American Navy in the period between the Leyte invasion last October and the present than in any previous period in its history.

During the Okinawa campaign, when our ship damages were at their peak, West Coast shipyards were glutted with ship repairs and some of the worst-damaged vessels were sent to East Coast yards.

Japanese suicide attacks probably were experienced by some ships one or two years ago. But they were not undertaken on a large scale and were unimportant in results achieved until the Leyte invasion. The Japanese Naval Air Force then commenced what it called "body-ramming" tactics with the "special attack" units of the Kamikaze, or "Divine Wind" squadrons, so named for the "divine wind" (typhoon) which, according to Japanese legend, broke up the fleet of Kublai Khan in 1281. The Japanese Army Air Force then undertook the organization of suicide squadrons, and the semi-fanatical, though care-

Continued on Page 32, Column 1

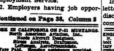

U. S. STATES TERMS

Insists on Free Election in Japan as Provided in Atlantic Charter

REPLY IS DUE TODAY

Truman's Answer Calls for Enemy Guarantee of Captives' Safety

By FELIX BELAIR Jr.
Special to THE NEW YORK TIMES.

WASHINGTON, Aug. 11—President Truman, in replying today on behalf of the United States, Great Britain, Soviet Russia and China to Japan's offer of surrender and her request for a clarification of the status of the Emperor, said the ruler would be permitted to remain on the throne for the time being subject to the commander of the Allied occupation forces.

On behalf of the Big Four the President further insisted that the future of the "Son of Heaven" be determined in a popular election "by the freely expressed will of the Japanese people," in accordance with provisions of the Atlantic Charter and the Potsdam ultimatum and that occupation forces remain in Japan until the democratic purposes of the ultimatum had been achieved.

Reply Made at 10:30 A. M.

The position of the Allied powers was set forth in a note by Secretary of State James F. Byrnes, which was delivered at 10:30 A. M. today to Max Grassli, Chargé d'Affaires of the Swiss Legation.

[*The notes on the Japanese surrender offer appear on Page 3.*]

No return communication had been received by this Government through the Swiss when the Federal establishment shut down for the night and none was expected before tomorrow.

But for all practical political purposes and except for the working out of occupation and formal surrender arrangements, the war with Japan that began the day after her sneak attack on Pearl Harbor on Dec. 7, 1941, was considered at an end.

There was no question of Japan's final answer to President Truman's final statement of the Allied position and not a great deal of interest in it either.

Says Japan Will Accept

As Senator Alben W. Barkley, majority leader, said as he left the White House, it did not make much difference what the Japanese thought of the discredited position of their Emperor nor what they had to say in reply to the President's note.

Senator Tom Connally made the flat prediction that "Japan will

Continued on Page 3, Column 4

Tokyo Communique Reports War Actions

A Japanese Imperial Headquarters communiqué, issued in a Domei agency broadcast at 3:30 P. M. Sunday, Japanese time, 2:30 A. M. Sunday, EWT, gave indication that enemy headquarters then considered the war still in progress.

The broadcast communiqué, recorded by the Federal Communications Commission, said a Japanese submarine unit had attacked an Allied convoy off Okinawa Saturday afternoon, sinking three craft.

The enemy also reported Red Army gains against "fierce fighting" by the Japanese in Manchuria.

"All the News That's Fit to Print"

The New York Times.

LATE CITY EDITION
Warm and humid; thunder showers this afternoon and tomorrow.
Temperatures Yesterday—Max., 85; Min., 69
Sunrise today, 6:03 A. M.; Sunset, 7:57 P. M.

VOL. XCIV..No. 31,978. Entered as Second-Class Matter, Postoffice, New York, N. Y. NEW YORK, MONDAY, AUGUST 13, 1945. THREE CENTS IN NEW YORK CITY

ALLIES TO LOOSE MIGHTY BLOWS ON JAPAN IF SURRENDER IS NOT MADE BY NOON TODAY; CARRIER PLANES RENEW TOKYO ATTACKS

ATTLEE ASSURES U.S. OF COOPERATION ON ATOMIC CONTROL

Pledges That Britain Will Help Guard Bomb's Secret Until It Can Be Fully Regulated

TO AVERT WORLD HAVOC

A Power for Peace Is Seen—Industrial Use of Force Within Decade Predicted

By The Associated Press.

LONDON, Aug. 12—Prime Minister Clement R. Attlee tonight pledged British cooperation with President Truman's proposal that the secret of the atomic bomb be guarded until complete control of the devastating weapon was assured.

The Prime Minister, back at 10 Downing Street after spending Saturday night at his Chequers country place, made this announcement:

"Since I issued the statement on the day of the release of the first atomic bomb a week ago, the vast and terrible effects of this new invention have made themselves felt.

"The last of our enemies has offered to surrender.

"The events of these tremendous days reinforce the words in that statement to the effect that we must pray that the discovery which led to the production of the atomic bomb will be made to conduce to peace among the nations, and that instead of wreaking measureless havoc upon the entire globe, it may become a perennial fountain of world prosperity.

Influence for Peace

"President Truman in his broadcast of Aug. 9 has spoken of the preparation of plans for the future control of this bomb, and of a request to the Congress to cooperate to the end that its production and use may be controlled and that its power may be made an overwhelming influence toward world peace.

"It is the intention of His Majesty's Government to put all their efforts into the promotion of the objects thus foreshadowed and they will lend their full cooperation to that end."

In Bangor, Wales, the National Council of the Independent Labor party, which is not affiliated with the Labor party Government, adopted a resolution declaring that the discovery of the use of atomic energy "could be of the greatest benefit ever vouchsafed to man" in a socialist world.

The resolution said the human race "must go forward to a new order of world socialism if it is to survive." The Independent Labor party has three seats in the new House of Commons.

Industrial Use in Decade Seen

WASHINGTON, Aug. 12 (UP)—Sir James Chadwick, chief British scientist in the atomic bomb project, said today there was a possibility that within about ten years atomic energy could be used for industrial purposes.

The Nobel Prize winner in physics in 1935 also declared that the atomic bomb was not strictly a British-American secret, asserting that any nation could learn the secret in about five years of experimentation, assuming it had access to the necessary raw materials.

"I think this is a very serious point," he said.

Sir James was chief scientific adviser to the British members of the American - British - Canadian policy committee that developed the bomb that wrecked Hiroshima and Nagasaki in Japan.

The work of this committee, he told a press conference, was confined to developing atomic energy for purely military purposes and very little attention was paid to the industrial possibilities. However, he said it would be "nearer

Continued on Page 10, Column 2

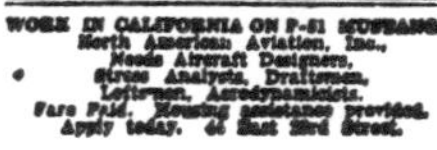

Expect Early End Of Clock War Time

By The United Press.

WASHINGTON, Aug. 12—War time is expected to be an early casualty of peace.

The clocks may go back one hour soon after Congress reconvenes and has time to pass a resolution.

The stepped-up schedule has not been popular with the legislators. Chairman Cannon, of Missouri, of the House Appropriations Committee, said recently that he intended to end it as soon as conditions permitted.

POLICE KILLING LAID TO 3 YOUNG GUNMEN

Gang Rounded Up After Series of Hold-Ups—Two Others Held as Confederates

Three young two-gun hoodlums, one a Navy deserter, who, according to the police, ran riot in a score of hold-ups and burglaries in one of which a policeman was killed, were rounded up early yesterday by Queens detectives. Seized also were two other members of the gang, their alleged driver and a fence who disposed of their loot.

Between July 15 and Aug. 9 the three thugs stole $8,000 in cash and $1,000 worth of jewelry. Specializing in robberies at dining places in Queens, they included forays also in the Bronx and Greenwich, Conn. Living riotously, they went through their money almost as quickly as they stole it. When their women friends, horse-race betting and liquor had taken their toll, they had hardly a dime left.

The three gunmen charged with homicide in the shooting of Patrolman Howard H. Hegerich on the morning of July 30 were: Victor (Vicki) Gelson, 25 years old, of 35-11 103d Street, Corona; Louis A. Boyce, called "Louis the Lip," 23, of 23-10 Steinway Street, Astoria, and Robert Fish, dubbed "Big Fish," 23, of Jamestown, N. Y.

Other Members of Gang

Gelson served a term in Elmira for a hold-up; Boyce was wanted for violating his parole from Sing Sing where he was sent in 1941 to serve four to eight years for assault and robbery, and Fish, a seaman first class, had been picked up in Flushing and was seized by police in the Navy brig at Harts Island.

The two other members of the band were Raffaele Pellegrino, 23, of 103-92 Fifty-second Avenue, Corona, a chauffeur charged with acting in concert, and Joseph Mancuso, 41, of 95-01 Roosevelt Avenue, Corona, charged with receiving stolen goods.

The importance police attached to their quarry was evident when the five were brought to Police Headquarters in Manhattan later in the day. They were placed under continuous guards, powerful lights were focused on their cells so their movements were under observation every minute, and they were stripped of every article that

Continued on Page 32, Column 3

WASHINGTON FACES WAR-END EXODUS OF ITS MIGRANTS

Many on the Swollen Staffs of Bureaus and in Services Are Glad to Return Home

GLAMOR ATTRACTS OTHERS

Emergency Agencies Will Not Expire for Some Time—Their Rules Continue in Effect

By The Associated Press.

WASHINGTON, Aug. 12—"Where do we go from here?"

This question was on the lips of thousands of Federal workers today as they concluded that the end of the war was at hand.

They were not alone with this question. Service men stationed in and around Washington, wives of service men marking time until their return and thousands of others who fall into no particular category were framing the same question.

For many the answer is:

"I'm going home."

Home for many in Washington is any city, town or hamlet in any far corner of the country, but not Washington.

The war, which began almost four years ago for this country, has drawn thousands into the nation's capital, where they came to a job to be done, but in few cases do these migrants consider Washington as their permanent home.

Reconversion at the Capital

Though thousands will be needed for many months to come to keep the wheels of the most complicated Government in the world rolling, others know that with the end of the war many agencies will die. And with them will go the jobs which brought so many people here.

Washington's reconversion program is unique. The city has no large factories, no shipyards, no aircraft plants. Reconversion here means the probable elimination of some wartime agencies, the trimming down of others and the return of numerous non-war bureaus crowded out of the capital and dispersed over the country.

The bustling city will never approach the position of becoming a ghost town, but such things as housing shortages, transportation jams and other discomforts brought on by overcrowding will diminish.

Mixed Feelings on Departure

Before the war, in 1940, Washington had a population of about 663,000. Now about a million persons make their home here. Many more commuting thousands live in near-by Virginia and Maryland.

Not all persons who plan to leave are unhappy about it. A certain Senator's secretary, whose job lasts only for the duration, had this to say:

"Washington is a funny town. It is a place where a person has to

Continued on Page 32, Column 6

DAWN STRIKE MADE

Fleet Goes Into Action While Our Land Planes Hit Kyushu Heavily

ENEMY GETS IN BLOW

Aerial Torpedo Damages Major U. S. Warship in Bay at Okinawa

By ROBERT TRUMBULL

By Wireless to The New York Times.

GUAM, Monday, Aug. 13—Admiral William F. Halsey's carriers are attacking the Tokyo area today (Monday, Japanese time), Fleet Admiral Chester W. Nimitz announced in his communiqué this morning. The attack started at dawn.

[Japanese planes were hitting back at Admiral Halsey's ships off Tokyo more strongly than before, a United Press correspondent with the fleet reported. At least one enemy torpedo plane was shot down early.

[Planes of our Far East Air Forces struck heavily at Kyushu cities on Saturday and continued attacks Sunday and Monday.]

Admiral Nimitz reported that a "major unit" of the Pacific Fleet was torpedoed Sunday night in Buckner Bay off Okinawa, with undetermined damage. The torpedo was dropped by a single low-flying plane.

A major unit would be either a battleship, heavy cruiser, large carrier or converted cruiser-type carrier.

After a respite while Admiral Halsey's Third Fleet with an attached British carrier task force moved southward after a two-day strike Thursday and Friday against northern Honshu, the sea and air war against the Japanese home islands for the Navy, as much as it ever was.

There were few details available this morning of the attack on the United States ship off Okinawa Sunday night. The attack occurred at about 10:45, Okinawa time,

Continued on Page 4, Column 3

THE WHOLE NATION JOINED IN THEIR VIGIL

Waiting outside the gates of the White House for news from Japan

Associated Press Wirephoto

CHIANG TELLS REDS TO OBEY HIS ORDERS

Reasserts Control Over Yenan Armies, Instructed by Own Chiefs to Disarm Japanese

By The United Press.

CHUNGKING, China, Aug. 12—Chinese Communist leaders, who issued instructions to their troops to disarm Japanese forces and occupy areas hitherto held by the enemy, were told by Generalissimo Chiang Kai-shek today to "remain in their posts and wait for further directions."

General Chiang ordered Gen. Chu Teh, commander of the Eighteenth Group Army, and his deputy, Peng Teh-huai, "never again to take independent action."

[Though nominally under com-

Continued on Page 5, Column 2

Russians Swarm Ashore To Win Korean Naval Base

By The Associated Press.

LONDON, Aug. 12—Russian marines, invading Korea under the protecting guns of the Soviet Pacific Fleet, captured the big Japanese naval base of Rashin and the near-by port of Yuki today after having stormed ashore ninety miles southwest of Vladivostok, the Soviet High Command announced. [This was the first Soviet announcement of the invasion of Korea, which Japan reported several days ago.]

The ports fell as Tokyo reported a massive new Russian drive in Manchuria that threatened to trap perhaps 500,000 Japanese troops in China, cutting them off from Manchuria and the Japanese homeland.

The Red Army drive, if substantiated, would threaten to split an estimated 1,500,000 Japanese troops on the Asiatic mainland into two huge pockets.

Headquarters of the Japanese Kwantung Army in Manchuria said that the drive was launched by Soviet troops striking from Outer Mongolia across Inner Mongolia toward the Yellow Sea northeast of Peiping, ancient capital of China.

The Russians were hammering across barren, mountainous terrain toward the road and air-base center of Linsi in southwestern Manchuria, lunging over an old caravan route from Wuchumutsin in Inner Mongolia 150 miles to the north, the enemy said.

Linsi is 240 miles northwest of the Yellow Sea coast. A drive to the coast would isolate the enemy in China. The town, 197 miles from the Chinese frontier, is only seventy miles north of the northernmost rail line linking central China with the Manchurian city of Mukden.

There was no confirmation of the Japanese report from the Soviet High Command, but Moscow's fourth Japanese war bulletin told

Continued on Page 2, Column 2

TOKYO NEWSPAPERS AGAIN URGE UNITY

Call Upon People to Obey Every Command of Emperor in Nation's 'Worst' Crisis

For the second day the Tokyo radio broadcast yesterday excerpts from editorials in the leading Tokyo newspapers stressing the need for national unity and obedience to the commands of the Emperor in what some of the newspapers described as the gravest crisis in Japan's history.

Before the editorials appeared Domei, the official Japanese news agency, broadcast and then retracted an "imperial" communiqué announcing that the Japanese "Army and Navy had begun an offensive along all fronts against enemy Allied armies."

One of the editorials quoted, that in the Yomiuri Hochi, warned the Japanese people that the "gravity of the situation is undoubtedly more than words signify" and called on them to "face the stark reality of the present crisis with the utmost calmness and composure."

"What we should do at this critical moment is to wait for the

Continued on Page 2, Column 4

War News Summarized

MONDAY, AUGUST 13, 1945

A tense world waited in vain yesterday for Japan's expected surrender. As Tokyo delayed its answer to the note by the four Allied Governments, in which it was agreed to permit Emperor Hirohito to retain his throne for the time being provided his authority was subject to that of a supreme Allied commander, the patience of the Allies grew thin. Unless the enemy's surrender is received by noon today, there was every expectation that the full might of the Allies would be unleashed against the harassed enemy. [1:8.]

A false "flash" that Japan had surrendered led to many premature celebrations throughout the United States and Canada last night. [1:6-7.]

A plea for national unity under "the great command from the throne" was the universal theme of gloomy Tokyo broadcasts that emphasized anew that the Japanese were confronted with the gravest crisis in their history. [1:7.] The Emperor's brother, Prince Takamatsu, was lavishly praised. [3:3-4.]

Hostilities continued. Admiral Halsey's powerful Third Fleet sent carrier planes to assault the Tokyo area at dawn Monday, Japanese Time, in the first offensive action against Japan since the Third Fleet broke off a two-day attack on northern Honshu on Friday. The Japanese succeeded in hitting a major American warship at Okinawa with an aerial torpedo. [1:4; map P. 4.]

More than 400 American Army planes under the command of General MacArthur struck targets on the Japanese homeland. The main objective was the Kurume supply and distribution center on Kyushu. [5:1.]

The Red Army also disregarded the apparent imminence of the end of World War II by initiating a new offensive as it sent amphibious forces into Korea. In the first official Russian announcement of the invasion of that Japanese-held territory, Moscow reported that Soviet troops had captured the ports of Yuki and Rashin, twelve and nineteen miles south of the Korean-Siberian border. Meanwhile other Russian armies far to the west smashed completely through the Great Hingan Mountains in their drive toward the major Japanese stronghold of Harbin. [1:6-7; map, P. 2.]

Chinese troops menaced the enemy's escape route up the Kwangsi-Hunan railway by reaching within five miles of the railway city of Tungan. [5:6.]

Generalissimo Chiang Kai-shek ordered Chinese Communist leaders who had issued instructions to their men to disarm Japanese troops and to occupy areas held by the enemy to "remain in their posts and wait for further directions." The Generalissimo condemned "independent action" by the Communist commanders. [1:5.]

Prime Minister Attlee pledged Britain's cooperation to guard the secret of the atomic bomb until complete control and use of it for the maintenance of peace had been assured. [1:1.]

General Eisenhower was the guest of Premier Stalin as the two men, together with high Russian Government dignitaries, stood atop Lenin's tomb in Moscow to watch a spectacular parade of 40,000 men and women athletes in the first mass civilian festival since the start of the war. [1:2-3.]

Eisenhower and Stalin Review Parade of 40,000 in Red Square

By BROOKS ATKINSON

By Wireless to The New York Times.

MOSCOW, Aug. 12—Forty thousand young people representing the entire Soviet Union participated today in a superbly designed and executed spectacle in honor of Premier Stalin and the nation's physical prowess.

It was the first sports day parade since the war against Germany broke out. It demonstrated the untapped human resources behind the Red Army. As the deep-toned bell of the Kremlin clock struck noon, Generalissimo Stalin, in a white uniform with red trim and gold braid, mounted a platform above Lenin's tomb in Red Square with members of the Politburo.

After they had been acclaimed by the crowd, Premier Stalin sent the Red Army's Chief of Staff, Gen. A. E. Antonoff, to invite Gen. Dwight D. Eisenhower; the American Ambassador, W. Averell Harriman, and Maj. Gen. John R. Deans, head of the American military mission, to join him on the reviewing platform. It is believed that they are the first foreigners to have shared with Premier Stalin the honor of reviewing a national spectacle from Russia's national shrine against the Kremlin wall.

They saw a stupendous parade and carnival. Red Square, one of

Continued on Page 6, Column 6

Erroneous 'Flash' of Surrender Starts Many Wild Celebrations

An erroneous news flash, carried to the public by radio, that Japan had accepted the surrender terms touched off wild celebrations in the United States, Canada and elsewhere last night although the report, transmitted over the leased wires of The United Press at 9:34 P. M., was "killed" two minutes later.

Hinting that someone had tampered with its circuits, The United Press announced that, although the message bore a Washington dateline, it had not been transmitted by its bureau there. It said that it had asked the Federal Bureau of Investigation and the Federal Communications Commission to "ascertain who could have cut into the UP's wire system with the intent to disseminate false information."

In addition, Hugh Baillie, president of The United Press, offered a reward of $5,000 for "information leading to the identification and conviction of the person who transmitted the mysterious flash over The UP circuit."

Long after last midnight crowds were still milling about major cities in the United States. They were no longer celebrating, but merely waiting near newsstands for morning papers, to find a full explanation of the erroneous radio report. This was the third major news event related to the war that was marred by a false radio report. The others were the first accounts of D-Day and V-E Day.

In New York and throughout the

Continued on Page 3, Column 6

U. S. IRKED AT DELAY

Truman Stays at Office All Day Vainly Waiting for Japanese Reply

REJECTION IS DOUBTED

Secretary to President Says V-J Day Will Not Come With Acceptance

By LANSING WARREN

Special to The New York Times.

WASHINGTON, Aug. 12—Unless a Japanese surrender, awaited fruitlessly today, has been received in Washington by tomorrow noon there was every prospect that all the pent-up fury of the overwhelming Allied strength, including more atomic bombs, would burst again with inconceivable violence on Japan.

The Allies set no time limit for a reply to their note to Japan but they have checked their assault to allow the enemy to consider the terms, even though fighting has not ceased. Russian forces were reported advancing through Manchuria, and our Third Fleet carrier aircraft attacked military targets around Tokyo today. But no atomic bomb has fallen in the Pacific since the second terrible missile dropped on Nagasaki, and the Allies have reduced the tempo of their blows.

U. S. Patience Running Out

In Washington tonight there was evidence that patience was beginning to run out, and it is understood that without warning the attack may be renewed with such an avalanche of power as the world has never seen.

From Saturday through Sunday Washington and other capitals waited in vain for Japan's reply to the note of Secretary of State James F. Byrnes that had been transmitted with all speed to Tokyo. In it the Allies gave the Japanese Emperor permission to remain, which was the only point the Japanese had raised. Prompt acceptance now is needed to avert the destruction that is poised and may perhaps make the surrender come too late.

At 10:30 P. M. Charles G. Ross, press secretary to the President, called in correspondents to deny formally a report that Japan had surrendered.

Calls Peace Report False

"The President has not announced that Japan has accepted surrender terms from the Allies," said Mr. Ross. "There has been nothing received by the State, War or Navy Departments, the President, or anyone else."

Mr. Ross also told the reporters that President Truman had retired shortly after 10 P. M., with the request that he be called should any word from Japan be received before midnight.

Shortly before midnight Mr. Ross told reporters that the White House was shutting down for the night, and that no news regarding Japanese acceptance of the Allies' surrender terms would be issued from there before 9 A. M. tomorrow.

[At 1:40 A. M. Monday [EWT], the Tokyo radio said that Emperor Hirohito had received Foreign Minister Shigenori Togo for the second time in two days, the Federal Communications Commission reported.

[Soon after FCC engineers heard a Tokyo wireless code station calling a similar post in Switzerland, through which any Tokyo reply would be forwarded.]

When the surrender is received President Truman does not expect to proclaim V-J Day at once, it was officially announced. This must await the formal signature of the armistice conditions that will be presented at once to the Japanese,

Continued on Page 3, Column 2

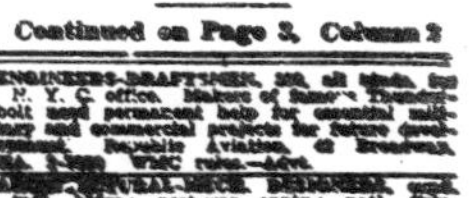

"All the News That's Fit to Print"

The New York Times.

EXTRA

Sunny, continued warm and humid today and tomorrow.

Temperatures Yesterday—Max., 82; Min., 70
Sunrise today, 6:05 A. M.; Sunset, 7:56 P. M.

VOL. XCIV—No. 31,979. Entered as Second-Class Matter, Postoffice, New York, N. Y. NEW YORK, TUESDAY, AUGUST 14, 1945. THREE CENTS NEW YORK CITY

JAPAN DECIDES TO SURRENDER, THE TOKYO RADIO ANNOUNCES AS WE RESUME HEAVY ATTACKS

WPB ACTS TO SPUR BUILDING OF PLANTS FOR CIVILIAN OUTPUT

Krug Reveals Plan to Aid Industrial Expansion and 'Create' Millions of Jobs

BASED ON PRIORITIES HELP

Army Urges Use of Broadcast to Halt War Production on V-J Day and Speed Shifts

Special to The New York Times.

WASHINGTON, Aug. 13—A program to speed the expansion of manufacturing capacity and the construction of new facilities for the production of civilian goods was made known today by the War Production Board. The plan is being furthered through the relaxation of its regulation, L-41, which has sharply limited construction and building for all except the most critical war purposes.

J. A. Krug, WPB chairman, described the move as "a major step toward clearing the way for industrial expansion that will create employment for millions."

Without predicting when the full effect of the relaxation would be felt, he asserted that industry knew we were "nearing the point when we can give the full green light."

"Emphasis is being placed," he declared, "on industrial expansion that will give employment to workers as fast as they are released from war production."

Scope of Priorities Aid

Priorities assistance for materials will be extended to builders of the following three general categories of construction:

1, additions to or alterations of existing facilities for making civilian goods; 2, facilities for production of certain "bottlenecks" materials or components holding up other aspects of production, war or civilian; and 3, facilities needed for essential civilian production.

Industry divisions of the WPB would "give every assistance" in locating supplies of scarce materials and parts, Mr. Krug said.

Other major developments in the task of swinging industry from a total war to a total peace economy were awaiting the official proclamation of Japanese surrender by President Truman.

The WPB "master plan" of reconversion, embodying five points laid down by the President in a letter to Mr. Krug last week, was still a highly secret document, understood to be prefaced by the warning that premature publication of its contents in detail would be subject to terms of the Espionage Act.

Early Releases Expected

This document, however, and another omnibus report by the Office of War Mobilization and Reconversion, "From War to Peace; a Challenge," are expected to be made public immediately upon the official announcement of V-J Day.

With War Department procurement machinery set for a quick halt as soon as the Japanese surrender, Army sources have proposed to the WPB a plan whereby much red tape can be eliminated in reconversion.

The plan, reported to have come from the Army Ordnance Department, is this:

Let the WPB issue preliminary instructions to war contractors advising them that formal notices will not be necessary for the cessation of war production. Then, as soon as V-J Day is proclaimed let Mr. Krug go on the air and broadcast the word for war production to stop.

The flow of raw materials into war production could immediately

Continued on Page 22, Column 5

THE GENERAL AND THE MARSHAL MEET AGAIN

Gen. Dwight D. Eisenhower (right) with Marshal Gregory K. Zhukoff (left) after the commander of American forces in Europe arrived in Moscow. The New York Times (Sovfoto Radiophoto)

ACHESON LEAVING STATE DEPARTMENT

Byrnes Accepts Resignation of His Assistant Secretary on the Latter's Request

By JAMES B. RESTON
Special to The New York Times.

WASHINGTON, Aug. 13—The expected reorganization of the Department of State started today. Dean Acheson, assistant secretary of state, has resigned and his resignation has been accepted by Secretary Byrnes.

The initiative was taken by Mr. Acheson, who had indicated even before the death of President Roosevelt that he wished to leave the department and was said to have rejected an appointment as Solicitor General. Other resignations are expected to be taken up before or soon after the first meeting in London on Sept. 1 of the Foreign Ministers Council of the Big Five.

Mr. Byrnes has in his hands the resignations of all other appointive officials in the department, including those of Under-Secretary and the other five assistant secretaries. These have been at his disposal ever since he took office, but he has been at the Potsdam Conference most of the time since then and he has had pressing tasks since he returned.

Consequently officials who have inquired, since Mr. Byrnes returned, where they stood, have been advised by his aides that the Secretary has not had an opportunity to complete reorganization of his department.

Other Changes Expected

Meanwhile Mr. Acheson sought an interview with Secretary Byrnes and is said to have expressed a desire to be relieved of his responsibilities so that he could return to private law practice. Mr. Byrnes granted the request.

Mr. Acheson has been in charge of the State Department's relations with Congress since the last reorganization of the department several months ago. He held this responsibility throughout the period when revision of reciprocal trade agreements, the Bretton Woods agreement and the United Nations' Charter were under consideration.

As to other and forthcoming changes in the State Department, all that is known at the moment is that Secretary Byrnes has a commission from the President to reorganize the department as he pleases; that Mr. Byrnes intends to reorganize the department at the assistant secretary level and elsewhere and that he has a detailed report which is critical of

Continued on Page 22, Column 2

Japanese Militarist Urged The Destruction of Allies

Before the Tokyo radio announced Japanese acceptance of the Allies' Potsdam terms Field Marshal Prince Norimasa Nashimoto, honorary president of the Japanese Imperial Reservists Association and Chief Priest of the Grand Shrines of Ise, called on the empire's reservists yesterday "ultimately to destroy completely the strong enemy" and "consummate the purpose of this holy war," in a special message beamed to Japanese-occupied territories by Domei, the official Japanese news agency and recorded by the Federal Communications Commission.

A short time later Domei broadcast excerpts from an editorial in the newspaper Tokyo, warning against a "fatal internal split"

Continued on Page 2, Column 8

RED ARMY DEEPENS MANCHURIAN BULGE

Races Toward Harbin, Cuts Rail Line—Russians Land in South Sakhalin, Tokyo Says

By The Associated Press.

LONDON, Aug. 13—Russian armies, lunging toward the arsenal city of Harbin, tore out gains up to twenty-eight miles in Manchuria today and cut a vital Japanese communication line. Tokyo reported a Soviet invasion of Sakhalin Island, which lies twenty-six miles north of the Japanese homeland.

Swift, tank-tipped Soviet thrusts threatened to disrupt the entire Japanese communication system in Manchuria, playing havoc with the enemy's supply and leaving pockets of enemy troops open to encirclement and annihilation.

Japanese broadcasts said that Russian marines had swarmed ashore on Karafuto, Japanese territory on the southern half of Sakhalin Island, and established two beachheads on the west coast in a swift follow-up of the seaborne invasion of Korea. There was no Soviet confirmation.

Moscow's broadcast communiqué announced that Marshal Alexander M. Vasilevsky's five-pronged drive toward Harbin had seized at least twenty-two strong points in converging sweeps into central Manchuria from the west, northwest, north, northeast and east.

The Russians ripped across one of Manchuria's three vital north-south rail lines and threatened another, the 950-mile line linking Dairen and Mukden with extreme northern Manchuria, Moscow's war bulletin disclosed.

The easternmost of Manchuria's north-south lines, running from the Korean port of Seishin to Kiamusze on the Sungari River, was severed when Marshal Kirill A. Meretskoff's First Far Eastern Army captured the rail junction of Linkow, 170 miles northwest of Vladivostok.

Capture of the three-way junction put the Russians 177 miles east of Harbin, great war-produc-

Continued on Page 5, Column 1

B-29'S BOMB AGAIN

Superforts' by Hundreds Attack Honshu—Rail Center First Target

ARSENALS BATTERED

Japanese Suicide Planes Jab at Third Fleet—Kenney Fliers Busy

By The Associated Press.

GUAM, Tuesday, Aug. 14—Superfortresses, already more than 400 strong and growing in numbers steadily, resumed the assault on Japan at noon today in a maximum effort that is still continuing. Fighters from our forward bases escorted some of the strikes.

It could be the greatest onslaught of the war, and gave sharp notice to the procrastinating enemy to make up his mind on his tentative surrender proposals. Three major attacks had been made by mid-afternoon.

After laying off since last Friday, the B-29's lashed out at southern Honshu, ending a period of watchful waiting induced by a conditional peace offer of the enemy—who had not halted his suicide-plane blows.

[Admiral William F. Halsey's American and British carrier planes of our Third Fleet smashed 117 Japanese planes on airfields in the Tokyo area Monday and twenty-one enemy planes that tried to attack the fleet were shot down. Kamikaze planes were striking at the Third Fleet on Tuesday, Japanese broadcasts said.

[Kyushu ports and airfields and ships off southern Japan were battered Sunday in a 600-plane attack by Gen. George C. Kenney's Far East Air Forces.]

The new B-29 attacks, warning

Continued on Page 4, Column 4

Guam Demand Rises For Occupation Map

By Wireless to The New York Times.

GUAM, Aug. 13—Army engineers of a topographic battalion attached to Fleet Admiral Chester W. Nimitz's staff here are being swamped with demands for maps to be used by occupation troops in Japan.

Maps had already been completed for new bombardments of Japan by Admiral William F. Halsey's Third Fleet, it was revealed by the topographic battalion's commander, Lieut. Col. M. C. Shetler of Clinton, Iowa.

TRUMAN MESSAGE DUE AFTER 9 A. M.

President Retires With No Official Word From Japan —No Hint on V-J Day

By The United Press.

WASHINGTON, Tuesday, Aug. 14—Although Tokyo broadcasts reported early today that Japan had accepted the Allied unconditional surrender demand, no Allied confirmation was likely before 9 A. M.

If the enemy reports were true, World War II was over except for the formal signing of surrender documents by the defeated Japanese.

It meant that the Japanese had given up 3 years 8 months and 1 week to the day after their infamy at Pearl Harbor plunged the United States into a two-front war that cost scores of thousands of lives and billions of dollars.

It meant that Japan could retain Emperor Hirohito but that he had to take orders from the Allied Supreme Commander to be named to administer Japan. Gen. Douglas MacArthur was expected by most quarters to be chosen for that role.

President Retired Early

President Truman, who retired early last night when no word had been received from Tokyo, planned to announce Japan's surrender to a nation-wide radio audience when the official word was received.

He will not proclaim V-J Day, however, until after the official surrender papers are signed.

The "lid was on" at the White House until 9 A. M. This meant that nothing was expected from that quarter until later in the morning. Reporters rushed to the White House, however, when the Tokyo broadcasts were received, to be prepared for any eventuality.

There was a possibility that no announcement would be made at 9 A. M. even if the Tokyo reports were true. It was presumed that the Japanese reply was on its way, but it normally requires twelve hours to transmit messages through neutral nations.

The Tokyo reports came as patience with the enemy's long delay in replying was growing thin and as Allied might strove to force Tokyo to a quick decision by unleashing devastating new blows against the already battered and broken enemy homeland.

Attlee at Work Early

LONDON, Aug. 13 (UP)—Prime Minister Attlee arrived at 10 Downing Street early today and a crowd gathered outside in hopes of hearing news of a Japanese surrender.

His only early caller was the Lord President of the Council, Herbert Morrison.

At the Foreign Office, Foreign Minister Ernest Bevin conferred with Alfred Duff Cooper, British Ambassador to Paris.

King George VI will broadcast to the British Empire on the evening of V-J Day, it was officially announced.

In Whitehall it was comparatively quiet. There was no Cabinet meeting.

War News Summarized

TUESDAY, AUGUST 14, 1945

At 2:49 P. M. today Tokyo time (1:49 A. M., EWT), Domei announced that Japan had decided to accept the Allies' surrender terms in the war that she had entered three years eight months and seven days earlier with the sneak attack on Pearl Harbor. Japan's announcement came more than sixty-three hours after the dispatch of the Allies' note setting forth their terms.

The disclosure that meant the end of the Second World War almost six years after it had been begun by Japan's Axis partner, Germany, followed growing American suspicions that the enemy was "stalling." Earlier, Tokyo had declared that the Allies' reply to its surrender offer had been delivered only yesterday morning but this was branded a lie by a Swiss Government spokesman. [All the foregoing, 1:8.]

Official Washington remained silent, however. President Truman will have no statement until at least 9 A. M. [1:6.]

Domei's promise of imminent peace followed by only a few hours its broadcast of a message from Field Marshal Prince Norimasa Nashimoto, held up since Saturday, urging enemy reservists "ultimately to destroy completely the strong enemy." This appeal had lent credence to some observers' belief that there was a serious rift among Japanese factions on the surrender issue. [1:3-4.]

The Allies were continuing their military action even as Domei announced the Government's decision. By mid-afternoon hundreds of B-29's with fighter escort had struck a rail yards, an army arsenal and a naval arsenal on Honshu. More than 600 other planes blasted enemy shipping and rail facilities at Kyushu and a heavy cruiser in Tsushima Strait. [1:4; map, P. 4.]

At dawn on Monday, Japanese time, carrier planes of the United States Third Fleet had smashed at airfields and military installations in the Tokyo area and destroyed or damaged 138 planes. [4:3.]

The Red Army sent five armor-tipped columns thundering through Manchuria on their way to the major Japanese stronghold of Harbin, and gains ranged to twenty-eight miles. The Russians seized at least twenty-two Japanese strong points, including Linkow, 177 miles east of Harbin. Tokyo said that Soviet marines had invaded Karafuto, Japanese-held southern half of Sakhalin Island. [1:3; map P. 5.]

Some time before Domei's announcement, it was reported, Japanese troops in Chekiang Province, south of Shanghai, had ceased firing after the first disclosure of their Government's surrender offer and had begun negotiating their capitulation. [8:3.]

Chungking is believed to be making plans to outwit the Communists by a rapid reoccupation of Japanese-held China, possibly with airborne troops, when Japan surrenders. Meanwhile Chinese Communist leaders hit back at Generalissimo Chiang Kai-shek and charged that his order to Communist General Chu Teh, condemning "independent action" by the Communists in accepting Japanese surrenders, indicated that he was plotting a civil war in china. [10:6.]

POTSDAM TERMS ACCEPTED, DOMEI SAYS

'An Imperial Message Is Forthcoming Soon,' Official News Agency Reports in Broadcast at 1:49 A. M.

DISCLOSES LONG SESSION BY CABINET

FCC Monitors Hear Code Dispatch Being Sent by Japanese to Switzerland—Washington Began to Suspect 'Stalling'

The Japanese Government has accepted the Allies' surrender formula embodied in the note dispatched to Tokyo by the United States, Domei, the Japanese news agency, said today [Tuesday] in a wireless dispatch recorded by the Federal Communications Commission.

"It is learned that an Imperial message accepting the Potsdam proclamation is forthcoming soon," the English-language wireless dispatch said, as directed to the American zone.

The Domei wireless dispatch was transmitted at 1:49 A. M., Eastern War Time, today.

Although the dispatch did not flatly say that Japan had surrendered and that the action was final, the fact that Domei put out such a statement indicated that that was in fact the case. Domei is controlled by the Japanese Government.

The statement was repeated a few moments later.

No other information was forthcoming from the Japanese immediately.

The Domei dispatch announcing that an Imperial message accepting surrender terms was expected soon followed by thirty-eight minutes another Domei dispatch reporting that the Japanese Government was deliberating on Allied surrender terms and that its reply probably would be available as soon as "legal procedures" had been completed.

Message to Switzerland Heard

The earlier Domei broadcast said:

"Immediately upon receipt of the Allied reply yesterday, Monday, the Japanese Government started deliberations upon its terms, which as a Reuter diplomatic correspondent pointed out 'created a very serious problem' for the Japanese people. The Cabinet has been in continuous session until late Monday night. It is understood the Japanese Government's reply probably will be available any time as soon as legal procedure is completed."

FCC engineers reported about the same time that a Tokyo code station had been sending long code messages to Switzerland since 12:48 A. M., Eastern war time, today.

Japanese press and radio transmissions did not elaborate immediately on the one-sentence Domei report. FCC monitors reported that the Tokyo radio in a Japanese-language broadcast to occupied Asia at 2 A. M. [EWT] had made no mention of surrender, indicating that the Japanese people in occupied territory were still being kept in the dark on the negotiations.

They also reported that there was no indication that the Japanese people in the home islands had been told of the surrender offer and the Allies' reply.

At the White House it was said that President Truman was asleep and that there was no intention of waking him up to inform him of the report from the Tokyo radio.

Cheering Greets Report in Guam

GUAM, Tuesday, Aug. 14 (AP)—The communications room of United States Pacific Fleet headquarters flashed word over the Guam radio today that the Tokyo radio had reported Japan had accepted the Potsdam ultimatum to surrender. There was no announcement as to where the broadcast was picked up.

Waves of cheering were heard as the Guam radio broke into a regular broadcast to make the announcement at 3:58 P. M. Guam time [1:58 A. M., EWT].

The news came as the United States Third Fleet—most powerful naval force in the world—was patroling just off Japan. It was believed that the fleet would head for Japanese ports shortly.

Capital Awaited Reply All Day

By FELIX BELAIR Jr.
Special to The New York Times.

WASHINGTON, Aug. 13—President Truman, as spokesman for the Allied powers, waited all day for Japan's acceptance of his surrender terms.

Some officials versed in the exactions of international law were beginning to suspect bad faith by the enemy in first requesting a clarification of the status of the Emperor in the note accepting the terms of the Potsdam Declaration.

In the long absence of word from the Japanese Government, therefore, they could only speculate that the delay was being caused by a Cabinet crisis or other machinations calculated to save face, probably through the

Continued on Page 3, Column 2

"All the News That's Fit to Print"

The New York Times.

LATE CITY EDITION
Thunderstorms, warm, humid; clear and cooler tonight. Fair tomorrow.
Temperatures Yesterday—Max., 84; Min., 71
Sunrise today, 6:06 A. M.; Sunset, 7:55 P. M.

VOL. XCIV..No. 31,980. Entered as Second-Class Matter, Postoffice, New York, N. Y. NEW YORK, WEDNESDAY, AUGUST 15, 1945. THREE CENTS IN NEW YORK CITY

JAPAN SURRENDERS, END OF WAR! EMPEROR ACCEPTS ALLIED RULE; M'ARTHUR SUPREME COMMANDER; OUR MANPOWER CURBS VOIDED

HIRING MADE LOCAL

Communities, Labor and Management Will Unite Efforts

6,000,000 AFFECTED

Draft Quotas Cut, Services to Drop 5,500,000 in 18 Months

By LEWIS WOOD
Special to THE NEW YORK TIMES.

WASHINGTON, Aug. 14—All manpower controls over employers and workers were abolished tonight, the War Manpower Commission announced, enabling employers to hire men where and when they pleased.

The end of the war threw on the Government the difficult task of trying to readjust perhaps 6,000,000 war workers into new employment. Nevertheless, the WMC said, all its facilities would be used to help workers find new places, with preference going to veterans, displaced migratory war workers and other preferentials.

At the same time President Truman announced that monthly inductions into the Army would be immediately slashed from 80,000 to 50,000, and said 5,000,00 to 5,500,000 men probably would be released from the service within the next year or eighteen months.

The induction rate of 50,000 monthly, the President said, would be sufficient to maintain the occupation forces and allow men of long service overseas to return to their homes.

Under the WMC program, the manpower controls are to be lifted at once and voluntary community action to hurry reconversion will be substituted. In every community, the number of displaced workers and returning veterans will be ascertained in cooperation with local management-labor groups. Full facilities of the United States Employment Service offices will be made available to all employers. Service for veterans will be enlarged.

The WMC program embraced these seven points:

1. All manpower controls are to be lifted at once and in their place voluntary community action to

Continued on Page 13, Column 3

Hirohito on Radio; Minister Ends Life

The Japanese Domei agency said at 11 o'clock last night that Emperor Hirohito had been "graciously pleased to personally read an imperial rescript accepting the Potsdam declaration."

The Domei English-language wireless dispatch, directed to the United States and recorded by the Federal Communications Commission, said that the Emperor had read the rescript over a nation-wide broadcast at noon Wednesday, Tokyo time.

Previously Domei had reported that weeping people had gathered before the Imperial Palace and "bowed to the very ground" in shame.

Japanese War Minister Korechika Anami committed suicide, Domei reported this morning. The wireless dispatch, directed to the American zone, said Anami had taken his life at his "official residence" to "atone for his failure in accomplishing his duties as His Majesty's Minister."

A complete story appears on Page 3.

Third Fleet Fells 5 Planes Since End

By The Associated Press.

GUAM, Wednesday, Aug. 15—Japanese aircraft are approaching the Pacific Fleet off Tokyo and are being shot down, Admiral Chester W. Nimitz announced today.

Five enemy planes have been destroyed since noon today, Japanese time, or 11 P. M. EWT.

Gen. Douglas MacArthur has been requested to tell the Japanese that American defense measures require the Third Fleet to destroy any Japanese planes approaching United States warships.

GUAM, Wednesday, Aug. 15 (U.P.)—When Admiral Halsey received word of Japan's capitulation today, he sent this message to his fliers:

"It looks like the war is over, but if any enemy planes appear shoot them down in friendly fashion."

SECRETS OF RADAR GIVEN TO WORLD

Its Role in War and Uses for Peacetime Revealed in Washington and London

By WILLIAM S. WHITE
Special to THE NEW YORK TIMES.

WASHINGTON, Aug. 14—The great drama of radar, the war's most powerful "secret weapon" until the atomic bomb was devised, was displayed before a world audience today.

The Joint Board on Scientific Information Policy permitted the Office of Scientific Research and Development, the War Department and the Navy Department to tell the story of a device of which millions had known vaguely for two years, a device which at least three times stood between survival or defeat by the Axis powers for the United States and Great Britain.

It was radar, short for "radio detection and range," that helped the small surviving British air squadrons to beat the German blitz of 1940, thus not only saving the home islands but preserving them as the essential Anglo-American base from which the continental invasion went forward on June 6, 1944.

It was radar, which "sees through the heaviest fog and the blackest night," that more than any other factor broke in 1942 the German submarine attack in the Atlantic which was threatening to starve and strangle the British homeland.

And it was radar that permitted the remnants of the blasted United States Pacific Fleet to stay alive

Continued on Page 14, Column 3

ALL CITY 'LETS GO'

Hundreds of Thousands Roar Joy After Victory Flash Is Received

TIMES SQ. IS JAMMED

Police Estimate Crowd in Area at 2,000,000—Din Overwhelming

By ALEXANDER FEINBERG

Five days of waiting, of rumor, intimation, fact, distortion—five agonizing days following the first indication of a Japanese surrender, days of alternately rising hopes and fears—came to an end for New York, as for the nation and the world, a moment or two after seven o'clock last night. And the metropolis exploded its emotions, harnessed for the most part during the day, with atomic force.

"Official — Truman announces Japanese surrender."

These were the magic words, flashed on the moving electric sign of the Times Tower, at 7:03 P. M. that touched off an unparalleled demonstration in Times Square, packed with half a million persons.

The victory roar that greeted the announcement beat upon the eardrums until it numbed the senses. For twenty minutes wave after wave of that joyous roar surged forth.

Restraint was thrown to the winds. Those in the crowds in the streets tossed hats, boxes and flags into the air. From those leaning perilously out of the windows of office buildings and hotels came a shower of paper, confetti, streamers. Men and women embraced—there were no strangers in New York yesterday. Some were hilarious, others cried softly.

By 7:30 P. M. the crowd in the Square had risen to 750,000 persons; by 8:45 it had swelled to 800,000 and the number continued to rise. People were packed solidly between Forty-third Street and Forty-fifth Street. Individual movement was virtually impossible; one moved not in the crowd but with it.

At 10 P. M. Chief Inspector John J. O'Connell estimated that 2,000,000 persons were in the Times Square area from Fortieth to Fifty-second Street, between Sixth and Eighth Avenues. This constitutes an all-time record, police officials said. At that hour people were still pouring into the Square from subways, buses and on foot.

Those at the north end of the

Continued on Page 5, Column 1

Two-Day Holiday Is Proclaimed; Stores, Banks Close Here Today

By The Associated Press.

WASHINGTON, Aug. 14—Tomorrow and Thursday are days off for Government workers and holidays for pay purposes for workers in general.

And V-J Day, when it comes, will be a premium pay day, too.

President Truman announced both rulings tonight.

He directed agency heads throughout the Government to cut their forces down to a bare skeleton staff Aug. 15 and 16 and not to charge the two days against the employes' annual leave. He said it was in "inadequate" recognition of the four-year efforts on "one of the hardest working groups of war workers."

For other workers under wage control, Wednesday and Thursday count like Christmas and the few other accepted holidays for purposes of overtime pay and in figuring the number of days worked in a week. Many employers already have obtained approval for regular time pay to workers who take the day off.

Postal service for the next two days will "approximate holiday service," the Postoffice Department said.

Local postmasters will have wide discretion in carrying out the President's wishes, it was indicated, and those postal employes required to work tomorrow and next day will have compensating time off at a later date.

It was presumed, but not specifically stated, that Government workers generally will be off on V-J Day, too.

The White House said that the next two days are to be regarded as legal holidays.

Preston Delano, Controller of the

Continued on Page 6, Column 7

PRESIDENT ANNOUNCING SURRENDER OF JAPAN

Mr. Truman reading the message in the White House. Seated are Admiral William D. Leahy, Secretary of State James F. Byrnes and former Secretary of State Cordell Hull. Standing (left to right) are Maj. Gen. Philip Fleming, head of the Federal Works Administration; William H. Davis, Economic Stabilizer; John W. Snyder, Reconversion Director; James Forrestal, Secretary of the Navy; Fred Vinson, Secretary of the Treasury; Tom Clark, Attorney General, and Lewis Schwellenbach, Secretary of Labor. Associated Press Wirephoto

PETAIN CONVICTED, SENTENCED TO DIE

Jurors Recommend Clemency Because of His Age—Long Indictment Upheld

By G. H. ARCHAMBAULT
By Wireless to THE NEW YORK TIMES.

PARIS, Wednesday, Aug. 15—Marshal Henri-Philippe Pétain was convicted at 4:15 A. M. today of intelligence with the enemy and sentenced to death. Because of his age—the former head of the Vichy regime is 89—the jury expressed the hope that the death sentence might not be carried out.

Guards had to arouse Pétain in

Continued on Page 15, Column 5

Terms Will Reduce Japan To Kingdom Perry Visited

By JAMES B. RESTON
Special to THE NEW YORK TIMES.

WASHINGTON, Aug. 14—The Allied terms of surrender will not only demobilize and demilitarize Japan but also deprive her of 80 per cent of the territory and nearly one-third of the population she held when she attacked Pearl Harbor. Thus these terms, already approved by President Truman and our major Allies, will not only destroy the vast empire she conquered in the first eighteen months of this war but also reduce her to little more than the territory she occupied when Commodore Perry introduced her to the western world in 1853.

The main terms of surrender, as

Continued on Page 11, Column 2

TREATY WITH CHINA SIGNED IN MOSCOW

Complete Agreement Reached With Chungking on All Points at Issue, Russians Say

By Cable to THE NEW YORK TIMES.

LONDON, Aug. 14—The Soviet Union and China have signed a treaty of friendship and alliance, the Moscow radio announced tonight, and have reached "full agreement on all other questions of common interest."

The broadcast said the treaty and "other agreements" would be published shortly after they had been ratified by the two countries.

These are the first fruits of the talks that have been proceeding in

Continued on Page 6, Column 3

World News Summarized

WEDNESDAY, AUGUST 15, 1945

World War II became a page in history last night.

President Truman announced at 7 P. M. that he had received the Japanese reply to the Allied note of last Saturday and that he deemed it full acceptance of the Potsdam declaration of July 26. The Chief Executive said that the Japanese surrender would be made to Gen. Douglas MacArthur in his capacity as Supreme Allied Commander in Chief. Allied military commanders were ordered to stop fighting, but the proclamation of V-J Day will await the signing of the peace treaties. [1:7-8.]

Simultaneously with the President's announcement, Admiral Nimitz flashed "cease fire" orders to all units under his command. [8:3-4.]

The official announcement that the Japanese sneak attack on Pearl Harbor had resulted three years and 250 days later in the inglorious end of the Japanese Empire touched off unrestrained celebrations throughout the Allied world. Here in New York the flash on the moving electric sign on the Times Tower, "Official—Truman announces Japanese surrender," signaled a wild demonstration. [1:3.]

Emperor Hirohito announced the Japanese surrender to his people in his first broadcast to the nation. Weeping Japanese gathered outside the Emperor's palace to bow to the ground in their shame because their "efforts were not enough." [3:2.]

The fury of Allied military might continued to strike the Japanese up to the very last. Even as the Tokyo radio announced that the Japanese reply to the Allied note of Saturday was on its way, our Superfortresses were winging from the Marianas to the Japanese homeland. More than 1,000 planes struck Honshu with 6,000 tons of bombs in a fourteen-hour assault ending early yesterday. [8:1.]

In the midst of rejoicing it was disclosed that the heavy cruiser Indianapolis had been sunk, presumably by an enemy submarine, shortly after she had delivered an atomic bomb cargo to Guam. All men aboard were casualties. [1:6-7.]

The Red Army unleashed fierce new attacks. Russian armored forces raced ninety-three miles unchecked across western Manchuria toward Harbin and other Soviet columns scored new gains all along the 2,300-mile front. [8:6; Pacific area map P. 8.]

The Soviet Union signed "a treaty of friendship and alliance" with China after an agreement had been reached between the two nations on all questions of common interest. [1:6.]

Chinese Communists informed the Generalissimo that they refused to accept his command to remain at their posts. [6:1.]

A French jury sentenced Marshal Pétain to death. [1:4.]

Cruiser Sunk, 1,196 Casualties; Took Atom Bomb Cargo to Guam

Special to THE NEW YORK TIMES.

WASHINGTON, Aug. 14—The American heavy cruiser Indianapolis was sunk by enemy action in the Philippine Sea with 1,196 casualties, every man aboard, the Navy announced today.

The 9,950-ton ship left San Francisco on July 16 on a special, high-speed run to deliver essential atomic bomb materials to Guam. The cargo was delivered. The cruiser was lost after having left Guam.

The sinking, which took one of the Navy's heaviest tolls of lives since Pearl Harbor, was disclosed a few minutes before President Truman announced Japan's surrender.

Casualties included five Navy dead, including one officer; 845 Navy missing, including sixty-three officers; 307 Navy wounded, including fifteen officers; thirty Marine missing, including two officers, and nine enlisted Marine wounded. Next of kin have been notified.

The skipper, Capt. Charles B. McVay 3d, 47, of Washington, was wounded.

The Navy Department also reported for the first time that in a previous action on March 31 the Indianapolis, flagship of the Fifth Fleet, was damaged by a suicide plane off Okinawa. She had been at the Mare Island, Calif., Navy

Continued on Page 10, Column 6

YIELDING UNQUALIFIED, TRUMAN SAYS

Japan Is Told to Order End of Hostilities, Notify Allied Supreme Commander and Send Emissaries to Him

MAC ARTHUR TO RECEIVE SURRENDER

Formal Proclamation of V-J Day Awaits Signing of Those Articles—Cease-Fire Order Given to the Allied Forces

By ARTHUR KROCK
Special to THE NEW YORK TIMES.

WASHINGTON, Aug. 14—Japan today unconditionally surrendered the hemispheric empire taken by force and held almost intact for more than two years against the rising power of the United States and its Allies in the Pacific war.

The bloody dream of the Japanese military caste vanished in the text of a note to the Four Powers accepting the terms of the Potsdam Declaration of July 26, 1945, which amplified the Cairo Declaration of 1943.

Like the previous items in the surrender correspondence, today's Japanese document was forwarded through the Swiss Foreign Office at Berne and the Swiss Legation in Washington. The note of total capitulation was delivered to the State Department by the Legation Charge d'Affaires at 6:10 P. M., after the third and most anxious day of waiting on Tokyo, the anxiety intensified by several premature or false reports of the finale of World War II.

Orders Given to the Japanese

The Department responded with a note to Tokyo through the same channel, ordering the immediate end of hostilities by the Japanese, requiring that the Supreme Allied Commander—who, the President announced, will be Gen. Douglas MacArthur—be notified of the date and hour of the order, and instructing that emissaries of Japan be sent to him at once—at the time and place selected by him—"with full information of the disposition of the Japanese forces and commanders."

President Truman summoned a special press conference in the Executive offices at 7 P. M. He handed to the reporters three texts.

The first—the only one he read aloud—was that he had received the Japanese note and deemed it full acceptance of the Potsdam Declaration, containing no qualification whatsoever; that arrangements for the formal signing of the peace would be made for the "earliest possible moment;" that the Japanese surrender would be made to General MacArthur in his capacity as Supreme Allied Commander in Chief; that Allied military commanders had been instructed to cease hostilities, but that the formal proclamation of V-J Day must await the formal signing.

The text ended with the Japanese note, in which the Four Powers (the United States, Great Britain, China and Russia) were officially informed that the Emperor of Japan had issued an imperial rescript of surrender, was prepared to guarantee the necessary signatures to the terms as prescribed by the Allies, and had instructed all his commanders to cease active operations, to surrender all

Continued on Page 2, Column 3

MacArthur Begins Orders to Hirohito

By Wireless to THE NEW YORK TIMES.

MANILA, Wednesday, Aug. 15—Gen. Douglas MacArthur in his first action as Allied Supreme Commander today directed Emperor Hirohito and the Japanese Government to furnish a radio station in the Tokyo area for "continuous use in handling radio communications between this headquarters and your headquarters." The message, sent in the clear, called for "the earliest practicable" arrangements to end hostilities.

"All the News That's Fit to Print"

The New York Times.

LATE CITY EDITION
Clearing early today; cooler. Clear and cool tomorrow.
Temperatures Yesterday—Max., 88; Min., 72
Sunrise today, 6:33 A. M.; Sunset, 7:28 P. M.

Section 1

NEWS INDEX, PAGE 33, THIS SECTION

Copyright, 1945, by The New York Times Company.

VOL. XCIV..No. 31,998. Entered as Second-Class Matter, Postoffice, New York, N. Y. NEW YORK, SUNDAY, SEPTEMBER 2, 1945. Including Magazine and Book Review. TEN CENTS New York City and Suburban Areas (15c Elsewhere)

JAPAN SURRENDERS TO ALLIES, SIGNS RIGID TERMS ON WARSHIP; TRUMAN SETS TODAY AS V-J DAY

HOLIDAY TRAFFIC NEAR 1941 LEVEL; 'GAS' IS PLENTIFUL

Exodus From City Is Greatest Since Pre-War Days but Congestion Is Avoided

GOOD WEATHER PROMISED

Near-by Resorts Do Capacity Business—3 Persons Die in Queens Accidents

America's millions, deprived since 1941 of the chance to cruise the highways of their nation, hit the road in traditional Labor Day week-end style yesterday.

There was a plentiful supply of gasoline, the sun shone warm out of blue skies, and everyone felt free from war worries. This combined to roll up traffic that continued heavy all day.

New York City's heat-ridden population took to car, train, bus and plane. The exodus to near-by mountain and seashore resorts was the greatest since that of 1941.

The weather formed a perfect lure. Not even the thunder showers predicted by the Weather Bureau for late afternoon took place. Today's prediction is for clearing weather early, followed by cooler, with the highest temperature around 80 degrees, and with fresh to strong northwest winds. A clear and cool Monday is forecast by the bureau. The temperature yesterday reached 88 degrees at 3:30 P. M. with the humidity at 52 per cent. The all-time high for the date was set in 1924 with 92.5 degrees and the low in 1872 with 51.

Many Cars Come Into City

Travel in the city was two-way. As cars streamed out of the city over bridges, on ferries and through tunnels, out-of-towners poured in. The main idea for Labor Day seemed to be change of scenery.

Thousands of automobiles, many of them looking as though they had just been taken off the jacks for the first time in years, formed a continuous procession along the main highways leading up-State, out on Long Island and to the South Jersey shore.

The Port of New York Authority reported that 69,400 automobiles had crossed the George Washington Bridge into New Jersey. Forty-five thousand cars passed through the Holland Tunnel during the sixteen hours preceding 6 o'clock last night. Lincoln Tunnel police said traffic was heavier than usual.

Few serious accidents were reported. "Maybe it's because the cars just don't have the pep," remarked a Westchester County parkway policeman.

Sights along the parkways bore out his contention. Many cars became pathetically silent as their drivers resignedly hauled them over to the side of the road to patch up tires or to fume over engine repairs.

Gasoline Supplies Abundant

Assured of as much gasoline as they wanted, motorists traveled leisurely and did not cause congestion. Filling station pumps received their heaviest workout in years. Station operators estimated that demands for gasoline ranged from 10 to 30 per cent over last week-end, but they reported there was no difficulty in obtaining supplies.

The Cities Service Oil Company said it was having difficulty in meeting orders for premium gasoline, ordinarily accounting for 25 per cent of sales, as the supply was limited, but no company reported shortages of non-premium gasoline. No motorist was forced to stay in town because of lack of fuel.

Trains, buses and airlines were crowded, as they have been all through the war. The airlines re-

Continued on Page 30, Column 2

Times Sq. Takes V-J News Quietly

Times Square throngs, which had greeted Japanese capitulation explosively last month, took the formal signing of terms in much calmer fashion last night.

Two hundred policemen, including twenty-five mounted patrolmen, who had been assigned to the area in case of another outburst of feeling, reported that the street crowds took the flashing of the bulletin from Times Tower at 10:04 P. M. with a few cheers and good-natured remarks, and did not attempt to start a celebration.

In numbers the crowd was no larger than an average Saturday night, and of the persons present perhaps half or more were out-of-town visitors here for the Labor Day week-end, the police estimated. Other parts of the city were similarly quiet.

Mayor La Guardia had said earlier that the people "have had their big time and are satisfied." He decided not to hold a celebration in Central Park today as had been planned.

PRESIDENT STRESSES LABOR DAY OF PEACE

But He Warns That After Six Holidays of Hostilities Great New Problems Lie Ahead

Special to THE NEW YORK TIMES.

WASHINGTON, Sept. 1—President Truman hailed the first Labor Day of peace in six years today and declared a grateful world would always remember the workers of all free nations for their contribution to victory.

Secretary Forrestal and J. A. Krug, chairman of the War Production Board, also lauded the men and women of labor, and Philip Murray, chairman of the Congress of Industrial Organizations, told a radio audience that America's vast war plant must be put to work on peacetime products which would give prosperity unlimited to this country.

Mr. Truman's statement said that six years ago today the workers of the United States, and of the world, awoke to a Labor Day in a world at war, and added:

"We in the United States had two years of grace, but the issue was squarely joined at that hour, as we now know. There was to be no peace until tyranny had been outlawed.

"Today we stand on the threshold of a new world. We must do our part in making this world what it should be, a world in which the bigotries of race and class and creed shall not be permitted to warp the souls of men.

"We enter upon an era of great problems, but to live is to face problems. Our men and women did not falter in the task of saving freedom. They will not falter now in the task of making freedom

Continued on Page 24, Column 3

HAILS ERA OF PEACE

President Calls On U.S. to Stride On Toward a World of Good-Will

SALUTES HEROIC DEAD

Cautions Jubilant Nation Hard Jobs Ahead Need Same Zeal as War

Text of the President's address proclaiming V-J Day, P. 4.

By WILLIAM S. WHITE
Special to THE NEW YORK TIMES.

WASHINGTON, Sept. 1—President Truman, in remembrance of all who have fallen and in an appeal to all Americans to go forward now in hope and fraternity toward "a new and better world of peace and international good-will," tonight solemnly proclaimed tomorrow to be V-J Day.

The moment that he began to speak was, in the official and historical sense, the first moment of peace this country had known since a December day nearly four years ago, when, at a sudden, a harsh and an incredible blow the whole of the Pacific world went into flames.

Into the human calendar of great American holidays, like the Fourth of July and the Eleventh of November, the President thus entered another date, the Second of September, although it does not technically signify the end of the "duration" and will have no basis as a legal end of the war. The termination of hostilities, for purposes of computing military service, for setting the limit to war agencies and for all other like formalities, will be set only by final decision of Congress.

Japanese Surrender Signaled

But Mr. Truman's speech was a speech to the heart of a country that had had the skill to make the atomic bomb and could now "use the same skill and energy and determination to overcome all the difficulties ahead," rather than to the keepers of its books of law.

It was notice from the White House, so long awaited, that nearly four years of war, a struggle of sacrificial grandeur such as the United States had never known, had at last come to an end, and that the terrible ledger opened at Pearl Harbor had now been balanced and closed.

The President spoke in this mood, a mood of valedictory and of dedication, as he proclaimed "this . . . victory of more than arms alone . . . this . . . victory of liberty over tyranny." He had just received the signal from across the world that the Japanese had signed, aboard the great battleship Missouri, the last, humiliat-

Continued on Page 4, Column 1

Public Gets Big Army Food Stocks; Whipping Cream Is Freed of Bans

Special to THE NEW YORK TIMES.

WASHINGTON, Sept. 1—The national food situation continued its steady improvement today as the Department of Agriculture, with four orders, increased the supplies of butter, canned salmon and ice cream and signalled the return of whipping cream.

This action was a direct consequence of the sharp reduction of military requirements of these foods. With the discontinuance of butter purchases by the armed forces, the Department explained, it is now possible to revoke the limitations on the sale of heavy cream and the use of butter fat in the production of all frozen desserts. Both these rulings will make whipping cream and ice cream of a higher butter fat content readily available.

In a simultaneous direction, the agency ordered released for civilian use all butter currently held by creameries and receivers for the armed forces and other Government buyers. Although as much as 20,000,000 pounds of butter may be returned to civilian consumers under this ruling, ration values will not be changed, it was indicated.

"At the time ration point values were established for September, the Office of Price Administration recognized the possibility of these

Continued on Page 33, Column 1

JAPANESE FOREIGN MINISTER SIGNING SURRENDER ARTICLES

Mamoru Shigemitsu (right, seated), on behalf of Emperor Hirohito, affixes his signature to document as Gen. Douglas MacArthur (left) and Lieut. Gen. Richard K. Sutherland (center) look on during ceremony aboard the Missouri in Tokyo Bay.

Associated Press Wirephoto (via Navy Radio from U. S. S. Iowa)

BYRNES FORESEES A PEACEFUL JAPAN

Says People Are Expected to Force Development—World Amity Vital, Hull Warns

Special to THE NEW YORK TIMES.

WASHINGTON, Sept. 1—Secretary of State James F. Byrnes declared tonight that with Japan's surrender we have entered the second phase of our war—"what might be called the spiritual disarmament of that nation, to make them want peace instead of wanting war."

The intention of this Govern-

Continued on Page 5, Column 1

Japan's Surrender Ordered Over Militarist Opposition

By FRANK L. KLUCKHOHN
By Wireless to THE NEW YORK TIMES.

TOKYO, Sept. 1—In the rubble of this once-proud imperial capital the story of how the Japanese Army opposed the surrender and how the Emperor made the final decision to capitulate after having heard the opinions of all his advisers, and how War Minister Korechika Anami had committed suicide was unfolded today by one of a handful of those in a position to know without bias what occurred.

It was also learned how the Japanese reacted step by step to wartime developments and how propaganda that Japan could win had been continued to the last moment, thus leaving the industrious long-

Continued on Page 7, Column 1

U. S. CHIEFS DIVIDED ON ITALY'S COLONIES

State Department Split Over Russia and Influence Zones Is Projected by Issue

By JAMES B. RESTON
Special to THE NEW YORK TIMES.

WASHINGTON, Sept. 1—A fundamental issue has developed in the Department of State over the future of the Italian colonies, particularly Eritrea, Libya and Italian Somaliland.

The issue is whether these colonies should go back to Italy as part of her sovereign territory, be taken from her and administered by the United States, Britain, France and the Soviet Union under the United Nations Organization or be administered by a neutral international commission under the United Nations.

The major powers that defeated Germany are soon to start draft-

Continued on Page 15, Column 1

TOKYO AIDES WEEP AS GENERAL SIGNS

Imperial Staff Chief Hastily Scrawls His Signature—Shigemitsu Is Anxious

By The Associated Press.

ABOARD U. S. S. MISSOURI in Tokyo Bay, Sunday, Sept. 2—The solemn surrender ceremony, on this battleship today, marking the first defeat in Japan's 2,600-year-old semi-legendary history, required only a few minutes as twelve signatures were affixed to the articles.

Surrounded by the might of the United States Navy and Army, and under the eyes of the American and British commanders they so ruthlessly defeated in the Philippines and Malaya, the Japanese representatives quietly made the marks on paper that ended the bloody Pacific conflict.

The Japanese delegation came aboard at 8:55 A. M., 7:55 P. M. Saturday, E. W. T., as scheduled. They reached the Missouri in personnel speed boats flying the American flag.

Foreign Minister Mamoru Shigemitsu led the delegation. He climbed stiffly up the ladder and limped forward on his right leg, which is artificial. He was wounded by a bomb tossed by a Korean terrorist in Shanghai many years ago.

On behalf of Emperor Hirohito, Mr. Shigemitsu signed first for

Continued on Page 9, Column 1

World News Summarized

SUNDAY, SEPTEMBER 2, 1945

The rulers of Japan, who set the Pacific ablaze nearly four years ago with their surprise attack on Pearl Harbor and hoped to culminate that assault with a peace dictated in the White House, formally signed their unconditional surrender to the Allied powers in Tokyo Bay. Foreign Minister Shigemitsu signed the historic document for his country in the shadow of the sixteen-inch gun muzzles of the battleship Missouri. General MacArthur, who signed in behalf of the Allies, said mankind hoped a better world would result from the solemn occasion. [1:8; map P. 12.]

President Truman proclaimed today as V-J Day. He urged the nation to observe the day of victory over Japan in a spirit of dedication and as a symbol of "victory of liberty over tyranny." He also asked his countrymen to remember "our departed gallant leader, Franklin D. Roosevelt." [1:3.]

Japan's decision to surrender was dictated by Emperor Hirohito after he had overruled a strong faction within the Cabinet and the army that wanted to keep on with the war in the belief that the Japanese could defeat an invasion of the homeland, according to well-informed observers in Tokyo. [1:5-6.]

Medical "experiments" recalling medieval sadism were carried out on dying American prisoners of war by young Japanese Army doctors, two American physicians interned with their compatriots said aboard a United States hospital ship. [1:6-7.]

With the Foreign Ministers' Council scheduled to meet in London next week to begin consideration of peace terms, it was learned that a serious division of opinion over the disposition of the Italian colonies had developed in the State Department. [1:6.]

Former Secretary of State Stettinius said in London that the development of the atomic bomb emphasized the need for "the speedy creation of the United Nations Organization to keep the peace of the world" and predicted that as soon as the organization began functioning it would appoint a military staff to deal with the use of atomic bombs, as well as all other types of force in preserving peace. [18:2.]

"ALL THE NEWS THAT'S FIT TO PRINT"

In the first eight months of this year, The Times published 6.092 more columns of news than any other newspaper. With World Peace still to be won, and reconversion a topic of daily import, The New York Times continues to print the complete news.

Enemy Tortured Dying Americans With Sadist Medical 'Experiments'

By ROBERT TRUMBULL
By Wireless to THE NEW YORK TIMES.

ABOARD THE HOSPITAL SHIP BENEVOLENCE, in Tokyo Bay, Sept. 1 — Seriously ailing American prisoners at Shinagawa, the only hospital serving 8,000 prisoners of war held in the Tokyo area, were guinea pigs for fantastic experiments recalling the sorcery and sadism of the middle ages, Drs. Mack L. Gottlieb and Harold W. Keschner, both of New York, told this correspondent today.

Both doctors are recuperating aboard this ship after their rescue from Shinagawa on Wednesday by a special Navy evacuation mission headed by Comdr. Harold A. Stassen, former Governor of Minnesota and now Assistant Chief of Staff and Flag Secretary to Admiral William F. Halsey, commander of the Third Fleet.

[In an interview in Tokyo the Japanese Army doctor to whom some of these practices were charged confirmed the cruel treatment of American prisoners.]

Dr. Gottlieb, who had his home and office at 307 East Forty-fourth Street, was a Naval officer captured at Guam. Dr. Keschner, of 451 West End Avenue, was taken with an Army force in the Philippines. Both are in good physical

Continued on Page 14, Column 1

WAR COMES TO END

Articles of Capitulation Endorsed by Countries in Pacific Conflict

M'ARTHUR SEES PEACE

Emperor Orders Subjects to Obey All Commands Issued by General

The texts of the surrender documents and statements, P. 3.

By The Associated Press.

ABOARD THE U. S. S. MISSOURI in Tokyo Bay, Sunday, Sept. 2—Japan surrendered formally and unconditionally to the Allies today in a twenty-minute ceremony which ended just as the sun burst through low-hanging clouds as a shining symbol to a ravaged world now done with war.

[A United Press dispatch said the leading Japanese delegate signed the articles at 9:03 A. M. Sunday, Tokyo time, and that General MacArthur signed them at 9:07 A. M.]

Twelve signatures, requiring only a few minutes to inscribe on the articles of surrender, ended the bloody Pacific conflict.

On behalf of Emperor Hirohito, Foreign Minister Mamoru Shigemitsu signed for the Government and Gen. Yoshijiro Umezu for the Imperial General Staff.

MacArthur Voices Peace Hope

Gen. Douglas MacArthur then accepted in behalf of the United Nations, declaring:

"It is my earnest hope and indeed the hope of all mankind that from this solemn occasion a better world shall emerge out of the blood and carnage of the past."

One by one the Allied representatives stepped forward and signed the document that blighted Japan's dream of empire built on bloodshed and tyranny.

First was Admiral Chester W. Nimitz for the United States, then the representatives of China, the United Kingdom, the Soviet, Australia, Canada, France, the Netherlands and New Zealand.

The flags of the United States, Britain, the Soviet and China fluttered from the veranda deck of the famed superdreadnaught, polished and scrubbed as never before. More than 100 high-ranking military and naval officers watched.

Pledges Justice and Tolerance

"As Supreme Commander for the Allied powers," General MacArthur told the Japanese, "I announce it my firm purpose, in the tradition of the countries I represent, to proceed in the discharge of my responsibilities with justice and tolerance, while taking all necessary dispositions to insure that the terms of surrender are fully, promptly and faithfully complied with."

All through this dramatic half hour, only those aboard the battleship knew of what was taking place, because the Missouri has no broadcasting facilities.

But recordings were rushed to the near-by communications ship Ancon, and the solemn words of General MacArthur beginning the ceremony—"We are gathered here, representatives of the major warring powers"—were flashed around the world.

The Japanese representatives were present at the command of Emperor Hirohito contained in a proclamation issued by order of the Supreme Allied Commander.

The Emperor further commanded his officials "to issue general orders to the military and naval forces in accordance with the direction of the Supreme Commander

Continued on Page 2, Column 3